TABLE OF CONTENTS

ACKNOWLEDGEMENTS

Larry Bigman (Frazetta-Williamson data); Glenn Bray (Kurtzman data); Dan Malan & Charles Heffelfinger (Classic Comics data); Gary Carter (DC data)); J. B. Clifford Jr. (E. C. data); Gary Coddington (Superman data); Wilt Conine (Fawcett data); Dr. S. M. Davidson (Cupples & Leon data); Al Dellinges (Kubert data); Kevin Hancer (Tarzan data); Charles Heffelfinger and Jim Ivey (March of Comics listing;); R. C. Holland and Ron Pussell (Seduction and Parade of Pleasure data); Grant Irwin (Quality data); Richard Kravitz (Kelly data); Phil Levine (giveaway data); Fred Nardelli (Frazetta data); Michelle Nolan (love comics); Mike Nolan (MLJ, Timely, Nedor data); George Olshevsky (Timely data); Don Rosa (Late 1940s to 1950s data); Richard Olson (LOA & R. F. Outcault data); Scott Pell ('50s data); Greg Robertson (National data); Mark Arnold (Harvey data); Frank Scigliano (Little Lulu data); Gene Seger (Buck Rogers data); Rick Sloane (Archie data); David F Smith, Archivist, Walt Disney Productions (Disney data); Don and Maggie Thompson (Four Color listing); Mike Tiefenbacher & Jerry Sinkovec (Atlas and National data); Raymond True (Classic Comics data); Jim Vadeboncoeur Jr. (Williamson and Atlas data); Kim Weston (Disney and Barks data); Cat Yronwode (Spirit data); Andrew Zerbe and Gary Behymer (M. E. data).

My appreciation must also be extended to Don Maris, John Snyder, Steve Geppi, Bruce Hamilton, Harry Thomas, Gary Carter, and especially to Hugh and Louise O'Kennon for their support and help. Special acknowledgement is also given to Ron Pussell, Michelle Nolan, Garth Wood, Terry Stroud, John Newberry, Tony Starks, Dan Kurdilla, Stephen Baer and Dave Puckett for submitting corrective data; to Dr. Richard Olson for grading information; to Larry Breed for his suggestions on re-organizing the introductory section; to Dan Malan for revamping the Classics section; to Terry Stroud, Ron Pussell, Hugh O'Kennon, Dave Smith, Rod Dyke, James Payette, John Snyder, Gary Carter, Sean Linkenback, Rick Frogge, Stephen Fishler, Jerry Weist, Walter Wang, Steve Geppi, Harley Yee, Joe Mannarino, Bruce Hamilton, John Verzyl, Gary Colabuono, Dave Anderson (OK) and Dave Anderson (VA.)-pricing; to Tom Inge for his "Chronology of the American Comic Book;" to Tom Andrae for his entertaining articles; to Carmine Infantino and Terry Austin for their inspired cover art; to Landon Chesney and Dave Noah for their work on the key comic book list; to L. B. Cole, Steve Saffel, and Jerry DeFuccio for their counsel and help; to Bill Spicer and Zetta DeVoe (Western Publishing Co.) for their contribution of data; and especially to Bill for his kind permission to reprint portions of his and Jerry Bails' America's Four Color Pastime; and to Jeff Overstreet and Tony Overstreet for their help in editing this volume.

I will always be indebted to Jerry Bails, Landon Chesney, Bruce Hamilton and Larry Bigman whose advice and concern have helped in making The Comic Book Price Guide a reality; to my wife for her encouragement and help in putting this reference work together; and to everyone who placed ads in this edition.

Acknowledgement is also due to the following people who have so generously contributed much needed data for this edition:

David Anderson III
Steve Andrew
Eric W. Augustin
Stephen Baer
Robbie Barker
Robert Barks
Tim Barnes
David Bates
Bruce Berges
Peter James Bilelis
John Binder M.D.
John Brillhart
Chris Bourassa
Larry Boyd
Douglas J. Brown
Richard M. Brown
Bart Bush
John E. Butt
Norman Camar
Brandon Carter
Douglas Chambers
Samuel M. Clevenger
Monte Cohen
Stephen W. Combs
Prof. David A. Cook

Stephen Couch
Ken & Janice Cross
Keith B. Darrell
Sterling Dashiell
Howard Leroy Davis
Craig Delich
John Doliber
Doris Elmore
Andrew Finch
Shawn Finlay
Brian Flota
Don French
Alex Frazer-Harrison
Rick Frogge
Michael T. Gilbert
David Harper
Donald Harper
Steve Haynie
Peter Healy
Daniel D. Hering
Anton Hermus
Jef Hinds
Alex Hloderwski
Bill Hoffmeister
Carl J. Horak

Bill Hutchison
Steven R. Johnson
Scott Jones
Ken Kaake
Lynne Keith
Gary Kirkland
Richard J. Kohman, Jr.
Richard Kolkman
Joe Krolik
Robert C. Kuhl
Dan Kurdilla
Graham Lockley
Dan Malan
Robert Manning
Rob Mathis
Sheila Mathis
Doug Mabry
James P McLoughlin
Ward McMillan
Harry W. Miller
Bill Mills
John Mlachnik
Lou Mougin
David Mulford
Bob Myers

Michael Naiman
John Newberry
Roger Newberry
Rick Norwood
Ed O'Brien
Steve O'Day
Hugh O'Kennon
Richard D. Olson
Buddy Paige
John Paige
John Pappas, JR.
Geoffrey Patterson
Don Phelps
Brian Powell
Dave Puckett
John Randall
Rob Rankin
Stanley Resnick
Wayne Richardson
Richard M. Rizza
Charlie Roberts
Jeremy Rogers
David Rosciszewski
John Russell
Andrew Schwartzbert

Adam Schultz
Randall W. Scott
Patrick Shaughnessy
David Sorochty
Sergei S. Sourfield
Steve Spence
Tony Starks
West Robert Stephan
Roger Taylor
Jason Thomas
Kim Thompson
Bill Tighe
Don Van Horn
E. Van Melkebeke
John K. Vavra
Laurie Wanser
Mark D. Warner
Justin S. Wehner
Jerome Wenker
Julian West
Allen Willford
Garth Wood
Dan Wright Ph.D.
James L. Wright
Terry Yakish

PREFACE

Comic book values listed in this reference work were recorded from convention sales, dealers' lists, adzines, and by special contact with dealers and collectors from coast to coast. Prices paid for rare comics vary considerably from one locale to another. We have attempted to list a realistic average between the lowest and highest range observed. The reader should keep in mind that the prices listed only reflect the market just prior to publication. Any new trends that have developed since the preparation of this book would not be shown.

The values listed are based on reports wherever possible. Each new edition of the guide is actually an average report of sales that occurred during the year; not an estimate of what we feel the books will be bringing next year. Even though many prices listed will remain current throughout the year, the wise user of this book would keep abreast of current market trends to get the fullest potential out of his invested dollar.

By the same token, many of the scarcer books are seldom offered for sale in top condition. This makes it difficult to arrive at a realistic market value. Some of the issues in this category are: Action #1, All-American #16, Batman #1, Large Feature Comic #20, Captain America #1, Captain Marvel #1, Detective #27, Double Action #2, the no number Feature Books, Green Giant #1, March of Comics #4, Marvel #1, More Fun #52, Famous Funnies #1s, Superman #1, Whiz #2 (#1), Amazing Man #5, New Fun #1, and Wow #1.

Some rare comics were published in a complete black and white format; i.e., All-New #15, Blood Is the Harvest, Boy Explorers #2, Eerie #1, If the Devil Would Talk, Is This Tomorrow, Flash #1, Thrill #1 and Stuntman #3. As we have learned in the case of Eerie #1, the collector or investor in these books would be well advised to give due consideration to the possibility of counterfeits before investing large sums of money.

This book is the most comprehensive listing of newsstand comic books ever attempted. Comic book titles, dates of first and last issues, publishing companies, origin and special issues are listed when known.

The Guide will be listing primarily American comic books due to space limitation. Some variations of the regular comic book format will be listed. These basically include those pre-1933 comic strip reprint books with varying size usually with cardboard covers, but sometimes with hardback. As forerunners of the modern comic book format, they deserve to be listed despite their obvious differences in presentation. Other books that will be listed are selected black and white comics of the 1980s, giveaway comics but only those that contain known characters, work by known collectible artists, or those of special interest.

All titles are listed as if they were one word, ignoring spaces, hyphens and apostrophes. Page counts listed will always include covers.

IMPORTANT. Prices listed in this book are in U. S. currency and are for your reference only. This book is not a dealer's price list, although some dealers may base their prices on the values listed. The true value of any comic book is what you are willing to pay. Prices listed herein are an indication of what collectors (not dealers) would probably pay. For one reason or another, these collectors might want certain books badly, or else need specific issues to complete their runs and so are willing to pay more. Dealers are not in a position to pay the full prices listed, but work on a percentage depending largely on the amount of investment required and the quality of material offered. Usually they will pay from 20 to 70 percent of the list price depending on how long it will take them to sell the collection after making the investment; the higher the demand and better the condition, the more the percentage. Most dealers are faced with expenses such as advertising, travel, telephone and mailing, rent, employee salaries, plus convention costs. These costs all go in before the books are sold. The high demand books usually sell right away but there are many other titles that are difficult to sell due to low demand. Sometimes a dealer will have cost tied up in this type of material for several years before finally moving it. Remember, his position is that of handling, demand and overhead. Most dealers are victims of these economics.

POLICY OF LISTING NEW COMIC BOOKS; The current market has experienced an explosion of publishers with hundreds of new titles appearing in black and white and color. Many of these comics are listed in this book, but not all due to space limitation. We will attempt to list complete information only on those titles that show some collector interest. The selection of titles to include is constantly being monitored by our board of advisors who work on our monthly magazine. Of course a much better coverage of recent books will be made in the monthly throughout the year. Please do not contact us to list your new comic books. Listings are determined by the marketplace. However, we are interested in receiving review copies of all new comic books published.

GRADING COMIC BOOKS

For complete, detailed information on grading and restoration, consult the Overstreet Comic Book Grading Guide. Copies are available through all normal distribution channels or can be ordered direct from the publisher by sending $12 postage paid.

The Overstreet Comic Book Grading Card, known as the **ONE** and **OWL Card** is also available. This card has two functions. The **ONE Card** (Overstreet's Numerical Equivalent is used to convert grading condition terms to the New numerical grading system. The **OWL Card** (Overstreet's Whiteness Level) is used for grading the whiteness of paper. The color scale on the **OWL Card** is simply placed over the interior comic book paper. The paper color is matched with the color on the card to get the **OWL** number. The **ONE/OWL Card** will be available through all normal distribution channels or may be ordered direct from the publisher by sending $2.75 per card, post paid.

Before a comic book's true value can be assessed, its condition or state of preservation must be determined. In all comic books the better the condition the more desirable and valuable the book. Comic books in **MINT** condition will bring several times the price of the same book in **POOR** condition. Therefore it is very important to be able to properly grade your books. Comics should be graded from the inside out, so the following comic book areas should be examined before assigning a final grade.

Check inside pages, inside spine and covers and outside spine and covers for any tears, markings, brittleness, tape, soiling, chunks out or other defects that would affect the grade. After all the above steps have been taken, then the reader can begin to consider an overall grade for his or her book. The grading of a comic book is done by simply looking at the book and describing its condition, which may range from absolutely perfect newsstand condition (MINT) to extremely worn, dirty, and torn (POOR.)

Numerous variables influence the evaluation of a comic book's condition and all must be considered in the final evaluation. As grading is the most subjective aspect of determining a comic's value, it is very important that the grader be careful and not allow wishful thinking to influence what the eyes see. It is also very important to realize that older comics in MINT condition are extremely scarce and are rarely advertised for sale; most of the higher grade comics advertised range from VERY FINE to NEAR MINT.

ABOUT RESTORED COMICS:

Our board of advisors suggests that **professionally restored comic books** are an accepted component of the comic book market; but only if the following criteria is met: 1–Must be professional work. 2–Complete disclosure of the extent and type of restoration. 3–Both parties are informed. 4–Priced accordingly depending on availability and demand. **Note:** A professionally restored book, reasonably priced, while not worth as much as the same book unrestored, will increase in value at the same rate. However, if you pay the unrestored price for a restored book, you would be paying a premium, which of course may not be a good investment.

Initial indications on sales and auction results suggests the following. Unrestored keys in Fine or better condition may prove in the future to be better investments, as their availability decreases, and should not be restored to an apparent higher grade. Restoration should be concentrated on books in less than Fine condition. **Warning:** Before getting restoration done, seek advise from a professional and avoid doing it yourself.

Many rare and expensive books are being repaired and restored by professionals and amateurs alike. If the book is expensive, there is a strong likelihood that some type of repair, cleaning or restoration has been done. In most cases, after restoration, these books are not actually higher grades, but are altered lower grade books. Note: Expert restoration is always preferable to amateur work and is sometimes very difficult to spot and can be easily missed when grading. In some cases, the work done is so good that it is impossible to spot. Depending upon the extent and type of restoration and the quality of what was done, you will have to decide whether the value has increased or decreased. In many cases we have observed in the market that the value has been increased on certain books that were originally in low grade before restoration where the appearance and structural integrity was greatly improved afterwards. Restoration on higher grade copies may or may not affect value depending on what is done. Of course, when a comic book is graded, everything must be taken into account in the final grade given.

To the novice grading will appear difficult at first; but, as experience is gained accuracy will improve. Whenever in doubt (after using the Overstreet Comic Book Grading Guide), consult with a reputable dealer or experienced collector in your area. The following grading guide is given to aid the collector.

GRADING DEFINITIONS

Note: This edition uses both the traditional grade abbreviations and the ONE number throughout the listings.

The Overstreet Numerical Equivalent (ONE spread range is given with each grade.)

MINT (MT) (ONE 100-98): Near perfect in every way. Only the most subtle bindery or printing defects are allowed. Cover is flat with no surface wear. Cover inks are bright with high reflectivity and minimal fading. Corners are cut square and sharp. Staples are generally centered, clean with no rust. Cover is generally well centered and firmly secured to interior pages. Paper is supple and fresh. Spine is tight and flat.

NEAR MINT (NM) (ONE 97-90): Nearly perfect with only minor imperfections such as tiny corner creases or staple stress lines, a few color flecks, bindery tears, tiny impact creases or a combination of the above where the overall eye appeal is less than Mint. Only the most subtle binding and/or printing defects allowed. Cover is flat with no surface wear. Cover inks are bright with high reflectivity and minimum of fading. Corners are cut square and sharp with ever so slight blunting permitted. Staples are generally centered, clean with no rust. Cover is well centered and firmly secured to interior pages. Paper is supple and like new. Spine is tight and flat.

VERY FINE (VF) (ONE 89-75): An excellent copy with outstanding eye-appeal. Sharp, bright and clean with supple pages. Cover is relatively flat with minimal surface wear beginning to show. Cover inks are generally bright with moderate to high reflectivity. Slight wear beginning to show including some minute wear at corners. Staples may show some discoloration. Spine may have a few transverse stress lines but is relatively flat. A light inch crease is acceptible. Pages and covers can be yellowish/tannish (at the least but not brown and will usually be off-white to white.

FINE (FN) (ONE 74-55): An exceptional, above-average copy that shows minor wear, but is still relatively flat and clean with no major creasing or other serious defects. Eye appeal is somewhat reduced because of noticeable surface wear and the accumulation of smaller defects, especially on the spine and edges. A Fine condition comic book appears to have been read many times and has been handled with moderate care. Compared to a VF, cover inks are beginning to show a significant reduction in reflectivity but is still highly collectible and desirable.

VERY GOOD (VG) (ONE 54-35): The average used comic book. A comic in this grade shows moderate wear, can have a reading or center crease or a rolled spine, but has not accumulated enough total defects to reduce eye appeal to the point where it is not a desirable copy. Some discoloration, fading and even minor soiling is allowed. No chunks can be missing but a small piece can be out at the corner or edge. Store stamps, name stamps, arrival dates, initials, etc. have no effect on this grade. Cover and interior pages can have minor tears and folds and the centerfold may be loose or detached. One or both staples might be loose, but cover is not completely detached. Common bindery and printing defects do not affect grade. Pages and inside covers may be brown but not brittle. Tape should never be used for comic book repair, however many VG condition comics have minor tape repair.

GOOD (GD) (ONE 34-15): A copy in this grade has all pages and covers, although there may be small pieces missing. Books in this grade are commonly creased, scuffed, abraded and soiled, but completely readable. Often paper quality is low but not brittle. Cover reflectivity is low and in some cases completely absent. Most collectors consider this the lowest collectible grade because comic books in lesser condition are usually incomplete and/or brittle. This grade can have a large accumulation of defects but still maintains its basic structural integrity.

FAIR (FR) (ONE 14-5): A copy in this grade has all pages and most of the covers, although there may be up to 1/3 of the front cover missing or all of the back cover, but not both. A comic in this grade is soiled, ragged and unattractive. Creases and folds are prevalent and paper quality may be very low. The centerfold may be missing if it does not affect a story. Spine may be completely split its entire length. Staples may be gone, and/or cover completely detached. Corners are commonly severely rounded or absent. Coupons may be cut from front cover and/or back cover and/or interior pages. These books are mostly readable although soiling, staining, tears, markings or chunks missing may interfere with reading the complete story. Very often paper quality is low and may even be brittle around the edges but not in the central portion of the pages.

POOR (PR) (ONE 4-1): Most comic books in this grade have been sufficiently degraded to where there is no longer any collector value. Copies in this grade typically have: Pages and/or more than approximately 1/3 of the front cover missing. They may have extremely severe stains, mildew or heavy cover abrasion to the point where cover inks are indistinct/absent. They may have been defaced with paints, varnishes, glues, oil, indelible markers or dyes. Other defects often include severe rips, tears, folding and creasing. Another common defect in this grade is moderate to severe brittleness, often to the point where the comic book literally "falls apart" when examined.

DUST JACKETS: Many of the early strip reprint comics were printed in hardback with dust jackets. Books with dust jackets are worth more. The value can increase from 20 to 50 percent depending on the rarity of book. Usually, the earlier the book, the greater the percentage. Unless noted, prices listed are without dust jackets. The condition of the dust jacket should be graded independently of the book itself.

SCARCITY OF COMIC BOOKS RELATED TO GRADE

1900-1933 Comics: Most of these books are bound with thick cardboard covers and are very rare to non-existent in fine or better condition. Due to their extreme age, paper browning is very common. Brittleness could be a problem.

1933-1940 Comics: There are many issues from this period that are very scarce in any condition, especially from the early to mid-1930s. Surviving copies of any particular issue range from a handful to several hundred. Near Mint to Mint copies are virtually non-existent with known examples of any particular issue limited to five or less copies. Most surviving copies are in FVF or less condition. Brittleness or browning of paper is fairly common and could be a problem.

1941-1952 Comics: Surviving comic books would number from less than 100 to several thousand copies of each issue. Near Mint to Mint copies are a little more common but are still relatively scarce with only a dozen or so copies in this grade existing of any particular issue. Exceptions would be recent warehouse finds of most Dell comics (6-100 copies, but usually 30 or less), and Harvey comics (1950s-1970s) surfacing. Due to low paper quality of the late 1940s and 1950s, many comics from this period are rare in Near Mint to Mint condition. Most remaining copies are VF or less. Browning of paper could be a problem.

1953-1959 Comics: As comic book sales continued to drop during the 1950s, production values were lowered resulting in cheaply printed comics. For this reason, high grade copies are extremely rare. Many Atlas and Marvel comics have chipping along the trimmed edges (Marvel chipping) which reduces even more the number of surviving high grade copies.

1960-1970 Comics: Early 60s comics are rare in Near Mint to Mint condition. Most copies of early 60s Marvels and DCs grade no higher than VF. Many early keys in NM or M exist in numbers less than 10-20 of each. Mid to late 60s books in high grade are more common due to the hoarding of comics that began in the mid-60s.

1970-Present: Comics of today are common in high grade. VF to NM is the standard rather than the exception.

When you consider how few Golden and Silver Age books exist compared to the current market, you will begin to appreciate the true rarity of these early books. In many cases less than 5-10 copies exist of a particular issue in Near Mint to Mint condition, while most of the 1930s books do not exist in this grade at all.

TERMINOLOGY

Many of the following terms and abbreviations are used in the comic book market and are explained here: (Note: Consult the Overstreet Comic Book Grading Guide for a more detailed list of terms).

a-Story art; **a(i)**-Story art inks; **a(p)**-Story art pencils; **a(r)**-Story art reprint.

Annual-A book that is published yearly.

Arrival date-Markings on a comic book cover (usually in pencil) made by either the newsstand dealer or the distributor. These markings denote the date the book was placed on the newsstand. Usually the arrival date is one to two months prior to the cover date.

Ashcan-A publisher's inhouse facsimile of a proposed new title. Most ashcans have black & white covers stapled to an existing coverless comic on the inside. Other ashcans are totally black and white.

B&W-Black and white art.

Bi-monthly-Published every two months.

Bi-weekly-Published every two weeks.

Bondage cover-Usually denotes a female in bondage.

Brittleness-The final stage of paper deterioration.

c-Cover art; **c(i)**-Cover inks; **c(p)**-Cover pencils; **c(r)**-Cover reprint.

Cameo-When a character appears briefly in one or two panels.

CCA-Comics Code Authority.

CCA seal-An emblem that was placed on the cover of all CCA approved comics beginning in April-May, 1955.

Centerfold-The two folded pages in the center of a comic at the terminal end of the staples.

Church, Edgar collection-A large high grade comic book collection discovered by Mile High Comics in Colorado (over 22,000 books).

Colorist-Artist that applies color to the black and white pen and ink art.

Comic book repair-When a tear, loose staple or centerfold has been mended without changing or adding to the original finish of the book. Repair may involve tape, glue or nylon gossamer and is easily detected. It is considered a defect.

Comic book restoration-Any attempt, whether professional or amateur, to enhance the appearance of a comic book. These procedures may include any or all of the following techniques: Recoloring, adding missing paper, stain, ink, dirt, tape removal, whitening, pressing out wrinkles, staple replacement, trimming, re-glossing, etc. Note: Unprofessional work can lower the value of a book. In all cases, a restored book can never be worth the same as an unrestored book in the same condition.

Comics Code Authority-In 1954 the major publishers joined together and formed a committee who set up guide lines for acceptable comic contents. It was their task to approve the contents of comics before publication.

Con-A Convention or public gathering of fans.

Cosmic Aeroplane-Refers to a large collection discovered by Cosmic Aeroplane Books.

Debut-The first time that a character appears anywhere.

Double cover-An error in the binding process which results in two or more covers being bound to a single book. Multiple covers are not considered a defect.

Drug propaganda story-Where comic makes an editorial stand about drug abuse.

Drug use story-Shows the actual use of drugs: shooting, taking a trip, harmful effects, etc.

Fanzine-An amateur fan publication.

File Copy-A high grade comic originating from the publisher's file. Not all file copies are in pristine condition. Note: An arrival date on the cover of a comic does not indicate that it is a file copy.

First app.-Same as debut.

Flashback-When a previous story is being recalled.

Four color-A printing process in which all primary colors plus black are used. Also refers to the Four Color series published by Dell.

Foxing-Tiny orange-brown spots on the cover or pages of a comic book.

G. A.-Golden Age.

Golden Age (G.A.)-The period beginning with Action #1 (June, 1938) and ending with World War II in 1945.

Headlight-Protruding breasts.

i-Art inks.

Indicia-Publishers title, issue number, date, copyright and general information statement usually located on the inside front cover, facing page or inside back cover.

Infinity cover-Shows a scene that repeats itself to infinity.

Inker-Artist that does the inking.

Intro-Same as debut.

JLA-Justice League of America.

JLI-Justice League International.

JSA-Justice Society of America.

Lamont Larson-Refers to a large high grade collection of comics. Many of the books have Lamont or Larson written on the cover.

Logo-The title of a strip or comic book as it appears on the cover or title page.

LSH-Legion of Super-Heroes.

Marvel chipping-A defect that occurred during the trimming process of 1950s & 1960s Marvels which produced a ragged edge around the comic cover. Usually takes the form of a tiny chip or chips along the right-hand edge of the cover.

Mile High-Refers to a large NM-Mint collection of comics originating from Denver, Colorado (Edgar Church collection).

nd-No date.

nn-No number.

N. Y. Legis. Comm.-New York Legislative Committee to Study the Publication of Comics (1951).

One-shot-When only one issue is published of a title, or when a series is published where each issue is a different title (i.e. Four Color).

Origin-When the story of the character's creation is given.

Over guide-When a comic book is priced at a value over guide list.

p-Art pencils.

Pedigree-A book from a famous collection, e.g. Allentown, Larson, Church/Mile High, Denver, San Francisco, Cosmic Aeroplane, etc. Note: Beware of non-pedigree collections being promoted as pedigree books. Only outstanding high grade collections similar to those listed qualify.

Penciler-Artist that does the pencils.

POP-Parade of Pleasure, book about the censorship of comics.

Post-Code-Comic books published with the CCA seal.

Post-Golden Age-Comic books published between 1945 and 1950.

Post-Silver Age-Comic books published from 1969 to present.

Poughkeepsie-Refers to a large collection of Dell Comics' "file copies" believed to have originated from the warehouse of Western Publishing in Poughkeepsie, N.Y.

Pre-Code-Comic books published before the CCA seal.

Pre-Golden Age-Comic books published prior to Action #1 (June, 1938).

Pre-Silver Age-Comic books published between 1950 and Showcase #4 (1956).

Printing defect-A defect caused by the printing process. Examples would include paper wrinkling, miscut edges, mis-folded spine, untrimmed pages, off-registered color, off-centered trimming, mis-folded and mis-bound pages. It should be noted that these are defects that lower the grade of the book.

Provenance-When the owner of a book is known and is stated for the purpose of authenticating and documenting the history of the book. Example: A book from the Stan Lee or Forrest Ackerman collection would be an example of a value-adding provenance.

Quarterly-Published every three months (four times a year).

R or r-Reprint.

Rare-10 to 20 copies estimated to exist.

Reprint comics-Comic books that contain newspaper strip reprints.

Rice paper-A thin, transparent paper commonly used by restorers to repair tears and replace small pieces on covers and pages of comic books.

S. A.-Silver Age.

S&K-Joe Simon and Jack Kirby (artists).

Scarce-20 to 100 copies estimated to exist.

Silver Age-Officially begins with Showcase #4 in 1956 and ends in 1969.

Silver proof-A black & white actual size print on thick glossy paper given to the colorist to indicate colors to the engraver.

SOTI-Seduction of the Innocent, book about the censorship of comics. Refer to listing in this guide.

Spine-The area representing the folded and stapled part of a comic book.

Spine roll-A defect caused by improper storage which results in uneven pages and the shifting or bowing of the spine.

Splash panel-A large panel that usually appears at the front of a comic story.

Squarebound-A comic book glue-bound with a square spined cover.

Stress lines-Light, tiny wrinkles occuring along the spine, projecting from the staples or appearing anywhere on the covers of a comic book.

Subscription crease-A center crease caused by the folding of comic books for mailing to subscribers. This is considered a defect.

3-D comic-Comic art that is drawn and printed in two-color layers, producing a true 3-D effect when viewed through special glasses.

3-D Effect comic-Comic art that is drawn to appear 3-D, but isn't.

Under guide-When a comic book is priced at a value less than guide list.

Very rare-1 to 10 copies estimated to exist.

Warehouse copy-Originating from a publisher's warehouse; similar to file copy.

X-over-When one character crosses over into another's strip.

Zine-See Fanzine.

Marvel comic books are cover coded for the direct sales (comic shop, newsstand, and foreign markets). They are all first printings, with the special coding being the only difference. The comics sold to the comic shops have to be coded differently, as they are sold on a no-return basis while newsstand comics are not. The Price Guide has not detected any price difference between these versions. Currently, the difference is easily detected by looking at the front cover bar code (a box located at the lower left. The bar code is filled in for newsstand sales and is left blank or contains a character for comic shop sales.

Marvel Reprints: In recent years Marvel has reprinted some of their comics. There has been confusion in identifying the reprints from the originals. However, in 99 percent of the cases, the reprints have listed "reprint," or "2nd printing," etc. in the indicia, along with a later copyright date in some cases. Some Marvel 2nd printings will have a gold logo. The only known exceptions are a few of the movie books such as Star Wars, the Marvel Treasury Editions, and tie-in books such as G. I. Joe. These books were reprinted and not identified as reprints. The Star Wars reprints have a large diamond with no date and a blank UPC symbol on the cover. The other reprints had some cover variation such as a date missing, different colors, etc. Beginning in mid-1990, all Marvel 2nd printings will have a gold logo.

Gold Key and other comics were also sold with a Whitman label. There are collectors who prefer the regular labels to Whitman, although the Price Guide does not differentiate in the price. Beginning in 1980, all comics produced by Western carried the Whitman label.

Many of the better artists are pointed out. When more than one artist worked on a story, their names are separated by a (/). The first name did the pencil drawings and the second did the inks. When two or more artists work on a story, only the most prominent will be noted in some cases. We wish all good artists could be listed, but due to space limitation, only the most popular can. The following list of artists are considered to be either the most collected in the comic field or are historically significant and should be pointed out. Artists designated below with an (*) indicate that only their most noted work will be listed. The rest will eventually have all their work shown as the information becomes available. This list could change from year to year as new artists come into prominence.

Adams, Arthur
Adams, Neal
*Aparo, Jim
*Austin, Terry
Baker, Matt
Barks, Carl
Beck, C. C.
*Brunner, Frank
*Buscema, John
Byrne, John
*Check, Sid
Cole, Jack
Cole, L. B.
Craig, Johnny
Crandall, Reed
Davis, Jack
Disbrow, Jayson
*Ditko, Steve
Eisner, Will
*Elder, Bill
Evans, George
Everett, Bill
Feldstein, Al
Fine, Lou
Foster, Harold
Fox, Matt
Frazetta, Frank
*Giffen, Keith
Golden, Michael
Gottfredson, Floyd
*Guardineer, Fred
Gustavson, Paul
*Heath, Russ
Howard, Wayne
Ingels, Graham
Jones, Jeff
Kamen, Jack
Kane, Bob
*Kane, Gil
Kelly, Walt
Kinstler, E. R.
Kirby, Jack
Krenkel, Roy
Krigstein, Bernie
*Kubert, Joe
Kurtzman, Harvey
*Lee, Jim
Manning, Russ
McFarlane, Todd
McWilliams, Al
*Meskin, Mort
Miller, Frank
Moreira, Ruben
*Morisi, Pete
*Newton, Don
Nostrand, Howard
Orlando, Joe
Pakula, Mac
*Palais, Rudy
*Perez, George
Powell, Bob
Raboy, Mac
Raymond, Alex
Ravielli, Louis
*Redondo, Nestor
Rogers, Marshall
Schomburg, Alex
Siegel & Shuster
Simon & Kirby (S&K)
*Simonson, Walt
Smith, Barry
Smith, Paul
Stanley, John
*Starlin, Jim
Steranko, Jim
Stevens, Dave
Torres, Angelo
Toth, Alex
Tuska, George
Ward, Bill
Williamson, Al
Woggon, Bill
Wolverton, Basil
Wood, Wallace
Wrightson, Bernie

The following abbreviations are used with the cover reproductions throughout the book for copyright credit purposes. The companies they represent are listed here:

AC -(Americomics)
ACE-Ace Periodicals
ACG-American Comics Group
AJAX-Ajax-Farrell
AP-Archie Publications
ATLAS-Atlas Comics (see below)
AVON-Avon Periodicals
BP-Better Publications
C & L-Cupples & Leon
CC-Charlton Comics
CEN-Centaur Publications
CCG-Columbia Comics Group
CG-Catechetical Guild
CHES-Harry 'A' Chesler
CLDS-Classic Det. Stories
CM-Comics Magazine
DC-DC Comics, Inc.
DELL-Dell Publishing Co.
DH-Dark Horse
DMP-David McKay Publishing
DS-D. S. Publishing Co.
EAS-Eastern Color Printing Co.
EC-E. C. Comics
ECL-Eclipse Comics
ENWIL-Enwil Associates
EP-Elliott Publications
ERB-Edgar Rice Burroughs
FAW-Fawcett Publications
FC-First Comics
FF-Famous Funnies
FH-Fiction House Magazines
FOX-Fox Features Syndicate
GIL-Gilberton
GK-Gold Key
GP-Great Publications
HARV-Harvey Publications
H-B-Hanna-Barbera
HILL-Hillman Periodicals
HOKE-Holyoke Publishing Co.
KING-King Features Syndicate
LEV-Lev Gleason Publications
ME-Magazine Enterprises
MEG-Marvel Ent. Group
MLJ-MLJ Magazines
MS-Mirage Studios
NOVP-Novelty Press
PG-Premier Group
PINE-Pines
PMI-Parents' Magazine Institute
PRIZE-Prize Publications
QUA-Quality Comics Group
REAL-Realistic Comics
RH-Rural Home
S & S-Street and Smith Publishers
SKY-Skywald Publications
STAR-Star Publications
STD-Standard Comics
STJ-St. John Publishing Co.
SUPR-Superior Comics
TC-Tower Comics
TM-Trojan Magazines
TOBY-Toby Press
UFS-United Features Syndicate
VITL-Vital Publications
WDC-The Walt Disney Company
WEST-Western Publishing Co.
WHIT-Whitman Publishing Co.
WHW-William H. Wise
WMG-William M. Gaines (E. C.)
WP-Warren Publishing Co.
YM-Youthful Magazines
Z-D-Ziff-Davis Publishing Co.

TIMELY/MARVEL/ATLAS COMICS. "A Marvel Magazine" and "Marvel Group" was the symbol used between December 1946 and May 1947 (not used on all titles/issues during period). The Timely Comics symbol was used between July 1942 and September 1942 (not on all titles/issues during period). The round "Marvel Comic" symbol was used between February 1949 and June 1950. Early comics code symbol (star and bar) was used between April 1952 and February 1955. The Atlas globe symbol was used between December 1951 and September 1957. The M over C symbol (beginning of Marvel Comics) was used between July 1961 until the price increased to 12 cents on February 1962.

TIMELY/MARVEL/ATLAS Publishers' Abbreviation Codes:

ACI-Animirth Comics, Inc.
AMI-Atlas Magazines, Inc.
ANC-Atlas News Co., Inc.
BPC-Bard Publishing Corp.
BFP-Broadcast Features Pubs.
CBS-Crime Bureau Stories
CIDS-Classic Detective Stories
CCC-Comic Combine Corp.
CDS-Current Detective Stories
CFI-Crime Files, Inc.
CmPI-Comedy Publications, Inc.
CmPS-Complete Photo Story
CnPC-Cornell Publishing Corp.
CPC-Chipiden Publishing Corp.
CPI-Crime Publications, Inc.
CPS-Canam Publishing Sales Corp.
CSI-Classics Syndicate, Inc.
DCI-Daring Comics, Inc.
EPC-Euclid Publishing Co.
EPI-Emgee Publications, Inc.
FCI-Fantasy Comics, Inc.
FPI-Foto Parade, Inc.
GPI-Gem Publishing, Inc.
HPC-Hercules Publishing Corp.
IPS-Interstate Publishing Corp.
JPI-Jaygee Publications, Inc.
LBI-Lion Books, Inc.
LCC-Leading Comic Corp.
LMC-Leading Magazine Corp.
MALE-Male Publishing Corp.
MAP-Miss America Publishing Corp.
MCI-Marvel Comics, Inc.
MgPC-Margood Publishing Corp.
MjMC-Marjean Magazine Corp.
MMC-Mutual Magazine Corp.
MPC-Medalion Publishing Corp.
MPI-Manvis Publications, Inc.
NPI-Newsstand Publications, Inc.
NPP-Non-Pareil Publishing Corp.
OCI-Official Comics, Inc.
OMC-Official Magazine Corp.
OPI-Olympia Publications, Inc.
PPI-Postal Publications, Inc.
PrPI-Prime Publications, Inc.
RCM-Red Circle Magazines, Inc.
SAI-Sports Actions, Inc.
SePI-Select Publications, Inc.
SnPC-Snap Publishing Co.
SPC-Select Publishing Co.
SPI-Sphere Publications, Inc.
TCI-Timely Comics, Inc.
TP-Timely Publications
20 CC-20th Century Comics Corp.
USA-U.S.A. Publications, Inc.
VPI-Vista Publications, Inc.
WFP-Western Fiction Publishing
WPI-Warwick Publications, Inc.
YAI-Young Allies, Inc.
ZPC-Zenith Publishing Co., Inc.

YOUR INFORMATION IS NEEDED: In order to make future Guides more accurate and complete, we are interested in any relevant information or facts that you might have. **Relevant and significant data includes:**

Works by the artists named elsewhere. **Caution:** Most artists did not sign their work and were imitated by others. When submitting this data, advise whether the work was signed or not. In many cases, it takes an expert to identify certain artists–so extreme caution should be observed in submitting this data.

Issues mentioned by Wertham and others in **Seduction, Parade...**, origin issues, first and last appearances of strips and characters, title continuity information, beginning and ending numbers of runs, atomic bomb, Christmas, Flag and infinity covers, swipes and photo covers.

To record something in the Guide, **documented** facts are needed. Please send a photo copy of indicia or page in question if possible.

Non-relevent data-Most giveaway comics will not be listed. Literally thousands of titles came out, many of which have educational themes. We will only list significant collectible giveaways such as March of Comics, Disney items, communist books (but not civil defense educational comics), and books that contain illustrated stories by top artists or top collected characters.

Good Luck and Happy Hunting. . . Robert M. Overstreet

STORAGE OF COMIC BOOKS

Proper storage is the most important factor in prolonging the life of your comic books. Exposure to oxygen and atmospheric pollutants as well as heat coupled with high humidity is believed to be the primary cause of aging and yellowing. Improper storage can accelerate the aging process.

The importance of storage is proven when looking at the condition of books from large collections that have surfaced over the past few years. In some cases, an entire collection has brown or yellowed pages approaching brittleness. Collections of this type were probably stored in too much heat or moisture, or exposed to atmospheric pollution (sulfur dioxide or light). On the other hand, other collections of considerable age (30 to 50 years) have emerged with creamy white, supple pages and little sign of aging. Thus we learn that proper storage is imperative to insure the long life of our comic book collections.

Store books in a dark, cool place with relative humidity of 40 - 75 percent and a temperature as cool as possible. Avoid excessive heat. Air conditioning is recommended. Do not use regular cardboard boxes, since most contain harmful acids. Use acid-free boxes instead. Seal books in Mylar or other suitable wrappings or bags and store them in the proper containers or cabinets, to protect them from heat, excessive dampness, ultraviolet light (use tungsten filament lights), polluted air, and dust.

Many collectors seal their books in plastic bags and store them in a cool dark room in cabinets or on shelving. Plastic bags should be changed every two to three years, since most contain harmful acids. Cedar chest storage is recommended, but the ideal method of storage is to stack your comics (preferably in Mylar bags vertically in acid-free boxes. The boxes can be arranged on shelving for easy access. Storage boxes, plastic bags, backing boards, Mylar bags, archival supplies, etc. are available from dealers. (See ads in this edition).

Some research has been done on deacidifying comic book paper, but no easy or inexpensive, clear-cut method is available to the average collector. In fact, it has not been proven whether deacidification is even necessary. The best and longest-lasting procedure involves soaking the paper in solutions or spraying each page with specially prepared solutions. These procedures should be left to experts. Covers of comics pose a special problem in deacidifying due to their varied composition of papers used.

Here is a list of persons who offer services in restoration or archival supplies:

– Bill Cole, P.O. Box 60, Randolph, MA 02368-0060. Archival supplies, storage protection, deacidification solutions.

– The Restoration Lab, Susan Cicconi, P.O. Box 632, New Town Branch, Boston, MA 02258.

– The Art Conservatory, Mark Wilson, P.O. Box 340, Castle Rock, WA 98611. Restoration.

– Comic Conservation Lab, Jef Hinds, P.O. Box 44803, Madison, WI 53744-4803. PH: (608) 277-8750. Restoration & preservation supplies.

– Lee Tennant Enterprises, P.O. Box 296, Worth, IL 60482. Preservation supplies.

Mylar is a registered trademark of the DuPont Company.

1992 MARKET REPORT
by Bob Overstreet

Prices continued their upward surge in the comic marketplace despite the extremely slow national economic recovery. The marketplace has maintained a solid rate of growth despite continued grim economic news. As the national economy gains momentum, long-term prospects for the marketplace appear very bullish.

Comic book prices in general have proven resistant to economic downturns of the past 20 years! This fact has gone unnoticed by professionals of other fields. As sales fell in other collectibles, several new dealers began to enter the comic marketplace. Since the supply of silver and golden age comics is limited, one can only expect additional price gains due to the increased competition.

All comic related fields registered strong growth and sales. Many factors influenced this. First, all the major auction houses are now selling rare comic books and related items (see the following special Christie's and Sotheby's auction reports). These auctions have received world-wide publicity and attention attracting new collectors and investors into our market. They sold an Action #1VF for $82,500. All major hobby magazines and financial publications published articles all year long. Comic character rings received much publicity, especially with the sale of a rare Superman ring bringing a record $125,000.00 (refer to the Overstreet Price Guide Companion for a complete ring pricing section with over 1,000 illustrations).

Many baseball card shops began stocking comic books and related items to increase profits from drooping sales in the card market. Baseball card show promoters are scheduling large card/comic shows beginning in 1993. This large influx of new collectors from the card market is already having impact in the comics market.

The **Overstreet Comic Book Grading Guide** and the **ONE/OWL** Comic Book Grading Card was released for the first time last year. This book and card remain current as updated versions will not be published for several years. It is our hope that these new tools for grading will make the job easier for the novice as well as the seasoned collector/dealer.

With the many changes occuring in the comics market today, **The Overstreet Comic Book Price Update** (published for 12 years) ceased publication. In its stead Overstreet Publications introduced the **Overstreet Comic Book Marketplace**, a brand new magazine with many new features for the collector.

The San Diego Comic Con again broke all previous records for attendance and size. The convention room was packed with people making it difficult getting around. Dealers with good inventory reported brisk sales. If you want to see the top artists, as well as all the professionals in the field, this is the conventon to attend.

SILVER AGE: Still one of the hottest areas of collecting. Books in high grade are still proving extremely difficult to locate in the marketplace and are usually sold at figures well above current guide levels. Books in the lower grades (less than fine) sell at a much slower pace at or below guide levels. DCs in high grade were almost impossible to keep in stock. DC and Marvel 15¢ and 20¢ covers are definitely starting to mature. Strong pickup in demand for this area of collecting.

GOLDEN AGE: Unlike silver age titles, golden age books in all grades sell very well at or above current guide levels. Given the large price increases in the silver age area, golden age titles seem poised for a major price increase. Scarce few nice golden age collections surfaced in 1992 while the market demand for these books kept increasing at a fast pace.

1920s Titles-Still very hard to find, remained in demand and sold well.

1930s Titles-Supply limitations once again governed the increases shown in this area of collecting. DC titles were still the most requested. *Adventure, Detective, More Fun, New Fun* and *New Adventure* remained very scarce. The few copies that did surface sold very quickly at and above guide list. A *Comics Magazine #1* in VF82 sold for $7,000, a *King Comics* #1 in FN55 brought $1,500. Other sales are: *Adventure Comics* #40-

FR5–$900, 48-FR14–$1300, *Amazing Man* #5-FR10–$950, *Detective Comics* #1-FR10–$3000, 1-PR4–$1800, 2-VG35–$1600, 27-FN68–$81,000. 27-FR10–$16,500, 27-FR5–$7000, 29-NM97(Allentown)–$15,000, 33-VG(R)50–$2700, 33-VG(R)–$2350, *Famous Funnies (Carnival)* vf(R)–$2100, *Merry Christmas From Mickey Mouse* nn-VF80 $600, *More Fun* #26-NM94–$750, *New York World's Fair 1939* FR12–$475, *Super Comics* #1-NM94–$850, *Superman* #1-FN65(R)–$19,000, 1-GD34(R)–$6,500, 2-FR32–$700.

1940s Titles-Superhero titles were the most popular, led by DC and followed very closely by Timely. Late '40s titles remained scarce, all publishers.

DC-Very strong demand. Prices will continue to rise in this most popular area of collecting. Batman, Superman, Flash, All Flash, Green Lantern, Sensation and Wonder Woman, late '40s issues of all superhero titles were in high demand. A few sales are: *Action* #15-VG40–$475, *Action* #32-VG45–$150, *Adventure* #48-FR14–$1300, 49-FN70–$425, 60-FN70–$400, *All American*-#16-FR10–$2900, 16-FR9–$2000, 16-PR2–$300, 18-VF(R)–$1770, 19-VG35–$900, 26-FN65–$550, *All Flash* #1-FN70–$1800, *All Star* #1-VF80–$4000, 3-NM97-$26,000, FN68(R)–$3600, 3-VG54–$3000, 8-FR14–$625 , 49-VF.82–$340, *Batman* #1-NM97–$40,000, 1-VF85–$18,000, 2-GD34–$995, 12-NM94–$1500, 27-VF82–$465, 47-VG50–$450, 47-GD25–$250, *Comic Cavalcade* #1-VG50–$700, *Detective* #47VF88–$700, *Flash Comics* #1-NM96–$20,000, 1-GD(R)25–$1550, 1-PR3–$900, *Fox & Crow* #1–VG50–$125, *Green Lantern* #1-VF(R)–$3400, *More Fun* #73-VG52–$1900, 73-GD34–$1100, 94, *Real Screen* #1-VF87–$385, *Sensation* #1-VG45–$700, *Superman* #10-VF88–$775, 76-FN70–$300, *Wonder Woman* #1-FR10–$500, 1-FN60–$1400, 20VF86–$200, 24-VF85–$175.

TIMELY-Increased demand for all titles led again by *Captain America* related titles. Sales were very brisk in all grades at prices over current guide levels. The previously large increases in the Centaur (pre-Timely) books has helped this area enormously. Some reported sales: *All Select* #1-VG52–$450, *All Winners* #1-VG52–$750, 1-VG40–$800, V2/1-VF80–$550, *Captain America* #1-FN74–$13,000, 1-GD32–$4000, 1-FR14–$2500, 1-PR3–$800, 2-VG52–$1250, 4-FN70–$875, 5-VF87–$1750, 9-FN72–$995, 13-FN73–$725, *Daring Mystery* #6-VG45–$375, 8-GD32–$250, *Human Torch* #5(Fall)-VF96–$1400, *Marvel Mystery* #16-VF82–$500, 33-NM94–$675, 52-FN70–$200, 62-FN65–$160, *Millie The Model* #3-NM94–$70, 5-VF82–$50, *Sub-Mariner*#1-GD30–$700, 2-VF82–$1250.

FAWCETT-Strong demand for *Captain Midnight, Ibis, Spy Smasher, Don Winslow* and *Captain Marvel* and related titles in all grades at or above current guide levels. *Captain Marvel Jr., Mary Marvel* and *Wow* had average sales. Mac Raboy cover issues sold well. The western titles slowed while the sports titles were still very hot and scarce. A *Bulletman* #1-VG52 sold for $395, *Nickel* #1-GD32–$250, *Special Edition* #1-GD32–$550.

CENTAUR- Very few copies were offered for sale. This company's books have average sales due to past price increases. An *Amazing Man* #5-FR10 sold for $950.

FOX-The early issues enjoyed good demand and remained scarce. The late '40s *Crimes By Women, Phantom Lady, Blue Beetle,* etc. were popular. A few sales: *All Top* #16-NM94–$200, 17-VF82–$150, *Zoot* #9-VF82–$150.

CLASSICS-High demand for VF or better early issues and LDC reprints. The later originals and reprints saw very slow growth. Interest in giveways, giants, boxes, etc. remained very high. Reported sales: #2(O)VF82–$900, Robin Hood Saks giveaway-VF82–$3000, Robin Hood Flour Co. Giveaway VF87–$1750, Gift Box "A" containing #1-5(O) average FN-VF65-82 sold for $5000.

FICTION HOUSE-Planet sold very well with average sales on other titles. Good girl artwork of this line continued to be very popular with collectors, with books selling at or above current guide levels in all conditions. Pickup in demand for all offbeat titles. Reported sales: *Firehair* #1-VF85–$150, *Jungle* #3-VF85–$325, continued to be the strongest title, selling well in all grades. All other titles enjoyed good solid sales. Early issues of Jumbo and Jungle remained hard to get. Sales: Planet #7-VF$550, 60-VF+$200, 70-VF+$125.

QUALITY-& MLJ- All titles had reported slow to average sales overall. Increased demand for all early Archie-related titles. Lou Fine issues are still in demand. *Military, Modern* and *Blackhawk* have a good following and showed a slight increase. Some of the offbeat titles like *Buccaneers* and *Lady Luck* sold very well. Reported sales: *Archie Annual* #1-VG50–$250, 2-VG50–$150, 3-VG–$65, *Police* 6-FN72–$400, 8-VF–$300, 10-VF–$400.

GLEASON-Slow to moderated sales overall with highest demand for *Daredevil, Boy* and *Silver Streak*. Early issues remained scarce. *Crime Does Not Pay* was very hot.

HARVEY-*All New* and *Green Hornet* were in high demand. Dick Tracy remained slow and all horror titles sold very well.

DISNEY-After five years of slow sales, reported sales on this company's books may be indicating a turnaround. There was high demand for all titles in all grades at guide levels. *Uncle Scrooge* was very hot. The Duck one-shots in NM or MT condition were in very high demand and impossible to find. The early issues of *Walt Disney's Comics & Stories* remained scarce.

FUNNY ANIMAL-All DC titles were very hot, esp. *Do Do & The Frog, Nutsy Squirrel* & *Real Screen. Looney Tunes* sold very well at guide price levels with the early issues seldom turning up. Dell, ACG, *Felix The Cat* and Timely titles remained popular. There is still a solid Pogo following. All TV characters' books were very hot: *Atom Ant, Flintstones, Augie Dogie, Quick Draw McGraw, Banana Splits, Rocky & His Friends, Milton The Monster, Peter Potomus, King Leonardo,* etc. Reported Sales: *Augie Dogie* #1-File copy–$60, *Banana Splits* #1-MT99–$30, *Barney & Betty* #1NM94–$20, *Clyde Crashcup* #2-NM94–$60, *King Leonardo* FC 1242-File copy–$70, *Mighty Heroes* #1-MT99–$75, *Mighty Hercules* #1-MT99–$75, *Milton The Monster* #1-File copy–$70, *Peter Potomus* #1-File copy–$40, *Quick Draw McGraw* FC1040-File copy–$75, *Rocky & His Friends* FC1166-File copy–$120.

NEDOR-Good sales overall. *Real Life* showed increased interest. Later issues of *Black Terror, Fighting Yank, Startling, America's Best,* etc. sold well in Fine or less. The early issues had average sales.

MISCELLANEOUS-*Supersnipe* was in high demand as well as *The Shadow, Doc Savage,* and *True Comics.* All books depicting Hitler, Tojo or Mussolini on the cover were very hot.

NEWSPAPER REPRINT-Average sales, esp. *Famous Funnies, Kerry Drake* and *Brenda Starr.*

1950s TITLES-The three hot publishers are DC, Atlas and EC. followed by ACG and Charlton.

ATLAS-All titles are very hot, esp. horror and science fiction. The #1 issues of *Strange Tales, Journey Into Mystery, Tales of Suspense, Tales to Astonish,* etc. are in very high demand. All early super hero prototype books are hot. The crime and offbeat titles sold well. Several White Mountain runs (*Mystery Tales,* etc.) sold at 2.5 times guide list. A few sales: *Journey Into Mystery* #3-VF82–$175, 60-VF86–$40, *Strange Tales* #10-FN70–$135, 12-VF87–$90, *Tales of Suspense* #1-VF89–$575, 12-FN70–$100, *Venus* #17-FN70–$160.

TV/MOVIE TITLES-Solid demand for movie titles but the big interest is focused on TV titles. The *Munsters, Jetsons, Astro Boy, Space Ghost, Star Trek, Dark Shadows, I Love Lucy* are very hot. Most other TV titles enjoyed good sales, especially whenever Dell or Gold Key file copies were offered. Increased demand for all Gold Key titles.

WESTERNS-Atlas titles were in high demand. Most Dell titles were slow to average sales. *Red Ryder* and the photo cover *Lone Rangers* had moderate sales. *Tim McCoy, Whip Wilson, Andy Devine,* and *Smiley Burnette* continued to be hot, with prices leveling on *Sunset Carson. Rawhide* was hot with good demand for the other TV titles. Reported sales: *Bob Steele* #1-FN70–$150, *Ken Maynard* #1-VF82–$225, 1-FN70–$175, *Roy Rogers* FC38-VG50–$150, *Smiley Burnette* #1-VF82–$200, 2-VF87–$140.

EC-Average sales overall, but Mad comics and mags were very hot. The war titles were slow to moderate. The popular HBO Tales From the Crypt is still keeping high interest in the horror mags. A Mad #1 in NM94 sold for $1750. All the Gaines EC sets sold in the recent Christie's auction bringing multiples of guide list.

GIANTS-Solid sales in lower grades if priced at guide. Higher grade copies, due to their scarcity sold very well at over guide.

3-D COMICS-Average sales were again reported.

ROMANCE COMICS-Small increases in demand, but still a relatively slow area of collecting.

ERB COMICS-Most Tarzan comics recorded slow sales.

HUMOR COMICS-All DC titles were in high demand, esp. *Advs. of Bob Hope, Jerry Lewis, Ozzie & Harriet, Sugar & Spike, Scribbly and Jackie Gleason* were hot. *Sad Sack, Dennis The Menace, Peanuts, Milt Gross, Big Daddy Roth* sold well. The Mad imitators, such as *Riot, Wild* and *Humbug,* etc. remained hot. All ACG titles remained in high demand.

GOOD-GIRL-ART COMICS-Remained very popular as it crosses over into humor, western, crime, horror and other genres.

1950s DC-Still the most popular single company collected from this period. All titles from super-hero to war to humor increased in value.

HORROR AND CRIME COMICS-Very hot in all grades, esp. pre-code issues.

SPORT COMICS-All titles are very, very hot, esp. the photo cover issues which are also very scarce. With sports card collectors coming into the comics market, look for even higher demand next year. Some examples are: *Jackie Robinson, Roy Campanella, Sports Action, Babe Ruth, Joe Louis,* etc.

ART COMICS-Kirby, Ditko and Wolverton were in high demand.

ORIGINAL ART-See the following Christie's and Sotheby's auction report. Congratulations to Avon Books and Jerry Weist for his new paperback price guide on original art available through all normal distribution channels.

SILVER AGE DC-This was the hottest area of collecting in the entire field with VF-MT copies fetching 150% of guide overall. Most popular: *Flash* #105-123, *Brave & Bold* #25-80, *Showcase* #1-85, *Mystery In Space* #53-90, *Strange Adventures* #71-180, *Star Spangled War Stories* #84-161, *House Of Secrets* #92. Selling at over double guide (high grade only) were: *House of Secrets* #61-80 and *Our Army At War*

#81-170. Lower grades were selling at or slightly above guide. Reported sales: Batman #171-NM94–$400, *Brave And The Bold* #28-FN56–$950, 30-FN72–$475, 34-FN60-$600, VF80–$750, *Flash* #105-VG45–$450, *Green Lantern* #1-NM94–$1500, 1-VG45–$365, *Jimmy Olsen* #1-FN60–$325, *Justice League* #1-VG40–$450, *Mystery In Space* #53-VF87–$500, *Showcase* #4-F(R)-$5000, 4-NM(R)–$6200, 8-VG45–$800, 13-VG45-$400, 14-GD30–$335, 17-VF82–$500, 18-VF78–$250, 22-VG50–$1000. 22-GD25–$325, 34-VF82–$525, 55-VF85–$125, *Superboy* #100-NM97–$125.

SILVER AGE MARVEL-There is still a very high demand for all mainstream titles in VF-MT condition, especially *Spider-Man. Amazing Fantasy* #15 was in very high demand. Other popular titles were: *Fantastic Four, Daredevil, Journey Into Mystery* #83, *X-Men* #1-66, *Marvel Spotlight* #2-12, *Fear* #20-30, *Iron Man* #1. Early *Spiderman* and *Fantastic Four* annuals were selling at over guide in NM condition. #1-50 is hot. There is always a short supply of early keys in high grade. Price resistance in the lower grades of most titles continued from last year. A few reported sales: *Amazing Fantasy* #15-VF–$8000, 15-VF–$7150, 15-VG(marvel chips)–$1500, 15-GD32–$700, *Amazing Spider Man* #1-VF75–$3500, 1-VG40–$900, 1-GD20–$500, 1-GD25–$625, 1-FR10–$225, 2-GD34–$300, 10-FN72–$210, 14-MT99–$1100, 129-NM96–$250, *Avengers* #1-FN65–$500, 1-VG45–$295, 3-NM94–$250, *Daredevil* #1-VF85–$700, *Fantastic Four* #1-VG50-$900, 1-GD25–$450, 1-FR14–$200, 48-VF82–$300, *Incredible Hulk* #1-VF(R)–$1575, 5-NM94–$500, *Journey Into Mystery* #83-FN70(R)–$900, *Tales of Suspense* #39-VF75–$900, 39-FN70–$550, *X-Men* #1-NM94–$1750, 1-FN55–$575, 1-VG40–$450.

SILVER AGE DELL/GOLD KEY-There is new emphasis on this area of collecting. Especially with the recent success of the new Valiant titles. *Doctor Solar, Magnus Robot Fighter, Turok, Space Family Robinson, Star Trek, M.A.R.S Patrol* and *Phantom* are popular titles.

SILVER AGE CHARLTON-Moderate sales on *Capt. Atom, Flash Gordon, Phantom, Thunderbolt, Space Adventures*, etc. The market is beginning to look at these books which are now over 20 years old.

SILVER AGE ACG-There is new demand for 1960s super hero issues of *Adventures Into The Unknown* and *Forbidden Worlds. Herbie* issues are also very hot.

1992 will always be remembered as the year Superman died. Beginning in October, an alien being, Doomsday and his henchmen invaded the Earth. For the next six weeks, the Doomsday saga unfolded, culminating in mid-November in *Superman* #75, with the Death of Superman. The following eight weeks brought us Funeral For a Friend, as Earth paid homage to its greatest fallen hero, Superman. Interest during the three month period reached new heights as news media covered the story from coast to coast. Sales were astonishing. Second and third printings were scheduled to attempt to satisfy a seemingly unquenchable thirst for the latest chapter of what was happening to everyone's favorite Super Hero. Emotion, frustration, anxiety, and profits kept pace with the growing interest as consumers, retailers, distributors and DC Comics scrambled to keep up with the demand. Although DC Comics, distributors and retailers all reacted quicker than a speeding bullet, no one anticipated how much the general public would be caught up with the news of the loss of Earth's greatest champion. This event undoubtedly brought more attention to the comic book industry than any other event ever. Sure, the Batman movie was great for the comic book industry but the attention was on the movie, the actors, the licensed product, the T-Shirts, and everything else related to Batman. This time the focus of everyone's attention was the comic books themselves!

The Death of Superman was not DC's only success of 1992. Batman returned to the silver screen in Batman Returns, the much anticipated sequel to the 1989 Batman movie. This time around, the anticipation far overshadowed the movie itself. Although the movie was a success, it was not as big a success as many hoped it would be and hence its success was diminished. On the other hand, the Animated Batman television series was much more successful than predicted and its weekly exposure helped increase public awareness of Batman and comics in general.

Perhaps DC's strongest departments are those that promote and support their editorial line. Much credit must be given to DC's public relations people who worked with the media to generate the interest in the Doomsday project. The consumer products area shined with highly acclaimed statues of Sandman, Batman and Lobo. The promotions programs were innovative with Green Lantern ring give-aways, Superman memorial arm bands, three dimensional pop ups and pop outs, blue prints, moving covers, holograms, and even a jeweled cover for Eclipso. And as always, Chris Demiris supported all the DC projects with an efficiently administered Co-op advertising program.

Meanwhile, on the other side of town, Marvel Comics was working hard to keep and increase their number one position in the comic field. The major event of 1992 for Marvel was their main man's 30th birthday. Yes, Spider-Man is now middle aged. Marvel celebrated the event with four hologram covers, one for each of the Spider-Man titles. Marvel also launched a new universe of the future in 1992. 2099 was the common denominator for Ravage by none other than Stan Lee, Spider-Man, Doom and Punisher. The first issues all sported foil covers and were well received by fandom. The X books had their share of the limelight with a mega crossover saga titled X-Cutioner's Song. Each issue was polybagged with a trading card and brought together X-Men, Uncanny X-Men, X-Factor and X-Force. Ren and Stimpy was Marvel's major attempt to go outside the traditional comic book marketplace and the title was an unexpected success, requiring a second printing of the first issue. Marvel made good and frequent use of cover enhancements to boost sales. Prism covers, embossed covers, foil covers, die cut covers, trading card inserts, trading card premiums and the like were all utilized by Marvel to generate casual reader interest in their product line.

The real attention grabbers of 1992 were two new kids on the block. Image and Valiant. Their development as comic book publishers is perhaps the most important long term event of 1992.

Valiant Comics, a division of Voyager Communications was the brain child of Jim Shooter and Steve Massarsky. They formed the comic book publishing company in 1989 after a failed attempt to purchase Marvel Comics. After two false starts in non Super Hero comics, Valiant licensed the popular but dormant, Western Publishing characters, including Solar, Magnus and Turok. They recruited creative talent such as Bob Layton, Don Perlin and Barry Windsor-Smith and marketing talent including Jon Hartz. They then re-launched their publishing efforts. They introduced many of their own creations, including Rai, X-O Manowar, Shadowman, the Harbinger kids, Bloodshot, Archer & Armstrong and Eternal Warrior and built a cohesive universe around all their characters. Good writing, good art, great marketing, and clearly the most innovative company in the industry launched Valiant to the forefront of fan interest. The eighteen issue Unity epic, involving the entire Valiant Universe for two months, with its marketing incentives brought Valiant into sharp focus for all of comic fandom. The gold editions of Archer & Armstrong, Eternal Warrior, HARD Corps, and Magnus quickly became some of the most desirable books in the hobby. The concept of #0 origin issues for Magnus, Rai and Harbinger was copied by several other publishers. The coupon redemption programs for Magnus #0 and Harbinger #0 created much sought after collectibles, while offering a second version available to everyone. The chromium cover of Bloodshot #1 made it as complete a sell through as Superman #75 (the Death issue) as both were released the same week in November. Sadly, in the summer of 1992, because of differences in their vision of where the company was going, Jim Shooter left Valiant. As often happens when a team loses a key player, the rest of the team worked a little harder and not only held together, but quickly demonstrated to all the doubting Thomases that nothing would stop Valiant in their rise to the top of the comic book publishing heap. Look for more new characters and titles from Valiant as well as new, creative marketing concepts to enhance their fine writing, art and editorial creativity as they continue to increase their sales and market.

The other huge growth company of 1992 was Image Comics. Image was formed as a loose union of disgruntled creators from Marvel Comics. The leaders of the upstart band were Jim (X-Men) Lee, Todd (Spider-Man) McFarlane, and Rob (X-Force) Liefeld. These three, who were the creative forces behind the three best selling comics ever, broke away from Marvel in 1992 and formed their own publishing company. Image's first publication was Rob Liefeld's Youngblood #1, which immediately broke the record for best selling independent. This record was short lived as Todd McFarlane's Spawn #1 surpassed it and his record was month's old when Jim Lee's Wild CATS #1 shattered it. Their success, as independent creators was immediate and overwhelming and soon attracted several more creators, including Erik (Savage Dragon) Larsen, Whilce (Wetworks) Portacio, Mark (Cyberforce) Silvestri and Jim (Shadowhawk) Valentino. More creators, with more projects were quick to join the ranks of Image and all had similar successes, if not quite the magnitude of these original creators. The main thing holding Image back from becoming a dominant force was their inability to produce their books on schedule. With a line average second to none, Image has the potential to rise to the top of the comic book ladder if they can publish more than four or five books a month. With their books rising rapidly in the secondary market, collectors and speculators alike look forward to each issue's appearance at their local comic book shop. Their prism and foil covers, their coupon redemptions, trading card inserts, limited editions and other borrowed marketing concepts have given them additional sales boosts. Keep your eye on Image to see if they can develop business skills comparable to their creative skills.

1992 saw the successful debut of Topps Comics as the trading card giant entered the comic book marketplace. Also Harris Comics entered the arena with a re-launch of former Warren titles, as well as new titles. Dark Horse increased their offerings significantly and held their market share, but many other independent publishers suffered greatly as the bigger, better staffed, better capitalized publishers raised the ante to stay in the comic publishing game. The black and white comics, adult oriented comics and other non mainstream comics all lost ground as the comic book consumer's attention and dollars shifted towards the bells and whistles supplied by the more marketing oriented publishers.

It is interesting that 1992 marked the 10th anniversary of the first creator owned Comic Book characters. Unlike all its predecessors, in 1982, Pacific Comics broke the mold with Captain Victory by the legendary Jack Kirby. The concept of the creator rather than the publisher owning or at least sharing the rights to his or her creation, has revolutionized the creative end of the Comic Book industry and has allowed creators to share the risks and rewards with the publishers. 1992 may eventually be looked upon as an equally important, historical turning point for Comic Books as the Death of Superman clearly demonstrated the potential audience for Comic Books. The velocity of the sell through on the Doomsday project may long be the benchmark for all publishers to aspire to. The broad and rapid acceptance of Valiant Comics and Image Comics by the readers, collectors, investors and speculators of Comic Books will be the model for new and old publishers to emulate for the coming decade. The quality of their editorial packages as well as the creativity of their marketing programs clearly indicate that the day of the loyal brand reader is behind us and to succeed in this market of the 90's publishers will have to offer the reader/collector the quality he/she demands.

With helpful assistance from Steve Geppi, Hugh O'Kennon, Ron Pussell, Sean Linkenback, Dan Malan, Rick Frogge, John Snyder, Terry Stroud, Gary Colabuono, Walter Wang, James Payette, Jerry Weist, Stephen Fishler, Harry Thomas, Bruce Hamilton, John Verzyl, Gary Carter, Mark Wilson and Joe Mannarino.

SOTHEBY'S SECOND COMIC AUCTION, FALL 1992 By Jerry Weist

The auction began with the Silver Age Comics and artwork, and of the first 150 lots only 14 did not sell. Record prices were brought on many pieces of artwork, and both DC and Marvel Silver Age groups sold for healthy prices. Three pages of Jack Kirby pre-hero art sold for $1,870. Jack Kirby/Dick Ayers cover for *Avengers* #23 sold for $3,300. *Hulk* #1-6 in VF sold for $5,500 and *Tales To Astonish* #27,35-101 sold for $5,225. Jack Kirby's cover to *Fantastic Four* #40 sold for $6,050, and a set of *Fantastic Four* #2-115 sold for $8,800. *Showcase Comics* #5,23-66 in VF sold for $5,500. Murphy Anderson's cover for *Showcase Comics* sold for $4,950 and his story for *Hawkman* #10 (sold after the auction) for $5,500. Joe Kubert's splash page for *Brave And The Bold* sold for $1,980, and a set of *Brave And The Bold Comics* (#28-69) sold for $4,125. The entire interior story to *Silver Surfer* #4 by John Buscema sold after the auction for $11,000. A pencil only Jack Kirby unpublished portrait drawing of Silver Surfer sold for $3,575. A later redo cover by Kirby/Lasick of *Amazing Fantasy* #15 sold for $5,500. Steve Ditko's unmasking page from *Amazing Spider-Man* #12 sold for a record $3,850 for a single page. Single pages from Jack Kirby for *Avengers* #1 and *Sgt. Fury* #2 (the splash) sold for $3,300 each! Kurt Schaffenberger's tryout page for Lois Lane sold for $3,575. Curt Swan's cover for *Superman* #180 sold for $3,025, and finally Jeff Jones' cover for *Wonder Woman* #199 sold for $3,850.

Most of the prices realized were within the estimates and many times prices realized were over the high end of the estimate. Many people have commented to me that they were amazed at both the depth of our Silver Age consignments and the very reasonable estimates that were assigned for this second auction. The single most remarkable fact from this part of our auction is that Jack Kirby is indeed the king! How could so much of his original artwork be offered at one time and bring such consistently high prices? The answer is in the quality of the selection and the strength of numbers of Jack's serious fans who showed up to bid, which is a tribute to this great artist. Everyone should remember that only one key piece of original artwork from the Silver Age passed, Murphy Anderson's cover for *Hawkman* #1 passed at $7,000.

The first half of Sotheby's second auction ended with above average sales for both science fiction artwork (a new experiment), Al Feldstein's S.F. oil painting sold for $4,400 and Michael Whelan's cover for Ray Bradbury's "The Martian Chronicles" sold for $12,000. The underground comic artwork was highlighted by Robert Crumb's "Fuzzy the Bunny" (six page story) selling for $5,500 and Bill Griffith's cover to *Yow Comics* #1 selling for $3,300. This first half ended with two passed sales on paintings by Frank Frazetta, and one sale of Carl Barks' "Red Bullet Valley" painting for $22,000.

Collectors should realize that Sotheby's has realized over $250,000 in post auction sales. Included are sales for Frank Frazetta's lot #359 "The Night They Raided Minsky's" for $48,400. Frank Frazetta's story for lot #358 did sell after the auction for $8,800, but the big news for fans will be the sale of our final lot #437, the Carl Barks painting "Who's Out There?" (the first money-bin painting to be offered in a long time) for $121,500. This stands as a new world record for a work of comic art sold at auction and along with Sotheby's world record price for the highest price ever paid for a comic book for the *Action Comics* #1 in VF at $82,500, represents an extraordinary success for comics in the present recession economy that we are experiencing.

The second half of Sotheby's auction featured what many people have since marked to be an historic offering of once in a lifetime originals along with key Golden Age comics that were on the average in higher grade than our first auction's offerings. Will Eisner's cover art to *Spirit* #15 sold for $3,300. The cover artwork to *Detective Comics* #59 sold for $13,200. *Detective Comics* #27 in VF sold for $38,500. The Mile High *Detective Comics* #8 sold for $4,125. The Mile High *More Fun Comics* sets of #57 and 62 (sold after the auction) sold for $5,775 and #63 and 66 sold for $4,675. An unrestored copy of *Batman* #1 in fine condition sold for $18,700. The cover to *Master Comics* #27 by Mac Raboy sold for $11,000. The October *Marvel Comics* (restored by Susan Cicconi) sold for $16,500 and the November copy of *Marvel Comics* #1 (restored by Susan Cicconi) sold for $15,500. The cover artwork to *Worlds Finest* #33 by Mortimer sold for $3,300, and a VF copy of *Action Comics* #1 sold for $82,500.

Collectors should remember that every key Golden Age comic sold except for *Superman* #1 (which nearly sold after the auction for the middle estimate). This is also remarkable during a recession when there were double copies offered of *Batman* #1 and *Marvel Comics* #1 and *Superman* #1. These sales in respectable numbers on double copy offerings should signal that Golden Age comics still have a strong and not a weak market.

Newspaper strip artwork and E.C. artwork with this auction showed mixed results. It appears that strip collectors require excellent examples of originals to bring brisk bidding as with our three Burne Hogarth originals which brought $7,125, $7,125 and $4,125 each. A Milton Caniff *Terry & the Pirates* Sunday with three daily stips brought $2,475. A *Dick Tracy* daily by Chester Gould sold for $1,650. A Hal Foster *Tarzan* Sunday sold for $5,500, and a Hal Foster *Prince Valiant* (sold after the auction) for $2,450, and two Alex Raymond *X-9* daily strips (sold after the auction) for $2,200. However lot #371 Alex Raymond's *Flash Gordon* Sunday passed at $21,000. With E.C. artwork the cover to Mad #5 by Bill Elder sold for $4,950, and the story by Jack Davis for "The Black Ferris" (by Ray Bradbury from Haunt #18) sold for $4,125.

For the second year in a row the A.C.G. (Committee for Authenticity, Certification and Grading), chairpersoned by Gary M. Carter functioned admirably under pressure. Pat Kohanek, Mark Wilson, Joe Dungan, Bill Howard, Jim Payette, Steve Geppi, Susan Cicconi and Roger Hill flew in from different points in America for the express purpose of making Sotheby's second comic auction safer, ethical and more secure for the buyers of this auction. We can note with pride that during the two auctions no buyer has attempted to return any original art or comic book for any reasons of dissapointment in the description of condition. There is a reason for this, the consultant along with the help of the A.C.G. committee are striving each year to set standards that are thorough and respect the rights of the buyers to spend with confidence.

Sotheby's is already planning its third comic book auction. We have signed already a beautiful watercolor original by George Herriman with the entire cast of characters, in a hand-made and embellished frame designed by Herriman, along with a full color original by R.F. Outcault of the *Yellow Kid* that measures over 24" tall. There will be major and historic offerings of Golden Age key first issues that will outdo our prior offerings. The Silver Age selection will continue to excite and amaze comic's fans with its continuing depth and quality. Forthcoming announcements and advertising will unfold future consignments and dates for comics fandom.

CHRISTIE'S SETS RECORDS AT AUCTION, Fall 1992 By Joe Mannarino

Christie's inaugural Halloween Comic Collectibles sale October 31, 1992 was highlighted by record prices.

Frank Frazetta's "Mastermind/Fighting Man of Mars", oil on masonite, sold for $82,500, a record at auction for a Frazetta.

Carl Barks oil on masonite, "Menace Out Of The Myths" which included two small preliminary paintings and four pencil studies sold for $77,000.

Floyd Gottfredson Mickey Mouse Sunday page with the matching Silly Symphonies topper from May 26, 1935 sold for a comic strip art record, at auction of $30,800. It was estimated at $18,000 - $24,000.

The auction was well attended with numerous phone and left bids. Reversing recent trends, Frazetta did extraordinarily well with 10 lots sold. Highlights beside the "Mastermind/Fighting Man of Mars" painting, included a science fiction landscape 8x15 1/2 oil which sold for $20,900 and "Cowboy and Indian" an oil on masonite which sold for $11,000. A Doubleday book club illustration sold for $6,600, and several illustrations sold for well over estimate.

Disney art did extremely well, aside from the Mickey Sunday page and the Barks painting, Walt Kelly's original cover from Walt Disney's Comics & Stories #42 sold for $9,900. A Silly Symphonies Donald Duck and Mickey Mouse Sunday, both from 1937, sold for $8,800 each. A Mickey daily 9/12/36 and 8/28/34 sold for $7,700 and $6,000 respectively, well over pre-sale estimates. A real surprise was a 26 page Uncle Scrooge story with cover by Don Rosa that sold for $8,250, double the pre-sale high estimate.

In comic books the William Gaines file copies, were the big hit. Fifteen lots were offered by title, including the classic horror, and sci-fi titles, *Vault Of Horror* and *Weird Science*. Sales ranged from approximately double Overstreet price guide to over four times guide. Highlights included: *Vault Of Horror* #12-40 along with *War Against Crime* #10 & 11 selling for $26,400; *Tales From The Crypt* #20-46 along with *Crypt Of Terror* #17-19 and *Crime Patrol* #15 & 16 sold for $26,400; *Panic* #1-12 sold for $2,240. The long running pop-culture classic, *Mad* (which began as a comic before converting to a magazine) was represented by the first 23 issues. Estimated at $13,000, the run sold for $17,600 which translates to triple guide.

High grade Silver Age remains very strong, a near mint *Amazing Spider-Man* #1 sold for $8,200 and runs of Silver Age Marvel titles sold for well above estimate. (ie: *X-Men* #2-20 estimated at $700 sold for $2200; *Avengers* lot, estimated at $600 sold for $1650, etc.).

High grade Golden Age key issues did very well also, examples include: *Green Lantern* #1 (GA) VF–$5280, *Silver Streak* #6 NM–$4400, *Plastic Man* #1, Mile High (Church collection)–$3,850, *Sensation* #1 VF–$3080, *Superboy* #1 VF–$2,640, *More Fun* #9 VG–$2200, *Thunda* #1, Mile High NM –$1320, *Lone Ranger* #1 NM–$1045. A copy of *Action Comics* #1 in VGF sold for $26,400 and a very good copy of *Detective* #27 sold for $24,200. Disney did well with a rare complete run of *Mickey Mouse Magazine* selling for $12,100 and the rare Bibo and Lang *Mickey Mouse Book* in FVF for $4840.

It was obvious that buyers had an eye on guide and the 10% buyers premium when it came to middle grade Gold and Silver Age books as bids consistently hovered near the pre-sale estimates. Lots that featured Church (Mile High) books without either notable characters nor from the big three publishers showed resistance at double guide.

Comic book art in general did extremely well, examples, aside from the aforementioned Disney art, include: Cover painting to *Savage Sword of Conan* #1 by Vallejo–$8,250, Kurtzman cover to *Mad* #6–$7150, Wrightson Frankenstein plate–$6600, Kirby 13 page Antman story from *Tales To Astonish* #36–$6600, Wally Wood six page V-Vampire story from *Mad* #3–$5280, *Teen-age Dope Slaves* #1 cover–$3850, Steranko *Strange Tales* #159 cover–$3300, *Captain America* #110 spash–$2200, Ditko page from *Spider-Man* #36–$2750 and the cover to *Creeper* #2–$1760. E.C. art did very well as did most Silver Age art. The Harvey archive material, sold in most cases for over current market prices but below pre-sale estimates. The pulp cover painting from *Amazing Stories*, Jan., 1944 sold for a record $14,300.

Comic strip art showed an interesting new trend. Humor strip art did very well as compared to the classic adventure strips which have dominated the market in recent years. Twelve of the top twenty lots were humor strips, led by Disney. Aside from the Disney art, a 1955 Schulz, Peanuts Sunday sold for $4620, a 1979 daily for $1540, a 1943 Herriman Krazy Kat for $4180, a 1936 Segar Popeye daily sold for $2090. Nine lots of McManus art all sold. In the adventure genre, a 1941 Hogarth Tarzan sold for $3300, a 1948 for $2090, a 1966 Prince Valiant sold for $2860 and twenty two lots of Dick Tracy by Gould sold, the highlight being a 5/10/34 daily selling for $2640. Serious questions can be raised about the adventure art market above the $10,000 level, particularly Alex Raymond material. A rare prime period 1935 full page Flash Gordon passed at $18,000, as did a beautiful example from 1939. A full page Jungle Jim from 1935, considered to be among the finest examples known, sold for a disappointing $9350. These examples, coupled with the results of the recent Sotheby's sale, raise questions as to the current veracity of this market.

The catalogue for the sale, promises to become an important reference work for years to come. It is still available, along with a list of prices realized from Christie's catalogue department for $25 in person or $30 by mail. To order the catalogue, send payment to Christie's Publications, 21-24 44th Avenue, Long Island City, NY 11101 or call 718/784/1480.

INVESTOR'S DATA

The following table denotes the rate of appreciation of the top 50 most valuable Golden Age books over the past year and the past five years (1988-1993). The retail value for a NM copy of each book in 1993 is compared to its value in 1992 and 1988. The 1971 values are also included as an interesting point of reference. The rate of return for 1993 over 1992, and the yearly average rate of return for each year since 1988, is given.

The place in rank is given for each comic by year, with its corresponding NM value. This table can be very useful in forecasting trends in the market place. For instance, the investor might want to know which book is yielding the best dividend from one year to the next, or one might just be interested in seeing how the popularity of books changes from year to year. For instance, All Star #1 was in 31st place in 1992 and has dropped to 34th place in 1993.

The following tables are meant as a guide to the investor and it is hoped that they might aid him in choosing books in which to invest. However, it should be pointed out that trends may change at anytime and that some books can meet market resistance with a slowdown in price increases, while others can develop into real comers from a presently dormant state. In the long run, if the investor sticks to the books that are appreciating steadily each year, he shouldn't go very far wrong.

The Silver Age titles continued to show movement, especially early issues of Marvels and DCs in high grade. Golden & Silver Age titles are continuing to appreciate faster than economic inflationary values during the same period.

The following tables show the rate of return of the 50 most valuable Golden Age books, and the 40 most valuable Silver Age books over the past year. It also shows the average yearly rate of return over the past five years (1993-1988). Comparisons can be made in the same way as in the previous table of the Top 50 titles. Ranking in many cases is relative since so many books have the same value. These books are listed alphabetically within the same value.

TOP 50 TITLES

TOP 50 TITLES & RATE OF INCREASE OVER 1992 AND 1988 GUIDE VALUES

Title	1993 Guide Rank	& Value	% Change from '92 Value	Avg. Yrly. Return '88-'93	1992 Guide Rank	& Value	1988 Guide Rank	& Value
Detective Comics #27	1	85,000	42%	65%	1	60,000	4	20,000
Action Comics #1	2	75,000	50%	32%	2	50,000	1	28,650
Superman #1	3	65,000	63%	43%	3	40,000	3	20,800
Marvel #1	4	63,000	58%	27%	3	40,000	2	27,000
Whiz Comics #1	5	42,000	71%	32%	5	24,500	5	16,250
Batman #1	6	33,500	68%	60%	6	20,000	8	8,400
All American #16	7	32,000	100%	88%	7	16,000	12	5,900
Captain America #1	8	30,000	100%	75%	8	15,000	10	6,300
More Fun #52	9	25,000	108%	39%	11	12,000	7	8,500
Detective Comics #1	10	20,000	43%	24%	10	14,000	6	9,100
Flash Comics #1	10	20,000	85%	71%	12	10,800	18	4,400
All Star #3	12	17,500	94%	41%	13	9,000	13	5,740
Detective Comics #33	13	17,000	118%	61%	17	7,800	21	4,200
New Fun #1	13	17,000	13%	61%	8	15,000	21	4,200
Capt. Marvel Adv. #1	15	16,000	93%	33%	15	8,300	11	6,000
Detective Comics #38	15	16,000	88%	56%	14	8,500	21	4,200
More Fun #53	17	15,500	89%	36%	16	8,200	14	5,500
Adventure #40	18	14,000	124%	147%	21	6,250	88	1,680
Famous Funnies	19	12,000	67%	112%	18	7,200	75	1,820
Detective Comics #29	20	11,000	90%	61%	23	5,800	40	2,700
Detective Comics #31	20	11,000	90%	68%	23	5,800	46	2,500
Detective Comics #32	20	11,000	340%	127%	95	2,500	103	1,500
Green Lantern #1	23	10,000	100%	60%	32	5,000	46	2,500
Amazing-Man #5	24	9,500	73%	34%	25	5,500	25	3,500
Famous Funnies #1	25	9,000	50%	97%	22	6,000	99	1,540
Marvel Mystery #2	26	8,500	57%	19%	27	5,400	18	4,400
NY World's Fair 1939	26	8,500	111%	80%	43	4,020	86	1,700
Wow Comics #1	28	8,000	48%	12%	27	5,400	15	5,000
Human Torch #1	29	7,800	86%	29%	40	4,200	28	3,200
Adventure #48	30	7,500	56%	73%	35	4,800	93	1,610
Century of Comics nn	30	7,500	50%	87%	32	5,000	114	1,400
Double Action Comics #2	30	7,500	10%	3%	19	6,800	9	6,500
Jumbo Comics #1	30	7,500	88%	46%	44	4,000	53	2,275
New Fun #2	30	7,500	15%	26%	20	6,500	27	3,250
All Star #1	35	7,000	37%	22%	31	5,100	26	3,300
Daring Mystery #1	35	7,000	59%	27%	39	4,400	32	3,000
Walt Disney C & S #1	37	6,700	72%	22%	49	3,900	28	3,200
All Star #8	38	6,500	81%	42%	54	3,600	57	2,100
Marvel Mystery Comics #5	38	6,500	71%	21%	50	3,800	30	3,185
Funnies On Parade	40	6,000	122%	80%	88	2,700	145	1,200
More Fun #55	40	6,000	88%	43%	61	3,200	71	1,900
Red Raven #1	40	6,000	50%	21%	44	4,000	35	2,900
Sub-Mariner #1	40	6,000	76%	28%	59	3,400	46	2,500
World's Best #1	40	6,000	82%	41%	60	3,300	68	1,960
Action Comics #2	45	5,600	8%	4%	30	5,200	17	4,725
Motion Pictures Funnies	46	5,500	0%	2%	25	5,500	15	5,000
Detective Comics #28	46	5,400	0%	5%	27	5,400	18	4,400
Batman #2	48	5,200	8%	22%	35	4,800	46	2,500
Big Book of Fun #1	49	5,000	19%	18%	40	4,200	43	2,625
Detective Comics #2	49	5,000	11%	16%	37	4,500	39	2,765
Donald Duck MOC #4	49	5,000	0%	13%	32	5,000	32	3,000
New Comics #1	49	5,000	11%	28%	37	4,500	57	2,100

TREND ANALYSIS

THOUSAND OF DOLLARS

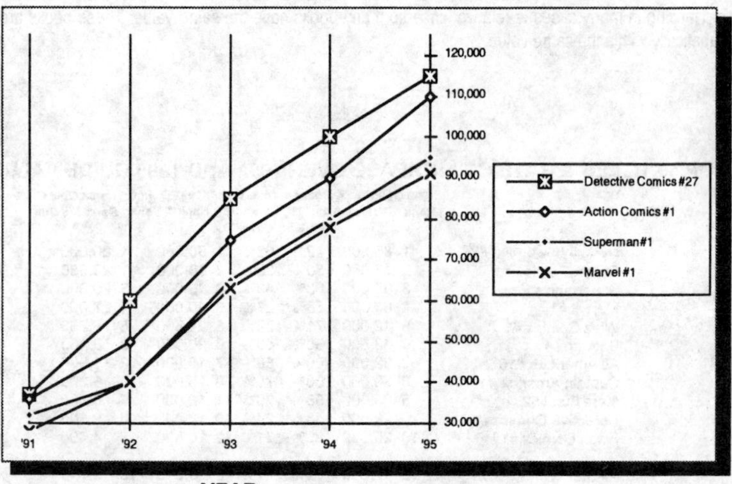

YEAR

The above trend analysis based on prices from the 1988-1993 Overstreet Price Guide.

40 MOST VALUABLE SILVER AGE BOOKS AND RATE OF RETURN

Title	1993 Guide Rank	1993 Guide Value	% Change from '92 Value	Avg. Yrly. Return '88-'93	1992 Guide Rank	1992 Guide Value	1988 Guide Rank	1988 Guide Value
Showcase #4	1	9,400	71%	110%	1	5,500	2	1,450
Fantastic Four #1	2	7,200	76%	84%	2	4,100	3	1,380
Amazing Fantasy #1	3	7,000	75%	73%	3	4,000	1	1,500
Amazing Spider-Man #1	4	6,800	74%	116%	4	3,900	5	1,000
Incredible Hulk #1	5	4,000	146%	101%	8	1,625	6	660
Showcase #8	6	3,800	117%	129%	6	1,750	16	510
Adventure #247	7	2,600	42%	19%	5	1,825	4	1,350
Brave & The Bold #28	7	2,600	53%	75%	7	1,700	10	550
Detective #225	9	2,500	56%	58%	9	1,600	7	640
Showcase #22	10	2,250	50%	71%	10	1,500	18	495
Journey Into Mystery #83	11	2,200	83%	73%	16	1,200	19	475
X-Men #1	12	2,150	43%	52%	10	1,500	8	600
Flash #105	13	2,000	33%	53%	10	1,500	10	550
Tales Of Suspense #39	13	2,000	33%	75%	10	1,500	25	420
Amazing Spider-Man #2	15	1,800	50%	75%	16	1,200	26	380
Justice League #1	16	1,750	40%	41%	14	1,250	9	575
Adventure #210	17	1,650	32%	66%	14	1,250	-	385
Fantastic Four #2	18	1,600	33%	38%	16	1,200	10	550
Showcase #13	18	1,600	33%	64%	16	1,200	26	380
Showcase #14	18	1,600	33%	64%	16	1,200	26	380
Showcase #1	21	1,500	114%	47%	34	700	20	450
Showcase #6	21	1,500	67%	66%	24	900	29	350
Tales To Astonish #27	21	1,500	36%	35%	21	1,100	10	550
Green Lantern #1	24	1,400	40%	44%	22	1,000	24	438
Showcase #9	24	1,400	100%	127%	34	700	57	190
Avengers #1	26	1,250	32%	28%	23	950	15	520
Fantastic Four #5	26	1,250	56%	73%	25	800	37	270
Brave & The Bold #1	28	1,200	50%	24%	25	800	14	540
Fantastic Four #4	28	1,200	50%	51%	25	800	30	340
Incredible Hulk #2	28	1,200	92%	78%	43	625	39	245
Superman's Pal J. Olsen #1	28	1,200	50%	28%	25	800	17	500
Amazing Spider-Man #3	32	1,000	33%	71%	31	750	42	220
Brave & The Bold #29	32	1,000	43%	71%	34	700	42	220
Brave & The Bold #30	32	1,000	43%	71%	34	700	42	220

40 MOST VALUABLE SILVER AGE BOOKS AND RATE OF RETURN (Cont.)

Title	1993 Guide Rank & Value		% Change from '92 Value	Avg. Yrly. Return '88-'93		1992 Guide Rank & Value		1988 Guide Rank & Value
Fantastic Four #3	32	1,000	25%	25%	25	800	21	440
Daredevil #1	32	1,000	29%	47%	30	775	34	300
Incredible Hulk #6	32	1,000	122%	136%	63	450	-	128
Showcase #10	32	1,000	54%	85%	40	650	57	190
Chall. of the Unknown #1	39	950	31%	40%	32	725	32	315
Showcase #17	39	950	46%	59%	40	650	40	240

TOP TEN ISSUES

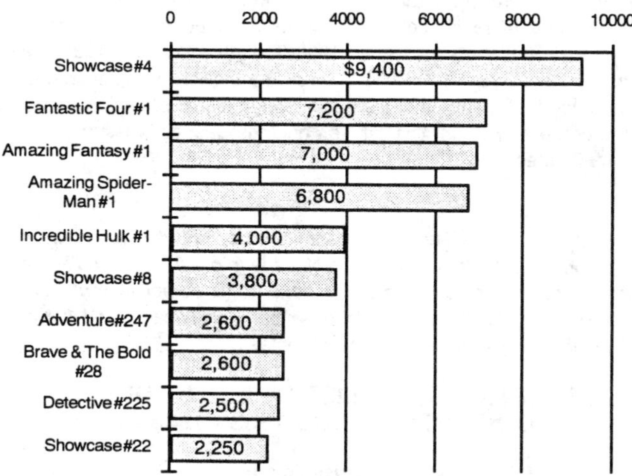

THE FIRST WAVE OF COMIC BOOKS 1933-1943 (Key books listed and ranked)

The first modern format comic book came out in 1933 and represents the beginning of comic books as we know them today. The impact of these early characters and ideas are today deeply engrained in American folklore and continue to feed and inspire this ever changing industry.

Over the years historians, collectors and bibliofiles have tried to make some sense out of this era. The question "what are considered to be the most important books?" has been a topic of discussion and debate for many years. With certain criteria considered, how would the top key issues be ranked in order of importance? How would they relate to each other? In an attempt to answer some of these questions, the following list has been prepared. The books are grouped chronologically in the order they were published. The most important books are ranked into seven tiers, with the top six designated with stars. The more important the book is, the more stars it receives. The following criteria were used to determine the importance and placement of each book in each tier:

a. Durability of Character(s)
b. Durability of title
c. Popularity of character(s)
d. First app. anywhere of a major character
e. First issue of a title
f. Originality of character (first of a type)
g. First or most significant work of a major artist
h. Starts a trend
i. First of a genre
j. Historical significance
k. First of a publisher
l. First appearance in comic books of a character from another medium

This list was compiled by several people * and represents a collective opinion of all. The list is not perfect by any means. Adjustments will be made over time as more input is received. The final ranking of a book depends greatly on the overall importance and impact of that book on the comic book market. Obviously, the further you get away from the top key books, the more difficult it becomes for proper ranking. For this reason, books ranked in the lower numbered tiers could change drastically. The final rating given a book is not based entirely on the quantity of points it receives, but rather the overall weight of the points it does receive. For example, the first appearance of The Fighting Yank is not as important as the first appearance of Superman who was a trend setting character and long lasting.

In the comics market there are several comics that have become high demand, valuable books due primarily to rarity. A list of the top key books ranked due to value, demand and rarity would look entirely different than what we have here. As we have learned in coins, stamps and other hobbies, rarity is an important factor that affects value and it is not our intention to demean the collectibility of any particular book that is rare. Quite the contrary. There are many rare books that would enhance anyone's collection. Consideration of rarity, for the ranking of books in this list has been kept at a minimum.

The following list covers the period 1933 through 1943 and includes every key book of this period of which we are currently aware. Any omissions will be added in future lists. It should be noted that many other issues, although highly collectible, were not considered important for the purpose of this list: i.e., origin issues, early issues in a run, special cover and story themes, etc.

**Special thanks is due Landon Chesney who contributed considerable energy and thought to the individual write-ups; to David Noah who polished and edited, and to the following people who contributed their time and ideas to the compilation of this list: Hugh O'Kennon, Steve Geppi, Richard Halegua, John Snyder, Joe Tricarichi, Walter Wang, Jon Warren, Bruce Hamilton, Ray Belden and Chuck Wooley.*

CHRONOLOGICAL LIST OF KEY COMIC BOOKS FOR PERIOD 1933 - 1943

(All first issues listed)

GENRE CODES (Main theme)

NOTE: The stars signify the ranking of books into seven different tiers of importance. The top (most important) books receive six stars (1st tier), dropping to no star (7th tier) as their significance diminishes. The following information is provided for each comic: 1. Ranking, 2. Title, 3. Issue number, 4. Date, 5. Publisher, 6. Genre code, 7. Description. 8. Criteria-codes.

An - Anthology (mixed)	**H** - Costumed/Superhero	**Mg** - Magic	**Sp** - Sport
Av - Aviation	**Hr** - Horror	**M** - Movie	**TA** - Teen-Age
Cr - Crime	**Hm** - Humor	**R** - Strip Reprints	**Tr** - True Fact
D - Detective	**J** - Jungle	**Re** - Religious	**W** - War
F - Funny	**Lit** - Literature	**SF** - Science Fiction	**Ws** - Western

PRE-GOLDEN AGE PERIOD

1933 ■

★★★★**FUNNIES ON PARADE** nn (1933, Eastern Color,- R)-The very first comic book in the modern format reprinting popular strip characters. Given away to test the feasibility of demand for repackaged Sunday newspaper funnies. (An 8-page tabloid folded down to 32 pages).
(a,c,d,e,h,i,j,k,l)

★★★★**FAMOUS FUNNIES, A CARNIVAL OF COMICS** nn (1933, Eastern Color, R)-The second comic book. Given away to test reader demand. Its success set up another test- to come in the following year to see if the public would actually pay 10 cents for this type of product (an 8-page tabloid folded down to 32 pages). The first of three first issues for this title.
(a,b,c,e,f,h,j)

★**CENTURY OF COMICS** nn (1933, Eastern Color, R) The third comic book. A 100-pager given away with three times the contents of the previous two books.
(e,j)

1934 ■

★**SKIPPY'S OWN BOOK OF COMICS** nn (1934, Eastern Color, R)-The fourth comic book. The first to feature a single character-this wasn't tried again until ***Superman*** No. 1.
(e,j)

★★★★**FAMOUS FUNNIES, SERIES I** (1934, Eastern Color, R)-The first comic book sold to the general public (through chain stores). The acid test, its unprecedented success set up the beginning of the first continuous series (anthology reprint) title in comics, and started the chain-reaction.
(a,b,c,e,f,h,j)

★★★★★**FAMOUS FUNNIES** No. 1 (7/34 Eastern Color, R)-Satisfied with the public response, this issue began the series and was the first comic book sold to the general public through newsstand distribution.
(a,b,c,e,f,h,j)

★**FAMOUS FUNNIES** No. 3 (9/34, Eastern Color, R)-This issue ushered in the famous and very popular Buck Rogers strip reprints. Not trend setting, but important for the survival of the run which lasted 22 years.

(a,b,c,f,i,j,l)

1935 ■

★★★★**NEW FUN COMICS** No. 1 (2/35, DC, An)-The first prototype of the modern comic in that it featured an anthology format of continuing characters and original rather than reprinted material. First of the DC line and the first tabloid-size book (albeit short-lived), surviving 13 years as ***More Fun Comics***.
(b,e,h,i,j,k)

★**MICKEY MOUSE MAGAZINE** No. 1 (Sum/35, K.K., F)— Magazine-size protocomic introducing the already legendary transfer characters to the fledgling comic book market. This title first appeared in 1933 as a black & white giveaway comic, and after going through format changes, eventually led to the ultimate "funny animal" comic, ***Walt Disney's Comics & Stories***, to come five years later.
(a,b,c,e,g,j,k)

★**NEW COMICS** No. 1 (12/35, DC, An)-DC felt enough confidence in the market to issue a second anthology title featuring original, continuing characters. It was second only to ***New Fun*** of its kind. Evolved into ***Adventure Comics***, warhorse of the DC line. DC parlayed the second most perfect comic book title (the first is Action) into a forty plus year run.
(b,e,h,j)

1936 ■

MORE FUN COMICS No. 7 (1/36, DC, An)-DC cancelled the title ***New Fun*** due to the appearance of ***New Comics***, continuing the series under this changed title.
(b,e,j)

★★★**POPULAR COMICS** No. 1 (2/36, Dell, R)-The second anthology format title of continuing reprint strips. First of the Dell line, the third publisher to enter the field. Featuring the first comic book appearance of *Dick Tracy, Little Orphan Annie, Terry & the Pirates* and others, lasting 13 years.
(a,b,c,e,j,k,l)

BIG BOOK OF FUN COMICS (Spr/36, DC, An)-The first annual in comics (56 pages, large size; reprints from New Fun No. 1-5).
(e,h,i,j)

★★★**KING COMICS** No. 1 (4/36, McKay, R)-Ties as the third continuous series reprint title. The first of a publisher (4th to enter the field). Showcase title of all the King Feature characters-the most popular and widely circulated in the world, featuring Segar's *Popeye* and Raymond's *Flash Gordon* series as the mainstay, lasting 16 years.
(a,b,c,e,j,k,l)

★★★**TIP TOP COMICS** No. 1 (4/36, UFS, R)-Ties as the third continuous series reprint anthology title. The first of a publisher (5th to enter the field). Featuring the Tarzan and Li'l Abner series and surviving 25 years.
(a,b,c,e,j,k,l)

★**COMICS MAGAZINE, THE** (Funny Pages) No. 1 (5/36, Comics Mag., An)-The third anthology format title of original material. The first of a publisher (6th to enter the field). This book is unique in that its cover and entire contents were purchased from DC. This material created gaps in the story line continuity of DC's titles ***More Fun*** and ***New Adventure*** from which it came.
(e,j,k)

WOW COMICS No. 1 (7/36, McKay, An)-The fourth anthology title of original material. McKay's second series (first with original contents), lasting only 4 issues to 11/36. The unpublished inventory formed the basis of the Eisner/Iger shop.
(e)

NEW BOOK OF COMICS No. 1 (6-8/36, DC, An)-The second annual in comics; 100 pages, reprinting popular strips from ***More Fun*** and ***New Comics.*** Second and last issue appeared in Spring of 1938.
(e)

FUNNIES, THE No. 1 (10/36, Dell, R)-Having published this title six years earlier as a tabloid, Dell brought it back as a regular comic book. Featuring more popular strip charcacters, this became Dell's second comic book title and ran for 6 years.
(b,e)

FUNNY PAGES No. 6 (11/36, Comics Mag., An)- Continued from ***The Comics Magazine***; introduced *The Clock*(?), the first masked hero (detective type, transition hero) in a comic book.
(a,b,c,d,e,f,h,i,j)

FUNNY PICTURE STORIES No. 1 (11/36, Comics Mag.,An)-Actually this company's second title, featuring their popular original character, The Clock, who appeared on the cover. Title continues for 3 years.
(e)

DETECTIVE PICTURE STORIES No. 1 (12/36, Comic Mag., D)-The first anthology comic title series devoted to a single theme and the first to focus on this subject. Popular in pulps, magazines and films of the time, lasted 7 issues.
(e,h,i,j)

1937 ■

NEW ADVENTURE COMICS No. 12 (1/37, DC, An)-Title change from ***New Comics***, continues series.
(e)

STAR COMICS No. 1 (2/37, Chesler, An)-Ties as first of a publisher. Anthology format of continuing original material, but short lived (2 years). Large-size format.
(e,k)

STAR RANGER No. 1 (2/37, Chesler, Ws)-Ties as first of a publisher, and as the first continuous series western anthology title (see **Western Picture Stories**). Large-size format of original material, lasting only 1 year.
(e,i,j,k)

WESTERN PICTURE STORIES No. 1 (2/37, Comics Mag,-Ws)-Ties with Star Ranger as the first anthology comic title of original material to focus on this subject, the second of a single theme, not lasting out the year.
(e,i,j)

COMICS, THE No. 1 (3/37, Dell, R)-Dell's third anthology reprint title. The first comic book appearance of Tom Mix, lasting only one year.
(e,d)

★★★**DETECTIVE COMICS** No. 1 (3/37, DC, D)-Inaugurated the longest run in comics. Initially a pulpy anthology of mystery men and private eyes, it emerged as the first important title on a single theme with the debut of the implacable *Batman* in '39 (Siegel and Shuster's *Slam Bradley* series is a flavorful example of title's '37-'38 period).
(a,b,c,e,f,h,i,j)

ACE COMICS No. 1 (4/37, McKay, R)-Due to the enormous success of McKay's first series, ***King Comics***, this companion title was published featuring, among others, Raymond's *Jungle Jim*, lasting 12 years.
(a,b,c,e,j,l)

WESTERN ACTION THRILLERS No. 1 (4/37, Dell, Ws)-The third title devoted to westerns. A one-shot of 100 pages.
(e)

FEATURE BOOK nn (Popeye)(1937, McKay, R)-A new concept. The first series of comic books representing a divergence from the normal anthology format. Each issue in the run is actually a one-shot devoted to a single character. More than one issue in the run can be devoted to the same character. These books began in a B&W, magazine-size format. Improvements on this concept came a year later with UFS's ***Single Series*** (in color, comic book size), and still a year later with Dell's ***Four Color*** series, the only one to last.
(a,b,c,e,h,i,j)

FEATURE FUNNIES No. 1 (10/37, Chesler, R)-Another reprint title to add to the list, surviving 13 years as ***Feature Comics***; carrying *Joe Palooka, Mickey Finn* and others.
(e)

100 PAGES OF COMICS No. 101 (1937, Dell, R)-Another 100-page reprint anthology book (Dell's 2nd) with a western cover. Only one issue.
(e)

1938 ■

ACE COMICS No. 11 (2/38, McKay, R)-First comic book appearance of *The Phantom*. Premiere mystery man and first costumed hero. The Ghost Who Walks never made the impact in comics that he enjoyed as a syndicated star.
(a,b,c,f,i,j,l)

FUNNY PAGES V2/6 (3/38, Centaur, An)-Ties with ***Funny Picture Stories, Star Comics*** and ***Star Ranger*** as first of a publisher. Series

picked up from Chesler, ending two years later.
(k)

FUNNY PICTURE STORIES V2/6 (3/38, Centaur, An)-Ties with ***Funny Pages, Star Comics***, and ***Star Ranger*** as first of a publisher. Series picked up from Comics Magazine, ending one year later.
(k)

STAR COMICS No. 10 (3/38, Centaur, An)-Ties with ***Funny Pages, Funny Picture Stories***, and ***Star Ranger*** as first of a publisher. Series picked up from Chesler, ending one year later.
(k)

STAR RANGER V2/10 (3/38, Centaur, Ws)-Ties with ***Funny Picture Stories, Star Ranger***, and ***Funny Pages*** as first of a publisher. Series picked up from Chesler, lasting 2 more issues.
(k)

COMICS ON PARADE No. 1 (4/38, UFS, R)-The second title of this publisher, featuring much the same reprint strips as ***Tip Top***, their first. This series survived 17 years.
(a,b,c,e,j)

MAMMOTH COMICS No. 1 (1938, Whitman, R)-First of a publisher, in the same format as the McKay **Feature Books**. Only one issue.
(e,k)

SUPER COMICS No. 1 (5/38, Dell, R)-A dynamic new title, Dell's fourth. Debuted with some of the heavy weights transferred from the already successful ***Popular Comics***. This new line-up of *Dick Tracy, Terry & The Pirates*, etc. proved to be a sound marketing strategy, lasting 11 years.
(a,b,c,e,j)

GOLDEN AGE PERIOD

1938 ■

★★★★★★**ACTION COMICS** No. 1 (6/38, DC, H)-The ultimate refinement of the anthology, continuing character title. The first appearance of Superman, the quintessential hero with extraordinary powers. Arguably the most imitated character in all of fiction. Standard bearer of the DC line. The most important comic book ever published, and in tandem with ***Superman***, one of the most influential, prevailed beyond four decades.
(a,b,c,d,e,f,h,i,j)

CIRCUS COMICS No. 1 (6/38, Globe, An)-A unique short-lived title featuring a top artist line-up. Introduced Wolverton's Spacehawks, later to appear in ***Target Comics*** as *Spacehawk*. First of a publisher.
(d,e,f,j,k)

CRACKAJACK FUNNIES No. 1 (6/38, Dell, R)-A new Dell title, replacing the defunct ***The Comics*** with a similar but different mix of reprint strips. Lasted 4 years.
(e)

COWBOY COMICS No. 13 (7/38, Centaur, Ws)-Continued from ***Star Ranger*** and lasted only two issues. The fourth western anthology title.
(e)

KEEN DETECTIVE FUNNIES No. 8 (7/38, Centaur, An)—Continued from ***Detective Picture Stories***, this title became one of Centaur's mainstays introducing the *Masked Marvel* one year later, lasting 2 years.
(e)

LITTLE GIANT COMICS No. 1 (7/38, Centaur, An)-Small—size diversion from the regular format and short-lived (4-issues).
(e)

AMAZING MYSTERY FUNNIES No. 1 (8/38, Centaur, An)—Standard bearer of the Centaur line. Top artist line-up due to its production by the Everett shop. Ran for two years.
(e,g)

LITTLE GIANT MOVIE FUNNIES No. 1 (8/38, Centaur, An)—A miniature-sized format comic lasting two issues. A small cartoon panel appears on the right edge of each page giving the illusion of motion when riffled (a flip book) (the cover is set up to represent a movie theater).
(e,i)

★**FUNNY PAGES** V2/10 (9/38, Centaur, H)-First appearance of *The Arrow* who is the very first costumed hero originating in the comic book (3 months after Superman). A primitive percursor of the more refined archers to come, The Arrow executed his adversaries with the medieval bluntness his uniform suggested.
(a,b,d,f,h,i,j)

★★★**JUMBO COMICS** No. 1 (9/38, FH, J)-Publisher of the most perused, but least read, of Golden Age comics, Fiction House did not so much initiate a trend as continue the trusty formula that sustained their line of pulps, cheesecake cast against a variety of single theme adventurous backgrounds (aviation, s/f, jungle & war). ***Jumbo*** was the pilot model of the FH line and the first of the exploitation comics. The debut of *Sheena, Queen of the Jungle* heralded hordes of jungle goddesses to follow. The line overall is perhaps best remembered as a showcase for Matt Baker's patented `calendar girl' art which, after Caniff and Raymond, was the most pervasive of Golden Age styles, enduring 15 years.
(a,b,c,e,f,h,i,j,k,l)

DETECTIVE COMICS No. 20 (10/38, DC, H)-First appearance of *The Crimson Avenger*, a *Shadow* look-a-like, who was the second comic book costumed hero (4 months after *Superman*).
(b,c,d,f,h,i,j)

LITTLE GIANT DETECTIVE FUNNIES No. 1 (10/38, Centaur, An)-Small-size format only lasting a few issues.
(e)

STAR RANGER FUNNIES No. 15 (10/38, Centaur, An)— Links to ***Star Ranger*** and ***Cowboy Comics***, only lasting a few months. (Packaged by the Iger Shop.)
(e)

★★★**DONALD DUCK** nn (1938, Whitman, F)-The first *Donald Duck*, as well as the first Walt Disney comic book; in the format of McKay's ***Feature Book*** (B&W with color cover), reprinting 1936 & 1937 Sunday comics. The first funny animal comic devoted to a single character. Precursor to great things to come for this character.
(a,b,c,e,f,i,j,l)

★★**SINGLE SERIES** nn (Captain & The Kids) (1938, UFS, R)-UFS refined McKay's one-shot ***Feature Book*** format by adding color and adopting the standard comic book size, resulting in a more marketable package. Dell adopted this format for their ***Four Color*** series, which started a year later. This is UFS' third continuous series title.
(e,f,h,i,j)

COCOMALT BIG BOOK OF COMICS No. 1 (1938, Chesler, An)-A one-shot mixed anthology Charles Biro creation, packaged by the Chesler shop (top-notch art).
(e)

NICKEL COMICS No. 1 (1938, Dell, An)-A small size divergent format one-shot, lasting only one issue.
(e)

1939 ■

ALL-AMERICAN COMICS No. 1 (4/39, DC, R)-DC finally bends to the reprint anthology format, but includes some original material for flavor. Scribbly by Mayer begins; a ten-year run.
(a,b,c,d,e,j)

★★**NEW YORK WORLD'S FAIR** (3-5/39, DC, H)-The first newsstand comic with a commercial tie-in, capitalizing on the enormous publicity of a real life public event, featuring DC's top characters. The first published appearance of *The Sandman*. The thick format, as well as the title segued into ***World's Finest Comics*** two years later.
(a,c,d,e,i,j)

★**MOVIE COMICS** No. 1 (4/39, DC, M)-A unique but short-lived idea. The notion of adapting films to comics in fumetti-form (the panels were half-tones of stills from the films) was a good one, but didn't work any better in '39 than it does today. (The first movie adaptation comic in standard comic book form and probably the first attempt at a fumetti continuity.)
(e,f,j,i)

★★★★★**DETECTIVE COMICS** No. 27 (5/39, DC, H)—Reliable but predictable 'funny paper' cops 'n robbers anthology came into focus with the debut of *The Batman*. DC's second powerhouse set another standard for the industry to follow. The 'dynamic' hero costumed athlete sans extraordinary powers proved a viable alternative for the burgeoning competition to mimic, but Bob Kane broke the mold. The character's unique personna defied any but the most oblique imitation. **Detective** shared standard bearer honors with **Action** and provided the initials by which the company was known. One of the top four comics.
(a,b,c,d,f,h,j)

KEEN KOMICS V2/1 (5/39, Centaur, An)-A large size mixed anthology comic changing to regular size with number two. Packaged by the Everett shop and lasting only three issues.
(e)

★★**WONDER COMICS** No. 1 (5/39, Fox, H)-Salutory effort of Fox (packaged by Eisner/Iger). First, and shortest-lived, of Superman imitations. Historically significant because the debut of Fox's *Wonder Man* prompted DC's first attempt to successfully defend their copyright on *Superman*. (A precedent that would prove decisive when the Man of Steel confronted a more formidable courtroom adversary a decade hence). Only one more issue followed.
(d,e,j,k)

★★★**MOTION PICTURE FUNNIES WEEKLY** No.1 (5/39?-Funnies, Inc., H)-Produced as a theatre giveaway, this title featured the first appearance of *Sub-Mariner*. His official newsstand debut occurred later in the year in ***Marvel Comics*** No. 1. Only seven known copies exist.
(a,c,d,e,f,g,h,i,j,k)

FEATURE COMICS No. 21 (6/39, Quality, An)-Continues from ***Feature Funnies*** of two years earlier. A discreet title change, indicating that original adventure comics were becoming a significant alternative to the formerly dominant reprints.
(b,e,k)

★★**ADVENTURE COMICS** No. 40 (7/39, DC, H)-First conceived story of *The Sandman*, a transition crime fighter who stuck tenaciously to the trusty regalia of the pulp heroes. Finally, the pressure to adopt modern togs was brought to bear. The original mystery man vanished into oblivion, replaced by a swashbuckling Kirby hero.
(a,b,c,j)

AMAZING MYSTERY FUNNIES V2/7 (7/39, Centaur, H)—Debut of *The Fantom of the Fair*, mystery man, whose headquarters were under the World's Fair (An unexpected attraction for Fair goers). Destined for extinction with the 1940 wind-up of the Fair. Top artist line-up and exciting cover concepts.
(c,d,j)

COMIC PAGES V3/4 (7/39, Centaur, An)-A mixed anthology series continuing from ***Funny Picture Stories*** of three years earlier, lasting 3 issues.
(e)

KEEN DETECTIVE FUNNIES V2/7 (7/39, Centaur, H)-*The Masked Marvel*, super sleuth, and his three confederates began a terror campaign against lawless gangs. His big amphibian plane, secret laboratory and projected red shadow were devices used in the strip, lasting one year.
(d,j)

★★★**MUTT AND JEFF** nn (Sum/39, DC, R)-This one shot represented a significant departure for DC. Formerly they had avoided the reprint title, preferring to develop their own original characters. This title was obviously a test to see if the market would support an entire book devoted to a single character (or in this case characters). This book has the honor of being the very first *newsstand* comic devoted to a single reprint strip. After a very slow start (four issues in four years), ***Mutt And Jeff*** was made a quarterly and soon became a popular run lasting 26 astounding years. It was the only successful reprint series of a single character to enjoy a respectable run. The syndicated *Mutt and Jeff* strip was, after *The Katzenjammer Kids*, the oldest continuously published newspaper strip.
(a,b,c,e,j)

★★★★★**SUPERMAN** No. 1 (Sum/39, DC, H)- This landmark issue signaled a major turning point for the industry. Arguably, the second most important comic ever published (***Action*** being the first), and possibly the most influential. *Superman* was the first original character promoted from heading an anthology title to starring in a book of his own. More importantly, this tandem exposure demonstrated to the industry that it could survive on its own original material, independent of the proven syndicated stars. As other publishers were attracted to the field in the months to come, they emulated not only *Superman*, but the tandem anthology/headline format that had contributed to his unprecedented success. A double trend setter. Contains reprint material from ***Action*** No. 1-4. Title has continued beyond four decades.
(a,b,c,e,h,i,j)

WONDERWORLD COMICS No. 3 (7/39, Fox, H)-After the *Wonder Man* debacle, Fox bounces back with a revised title and a new lead character (courtesy of the Iger shop). *The Flame* got off to a brilliant start, but was snuffed out when Iger and Fox parted company, lasting 3 years.
(a,c,d,e,j)

MAGIC COMICS No. 1 (8/39, McKay, R)-King Features' third reprint anthology (after ***King*** and ***Ace Comics***) featured such popular syndicated stars as *Mandrake, Henry, and Blondie*. By 1940 *Blondie* had become the most widely syndicated newspaper strip in the world, and became the prime cover feature for the balance of the run, title enduring 10 years.
(a,b,c,e,j)

★**MYSTERYMEN COMICS** No. 1 (8/39, Fox, H)-Fox was on firm ground with a trio of potential contenders: ***Wonderworld's*** *The Flame* and, debuting in this title, *The Blue Beetle* and *The Green Mask*. These early products of the Eisner/Iger shop are worth a second look. Potential glows from every page. Soon, due to the E/I and Fox break up, the characters sank into hack oblivion.
(a,c,d,e,j)

SMASH COMICS No. 1 (8/39, Quality, An)-This is the first title that Quality developed entirely on their own, (previous titles having been purchased from other publishers). The series lacked originality until the debut of Lou Fine's *Ray* which began in issue No. 14.
(b,e,j)

AMAZING MAN COMICS No. 5 (9/39, Centaur, H)-Everett's *A-Man* was launched here, the first Centaur character to headline his own title. The first costumed hero to shrink (*Minimidget*) begins. (This concept was better used later in Quality's *Doll Man*.) Top artist line-up in this series which ended in early 1942. The standard bearer of the Centaur line.
(e,j)

SPEED COMICS No. 1 (10/39, Harvey, H)-First of a publisher. *Shock Gibson* is the main hero. The characters in this series lacked the charisma of the competition's best; had a few bright moments when top artists entered the line-up, surviving as an average run for 7 years.
(a,b,e,k)

BEST COMICS No. 1 (11/39, BP, H)-First of a publisher. Debut of the *Red Mask*. An experimental large format book that read sideways; it failed to find an audience after four issues and folded.
(e,j,k)

BLUE RIBBON COMICS No. 1 (11/39, MLJ, An)-First of a publisher. Contents unremarkable (*Rang-A-Tang, The Wonder Dog*, for example). An MLJ anthology that failed to survive beyond 1942 despite the influx of super heroes.
(e,j,k)

★★★★★**MARVEL COMICS** No. 1 (11/39, Timely, H)—Timely, the first publisher to hit with a smash twin bill in their inaugural title (courtesy of the Everett shop). From the onset, the formula of iconoclast as hero would prove to be Timely's most successful newsstand strategy. *The Human Torch* and *Sub-Mariner* won immediate reader approval, paving the way for more marvels to come from the pre-eminent Thrill Factory of comicdom. Possibly the most sought after of all Golden Age comics. Title lasted 10 years.
(a,b,c,d,e,f,g,h,i,j,k)

CHAMPION COMICS No. 2 (12/39, Harvey, An)-Early transitional anthology title with a sports theme, changing over to costumed heroes early on. None of the characters caught on enough to sustain the run for more than four years.
(e)

FANTASTIC COMICS No. 1 (12/39, Fox, H)-Biblical character *Samson* debuts. This series is more noted for the Lou Fine covers (Iger Shop). *Stardust* begins, one of the most bizarre super heroes in comics (almost childlike, almost surrealistic art and plotting). He assassinated wrong doers regularly.
(e)

★★**FEATURE COMICS** No. 27 (12/39, Quality, H)-Debut of the *Dollman* (Quality's first super hero), who was the second, but most significant, with the power to shrink (See ***Amazing Man***). The stories were generally undistinguished but Quality's high standards of illustration (Eisner in this case) lent the strip a credibility that would have been lacking in lesser hands. This title lasted 11 years.
(a,b,c,d,j)

★**SILVER STREAK COMICS** No. 1 (12/39, Lev, An)-First of a publisher. Debut of *The Claw*, one of the most bizarre villains in the annals of comics. Standing 100 feet tall with claws and fangs was the ultimate refinement of the 'yellow-peril' theme from the pulps. Such a formidable figure had to have an adversary to match (See *Silver Streak* No. 7). The first comic book to display a metallic silver logo to insure prominence on the stands.
(a,c,d,e,f,k)

TOP-NOTCH COMICS No. 1 (12/39, MLJ, H)-*The Wizard*, one of MLJ's top characters debuted. Their second anthology title, lasting 4 years.
(a,b,c,d,e,j)

LARGE FEATURE COMIC nn (1939, Dell, R)-Black and white, magazine size, one-shot series with color covers (identical to McKay ***Feature Books*** of two years earlier), lasting four years.
(a,c,e)

CAPTAIN EASY nn (1939, Hawley, R)-First of a publisher. A one-shot reprint comic devoted to a single character, already proven successful by other publishers.
(a,c,e,k)

★★**FOUR COLOR** No. 1 (Dick Tracy)(1939, Dell, R)-Exact format of UFS's ***Single Series*** of one year earlier. The most successful of the one-shot continuity titles, lasting 23 years. This series also provided a testing arena for new characters and concepts.
(a,b,c,e,j)

LONE RANGER COMICS, THE nn (1939, giveaway, Ws)—Fifth western title, first of a major character and first devoted to a single western character. This one-shot may have had newsstand distribution as price (10 cents) was stamped on cover.
(a,c,e)

1940 ■

★★**BLUE BEETLE, THE** No. 1 (Wint/39-40, Fox, H)-The star of the second continuous series title devoted to a single character exemplified the pioneer 'crime fighter' of the early comics. His uniform was as simple and direct as the four-color medium itself—unadorned, form-fitting chain mail. Disdaining cloak, cape and the cover of night, *Blue Beetle* trounced crime where he found it, usually in the street and in broad daylight. Striking figure made an indelible impression on readers and, had Fox been more committed to long term development, would have doubtless gone the distance. The series eventually succumbed to tepid scripts and lack-lustre art, but the character was of sufficient personal appeal to survive, in memory, not only the demise of his title but legions of better produced, longer tenured heroes.
(a,b,c,e,j)

★★★★★**FLASH COMICS** No. 1 (1/40, DC, H)-DC reinforced its arsenal with two more dynamos: *The Flash* (first, and most significant hero with lightning speed), and *The Hawkman* (first and most significant winged hero). Both trend setters, with series lasting beyond 40 years.
(a,b,c,d,e,f,h,i,j)

★★**FLASH COMICS** No. 1 (1/40, Faw, H)-An in-house b&w proof produced to secure pre-publication copyright. Important changes made before the book was officially released were, a title change from ***Flash*** to ***Whiz*** (DC had already gone to press with their ***Flash Comics***), and the name of the lead character was changed from *Captain Thunder* to *Captain Marvel*. (8 known copies exist.)
(e,f,g,j,k)

THRILL COMICS No. 1 (1/40, Faw, H)-Identical to ***Flash Comics*** listed above, only a different title. Only three known copies exist.
(e,f,g,j,k)

JUNGLE COMICS No. 1 (1/40, FH, J)-The second single theme anthology series of this subject (cloned from ***Jumbo***). The title more perfectly suggested the 'jungle' theme with format selling rather than strong characters. Third series of a publisher, lasting as long as its parent (14 years), with no competition until six years later.
(a,b,c,d,e,j)

FIGHT COMICS No. 1, (1/40, FH, Sp)-Sports theme anthology comic produced by the Iger shop. Later adapted to a war theme, and finally to a jungle theme. The usual house style of cheesecake covers/stories was adhered to resolutely throughout. Duration 13 years.
(a,b,e)

★★**PEP COMICS** No. 1 (1/40, MLJ, H)-Debut of *The Shield*, the first patriotic hero, later eclipsed by Simon & Kirby's *Captain America*, the bombshell of 1941. MLJ's third and longest lasting (over 40 years) anthology title. *Archie* eventually takes over the series.
(a,b,c,d,e,f,h,i,j)

★★★★**PLANET COMICS** No. 1 (1/40, FH, SF)-The publisher's fourth anthology title of continuing characters. The first and by far the most successful science fiction run in comics. As with ***Jumbo*** and ***Jungle***, this title had no competition for many years. Fiction House's style of action-packed covers and art made up for the routine plotting, lasting 14 years.
(a,b,c,e,f,h,i,j)

MIRACLE COMICS No. 1 (2/40, Hillman, H)-A mixed anthology series similar to ***Rocket Comics*** published a month later. First of a publisher. Covers have good eye-appeal, ending with the fourth issue.
(e,k)

★★★**MORE FUN COMICS** No. 52,53 (2,3/40, DC, H)-DC modernizes its first anthology title, introducing the ominous *Spectre* in this two-part origin series. This frightening ethereal hero was too much a match for his adversaries, but gave DC an exciting alternative to their swelling ranks of wondermen. A trend setter, lasting 4 years in this title.
(a,b,c,d,f,h,i,j)

SCIENCE COMICS No. 1 (2/40, Fox, SF)-With qualifications, the second science fiction anthology title (very few of the stories dealt with outer space). Aside from the Lou Fine covers (No. 1 & 2), the artwork was not attractive and the series died after eight issues. First *Eagle* (the second winged hero).
(e)

TARGET COMICS No. 1 (2/40, Novelty, H)-First of a publisher. An early Everett shop super hero production. First *White Streak* by Burgos (the second android super hero). Top artist line-up featuring above average covers and stories, lasting 10 years.
(b,e,k)

THRILLING COMICS No. 1 (2/40, Better, H)-The first successful anthology title by this publisher (their second series). Debut of *Dr. Strange*. Logo carried over from the pulp. The Schomburg covers are the highlight of the run. The title lasted 11 years, switching to a jungle theme near the end.
(a,b,c,e,j)

★★★★★**WHIZ COMICS** No. 2 (2/40, Faw, H)-After ***Action***, the most significant of all hero/adventure anthologies was this late entry from Fawcett. Origin, first appearance of *Captain Marvel*, humor hero par excellence. The most accessible of miracle men came from behind to eclipse the competition's best. He also founded the industry's first character dynasty (Marvel's *Junior*, *Mary* and even *Bunny*), a tactic that would prove as fundamental to comics' merchandising as DC's hero team concept. Landmark first issue also introduced such secondary stalwarts as *Sivana, Old Shazam, Spy Smasher* (the definitive aviator/mysteryman), and *Ibis the Invincible*, most memorable of comic book sorcerers. Flagship of the Fawcett line and a perennial favorite for 13 years.
(a,b,c,d,e,f,g,j,k)

ZIP COMICS No. 1 (2/40, MLJ, H)-MLJ's fourth anthology title (featuring *Steel Sterling*). Interesting stylized covers and art. Series lasted four years. With the exception of *Wilbur* (an *Archie* clone), none of the characters reached their own titles.
(a,b,c,d,j)

★★**ADVENTURE COMICS** No. 48 (3/40, DC, H)-Debut of *The Hourman*. A substantial secondary feature that sold a few books for DC, but never received adequate creative support. Interesting premise came to dominate all the stories resulting in monotonous repetition.
(a,b,c,d,e,j)

COLOSSUS COMICS No. 1 (3/40, Sun, H)-An early esoteric book which ties to the esoteric ***Green Giant*** comic.
(e)

★★★**DONALD DUCK FOUR COLOR** No. 4 (3/40?, Dell,-F)-The first comic book devoted to this important transfer character. Still confined to one page gag strips. Full potential not yet reached.
(a,b,c,j)

MASTER COMICS No. 1 (3/40, Faw, H)-An experimental format at first (magazine size, priced at 15¢ and 52 pages). Debut of *Master Man*, an imitation of *Superman*, killed by DC after six issues; just in time for *Bulletman* to become the lead figure with issue no. 7, transferred from the defunct ***Nickel Comics***.
(b,e,j,k)

MYSTIC COMICS No. 1 (3/40, Timely, H)-Unusual anthology title (their third) in that each issue featured a practically new line-up of costumed heroes. High impact covers and art, lasting only 10 issues.
(e)

PRIZE COMICS No. 1 (3/40, Prize, H)-High quality anthology series with the debut of *Power Nelson*. First of a publisher. Dick Briefer's unique *Frankenstein* was introduced in No. 7 as well as Simon & Kirby's *Black Owl*. The covers have tremendous eye-appeal.
(a,b,e,j,k)

ROCKET COMICS No. 1 (3/40, Hillman, H)-The title is misleading. This

is actually a mixed anthology title with science fiction covers; short-lived with only three issues. Companion mag to ***Miracle Comics***. The second Hillman title.
(e)

★**SHADOW COMICS** No. 1 (3/40, S&S, H)-The venerable pulp publisher tested the comic waters with a heavyweight who had dominated both the pulp and radio markets but never quite found his metier in a medium that relied on action over ethereal atmosphere. *Doc Savage*, another renowned pulp character, debuted in this issue. A respectable but undistinguished run (9 years) probably sustained by popularity of radio program.
(a,b,c,e,f,i,j,k,l)

SLAM BANG COMICS No. 1 (3/40, Faw, An)-Fawcett's third title was an ill conceived adventure anthology starring civilian heroes. This formula had gone out two years before with the appearance of *Superman*. The title was retired after 8 issues.
(e)

SUN FUN KOMIKS No. 1 (3/40, Sun, Hm)-An esoteric one-shot printed in black and red. A satire on comic books. The first of its kind not to be fully developed until ***Mad*** of 12 years hence.
(e,i,j)

★★★★**DETECTIVE COMICS** No. 38 (4/40, DC, H)-DC initiates yet another breakthrough concept–the apprentice costumed hero. Origin, first appearance of *Robin*, the first and most enduring juvenile aide. For the first time in popular literature, the youthful apprentice was accepted as an equal by his partner. Bob Kane set another standard for the industry to mimic. The foreboding and enigmatic Batman was never the same after this issue.
(a,b,c,d,f,h,i,j)

EXCITING COMICS No. 1 (4/40, Better, H)-A sister anthology title to ***Thrilling***, becoming Better's second successful series. This title launched *The Black Terror* in No. 9, with Schomburg doing the covers early on (a poor man's Timely). Title lasted 9 years with jungle theme covers at the end.
(b,e,j)

★★**NEW YORK WORLD'S FAIR** (3-5/40, DC, H)-The second comic book produced for a public event, ending the series. The first book to feature *Superman* and *Batman* together on a cover, as well as the first to showcase all of a company's stars, all in one book.
(a,c,j)

SUPERWORLD COMICS No. 1 (4/40, Gernsback, SF)—Following the success of ***Planet***, this title takes the honors as the third continuous series science fiction anthology. But Gernsback soon learned that 'raw' science fiction without a unique art style or gimmick (cheesecake) wouldn't sell. Disappeared after only three issues.
(e,k)

WEIRD COMICS No. 1 (4/40, Fox, H)-Another mixed anthology title with costumed heroes. The first to capitalize on this title, which became more common a decade later. Early issues by the Iger shop. First *Birdman* (the third winged hero). First *Thor*, from Greek mythology. Title lasted 2 years.
(e)

BIG SHOT COMICS No. 1 (5/40, CCG, Av)-First *Skyman*, the second aviation hero (noted for his flying wing)(See ***Whiz***). The first of a publisher. Mixed anthology series with original and reprint strips (*Joe Palooka*), lasting 9 years.
(a,b,c,d,e,j,k)

CRACK COMICS No. 1 (5/40, Quality, H)-Debut of Fine's *Black Condor* (the fourth winged hero). *Madame Fatal* begins, a bizarre hero who dresses as a woman to fight crime. A top quality series, lasting 9 years.
(a,b,c,d,e)

CRASH COMICS No. 1 (5/40, Tem/Holyoke, H)-The first Simon & Kirby art team-up, whose loose style of action reached maturity a year later with *Captain America*. Kirby was on his way to becoming one of the most influencial artists in comics. First of a publisher. A short lived mixed anthology series with costumed heroes, lasting 5 issues.
(e,g,k)

DOC SAVAGE COMICS No. 1 (5/40, S&S, H)-The legendary Man of Bronze headlined Street & Smith's second comic title. But it soon became evident that the original 'superman' was out of his depth. His prose adventures, which crackled with vitality in the pulps, seemed bland and derivative in the four-color medium. Outclassed by the characters he inspired, Doc and his title were retired after 3 years of so-so performance.
(c,e)

HYPER MYSTERY COMICS No. 1 (5/40, Hyper, H)-First of a publisher. A costumed hero anthology title which could not compete with the many heroes on the market at this time, lasting 2 issues.
(e,k)

★**MORE FUN COMICS** No. 55 (5/40, DC, H)-First *Dr. Fate*, DC's second supernatural hero was given immediate cover exposure. Above average art and stories; colorful costume, lasting 3 years and not achieving his own title.
(a,b,c,d,j)

★★★**NICKEL COMICS** No. 1 (5/40, Faw, H)-Introduced *Bulletman*, Fawcett's third costumed hero. This book was experimental, selling for 5 cents, coming out biweekly, and lasting only 8 issues. (After *Bulletman* was moved to ***Master Comics***, he won his own title in 1941.)
(a,c,d,e,j)

WAR COMICS No. 1 (5/40, Dell, W)-The first single theme anthology series devoted to war. The combat genre did not find a significant market until the outbreak of the Korean conflict a decade later.
(e,i,j)

AMAZING ADVENTURE FUNNIES No. 1 (6/40, Centaur,H)-Outstanding collection of Centaur's best characters reprinted from earlier titles. Centaur was increasingly thrown back to all reprint books. Conjecture is that Timely's sudden success pre-empted all of the Everett shop's time.
(c,e)

★★★★**BATMAN** No. 1 (Spr/40, DC, H)-Has arrival date of 4/25/40. DC's second strongest character achieved stardom and was given his own title. Assembled from Detective Comics' inventory, containing the last solo appearance of *The Batman*. *The Joker* and T*he Cat* debut. Title has run uninterrupted over four decades.
(a,b,c,e,j)

BLUE BOLT No. 1 (6/40, Novelty, H)-Second of a publisher. Costumed hero anthology title. Important early Simon & Kirby development began in No. 3. The heroes in this series could not be sustained, with Dick Cole eventually taking over, lasting 9 years.
(a,b,c,d,e,j)

CYCLONE COMICS No. 1 (6/40, Bilbara, An)-An anthology title with emphasis on subjects other than costumed hero. First of a publisher, expiring after 5 issues.
(e,j,k)

FUTURE COMICS No. 1 (6/40, McKay, R)-McKay's first new title in about a year. A reprint anthology with a science fiction theme (the fourth ever). This issue is noted for *The Phantom's* origin and science fiction cover. Went down for the count after 4 issues.
(e)

★★★**SPIRIT, THE** No. 1 (6/2/40, Eisner, D)-A weekly comic book (the only in comics) featuring the blockbuster strip distributed through newspapers. Notably, one of the best written and illustrated strips ever. A trend setter. Ingenious themes; capital atmospheric art with movie-like continuity and humorous plotting. Focus on special effects, lighting and unusual angles, lasting 12 years and endlessly revived.
(a,b,c,d,e,f,h,i,j)

STARTLING COMICS No. 1 (6/40, Better, H)-Better's third companion anthology series; *Wonder Man* and *Captain Future* begin. *The Fighting Yank* debuted in No. 10. Schomburg covers began early giving the books more impact. Cover theme changed to science fiction at the end.
(a,b,c,e,j)

SURE-FIRE COMICS No. 1 (6/40, Ace, H)-First of a publisher. A super hero anthology title of average quality lasting 4 issues before a title change.
(e,k)

WHIRLWIND COMICS No. 1 (6/40, Nita, H)-First of a publisher. A three-issue run of mediocre quality with no sustaining characters.
(e,k)

★★★★**ALL-AMERICAN COMICS** No. 16 (7/40,DC, H)—DC scored with another winning variation on the mystery-man/adventure theme. Origin and first appearance of most enduring of DC's magic oriented heroes. The ancient fable of the magic lamp was transformed into a modern and more accessible, more mysterious form. *The Green Lantern's* chant became a staple of school boy mythology and another great career was launched. Series ended in 1949, although the name continued beyond 4 decades.
(a,b,c,d,j)

★★★**ALL-STAR COMICS** No. 1 (Sum/40, DC, H)-The first continuous series showcase comic (see ***New York World's Fair***, 1940) for giving more exposure to top characters, who all headlined anthology series but as yet were not strong enough to have titles of their own. (This abundance of popular characters was unique to DC, forcing them to come up with this new format.)
(a,b,c,e)

FLAME, THE No. 1 (Sum/40, Fox, H)-One of Fox's top characters given prominence, reprinted from ***Wonderworld***. Lou Fine art in this issue, but the quality dropped early on, with the title lasting only 1-1/2 years.
(c,e)

GREEN MASK, THE No. 1 (Sum/40, Fox, H)-Fox's emerald mystery man achieved stardom, but was squelched early on due to sub-standard art. An intriguing concept that was resurrected several times over the next 15 years, none of which were successful.
(c,e)

★**MARVEL MYSTERY COMICS** No. 9 (7/40, Timely, H)—Epic battle issue. The first time in comics that two super heroes appeared together in one story. *Sub-Mariner* and *The Human Torch* each give up their usual space and battle for 22 pages. A coming together of the ancient basic elements, Water and Fire. Ignited newsstands everywhere.
(a,b,c,h,j)

HIT COMICS No. 1 (7/40, Quality, H)-Quality's fourth anthology title. Distinguished primarily by Iger shop graphics (Lou Fine). Non-memorable characters until *Kid Eternity* took over as main feature two years later. Series lasted 10 years.
(a,b,e,j)

NATIONAL COMICS No. 1 (7/40, Quality, H)-Of equal quality to ***Hit***, Lou Fine at his very best (covers and story art). Debut of *Uncle Sam*, Quality's top patriot. Legendary artist line-up with series lasting 9 years.
(a,b,c,d,e,f,j)

OKAY COMICS No. 1 (7/40, UFS, R)-Not having published a new title since 1938 (***Single Series***), United decides to make a comeback. Three new titles are released simultaneously with a fourth the following month. This one-shot issue features *The Captain and the Kids* and *Hawkshaw the Detective*.
(e)

OK COMICS No. 1 (7/40, UFS, H)-United tries their first super hero anthology title, but the characters were not strong enough to endure the stiff competition, lasting only two issues. Their second new title for the month.
(e)

SHIELD-WIZARD COMICS No. 1 (Sum/40, MLJ, H)-MLJ gave their top two characters joint stardom. A unique concept, titling a book after more than one character to insure its survival–a first in comics. The series lasted 4 years (the dual title wasn't enough).
(c,e)

SPARKLER COMICS No. 1 (7/40, UFS, R)-A two-issue reprint anthology series featuring *Jim Hardy* in No. 1 and *Frankie Doodle* in No. 2. United's third new title for the month.
(c,e)

SUPER-MYSTERY COMICS No. 1 (7/40, Ace, H)-Ace's second title, featuring more prominent characters and art, becoming their mainstay run. The series lasted 9 years, sustained by colorful covers and top artists.
(a,b,c,e)

FANTOMAN No. 2 (8/40, Centaur, H)-Centaur's second title reprinting their top characters and lasting three issues. Their second series of repackaged material.
(e)

HEROIC COMICS No. 1 (8/40, Eastern Color, H)-Seven years after introducing **Famous Funnies**, Eastern came out with their second anthology title (their third ever). Original rather than reprinted material. *Hydroman*, a spin-off of the *Sub-Mariner* debuted. Eventually the format was changed to true stories of heroism, lasting 15 years. Top artists included throughout the run.
(e)

RED RAVEN COMICS No. 1 (8/40, Timely, H)-A one-shot esoteric super hero book featuring Kirby art. Highly sought after due to its lineage and rarity. Timely's fourth title.
(e)

★★★★**SPECIAL EDITION COMICS** No. 1 (8/40, Fawcett, H)-Due to the enormous popularity of ***Whiz's*** explosive character, a single theme (Fawcett's first) anthology one-shot of *Captain Marvel* was published. A few months later, he began his own series. Beck cover and story art–high quality throughout.
(a,c,e,j)

UNITED COMICS No. 1 (8/40, UFS, R)-The popular Fritzi Ritz strip was featured and sustained the run for 12 years. United's fourth and only successful title in their recent comeback attempt beginning a month earlier. The first comic book series to focus on the career girl theme (prototype of *Katy Keene*).
(a,b,c,e)

CRASH COMICS No. 4(9/40, Holyoke, H)-*Catman* debuted for two issues then stayed dormant for six months before appearing in his own title.
(a,c,d,j)

MASKED MARVEL No. 1 (9/40, Centaur, H)-After exposure in ***Keen Detective Funnies***, the crimson sleuth was given his own title, lasting only 3 issues.
(e)

★**MICKEY MOUSE MAGAZINE** V5/12, (9/40, K.K. F)-This historically significant publication was one step removed from becoming the first official funny animal series. As a magazine, it had evolved through various sizes and formats to finally become a full-fledged comic book. The following month, a title change to ***Walt Disney's Comics & Stories*** completed the transition.
(a,c,h,j)

PRIZE COMICS No. 7 (9/40, Prize, H)-Debut of Dick Briefer's *Frankenstein* series, and *The Black Owl* by Simon & Kirby. Above average strips with eye catching covers.
(a,b,c,d,j)

★**RED RYDER COMICS** No. 1 (9/40, Hawley/Dell, Ws)-A one-shot devoted to the popular strip character by Fred Harman, not becoming a continuous series until Dell picked up the title a year later. Ties with ***Tom Mix*** as the second book devoted to a single western character, but the first to receive widespread newsstand distribution. Lasted 17 years due to popular movie series. The second title of a publisher.
(a,b,c,e,f,h,i,j,l)

★★★**SILVER STREAK COMICS** No. 6 (9/40, Lev, H)-High impact cover of *The Claw* by Jack Cole. Debut of *Daredevil* with his unprecedented costume of dichromatic symmetry. (See Silver Streak no.7.)
(a,b,c,d,f,j)

SKY BLAZERS No. 1 (9/40, Hawley, Av)-Ties with Red Ryder as 2nd of a publisher. Inspired by the radio show, not lasting beyond 2 issues.
(e)

★★**TOM MIX** No. 1 (9/40, Ralston, Ws)-The first continuous series single theme western comic, but a giveaway by Ralston not sold on the stands.
(a,b,c,e,j,k)

★**WINGS COMICS** No. 1 (9/40, FH, Av)-The publisher's fifth single theme anthology title. The first to focus entirely on aviation (a subject of high appeal to boys of the era). With no competition, the series lasted 14 years.
(a,b,c,e,h,i,j)

ALL-AMERICAN COMICS No. 19 (10/40, DC, H)-Debut of *The Atom* (a hero for short people). Good filler material as a back-up to the main feature, who lasted 4 years.
(a,b,c,d,f,h,j)

ARROW, THE No. 1 (10/40, Centaur, H)-The very first costume hero (pre-*Batman*) was given prominence after a two-year run in ***Funny Pages***. Folded after 3 issues (Centaur phasing out).
(e)

BIG 3 No. 1 (Fall/40, Fox, H)-Fox's first showcase anthology title featuring their top characters together in one magazine. A good idea, but not surviving more than 7 issues.
(e)

BILL BARNES COMICS No. 1 (10/40, S&S, Av)-The celebrated pulp ace got his own comic title, but after three years failed to find an audience. Street & Smith's third title.
(c,e,l)

CHAMP COMICS No. 11 (10/40, Harvey, H)-Continued from ***Champion***, now featuring super heroes in full swing. Later on the popular and saleable Simon & Kirby art style was copied as an attempt to sustain the run. The title ended in 1944.
(e)

★★★**HUMAN TORCH, THE** No. 2(Fall/40, Timely, H)—From the pages of ***Marvel Mystery***, the android flies into his own title. Inspired concept. High impact, eye-catching character, making appearances over the next 40 years.
(a,b,c,e,j)

REX DEXTER OF MARS No. 1 (Fall/40, Fox, SF)-A modest success in ***Mysterymen***, but not important enough to carry a title of his own. Expired after one issue.
(e)

SAMSON No. 1 (Fall/40, Fox, H)-One of Fox's top characters from ***Fantastic*** achieves stardom. Lack-luster art leads to the early death of the run the following year.
(e)

SPORT COMICS No. 1 (10/40, S&S, Sp)-A good idea 'real life' comic series featuring notable sport figures and lasting (through a title change) for 9 years. The first comic series devoted entirely to this theme (see ***Champion*** and ***Fight***).
(b,c,e,h,i,j)

SUPER SPY No. 1 (10/40, Centaur, H)-Late Centaur superhero anthology title, introducing *The Sparkler*. Interesting early vintage comic with only two issues published.
(e)

TOP-NOTCH COMICS No. 9 (10/40, MLJ, H)-Debut of *The Black Hood*, key MLJ hero. One of the few at MLJ to later star in his own title. The costume had eye appeal which sustained the character, lasting 3 years.
(c,d,j)

★★★★★**WALT DISNEY'S COMICS AND STORIES** No. 1 (10/40, Dell, F)-The first funny animal continuous series comic book title. Miscellaneous collection of proven Disney characters began to come into focus around consistently high quality strips by Taliaferro and Gottfredson, who consistently delivered the goods. The definitive funny animal anthology comic after which all others were modeled. A trend setter. Suspected to have achieved the highest circulation of any comic, lasting beyond 40 years.
(a,b,c,e,h,i,j)

WESTERN DESPERADO COMICS No. 8 (10/40, Fawcett, Ws)-Fawcett's first western theme anthology title, only one issue.
(e)

DETECTIVE EYE No. 1 (11/40, Centaur, H)-More exposure for characters from ***Keen Detective Funnies***, lasting 2 issues.
(e)

HI-SPOT COMICS No. 2 (11/40, Hawley, An)-A one-shot book featuring an Edgar Rice Burroughs strip, *David Innes of Pellucidar*.
(e)

WHAM COMICS No. 1 (11/40, Centaur, H)-Another short-lived anthology title, similar to ***Super Spy*** (reprinting earlier material).
(e)

★★**GREEN HORNET COMICS** No. 1 (12/40, Harvey, H)-The respected radio and movie hero tried his wings in comics. Intriguing concept, with a few high points of good artists in the run. He never excelled in the medium, but did present a respectable run of 9 years–probably sustained by the popularity of the radio program.
(a,b,c,e,l)

LIGHTNING COMICS No. 4 (12/40, Ace, H)-Continued from ***Sure-Fire***, becoming Ace's third title. Colorful covers (some exceptional) could not sustain the run beyond 18 months.
(e)

DOUBLE COMICS (1940, Elliot, H)-The first attempt at repackaging (and remarketing) remaindered comics. First of a publisher. Elliot produced these unique books for four years, taking advantage of the insatiable public demand for comics.
(e,h,j,k)

GREEN GIANT COMICS No. 1 (1940, Funnies, Inc., H)-A very rare one-shot test comic. Conjecture is that its circulation was limited to the New York City area only.
(e,j)

1941 ■

★★★★★**ALL-STAR COMICS** No. 3 (Wint/40-41, DC, H)—A breakthrough concept, second in importance only to the creation of the super hero. For the first time in comics, top characters come together in one book to form a crime fighting organization *The Justice Society*. A trend setter. Unprecedented in all of literature (the gods of Mt. Olympus weren't on speaking terms; the Knights of the Round Table didn't gather to confront a common foe). Forerunner of *The Justice League*, and inspiration for many hero groups that followed.
(a,b,c,f,h,i,j)

BUCK ROGERS No. 1 (Wint/40-41, FF, R)-Due to the enormous popularity of the strip in ***Famous Funnies***, he earned his own title, which is the first continuous title devoted to a reprint character. Unfortunately, like many other transfer characters, the series didn't last, running only 6 issues.
(a,c,e)

SILVER STREAK COMICS No. 7 (1/41, Lev, H)-Epic clash between *Daredevil* and *The Claw* began in this issue. (Rivaled only by the *Torch-Sub-Mariner* brouhaha). Early enthusiastic work by Jack Cole. *DD's* costume colors change to red and blue, giving him a sinister, demonic appearance (unforgettable). Smash hit series launched *DD* to stardom with own title.
(a,c,f,j)

WOW COMICS No. 1 (Wint/40-41, Faw, H)-Featuring the costumed hero *Mr. Scarlet* (imitation of *Batman*), drawn by Kirby. Included other features with small impact to the comic scene. The major feature of this title was *Mary Marvel*, a *Captain Marvel* clone, who dominated from No. 9 on. This particular issue is highly prized due to its rarity and early Kirby art.
(b,e)

★★★★**CAPTAIN MARVEL ADVENTURES** nn (1-2/41?, Faw, H)-Following the wake of ***Special Edition***, the celebrated character started his own series (this issue illustrated by Kirby), reaching a two-week publication frequency at one point, lasting 13 years.
(a,b,c,e,j)

BLUE RIBBON COMICS No. 9 (2/41, MLJ, H)-Inspired by DC's The *Spectre, Mr. Justice* began this issue and survived to the end of the run (1942).
(d)

★★★★★**CAPTAIN AMERICA COMICS** No. 1 (3/41, Timely, H)-Simon & Kirby's most classic creation; a patriotic paragon (the second but foremost of patriotic heroes) that set the comics market reeling. A trend setter. One of the top ten most sought after books. With a few interruptions, the character has survived beyond 40 years.
(a,b,c,d,e,g,j)

JACKPOT COMICS No. 1 (Spr/41, MLJ, H)-MLJ's first showcase title to give more exposure to their top characters. The mediocre scripts and art could only keep the run alive for 2 years.
(c,e)

★★★**SUB-MARINER COMICS** No. 1 (Spr/41, Timely, H)—The aquatic anti-hero is given prominence. The potential of the character was never fully realized. High impact covers, sustaining the run for 8 years.
(a,b,c,e,j)

★★★**WORLD'S BEST COMICS** No. 1 (Spr/41, DC, H)—Using the successful format of ***The World's Fair*** books, DC created this title to feature their top two attractions, *Batman* and *Superman*. This was the first thick format continuous series comic (as ***World's Finest***). Series lasted beyond 40 years without interruption.
(a,b,c,e,h,j)

★★★**MICKEY MOUSE FOUR COLOR** No. 16 (4/41?, Dell, F)-The first comic devoted to this world-renowned character. The subject of this landmark issue was Gottfredson's classic, *The Phantom Blot*.
(a,b,c,j)

★★**ADVENTURE COMICS** No. 61 (4/41, DC, H)-*Starman* was introduced as DC continued to create new characters. Visually, an intriguing alternative with enough appeal to last 3 years in this run, but not quite strong enough to appear in his own title.
(a,b,c,d,j)

TRUE COMICS No. 1 (4/41, PM, TR)-The second anthology series based on true stories (see ***Sport Comics***). The first of a publisher, lasting 9 years.
(b,e,h,i,h,k)

AMERICA'S GREATEST COMICS No. 1 (5/41?, Faw, H)-Fawcett's first showcase anthology title (in thick format) featuring their top characters, lasting 8 issues.
(a,c,e)

ARMY AND NAVY No. 1 (5/41, S&S, W)-S&S's fifth anthology title, the second ever with a war theme, lasting 5 issues.
(e)

CATMAN COMICS No. 1 (5/41, Holyoke, H)-Continued from ***Crash***, *Catman* got his own series. Second of a publisher. Adequate, but unexceptional covers and stories. Expired after 5 years.
(a,b,c,e)

EXCITING COMICS No. 9 (5/41, BP, H)-Debut of *The Black Terror*, nemesis of crime. Editors never adequately capitalized on the tremendous eye-appeal of the character. Indifferent scripts, lack-luster art disappointed more often than not. The indomitable character endured despite lack of staff support. Logical yet striking appearance of costume sustained character.
(a,b,c,d,j)

STARS AND STRIPES COMICS No. 2 (5/41, Centaur, H)—After the failure of Centaur's last flurry of reprint books a year earlier, they tried to make a comeback. Following Timely's newsstand hit, Centaur picked up on the patriotic theme with the first of three books of this type, lasting only 5 issues.
(e)

SUPER MAGIC No. 1 (5/41, S&S, Mg)-A one-shot book featuring *Blackstone the Magician* and *Rex King*. The first title to focus on magicians. The title was modified to ***Super Magician*** and the series lasted 6 years.
(b,e,i,j)

LIBERTY SCOUTS No. 2 (6/41, Centaur, H)-Centaur's second patriotic theme series lasted only two issues.
(e)

★★★**ALL FLASH COMICS** No. 1 (Sum/41, DC, H)-The hero of speed achieved stardom and was given his own title. Momentarily retired after 6 years.
(a,b,c,e)

★**ALL WINNERS COMICS** No. 1 (Sum/41, Timely, H)-First Timely showcase title to give more exposure to their top characters. High impact covers and characters sustained run for 5 years.
(a,c,e)

★★**BULLETMAN** No. 1 (7/41, Faw, H)-The hit of ***Master Comics***, receives his own title, lasting 5 years. The Raboy cover and silver logo gets the series off to a good start.
(a,c,e)

CAPTAIN BATTLE COMICS No. 1 (Sum/41, Lev, H)-The third patriotic hero (see ***Pep Comics*** and ***Captain America***) from ***Silver Streak*** is given his own title. Lacked necessary distinctiveness to compete, folding with the second issue.
(e)

★★**DAREDEVIL COMICS** No. 1 (7/41, Lev, H)-High impact cover, inspired costume design and massive support from Biro's strong, complex plotting sustained momentum of "The Greatest Name in Comics" splash debut. Immediately stood out from the hordes of rival strongmen glutting the stands. Series prevailed for 15 years.
(a,b,c,e,j)

EAGLE, THE No. 1 (7/41, Fox, H)-Another publisher on the patriotic band wagon. *The Eagle* only flew for four issues.
(e)

FUNNIES, THE No. 57 (7/41, Dell, H)-Debut of *Captain Midnight*, a patriotic aviation hero who was an established attraction on radio. He was also featured in Dell's ***Popular Comics*** before being picked up by Fawcett as a regular series.
(a,c,d,j)

MINUTEMAN No. 1 (7/41, Faw, H)-Fawcett's answer to a patriotic hero who began in ***Master Comics***. This less than distinguished hero only lasted three issues in his own title.
(e)

PEP COMICS No. 17 (7/41, MLJ, H)-Landmark issue. The first time in comics that a major character (*The Comet*) actually died, and a new character (*The Hangman*) was created in the same story.
(a,b,c,d,h)

SPARKLER COMICS No. 1 (7/41, UFS, R)-After three years of costumed heroes glutting the stands, UFS tries its second costumed hero series. Debut of *Sparkman*, a colorful character who eventually gave way to *Tarzan* and other reprint characters, title proved competitive through 14 years.
(a,b,c,e,j)

★**YOUNG ALLIES** No. 1 (Sum/41, Timely, H)-The first sidekick group in comics. *The Red Skull* guest-starred to give the title a good send-off. Proto-type of the more successful *Teen Titans* of 25 years hence, it managed a respectable run of 5 years.
(e,f,h,i,j)

CAPTAIN FEARLESS No. 1 (8/41, Helnit, H)-Third of a publisher. An interesting mix of super patriots not lasting beyond the second issue.
(e)

★★★★**MILITARY COMICS** No. 1 (8/41, Qua, Av)-Otherwise predictable war-theme anthology (the third of its kind) sparked by debut of aviation feature of geniune classic proportions. The crack *Blackhawk* team took command of the series and continued at the helm 9 years after a title change (to ***Modern Comics***) indicated the public had grown jaded with war-themes generally. Ace concept (airborne privateers meet the axis on its own terms) backed by sterling Iger graphics (the shop's *piece de resistance*) and top-drawer scripting propelled feature into its own title and a phenomenal 40 year run (with interruptions). The introduction of *Blackhawk*, and *Plastic Man* later the same month, lifted Quality into the first rank of comics publishers. A masterpiece of collaborative art.
(a,b,c,d,e,f,h,i,j)

OUR FLAG COMICS No. 1 (8/41, Ace, H)-Ace joined the other publishers with a host of patriotic strongmen debuting in this book. High impact patriotic cover. Series lasted 5 issues.
(e,j)

POCKET COMICS No. 1 (8/41, Harv, H)-An experimental pocket size comic book series featuring Harvey's top characters. Most divergent forms didn't last long and this was no exception, expiring after 4 issues.
(e)

★★★★**POLICE COMICS** No. 1 (8/41, Quality, H)-Debut of one of the most ingenious super heroes in comics, *Plastic Man*. An original concept, fully exploited by Jack Cole in the ensuing years. Sheer entertainment with the incomparable Cole at the top of his form. Shares standard bearer honors with *Military*, lasting 12 years.
(a,b,c,d,e,f,i,j)

★**RED RYDER COMICS** No. 3 (8/41, Hawley, Ws)-The first continuous series single theme western comic for newsstand sales. Ties back to a one-shot issue of a year earlier. Title lasted 16 years due to popular movie series.
(a,b,c,e,f,h,i,j)

SPITFIRE COMICS No. 1 (8/41, Harvey, Av)-An experimental aviation pocket size comic book, lasting 2 issues.
(e)

★**UNCLE SAM QUARTERLY** No. 1 (8/41, Qua, H)-Eisner's version of a patriotic hero, the star of ***National Comics***, is given his own book, lasting 8 issues. Usual Iger shop excellence.
(e)

USA COMICS No. 1 (8/41, Timely, H)-Timely, extending the patriotic theme, created another showcase title for introducing new characters. After five issues, their trend setting *Captain America* was brought in to save the run and it endured 4 years.
(a,c,e)

VICTORY COMICS No. 1 (8/41, Hill, H)-Classic Everett Nazi war cover. Hillman tried their third title, this time with a patriotic costumed hero theme, again unsuccessfully. It lasted only 4 issues.
(e)

BANNER COMICS No. 3 (9/41, Ace, H)-Debut of *Captain Courageous*, a derivative patriotic hero not prominent enough to survive more than 3 issues.
(e)

CALLING ALL GIRLS No. 1 (9/41, PMI, TR)-Second of a publisher. The true fact anthology, with biographies of famous persons and sketches of historic events (occasionally mixed with magazine-type photo features), was a comics format pioneered by Parent's Magazine Institute. Here the target audience was adolescent girls. Similar titles were cloned later on. Enjoyed a run of 7 years.
(b,e,f,h,i,j)

FOUR FAVORITES No. 1 (9/41, Ace, H)-Ace's first showcase title featuring their top characters together in one book, lasting 6 years.
(e)

REAL HEROES COMICS No. 1 (9/41, PMI, TR)-With the success of ***True Comics***, the publisher attempted another title based on true stories. Their third series, lasting 5 years. ***Heroic Comics*** was later converted to this theme.
(e)

REAL LIFE COMICS No. 1 (9/41, BP, TR)-Inspired by the newsstand success of PMI's ***True Comics***, this publisher came out with their ver-

sion, lasting 11 years.
(b,e)

STARTLING COMICS No. 10 (9/41, BP, H)-Debut of *The Fighting Yank*, America's super patriot. Interesting variation on the patriotic theme in that he could call up heroes from the American revolution to assist in the modern fight against crime. Tremendous eye-appeal of character never fully realized due to low standard story art. High impact Schomburg covers sustained the run.
(a,b,c,d,j)

SUPER MAGICIAN COMICS No. 2 (9/41, S&S, Mg)-The first continuous series anthology title on the subject of magic, continuing from ***Super Magic*** and lasting 6 years.
(e,j)

YANKEE COMICS No. 1 (9/41, Chesler, H)-Chesler re-entered the comic market with this patriotic title. Debut of *Yankee Doodle Jones*. Sensational patriotic cover. Despite its visual appeal, it endured only 4 issues.
(e)

★★★★CLASSIC COMICS No. 1 (10/41, Gil, Lit)-First and most enduring of 'educational' theme comics, Gilberton drew on works of great literature for their highly visible newsstand product. One of the few lines that could be endorsed without reservation by parents and educators, its marketing success was not tied to single theme titles or continuing characters. Variable art quality somewhat diminished the overall impact of the line. The only comic publisher to place each issue into endless reprints while continuing to publish new titles on a monthly basis, lasting 30 years.
(a,b,c,e,f,h,i,j,k)

DOLL MAN No. 1 (Fall/41, Qua, H)-After a successful two-year run in ***Feature***, the mighty mite leaped into his own title, lasting 12 years. The proto-type of the Silver Age Atom.
(a,b,c,e,j)

DYNAMIC COMICS No. 1 (10/41, Chesler, H)-Chesler's second patriotic super hero series. Debut of *Major Victory*. Suspended after three issues and brought back with a format change in 1944, lasting four more years.
(e)

★★★GREEN LANTERN No. 1 (Fall/41, DC, H)-Having headlined ***All-American*** for one year, one of DC's foremost heroes achieved the distinction of his own title. It ran for 8 years and went on to become one of the key revival characters of the Silver Age.
(a,b,c,e)

★★★★LOONEY TUNES & MERRY MELODIES No. 1 (Fall/41, Dell, F)-The companion title to the enormously successful ***WDC&S***. Dell's second funny animal anthology featured *Bugs Bunny*, *Porky Pig* and *Elmer Fudd*. This was the first comic book appearance of Warner Brothers film characters. The series ran for 21 years.
(a,b,c,e,h,j,l)

RANGERS COMICS No. 1 (10/41, FH, W)-The publisher's sixth single theme anthology title (war theme). Standard FH style of cheesecake art and covers, lasting 11 years.
(a,b,c,e)

SKYMAN No. 1 (Fall/41, CCG, Av)-After a year's successful run in ***Big Shot***, he was given his own title. Second of a publisher, lasting only 4 issues. (He remained the main feature in ***Big Shot*** for 9 years.)
(a,c,e)

★★SPYSMASHER No. 1 (Fall/41, Faw, Av)-Popular war hero graduating from ***Whiz*** into his own title, lasting 2 years. Maiden issue featured unusual logo printed in metallic silver.
(a,c,e)

STAR SPANGLED COMICS No. 1(10/41, DC, H)-DC's first patriotic theme title featuring the *Star Spangled Kid*. Due to the weak contents, the title had a dramatic format change with No. 7 when *The Guardian* and *The Newsboy Legion* were introduced.
(b,e)

WORLD FAMOUS HEROES MAGAZINE No. 1 (10/41, Comic Corp, TR)-Similar theme to PMI's ***Real Heroes***, and Eastern's ***Heroic***, with stories of famous people, lasting 4 issues.
(e)

AIRFIGHTERS COMICS No. 1 (11/41, Hill, Av)-An early attempt at an aviation theme comic (like ***Wings***), lasting only one issue. A year later the title was revived more successfully with a new 'dynamic' character in *Airboy*.
(e)

GREAT COMICS No. 1 (11/41, Great, H)-First of a publisher, featuring super heroes. The third and last issue is a classic: *Futuro* takes *Hitler* to Hell.
(e,k)

MAN OF WAR No. 1 (11/41, Centaur, H)-Centaur's third and last patriotic theme title, lasting 2 issues. Conjecture is that Centaur itself expired with this book.
(e)

SCOOP COMICS No. 1 (11/41, Chesler, H)-Chesler's third attempt at a comeback with this anthology of super heroes. Debut of *Rocketman* and *Rocketgirl*, lasting 8 issues.
(e)

U.S. JONES No. 1 (11/41, Fox, H)-Fox's second patriotic theme title, lasting 2 issues.
(e)

★★★★ALL-STAR COMICS No. 8 (11-12/41, DC, H)—*Wonder Woman*, the first super heroine, created by Charles Moulton and drawn by H.G. Peter, debuted in this issue as an 8 page add-on. Her origin continued in ***Sensation*** No. 1, where she becomes the lead feature. A trend setter.
(a,b,c,d,f,h,i,j)

BANG-UP COMICS No. 1 (12/41, Progressive, H)-A new publisher entered the field. This series was mediocre in its content only surviving 3 issues.
(e,k)

CAPTAIN AERO COMICS No. 7 (12/41, Hoke, Av)-Cashing in on the popularity of *Spy Smasher* and *Captain Midnight*, this publisher began with another aviation hero. With strong, colorful covers, the series lasted 5 years.
(e)

CHOICE COMICS No. 1 (12/41, Great, H)-The publisher's second title. A mixed anthology, lasting 3 issues.
(e)

MASTER COMICS No. 21 (12/41, Faw, H)-*Captain Marvel* and *Bulletman* team-up to fight *Captain Nazi*. A classic battle sequence, rare in comics at this time. High impact (classic) Raboy cover and story art.
(a,b,c)

PIONEER PICTURE STORIES No. 1 (12/41, S&S, TR)-An anthology of true stories about heroes (ala ***Heroic Comics***), lasting 9 issues.
(e)

★★★★PEP COMICS No. 22 (12/41, MLJ, TA)-The eternal sophomore and his friends began the first of over forty consecutive terms at Riverdale High. Never rose above pat formula, but survived vagaries of shifting market that did in a host of illustrious predecessors and glut of imitators (many of which originated at MLJ itself). Auxillary characters achieved stardom with their own titles. Trend setter, lasting beyond 40 years.
(a,b,c,d,f,h,i,j)

PUNCH COMICS No. 1 (12/41, Chesler, H)-Chesler's fourth attempt to get back into the market. A mixed anthology series with a successful format, lasting 6 years.
(e)

★★★WHIZ COMICS No. 25 (12/12/41, Faw, H)-*Captain Marvel* was cloned for the second time (see *Lt. Marvels*) into a junior size as *Captain Marvel Jr.* Classic art by Mac Raboy gave the character a slick streamlined 'Raymond' look. He was given immediate headlining in *Master Comics*. This was the first significant character cloned.
(a,b,c,d,j)

X-MAS COMICS No. 1 (12/41, Faw, H)-A new concept. Earlier in the year, Fawcett began over-running certain selected comics with indicias, page numbers, etc. removed. These comics were then bound up into a thick book (324-pgs.) to be sold as a special comic for Christmas. This successful format evolved into several other titles and lasted for 11 years.
(a,b,c,e,f,h,j)

CAPTAIN MARVEL THRILL BOOK nn (1941, Faw, H)-A large-size black & white comic reprinting popular *Captain Marvel* stories, lasting one issue. (Half text, half illustration.)
(e)

DICKIE DARE No. 1 (1941, Eastern, R)-Another single theme anthology title of the popular strip, lasting 4 issues.
(e)

DOUBLE UP nn (1941, Elliott, H)-The same idea as ***Double***, except this

was a one-shot remarketing of remaindered digest-sized issues of ***Speed, Spitfire*** and ***Pocket***. Probably a special deal to Elliott due to heavy returns?
(e)

FACE, THE No. 1 (1941, CCG, H)-The popular strip from ***Big Shot*** achieved brief stardom, lasting only two issues.
(e)

KEY RING COMICS (1941, Dell, An)-A special formatted comic series of 16 pages each to put in a two-ring binder (sold as a set of five).
(e)

TRAIL BLAZERS No. 1 (1941, S&S, TR)-True fact anthology of heroic deeds, lasting 4 issues.
(e)

USA IS READY No. 1 (1941, Dell, W)-Dell's second war title lasting one issue.
(e)

★★★**ANIMAL COMICS** No. 1 (12-1/41-42, Dell, F)-Debut of Walt Kelly's classic character, *Pogo*, which became syndicated in 1948. Dell's third funny animal single theme anthology title following the success of ***WDC&S*** and ***Looney Tunes***. The first funny animal comic with original characters at Dell.
(a,c,d,e,j)

1942■

FOUR MOST No. 1 (Wint/41-42, Novelty, H)-A showcase title featuring Novelty's best characters from ***Target*** and ***Blue Bolt***. Series taken over by Dick Cole with No. 3 on. Their third title.
(a,b,c,e)

★**LEADING COMICS** No. 1 (Wint/41-42, DC, H)-Like ***All-Star***, this title provided a showcase for DC's secondary heroes (a poor man's *All-Star*). Series ran 14 issues then changed to a funny animal format for the rest of its 7 year existence.
(e)

★★★★★**SENSATION COMICS** No. 1 (1/42, DC, H)-*Wonder Woman's* origin continued from ***All-Star*** No. 8 (her first appearance). A very strong character from the onset, achieving stardom instantly as a headline feature of this series. She won her own title within a few months which has run uninterrupted for over 40 years. (One of the few characters to achieve this kind of exposure.)
(a,b,c,e,f,h,j)

SPECIAL COMICS No. 1 (Wint/41-42, MLJ, H)-A one-shot special featuring *The Hangman* from ***Pep Comics***. A hit on the stands, the character was launched into his own series with No. 2.
(c,e)

V...- COMICS No. 1 (1/42, Fox, H)-another short-lived title from Fox. Their third patriotic theme comic. Introduced *V-Man*, lasted only two issues.
(e)

AMERICA'S BEST COMICS No. 1 (2/42, BP, H)-A showcase title to give more exposure to their top characters. The high impact covers (many by Schomburg) sustained the run, lasting 7 years.
(a,b,c,e)

CAMP COMICS No. 1 (2/42, Dell, Hm)-A mixed (humorous) anthology title with pretty girl photo covers. An unusual format slanted to the soldier boys at camp.
(e)

★★**GENE AUTRY COMICS** No. 1 (2/42, Faw, Ws)-The second newsstand continuous series western title devoted to a single character. *Gene* ties with *Roy Rogers* as the most popular cowboy star of the sound era. Title survived 18 years.
(a,b,c,e,h,j,l)

JINGLE JANGLE COMICS No. 1 (2/42, Eastern Color, Hm)-A young children's comic, containing illustrations and script by George Carlson, a children's book heavyweight (*Uncle Wiggily*). Eastern's second anthology title of original material (see ***Heroic***), lasting 7 years.
(a,b,e,j)

TRUE SPORT PICTURE STORIES No. 5 (2/42, S&S, Sp)-Continued from *Sport Comics*, lasting 7 years.
(e)

CAPTAIN COURAGEOUS COMICS No. 6 (3/42, Ace, H)-Introduced in ***Banner***, the character was given his own title but lasted only one issue.
(e)

TOUGH KID SQUAD No. 1 (3/42, Timely, H)-Timely's second series devoted to sidekicks (see ***Young Allies***). Highly prized due to its rarity.
(e)

★★**BOY COMICS** No. 3 (4/42, Lev, H)-Gleason's second successful title, introducing *Crimebuster*. This series survived 14 years due to Biro's strong, complex plotting.
(a,b,c,d,e,j)

COMEDY COMICS No. 9 (4/42, Timely, H)-The title is misleading. A super hero anthology title changing to a humorous and funny animal format early on.
(e)

HANGMAN COMICS No. 2 (Spr/42, MLJ, H)-The smash hit of ***Pep Comics*** received his own series, but lasted only 7 issues.
(e)

★**JOKER COMICS** No. 1 (4/42, Timely, Hm)-First *Powerhouse Pepper* by Wolverton. Wolverton, an original if there ever was one, stood totally aloof from the mainstream of comic art. His effect on later comics ranging from the original ***Mad*** to the sixties undergrounds, is incalculable. (He tried to fit in, but the effect of playing it straight made his work even more bizzarre.)
(a,b,c,d,e,f,g,j)

SHEENA, QUEEN OF THE JUNGLE No. 1 (Spr/42, FH, J)-After three years exposure in ***Jumbo Comics***, *Sheena* finally graduated to her own title, lasting 18 issues spread over 11 years.
(a,b,c,e)

★★**STAR SPANGLED COMICS** No. 7 (4/42, DC, H)-Debut of *The Guardian* and *The Newsboy Legion* by Simon and Kirby (vintage). Title lasted 11 years.
(a,b,c,d,j)

WAMBI, JUNGLE BOY No. 1 (Spr/42, FH, J)-From ***Jungle Comics***. Not strong enough to carry his own title which had erratic publishing (18 issues in 11 years).
(e)

★★★★**CRIME DOES NOT PAY** No. 22 (6/42, Lev, C)-Aside from being the first crime comic, this title was the first of many to be deliberately targeted at the adult reader. Inspired by the widely read ***True Detective*** - style magazines of the time. Implicit and unsavory subject matter, in the context of what was popularly understood as publications for children, assured the attention and disapproval of Wertham and others. Established conventions of graphically depicted violence that would be exploited to the extreme in the horror comics of a decade later. Arguably the third most influential comic ever published (after ***Action*** and ***Superman***), ***CDNP*** was a belated trend setter. Gleason had the field all to himself for six years. Then, in 1948 the industry suffered a severe slump in sales. In desperation, publishers turned *en masse* to the formerly untapped 'crime' market. This move was abetted in part by Gleason himself. In mid-1947 he had begun publishing circulation figures on the covers of ***CDNP***, reporting sales of 5 million - 6 million copies (per issue?), an astounding record for a comics periodical and, an open invitation to imitation.
(a,b,c,e,f,h,i,j)

★**DETECTIVE COMICS** No. 64 (6/42, DC, H)-Simon and Kirby introduce the *Boy Commandos*. A more timely version of the *Newsboy Legion*, this popular series found the Axis plagued with a platoon of wise-cracking juveniles. An immediate hit, the lads were rewarded with a quarterly of their own within a matter of months.
(a,c,d,j)

FAIRY TALE PARADE No. 1 (6-7/42, Dell, F)-Dell's second continuous series funny animal title with original characters. Its popularity was carried entirely by the imaginative illustrative genius of Walt Kelly.
(c,e)

BIG CHIEF WAHOO No. 1 (7/42, Eastern, R)-Popular transfer strip debuts in his own comic series, lasting 23 issues.
(c,e)

DIXIE DUGAN No. 1 (7/42, CCG, R)-Popular strip character given own title, lasting 7 years (13 issues).
(e)

KRAZY KOMICS No. 1 (7/42, Timely, F)-With four funny animal anthology titles on the stands (all by Dell), Timely entered this new developing field. This series had a humorous format with no strong characters, lasting 4 years. The second publisher in this genre.
(e)

NAPOLEON AND UNCLE ELBY No. 1 (7/42), Eastern Color, R)-A one-shot single theme anthology title of the popular transfer strip.
(e)

NEW FUNNIES No. 65 (7/42, Dell, F)-The funny animal fever was catching on as Dell gave stardom to their newly acquired characters, *Andy Panda* and *Woody Woodpecker.* Lantz created these characters who became an instant success for Dell's ***The Funnies***. This was Dell's fifth funny animal series (with only six on the stands).
(a,b,c,e,j)

OAKY DOAKS No. 1 (7/42, Eastern Color, R)-A one-shot strip reprint book which couldn't compete on the stands.
(e)

STRICTLY PRIVATE No. 1 (7/42), Eastern Color, R)-A two-issue run of the famous strip, not surviving as a comic book.
(e)

WAR VICTORY ADVENTURES No. 1 (Sum/42, Harv, W)—A unique super hero title produced to promote purchase of war savings bonds, lasting 3 issues.
(e)

★★★★WONDER WOMAN No. 1 (Sum/42, DC, H)-One of the few characters in comics to make her own title just months from her debut in ***All-Star*** No. 8. The only mythological character to flourish in the comics format, her only concession to the present was adopting a modern costume. The amazing Amazon was a trend setter whose popularity has lasted beyond 40 years.
(a,b,c,e,j)

WAR HEROES No. 1 (7-9/42, Dell, W)-Dell's third war title, lasting 11 issues.
(e)

★CAPTAIN MIDNIGHT No. 1 (9/42, Faw, Av)-This book heralds one of the most changed transfer characters adapted successfully to the comic book format. Fawcett's version of the character is the most memorable (see ***The Funnies*** No. 57), lasting 6 years. Kept alive by the longlasting radio series and a movie serial. A spin-off of Spy Smasher.
(a,b,c,e)

FIGHTING YANK No. 1 (9/42, BP, H)-After a year's exposure in ***Startling***, the colonial hero was given his own series. The outstanding Schomburg covers sustained the run, lasting 7 years.
(a,b,c,e,j)

OUR GANG COMICS No. 1 (9-10/42, Dell, F)-A strong early licensed group from MGM films who didn't quite come across as well in the comic medium due to necessary changes in the stereotyping of *Buckwheat* and others. The comic version is mainly collected due to the outstanding art by Walt Kelly and the back-up strips by Carl Barks.
(a,b,c,e,f,j,l)

★COO COO COMICS No. 1 (10/42, BP, F)-Seeing the stands beginning to swell with Dell's funny animal titles (5), Better got on the band wagon. *Super Mouse* debuted, the first funny animal super hero (cloned from *Superman*). (7 funny animal titles now on the stands.)
(a,b,c,d,e,f,h,i,j)

★★★★★DONALD DUCK FOUR COLOR No. 9 (10/42, Dell, F)-Debut of anonymous artist, who breathed life into the character and turned the strip into full length adventure stories. Carl Barks' successful adaptation won him the position as *Donald Duck's* biographer for almost three decades beginning with ***Walt Disney's Comics and Stories*** No. 31.
(a,b,c,g,h,j)

★JUNGLE GIRL No. 1 (Fall/42, Faw, J)-Inspired by the popular film serial, *Perils of Nyoka*, this one-shot introduced the jungle heroine to comics. The series was picked up again in 1945 (retitled ***Nyoka***), lasting 8 years.
(a,b,c,e,f,j,l)

PICTURE STORIES FROM THE BIBLE No. 1 (Fall/42, DC, TR)-The pilot model of M. C. Gaines' projected 'educational comics' line was laudable in concept but squelched at the stands by abysmal art, pedantic scripting and the normal resistance of kids to anything even remotely preachy. Sustained primarily by lot sales to educators and church groups. Ironically, the first comic ever to bear the EC seal.
(a,c,e,i,j,l)

SUPERSNIPE COMICS No. 6 (10/42, S&S, H)-Probably the best, and certainly the most original comic book character of this pulp publisher. A super hero parody lasting 7 years.
(a,b,c,e,f,j)

★TERRY-TOONS COMICS No. 1 (10/42, Timely, F)-20th Century Fox's characters enter the comic field with this book. Timely's second funny animal anthology series (8 titles are now on the stands). 20th Century Fox's *Mighty Mouse* appeared in films the following year and entered this run with No. 38.
(a,b,c,e,j,l)

★AIR FIGHTERS No. 2 (11/42, Hill, Av)-First appearance of one of the top aviation features also marked Hillman's first successful title. Engaging origin featured air-minded monk who designed and built the premier imaginary aircraft in all of comics. At the controls of the unusual bat-winged orinthopter, dubbed *Birdie*, was the youth who would become known as *Airboy*. He managed to make the standard garb of the pilot goggles, scarf, flight jacket, *et al*-look as if they were designed expressly for him. Thoughtful scripting and complimentary art (ala Caniff) propelled this feature through the war years and beyond. Duration 11 years. (*The Heap*, one of the most original characters in comics, began in the next issue.)
(a,b,c,d,j)

★★CAPTAIN MARVEL JR No. 1 (11/42, Faw, H)-Fawcett's second most popular hero (from ***Master***) was given his own series. Raboy classic covers/story art sustained the run, lasting 11 years.
(a,b,c,e)

MICKEY FINN No. 1 (11/42, Eastern Color, R)-The popular transfer character tried his wings in a title of his own. Like *Sparky Watts*, only 17 issues came out in a 10 year period.
(a,c,e)

SPARKY WATTS No. 1 (11/42, CCG, R)-Humorous, offbeat character (proven in ***Big Shot***) is given own title, struggling through 10 issues in 7 years.
(a,c,e)

TOPIX No. 1 (11/42, CG, Re)-The first continuous series comic with a religious theme, lasting 10 years. First of a publisher.
(b,e,i,j,k)

★CAPTAIN MARVEL ADVENTURES No. 18 (12/11/42, Faw, H)-*Captain Marvel* is cloned again. Debut of *Mary Marvel* and *The Marvel Family. Mary Marvel* was given instant stardom in ***Wow***.
(a,b,c,d,j)

FAWCETT'S FUNNY ANIMAL COMICS No. 1 (12/42, Faw, F)-The first appearance of *Hoppy The Marvel Bunny*, (cloned from *Captain Marvel*), lasting 13 years. The second funny animal super hero (see ***Coo Coo***). Fawcett joined Dell, Timely and Better entering the funny animal market (10 titles now on the stands). (*Captain Marvel* himself introduced *Hoppy* on the cover.)
(a,b,c,d,e,h,j)

FUNNY BOOK No. 1 (12/42, PMI, F)-Another publisher entered the funny animal market with this book. Weak concepts overall, the title lasting 9 issues over 4 years (10 titles now on the stands).
(e)

GIFT COMICS No. 1 (12/42, Faw, H)-Fawcett's second thick-format title containing original comics to be released at Christmas with ***Holiday*** and ***Xmas*** for 50¢.
(a,c,e)

HIT COMICS No. 25 (12/42, Qua, H)-*Kid Eternity* debuts. Recurring war-era theme of life after life was given novel twist in this long-running series. Youthful hero, dying ahead of his appointed time, was not only miraculously restored to life but granted the ability to call on all the great heroes of the past for assistance in solving crimes (see *The Fighting Yank*). Intriguing concept was given usual stellar Iger shop treatment.
(a,b,c,d,j)

HOLIDAY COMICS No. 1 (12/42, Faw, H)-Fawcett's third thick-format title of original comics to be released at Christmas with ***Gift*** and ***Xmas*** for 25¢.
(a,c,e)

SANTA CLAUS FUNNIES No. 1 (12/42, Dell, F)-A special Christmas book illustrated by Kelly. A successful concept that was repeated annually for 20 years.
(a,b,c,e)

AMERICA IN ACTION nn (1942, Dell, W)-A one-shot war anthology book.
(e)

FAMOUS STORIES No. 1 (1942, Dell, Lit)-An educational theme comic, similar to ***Classic Comics***, not lasting beyond the 2nd issue.
(e)

JOE PALOOKA No. 1 (1942, CCG, R)-With proven success in ***Big***

Shot (not to mention syndication), the character became a star in his own title. Early issues boast "over 1,000,000 copies sold." The series lasted 19 years.
(a,b,c,e)

WAR STORIES No. 1 (1942, Dell, W)-Dell's fourth war theme anthology title, lasting 8 issues. *Night Devils*, a mysterious costumed war team debuted in No. 3.
(e)

1943 ■

ALL NEW COMICS No. 1 (1/43, Harv, H)-A super hero anthology title of mediocre quality, lasting 15 issues.
(e)

★★★**ARCHIE COMICS** No. 1 (Wint/42-43, AP, TA)-Early stardom for a non-super hero theme. A successful formula with many spin-off characters, lasting beyond 40 years.
(a,b,c,d,e,h,i,j)

BLACK TERROR No. 1 (Wint/42-43, BP, H)-Fighting his way from ***Exciting***, the character begins his own series. Sterling costume. High impact Schomburg covers mislead the buyer as to the quality of the contents. Lasted 7 years.
(a,b,c,e,j)

BOY COMMANDOS No. 1 (Wint/42-43, DC, W)-After *Captain America*, this was the second title that Simon and Kirby had all to themselves. Pat variation of favorite S&K- theme: Kid group with adult mentor. Seldom rose above the expected, but S&K were at their loosest and the strip conveys the sense of fun they probably had doing it. Earlier covers, sans redundant blurbs and intrusive dialogue balloons, are superb poster art.
(a,b,c,e,j)

CAPTAIN BATTLE No. 3 (Wint/42-43, Mag. Press, H)-After a year's delay, the character from ***Silver Streak*** was given another chance, only lasting 3 issues.
(e)

CLUE COMICS No. 1 (1/43, Hill, H)-Hillman's second most successful title. Unusual heroes and bizarre villains sustained run for four years.
(e)

COMIC CAVALCADE No. 1 (Wint/42-43, DC, H)-Following the success of ***World's Finest***, DC launched this companion book in thick format featuring their next tier of top characters, *Wonder Woman, The Flash* and *Green Lantern*.
(a,b,c,e)

COMICS DIGEST No. 1 (Wint/42-43, PMI, TR)-A one-shot war theme reprint anthology (pocket size) from ***True Comics***.
(e)

FLYING CADET No. 1 (1/43, Flying Cadet, Av)-A true theme World War II aviation anthology (with real photos), lasting 4 years.
(e)

GOLDEN ARROW No. 1 (Wint/42-43, Faw, Ws)-Fawcett's original western character from ***Whiz*** finally given own title, lasting 6 issues.
(a,e)

HELLO PAL COMICS No. 1 (1/43, Harv, An)-Unusual format featuring photographic covers of movie stars. *Rocketman* and *Rocketgirl* appear (see ***Scoop***), lasting 3 issues.
(e)

MISS FURY COMICS No. 1 (Wint/42-43, Timely, H)-A strong transfer character by Tarpe Mills. Noteworthy and unique in that she rarely appeared in costume.
(a,c,e,f,j)

MAJOR HOOPLE COMICS No. 1 (1/43, BP, R)-A one-shot comic of the famous strip character, as Better tried to enter the reprint market.
(e)

REAL FUNNIES No. 1 (1/43, Nedor, F)-The publisher's second funny animal title (11 titles now on stands), only lasting 3 issues. First appearance of *The Black Terrier* (cloned from *The Black Terror*), the third funny animal super hero.
(e)

RED DRAGON COMICS No. 5 (1/43, S&S, An)-Pulpy anthology series not strong enough to last over 5 issues.
(e)

DON WINSLOW OF THE NAVY No. 1 (2/43, Faw, W)-His comic book career was launched here with an introduction by *Captain Marvel* himself. Successful adaptation of this popular transfer character, lasting 12 years.
(a,b,c,e,j,l)

HEADLINE COMICS No. 1 (2/43, Prize, TR)-Taking up the "True" theme of PMI's ***True*** and ***Real Heroes*** and Better's **Real Life**, Prize entered the field with this, their second title, which lasted 13 years.
(b,e)

HOPALONG CASSIDY No. 1 (2/43, Faw, Ws)-A one-shot issue continuing as a series three years later. The third continuous series newsstand western title, lasting 16 years. A transfer character kept alive by William Boyd's strong following in the movies and on TV.
(a,b,c,e)

IBIS, THE INVINCIBLE No. 1 (2/43, Faw, Mg)-As a solid back-up feature in ***Whiz***, he was invincible, but not invincible enough to support a title of his own. The title expired after 6 issues.
(e)

KID KOMICS No. 1 (2/43, Timely, H)-Timely's third series devoted to sidekicks. The Schomburg covers and guest appearances of secondary characters sustained the run through 10 issues.
(e)

ALL HERO COMICS No. 1 (3/43, Faw, H)-Fawcett's second title that showcased their top characters (see ***America's Greatest***). A thick format one shot.
(a,c,e)

CAPTAIN MARVEL ADVENTURES No. 22 (3/43, Faw, H)—Begins the 25-issue *Mr. Mind* serial which captured nationwide attention at the time. Tremendous and brilliant marketing strategy by Fawcett. An epic by any standard, unmatched before or since.
(c,d,f,h,i,j)

COMEDY COMICS No. 14 (3/43, Timely, F)-The first *Super Rabbit* (the fourth funny animal super hero) (the 12th title on the stands). Given his own title the following year. (An imitation of ***Hoppy The Marvel Bunny***.)
(a,c,d,e,j)

FUNNY FUNNIES No. 1 (4/43, BP, F)-A one-shot funny animal title (their third) (13 titles now on the stands). No enduring characters.
(e)

★★★★**WALT DISNEY'S COMICS AND STORIES** No. 31 (4/43, Dell, F)-Anonymous staffer who defined what funny animal continuity is all about began this issue (2nd Barks *DD* story; see ***DD Four Color*** No. 9). Cinched long-term success of Disney anthology. One of a half-dozen absolute masters of the form, Carl Barks' achievement on individual stories is exceeded only by remarkable consistency of the series over the length of its run (over 40 years).
(a,b,c,j)

GOOFY COMICS No. 1 (6/43, Nedor, F)-Nedor's fourth funny animal title and one of the most enduring, lasting 10 years. No memorable characters. (13 funny animal titles on the stands.)
(b,e)

JOLLY JINGLES No. 10 (Sum/43, MLJ, F)-A new publisher tried their hand at funny animals, introducing *Super Duck* (the fifth funny animal super hero). (A hybrid of *Superman* and *Donald Duck*.) (14 titles on the stands.)
(a,c,d,e,j)

★★**PLASTIC MAN** No. 1 (Sum/43, Qua, H)-After a slow start, this title outlasts ***Police Comics***, surviving 13 years. One of the top hero concepts carried by the exciting plotting/art of Jack Cole.
(a,b,c,e)

HAPPY COMICS No. 1 (8/43, Standard, F)-Their fifth funny animal title. No memorable characters, lasting 7 years (14 titles on the stands.)
(b,e)

ALL-SELECT COMICS No. 1 (Fall/43, Timely, H)-Timely's second showcase title featuring their top three characters (see ***All Winners***). Series carried by Schomburg covers (a proven sales feature), lasting 3 years.
(a,c,e)

ALL SURPRISE No. 1 (Fall/43, Timely, F)-Timely's fourth funny animal title, giving more exposure to their leading character, *Super Rabbit*, lasting 4 years. (15 titles on the stands.)
(e)

SUPER RABBIT No. 1 (Fall/43, Timely, F)-After his debut in ***Comedy Comics***, *Super Rabbit* is given his own title, lasting 5 years. (15 titles on the stands.)
(e)

CAPTAIN BATTLE JR No. 1 (Fall/43, Comic House, H)—Clone of *Captain Battle. The Claw vs. The Ghost*, lasting 2 issues.
(e)

GIGGLE COMICS No. 1 (10/43, ACG, F)-Ties as first title of a new publisher, reinforcing the trend to funny animals. The quality and style of ACG's whole line was heavily influenced by the mastery of the teacher-artist of Ken Hultgren, the series' artist (beginning in 1944). This title lasted 12 years. (17 titles on the stands.)
(a,b,c,e,j,k)

HA HA COMICS No. 1 (10/43, ACG, F)-Ties as first title of a new publisher, reinforcing the trend to funny animals. A double impact–with sister title on the stands. Ingenious plotting and art by Ken Hultgren begins the following year. This series lasted 12 years. (17 titles on the stands.)
(a,b,c,e,j,k)

SUSPENSE COMICS No. 1 (12/43, Continental, D)-Debut of *The Grey Mask* (imitation of *The Spirit*). Atmospheric radio drama in a comic book form, lasting 3 years.
(e)

AVIATION CADETS nn (1943, S&S, Av)-A World War II aviation anthology one-shot. Navy pre-flight training involving sports.
(e)

COLUMBIA COMICS No. 1 (1943, Wise, R)-More exposure for Columbia's reprint characters, *Joe Palooka, Dixie Duggan*, etc., lasting 4 issues.
(e)

POWERHOUSE PEPPER No. 1 (1943, Timely, Hm)-The protagonist of ***Joker Comics*** of a year earlier, Wolverton's humorous plotting made this character a memorable one. Popular enough to receive his own title.
(a,c,e,j)

TINY TOTS COMICS No. 1 (1943, Dell, F)-A one-shot anthology book of funny animals with Walt Kelly art.
(e)

TREASURE COMICS nn (1943, Prize, H)-Rebinding of coverless copies of ***Prize*** No. 7-11 from 1942. A very rare book with only one copy known to exist.
(e)

UNITED STATES MARINES nn (1943, Wise, W)-A documentary style war anthology series mixed with magazine-type photo features from the front, surviving one year. The title was resurrected for a brief period after the Korean conflict.
(e)

ALL FUNNY COMICS No. 1 (Wint/43-44, DC, Hm)-DC's first all funny anthology title. A popular series with the humorous plotting of *Genius Jones*, lasting 4 years.
(e,j)

BLACK HOOD COMICS No. 9 (Wint/43-44, MLJ, H)-The Man of Mystery graduates from ***Top-Notch*** into his own title, lasting 11 issues.
(e)

CHRONOLOGICAL LIST OF COMIC BOOK TITLES BY PUBLISHER FOR PERIOD 1933 - 1943

(The indented titles are key books other than No. 1's)

ACE MAGAZINES
Sure-Fire No. 1, 6/40
Super Mystery No. 1, 7/40
Lightning No. 4, 12/40
Our Flag No. 1, 8/41
Banner No. 3, 9/41
Four Favorites No. 1, 9/41
Captain Courageous No. 6, 3/42

AMERICAN COMICS GROUP
Giggle No. 1, 10/43
Ha Ha No. 1, 10/43

BETTER PUBL. (Standard)
Best No. 1, 11/39
Thrilling No. 1, 2/40
Exciting No. 1, 4/40
Exciting No. 9, 5/41
Startling No. 1, 6/40
Real Life No. 1, 9/41
Startling No. 10, 9/41
America's Best No. 1, 2/42
Fighting Yank No. 1, 9/42
Coo Coo No. 1, 10/42
Black Terror No. 1, Wint/42-43
Major Hoople No. 1, 1/43
Real Funnies No. 1, 1/43
Funny Funnies No. 1, 4/43
Goofy No. 1, 6/43
Happy No. 1, 8/43

BILBARA PUBLISHING CO.
Cyclone No. 1, 6/40

CENTAUR PUBLICATIONS
Funny Pages V2/6, 3/38
Funny Pic. Stories V2/6, 3/38
Star Comics No. 10, 3/38
Star Ranger No. 10, 3/38
Cowboy No. 13, 7/38
Keen Detective No. 8, 7/38
Little Giant No. 1, 7/38
Amazing Mystery Funnies No. 1,8/38
Little Giant Movie No. 1, 8/38
Funny Pages V2/10, 9/38
Star Ranger Funnies No. 15, 10/38
Little Giant Det. No. 1, 10/38
Keen Komics V2/1, 5/39
Amazing Mystery Funnies V2/7, 7/39
Comic Pages V3/4, 7/39
Keen Detective V2/7, 7/39
Amazing Man No. 5, 9/39
Amazing Adventure Funnies No. 1, 6/40
Fantoman No. 2, 8/40
Masked Marvel No. 1, 9/40
Arrow, The No. 1, 10/40
Super Spy No. 1, 10/40
Detective Eye No. 1, 11/40
Wham No. 1, 11/40
Stars and Stripes No. 2, 5/41
Liberty Scouts No. 2, 6/41
World Famous Heroes No. 1, 10/41
Man Of War No. 1, 11/41

CATECHETICAL GUILD
Topix No. 1, 11/42

HARRY 'A' CHESLER
Star No. 1, 2/37
Star Ranger No. 1, 2/37
Feature Funnies No. 1, 10/37
Cocomalt Big Book No. 1, 1938
Yankee No. 1, 9/41
Dynamic No. 1, 10/41
Scoop No. 1, 11/41
Punch No. 1, 12/41

COLUMBIA COMICS GROUP
Big Shot No. 1, 5/40
Skyman No. 1, Fall/41
Face, The No. 1, 1941
Dixie Duggan No. 1, 7/42
Joe Palooka No. 1, 1942
Sparky Watts No. 1, 11/42

COMICS MAGAZINE
Comics Magazine No. 1, 5/36
Funny Pages No. 6, 11/36
Funny Picture Stories No. 1, 11/36
Detective Picture Stories No. 1, 12/36
Western Picture Stories No. 1, 2/37

DC COMICS
New Fun No. 1, 2/35
New Comics No. 1, 12/35
More Fun No. 7, 1/36
Big Book of Fun No. 1, Spr/36
New Book of Comics No. 1, 6-8/36
New Adventure No. 12, 1/37
Detective No. 1, 3/37
Action No. 1, 6/38
Detective No. 20, 10/38
Adventure No. 32, 11/38
All-American No. 1, 4/39
New York World's Fair, 3-5/39
Movie No. 1, 4/39
Detective No. 27, 5/39
Adventure No. 40, 7/39
Mutt and Jeff No. 1, Sum/39
Superman No. 1, Sum/39
Double Action No. 2, 1/40
Flash No. 1, 1/40
More Fun No. 52,53, 2,3/40
Adventure No. 48, 3/40
Batman No. 1, Spr/40
New York World's Fair, 3-5/40
More Fun No. 55, 5/40
All-American No. 16, 7/40
All-Star No. 1, Sum/40
All-American No. 19, 10/40
All-Star No. 3, Wint/40-41
Adventure No. 61, 4/41
World's Best No. 1, Spr/41
All Flash No. 1, Sum/41
World's Finest No. 2, Sum/41
Green Lantern No. 1, Fall/41
Star Spangled No. 1, 10/41
All-Star No. 8, 11-12/41
Leading No. 1, Wint/41-42
Sensation No. 1, 1/42
Star Spangled No. 7, 4/42
Detective No. 64, 6/42
Wonder Woman No. 1, Sum/42
Pic. Stories/Bible No. 1, Fall/42
Boy Commandos No. 1, Wint/42-43
Comic Cavalcade No. 1, Wint/42-43
All Funny No. 1, Wint/43-44

DELL PUBLISHING CO.
Popular No. 1, 2/36
Funnies No. 1, 10/36
Comics No. 1, 3/37
West. Action Thrillers No. 1, 4/37
100 Pages of Comics No. 1, 1937
Super No. 1, 5/38
Crackajack No. 1, 6/38
Nickel No. 1, 1938
Large Feature Comic No. 1, 1939
Four-Color No. 1, 1939
Donald Duck 4-Color No. 4, 3/40?
War No. 1, 5/40
W.D.'s Comics & Stories No. 1, 10/40
Mickey Mouse 4-Color No. 16, 4/41
Funnies No. 57, 7/41
Red Ryder No. 3, 8/41
Looney Tunes No. 1, Fall/41
Key Ring No. 1, 1941
Large Feature No. 1, 1941
USA Is Ready No. 1, 1941
Animal No. 1, 12-1/41-42
Camp No. 1, 2/42
Fairy Tale Parade No. 1, 6-7/42
New Funnies No. 65, 7/42
War Heroes No. 1, 7-9/42
Our Gang No. 1, 9-10/42
Santa Claus Funnies No. 1, 12/42
America In Action No. 1, 1942
Donald Duck 4-Color No. 9, 1942
Famous Stories No. 1, 1942
War Stories No. 1, 1942
W.D. Comics & Stories No. 31, 4/43
Tiny Tots No. 1, 1943

EASTERN COLOR
Funnies On Parade nn, 1933
F. F., A Carnival— nn, 1933
Century Of Comics nn, 1933
Skippy's Own Book nn, 1934
Famous Funnies Series 1, 1934
Famous Funnies No. 1, 7/34
Heroic No. 1, 8/40
Buck Rogers No. 1, Wint/40-41
Dickie Dare No. 1, 1941
Big Chief Wahoo No. 1, Wint/41-42
Jingle Jangle No. 1, 2/42
Oaky Doaks No. 1, 7/42
Mickey Finn No. 1, 11/42
Napoleon & Uncle Elby No. 1, 11/42
Strictly Private No. 1, 11/42
Tiny Tots No. 1, 1943

WILL EISNER
Spirit No. 1, 6/2/40

ELLIOT PUBLICATIONS
Double 1940
Double Up 1941

FAWCETT PUBLICATIONS
Flash No. 1, 1/40
Whiz No. 2, 2/40
Master No. 1, 3/40
Slam Bang No. 1, 3/40
Nickel No. 1, 5/40
Special Edition No. 1, 8/40
Western Desperado No. 8, 10/40
Wow No. 1, Wint/40-41
Captain Marvel No. 1, 1-2/41
America's Greatest No. 1, 5/41
Bulletman No. 1, 7/41
Minuteman No. 1, 7/41
Capt. Marvel Thrill Book 1941
Gene Autry No. 1, Fall/41
Spysmasher No. 1, Fall/41
Master No. 21, 12/41
Whiz No. 25, 12/12/41
Xmas No. 1, 12/41
Captain Midnight No. 1, 9/42
Jungle Girl No. 1, Fall/42
Captain Marvel Jr. No. 1, 11/42
Captain Marvel No. 18, 12/11/42
Fawcett's Funny Animals No. 1, 12/42
Gift No. 1, 12/42
Holiday No. 1, 12/42
Golden Arrow No. 1, Wint/42-43
Don Winslow No. 1, 2/43
Hopalong Cassidy No. 1, 2/43
Ibis No. 1, 2/43
All Hero No. 1, 3/43
Captain Marvel No. 22, 3/43

FICTION HOUSE
Jumbo No. 1, 9/38
Fight No. 1, 1/40
Jungle No. 1, 1/40
Planet No. 1, 1/40
Wings No. 1, 9/40
Rangers No. 1, 10/41
Sheena No. 1, Spr/42
Wambi No. 1, Spr/42

FLYING CADET
Flying Cadet No. 1, 1/43

FOX FEATURES SYNDICATE
Wonder No. 1, 5/39
Wonderworld No. 3, 7/39
Mysterymen No. 1, 8/39
Fantastic No. 1, 12/39
Blue Beetle No. 1, Wint/39-40
Science No. 1, 2/40
Weird No. 1, 4/40
Flame, The No. 1, Sum/40
Green Mask No. 1, Sum/40
Big 3 No. 1, Fall/40
Rex Dexter No. 1, Fall/40
Samson No. 1, Fall/40
Eagle, The No. 1, 7/41
U.S. Jones No. 1, 11/41
V-Comics No. 1, 1/42

FUNNIES, INC.
Motion Pic. Funn. Weekly No. 1, 5/39?
Green Giant No. 1, 1940

LEV GLEASON
Silver Streak No. 1, 12/39
Silver Streak No. 6, 9/40
Silver Streak No. 7, 1/41
Captain Battle No. 1, Sum/41
Daredevil No. 1, 7/41
Boy No. 3, 4/42
Crime Does Not Pay No. 22, 6/42
Captain Battle No. 3, Wint/42-43
Captain Battle Jr. No. 1, Fall/43

HUGO GERNSBACK
Superworld No. 1, 4/40

GILBERTON PUBLICATIONS
Classic No. 1, 10/41

GLOBE SYNDICATE
Circus No. 1, 6/38

GREAT PUBLICATIONS
Great No. 1, 11/41
Choice No. 1, 12/41

HARVEY PUBL. (Helnit)
Speed No. 1, 10/39
Champion No. 2, 12/39
Champ No. 11, 10/40
Green Hornet No. 1, 12/40
Pocket No. 1, 8/41
War Victory No. 1, Sum/42
All New No. 1, 1/43
Hello Pal No. 1, 1/43

HAWLEY PUBLICATIONS
Captain Easy nn, 1939
Red Ryder No. 1, 9/40
Sky Blazers No. 1, 9/40
Hi-Spot No. 2, 11/40

HILLMAN PERIODICALS
Miracle No. 1, 2/40
Rocket No. 1, 3/40
Victory No. 1, 8/41
Air Fighters No. 1, 11/41
Air Fighters No. 2, 11/42
Clue No. 1, 1/43

HOLYOKE (Continental)
Crash No. 1, 5/40
Crash No. 4, 9/40
Catman No. 1, 5/41
Captain Fearless No. 1, 8/41
Captain Aero No. 7, 12/41
Suspense No. 1, 12/43

HYPER PUBLICATIONS
Hyper Mystery No. 1, 5/40

K.K. PUBLICATIONS
Mickey Mouse Mag. No. 1, Sum/35
Mickey Mouse Mag. V5/12, 9/40

DAVID MCKAY PUBL.
King No. 1, 4/36
Wow No. 1, 5/36
Ace No. 1, 4/37
Feature Book nn, 1-4/37
Magic No. 1, 8/39
Future No. 1, 6/40

MLJ MAGAZINES
Blue Ribbon No. 1, 11/39
Top-Notch No. 1, 12/39
Pep No. 1, 1/40
Zip No. 1, 2/40
Shield-Wizard No. 1, Sum/40
Top-Notch No. 9, 10/40
Blue Ribbon No. 9, 2/41
Jackpot No. 1, Spr/41
Pep No. 17, 7/41
Pep No. 22, 12/41
Special No. 1, Wint/41-42
Hangman No. 2, Spr/42
Archie No. 1, Wint/42-43
Jolly Jingles No. 10, Sum/43
Black Hood No. 9, Wint/43-44

NITA PUBLICATIONS
Whirlwind No. 1, 6/40

NOVELTY PUBLICATIONS
Target No. 1, 2/40
Blue Bolt No. 1, 6/40
Four Most No. 1, Wint/41-42

PARENT'S MAGAZINE INST.
True No. 1, 4/41
Calling All Girls No. 1, 9/41
Real Heroes No. 1, 9/41
Funny Book No. 1, 12/42
Comics Digest No. 1, Wint/42-43

PRIZE PUBLICATIONS
Prize No. 1, 3/40
Prize No. 7, 9/40
Headline No. 1, 2/43
Treasure nn, 1943

PROGRESSIVE PUBLISHERS
Bang-Up No. 1, 12/41

QUALITY COMICS GROUP
Feature No. 21, 6/39
Smash No. 1, 8/39
Feature No. 27, 12/39
Crack No. 1, 5/40
Hit No. 1, 7/40
National No. 1, 7/40
Military No. 1, 8/41
Police No. 1, 8/41
Uncle Sam No. 1, 8/41
Doll Man No. 1, Fall/41
Hit No. 25, 12/42
Plastic Man No. 1, Sum/43

RALSTON-PURINA CO.
Tom Mix No. 1, 9/40

STREET AND SMITH PUBL.
Shadow No. 1, 3/40
Doc Savage No. 1, 5/40
Bill Barnes No. 1, 10/40
Sport No. 1, 10/40
Army and Navy No. 1, 5/41
Super Magic No. 1, 5/41
Super Magician No. 2, 9/41
Pioneer Pic. Stories No. 1, 12/41
Trail Blazers No. 1, 1941
True Sport Pic. Stories No. 5, 2/42
Supersnipe No. 6, 10/42
Devil Dogs No. 1, 1942
Remember Pearl Harbor nn, 1942
Red Dragon No. 5, 1/43
Aviation Cadets No. 1, 1943

SUN PUBLICATIONS
Colossus No. 1, 3/40
Sun Fun No. 1, 3/40

TIMELY COMICS (Marvel)
Marvel No. 1, 11/39
Marvel Mystery No. 2, 12/39
Daring Mystery No. 1, 1/40
Mystic No. 1, 3/40
Marvel Mystery No. 9, 7/40
Red Raven No. 1, 8/40
Human Torch No. 2, Fall/40
Captain America No. 1, 3/41
Sub-Mariner No. 1, Spr/41
All-Winners No. 1, Sum/41
Young Allies No. 1, Sum/41
USA No. 1, 8/41
Tough Kid Squad No. 1, 3/42
Comedy No. 9, 4/42
Joker No. 1, 4/42
Krazy No. 1, 7/42
Terry-Toons No. 1, 10/42
Miss Fury No. 1, Wint/42-43
Kid Komics No. 1, 2/43
Comedy No. 14, 3/43
All-Select No. 1, Fall/43
All-Surprise No. 1, Fall/43
Super Rabbit No. 1, Fall/43
Powerhouse Pepper No. 1, 1943

UNITED FEATURES SYND.
Tip Top No. 1, 4/36
Comics On Parade No. 1, 4/38
Single Series No. 1, 1938
Okay No. 1, 7/40
O.K. No. 1, 7/40
Sparkler No. 1, 7/40
United No. 1, 8/40
Sparkler No. 1, 7/41

WHITMAN PUBLISHING CO.
Mammoth No. 1, 1937
Donald Duck nn, 1938

WILLIAM H. WISE
Columbia Comics No. 1, 1943
United States Marines No. 1, 1943

COMICS WITH LITTLE IF ANY VALUE

There exists in the comic book market, as in all other collector's markets, items, usually of recent origin, that have relatively little if any value. Why even mention it? We wouldn't, except for one thing–this is where you could probably take your worst beating, investment-wise. Since these books are listed by dealers in such profusion, at prices which will vary up to 500 percent from one dealer's price list to another, determining a realistic "market" value is almost impossible. And since the same books are listed repeatedly, list after list, month after month, it is difficult to determine whether or not these books are selling. In some cases, it is doubtful that they are even being collected. Most dealers must get a minimum price for their books; otherwise, it would not be profitable to handle. This will sometimes force a value on an otherwise valueless item. Most dealers who handle new comics get a minimum price of at least 75 cents- to $2.00 per copy. This is the **available** price to obtain a **reading** copy. However, this is not what dealers will pay to restock. Since many of these books are not yet collector's items, their salvage value would be very low. You may not get more than 5 cents to 10 cents per copy selling them back to a dealer. This type of material, from an investment point of view, would be of maximum risk since the salvage value is so low. For this reason, recent comics should be bought for enjoyment as reading copies and if they go up in value, consider it a bonus.

COLLECTING FOREIGN COMICS AND AMERICAN REPRINTS

One extremely interesting source of comics of early vintage–one which does not necessarily have to be expensive–is the foreign market. Many American strips, from both newspapers and magazines, are reprinted abroad (both in English and in other languages) months and even years after they appear in the states. By working out trade agreements with foreign collectors, one can obtain, for practically the cover price, substantial runs of a number of newspaper strips and reprints of American comic books dating back five, ten, or occasionally even twenty or more years. These reprints are often in black and white, and sometimes the reproduction is poor, but this is not always the case. In any event, this is a source of material that every serious collector should look into.

Once the collector discovers comics published in foreign lands, he often becomes fascinated with the original strips produced in these countries. Many are excellent, and have a broader range of appeal than those of American comic books.

CANADIAN REPRINTS (E.C.s: by J. B. Clifford)

Several E.C. titles were published in Canada by Superior Comics from 1949 to at least 1953. Canadian editions of the following E.C. titles are known: (Pre-Trend) *Saddle Romances, Moon Girl, A Moon A Girl. . .Romance, Modern Love, Saddle Justice*; (New-Trend) *Crypt of Terror, Tales From the Crypt, Haunt of Fear, Vault of Horror, Weird Science, Weird Fantasy, Two-Fisted Tales, Frontline Combat,* and *Mad. Crime SuspenStories* was also published in Canada under the title *Weird SuspenStories* (Nos. 1-3 known). No reprints of Shock SuspenStories by Superior are known, nor have any "New Direction" reprints ever been reported. No reprints later than January 1954 are known. Canadian reprints sometimes exchanged cover and contents with adjacent numbers (e.g., a *Frontline Combat* 12 with a *Frontline Combat* No. 11 cover). They are distinguished both in cover and contents. As the interior pages are always reprinted poorly, these comics are of less value (about 1/2) than the U.S. editions; they were printed from asbestos plates made from the original plates. On some reprints, the Superior seal replaces the E.C. seal. Superior publishers took over Dynamic in 1947.

CANADIAN REPRINTS (Dells: by Ronald J. Ard)

Canadian editions of Dell comics, and presumably other lines (Fiction House, Atlas/Marvel, Superior, etc.), began in March-April, 1948 and lasted until February-March, 1951. They were a response to the great Canadian dollar crisis of 1947. Intensive development of the post-war Canadian economy was financed almost entirely by American capital. This massive import or money reached such a level that Canada was in danger of having grossly disproportionate balance of payments which could drive it into technical bankruptcy in the midst of the biggest boom in its history. The Canadian government responded by banning a long list of imports. Almost 500 separate items were involved. Alas, the consumers of approximately 499 of them were politically more formidable than the consumers of comic books.

Dell responded by publishing its titles in Canada, through an arrangement with Wilson Publishing Company of Toronto. This company had not existed for a number of years and it is reasonable to assume that its sole business was the production and distribution of Dell titles in Canada. There is no doubt that they had a captive market. If you check the publication data on the U. S. editions of the period you will see the sentence "Not for sale in Canada." Canada was thus the only area of the Free World in those days technically beyond the reach of the American comic book industry.

We do not know whether French editions existed of the Dell titles put out by Wilson. The English editions were available nationwide. They were priced at 10 cents and were all 36 pages in length, at a time when their American parents were 52 pages. The covers were made of coarser paper, similar to that used in the Dell Four Color series in 1946 and 1947 and were abandoned as the more glossy cover paper became more economical. There was also a time lag of from six to eight weeks between, say, the date an American comic appeared and the date that the Canadian edition appeared.

Many Dell covers had seasonal themes and by the time the Canadian edition came out (two months later) the season was over. Wilson solved this problem by switching covers around so that the appropriate season would be reflected when the books hit the stands. Most Dell titles were published in Canada during this period including the popular Atom Bomb giveaway, *Walt Disney Comics and Stories* and the *Donald Duck* and *Mickey Mouse* Four Color one-shots. The quality of the Duck one-shots is equal to that of their American counterparts and generally bring about 30 percent less.

By 1951 the Korean War had so stimulated Canadian exports that the restrictions on comic book importation, which in any case were an offense against free trade principle, could be lifted without danger of economic collapse. Since this time Dell, as well as other companies, have been shipping direct into Canada.

CANADIAN REPRINTS (DCs: by Doug A. England)

Many DC comics were reprinted in Canada by National Comics Publications Limited and Simcoe Publishing and Distributing Co., both of Toronto, for years 1948-1950 at least. Like the Dells, these issues were 36 pages rather than the 52 pages offered in the U.S. editions, and the inscription "Published in Canada" would appear in place of "A 52 Page Magazine" or "52 Big Pages" appearing on U.S. editions. These issues contained no advertisements and some had no issue numbers.

HOW TO START COLLECTING

Most collectors of comic books begin by buying new issues in mint condition directly off the newsstand or from their local comic store. (Subscription copies are available from several mail-order services.) Each week new comics appear on the stands that are destined to become true collectors items. The trick is to locate a store that carries a complete line of comics. In several localities this may be difficult. Most panelologists frequent several magazine stands in order not to miss something they want. Even then, it pays to keep in close contact with collectors in other areas. Sooner or later, nearly every collector has to rely upon a friend in Fandom to obtain for him an item that is unavailable locally.

Before you buy any comic to add to your collection, you should carefully inspect its condition. Unlike stamps and coins, defective comics are generally not highly prized. The cover should be properly cut and printed. Remember that every blemish or sign of wear depreciates the beauty and value of your comics.

The serious panelologist usually purchases extra copies of popular titles. He may trade these multiples for items unavailable locally (for example, foreign comics), or he may store the multiples for resale at some future date. Such speculation is, of course, a gamble, but unless collecting trends change radically in the future, the value of certain comics in mint condition should appreciate greatly, as new generations of readers become interested in collecting.

COLLECTING BACK ISSUES

In addition to current issues, most panelologists want to locate back issues. Some energetic collectors have had great success in running down large hoards of rare comics in their home towns. Occasionally, rare items can be located through agencies that collect old papers and magazines, such as the Salvation Army. The lucky collector can often buy these items for much less than their current market value. Placing advertisements in trade journals, newspapers, etc., can also produce good results. However, don't be discouraged if you are neither energetic nor lucky. Most panelologists build their collections slowly but systematically by placing mail orders with dealers and other collectors.

Comics of early vintage are extremely expensive if they are purchased through a regular dealer or collector, and unless you have unlimited funds to invest in your hobby, you will find it necessary to restrict your collecting in certain ways. However you define your collection, you should be careful to set your goals well within your means.

PROPER HANDLING OF COMIC BOOKS

Before picking up an old rare comic book, caution should be exercised to handle it properly. Old comic books are very fragile and can be easily damaged. Because of this, many dealers hesitate to let customers personally handle their rare comics. They would prefer to remove the comic from its bag and show it to the customer themselves. In this way, if the book is damaged, it would be the dealer's responsibility–not the customer's. Remember, the slightest crease or chip could render an otherwise Mint book to Near Mint or even Very Fine. The following steps are provided to aid the novice in the proper handling of comic books: 1. Remove the comic from its protective sleeve or bag very carefully. 2. Gently lay the comic (unopened) in the palm of your hand so that it will stay relatively flat and secure. 3. You can now leaf through the book by carefully rolling or flipping the pages with the thumb and forefinger of your other hand. Caution: Be sure the book always remains relatively flat or slightly rolled. Avoid creating stress points on the covers with your fingers and be particularly cautious in bending covers back too far on Mint books. 4. After examining the book, carefully insert it back into the bag or protective sleeve. Watch corners and edges for folds or tears as you replace the book.

HOW TO SELL YOUR COMICS

If you have a collection of comics for sale, large or small, the following steps should be taken. (1) Make a detailed list of the books for sale, being careful to grade them accurately, showing any noticeable defects; i.e., torn or missing pages, centerfolds, etc. (2) Decide whether to sell or trade wholesale to a dealer all in one lump or to go through the long laborious process of advertising and selling piece by piece to collectors. Both have their advantages and disadvantages.

In selling to dealers, you will get the best price by letting everything go at once-the good with the bad–all for one price. Simply select names either from ads in this book or from some of the adzines mentioned below. Send them your list and ask for bids. The bids received will vary depending on the demand, rarity and condition of the books you have. The more in demand, and better the condition, the higher the bids will be.

On the other hand, you could become a "dealer" and sell the books yourself. Order a copy of one or more of the adzines. Take note how most dealers lay out their ads. Type up your ad copy, carefully pricing each book (using the Guide as a reference). Send finished ad copy with payment to adzine editor to be run. You will find that certain books will sell at once while others will not sell at all. The ad will probably have to be retyped, remaining books repriced, and run again. Price books according to how fast you want them to move. If you try to get top dollar, expect a much longer period of time. Otherwise, the better deal you give the collector, the faster they will move. Remember, in being your own dealer, you will have overhead expenses in postage, mailing supplies and advertising cost. Some books might even be returned for refund due to misgrading, etc.

In selling all at once to a dealer, you get instant cash, immediate profit, and eliminate the long process of running several ads to dispose of the books; but if you have patience, and a small amount of business sense, you could realize more profit selling them directly to collectors yourself.

WHERE TO BUY AND SELL

Throughout this book you will find the advertisements of many reputable dealers who sell back-issue comics magazines. If you are an inexperienced collector, be sure to compare prices before you buy. When a dealer is selected (ask for references), send him a small order (under $100) first to check out his grading accuracy, promptness in delivery, guarantees of condition advertised, and whether he will accept returns when dissatisfied. Never send large sums of cash through the mail. Send money orders or checks for your personal protection. Beware of bargains, as the items advertised sometimes do not exist, but are only a fraud to get your money.

The Price Guide is indebted to everyone who placed ads in this volume, whose support has helped in curbing printing costs. Your mentioning this book when dealing with the advertisers would be greatly appreciated.

THE COMICS BUYERS GUIDE, Krause Publications, 700 E. State St., Iola, WI 54990 PH: (715) 445-2214.

COLLECTORS' CLASSIFIED, P.O. Box 347, Holbrook, MA 02343.

OVERSTREET'S COMIC BOOK MARKETPLACE, P. O. Box 2610, Cleveland, TN 37320-2610, (615) 472-4135. Subscription rate: $14.95 (5 iss.), $24.95 (10 iss.).

The Price Guide highly recommends the above adzines, which are full of ads buying and selling comics, pulps, radio tapes, premiums, toys and other related items. You can also place ads to buy or sell your comics in the above publications.

COMIC BOOK MAIL ORDER SERVICES

Order your comics through the mail. Write for rates and details:

AT YOUR SERVICE SUB., P.O. Box 867434, Plano, TX. 75093, (214) 964-0766

COLLECTOR'S CHOICE, 1503 S. Ocoee, Cleveland, TN 37311. (615) 476-2501

THE COMIC SOURCE, Bruce B. Brittain, P.O. Box 863605, Plano, TX 75086-3605

COMICS TO ASTONISH, 4001-C Country Club Rd., Winston-Salem, NC 27104 (919) 765-0400

COMIC COLLECTIBLES, P. O. Box 536, East Brunswick, NJ 08816, (908) 238-9023.

DAVE'S COMICS, 1240 Harvard Ave., Salt Lake City, UT 84105

DOUG SULIPA'S COMIC WORLD, 374 Donald St., Winnipeg, Man., Canada R3B 2J2

FANTACO ENTERPRISES, INC., 21 Central Ave., Albany, NY 12210-1391. PH: (518) 463-1400

FRIENDLY FRANK'S Distribution, Inc., 3990 Broadway, Gary IN 46408-2705 (219)884-5052 or 884-5053 1025 North Vigo, Gary, IN 46403

GEPPI'S SUBSCRIPTION SERVICE, 1720 Belmont Ave., Bay-C, Baltimore, MD 21207

HALLEY'S COMICS SERVICE, 345/347 Mountain Road, Moncton, New Brunswick, Canada E1C 2M5, (506) 855-0056.

HEROES AREN'T HARD TO FIND, 1214 Thomas Ave., Charlotte, NC 28205

M&M, P.O. Box 6, Orland Park, IL 60462. PH: 312-349-2486

MEMBERS ONLY COMIC SERVICE, 6257 Yale St., Halifax, Nova Scotia, Canada, B3L 1C9, PH:902-423-MOCS

MOUNTAIN EMPIRE COLLECTIBLES, 509 State St., 2nd Floor, Bristol, VA 24201, (703) 466-6337.

MR. MONSTERS COMIC CRYPT, 1805 Wash, Blvd, Easton, PA 18042

PRESIDENTIAL COMIC BOOK SERVICE, P. O. Box 41, Scarsdale, NY 10583

COMICS AMERICA, #10 62 Scurfield, Winnipeg, Manitoba, Canada (204) 489-0580, FAX (204) 489-0589 (A div. of Styx International).

LEE TENNANT, THE COMIC SHOP, P.O. Box 296, Worth, IL 60482-(312) 448-2937

THE WESTFIELD COMPANY, 8608 University Green, P.O. Box 470, Middleton, WI 53562 (608)836-1945

COMIC BOOK CONVENTIONS

As is the case with most other aspects of comic collecting, comic book conventions, or cons as they are referred to, were originally conceived as the comic-book counterpart to science-fiction fandom conventions. There were many attempts to form successful national cons prior to the time of the first one that materialized, but they were all stillborn. It is interesting that after only three relatively organized years of existence, the first comic con was held. Of course, its magnitude was nowhere near as large as most established cons held today.

What is a comic con? As might be expected, there are comic books to be found at these gatherings. Dealers, collectors, fans, whatever they call themselves can be found trading, selling, and buying the adventures of their favorite characters for hours on end. Additionally if at all possible, cons have guests of honor, usually professionals in the field of comic art, either writers, artists, or editors. The committees put together panels for the con attendees where the assembled pros talk about certain areas of comics, most of the time fielding questions from the assembled audience. At cons one can usually find displays of various and sundry things, usually original art. There might be radio listening rooms; there is most certainly a daily showing of different movies, usually science-fiction or horror type. Of course there is always the chance to get together with friends at cons and just talk about comics; one also has a good opportunity to make new friends who have similar interests and with whom one can correspond after the con.

It is difficult to describe accurately what goes on at a con. The best way to find out is to go to one or more if you can.

The addresses below are those currently available for conventions to be held in the upcoming year. Unfortunately, addresses for certain major conventions are unavailable as this list is being compiled. Once again, the best way to keep abreast of conventions is through the various adzines. Please remember when writing for convention information to include a self addressed, stamped envelope for reply. Most conventions are non-profit, so they appreciate the help. Here is the list:

COMIC BOOK CONVENTIONS FOR 1993

(**Note**: All convention listings must be submitted to us by December 15th of each year)

ATLANTA FANTASY FAIR, Jul., 1993, Atlanta Hilton & Towers, Atlanta, GA. Info: Atlanta Fantasy Fair, 4175 Eliza Ct., Lithonia, GA 30058. PH: (404) 985-1230.

BIG-D Super Comic & Collectibles Show (Formally CHILDHOOD TREASURES) July, 1993-Dallas Sheraton Park Central Hotel, Hwy 635 & Coit Rd. Write Don Maris, Box 111266 Arlington, TX 76007. (817) 261-8745

CAROLINA COMIC BOOK FAIR–For info contact New Dimension Comics, 2609 Central Ave., Charlotte, NC 28205. PH: (704) 372-4376.

CAROLINA CON–Sponsored by The Carolina Pictorial Fiction Assn. Send SASE to Steve Harris, 100 E. Augusta Place, Greenville, SC 29605.

CENTRAL NEW JERSEY COMIC BOOK SHOW–Held monthly on Sundays at the Washington Twp. Volunteer Fire Dept., Rt. 130, Robbinsville. Contact Michael Chaudhuri of EMCEE Conventions, P.O. Box 151, Hightstown, NJ 08520. PH: (609) 448-7585.

CHATTANOOGA, TN. Spring Comics & Collectibles Show–contact Mark Derrick, 3244 Castle Ave, East Ridge, TN 37412. PH: 615/624-3702, before 10:00 p.m.

CHICAGO - Baseball Card & Comic Book Show. Held monthly at University of Illinois at Chicago. For more info call Rich at (312) 733-2266.

CHICAGO COMICON–July 2-4, 1993, Larry Charet, 1219-A West Devon Ave., Chicago, IL 60660. Phone (312)-274-1832.

COMIC BOOK AND ART EXPO–Rosemont Ohare Exposition Center, River Rd. & Kennedy Exp, Rosemont, IL, Midwest Shows, 7516 W. Douglas, Summit, IL 60501, PH: 708/496-8881.

COMICFEST '93–October 8-11, 1993, Philadelphia Civic Center, Philadelphia, PA. For more info: Comicfest '93, 614 Corporate Way, Valley Cottage, NY 10989, (914) 268-3600.

CROWN POINT'S PREMIERE MONTHLY CARD AND COMIC SHOW–Crown Point, IN, Knight's of Columbus, 700 Merrillville Rd. Contact Marilyn Hall, P.O. Box 507, Crown Point, IN. 46307. PH: 219-663-8561.

DALLAS FANTASY FAIR, A Bulldog Prod. Convention. For info: Lary Lankford, P.O. Box 820488, Dallas, TX 75382, PH: (214) 349-3367.

DETROIT AREA COMIC BOOK/BASEBALL CARD SHOWS. Held every 2-3 weeks in Royal Oak and Livonia Mich., write: Michael Goldman, Suite 231, 19785 W. 12 Mile Rd., Southfield, MI 48076. PH: (313) 350-2633.

DEF-CON CONVENTIONS–2681 Monroeville Blvd., Monroeville, PA 15146, PH:412/372-4774. Holds cons in the following cities: Pittsburgh, Erie, State College, Charleston, Morgantown, Elmira, Scranton.

EL PASO FANTASY FESTIVAL–c/o Rita's Fantasy Shop, No. 34 Sunrise Center, El Paso, TX 79904. PH: (915)-757-1143. Late July-Early August.

FOUR COLOR COMIC ART CONVENTIONS™ P. O. Box 11234, New Brunswick, NJ 08906-1234. (908) 828-5955. (Monthly shows throughout New Jersey).

GREAT EASTERN CONVENTIONS, 225 Everitts Road, Ringoes, NJ 08551, PH: (201) 788-6845. Holds cons in the following cities: Atlanta, Boston, Chicago, Los Angeles, New York and San Francisco.

HEROES CONVENTION–Charlotte Apparel Center, 200 N. College St, Charlotte, NC. Contact H. Shelton Drum, P. O. Box 9181, Charlotte, NC 28299, PH: (704) 376-5766 or 1-800-321-4370.

HIGHLAND INDIANA MONTHLY CARD & COMIC SHOW. Wicker Park Social Center, Ridge Rd. at Indianapolis Blvd., Marilyn Hall, P.O. Box 507, Crown Point, Indiana 46307, PH: 219/663-8561

ILLINOIS/INDIANA–Pinsky Baseball Card & Comic Book Supershow, c/o Louis Pinsky, P.O. Box 1072, Lombard, IL 60148-8072, PH: (708) 620-0865. Holds conventions in these cities: Illinois: Alsip, Carol Stream, Countryside/LaGrange, Crystal Lake, Downers Grove, Elgin, Glen Ellyn/Lombard, Itasca, Oakbrook Terrace, Willowbrook/Hinsdale. Indiana: Merrillville.

ISLAND NOSTALGIA ALL CARD AND COMIC SHOWS (Since 1980), Ronkonkoma, N.Y.-Holiday Inn 3845 Vets Hwy., 10a.m.-4p.m. For more info call Dennis (516) 724-7422 daily for next show dates.

KANSAS CITY COMIC CONVENTION (Formally MO-KAN COMICS FESTIVAL) c/o Kansas City Comic Book Club, 734 North 78th St., Kansas City, KS 66112.

LONG ISLAND COMIC BOOK & COLLECTOR'S CONVENTION–(Held monthly). Rockville Centre, Holiday Inn, 173 Sunrise Hwy, Long Island, NY.For info: Cosmic Comics & Books of Rockville Centre, 139 N. Park Ave., Rockville Centre, NY 11570. (516) 763-1133.

LOS ANGELES COMIC BOOK & SCIENCE FICTION CONVENTION, held monthly. For information contact: Bruce Schwartz, 1802 West Olive Ave., Burbank, CA 91506. PH: (818) 954-8432.

MICHIANA COMICON: South Bend, IN. Contact Jim Rossow, 53100 Poppy Rd., South Bend, IN 46628. PH: (219) 232-8129.

MOBI-CON 93, June 11-13, 1993, comics, gaming, & sf; The Days Inn 3650 Airport Blvd., Mobile, AL. For more info: Mobi-Con, P.O. Box 161257, Mobile, AL 36616.

MOTOR CITY COMIC CON, Dearborn, MI. Held at the Dearborn Civic Center, 15801 Michigan Ave. Contact Michael Goldman, Suite 231, 19785 W. 12 Mile Rd., Southfield, MI 48076. PH: (313) 350-2633.

NORTHERN ILLINOIS SEASONAL COMIC SHOW–Rockford, IL, contact Mick at Hotstuff Comics, 3833 E. State St., Rockford, IL 61108, PH: 815/227 XMEN (9636).

NOSTALIGA CON–Held in Elizabeth, NJ, Lyndhurst, NJ, Hempstead, NY. Contact George Downes, G.A.

Corp., Box 572, Nutley, NJ 07110. PH: (201) 661-3358.

THE ORIGINAL LONG ISLAND MONTHLY COMIC BOOK & BASEBALL CARD SHOW, Held 1st Sunday each month (2nd Sunday in July, 1993) at the Coliseum Motor Inn, 1650 Hempstead Turnpike, East Meadow, Long Island, NY. Contact: Perry Albert, P.O. Box 66, Fredonia, NY 14063. PH:(716) 672-2913.

ORLANDO CON, International Inn, Orlando, FL. Info: Jim Ivey, 4300 S. Semoran, Suite 109, Orlando, FL 32822-2453, PH: (407) 273-0141.

SAN DIEGO COMIC-CON–Box 17066, San Diego, CA 92117. Aug 19-22, 1993, San Diego Convention Center.

SEATTLE CENTER CON, Box 2043, Kirkland, Wash, 98033. Phone (206) 822-5709 or 827-5129.

SEATTLE QUEST NORTHWEST, Seattle, Wash. Write: Ron Church or Steve Sibra, P.O. Box 82676, Kenmore, WA 98028.

WESTERN NEW YORK COMIC BOOK BASEBALL CARD & COLLECTIBLES SHOW–(held monthly), Masonic Lodge, 321 E. Main St., Fredonia, NY. Contact: Perry Albert, P.O. Box 66, Fredonia, NY 14063. PH: (716) 672-2913.

COMIC BOOK CLUBS

ALABAMA–The Mobile Panelology Assoc. Meets 1st Monday of each month at 2301 Airport Blvd. (Back Bldg. Mobile Recreation Dept.), Mobile, Ala.; 7:00 p.m. to 9:00 p.m. Club business address: 161 West Grant St., Chickasaw, AL 36611. (205) 456-4514. Founded 1973.

CALIFORNIA–The California Comic Book Collectors Club, c/o Matt Ornbaun, 23601 Hwy. 128, Yorkville, CA 95494. Send 50 cents and SASE for information and enrollment.

Alpha Omega, c/o Harry W. Miller, 1106 Jones Ave., Bowling Green, KY 42104. PH: (502) 843-2300.

USC Comics Club, University of Southern California Intramural Recreation Dept., Heritage Hall 103, University Park, Los Angeles, CA 90089-0601. PH 213-743-5127.

West Coast Comic Club, c/o Frank Como, 2536 Terrace, Anaheim, CA 92806-1656. Meets the second Saturday of the month at the community meeting hall in the City Mall at 7:00 p.m.

CONNETICUT–Collectors' Club, c/o Susan Dorne, President, 551 Park Ave., Windsor, CT 06095. Publishes a bi-monthly newsletter.

GEORGIA–The Defenders of Dreams, Inc., World Headquarters, c/o Will Rose, Chairman of the Board, 3121-Shady Grove Rd., Carrollton, GA 30117. (Publishes own fanzine *Just Imagine...*bi-monthly and a pulpzine *Pulp Adventures* quarterly.) Please send business size SASE for details.

IDAHO–Mr. O's Comic Book Collectors Club, S. 1200 Agate Rd., Coeur D'Alene, Idaho 83814.

MASSACHUSETTS–The Gloo Club, c/o Ron Holmes, 140 Summit St., New Bedford, Mass. 02740. Write for details and send SASE. (This club is both national and international.)

MINNESOTA–The Pogo Fan Club. A mail club dedicated to Walt Kelly's career. Puts out a bi-monthly "*The Fort Mudge Most.*" Write: Steve Thompson, 6908 Wentworth Ave. So., Richfield, MN 55423.

OHIO–International Comics Club, meets monthly at Cleveland Hts., University Hts. Library, 2345 Lee Rd., Cleveland Hts., Ohio on 1st Monday of each month, 7p.m. Contact: Richard Bennett, 6204 Fullerton Ave., Apt. 3, Cleveland, OH 44105.

OKLAHOMA–Fandom International. For information, write to: Dan DePalma, 5823 E. 22 St., Tulsa, OK 74114. Phone 834-8035.

TEXAS–The Gulf Coast Comic Collectors' Society (GCCCS). Write to GCCCS Headquarters, c/o Mike Mills, 4318 Iroquois St., Houston, TX 77504.

CANADA–The Collectors' Club. Write: T.M. Maple, Box 1272, Station B., Weston, Ontario M9L 2R9 Canada. Bimonthly newsletter.

THE HISTORY OF COMICS FANDOM

At this time it is possible to discern two distinct and largely unrelated movements in the history of Comics Fandom. The first of these movements began about 1953 as a response to the then popular, trend setting EC lines of comics. The first true comics fanzines of this movement were short lived. Bob Stewart's EC FAN BULLETIN was a hectographed newsletter that ran two issues about six months apart; and Jimmy Taurasi's FANTASY COMICS, a newsletter devoted to all science-fiction comics of the period, was a monthly that ran for about six months. These were followed by other newsletters, such as Mike May's EC FAN JOURNAL, and George Jennings' EC WORLD PRESS. EC fanzines of a wider and more critical scope appeared somewhat later. Two of the finest were POTRZEBIE, the product of a number of fans, and Ron Parker's HOOHAH. Gauging from the response that POTRZEBIE received from a plug in an EC letter column, Ted White estimated the average age of EC fans to lie in the range of 9 to 13, while many EC fans were in their mid-teens. This fact was taken as discouraging to many of the faneds, who had hoped to reach an older audience. Consequently, many of them gave up their efforts in behalf of Comics Fandom, especially with the demise of the EC groups, and turned their attention to science-fiction fandom with its longer tradition and older membership. While the flourish of fan activity in response to the EC comics was certainly noteworthy, it is fair to say that it never developed into a full-fledged, independent, and self-sustaining movement.

The second comics fan movement began in 1960. It was largely a response to (though it later became a stimulus for) the Second Heroic Age of Comics. Most fan historians date the Second Heroic Age from the appearance of the new FLASH comics magazine (numbered 105 and dated February 1959). The letter departments of Julius Schwartz (editor at National Periodicals), and later those of Stan Lee (Marvel Group) and Bill Harris (Gold Key) were most influential in bringing comics readers into Fandom. Beyond question, it was the reappearance of the costumed hero that sparked the comics fan movement of the sixties. Sparks were lit among some science-fiction fans first, when experienced fan writers, who were part of an established tradition, produced the first in a series of articles on the comics of the forties–ALL IN COLOR FOR A DIME. The series was introduced in XERO No. 1 (September 1960), a general fanzine for science-fiction fandom edited and published by Dick Lupoff.

Meanwhile, outside science-fiction fandom, Jerry Bails and Roy Thomas, two strictly comics fans of long-standing, conceived the first true comics fanzine in response to the Second Heroic Age. The fanzine, ALTER EGO, appeared in March 1961. The first several issues were widely circulated among comics fans, and were to influence profoundly the comics fan movement to follow. Unlike the earlier EC fan movement, this new movement attracted many fans in their twenties and thirties. A number of these older fans had been active collectors for years but had been largely unknown to each other. Joined by scores of new, younger fans, this group formed the nucleus of a new movement that is still growing and shows every indication of being self-sustaining. Although it has borrowed a few of the more appropriate terms coined by science-fiction fans, Comics Fandom of the Sixties was an independent if fledging movement, without, in most cases, the advantages and disadvantages of a longer tradition. What Comics Fandom did derive from science-fiction fandom it did so thanks largely to the fanzines produced by so-called double fans. The most notable of this type is COMIC ART, edited and published by Don and Maggie Thompson.

The ROCKETS BLAST COMIC COLLECTOR, by G.B. Love was the first sucessful adzine in the early 1960s and was instrumental and important in the early development of the comics market. G.B. remembers beginning his fanzine THE ROCKET'S BLAST in late 1961. Only six copies of the first issue was printed and consisted of only 4 pages. Shortly thereafter Mr. Love had a letter published in MYSTERY IN SPACE, telling all about his new fanzine. His circulation began to grow. Buddy Saunders, a well known comic book store owner, designed the first ROCKET'S BLAST logo, and was an artist for this publication for many years thereafter. With issue #29 he took over THE COMICOLLECTOR fanzine from Biljo White and combined it with the ROCKET'S BLAST to from the RBCC. He remembers that the RBCC hit its highest circulation of 2500 around 1971. Many people who wrote, drew or otherwise contributed to the RBCC went on to become well known writers, artists, dealers and store-owners in the comics field.

HOW TO SELECT FANZINES

In the early 1960s, only a few comic fanzines were being published. A fan could easily afford to subscribe to them all. Today, the situation has radically changed, and it has become something of a problem to decide which fanzines to order.

Fanzines are not all of equal quality or general interest. Even different issues of the same fanzine may vary significantly. To locate issues that will be of interest to you, learn to look for the names of outstanding amateur artists, writers, and editors and consult fanzine review columns. Although you may not always agree with the judgements of the reviewers, you will find these reviews to be a valuable source of information about the content and quality of the current fanzines.

When ordering a fanzine, remember that print runs are small and the issue you may want may be out of print (OP). Ordinarily in this case, you will receive the next issue. Because of irregular publishing schedules that nearly all fanzines must, of necessity, observe, allow up to 90 days or more for your copy to reach you. It is com mon courtesy when addressing an inquiry to an ama-publisher to enclose a self-addressed, stamped envelope.

NOTE: We must be notified each year by December 1 for listing to be included, due to changes of address, etc. Please send sample copy.

ALPHA OMEGA–(APA) For christian comics artists, cartoonists, writers and fans. Bi-Monthly issues for members, send SASE to: Harry W. Miller, 1106 Jones Ave., Bowling Green, KY 42104, PH: 502/843 2300.

ANNIE PEOPLE–Jon Merrill, P.O. Box 431, Cedar Knolls, NJ 07927. Bi-monthly Little Orphan Annie newsletter.

THE ARCHIE FANZINE–Mary Smith, 185 Ashland St., Holliston, MA 01746. Monthly fanzine about Archie and the people behind the books plus news and opinions. Sample copy: $3.00. 6 issue subscription: $15.00.

THE BATMANIAC'S INDEX–Randy Lee Prinslow, 10116 NE Notchlog Dr. #205, Vancouver, WA 98665. An 80-page fanzine devoted to chronicling the Caped Crusader's comic book history. $5.50 postpaid for publications and free newsletter.

CANIFFITES–Carl Horak, 1319 108th Ave. S.W., Calgary, Alberta, Canada T2W 0C6. Fanzine devoted to the art of Milton Caniff. Sample copy of newsletter: $1.50. 6 issue subscription: $6.00.

COMIC ART AND FANTASY–Stephen Barrington, 161 West Grant Street, Chickasaw, AL 36611. Published quarterly for comics, gaming & sf fans. $1.00 for two issues.

THE COMICOL MONTHLY–Todd Estes, Rt. 1, Box 22, Brilliant, AL 35548. Features news and reviews on everything; the big two, the independents and the small press. Either a stamp or SASE gets you complete info.

COMICS INTERVIEW–c/o Fictioneer Books Ltd., #1 Screamer Mtn., Clayton, GA 30525.

THE COMPLETE EC LIBRARY–Russ Cochran, P. O. Box 437, West Plains, MO 65775. (A must for all EC collectors. Reprinting of the complete EC line is planned. Write for details.)

DITKOMANIA–A Ditko-devoted digest. This year presenting the Complete Chronological Checklist plus a myriad of art and articles. $1 for a sample copy. Write: Bill Hall, 556 Main St., Cromwell, CT 05416.

THE DUCKBURG TIMES–Barks/Disney fanzine. Sample copy $3.00, Dana Gabbard, 3010 Wilshire Blvd., #362, Los Angeles, CA 90010.

FANTACO NOOZ–FantaCo. Enterprises Inc., 21 Central Ave., Albany, NY 12210. Free with SASE.

FCA & ME TOO!–Bill & Teresa Harper, 301 E. Buena Vista Ave., North Augusta, SC 29841. Covers Golden Age Fawcett and Magazine Enterprises. Sample $1.00. 4 issue subscription, $5. Now in it's 17th year.

FORT MUDGE MOST–Bi monthly magazine of the Pogo Fan Club. Subscription: $15/yr. Sample $3. Spring Hollow Books, 6908 Wentworth Ave. So., Richfield, MN 55423.

THE HARVEYVILLE FUN TIMES!–Mark Arnold, 1464 La Playa #105, San Francisco, CA 94122. Fanzine dedicated to the Harvey World. Published quarterly. Subscriptions are $6.00 for 4 issues and $11.00 for 8. Sample: $2.00

HISTORY OF COMICS–Robin Snyder, 255 N. Forest #455, Bellingham, WA 98225-5833 (Magazine, write for subscription rates).

THE HOLLYWOOD ECLECTERN–Ed Buchman, P. O. Box 4215, Fullerton CA 92634. Little Lulu related fanzine.

INSIDE REVIEW on comics–J.E. Essick, Rt. 10, Box 369D, Winston-Salem, NC 27127. Monthly current comics newsletter. Sample 90 cents, 1 year subs-$9. Checks only.

IT'S A FANZINE–Gene Kehoe, 2424 Adams Ave., Des Moines, IA 50310. Lively '60s style comic fanzine now in it's 13th year. Sample copy: $1.50 ppd. Subscription: 4 issues for $5.00.

THE MAD PANIC–Ed Norris, 91 Kelly Dr., Lancaster, MA 01523. Fanzine for Mad/Panic/Alfred E. Neuman fans. Sample issue: $1.00. 6 issue subscription is $5.00

MARVEL SERIES NOTIZIARIO–c/o Claudio Piccinini, V.LE Amendola 471, 41100 Modena, Italy. Covers all aspects of Italian comics, with articles on European, English and American comics. Text in Italian.

POW-POW–Bill & Teresa Harper, 301 E. Buena Vista Ave., North Augusta, SC 29841. Fanzine covering the Straight Arrow radio show, comics & strip reprints. Sample copy: $1.00. 4 issue subscription: $5.00.

VERTICAL HOLD–85 Burnie St., Lyons, ACT Australia 2606. Fanzine mainly about cult television series, also covering comic books.

THE YELLOW KID NOTES–The Yellow Kid Society, 103 Doubloon Dr., Slidell, LA 70461. PH: 504-641-5173.

COLLECTING STRIPS

Collecting newspaper comic strips is somewhat different than collecting magazines, although it can be equally satisfying.

Obviously, most strip collectors begin by clipping strips from their local paper, but many soon branch out to strips carried in out-of-town papers. Naturally this can become more expensive and it is often frustrating, because it is easy to miss editions of out-of-town papers. Consequently, most strip collectors work out trade agreements with collectors in other cities in order to get an uninterrupted supply of the strips they want. This usually necessitates saving local strips to be used for trade purposes only.

Back issues of strips dating back several decades are also available from time to time from dealers. The prices per panel vary greatly depending on the age, condition, and demand for the strip. When the original strips are unavailable, it is sometimes possible to get photostatic copies from collectors, libraries, or newspaper morgues.

COLLECTING ORIGINAL ART

In addition to magazines and strips, some enthusiasts also collect the original art for the comics. These black and white, inked drawings are usually done on illustration paper at about 30 percent up (i.e., 30 percent larger than the original printed panels). Because original art is a one-of-a kind article, it is highly prized and often difficult to obtain.

Interest in original comic art has increased tremendously in the past several years. Many companies now return the originals to the artists who have in turn offered them for sale, usually at cons but sometimes through agents and dealers. As with any other area of collecting, rarity and demand governs value. Although the masters' works bring fine art prices, most art is available at moderate prices. Comic strips are the most popular facet with collectors, followed by comic book art. Once scarce, current and older comic book art has surfaced within the last few years. In 1974 several original painted covers of vintage comic books and coloring books turned up from Dell, Gold Key, Whitman, and Classic Comics.

The following are sources for original art:

Abraxas Graphix, 9847 Belair Rd., Perry Hall, MD 21128.

Artman, Bruce Bergstrom, 1620 Valley St., Fort Lee, NJ 07024.

Cartoon Carnival, 408 Bickmore Dr., Wallingford, PA 19086, PH: (215) 566-1292.

The Cartoon Museum, Jim Ivey, 4300 S. Semoran, Suite 109, Orlando, FL 32822-2453. PH: (407) 273-0141.

Russ Cochran, P.O. Box 437, West Plains, MO 65775.

Collectors Paradise Gallery, Harry Kleinman, P.O. Box 1540, Studio City, CA 91604.

The Comic Character Shop, Old Firehouse Antiques, 110 Alaskan Way S., Seattle, WA 98104. (206) 283-0532.

Tony Dispoto, Comic Art Showcase, P. O. Box 425, Lodi, NJ 07644.

Scott Dunbier, P.O. Box 1446, Gracie Station, New York, NY, 10028. PH: (212) 666-0982, FAX: (212) 662-8732.

Graphic Collectibles, Mitch Itkowitz, P.O. Box 683, Staten Island, NY 10302. PH: (718) 273-3685.

Richard Halegua, Comic Art & Graffix Gallery, 2033 Madison Rd., Cincinnati, OH 45208. PH: (513) 321-4208.

Steve Herrington, 30 W. 70th St., New York, NY 10023.

Carsten Lagua, Havensteinstr. 54, 1000 Berlin 46, West Germany, Tel. 030/7734665.

Museum Graphics, Jerome K. Muller, Box 743, Costa Mesa, CA 92627.

Original Artwork, Martin Hilland, SteinstraBe 135, 4150 Krefeld Germany.

San Mateo Comic Books/Original art, 306 Baldwin Ave. San Mateo, CA 94401. PH: (415) 344-1536.

TRH Gallery (Tom Horvitz), 255 N. Cielo #601, Palm Springs, CA 92263. PH: (619) 341-8592.

A Chronology of the Development of THE AMERICAN COMIC BOOK

By
M. Thomas Inge*

Precursors: The facsimile newspaper strip reprint collections constitute the earliest "comic books." The first of these was a collection of Richard Outcault's **Yellow Kid** from the Hearst New York American in March 1897. Commercial and promotional reprint collections, usually in cardboard covers, appeared through the 1920s and featured such newspaper strips as **Mutt and Jeff, Foxy Grandpa, Buster Brown**, and **Barney Google**. During 1922 a reprint magazine, **Comic Monthly**, appeared with each issue devoted to a separate strip, and from 1929 to 1930 George Delacorte published 36 issues of **The Funnies** in tabloid format with original comic pages in color, becoming the first four-color comic newsstand publication.

1933: The Ledger syndicate published a small broadside of their Sunday comics on 7" by 9" plates. Employees of Eastern Color Printing Company in New York, sales manager Harry I. Wildenberg and salesman Max C. Gaines, saw it and figured that two such plates would fit a tabloid page, which would produce a book about 7-1/2" x 10" when folded. Thus 10,000 copies of **Funnies on Parade**, containing 32 pages of Sunday newspaper reprints, was published for Proctor and Gamble to be given away as premiums. Some of the strips included were: **Joe Palooka, Mutt and Jeff, Hairbreadth Harry**, and **Reg'lar Fellas**. M. C. Gaines was very impressed with this book and convinced Eastern Color that he could sell a lot of them to such big advertisers as Milk-O-Malt, Wheatena, Kinney Shoe Stores, and others to be used as premiums and radio give-aways. So, Eastern Color printed **Famous**

Funnies: A Carnival of Comics, and then **Century of Comics**, both as before, containing Sunday newspaper reprints. Mr. Gaines sold these books in quantities of 100,000 to 250,000.

1934: The give-away comics were so successful that Mr. Gaines believed that youngsters would buy comic books for ten cents like the "Big Little Books" coming out at that time. So, early in 1934, Eastern Color ran off 35,000 copies of **Famous Funnies, Series 1**, 64 pages of reprints for Dell Publishing Company to be sold for ten cents in chain stores. Since it sold out promptly on the stands, Eastern Color, in May 1934, issued **Famous Funnies** No. 1 (dated July 1934) which became, with issue No. 2 in July, the first monthly comic magazine. The title continued for over 20 years through 218 issues, reaching a circulation peak of over 400,000 copies a month. At the same time, Mr. Gaines went to the sponsors of Percy Crosby's **Skippy,** who was on the radio, and convinced them to put out a Skippy book, advertise it on the air, and give away a free copy to anyone who bought a tube of Phillip's toothpaste. Thus 500,000 copies of **Skippy's Own Book of Comics** was run off and distributed through drug stores everywhere. This was the first four-color comic book of reprints devoted to a single character.

1935: Major Malcolm Wheeler-Nicholson's National Periodical Publications issued in February a tabloid-sized comic publication called **New Fun**, which became **More Fun** after the sixth issue and converted to the normal comic-book size after issue eight. **More Fun** was the first comic book of a standard size to publish original material and continued publication until 1949. **Mickey Mouse Magazine** began in the summer, to become **Walt Disney's Comics and Stories** in 1940, and combined original material with reprinted newspaper strips in most issues.

1936: In the wake of the success of **Famous Funnies**, other publishers, in conjunction with the major newspaper strip syndicates, inaugurated more reprint comic books: **Popular Comics** (News Tribune, February), **Tip Top Comics** (United Features, April), **King Comics** (King Features, April), and **The Funnies** (new series, NEA, October). Four issues of **Wow Comics**, from David McKay and Henle Publications, appeared, edited by S. M. Iger and including early art by Will Eisner, Bob Kane, and Alex Raymond. The first non-reprint comic book devoted to a single theme was **Detective Picture Stories** issued in December by The Comics Magazine Company.

1937: The second single theme title, **Western Picture Stories**, came in February from The Comics Magazine Company, and the third was **Detective Comics**, an offshoot of **More Fun**, which began in March to be published to the present. The book's initials, "D.C.," have long served to refer to National Periodical Publications, which was purchased from Major Nicholson by Harry Donenfeld late this year.

1938: "DC" copped a lion's share of the comic book market with the publication of **Action Comics** No. 1 in June which contained the first appearance of Superman by writer Jerry Siegel and artist Joe Shuster, a discovery of Max C. Gaines. The "man of steel" inaugurated the "Golden Era" in comic book history. Fiction House, a pulp publisher, entered the comic book field in September with **Jumbo Comics**, featuring Sheena, Queen of the Jungle, and appearing in over-sized format for the first eight issues.

1939: The continued success of "DC" was assured in May with the publication of **Detective Comics** No. 27 containing the first episode of Batman by artist Bob Kane and writer Bill Finger. **Superman Comics** appeared in the summer. Also, during the summer, a black and white premium comic titled **Motion Picture Funnies Weekly** was published to be given away at motion picture theatres. The plan was to issue it weekly and to have continued stories so that the kids would come back week after week not to miss an episode. Four issues were planned but only one came out. This book contains the first appearance and origin of the Sub-Mariner by Bill Everett (8 pages) which was later reprinted in **Marvel Comics**. In November, the first issue of **Marvel Comics** came out, featuring the Human Torch by Carl Burgos and the Sub-Mariner reprint with color added.

1940: The April issue of **Detective Comics** No. 38 introduced Robin the Boy Wonder as a sidekick to Batman, thus establishing the "Dynamic Duo" and a major precedent for later costumed heroes who would also have boy companions. **Batman Comics** began in the spring. Over 60 different comic book titles were being issued, including **Whiz Comics** begun in February by Fawcett Publications. A creation of writer Bill Parker and artist C. C. Beck, Whiz's Captain Marvel was the only superhero ever to surpass Superman in comic book sales. Drawing on their own popular pulp magazine heroes, Street and Smith Publications introduced **Shadow**

Preserve Your Comic Books Virtually Forever with Archival Quality Preservation Supplies from Bill Cole Enterprises.

Step 2: Protect

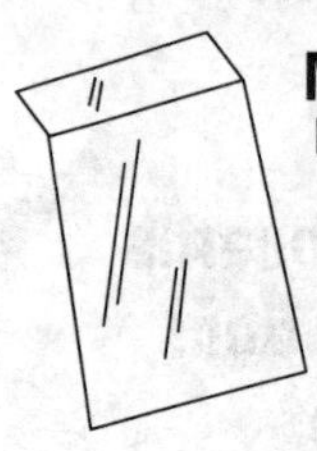

Mylites™
Designed to fit tight budgets these are BCE's lightest weight sleeve, only 1 mil. thick.

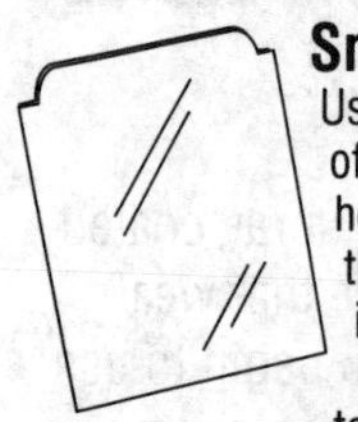

Snugs™
Used by the Library of Congress, these heavy-duty, 4 mil. thick, sleeves are ideal for permanent storage or to display your more valuable comics.

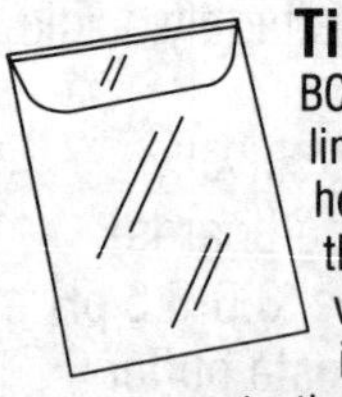

Time-Lok® IIs
BCE's top-of-the-line sleeves. These heavy-duty, 4 mil. thick sleeves, provide optimum investment protection. Ideal for collectibles that you buy and never want to touch.

Beware of advertisements that depict polypropylene bags as being archivally sound. It's a lie!

For years collectors have stored their comic books in inexpensive polyethylene and polypropylene bags. These plastics are coated with chemicals and contain additives that migrate into paper and cause premature aging.

Even the manufacturers of polypropylene warn that only uncoated and untreated Mylar®D is suitable for archival protection. This exceptionally strong transparent film will resist moisture, pollutants, oils and acids.

BCE offers three types of protective sleeves in varying thicknesses and styles. All three are made entirely of MYLAR®D with our exclusive UltraWeld™ for the strongest seams in the industry.

Snugs™ and Mylites™ are trademarks of E. Gerber Products, Inc., with exclusive rights to Bill Cole Enterprises, Inc. Time-Lok II® is a registered trademark of Bill Cole Enterprises, Inc. Thin-X-Tenders™, Time-X-Tenders™, and Ultra-Weld™ are trademarks of Bill Cole Enterprises, Inc. All references to Mylar® refer to archival quality polyester film such as Mylar® type D by DuPont Co., or equivalent material such as Melinex®516 by ICI Corp.

BUYING

1920 through 1964 Wanted
Paying up to 100% of

© DC Comics, Inc.

• We are the World's largest mail order comic book dealer, specializing in comic books dated from 1920 through 1964.
Being a mail order company we are not dependent on any one local economy to support our business. Our customer base consists of the entire United States, as well as Canada,
Europe, Australia, Japan, and other countries.
Our large customer base allows us to buy at much higher prices than any other dealer.

© Marvel

<u>* WE PAY MORE BECAUSE WE CAN SELL MORE *</u>

• We offer immediate immediate payment.
How fast? For books and collections shipped to us we can send payment to you within 24 hours!
If we travel to you for large valuable collections, payment is made immediately.

• If you ship your books to us **WE** pay the cost!
Please call before you ship. This allows us to give you complete and thorough shipping instructions. You can <u>expect</u> a reply the same day we receive your package.

© Marvel Comics

• <u>You are under NO risk or obligation at any time</u>. If you do not except our offer we will return your books at our expense within 24 hours.

WORLD'S FINEST COMICS & COLLECTIBLES
"The Right Choice"
• Dedicated to customer service since 1985 •

COMICS

Immediate Payment!

Price Guide Value!

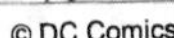
© DC Comics

- We have worked hard to build a reputation of complete customer satisfaction, and welcome any inquiries you may have. We invite you to contact the author of this Price Guide as a reference.

- We are expert in accurately grading and pricing your books. We use the standards that are written in this Price Guide, and will be happy to go over the grading procedure with you.

© DC Comics

- Don't be afraid to ask questions. We understand that this process might be something you have never done before. We are here to help you. That's good business.

- We offer a TOLL FREE number to call at any time, day or night. (800) 225-4189.

- Our hours are 9:00 to 5:30 PST, Monday - Friday. We are in & out on Saturday. When we are not in a recording will receive your call. We return calls promptly.

© Standard

- We travel most ANYWHERE to purchase larger collections.

- We are an advisor to the Overstreet Price Guide, the Overstreet Grading Guide, and the Overstreet Marketplace Update.

Phone- **(800) 225-4189 Or (206) 274-916**

Address: P.O. Box 340
Castle Rock, WA. 98611

FAX - (206) 274-9174

BUYING CARTOON POSTERS

ORIGINALS ONLY

- **Highest Prices Paid**
- **Immediate Payment**
- **Free Appraisal**

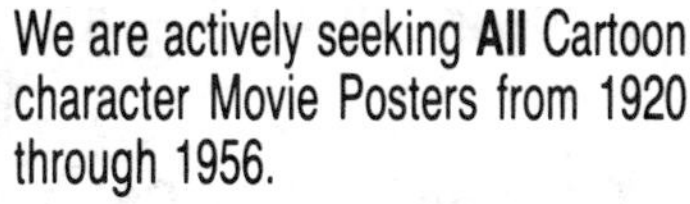
We are actively seeking **All** Cartoon character Movie Posters from 1920 through 1956.

Including:
All Disney Full Feature Cartoons & Shorts
All Fleisher Cartoons
All Super hero Cartoons & Serials
All Warner Brothers Cartoons
All MGM, Universal & Columbia Cartoons

If you have a Cartoon Poster—**We'll buy it!** Lobby Cards too!

Give us a call today at (206) 274-9163 or write:

WORLD'S FINEST COMICS & COLLECTIBLES
P.O. Box 340
Castle Rock, WA 98611

Have any Old Movie Posters with Real People? We buy those too

Earth's Mightiest
Super Heroes.
America's Favorite Mutants.
MARVEL®
COMICS
WHERE
THE
HEROES
ARE.

Celebrating 30 years of
The X-Men and The Avengers
Mark S. Pacella '92
Mark McKenna

Action Comics #267, 1960 © DC. 3rd app. Legion of Super-Heroes

Adventure Comics #47, 1939 © DC. 1st Steve Conrad Adventurer.

Adventure Comics # 267, 1959, © DC. 2nd App. Legion of Super-Heroes

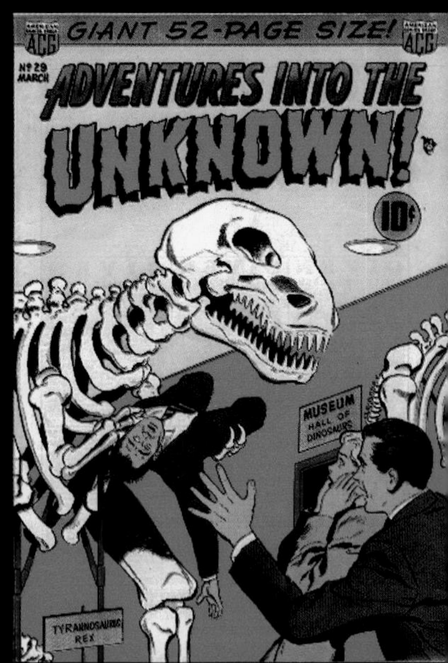

Adventures into the Unknown #29, 1952 © ACG

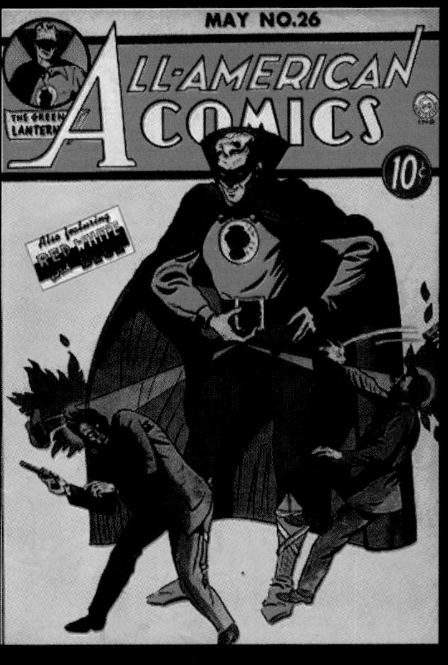

All-American #26, 1941, © DC.
Origin Sargon, the Sourcerer.

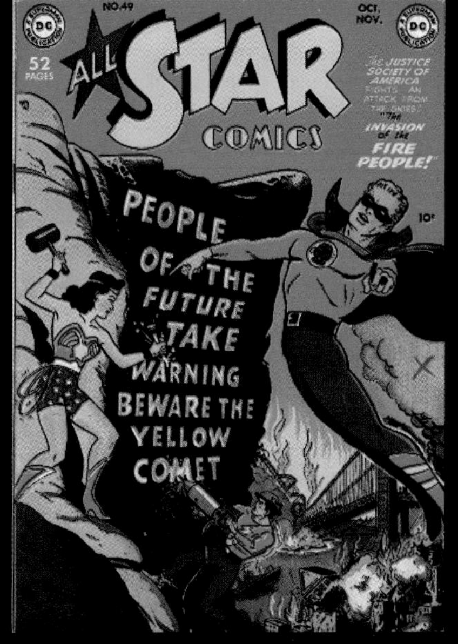

All-Star #49, 1949, © DC.

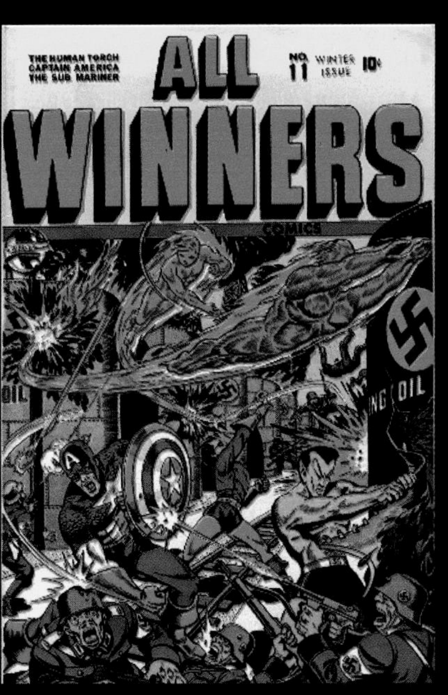

All-Winners #11, 1943, © Marvel.

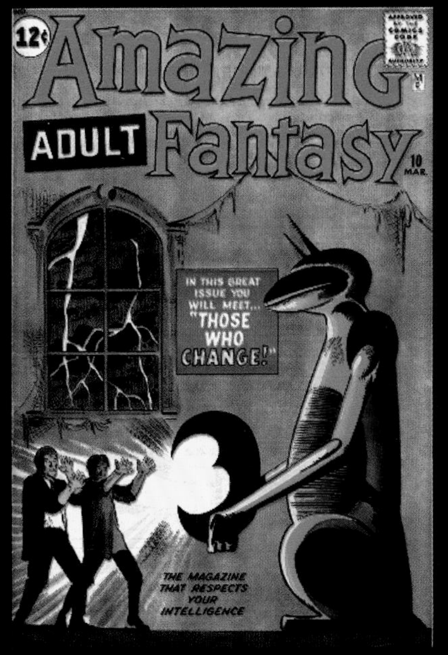

Amazing Adult Fantasy #10,
1961, © Marvel

Amazing Spider-Man #101, 1971, © Marvel. 1st app. Morbius.

America's Greatest Comics #5, 1942, © Fawcett.

Aquaman #1, 1962, © DC. Intro Quisp.

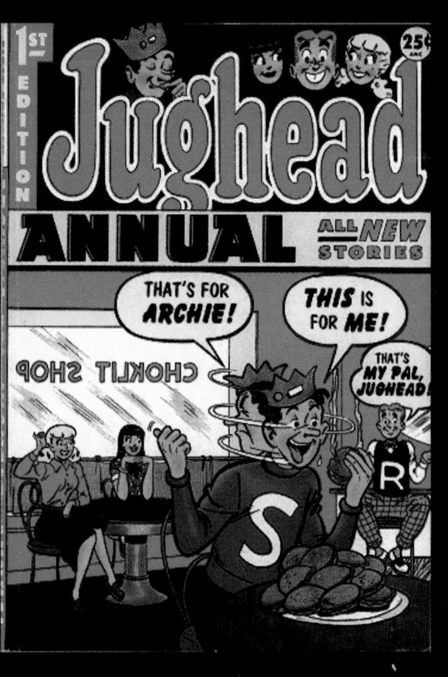

Archie's Pal Jughead Annual #1, 1953, © Archie

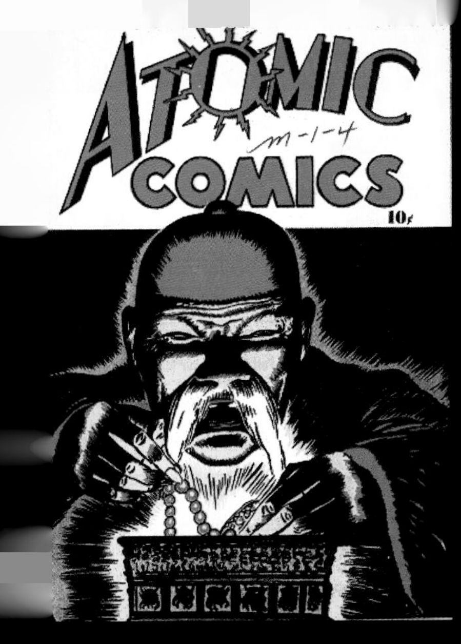

Atomic Comics #1, 1946, © Green Publishing Co.

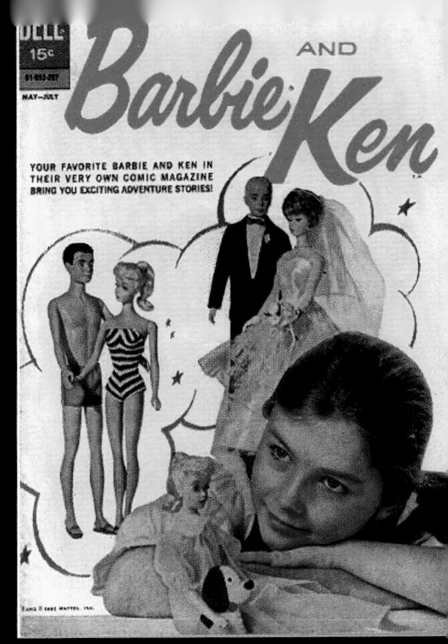

Barbie and Ken #1, 1962, © Mattel.

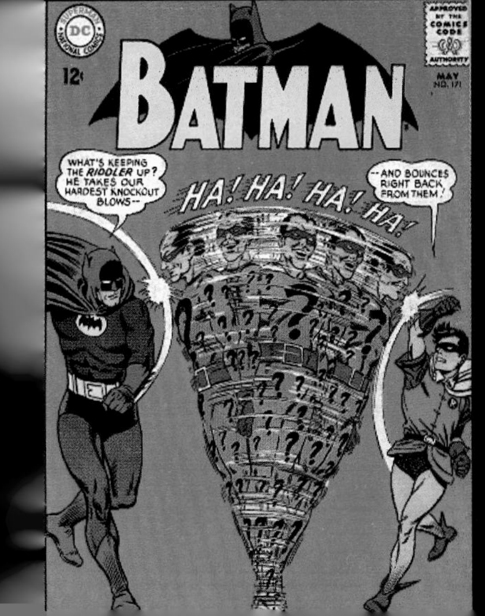

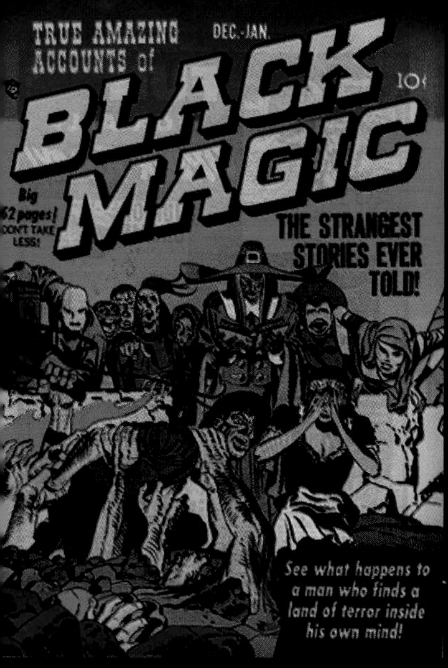

Black Magic #2, 1950, © Crestwood

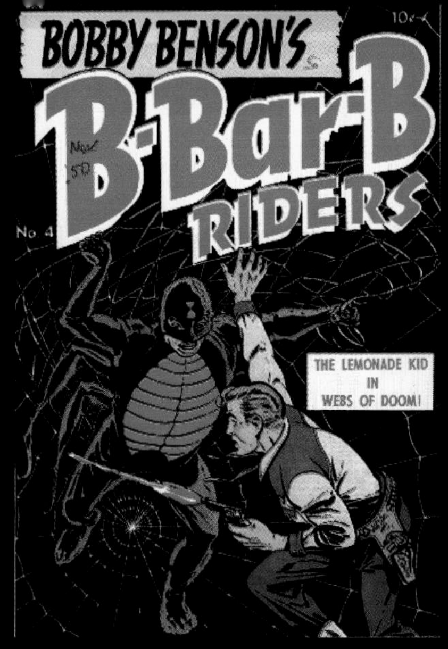

Bobby Benson's B-Bar-B Riders #4, 1950, © Magazine Ent.

Comic Cavalcade #12, 1945, © DC.
Last Red, White, & Blue.

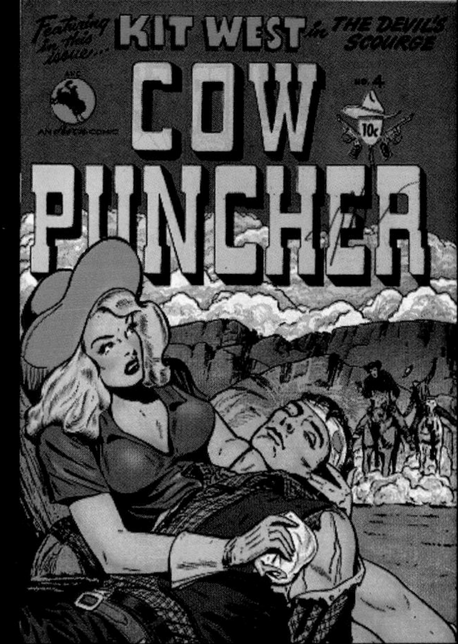

Cow Puncher Comics #4, 1948, © Avon

Crackajack Funnies #2, 1938, © Dell

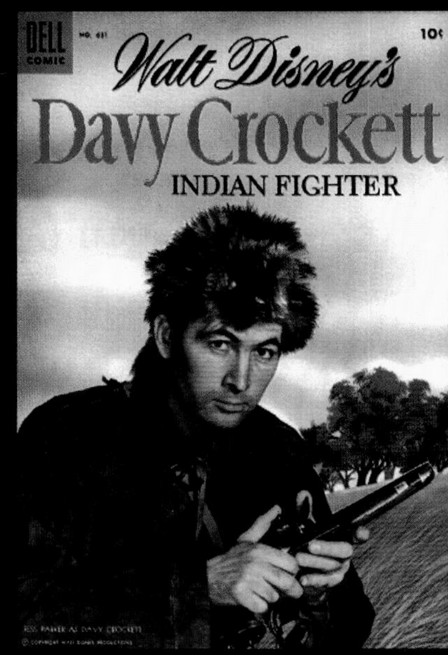

Davy Crocket #1, 1955, © Walt Disney

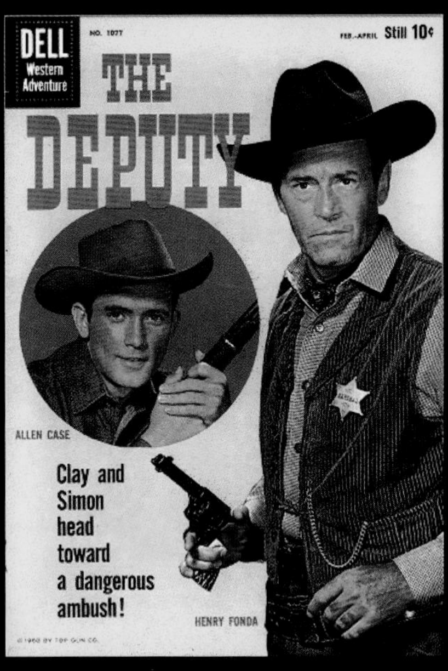

The Deputy (Four Color) #1077, 1960, © Top Gun Co.

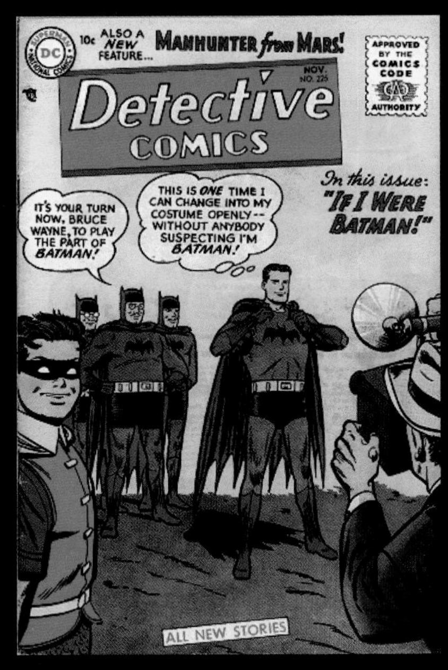

Detective #225, 1955, © DC. 1st app. Martian Manhunter.

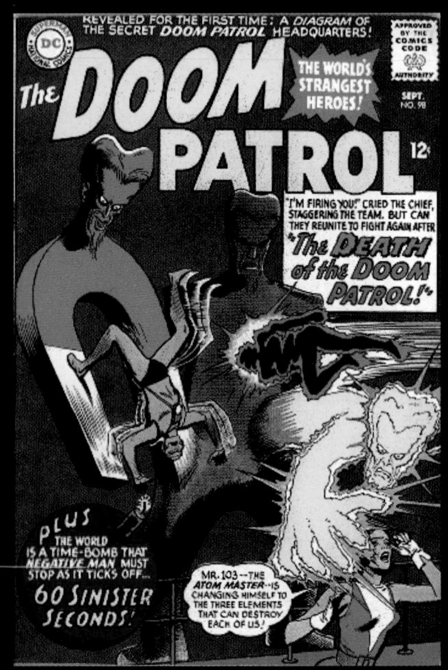

Doom Patrol #98, 1965, © DC

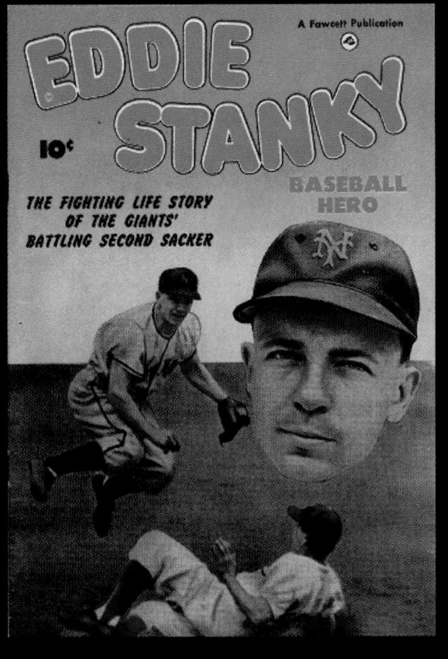

Eddie Stanky nn, 1951, © Fawcett

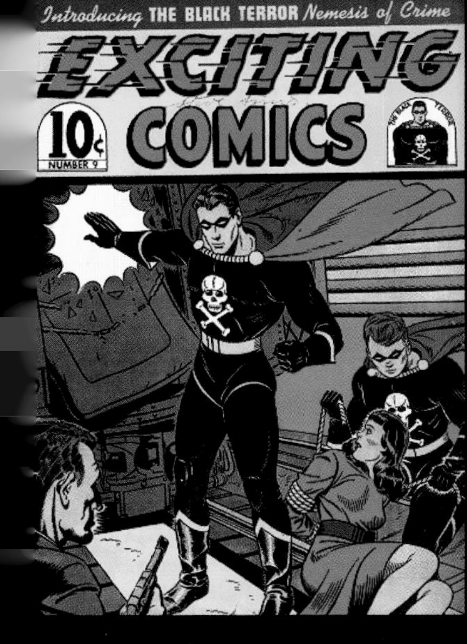

Exciting Comics #9, 1941, © Standard Comics. Origin/1st app. Black Terror.

Fantastic Four #13, 1962, © Marvel. Intro. The Watcher, 1st app. Red Ghost

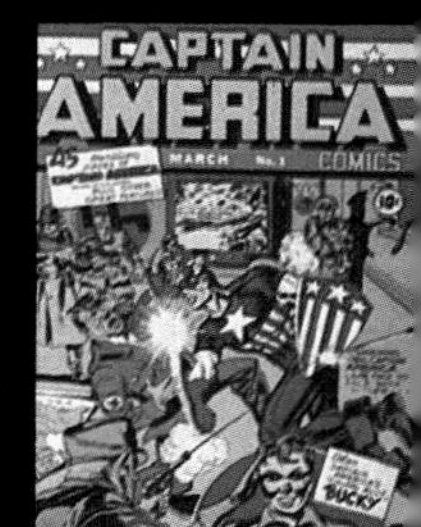
CAPTAIN AMERICA
COMICS
MARCH

WHIZ COMICS
GANGWAY FOR CAPTAIN MARVEL!

NO.1-JAN.
FLASH Comics

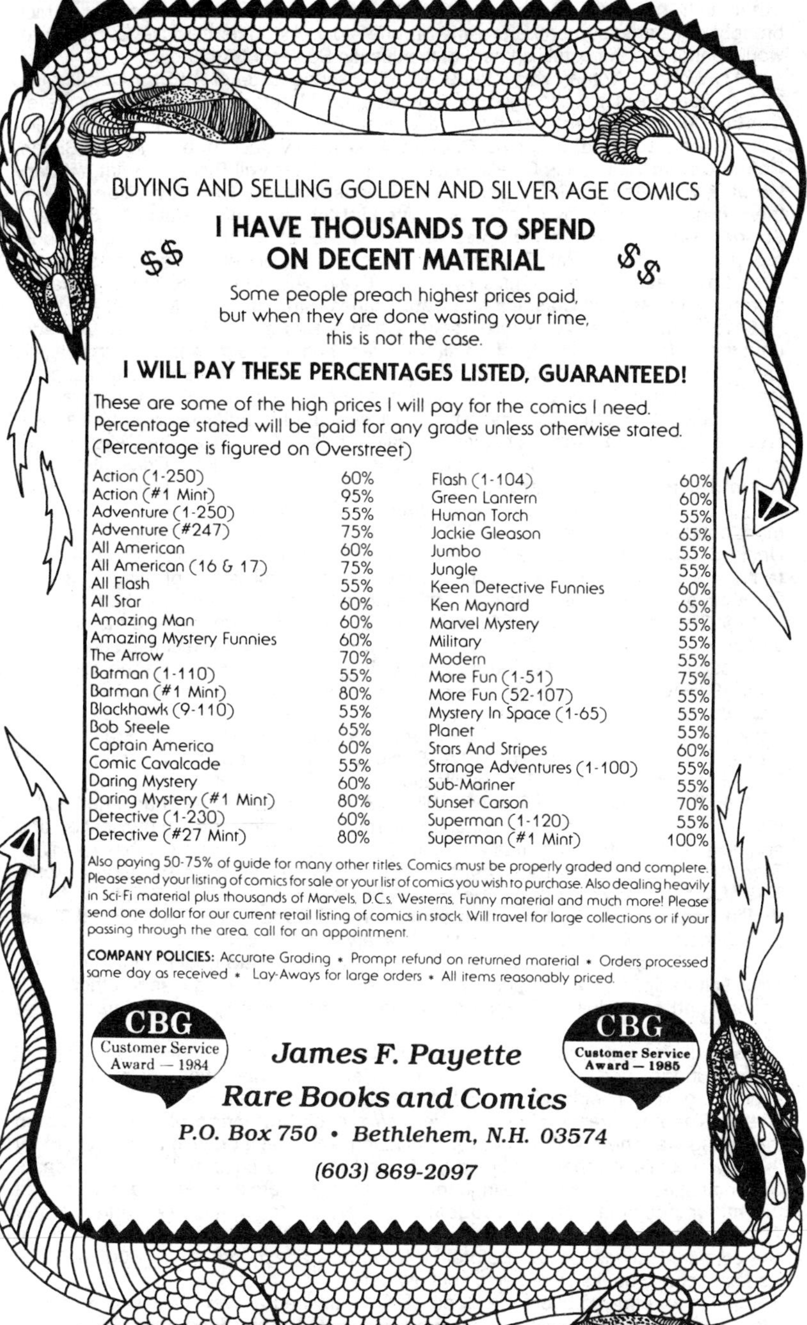

BUYING AND SELLING GOLDEN AND SILVER AGE COMICS
I HAVE THOUSANDS TO SPEND ON DECENT MATERIAL
$$ $$
Some people preach highest prices paid, but when they are done wasting your time, this is not the case.
I WILL PAY THESE PERCENTAGES LISTED, GUARANTEED!
These are some of the high prices I will pay for the comics I need. Percentage stated will be paid for any grade unless otherwise stated. (Percentage is figured on Overstreet)
Action (1-250) 60%
Action (#1 Mint) 95%
Adventure (1-250) 55%
Adventure (#247) 75%
All American 60%
All American (16 & 17) 75%
All Flash 55%
All Star 60%
Amazing Man 60%
Amazing Mystery Funnies 60%
The Arrow 70%
Batman (1-110) 55%
Batman (#1 Mint) 80%
Blackhawk (9-110) 55%
Bob Steele 65%
Captain America 60%
Comic Cavalcade 55%
Daring Mystery 60%
Daring Mystery (#1 Mint) 80%
Detective (1-230) 60%
Detective (#27 Mint) 80%
Flash (1-104) 60%
Green Lantern 60%
Human Torch 55%
Jackie Gleason 65%
Jumbo 55%
Jungle 55%
Keen Detective Funnies 60%
Ken Maynard 65%
Marvel Mystery 55%
Military 55%
Modern 55%
More Fun (1-51) 75%
More Fun (52-107) 55%
Mystery In Space (1-65) 55%
Planet 55%
Stars And Stripes 60%
Strange Adventures (1-100) 55%
Sub-Mariner 55%
Sunset Carson 70%
Superman (1-120) 55%
Superman (#1 Mint) 100%
Also paying 50-75% of guide for many other titles. Comics must be properly graded and complete. Please send your listing of comics for sale or your list of comics you wish to purchase. Also dealing heavily in Sci-Fi material plus thousands of Marvels, D.C.s, Westerns, Funny material and much more! Please send one dollar for our current retail listing of comics in stock. Will travel for large collections or if your passing through the area, call for an appointment.
COMPANY POLICIES: Accurate Grading • Prompt refund on returned material • Orders processed same day as received • Lay-Aways for large orders • All items reasonably priced.
CBG Customer Service Award — 1984
James F. Payette
CBG Customer Service Award — 1985
Rare Books and Comics
P.O. Box 750 • Bethlehem, N.H. 03574
(603) 869-2097

Comics in March and **Doc Savage Comics** in May. A second trend was established with the summer appearance of the first issue of **All Star Comics**, which brought several superheroes together in one story and in its third issue that winter would announce the establishment of the Justice Society of America.

1941: Wonder Woman was introduced in the spring issue of **All Star Comics** No. 8, the creation of psychologist William Moulton Marston and artist Harry Peter. **Captain Marvel Adventures** began this year. By the end of 1941, over 160 titles were being published, including **Captain America** by Jack Kirby and Joe Simon, **Police Comics** with Jack Cole's Plastic Man and later Will Eisner's Spirit, **Military Comics** with Blackhawk by Eisner and Charles Cuidera, **Daredevil Comics** with the original character by Charles Biro, **Air Fighters** with Airboy also by Biro, and **Looney Tunes & Merrie Melodies** with Porky Pig, Bugs Bunny, and Elmer Fudd, reportedly created by Bob Clampett for the Leon Schlesinger Productions animated films and drawn for the comics by Chase Craig. Also, Albert Kanter's Gilberton Company initiated the **Classics Illustrated** series with The Three Musketeers.

1942: Crime Does Not Pay by editor Charles Biro and publisher Lev Gleason, devoted to factual accounts of criminals' lives, began a different trend in realistic crime stories. **Wonder Woman** appeared in the summer. John Goldwater's character Archie, drawn by Bob Montana, first published in **Pep Comics**, was given his own magazine **Archie Comics**, which has remained popular over 40 years. The first issue of **Animal Comics** contained Walt Kelly's "Albert Takes the Cake," featuring the new character of Pogo. In mid-1942, the undated Dell Four Color title, No. 9, **Donald Duck Finds Pirate Gold**, appeared with art by Carl Barks and Jack Hannah. Barks, also featured in **Walt Disney's Comics and Stories**, remained the most popular delineator of Donald Duck and later introduced his greatest creation, Uncle Scrooge, in **Christmas on Bear Mountain** (Dell Four Color No. 178). The fantasy work of George Carlson appeared in the first issue of **Jingle Jangle Comics**, one of the most imaginative titles for children ever to be published.

1945: The first issue of **Real Screen Comics** introduced the Fox and the Crow by James F. Davis, and John Stanley began drawing the **Little Lulu** comic book based on a popular feature in the **Saturday Evening Post** by Marjorie Henderson Buell from 1935 to 1944. Bill Woggon's Katy Keene appears in issue No. 5 of **Wilbur Comics** to be followed by appearances in **Laugh, Pep, Suzie** and her own comic book in 1950. The popularity of Dick Briefer's satiric version of the Frankenstein monster, originally drawn for **Prize Comics** in 1941, led to the publication of **Frankenstein Comics** by Prize publications.

1950: The son of Max C. Gaines, William M. Gaines, who earlier had inherited his father's firm Educational Comics (later Entertaining Comics), began publication of a series of well-written and masterfully drawn titles which would establish a "New Trend" in comics magazines: **Crypt of Terror** (later **Tales from the Crypt**, April), **The Vault of Horror** (April), **The Haunt of Fear** (May), **Weird Science** (May), **Weird Fantasy** (May), **Crime SuspenStories** (October), and **Two Fisted Tales** (November), the latter stunningly edited by Harvey Kurtzman.

1952: In October "E.C." published the first number of **Mad** under Kurtzman's creative editorship, thus establishing a style of humor which would inspire other publications and powerfully influence the underground comic book movement of the 1960s.

1953: All Fawcett titles featuring Captain Marvel were ceased after many years of litigation in the courts during which National Periodical Publications claimed that the super-hero was an infringement on the copyrighted Superman.

1954: The appearance of Fredric Wertham's book **Seduction of the Innocent** in the spring was the culmination of a continuing war against comic books fought by those who believed they corrupted youth and debased culture. The U. S. Senate Subcommittee on Juvenile Delinquency investigated comic books and in response the major publishers banded together in October to create the Comics Code Authority and adopted, in their own words, "the most stringent code in existence for any communications media." Before the Code took effect, more than 1,000,000,000 issues of comic books were being sold annually.

1955: In an effort to avoid the Code, "E.C." launched a "New Direction" series of titles, such as **Impact, Valor, Aces High, Extra, M.D.,** and **Psychoanalysis**, none of which lasted beyond the year. **Mad** was changed into a larger magazine format with issue No. 24 in July to escape the Comics Code entirely, and "E.C." closed down its line of comic books altogether.

1956: Beginning with the Flash in **Showcase** No. 4, Julius Schwartz began a popular revival of "DC" superheroes which would lead to the "Silver Age" in comic book history.

1957: Atlas reduced the number of titles published by two-thirds, with **Journey into Mystery** and **Strange Tales** surviving, while other publishers did the same or went out of business. Atlas would survive as a part of the Marvel Comics Group.

1960: After several efforts at new satire magazines (**Trump** and **Humbug**), Harvey Kurtzman, no longer with Gaines, issued in August the first number of another abortive effort, **Help!**, where the early work of underground cartoonists Jay Lynch, Skip Williamson, Gilbert Shelton, and Robert Crumb appeared.

1961: Stan Lee edited in November the first **Fantastic Four**, featuring Mr. Fantastic, the Human Torch, the Thing, and the Invisible Girl, and inaugurated an enormously popular line of titles from Marvel Comics featuring a more contemporary style of superhero.

1962: Lee introduced **The Amazing Spider-Man** in August, with art by Steve Ditko, **The Hulk** in May and **Thor** in August, the last two produced by Dick Ayers and Jack Kirby.

1963: Marvel's **The X-Men**, with art by Jack Kirby, began a successful run in November, but the title would experience a revival and have an even more popular reception in the 1980s.

1965: James Warren issued **Creepy**, a larger black and white comic book, outside Comics Code's control, which emulated the "E.C." horror comic line. Warren's **Eerie** began in September and **Vampirella** in September 1969.

1967: Robert Crumb's **Zap** No. 1 appeared, the first underground comic book to achieve wide popularity, although the undergrounds had begun in 1962 with **Adventures of Jesus** by Foolbert Sturgeon (Frank Stack) and 1964 with **God Nose** by Jack Jackson.

1970: Editor Roy Thomas at Marvel begins **Conan the Barbarian** based on fiction by Robert E. Howard with art by Barry Smith, and Neal Adams began to draw for "DC" a series of **Green Lantern/Green Arrow** stories which would deal with relevant social issues such as racism, urban poverty, and drugs.

1972: The Swamp Thing by Berni Wrightson begins in November from "DC."

1973: In February, "DC" revived the original **Captain Marvel** with new art by C. C. Beck and reprints in the first issue of **Shazam** and in October **The Shadow** with scripts by Denny O'Neil and art by Mike Kaluta.

1974: "DC" began publication in the spring of a series of over-sized facsimile reprints of the most valued comic books of the past under the general title of "Famous First Editions," beginning with a reprint of **Action** No. 1 and including afterwards **Detective Comics** No. 27, **Sensation Comics** No. 1, **Whiz Comics** No. 2, **Batman** No. 1, **Wonder Woman** No. 1, **All-Star Comics** No. 3, **Flash Comics** No. 1, and **Superman** No. 1. Mike Friedrich, an independent publisher, released **Star★Reach** with work by Jim Starlin, Neal Adams, and Dick Giordano, with ownership of the characters and stories invested in the creators themselves.

1975: In the first collaborative effort between the two major comic book publishers of the previous decade, Marvel and "DC" produced together an over-sized comic book version of MGM's **Marvelous Wizard of Oz** in the fall, and then the following year in an unprecedented cross-over produced **Superman vs. the Amazing Spider-Man**, written by Gerry Conway, drawn by Ross Andru, and inked by Dick Giordano.

1976: Frank Brunner's Howard the Duck, who had appeared earlier in Marvel's **Fear** and **Man-Thing**, was given his own book in January, which because of distribution problems became an overnight collector's item. After decades of litigation, Jerry Siegel and Joe Shuster were given financial recompense and recognition by National Periodical Publications for their creation of Superman, after several friends of the team made a public issue of the case.

1977: Stan Lee's **Spider-Man** was given a second birth, fifteen years after his first, through a highly successful newspaper comic strip, which began syndication on January 3 with art by John Romita. This invasion of the comic strip by comic book characters continued with the appearance on June 6 of Marvel's **Howard the Duck**, with story by Steve Gerber and visuals by Gene Colan. In an unusually successful collaborative effort, Marvel began publication of the comic book adaption of the George Lucas film **Star Wars**, with script by Roy Thomas and art by Howard Chaykin, at least three months before the film was released nationally on May 25. The demand was so great that all six issues of **Star Wars** were reprinted at least seven times, and the installments were reprinted in two volumes of an over-sized

Marvel Special Edition and a single paperback volume for the book trade. Dave Sim, with an issue dated December, began self-publication of his **Cerebus the Aardvark**, the success of which would help establish the independent market for non-traditional black-and-white comics.

1978: In an effort to halt declining sales, Warner Communications drastically cut back on the number of "DC" titles and overhauled its distribution process in June. The interest of the visual media in comic book characters reached a new high with the Hulk, Spider-Man, and Doctor Strange, the subjects of television shows; with various projects begun to produce film versions of Flash Gordon, Dick Tracy, Popeye, Conan, The Phantom, and Buck Rogers; and with the movement reaching an outlandish peak of publicity with the release of **Superman** in December. Two significant applications of the comic book format to traditional fiction appeared this year: **A Contract with God and Other Tenement Stories** by Will Eisner and **The Silver Surfer** by Stan Lee and Jack Kirby. Eclipse Enterprises published Don McGregor and Paul Gulacy's **Sabre**, the first graphic album produced for the direct sales market, and initiated a policy of paying royalties and granting copyrights to comic book creators. Wendy and Richard Pini's **Elfquest**, a self-publishing project begun this year, eventually became so popular that it achieved bookstore distribution. The magazine **Heavy Metal** brought to American attention the avant-garde comic book work of European artists.

1980: Publication of the November premier issue of **The New Teen Titans**, with art by George Perez and story by Marv Wolfman, brought back to widespread popularity a title originally published by "DC" in 1966.

1981: The distributor Pacific Comics began publishing titles for direct sales through comic shops with the inaugural issue of Jack Kirby's **Captain Victory and the Galactic Rangers** and offered royalties to artists and writers on the basis of sales. "DC" would do the same for regular newsstand comics in November (with payments retroactive to July 1981), and Marvel followed suit by the end of the year. The first issue of **Raw**, irregularly published by Art Spiegelman and Francoise Mouly, carried comic book art into new extremes of experimentation and innovation with work by European and American artists. With issue No. 158, Frank Miller began to write and draw Marvel's **Daredevil** and brought a vigorous style of violent action to comic book pages.

1982: The first slick format comic book in regular size appeared, **Marvel Fanfare** No. 1, with a March date. Fantagraphics Books began publication in July of **Love and Rockets** by Mario, Gilbert, and Jaime Hernandez and brought a new ethnic sensibility and sophistication in style and content to comic book narratives for adults.

1983: This year saw more comic book publishers, aside from Marvel and DC, issuing more titles than had existed in the past 40 years, most small independent publishers relying on direct sales, such as Americomics, Capital, Eagle, Eclipse, First, Pacific, and Red Circle, and with Archie, Charlton, and Whitman publishing on a limited scale. Frank Miller's mini-series **Ronin** demonstrated a striking use of sword play and martial arts typical of Japanese comic book art, and Howard Chaykin's stylish but controversial **American Flagg** appeared with an October date on its first issue.

1984: A publishing, media, film, and merchandising phenomenon began with the first issue of **Teenage Mutant Ninja Turtles** from Mirage Studios by Kevin Eastman and Peter Laird.

1985: Ohio State University's Library of Communication and Graphic Arts hosted the first major exhibition devoted to the comic book May 19 through August 2. In what was billed as an irreversible decision, the silver age superheroine Supergirl was killed in the seventh (October) issue of **Crisis on Infinite Earths**, a limited series intended to reorganize and simplify the DC universe on the occasion of the publisher's 50th anniversary.

1986: In recognition of its twenty-fifth anniversary, Marvel began publication of several new ongoing titles comprising Marvel's ``New Universe," a self-contained fictional world. DC attracted extensive publicity and media coverage with its revisions of the character of **Superman** by John Byrne and of **Batman** in the **Dark Knight** series by Frank Miller. **Watchmen**, a limited-series graphic novel by Alan Moore and artist Dave Gibbons, began publication with a September issue from DC and Marvel's **The `Nam**, written by Vietnam veteran Doug Murray and penciled by Michael Golden, began with its December issue. DC issued guidelines in December for labelling their titles as either for mature readers or for readers of all ages; in response, many artists and writers publicly objected or threatened to resign.

1987: Art Spiegelman's **Maus: A Survivor's Tale** was nominated for the National Book Critics Circle Award in biography, the first comic book to be so honored. A celebration of Superman's fiftieth Birthday began with the opening of an exhibition on his history at the Smithsonian's Museum of American History in Washington, D.C., in June and a symposium on "The Superhero in America" in October.

1988: Superman's birthday celebration continued with a public party in New York and a CBS television special in February, a cover story in Time magazine in March (the first comic book character to appear on the cover), and an international exposition in Cleveland in June. With issue number 601 for May 24, **Action Comics** became the first modern weekly comic book, which ceased publication after 42 issues with the December 13 number. In August, DC initiated a new policy of allowing creators of new characters to retain ownership of them rather than rely solely on work-for-hire.

1989: The fiftieth anniversary of Batman was marked by the release of the film **Batman**, starring Michael Keaton as Bruce Wayne and Jack Nicholson as the Joker; it grossed more money in the weekend it opened than any other motion picture in film history to that time.

1990: The publication of a new **Classics Illustrated** series began in January from Berkley/First with adaptations of Poe's **The Raven and Other Poems** by Gahan Wilson, Dickens' **Great Expectations** by Rick Geary, Carroll's **Through the Looking Glass** by Kyle Baker, and Melville's **Moby Dick** by Bill Sienkiewicz, with extensive media attention. The adaptation of characters to film continued with the most successful in terms of popularity and box office receipts being **Teenage Mutant Ninja Turtles** and Warren Beatty's **Dick Tracy**. In November, the engagement of Clark Kent and Lois Lane was announced in **Superman** No. 50 which brought public fanfare about the planned marriage.

1991: One of the first modern comic books to appear in the Soviet Union was a Russian version of **Mickey Mouse** published in Moscow on May 16 in a printing of 200,000 copies which were sold out within hours. Issue number one of a new series of Marvel's **X-Men**, with story and art by Chris Claremont and Jim Lee, was published in October in five different editions with a print run of eight million copies, the highest circulation title in the history of the comic book. On December 18, Sotheby's of New York held its first auction of comic book material.

1992: The opening weekend for **Batman Returns** in June was the biggest in film box office history, bringing in over 46 million dollars, exceeding the record set by **Batman** in 1989. In November the death of **Superman** generated considerable media attention. A record number of over 100 publishers of comic books and graphic albums issued titles this year, some of the most prominent being Archie, Caliber, DC, Dark Horse, Disney, Eclipse, Fantagraphics, Gladstone, Harvey, Innovation, Kitchen Sink, Malibu, Marvel, Now, Personality, Revolutionary, Tundra, Viz, and Voyager.

COMIC CHARACTER RINGS, A NEW HOT COLLECTIBLE–THE TOP 50

Value	Rank & Ring Type
$100,000	1 Supermen of America (prize)
$70,000	2 Superman Secret Compart.(candy)
$70,000	3 Superman Secret Compart.(gum)
$15,000	4 Radio Orphan Annie Altascope
$15,000	4 Superman Tim
$14,000	6 Operator Five
$9,000	7 Cisco Kid Secret Compartment
$5,500	8 Valric The Viking
$5,000	9 Howdy Doody Jack in Box
$5,000	9 Tom Mix Deputy
$4,500	11 Lone Ranger Meteorite
$4,000	12 Radio Orphan Annie Magnifying
$4,000	12 Radio Orphan Annie Initial
$3,500	14 Frank Buck Black Leopard (W Fair)
$3,000	15 Lone Ranger (ice cream)
$2,500	16 Frank Buck Black Leopard (bronze)
$2,400	17 Buck Rogers Sylvania Bulb
$2,000	18 Captain Marvel
$2,000	18 Captain Midnight Mystic Sun God
$2,000	18 Tonto (ice cream)
$2,000	18 Buck Rogers Repeller Ray
$1,800	22 Knights of Columbus
$1,600	23 Green Hornet (plastic)
$1,500	24 Quisp Figura
$1,500	24 Dick Tracy Monogram
$1,500	24 Lone Ranger Photo (test)
$1,500	24 Frank Buck Black Leopard (silver)
$1,500	24 Joe Louis Face
$1,500	24 U.S.A. (KKK)
$1,200	31 Captain Video Flying Saucer
$1,200	31 Captain Hawks/Melvin Purvis Scarab
$1,000	33 Shadow Carey Salt
$1,000	33 Green Hornet Secret Compt
$1,000	33 Don Winslow Member
$1,000	33 Whistle Bomb
$1,000	33 Howdy Doody T.V. Flicker
$1,000	33 Clarabelle Face/Hat
$1,000	33 Tom Mix Spinner
$1,000	33 Radio Orphan Annie Triple Mystery
$950	41 B. Collins/Dark Shadows
$900	42 Captain Video Pendant
$850	43 Buck Rogers Ring of Saturn
$800	44 Sky King Aztec
$800	44 Captain Midnight Signet
$800	44 Space Patrol Cosmic Glow
$800	44 Ted Williams Baseball
$800	44 Jack Armstrong Crocodile
$800	44 Roy Rogers Hat
$750	50 Rocket to Moon

The above rings represent the current most valuable. Consult **the Overstreet Price Guide Companion** for a complete listing of these fabulous collectible rings.

IN BRIGHTEST DAY... IN BLACKEST NIGHT... NO EVIL SHALL ESCAPE MY SIGHT... LET THOSE WHO WORSHIP EVIL'S MIGHT... BEWARE MY POWER...

Green Lantern's Light!

A History by Thomas Andrae with Keif Fromm

The introduction of Superman in 1938 launched not only a new comic book hero but a new type of protagonist – the superhero. A year later, Bob Kane and Bill Finger put a new spin on this mythos creating Batman, the first costumed hero without super powers. Inspired by the great success of these two heroes, artists and writers created scores of new supermen (and superwomen) in the pre-war and wartime years which followed. The boom in sales revolutionized comic book publishing, transforming it from a cottage industry into a multimillion dollar business.

One of the men who jumped onto the superhero bandwagon was M. C. Gaines, father of EC/Mad publisher William Gaines, and one of the discoverers of Superman. In 1939, Gaines decided to publish a new line of comic books, All-American Comics, which would be linked with, but retain an independent relationship to DC Comics, publishers of Superman and Batman. The two companies would share advertising and company logo but be owned separately. With the aid of chief editor Sheldon Mayer, Gaines built his own stable of superheroes which included The Flash, Wonder Woman, The Justice Society of America–and Green Lantern. While not as popular as Superman or Batman, these heroes would become some of the most beloved and enduring characters in the history of comics.

The Golden Age Green Lantern; A Modern Aladdin

Green Lantern was created in 1940 by an aspiring young artist named Martin Nodell. In 1937 Nodell came to New York to make his fortune: "I came to New York from Chicago after extensive art education. I came packed full of letters to see about getting into advertising, for which I was trained. But, I found that jobs were not easy to get because of the Depression." However, Nodell had the good fortune of being in the right place at the right time. The comic book industry soon experienced an explosion in sales due to the creation of Superman. "I found there was a new thing going around, and that was comics. So, I did some individual free-lance comics for independent publishers. After I got used to comics, I went to see the publishers of DC comics. Sheldon Mayer, the editor, told me that they had a need for a new title. If I were to think of something, fine, they'd consider it." The seed was planted for the birth of Green Lantern.

Nodell describes his creation of the character this way: "On the way home that very day, on the train, I saw a trainman in the trough of the subway in New York waving a green lantern. That meant 'train stop,' or 'I'm down here doing repairs'. Then he waved a green lantern. That sounded good. On the way home, I made notes. I couldn't think of a better title. I came up with 'Green Lantern' and nothing else. I was interested in both Greek mythology and ancient Chinese lore, so I put all these elements together with the green lantern." Nodell then contacted Mayer, showing him some Green Lantern art, two or three pages of storyline, and a sketch of the character's philosophy.

Mayer was not overly impressed: "Nodell's drawing was crude," he recalled. "What he did have , crude as he was apt to be in his drawing, was an effective first page. He had taken the lead from the Superman motif and applied the Aladdin formula to that. I don't know if he included the ring, but he did have the hero with the magical lantern. I didn't want to take it. I thought, what the hell, this is a direction we're already going in, and Nodell didn't seem good enough to handle the feature, and yet he had walked in with the idea. I wasn't going to use Green Lantern and do it with somebody else. So Bill Finger and I fleshed out the concept... as for Nodell, he made an intense effort to improve."

Finger created an alter ego for Green Lantern, initially calling him Alan Ladd (an amalgam of Aladdin). "That's ridiculous, Mayer said when he heard the name, "who'd believe that?" Two years later a young actor Alan Ladd would make his screen debut as a confused killer in the Film noir classic "This Gun for Hire". Due to Mayer's objections, Finger changed the name of GL's civilian identity to Alan Scott.

Green Lantern debuted in All-American Comics #16 (July, 1940) written by Finger and drawn by Nodell (under the pseudonym Mart Dellon). Finger spun a mystical legend around Nodell's allusion to Chinese lore. Falling to Earth in ancient China, a meteor bursts open to reveal a fiery green metal. A mysterious voice from the green flame utters a prophecy: "Three times shall I flame green: first to bring death, second to bring life, third to bring power." The metal is fashioned into a lamp by its original discoverer and passed down through the centuries. Alan Scott, a young engineer, finds the lamp and is beneficiary of its third prophecy. The lantern commands Scott to make a ring from its metal which he can carry when he needs to use its power. This ring must be charged every twenty four hours by touching it to the lantern.

The ring gives Scott almost supernatural powers: he can fly at the speed of light, walk through walls and other objects, and is immune to metals, making him invulnerable to assailants' bullets. Later, Finger would give him an Achilles heel: his ring would have no power over objects made of wood.

Because of its dependence on magic, Green Lantern inspired writers and artists to create extravagant fantasies and graphics which stirred readers' imaginations. For the ring could metamorphose into anything from fiery swirls of light which dissolved bullets in mid-air to the claws of a giant derrick which clasped villains in its jaws and deposited them unceremoniously in jail. The lamp could even function as a mystic television set (this before TV was available on

All-American Comics #16, The first appearance of the Green Lantern. (July, 1940). © DC.

the market) so that GL could spy on events at a distance.

All-American Comics #27, The introduction of Doiby Dickles (June,1941). © DC.

The idea of a modern Aladdin, in itself, was imaginative enough to elevate Green Lantern above more pedestrian superheroes. But Finger realized the value of adding colorful secondary characters to his casts. In 1940, he and Bob Kane had teamed Batman and Robin, the Boy Wonder, transforming the grim vigilante into a father figure and trusted buddy. Shortly thereafter, the Batman scripter hit upon a similar idea for Green Lantern; he created a comic sidekick for GL who idolized and assisted him like Robin worshipped and aided Batman. His name was Doiby Dickles. Doiby was a cabby who summoned Green Lantern by sending up green flares in the sky, an obvious influence from Finger's work on Batman in which the Caped Crusader was called into action by flashing the famed Bat-signal into the heavens. Astonishingly, Green Lantern even operated in the same Gotham City as Batman.

Doiby was one of the most endearing sidekicks in comics adding a touch of warmth, charm, and humor to Green Lantern that was often lacking in other superhero strips. The chubby cab driver was modeled after film character actor Edward Brophy. Brophy typically played small-time gangsters or dumb cops, and appeared as The Falcon's manservant/sidekick in the series about the debonair sleuth. Finger was a mystery buff and may have gotten the idea for Doiby from Brophy's role in The Thin Man, starring William Powell and Myrna Loy as the fun-loving detective and his wife, Nick and Nora Charles. In that film Brophy wears a derby and his small, pudgy body and bald pate make him the spitting image of Doiby. Like Brophy, Doiby spoke pure Brooklynese, peppering his sentences with "dese" and "dose" and various malapropisms. Doiby's dialect was immortalized in his motto: "Soivice what don't make you noivous."

Doiby first appeared in All-American #27 (June, 1941) and was shown on the cover wearing an ill-fitting Green Lantern costume, beaning a villain with a wrench. In subsequent stories, he would occasionally wear a similar make-shift outfit, wanting to emulate his idol. In this tale Doiby becomes a hero, albeit a humorous one, who rescues Irene Miller, Alan Scott's girlfriend, from being abducted. Doiby's deed comes to the attention of the Green Lantern who offers him a partnership. The relationship was solidified in All-American #35, Doiby's second appearance, in which he accidentally discovers GL's secret identity. Finger could not help putting some of the Dynamic Duo's fighting tactics into the action: Doiby swings down on the criminals from an overhanging hoist, commenting, "I seen some Boy Wonder kid do this once in a comic book!" and emulates Robin's playful banter with the bad guys, "Greetin's, fellers! An wot's new wid youse?"

Green Lantern boasted some of comics' finest writers, making the stories some of the best plotted in the medium. Finger himself was one of the best scripters in comics; but, he was only one of the major writing talents to work on Green Lantern. When he was drafted in 1942 he was replaced by eminent science fiction author Alfred Bester. Bester had won the very first Hugo award, science fiction's most prestigious prize, for his novel The Demolished Man. A later book, My Stars, My Destination, is considered one of the best science fiction novels ever written.

When he was first hired, Bester was unfamiliar with comics and did not know how to write a comic book script. DC editor Mort Weisinger introduced Bester to Finger who gave him a crash course in comics writing, teaching him what panels, balloons, and captions were. Bester's contribution to Green Lantern was enormous for he created one of the medium's most memorable villains – Solomon Grundy.

Grundy first appeared in All-American #61 (Oct., 1944) in a story entitled "Fighters Never Quit!" It was drawn by Paul Reinman who, with Irvin Hasen, was the major Golden Age Green Lantern artist besides Nodell. Grundy's name was inspired by a nursery rhyme which was featured in the opening legend of the story: "This is a tale of Solomon Grundy, born on Monday, got a mob on Tuesday, robbed on Wednesday, looted on Thursday, murdered on Friday, trapped on Saturday, and Sunday??. . ." The verse is chilling because it uses something associated with innocence, a childhood rhyme, and turns it into a tale of murder and evil. This is also part of our fascination with Grundy who, like the Frankenstein monster which inspired him, is like a newborn child with no experience or morality. He is an artificially created being, the product of a chemical reaction produced on the skeleton of a murdered man, Cyrus Gold, by the decomposition of rotten wood and leaves in Slaughter's Swamp. Born with no name, Grundy adopts that of the nursery rhyme because he was born on the day he heard it. His mind is a tabula rasa and he is taught to rob and kill by a criminal gang who make him their leader.

Undoubtedly Bester saw Grundy as a way of filling a hole in the Green Lantern corpus: GL's power ring had made him almost omnipotent. Grundy's strength and indestructibility (and the fact that he is made of wood, the one element GL's ring is helpless against) made him GL's greatest nemesis. Indeed, Bester had to think up new ways for GL to use his ring to avoid being harmed. When the monster almost kills him by throwing him over a balcony, Bester resorts to a contrivance: although GL is unconscious and cannot activate his ring, his lantern activates it for him and cushions his fall.

In the final confrontation GL forgets his ring and must defeat Grundy in a physical contest. This was a frequent occurrence throughout GL's career as writers strove to prove that GL could be physically powerful and courageous without the aid of his ring. GL defeats Grundy by flipping him into the path of an oncoming train. The story ends with a quizzical GL musing about

All-American Comics #61, Solomon Grundy is born (October, 1944). © DC.

whether or not his arch-foe will return. Return he does in Comic Cavalcade #13 in which he is resurrected when a scientist feeds him concentrated chlorophyll. This changes his physical structure making him more vulnerable to GL's ring. Although GL imprisons him in an energy bubble, he would return to haunt the Emerald Crusader in many subsequent adventures.

Not only was Bester responsible for creating memorable villains and stories, he left his mark by transforming GL's original oath, "And I shall shed my light over the dark evil... for the dark cannot stand the light of the Green Lantern!" into the familiar rhyming verse still used by Hal Jordan: "In brightest day, in blackest night, no evil shall escape my sight! Let those who worship evil's might, beware my power, Green Lantern's light."

Bester was a client of literary agent Julius Schwartz. On Bester's recommendation, Schwartz was hired in 1944 to edit the All-American line. "The first script Shelly Mayer gave me to edit," Schwartz recalls, "was a Green Lantern script by Alfred Bester. I was told to make whatever editorial changes I thought necessary. Bester was such a wonderful writer that the only thing I found wrong with the script was that Bester's spelling was lousy - L-O-U-S-Y. It showed me all I had to know about script editing."

In honor of his long friendship with Schwartz, Bester made and kept a promise to stay on Green Lantern for one more year, after which he would leave to move further into prose fiction and radio drama. While Bester was still writing Green Lantern, Schwartz went hunting for another writer. He settled on another well-known science fiction author and also a client,

All-American Comics #89, Robert Kanigher's The Harlequin appears (Sept., 1947), © DC

Henry Kuttner. To Schwartz's dismay Kuttner turned the job down, saying that he knew nothing about comics. "I pleaded with him to read Green Lantern," Schwartz remembers. "He liked it but still didn't want to do it. Fortunately, his beautiful wife (famed fantasy writer C. L. Moore) read it too and said, "Hank, you must do it - I love Doiby Dickles!"

About a year later Kuttner, like Bester, left comics to further his science fiction career, leaving Green Lantern again without an author. In the late forties another science fiction writer, John Broome, took over the scripting chores. Thus began a twenty five year association with Green Lantern that would reach its peak in the Silver Age when Broome would become responsible for totally revamping the character.

Before that could happen, comics had to traverse the second world war and one of the writers who carried readers through these changing times was Robert Kanigher. Kanigher created the villainess who became GL's most important opponent during this period – The Harlequin. She first appeared in All-American #89 (Sept., 1947). This story embodied the upheaval in gender roles produced when women went into the workplace to fill the shoes of men drafted into the army. Once seen primarily as wives and mothers, women became truck drivers, welders, and riveters, jobs formerly occupied exclusively by men. This undermined traditional definitions of masculinity and femininity creating a cultural crisis which peaked after the war when women were told to give up their jobs to returning service men and return to the home.

This transformation aroused male anxieties and, as a result, the media were saturated with images of women as femme fatales and destroyers of men. Seen through the lens of male fears, the emergence of more powerful, independent women were perceived as the threat of emasculation and feminine dominance. The cover of All-American #89 invokes this threat, showing GL holding a picture of a huge, mandolin-playing, jester-garbed woman standing over a diminutive GL imprisoned within a fishbowl. The caption reads, "Warning - this is your fate! Signed The Harlequin."

The Harlequin's alter ego was Molly Mayne, Alan Scott's secretary, who is secretly in love with Green Lantern. By this time, Scott had abandoned his identity as an engineer to become a radio broadcaster. Scott plans to do a radio drama starring the Emerald Crusader and a fictional villain called the Harlequin. Thinking this would be a way of meeting GL, Molly decides to play the role both on stage - and off.

Male fears of female power provide the subtext of the story; like women before the war Molly has had to hide her abilities to accommodate male stereotypes: "I never had a date," she laments, "because I was too athletic - no man could beat me at sports - I had to hide my talents... become a mousy secretary." However, when women began to assert their capabilities and become more equal to men, a male-dominated society cast them as deviants who threaten social order. Once ignored by men, Molly becomes a power over them, becoming the boss of a criminal gang whom she mesmerizes with her hypnotic spectacles. However, The Harlequin does not want to harm GL, only get his attention and prove she is his equal. When she captures him and hangs him by his heels, she puts a pillow below his head so that he will not be hurt if he falls. Although apparently killed in a bomb blast set off by her gang, she turns up again in her role as Alan Scott's secretary, vowing to prove to GL that she is his "match".

The Harlequin became GL's most popular adversary in the post-war years, appearing in more stories in this period than any other villain. GL would use her desire to marry him as a ploy to make her give up her criminal career in All-American #91, but the wedding would never take place. Years later Molly Mayne would actually marry Alan Scott, fulfilling her dream of wedding the Green Lantern.

Gaines unique relationship with DC Comics continued to the end of the war when personality conflicts led him to sell the All-American line to DC publisher Harry Donenfeld. DC would publish the combined stable of superheroes to the end of the forties. But, by this time, the superhero craze of the war years was petering out. In 1948 DC discontinued All-American Comics and its regular Green Lantern feature. With issue #103 the title was changed to All-American Western. This reflected a new trend in comics: as superheroes died out they were replaced by comics devoted to other genres such as crime, horror, romance, and westerns. In the forties, Green Lantern appeared in All-Star Comics as a member of the superhero team, The Justice Society of America, and continued his appearances in that magazine until 1951. But, by the middle of the decade only Superman, Batman, and Wonder Woman remained of the great All-American/DC heroes. Most of these heroes would stay in limbo until events coalesced to bring about a second boom in superheroes - the so-called Silver Age of comics.

The Silver Age Green Lantern

In the fifties, when American military might and technology geared up to fight the cold war, science fiction became a popular comic book genre. EC science fiction anthologies like Weird Science and Weird Science-Fantasy set a trend towards more sophisti-

Showcase #22, 1st Silver Age appearance of Green Lantern (October, 1959), © DC

cated stories aimed at mature readers. Interest increased even more when, in 1957, the Russians launched their first satellite, Sputnik, into outer space. As historian Eric Goldman writes, this event shattered Americans out of their Eisenhower-era complacency: "The chief thing in which Americans had depended for their national security and for victory in a competitive battle with communism - the superiority of American technical know-how - had been blatantly challenged." As a result, the U.S. resolved to win the race for space founding NASA in 1958. Putting a man on the moon became a matter of national prestige as well as military superiority. Science and technology became all the rage, and science education a patriotic duty.

The Space Age demanded standard bearers and Julius Schwartz would be a major figure in creating a new breed of techno-supermen. Schwartz had been a long-time science fiction fan and, at age 16, had helped publish the first nationally distributed SF fanzine, The Time Traveler (Jan., 1932). In 1934 Schwartz and fellow fan Mort Weisinger founded Solar Sales Service, the first science fiction literary agency, which specialized in selling stories to the growing number of SF pulps in the 1930s. Schwartz's clients included Ray Bradbury, H. P. Lovecraft, Robert Bloch, and other renowned science fiction authors many of whom he recruited to write Green Lantern. In the early fifties, he launched DC's first science fiction titles, Mystery In Space and Strange Adventures. The latter starred Adam Strange, billed as "America's first spaceman."

In the mid-fifties Schwartz and Robert Kanigher came with the idea of a Showcase comic book which premiered new characters, to see if they might be popular enough to spin off into their own series. Showcase #4 (Sept., 1956) featured a revamped version of The Flash and is usually regarded as marking the revival of reader interest in superheroes, and the dawning of comics' Silver Age. Schwartz felt that the time was ripe again for superheroes: "I assumed our comics had an 8 - 12 year-old readership. Flash Comics died in 1950. I felt that there would hardly be any readers who would remember Flash." After Flash appeared four times in Showcase, each time garnering substantial sales, he was given his own title.

Once Flash's star status was assured, Schwartz decided to try one more 1940s revival. Green Lantern had been the second most popular character in the All-American line so Schwartz gave him a tryout in Showcase #22-24 (Oct., 1959 - Feb., 1960). John Broome was brought in to do the writing, Gil Kane to do the pencils, and Joe Giella to do the inking.

In order to make them look like new characters, Schwartz decided that all his revamped heroes would have new origins, secret identities, and costumes, while their powers would stay essentially the same. This also allowed Schwartz to remold them to fit his interest in science fiction. All the alter egos of his heroes would have Space Age occupations: The Flash doubled as police scientist Barry Allen, The Atom was government research scientist Ray Palmer, and Green Lantern's new secret identity was that of Hal Jordan, test pilot.

Their costumes would be remodeled to fit the high-tech mystique. While the Golden Age Flash's costume was modeled after that of the Greek god Mercury, his Silver Age counterpart wore a sleek red jumpsuit that looked like it was molded to his body, and no cape or tights, giving him a dynamic, streamlined look. Gil Kane designed a similar outfit for Green Lantern. "I don't like to break up my costumes with a belt or tights a la the standard superhero," Kane explained. "I always design using the configurations of the body, and what I did with Green Lantern's uniform was to make it an hourglass shape that started at the point of the shoulders and wound to a narrow point at mid-chest and went out again at the waistline. I was trying for a balance between power and lyricism."

But Kane did not like the way his design was rendered in print. "The inkers and colorists' didn't follow my suggestions. Only once or twice in the whole run did my color scheme get used. I wanted green the way they have it, but I wanted blue in the black portion, not gray. They insisted on using gray or light purple on the theory that if they withheld the blue, it gave them the option to use blue as a background color. Which was ridiculous because Superman, God knows, has blue, red, and yellow in his costume... and the inkers didn't understand how I was accenting the costume with a kind of diamond shape, and they always made it look like a sleeveless sweater which bothered me no end."

Kane also streamlined GL's body, abandoning the heavy musculature and bulky costumes for a smooth, lithe look. GL even seemed to float rather than fly. However, Kane had no say in contouring GL's face; he was told to model his features on those of then hot film star Paul Newman.

Showcase #22, which introduced the new Green Lantern, drew heavily upon science fiction. Looking for inspiration for a story to launch the series, Schwartz remembered the pulps he had enjoyed as a youth and the star-spanning adventures of E. E. "Doc" Smith's Skylark Smith. What if an alien gave his power ring to an earthling? he mused. The idea found its way into the first story in which Abin Sur, a red-skinned, bald-domed alien crashes his spaceship on Earth and must pass his power battery onto "one who is without fear." Sur's green power beam traverses the Earth finally locating Hal Jordan, who is sitting in his training plane, and whisks him, plane and all, to his spaceship. This is "a battery of power, given only to select space-patrolmen in the super-galactic system," the dying alien tells him, "to be used as a weapon against the forces of evil and injustice." Sur explains that the battery will give him power over everything except that which is yellow, explaining that the battery has a yellow impurity in it which cannot be removed without losing its power. In this way, Broome updated Green Lantern's earlier vulnerability to wood, choosing yellow because of its association with fear, a quality a man with the "right stuff" could not have.

The Showcase debut also featured two other stories, "Secret of the Flaming Spear" and "Menace of the Runaway Missile." In these tales we are introduced to Hal's girlfriend, Carol Ferris, whose father owns the aircraft company for which Hal works. When her father leaves for a two-year sabbatical, Carol is left in charge, becoming Hal's boss. This crimps Hal's love life, for Carol vows not to get romantically involved with employees. Determined to see her, Hal dons his Green Lantern costume and sweeps her off her feet at a celebrity dance. However, the romance is stalled when GL takes off after a runaway missile, leaving Carol in mid-kiss. With Carol angry at GL's intermittent attention and holding Hal at arms length, Hal's love life is in a quandary. In effect, Hal had created a rivalry with himself and Carol's love for GL would create a constant tension in his love life.

The first three Showcase issues set a pattern for GL's own title. The lead story would feature a science fiction adventure or battle with a super-villain followed by a shorter human interest story focusing on Hal's personal life or that of one of the supporting cast. Even in the occasional book-length epics, a secondary background story would parallel the major narrative. This format allowed Schwartz to introduce a great degree of character development into the GL corpus, making Hal a more complex character than the one-dimensional heroes of the Golden Age. It also allowed Schwartz to evolve a vast panoply of characters. As Bob Hughes notes, with 6500 members in the Green Lantern Corps, Green Lantern has the largest supporting cast in comic book history.

In Showcase #22 Abin Sur had only described himself as a member of an anonymous group of intergalactic policemen. The Guardians who ruled this police force were not even mentioned until Green Lantern had become successful enough to merit having his own title. "Originally," Schwartz explained, "Broome and I didn't have much of an idea about the Guardians. We took the name from an old Captain Comet story Broome had scripted (Strange Adventures #22: "Guardians of the Clockwork Universe"). We decided that all the Guardians should look alike. That was our little inside joke. Gil Kane based their appearance on the prime minister of Israel at the time, Ben-Gurion."

Broome and Schwartz began to answer some of the questions in Green Lantern #1. In the first story in that issue, Hal is forced to bail out while testing an experimental plane. In that brief instant, The Guardians pull his "energy duplicate" to Oa, a far distant planet in another galaxy. Perturbed by the unorthodox way Hal had become a Green Lantern, the Guardians decide to return him to Earth for a probationary period during which they erase all memories of their existence from his mind. However, they continue to send him instruction through his power battery.

The second issue introduced the anti-matter universe of Qward which is inhabited by a strange warrior race called the Weaponers who are devoted solely to evil. Morality on Qward is the exact opposite of Earth's: there it is legal to do evil but illegal to do good. Because they refused to become robbers, a small band of honest people have formed an underground and are pursued by the police. By fashioning an inter-dimensional bridge, GL is able to rescue these renegades and transport them to Earth. Although GL blocks the passage with a blast from his ring, the Qwardians would find ways to escape and returned to battle him in subsequent tales.

The second story in this issue, "Riddle of the Frozen Ghost Town," introduced a young Eskimo man named Thomas Kalmaku, Carol Ferris' mechanic. Tom discovers GL's identity and becomes his helper and "unofficial biographer". Ethnic sidekicks had traditionally been humorous stereotypes who mangled English like Ebony White, The Spirit's black helper in Will Eisner's famed comic strip. However, Tom was neither funny nor spoke with an accent. But he was saddled with the demeaning nickname "Pieface" and his dialogue was interlaced with the ridiculous exclamation, "Jumpin' fish hooks!" The sobriquet may have derived from the ice cream bar Eskimo Pie, but was, in the sixties, an embarrassing anachronism and was soon dropped.

Green Lantern #7 introduced the Emerald Crusader's arch-nemesis in the Silver Age - Sinestro. The former Green Lantern of Space Sector 1417, Sinestro was the only renegade in the history of the Green Lantern Corps. The Guardians banished him to the planet of Qward for using his power ring to make himself monarch of his home planet, Koriegar. On Qward Sinestro tries to make himself ruler by promising to capture GL. To accomplish this the renegade transports an entire city from the planet Oa, mistakenly believing that GL is there. After being warned by the Guardians, GL captures Sinestro and returns the city. Thinking GL has proven himself, the Guardians allow him to retain his memory of his visit to Oa.

Broome decided to make GL's rival more formidable and, in issue #9, Sinestro reappears possessing a yellow power ring which worked by drawing power from the Guardian's power battery. Waylaying Green Lantern, Sinestro assumes his place at the very first meeting of the Green Lantern Corps. This convocation of Green Lanterns from outer space provided Gil Kane the opportunity to stretch his imagination the fullest and included such weird creatures as the insect Xax from Xaos, a water breathing, fish-headed Green Lantern, and the Green Lantern of T41A, which looked like a one-eyed beet with six legs, tentacles, and a fright wig. It's no wonder that Kane soon tired of drawing aliens which he derisively describes as "cockroaches with masks."

Because GL's ring had no power over yellow objects, it should not have had any effect on Sinestro's yellow beam. However, when the two fought, the rays from their rings seemed to cancel each other out. Creating a yellow ring obviously posed problems for writers who had to both create a dramatic contest between the opponents and hew to the formula that GL must always triumph in the end. To accommodate this formula, scripters gave Sinestro's ring a number of powers which were inconsistent from story to story. Consequently, the duel between two power rings never reached the epic proportions such a match-up promised.

Green Lantern #59, 1st appearance of Guy Gardner.
© DC

Green Lantern was more successful in its pioneering attempt to develop more characterization in its stories. Schwartz had always been disgruntled because "we never got to know about a hero's family" in superhero tales. So, in the back-up story to Green Lantern #10, "Green Lantern's Brother Act," he and Broome gave GL twin brothers, an older brother named Jack and a carefree younger brother named Jim. When Jack asks for help in raising money for his campaign to become district attorney, GL distributes campaign literature with his power ring. Because of a series of coincidences, a young reporter covering the campaign decides that Jim is really Green Lantern and Jim's girlfriend Sue comes to share his belief. Sue and Jim reappear in a number of later stories which describe their courtship, marriage, and the birth of their son, and all the while Sue continues to believe that Jim is Green Lantern.

Schwartz and Broome greatly expanded the narrative possibilities of their stories by introducing complete parallel universes and making GL a "time-hopper." A series of tales dealt with the Emerald Avenger's adventures in the world of 5700 A.D. The date came from the DC phone number at the time: Plaza 9-5700. Creating an alternative time dimension allowed GL to have two different, but simultaneously existing lives, including two secret identities.

The series was introduced in Green Lantern #8 in which GL was spirited into the 58th century by the Solar Council, who decreed that only the legendary hero could defeat the menace they faced. They implanted a set of false memories in Hal's mind that implied that he had always lived in the 58th century, for the time travel process created total amnesia. Hal was led to believe that he was, in reality, space explorer Pol Manning and that he was in love with Solar Council member Iola Vale. After defeating a race of giant gila monster, GL was returned to the present but retained no memory of his trip to the future. Broome brought the 5700 A.D. storyline to a conclusion in issue #66. In that story, GL uses his power ring to find out where a group of mysterious objects he had found in his clothes came from and was told by the ring that they all came from the distant future. Traveling there by means of his power ring, Hal arrives to find that his future alter ego, Pol Manning, had attempted to take over Earth. However, it turned out that Pol Manning was only a creation of Hal's power ring, a mental distortion which was a side effect of the time travel system he used. From this point on, Hal would remember his visits to the 58th century.

The notion of parallel dimensions was also explored in a series of superhero team-up tales. In a two-part story, "Crisis on Earths One and Two" (Justice League #21-22), GL discovered the existence of duplicate Earths and Hal Jordan first encounters his Golden Age counterpart Alan Scott.

John Broome paired the two Green Lanterns for the first time in a story which also explained the origin of the Guardians (GL #40). Alan Scott begins to think that, due to the rays of a meteor, his power ring has gained power over wood. Enthused, he brings the meteor to Hal to see if it might also cure his ring of its yellow impurity. Puzzled when this fails, they ask the ring to explain. It reveals that the meteor was actually the prison of Krona, a renegade Guardian who had tried to discover the origin of the universe. Krona had transformed Scott's ring as a ruse to get Scott to return him to his own universe. Krona's return caused such havoc that the Guardians themselves come to Earth to combat him, revealing their existence for the first time. Alan and Hal defeat Krona by switching rings and confusing him about which ring has the yellow weakness.

Schwartz also introduced what he called 'what if' stories; imaginary tales about what would have happened if certain things in the past were altered. Broome utilized the concept in "Earth's Other Green Lantern," (GL #59) which introduced Guy Gardner. The cover depicted Gardner defiantly standing over Jordan's prone body screaming, "Get off this Earth, Hal Jordan! There's room for only one Green Lantern - me!" While the cover implied a shocking confrontation over who would be Earth's Green Lantern, the story inside was a mild imaginary tale about what would have happened if Abin Sur had given his ring to someone else. Broome had envisioned Gardner as a one-shot character so there was no mention of making him Earth's stand-by Green Lantern. Only when Denny O'Neil revived Gardner in the 1970s would he assume that position. This was Broome's final issue as a regular scripter. Likewise, Gil Kane would be replaced a month later.

The Green Lantern/Green Arrow Team-Ups... And Beyond

New artists and writers would take the second Green Lantern in totally new directions never envisioned by his Silver Age creators. This radical approach would come from a young generation of artists and writers who had not been part of the comic book industry when patriotic heroism was *de riguer*. Leading this departure was writer Denny O'Neil who liberalized storylines in Green Lantern, orienting them around social issues, and teaming the Emerald Gladiator with a revamped Green Arrow. He would be joined by artist Neal Adams, who had gained recognition for his revamping of Batman in The Brave and the Bold.

Green Lantern-Green Arrow #76, © DC

The first team-up was in "No Evil Shall Escape My Sight!" (GL/GA #76), a pathbreaking story which shattered comic book conventions with its gritty realism. O'Neil also subverted superhero convention by stressing the importance of combating social evils and not just evil doers. Throughout the series he made it clear that his heroes could not resolve the complex social problems his stories dramatized.

Neal Adams' art perfectly complemented O'Neil's scripts and brought new techniques to comics which revolutionized the medium. His hyper-realistic rendering of anatomy and facial expressions made Adams' characters seethe with emotional intensity. Many comic art historians have suggested that no other comic book artist could make anger, rage, and passion so palpable. Adams also began to take the design of the whole page more into account, giving comics a radical new look. He broke out of the row-like uniformity comics had been heir to by drastically altering the size and shape of panels for dramatic effect. His cinematic page layouts broke scenes down into microseconds of action, seen from different perspectives, to intensify the emotional impact of a scene. And, he used what might be called sequential montage, the superimposition of panels over other images, giving the page a multi-layered set of meanings.

The GL/GA series was highly successful, winning awards for writer and artist. It was praised in Newsweek and The New York Times and Adams and O'Neil appeared on many radio and television talk shows. This acclaim was a landmark, the beginning of public recognition that comic books should be considered a serious art form, and paved the way for the success of the avant-garde comic books of the present.

However, the title's sales continued to be low. As Schwartz puts it, "There was a lot of media interest, but no commensurate increase in sales. Green Lantern/Green Arrow gained a lot of swell publicity and didn't lose money, but the young readers didn't want the relevance. They wanted entertainment, and for them the two didn't match up." DC killed the book with #89 and the story slated for #90 was serialized in the back of The Flash.

GL continued as a solo feature before regaining his own title. O'Neil would continue to write the Emerald Avenger's adventures for eight more years, but never again experimented with comics as a form of 'new journalism.' Occasionally Adams did one shots, yet never again did series work for the major companies. He would continue to create new characters for his own publishing firm, Continuity Comics.

Green Lantern itself has undergone a renaissance in recent years under the leadership of editor Kevin Dooley and chief scripter Gerard Jones. The comics now feature three Emerald Crusaders with Hal Jordan as the battered veteran, John Stewart as the Green Lantern of a multicultural universe (in the Mosaic series), and Guy Gardner as the egotistical renegade.

An epic spanning eons, a myriad of universes, and five incredible decades of publication, it's amazing to consider that the Green Lantern saga has really just begun!

Thanks to Craig Delich, world's foremost authority on Green Lantern and All-Star Comics, Fantagraphic Books, Fantasy Distribution, Gabe Essoe, Denny O'Neil, Neil Adams, and Geoffrey Blum.

SILVER SAGAS
of the
Scarlet Speedster
Whirlwind Adventures of the Fastest Man Alive! 1956-1960
by Gary M. Carter

The story of the Silver Age Flash actually begins in the late 1930s. Beginning with Superman, Batman, Captain America, Captain Marvel, and even the original Flash, the costumed super hero dominated the scene for about eight years and then this "Golden Age" began to lose its grip on the heart of America, just as the first boom of post-war babies began. For another decade or so, comics nearly deserted the costumed hero and by the mid-fifties many in the industry predicted they would never rise again.

Little did they know.

Millions of comparatively literate, idea-hungry young consumers were waiting to latch onto just one really good idea. And that idea finally arrived at the corner market, the drug store, the soda fountain, and the newsstand during the sizzling hot summer of 1956, just as these youngsters were about to return to the drudgery of another school year. Like some red demon adorned with lightning, *The Flash* was re-born in the pages of the most famous and historic comic of the 1950's. *Showcase Comics* #4 announced its presence in hamlet and city across the country with an almost "audible" shock wave. The long dead costumed hero was "reincarnated" in one single incredible summer's day and the epic Silver Age of comics was born. The rest, so to speak, is comic book history.

Yet how many have ever considered the vast amount of great Flash material published in the remainder of that first Silver Decade. Many collectors have yet to be introduced to the interesting content and history of the Silver Age Flash's first four years. Conceptualized by editor Julius Schwartz, originally written by Robert Kanigher and later John Broome, and drawn by Carmine Infantino, the first four years of Flash episodes are among DC's greatest Silver Age treasures! Consider the following roll call of classics: (* indicates cover story.)

Showcase #4 (Sep-Oct 1956)

"Mystery Of The Human Thunderbolt!" (12 pgs) - The momentous origin story of the Silver Age Flash shows a mock cover of an issue of the Golden Age *Flash Comics* (#13, January 1941) with the original mercury helmeted Flash on the cover. Actually, *Flash Comics* #13 featured a Hawkman cover. The story also contains the 1st mention of: Central City, Barry's girlfriend Iris, his famous uniform (which is expelled from Barry Allen's ring and expands to life size in the twinkling of an eye), his ability to run down the side of a building and to run across water, and the 1st Flash villain, Turtle Man, the slowest man on Earth.

"The Man Who Broke The Time Barrier". (10 pgs) - 1st mention of the official name of the police laboratory that Barry Allen works for: Scientific Detection Bureau. Origin and first appearance of Mazdan, villain from the distant future. 1st use of Flash's most catchy nickname when Mazdan refers to him as "The Scarlet Speedster". 1st Flash time travel story.

Showcase #8 (May-Jun 1957)

"The Secret of the Empty Box!" (12 pgs) - 1st mention of Iris' last name, West, and her occupation, reporter for *Picture News.* This curious story stars a villain who wears a black top hat and tails and a yellow mask and who turns out to be identical triplets. Amazingly, we never learn anything about this early villain(s), not even a name(s)!

"The Coldest Man On Earth!" (12 pgs) - Superbly written and illustrated origin and 1st appearance of one of Flash's most enduring villains, Len Snart alias Captain Cold, and his famous Cold-Gun.

"The Race Of Wheel And Keel" (3 pgs) - "factually" based filler story about the history of American transportation.

Showcase #13 (Mar-Apr 1958)

**"Around The World In 80 Minutes!"* (13

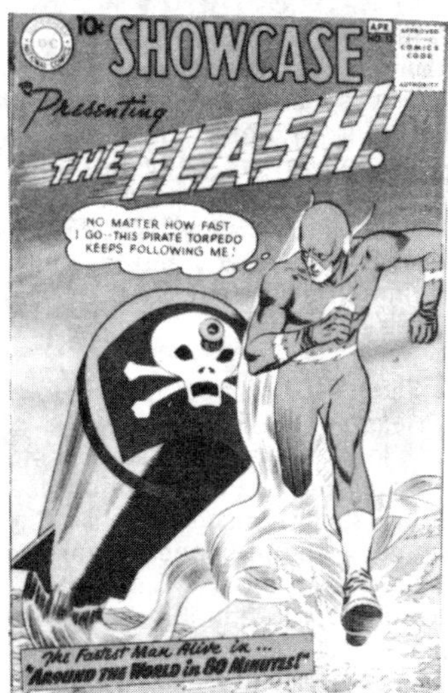

Showcase #13, © DC

& 2/3 pgs) - Fast paced and nicely drawn story in which Flash battles and overcomes criminals and natural disasters all over the world in less than an hour and twenty minutes; including the atom bomb toting Le Chat Noir (The Black Cat) in Paris, bandit Chief and kidnapper El Claw in Cairo, a devastating avalanche on Mt. Everest, and a deadly torpedo fired by gold bullion stealing pirate sub in the mid Pacific Ocean. In the splash panel, Central City is misspelled "Center City".

"Master of the Elements!" (12 pgs) - Origin and 1st appearance of Flash villain Mr. Element. Flash meets and defeats the garishly garbed Mr. Element and his six henchmen, (Argon, Radon, Xenon, Krypton, etc.) who are all named after the six inert elements! Mr. Element's crimes and tricks are always based on (you guessed it) the various elements of the periodic table.

Showcase #14 (May-Jun 1958)

*****"Giants of the Time-World!"* (13 pgs) - Great inter-dimensional/ time travel story, 1st face to face meeting between the Flash and Iris West, and the 1st mention of Barry's powerful wrist-TV set (a la Dick Tracy). Iris West's vocation is said to be Picture News photographer instead of reporter, as stated in previous stories.

"The Man Who Changed Earth!" (12 pgs) - the villainous Mr. Element ("...my most dangerous foe!") returns in a new guise; Dr. Alchemy! To make matters worse for the Flash, the "good" Doctor gains possession of the legendary Philosophers Stone and begins a new wave of havoc and crime. The place where Barry works is referred to as the Police Technical Laboratory instead of the Scientific Detection Bureau as stated in an earlier story.

The Flash #105 (Feb-Mar 1959)

Really a #1 issue, DC decides to continue the numbering sequence from the Golden Age series. This approach caused so much confusion on the part of readers that the technique was never used again for any other Silver Age title.

"Conqueror From 8 Million B.C.!" (11 & 2/3 pgs) - Positively brilliant story of "Katmos, survivor of a super scientific civilization that existed eight million years ago on Earth! Absolute monarch of the world in that prehistoric era, Katmos begins an amazing campaign to regain his former exalted position!". Artist Carmine Infantino draws particularly breathtaking panoramas and vistas throughout this epic science fiction saga. This issue also retells Flash's origin in seven panels. Even though 2 and 1/2 years have passed since Flash's origin was published in Showcase #4, the preface to this retold origin suggests that only one year has passed since the fateful day a lightning bolt bathed Barry Allen in the random assortment of chemicals which gave him super speed. Also in this story, Barry Allen once again works for the Scientific Detection Bureau.

**"The Master Of Mirrors!"* (12 & 2/3 pgs) - Origin and 1st appearance of the greatest of the Flash costumed villains, The Mirror-Master. An ex con named Scudder makes amazing new discoveries about the properties of mirrors, thus his alter identity as costumed villain. During the fray, Flash does battle with three dimensional "mirror" images in the form a giant mosquito and a minotaur. The historic episode also includes the 1st time Flash demonstrates his ability to pass through a solid wall without damaging himself or it.

The Flash #106 (Apr-May 1959)

"Menace of the Super-Gorilla!" (14 & 2/3 pgs) - Origin and 1st appearance of Grodd The Super Gorilla and the first installment of a three part epic which continues in the next two issues. The plot of this exceptional fiction is nothing short of a science fiction masterpiece, and introduces us to the secret "Gorilla City" hidden in central Africa as well as its gorilla leader,

Solovar. And equal to the quality scripting is the masterful art of Carmine Infantino at his zenith! No one, absolutely no one in comic art history can draw simians with the flair, style, and personality that Infantino imparts to his anthrapoidal creations. Many readers of these early Grodd epics tell a similar story, of being literally spellbound by these early episodes of the Flash, and then remembering, after decades, the complex story lines with clarity, as if they read them yesterday! As just one excellent example of Infantino's graphic mastery, consider the large panel at the top of page 13. It depicts a legion of gorilla soldiers, each armed with a futuristic helmet and rifle, standing before the Gorilla city throne. But the most important element of this masterful panorama is the varying facial features and expressions of each and every gorilla soldier. This incredible attention to detail further supports the illusion of intelligent gorilla individuals and the credibility of the entire plot. In spite of the fact that Flash #106 is considered by Silver Age collectors to be the rarest issue of the run, the effort required to locate it is well spent. Additionally, some comic book historians have speculated that the pioneering Grodd "trilogy" may have been the inspiration for the "Planet Of The Apes" series, so popular in years to come.

"The Pied Piper Of Peril" (9 & 2/3 pgs) - Origin and 1st appearance of the second costumed Flash villain - The Pied Piper, master of sound, and possessor of the super-sonic flute. Infantino again demonstrates his artistic expertise with his detailed renderings of moving water and tidal waves that almost splash right off the page. His aqueous creations are not benign, however. They are the very embodiment of villainy, like the "Piper" who created them. This story also advances the relation between Barry and Iris and is the 1st time Iris is described as Barry's Fiancee'.

Flash #106, © DC

The Flash #107 (Jun-Jul 1959)

"Return of the Super-Gorilla!" (14 & 2/3 pgs) - In the sensational second story of the Super-Gorilla trilogy, Grodd escapes from his special prison in Gorilla City and discovers a subterranean world miles below the Earth's crust. Grodd causes the bird-people who inhabit the cavernous depths to fall under the spell of his Force-Of-Mind power and makes them unwitting pawns in his plot to rule the world. His heinous plot also includes plans to expose the other intelligent gorillas to the rays of the De-Evolutionizer, which will cause them to revert to "primitive primates no different from the other dumb gorillas of Earth".

"The Amazing Race Against Time!" (9 & 2/3 pgs) - Flash meets Kyri, an automaton under the direction of the "Rulers Of The Galaxy" and endowed with "super swift cosmic forces", who crash lands on Earth. Because of amnesia, Kyri forgets who he is and his important mission. Flash helps him regain his memory via shock treatments, and then helps him complete his Galaxy-saving mission to repair the "weak spot where the terrible forces of another dimension threaten to break through!"

The Flash #108 (Aug-Sep 1959)

"The Speed of Doom!" (10 pgs) - Flash battles the super fast "Mohruvians...mysterious, unearthly creatures whose sole purpose on Earth is to steal objects struck by lightning!" Interdimensional criminal Kee Feleg of the world of Mohru tricks Flash into getting on a deadly treadmill. Flash escapes by exceeding the speed of light, thus this story establishes an important precedent in the Flash mythos.

"The Super-Gorilla's Secret Identity!" (13 & 2/3 pgs) - In the final (and possibly most beautifully drawn) episode of the Grodd trilogy, the power-mad gorilla genius develops the power of mind over matter. Using the drill-like "quadromobile" (so named because it can travel in four mediums; on the ground, under the ground, through the air, and under water) Grodd

escapes for a third time. Bathing in the multi-colored rays of his Evolution-Accelerator, Grodd advances his super-brain far along the evolutionary track and becomes a human, temporarily. Eventually Flash prevails and Grodd is taken back to Gorilla City. The ominous closing statement of this historical conclusion suggests that Grodd will be back!

The Flash #109 (Oct-Nov 1959)

*"*Return of the Mirror Master!"* (13 pgs) - In a story containing the 1st time (other than Grodd) that a Flash villain returns, Flash is reduced in size by the mirror master's diabolical Mirror-Reducer in a story that hints of a DC revival hero yet to come (The Atom). In an interesting sub plot, Iris is fed up with Barry Allen's perpetual lateness and vows never to see him again. The reader is left with the threat of their relationship ending as Iris proclaims in the last panel of the story "Thirty minutes late! This is the end! I will never make a date with Barry Allen again — NEVER!" DC was flooded with letters from worried readers pleading for the estranged couple to make up. This confirmed that the character of Barry Allen was as important to the story line as the Flash himself. The story also retells the origin of the Mirror Master in three panels.

"Secret of the Sunken Satellite!" (12 pgs) - A great sci fi sleeper, this story has all the elements of a classic. Not only does it include an early and realistic astronaut only two years after Sputnik, but it also stars ray-gun toting, vicious, and fish-like "Maugites" who threaten the Flash as they attempt to conquer the underwater city of Sareme and its elegant and alien inhabitants, the Saremites. The ethereal look of the Saremites is in the quintessential style of Infantino aliens. Also Flash demonstrates that he can use his super abilities under water.

The Flash #110 (Dec 1959-Jan 1960)

*"*The Challenge Of The Weather Wizard!"* (12 & 2/3 pgs) - Origin and 1st appearance of the third costumed villain, Mark Marden alias The Weather Wizard and his electro-vibrator wand or "Weather Stick". After overcoming The Wizard Of Weather, Flash races to keep his date at the theater with Iris West. Absent-mindedly, Barry shows up in his Flash costume, giving Iris an opportunity to be very suspicious.

"Meet Kid Flash!" (11 & 2/3 pgs) - Origin and 1st appearance of Kid Flash. In the tradition of Robin, Speedy, Aqualad, and Wonder Girl, a young "sidekick" for the Silver Age Flash is introduced in the first episode of the Kid Flash trilogy. Iris West's red-haired and freckle-faced nephew, Wally, is the president of the Flash Fan Club. In a lab in Barry's apartment (just like the one Barry's has at police headquarters), The Flash explains his origin to Wally "it was two years ago..." (even though Showcase #4 was published over three years ago). Suddenly a lightning bolt smashes the chemicals above Wally's head, bathing him in the unknown mixture in just the same way as the "freak" accident that created The Flash. And so is born the character who will eventually assume the role of the Flash in the distant future.

The Flash #111 (Feb-Mar 1960)

*"*The Invasion Of The Cloud Creatures!"* (12 & 2/3 pgs) - One of the all time classic Flash yarns once again is a sci fi odyssey so novel and original, that it might have appeared without the Flash as a feature story in Strange Adventures or Mystery In Space. The high quality scripting and beautiful art come at a time that is considered a high water mark for DC. Dr. Wiley Summers (a former college classmate of Barry Allen), while investigating Mt. Lassen (the only active volcano in the continental United States) develops the theory that "a civilization of evil cloud creatures exists within the Earth, and that volcanoes and earthquakes are their attempts to annihilate us surface creatures!" After Flash destroys the evil cloud creatures, Iris develops a crush on the good Doctor Summers. The continuing "soap opera" between Barry and Iris takes a twist when Barry contemplates in the last panel "...looks like I may have a rival for Iris's affection!"

"The Flash Presents Kid Flash...The Challenge of the Crimson Crows!" (12 pgs) - Second Installment in the Kid Flash trilogy, this story addresses the question of teenage gangs as well as retells Kid Flash's origin in 5 panels. It also mentions for the first time Wally's home town of Blue Valley where he attends Blue Valley High School.

The Brave and the Bold #28 (Feb-Mar 1960)

*"*Starro the Conqueror!"* (25 & 2/3 pgs) - This important Flash appearance was published the same month as the seventh Flash magazine (#111). It should be noted

Brave And The Bold #28, © DC

by fans and historians alike that The Flash was the first chairman of the Justice League and seemed to dominate much of the action. He was charged with handing out the assignments and deciding which members would team up and which members would get solo assignments. The 6 page chapter entitled "Starro VS. The Flash" is interesting for two reasons. First, it is the longest solo chapter and obviously reflects the belief of the editor that The Flash is the most popular and dynamic character of the group (along with the newly introduced Green Lantern who appears as a member of the JLA after only three Showcase tryouts and having no magazine of his own). Secondly, the Flash chapter brings the Scarlet Speedster to the coastal town of Happy Harbor, where he is the first JLA member to meet a character named Snapper Carr, who will eventually become the only "non super" member of the esteemed crime fighting organization. Flash actually saves Snapper from a deadly atomic blast, thus introducing the team for the first time. By making The Flash by far the most visible and dominant character in this historical premiere, it seems clear that writer and editor were depending on his already phenomenal popularity to help ensure the success of the JLA.

The Flash #112 (Apr-May 1960)

This issue begins the noble tradition of the letter column for Flash comics, with the first installment of "Flash Grams". The last paragraph of this important page contains a memorable and nostalgic message, reminiscent of the '40s and hinting at the Marvel approach so expertly exploited by Stan Lee in the remaining years of the decade. Even the absence of a ZIP code in the address transports us back to the spirit of the times. "We have to flash off now, friends! Remember - as a reader of this magazine you automatically become a member of the FLASH FANS FRATERNITY! We'd like to hear from you! Address all communications - FLASH-GRAMS - to THE FLASH, c/o National Comics, 575 Lexington Avenue, New York 22, New York.

**"The Mystery of the Elongated Man!"* (13 pgs) - No doubt inspired by Plastic Man, and soon to be an inspiration for the Fantastic Four's Mr. Fantastic, the rubber limbed Elongated man actually had a number of unique story elements to set him apart from both his Quality Comics predecessor and his Marvel Comics successor. One of these was the way Infantino drew the stretchy hero. The sleek fluidity of his style, plus his ability to suggest movement (so expertly done in each Flash story) made the character of the Elongated Man that much more believable to young readers and fans. Another was the fact that the Elongated Man openly shared his civilian identity, Ralph Dibny, with the public. This was a very new twist in the world of costumed heroes and alter identities. And finally (almost absurdly), later Elongated Man stories contained sequences in which Ralph Dibny would publicly discuss the derivative of the Gingold tree as the source of his special abilities. As a young reader barely past my eleventh birthday, this was really "stretching" the limits of credibility. I often wondered why every would-be crime fighter in the Flash universe didn't immediately run out to the nearest nursery, plant a specimen of the wondrous tree, consume its fruit, and begin their own careers as highly flexible crime fighters. Even after The Elongated man became the back-up feature for the "new-look" Batman in Detective Comics approximately four years later, this unanswered nagging question plagued the credibility of the story line.

"The Flash Presents Kid Flash...Danger On Wheels!" (12 pgs) - Third Installment in the Kid Flash trilogy with somewhat confusing story elements. The title suggests that the anti go-cart theme proposed in the title would be the focus of the plot. However, the theme of the story actually revolves around a scam to build a substandard school, which the boy speedster eventually

foils just like many *Showcase* tryout threesomes, the trio of Kid Flash novelettes in Flash 110, 111, and 112 were meant to provide readers with enough stories to decide whether they liked the new feature. They did, and Kid Flash would continue to claim an ever increasing role in the Flash mythos.

Brave and the Bold #29 (Apr-May 1960)

*"*Challenge of the Weapons Master!"* (26 pgs) - This second "tryout" for the JLA, like the first, relied heavily on the character of The Flash as a key story element. Not only does he dominate the cover with his strategic foreground position, but he is the only hero to have an entire chapter devoted to his solo battle with the arch-criminal Xotar, The Weapons Master.

The Flash #113 (Jun-Jul 1960)

The second page of Flash Grams appears in this noteworthy issue. A historically important letter from reader John Ferrazzano asks about Flash's Showcase appearances, about the availability of back issues, and most importantly about the strangely high issue numbers which suggest that the Silver Age Flash "must have been around for at least 18 years...". This historic letter and the editors equally historic response was the first time most young Silver Agers had ever considered the idea that comics even existed prior to the 50s! Consider the implications of that fateful response for young Flash collectors of the early 1960s when, with eyes wide and mouth open, they read the following: "...The original FLASH made his debut twenty years ago in FLASH COMICS . . and ran through 104 issues, when publication ceased. After a lapse of several years, we thought that the time was ripe to reissue *Flash* for the new generation of readers who had never thrilled to his whirlwind exploits. To put the theory to the test, we revived *Flash* (in a new and more up-to-date version) in DC's experimental magazine, SHOWCASE. *Flash's* one-shot reappearance was in SHOWCASE No. 4. When the sales reports came in they proved encouraging enough to bring *Flash* back again in SHOWCASE No. 8, and again in SHOWCASE No. 13 and No. 14. When all the returns were in, we were convinced that *Flash* should appear in a magazine exclusively his own - and to preserve the continuity of the "last" *Flash*, the issue was dated No. 105. Unfortunately, no back issues of FLASH COMICS are available.-Editor"

Unfortunate is right...imagine if an army of avid pre-teen collectors could have ordered back issues of the Golden Age *Flash Comics* #1-104 from DC for cover price plus postage? The fantasy thrilled us, the reality simply hardened our collecting resolve to find somewhere, anywhere, the elusive 104 back issues of the Scarlet Speedster's predecessor from the 1940s.

*"*Danger In The Air!"* (12 pgs) - Origin and 1st appearance of The Trickster, whose real name, James Jesse, is the reverse of his idol, the outlaw Jesse James. Somewhat like Batman's Riddler, The Trickster's slim form makes a striking villain in his striped, Harlequin-like uniform.

"The Man Who Claimed The Earth!" (13 pgs) - Flash's old college classmate, Dr. Wiley Summers, appears for the second time (see #111) in an excellent science fiction story based on Greek mythology. It turns out that the Earth is a "lost planet", previously "discovered" by the Galactic Universe of Olimpus (sic), located in the "Fourth Quadrangle of Space." Po-Siden (sic) is given the task of reclaiming Earth and has the power to do it. Flash finally defeats him and he returns to his home planet to report to "Zus". In a show of "generosity" Zus (sic) acknowledges the "independence" of the Earth. Good thing, too. Stan still needed to borrow this theme for Journey Into Mystery #83!

Brave And The Bold #30, © DC

Brave and the Bold #30 (Jun-Jul 1960)

"The Case Of The Stolen Super Powers!" (27 pgs) - The last JLA tryout again focuses on Flash as the primary hero, and has his character send out the special signal which calls the JLA in case of emergencies. In an especially symbolic panel at the bottom of page 5, Flash is seen as the central figure (around which the other members are positioned) as Flash commandingly thinks, "This is a job for the Justice League of America to deal with!" Later, at JLA headquarters, Flash is the one to analyze the case, hand out pertinent information, but unlike the previous two JLA adventures, Flash teams up with J'onn J'onzz, Manhunter From Mars. Not only that, but it's Green Lantern who saves the day and the Scarlet Speedster is among the rescued.

The Flash #114 (Aug 1960)

With this issue, the title increases its publication frequency from six times a year to eight times a year.

"The Big Freeze!" (13 pgs) - The fastest man on Earth battles the coldest man on Earth as Captain Cold (alias Len Snart) makes his second sinister appearance. The good Captain not only proposes to Iris, but puts the entire city into suspended animation.

"The Flash Presents Kid Flash...King of the Beatniks!" (11 & 2/3 pgs) - Fourth Kid Flash entry with the intriguing plot of a gang that disguises themselves as, you guessed it, Beatniks! Kid Flash eventually routs the gang and rescues his track star friend, thereby helping Blue Valley High School to win the state track meet!

The Flash #115 (Sep 1960)

"The Day Flash Weighed 1000 Pounds!" (12 & 2/3 pgs) - Flash's most dangerous villain, Grodd The Super-Gorilla, takes over the body of William Dawson as he returns for his fourth appearance. He aims a new ray weapon at the Flash, causing him to absorb moisture from the air, swell like a balloon, and endure the world's worst case of water weight gain. Of course Flash eventually prevails and is "dehydrated" back to his original size.

"The Elongated Man's Secret Weapon!" (12 pgs) - Ralph Dibney returns for the second time in a great sci fi outing. In the jungles of Mexico, The Elongated Man discovers aliens plotting to conquer Earth with their miniaturizing weapon. With the help of the Flash the aliens are defeated and the Earth is saved.

As you review these entertaining examples of early Silver Age Flash, it's difficult to imagine the volume of work, talent, and imagination packed into each incredible issue. The comic book greats responsible for recruiting a whole new army of fans are still amazed that their creations so deeply and profoundly affected such a large legion of freckle-face, mid-pubic fans from coast to coast! The astonishingly sophisticated, entertaining plots in the early Silver Age Flash are now permanently enshrined in the comic book "hall of fame" as well as in the fond memories of millions of loyal collectors.

Of course, Flash would continue for many years... yet somehow these early stories reflect the creative cornucopia of the time. The "just right" combination of story and art, along with the explosion of scientific events in the real world, combined to create a comic book masterpiece that can never be re-created.

Whether he is remembered as The World's Fastest Human, The King Of Super Speed, The Fastest Man Alive, The Champion Of Justice, The Crimson Comet, The Human Hurricane, The Sultan Of Speed, The Human Whirlwind, or The Human Comet... Baby Boomers will always affectionately recall those amazing and wonderful...Silver Sagas of the Scarlet Speedster!

The first comic book Gary M. Carter ever purchased from the stands was Showcase #4. He has been an avid fan ever since...

DIRECTORY OF COMIC AND NOSTALGIA SHOPS

This is a current up-to-date list, but is not all-inclusive. We cannot assume any responsibility in your dealings with these shops. This list is provided for your information only. When planning your trips, it would be advisable to make appointments in advance. To get your shop included in the next edition, write for rates. Items stocked by these shops are listed just after the telephone numbers and are coded as follows:

(a) Golden Age Comics
(b) Silver Age Comics
(c) New comics, magazines
(d) Pulps
(e) Paperbacks
(f) Big Little Books
(g) Magazines (old)
(h) Books (old)
(i) Movie Posters, Lobby Cards
(j) Original Art
(k) Toys (old)
(l) Records (old)
(m) Trading Cards
(n) Underground Comics
(o) Video Tapes
(p) Premiums
(q) Comic Related Posters
(r) Comic Supplies
(s) Role Playing Games
(t) Star Trek Items
(u) Dr. Who Items
(v) Japanimation Items

ALABAMA

Discount Comic Book Shop
1301 Noble St.
Anniston, AL 36201
PH: 205-238-8373 (a-c,e,m,q,r)

Wizard's Comics
324 N. Court St.
Florence, AL 35630
PH: 205-766-6821 (a-c,e,g-k,m-v)

Sincere Comics
3738 Airport Blvd.
Mobile, AL 36608
PH: 205-342-2603 (a-c,e,f,m,q-t)

Hellen's Comics
113 Mill St.
Oxford, AL 36203
PH: 205-835-3040 (b,c,e,h,k-m)

ARIZONA

Atomic Comics
1318 W. Southern Suite #1
Mesa, AZ 85202
PH: 602-649-0807 (a-c,f,g,i-k,m-v)

Ed Kalb – Comics Wanted
(Mail Order Only)
1353 S. Los Alamos
Mesa, AZ 85204 (a-i,k,m)

AAA Best Comics Etc.
9226 N. 7th St. Suite #A
Phoenix, AZ 85020
PH: 602-997-4012 (b,c,m,q,r)

Lost Dutchman Comics
5805 N. 7th St.
Phoenix, AZ 85014
PH: 602-249-1650 (a-c,e,g,h,l-n,r,t)

ARKANSAS

Paperbacks Plus
2207 Rogers Avenue
Fort Smith, AR 72901
PH: 501-785-5642 (a-c,e-i,m,n,q-s)

The Comic Book Store
9307 Treasure Hill
Little Rock, AR 72207
PH: 501-227-9777
(a-c,e,g,h,m,o,q-v)

Collector's Edition Comics
3217 John F. Kennedy
N. Little Rock, AR 72116
PH: 501-791-4222
(a-c,e,g,h,m,o,q-v)

TNT Collectors Hut
503 West Hale Ave.
Osceola, AR 72370
PH: 501-563-5760 (c,m,r)

CALIFORNIA

Heroes + Legends
5290 Kanan Road
Agoura Hills, CA 91301
PH: 818-991-5979 (a-j,m,n,p-v)

Comic Heaven
24 W. Main Street
Alhambra, CA 91801
PH: 818-289-3945 (a-c,g,j,q-t)

Comic Relief
2138 University Avenue
Berkeley, CA 94704
PH: 415-843-5002 (a-d,f-h,j,n,q,r,v)

Comics & Comix, Inc.
2461 Telegraph Ave.
Berkeley, CA 94704
PH: 510-845-4091

Fantasy Kingdom
1802 West Olive Ave.
Burbank, CA 91506
PH: 818-954-8432
(a-c,f,g,i,k,m,o,q,r,t-v)

Crush Comics & Cards
2785 Castro Valley Blvd.
Castro Valley, CA 94546
PH: 510-581-4779 (a-c,g,k,m,q,r)

Comics Unlimited
11900 South Street
Cerritos, CA 90701
PH:310-403-1521
(a-c,e,f,k,m,o,q,r,t,v)

Collectors Ink
932-A W. 8th Ave.
Chico, CA 95926
PH: 916-345-0958
(a-c,g,m-p,q,r,t-v)

Comics & Comix, Inc.
6135 Sunrise Blvd.
Citrus Heights, CA 95610
PH: 916-969-0717

Flying Colors Comics & Other Cool Stuff
2980 Treat Blvd.
Oak Grove Plaza
Concord, CA 94518
PH: 510-825-5410 (a-c,i,m,o,q-t,v)

Comic Gallery
322-J W. El Norte Parkway
Escondido, CA 92026
PH: 619-745-5660 (b,c,j,m,n,q-t,v)

Comics & Comix, Inc.
1350 Travis Blvd.
Fairfield, CA 94533
PH: 707-427-1202

Geoffrey's Comics
15530 Crenshaw
Gardena, CA 90249
PH: 213-538-3198
(a-c,g,j,m-o,q-s,v)

Comics Unlimited
12913 Harbor Blvd.
Garden Grove, CA 92640
PH: 714-638-2040
(a-c,e,g,m,o,q-s,v)

Shooting Star Comics & Games
618 E. Colorado Blvd.
Glendale, CA 91205
PH: 818-502-1535 (b,c,m-o,q-s,v)

Bud Plant Comic Art
(Free Catalog)
P. O. Box 1689-P
Grass Valley, CA 95945
PH: 916-273-2166 (c,h,n,o,q,r,v)

The Comic Shop
23986 Aliso Creek Rd.
Laguna Niguel, CA 92656
PH: 714-831-6149 (b,c,g,m,o,r)

The American Comic Book Co.
3972 Atlantic Avenue
Long Beach, CA 90807
PH: 310-426-0393 (a-f,j,m,n)

Cheap Comics
7779 Melrose Ave.
Los Angeles, CA 90046
PH: 213-655-9323 (a-d,g,i,k,m,t,v)

Golden Apple Comics
7711 Melrose Avenue
Los Angeles, CA 90046
PH: 213-658-6047 (a-c,e,m-o,q,r,u)

Golden Apple Comics
8934 West Pico Blvd.
Los Angeles, CA 90034
PH: 310-274-2008 (c,m-o,q-s,v)

Graphitti - Westwood - UCLA
960 Gayley Ave.
Los Angeles, CA 90024
PH: 310-824-3656 (a-c,g-i,m,n,q-t)

Pacific Comic Exchange, Inc.
(By Appointment Only)
P. O. Box 34849
Los Angeles, CA 90034
PH: 310-836-PCEI (a,b)

Golden Apple Comics
8962 Reseda Blvd.
Northridge, CA 91324
PH: 818-993-7804 (a-c,e,j-o,q,r,v)

Freedonia Funnyworks
350 S. Tustin Ave.
Orange, CA 92666
PH: 714-639-5830 (a-h,j,k,m-r,v)

Bud Plant Illustrated Books
c/o Jim Vadeboncoeur, Jr.
3809-C Laguna Avenue
Palo Alto, CA 94306
PH: 415-493-1191 (evenings, weekends)(g,h)

Comics & Comix, Inc.
405 California Avenue
Palo Alto, CA 94306
PH: 415-328-8100

Discount Comics and Sportscards
3485 University Ave.
Riverside, CA 92501
PH: 909-684-8544 (a-c,f,g,m,n,r)

Comics & Comix, Inc.
5050 Rocklin Rd. #9
Rocklin, CA 95677
PH: 916-632-2389

Comics & Comix, Inc.
921 K Street
Sacramento, CA 95814
PH: 916-442-5142

Comic Gallery
4224 Balboa Ave.
San Diego, CA 92117
PH: 619-483-4853 (b,c,j,m,n,q-t,v)

Comic Gallery
9460-G Mira Mesa Blvd.
San Diego, CA 92126
PH: 619-578-9444 (b,c,j,m,n,q-t,v)

Comic Relief
1597 Haight Street
San Francisco, CA 94117
PH: 415-552-9010 (a-d,f-h,j,n,q,r,v)

Comics & Comix, Inc.
650 Irving
San Francisco, CA 94122
PH: 415-665-5888

Comics & Comix, Inc.
700 Lombard Street
San Francisco, CA 94133
PH: 415-982-3511

Comics And Da-Kind
1643 Noriega Street
San Francisco, CA 94122
PH: 415-753-9678 (a,b,g,r)

Comics And Da-Kind
1653 Noriega Street
San Francisco, CA 94122
PH: 415-753-9678 (c,m,o,q,r,t,v)

The Funny Papers
5957 Geary Blvd.
San Francisco, CA 94121
PH: 415-752-1914
(a-d,f,g,j,k,m,q-t)

Comics Pendragon
1189 Branham Lane
San Jose, CA 95118
PH: 408-265-3233
(a-c,f,g,m-o,q,r,v)

Brian's Books
2765 El Camino
Santa Clara, CA 95051
PH: 408-985-7481 (a-h,m,n,q,r)

San Mateo Comic Books, Baseball Cards, & Original Art
106 South B Street
San Mateo, CA 94401
PH: 415-344-1536 (a-c,g,j,m,n,q,r)

Graphitti- World Wide Mail Order
(Free Catalog-USA & Canada)
P. O. Box 5021, Dept. PG
Santa Monica, CA 90409
FAX: 310-824-7737

Hi De Ho Comics & Fantasy
525 Santa Monica Blvd.
Santa Monica, CA 90401
PH: 310-394-2820 (a-j,m-o,q-v)

Forbidden Planet
14513 Ventura Blvd.
Sherman Oaks, CA 91403
PH: 818-995-0151
(a-c,e,g-j,m-o,q-v)

R & K Comics and Cards
568 A El Camino Real
Sunnyvale, CA 94087
PH: 408-732-8775
(a-c,f,g,m-o,q,r,v)

Pantechnicon
1165 E. Thousand Oaks Blvd.
Thousand Oaks, CA 91360
PH: 805-495-0299 (a-j,m,n,p-v)

Silver City Comics
4671 Torrance Blvd.
Torrance, CA 90503
PH: 310-542-8034 (a-c,i,m,o,q-t,v)

Graphitti - South Bay!
Airport/Marina Hotel (Rear)
8639 Lincoln Blvd. No. 102
Westchester (L.A.), CA 90045
PH: 310-641-8661
(b,c,e,g,h,m,n,q-s)

Comics Unlimited
16344 Beach Blvd.
Westminster, CA 92683
PH: 714-841-6646
(a-c,e-g,m,o,q-t,v)

COLORADO

Heroes & Dragons #2
The Citadel #2158
Colorado Springs, CO 80909
PH: 719-550-9570 (b,c,e,m,o,q-t,v)

Heroes & Dragons #1
220 N. Tejon St.
Colorado Springs, CO 80903
PH: 719-635-2516 (a-c,e,m-o,q-v)

CONNECTICUT

The Dragon's Den
43 Greenwich Ave.
Greenwich, CT 06830
PH: 203-622-1171 (b,c,g,m,q-t,v)

X-Pressions Mail Order Comics
11 Dix Street
Hamden, CT 06514
PH: 203-498-9445 (c,j,k-q,t)

A Timeless Journey
2538 Summer St.
Stamford, CT 06905
PH: 203-353-1720 (a-c,g,k,m,q,r,t)

DELAWARE

Captain Blue Hen Comics
Baycourt Plaza, Rte. 113
Dover, DE 19901
PH: 302-734-3222 (b,c,g,m-o,q-s)

DISTRICT OF COLUMBIA

Another Universe
1504 Wisconsin Ave. NW
Washington, DC 20007
PH: 202-333-8651 (a-c,e,m,o,q-t,v)

FLORIDA

Cliff's Books
209 N. Woodland Blvd. (17-92)
Deland, FL 32720
PH: 904-738-9464 (a-h,k-o,q-t)

Family Book Shop, Inc.
1301 N. Woodland Blvd.
DeLand, FL 32720
PH: 904-736-6501 (b,c,e,h,m,r)

Comics Plus
1117 W. University Avenue
Gainesville, FL 32601
PH: 904-373-3790
(a-c,i-k,m,o,q,s,t,v)

Charlie's Comics #1
801 W. 49 St. #105
Hialeah, FL 33012
PH: 305-557-5994 (b,c,g,i,n,q-s)

Absolute Comics
6034 Merrill Rd.
Jacksonville, FL 32211
PH: 904-744-1985 (b,c,m,q,s)

Coliseum of Comics
1180 E. Vine St.
Kissimmee, FL 34744
PH: 407-870-5322 (b,c,e,g,m,q-s)

Charlie's Comics #2
7600 N.W. 106 St.
Miami, FL 33015
PH: 305-828-2665 (b,c,g,i,n,q-s)

Comic Warehouse
1029 Airport Rd.
Naples, FL 33942
PH: 813-643-1020 (b,c,e,m,q-t)

Tropic Comics South, Inc.
743 N.E. 167th St.
N. Miami Beach, FL 33162
PH: 305-940-8700 (a-d,j,n,r,v)

The Cartoon Museum
4300 S. Semoran - Suite 109
Orlando, FL 32822
PH: 407-273-0141 (a-n,p,q)

Coliseum of Comics
4103 S. Orange Blossom Trail
Orlando, FL 32839
PH: 407-422-5757 (b,c,g,m,q-s)

Enterprise 1701
2814 Corrine Dr.
Orlando, FL 32803
PH: 407-896-1701 (b,c,e,j,m-o,q-v)

Sincere Comics
3330 N. Pace Blvd.
Pensacola, FL 32505
PH: 904-432-1352 (a-c,e,f,m,q-t)

Tropic Comics
313 S. State Rd. 7
Plantation, FL 33317
PH: 305-587-8878 (a-d,j,n,q,r,v)

Comic & Gaming Exchange
8432 W. Oakland Park Blvd.
Sunrise, FL 33351
PH: 305-742-0777 (b-e,g,i,k,m-v)

Absolute Comics
5025 E. Fowler Avenue
Store #8
Tampa, FL 33617
PH: 813-985-5080
(a-c,i-k,m,o,q,s,t,v)

Tropic Comics North, Inc.
1018 - 21st St. (U.S. 1)
Vero Beach, FL 32960
PH: 407-562-8501 (a-c,j,n,q-s)

GEORGIA

Showcase Collectibles
2880 Holcomb Bridge Rd. #19
Alpharetta, GA 30202
PH: 404-594-0778 (a-c,g,i,q-s)

Titan Games & Comics
5436 Riverdale Road
College Park, GA 30349
PH: 404-996-9129 (a-d,g,m,o-v)

Comic Company
1058 Mistletoe Road
Decatur, GA 30033
PH: 404-248-9846 (a-d,g,m,n,r)

Titan Games & Comics IV
2131 Pleasant Hill Road
Duluth, GA 30136
PH: 404-497-0202 (a-c,g,k,m,o,q-v)

Titan Games & Comics V
937 North Glynn Street #13
Fayetteville, GA 30214
PH: 404-461-9432 (a-c,g,m,o,q-v)

Odin's Cosmic Bookshelf
4760 Hwy. 29, Suite A-1
Lilburn, GA 30247
PH: 404-923-0123 (a-c,e,h,m,r,s)

Showcase Collectibles
5920 Roswell Rd.
Sandy Springs, GA
PH: 404-255-5170 (a-c,g,i,o,q-s,v)

Titan Games & Comics III
2585 Spring Road
Smyrna, GA 30080
PH: 404-433-8226 (a-c,g,m,o,q-v)

Titan Games & Comics II
3853-C Lawrenceville Hwy.
Tucker, GA 30084
PH: 404-491-8067 (a-c,g,k,m,o,q-v)

HAWAII

Compleat Comics Company
1728 Kaahumanu Ave.
Wailuku, HI 96793
PH: 808-242-5875 (b,c,m,n,q-t)

IDAHO

King's Komix Kastle
1706 N. 18th St. (By Appointment)
Boise, ID 83702
PH: 208-343-7142 (a-i,m,n,q,r)
King's Komix Kastle II
2560 Leadville (Drop-In)
Mail: 1706 N. 18th
Boise, ID 83702
PH: 208-343-7055 (a-i,m,n,q,r)
New Mythology Comics & Science Fiction
1725 Broadway
Boise, ID 83706
PH: 208-344-6744 (a-c,e,m,n,q-t)

ILLINOIS

Friendly Frank's Comics
11941 S. Cicero
Alsip, IL 60658
PH: 708-371-6760
(a-d,f,g,i,j,m-o,q,r,u,v)
All-American Comic Shops 3
9118 Ogden Avenue
Brookfield, IL 60513
PH: 708-387-9588 (a-c,e,j,m,q,r)
AF Books/Amazing Fantasy
582 Torrence Ave.
Calumet City, IL 60409
PH: 708-891-2260 (a-c,e,m,o-s)
All-American Comic Shops 7
15 River Oaks Drive
Calumet City, IL 60409
PH: 708-891-0845 (a-c,e,j,m,q,r)
Comic Cavalcade
502 East John
Champaign, IL 61820
PH: 217-384-2211 (a-c,g,i,j,m,n,q,r)
All-American Comic Shops 6
6457 W. Archer Avenue
Chicago, IL 60638
PH: 312-586-5090 (a-c,e,j,m,q,r)
Chicago Comics
2936 N. Clark Street
Chicago, IL 60657
PH: 312-528-1983
(a-c,k,m,o,p,q,r,t)
Comics For Heroes
1702 W. Foster
Chicago, IL 60640
PH: 312-769-3494 (a-c,m,n,q-u)
Joe Sarno's Comic Kingdom
5941 West Irving Park Rd.
Chicago, IL 60634
PH: 312-545-2231 (a-d,j,m,r)
Larry's Comic Book Store
1219 W. Devon Ave.
Chicago, IL 60660
PH: 312-274-1832 (a-c,n,r,t-v)
Larry Laws
(by appointment only-call first)
831 Cornelia
Chicago, IL 60657
PH: 312-477-9247 (e,g,h,m,o)
Mikes on Mars
(An All-American Affiliate 8)
1753 W. 69th Street
Chicago, IL 60637
PH: 312-778-6990 (a-c,e,j,m,q,r)
Moondog's
7601 S. Cicero
Ford City Shopping Center
Chicago, IL 60652
PH: 312-581-6060 (b,c,e,m,o,q-v)
Moondog's
2301 N. Clark Street
Chicago, IL 60614
PH: 312-248-6060 (a-c,e,m-o,q-v)
Toon Town Comics Co.
Brickyard Mall
6465 West Diversey
Chicago, IL 60635
PH: 312-804-9557 (b,c,i,k,m,q-t)
Toon Town Comic Co.
3946 N. Southport
Chicago, IL 60613
PH: 312-549-6430 (b,c,i,k,m,q-t)
Yesterday
1143 W. Addison St.
Chicago, IL 60613
PH: 312-248-8087 (a,b,d-g,i-n,r,t)
All-American Comic Shops 5
1701 N. Larkin Avenue
Hillcrest Shopping Center
Crest Hill, IL 60435
PH: 815-744-2094 (a-c,e,j,m,q,r)
Moondog's Outlet
114 S. Waukegan Rd.
Deerfield, IL 60015
PH: 708-272-6080 (b,c,e,m,o,q-v)
The Paper Escape
205 W. First Street
Dixon, IL 61021
PH: 815-284-7567 (c,e,m,q,s,t)
GEM Comics
156 N. York Rd.
Elmhurst, IL 60126
PH: 708-833-8787 (b,c,q-s)
All-American Comics Shops, Ltd.
3514 W. 95th Street
Evergreen Park, IL 60642
PH: 708-425-7555 (a-c,e,j,m,q,r)
AF Books/Amazing Fantasy
47 E. Lincoln Hwy.
Franfort, IL 60423
PH: 815-469-5092 (a-c,e,m,o-s)
Comics Galore
725 W. Hillgrove
LaGrange, IL 60525
PH: 708-354-9570 (c,e,q-u)
Friendly Frank's Distribution
820 N. Ridge Rd., Unit H
Lombard, IL 60148
PH: 708-916-0117 (c,e,m-o,q-v)
Moondog's
139 W. Prospect Ave.
Mt. Prospect, IL 60056
PH: 708-398-6060 (a-c,e,m,o,q-v)
Moondog's
Randhurst Shopping Center
999 Elmhurst Road
Mt. Prospect, IL 60056
PH: 708-577-8668 (b,c,e,m,o,q-v)
Tenth Planet, Inc.
9513 S. Cicero
Oak Lawn, IL 60453
PH: 708-636-0806 (b,c,e,m,o,q-u)
All-American Comic Shops 2
14620 S. LaGrange Rd.
Orland Park, IL 60462
PH: 708-460-5556 (a-c,e,j,m,q,r)
All-American Comic Shops 4
22305 S. Central Park Ave.
Park Forest, IL 60466
PH: 708-748-2509 (a-c,e,j,m,q,r)
Comic Quest
503 Lockport
Plainfield, IL 60544
PH: 815-439-2735 (a-c,g,m,q,r)
Tomorrow Is Yesterday
5600 N. 2nd Street
Rockford, IL 61111
PH: 815-633-0330 (a-j,m-o,q-v)
Moondog's
1455 W. Schaumburg Rd.
Schaumburg, IL 60194
PH: 708-529-6060 (a-c,e,m,o,q-v)
Unicorn Comics & Cards
216 S. Villa Avenue
Villa Park, IL 60181
PH: 708-279-5777
(a-c,e,g,h,j,l-n,q-s)

INDIANA

25th Century Five & Dime
106 East Kirkwood Ave.
P. O. Box 7
Bloomington, IN 47402
PH: 812-332-0011 (b,c,g,m,n,q-t)
The Book Broker
2127 S. Weinbach (Fairlawn Ctr.)
Evansville, IN 47714
PH: 812-479-5647 (a-c,e-h,l-o,q-t)
Friendly Frank's Distribution
3990 Broadway
Gary, IN 46408
PH: 219-884-5052 (c,e,m-o,q-v)
Friendly Frank's Comics
220 Main Street
Hobart, IN 46342
PH: 219-942-6020
(a-d,f,g,i,j,m-o,q,r,u,v)
Blue Moon Comics & Games
8336 West 10th St. Suite #E
Indianapolis, IN 46234
PH: 317-271-1479
(b,c,e,g,j,m,o,q-v)
Comic Carnival & Nostalgia Emporium
7311 U.S. 31 South
Indianapolis, IN 46227
PH: 317-889-8899 (a-j,m-u)
Comic Carnival & Nostalgia Emporium
6265 N. Carollton Avenue
Indianapolis, IN 46220
PH: 317-253-8882 (a-j,m-u)
Comic Carnival & Nostalgia Emporium
5002 S. Madison Avenue
Indianapolis, IN 46227
PH: 317-787-3773 (a-j,m-u)
Comic Carnival & Nostalgia Emporium
982 N. Mitthoeffer Rd.
Indianapolis, IN 46229
PH: 317-898-5010 (a-j,m-u)
Comic Carnival & Nostalgia Emporium
3837 N. High School Rd.
Indianapolis, IN 46254
PH: 317-293-4386 (a-j,m-u)
Tenth Planet, Inc.
204 W. Lincoln Hwy. (Rt. 30)
Schererville, IN 46375
PH: 219-322-2902 (b,c,e,m,o,q-u)
Galactic Greg's
1407 E. Lincolnway
Valparaiso, IN 46383
PH: 219-464-0119 (a-c,m,n,q-s)

IOWA

Mayhem Collectibles
2532 Lincoln Way
Ames, IA 50010
PH: 515-292-3510 (b,c,e,m,q-u)
Oak Leaf Comics
1926 Valley Park Drive
Cedar Falls, IA 50613
PH: 319-277-1835 (a-c,f,k,m,n,q-v)
Comic World & Sports Cards
1626 Central Ave.
Dubuque, IA 52001
PH: 319-557-1897 (a-c,g,m,n,q-v)

Oak Leaf Comics
23 5th SW
Mason City, IA 50401
PH: 515-424-0333 (a-c,f,j-v)

KANSAS

Friendly Frank's Distribution
1401 Fairfax Trafficway 220D Bldg.
Kansas City, KS 66115
PH: 913-371-0333 (c,e,m-o,q-v)
Kwality Comics
1111 Massachusetts
Lawrence, KS 66044
PH: 913-843-7239 (a-c,e,i,m,q-s,v)
Prairie Dog Comics West
7130 West Maple, Suite 240
Wichita, KS 67209
PH: 316-942-3456 (a-v)
Prairie Dog Comics East
Oxford Square Mall
6100 E. 21st St., Suite 190
Wichita, KS 67208
PH: 316-688-5576 (a-n,p-s)

KENTUCKY

Pac-Rat's, Inc.
1051 Bryant Way
Bowling Green, KY 42103
PH: 502-782-8092 (a-c,l,m,o-t)
Comic Book World
7130 Turfway Road
Florence, KY 41042
PH: 606-371-9562 (a-c,m,o,q-v)
Comic Book World
6905 Shepherdsville Road
Louisville, KY 40219
PH: 502-964-5500 (a-c,m,o,q-v)
The Great Escape
2433 Bardstown Road
Louisville, KY 40205
PH: 502-456-2216
(a-c,e,g,i,j,l-o,q-v)

LOUISIANA

B.T. & W.D. Giles
P. O. Box 271
Keithville, LA 71047
PH: 318-925-6654 (a,b,d,e,f,h)
Bookworm N.O.E.
7011 Read Blvd.
New Orleans, LA 70129
PH: 504-242-7608 (a-c,e,m,o,q-s,v)
Comix Plus
248 West Hall Avenue
Slidell, LA 70460
PH: 504-649-4376 (b,c,r)

MAINE

Lippincott Books
624 Hammond St.
Bangor, ME 04401
PH: 207-942-4398 (a,b,d-h,n,t)
Moonshadow Comics
359 Maine Mall Road
S. Portland, ME 04210
PH: 207-772-4605
(a-c,g,i,j,m,n,q-u)

MARYLAND

Universal Comics
5300 East Drive
Arbutus, MD 21227
PH: 410-242-4578 (b,c,k,m,r)
ABC Comics & Cards
4415 Kenwood Avenue
Baltimore, MD 21206
PH: 410-665-3065 or 800-225-9232
(a-v)
Comic Book Kingdom, Inc.
4307 Harford Road
Baltimore, MD 21214
PH: 410-426-4529 (a-i,k,m,q,r,t)
Geppi's Comic World
7019 Security Blvd.
Hechinger's Square at Security Mall
Baltimore, MD 21214
PH: 301-208-1758 (a-c,f)
Geppi's Comic World
Upper Level, Light St. Pavilion
301 Light Street
Baltimore, MD 21202
PH: 301-547-0910 (a-c,f)
Alternate Worlds
72 Cranbrook-Yorktowne Plaza
Cockeysville, MD 21030
PH: 410-666-3290 (b,c,m,n,q-v)
The Closet of Comics
7319 Baltimore Avenue
College Park, MD 20740
PH: 301-699-0498 (b,c,m,n,o,r)
ABC Comics & Toys
59 Shipping Place
Dundalk, MD 21222
PH: 410-282-4737 (a-v)
Comic Classics
203 E. Main Street
Frostburg, MD 21532
PH: 301-689-1823 (a-c,m-o,q-v)
ABC Comics & Collectibles
6711 Ritchie Highway
Glen Burnie Mall
Glen Burnie, MD 21061
PH: 410-760-1206 (a-v)
Comic Classics
365 Main Street
Laurel, MD 20707
PH: 301-792-4744 or
410-490-9811 (a-c,e,m-o,q-v)
Zenith Comics & Collectibles
18200 P Georgia Avenue
Olney, MD 20852
PH: 301-774-1345
(a-c,f,j,k,m,o,q-v)
Geppi's Comic World
8317 Fenton Street
Silver Spring, MD 20910
PH: 301-588-2546 (a-c,e,f)

MASSACHUSETTS

New England Comics
170 Harvard Avenue
Allston, MA 02134
PH: 617-783-1848 (a-c,e,m,o,q-v)
New England Comics
168 Harvard Ave.
Boston, MA 02134
PH: 617-783-1848 (a-c,e,m,o,q-v)
New England Comics
748 Crescent Street
East Crossing Plaza
Brockton, MA 02402
PH: 508-559-5068
(a-c,e,m,o,q,r,t-v)
New England Comics
316 Harvard Street
Brookline, MA 02146
PH: 617-566-0115 (a-c,e,m,o,q-v)
New England Comics
12B Eliot Street
Cambridge, MA 02138
PH: 617-354-5352 (a-c,e,m,o,q-s,v)
That's Entertainment II
387 Main Street
Fitchburg, MA 01420
PH: 508-342-8607 (a-v)
Bop City Comics
Route 9, Marshalls Plaza
Framingham, MA 01701
PH: 508-872-2317
New England Comics
12A Pleasant Street
Malden, MA 02148
PH: 617-322-2404 (a-c,e,m,o,q-s,v)
Colton's Comics
19 N. Main Street, Suite "B"
Millbury, MA 01527
PH: 508-865-4998 (a-c,m,o,q,r,t)
Dan's Comics & Cards
276 W. Main St. (Rt. 20)
Northboro, MA 01532
PH: 508-393-1395 (a-d,g,i,j,l-o,r,t,u)
New England Comics
732 Washington Street
Norwood, MA 02062
PH: 617-769-4552 (a-c,e,m,o,q-s,v)
Outer Limits Limited
377 Court Street, Rt. 3A
Cordage Park, Bldg. 3
N. Plymouth, MA 02360
PH: 508-747-2550 (b,c,g,m,q,r,t)
New England Comics
11 Court Street
Plymouth, MA 02360
PH: 508-746-8797 (a-c,m,o,q,r,v)
New England Comics
1511 Hancock Street
Quincy, Ma 02169
PH: 617-770-1848 (a-c,e,m,o,q-s,v)
Fabulous Fiction Comics & Games
Rt. 131, Fiske Hill Plaza
Sturbridge, MA 01566
PH: 508-347-8088 (b,c,e,o,q-v)
The Outer Limits
457 Moody Street
Waltham, MA 02154
PH: 617-891-0444 (a-k,m-v)
Mayo Beach Bookstore
Kendrick Avenue
Box 502
Wellfleet, MA 02667
PH: 508-349-3154 (a-i)
Stan's Toy Chest
8 West Main Street
Westboro, MA 01581
PH: 508-366-5091 (a-c,i-t,v)
Best Comic Shop Of Worcester
244 Park Avenue
Worcester, MA 01609
PH: 508-755-4207 (a-v)
Fabulous Fiction Book Store
984 Main Street
Worcester, MA 01603
PH: 508-754-8826 (a-g,o,q-v)
That's Entertainment
244 Park Avenue
Worcester, MA 01609
PH: 508-755-4207 (a-v)

MICHIGAN

Tom & Terry Comics
508 Lafayette Ave.
Bay City, MI 48708
PH: 517-895-5525 (b,c,e,m,o,q-t)
Argos Book Shop
1405 Robinson Rd. S.E.
Grand Rapids, MI 49806
PH: 616-454-0111 (a-k,m-v)
Tardy's Collector's Corner, Inc.
2009 Eastern Ave. S.E.
Grand Rapids, MI 49507
PH: 616-247-7828 (a-c,m,n,q,r)

Curious Book Shop
307 E. Grand River
E. Lansing, MI 48823
PH: 517-332-0112 (d,e-k,m,p,t,v)

Curious Book Shop
210 M. A. C. Ave.
E. Lansing, MI 48823
PH: 517-332-0222

Friendly Frank's Distribution
28055 Dequindre
Madison Heights, MI 48071
PH: 313-542-2525 (c,e,m-o,q-v)

MINNESOTA

Collector's Connection
21 East Superior Street
Duluth, MN 55802
PH: 218-722-9551 (b,c,m,r-t)

Collector's Connection II
1600 Miller Trunk Highway
Miller Hill Mall
Duluth, MN 55811
PH: 218-726-1360 (b,c,m,r-t)

College Of Comic Book Knowledge
3151 Hennepin Avenue S.
Minneapolis, MN 55408
PH: 612-822-2309
(a-c,e-i,k-n,p-r,t-v)

Midway Book & Comic
1579 University Ave.
St. Paul, MN 55104
PH: 612-644-7605 (a-h,m,n,q,r)

MISSISSIPPI

Star Store
4212 N. State Street
Jackson, MS 39206
PH: 601-362-8001 (a-t)

MISSOURI

Mo's Comics & Stories
4573 Gravois
St. Louis, MO 63116
PH: 314-353-9500 (a-d,f,p,r,t)

NEVADA

Fandom's Comicworld of Reno
2001 East Second Street
Reno, NV 89502
PH: 702-786-6663 (a-c,j,m,q,r)

West Coast Comics Supplies
2001 East Second Street
Reno, NV 89502
PH: 702-323-2623 or
800-444-7371

NEW HAMPSHIRE

James F. Payette
P. O. Box 750
Bethlehem, NH 03574
PH: 603-869-2097 (a,b,d-h)

21st Century Collectibles
13 Roxbury Street
Keene, NH 03431
PH: 603-352-2755 (c,e,l,m,n,q-u)

Club Comics
45 Hanover Street
Lebanon, NH 03766
PH: 603-448-0130
(b,c,e,j,m-o,q-s,u)

Comic Store
643 Elm Street
Manchester, NH 03101
PH: 603-668-6705 (a-c,g,j,m-o,q-v)

Comic Store
300 Main Street
Nashua, NH 03060
PH: 603-881-4855 (a-c,g,j,m-o,q-v)

Granite State Collectable$
369 Gage Hill Rd. (Rt. 38)
Pelham, NH 03076
PH: 603-898-5086 (a-d,g,i,j,l-o,r,t,u)

NEW JERSEY

Cards & Comics
17 Olcott Square
Bernardsville, NJ 07924
PH: 908-953-8101 (c,m,q-s)

Comics Plus
Laurel Square
Hwy. 70 & 88
Brick, NJ 08723
PH: 908-206-1070 (a-c,g,h,k,m,q,r)

Grafik XS
288 Parker Ave.
Clifton, NJ 07011
PH: 201-340-5255 (b,c,e,i-k,m-v)

Steve's Comic Relief
1555 St. George Ave.
Colonia, NJ 07067
PH: 908-382-3736 (a-c,j,n,q,r,t-v)

Steve's Comic Relief
24 Heritage Square
Delran, NJ 08075
PH: 609-461-1770 (a-c,j,n,q,r,t-v)

Shore Video Comics & BB Cards
615 Lacey Road
Forked River, NJ 08734
PH: 609-693-3831 (a-c,m,o,r)

Comic Relief of Freehold
Freehold Raceway Mall
Freehold, NJ 07728
PH: 908-577-1601 (a-c,j,n,q,r,t-v)

Star Spangled Comics
Rt. 22 & Green Brook Rd.
King George Plaza
Green Brook, NJ 08812
PH: 908-356-8338 (a-c,j,m,q-s,v)

Dreamer's Comics
229-235 Main Street
Hackettstown, NJ 07840
PH: (908) 850-5255 (a-e,k,m,q,r)

Steve's Comic Relief
165 Mercer Mall
Lawrenceville, NJ 08648
PH: 609-452-7548 (a-c,j,n,q,r,t-v)

Philly Sportsfan
Hamilton Mall
Mays Landing, NJ 08330
PH: 609-646-4577 (c,m,q-s)

Comics Plus
Squire Plaza
1300 Hwy. 35
Middletown, NJ 07748
PH: 908-706-0102 (a-c,g,h,k,m,q,r)

Comic Museum
434 Pine Street
Mount Holly, NJ 08060
PH: 609-261-0996
(a-c,e,m,n,q,r,u,v)

Passaic Book Center
594 Main Ave.
Passaic, NJ 07055
PH: 201-778-6646 (a-h,l-o,q-v)

Steve's Comic Relief
635 Bay Avenue
Toms River, NJ 08753
PH: 908-244-5003 (a-c,j,n,q,r,t-v)

Mr. Collector
327 Union Blvd.
Totowa, NJ 07512
PH: 201-595-0900 (a-c,m,r)

Thunder Road Sportscards & Comics
3694 Nottingham Way
Trenton, NJ 08619
PH: 609-587-5353 (a-c,m,r)

Thunder Road Sportscards & Comics
1973 N. Olden Ave.
Trenton, NJ 08618
PH: 609-771-1055 (a-c,m,r)

Temdee
1201 Black Horse Pike
Turnersville, NJ 08012
PH: 609-228-8645 (a-d,f,g,k-v)

Comics Plus
Ocean Plaza
Hwy. 35 & Sunset Ave.
Wanamassa, NJ 07712
PH: 908-922-3308 (a-c,g,h,k,m,q,r)

JHV Associates
(Appointment Only)
P. O. Box 317
Woodbury Hts., NJ 08097
PH: 609-845-4010 (a,b,d)

NEW MEXICO

Bruce's Comics
2432 Cerrillos Rd.
Santa Fe, NM 87501
PH: 505-474-0494 (a-c,g,j,n,q,r)

NEW YORK

Earthworld Comics
327 Central Avenue
Albany, NY 12206
PH: 518-465-5495 (a-c,m-o,q-v)

FantaCo Enterprises Inc.
21 Central Ave.
Albany, NY 12210
PH: 518-463-1400
(b,c,e,g,i,m-o,q-v)

Long Island Comics
1670-D Sunrise Hwy.
Bay Shore, NY 11706
PH: 516-665-4342 (a-c,g,j,q-t)

Wow Comics
652 East 233rd Street
Bronx, NY 10467
PH: 212-231-0913 (a-c,k,m,q-s)

Wow Comics
642 Pelham Parkway South
Bronx, NY 10462
PH: 212-829-0461 (a-c,k,m,q-s)

Pinocchio Discounts
1814 McDonald Ave.
Brooklyn, NY 11223
PH: 718-645-2573 (a,b,c)

Comics For Collectors
60 East Market St.
Corning, NY 14830
PH: 607-936-3994 (a-c,j,m,n,q-v)

The Book Stop
384 East Meadow Avenue
East Meadow, NY 11554
PH: 516-794-9129 (a-d,g,h,n,r,v)

Comics For Collectors
211 West Water St.
Elmira, NY 14901
PH: 607-732-2299 (a-c,j,m,n,q-v)

Comics For Collectors
148 The Commons
Ithaca, NY 14850
PH: 607-272-3007 (a-c,j,m,n,q-v)

Long Beach Books Inc.
17 East Park Ave.
Long Beach, NY 11561
PH: 516-432-2265 and 432-0063
(b-h,m-o,r-u)

Comics And Hobbies
(Mail Order Available)
156 Mamaroneck Ave.
Mamaroneck, NY 10543
PH: 914-698-9473 (c,h,m,q,r)

Port Comics & Cards
3120 Rt. 112
Medford, NY 11763
PH: 516-732-9143 (a-c,g,j,m,o,r,t)

Funny Business
656 Amsterdam Ave.
New York, NY 10025
PH: 212-799-9477 (b,c,m,n,q,r)

Jerry Ohlinger's Movie Material Store, Inc.
242 W. 14th St.
New York, NY 10011
PH: 212-989-0869 (g,i)

Jim Hanley's Universe
126 West 32nd Street
(between 6th and 7th Aves.)
New York, NY 10001
PH: 212-268-7088
(a-c,e,g,m-o,q-v)

Jim Hanley's Universe
166 Chambers Street
(at Greenwich St.)
New York, NY 10007
PH: 212-349-2930
(a-c,e,g,m-o,q-v)

Supersnipe Comic Book Euphorium
Gracie Station
P. O. Box 1102
New York, NY 10028
(a-h,j,n,r,t,u)

Fantastic Planet
24 Oak Street
Plattsburgh, NY 12901
PH: 518-563-2946
(b,c,e,g,m,q,r,t-v)

Flash Point Comics • Cards • Toys
320 Main Street
Port Jefferson, NY 11777
(Long Island)
PH: 516-331-9401 (b,c,e,k,m,n,q-u)

Queensboro Comics
99-17 Queens Blvd., Forest Hills
Queens, NY 11374
PH: 718-268-0146 (a-c,k,m,q-s)

Amazing Comics
12 Gillette Avenue
Sayville, NY 11782
PH: 516-567-8069
(a-c,e,j,m,o,q-s,v)

One If By Cards, Two If By Comics
1107 Central Park Ave.
Scarsdale, NY 10583
PH: 914-725-2225 (b,c,g,m,r-t)

Electric City Comics
1704 Van Vranken Ave.
Schenectady, NY 12308
PH: 518-377-1500
(a-c,g,j,m,n,q,r,t-v)

Electric City Comics-Rotterdam
2801 Guilderland Avenue
Schenectady, NY 12306
PH: 518-356-1361 (b,c,g,m,q,r)

Jim Hanley's Universe
350 New Dorp Lane
(near Hylan Blvd.)
Staten Island, NY 10306
PH: 718-351-6299
(a-c,e,g,m-o,q-v)

Comic Book Heaven
48-14 Skillman Avenue
Sunnyside (Queens), NY 11104
PH: 718-899-4175 (b,c,g,q-s)

Twilight Book & Game Emporium, Inc.
1401 N. Salina St.
Syracuse, NY 13208
PH: 315-471-3139 (a-c,e,m-o,q-v)

Twilight Book & Game Emporium, Inc.
Carousel Center
Syracuse, NY 13290
PH: 315-466-1601 (c,e,m,q-u)

Ravenswood, Inc.
263 Genesee St.
Utica, NY 13501
PH: 315-735-3699 (a-c,g,k,m,q-u)

The Dragon's Den
2614 Central Ave.
Yonkers, NY 10710
PH: 914-793-4630 (b,c,g,m,q-t,v)

NORTH CAROLINA

Dragon's Hoard
344 Merrimon Ave.
Asheville, NC 28801
PH: 704-254-3829 (e,i,m,o,s-v)

Super Giant Comics
273-A Tunnel Rd.
Asheville, NC 28805
PH: 704-253-6188 (a-eg,h,j,l-n,q,r)

Heroes Aren't Hard To Find
Corner Central Ave. & The Plaza
P. O. Box 9181
Charlotte, NC 28299
PH: 704-375-7462
(a-c,g,j,k,m-o,q-t,v)

Heroes Aren't Hard To Find
(Mail Order & Wholesale)
P. O. Box 9181
Charlotte, NC 28299
PH: 704-376-5766, 800-321-4370
(a-c,g,j,k,m-o,q-t,v)

Lee's Book Exchange
329 S.E. Blvd.
Clinton, NC 28328
PH: 919-592-6539 (a-c,e)

Heroes Are Here
208 S. Berkeley Blvd.
Goldsboro, NC 27534
PH: 919-751-3131 (a-c,m,q,r)

Parts Unknown: The Comic Book Store
801 Merritt Drive
The Cottonmill Square
Greensboro, NC 27407
PH; 919-294-0091 (a-c,m,r)

Heroes Are Here, Too
116 E. Fifth St.
Greenville, NC 27834
PH: 919-757-0948 (a-c,m,q,r)

The Nostalgia News Stand
919 Dickinson Avenue
Greenville, NC 27834
PH: 919-758-6909 (b,c,e,n,q,r)

Tales Resold
3936 Atlantic Ave.
Raleigh, NC 27604
PH: 919-878-8551
(a-c,e,g,h,j,q,r,t,u)

The Booktrader
121 Country Club Drive
Rocky Mount, NC 27801
PH: 919-443-3993 (b,c,e,r)

Bargain Bookstore II
2001 Delwood Rd.
Waynesville, NC 28786
PH: 704-452-2539 (b,c,e,g,h,m,r)

Heroes Aren't Hard To Find
Silas Creek Shopping Center
3234 Silas Creek Parkway
Winston-Salem, NC 27103
PH: 919-765-4370
(a-c,g,j,k,m-o,q-t,v)

OHIO

Dark Star III Books & Comics
1273 N. Fairfield Rd.
Beavercreek, OH 45432
PH: 513-427-3213 (b,c,e,h,m,q-v)

Comics, Cards, & Collectables
533 Market Ave. N.
Canton, OH 44702
PH: 216-456-8907 (b,c,g,k,m,n,r,t)

Comic Book World
4016 Harrison Avenue
Cincinnati, OH 45211
PH: 513-661-6300 (a-c,m,o,q-v)

Collectors Warehouse Inc.
5437 Pearl Road
Cleveland, OH 44129
PH: 216-842-2896 (a-i,l-m,q-t)

Bookery Fantasy & Comics
35 N. Broad Street
Fairborn, OH 45324
PH: 513-879-1408 (a-c,e-k,m-o,q-v)

Bookery Collectibles Division
608 Middle Street
Fairborn, OH 45324
PH: 513-878-0144 (a,b,e)

Dark Star II Books & Comics
1410 W. Dorothy Lane
Kettering, OH 45409
PH: 513-293-7307 (b,c,e,h,m,q-v)

Rich's Comic Shoppe
2441 North Verity Parkway
Middletown, OH 45042
PH: 513-424-1095 (b,c,m,o,q-s)

Monarch Cards & Comics
2620 Airport Highway
Toledo, OH 43609
PH: 419-382-1451 (b,c,m,q,r)

Funnie Farm Bookstore
328 N. Dixie Drive
Vandalia, OH 45377
PH: 513-898-2794 (a-c,m,q-s)

Dark Star Books & Comics
237 Xenia Ave.
Yellow Springs, OH 45387
PH: 513-767-9400
(a-c,e-h,m,n,q-v)

OKLAHOMA

New World Comics & Games
2203 W. Main #10
Norman, OK 73069
PH: 405-321-7445 (a-h,m-o,q-v)

New World Comics & Games
6219 N. Meridian
Oklahoma City, OK 73112
PH: 405-721-7634 (a-h,m-o,q-v)

New World Comics & Games
4420 SE 44th St.
Oklahoma City, OK 73135
PH: 405-677-2559 (a-h,m-o,q-v)

The Comic Empire of Tulsa
3122 S. Mingo Rd.
Tulsa, OK 74146
PH: 918-664-5808 (a-c,n,q,r)

Starbase 21
2130 S. Sheridan Rd.
Tulsa, OK 74129
PH: 918-838-3388
(a-c,e,g,i,k,m,q-v)

Want List Comics
(Appointment Only)
P. O. Box 701932
Tulsa, OK 74170-1932
PH: 918-299-0440 (a,b,f,h-k,m)

OREGON

Pegasus Books
4390 S.W. Lloyd Street
Beaverton, OR 97005
PH: 503-643-4222
(a-c,e,f,k,m,n,q-t)

Emerald City Comics
770 E. 13th
Eugene, OR 97401
PH: 503-345-2568 (c,e,m,o,p,q-s,v)

Nostalgia Collectibles
527 Willamette St.
Eugene, OR 97401
PH: 503-484-9202 (a-g,i-n,q,r,t)

It Came From Outer Space
Milwaukie Marketplace
10812 S.E. Oak
Milwaukie, OR 97222
PH: 503-786-0865
(a-c,e,f,k,m,n,q-t)

Pegasus Books
10902 S.E. Main St.
Milwaukie, OR 97222
PH: 503-652-2752
(a-c,e,f,k,m,n,q-t)

Future Dreams Burnside
1800 East Burnside\
Portland, OR 97214-1599
PH: 503-231-8311 (a-e,g,i,n,q,r,t,v)

Future Dreams Comic Art Library
10506 N.E. Halsey
Portland, OR 97220
PH: 503-256-1885
(Reading Library)

Future Dreams Gateway
10508 N.E. Halsey
Portland, OR 97220
PH: 503-255-5245 (b-e,g,i,q,r)

It Came From Outer Space II
Plaza 205 Ste. P
9738 S.E. Washington
Portland, OR 97216
PH: 503-257-2701
(a-c,e,f,k,m,n,q-t)

Pegasus Books
4161 N.E. Sandy
Portland, OR 97232
PH: 503-284-4693
(a-c,e,f,k,m,n,q-t)

Pegasus Books
1401 S.E. Division Street
Portland, OR 97214
PH: 503-233-0768
(a-c,e,f,k,m,n,q-t)

PENNSYLVANIA

Cap's Comic Cavalcade
1894 Catasauqua Rd.
Allentown, PA 18103
PH: 215-264-5540 (a-c,g,k,m-v)

Dreamscape Comics
404 West Broad Street
Bethlehem, PA 18018
PH: 215-867-1178 (a-c,m,q-s)

Time Tunnel Collectibles
1001 Castle Shannon Blvd.
Castle Shannon, PA 15234
PH: 412-531-8833 (a-c,g,j,m,q,r)

Dreamscape Comics
25th Street Shopping Center
Easton, PA 18042
PH: 215-250-9818 (a-c,m,q-s)

New Dimension Comics
311 5th Street
Ellwood City, PA 16117
PH: 412-752-9483 (a-c,k,m,r)

New Dimension Comics
20550 Route 19 - Piazza Plaza
Cranberry Township
Evans City, PA 16033
PH: 412-776-0433 (a-c,k,m,r)

Golden Unicorn Comics
860 Alter St.
Hazleton, PA 18201
PH: 717-455-4645 (b,c,n,q-s)

Ott's Trading Post
201 Allegheny St.
Hollidaysburg, PA 16648
PH: 814-696-9139 (a-g,l-n,r)

Charlie's Collectors Corner
100 D West Second St.
Hummelstown, PA 17036
PH: 717-566-7216 (b,c,m,r)

Captain Blue Hen Comics
1800 Lincoln Highway East
Lancaster, PA 17602
PH: 717-397-8011 (a-e,g-i,m-o,q-t)

Comic Express
Silver Spring Plaza
3545 Marietta Ave.
Lancaster, PA 17601
PH: 717-285-3040 (b,c,e,g,h,m,q,r)

The Comic Store
2481 Lincoln Hwy. E.
Quality Centers
Lancaster, PA 17602
PH: 717-397-8636 (b,c,e,m,n,q-s)

The Comic Store
Station Square
28 McGovern Ave.
Lancaster, PA 17602
PH: 717-397-8737 (a-c,e,m-o,q-s)

Steve's Comic Relief
4153 Woerner Avenue
Levittown, PA 19057
PH: 215-945-7954 (a-c,j,n,q,r,t-v)

Steve's Comic Relief
2114 S. Eagle Road
Newtown, PA 18940
PH: 215-579-9225 (a-c,j,n,q,r,t-v)

Steve's Comic Relief
1248 Franklin Mills Cl.
Philadelphia, PA 19154
PH: 215-281-3730 (a-c,j,n,q,r,t-v)

Adventures In Comics
3279 West Liberty Ave.
Pittsburgh, PA 15216
PH: 412-531-5644 (a-c,g,k,m,o,q-t)

Eide's Entertainment
1111 Penn Ave.
Pittsburgh, PA 15222
PH: 412-261-0900 (a-v)

The Comic Store - West
Northwest Plaza
915 Loucks Road
York, PA 17404 (b,c,e,m,n,q-s)

SOUTH CAROLINA

Super Giant Comics
3464 Cinema Center
Anderson, SC 29621
PH: 803-225-9024 (a-c,g,j,l-n,q,r,t)

Heroes Aren't Hard To Find
1415-A Laurens Road
Greenville, SC 29607
PH: 803-235-3488
(a-c,g,j,k,m-o,q-t,v)

Heroes Aren't Hard To Find
Westgate Mall
I-26 & US 29
Spartanburg, SC 29301
PH: 803-574-1713
(a-c,g,j,k,m-o,q-t,v)

Super Giant Comics
Franklin Square
Wal-Mart Plaza
7600 Greenville Hwy.
Spartanburg, SC 29301
PH: 803-576-4990 (a-c,g,j,m,n,q-t)

SOUTH DAKOTA

Storyteller Book Shoppe
520 Sixth Street
Rapid City, SD 57701
PH: 605-348-7242 (a-c,e,g-i,m,q-u)

TENNESSEE

American Collectors Exchange
2401 Broad St.
Chattanooga, TN 37408
PH: 615-265-5515 (a-c,e,f,i,m,q,r)

Collector's Choice
3405 Keith Street, Shoney's Plaza
Cleveland, TN 37311
PH: 615-472-6649 (c,i,m,q-t)

Comics Universe
1869 Hwy. 45 By-Pass
Jackson, TN 38305
PH: 901-664-9131 (a-c,j,m,o,q-s)

Mountain Empire Collectibles III
1210 North Roan Street
Johnson City, TN 37601
PH: 615-929-8245 (a-i,l-n,q-t,v)

Mountain Empire Collectibles II
1451 East Center Street
Kingsport, TN 37664
PH: 615-245-0364 (a-e,g,i,m,n,q-t,v)

Collector's Choice
2104 Cumberland Avenue
Knoxville, TN 37916
PH: 615-546-2665 (c,i,m,q-t)

Collector's World
Commons S/C-165 N. Peters Rd.
Knoxville, TN 37923
PH: 615-531-2943 (a-g,i-m,o-v)

The Great Escape
111-B Gallatin Road North
Madison, TN 37115
PH: 615-865-8052 (a-g,k-m,o-t)

Comics & Collectibles
4730 Poplar Ave. #2
Memphis, TN 38117
PH: 901-683-7171 (a-c,g,m-o,q-s,v)

Memphis Comics & Records
665 S. Highland
Memphis, TN 38111
PH: 901-452-1304 (a-t)

Collector's World
1511 East Main Street
Murfreesboro, TN 37130
PH: 615-895-1120 (a-g,i-m,o-v)

Collector's World
5751 Nolensville Rd.
Nashville, TN 37211
PH: 615-333-9458 (a-g,i-m,o-v)

The Great Escape
1925 Broadway
Nashville, TN 37203
PH: 615-327-0646 (a-g,k-m,o-t)

Walt's
2604 Franklin Road
Nashville, TN 37204
PH: 615-298-2506 (b,c,e,o,r,s)

TEXAS

Lone Star Comics, Books, & Games
511 East Abram St.
Arlington, TX 76010
PH: 817-Metro 265-0491
(a-c,e,g,k,m,q-t,v)

Lone Star Comics, Books, & Games
3415 South Cooper St., #141
Arlington, TX 76015
PH: 817-557-5252 (b,c,g,k,m,q-t,v)

Friendly Frank's Distribution
2959 Ladybird Lane
Dallas, TX 75220
PH: 214-351-3131 (c,e,m-o,q-v)

Lone Star Comics, Books, & Games
11661 Preston Forest Village
Dallas, TX 75230
PH: 214-373-0934
(a-c,e,k,m,n,q-t,v)

Remember When
2431 Valwood Parkway
Dallas, TX 75234
PH: 214-243-3439
(a-c,g,i,j,m,n,q,r,t,u)

Lone Star Comics, Books, & Games
6312 Hulen Bend Blvd.
Ft. Worth, TX 76132
PH: 817-346-7773
(a-c,e,g,k,m,q-t,v)

Third Planet
2718 Southwest Freeway
Houston, TX 77098
PH: 713-528-1067 (a-v)

Lone Star Comics, Books, & Games
931 Melbourne
Hurst, TX 76053
PH: 817-595-4375
(a-c,e,g,k,m,q-t,v)

Lone Star Comics, Books, & Games
2550 N. Beltline Rd.
Irving, TX 75062
PH: 817-659-0317
(a-c,e,g,k,m,q-t,v)

Lone Star Comics, Books, & Games
3600 Gus Thomasson, Suite 107
Mesquite, TX 75150
PH: 214-681-2040 (b,c,e,k,m,q-t,v)

Lone Star Comics, Books, & Games
1900 Preston Rd. #345
Plano, TX 75093
PH: 214-985-1953 (a-c,e,g,m,q-t,v)

Comics Unlimited
4 convenient locations in
San Antonio, TX
PH: 210-522-9063
(a-c,e,i-m,o,q-t,v)

Heroes & Fantasies
4 convenient locations in
San Antonio, TX
PH: 210-341-5567
(a-c,e,i-m,o,q-t,v)

UTAH

The Bookshelf
2456 Washington Blvd.
Ogden, UT 84401
PH: 801-621-4752 (b-e,h,l-o,q-s,v)

VERMONT

Comics Outpost
27 Granite Street
Barre, VT 05641
PH: 802-476-4553 or Toll-free VT only 800-564-4553 (a-c,m,q-t)

Comics City, Inc.
6 North Winooski Ave.
Burlington, VT 05401
PH: 802-865-3828
(b,c,e,j,m,n,p,q-v)

Westside Comics
P. O. Box 148, Rte. 4
Ctr. Rutland, VT 05736
PH: 802-773-9539 or 802-773-9480 (a-c,m,q,r)

Comics Route
Green Mtn. Village Shops
Rt. 7A - N. Main St.
Manchester Ctr., VT 05255
PH: 802-362-3698 (c,e,g,j,m,o,q,r,t)

Comics And Collectibles
Merchants Row
Middlebury, VT 05753
PH: 802-388-9953 (a-c,m,o,r-t,v)

Comics City, Inc.
67 Eastern Ave.
St. Johnsbury, VT 05819
PH: 802-748-3060 (b,c,j,m,p,q-v)

M & M Sportscards and Comics
6 North Main Street
White River Jct., VT 05001
PH: 802-295-3730 (a,b,m,r)

VIRGINIA

Capital Comics Center & Card Collectorama
(Greater D.C. Area)
2008 Mt. Vernon Ave.
Alexandria, VA 22301
PH: 703-548-3466 (a-c,f,m,o,q-u)

Mountain Empire Collectibles I
509 State Street
Bristol, VA 24201
PH; 703-466-6337 (a-e,g,i,m,n,q-t)

Burke Centre Used Books & Comics
5741 Burke Centre Parkway
Burke, VA 22015
PH: 703-250-5114 (a-h,m,q-u)

Trilogy Shop #3
3916-A6 Portsmouth Blvd.
Chesapeake, VA 23321
PH: 804-488-6578 (c,m,o,q-s,v)

Hole In The Wall Books
905 W. Broad St.
Falls Church, VA 22046
PH: 703-536-2511 (b-e,g,h,l,n,q-v)

Marie's Books And Things
1701 Princess Anne Street
Fredericksburg, VA 22401
PH: 703-373-5196 (a-c,e-i,l,m,q,r)

Franklin Farm Used Books & Comics
13340-B Franklin Farm Rd.
Herndon, VA 22071
PH: 703-437-9530 (a-h,m,q-u)

Cosmic Bookstore
10953 Lute Court
Manassas, VA 22110
PH: 703-330-8573 (b-e,g,h,j,l,q-u)

Trilogy Shop #2
700 E. Little Creek Rd.
Norfolk, VA 23518
PH: 804-587-2540 (c,m,o,q-v)

Trilogy Shop #5
Airline Flea Fair
3535 Airline Blvd.
Portsmouth, VA 23701
(c,m,r)

Dave's Comics
7019 Three Chopt. Rd.
Richmond, VA 23226
PH: 804-282-1211 (b,c,m,q-t,v)

Nostalgia Plus
1601 Willow Lawn Drive
Richmond, VA 23230
PH: 804-282-5532 (a-c,m,n,q,r)

Trilogy Shop #1
5773 Princess Anne Rd.
Virginia Beach, VA 23462
PH: 804-490-2205 (a-c,e,i,m,o,q-v)

Trilogy Shop #4
857 S. Lynnhaven Rd.
Virginia Beach, VA 23452
PH: 804-468-0412 (c,m,o,q-s,v)

WASHINGTON

Psycho 5 Comics & Cards
221 Bellevue Way N.E.
Bellevue, WA 98004
PH: 206-462-2869 (a-c,m,o,q-s,v)

Platinum Comic X-Change
830 S.W. 152nd
Burien, WA 98166
PH: 206-431-1415 or 762-8895
(b,c,m,n,p,q,r,t)

The Comic Character Shop
110 Alaskan Way South
Seattle, WA 98104
PH: 206-283-0532 (a,b,f,h-k,q)

Corner Comics
6565 N.E. 181
Seattle, WA 98155
PH: 206-486-XMEN (a-c,m,n,q)

Corner Comics II
5226 University Way N.E.
Seattle, WA 98105
PH: 206-525-9394 (b,c,m,q)

Golden Age Collectables, Ltd.
1501 Pike Place Market
401 Lower Level
Seattle, WA 98101
PH: 206-622-9799 (a-g,i-k,m-o,q-v)

Psycho 5 Comics & Cards
12513 Lake City Way N.E.
Seattle, WA 98125
PH: 206-367-1620 (a-c,m,o,q-s,v)

Rocket Comics
8544 Greenwood N.
Seattle, WA 98103
PH: 206-784-7300 (a-c,k,m,q)

Collectors Nook
213 N. I St.
Tacoma, WA 98403
PH: 206-272-9828 (b,e,g,h,m)

Lady Jayne's Comics & Books
5969 - 6th Ave.
Tacoma, WA 98406
PH: 206-564-6168 (c,e,m,q-u)

Lady Jayne's Comics & Books
440 E. 25th St.
Tacoma, WA 98421
PH: 206-572-4368 (c,e,r,s)

Pegasus Books
813 Grand
Vancouver, WA 98661
PH: 206-693-1240
(a-c,e,f,k,m,n,q-t)

WEST VIRGINIA

Comic Castle
314 Neville St.
Beckley, WV 25801
PH: 304-253-1974 (b,c,k,m-o,q,r)

All Star Sportscards/Triple Play
5206 MacCorkle Ave. SE
Charleston, WV 25302
PH: 304-925-3060 (a-c,m,o,q-s)

Comic World
613 W. Lee St.
Charleston, WV 25302
PH: 304-343-3874 (a-c,m,q,r)

Comic World
1204 - 4th Ave.
Huntington, WV 25701
PH: 304-522-3923 (a-c,m,q,r)

Triple Play Cards, Comics, & Collectibles/Fielders Choice
414 Stratton Street
Logan, WV 25601
PH: 304-752-9315 (a-c,m,o,q-s)

Triple Play Cards, Comics, & Collectibles
335 4th Ave.
South Charleston, WV 25303
PH: 304-744-2602 (a-c,m,o,q-s)

WISCONSIN

Incredible Comics
4429 W. Lisbon Ave.
Milwaukee, WI 53208
PH: 414-445-7006 (a-c,e-i,m,n,q,r)

CANADA
ALBERTA

Another Dimension Comics
7610 Elbow Drive S.W.
Calgary, Alberta, T2V 1K2
PH: 403-255-2588 (b,c,e,j,m,n,q-t)

Another Dimension Comics
4625 Varsity Drive, N.W.
Calgary, Alberta, T2A 0Z9
PH: 403-288-1802 (b,c,e,m,q,r,t)

Another Dimension Comics
2640-52 Street N.E.
Calgary, Alberta
PH: 403-293-1272 (b,c,e,m,q-t)

Another Dimension Comics
324-10 Street N.W.
Calgary, Alberta, T2N 1V8
PH: 403-283-7078 (b,c,e,j,m,n,q-t)

Comic Legends Ltd.
#205-908-17 Ave. SW
Calgary, Alberta, T2T 0A3
PH: 403-245-5884 (a-c,m,q,r,u)

Scorpio Comics, Books, And Sports Cards
7640 Fairmount Dr. S.E.
Calgary, Alberta, T2M 0X8
PH: 403-258-0035 (a-c,e-i,k,m,t,u)

Comic Legends Ltd.
1275 3rd Ave. S.
Lethbridge, Alberta
PH: 403-327-8558 (a-c,m,q,r,u)

Canadian Comics & Collectibles Express
P. O. Box 5169
Peace River, Alberta T8S 1B2
PH: 403-624-1224
'Subscription Service' (b,c,m,o,q-t)

BRITISH COLUMBIA

Page After Page
1771 Harvey Avenue
Kelowna, B.C. V1Y 6G4
PH: 604-860-6554 (a,c,e,h,q,r)

Golden Age Collectables
830 Granville Street
Vancouver, B.C., Can. V3Z 1K3
PH: 604-683-2819 (a-d,f,i,j,n,o)

MANITOBA

The Collector's Slave
156 Imperial Ave.
Winnipeg, Manitoba, R2M 0K8
PH: 204-237-4428 (a-g, k-n, p-r, t)

NEW BRUNSWICK

Halley's Comics/United Bookstores
345/347 Mountain Road
Moncton,New Brunswick E1C 2M7
PH: 506-855-0056 (b,c,e,m,o,q-t)

QUEBEC

Capitaine Quebec - Centre-Ville
1837 St. Catherine O.
Montreal, Quebec, H3H 1M2
PH:514-939-9970 (a-c,e,g,m,n,q-v)

Capitaine Quebec - Snowdon
5108 Decarie
Montreal, Quebec H3X 2H9
PH:514-487-0970 (a-c,e,g,m,n,q-v)

Cosmix
931 Decarie
St. Laurent, Quebec, H4L 3M3
PH: 514-744-9494 (a-c,e,m,o,q-t,v)

Komico
4210 Decarie Blvd.
Montreal, Quebec H4A 3K3
PH: 514-489-4009 (a-c,g,j,m,q,r,t)

Premiere Issue
27- A D'Auteuil
Quebec City (Vieux-Quebec) G1R 4B9
PH: 418-692-3985 (a-c,e,i,m,q-u)

Capitaine Quebec - Verdun
4422 Wellington
Verdun, Quebec H4G 1W5
PH:514-768-1351 (a-c,e,g,m,n,q-v)

FRANCE

Dangereuses Visions
81 Rue De La Monnaie
59800 Lille France
PH: 20-06-51-51
(b,c,e,g,i,j,m-o,q-t,v)

DIRECTORY OF ADVERTISERS (Cl = Classified, c = color)

DIRECTORY OF ADVERTISERS (Continued)

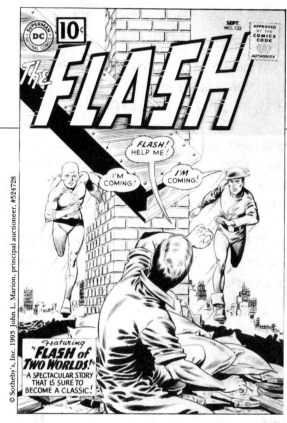

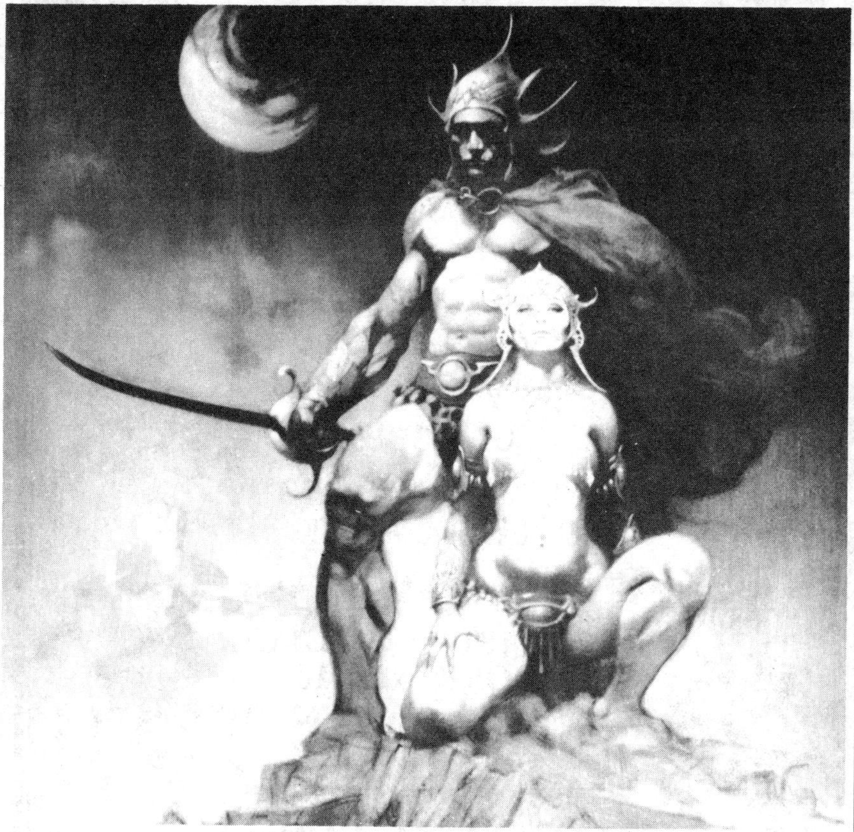

©DC

COMIC BOOKS WANTED

©MCG

NO ONE PAYS MORE!

IF YOU HAVE ANY COMIC BOOKS TO SELL

CONTACT US!

WE WILL TRAVEL TO VIEW LARGE COLLECTIONS

©MCG

©CEN

METROPOLIS COMICS

7 W. 18TH STREET
NEW YORK, N.Y. 10011
(212) 627-9691 FAX: (212) 627-5947

(BY APPOINTMENT ONLY)

©MCG

©DC

METROPOLIS COMICS

★ Accurate Grading ★ Competitive Pricing ★ Large Selection Of Golden And Silver Age ★ Complete Want List Service ★ New Approval Policy (Available To Want List Customers Only) Will Ship All Books Under $5000 To Any Want List Customer Without Pre-Payment. Payment Due Within 7 Days Unless Other Arrangements Are Made ★ Time Payments Possible

©MCG

©DC

7 W. 18TH STREET
NEW YORK, N.Y. 10011
(212) 627-9691 FAX: (212) 627-5947

(BY APPOINTMENT ONLY)

©FAW

©DIS

Quite Simply the Best in Brooklyn for your Golden and Silver Age "HARD TO FIND" COMICS

We sell Marvel, D.C., and Independent comics, which come in every Thursday. Magazine bags, comic bags, mylars, paperbacks, backboards, posters, comic and magazine boxes, rollplaying games, baseball cards (old & new), football cards etc.

We have spent $250,000 this year in comics and collections. Make us even happier by spending double this year or more.

We are located at: 1301 Prospect Ave. Brooklyn, NY 11218. Easy to get to by train or bus. Take F train to the Ft. Hamilton Parkway Station or buses #33 to Prospect Ave. or the #68 to Greenwood Ave.

OPEN MON. THRU SAT.
FROM 12 NOON TO 7:30PM
TEL. (718) 438-1335.
FAX. (718) 871-6948

We are always interested in early Golden Age & Silver Age books, Marvel's & D.C's, etc. for immediate cash.

COMIC BOOKS WANTED

The following prices represent a small sample of the prices that we will pay for your comic books. Other dealers say that they will pay top dollar, but when it really comes down to it, they simply do not. If you have comics to sell, we invite you to contact every comic dealer in the country to get their offers. Then come to us to get your best offer. **Metropolis Comics** is not a store. We are a Golden and Silver Age mail-order comic company. We can afford to pay the highest price for your Golden and Silver Age comics because that is all we sell. If you wish to sell us your comic books, please either ship us the books securely via Registered U.S. Mail or UPS. However, if your collection is too large to ship, kindly send us a detailed list of what you have and we will travel directly to you. The prices below are for NM/M copies.

Action #1 .... $70,000
Action #242 .... $850
Adventure #40 .... $8,000
Adventure #48 .... $5,200
Adventure #61 .... $3,800
Adventure #210 .... $1,000
All-American #16 ..... $18,000
All-American #19 ...... $4,000
All-Star #3 .... $9,000
Amazing Fantasy #15.. $6,200
Amaz.Spiderman #1..... $4,900
Amaz.Spiderman #6 ...... $600
Arrow #1 .... $1,000
Atom #1 .... $400
Batman #1 .... $24,000
Brave & the Bold #28. $2,200
Brave & the Bold #34 .. . $700
Captain America #1... $17,000
Classic Comics #1 .... $3,000
Detective #1 .... $29,000
Detective #27............. $80,000
Detective #35............. $3,400
Detective #38 .... $12,000
Detective #40 .... $2,800
Detective #168 .... $1,700
Detective #225 .... $2,100
Detec. Picture Stories #1 $1,500
Donald Duck #9 .... $2,400
Famous Funnies #1 .... $5,300

Famous Funnies Series #1. paying $11,000 for Very Fine copy!!!

Fantastic Four #1 .... $5,800
Fantastic Four #4 .... $850
Fantastic Four #5 .... $800
Flash #105 .... $2,200
Flash #110 .... $450
Flash Comics #1 .... $15,000
Funnies On Parade....... $4,000
Funny Pages 2#10 ...... $1,500
Green Hornet #1 .... $1,200
Green Lantern #1 (GA) . $5,000
Green Lantern #1 (SA) .. $1,400
Human Torch #2(#1) .. $3,900
Incredible Hulk #1 .... $2,900
Journey into Myst. #83.. $1,800
Justice League #1 .... $1,700
Jumbo Comics #1 .... $7,000
March of Comics #4..... $2,100
Marvel Comics #1 ...... $25,000
More Fun #52 .... $14,000
More Fun #53 .... $8,000
More Fun #54 .... $4.000
More Fun #55 .... $4,000
More Fun #73 .... $3,300
More Fun #101 .... $2,600
New Comics #1 .... $5,200
New Fun #1 .... $25,000
NY World's Fair '39 ... $5,000

New Fun #2 .... $8,000
New Fun #6 .... $10,000
Pep Comics #22 .... $2,000
Real Fact Comics #5 .... $600
Science Fict. Fanzine $12,000
Showcase #4 .... $10,500
Showcase #8 .... $3,000
Showcase #13 .... $2,000
Showcase #22 .... $2,000
Showcase #34 .... $700
Superboy #1 .... $2,500
Superman #1 .... $40,000
Superman #14 .... $1,500
Suspense Comics #3 .... $900
Tales of Suspense #1 .... $400
Tales of Suspense #39 $1,900
Tales to Astonish #27 $1,500
Target Comics V1#7 ..... $1,400
Thing #15 .... $300
Walt Disney C&S #1 .. $5,700
Weird Fantasy #13(#1) .. $600
Whiz #2 (#1) $20,000
Wonder Woman #1 ...... $3,300
Wow #1 (1936) $4,000
Young Allies #1 .... $2,000
X-Men #1.................... $1,700

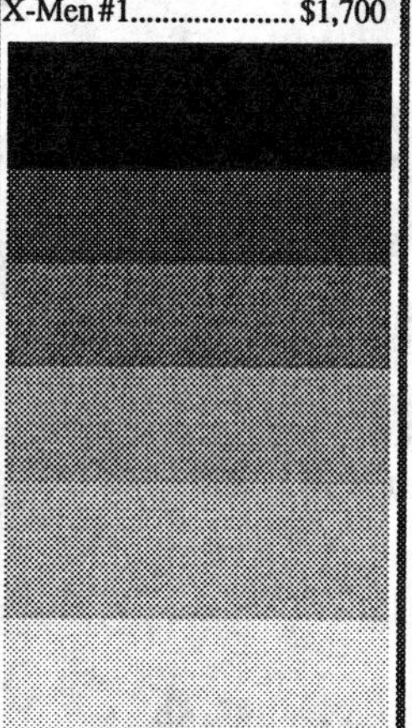

METROPOLIS COMICS

7 W. 18th Street
New York, NY 10011
212-627-9691
Fax:212-627-5947

The following is a sample of the books we are purchasing:

Action Comics	#1-300
Adventure Comics	#32-320
All-American Comics	#1-102
All-Flash Quarterly	#1-32
All-Select	#1-11
All-Star Comics	#1-57
All-Winners	#1-21
Amazing Spiderman	#1-50
Amazing Man	#5-26
Amaz. Mystery Funnies	#1-24
Avengers	#1-20
Batman	#1-200
Blackhawk	#9-130
Boy Commandos	#1-32
Brave & the Bold	#1-50
Captain America	#1-78
Captain Marvel Advs.	#1-150
Challengers	#1-25
Classic Comics	#1-169
Comic Cavalcade	#1-63
Daredevil Comics	#1-60
Daredevil (MCG)	#1-15
Daring Mystery	#1-8
Detective Comics	#1-350
Donald Duck 4-Colors	#4-up
Fantastic Four	#1-50
Fight Comics	#1-86
Flash	#105-150
Flash Comics	#1-104
Funny Pages	#6-42
Green Lantern (GA)	#1-32
Green Lantern (SA)	#1-59
Hit Comics	#1-65
Human Torch	#2(#1)-38
Incredible Hulk	#1-6
Journey Into Mystery	#1-125
Jumbo Comics	#1-167
Jungle Comics	#1-163
Justice League	#1-50
Mad	#1-30
Marvel Mystery	#1-92
Military Comics	#1-43
More Fun Comics	#7-127
Mystery in Space	#1-75
Mystic Comics	#1-up
New Adventure	#12-31
New Fun Comics	#1-6
Planet Comics	#1-73
Rangers Comics	#1-69
Sensation Comics	#1-116
Showcase	#1-75
Star-Spangled Comics	#1-130
Strange Tales	#1-145
Sub-Mariner	#1-42
Superboy	#1-110
Superman	#1-175
Tales of Suspense	#1-80
Tales to Astonish	#1-80
USA Comics	#1-17
Wings Comics	#1-124
Whiz Comics	#1-155
Wonder Woman	#1-120
World's Finest	#1-100
X-Men	#1-30

Cash Paid For Historic "Ashcans!"

Do you have an unidentifiable comic with an odd black & white cover and color interior?

It may be an historic "ashcan!"

In the early days of comic book publishing, there was a never-ending battle between highly competitive businessmen to lay claim to every conceivable comic book title. In order to properly register the title with the copyright office in Washington DC, publication of the book was required.

In the heat of competition, crafty comic book publishers developed a system to fool the government into believing that the book had been produced. They produced "ashcan" comics! These "imposters" existed only for legal registration and were never sold.

"Ashcans" usually had black and white covers (often Velox prints) stapled to color interiors from previously printed comics.

One "ashcan" comic was rushed to the copyright office in Washington DC to register the title and logo art. Another was placed in the publisher's files. Often extra "ashcans" were made and given to editors and other employees as souvenirs. Sometimes these rarities surface in today's comics collector marketplace.

Recently signed and numbered limited edition "ashcans" have appeared on the collectors market. Though highly desirable, these modern-day collectibles are not traditional "ashcan" editions.

Genuine historical "ashcans" are by definition among the rarest of comic books.

If you aren't sure that the book you have is an "ashcan" or not — please call me toll-free at **800-344-6060**. I'll help you identify your book and gladly make an offer.

Gary Colabuono

Moondog's

1201 Oakton St.
Elk Grove Village, IL 60007

(800) 344-6060

SILVER
WHEN YOU'RE IN NEW YORK CITY—
COME VISIT OUR BRAND NEW SHOWROOM!
OPEN WEEKDAYS, 10 AM TO 5 PM: BY APPOINTMENT ONLY
THE INCREDIBLE HULK
THE AMAZING SPIDER-MAN
Fantastic Four
THE CHAMELEON STRIKES!
AMAZING FANTASY
SPIDER MAN
SHOWCASE
THE FLASH
THE FLASH
MASTER OF MIRRORS!
THE BRAVE AND THE BOLD
JUSTICE LEAGUE of AMERICA
STARRO THE CONQUEROR!
SHOWCASE
THE FLASH!
DESIGN: ARNIE SAWYER
All artwork © DC COMICS, © MARVEL ENTERTAINMENT GROUP, INC

COMICS

617 391 5614

LARRY CURCIO
P.O. Box 821
Medford, MA 02155

MAIL ORDER
SPECIALIST
SELLING
PLEASE SEND
$1 FOR CATALOG

©DC

©MCG

Buying
Golden Age
Silver Age

©MCG

©DC

I offer the following to all customers:

BUYING:

- Top Prices Paid
- Immediate Cash
- Will travel to view large collections
- Experience

©DC

©FH

SELLING:

- Accurate Grading
- Reasonable Prices
- Dependable Service
- Large Selection
- Experience

©CEN

©DC

Send For Latest List

©DC

HARLEY YEE
P.O. Box 19578
Detroit, MI 48219-0578

(313) 533-2731

©MCG

SHOCK
BONZAI COMICS
WE SPECIALIZE IN THE
RARE,OBSCURE,HARD TO FIND
UNDERGROUNDS·GOLD AND SILVER AGE
WE HAVE IN STOCK HIGH GRADE COPIES OF
SUPERMAN #1 · CAPT. AMERICA #1 · AMAZING FANTASY #15
RUNS OF SPIDERMAN #1-100 —— FANTASTIC FOUR #1-100
CALL IN YER WANTS
212·502·3991★BUYING & SELLING

ORIGINAL ART

BUY - SELL - TRADE

Specializing in ORIGINAL COMIC BOOK & COMIC STRIP ART I have a selection of THOUSANDS of ORIGINALS in stock. Possibly the LARGEST SELECTION of classic, quality comic art IN THE WORLD!

From ALEX RAYMOND's "Flash Gordon" & HAL FOSTER's "Prince Valiant" & "Tarzan", to JACK KIRBY's "Fantastic Four" or DITKO's "Spider-man". SEGAR's "Popeye", WAYNE BORING or CURT SWAN's "Superman", SCHULZ's "Peanuts", GEORGE HERRIMAN's "Krazy Kat", CANIFF's "Terry" or "Steve Canyon". WILL EISNER, LOU FINE, BERNI WRIGHTSON, JOE KUBERT, CARMINE INFANTINO, WALLY WOOD, FRANK FRAZETTA, AL WILLIAMSON, R. CRUMB, STERRETT, SPRANG, FINLAY, BOK and on and on....

If original comic art & other graphic media are your hobby, then you should call or write me. If you are interested in buying, trading or selling fine quality originals, I HAVE MORE THAN ANYONE ELSE!! Contact me today....

My interests are: SILVER AGE DC & MARVEL; CLASSIC COMIC STRIPS; PIN-UP, PULP & PAPERBACK ART; MOVIE POSTER ART and UNDERGROUND COMIC ART.

Send $2. in stamps for my current catalog, $4. Foreign & Canada.

above: JACK KIRBY DC splash. One of 2 known, inked by WALLY WOOD. below: HERRIMAN's Krazy Kat

RICHARD HALEGUA

P.O.BOX 8256 CINCINNATI, OHIO 45208

phone 513-321-4208

Visit Our Fantastic

FOUR Locations!!!

• Best Selection!

• Reliable Service!

• Friendly, Knowledgable People!

We Always Buy & Sell

The Best In Collectible &

Back Issue Comics!!

Send Us Your Want List, List Of

Books To Sell, Or Call Us!

Plan To Attend

HEROES CONVENTION '93!

June 11-13, 1992

Charlotte International Trade Center

(formerly Charlotte Apparel Center)

HEROES AREN'T HARD TO FIND

Midwood Corners Shopping Center Corner of Central Avenue & The Plaza Charlotte NC (704) 375 7462	Silas Creek Crossing Shopping Center 3204 Silas Creek Parkway Winston-Salem NC 27106 (919) 765 4370 (HERØ)	Heroes Plaza Shopping Center 1415-A Laurens Road Greenville SC 29607 (803) 235 3488	Westgate Mall At The Intersection Of I-26 & U.S. 29 Spartanburg SC 29301 (803) 574 1713

For Convention Info: PO Box 9181, Charlotte NC 28299-9181 or 1-800-321-4370 (HERØ)

For The Latest Information About New Comics, Special Events, & Other Surprises, Call The HEROES HOTLINE!!!
Dial 704 372 4370 (HERØ) Around The Clock In Charlotte, After-Hours At The Regular Numbers Everywhere Else!!

OUR CARDS AND MARVEL COMICS WILL MAKE *YOUR* MOUTH WATER

OPEN EVERYDAY

MAIL ORDERS WELCOME

1107 CENTRAL PARK AVEUE (NEXT TO NBO)
SCARSDALE, NY 10583 (914) 725-2225

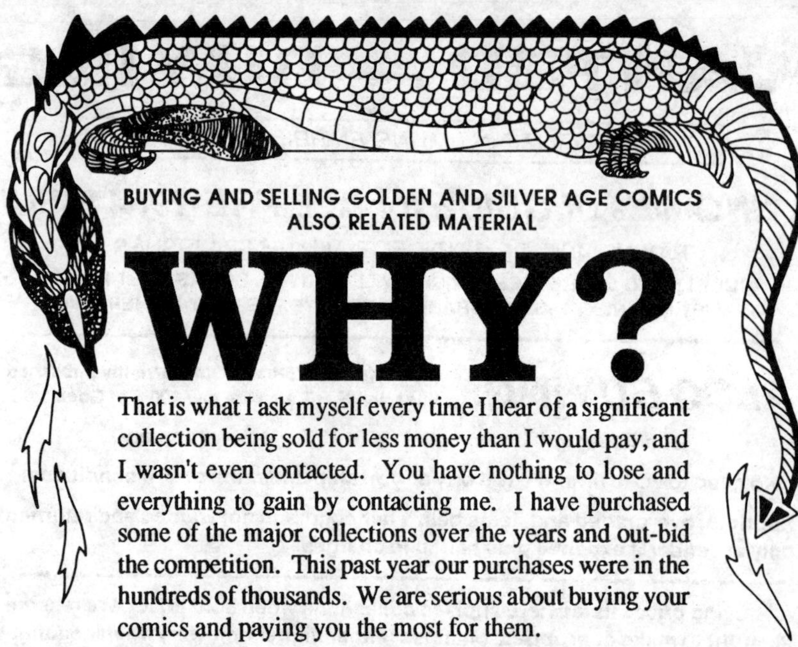

BUYING AND SELLING GOLDEN AND SILVER AGE COMICS
ALSO RELATED MATERIAL

WHY?

That is what I ask myself every time I hear of a significant collection being sold for less money than I would pay, and I wasn't even contacted. You have nothing to lose and everything to gain by contacting me. I have purchased some of the major collections over the years and out-bid the competition. This past year our purchases were in the hundreds of thousands. We are serious about buying your comics and paying you the most for them.

If you have comics or related items for sale please call or send a list for my quote. Or if you would like, just send me your comics and figure them by the percentages below. If your grading is by Overstreets standards you can expect the percentages paid by grade. Before I send any checks I will call to verify your satisfaction with the price. If we cannot reach a price we are both happy and I will ship your books back at my expense that day. Remember, no collection is too large or small, even if it's one hundred thousand or more.

These are some of the high prices I will pay for comics I need. Percentages stated will be paid for any grade unless otherwise stated. Percentages should be based on this guide.

– JAMES F. PAYETTE

Action (1-225)	70%
Action (#1 Mint)	95%
Adventure (247)	75%
All American (16 & 17)	75%
All Star (3 & 8)	70%
Amazing Man	70%
Amazing Mustery Funnies	70%
The Arrow	70%
Batman (1-125)	70%
Batman (#1 Mint)	85%
Bob Steele	70%
Captain Marvel (#1)	70%
Detective (1-225)	70%
Detective (#27 Mint)	80%
Green Lantern (#1 Mint)	85%
Jackie Gleason (1-12)	70%
Keen Detective Funnies	70%
Ken Maynard	70%
More Fun (7-51)	70%
New Adventure (12-31)	70%
New Comics (1-11)	70%
New Fun (1-6)	70%
Sunset Carson	70%
Superman (#1 Mint)	95%
Whip Wilson	70%

We are paying 65% of guide for the following:

Andy Devine
Congo Bill
Detective Eye
Detec. Picture Stories
Funny Pages
Funny Picture Stories
Green Lantern (1st)
Hangman
Hoot Gibson
Jumbo (1-10)
Smiley Burnette
Start & Stripes
Tales of the Unexpected
Tim McCoy
Wonder Comics (Fox-1&2)

We are paying 60% of guide for the following:

Adventure (32-267)
Adv. of Bob Hope (1-50)
Adv. of Jerry Lewis (1-50)
Adv. of Ozzie & Harriet
All American
All Flash
All New
All Top (8-18)
Blackhawk (9-110)
Blue Beetle (47-57)
Captain America (1st)
Flash (1st)
Hit (1-20)
House of Mystery (1-50)
House of Secrets (1-25)
Leading (1-14)
Legend of Dan'l Boone
Mary Marvel
Military
Movie Comics (D.C.)
My Greatest Adventure (1-50)
Mystery Men
National (1-23)
New Book of Comics
Phantom Stranger
Science (Fox)
Shadow (Fox)
Showcase (1-30)
Speed (1-20)
Superman (1-125)
Superman's Pal (1-30)

We are paying 55% of guide for the following:

Airboy
Air Fighters
All Select
All Star
All Winners
Amazing Spiderman (1-20)
America's Greatest
Blonde Phamtom
Brave & the Bold (1-30)
Brenda Starr (1-12)
Bulletman
Captain Marvel
Captain Marvel Jr.
Captain Midnight
Catman
Challengers of the Unknown (1-10)
Classics Comics (1st 1-20)
Comic Cavalcade (1-29)
Crash
Daredevil (1st 1-20)
Daring Mystery
Dollman
Fantastic
Fantastic Four (1-20)
Frontier Fighters
Green Hornet (1-20)
Human Torch
Ibis
John Wayne
JO-JO (7-29)
Journey into Mystery (1-85)
Jungle (1-10)
Kid Komics
Lash Larue (1-46)
Marvel Family
Marvel Mystery
Master
Miss Fury
Modern
More Fun (52-107)
Mystery In Space (1-90)
Mystic (1st)
Nickel
Pep (1-40)
Phamtom Lady
Planet
Pogo Possum
Police (1-20)
Rangers (1-20)
Rulah
Saint
Sensation
Shield Wizard
Silver Streak (1-17)
Smash
Spy Smasher
Star Spangled
Strange Adventure (1-120)
Strange Tales (1-100)
Sub-Mariner (1st)
Superboy (1-50)
Tomahawk (1-30)
Top-Notch
U.S.A.
W.D. Comics & Stories (1-40)
Weird Comics
Whiz
World's Finest (1-110)
Young Allies
Zip (1-39)
Zoot (7-16)

We are also paying 50-75% of guide for many other titles. Comics must be properly graded and complete. Please send your listing of comics for sale or your list of comics you wish to purchase. We are also dealing heavily in Sci-Fi material plus thousands of Marvels, D.C.'s Western, Funny Material and Much More! Please Send one dollar for our current retail listing of comics in stock. Will Travel for Large Collections or if you're passing through the area call for an appointment.

JAMES F. PAYETTE
RARE BOOKS AND COMICS
P.O. BOX 750, BETHLEHEM, NH 03574
(603) 869-2097

PACIFIC COMIC EXCHANGE, INC.

The Pacific Comic Exchange, Inc. (PCE) is the first computerized *"on-line"* comic book trading company specializing in Golden and Silver Age comics from 1933-1969. All comics listed on *"The Exchange"* have been graded and certified by the Comic Grading Service of America (CGSA), which has developed a new standardized numerical grading system that ensures an unprecedented degree of accuracy and consistency.

CGSA	M	NM/M	NM	VFN/NM	VFN	FN/VFN	FN	VG/FN	VG	G/VG	G	Fr	Pr
	100,99,98,97,96,95,94,93,92,91	90	88,85,80,75	70	65,60,55	50	45,40,35	30	25,20	15	10	6	3
PgQ	0 1 2 2.5	3	3.3 4	5	6	6.5	7	7.5	8	8.5	9	9.5	10

LIQUIDITY

- ❖ **PCE** is an international network of dealers, collectors, and retailers,
- ❖ Providing an excellent selection of Golden and Silver Age comics,
- ❖ Negotiable prices, prompt payment to Sellers.
- ❖ Sellers enjoy the lowest brokerage commissions (8% to 13%) in the industry.

CONFIDENCE AND PROTECTION

- ❖ **CGSA** certified books are guaranteed to be in stated condition.
- ❖ Full disclosure of any restoration, is certified by such respected experts as **Susan Ciccone** of **The Restoration Lab.**
- ❖ All books are uniquely identified and catalogued - Buyers and Sellers are protected from fraudulent substitution or damage.

ACCESS

- ❖ *"The Exchange"* is accessible via phone, computer or mail.
- ❖ Detailed monthly reports (available through subscription) of sales data, updated listings, special market analyses, etc., help Buyers and Sellers make informed decisions.
- ❖ Buyers have access to a large selection of Golden and Silver age comics at negotiable prices.

COMPREHENSIVE ON-LINE SERVICE

- ❖ All statistics available *"on-line"*: prices, market trends, grading, restoration information, etc.
- ❖ "Want Lists" link Sellers with interested Buyers.
- ❖ Buyers and Sellers can utilize extended "after hours" trading.

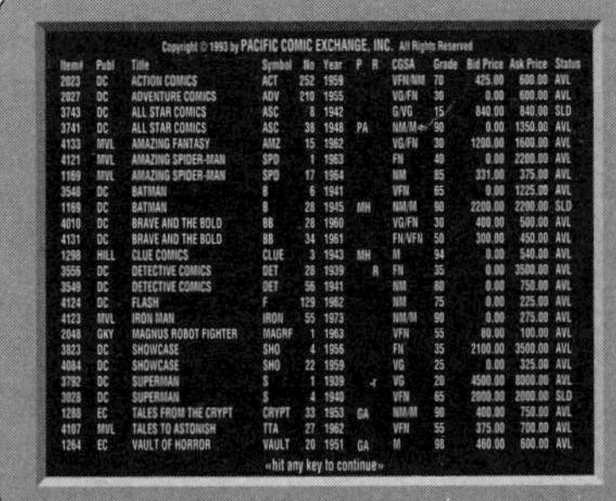

Copyright © 1993 by PACIFIC COMIC EXCHANGE, INC. All Rights Reserved

Item#	Publ	Title	Symbol	No	Year	P	R	CGSA	Grade	Bid Price	Ask Price	Status
2023	DC	ACTION COMICS	ACT	252	1959			VFN/NM	70	425.00	600.00	AVL
2027	DC	ADVENTURE COMICS	ADV	210	1955			VG/FN	30	0.00	600.00	AVL
3743	DC	ALL STAR COMICS	ASC	8	1942			G/VG	15	840.00	840.00	SLD
3741	DC	ALL STAR COMICS	ASC	38	1948	PA		NM/M	90	0.00	1350.00	AVL
4133	MVL	AMAZING FANTASY	AMZ	15	1962			VG/FN	30	1200.00	1600.00	AVL
4121	MVL	AMAZING SPIDER-MAN	SPD	1	1963			FN	40	0.00	2200.00	AVL
1169	MVL	AMAZING SPIDER-MAN	SPD	17	1964			NM	85	331.00	375.00	AVL
3548	DC	BATMAN	B	6	1941			VFN	65	0.00	1225.00	AVL
1169	DC	BATMAN	B	28	1945	MH		NM/M	90	2200.00	2200.00	SLD
4010	DC	BRAVE AND THE BOLD	BB	28	1960			VG/FN	30	400.00	500.00	AVL
4131	DC	BRAVE AND THE BOLD	BB	34	1961			FN/VFN	50	300.00	450.00	AVL
1298	HILL	CLUE COMICS	CLUE	3	1943	MH		M	94	0.00	540.00	AVL
3556	DC	DETECTIVE COMICS	DET	28	1939		R	FN	35	0.00	3500.00	AVL
3549	DC	DETECTIVE COMICS	DET	56	1941			NM	80	0.00	750.00	AVL
4124	DC	FLASH	F	129	1962			NM	75	0.00	225.00	AVL
4123	MVL	IRON MAN	IRON	55	1973			NM/M	90	0.00	275.00	AVL
2048	GKY	MAGNUS ROBOT FIGHTER	MAGRF	1	1963			VFN	55	80.00	100.00	AVL
3823	DC	SHOWCASE	SHO	4	1956			FN	35	2100.00	3500.00	AVL
4084	DC	SHOWCASE	SHO	22	1959			VG	25	0.00	325.00	AVL
3792	DC	SUPERMAN	S	1	1939			VG	20	4500.00	8000.00	AVL
3028	DC	SUPERMAN	S	4	1940			VFN	65	2000.00	2000.00	SLD
1288	EC	TALES FROM THE CRYPT	CRYPT	33	1953	GA		NM/M	90	400.00	750.00	AVL
4107	MVL	TALES TO ASTONISH	TTA	27	1962			VFN	55	375.00	700.00	AVL
1264	EC	VAULT OF HORROR	VAULT	20	1951	GA		M	98	460.00	600.00	AVL

«hit any key to continue»

TRADE WITH CONFIDENCE, TRADE WITH PCE

Call or write (include your telephone number) for more information about opening a free trading account, viewing a demonstration of the **PCE** *"on-line"* service, or selling comics on *"The Exchange."*

Meetings and consultations are arranged by appointment only.

Pacific Comic Exchange, Inc.
P.O. Box 34849 ❖ Los Angeles, CA ❖ 90034
Tel: (310) 836-PCEI Fax: (310) 836-7127 Modem: (310) 836-3076

DET27 25$29850 MFC52 15$3575 S1 20$7700 B1 15$5500 BB28 65$2750 SHO4 25$2300 AMZ15 40$2200

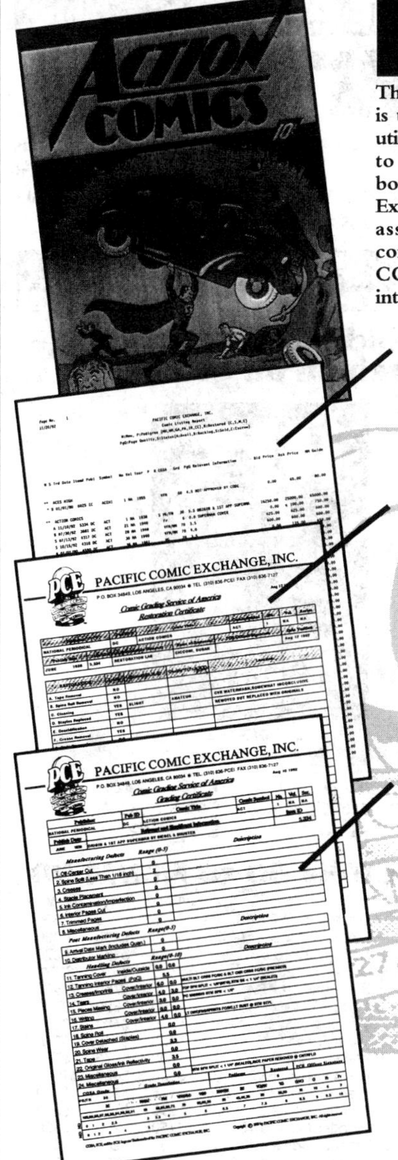

THE COMIC GRADING SERVICE OF AMERICA

The Comic Grading Service of America (CGSA) is the first professional comic grading service to utilize a revolutionary, scientific grading system to assure accurately and consistently graded books. All books listed on the Pacific Comic Exchange (PCE) are graded in this fashion and assure that your purchase is made with confidence and knowledge. Alternatively, the CGSA will certify your books or act as an intermediary between Buyer and Seller.

THE COMIC LISTING REPORT

❖ Every month **PCE** issues a report (available through subscription) about the comic books available for sale. Each book is listed with a grade (verified by **CGSA**), Bid and Ask prices, and other relevant information.

CGSA RESTORATION CERTIFICATE

❖ The **CGSA** in collaboration with **Susan Ciccone** of **The Restoration Lab**, requires all restored books undergo a complete evaluation before being listed on *"The Exchange."* This certificate records, in depth, any change or modification made to the book. This procedure insures that the buyer is informed of the "true" condition of the restored book and protected against fraud. This information is also available *"on-line"* or upon request to users of *"The Exchange."*

CGSA GRADING CERTIFICATE

❖ **PCE** prides itself for using the first ever 100 point scale grading system (provided by the **CGSA**). Each book is examined on a defect-by-defect basis with a description and numerical value assigned for every defect. These values are used to create an accurate assessment of the books condition.

❖ Each book is evaluated independently by a team of expert graders who use the 100 point system to arrive at a final grade. This ensures Buyer and Seller an objective and accurate final grade.

❖ The **CGSA** system is the "state of the art" in comic book grading. Grading is now a science and no longer an "eye of the beholder" art.

Pacific Comic Exchange, Inc.
P.O. Box 34849 ❖ Los Angeles, CA ❖ 90034
Tel: (310) 836-PCEI Fax: (310) 836-7127 Modem: (310) 836-3076

DET27 25$29850 MFC52 15$3575 S1 20$7700 B1 15$5500 BB28 65$2750 SH04 25$2300 AMZ15 40$2200

Title/Issue #	Good	V/Good	Fine	F/VF	V/Fine	VF/NM	N/Mint	NM/M	Mint
177-224,226-230,233,235	18	38	60	80	120	145	175	210	260
231,232,234,236-240	13	27	42	55	80	100	120	145	185
241-260	10	21	34	45	65	75	85	100	130
Fantastic Four 1	325	675	1050	1475	2200	2750	3300	4200	6000
2	85	170	285	370	550	675	800	1000	1300
3-5	60	125	215	275	420	510	600	750	950
6-10	34	68	110	145	210	250	300	380	475
11-20,25,26,48,ann.1	15	30	48	65	85	100	125	150	190
Flash 104,105	120	260	425	560	825	1000	1200	1700	2400
86-103,106	35	75	125	170	260	325	400	480	600
21-85,107-110,123	24	48	80	105	150	180	225	270	340
111-120,129,137	8	18	30	40	60	70	85	100	130
121,122,124-140	3	7	12	16	24	29	35	42	52
Green Lantern 1	90	180	300	400	600	725	900	1100	1400
1st series21-38,2nd series2	35	75	115	150	230	285	350	425	550
2nd series3-5, 40	10	21	33	45	65	80	100	115	150
Hulk 1	125	275	450	600	900	1100	1400	1700	2200
2	50	105	165	225	335	400	500	600	750
Hulk 3-6, Iron Man 1	24	50	85	115	175	200	240	270	340
Journey into Mystery 83	95	200	325	450	650	800	1000	1175	1500
84	25	52	80	110	170	205	260	315	400
85-89	10	22	34	45	65	80	100	115	150
Justice League 1	100	225	340	450	650	800	1000	1250	1600
2	33	68	110	150	225	275	350	420	525
3,4,9	16	34	55	75	115	140	175	210	260
5-8,10,21,22	11	23	37	50	75	90	115	135	170
Showcase 4	450	950	1500	2100	3200	3750	5000	6200	8000
8,22	125	275	400	550	850	1050	1400	1700	2200
6,13,14	75	165	250	340	525	650	800	950	1200
1,9,10,17,34	55	115	180	240	360	435	550	650	850
23,24	45	95	155	210	310	380	475	550	750
7,11,12,15	28	60	95	135	200	240	300	360	450
2-5,16-20,27,30,37,43	23	48	75	100	150	180	225	270	340
21,28,29,35,36	12	25	38	53	80	95	120	140	180
25,26,31-33,38-40	8	17	27	36	55	67	85	100	125
Strange Tales 101,110	30	63	100	135	200	240	300	360	450
102-105,111,114,115	9	19	30	40	60	72	90	110	140
Superman 51-95	15	31	49	66	100	118	150	175	220
96-120	9	19	30	40	60	75	95	110	135
121-140,146,147,149	5	11	18	24	36	44	55	65	80
Tales of Suspense 39	115	240	385	525	800	950	1200	1500	1900
40	53	110	170	230	350	420	525	635	800
1,41	27	57	90	120	180	220	275	340	425
Tales to Astonish 27	85	175	275	375	575	700	900	1150	1500
35	57	118	185	250	375	465	575	700	875
X-Men 1	100	220	350	485	750	900	1150	1400	1750
2	36	75	120	165	250	300	375	450	550
3,4	16	34	54	72	110	130	160	190	240
5-10,94	9	20	31	42	65	80	100	115	150

THE CAPITAL ADVANTAGE:™

1) Commitment to customer service. Every Capital City employee has customer service as their #1 priority. We work hard to make the everyday things easy, so you can spend your time running your business.

2) We don't sell retail. We don't sell mail order. We don't sell at conventions. We don't run a back issue service. We don't have a chain of retail stores. We don't compete with our customers for consumer dollars.

3) We have the largest product line. We offer over 2,100 items every month in *Advance Comics*,® our *inside-the-industry* source book.

4) We give you the information you need to make your business successful. Our publications, like *Advance Comics* and *New Weekly Releases*® give you the product knowledge you need, and *Internal Correspondence*® provides news and market reports that keep you on top of the comics business. We also have *Orderpak-On-Disk*,® customized to your computer system, and *The Capital City Bulletin Board System*, for retailers with a computer and a modem.

5) Commitment to backlist. Capital City has the deepest backlist of any comics distributor and the widest breadth of product selection. We also have *Reorder Confirmation* to let you know what backstock items(current and older titles) will be in your next shipment.

6) Investment in infrastructure. You're in this business for the long haul and so are we. That's why we built our state-of-the-art distribution center and our new corporate headquarters. We also have a huge fleet of trucks to keep our shipping costs low and our delivery speed high.

7) Comprehensive supply program. Our supply line, *Comic Defense System*,® is stocked in every one of our 19 locations. We support your sales of these products with heavy consumer advertising. And remember, these products are only available through our retailers. We don't sell them any other way!

8) CASH BACK! Every month every Capital City customer who stays within their terms gets a rebate check from Capital City. Not just on current orders, but <u>every</u> reorder and supply purchase is included, too!

GROUNDS FOR A CHANGE!™

Don't be afraid to compare.
Take the Capital City Coffee Challenge.

Send us your most recent monthly order form from any other distributor. We'll do a price comparison and show you exactly how much you'll be spending with them, and how much the same purchases would cost from us. We'll also compare other factors that affect your costs. All information you send us and the results of the comparison will be kept strictly confidential.

We'll send you a Capital City mug and gourmet coffee FREE, just for accepting the challenge! Brew yourself a fresh cup, on us, while you study the results!

That's it! If you want to know all your options, if you want to know whether you're getting the best deal — not to mention a fresh cup of coffee — then take the Capital City Coffee Challenge! No risks, no costs, and no way should you miss this opportunity to let us show you what we have to offer. Send your order form(which will be kept strictly confidential) to:

Capital City Coffee Challenge
P.O. Box 8156
Madison, WI 53708

If you'd like more information before sending your order form, call 608/223-2000 and ask for customer service.

Protect Your Investment with "Comic Defense System®"

Bag 'em™

Probags® are made of polypropylene, super-clear with superior preservation qualities. Probags® come in color-coded packages of 100. Available in four sizes.

Board 'em™

Comic Defense System® All-White Backer Boards are acid-free at the time of manufacture and will protect your comics and magazines from bends and folds. All-White Backer Boards come in color-coded packages. Available in four sizes.

Box 'em™

Comic Defense System® boxes are constructed with double-wall cardboard and double-wall lids for easy stacking. They are simple to assemble and require no tape. Handles are provided for easy moving. Available in long comic, regular comic, and magazine sizes.

Comic Defense System® products are available from your local comic store — ask for them by name!

Ball Four® Pages

Card protection you can depend on™

These new, 9-pocket pages are crystal clear, extremely strong, and archival safe. Made from virgin polypropylene, they feature solid double bar sealed front and back for added durability and a contoured design for easy page turning.

Capital™

Look for the colorful display box on the counter of a store near you.

Ask for Ball Four mylars and binders too.

Comic Books Wanted!

Before you sell, check me out!
Immediate Cash!
Will Travel to View Large Collections

I'm paying the following percentages, GUARANTEED!

(Based on Over Street Price Guide)

Title	%	Title	%
Action (1-280)	65	Human Torch	60
Adventure (1-260)	60	Jackie Gleason	75
All American (1-102)	65	John Wayne	70
All Flash	60	Journey into Mystery (1-110)	60
All Select	60	Jumbo	55
All Star	65	Justice League (1-30)	65
All Winners	60	Ken Maynard	65
Avengers (1-20)	60	Marvel Mystery	60
Batman (1-150)	65	Military	60
Blackhawk (9-110)	60	More Fun (1-107)	65
Brave and the Bold (1-44)	65	Mystery Men	55
Captain America	65	Planet	60
Captain Midnight	55	Shadow	65
Centaurs (All)	80	Showcase (1-43)	65
Comic Cavalcade (1-23)	60	Spiderman (1-30)	60
Daredevil (1-10)	60	Star Spangled (1-127)	55
Daring Mystery	65	Strange Tales (1-115)	60
Detective (1-280)	60	Submariner	60
Famous Funnies (1-60)	60	Superman (1-150)	60
Fantastic Four (1-30)	60	Tales of Suspense (1-50)	60
Fight	55	Tales to Astonish (1-40)	60
Flash (1-125)	65	Top Notch	55
Green Lantern (1-38, 1-20)	65	Wings	60
Hulk (1-6)	60	X-Men (1-20)	60

BUYING: Paying high prices, 50-80% for other DC, Timely, Fiction House, Fox, MLJ and Fawcetts. Books must be accurately graded and complete. Send for immediate payment or write.

SELLING: I Offer • Accurate Grading • Reasonable Prices • Large Selection • Satisfaction Guaranteed • Send for Latest List •

HARLEY YEE
P.O. Box 19578
Detroit, MI 48219-0578
Phone: (313) 533-2731

DOUG SULIPA'S

comic world

374 Donald St., Winnipeg, Manitoba Canada R3B 2J2
PH: (204) 943-3642

Over 1 MILLION comics in stock, 1950-1989. Send 50 cents for my catalogue of Marvels and DC's from 1960 to 1989. We have a large stock of Alternatives, Harvey, Dell, Gold Key, Mad, Archies, Disneys, Charlton, Playboys, Warren Mags, Digests, Star Trek, National Lampoon, Life Mags, etc.—Send WANT LIST. WE also specialize in rare paperbacks (SF, Mystery, Harlequin, TV, etc.)—Inquire. Send 50 cents for our huge Records catalogue (10,000 albums, all types 1950-1989).

FANTASY EXPRESS

NEW COMIC SUBSCRIPTIONS

20% OFF EVERYTHING TO ANYONE! 30% off if over $100.00 a month.

The most efficient, fast and progressive service with the best selection!!

THIRD PLANET

Comics • Books • Sci-Fi

2718 SOUTHWEST FREEWAY
HOUSTON, TX 77098
713-528-1067

THIRD PLANET is proud to announce the purchase of it's own building making us one of the worlds largest nostalgia shop with over 7600 square feet of space.

With over 1,000,000 comics, 50,000 45 records, 10,000 movie posters, 800 different models, 1,000's of comic and sci-fi related posters, a complete art gallery of limited edition art prints by some of the greatest artist around (Olivia, Canty, Adams, Smith, etc.) as well as custom framing and matting, giant video tape room with all Japamation tapes in stock, a large selection of the finest sci-fi pewter and porcelain, Dr. Who, Star Trek and Star Wars selections of large proportions and a mail order service available as well as many other fine products very few stores can compare to.

THIRD PLANET also wholesales to full time professional dealers.

So deal with the people who have over 17 years experience in the business and know how to fill your every need. If we do not have it and can not get it for you we will travel to the far reaches of the galaxy to get it anyway.

CA$H for Vintage Comic Books

Buy • Sell

Gold & Silver Age Specialist
1933-1965

I will buy entire
collections, or
individual pieces.
Immediate CASH.

I have an extensive
Free Catalogue
with many
hard to find
Pre-1965 Comics
for sale.

Experienced Professional Service

For a Quick Reply
Call or fax
1-608-277-8750
or write:

Jef Hinds
P.O. Box 44803 • Madison, WI 53744-4803

ORIGINAL ROCK ART • TOYS • ROCK POSTERS

2801 LEAVENWORTH ST · SAN FRANCISCO · 94133 · TEL (415) 771-9247 · FAX (415) 771-8047

1-800-775-1966

HANDBILLS • COLLECTIBLES • COMICS

ROCK ARTIST'S WORK RETURNS TO THE CANNERY

San Francisco --After a year long probate battle, the original art from the late Rick Griffin, one of the innovators of 60's and 70's rock poster art, has been released, and will be available for view and sale at Best Comics and Rock Art Gallery, Ltd., located at The Cannery, the historic renovated former peach factory. Original works by Mr. Griffin featured, will include, full color Grateful Dead oil paintings, surf art of the early sixties, psychedelic art, pen and ink works, and comic art for Zap Comics.

Rick Griffin's art remains highly regarded by the public and his contemporaries alike. As Ron Turner, publisher of Zap Comics, has said, "His art went well beyond the psychedelic era. He was a serious surrealist...a visionary who was able to share that vision with the rest of us." Fellow poster/album cover artist Stanley Mouse, who recently saw a fine retrospective of his own career published, said, "Out of all my contemporaries, Rick was the one I looked up to the most. Losing Rick was a national, if not worldwide, loss. Rick was a national treasure." Victor Moscoso, another of Rick Griffin's contemporaries had this to say, "It's the passing of a master. Rick's place in history is coming up fast."

Best Comics & Rock Art Gallery Ltd. opened its doors in early 1991 as a showcase for the finest of San Francisco's rock art graphic artists.

Best Comics & Rock Art Gallery Ltd. open: Monday thru Saturday 10 AM - 6 PM Sunday 11 AM - 6 PM. 415-771-9247. The Cannery, 2801 Leavenworth, S.F. 94133

Jim Hanley's
UNIVERSE

PHILIP WEISS AUCTIONS

Four mail phone auctions yearly.

Comics, pulps, original comic art, animation art, non-sports cards, Disneyana, toys, Big Little books, science fiction books and all related items.

Don't settle for less!

Auction your collections for competitive top prices at competitive rates. Prompt service and payment. Professional grading. Items purchased outright as well. Call for more information. Fully illustrated catalogues $8.00 each. Yearly subscription $30.00. Canada $10 & $36. Foreign $12 & $40.

PHILIP WEISS AUCTIONS
P. O. Box 278
East Rockaway, NY 11518-0278
(516) 594-0731 FAX: (516) 594-9414

THERE'S SOMETHING NEW IN THE AIR. . .

OVER 500 NEW ISSUE TITLES – MARVEL, DC, INDEPENDENTS ★ HUGE SELECTION GOLDEN AGE AND SILVER AGE ★ GRAPHIC NOVELS ★ BASEBALL CARDS ★ ROLE-PLAYING GAMES ★ JAPANESE ANIMATION ★ POSTERS ★ T-SHIRTS ★ STAR TREK MEMORABILIA ★ COLLECTING SUPPLIES ★ CATALOGS AVAILABLE ($1.00)

ALL THIS AND SKATEBOARDS TOO!

OPEN 7 DAYS

MON-SAT 11:00am-7:00pm SUN 11:00am-6:00pm

SILVER CITY COMICS

4671 TORRANCE BOULEVARD
TORRANCE, CA 90503
(310) 542-8034
CORNER OF TORRANCE AND ANZA

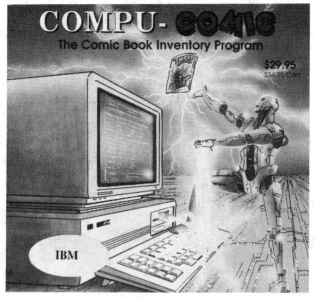

JUST KIDS NOSTALGIA

326 MAIN STREET
HUNTINGTON, NY 11743
(516) 423-8449

SALES AND AUCTIONS

326 MAIN STREET, HUNTINGTON, NY 11743 • (516) 423-8449 • FAX (516) 423-4326

VISIT OUR STORE

ALWAYS BUYING

DON'T MISS OUT! SEND $4.00 FOR COMPLETE CATALOG

- CHARACTER WATCHES
- RADIO PREMIUMS
- COWBOYS (LONE RANGER-HOPPY-ROY
- ADVERTISING
- ORIGINAL COMIC ART
- ROCK & ROLL
- TV GUIDES
- TONS OF 50'S & 60'S TV
- TOYS-TOYS-MORE TOYS
- MOVIE POSTERS & CELEBRITY ITEMS
- SCI-FI & MONSTER MATERIAL
- CEREAL BOXES & PRIZES
- SUPER HEROES
- BASEBALL/SPORTS
- LOTS OF INTERESTING CARTOON CHARACTER ITEMS
- EARLY DISNEY-WARNER BROS.
- FLINTSTONES, ETC.
- DOLLS/ACTION FIGURES
- PLAYSETS

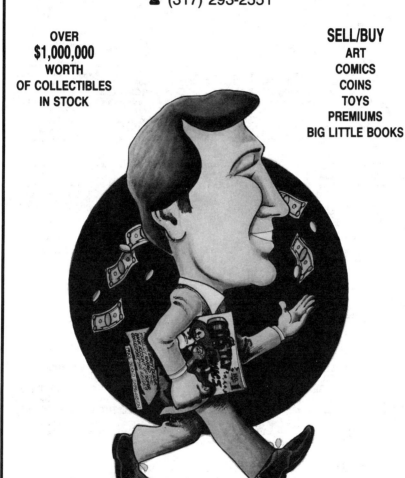

A BRIEF HISTORICAL NOTE ABOUT "COMIC HEAVEN"

John Verzyl started collecting comic books in 1965, and within ten years, he had amassed thousands of Golden and Silver Age comic books. In 1979, with his wife Nanette, he opened "COMIC HEAVEN", a retail store devoted entirely to the buying and selling of comic books.

Over the years, John Verzyl has come to be recognized as an authority in the field of comic books,. He has served as an advisor to the "Overstreet Price Guide". Thousands of his "mint" comics were photographed for Ernst Gerbers newly-released "Photo-Journal Guide To Comic Books". His tables and displays at the annual San Diego Comic Convention draw customers from all over the country.

The first COMIC HEAVEN AUCTION was held in 1987, and today his Auction Catalogs are mailed out to more then ten thousand interested collectors (and dealers).

Gary K. Wolf, Harvard, MA (Author and creator of Roger Rabbit Characters)
"Your Photo - Journal Guide to Comic Books is one of the best pieces of research material I've ever encountered. I shudder to think of the work that must have gone into it."

Robert Rentzer, Encino, CA, Attorney
"A lawyer should not be at a loss for words but I find myself unable to adequately describe the task you set for yourself and your having accomplished it so magnificently...your book occupies an important place in my den and an even more important place in my heart..."

Malcolm Willits, Owner, Collectors Book Store - Hollywood, CA
"I will admit your Photo - Journal is the greatest undertaking in comic book history, and will probably remain so for the end of time..."

Richard Wokurka, St. Louis, MO
It is difficult to tell you how very much impressed I am with your book...Not only is the workmanship 1st class, and the colors so vibrant, but the way you authored the text makes for enjoyable and informative reading."

Joseph B. Lambert, Professor - Evanston, IL
I just received Volume I and it is a work of art. I have just begun to tap the potential of the contents. It will provide me with many enjoyable hours, not to mention its reference value...

John Stanley, Editor - Publisher, Pacifica, CA
"Just last week I purchased a copy of The Photo - Journal Guide and must confess it is the most overwhelming publication ever about comic books."

Michael Law - Indianapolis, IN
I have to admit, at times I was skeptical that such an ambitious project could be carried out. Such skepticism is not unusual in a world where vision, passion and sharing have been replaced by profit as the seed of such ventures. Your Photo - Journal is a labor of love, it is a product of your vision, your passion, and your desire to share with others something beautiful you have found in the world. I look at my Photo - Journal Guide every day. Thank you for sharing your dream and creating a rare and beautiful thing.

" THE MOST IMPORTANT BOOKS EVER PUBLISHED ABOUT COMICS! "

CBG Customer Service Award - 1992

(Distributed by Diamond Comics) (Published by Gerber Publishing Co., Inc.)

NOW AT AFFORDABLE PRICES !

THE PHOTO - JOURNAL GUIDE TO COMICS, Volumes 1 thru 4

	PER BOOK PRICES NEW WAS	NEW IS NOW	BLEMISHED COPIES
Vol. 1 and 2 22,000 Photos of Rare comics, 1933 - 1963 Plus loads of reference information, including Scarcity Index.	$75.00 ea.	$47.00 ea.	$29.00 ea.
Vol. 3 and 4 8,000 Photos of all Marvel Comics, 1961 -1990 A MUST reference tool for Marvel Collectors	$30.00 ea.	$24.50 ea.	$15.00 ea.
Deluxe Vol 3 & 4 Set	$130.00 set	$89.00 set	$54.00 set

★ Blemished Copies. These are like new, except previously opened or slightly blemished. Return guarantee, if not satisfied with condition. (Shipping charges not refunded)

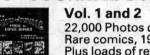

Add $4.00 per volume, shipping/handling charges

Send Check, Money Order, or order with VISA, MasterCard to:

GERBER PUBLISHING CO., INC.

P.O. Box 906, Minden, NV 89423 • Ph. 702-883-4100

Grover De Luca, Manager, Oxford Too Books, Atlanta, GA
"Having just seen and perused your book, I am so overwhelmed by it that I had to stop and tell you that it is one of the most wonderful books I've ever seen, and I've seen plenty-...How you plan to make a dime on so lavish a production at so low a price is beyond me, but I hope you do!"

Leonard Rifas, Owner, EduComics, Seattle, WA
"The Photo - Journal is a great boon to comic book researchers. I found useful information for my master's thesis on cold war comics in just a few minutes with your guide that I had not discovered in days of research at the best library collections in the country...it's a beautifully done book. I want libraries especially to know that this is a marvelous reference tool which is also a delight for casual browsers."

James Payette, Rare Books & Comics - Bethlehem, NH
There are books published in many collectible fields, and few are milestones. The Photo - Journal Guide is one of these rare milestone books. This book will change the way we view and are viewed as a collectible field. This book is a must, and will always come highly recommended. To sum up the Photo - Journal, it is not just a book, it is a publishing event.

Frank Nuessel, Professor, University of Louisville, KY
"At first I wasn't sure that I wanted to spend that much on a book. Now, however, I know that my money was well spent. You have done an excellent job and you really know comics. Thanks for this important contribution to the field."

Richard Gray, Enfield, NH, Editor "Current Comics"
"Until you see it, this book is unbelievable. After you se it, it is still unbelievable! OH WOW! describes it very nicley."

Donald Berhent, Willowick, OH
"The deluxe limited edition is the finest book on comics not only in content, but in quality of materials used...I have purchased many so - called Collector's Limited Editions, but yours truly lives up to its title."

William Harroff, Roxana, IL
I was really surprised at the quality of the work. The color was superb, as was the overall condition of the covers. It truly is one of the most beautiful books I possess in a sizable collection. Librarians and collectors who miss this reference work will be kicking themselves for years.

Don Wilmoth, Author, Stanton, CA
Recieved by Photo - Journal and I'm delighted. What a book! Looking at it, I still am saying to myself, there is no way this can be done. Truly a work of art. My hat's off to you.

Steve Geppi, Diamond Distributors - Baltimore, MD
Dear Ernie, Thanks for publishing the best book ever in the history of comic book collecting. I am particularly excited about your book since I had often noted in the past how the comic industry could use such a book but doubted that it would ever become a reality, and now it is!!!

Donald R. Petterson, Essex Junction, VT
"May I say, as a 60-year-old enthusiast, that many of the comics illustrated I read as a youngster. It is enjoyable to relive memories when viewing covers of comics way back. This Photo - Journal is Excellent in every way. Bravo for a job well done."

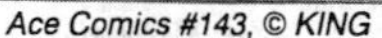
Ace Comics #143, © KING

Abbie & Slats #3, © UFS

Action Comics #1, © DC

	GD25	FN65	NM94

The correct title listing for each comic book can be determined by consulting the indicia (publication data) on the beginning interior pages of the comic. The official title is determined by those words of the title in capital letters only, and not by what is on the cover.

Titles are listed in this book as if they were one word, ignoring spaces hyphens, and apostrophes, to make finding titles easier.

Comic publishers are invited to send us sample copies for possible inclusion in future guides.

Near Mint is the highest value listed in this price guide. True mint books from the 1970s and 1980s do exist, so the Near Mint value listed should be interpreted as a Mint value for those books.

A-1 (See A-One)

ABBIE AN' SLATS (...With Becky No. 1-4) (See Comics On Parade, Fight for Love, Giant Comics Edition 2, Sparkler Comics, Tip Topper, Treasury of Comics, & United Comics)
1940; March, 1948 - No. 4, Aug, 1948 (Reprints)
United Features Syndicate

	GD25	FN65	NM94
Single Series 25 ('40)	23.00	70.00	160.00
Single Series 28	20.00	60.00	140.00
1 (1948)	11.00	32.00	75.00
2-4: 3-r/Sparkler #68-72	5.85	17.50	35.00

ABBOTT AND COSTELLO (...Comics)(See Treasury of Comics)
Feb, 1948 - No. 40, Sept, 1956 (Mort Drucker art in most issues)
St. John Publishing Co.

	GD25	FN65	NM94
1	30.00	90.00	210.00
2	14.00	43.00	100.00
3-9 (#8, 8/49; #9, 2/50)	10.00	30.00	60.00
10-Son of Sinbad story by Kubert (new)	13.00	40.00	90.00
11,13-20 (#11, 10/50; #13, 8/51; #15, 12/52)	6.35	19.00	38.00
12-Movie issue	8.35	25.00	50.00
21-30: 28-r/#8. 30-Painted-c	5.35	16.00	32.00
31-40: 33,38-Reprints	4.35	13.00	26.00
3-D #1 (11/53)-Infinity-c	23.00	70.00	160.00

ABBOTT AND COSTELLO (TV)
Feb, 1968 - No. 22, Aug, 1971 (Hanna-Barbera)
Charlton Comics

	GD25	FN65	NM94
1	4.35	13.00	26.00
2-10	2.40	6.00	12.00
11-22	1.60	4.00	8.00

ABC (See America's Best TV Comics)

ABRAHAM LINCOLN LIFE STORY (See Dell Giants)

ABSENT-MINDED PROFESSOR, THE (See 4-Color Comics No.1199)

ABYSS, THE (Dark Horse)(Value: cover or less)

ACE COMICS
April, 1937 - No. 151, Oct-Nov, 1949
David McKay Publications

	GD25	FN65	NM94
1-Jungle Jim by Alex Raymond, Blondie, Ripley's Believe It Or Not, Krazy Kat begin	200.00	600.00	1200.00
2	67.00	200.00	400.00
3-5	47.00	142.00	285.00
6-10	35.00	105.00	210.00
11-The Phantom begins(in brown costume, 2/38)	44.00	132.00	265.00
12-20	27.00	80.00	160.00
21-25,27-30	22.00	68.00	135.00
26-Origin Prince Valiant (begins series?)	61.00	182.00	365.00
31-40: 37-Krazy Kat ends	16.00	48.00	95.00
41-60	13.00	40.00	80.00
61-64,66-76-(7/43; last 68 pgs.)	12.00	35.00	70.00
65-(8/42)-Flag-c	12.50	38.00	75.00
77-84 (3/44; all 60 pgs.)	10.00	30.00	60.00
85-99 (52 pgs.)	8.00	24.00	48.00
100 (7/45; last 52 pgs.)	9.15	27.50	55.00
101-134: 128-(11/47)-Brick Bradford begins. 134-Last Prince Valiant (all 36 pgs.)	6.70	20.00	40.00
135-151: 135-(6/48)-Lone Ranger begins	5.35	16.00	32.00

ACE KELLY (See Tops Comics & Tops In Humor)

ACE KING (See Adventures of the Detective)

ACES (Eclipse)(Value: cover or less)

ACES HIGH
Mar-Apr, 1955 - No. 5, Nov-Dec, 1955
E.C. Comics

	GD25	FN65	NM94
1-Not approved by code	12.00	36.00	85.00
2	10.00	30.00	60.00
3-5	8.35	25.00	50.00

NOTE: *All have stories by* ***Davis, Evans, Krigstein,*** *and* ***Wood; Evans*** *c-1-5.*

ACTION ADVENTURE (War) (Formerly Real Adventure)
V1#2, June, 1955 - No. 4, Oct, 1955
Gillmor Magazines

	GD25	FN65	NM94
V1#2-4	2.80	7.00	14.00

ACTION COMICS (...Weekly #601-642; also see The Comics Magazine #1, More Fun #14-17 & Special Edition)
6/38 - No. 583, 9/86; No. 584, 1/87 - Present
National Periodical Publ./Detective Comics/DC Comics

	GD25	FN65	VF82	NM94
1-Origin & 1st app. Superman by Siegel & Shuster, Marco Polo, Tex Thompson, Pep Morgan, Chuck Dawson & Scoop Scanlon; 1st app. Zatara & Lois Lane; Superman story missing 4 pgs. which were included when reprinted in Superman #1; Clark Kent works for Daily Star; story continued in #2	8,335.00	25,000.00	50,000.00	75,000.00

(Estimated up to 75+ total copies exist, 4 in NM/Mint)
(Issues 1 through 10 are all scarce to rare)

1-Reprint, Oversize 13½"x10." **WARNING:** This comic is an exact reprint of the original except for its size. DC published it in 1974 with a second cover titling it as a Famous First Edition. There have been many reported cases of the outer cover being removed and the interior sold as the original edition. The reprint with the new outer cover removed is practically worthless.

	GD25	FN65	NM94
1(1976,1983)-Giveaway; paper cover, 16pgs. in color; reprints complete Superman story from #1 ('38)	2.40	6.00	12.00
1(1987 Nestle Quik giveaway; 1988, 50 cent-c)		.25	.50
2	935.00	2800.00	5600.00
3 (Scarce)-Superman apps. in costume in only one panel	750.00	2250.00	4600.00
4-6: 6-1st Jimmy Olsen (called office boy)	500.00	1500.00	3000.00
7-Superman cover	700.00	2100.00	4200.00
8,9	435.00	1300.00	2600.00
10-Superman cover	635.00	1900.00	3800.00
11,12,14: 14-Clip Carson begins, ends #41	235.00	700.00	1400.00
13-Superman cover; last Scoop Scanlon	370.00	1100.00	2200.00
15-Superman cover	317.00	950.00	1900.00
16	167.00	500.00	1000.00
17-Superman cover; last Marco Polo	260.00	775.00	1550.00
18-Origin 3 Aces; 1st X-Ray Vision?	167.00	500.00	1000.00
19-Superman covers begin	235.00	700.00	1400.00
20-'S' left off Superman's chest; Clark Kent works at 'Daily Star'	217.00	650.00	1300.00
21,22,24,25: 24-Kent at Daily Planet. 25-Last app. Gargantua T. Potts, Tex Thompson's sidekick	135.00	400.00	800.00

23-1st app. Luthor (w/red hair) & Black Pirate; Black Pirate by Moldoff; 1st

	GD25	FN65	NM94
mention of The Daily Planet (4/40)	200.00	600.00	1200.00
26-30	108.00	325.00	650.00
31,32: 32-Intro/1st app. Krypto Ray Gun in Superman story by Burnley	83.00	250.00	500.00
33-Origin Mr. America	100.00	300.00	600.00
34-40: 37-Origin Congo Bill. 40-Intro/1st app. Star Spangled Kid & Stripesy	83.00	250.00	500.00
41	75.00	225.00	450.00
42-1st app./origin Vigilante; Bob Daley becomes Fat Man; origin Mr. America's magic flying carpet; The Queen Bee & Luthor app; Black Pirate ends; not in #41	110.00	335.00	665.00
43-46,48-50: 44-Fat Man's i.d. revealed to Mr. America. 45-1st app. Stuff (Vigilante's oriental sidekick)	75.00	225.00	450.00
47-1st Luthor cover in comics (4/42)	92.00	275.00	550.00
51-1st app. The Prankster	75.00	225.00	450.00
52-Fat Man & Mr. America become the Ameri-commandos; origin Vigilante retold	79.00	240.00	475.00
53-60: 56-Last Fat Man. 59-Kubert Vigilante begins?, ends #70. 60-First app. Lois Lane as Superwoman	54.00	165.00	325.00
61-63,65-70: 63-Last 3 Aces	47.00	140.00	280.00
64-Intro Toyman	57.00	170.00	340.00
71-79: 74-Last Mr. America	44.00	135.00	265.00
80-2nd app. & 1st Mr. Mxyztplk-c (1/45)	70.00	210.00	420.00
81-90: 83-Intro Hocus & Pocus	44.00	135.00	265.00
91-99: 93-XMas-c. 99-1st small logo (7/46)	41.00	125.00	245.00
100	92.00	275.00	550.00
101-Nuclear explosion-c	54.00	165.00	325.00
102-120: 105,117-X-Mas-c	39.00	118.00	235.00
121-126,128-140: 135,136,138-Zatara by Kubert	37.00	112.00	225.00
127-Vigilante by Kubert; Tommy Tomorrow begins	47.00	145.00	285.00
141-157,159-161: 151-Luthor/Mr. Mxyztplk/Prankster team-up. 156-Lois Lane as Super Woman. 160- Last 52 pgs.	37.00	110.00	225.00
158-Origin Superman retold	67.00	200.00	400.00
162-180: 168,176-Used in **POP**, pg. 90	29.00	90.00	175.00
181-201: 191-Intro. Janu in Congo Bill. 198-Last Vigilante. 201-Last pre-code issue	29.00	90.00	175.00
202-220	22.00	65.00	150.00
221-240: 224-1st Golden Gorilla story	17.00	52.00	120.00
241,243-251: 241-Batman x-over. 248-Congo Bill becomes Congorilla. 251-Last Tommy Tomorrow	13.00	40.00	90.00
242-Origin & 1st app. Brainiac (7/58); 1st mention of Shrunken City of Kandor	93.00	280.00	650.00
252-Origin & 1st app. Supergirl (5/59); Re-intro Metallo (his 2nd app. since Superboy #49)	107.00	320.00	750.00
253-2nd app. Supergirl	22.00	65.00	150.00
254-1st meeting of Bizarro & Superman-c/story	19.00	58.00	135.00
255-1st Bizarro Lois Lane-c/story & both Bizarros leave Earth to make Bizarro World	13.00	40.00	90.00
256-261: 259-Red Kryptonite used. 261-1st X-Kryptonite which gave Streaky his powers; last Congorilla in Action; origin & 1st app. Streaky The Super Cat	10.00	30.00	60.00
262,264-266,268-270	7.50	22.50	45.00
263-Origin Bizarro World	10.00	30.00	65.00
267(8/60)-3rd Legion app; 1st app. Chameleon Boy, Colossal Boy, & Invisible Kid	39.00	120.00	275.00
271-275,277-282: Last 10 cent issue	6.70	20.00	40.00
276(5/61)-6th Legion app; 1st app. Brainiac 5, Phantom Girl, Triplicate Girl, Bouncing Boy, Sun Boy, & Shrinking Violet; Supergirl joins Legion	17.00	52.00	120.00
283(12/61)-Legion of Super-Villains app.	8.35	25.00	50.00
284(1/62)-Mon-el app.	8.35	25.00	50.00
285(2/62)-12th Legion app; Brainiac 5 cameo; Supergirl's existence revealed to world	8.35	25.00	50.00
286(3/62)-Legion of Super Villains app.	4.35	13.00	26.00
287(4/62)-14th Legion app.(cameo)	4.35	13.00	26.00

	GD25	FN65	NM94
288-Mon-el app.; r-origin Supergirl	4.35	13.00	26.00
289(6/62)-16th Legion app.(Adult); Lightning Man & Saturn Woman's marriage 1st revealed	4.35	13.00	26.00
290(7/62)-17th Legion app; Phantom Girl app.	4.35	13.00	26.00
291,292,294-299: 290-1st Supergirl emergency squad. 291-1st meeting Supergirl & Mr. Mxyzptlk. 292-2nd app. Superhorse (see Adv. #293). 297-Mon-el app; 298-Legion app.	3.60	9.00	18.00
293-Origin Comet(Superhorse)	6.35	19.00	38.00
300-(5/63)	4.00	10.00	20.00
301-303,305-308,310-320: 306-Brainiac 5, Mon-el app. 307-Saturn Girl app. 314-r-origin Supergirl; J.L.A. x-over. 317-Death of Nor-Kan of Kandor. 319-Shrinking Violet app.	2.40	6.00	12.00
304-Origin & 1st app. Black Flame	3.00	7.50	15.00
309-Legion app.; Batman & Robin-c & cameo	2.80	7.00	14.00
321-333,335-340: 336-Origin Akvar(Flamebird). 340-Origin, 1st app. Parasite	1.80	4.50	9.00
334-Giant G-20; origin Supergirl, Streaky, Superhorse & Legion (all-r)	3.20	8.00	16.00
341-346,348-359: 344-Batman x-over. 350-Batman, Green Arrow & Green Lantern app. in Supergirl back-up story	1.30	3.25	6.50
347,360-Giant Supergirl G-33,G-45; 347-Origin Comet-r plus 3 Bizarro stories. 360-Legion-r; r/origin Supergirl	2.00	5.00	10.00
361-372,374-380: 365-Legion app. 370-New facts about Superman's origin. 376-Last Supergirl in Action. 377-Legion begins	1.00	2.50	5.00
373-Giant Supergirl G-57; Legion-r	1.60	4.00	8.00
381-402: 392-Last Legion in Action. Saturn Girl gets new costume. 393-402-All Superman issues	.80	2.00	4.00
403-413: All 52pg. issues; 411-Origin Eclipso-(r). 413- Metamorpho begins, ends #418	.80	2.00	4.00
414-424: 419-Intro. Human Target. 421-Intro Capt. Strong; Green Arrow begins. 422,423-Origin Human Target	.80	2.00	4.00
425-Neal Adams-a(p); The Atom begins	1.20	3.00	6.00
426-436,438,439: 432-1st S.A. app. The Toyman	.60	1.50	3.00
437,443-100 pg. giants	1.00	2.50	5.00
440-1st Grell-a on Green Arrow	1.20	3.00	6.00
441-Grell-a on Green Arrow continues	1.00	2.50	5.00
442,444-499: 454-Last Atom. 458-Last Green Arrow. 484-Earth II Superman & Lois Lane wed. 487,488-(44pgs.). 487-1st app. Microwave Man; origin Atom retold	.50	1.25	2.50
500-($1.00, 68 pgs.)-Infinity-c; Superman life story; shows Legion statues in museum	.40	1.00	2.00
501-551,554-582: 511-514-Airwave II solo stories. 513-The Atom begins. 517 Aquaman begins; ends #541. 521-1st app. The Vixen. 532,536-New Teen Titans cameo. 535,536- Omega Men app. 544- (Mando paper, 68 pgs.)-Origins new Luthor & Brainiac; Omega Men cameo. 546-J.L.A., New Teen Titans app. 551-Starfire becomes Red-Star	.30	.75	1.50
552,553-Animal Man-c & app. (2/84 & 3/84)	1.20	3.00	6.00
583-Alan Moore scripts	1.40	3.50	7.00
584-Byrne-a begins; New Teen Titans app.	.30	.75	1.50
585-599: 586-Legends x-over. 596-Millennium x-over. 598-1st app. Checkmate		.50	1.00
600-($2.50, 84 pgs., 5/88)	.80	2.00	4.00
601-642-Weekly issues ($1.50, 52 pgs.): 601-Re-intro The Secret Six. 611-614: Catwoman stories (new costume in #611). 613-618: Nightwing stories	.30	.75	1.50
643-Superman & monthly issues begin again; Perez- c/a/scripts begin; swipes cover to Superman #1	.30	.75	1.50
644-649,651-661,663-666,668-679: 654-Part 3 of Batman storyline. 655-Free extra 8 pgs. 660-Death of Lex Luthor. 661-Begin $1.00-c. 674-Supergirl logo & c/story (reintro). 675-Deathstroke cameo. 679-Last $1.00 issue		.50	1.00
650-($1.50, 52 pgs.)-Lobo cameo (last panel)	.30	.75	1.50
662-Clark Kent reveals i.d. to Lois Lane; story continued in Superman #53	.50	1.25	2.50
667-($1.75, 52 pgs.)	.35	.90	1.75
680-682		.60	1.25

Action Comics #17, © DC

Action Comics #50, © DC

Action Comics #351, © DC

Action Comics #662, © DC

Adam-12 #10, © Adam-12 Productions

Adventure Comics #46, © DC

	GD25	FN65	NM94
683-Doomsday cameo	.60	1.50	3.00
683-2nd printing		.60	1.25
684-Doomsday battle issue	.80	2.00	4.00
685,686-Funeral for a Friend issues	.40	1.00	2.00
685-2nd & 3rd printings		.60	1.25
Annual 1(1987)-Art Adams-c/a(p)	1.20	3.00	6.00
Annual 2(1989, $1.75, 68 pgs.)-Perez-c/a(i)	.40	1.00	2.00
Annual 3('91, $2.00, 68 pgs.)-Armageddon 2001	.40	1.00	2.00
Annual 4('92, $2.50, 68 pgs.)-Eclipso vs. Shazam	.50	1.25	2.50
Theater Giveaway (1947, 32 pgs., 6 1/2 x 8 1/4", nn)- Vigilante story based on Vigilante Columbia serial; no Superman-c or story	64.00	192.00	450.00

NOTE: ***Supergirl's*** *origin in 262, 280, 285, 291, 305, 309.* ***N. Adams*** *c-356, 358, 359, 361-364, 366, 367, 370-374, 377-379i, 398-400, 402, 404-406, 419p, 466, 468, 473i, 485.* ***Austin*** *c/a-682i.* ***Baily*** *a-24, 25.* ***Burnley*** *a-28-33; c-48?, 53-55, 58, 59?, 60-63, 65, 66p, 67p, 70p, 71p, 79p, 82p, 84-86p, 90-92p, 93p?, 94p, 107p, 108p.* ***Byrne*** *a-584-598p, 599i, 600p; c-596-600.* ***Giffen*** *a-560, 563, 565, 577, 579; c-539, 560, 563, 565, 577, 579.* ***Grell*** *a-440-442, 444-446, 450-452, 456-458; c-456.* ***Guardineer*** *a-24, 25; c-8, 11, 12, 14-16, 18. 25.* ***Guice*** *a(p)-677-681, 683; c-683.* ***Bob Kane's*** *Clip Carson-14-41.* ***Gil Kane*** *a-443r, 493r, 539-541, 544-546, 551-554, 601-605; c-535p, 540, 541, 544p, 545-549, 551-554.* ***Meskin*** *a-42-121(most).* ***Moldoff*** *a-23-25, 443r.* ***Mooney*** *a-667p.* ***Mortimer*** *c-153, 154, 159-172, 174, 178-181, 184, 186-189, 191-193, 196, 200, 206.* ***Perez*** *a-600i, 643-652p; c-529p, 643-651.* ***Fred Ray*** *c-34, 36-46, 50, 52.* ***Siegel & Shuster*** *a-1-27.* ***Starlin*** *a-509.* ***Leonard Starr*** *a-597i(part).* ***Staton*** *a-525p, 526p, 531p, 535p, 536p.* ***Toth*** *a-406, 407, 413, 431.* ***Tuska*** *a-486p, 550.* ***Williamson*** *a-568i.*

ACTION FORCE (Marvel) (Value: cover or less)

ACTUAL CONFESSIONS (Formerly Love Adventures)
No. 13, October, 1952 - No. 14, December, 1952
Atlas Comics (MPI)

	GD25	FN65	NM94
13,14	2.80	7.00	14.00

ACTUAL ROMANCES (Becomes True Secrets #3 on?)
October, 1949 - No. 2, Jan, 1950 (52 pgs.)
Marvel Comics (IPS)

	GD25	FN65	NM94
1	5.85	17.50	35.00
2-Photo-c	4.00	10.00	20.00

ADAM AND EVE (Spire Christian) (Value: cover or less)

ADAM STRANGE (DC) (Value: cover or less) (See Green Lantern #132, Mystery In Space #53 & Showcase #17)

ADAM-12 (TV)
Dec, 1973 - No. 10, Feb, 1976 (Photo covers)
Gold Key

	GD25	FN65	NM94
1	3.60	9.00	18.00
2-10	1.60	4.00	8.00

ADDAMS FAMILY (TV cartoon)
Oct, 1974 - No. 3, Apr, 1975 (Hanna-Barbera)
Gold Key

	GD25	FN65	NM94
1	5.00	15.00	30.00
2,3	3.60	9.00	18.00

ADLAI STEVENSON
December, 1966
Dell Publishing Co.

	GD25	FN65	NM94
12-007-612-Life story; photo-c	3.00	9.00	18.00

ADOLESCENT RADIOACTIVE BLACK BELT HAMSTERS (Eclipse) (Value: cover or less)

ADULT TALES OF TERROR ILLUSTRATED (See Terror Illustrated)

ADVANCED DUNGEONS & DRAGONS (DC) (Value: cover or less)

ADVENTURE BOUND (See 4-Color Comics No. 239)

ADVENTURE COMICS (Formerly New Adventure) (...Presents Dial H For Hero #479-490)
No. 32, 11/38 - No. 490, 2/82; No. 491, 9/82 - No. 503, 9/83
National Periodical Publications/DC Comics

	GD25	FN65	NM94
32-Anchors Aweigh (ends #52), Barry O'Neil (ends #60, not in #33), Captain Desmo (ends #47), Dale Daring (ends #47), Federal Men (ends #70), The Golden Dragon (ends #36), Rusty & His Pals (ends #52) by Bob Kane, Todd Hunter (ends #38) and Tom Brent (ends #39) begin	142.00	425.00	850.00
33-38: 37-Cover used on Double Action #2	83.00	225.00	500.00
39(1/39):-Jack Wood begins, ends #42; 1st mention of Marijuana in comics	92.00	295.00	550.00

	GD25	FN65	VF82	NM94
40-(Rare, 7/39, on stands 6/10/39)-The Sandman begins; believed to be 1st conceived story (see N.Y. World's Fair for 1st publ. app.); Socko Strong begins, ends #54	1750.00	5250.00	9600.00	14,000.00

	GD25	FN65	NM94
41	235.00	700.00	1400.00
42,44: Sandman-c by Flessel. 44-Opium story	300.00	900.00	1800.00
43,45	150.00	450.00	900.00
46,47-Sandman covers by Flessel. 47-Steve Conrad Adventurer begins, ends #76	233.00	700.00	1400.00

	GD25	FN65	VF82	NM94
48-Intro & 1st app. The Hourman by Bernard Bailey (Hourman c-48,50,52-59)	940.00	2800.00	5150.00	7500.00

(Estimated up to 80 total copies exist, 5 in NM/Mint)

	GD25	FN65	NM94
49,50: 50-Cotton Carver by Jack Lehti begins, ends #64	135.00	400.00	800.00
51,60-Sandman-c	170.00	500.00	1000.00
52-59: 53-1st app. Jimmy "Minuteman" Martin & the Minutemen of America in Hourman; ends #78. 58-Paul Kirk Manhunter begins (1st app.), ends #72	116.00	350.00	700.00

	GD25	FN65	VF82	NM94
61-1st app. Starman by Jack Burnley; Starman c-61-72	650.00	1950.00	3600.00	5200.00

(Estimated up to 100+ total copies exist, 7 in NM/Mint)

	GD25	FN65	NM94
62-65,67,68,70: 67-Origin The Mist. 70-Last Federal Men	108.00	325.00	650.00
66-Origin/1st app. Shining Knight	138.00	410.00	825.00
69-1st app. Sandy the Golden Boy (Sandman's sidekick) by Bob Kane; Sandman dons new costume	128.00	388.00	775.00
71-Jimmy Martin becomes costume aide to the Hourman; 1st app.Hourman's Miracle Ray machine	100.00	300.00	600.00

	GD25	FN65	VF82	NM94
72-1st Simon & Kirby Sandman	500.00	1500.00	2800.00	4000.00

(Estimated up to 100+ total copies exist, 8 in NM/Mint)

	GD25	FN65	VF82	NM94
73-(Scarce)-Origin Manhunter by Simon & Kirby; begin new series; Manhunter-c	565.00	1700.00	3100.00	4500.00

(Estimated up to 100+ total copies exist, 7 in NM/Mint)

	GD25	FN65	NM94
74-80: 74-Thorndyke replaces Jimmy, Hourman's assistant; new Manhunter-c begin by S&K. 77-Origin Genius Jones; Mist story. 79-Manhunter-c. 80-Last S&K Manhunter & Burnley Starman	130.00	390.00	780.00
81-90: 83-Last Hourman. 84-Mike Gibbs begins, ends #102	83.00	250.00	500.00
91-Last Simon & Kirby Sandman	75.00	225.00	450.00
92-99,101,102: 92-Last Manhunter. 102-Last Starman, Sandman, & Genius Jones. Most-S&K-c	57.00	170.00	340.00
100	92.00	275.00	550.00
103-Aquaman, Green Arrow, Johnny Quick & Superboy begin; Superboy-c begin; 1st small logo (4/46)	217.00	650.00	1300.00
104	67.00	200.00	400.00
105-110	54.00	162.00	325.00
111-120: 113-X-Mas-c	50.00	150.00	300.00

121-126,128-130: 128-1st meeting Superboy & Lois Lane

	GD25	FN65	NM94
	42.00	125.00	250.00
127-Brief origin Shining Knight retold	44.00	132.00	265.00
131-141,143-149: 132-Shining Knight 1st return to King Arthur time;origin aide Sir Butch	35.00	105.00	210.00
142-Origin Shining Knight & Johnny Quick retold	40.00	120.00	240.00
150,151,153,155,157,159,161,163-All have 6 pg. Shining Knight stories by Frank Frazetta. 159-Origin Johnny Quick	47.00	140.00	280.00
152,154,156,158,160,162,164-169: 166-Last Shining Knight. 168-Last 52 pg. issue	25.00	75.00	175.00
170-180	23.00	70.00	160.00
181-199: 189-B&W and color illo in **POP**	21.00	63.00	145.00
200 (5/54)	39.00	120.00	275.00
201-209: 207-Last Johnny Quick (not in 205). 209-Last Pre-code issue; origin Speedy	27.00	81.00	190.00
210-1st app. Krypto (Superdog)	235.00	705.00	1650.00
211-213,215-220: 220-Krypto app.	22.00	65.00	150.00
214-2nd app. Krypto	23.00	70.00	160.00
221-246: 237-1st Intergalactic Vigilante Squadron (Legion tryout)	19.00	57.00	130.00
247(4/58)-1st Legion of Super Heroes app.; 1st app. Cosmic Boy, Lightning Boy (later Lightning Lad in #267), & Saturn Girl (origin)	325.00	975.00	2600.00
248-252,254,255: All Kirby Green Arrow. 255-Intro. Red Kryptonite in Superboy (used in #252 but w/no effect)	13.50	41.00	95.00
253-1st meeting of Superboy & Robin; Green Arrow by Kirby	19.00	57.00	130.00
256-Origin Green Arrow by Kirby	54.00	160.00	375.00
257-259	12.00	36.00	85.00
260-1st Silver-Age origin Aquaman (5/59)	54.0	160.00	375.00
261-266,268,270: 262-Origin Speedy in Green Arrow. 270-Congorilla begins, ends #281,283	10.00	30.00	60.00
267(12/59)-2nd Legion of Super Heroes; Lightning Boy now called Lightning Lad; new costumes for Legion	82.00	245.00	575.00
269-Intro. Aqualad; last Green Arrow (not in #206)	18.00	54.00	125.00
271-Origin Luthor	20.00	60.00	140.00
272-274,277-280: 279-Intro White Kryptonite in Superboy. 280-1st meeting Superboy-Lori Lemaris	7.50	22.50	45.00
275-Origin Superman-Batman team retold (see World's Finest #94)	14.00	43.00	100.00
276-(9/60) Re-intro Metallo (3rd app?); story similar to Superboy #49	7.50	22.50	45.00
281,284,287-289: 281-Last Congorilla. 284-Last Aquaman in Adv. 287,288-Intro. Dev-Em, the Knave from Krypton. 287-1st Bizarro Perry White & J. Olsen. 288-Bizarro-c. 289-Legion cameo (statues)	6.70	20.00	40.00
282(3/61)-5th Legion app; intro/origin Star Boy	14.00	43.00	100.00
283-Intro. The Phantom Zone	10.00	30.00	65.00
285-1st Tales of the Bizarro World-c/story (ends #299) in Adv. (see Action #255)	10.00	30.00	70.00
286-1st Bizarro Mxyzptlk; Bizarro-c	10.00	30.00	60.00
290(11/61)-8th Legion app; origin Sunboy in Legion (last 10 cent issue)	13.00	40.00	90.00
291,292,295-298: 292-1st Bizarro Lana Lang & Lucy Lane. 295-1st Bizarro Titano	5.00	15.00	30.00
293(2/62)-13th Legion app; Mon-el & Legion Super Pets (1st app. & origin) app. (1st Superhorse). 1st Bizarro Luthor & Kandor	10.00	30.00	60.00
294-1st Bizarro M. Monroe, Pres. Kennedy	10.00	30.00	60.00
299-1st Gold Kryptonite (8/62)	5.00	15.00	35.00
300-Tales of the Legion of Super-Heroes series begins (9/62); Mon-el leaves Phantom Zone (temporarily), joins Legion	38.00	115.00	265.00
301-Origin Bouncing Boy	11.50	34.00	80.00
302-305: 303-1st app. Matter Eater Lad. 304-Death of Lightning Lad in Legion	8.35	25.00	50.00
306-310: 306-Intro. Legion of Substitute Heroes. 307-1st app. Element Lad in Legion. 308-1st app. Lightning Lass in Legion	6.35	19.00	38.00
311-320: 312-Lightning Lad back in Legion. 315-Last new Superboy story; Colossal Boy app. 316-Origins & powers of Legion given. 317-Intro. Dream Girl in Legion; Lightning Lass becomes Light Lass; Hall of Fame series begins. 320-Dev-Em 2nd app.	4.70	14.00	28.00
321-Intro Time Trapper	4.00	11.00	22.00
322-330: 327-Intro/1st app. Timber Wolf in Legion. 329-Intro The Bizarro Legionnaires	4.00	10.00	20.00
331-340: 337-Chlorophyll Kid & Night Girl app. 340-Intro Computo in Legion	3.20	8.00	16.00
341-Triplicate Girl becomes Duo Damsel	2.40	6.00	12.00
342-345,347,350,351: 345-Last Hall of Fame; returns in 356,371. 351-1st app. White Witch	1.80	4.50	9.00
346,348,349: 346-1st app. Karate Kid, Princess Projectra, Ferro Lad, & Nemesis Kid. 348-Origin Sunboy; intro Dr. Regulus in Legion. 349-Intro Universo & Rond Vidar	2.00	5.00	10.00
352,354-360: 355-Insect Queen joins Legion (4/67)	1.60	4.00	8.00
353-Death of Ferro Lad in Legion	2.60	6.50	13.00
361-364,366,368-370: 369-Intro Mordru in Legion	1.20	3.00	6.00
365,367,371,372: 365-Intro Shadow Lass; lists origins & powers of L.S.H. 367-New Legion headquarters. 371-Intro. Chemical King. 372-Timber Wolf & Chemical King join	1.40	3.50	7.00
373,374,376-380: Last Legion in Adventure	1.20	3.00	6.00
375-Intro Quantum Queen & The Wanderers	1.40	3.50	7.00
381-389,391-400: 381-Supergirl begins; 1st full length Supergirl story & her 1st solo book (6/69). 399-Unpubbed G.A. Black Canary story. 400-New costume for Supergirl	.40	1.00	2.00
390-Giant Supergirl G-69	1.20	3.00	6.00
401,402,404-410: 409-420-(52 pg. issues)	.40	1.00	2.00
403-68pg. Giant G-81; Legion-r/#304,305,308,312	1.00	2.50	5.00
411,413: 413-Hawkman by Kubert; G.A. Robotman-r/Det. #178; Zatanna begins, ends #421		.50	1.00
412-Reprints origin/1st app. Animal Man/Strange Adventures #180	.80	2.00	4.00
414-Reprints 2nd Animal Man/Str. Advs. #184	.60	1.50	3.00
415,420-Animal Man reprints from Strange Adventures #190 (origin recap) & #195	.30	.75	1.50
416-Giant DC-100 Pg. Super Spect. #10; GA-r		.60	1.20
417-Morrow Vigilante; Frazetta Shining Knight-r/Adv. #161; origin The Enchantress		.60	1.20
418,419,421-424: Last Supergirl in Adv.		.50	1.00
425-New look, content change to adventure; Toth-a, origin Capt. Fear	.30	.75	1.50
426-458: 426-1st Adventurers Club. 427-Last Vigilante. 428-430-Black Orchid app. (428-1st app?). 431-440-Spectre app. 433-437-Cover title is Weird Adv. Comics. 435-Mike Grell's 1st comic work (9-10/74). 440-New Spectre origin. 441-452-Aquaman app. 445-447-The Creeper app. 449-451-Martian Manhunter app. 453-458-Superboy app. 453-Intro Mighty Girl. 457,458-Eclipso app.		.50	1.00
459,460,463-466($1.00 size, 68pgs.): 459-Flash (ends 466), Deadman (ends 466), Wonder Woman (ends 464), Gr. Lantern (ends 460), New Gods begin (ends 460). 460-Aquaman begins; ends 478		.50	1.00
461,462: 461-Justice Society begins; ends 466. 461,462-Death Earth II Batman (both $1.00, 68 pgs.)	.80	2.00	4.00
467-490: 467-Starman by Ditko, Plastic Man begin, end 478. 469,470-Origin Starman. 479-Dial 'H' For Hero begins, ends #490		.50	1.00
491-499: 488,489-Deathstroke-c/cameos. 491-100pg. Digest size begins; r-Legion of Super Heroes/Adv. #247,267; Spectre, Aquaman, Superboy, S&K Sandman, Bl. Canary-r & new Shazam by Newton begin. 493-Challengers of the Unknown begins by Tuska w/brief origin. 492,495,496, 499-S&K Sandman- r/Adventure in all; 494-499-Spectre-r/Spectre 1-3, 5-7. 493-495,497-499-G.A. Captain Marvel-r. 498-Plastic Man-r begin; origin Bouncing Boy-r/#301		.60	1.20
500-All Legion-r (Digest size, 148 pgs.)	.30	.80	1.60
501-503-G.A.-r		.60	1.20

Adventure Comics #62, © DC

Adventure Comics #130, © DC

Adventure Comics #344 © DC

Adventures For Boys #1, © Bailey Ent.

Adventures In 3-D #2, © HARV

Adventures Into Darkness #6, © STD

GD25 FN65 NM94

NOTE: *Bizarro covers-285, 286, 288, 294, 295, 329. Vigilante app.-420, 426, 427.* ***N. Adams*** *a(r)-495i-498i; c-365-369, 371-373, 375-379, 381-383.* ***Austin*** *a-449i 451i.* ***Bernard Baily*** *c-48, 50, 52-59.* ***Bolland*** *c-475.* ***Burnley*** *c-61-72, 116-120p.* ***Ditko*** *a-467p-478p; c-467p.* ***Craig Flessel*** *c-32, 33, 40, 42, 44, 46, 47, 51, 60.* ***Giffen*** *c-491p-494p, 500p.* ***Grell*** *a-435-437, 440.* ***Guardineer*** *c-34, 35, 45.* ***Kaluta*** *c-425.* ***Bob Kane*** *a-38.* ***G. Kane*** *a-414r, 425; c-496-499, 537.* ***Kirby*** *a-250-256.* ***Kubert*** *a-413.* ***Meskin*** *a-81,127.* ***Moldoff*** *a-494i; c-49.* ***Morrow*** *a-413-415, 417, 422, 502r, 503r.* ***Newton*** *a-459-461, 464-466, 491p, 492p.* ***Orlando*** *a-457p, 458p.* ***Perez*** *c-484-486, 490p.* ***Simon/Kirby****c-73-97, 100-102.* ***Starlin*** *c-471.* ***Staton*** *a-445-447i, 456-458p, 459, 460, 461p-465p, 466,467p-478p, 502p(r); c-458, 461(back).* ***Toth*** *a-418, 419, 425, 431, 495p-497p.* ***Tuska*** *a494p.*

ADVENTURE COMICS
No date (early 1940s) Paper cover, 32 pgs.
IGA

Two different issues; Super-Mystery reprints from 1941
17.00 51.00 120.00

ADVENTURE IN DISNEYLAND (Giveaway)
May, 1955 (16 pgs., soft-c) (Dist. by Richfield Oil)
Walt Disney Productions

nn 4.00 11.00 22.00

ADVENTURE INTO FEAR
1951
Superior Publ. Ltd.

1-Exist? 9.15 27.50 55.00

ADVENTURE INTO MYSTERY
May, 1956 - No. 8, July, 1957
Atlas Comics (BFP No. 1/OPI No. 2-8)

1-Powell s/f-a; Forte-a; Everett-c 16.00 48.00 110.00
2-Flying Saucer story 9.15 27.50 55.00
3,6,8: 3,6-Everett-c 7.50 22.50 45.00
4-Williamson-a, 4 pgs; Powell-a 9.15 27.50 55.00
5-Everett-c/a, Orlando-a 7.50 22.50 45.00
7-Torres-a; Everett-c 7.50 22.50 45.00
8-Moriera, Sale, Torres, Woodbridge-a, Severin-c
7.50 22.50 45.00

ADVENTURE IS MY CAREER
1945 (44 pgs.)
U.S. Coast Guard Academy/Street & Smith

nn-Simon, Milt Gross-a 10.00 30.00 60.00

ADVENTURERS, THE (Aircel) (Value: cover or less)

ADVENTURES (No. 2 Spectacular... on cover)
Nov, 1949 - No. 2, Feb, 1950 (No. 1 ...in Romance on cover)
St. John Publishing Co. (Slightly large size)

1(Scarce); Bolle, Starr-a(2) 14.00 43.00 100.00
2(Scarce)-Slave Girl; China Bombshell app.; Bolle, L. Starr-a
23.00 70.00 160.00

ADVENTURES FOR BOYS
December, 1954
Bailey Enterprises

nn-Comics, text, & photos 3.60 9.00 18.00

ADVENTURES IN PARADISE (See 4-Color No. 1301)

ADVENTURES IN ROMANCE (See Adventures)

ADVENTURES IN SCIENCE (See Classics Illustrated Special Issue)

ADVENTURES IN 3-D
Nov, 1953 - No. 2, Jan, 1954
Harvey Publications

1-Nostrand, Powell-a, 2-Powell-a 11.50 34.00 80.00

ADVENTURES INTO DARKNESS (See Seduction of the Innocent 3-D)
No. 5, Aug, 1952 - No. 14, 1954
Better-Standard Publications/Visual Editions

GD25 FN65 NM94

5-Katz-c/a; Toth-a(p) 12.00 36.00 85.00
6-Tuska, Katz-a 8.35 25.00 50.00
7-Katz-c/a 9.15 27.50 55.00
8,9-Toth-a(p) 10.00 30.00 60.00
10,11-Jack Katz-a 7.50 22.50 45.00
12-Toth-a?; lingerie panels 7.50 22.50 45.00
13-Toth-a(p); Cannibalism story cited by T. E. Murphy articles
10.00 30.00 60.00
14 6.70 20.00 40.00

NOTE: ***Fawcette*** *a-13.* ***Moriera*** *a-5.* ***Sekowsky*** *a-10, 11, 13(2).*

ADVENTURES INTO TERROR (Formerly Joker Comics)
No. 43, Nov, 1950 - No. 31, May, 1954
Marvel/Atlas Comics (CDS)

43(#1) 22.00 65.00 150.00
44(#2, 2/51)-Sol Brodsky-c 14.00 43.00 100.00
3(4/51), 4 10.00 30.00 70.00
5-Wolverton-c panel/Mystic #6; Rico-c panel also; Atom Bomb story
11.00 32.00 75.00
6,8: 8-Wolverton text illo r-/Marvel Tales #104 10.00 30.00 60.00
7-Wolverton-a "Where Monsters Dwell", 6 pgs.; Tuska-c; Maneely-c panels
25.00 75.00 175.00
9,10,12-Krigstein-a. 9-Decapitation panels 10.00 30.00 60.00
11,13-20 6.70 20.00 40.00
21-24,26-31 5.85 17.50 35.00
25-Matt Fox-a 8.35 25.00 50.00

NOTE: ***Ayers*** *a-21.* ***Colan*** *a-3, 5, 14, 21, 24, 25, 28, 29; c-27.* ***Colletta*** *a-30.* ***Everett*** *c-13, 21, 25.* ***Fass*** *a-28, 29.* ***Forte*** *a-28.* ***Heath*** *a-43, 44, 4-6, 22, 24, 26; c-43, 9, 11.* ***Lazarus*** *a-7.* ***Maneely*** *a-7(3 pg.), 10, 11, 21. c-15, 29.* ***Don Rico*** *a-4, 5(3 pg.).* ***Sekowsky*** *a-43, 3, 4.* ***Sinnott*** *a-8, 9, 11, 28.* ***Tuska*** *a-14; c-7.*

ADVENTURES INTO THE UNKNOWN
Fall, 1948 - No. 174, Aug, 1967 (No. 1-33: 52 pgs.)
American Comics Group

(1st continuous series horror comic; see Eerie #1)

1-Guardineer-a; adapt. of 'Castle of Otranto' by Horace Walpole
77.00 230.00 540.00
2 34.00 105.00 240.00
3-Feldstein-a (9 pgs) 37.00 110.00 260.00
4,5 19.00 58.00 135.00
6-10 15.00 45.00 105.00
11-16,18-20: 13-Starr-a 11.00 32.00 75.00
17-Story similar to movie 'The Thing' 13.50 42.00 95.00
21-26,28-30 9.30 28.00 65.00
27-Williamson/Krenkel-a (8 pgs.) 16.00 48.00 110.00
31-50: 38-Atom bomb panels 8.35 25.00 50.00
51(1/54) - 58 (3-D effect-c/stories). 52-E.C. swipe/Haunt Of Fear #14
16.00 48.00 110.00
59-3-D effect story only 10.00 30.00 70.00
60-Woodesque-a by Landau 6.70 20.00 40.00
61-Last pre-code issue (1-2/55) 5.85 17.50 35.00
62-70 4.20 12.50 25.00
71-90 3.60 9.00 18.00
91,96(#95 on inside),107,116-All contain Williamson-a
4.20 12.50 25.00
92-95,97-99,101-106,108-115,117-127: 109-113,118-Whitney painted-c
3.20 8.00 16.00
100 4.00 10.00 20.00
128-Williamson/Krenkel/Torres-a(r)/Forbidden Worlds #63; last 10 cent issue
3.20 8.00 16.00
129-150 2.80 7.00 14.00
151-153: 153-Magic Agent app. 2.40 6.00 12.00
154-Nemesis series begins (origin), ends #170 3.20 8.00 16.00
155-167,169-174: 157-Magic Agent app. 2.40 6.00 12.00
168-Ditko-a(p) 2.80 7.00 14.00

NOTE: *"Spirit of Frankenstein" series in 5, 6, 8-10, 12, 16.* ***Buscema*** *a-100, 106, 108-110,*

158r, 165r. ***Craig*** *a-152, 160.* ***Goode*** *a-45, 47, 60.* ***Landau*** *a-51, 59-63.* ***Lazarus*** *a-48, 51, 52, 58, 79, 87; c-31-58.* ***Reinman*** *a-102, 111, 112, 115-118, 124, 130, 137, 141, 145, 164.* ***Whitney*** *c-12-30, 59-on (most.)* ***Torres/Williamson*** *a-116.*

ADVENTURES INTO WEIRD WORLDS
Jan, 1952 - No. 30, June, 1954
Marvel/Atlas Comics (ACI)

	GD25	FN65	NM94
1-Atom bomb panels	20.00	60.00	140.00
2-Sci/fic stories (2); one by Maneely	13.00	40.00	90.00
3-10: 7-Tongue ripped out. 10-Krigstein, Everett-a	10.00	30.00	60.00
11-21: 21-Hitler in Hell story	8.35	25.00	50.00
22-26: 24-Man holds hypo & splits in two	5.85	17.50	35.00
27-Matt Fox end of world story-a; severed head cover	13.00	40.00	90.00
28-Atom bomb story; decapitation panels	8.35	25.00	50.00
29,30	4.70	14.00	28.00

NOTE: ***Ayers*** *a-8, 26.* ***Everett*** *a-4, 5; c-6, 8, 10-13, 18, 19, 22, 24, 25; a-4, 25.* ***Fass*** *a-7.* ***Forte*** *a-21, 24.* ***Al Hartley*** *a-2.* ***Heath*** *a-1, 4, 17, 22; c-7, 9, 20.* ***Maneely*** *a-2, 3, 11, 20, 22, 23, 25; c-1, 3, 25-27, 29.* ***Reinman*** *a-24, 28.* ***Rico*** *a-13.* ***Robinson*** *a-13.* ***Sinnott*** *a-25, 30.* ***Tuska*** *a-1, 2, 12, 15.* ***Whitney*** *a-7.* ***Wildey*** *a-28. Bondage c-22.*

ADVENTURES IN WONDERLAND
April, 1955 - No. 5, Feb, 1956 (Jr. Readers Guild)
Lev Gleason Publications

	GD25	FN65	NM94
1-Maurer-a	5.00	15.00	30.00
2-4	4.00	10.00	20.00
5-Christmas issue	4.00	11.00	22.00

ADVENTURES OF ALAN LADD, THE
Oct-Nov, 1949 - No. 9, Feb-Mar, 1951 (All 52 pgs.)
National Periodical Publications

	GD25	FN65	NM94
1-Photo-c	57.00	170.00	400.00
2-Photo-c	36.00	108.00	250.00
3-6: Last photo-c	27.00	79.00	185.00
7-9	22.00	65.00	150.00

NOTE: ***Dan Barry*** *a-1.* ***Moreira*** *a-3-7.*

ADVENTURES OF ALICE
1945 (Also see Alice in Wonderland & ...at Monkey Island)
Civil Service Publ./Pentagon Publishing Co.

	GD25	FN65	NM94
1	7.00	21.00	50.00
2-Through the Magic Looking Glass	6.70	20.00	40.00

ADVENTURES OF BARON MUNCHAUSEN, THE (Now) (Value: cover or less)

ADVENTURES OF BAYOU BILLY, THE
Sept, 1989 - No. 5, June, 1990 ($1.00, color)
Archie Comics

	GD25	FN65	NM94
1-5: Esposito-c/a(i). 5-Kelley Jones-c		.50	1.00

ADVENTURES OF BOB HOPE, THE (Also see True Comics #59)
Feb-Mar, 1950 - No. 109, Feb-Mar, 1968 (#1-10: 52pgs.)
National Periodical Publications

	GD25	FN65	NM94
1-Photo-c	86.00	260.00	600.00
2-Photo-c	43.00	130.00	300.00
3,4-Photo-c	29.00	85.00	200.00
5-10	22.00	65.00	150.00
11-20	13.00	40.00	90.00
21-31 (2-3/55; last precode)	10.00	30.00	60.00
32-40	8.35	25.00	50.00
41-50	6.70	20.00	40.00
51-70	4.35	13.00	26.00
71-93,95-105	2.80	7.00	14.00
94-Aquaman cameo	3.20	8.00	16.00
106-109-All monster-c/stories by N. Adams-c/a	4.35	13.00	26.00

NOTE: *Buzzy in #34. Kitty Karr of Hollywood in #15, 17-20, 23, 28. Liz in #26, 109. Miss Beverly Hills of Hollywood in #7, 8, 10, 13, 14. Miss Melody Lane of Broadway in #15. Rusty in #23, 25. Tommy in #24. No 2nd feature in #2-4, 6, 8, 11, 12, 28-108.*

ADVENTURES OF CAPTAIN AMERICA
Sept, 1991 - No. 4, Jan, 1992 ($4.95, color, mini-series, 52 pgs.)
Marvel Comics

GD25 FN65 NM94

	GD25	FN65	NM94
1-4: 1-Embossed-c. 2-4-Austin-c/a(i)	1.00	2.50	5.00

ADVENTURES OF CHRISSIE CLAUS, THE (Hero) (Value: cover or less)

ADVENTURES OF DEAN MARTIN AND JERRY LEWIS, THE
(The Adventures of Jerry Lewis No. 41 on)
July-Aug, 1952 - No. 40, Oct, 1957
National Periodical Publications

	GD25	FN65	NM94
1	57.00	170.00	400.00
2	29.00	85.00	200.00
3-10: 3-3 pg origin on how they became a team	13.00	40.00	90.00
11-19: Last precode (2/55)	9.15	27.50	55.00
20-30	7.00	21.00	42.00
31-40	5.00	15.00	30.00

ADVENTURES OF FELIX THE CAT, THE
May, 1992 -Present ($1.25, color, quarterly)
Harvey Comics

	GD25	FN65	NM94
1,2-Messmer-r		.60	1.25

ADVENTURES OF FORD FAIRLANE, THE
May, 1990 - No. 4, Aug, 1990 ($1.50, mini-series, mature readers)
DC Comics

	GD25	FN65	NM94
1-4: Movie tie-in; Don Heck inks	.30	.75	1.50

ADVENTURES OF G. I. JOE
1969 (3-1/4x7") (20 & 16 pgs.)
Giveaways

First Series: 1-Danger of the Depths. 2-Perilous Rescue. 3-Secret Mission to Spy Island. 4-Mysterious Explosion. 5-Fantastic Free Fall. 6-Eight Ropes of Danger. 7-Mouth of Doom. 8-Hidden Missile Discovery. 9-Space Walk Mystery. 10-Fight for Survival. 11-The Shark's Surprise. **Second Series:** 2-Flying Space Adventure. 4-White Tiger Hunt. 7-Capture of the Pygmy Gorilla. 12-Secret of the Mummy's Tomb. Third Series: Reprinted surviving titles of First Series. Fourth Series: 13-Adventure Team Headquarters. 14-Search For the Stolen Idol.

	GD25	FN65	NM94
each....		.40	.80

ADVENTURES OF HAWKSHAW (See Hawkshaw The Detective)
1917 (9-3/4x13", 48 pgs., Color & two-tone)
The Saalfield Publishing Co.

	GD25	FN65	NM94
nn-By Gus Mager (only 24 pgs. of strips, reverse of each page is blank)	20.00	60.00	140.00

ADVENTURES OF HOMER COBB, THE
September, 1947 (Oversized)
Say/Bart Prod. (Canadian)

	GD25	FN65	NM94
1-(Scarce)-Feldstein-a	18.00	54.00	125.00

ADVENTURES OF HOMER GHOST (See Homer The Happy Ghost)
June, 1957 - No. 2, August, 1957
Atlas Comics

	GD25	FN65	NM94
V1#1,2	3.60	9.00	18.00

ADVENTURES OF JERRY LEWIS, THE (Advs. of Dean Martin & Jerry Lewis No. 1-40)(See Super DC Giant)
No. 41, Nov, 1957 - No. 124, May-June, 1971
National Periodical Publications

	GD25	FN65	NM94
41-60	4.20	12.50	25.00
61-80: 68,74-Photo-c	4.00	10.00	20.00
81-91,93-96,98-100: 89-Bob Hope app.	2.40	6.00	12.00
92-Superman cameo	3.20	8.00	16.00
97-Batman/Robin/Joker-c/story; Riddler & Penguin app.	4.20	12.50	25.00
101,103,104-Neal Adams-c/a;	4.00	10.00	20.00
102-Beatles app.; Neal Adams c/a	4.00	12.00	24.00
105-Superman x-over	2.80	7.00	14.00
106-111,113-116	1.20	3.00	6.00
112-Flash x-over	2.80	7.00	14.00
117-Wonder Woman x-over	1.60	4.00	8.00
118-124	1.00	2.50	5.00

Adventures Into Weird Worlds #1 © MEG

Adventures of Bob Hope #4, © DC

Adventures of Jerry Lewis #94, © DC

Adventures of Mighty Mouse #166
© Viacom Enterprises

Adventures of Pipsqueak #37,
© AP

Adventures of Superman #463
© DC

ADVENTURES OF JO-JOY, THE (See Jo-Joy)

ADVENTURES OF LUTHER ARKWRIGHT, THE (Dark Horse) (Value: cover or less)

ADVENTURES OF MARGARET O'BRIEN, THE
1947 (20 pgs. in color; slick cover; regular size) (Premium)
Bambury Fashions (Clothes)

	GD25	FN65	NM94
In "The Big City"-movie adaptation (scarce)	13.00	40.00	90.00

ADVENTURES OF MIGHTY MOUSE (Mighty Mouse Advs. No. 1)
No. 2, Jan, 1952 - No. 18, May, 1955
St. John Publishing Co.

	GD25	FN65	NM94
2	13.00	40.00	90.00
3-5	8.35	25.00	50.00
6-18	5.85	17.50	35.00

ADVENTURES OF MIGHTY MOUSE (2nd Series)
(Two No. 144's; formerly Paul Terry's Comics; No. 129-137 have nn's)
(Becomes Mighty Mouse No. 161 on)
No. 126, Aug, 1955 - No. 160, Oct, 1963
St. John/Pines/Dell/Gold Key

	GD25	FN65	NM94
126(8/55), 127(10/55), 128(11/55)-St. John	4.00	10.00	20.00
nn(129, 4/56)-144(8/59)-Pines	3.20	8.00	16.00
144(10-12/59)-155(7-9/62) Dell	2.80	7.00	14.00
156(10/62)-160(10/63) Gold Key	2.80	7.00	14.00

NOTE: *Early issues titled "Paul Terry's Adventures of ...."*

ADVENTURES OF MIGHTY MOUSE (Formerly Mighty Mouse)
No. 166, Mar, 1979 - No. 172, Jan, 1980
Gold Key

	GD25	FN65	NM94
166-172	1.00	2.50	5.00

ADVS. OF MR. FROG & MISS MOUSE (See Dell Junior Treasury No. 4)

ADVENTURES OF OZZIE AND HARRIET, THE (Radio)
Oct-Nov, 1949 - No. 5, June-July, 1950
National Periodical Publications

	GD25	FN65	NM94
1-Photo-c	54.00	160.00	375.00
2	29.00	85.00	200.00
3-5	26.00	78.00	180.00

ADVENTURES OF PATORUZU
Aug, 1946 - Winter, 1946
Green Publishing Co.

	GD25	FN65	NM94
nn's-Contains Animal Crackers reprints	3.60	9.00	18.00

ADVENTURES OF PINKY LEE, THE (TV)
July, 1955 - No. 5, Dec, 1955
Atlas Comics

	GD25	FN65	NM94
1	16.00	48.00	110.00
2-5	10.00	30.00	65.00

ADVENTURES OF PIPSQUEAK, THE (Formerly Pat the Brat)
No. 34, Sept, 1959 - No. 39, July, 1960
Archie Publications (Radio Comics)

	GD25	FN65	NM94
34	4.00	10.00	20.00
35-39	2.80	7.00	14.00

ADVENTURES OF QUAKE & QUISP, THE (See Quaker Oats "Plenty of Glutton")

ADVENTURES OF REX THE WONDER DOG, THE (Rex...No. 1)
Jan-Feb, 1952 - No. 45, May-June, 1959; No. 46, Nov-Dec, 1959
National Periodical Publications

	GD25	FN65	NM94
1-(Scarce)-Toth-c/a	75.00	225.00	525.00
2-(Scarce)-Toth-c/a	36.00	108.00	250.00
3-(Scarce)-Toth-a	29.00	85.00	200.00
4,5	20.00	60.00	140.00
6-10	14.00	43.00	100.00
11-Atom bomb-c/story	16.00	48.00	110.00
12-19: 19-Last precode (1-2/55)	9.15	27.50	55.00
20-46	6.70	20.00	40.00

NOTE: ***Infantino, Gil Kane** art in 5-19 (most)*

ADVENTURES OF ROBIN HOOD, THE (Formerly Robin Hood)
No. 7, 9/57 - No. 8, 11/57 (Based on Richard Greene TV Show)
Magazine Enterprises (Sussex Publ. Co.)

	GD25	FN65	NM94
7,8-Richard Greene photo-c. 7-Powell-a	8.35	25.00	50.00

ADVENTURES OF ROBIN HOOD, THE
March, 1974 - No. 7, Jan, 1975 (Disney cartoon) (36 pgs.)
Gold Key

	GD25	FN65	NM94
1(90291-403)-Part-r of $1.50 editions	1.00	2.50	5.00
2-7: 1-7 are part-r	.60	1.50	3.00

ADVENTURES OF SLIM AND SPUD, THE
1924 (3-3/4x 9-3/4")(104 pg. B&W strip reprints)
Prairie Farmer Publ. Co.

	GD25	FN65	NM94
nn	13.00	40.00	80.00

ADVENTURES OF STUBBY, SANTA'S SMALLEST REINDEER, THE
nd (early 1940s) 12 pgs.
W. T. Grant Co. (Giveaway)

	GD25	FN65	NM94
nn	3.60	9.00	18.00

ADVENTURES OF SUPERBOY, THE (See Superboy, 2nd series)

ADVENTURES OF SUPERMAN (Formerly Superman)
No. 424, Jan, 1987 - Present
DC Comics

	GD25	FN65	NM94
424	.30	.75	1.50
425-449: 426-Legends x-over. 432-1st app. Jose Delgado who becomes Gangbuster in #434. 436-Byrne scripts begin. 436,437-Millennium x-over. 438-New Brainiac app. 440-Batman app.		.50	1.00
450-463,465-479,481-491: 457-Perez plots. 463-Superman/Flash race; cover swipe/Superman #199. 467-Part 2 of Batman story. 473-Hal Jordan, Guy Gardner x-over. 474-Begin $1.00-c. 477-Legion app. 491-Last $1.00-c		.50	1.00
464-Lobo-c & app. (pre-dates Lobo #1)	.80	2.00	4.00
480-($1.75, 52 pgs.)-Mooney part pencils	.35	.90	1.75
492-495: 495-Forever People-c/story		.60	1.25
496-Doomsday cameo	.60	1.50	3.00
496,497-2nd printings		.60	1.25
497-Doomsday battle issue	1.00	2.50	5.00
498-Funeral for a Friend	.60	1.50	3.00
498-2nd printing		.60	1.25
499-Funeral for a Friend	.40	1.00	2.00
Annual 1 (1987, $1.25, 52 pgs.)-Starlin-c	.25	.75	1.40
Annual 2,3 (1990, 1991, $2.00, 68 pgs.): 2-Byrne-c/a(i); Legion '90 (Lobo) app. 3-Armageddon 2001 x-over	.40	1.00	2.00
Annual 4 (1992, $2.50, 68 pgs.)-Guy Gardner/Lobo-c/story; Eclipso storyline; Quesada-c(p)	.50	1.25	2.50

ADVENTURES OF THE BIG BOY (Giveaway)
1956 - Present (East & West editions of early issues)
Timely Comics/Webs Adv. Corp./Illus. Features

	GD25	FN65	NM94
1-Everett-a	45.00	135.00	315.00
2-Everett-a	22.00	65.00	154.00
3-5	8.35	25.00	50.00
6-10: 6-Sci/fic issue	5.00	15.00	30.00
11-20	3.00	7.50	15.00
21-30	1.60	4.00	8.00
31-50	.80	2.00	4.00
51-100	.40	1.00	2.00
101-150		.50	1.00
151-240		.20	.40
241-417: 266-Superman x-over. 417-(1992)			.10

	GD25	FN65	NM94
1-50 ('76-'84,Paragon Prod.)		.10	.20
Summer, 1959 issue, large size	3.00	7.50	15.00

ADVENTURES OF THE DETECTIVE
No date (1930's) 36 pgs.; 9-1/2x12"; B&W (paper cover)
Humor Publ. Co.

	GD25	FN65	NM94
nn-Not reprints; Ace King by Martin Nadle	10.00	30.00	60.00
2nd version (printed in red & blue)	10.00	30.00	60.00

ADVENTURES OF THE DOVER BOYS
September, 1950 - No. 2, 1950 (No month given)
Archie Comics (Close-up)

	GD25	FN65	NM94
1,2	5.85	17.50	35.00

ADVENTURES OF THE FLY (The Fly #1-6; Fly Man No. 32-39; See The Double Life of Private Strong & Laugh Comics)
Aug, 1959 - No. 30, Oct, 1964; No. 31, May, 1965
Archie Publications/Radio Comics

	GD25	FN65	NM94
1-Shield app.; origin The Fly; S&K-c/a	47.00	140.00	325.00
2-Williamson, S&K-a	25.00	75.00	175.00
3-Origin retold; Davis, Powell-a	17.00	52.00	120.00
4-Neal Adams-a(p)(1 panel); S&K-c; Powell-a; 2 pg. Shield story	11.50	34.00	80.00
5-10: 7-Black Hood app. 8,9-Shield x-over. 9-1st app. Cat Girl. 10-Black Hood app.	8.70	26.00	52.00
11-13,15-20: 13-1st app. Fly Girl w/o costume. 16-Last 10 cent issue. 20-Origin Fly Girl retold	5.35	16.00	32.00
14-Origin & 1st app. Fly Girl in costume	7.50	22.50	45.00
21-30: 23-Jaguar cameo. 27-29-Black Hood 1 pg. strips. 30-Comet x-over in Fly Girl	4.00	11.00	22.00
31-Black Hood, Shield, Comet app.	4.20	12.50	25.00

NOTE: ***Simon*** *c-2-4.* ***Tuska*** *a-1. Cover title to #31 is Flyman; Advs. of the Fly inside.*

ADVENTURES OF THE JAGUAR, THE (See Blue Ribbon Comics, Laugh Comics & Mighty Crusaders)
Sept, 1961 - No. 15, Nov, 1963
Archie Publications (Radio Comics)

	GD25	FN65	NM94
1-Origin Jaguar(1st app?); by J.Rosenberger	16.00	48.00	110.00
2,3: 3-Last 10 cent issue	9.15	27.50	55.00
4-6-Catgirl app. (#4's-c is same as splash pg.)	6.70	20.00	40.00
7-10	4.70	14.00	28.00
11-15:13,14-Catgirl,Black Hood app. in both	4.00	11.00	22.00

ADVENTURES OF THE OUTSIDERS, THE (Formerly Batman & The Outsiders; also see The Outsiders)
No. 33, May, 1986 - No. 46, June, 1987
DC Comics

	GD25	FN65	NM94
33-46		.50	1.00

ADVENTURES OF THE SUPER MARIO BROTHERS
1990 - No. 9?, 1990? ($1.50, color) (Also see Super Mario Brothers)
Valiant

	GD25	FN65	NM94
V2#1-9	.30	.75	1.50

ADVENTURES OF THE THING, THE (Also see The Thing)
Apr, 1992 - No. 4, July, 1992, ($1.25, color, mini-series)
Marvel Comics

	GD25	FN65	NM94
1-4: 1-r/Marvel Two-In-One #50 by Byrne; Kieth-c. 2-4-r/Marvel Two-In-One #80,51 & 77; 2-Ghost Rider-c/story. 3-Miller-r		.60	1.25

ADVENTURES OF TINKER BELL (See 4-Color No. 982)

ADVENTURES OF TOM SAWYER (See Dell Junior Treasury No. 10)

ADVENTURES OF WILLIE GREEN, THE
1915 (8X16, 50 cents, B&W, soft-c)
Frank M. Acton Co.

	GD25	FN65	NM94
Book 1-By Harris Brown; strip-r	12.00	36.00	85.00

ADVENTURES OF YOUNG DR. MASTERS, THE
Aug, 1964 - No. 2, Nov, 1964
Archie Comics (Radio Comics)

	GD25	FN65	NM94
1,2	1.20	3.00	6.00

ADVENTURES ON OTHER WORLDS (See Showcase #17 & 18)

ADVENTURES ON THE PLANET OF THE APES
Oct, 1975 - No. 11, Dec, 1976
Marvel Comics Group

	GD25	FN65	NM94
1-Planet of the Apes-r in color; Starlin-c	.60	1.50	3.00
2-5	.45	1.10	2.20
6-11	.35	.90	1.80

NOTE: ***Alcala*** *a-6-11r.* ***Buckler*** *c-2p.* ***Nasser*** *c-7.* ***Starlin*** *c-6.* ***Tuska*** *a-1-5r.*

ADVENTURES WITH SANTA CLAUS
No date (early 50's) (24 pgs.; 9-3/4x 6-3/4"; paper cover) (Giveaway)
Promotional Publ. Co. (Murphy's Store)

	GD25	FN65	NM94
nn-Contains 8 pgs. ads	4.00	10.00	21.00
16 page version	4.00	10.00	21.00

AFRICA
1955
Magazine Enterprises

	GD25	FN65	NM94
1(A-1#137)-Cave Girl,Thun'da;Powell-c/a(4)	13.00	40.00	90.00

AFRICAN LION (See 4-Color No. 665)

AFTER DARK
No. 6, May, 1955 - No. 8, Sept, 1955
Sterling Comics

	GD25	FN65	NM94
6-8-Sekowsky-a in all	4.35	13.00	26.00

AGAINST BLACKSHARD 3-D (Sirius) (Value: cover or less)

AGENT LIBERTY SPECIAL
1992 ($2.00, color, 52 pgs.)
DC Comics

	GD25	FN65	NM94
1-From Superman; 1st solo adv.; Guice-c/a(i)	.40	1.00	2.00

AGGIE MACK
Jan, 1948 - No. 8, Aug, 1949
Four Star Comics Corp./Superior Comics Ltd.

	GD25	FN65	NM94
1-Feldstein-a, "Johnny Prep"	13.00	40.00	90.00
2,3-Kamen-c	7.50	22.50	45.00
4-Feldstein "Johnny Prep"; Kamen-c	10.00	30.00	60.00
5-8-Kamen-c/a	7.50	22.50	45.00

AGGIE MACK (See 4-Color Comics No. 1335)

AIN'T IT A GRAND & GLORIOUS FEELING?
1922 (52 pgs.; 9x9³/4"; stiff cardboard cover)
Whitman Publishing Co.

	GD25	FN65	NM94
nn-1921 daily strip-r; B&W, color-c; Briggs-a	12.00	36.00	85.00

AIR ACE (Formerly Bill Barnes No. 1-12)
V2#1, Jan, 1944 - V3#8(No. 20), Feb-Mar, 1947
Street & Smith Publications

	GD25	FN65	NM94
V2#1	11.00	32.00	75.00
V2#2-12: 7-Powell-a	6.35	19.00	38.00
V3#1-6	4.20	12.50	25.00
V3#7-Powell bondage-c/a; all atomic issue	10.00	30.00	60.00
V3#8 (V5#8 on-c)-Powell-c/a	5.00	15.00	30.00

AIRBOY (Eclipse) (Value: cover or less)

AIRBOY COMICS (Air Fighters Comics No. 1-22)
V2#11, Dec, 1945 - V10#4, May, 1953 (No V3#3)
Hillman Periodicals

	GD25	FN65	NM94
V2#11	40.00	125.00	250.00
12-Valkyrie app.	28.00	85.00	170.00
V3#1,2(no #3)	24.00	72.00	145.00
4-The Heap app. in Skywolf	21.00	62.00	125.00
5-8,10,11: 6-Valkyrie app.	17.00	52.00	105.00

Adventures of the Fly #27, © AP

Aggie Mack #1, © SUPR

Air Ace #12, © S&S

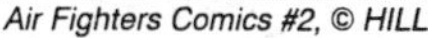
Air Fighters Comics #2, © HILL

Air War Stories #2, © DELL

Alarming Adventures #1, © HARV

	GD25	FN65	NM94
9-Origin The Heap	21.00	62.00	125.00
12-Skywolf & Airboy x-over; Valkyrie app.	22.00	68.00	135.00
V4#1-Iron Lady app.	21.00	62.00	125.00
2,3,12: 2-Rackman begins	12.00	38.00	75.00
4-Simon & Kirby-c	14.00	42.00	85.00
5-11-All S&K-a	18.00	55.00	110.00
V5#1-11: 4-Infantino Heap. 5-Skull-c. 10-Origin The Heap	10.00	30.00	60.00
12-Krigstein-a(p)	12.00	35.00	70.00
V6#1-3,5-12: 6,8-Origin The Heap	10.00	30.00	60.00
4-Origin retold	11.00	32.00	65.00
V7#1-12: 7,8,10-Origin The Heap	10.00	30.00	60.00
V8#1-3,6-12	8.35	25.00	50.00
4-Krigstein-a	10.00	30.00	60.00
5(#100)	9.15	27.50	55.00
V9#1-12: 2-Valkyrie app. 7-One pg. Frazetta ad	7.50	22.50	45.00
V10#1-4	7.50	22.50	45.00

NOTE: ***Barry** a-V2#3, 7. **Bolle** a-V4#12. **McWilliams** a-V3#7, 9. **Powell** a-V7#2, 3, V8#1, 6. **Starr** a-V5#1, 12. **Dick Wood** a-V4#12. Bondage-c V5#8.*

AIR FIGHTERS CLASSICS (Eclipse) (Value: cover or less)

AIR FIGHTERS COMICS (Airboy Comics #23 (V2#11) on)
Nov, 1941; No. 2, Nov, 1942 - V2#10, Fall, 1945
Hillman Periodicals

	GD25	FN65	NM94
V1#1-(Produced by Funnies, Inc.); Black Commander only app.	133.00	400.00	800.00
2(11/42)-(Produced by Quality artists & Biro for Hillman); Origin Airboy & Iron Ace; Black Angel, Flying Dutchman & Skywolf begin; Fuje-a; Biro-c/a	217.00	650.00	1300.00
3-Origin The Heap & Skywolf	108.00	325.00	650.00
4	75.00	225.00	450.00
5,6	57.00	172.00	345.00
7-12	43.00	130.00	260.00
V2#1,3-9: 5-Flag-c; Fuje-a. 7-Valkyrie app.	41.00	122.00	245.00
2-Skywolf by Giunta; Flying Dutchman by Fuje; 1st meeting Valkyrie & Airboy (She worked for the Nazis in beginning)	52.00	158.00	315.00
10-Origin The Heap & Skywolf	50.00	150.00	300.00

NOTE: ***Fuje** a-V1#2, 5, 7, V2#2, 3, 5, 7-9. **Giunta** a-V2#2, 3, 7, 9.*

AIRFIGHTERS MEET SGT. STRIKE SPECIAL, THE (Eclipse) (Value: cover or less)

AIR FORCES (See American Air Forces)

AIRMAIDENS SPECIAL (Eclipse) (Value: cover or less)

AIR POWER (CBS TV & the U.S. Air Force Presents)
1956 (32pgs, 5-1/4x7-1/4", soft-c)
Prudential Insurance Co. giveaway

	GD25	FN65	NM94
nn-Toth-a? Based on 'You Are There' TV program by Walter Cronkite	6.70	20.00	40.00

AIR RAIDERS (Marvel) (Value: cover or less)

AIR WAR STORIES
Sept-Nov, 1964 - No. 8, Aug, 1966
Dell Publishing Co.

	GD25	FN65	NM94
1-Painted-c; Glanzman-c/a begins	3.20	8.00	16.00
2-8: 2-Painted-c (all painted?)	1.80	4.50	9.00

AKIRA
Sept, 1988 - Present ($3.50-$3.75, color, deluxe, 68 pgs.)
Epic Comics (Marvel)

	GD25	FN65	NM94
1	4.00	10.00	20.00
1,2-2nd printings ('89, $3.95)	.80	2.00	4.00
2	2.40	6.00	12.00
3-5	1.80	4.50	9.00
6-15	1.10	2.75	5.50
16-35: 17-Begin $3.95-c	.80	2.00	4.00
36 ($4.50-c)	.90	2.25	4.50

ALADDIN (Disney Comics) (Value: cover or less) (Also see Dell Junior Treasury No. 2)

ALAN LADD (See The Adventures of ...)

ALARMING ADVENTURES
Oct, 1962 - No. 3, Feb, 1963
Harvey Publications

	GD25	FN65	NM94
1-Crandall/Williamson-a	4.70	14.00	28.00
2,3: 2-Williamson/Crandall-a	3.60	9.00	18.00

NOTE: ***Bailey** a-1, 3. **Crandall** a-1p, 2i. **Powell** a-2(2). **Severin** c-1-3. **Torres** a-2? **Tuska** a-1. **Williamson** a-1i, 2p, 3.*

ALARMING TALES
Sept, 1957 - No. 6, Nov, 1958
Harvey Publications (Western Tales)

	GD25	FN65	NM94
1-Kirby-c/a(4)	9.15	27.50	55.00
2-Kirby-a(4)	8.35	25.00	50.00
3,4-Kirby-a. 4-Powell, Wildey-a	5.85	17.50	35.00
5-Kirby/Williamson-a; Wildey-a; Severin-c	6.70	20.00	40.00
6-Williamson-a?; Severin-c	5.00	15.00	30.00

ALBEDO
April, 1985 - No. 14, Spring, 1989 (B&W)
Thoughts And Images

	GD25	FN65	NM94
0-Yellow cover; 50 copies	7.50	22.50	45.00
0-White cover, 450 copies	5.85	17.50	35.00
0-Blue, 1st printing, 500 copies	2.40	6.00	12.00
0-Blue, 2nd printing, 1000 copies	1.60	4.00	8.00
0-3rd printing	.40	1.00	2.00
0-4th printing		.60	1.20
1-Dark red; 1st app. Usagi Yojimbo	1.80	4.50	9.00
1-Bright red	1.80	4.50	9.00
2	1.20	3.00	6.00
3-14	.40	1.00	2.00

ALBERTO (See The Crusaders)

ALBERT THE ALLIGATOR & POGO POSSUM (See 4-Color Comics #105, 148)

ALBUM OF CRIME (See Fox Giants)

ALBUM OF LOVE (See Fox Giants)

AL CAPP'S DOGPATCH (Also see Mammy Yokum)
No. 71, June, 1949 - No. 4, Dec, 1949
Toby Press

	GD25	FN65	NM94
71(#1)-Reprints from Tip Top #112-114	19.00	58.00	135.00
2-4: 4-Reprints from Li'l Abner #73	13.00	40.00	90.00

AL CAPP'S SHMOO (Also see Oxydol-Dreft)
July, 1949 - No. 5, April, 1950 (None by Al Capp)
Toby Press

	GD25	FN65	NM94
1	26.00	78.00	180.00
2-5: 3-Sci-fi trip to moon. 4-X-Mas-c; origin/1st app. Super-Shmoo	19.00	56.00	130.00

AL CAPP'S WOLF GAL
1951 - No. 2, 1952
Toby Press

	GD25	FN65	NM94
1,2-Edited-r from Li'l Abner #63,64	26.00	78.00	180.00

ALEXANDER THE GREAT (See 4-Color No. 688)

ALF (TV) (See Star Comics Digest)
Mar, 1988 - No. 50, Feb, 1992 ($1.00, color)
Marvel Comics

	GD25	FN65	NM94
1-49		.50	1.00
50-($1.75, 52 pgs.)-Final issue; photo-c	.35	.90	1.75
Annual 1-3	.40	1.00	2.00
...Comics Digest 1 (1988)-Reprints Alf #1,2	.30	.75	1.50

Holiday Special 1 ($1.75, 1988, 68 pgs.) .35 .90 1.75
Holiday Special 2 ($2.00, Winter, 1989, 68 pgs.) .40 1.00 2.00
Spring Special 1 (Spr/89, $1.75, 68 pgs.) .35 .90 1.75

ALGIE
Dec, 1953 - No. 3, 1954
Timor Publ. Co.
1-Teenage 3.20 8.00 16.00
2,3 2.40 6.00 12.00
Accepted Reprint #2(nd) 1.40 3.50 7.00
Super Reprint #15 1.20 3.00 6.00

ALIAS: (Now)(Value: cover or less)

ALICE (New Adventures in Wonderland)
No. 10, 7-8/51 - No. 2, 11-12/51
Ziff-Davis Publ. Co.
10-Painted-c (spanking scene); Berg-a 13.00 40.00 90.00
11-Dave Berg-a 7.50 22.50 45.00
2-Dave Berg-a 5.85 17.50 35.00

ALICE AT MONKEY ISLAND (See The Adventures of Alice)
No. 3, 1946
Pentagon Publ. Co. (Civil Service)
3 5.35 16.00 32.00

ALICE IN BLUNDERLAND
1952 (Paper cover, 16 pages in color)
Industrial Services
nn-Facts about big government waste and inefficiency
12.00 36.00 84.00

ALICE IN WONDERLAND (See Advs. of Alice, 4-Color No. 331,341, Dell Jr. Treasury No. 1, The Dreamery, Movie Comics, Single Series No. 24, Walt Disney Showcase No. 22, and World's Greatest Stories)

ALICE IN WONDERLAND
1965; 1982
Western Printing Company/Whitman Publ. Co.
Meets Santa Claus(1950s), nd, 16 pgs. 3.60 9.00 18.00
Rexall Giveaway(1965, 16 pgs., 5x7-1/4) Western Printing (TV, Hanna-Barbera) 2.80 7.00 14.00
Wonder Bakery Giveaway(16 pgs, color, nn, nd) (Continental Baking Company, 1969) 2.80 7.00 14.00
1-(Whitman; 1982)-r/4-Color #331 .60 1.20

ALICE IN WONDERLAND MEETS SANTA
nd (16 pgs., 6-5/8x9-11/16", paper cover)
No publisher (Giveaway)
nn 10.00 30.00 65.00

ALIEN ENCOUNTERS (Eclipse)(Value: cover or less)

ALIEN LEGION (See Epic & Marvel Graphic Novel #25)
April, 1984 - No. 20, Sept, 1987
Epic Comics (Marvel)
1-$2.00 cover, high quality paper .40 1.00 2.00
2-20 .30 .75 1.50

ALIEN LEGION (2nd series)
Aug, 1987 (indicia) (10/87 on-c) - No. 18, Aug, 1990 ($1.25, color)
Epic Comics (Marvel)
V2#1-6 .60 1.25
7-18: 7-Begin $1.50 cover .30 .75 1.50

ALIEN LEGION: JUGGER GRIMROD
Aug, 1992 ($5.95, color, one-shot, 52 pgs.)
Epic Comics (Marvel)
Book One 1.20 3.00 6.00

ALIEN LEGION: ON THE EDGE (The... #2 & 3)
Nov, 1990 - No. 3, Jan, 1991 ($4.50, color, mini-series, 52 pgs.)
Epic Comics (Marvel)
1-3 .90 2.25 4.50

ALIEN LEGION: TENNANTS OF HELL
1991 - No. 2, 1991 ($4.50, color, squarebound, 52 pgs.)
Epic Comics (Marvel)
Book 1,2-Stroman-c/a(p) .90 2.25 4.50

ALIEN NATION
Dec, 1988 ($2.50; 68 pgs.)
DC Comics
1-Adapts movie; painted-c .50 1.25 2.50

ALIENS, THE (Captain Johner and...)(Also see Magnus Robot...)
Sept-Dec, 1967; No. 2, May, 1982
Gold Key
1-Reprints from Magnus #1,3,4,6-10, all by Russ Manning
3.00 7.50 15.00
2-Reprints from Magnus #1 by Manning .80 2.00 4.00

ALIENS (See Alien: The Illustrated... & Dark Horse Presents #24)
May, 1988 - No. 6, July, 1989 ($1.95, B&W, mini-series)
V2#1, Aug, 1989 - No. 4, 1990 ($2.25, color, mini-series)
Dark Horse Comics
1-Based on movie sequel; 1st app. Aliens 5.50 16.50 33.00
1-2nd printing 1.80 4.50 9.00
1-3rd - 6th printings; 4th w/new inside front-c .40 1.00 2.00
2 4.00 12.00 24.00
2-2nd printing .80 2.00 4.00
2-3rd printing w/new inside f/c .40 1.00 2.00
3 2.40 6.00 12.00
4 1.60 4.00 8.00
5,6 1.20 3.00 6.00
3-6-2nd printings .40 1.00 2.00
Mini Comic #1 (2/89, 4x6")-Was included with Aliens Portfolio
2.00 5.00 10.00
...Collection 1 ($10.95,)-r/1-6 plus Dark Horse Presents #24 plus new-a
2.20 5.50 11.00
...Collection 1-2nd printing (1991, $11.95)-Printed on higher quality paper than 1st print; Dorman painted-c 2.40 6.00 12.00
Hardcover ('90, $24.95, B&W)-r/1-6, DHP #24 4.20 12.50 25.00
V2#1 ($2.25, color)-Adapts sequel 2.40 6.00 12.00
1-2nd printing ($2.25) .45 1.10 2.25
2-4 1.20 3.00 6.00

ALIENS: EARTH WAR
June, 1990 - No. 4, Oct, 1990 ($2.50, color, mini-series)
Dark Horse Comics
1-All have Sam Kieth-a & Bolton painted-c 2.00 5.00 10.00
1-2nd printing .50 1.25 2.50
2 1.60 4.00 8.00
3,4 1.30 3.25 6.50

ALIENS: GENOCIDE
Nov, 1991 - No. 4, Feb, 1992 ($2.50, color, mini-series)
Dark Horse Comics
1-4: All have Arthur Suydam painted-c .50 1.25 2.50

ALIENS: HIVE
Feb, 1992 - No. 4, May, 1992 ($2.50, color, mini-series)
Dark Horse Comics
1-4: Kelley Jones-c-a in all .50 1.25 2.50

ALIENS: NEWT'S TALE (Dark Horse)(Value: cover or less)

ALIENS VS. PREDATOR (See Dark Horse Presents #36)
June, 1990 - No. 4, Dec, 1990, ($2.50, color, mini-series)
Dark Horse Comics
1-Painted-c 2.00 5.00 10.00

Alien Legion #7, © MEG

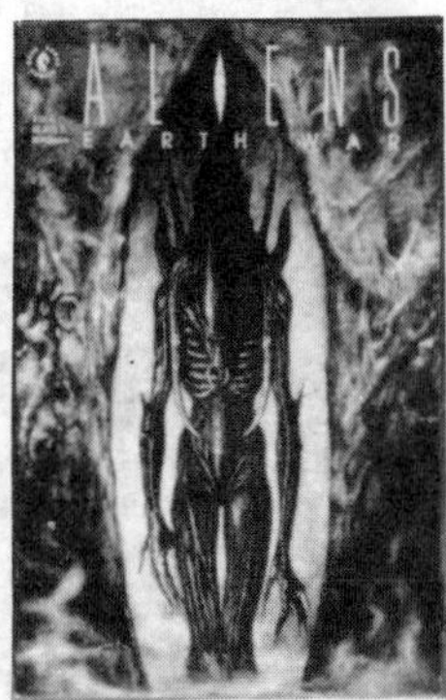

Aliens: Earth War #3, © 20th Century Fox

Aliens Vs. Predator #0, © 20th Century Fox

All-American Comics #36, © DC

All American Men of War #13, © DC

All American Western #104, © DC

GD25 FN65 NM94

1-4-2nd printings .50 1.25 2.50
0-(7/90, $1.95, B&W)-r/Dark Horse Pres. #34-36 2.40 6.00 12.00
2,3 1.20 3.00 6.00
4-Dave Dorman painted-c .80 2.00 4.00

ALIEN TERROR (See 3-D Alien Terror)

ALIEN: THE ILLUSTRATED STORY (Also see Aliens)
1980 ($3.95, color, soft-c, 8X11")
Heavy Metal Books

nn-Movie adaptation; Simonson-a .80 2.00 4.00

ALIEN^3
June, 1992 - No. 3, July, 1992 ($2.50, color, mini-series)
Dark Horse Comics

1-3: Adapts 3rd movie; Suydam painted-c .50 1.25 2.50

ALIEN WORLDS (Pacific) (Value: cover or less) (See Eclipse Graphic Album #22)

ALL-AMERICAN COMICS (...Western #103-126, ...Men of War #127 on; Also see The Big All-American Comic Book)
April, 1939 - No. 102, Oct, 1948
All-American/National Periodical Publications

1-Hop Harrigan, Scribbly by Mayer, Toonerville Folks, Ben Webster, Spot Savage, Mutt & Jeff, Red White & Blue, Adv. in the Unknown, Tippie, Reg'lar Fellers, Skippy, Bobby Thatcher, Mystery Men of Mars, Daiseybelle, & Wiley of West Point begin 350.00 1050.00 2100.00
2-Ripley's Believe It or Not begins, ends #24 110.00 325.00 650.00
3-5: 5-The American Way begins, ends #10 80.00 240.00 475.00
6,7: 6-Last Spot Savage; Popsicle Pete begins, ends #26, 28. 7-Last Bobby Thatcher 67.00 200.00 400.00
8-The Ultra Man begins 100.00 300.00 600.00
9,10: 10-X-Mas-c 70.00 210.00 425.00
11-15: 12-Last Toonerville Folks. 15-Last Tippie & Reg'lar Fellars 63.00 170.00 375.00

GD25 FN65 VF82 NM94

16-(Rare)-Origin/1st app. Green Lantern by Sheldon Mayer (c/a)(7/40) & begin series; appears in costume on-c & only one panel inside; created by Martin Nodell. Inspired by Aladdin's Lamp; the suggested alter ego name Alan Ladd, was never capitalized on. It was changed to Alan Scott before Alan Ladd became a major film star (he was in two films before this issue) 3,200.00 9,600.00 19,200.00 32,000.00
(Estimated up to 35+ total copies exist, 3 in NM/Mint)

GD25 FN65 NM94

17-(Scarce)-2nd Green Lantern 780.00 2350.00 4700.00
18-N.Y. World's Fair-c/story 585.00 1750.00 3500.00

GD25 FN65 VF82 NM94

19-Origin/1st app. The Atom (10/40); last Ultra Man 690.00 2060.00 3800.00 5500.00
(Estimated up to 80 total copies exist, 5 in NM/Mint)

GD25 FN65 NM94

20-Atom dons costume; Ma Hunkle becomes Red Tornado (1st app.)(1st DC costumed heroine, before Wonder Woman, 11/40); Rescue on Mars begins, ends #25; 1 pg. origin Green Lantern 235.00 700.00 1400.00
21-23: 21-Last Wiley of West Point & Skippy. 23-Last Daiseybelle; 3 Idiots begin, end #82 150.00 450.00 900.00
24-Sisty & Dinky become the Cyclone Kids; Ben Webster ends. Origin Dr. Mid-Nite & Sargon, The Sorcerer in text with app. 185.00 550.00 1100.00

GD25 FN65 VF82 NM94

25-Origin & 1st story app. Dr. Mid-Nite by Stan Asch; Hop Harrigan becomes Guardian Angel; last Adventure in the Unknown 440.00 1300.00 2400.00 3500.00
(Estimated up to 120 total copies exist, 6 in NM/Mint)

GD25 FN65 NM94

26-Origin/1st story app. Sargon, the Sorcerer 192.00 480.00 1150.00
27: #27-32 are misnumbered in indicia with correct No. appearing on-c. Intro. Doiby Dickles, Green Lantern's sidekick 245.00 725.00 1450.00
28-Hop Harrigan gives up costumed i.d. 100.00 300.00 600.00
29,30 100.00 300.00 600.00
31-40: 35-Doiby learns Green Lantern's i.d. 75.00 225.00 450.00
41-50: 50-Sargon ends 67.00 200.00 400.00
51-60: 59-Scribbly & the Red Tornado ends 57.00 170.00 340.00
61-Origin/1st app. Solomon Grundy 200.00 600.00 1200.00
62-70: 70-Kubert Sargon; intro Sargon's helper, Maximillian O'Leary 48.00 145.00 285.00
71-88,90-99: 71-Last Red White & Blue. 72-Black Pirate begins (not in #74-82); last Atom. 73-Winky, Blinky & Noddy begins, ends #82. 90-Origin Icicle. 99-Last Hop Harrigan 42.00 125.00 250.00
89-Origin Harlequin 50.00 150.00 300.00
100-1st app. Johnny Thunder by Alex Toth 83.00 250.00 500.00
101-Last Mutt & Jeff 67.00 200.00 400.00
102-Last Green Lantern, Black Pirate & Dr. Mid-Nite 83.00 250.00 500.00

NOTE: *No Atom in 47, 62-69.* ***Kinstler*** *Black Pirate-89.* ***Stan Aschmeier*** *a (Dr. Mid-Nite) 25-84; c-7.* ***Mayer*** *c-1, 2(part), 6, 10.* ***Moldoff*** *c-16-23.* ***Nodell*** *c-31.* ***Paul Reinman*** *a (Green Lantern)-53-55p, 56-84, 87; (Black Pirate)-83-88, 90; c-52, 55-76, 78, 80, 81, 87.* ***Toth*** *a-88, 92, 96, 98-102; c(p)-92, 96-102. Scribbly by* ***Mayer*** *in #1-59. Ultra Man by* ***Mayer*** *in #8-19.*

ALL-AMERICAN MEN OF WAR (Previously All-American Western)
No. 127, Aug-Sept, 1952 - No. 117, Sept-Oct, 1966
National Periodical Publications

127 (#1, 1952) 57.00 170.00 400.00
128 (1952) 39.00 120.00 275.00
2(12-1/'52-53)-5 32.00 95.00 225.00
6-10 19.00 58.00 135.00
11-18: Last precode (2/55) 18.00 54.00 125.00
19-28 12.00 36.00 85.00
29,30,32-Wood-a 13.50 41.00 95.00
31,33-40 10.00 30.00 65.00
41-50 8.70 26.00 52.00
51-56,58-70 6.70 20.00 40.00
57-1st Gunner & Sarge by Andru 10.00 30.00 70.00
71-80 4.35 13.00 26.00
81-100: 82-Johnny Cloud begins, ends #111,114,115. 86-Last 10 cent issue? 3.20 8.00 16.00
101-117: 112-Balloon Buster series begins, ends #114,116; 115-Johnny Cloud app. 2.00 5.00 10.00

NOTE: ***Colan*** *a-112.* ***Drucker*** *a-47, 65, 71, 74, 77.* ***Grandenetti*** *c(p)-127, 128, 2-17(most).* ***Heath*** *a-27, 32, 47, 71, 95, 111, 112; c-85, 91, 94-96, 100, 101, 112, others?* ***Krigstein*** *a-128('52), 2, 3, 5.* ***Kirby*** *a-29.* ***Kubert*** *a-29, 36, 38, 41, 43, 47, 49, 50, 52, 53, 55, 56, 60, 63, 65, 69, 71-73, 102, 103, 105, 106, 108, 114; c-41, 77, 102, 103, 105, 106, 108, 114, others? Tank Killer in 69, 71, 76 by* ***Kubert. P. Reinman*** *c-55, 57, 61, 62, 71, 72, 74-76, 80.*

ALL-AMERICAN SPORTS
October, 1967
Charlton Comics

1 1.40 3.50 7.00

ALL-AMERICAN WESTERN (Formerly All-American Comics; Becomes All-American Men of War)
No. 103, Nov, 1948 - No. 126, June-July, 1952 (103-121: 52 pgs.)
National Periodical Publications

103-Johnny Thunder & his horse Black Lightning continues by Toth, ends #126; Foley of The Fighting 5th, Minstrel Maverick, & Overland Coach begin; Captain Tootsie by Beck; mentioned in Love and Death 32.00 95.00 225.00
104-Kubert-a 23.00 70.00 160.00
105,107-Kubert-a 18.50 56.00 130.00
106,108-110,112: 112-Kurtzman "Pot-Shot Pete," (1 pg.) 14.00 43.00 100.00
111,114-116-Kubert-a 16.50 50.00 115.00
113-Intro. Swift Deer, J. Thunder's new sidekick; classic Toth-c; Kubert-a 18.00 54.00 125.00

	GD25	FN65	NM94
117-126: 121-Kubert-a	11.50	34.00	80.00

NOTE: *G. Kane c(p)-119, 120, 123. Kubert a-103-105, 107, 111, 112(1 pg.), 113-116, 121. Toth a 103-126; c(p)-103-116, 121, 122, 124-126.*

ALL COMICS
1945
Chicago Nite Life News

1	8.35	25.00	50.00

ALLEY OOP (See The Comics, 4-Color #3, The Funnies, Red Ryder and Super Book #9)

ALLEY OOP
No. 10, 1947 - No. 18, Oct, 1949
Standard Comics

10	16.00	48.00	110.00
11-18: 17,18-Schomburg-c	11.50	34.00	80.00

ALLEY OOP
Nov, 1955 - No. 3, March, 1956 (Newspaper reprints)
Argo Publ.

1	11.00	32.00	75.00
2,3	9.15	27.50	55.00

ALLEY OOP
12-2/62-63 - No. 2, 9-11/63
Dell Publishing Co.

1,2	6.70	20.00	40.00

ALL-FAMOUS CRIME (Formerly Law Against Crime #1-3; becomes All-Famous Police Cases #6 on)
No. 4, 2/50 - No. 5, 5/50; No. 8, 5/51 - No. 10, 11/51
Star Publications

4(#1-1st series)-Formerly Law-Crime	7.50	22.50	45.00
5(#2)	4.20	12.50	25.00
8 (#3-2nd series)	6.70	20.00	40.00
9-(#4)-Used in **SOTI**, illo-"The wish to hurt or kill couples in lovers' lanes is a not uncommon perversion;" L.B. Cole-c/a(r)/Law-Crime #3	11.00	32.00	75.00
10 (#5)-Becomes All-Famous Police Cases #6	4.20	12.50	25.00

NOTE: *All have **L.B. Cole** covers.*

ALL FAMOUS CRIME STORIES (See Fox Giants)

ALL-FAMOUS POLICE CASES (Formerly All Famous Crime #10 [#5])
No. 6, Feb, 1952 - No. 16, Sept, 1954
Star Publications

6	5.85	17.50	35.00
7,8: 7-Kubert-a. 8-Marijuana story	4.70	14.00	28.00
9-16	4.00	11.00	22.00

NOTE: *L. B. Cole c-all; a-15, 1pg. Hollingsworth a-15.*

ALL-FLASH (...Quarterly No. 1-5)
Summer, 1941 - No. 32, Dec-Jan, 1947-48
National Periodical Publications/All-American

	GD25	FN65	VF82	NM94
1-Origin The Flash retold by E. E. Hibbard; Hibbard c-1-10,12-14,16,31p	625.00	1825.00	3440.00	5000.00

(Estimated up to 200 total copies exist, 11 in NM/Mint)

	GD25	FN65	NM94
2-Origin recap	154.00	465.00	925.00
3,4	104.00	315.00	625.00
5-Winky, Blinky & Noddy begins, ends #32	80.00	240.00	475.00
6-10	62.00	190.00	375.00
11-13: 12-Origin The Thinker. 13-The King app.	56.00	170.00	335.00
14-Green Lantern cameo	64.00	190.00	385.00
15-20: 18-Mutt & Jeff begins, ends #22	50.00	150.00	300.00
21-31	40.00	120.00	240.00
32-Origin The Fiddler; 1st Star Sapphire	63.00	185.00	375.00

NOTE: *Book length stories in 2-13, 16. Bondage c-31, 32. **Martin Naydell** c-15, 17-28.*

ALL FOR LOVE (Young Love V3#5-on)
Apr-May, 1957 - V3#4, Dec-Jan, 1959-60
Prize Publications

	GD25	FN65	NM94
V1#1	4.70	14.00	28.00
2-6: 5-Orlando-c	3.00	7.50	15.00
V2#1-5(1/59), 5(3/59)	2.00	5.00	10.00
V3#1(5/59), 1(7/59)-4: 2-Powell-a	1.40	3.50	7.00

ALL FUNNY COMICS
Winter, 1943-44 - No. 23, May-June, 1948
Tilsam Publ./National Periodical Publications (Detective)

1-Genius Jones, Buzzy (ends #4), Dover & Clover begin; Bailey-a	32.00	95.00	225.00
2	13.00	40.00	90.00
3-10	10.00	30.00	60.00
11-13,15,18,19-Genius Jones app.	7.00	21.00	42.00
14,17,20-23	3.20	16.00	32.00
16-DC Super Heroes app.	17.00	52.00	120.00

ALL GOOD
Oct, 1949 (260 pgs., 50 cents)
St. John Publishing Co.

(8 St. John comics bound together)	50.00	150.00	350.00

NOTE: *Also see Li'l Audrey Yearbook & Treasury of Comics.*

ALL GOOD COMICS (See Fox Giants)
Spring, 1946 (36 pgs.)
Fox Features Syndicate

1-Joy Family, Dick Transom, Rick Evans, One Round Hogan	12.00	35.00	70.00

ALL GREAT (See Fox Giants)
1946 (36 pgs.)
Fox Feature Syndicate

1-Crazy House, Bertie Benson Boy Detective, Gussie the Gob	10.00	30.00	60.00

ALL GREAT
nd (1945?) (132 pgs.)
William H. Wise & Co.

nn-Capt. Jack Terry, Joan Mason, Girl Reporter, Baron Doomsday; Torture scenes	27.00	80.00	160.00

ALL GREAT COMICS (Formerly Phantom Lady #13? Dagar, Desert Hawk No. 14 on)
No. 14, Oct, 1947 - No. 13, Dec, 1947
Fox Features Syndicate

14-Brenda Starr-r (Scarce)	28.00	82.00	165.00
13-Origin Dagar, Desert Hawk; Brenda Starr (all-r); Kamen-c	23.00	70.00	140.00

ALL-GREAT CONFESSIONS (See Fox Giants)

ALL GREAT CRIME STORIES (See Fox Giants)

ALL GREAT JUNGLE ADVENTURES (See Fox Giants)

ALL HALLOW'S EVE (Innovation)(Value: cover or less)

ALL HERO COMICS
March, 1943 (100 pgs.) (Cardboard cover)
Fawcett Publications

1-Captain Marvel Jr., Capt. Midnight, Golden Arrow, Ibis the Invincible, Spy Smasher, & Lance O'Casey	100.00	300.00	600.00

ALL HUMOR COMICS
Spring, 1946 - No. 17, December, 1949
Quality Comics Group

1	12.00	35.00	70.00
2-Atomic Tot story; Gustavson-a	5.85	17.50	35.00
3-9: 5-1st app. Hickory? 8-Gustavson-a	4.00	10.00	20.00
10-17	2.80	7.00	14.00

All-Famous Crime #4, © STAR

All-Flash Quarterly #1, © DC

All Funny Comics #5, © DC

All-New Comics #1, © HARV

All Select Comics #4, © MEG

All Star Comics #7, © DC

ALL LOVE (...Romances No. 26)(Formerly Ernie Comics)
No. 26, May, 1949 - No. 32, May, 1950
Ace Periodicals (Current Books)

	GD25	FN65	NM94
26(No. 1)-Ernie, Lily Belle app.	4.70	14.00	28.00
27-L. B. Cole-a	5.00	15.00	30.00
28-32	3.00	7.50	15.00

ALL-NEGRO COMICS
June, 1947 (15 cents)
All-Negro Comics

	GD25	FN65	NM94
1 (Rare)	135.00	400.00	800.00

NOTE: *Seldom found in fine or mint condition; many copies have brown pages.*

ALL-NEW COLLECTORS' EDITION (Formerly Limited ...)
Jan, 1978 - Vol. 8, No. C-62, 1979 (No. 54-58: 76 pgs.)
DC Comics, Inc.

	GD25	FN65	NM94
C-53-Rudolph the Red-Nosed Reindeer	.30	.75	1.50
C-54-Superman Vs. Wonder Woman	.40	1.00	2.00
C-55-Superboy & the Legion of Super-Heroes	1.00	2.50	5.00
C-56-Superman Vs. Muhammad Ali: story & wraparound N. Adams-c	.60	1.50	3.00
C-58-Superman Vs. Shazam	.40	1.00	2.00
C-60-Rudolph's Summer Fun(8/78)	.40	1.00	2.00
C-61-See Famous First Edition			
C-62-Superman the Movie (68 pgs.; 1979)-Photo-c from movie plus photos inside (also see DC Special Series #25)	.40	1.00	2.00

ALL-NEW COMICS (...Short Story Comics No. 1-3)
Jan, 1943 - No. 14, Nov, 1946; No. 15, Mar-Apr, 1947 (10 x 13-1/2")
Family Comics (Harvey Publications)

	GD25	FN65	NM94
1-Steve Case, Crime Rover, Johnny Rebel, Kayo Kane, The Echo, Night Hawk, Ray O'Light, Detective Shane begin; Red Blazer on cover only; Sultan-a	92.00	275.00	550.00
2-Origin Scarlet Phantom by Kubert	42.00	125.00	250.00
3	33.00	100.00	200.00
4,5	30.00	90.00	180.00
6-The Boy Heroes & Red Blazer (text story) begin, end #12; Black Cat app.; intro. Sparky in Red Blazer	33.00	100.00	200.00
7-Kubert, Powell-a; Black Cat & Zebra app.	33.00	100.00	200.00
8,9: 8-Shock Gibson app.; Kubert, Powell-a; Schomburg bondage-c. 9-Black Cat app.; Kubert-a	33.00	100.00	200.00
10-12: 10-The Zebra app.; Kubert-a(3). 11-Girl Commandos, Man In Black app. 12-Kubert-a	28.00	85.00	170.00
13-Stuntman by Simon & Kirby; Green Hornet, Joe Palooka, Flying Fool app.; Green Hornet-c	33.00	100.00	200.00
14-The Green Hornet & The Man in Black Called Fate by Powell, Joe Palooka app.; J. Palooka-c by Ham Fisher	28.00	85.00	170.00

15-(Rare)-Small size (5-1/2x8-1/2"; B&W; 32 pgs.). Distributed to mail subscribers only. Black Cat and Joe Palooka app.Estimated value....$200-250

NOTE: *Also see Boy Explorers No. 2, Flash Gordon No. 5, and Stuntman No. 3.* ***Powell*** *a-11.* ***Schomburg*** *c-5, 7-11.*

ALL-OUT WAR
Sept-Oct, 1979 - No. 6, Aug, 1980 ($1.00, 68 pgs.)
DC Comics

	GD25	FN65	NM94
1-6: 1-The Viking Commando(origin), Force Three(origin), & Black Eagle Squadron begin	.30	.75	1.50

NOTE: ***Ayers*** *a(p)-1-6.* ***Elias*** *r-2.* ***Evans*** *a-1-6.* ***Kubert*** *c-16.*

ALL PICTURE ADVENTURE MAGAZINE
Oct, 1952 - No. 2, Nov, 1952 (100 pg. Giants, 25 cents, squarebound)
St. John Publishing Co.

	GD25	FN65	NM94
1-War comics	16.00	48.00	110.00
2-Horror-crime comics	22.00	65.00	150.00

NOTE: *Above books contain three St. John comics rebound; variations possible.* ***Baker*** *art known in both.*

ALL PICTURE ALL TRUE LOVE STORY
October, 1952 (100 pages)
St. John Publishing Co.

	GD25	FN65	NM94
1-Canteen Kate by Matt Baker	29.00	85.00	200.00

ALL-PICTURE COMEDY CARNIVAL
October, 1952 (100 pages, 25 cents)(Contains 4 rebound comics)
St. John Publishing Co.

	GD25	FN65	NM94
1-Contents can vary; Baker-a	29.00	85.00	200.00

ALL REAL CONFESSION MAGAZINE (See Fox Giants)

ALL ROMANCES (Mr. Risk No. 7 on)
Aug, 1949 - No. 6, June, 1950
A. A. Wyn (Ace Periodicals)

	GD25	FN65	NM94
1	5.35	16.00	32.00
2	2.80	7.00	14.00
3-6	2.40	6.00	12.00

ALL-SELECT COMICS (Blonde Phantom No. 12 on)
Fall, 1943 - No. 11, Fall, 1946
Timely Comics (Daring Comics)

	GD25	FN65	NM94
1-Capt. America (by Rico #1), Human Torch, Sub-Mariner begin; Black Widow story (4 pgs.)	284.00	850.00	1700.00
2-Red Skull app.	125.00	375.00	750.00
3-The Whizzer begins	85.00	250.00	500.00
4,5-Last Sub-Mariner	64.00	190.00	385.00
6-9: 6-The Destroyer app. 8-No Whizzer	57.00	165.00	330.00
10-The Destroyer & Sub-Mariner app.; last Capt. America & Human Torch issue	57.00	165.00	330.00
11-1st app. Blonde Phantom; Miss America app.; all Blonde Phantom-c by Shores	92.00	275.00	550.00

NOTE: ***Schomburg*** *c-1-10.* ***Sekowsky*** *a-7. #7 & 8 show 1944 in indicia, but should be 1945.*

ALL SPORTS COMICS (Formerly Real Sports Comics; becomes All Time Sports Comics No. 4 on)
No. 2, Dec-Jan, 1948-49; No. 3, Feb-Mar, 1949
Hillman Periodicals

	GD25	FN65	NM94
2-Krigstein-a(p), Powell, Starr-a	18.00	55.00	110.00
3-Mort Lawrence-a	14.00	42.00	85.00

ALL STAR COMICS (All Star Western No. 58 on)
Sum, '40 - No. 57, Feb-Mar, '51; No. 58, Jan-Feb, '76 -No. 74, Sept-Oct, '78
National Periodical Publ./All-American/DC Comics

	GD25	FN65	VF82	NM94
1-The Flash(#1 by Harry Lampert), Hawkman(by Shelly), Hourman, The Sandman, The Spectre, Biff Bronson, Red White & Blue(ends #2?) begin; Ultra Man's only app. (#1-3 are quarterly; #4 begins bi-monthly issues)	875.00	2625.00	4800.00	7000.00

(Estimated up to 200+ total copies exist, 6 in NM/Mint)

	GD22	FN65	NM94
2-Green Lantern, Johnny Thunder begin	400.00	1200.00	2400.00

	GD25	FN65	VF82	NM94
3-Origin & 1st app. The Justice Society of America; Dr. Fate & The Atom begin, Red Tornado cameo; reprinted in Famous First Edition	1750.00	5250.00	10,500.00	17,500.00

(Estimated up to 150+ total copies exist, 6 in NM/Mint)

	GD25	FN65	NM94
4-1st adventure for J.S.A.	383.00	1150.00	2300.00
5-1st app. Shiera Sanders as Hawkgirl	400.00	1200.00	2400.00
6-Johnny Thunder joins JSA	267.00	800.00	1600.00
7-Batman, Superman, Flash cameo; last Hourman; Doiby Dickles app.	285.00	850.00	1700.00

	GD25	FN65	VF82	NM94

8-Origin & 1st app. Wonder Woman (12-1/41-42)(added as 9pgs. making book 76 pgs.; origin cont'd in Sensation #1; see W.W. #1 for more detailed origin); Dr. Fate dons new helmet; Hop Harrigan text stories & Starman

begin; Shiera app.; Hop Harrigan JSA guest; Starman & Dr. Midnite become members 815.00 2450.00 4500.00 6500.00
(Estimated up to 150 total copies exist, 6 in NM/Mint)

	GD25	FN65	NM94
9,10: 9-Shiera app. 10-Flash, Green Lantern cameo, Sandman new costume	235.00	700.00	1400.00
11,12: 11-Wonder Woman begins; Spectre cameo; Shiera app. 12- Wonder Woman becomes JSA Secretary	200.00	600.00	1200.00
13-15: Sandman w/Sandy in #14 & 15; 15-Origin Brain Wave; Shiera app.	185.00	550.00	1100.00
16-20: 19-Sandman w/Sandy. 20-Dr. Fate & Sandman cameo	135.00	400.00	800.00
21-23: 21-Spectre & Atom cameo; Dr. Fate by Kubert; Dr. Fate, Sandman end. 22-Last Hop Harrigan; Flag-c. 23-Origin Psycho Pirate; last Spectre & Starman	115.00	350.00	700.00
24-Flash & Green Lantern cameo; Mr. Terrific only app.; Wildcat, JSA guest; Kubert Hawkman begins	115.00	350.00	700.00
25-27: 25-The Flash & Green Lantern start again. 27-Wildcat, JSA guest	110.00	325.00	650.00
28-32	96.00	290.00	575.00
33-Solomon Grundy & Doiby Dickles app; classic Solomon Grundy cover	215.00	650.00	1300.00
34,35-Johnny Thunder cameo in both	88.00	260.00	525.00
36-Batman & Superman JSA guests	200.00	600.00	1200.00
37-Johnny Thunder cameo; origin Injustice Society; last Kubert Hawkman	130.00	325.00	650.00
38-Black Canary begins; JSA Death issue	150.00	375.00	750.00
39,40: 39-Last Johnny Thunder	100.00	250.00	500.00
41-Black Canary joins JSA; Injustice Society app.	97.00	242.00	485.00
42-Atom & the Hawkman don new costumes	100.00	250.00	500.00
43-49,51-56: 55-Sci/Fi story	100.00	250.00	500.00
50-Frazetta art, 3 pgs.	110.00	275.00	550.00
57-Kubert-a, 6 pgs. (Scarce)	120.00	300.00	600.00
V12#58-74(1976-78)-Flash, Hawkman, Dr. Mid-Nite, Wildcat, Dr. Fate, Green Lantern, Star Spangled Kid, & Robin app.; intro Power Girl. 58-JSA app. 69-1st app. Huntress		.60	1.25

NOTE: *No Atom-27, 36; no Dr. Fate-13; no Flash-8, 9, 11-23; no Green Lantern-8, 9,11-23; Hawkman in 1-57; no Johnny Thunder-5, 36; no Wonder Woman-9, 10, 23. Book length stories in 4-9, 11-14, 18-22, 25, 26, 29, 30, 32-36, 42, 43. Johnny Peril in #42-46, 48, 49, 51, 52,54-57.* ***Baily*** *a-1-10, 12, 13, 14i, 15-20.* ***Burnley*** *Starman-8-13; c-12, 13.* ***Grell*** *c-58.* ***E.E. Hibbard*** *c-3, 4, 6-10.* ***Kubert*** *Hawkman-24-30, 33-37.* ***Lampert/Baily/Flessel*** *c-1, 2.* ***Moldoff*** *Hawkman-3-23; c-11.* ***Mart Naydell*** *c-25i, 26i, 27-32.* ***Simon & Kirby*** *Sandman 14-17, 19.* ***Staton*** *a-66-74p. c-74p.* ***Toth*** *a-37(2), 38(2), 40, 41; c-38, 41.* ***Wood*** *a-58i-63i, 64, 65; c-63i, 64, 65.*

ALL STAR INDEX, THE (Eclipse) (Value: cover or less)

ALL-STAR SQUADRON (See Justice League of America #193)
Sept, 1981 - No. 67, March, 1987
DC Comics

	GD25	FN65	NM94
1-Original Atom, Hawkman, Dr. Mid-Nite, Robotman (origin), Plastic Man, Johnny Quick, Liberty Belle, Shining Knight begin		.50	1.00
2-24: 5-Danette Reilly becomes new Firebrand. 8-Re-intro Steel, the Indestructable Man. 12-Origin G.A. Hawkman retold. 23-Origin/1st app. The Amazing Man. 24-Batman app.		.50	1.00
25-1st app. Infinity, Inc. (9/83)		.50	1.00
26-Origin Infinity, Inc. (2nd app.); Robin app.		.50	1.00
27-46,48,49: 33-Origin Freedom Fighters of Earth-X. 41-Origin Starman		.50	1.00
47-Origin Dr. Fate; McFarlane-a (1st full story)/part-c (7/85)	.50	1.50	3.00
50-Double size; Crisis x-over		.50	1.00
51-67: 51-56-Crisis x-over. 61-Origin Liberty Belle. 62-Origin The Shining Knight. 63-Origin Robotman. 65-Origin Johnny Quick. 66-Origin Tarantula		.50	1.00
Annual 1-3: 1(11/82)-Retells origin of G.A. Atom, Guardian & Wildcat. 2(11/83)-Infinity, Inc. app. 3(9/84)		.50	1.00

NOTE: ***Kubert*** *c-2, 7-18. JLA app. in 14, 15. JSA app. in 4, 14, 15, 19, 27, 28.*

ALL-STAR STORY OF THE DODGERS, THE
April, 1979 (Full Color) ($1.00)
Stadium Communications

	GD25	FN65	NM94
1		.50	1.00

ALL STAR WESTERN (Formerly All Star Comics No. 1-57)
No. 58, Apr-May, 1951 - No. 119, June-July, 1961
National Periodical Publications

	GD25	FN65	NM94
58-Trigger Twins (ends #116), Strong Bow, The Roving Ranger & Don Caballero begin	31.00	93.00	215.00
59,60: Last 52 pgs	14.00	43.00	100.00
61-66: 61-64-Toth-a	11.50	34.00	80.00
67-Johnny Thunder begins; Gil Kane-a	14.00	43.00	100.00
68-81: Last precode (2-3/55)	7.50	22.50	45.00
82-98	6.35	19.00	38.00
99-Frazetta-r/Jimmy Wakely #4	7.50	22.50	45.00
100	7.00	21.00	42.00
101-107,109-116,118,119	4.70	14.00	28.00
108-Origin Johnny Thunder	11.00	32.00	75.00
117-Origin Super Chie	8.35	25.00	50.00

NOTE: ***G. Kane*** *c(p)-58, 59, 61, 63, 64, 68, 69, 70-95(most), 97-199(most).* ***Infantino*** *art in most issues. Madame .44 app.-#117-119.*

ALL-STAR WESTERN (Weird Western Tales No. 12 on)
Aug-Sept, 1970 - No. 11, Apr-May, 1972
National Periodical Publications

	GD25	FN65	NM94
1-Pow-Wow Smith-r; Infantino-a	2.00	5.00	10.00
2-8: 2-Outlaw begins; El Diablo by Morrow begins; has cameos by Williamson, Torres, Gil Kane, Giordano & Phil Seuling. 3-Origin El Diablo. 5-Last Outlaw issue. 6-Billy the Kid begins, ends #8	.70	1.75	3.50
9-Frazetta-a, 3pgs.(r)	1.00	2.50	5.00
10-Jonah Hex begins (1st app., 2-3/72)	6.35	19.00	38.00
11	2.00	5.00	10.00

NOTE: ***Neal Adams*** *c-1-5;* ***Aparo*** *a-5.* ***G. Kane*** *a-3, 4, 6, 8.* ***Kubert*** *a-4r, 7-9r.* ***Morrow*** *a-2-4, 10, 11. No. 7-11 have 52 pages.*

ALL SURPRISE (Becomes Jeanie #13 on)
Fall, 1943 - No. 12, Winter, 1946-47
Timely/Marvel (CPC)

	GD25	FN65	NM94
1-Super Rabbit & Gandy & Sourpuss	17.00	50.00	100.00
2	7.50	22.50	45.00
3-10,12	5.00	15.00	30.00
11-Kurtzman "Pigtales" art	7.50	22.50	45.00

ALL TEEN (Formerly All Winners; All Winners & Teen Comics No. 21 on)
No. 20, January, 1947
Marvel Comics (WFP)

	GD25	FN65	NM94
20-Georgie, Mitzi, Patsy Walker, Willie app.; Syd Shores-c	5.35	16.00	32.00

ALL THE FUNNY FOLKS
1926 (hardcover, 112 pgs., 11-1/2x3-1/2") (Full color)
World Press Today, Inc.

	GD25	FN65	NM94
nn-Barney Google, Spark Plug, Jiggs & Maggie, Tillie The Toiler, Happy Hooligan, Hans & Fritz, Toots & Casper, etc.	30.00	90.00	180.00

ALL-TIME SPORTS COMICS (Formerly All Sports Comics)
V2No. 4, Apr-May, 1949 - V2No. 7, Oct-Nov, 1949 (All 52 pgs.)
Hillman Periodicals

	GD25	FN65	NM94
V2#4	13.00	32.00	75.00
5-7: 5-Powell-a. 7-Krigstein-a(p)	9.15	27.50	55.00

ALL TOP
1944 (132 pages)
William H. Wise Co.

	GD25	FN65	NM94
Capt. V, Merciless the Sorceress, Red Robbins, One Round Hogan, Mike the M.P., Snooky, Pussy Katnip app.	20.00	60.00	120.00

ALL TOP COMICS (My Experience No. 19 on)

All Star Comics #55, © DC

All-Star Western #1, © DC

All-Time Sports Comics #7, © HILL

All-True Detective Cases #2, © AVON

All True Romance #20, © AJAX

All Winners #5, © MEG

1945; No. 2, Sum, 1946 - No. 18, Mar, 1949; 1957 - 1959
Fox Features Synd./Green Publ./Norlen Mag.

	GD25	FN65	NM94
1-Cosmo Cat & Flash Rabbit begin	14.00	42.00	85.00
2 (#1-7 are funny animal)	7.00	21.00	42.00
3-7	5.35	16.00	32.00
8-Blue Beetle, Phantom Lady, & Rulah, Jungle Goddess begin (11/47); Kamen-c	92.00	275.00	550.00
9-Kamen-c	55.00	165.00	330.00
10-Kamen bondage-c	58.00	1755.00	350.00
11-13,15-17: 15-No Blue Beetle	40.00	120.00	240.00
14-No Blue Beetle; used in **SOTI**, illo-"Corpses of colored people strung up by their wrists"	50.00	150.00	300.00
18-Dagar, Jo-Jo app; no Phantom Lady or Blue Beetle	32.00	95.00	190.00
6(1957-Green Publ.)-Patoruzu the Indian; Cosmo Cat on cover only	2.40	6.00	12.00
6(1958-Literary Ent.)-Muggy Doo; Cosmo Cat on cover only	2.40	6.00	12.00
6(1959-Norlen)-Atomic Mouse; Cosmo Cat on cover only	2.40	6.00	12.00
6(1959)-Little Eva	2.40	6.00	12.00
6(Cornell)-Supermouse on-c	2.40	6.00	12.00

NOTE: *Jo-Jo by **Kamen**-12,18.*

ALL TRUE ALL PICTURE POLICE CASES
Oct, 1952 - No. 2, Nov, 1952 (100 pages)
St. John Publishing Co.

	GD25	FN65	NM94
1-Three rebound St. John crime comics	25.00	75.00	175.00
2-Three comics rebound	20.00	60.00	140.00

NOTE: *Contents may vary*

ALL-TRUE CRIME (...Cases No. 26-35; formerly Official True Crime Cases)
No. 26, Feb, 1948 - No. 52, Sept, 1952
Marvel/Atlas Comics(OFI No. 26,27/CFI No. 28,29/LCC No. 30-46/LMC No. 47-52)

	GD25	FN65	NM94
26(#1)-Syd Shores-c	10.00	30.00	70.00
27(4/48)-Electric chair-c	9.15	27.50	55.00
28-41,43-48,50-52: 36-Photo-c	4.00	10.00	20.00
42,49-Krigstein-a. 49-Used in **POP**, Pg 79	5.00	15.00	30.00

NOTE: ***Robinson** a-47, 50. **Shores** c-26. **Tuska** a-48(3).*

ALL-TRUE DETECTIVE CASES (Kit Carson No. 5 on)
Feb-Mar, 1954 - No. 4, Aug-Sept, 1954
Avon Periodicals

	GD25	FN65	NM94
1	12.00	36.00	80.00
2-Wood-a	11.00	32.00	75.00
3-Kinstler-c	5.35	16.00	32.00
4-Wood(?), Kamen-a	9.30	28.00	65.00
nn(100 pgs.)-7 pg. Kubert-a, Kinstler back-c	21.50	65.00	150.00

ALL TRUE ROMANCE (...Illustrated No. 3)
3/51 - No. 20, 12/54; No. 22, 3/55 - No. 30?, 7/57; No. 3(#31), 9/57 No. 4(#32), 11/57; No. 33, 2/58 - No. 34, 3/58
Artful Publ. #1-3/Harwell(Comic Media) #4-20?/Ajax-Farrell(Excellent Publ.) No. 22 on/Four Star Comic Corp.

	GD25	FN65	NM94
1 (3/51)	9.15	27.50	55.00
2 (10/51; 11/51 on-c)	5.35	16.00	32.00
3(12/51) - #5(5/52)	4.35	13.00	26.00
6-Wood-a, 9 pgs. (exceptional)	11.00	32.00	75.00
7-10	4.00	10.00	20.00
11-13,16-19 (2/54)	3.20	8.00	16.00
14-Marijuana story	3.60	9.00	18.00
20,22: Last precode issue (Ajax, 3/55)	2.60	6.50	13.00
23-27,29,30	2.20	5.50	11.00
28 (9/56)-L. B. Cole, Disbrow-a	4.00	12.00	24.00
3,4,33,34 (Farrell, '57-'58)	1.40	3.50	7.00

ALL WESTERN WINNERS (Formerly All Winners; becomes Western Winners with No. 5; see Two-Gun Kid No. 5)
No. 2, Winter, 1948-49 - No. 4, April, 1949
Marvel Comics(CDS)

	GD25	FN65	NM94
2-Black Rider (Origin & 1st app.) & his horse Satan, Kid Colt & his horse Steel, & Two-Gun Kid & his horse Cyclone begin; Shores c-2-4	30.00	90.00	210.00
3-Anti-Wertham editorial	20.00	60.00	140.00
4-Black Rider i.d. revealed; Heath, Shores-a	20.00	60.00	140.00

ALL WINNERS COMICS (All Teen #20)
Summer, 1941 - No. 19, Fall, 1946; No. 21, Winter, 1946-47 (no No. 20) (No. 21 continued from Young Allies No. 20)
USA No. 1-7/WFP No. 10-19/YAI No. 21

	GD25	FN65	VF82	NM94
1-The Angel & Black Marvel only app.; Capt. America by Simon & Kirby, Human Torch & Sub-Mariner begin (#1 was advertised as All Aces)	500.00	1500.00	2750.00	4000.00

	GD25	FN65	NM94
2-The Destroyer & The Whizzer begin; Simon & Kirby Captain America &-c	200.00	600.00	1200.00
3	150.00	450.00	900.00
4-Classic War-c by Al Avison	170.00	510.00	1025.00
5	100.00	300.00	600.00
6-The Black Avenger only app.; no Whizzer story; Hitler, Hirohito & Mussolini-c	112.00	335.00	675.00
7-10	84.00	250.00	500.00
11,13-18: 14-16-No Human Torch	56.00	165.00	335.00
12-Red Skull story; last Destroyer; no Whizzer story	58.00	175.00	350.00
19-(Scarce)-1st app. & origin All Winners Squad (Capt. America & Bucky, Human Torch & Toro, Sub-Mariner, Whizzer, & Miss America; r-in Fantasy Masterpieces #10	128.00	380.00	765.00
21-(Scarce)-All Winners Squad; bondage-c	116.00	350.00	700.00

NOTE: ***Everett** Sub-Mariner-1, 3, 4; **Burgos** Torch-1, 3, 4. **Schomburg** c-1, 7-18. **Shores** c-19p, 21.*

(2nd Series - August, 1948, Marvel Comics (CDS))
(Becomes All Western Winners with No. 2)

	GD25	FN65	NM94
1-The Blonde Phantom, Capt. America, Human Torch, & Sub-Mariner app.	104.00	310.00	625.00

ALL YOUR COMICS (See Fox Giants)
Spring, 1946 (36 pages)
Fox Feature Syndicate (R. W. Voight)

	GD25	FN65	NM94
1-Red Robbins, Merciless the Sorceress app.	9.15	27.50	55.00

ALMANAC OF CRIME (See Fox Giants)

AL OF FBI (See Little Al of the FBI)

ALONG THE FIRING LINE WITH ROGER BEAN
1916 (Hardcover, B&W) (6x17") (66 pages)
Chas. B. Jackson

	GD25	FN65	NM94
3-by Chic Jackson (1915 daily strips)	13.50	40.00	80.00

ALPHA AND OMEGA (Spire Christian) (Value: cover or less)

ALPHA FLIGHT (See X-Men #120,121 & X-Men/Alpha Flight)
Aug, 1983 - Present (#52-on are direct sale only)
Marvel Comics Group

	GD25	FN65	NM94
1-Byrne-a begins (52pgs.)-Wolverine & Nightcrawler cameo	.80	2.00	4.00
2-Vindicator becomes Guardian; origin Marrina & Alpha Flight	.40	1.00	2.00
3-11: 3-Concludes origin Alpha Flight. 6-Origin Shaman. 7-Origin Snowbird. 10,11-Origin Sasquatch	.40	1.00	2.00
12-Double size; death of Guardian	.40	1.00	2.00

	GD25	FN65	NM94
13-Wolverine app.	2.40	6.00	12.00
14-16: 16-Wolverine cameo	.30	.75	1.50
17-X-Men x-over; Wolverine cameo	1.20	3.00	6.00
18-28: 20-New headquarters. 25-Return of Guardian. 28-Last Byrne issue	.30	.75	1.50
29-32,35-49		.60	1.25
33,34: 33-X-Men (Wolverine) app. 34-Origin Wolverine	1.40	3.50	7.00
50-Double size	.30	.75	1.50
51-Jim Lee's 1st work at Marvel (10/87); Wolverine cameo; 1st Lee Wolverine	1.80	4.50	9.00
52,53-Wolverine app.; Lee-a on Wolverine; 53-Lee/Portacio-a	1.00	2.50	5.00
54,63,64-No Jim Lee-a		.60	1.25
55-62-Jim Lee-a(p)	.80	2.00	4.00
65-74,76-86: 65-Begin $1.50-c. 71-Intro The Sorcerer (villain). 74-Wolverine, Spider-Man & The Avengers app. 89-Original Guardian returns	.30	.75	1.50
75-Double size ($1.95, 52 pgs.)	.40	1.00	2.00
87-90-Wolverine 4 part story w/Jim Lee covers	1.20	3.00	6.00
91-99,101-104: 91-Dr. Doom app. 94-F.F. x-over. 99-Galactus, Avengers app. 102-Intro Weapon Omega. 104-Last $1.50-c	.35	.90	1.75
100-($2.00, 52 pgs.)-Avengers & Galactus app.	.40	1.00	2.00
105,107-119: 107-X-Factor x-over. 110-112-Infinity War x-overs. 110,111-Wolverine app. (brief). 111-Thanos cameo	.35	.90	1.75
106-Northstar revelation issue	1.40	3.50	7.00
106-2nd printing (direct sale only)	.40	1.00	2.00
120-($2.25)-Polybagged w/Superpowers poster	.45	1.10	2.25
Annual 1 (9/86, $1.25)	.35	.90	1.75
Annual 2(12/87, $1.25)		.65	1.25
Special V2#1(6/92, $2.50, 52 pgs.)-Wolverine-c/s	.50	1.25	2.50

NOTE: ***Austin*** *c-1i, 2i, 53i.* ***Byrne*** *c-81, 82.* ***Guice*** *c-85, 91-99.* ***Jim Lee*** *a(p)-51, 53, 55-62, 64; c-53, 87-90.* ***Whilce Portacio*** *a(i)-39-47, 49-54.*

ALPHA FLIGHT SPECIAL
July, 1991 - No. 4, Oct, 1991 ($1.50, color, limited series)
Marvel Comics

	GD25	FN65	NM94
1-3: Reprints Alpha Flight #97-99 w/covers	.30	.75	1.50
4 ($2.00, 52 pgs.)-Reprints Alpha Flight #100	.40	1.00	2.00

ALPHA WAVE (Darkline) (Value: cover or less)

ALPHONSE & GASTON & LEON
1903 (15x10", Sunday strip reprints in color)
Hearst's New York American & Journal

	GD25	FN65	NM94
nn-by Fred Opper	47.00	140.00	325.00

ALTER EGO (First) (Value: cover or less)

ALVIN (TV) (See 4-Color Comics No. 1042)
Oct-Dec, 1962 - No. 28, Oct, 1973
Dell Publishing Co.

	GD25	FN65	NM94
12-021-212 (#1)	10.00	30.00	60.00
2	5.85	17.50	35.00
3-10	4.20	12.50	25.00
11-28	4.00	10.50	21.00
Alvin For President (10/64)	3.20	8.00	16.00
...& His Pals in Merry Christmas with Clyde Crashcup & Leonardo 1 (02-120-402)-(12-2/64), reprinted in 1966 (12-023-604)	4.70	14.00	28.00

AMAZING ADULT FANTASY (Formerly Amazing Adventures #1-6; becomes Amazing Fantasy #15)
No. 7, Dec, 1961 - No. 14, July, 1962
Marvel Comics Group (AMI)

	GD25	FN65	NM94
7-Ditko-c/a begins, ends #14	32.00	95.00	225.00
8-Last 10 cent issue	27.00	80.00	185.00
9-13: 12-1st app. Mailbag. 13-Anti-communist story	23.00	70.00	160.00
14-Professor X prototype	26.00	78.00	180.00

AMAZING ADVENTURE FUNNIES (Fantoman No. 2 on)
June, 1940 - No. 2, Sept. 1940
Centaur Publications

	GD25	FN65	NM94
1-The Fantom of the Fair by Gustavson (r/Amaz. Mystery Funnies V2#7, V2#8), The Arrow, Skyrocket Steele From the Year X by Everett (r/AMF #2); Burgos-a	135.00	400.00	800.00
2-Reprints; Published after Fantoman #2	92.00	275.00	550.00

NOTE: ***Burgos*** *a-1(2).* ***Everett*** *a-1(3).* ***Gustavson*** *a-1(5), 2(3).* ***Pinajian*** *a-2.*

AMAZING ADVENTURES (Also see Boy Cowboy & Science Comics)
1950; No. 1, Nov, 1950 - No. 6, Fall, 1952 (Painted covers)
Ziff-Davis Publ. Co.

	GD25	FN65	NM94
1950 (no month given) (8-1/2x11) (8 pgs.) Has the front & back cover plus Schomburg story used in Amazing Advs. #1 (Sent to subscribers of Z-D s/f magazines & ordered through mail for 10 cents. Used to test market) Estimated value....			190.00
1-Wood, Schomburg, Anderson, Whitney-a	37.00	110.00	260.00
2-5: 2,4,5-Anderson-a. 3,5-Starr-a	14.00	43.00	100.00
6-Krigstein-a	19.00	58.00	135.00

AMAZING ADVENTURES (Becomes Amazing Adult Fantasy #7 on)
June, 1961 - No. 6, Nov, 1961
Atlas Comics (AMI)/Marvel Comics No. 3 on

	GD25	FN65	NM94
1-Origin Dr. Droom (1st Marvel-Age Superhero) by Kirby; Ditko & Kirby-a in all; Kirby c-1-6	72.00	215.00	500.00
2	39.00	120.00	275.00
3-6: 6-Last Dr. Droom	32.00	95.00	225.00

AMAZING ADVENTURES
Aug, 1970 No. 39, Nov, 1976
Marvel Comics Group

	GD25	FN65	NM94
1-Inhumans by Kirby(p) & Black Widow (1st app. in Tales of Suspense #52) double feature begins	2.40	6.00	12.00
2-4: 2-F.F. brief app. 4-Last Kirby Inhumans	1.00	2.50	5.00
5-8-Neal Adams-a(p); 8-Last Black Widow	1.40	3.50	7.00
9,10: Magneto app. 10-Last Inhumans (origin-r by Kirby)	1.00	2.50	5.00
11-New Beast begins(origin in flashback); X-Men cameo in flashback (11-17 are all X-Men tie-ins)	2.00	5.00	10.00
12-17: 13-Brotherhood of Evil Mutants x-over from X-Men. 15-X-Men app. 17-Last Beast (origin); X-Men app.	1.40	3.50	7.00
18-War of the Worlds begins; 1st app. Killraven; Neal Adams-a(p)	2.40	6.00	12.00
19-39: 35-Giffen's first published story (art); along with Deadly Hands of Kung-Fu #22 (3/76)	.70	1.75	3.50

NOTE: ***N. Adams*** *c-6-8.* ***Buscema*** *a-1p, 2p.* ***Colan*** *a-3-5p, 26p.* ***Ditko*** *a-24r.* ***Everett*** *a(i)3-5, 7-9.* ***Giffen*** *a-35i, 38p.* ***G. Kane*** *c-11, 25p, 29p.* ***Ploog*** *a-12i.* ***Russell*** *a-27-32, 34-37, 39; c-28, 30-32, 33i, 34, 35, 37, 39i.* ***Starliing*** *a-17.* ***Starlin*** *c-15p, 16, 17, 27.* ***Sutton*** *a-11-15p.*

AMAZING ADVENTURES
December, 1979 - No. 14, January, 1981
Marvel Comics Group

	GD25	FN65	NM94
V2#1-Reprints story/X-Men #1 & 38 (origins)	.80	2.00	4.00
2-14: 2-6-Early X-Men-r. 7,8-Origin Iceman	.60	1.50	3.00

NOTE: ***Byrne*** *c-6p, 9p.* ***Kirby*** *a-1-14r; c-7, 9.* ***Steranko*** *a-12r.* ***Tuska*** *a-7-9.*

AMAZING ADVENTURES
July, 1988 ($4.95, One-shot, color, squarebound, 80 pgs.)
Marvel Comics

	GD25	FN65	NM94
1-Anthology; Austin, Golden-a	1.00	2.50	5.00

AMAZING ADVENTURES OF CAPTAIN CARVEL AND HIS CARVEL CRUSADERS, THE (See Carvel Comics)

AMAZING CHAN & THE CHAN CLAN, THE (TV)
May, 1973 - No. 4, Feb, 1974 (Hanna-Barbera)
Gold Key

	GD25	FN65	NM94
1	2.00	5.00	10.00

Alpha Flight #88, © MEG

Amazing Adventure Funnies #1, © CEN

Amazing Adventures #5 (10/61), © MEG

Amazing Man Comics #16, © CEN

Amazing Mystery Funnies V2#8, © CEN

Amazing Spider-Man #3, © MEG

GD25 FN65 NM94

2-4 1.20 3.00 6.00

AMAZING COMICS (Complete Comics No. 2)
Fall, 1944
Timely Comics (EPC)

1-The Destroyer, The Whizzer, The Young Allies (by Sekowsky), Sergeant Dix; Schomburg-c 100.00 300.00 600.00

AMAZING DETECTIVE CASES (Formerly Suspense No. 2?)
No. 3, Nov, 1950 - No. 14, Sept, 1952
Marvel/Atlas Comics (CCC)

3 11.00 32.00 75.00
4-6 6.00 18.00 36.00
7-10 4.70 14.00 28.00
11,14: 11-(3/52)-change to horror 7.50 22.50 45.00
12-Krigstein-a 7.50 22.50 45.00
13-(Scarce)-Everett-a; electrocution-c/story 10.00 30.00 60.00

NOTE: ***Colan** a-9. **Maneely** c-13. **Sekowsky** a-12. **Sinnott** a-13. **Tuska** a-10.*

AMAZING FANTASY (Formerly Amazing Adult Fantasy #7-14)
No. 15, Aug, 1962 (Sept, 1962 shown in indicia)
Marvel Comics Group (AMI)

15-Origin/1st app. of Spider-Man by Ditko (11 pgs.); 1st app. Aunt May & Uncle Ben; Kirby/Ditko-c 875.00 2625.00 7000.00

AMAZING GHOST STORIES (Formerly Nightmare)
No. 14, Oct, 1954 - No. 16, Feb, 1955
St. John Publishing Co.

14-Pit & the Pendulum story by Kinstler; Baker-c 13.00 40.00 90.00
15-r/Weird Thrillers #5; Baker-c, Powell-a 10.00 30.00 65.00
16-Kubert reprints of Weird Thrillers #4; Baker-c; Roussos, Tuska-a; Kinstler-a (1 pg.) 10.00 30.00 70.00

AMAZING HIGH ADVENTURE
8/84; No. 2, 10/85; No. 3, 10/86 - No. 5, 1987 (Baxter No. 3,4)($2.00)
Marvel Comics

1-5 .40 1.00 2.00

NOTE: ***Bissette** a-4. **Bolton** c/a-4. **Severin** a-1, 3. **P. Smith** a-2. **Williamson** a-2i.*

AMAZING-MAN COMICS (Formerly Motion Picture Funnies Weekly?)
(Also see Stars And Stripes Comics)
No. 5, Sept, 1939 - No. 27, Feb, 1942
Centaur Publications

GD25 FN65 VF82 NM94

5(#1)(Rare)-Origin/1st app. A-Man the Amazing Man by Bill Everett; The Cat-Man by Tarpe Mills (also #8), Mighty Man by Filchock, Minimidget & sidekick Ritty, & The Iron Skull by Burgos begins
1190.00 3560.00 6550.00 9500.00
(Estimated up to 60 total copies exist, 3 in NM/Mint)

GD25 FN65 NM94

6-Origin The Amazing Man retold; The Shark begins; Ivy Menace by Tarpe Mills app. 267.00 800.00 1600.00
7-Magician From Mars begins; ends #11 158.00 475.00 950.00
8-Cat-Man dresses as woman 117.00 350.00 700.00
9-Magician From Mars battles the 'Elemental Monster,' swiped into The Spectre in More Fun #54 & 55 117.00 350.00 700.00
10,11: 11-Zardi, the Eternal Man begins; ends #16; Amazing Man dons costume; last Everett issue 100.00 300.00 600.00
12,13 96.00 285.00 575.00
14-Reef Kinkaid, Rocke Wayburn (ends #20), & Dr. Hypno (ends #21) begin; no Zardi or Chuck Hardy 75.00 225.00 450.00
15,17-20: 15-Zardi returns; no Rocke Wayburn. 17-Dr. Hypno returns; no Zardi 58.00 175.00 350.00
16-Mighty Man's powers of super strength & ability to shrink & grow explained; Rocke Wayburn returns; no Dr. Hypno; Al Avison (a character) begins, ends #18 (a tribute to the famed artist) 63.00 185.00 375.00
21-Origin Dash Dartwell (drug-use story); origin & only app. T.N.T. 58.00 175.00 350.00
22-Dash Dartwell, the Human Meteor & The Voice app; last Iron Skull & The Shark; Silver Streak app. 58.00 175.00 350.00
23-Two Amazing Man stories; intro/origin Tommy the Amazing Kid; The Marksman only app. 63.00 185.00 375.00
24,27: 24-King of Darkness, Nightshade, & Blue Lady begin; end #26; 1st app. Super-Ann 58.00 175.00 350.00
25,26 (Scarce)-Meteor Martin by Wolverton in both; 26-Electric Ray app. 78.00 235.00 550.00

NOTE: ***Everett** a-5-11; c-5-11. **Gilman** a-14-20. **Giunta/Mirando** a-7-10. **Sam Glanzman** a-14-16, 18-21, 23. **Louis Glanzman** a-6, 9-11, 14-21; c-13-19, 21. **Robert Golden** a-9. **Gustavson** a-6; c-22, 23. **Lubbers** a-14-21. **Simon** a-10. **Frank Thomas** a-6, 9-11, 14, 15, 17-21.*

AMAZING MYSTERIES (Formerly Sub-Mariner Comics No. 31)
No. 32, May, 1949 - No. 35, Jan, 1950
Marvel Comics (CCC)

32-The Witness app; 1st Marvel horror comic 37.00 110.00 265.00
33-Horror format 13.00 40.00 90.00
34,35-Change to Crime. 34,35-Photo-c 10.00 30.00 60.00

AMAZING MYSTERY FUNNIES
Aug, 1938 - No. 24, Sept, 1940 (All 52 pgs.)
Centaur Publications

V1#1-Everett-c(1st); Dick Kent Adv. story; Skyrocket Steele in the Year X on cover only 265.00 800.00 1600.00
2-Everett 1st-a (Skyrocket Steele) 125.00 375.00 750.00
3 70.00 210.00 425.00
3(#4, 12/38)-nn on cover, #3 on inside; bondage-c 60.00 175.00 350.00
V2#1-4,6: 2-Drug use story. 3-Air-Sub DX begins by Burgos. 4-Dan Hastings, Hastings, Sand Hog begins (ends #5). 6-Last Skyrocket Steele 54.00 160.00 325.00
5-Classic Everett-c 73.00 215.00 435.00
7 (Scarce)-Intro. The Fantom of the Fair; Everett, Gustavson, Burgos-a 265.00 800.00 1600.00
8-Origin & 1st app. Speed Centaur 105.00 310.00 625.00
9-11: 11-Self portrait and biog. of Everett; Jon Linton begins 60.00 175.00 350.00
12 (Scarce)-1st Space Patrol; Wolverton-a (12/39) 132.00 400.00 800.00
V3#1(#17, 1/40)-Intro. Bullet; Tippy Taylor serial begins, ends #24 (continued in The Arrow #2) 60.00 175.00 350.00
18,20: 18-Fantom of the Fair by Gustavson 54.00 160.00 325.00
19,21-24-Space Patrol by Wolverton in all 80.00 240.00 485.00

NOTE: ***Burgos** a-V2#3-9. **Eisner** a-V1#2, 3(2). **Everett** a-V1#2-4, V2#1, 3-6; c-V1#1-4,V2#3, 5, 18. **Filchock** a-V2#9. **Flessel** a-V2#6. **Guardineer** a-V1#4, V2#4-6; **Gustavson** a-V2#4, 5, 9-12, V3#1, 18, 19; c-V2#7, 9, 12, V3#1, 21, 22; **McWilliams** a-V2#9, 10. **TarpeMills** a-V2#2, 4-6, 9-12, V3#1. **Leo Morey**(Pulp artist) c-V2#10; text illo-V2#11. **FrankThomas** a-6-V2/11. **Webster** a-V2#4.*

AMAZING SAINTS (Logos)(Value: cover or less)

AMAZING SPIDER-MAN, THE (See All Detergent Comics, Amazing Fantasy, America's Best TV Comics, Aurora, Deadly Foes of Spider-Man, Giant-Size Spider-Man, Giant Size Super-Heroes Feat...., Marvel Coll. Item Classics, Marvel Fanfare, Marvel Graphic Novel, Marvel Spec. Ed., Marvel Tales, Marvel Team-Up, Marvel Treasury Ed., Nothing Can Stop the Juggernaut, Official Marvel Index To..., Power Record Comics, Spectacular..., Spider-Man, Spider-Man Digest, Spider-Man Saga, Spider-Man 2099, Spider-Man Vs. Wolverine, Spidey Super Stories, Strange Tales Annual #2, Superman Vs. ..., Try-Out Winner Book, Web of Spider- Man & Within Our Reach)

AMAZING SPIDER-MAN, THE
March, 1963 - Present
Marvel Comics Group

1-Retells origin by Steve Ditko; 1st Fantastic Four x-over; intro. John Jameson & The Chameleon; Spider-Man's 2nd app.; Kirby-c 850.00 2550.00 6800.00
1-Reprint from the Golden Record Comic set 11.00 32.00 75.00
with record (mid-'60s)(still sealed) 22.00 65.00 150.00

GD25 FN65 NM94

2-1st app. the Vulture & the Terrible Tinkerer 257.00 770.010 1800.00
3-1st full-length story; Human Torch cameo; intro. & 1st app. Doc Octopus; Dr. Doom & Ant-Man app. 143.00 430.00 1000.00
4-Origin & 1st app. The Sandman (see Strange Tales #115 for 2nd app.); Intro. Betty Brant & Liz Allen 115.00 345.00 800.00
5-Dr. Doom app. 100.00 300.00 700.00
6-1st app. Lizard 100.00 300.00 700.00
7,8,10: 7-Vs. The Vulture; 1st monthly issue. 8-Fantastic Four app. in back-up story by Ditko/Kirby. 10-1st app. Big Man & The Enforcers 64.00 192.00 450.00
9-Origin & 1st app. Electro (2/64) 72.00 215.00 500.00
11,12: 11-1st app. Bennett Brant 37.00 112.00 260.00
13-1st app. Mysterio 50.00 150.00 350.00
14-(7/64)-1st app. The Green Goblin (c/story)(Norman Osborn); Hulk x-over 125.00 375.00 875.00
15-1st app. Kraven the Hunter; 1st mention of Mary Jane Watson (not shown) 43.00 130.00 300.00
16-Spider-Man battles Daredevil (1st x-over 9/64); still in old yellow costume 30.00 90.00 210.00
17-2nd app. Green Goblin (c/story); Human Torch x-over (also in #18 & #21) 54.00 160.00 375.00
18-1st app. Ned Leeds who later becomes Hobgoblin; Fantastic Four back-up story; 3rd app. Sandman 32.00 95.00 225.00
19-Sandman app. 27.00 80.00 185.00
20-Origin & 1st app. The Scorpion 32.00 95.00 225.00
21-1st app. The Beetle 22.00 65.00 150.00
22-1st app. Princess Python 19.00 58.00 135.00
23-3rd app. The Green Goblin (c/story) 32.00 95.00 225.00
24 18.00 54.00 125.00
25-(6/65)-1st app. Mary Jane Watson (cameo; face not shown); 1st app. Spencer Smythe 22.00 67.00 155.00
26-4th app. The Green Goblin (c/story); 1st app. Crime Master; dies in #27 25.00 75.00 175.00
27-5th app. The Green Goblin (c/story) 23.00 70.00 160.00
28-Origin & 1st app. Molten Man (scarcer in high grade) 29.00 85.00 200.00
29,30 17.00 50.00 115.00
31-38: 31-1st app. Harry Osborn who later becomes 2nd Green Goblin, Gwen Stacy & Prof. Warren. 34-2nd app. Kraven the Hunter. 36-1st app. Looter. 37-Intro. Norman Osborn. 38-(7/66)-2nd app. Mary Jane Watson (cameo; face not shown); last Ditko issue 13.00 40.00 90.00
39-The Green Goblin-c/story; Green Goblin's i.d. revealed as Norman Osborn 17.00 50.00 115.00
40-1st told origin The Green Goblin (c/story) 24.00 72.00 165.00
41-1st app. Rhino 11.00 32.00 75.00
42-(11/66)-3rd app. Mary Jane Watson (cameo in last 2 panels); 1st time face is shown 11.00 32.00 75.00
43-49: 44,45-2nd & 3rd app. The Lizard. 46-Intro. Shocker. 47-M. J. Watson & Peter Parker 1st date. 47,49-3rd & 4th app. Kraven the Hunter 8.35 25.00 50.00
50-1st app. Kingpin (7/67) 32.00 95.00 225.00
51-2nd app. Kingpin 12.00 36.00 85.00
52-60: 52-1st app. Joe Robertson & 3rd app. Kingpin. 56-1st app. Capt. George Stacy. 57-1st-c app. M. J. Watson. 57,58-Ka-Zar app. 59-1st app. Brainwasher (alias Kingpin) 6.70 20.00 40.00
61-74: 67-1st app. Randy Robertson. 69-Kingpin app. 73-1st app. Silvermane. 74-Last 12 cent issue. 5.70 17.00 34.00
75-89,91-93,95,99: 83-1st app. Schemer & Vanessa (Kingpin's wife). 84,85-Kingpin-c/story. 93-1st app. Arthur Stacy . 78,79-1st app. The Prowler 4.70 14.00 28.00
90-Death of Capt. Stacey 5.70 17.00 34.00
94-Origin retold 7.50 22.50 45.00
96-98-Green Goblin app. (97,98-Green Goblin-c); drug books not approved by CCA 10.00 30.00 60.00
100-Anniversary issue (9/71); Green Goblin cameo (2 pgs.) 16.00 48.00 110.00

GD25 FN65 NM94

101-1st app. Morbius the Living Vampire; last 15 cent issue 17.00 52.00 120.00
101-Silver ink 2nd printing (9/92, $1.75) .40 1.00 2.00
102-Origin Morbius (25 cents, 52 pgs.) 13.00 40.00 90.00
103-118: 104,111-Kraven the Hunter-c/stories. 108-1st app. Sha-Shan. 109-Dr. Strange-c/story (6/72). 110-1st app. Gibbon. 113-1st app. Hammerhead 3.60 9.00 18.00
119,120-Spider-Man vs. Hulk 4.70 14.00 28.00
121-Death of Gwen Stacy (killed by Green Goblin) (reprinted in Marvel Tales #98 & 192) 11.00 32.00 75.00
122-Death of The Green Goblin (c/story) (reprinted in Marvel Tales #99 & 192) 14.00 43.00 100.00
123-128: 124-1st app. Man-Wolf, origin in #125. 127-1st mention of Harry Osborn becoming Green Goblin 3.60 9.00 18.00
129-1st app. Jackal & The Punisher (2/74) 40.00 122.00 285.00
130-133,138-160: 131-Last 20 cent issue. 139-1st app. Grizzly. 140-1st app. Glory Grant. 143-1st app. Cyclone. 159-Last 25 cent issue 2.40 6.00 12.00
134-Punisher cameo (7/74); 1st app. Tarantula 4.00 11.00 22.00
135-2nd full Punisher app. (8/74) 10.00 30.00 65.00
136-Reappearance of The Green Goblin (Harry Osborn; Norman Osborn's son) 4.20 12.50 25.00
137-Green Goblin-c/story (2nd Harry Osborn) 3.00 7.50 15.00
161-Nightcrawler app. from X-Men; Punisher cameo 2.40 6.00 12.00
162-Punisher, Nightcrawler app. 4.00 11.00 22.00
163-173,181-190: 167-1st app. Will O' The Wisp. 171-Nova app. 181-Origin retold; gives life history of Spidey; Punisher cameo in flashback (1 panel) 182-(7/78)-Peter proposes to Mary Jane for 1st time, but she refuses 1.40 3.50 7.00
174,175-Punisher app. 3.60 9.00 18.00
176-180-Green Goblin app 2.40 6.00 12.00
191-193,195-199,203-208,210-219: 193-Peter & Mary Jane break up. 196-Faked death of Aunt May. 203-2nd app. Dazzler. 209-1st app. Calypso (Kraven's girlfriend). 210-1st app. Madame Web. 212-1st app. Hydro Man; origin Sandman 1.20 3.00 6.00
194-1st app. Black Cat 2.40 6.00 12.00
200-Giant origin issue (1/80) 4.00 10.00 20.00
201,202-Punisher app. 4.00 11.00 22.00
209-Origin & 1st app. Calypso 1.60 4.00 8.00
220-237: 225-Foolkiller app. 226,227-Black Cat returns. 236-Tarantula dies. 234-Free 16 pg. insert "Marvel Guide to Collecting Comics." 235-Origin Will-'O-The-Wisp 1.20 3.00 6.00
238-(3/83)-1st app. Hobgoblin (Ned Leeds); came with skin "Tattooz" decal 10.00 30.00 60.00
238-Without tattooz decal 4.00 12.00 24.00
239-2nd app. Hobgoblin & 1st battle w/Spidey 5.85 17.50 35.00
240-243,246-248: 241-Origin The Vulture. 243-Reintro Mary Jane Watson after 4 year absence 1.20 3.00 6.00
244-3rd app. Hobgoblin (cameo only) 1.80 4.50 9.00
245-4th app. Hobgoblin (cameo only); Lefty Donovan gains powers of Hobgoblin & battles Spider-Man 2.80 7.00 14.00
249-251: 3 part Hobgoblin/Spider-Man battle. 249-Retells origin & death of 1st Green Goblin. 251-Last old costume 2.40 6.00 12.00
252-Spider-Man dons new black costume (5/84); ties with Marvel Team-Up #141 & Spectacular Spider-Man #90 for 1st new costume (See Marvel S-H Secret Wars #8) 4.00 10.00 20.00
253-1st app. The Rose 1.40 3.50 7.00
254 1.00 2.50 5.00
255,263,264,266-273,277-280,282,283: 279-Jack O'Lantern-c/story. 282-X-Factor x-over .70 1.75 3.50
256-1st app. Puma .80 2.00 4.00
257-Hobgoblin cameo; 2nd app. Puma; M. J. Watson reveals she knows Spidey's i.d. 1.80 4.50 9.00
258-Hobgoblin app. (minor) 2.40 6.00 12.00
259-Full Hobgoblin app.; Spidey back to old costume; origin Mary Jane

Amazing Spider-Man #40, © MEG

Amazing Spider-Man #101, © MEG

Amazing Spider-Man #136, © MEG

Amazing Spider-Man #299, © MEG

Amazing Spider-Man #350, © MEG

Amazing Spider-Man Annual #23, © MEG

	GD25	FN65	NM94
Watson	2.80	7.00	14.00
260-Hobgoblin app.	1.80	4.50	9.00
261-Hobgoblin-c/story; painted-c by Vess	2.00	5.00	10.00
262-Spider-Man unmasked; photo-c	1.20	3.00	6.00
265-1st app. Silver Sable	2.40	6.00	12.00
265-Silver ink 2nd printing ($1.25)	.60	1.50	3.00
274-Zarathos (The Spirit of Vengeance) app. (3/86)	.80	2.00	4.00
275-($1.25, 52 pgs.)-Hobgoblin-c/story; origin-r by Ditko	2.40	6.00	12.00
276-Hobgoblin app.	1.80	4.50	9.00
281-Hobgoblin battles Jack O'Lantern	2.00	5.00	10.00
284-Punisher cameo; Gang War story begins; Hobgoblin-c/story	1.80	4.50	9.00
285-Punisher app.; minor Hobgoblin app.	3.60	9.00	18.00
286,287: 286-Hobgoblin-c & app. (minor). 287-Hobgoblin app. (minor)	1.20	3.00	6.00
288-Full Hobgoblin app.; last Gang War	1.60	4.00	8.00
289-($1.25, 52 pgs.)-Hobgoblin's i.d. revealed as Ned Leeds; death of Ned Leeds; Macendale (Jack O'Lantern) becomes new Hobgoblin	4.00	11.00	22.00
290-292: 290-Peter proposes to Mary Jane. 292-She accepts; leads into Amazing Spider-Man Annual #21	.90	2.25	4.50
293,294-Part 2 & 5 of Kraven story from Web of Spider-Man. 294-Death of Kraven	1.60	4.00	8.00
295-297	1.10	2.75	5.50
298-Todd McFarlane-c/a begins; 1st app. Venom w/o costume (cameo on last pg.)	5.00	15.00	30.00
299-1st Venom with costume (cameo)	3.20	8.00	16.00
300 ($1.50, 52 pgs.; 25th Anniversary)-1st full Venom app.; last black costume	6.70	20.00	40.00
301-305: 301 ($1.00 issues begin). 304-1st bi-weekly issue	3.00	7.50	15.00
306-311,313,314: 306-Swipes-c from Action #1. 315-317-Venom app.	2.00	5.00	10.00
312-Hobgoblin battles Green Goblin	3.60	9.00	18.00
315-317-Venom app.	3.00	7.50	15.00
318-323,325: 319-Bi-weekly begins again	1.40	3.50	7.00
324-Sabretooth app.; McFarlane cover only	2.40	6.00	12.00
326,327,329: 327-Cosmic Spidey continues from Spectacular Spider-Man (no McFarlane-c/a)	.70	1.75	3.50
328-Hulk x-over; last McFarlane issue	1.50	3.75	7.50
330,331-Punisher app. 331-Minor Venom app.	.80	2.00	4.00
332-336,338-343: 332,333-Venom-c/story. 341-Tarantula app.	.50	1.25	2.50
337-Hobgoblin app.	.70	1.75	3.50
344-1st app. Cletus Kasady (Carnage)	1.40	3.50	7.00
345-1st full app. Cletus Kasady; Venom cameo on last pg.	2.00	5.00	10.00
346,347-Venom app.	1.40	3.50	7.00
348,349,351-359: 348-Avengers x-over. 351,352-Nova of New Warriors app. 353-Darkhawk app.; brief Punisher app. 354-Punisher cameo & Nova, Night Thrasher (New Warriors), Darkhawk & Moon Knight app. 357,358-Punisher, Darkhawk, Moon Knight, Night Thrasher, Nova x-over. 358-3 part gatefold-c; last $1.00-c. 360-Carnage cameo	.40	1.00	2.00
350-($1.50, 52pgs.)-Origin retold; Spidey vs. Dr. Doom; pin-ups	.60	1.50	3.00
360-Carnage cameo	1.00	2.50	5.00
361-Intro Carnage (the Spawn of Venom); begin 3 part story; recap of how Spidey's alien costume became Venom	2.20	5.50	11.00
361-2nd printing ($1.25)	.40	1.00	2.00
362,363-Carnage & Venom-c/story	1.20	3.00	6.00
362-2nd printing	.30	.75	1.50
364,366-374,376-378: 364-The Shocker app. (old villain). 366-Peter's parents-c/story. 369-Harry Osborn back-up (Gr. Goblin II)		.60	1.25
365-($3.95, 84 pgs.)-30th anniversary issue w/hologram-c; Spidey/Venom/Carnage pull-out poster; contains 5 pg. preview of Spider-Man 2099 (1st app.); Spidey's origin retold; Lizard app.; reintro Peter's parents in Stan Lee 3 pg. text w/illo (saga continues thru #370)	1.20	3.00	6.00
375-($3.95, 68 pgs.)-Metallic holo-grafx-c; Venom story ties into Venom #1	.80	2.00	4.00
Annual 1 (1964, 72 pgs.)-Origin Spider-Man; 1st app. Sinister Six (Dr. Octopus, Electro, Kraven the Hunter, Mysterio, Sandman, Vulture) (41 pg. story); plus gallery of Spidey foes	35.00	107.00	250.00
Annual 2 (1965, 25 cents, 72 pgs.)-Reprints from #1,2,5 plus new Doctor Strange story	13.50	41.00	95.00
Special 3 (11/66, 25 cents, 72 pgs.)-Avengers & Hulk x-over; Doctor Octopus-r from #11,12; Romita/Heath-a	6.35	19.00	38.00
Special 4 (11/67, 25 cents, 68 pgs.)-Spidey battles Human Torch (new 41 pg. story)	7.50	22.50	45.00
Special 5 (11/68, 25 cents, 68 pgs.)-New 40 pg. Red Skull story; 1st app. Peter Parker's parents	8.35	25.00	50.00
Special 6 (11/69, 25 cents, 68 pgs.)-New 41 pg. Sinister Six story plus 2 Kirby/Ditko stories	3.60	9.00	18.00
Special 7 (12/70, 25 cents, 68 pgs.)-All-r(#1,2)	3.60	9.00	18.00
Special 8 (12/71)	3.60	9.00	18.00
King Size 9 ('73)-Reprints Spectacular Spider-Man (mag.) #2; 40 pg. Green Goblin-c/story (re-edited from 58 pgs.)	3.60	9.00	18.00
Annual 10 (1976)-Origin Human Fly (vs. Spidey)	1.40	3.50	7.00
Annual 11,12: 11 (1977). 12 (1978)-Spider-Man vs. Hulk-r/#119,120	1.15	3.50	7.00
Annual 13 (1979)-Byrne/Austin-a (new)	1.60	4.00	8.00
Annual 14 (1980)-Miller-c/a(p), 40pgs.	1.80	4.50	9.00
Annual 15 (1981)-Miller-c/a(p); Punisher app.	4.00	11.00	22.00
Annual 16-20: 16 (1982)-Origin/1st app. new Capt. Marvel (female heroine). 17 (1983). 18 (1984). 19 (1985). 20 (1986)-Origin Iron Man of 2020	1.20	3.00	6.00
Annual 21 (1987)-Special wedding issue; newsstand & direct sale versions exist & are worth same	1.60	4.00	8.00
Annual 22 (1988, $1.75, 68 pgs.)-1st app. Speedball; Evolutionary War x-over	1.60	4.00	8.00
Annual 23 (1989, $2.00, 68 pgs.)-Atlantis Attacks; origin Spider-Man retold; She-Hulk app.; Byrne-c; Liefeld-a(p), 23 pgs.	1.20	3.00	6.00
Annual 24 (1990, $2.00, 68 pgs.)-Ant-Man app.	.70	1.75	3.50
Annual 25 (1991, $2.00, 68 pgs.)-3 pg. origin recap; Iron Man app.; 1st Venom solo story; Ditko-a (6 pgs.)	1.40	3.50	7.00
Annual 26 (1992, $2.25, 68 pgs.)-New Warriors-c/story; Venom solo story cont'd in Spectacular Spider-Man Annual #12	1.00	2.50	5.00
Soul of the Hunter nn (8/92, $5.95, 52pgs.)-	1.00	3.00	6.00
...: Skating on Thin Ice 1(1990, $1.25, Canadian)-McFarlane-c; anti-drug issue	.80	2.00	4.00
...: Double Trouble 2 (1990, $1.25, Canadian)	.60	1.50	3.00
...: Hit and Run 3 (1990, $1.25, Canadian)-Ghost Rider-c/story	.60	1.50	3.00
Parallel Lives (graphic novel, 1990, $8.95, 68pgs.)	1.80	4.50	9.00
Aim Toothpaste giveaway(36pgs., reg. size)-1 pg. origin recap; Green Goblin-c/story	1.20	3.00	6.00
Aim Toothpaste giveaway (16pgs., reg. size)-Dr. Octopus app.	1.00	2.50	5.00
All Detergent Giveaway (1979, 36 pgs.), nn-Origin-r	2.00	5.00	10.00
Giveaway-Acme & Dingo Children's Boots (1980)-Spider-Woman app.	.80	2.00	4.00
...& Power Pack (1984, nn)(Nat'l Committee for Prevention of Child Abuse (two versions, mail offer & store giveaway)-Mooney-a; Byrne-c		.50	1.00
...& The Hulk (Special Edition)(6/8/80; 20 pgs.); Supplement to Chicago Tribune (giveaway)	1.60	4.00	8.00

...& The Incredible Hulk (1981, 1982; 36 pgs.), Sanger Harris supplement to Dallas Times, Dallas Herald, Denver Post, Kansas City Star, Tulsa World; The Jones Store-giveaway (1983, 16 pgs.) 2.00 5.00 10.00
..., Captain America, The Incredible Hulk, & Spider-Woman (1981) (7-11 Stores giveaway; 36 pgs.) 1.00 2.50 5.00
...: Christmas In Dallas (1983) (Supplement to Dallas Times Herald) giveaway 1.00 2.50 5.00
..., Fire-Star, and Iceman At the Dallas Ballet Nutcracker (1983; supplement to Dallas Times Herald)-Mooney-p 1.00 2.50 5.00
Giveaway-Esquire & Eye Magazines(2/69)-Miniature-Still attached 8.35 25.00 50.00
..., Storm & Powerman (1982; 20 pgs.)(American Cancer Society) giveaway 1.00 2.50 5.00
...Vs. The Hulk (Special Edition; 1979, 20 pgs.)(Supplement to Columbus Dispatch)-Giveaway 1.00 2.50 5.00
...vs. the Prodigy Giveaway, 16 pgs. in color (1976, 5x6-1/2")-Sex education; (1 million printed; 35-50 cents) .60 1.50 3.00

NOTE: ***Austin*** *a(i)-248, 335, 337, Annual 13; c(i)-188, 241, 242, 248, 331, 334, 343, Annual 25i. J.* ***Buscema*** *a(p)-72, 73, 76-81, 84, 85.* ***Byrne*** *a-189p, 190p, 206p, Annual 3r, 6r, 7r, 13p; c-189p, 268, 296, Annual 12.* ***Ditko*** *a-1-38, Annual 1, 2, 24(2); c-1-38.* ***Guice*** *c/a-Annual 18i.* ***Gil Kane*** *a(p)-89-105, 120-124, 150, Annual 10, 12i, 24p; c-90p, 96, 98, 99, 101-105p, 129p, 131p, 132p, 137-140p, 143p, 148p, 149p, 151p, 153p, 160p, 161p, Annual 10p, 24.* ***Kirby*** *a-8.* ***McFarlane*** *a-298p, 299p, 300-303, 304-323p, 325p, 328; c-298-325, 328.* ***Miller*** *c-218, 219.* ***Mooney*** *a-65i, 67-82i, 84-88i, 173i, 178i, 189i, 190i, 192i, 193i, 196-202i, 207i, 211-219i, 221i, 222i, 226i, 227i, 229-233i, Annual 11i, 17i.* ***Nasser*** *c-228p.* ***Nebres*** *a-Annual 24i.* ***Russell*** *c-357i.* ***Simonson*** *c-222, 337i.* ***Starlin*** *a-113i, 114i, 187p.*

AMAZING WILLIE MAYS, THE
No date (Sept, 1954)
Famous Funnies Publ.

nn 50.00 150.00 350.00

AMAZING WORLD OF SUPERMAN (See Superman)

AMAZON, THE (Comico)(Value: cover or less)

AMAZON ATTACK 3-D (3-D Zone)(Value: cover or less)

AMBUSH (See 4-Color Comics No. 314)

AMBUSH BUG (Also see Son of...)
June, 1985 - No. 4, Sept, 1985 (75 cents, mini-series)
DC Comics

1-4: Giffen-c/a in all .50 1.00
...Nothing Special 1 (9/92, $2.50, 68pg.)-Giffen-c/a .50 1.25 2.50
...Stocking Stuffer (2/86, $1.25)-Giffen-c/a .65 1.30

AMERICA IN ACTION
1942; Winter, 1945 (36 pages)
Dell(Imp. Publ. Co.)/Mayflower House Publ.

1942-Dell-(68 pages) 12.50 37.50 75.00
1(1945)-Has 3 adaptations from American history; Kiefer, Schrotter & Webb-a 8.35 25.00 50.00

AMERICA MENACED!
1950 (Paper cover)
Vital Publications
nn-Anti-communism estimated value.... 175.00

AMERICAN, THE
July, 1987 - No. 8, 1989 ($1.50-$1.75, B&W)
Dark Horse Comics

1 ($1.50) 1.00 2.50 5.00
2-Begin $1.75-c? .70 1.75 3.50
3-5 .60 1.50 3.00
6-9 .35 .90 1.75
...Collection ($5.95, B&W)-reprints 1.20 3.00 6.00
...Special 1 (1990, $2.25, B&W) .45 1.15 2.25

AMERICAN AIR FORCES, THE (See A-1 Comics)
Sept-Oct, 1944 - No. 4, 1945; No. 5, 1951 - No. 12, 1954
William H. Wise(Flying Cadet Publ. Co./Hasan(No.1)/Life's Romances/Magazine Ent. No. 5 on)

1-Article by Zack Mosley, creator of Smilin' Jack 8.35 25.00 50.00
2-4 5.35 16.00 32.00

NOTE: *All part comic, part magazine. Art by* ***Whitney, Chas. Quinlan, H. C. Kiefer,*** *and* ***Tony Dipreta.***

5(A-1 45)(Formerly Jet Powers), 6(A-1 54), 7(A-1 58), 8(A-1 65), 9(A-1 67), 10(A-1 74), 11(A-1 79), 12(A-1 91) 4.00 10.50 21.00

NOTE: ***Powell*** *c/a-5-12.*

AMERICAN COMICS
1940's
Theatre Giveaways (Liberty Theatre, Grand Rapids, Mich. known)

Many possible combinations. "Golden Age" superhero comics with new cover added and given away at theaters. Following known: Superman #59, Capt. Marvel #20, Capt. Marvel Jr. #5, Action #33, Classics Comics #8, Whiz #39. Value would vary with book and should be 70-80 percent of the original.

AMERICAN FLAGG! (First)(Value: cover or less)

AMERICAN GRAPHICS
No. 1, 1954; No. 2, 1957 (25 cents)
Henry Stewart

1-The Maid of the Mist, The Last of the Eries (Indian Legends of Niagara) (sold at Niagara Falls) 6.35 19.00 38.00
2-Victory at Niagara & Laura Secord (Heroine of the War of 1812) 4.00 12.00 24.00

AMERICAN INDIAN, THE (See Picture Progress)

AMERICAN LIBRARY
No. 3, 1944 - No. 6, 1944 (68 pages) (15 cents, B&W, text & pictures)
David McKay Publications

3-6: 3-Look to the Mountain. 4-Case of the Crooked Candle (Perry Mason). 5-Duel in the Sun. 6-Wingate's Raiders 10.00 30.00 60.00

NOTE: *Also see Guadalcanal Diary & Thirty Seconds Over Tokyo (part of series?).*

AMERICAN: LOST IN AMERICA, THE (Dark Horse)(Value: cover or less)

AMERICAN TAIL: FIEVEL GOES WEST, AN
Early Jan, 1992 - No. 3, Early Feb, 1992 ($1.00, color, mini-series)
Marvel Comics

1-Adapts Universal animated movie; Wildman-a .50 1.00

AMERICA'S BEST COMICS
Feb, 1942 - No. 31, July, 1949
Nedor/Better/Standard Publications

1-The Woman in Red, Black Terror, Captain Future, Doc Strange, The Liberator, & Don Davis, Secret Ace begin 92.00 275.00 550.00
2-Origin The American Eagle; The Woman in Red ends 46.00 140.00 275.00
3-Pyroman begins 35.00 105.00 210.00
4 29.00 85.00 175.00
5-Last Captain Future (not in #4); Lone Eagle app. 25.00 75.00 150.00
6,7: 6-American Crusader app. 7-Hitler, Mussolini & Hirohito-c 22.00 65.00 135.00
8-Last Liberator 18.00 55.00 110.00
9-The Fighting Yank begins; The Ghost app. 20.00 60.00 120.00
10-14: 10-Flag-c. 14-American Eagle ends 17.00 50.00 100.00
15-20 22.00 45.00 90.00
21,22: 21-Infinity-c. 22-Capt. Future app. 13.00 40.00 80.00
23-Miss Masque begins; last Doc Strange 17.00 50.00 100.00
24-Miss Masque bondage-c 15.00 45.00 90.00
25-Last Fighting Yank; Sea Eagle app. 13.50 40.00 80.00
26-31: 26-The Phantom Detective & The Silver Knight app.; Frazetta text illo & some panels in Miss Masque. 27,28-Commando Cubs. 27-Doc Strange. 28-Tuska Black Terror. 29-Last Pyroman 17.00 50.00 100.00

NOTE: *American Eagle not in 3, 8, 9, 13. Fighting Yank not in 10, 12. Liberator not in 2, 6, 7. Pyroman not in 9, 11, 14-16, 23, 25-27.* ***Schomburg (Xela)*** *c-5, 7-31. Bondage c-18, 24.*

AMERICA'S BEST TV COMICS (TV)
1967 (Produced by Marvel Comics) (25 cents, 68 pgs.)
American Broadcasting Company

The Amazing Willie Mays nn, © FF

The American Air Forces #6, © WHW

America's Best Comics #19, © STD

America's Greatest Comics #5, © FAW

America Vs. The Justice Society #1, © DC

Andy Hardy (Bendix Giveaway), © WEST

	GD25	FN65	NM94
1-Spider-Man, Fantastic Four (by Kirby/Ayers), Casper, King Kong, George of the Jungle, Journey to the Center of the Earth stories (promotes new TV cartoon show)	6.70	20.00	40.00

AMERICA'S BIGGEST COMICS BOOK
1944 (196 pages) (One Shot)
William H. Wise

	GD25	FN65	NM94
1-The Grim Reaper, The Silver Knight, Zudo, the Jungle Boy, Commando Cubs, Thunderhoof app.	33.00	100.00	200.00

AMERICA'S FUNNIEST COMICS
1944 - No. 2, 1944 (80 pages) (15 cents)
William H. Wise

	GD25	FN65	NM94
nn(#1), 2	18.00	55.00	110.00

AMERICA'S GREATEST COMICS
May?, 1941 - No. 8, Summer, 1943 (100 pgs.) (Soft cardboard covers)
Fawcett Publications (15 cents)

	GD25	FN65	NM94
1-Bulletman, Spy Smasher, Capt. Marvel, Minute Man & Mr. Scarlet begin; Mac Raboy-c	192.00	575.00	1150.00
2	92.00	275.00	550.00
3	71.00	210.00	425.00
4,5: 4-Commando Yank begins; Golden Arrow, Ibis the Invincible & Spy Smasher cameo in Captain Marvel	56.00	165.00	335.00
6,7: 7-Balbo the Boy Magician app.; Captain Marvel, Bulletman cameo in Mr. Scarlet	42.00	125.00	250.00
8-Capt. Marvel Jr. & Golden Arrow app.; Spy Smasher x-over in Capt. Midnight; no Minute Man or Commando Yank	42.00	125.00	250.00

AMERICA'S SWEETHEART SUNNY (See Sunny, ...)

AMERICA VS. THE JUSTICE SOCIETY
Jan, 1985 - No. 4, Apr, 1985 ($1.00, mini-series)
DC Comics

	GD25	FN65	NM94
1-Double size; Alcala-a(i) in all	.30	.75	1.50
2-4		.50	1.00

AMERICOMICS (Americomics) (Value: cover or less)

AMETHYST
Jan, 1985 - No. 16, Aug, 1986 (75 cents)
DC Comics

	GD25	FN65	NM94
1-16: 8-Fire Jade's i.d. revealed		.50	1.00
Special 1 (10/86, $1.25)		.65	1.30

AMETHYST
Nov, 1987 - No. 4, Feb, 1988 ($1.25, color, mini-series)
DC Comics

	GD25	FN65	NM94
1-4		.60	1.25

AMETHYST, PRINCESS OF GEMWORLD
May, 1983 - No. 12, April, 1984 (12 issue maxi-series)
DC Comics

	GD25	FN65	NM94
1-60 cent cover		.50	1.00
1,2-35 cent-tested in Austin & Kansas City	3.00	7.50	15.00
2-12: Perez-c(p) #6-11		.50	1.00
Annual 1 (9/84)		.60	1.25

ANARCHO DICTATOR OF DEATH (See Comics Novel)

ANCHORS ANDREWS (The Saltwater Daffy)
Jan, 1953 - No. 4, July, 1953 (Anchors the Saltwater... No. 4)
St. John Publishing Co.

	GD25	FN65	NM94
1-Canteen Kate by Matt Baker (9 pgs.)	10.00	30.00	70.00
2-4	4.00	10.00	20.00

ANDY & WOODY (See March of Comics No. 40, 55, 76)

ANDY BURNETT (See 4-Color Comics No. 865)

ANDY COMICS (Formerly Scream Comics; becomes Ernie Comics)
No. 20, June, 1948 - No. 21, Aug, 1948
Current Publications (Ace Magazines)

	GD25	FN65	NM94
20,21-Archie-type comic	4.00	11.00	22.00

ANDY DEVINE WESTERN
Dec, 1950 - No. 2, 1951
Fawcett Publications

	GD25	FN65	NM94
1	36.00	108.00	250.00
2	27.00	80.00	190.00

ANDY GRIFFITH SHOW, THE (See 4-Color No. 1252, 1341)

ANDY HARDY COMICS (See Movie Comics No. 3 by Fiction House)
April, 1952 - No. 6, Sept-Nov, 1954
Dell Publishing Co.

	GD25	FN65	NM94
4-Color 389 (#1)	3.60	9.00	18.00
4-Color 447,480,515,5,6	2.40	6.00	12.00
...& the New Automatic Gas Clothes Dryer (1952, 16 pgs., 5x7-1/4") Bendix Giveaway (soft-c)	3.60	9.00	18.00

ANDY PANDA (Also see Crackajack Funnies #39, The Funnies, New Funnies & Walter Lantz ...)
1943 - No. 56, Nov-Jan, 1961-62 (Walter Lantz)
Dell Publishing Co.

	GD25	FN65	NM94
4-Color 25(#1, 1943)	34.00	100.00	240.00
4-Color 54('44)	22.00	65.00	150.00
4-Color 85('45)	13.00	40.00	90.00
4-Color 130('46),154,198	8.35	25.00	50.00
4-Color 216,240,258,280,297	5.00	15.00	30.00
4-Color 326,345,358	3.60	9.00	18.00
4-Color 383,409	2.80	7.00	14.00
16(11-1/52-53) - 30	1.60	4.00	8.00
31-56	1.20	3.00	6.00

(See March of Comics #5, 22, 79, & Super Book #4, 15, 27.)

ANGEL
Aug, 1954 - No. 16, Nov-Jan, 1958-59
Dell Publishing Co.

	GD25	FN65	NM94
4-Color 576(#1, 8/54)	2.40	6.00	12.00
2(5-7/55) - 16	1.60	4.00	8.00

ANGEL AND THE APE (Meet Angel No. 7) (See Limited Collector's Edition C-34 & Showcase No. 77)
Nov-Dec, 1968 - No. 6, Sept-Oct, 1969
National Periodical Publications

	GD25	FN65	NM94
Showcase #77 (11-12/67)-1st app. Angel & the Ape	5.00	15.00	30.00
1-(11-12/68)-Not Wood-a	4.00	10.00	20.00
2-6-Wood inks in all	2.40	6.00	12.00

ANGEL AND THE APE (2nd series)
Mar, 1991 - No. 4, June, 1991 ($1.00, color, mini-series)
DC Comics

	GD25	FN65	NM94
1-4		.50	1.00

ANGELIC ANGELINA
1909 (11-1/2x17"; 30 pgs.; 2 colors)
Cupples & Leon Company

	GD25	FN65	NM94
nn-By Munson Paddock	22.00	65.00	130.00

ANGEL LOVE
Aug, 1986 - No. 8, Mar, 1987 (75 cents, mini-series)
DC Comics

	GD25	FN65	NM94
1-8		.50	1.00
Special 1 (1987, $1.25, 52 pgs.)		.60	1.25

ANGEL OF LIGHT, THE (See The Crusaders)

ANIMAL ADVENTURES

Dec, 1953 - No. 3, Apr?, 1954
Timor Publications/Accepted Publications (reprints)

	GD25	FN65	NM94
1	2.80	7.00	14.00
2,3	1.80	4.50	9.00
1-3 (reprints, nd)	1.40	3.50	7.00

ANIMAL ANTICS (Movie Town... No. 24 on)
Mar-Apr, 1946 - No. 23, Nov-Dec, 1949 (All 52 pgs.?)
National Periodical Publications

	GD25	FN65	NM94
1-Raccoon Kids begins by Otto Feur; some-c by Grossman; Seaman Sy Wheeler by Kelly in some issues	36.00	108.00	215.00
2	17.50	52.00	105.00
3-10: 10-Post-c/a	10.00	30.00	65.00
11-23: 14,15,18,19-Post-a	6.35	19.00	38.00

ANIMAL COMICS
Dec-Jan, 1941-42 - No. 30, Dec-Jan, 1947-48
Dell Publishing Co.

	GD25	FN65	NM94
1-1st Pogo app. by Walt Kelly (Dan Noonan art in most issues)	89.00	270.00	625.00
2-Uncle Wiggily begins	38.00	115.00	265.00
3,5	26.00	78.00	180.00
4,6,7-No Pogo	15.00	45.00	105.00
8-10	18.00	54.00	125.00
11-15	11.50	34.00	80.00
16-20	8.70	26.00	52.00
21-30: 25-30-"Jigger" by John Stanley	6.35	19.00	38.00

NOTE: ***Dan Noonan** a-18-30. **Gollub** art in most later issues; c-29, 30. **Kelly** c-7-26.*

ANIMAL CONFIDENTIAL (Dark Horse)(Value: cover or less)

ANIMAL CRACKERS (Also see Adventures of Patoruzu)
1946; No. 31, July, 1950; 1959
Green Publ. Co./Norlen/Fox Feat.(Hero Books)

	GD25	FN65	NM94
1-Super Cat begins	8.35	25.00	50.00
2	4.70	14.00	28.00
3-10 (Exist?)	2.00	5.00	10.00
31(Fox)-Formerly My Love Secret	4.00	10.50	21.00
9(1959-Norlen)	1.80	4.50	9.00
nn, nd ('50s), no publ.; infinity-c	1.80	4.50	9.00

ANIMAL FABLES
July-Aug, 1946 - No. 7, Nov-Dec, 1947
E. C. Comics(Fables Publ. Co.)

	GD25	FN65	NM94
1-Freddy Firefly (clone of Human Torch), Korky Kangaroo, Petey Pig, Danny Demon begin	29.00	85.00	200.00
2-Aesop Fables begin	18.00	54.00	125.00
3-6	14.00	43.00	100.00
7-Origin Moon Girl	47.00	140.00	325.00

ANIMAL FAIR (Fawcett's...)
March, 1946 - No. 11, Feb, 1947
Fawcett Publications

	GD25	FN65	NM94
1	14.00	43.00	100.00
2	8.35	25.00	50.00
3-6	5.85	17.50	35.00
7-11	4.00	12.00	24.00

ANIMAL FUN
1953
Premier Magazines

	GD25	FN65	NM94
1-(3-D)	27.00	80.00	190.00

ANIMAL MAN (See Action Comics #552, 553, DC Comics presents #77, 78, Secret Origins #39, Strange Adventures #180 & Wonder Woman #267, 268)
Sept, 1988 - Present ($1.25-$1.50, color)
DC Comics

	GD25	FN65	NM94
1-Bolland c-all; Grant Morrison scripts begin	3.00	7.50	15.00
2-Superman cameo	2.00	5.00	10.00
3,4	1.20	3.00	6.00
5-10: 6-Invasion tie-in. 9-Manhunter-c/story	.80	2.00	4.00
11-20: 11-Begin $1.50-c	.60	1.50	3.00
21-26: 24-Arkham Asylum story; Bizarro Superman app. 25-Inferior Five app. 26-Last Morrison scripts; Morrison apps. in story; part photo-c (of Morrison?)	.50	1.25	2.50
27-49,51-55,57-60: 41-Begin $1.75-c	.35	.90	1.75
50-($2.95, 52 pgs.)-Last issue w/Veitch scripts	.60	1.50	3.00
56-($3.50, 68 pgs.)	.70	1.75	3.50

ANIMAL WORLD, THE (See 4-Color Comics No. 713)

ANIMATED COMICS
No date given (Summer, 1947?)
E. C. Comics

	GD25	FN65	NM94
1 (Rare)	62.00	186.00	425.00

ANIMATED FUNNY COMIC TUNES (See Funny Tunes)

ANIMATED MOVIE-TUNES (Movie Tunes No. 3)
Fall, 1945 - No. 2, Sum, 1946
Margood Publishing Corp. (Timely)

	GD25	FN65	NM94
1,2-Super Rabbit, Ziggy Pig & Silly Seal	11.00	32.00	75.00

ANIMAX
Dec, 1986 - No. 4, June, 1987
Star Comics (Marvel)

	GD25	FN65	NM94
1-4: Based on toys		.50	1.00

ANNE RICE'S THE MUMMY OR RAMSES THE DAMNED
Oct, 1990 - No. 12, 1991 ($2.50, color, high quality, mini-series)
Millennium Publications

	GD25	FN65	NM94
1-12: Adapts novel; Mooney-p in all	.50	1.50	2.50

ANNETTE (See 4-Color Comics No. 905)

ANNETTE'S LIFE STORY (See 4-Color No. 1100)

ANNIE
Oct, 1982 - No. 2, Nov, 1982 (60 cents)
Marvel Comics Group

	GD25	FN65	NM94
1,2-Movie adaptation		.60	1.25
Treasury Edition ($2.00, tabloid size)	.40	1.00	2.00

ANNIE OAKLEY (See Tessie The Typist #19, Two-Gun Kid & Wild Western)
Spring, 1948 - No. 4, 11/48; No. 5, 6/55 - No. 11, 6/56
Marvel/Atlas Comics(MPI No. 1-4/CDS No. 5 on)

	GD25	FN65	NM94
1 (1st Series, 1948)-Hedy Devine app.	25.00	75.00	175.00
2 (7/48, 52 pgs.)-Kurtzman-a, "Hey Look," 1 pg; Intro. Lana; Hedy Devine app; Captain Tootsie by Beck	16.00	48.00	110.00
3,4	13.00	40.00	90.00
5 (2nd Series, 1955)-Reinman-a ; Maneely-c	10.00	30.00	60.00
6-9: 6,8-Woodbridge-a. 9-Williamson-a (4 pgs.)	8.35	25.00	50.00
10,11: 11-Severin-c	6.70	20.00	40.00

ANNIE OAKLEY AND TAGG (TV)
1953 - No. 18, Jan-Mar, 1959; July, 1965 (Photo-c #3 on)
Dell Publishing Co./Gold Key

	GD25	FN65	NM94
4-Color 438 (#1)	11.00	32.00	75.00
4-Color 481,575 (#2,3)	7.50	22.50	45.00
4(7-9/55)-10	6.35	19.00	38.00
11-18(1-3/59)	5.00	15.00	30.00
1(7/65-Gold Key)-Photo-c	4.35	13.00	26.00

NOTE: ***Manning** a-13. Photo back c-4, 9, 11.*

ANOTHER WORLD (See Strange Stories From...)

ANTHRO (See Showcase #74)
July-Aug, 1968 - No. 6, July-Aug, 1969
National Periodical Publications

	GD25	FN65	NM94
Showcase #74 (5-6/67)-1st app. Anthro; Post-c/a	7.00	21.00	42.00
1-(7-8/68)-Howie Post-a in all	5.00	15.00	30.00

Animal Adventures #2, © Timor Publ.

Animal Man #4, © DC

Annie Oakley and Tagg # 5, © DELL

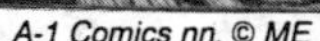
A-1 Comics nn, © ME

A-1 Comics #50, © ME

A-1 Comics #106, © ME

	GD25	FN65	NM94
2-6: 6-Wood-c/a (inks)	3.20	8.00	16.00
ANTONY AND CLEOPATRA (See Ideal, a Classical Comic)			
ANYTHING GOES			
Oct, 1986 - No. 6, 1987 ($2.00, mini-series, mature readers)			
Fantagraphics Books (#1-5: color & B&W; #6: B&W)			
1-Flaming Carrot app. (1st in color?); G. Kane-c	.60	1.50	3.00
2-4,6: 2-Miller-c(p); Alan Moore scripts; early Sam Kieth-a (2 pgs.). 3-Capt. Jack, Cerebus app.; Cerebus-c by N. Adams. 4-Perez-c	.40	1.00	2.00
5-2nd color Teenage Mutant Ninja Turtles app.	.60	1.50	3.00
A-1			
1992 - No. 4, 1993 ($5.95, color, mini-series, mature readers)			
Epic Comics (Marvel)			
1-4: 3-Bisley-c	1.20	3.00	6.00
A-1 COMICS (A-1 appears on covers No. 1-17 only)(See individual title listings. 1st two issues not numbered.)			
1944 - No. 139, Sept-Oct, 1955 (No #2)			
Life's Romances Publ.-No. 1/Compix/Magazine Ent.			
nn-Kerry Drake, Johnny Devildog, Rocky, Streamer Kelly (slightly large size)	16.00	48.00	110.00
1-Dotty Dripple (1 pg.), Mr. Ex, Bush Berry, Rocky, Lew Loyal (20 pgs.)	8.35	25.00	50.00
3-8,10-Texas Slim & Dirty Dalton, The Corsair, Teddy Rich, Dotty Dripple, Inca Dinca, Tommy Tinker, Little Mexico & Tugboat Tim, The Masquerader & others. 8-Intro. Rodeo Ryan	4.00	10.00	20.00
9-Texas Slim (all)	4.00	10.00	20.00
11-Teena	5.00	15.00	30.00
12,15-Teena	4.20	12.50	25.00
13-Guns of Fact & Fiction (1948). Used in **SOTI**, pg. 19; Ingels & Johnny Craig-a	16.00	48.00	110.00
14-Tim Holt Western Adventures #1 (1948)	41.00	122.00	285.00
16-Vacation Comics	3.20	8.00	16.00
17-Tim Holt #2. Last issue to carry A-1 on cover (9-10/48)	25.00	75.00	175.00
18,20-Jimmy Durante; photo covers	24.00	70.00	165.00
19-Tim Holt #3	17.00	52.00	120.00
21-Joan of Arc(1949)-Movie adaptation; Ingrid Bergman photo-covers & interior photos; Whitney-a	17.00	52.00	120.00
22-Dick Powell(1949)	16.00	48.00	110.00
23-Cowboys and Indians #6	5.00	15.00	30.00
24-Trail Colt #1-Frazetta, r-in Manhunt #13; Ingels-c; L. B. Cole-a	29.00	85.00	200.00
25-Fibber McGee & Molly(1949) (Radio)	6.70	20.00	40.00
26-Trail Colt #2-Ingels-c	23.00	70.00	160.00
27-Ghost Rider #1(1950)-Origin Ghost Rider	43.00	130.00	300.00
28-Christmas-(Koko & Kola #6)(1950)	3.60	9.00	18.00
29-Ghost Rider #2-Frazetta-c (1950)	40.00	120.00	285.00
30-Jet Powers #1-Powell-a	20.00	60.00	140.00
31-Ghost Rider #3-Frazetta-c & origin ('51)	40.00	120.00	285.00
32-Jet Powers #2	14.00	43.00	100.00
33-Muggsy Mouse #1('51)	4.20	12.50	25.00
34-Ghost Rider #4-Frazetta-c (1951)	40.00	120.00	285.00
35-Jet Powers #3-Williamson/Evans-a	24.00	72.00	165.00
36-Muggsy Mouse #2; Racist-c	5.85	17.50	35.00
37-Ghost Rider #5-Frazetta-c (1951)	40.00	120.00	285.00
38-Jet Powers #4-Williamson & Wood-a	24.00	72.00	165.00
39-Muggsy Mouse #3	2.40	6.00	12.00
40-Dogface Dooley #1('51)	4.00	12.00	24.00
41-Cowboys 'N' Indians #7	4.00	11.00	22.00
42-Best of the West #1-Powell-a	29.00	85.00	200.00
43-Dogface Dooley #2	3.20	8.00	16.00
44-Ghost Rider #6	16.00	48.00	110.00

	GD25	FN65	NM94
45-American Air Forces #5-Powell-c/a	4.00	10.50	21.00
46-Best of the West #2	13.00	40.00	90.00
47-Thun'da, King of the Congo #1-Frazetta-c/a('52)	83.00	250.00	580.00
48-Cowboys 'N' Indians #8	4.00	11.00	22.00
49-Dogface Dooley #3	3.20	8.00	16.00
50-Danger Is Their Business #11 ('52)-Powell-a	8.35	25.00	50.00
51-Ghost Rider #7 ('52)	16.00	48.00	110.00
52-Best of the West #3	11.50	34.00	80.00
53-Dogface Dooley #4	3.20	8.00	16.00
54-American Air Forces #6(8/52)-Powell-a	4.00	10.50	21.00
55-U.S. Marines #5-Powell-a	4.00	10.00	20.00
56-Thun'da #2-Powell-c/a 1	2.00	36.00	84.00
57-Ghost Rider #8	13.50	41.00	95.00
58-American Air Forces #7-Powell-a	4.00	10.50	21.00
59-Best of the West #4	11.00	34.00	80.00
60-The U.S. Marines #6-Powell-a	4.00	10.00	20.00
61-Space Ace #5(1953)-Guardineer-a	29.00	86.00	200.00
62-Starr Flagg, Undercover Girl #5 (#1)	26.00	77.00	180.00
63-Manhunt #13-Frazetta reprinted from A-1 #24	19.00	57.00	130.00
64-Dogface Dooley #5	3.20	8.00	16.00
65-American Air Forces #8-Powell-a	4.00	10.50	21.00
66-Best of the West #5	11.50	34.00	80.00
67-American Air Forces #9-Powell-a	4.00	10.50	21.00
68-U.S. Marines #7-Powell-a	4.00	10.00	20.00
69-Ghost Rider #9(10/52)	13.50	41.00	95.00
70-Best of the West #6	10.00	30.00	60.00
71-Ghost Rider #10(12/52)	13.50	41.00	95.00
72-U.S. Marines #8-Powell-a(3)	4.00	10.00	20.00
73-Thun'da #3-Powell-c/a	9.00	27.00	62.00
74-American Air Forces #10-Powell-a	4.00	10.50	21.00
75-Ghost Rider #11(3/52)	11.50	34.00	80.00
76-Best of the West #7	10.00	30.00	60.00
77-Manhunt #14	13.00	40.00	90.00
78-Thun'da #4-Powell-c/a	9.00	27.00	62.00
79-American Air Forces #11-Powell-a	4.00	10.50	21.00
80-Ghost Rider #12(6/52)	11.50	34.00	80.00
81-Best of the West #8	10.00	30.00	60.00
82-Cave Girl #11(1953)-Powell-c/a; origin (#1)	27.00	80.00	185.00
83-Thun'da #5-Powell-c/a	8.00	24.00	56.00
84-Ghost Rider #13(7-8/53)	11.50	34.00	80.00
85-Best of the West #9	10.00	30.00	60.00
86-Thun'da #6-Powell-c/a	8.00	24.00	56.00
87-Best of the West #10(9-10/53)	10.00	30.00	60.00
88-Bobby Benson's B-Bar-B Riders #20	4.50	14.00	32.00
89-Home Run #3-Powell-a; Stan Musial photo-c	14.00	43.00	100.00
90-Red Hawk #11(1953)-Powell-c/a	8.35	25.00	50.00
91-American Air Forces #12-Powell-a	4.00	10.50	21.00
92-Dream Book of Romance #5-photo-c; Guardineer-a	5.00	15.00	30.00
93-Great Western #8('54)-Origin The Ghost Rider; Powell-a	13.00	40.00	90.00
94-White Indian #11-Frazetta-a(r); Powell-c	16.00	48.00	110.00
95-Muggsy Mouse #4	2.40	6.00	12.00
96-Cave Girl #12, with Thun'da; Powell-c/a	20.00	60.00	140.00
97-Best of the West #11	10.00	30.00	60.00
98-Undercover Girl #6-Powell-c	24.00	70.00	165.00
99-Muggsy Mouse #5	2.40	6.00	12.00
100-Badmen of the West #1-Meskin-a(?)	14.00	43.00	100.00
101-White Indian #12-Frazetta-a(r)	16.00	48.00	110.00
101-Dream Book of Romance #6 (4-6/54); Marlon Brando photo-c; Powell, Bolle, Guardineer-a	10.00	30.00	70.00
103-Best of the West #12-Powell-a	10.00	30.00	60.00
104-White Indian #13-Frazetta-a(r)('54)	16.00	48.00	110.00

	GD25	FN65	NM94
105-Great Western #9-Ghost Rider app.; Powell-a, 6 pgs.; Bolle-c	7.50	22.50	45.00
106-Dream Book of Love #1 (6-7/54)-Powell, Bolle-a; Montgomery Clift, Donna Reed photo-c	6.70	20.00	40.00
107-Hot Dog #1	4.20	12.50	25.00
108-Red Fox #15 (1954)-L.B. Cole c/a; Powell-a	10.00	30.00	70.00
109-Dream Book of Romance #7 (7-8/54). Powell-a; photo-c	4.20	12.50	25.00
110-Dream Book of Romance #8 (10/54)	4.20	12.50	25.00
111-I'm a Cop #1 ('54); drug mention story; Powell-a	8.35	25.00	50.00
112-Ghost Rider #14 ('54)	11.50	34.00	80.00
113-Great Western #10; Powell-a	6.70	20.00	40.00
114-Dream Book of Love #2-Guardineer, Bolle-a; Peter Lorre, Victor Mature photo-c	4.70	14.00	28.00
115-Hot Dog #3	3.20	8.00	16.00
116-Cave Girl #13-Powell-c/a	20.00	60.00	140.00
117-White Indian #14	8.35	25.00	50.00
118-Undercover Girl #7-Powell-c	24.00	70.00	165.00
119-Straight Arrow's Fury #1 (origin); Fred Meagher-c/a	8.35	25.00	50.00
120-Badmen of the West #2	10.00	30.00	60.00
121-Mysteries of Scotland Yard #1; reprinted from Manhunt (5 stories)	10.00	30.00	60.00
122-Black Phantom #1(11/54)	22.00	65.00	150.00
123-Dream Book of Love #3(10-11/54)	4.20	12.50	25.00
124-Dream Book of Romance #8(10-11/54)	4.20	12.50	25.00
125-Cave Girl #14-Powell-c/a	20.00	60.00	140.00
126-I'm a Cop #2-Powell-a	4.70	14.00	28.00
127-Great Western #11('54)-Powell-a	7.50	22.50	45.00
128-I'm a Cop #3-Powell-a	4.70	14.00	28.00
129-The Avenger #1('55)-Powell-c	22.00	65.00	150.00
130-Strongman #1-Powell-a	12.00	36.00	75.00
131-The Avenger #2('55)-Powell-c/a	13.00	40.00	90.00
132-Strongman #2	11.00	32.00	75.00
133-The Avenger #3-Powell-c/a	13.00	40.00	90.00
134-Strongman #3	11.00	32.00	75.00
135-White Indian #15	8.35	25.00	50.00
136-Hot Dog #4	3.20	8.00	16.00
137-Africa #1-Powell-c/a(4)	13.00	40.00	90.00
138-The Avenger #4-Powell-c/a	13.00	40.00	90.00
139-Strongman #4-Powell-a	11.00	32.00	75.00

NOTE: ***Bolle** a-110. Photo-c-110.*

APACHE
1951
Fiction House Magazines

	GD25	FN65	NM94
1-Baker-c	11.50	34.00	80.00
I.W. Reprint No. 1-r/#1 above	2.00	5.00	10.00

APACHE HUNTER
1954 (18 pgs. in color) (promo copy) (saddle stitched)
Creative Pictorials

	GD25	FN65	NM94
nn-Severin, Heath stories	14.00	43.00	100.00

APACHE KID (Formerly Reno Browne; Western Gunfighters #20 on)
(Also see Two-Gun Western & Wild Western)
No. 53, 12/50 - No. 10, 1/52; No. 11, 12/54 - No. 19, 4/56
Marvel/Atlas Comics(MPC No. 53-10/CPS No. 11 on)

	GD25	FN65	NM94
53(#1)-Apache Kid & his horse Nightwind (origin), Red Hawkins by Syd Shores begins	16.00	48.00	110.00
2(2/51)	8.35	25.00	50.00
3-5	5.85	17.50	35.00
6-10 (1951-52)	4.35	13.00	26.00
11-19 (1954-56)	4.00	12.00	21.00

NOTE: ***Heath** c-11, 13. **Maneely** a-53; c-53(#1), 12, 14-16. **Powell** a-14. **Severin** c-17.*

APACHE MASSACRE (See Chief Victorio's...)

APACHE TRAIL
Sept, 1957 - No. 4, June, 1958
Steinway/America's Best

	GD25	FN65	NM94
1	5.35	16.00	32.00
2-4: 2-Tuska-a	3.60	9.00	18.00

APPLESEED
Sept, 1988 - Book 4, Vol. 4, Aug, 1991 (B&W, $2.50-$2.75, 52 pgs)
Eclipse Comics

	GD25	FN65	NM94
Book One, Volume 1 ($2.50)	2.40	6.00	12.00
Book One, Volume 2-5: 5-(1/89, $2.75 cover)	.60	1.50	3.00
Book Two, Vol. 1(2/89) -5(7/89): Art Adams-c	.55	1.40	2.75
Book Three, Volume 1(8/89) -4 ($2.75)	.55	1.40	2.75
Book Three, Volume 5 ($3.50)	.70	1.75	3.50
Book Four, Volume 1(1/91) -4 (3.50, 68 pgs.)	.70	1.75	3.50

APPROVED COMICS
March, 1954 - No. 12, Aug, 1954 (All painted-c)
St. John Publishing Co. (Most have no c-price)

	GD25	FN65	NM94
1-The Hawk #5-r	5.35	16.00	32.00
2-Invisible Boy-r(3/54)-Origin; Saunders-c	10.00	30.00	65.00
3-Wild Boy of the Congo #11-r(4/54)	5.35	16.00	32.00
4,5: 4-Kid Cowboy-r. 5-Fly Boy-r	5.35	16.00	32.00
6-Daring Adv.-r(5/54); Krigstein-a(2); Baker-c	7.50	22.50	45.00
7-The Hawk #6-r	5.35	16.00	32.00
8-Crime on the Run (6/54); Powell-a; Saunders-c	5.35	16.00	32.00
9-Western Bandit Trails #3-r, with new-c; Baker-c/a	7.50	22.50	45.00
11-Fightin' Marines #3-r; Canteen Kate app; Baker-c/a	8.00	24.00	48.00
12-North West Mounties #4-r(8/54); new Baker-c	8.35	25.00	50.00

AQUAMAN (See Adventure #260, Brave & the Bold, DC Comics Presents #5, DCSpecial #28, DC Special Series #1, DC Super Stars #7, Detective, Justice League of America, More Fun #73, Showcase #30-33, Super DC Giant, Super Friends, and World's Finest Comics)

AQUAMAN
Jan-Feb, 1962 - No. 56, Mar-Apr, 1971; No. 57, Aug-Sept, 1977 - No. 63, Aug-Sept, 1978
National Periodical Publications/DC Comics

	GD25	FN65	NM94
Showcase #30 (1-2/61)-Origin S.A. Aquaman	54.00	160.00	375.00
Showcase #31-33 (3-4/61 - 7-8/61)-Aquaman	26.00	78.00	180.00
1-(1-2/62)-Intro. Quisp	40.00	120.00	280.00
2	17.00	52.00	120.00
3-5	12.00	36.00	85.00
6-10	10.00	30.00	60.00
11-20: 11-1st app. Mera. 18-Aquaman weds Mera; JLA cameo	7.50	22.50	45.00
21-32,34-40: 23-Birth of Aquababy. 26-Huntress app.(3-4/66). 29-1st app. Ocean Master, Aquaman's step-brother. 30-Batman & Superman-c & cameo	4.70	14.00	28.00
33-1st app. Aqua-Girl	6.70	20.00	40.00
41-47,49	2.40	6.00	12.00
48-Origin reprinted	3.20	8.00	16.00
50-52-Deadman by Neal Adams	4.00	11.00	22.00
53-56('71): 56-1st app. Crusader	1.40	3.50	7.00
57('77)-63: 58-Origin retold	.90	2.25	4.50

NOTE: ***Aparo** a-40-59; c-57-60, 63. **Nick Cardy** c-1-39. **Newton** a-60-63.*

AQUAMAN
Feb, 1986 - No. 4, May, 1986 (Mini-series)
DC Comics

	GD25	FN65	NM94
1-New costume	.80	2.00	4.00
2-4	.50	1.25	2.50
Special 1 ('88, $1.50, 52 pgs.)	.40	1.00	2.00

AQUAMAN
June, 1989 - No. 5, Oct, 1989 ($1.00, mini-series)
DC Comics

A-1 Comics #119, © ME

Apache Kid #5, © MEG

Aquaman #4 (8/62), © DC

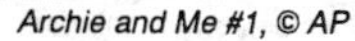
Archie and Me #1, © AP

Archie Comics #38, © AP

Archie Comics Annual #5, © AP

	GD25	FN65	NM94
1-5: Giffen plots/breakdowns; Swan-p		.50	1.00
Special 1 (Legend of..., $2.00, 1989, 52 pgs.)-Giffen plots/breakdowns; Swan-p	.40	1.00	2.00

AQUAMAN
Dec, 1991 - No. 12, Nov, 1992 ($1.00/$1.25, color)
DC Comics

	GD25	FN65	NM94
1	.50	1.25	2.50
2-5: 5-Last $1.00-c	.30	.75	1.50
6-12: 9-Sea Devils app.		.60	1.25

AQUANAUTS (See 4-Color No. 1197)

ARABIAN NIGHTS (See Cinema Comics Herald)

ARACHNOPHOBIA
1990 ($5.95, color. 68 pg. graphic novel)
Hollywood Comics (Disney Comics)

	GD25	FN65	NM94
nn-Movie adaptation; Spiegle-a	1.00	3.00	6.00
Comic edition ($2.95, 68 pgs.)	.50	1.50	3.00

ARAK/SON OF THUNDER (See Warlord #48)
Sept, 1981 - No. 50, Nov, 1985
DC Comics

	GD25	FN65	NM94
1-50: 1-Origin; 1st app. Angelica, Princess of White Cathay. 3-Intro Valda, The Iron Maiden. 12-Origin Valda. 20-Origin Angelica. 24-$1.00 size. 50-Double size		.50	1.00
Annual 1(10/84)		.50	1.00

ARCHER & ARMSTRONG
July (June inside), 1992 - Present ($2.50, color)
Valiant

	GD25	FN65	NM94
0-(7/92)-B. Smith-c/a; Reese-i assists	1.80	4.50	9.00
0-(Gold Logo)	12.00	36.00	85.00
1-(8/92)-Miller-c; B. Smith/Layton-a	2.00	5.00	10.00
2-2nd app. Turok(c/story); Smith/Layton-a;	2.40	6.00	12.00
3,4-Smith-c&a(p) & scripts	1.00	2.50	5.00
5-7,9-12: 2-2nd app. Turok (c/story); Smith/Layton-a; Simonson-c. 3,4-B. Smith-c & a(p) & scripts	.50	1.25	2.50
8-($4.50, 52 pgs.)-Combined with Eternal Warrior #8; B. Smith-a	.90	2.25	4.50

ARCHIE AND BIG ETHEL (Spire Christian)(Value: cover or less)

ARCHIE & FRIENDS
Dec, 1992 - Present ($1.25, color)
Archie Comics

	GD25	FN65	NM94
1-4		.60	1.25

ARCHIE AND ME (See Archie Giant Series Mag. #578, 591, 603, 616, 626)
Oct, 1964 - No. 161, Feb, 1987
Archie Publications

	GD25	FN65	NM94
1	13.00	40.00	90.00
2	7.50	22.50	45.00
3-5	4.00	11.00	22.00
6-10	2.40	6.00	12.00
11-20	1.20	3.00	6.00
21-30: 26-X-Mas-c	.80	2.00	4.00
31-63: 43-63-(All Giants)	.50	1.25	2.50
64-162-(Regular size)		.50	1.00

ARCHIE AND MR. WEATHERBEE
1980 (59 cents)
Spire Christian Comics (Fleming H. Revell Co.)

	GD25	FN65	NM94
nn		.50	1.00

ARCHIE...ARCHIE ANDREWS, WHERE ARE YOU? (...Comics Digest #9, 10; ...Comics Digest Mag. No. 11 on)
Feb, 1977 - Present (Digest size, 160-128 pages)
Archie Publications

	GD25	FN65	NM94
1	.80	2.00	4.00
2,3,5,7-9-N. Adams-a; 8-r-/origin The Fly by S&K. 9-Steel Sterling-r	.60	1.50	3.00
4,6,10-50 ($1.00-$1.50): 17-Katy Keene story	.50	1.00	2.00
51-88	.30	.75	1.50

ARCHIE AS PUREHEART THE POWERFUL
Sept, 1966 - No. 6, Nov, 1967
Archie Publications (Radio Comics)

	GD25	FN65	NM94
1	8.35	25.00	50.00
2	5.00	15.00	30.00
3-6	4.00	10.00	20.00

NOTE: *Evilheart cameos in all. Title: ...As Capt. Pureheart the PowerfulNo. 4, 6; ...As Capt. Pureheart-No. 5.*

ARCHIE AT RIVERDALE HIGH (See Archie Giant Series Magazine #573, 586, 604 & Riverdale High)
Aug, 1972 - No. 113, Feb, 1987
Archie Publications

	GD25	FN65	NM94
1	4.70	14.00	28.00
2	2.40	6.00	12.00
3-5	1.20	3.00	6.00
6-10	.70	1.75	3.50
11-30	.50	1.00	2.00
31-114: 96-Anti-smoking issue		.50	1.00

ARCHIE COMICS (Also see Christmas & Archie, Everything's..., Explorers of the Unknown, Jackpot, Little..., Oxydol-Dreft, Pep, Riverdale High, Teenage Mutant Ninja Turtles Adventures & To Riverdale and Back Again)

ARCHIE COMICS (Archie #158 on)(First Teen-age comic)(Radio show 1st aired 6/2/45, by NBC)
Winter, 1942-43 - No. 19, 3-4/46; No. 20, 5-6/46 - Present
MLJ Magazines No. 1-19/Archie Publ.No. 20 on

	GD25	FN65	VF82	NM94
1 (Scarce)-Jughead, Veronica app.	500.00	1500.00	3250.00	5000.00

(Estimated up to 50+ total copies exist, 5 in NM/Mint)

	GD25	FN65	NM94
2	137.00	410.00	950.00
3 (60 pgs.)	100.00	300.00	700.00
4,5: 4-Article about Archie radio series	67.00	200.00	475.00
6-10	47.00	140.00	330.00
11-20: 15,17,18-Dotty & Ditto by Woggon. 16-Woggon-a	30.00	90.00	210.00
21-30: 23-Betty & Veronica by Woggon. 25-Woggon-a	22.00	65.00	150.00
31-40	13.00	40.00	90.00
41-50	10.00	30.00	60.00
51-70 (1954): 51,65-70-Katy Keene app.	5.85	17.50	35.00
71-99: 72-74-Katy Keene app.	4.00	12.00	24.00
100	4.70	14.00	28.00
101-130 (1962)	2.40	6.00	12.00
131-160	1.20	3.00	6.00
161-200	.70	1.75	3.50
201-240	.35	.85	1.75
241-282	.25	.70	1.40
283-Cover/story plugs "International Children's Appeal" which was a fraudulent charity, according to TV's 20/20 news program broadcast July 20, 1979	.40	1.00	2.00
284-412: 300-Anniversary issue		.60	1.20
Annual 1('50)-116 pgs. (Scarce)	117.00	350.00	700.00
Annual 2('51)	50.00	150.00	350.00
Annual 3('52)	32.00	95.00	225.00
Annual 4,5(1953-54)	25.00	75.00	175.00
Annual 6-10(1955-59)	13.00	40.00	90.00

Annual 11-15(1960-65) 5.85 17.50 35.00
Annual 16-20(1966-70) 2.80 7.00 14.00
Annual 21-26(1971-75) 1.00 2.50 5.00
Annual Digest 27('75)-62('83-'93, $1.50)(...Magazine #35 on)
.50 1.25 2.50
...All-Star Specials(Winter '75)-$1.25; 6 remaindered Archie comics rebound in each; titles: "The World of Giant Comics" "Giant Grab Bag of Comics," "Triple Giant Comics," and "Giant Spec. Comics
1.00 2.50 5.00
Mini-Comics (1970-Fairmont Potato Chips Giveaway-Miniature)(8 issues-nn's., 8 pgs. each) 2.00 5.00 10.00
Official Boy Scout Outfitter(1946)-9-1/2x6-1/2, 16 pgs., B. R. Baker Co. (Scarce) 36.00 108.00 250.00
Shoe Store giveaway (1948, Feb?) 11.00 32.00 75.00

ARCHIE COMICS DIGEST (...Magazine No. 37-95)
Aug, 1973 - Present (Small size, 160-128 pages)
Archie Publications

1 4.20 12.50 25.00
2 2.80 7.00 14.00
3-5 1.40 3.50 7.00
6-10 .80 2.00 4.00
11-33: 32,33-The Fly-r by S&K .50 1.25 2.50
34-122: 36-Katy Keene story .30 .75 1.50
NOTE: ***Neal Adams** a-1, 2, 4, 5, 19-21, 24, 25, 27, 29, 31, 33. X-mas c-88, 94, 100, 106.*

ARCHIE GETS A JOB (Spire Christian)(Value: cover or less)

ARCHIE GIANT SERIES MAGAZINE
1954 - Present (No No. 36-135, no No. 252-451)(#1 not code approved)
Archie Publications

1-Archie's Christmas Stocking 75.00 225.00 450.00
2-Archie's Christmas Stocking('55) 42.00 125.00 250.00
3-6-Archie's Christmas Stocking('56-'59) 25.00 75.00 150.00
7-10: 7-Katy Keene Holiday Fun(9/60). 8-Betty & Veronica Summer Fun (10/60). 9-The World of Jughead (12/60). 10-Archie's Christmas Stocking (1/61) 14.00 43.00 100.00
11,13,16,18: 11-Betty & Veronica Spectacular (6/61). 13-Betty & Veronica Summer Fun (10/61). 16-Betty & Veronica Spectacular (6/62). 18-Betty & Veronica Summer Fun (10/62) 13.00 40.00 90.00
12,14,15,17,19,20: 12-Katy Keene Holiday Fun (9/61). 14-The World of Jughead (12/61). 15-Archie's Christmas Stocking (1/62). 17-Archie's Jokes (9/62); Katy Keene app. 19-The World of Jughead (12/62). 20-Archie's Christmas Stocking (1/63) 10.00 30.00 70.00
21,23,26,28: 21-Betty & Veronica Spectacular (6/63). 23-Betty & Veronica Summer Fun (10/63). 26-Betty & Veronica Spectacular (6/64). 28-Betty & Veronica Summer Fun (9/64) 8.35 25.00 50.00
22,24,25,27,29,30: 22-Archie's Jokes (9/63). 24-The World of Jughead (12/63). 25-Archie's Christmas Stocking (1/64). 27-Archie's Jokes (8/64). 29-Around the World with Archie (10/64). 30-The World of Jughead (12/64)
5.85 17.50 35.00
31-35,136-141: 31-Archie's Christmas Stocking (1/65). 32-Betty & Veronica Spectacular (6/65). 33-Archie's Jokes (8/65). 34-Betty & Veronica Summer Fun (9/65). 35-Around the World with Archie (10/65). 136-The World of Jughead (12/65). 137-Archie's Christmas Stocking (1/66). 138-Betty & Veronica Spectacular (6/66). 139-Archie's Jokes (6/66). 140-Betty & Veronica Summer Fun (8/66). 141-Around the World with Archie (9/66)
4.00 12.00 24.00
142-Archie's Super-Hero Special (10/66)-Origin Capt. Pureheart, Capt. Hero, and Evilheart 4.70 14.00 28.00
143-160: 143-The World of Jughead (12/66). 144-Archie's Christmas Stocking (1/67). 145-Betty & Veronica Spectacular (6/67). 146-Archie's Jokes (6/67). 147-Betty & Veronica Summer Fun (8/67) 148-World of Archie (9/67). 149-World of Jughead (10/67). 150-Archie's Christmas Stocking (1/68). 151-World of Archie (2/68). 152-World of Jughead (2/68). 153-Betty & Veronica Spectacular (6/68). 154-Archie Jokes (6/68). 155-Betty & Veronica Summer Fun (8/68). 156-World of Archie (10/68). 157-World of Jughead (12/68). 158-Archie's Christmas Stocking (1/69). 159-Betty & Veronica Christmas Spectacular (1/69). 160-World of Archie (2/69) 2.40 6.00 12.00
161-200: 161-World of Jughead (2/69). 162-Betty & Veronica Spectacular (6/69). 163-Archie's Jokes(8/69). 164-Betty & Veronica Summer Fun (9/69). 165-World of Archie (9/69). 166-World of Jughead (9/69). 167-Archie's Christmas Stocking (1/70). 168-Betty & Veronica Christmas Spect. (1/70). 169-Archie's Christmas Love-In (1/70). 170-Jughead's Eat-Out Comic Book Mag. (12/69). 171-World of Archie (2/70). 172-World of Jughead (2/70). 173-Betty & Veronica Spectacular (6/70). 174-Archie's Jokes (8/70). 175-Betty & Veronica Summer Fun (9/70). 176-Li'l Jinx Giant Laugh-Out (8/70). 177-World of Archie (9/70). 178-World of Jughead (9/70). 179-Archie's Christmas Stocking (1/71). 180-Betty & Veronica Christmas Spect. (1/71). 181-Archie's Christmas Love-In (1/71). 182-World of Archie (2/71). 183-World of Jughead (2/71). 184-Betty & Veronica Spectacular (6/71). 185-Li'l Jinx Giant Laugh-Out (6/71). 186-Archie's Jokes (8/71). 187-Betty & Veronica Summer Fun (9/71). 188-World of Archie (9/71). 189-World of Jughead (9/71). 190-Archie's Christmas Stocking (12/71). 191-Betty & Veronica Christmas Spectacular (2/72). 192-Archie's Christmas Love-In (1/72). 193-World of Archie (3/72). 194-World of Jughead (4/72). 195-Li'l Jinx Christmas Bag (1/72). 196-Sabrina's Christmas Magic (1/72). 197-Betty & Veronica Spectacular (6/72). 198-Archie's Jokes (8/72). 199-Betty & Veronica Summer Fun (9/72). 200-World of Archie (10/72) .80 2.00 4.00
201-251: 201-Betty & Veronica Spectacular (10/72). 202-World of Jughead (11/72). 203-Archie's Christmas Stocking (12/72). 204-Betty & Veronica Christmas Spectacular (2/73). 205-Archie's Christmas Love-In (1/73). 206-Li'l Jinx Christmas Bag (12/72). 207-Sabrina's Christmas Magic (12/72). 208-World of Archie (3/73). 209-World of Jughead (4/73). 210-Betty & Veronica Spectacular (6/73). 211-Archie's Jokes (8/73). 212-Betty & Veronica Summer Fun (9/73). 213-World of Archie (10/73). 214-Betty & Veronica Spectacular (10/73). 215-World of Jughead (11/73). 216-Archie's Christmas Stocking (12/73). 217-Betty & Veronica Christmas Spectacular (2/74). 218-Archie's Christmas Love-In (1/74). 219-Li'l Jinx Christmas Bag (12/73). 220-Sabrina's Christmas Magic (12/73). 221-Betty & Veronica Spectacular (Advertised as World of Archie) (6/74). 222-Archie's Jokes (advertised as World of Jughead) (8/74). 223-Li'l Jinx (8/74). 224-Betty & Veronica Summer Fun (9/74). 225-World of Archie (9/74). 226-Betty & Veronica Spectacular (10/74). 227-World of Jughead (10/74). 228-Archie's Christmas Stocking (12/74). 229-Betty & Veronica Christmas Spectacular (12/74). 230-Archie's Christmas Love-In (1/75). 231-Sabrina's Christmas Magic (1/75). 232-World of Archie (3/75). 233-World of Jughead (4/75). 234-Betty & Veronica Spectacular (6/75). 235-Archie's Jokes (8/75). 236-Betty & Veronica Summer Fun (9/75). 237-World of Archie (9/75) 238-Betty & Veronica Spectacular (10/75). 239-World of Jughead (10/75). 240-Archie's Christmas Stocking (12/75). 241-Betty & Veronica Christmas Spectacular (12/75). 242-Archie's Christmas Love-In (1/76). 243-Sabrina's Christmas Magic (1/76). 244-World of Archie (3/76). 245-World of Jughead (4/76). 246-Betty & Veronica Spectacular (6/76). 247-Archie's Jokes (8/76). 248-Betty & Veronica Summer Fun (9/76). 249-World of Archie (9/76). 250-Betty & Veronica Spectacular (10/76). 251-World of Jughead
.40 1.00 2.00
452-500: 452-Archie's Christmas Stocking (12/76). 453-Betty & Veronica Christmas Spectacular (12/76). 454-Archie's Christmas Love-In (1/77). 455-Sabrina's Christmas Magic (1/77). 456-World of Archie (3/77). 457-World of Jughead (4/77). 458-Betty & Veronica Spectacular (6/77). 459-Archie's Jokes (8/77)-Shows 8/76 in error. 460-Betty & Veronica Summer Fun (9/77). 461-World of Archie (9/77). 462-Betty & Veronica Spectacular (10/77). 463-World of Jughead (10/77). 464-Archie's Christmas Stocking (12/77). 465-Betty & Veronica Christmas Spectacular (12/77). 466-Archie's Christmas Love-In (1/78). 467-Sabrina's Christmas Magic (1/78). 468-World of Archie (2/78). 469-World of Jughead (2/78). 470-Betty & Veronica Spectacular(6/78). 471-Archie's Jokes (8/78). 472-Betty & Veronica Summer Fun (9/78). 473-World of Archie (9/78). 474-Betty & Veronica Spectacular (10/78). 475-World of Jughead (10/78). 476-Archie's Christmas Stocking (12/78). 477-Betty & Veronica Christmas Spectacular (12/78). 478-Archie's Christmas Love-In (1/79). 479-Sabrina Christmas Magic (1/79). 480-The World of Archie (3/79). 481-World of Jughead

Archie Giant Series Magazine #1, © AP

Archie Giant Series Magazine #19, © AP

Archie Giant Series Magazine #587 © AP

Archie Giant Series Magazine #599, © AP

Archie Giant Series Magazine #601, © AP

Archie's Girls, Betty & Veronica #1, © AP

	GD25	FN65	NM94
(4/79). 482-Betty & Veronica Spectacular (6/79). 483-Archie's Jokes (8/79). 484-Betty & Veronica Summer Fun(9/79). 485-The World of Archie (9/79). 486-Betty & Veronica Spectacular(10/79). 487-The World of Jughead (10/79). 488-Archie's Christmas Stocking (12/79). 489-Betty & Veronica Christmas Spectacular (1/80). 490-Archie's Christmas Love-in (1/80). 491-Sabrina's Christmas Magic (1/80).492-The World of Archie (2/80). 493-The World of Jughead (4/80). 494-Betty & Veronica Spectacular (6/80). 495-Archie's Jokes (8/80). 496-Betty & Veronica Summer Fun (9/80). 497-The World of Archie (9/80). 498-Betty & Veronica Spectacular (10/80). 499-The World of Jughead (10/80). 500-Archie's Christmas Stocking (12/80) each...	.30	.75	1.50
501-550: 501-Betty & Veronica Christmas Spectacular (12/80). 502-Archie's Christmas Love-in (1/81). 503-Sabrina Christmas Magic (1/81). 504-The World of Archie (3/81). 505-The World of Jughead (4/81). 506-Betty & Veronica Spectacular (6/81). 507-Archie's Jokes (8/81). 508-Betty & Veronica Summer Fun (9/81). 509-The World of Archie (9/81). 510-Betty & Vernonica Spectacular (9/81). 511-The World of Jughead (10/81). 512-Archie's Christmas Stocking (12/81). 513-Betty & Veronica Christmas Spectacular (12/81). 514-Archie's Christmas Love-in (1/82). 515-Sabrina's Christmas Magic (1/82). 516-The World of Archie (3/82). 517-The World of Jughead (4/82). 518-Betty & Veronica Spectacular (6/82). 519-Archie's Jokes (8/82). 520-Betty & Veronica Summer Fun (9/82). 521-The World of Archie (9/82). 522-Betty & Veronica Spectacular (10/82). 523-The World of Jughead (10/82). 524-Archie's Christmas Stocking (1/83). 525-Betty and Veronica Christmas Spectacular (1/83). 526-Betty and Veronica Spectacular (5/83). 527-Little Archie (8/83). 528-Josie and the Pussycats (8/83). 529-Betty and Veronica Summer Fun (8/83). 530-Betty and Veronica Spectacular (9/83). 531-The World of Jughead (9/83). 532-The World of Archie (10/83). 533-Space Pirates by Frank Bolling (10/83). 534-Little Archie (1/84). 535-Archie's Christmas Stocking (1/84). 536-Betty and Veronica Christmas Spectacular (1/84). 537-Betty and Veronica Spectacular (6/84). 538-Little Archie (8/84). 539-Betty and Veronica Summer Fun (8/84). 540-Josie and the Pussycats (8/84). 541-Betty and Veronica Spectacular (9/84). 542-The World of Jughead (9/84). 543-The World of Archie (10/84). 544-Sabrina the Teen-Age Witch (10/84). 545-Little Archie (12/84). 546-Archie's Christmas Stocking (12/84). 547-Betty and Veronica Christmas Spectacular (12/84). 548-? 549-Little Archie. 550-Betty and Veronica Summer Fun each...		.60	1.25
551-600: 551-Josie and the Pussycats. 552-Betty and Veronica Spectacular. 553-The World of Jughead. 554-The World of Archie. 555-Betty's Diary. 556-Little Archie (1/86). 557-Archie's Christmas Stocking (1/86). 558-Betty & Veronica Christmas Spectacular (1/86). 559-Betty & Veronica Spectacular. 560-Little Archie. 561-Betty & Veronica Summer Fun. 562-Josie and the Pussycats. 563-Betty & Veronica Spectacular. 564-World of Jughead. 565-World of Archie. 566-Little Archie. 567-Archie's Christmas Stocking. 568-Betty & Veronica Christmas Spectacular. 569-Betty & Veronica Spring Spectacular. 570-Little Archie. 571-Josie & the Pussycats. 572-Betty & Veronica Summer Fun. 573-Archie At Riverdale High. 574-World of Archie. 575-Betty & Veronica Spectacular. 576-Pep. 577-World of Jughead. 578-Archie And Me. 579-Archie's Christmas Stocking. 580-Betty and Veronica Christmas Spectacular. 581-Little Archie Christmas Special. 582-Betty & Veronica Spring Spectacular. 583-Little Archie. 584-Josie and the Pussycats. 585-Betty & Veronica Summer Fun. 586-Archie At Riverdale High. 587-The World of Archie (10/88); 1st app. Explorers of the Unknown. 588-Betty & Veronica Spectacular. 589-Pep (10/88). 590-The World of Jughead. 591-Archie & Me. 592-Archie's Christmas Stocking. 593-Betty & Veronica Christmas Spectacular. 594-Little Archie. 595-Betty & Veronica Spring Spectacular. 596-Little Archie. 597-Josie and the Pussycats. 598-Betty & Veronica Summer Fun. 599-The World of Archie (10/89); 2nd app. Explorers of the Unknown. 600-Betty and Veronica Spectacular each....		.50	1.00
601-630: 601-Pep. 602-The World of Jughead. 603-Archie and Me. 604-Archie at Riverdale High. 605-Archie's Christmas Stocking. 606-Betty and Veronica Christmas Spectacular. 607-Little Archie. 608-Betty and Veronica Spectacular. 609-Little Archie. 610-Josie and the Pussycats. 611-Betty and Veronica Summer Fun. 612-The World of Archie. 613-Betty and Veronica Spectacular. 614-Pep (10/90). 615-Veronica's Summer Special. 616-Archie and Me. 617-Archie's Christmas Stocking. 618-Betty & Veronica Christmas Spectacular. 619-Little Archie. 620-Betty and Veronica Spectacular. 621-Betty and Veronica Summer Fun. 622-Josie & the Pussycats; not published. 623-Betty and Veronica Spectacular. 624-Pep Comics. 625-Veronica's Summer Special. 626-Archie and Me. 627-World of Archie. 628-Archie's Pals 'n' Gals Holiday Special. 629-Betty & Veronica Christmas Spectacular. 630-Archie's Christmas Stocking each....		.50	1.00

ARCHIE'S ACTIVITY COMICS DIGEST MAGAZINE
1985 - No. 4? (Annual, 128 pgs.; digest size)
Archie Enterprises

	GD25	FN65	NM94
1-4	.30	.75	1.50

ARCHIE'S CAR (Spire Christian) (Value: cover or less)

ARCHIE'S CHRISTMAS LOVE-IN (See Archie Giant Series Mag. No. 169, 181, 192, 205, 218, 230, 242, 454, 466, 478, 490, 502, 514)

ARCHIE'S CHRISTMAS STOCKING (See Archie Giant Series Mag. No. 1-6, 10, 15, 20, 25, 31, 137, 144, 150, 158, 167, 179, 190, 203, 216, 228, 240, 452, 464, 476, 488, 500, 512, 524, 535, 546, 557, 567, 579, 592, 605, 617, 630)

ARCHIE'S CLEAN SLATE (Spire Christian) (Value: cover or less)

ARCHIE'S DATE BOOK (Spire Christian) (Value: cover or less)

ARCHIE'S DOUBLE DIGEST QUARTERLY MAGAZINE
1981 - Present ($1.95-$2.50, 256pgs.) (A.D.D. Magazine No. 10 on)
Archie Comics

	GD25	FN65	NM94
1-30: 6-Katy Keene story. 29-Pureheart story	.60	1.50	3.00
31-66	.50	1.25	2.50

ARCHIE'S FAMILY ALBUM (Spire Christian) (Value: cover or less)

ARCHIE'S FESTIVAL (Spire Christian) (Value: cover or less)

ARCHIE'S GIRLS, BETTY AND VERONICA (Becomes Betty & Veronica)
1950 - No. 347, April, 1987 (Also see Veronica)
Archie Publications (Close-Up)

	GD25	FN65	NM94
1	87.00	260.00	600.00
2	43.00	130.00	300.00
3-5	25.00	75.00	175.00
6-10: 10-2pg. Katy Keene app.	19.00	58.00	135.00
11-20: 11,13,14,17-19-Katy Keene app. 17-Last pre-code issue. 20-Debbie's Diary, 2 pgs.	13.00	40.00	90.00
21-30: 27-Katy Keene app.	10.00	30.00	70.00
31-50	8.35	25.00	50.00
51-74	5.85	17.50	35.00
75-Betty & Veronica sell souls to Devil	9.30	28.00	65.00
76-99	3.60	9.00	18.00
100	4.20	12.50	25.00
101-140: 118-Origin Superteen. 119-Last Superteen story	1.60	4.00	8.00
141-180	.70	1.75	3.50
181-220	.35	.85	1.75
221-347: 300-Anniversary issue		.60	1.20
Annual 1 (1953)	53.00	160.00	375.00
Annual 2(1954)	24.50	73.00	170.00
Annual 3-5 ('55-'57)	18.00	54.00	125.00
Annual 6-8 ('58-'60)	12.00	36.00	85.00

ARCHIE SHOE-STORE GIVEAWAY
1944-49 (12-15 pgs. of games, puzzles, stories like Superman-Tim books, No nos. - came out monthly)
Archie Publications

	GD25	FN65	NM94
(1944-47)-issues	10.00	30.00	70.00
2/48-Peggy Lee photo-c	8.35	25.00	50.00

	GD25	FN65	NM94
3/48-Marylee Robb photo-c	7.50	22.50	45.00
4/48-Gloria De Haven photo-c	7.50	22.50	45.00
5/48,6/48,7/48	7.50	22.50	45.00
8/48-Story on Shirley Temple	8.35	25.00	50.00
10/48-Archie as Wolf on cover	8.35	25.00	50.00
5/49-Kathleen Hughes photo-c	5.85	17.50	35.00
7/49	5.85	17.50	35.00
8/49-Archie photo-c from radio show	10.00	30.00	60.00
10/49-Gloria Mann photo-c from radio show	8.35	25.00	50.00
11/49,12/49	5.85	17.50	35.00

ARCHIE'S JOKEBOOK COMICS DIGEST ANNUAL (See Jokebook...)

ARCHIE'S JOKE BOOK MAGAZINE (See Joke Book ...)
1953 - No. 3, Sum, 1954; No. 15, Fall, 1954 - No. 288, 11/82
Archie Publications

	GD25	FN65	NM94
1953-One Shot (#1)	50.00	150.00	350.00
2	29.00	85.00	200.00
3 (no #4-14)	19.30	58.00	135.00
15-20: 15-Formerly Archie's Rival Reggie #14; last pre-code issue. 15-17-Katy Keene app.	14.00	43.00	100.00
21-30	10.00	30.00	65.00
31-40,42,43	5.85	17.50	35.00
41-1st professional comic work by Neal Adams ('59), 1 pg.	16.00	48.00	110.00
44-47-N. Adams-a in all, 1-2 pgs.	9.15	27.50	55.00
48-Four pgs. N. Adams-a	9.15	27.50	55.00
49-60 (1962)	3.20	8.00	16.00
61-80	1.80	4.50	9.00
81-100	.80	2.00	4.00
101-140	.50	1.00	2.00
141-200	.30	.75	1.50
201-288		.50	1.00
Drug Store Giveaway (No. 39 w/new-c)	2.80	7.00	14.00

ARCHIE'S JOKES (See Archie Giant Series Mag. No. 17, 22, 27, 33, 139, 146, 154, 163, 174, 186, 198, 211, 222, 235, 247, 459, 471, 483, 495, 519)

ARCHIE'S LOVE SCENE (Spire Christian) (Value: cover or less)

ARCHIE'S MADHOUSE (Madhouse Ma-ad No. 67 on)
Sept, 1959 - No. 66, Feb, 1969
Archie Publications

	GD25	FN65	NM94
1-Archie begins	22.00	65.00	150.00
2	10.00	30.00	70.00
3-5	8.35	25.00	50.00
6-10	5.85	17.50	35.00
11-16 (Last w/regular characters)	4.00	12.00	24.00
17-21,23-30 (New format)	1.80	4.50	9.00
22-1st app. Sabrina, the Teen-age Witch (10/62)	6.70	20.00	40.00
31-40	.80	2.00	4.00
41-66: 43-Mighty Crusaders cameo. 44-Swipes Mad #4 (Super-Duperman) in "Bird Monsters From Outer Space"	.50	1.00	1.50
Annual 1 (1962-63)	5.85	17.50	35.00
Annual 2 (1964)	3.60	9.00	18.00
Annual 3 (1965)-Origin Sabrina The Teen-Age Witch	1.80	4.50	9.00
Annual 4-6('66-69) (Becomes Madhouse Ma-ad Annual #7 on)	1.20	3.00	6.00

NOTE: *Cover title to 61-65 is "Madhouse" and to 66 is "Madhouse Ma-ad Jokes."*

ARCHIE'S MECHANICS
Sept, 1954 - No. 3, 1955
Archie Publications

	GD25	FN65	NM94
1-(15 cents; 52 pgs.)	68.00	205.00	475.00
2-(10 cents)	40.00	120.00	280.00
3-(10 cents)	35.00	105.00	240.00

ARCHIE'S ONE WAY (Spire Christian) (Value: cover or less)

ARCHIE'S PAL, JUGHEAD (Jughead No. 122 on)
1949 - No. 126, Nov, 1965
Archie Publications

	GD25	FN65	NM94
1 (1949)	80.00	240.00	550.00
2 (1950)	40.00	120.00	275.00
3-5	25.00	75.00	175.00
6-10: 7-Suzie app.	15.00	45.00	105.00
11-20	11.50	34.00	80.00
21-30: 23-25,28-30-Katy Keene app. 28-Debbie's Diary app.	9.15	27.50	55.00
31-50	5.35	16.00	32.00
51-70	4.00	10.00	20.00
71-100	2.00	5.00	10.00
101-126	1.40	3.50	7.00
Annual 1 (1953)	37.00	110.00	265.00
Annual 2 (1954)	23.00	70.00	160.00
Annual 3-5 (1955-57)	16.00	48.00	110.00
Annual 6-8 (1958-60)	11.00	32.00	75.00

ARCHIE'S PALS 'N' GALS (Also see Archie Giant Series Mag. #628)
1952-53 - No. 6, 1957-58; No. 7, 1958 - No. 231, May, 1992
Archie Publications

	GD25	FN65	NM94
1-(116 pages)	47.00	140.00	325.00
2(Annual)('53-'54)	27.00	80.00	190.00
3-5(Annual, '54-57): 3-Last pre-code issue	18.00	54.00	125.00
6-10('58-'60)	10.00	30.00	65.00
11-20	5.35	16.00	32.00
21-28,30-40	3.60	9.00	18.00
29-Beatles satire	4.20	12.50	25.00
41-60	1.40	3.50	7.00
61-80	.70	1.75	3.50
81-110	.40	1.00	2.00
111-231: Later issues $1.00 cover. 197-G. Colan-a		.50	1.00

ARCHIE'S PARABLES
1973, 1975 (36 pages, 39-49 cents)
Spire Christian Comics (Fleming H. Revell Co.)

	GD25	FN65	NM94
nn-By Al Hartley		.50	1.00

ARCHIE'S R/C RACERS
Sept, 1989 - No. 10, Mar, 1991 (95 cents, $1.00, color)
Archie Comics

	GD25	FN65	NM94
1-10: Radio control cars		.50	1.00

ARCHIE'S RIVAL REGGIE (Reggie & Archie's Joke Book #15 on)
1950 - No. 14, Aug, 1954
Archie Publications

	GD25	FN65	NM94
1	53.00	160.00	375.00
2	26.30	79.00	185.00
3-5	19.00	57.00	130.00
6-10	12.00	36.00	85.00
11-14: Katy Keene in No. 10-14, 1-2pgs.	10.00	30.00	65.00

ARCHIE'S ROLLER COASTER (Spire Christian) (Value: cover or less)

ARCHIE'S SOMETHING ELSE (Spire Christian) (Value: cover or less)

ARCHIE'S SONSHINE (Spire Christian) (Value: cover or less)

ARCHIE'S SPORTS SCENE (Spire Christian) (Value: cover or less)

ARCHIE'S STORY & GAME COMICS DIGEST MAGAZINE
Nov, 1986 - Present (Digest size, $1.25, $1.35, $1.50, 128 pgs.)
Archie Enterprises

	GD25	FN65	NM94
1-25	.40	1.00	2.00

ARCHIE'S SUPER HERO SPECIAL (See Archie Giant Series Mag. No. 142)

ARCHIE'S SUPER HERO SPECIAL (...Comics Digest Mag. 2)
Jan, 1979 - No. 2, Aug, 1979 (148 pages, 95 cents)
Archie Publications (Red Circle)

1-Simon & Kirby r-/Double Life of Pvt. Strong #1,2; Black Hood, The Fly,

Archie's Mad House #12, © AP

Archie's Pal Jughead #2, © AP

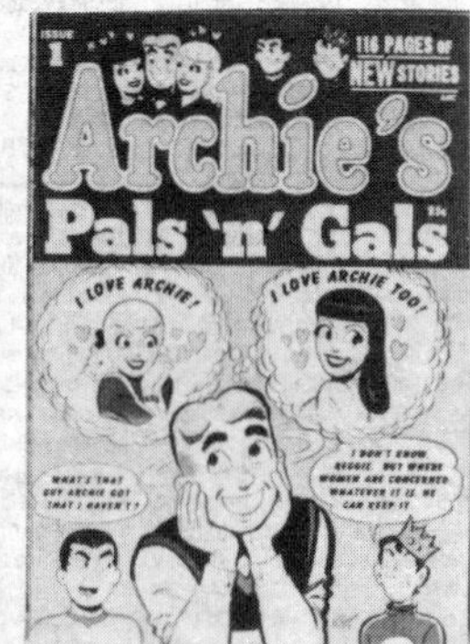

Archie's Pals 'N' Gals #1, © AP

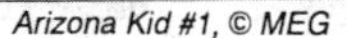
Arizona Kid #1, © MEG

Army & Navy #5, © S&S

The Arrow #1, © CEN

	GD25	FN65	NM94
Jaguar, The Web app.		.50	1.00
2-Contains contents to the never published Black Hood #1; origin Black Hood; N. Adams, Wood, McWilliams, Morrow, S&K-a(r); N. Adams-c. The Shield, The Fly, Jaguar, Hangman, Steel Sterling, The Web, The Fox-r		.50	1.00

ARCHIE'S TV LAUGH-OUT
Dec, 1969 - No. 106, April, 1986
Archie Publications

	GD25	FN65	NM94
1	4.70	14.00	28.00
2	2.00	5.00	10.00
3-5	1.00	2.50	5.00
6-10	.50	1.20	2.00
11-20	.50	1.00	1.50
21-106		.50	1.00

ARCHIE'S WORLD (Spire Christian)(Value: cover or less)

ARCHIE 3000
May, 1989 - No. 15, May, 1991 (75 & 95 cents, $1.00, color)
Archie Comics

	GD25	FN65	NM94
1-15: 6-X-Mas-c		.50	1.00

AREA 88 (Eclipse)(Value: cover or less)

ARENA (Alchemy)(Value: cover or less)

ARIANE AND BLUEBEARD (See Night Music #8)

ARIEL & SEBASTIAN (See Cartoon Tales & The Little Mermaid)

ARION, LORD OF ATLANTIS (Also see Warlord #55)
Nov, 1982 - No. 35, Sept, 1985
DC Comics

	GD25	FN65	NM94
1-35: 1-Story cont'd from Warlord #62		.50	1.00
Special #1 (11/85)		.50	1.00

ARION THE IMMORTAL
July, 1992 - No. 6, Dec, 1992 ($1.50, color, limited series)
DC Comics

	GD25	FN65	NM94
1-6: 4-Gustovich-a(i)	.30	.75	1.50

ARISTOCATS (See Movie Comics & Walt Disney Showcase No. 16)

ARISTOKITTENS, THE (...Meet Jiminy Cricket No. 1)(Disney)
Oct, 1971 - No. 9, Oct, 1975 (No. 6: 52 pages)
Gold Key

	GD25	FN65	NM94
1	3.00	7.50	15.00
2-9	1.60	4.00	8.00

ARIZONA KID, THE (Also see The Comics & Wild Western)
March, 1951 - No. 6, Jan, 1952
Marvel/Atlas Comics(CSI)

	GD25	FN65	NM94
1	11.50	34.00	80.00
2-4: 2-Heath-a(3)	6.70	20.00	40.00
5,6	6.00	18.00	36.00

NOTE: ***Heath*** *a-1-3; c-1-3.* ***Maneely*** *c-4-6.* ***Morisi*** *a-4-6.* ***Sinnott*** *a-6.*

ARK, THE (See The Crusaders)

ARKHAM ASYLUM (Also see Animal Man #24, Black Orchid #2 & The Saga of Swamp Thing #52, 53)
1989 ($24.95, hard-c, mature readers, 132 pgs.)
DC Comics

	GD25	FN65	NM94
nn-Joker-c/story; Grant Morrison scripts	6.00	15.00	30.00
nn-Soft cover reprint ($14.95)	3.00	7.50	15.00

ARMAGEDDON: ALIEN AGENDA
Nov, 1991 - No. 4, Feb, 1992 ($1.00, color, mini-series)
DC Comics

	GD25	FN65	NM94
1-4		.50	1.00

ARMAGEDDON FACTOR, THE (AC)(Value: cover or less)

ARMAGEDDON: INFERNO
Apr, 1992 - No. 4, July, 1992 ($1.00, color, mini-series)
DC Comics

	GD25	FN65	NM94
1-4: Many DC heroes app. 3-A. Adams/Austin-a		.50	1.00

ARMAGEDDON 2001
May, 1991 - No. 2, Oct, 1991 ($2.00, squarebound, 68 pgs.)
DC Comics

	GD25	FN65	NM94
1-Features many DC heroes; intro Waverider	.80	2.00	4.00
1-2nd & 3rd printings; 3rd has silver ink-c	.40	1.00	2.00
2	.50	1.25	2.50

ARMOR (Continuity Comics)(Value: cover or less)

ARMY AND NAVY COMICS (Supersnipe No. 6 on)
May, 1941 - No. 5, July, 1942
Street & Smith Publications

	GD25	FN65	NM94
1-Cap Fury & Nick Carter	35.00	105.00	210.00
2-Cap Fury & Nick Carter	17.50	52.00	105.00
3,4	12.50	37.50	75.00
5-Supersnipe app.; see Shadow V2#3 for 1st app.; Story of Douglas MacArthur; George Marcoux-c/a	33.00	100.00	200.00

ARMY ATTACK
July, 1964 - No. 4, Feb, 1965; V2#38, July, 1965 - No. 47, Feb, 1967
Charlton Comics

	GD25	FN65	NM94
V1#1	2.40	6.00	12.00
2-4(2/65)	1.20	3.00	6.00
V2#38(7/65)-47 (formerly U.S. Air Force #1-37)	1.20	3.00	6.00

NOTE: ***Glanzman*** *a-1-3.* ***Montes/Bache*** *a-44.*

ARMY AT WAR (Also see Our Army at War & Cancelled Comic Cavalcade)
Oct-Nov, 1978
DC Comics

	GD25	FN65	NM94
1-Kubert-c	.40	1.00	2.00

ARMY SURPLUS KOMIKZ FEATURING CUTEY BUNNY
1982 - No. 5, 1985 ($1.50, B&W)
Army Surplus Komikz/Eclipse Comics No. 5

	GD25	FN65	NM94
1-Cutey Bunny begins	.40	1.00	2.00
2-5: 5-JLA/X-Men/Batman parody	.30	.75	1.50

ARMY WAR HEROES (Also see Iron Corporal)
Dec, 1963 - No. 38, June, 1970
Charlton Comics

	GD25	FN65	NM94
1	2.40	6.00	12.00
2-38: 22-Origin & 1st app. Iron Corporal series by Glanzman. 24-Intro. Archer & Corp. Jack series	.80	2.00	4.00
Modern Comics Reprint 36 ('78)	.40	1.00	2.00

NOTE: ***Montes/Bache*** *a-1, 16, 17, 21, 23-25, 27-30.*

AROUND THE BLOCK WITH DUNC & LOO (See Dunc and Loo)

AROUND THE WORLD IN 80 DAYS (See Four Color Comics #784 and A Golden Picture Classic)

AROUND THE WORLD UNDER THE SEA (See Movie Classics)

AROUND THE WORLD WITH ARCHIE (See Archie Giant Series Mag. #29, 35, 141)

AROUND THE WORLD WITH HUCKLEBERRY & HIS FRIENDS (See Dell Giant No. 44)

ARRGH! (Satire)
Dec, 1974 - No. 5, Sept, 1975
Marvel Comics Group

	GD25	FN65	NM94
1	.80	2.00	4.00
2-5	.40	1.00	2.00

NOTE ***Alcala*** *a-2; c-3.* ***Everett*** *a-1r, 2r.* ***Maneely*** *a-4r.* ***Sekowsky*** *a-1p.* ***Sutton*** *a-1, 2.*

ARROW, THE (See Funny Pages)
Oct, 1940 - No. 2, Nov, 1940; No. 3, Oct, 1941

GD25 FN65 NM94

Centaur Publications

1-The Arrow begins(r/Funny Pages) 135.00 400.00 800.00
2,3: 2-Tippy Taylor serial continues from Amazing Mystery Funnies #24. 3-Origin Dash Dartwell, the Human Meteor; origin The Rainbow-r; bondage-c 80.00 240.00 475.00

NOTE: ***Gustavson** a-1, 2; c-3.*

ARROWHEAD (See Black Rider and Wild Western)
April, 1954 - No. 4, Nov, 1954
Atlas Comics (CPS)

1-Arrowhead & his horse Eagle begin 9.15 27.50 55.00
2-4: 4-Forte-a 5.85 17.50 35.00

NOTE: ***Heath** c-3. **Jack Katz** a-3. **Maneely** c-2. **Pakula** a-2. **Sinnott** a-1-4; c-1.*

ASSASSINS, INC. (Silverline)(Value: cover or less)

ASTONISHING (Formerly Marvel Boy No. 1, 2)
No. 3, April, 1951 - No. 63, Aug, 1957
Marvel/Atlas Comics(20CC)

3-Marvel Boy continues; 3-5-Marvel Boy-c 43.00 130.00 300.00
4-6-Last Marvel Boy; 4-Stan Lee app. 30.00 90.00 210.00
7-10: 7-Maneely s/f story. 10-Sinnott s/f story 10.00 30.00 70.00
11,12,15,17,20 9.15 27.50 55.00
13,14,16,19-Krigstein-a 10.00 30.00 60.00
18-Jack The Ripper story 10.00 30.00 65.00
21,22,24 7.50 22.50 45.00
23-E.C. swipe-"The Hole In The Wall" from Vault Of Horror #16 9.15 27.50 55.00
25-Crandall-a 9.15 27.50 45.00
26-28 6.70 20.00 40.00
29-Decapitation-c 7.50 22.50 45.00
30-Tentacled eyeball story 10.00 30.00 65.00
31-37-Last pre-code issue 5.85 17.50 35.00
38-43,46,48-52,56,58,59,61 4.20 12.50 25.00
44-Crandall swipe/Weird Fantasy #22 6.35 19.00 38.00
45,47-Krigstein-a 6.35 19.00 38.00
53,54: 53-Crandall, Ditko-a. 54-Torres-a 5.00 15.00 30.00
55-Crandall, Torres-a 6.35 19.00 38.00
57-Williamson/Krenkel-a (4 pgs.) 7.50 22.50 45.00
60-Williamson/Mayo-a (4 pgs.) 7.50 22.50 45.00
62-Torres, Powell-a 4.35 13.00 26.00
63-Last issue; Woodbridge-a 4.35 13.00 26.00

NOTE: ***Ayers** a-16. **Berg** a-36, 53, 56. **Cameron** a-50. **Gene Colan** a-12, 20, 29, 56. **Ditko** a-50, 53. **Drucker** a-41, 62. **Everett** a-3-6(3), 6, 10, 12, 37, 47, 48, 58; c-3-5, 13,15, 16, 18, 29, 47, 49, 51, 53-55, 57, 59-63. **Fass** a-11, 34. **Forte** a-53, 58, 60. **Fuje** a-11. **Heath** a-8, 29; c-8, 9, 19, 22, 25, 26. **Kirby** a-56. **Lawrence** a-28, 37, 38, 42. **Maneely** a-7(2); c-7, 31, 33, 34, 56. **Moldoff** a-33. **Morisi** a-10, 60. **Morrow** a-52, 61. **Orlando** a-47, 58, 61. **Pakula** a-10. **Powell** a-43, 44, 48. **Ravielli** a-28. **Reinman** a-32, 34, 38. **Robinson** a-20. **J. Romita** a-7, 18, 24, 43, 57,61. **Roussos** a-55. **Sale** a-28, 38, 59; c-32. **Sekowsky** a-13. **Severin** c-46. **Shores** a-16, 60. **Sinnott** a-11, 30. **Whitney** a-13. **Ed Win** a-20. Canadian reprints exist.*

ASTONISHING TALES (See Ka-Zar)
Aug, 1970 - No. 36, July, 1976 (#1-7: 15 cents; #8: 25 cents)
Marvel Comics Group

1-Ka-Zar by Kirby(p) & Dr. Doom by Wood double feature begins; Kraven the Hunter-c/story; Nixon cameo 4.00 10.00 20.00
2-Kraven the Hunter-c/story; Kirby, Wood-a 2.00 5.00 10.00
3-6: B. Smith-p; Wood-a-#3,4. 5-Red Skull app. 3.60 9.00 18.00
7,8: 8-(52 pgs.)-Last Dr. Doom & Kirby-a 2.00 5.00 10.00
9-Lorna-r/Lorna #14 .80 2.00 4.00
10-B. Smith-a(p). 1.60 4.00 8.00
11-Origin Ka-Zar & Zabu 1.40 3.50 7.00
12-Man-Thing by Neal Adams (apps. #13 also) 1.40 3.50 7.00
13-24: 20-Last Ka-Zar. 21-It! the Living Colossus begins, ends #24 .50 1.25 2.50
25-1st app. Deathlok the Demolisher; full length stories begin, end #36; Perez's 1st work, 2 pgs. (8/74) 14.00 43.00 100.00
26-28,30 4.70 14.00 28.00
29-r/origin/1st app. Guardians of the Galaxy from Marvel Super-Heroes #18 plus-c w/4 pgs. omitted; no Deathlok story 4.70 14.00 28.00
31-36: 31-Watcher-r/Silver Surfer #3 3.60 9.00 18.00

NOTE: ***Buckler** a-13i, 16p, 25, 26p, 27p, 28, 29p-36p; c-13, 25p, 26-30, 32-35p, 36. **John Buscema** a-9, 12p-14p, 16p; c-4-6p, 12p. **Colan** a-7p, 8p. **Ditko** a-21r. **Everett** a-6i. **G. Kane** a-11p, 15p; c-9, 10p, 11p, 14, 15p, 21p. **McWilliams** a-30i. **Starlin** a-19p; c-16p. **Sutton & Trimpe** a-8. **Tuska** a-5p, 6p, 8p. **Wood** a-1-4. **Wrightson** c-31i.*

ASTRO BOY (TV) (See March of Comics #285 & The Original...)
August, 1965 (12 cents)
Gold Key

1(10151-508)-1st app. Astro Boy in comics 29.00 85.00 200.00

ASTRO COMICS
1969 - 1979 (Giveaway)
American Airlines (Harvey)

nn-Harvey's Casper, Spooky, Hot Stuff, Stumbo the Giant, Little Audrey, Little Lotta, & Richie Rich reprints .80 2.00 4.00

ATARI FORCE
1982; Jan, 1984 - No. 20, Aug, 1985 (Mando paper)
DC Comics

1-3 (1982, color, 52 pgs., 5X7")-Given away with Atari games .50 1.00
1-20: 1-(1/84)-1st app. Tempest, Packrat, Babe, Morphea, & Dart .50 1.00
Special 1 (4/86) .50 1.00

NOTE: ***Byrne** c-Special 1i. **Giffen** a-12p, 13i. **Rogers** a-18p, Special 1p.*

A-TEAM, THE (TV)
March, 1984 - No. 3, May, 1984
Marvel Comics Group

1-3 .50 1.00

ATLANTIS CHRONICLES, THE
Mar, 1990 - No. 7, Sept, 1990 ($2.95, mini-series, 52 pgs.)
DC Comics

1-7: 7-Nudity panels .60 1.50 3.00

ATLANTIS, THE LOST CONTINENT (See 4-Color No. 1188)

ATLAS (See 1st Issue Special)

ATOM, THE (See Action, All-American #19, Brave & the Bold, D.C. Special Series #1, Detective, Flash Comics #80, Power Of The Atom, Showcase #34, Super Friends, Sword of The Atom & World's Finest)

ATOM, THE (...& the Hawkman No. 39 on)
June-July, 1962 - No. 38, Aug-Sept, 1968
National Periodical Publications

Showcase #34 (9-10/61)-Origin & 1st app. Silver Age Atom by Kane & Anderson 120.00 365.00 850.00
Showcase #35 (11-12/61)-2nd app. Atom by Gil Kane; last 10 cent issue 68.00 205.00 475.00
Showcase #36 (1-2/62)-3rd app. Atom by Kane 50.00 150.00 350.00
1-(6-7/62)-Intro Plant-Master; 1st app. Maya 77.00 230.00 540.00
2 27.00 80.00 185.00
3-1st Time Pool story; 1st app. Chronos (origin) 17.00 52.00 120.00
4,5: 4-Snapper Carr x-over 12.00 36.00 85.00
6,8-10: 8-Justice League, Dr. Light app. 10.00 30.00 70.00
7-Hawkman x-over (6-7/63; 1st Atom & Hawkman team-up); 1st app. Hawkman since Brave & the Bold tryouts 22.00 65.00 150.00
11-15: 13-Chronos-c/story 8.00 24.00 48.00
16-20: 19-Zatanna x-over 5.35 16.00 32.00
21-28,30: 28-Chronos-c/story 4.00 11.00 22.00
29-1st solo Golden Age Atom x-over in S.A. 11.50 34.00 80.00
31-35,37,38: 31-Hawkman x-over. 37-Intro. Major Mynah; Hawkman cameo 4.00 11.00 22.00
36-G.A. Atom x-over 4.70 14.00 28.00

NOTE: ***Anderson** a-1-11i, 13i; c-inks-1-25, 31-35, 37. **Sid Greene** a-8i-38i. **Gil Kane** a-1p-38p; c-1p-28p, 29, 33p, 34. Time Pool stories also in 6, 9,12, 17, 21, 27, 35.*

ATOM AGE (See Classics Illustrated Special Issue)

Astonishing #29, © MEG

Astonishing Tales #1, © MEG

The Atom #3, © DC

Atoman #2, © Spark Publ.

Atomic Bunny #17, © CC

Atomic Rabbit #1, © CC

ATOM-AGE COMBAT
June, 1952 - No. 5, April, 1953; Feb, 1958
St. John Publishing Co.

	GD25	FN65	NM94
1	25.00	75.00	175.00
2	14.00	43.00	100.00
3,5: 3-Mayo-a (6 pgs.)	11.00	32.00	75.00
4 (Scarce)	13.00	40.00	90.00
1(2/58-St. John)	10.00	30.00	60.00

ATOM-AGE COMBAT
Nov, 1958 - No. 3, March, 1959
Fago Magazines

	GD25	FN65	NM94
1-All have Dick Ayers-c/a	13.00	40.00	90.00
2,3	10.00	30.00	60.00

ATOMAN
Feb, 1946 - No. 2, April, 1946
Spark Publications

	GD25	FN65	NM94
1-Origin Atoman; Robinson/Meskin-a; Kidcrusaders, Wild Bill Hickok, Marvin the Great app.	33.00	100.00	200.00
2: Robinson/Meskin-a; Robinson c-1,2	25.00	75.00	150.00

ATOM & HAWKMAN, THE (Formerly The Atom)
No. 39, Oct-Nov, 1968 - No. 45, Oct-Nov, 1969
National Periodical Publications

	GD25	FN65	NM94
39-45: 43-Last 12 cent issue; 1st app. Gentlemen Ghost, origin in #44	3.60	9.00	18.00

NOTE: ***M. Anderson** a-39, 40i, 41i, 43, 44. **Sid Greene** a-40i-45i. **Kubert** a-40p, 41p; c-39-45.*

ATOM ANT (TV)
January, 1966 (Hanna-Barbera)
Gold Key

	GD25	FN65	NM94
1(10170-601)	11.00	32.00	75.00

ATOMIC AGE
Nov, 1990 - No. 4, Feb, 1991 ($4.50, mini-series, squarebound, 52 pgs.)
Epic Comics (Marvel)

	GD25	FN65	NM94
1-4: Williamson-a(i)	.90	2.25	4.50

ATOMIC ATTACK (Formerly Attack, first series)
No. 5, Jan, 1953 - No. 8, Oct, 1953
Youthful Magazines

	GD25	FN65	NM94
5-Atomic bomb-c	17.00	52.00	120.00
6-8	10.00	30.00	70.00

ATOMIC BOMB
1945 (36 pgs.)
Jay Burtis Publications

	GD25	FN65	NM94
1-Airmale & Stampy	27.00	80.00	160.00

ATOMIC BUNNY (Formerly Atomic Rabbit)
No. 12, Aug, 1958 - No. 19, Dec, 1959
Charlton Comics

	GD25	FN65	NM94
12	8.35	25.00	50.00
13-19	4.70	14.00	28.00

ATOMIC COMICS
1946 - No. 4, 1946 (Reprints)
Daniels Publications (Canadian)

	GD25	FN65	NM94
1-Rocketman, Yankee Boy, Master Key; bondage-c	13.00	40.00	90.00
2-4	10.00	30.00	60.00

ATOMIC COMICS
Jan, 1946 - No. 4, July-Aug, 1946 (#1-4 were printed without cover gloss)
Green Publishing Co.

	GD25	FN65	NM94
1-Radio Squad by Siegel & Shuster; Barry O'Neal app.; Fang Gow cover-r/Det. Comics	67.00	200.00	400.00
2-Inspector Dayton; Kid Kane by Matt Baker; Lucky Wings, Congo King, Prop Powers (only app.) begin	35.00	105.00	210.00
3,4: 3-Zero Ghost Detective app.; Baker-a(2) each; 4-Baker-c	20.00	60.00	120.00

ATOMIC MOUSE (TV, Movies) (See Blue Bird, Funny Animals, Giant Comics & Wotalife Comics)
3/53 - No. 54, 6/63; No. 1, 12/84; V2/10, 9/85 - No. 13, ?/86
Capitol Stories/Charlton Comics

	GD25	FN65	NM94
1-Origin; Al Fago c/a	13.00	40.00	90.00
2	7.50	22.50	45.00
3-10: 5-Timmy The Timid Ghost app.; see Zoo Funnies	5.00	15.00	30.00
11-13,16-25	3.60	9.00	18.00
14,15-Hoppy The Marvel Bunny app.	4.70	14.00	28.00
26-(68 pages)	6.35	19.00	38.00
27-40: 36,37-Atom The Cat app.	2.80	7.00	14.00
41-54	1.40	3.50	7.00
1 (1984)		.50	1.00
V2#10 (10/85) -13-Fago-r. #12(1/86)		.50	1.00

ATOMIC RABBIT (Atomic Bunny No. 12 on; see Wotalife Comics)
August, 1955 - No. 11, March, 1958
Charlton Comics

	GD25	FN65	NM94
1-Origin; Al Fago-a	12.00	36.00	85.00
2	6.70	20.00	40.00
3-10-Fago-a in most	4.70	14.00	28.00
11-(68 pages)	6.70	20.00	40.00

ATOMIC SPY CASES
Mar-Apr, 1950 (Painted-c)
Avon Periodicals

	GD25	FN65	NM94
1-No Wood-a; A-bomb blast panels; Fass-a	17.00	52.00	120.00

ATOMIC THUNDERBOLT, THE
Feb, 1946 (One shot)
Regor Company

	GD25	FN65	NM94
1-Intro. Atomic Thunderbolt & Mr. Murdo	28.00	85.00	170.00

ATOMIC WAR!
Nov, 1952 - No. 4, April, 1953
Ace Periodicals (Junior Books)

	GD25	FN65	NM94
1-Atomic bomb-c	43.00	130.00	300.00
2,3: 3-Atomic bomb-c	32.00	95.00	225.00
4-Used in **POP**, pg. 96 & illo.	32.00	95.00	225.00

ATOM THE CAT (Formerly Tom Cat)
No. 9, Oct, 1957 - No. 17, Aug, 1959
Charlton Comics

	GD25	FN65	NM94
9	5.00	15.00	30.00
10,13-17	3.20	8.00	16.00
11,12: 11(64pgs)-Atomic Mouse app. 12(100pgs)	6.70	20.00	40.00

ATTACK
May, 1952 - No. 4, Nov, 1952; No. 5, Jan, 1953 - No. 5, Sept, 1953
Youthful Mag./Trojan No. 5 on

	GD25	FN65	NM94
1-(1st series)-Extreme violence	11.00	32.00	75.00
2,3: 3-Harrison-c/a; bondage, whipping	5.85	17.50	35.00
4-Krenkel-a (7 pgs.); Harrison-a (becomes Atomic Attack #5 on)	6.70	20.00	40.00
5-(#1, Trojan, 2nd series)	5.85	17.50	35.00
6-8 (#2-4), 5	4.20	12.50	25.00

ATTACK
No. 54, 1958 - No. 60, Nov, 1959
Charlton Comics

	GD25	FN65	NM94
54 (100 pages)	5.35	16.00	32.00

	GD25	FN65	NM94
55-60	1.80	4.50	9.00

ATTACK!
1962 - No. 15, 3/75; No. 16, 8/79 - No. 48, 10/84
Charlton Comics

	GD25	FN65	NM94
nn(#1)-('62) Special Edition	2.40	6.00	12.00
2('63), 3(Fall, '64)	1.60	4.00	8.00
V4#3(10/66), 4(10/67)-(Formerly Special War Series #2; becomes Attack At Sea V4#5)	1.00	2.50	5.00
1(9/71)	.80	2.00	4.00
2-15(3/75): 4-American Eagle app.	.40	1.00	2.00
16(8/79) - 47		.60	1.20
48(10/84)-Wood-r; S&K-c	.30	.75	1.50
Modern Comics 13('78)-r		.50	1.00

ATTACK! (Spire Christian)(Value: cover or less)

ATTACK AT SEA (Formerly Attack!, 1967)
V4#5, October, 1968
Charlton Comics

	GD25	FN65	NM94
V4#5	1.00	2.50	5.00

ATTACK ON PLANET MARS (See Strange Worlds #18)
1951
Avon Periodicals

	GD25	FN65	NM94
nn-Infantino, Fawcette, Kubert & Wood-a; adaptation of Tarrano the Conqueror by Ray Cummings	49.00	145.00	340.00

AUDREY & MELVIN (Formerly Little...)(See Little Audrey & Melvin)
No. 62, September, 1974
Harvey Publications

	GD25	FN65	NM94
62	.40	1.00	2.00

AUGIE DOGGIE (TV) (See Spotlight #2 & Whitman Comic Books)
October, 1963 (Hanna-Barbera)
Gold Key

	GD25	FN65	NM94
1	10.00	30.00	60.00

AURORA COMIC SCENES INSTRUCTION BOOKLET
1974 (Slick paper, 8 pgs.)(6-1/4x9-1/4")(in full color)
(Included with superhero model kits)
Aurora Plastics Co.

	GD25	FN65	NM94
181-140-Tarzan; Neal Adams-a	.80	2.00	4.00
182-140-Spider-Man. 183-140-Tonto(Gil Kane art). 184-140-Hulk. 185-140-Superman. 186-140-Superboy. 187-140-Batman. 188-140-The Lone Ranger(1974-by Gil Kane). 192-140-Captain America(1975). 193-140-Robin each....	.60	1.50	3.00

AUTHENTIC POLICE CASES
2/48 - No. 6, 11/48; No. 7, 5/50 - No. 38, 3/55
St. John Publishing Co.

	GD25	FN65	NM94
1-Hale the Magician by Tuska begins	16.00	48.00	110.00
2-Lady Satan, Johnny Rebel app.	10.00	30.00	70.00
3-Veiled Avenger app.; blood drainage story plus 2 Lucky Coyne stories; used in **SOTI**, illo. from Red Seal #16	22.00	65.00	150.00
4,5: 4-Masked Black Jack app. 5-Late 1930s Jack Cole-a(r); transvestism story	10.00	30.00	65.00
6-Matt Baker-c; used in **SOTI**, illo-"An invitation to learning", r-in Fugitives From Justice #3; Jack Cole-a; also used by the N.Y. Legis. Comm.	22.00	65.00	150.00
7,8,10-14: 7-Jack Cole-a; Matt Baker art begins #8, ends #?; Vic Flint in #10-14. 11-Baker-a(2)	10.00	30.00	60.00
9-No Vic Flint	8.35	25.00	50.00
15-Drug-c/story; Vic Flint app.; Baker-c	10.00	30.00	60.00
16,18,20,21,23	5.35	16.00	32.00
17,19,22-Baker-c	5.85	17.50	35.00
24-28 (All 100 pages): 26-Transvestism	11.50	34.00	80.00
29,30	4.00	11.00	22.00
31,32,37-Baker-c	4.20	12.50	25.00
33-Transvestism; Baker-c	5.00	15.00	30.00
34-Baker-c	5.00	15.00	30.00
35-Baker-c/a(2)	4.70	14.00	28.00
36-r/#11; Vic Flint strip-r; Baker-c/a(2) unsigned	5.00	15.00	30.00
38-Baker-c/a	5.00	15.00	30.00

NOTE: ***Matt Baker** c-6-16, 17, 19, 22, 27, 29, 31-38; a-13, 16. Bondage c-1, 3.*

AUTUMN ADVENTURES (Walt Disney's)
Autumn, 1990; No2, Aut, 1991 ($2.95, color, quarterly, 68 pgs.)
Disney Comics

	GD25	FN65	NM94
1-Donald Duck-r(2) by Barks, Pluto-r, & new-a	.60	1.50	3.00
2-D. Duck-r by Barks; new Super Goof story	.60	1.50	3.00

AVATAR
Feb, 1991 - No. 3, Apr, 1991 ($5.95, color, mini-series, 100 pgs.)
DC Comics

	GD25	FN65	NM94
1-3: Based on TSR's Forgotten Realms	1.20	3.00	6.00

AVENGER, THE (See A-1 Comics)
1955 - No. 4, Aug-Sept, 1955
Magazine Enterprises

	GD25	FN65	NM94
1(A-1 #129)-Origin	22.00	65.00	150.00
2(A-1 #131), 3(A-1 #133), 4(A-1 #138)	13.00	40.00	90.00
IW Reprint #9('64)-Reprints #1 (new cover)	2.40	6.00	12.00

NOTE: ***Powell** a-2-4; c-1-4.*

AVENGERS, THE (See Giant-Size..., Kree/Skrull War Starring..., Marvel Graphic Novel #27, Marvel Super Action, Marvel Super Heroes('66), Marvel Treasury Ed., Marvel Triple Action, Solo Avengers, Tales Of Suspense, West Coast Avengers & X-Men Vs....)

AVENGERS, THE (The Mighty Avengers on cover only #63-69)
Sept, 1963 - Present
Marvel Comics Group

	GD25	FN65	NM94
1-Origin & 1st app. The Avengers (Thor, Iron Man, Hulk, Ant-Man, Wasp); Loki app.	180.00	535.00	1250.00
2-Hulk leaves	57.00	170.00	400.00
3-1st Sub-Mariner x-over (outside the F.F.); Hulk & Sub-Mariner team-up & battle Avengers	36.00	107.00	250.00
4-Revival of Captain America who joins the Avengers; 1st Silver Age app. of Captain America & Bucky (3/64)	90.00	270.00	625.00
4-Reprint from the Golden Record Comic set	9.15	27.50	55.00
With Record (still sealed)	14.00	43.00	100.00
5-Hulk app.	22.00	65.00	150.00
6-8: 6-Intro. The Masters of Evil. 8-Intro Kang.	17.00	52.00	120.00
9-Intro Wonder Man who dies in same story.	18.00	54.00	125.00
10-Early Hercules app.	14.00	43.00	110.00
11-Spider-Man-c & x-over (12/64)	18.00	54.00	125.00
12-16: 15-Death of Zemo. 16-New Avengers line-up (Hawkeye, Quicksilver, Scarlet Witch join; Thor, Iron Man, Giant-Man, Wasp leave.)	11.00	32.00	75.00
17-19: 19-Intro. Swordsman; origin Hawkeye	9.15	27.50	55.00
20-22: Wood inks	5.85	17.50	35.00
23-30: 28-Giant-Man becomes Goliath	4.20	12.50	25.00
31-40	3.60	9.00	18.00
41-52,54-56: 43,44-1st app. Red Guardian. 46-Ant-Man returns. 47-Magneto c/story. 48-Origin/1st app. new Black Knight. 52-Black Panther joins; 1st app. The Grim Reaper. 54-1st app. new Masters of Evil	2.80	7.00	14.00
53-X-Men app.	3.60	9.00	18.00
57-1st app. S.A. Vision	6.70	20.00	40.00
58-Origin The Vision	5.00	15.00	30.00
59-65: 59-Intro. Yellowjacket. 60-Wasp & Yellowjacket wed. 63-Goliath becomes Yellowjacket; Hawkeye becomes the new Goliath. 65-Last 12 cent issue.	3.20	8.00	16.00
66,67: B. Smith-a	3.00	7.50	15.00
68-70	2.00	5.00	10.00
71-1st app. The Invaders; 1st app. Nighthawk; Black Knight joins	2.40	6.00	12.00

72-82,84-86,88-91: 80-Intro. Red Wolf. 82-Daredevil app. 88-Written by

Attack on Planet Mars #1, © AVON

Authentic Police Cases #35, © STJ

The Avengers #5, © MEG

The Avengers #92, © MEG

The Avengers King Size Special #4, © MEG

Awful Oscar #12, © MEG

	GD25	FN65	NM94
Harlan Ellison	1.80	4.50	9.00
83-Intro. The Liberators (Wasp, Valkyrie, Scarlet Witch, Medusa & the Black Widow)	2.00	5.00	10.00
87-Origin The Black Panther	4.00	10.00	20.00
92-Last 15 cent issue; Neal Adams-c	2.20	5.50	11.00
93-(52 pgs.)-Neal Adams-c/a	6.70	20.00	40.00
94-96-Neal Adams-c/a	4.35	13.00	26.00
97-G.A. Capt. America, Sub-Mariner, Human Torch, Patriot, Vision, Blazing Skull, Fin, Angel, & new Capt. Marvel x-over	2.20	5.50	11.00
98-Goliath becomes Hawkeye; Smith c/a(i)	4.00	11.00	22.00
99-Smith/Sutton-a	4.00	11.00	22.00
100-(6/72)-Smith-c/a; featuring everyone who was an Avenger	6.70	20.00	40.00
101-106,108,109: 101-Harlan Ellison scripts	1.40	3.50	7.00
107-Starlin-a(p)	2.00	5.00	10.00
110,111-X-Men app.	3.00	7.50	15.00
112-1st app. Mantis	2.00	5.00	10.00
113-120: 116-118-Defenders/Silver Surfer app.	1.20	3.00	6.00
121-124,126-130: 123-Origin Mantis	1.20	3.00	6.00
125-Thanos-c & brief app.	3.00	7.50	15.00
131-140: 136-Ploog-r/Amazing Advs. #12	1.00	2.50	5.00
141-163: 144-Origin & 1st app. Hellcat. 146-25 & 30 cent variants exist. 150-Kirby-a(r); new line-up: Capt. America, Scarlet Witch, Iron Man, Wasp, Yellowjacket, Vision & The Beast. 151-Wonderman returns w/new costume	.80	2.00	4.00
164-166: Byrne-a	1.00	2.50	5.00
167-180: 174-Thanos cameo. 176-Starhawk app.	.60	1.50	3.00
181-191: Byrne-a. 181-New line-up: Capt. America, Scarlet Witch, Iron Man, Wasp, Vision, Beast & The Falcon. 183-Ms. Marvel joins. 185-Origin Quicksilver & Scarlet Witch	.60	1.50	3.00
192-202: Perez-a. 195-1st Taskmaster. 200-Double size; Ms. Marvel leaves	.40	1.00	2.00
203-213,215-262: 211-New line-up: Capt. America, Iron Man, Tigra, Thor, Wasp & Yellowjacket. 213-Yellowjacket leaves. 215,216-Silver Surfer app. 216-Tigra leaves. 217-Yellowjacket & Wasp return. 221-Hawkeye & She-Hulk join. 227-Capt. Marvel (female) joins; origins of Ant-Man, Wasp, Giant-Man, Goliath, Yellowjacket, & Avengers. 230-Yellowjacket quits. 231-Iron Man leaves. 232-Starfox (Eros) joins. 234-Origin Quicksilver, Scarlet Witch. 236-New logo. 238-Origin Blackout. 240-Spider-Woman revived. 250-($1.00, 52 pgs.)	.40	1.00	2.00
214-Ghost Rider-c/story	1.00	2.50	5.00
263-1st app. X-Factor (1/86)(story continues in Fantastic Four #286)	1.00	2.50	5.00
264-299: 272-Alpha Flight app. 291-$1.00 issues begin. 297-Black Knight, She-Hulk & Thor resign. 298-Inferno tie-in	.30	.75	1.50
300 ($1.75, 68 pgs.)-Thor joins; Simonson-a	.50	1.25	2.50
301-304,306-325,327,329-343: 302-Re-intro Quasar. 314-318-Spider-Man x-over. 320-324-Alpha Flight app. (320-cameo). 341,342-New Warriors app. 343-Last $1.00-c		.50	1.00
305-Byrne scripts begin	.40	1.00	2.00
326-1st app. Rage	1.20	3.00	6.00
328-Origin Rage	1.00	2.50	5.00
344-346,348,349,351-362		.60	1.25
347-($1.75, 56 pgs.)	.35	.90	1.75
350-($2.50, 68 pgs.)-Double gatefold-c showing-c to #1; r/#53 w/cover in flip book format; vs. The Starjammers	.50	1.25	2.50
Special 1(9/67, 25 cents, 68 pgs.)-New-a; original & new Avengers team-up	5.85	17.50	35.00
Special 2(9/68, 25 cents, 68 pgs.)-New-a; original vs. new Avengers	2.40	6.00	12.00
Special 3(9/69, 25 cents, 68 pgs.)-r/Avengers #4 plus 3 Capt. America stories by Kirby-a; origin Red Skull	3.00	7.50	15.00
Special 4,5: 4(1/71, 25 cents, 68 pgs.)-New Kirby-a (23 pgs.) plus Kirby reprints (23 pgs.). 5(1/72)-Spider-Man x-over	1.20	3.00	6.00
Annual 6(11/76)	1.00	2.50	5.00
Annual 7(11/77)-Starlin-c/a; Warlock dies; Thanos app.	4.70	14.00	28.00
Annual 8(1978)-Dr. Strange, Ms. Marvel app.	.90	2.25	4.50
Annual 9(1979)-Newton-a(p)	.70	1.75	3.50
Annual 10(1981)-Golden-p; X-Men cameo; 1st app. Rogue & Madelyne Pryor	1.60	4.00	8.00
Annual 11-16: 11(1982)-Vs. The Defenders. 12(1983). 13(1984). 14(1985). 15(1986). 16(1987)	.70	1.75	3.50
Annual 17(1988)-Evolutionary War x-over	.80	2.00	4.00
Annual 18(1989, $2.00, 68 pgs.)-Atlantis Attacks	.60	1.50	3.00
Annual 19,20(1990, 1991)(both $2.00, 68 pgs.)	.50	1.25	2.50
Annual 21(1992, $2.25, 68 pgs.)	.45	1.15	2.25

NOTE: ***Austin*** *c(i)-157, 167, 168, 170-177, 181, 183-188, 198-201, Annual 8.* ***John Buscema*** *a-41-44p, 46p, 47p, 49, 50, 51-62p, 74-77, 79-85, 87-91, 97, 105p, 121p, 124p,125p, 152, 153p, 255-279p, 281-302p; c-41-66, 68-71, 73-91, 97-99, 178, 256-259p, 261-279p, 281-302p.* ***Byrne*** *a-164-166p, 181-191p, 233p, Annual 13, 14p; c-186-190p, 233p, 260, 305p; scripts-305-312.* ***Colan*** *a(p)-63-65, 111, 206-208, 210, 211; c(p)-65, 206-208, 210, 211.* ***Guice*** *a-Annual 12p.* ***Kane*** *c-37p, 159p.* ***Kane/Everett*** *c-97.* ***Kirby*** *a-1-8p, Special 3r, 4r(p); c-1-30, 148, 151-158; layouts-14-16.* ***Miller*** *c-193p.* ***Mooney*** *a-86i, 179p, 180p.* ***Nebres*** *a-178i; c-179i.****Newton*** *a-204p, Annual 9p.* ***Perez*** *a(p)-141, 143, 144, 148, 154, 155, 160, 161, 162, 167,168, 170, 171, 194, 195, 196, 198-202, Annual 6, 8; c(p)-160-162, 164-166, 170-174, 181,183-185, 191, 192, 194-201, Annual 8.* ***Starlin*** *c-121, 135.* ***Staton*** *a-127-134i.* ***Tuska*** *a-47i,48i, 51i, 53i, 54i, 106p, 107p, 135p, 137-140p, 163p. Guardians of the Galaxy app. in #167, 168, 170, 173, 175, 181.*

AVENGERS, THE (TV)(Also see Steed and Mrs. Peel)
Nov, 1968 ("John Steed & Emma Peel" cover title) (15 cents)
Gold Key

	GD25	FN65	NM94
1-Photo-c	22.00	65.00	150.00

AVENGERS SPOTLIGHT (Formerly Solo Avengers #1-20)
No. 21, Aug, 1989 - No. 40, Jan, 1991 (.75-$1.00, color)
Marvel Comics

	GD25	FN65	NM94
21 (75 cents)-Byrne-c/a		.50	1.00
22-40 ($1.00): 26-Acts of Vengeance story. 31-34-U.S. Agent series. 36-Heck-i. 37-Mortimer-i. 40-The Black Knight app.		.50	1.00

AVENGERS WEST COAST (Formerly West Coast Avengers)
No. 48, Sept, 1989 - Present ($1.00-$1.25, color)
Marvel Comics

	GD25	FN65	NM94
48,49: Byrne-c/a & scripts continue thru #57		.55	1.10
50-Re-intro original Human Torch	.30	.75	1.50
51-74,76-94: 54-Cover swipe/F.F. #1. 70-Spider-Woman app. 78-Last $1.00-c. 79-Dr. Strange x-over. 84-Origin Spider-Woman retold; Spider-Man app. (also in #85,86). 87,88-Wolverine-c/story		.60	1.25
75-($1.50, 52 pgs.)-Fantastic Four x-over	.30	.75	1.50

AVIATION ADVENTURES AND MODEL BUILDING
No. 16, Dec, 1946 - No. 17, Feb, 1947 (True Aviation Adv...No. 15)
Parents' Magazine Institute

	GD25	FN65	NM94
16,17-Half comics and half pictures	4.70	14.00	28.00

AVIATION CADETS
1943
Street & Smith Publications

	GD25	FN65	NM94
nn	10.00	30.00	60.00

A-V IN 3-D
Dec, 1984 (28 pgs. w/glasses)
Aardvark-Vanaheim

	GD25	FN65	NM94
1-Cerebus, Flaming Carrot, Normalman & Ms. Tree	.70	1.75	3.50

AWFUL OSCAR (Formerly & becomes Oscar Comics with No. 13)
No. 11, June, 1949 - No. 12, Aug, 1949
Marvel Comics

	GD25	FN65	NM94
11,12	4.70	14.00	28.00

AXA (Eclipse)(Value: cover or less)

AXEL PRESSBUTTON (Eclipse) (Value: cover or less)

AZTEC ACE (Eclipse) (Value: cover or less)

BABE (...Darling of the Hills, later issues) (See Big Shot and Sparky Watts)
June-July, 1948 - No. 11, Apr-May, 1950
Prize/Headline/Feature

	GD25	FN65	NM94
1-Boody Rogers-a	11.00	32.00	75.00
2-Boody Rogers-a	8.35	25.00	50.00
3-11-All by Boody Rogers	6.70	20.00	40.00

BABE AMAZON OF OZARKS
No. 5, 1948
Standard Comics

	GD25	FN65	NM94
5-Exist?	4.70	14.00	28.00

BABE RUTH SPORTS COMICS
April, 1949 - No. 11, Feb, 1951
Harvey Publications

	GD25	FN65	NM94
1-Powell-a	22.00	65.00	130.00
2-Powell-a	17.00	50.00	100.00
3-11: Powell-a in most	14.00	42.50	85.00

NOTE: *Baseball c-2-4, 9. Basketball c-1, 6. Football c-5. Yogi Berra c/story-8. Joe DiMaggio c/story-3. Bob Feller c/story-4. Stan Musial c-9.*

BABES IN TOYLAND (See 4-Color No. 1282 & Golden Pix Story Book ST-3)

BABY HUEY
1991 - Present ($1.00/$1.25, color)
Harvey Comics

	GD25	FN65	NM94
1-5		.60	1.25

BABY HUEY AND PAPA (See Paramount Animated...)
May, 1962 - No. 33, Jan, 1968 (Also see Casper The Friendly Ghost)
Harvey Publications

	GD25	FN65	NM94
1	11.00	32.00	75.00
2	5.35	16.00	32.00
3-5	3.20	8.00	16.00
6-10	2.00	5.00	10.00
11-20	1.20	3.00	6.00
21-33	1.00	2.50	5.00

BABY HUEY DUCKLAND
Nov, 1962 - No. 15, Nov, 1966 (25 cent Giants) (all 68 pgs.)
Harvey Publications

	GD25	FN65	NM94
1	7.50	22.50	45.00
2-5	3.20	8.00	16.00
6-15	1.60	4.00	8.00

BABY HUEY, THE BABY GIANT (Also see Big Baby Huey, Casper, Harvey Hits #22, Harvey Comics Hits #60, & Paramount Animated Comics)
9/56 - #97, 10/71; #98, 10/72; #99, 10/80; #100, 10/90 - #102?
Harvey Publications

	GD25	FN65	NM94
1-Infinity-c	26.00	78.00	180.00
2	13.00	40.00	90.00
3-Baby Huey takes anti-pep pills	9.15	27.50	55.00
4,5	6.70	20.00	40.00
6-10	4.00	10.00	20.00
11-20	2.40	6.00	12.00
21-40	2.00	5.00	10.00
41-60	1.40	3.50	7.00
61-79(12/67)	1.00	2.50	5.00
80(12/68) - 95-All 68 pg. Giants	1.20	3.00	6.00
96,97-Both 52 pg. Giants	1.00	2.50	5.00
98-99: Regular size	.60	1.50	3.00
100-102 ($1.00)		.50	1.00

BABY SNOOTS (Also see March of Comics No. 359, 371, 396, 401, 419, 431, 443, 450, 462, 474, 485)
Aug, 1970 - No. 22, Nov, 1975
Gold Key

	GD25	FN65	NM94
1	1.60	4.00	8.00
2	.60	1.50	3.00
3-22: 22-Titled Snoots, the Forgetful Elefink	.40	1.00	2.00

BACHELOR FATHER (TV)
No. 1332, 4-6/62 - No. 2, 1962
Dell Publishing Co.

	GD25	FN65	NM94
4-Color 1332 (#1)	7.50	22.50	45.00
2-Written by Stanley	7.50	22.50	45.00

BACHELOR'S DIARY
1949
Avon Periodicals

	GD25	FN65	NM94
1(Scarce)-King Features panel cartoons & text-r; pin-up, girl wrestling photos	23.00	70.00	160.00

BACK DOWN THE LINE
1991 (Mature adults, 8-1/2 x 11", 52 pgs.)
Eclipse Books

	GD25	FN65	NM94
nn (Soft-c, $8.95)-Bolton-c/a	1.80	4.50	9.00
nn (Limited hard-c, $29.95)	5.00	15.00	30.00

BACK TO THE FUTURE (TV cartoon)
Nov, 1991 - Present ($1.25, color)
Harvey Comics

	GD25	FN65	NM94
1-4: 1,2-Gil Kane-c; based on animated cartoon		.60	1.25
Special nn (1991, 20 pgs.)-Brunner-c; given away at Universal Studios in Florida		.50	1.00

BACK TO THE FUTURE: FORWARD TO THE FUTURE
Oct, 1992 - No. 3, Feb, 1993 ($1.50, color, mini-series)
Harvey Comics

	GD25	FN65	NM94
1-3	.30	.75	1.50

BAD COMPANY
Aug, 1988 - Present ($1.50-$1.75, color, high quality paper)
Quality Comics/Fleetway Quality #15 on

	GD25	FN65	NM94
1-15: 5,6-Guice-c	.30	.75	1.50
16-18: ($1.75-c)	.35	.90	1.75

BADGE OF JUSTICE
No. 22, 1/55 - No. 23, 3/55; 4/55 - No. 4, 10/55
Charlton Comics

	GD25	FN65	NM94
22(1/55)	5.00	15.00	30.00
23(3/55), 1	4.00	10.00	20.00
2-4	2.80	7.00	14.00

BADGER, THE (First) (Value: cover or less)

BADGER GOES BERSERK (First) (Value: cover or less)

BADLANDS (Vortex) (Value: cover or less)

BADLANDS (Dark Horse) (Value: cover or less)

BADMEN OF THE WEST
1951 (Giant - 132 pages) (Painted-c)
Avon Periodicals

	GD25	FN65	NM94
1-Contains rebound copies of Jesse James, King of the Bad Men of Deadwood, Badmen of Tombstone; other combinations possible. Issues with Kubert-a...	22.00	65.00	150.00

BADMEN OF THE WEST! (See A-1 Comics)
1953 - No. 3, 1954
Magazine Enterprises

	GD25	FN65	NM94
1(A-1 100)-Meskin-a?	14.00	43.00	100.00
2(A-1 120), 3: 2-Larsen-a	10.00	30.00	60.00

BADMEN OF TOMBSTONE
1950
Avon Periodicals

	GD25	FN65	NM94
nn	10.00	30.00	60.00

Babe Ruth Sports #1, © HARV

Baby Huey, the Baby Giant #1, © HARV

Badmen of the West #1, © ME

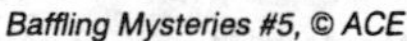
Baffling Mysteries #5, © ACE

Bang-Up Comics #3, © Prog. Publ.

Banner Comics #4, © ACE

GD25 FN65 NM94

BAFFLING MYSTERIES (Formerly Indian Braves No. 1-4; Heroes of the Wild Frontier No. 26-on)
No. 5, Nov, 1951 - No. 26, Oct, 1955
Periodical House (Ace Magazines)

5 — 13.00 40.00 90.00
6-24: 8-Woodish-a by Cameron. 10-E.C. Crypt Keeper swipe on-c. 24-Last pre-code issue — 9.15 27.50 55.00
25-Reprints; surrealistic-c — 6.70 20.00 40.00
26-Reprints — 5.00 15.00 30.00
NOTE: ***Cameron** a-8, 10, 16-18, 20-22. **Colan** a-5, 11, 25r/5. **Sekowsky** a-5, 6, 22. Bondage c-20. Reprints in 18(1), 19(1), 24(3).*

BALBO (See Master Comics #33 & Mighty Midget Comics)

BALDER THE BRAVE
Nov, 1985 - No. 4, 1986 (Mini-series)
Marvel Comics Group

1-4: Simonson-c/a; character from Thor — .50 1.00

BALLAD OF HALO JONES, THE (Quality)(Value: cover or less)

BALLOONATIKS SUPER HEROES, THE (Best)(Value: cover or less)

BALOO & LITTLE BRITCHES
April, 1968 (Walt Disney)
Gold Key

1-From the Jungle Book — 2.40 6.00 12.00

BALTIMORE COLTS
1950 (Giveaway)
American Visuals Corp.

nn-Eisner-c — 40.00 120.00 275.00

BAMBI (See 4-Color No. 12,30,186, Movie Classics, Movie Comics, and Walt Disney Showcase No. 31)

BAMBI (Disney)
1941, 1942, 1984
K. K. Publications (Giveaways)/Whitman Publ. Co.

1941-Horlick's Malted Milk & various toy stores; text & pictures; most copies mailed out with store stickers on-c — 14.00 43.00 100.00
1942-Same as 4-Color #12, but no price (Same as '41 issue?) (Scarce) — 22.00 65.00 150.00
1-(Whitman, 1984; 60 cents)-r/4-Color #186 — .50 1.00

BAMM BAMM & PEBBLES FLINTSTONE (TV)
Oct, 1964 (Hanna-Barbera)
Gold Key

1 — 5.35 16.00 32.00

BANANA OIL
1924 (52 pages)(Black & White)
MS Publ. Co.

nn-Milt Gross-a; not reprints — 22.00 65.00 150.00

BANANA SPLITS, THE (TV) (See March of Comics No. 364)
June, 1969 - No. 8, Oct, 1971 (Hanna-Barbera)
Gold Key

1-Photo-c — 3.00 7.50 15.00
2-8 — 1.60 4.00 8.00

BAND WAGON (See Hanna-Barbera Band Wagon)

BANG-UP COMICS
Dec, 1941 - No. 3, June, 1942
Progressive Publishers

1-Cosmo Mann & Lady Fairplay begin; Buzz Balmer by Rick Yager in all (origin #1) — 58.00 175.00 350.00
2,3 — 35.00 105.00 210.00

BANNER COMICS (Captain Courageous No. 6)
No. 3, Sept, 1941 - No. 5, Jan, 1942
Ace Magazines

3-Captain Courageous & Lone Warrior & Sidekick Dicky begin — 75.00 225.00 450.00
4,5: 4-Flag-c — 50.00 150.00 300.00

BARBARIANS, THE
June, 1975
Atlas Comics/Seaboard Periodicals

1-Origin, only app. Andrax; Iron Jaw app. — .50 1.00

BARBIE
Jan, 1991 - Present ($1.00/$1.25, color)
Marvel Comics

1-Sealed in plastic bag w/Barbie Pink Card; Romita-c — .70 1.75 3.50
2-30: 13-Last $1.00-c — .60 1.25

BARBIE & KEN
May-July, 1962 - No. 5, Nov-Jan, 1963-64
Dell Publishing Co.

01-053-207(#1)-Based on Mattel toy dolls — 28.00 86.00 200.00
2-4 — 22.00 65.00 150.00
5 (Rare) — 25.00 75.00 175.00

BARBIE FASHION
Jan, 1991 - Present ($1.00/$1.25, color)
Marvel Comics

1-Sealed in plastic bag w/doorknob hanger — .50 1.25 2.50
2-30: 4-Contains preview to Sweet XVI. 13-Last $1.00-c — .60 1.25

BARKER, THE (Also see National Comics #42)
Autumn, 1946 - No. 15, Dec, 1949
Quality Comics Group/Comic Magazine

1 — 11.00 32.00 75.00
2 — 5.35 16.00 32.00
3-10 — 4.00 11.00 22.00
11-14 — 3.60 9.00 18.00
15-Jack Cole-a(p) — 4.35 13.00 26.00
NOTE: ***Jack Cole** art in some issues.*

BARNEY AND BETTY RUBBLE (TV) (Flintstones' Neighbors)
Jan, 1973 - No. 23, Dec, 1976 (Hanna-Barbera)
Charlton Comics

1 — 4.00 10.00 20.00
2-10 — 1.80 4.50 9.00
11-23: 11(2/75)-1st Mike Zeck-a (illos) — 1.00 2.50 5.00

BARNEY BAXTER (Also see Magic Comics)
1938 - No. 2, 1956
David McKay/Dell Publishing Co./Argo

Feature Books 15(McKay-1938) — 22.00 65.00 150.00
4-Color 20(1942) — 20.00 60.00 140.00
4,5 — 10.00 30.00 70.00
1,2(1956-Argo) — 5.00 15.00 30.00

BARNEY BEAR ... (Spire Christian)(Value: cover or less)

BARNEY GOOGLE AND SPARK PLUG (See Comic Monthly & Giant Comic Album)
1923 - No. 6, 1928 (Daily strip reprints; B&W) (52 pages)
Cupples & Leon Co.

1-By Billy DeBeck — 24.00 72.00 165.00
2-6 — 16.00 48.00 110.00
NOTE: *Started in 1918 as newspaper strip; Spark Plug began 1922, 1923.*

BARNEY GOOGLE & SNUFFY SMITH

GD25 FN65 NM94

1942 - 1943; April, 1964
Dell Publishing Co./Gold Key

4-Color 19('42) 32.00 95.00 220.00
4-Color 40('44) 17.00 51.00 120.00
Large Feature Comic 11(1943) 17.00 51.00 120.00
1(10113-404)-Gold Key (4/64) 3.60 9.00 18.00

BARNEY GOOGLE & SNUFFY SMITH
June, 1951 - No. 4, Feb, 1952 (Reprints)
Toby Press

1 10.00 30.00 60.00
2,3 5.35 16.00 32.00
4-Kurtzman-a "Pot Shot Pete," 5 pgs.; reprints John Wayne #5
6.70 20.00 40.00

BARNEY GOOGLE AND SNUFFY SMITH
March, 1970 - No. 6, Jan, 1971
Charlton Comics

1 2.40 6.00 12.00
2-6 1.60 4.00 8.00

BARNYARD COMICS (Dizzy Duck No. 32 on)
June, 1944 - No. 31, Sept, 1950; No. 10, 1957
Nedor/Polo Mag./Standard(Animated Cartoons)

1(nn, 52 pgs.) 11.00 32.00 75.00
2 (52 pgs.) 5.85 17.50 35.00
3-5 4.20 12.50 25.00
6-12,16 4.00 10.00 20.00
13-15,17,21,23,26,27,29-All contain Frazetta text illos
4.20 12.50 25.00
18-20,22,24,25-All contain Frazetta-a & text illos 10.00 30.00 60.00
28,30,31 2.40 6.00 12.00
10(1957)(Exist?) 1.40 3.50 7.00

BARRY M. GOLDWATER
March, 1965 (Complete life story)
Dell Publishing Co.

12-055-503-Photo-c 3.60 9.00 18.00

BASEBALL COMICS
Spring, 1949 (Reprinted later as a Spirit section)
Will Eisner Productions

1-Will Eisner-c/a 53.00 160.00 375.00

BASEBALL COMICS (Kitchen Sink)(Value: cover or less)

BASEBALL GREATS (Dark Horse)(Value: cover or less)

BASEBALL HEROES
1952 (One Shot)
Fawcett Publications

nn (Scarce)-Babe Ruth photo-c; baseball's Hall of Fame biographies
55.00 165.00 385.00

BASEBALL'S GREATEST HEROES
Dec, 1991 - No. 2, May, 1992 ($1.75, color)
Magnum Comics

1-Mickey Mantle #1; photo-c; Sinnott-a(p) .35 .90 1.75
2-Brooks Robinson #1; photo-c; Sinnott-a(i) .35 .90 1.75

BASEBALL THRILLS
No. 10, Sum, 1951 - No. 3, Sum, 1952 (Saunders painted-c No.1,2)
Ziff-Davis Publ. Co.

10(#1) 25.00 75.00 175.00
2-Powell-a(2)(Late Sum, '51) 17.00 52.00 120.00
3-Kinstler-c/a 17.00 52.00 120.00

BASEBALL THRILLS 3-D (3-D Zone)(Value: cover or less)

BASICALLY STRANGE (Magazine)
December, 1982 (B&W, $1.95)

GD25 FN65 NM94

John C. Comics (Archie Comics Group)
1-(21,000 printed; all but 1,000 destroyed; pages out of sequence)
.40 1.00 2.00
1-Wood, Toth-a; Corben-c. Reprints & new art .40 1.00 2.00

BASIC HISTORY OF AMERICA ILLUSTRATED
1976 (B&W) (Soft-c $1.50; Hard-c $4.50)
Pendulum Press

07-1999-America Becomes a World Power 1890-1920. 07-2251-The Industrial Era 1865-1915. 07-226x-Before the Civil War 1830-1860. 07-2278-Americans Move Westward 1800-1850. 07-2286-The Civil War 1850-1876; Redondo-a. 07-2294-The Fight for Freedom 1750-1783. 07-2308-The New World 1500-1750. 07-2316-Problems of the NewNation 1800-1830. 07-2324-Roaring Twenties and the Great Depression 1920-1940. 07-2332-The United States Emerges 1783-1800. 07-2340-America Today 1945-1976. 07-2359-World War II 1940-1945

BASIL (...the Royal Cat)
Jan, 1953 - No. 4, Sept, 1953
St. John Publishing Co.

1 3.60 9.00 18.00
2-4 2.00 5.00 10.00
I.W. Reprint 1 .80 2.00 4.00

BASIL WOLVERTON'S GATEWAY TO HORROR (Dark Horse)(Value: cover or less)

BASIL WOLVERTON'S PLANET OF TERROR (Dark Horse)(Value: cover or less)

BATGIRL SPECIAL (See Teen Titans #50)
1988 ($1.50, color, one-shot, 52 pgs)
DC Comics

1 .80 2.00 4.00

BAT LASH (See DC Special Series #16, Showcase #76 & Weird Western Tales)
Oct-Nov, 1968 - No. 7, Oct-Nov, 1969
National Periodical Publications

Showcase #76 (9-10/67)-1st app. Bat Lash 4.70 14.00 28.00
1-(10-11/68) 2.40 6.00 12.00
2-7 1.40 3.50 7.00

BATMAN (See Arkham Asylum, Aurora, The Best of DC #2, Blind Justice, The Brave & the Bold, Cosmic Odyssey, DC 100-Page Super Spec. #14,20, DC Special, DC Special Series, Detective, Dynamic Classics, 80-Page Giants, Gotham By Gaslight, Gotham Nights, Greatest Batman Stories Ever Told, Greatest Joker Stories Ever Told, Heroes Against Hunger, The Joker, Justice League of America #250, Justice League Int., Legends of the Dark Knight, Limited Coll. Ed., Man-Bat, Power Record Comics, Real Fact #5, Saga of Ra's Al Ghul, Shadow of the..., Star Spangled, Super Friends, 3-D Batman, Untold Legend of..., Wanted... & World's Finest Comics)

BATMAN
Spring, 1940 - Present (#1-5 were quarterly)
National Periodical Publ./Detective Comics/DC Comics

GD25 FN65 VF82 NM94

1-Origin The Batman retold by Bob Kane; see Detective #33 for 1st origin; 1st app. Joker (2 stories which count as 1st & 2nd app.); 1st app. The Cat (Catwoman); has Batman story without Robin originally planned for Detective #38. This book was created entirely from the inventory of Det. Comics; 1st Batman/Robin pin-up on back-c
3,350.00 10,000.00 20,000.00 33,500.00
(Estimated up to 250+ total copies exist, 16 in NM/Mint)

1-Reprint, oversize 13-1/2x10. **WARNING**: This comic is an exact duplicate reprint of the original except for its size. DC published it in 1974 with a second cover titling it as a Famous First Edition. There have been many reported cases of the outer cover being removed and the interior sold as the original edition. The reprint with the new outer cover removed is practically worthless.

GD25 FN65 NM94

2-3rd app. The Joker; 2nd app. Catwoman (out of costume) in Joker story; 1st time called Catwoman 870.00 2600.00 5200.00
3-3rd app Catwoman (1st in costume); 1st Puppet Master app.
617.00 1850.00 3700.00
4-5th app. The Joker (see Det. #45 for 4th) 467.00 1400.00 2800.00
5-1st app. of the Batmobile with its bat-head front
350.00 1050.00 2100.00

Barnyard Comics #6, © STD

Baseball Heroes, © FAW

Batman #2, © DC

Batman #12, © DC

Batman #68, © DC

Batman #150, © DC

	GD25	FN65	NM94
6-10: 8-Infinity-c. 9-1st Batman x-mas story; Fred Ray-c. 10-Cat-Woman story (gets new costume)	260.00	775.00	1550.00
11-Classic Joker-c (3rd Joker-c, 6-7/42); Joker & Penguin app.	290.00	875.00	1750.00
12,13,15: 13-Jerry Siegel, creator of Superman appears in a Batman story. 15-New costume Catwoman	210.00	625.00	1250.00
14-2nd Penguin-c; Penguin app. (12-1/42-43)	235.00	700.00	1400.00
16-Intro/origin Alfred (4-5/43)	470.00	1400.00	2800.00
17-20: 17-Penguin app. 18-Hitler, Hirohito, Mussolini-c	135.00	400.00	800.00
21,22,24,26,28-30: 21-1st skinny Alfred in Batman (2-3/44). 21,30-Penguin app. 22-1st Alfred solo-c/story (Alfred solo stories in 22-32,36); Catwoman app.; 2nd app. The Cavalier	108.00	325.00	650.00
23-Joker-c/story	167.00	500.00	1000.00
25-Only Joker/Penguin team-up; 1st team-up between two major villains	160.00	475.00	950.00
27-Burnley Christmas-c; Penguin app.	140.00	410.00	825.00
31,32,34-36,39: 31-Infinity logo-c. 32-Origin Robin retold. 35-Catwoman story (in new costume w/o cat head mask). 36-Penguin app.	80.00	240.00	475.00
33-Christmas-c	96.00	290.00	575.00
37,40,44-Joker-c/stories	108.00	325.00	650.00
38-Penguin-c	92.00	275.00	550.00
41,45,46: 41-Penguin app. 45-Christmas-c/story; Catwoman story; Vicki Vale app.	62.00	185.00	375.00
42-2nd Catwoman-c (1st in Batman)(8-9/47); Catwoman story also	78.00	230.00	460.00
43-Penguin-c/story	78.00	230.00	460.00
47-1st detailed origin The Batman (6-7/48)	216.00	650.00	1300.00
48-1000 Secrets of the Batcave; r-in #203; Penguin story	75.00	225.00	450.00
49-Joker-c/story; 1st Vicki Vale & Mad Hatter	108.00	325.00	650.00
50-Two-Face impostor app.	70.00	210.00	425.00
51,54,56,57,59,60: 57-Centerfold is a 1950 calendar. 59-1st app. Deadshot	62.00	185.00	375.00
52,55-Joker-c/stories	75.00	225.00	450.00
53-Joker story	67.00	200.00	400.00
58-Penguin-c	67.00	200.00	400.00
61-Origin Batman Plane II	62.00	185.00	375.00
62-Origin Catwoman; Catwoman-c	84.00	250.00	500.00
63,80-Joker stories. 63-Flying saucer story (2-3/51)	54.00	162.00	325.00
64,67,70-72,74-77,79: 72-Last 52 pg. issue. 74-Used in **POP**, Pg. 90. 79-Vicki Vale in "The Bride of Batman"	50.00	150.00	300.00
65,69,84-Catwoman-c/stories. 84-Two-Face app.	54.00	160.00	325.00
66,73-Joker-c/stories. 73-Vicki Vale story	62.00	185.00	375.00
68,81-Two-Face-c/stories	50.00	150.00	300.00
78-(8-9/53)-Roh Kar, The Man Hunter from Mars story-the 1st lawman of Mars to come to Earth (green skinned)	62.00	185.00	375.00
82,83,85-89: 86-Intro Batmarine (Batman's submarine). 89-Last pre-code issue	48.00	142.00	285.00
90,91,93-99: 97-2nd app. Bat-Hound-c/story; Joker app.	34.00	100.00	200.00
92-1st app. Bat-Hound-c/story	44.00	132.00	265.00
100 (6/56)	167.00	500.00	1000.00
101-104,106-109: 103-3rd Bat-Hound-c/story	33.00	100.00	230.00
105-1st Batwoman in Batman (2nd anywhere)	43.00	130.00	300.00
110-Joker story	34.00	102.00	240.00
111-120: 112-1st app. Signalman (super villain). 113-1st app. Fatman	24.00	72.00	170.00
121,122,124-126,128,130	17.00	52.00	120.00
123-Joker story; Bat-Hound app.	20.00	60.00	140.00
127-Joker story; Superman cameo	20.00	60.00	140.00
129-Origin Robin retold; bondage-c	22.00	65.00	150.00

	GD25	FN65	NM94
131-135,137-139,141-143: 131-Intro 2nd Batman & Robin series. 133-1st Bat-Mite in Batman (3rd app. anywhere). 134-Origin The Dummy. 139-Intro old Bat-Girl; only app. Signalman as the Blue Bowman. 141-2nd app. old Bat-Girl. 143-Last 10 cent issue	12.00	36.00	85.00
136-Joker-c/story	18.00	54.00	125.00
140,144-Joker stories. 140-Batgirl-c & cameo; Superman cameo	12.00	36.00	85.00
145,148-Joker-c/stories	14.00	43.00	100.00
146,147,149,150	10.00	30.00	65.00
151,153,154,156-158,160-162,164-168,170: 164-New Batmobile (6/64); new look & Mystery Analysts series begins	7.50	22.50	45.00
152-Joker story	7.50	22.50	45.00
155-1st S.A. app. The Penguin (4/63)	29.00	85.00	200.00
159,163-Joker-c/stories	10.00	30.00	60.00
169-Early SA Penguin app.	11.50	34.00	80.00
171-1st Riddler app.(5/65) since Dec. 1948	43.00	130.00	300.00
172-175,177,178,180,181.183,184: 181-Batman & Robin poster insert; intro. Poison Ivy	5.00	15.00	30.00
176-(80-Pg. Giant G-17); Joker-c/story; Penguin app. in strip-r; Catwoman reprint	6.70	20.00	40.00
179-2nd app. Silver Age Riddler	10.00	30.00	70.00
182,187-(80 Pg. Giants G-24, G-30); Joker-c/stories	4.50	14.00	32.00
185-(80 Pg. Giant G-27)	4.00	12.00	28.00
186-Joker-c/story	2.85	8.50	20.00
188,189,191,192,194-196,199: 189-1st S.A. app. Scarecrow. 190-2nd app. S.A. Penguin?	2.15	6.50	15.00
190-Penguin app.	4.00	10.00	20.00
193-(80-Pg. Giant G-37)	3.60	9.00	18.00
197-4th S.A. Catwoman app. cont'd from Det. #369; 1st new Batgirl app. in Batman (4th anywhere)	5.85	17.50	40.00
198-(80-Pg. Giant G-43); Joker-c/story-r/World's Finest #61; Catwoman-r/ Det. #211; Penguin-r; origin-r/#47	7.50	22.50	45.00
200-(3/68)-Joker-story; retells origin of Batman & Robin; 1st Neal Adams work this title (cover only)	15.00	45.00	105.00
201-Joker story	3.60	9.00	18.00
202,204-207,209,210	2.00	5.00	10.00
203-(80 Pg. Giant G-49); r/#48, 61, & Det. 185; Batcave Blueprints	2.80	7.00	14.00
208-(80 Pg. Giant G-55); New origin Batman by Gil Kane plus 3 G.A. Batman reprints w/Catwoman, Vicki Vale & Batwoman	3.60	9.00	18.00
211,212,214-217: 212-Last 12 cent issue. 214-Alfred given a new last name-"Pennyworth" (see Detective #96)	2.00	5.00	10.00
213-(80-Pg. Giant G-61); 30th anniversary issue (7-8/69); origin Alfred (r/Batman #16), Joker(r/Det. #168), Clayface; new origin Robin with new facts	5.35	16.00	32.00
218-(80-Pg. Giant G-67)	2.80	7.00	14.00
219-Neal Adams-a	4.00	10.00	20.00
220,221,224-227,229-231	1.80	4.50	9.00
222-Beatles take-off	3.60	9.00	18.00
223,228,233-(80-Pg. Giants G-73,G-79,G-85)	2.20	5.50	11.00
232,237-N. Adams-a. 232-Intro/1st app. Ras Al Ghul; origin Batman & Robin retold. 237-G.A. Batman-r/Det. #37; 1st app. The Reaper; Wrightson/ Ellison plots	4.00	11.00	22.00
234-1st S.A. app. Two-Face; N. Adams-a; 52 pg. issues begin, end #242	6.70	20.00	40.00
235,236,239-242: 239-XMas-c. 241-Reprint/#5	1.60	4.00	8.00
238-DC-8 100 pg. Super Spec.; G.A. Atom, Sargon (r/Sensation #57), Plastic Man (r/Police #14) stories; Doom Patrol origin-r; Batman, Legion, Aquaman-r; N. Adams-c	1.80	4.50	9.00
243-245-Neal Adams-a	3.20	8.00	16.00
246-250,252,253: 253-Shadow app.	1.60	4.00	8.00
251-N. Adams-c/a; Joker-c/story	4.50	14.00	32.00
254,256-259,261-All 100 pg. editions; part-r. 258-Joker app.			

	GD25	FN65	NM94
	1.80	4.50	9.00
255-N. Adams-c/a; tells of Bruce Wayne's father who wore bat costume & fought crime (100 pgs.); r/story Batman #22	2.80	7.00	14.00
260-Joker-c/story (100 pgs.)	4.00	11.00	22.00
262-285,287-290,292,293,295-299: 262-(68pgs.). 266-Catwoman back to old costume	1.00	2.50	5.00
286,291,294-Joker-c/stories	1.40	3.50	7.00
300-Double-size	1.40	3.50	7.00
301-320,322-352,354-356,358,360-365,367,369,370: 304-(44 pgs.). 310-1st app. The Gentleman Ghost. 311-Batgirl reteams w/Batman. 313,314-Two-Face-c/stories. 316-Robin returns. 322-324-Catwoman (Selina Kyle) app. 322,323-Cat-Man cameos (1st in Batman, 1 panel each). 323-1st meeting Catwoman & Cat-Man. 332-Catwoman's 1st solo. 325-Death of Comm. Gordon. 345-1st app. new Dr. Death. 357,358-1st app. Killer Croc. 361-1st app. Harvey Bullock	1.00	2.50	5.00
321,353,359-Joker-c/stories	1.40	3.50	7.00
357-1st app. Jason Todd (3/83); see Det. 524	1.60	4.00	8.00
366-Jason Todd 1st in Robin costume; Joker-c/story	4.20	12.50	25.00
368-1st new Robin in costume (Jason Todd)	4.00	10.00	20.00
371-399,401-403: 386,387-Intro Black Mask (villain). 401-2nd app. Magpie. 403-Joker cameo	.50	1.25	2.50

NOTE: *Most issues between 397 & 432 were reprinted in 1989 and sold in multi-packs. Some are not identified as reprints but have newer ads copyrighted after cover dates. 2nd and 3rd printings exist.*

	GD25	FN65	NM94
400 ($1.50, 64pgs.)-Dark Knight special; intro by Stephen King; Art Adams/Austin-a	3.00	7.50	15.00
404-Miller scripts begin (end 407); Year 1; 1st modern app. Catwoman	2.40	6.00	12.00
405-407: 407-Year 1 ends (See Det. for Year 2)	1.00	2.50	5.00
408-410: New Origin Jason Todd (Robin)	1.00	2.50	5.00
411-416,421-425: 412-Origin/1st app. Mime. 414-Starlin scripts begin, end #429. 416-Nightwing-c/story	.50	1.20	2.35
417-420: "Ten Nights of the Beast" storyline	2.00	5.00	10.00
426-($1.50, 52 pgs.)-"A Death In The Family" storyline begins, ends #429	1.40	3.50	7.00
427-"A Death In The Family" part 2	1.20	3.00	6.00
428-Death of Robin (Jason Todd)	1.30	3.25	6.50
429-Joker-c/story; Superman app.	1.00	2.50	5.00
430-432	.30	.75	1.50
433-435-"Many Deaths of the Batman" story by John Byrne-c/scripts	.50	1.25	2.50
436-Year 3 begins (ends #439); origin original Robin retold by Nightwing (Dick Grayson); 1st app. Timothy Drake	.90	2.25	4.50
436-2nd print		.50	1.00
437-439: 437-Origin Robin continued	.50	1.25	2.50
440,441: "A Lonely Place of Dying" Parts 1 & 3		.50	1.00
442-1st app. Timothy Drake in Robin costume	.90	2.25	4.50
443-456,458,459,462-464: 445-447-Batman goes to Russia. 448,449-"The Penguin Affair" parts 1 & 3. 450,451-Joker-c/stories. 452-454-"Dark Knight Dark City" storyline; Riddler app. 455-Alan Grant scripts begin, ends #466, 470. 464-Last solo Batman story; free 16 pg. preview of Impact Comics line	.30	.75	1.50
457-Timothy Drake officially becomes Robin & dons new costume	1.60	4.00	8.00
457-2nd printing (has #000 in indicia)	1.00	2.50	5.00
460,461-Two part Catwoman story	.40	1.00	2.00
465-Robin returns to action with Batman	.30	.75	1.50
466-492: 470-War of the Gods x-over. 475,476-The return of Scarface-c/story. 476-Last $1.00-c. 477,478-Photo-c. 488-Cont'd from Batman: Sword of Azreal #4 & cont'd in Scarlett #1		.60	1.25
Annual 1(8-10/61)-Swan-c	35.00	107.00	250.00
Annual 2	16.00	48.00	110.00
Annual 3(Summer, '62)-Joker-c/story	17.00	52.00	120.00
Annual 4,5	8.00	24.00	48.00
Annual 6,7(7/64, 25 cents, 80 pgs.)	6.35	19.00	38.00

	GD25	FN65	NM94
Annual V5#8(1982)-Painted-c	1.00	2.50	5.00
Annual 9,10,12: 9(7/85). 10(1986). 12(1988, $1.50)	.65	1.65	3.30
Annual 11(1987, $1.25)-Penguin-c/story; Alan Moore scripts	1.20	3.00	6.00
Annual 13(1989, $1.75, 68 pgs.)-Gives history of Bruce Wayne, Dick Grayson, Jason Todd, Alfred, Comm. Gordon, Barbara Gordon (Batgirl) & Vicki Vale; Morrow-i	.45	1.10	2.20
Annual 14('90, $2.00, 68 pgs.)-Origin Two-Face	.40	1.00	2.00
Annual 15('91, $2.00, 68 pgs.)-Armageddon 2001 x-over; Joker app.; 2nd printing exists	.40	1.00	2.00
Annual 16('92, $2.50, 68 pgs.)-Joker-c/s; Kieth-c	.50	1.25	2.50
Special 1 (4/84)-Golden-c/a	1.00	2.50	5.00
...And Dracula: Red Rain nn(1991, $24.95)-Hard-c; Elseworlds storyline	7.50	22.50	45.00
...And Dracula: Red Rain nn(1992, $9.95)-Soft-c	1.70	5.00	10.00
Blind Justice nn (1992, $7.50)-r/Det. #598-600	1.25	3.75	7.50
Death In The Family trade paperback (1988, $3.95)-r/Batman #426-429 by Aparo	.85	2.50	5.00
Death In The Family: 2nd - 5th printings	.70	2.00	4.00
Digital Justice nn (1990, $24.95, hardcover)-Computer generated art	4.20	12.50	25.00
Full Circle nn (1991, $5.95, stiff-c, 68 pgs.)-Sequel to Batman: Year Two	1.20	3.00	6.00
...Gothic nn (1992, $12.95)-r/Legends of the Dark Knight #6-10	2.60	6.50	13.00
.../Green Arrow: The Poison Arrow nn (1992, $5.95, squarebound, 68 pgs.)-Netzer-c/a	1.20	3.00	6.00
Holy Terror nn (1991, $4.95, 52 pgs.)-Elseworlds	1.20	3.00	6.00
Lonely Place of Dying (1990, $3.95, 132 pgs.)-r/Batman #440-442 & New Titans #60,61; Perez-c	.80	2.00	4.00
...: Seduction of the Gun nn (1992, $2.50, 68 pgs.)	.50	1.25	2.50
...: The Blue, the Grey, & the Bat nn (1992, $5.95, 68 pgs.)-Weiss/Lopez-a	1.20	3.00	6.00
...: The Many Deaths of the Batman nn (1992, $3.95, 84 pgs.)-r/Batman #433-435 w/new Byrne-c	.80	2.00	4.00
...: Master of the Future nn (1991, $5.95, 68 pgs.)-Elseworlds storyline; sequel to Gotham By Gaslight; embossed-c	1.20	3.00	6.00
...: Vengeance of Bane Special 1 (1992, $2.50, 68 pgs.)	.50	1.25	2.50
Year One Hardcover (1988, $12.95)	3.00	7.50	15.00
Year One trade paperback (1988, $9.95)-r/Batman #404-407 by Miller; introduction by Miller	2.40	6.00	12.00
Year One trade paperback: 2nd & 3rd prints	2.00	5.00	10.00
Year Two trade paperback (1990, $9.95)-r/Det. 575-578 by McFarlane; wraparound-c	2.00	5.00	10.00
Pizza Hut giveaway(12/77)-exact-r of #122,123; Joker-c/story	.40	1.00	2.00
Prell Shampoo giveaway(1966, 16 pgs.)-"The Joker's Practical Jokes" (6-7/8x3-3/8")	2.80	7.00	14.00

NOTE: ***Art Adams** a-400p. **Neal Adams** c-200, 203, 210, 217, 219-222, 224-227, 229, 230, 232, 234, 236-241, 243-246, 251, 255, Annual 14. **Bolland** c-445-447. **Burnley** a-10, 12-18, 20, 25, 27; c-9, 27, 28p, 40p, 42p. **Byrne** c-401, 433-435, 533-535, Annual 11. **Colan** a-340p, 343-345p, 348-351p, 373p, 383p; c-343p, 345p, 350p. **J. Cole** a-238r. **Cowan** a-Annual 10p. **Golden** a-295p, 303p. **Alan Grant** scripts-455-466, 470, 474-476, 479, 480, Annual 16(part). **Grell** a-287, 288p, 289p, 290; c-287-290. **Infantino/Anderson** c-167, 173, 175, 181, 186, 191, 192, 194, 195, 198, 199. **Kaluta** c-242, 2G. **Kane/Anderson** c-178-180. 48, 253, Annual 12. **Bob Kane** a-1, 2, 5; c-1-5, 7, 17. **G. Kane** a-(r)-254, 255, 259, 261, 353i. **Kubert** a-238r, 400; c-310, 319p, 327, 328, 344. **McFarlane** c-423. **Moldoff/Giella** a-164-175, 177-181, 183, 184, 186. **Moldoff/Greene** a-169, 172-174, 177-179, 181, 184. **Mooney** a-255r. **Newton** a-305, 306, 328p, 331p, 332p, 337p, 338p, 346p, 352-357p, 360-372p, 374-378p; c-374p, 378p. **Nino** a-Annual 9. **Irv Novick** c-201, 202. **Perez** a-400; c-436-442. **Robinson/Roussos** a-12-17, 20, 22, 24, 25, 27, 28, 31, 33, 37. **Robinson** a-12, 14, 18, 22-32,34, 36, 37, 255r, 260r, 261r; c-6, 8, 10, 12-15, 18, 21, 24, 26, 30, 37, 39. **Simonson** a-300p, 312p, 321p; c-300p, 312p, 366, 413i. **P. Smith** a-Annual 9. **Dick Sprang** c-19, 20, 22, 23, 29, 31-36, 38, 51, 55, 66, 73, 76. **Starlin** c/a-402. **Staton** a-334. **Wrightson** a-265i, 400; c-320r. Catwoman back-ups in 332, 345, 346, 348-351. Joker app. in 1, 2, 4, 5, 7-9, 11-13, 19, 20, 23, 25, 28, 32 & many more. Robin solo back-up stories in 337-339, 341-343.*

BATMAN (Kellogg's Poptarts comics)
1966 (set of 6) (16 pages)

Batman #442, © DC

Batman #465, © DC

Batman Annual #11, © DC

Batman and the Outsiders #1, © DC

Batman Family #20, © DC

Batman: The Cult #3, © DC

GD25 FN65 NM94

National Periodical Publications

"The Man in the Iron Mask," "The Penguin's Fowl Play," "The Joker's Happy Victims," "The Catwoman's Catnapping Caper," "The Mad Hatter's Hat Crimes," "The Case of the Batman II" each.... 2.80 7.00 14.00

NOTE: *All above were folded and placed in Poptarts boxes.* ***Infantino*** *art on Catwoman and Joker issues.*

BATMAN ADVENTURES, THE (TV cartoon)
Oct, 1992 - Present (1.25, color)
DC Comics

1-8: Based on Fox TV cartoon. 1-Penguin-c/story. 2-Catwoman-c/story. 3-Joker-c/story. 5-Scarecrow .60 1.25

BATMAN AND OTHER DC CLASSICS
1989 (Giveaway)
DC Comics/Diamond Comic Distributors

1-Batman origin-r/Batman #47, Camelot 3000-r by Bolland, Justice League-r('87), New Teen Titans-r by Perez .50 1.00

BATMAN AND THE OUTSIDERS (The Adventures of the Outsiders#33 on) (Also see Brave & The Bold #200 & The Outsiders)
Aug, 1983 - No. 32, Apr, 1986 (Mando paper #5 on)
DC Comics

1-32: 1-Batman, Halo, Geo-Force, Katana, Metamorpho & Black Lightning begin. 5-New Teen Titans x-over. 9-Halo begins. 11,12-Origin Katana. 18-More facts about Metamorpho's origin. 28-31-Lookers origin. 32-Team disbands .50 1.00
Annual 1(9/84)-Miller/Aparo-c; Aparo-i .50 1.00
Annual 2(9/85)-Metamorpho & Sapphire Stagg wed; Aparo-c .50 1.00

NOTE: ***Aparo*** *a-1-9, 11, 12p, 16-20; c-1-4, 5i, 6-21.* ***B. Kane*** *a-3r.* ***Layton*** *a-19i, 20i.* ***Lopez*** *a-3p.* ***Perez*** *c-5p.* ***B. Willingham*** *a-14p.*

BATMAN: BRIDE OF THE DEMON
1990 ($19.95, hard cover w/dust jacket)
DC Comics

nn 4.00 10.00 20.00

BATMAN: CATWOMAN DEFIANT
1992 ($4.95, color, one-shot, prestige format)
DC Comics

nn-Milligan scripts; c-interlocks w/Batman: Penguin Triumphant; special foil logo 1.00 2.50 5.00

BATMAN FAMILY, THE
Sept-Oct, 1975 - No. 20, Oct-Nov, 1978 (No.1-4, 17-on: 68 pages)
(Combined with Detective Comics with No. 481)
National Periodical Publications/DC Comics

1-Origin Batgirl-Robin team-up (The Dynamite Duo); reprints plus one new story begins; N. Adams-a(r) 1.00 2.50 5.00
2-5: 3-Batgirl & Robin learn each's i.d. .60 1.50 3.00
6,9-Joker's daughter on cover (1st app?) .80 2.00 4.00
7,8,10,14-16: 10-1st revival Batwoman .60 1.50 3.00
11-13: Rogers-a(p). 11-New stories begin; Man-Bat begins 1.00 2.50 5.00
17-($1.00 size)-Batman, Huntress begin .60 1.50 3.00
18-20: Huntress by Staton in all. 20-Origin Ragman retold .35 .90 1.75

NOTE: ***Aparo*** *a-17; c-11-16.* ***Austin*** *a-12i.* ***Chaykin*** *a-14p.* ***Michael Golden*** *a-15-17,18-20p.* ***Grell*** *a-1; c-1.* ***Gil Kane*** *a-2r.* ***Kaluta*** *c-17, 19.* ***Newton*** *a-13.* ***Robinson*** *a-1r, 3i(r), 9r.* ***Russell*** *a-18i, 19i.* ***Starlin*** *a-17; c-18, 20.*

BATMAN GALLERY, THE
1992 ($2.95, color, glossy stock)
DC Comics

1-Reprints covers & art from 1939-1992 .50 1.25 2.50

BATMAN - JUDGE DREDD: JUDGEMENT ON GOTHAM
1991 ($5.95, color, 68 pgs.)
DC Comics/Fleetway

nn-Grant/Wagner scripts; Simon Bisley-c/a 1.40 3.50 7.00
nn-2nd printing 1.20 3.00 6.00

BATMAN: LEGENDS OF THE DARK KNIGHT (See Legends of the...)

BATMAN MINIATURE (See Batman Kellogg's)

BATMAN: PENGUIN TRIUMPHANT
1992 ($4.95, color, one-shot, prestige format)
DC Comics

nn-Staton-a(p); special foil logo 1.00 2.50 5.00

BATMAN RECORD COMIC
1966 (One Shot)
National Periodical Publications

1-With record (still sealed) 13.00 40.00 90.00
Comic only 2.40 6.00 12.00

BATMAN RETURNS: THE OFFICIAL COMIC ADAPTATION OF THE WARNER BROS. MOTION PICTURE
1992
DC Comics

nn-($3.95, regular format)-Adapts movie sequel .80 2.00 4.00
nn-($5.95, squarebound) 1.20 3.00 6.00

BATMAN: RUN, RIDDLER, RUN
1992 - Book 3, 1992 ($4.95, color, mini-series)
DC Comics

Book 1-3: Mark Badger-a & plot 1.00 2.50 5.00

BATMAN: SHADOW OF THE BAT
June, 1992 - Present ($1.50, color)
DC Comics

1-The Last Arkham-c/story begins, ends #4 .60 1.50 3.00
1-Deluxe edition(polybagged w/poster, pop-up, book mark, 2.50-c 1.00 2.50 5.00
2-12 .30 .75 1.50

BATMAN: SON OF THE DEMON
Sept, 1987 ($14.95, hardcover, 80 pgs.)
DC Comics

1-Hardcover 9.50 28.50 57.00
Limited signed & numbered hard-c (1,700) 14.00 42.50 85.00
Softcover w/new-c ($8.95) 2.80 7.00 14.00
Softcover, 2nd print (1989, $9.95)-4th print 2.00 5.00 10.00

BATMAN SPECTACULAR (See DC Special Series No. 15)

BATMAN: SWORD OF AZRAEL
Oct, 1992 - No. 4, Jan, 1993 ($1.75, color, mini-series)
DC Comics

1-Wraparound gatefold-c; Quesada-c/a(p). .45 1.10 2.25
2-4: 4-Cont'd in Batman #488 .35 .90 1.75

BATMAN: TALES OF THE DEMON
1991 ($17.95, 212 pgs.)
DC Comics

nn-Intro by Sam Hamm; reprints by Neal Adams(3), Newton(3), & Golden; contains Saga of Ra's Al Ghul #1 3.60 9.00 18.00

BATMAN: THE CULT
1988 - No. 4, Nov, 1988 ($3.50, color, deluxe mini-series)
DC Comics

1-Wrightson-a/painted-c in all 1.40 3.50 7.00
2-4 .80 2.00 4.00
Trade Paperback ('91, $14.95)-New Wrightson-c 3.00 7.50 15.00

BATMAN: THE DARK KNIGHT

	GD25	FN65	NM94

March, 1986 - No. 4, 1986
DC Comics

	GD25	FN65	NM94
1-Miller story & c/a(p); set in the future	3.60	9.00	18.00
1-2nd & 3rd printings	.60	1.50	3.00
2-Carrie Kelly becomes Robin (female)	1.80	4.50	9.00
2-2nd & 3rd printings	.60	1.50	3.00
3-Death of Joker; Superman app.	1.20	3.00	6.00
3-2nd printing	.60	1.50	3.00
4-Death of Alfred; Superman app.	.80	2.00	4.00
Hardcover, signed & numbered edition ($40.00)(4000 copies)	29.00	85.00	200.00
Hardcover, trade edition	8.35	25.00	50.00
Softcover, trade edition (1st printing only)	3.00	7.50	15.00
Softcover, trade edition (2nd thru 8th printings)	2.60	6.50	13.00

NOTE: *The #2 second printings can be identified by matching the grey background colors on the inside front cover and facing page. The inside front cover of the second printing has a dark grey background which does not match the lighter grey of the facing page. On the true 1st printings, the backgrounds are both light grey. All other issues areclearly marked.*

BATMAN: THE KILLING JOKE
1988 ($3.50, 52pgs. color, deluxe, adults)
DC Comics

	GD25	FN65	NM94
1-Bolland-c/a; Alan Moore scripts	2.40	6.00	12.00
1-2nd thru 8th printings	.70	1.75	3.50

BATMAN: THE OFFICIAL COMIC ADAPTATION OF THE WARNER BROS. MOTION PICTURE
1989 ($2.50, $4.95, 68 pgs.) (Movie adaptation)
DC Comics

	GD25	FN65	NM94
1-Regular format ($2.50)-Ordway-c/a	.80	2.00	4.00
1-Prestige format ($4.95)-Diff.-c, same insides	1.20	3.00	6.00

BATMAN 3-D (Also see 3-D Batman)
1990 ($9.95, w/glasses, 8-1/8x10-3/4")
DC Comics

	GD25	FN65	NM94
nn-Byrne-a/scripts; Riddler, Joker, Penguin & Two-Face app. plus r/1953 3-D Batman; pin-ups by many artists	2.00	5.00	10.00

BATMAN VERSUS PREDATOR
1991 - No. 3, 1992 (Mini-series, color)
DC Comics/Dark Horse Comics

	GD25	FN65	NM94
1 (Prestige format, $4.95)-1 & 3 contain 8 Batman/Predator trading cards; Andy & Adam Kubert-a; Suydam painted-c	1.40	3.50	7.00
1 (Regular format, $1.95)-No trading cards	.80	2.00	4.00
2-(Prestige)-Extra pin-ups inside; Suydam-c	1.20	3.00	6.00
2-(Regular)-Without cards	.70	1.75	3.50
3-(Prestige)-Suydam-c	1.20	3.00	6.00
3-(Regular)-Without cards	.60	1.50	3.00
Trade paperback nn (1992, $5.95, 132pgs.)-r/#1-3 w/new introductions & forward plus new wraparound-c by Gibbons	1.20	3.00	6.00

BATMAN VS. THE INCREDIBLE HULK (See DC Special Series No. 27)

BAT MASTERSON (TV) (Also see Tim Holt #28)
Aug-Oct, 1959; Feb-Apr, 1960 - No. 9, Nov-Jan, 1961-62
Dell Publishing Co.

	GD25	FN65	NM94
4-Color 1013 (8-10/59)	8.35	25.00	50.00
2-9: Gene Barry photo-c on all	5.35	16.00	32.00

BATS (See Tales Calculated to Drive You Bats)

BATS, CATS & CADILLACS (Now)(Value: cover or less)

BATTLE
March, 1951 - No. 70, June, 1960
Marvel/Atlas Comics(FPI No. 1-62/Male No. 63 on)

	GD25	FN65	NM94
1	10.00	30.00	65.00
2	4.70	14.00	28.00
3-10: 4-1st Buck Pvt. O'Toole. 10-Pakula-a	4.00	11.00	22.00
11-20: 11-Check-a	3.60	9.00	18.00
21,23-Krigstein-a	4.35	13.00	26.00
22,24-36: 32-Tuska-a. 36-Everett-a	2.80	7.00	14.00
37-Kubert-a (Last precode, 2/55)	3.20	8.00	16.00
38-40,42-48	2.40	6.00	12.00
41-Kubert/Moskowitz-a	3.20	8.00	16.00
49-Davis-a	3.60	9.00	18.00
50-54,56-58	2.40	6.00	12.00
55-Williamson-a (5 pgs.)	4.20	12.50	25.00
59-Torres-a	2.80	7.00	14.00
60-62: 60,62-Combat Kelly app. 61-Combat Casey app.	2.00	5.00	10.00
63-66: 63-Ditko-a. 64-66-Kirby-a. 66-Davis-a; has story of Fidel Castro in pre-Communism days (an admiring profile)	4.35	13.00	26.00
67,68: 67-Williamson/Crandall-a (4 pgs.); Kirby, Davis-a. 68-Kirby/Williamson-a (4 pgs.); Kirby/Ditko-a	5.00	15.00	30.00
69,70: 69-Kirby-a. 70-Kirby/Ditko-a	4.00	12.00	24.00

NOTE: ***Andru** a-37. **Berg** a-38, 14, 60-62. **Colan** a-33, 55. **Everett** a-36, 50, 70; c-56, 57. **Heath** a-6, 9, 13, 31, 69; c-6, 9, 12, 26, 35, 37. **Kirby** c-64-69. **Maneely** a-4, 6, 31, 61; c-4, 33, 59, 61. **Orlando** a-47. **Powell** a-53, 55. **Reinman** a-8, 9, 26, 32. **Robinson** a-9, 39. **Romita** a-26. **Severin** a-28, 32-34, 66-69; c-36, 55. **Sinnott** a-33, 37. **Woodbridge** a-52, 55.*

BATTLE ACTION
Feb, 1952 - No. 12, 5/53; No. 13, 11/54 - No. 30, 8/57
Atlas Comics (NPI)

	GD25	FN65	NM94
1-Pakula-a	10.00	30.00	65.00
2	4.70	14.00	28.00
3,4,6,7,9,10: 6-Robinson-c/a. 7-Partial nudity	4.00	10.00	20.00
5-Used in **POP**, pg. 93,94	3.60	9.00	18.00
8-Krigstein-a	4.20	12.50	25.00
11-15 (Last precode, 2/55)	3.60	9.00	18.00
16-26,28,29	2.40	6.00	12.00
27,30-Torres-a	3.20	8.00	16.00

NOTE: *Battle Brady app. 5-7, 10-12. **Berg** a-3. **Check** a-11. **Everett** a-7; c-13, 25. **Heath** a-3, 8; c-3,15, 21. **Maneely** a-1; c-5. **Reinman** a-1. **Robinson** a-6, 7; c-6. **Shores** a-7(2). **Sinnott** a-3. **Woodbridge** a-28, 30.*

BATTLE ATTACK
Oct, 1952 - No. 8, Dec, 1955
Stanmor Publications

	GD25	FN65	NM94
1	5.00	15.00	30.00
2	3.00	7.50	15.00
3-8: 3-Hollingsworth-a	2.00	5.00	10.00

BATTLE BEASTS (Blackthorne)(Value: cover or less)

BATTLE BRADY (Formerly Men in Action No. 1-9; see 3-D Action)
No. 10, Jan, 1953 - No. 14, June, 1953
Atlas Comics (IPC)

	GD25	FN65	NM94
10: 10-12-Syd Shores-c	6.70	20.00	40.00
11-Used in **POP**, pg. 95 plus B&W & color illos	4.20	12.50	25.00
12-14	3.60	9.00	18.00

BATTLE CLASSICS (See Cancelled Comic Cavalcade)
Sept-Oct, 1978 (44 pages)
DC Comics

	GD25	FN65	NM94
1-Kubert-r; new Kubert-c		.50	1.00

BATTLE CRY
1952(May) - No. 20, Sept, 1955
Stanmor Publications

	GD25	FN65	NM94
1	5.85	17.50	35.00
2	3.60	9.00	18.00
3,5-10: 8-Pvt. Ike begins, ends #13,17	2.00	5.00	10.00
4-Classic E.C. swipe	3.60	9.00	18.00
11-20	1.60	4.00	8.00

NOTE: ***Hollingsworth** a-9; c-20.*

BATTLEFIELD (War Adventures on the...)
April, 1952 - No. 11, May, 1953
Atlas Comics (ACI)

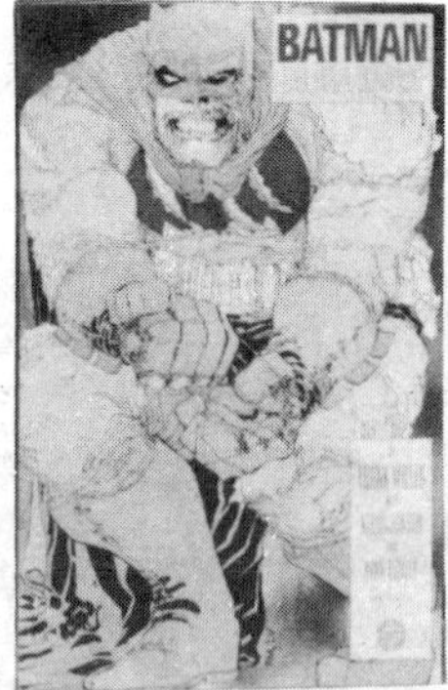

Batman: The Dark Knight #2, © DC

Bat Masterson #9, © ZIV TV Programs

Battle Action #1, © MEG

Battle Fire #1, © Aragon Mag.

Battlefront #1, © MEG

Battlestar Galactica #1, © Universal City Studios

	GD25	FN65	NM94
1-Pakula, Reinman-a	9.15	27.50	55.00
2-5: 2-Heath, Maneely, Pakula, Reinman-a	4.20	12.50	25.00
6-11	2.80	7.00	14.00

NOTE: ***Colan** a-11. **Everett** a-8. **Heath** a-1, 2, 5p; c-2, 8, 9, 11. **Ravielli** a-11.*

BATTLEFIELD ACTION (Formerly Foreign Intrigues)
No. 16, Nov, 1957 - No. 62, 2-3/66; No. 63, 7/80 - No. 89, 11/84
Charlton Comics

	GD25	FN65	NM94
V2#16	3.00	7.50	15.00
17,20-30	1.20	3.00	6.00
18,19-Check-a (2 stories in #18)	1.60	4.00	8.00
31-62(1966)	1.00	2.50	5.00
63-89(1983-'84)		.50	1.00

NOTE: ***Montes/Bache** a-43, 55, 62. **Glanzman** a-87r.*

BATTLE FIRE
April, 1955 - No. 7, 1955
Aragon Magazine/Stanmor Publications

	GD25	FN65	NM94
1	4.00	11.00	22.00
2	2.40	6.00	12.00
3-7	1.60	4.00	8.00

BATTLE FOR A THREE DIMENSIONAL WORLD (3D Cosmic) (Value: cover or less)

BATTLEFORCE
Nov, 1987 - No. 2?, 1988 ($1.75) (#1: color; #2: B&W)
Blackthorne Publishing

	GD25	FN65	NM94
1,2-Based on game	.35	.90	1.75

BATTLE FOR THE PLANET OF THE APES (See Power Record Comics)

BATTLEFRONT
June, 1952 - No. 48, Aug, 1957
Atlas Comics (PPI)

	GD25	FN65	NM94
1-Heath-c	12.50	37.50	75.00
2-Robinson-a(4)	6.35	19.00	38.00
3-5-Robinson-a(4) in each	5.00	15.00	30.00
6-10: Combat Kelly in No. 6-10	4.20	12.50	25.00
11-22,24-28: 14,16-Battle Brady app. 22-Teddy Roosevelt & His Rough Riders story. 28-Last pre-code (2/55)	2.80	7.00	14.00
23,43-Check-a	3.60	9.00	18.00
29-39,41,44-47	2.40	6.00	12.00
40,42-Williamson-a	4.00	11.00	22.00
48-Crandall-a	3.60	9.00	18.00

NOTE: ***Ayers** a-19, 32. **Berg** a-44. **Colan** a-21, 22, 32, 33, 40. **Drucker** a-28, 29. **Everett** a-44.**Heath** c-23, 26, 27, 29, 32. **Maneely** a-22, 23; c-2, 13, 22, 35. **Morisi** a-42. **Morrow** a-41.**Orlando** a-47. **Powell** a-19, 21, 25, 29, 32, 40, 47. **Robinson** a-1-4, 5(4); c-4, 5. **Robert Sale** a-19.**Severin** a-32; c-40. **Woodbridge** a-45, 46.*

BATTLEFRONT
No. 5, June, 1952
Standard Comics

	GD25	FN65	NM94
5-Toth-a	9.15	27.50	55.00

BATTLE GROUND
Sept, 1954 - No. 20, Aug, 1957
Atlas Comics (OMC)

	GD25	FN65	NM94
1	10.00	30.00	60.00
2-Jack Katz-a	5.00	15.00	30.00
3,4-Last precode (3/55)	4.00	10.00	20.00
5-8,10	3.60	9.00	18.00
9-Krigstein-a	4.20	12.50	25.00
11,13,18-Williamson-a in each	4.20	12.50	25.00
12,15-17,19,20	2.80	7.00	14.00
14-Kirby-a	4.00	11.00	22.00

NOTE: ***Ayers** a-13. **Colan** a-11, 13. **Drucker** a-7, 12, 13, 20. **Heath** c-2, 5, 13. **Maneely** a-19; c-1, 19. **Orlando** a-17.**Pakula** a-11. **Severin** a-5, 12, 19. c-20. **Tuska** a-11.*

BATTLE HEROES
Sept, 1966 - No. 2, Nov, 1966 (25 cents)
Stanley Publications

	GD25	FN65	NM94
1,2	1.00	2.50	5.00

BATTLE OF THE BULGE (See Movie Classics)

BATTLE OF THE PLANETS (TV)
6/79 - No. 10, 12/80 (Based on syndicated cartoon by Sandy Frank)
Gold Key/Whitman No. 6 on

	GD25	FN65	NM94
1	.30	.75	1.50
2-10: Mortimer a-1-4,7-10		.50	1.00

BATTLE REPORT
Aug, 1952 - No. 6, June, 1953
Ajax/Farrell Publications

	GD25	FN65	NM94
1	4.20	12.50	25.00
2-6	3.20	8.00	16.00

BATTLE SQUADRON
April, 1955 - No. 5, Dec, 1955
Stanmor Publications

	GD25	FN65	NM94
1	3.60	9.00	18.00
2-5: 3-Iwo Jima & flag-c	2.00	5.00	10.00

BATTLESTAR GALACTICA (TV)(Also see Marvel Super Special #8)
March, 1979 - No. 23, January, 1981
Marvel Comics Group

	GD25	FN65	NM94
1: 1-5 adapt TV episodes	.40	1.00	2.00
2-23: 1-3-Partial-r	.30	.75	1.50

NOTE: ***Austin** c-9i, 10i. **Golden** c-18. **Simonson** a(p)-4, 5, 11-13, 15-20, 22, 23; c(p)-4, 5,11-17, 19, 20, 22, 23.*

BATTLE STORIES (See XMas Comics)
Jan, 1952 - No. 11, Sept, 1953
Fawcett Publications

	GD25	FN65	NM94
1-Evans-a	8.35	25.00	50.00
2	4.20	12.50	25.00
3-11	3.60	9.00	18.00

BATTLE STORIES
1963 - 1964
Super Comics

	GD25	FN65	NM94
Reprints #10-12,15-18: 10-r/U.S Tank Commandos #? 11-r/? 12,17-r/ Monty Hall #?; 15-r/American Air Forces #7 by Powell; Bolle-r	.60	1.75	3.00

BATTLETECH (Blackthorne) (Value: cover or less)

BATTLETIDE (Death's Head II & Killpower...)
Dec, 1992 - No. 4, Mar, 1993 ($1.75, color, mini-series)
Marvel Comics UK, Ltd.

	GD25	FN65	NM94
1-4: Wolverine, Psylocke, Dark Angel app.	.35	.90	1.75

BEACH BLANKET BINGO (See Movie Classics)

BEAGLE BOYS, THE (Walt Disney) (See The Phantom Blot)
11/64; No. 2, 11/65; No. 3, 8/66 - No. 47, 2/79 (See WDC&S #134)
Gold Key

	GD25	FN65	NM94
1	3.60	9.00	18.00
2-5	1.80	4.50	9.00
6-10	1.20	3.00	6.00
11-20: 11,14,19-r	.80	2.00	4.00
21-47: 27-r	.40	1.00	2.00

BEAGLE BOYS VERSUS UNCLE SCROOGE
March, 1979 - No. 12, Feb, 1980
Gold Key

	GD25	FN65	NM94
1	.40	1.00	2.00
2-12: 9-r		.50	1.00

	GD25	FN65	NM94
BEANBAGS			
Winter, 1951 - No. 2, Spring, 1952			
Ziff-Davis Publ. Co. (Approved Comics)			
1,2	5.85	17.50	35.00
BEANIE THE MEANIE			
1958 - No. 3, May, 1959			
Fago Publications			
1-3	2.80	7.00	14.00
BEANY AND CECIL (TV) (Bob Clampett's...)			
Jan, 1952 - 1955; July-Sept, 1962 - No. 5, July-Sept, 1963			
Dell Publishing Co.			
4-Color 368	17.00	51.00	120.00
4-Color 414,448,477,530,570,635(1/55)	14.00	43.00	100.00
01-057-209 (#1)	13.00	40.00	90.00
2-5	10.00	30.00	70.00

BEAR COUNTRY (Disney) (See 4-Color No. 758)

BEATLES, THE (See Girls' Romances #109, Go-Go, Heart Throbs #101, Herbie #5, Howard the Duck Mag. #4, Laugh #166, Marvel Comics Super Special #4, My LittleMargie #54, Not Brand Echh, Strange Tales #130, Summer Love, Superman's Pal Jimmy Olsen #79, Teen Confessions #37, Tippy's Friends & Tippy Teen)

	GD25	FN65	NM94
BEATLES, THE (Life Story)			
Sept-Nov, 1964 (35 cents)			
Dell Publishing Co.			
1-(Scarce)-Stories with color photo pin-ups	50.00	150.00	350.00
BEATLES EXPERIENCE, THE			
Mar, 1991 - No. 8, 1991 ($2.50, B&W, limited series)			
Revolutionary Comics			
1-8: 1-Gold logo	.50	1.25	2.50

BEATLES YELLOW SUBMARINE (See Movie Comics under Yellow...)

	GD25	FN65	NM94
BEAUTIFUL STORIES FOR UGLY CHILDREN			
1989 - Present ($2.00-$2.50, B&W, mature readers)			
Piranha Press (DC Comics)			
Vol. 1-11 ($2.00)	.40	1.00	2.00
12-30 ($2.50)	.50	1.25	2.50
BEAUTY AND THE BEAST, THE			
Jan, 1985 - No. 4, Apr, 1985 (Mini-series)			
Marvel Comics Group			
1-4: Dazzler & the Beast from X-Men	.30	.75	1.50
BEAUTY AND THE BEAST (Graphic novel)(Also see Cartoon Tales & Disney's New Adventures of...)			
1992			
Disney Comics			
nn-($4.95, prestige edition)-Adapts animated film	1.00	2.50	5.00
nn-($2.50, newsstand edition)	.50	1.25	2.50
BEAUTY AND THE BEAST: PORTRAIT OF LOVE (TV)			
May, 1989 - No. 2, Mar, 1990 ($5.95, 60 pgs., color, squarebound)			
First Comics			
1-Based on TV show, Wendy Pini-a/scripts	1.20	3.00	6.00
2-...: Night of Beauty; by Wendy Pini	1.20	3.00	6.00

BEAVER VALLEY (See 4-Color No. 625)

BEDKNOBS AND BROOMSTICKS (See Walt Disney Showcase No. 6 & 50)

BEDLAM! (Eclipse)(Value: cover or less)

BEDTIME STORY (See Cinema Comics Herald)

	GD25	FN65	NM94
BEEP BEEP, THE ROAD RUNNER (TV)(See Daffy & Kite Fun Book)			
July, 1958 - No. 14, Aug-Oct, 1962; Oct, 1966 - No. 105, 1983			
Dell Publishing Co./Gold Key No. 1-88/Whitman No. 89 on			
4-Color 918 (#1, 7/58)	7.50	22.50	45.00
4-Color 1008,1046 (11-1/59-60)	4.20	12.50	25.00
4(2-4/60)-14(Dell)	3.60	9.00	18.00
1(10/66, Gold Key)	4.00	10.50	21.00
2-5	2.40	6.00	12.00
6-14 (1962)	1.60	4.00	8.00
15-18,20-40	1.20	3.00	6.00
19-w/pull-out poster	2.40	6.00	12.00
41-60	.50	1.25	2.50
61-105	.30	.75	1.50

NOTE: *See March of Comics #351, 353, 375, 387, 397, 416, 430, 442, 455. #5, 8-10, 35, 53, 59-62, 68-r; 96-102, 104 are 1/3-r.*

	GD25	FN65	NM94
BEETLE BAILEY (See Comics Reading Library, Giant Comic Album & Sarge Snorkel)			
#459, 5/53 - #38, 5-7/62; #39, 11/62 - #53, 5/66; #54, 8/66 - #65, 12/67; #67, 2/69 - #119, 11/76; #120, 4/78 - #132, 4/80			
Dell Publishing Co./Gold Key #39-53/King #54-66/Charlton #67-119/ Gold Key #120-131/Whitman #132			
4-Color 469 (#1)-By Mort Walker	8.35	25.00	50.00
4-Color 521,552,622	4.20	12.50	25.00
5(2-4/56)-10(5-7/57)	3.60	9.00	18.00
11-20(4-5/59)	2.40	6.00	12.00
21-38(5-7/62)	1.50	3.75	7.50
39-53(5/66)	.90	2.25	4.50
54-119 (No. 66 publ. overseas only?)	.50	1.25	2.50
120-132	.30	.75	1.50
Bold Detergent Giveaway('69)-same as regular issue (#67) minus price	.40	1.00	2.00
Cerebral Palsy Assn. Giveaway V2#71('69)-V2#73; (#1), 1/70 (Charlton)	.40	1.00	2.00
Red Cross Giveaway, 16pp, 5x7", 1969, paper-c	.40	1.00	2.00
BEETLE BAILEY			
Sept, 1992 - Present ($1.25, color)			
Harvey Comics			
V2#1-4		.60	1.25
...Giant Size V2#1(10/92),2 (Both $2.25, 68 pgs.)	.45	1.15	2.25
BEETLEJUICE (TV)			
Oct, 1991 - No. 2? ($1.25, color, quarterly)			
Harvey Comics			
1,2		.60	1.25
BEETLEJUICE CRIMEBUSTERS ON THE HAUNT			
Sept, 1992 - No. 3, Jan, 1993 ($1.50, color, mini-series)			
Harvey Comics			
1-3	.30	.75	1.50
BEE 29, THE BOMBARDIER			
Feb, 1945			
Neal Publications			
1-(Funny animal)	10.00	30.00	70.00
BEHIND PRISON BARS			
1952			
Realistic Comics (Avon)			
1-Kinstler-c	17.00	52.00	1200.00
BEHOLD THE HANDMAID			
1954 (Religious) (25 cents with a 20 cent sticker price)			
George Pflaum			
nn	3.20	8.00	16.00

BELIEVE IT OR NOT (See Ripley's...)

BEN AND ME (See 4-Color No. 539)

	GD25	FN65	NM94
BEN BOWIE AND HIS MOUNTAIN MEN			
1952 - No. 17, Nov-Jan, 1958-59			
Dell Publishing Co.			
4-Color 443 (#1)	6.70	20.00	40.00

Beep Beep, the Road Runner #5, © Warner Bros.

Beetle Bailey #12, © KING

Behind Prison Bars #1, © AVON

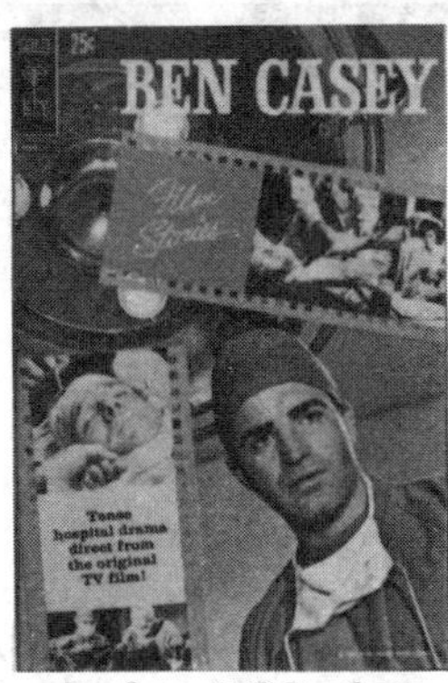

Ben Casey #1, © Bing Crosby Prod.

The Berrys #1, © Argo Publ.

Best Comics #4, © BP

	GD25	FN65	NM94
4-Color 513,557,599,626,657	4.00	10.50	21.00
7(5-7/56)-11: 11-Intro/origin Yellow Hair	3.20	8.00	16.00
12-17	2.40	6.00	12.00

BEN CASEY (TV)
June-July, 1962 - No. 10, June-Aug, 1965 (Photo-c)
Dell Publishing Co.

	GD25	FN65	NM94
12-063-207 (#1)	4.35	13.00	26.00
2(10/62)-10: 4-Marijuana & heroin use story	3.20	8.00	16.00

BEN CASEY FILM STORY (TV)
November, 1962 (25 cents) (Photo-c)
Gold Key

	GD25	FN65	NM94
30009-211-All photos	7.50	22.50	45.00

BENEATH THE PLANET OF THE APES (See Movie Comics & Power Record Comics)

BEN FRANKLIN (See Kite Fun Book)

BEN HUR (See 4-Color No. 1052)

BEN ISRAEL (Logos Int.)(Value: cover or less)

BEOWULF (See First Comics Graphic Novel #1)
April-May, 1975 - No. 6, Feb-Mar, 1976
National Periodical Publications

	GD25	FN65	NM94
1	.30	.75	1.50
2-6: 5-Flying saucer-c/story		.50	1.00

BERNI WRIGHTSON, MASTER OF THE MACABRE
July, 1983 - No. 5, Nov, 1984 ($1.50; Baxter paper)
Pacific Comics/Eclipse Comics No. 5

	GD25	FN65	NM94
1-5: Wrightson-c/a(r). 4-Jeff Jones-r (11 pgs.)	.30	.75	1.50

BERRYS, THE (Also see Funny World)
May, 1956
Argo Publ.

	GD25	FN65	NM94
1-Reprints daily & Sunday strips & daily Animal Antics by Ed Nofziger	4.00	11.00	22.00

BEST COMICS
Nov, 1939 - No. 4, Feb, 1940 (large size, reads sideways)
Better Publications

	GD25	FN65	NM94
1-(Scarce)-Red Mask begins	50.00	150.00	300.00
2-4: 4-Cannibalism story	30.00	92.00	185.00

BEST FROM BOY'S LIFE, THE
Oct, 1957 - No. 5, Oct, 1958 (35 cents)
Gilberton Company

	GD25	FN65	NM94
1-Space Conquerors & Kam of the Ancient Ones begin, end #5	5.85	17.50	35.00
2,3,5	3.60	9.00	18.00
4-L.B. Cole-a	4.00	10.50	21.00

BEST LOVE (Formerly Sub-Mariner Comics No. 32)
No. 33, Aug, 1949 - No. 36, April, 1950 (Photo-c 33-36)
Marvel Comics (MPI)

	GD25	FN65	NM94
33-Kubert-a	7.00	21.00	42.00
34	3.60	9.00	18.00
35,36-Everett-a	4.70	14.00	28.00

BEST OF BUGS BUNNY, THE
Oct, 1966 - No. 2, Oct, 1968
Gold Key

	GD25	FN65	NM94
1,2-Giants	2.50	7.50	20.00

BEST OF DC, THE (Blue Ribbon Digest) (See Limited Coll. Ed. C-52)
Sept-Oct, 1979 - No. 71, Apr, 1986 (100-148 pgs; all reprints)
DC Comics

	GD25	FN65	NM94
1-17,19-34,36-71: 34-Has #497 on-c from Adv. Comics. 60-Plop!; Wood-c(r) & Aragones-r (5/85)		.50	1.00
18-The New Teen Titans	.30	.80	1.60
35-The Year's Best Comics Stories(148 pgs.)		.60	1.20

NOTE: ***N. Adams** a-26, 51. **Aparo** a-9, 14, 26, 30; c-9, 14, 26. **Austin** a-51i. **Buckler** a-40p; c-22. **Giffen** a-50, 52; c-33p. **Grell** a-33p. **Grossman** a-37. **Heath** a-26. **Kaluta** a-40. **G. Kane** c-40, 44. **Kubert** a-21, 26. **Layton** a-21. **S. Mayer** c-29, 37, 41, 43, 47; a-28, 29, 37, 41, 43, 47, 58, 65, 68. **Moldoff** c-64p. **Morrow** a-40; c-40. **W. Mortimer** a-39p. **Newton** a-5, 51. **Perez** a-24, 50p; c-18, 21, 23. **Rogers** a-14, 51p. **Spiegle** a-52. **Starlin** a-51. **Staton** a-5, 21. **Tuska** a-24. **Wolverton** a-60. **Wood** a-60, 63; c-60, 63. **Wrightson** a-60. New art in #14, 18, 24.*

BEST OF DENNIS THE MENACE, THE
Summer, 1959 - No. 5, Spring, 1961 (100 pages)
Hallden/Fawcett Publications

	GD25	FN65	NM94
1-All reprints; Wiseman-a	5.00	15.00	30.00
2-5	4.00	11.00	22.00

BEST OF DONALD DUCK, THE
Nov, 1965 (12 cents, 36 pages)(Says 2nd printing in indicia)
Gold Key

	GD25	FN65	NM94
1-Reprints 4-Color #223 by Barks	5.00	15.00	30.00

BEST OF DONALD DUCK & UNCLE SCROOGE, THE
Nov, 1964 - No. 2, Sept, 1967 (25 cent giant)
Gold Key

	GD25	FN65	NM94
1(30022-411)('64)-Reprints 4-Color #189 & 408 by Carl Barks; cover of F.C. #189 redrawn by Barks	5.00	15.00	35.00
2(30022-709)('67)-Reprints 4-Color #256 & "Seven Cities of Cibola" & U.S. #8 by Barks	4.00	12.00	28.00

BEST OF HORROR AND SCIENCE FICTION COMICS (Webster)(Value: cover or less)

BEST OF MARMADUKE, THE
1960 (A dog)
Charlton Comics

	GD25	FN65	NM94
1-Brad Anderson's strip reprints	2.40	6.00	12.00

BEST OF MS. TREE, THE (Pyramid)(Value: cover or less)

BEST OF THE BRAVE AND THE BOLD, THE (See Super DC Giant)
Oct, 1988 - No. 6, Jan, 1989 ($2.50, color, mini-series)
DC Comics

	GD25	FN65	NM94
1-6: Neal Adams-r in all	.50	1.25	2.50

BEST OF THE WEST (See A-1 Comics)
1951 - No. 12, April-June, 1954
Magazine Enterprises

	GD25	FN65	NM94
1(A-1 42)-Ghost Rider, Durango Kid, Straight Arrow, Bobby Benson begin	29.00	85.00	200.00
2(A-1 46)	13.00	40.00	90.00
3(A-1 52), 4(A-1 59), 5(A-1 66)	11.50	34.00	80.00
6(A-1 70), 7(A-1 76), 8(A-1 81), 9(A-1 85), 10(A-1 87), 11(A-1 97), 12(A-1 103)	10.00	30.00	60.00

NOTE: ***Bolle** a-9. **Borth** a-12. **Guardineer** a-5, 12. **Powell** a-1, 12.*

BEST OF UNCLE SCROOGE & DONALD DUCK, THE
November, 1966 (25 cents)
Gold Key

	GD25	FN65	NM94
1(30030-611)-Reprints part 4-Color #159 & 456 & Uncle Scrooge #6,7 by Carl Barks	5.85	17.50	35.00

BEST OF WALT DISNEY COMICS, THE
1974 (In color; $1.50; 52 pages) (Walt Disney)
(8-1/2x11" cardboard covers; 32,000 printed of each)
Western Publishing Co.

	GD25	FN65	NM94
96170-Reprints 1st two stories less 1 pg. each from 4-Color #62	1.60	4.00	8.00
96171-Reprints Mickey Mouse and the Bat Bandit of Inferno Gulch from 1934 (strips) by Gottfredson	1.60	4.00	8.00

96172-Reprints Uncle Scrooge #386 & two other stories
1.60 4.00 8.00

96173-Reprints "Ghost of the Grotto" (from 4-Color #159) & "Christmas on Bear Mtn." (from 4-Color #178) 1.60 4.00 8.00

BEST ROMANCE
No. 5, Feb-Mar, 1952 - No. 7, Aug, 1952
Standard Comics (Visual Editions)

5-Toth-a; photo-c 8.35 25.00 50.00
6,7-Photo-c 3.60 9.00 18.00

BEST SELLER COMICS (See Tailspin Tommy)

BEST WESTERN (Formerly Terry Toons? or Miss America Magazine V7#24(#57)? ; Western Outlaws & Sheriffs No. 60 on)
No. 58, June, 1949 - No. 59, Aug, 1949
Marvel Comics (IPC)

58,59-Black Rider, Kid Colt, Two-Gun Kid app.; both have Syd Shores-c
10.00 30.00 70.00

BETTY
Sept, 1992 - Present ($1.25, color)
Archie Comics

1-6 .60 1.25

BETTY AND HER STEADY (Going Steady with Betty No. 1)
No. 2, Mar-Apr, 1950
Avon Periodicals

2 6.70 20.00 40.00

BETTY AND ME
Aug, 1965 - Present
Archie Publications

1 10.00 30.00 65.00
2 5.35 16.00 32.00
3-5: 3-Origin Superteen. Superteen in new costume #4-7; dons new helmet #5, ends #8 3.60 9.00 18.00
6-10 1.80 4.50 9.00
11-30 .80 2.00 4.00
31-55 (52 pages #36-55) .40 1.00 2.00
56-100 .30 .75 1.50
101-198: Later issues $1.00 cover .50 1.00

BETTY AND VERONICA (Also see Archie's Girls...)
June, 1987 - Present (75 cents - $1.25)
Archie Enterprises

1-64 .60 1.25

BETTY & VERONICA ANNUAL DIGEST (...Digest Mag. #2-4, 44 on; ...Comics Digest Mag. #5-43)
November, 1980 - No. 54?, 1992 ($1.00 - 1.50, digest size)
Archie Publications

1, 2(11/81-Katy Keene story), 3(8/82) - 62('93) .30 .75 1.50

BETTY & VERONICA ANNUAL DIGEST (... Magazine #3 on)
Aug?, 1989 - Present? ($1.50, 128 pgs.)
Archie Comics

1-6 .30 .75 1.50

BETTY & VERONICA CHRISTMAS SPECTACULAR (See Archie Giant Series Magazine #159, 168, 180, 191, 204, 217, 229, 241, 453, 465, 477, 489, 501, 513, 525, 536, 547, 558, 568, 580, 593, 606, 618)

BETTY & VERONICA DOUBLE DIGEST MAGAZINE
1987 - Present (Digest size, 256 pgs., $2.25)(...Digest #12 on)
Archie Enterprises

1-38: 5,17-Xmas-c. 16-Capt. Hero story .45 1.10 2.25

BETTY & VERONICA SPECTACULAR (See Archie Giant Series Mag. #11, 16, 21, 26, 32, 138, 145, 153, 162, 173, 184, 197, 201, 210, 214, 221, 226, 234, 238, 246, 250, 458, 462, 470, 482, 486, 494, 498, 506, 510, 518, 522, 526, 530, 537, 552, 559, 563, 569, 575, 582, 588, 600, 608, 613, 620, 623)

BETTY AND VERONICA SPECTACULAR
Oct, 1992 - Present ($1.25, color)
Archie Comics

1-4: 1-Dan DeCarlo-c/a .60 1.25

BETTY & VERONICA SPRING SPECTACULAR (See Archie Giant Series Magazine #569, 582, 595)

BETTY & VERONICA SUMMER FUN (See Archie Giant Series Mag. #8, 13, 18, 23, 28, 34, 140, 147, 155, 164, 175, 187, 199, 212, 224, 236, 248, 460, 484, 496, 508, 520, 529, 539, 550, 561, 572, 585, 598, 611, 621)

BETTY BOOP'S BIG BREAK (First)(Value: cover or less)

BETTY PAGE 3-D COMICS (3-D Zone)(Value: cover or less)

BETTY'S DIARY (See Archie Giant Series Magazine No. 555)
April, 1986 - No. 40, 1991 (75 & 95 cents)
Archie Enterprises

1-40 .50 1.00

BEVERLY HILLBILLIES (TV)
4-6/63 - No. 18, 8/67; No. 19, 10/69; No. 20, 10/70; No. 21, Oct, 1971
Dell Publishing Co.

1-Photo-c 11.50 34.00 85.00
2-Photo-c 6.70 20.00 40.00
3-9: All have photo covers 4.70 14.00 28.00
10: No photo cover 3.20 8.00 16.00
11-21: All have photo covers. 18-Last 12 cent-c 4.00 11.00 22.00
NOTE: *#1-9, 11-21 are photo covers. #19 reprints cover to #1, but not insides.*

BEWARE (Formerly Fantastic; Chilling Tales No. 13 on)
No. 10, June, 1952 - No. 12, Oct, 1952
Youthful Magazines

10-E.A. Poe's Pit & the Pendulum adaptation by Wildey; Harrison/Bache-a; atom bomb and shrunken head-c 17.00 52.00 120.00
11-Harrison-a; Ambrose Bierce adapt. 13.00 40.00 90.00
12-Used in **SOTI**, pg. 388; Harrison-a 13.00 40.00 90.00

BEWARE
No. 13, 1/53 - No. 16, 7/53; No. 5, 9/53 - No. 15, 5/55
Trojan Magazines/Merit Publ. No. ?

13(#1)-Harrison-a 16.00 48.00 110.00
14(#2, 3/53)-Krenkel/Harrison-c; dismemberment, severed head panels
11.50 34.00 80.00
15,16(#3, 5/53; #4, 7/53)-Harrison-a 10.00 30.00 60.00
5,9,12,13 10.00 30.00 60.00
6-Ill. in **SOTI**-"Children are first shocked and then desensitized by all this brutality." Corpse on cover swipe/V.O.H. #26; girl on cover swipe/Advs. Into Darkness #10 19.30 58.00 130.00
7,8-Check-a 10.00 30.00 70.00
10-Frazetta/Check-c; Disbrow, Check-a 30.00 90.00 210.00
11-Disbrow-a; heart torn out, blood drainage 11.50 34.00 80.00
14,15: 14-Myron Fass-c. 15-Harrison-a 10.00 30.00 60.00
NOTE: ***Fass** a-5, 6, 8; c-6, 11, 14. **Forte** a-8. **Hollingsworth** a-15(#3), 16(#4), 9; c-16(#4), 8, 9. **Kiefer** a-16(#4), 5, 6, 10.*

BEWARE (Becomes Tomb of Darkness No. 9 on)
March, 1973 - No. 8, May, 1974 (All reprints)
Marvel Comics Group

1-Everett-c; Sinnott-r ('54) .80 2.00 4.00
2-8: 2-Forte, Colan-r. 6-Tuska-a. 7-Torres-r/Mystical Tales #7
.40 1.00 2.00

BEWARE TERROR TALES
May, 1952 - No. 8, July, 1953
Fawcett Publications

1-E.C. art swipe/Haunt of Fear #5 & Vault of Horror #26
17.00 52.00 120.00
2 10.00 30.00 70.00
3-8: 8-Tothish-a 10.00 30.00 600.00

Best Western #59, © MEG

Beverly Hillbillies #21, © Filmways

Beware Terror Tales #1, © FAW

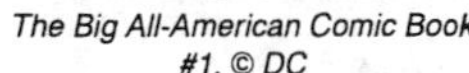
The Big All-American Comic Book #1, © DC

Big Chief Wahoo #1, © EAS

Big Shot #43, © CCG

	GD25	FN65	NM94

NOTE: ***Andru** a-2. **Bernard Bailey** a-1; c-1-5. **Powell** a-1, 2, 8. **Sekowsky** a-2.*

BEWARE THE CREEPER (See Adventure, Best of the Brave & the Bold, Brave & the Bold, First Issue Special, Flash #318-323, Showcase, and World's Finest #249)
May-June, 1968 - No. 6, March-April, 1969
National Periodical Publications

	GD25	FN65	NM94
Showcase #73 (3-4/67)-Origin & 1st app. The Creeper; Ditko-c/a	9.15	27.50	55.00
1-(5-6/68)-Ditko-a in all; c-1-5	6.35	19.00	38.00
2-6: 6-G. Kane-c	4.20	12.50	25.00

BEWITCHED (TV)
4-6/65 - No. 11, 10/67; No. 12, 10/68 - No. 13, 1/69; No. 14, 10/69
Dell Publishing Co.

	GD25	FN65	NM94
1-Photo-c	11.50	34.00	80.00
2-No photo-c	6.70	20.00	40.00
3-13-All have photo-c	4.70	14.00	28.00
14-No photo-c	4.00	11.00	22.00

BEYOND, THE
Nov, 1950 - No. 30, Jan, 1955
Ace Magazines

	GD25	FN65	NM94
1-Bakerish-a(p)	19.30	58.00	130.00
2-Bakerish-a(p)	10.00	30.00	70.00
3-10: 10-Woodish-a by Cameron	7.50	22.50	45.00
11-20: 18-Used in **POP**, pgs. 81,82	6.00	18.00	36.00
21-26,28-30	5.35	16.00	32.00
27-Used in **SOTI**, pg. 111	5.85	17.50	35.00

NOTE: ***Cameron** a-10, 11p, 12p, 15, 16, 21-27, 30; c-20. **Colan** a-6, 13, 17. **Sekowsky** a-2, 3, 5, 7, 11, 14, 27r. No. 1 was to appear as Challenge of the Unknown No. 7.*

BEYOND THE GRAVE
July, 1975 - No. 6, June, 1976; No. 7, Jan, 1983 - No. 17, Oct, 1984
Charlton Comics

	GD25	FN65	NM94
1-Ditko-a (6 pgs.); Sutton painted-c	.80	2.00	4.00
2-6: 2-5-Ditko-a; Ditko c-2,3,6	.40	1.00	2.00
7-17: ('83-'84) Reprints. 15-Sutton-c		.60	1.25
Modern Comics Reprint 2('78)		.50	1.00

BIBLE TALES FOR YOUNG FOLK (...Young People No. 3-5)
Aug, 1953 - No. 5, Mar, 1954
Atlas Comics (OMC)

	GD25	FN65	NM94
1	11.50	34.00	80.00
2-Everett, Krigstein-a	9.30	28.00	65.00
3-5: 4-Robinson-c	7.50	22.50	45.00

BIG (Hit) (Value: cover or less)

BIG ALL-AMERICAN COMIC BOOK, THE
1944 (One Shot) (132 pages)
All-American/National Periodical Publ.

GD25	FN65	VF82	NM94

1-Wonder Woman, Green Lantern, Flash, The Atom, Wildcat, Scribbly, The Whip, Ghost Patrol, Hawkman by Kubert (1st on Hawkman), Hop Harrigan, Johnny Thunder, Little Boy Blue, Mr. Terrific, Mutt & Jeff app.; Sargon on cover only; cover by Kubert/Hibbard/Mayer/others

GD25	FN65	VF82	NM94
550.00	1650.00	3300.00	5500.00

(Estimated up to 80+ total copies exist, 6 in NM/Mint)

BIG BABY HUEY (Also see Baby Huey)
Oct, 1991 - Present ($1.00, color, quarterly)
Harvey Comics

	GD25	FN65	NM94
1-4		.50	1.00

BIG BOOK OF FUN COMICS (See New Book of Comics)
Spring, 1936 (52pgs., large size) (1st comic book annual & DC annual)
National Periodical Publications

	GD25	FN65	VF82
1 (Very rare)-r/New Fun #1-5	1000.00	2500.00	5000.00

(Estimated up to 15 total copies exist, none in NM/Mint)

BIG BOOK ROMANCES
February, 1950 (no date given) (148 pages)
Fawcett Publications

	GD25	FN65	NM94
1-Contains remaindered Fawcett romance comics - several combinations possible	22.00	65.00	150.00

BIG BOY (See Adventures of the Big Boy)

BIG CHIEF WAHOO
July, 1942 - No. 23, 1945? (Quarterly)
Eastern Color Printing/George Dougherty (distr. by Fawcett)

	GD25	FN65	NM94
1-Newspaper-r (on sale 6/15/42)	26.00	78.00	180.00
2-Steve Roper app.	13.00	40.00	90.00
3-5: 4-Chief is holding a Katy Keene comic	10.00	30.00	65.00
6-10: 8-23-Exist?	7.50	22.50	45.00
11-23	5.35	16.00	32.00

NOTE: *Kerry Drake in some issues.*

BIG CIRCUS, THE (See 4-Color No. 1036)

BIG COUNTRY, THE (See 4-Color No. 946)

BIG DADDY ROTH
Oct-Nov, 1964 - No. 4, Apr-May, 1965 (35 cents, magazine)
Millar Publications

	GD25	FN65	NM94
1-Toth-a	14.00	43.00	100.00
2-4-Toth-a	10.00	30.00	70.00

BIG HERO ADVENTURES (See Jigsaw)

BIG JIM'S P.A.C.K.
No date (16 pages)
Mattel, Inc. (Marvel Comics)

	GD25	FN65	NM94
nn-Giveaway with Big Jim doll		.15	.30

BIG JON & SPARKIE (Radio) (Formerly Sparkie, Radio Pixie)
No. 4, Sept-Oct, 1952 (Painted-c)
Ziff-Davis Publ. Co.

	GD25	FN65	NM94
4-Based on children's radio program	10.00	30.00	70.00

BIG LAND, THE (See 4-Color No. 812)

BIG RED (See Movie Comics)

BIG SHOT COMICS
May, 1940 - No. 104, Aug, 1949
Columbia Comics Group

	GD25	FN65	NM94
1-Intro. Skyman; The Face (Tony Trent), The Cloak (Spy Master), Marvelo, Monarch of Magicians, Joe Palooka, Charlie Chan, Tom Kerry, Dixie Dugan, Rocky Ryan begin	115.00	350.00	700.00
2	46.00	132.00	275.00
3-The Cloak called Spy Chief; Skyman-c	40.00	120.00	240.00
4,5	33.00	100.00	200.00
6-10: 8-Christmas-c	29.00	85.00	175.00
11-14: 14-Origin Sparky Watts	25.00	75.00	150.00
15-Origin The Cloak	29.00	75.00	175.00
16-20	18.00	55.00	110.00
21-27,29,30: 24-Tojo-c. 29-Intro. Capt. Yank; Bo (a dog) newspaper strip reprints by Frank Beck begin, ends #104. 30-Christmas-c	14.00	42.00	85.00
28-Hitler, Tojo & Mussolini-c	17.00	50.00	100.00
31,33-40	10.00	30.00	65.00
32-Vic Jordan newspaper strip reprints begin, ends #52; Hitler, Tojo & Mussolini-c	12.50	37.50	75.00
41-50: 42-No Skyman. 43,46-Hitler-c. 50-Origin The Face retold	9.15	27.50	55.00
51-60	7.00	21.00	42.00
61-70: 63 on-Tony Trent, the Face	5.85	17.50	35.00

71-80: 73-The Face cameo. 74-(2/47)-Mickey Finn begins. 74,80-The Face

	GD25	FN65	NM94
app. in Tony Trent. 78-Last Charlie Chan strip reprints	5.00	15.00	30.00
81-90: 85-Tony Trent marries Babs Walsh. 86-Valentines-c	4.35	13.00	26.00
91-99,101-104: 69-94-Skyman in Outer Space. 96-Xmas-c	4.00	11.00	22.00
100	5.00	15.00	30.00

NOTE: ***Mart Bailey** art on "The Face"-No. 1-104. **Guardineer** a-5. Sparky Watts by **Boody Rogers**-No. 14-42, 77-104, (by others No. 43-76). Others than Tony Trent wear` 'The Face" mask in No. 46-63, 93. Skyman by **Ogden Whitney**-No. 1, 2, 4, 12-37, 49, 70-101. Skyman covers-No. 1, 3, 7-12, 14, 16, 20, 27, 89, 95, 100.*

BIG TEX
June, 1953
Toby Press

	GD25	FN65	NM94
1-Contains (3) John Wayne stories-r with name changed to Big Tex	5.85	17.50	35.00

BIG-3
Fall, 1940 - No. 7, Jan, 1942
Fox Features Syndicate

	GD25	FN65	NM94
1-Blue Beetle, The Flame, & Samson begin	115.00	340.00	680.00
2	50.00	150.00	300.00
3-5	40.00	120.00	240.00
6-Last Samson; bondage-c	33.00	100.00	200.00
7-V-Man app.	33.00	100.00	200.00

BIG TOP COMICS, THE (TV's Great Circus Show)
1951 - No. 2, 1951 (no month)
Toby Press

	GD25	FN65	NM94
1,2	4.35	13.00	26.00

BIG TOWN (Radio/TV)
Jan, 1951 - No. 50, Mar-Apr, 1958 (No. 1-9: 52pgs.)
National Periodical Publications

	GD25	FN65	NM94
1-Dan Barry-a begins	34.00	102.00	240.00
2	16.50	50.00	115.00
3-10	10.00	30.00	70.00
11-20	8.35	25.00	50.00
21-31: Last pre-code (1-2/55)	5.85	17.50	35.00
32-50	4.20	12.50	25.00

BIG VALLEY, THE (TV)
June, 1966 - No. 5, Oct, 1967; No. 6, Oct, 1969
Dell Publishing Co.

	GD25	FN65	NM94
1: Photo-c #1-5	4.70	14.00	28.00
2-6: 6-Reprints #1	2.80	7.00	14.00

BILL & TED'S BOGUS JOURNEY
Sept, 1991 ($2.95, color, squarebound, 84 pgs.)
Marvel Comics

	GD25	FN65	NM94
1-Adapts movie sequel	.60	1.50	3.00

"BILL AND TED'S EXCELLENT ADVENTURE" MOVIE ADAPTATION
1989 (No cover price, color)
DC Comics

	GD25	FN65	NM94
nn-Torres-a		.50	1.00

BILL & TED'S EXCELLENT COMIC BOOK
Dec, 1991 - No. 12, 1992 ($1.00/$1.25, color)
Marvel Comics

	GD25	FN65	NM94
1,2: 2-Last $1.00-c		.50	1.00
3-12		.60	1.25

BILL BARNES COMICS (...America's Air Ace Comics No. 2 on)
(Becomes Air Ace V2#1 on; also see Shadow Comics)
Oct, 1940(No. month given) - No. 12, Oct, 1943
Street & Smith Publications

	GD25	FN65	NM94
1-23 pgs.-comics; Rocket Rooney begins	57.00	170.00	340.00
2-Barnes as The Phantom Flyer app.; Tuska-a	33.00	100.00	200.00
3-5	25.00	75.00	150.00
6-12	21.00	62.00	125.00

BILL BATTLE, THE ONE MAN ARMY (Also see Master Comics No. 133)
Oct, 1952 - No. 4, Apr, 1953 (All photo-c)
Fawcett Publications

	GD25	FN65	NM94
1	5.00	15.00	30.00
2	3.20	8.00	16.00
3,4	2.60	6.50	13.00

BILL BLACK'S FUN COMICS (Americomics)(Value: cover or less)

BILL BOYD WESTERN (Movie star; see Hopalong Cassidy & Western Hero)
Feb, 1950 - No. 23, June, 1952 (1-3,7,11,14-on: 36 pgs.)
Fawcett Publications

	GD25	FN65	NM94
1-Bill Boyd & his horse Midnite begin; photo front/back-c	32.00	95.00	225.00
2-Painted-c	17.00	50.00	115.00
3-Photo-c begin, end #23; last photo back-c	14.00	43.00	100.00
4-6(52pgs.)	11.50	34.00	80.00
7,11(36pgs.)	10.00	30.00	65.00
8-10,12,13(52pgs.)	10.00	30.00	70.00
14-22	10.00	30.00	60.00
23-Last issue	10.00	30.00	70.00

BILL BUMLIN (See Treasury of Comics No. 3)

BILL ELLIOTT (See Wild Bill Elliott)

BILLI 99 (Dark Horse)(Value: cover or less)

BILL STERN'S SPORTS BOOK
Spring-Summer, 1951 - V2#2, Winter, 1952
Ziff-Davis Publ. Co.(Approved Comics)

	GD25	FN65	NM94
V1#10(1951)	11.00	32.00	75.00
2(Sum'52-reg. size)	10.00	30.00	60.00
V2#2(1952,96 pgs.)-Krigstein, Kinstler-a	11.00	32.00	75.00

BILLY AND BUGGY BEAR
1958; 1964
I.W. Enterprises/Super

	GD25	FN65	NM94
I.W. Reprint #1(early Timely funny animal-r), #7(1958)	.60	1.50	3.00
Super Reprint #10(1964)	.60	1.50	3.00

BILLY BUCKSKIN WESTERN (2-Gun Western No. 4)
Nov, 1955 - No. 3, March, 1956
Atlas Comics (IMC No. 1/MgPC No. 2,3)

	GD25	FN65	NM94
1-Mort Drucker-a; Maneely-c/a	10.00	30.00	60.00
2-Mort Drucker-a	6.70	20.00	40.00
3-Williamson, Drucker-a	7.00	21.00	42.00

BILLY BUNNY (Black Cobra No. 6 on)
Feb-Mar, 1954 - No. 5, Oct-Nov, 1954
Excellent Publications

	GD25	FN65	NM94
1	4.20	12.50	25.00
2	3.00	7.50	15.00
3-5	2.00	5.00	10.00

BILLY BUNNY'S CHRISTMAS FROLICS
1952 (100 pages, 25 cent giant)
Farrell Publications

	GD25	FN65	NM94
1	10.00	30.00	60.00

BILLY MAKE BELIEVE (See Single Series No. 14)

BILLY NGUYEN, PRIVATE EYE (Caliber Press)(Value: cover or less)

BILLY THE KID (Formerly The Masked Raider; also see Doc Savage Comics & Return of the Outlaw)
No. 9, Nov, 1957 - No. 121, Dec, 1976; No. 122, Sept, 1977 - No. 123, Oct, 1977; No. 124, Feb, 1978 - No. 153, Mar, 1983
Charlton Publ. Co.

Big 3 #2, © FOX

Big Town #2, © DC

Billy Bunny's Christmas Frolics #1, © AJAX

Billy The Kid #21 (3/60), © CC

Bingo, The Monkey Doodle Boy #1 ('51), © STJ

Black Cat Comics #1, © HARV

	GD25	FN65	NM94
9	5.85	17.50	35.00
10,12,14,17-19	4.00	10.50	21.00
11-(68 pgs., origin, 1st app. The Ghost Train)	4.35	13.00	26.00
13-Williamson/Torres-a	5.00	15.00	30.00
15-Origin; 2pgs. Williamson-a	5.00	15.00	30.00
16-Two pgs. Williamson	5.00	15.00	30.00
20-26-Severin-a(3-4 each)	5.00	15.00	30.00
27-30	3.20	8.00	16.00
31-40	2.00	5.00	10.00
41-60	1.40	3.50	7.00
61-80: 66-Bounty Hunter series begins. Not in #79,82,84-863	.70	1.75	3.50
81-99,101-123: 87-Last Bounty Hunter. 111-Origin The Ghost Train. 117-Gunsmith & Co., The Cheyenne Kid app.	.50	1.25	2.50
100	.40	1.00	2.00
124(2/78)-153	.30	.75	1.50
Modern Comics 109 (1977 reprint)		.60	1.20

NOTE: ***Severin** a(r)-121-129, 134; c-23, 25. **Sutton** a-111.*

BILLY THE KID ADVENTURE MAGAZINE
Oct, 1950 - No. 30, 1955
Toby Press

	GD25	FN65	NM94
1-Williamson/Frazetta-a (2 pgs); photo-c	18.00	54.00	125.00
2-Photo-c	5.85	17.50	35.00
3-Williamson/Frazetta "The Claws of Death," 4 pgs. plus Williamson art	19.30	58.00	135.00
4,5,7,8,10: 4,7-Photo-c	4.20	12.50	25.00
6-Frazetta story assist on "Nightmare;" photo-c	9.15	27.50	55.00
9-Kurtzman Pot-Shot Pete; photo-c	8.35	25.00	50.00
11,12,15-20: 11-Photo-c	4.00	10.50	21.00
13-Kurtzman-r/John Wayne #12 (Genius)	4.20	12.50	25.00
14-Williamson/Frazetta; r-of #1 (2 pgs.)	6.35	19.00	38.00
21,23-30	3.20	8.00	16.00
22-Williamson/Frazetta-r(1pg.)/#1; photo-c	4.20	12.50	25.00

BILLY THE KID AND OSCAR (Also see Fawcett's Funny Animals)
Winter, 1945 - No. 3, Summer, 1946 (Funny animal)
Fawcett Publications

	GD25	FN65	NM94
1	8.35	25.00	50.00
2,3	5.00	15.00	30.00

BILLY WEST (Bill West No. 9,10)
1949 - No. 9, Feb, 1951; No. 10, Feb, 1952
Standard Comics (Visual Editions)

	GD25	FN65	NM94
1	5.85	17.50	35.00
2	3.60	9.00	18.00
3-10: 7,8-Schomburg-c	2.80	7.00	14.00

NOTE: ***Celardo** a-1-6, 9; c-1-3. **Moreira** a-3. **Roussos** a-2.*

BING CROSBY (See Feature Films)

BINGO (...Comics) (H. C. Blackerby)
1945 (Reprints National material)
Howard Publ.

	GD25	FN65	NM94
1-L. B. Cole opium-c	13.00	40.00	90.00

BINGO, THE MONKEY DOODLE BOY
Aug, 1951; Oct, 1953
St. John Publishing Co.

	GD25	FN65	NM94
1(8/51)-By Eric Peters	4.00	12.00	24.00
1(10/53)	3.60	9.00	18.00

BINKY (Formerly Leave It to...)
No. 72, 4-5/70 - No. 81, 10-11/71; No. 82, Summer/77
National Periodical Publ./DC Comics

	GD25	FN65	NM94
72-81	.80	2.00	4.00
82('77)-(One Shot)	.40	1.00	2.00

BINKY'S BUDDIES
Jan-Feb, 1969 - No. 12, Nov-Dec, 1970
National Periodical Publications

	GD25	FN65	NM94
1	1.40	3.50	7.00
2-12	.80	2.00	4.00

BIONIC WOMAN, THE (TV)
October, 1977 - No. 5, June, 1978
Charlton Publications

	GD25	FN65	NM94
1-5		.60	1.25

BIZARRE ADVENTURES (Formerly Marvel Preview)
No. 25, 3/81 - No. 34, 2/83 (#25-33: Magazine-$1.50)
Marvel Comics Group

	GD25	FN65	NM94
25-Lethal Ladies. 26-King Kull		.60	1.25
27-Phoenix, Iceman & Nightcrawler app. 28-The Unlikely Heroes; Elektra by Miller; Neal Adams-a	.30	.75	1.50
29-Horror. 30-Tomorrow. 31-After The Violence Stops; new Hangman story; Miller-a. 32-Gods. 33-Horror; photo-c		.60	1.25
34 ($2.00, Baxter paper, comic size)-Son of Santa; Christmas spec.; Howard the Duck by Paul Smith	.30	.75	1.50

NOTE: ***Alcala** a-27i. **Austin** a-25i, 28i. **J. Buscema** a-27p, 29, 30p; c-26. **Byrne** a-31 (2 pg.). **Golden** a-25p, 28p. **Perez** a-27p. **Rogers** a-25p. **Simonson** a-29; c-29. **Paul Smith** a-34.*

BLACK AND WHITE (See Large Feature Comic, Series I)

BLACK & WHITE MAGIC (Innovation)(Value: cover or less)

BLACKBEARD'S GHOST (See Movie Comics)

BLACK BEAUTY (See 4-Color No. 440)

BLACK CANARY
Nov, 1991 - No. 4, Feb, 1992 ($1.75, color, mini-series)
DC Comics

	GD25	FN65	NM94
1-4	.35	.90	1.75

BLACK CANARY
Jan, 1993 - Present ($1.75, color)
DC Comics

	GD25	FN65	NM94
1-5	.35	.90	1.75

BLACK CAT COMICS (...Western #16-19; ...Mystery #30 on)
(See All-New #7,9, The Original Black Cat, Pocket & Speed Comics)
June-July, 1946 - No. 29, June, 1951
Harvey Publications (Home Comics)

	GD25	FN65	NM94
1-Kubert-a; Joe Simon c-1-3	40.00	120.00	240.00
2-Kubert-a	21.00	62.00	125.00
3,4: 4-The Red Demons begin (The Demon #4 & 5)	15.00	45.00	90.00
5,6-The Scarlet Arrow app. in ea. by Powell; S&K-a in both. 6-Origin Red Demon	20.00	60.00	120.00
7-Vagabond Prince by S&K plus 1 more story	20.00	60.00	120.00
8-S&K-a; Kerry Drake begins, ends #13	17.50	52.00	105.00
9-Origin Stuntman (r/Stuntman #1)	21.00	62.00	125.00
10-20: 14,15,17-Mary Worth app. plus Invisible Scarlet O'Neil-#15,20,24	12.50	37.50	75.00
21-26	10.00	30.00	65.00
27-Used in **SOTI**, pg. 193; X-Mas-c; 2 pg. John Wayne story	12.50	37.50	75.00
28-Intro. Kit, Black Cat's new sidekick	12.50	37.50	75.00
29-Black Cat bondage-c; Black Cat stories	10.00	30.00	70.00

BLACK CAT MYSTERY (Formerly Black Cat; ...Western Mystery #54; ...Western #55,56; ...Mystery #57; ...Mystic #58-62; Black Cat #63-65)
No. 30, Aug, 1951 - No. 65, April, 1963
Harvey Publications

	GD25	FN65	NM94
30-Black Cat on cover only	10.00	30.00	65.00
31,32,34,37,38,40	7.00	21.00	42.00

GD25 FN65 NM94

33-Used in **POP**, pg. 89; electrocution-c 7.50 22.50 45.00
35-Atomic disaster cover/story 9.15 27.50 55.00
36,39-Used in **SOTI**: #36-Pgs. 270,271; #39-Pgs. 386-388
10.00 30.00 70.00
41-43 6.70 20.00 40.00
44-Eyes, ears, tongue cut out; Nostrand-a 7.50 22.50 45.00
45-Classic "Colorama" by Powell; Nostrand-a 11.50 34.00 80.00
46-49,51-Nostrand-a in all 7.50 22.50 45.00
50-Check-a; Warren Kremer?-c showing a man's face burning away
11.00 32.00 75.00
52,53 (r/#34 & 35) 5.00 15.00 30.00
54-Two Black Cat stories (2/55, last pre-code) 8.35 25.00 50.00
55,56-Black Cat app. 5.35 16.00 32.00
57(7/56)-Kirby-c 4.20 12.50 25.00
58-60-Kirby-a(4). 58,59-Kiurby-c. 60,61-Simon-c 7.50 22.50 45.00
61-Nostrand-a; "Colorama" r/#45 5.85 17.50 35.00
62(3/58)-E.C. story swipe 4.35 13.00 26.00
63-Giant(10/62); Reprints; Black Cat app.; origin Black Kitten
6.70 20.00 40.00
64-Giant(1/63); Reprints; Black Cat app. 6.70 20.00 40.00
65-Giant(4/63); Reprints; Black Cat app. 6.70 20.00 40.00

NOTE: ***Kremer** a-37, 39, 43; c-36, 37, 47. **Meskin** a-51. **Palais** a-30, 31(2), 32(2), 33-35, 37-40. **Powell** a-32-35, 36(2), 40, 41, 43-53, 57. **Simon** c-63-65. **Sparling** a-44. Bondage-c No. 32, 34, 43.*

BLACK COBRA (Bride's Diary No. 4 on)
No. 1, 10-11/54; No. 6(No. 2), 12-1/54-55; No. 3, 2-3/55
Ajax/Farrell Publications(Excellent Publ.)

1-1st app. Black Cobra & The Cobra Kid (costumed heroes)
14.00 43.00 100.00
6(#2)-Formerly Billy Bunny 10.00 30.00 60.00
3-(Pre-code)-Torpedoman app. 10.00 30.00 60.00

BLACK CONDOR (Also see Crack Comics)
June, 1992 - Present ($1.25, color)
DC Comics

1-12: 1-3-Heath-c. 9,10-The Ray guest stars .60 1.25

BLACK CROSS SPECIAL (Dark Horse)(Value: cover or less)(See Dark Horse Presents)

BLACK DIAMOND (Americomics)(Value: cover or less)

BLACK DIAMOND WESTERN (Formerly Desperado No. 1-8)
No. 9, Mar, 1949 - No. 60, Feb, 1956 (No. 9-28: 52 pgs.)
Lev Gleason Publications

9-Black Diamond & his horse Reliapon begin; origin Black Diamond
11.00 32.00 75.00
10 6.35 19.00 38.00
11-15 4.70 14.00 28.00
16-28(11/49-11/51)Wolverton's Bing Bang Buster 6.70 20.00 40.00
29-40: 31-One pg. Frazetta anti drug ad 3.60 9.00 18.00
41-50,53-59 3.00 7.50 15.00
51-3-D effect-c/story 8.35 25.00 50.00
52-3-D effect story 7.00 21.00 42.00
60-Last issue 4.00 10.00 20.00

NOTE: ***Biro** c-9-35?. **Fass** a-58, c-54-56, 58. **Guardineer** a-9, 15, 18. **Kida** a-9. **Maurer** a-10. **Ed Moore** a-16. **Morisi** a-55. **Tuska** a-10, 48.*

BLACK DRAGON, THE
May, 1985 - No. 6, Oct, 1985 (Baxter paper; mini-series; adults only)
Epic Comics (Marvel)

1-Bolton-c/a in all .40 1.00 2.00
2-6 .50 1.00

BLACK FURY (Becomes Wild West No. 58) (See Blue Bird)
May, 1955 - No. 57, Mar-Apr, 1966 (Horse stories)
Charlton Comics Group

1 4.00 12.00 24.00
2 2.40 6.00 12.00
3-10 1.60 4.00 8.00

GD25 FN65 NM94

11-15,19,20 1.20 3.00 6.00
16-18-Ditko-a 4.20 12.50 25.00
21-30 .90 2.25 4.50
31-57 .70 1.75 3.50

BLACK GOLD
1945? (8 pgs. in color)
Esso Service Station (Giveaway)

nn-Reprints from True Comics 4.00 11.00 22.00

BLACK GOLIATH
Feb, 1976 - No. 5, Nov, 1976
Marvel Comics Group

1: 1-3-Tuska-a(p) 1.00 2.50 5.00
2-5 .60 1.50 3.00

BLACKHAWK (Formerly Uncle Sam #1-8; see Military & Modern Comics)
No. 9, Winter, 1944 - No. 243, 10-11/68; No. 244, 1-2/76 - No. 250, 1-2/77; No. 251, 10/82 - No. 273, 11/84
Comic Magazines(Quality)No. 9-107(12/56); National Periodical Publ. No. 108(1/57)-250; DC Comics No. 251 on

9 (1944) 200.00 600.00 1200.00
10 (1946) 75.00 225.00 450.00
11-15: 14-Ward-a; 13,14-Fear app. 54.00 160.00 325.00
16-20: 20-Ward Blackhawk 46.00 140.00 275.00
21-30 33.00 100.00 200.00
31-40: 31-Chop Chop by Jack Cole 24.00 122.00 145.00
41-49,51-60 19.00 55.00 115.00
50-1st Killer Shark; origin in text 22.00 65.00 130.00
61-Used in **POP**, pg. 91 17.00 50.00 100.00
62-Used in **POP**, pg. 92 & color illo 17.00 50.00 100.00
63-70,72-80: 65-H-Bomb explosion panel. 66-B&W and color illos **POP**. 70-Return of Killer Shark. 75-Intro. Blackie the Hawk
15.00 45.00 90.00
71-Origin retold; flying saucer-c; A-Bomb panels 18.00 55.00 110.00
81-86: Last precode (3/55) 14.00 42.50 85.00
87-92,94-99,101-107 12.00 35.00 70.00
93-Origin in text 12.50 37.50 75.00
100 15.00 45.00 90.00
108-1st DC issue (1/57); re-intro. Blackie, the Hawk, their mascot; not in #115 39.00 120.00 275.00
109-117 11.50 34.00 80.00
118-Frazetta-r/Jimmy Wakely #4 (3 pgs.) 12.00 36.00 85.00
119-130 10.00 30.00 60.00
131-140: 133-Intro. Lady Blackhawk 7.50 22.50 45.00
141-163,165,166: 143-Kurtzman-r/Jimmy Wakely #4. 166-Last 10 cent issue
5.35 16.00 32.00
164-Origin retold 4.70 14.00 28.00
167-180 2.40 6.00 12.00
181-190 1.60 4.00 8.00
191-197,199-202,204-210: Combat Diary series begins. 197-New look for Blackhawks 1.20 3.00 6.00
198-Origin retold 1.60 4.00 8.00
203-Origin Chop Chop (12/64) 1.40 3.50 7.00
211-243(1968): 228-Batman, Green Lantern, Superman, The Flash cameos. 230-Blackhawks become superheroes. 242-Return to old costumes
1.00 2.50 5.00
244 ('76) -250: 250-Chuck dies .40 1.00 2.00
251-273: 251-Origin retold; Black Knights return. 252-Intro Domino. 253-Part origin Hendrickson. 258-Blackhawk's Island destroyed. 259-Part origin Chop-Chop. 265-273 (75 cent cover price) .50 1.00

NOTE: ***Chaykin** a-260; c-257-260, 262. **Crandall** a-10, 11, 13, 16?, 18-20, 22-26, 30-33, 35p, 36(2), 37, 38?, 39-44, 46-50, 52-58, 60, 63, 64, 66, 67; c-14-20, 22-63(most except #28-33, 36, 37, 39). **Evans** a-244, 245,246i, 248-250i. **G. Kane** c-263, 264. **Kubert** c-244, 245. **Newton** a-266p. **Severin** a-257.**Spiegle** a-261-267, 269-273; c-265-272. **Toth** a-260p. **Ward** a-16-27(Chop Chop, 8pgs. ea.); pencilled stories-No. 17-63(approx.). **Wildey** a-268. Chop Chop solo stories in #10-95?*

BLACKHAWK

Black Cobra #6, © AJAX

Black Diamond Western #50, © LEV

Blackhawk #114, © DC

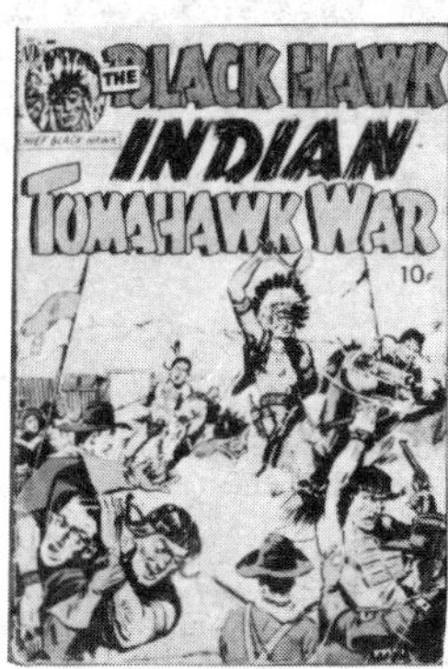

Blackhawk Indian Tomahawk War nn, © AVON

Black Hood Comics #9, © AP

Black Magic #27, © Crestwood

	GD25	FN65	NM94

Mar, 1988 - No. 3, May, 1988 ($2.95, mini-series)
DC Comics

	GD25	FN65	NM94
1-3: Chaykin painted-c/a	.60	1.50	3.00

BLACKHAWK
March, 1989 - No. 16, Aug, 1990 ($1.50, color, mature readers)
DC Comics

	GD25	FN65	NM94
1-6,8-16: 16-Crandall-c swipe	.30	.75	1.50
7-($2.50, 52 pgs.)-Story-r/Military #1	.50	1.25	2.50
Annual 1 (1989, $2.95, 68 pgs.)-Recaps origin of Blackhawk, Lady Blackhawk, and others	.60	1.50	3.00
Special 1 (1992, $3.50, 68 pgs.)-Mature readers	.70	1.75	3.50

BLACKHAWK INDIAN TOMAHAWK WAR, THE
1951
Avon Periodicals

	GD25	FN65	NM94
nn-Kinstler-c; Kit West story	10.00	30.00	65.00

BLACK HOLE (See Walt Disney Showcase #54)
March, 1980 - No. 4, September, 1980 (Disney movie)
Whitman Publishing Co.

	GD25	FN65	NM94
11295(#1)-Photo-c; Spiegle-a		.50	1.00
2-4-Spiegle-a. 3-McWilliams-a; photo-c		.50	1.00

BLACK HOOD, THE (See Blue Ribbon, Flyman & Mighty Comics)
June, 1983 - No. 3, Oct, 1983 (Printed on Mandell paper)
Red Circle Comics (Archie)

	GD25	FN65	NM94
1-Morrow, McWilliams, Wildey-a; Toth-c	.30	.75	1.50
2,3: MLJ's The Fox by Toth, c/a. 3-Morrow-a		.50	1.00

(Also see Archie's Super-Hero Special Digest #2)

BLACK HOOD
Dec, 1991 - No. 12, Dec, 1992 ($1.00, color)
DC/Impact Comics

	GD25	FN65	NM94
1-12: 11-Intro The Fox		.50	1.00
Annual 1 (1992, $2.50, 68 pgs.)-W/Trading card	.50	1.25	2.50

BLACK HOOD COMICS (Formerly Hangman #2-8; Laugh Comics #20 on; also see Black Swan, Jackpot, Roly Poly & Top-Notch #9)
No. 9, Winter, 1943-44 - No. 19, Summer, 1946 (on radio in 1943)
MLJ Magazines

	GD25	FN65	NM94
9-The Hangman & The Boy Buddies cont'd	54.00	160.00	325.00
10-The Hangman & Dusty, the Boy Detective app.	25.00	75.00	150.00
11-Dusty app.; no Hangman	19.00	58.00	115.00
12-18: 14-Kinstler blood-c. 17-Hal Foster swipe from Prince Valiant	19.00	58.00	115.00
19-I.D. exposed	25.00	75.00	150.00

NOTE: *Hangman by Fuje in 9, 10.* ***Kinstler*** *a-15, c-14-16.*

BLACK JACK (Rocky Lane's..., formerly Jim Bowie)
No. 20, Nov, 1957 - No. 30, Nov, 1959
Charlton Comics

	GD25	FN65	NM94
20	4.70	14.00	28.00
21,27,29,30	2.80	7.00	14.00
22-(68 pages)	4.00	11.00	22.00
23-Williamson/Torres-a	4.35	13.00	26.00
24-26,28-Ditko-a	5.00	15.00	30.00

BLACK KNIGHT, THE
May, 1953; 1963
Toby Press

	GD25	FN65	NM94
1-Bondage-c	11.50	34.00	80.00
Super Reprint No. 11 (1963)-Reprints 1953 issue	2.40	6.00	12.00

BLACK KNIGHT, THE (Also see The Avengers #48, Marvel Super Heroes & Tales To Astonish #52)
May, 1955 - No. 5, April, 1956
Atlas Comics (MgPC)

	GD25	FN65	NM94
1-Origin Crusader; Maneely-c/a	54.00	160.00	375.00
2-Maneely-c/a(4)	40.00	120.00	275.00
3-5: 4-Maneely-c/a. 5-Maneely-c, Shores-a	32.00	96.00	225.00

BLACK KNIGHT
June, 1990 - No. 4, Sept, 1990 ($1.50, mini-series)
Marvel Comics

	GD25	FN65	NM94
1-4: 1-Original Black Knight returns	.30	.75	1.50

BLACK LIGHTNING (See Brave & The Bold, Cancelled Comic Cavalcade, DC Comics Presents #16, Detective #490 and World's Finest)
April, 1977 - No. 11, Sept-Oct, 1978
National Periodical Publications/DC Comics

	GD25	FN65	NM94
1	.60	1.50	3.00
2-11: 4-Intro Cyclotronic Man. 11-The Ray app.	.30	.75	1.50

NOTE: ***Buckler*** *c-1-3p, 6-11p. #11 is 44 pgs.*

BLACK MAGIC (...Magazine) (Becomes Cool Cat V8#6 on)
10-11/50 - V4#1, 6-7/53: V4#2, 9-10/53 - V5#3, 11-12/54; V6#1, 9-10/57 - V7#2, 11-12/58: V7#3, 7-8/60 - V8#5, 11-12/61
(V1#1-5, 52pgs.; V1#6-V3#3, 44pgs.)
Crestwood Publ. V1#1-4,V6#1-V7#5/Headline V1#5-V5#3,V7#6-V8#5

	GD25	FN65	NM94
V1#1-S&K-a, 10 pgs.; Meskin-a(2)	43.00	130.00	300.00
2-S&K-a, 17 pgs.; Meskin-a	20.00	60.00	140.00
3-6(8-9/51)-S&K, Roussos, Meskin-a	16.00	48.00	110.00
V2#1(10-11/51),4,5,7(#13),9(#15),12(#18)-S&K-a	11.50	34.00	80.00
2,3,6,8,10,11(#17)	8.35	25.00	50.00
V3#1(#19, 12/52) - 6(#24, 5/53)-S&K-a	10.00	30.00	65.00
V4#1(#25, 6-7/53), 2(#26, 9-10/53)-S&K-a(3-4)	10.00	30.00	70.00
3(#27, 11-12/53)-S&K-a; Ditko-a(1st in comics); also see Captain 3-D & Fantastic Fears #5	24.00	72.00	165.00
4(#28)-Eyes ripped out/story-S&K, Ditko-a	14.00	43.00	100.00
5(#29, 3-4/54)-S&K, Ditko-a	11.50	34.00	80.00
6(#30, 5-6/54)-S&K, Powell?-a	7.50	22.50	45.00
V5#1(#31, 7-8/54 - 3(#33, 11-12/54)-S&K-a	6.70	20.00	40.00
V6#1(#34, 9-10/57), 2(#35, 11-12/57)	4.00	11.00	22.00
3(1-2/58) - 6(7-8/58)	4.00	11.00	22.00
V7#1(9-10/58) - 3(7-8/60)	3.60	9.00	18.00
4(9-10/60), 5(11-12/60)-Torres-a	4.20	12.50	25.00
6(1-2/61)-Powell-a(2)	3.60	9.00	18.00
V8#1(3-4/61)-Powell-c/a	3.60	9.00	18.00
2(5-6/61)-E.C. story swipe/W.F. #22; Ditko, Powell-a	4.20	12.50	25.00
3(7-8/61)-E.C. story swipe/W.F. #22; Powell-a(2)	4.00	11.00	22.00
4(9-10/61)-Powell-a(5)	3.60	9.00	18.00
5-E.C. story swipe/W.S.F. #28; Powell-a(3)	4.00	11.00	22.00

NOTE: ***Bernard Baily*** *a-V4#6?, V5#3(2).* ***Grandenetti*** *a-V2#3, 11.* ***Kirby*** *c-V1#1-6, V2#1-12, V3#1-6, V4#1, 2, 4-6, V5#1-3.* ***McWilliams*** *a-V3#2i.* ***Meskin*** *a-V1#1(2), 2, 3, 4(2), 5(2), 6, V2/1, 2, 3(2), 4(3), 5, 6(2), 7-9, 11, 12i, V3#1(2), 5, 6, V5#1(2), 2.* ***Orlando*** *a-V6#1, 4, V7#2; c-V6/1-6.* ***Powell*** *a-V5#1?.* ***Roussos*** *a-V1#3-5, 6(2), V2#3(2), 4, 5(2), 6, 8, 9, 10(2), 11, 12p, V3#1(2), 2i, 5, V5#2.* ***Simon*** *a-V2#12, V3#2, V7#5? c-V4#3?, V7#3?, 4, 5?, 6?, V8#1-5.* ***Simon & Kirby*** *a-V1#1, 2(2), 3-6, V2#1, 4, 5, 7, 9, 12, V3#1-6, V4#1(3), 2(4), 3(2), 4(2), 5, 6, V5#1-3; c-V2#1.* ***Leonard Starr*** *a-V1#1.* ***Tuska*** *a-V6#3, 4.* ***Woodbridge*** *a-V7#4.*

BLACK MAGIC
Oct-Nov, 1973 - No. 9, Apr-May, 1975
National Periodical Publications

	GD25	FN65	NM94
1-S&K reprints	.40	1.00	2.00
2-9-S&K reprints	.30	.75	1.50

BLACK MAGIC (Eclipse)(Value: cover or less)

BLACKMAIL TERROR (See Harvey Comics Library)

BLACK ORCHID (See Adventure Comics #428 & Phantom Stranger)
Holiday, 1988-'89 - No. 3, 1989 ($3.50, mini-series, prestige format)
DC Comics

GD25 FN65 NM94

Book 1,3: Gaiman (Sandman) scripts & McKean-a in all
1.00 2.50 5.00
Book 2-Arkham Asylum story; Batman app. 1.40 3.50 7.00

BLACKOUTS (See Broadway Hollywood...)

BLACK PANTHER, THE (Also see Avengers #52, Fantastic Four #52, Jungle Action & Marvel Premiere #51-53)
Jan, 1977 - No. 15, May, 1979
Marvel Comics Group

1 1.60 4.00 8.00
2 1.00 2.50 5.00
3-10 .70 1.75 3.50
11-15: 14,15-Avengers x-over .60 1.50 3.00
NOTE: ***J. Buscema** c-15p. **Kirby** c/a-1-14. **Layton** c-13i.*

BLACK PANTHER
July, 1988 - No. 4, Oct, 1988 ($1.25, color)
Marvel Comics Group

1-4 .30 .75 1.50

BLACK PANTHER: PANTHER'S PREY
1991 - No. 4, 1991 ($4.95, squarebound, mini-series, 52 pgs.)
Marvel Comics

1-4 1.00 2.50 5.00

BLACK PHANTOM (See Tim Holt #25, 38)
Nov, 1954 (One shot) (Female outlaw)
Magazine Enterprises

1 (A-1 #122)-The Ghost Rider story plus 3 Black Phantom stories;
Headlight-c/a 22.00 65.00 150.00

BLACK PHANTOM
1989 - No. 3, 1990 ($2.50, B&W; #2 color)(Reprints & new-a)
AC Comics

1,2: 1-Ayers-r, Bolle-r/B.P. #1. 2-Redmask-r .50 1.25 2.50
3 ($2.75, B&W)-B.P., Redmask-r & new-a .55 1.40 2.75

BLACK PHANTOM, RETURN OF THE (See Wisco)

BLACK RIDER (Formerly Western Winners; Western Tales of Black Rider #28-31; Gunsmoke Western #32 on)(Also see All Western Winners, Best Western, Kid Colt, Outlaw Kid, Rex Hart, Two-Gun Kid, Two-Gun Western, Western Gunfighters, Western Winners, & Wild Western)
No. 8, 3/50 - No. 18, 1/52; No. 19, 11/53 - No. 27, 3/55
Marvel/Atlas Comics(CDS No. 8-17/CPS No. 19 on)

8 (#1)-Black Rider & his horse Satan begin; 36 pgs; Stan Lee photo-c (as Black Rider) 25.00 75.00 175.00
9-52 pgs. begin, end #14 12.00 36.00 85.00
10-Origin Black Rider 15.00 45.00 105.00
11-14(Last 52pgs.) 10.00 30.00 60.00
15-19: 19-Two-Gun Kid app. 9.50 29.50 55.00
20-Classic-c; Two-Gun Kid app. 10.00 30.00 60.00
21-26: 21-23-Two-Gun Kid app. 24,25-Arrowhead app. 26-Kid Colt app.
7.50 22.50 50.00
27-Last issue; last precode. Kid Colt app. The Spider (a villain) burns to death
8.35 25.00 50.00
NOTE: ***Ayers** c-22. **Jack Keller** a-15, 26, 27. **Maneely** a-14; c-16, 17, 25, 27. **Syd Shores** a-19, 21, 22, 23(3), 24(3), 25-27; c-19, 21, 23. **Sinnott** a-24, 25. **Tuska** a-12, 19-21.*

BLACK RIDER RIDES AGAIN!, THE
September, 1957
Atlas Comics (CPS)

1-Kirby-a(3); Powell-a; Severin-c 13.00 40.00 90.00

BLACKSTONE (See Super Magician Comics & Wisco Giveaways)

BLACKSTONE, MASTER MAGICIAN COMICS
Mar-Apr, 1946 - No. 3, July-Aug, 1946
Vital Publications/Street & Smith Publ.

1 14.00 43.00 100.00
2,3 11.00 32.00 75.00

BLACKSTONE, THE MAGICIAN (...Detective on cover only #3 & 4)
No. 2, May, 1948 - No. 4, Sept, 1948 (No #1)
Marvel Comics (CnPC)

2-The Blonde Phantom begins 34.00 102.00 240.00
3,4-Bondage-c. 3-Blonde Phantom by Sekowsky 22.00 65.00 150.00

BLACKSTONE, THE MAGICIAN DETECTIVE FIGHTS CRIME
Fall, 1947
E. C. Comics

1-1st app. Happy Houlihans 32.00 95.00 225.00

BLACK SWAN COMICS
1945
MLJ Magazines (Pershing Square Publ. Co.)

1-The Black Hood reprints from Black Hood No. 14; Bill Woggon-a; Suzie app. 11.50 34.00 80.00

BLACK TARANTULA (See Feature Presentations No. 5)

BLACK TERROR (See America's Best Comics & Exciting Comics)
Wint, 1942-43 - No. 27, June, 1949
Better Publications/Standard

1-Black Terror, Crime Crusader begin 100.00 300.00 600.00
2 46.00 138.00 225.00
3 35.00 105.00 210.00
4,5 28.00 82.00 165.00
6-10: 7-The Ghost app. 21.00 62.00 125.00
11-20: 20-The Scarab app. 17.50 52.00 105.00
21-Miss Masque app. 18.00 55.00 110.00
22-Part Frazetta-a on one Black Terror story 20.00 60.00 120.00
23,25-27 17.00 50.00 100.00
24-Frazetta-a (1/4 pg.) 17.50 52.00 105.00
NOTE: ***Schomburg (Xela)** c-2-27; bondage c-2, 17, 24. **Meskin** a-27. **Moreira** a-27.**Robinson/Meskin** a-23, 24(3), 25, 26. **Roussos/Mayo** a-24. **Tuska** a-26, 27.*

BLACK TERROR, THE (Eclipse) (Value: cover or less) (Also see Total Eclipse)

BLACKTHORNE 3-D SERIES (Blackthorne)(Value: cover or less)

BLACK ZEPPELIN (See Gene Day's...)

BLADE RUNNER
Oct, 1982 - No. 2, Nov, 1982 (Movie adaptation)
Marvel Comics Group

1,2-r/Marvel Super Special #22; 1-Williamson-c/a. 2-Williamson-a
.50 1.00

BLAKE HARPER (See City Surgeon...)

BLAST (Satire Magazine)
Feb, 1971 - No. 2, May, 1971
G & D Publications

1-Wrightson & Kaluta-a 3.00 7.50 15.00
2-Kaluta-a 2.40 6.00 12.00

BLASTERS SPECIAL
1989 ($2.00, one-shot)
DC Comics

1-Invasion spin-off .40 1.00 2.00

BLAST-OFF (Three Rocketeers)
October, 1965
Harvey Publications (Fun Day Funnies)

1-Kirby/Williamson-a(2); Williamson/Crandall-a; Williamson/Torres/Krenkel-a; Kirby/Simon-c 4.00 11.00 22.00

BLAZE CARSON (Becomes Rex Hart No. 6 on)(See Kid Colt, Tex Taylor, Wild Western, Wisco)
Sept, 1948 - No. 5, June, 1949
Marvel Comics (USA)

1: 1,2-Shores-c 14.00 43.00 100.00

Black Panther #1, © MEG

Black Phantom #1, © ME

Black Rider #1 (1957), © MEG

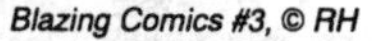
Blazing Comics #3, © RH

Blazing West #2, © ACG

Blonde Phantom #12, © MEG

	GD25	FN65	NM94
2,4,5: 4-Two-Gun Kid app. 5-Tex Taylor app.	10.00	30.00	65.00
3-Used by N.Y. State Legis. Comm. (injury to eye splash); Tex Morgan app.	11.00	32.00	75.00

BLAZE THE WONDER COLLIE (Formerly Molly Manton's Romances #1?)
No. 2, Oct, 1949 - No. 3, Feb, 1950 (Both have photo covers)
Marvel Comics(SePI)

	GD25	FN65	NM94
2(#1), 3-(Scarce)	13.00	40.00	90.00

BLAZING BATTLE TALES
July, 1975
Seaboard Periodicals (Atlas)

	GD25	FN65	NM94
1-Intro. Sgt. Hawk & the Sky Demon; Severin, McWilliams, Sparling-a; Thorne-c		.50	1.00

BLAZING COMBAT (Magazine)
Oct, 1965 - No. 4, July, 1966 (Black & White, 35 cents)
Warren Publishing Co.

	GD25	FN65	NM94
1-Frazetta painted-c on all	9.30	28.00	56.00
2	3.00	7.50	15.00
3,4: 4-Frazetta pg. ad	2.00	5.00	10.00
...Anthology (reprints from No. 1-4)	.80	2.00	4.00

NOTE: *Above has art by **Colan, Crandall, Evans, Morrow, Orlando, Severin, Torres, Toth, Williamson,** and **Wood.***

BLAZING COMICS
6/44 - #3, 9/44; #4, 2/45; #5, 3/45; #5(V2#2), 3/55 - #6(V2#3), 1955?
Enwil Associates/Rural Home

	GD25	FN65	NM94
1-The Green Turtle, Red Hawk, Black Buccaneer begin; origin Jun-Gal	31.00	90.00	185.00
2-5: 3-Briefer-a. 5-(V2#2 inside)	18.00	55.00	110.00
5(3/55, V2#2-inside)-Black Buccaneer-c, 6(V2#3-inside, 1955)-Indian/Jap-c	6.70	20.00	40.00

NOTE: *No. 5 & 6 contain remaindered comics rebound and the contents can vary. Cloak & Daggar, Will Rogers, Superman 64, Star Spangled 130, Kaanga known. Value would be half of contents.*

BLAZING SIXGUNS
December, 1952
Avon Periodicals

	GD25	FN65	NM94
1-Kinstler-c/a; Larsen/Alascia-a(2), Tuska?-a; Jesse James, Kit Carson, Wild Bill Hickok app.	10.00	30.00	60.00

BLAZING SIXGUNS
1964
I.W./Super Comics

	GD25	FN65	NM94
I.W. Reprint #1,8,9: 1-r/Wild Bill Hickok #26 & Blazing Sixguns #1 by Avon; Kinstler-c. 8-r/Blazing Western #?; Kinstler-c. 9-r/Blazing Western #1; Ditko-r	1.40	3.50	7.00
Super Reprint #10,11,15,16: 10,11-r/The Rider #2,1. 15-r/Silver Kid Western #?. 16-r/Buffalo Bill #?; Wildey-r; Severin-c. 17(1964)-r/Western True Crime #?	1.20	3.00	6.00
12-Reprints Bullseye #3; S&K-a	3.20	8.00	16.00
18-r/Straight Arrow #? by Powell; Severin-c	1.60	4.00	8.00

BLAZING SIX-GUNS (Also see Sundance Kid)
Feb, 1971 - No. 2, April, 1971 (52 pages)
Skywald Comics

	GD25	FN65	NM94
1-The Red Mask, Sundance Kid begin, Avon's Geronimo reprint by Kinstler; Wyatt Earp app.	.80	2.00	4.00
2-Wild Bill Hickok, Jesse James, Kit Carson-r	.40	1.00	2.00

BLAZING WEST (Also see The Hooded Horseman)
Fall, 1948 - No. 22, Mar-Apr, 1952
American Comics Group(B&I Publ./Michel Publ.)

	GD25	FN65	NM94
1-Origin & 1st app. Injun Jones, Tenderfoot & Buffalo Belle; Texas Tim & Ranger begins, ends #13	11.50	34.00	80.00
2,3	6.70	20.00	40.00
4-Origin & 1st app. Little Lobo; Starr-a	5.00	15.00	30.00
5-10: 5-Starr-a	4.20	12.50	25.00
11-13	3.60	9.00	18.00
14-Origin & 1st app. The Hooded Horseman	6.70	20.00	40.00
15-22: 15,16,18,19-Starr-a	4.70	14.00	28.00

BLAZING WESTERN
Jan, 1954 - No. 5, Sept, 1954
Timor Publications

	GD25	FN65	NM94
1-Ditko-a; Text story by Bruce Hamilton	10.00	30.00	60.00
2-4	4.00	11.00	22.00
5-Disbrow-a	4.70	14.00	28.00

BLESSED PIUS X
No date (32 pages; text, comics) (Paper cover)
Catechetical Guild (Giveaway)

	GD25	FN65	NM94
nn	3.20	8.00	16.00

BLIND JUSTICE (Also see Batman: Blind Justice)
1989 (Giveaway, squarebound)
DC Comics/Diamond Comic Distributors

	GD25	FN65	NM94
nn-Contains Detective #598-600 by Batman movie writer Sam Hamm, w/covers; published same time as originals?	.40	1.00	2.00

BLITZKRIEG
Jan-Feb, 1976 - No. 5, Sept-Oct, 1976
National Periodical Publications

	GD25	FN65	NM94
1-Kubert-c on all	.30	.75	1.50
2-5		.50	1.00

BLONDE PHANTOM (Formerly All-Select #1-11; Lovers #23 on)(Also see Blackstone, Marvel Mystery, Millie The Model #2, Sub-Mariner Comics #25 & Sun Girl)
No. 12, Winter, 1946-47 - No. 22, March, 1949
Marvel Comics (MPC)

	GD25	FN65	NM94
12-Miss America begins, ends #14	75.00	225.00	450.00
13-Sub-Mariner begins (not in #16)	50.00	150.00	300.00
14,15; 14-Male bondage-c; Namora app. 15-Kurtzman's "Hey Look"	42.00	125.00	250.00
16-Captain America with Bucky story by Rico(p), 6 pgs.; Kurtzman's "Hey Look" (1 pg.)	54.00	162.00	325.00
17-22: 22-Anti Wertham editorial	38.00	115.00	230.00

NOTE: ***Shores** c-12-18.*

BLONDIE (See Ace Comics, Comics Reading Libraries, Dagwood, Daisy & Her Pups, Eat Right to Work..., King & Magic Comics)
1942 - 1946
David McKay Publications

	GD25	FN65	NM94
Feature Books 12 (Rare)	47.00	140.00	325.00
Feature Books 27-29,31,34(1940)	11.00	32.00	75.00
Feature Books 36,38,40,42,43,45,47	10.00	30.00	70.00
...1944 (Hard-c, 1938, B&W, 128 pgs.)-1944 daily strip-r	10.00	30.00	70.00

BLONDIE & DAGWOOD FAMILY
Oct, 1963 - No. 4, Dec, 1965 (68 pages)
Harvey Publications (King Features Synd.)

	GD25	FN65	NM94
1	3.00	7.50	15.00
2-4	1.80	4.50	9.00

BLONDIE COMICS (...Monthly No. 16-141)
Spring, 1947 - No. 163, Nov, 1965; No. 164, Aug, 1966 - No. 175, Dec, 1967; No. 177, Feb, 1969 - No. 222, Nov, 1976
David McKay #1-15/Harvey #16-163/King #164-175/Charlton #177 on

	GD25	FN65	NM94
1	13.00	40.00	90.00
2	7.50	22.50	45.00
3-5	5.00	15.00	30.00

	GD25	FN65	NM94
6-10	4.00	12.00	24.00
11-15	3.20	8.00	16.00
16-(3/50; 1st Harvey issue)	3.50	10.50	21.00
17-20	2.80	7.00	14.00
21-30	2.00	5.00	10.00
31-50	1.60	4.00	8.00
51-80	1.40	3.50	7.00
81-124,126-130	1.20	3.00	6.00
125 (80 pgs.)	1.60	4.00	8.00
131-136,138,139	1.00	2.50	5.00
137,140-(80 pages)	1.40	3.50	7.00
141-167(#148,155,157-159,161-163 are 68 pgs.)	1.40	3.50	7.00
168-175,177-222 (no #176)	.60	1.50	3.00
Blondie, Dagwood & Daisy 1(100 pgs., 1953)	10.00	30.00	70.00
1950 Giveaway	2.80	7.00	14.00
1962,1964 Giveaway	.80	2.00	4.00
N. Y. State Dept. of Mental Hygiene Giveaway-('50,'56,'61) Regular size (Diff. issues) 16 pages; no #	1.40	3.50	7.00

BLOOD
Feb, 1988 - No. 4, Apr, 1988 ($3.25, adults)
Epic Comics (Marvel)

	GD25	FN65	NM94
1-4	.65	1.65	3.25

BLOOD AND GLORY (Punisher & Captain America)
Oct, 1992 - No. 3, Dec, 1992 ($5.95, color, mini-series)
Marvel Comics

	GD25	FN65	NM94
1-3: 1-Embossed wraparound-c	1.20	3.00	6.00

BLOOD IS THE HARVEST
1950 (32 pages) (paper cover)
Catechetical Guild

	GD25	FN65	NM94
(Scarce)-Anti-communism (13 known copies)	75.00	225.00	525.00
Black & white version (5 known copies), saddle stitched	30.00	90.00	200.00

Untrimmed version (only one known copy); estimated value-$600
NOTE: *In 1979 nine copies of the color version surfaced from the old Guild's files plus the five black & white copies.*

BLOOD IS THE HARVEST (Eclipse) (Value: cover or less)

BLOODLINES: A TALE FROM THE HEART OF AFRICA
1992 ($5.95, color, 52 pgs.) (See Tales From the Heart of Africa)
Epic Comics (Marvel)

	GD25	FN65	NM94
1-Story cont'd from Tales From...	1.20	3.00	6.00

BLOOD OF DRACULA
Nov, 1987 - Present ($1.75-$1.95, B&W) ($2.25 #14,16 on)
Apple Comics

	GD25	FN65	NM94
1-13: 6-Begin $1.95-c. 10-Chadwick-c	.40	1.00	2.00
14,16-20 ($2.25): 14,16-19-Lost Frankenstein pages by Wrightson	.45	1.35	2.25
15-Contains stereo flexidisc ($3.75)	.75	1.90	3.75

BLOOD OF THE INNOCENT (WaRP) (Value: cover or less)

BLOODSCENT (Comico) (Value: cover or less)

BLOODSHOT (See Eternal Warrior #4 & Rai #0)
Feb, 1993 - Present ($2.50, color)
Valiant

	GD25	FN65	NM94
1-($3.50)-Chromium embossed-c by B. Smith w/poster	1.60	4.00	8.00
2	.70	1.75	3.50
3-6	.50	1.25	2.50

BLOOD SWORD, THE (Jademan) (Value: cover or less)

BLOOD SWORD DYNASTY (Jademan) (Value: cover or less)

BLUE BEETLE, THE (Also see All Top, Big-3, Mystery Men & Weekly Comic Magazine)
Winter, 1939-40 - No. 57, 7/48; No. 58, 4/50 - No. 60, 8/50
Fox Publ. No. 1-11, 31-60; Holyoke No. 12-30

	GD25	FN65	NM94
1-Reprints from Mystery Men 1-5; Blue Beetle origin; Yarko the Great-r/from Wonder/Wonderworld 2-5 all by Eisner; Master Magician app.; (Blue Beetle in 4 different costumes)	200.00	600.00	1200.00
2-K-51-r by Powell/Wonderworld 8,9	83.00	215.00	500.00
3-Simon-c	58.00	150.00	350.00
4-Marijuana drug mention story	42.00	125.00	250.00
5-Zanzibar The Magician by Tuska	35.00	105.00	210.00
6-Dynamite Thor begins; origin Blue Beetle	33.00	100.00	200.00
7,8-Dynamo app. in both. 8-Last Thor	30.00	90.00	180.00
9,10-The Blackbird & The Gorilla app. in both. 10-Bondage/hypo-c	28.00	85.00	170.00
11(2/42)-The Gladiator app.	28.00	85.00	170.00
12(6/42)-The Black Fury app.	28.00	85.00	170.00
13-V-Man begins, ends #18; Kubert-a	33.00	100.00	200.00
14,15-Kubert-a in both. 14-Intro. side-kick (c/text only), Sparky (called Spunky #17-19)	32.00	95.00	190.00
16-18	25.00	75.00	150.00
19-Kubert-a	27.00	80.00	160.00
20-Origin/1st app. Tiger Squadron; Arabian Nights begin	29.00	85.00	175.00
21-26: 24-Intro. & only app. The Halo. 26-General Patton story & photo	18.00	55.00	110.00
27-Tamaa, Jungle Prince app.	17.00	50.00	100.00
28-30(2/44)	14.00	42.00	85.00
31(6/44), 33-40: "The Threat from Saturn" serial in #34-38	10.00	30.00	65.00
32-Hitler-c	13.00	40.00	80.00
41-45	9.15	27.50	55.00
46-The Puppeteer app.	10.00	30.00	60.00
47-Kamen & Baker-a begin	54.00	160.00	325.00
48-50	42.00	125.00	250.00
51,53	37.00	110.00	225.00
52-Kamen bondage-c	54.00	160.00	325.00
54-Used in **SOTI**. Illo-"Children call these 'headlights' comics"	75.00	225.00	450.00
55,57(7/48)-Last Kamen issue; becomes Western Killers?	35.00	105.00	210.00
56-Used in **SOTI**, pg. 145	35.00	105.00	210.00
58(4/50)-60-No Kamen-a	7.50	22.50	45.00

NOTE: ***Kamen** a-47-51, 53, 55-57; c-47, 49-52. **Powell** a-4(2). Bondage-c 9-12, 46, 52.*

BLUE BEETLE (Formerly The Thing; becomes Mr. Muscles No. 22 on) (See Charlton Bullseye & Space Adventures)
No. 18, Feb, 1955 - No. 21, Aug, 1955
Charlton Comics

	GD25	FN65	NM94
18,19-(Pre-1944-r). 19-Bouncer, Rocket Kelly-r	10.00	30.00	65.00
20-Joan Mason by Kamen	12.00	35.00	70.00
21-New material	8.35	25.00	50.00

BLUE BEETLE (Unusual Tales #1-49; Ghostly Tales #55 on) (Also see Captain Atom & Charlton Bullseye)
V2#1, June, 1964 - V2#5, Mar-Apr, 1965; V3#50, July, 1965 - V3#54, Feb-Mar, 1966; #1, June, 1967 - #5, Nov, 1968
Charlton Comics

	GD25	FN65	NM94
V2#1-Origin Dan Garrett-Blue Beetle	6.70	20.00	40.00
2-5,V3#50-54: 5-Weiss illo; 1st published-a?	4.70	14.00	28.00
1(1967)-Question series begins by Ditko	10.00	30.00	60.00
2-Origin Ted Kord-Blue Beetle (see Capt. Atom #83 for 1st Ted Kord Blue Beetle); Dan Garrett x-over	4.20	12.50	25.00
3-5 (All Ditko-c/a in #1-5)	3.60	9.00	18.00
1,3(Modern Comics-1977)-Reprints		.50	1.00

NOTE: *#6 only appeared in the fanzine 'The Charlton Portfolio.'*

BLUE BEETLE (Also see Americomics & Crisis On Infinite Earths)
June, 1986 - No. 24, May, 1988

Blondie Comics #15, © KING

Blood Is The Harvest, © CG

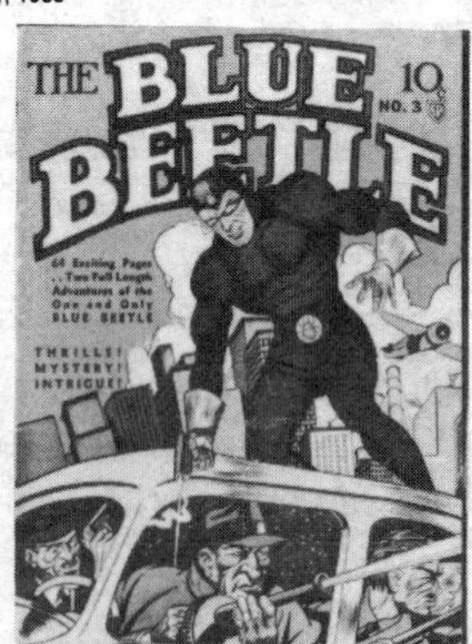

Blue Beetle #3, © FOX

Blue Bolt #5, © STAR

Blue Bolt #107, © STAR

Blue Circle Comics #2, © RH

GD25 FN65 NM94

DC Comics
1-Origin retold; intro. Firefist .50 1.00
2-24: 2-Origin Firefist. 5-7-The Question app. 11-14-New Teen Titans x-over. 18-Begin $1.00-c. 20-Justice League app. 20,21-Millennium tie-ins .50 1.00

BLUEBERRY (See Lt. Blueberry & Marshal Blueberry)
1989 - No. 5, 1990 ($12.95/$14.95, color, graphic novel)
Epic Comics (Marvel)
1,3,4,5-($12.95)-Moebius-a in all 2.60 6.50 13.00
2-($14.95) 3.00 7.50 15.00

BLUE BIRD COMICS
Late 1940's - 1964 (Giveaway)
Various Shoe Stores/Charlton Comics
nn(1947-50)(36 pgs.)-Several issues; Human Torch, Sub-Mariner app. in some 5.85 17.50 35.00
1959-Li'l Genius, Timmy the Timid Ghost, Wild Bill Hickok (All #1) 1.40 3.50 7.00
1959-(6 titles; all #2) Black Fury #1,4,5, Freddy #4, Li'l Genius, Timmy the Timid Ghost #4, Masked Raider #4, Wild Bill Hickok (Charlton) 1.40 3.50 7.00
1959-(#5) Masked Raider #21 1.40 3.50 7.00
1960-(6 titles)(All #4) Black Fury #8,9, Masked Raider, Freddy #8,9, Timmy the Timid Ghost #9, Li'l Genius #7,9 (Chartl.) 1.40 3.50 7.00
1961,1962-(All #10's) Atomic Mouse #12,13,16, Black Fury #11,12, Freddy, Li'l Genius, Masked Raider, Six Gun Heroes, Texas Rangers in Action, Timmy the Ghost, Wild Bill Hickok, Wyatt Earp #3,11-13,16-18 (Charlton) 1.20 3.00 6.00
1963-Texas Rangers #17 (Charlton) .60 1.75 3.00
1964-Mysteries of Unexplored Worlds #18, Teenage Hotrodders #18, War Heroes #18 (Charlton) .80 2.00 4.00
1965-War Heroes #18 .40 1.00 2.00
NOTE: *More than one issue of each character could have been published each year. Numbering is sporadic.*

BLUE BIRD CHILDREN'S MAGAZINE, THE
V1#2, 1957 - No. 10 1958 (16 pages; soft cover; regular size)
Graphic Information Service
V1#2-10: Pat, Pete & Blue Bird app. .80 2.00 4.00

BLUE BOLT
June, 1940 - No. 101 (V10No.2), Sept-Oct, 1949
Funnies, Inc. No. 1/Novelty Press/Premium Group of Comics
V1#1-Origin Blue Bolt by Joe Simon, Sub-Zero, White Rider & Super Horse, Dick Cole, Wonder Boy & Sgt. Spook 167.00 500.00 1000.00
2-Simon-a 83.00 250.00 500.00
3-1 pg. Space Hawk by Wolverton; S&K-a 67.00 200.00 400.00
4,5-S&K-a in each; 5-Everett-a begins on Sub-Zero 63.00 185.00 375.00
6,8-10-S&K-a 58.00 175.00 350.00
7-S&K-c/a 63.00 185.00 375.00
11,12 27.50 185.00 375.00
V2#1-Origin Dick Cole & The Twister; Twister x-over in Dick Cole, Sub-Zero, & Blue Bolt; origin Simba Karno who battles Dick Cole through V2#5 & becomes main supporting character V2#6 on; battle-c 18.00 55.00 110.00
2-Origin The Twister retold in text 14.00 42.00 85.00
3-5: 5-Intro. Freezum 12.00 32.50 70.00
6-Origin Sgt. Spook retold 10.00 30.00 65.00
7-12: 7-Lois Blake becomes Blue Bolt's costume aide; last Twister 8.35 25.00 50.00
V3#1-3 6.35 19.00 38.00
4-12: 4-Blue Bolt abandons costume 5.00 15.00 30.00
V4#1-Hitler, Tojo, Mussolini-c 6.35 19.00 38.00
V4#2-12: 3-Shows V4#3 on-c, V4#4 inside (9-10/43). 5-Infinity-c. 8-Last Sub-Zero 4.35 13.00 26.00
V5#1-8, V6#1-3,5-10, V7#1-12 3.60 9.00 18.00
V6#4-Racist cover 4.70 14.00 28.00
V8#1-6,8-12, V9#1-5,7,8 3.20 8.00 16.00
V8#7,V9#6,9-L. B. Cole-c 3.50 10.50 21.00
V10#1(#100) 3.60 9.00 18.00
V10#2(#101)-Last Dick Cole, Blue Bolt 3.60 9.00 18.00
NOTE: ***Everett*** *c-V1#4, 11, V2#1, 2.* ***Gustavson*** *a-V1#1-12, V2#1-7.* ***Kiefer*** *c-V3#1.* ***Rico*** *a-V6#10, V7#4. Blue Bolt not in V9#8.*

BLUE BOLT (Becomes Ghostly Weird Stories #120 on; continuation of Novelty Blue Bolt) (...Weird Tales #112-119)
No. 102, Nov-Dec, 1949 - No. 119, May-June, 1953
Star Publications
102-The Chameleon, & Target app. 13.00 40.00 90.00
103,104-The Chameleon app.; last Target-#104 11.50 34.00 80.00
105-Origin Blue Bolt (from #1) retold by Simon; Chameleon & Target app.; opium den story 25.00 75.00 175.00
106-Blue Bolt by S&K begins; Spacehawk reprints from Target by Wolverton begins, ends #110; Sub-Zero begins; ends #109 21.00 63.00 145.00
107-110: 108-Last S&K Blue Bolt reprint. 109-Wolverton-c(r)/inside Spacehawk splash. 110-Target app. 21.00 63.00 145.00
111-Red Rocket & The Mask-r; last Blue Bolt; 1pg. L. B. Cole-a 20.00 60.00 135.00
112-Last Torpedo Man app. 19.00 57.00 130.00
113-Wolverton's Spacehawk-r/Target V3#7 20.00 60.00 140.00
114,116: 116-Jungle Jo-r 19.00 57.00 130.00
115-Sgt. Spook app. 21.00 63.00 145.00
117-Jo-Jo & Blue Bolt-r 19.00 57.00 130.00
118-"White Spirit" by Wood 21.00 63.00 145.00
119-Disbrow/Cole-c; Jungle Jo-r 19.00 57.00 130.00
Accepted Reprint #103(1957?, nd) 4.70 14.00 28.00
NOTE: ***L. B. Cole*** *c-102-108, 110 on.* ***Disbrow*** *a-112(2), 113(3), 114(2), 115(2), 116-118.* ***Hollingsworth*** *a-117.* ***Palais*** *a-112r. Sci/Fi c-105-110. Horror c-111.*

BLUE BULLETEER, THE (AC)(Value: cover or less)

BLUE CIRCLE COMICS (Also see Roly Poly Comic Book)
June, 1944 - No. 5, Mar, 1945
Enwil Associates/Rural Home
1-The Blue Circle begins; origin Steel Fist 13.00 40.00 80.00
2,3: 3-Hitler parody-c 8.35 25.00 50.00
4,5: 5-Last Steel Fist 5.35 16.00 32.00
6-(1950s)-Colossal Features-r 5.35 16.00 32.00

BLUE DEVIL (See Fury of Firestorm #24)
June, 1984 - No. 31, Dec, 1986 (75 cents)
DC Comics
1-30: 4-Origin Nebiros. 7-Gil Kane-a. 8-Giffen-a. 17-19: Crisis x-over .50 1.00
31-($1.25, 52 pgs.) .60 1.25
Annual 1 (11/85)-Team-ups w/Black Orchid, Creeper, Demon, Madame Xanadu, Man-Bat & Phantom Stranger .60 1.25

BLUE PHANTOM, THE
June-Aug, 1962
Dell Publishing Co.
1(01-066-208)-by Fred Fredericks 3.60 9.00 18.00

BLUE RIBBON COMICS (...Mystery Comics No. 9-18)
Nov, 1939 - No. 22, March, 1942 (1st MLJ series)
MLJ Magazines
1-Dan Hastings, Richy the Amazing Boy, Rang-A-Tang the Wonder Dog begin; Little Nemo app. (not by W. McCay); Jack Cole-a(3) 175.00 525.00 1050.00
2-Bob Phantom, Silver Fox (both in #3), Rang-A-Tang Club & Cpl. Collins

	GD25	FN65	NM94
begin; Jack Cole-a	75.00	225.00	450.00
3-J. Cole-a	50.00	150.00	300.00
4-Doc Strong, The Green Falcon, & Hercules begin; origin & 1st app. The Fox & Ty-Gor, Son of the Tiger	54.00	162.00	325.00
5-8: 8-Last Hercules; 6,7-Biro, Meskin-a. 7-Fox app. on-c	37.00	110.00	225.00
9-(Scarce)-Origin & 1st app. Mr. Justice	133.00	400.00	800.00
10-13: 12-Last Doc Strong. 13-Inferno, the Flame Breather begins, ends #19; Devil-c	63.00	185.00	375.00
14,15,17,18: 15-Last Green Falcon	54.00	160.00	325.00
16-Origin & 1st app. Captain Flag	100.00	300.00	600.00
19-22: 20-Last Ty-Gor. 22-Origin Mr. Justice retold	50.00	150.00	300.00

NOTE: ***Biro** c-3-5; a-2 (Cpl. Collins & Scoop Cody). **S. Cooper** c-9-17. 20-22 contain "Tales From the Witch's Cauldron" (same strip as "Stories of the Black Witch" in Zip Comics).*

BLUE RIBBON COMICS (Becomes Teen-Age Diary Secrets #4)
Feb, 1949 - No. 6, Aug, 1949 (See Heckle & Jeckle)
Blue Ribbon (St. John)

	GD25	FN65	NM94
1,3-Heckle & Jeckle	5.35	16.00	32.00
2(4/49)-Diary Secrets; Baker-c	8.35	25.00	50.00
4(6/49)-Teen-Age Diary Secrets; Baker c/a(2)	9.15	22.50	55.00
5(8/49)-Teen-Age Diary Secrets; Oversize; photo-c; Baker-a(2)- Continues as Teen-Age Diary Secrets	11.00	32.00	75.00
6-Dinky Duck(8/49)	2.40	6.00	12.00

BLUE-RIBBON COMICS
Nov, 1983 - No. 14, Dec, 1984
Red Circle Prod./Archie Ent. No. 5 on

	GD25	FN65	NM94
1-S&K-r/Advs. of the Fly #1,2; Williamson/Torres-r/Fly #2; Ditko-c		.50	1.00
2-14: 3-Origin Steel Sterling. 5-S&K Shield-r. 6,7-The Fox app. 8-Toth centerspread. 8,11-Black Hood. 12-Thunder Agents. 13-Thunder Bunny. 14-Web & Jaguar		.50	1.00

NOTE: ***N. Adams** a(r)-8. **Buckler** a-4i. **Nino** a-2i. **McWilliams** a-8. **Morrow** a-8.*

BLUE STREAK (See Holyoke One-Shot No. 8)

BLYTHE (See 4-Color No. 1072)

B-MAN (See Double-Dare Adventures)

BO (Tom Cat #4 on; also see Big Shot #29 & Dixie Dugan)
June, 1955 - No. 3, Oct, 1955 (a dog)
Charlton Comics Group

	GD25	FN65	NM94
1-3-Newspaper reprints by Frank Beck	5.00	15.00	30.00

BOATNIKS, THE (See Walt Disney Showcase No. 1)

BOB & BETTY & SANTA'S WISHING WELL
1941 (12 pages) (Christmas giveaway)
Sears Roebuck & Co.

	GD25	FN65	NM94
nn	7.50	22.50	45.00

BOBBY BENSON'S B-BAR-B RIDERS (Radio) (See Best of The West, The Lemonade Kid & Model Fun)
May-June, 1950 - No. 20, May-June, 1953
Magazine Enterprises

	GD25	FN65	NM94
1-The Lemonade Kid begins; Powell-a	18.00	54.00	125.00
2	10.00	30.00	60.00
3-5: 4,5-Lemonade Kid-c (#4-Spider-c)	8.35	25.00	50.00
6-8,10	7.00	21.00	42.00
9,11,13-Frazetta-c; Ghost Rider in #13-15 by Ayers-a. 13-Ghost Rider-c	17.00	52.00	120.00
12,17-20: 20-(A-1 #88)	5.85	17.50	35.00
14-Decapitation/Bondage-c & story; horror-c	9.15	27.50	55.00
15-Ghost Rider-c	10.00	30.00	60.00
16-Photo-c	8.35	25.00	50.00
...in the Tunnel of Gold-(1936, 5-3/4x8"; 100 pgs.) Radio giveaway by Hecker-H.O. Company(H.O. Oats); contains 22 color pages of comics, rest in novel form	7.50	22.50	45.00
...And The Lost Herd-same as above	7.50	22.50	45.00

NOTE: ***Ayers** a-13-15, 20. **Powell** a-1-12(4 ea.), 13(3), 14-16(Red Hawk only); c-1-8,10,12. Lemonade Kid in most 1-13.*

BOBBY COMICS
May, 1946
Universal Phoenix Features

	GD25	FN65	NM94
1-By S. M. Iger	5.35	16.00	32.00

BOBBY SHELBY COMICS
1949
Shelby Cycle Co./Harvey Publications

	GD25	FN65	NM94
nn	3.20	8.00	16.00

BOBBY SHERMAN (TV)
Feb, 1972 - No. 7, Oct, 1972 (Photo-c, 4)
Charlton Comics

	GD25	FN65	NM94
1-Based on TV show "Getting Together"	2.80	7.00	14.00
2-7	1.60	4.00	8.00

BOBBY THATCHER & TREASURE CAVE
1932 (86 pages; B&W; hardcover; 7x9")
Altemus Co.

	GD25	FN65	NM94
nn-Reprints; Storm-a	7.50	22.50	45.00

BOBBY THATCHER'S ROMANCE
1931 (7x8-3/4)
The Bell Syndicate/Henry Altemus Co.

	GD25	FN65	NM94
nn-By Storm	7.50	22.50	45.00

BOB COLT (Movie star)(See XMas Comics)
Nov, 1950 - No. 10, May, 1952
Fawcett Publications

	GD25	FN65	NM94
1-Bob Colt, his horse Buckskin & sidekick Pablo begin; photo front/back-c begin	27.00	85.00	200.00
2	18.00	54.00	125.00
3-5	16.00	48.00	110.00
6-Flying Saucer story	13.00	40.00	90.00
7-10: 9-Last photo back-c	11.50	34.00	80.00

BOB HOPE (See Adventures of...)

BOB POWELL'S TIMELESS TALES (Eclipse)(Value: cover or less)

BOB SCULLY, TWO-FISTED HICK DETECTIVE
No date (1930's) (36 pages; 9-1/2x12"; B&W; paper cover)
Humor Publ. Co.

	GD25	FN65	NM94
nn-By Howard Dell; not reprints	8.35	25.00	50.00

BOB SON OF BATTLE (See 4-Color No. 729)

BOB STEELE WESTERN (Movie star)
Dec, 1950 - No. 10, June, 1952; 1990
Fawcett Publications/AC Comics

	GD25	FN65	NM94
1-Bob Steele & his horse Bullet begin; photo front/back-c begin	32.00	95.00	225.00
2	18.00	54.00	125.00
3-5: 4-Last photo back-c	14.00	43.00	100.00
6-10: 10-Last photo-c	11.50	34.00	80.00
1 (1990, $2.75, B&W)-Bob Steele & Rocky Lane reprints; photo-c & inside covers	.55	1.60	2.75

BOB SWIFT (Boy Sportsman)
May, 1951 - No. 5, Jan, 1952
Fawcett Publications

	GD25	FN65	NM94
1	5.00	15.00	30.00
2-5: Saunders painted-c #1-5	3.60	9.00	18.00

BOLD ADVENTURES (Pacific)(Value: cover or less)

BOLD STORIES (Also see Candid Tales & It Rhymes With Lust)
Mar, 1950 - July, 1950 (Digest size; 144 pgs.; full color)
Kirby Publishing Co.

Blue Ribbon Comics #10, © AP

Bobby Benson's B-Bar-B Riders #3, © ME

Bob Steele Western #9, © FAW

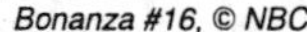
Bonanza #16, © NBC

Boots and her Buddies #1, © NEA Service

Border Patrol #1, © P.L. Publ.

	GD25	FN65	NM94
March issue (Very Rare) - Contains "The Ogre of Paris" by Wood	43.00	130.00	300.00
May issue (Very Rare) - Contains "The Cobra's Kiss" by Graham Ingels (21 pgs.)	32.00	95.00	225.00
July issue (Very Rare) - Contains "The Ogre of Paris" by Wood	36.00	108.00	250.00

BOLT AND STAR FORCE SIX (Americomics)(Value: cover or less)

BOMBARDIER (See Bee 29, the Bombardier & Cinema Comics Herald)

BOMBA THE JUNGLE BOY (TV)
Sept-Oct, 1967 - No. 7, Sept-Oct, 1968 (12 cents)
National Periodical Publications

	GD25	FN65	NM94
1-Intro. Bomba; Infantino/Anderson-c	2.80	7.00	14.00
2-7	1.40	3.50	7.00

BOMBER COMICS
March, 1944 - No. 4, Winter, 1944-45
Elliot Publ. Co./Melverne Herald/Farrell/Sunrise Times

	GD25	FN65	NM94
1-Wonder Boy, & Kismet, Man of Fate begin	27.00	82.00	165.00
2-4: 2-4-Have Classics Comics ad to HRN 20	10.00	55.00	110.00

BONANZA (TV)
June-Aug, 1960 - No. 37, Aug, 1970 (All Photo-c)
Dell/Gold Key

	GD25	FN65	NM94
4-Color 1110 (6-8/60)	29.00	85.00	200.00
4-Color 1221,1283, & #01070-207, 01070-210	14.00	43.00	100.00
1(12/62-Gold Key)	14.00	43.00	100.00
2	7.50	22.50	45.00
3-10	4.20	12.50	25.00
11-20	3.60	9.00	18.00
21-37: 29-Reprints	2.40	6.00	12.00

BONGO (See Story Hour Series)

BONGO & LUMPJAW (See 4-Color #706,886, & Walt Disney Showcase #3)

BON VOYAGE (See Movie Classics)

BOOK AND RECORD SET (See Power Record Comics)

BOOK OF ALL COMICS
1945 (196 pages)
William H. Wise

	GD25	FN65	NM94
nn-Green Mask, Puppeteer	28.00	85.00	170.00

BOOK OF COMICS, THE
No date (1944) (132 pages) (25 cents)
William H. Wise

	GD25	FN65	NM94
nn-Captain V app.	28.00	85.00	170.00

BOOK OF LOVE (See Fox Giants)

BOOK OF NIGHT, THE (Dark Horse)(Value: cover or less)

BOOKS OF MAGIC
1990 - No. 4, 1991 ($3.95, color, mini-series, mature readers, 52 pgs.)
DC Comics

	GD25	FN65	NM94
1-Bolton painted-c/a; Phantom Stranger app.	1.00	2.50	5.00
2-4: 2-John Constantine, Dr. Fate, Spectre, Deadman app. 3-Dr. Occult app.	.80	2.00	4.00

BOOSTER GOLD (See Justice League #4)
Feb, 1986 - No. 25, Feb, 1988 (75 cents)
DC Comics

	GD25	FN65	NM94
1-25: 4-Rose & Thorn app. 6-Origin. 6,7,23-Superman app. 8,9-LSH app. 22-JLI app. 24,25-Millennium tie-ins		.50	1.00

NOTE: *Austin c-22i. Byrne c-23i.*

BOOTS AND HER BUDDIES
No. 5, 9/48 - No. 9, 9/49; 12/55 - No. 3, 1956
Standard Comics/Visual Editions/Argo (NEA Service)

	GD25	FN65	NM94
5-Strip-r	10.00	30.00	65.00
6,8	6.70	20.00	40.00
7-(Scarce)-Spanking panels(3)	8.35	25.00	50.00
9-(Scarce)-Frazetta-a (2 pgs.)	17.00	51.00	120.00
1-3(Argo-1955-56)-Reprints	3.60	9.00	18.00

BOOTS & SADDLES (See 4-Color No. 919, 1029, 1116)

BORDER PATROL
May-June, 1951 - No. 3, Sept-Oct, 1951
P. L. Publishing Co.

	GD25	FN65	NM94
1	6.70	20.00	40.00
2,3	4.20	12.50	25.00

BORDER WORLDS (Kitchen Sink)(Value: cover or less)

BORIS KARLOFF TALES OF MYSTERY (TV) (...Thriller No. 1,2)
No. 3, April, 1963 - No. 97, Feb, 1980
Gold Key

	GD25	FN65	NM94
3-8,10-(Two #5's, 10/63,11/63)	2.80	7.00	14.00
9-Wood-a	3.60	9.00	18.00
11-Williamson-a, Orlando-a, 8 pgs.	3.60	9.00	18.00
12-Torres, McWilliams-a; Orlando-a(2)	2.40	6.00	12.00
13,14,16-20	1.80	4.50	9.00
15-Crandall,Evans-a	2.00	5.00	10.00
21-Jeff Jones-a(3 pgs.) "The Screaming Skull"	2.00	5.00	10.00
22-30: 23-Reprint; photo-c	1.40	3.50	7.00
31-50	.80	2.00	4.00
51-74: 74-Origin & 1st app. Taurus	.60	1.50	3.00
75-97: 80-86-(52 pages)	.40	1.00	2.00
Story Digest 1(7/70-Gold Key)-All text	1.40	3.50	7.00

(See Mystery Comics Digest No. 2, 5, 8, 11, 14, 17, 20, 23, 26)

NOTE: ***Bolle** a-51-54, 56, 58, 59. **McWilliams** a-12, 14, 18, 19, 80, 81, 93. **Orlando** a-11-15, 21. Reprints: 78, 81-86, 88, 90, 92, 95, 97.*

BORIS KARLOFF THRILLER (TV) (Becomes Boris Karloff Tales...)
Oct, 1962 - No. 2, Jan, 1963 (80 pages)
Gold Key

	GD25	FN65	NM94
1-Photo-c	5.85	17.50	35.00
2	4.70	14.00	28.00

BORIS THE BEAR INSTANT COLOR CLASSICS (Dark Horse)(Value: cover or less)

BORN AGAIN (Spire Christian)(Value: cover or less)

BOUNCER, THE (Formerly Green Mask #9)
1944 - No. 14, Jan, 1945
Fox Features Syndicate

	GD25	FN65	NM94
nn(1944, #10?)	14.00	42.00	85.00
11(#1)(9/44)-Origin; Rocket Kelly, One Round Hogan app.	11.00	32.00	75.00
12-14: 14-Reprints no # issue	10.00	30.00	60.00

BOUNTY GUNS (See 4-Color No. 739)

BOY AND HIS 'BOT, A (Now)(Value: cover or less)

BOY AND THE PIRATES, THE (See 4-Color No. 1117)

BOY COMICS (Captain Battle No. 1 & 2; Boy Illustories No. 43-108)
(Stories by Charles Biro)
No. 3, April, 1942 - No. 119, March, 1956
Lev Gleason Publications (Comic House)

	GD25	FN65	NM94
3(No.1)-Origin Crimebuster, Bombshell & Young Robin Hood; Yankee Longago, Case 1001-1008, Swoop Storm, & Boy Movies begin; 1st app. Iron Jaw	167.00	500.00	1000.00
4-Hitler, Tojo, Mussolini-c	58.00	205.00	410.00
5	47.00	160.00	325.00
6-Origin Iron Jaw; origin & death of Iron Jaw's son; Little Dynamite begins, ends #39	125.00	375.00	750.00

	GD25	FN65	NM94
7,9: 7-Flag & Hitler, Tojo, Mussolini-c	46.00	135.00	275.00
8-Death of Iron Jaw	50.00	150.00	300.00
10-Return of Iron Jaw; classic Biro-c	67.00	200.00	400.00
11-14: 11-Classic Iron Jaw-c. 14-Iron Jaw-c	32.00	95.00	190.00
15-Death of Iron Jaw	37.00	110.00	225.00
16,18-20	21.00	62.00	125.00
17-Flag-c	23.00	70.00	140.00
21-26	15.00	45.00	90.00
27-29,31,32-(All 68 pages). 28-Yankee Longago ends. 32-Swoop Storm & Young Robin Hood end	15.00	45.00	90.00
30-(68 pgs.)-Origin Crimebuster retold	20.00	60.00	120.00
33-40: 34-Crimebuster story(2); suicide-c/story	10.00	30.00	60.00
41-50	7.00	21.00	42.00
51-59: 57-Dilly Duncan begins, ends #71	5.85	17.50	35.00
60-Iron Jaw returns	7.50	22.50	45.00
61-Origin Crimebuster & Iron Jaw retold	8.35	25.00	50.00
62-Death of Iron Jaw explained	8.35	25.00	50.00
63-73: 73-Frazetta 1-pg. ad	5.85	17.50	35.00
74-88: 80-1st app. Rocky X of the Rocketeers; becomes "Rocky X" #101; Iron Jaw, Sniffer & the Deadly Dozen begins, ends #118	5.00	15.00	30.00
89-92-The Claw serial app. in all	5.85	17.50	35.00
93-Claw cameo; Rocky X by Sid Check	5.85	17.50	35.00
94-97,99	4.00	12.00	24.00
98-Rocky X by Sid Check	5.00	15.00	30.00
100	5.00	15.00	30.00
101-107,109,111,119: 111-Crimebuster becomes Chuck Chandler. 119-Last Crimebuster	4.00	12.00	24.00
108,110,112-118-Kubert-a	5.00	15.00	30.00

(See Giant Boy Book of Comics)

NOTE: *Boy Movies in 3-5,40,41. Iron Jaw app.-3, 4, 6, 8, 10, 11, 13-15; returns-60-62, 68, 69, 72-79, 81-118.* ***Biro*** *c-all.* ***Briefer*** *a-5, 13, 14, 16-20 among others.* ***Fuje*** *a-55, 18 pgs.* ***Palais*** *a-14, 16, 17, 19, 20 among others*

BOY COMMANDOS (See Detective #64 & World's Finest Comics #8)
Winter, 1942-43 - No. 36, Nov-Dec, 1949
National Periodical Publications

	GD25	FN65	NM94
1-Origin Liberty Belle; The Sandman & The Newsboy Legion x-over in Boy Commandos; S&K-a, 48 pgs.	270.00	800.00	1500.00
2-Last Liberty Belle; Hitler-c; S&K-a, 46 pgs.	92.00	275.00	550.00
3-S&K-a, 45 pgs.	67.00	200.00	400.00
4,5	41.00	122.00	245.00
6-8,10: 6-S&K-a	29.00	86.00	175.00
9-No S&K-a	20.00	60.00	120.00
11-Infinity-c	20.00	60.00	120.00
12-16,18-20	15.00	45.00	90.00
17-Sci/fi-c/story	17.00	50.00	100.00
21,22,24,25: 22-Judy Canova x-over	12.00	35.00	70.00
23-S&K-c/a(all)	13.00	40.00	80.00
26-Flying Saucer story (3-4/48)-4th of this theme	12.50	37.50	75.00
27,28,30: 30-Cleveland Indians story	12.00	35.00	70.00
29-S&K story (1)	12.50	37.50	75.00
31-35: 32-Dale Evans app. on-c & in story. 34-Intro. Wolf, their mascot	12.00	35.00	70.00
36-Intro The Atomobile c/sci-fi story	14.00	42.50	85.00

NOTE: *Most issues signed by* ***Simon & Kirby*** *are not by them.* ***S&K*** *c-1-9, 13, 14, 17, 21, 23, 30-32.* ***Feller*** *c-30.*

BOY COMMANDOS
Sept-Oct, 1973 - No. 2, Nov-Dec, 1973 (G.A. S&K reprints)
National Periodical Publications

	GD25	FN65	NM94
1,2: 1-Reprints story from Boy Commandos #1 plus-c & Detective #66 by S&K. 2-Infantino/Orlando-c	.40	1.00	2.00

BOY COWBOY (Also see Amazing Adventures & Science Comics)
1950 (8 pgs. in color)
Ziff-Davis Publ. Co.

nn-Sent to subscribers of Ziff-Davis mags. & ordered through mail for 10 cents; used to test market for Kid Cowboy
Estimated value 120.00

BOY DETECTIVE
May-June, 1951 - No. 4, May, 1952
Avon Periodicals

	GD25	FN65	NM94
1	11.00	32.00	75.00
2,3: 3-Kinstler-c	7.00	21.00	42.00
4-Kinstler-c/a	10.00	30.00	65.00

BOY EXPLORERS COMICS (Terry and The Pirates No. 3 on)
May-June, 1946 - No. 2, Sept-Oct, 1946
Family Comics (Harvey Publications)

	GD25	FN65	NM94
1-Intro The Explorers, Duke of Broadway, Calamity Jane & Danny Dixon...Cadet; S&K-c/a, 24 pgs	52.00	155.00	310.00

2-(Scarce)-Small size (5x8"; B&W; 32 pgs.) Distributed to mail subscribers only; S&K-a Estimated value $250.00-$400.00

(Also see All New No. 15, Flash Gordon No. 5, and Stuntman No. 3)

BOY ILLUSTORIES (See Boy Comics)

BOY LOVES GIRL (Boy Meets Girl No. 1-24)
No. 25, July, 1952 - No. 57, June, 1956
Lev Gleason Publications

	GD25	FN65	NM94
25(#1)	4.00	12.00	24.00
26,27,29-42: 30-33-Serial, 'Loves of My Life.' 39-Lingerie panels	2.40	6.00	12.00
28-Drug propaganda story	3.20	8.00	16.00
43-Toth-a	4.35	13.00	26.00
44-50: 50-Last pre-code (2/55)	1.80	4.50	9.00
51-57: 57-Ann Brewster-a	1.40	3.50	7.00

BOY MEETS GIRL (Boy Loves Girl No. 25 on)
Feb, 1950 - No. 24, June, 1952 (No. 1-17: 52 pgs.)
Lev Gleason Publications

	GD25	FN65	NM94
1-Guardineer-a	4.00	12.00	24.00
2	2.40	6.00	12.00
3-10	1.80	4.50	9.00
11-24	1.60	4.00	8.00

NOTE: ***Briefer*** *a-24.* ***Fuje*** *c-3,7. Painted-c 1-17. Photo-c 19-21, 23.*

BOYS' AND GIRLS' MARCH OF COMICS (See March of Comics)

BOYS' RANCH (Also see Western Tales & Witches' Western Tales)
Oct, 1950 - No. 6, Aug, 1951 (No.1-3, 52 pgs.; No. 4-6, 36 pgs.)
Harvey Publications

	GD25	FN65	NM94
1-S&K-c/a(3)	40.00	120.00	280.00
2-S&K-c/a(3)	30.00	90.00	210.00
3-S&K-c/a(2); Meskin-a	26.30	79.00	185.00
4-S&K-c/a, 5 pgs.	22.00	65.00	150.00
5,6-S&K-c, splashes & centerspread only; Meskin-a	13.00	40.00	90.00
Shoe Store Giveaway #5,6 (Identical to regular issues except S&K centerfold replaced with ad)	11.00	32.00	75.00

BOZO (Larry Harmon's Bozo, the World's Most Famous Clown)
1992 ($6.95, color, 68 pgs.)
Innovation Publishing

	GD25	FN65	NM94
1-Reprints Four Color #285(#1)	1.40	3.50	7.00

BOZO THE CLOWN (TV) (Bozo No. 7 on)
July, 1950 - No. 4, Oct-Dec, 1963
Dell Publishing Co.

	GD25	FN65	NM94
4-Color 285(#1)	11.50	34.00	80.00
2(7-9/51)-7(10-12/52)	9.15	27.50	55.00
4-Color 464,508,551,594(10/54)	9.15	27.50	55.00
1(nn, 5-7/62) - 4(1963)	5.00	15.00	30.00
Giveaway-1961, 16 pgs., 3-1/2x7-1/4", Apsco Products	3.60	9.00	18.00

BOZZ CHRONICLES, THE

Boy Comics #3, © LEV

Boy Commandos #17, © DC

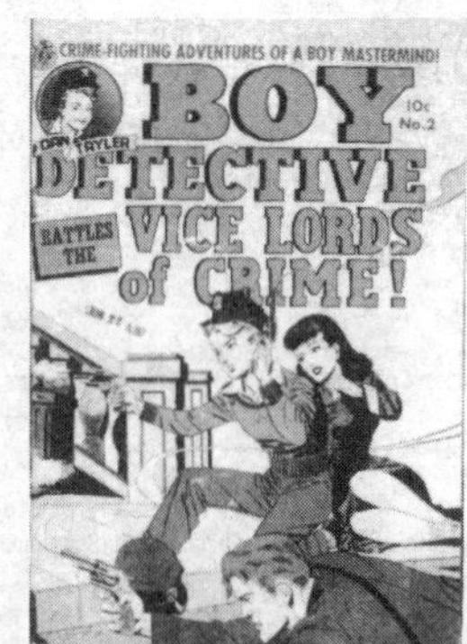

Boy Detective #2, © AVON

The Brave and the Bold #23, © DC

The Brave and the Bold #29, © DC

The Brave and the Bold #182, © DC

	GD25	FN65	NM94
Dec, 1985 - No. 6, 1986 (Adults only)(Mini-series) Epic Comics (Marvel)			
1-6	.30	.75	1.50

BRADY BUNCH, THE (TV)(See Kite Fun Book)
Feb, 1970 - No. 2, May, 1970
Dell Publishing Co.

	GD25	FN65	NM94
1,2	4.70	14.00	28.00

BRAIN, THE
Sept, 1956 - No. 7, 1958
Sussex Publ. Co./Magazine Enterprises

	GD25	FN65	NM94
1-Dan DeCarlo-a in all including reprints	4.20	12.50	25.00
2,3	2.40	6.00	12.00
4-7	1.60	4.00	8.00
I.W. Reprints #1-4,8-10('63),14: 2-Reprints Sussex #2 with new cover added	1.00	2.50	5.00
Super Reprint #17,18(nd)	1.00	2.50	5.00

BRAIN BOY
April-June, 1962 - No. 6, Sept-Nov, 1963 (Painted c-5,6)
Dell Publishing Co.

	GD25	FN65	NM94
4-Color 1330(#1)-Gil Kane-a; origin	6.70	20.00	40.00
2(7-9/62),3-6: 4-Origin retold	4.20	12.50	25.00

BRAND ECHH (See Not Brand Echh)

BRAND OF EMPIRE (See 4-Color No. 771)

BRAVADOS, THE (See Wild Western Action)
August, 1971 (52 pages) (One-Shot)
Skywald Publ. Corp.

	GD25	FN65	NM94
1-Red Mask, The Durango Kid, Billy Nevada-r	.30	.75	1.50

BRAVE AND THE BOLD, THE (See Best Of... & Super DC Giant)
Aug-Sept, 1955 - No. 200, July, 1983
National Periodical Publications/DC Comics

	GD25	FN65	NM94
1-Viking Prince by Kubert, Silent Knight, Golden Gladiator begin; part Kubert-c	170.00	515.00	1200.00
2	65.00	195.00	450.00
3,4	37.00	110.00	260.00
5-Robin Hood begins	39.00	120.00	275.00
6-10: 6-Robin Hood by Kubert; Golden Gladiator last app.; Silent Knight; no Viking Prince	29.00	85.00	200.00
11-22,24: 22-Last Silent Knight. 24-Last Viking Prince by Kubert	22.00	65.00	150.00
23-Viking Prince origin by Kubert; 1st B&B single theme issue	27.00	81.00	190.00
25-1st app. Suicide Squad (8-9/59)	29.00	85.00	200.00
26,27-Suicide Squad	22.00	65.00	150.00
28-(2-3/60)-Justice League intro./1st app.; origin Snapper Carr	325.00	975.00	2600.00
29,30-Justice League	143.00	430.00	1000.00
31-1st app. Cave Carson (8-9/60)	17.00	52.00	120.00
32-33-Cave Carson	13.50	41.00	95.00
34-Origin/1st app. Silver-Age Hawkman & Byth by Kubert (2-3/61); 1st S.A. Hawkman tryout series	115.00	345.00	800.00
35,36-Hawkman by Kubert; origin Shadow Thief #36 (6-7/61)	32.00	95.00	225.00
37-Suicide Squad (2nd tryout series)	19.00	57.00	130.00
38,39-Suicide Squad. 38-Last 10 cent issue	16.00	48.00	110.00
40,41-Cave Carson Inside Earth. 40-Kubert-a. 41-Meskin-a	11.00	32.00	75.00
42,44-Hawkman by Kubert (2nd tryout series)	16.00	48.00	110.00
43-Origin Hawkman by Kubert retold	19.00	57.00	130.00
45-49-Strange Sports Stories by Infantino	4.70	14.00	28.00
50-The Green Arrow & Manhunter From Mars (10-11/63); team-ups begin	12.00	36.00	85.00
51-Aquaman & Hawkman (12-1/63-64); pre-dates Hawkman #1	7.50	22.50	45.00
52-3 Battle Stars; Sgt. Rock, Haunted Tank, Johnny Cloud, & Mlle. Marie team-up for 1st time by Kubert (c/a)	5.85	17.50	35.00
53-Atom & The Flash by Toth	5.00	15.00	30.00
54-Kid Flash, Robin & Aqualad; 1st app./origin Teen Titans (6-7/64)	25.00	75.00	175.00
55-Metal Men & The Atom	3.60	9.00	18.00
56-The Flash & Manhunter From Mars	3.60	9.00	18.00
57-Origin & 1st app. Metamorpho (12-1/64-65)	13.00	40.00	90.00
58-Metamorpho by Fradon	6.70	20.00	40.00
59-Batman & Green Lantern; 1st Batman team-up in Brave and the Bold	10.00	30.00	60.00
60-Teen Titans (2nd app.)-1st app. new Wonder Girl (Donna Troy), who joins Titans (6-7/65)	10.00	30.00	60.00
61,62-Origin Starman & Black Canary by Anderson. 62-1st S.A. app. Wildcat (10-11/65); Huntress app.	5.85	17.50	35.00
63-Supergirl & Wonder Woman	2.40	6.00	12.00
64-Batman Versus Eclipso (see H.O.S. #61)	6.70	20.00	40.00
65-Flash & Doom Patrol	2.00	5.00	10.00
66-Metamorpho & Metal Men	2.00	5.00	10.00
67-Batman & The Flash by Infantino; Batman team-ups begin, end #200	4.20	12.50	25.00
68-Batman/Joker/Riddler/Penguin-c/story; Batman as Bat-Hulk (Hulk parody)	7.50	22.50	45.00
69-71: Batman team-ups	3.60	9.00	18.00
72,73: 72-Spectre-Flash. 73-Aquaman-Atom	3.00	7.50	15.00
74-78-Batman team-ups. 78-Batgirl app.	3.00	7.50	15.00
79-Batman-Deadman by Neal Adams	4.20	12.50	25.00
80-Batman-Creeper; N. Adams-a	4.00	12.00	24.00
81-Batman-Flash; N. Adams-a	4.00	12.00	24.00
82-Batman-Aquaman; N. Adams-a; origin Ocean Master retold	4.00	12.00	24.00
83-Batman-Teen Titans; N. Adams-a	5.70	17.00	34.00
84-Batman(GA)-Sgt. Rock; N. Adams-a	4.00	12.00	24.00
85-Batman-Green Arrow; 1st new costume for Green Arrow by Neal Adams	4.00	12.00	24.00
86-Batman-Deadman; N. Adams-a	4.00	12.00	24.00
87-92: Batman team-ups	3.20	8.00	16.00
93-Batman-House of Mystery; N. Adams-a	4.00	11.00	22.00
94-Batman-Teen Titans	1.80	4.50	9.00
95-99: 97-Origin Deadman-r	1.40	3.50	7.00
100-(25 cents, 52 pgs.)-Batman-Green Lantern-Green Arrow-Black Canary-Robin; Deadman-r by N. Adams	4.00	10.00	20.00
101-Batman-Metamorpho; Kubert Viking Prince	.80	2.00	4.00
102-Batman-Teen Titans; N. Adams-a(p)	1.40	3.50	7.00
103-110: Batman team-ups	.80	2.00	4.00
111-Batman/Joker-c/story	2.00	5.00	10.00
112-117: All 100 pgs.; Batman team-ups. 113-Reprints Brave and the Bold #34	1.20	3.00	6.00
118-Batman/Wildcat/Joker-c/story	1.80	4.50	9.00
119-128,131-140: Batman team-ups. 131-Batman & Wonder Woman vs. Catwoman-c/story	.60	1.50	3.00
129,130-Batman/Joker-c/stories	2.00	5.00	10.00
141-Batman vs. Joker-c/story	1.80	4.50	9.00
142-190,192-199: 143,144-(44 pgs.). 148-XMas-c. 149-Batman-Teen Titans. 150-Anniversary issue; Superman. 157-Kamandi (ties into Kamandi #59). 166-Penguin-c/story. 179-LSH. 181-Hawk & Dove. 182-Batman/Robin. 182,197-1st & 2nd S.A. app. of G.A. Batwoman. 183-Riddler. 187-Metal Men. 196-Origin Ragman retold. 197-Earth II Batman & Catwoman marry	.60	1.50	3.00
191-Batman/Joker-c/story	1.40	3.50	7.00
200-Double-sized (64 pgs.); printed on Mando paper; Earth One & Earth Two			

Batman team-up; Intro/1st app. Batman & The Outsiders
1.60 4.00 8.00

NOTE: ***Neal Adams** a-79-86, 93, 100r, 102; c-75, 76, 79-86, 88-90, 93, 95, 99, 100r. **M. Anderson** a-115r; c-72i, 96i. **Andru/Esposito** c-25-27. **Aparo** a-98, 100-102, 104-125, 126i, 127-136, 138-145, 147, 148i, 149-152, 154, 155, 157-162, 168-170, 173-178, 180-182, 184, 186i-189i, 191i-193i, 195, 196, 200; c-105-109, 111-136, 137i, 138-175, 177, 180-184, 186-200. **Austin** a-166i. **Bernard Baily** c-32, 33. **Buckler** a-185, 186p; c-137, 178p, 185p, 186p. **Giordano** a-143, 144. **Infantino** a-67p, 72p, 97r, 98r, 172p, 183p, 190p, 194p; c-45-49, 67p, 69p, 70p, 72p, 96p, 98r. **Kaluta** c-176. **Kane** a-115r. **Kubert** &/or **Heath** a-1-24; reprints-101, 113, 115, 117. **Kubert** c-22-24, 34-36, 40, 42-44, 52. **Mooney** a-114r. **Newton** a-153p, 156p, 165p. **Irv Novick** c-1(part), 2-21. **Roussos** a-114r. **Staton** 148p. 52 pgs.-97, 100; 64 pgs.-120; 100 pgs.-112-117.*

BRAVE AND THE BOLD, THE
Dec, 1991 - No. 6, June, 1992 ($1.75, color, mini-series)
DC Comics

1-6: Green Arrow, The Butcher, The Question in all; Grell scripts in all; Grell c-3,4,6 .35 .90 1.75

BRAVE AND THE BOLD SPECIAL, THE (See DC Special Series No. 8)

BRAVE EAGLE (See 4-Color No. 705, 770, 816, 879, 929)

BRAVE ONE, THE (See 4-Color No. 773)

BREATHTAKER
1990 - No. 4, 1990 ($4.95, prestige format, mature readers, 52 pgs.)
DC Comics

Book 1-4: By Hempel & Wheatley painted-c/a 1.00 2.50 5.00

BREEZE LAWSON, SKY SHERIFF (See Sky Sheriff)

BRENDA LEE STORY, THE
September, 1962
Dell Publishing Co.

01-078-209 9.15 27.50 55.00

BRENDA STARR (Also see All Great)
No. 13, 9/47; No. 14, 3/48; V2#3, 6/48 - V2#12, 12/49
Four Star Comics Corp./Superior Comics Ltd.

	GD25	FN65	NM94
V1#13-By Dale Messick	43.00	130.00	300.00
14-Kamen bondage-c	43.00	130.00	300.00
V2#3-Baker-a?	36.00	108.00	250.00
4-Used in **SOTI**, pg. 21; Kamen bondage-c	40.00	120.00	275.00
5-10	32.00	95.00	225.00
11,12 (Scarce)	36.00	108.00	250.00

NOTE: *Newspaper reprints plus original material through #6. All original #7 on.*

BRENDA STARR (...Reporter)(Young Lovers No. 16 on?)
No. 13, June, 1955 - No. 15, Oct, 1955
Charlton Comics

13-15-Newspaper-r 22.00 65.00 150.00

BRENDA STARR REPORTER
October, 1963
Dell Publishing Co.

1 16.00 48.00 110.00

BRER RABBIT (See 4-Color No. 129, 208, 693, Kite Fun Book, Walt Disney Showcase #28 and Wheaties)

BRER RABBIT IN "ICE CREAM FOR THE PARTY"
1955 (16 pages, 5x7-1/4", soft-c) (Walt Disney) (Premium)
American Dairy Association

nn-(Rare) 11.00 32.00 75.00

BRIAN BOLLAND'S BLACK BOOK (Eclipse) (Value: cover or less)

BRICK BRADFORD (Also see Ace Comics & King Comics)
No. 5, July, 1948 - No. 8, July, 1949 (Ritt & Grey reprints)
King Features Syndicate/Standard

	GD25	FN65	NM94
5	10.00	30.00	70.00
6-8: 7-Schomburg-c. 8-Says #7 inside, #8 on-c	9.15	27.50	55.00

BRIDE'S DIARY (Formerly Black Cobra No. 3)
No. 4, May, 1955 - No. 10, Aug, 1956
Ajax/Farrell Publ.

	GD25	FN65	NM94
4 (#1)	4.35	13.00	26.00
5-8	3.00	7.50	15.00
9,10-Disbrow-a	4.35	13.00	26.00

BRIDES IN LOVE (Hollywood Romances & Summer Love No. 46 on)
Aug, 1956 - No. 45, Feb, 1965
Charlton Comics

	GD25	FN65	NM94
1	4.00	11.00	22.00
2	2.40	6.00	12.00
3-10	1.60	4.00	8.00
11-20	1.00	2.50	5.00
21-45	.70	1.75	3.50

BRIDES ROMANCES
Nov, 1953 - No. 23, Dec, 1956
Quality Comics Group

	GD25	FN65	NM94
1	7.50	22.50	45.00
2	4.00	11.00	22.00
3-10: Last precode (3/55)	2.80	7.00	14.00
11-14,16,17,19-22	1.80	4.50	9.00
15-Baker-a(p); Colan-a	2.00	5.00	10.00
18-Baker-a	2.80	7.00	14.00
23-Baker-c/a	4.00	11.00	22.00

BRIDE'S SECRETS
Apr-May, 1954 - No. 19, May, 1958
Ajax/Farrell(Excellent Publ.)/Four-Star Comic

	GD25	FN65	NM94
1	6.35	19.00	38.00
2	4.00	10.00	20.00
3-6: Last precode (3/55)	2.80	7.00	14.00
7-19: 12-Disbrow-a. 18-Hollingsworth-a	4.00	5.00	10.00

BRIDE-TO-BE ROMANCES (See True...)

BRIGADE
Aug, 1992 - No. 4, 1992 ($1.95, color, mini-series)
Image Comics

	GD25	FN65	NM94
1-Liefeld part plots/scripts in all, Liefeld-c(p); contains 2 Brigade trading cards	.50	1.25	2.50
1-Gold embossed cover	4.20	12.50	25.00
2-Contains coupon for Image Comics #0 & 2 trading cards	1.00	2.50	5.00
2-With coupon missing	.40	1.00	2.00
3,4	.40	1.00	2.00

BRIGAND, THE (See Fawcett Movie Comics No. 18)

BRINGING UP FATHER (See 4-Color #37 & Large Feature Comic #9)

BRINGING UP FATHER
1917 (16-1/2x5-1/2"; cardboard cover; 100 pages; B&W)
Star Co. (King Features)

nn-(Rare) Daily strip reprints by George McManus (no price on-c)
40.00 120.00 275.00

BRINGING UP FATHER
1919 - 1934 (by George McManus)(No. 22 is 9-1/4x9-1/2")
(10x10"; stiff cardboard covers; B&W; daily strip reprints; 52 pgs.)
Cupples & Leon Co.

	GD25	FN65	NM94
1	32.00	95.00	225.00
2-10	16.00	48.00	110.00
11-26 (Scarcer)	24.00	72.00	165.00
The Big Book 1(1926)-Thick book (hardcover); 10-1/4x10-1/4", 142pgs.	40.00	120.00	275.00
The Big Book 2(1929)	32.00	95.00	225.00

NOTE: *The Big Books contain 3 regular issues rebound and probably w/dust jackets.*

BRINGING UP FATHER, THE TROUBLE OF

Brenda Starr #12, © SUPR

Bride's Diary #5, © AJAX

Bride's Secrets #1, © AJAX

Bruce Gentry #6, © STD

Buccaneers #23, © QUA

Buck Jones #3,
© Mrs. Odille D. Jones

1921 (9x15") (Sunday reprints in color)
Embee Publ. Co.

	GD25	FN65	NM94
nn-(Rare)	40.00	120.00	275.00

BROADWAY HOLLYWOOD BLACKOUTS
Mar-Apr, 1954 - No. 3, July-Aug, 1954
Stanhall

	GD25	FN65	NM94
1	7.00	21.00	42.00
2,3	4.70	14.00	28.00

BROADWAY ROMANCES
January, 1950 - No. 5, Sept, 1950
Quality Comics Group

	GD25	FN65	NM94
1-Ward-c/a (9 pgs.); Gustavson-a	16.00	48.00	110.00
2-Ward-a (9 pgs.); photo-c	10.00	30.00	70.00
3-5: 4,5-Photo-c	5.85	17.50	35.00

BROKEN ARROW (See 4-Color No. 855,947)

BROKEN CROSS, THE (See The Crusaders)

BRONCHO BILL (See Comics On Parade, Sparkler & Tip Top Comics)
1939 - 1940; No. 5, 1?/48 - No. 16, 8?/50
United Features Syndicate/Standard(Visual Editions) No. 5-on

	GD25	FN65	NM94
Single Series 2 ('39)	32.00	95.00	225.00
Single Series 19 ('40)(#2 on cvr)	26.00	77.00	180.00
5	7.00	21.00	42.00
6(4/48)-10(4/49)	4.20	12.50	25.00
11(6/49)-16	3.60	9.00	18.00

NOTE: ***Schomburg** c-6, 7, 9-13, 16.*

BROOKS ROBINSON (See Baseball's Greatest Heroes #2)

BROTHER POWER, THE GEEK (See Saga of Swamp Thing Annual)
Sept-Oct, 1968 - No. 2, Nov-Dec, 1968
National Periodical Publications

	GD25	FN65	NM94
1-Origin; Simon-c(i?)	4.20	12.50	25.00
2	3.60	9.00	18.00

BROTHERS, HANG IN THERE, THE (Spire Christian)(Value: cover or less)

BROTHERS OF THE SPEAR (Also see Tarzan)
June, 1972 - No. 17, Feb, 1976; No. 18, May, 1982
Gold Key/Whitman No. 18 on

	GD25	FN65	NM94
1	2.40	6.00	12.00
2-Painted-c begin, end #17	1.40	3.50	7.00
3-10	.90	2.25	4.50
11-17: 13-17-Spiegle-a	.40	1.00	2.00
18-Manning-r/#2; Leopard Girl-r		.50	1.00

BROTHERS, THE CULT ESCAPE, THE (Spire Christian)(Value: cover or less)

BROWNIES (See 4-Color No. 192, 244, 293, 337, 365, 398, 436, 482, 522, 605 & New Funnies)

BROWN'S BLUE RIBBON BOOK OF JOKES AND JINGLES (See Buster Brown's...)

BRUCE GENTRY
Jan, 1948 - No. 2, Nov, 1948; No. 3, Jan, 1949 - No. 8, July, 1949
Better/Standard/Four Star Publ./Superior No. 3

	GD25	FN65	NM94
1-Ray Bailey strip reprints begin, end #3; E. C. emblem appears as a monogram on stationery in story; negligee panels	24.00	72.00	165.00
2,3	18.00	54.00	125.00
4-8	12.00	36.00	85.00

NOTE: ***Kamenish** a-2-7; c-1-8.*

BRUTE, THE
Feb, 1975 - No. 3, July, 1975
Seaboard Publ. (Atlas)

	GD25	FN65	NM94
1-Origin & 1st app; Sekowsky-a(p)	.30	.75	1.50
2,3: 2-Sekowsky-a(p). 3-Weiss-a(p)		.50	1.00

BRUTE FORCE
Aug, 1990 - No. 4, Nov, 1990 ($1.00, color, limited series)
Marvel Comics

	GD25	FN65	NM94
1-4: Animal super-heroes		.50	1.00

BUCCANEER
No date (1963)
I. W. Enterprises

	GD25	FN65	NM94
I.W. Reprint #1(r-/Quality #20), #8(r-/#23): Crandall-a in each	2.80	7.00	14.00

BUCCANEERS (Formerly Kid Eternity)
No. 19, Jan, 1950 - No. 27, May, 1951 (No. 24-27: 52 pages)
Quality Comics Group

	GD25	FN65	NM94
19-Captain Daring, Black Roger, Eric Falcon & Spanish Main begin; Crandall-a	30.00	90.00	210.00
20,23-Crandall-a	22.00	65.00	150.00
21-Crandall-c/a	26.00	78.00	180.00
22-Bondage-c	16.00	48.00	110.00
24-26: 24-Adam Peril, U.S.N. begins. 25-Origin & 1st app. Corsair Queen. 26-last Spanish Main	13.00	40.00	90.00
27-Crandall-c/a	22.00	65.00	150.00
Super Reprint #12 (1964)-Crandall-r/#21	2.80	7.00	14.00

BUCCANEERS, THE (See 4-Color No. 800)

BUCKAROO BANZAI
Dec, 1984 - No. 2, Feb, 1985 (Movie adaptation)
Marvel Comics Group

	GD25	FN65	NM94
1,2-r/Marvel Super Special #33		.50	1.00

BUCK DUCK
June, 1953 - No. 4, Dec, 1953
Atlas Comics (ANC)

	GD25	FN65	NM94
1-Funny animal stories in all	5.85	17.50	35.00
2-4: 2-Ed Win-a(5)	3.60	9.00	18.00

BUCK JONES (Also see Crackajack Funnies, Famous Feature Stories & Master Comics #7)
No. 299, Oct, 1950 - No. 850, Oct, 1957 (All Painted-c)
Dell Publishing Co.

	GD25	FN65	NM94
4-Color 299(#1)-Buck Jones & his horse Silver-B begin; painted back-c begins, ends #5	11.50	34.00	80.00
2(4-6/51)	6.70	20.00	40.00
3-8(10-12/52)	5.00	15.00	30.00
4-Color 460,500,546,589	4.70	14.00	28.00
4-Color 652,733,850	3.60	9.00	18.00

BUCK ROGERS (In the 25th Century)
1933 (36 pages in color) (6x8")
Kelloggs Corn Flakes Giveaway

	GD25	FN65	NM94
370A-By Phil Nowlan & Dick Calkins; 1st Buck Rogers radio premium (tells origin)	43.00	130.00	300.00

BUCK ROGERS (Also see Famous Funnies, Pure Oil Comics, Salerno Carnival of Comics, 24 Pages of Comics, & Vicks Comics)
Winter, 1940-41 - No. 6, Sept, 1943
Famous Funnies

	GD25	FN65	NM94
1-Sunday strip reprints by Rick Yager; begins with strip #190; Calkins-c	167.00	500.00	1000.00
2 (7/41)-Calkins-c	100.00	300.00	600.00
3 (12/41), 4 (7/42)	83.00	250.00	500.00
5-Story continues with Famous Funnies No. 80; Buck Rogers, Sky Roads	75.00	225.00	450.00
6-Reprints of 1939 dailies; contains B.R. story "Crater of Doom" (2 pgs.) by Calkins not-r from Famous Funnies	75.00	225.00	450.00

BUCK ROGERS

No. 100, Jan, 1951 - No. 9, May-June, 1951
Toby Press

	GD25	FN65	NM94
100(#7)	20.00	60.00	120.00
101(#8), 9-All Anderson-a('47-'49-r/dailies)	15.00	45.00	105.00

BUCK ROGERS (...in the 25th Century No. 5 on) (TV)
Oct, 1964; No. 2, July, 1979 - No. 16, May, 1982 (No #10)
Gold Key/Whitman No. 7 on

	GD25	FN65	NM94
1(10128-410)-Painted-c; 12 cents	4.20	12.50	25.00
2(8/79)-Movie adaptation	.50	1.25	2.50
3-9,11-16: 3,4-Movie adaptation; 5-new stories	.30	.75	1.50
Giant Movie Edition 11296(64pp, Whitman, $1.50), reprints GK #2-4 minus cover; tabloid size	.40	1.00	2.00
Giant Movie Edition 02489(Western/Marvel, $1.50), reprints GK #2-4 minus cover	.40	1.00	2.00

NOTE: ***Bolle** a-2-4p, Movie Ed.(p). **McWilliams** a-2-4i, 5-11, Movie Ed.(i). Painted c-1-9,11-13.*

BUCK ROGERS (TSR)(Value: cover or less)

BUCK ROGERS ADVENTURE BOOK
1933 (premium)
Cocomalt

	GD25	FN65	NM94
nn-(rare)	670.00	2000.00	4000.00

BUCKSKIN (Movie) (See 4-Color No. 1011,1107)

BUCKY O'HARE (Continuity)(Value: cover or less)

BUDDIES IN THE U.S. ARMY
Nov, 1952 - No. 2, 1953
Avon Periodicals

	GD25	FN65	NM94
1-Lawrence-c	7.50	22.50	45.00
2-Mort Lawrence-c/a	5.35	16.00	32.00

BUDDY TUCKER & HIS FRIENDS (Also see Buster Brown)
1906 (11x17") (In color)
Cupples & Leon Co.

	GD25	FN65	NM94
1905 Sunday strip reprints by R. F. Outcault	38.00	110.00	225.00

BUFFALO BEE (See 4-Color No. 957, 1002, 1061)

BUFFALO BILL (Also see Frontier Fighters, Super Western Comics & Western Action Thrillers)
No. 2, Oct, 1950 - No. 9, Dec, 1951
Youthful Magazines

	GD25	FN65	NM94
2-Annie Oakley story	6.70	20.00	40.00
3-9: 2-4-Walter Johnson-c/a. 9-Wildey-a	3.50	10.50	21.00

BUFFALO BILL CODY (See Cody of the Pony Express)

BUFFALO BILL, JR. (TV) (See Western Roundup under Dell Giants)
Jan, 1956 - No. 13, Aug-Oct, 1959; 1965 (All photo-c)
Dell Publishing Co./Gold Key

	GD25	FN65	NM94
4-Color 673 (#1)	5.85	17.50	35.00
4-Color 742,766,798,828,856(11/57)	4.00	12.00	24.00
7(2-4/58)-13	3.60	9.00	18.00
1(6/65-Gold Key)	2.40	6.00	12.00

BUFFALO BILL PICTURE STORIES
June-July, 1949 - No. 2, Aug-Sept, 1949
Street & Smith Publications

	GD25	FN65	NM94
1,2-Wildey, Powell-a in each	7.50	22.50	45.00

BUFFALO BILL'S PICTURE STORIES
1909 (Soft cardboard cover)
Street & Smith Publications

	GD25	FN65	NM94
nn	14.00	43.00	100.00

BUGALOOS (TV)
Sept, 1971 - No. 4, Feb, 1972
Charlton Comics

	GD25	FN65	NM94
1-4	.80	2.00	4.00

NOTE: No. 3(1/72) went on sale late in 1972 (after No. 4) with the 1/73 issues.

BUGHOUSE (Satire)
Mar-Apr, 1954 - No. 4, Sept-Oct, 1954
Ajax/Farrell (Excellent Publ.)

	GD25	FN65	NM94
V1#1	10.00	30.00	65.00
2-4	6.35	19.00	38.00

BUGHOUSE FABLES
1921 (48 pgs.) (4x4-1/2") (10 cents)
Embee Distributing Co. (King Features)

	GD25	FN65	NM94
1-Barney Google	11.50	34.00	80.00

BUG MOVIES
1931 (52 pages) (B&W)
Dell Publishing Co.

	GD25	FN65	NM94
nn-Not reprints; Stookie Allen-a	11.00	32.00	75.00

BUGS BUNNY (See The Best of..., Camp Comics, Comic Album #2, 6, 10, 14, Dell Giant #28, 32, 46, Dynabrite, Golden Comics Digest #1, 3, 5, 6, 8, 10, 14, 15, 17, 21, 26, 30, 34, 39, 42, 47, Kite Fun Book, Large Feature Comic #8, Looney Tunes and Merry Melodies, March of Comics #44, 59, 75, 83, 97, 115, 132, 149, 160, 179, 188, 201, 220, 231, 245, 259, 273, 287, 301, 315, 329, 343, 363, 367, 380, 392, 403, 415, 428, 440, 452, 464, 476, 487, Porky Pig, Puffed Wheat, Story Hour Series #802, Super Book #14, 26 and Whitman Comic Books)

BUGS BUNNY (See Dell Giants for annuals)
1942 - No. 245, 1983
Dell Publishing Co./Gold Key No. 86-218/Whitman No. 219 on

	GD25	FN65	NM94
Large Feature Comic 8(1942)-(Rarely found in fine-mint condition)	72.00	215.00	500.00
4-Color 33 ('43)	47.00	140.00	325.00
4-Color 51	25.00	75.00	175.00
4-Color 88	16.00	48.00	110.00
4-Color 123('46),142,164	10.00	30.00	65.00
4-Color 187,200,217,233	9.15	27.50	55.00
4-Color 250-Used in **SOTI**, pg. 309	9.15	27.50	55.00
4-Color 266,274,281,289,298('50)	7.50	22.50	45.00
4-Color 307,317(#1),327(#2),338,347,355,366,376,393	6.35	19.00	38.00
4-Color 407,420,432	4.70	14.00	28.00
28(12-1/52-53)-30	3.00	7.50	15.00
31-50	1.60	4.00	8.00
51-85(7-9/62)	1.40	3.50	7.00
86(10/62)-88-Bugs Bunny's Showtime-(80 pgs.)(25 cents)	4.70	14.00	28.00
89-100	1.20	3.00	6.00
101-120	.80	2.00	4.00
121-140	.60	1.50	3.00
141-170	.50	1.25	2.50
171-245: 229-Swipe of Barks story/WDC&S #223	.30	.75	1.50

NOTE: *Reprints-100, 102, 104, 123, 143, 144, 147, 167, 173, 175-177, 179-185, 187, 190.*

	GD25	FN65	NM94
Comic-Go-Round 11196-(224 pgs.)($1.95)(Golden Press, 1979)	.60	1.50	3.00
Winter Fun 1(12/67-Gold Key)-Giant	2.50	7.50	20.00

BUGS BUNNY (Puffed Rice Giveaway)
1949 (32 pages each, 3-1/8x6-7/8")
Quaker Cereals

A1-Traps the Counterfeiters, A2-Aboard Mystery Submarine, A3- Rocket to the Moon, A4-Lion Tamer, A5-Rescues the Beautiful Princess, B1-Buried Treasure, B2-Outwits the Smugglers, B3-Joins the Marines, B4-Meets the Dwarf Ghost, B5-Finds Aladdin's Lamp, C1-Lost in the Frozen North, C2-Secret Agent, C3-Captured by Cannibals, C4-Fights the Man from Mars, C5-And the Haunted Cave

	GD25	FN65	NM94
each....	5.00	15.00	30.00

BUGS BUNNY (3-D)
1953 (Pocket size) (15 titles)
Cheerios Giveaway

	GD25	FN65	NM94
each....	6.70	20.00	40.00

Buck Rogers #2 (F.F.), © Nat'l Newspaper Synd.

Buffalo Bill, Jr. #1, © Tie-Ups Co.

Bughouse #2, © AJAX

Bugs Bunny and Porky Pig #1, © Warner Bros.

Bulletman #4, © FAW

Bulls Eye Comics #11, © CHES

	GD25	FN65	NM94
BUGS BUNNY			
June, 1990 - No. 3, Aug, 1990 ($1.00, color, mini-series)			
DC Comics			
1-3: Daffy Duck, Elmer Fudd, others app.		.50	1.00
BUGS BUNNY & PORKY PIG			
Sept, 1965 (100 pages; paper cover; giant)			
Gold Key			
1(30025-509)	5.00	15.00	30.00
BUGS BUNNY'S ALBUM (See 4-Color No. 498,585,647,724)			
BUGS BUNNY LIFE STORY ALBUM (See 4-Color No. 838)			
BUGS BUNNY MERRY CHRISTMAS (See 4-Color No. 1064)			
BULLET CROW, FOWL OF FORTUNE (Eclipse) (Value: cover or less)			
BULLETMAN (See Fawcett Miniatures, Master Comics, Mighty Midget Comics, Nickel Comics & XMas Comics)			
Sum, 1941 - #12, 2/12/43; #14, Spr, 1946 - #16, Fall, 1946 (nn 13)			
Fawcett Publications			
1	200.00	600.00	1200.00
2	100.00	300.00	600.00
3	72.00	218.00	435.00
4,5	62.00	188.00	375.00
6-10: 7-Ghost Stories as told by the night watchman of the cemetery begins; Eisnerish-a	54.00	162.00	325.00
11,12,14-16 (nn 13)	46.00	138.00	275.00
Well Known Comics (1942)-Paper-c, glued binding; printed in red (Bestmaid/Samuel Lowe giveaway)	12.50	37.50	75.00

NOTE: *Mac Raboy c-1-3, 5, 6, 10. "Bulletman the Flying Detective" on cover #8 on.*

	GD25	FN65	NM94
BULLS-EYE (Cody of The Pony Express No. 8 on)			
7-8/54 - No. 5, 3-4/55; No. 6, 6/55; No. 7, 8/55			
Mainline No. 1-5/Charlton No. 6,7			
1-S&K-c, 2 pages-a	37.00	110.00	225.00
2-S&K-c/a	32.00	100.00	195.00
3-5-S&K-c/a(2 each)	23.00	70.00	140.00
6-S&K-c/a	18.00	55.00	110.00
7-S&K-c/a(3)	23.00	70.00	140.00
Great Scott Shoe Store giveaway-Reprints #2 with new cover	12.50	37.50	75.00
BULLS-EYE COMICS (Formerly Komik Pages #10; becomes Kayo #12)			
No. 11, 1944			
Harry 'A' Chesler			
11-Origin K-9, Green Knight's sidekick, Lance; The Green Knight, Lady Satan, Yankee Doodle Jones app.	20.00	60.00	120.00
BULLWHIP GRIFFIN (See Movie Comics)			
BULLWINKLE (TV) (...and Rocky No. 20 on; See March of Comics #233 and Rocky & Bullwinkle) (Jay Ward)			
3-5/62 - #11, 4/74; #12, 6/76 - #19, 3/78; #20, 4/79 - #25, 2/80			
Dell/Gold Key			
4-Color 1270 (3-5/62)	12.00	36.00	85.00
01-090-209 (Dell, 7-9/62)	12.00	36.00	85.00
1(11/62, Gold Key)	10.00	30.00	70.00
2(2/63)	9.15	27.50	55.00
3(4/72)-11(4/74-Gold Key)	4.00	10.00	20.00
12(6/76)-Reprints	2.00	5.00	10.00
13(9/76), 14-New stories	2.40	6.00	12.00
15-25	1.60	4.00	8.00
Mother Moose Nursery Pomes 01-530-207 (5-7/62-Dell)	10.00	30.00	65.00

NOTE: *Reprints: 6, 7, 20-24.*

	GD25	FN65	NM94
BULLWINKLE (...& Rocky No. 2 on)(TV)			
July, 1970 - No. 7, July, 1971			
Charlton Comics			
1	4.20	12.50	25.00
2-7	3.00	7.50	15.00
BULLWINKLE AND ROCKY			
Nov, 1987 - No. 9, Mar, 1989			
Star Comics/Marvel Comics No. 3 on			
1-9		.50	1.00
BUNNY (Also see Rock Happening)			
Dec, 1966 - No. 20, Dec, 1971; No. 21, Nov, 1976			
Harvey Publications			
1: 68 pg. Giant	2.40	6.00	12.00
2-18: 68 pg. Giants	2.00	5.00	10.00
19-21: 52 pg. Giants	1.80	4.50	9.00
BURKE'S LAW (TV)			
1-3/64; No. 2, 5-7/64; No. 3, 3-5/65 (Gene Barry photo-c, all)			
Dell Publishing Co.			
1-Photo-c	4.20	12.50	25.00
2,3-Photo-c	3.20	8.00	16.00
BURNING ROMANCES (See Fox Giants)			
BUSTER BEAR			
Dec, 1953 - No. 10, June, 1955			
Quality Comics Group (Arnold Publ.)			
1-Funny animal	4.70	14.00	28.00
2	2.80	7.00	14.00
3-10	2.00	5.00	10.00
I.W. Reprint #9,10 (Super on inside)	1.00	2.50	5.00

BUSTER BROWN (Also see Brown's Blue Ribbon Book of Jokes and Jingles & Buddy Tucker & His Friends)
1903 - 1916 (11x17" strip reprints in color)
Frederick A. Stokes Co.

	GD25	FN65	VF82
...& His Resolutions (1903) by R. F. Outcault	75.00	225.00	450.00
...Abroad (1904)-86 pgs.; hardback; 8x10-1/4"; B&W; by R. F. Outcault (76 pgs.)	58.00	175.00	350.00
...His Dog Tige & Their Troubles (1904)	58.00	175.00	350.00
...Pranks (1905)	58.00	175.00	350.00
...Antics (1906)-11x17", 66 pgs.	58.00	175.00	350.00
...And Company (1906)-11x17" in color	58.00	175.00	350.00
...Mary Jane & Tige (1906)	58.00	175.00	350.00
...My Resolutions (1906)-68 pgs.; B&W; hardcover; Sunday panel reprints	58.00	175.00	350.00
Collection of Buster Brown Comics (1908)	58.00	175.00	350.00
Buster Brown Up to Date (1910)	58.00	175.00	350.00
...The Fun Maker (1912)	58.00	175.00	350.00
...The Little Rogue (1916) (10x15-3/4," 62 pgs., in color)	46.00	135.00	275.00

NOTE: *Rarely found in fine or mint condition.*

BUSTER BROWN
1904 - 1912 (3x5" to 5x7"; sizes vary) (Advertising premium booklets)
Various Publishers

The Brown Shoe Company, St. Louis, USA
(Color, 5x7", 16 pgs.set of five books)

	GD25	FN65	VF82
Brown's Blue Ribbon Book of Jokes and Jingles Book 1 (nn, 1904)-By R. F. Outcault; Buster Brown & Tige, Little Tommy Tucker, Jack & Jill, Little Boy Blue, Dainty Jane; The Yellow Kid app. on back-c (1st comic book premium)	200.00	600.00	1400.00
Buster Brown's Blue Ribbon Book of Jokes and Jingles Book 2 (1905)-Original color art by Outcault	170.00	510.00	1200.00
Buster's Book of Jokes & Jingles Book 3 (1909)-r/Blue Ribbon post cards not signed by R.F. Outcault	170.00	510.00	1200.00

	GD25	FN65	NM94
Buster's Book of Instructive Jokes and Jingles Book 4 (1910)-original color art not signed by R.F. Outcault	170.00	510.00	1200.00
...Book of Travels nn (1912, 3x5")-Original color art not signed by Outcault	72.00	215.00	500.00

NOTE: *Estimated 5 to 6 known copies exist of books #1-4.*

The Buster Brown Bread Company

"Buster Brown" Bread Book of Rhymes, The nn (1904, 4x6", 12 pgs.)-Original color art not signed by R.F. Outcault	100.00	300.00	700.00

The Buster Brown Stocking Company

Buster Brown Drawing Book, The nn (nd, 5x6", 20 pgs.)-B&W reproductions of 1903 R.F. Outcault art to trace	43.00	130.00	300.00

Collins Baking Company

Buster Brown Drawing Book nn (1904, 3x5", 12 pgs.)-Original B&W art to trace not signed by R.F. Outcault	43.00	130.00	300.00

C. H. Morton, St. Albans, VT

Merry Antics of Buster Brown, Buddy Tucker & Tige nn (nd, 3-1/2x5-1/2", 16 pgs.)-Original B&W art by R.F. Outcault	43.00	130.00	300.00

Pond's Extract

Buster Brown's Experiences With Pond's Extract nn (1904, 4-1/2x6-3/4", 28 pgs.)-Original color art by R.F. Outcault	72.00	215.00	500.00

Ringen Stove Company

Quick Meal Steel Ranges nn (nd, 3x5", 16 pgs.)-Origiinal B&W art not signed by R.F. Outcault	43.00	130.00	300.00

No Publisher Listed

The Drawiing Book nn (1906, 3-9/16x5", 8 pgs.)-Original B&W art to trace not signed by R.F. Outcault	43.00	130.00	300.00

BUSTER BROWN
1906 - 1917 (11x17" strip reprints in color)
Cupples & Leon Co./N. Y. Herald Co.
(By R. F. Outcault)

	GD25	FN65	VF82
...His Dog Tige & Their Jolly Times (1906, 58 pgs.)	54.00	160.00	325.00
...Latest Frolics (1906, 58 pgs.)	54.00	160.00	325.00
...Amusing Capers (1908, 46 pgs.)	54.00	160.00	325.00
...And His Pets (1909)	54.00	160.00	325.00
...On His Travels (1910)	54.00	160.00	325.00
...Happy Days (1911)	54.00	160.00	325.00
...In Foreign Lands (1912)	46.00	135.00	275.00
...And the Cat (1917)	46.00	135.00	275.00

NOTE: *Rarely found in fine or mint condition.*

BUSTER BROWN COMICS (Radio)(Also see My Dog Tige)
1945 - No. 43, 1959 (No. 5: paper cover)
Brown Shoe Co.

nn, nd (#1)-Covers mention diff. shoe stores	37.00	110.00	225.00
2	15.00	45.00	90.00
3-10	8.35	25.00	50.00
11-20	5.35	16.00	32.00
21-24,26-29	4.00	11.00	22.00
25,33-37,40-43-Crandall-a in all	8.35	25.00	50.00
30-32-"Interplanetary Police Vs. the Space Siren" by Crandall (also in #29 but not by Crandall)	8.35	25.00	50.00
38,39	4.00	12.00	24.00
...Goes to Mars (2/58-Western Printing), slick-c, 20 pgs., reg. size	6.70	20.00	40.00
...In "Buster Makes the Team!" (1959-Custom Comics)	4.70	14.00	28.00
...In The Jet Age ('50s), slick-c, 20 pgs., 5x7-1/4"	6.70	20.00	40.00
...Of the Safety Patrol ('60-Custom Comics)	3.60	9.00	18.00
...Out of This World ('59-Custom Comics)	4.70	14.00	28.00
...Safety Coloring Book (1958, 16 pgs.)-Slick paper	4.70	14.00	28.00

BUSTER BUNNY
Nov, 1949 - No. 16, Oct, 1953
Standard Comics(Animated Cartoons)/Pines

1-Frazetta 1 pg. text illo.	4.70	14.00	28.00
2	2.80	7.00	14.00
3-16: 15-Racist-c	2.00	5.00	10.00

BUSTER CRABBE (TV)
Nov, 1951 - No. 12, 1953
Famous Funnies Publ.

1-Frazetta anti-drug ad; text story about Buster Crabbe & Billy the Kid	22.00	65.00	150.00
2-Williamson/Evans-c; text story about Wild Bill Hickok & Pecos Bill	23.00	70.00	160.00
3-Williamson/Evans-c/a	26.00	77.00	180.00
4-Frazetta-c/a, 1pg.; bondage-c	30.00	90.00	210.00
5-Frazetta-c; Williamson/Krenkel/Orlando-a, 11pgs. (per Mr. Williamson)	85.00	255.00	600.00
6-12: 7,9-One pg. Frazetta ad in each	7.00	21.00	42.00

BUSTER CRABBE (The Amazing Adventures of..)
Dec, 1953 - No. 4, June, 1954
Lev Gleason Publications

1,4: 1-Photo-c. 4-Flash Gordon-c	10.00	30.00	70.00
2,3-Toth-a	13.00	40.00	90.00

BUTCH CASSIDY
June, 1971 - No. 3, Oct, 1971 (52 pages)
Skywald Comics

1-Red Mask reprint, retitled Maverick; Bolle-a	.40	1.00	2.00
2,3: 2-Whip Wilson-r. 3-Dead Canyon Days reprint/Crack Western No. 63; Sundance Kid app.; Crandall-a	.30	.75	1.50

BUTCH CASSIDY (...& the Wild Bunch)
1951
Avon Periodicals

1-Kinstler-c/a	11.00	32.00	75.00

NOTE: *Reinman story; Issue number on inside spine.*

BUTCH CASSIDY (See Fun-In No. 11 & Western Adventure Comics)

BUTCHER, THE (Also see Brave and the Bold, 2nd series)
May, 1990 - No. 5, Sept, 1990 ($1.50, color, mature readers)
DC Comics

1-5: 1-No indicia inside	.30	.75	1.50

BUZ SAWYER (Sweeney No. 4 on)
June, 1948 - No. 3, 1949
Standard Comics

1-Roy Crane-a	13.00	40.00	90.00
2-Intro his pal Sweeney	9.15	27.50	55.00
3	7.50	22.50	45.00

BUZ SAWYER'S PAL, ROSCOE SWEENEY (See Sweeney)

BUZZY (See All Funny Comics)
Winter, 1944-45 - No. 75, 1-2/57; No. 76, 10/57; No. 77, 10/58
National Periodical Publications/Detective Comics

1 (52 pgs. begin)	19.00	57.00	135.00
2	10.00	30.00	65.00
3-5	5.85	17.50	35.00
6-10	4.70	14.00	28.00
11-20	4.00	10.50	21.00
21-30	3.20	8.00	16.00
31,35-38	2.80	7.00	14.00
32-34,39-Last 52 pgs. Scribbly story by Mayer in each (these four stories were done for Scribbly #14 which was delayed for a year)	3.20	8.00	16.00
40-77: 62-Last precode (2/55)	2.40	6.00	12.00

Buster Brown #1 (1904), © Buster Brown

Buster Crabbe #9, © FF

Butch Cassidy #1, © AVON

Camera Comics #1, © U.S. Camera Publ.

Calling All Girls #11, © PMI

Camp Comics #3, © DELL

BUZZY THE CROW (See Harvey Hits #18 & Paramount Animated Comics #1)

CABLE - BLOOD AND METAL (See Ghost Rider &..., & New Mutants #87)
Oct, 1992 - No. 2, Nov, 1992 ($2.50, color, mini-series, 52 pgs.)
Marvel Comics

	GD25	FN65	NM94
1-Wraparound-c; Cable vs. Stryfe; Romita, Jr.-c/a in both	.60	1.50	3.00
2-Prelude to X-Cutioner's Song x-overs	.50	1.25	2.50

CADET GRAY OF WEST POINT (See Dell Giants)

CADILLACS & DINOSAURS
Nov, 1990 - No. 6, Apr, 1991 ($2.50, color, limited series, coated paper)
Epic Comics (Marvel)

	GD25	FN65	NM94
1-6: r/Xenozoic Tales in color w/new-c	.50	1.25	2.50
...In 3-D #1 (7/92, $3.95, Kitchen Sink)-W/glasses	.80	2.00	4.00

CAGE (Also see Hero for Hire, Power Man & Punisher)
Apr, 1992 - Present ($1.25, color)
Marvel Comics

	GD25	FN65	NM94
1-($1.50)-Has extra color on-c	.40	1.00	2.00
2-11,13-15: 3-Punisher-c & minor app. 9-Rhino-c/story; Hulk cameo. 10-Rhino & Hulk-c/story		.60	1.25
12-($1.75, 52 pgs.)-Iron Fist app.	.35	.90	1.75

CAGES
1991 - No. 10 ($3.50/$3.95, color, limited series)
Tundra Publ.

	GD25	FN65	NM94
1-Dave McKean-c/a in all	2.40	6.00	12.00
2-Misprint exists	1.80	4.50	9.00
3,4	1.20	3.00	6.00
5-10: 5-Begin $3.95-c	.80	2.00	4.00

CAIN'S HUNDRED (TV)
May-July, 1962 - No. 2, Sept-Nov, 1962
Dell Publishing Co.

	GD25	FN65	NM94
nn(01-094-207)	2.80	7.00	14.00
2	1.80	4.50	9.00

CALIBER PRESENTS
Jan, 1989 - No. 24?, 1991 ($1.95-$2.50, B&W, 52 pgs.)
Caliber Press

	GD25	FN65	NM94
1-Anthology; The Crow, others; Tim Vigil-c/a	1.20	3.00	6.00
2-Deadworld story; Tim Vigil-a	.80	2.00	4.00
3-14: 9-Begin $2.50-c	.60	1.50	3.00
15-24 ($3.50, 68 pgs.)	.70	1.75	3.50

CALIFORNIA GIRLS
June, 1987 - No. 8, May, 1988 ($2.00, B&W, 40pgs)
Eclipse Comics

	GD25	FN65	NM94
1-8: All contain color paper dolls	.40	1.00	2.00

CALL FROM CHRIST
1952 (36 pages) (Giveaway)
Catechetical Educational Society

	GD25	FN65	NM94
nn	2.00	5.00	10.00

CALLING ALL BOYS (Tex Granger No. 18 on)
Jan, 1946 - No. 17, May, 1948 (Photo c-1-5,7,8)
Parents' Magazine Institute

	GD25	FN65	NM94
1	4.70	14.00	28.00
2	2.80	7.00	14.00
3-7,9,11,14-17: 6-Painted-c. 11-Rin Tin Tin photo on-c. 14-J. Edgar Hoover photo on-c	2.00	5.00	10.00
8-Milton Caniff story	4.00	10.50	21.00
10-Gary Cooper photo on-c	4.00	11.00	22.00
12-Bob Hope photo on-c	5.00	15.00	30.00
13-Bing Crosby photo on-c	4.20	12.50	25.00

CALLING ALL GIRLS
Sept, 1941 - No. 89, Sept, 1949 (Part magazine, part comic)
Parents' Magazine Institute

	GD25	FN65	NM94
1	7.50	22.50	45.00
2-Photo-c	4.00	11.00	22.00
3-Shirley Temple photo-c	5.35	16.00	32.00
4-10: 4,5,7,9-Photo-c. 9-Flag-c	2.80	7.00	14.00
11-20: 11-Photo-c	2.00	5.00	10.00
21-39,41-43(10-11/45)-Last issue with comics	1.60	4.00	8.00
40-Liz Taylor photo-c	5.35	16.00	32.00
44-51(7/46)-Last comic book size issue	1.20	3.00	6.00
52-89	1.00	2.50	5.00

NOTE: ***Jack Sparling** art in many issues; becomes a girls' magazine "Senior Prom" with #90.*

CALLING ALL KIDS (Also see True Comics)
Dec-Jan, 1945-46 - No. 26, Aug, 1949
Parents' Magazine Institute

	GD25	FN65	NM94
1-Funny animal	4.35	13.00	26.00
2	2.80	7.00	14.00
3-10	1.60	4.00	8.00
11-26	1.20	3.00	6.00

CALVIN (See Li'l Kids)

CALVIN & THE COLONEL (TV)
No. 1354, Apr-June, 1962 - No. 2, July-Sept, 1962
Dell Publishing Co.

	GD25	FN65	NM94
4-Color 1354(#1)	6.70	20.00	40.00
2	5.00	15.00	30.00

CAMELOT 3000
12/82 - No. 11, 7/84; No. 12, 4/85 (Direct Sale; Mando paper)
DC Comics (Maxi-series)

	GD25	FN65	NM94
1-12: 5-Intro Knights of New Camelot	.50	1.25	2.50

NOTE: ***Austin** a-7i-12i. **Bolland** a-1-12p; c-1-12.*

CAMERA COMICS
July, 1944 - No. 9, Summer, 1946
U.S. Camera Publishing Corp./ME

	GD25	FN65	NM94
nn (7/44)	13.00	40.00	90.00
nn (9/44)	10.00	30.00	70.00
1(10/44)-The Grey Comet	10.00	30.00	70.00
2	8.35	25.00	50.00
3-Nazi WW II-c; photos	7.50	22.50	45.00
4-9: All photos	6.70	20.00	40.00

CAMP CANDY (TV)
May, 1990 - No. 6, Oct, 1990 ($1.00, color)
Marvel Comics

	GD25	FN65	NM94
1-6: Post-c/a(p); featuring John Candy		.50	1.00

CAMP COMICS
Feb, 1942 - No. 3, April, 1942 (All have photo-c)
Dell Publishing Co.

	GD25	FN65	NM94
1-"Seaman Sy Wheeler" by Kelly, 7 pgs.; Bugs Bunny app.; Mark Twain adaptation	35.00	105.00	250.00
2-Kelly-a, 12 pgs.; Bugs Bunny app.	27.00	80.00	190.00
3-(Scarce)-Dave Berg & Walt Kelly-a	35.00	105.00	250.00

CAMP RUNAMUCK (TV)
April, 1966
Dell Publishing Co.

	GD25	FN65	NM94
1-Photo-c	2.80	7.00	14.00

CAMPUS LOVES
Dec, 1949 - No. 5, Aug, 1950
Quality Comics Group (Comic Magazines)

	GD25	FN65	NM94
1-Ward-c/a (9 pgs.)	16.00	48.00	110.00

2-Ward-c/a 11.50 34.00 80.00
3-5: 5-Spanking panels (2) 6.35 19.00 38.00
NOTE: *Gustavson a-1-5. Photo c-3-5.*

CAMPUS ROMANCE (...Romances on cover)
Sept-Oct, 1949 - No. 3, Feb-Mar, 1950
Avon Periodicals/Realistic

1-Walter Johnson-a; c-/Avon paperback 348 11.50 34.00 80.00
2-Grandenetti-a; c-/Avon paperback 151 10.00 30.00 65.00
3-c-/Avon paperback 201 10.00 30.00 65.00
Realistic reprint 4.35 13.00 26.00

CANADA DRY PREMIUMS (See Swamp Fox, The & Terry & The Pirates)

CANCELLED COMIC CAVALCADE
Summer, 1978 - No. 2, Fall, 1978 (8-1/2x11"; B&W)
(Xeroxed pages on one side only w/blue cover and taped spine)
DC Comics, Inc.

1-(412 pages) Contains xeroxed copies of art for: Black Lightning #12, cover to #13; Claw #13,14; The Deserter #1; Doorway to Nightmare #6; Firestorm #6; The Green Team #2,3.
2-(532 pages) Contains xeroxed copies of art for: Kamandi #60 (including Omac), #61; Prez #5; Shade #9 (including The Odd Man); Showcase #105 (Deadman), 106 (The Creeper); The Vixen #1; and covers to Army t War #2, Bat#tle Classics #3, Demand Classics #1 & 2, Dynamic Classics #3, Mr. Miracle #26, Ragman #6, Weird Mystery #25& 26, & Western Classics #1 & 2. (Rare)
(One set sold in 1989 for $1,200.00)
NOTE: *In June, 1978, DC cancelled several of their titles. For copyright purposes, the unpublished original art for these titles was xeroxed, bound in the above books, published and distributed. Only 35 copies were made.*

CANDID TALES (Also see Bold Stories & It Rhymes With Lust)
April, 1950; June, 1950 (Digest size) (144 pages) (Full color)
Kirby Publishing Co.

nn-(Scarce) Contains Wood female pirate story, 15 pgs., and 14 pgs. in June issue; Powell-a 47.00 140.00 325.00
NOTE: *Another version exists with Dr. Kilmore by Wood; no female pirate story.*

CANDY
Fall, 1944 - No. 3, Spring, 1945
William H. Wise & Co.

1-Two Scoop Scuttle stories by Wolverton 18.00 54.00 125.00
2,3-Scoop Scuttle by Wolverton, 2-4 pgs. 14.00 43.00 100.00

CANDY (Teen-age)(Also see Police Comics #37)
Autumn, 1947 - No. 64, July, 1956
Quality Comics Group (Comic Magazines)

1-Gustavson-a 10.00 30.00 70.00
2-Gustavson-a 5.85 17.50 35.00
3-10 4.00 11.00 22.00
11-30 2.80 7.00 14.00
31-63 2.40 6.00 12.00
64-Ward-c(p)? 3.00 7.50 15.00
Super Reprint No. 2,10,12,16,17,18('63-'64) 1.20 3.00 6.00
NOTE: *Jack Cole 1-2 pg. art in many issues.*

CANNONBALL COMICS
Feb, 1945 - No. 2, Mar, 1945
Rural Home Publishing Co.

1-The Crash Kid, Thunderbrand, The Captive Prince & Crime Crusader begin; skull-c 37.00 110.00 220.00
2-Devil-c 28.00 85.00 170.00

CANTEEN KATE (See All Picture All True Love Story & Fightin' Marines)
June, 1952 - No. 3, Nov, 1952
St. John Publishing Co.

1-Matt Baker-c/a 26.00 77.00 180.00
2-Matt Baker-c/a 22.00 65.00 150.00
3-(Rare)-Used in **POP**, pg. 75; Baker-c/a 26.00 77.00 180.00

CAP'N CRUNCH COMICS (See Quaker Oats)
1963; 1965 (16 pgs.; miniature giveaways; 2x6")
Quaker Oats Co.

(1963 titles)-"The Picture Pirates," "The Fountain of Youth," "I'm Dreaming of a Wide Isthmus." (1965 titles)-"Bewitched, Betwitched, & Betweaked," "Seadog Meets the Witch Doctor" (another 1965 title suspected) 3.00 7.50 15.00

CAP'N QUICK & A FOOZLE (Eclipse)(Value: cover or less)

CAPTAIN ACTION
Oct-Nov, 1968 - No. 5, June-July, 1969 (Based on Ideal toy)
National Periodical Publications

1-Origin; Wood-a; Superman-c app. 6.70 20.00 40.00
2,3,5-Kane/Wood-a 4.20 12.50 25.00
4 4.00 10.00 20.00
...& Action Boy('67)-Ideal Toy Co. giveaway 7.50 22.50 45.00

CAPTAIN AERO COMICS (Samson No. 1-6; also see Veri Best Sure Fire & Veri Best Sure Shot Comics)
V1#7(#1), Dec, 1941 - V2#4(#10), Jan, 1943; V3#9(#11), Sept, 1943 - V4#3(#17), Oct, 1944; #21, Dec, 1944 - #26, Aug, 1946 (No #18-20)
Holyoke Publishing Co.

V1#7(#1)-Flag-Man & Solar, Master of Magic, Captain Aero, Cap Stone, Adventurer begin 75.00 225.00 450.00
8(#2)-Pals of Freedom app. 42.00 125.00 250.00
9(#3)-Alias X begins; Pals of Freedom app. 42.00 125.00 250.00
10(#4)-Origin The Gargoyle; Kubert-a 42.00 125.00 250.00
11,12(#5,6)-Kubert-a; Miss Victory in #6 35.00 105.00 210.00
V2#1,2(#7,8): 8-Origin The Red Cross; Miss Victory app. 20.00 60.00 120.00
3(#9)-Miss Victory app. 15.00 45.00 90.00
4(#10)-Miss Victory app. 12.00 35.00 70.00
V3#9 - V3#13(#11-15): 11,15-Miss Victory app. 9.15 27.50 55.00
V4#2, V4#3(#16,17) 7.50 22.50 45.00
21-24,26-L. B. Cole covers. 22-Intro/origin Mighty Mite 10.00 32.00 65.00
25-L. B. Cole S/F-c 13.00 40.00 80.00
NOTE: ***L.B. Cole** c-17. **Hollingsworth** a-23. **Infantino** a-23. **Schomburg** c-15, 16*

CAPTAIN AMERICA (See Adventures of..., All-Select, All Winners, Aurora, Avengers #4, Blood and Glory, Giant-Size..., The Invaders, Marvel Double Feature, Marvel Fanfare, Marvel Mystery, Marvel Super-Action, Marvel Super Heroes V2#3, Marvel Team-Up, Marvel Treasury Special, Power Record Comics, USA Comics, Young Allies & Young Men)

CAPTAIN AMERICA (Formerly Tales of Suspense #1-99; Captain America and the Falcon #134-223 on cover only)
No. 100, April, 1968 - Present
Marvel Comics Group

100-Flashback on Cap's revival with Avengers & Sub-Mariner; story continued from Tales of Suspense #99 40.00 122.00 285.00
101 10.00 30.00 65.00
102-108 6.70 20.00 40.00
109-Origin Capt. America 8.35 25.00 50.00
110,111,113-Steranko-c/a. 110-Rick becomes Cap's partner; Hulk x-over; 1st app. Viper. 111-Death of Steve Rogers. 113-Cap's funeral 8.35 25.00 50.00
112-Origin retold 4.00 11.00 22.00
114-116,118-120: 115-Last 12 cent issue 3.20 8.00 16.00
117-1st app. The Falcon (9/69) 4.70 14.00 28.00
121-140: 121-Retells origin. 133-The Falcon becomes Cap's partner; origin Modok. 137,138-Spider-Man x-over. 140-Origin Grey Gargoyle retold 1.80 4.50 9.00
141-153,155-171,176-179: 142-Last 15 cent issue. 143-(52 pgs.). 153-1st app. (cameo) Jack Monroe. 155-Origin; redrawn with Falcon added; origin Jack Monroe. 160-1st app. Solarr. 164-1st app. Nightshade. 176-End of Capt. America 1.20 3.00 6.00
154-1st full app. Jack Monroe (Nomad)(10/72) 1.60 4.00 8.00
172-175-X-Men x-over 2.20 5.50 11.00
180,181,183: 180-Intro/origin of Nomad; Steve Rogers becomes Nomad. 181-Intro & origin of new Capt. America. 183-Death of New Cap; Nomad

Canteen Kate #3, © STJ

Captain Aero #25, © HOKE

Captain America #107, © MEG

Captain America #235, © MEG

Captain America Comics #1, © MEG

Captain America Comics #59, © MEG

GD25 FN65 NM94

becomes Cap 1.00 2.50 5.00
182,184-200(8/76): 186-True origin The Falcon .80 2.00 4.00
201-240,242-246: 215-Retells Cap's origin. 216-r/story from Strange Tales #114. 217-1st app. Marvel Man (later Quasar). 229-Marvel Man app. 230-Battles Hulk-c/story cont'd in Hulk #232. 233-Death of Sharon Carter. 234, 235-Daredevil x-over; 235(7/79)-Miller pencils. 244,245-Miller-c .60 1.50 3.00
241-Punisher app.; Miller-c 8.35 25.00 50.00
247-255-Byrne-a. 255-Origin; Miller-c .70 1.75 3.50
256-281,284,285,289-322,324-326,329-331: 264-Old X-Men cameo in flash-back. 265,266-Nick Fury & Spider-Man app. 267-1st app. Everyman. 269-1st Team America. 281-'50s Bucky returns. 284-Patriot (Jack Mace) app. 285-Death of Patriot. 298-Origin Red Skull .40 1.00 2.00
282-Bucky becomes new Nomad (Jack Monroe) 1.60 4.00 8.00
282-Silver ink 2nd print ($1.75) w/orig. date (6/83) .35 .90 1.75
283-2nd app. Nomad .80 2.00 4.00
286-288-Deathlok app. .60 1.50 3.00
323-1st app. new Super Patriot (see Nick Fury) .80 2.00 4.00
327-Captain America battles Super Patriot .60 1.50 3.00
328-Origin & 1st app. D-Man .60 1.50 3.00
332-Old Cap resigns 2.00 5.00 10.00
333-Intro new Captain (Super Patriot) 1.40 3.50 7.00
334 1.10 2.75 5.50
335-340: 339-Fall of the Mutants tie-in 1.00 2.50 5.00
341-343,345-349 .35 .85 1.70
344-($1.50, 52 pgs.) .45 1.10 2.20
350-($1.75, 68 pgs.)-Return of Steve Rogers (original Cap) to original costume .90 2.25 4.50
351-354: 351-Nick Fury app. 354-1st app. U.S. Agent (see Avengers West Coast) .35 .85 1.70
355-382,384-396: 373-Bullseye app. 375-Daredevil app. 386-U.S. Agent app. 387-389-Red Skull back-up stories. 396-Last $1.00-c. 396,397-1st app. all new Jack O'Lantern .30 .75 1.50
383-($2.00, 68 pgs.)-50th anniversary issue; Red Skull story; Jim Lee-c(i) 1.00 2.50 5.00
397-399,401-416: 402-Begin 6 part Man-Wolf story w/Wolverine in #403-407. 405-410-New Jack O'Lantern app. 406-Cable & Shatterstar cameo. 407-Capwolf vs. Cable-c/story. 408-Infinity War x-over; Falcon solo back-up .60 1.25
400-($2.25, 84 pgs.)-Flip book format w/double gatefold-c; r/Avengers #4 plus-c; contains cover pin-ups .70 1.75 3.50
Special 1(1/71)-Origin retold 3.00 7.50 15.00
Special 2(1/72)-Colan-r/Not Brand Echh; all-r 2.40 12.00 12.00
Annual 3-7: 3(1976). 4(1977, 52pgs.)-Kirby-c/a(new); Magneto app. 5('81, 52pgs.). 6('82, 52pgs.). 7('83, 52pgs.) .50 1.25 2.50
Annual 8(9/86)-Wolverine-c/story 7.50 22.50 45.00
Annual 9(1990, $2.00, 68 pgs.)-Nomad back-up 1.00 2.50 5.00
Annual 10('91, $2.00, 68 pgs.)-Origin retold(2 pgs.) .40 1.00 2.00
Annual 11(1992, $2.25, 68 pgs.)-Falcon solo story .45 1.15 2.25
...: The Movie Special nn (5/92, $3.50, 52 pgs.)-Adapts movie; printed on coated stock; The Red Skull app. .70 1.75 3.50
...& The Campbell Kids (1980, 36pg. giveaway, Campbell's Soup/U.S. Dept. of Energy) .40 1.00 2.00
...Fights in the War Against Drugs (1990, no #, giveaway)-Distributed to direct sales shops; 2nd printing exists .50 1.00
...Meets the Asthma Monster (1987, no #, giveaway, Your Physician and Glaxo, Inc.) .50 1.00
...Vs. Asthma Monster (1990, no #, giveaway, Your Physician & Allen & Hanbury's) .50 1.00

NOTE: ***Austin*** *c-225i, 239i, 246i.* ***Buscema*** *a-115p, 217p; c-136p, 217.* ***Byrne*** *c-223(part), 238, 239, 247p-254p, 290, 291, 313p; a-247-254p, 255, 313p, 350.* ***Colan*** *a(p)-116-137, 256, Annual 5; c(p)-116-123, 126, 129.* ***Everett*** *a-136i, 137i; c-126i.* ***Gil Kane*** *a-145p; c-147p, 149p, 150p, 170p, 172-174, 180, 181p, 183-190p, 215, 216, 220, 221.* ***Kirby*** *a(p)-100-109, 112, 193-214, 216, Special 1, 2(layouts), Annual 3, 4; c-100-109, 112, 126p, 193-214.* ***Ron Lim*** *a(p)-366, 368-378, 380-386; c-366p, 368-378p, 379, 380-393p.* ***Miller*** *c-241p, 244p, 245p, 255p, Annual 5.* ***Mooney*** *a-149i.* ***Morrow*** *a-144.* ***Perez*** *c-243p, 246p.* ***Robbins*** *c(p)-183-187, 189-192, 225.* ***Roussos*** *a-140i, 168i.* ***Starlin/Sinnott*** *c-162.* ***Sutton*** *a-244i.* ***Tuska*** *a-112i, 215p, Special 2.* ***Williamson*** *a-313i.* ***Wood*** *a-127i.*

CAPTAIN AMERICA COMICS

Mar, 1941 - No. 75, Jan, 1950; No. 76, 5/54 - No. 78, 9/54
(No. 74 & 75 titled Capt. America's Weird Tales)
Timely/Marvel Comics (TCI 1-20/CmPS 21-68/MjMC 69-75/Atlas Comics (PrPI 76-78)

GD25 FN65 VF82 NM94

1-Origin & 1st app. Captain America & Bucky by S&K; Hurricane, Tuk the Caveboy begin by S&K; Red Skull app. Hitler-c 3,000.00 9,000.00 18,000.00 30,000.00
(Estimated up to 180 total copies exist, 8 in NM/Mint)

GD25 FN65 NM94

2-S&K Hurricane; Tuk by Avison (Kirby splash); classic Hitler-c 750.00 2250.00 4500.00
3-Red Skull-c & app; Stan Lee's 1st text (1st work for Marvel) 500.00 1500.00 3000.00
4-1st full page panel in comics 350.00 1050.00 2100.00
5 317.00 950.00 1900.00
6-Origin Father Time; Tuk the Caveboy ends 240.00 800.00 1600.00
7-Red Skull app.; classic-c 283.00 850.00 1700.00
8-10-Last S&K issue, (S&K centerfold #6-10) 217.00 650.00 1300.00
11-Last Hurricane, Headline Hunter; Al Avison Captain America begins, ends #20; Avison-c(p) 175.00 525.00 1050.00
12-The Imp begins, ends #16; last Father Time 167.00 500.00 1000.00
13-Origin The Secret Stamp; classic-c 183.00 550.00 1100.00
14,15 167.00 500.00 1000.00
16-Red Skull unmasks Cap 192.00 575.00 1150.00
17-The Fighting Fool only app. 145.00 435.00 875.00
18,19-Human Torch begins #19 125.00 375.00 750.00
20-Sub-Mariner app.; no H. Torch 125.00 375.00 750.00
21-25: 25-Cap drinks liquid opium 117.00 350.00 700.00
26-30,36: 27-Last Secret Stamp; last 68 pg. issue? 28-60 pg. issues begin? 36-Hitler-c 110.00 325.00 650.00
31-35,38-40: 34-Centerfold poster of Cap 92.00 275.00 550.00
37-Red Skull app. 100.00 300.00 600.00
41-47: 41-Last Jap War-c. 46-German Holocaust-c. 47-Last German War-c 80.00 235.00 475.00
48-58,60 75.00 225.00 450.00
59-Origin retold 150.00 450.00 900.00
61-Red Skull-c/story 125.00 375.00 750.00
62,64,65: 65-"Hey Look" by Kurtzman 80.00 235.00 475.00
63-Intro/origin Asbestos Lady 83.00 250.00 500.00
66-Bucky is shot; Golden Girl teams up with Captain America & learns his i.d; origin Golden Girl 92.00 275.00 550.00
67-Captain America/Golden Girl team-up; Mxyztplk swipe; last Toro in Human Torch 75.00 225.00 450.00
68,70-Sub-Mariner/Namora, and Captain America/Golden Girl team-up in each. 70-Science fiction-c/story 75.00 225.00 450.00
69,71-73: 69-Human Torch/Sun Girl team-up. 71-Anti Wertham editorial; The Witness, Bucky app. 75.00 225.00 450.00
74-(Scarce)(1949)-Titled "C.A.'s Weird Tales;" Red Skull app. 125.00 375.00 750.00
75(2/50)-Titled "C.A.'s Weird Tales;" no C.A. app.; horror cover/stories 75.00 225.00 450.00
76-78(1954): Human Torch/Toro stories 50.00 150.00 300.00
132-Pg. Issue (B&W-1942)(Canadian)-Has blank inside-c and back-c; contains Marvel Mystery #33 & Capt. America #18 w/cover from Capt. America #22; same contents as Marvel Mystery annual 467.00 1400.00 2800.00
Shoestore Giveaway #77 27.50 82.00 165.00

NOTE: ***Crandall*** *a-2i, 3i, 9i, 10i.* ***Kirby*** *c-8p.* ***Rico*** *c-69-71.* ***Romita*** *c-77, 78.* ***Schomburg*** *c-3, 4, 26-29, 31, 33, 37-39, 41, 42, 45-54, 58.* ***Sekowsky*** *c-55, 56.* ***Shores*** *c-1, 2, 5-7, 11i, 20-25, 30, 32, 34, 35, 40, 57, 59-67.* ***S&K*** *c-1, 2, 5-7, 9, 10. Bondage c-3, 7, 15, 16, 34, 38.*

CAPTAIN AMERICA SPECIAL EDITION

Feb, 1984 - No. 2, Mar, 1984 ($2.00, Baxter paper)
Marvel Comics Group
1,2-Steranko-c/a(r) .50 1.25 2.50

CAPTAIN AND THE KIDS, THE (See Famous Comics Cartoon Books)

CAPTAIN AND THE KIDS, THE (See Comics on Parade, Okay Comics & Sparkler Comics)
1938 -12/39; Sum, 1947 - No. 32, 1955; 4-Color No. 881, Feb, 1958
United Features Syndicate/Dell Publ. Co.
Single Series 1('38) 54.00 160.00 375.00
Single Series 1(Reprint)(12/39-"Reprint" on-c) 30.00 90.00 210.00
1(Summer, 1947-UFS) 9.15 27.50 55.00
2 5.00 15.00 30.00
3-10 4.00 10.50 21.00
11-20 3.20 8.00 16.00
21-32(1955) 2.40 6.00 12.00
50th Anniversary issue('48)-Contains a 2 page history of the strip, including an account of the famous Supreme Court decision allowing both Pulitzer & Hearst to run the same strip under different names 5.35 16.00 32.00
Special Summer issue, Fall issue (1948) 4.00 11.00 22.00
4-Color 881 (Dell) 3.20 8.00 16.00

CAPTAIN ATOM
1950 - No. 7, 1951 (5x7-1/4") (5 cents, 52 pgs.)
Nationwide Publishers
1-Sci/fic 14.00 43.00 100.00
2-7 9.15 27.50 55.00
...- Secret of the Columbian Jungle (16 pgs. in color, paper-c, 3-3/4x5-1/8")-Fireside Marshmallow giveaway 3.20 800 16.00

CAPTAIN ATOM (Formerly Strange Suspense Stories No. 77)
V2#78, Dec, 1965 - V2#89, Dec, 1967 (Also see Space Adventures)
Charlton Comics
78-Origin retold; Bache-a (3 pgs.) 8.35 25.00 50.00
79-82: 82-Intro. Nightshade (9/66) 5.00 15.00 30.00
83-86: Ted Kord Blue Beetle in all. 83-(11/66)-1st app. Ted Kord. 84-1st app. new Captain Atom 4.20 12.50 25.00
87-89-Nightshade by Aparo in all 4.20 12.50 25.00
83-85(Modern Comics-1977)-reprints .50 1.00
NOTE: ***Aparo** a-87-89. **Ditko** c/a(p) 78-89. #90 only published in fanzine 'The Charlton Bullseye' #1, 2*

CAPTAIN ATOM (Also see Americomics & Crisis On Infinite Earths)
March, 1987 - No. 57, Sept, 1991 (Direct sale only #35 on)
DC Comics
1-(44 pgs.)-Origin/1st app. with new costume .40 1.00 2.00
2-49: 5-Firestorm x-over. 6-Intro. new Dr. Spectro. 11-Millennium tie-in. 14-Nightshade app. 16-Justice League app. 17-$1.00-c begins; Swamp Thing app. 20-Blue Beetle x-over .60 1.20
50-($2.00, 52 pgs.) .40 1.00 2.00
51-57: 57-War of the Gods x-over .50 1.00
Annual 1 (1988, $1.25)-Intro Major Force .30 .75 1.50
Annual 2 (1988, $1.50) .30 .75 1.50

CAPTAIN BATTLE (Boy Comics #3 on) (See Silver Streak Comics)
Summer, 1941 - No. 2, Fall, 1941
New Friday Publ./Comic House
1-Origin Blackout by Rico; Captain Battle begins 75.00 225.00 450.00
2 50.00 150.00 300.00

CAPTAIN BATTLE (2nd Series)
No. 3, Wint, 1942-43 - No. 5, Sum, 1943 (#3: 52pgs., nd)(#5: 68pgs.)
Magazine Press/Picture Scoop No. 5
3-Origin Silver Streak-r/SS#3; Origin Lance Hale-r/Silver Streak; Simon-a(r) 46.00 135.00 275.00
4,5: 5-Origin Blackout retold 33.00 100.00 200.00

CAPTAIN BATTLE, JR.
Fall, 1943 - No. 2, Winter, 1943-44
Comic House (Lev Gleason)
1-The Claw vs. The Ghost 63.00 185.00 375.00
2-Wolverton's Scoop Scuttle; Don Rico-c/a; The Green Claw story is reprinted from Silver Streak #6 50.00 150.00 300.00

CAPTAIN BRITAIN (Also see Marvel Team-Up No. 65,66)
Oct. 13, 1976 - No. 39, July 6, 1977 (Weekly)
Marvel Comics International
1-Origin; with Capt. Britain's face mask inside 1.00 2.50 5.00
2-Origin, conclusion; Capt. Britain's Boomerang inside .70 1.80 3.60
3-8: 3,8-Vs. Bank Robbers. 4-7-Vs. Hurricane .40 1.00 2.00
9-15: 9-13-Vs. Dr. Synne. 14,15-Vs. Mastermind .35 .90 1.80
16-20-With Capt. America; 17 misprinted & color section reprinted in #18 .35 .90 1.80
21-23,25,26-With Capt. America .35 .90 1.80
24-With C.B.'s Jet Plane inside .70 1.80 3.60
27,33-35: 27-Origin retold. 33-35-More on origin .35 .90 1.80
28-32,36-39: 28-32-Vs. Lord Hawk. 36-Star Sceptre. 37-39-Vs. Highwayman & Munipulator .30 .75 1.50
Annual (1978, Hardback, 64 pgs.)-Reprints #1-7 with pin-ups of Marvel characters 1.60 4.00 8.00
Summer Special (1980, 52 pgs.)-Reprints .40 1.00 2.00
NOTE: *No. 1, 2, & 24 are rarer in mint due to inserts. Distributed in Great Britain only. Nick Fury-r by **Steranko** in 1-20, 24-31, 35-37. Fantastic Four-r by **J. Buscema** in all. New **Buscema**-a in 24-30. Story from No. 39 continues in Super Spider-Man (British weekly) No. 231-247. Following cancellation of his series, new Captain Britain stories appeared in 'Super Spider-Man" (British weekly) No. 231-247. Captain Britain stories which appear in Super-Spider-Man No 248-253 are reprints of Marvel Team-Up No. 65&66. Capt. Britain strips also appeared in Hulk Comic (weekly) 1, 3-30, 42-55, 57-60, in Marvel Superheroes (monthly) 377-388, in Daredevils (monthly) 1-11, Mighty World of Marvel (monthly) 7-16 & Captain Britain (monthly) 1-present.*

CAPTAIN CANUCK
7/75 - No. 4, 7/77; No. 4, 7-8/79 - No. 14, 3-4/81
Comely Comix (Canada) (All distr. in U. S.)
1-1st app. Bluefox .50 1.25 2.50
2-1st app. Dr. Walker, Redcoat & Kebec .35 .90 1.80
3(5-7/76)-1st app. Heather .35 .90 1.80
4(1st printing-2/77)-10x14-1/2"; (5.00); B&W; 300 copies serially numbered and signed with one certificate of authenticity 3.00 7.50 15.00
4(2nd printing-7/77)-11x17", B&W; only 15 copies printed; signed by creator Richard Comely, serially #'d and two certificates of authenticity inserted; orange cardboard covers (Very Rare) 5.00 15.00 30.00
4-14: 4(7-8/79)-1st app. Tom Evans & Mr. Gold; origin The Catman. 5-Origin Capt. Canuck's powers; 1st app. Earth Patrol & Chaos Corps. 8-Jonn 'The Final Chapter'. 9-1st World Beyond. 11-1st 'Chariots of Fire' story .50 1.00
Summer Special 1(7-9/80, 95 cents, 64pgs.) .50 1.00
NOTE: *30,000 copies of No. 2 were destroyed in Winnipeg.*

CAPTAIN CARROT AND HIS AMAZING ZOO CREW
March, 1982 - No. 20, Nov, 1983 (Also see New Teen Titans)
DC Comics
1-20: 1-Superman app. 3-Re-intro Dodo & The Frog. 9-Re-intro Three Mouseketeers, the Terrific Whatzit. 10,11- Pig Iron reverts back to Peter Porkchops. 20-The Changeling app. .50 1.00

CAPTAIN CARVEL AND HIS CARVEL CRUSADERS (See Carvel Comics)

CAPTAIN CONFEDERACY
Nov, 1991 - No. 4, Feb, 1992 ($1.95, color)
Epic Comics (Marvel)
1-4: All new stories .40 1.00 2.00

CAPTAIN COURAGEOUS COMICS (Banner No. 3-5)
No. 6, March, 1942
Periodical House (Ace Magazines)

Captain and the Kids #17, © UFS

Captain Atom #86 (Charlton), © DC

Captain Battle #5, © LEV

Captain Flash #2, © Sterling Comics

Captain Flight #11, © Four Star

Captain Gallant #2, © CC

GD25 FN65 NM94

6-Origin & 1st app. The Sword; Lone Warrior, Capt. Courageous app. 54.00 162.00 325.00

CAPT'N CRUNCH COMICS (See Cap'n...)

CAPTAIN DAVY JONES (See 4-Color No. 598)

CAPTAIN EASY (See The Funnies & Red Ryder #3-32)
1939 - No. 17, Sept, 1949; April, 1956
Hawley/Dell Publ./Standard(Visual Editions)/Argo

nn-Hawley(1939)-Contains reprints from The Funnies & 1938 Sunday strips by Roy Crane 43.00 130.00 300.00
4-Color 24 (1943) 29.00 86.00 200.00
4-Color 111(6/46)-Spanking panels 11.00 32.00 75.00
10(Standard-10/47) 6.70 20.00 40.00
11-17: All contain 1930's & '40's strip-r 4.70 14.00 28.00
Argo 1(4/56)-Reprints 4.70 14.00 28.00
NOTE: *Schomburg c-13, 16.*

CAPTAIN EASY & WASH TUBBS (See Famous Comics Cartoon Books)

CAPTAIN ELECTRON (Brick Computer)(Value: cover or less)

CAPTAIN EO 3-D (Eclipse)(Value: cover or less) (Disney)

CAPTAIN FEARLESS COMICS (Also see Holyoke One-Shot #6, Old Glory Comics & Silver Streak #1)
August, 1941 - No. 2, Sept, 1941
Helnit Publishing Co. (Holyoke Publishing Co.)

1-Origin Mr. Miracle, Alias X, Captain Fearless, Citizen Smith Son of the Unknown Soldier; Miss Victory begins (1st patriotic heroine? before Wonder Woman) 50.00 150.00 300.00
2-Grit Grady, Captain Stone app. 30.00 90.00 180.00

CAPTAIN FLASH
Nov, 1954 - No. 4, July, 1955
Sterling Comics

1-Origin; Sekowsky-a; Tomboy (female super hero) begins; last pre-code issue 17.00 52.00 120.00
2-4 10.00 30.00 70.00

CAPTAIN FLEET
Fall, 1952
Ziff-Davis Publishing Co.

1-Painted-c 10.00 30.00 60.00

CAPTAIN FLIGHT COMICS
Mar, 1944 - No. 10, Dec, 1945; No. 11, Feb-Mar, 1947
Four Star Publications

nn 14.00 41.00 95.00
2 8.35 25.00 50.00
3,4: 4-Rock Raymond begins, ends #7 7.50 22.50 45.00
5-Bondage, torture-c; Red Rocket begins; the Grenade app. 10.00 30.00 65.00
6,7: 7-L. B. Cole covers begin, end #11 8.35 25.00 50.00
8,9: 8-Yankee Girl, Black Cobra begin; intro. Cobra Kid. 9-Torpedoman app.; last Yankee Girl; Kinstler-a 13.00 40.00 80.00
10-Deep Sea Dawson, Zoom of the Jungle, Rock Raymond, Red Rocket, & Black Cobra app; bondage-c 13.00 40.00 80.00
11-Torpedoman, Blue Flame app.; last Black Cobra, Red Rocket; L. B. Cole-c 13.00 40.00 80.00

CAPTAIN FORTUNE PRESENTS
1955 - 1959 (16 pages; 3-1/4x6-7/8") (Giveaway)
Vital Publications

"Davy Crockett in Episodes of the Creek War," "Davy Crockett at the Alamo," "In Sherwood Forest Tells Strange Tales of Robin Hood" ('57), "Meets Bolivar the Liberator" ('59), "Tells How Buffalo Bill Fights the Dog Soldiers" ('57), "Young Davy Crockett" 1.60 4.00 8.00

CAPTAIN GALLANT (...of the Foreign Legion) (TV)
(Texas Rangers in Action No. 5 on?)
1955: No. 2, Jan, 1956 - No. 4, Sept, 1956
Charlton Comics

Heinz Foods Premium (#1?)(1955; regular size)-U.S. Pictorial; contains Buster Crabbe photos; Don Heck-a 1.60 4.00 8.00
Non-Heinz version (same as above except pictures of show replaces ads) (#1)-Buster Crabbe photo on-c 6.70 20.00 40.00
2-4: Buster Crabbe in all 5.85 17.50 35.00

CAPTAIN HERO (See Jughead as...)

CAPTAIN HERO COMICS DIGEST MAGAZINE
Sept, 1981
Archie Publications

1-Reprints of Jughead as Super-Guy .50 1.00

CAPTAIN HOBBY COMICS
Feb, 1948 (Canadian)
Export Publication Ent. Ltd. (Dist. in U.S. by Kable News Co.)

1 4.20 12.50 25.00

CAPT. HOLO IN 3-D (See Blackthorne 3-D Series #65)

CAPTAIN HOOK & PETER PAN (See 4-Color No. 446 and Peter Pan)

CAPTAIN JET (Fantastic Fears No. 7 on)
May, 1952 - No. 5, Jan, 1953
Four Star Publ./Farrell/Comic Media

1-Bakerish-a 10.00 30.00 65.00
2 7.50 22.50 45.00
3-5,6(?) 4.70 14.00 28.00

CAPTAIN JUSTICE
March, 1988 - No. 2, April, 1988
Marvel Comics

1,2-Based on TV series, True Colors .60 1.25

CAPTAIN KANGAROO (See 4-Color No. 721, 780, 872)

CAPTAIN KIDD (Formerly Dagar; My Secret Story #26 on)(Also see Comic Comics & Fantastic Comics)
No. 24, June, 1949 - No. 25, Aug, 1949
Fox Feature Syndicate

24,25 10.00 30.00 60.00

CAPTAIN MARVEL (See All Hero, All-New Collectors' Ed., America's Greatest, Fawcett Min., Gift, Legends, Limited Collectors' Ed., Marvel Family, Master No. 21, Mighty Midget Comics, Shazam, Special Edition Comics, Whiz, Wisco, and XMas Comics)

CAPTAIN MARVEL (Becomes ...Presents the Terrible 5 No. 5)
April, 1966 - No. 4, Nov, 1966 (25 cent Giants)
M. F. Enterprises

nn-(#1 on pg. 5)-Origin; created by Carl Burgos 2.80 7.00 14.00
2-4: 3-(#3 on page 4)-Fights the Bat 1.60 4.00 8.00

CAPTAIN MARVEL (See Giant-Size..., Life Of..., Marvel Graphic Novel #1, Marvel Spotlight V2#1 & Marvel Super-Heroes #12)
May, 1968 - No. 19, Dec, 1969; No. 20, June, 1970 - No. 21, Aug, 1970; No. 22, Sept, 1972 - No. 62, May, 1979
Marvel Comics Group

1 13.00 40.00 90.00
2 4.70 14.00 28.00
3-5: 4-Captain Marvel battles Sub-Mariner 3.60 9.00 18.00
6-11: 11-Capt. Marvel given great power by Zo the Ruler; Smith/Trimpe-c; Death of Una 2.40 6.00 12.00
12-24: 14-Capt. Marvel vs. Iron Man; last 12 cent issue. 16,17-New costume. 21-Capt. Marvel battles Hulk; last 15 cent issue 1.80 4.50 9.00
25-Starlin-c/a begins; Starlin's 1st Thanos saga begins (3/73), ends #34; Thanos cameo (5 panels) 4.70 14.00 28.00
26-2nd full app. Thanos (see Iron Man #55); 1st Thanos-c

	GD25	FN65	NM94
	5.85	17.50	35.00
27,28-3rd & 4th app. Thanos. 28-Thanos-c	4.20	12.50	25.00
29,30-Thanos cameos. 29-C.M. gains more powers	2.00	5.00	10.00
31,32: Thanos app. 31-Last 20 cent issue. 32-Thanos-c	3.00	7.50	15.00
33-Thanos-c & app.; Capt. Marvel battles Thanos; 1st origin Thanos	5.00	15.00	30.00
34-1st app. Nitro; C.M. contracts cancer which eventually kills him last; Starlin-c/a & last 20 cent issue	1.40	3.50	7.00
35,37-56,58-62: 39-Origin Watcher. 41,43-Wrightson part inks; #43-c(i). 49-Starlin & Weiss-p assists	.30	.75	1.50
36-Reprints origin/1st app. Capt. Marvel from Marvel Super-Heroes #12; Starlin-a (3 pgs.)	1.00	2.50	5.00
57-Thanos appears in flashback	1.40	3.50	7.00

NOTE: ***Alcala** a-35. **Austin** a-46i, 49-53i; c-52i. **Buscema** a-18p-21p. **Colan** a(p)-1-4; c(p)-1-4, 8, 9. **Heck** a-5p-10p, 16p. **Gil Kane** a-17-21p; c-17-24p, 37p, 53. **McWilliams** a-40i. #25-34 were reprinted in The Life of Captain Marvel.*

CAPTAIN MARVEL
Nov, 1989 ($1.50, color, one-shot, 52 pgs.)
Marvel Comics

	GD25	FN65	NM94
1-Super-hero from Avengers; new powers	.30	.75	1.50

CAPTAIN MARVEL ADVENTURES (See Special Edition Comics for pre #1)
1941 (March) - No. 150, Nov, 1953 (#1 on stands 1/16/41)
Fawcett Publications

	GD25	FN65	VF82	NM94
nn(#1)-Captain Marvel & Sivana by Jack Kirby. The cover was printed on unstable paper stock and is rarely found in Fine or Mint condition; blank blank inside-c	1600.00	4800.00	9600.00	16,000.00

(Estimated up to 140 total copies exist, 3 in NM/Mint)

	GD25	FN65	NM94
2-(Advertised as #3, which was counting Special Edition Comics as the real #1); Tuska-a	267.00	800.00	1600.00
3-Metallic silver-c	167.00	500.00	1000.00
4-Three Lt. Marvels app.	117.00	350.00	700.00
5	92.00	275.00	550.00
6-10: 9-1st Otto Binder scripts on Capt. Marvel	67.00	200.00	400.00
11-15: 13-Two-pg. Capt. Marvel pin-up. 15-Comic cards on back-c begin, end #26	54.00	162.00	325.00
16,17: 17-Painted-c	50.00	150.00	300.00
18-Origin & 1st app. Mary Marvel & Marvel Family (12/11/42); painted-c; Mary Marvel by Marcus Swayze	83.00	250.00	500.00
19-Mary Marvel x-over; Christmas-c	46.00	138.00	275.00
20,21-Attached to the cover, each has a miniature comic just like the Mighty Midget Comics #11, except that each has a full color promo ad on the back cover. Most copies were circulated without the miniature comic. These issues with miniatures attached are very rare, and should not be mistaken for copies with the similar Mighty Midget glued in its place. The Mighty Midgets had blank back covers except for a small victory stamp seal. Only the Capt. Marvel and Captain Marvel Jr. No. 11 miniatures have been positively documented as having been affixed tothese covers. Each miniature was only partially glued by its back cover to the Captain Marvel comic making it easy to see if it's the genuine miniature rather than a Mighty Midget. with comic attached....	250.00	750.00	1500.00
20,21-Without miniature	42.00	125.00	250.00
22-Mr. Mind serial begins	62.00	188.00	375.00
23-25	42.00	125.00	250.00
26-30: 26-Flag-c	33.00	100.00	200.00
31-35: 35-Origin Radar	29.00	88.00	175.00
36-40: 37-Mary Marvel x-over	25.00	75.00	150.00
41-46: 42-Christmas-c. 43-Capt. Marvel 1st meets Uncle Marvel; Mary Batson cameo. 46-Mr. Mind serial ends	22.00	65.00	130.00
47-50	18.00	55.00	110.00
51-53,55-60: 52-Origin & 1st app. Sivana Jr.; Capt. Marvel Jr. x-over	15.00	45.00	90.00
54-Special oversize 68 pg. issue	17.00	50.00	100.00
61-The Cult of the Curse serial begins	20.00	60.00	120.00
62-66-Serial ends; Mary Marvel x-over in #65. 66-Atomic War-c	15.00	45.00	90.00
67-77,79: 69-Billy Batson's Christmas; Uncle Marvel, Mary Marvel, Capt. Marvel Jr. x-over. 71-Three Lt. Marvels app. 79-Origin Mr. Tawny	14.00	42.00	85.00
78-Origin Mr. Atom	17.00	50.00	100.00
80-Origin Capt. Marvel retold	29.00	88.00	175.00
81-84,86-90: 81,90-Mr. Atom app. 82-Infinity-c. 86-Mr. Tawny app.	13.00	40.00	80.00
85-Freedom Train issue	17.00	50.00	100.00
91-99: 96-Mr. Tawny app.	12.50	37.50	75.00
100-Origin retold	25.00	75.00	150.00
101-120: 116-Flying Saucer issue (1/51)	12.00	35.00	70.00
121-Origin retold	17.00	50.00	100.00
122-149: 138-Flying Saucer issue (11/52). 141-Pre-code horror story "The Hideous Head-Hunter." 142-Used in **POP**, pgs. 92,96	12.00	35.00	70.00
150-(Low distribution)	17.00	50.00	100.00
Bond Bread Giveaways-(24 pgs.; pocket size-7-1/4x3"; paper cover): "...& the Stolen City" ('48), "The Boy Who Never Heard of Capt. Marvel," "Meets the Weatherman"-(1950)(reprint) each....	23.00	68.00	135.00
...Well Known Comics (1944; 12 pgs.; 8x10")-printed in red & in blue; soft-c; glued binding)-Bestmaid/Samuel Lowe Co. giveaway	17.00	50.00	100.00

NOTE: ***Swayze** a-12, 14, 15, 18, 19, 40; c-12, 15, 19.*

CAPTAIN MARVEL ADVENTURES
1945 (6x8") (Full color, paper cover)
Fawcett Publications (Wheaties Giveaway)

	GD25	FN65	–
nn-"Captain Marvel & the Threads of Life" plus 2 other stories (32 pgs.)	60.00	240.00	–

NOTE: *All copies were taped at each corner to a box of Wheaties and are never found in Fine or Mint condition.*

CAPTAIN MARVEL AND THE GOOD HUMOR MAN (Movie)
1950
Fawcett Publications

	GD25	FN65	NM94
nn-Partial photo-c w/Jack Carson & the Captain Marvel Club Boys	30.00	90.00	180.00

CAPTAIN MARVEL AND THE LTS. OF SAFETY
1950 - 1951 (3 issues - no No.'s)
Ebasco Services/Fawcett Publications

	GD25	FN65	NM94
"Danger Flies a Kite" ('50), "Danger Takes to Climbing" ('50), "Danger Smashes Street Lights" ('51)	16.00	48.00	110.00

CAPTAIN MARVEL COMIC STORY PAINT BOOK (See Comic Story....)

CAPTAIN MARVEL, JR. (See Fawcett Miniatures, Marvel Family, Master Comics, Mighty Midget Comics, Shazam & Whiz Comics)

CAPTAIN MARVEL, JR.
Nov, 1942 - No. 119, June, 1953 (nn 34)
Fawcett Publications

	GD25	FN65	NM94
1-Origin Capt. Marvel Jr. retold (Whiz No. 25); Capt. Nazi app.	208.00	625.00	1250.00
2-Vs. Capt. Nazi; origin Capt. Nippon	92.00	275.00	550.00
3,4	63.00	186.00	375.00
5-Vs. Capt. Nazi	58.00	175.00	350.00
6-10: 8-Vs. Capt. Nazi. 9-Flag-c. 10-Hitler-c	46.00	135.00	275.00
11,12,15-Capt. Nazi app.	37.00	110.00	225.00
13,14,16-20: 13-Hitler-c. 14-X-Mas-c. 16-Capt. Marvel & Sivana x-over. 19-Capt. Nazi & Capt. Nippon app.	30.00	90.00	180.00
21-30: 25-Flag-c	18.00	55.00	110.00
31-33,36-40: 37-Infinity-c	12.50	37.50	75.00
35-#34 on inside; cover shows origin of Sivana Jr. which is not on inside. Evidently the cover to #35 was printed out of sequence and bound with contents to #34	12.50	37.50	75.00
41-70: 53-Atomic Bomb-c/story	8.35	25.00	50.00
71-99,101-104: 104-Used in **POP**, pg. 89	5.85	17.50	35.00
100	6.70	20.00	40.00

Captain Marvel #31, © MEG

Captain Marvel Adventures #5, © FAW

Captain Marvel Adventures #100, © FAW

Captain Marvel Story Book #1, © FAW

Captain Midnight #12, © The Wander Co.

Captain Steve Savage #8 (1st series), © AVON

	GD25	FN65	NM94
105-114,116-119: 116-Vampira, Queen of Terror app. 119-Electric chair-c	5.85	17.50	35.00
115-Injury to eye-c; Eyeball story w/injury-to-eye panels	8.35	25.00	50.00
...Well Known Comics (1944; 12 pgs.; 8x10")(Printed in blue; paper-c, glued binding)-Bestmaid/Samuel Lowe Co. giveaway	13.00	40.00	80.00

NOTE: ***Mac Raboy** c-1-10, 12-14, 16, 19, 21, 22, 25, 27, 28, 30-33, 57 among others.*

CAPTAIN MARVEL PRESENTS THE TERRIBLE FIVE
Aug, 1966; V2#5, Sept, 1967 (No #2-4) (25 cents)
M. F. Enterprises

	GD25	FN65	NM94
1	2.80	7.00	14.00
V2#5-(Formerly Captain Marvel)	1.60	4.00	8.00

CAPTAIN MARVEL'S FUN BOOK
1944 (1/2" thick) (cardboard covers)
Samuel Lowe Co.

	GD25	FN65	NM94
nn-Puzzles, games, magic, etc.; infinity-c	22.00	65.00	135.00

CAPTAIN MARVEL SPECIAL EDITION (See Special Edition)

CAPTAIN MARVEL STORY BOOK
Summer, 1946 - No. 4, Summer?, 1948
Fawcett Publications

	GD25	FN65	NM94
1-Half text	42.00	125.00	250.00
2-4	29.00	86.00	175.00

CAPTAIN MARVEL THRILL BOOK (Large-Size)
1941 (Black & White; color cover)
Fawcett Publications

	GD25	FN65	VF88
1-Reprints from Whiz #8,10, & Special Edition #1 (Rare)	200.00	600.00	1200.00

NOTE: *Rarely found in Fine or Mint condition.*

CAPTAIN MIDNIGHT (Radio, films, TV) (See The Funnies & Popular Comics) (Becomes Sweethearts No. 68 on)
Sept, 1942 - No. 67, Fall, 1948 (#1-14: 68 pgs.)
Fawcett Publications

	GD25	FN65	NM94
1-Origin Captain Midnight; Captain Marvel cameo on cover	150.00	450.00	900.00
2	75.00	225.00	450.00
3-5	50.00	150.00	300.00
6-10: 9-Raboy-c. 10-Raboy Flag-c	37.00	110.00	225.00
11-20: 11,17,18-Raboy-c	25.00	75.00	150.00
21-30	19.00	57.00	115.00
31-40	14.00	42.50	85.00
41-59,61-67: 54-Sci/fi theme begins?	12.00	35.00	70.00
60-Flying Saucer issue (2/48)-3rd of this theme; see Shadow Comics V7#10 & Boy Commandos #26	17.00	50.00	100.00

CAPTAIN NICE (TV)
Nov, 1967 (One Shot)
Gold Key

	GD25	FN65	NM94
1(10211-711)-Photo-c	4.70	14.00	28.00

CAPTAIN N: THE GAME MASTER (TV)
1990 - No. 6? ($1.95, color, thick stock, coated-c)
Valiant Comics

	GD25	FN65	NM94
1-6: 4-6-Layton-c	.50	1.20	2.00

CAPTAIN PARAGON (Americomics) (Value: cover or less)

CAPTAIN PARAGON AND THE SENTINELS OF JUSTICE (AC) (Value: cover or less)

CAPTAIN PLANET AND THE PLANETEERS (TV)
Oct, 1991 - No. 12, Oct, 1992 ($1.00/$1.25, color, based on cartoon series)
Marvel Comics

	GD25	FN65	NM94
1-12: 1-N. Adams painted-c. 3-Romita-c		.60	1.25

CAPTAIN POWER AND THE SOLDIERS OF THE FUTURE (TV) (Continuity) (Value: cover or less)

CAPTAIN PUREHEART (See Archie as...)

CAPTAIN ROCKET
November, 1951
P. L. Publ. (Canada)

	GD25	FN65	NM94
1	22.00	65.00	150.00

CAPT. SAVAGE AND HIS LEATHERNECK RAIDERS
Jan, 1968 - No. 19, Mar, 1970 (See Sgt. Fury No. 10)
Marvel Comics Group (Animated Timely Features)

	GD25	FN65	NM94
1-Sgt. Fury & Howlers cameo	2.40	6.00	12.00
2-10: 2-Origin Hydra. 1-5,7-Ayers/Shores-a	1.20	3.00	6.00
11-19	1.00	2.50	5.00

CAPTAIN SCIENCE (Fantastic No. 8 on)
Nov, 1950 - No. 7, Dec, 1951
Youthful Magazines

	GD25	FN65	NM94
1-Wood-a; origin	50.00	150.00	350.00
2	24.00	70.00	165.00
3,6,7; 3,6-Bondage c-swipes/Wings #94,91	21.00	62.00	145.00
4,5-Wood/Orlando-c/a(2) each	47.00	140.00	325.00

NOTE: ***Fass** a-4. Bondage c-3, 6, 7.*

CAPTAIN SILVER'S LOG OF SEA HOUND (See Sea Hound)

CAPTAIN SINDBAD (Movie Adaptation) (See Fantastic Voyages of... & Movie Comics)

CAPTAIN STEVE SAVAGE (...& His Jet Fighters, No. 2-13)
1950 - No. 8, 1/53; No. 5, 9-10/54 - No. 13, 5-6/56
Avon Periodicals

	GD25	FN65	NM94
nn(1st series)-Wood art, 22 pgs. (titled "...Over Korea")	26.00	77.00	180.00
1(4/51)-Reprints nn issue (Canadian)	11.00	32.00	75.00
2-Kamen-a	8.35	25.00	50.00
3-11 (#6, 9-10/54, last precode)	4.70	14.00	28.00
12-Wood-a (6 pgs.)	9.15	27.50	55.00
13-Check, Lawrence-a	5.85	17.50	35.00

NOTE: ***Kinstler** c-2-5, 7-9, 11. **Lawrence** a-8. **Ravielli** a-5, 9.*

	GD25	FN65	NM94
5(9-10/54-2nd series)(Formerly Sensational Police Cases)	4.70	14.00	28.00
6-Reprints nn issue; Wood-a	7.50	22.50	45.00
7-13: 13 reprints cover to #8 (1st series)	3.20	8.00	16.00

CAPTAIN STONE (See Holyoke One-Shot No. 10)

CAPT. STORM (Also see G. I. Combat #138)
May-June, 1964 - No. 18, Mar-Apr, 1967
National Periodical Publications

	GD25	FN65	NM94
1-Origin	3.60	9.00	18.00
2-18: 3,6,13-Kubert-a. 12-Kubert-c	2.00	5.00	10.00

CAPTAIN 3-D
December, 1953
Harvey Publications

	GD25	FN65	NM94
1-Kirby/Ditko-a (Ditko's 2nd work, see Black Magic & Fantastic Fears)	5.85	17.50	35.00

CAPTAIN THUNDER AND BLUE BOLT (Hero) (Value: cover or less)

CAPTAIN TOOTSIE & THE SECRET LEGION (Advs. of..) (Also see Monte Hale #30,39 & Real Western Hero)
Oct, 1950 - No. 2, Dec, 1950
Toby Press

	GD25	FN65	NM94
1-Not Beck-a	16.00	48.00	110.00
2-The Rocketeer Patrol app.; not Beck-a	10.00	30.00	65.00

CAPTAIN VENTURE & THE LAND BENEATH THE SEA
Oct, 1968 - No. 2, Oct, 1969 (See Space Family Robinson)

	GD25	FN65	NM94

Gold Key

	GD25	FN65	NM94
1,2: 1-r/Space Family Robinson serial; Spiegle-a in both	4.20	12.50	25.00

CAPTAIN VICTORY AND THE GALACTIC RANGERS (Pacific)(Value: cover or less)

CAPTAIN VIDEO (TV) (See XMas Comics)
Feb, 1951 - No. 6, Dec, 1951 (No. 1,5,6-36pgs.; 2-4, 52pgs.)
Fawcett Publications

	GD25	FN65	NM94
1-George Evans-a(2)	47.00	140.00	325.00
2-Used in **SOTI**, pg. 382	36.00	107.00	250.00
3-6-All Evans-a	30.00	90.00	210.00

NOTE: *Minor* ***Williamson*** *assists on most issues. Photo c-1, 5, 6; painted c-2-4.*

CAPTAIN WILLIE SCHULTZ (Also see Fightin' Army)
No. 76, Oct, 1985 - No. 77, Jan, 1986
Charlton Comics

	GD25	FN65	NM94
76,77		.50	1.00

CAPTAIN WIZARD COMICS (Also see Meteor & Red Band Comics)
1946
Rural Home

	GD25	FN65	NM94
1-Capt. Wizard dons new costume; Impossible Man, Race Wilkins app.	15.00	45.00	90.00

CARAVAN KIDD (Dark Horse)(Value: cover or less)

CARDINAL MINDSZENTY (The Truth Behind the Trial of...)
1949 (24 pages; paper cover, in color)
Catechetical Guild Education Society

	GD25	FN65	NM94
nn-Anti-communism	5.85	17.50	35.00
Press Proof-(Very Rare)-(Full color, 7-1/2x11-3/4", untrimmed) Only two known copies			150.00
Preview Copy (B&W, stapled), 18 pgs.; contains first 13 pgs. of Cardinal Mindszenty and was sent out as an advance promotion. Only one known copy		150.00 - 200.00	

NOTE: *Regular edition also printed in French. There was also a movie released in 1949 called "Guilty of Treason" which is a fact-based account of the trial and imprisonmentof Cardinal Mindszenty by the Communist regime in Hungary.*

CARE BEARS (TV, Movie)(See Star Comics Magazine)
Nov, 1985 - No. 20, Jan, 1989 ($1.00 #11 on)
Star Comics/Marvel Comics No. 15 on

	GD25	FN65	NM94
1-20: Post-a begins		.50	1.00

CAREER GIRL ROMANCES (Formerly Three Nurses)
June, 1964 - No. 78, Dec, 1973
Charlton Comics

	GD25	FN65	NM94
V4#24-31,33-50	.80	2.00	4.00
32-Elvis Presley, Hermans Hermits, Johnny Rivers line drawn-c	5.00	15.00	30.00
51-78	.40	1.00	2.00

CAR 54, WHERE ARE YOU? (TV)
Mar-May, 1962 - No. 7, Sept-Nov, 1963; 1964 - 1965 (All photo-c)
Dell Publishing Co.

	GD25	FN65	NM94
4-Color 1257(#1, 3-5/62)	6.35	19.00	38.00
2(6-8/62)-7	4.00	11.00	22.00
2,3(10-12/64), 4(1-3/65)-Reprints #2,3,&4 of 1st series	3.20	8.00	16.00

CARL BARKS LIBRARY OF WALT DISNEY'S COMICS AND STORIES IN COLOR, THE
No date (1991) - Present ($8.95, color, 60 pgs., 8-1/2x11")
Gladstone Publishing

	GD25	FN65	NM94
..1-13: 1-Barks Donald Duck-r/WDC&S #31-35. 2-r/#36,38-41. 3-r/#47-51. 4-r/#47-51. 5-r/#52-56. 6-r/#57-61. 7-r/#62-66. 8-r/#67-71. 9-r/#72-76. 10-r/#77-81. 11-r/#82-86. 12-r/#87-91. 13-r/#92-96. All contain one trading card each	1.80	4.50	9.00

CARL BARKS LIBRARY OF WALT DISNEY'S UNCLE SCROOGE COMICS ONE PAGERS IN COLOR
1992 - No. 2, 1992 ($8.95, color, 60 pgs., 8-1/2x11")
Gladstone Publishing

	GD25	FN65	NM94
1,2-Carl Barks one page reprints	1.80	4.50	9.00

CARNATION MALTED MILK GIVEAWAYS (See Wisco)

CARNIVAL COMICS (Formerly Kayo #12; becomes Red Seal Comics #14)
1945
Harry 'A' Chesler/Pershing Square Publ. Co.

	GD25	FN65	NM94
nn (#13)-Guardineer-a	9.15	27.50	55.00

CARNIVAL OF COMICS
1954 (Giveaway)
Fleet-Air Shoes

	GD25	FN65	NM94
nn-Contains a comic bound with new cover; several combinations possible; Charlton's Eh! known	2.00	5.00	10.00

CAROLINE KENNEDY
1961 (One Shot)
Charlton Comics

	GD25	FN65	NM94
nn	7.50	22.50	45.00

CAROUSEL COMICS
V1#8, April, 1948
F. E. Howard, Toronto

	GD25	FN65	NM94
V1#8	4.00	11.00	22.00

CARTOON KIDS
1957 (no month)
Atlas Comics (CPS)

	GD25	FN65	NM94
1-Maneely-c/a; Dexter The Demon, Willie The Wise-Guy, Little Zelda app.	4.70	14.00	28.00

CARTOON TALES (Disney's...)
No date (1992) - Presents ($2.95, color, 6-5/8x9-1/2", 52 pgs.)
W.D. Publications (Disney)

	GD25	FN65	NM94
nn-Ariel & Sebastian - Serpent Teen	.60	1.50	3.00
nn-Beauty and the Beast - A Tale of Enchantment	.60	1.50	3.00
nn-Darkwing Duck - Just Us Justice Ducks	.60	1.50	3.00
nn-101 Dalmations - Canine Classics	.60	1.50	3.00
nn-Tale Spin - Surprise in the Skies	.60	1.50	3.00
nn-Uncle Scrooge - Blast to the Past	.60	1.50	3.00

CARVEL COMICS (Amazing Advs. of Capt. Carvel)
1975 - No. 5, 1976 (25 cents; #3-5: 35 cents) (#4,5: 3-1/4x5")
Carvel Corp. (Ice Cream)

	GD25	FN65	NM94
1-3		.50	1.00
4,5(1976)-Baseball theme	1.20	3.00	6.00

CAR WARRIORS
June, 1991 - No. 4, Sept, 1991 ($2.25, color, mini-series)
Epic Comics (Marvel)

	GD25	FN65	NM94
1-4: 1-Says April in indicia	.45	1.15	2.25

CASE OF THE SHOPLIFTER'S SHOE (Perry Mason) (See Feature Book No.50)

CASE OF THE WASTED WATER, THE
1972? (Giveaway)
Rheem Water Heating

	GD25	FN65	NM94
nn-Neal Adams-a	4.00	10.50	21.00

CASE OF THE WINKING BUDDHA, THE
1950 (132 pgs.; 25 cents; B&W; 5-1/2x7-5-1/2x8")
St. John Publ. Co.

	GD25	FN65	NM94
nn-Charles Raab-a; reprinted in Authentic Police Cases No. 25	14.00	43.00	100.00

CASEY-CRIME PHOTOGRAPHER (Two-Gun Western No. 5 on)
Aug, 1949 - No. 4, Feb, 1950 (Radio)

Captain Video #1, © FAW

Captain Wizard Comics #1, © RH

Car 54, Where Are You? #5 (1962) © Eupolis Prod.

Casey-Crime Photographer #4, © MEG

Casper Cat #1, © I.W.

Casper, the Friendly Ghost #18, © Paramount

	GD25	FN65	NM94
Marvel Comics (BFP)			
1-Photo-c; 52 pgs.	10.00	30.00	60.00
2-4: Photo-c	7.50	22.50	45.00

CASEY JONES (See 4-Color No. 915)

CASPER ADVENTURE DIGEST
Oct, 1992 - Present ($1.75, color, digest-size)
Harvey Comics

V2#1,2-Casper, Richie Rich, Spooky, Wendy	.35	.90	1.75

CASPER AND...
Nov, 1987 - No. 12, June, 1990 (.75-$1.00, all reprints)
Harvey Comics

1-10: 1-Ghostly Trio. 2-Spooky; begin $1.00-c. 3-Wendy. 4-Nightmare. 5-Ghostly Trio. 6-Spooky. 7-Wendy. 8-Hot Stuff. 9-Baby Huey. 10-Wendy. 11-Ghostly Trio. 12-Spooky		.50	1.00

CASPER AND FRIENDS
Oct, 1991 - No. 5?, 1992 ($1.00/$1.25 #5, color)
Harvey Comics

1-5: Nightmare, Ghostly Trio, Wendy, Spooky		.60	1.25

CASPER AND NIGHTMARE (See Harvey Hits# 37, 45, 52, 56, 59, 62, 65, 68,71, 75)

CASPER AND NIGHTMARE (Nightmare & Casper No. 1-5)
No. 6, 11/64 - No. 44, 10/73; No. 45, 6/74 - No. 46, 8/74 (25 cents)
Harvey Publications

6: 68 pg. Giants begin, ends #32	3.60	9.00	18.00
7-10	1.80	4.50	9.00
11-20	1.00	2.50	5.00
21-46: 33-37-(52 pg. Giants)	.80	2.00	4.00

NOTE: *Many issues contain reprints.*

CASPER AND SPOOKY (See Harvey Hits No. 20)
Oct, 1972 - No. 7, Oct, 1973
Harvey Publications

1	1.20	3.00	6.00
2-7	.60	1.50	3.00

CASPER AND THE GHOSTLY TRIO
Nov, 1972 - No. 7, Nov, 1973; No. 8, Aug, 1990 - No. 10, Dec, 1990
Harvey Publications

1	1.20	3.00	6.00
2-7	.60	1.50	3.00
8-10		.50	1.00

CASPER AND WENDY
Sept, 1972 - No. 8, Nov, 1973
Harvey Publications

1: 52 pg. Giant	1.20	3.00	6.00
2-8	.60	1.50	3.00

CASPER CAT (See Dopey Duck)
1958; 1963
I. W. Enterprises/Super

1,7-Reprint, Super No. 14('63)	.60	1.50	3.00

CASPER DIGEST (... Magazine #?; ...Halloween Digest #8, 10)
Oct, 1986 - No. 20? ($1.25-$1.75, digest-size)
Harvey Publications

1-20: 11-Valentine-c. 18-Halloween-c	.30	.75	1.50

CASPER DIGEST
1991 - Present ($1.75, color, digest-size)
Harvey Comics

1-6	.35	.90	1.75

CASPER DIGEST STORIES
Feb, 1980 - No. 4, Nov, 1980 (95 cents; 132 pgs.; digest size)
Harvey Publications

	GD25	FN65	NM94
1	.60	1.50	3.00
2-4	.40	1.00	2.00

CASPER DIGEST WINNERS
April, 1980 - No. 3, Sept, 1980 (95 cents; 132 pgs.; digest size)
Harvey Publications

1	.40	1.00	2.00
2,3	..30	.75	1.50

CASPER ENCHANTED TALES DIGEST
May, 1992 - No. 2? ($1.75, color, digest-size, 98 pgs.)
Harvey Comics

1,2-Casper, Spooky, Wendy stories	.35	.90	1.75

CASPER GHOSTLAND
May, 1992 ($1.25, color)
Harvey Comics

1		.60	1.25

CASPER GIANT SIZE
Oct, 1992 - Present ($2.25, color, 68 pgs.)
Harvey Comics

V2#1-Casper, Wendy, Spooky stories	.45	1.15	2.25

CASPER HALLOWEEN TRICK OR TREAT
January, 1976 (52 pgs.)
Harvey Publications

1	.60	1.50	3.00

CASPER IN SPACE (Formerly Casper Spaceship)
No. 6, June, 1973 - No. 8, Oct, 1973
Harvey Publications

6-8	.60	1.50	3.00

CASPER'S GHOSTLAND
Winter, 1958-59 - No. 97, 12/77; No. 98, 12/79 (25 cents)
Harvey Publications

1: 68 pgs. begin, ends #61	11.50	34.00	80.00
2	6.70	20.00	40.00
3-10	4.35	13.00	26.00
11-20: 13-X-Mas-c	3.20	8.00	16.00
21-40	2.40	6.00	12.00
41-61: Last 68 pg. issue	1.60	4.00	8.00
62-77: All 52 pgs.	1.00	2.50	5.00
78-98: 94-X-Mas-c	.80	2.00	4.00

NOTE: *Most issues contain reprints.*

CASPER SPACESHIP (Casper in Space No. 6 on)
Aug, 1972 - No. 5, April, 1973
Harvey Publications

1: 52 pg. Giant	1.20	3.00	6.00
2-5	.60	1.50	3.00

CASPER SPECIAL
nd (Dec., 1990) (Giveaway with $1.00 cover)
Target Stores (Harvey)

Three issues-Given away with Casper video		.50	1.00

CASPER STRANGE GHOST STORIES
October, 1974 - No. 14, Jan, 1977 (All 52 pgs.)
Harvey Publications

1	1.00	2.50	5.00
2-14	.40	1.00	2.00

CASPER, THE FRIENDLY GHOST (See America's Best TV Comics, Famous TV Funday Funnies, The Friendly Ghost..., Nightmare &..., Richie Rich and..., Tastee-Freez, Treasury of Comics & Wendy the Good Little Witch)

CASPER, THE FRIENDLY GHOST (Becomes Harvey Comics Hits No. 61 (No. 6), and then continued with Harvey issue No. 7)
9/49 - No. 3, 8/50; 9/50 - No. 5, 5/51
St. John Publishing Co.

	GD25	FN65	NM94
1(1949)-Origin & 1st app. Baby Huey & Herman the Mouse	61.00	182.00	425.00
2,3	36.00	107.00	250.00
1(9/50)	40.00	120.00	275.00
2-5	25.00	75.00	175.00

CASPER, THE FRIENDLY GHOST (Paramount Picture Star...)
No. 7, Dec, 1952 - No 70, July, 1958
Harvey Publications (Family Comics)
Note: No. 6 is Harvey Comics Hits No. 61 (10/52)

	GD25	FN65	NM94
7-Baby Huey begins, ends #9	21.00	62.00	145.00
8,9	10.00	30.00	70.00
10-Spooky begins(1st app.), ends #70?	11.50	34.00	80.00
11-18	7.50	22.50	45.00
19-1st app. Nightmare (4/54)	9.15	27.50	55.00
20-Wendy the Witch begins (1st app., 5/54)	10.00	30.00	65.00
21-30: 24-Infinity-c	5.85	17.50	35.00
31-40	4.35	13.00	26.00
41-50	4.00	10.50	21.00
51-70	3.20	8.00	16.00
American Dental Association (Giveaways):			
...'s Dental Health Activity Book-1977	.40	1.00	2.00
...Presents Space Age Dentistry-1972	.60	1.50	3.00
..., His Den, & Their Dentist Fight the Tooth Demons-1974	.60	1.50	3.00

CASPER THE FRIENDLY GHOST (Formerly The Friendly Ghost...)
No. 254, July, 1990 - No. 260, Jan, 1991 ($1.00, color)
Harvey Comics

	GD25	FN65	NM94
254-260		.50	1.00

CASPER THE FRIENDLY GHOST
Mar, 1991 - 8? ($1.00/$1.25, color)
V2#1, Aug, 1992 - Present ($1.95, color, 52 pgs.)
Harvey Comics

	GD25	FN65	NM94
1-8: 1-Casper becomes Mighty Ghost; Spooky & Wendy app. 7-Last $1.00-c. 7,8-Post-a		.60	1.25
V2#1-Cover says "Casper Big Book"; Spooky app.	.40	1.00	2.00

CASPER T.V. SHOWTIME
Jan, 1980 - No. 5, Oct, 1980
Harvey Comics

	GD25	FN65	NM94
1	.40	1.00	2.00
2-5		.50	1.00

CASSETTE BOOKS
(Classics Illustrated)
1984 (48 pgs, b&w comic with cassette tape)
Cassette Book Co./I.P.S. Publ.

NOTE: *This series was illegal. The artwork was illegally obtained, and the Classics Illustrated copyright owner, Twin Circle Publ. sued to get an injunction to prevent the continued sale of this series. Many C.I. collectors obtained copies before the 1987 injunction, but now they are already scarce. Here again the market is just developing, but sealed mint copies of com ic and tape should be worth at least $25.*

1001 (CI#1-A2)New-PC 1002(CI#3-A2)CI-PC 1003(CI#13-A2)CI-PC
1004(CI#25)CI-LDC 1005(CI#10-A2)New-PC 1006(CI#64)CI-LDC

CASTILIAN (See Movie Classics)

CAT, T.H.E. (TV) (See T.H.E. Cat)

CAT, THE (See Movie Classics)

CAT, THE
Nov, 1972 - No. 4, June, 1973
Marvel Comics Group

	GD25	FN65	NM94
1-Origin & 1st app. The Cat (who later becomes Tigra); Mooney-a(i); Wood-c(i)/a(i)	2.40	6.00	12.00
2,3: 2-Mooney-a(i). 3-Everett inks	1.60	4.00	8.00
4-Starlin/Weiss-a(p)	1.60	4.00	8.00

CAT & MOUSE
Dec, 1988 ($1.75, color w/part B&W)
EF Graphics (Silverline)

	GD25	FN65	NM94
1-1st printing (12/88, 32 pgs.)	.35	.90	1.75
1-2nd printing (5/89, 36 pgs.)	.35	.90	1.75

CAT FROM OUTER SPACE (See Walt Disney Showcase #46)

CATHOLIC COMICS (See Heroes All Catholic...)
June, 1946 - V3No.10, July, 1949
Catholic Publications

	GD25	FN65	NM94
1	13.00	40.00	90.00
2	7.50	22.50	45.00
3-13(7/47)	5.85	17.50	35.00
V2#1-10	3.60	9.00	18.00
V3#1-10: Reprints 10-part Treasure Island serial from Target V2#2-11 (see Key Comics #5)	4.20	12.50	25.00

CATHOLIC PICTORIAL
1947
Catholic Guild

	GD25	FN65	NM94
1-Toth-a(2) (Rare)	22.00	65.00	150.00

CATMAN COMICS (Formerly Crash Comics No. 1-5)
5/41 - No. 17, 1/43; No. 18, 7/43 - No. 22, 12/43; No. 23, 3/44 - No. 26, 11/44; No. 27, 4/45 - No. 30, 12/45; No. 31, 6/46 - No. 32, 8/46
Holyoke Publishing Co./Continental Magazines V2#12, 7/44 on

	GD25	FN65	NM94
1(V1#6)-Origin The Deacon & Sidekick Mickey, Dr. Diamond & Rag-Man; The Black Widow app.; The Catman by Chas. Quinlan & Blaze Baylor begin	100.00	300.00	600.00
2(V1#7)	50.00	150.00	300.00
3(V1#8), 4(V1#9): 3-The Pied Piper begins	37.00	110.00	220.00
5(V2#10)-Origin Kitten; The Hood begins (c-redated), 6,7(V2#11,12)	29.00	86.00	175.00
8(V2#13,3/42)-Origin Little Leaders; Volton by Kubert begins (his 1st comic book work)	42.00	125.00	250.00
9,10(V2#14,15): 10-Origin Blackout; Phantom Falcon begins	27.00	82.00	165.00
11(V3#1)-Kubert-a	27.00	82.00	165.00
12(V3#2) - 15, 17, 18(V3#8, 7/43)	21.00	62.00	125.00
16 (V3#5)-Hitler, Tojo, Mussolini, Stalin-c	25.00	75.00	150.00
19 (V2#6)-Hitler, Tojo, Mussolini-c	25.00	75.00	150.00
20(V2#7) - 23(V2#10, 3/44): 20-Hitler-c	21.00	62.00	125.00
nn(V3#13, 5/44)-Rico-a; Schomburg bondage-c	18.00	55.00	110.00
nn(V2#12, 7/44)	18.00	55.00	110.00
nn(V3#1, 9/44)-Origin The Golden Archer; Leatherface app.;	18.00	55.00	110.00
nn(V3#2, 11/44)-L. B. Cole-c	25.00	75.00	150.00
27-Origin Kitten retold; L. B. Cole Flag-c	27.00	82.00	165.00
28-Catman learns Kitten's I.D.; Dr. Macabre, Deacon app.; L. B. Cole c/a	29.00	86.00	175.00
29-32-L. B. Cole-c; bondage-#30	25.00	75.00	150.00

NOTE: ***Fuje** a-11, 29(3), 30. **Palais** a-11, 29(2), 30; c-25(7/44). **Rico** a-11(2).*

CAT TALES (3-D)
April, 1989 ($2.95)
Eternity Comics

	GD25	FN65	NM94
1-Felix the Cat-r in 3-D	.60	1.50	3.00

CATWOMAN (Also see Action Comics Weekly #611, Batman #1, Detective Comics, Showcase '93 & Superman's Girlfriend Lois Lane #70, 71)
Feb, 1989 - No. 4, May, 1989 ($1.50, mini-series, mature readers)
DC Comics

	GD25	FN65	NM94
1	1.60	4.00	8.00

The Cat #1, © MEG

Catholic Comics V2#10, © Catholic Publ.

Catman Comics #10, © HOKE

Catwoman #4, © DC

Century of Comics, © EAS

Challenge of the Unknown #6, © ACE

	GD25	FN65	NM94
2	1.00	2.50	5.00
3,4: 3-Batman cameo. 4-Batman app.	.60	1.50	3.00
...: Her Sister's Keeper (1991, $9.95)-r/#1-4	2.00	5.00	10.00

CAUGHT
Aug, 1956 - No. 5, April, 1957
Atlas Comics (VPI)

	GD25	FN65	NM94
1	10.00	30.00	60.00
2,4: 4-Maneely-a (4 pgs.)	4.70	14.00	28.00
3-Maneely, Pakula, Torres-a	5.00	15.00	30.00
5-Crandall, Krigstein-a	6.35	19.00	38.00

NOTE: ***Drucker** a-2. **Heck** a-4. **Severin** c-1, 2, 4, 5. **Shores** a-4.*

CAVALIER COMICS
1945; 1952 (Early DC reprints)
A. W. Nugent Publ. Co.

	GD25	FN65	NM94
2(1945)-Speed Saunders, Fang Gow	10.00	30.00	65.00
2(1952)	5.35	16.00	32.00

CAVE GIRL (Also see Africa)
No. 11, 1953 - No. 14, 1954
Magazine Enterprises

	GD25	FN65	NM94
11(A-1 82)-Origin; all Cave Girl stories	27.00	80.00	185.00
12(A-1 96), 13(A-1 116), 14(A-1 125)-Thunda by Powell in each	20.00	60.00	140.00

NOTE: ***Powell** c/a in all.*

CAVE GIRL
1988 ($2.95, 44 pgs., 16 pgs. of color, rest B&W)
AC Comics

	GD25	FN65	NM94
1-Powell-r/Cave Girl #11; Nyoka photo back-c from movie; Powell/Bill Black-c; Special Limited Edition on-c	.60	1.50	3.00

CAVE KIDS (TV)
Feb, 1963 - No. 16, Mar, 1967 (Hanna-Barbera)
Gold Key

	GD25	FN65	NM94
1	3.60	9.00	18.00
2-5	2.40	6.00	12.00
6-16: 7,12-Pebbles & Bamm Bamm app.	1.60	4.00	8.00

CENTURION OF ANCIENT ROME, THE
1958 (no month listed) (36 pages) (B&W)
Zondervan Publishing House

	GD25	FN65	NM94
(Rare) All by Jay Disbrow Estimated Value....			200.00

CENTURIONS
June, 1987 - No. 4, Sept, 1987 (75 cents, mini-series)
DC Comics

	GD25	FN65	NM94
1-4		.50	1.00

CENTURY OF COMICS
1933 (100 pages) (Probably the 3rd comic book)
Eastern Color Printing Co.

Bought by Wheatena, Milk-O-Malt, John Wanamaker, Kinney Shoe Stores, & others to be used as premiums and radio giveaways. No publisher listed.

	GD25	FN65	VF82
nn-Mutt & Jeff, Joe Palooka, etc. reprints	1500.00	4500.00	7500.00

(Estimated up to 20 total copies exist, none in NM-Mint)

CEREBUS BI-WEEKLY
Dec. 2, 1988 - No. 26, Nov. 11, 1989 ($1.25, B&W)
Aardvark-Vanaheim

	GD25	FN65	NM94
1-26: Reprints Cerebus #1-26		.60	1.25

CEREBUS: CHURCH & STATE
Feb, 1991 - No. 30, Apr, 1992 ($2.00, B&W, bi-weekly)
Aardvark-Vanaheim

	GD25	FN65	NM94
1-30: r/Cerebus #51-80	.40	1.00	2.00

CEREBUS: HIGH SOCIETY
Feb, 1990 - No. 25, 1991 ($1.70, B&W)
Aardvark-Vanaheim

	GD25	FN65	NM94
1-25: r/Cerebus #26-50	.35	.85	1.70

CEREBUS JAM
Apr, 1985
Aardvark-Vanaheim

	GD25	FN65	NM94
1-Eisner, Austin-a	.60	1.50	3.00

CEREBUS THE AARDVARK (See A-V in 3-D, Nucleus, Power Comics)
Dec, 1977 - Present ($1.70-$2.00, B&W)
Aardvark-Vanaheim

	GD25	FN65	NM94
1-2000 print run; most copies poorly printed	18.00	54.00	125.00

Note: *There is a counterfeit version known to exist. It can be distinguished from the original in the following ways: inside cover is glossy instead of flat, black background on the front cover is blotted or spotty.*

	GD25	FN65	NM94
2-Dave Sim art in all	10.00	30.00	60.00
3-Origin Red Sophia	8.35	25.00	50.00
4-Origin Elrod the Albino	5.00	15.00	30.00
5,6	4.00	12.00	24.00
7-10	3.20	8.00	16.00
11,12: 11-Origin Capt. Coachroach	3.60	9.00	18.00
13-15: 14-Origin Lord Julius	1.80	4.50	9.00
16-20	1.20	3.00	6.00
21-Scarcer	5.85	17.50	35.00
22-Low distribution; no cover price	2.40	6.00	12.00
23-30: 26-High Society storyline begins	1.00	2.50	5.00
31-Origin Moonroach	1.40	3.50	7.00
32-40	.80	2.00	4.00
41-50,52: 52-Cutey Bunny app.	.60	1.50	3.00
51-Not reprinted; Cutey Bunny app.	2.40	6.00	12.00
53-Intro. Wolveroach (cameo)	1.00	2.50	5.00
54-1st full Wolveroach story	1.40	3.50	7.00
55,56-Wolveroach app.	1.00	2.50	5.00
57-79: 61,62: Flaming Carrot app.	.50	1.25	2.50
80-168: 104-Flaming Carrot app. 112/113-Double issue. 137-Begin $2.25-c. 151-153-2nd printings exist	.40	1.15	2.25

CHALLENGE OF THE UNKNOWN (Formerly Love Experiences)
No. 6, Sept, 1950 (See Web Of Mystery No. 19)
Ace Magazines

	GD25	FN65	NM94
6-"Villa of the Vampire" used in N.Y. Joint Legislative Comm. Publ; Sekowsky-a	11.00	32.00	75.00

CHALLENGER, THE
1945 - No. 4, Oct-Dec, 1946
Interfaith Publications/T.C. Comics

	GD25	FN65	NM94
nn; nd; 32 pgs.; Origin the Challenger Club; Anti-Fascist with funny animal filler	17.00	52.00	120.00
2-4-Kubert-a; 4-Fuje-a	15.00	45.00	105.00

CHALLENGERS OF THE UNKNOWN (See Showcase #6, 7, 11, 12, Super DC Giant, and Super Team Family)
4-5/58 - No. 77, 12-1/70-71; No. 78, 2/73 - No. 80, 6-7/73;
No. 81, 6-7/77 - No. 87, 6-7/78
National Periodical Publications/DC Comics

	GD25	FN65	NM94
Showcase #6 (1-2/57)-Origin & 1st app. Challengers of the Unknown by Kirby (1st Silver Age super-hero team) (1st original concept S.A. series)	215.00	650.00	1500.00
Showcase #7 (3-4/57)-2nd app. by Kirby	107.00	320.00	750.00
Showcase #11,12 (11-12/57, 1-2/58)-3rd & 4th app. Challengers by Kirby (2nd tryout series)	90.00	270.00	625.00
1-(4-5/58)-Kirby/Stein-a(2)	135.00	405.00	950.00
2-Kirby/Stein-a(2)	68.00	205.00	475.00

	GD25	FN65	NM94
3-Kirby/Stein-a(2)	55.00	165.00	385.00
4-8-Kirby/Wood-a plus c-#8	47.00	140.00	325.00
9,10	24.00	72.00	165.00
11-15: 14-Origin Multi-Man	15.00	45.00	105.00
16-22: 18-Intro. Cosmo, the Challengers Spacepet. 22-Last 10 cent issue	12.00	36.00	85.00
23-30	7.50	22.50	45.00
31-Retells origin of the Challengers	8.35	25.00	50.00
32-40	4.00	11.00	22.00
41-60: 43-New look begins. 48-Doom Patrol app. 49-Intro. Challenger Corps. 51-Sea Devils app. 55-Death of Red Ryan. 60-Red Ryan returns	2.20	5.50	11.00
61-73,75-77: 64,65-Kirby origin-r, parts 1 & 2. 66-New logo. 68-Last 12 cent issue. 69-1st app. Corinna	.80	2.00	4.00
74-Deadman by Tuska/N. Adams	2.40	6.00	12.00
78-87: 82-Swamp Thing begins	.60	1.50	3.00

NOTE: ***N. Adams** c-67, 68, 70, 72, 74i, 81i. **Buckler** c-83-86p. **Giffen** a-83-87p. **Kirby** a-75-80r; c-75, 77, 78. **Kubert** c-64, 66, 69, 76, 79. **Nasser** c/a-81p, 82p. **Tuska** a-73. **Wood** r-76.*

CHALLENGERS OF THE UNKNOWN
Mar, 1991 - No. 8, Oct, 1991 ($1.75, color, limited series)
DC Comics

	GD25	FN65	NM94
1-Bolland-c	.50	1.25	2.50
2-8: 6-G. Kane-c(p). 7-Steranko-c swipe by Arthur Adams	.35	.90	1.75

CHALLENGE TO THE WORLD
1951 (36 pages) (10 cents)
Catechetical Guild

	GD25	FN65	NM94
nn	3.20	8.00	16.00

CHAMBER OF CHILLS (...of Clues No. 27 on)
No. 21, June, 1951 - No. 26, Dec, 1954
Harvey Publications/Witches Tales

	GD25	FN65	NM94
21 (#1)	14.00	43.00	100.00
22,24 (#2,3)	8.35	25.00	50.00
23 (#4)-Excessive violence; eyes torn out	10.00	30.00	65.00
5(2/52)-Decapitation, acid in face scene	10.00	30.00	65.00
6-Woman melted alive	10.00	30.00	60.00
7-Used in **SOTI**, pg. 389; decapitation/severed head panels	8.35	25.00	50.00
8-10: 8-Decapitation panels	7.50	22.50	45.00
11,12,14	5.35	16.00	32.00
13,15-24-Nostrand-a in all. 13,21-Decapitation panels. 18-Atom bomb panels. 20-Nostrand-c	9.15	27.50	55.00
25,26	4.35	13.00	26.00

NOTE: *About half the issues contain bondage, torture, sadism, perversion, gore, cannabalism, eyes ripped out, acid in face, etc. **Elias** c-4-11, 14-19, 21-26. **Kremer** a-12, 17. **Palais** a-21(1), 23. **Nostrand/Powell** a-13, 15, 16. **Powell** a-21, 23, 24('51), 5-8, 11, 13, 18-21, 23-25. Bondage-c-21, 24('51), 7. 25-r/#5; 26-r/#9.*

CHAMBER OF CHILLS
Nov, 1972 - No. 25, Nov, 1976
Marvel Comics Group

	GD25	FN65	NM94
1-Harlan Ellison adaptation	.80	2.00	4.00
2-25	.40	1.00	2.00

NOTE: ***Adkins** a-1i, 2i. **Brunner** a-2-4; c-4. **Ditko** r-14, 16, 19, 23, 24. **Everett** a-3i, 11r,21r. **Heath** a-1r. **Gil Kane** c-2p. **Powell** a-13r. **Russell** a-1p, 2p. **Williamson/Mayo** a-13r. **Robert E. Howard** horror story adaptation-2, 3.*

CHAMBER OF CLUES (Formerly Chamber of Chills)
No. 27, Feb, 1955 - No. 28, April, 1955
Harvey Publications

	GD25	FN65	NM94
27-Kerry Drake-r/#19; Powell-a; last pre-code	6.70	20.00	40.00
28-Kerry Drake	4.00	11.00	22.00

CHAMBER OF DARKNESS (Monsters on the Prowl #9 on)
Oct, 1969 - No. 8, Dec, 1970
Marvel Comics Group

	GD25	FN65	NM94
1-Buscema-a(p)	5.85	17.50	35.00
2-Neal Adams scripts	2.40	6.00	12.00
3-Smith, Buscema-a	2.40	6.00	12.00
4-A Conanesque tryout by Smith (4/70); reprinted in Conan #16; Marie Severin/Everett-c	6.70	20.00	40.00
5,6,8: 5-H.P. Lovecraft adaptation	1.00	2.50	5.00
7-Wrightson-c/a, 7pgs. (his 1st work at Marvel); Wrightson draws himself in 1st & last panels; Kirby/Ditko-r	3.00	7.50	15.00
1-(1/72; 25 cent Special)	1.40	3.50	7.00

NOTE: ***Adkins/Everett** a-8. **Craig** a-5. **Ditko** a-6-8r. **Kirby** a(p)-4, 5, 7r. **Kirby/Everett** c-5. **Severin/Everett** c-6. **Wrightson** c-7, 8.*

CHAMP COMICS (Formerly Champion No. 1-10)
No. 11, Oct, 1940 - No. 29, March, 1944
Worth Publ. Co./Champ Publ./Family Comics(Harvey Publ.)

	GD25	FN65	NM94
11-Human Meteor cont'd.	50.00	150.00	300.00
12-20: 14,15-Crandall-c. 18,19-Kirbyish-c. 19-The Wasp app. 20-The Green Ghost app.	39.00	115.00	235.00
21-29: 22-The White Mask app. 23-Flag-c	32.00	95.00	190.00

CHAMPION (See Gene Autry's...)

CHAMPION COMICS (Champ No. 11 on)
No. 2, Dec, 1939 - No. 10, Aug, 1940 (no No.1)
Worth Publ. Co.(Harvey Publications)

	GD25	FN65	NM94
2-The Champ, The Blazing Scarab, Neptina, Liberty Lads, Jungleman, Bill Handy, Swingtime Sweetie begin	75.00	225.00	450.00
3-7: 7-The Human Meteor begins?	37.00	110.00	225.00
8-10-Kirbyish-c; bondage #10	42.00	125.00	250.00

CHAMPIONS, THE
October, 1975 - No. 17, Jan, 1978
Marvel Comics Group

	GD25	FN65	NM94
1-Origin & 1st app. The Champions (The Angel, Black Widow, Ghost Rider, Hercules, Ice Man); Venus x-over	3.60	9.00	18.00
2-10,16: 2,3-Venus x-over	2.00	5.00	10.00
11-15,17-Byrne-a	2.40	6.00	12.00

NOTE: ***Buckler/Adkins** c-3. **Kane/Adkins** c-1. **Kane/Layton** c-11. **Tuska** a-3p, 4p, 6p. Ghost Rider c-1-4, 7, 8, 10, 14, 16, 17 (4, 10, 14 are more prominent).*

CHAMPIONS (Eclipse) (Value: cover or less)

CHAMPIONS (Hero) (Value: cover or less)

CHAMPION SPORTS
Oct-Nov, 1973 - No. 3, Feb-Mar, 1974
National Periodical Publications

	GD25	FN65	NM94
1-3	.30	.75	1.50

CHAOS (See The Crusaders)

CHARLIE CHAN (See Big Shot Comics, Columbia Comics, Feature Comics & The New Advs. of...)

CHARLIE CHAN (The Adventures of...) (Zaza The Mystic No. 10 on)
6-7/48 - No.5, 2-3/49; No.6, 6/55 - No.9, 3/56
Crestwood(Prize) No. 1-5; Charlton No. 6(6/55) on

	GD25	FN65	NM94
1-S&K-c, 2 pages; Infantino-a	36.00	107.00	250.00
2-S&K-c	22.00	65.00	150.00
3-5-All S&K-c (#3-S&K-c/a)	19.00	58.00	135.00
6(6/55-Charlton)-S&K-c	14.00	43.00	100.00
7-9	10.00	30.00	60.00

CHARLIE CHAN
Oct-Dec, 1965 - No. 2, Mar, 1966
Dell Publishing Co.

	GD25	FN65	NM94
1-Springer-a	3.00	7.50	15.00
2	2.00	5.00	10.00

CHARLIE CHAPLIN
1917 (9x16"; large size; softcover; B&W)
Essanay/M. A. Donohue & Co.

Series 1, #315-Comic Capers (9-3/4"x15-3/4")-18pp by Segar, Series 1,

Challengers of the Unknown #31, © DC

Chamber of Chills #21 (#1), © HARV

Champ Comics #12, © HARV

Charlie McCarthy #5, © Edgar Bergen

Charlton Premiere #2, © CC

Checkmate #2, © Jamco Prod.

	GD25	FN65	NM94
#316-In the Movies	79.00	235.00	475.00
Series 1, #317-Up in the Air. 318-In the Army	79.00	235.00	475.00
Funny Stunts-(12-1/2x16-3/8") in color	58.00	175.00	350.00

NOTE: *All contain **Segar** -a; pre-Thimble Theatre.*

CHARLIE McCARTHY (See Edgar Bergen Presents...)
No. 171, Nov, 1947 - No. 571, July, 1954 (See True Comics #14)
Dell Publishing Co.

	GD25	FN65	NM94
4-Color 171	13.00	40.00	90.00
4-Color 196-Part photo-c; photo back-c	11.50	34.00	80.00
1(3-5/49)-Part photo-c; photo back-c	11.50	34.00	80.00
2-9(7/52; #5,6-52 pgs.)	5.85	17.50	35.00
4-Color 445,478,527,571	4.20	12.50	25.00

CHARLTON BULLSEYE
1975 - No. 5, 1976 ($1.50, B&W, bi-monthly, magazine format)
CPL/Gang Publications

	GD25	FN65	NM94
1: 1 & 2 are last Capt. Atom by Ditko/Byrne intended for the never published Capt. Atom #90; Nightshade app.; Jeff Jones-a	1.60	4.00	8.00
2-Part 2 Capt. Atom story by Ditko/Byrne	1.60	4.00	8.00
3-Wrong Country by Sanho Kim	1.00	2.50	5.00
4-Doomsday [1 by John Byrne	1.60	4.00	8.00
5-Doomsday [1 by Byrne, The Question by Toth; Neal Adams back-c; Toth-c	2.00	5.00	10.00

CHARLTON BULLSEYE
June, 1981 - No. 10, Dec, 1982; Nov, 1986 (Color)
Charlton Publications

	GD25	FN65	NM94
1-Blue Beetle, The Question app.; 1st app. Rocket Rabbit	.40	1.00	2.00
2-10: 2-1st app. Neil The Horse; Rocket Rabbit app. 6-Origin & 1st app. Thunderbunny	.30	.75	1.50
Special 1(11/86)(-in B&W)	.60	1.50	3.00
Special 2-Atomic Mouse app. ('87)	.40	1.00	2.00

CHARLTON CLASSICS
April, 1980 - No. 9, Aug, 1981
Charlton Comics

	GD25	FN65	NM94
1	.40	1.00	2.00
2-9		.50	1.00

CHARLTON CLASSICS LIBRARY (1776)
V10No.1, March, 1973 (One Shot)
Charlton Comics

	GD25	FN65	NM94
1776 (title) - Adaptation of the film musical "1776"; given away at movie theatres	.60	1.50	3.00

CHARLTON PREMIERE (Formerly Marine War Heroes)
V1#19, July, 1967; V2#1, Sept, 1967 - No. 4, May, 1968
Charlton Comics

	GD25	FN65	NM94
V1#19-Marine War Heroes, V2#1-Trio; intro. Shape, Tyro Team, & Spookman, 2-Children of Doom, 3-Sinistro Boy Fiend; Blue Beetle & Peacemaker x-over, 4-Unlikely Tales; Ditko-a	.60	1.50	3.00

CHARLTON SPORT LIBRARY - PROFESSIONAL FOOTBALL
Winter, 1969-70 (Jan. on cover) (68 pages)
Charlton Comics

	GD25	FN65	NM94
1	2.00	5.00	10.00

CHASING THE BLUES
1912 (52 pages) (7-1/2x10"; B&W; hardcover)
Doubleday Page

	GD25	FN65	NM94
nn-by Rube Goldberg	50.00	150.00	300.00

CHECKMATE (TV)
Oct, 1962 - No. 2, Dec, 1962
Gold Key

	GD25	FN65	NM94
1,2-Photo-c	4.00	11.00	22.00

CHECKMATE (See Action Comics #598)
April, 1988 - No. 33, Jan, 1991 ($1.25)
DC Comics

	GD25	FN65	NM94
1-12		.60	1.25
13-33: $1.50-$2.00, new format	.30	.75	1.50

NOTE: ***Gil Kane** c-2, 4, 7, 8, 10, 11, 15-19.*

CHEERIOS PREMIUMS (Disney)
1947 (32 pages) (Pocket size; 16 titles)
Walt Disney Productions

	GD25	FN65	NM94
Set "W"			
W1-Donald Duck & the Pirates	4.50	13.50	27.00
W2-Bucky Bug & the Cannibal King	3.00	7.50	15.00
W3-Pluto Joins the F.B.I.	3.00	7.50	15.00
W4-Mickey Mouse & the Haunted House	4.00	12.00	24.00
Set "X"			
X1-Donald Duck, Counter Spy	4.00	10.50	21.00
X2-Goofy Lost in the Desert	3.00	7.50	15.00
X3-Br'er Rabbit Outwits Br'er Fox	3.00	7.50	15.00
X4-Mickey Mouse at the Rodeo	4.00	12.00	24.00
Set "Y"			
Y1-Donald Duck's Atom Bomb by Carl Barks; on Disney's reprint banned list	54.00	160.00	375.00
Y2-Br'er Rabbit's Secret	3.00	7.50	15.00
Y3-Dumbo & the Circus Mystery	4.00	10.50	21.00
Y4-Mickey Mouse Meets the Wizard	4.00	12.00	24.00
Set "Z"			
Z1-Donald Duck Pilots a Jet Plane (not by Barks)	4.00	10.50	21.00
Z2-Pluto Turns Sleuth Hound	3.00	7.50	15.00
Z3-The Seven Dwarfs & the Enchanted Mtn.	4.00	10.50	21.00
Z4-Mickey Mouse's Secret Room	4.00	12.00	24.00

CHEERIOS 3-D GIVEAWAYS (Disney)
1954 (Pocket size) (24 titles)
Walt Disney Productions

(Glasses were cut-outs on boxes)

	GD25	FN65	NM94
Glasses only....	6.70	20.00	40.00
(Set 1)			
1-Donald Duck & Uncle Scrooge, the Firefighters			
2-Mickey Mouse & Goofy, Pirate Plunder			
3-Donald Duck's Nephews, the Fabulous Inventors			
4-Mickey Mouse, Secret of the Ming Vase			
5-Donald Duck with Huey, Dewey, & Louie; ...the Seafarers (title on 2nd page)			
6-Mickey Mouse, Moaning Mountain			
7-Donald Duck, Apache Gold			
8-Mickey Mouse, Flight to Nowhere (per book)....	8.35	25.00	50.00
(Set 2)			
1-Donald Duck, Treasure of Timbuktu			
2-Mickey Mouse & Pluto, Operation China			
3-Donald Duck in the Magic Cows			
4-Mickey Mouse & Goofy, Kid Kokonut			
5-Donald Duck, Mystery Ship			
6-Mickey Mouse, Phantom Sheriff			
7-Donald Duck, Circus Adventures			
8-Mickey Mouse, Arctic Explorers (per book)....	8.35	25.00	50.00
(Set 3)			
1-Donald Duck & Witch Hazel			
2-Mickey Mouse in Darkest Africa			
3-Donald Duck & Uncle Scrooge, Timber Trouble			
4-Mickey Mouse, Rajah's Rescue			
5-Donald Duck in Robot Reporter			

	GD25	FN65	NM94
6-Mickey Mouse, Slumbering Sleuth			
7-Donald Duck in the Foreign Legion			
8-Mickey Mouse, Airwalking Wonder (per book)....	8.35	25.00	50.00

CHESTY AND COPTIE
1946 (4 pages) (Giveaway) (Disney)
Los Angeles Community Chest

	GD25	FN65	NM94
nn-(Very Rare) by Floyd Gottfredson	50.00	150.00	350.00

CHESTY AND HIS HELPERS
1943 (12 pgs., Disney giveaway, 5-1/2"x7-1/4")
Los Angeles War Chest

	GD25	FN65	NM94
nn-Chesty & Coptie	54.00	160.00	375.00

CHEVAL NOIR
1989 - Present ($3.50, B&W, 68 pgs.)
Dark Horse Comics

	GD25	FN65	NM94
1-8,10 ($3.50): 6-Moebius poster insert	.70	1.75	3.50
9,11,13,15,17,20,22 ($4.50, 84 pgs.)	.90	2.25	4.50
12,18,19,21,23,25,26 ($3.95): 12-Geary-a; Mignola-c. 26-Moebius-a begins	.80	2.00	4.00
14 ($4.95, 76 pgs.)(7 pgs. color)	1.00	2.50	5.00
16,24 ($3.75): 16-19-Contain trading cards	.75	1.90	3.75
27-38 ($2.95)	.60	1.50	3.00

NOTE: ***Bolland** a-2, 6, 7, 13, 14. **Bolton** a-2, 4; c-4, 20. **Chadwick** c-13. **Dorman** c-16 (painted). **Geary** a-13, 14. **Kaluta** a-6; c-6, 18. **Moebius** c-5, 9. **Dave Stevens** c-1, 7. **Sutton** painted c-36.*

CHEYENNE (TV)
No. 734, Oct, 1956 - No. 25, Dec-Jan, 1961-62
Dell Publishing Co.

	GD25	FN65	NM94
4-Color 734(#1)-Clint Walker photo-c	11.50	34.00	80.00
4-Color 772,803: Clint Walker photo-c	6.70	20.00	40.00
4(8-10/57) - 12: 4-9-Clint Walker photo-c. 10-12-Ty Hardin photo-c	5.00	15.00	30.00
13-25 (All Clint Walker photo-c)	4.20	12.50	25.00

CHEYENNE AUTUMN (See Movie Classics)

CHEYENNE KID (Formerly Wild Frontier No. 1-7)
No. 8, July, 1957 - No. 99, Nov, 1973
Charlton Comics

	GD25	FN65	NM94
8 (#1)	4.70	14.00	28.00
9,15-17,19	2.80	7.00	14.00
10-Williamson/Torres-a(3); Ditko-c	6.70	20.00	40.00
11,12-Williamson/Torres-a(2) ea.; 11-(68 pgs.)-Cheyenne Kid meets Geronimo	6.70	20.00	40.00
13-Williamson/Torres-a, 5 pgs.	4.35	13.00	26.00
14,18-Williamson-a, 5 pgs.?	4.35	13.00	26.00
20-22,24,25-Severin c/a(3) each	3.20	8.00	16.00
23,27-29	1.60	4.00	8.00
26,30-Severin-a	2.40	6.00	12.00
31-59	1.00	2.50	5.00
60-99: 66-Wander by Aparo begins, ends #87. Apache Red begins #88, origin in #89	.60	1.50	3.00
Modern Comics Reprint 87,89(1978)		.50	1.00

CHICAGO MAIL ORDER (See C-M-O Comics)

CHIEF, THE (Indian Chief No. 3 on)
No. 290, Aug, 1950 - No. 2, Apr-June, 1951
Dell Publishing Co.

	GD25	FN65	NM94
4-Color 290(#1), 2	4.70	14.00	28.00

CHIEF CRAZY HORSE (See Wild Bill Hickok #21)
1950
Avon Periodicals

	GD25	FN65	NM94
nn-Fawcette-c	13.00	40.00	90.00

CHIEF VICTORIO'S APACHE MASSACRE
1951
Avon Periodicals

	GD25	FN65	NM94
nn-Williamson/Frazetta-a, 7 pgs.; Larsen-a; Kinstler-c	27.00	80.00	190.00

CHILDREN OF FIRE (Fantagor) (Value: cover or less)

CHILDREN'S BIG BOOK
1945 (68 pages; stiff covers) (25 cents)
Dorene Publ. Co.

	GD25	FN65	NM94
nn-Comics & fairy tales; David Icove-a	8.35	25.00	50.00

CHILD'S PLAY: THE SERIES (Innovation) (Value: cover or less)

CHILD'S PLAY 2 THE OFFICIAL MOVIE ADAPTATION (Innovation) (Value: cover or less)

CHILI (Millie's Rival)
5/69 - No. 17, 9/70; No. 18, 8/72 - No. 26, 12/73
Marvel Comics Group

	GD25	FN65	NM94
1	3.20	8.00	16.00
2-5	1.60	4.00	8.00
6-17	1.40	3.50	7.00
18-26	1.00	2.50	5.00
Special 1(12/71)	1.60	4.00	8.00

CHILLING ADVENTURES IN SORCERY (...as Told by Sabrina #1, 2) (Red Circle Sorcery No. 6 on)
9/72 - No. 2, 10/72; No. 3, 10/73 - No. 5, 2/74
Archie Publications (Red Circle Prod.)

	GD25	FN65	NM94
1,2-Sabrina cameo in both	1.00	2.50	5.00
3-Morrow-c/a, all	.60	1.50	3.00
4,5-Morrow-c/a, 5,6 pgs.	.60	1.50	3.00

CHILLING TALES (Formerly Beware)
No. 13, Dec, 1952 - No. 17, Oct, 1953
Youthful Magazines

	GD25	FN65	NM94
13(No.1)-Harrison-a; Matt Fox-c/a	20.00	60.00	140.00
14-Harrison-a	11.50	34.00	80.00
15-Has #14 on-c; Matt Fox-c; Harrison-a	13.50	41.00	95.00
16-Poe adapt.-'Metzengerstein'; Rudyard Kipling adapt.-'Mark of the Beast,' by Kiefer; bondage-c	11.00	32.00	75.00
17-Matt Fox-c; Sir Walter Scott & Poe adapt.	13.50	41.00	95.00

CHILLING TALES OF HORROR (Magazine)
V1#1, 6/69 - V1#7, 12/70; V2#2, 2/71 - V2#5, 10/71
(52 pages; black & white) (50 cents)
Stanley Publications

	GD25	FN65	NM94
V1#1	3.20	8.00	16.00
2-7: 7-Cameron-a	1.60	4.00	8.00
V2#2,3,5: 2-Spirit of Frankenstein-r/Adventures into the Unknown #16	1.60	4.00	8.00
V2#4-r/9 pg. Feldstein-a from Adventures into the Unknown #3	1.80	4.50	9.00

NOTE: *Two issues of V2#2 exist, Feb, 1971 and April, 1971.*

CHILLY WILLY (See 4-Color #740, 852, 967, 1017, 1074, 1122, 1177, 1212, 1281)

CHINA BOY (See Wisco)

CHIP 'N' DALE (Walt Disney) (See Walt Disney's C&S #204)
Nov, 1953 - No. 30, June-Aug, 1962; Sept, 1967 - No. 83, 1982
Dell Publishing Co./Gold Key/Whitman No. 65 on

	GD25	FN65	NM94
4-Color 517(#1)	4.00	10.50	21.00
4-Color 581,636	2.40	6.00	12.00
4(12/55-2/56)-10	1.80	4.50	9.00
11-30	1.40	3.50	7.00
1(Gold Key, 1967)-Reprints	2.00	5.00	10.00
2-10	.80	2.00	4.00
11-20	.60	1.50	3.00
21-83	.30	.75	1.50

Cheyenne #11, © Warner Bros.

Cheyenne Kid #47, © CC

Children's Big Book nn, © Dorene Publ.

Choice Comics #3, © GP

A Christmas Carol (1940's), © Sears

A Christmas Dream (1952)

	GD25	FN65	NM94

NOTE: *All Gold Key/Whitman issues have reprints except No. 32-35, 38-41, 45-47. No. 23-28, 30-42, 45-47, 49 have new covers.*

CHIP 'N DALE RESCUE RANGERS
June, 1990 - No. 19, Dec, 1991 ($1.50, color)
Disney Comics

	GD25	FN65	NM94
1-19: New stories; 1,2-Origin	.30	.75	1.50

CHITTY CHITTY BANG BANG (See Movie Comics)

CHOICE COMICS
Dec, 1941 - No. 3, Feb, 1942
Great Publications

	GD25	FN65	NM94
1-Origin Secret Circle; Atlas the Mighty app.; Zomba, Jungle Fight, Kangaroo Man, & Fire Eater begin	71.00	210.00	425.00
2	46.00	135.00	275.00
3-Double feature; Features movie "The Lost City" (classic cover); continued from Great Comics #3	63.00	185.00	375.00

CHOO CHOO CHARLIE
Dec, 1969
Gold Key

	GD25	FN65	NM94
1-John Stanley-a (scarce)	10.00	30.00	60.00

CHRISTIAN HEROES OF TODAY
1964 (36 pages)
David C. Cook

	GD25	FN65	NM94
nn	.80	2.00	4.00

CHRISTMAS (See A-1 No. 28)

CHRISTMAS ADVENTURE, A (See Classics Comics Giveaways, 12/69)

CHRISTMAS ADVENTURE, THE
1963 (16 pages)
S. Rose (H. L. Green Giveaway)

	GD25	FN65	NM94
nn	1.20	3.00	6.00

CHRISTMAS ALBUM (See March of Comics No. 312)

CHRISTMAS & ARCHIE ($1.00)
Jan, 1975 (68 pages) (10-1/4"x13-1/4")
Archie Comics

	GD25	FN65	NM94
1	2.40	6.00	12.00

CHRISTMAS AT THE ROTUNDA (Titled Ford Rotunda Christmas Book 1957 on) (Regular size)
Given away every Christmas at one location
1954 - 1961
Ford Motor Co. (Western Printing)

	GD25	FN65	NM94
1954-56 issues (nn's)	4.00	11.00	22.00
1957-61 issues (nn's)	3.60	9.00	18.00

CHRISTMAS BELLS (See March of Comics No. 297)

CHRISTMAS CARNIVAL
1952 (100 pages, 25 cents) (One Shot)
Ziff-Davis Publ. Co./St. John Publ. Co. No. 2

	GD25	FN65	NM94
nn	13.00	40.00	90.00
2-Reprints Ziff-Davis issue plus-c	10.00	30.00	60.00

CHRISTMAS CAROL, A (See March of Comics No. 33)

CHRISTMAS CAROL, A
No date (1942-43) (32 pgs.; 8-1/4x10-3/4"; paper cover)
Sears Roebuck & Co. (Giveaway)

	GD25	FN65	NM94
nn-Comics & coloring book	6.70	20.00	40.00

CHRISTMAS CAROL, A
1940s ? (20 pgs.)
Sears Roebuck & Co. (Christmas giveaway)

	GD25	FN65	NM94
nn-Comic book & animated coloring book	5.00	15.00	30.00

CHRISTMAS CAROLS
1959 ? (16 pgs.)
Hot Shoppes Giveaway

	GD25	FN65	NM94
nn	2.00	5.00	10.00

CHRISTMAS COLORING FUN
1964 (20 pgs.; slick cover; B&W inside)
H. Burnside

	GD25	FN65	NM94
nn	1.00	2.50	5.00

CHRISTMAS DREAM, A
1950 (16 pages) (Kinney Shoe Store Giveaway)
Promotional Publishing Co.

	GD25	FN65	NM94
nn	2.00	5.00	10.00

CHRISTMAS DREAM, A
1952? (16 pgs.; paper cover)
J. J. Newberry Co. (Giveaway)

	GD25	FN65	NM94
nn	2.00	5.00	10.00

CHRISTMAS DREAM, A
1952 (16 pgs.; paper cover)
Promotional Publ. Co. (Giveaway)

	GD25	FN65	NM94
nn	2.00	5.00	10.00

CHRISTMAS EVE, A (See March of Comics No. 212)

CHRISTMAS FUN AROUND THE WORLD
No date (early 50's) (16 pages; paper cover)
No publisher

	GD25	FN65	NM94
nn	3.20	8.00	16.00

CHRISTMAS IN DISNEYLAND (See Dell Giants)

CHRISTMAS JOURNEY THROUGH SPACE
1960
Promotional Publishing Co.

	GD25	FN65	NM94
nn-Reprints 1954 issue Jolly Christmas Book with new slick cover	3.60	9.00	18.00

CHRISTMAS ON THE MOON
1958 (20 pgs.; slick cover)
W. T. Grant Co. (Giveaway)

	GD25	FN65	NM94
nn	4.00	11.00	22.00

CHRISTMAS PARADE (See Dell Giant No. 26, Dell Giants, March of Comics No. 284, Walt Disney Christmas Parade & Walt Disney's...)

CHRISTMAS PARADE (Walt Disney's)
1/63 (no month) - No. 9, 1/72; Wint/88 (#1,5: 80pgs.; #2-4,7-9: 36pgs.)
Gold Key

	GD25	FN65	NM94
1 (30018-301)-Giant	5.85	17.50	35.00
2-6: 2-r/F.C. #367 by Barks. 3-r/F.C. #178 by Barks. 4-r/F.C. #203 by Barks. 5-r/Christ. Parade #1 (Dell) by Barks; giant. 6-r/Christmas Parade #2 (Dell) by Barks (64 pgs.); giant	5.35	15.00	32.00
7,9: 7-Pull-out poster	3.20	8.00	16.00
8-r/F.C. #367 by Barks; pull-out poster	5.35	16.00	32.00

CHRISTMAS PARTY (See March of Comics No. 256)

CHRISTMAS PLAY BOOK
1946 (16 pgs.; paper cover)
Gould-Stoner Co. (Giveaway)

	GD25	FN65	NM94
nn	4.00	11.00	22.00

CHRISTMAS ROUNDUP
1960
Promotional Publishing Co.

	GD25	FN65	NM94
nn-Marv Levy-c/a	1.60	4.00	8.00

CHRISTMAS STORIES (See 4-Color No. 959, 1062)

CHRISTMAS STORY (See March of Comics No. 326)

CHRISTMAS STORY BOOK (See Woolworth's Christmas Story Book)

CHRISTMAS STORY CUT-OUT BOOK, THE
1951 (36 pages) (15 cents)
Catechetical Guild

393- text & comics 4.00 11.00 22.00

CHRISTMAS TREASURY, A (See Dell Giants & March of Comics No. 227)

CHRISTMAS USA (Through 300 Years) (Also see Uncle Sam's...)
1956
Promotional Publ. Co. (Giveaway)

nn-Marv Levy-c/a 1.60 4.00 8.00

CHRISTMAS WITH ARCHIE
1973, 1974 (52 pages) (49 cents)
Spire Christian Comics (Fleming H. Revell Co.)

nn .40 1.00 2.00

CHRISTMAS WITH MOTHER GOOSE (See 4-Color No. 90, 126, 172, 201, 253)

CHRISTMAS WITH SANTA (See March of Comics No. 92)

CHRISTMAS WITH SNOW WHITE AND THE SEVEN DWARFS
1953 (16 pages, paper cover)
Kobackers Giftstore of Buffalo, N.Y.

nn 4.20 12.50 25.00

CHRISTMAS WITH THE SUPER-HEROES (See Limited Collectors' Edition)
1988; No. 2, 1989 ($2.95)(#2-All new, 68 pgs.)
DC Comics

1-(100 pgs.)-All reprints; N. Adams-r, Byrne-c; Batman, Superman, JLA, LSH Christmas stories; r-Miller's 1st Batman/DC Special Series #21 .60 1.50 3.00
2-Superman by Chadwick, Batman, Wonder Woman, Deadman, Gr. Lantern, Flash app.; Enemy Ace by Byrne .60 1.50 3.00

CHRISTOPHERS, THE
1951 (36 pages) (Some copies have 15 cent sticker)
Catechetical Guild (Giveaway)

nn-Stalin as Satan in Hell 19.00 57.00 130.00

CHROMA-TICK, THE (Special Edition) (Also see The Tick)
Feb, 1992 ($3.95, color, 44 pgs.)
New England Comics Press

1-Includes serially numbered trading card set .80 2.00 4.00

CHROME (Hot)(Value: cover or less)

CHRONICLES OF CORUM, THE (First)(Value: cover or less)

CHUCKLE, THE GIGGLY BOOK OF COMIC ANIMALS
1945 (132 pages) (One Shot)
R. B. Leffingwell Co.

1-Funny animal 14.00 43.00 100.00

CHUCK NORRIS (TV)
Jan, 1987 - No. 3, Sept, 1987
Star Comics (Marvel)

1-3: 1-Ditko-a .50 1.00

CHUCK WAGON (See Sheriff Bob Dixon's...)

CICERO'S CAT
July-Aug, 1959 - No. 2, Sept-Oct, 1959
Dell Publishing Co.

1,2-Cat from Mutt & Jeff 3.60 9.00 18.00

CIMARRON STRIP (TV)
January, 1968
Dell Publishing Co.

1 3.60 9.00 18.00

CINDER AND ASHE
May, 1988 - No. 4, Aug, 1988 ($1.75, mini-series)
DC Comics

1-4: Mature readers .35 .90 1.75

CINDERELLA (See 4-Color No. 272, 786, & Movie Comics)

CINDERELLA
April, 1982
Whitman Publishing Co.

nn-Reprints 4-Color #272 .50 1.00

CINDERELLA IN "FAIREST OF THE FAIR"
1955 (16 pages, 5x7-1/4", soft-c) (Walt Disney)
American Dairy Association (Premium)

nn 7.50 22.50 45.00

CINDERELLA LOVE
No. 10, 1950; No. 11, 4-5/51; No. 12, 9/51; No. 4, 10-11/51 - No. 11, Fall, 1952; No. 12, 10/53 - No. 15, 8/54; No. 25, 12/54 - No. 29, 10/55 (No #16-24)
Ziff-Davis/St. John Publ. Co. No. 12 on

10(#1)(1st Series, 1950) 7.50 22.50 45.00
11(#2, 4-5/51)-Crandall-a; Saunders painted-c 5.00 15.00 30.00
12(#3, 9/51) 4.00 11.00 22.00
4-8: 4,7-Photo-c 3.60 9.00 18.00
9-Kinstler-a; photo-c 4.20 12.50 25.00
10,11(Fall/'52): 10-Whitney painted-c. 11-Photo-c 4.00 11.00 22.00
12(St. John-10/53)-#14:13-Painted-c.14-Baker-a? 3.20 8.00 16.00
15 (8/54)-Matt Baker-c 4.00 11.00 22.00
25(2nd Series)(Formerly Romantic Marriage) 2.80 7.00 14.00
26-Baker-c; last precode (2/55) 4.00 11.00 22.00
27,29-Matt Baker-c 4.00 11.00 22.00
28 2.40 6.00 12.00

CINDY COMICS (...Smith No. 39,40; Crime Can't Win No. 41 on)
(Formerly Krazy Komics)(See Teen Comics)
No. 27, Fall, 1947 - No. 40, July, 1950
Timely Comics

27-Kurtzman-a, 3 pgs: Margie, Oscar begin 10.00 30.00 60.00
28-31-Kurtzman-a 6.70 20.00 40.00
32-40: 33-Georgie story; anti-Wertham editorial 4.20 12.50 25.00
NOTE: *Kurtzman's "Hey Look"-#27(3), 29(2), 30(2), 31; "Giggles 'N' Grins"-28.*

CINEMA COMICS HERALD
1941 - 1943 (4-pg. movie "trailers," paper-c, 7x10")(Giveaway)
Paramount Pictures/Universal/RKO/20th Century Fox/Republic

"Mr. Bug Goes to Town"-(1941) 4.00 10.00 20.00
"Bedtime Story" 4.00 10.00 20.00
"Lady For A Night," John Wayne, Joan Blondell (1942) 5.85 17.50 35.00
"Reap The Wild Wind" (1942) 4.00 10.00 20.00
"Thunder Birds" (1942) 4.00 10.00 20.00
"They All Kissed the Bride" 4.00 10.00 20.00
"Arabian Nights," (nd) 4.20 12.50 25.00
"Bombardie" (1943) 4.00 10.00 20.00
"Crash Dive" (1943)-Tyrone Power 4.20 12.50 25.00
NOTE: *The 1941-42 issues contain line art with color photos. 1943 issues are line art.*

CIRCUS (...the Comic Riot)
June, 1938 - No. 3, Aug, 1938
Globe Syndicate

1-(Scarce)-Spacehawks (2 pgs.), & Disk Eyes by Wolverton (2 pgs.), Pewee Throttle by Cole (2nd comic book work; see Star Comics V1#11), Beau Gus, Ken Craig & The Lords of Crillon, Jack Hinton by Eisner, Van Bragger by Kane 283.00 850.00 1700.00
2,3-(Scarce)-Eisner, Cole, Wolverton, Bob Kane-a in each 150.00 450.00 900.00

Cinderella Love #7, © Z-D

Cindy #40, © MEG

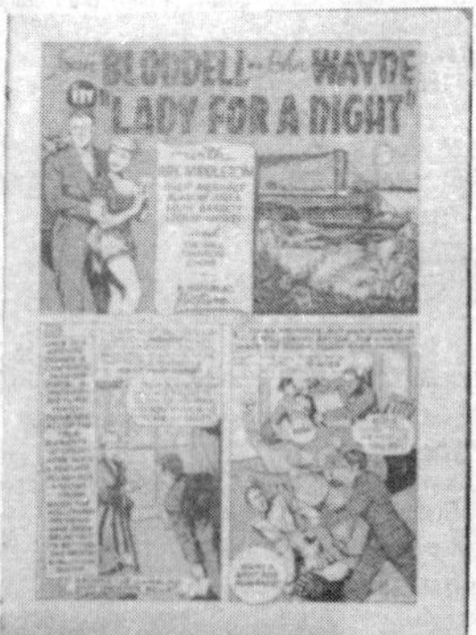

Cinema Comics Herald © Universal

Circus of Fun Comics #3, © A.W. Nugent

Cisco Kid #20, © DELL

Claire Voyant #1, © STD

	GD25	FN65	NM94

CIRCUS BOY (See 4-Color No. 759, 785, 813)

CIRCUS COMICS
1945 - No. 2, June, 1945; Winter, 1948-49
Farm Women's Publishing Co./D. S. Publ.

	GD25	FN65	NM94
1-Funny animal	6.70	20.00	40.00
2	4.70	14.00	28.00
1(1948)-D.S. Publ.; 2 pgs. Frazetta	14.00	43.00	100.00

CIRCUS OF FUN COMICS
1945 - No. 3, Dec, 1947 (a book of games & puzzles)
A. W. Nugent Publishing Co.

	GD25	FN65	NM94
1	8.35	25.00	50.00
2,3	5.35	16.00	32.00

CIRCUS BOY (See Movie Classics)

CISCO KID, THE (TV)
July, 1950 - No. 41, Oct-Dec, 1958
Dell Publishing Co.

	GD25	FN65	NM94
4-Color 292(#1)-Cisco Kid, his horse Diablo, & sidekick Pancho & his horse Loco begin; painted-c begin	16.00	48.00	110.00
2(1/51)-5	8.35	25.00	50.00
6-10	6.70	20.00	40.00
11-20	5.00	15.00	30.00
21-36-Last painted-c	4.20	12.50	25.00
37-41: All photo-c	8.35	25.00	50.00

NOTE: ***Buscema** a-40. **Ernest Nordli** painted-c-5-16, 20, 35.*

CISCO KID COMICS
Winter, 1944 - No. 3?, 1945
Bernard Bailey/Swappers Quarterly

	GD25	FN65	NM94
1-Illustrated Stories of the Operas: Faust; Funnyman by Giunta; Cisco Kid begins	29.00	86.00	200.00
2,3 (Exist?)	22.00	65.00	150.00

CITIZEN SMITH (See Holyoke One-Shot No. 9)

CITY OF THE LIVING DEAD (See Fantastic Tales No. 1)
1952
Avon Periodicals

	GD25	FN65	NM94
nn-Hollingsworth-c/a	22.00	65.00	150.00

CITY SURGEON (Blake Harper...)
August, 1963
Gold Key

	GD25	FN65	NM94
1(10075-308)-Painted-c	2.00	5.00	10.00

CIVIL WAR MUSKET, THE (Kadets of America Handbook)
1960 (36 pages) (Half-size; 25 cents)
Custom Comics, Inc.

	GD25	FN65	NM94
nn	2.40	6.00	12.00

CLAIRE VOYANT (Also see Keen Teens)
1946 - No. 4, 1947 (Sparling strip reprints)
Leader Publ./Standard/Pentagon Publ.

	GD25	FN65	NM94
nn	32.00	95.00	220.00
2,4: 2-Kamen-c. 4-Kamen bondage-c	25.00	75.00	175.00
3-Kamen bridal-c; contents mentioned in Love and Death, a book by Gershom Legman('49) referenced by Dr. Wertham	29.00	85.00	200.00

CLANCY THE COP
1930 - No. 2, 1931 (52 pages; B&W) (not reprints) (10"x10")
Dell Publishing Co. (Soft cover)

	GD25	FN65	NM94
1,2-Vep-a	12.00	36.00	85.00

CLASH
1991 - No. 3, 1991 ($4.95, color, mini-series, 52 pgs.)
DC Comics

	GD25	FN65	NM94
Book One - Three: Adam Kubert-c/a	1.00	2.50	5.00

CLASSIC COMICS/ILLUSTRATED - INTRODUCTION
by Dan Malan

Further revisions have been made to help in understanding the **Classics** section. **Classics** reprint editions prior to 1963 had either incorrect dates or no dates listed. Those reprint editions should be identified only by the highest number on the reorder list (HRN). Past price guides listed what were calculated to be approximately correct dates, but many people found it confusing for the price guide to list a date not listed in the comic itself.

We have also attempted to clear up confusion about edition variations, such as color, printer, etc. Such variations will be identified by letters. Editions will now be determined by three categories. Original edition variations will be Edition 1A, 1B, etc. All reprint editions prior to 1963 will be identified by HRN only. All reprint editions from 9/63 on will be identified by the correct date listed in the comic.

We have also included new information on four recent reprintings of **Classics** not previously listed. From 1968-1976 Twin Circle, the Catholic newspaper, serialized over 100 **Classics** titles. That list can be found under non-series items at the end of this section. In 1972 twelve **Classics** were reissued as **Now Age Books Illustrated**. They are listed under **Pendulum Illustrated Classics**. In 1982, 20 **Classics** were reissued, adapted for teaching English as a second language. They are listed under **Regents Illustrated Classics**. Then in 1984, six **Classics** were reissued with cassette tapes. See the listing under **Cassette Books**.

UNDERSTANDING CLASSICS ILLUSTRATED
by Dan Malan

Since **Classics Illustrated** is the most complicated comic book series, with all its reprint editions and variations, with changes in covers and artwork, with a variety of means of identifying editions, and with the most extensive worldwide distribution of any comic-book series; therefore this introductory section is provided to assist you in gaining expertise about this series.

THE HISTORY OF CLASSICS

The **Classics** series was the brain child of Albert L. Kanter, who saw in the new comic-book medium a means of introducing children to the great classics of literature. In October of 1941 his Gilberton Co. began the **Classic Comics** series with **The Three Musketeers**, with 64 pages of storyline. In those early years, the struggling series saw irregular schedules and numerous printers, not to mention variable art quality and liberal story adaptations. With No.13 the page total was reduced to 56 (except for No. 33, originally scheduled to be No. 9), and with No. 15 the coming-next ad on the outside back cover moved inside. In 1945 the Jerry Iger Shop began producing all new CC titles, beginning with No. 23. In 1947 the search for a classier logo resulted in **Classics Illustrated**, beginning with No. 35, The **Last Days of Pompeii**. With No. 45 the page total dropped again to 48, which was to become the standard.

Two new developments in 1951 had a profound effect upon the success of the series. One was the introduction of painted covers, instead of the old line drawn covers, beginning with No. 81, **The Odyssey**. The second was the switch to the major national distributor Curtis. They raised the cover price from 10 to 15 cents, making it the highest priced comic-book, but it did not slow the growth of the series, because they were marketed as books, not comics. Because of this higher quality image, **Classics** flourished during the fifties while other comic series were reeling from outside attacks. They diversified with their new **Juniors**, **Specials**, and **World Around Us** series.

Classics artwork can be divided into three distinct periods. The pre-Iger era (1941-44) was mentioned above for its variable art quality. The Iger era (1945-53) was a major improvement in art quality and adaptations. It came to be dominated by artists Henry Kiefer and Alex Blum, together accounting for some 50 titles. Their styles gave the first real personality to the series. The EC era (1954-62) resulted from the demise of the EC horror series, when many of their artists made the major switch to classical art.

But several factors brought the production of new CI titles to a complete halt in 1962. Gilberton lost its 2nd class mailing permit. External factors like television, cheap paperback books, and Cliff Notes were all eating away at their market. Production halted with No.167, **Faust**, even though many more titles were already in the works. Many of those found their way into foreign series, and are very desirable to collectors. In 1967, **Classics Illustrated** was sold to Patrick Frawley and his Catholic publication, Twin Circle. They issued two new titles in 1969 as part of an attempted revival, but succumbed to major distribution problems in 1971. In 1988, the trio: First Publishing, Berkley Press, and Classics Media Group acquired the use rights for the old CI series art, logo, and name from the Frawley Group. So far they have used only the name in the new series, but do have plans to reprint the old CI.

One of the unique aspects of the **Classics Illustrated** (CI) series was the proliferation of reprint variations. Some titles had as many as 25 editions. Reprinting began in 1943. Some **Classic Comics** (CC) reprints (r) had the logo format revised to a banner logo, and added a motto under the banner. In 1947 CC titles changed to the CI logo, but kept their line drawn covers (LDC). In 1948, Nos. 13, 18, 29 and 41 received second covers (LDC2), replacing covers considered too violent, and reprints of Nos. 13-44 had pages reduced to 48, except for No. 26, which had 48 pages to begin with.

Starting in the mid-1950s, 70 of the 80 LDC titles were reissued with new painted covers (PC). Thirty of them also received new interior artwork (A2). The new artwork was generally higher quality with larger art panels and more faithful but abbreviated storylines. Later on, there were 29 second painted covers (PC2), mostly by Twin Circle. Altogether there were 199 interior art variations (169 (O)s and 30 A2 editions) and 272 different covers (169 (O)s, four LDC2s, 70 new PCs of LDC (O)s, and 29 PC2s). It is mildly astounding to realize that there are nearly 1400 different editions in the U.S. CI series.

FOREIGN CLASSICS ILLUSTRATED

If U.S. **Classics** variations are mildly astounding, the veritable plethora of foreign CI variations will boggle your imagination. While we still anticipate additional discoveries, we presently know about series in 25 languages and 27 countries. There were 250 new CI titles in foreign series, and nearly 400 new foreign covers of U.S. titles. The 1400 U.S. CI editions pale in comparison to the 4000[foreign editions. The very nature of CI lent itself to flourishing as an international series. Worldwide, they published over one billion copies! The first foreign CI series consisted of six Canadian **Classic Comic** reprints in 1946.

Here is a chart showing when CI series first began in each country:

1946: Canada. 1947: Australia. 1948: Brazil/The Netherlands. 1950: Italy. 1951: Greece/Japan/Hong Kong(?)/England/Argentina/Mexico. 1952: West Germany. 1954: Norway. 1955: New Zealand/South Africa. 1956:: Denmark/Sweden/Iceland. 1957: Finland/France. 1962: Singapore(?). 1964: India (8 languages). 1971: Ireland (Gaelic). 1973:Belgium(?) /Philippines(?) /Malaysia(?).

Significant among the early series were Brazil and Greece. In 1950, Brazil was the first country to begin doing its own new titles. They issued nearly 80 new CI titles by Brazilian authors. In Greece in 1951 they actually had debates in parliament about the effects of **Classics Illustrated** on Greek culture, leading to the inclusion of 88 new Greek History & Mythology titles in the CI series.

But by far the most important foreign CI development was the joint European series which began in 1956 in 10 countries simultaneously. By 1960, CI had the largest European distribution of any American publication, not just comics! So when all the problems came up with U.S. distribution, they literally moved the CI operation to Europe in 1962, and continued producing new titles in all four CI series. Many of them were adapted and drawn in the U.S., the most famous of which was the British CI #158A. Dr. No, drawn by Norman Node!. Unfortunately, the British CI series ended in late 1963, which limited the European CI titles available in English to 15. Altogether there were 82 new CI art titles in the joint European series, which ran until 1976.

CLASSICS REFERENCE INFORMATION

The Classics Collector Magazine (formerly **Worldwide Classics Newsletter**) (1987-1993) Dan Malan, Editor/Publisher. This magazine is the nerve center of the classics-collecting hobby, with subscribers in 22 countries. It covers the official CI series (old and new), related classical comic-book series, foreign series, various memorabilia collectibles, and even illustrated books. Features include new discoveries, market analysis, interviews, pictorials, artist info, and classical ads. It is available by subscription directly from the publisher at 7519 Lindbergh Dr., St. Louis, MO 63117, or at local comic specialty shops.

(Note: CI reference works such as **The Classics Handbook** are now out of print, and the anticipated **Complete Guide to Classics Collectibles** will be out in 1993. Vol. 1 by Dan Malan contains nearly 800 full color photos, plus more historical information & market analysis than covered here. Future volumes will cover Foreign Classics, related series & old illustrated books. For current info on CI reference books, refer to TCC magazine)

IDENTIFYING CLASSICS EDITIONS

HRN: This is the highest number on the reorder list. It should be listed in ( ) after the title number. It is crucial to understanding various CI editions.

ORIGINALS (O): This is the all-important First Edition. To determine (O)s,there is one primary rule and two secondary rules (with exceptions):

Rule No. 1: All (O)s and only (O)s have coming-next ads for the next number. **Exceptions**: No. 14(15) (reprint) has an ad on the last inside text page only. No. 14(0) also has a full-page outside back cover ad (also rule 2). Nos.55(75) and 57(75) have coming-next ads. (Rules 2 and 3 apply here). Nos. 168(0) and 169(0) do not have coming-next ads. No.168 was never reprinted; No. 169(0) has HRN (166). No. 169(169) is the only reprint.

Rule No. 2: On nos.1-80, all (O)s and only (O)s list 10c on the front cover. **Exceptions**: Reprint variations of Nos. 37(62), 39(71), and 46(62) list 10c on the front cover. (Rules 1 and 3 apply here.)

Rule No. 3: All (O)s have HRN close to that title No. **Exceptions**: Some reprints also have HRNs close to that title number: a few CC(r)s, 58(62), 60(62), 149(149), 152(149) 153(149), and title nos. in the 160's. (Rules 1 and 2 apply here.)

DATES: Many reprint editions list either an incorrect date or no date. Since Gilberton apparently kept track of CI editions by HRN, they often left the (O) date on reprints. Often, someone with a CI collection for sale will swear that all their copies are originals. That is why we are so detailed in pointing out how to identify original editions. Except for original editions, which should have a coming-next ad, etc., all CI dates prior to 1963 are incorrect! So you want to go by HRN only if it is (165) or below, and go by listed date if it is 1963 or later. There are a few (167) editions with incorrect dates. They could be listed either as (167) or (62/3), which is meant to indicate that they were issued sometime between late 1962 and early 1963.

COVERS: A change from CC to LDC indicates a logo change, not a cover change; while a change from LDC to LDC2, LDC to PC, or from PC to PC2 does indicate a new cover. New PCs can be identified by HRN, and PC2s can be identified by HRN and date. Several covers had color changes, particularly from purple to blue.

Notes: If you see 15 cents in Canada on a front cover, it does not necessarily indicate a Canadian edition. Editions with an HRN between 44 and 75, with 15 cents on the cover are Canadian. Check the publisher's address. An HRN listing two numbers with a / between them indicates that there are two different reorder lists in the front and back covers. Official Twin Circle editions have a full-page back cover ad for their TC magazine, with no CI reorder list. Any CI with just a Twin Circle sticker on the front is not an official TC edition.

TIPS ON LISTING CLASSICS FOR SALE

It may be easy to just list Edition 17, but Classics collectors keep track of CI editions in terms of HRN and/or date, (O) or (r), CC or LDC, PC or PC2, A1 or A2, soft or stiff cover, etc. Try to help them out. For originals, just list (0), unless there are variations such as color (Nos. 10 and 61), printer (Nos. 18-22), HRN (Nos. 95, 108, 160), etc. For reprints, just list HRN if its (165) or below. Above that, list HRN and date. Also, please list type of logo/cover/art for the convenience of buyers. They will appreciate it.

CLASSIC COMICS (Also see Best from Boys Life, Cassette Books, Famous Stories, Fast Fiction, Golden Picture Classics, King Classics, Marvel Classics Comics, Pendulum Illustrated Classics, Picture Parade, Picture Progress, Regents Ill. Classics, Stories by Famous Authors, Superior Stories, and World Around Us.)

CLASSIC COMICS (Classics Illustrated No. 35 on)
10/41 - No. 34, 2/47; No. 35, 3/47 - No. 169, Spring 1969
(Reprint Editions of almost all titles 5/43 - Spring 1971)
(Painted Covers (0)s No. 81 on, and (r)s of most Nos. 1-80)
Elliot Publishing #1-3 (1941-1942)/Gilberton Publications #4-167 (1942-

Classic Comics #1, © GIL

1967)/Twin Circle Pub. (Frawley) #168-169 (1968-1971)

Abbreviations:
A–Art; C or c–Cover; CC–Classic Comics; CI–Classics Ill.;
Ed–Edition; LDC–Line Drawn Cover; PC–Painted Cover; r–Reprint

1. The Three Musketeers

Ed	HRN	Date	Details	A	C			
1	–	10/41	Date listed-1941; Elliot Pub; 68 pgs.	1	1	400.00	1200.00	2800.00
2	10	–	10¢ price removed on all (r)s; Elliot Pub; CC-r	1	1	25.00	75.00	175.00
3	15	–	Long Isl. Ind. Ed.; CC-r	1	1	18.00	54.00	125.00
4	18/20	–	Sunrise Times Ed.; CC-r	1	1	14.00	43.00	100.00
5	21	–	Richmond Courier Ed.; CC-r	1	1	13.00	40.00	90.00
6	28	1946	CC-r	1	1	10.00	30.00	65.00

Classic Comics #2 (HRN-18), © GIL

Classic Comics #3 (HRN-20), © GIL

Classic Comics #4 (Orig?), © GIL

Ed	HRN	Date	Details	A	C	GD25	FN65	NM94
7	36	–	LDC-r	1	1	5.35	16.00	32.00
8	60	–	LDC-r	1	1	4.00	11.00	22.00
9	64	–	LDC-r	1	1	3.60	9.00	18.00
10	78	–	C-price 15¢;LDC-r	1	1	3.20	8.00	16.00
11	93	–	LDC-r	1	1	3.20	8.00	16.00
12	114	–	Last LDC-r	1	1	2.40	6.00	12.00
13	134	–	New-c; old-a; 64 pg. PC-r	1	2	2.40	6.00	12.00
14	143	–	Old-a; PC-r; 64 pg.	1	2	2.00	5.00	10.00
15	150	–	New-a; PC-r; Evans/Crandall-a	2	2	2.40	6.00	12.00
16	149	–	PC-r	2	2	1.25	2.50	5.00
17	167	–	PC-r	2	2	1.25	2.50	5.00
18	167	4/64	PC-r	2	2	1.25	2.50	5.00
19	167	1/65	PC-r	2	2	1.25	2.50	5.00
20	167	3/66	PC-r	2	2	1.25	2.50	5.00
21	166	11/67	PC-r	2	2	1.25	2.50	5.00
22	166	Spr/69	C-price 25¢ ; stiff-c; PC-r	2	2	1.25	2.50	5.00
23	169	Spr/71	PC-r; stiff-c	2	2	1.25	2.50	5.00

2. Ivanhoe

Ed	HRN	Date	Details	A	C	GD25	FN65	NM94
1	(O)	12/41?	Date listed-1941; Elliot Pub; 68 pgs.	1	1	157.00	471.00	1100.00
2	10	–	Price & 'Presents' removed; Elliot Pub; CC-r	1	1	22.00	65.00	150.00
3	15	–	Long Isl. Ind. ed.; CC-r	1	1	16.00	48.00	110.00
4	18/20		Sunrise Times ed.; CC-r	1	1	14.00	43.00	100.00
5	21	–	Richmond Courier ed.; CC-r	1	1	13.00	40.00	90.00
6	28	1946	Last 'Comics'-r	1	1	10.00	30.00	65.00
7	36	–	1st LDC-r	1	1	5.35	16.00	32.00
8	60	–	LDC-r	1	1	4.00	11.00	22.00
9	64	–	LDC-r	1	1	4.00	10.00	20.00
10	78	–	C-price 15¢; LDC-r	1	1	3.20	8.00	16.00
11	89	–	LDC-r	1	1	2.80	7.00	14.00
12	106	–	LDC-r	1	1	2.40	6.00	12.00
13	121	–	Last LDC-r	1	1	2.40	6.00	12.00
14	136	–	New-c&a; PC-r	2	2	2.80	7.00	14.00
15	142	–	PC-r	2	2	1.25	2.50	5.00
16	153	–	PC-r	2	2	1.25	2.50	5.00
17	149	–	PC-r	2	2	1.25	2.50	5.00
18	167	–	PC-r	2	2	1.25	2.50	5.00
19	167	5/64	PC-r	2	2	1.25	2.50	5.00
20	167	1/65	PC-r	2	2	1.25	2.50	5.00
21	167	3/66	PC-r	2	2	1.25	2.50	5.00
22A	166	9/67	PC-r	2	2	1.25	2.50	5.00
22B	166	–	Center ad for Children's Digest & Young Miss; rare; PC-r	2	2	8.35	25.00	50.00
23	166	R/68	C-Price 25¢; PC-r	2	2	1.25	2.50	5.00
24	169	Win/69	Stiff-c	2	2	1.25	2.50	5.00
25	169	Win/71	PC-r; stiff-c	2	2	1.25	2.50	5.00

3. The Count of Monte Cristo

Ed	HRN	Date	Details	A	C	GD25	FN65	NM94
1	(O)	3/42	Elliot Pub; 68 pgs.	1	1	110.00	332.00	775.00
2	10	–	Conray Prods; CC-r	1	1	22.00	65.00	150.00
3	15	–	Long Isl. Ind. ed.; CC-r	1	1	16.00	48.00	110.00
4	18/20		Sunrise Times ed.; CC-r	1	1	14.00	43.00	100.00
5	20	–	Sunrise Times ed.; CC-r	1	1	13.00	40.00	90.00
6	21	–	Richmond Courier ed.; CC-r	1	1	12.00	36.00	85.00
7	28	1946	CC-r; new Banner logo	1	1	10.00	30.00	65.00
8	36	–	1st LDC-r	1	1	5.35	16.00	32.00
9	60	–	LDC-r	1	1	4.00	11.00	22.00
10	62	–	LDC-r	1	1	4.35	13.00	26.00
11	71	–	LDC-r	1	1	3.60	9.00	18.00
12	87	–	C-price 15¢; LDC-r	1	1	3.20	8.00	16.00
13	113	–	LDC-r	1	1	2.40	6.00	12.00
14	135	–	New-c&a; PC-r	2	2	2.40	6.00	12.00
15	143	–	PC-r	2	2	1.25	2.50	5.00
16	153	–	PC-r	2	2	1.25	2.50	5.00
17	161	–	PC-r	2	2	1.25	2.50	5.00
18	167	–	PC-r	2	2	1.25	2.50	5.00
19	167	7/64	PC-r	2	2	1.25	2.50	5.00
20	167	7/65	PC-r	2	2	1.25	2.50	5.00
21	167	7/66	PC-r	2	2	1.25	2.50	5.00
22	166	R/68	C-price 25¢; PC-r	2	2	1.25	2.50	5.00
23	169	–	Win/69 Stiff-c;PC-r	2	2	1.25	2.50	5.00

4. The Last of the Mohicans

Ed	HRN	Date	Details	A	C	GD25	FN65	NM94
1	(O)	8/42?	Date listed-1942; Gilberton #4(0) on; 68 pgs.	1	1	96.00	290.00	675.00
2	12	–	Elliot Pub; CC-r	1	1	20.00	60.00	140.00
3	15	–	Long Isl. Ind. ed.; CC-r	1	1	16.00	48.00	110.00
4	20	–	Long Isl. Ind. ed.; CC-r; banner logo	1	1	14.00	43.00	100.00
5	21	–	Queens Home News ed.; CC-r	1	1	13.00	40.00	90.00
6	28	1946	Last CC-r; new	1	1	10.00	30.00	65.00
7	36	–	1st LDC-r	1	1	5.35	16.00	32.00
8	60	–	LDC-r	1	1	4.00	11.00	22.00
9	64	–	LDC-r	1	1	3.60	9.00	18.00
10	78	–	C-price 15¢; LDC-r	1	1	3.20	8.00	16.00
11	89	–	LDC-r	1	1	2.80	7.00	14.00
12	117	–	Last LDC-r	1	1	2.40	6.00	12.00
13	135	–	New-c; PC-r	1	2	2.40	6.00	12.00
14	141	–	PC-r	1	2	2.00	5.00	10.00
15	150	–	New-a; PC-r; Severin, L.B. Cole-a	2	2	2.40	6.00	12.00
16	161	–	PC-r	2	2	1.25	2.50	5.00
17	167	–	PC-r	2	2	1.25	2.50	5.00
18	167	6/64	PC-r	2	2	1.25	2.50	5.00
19	167	8/65	PC-r	2	2	1.25	2.50	5.00
20	167	8/66	PC-r	2	2	1.25	2.50	5.00
21	166	R/67	C-price 25¢; PC-r	2	2	1.25	2.50	5.00
22	169	Spr/69	Stiff-c; PC-r	2	2	1.25	2.50	5.00

5. Moby Dick

Ed	HRN	Date	Details	A	C	GD25	FN65	NM94
1	(O)	9/42?	Date listed-1942; Gilberton; 68 pgs.	1	1	115.00	343.00	800.00
2	10	–	Conray Prods; Pg. 64 changed from 105 title list to letter from Editor; CC-r	1	1	22.00	65.00	150.00

Ed	HRN	Date	Details	A	C			
3	15	–	Long Isl. Ind. ed.; Pg. 64 changed from Letter to the Editor to Ill. poem-Concord Hymn; CC-r	1	1	16.00	48.00	110.00
4	18/20	–	Sunrise Times ed.; CC-r	1	1	15.00	45.00	105.00
5	20	–	Sunrise Times ed.; CC-r	1	1	14.00	43.00	100.00
6	21	–	Sunrise Times ed.; CC-r	1	1	13.00	40.00	90.00
7	28	1946	CC-r; new banner logo	1	1	10.00	30.00	65.00
8	36	–	1st LDC-r	1	1	5.35	16.00	32.00
9	60	–	LDC-r	1	1	4.00	11.00	22.00
10	62	–	LDC-r	1	1	4.35	13.00	26.00
11	71	–	LDC-r	1	1	3.60	9.00	18.00
12	87	–	C-price 15¢; LDC-r	1	1	3.20	8.00	16.00
13	118	–	LDC-r	1	1	2.40	6.00	12.00
14	131	–	New c&a; PC-r	2	2	2.40	6.00	12.00
15	138	–	PC-r	2	2	1.25	2.50	5.00
16	148	–	PC-r	2	2	1.25	2.50	5.00
17	158	–	PC-r	2	2	1.25	2.50	5.00
18	167	–	PC-r	2	2	1.25	2.50	5.00
19	167	6/64	PC-r	2	2	1.25	2.50	5.00
20	167	7/65	PC-r	2	2	1.25	2.50	5.00
21	167	3/66	PC-r	2	2	1.25	2.50	5.00
22	166	9/67	PC-r	2	2	1.25	2.50	5.00
23	166	Win/69	New-c & c-price 25¢; Stiff-c; PC-r	2	3	2.00	5.00	10.00
24	169	Win/71	PC-r	2	3	2.00	5.00	10.00

6. A Tale of Two Cities

Ed	HRN	Date	Details	A	C			
1	(O)	10/42	Date listed-1942; 68 pgs. Zeckerberg c/a	1	1	100.00	300.00	700.00
2	14	–	Elliot Pub; CC-r	1	1	19.00	57.00	130.00
3	18	–	Long Isl. Ind. ed.; CC-r	1	1	16.00	48.00	110.00
4	20	–	Sunrise Times ed.; CC-r	1	1	14.00	43.00	100.00
5	28	1946	Last CC-r; new banner logo	1	1	10.00	30.00	65.00
6	51	–	1st LDC-r	1	1	4.70	14.00	28.00
7	64	–	LDC-r	1	1	4.00	10.50	21.00
8	78	–	C-price 15¢; LDC-r	1	1	3.20	8.00	16.00
9	89	–	LDC-r	1	1	2.40	6.00	12.00
10	117	–	LDC-r	1	1	2.40	6.00	12.00
11	132	–	New-c&a; PC-r; Joe Orlando-a	2	2	2.40	6.00	12.00
12	140	–	PC-r	2	2	1.25	2.50	5.00
13	147	–	PC-r	2	2	1.25	2.50	5.00
14	152	–	PC-r; very rare	2	2	11.50	34.00	80.00
15	153	–	PC-r	2	2	1.25	2.50	5.00
16	149	–	PC-r	2	2	1.25	2.50	5.00
17	167	–	PC-r	2	2	1.25	2.50	5.00
18	167	6/64	PC-r	2	2	1.25	2.50	5.00
19	167	8/65	PC-r	2	2	1.25	2.50	5.00
20	166	5/67	PC-r	2	2	1.25	2.50	5.00
21	166	Fall/68	New-c & 25¢; PC-r	2	3	2.00	5.00	10.00
22	169	Sum/70	Stiff-c; PC-r	2	3	2.00	5.00	10.00

7. Robin Hood

Ed	HRN	Date	Details	A	C			
1	(O)	12/42	Date listed-1942; first Gift Box ad-bc; 68 pgs.	1	1	79.00	235.00	550.00
2	12	–	Elliot Pub; CC-r	1	1	19.00	57.00	130.00
3	18	–	Long Isl. Ind. ed.; CC-r	1	1	15.00	45.00	105.00
4	20	–	Nassau Bulletin ed.; CC-r	1	1	14.00	43.00	100.00
5	22	–	Queens Cty. Times ed.; CC-r	1	1	13.00	40.00	90.00
6	28	–	CC-r	1	1	10.00	30.00	65.00
7	51	–	LDC-r	1	1	4.70	14.00	28.00
8	64	–	LDC-r	1	1	4.00	10.50	21.00
9	78	–	LDC-r	1	1	3.20	8.00	16.00
10	97	–	LDC-r	1	1	2.80	7.00	14.00
11	106	–	LDC-r	1	1	2.40	6.00	12.00
12	121	–	LDC-r	1	1	2.40	6.00	12.00
13	129	–	New-c; PC-r	1	2	2.40	6.00	12.00
14	136	–	New-a; PC-r	2	2	2.40	6.00	12.00
15	143	–	PC-r	2	2	1.25	2.50	5.00
16	153	–	PC-r	2	2	1.25	2.50	5.00
17	164	–	PC-r	2	2	1.25	2.50	5.00
18	167	–	PC-r	2	2	1.25	2.50	5.00
19	167	6/64	PC-r	2	2	1.50	3.00	6.00
20	167	5/65	PC-r	2	2	1.25	2.50	5.00
21	167	7/66	PC-r	2	2	1.25	2.50	5.00
22	166	12/67	PC-r	2	2	1.50	3.00	6.00
23	169	Sum/69	Stiff-c; c-price 25¢; PC-r	2	2	1.25	2.50	5.00

8. Arabian Nights

Ed	HRN	Date	Details	A	C			
1	(O)	2/43	Original; 68 pgs. Lilian Chestney-c/a	1	1	200.00	600.00	1400.00
2	17	–	Long Isl. ed.; pg. 64 changed from Gift Box ad to Letter from British Medical Worker; CC-r	1	1	79.00	235.00	550.00
3	20	–	Nassau Bulletin; Pg. 64 changed from letter to article-Three Men Named Smith; CC-r	1	1	64.00	192.00	450.00
4	28	1946	CC-r; new banner logo	1	1	47.00	140.00	325.00
5	51	–	LDC-r	1	1	25.00	75.00	175.00
6	64	–	LDC-r	1	1	19.00	57.00	130.00
7	78	–	LDC-r	1	1	17.00	51.00	120.00
8	164	–	New-c&a; PC-r	2	2	14.00	43.00	100.00

9. Les Miserables

Ed	HRN	Date	Details	A	C			
1A	(O)	3/43	Original; slick paper cover; 68 pgs.	1	1	68.00	205.00	475.00
1B	(O)	3/43	Original; rough, pulp type-c; 68 pgs.	1	1	72.00	215.00	500.00
2	14	–	Elliot Pub; CC-r	1	1	22.00	65.00	150.00
3	18	3/44	Nassau Bul. Pg. 64 changed from Gift Box ad to Bill of Rights article; CC-r	1	1	17.00	52.00	120.00
4	20	–	Richmond Courier ed.; CC-r	1	1	14.00	43.00	100.00
5	28	1946	Gilberton; pgs. 60-64 rearranged/ illos added; CC-r	1	1	11.00	32.00	75.00
6	51	–	LDC-r	1	1	5.85	17.50	35.00
7	71	–	LDC-r	1	1	4.35	13.00	26.00

Classic Comics #5 (HRN-36), © GIL

Classic Comics #6 (HRN-20), © GIL

Classic Comics #9 (Orig?), © GIL

Classic Comics #11 (Orig.), © GIL

Classics Illustrated #12 (HRN-167), © GIL

Classics Illustrated #15 (HRN-53), © GIL

Ed	HRN	Date	Details	A	C	GD25	FN65	NM94
8	87	–	C-price 15¢; LDC-r	1	1	4.00	10.50	21.00
9	161	–	New-c&a; PC-r	2	2	4.00	12.00	24.00
10	167	9/63	PC-r	2	2	3.20	8.00	16.00
11	167	12/65	PC-r	2	2	3.20	8.00	16.00
12	166	R/1968	New-c & price 25¢; PC-r	2	3	3.60	9.00	18.00

10. Robinson Crusoe (Used in **SOTI**, pg. 142)

Ed	HRN	Date	Details	A	C	GD25	FN65	NM94
1A	(O)	4/43	Original; Violet-c; 68 pgs; Zuckerberg c/a	1	1	68.00	205.00	475.00
1B	(O)	4/43	Original; blue-grey -c, 68 pgs.	1	1	72.00	215.00	500.00
2A	14	–	Elliot Pub; violet-c; 68 pgs; CC-r	1	1	19.00	57.00	130.00
2B	14	–	Elliot Pub; blue-grey-c; CC-r	1	1	20.00	60.00	140.00
3	18	–	Nassau Bul. Pg. 64 changed from Gift Box ad to Bill of Rights article; CC-r	1	1	15.00	45.00	105.00
4	20	–	Queens Home News ed.; CC-r	1	1	13.00	40.00	90.00
5	28	1946	Gilberton; pg. 64 changes from Bill-Rights to WWII article-One Leg Shot Away; last CC-r	1	1	10.00	30.00	65.00
6	51	–	LDC-r	1	1	4.70	14.00	28.00
7	64	–	LDC-r	1	1	4.00	10.50	21.00
8	78	–	C-price 15¢; LDC-r	1	1	3.20	8.00	16.00
9	97	–	LDC-r	1	1	2.80	7.00	14.00
10	114	–	LDC-r	1	1	2.40	6.00	12.00
11	130	–	New-c; PC-r	1	2	2.40	6.00	12.00
12	140	–	New-a; PC-r	2	2	2.40	6.00	12.00
13	153	–	PC-r	2	2	1.25	2.50	5.00
14	164	–	PC-r	2	2	1.25	2.50	5.00
15	167	–	PC-r	2	2	1.25	2.50	5.00
16	167	7/64	PC-r	2	2	1.25	2.50	5.00
17	167	5/65	PC-r	2	2	1.80	4.50	9.00
18	167	6/66	PC-r	2	2	1.25	2.50	5.00
19	166	Fall/68	C-price 25¢; PC-r	2	2	1.25	2.50	5.00
20	166	R/68	(No Twin Circle ad)	2	2	1.50	3.00	6.00
21	169	Sm/70	Stiff-c; PC-r	2	2	1.50	3.00	6.00

11. Don Quixote

Ed	HRN	Date	Details	A	C	GD25	FN65	NM94
1	10	5/43	First (O) with HRN list; 68 pgs.	1	1	72.00	215.00	500.00
2	18	–	Nassau Bulletin ed.; CC-r	1	1	19.00	57.00	130.00
3	21	–	Queens Home News ed.; CC-r	1	1	14.00	43.00	100.00
4	28	–	CC-r	1	1	10.00	30.00	65.00
5	110	–	New-PC; PC-r	1	2	4.00	10.00	20.00
6	156	–	Pgs. reduced 68 to 52; PC-r	1	2	2.40	6.00	12.00
7	165	–	PC-r	1	2	1.75	3.50	7.00
8	167	1/64	PC-r	1	2	1.75	3.50	7.00
9	167	11/65	PC-r	1	2	1.75	3.50	7.00
10	166	R/1968	New-c & price 25¢; PC-r	1	3	2.80	7.00	14.00

12. Rip Van Winkle and the Headless Horseman

Ed	HRN	Date	Details	A	C	GD25	FN65	NM94
1	11	6/43	Original; 68 pgs.	1	1	72.00	215.00	500.00
2	15	–	Long Isl. Ind. ed.; CC-r	1	1	20.00	60.00	140.00
3	20	–	Long Isl. Ind. ed.;	1	1	15.00	45.00	105.00
4	22	–	Queens Cty. Times ed.; CC-r	1	1	13.00	40.00	90.00
5	28	–	CC-r	1	1	10.00	30.00	65.00
6	60	–	1st LDC-r	1	1	4.20	12.50	25.00
7	62	–	LDC-r	1	1	4.00	11.00	22.00
8	71	–	LDC-r	1	1	3.20	8.00	16.00
9	89	–	C-price 15¢; LDC-r	1	1	2.80	7.00	14.00
10	118	–	LDC-r	1	1	2.40	6.00	12.00
11	132	–	New-c; PC-r	1	2	2.40	6.00	12.00
12	150	–	New-a; PC-r	2	2	2.40	6.00	12.00
13	158	–	PC-r	2	2	1.25	2.50	5.00
14	167	–	PC-r	2	2	1.25	2.50	5.00
15	167	12/63	PC-r	2	2	1.25	2.50	5.00
16	167	4/65	PC-r	2	2	1.50	3.00	6.00
17	167	4/66	PC-r	2	2	1.25	2.50	5.00
18	166	R/1968	New-c&price 25¢; PC-r; stiff-c	2	3	2.00	5.00	10.00
19	169	Sm/70	PC-r; stiff-c	2	3	2.00	5.00	10.00

13. Dr. Jekyll and Mr. Hyde (Used in **SOTI**, pg. 143)

Ed	HRN	Date	Details	A	C	GD25	FN65	NM94
1	12	8/43	Original 60 pgs.	1	1	86.00	257.00	600.00
2	15	–	Long Isl. Ind. ed.; CC-r	1	1	23.00	70.00	160.00
3	20	–	Long Isl. Ind. ed.; CC-r	1	1	16.00	48.00	110.00
4	28	–	No c-price; CC-r	1	1	13.00	40.00	90.00
5	60	–	New-c; Pgs. reduced from 60 to 52; H.C. Kiefer-c; LDC-r	1	2	4.70	14.00	28.00
6	62	–	LDC-r	1	2	4.00	12.00	24.00
7	71	–	LDC-r	1	2	3.60	9.00	18.00
8	87	–	Date returns (erroneous); LDC-r	1	2	3.20	8.00	16.00
9	112	–	New-c&a; PC-r	2	3	3.20	8.00	16.00
10	153	–	PC-r	2	3	1.25	2.50	5.00
11	161	–	PC-r	2	3	1.25	2.50	5.00
12	167	–	PC-r	2	3	1.25	2.50	5.00
13	167	8/64	PC-r	2	3	1.25	2.50	5.00
14	167	11/65	PC-r	2	3	1.25	2.50	5.00
15	166	R/68	C-price 25¢; PC-r	2	3	1.50	3.00	6.00
16	169	Wn/69	PC-r; stiff-c	2	3	1.25	2.50	5.00

14. Westward Ho!

Ed	HRN	Date	Details	A	C	GD25	FN65	NM94
1	13	9/43	Original; last outside bc coming-next ad; 60 pgs.	1	1	150.00	450.00	1050.00
2	15	–	Long Isl. Ind. ed.; CC-r	1	1	64.00	193.00	450.00
3	21	–	Queens Home News; Pg. 56 changed from coming-next ad to Three Men Named Smith; CC-r	1	1	50.00	150.00	350.00
4	28	1946	Gilberton; Pg. 56 changed again to WWII article-Speaking for America; last CC-r	1	1	40.00	120.00	280.00
5	53	–	Pgs. reduced from 60 to 52; LDC-r	1	1	32.00	95.00	225.00

15. Uncle Tom's Cabin (Used in **SOTI**, pgs. 102, 103)

Ed	HRN	Date	Details	A	C	GD25	FN65	NM94
1	14	11/43	Original; Outside-bc ad: 2 Gift Boxes; 60 pgs.	1	1	60.00	182.00	425.00
2	15	–	Long Isl. Ind. listed- bottom inside-fc; also Gilberton listed bottom-pg. 1; CC-r	1	1	22.00	65.00	150.00
3	21	–	Nassau Bulletin ed.; CC-r	1	1	18.00	54.00	125.00
4	28	–	No c-price; CC-r	1	1	11.00	32.00	75.00
5	53	–	Pgs. reduced 60 to 52; LDC-r	1	1	5.00	15.00	30.00
6	71	–	LDC-r	1	1	4.00	11.00	22.00
7	89	–	C-price 15¢; LDC-r	1	1	4.00	10.00	20.00
8	117	–	New-c/lettering changes; PC-r	1	2	2.40	6.00	12.00
9	128	–	'Picture Progress' promo; PC-r	1	2	1.60	4.00	8.00
10	137	–	PC-r	1	2	1.25	2.50	5.00
11	146	–	PC-r	1	2	1.25	2.50	5.00
12	154	–	PC-r	1	2	1.25	2.50	5.00
13	161	–	PC-r	1	2	1.25	2.50	5.00
14	167	–	PC-r	1	2	1.25	2.50	5.00
15	167	6/64	PC-r	1	2	1.25	2.50	5.00
16	167	5/65	PC-r	1	2	1.25	2.50	5.00
17	166	5/67	PC-r	1	2	1.25	2.50	5.00
18	166	Wn/69	New-stiff-c; PC-r	1	3	2.00	5.00	10.00
19	169	Sm/70	PC-r; stiff-c	1	3	2.00	5.00	10.00

16. Gullivers Travels

Ed	HRN	Date	Details	A	C	GD25	FN65	NM94
1	15	12/43	Original-Lilian Chestney c/a; 60 pgs.	1	1	54.00	161.00	375.00
2	18/20	–	Price deleted; Queens Home News ed; CC-r	1	1	18.00	54.00	125.00
3	22	–	Queens Cty. Times ed.; CC-r	1	1	14.00	43.00	100.00
4	28	–	CC-r	1	1	10.00	30.00	65.00
5	60	–	Pgs. reduced to 48; LDC-r	1	1	4.00	11.00	22.00
6	62	–	LDC-r	1	1	4.00	10.00	20.00
7	78	–	C-price 15¢; LDC-r	1	1	3.20	8.00	16.00
8	89	–	LDC-r	1	1	2.40	6.00	12.00
9	155	–	New-c; PC-r	1	2	2.40	6.00	12.00
10	165	–	PC-r	1	2	1.25	2.50	5.00
11	167	5/64	PC-r	1	2	1.25	2.50	5.00
12	167	11/65	PC-r	1	2	1.25	2.50	5.00
13	166	R/1968	C-price 25¢; PC-r	1	2	1.25	2.50	5.00
14	169	Wn/69	PC-r; stiff-c	1	2	1.25	2.50	5.00

17. The Deerslayer

Ed	HRN	Date	Details	A	C	GD25	FN65	NM94
1	16	1/44	Original; Outside-bc ad: 3 Gift Boxes; 60 pgs.	1	1	50.00	150.00	350.00
2A	18	–	Queens Cty Times (inside-fc); CC-r	1	1	17.00	52.00	120.00
2B	18	–	Gilberton (bottom-pg. 1); CC-r; Scarce	1	1	24.00	72.00	165.00
3	22	–	Queens Cty. Times ed.; CC-r	1	1	14.00	43.00	100.00
4	28	–	CC-r	1	1	10.00	30.00	65.00
5	60	–	Pgs.reduced to 52; LDC-r	1	1	4.00	11.00	22.00
6	64	–	LDC-r	1	1	3.60	9.00	18.00
7	85	–	C-price 15¢; LDC-r	1	1	2.80	7.00	14.00
8	118	–	LDC-r	1	1	2.40	6.00	12.00
9	132	–	LDC-r	1	1	2.40	6.00	12.00
10	167	11/66	Last LDC-r	1	1	2.00	5.00	10.00
11	166	R/1968	New-c & price 25¢; PC-r	1	2	2.40	6.00	12.00
12	169	Spr/71	Stiff-c; letters from parents & educators; PC-r	1	2	2.00	5.00	10.00

18. The Hunchback of Notre Dame

Ed	HRN	Date	Details	A	C	GD25	FN65	NM94
1A	17	3/44	Orig.; Gilberton ed; 60 pgs.	1	1	64.00	193.00	450.00
1B	17	3/44	Orig.; Island Pub. Ed.; 60 pgs.	1	1	57.00	171.00	400.00
2	18/20	–	Queens Home News ed.; CC-r	1	1	19.00	56.00	130.00
3	22	–	Queens Cty. Times ed.; CC-r	1	1	14.00	43.00	100.00
4	28	–	CC-r	1	1	11.00	32.00	75.00
5	60	–	New-c; 8pgs. deleted; Kiefer-c; LDC-r	1	2	4.00	12.00	24.00
6	62	–	LDC-r	1	2	3.60	9.00	18.00
7	78	–	C-price 15¢; LDC-r	1	2	3.20	8.00	16.00
8A	89	–	H.C.Kiefer on bottom right-fc; LDC-r	1	2	2.80	7.00	14.00
8B	89	–	Name omitted; LDC-r	1	2	3.60	9.00	18.00
9	118	–	LDC-r	1	2	2.80	7.00	14.00
10	140	–	New-c; PC-r	1	3	4.00	10.00	20.00
11	146	–	PC-r	1	3	3.20	8.00	16.00
12	158	–	New-c&a; PC-r; Evans/Crandall-a	2	4	2.80	7.00	14.00
13	165	–	PC-r	2	4	1.50	3.00	6.00
14	167	9/63	PC-r	2	4	1.50	3.00	6.00
15	167	10/64	PC-r	2	4	1.50	3.00	6.00
16	167	4/66	PC-r	2	4	1.25	2.50	5.00
17	166	R/1968	New price 25¢; PC-r	2	4	1.25	2.50	5.00
18	169	Sp/70	Stiff-c; PC-r	2	4	1.25	2.50	5.00

19. Huckleberry Finn

Ed	HRN	Date	Details	A	C	GD25	FN65	NM94
1A	18	4/44	Orig.; Gilberton ed.; 60 pgs.	1	1	43.00	130.00	300.00
1B	18	4/44	Orig.; Island Pub.; 60 pgs.	1	1	47.00	140.00	325.00
2	18	–	Nassau Bulletin ed.; fc-price 15¢-Canada; no coming-next ad; CC-r	1	1	18.00	54.00	125.00
3	22	–	Queens Cty. Times ed.; CC-r	1	1	14.00	43.00	100.00
4	28	–	CC-r	1	1	10.00	30.00	65.00
5	60	–	Pgs. reduced to 48; LDC-r	1	1	4.00	11.00	22.00
6	62	–	LDC-r	1	1	4.00	10.00	20.00
7	78	–	LDC-r	1	1	3.20	8.00	16.00
8	89	–	LDC-r	1	1	2.80	7.00	14.00
9	117	–	LDC-r	1	1	2.40	6.00	12.00
10	131	–	New-c&a; PC-r	2	2	2.40	6.00	12.00
11	140	–	PC-r	2	2	1.25	2.50	5.00
12	150	–	PC-r	2	2	1.25	2.50	5.00
13	158	–	PC-r	2	2	1.25	2.50	5.00

Classic Comics #16, © GIL

Classic Comics #18, © GIL

Classic Comics #19, © GIL

Classic Comics #21, © GIL

Classics Illustrated #23 (HRN-85?), © GIL

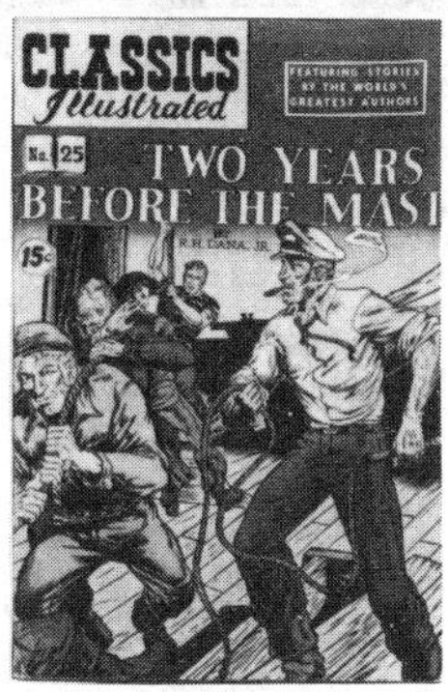

Classics Illustrated #25 (HRN-85?), © GIL

Ed	HRN	Date	Details	A	C	GD25	FN65	NM94
14	165	–	PC-r	2	2	1.25	2.50	5.00
15	167	–	PC-r	2	2	1.25	2.50	5.00
16	167	6/64	PC-r	2	2	1.25	2.50	5.00
17	167	6/65	PC-r	2	2	1.25	2.50	5.00
18	167	10/65	PC-r	2	2	1.25	2.50	5.00
19	166	9/67	PC-r	2	2	1.25	2.50	5.00
20	166	Win/69	C-price 25¢; PC-r; stiff-c	2	2	1.25	2.50	5.00
21	169	Sm/70	PC-r; stiff-c	2	2	1.25	2.50	5.00

20. The Corsican Brothers

Ed	HRN	Date	Details	A	C	GD25	FN65	NM94
1A	20	6/44	Orig.; Gilberton ed.; bc-ad: 4 Gift Boxes; 60 pgs.	1	1	50.00	150.00	350.00
1B	20	6/44	Orig.; Courier ed.; 60 pgs.	1	1	47.00	140.00	325.00
1C	20	6/44	Orig.; Long Island Ind. ed.; 60 pgs.	1	1	47.00	140.00	325.00
1D	20	6/44	Orig.; Both Gilberton & Long Isl. Ind.; 60 pgs.(rare)	1	1	57.00	171.00	400.00
2	22	–	Queens Cty. Times ed.; white logo banner; CC-r	1	1	22.00	65.00	150.00
3	28	–	CC-r	1	1	19.00	57.00	130.00
4	60	–	CI logo; no price; 48 pgs.; LDC-r	1	1	15.00	45.00	105.00
5A	62	–	LDC-r; Classics Ill. logo at top of pgs.	1	1	13.50	41.00	95.00
5B	62	–	w/o logo at top of pg. (scarcer)	1	1	13.50	41.00	95.00
6	78	–	C-price 15¢; LDC-r	1	1	12.00	36.00	85.00
7	97	–	LDC-r	1	1	11.00	32.00	65.00

21. 3 Famous Mysteries ("The Sign of the 4," "The Murders in the Rue Morgue," "The Flayed Hand")

Ed	HRN	Date	Details	A	C	GD25	FN65	NM94
1A	21	7/44	Orig.; Gilberton ed.; 60 pgs.	1	1	79.00	235.00	550.00
1B	21	7/44	Orig. Island Pub. Co.; 60 pgs.	1	1	82.00	246.00	575.00
1C	21	7/44	Original; Courier Ed.; 60 pgs.	1	1	71.00	215.00	500.00
2	22	–	Nassau Bulletin ed.; CC-r	1	1	31.00	93.00	215.00
3	30	–	CC-r	1	1	24.50	73.00	170.00
4	62	–	LDC-r; 8 pgs. deleted; LDC-r	1	1	19.00	57.00	130.00
5	70	–	LDC-r	1	1	17.00	52.00	120.00
6	85	–	C-price 15¢; LDC-r	1	1	15.00	45.00	105.00
7	114	–	New-c; PC-r	1	2	15.00	45.00	105.00

22. The Pathfinder

Ed	HRN	Date	Details	A	C	GD25	FN65	NM94
1A	22	10/44	Orig.; No printer listed; ownership statement inside fc lists Gilberton & date; 60 pgs.	1	1	39.00	118.00	275.00
1B	22	10/44	Orig.; Island Pub. ed.; 60 pgs.	1	1	34.00	100.00	235.00
1C	22	10/44	Orig.; Queens Cty Times ed. 60 pgs.	1	1	34.00	100.00	235.00
2	30	–	C-price removed; CC-r	1	1	10.00	30.00	70.00
3	60	–	Pgs. reduced to 52; LDC-r	1	1	4.00	11.00	22.00
4	70	–	LDC-r	1	1	4.00	10.00	20.00
5	85	–	C-price 15¢; LDC-r	1	1	3.20	8.00	16.00
6	118	–	LDC-r	1	1	2.80	7.00	14.00
7	132	–	LDC-r	1	1	2.40	6.00	12.00
8	146	–	LDC-r	1	1	2.40	6.00	12.00
9	167	11/63	New-c; PC-r	1	2	4.00	10.00	20.00
10	167	12/65	PC-r	1	2	2.80	7.00	14.00
11	166	8/67	PC-r	1	2	2.80	7.00	14.00

23. Oliver Twist (1st Classic produced by the Iger Shop)

Ed	HRN	Date	Details	A	C	GD25	FN65	NM94
1	23	7/45	Original; 60 pgs.	1	1	32.00	95.00	225.00
2A	30	–	Printers Union logo on bottom left-fc same as 23(Orig.) (very rare); CC-r	1	1	22.00	65.00	150.00
2B	30	–	Union logo omitted; CC-r	1	1	10.00	30.00	70.00
3	60	–	Pgs. reduced to 48; LDC-r	1	1	4.00	11.00	22.00
4	62	–	LDC-r	1	1	4.00	10.00	20.00
5	71	–	LDC-r	1	1	3.20	8.00	16.00
6	85	–	C-price 15¢; LDC-r	1	1	2.80	7.00	14.00
7	94	–	LDC-r	1	1	2.40	6.00	12.00
8	118	–	LDC-r	1	1	2.40	6.00	12.00
9	136	–	New-PC, old-a; PC-r	1	2	2.40	6.00	12.00
10	150	–	Old-a; PC-r	1	2	1.80	4.50	9.00
11	164	–	Old-a; PC-r	1	2	1.80	4.50	9.00
12	164	–	New-a; PC-r; Evans/Crandall-a	2	2	2.80	7.00	14.00
13	167	–	PC-r	2	2	1.80	4.50	9.00
14	167	8/64	PC-r	2	2	1.25	2.50	5.00
15	167	12/65	PC-r	2	2	1.25	2.50	5.00
16	166	R/1968	New 25¢; PC-r	2	2	1.00	2.00	5.00
17	169	Win/69	Stiff-c; PC-r	2	2	1.25	2.50	5.00

24. A Connecticut Yankee in King Arthur's Court

Ed	HRN	Date	Details	A	C	GD25	FN65	NM94
1	9/45	–	Original	1	1	32.00	95.00	225.00
2	30	–	No price circle; CC-r	1	1	10.00	30.00	70.00
3	60	–	8 pgs. deleted; LDC-r	1	1	4.00	11.00	22.00
4	62	–	LDC-r	1	1	4.00	10.00	20.00
5	71	–	LDC-r	1	1	3.20	8.00	16.00
6	87	–	C-price 15¢; LDC-r	1	1	2.80	7.00	14.00
7	121	–	LDC-r	1	1	2.40	6.00	12.00
8	140	–	New-c&a; PC-r	2	2	2.40	6.00	12.00
9	153	–	PC-r	2	2	1.25	2.50	5.00
10	164	–	PC-r	2	2	1.25	2.50	5.00
11	167	–	PC-r	2	2	1.25	2.50	5.00
12	167	7/64	PC-r	2	2	1.25	2.50	5.00
13	167	6/66	PC-r	2	2	1.25	2.50	5.00
14	166	R/1968	C-price 25¢; PC-r	2	2	1.25	2.50	5.00
15	169	Spr/71	PC-r; stiff-c	2	2	1.25	2.50	5.00

25. Two Years Before the Mast

Ed	HRN	Date	Details	A	C	GD25	FN65	NM94
1	10/45	–	Original; Webb/Heames-a&c	1	1	32.00	95.00	225.00
2	30	–	Price circle blank;	1	1	11.00	32.00	75.00

Ed	HRN	Date	Details	A	C	GD25	FN65	NM94
			CC-r					
3	60	–	8 pgs. deleted; LDC-r	1	1	4.00	12.00	24.00
4	62	–	LDC-r	1	1	4.00	10.50	21.00
5	71	–	LDC-r	1	1	3.20	8.00	16.00
6	85	–	C-price 15¢; LDC-r	1	1	2.80	7.00	14.00
7	114	–	LDC-r	1	1	2.40	6.00	12.00
8	156	–	3 pgs. replaced by fillers; new-c; PC-r	1	2	2.40	6.00	12.00
9	167	12/63	PC-r	1	2	1.25	2.50	5.00
10	167	12/65	PC-r	1	2	1.25	2.50	5.00
11	166	9/67	PC-r	1	2	1.25	2.50	5.00
12	169	Win/69	C-price 25¢; stiff-c PC-r	1	2	1.25	2.50	5.00

26. Frankenstein

Ed	HRN	Date	Details	A	C	GD25	FN65	NM94
1	26	12/45	Orig.; Webb/Brewster a&c; 52 pgs.	1	1	779.00	235.00	550.00
2A	30	–	Price circle blank; no indicia; CC-r	1	1	23.00	70.00	160.00
2B	30	–	With indicia; scarce; CC-r	1	1	27.00	80.00	190.00
3	60	–	LDC-r	1	1	6.70	20.00	40.00
4	62	–	LDC-r	1	1	10.00	30.00	60.00
5	71	–	LDC-r	1	1	4.20	12.50	25.00
6A	82	–	C-price 15¢; soft-c LDC-r	1	1	4.00	11.00	22.00
6B	82	–	Stiff-c; LDC-r	1	1	4.70	14.00	28.00
7	117	–	LDC-r	1	1	2.80	7.00	14.00
8	146	–	New Saunders-c; PC-r	1	2	2.80	7.00	14.00
9	152	–	Scarce; PC-r	1	2	4.00	12.00	24.00
10	153	–	PC-r	1	2	1.25	2.50	5.00
11	160	–	PC-r	1	2	1.25	2.50	5.00
12	165	–	PC-r	1	2	1.25	2.50	5.00
13	167	–	PC-r	1	2	1.25	2.50	5.00
14	167	6/64	PC-r	1	2	1.25	2.50	5.00
15	167	6/65	PC-r	1	2	1.25	2.50	5.00
16	167	10/65	PC-r	1	2	1.25	2.50	5.00
17	166	9/67	PC-r	1	2	1.25	2.50	5.00
18	169	Fall/69	C-price 25¢; stiff-c PC-r	1	2	1.25	2.50	5.00
19	169	Spr/71	PC-r; stiff-c	1	2	1.25	2.50	5.00

27. The Adventures of Marco Polo

Ed	HRN	Date	Details	A	C	GD25	FN65	NM94
1	4/46	–	Original	1	1	32.00	95.00	225.00
2	30	–	Last 'Comics' reprint; CC-r	1	1	10.00	30.00	70.00
3	70	–	8 pgs. deleted; no c-price; LDC-r	1	1	4.00	10.50	21.00
4	87	–	C-price 15¢; LDC-r	1	1	3.20	8.00	16.00
5	117	–	LDC-r	1	1	2.40	6.00	12.00
6	154	–	New-c; PC-r	1	2	2.40	6.00	12.00
7	165	–	PC-r	1	2	1.25	2.50	5.00
8	167	4/64	PC-r	1	2	1.25	2.50	5.00
9	167	6/66	PC-r	1	2	1.25	2.50	5.00
10	169	Spr/69	New price 25¢; stiff-c; PC-r	1	2	1.25	2.50	5.00

28. Michael Strogoff

Ed	HRN	Date	Details	A	C	GD25	FN65	NM94
1	6/46	–	Original	1	1	34.00	103.00	240.00
2	51	–	8 pgs. cut; LDC-r	1	1	10.00	30.00	70.00
3	115	–	New-c; PC-r	1	2	3.20	8.00	16.00
4	155	–	PC-r	1	2	1.60	4.00	8.00
5	167	11/63	PC-r	1	2	1.60	4.00	8.00
6	167	7/66	PC-r	1	2	1.60	4.00	8.00
7	169	Sm/69	C-price 25¢; stiff-c PC-r	1	3	2.00	5.00	10.00

29. The Prince and the Pauper

Ed	HRN	Date	Details	A	C	GD25	FN65	NM94
1	7/46	–	Orig.; "Horror"-c	1	1	57.00	170.00	400.00
2	60	–	8 pgs. cut; new-c by Kiefer; LDC-r	1	2	4.00	11.00	22.00
3	62	–	LDC-r	1	2	4.00	11.00	22.00
4	71	–	LDC-r	1	2	3.20	8.00	16.00
5	93	–	LDC-r	1	2	2.80	7.00	14.00
6	114	–	LDC-r	1	2	2.40	6.00	12.00
7	128	–	New-c; PC-r	1	3	2.40	6.00	12.00
8	138	–	PC-r	1	3	1.25	2.50	5.00
9	150	–	PC-r	1	3	1.25	2.50	5.00
10	164	–	PC-r	1	3	1.25	2.50	5.00
11	167	–	PC-r	1	3	1.25	2.50	5.00
12	167	7/64	PC-r	1	3	1.25	2.50	5.00
13	167	11/65	PC-r	1	3	1.25	2.50	5.00
14	166	R/68	C-price 25; PC-r	1	3	1.25	2.50	5.00
15	169	Sm/70	PC-r; stiff-c	1	3	1.25	2.50	5.00

30. The Moonstone

Ed	HRN	Date	Details	A	C	GD25	FN65	NM94
1	9/46	–	Original; Rico-c/a	1	1	32.00	95.00	225.00
2	60	–	LDC-r; 8pgs. cut	1	1	4.70	14.00	28.00
3	70	–	LDC-r	1	1	4.00	10.50	21.00
4	155	–	New L.B. Cole-c; PC-r	1	2	5.85	17.50	35.00
5	165	–	PC-r; L.B. Cole-c	1	2	2.80	7.00	14.00
6	167	1/64	PC-r; L.B. Cole-c	1	2	1.60	4.00	8.00
7	167	9/65	PC-r; L.B. Cole-c	1	2	1.50	3.00	6.00
8	166	R/1968	C-price 25¢; PC-r	1	2	1.25	2.50	5.00

31. The Black Arrow

Ed	HRN	Date	Details	A	C	GD25	FN65	NM94
1	10/46	–	Original	1	1	29.00	86.00	200.00
2	51	–	CI logo; LDC-r 8pgs. deleted	1	1	4.35	13.00	26.00
3	64	–	LDC-r	1	1	3.60	9.00	18.00
4	87	–	C-price 15¢; LDC-r	1	1	3.20	8.00	16.00
5	108	–	LDC-r	1	1	2.80	7.00	14.00
6	125	–	LDC-r	1	1	2.40	6.00	12.00
7	131	–	New-c; PC-r	1	2	2.40	6.00	12.00
8	140	–	PC-r	1	2	1.25	2.50	5.00
9	148	–	PC-r	1	2	1.25	2.50	5.00
10	161	–	PC-r	1	2	1.25	2.50	5.00
11	167	–	PC-r	1	2	1.25	2.50	5.00
12	167	7/64	PC-r	1	2	1.25	2.50	5.00
13	167	11/65	PC-r	1	2	1.25	2.50	5.00
14	166	R/1968	C-price 25¢; PC-r	1	2	1.25	2.50	5.00

32. Lorna Doone

Ed	HRN	Date	Details	A	C	GD25	FN65	NM94
1	12/46	–	Original; Matt Baker c&a	1	1	32.00	95.00	225.00
2	53/64	–	8 pgs. deleted; LDC-r	1	1	5.35	16.00	32.00
3	85	–	C-price 15¢; LDC-r; Baker c&a	1	1	4.00	12.00	24.00
4	118	–	LDC-r	1	1	3.20	8.00	16.00
5	138	–	New-c; old-c becomes new title pg.; PC-r	1	2	2.40	6.00	12.00
6	150	–	PC-r	1	2	1.25	2.50	5.00

Classics Illustrated #26 (HRN-167), © GIL

Classic Comics #28, © GIL

Classics Illustrated #30 (HRN-167), © GIL

Classics Illustrated #38 (Orig.), © GIL

Classics Illustrated #39, © GIL

Classics Illustrated #41 (Orig.), © GIL

						GD25	FN65	NM94
7	165	–	PC-r	1	2	1.25	2.50	5.00
8	167	1/64	PC-r	1	2	1.25	2.50	5.00
9	167	11/65	PC-r	1	2	1.25	2.50	5.00
10	166	R/1968	New-c; PC-r	1	3	2.40	6.00	12.00

33. The Adventures of Sherlock Holmes

Ed	HRN	Date	Details	A	C	GD25	FN65	NM94
1	33	1/47	Original; Kiefer-c; contains Study in Scarlet & Hound of the Baskervilles; 68 pgs.	1	1	100.00	300.00	700.00
2	53	–	'A Study in Scarlet' (17 pgs.) deleted; LDC-r	1	1	38.00	115.00	265.00
3	71	–	LDC-r	1	1	28.00	86.00	200.00
4A	89	–	C-price 15¢; LDC-r	1	1	23.00	70.00	160.00
4B	89	–	Kiefer's name omitted from-c	1	1	23.00	70.00	160.00

34. Mysterious Island (Last "Classic Comic")

Ed	HRN	Date	Details	A	C	GD25	FN65	NM94
1	2/47	–	Original; Webb/ Heames-c/a	1	1	32.00	95.00	225.00
2	60	–	8 pgs. deleted; LDC-r	1	1	4.00	11.00	22.00
3	62	–	LDC-r	1	1	4.00	10.00	20.00
4	71	–	LDC-r	1	1	4.35	13.00	26.00
5	78	–	C-price 15¢ in circle; LDC-r	1	1	3.20	8.00	16.00
6	92	–	LDC-r	1	1	2.80	7.00	14.00
7	117	–	LDC-r	1	1	2.40	6.00	12.00
8	140	–	New-c; PC-r	1	2	2.40	6.00	12.00
9	156	–	PC-r	1	2	1.25	2.50	5.00
10	167	10/63	PC-r	1	2	1.25	2.50	5.00
11	167	5/64	PC-r	1	2	1.25	2.50	5.00
12	167	6/66	PC-r	1	2	1.25	2.50	5.00
13	166	R/1968	C-price 25¢; PC-r	1	2	1.25	2.50	5.00

35. Last Days of Pompeii (First "Classics Illustrated")

Ed	HRN	Date	Details	A	C	GD25	FN65	NM94
1	–	3/47	Original; LDC; Kiefer-c/a	1	1	32.00	95.00	225.00
2	161	–	New c&a; 15¢; PC-r; Jack Kirby-a	2	2	3.60	9.00	18.00
3	167	1/64	PC-r	2	2	1.60	4.00	8.00
4	167	7/66	PC-r	2	2	1.60	4.00	8.00
5	169	Spr/70	New price 25¢; stiff-c; PC-r	2	2	1.60	4.00	8.00

36. Typee

Ed	HRN	Date	Details	A	C	GD25	FN65	NM94
1	4/47	–	Original	1	1	16.00	48.00	110.00
2	64	–	No c-price; 8 pg. ed.; LDC-r	1	1	4.35	13.00	26.00
3	155	–	New-c; PC-r	1	2	2.40	6.00	12.00
4	167	9/63	PC-r	1	2	1.40	3.50	7.00
5	167	7/65	PC-r	1	2	1.40	3.50	7.00
6	169	Sm/69	C-price 25¢; stiff-c PC-r	1	2	1.50	3.50	7.00

37. The Pioneers

Ed	HRN	Date	Details	A	C	GD25	FN65	NM94
1	37	5/47	Original; Palais-c/a	1	1	16.00	48.00	110.00
2A	62	–	8 pgs. cut; LDC-r; price circle blank	1	1	4.00	11.00	22.00
2B	62	–	10 cent-c; LDC-r;	1	1	10.00	30.00	70.00
3	70	–	LDC-r	1	1	3.20	8.00	16.00
4	92	–	15 cent-c; LDC-r	1	1	2.80	7.00	14.00
5	118	–	LDC-r	1	1	2.40	6.00	12.00
6	131	–	LDC-r	1	1	2.40	6.00	12.00
7	132	–	LDC-r	1	1	2.40	6.00	12.00
8	153	–	LDC-r	1	1	2.00	5.00	10.00
9	167	5/64	LDC-r	1	1	1.60	4.00	8.00
10	167	6/66	LDC-r	1	1	1.60	4.00	8.00
11	166	R/1968	New-c; 25 cent-c; PC-r	1	2	3.20	8.00	16.00

38. Adventures of Cellini

Ed	HRN	Date	Details	A	C	GD25	FN65	NM94
1	6/47	–	Original; Froehlich c/a	1	1	27.00	80.00	190.00
2	164	–	New-c&a; PC-r	2	2	2.80	7.00	14.00
3	167	12/63	PC-r	2	2	1.60	4.00	8.00
4	167	7/66	PC-r	2	2	1.60	4.00	8.00
5	169	Spr/70	Stiff-c; new price 25¢; PC-r	2	2	1.60	4.00	8.00

39. Jane Eyre

Ed	HRN	Date	Details	A	C	GD25	FN65	NM94
1	7/47	–	Original	1	1	22.00	65.00	150.00
2	60	–	No c-price; 8 pgs. cut; LDC-r	1	1	4.00	12.00	24.00
3	62	–	LDC-r	1	1	4.00	10.50	21.00
4	71	–	LDC-r; c-price 10¢	1	1	3.00	9.00	18.00
5	92	–	C-price 15¢; LDC-r	1	1	2.80	7.00	14.00
6	118	–	LDC-r	1	1	2.40	6.00	12.00
7	142	–	New-c; old-a; PC-r	1	2	2.80	7.00	14.00
8	154	–	Old-a; PC-r	1	2	2.40	6.00	12.00
9	165	–	New-a; PC-r	2	2	2.80	7.00	14.00
10	167	12/63	PC-r	2	2	2.80	7.00	14.00
11	167	4/65	PC-r	2	2	2.40	6.00	12.00
12	167	8/66	PC-r	2	2	2.40	6.00	12.00
13	166	R/1968	New-c; PC-r	2	3	4.70	14.00	28.00

40. Mysteries ("The Pit and the Pendulum," "The Advs. of Hans Pfall" & "The Fall of the House of Usher")

Ed	HRN	Date	Details	A	C	GD25	FN65	NM94
1	8/47	–	Original; Kiefer-c/a, Froehlich, Griffiths-a	1	1	61.00	182.00	425.00
2	62	–	LDC-r; 8pgs cut	1	1	22.00	65.00	150.00
3	75	–	LDC-r	1	1	19.30	58.00	135.00
4	92	–	C-price 15¢; LDC-r	1	1	14.00	43.00	100.00

41. Twenty Years After

Ed	HRN	Date	Details	A	C	GD25	FN65	NM94
1	9/47	–	Original; 'horror'-c	1	1	43.00	130.00	300.00
2	62	–	New-c; no c-price 8 pgs. cut; LDC-r; Kiefer-c	1	2	4.00	12.00	24.00
3	78	–	C-price 15¢; LDC-r	1	2	3.60	9.00	18.00
4	156	–	New-c; PC-r	1	3	2.40	6.00	12.00
5	167	12/63	PC-r	1	3	1.20	3.00	6.00
6	167	11/66	PC-r	1	3	1.20	3.00	6.00
7	169	Spr/70	New price 25¢; stiff-c; PC-r	1	3	1.20	2.50	5.00

42. Swiss Family Robinson

Ed	HRN	Date	Details	A	C	GD25	FN65	NM94
1	42	10/47	Orig.; Kiefer-c&a;	1	1	16.00	48.00	110.00
2A	62	–	8 pgs. cut; outside	1	1	4.00	11.00	22.00

Ed	HRN	Date	Details	A	C	GD25	FN65	NM94
			bc: Gift Box ad; LDC-r					
2B	62	–	8 pgs. cut; outside-bc: Reorder list; scarce; LDC-r	1	1	7.50	22.50	45.00
3	75	–	LDC-r	1	1	3.20	8.00	16.00
4	93	–	LDC-r	1	1	2.80	7.00	14.00
5	117	–	LDC-r	1	1	2.40	6.00	12.00
6	131	–	New-c; old-a; PC-r	1	2	2.40	6.00	12.00
7	137	–	Old-a; PC-r	1	2	2.00	5.00	10.00
8	141	–	Old-a; PC-r	1	2	2.00	5.00	10.00
9	152	–	New-a; PC-r	2	2	2.40	6.00	12.00
10	158	–	PC-r	2	2	1.25	2.50	5.00
11	165	–	PC-r	2	2	1.80	4.50	9.00
12	167	12/63	PC-r	2	2	1.50	3.00	6.00
13	167	4/65	PC-r	2	2	1.50	3.00	6.00
14	167	5/66	PC-r	2	2	1.50	3.00	6.00
15	166	11/67	PC-r	2	2	1.25	2.50	5.00
16	169	Spr/69	PC-r; stiff-c	2	2	1.25	2.50	5.00

43. Great Expectations (Used in **SOTI**, pg. 311)

Ed	HRN	Date	Details	A	C	GD25	FN65	NM94
1	11/47	–	Original; Kiefer-a/c	1	1	72.00	215.00	500.00
2	62	–	No c-price; 8 pgs. cut; LDC-r	1	1	43.00	130.00	300.00

44. Mysteries of Paris (Used in **SOTI**, pg. 323)

Ed	HRN	Date	Details	A	C	GD25	FN65	NM94
1A	44	12/47	Original; 56 pgs.; Kiefer-c/a	1	1	54.00	160.00	375.00
1B	44	12/47	Orig.; printed on white/heavier paper; (rare)	1	1	57.00	170.00	400.00
2A	62	–	8 pgs. cut; outside-bc: Gift Box ad; LDC-r	1	1	22.00	65.00	150.00
2B	62	–	8 pgs. cut; outside-bc: reorder list; LDC-r	1	1	22.00	65.00	150.00
3	78	–	C-price 15¢; LDC-r	1	1	19.30	58.00	135.00

45. Tom Brown's School Days

Ed	HRN	Date	Details	A	C	GD25	FN65	NM94
1	44	1/48	Original; 1st 48pg. issue	1	1	11.00	32.00	75.00
2	64	–	No c-price; LDC-r	1	1	4.70	14.00	28.00
3	161	–	New-c&a; PC-r	2	2	2.40	6.00	12.00
4	167	2/64	PC-r	2	2	1.60	4.00	8.00
5	167	8/66	PC-r	2	2	1.60	4.00	8.00
6	166	R/1968	C-price 25¢; PC-r	2	2	1.60	4.00	8.00

46. Kidnapped

Ed	HRN	Date	Details	A	C	GD25	FN65	NM94
1	47	4/48	Original; Webb-c/a	1	1	11.00	32.00	75.00
2A	62	–	Price circle blank; LDC-r	1	1	4.00	11.00	22.00
2B	62	–	C-price 10¢; rare; LDC-r	1	1	11.00	32.00	75.00
3	78	–	C-price 15¢; LDC-r	1	1	3.20	8.00	16.00
4	87	–	LDC-r	1	1	2.80	7.00	14.00
5	118	–	LDC-r	1	1	2.40	6.00	12.00
6	131	–	New-c; PC-r	1	2	2.40	6.00	12.00
7	140	–	PC-r	1	2	1.25	2.50	5.00
8	150	–	PC-r	1	2	1.25	2.50	5.00
9	164	–	Reduced pg.width; PC-r	1	2	1.25	2.50	5.00
10	167	–	PC-r	1	2	1.25	2.50	5.00
11	167	3/64	PC-r	1	2	1.25	2.50	5.00
12	167	6/65	PC-r	1	2	1.25	2.50	5.00
13	167	12/65	PC-r	1	2	1.25	2.50	5.00
14	166	9/67	PC-r	1	2	1.25	2.50	5.00
15	166	Win/69	New price 25¢; PC-r; stiff-c	1	2	1.25	2.50	5.00
16	169	Sm/70	PC-r; stiff-c	1	2	1.25	2.50	5.00

47. Twenty Thousand Leagues Under the Sea

Ed	HRN	Date	Details	A	C	GD25	FN65	NM94
1	47	5/48	Orig.; Kiefer-a&c;	1	1	11.00	32.00	75.00
2	64	–	No c-price; LDC-r	1	1	4.00	11.00	22.00
3	78	–	C-price 15¢; LDC-r	1	1	3.20	8.00	16.00
4	94	–	LDC-r	1	1	2.80	7.00	14.00
5	118	–	LDC-r	1	1	2.40	6.00	12.00
6	128	–	New-c; PC-r	1	2	2.40	6.00	10.00
7	133	–	PC-r	1	2	1.80	4.50	9.00
8	140	–	PC-r	1	2	1.25	2.50	5.00
9	148	–	PC-r	1	2	1.25	2.50	5.00
10	156	–	PC-r	1	2	1.25	2.50	5.00
11	165	–	PC-r	1	2	1.25	2.50	5.00
12	167	–	PC-r	1	2	1.25	2.50	5.00
13	167	3/64	PC-r	1	2	1.25	2.50	5.00
14	167	8/65	PC-r	1	2	1.25	2.50	5.00
15	167	10/66	PC-r	1	2	1.25	2.50	5.00
16	166	R/1968	C-price 25¢; new-c PC-r	1	3	2.00	5.00	10.00
17	169	Spr/70	Stiff-c; PC-r	1	3	2.00	5.00	10.00

48. David Copperfield

Ed	HRN	Date	Details	A	C	GD25	FN65	NM94
1	47	6/48	Original; Kiefer-c/a	1	1	11.00	32.00	75.00
2	64	–	Price circle replaced by motif of boy reading; LDC-r	1	1	4.00	11.00	22.00
3	87	–	C-price 15¢; LDC-r	1	1	3.20	8.00	16.00
4	121	–	New-c; PC-r	1	2	2.40	6.00	12.00
5	130	–	PC-r	1	2	1.50	3.00	6.00
6	140	–	PC-r	1	2	1.50	3.00	6.00
7	148	–	PC-r	1	2	1.50	3.00	6.00
8	156	–	PC-r	1	2	1.50	3.00	6.00
9	167	–	PC-r	1	2	1.25	2.50	5.00
10	167	4/64	PC-r	1	2	1.25	2.50	5.00
11	167	6/65	PC-r	1	2	1.25	2.50	5.00
12	166	5/67	PC-r	1	2	1.25	2.50	5.00
13	166	R/67	PC-r; C-price 25¢	1	2	1.80	4.50	9.00
14	166	Spr/69	C-price 25¢; stiff-c PC-r	1	2	1.25	2.50	5.00
15	169	Win/69	Stiff-c; PC-r	1	2	1.25	2.50	5.00

49. Alice in Wonderland

Ed	HRN	Date	Details	A	C	GD25	FN65	NM94
1	47	7/48	Original; 1st Blum a & c	1	1	14.00	43.00	100.00
2	64	–	No c-price; LDC-r	1	1	4.70	14.00	28.00
3A	85	–	C-price 15¢; soft-c LDC-r	1	1	4.00	10.50	21.00
3B	85	–	Stiff-c; LDC-r	1	1	4.00	12.00	24.00
4	155	–	New PC, similar to orig.; PC-r	1	2	4.00	10.50	21.00
5	165	–	PC-r	1	2	3.20	8.00	16.00
6	167	3/64	PC-r	1	2	2.80	7.00	14.00
7	167	6/66	PC-r	1	2	2.80	7.00	14.00
8A	166	Fall/68	New-c; soft-c; 25¢ c-price; PC-r	1	3	4.00	10.00	20.00
8B	166	Fall/68	New-c; stiff-c; 25¢ c-price; PC-r	1	3	5.85	17.50	35.00

Classics Illustrated #43 (Orig.), © GIL

Classics Illustrated #45 (Orig.), © GIL

Classics Illustrated #48 (Orig.), © GIL

Classics Illustrated #52 (Orig.), © GIL

Classics Illustrated #54 (Orig.), © GIL

Classics Illustrated #56 (Orig.), © GIL

50. Adventures of Tom Sawyer (Used in **SOTI**, pg. 37)

Ed	HRN	Date	Details	A	C	GD25	FN65	NM94
1A	51	8/48	Orig.; Aldo Rubano a&c	1	1	11.00	32.00	75.00
1B	51	9/48	Orig.; Rubano c&a	1	1	11.50	34.00	80.00
1C	51	9/48	Orig.; outside-bc: blue & yellow only; rare	1	1	16.00	48.00	110.00
2	64	–	No c-price; LDC-r	1	1	4.00	10.00	20.00
3	78	–	C-price 15¢; LDC-r	1	1	2.80	7.00	14.00
4	94	–	LDC-r	1	1	2.40	6.00	12.00
5	117	–	LDC-r	1	1	2.00	5.00	10.00
6	132	–	LDC-r	1	1	2.00	5.00	10.00
7	140	–	New-c; PC-r	1	2	2.00	5.00	10.00
8	150	–	PC-r	1	2	1.60	4.00	8.00
9	164	–	New-a; PC-r	2	2	2.00	5.00	10.00
10	167	–	PC-r	2	2	1.25	2.50	5.00
11	167	1/65	PC-r	2	2	1.25	2.50	5.00
12	167	5/66	PC-r	2	2	1.25	2.50	5.00
13	166	12/67	PC-r	2	2	1.25	2.50	5.00
14	169	Fall/69	C-price 25¢; stiff-c; PC-r	2	2	1.25	2.50	5.00
15	169	Win/71	PC-r	2	2	1.25	2.50	5.00

51. The Spy

Ed	HRN	Date	Details	A	C	GD25	FN65	NM94
1A	51	9/48	Original; inside-bc illo: Christmas Carol	1	1	11.00	32.00	75.00
1B	51	9/48	Original; inside-bc illo: Man in Iron Mask	1	1	11.00	32.00	75.00
1C	51	8/48	Original; outside-bc: full color	1	1	11.00	32.00	75.00
1D	51	8/48	Original; outside-bc: blue & yellow only; scarce	1	1	14.00	43.00	100.00
2	89	–	C-price 15¢; LDC-r	1	1	3.60	9.00	18.00
3	121	–	LDC-r	1	1	2.80	7.00	14.00
4	139	–	New-c; PC-r	1	2	2.40	6.00	12.00
5	156	–	PC-r	1	2	1.25	2.50	5.00
6	167	11/63	PC-r	1	2	1.25	2.50	5.00
7	167	7/66	PC-r	1	2	1.25	2.50	5.00
8A	166	Win/69	C-price 25¢; soft-c; scarce; PC-r	1	2	2.40	6.00	12.00
8B	166	Win/69	C-price 25¢; stiff-c; PC-r	1	2	1.25	2.50	5.00

52. The House of the Seven Gables

Ed	HRN	Date	Details	A	C	GD25	FN65	NM94
1	53	10/48	Orig.; Griffiths a&c	1	1	10.00	30.00	70.00
2	89	–	C-price 15¢; LDC-r	1	1	3.60	9.00	18.00
3	121	–	LDC-r	1	1	2.80	7.00	14.00
4	142	–	New-c&a; PC-r; Woodbridge-a	2	2	2.40	6.00	12.00
5	156	–	PC-r	2	2	1.25	2.50	5.00
6	165	–	PC-r	2	2	1.25	2.50	5.00
7	167	5/64	PC-r	2	2	1.25	2.50	5.00
8	167	3/66	PC-r	2	2	1.25	2.50	5.00
9	166	R/1968	C-price 25¢; PC-r	2	2	1.25	2.50	5.00
10	169	Spr/70	Stiff-c; PC-r	2	2	1.25	2.50	5.00

53. A Christmas Carol

Ed	HRN	Date	Details	A	C	GD25	FN65	NM94
1	53	11/48	Original & only ed; Kiefer-c/a	1	1	11.50	34.00	80.00

54. Man in the Iron Mask

Ed	HRN	Date	Details	A	C	GD25	FN65	NM94
1	55	12/48	Original; Froehlich-a, Kiefer-c	1	1	10.00	30.00	70.00
2	93	–	C-price 15¢; LDC-r	1	1	3.60	9.00	18.00
3A	111	–	(O) logo lettering; scarce; LDC-r	1	1	4.00	12.00	24.00
3B	111	–	New logo as PC; LDC-r	1	1	3.20	8.00	16.00
4	142	–	New-c&a; PC-r	2	2	2.40	6.00	12.00
5	154	–	PC-r	2	2	1.25	2.50	5.00
6	165	–	PC-r	2	2	1.25	2.50	5.00
7	167	5/64	PC-r	2	2	1.25	2.50	5.00
8	167	4/66	PC-r	2	2	1.25	2.50	5.00
9A	166	Win/69	C-price 25¢; soft-c PC-r	2	2	2.80	7.00	14.00
9B	166	Win/69	Stiff-c	2	2	1.25	2.50	5.00

55. Silas Marner (Used in **SOTI**, pgs. 311, 312)

Ed	HRN	Date	Details	A	C	GD25	FN65	NM94
1	55	1/49	Original-Kiefer-c	1	1	10.00	30.00	70.00
2	75	–	Price circle blank; 'Coming Next' ad; LDC-r	1	1	4.00	11.00	22.00
3	97	–	LDC-r	1	1	2.80	7.00	14.00
4	121	–	New-c; PC-r	1	2	2.40	6.00	12.00
5	130	–	PC-r	1	2	1.25	2.50	5.00
6	140	–	PC-r	1	2	1.25	2.50	5.00
7	154	–	PC-r	1	2	1.25	2.50	5.00
8	165	–	PC-r	1	2	1.25	2.50	5.00
9	167	2/64	PC-r	1	2	1.25	2.50	5.00
10	167	6/65	PC-r	1	2	1.25	2.50	5.00
11	166	5/67	PC-r	1	2	1.25	2.50	5.00
12A	166	Win/69	C-price 25¢; soft-c PC-r	1	2	2.80	7.00	14.00
12B	166	Win/69	C-price 25¢; stiff-c PC-r	1	2	1.25	2.50	5.00

56. The Toilers of the Sea

Ed	HRN	Date	Details	A	C	GD25	FN65	NM94
1	55	2/49	Original; A.M. Froehlich-c/a	1	1	15.00	45.00	105.00
2	165	–	New-c&a; PC-r; Angelo Torres-a	2	2	4.00	10.50	21.00
3	167	3/64	PC-r	2	2	2.80	7.00	14.00
4	167	10/66	PC-r	2	2	2.80	7.00	14.00

57. The Song of Hiawatha

Ed	HRN	Date	Details	A	C	GD25	FN65	NM94
1	55	3/49	Original; Alex Blum a&c	1	1	10.00	30.00	65.00
2	75	–	No c-price; 'Coming Next' ad; LDC-r	1	1	4.00	11.00	22.00
3	94	–	C-price 15¢; LDC-r	1	1	3.20	8.00	16.00
4	118	–	LDC-r	1	1	2.80	7.00	14.00
5	134	–	New-c; PC-r	1	2	2.40	6.00	12.00
6	139	–	PC-r	1	2	1.25	2.50	5.00
7	154	–	PC-r	1	2	1.25	2.50	5.00
8	167	–	Has orig.date; PC-r	1	2	1.25	2.50	5.00
9	167	9/64	PC-r	1	2	1.25	2.50	5.00
10	167	10/65	PC-r	1	2	1.25	2.50	5.00
11	166	F/1968	C-price 25¢; PC-r	1	2	1.25	2.50	5.00

58. The Prairie

Ed	HRN	Date	Details	A	C

Ed	HRN	Date	Details	A	C	GD25	FN65	NM94
1	60	4/49	Original; Palais c/a	1	1	10.00	30.00	65.00
2	62	–	No c-price; no coming-next ad; LDC-r	1	1	5.85	17.50	35.00
3	78	–	C-price 15¢ in dbl. circle; LDC-r	1	1	3.60	9.00	18.00
4	114	–	LDC-r	1	1	2.80	7.00	14.00
5	131	–	LDC-r	1	1	2.40	6.00	12.00
6	132	–	LDC-r	1	1	2.40	6.00	12.00
7	146	–	New-c; PC-r	1	2	2.40	6.00	12.00
8	155	–	PC-r	1	2	1.25	2.50	5.00
9	167	5/64	PC-r	1	2	1.25	2.50	5.00
10	167	4/66	PC-r	1	2	1.25	2.50	5.00
11	169	Sm/69	New price 25¢; stiff-c; PC-r	1	2	1.25	2.50	5.00

59. Wuthering Heights

Ed	HRN	Date	Details	A	C	GD25	FN65	NM94
1	60	5/49	Original; Kiefer-c/a	1	1	10.00	30.00	70.00
2	85	–	C-price 15¢; LDC-r	1	1	4.00	12.00	24.00
3	156	–	New-c; PC-r	1	2	2.40	6.00	12.00
4	167	1/64	PC-r	1	2	1.50	3.00	6.00
5	167	10/66	PC-r	1	2	1.50	3.00	6.00
6	169	Sm/69	C-price 25¢; stiff-c; PC-r	1	2	1.25	2.50	5.00

60. Black Beauty

Ed	HRN	Date	Details	A	C	GD25	FN65	NM94
1	62	6/49	Original; Froehlich-c/a	1	1	10.00	30.00	65.00
2	62	–	No c-price; no coming-next ad; LDC-r (rare)	1	1	10.00	30.00	70.00
3	85	–	C-price 15¢; LDC-r	1	1	4.00	10.00	20.00
4	158	–	New L.B. Cole-c/aPC-r	2	2	3.60	9.00	18.00
5	167	2/64	PC-r	2	2	2.40	6.00	12.00
6	167	3/66	PC-r	2	2	2.40	6.00	12.00
7	166	R/1968	New-c&price, 25¢; PC-r	2	3	5.85	17.50	35.00

61. The Woman in White

Ed	HRN	Date	Details	A	C	GD25	FN65	NM94
1A	62	7/49	Original; Blum-c/a fc-purple; bc: top illos light blue	1	1	10.00	30.00	65.00
1B	62	7/49	Original; Blum-c/a fc-pink; bc: top illos light violet	1	1	10.00	30.00	65.00
2	156	–	New-c; PC-r	1	2	3.20	8.00	16.00
3	167	1/64	PC-r	1	2	2.40	6.00	12.00
4	166	R/1968	C-price 25¢; PC-r	1	2	2.40	6.00	12.00

62. Western Stories ("The Luck of Roaring Camp" and "The Outcasts of Poker Flat")

Ed	HRN	Date	Details	A	C	GD25	FN65	NM94
1	62	8/49	Original; Kiefer-c/a	1	1	10.00	30.00	65.00
2	89	–	C-price 15¢; LDC-r	1	1	4.00	10.00	20.00
3	121	–	LDC-r	1	1	3.20	8.00	16.00
4	137	–	New-c; PC-r	1	2	2.40	6.00	12.00
5	152	–	PC-r	1	2	1.50	3.00	6.00
6	167	10/63	PC-r	1	2	1.50	3.00	6.00
7	167	6/64	PC-r	1	2	1.25	2.50	5.00
8	167	11/66	PC-r	1	2	1.25	2.50	5.00
9	166	R/1968	New-c&price 25¢; PC-r	1	3	2.80	7.00	14.00

63. The Man Without a Country

Ed	HRN	Date	Details	A	C	GD25	FN65	NM94
1	62	9/49	Original; Kiefer-c/a	1	1	10.00	30.00	65.00
2	78	–	C-price 15¢ in double circle; LDC-r	1	1	4.00	11.00	22.00
3	156	–	New-c, old-a; PC-r	1	2	3.20	8.00	16.00
4	165	–	New-a & text pgs.; PC-r; A. Torres-a	2	2	2.40	6.00	12.00
5	167	3/64	PC-r	2	2	1.25	2.50	5.00
6	167	8/66	PC-r	2	2	1.25	2.50	5.00
7	169	Sm/69	New price 25¢; stiff-c; PC-r	2	2	1.25	2.50	5.00

64. Treasure Island

Ed	HRN	Date	Details	A	C	GD25	FN65	NM94
1	62	10/49	Original; Blum-c/a	1	1	10.00	30.00	65.00
2A	82	–	C-price 15¢; soft-c LDC-r	1	1	4.00	10.00	20.00
2B	82	–	Stiff-c; LDC-r	1	1	4.00	11.00	22.00
3	117	–	LDC-r	1	1	3.20	8.00	16.00
4	131	–	New-c; PC-r	1	2	2.40	6.00	12.00
5	138	–	PC-r	1	2	1.25	2.50	5.00
6	146	–	PC-r	1	2	1.25	2.50	5.00
7	158	–	PC-r	1	2	1.25	2.50	5.00
8	165	–	PC-r	1	2	1.25	2.50	5.00
9	167	–	PC-r	1	2	1.25	2.50	5.00
10	167	6/64	PC-r	1	2	1.25	2.50	5.00
11	167	12/65	PC-r	1	2	1.25	2.50	5.00
12A	166	10/67	PC-r	1	2	1.80	4.50	9.00
12B	166	10/67	w/Grit ad stapled in book	1	2	10.00	30.00	60.00
13	169	Spr/69	New price 25¢; stiff-c; PC-r	1	2	1.25	2.50	5.00
14	–	1989	Long John Silver's Seafood Shoppes; $1.95, First/Berkley Publ.; Blum-r	1	2	.40	1.00	2.00

65. Benjamin Franklin

Ed	HRN	Date	Details	A	C	GD25	FN65	NM94
1	64	11/49	Original; Kiefer-c Iger Shop-a	1	1	10.00	30.00	65.00
2	131	–	New-c; PC-r	1	2	2.80	7.00	14.00
3	154	–	PC-r	1	2	1.25	2.50	5.00
4	167	2/64	PC-r	1	2	1.25	2.50	5.00
5	167	4/66	PC-r	1	2	1.25	2.50	5.00
6	169	Fall/69	New price 25¢; stiff-c; PC-r	1	2	1.25	2.50	5.00

66. The Cloister and the Hearth

Ed	HRN	Date	Details	A	C	GD25	FN65	NM94
1	67	12/49	Original & only ed; Kiefer-a & c	1	1	22.00	65.00	150.00

67. The Scottish Chiefs

Ed	HRN	Date	Details	A	C	GD25	FN65	NM94
1	67	1/50	Original; Blum-a&c	1	1	10.00	30.00	60.00
2	85	–	C-price 15¢; LDC-r	1	1	4.00	10.00	20.00
3	118	–	LDC-r	1	1	3.20	8.00	16.00
4	136	–	New-c; PC-r	1	2	2.40	6.00	12.00
5	154	–	PC-r	1	2	1.60	4.00	8.00
6	167	11/63	PC-r	1	2	1.60	4.00	8.00
7	167	8/65	PC-r	1	2	1.60	4.00	8.00

68. Julius Caesar (Used in **SOTI**, pgs. 36, 37)

Ed	HRN	Date	Details	A	C	GD25	FN65	NM94
1	70	2/50	Original; Kiefer-c/a	1	1	10.00	30.00	65.00
2	85	–	C-price 15¢; LDC-r	1	1	4.00	10.00	20.00

Classics Illustrated #61, © GIL

Classics Illustrated #64 (Orig.), © GIL

Classics Illustrated #67 (Orig.), © GIL

Classics Illustrated #72 (Orig.), © GIL

Classics Illustrated #73, © GIL

Classics Illustrated #78 (HRN-128), © GIL

Ed	HRN	Date	Details	A	C	GD25	FN65	NM94
3	108	–	LDC-r	1	1	3.20	8.00	16.00
4	156	–	New L.B. Cole-c; PC-r	1	2	3.20	8.00	16.00
5	165	–	New-a by Evans, Crandall; PC-r	2	2	3.20	8.00	16.00
6	167	2/64	PC-r	2	2	1.25	2.50	5.00
7	167	10/65	Tarzan books inside cover; PC-r	2	2	1.25	2.50	5.00
8	166	R/1967	PC-r	2	2	1.25	2.50	5.00
9	169	Win/69	PC-r; stiff-c	2	2	1.25	2.50	5.00

69. Around the World in 80 Days

Ed	HRN	Date	Details	A	C	GD25	FN65	NM94
1	70	3/50	Original; Kiefer-c/a	1	1	10.00	30.00	65.00
2	87	–	C-price 15¢; LDC-r	1	1	4.00	10.00	20.00
3	125	–	LDC-r	1	1	3.20	8.00	16.00
4	136	–	New-c; PC-r	1	2	2.40	6.00	12.00
5	146	–	PC-r	1	2	1.25	2.50	5.00
6	152	–	PC-r	1	2	1.25	2.50	5.00
7	164	–	PC-r	1	2	1.25	2.50	5.00
8	167	–	PC-r	1	2	1.25	2.50	5.00
9	167	7/64	PC-r	1	2	1.25	2.50	5.00
10	167	11/65	PC-r	1	2	1.25	2.50	5.00
11	166	7/67	PC-r	1	2	1.25	2.50	5.00
12	169	Spr/69	C-price 25¢; stiff-c; PC-r	1	2	1.25	2.50	5.00

70. The Pilot

Ed	HRN	Date	Details	A	C	GD25	FN65	NM94
1	71	4/50	Original; Blum-c/a	1	1	8.35	25.00	50.00
2	92	–	C-price 15¢; LDC-r	1	1	4.00	10.00	20.00
3	125	–	LDC-r	1	1	3.20	8.00	16.00
4	156	–	New-c; PC-r	1	2	2.40	6.00	12.00
5	167	2/64	PC-r	1	2	1.60	4.00	8.00
6	167	5/66	PC-r	1	2	1.60	4.00	8.00

71. The Man Who Laughs

Ed	HRN	Date	Details	A	C	GD25	FN65	NM94
1	71	5/50	Original; Blum-c/a	1	1	12.00	36.00	85.00
2	165	–	New-c&a; PC-r	2	2	8.35	25.00	50.00
3	167	4/64	PC-r	2	2	6.70	20.00	40.00

72. The Oregon Trail

Ed	HRN	Date	Details	A	C	GD25	FN65	NM94
1	7	6/50	Original; Kiefer-c/a	1	1	8.35	25.00	50.00
2	89	–	C-price 15¢; LDC-r	1	1	4.00	10.00	20.00
3	121	–	LDC-r	1	1	3.20	8.00	16.00
4	131	–	New-c; PC-r	1	2	2.40	6.00	12.00
5	140	–	PC-r	1	2	1.50	3.00	6.00
6	150	–	PC-r	1	2	1.25	2.50	5.00
7	164	–	PC-r	1	2	1.25	2.50	5.00
8	167	–	PC-r	1	2	1.25	2.50	5.00
9	167	8/64	PC-r	1	2	1.25	2.50	5.00
10	167	10/65	PC-r	1	2	1.25	2.50	5.00
11	166	R/1968	C-price 25¢; PC-r	1	2	1.25	2.50	5.00

73. The Black Tulip

Ed	HRN	Date	Details	A	C	GD25	FN65	NM94
1	75	7/50	1st & only ed.; Alex Blum-c/a	1	1	25.00	75.00	175.00

74. Mr. Midshipman Easy

Ed	HRN	Date	Details	A	C	GD25	FN65	NM94
1	75	8/50	1st & only edition	1	1	25.00	75.00	175.00

75. The Lady of the Lake

Ed	HRN	Date	Details	A	C	GD25	FN65	NM94
1	75	9/50	Original; Kiefer-c/a	1	1	7.50	22.50	45.00
2	85	–	C-price 15¢; LDC-r	1	1	4.00	10.00	20.00
3	118	–	LDC-r	1	1	3.20	8.00	16.00
4	139	–	New-c; PC-r	1	2	2.40	6.00	12.00
5	154	–	PC-r	1	2	1.25	2.50	5.00
6	165	–	PC-r	1	2	1.25	2.50	5.00
7	167	4/64	PC-r	1	2	1.25	2.50	5.00
8	167	5/66	PC-r	1	2	1.25	2.50	5.00
9	169	Spr/69	New price 25¢; stiff-c; PC-r	1	2	1.25	2.50	5.00

76. The Prisoner of Zenda

Ed	HRN	Date	Details	A	C	GD25	FN65	NM94
1	75	10/50	Original; Kiefer-c/a	1	1	7.50	22.50	45.00
2	85	–	C-price 15¢; LDC-r	1	1	4.00	10.00	20.00
3	111	–	LDC-r	1	1	3.20	8.00	16.00
4	128	–	New-c; PC-r	1	2	2.40	6.00	12.00
5	152	–	PC-r	1	2	1.25	2.50	5.00
6	165	–	PC-r	1	2	1.25	2.50	5.00
7	167	4/64	PC-r	1	2	1.25	2.50	5.00
8	167	9/66	PC-r	1	2	1.25	2.50	5.00
9	169	Fall/69	New price 25¢; stiff-c; PC-r	1	2	1.25	2.50	5.00

77. The Iliad

Ed	HRN	Date	Details	A	C	GD25	FN65	NM94
1	78	11/50	Original; Blum-c/a	1	1	7.50	22.50	45.00
2	87	–	C-price 15¢; LDC-r	1	1	4.00	10.00	20.00
3	121	–	LDC-r	1	1	3.20	8.00	16.00
4	139	–	New-c; PC-r	1	2	2.40	6.00	12.00
5	150	–	PC-r	1	2	1.25	2.50	5.00
6	165	–	PC-r	1	2	1.25	2.50	5.00
7	167	10/63	PC-r	1	2	1.25	2.50	5.00
8	167	7/64	PC-r	1	2	1.25	2.50	5.00
9	167	5/66	PC-r	1	2	1.25	2.50	5.00
10	166	R/1968	C-price 25¢; PC-r	1	2	1.25	2.50	5.00

78. Joan of Arc

Ed	HRN	Date	Details	A	C	GD25	FN65	NM94
1	78	12/50	Original; Kiefer-c/a	1	1	7.50	22.50	45.00
2	87	–	C-price 15¢; LDC-r	1	1	4.00	10.00	20.00
3	113	–	LDC-r	1	1	3.20	8.00	16.00
4	128	–	New-c; PC-r	1	2	2.40	6.00	12.00
5	140	–	PC-r	1	2	1.25	2.50	5.00
6	150	–	PC-r	1	2	1.25	2.50	5.00
7	159	–	PC-r	1	2	1.25	2.50	5.00
8	167	–	PC-r	1	2	1.25	2.50	5.00
9	167	12/63	PC-r	1	2	1.25	2.50	5.00
10	167	6/65	PC-r	1	2	1.25	2.50	5.00
11	166	6/67	PC-r	1	2	1.25	2.50	5.00
12	166	Win/69	New-c&price, 25¢; PC-r; stiff-c	1	3	2.40	6.00	12.00

79. Cyrano de Bergerac

Ed	HRN	Date	Details	A	C	GD25	FN65	NM94
1	78	1/51	Orig.; movie promo inside front-c; Blum-a & c	1	1	7.50	22.50	45.00
2	85	–	C-price 15¢; LDC-r	1	1	4.00	10.00	20.00
3	118	–	LDC-r	1	1	3.20	8.00	16.00
4	133	–	New-c; PC-r	1	2	2.80	7.00	14.00
5	156	–	PC-r	1	2	2.00	5.00	10.00
6	167	8/64	PC-r	1	2	2.00	5.00	10.00

80. White Fang (Last line drawn cover)

Ed	HRN	Date	Details	A	C

Ed	HRN	Date	Details	A	C	GD25	FN65	NM94
1	79	2/51	Orig.; Blum-c/a	1	1	7.50	22.50	45.00
2	87	–	C-price 15¢; LDC-r	1	1	4.00	10.00	20.00
3	125	–	LDC-r	1	1	3.20	8.00	16.00
4	132	–	New-c; PC-r	1	2	2.40	6.00	12.00
5	140	–	PC-r	1	2	1.25	2.50	5.00
6	153	–	PC-r	1	2	1.25	2.50	5.00
7	167	–	PC-r	1	2	1.25	2.50	5.00
8	167	9/64	PC-r	1	2	1.25	2.50	5.00
9	167	7/65	PC-r	1	2	1.25	2.50	5.00
10	166	6/67	PC-r	1	2	1.25	2.50	5.00
11	169	Fall/69	New price 25¢; PC-r; stiff-c	1	2	1.25	2.50	5.00

81. The Odyssey (1st painted cover)

Ed	HRN	Date	Details	A	C	GD25	FN65	NM94
1	82	3/51	First 15¢ Original; Blum-c	1	1	5.00	15.00	30.00
2	167	8/64	PC-r	1	1	2.00	5.00	10.00
3	167	10/66	PC-r	1	1	2.00	5.00	10.00
4	169	Spr/69	New, stiff-c; PC-r	1	2	2.40	6.00	12.00

82. The Master of Ballantrae

Ed	HRN	Date	Details	A	C	GD25	FN65	NM94
1	82	4/51	Original; Blum-c	1	1	5.00	15.00	30.00
2	167	8/64	PC-r	1	1	2.40	6.00	12.00
3	166	Fall/68	New, stiff-c; PC-r	1	2	2.40	6.00	12.00

83. The Jungle Book

Ed	HRN	Date	Details	A	C	GD25	FN65	NM94
1	85	5/51	Original; Blum-c Bossert/Blum-a	1	1	5.00	15.00	30.00
2	110	–	PC-r	1	1	1.40	3.50	7.00
3	125	–	PC-r	1	1	1.25	2.50	5.00
4	134	–	PC-r	1	1	1.25	2.50	5.00
5	142	–	PC-r	1	1	1.25	2.50	5.00
6	150	–	PC-r	1	1	1.25	2.50	5.00
7	159	–	PC-r	1	1	1.25	2.50	5.00
8	167	–	PC-r	1	1	1.25	2.50	5.00
9	167	3/65	PC-r	1	1	1.25	2.50	5.00
10	167	11/65	PC-r	1	1	1.25	2.50	5.00
11	167	5/66	PC-r	1	1	1.25	2.50	5.00
12	166	R/1968	New c&a; stiff-c; PC-r	2	2	2.40	6.00	12.00

84. The Gold Bug and Other Stories ("The Gold Bug," "The Tell-Tale Heart," "The Cask of Amontillado")

Ed	HRN	Date	Details	A	C	GD25	FN65	NM94
1	85	6/51	Original; Blum-c/a; Palais, Laverly-a	1	1	11.00	32.00	75.00
2	167	7/64	PC-r	1	1	6.70	20.00	40.00

85. The Sea Wolf

Ed	HRN	Date	Details	A	C	GD25	FN65	NM94
1	85	7/51	Original; Blum-c/a	1	1	4.00	11.00	22.00
2	121	–	PC-r	1	1	1.00	2.00	4.00
3	132	–	PC-r	1	1	1.00	2.00	4.00
4	141	–	PC-r	1	1	1.00	2.00	4.00
5	161	–	PC-r	1	1	1.00	2.00	4.00
6	167	2/64	PC-r	1	1	1.00	2.00	4.00
7	167	11/65	PC-r	1	1	1.00	2.00	4.00
8	169	Fall/69	New price 25¢; stiff-c; PC-r	1	1	1.00	2.00	4.00

86. Under Two Flags

Ed	HRN	Date	Details	A	C	GD25	FN65	NM94
1	87	8/51	Original; first delBourgo-a	1	1	4.00	11.00	22.00
2	117	–	PC-r	1	1	1.00	2.00	4.00
3	139	–	PC-r	1	1	1.00	2.00	4.00
4	158	–	PC-r	1	1	1.00	2.00	4.00
5	167	2/64	PC-r	1	1	1.00	2.00	4.00
6	167	8/66	PC-r	1	1	1.00	2.00	4.00
7	169	Sm/69	New price 25¢; stiff-c; PC-r	1	1	1.00	2.00	4.00

87. A Midsummer Nights Dream

Ed	HRN	Date	Details	A	C	GD25	FN65	NM94
1	87	9/51	Original; Blum c/a	1	1	4.00	11.00	22.00
2	161	–	PC-r	1	1	1.25	2.50	5.00
3	167	4/64	PC-r	1	1	1.00	2.00	4.00
4	167	5/66	PC-r	1	1	1.00	2.00	4.00
5	169	Sm/69	New price 25¢; stiff-c; PC-r	1	1	1.00	2.00	4.00

88. Men of Iron

Ed	HRN	Date	Details	A	C	GD25	FN65	NM94
1	89	10/51	Original	1	1	4.00	12.00	24.00
2	154	–	PC-r	1	1	1.25	2.50	5.00
3	167	1/64	PC-r	1	1	1.25	2.50	5.00
4	166	R/1968	C-price 25¢; PC-r	1	1	1.25	2.50	5.00

89. Crime and Punishment (Cover illo. in **POP**)

Ed	HRN	Date	Details	A	C	GD25	FN65	NM94
1	89	11/51	Original; Palais-a	1	1	4.00	12.00	24.00
2	152	–	PC-r	1	1	1.00	2.00	4.00
3	167	4/64	PC-r	1	1	1.00	2.00	4.00
4	167	5/66	PC-r	1	1	1.00	2.00	4.00
5	169	Fall/69	New price 25¢ stiff-c; PC-r	1	1	1.00	2.00	4.00

90. Green Mansions

Ed	HRN	Date	Details	A	C	GD25	FN65	NM94
1	89	12/51	Original; Blum-c/a	1	1	4.35	13.00	26.00
2	148	–	New L.B. Cole-c; PC-r	1	2	2.00	5.00	10.00
3	165	–	PC-r	1	2	1.00	2.00	4.00
4	167	4/64	PC-r	1	2	1.00	2.00	4.00
5	167	9/66	PC-r	1	2	1.00	2.00	4.00
6	169	Sm/69	New price 25¢; stiff-c; PC-r	1	2	1.00	2.00	4.00

91. The Call of the Wild

Ed	HRN	Date	Details	A	C	GD25	FN65	NM94
1	92	1/52	Orig.; delBourgo-a	1	1	4.00	11.00	22.00
2	112	–	PC-r	1	1	1.25	2.50	5.00
3	125	–	'Picture Progress' on back-c; PC-r	1	1	1.00	2.00	4.00
4	134	–	PC-r	1	1	1.00	2.00	4.00
5	143	–	PC-r	1	1	1.00	2.00	4.00
6	165	–	PC-r	1	1	1.00	2.00	4.00
7	167	–	PC-r	1	1	1.00	2.00	4.00
8	167	4/65	PC-r	1	1	1.00	2.00	4.00
9	167	3/66	PC-r	1	1	1.00	2.00	4.00
10	166	11/67	PC-r	1	1	1.00	2.00	4.00
11	169	Spr/70	New price 25¢; stiff-c; PC-r	1	1	1.00	2.00	4.00

92. The Courtship of Miles Standish

Ed	HRN	Date	Details	A	C	GD25	FN65	NM94
1	92	2/52	Original; Blum-c/a	1	1	4.00	11.00	22.00
2	165	–	PC-r	1	1	1.00	2.00	4.00
3	167	3/64	PC-r	1	1	1.00	2.00	4.00
4	166	5/67	PC-r	1	1	1.00	2.00	4.00
5	169	Win/69	New price 25¢ stiff-c; PC-r	1	1	1.00	2.00	4.00

93. Pudd'nhead Wilson

Classics Illustrated #80, © GIL

Classics Illustrated #87 (Orig.), © GIL

Classics Illustrated #91 (HRN-112), © GIL

Classics Illustrated #98 (Orig.), © GIL

Classics Illustrated #100 (Orig.), © GIL

Classics Illustrated #103, © GIL

Ed	HRN	Date	Details	A	C	GD25	FN65	NM94
1	94	3/52	Orig.; Kiefer-c/a;	1	1	4.35	13.00	26.00
2	165	–	New-c; PC-r	1	2	1.80	4.50	9.00
3	167	3/64	PC-r	1	2	1.40	3.50	7.00
4	166	R/1968	New price 25¢; soft-c; PC-r	1	2	1.40	3.50	7.00

94. David Balfour

Ed	HRN	Date	Details	A	C	GD25	FN65	NM94
1	94	4/52	Original; Palais-a	1	1	4.35	13.00	26.00
2	167	5/64	PC-r	1	1	2.00	5.00	10.00
3	166	R/1968	C-price 25¢; PC-r	1	1	2.00	5.00	10.00

95. All Quiet on the Western Front

Ed	HRN	Date	Details	A	C	GD25	FN65	NM94
1A	96	5/52	Orig.; del Bourgo-a	1	1	9.15	27.50	55.00
1B	99	5/52	Orig.; del Bourgo-a	1	1	8.35	25.00	50.00
2	167	10/64	PC-r	1	1	2.80	7.00	14.00
3	167	11/66	PC-r	1	1	2.80	7.00	14.00

96. Daniel Boone

Ed	HRN	Date	Details	A	C	GD25	FN65	NM94
1	97	6/52	Original; Blum-a	1	1	4.00	11.00	22.00
2	117	–	PC-r	1	1	1.00	2.00	4.00
3	128	–	PC-r	1	1	1.00	2.00	4.00
4	132	–	PC-r	1	1	1.00	2.00	4.00
5	134	–	"Story of Jesus" on back-c; PC-r	1	1	1.00	2.00	4.00
6	158	–	PC-r	1	1	1.00	2.00	4.00
7	167	1/64	PC-r	1	1	1.00	2.00	4.00
8	167	5/65	PC-r	1	1	1.00	2.00	4.00
9	167	11/66	PC-r	1	1	1.00	2.00	4.00
10	166	Win/69	New-c; price 25¢; PC-r; stiff-c	1	2	2.00	5.00	10.00

97. King Solomon's Mines

Ed	HRN	Date	Details	A	C	GD25	FN65	NM94
1	96	7/52	Orig.; Kiefer-a	1	1	4.00	11.00	22.00
2	118	–	PC-r	1	1	1.50	3.50	7.00
3	131	–	PC-r	1	1	1.00	2.00	4.00
4	141	–	PC-r	1	1	1.00	2.00	4.00
5	158	–	PC-r	1	1	1.00	2.00	4.00
6	167	2/64	PC-r	1	1	1.00	2.00	4.00
7	167	9/65	PC-r	1	1	1.00	2.00	4.00
8	169	Sm/69	New price 25¢; stiff-c; PC-r	1	1	1.25	2.50	5.00

98. The Red Badge of Courage

Ed	HRN	Date	Details	A	C	GD25	FN65	NM94
1	98	8/52	Original	1	1	4.00	11.00	22.00
2	118	–	PC-r	1	1	1.00	2.00	4.00
3	132	–	PC-r	1	1	1.00	2.00	4.00
4	142	–	PC-r	1	1	1.00	2.00	4.00
5	152	–	PC-r	1	1	1.00	2.00	4.00
6	161	–	PC-r	1	1	1.00	2.00	4.00
7	167	–	Has orig.date; PC-r	1	1	1.00	2.00	4.00
8	167	9/64	PC-r	1	1	1.00	2.00	4.00
9	167	10/65	PC-r	1	1	1.00	2.00	4.00
10	166	R/1968	New-c&price 25¢; PC-r; stiff-c	1	2	2.40	6.00	12.00

99. Hamlet (Used in **POP**, pg. 102)

Ed	HRN	Date	Details	A	C	GD25	FN65	NM94
1	98	9/52	Original; Blum-a	1	1	4.00	12.00	24.00
2	121	–	PC-r	1	1	1.00	2.00	4.00
3	141	–	PC-r	1	1	1.00	2.00	4.00
4	158	–	PC-r	1	1	1.00	2.00	4.00
5	167	–	Has orig.date; PC-r	1	1	1.00	2.00	4.00
6	167	7/65	PC-r	1	1	1.00	2.00	4.00
7	166	4/67	PC-r	1	1	1.00	2.00	4.00
8	169	Spr/69	New-c&price 25¢; PC-r; stiff-c	1	2	2.00	5.00	10.00

100. Mutiny on the Bounty

Ed	HRN	Date	Details	A	C	GD25	FN65	NM94
1	100	10/52	Original	1	1	4.00	11.00	22.00
2	117	–	PC-r	1	1	1.00	2.00	4.00
3	132	–	PC-r	1	1	1.00	2.00	4.00
4	142	–	PC-r	1	1	1.00	2.00	4.00
5	155	–	PC-r	1	1	1.00	2.00	4.00
6	167	–	Has orig. date;PC-r	1	1	1.00	2.00	4.00
7	167	5/64	PC-r	1	1	1.00	2.00	4.00
8	167	3/66	PC-r	1	1	1.00	2.00	4.00
9	169	Spr/70	PC-r; stiff-c	1	1	1.00	2.00	4.00

101. William Tell

Ed	HRN	Date	Details	A	C	GD25	FN65	NM94
1	101	11/52	Original; Kiefer-c delBourgo-a	1	1	4.00	11.00	22.00
2	118	–	PC-r	1	1	1.00	2.00	4.00
3	141	–	PC-r	1	1	1.00	2.00	4.00
4	158	–	PC-r	1	1	1.00	2.00	4.00
5	167	–	Has orig.date; PC-r	1	1	1.00	2.00	4.00
6	167	11/64	PC-r	1	1	1.00	2.00	4.00
7	166	4/67	PC-r	1	1	1.00	2.00	4.00
8	169	Win/69	New price 25¢; stiff-c; PC-r	1	1	1.00	2.00	4.00

102. The White Company

Ed	HRN	Date	Details	A	C	GD25	FN65	NM94
1	101	12/52	Original; Blum-a	1	1	6.70	20.00	40.00
2	165	–	PC-r	1	1	3.60	9.00	18.00
3	167	4/64	PC-r	1	1	3.60	9.00	18.00

103. Men Against the Sea

Ed	HRN	Date	Details	A	C	GD25	FN65	NM94
1	104	1/53	Original; Kiefer-c; Palais-a	1	1	4.35	13.00	26.00
2	114	–	PC-r	1	1	2.80	7.00	14.00
3	131	–	New-c; PC-r	1	2	2.00	5.00	10.00
4	158	–	PC-r	1	2	2.00	5.00	10.00
5	149	–	White reorder list; came after HRN-158; PC-r	1	2	3.60	9.00	18.00
6	167	3/64	PC-r	1	2	1.40	3.50	7.00

104. Bring 'Em Back Alive

Ed	HRN	Date	Details	A	C	GD25	FN65	NM94
1	105	2/53	Original; Kiefer c/a	1	1	4.00	10.50	21.00
2	118	–	PC-r	1	1	1.00	2.00	4.00
3	133	–	PC-r	1	1	1.00	2.00	4.00
4	150	–	PC-r	1	1	1.00	2.00	4.00
5	158	–	PC-r	1	1	1.00	2.00	4.00
6	167	10/63	PC-r	1	1	1.00	2.00	4.00
7	167	9/65	PC-r	1	1	1.00	2.00	4.00
8	169	Win/69	New price 25¢; stiff-c; PC-r	1	1	1.00	2.00	4.00

105. From the Earth to the Moon

Ed	HRN	Date	Details	A	C	GD25	FN65	NM94
1	106	3/53	Original; Blum-a	1	1	4.00	10.50	21.00
2	118	–	PC-r	1	1	1.00	2.00	4.00

Ed	HRN	Date	Details	A	C	GD25	FN65	NM94
3	132	–	PC-r	1	1	1.00	2.00	4.00
4	141	–	PC-r	1	1	1.00	2.00	4.00
5	146	–	PC-r	1	1	1.00	2.00	4.00
6	156	–	PC-r	1	1	1.00	2.00	4.00
7	167	–	Has orig. date;PC-r	1	1	1.00	2.00	4.00
8	167	5/64	PC-r	1	1	1.00	2.00	4.00
9	167	5/65	PC-r	1	1	1.00	2.00	4.00
10A	166	10/67	PC-r	1	1	1.00	2.00	4.00
10B	166	10/67	w/Grit ad stapled in book	1	1	9.35	28.00	56.00
11	169	Sm/69	New price 25¢; stiff-c; PC-r	1	1	1.00	2.00	4.00
12	169	Spr/71	PC-r	1	1	1.00	2.00	4.00

106. Buffalo Bill

Ed	HRN	Date	Details	A	C	GD25	FN65	NM94
1	107	4/53	Orig.; delBourgo-a	1	1	4.00	10.50	21.00
2	118	–	PC-r	1	1	1.00	2.00	4.00
3	132	–	PC-r	1	1	1.00	2.00	4.00
4	142	–	PC-r	1	1	1.00	2.00	4.00
5	161	–	PC-r	1	1	1.00	2.00	4.00
6	167	3/64	PC-r	1	1	1.00	2.00	4.00
7	166	7/67	PC-r	1	1	1.00	2.00	4.00
8	169	Fall/69	PC-r; stiff-c	1	1	1.00	2.00	4.00

107. King of the Khyber Rifles

Ed	HRN	Date	Details	A	C	GD25	FN65	NM94
1	108	5/53	Original	1	1	4.00	11.00	22.00
2	118	–	PC-r	1	1	1.00	2.00	4.00
3	146	–	PC-r	1	1	1.00	2.00	4.00
4	158	–	PC-r	1	1	1.00	2.00	4.00
5	167	–	Has orig.date; PC-r	1	1	1.00	2.00	4.00
6	167	–	PC-r	1	1	1.00	2.00	4.00
7	167	10/66	PC-r	1	1	1.00	2.00	4.00

108. Knights of the Round Table

Ed	HRN	Date	Details	A	C	GD25	FN65	NM94
1A	108	6/53	Original; Blum-a	1	1	4.00	11.00	22.00
1B	109	6/53	Original; scarce	1	1	5.35	16.00	32.00
2	117	–	PC-r	1	1	1.00	2.00	4.00
3	165	–	PC-r	1	1	1.00	2.00	4.00
4	167	4/64	PC-r	1	1	1.00	2.00	4.00
5	166	4/67	PC-r	1	1	1.00	2.00	4.00
6	169	Sm/69	New price 25¢; stiff-c; PC-r	1	1	1.00	2.00	4.00

109. Pitcairn's Island

Ed	HRN	Date	Details	A	C	GD25	FN65	NM94
1	110	7/53	Original; Palais-a	1	1	4.00	12.00	24.00
2	165	–	PC-r	1	1	1.50	3.50	7.00
3	167	3/64	PC-r	1	1	1.50	3.50	7.00
4	166	6/67	PC-r	1	1	1.50	3.50	7.00

110. A Study in Scarlet

Ed	HRN	Date	Details	A	C	GD25	FN65	NM94
1	111	8/53	Original	1	1	11.00	32.00	75.00
2	165	–	PC-r	1	1	7.00	21.00	42.00

111. The Talisman

Ed	HRN	Date	Details	A	C	GD25	FN65	NM94
1	112	9/53	Original; last H.C. Kiefer-a	1	1	5.35	16.00	32.00
2	165	–	PC-r	1	1	1.25	2.50	5.00
3	167	5/64	PC-r	1	1	1.25	2.50	5.00
4	166	Fall/68	C-price 25¢; PC-r	1	1	1.25	2.50	5.00

112. Adventures of Kit Carson

Ed	HRN	Date	Details	A	C	GD25	FN65	NM94
1	113	10/53	Original; Palais-a	1	1	5.35	16.00	32.00
2	129	–	PC-r	1	1	1.00	2.00	4.00
3	141	–	PC-r	1	1	1.00	2.00	4.00
4	152	–	PC-r	1	1	1.00	2.00	4.00
5	161	–	PC-r	1	1	1.00	2.00	4.00
6	167	–	PC-r	1	1	1.00	2.00	4.00
7	167	2/65	PC-r	1	1	1.00	2.00	4.00
8	167	5/66	PC-r	1	1	1.00	2.00	4.00
9	166	Win/69	New-c&price 25¢; PC-r; stiff-c	1	2	2.00	5.00	10.00

113. The Forty-Five Guardsmen

Ed	HRN	Date	Details	A	C	GD25	FN65	NM94
1	114	11/53	Orig.; delBourgo-a	1	1	7.50	22.50	45.00
2	166	7/67	PC-r	1	1	4.00	10.50	21.00

114. The Red Rover

Ed	HRN	Date	Details	A	C	GD25	FN65	NM94
1	115	12/53	Original	1	1	7.50	22.50	45.00
2	166	7/67	PC-r	1	1	4.00	10.50	21.00

115. How I Found Livingstone

Ed	HRN	Date	Details	A	C	GD25	FN65	NM94
1	116	1/54	Original	1	1	7.50	22.50	45.00
2	167	1/67	PC-r	1	1	4.00	10.50	21.00

116. The Bottle Imp

Ed	HRN	Date	Details	A	C	GD25	FN65	NM94
1	117	2/54	Orig.; Cameron-a	1	1	7.50	22.50	45.00
2	167	1/67	PC-r	1	1	4.00	10.50	21.00

117. Captains Courageous

Ed	HRN	Date	Details	A	C	GD25	FN65	NM94
1	118	3/54	Orig.; Costanza-a	1	1	6.35	19.00	38.00
2	167	2/67	PC-r	1	1	2.40	6.00	12.00
3	169	Fall/69	New price 25¢; stiff-c; PC-r	1	1	2.00	5.00	10.00

118. Rob Roy

Ed	HRN	Date	Details	A	C	GD25	FN65	NM94
1	119	4/54	Original; Rudy & Walter Palais-a	1	1	7.50	22.50	45.00
2	167	2/67	PC-r	1	1	4.00	10.50	21.00

119. Soldiers of Fortune

Ed	HRN	Date	Details	A	C	GD25	FN65	NM94
1	120	5/54	Original Shaffenberger-a	1	1	7.00	21.00	42.00
2	166	3/67	PC-r	1	1	2.80	7.00	14.00
3	169	Spr/70	New price 25¢; stiff-c; PC-r	1	1	2.00	5.00	10.00

120. The Hurricane

Ed	HRN	Date	Details	A	C	GD25	FN65	NM94
1	121	6/54	Orig.; Cameron-a	1	1	7.50	22.50	45.00
2	166	3/67	PC-r	1	1	4.00	12.00	24.00

121. Wild Bill Hickok

Ed	HRN	Date	Details	A	C	GD25	FN65	NM94
1	122	7/54	Original	1	1	4.00	11.00	22.00
2	132	–	PC-r	1	1	1.00	2.00	4.00
3	141	–	PC-r	1	1	1.00	2.00	4.00
4	154	–	PC-r	1	1	1.00	2.00	4.00
5	167	–	PC-r	1	1	1.00	2.00	4.00
6	167	8/64	PC-r	1	1	1.00	2.00	4.00
7	166	4/67	PC-r	1	1	1.00	2.00	4.00
8	169	Win/69	PC-r; stiff-c	1	1	1.00	2.00	4.00

122. The Mutineers

Classics Illustrated #107 (HRN-167),© GIL

Classics Illustrated #109, © GIL

Classics Illustrated #115 (Orig.), © GIL

Classics Illustrated #124 (HRN-167), © GIL

Classics Illustrated #127 (Orig.), © GIL

Classics Illustrated #130 (Orig.), © GIL

Ed	HRN	Date	Details	A	C	GD25	FN65	NM94
1	123	9/54	Original	1	1	4.00	11.00	22.00
2	136	–	PC-r	1	1	1.00	2.00	4.00
3	146	–	PC-r	1	1	1.00	2.00	4.00
4	158	–	PC-r	1	1	1.00	2.00	4.00
5	167	11/63	PC-r	1	1	1.00	2.00	4.00
6	167	3/65	PC-r	1	1	1.00	2.00	4.00
7	166	8/67	PC-r	1	1	1.00	2.00	4.00

123. Fang and Claw

Ed	HRN	Date	Details	A	C	GD25	FN65	NM94
1	124	11/54	Original	1	1	4.00	11.00	22.00
2	133	–	PC-r	1	1	1.00	2.00	4.00
3	143	–	PC-r	1	1	1.00	2.00	4.00
4	154	–	PC-r	1	1	1.00	2.00	4.00
5	167	–	Has orig.date; PC-r	1	1	1.00	2.00	4.00
6	167	9/65	PC-r	1	1	1.00	2.00	4.00

124. The War of the Worlds

Ed	HRN	Date	Details	A	C	GD25	FN65	NM94
1	125	1/55	Original; Cameron-c/a	1	1	5.00	15.00	30.00
2	131	–	PC-r	1	1	1.40	3.50	7.00
3	141	–	PC-r	1	1	1.40	3.50	7.00
4	148	–	PC-r	1	1	1.40	3.50	7.00
5	156	–	PC-r	1	1	1.40	3.50	7.00
6	165	–	PC-r	1	1	1.40	3.50	7.00
7	167	–	PC-r	1	1	1.40	3.50	7.00
8	167	11/64	PC-r	1	1	1.40	3.50	7.00
9	167	11/65	PC-r	1	1	1.40	3.50	7.00
10	166	R/1968	C-price 25¢; PC-r	1	1	1.40	3.50	7.00
11	169	Sm/70	PC-r; stiff-c	1	1	1.40	3.50	7.00

125. The Ox Bow Incident

Ed	HRN	Date	Details	A	C	GD25	FN65	NM94
1	3/55	–	Original; Picture Progress replaces reorder list	1	1	4.00	11.00	22.00
2	143	–	PC-r	1	1	1.00	2.00	4.00
3	152	–	PC-r	1	1	1.00	2.00	4.00
4	149	–	PC-r	1	1	1.00	2.00	4.00
5	167	–	PC-r	1	1	1.00	2.00	4.00
6	167	11/64	PC-r	1	1	1.00	2.00	4.00
7	166	4/67	PC-r	1	1	1.00	2.00	4.00
8	169	Win/69	New price 25¢; stiff-c; PC-r	1	1	1.00	2.00	4.00

126. The Downfall

Ed	HRN	Date	Details	A	C	GD25	FN65	NM94
1	5/55	–	Orig.; 'Picture Progress' replaces reorder list; Cameron-c/a	1	1	4.00	11.00	22.00
2	167	8/64	PC-r	1	1	1.60	4.00	8.00
3	166	R/1968	C-price 25¢; PC-r	1	1	1.60	4.00	8.00

127. The King of the Mountains

Ed	HRN	Date	Details	A	C	GD25	FN65	NM94
1	128	7/55	Original	1	1	4.00	11.00	22.00
2	167	6/64	PC-r	1	1	1.60	4.00	8.00
3	166	F/1968	C-price 25¢; PC-r	1	1	1.60	4.00	8.00

128. Macbeth (Used in **POP**, pg. 102)

Ed	HRN	Date	Details	A	C	GD25	FN65	NM94
1	128	9/55	Orig.; last Blum-a	1	1	4.00	11.00	22.00
2	143	–	PC-r	1	1	1.00	2.00	4.00
3	158	–	PC-r	1	1	1.00	2.00	4.00
4	167	–	PC-r	1	1	1.00	2.00	4.00
5	167	6/64	PC-r	1	1	1.00	2.00	4.00
6	166	4/67	PC-r	1	1	1.00	2.00	4.00
7	166	R/1968	C-Price 25¢; PC-r	1	1	1.00	2.00	4.00
8	169	Spr/70	Stiff-c; PC-r	1	1	1.00	2.00	4.00

129. Davy Crockett

Ed	HRN	Date	Details	AC		GD25	FN65	NM94
1	129	11/55	Orig.; Cameron-a	1	1	9.15	27.50	55.00
2	167	9/66	PC-r	1	1	5.35	16.00	32.00

130. Caesar's Conquests

Ed	HRN	Date	Details	A	C	GD25	FN65	NM94
1	130	1/56	Original; Orlando-a	1	1	4.00	11.00	22.00
2	142	–	PC-r	1	1	1.00	2.00	4.00
3	152	–	PC-r	1	1	1.00	2.00	4.00
4	149	–	PC-r	1	1	1.00	2.00	4.00
5	167	–	PC-r	1	1	1.00	2.00	4.00
6	167	10/64	PC-r	1	1	1.00	2.00	4.00
7	167	4/66	PC-r	1	1	1.00	2.00	4.00

131. The Covered Wagon

Ed	HRN	Date	Details	A	C	GD25	FN65	NM94
1	131	3/56	Original	1	1	4.00	11.00	22.00
2	143	–	PC-r	1	1	1.00	2.00	4.00
3	152	–	PC-r	1	1	1.00	2.00	4.00
4	158	–	PC-r	1	1	1.00	2.00	4.00
5	167	–	PC-r	1	1	1.00	2.00	4.00
6	167	11/64	PC-r	1	1	1.00	2.00	4.00
7	167	4/66	PC-r	1	1	1.00	2.00	4.00
8	169	Win/69	New price 25¢; stiff-c; PC-r	1	1	1.00	2.00	4.00

132. The Dark Frigate

Ed	HRN	Date	Details	A	C	GD25	FN65	NM94
1	132	5/56	Original	1	1	4.00	11.00	22.00
2	150	–	PC-r	1	1	1.40	3.50	7.00
3	167	1/64	PC-r	1	1	1.40	3.50	7.00
4	166	5/67	PC-r	1	1	1.40	3.50	7.00

133. The Time Machine

Ed	HRN	Date	Details	A	C	GD25	FN65	NM94
1	132	7/56	Orig.; Cameron-a	1	1	5.00	15.00	30.00
2	142	–	PC-r	1	1	1.40	3.50	7.00
3	152	–	PC-r	1	1	1.40	3.50	7.00
4	158	–	PC-r	1	1	1.40	3.50	7.00
5	167	–	PC-r	1	1	1.40	3.50	7.00
6	167	6/64	PC-r	1	1	1.40	3.50	7.00
7	167	3/66	PC-r	1	1	1.40	3.50	7.00
8	166	12/67	PC-r	1	1	1.40	3.50	7.00
9	169	Win/71	New price 25¢; stiff-c; PC-r	1	1	1.40	3.50	7.00

134. Romeo and Juliet

Ed	HRN	Date	Details	A	C	GD25	FN65	NM94
1	134	9/56	Original; Evans-a	1	1	4.00	11.00	22.00
2	161	–	PC-r	1	1	1.00	2.00	4.00
3	167	9/63	PC-r	1	1	1.00	2.00	4.00
4	167	5/65	PC-r	1	1	1.00	2.00	4.00
5	166	6/67	PC-r	1	1	1.00	2.00	4.00
6	166	Win/69	New c&price 25¢; stiff-c; PC-r	1	2	3.60	9.00	18.00

135. Waterloo

Ed	HRN	Date	Details	A	C	GD25	FN65	NM94
1	135	11/56	Orig.; G. Ingels-a	1	1	4.00	11.00	22.00

Ed	HRN	Date	Details	A	C	GD25	FN65	NM94
2	153	–	PC-r	1	1	1.00	2.00	4.00
3	167	–	PC-r	1	1	1.00	2.00	4.00
4	167	9/64	PC-r	1	1	1.00	2.00	4.00
5	166	R/1968	C-price 25¢; PC-r	1	1	1.00	2.00	4.00

136. Lord Jim

Ed	HRN	Date	Details	A	C	GD25	FN65	NM94
1	136	1/57	Original; Evans-a	1	1	4.00	11.00	22.00
2	165	–	PC-r	1	1	1.00	2.00	4.00
3	167	3/64	PC-r	1	1	1.00	2.00	4.00
4	167	9/66	PC-r	1	1	1.00	2.00	4.00
5	169	Sm/69	New price 25 ¢; stiff-c; PC-r	1	1	1.00	2.00	4.00

137. The Little Savage

Ed	HRN	Date	Details	A	C	GD25	FN65	NM94
1	136	3/57	Original; Evans-a	1	1	4.00	11.00	22.00
2	148	–	PC-r	1	1	1.00	2.00	4.00
3	156	–	PC-r	1	1	1.00	2.00	4.00
4	167	–	PC-r	1	1	1.00	2.00	4.00
5	167	10/64	PC-r	1	1	1.00	2.00	4.00
6	166	8/67	PC-r	1	1	1.00	2.00	4.00
7	169	Spr/70	New price 25 ¢; stiff-c; PC-r	1	1	1.00	2.00	4.00

138. A Journey to the Center of the Earth

Ed	HRN	Date	Details	A	C	GD25	FN65	NM94
1	136	5/57	Original	1	1	4.70	14.00	28.00
2	146	–	PC-r	1	1	1.25	2.50	5.00
3	156	–	PC-r	1	1	1.25	2.50	5.00
4	158	–	PC-r	1	1	1.25	2.50	5.00
5	167	–	PC-r	1	1	1.25	2.50	5.00
6	167	6/64	PC-r	1	1	1.25	2.50	5.00
7	167	4/66	PC-r	1	1	1.25	2.50	5.00
8	166	R/68	C-price 25 ¢; PC-r	1	1	1.25	2.50	5.00

139. In the Reign of Terror

Ed	HRN	Date	Details	A	C	GD25	FN65	NM94
1	139	7/57	Original; Evans-a	1	1	4.00	11.00	22.00
2	154	–	PC-r	1	1	1.00	2.00	4.00
3	167	–	Has orig.date; PC-r	1	1	1.00	2.00	4.00
4	167	7/64	PC-r	1	1	1.00	2.00	4.00
5	166	R/1968	C-price 25¢; PC-r	1	1	1.00	2.00	4.00

140. On Jungle Trails

Ed	HRN	Date	Details	A	C	GD25	FN65	NM94
1	140	9/57	Original	1	1	4.00	11.00	22.00
2	150	–	PC-r	1	1	1.00	2.00	4.00
3	160	–	PC-r	1	1	1.00	2.00	4.00
4	167	9/63	PC-r	1	1	1.00	2.00	4.00
5	167	9/65	PC-r	1	1	1.00	2.00	4.00

141. Castle Dangerous

Ed	HRN	Date	Details	A	C	GD25	FN65	NM94
1	141	11/57	Original	1	1	4.00	11.00	22.00
2	152	–	PC-r	1	1	1.25	2.50	5.00
3	167	–	PC-r	1	1	1.25	2.50	5.00
4	166	7/67	PC-r	1	1	1.25	2.50	5.00

142. Abraham Lincoln

Ed	HRN	Date	Details	A	C	GD25	FN65	NM94
1	142	1/58	Original	1	1	4.00	11.00	22.00
2	154	–	PC-r	1	1	1.00	2.00	4.00
3	158	–	PC-r	1	1	1.00	2.00	4.00
4	167	10/63	PC-r	1	1	1.00	2.00	4.00
5	167	7/65	PC-r	1	1	1.00	2.00	4.00
6	166	11/67	PC-r	1	1	1.00	2.00	4.00
7	169	Fall/69	New price 25¢; stiff-c; PC-r	1	1	1.00	2.00	4.00

143. Kim

Ed	HRN	Date	Details	A	C	GD25	FN65	NM94
1	143	3/58	Original; Orlando-a	1	1	4.00	11.00	22.00
2	165	–	PC-r	1	1	1.00	2.00	4.00
3	167	11/63	PC-r	1	1	1.00	2.00	4.00
4	167	8/65	PC-r	1	1	1.00	2.00	4.00
5	169	Win/69	New price 25¢; stiff-c; PC-r	1	1	1.00	2.00	4.00

144. The First Men in the Moon

Ed	HRN	Date	Details	A	C	GD25	FN65	NM94
1	143	5/58	Original; Woodbridge/Williamson/Torres-a	1	1	4.70	14.00	28.00
2	152	–	(Rare)-PC-r	1	1	5.85	17.50	35.00
3	153	–	PC-r	1	1	1.25	2.50	5.00
4	161	–	PC-r	1	1	1.25	2.50	5.00
5	167	–	PC-r	1	1	1.25	2.50	5.00
6	167	12/65	PC-r	1	1	1.25	2.50	5.00
7	166	Fall/68	New-c&price 25¢; PC-r; stiff-c	1	2	1.80	4.50	9.00
8	169	Win/69	Stiff-c; PC-r	1	2	1.80	4.50	9.00

145. The Crisis

Ed	HRN	Date	Details	A	C	GD25	FN65	NM94
1	143	7/58	Original; Evans-a	1	1	4.00	11.00	22.00
2	156	–	PC-r	1	1	1.00	2.00	4.00
3	167	10/63	PC-r	1	1	1.00	2.00	4.00
4	167	3/65	PC-r	1	1	1.00	2.00	4.00
5	166	R/68	C-price 25¢; PC-r	1	1	1.00	2.00	4.00

146. With Fire and Sword

Ed	HRN	Date	Details	A	C	GD25	FN65	NM94
1	143	9/58	Original; Woodbridge-a	1	1	4.00	11.00	22.00
2	156	–	PC-r	1	1	1.40	3.50	7.00
3	167	11/63	PC-r	1	1	1.40	3.50	7.00
4	167	3/65	PC-r	1	1	1.40	3.50	7.00

147. Ben-Hur

Ed	HRN	Date	Details	A	C	GD25	FN65	NM94
1	147	11/58	Original; Orlando-a	1	1	4.00	11.00	22.00
2	152	–	Scarce; PC-r	1	1	4.00	12.00	24.00
3	153	–	PC-r	1	1	1.00	2.00	4.00
4	158	–	PC-r	1	1	1.00	2.00	4.00
5	167	–	Orig.date; but PC-r	1	1	1.00	2.00	4.00
6	167	2/65	PC-r	1	1	1.00	2.00	4.00
7	167	9/66	PC-r	1	1	1.00	2.00	4.00
8A	166	Fall/68	New-c&price 25¢; PC-r; soft-c	1	2	2.40	6.00	12.00
8B	166	Fall/68	New-c&price 25¢; PC-r; stiff-c; scarce	1	2	4.00	12.00	24.00

148. The Buccaneer

Ed	HRN	Date	Details	A	C	GD25	FN65	NM94
1	148	1/59	Orig.; Evans/Jenny-a; Saunders-c	1	1	4.00	11.00	22.00
2	568	–	Juniors list only PC-r	1	1	1.40	3.50	7.00
3	167	–	PC-r	1	1	1.00	2.00	4.00
4	167	9/65	PC-r	1	1	1.00	2.00	4.00
5	169	Sm/69	New price 25¢; PC-r; stiff-c	1	1	1.00	2.00	4.00

149. Off on a Comet

Ed	HRN	Date	Details	A	C

Classics Illustrated #133 (HRN-167), © GIL

Classics Illustrated #138, © GIL

Classics Illustrated #148 (Orig?), © GIL

Classics Illustrated #160 (Orig.), © GIL

Classics Illustrated #161 (HRN-167), © GIL

Classics Illustrated #162 (HRN-167), © GIL

Ed	HRN	Date	Details	A	C	GD25	FN65	NM94
1	149	3/59	Orig.;G.McCann-a; blue reorder list	1	1	4.00	11.00	22.00
2	155	–	PC-r	1	1	1.00	2.00	4.00
3	149	–	PC-r; white reorder list; no coming-next ad	1	1	1.00	2.00	4.00
4	167	12/63	PC-r	1	1	1.00	2.00	4.00
5	167	2/65	PC-r	1	1	1.00	2.00	4.00
6	167	10/66	PC-r	1	1	1.00	2.00	4.00
7	166	Fall/68	New-c&price 25¢; PC-r	1	2	2.40	6.00	12.00

150. The Virginian

Ed	HRN	Date	Details	A	C	GD25	FN65	NM94
1	150	5/59	Original	1	1	5.00	15.00	30.00
2	164	–	PC-r	1	1	2.40	6.00	12.00
3	167	10/63	PC-r	1	1	2.00	5.00	10.00
4	167	12/65	PC-r	1	1	2.00	5.00	10.00

151. Won By the Sword

Ed	HRN	Date	Details	A	C	GD25	FN65	NM94
1	150	7/59	Original	1	1	5.00	15.00	30.00
2	164	–	PC-r	1	1	2.00	5.00	10.00
3	167	10/63	PC-r	1	1	1.80	4.50	9.00
4	166	7/67	PC-r	1	1	1.80	4.50	9.00

152. Wild Animals I Have Known

Ed	HRN	Date	Details	A	C	GD25	FN65	NM94
1	152	9/59	Orig.; L.B. Cole c/a	1	1	5.00	15.00	30.00
2A	149	–	PC-r; white reorder list; no coming-next ad; IBC: Jr. list #572	1	1	1.25	2.50	5.00
2B	149	–	PC-r; inside-bc: Jr. list to #555	1	1	1.40	3.50	7.00
2C	149	–	PC-r; inside-bc: has World Around Us ad; scarce	1	1	2.80	7.00	14.00
3	167	9/63	PC-r	1	1	1.00	2.00	4.00
4	167	8/65	PC-r	1	1	1.00	2.00	4.00
5	169	Fall/69	New price 25¢; stiff-c; PC-r	1	1	1.00	2.00	4.00

153. The Invisible Man

Ed	HRN	Date	Details	A	C	GD25	FN65	NM94
1	153	11/59	Original	1	1	5.00	15.00	30.00
2A	149	–	PC-r; white reorder list; no coming-next ad; inside-bc: Jr. list to #572	1	1	1.25	2.50	5.00
2B	149	–	PC-r; inside-bc: Jr. list to #555	1	1	1.40	3.50	7.00
3	167	–	PC-r	1	1	1.00	2.00	4.00
4	167	2/65	PC-r	1	1	1.00	2.00	4.00
5	167	9/66	PC-r	1	1	1.00	2.00	4.00
6	166	Win/69	New price 25¢; PC-r; stiff-c	1	1	1.00	2.00	4.00
7	169	Spr/71	Stiff-c; letters spelling 'Invisible Man' are 'solid' not 'invisible;' PC-r	1	1	1.00	2.00	4.00

154. The Conspiracy of Pontiac

Ed	HRN	Date	Details	A	C	GD25	FN65	NM94
1	154	1/60	Original	1	1	5.00	15.00	30.00
2	167	11/63	PC-r	1	1	2.40	6.00	12.00
3	167	7/64	PC-r	1	1	2.40	6.00	12.00
4	166	12/67	PC-r	1	1	2.40	6.00	12.00

155. The Lion of the North

Ed	HRN	Date	Details	A	C	GD25	FN65	NM94
1	154	3/60	Original	1	1	4.35	13.00	26.00
2	167	1/64	PC-r	1	1	2.00	5.00	10.00
3	166	R/1967	C-price 25¢; PC-r	1	1	1.80	4.50	9.00

156. The Conquest of Mexico

Ed	HRN	Date	Details	A	C	GD25	FN65	NM94
1	156	5/60	Orig.; Bruno Premiani-c/a	1	1	4.35	13.00	26.00
2	167	1/64	PC-r	1	1	1.40	3.50	7.00
3	166	8/67	PC-r	1	1	1.40	3.50	7.00
4	169	Spr/70	New price 25¢; stiff-c; PC-r	1	1	1.25	2.50	5.00

157. Lives of the Hunted

Ed	HRN	Date	Details	A	C	GD25	FN65	NM94
1	156	7/60	Orig.; L.B. Cole-c	1	1	5.00	15.00	30.00
2	167	2/64	PC-r	1	1	2.40	6.00	12.00
3	166	10/67	PC-r	1	1	2.40	6.00	12.00

158. The Conspirators

Ed	HRN	Date	Details	A	C	GD25	FN65	NM94
1	156	9/60	Original	1	1	5.00	15.00	30.00
2	167	7/64	PC-r	1	1	2.40	6.00	12.00
3	166	10/67	PC-r	1	1	2.40	6.00	12.00

159. The Octopus

Ed	HRN	Date	Details	A	C	GD25	FN65	NM94
1	159	11/60	Orig.; Gray Morrow & Evans-a; L.B. Cole-c	1	1	4.70	14.00	28.00
2	167	2/64	PC-r	1	1	2.00	5.00	10.00
3	166	R/1967	C-price 25¢; PC-r	1	1	2.00	5.00	10.00

160. The Food of the Gods

Ed	HRN	Date	Details	A	C	GD25	FN65	NM94
1A	159	1/61	Original	1	1	4.70	14.00	28.00
1B	160	1/61	Original; same, except for HRN	1	1	4.70	14.00	28.00
2	167	1/64	PC-r	1	1	2.00	5.00	10.00
3	166	6/67	PC-r	1	1	2.00	5.00	10.00

161. Cleopatra

Ed	HRN	Date	Details	A	C	GD25	FN65	NM94
1	161	3/61	Original	1	1	5.85	17.50	35.00
2	167	1/64	PC-r	1	1	2.80	7.00	14.00
3	166	8/67	PC-r	1	1	2.80	7.00	14.00

162. Robur the Conqueror

Ed	HRN	Date	Details	A	C	GD25	FN65	NM94
1	162	5/61	Original	1	1	4.70	14.00	28.00
2	167	7/64	PC-r	1	1	2.00	5.00	10.00
3	166	8/67	PC-r	1	1	2.00	5.00	10.00

163. Master of the World

Ed	HRN	Date	Details	A	C	GD25	FN65	NM94
1	163	7/61	Original; Gray Morrow-a	1	1	4.70	14.00	28.00
2	167	1/65	PC-r	1	1	2.00	5.00	10.00
3	166	R/1968	C-price 25¢; PC-r	1	1	2.00	5.00	10.00

164. The Cossack Chief

Ed	HRN	Date	Details	A	C	GD25	FN65	NM94
1	164	(1961)	Orig.; nd(10/61?)	1	1	5.00	15.00	30.00
2	167	4/65	PC-r	1	1	2.00	5.00	10.00

Ed	HRN	Date	Details	A	C	GD25	FN65	NM94
3	166	Fall/68	C-price 25¢; PC-r	1	1	2.00	5.00	10.00

165. The Queen's Necklace

Ed	HRN	Date	Details	A	C	GD25	FN65	NM94
1	164	1/62	Original; Morrow-a	1	1	5.00	15.00	30.00
2	167	4/65	PC-r	1	1	2.00	5.00	10.00
3	166	Fall/68	C-price 25¢; PC-r	1	1	2.00	5.00	10.00

166. Tigers and Traitors

Ed	HRN	Date	Details	A	C	GD25	FN65	NM94
1	165	5/62	Original	1	1	7.50	22.50	45.00
2	167	2/64	PC-r	1	1	3.60	9.00	18.00
3	167	11/66	PC-r	1	1	3.60	9.00	18.00

167. Faust

Ed	HRN	Date	Details	A	C	GD25	FN65	NM94
1	165	8/62	Original	1	1	10.00	30.00	70.00
2	167	2/64	PC-r	1	1	5.35	16.00	32.00
3	166	6/67	PC-r	1	1	5.35	16.00	32.00

168. In Freedom's Cause

Ed	HRN	Date	Details	A	C	GD25	FN65	NM94
1	169	Win/69	Original; Evans/ Crandall-a; stiff-c; 25¢; no coming-next ad;	1	1	10.00	30.00	65.00

169. Negro AmericansThe Early Years

Ed	HRN	Date	Details	A	C	GD25	FN65	NM94
1	166	Spr/69	Orig. & last issue; 25¢; Stiff-c; no coming-next ad; other sources indicate publication date of 5/69	1	1	10.00	30.00	65.00
2	169	Spr/69	Stiff-c	1	1	6.35	19.00	38.00

NOTE: *Many other titles were prepared or planned but were only issued in British/European series.*

CLASSICS GIVEAWAYS (Arranged in chronological order)

12/41–Walter Theatre Enterprises (Huntington, WV) giveaway containing #2 (orig.) w/new generic-c (only 1 known copy) 85.00 257.00 600.00

1942–Double Comics containing CC#1 (orig.) (diff. cover) (not actually a giveaway) (very rare) (also see Double Comics) (only one known copy) 186.00 557.00 1300.00

12/42–Saks 34th St. Giveaway containing CC#7 (orig.) (diff. cover) (very rare; only 6 known copies) 571.00 1715.00 4000.00

2/43–American Comics containing CC#8 (orig.) (Liberty Theatre giveaway) (different cover) (only one known copy) (see American Comics) 121.00 365.00 850.00

12/44–Robin Hood Flour Co. Giveaway - #7-CC(R) (diff. cover) (rare) (edition probably 5 [22]) 229.00 685.00 1600.00

NOTE: *How are above editions determined without CC covers? 1942 is dated 1942. and CC#1-first reprint did not come out until 5/43. 12/42 and 2/43 are determined by blue note at bottom of first text page only in original edition. 12/44 is estimated from page width each reprint edition had progressively slightly smaller page width.*

1951–Shelter Thru the Ages (C.I. Educational Series) (actually Giveaway by the Ruberoid Co.) (16 pgs.) (contains original artwork by H. C. Kiefer) (there are back cover ad variations)(scarce) 64.00 193.00 450.00

1952–George Daynor Biography Giveaway (CC logo) (partly comic book/ pictures/newspaper articles) (story of man who built Palace Depression out of junkyard swamp in NJ) (64 pgs.)(very rare; only 2 known copies, one missing-bc) 785.00 2360.00 5500.00

1953–Westinghouse/Dreams of a Man (C.I. Educational Series) (Westinghouse bio./Westinghouse Co. giveaway) (contains original artwork by H. C. Kiefer) (16 pgs.) (also French/Spanish/Italian versions) (scarce) 72.00 215.00 500.00

NOTE: *Reproductions of 1951, 1952, and 1953 exist color photocopy covers and black & white photocopy interior ("W.C.N. Reprint")*

	GD25	FN65	NM94
	2.00	5.00	10.00

1951-53–Coward Shoe Giveaways (all editions very rare); 2 variations of back-c ad exist:

With back-c photo ad: 5 (87), 12 (89), 22 (85), 49 (85), 69 (87), 72 (no HRN), 80 (0), 91 (0), 92 (0), 96 (0), 98 (0), 100 (0), 101 (0), 103-105 (all Os) 32.00 95.00 225.00

With back-c cartoon ad: 106-109 (all 0s), 110 (111), 112 (0) 40.00 120.00 280.00

1956–Ben Franklin 5-10 Store Giveaway (#65-PC with back cover ad) (scarce) 27.00 81.00 190.00

1956–Ben Franklin Insurance Co. Giveaway (#65-PC with diff. back cover ad) (very rare) 64.00 193.00 450.00

11/56–Sealtest Co. Edition - #4 (135) (identical to regular edition except for Sealtest logo printed, not stamped, on front cover) (only two copies known to exist) 32.00 95.00 225.00

1958–Get-Well Giveaway containing #15-CI (new cartoon-type cover) (Pressman Pharmacy) (only one copy known to exist) 32.00 95.00 225.00

1967-68–Twin Circle Giveaway Editions - all HRN 166, with back cover ad for National Catholic Press.

	GD25	FN65	NM94
2(R68), 4(R67), 10(R68), 13(R68)	4.00	11.00	22.00
48(R67), 128(R68), 535(576-R68)	4.70	14.00	28.00
16(R68), 68(R67)	6.35	19.00	38.00

12/69–Christmas Giveaway ("A Christmas Adventure") (reprints Picture Parade #4-1953, new cover) (4 ad variations)

	GD25	FN65	NM94
Stacy's Dept. Store	3.60	9.00	18.00
Anne & Hope Store	6.70	20.00	40.00
Gibson's Dept. Store (rare)	6.70	20.00	40.00
"Merry Christmas" & blank ad space	3.60	9.00	18.00

CLASSICS ILLUSTRATED GIANTS
October, 1949 (One-Shots - "OS")
Gilberton Publications

These Giant Editions, all with new Kiefer front and back covers, were advertised from 10/49 to 2/52. They were 50 cents on the newsstand and 60 cents by mail. They are actually four-classics in one volume. All the stories are reprints of the Classics Illustrated Series. NOTE: *There were also British hardback Adventure & Indian Giants in 1952, with the same covers but different contents: Adventure - 2, 7, 10; Indian - 17, 22, 37, 58. They are also rare.*

"An Illustrated Library of Great Adventure Stories" - reprints of No. 6,7,8,10 (Rare); Kiefer-c 100.00 300.00 700.00

"An Illustrated Library of Exciting Mystery Stories" - reprints of No. 30,21,40, 13 (Rare) 107.00 320.00 750.00

"An Illustrated Library of Great Indian Stories" - reprints of No. 4,17,22,37 (Rare) 93.00 280.00 650.00

INTRODUCTION TO CLASSICS ILLUSTRATED JUNIOR

Collectors of Juniors can be put into one of two categories those who want any copy of each title, and those who want all the originals. Those seeking every original and reprint edition are a limited group, primarily because Juniors have no changes in art or covers to spark interest, and because reprints are so low in value it is difficult to get dealers to look for specific reprint editions. Anyone interested in information about the full scope of Junior editions should write to **Jim McLoughlin, 28 Mercury Ave., East Patchogue, NY 11772**. He has been doing research in this area for several years.

In recent years it has become apparent that most serious Classics collectors seek Junior originals. Those seeking reprints seek them for low cost. This has made the previous note about the comparative market value of reprints inadequate. Most dealers report difficulty in moving reprints for more than $2-$4 for mint copies. Some may be worth $5-$7, just because of the popularity of the title, such as Snow White, Sleeping Beauty, and Wizard of Oz. Others may be worth $5-$7, because of the scarcity of particular title nos., such as 514, 560, 562, 575 & 576. Three particular reprint editions are worth even more. For the 535-Twin Circle edition, see Giveaways. There are also reprint editions of 501 and 503 which have a full-page bc ad for the very rare Junior record. Those may sell as high as $10-$15 in mint. Original editions of 557 and 558 also have that ad.

Classics Illustrated #169 (Orig.), © GIL

Classics Giveaways, 1952 George Daynor, © GIL

Classics Illustrated Giants (Exciting...), © GIL

Classics Illustrated Junior #518 (Orig.), © GIL

Classics Illustrated Special Issue #132A, © GIL

Classics Illustrated Special Issue #167A, © GIL

GD25 FN65 NM94

There are no reprint editions of 577. The only edition, from 1969, is a 25 cent stiff-cover edition with no ad for the next issue. All other original editions have coming-next ad. But 577, like C.I. #168, was prepared in 1962 but not issued. Copies of 577 can be found in 1963 British/European series, which then continued with dozens of additional new Junior titles.

PRICES LISTED BELOW ARE FOR ORIGINAL EDITIONS, WHICH HAVE AN AD FOR THE NEXT ISSUE.

CLASSICS ILLUSTRATED JUNIOR
Oct, 1953 - Spring, 1971
Famous Authors Ltd. (Gilberton Publications)

501-Snow White & the Seven Dwarfs; Alex Blum-a 9.35 28.00 56.00
502-The Ugly Duckling 5.85 17.50 35.00
503-Cinderella 4.00 10.50 21.00
504-512: 504-The Pied Piper. 505-The Sleeping Beauty. 506-The Three Little Pigs. 507-Jack & the Beanstalk. 508-Goldilocks & the Three Bears. 509-Beauty and the Beast. 510-Little Red Riding Hood. 511-Puss-N Boots. 512-Rumpel Stiltskin 2.80 7.00 14.00
513-Pinocchio 4.00 10.50 21.00
514-The Steadfast Tin Soldier 4.70 14.00 28.00
515-Johnny Appleseed 2.80 7.00 14.00
516-Aladdin and His Lamp 4.00 10.50 21.00
517-519: 517-The Emperor's New Clothes. 518-The Golden Goose. 519-Paul Bunyan 2.80 7.00 14.00
520-Thumbelina 4.00 10.50 21.00
521-King of the Golden River 2.80 7.00 14.00
522-530: 522-The Nightingale. 523-The Gallant Tailor. 524-The Wild Swans. 525-The Little Mermaid. 526-The Frog Prince. 527-The Golden-Haired Giant. 528-The Penny Prince. 529-The Magic Servants. 530-The Golden Bird 2.00 5.00 10.00
531-Rapunzel 2.80 7.00 14.00
532-534: 532-The Dancing Princesses. 533-The Magic Fountain. 534-The Golden Touch 2.00 5.00 10.00
535-The Wizard of Oz 4.70 14.00 28.00
536-538: 536-The Chimney Sweep. 537-The Three Fairies. 538-Silly Hans 2.00 5.00 10.00
539-The Enchanted Fish 4.00 10.50 21.00
540-The Tinder-Box 4.00 10.50 21.00
541-Snow White & Rose Red 2.80 7.00 14.00
542-The Donkey's Tale 2.80 7.00 14.00
543-The House in the Woods 2.00 5.00 10.00
544-The Golden Fleece 4.70 14.00 28.00
545-The Glass Mountain 2.80 7.00 14.00
546-The Elves & the Shoemaker 2.80 7.00 14.00
547-551: 547-The Wishing Table. 548-The Magic Pitcher. 549-Simple Kate. 550-The Singing Donkey. 551-The Queen Bee 2.00 5.00 10.00
552-The Three Little Dwarfs 2.80 7.00 14.00
553-556: 553-King Thrushbeard. 554-The Enchanted Deer. 555-The Three Golden Apples. 556-The Elf Mound 2.00 5.00 10.00
557-Silly Willy 4.00 10.50 21.00
558-The Magic Dish; L.B. Cole-c; soft and stiff-c exist on original 4.00 10.50 21.00
559-The Japanese Lantern; 1 pg. Ingels-a; L.B. Cole-c 4.00 10.50 21.00
560-The Doll Princess; L.B. Cole-c 4.00 10.50 21.00
561-Hans Humdrum; L.B. Cole-c 2.00 5.00 10.00
562-The Enchanted Pony; L.B. Cole-c 4.00 10.50 21.00
563-570: 563-The Wishing Well; L.B. Cole-c. 564-The Salt Mountain; L.B.Cole-c. 565-The Silly Princess; L.B. Cole-c. 566-Clumsy Hans; L.B. Cole-c. 567-The Bearskin Soldier; L.B. Cole-c. 568-The Happy Hedgehog; L.B. Cole-c. 569-The Three Giants. 570-The Pearl Princess 2.00 5.00 10.00
571-574: 571-How Fire Came to the Indians. 572-The Drummer Boy. 573-The Crystal Ball. 574-Brightboots 2.40 6.00 12.00
575-The Fearless Prince 2.80 7.00 14.00
576-The Princess Who Saw Everything 4.00 10.50 21.00
577-The Runaway Dumpling 4.70 14.00 28.00

NOTE: *Prices are for original editions. Last reprint - Spring, 1971.* ***Costanza & Shaffenberger*** *art in many issues.*

CLASSICS ILLUSTRATED SPECIAL ISSUE
Dec, 1955 - July, 1962 (100 pages) (35 cents)
Gilberton Co. (Came out semi-annually)

129-The Story of Jesus (titled ...Special Edition) "Jesus on Mountain" cover 5.00 15.00 30.00
"Three Camels" cover (12/58) 7.50 22.50 45.00
"Mountain" cover (no date)-Has checklist on inside b/c to HRN #161 & different testimonial on back-c 4.00 11.00 22.00
"Mountain" cover (1968 re-issue; has white 50 cent circle) 3.60 9.00 18.00
132A-The Story of America (6/56) 4.35 13.00 26.00
135A-The Ten Commandments(12/56) 5.35 16.00 32.00
138A-Adventures in Science(6/57); HRN to 137 4.35 13.00 26.00
138A-(6/57)-2nd version w/HRN to 149 4.00 11.00 22.00
138A-(12/61)-3rd version w/HRN to 149 4.00 10.00 20.00
141A-The Rough Rider (Teddy Roosevelt)(12/57); Evans-a 4.35 13.00 26.00
144A-Blazing the Trails West(6/58)- 73 pages of Crandall/Evans plus Severin-a 4.35 13.00 26.00
147A-Crossing the Rockies(12/58)-Crandall/Evans-a 5.35 16.00 32.00
150A-Royal Canadian Police(6/59)-Ingels, Sid Check-a 5.35 16.00 32.00
153A-Men, Guns & Cattle(12/59)-Evans-a, 26 pgs.; Kinstler-a 5.35 16.00 32.00
156A-The Atomic Age(6/60)-Crandall/Evans, Torres-a 4.35 13.00 26.00
159A-Rockets, Jets and Missiles(12/60)-Evans, Morrow-a 4.35 13.00 26.00
162A-War Between the States(6/61)-Kirby & Crandall/Evans-a; Ingels-a 10.00 30.00 60.00
165A-To the Stars(12/61)-Torres, Crandall/Evans, Kirby-a 4.35 13.00 26.00
166A-World War II('62)-Torres, Crandall/Evans, Kirby-a 5.85 17.50 35.00
167A-Prehistoric World(7/62)-Torres & Crandall/Evans-a; two versions exist (HRN to 165 & HRN to 167) 5.85 17.50 35.00
nn Special Issue-The United Nations (1964; 50 cents; scarce); This is actually part of the European Special Series, which continued on after the U.S. series stopped issuing new titles in 1962. This English edition was prepared specifically for sale at the U.N. It was printed in Norway 29.00 85.00 200.00

NOTE: *There was another U.S. Special Issue prepared in 1962 with artwork by* ***Torres*** *entitled World War I. Unfortunately, it was never issued in any English-language edition. It was issued in 1964 in West Germany, The Netherlands, and some Scandanavian countries, with another edition in 1974 with a new cover.*

CLASSIC PUNISHER (Also see Punisher)
Dec, 1989 ($4.95, B&W, deluxe format, 68 pgs.)
Marvel Comics

1-Reprints Marvel Super Action #1 & Marvel Preview #2 plus new story 1.10 2.75 5.50

CLASSICS ILLUSTRATED
Feb, 1990 - No. 27, July?, 1991 ($3.75-$3.95, color, 52 pgs.)
First Publishing/Berkley Publishing

1-17: 1-Gahan Wilson-c/a. 4-Sienkiewicz painted-c/a. 6-Russell scripts/ layouts. 7-Spiegle-a. 9-Ploog-c/a. 16-Staton-a .75 1.90 3.75
18-27: 18-Gahan Wilson-c/a; begin $3.95-c. 20-Geary-a. 26-Aesop's Fables

(6/91). 26,27-Direct sale only .80 2.00 4.00

CLASSICS LIBRARY (See King Classics)

CLASSIC STAR WARS (Also see Star Wars)
Aug, 1992 - Present ($2.50, color)
Dark Horse Comics

1-6-Star Wars strip-r by Williamson w/new Williamson-c; Williamson redrew portions of the panels to fit comic book format .50 1.25 2.50

CLASSIC X-MEN (Becomes X-Men Classic #46 on)
Sept, 1986 - No. 45, Mar, 1990 (#27 on: $1.25)
Marvel Comics Group

	GD25	FN65	NM94
1-Begins-r of New X-Men	1.40	3.50	7.00
2-4	1.00	2.50	5.00
5-9	.80	2.00	4.00
10-Sabretooth app.	1.00	2.50	5.00
11-15	.60	1.50	3.00
16,18-20	.50	1.25	2.50
17-Wolverine-c	1.00	2.50	5.00
21-25,27-30: 27-r/X-Men #121	.40	1.00	2.00
26-r/X-Men #120; Wolverine-c/app.	1.00	2.50	5.00
31-38,40-42,44,45: 35-r/X-Men #129	.35	.90	1.75
39-New Jim Lee back-up story (2nd-a on X-Men)	1.20	3.00	6.00
43-Byrne-c/a(r); $1.75, double-size	.50	1.25	2.50

NOTE: ***Art Adams*** *c(p)-1-10, 12-16, 18, 19, 25.* ***Austin*** *c-19i.* ***Bolton*** *back up stories in 1-28 at least.* ***Williamson*** *c-12-14i.*

CLAW THE UNCONQUERED (See Cancelled Comic Cavalcade)
5-6/75 - No. 9, 9-10/76; No. 10, 4-5/78 - No. 12, 8-9/78
National Periodical Publications/DC Comics

	GD25	FN65	NM94
1	.40	1.00	2.00
2,3: 3-Nudity panel	.30	.75	1.50
4-12: 9-Origin		.60	1.20

NOTE: ***Giffen*** *a-8-12p.* ***Kubert*** *c-10-12.* ***Layton*** *a-9i, 12i.*

CLAY CODY, GUNSLINGER
Fall, 1957
Pines Comics

1-Painted-c 3.60 9.00 18.00

CLEAN FUN, STARRING "SHOOGAFOOTS JONES"
1944 (24 pgs.; B&W; oversized covers) (10 cents)
Specialty Book Co.

nn-Humorous situations involving Negroes in the Deep South

	GD25	FN65	NM94
White cover issue....	3.20	8.00	16.00
Dark grey cover issue....	3.60	9.00	18.00

CLEMENTINA THE FLYING PIG (See Dell Jr. Treasury)

CLEOPATRA (See Ideal, a Classical Comic No. 1)

CLIFF MERRITT SETS THE RECORD STRAIGHT
Giveaway (2 different issues)
Brotherhood of Railroad Trainsmen

	GD25	FN65	NM94
...and the Very Candid Candidate by Al Williamson	.60	1.50	3.00
...Sets the Record Straight by Al Williamson (2 different-c: one by Williamson, the other by McWilliams)	.60	1.50	3.00

CLIFFORD MCBRIDE'S IMMORTAL NAPOLEON & UNCLE ELBY
1932 (12x17"; softcover cartoon book)
The Castle Press

nn-Intro. by Don Herod 10.00 30.00 65.00

CLIMAX!
July, 1955 - No. 2, Sept, 1955
Gillmor Magazines

1,2 (Mystery) 7.50 22.50 45.00

CLINT (Elcipse)(Value: cover or less)

CLINT & MAC (See 4-Color No. 889)

CLIVE BARKER'S BOOK OF THE DAMNED: A HELLRAISER COMPANION
Oct, 1991 - Present ($4.95, color, bi-annual, 52 pgs.)
Epic Comics (Marvel)

Volume One,Two: 1-Simon Bisley-c. 2-(4/92) 1.00 2.50 5.00

CLIVE BARKER'S HELLRAISER (Also see Epic, Hellraiser Nightbreed – Jihad, Revelations, Son of Celluloid, Tapping the Vein & Weaveworld)
1989 - Present ($4.95, color, mature readers, quarterly, 68 pgs.)
Epic Comics (Marvel)

	GD25	FN65	NM94
Book 1-Based on Hellraiser & Hellbound movies; Bolton-c/a; Spiegle & Wrightson-a (graphic album)	1.40	3.50	7.00
Book 2-4,14-20 ($4.95): 20-By Gaiman McKean	1.00	2.50	5.00
Book 5-9 ($5.95): 7-Bolton-a. 8-Morrow-a	1.20	3.00	6.00
Book 10,11 ($4.50, 52 pgs.): 11-Guice-p.	.90	2.25	4.50
Book 12-Sam Kieth-a	1.00	2.50	5.00
Book 13-16 ($4.95)	1.00	2.50	5.00
...Summer Special 1 (1992, $5.95, 68 pgs.)	1.20	3.00	6.00

CLIVE BARKER'S NIGHTBREED (Also see Epic)
Apr, 1990 - Present ($1.95/$2.25/$2.50, color, adults)
Epic Comics (Marvel)

	GD25	FN65	NM94
1: 1-4-Adapt horror movie	.70	1.75	3.50
2-6: 5-New stories & $2.25-c begin; Guice-a(p)	.50	1.25	2.50
7-19	.45	1.15	2.25
20-28: 20-Begin $2.50-c	.50	1.25	2.50

CLOAK AND DAGGER
Fall, 1952
Ziff-Davis Publishing Co.

1-Saunders painted-c 13.00 40.00 90.00

CLOAK AND DAGGER (Also see Marvel Fanfare)
Oct, 1983 - No. 4, Jan, 1984 (Mini-series)(See Spectacular Spider-Man #64)
Marvel Comics Group

1-4-Austin-c/a(i) in all. 4-Origin .30 .75 1.50

CLOAK AND DAGGER (Also see Marvel Graphic Novel #34, Mutant Misadventures Of... & Strange Tales, 2nd series)
July, 1985 - No. 11, Jan, 1987
Marvel Comics Group

	GD25	FN65	NM94
1	.30	.75	1.50
2-8,10,11		.50	1.00
9-Art Adams-p	.40	1.00	2.00
...And Power Pack (1990, $7.95, 68 pgs.)	1.60	4.00	8.00

CLONEZONE SPECIAL
1989 ($2.00, B&W)
Dark Horse Comics/First Comics

1-Back-up series from Badger & Nexus .40 1.00 2.00

CLOSE ENCOUNTERS (See Marvel Comics Super Special & Marvel Special Edition)

CLOSE SHAVES OF PAULINE PERIL, THE (TV?)
June, 1970 - No. 4, March, 1971 (Jay Ward?)
Gold Key

	GD25	FN65	NM94
1	1.60	4.00	8.00
2-4	1.00	2.50	5.00

CLOWN COMICS (No. 1 titled Clown Comic Book)
1945 - No. 3, Wint, 1946
Clown Comics/Home Comics/Harvey Publ.

	GD25	FN65	NM94
nn (#1)	5.35	16.00	32.00
2,3	4.00	10.00	20.00

CLUBHOUSE RASCALS (#1 titled ...Presents?)
June, 1956 - No. 2, Oct, 1956 (Also see Three Rascals)
Sussex Publ. Co. (Magazine Enterprises)

1,2: The Brain app. 3.60 9.00 18.00

Classic X-Men #41, © MEG

The Claw #1, © DC

Clubhouse Rascals #1, © ME

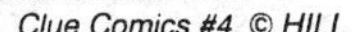

Clue Comics #4, © HILL

The Clutching Hand #1, © ACG

C-M-O Comics nn, © Chicago Mail Order

	GD25	FN65	NM94
CLUB "16" June, 1948 - No. 4, Dec, 1948 Famous Funnies			
1-Teen-age humor	7.00	21.00	42.00
2-4	4.00	11.00	22.00
CLUE COMICS (Real Clue Crime V2#4 on) Jan, 1943 - No. 15(V2#3), May, 1947 Hillman Periodicals			
1-Origin The Boy King, Nightmare, Micro-Face, Twilight, & Zippo	63.00	185.00	375.00
2	31.00	92.00	185.00
3-5	22.00	65.00	130.00
6,8,9: 8-Palais-c/a(2)	14.00	42.00	85.00
7-Classic torture-c	20.00	60.00	120.00
10-Origin/1st app. The Gun Master & begin series; content changes to crime	15.00	45.00	90.00
11	10.00	30.00	60.00
12-Origin Rackman; McWilliams-a, Guardineer-a(2)	13.00	40.00	80.00
V2#1-Nightmare new origin; Iron Lady app.; Simon & Kirby-a	20.00	60.00	120.00
V2#2-S&K-a(2)-Bondage/torture-c; man attacks & kills people with electric iron. Infantino-a	20.00	60.00	120.00
V2#3-S&K-a(3)	20.00	60.00	120.00
CLUTCHING HAND, THE July-Aug, 1954 American Comics Group			
1	14.00	43.00	100.00
CLYDE BEATTY COMICS (Also see Crackajack Funnies) October, 1953 (84 pages) Commodore Productions & Artists, Inc.			
1-Photo front/back-c; includes movie scenes and comics	17.00	52.00	120.00
...African Jungle Book('56)-Richfield Oil Co. 16 pg. giveaway, soft-c	7.00	21.00	42.00
CLYDE CRASHCUP (TV) Aug-Oct, 1963 - No. 5, Sept-Nov, 1964 Dell Publishing Co.			
1-All written by John Stanley	10.00	30.00	60.00
2-5	6.70	20.00	40.00
C-M-O COMICS 1942 - No. 2, 1942 (68 pages, full color) Chicago Mail Order Co.(Centaur)			
1-Invisible Terror, Super Ann, & Plymo the Rubber Man app. (all Centaur costume heroes)	58.00	175.00	350.00
2-Invisible Terror, Super Ann app.	39.00	116.00	235.00
COBALT BLUE (Innovation)(Value: cover or less)			
COCOMALT BIG BOOK OF COMICS 1938 (Regular size; full color; 52 pgs.) Harry 'A' Chesler (Cocomalt Premium)			
1-(Scarce)-Biro-c/a; Little Nemo by Winsor McCay Jr., Dan Hastings; Jack Cole, Guardineer, Gustavson, Bob Wood-a	117.00	350.00	700.00
CODE NAME: ASSASSIN (See 1st Issue Special)			
CODENAME: DANGER (Lodestone)(Value: cover or less)			
CODENAME SPITFIRE (Formerly Spitfire And The Troubleshooters) No. 10, July, 1987 - No. 13, Oct, 1987 Marvel Comics Group			
10-13: 10-Rogers-c/a		.50	1.00

	GD25	FN65	NM94
CODE NAME: TOMAHAWK Sept, 1986 ($1.75, color, high quality paper) Fantasy General Comics			
1-Sci/fi	.35	.90	1.75
CODY OF THE PONY EXPRESS (See Colossal Features Magazine) Sept, 1950 - No. 3, Jan, 1951 (See Women Outlaws) Fox Features Syndicate			
1-3 (Actually #3-5). 1-Painted-c	7.50	22.50	45.00
CODY OF THE PONY EXPRESS (Buffalo Bill...) (Outlaws of the West #11 on; Formerly Bullseye) No. 8, Oct, 1955; No. 9, Jan, 1956; No. 10, June, 1956 Charlton Comics			
8-Bullseye on splash pg; not S&K-a	4.35	13.00	26.00
9,10: 10-Buffalo Bill app.	3.60	9.00	18.00
CODY STARBUCK (1st app. in Star Reach #1) July, 1978 (Color, 2nd printing exists) Star Reach Productions			
nn-Howard Chaykin-c/a	.40	1.00	2.00
CO-ED ROMANCES November, 1951 P. L. Publishing Co.			
1	4.00	11.00	22.00
COLLECTORS ITEM CLASSICS (See Marvel Collectors Item Classics)			
COLOSSAL FEATURES MAGAZINE (Formerly I Loved) (See Cody of the Pony Express) No. 33, May, 1950 - No. 34, July, 1950; No. 3, Sept, 1950 Fox Features Syndicate			
33,34-Cody of the Pony Express begins (based on Columbia serial). 33-Painted-c; 34-Photo-c	6.70	20.00	40.00
3-Authentic criminal cases	6.70	20.00	40.00
COLOSSAL SHOW, THE (TV) October, 1969 Gold Key			
1	4.00	11.00	22.00
COLOSSUS COMICS (See Green Giant & Motion Picture Funnies Weekly) March, 1940 Sun Publications (Funnies, Inc.?)			
1-(Scarce)-Tulpa of Tsang(hero); Colossus app.	145.00	436.00	875.00
NOTE: *Cover by artist that drew Colossus in Green Giant Comics.*			
COLOUR OF MAGIC, THE (Terry Pratchett's...) 1991 - No. 4, 1991 ($2.50, color, mini-series) Innovation Publishing			
1-4: Adapts 1st novel of the Discworld series	.50	1.25	2.50
COLT .45 (TV) No. 924, 8/58 - No. 1058, 11-1/59-60; No. 4, 2-4/60 - No. 9, 5-7/61 Dell Publishing Co.			
4-Color 924(#1)-Wayde Preston photo-c on all	9.15	27.50	55.00
4-Color 1004,1058; #4,5,7-9	6.70	20.00	40.00
6-Toth-a	7.50	22.50	45.00
COLUMBIA COMICS 1943 William H. Wise Co.			
1-Joe Palooka, Charlie Chan, Capt. Yank, Sparky Watts, Dixie Dugan app.	17.00	52.00	120.00
COLUMBUS Sept, 1992 ($2.50, B&W, one-shot) Dark Horse Comics			

	GD25	FN65	NM94
1-Yeates painted-c	.50	1.25	2.50

COMANCHE (See 4-Color No. 1350)

COMANCHEROS, THE (See 4-Color No. 1300)

COMBAT
June, 1952 - No. 11, April, 1953
Atlas Comics (ANC)

	GD25	FN65	NM94
1	9.15	27.50	55.00
2-Heath-c/a	4.35	13.00	26.00
3,5-9,11: 9-Robert Q. Sale-a	3.60	9.00	18.00
4-Krigstein-a	4.20	12.50	25.00
10-B&W and color illos. in **POP**	4.00	11.00	22.00

NOTE: *Combat Casey in 7-11.* ***Heath*** *c-1, 2, 9.* ***Maneely*** *a-1; c-3.* ***Pakula*** *a-1.* ***Reinman*** *a-1.*

COMBAT
Oct-Nov, 1961 - No. 40, Oct, 1973 (No #9)
Dell Publishing Co.

	GD25	FN65	NM94
1	4.20	12.50	25.00
2-5: 4-John F. Kennedy c/story (P.T. 109)	2.40	6.00	12.00
6,7,8(4-6/63), 8(7-9/63)	1.80	4.50	9.00
10-27	1.60	4.00	8.00
28-40(reprints #1-14). 30-r/#4	1.20	3.00	6.00

NOTE: ***Glanzman*** *c/a-1-27, 28-40r.*

COMBAT CASEY (Formerly War Combat)
No. 6, Jan, 1953 - No. 34, July, 1957
Atlas Comics (SAI)

	GD25	FN65	NM94
6 (Indicia shows 1/52 in error)	6.35	19.00	38.00
7-Spanking panel	4.70	14.00	28.00
8-Used in **POP**, pg. 94	3.60	9.00	18.00
9	3.20	8.00	16.00
10,13-19-Violent art by R. Q. Sale; Battle Brady x-over #10	4.20	12.50	25.00
11,12,20-Last Precode (2/55)	3.00	7.50	15.00
21-34	2.40	6.00	12.00

NOTE: ***Everett*** *a-6.* ***Heath*** *c-10, 17, 19, 30.* ***Maneely*** *c-6, 8.* ***Powell*** *a-29(5), 30(5), 34.* ***Severin*** *c-26, 33.*

COMBAT KELLY
Nov, 1951 - No. 44, Aug, 1957
Atlas Comics (SPI)

	GD25	FN65	NM94
1-Heath-a	11.00	32.00	75.00
2	5.35	16.00	32.00
3-10	4.00	10.50	21.00
11-Used in **POP**, pages 94,95 plus color illo.	3.60	9.00	18.00
12-Color illo. in **POP**	3.60	9.00	18.00
13-16	2.40	6.00	12.00
17-Violent art by R. Q. Sale; Combat Casey app.	4.70	14.00	28.00
18-20,22-44: 18-Battle Brady app. 28-Last precode (1/55). 38-Green Berets story (8/56)	2.40	6.00	12.00
21-Transvestism-c	4.00	10.00	20.00

NOTE: ***Berg*** *a-8, 12-14, 16, 17, 19-23, 25, 26, 28, 31-36, 42-44; c-2.* ***Colan*** *a-42.* ***Heath*** *a-4; c-31.* ***Lawrence*** *a-23.* ***Maneely*** *a-4(2), 6, 7(3), 8; c-4, 5, 7, 8, 10, 25.* ***R.Q. Sale*** *a-17, 25.* ***Severin*** *c-41, 42.* ***Whitney*** *a-5.*

COMBAT KELLY (...and the Deadly Dozen)
June, 1972 - No. 9, Oct, 1973
Marvel Comics Group

	GD25	FN65	NM94
1-Intro & origin Combat Kelly; Ayers/Mooney-a; Severin-c (20 cent-c)	.60	1.50	3.00
2-9	.30	.75	1.50

COMBINED OPERATIONS (See The Story of the Commandos)

COMEDY CARNIVAL
no date (1950's) (100 pages)
St. John Publishing Co.

	GD25	FN65	NM94
nn-Contains rebound St. John comics	22.00	65.00	150.00

COMEDY COMICS (1st Series) (Formerly Daring Mystery No. 1-8)
(Becomes Margie Comics No. 35 on)
No. 9, April, 1942 - No. 34, Fall, 1946
Timely Comics (TCI 9,10)

	GD25	FN65	NM94
9-(Scarce)-The Fin by Everett, Capt. Dash, Citizen V, & The Silver Scorn app.; Wolverton-a; 1st app. Comedy Kid; satire on Hitler & Stalin	133.00	400.00	800.00
10-(Scarce)-Origin The Fourth Musketeer, Victory Boys; Monstro, the Mighty app.	92.00	275.00	550.00
11-Vagabond, Stuporman app.	27.00	80.00	190.00
12,13	9.15	27.50	55.00
14-Origin & 1st app. Super Rabbit	30.00	90.00	210.00
15-20	7.50	22.50	45.00
21-32	5.35	16.00	32.00
33-Kurtzman-a (5 pgs.)	7.50	22.50	45.00
34-Intro Margie; Wolverton-a (5 pgs.)	10.00	30.00	65.00

COMEDY COMICS (2nd Series)
May, 1948 - No. 10, Jan, 1950
Marvel Comics (ACI)

	GD25	FN65	NM94
1-Hedy, Tessie, Millie begin; Kurtzman's "Hey Look" (he draws himself)	19.00	57.00	130.00
2	7.50	22.50	45.00
3,4-Kurtzman's "Hey Look"(?&3)	10.00	30.00	60.00
5-10	4.00	12.00	24.00

COMET, THE (See The Mighty Crusaders & Pep Comics #1)
Oct, 1983 - No. 2, Dec, 1983
Red Circle Comics (Archie)

	GD25	FN65	NM94
1,2: 1-Re-intro & origin The Comet; The American Shield begins. 2-Origin continues		.50	1.00

COMET, THE
July, 1991 - No. 18, Dec, 1992 ($1.00/$1.25, color)
Impact Comics (DC)

	GD25	FN65	NM94
1-13: 4-Black Hood app. 6-Re-intro Hangman. 8-Web x-over. 10-Contains Crusaders trading card. 13-Last $1.00-c		.50	1.00
14-18: 14-Origin. Netzer(Nasser) c(p)-11,14-17		.60	1.25
Annual 1 (1992, $2.50, 68 pgs.)-Contains Impact trading card; Shield back-up story	.40	1.25	2.50

COMET MAN, THE
Feb, 1987 - No. 6, July, 1987 (Mini-series)
Marvel Comics Group

	GD25	FN65	NM94
1-6		.50	1.00

COMIC ALBUM (Also see Disney Comic Album)
Mar-May, 1958 - No. 18, June-Aug, 1962
Dell Publishing Co.

	GD25	FN65	NM94
1-Donald Duck	4.70	14.00	28.00
2-Bugs Bunny	3.20	8.00	16.00
3-Donald Duck	4.00	12.00	24.00
4-6,8-10: 4-Tom & Jerry. 5-Woody Woodpecker. 6,10-Bugs Bunny. 8-Tom & Jerry. 9-Woody Woodpecker	2.80	7.00	14.00
7,11: 7-Popeye (9-11/59). 11-Popeye (9-11/60)	4.00	10.00	20.00
12-14: 12-Tom & Jerry. 13-Woody Woodpecker. 14-Bugs Bunny	2.40	6.00	12.00
15-Popeye	4.00	10.00	20.00
16-Flintstones (12-2/61-62)-3rd app.	5.35	16.00	32.00
17-Space Mouse (3rd app.)	3.60	9.00	18.00
18-Three Stooges; photo-c	7.00	21.00	42.00

COMIC BOOK (Also see Comics From Weatherbird)
1954 (Giveaway)
American Juniors Shoe

Contains a comic rebound with new cover. Several combinations possible. Contents determines price.

COMIC BOOK MAGAZINE

Combat Casey #11, © MEG

Combat Kelly #22, © MEG

Comedy Comics #1 (5/48), © MEG

Comic Cavalcade #52, © DC

Comic Pages V3/#6, © CEN

The Comics #1, © DELL

	GD25	FN65	NM94

1940 - 1943 (Similar to Spirit Sections)
(7-3/4x10-3/4"; full color; 16-24 pages each)
Chicago Tribune & other newspapers

	GD25	FN65	NM94
1940 issues	5.85	17.50	35.00
1941, 1942 issues	4.70	14.00	28.00
1943 issues	4.00	12.00	24.00

NOTE: *Published weekly. Texas Slim, Kit Carson, Spooky, Josie, Nuts & Jolts, Lew Loyal, Brenda Starr, Daniel Boone, Captain Storm, Rocky, Smokey Stover, Tiny Tim, Little Joe, Fu Manchu appear among others. Early issues had photo stories with pictures from the movies; later issues had comic art.*

COMIC BOOKS (Series 1)
1950 (16 pgs.; 5-1/4x8-1/2"; full color; bound at top; paper cover)
Metropolitan Printing Co. (Giveaway)

	GD25	FN65	NM94
1-Boots and Saddles; intro. The Masked Marshal	4.70	14.00	28.00
1-The Green Jet; Green Lama by Raboy	25.00	75.00	175.00
1-My Pal Dizzy (Teen-age)	2.40	6.00	12.00
1-New World; origin Atomaster (costumed hero)	8.35	25.00	50.00
1-Talullah (Teen-age)	2.40	6.00	12.00

COMIC CAPERS
Fall, 1944 - No. 6, Summer, 1946
Red Circle Mag./Marvel Comics

	GD25	FN65	NM94
1-Super Rabbit, The Creeper, Silly Seal, Ziggy Pig, Sharpy Fox begin	13.00	40.00	90.00
2	7.00	21.00	42.00
3-6	5.35	16.00	32.00

COMIC CAVALCADE
Winter, 1942-43 - No. 63, June-July, 1954
(Contents change with No. 30, Dec-Jan, 1948-49 on)
All-American/National Periodical Publications

	GD25	FN65	VF82	NM94
1-The Flash, Green Lantern, Wonder Woman, Wildcat, The Black Pirate by Moldoff (also #2), Ghost Patrol, and Red White & Blue begin; Scribbly app., Minute Movie	440.00	1310.00	2400.00	3500.00

(Estimated up to 175 total copies exist, 6 in NM/Mint)

	GD25	FN65	NM94
2-Mutt & Jeff begin; last Ghost Patrol & Black Pirate; Minute Movies	147.00	440.00	880.00
3-Hop Harrigan & Sargon, the Sorcerer begin; The King app.	108.00	325.00	650.00
4,5: 4-The Gay Ghost, The King, Scribbly, & Red Tornado app. 5-Christmas-c	94.00	282.00	565.00
6-10: 7-Red Tornado & Black Pirate app.; last Scribbly. 9-Fat & Slat app.; X-mas-c	75.00	225.00	450.00
11,12,14-20: 12-Last Red White & Blue. 15-Johnny Peril begins, ends #29. 19-Christmas-c	64.00	192.00	385.00
13-Solomon Grundy app.; X-mas-c	108.00	325.00	650.00
21-23: 23-Harry Lampert-c (Toth swipes)	64.00	192.00	385.00
24-Solomon Grundy x-over in Green Lantern	75.00	225.00	450.00
25-28: 25-Black Canary app.; X-mas-c. 26-28-Johnny Peril app. 28-Last Mutt & Jeff	48.00	145.00	290.00
29-(10-11/48)-Last Flash, Wonder Woman, Green Lantern & Johnny Peril; Wonder Woman invents "Thinking Machine;" 1st computer in comics?; Leave it to Binky story (early app.)	54.00	162.00	325.00
30-(12-1/48-49)-The Fox & the Crow, Dodo & the Frog & Nutsy Squirrel begin	33.00	100.00	200.00
31-35	15.00	45.00	900.00
36-49	10.00	30.00	65.00
50-62(Scarce)	14.00	42.00	85.00
63(Rare)	22.00	68.00	135.00
Giveaway (1944, 8 pgs., paper-c, in color)-One Hundred Years of Co-operation-r/Comic Cavalcade #9	54.00	162.00	325.00
Giveaway (1945, 16 pages, paper-c, in color)-Movie "Tomorrow The World" (Nazi theme); r/Comic Cavalcade #10	79.00	238.00	475.00
Giveaway (c. 1944-45; 8 pgs, paper-c, in color)-The Twain Shall Meet-r/ Comic Cavalcade #8	71.00	212.00	425.00

NOTE: ***Grossman** a-30-63. **E.E. Hibbard** c-(Flash only)-1-4, 7-14, 16-19, 21. **Sheldon Mayer** a(2-3)-40-63. **Moulson** c(G.L.)-7, 15. **Nodell** c(G.L.)-9. **H.G. Peter** c(W. Woman only)-1, 3-21, 24. **Post** a-31, 36. **Purcell** c(G.L.)-2-5, 10. **Reinman** a(Green Lantern)-4-6, 8, 9, 13, 15-21; c(Gr. Lantern)-6, 8, 19. **Toth** a(Green Lantern)-26-28; c-27. Atom app.-22, 23.*

COMIC COMICS
April, 1946 - No. 10, Feb, 1947
Fawcett Publications

	GD25	FN65	NM94
1-Captain Kidd; Nutty Comics #1 in indicia	7.00	21.00	42.00
2-10-Wolverton-a, 4 pgs. each. 5-Captain Kidd app.	9.15	27.50	55.00

COMIC CUTS (Also see The Funnies)
5/19/34 - 7/28/34 (5 cents; 24 pages) (Tabloid size in full color)
(Not reprints; published weekly; created for newsstand sale)
H. L. Baker Co., Inc.

	GD25	FN65	NM94
V1#1 - V1#7(6/30/34), V1#8(7/14/34), V1#9(7/28/34)-Idle Jack strips	8.70	26.00	52.00

COMIC LAND
March, 1946
Fact and Fiction Publ.

	GD25	FN65	NM94
1-Sandusky & the Senator, Sam Stupor, Sleuth, Marvin the Great, Sir Passer, Phineas Gruff app.; Irv Tirman & Perry Williams art	7.50	22.50	45.00

COMIC MONTHLY
Jan, 1922 - No. 12, Dec, 1922 (32 pgs.)(8x9")(10 cents)
(1st monthly newsstand comic publication) (Reprints 1921 B&W dailies)
Embee Dist. Co.

	GD25	FN65	NM94
1-Polly & Her Pals	58.00	175.00	350.00
2-Mike & Ike	12.50	37.50	75.00
3-S'Matter, Pop?	12.50	37.50	75.00
4-Barney Google	25.00	75.00	150.00
5-Tillie the Toiler	17.00	50.00	100.00
6-12: 6-Indoor Sports. 7-Little Jimmy. 8-Toots and Casper. 9,10-Foolish Questions. 11-Barney Google & Spark Plug in the Abadaba Handicap. 12-Polly & Her Pals	11.00	32.00	65.00

COMICO CHRISTMAS SPECIAL (Comico)(Value: cover or less)

COMICO PRIMER (See Primer)

COMIC PAGES (Formerly Funny Picture Stories)
V3#4, July, 1939 - V3#6, Dec, 1939
Centaur Publications

	GD25	FN65	NM94
V3#4-Bob Wood-a	46.00	136.00	275.00
5,6	32.00	95.00	190.00

COMIC PAINTING AND CRAYONING BOOK
1917 (32 pages)(10x13-1/2")(No price on cover)
Saalfield Publ. Co.

	GD25	FN65	NM94
nn-Tidy Teddy by F. M. Follett, Clarence the Cop, Mr. & Mrs. Butt-In. Regular comic stories to read or color	15.00	45.00	90.00

COMICS (See All Good)

COMICS, THE
March, 1937 - No. 11, Nov, 1938 (Newspaper strip-r; bi-monthly)
Dell Publishing Co.

	GD25	FN65	NM94
1-1st app. Tom Mix in comics; Wash Tubbs, Tom Beatty, Myra North, Arizona Kid, Erik Noble & International Spy w/Doctor Doom begin	100.00	300.00	600.00
2	54.00	160.00	325.00
3-11: 3-Alley Oop begins	46.00	136.00	275.00

COMICS AND STORIES (See Walt Disney's Comics and Stories)

COMICS CALENDAR, THE (The 1946...)

	GD25	FN65	NM94

1946 (116 pgs.; 25 cents)(Stapled at top)
True Comics Press (ordered through the mail)

	GD25	FN65	NM94
nn-(Rare) Has a "strip" story for every day of the year in color	32.00	95.00	190.00

COMICS DIGEST (Pocket size)
Winter, 1942-43 (100 pages) (Black & White)
Parents' Magazine Institute

	GD25	FN65	NM94
1-Reprints from True Comics (non-fiction World War II stories)	6.70	20.00	40.00

COMIC SELECTIONS (Shoe store giveaway)
1944-46 (Reprints from Calling All Girls, True Comics, True Aviation, & Real Heroes)
Parents' Magazine Press

	GD25	FN65	NM94
1	3.00	7.50	15.00
2-5	2.40	6.00	12.00

COMICS EXPRESS (Eclipse) (Value: cover or less)

COMICS FOR KIDS
1945 (no month); No. 2, Sum, 1945 (Funny animal)
London Publishing Co./Timely

	GD25	FN65	NM94
1,2-Puffy Pig, Sharpy Fox	8.35	25.00	50.00

COMICS FROM WEATHER BIRD (Also see Comic Book, Edward's Shoes, Free Comics to You & Weather Bird)
1954 - 1957 (Giveaway)
Weather Bird Shoes

Contains a comic bound with new cover. Many combinations possible. Contents would determine price. Some issues do not contain complete comics, but only parts of comics. Value equals 40 to 60 percent of contents.

COMICS HITS (See Harvey Comics Hits)

COMICS MAGAZINE, THE (...Funny Pages #3)(Funny Pages #6 on)
May, 1936 - No. 5, Sept, 1936 (Paper covers)
Comics Magazine Co.

	GD25	FN65	VF82
1-Dr. Mystic, The Occult Detective (1st Superman prototype) by Siegel & Shuster (1st episode of "The Koth and the Seven;" continues in More Fun #14); note: DC sold this material to Comics Magazine from the More Fun inventory; 1 pg. Kelly-a; Sheldon Mayer-a	915.00	2750.00	5500.00

(Estimated up to 10 total copies exist)

	GD25	FN65	NM94
2-Federal Agent (a.k.a. Federal Men) by Siegel & Shuster; 1 pg. Kelly-a	133.00	400.00	800.00
3-5	117.00	350.00	700.00

COMICS NOVEL (Anarcho, Dictator of Death)
1947
Fawcett Publications

	GD25	FN65	NM94
1-All Radar	19.00	57.00	135.00

COMICS ON PARADE (No. 30 on are a continuation of Single Series)
April, 1938 - No. 104, Feb, 1955
United Features Syndicate

	GD25	FN65	NM94
1-Tarzan by Foster; Captain & the Kids, Little Mary Mixup, Abbie & Slats, Ella Cinders, Broncho Bill, Li'l Abner begin	183.00	550.00	1100.00
2	83.00	250.00	500.00
3	67.00	200.00	400.00
4,5	50.00	150.00	300.00
6-10	37.00	110.00	220.00
11-20	30.00	90.00	180.00
21-29: 22-Son of Tarzan begins. 29-Last Tarzan issue	25.00	75.00	150.00
30-Li'l Abner	17.50	52.00	105.00
31-The Captain & the Kids	12.50	37.50	75.00
32-Nancy & Fritzi Ritz	10.00	30.00	60.00
33-Li'l Abner	15.00	45.00	90.00
34-The Captain & the Kids (10/41)	12.00	35.00	70.00
35-Nancy & Fritzi Ritz	10.00	30.00	60.00
36-Li'l Abner	15.00	45.00	90.00
37-The Captain & the Kids (6/42)	12.00	35.00	70.00
38-Nancy & Fritzi Ritz; infinity-c	10.00	30.00	60.00
39-Li'l Abner	15.00	45.00	90.00
40-The Captain & the Kids (3/43)	12.00	35.00	70.00
41-Nancy & Fritzi Ritz	7.50	22.50	45.00
42-Li'l Abner	15.00	45.00	90.00
43-The Captain & the Kids	12.00	35.00	70.00
44-Nancy & Fritzi Ritz (3/44)	7.50	22.50	45.00
45-Li'l Abner	12.00	35.00	70.00
46-The Captain & the Kids	10.00	30.00	60.00
47-Nancy & Fritzi Ritz	7.50	22.50	45.00
48-Li'l Abner (3/45)	12.00	35.00	70.00
49-The Captain & the Kids	10.00	30.00	60.00
50-Nancy & Fritzi Ritz	7.50	22.50	45.00
51-Li'l Abner	10.00	30.00	60.00
52-The Captain & the Kids (3/46)	6.70	20.00	40.00
53-Nancy & Fritzi Ritz	6.70	20.00	40.00
54-Li'l Abner	10.00	30.00	60.00
55-Nancy & Fritzi Ritz	6.70	20.00	40.00
56-The Captain & the Kids (r-/Sparkler)	6.70	20.00	40.00
57-Nancy & Fritzi Ritz	6.70	20.00	40.00
58-Li'l Abner	10.00	30.00	60.00
59-The Captain & the Kids	5.85	17.50	35.00
60-70-Nancy & Fritzi Ritz	5.85	17.50	35.00
71-76-Nancy only	4.20	12.50	25.00
77-99,101-104-Nancy & Sluggo	4.20	12.50	25.00
100-Nancy & Sluggo	5.35	16.00	32.00
Special Issue, 7/46; Summer, 1948 - The Captain & the Kids app.	4.20	12.50	25.00
NOTE: Bound Volume (Very Rare) includes No. 1-12; bound by publisher in pictorial comic boards & distributed at the 1939 World's Fair and through mail order from ads in comic books (also see Tip Top)	208.00	625.00	1250.00

NOTE: *Li'l Abner reprinted from Tip Top.*

COMICS READING LIBRARIES (Educational Series)
1973, 1977, 1979 (36 pages in color) (Giveaways)
King Features (Charlton Publ.)

	GD25	FN65	NM94
R-01-Tiger, Quincy	.40	1.00	2.00
R-02-Beetle Bailey, Blondie & Popeye	.40	1.00	2.00
R-03-Blondie, Beetle Bailey	.40	1.00	2.00
R-04-Tim Tyler's Luck, Felix the Cat	2.00	5.00	10.00
R-05-Quincy, Henry	.40	1.00	2.00
R-06-The Phantom, Mandrake	3.20	8.00	16.00
1977 reprint(R-04)	1.00	2.50	5.00
R-07-Popeye, Little King	1.00	2.50	5.00
R-08-Prince Valiant(Foster), Flash Gordon	4.00	12.00	24.00
1977 reprint	1.60	4.00	8.00
R-09-Hagar the Horrible, Boner's Ark	.40	1.00	2.00
R-10-Redeye, Tiger	.40	1.00	2.00
R-11-Blondie, Hi & Lois	.40	1.00	2.00
R-12-Popeye-Swee'pea, Brutus	1.20	3.00	6.00
R-13-Beetle Bailey, Little King	.40	1.00	2.00
R-14-Quincy-Hamlet	.40	1.00	2.00
R-15-The Phantom, The Genius	3.20	8.00	16.00
R-16-Flash Gordon, Mandrake	4.00	12.00	24.00
1977 reprint	1.60	4.00	8.00
Other 1977 editions....		.50	1.00
1979 editions(68pgs.)		.50	1.00

NOTE: *Above giveaways available with purchase of $45.00 in merchandise. Used as a reading skills aid for small children.*

COMICS REVUE
June, 1947 - No. 5, Jan, 1948
St. John Publ. Co. (United Features Synd.)

	GD25	FN65	NM94
1-Ella Cinders & Blackie	7.50	22.50	45.00
2-Hap Hopper (7/47)	5.00	15.00	30.00

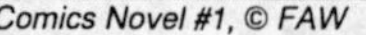
Comics Novel #1, © FAW

Comics On Parade #17, © UFS

Comics Revue #5, © UFS

Comic Story Paint Book #1055, © FAW

Commander Battle #4, © ACG

Complete Comics #2, © MEG

	GD25	FN65	NM94
3-Iron Vic (8/47)	4.20	12.50	25.00
4-Ella Cinders (9/47)	5.00	15.00	30.00
5-Gordo No. 1 (1/48)	4.20	12.50	25.00

COMIC STORY PAINT BOOK
1943 (68 pages) (Large size)
Samuel Lowe Co.

1055-Captain Marvel & a Captain Marvel Jr. story to read & color; 3 panels in color per page (reprints) 45.00 132.00 265.00

COMIX BOOK (B&W Magazine - $1.00)
1974 - No. 5, 1976
Marvel Comics Group/Krupp Comics Works No. 4,5

	GD25	FN65	NM94
1-Underground comic artists; 2 pgs. Wolverton-a	.80	2.00	4.00
2-Wolverton-a (1 pg.)	.40	1.00	2.00
3-Low distribution (3/75)	.60	1.50	3.00
4(2/76), 4(5/76), 5	.40	1.00	2.00

NOTE: *Print run No. 1-3: 200-250M; No. 4&5: 10M each.*

COMIX INTERNATIONAL
July, 1974 - No. 5, Spring, 1977 (Full color)
Warren Magazines

	GD25	FN65	NM94
1-Low distribution; all Corben remainders from Warren	4.00	12.00	24.00
2-Wood, Wrightson-r	1.40	3.50	7.00
3-5: 4-Crandall-a	.80	2.00	4.00

NOTE: *No. 4 had two printings with extra **Corben** story in one. No. 3 may also have a variation. No. 3 has two Jeff Jones reprints from Vampirella.*

COMMANDER BATTLE AND THE ATOMIC SUB
July-Aug, 1954 - No. 7, Aug-Sept, 1955
American Comics Group (Titan Publ. Co.)

	GD25	FN65	NM94
1 (3-D effect)	25.00	75.00	175.00
2,4-7: 4-(1-2/55)-Last pre-code; Landau-a. 5-3-D effect story (2 pgs.). 6,7-Landau-a	11.50	34.00	80.00
3-H-Bomb-c; Atomic Sub becomes Atomic Spaceship	13.50	41.00	95.00

COMMANDMENTS OF GOD
1954, 1958
Catechetical Guild

300-Same contents in both editions; diff-c 2.00 5.00 10.00

COMMANDO ADVENTURES
June, 1957 - No. 2, Aug, 1957
Atlas Comics (MMC)

1,2-Severin-c; 2-Drucker-a? 4.00 12.00 24.00

COMMANDO YANK (See The Mighty Midget Comics & Wow Comics)

COMPLETE BOOK OF COMICS AND FUNNIES
1944 (196 pages) (One Shot) (25 cents)
William H. Wise & Co.

1-Origin Brad Spencer, Wonderman; The Magnet, The Silver Knight by Kinstler, & Zudo the Jungle Boy app. 30.00 90.00 180.00

COMPLETE BOOK OF TRUE CRIME COMICS
No date (Mid 1940's) (132 pages) (25 cents)
William H. Wise & Co.

nn-Contains Crime Does Not Pay rebound (includes #22) 61.00 182.00 425.00

COMPLETE COMICS (Formerly Amazing Comics No. 1)
No. 2, Winter, 1944-45
Timely Comics (EPC)

2-The Destroyer, The Whizzer, The Young Allies & Sergeant Dix; Schomburg-c 80.00 240.00 475.00

COMPLETE LOVE MAGAZINE (Formerly a pulp with same title)
V26#2, May-June, 1951 - V32#4(#191), Sept, 1956
Ace Periodicals (Periodical House)

	GD25	FN65	NM94
V26#2-Painted-c (52 pgs.)	3.00	9.00	18.00
V26#3-6(2/52), V27#1(4/52)-6(1/53)	2.40	6.00	12.00
V28#1(3/53), V28#2(5/53), V29#3(7/53)-6(12/53)	2.00	5.00	10.00
V30#1(2/54), V30#1(#176, 4/54),2,4-6(#181, 1/55)	2.00	5.00	10.00
V30#3(#178)-Rock Hudson photo-c	2.80	7.00	14.00
V31#1(#182, 3/55)-Last precode	1.80	4.50	9.00
V31#2(5/55)-6(#187, 1/56)	1.40	3.50	7.00
V32#1(#188, 3/56)-4(#191, 9/56)	1.40	3.50	7.00

NOTE: *(34 total issues). Photo-c V27#5-on. Painted-c V26#3.*

COMPLETE MYSTERY (True Complete Mystery No. 5 on)
Aug, 1948 - No. 4, Feb, 1949 (Full length stories)
Marvel Comics (PrPI)

	GD25	FN65	NM94
1-Seven Dead Men	19.00	58.00	135.00
2-Jigsaw of Doom!	14.00	43.00	100.00
3-Fear in the Night; Burgos-c/a (28 pgs.)	14.00	43.00	100.00
4-A Squealer Dies Fast	14.00	43.00	100.00

COMPLETE ROMANCE
1949
Avon Periodicals

1-(Scarce)-Reprinted as Women to Love 25.00 75.00 175.00

COMPLIMENTARY COMICS
No date (1950's)
Sales Promotion Publ. (Giveaway)

1-Strongman by Powell, 3 stories 4.70 14.00 28.00

CONAN (See Chamber of Darkness #4, Giant-Size..., Handbook of..., King Conan, Marvel Graphic Novel #19, 28, Marvel Treasury Ed., Power Record Comics, Robert E. Howard's..., Savage Sword of Conan, and Savage Tales)

CONAN SAGA, THE
June, 1987 - Present ($2.00-$2.25, B&W magazine)
Marvel Comics

	GD25	FN65	NM94
1-Barry Smith-r begin	.40	1.00	2.00
2-27: 13,15-Boris-c. 22-r/Giant-Size Conan 1,2	.40	1.00	2.00
28-74 ($2.25): 31-Red Sonja-r by N. Adams/SSOC #1. 32-Newspaper strip-r begin by Buscema. 33-Smith/Conrad-a. 39-r/Kull #1('71) by Andru/Wood. 44-Swipes-c/Savage Tales #1. 57-Brunner-r/SSOC #30. 66-r/Conan Annual #2 by Buscema	.45	1.15	2.25

NOTE: ***J. Buscema** r-32-on. **Chaykin** r-34. **Chiodo** painted c-63, 65, 66. **G. Colan** a-47p. **Jusko** painted c-64. **Nino** a-37. **Ploog** a-50. **N. Redondo** painted c-48, 50, 51, 53, 57, 62. **Simonson** r-50-54, 56. **B. Smith** r-51. **Starlin** c-34. **Williamson** r-50i.*

CONAN THE BARBARIAN
Oct, 1970 - Present
Marvel Comics Group

	GD25	FN65	NM94
1-Origin/1st app. Conan (in comics) by Barry Smith; Kull app.; #1-9 are 15 cent issues	27.00	80.00	185.00
2	10.00	30.00	65.00
3-(Low distribution in some areas)	17.00	52.00	120.00
4,5	9.15	27.50	55.00
6-9: 8-Hidden panel message, pg. 14	5.85	17.50	35.00
10,11 (25 cent giants): 10-Black Knight-r; Kull story by Severin	7.00	21.00	42.00
12,13: 12-Wrightson-c(i)	4.20	12.50	25.00
14,15-Elric app.	6.35	19.00	38.00
16,19,20: 16-Conan-r/Savage Tales #1	4.00	11.00	22.00
17,18-No Barry Smith-a	2.00	5.00	10.00
21,22: 22-Has reprint from #1	4.00	10.00	20.00
23-1st app. Red Sonja (2/73)	4.70	14.00	28.00
24-1st full Red Sonja story; last Smith-a	4.00	12.00	24.00
25-John Buscema-c/a begins	1.80	4.50	9.00
26-30	1.00	2.50	5.00

31-36,38-40 .60 1.50 3.00
37-Neal Adams-c/a; last 20 cent issue; contains pull-out subscription form
1.20 3.00 6.00
41-57,59,60: 44,45-N. Adams-i(Crusty Bunkers). 45-Adams-c. 48-Origin retold. 59-Origin Belit .40 1.00 2.00
58-2nd Belit app. (see Giant-Size Conan #1) .60 1.50 3.00
61-99: 68-Red Sonja story cont'd from Marvel Feature #7. 84-Intro. Zula. 85-Origin Zula. 87-r/Savage Sword of Conan #3 in color .50 1.00
100-(52 pg. Giant)-Death of Belit .50 1.25 2.50
101-114,116-199: 116-r/Power Record Comic PR31 .50 1.00
115-Double size .60 1.20
201-249,251,252: 232-Young Conan storyline begins; Conan is born. 244-Return of Zula. 252-Last $1.00-c .50 1.00
200,250 ($1.50): 200-(52 pgs.). 250-(60 pgs.) .30 .75 1.50
253-268: 262-Adapted from R.E. Howard story .60 1.25
King Size 1(1973, 35 cents)-Smith-r/#2,4; Smith-c 1.60 4.00 8.00
Annual 2(1976, 50 cents)-New full length story .70 1.75 3.50
Annual 3(1978)-Chaykin/N. Adams-r/SSOC #2 .40 1.00 2.00
Annual 4,5: 4(1978)-New full length story. 5(1979)-New full length Buscema story & part-c .30 .75 1.50
Annual 6(1981)-Kane-c/a .30 .75 1.50
Annual 7-9: 7(1982)-Based on novel "Conan of the Isles" (new-a). 8(1984). 9(1984) .60 1.25
Annual 10-12: 10(1986). 11(1986). 12(1987) .60 1.25
Special Edition 1 (Red Nails) .70 1.75 3.50

NOTE: ***Arthur Adams*** *c-248, 249.* ***Neal Adams*** *a-116r(i); c-49i.* ***Austin*** *a-125, 126; c-125i, 126i.* ***Brunner*** *c-17i. c-40.* ***Buscema*** *a-25-36p, 38, 39, 41-56p, 58-63p, 65-67p, 68, 70-78p, 84-86p, 88-91p, 93-126p, 136p, 140, 141-144p. 146-158p, 159, 161, 162, 163p, 165-185p. 187-190p. Annual 2(3pgs.). 3-5p, 7p; c(p)-26. 36, 44, 46, 52, 56. 58. 59. 64, 65, 72, 78-80, 83-91, 93-103, 105-126, 136-151. 155-159. 161. 162, 168. 169, 171, 172. 174, 175. 178-185, 188, 189, Annual 4, 5, 7.* ***Chaykin*** *a-79-83.* ***Golden*** *c-152.* ***Kaluta*** *c-167.* ***Gil Kane*** *a-12p, 17p, 18p, 127-130, 131-134p; c-12p. 17p. 18p. 23, 25, 27-32, 34, 35. 38, 39. 41-43. 45-51, 53-55, 57, 60-63, 65-71, 73p, 76p, 127-134.* ***Jim Lee*** *c-242.* ***McFarlane*** *c-241p.* ***Ploog*** *a-57.* ***Russell*** *a-21; c-251i.* ***Simonson*** *c-135. B.* ***Smith*** *a-1-11p, 12, 13-15p, 16, 19-21, 23, 24; c-1-11, 13-16, 19-24p.* ***Starlin*** *a-64.* ***Wood*** *a-47r. Issue Nos. 3-5, 7-9, 11, 16-18, 21, 23, 25, 27-30. 35. 37, 38, 42, 45, 52, 57, 58, 65, 69-71, 73, 79-83, 99, 100, 104, 114, Annual 2 have original Robert E. Howard stories adapted. Issues #32-34 adapted from Norvell Page's novel* ***Flame Winds****.*

CONAN THE BARBARIAN MOVIE SPECIAL
Oct, 1982 - No. 2, Nov, 1982
Marvel Comics Group

1,2-Movie adaptation; Buscema-a .50 1.00

CONAN THE DESTROYER
Jan, 1985 - No. 2, Mar, 1985 (Movie adaptation)
Marvel Comics Group

1,2-r/Marvel Super Special .50 1.00

CONAN THE KING (Formerly King Conan)
No. 20, Jan, 1984 - No. 55, Nov, 1989
Marvel Comics Group

20-55: 48-55 ($1.50) .30 .75 1.50

NOTE: ***Kaluta*** *c-20-23, 24i, 26, 27, 30, 50, 52.* ***Williamson*** *a-37i; c-37i, 38i.*

CONCRETE (Also see Dark Horse Presents & Within Our Reach)
March, 1987 - No. 10, Nov, 1988 ($1.50, B&W)
Dark Horse Comics

1-Paul Chadwick-c/a in all 1.60 4.00 8.00
1-2nd print .40 1.00 2.00
2 1.00 2.50 5.00
3-Origin .60 1.50 3.00
4-10 .40 1.00 2.00
...: A New Life 1 (1989, $2.95, B&W)-r/#3,4 plus new-a (11 pgs.)
.60 1.50 3.00
...: Land And Sea 1 (2/89, $2.95, B&W)-r/#1,2 .60 1.50 3.00
...Color Special 1 (2/89, $2.95, 44 pgs.)-r/1st two Conrete apps. from Dark Horse Presents #1,2 plus new-a .60 1.50 3.00
...Celebrates Earth Day 1990 ($3.50, color, 52 pgs.)-Moebius, Vess & Chadwick-a .70 1.75 3.50
.... Odd Jobs 1 (7/90, $3.50)-r/5,6 plus new-a .70 1.75 3.50

CONCRETE: FRAGILE CREATURE
June, 1991 - No. 4, Feb, 1992 ($2.50, color, mini-series)
Dark Horse Comics

1-4: By Paul Chadwick .50 1.25 2.50

CONDORMAN (Walt Disney)
Oct, 1981 - No. 3, Jan, 1982
Whitman Publishing

1-3: 1,2-Movie adaptation; photo-c .50 1.00

CONFESSIONS ILLUSTRATED (Magazine)
Jan-Feb, 1956 - No. 2, Spring, 1956
E. C. Comics

1-Craig, Kamen, Wood, Orlando-a 10.00 30.00 65.00
2-Craig, Crandall, Kamen, Orlando-a 9.15 27.50 55.00

CONFESSIONS OF LOVE
Apr, 1950 - No. 2, July, 1950 (25 cents; 132 pgs. in color)(7-1/4x5-1/4)
Artful Publ.

1-Bakerish-a 19.00 58.00 135.00
2-Art & text; Bakerish-a 11.00 32.00 75.00

CONFESSIONS OF LOVE (Formerly Startling Terror Tales #10; becomes Confessions of Romance No. 7 on)
No. 11, 7/52 - No. 14, 1/53; No. 4, 3/53- No. 6, 8/53
Star Publications

11-13: 12,13-Disbrow-a 5.85 17.50 35.00
14,5,6 4.00 10.00 20.00
4-Disbrow-a 4.35 13.00 26.00

NOTE: *All have* ***L. B. Cole*** *covers.*

CONFESSIONS OF ROMANCE (Formerly Confessions of Love)
No. 7, Nov, 1953 - No. 11, Nov, 1954
Star Publications

7 5.00 15.00 30.00
8 4.00 10.00 20.00
9-Wood-a 7.50 22.50 45.00
10,11-Disbrow-a 4.35 13.00 26.00

NOTE: *All have* ***L. B. Cole*** *covers.*

CONFESSIONS OF THE LOVELORN (Formerly Lovelorn)
No. 52, Aug, 1954 - No. 114, June-July, 1960
American Comics Group (Regis Publ./Best Synd. Features)

52 (3-D effect) 13.00 40.00 90.00
53,55 4.00 10.00 20.00
54 (3-D effect) 12.00 36.00 85.00
56-Anti-communist propaganda story, 10 pgs; last pre-code (2/55)
4.70 14.00 28.00
57-90 2.40 6.00 12.00
91-Williamson-a 4.70 14.00 28.00
92-99,101-114 1.80 4.50 9.00
100 2.40 6.00 12.00

NOTE: ***Whitney*** *a-most issues; c-52, 53. Painted c-106, 107.*

CONFIDENTIAL DIARY (Formerly High School Confidential Diary; Three Nurses No. 18 on)
No. 12, May, 1962 - No. 17, March, 1963
Charlton Comics

12-17 1.00 2.50 5.00

CONGO BILL (See Action Comics & More Fun Comics #56)
Aug-Sept, 1954 - No. 7, Aug-Sept, 1955
National Periodical Publication

	GD25	FN65	VF82
1-(Scarce)	50.00	150.00	350.00
2,7 (Scarce)	43.00	130.00	300.00
3-6 (Scarce), 4-Last pre-code issue	36.00	107.00	250.00

NOTE: *(Rarely found in fine to mint condition.)* ***Nick Cardy*** *c-1-7.*

Conan The Barbarian #8, © MEG

Confessions Of Love #6, © STAR

Congo Bill #5, © DC

Conqueror Comics #1 (1945), © Albrecht Publ.

Coo Coo Comics #28, © STD

Cookie #2, © ACG

	GD25	FN65	NM94

CONGORILLA (Also see Actions Comics #224)
Nov, 1992 - No. 4, Feb, 1993 ($1.75, color, mini-series)
DC Comics

	GD25	FN65	NM94
1-4: All have Brian Bolland-c	.35	.90	1.75

CONNECTICUT YANKEE, A (See King Classics)

CONQUEROR, THE (See 4-Color No. 690)

CONQUEROR COMICS
Winter, 1945
Albrecht Publishing Co.

nn	10.00	30.00	60.00

CONQUEROR OF THE BARREN EARTH
Feb, 1985 - No. 4, May, 1985 (Mini-series)
DC Comics

1-4: Back-up series from Warlord		.50	1.00

CONQUEST
1953 (6 cents)
Store Comics

1-Richard the Lion Hearted, Beowulf, Swamp Fox	4.00	10.00	20.00

CONQUEST
Spring, 1955
Famous Funnies

1-Crandall-a, 1 pg.; contains contents of 1953 issue	3.00	7.50	15.00

CONTACT COMICS
July, 1944 - No. 12, May, 1946
Aviation Press

nn-Black Venus, Flamingo, Golden Eagle, Tommy Tomahawk begin	20.00	60.00	120.00
2-5: 3-Last Flamingo. 3,4-Black Venus by L. B. Cole. 5-The Phantom Flyer app.	14.00	42.50	85.00
6,11-Kurtzman's Black Venus; 11-Last Golden Eagle, last Tommy Tomahawk; Feldstein-a	18.00	55.00	110.00
7-10,12: 12-Sky Rangers, Air Kids, Ace Diamond app.	12.00	35.00	70.00

NOTE: *L. B. Cole a-9; c-1-12.* ***Giunta*** *a-3.* ***Hollingsworth*** *a-5, 7, 10.* ***Palais*** *a-11, 12.*

CONTEMPORARY MOTIVATORS
1977 - 1978 (5-3/8x8")(31 pgs., B&W, $1.45)
Pendelum Press

14-3002 The Caine Mutiny; 14-3010 Banner in the Sky; 14-3029 God Is My Co-Pilot;14-3037 Guadalcanal Diary; 14-3045 Hiroshima; 14-3053 Hot Rod; 14-3061 Just Dial a Number; 14-307x Star Wars; 14-3088 The Diary of Anne Frank; 14-3096 Lost Horizon — 1.50

NOTE: *Also see Now Age Illustrated. Above may have been distributed the same.*

CONTEST OF CHAMPIONS (See Marvel Super-Hero...)

CONTRACTORS (Eclipse) (Value: cover or less)

COO COO COMICS (... the Bird Brain No. 57 on)
Oct, 1942 - No. 62, April, 1952
Nedor Publ. Co./Standard (Animated Cartoons)

1-Origin/1st app. Super Mouse & begin series (cloned from Superman); the first funny animal super hero series (see Looney Tunes #5 for 1st funny animal super hero)	15.00	45.00	105.00
2	8.35	25.00	50.00
3-10 (3/44)	4.70	14.00	28.00
11-33: 33-1 pg. Ingels-a	4.00	10.00	20.00
34-40,43-46,48-50-Text illos by Frazetta in all	4.70	14.00	28.00
41-Frazetta-a(2)	10.00	30.00	60.00
42,47-Frazetta-a & text illos.	7.00	21.00	42.00
51-62: 56-Last Supermouse?	2.80	7.00	14.00

"COOKIE" (Also see Topsy-Turvy)
April, 1946 - No. 55, Aug-Sept, 1955
Michel Publ./American Comics Group(Regis Publ.)

	GD25	FN65	NM94
1-Teen-age humor	11.00	32.00	75.00
2	6.35	19.00	38.00
3-10	4.70	14.00	28.00
11-20	4.00	11.00	22.00
21-23,26,28-30	3.20	8.00	16.00
24,25,27-Starlet O'Hara stories	3.60	9.00	18.00
31-34,37-55	2.80	7.00	14.00
35,36-Starlett O'Hara stories	3.20	8.00	16.00

COOL CAT (Formerly Black Magic)
V8#6, Mar-Apr, 1962 - V9#2, July-Aug, 1962
Prize Publications

V8#6, nn(V9#1, 5-6/62), V9#2	3.20	8.00	16.00

COOL WORLD
Apr, 1992 - No. 4, Sept, 1992 ($1.75, color, mini-series)
DC Comics

1-4: Prequel to animated/live action movie by Ralph Bakshi. 1-Bakshi-c. Bill Wray inks in all	.35	.90	1.80
...Movie Adaptation nn ('92, $3.50, 68pg.)-Bakshi-c	.70	1.75	3.50

COPPER CANYON (See Fawcett Movie Comics)

COPS (TV)
Aug, 1988 - No. 15, Aug, 1989 ($1.00, color)
DC Comics

1 ($1.50, 52 pgs.)-Based on Hasbro Toys	.30	.75	1.50
2-15: 14-Orlando-c(p)		.50	1.00

COPS: THE JOB
June, 1992 - No. 4, Sept, 1992 ($1.25, color, mini-series)
Marvel Comics

1-4: All have Jusko scripts & Golden-c		.60	1.25

CORBEN SPECIAL, A (Pacific) (Value: cover or less)

CORKY & WHITE SHADOW (See 4-Color No. 707)

CORLISS ARCHER (See Meet Corliss Archer)

CORMAC MAC ART (Dark Horse) (Value: cover or less)

CORPORAL RUSTY DUGAN (See Holyoke One-Shot #2)

CORPSES OF DR. SACOTTI, THE (See Ideal a Classical Comic)

CORSAIR, THE (See A-1 Comics No. 5, 7, 10)

CORUM: THE BULL AND THE SPEAR (First) (Value: cover or less)

COSMIC BOOK, THE (Ace) (Value: cover or less)

COSMIC BOY (See The Legion of Super-Heroes)
Dec, 1986 - No. 4, Mar, 1987 (Mini-series)
DC Comics

1-4: Legends tie-in, all issues		.50	1.00

COSMIC ODYSSEY
1988 - No. 4, 1988 ($3.50, color, squarebound)
DC Comics

1-4: Superman, Batman, Green Lantern app.	.70	1.75	3.50

COSMO CAT (Becomes Sunny #11 on; also see Wotalife Comics)
July-Aug, 1946 - No. 10, Oct, 1947; 1957; 1959
Fox Publications/Green Publ. Co./Norlen Mag.

1	10.00	30.00	70.00
2	5.85	17.50	35.00
3-Origin (11-12/46)	7.00	21.00	42.00
4-10	4.70	14.00	28.00
2-4(1957-Green Publ. Co.)	2.40	6.00	12.00

GD25 FN65 NM94

2-4(1959-Norlen Mag.) 1.60 4.00 8.00
I.W. Reprint #1 1.20 3.00 6.00

COSMO THE MERRY MARTIAN
Sept, 1958 - No. 6, Oct, 1959
Archie Publications (Radio Comics)

1-Bob White-a in all 10.00 30.00 65.00
2-6 7.00 21.00 42.00

COTTON WOODS (See 4-Color No. 837)

COUGAR, THE (Cougar No. 2)
April, 1975 - No. 2, July, 1975
Seaboard Periodicals (Atlas)

1,2: 1-Adkins-a(p). 2-Origin; Buckler-c(p) .50 1.00

COUNTDOWN (See Movie Classics)

COUNT DUCKULA (TV)
Nov, 1988 - No. 15, Jan, 1991 ($1.00, color)
Marvel Comics

1-15: Dangermouse back-ups. 8-Geraldo Rivera photo-c .50 1.00

COUNT OF MONTE CRISTO, THE (See 4-Color No. 794)

COURAGE COMICS
1945
J. Edward Slavin

1,2,77 5.85 17.50 35.00

COURTSHIP OF EDDIE'S FATHER (TV)
Jan, 1970 - No. 2, May, 1970
Dell Publishing Co.

1,2-Bill Bixby photo-c 3.60 9.00 18.00

COVERED WAGONS, HO (See 4-Color No. 814)

COWBOY ACTION (Formerly Western Thrillers No. 1-4; Becomes Quick-Trigger Western No. 12 on)
No. 5, March, 1955 - No. 11, March, 1956
Atlas Comics (ACI)

5 6.70 20.00 40.00
6-10: 6-8-Heath-c 4.35 13.00 26.00
11-Williamson-a (4 pgs.); Baker-a 5.00 15.00 30.00

NOTE: ***Ayers*** *a-8.* ***Drucker*** *a-6.* ***Maneely*** *c/a-5, 6.* ***Severin*** *c-10.* ***Shores*** *a-7.*

COWBOY COMICS (...Stories No. 14; formerly Star Ranger)(Star Ranger Funnies No. 15 on)
No. 13, July, 1938 - No. 14, Aug, 1938
Centaur Publishing Co.

13-(Rare)-Ace and Deuce, Lyin Lou, Air Patrol, Aces High, Lee Trent, Trouble Hunters begin 75.00 225.00 450.00
14-Filchock-c 54.00 162.00 325.00

NOTE: ***Guardineer*** *a-13, 14.* ***Gustavson*** *a-13, 14.*

COWBOY IN AFRICA (TV)
March, 1968
Gold Key

1(10219-803)-Chuck Connors photo-c 4.00 10.50 21.00

COWBOY LOVE (Becomes Range Busters?)
7/49 - V2#10, 6/50; No. 11, 1951; No. 28, 2/55 - No. 31, 8/55
Fawcett Publications/Charlton Comics No. 28 on

V1#1-Rocky Lane photo back-c 10.00 30.00 65.00
2 3.60 9.00 18.00
V1#3,4,6 (12/49) 3.20 8.00 16.00
5-Bill Boyd photo back-c (11/49) 4.70 14.00 28.00
V2#7-Williamson/Evans-a 5.85 17.50 35.00
V2#8-11 2.80 7.00 14.00
V1#28 (Charlton)-Last precode (2/55) (Formerly Romantic Story?) 2.80 7.00 14.00
V1#29-31 (Charlton; becomes Sweetheart Diary #32 on) 2.40 6.00 12.00

NOTE: ***Powell*** *a-10.* ***Marcus Swayze*** *a-2, 3. Photo c-1-11. No. 1-3, 5-7, 9, 10 are 52 pgs.*

COWBOY ROMANCES (Young Men No. 4 on)
Oct, 1949 - No. 3, Mar, 1950
Marvel Comics (IPC)

1-Photo-c 11.50 34.00 80.00
2-William Holden, Mona Freeman 'Streets of Laredo' photo-c 10.00 30.00 60.00
3 7.50 22.50 45.00

COWBOYS 'N' INJUNS (...and Indians No. 6 on)
1946 - No. 5, 1947; No. 6, 1949 - No. 8, 1952
Com No. 1-5/Magazine Enterprises No. 6 on

1 5.35 16.00 32.00
2-5-All funny animal western 4.00 10.50 21.00
6(A-1 23)-Half violent, half funny; Ayers-a 5.00 15.00 30.00
7(A-1 41, 1950), 8(A-1 48)-All funny 4.00 10.50 21.00
I.W. Reprint No. 1,7 (Reprinted in Canada by Superior, No. 7) .80 2.00 4.00
Super Reprint #10 (1963) .80 2.00 4.00

COWBOY WESTERN COMICS (Formerly Jack In The Box; Becomes Space Western No. 40-45 & Wild Bill Hickok & Jingles No. 68 on; title: ...Heroes No. 47 & 48; Cowboy Western No. 49 on (TV))
No. 17, 7/48 - No. 39, 8/52; No. 46, 10/53; No. 47, 12/53; No. 48, Spr, '54; No. 49, 5-6/54 - No. 67, 3/58 (nn 40-45)
Charlton (Capitol Stories)

17-Jesse James, Annie Oakley, Wild Bill Hickok begin; Texas Rangers app. 10.00 30.00 65.00
18,19-Orlando-c/a 6.35 19.00 38.00
20-25: 24-Joel McCrea photo-c and adaptation from movie "Three Faces West." 25-Photo-c and adaptation from movie "Northwest Stampede" 4.70 14.00 28.00
26-George Montgomery photo-c and adaptation from movie "Indian Scout;" 1 pg. bio on Will Rogers 7.50 22.50 45.00
27-Sunset Carson photo-c & adapts movie "Sunset Carson Rides Again" plus 1 other Sunset Carson story 47.00 140.00 325.00
28-Sunset Carson line drawn-c; adapts movies "Battling Marshal" & "Fighting Mustangs" starring Sunset Carson 20.00 60.00 140.00
29-Sunset Carson line drawn-c; adapts movies "Rio Grande" with Sunset Carson & "Winchester 73" w/James Stewart plus 5 pg. life history of Sunset Carson featuring Tom Mix 20.00 60.00 140.00
30-Sunset Carson photo-c; adapts movie "Deadline" starring Sunset Carson plus 1 other Sunset Carson story 47.00 140.00 325.00
31-34,38,39,47-50 (no #40-45): 50-Golden Arrow, Rocky Lane & Blackjack (r?) stories 4.00 12.00 24.00
35,36-Sunset Carson-c/stories (2 in each). 35-Inside front-c photo of Sunset Carson plus photo on-c 20.00 60.00 140.00
37-Sunset Carson stories (2) 10.00 30.00 65.00
46-(Formerly Space Western)-Space western story 10.00 30.00 65.00
51-57,59-66: 51-Golden Arrow(r?) & Monte Hale-r renamed Rusty Hall. 53,54-Tom Mix-r. 55-Monte Hale story(r?). 66-Young Eagle story 3.20 8.00 16.00
58-(68 pgs.)-Wild Bill Hickok & Jingles (Guy Madison & Andy Devine) line drawn cover/stories begin, end #67 4.00 11.00 22.00
67-(68 pgs.)-Williamson/Torres-a, 5 pgs. 5.85 17.50 35.00

NOTE: *Many issues trimmed 1" shorter.* ***Maneely*** *c/a-67(5). Inside front/back photo-c #29.*

COWGIRL ROMANCES (Formerly Jeanie Comics)
No. 28, Jan, 1950 (52 pgs.)
Marvel Comics (CCC)

28(#1)-Photo-c 12.00 36.00 85.00

COWGIRL ROMANCES
1950 - No. 12, Winter, 1952-53 (No. 1-3: 52 pgs.)
Fiction House Magazines

Cowboy Romances #1, © MEG

Cowboys 'N' Injuns Comics #1, © ME

Cowboy Western #30, © CC

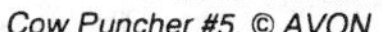

Cow Puncher #5, © AVON

Crackajack Funnies #2, DELL

Crack Comics #1, © QUA

	GD25	FN65	NM94
1-Kamen-a	17.00	52.00	120.00
2	10.00	30.00	65.00
3-5: 5-12-Whitman-c (most)	9.15	27.50	55.00
6-9,11,12	7.50	22.50	45.00
10-Frazetta?/Williamson-a; Kamen/Baker-a	17.00	52.00	120.00

COW PUNCHER (...Comics)
Jan, 1947; No. 2, Sept, 1947 - No. 7, 1949
Avon Periodicals

	GD25	FN65	NM94
1-Clint Cortland, Texas Ranger, Kit West, Pioneer Queen begin; Kubert-a; Alabam stories begin (1st Avon comic?)	23.00	70.00	160.00
2-Kubert, Kamen/Feldstein-a; Kamen-c	19.00	57.00	135.00
3-5,7: 3-Kiefer story	12.00	36.00	85.00
6-Opium drug mention story; bondage, headlight-c; Reinman-a	14.00	43.00	100.00

COWPUNCHER
1953 (nn) (Reprints Avon's No. 2)
Realistic Publications

	GD25	FN65	NM94
nn-Kubert-a	7.50	22.50	45.00

COWSILLS, THE (See Harvey Pop Comics)

COYOTE (Marvel) (Value: cover or less)

CRACKAJACK FUNNIES (Giveaway)
1937 (32 pgs.; full size; soft cover; full color) (Before No. 1?)
Malto-Meal

	GD25	FN65	NM94
nn-Features Dan Dunn, G-Man, Speed Bolton, Freckles, Buck Jones, Clyde Beatty, The Nebbs, Major Hoople, Wash Tubbs	63.00	186.00	375.00

CRACKAJACK FUNNIES
June, 1938 - No. 43, Jan, 1942
Dell Publishing Co.

	GD25	FN65	NM94
1-Dan Dunn, Freckles, Myra North, Wash Tubbs, Apple Mary, The Nebbs, Don Winslow, Tom Mix, Buck Jones, Major Hoople, Clyde Beatty, Boots begin	125.00	375.00	750.00
2	58.00	175.00	350.00
3	42.00	125.00	250.00
4,5: 5-Nude woman on cover	33.00	100.00	200.00
6-8,10: 8-Speed Bolton begins	27.00	82.00	165.00
9-(3/39)-Red Ryder strip-r begin by Harman; 1st app. in comics & 1st cover app.	37.00	112.00	225.00
11-14	25.00	75.00	150.00
15-Tarzan text feature begins by Burroughs (9/39); not in #26,35	27.00	82.00	165.00
16-24: 18-Stratosphere Jim begins. 23-Ellery Queen begins (1st comic book app?)	18.00	55.00	110.00
25-The Owl begins; in new costume #26 by Frank Thomas	42.00	125.00	250.00
26-30: 28-Part Owl-c	33.00	100.00	200.00
31-Owl covers begin, end #42	29.00	88.00	175.00
32-Origin Owl Girl	37.00	110.00	220.00
33-38: 36-Last Tarzan issue	22.00	65.00	130.00
39-Andy Panda begins (intro/1st app.)	25.00	75.00	150.00
40-43: 42-Last Owl-c. 43-Terry & the Pirates-r	20.00	60.00	120.00

NOTE: ***McWilliams*** *art in most issues.*

CRACK COMICS (Crack Western No. 63 on)
May, 1940 - No. 62, Sept, 1949
Quality Comics Group

	GD25	FN65	NM94
1-Origin The Black Condor by Lou Fine, Madame Fatal, Red Torpedo, Rock Bradden & The Space Legion; The Clock, Alias the Spider (by Gustavson), Wizard Wells, & Ned Brant begin; Powell-a; Note: Madame Fatal is a man dressed as a woman	250.00	750.00	1500.00
2	117.00	350.00	700.00
3	83.00	250.00	500.00
4	75.00	225.00	450.00
5-10: 5-Molly The Model begins. 10-Tor, the Magic Master begins	58.00	175.00	350.00
11-20: 13-1 pg. J. Cole-a. 18-1st app. Spitfire?	50.00	150.00	300.00
21-24-Last Fine Black Condor	40.00	120.00	240.00
25,26	27.00	82.00	165.00
27-(1/43)-Intro & origin Captain Triumph by Alfred Andriola (Kerry Drake artist) & begin series	58.00	175.00	350.00
28-30	23.00	70.00	140.00
31-39: 31-Last Black Condor	13.00	40.00	80.00
40-46	10.00	30.00	60.00
47-57,59.60-Capt. Triumph by Crandall	10.00	30.00	65.00
58,61,62-Last Captain Triumph	8.35	25.00	50.00

NOTE: *Black Condor by* ***Fine****: No. 1, 2, 4-6, 8, 10-24; by* ***Sultan****: No. 3, 7; by* ***Fugitani****: No. 9.* ***Cole*** *a-34.* ***Crandall*** *a-61(unsigned); c-48, 49, 51-61.* ***Guardineer*** *a-17.* ***Gustavson*** *a-1, 17.* ***McWilliams*** *a-15-27.*

CRACKED (Magazine) (Satire) (Also see The 3-D Zone #19)
Feb-Mar, 1958 - Present
Major Magazines

	GD25	FN65	NM94
1-One pg. Williamson-a	11.00	32.00	75.00
2-1st Shut-Ups & Bonus Cut-Outs	5.00	15.00	30.00
3-6	3.60	9.00	18.00
7-10: 7-Reprints 1st 6 covers on-c	2.80	7.00	14.00
11-12, 13(nn,3/60), 14-17, 18(nn,2/61), 19,20	2.40	6.00	12.00
21-27(11/62), 27(No.28, 2/63; mis-#d), 29(5/63)	2.00	5.00	10.00
31-60	1.40	3.50	7.00
61-98,100	1.00	2.50	5.00
99-Alfred E. Neuman on-c	3.00	7.50	15.00
101-200: 234-Don Martin-a begins ($1.75 #? on)	.60	1.50	3.00
201-270	.40	1.00	2.00
Biggest...(Winter, 1977)	1.40	3.50	7.00
Biggest, Greatest...nn('65)	3.60	9.00	18.00
Biggest, Greatest...2('66) - #12('76)	1.80	4.50	9.00
...Blockbuster 1,2('88)	.55	1.60	2.75
...Digest 1(Fall, '86, 148 pgs.) - #5	.40	1.00	2.00
...Collectors' Edition 4 ('73; formerly ...Special)	1.40	3.50	7.00
5-70: 23-Ward-a	.60	1.50	3.00
71-84: 83-Elvis, Batman parodies	.70	1.75	3.50
...Party Pack 1,2('88)	.70	1.75	3.50
...Shut-Ups (2/72-'72; Cracked Spec. #3) 1,2	1.20	3.00	6.00
...Special 3('73; formerly Cracked Shut-Ups; ...Collectors' Edition#4 on)	1.20	3.00	6.00
Extra Special...1('76), 2('76)	.60	1.50	3.00
Giant...nn('65)	3.00	7.50	15.00
Giant...2('66)-12('76), nn(9/77)-48('87)	2.00	5.00	10.00
King Sized...1('67)	4.20	12.50	25.00
King Sized...2('68)-11('77)	3.00	7.50	15.00
King Sized...12-22 (Sum/'86)	.40	1.00	2.00
Super...1('68)	4.00	10.50	21.00
Super...2('69)-24('88)	3.00	7.50	15.00
Super...1('87, 100 pgs.)-Severin & Elder-a	.55	1.40	2.75

NOTE: ***Burgos*** *a-1-10.* ***Colan*** *a-257.* ***Davis*** *a-5, 11-17, 24, 40, 80; c-12-14, 16.* ***Elder*** *a-5, 6, 10-13; c-10.* ***Everett*** *a-1-10, 23-25, 61; c-1.* ***Heath*** *a-1-3, 6, 13, 14, 17, 110; c-6.* ***Jaffee*** *a-5, 6.* ***Don Martin*** *c-235, 244, 247, 259, 261, 264.* ***Morrow*** *a-8-10.* ***Reinman*** *a-1-4.* ***Severin*** *c/a-in most all issues.* ***Shores*** *a-3-7.* ***Torres*** *a-7-10.* ***Ward*** *a-22-24, 27, 35, 40, 143, 144, 149, 150, 152, 153, 156.* ***Williamson*** *a-1 (1 pg.).* ***Wolverton*** *a-10 (2 pgs.), Giant nn('65).* ***Wood*** *a-27, 35, 40. Alfred E. Neuman c-177, 200, 202. Batman c-234, 248, 249, 256. Captain America c-256. Christmas c-234, 243. Spider-Man c-260. Star Trek c-127, 169, 207, 228. Star Wars c-145, 146, 148, 149, 152, 155, 173, 174, 199. Superman c-183, 233. #144, 146 have free full-color pre-glued stickers. #145, 147, 155, 163 have free full-color postcards. #123, 137, 154, 157 have free iron-ons.*

CRACK WESTERN (Formerly Crack Comics; Jonesy No. 85 on)
No. 63, Nov, 1949 - No. 84, May, 1953 (36pgs., 63-68,74-on)
Quality Comics Group

63(#1)-Two-Gun Lil (origin & 1st app.)(ends #84), Arizona Ames, his horse

Thunder (with sidekick Spurs & his horse Calico), Frontier Marshal (ends #70), & Dead Canyon Days (ends #69) begin; Crandall-a 13.00 40.00 90.00
64,65-Crandall-a 11.00 32.00 75.00
66,68-Photo-c. 66-Arizona Ames becomes A. Raines (ends #84) 10.00 30.00 65.00
67-Randolph Scott photo-c; Crandall-a 11.00 32.00 75.00
69(52pgs.)-Crandall-a 10.00 30.00 65.00
70(52pgs.)-The Whip (origin & 1st app.) & his horse Diablo begin (ends #84); Crandall-a 10.00 30.00 65.00
71(52pgs.)-Frontier Marshal becomes Bob Allen F. Marshal (ends #84); Crandall-c/a 11.00 32.00 75.00
72(52pgs.)-Tim Holt photo-c 10.00 30.00 60.00
73(52pgs.)-Photo-c 6.70 20.00 40.00
74-76,78,79,81,83-Crandall-c. 83-Crandall-a(p) 8.35 25.00 50.00
77,80,82 5.00 15.00 30.00
84-Crandall-c/a 10.00 30.00 65.00
NOTE: ***Crandall** c-71p, 74-81, 83p(w/**Cuidera**-i).*

CRASH COMICS (Catman Comics No. 6 on)
May, 1940 - No. 5, Nov, 1940
Tem Publishing Co.

1-The Blue Streak, Strongman (origin), The Perfect Human, Shangra begin; Kirby-a 146.00 436.00 875.00
2-Simon & Kirby-a 75.00 225.00 450.00
3,5-Simon & Kirby-a 58.00 175.00 350.00
4-Origin & 1st app. The Catman; S&K-a 96.00 286.00 575.00
NOTE: *Solar Legion by **Kirby** No. 1-5 (5 pgs. each).*

CRASH DIVE (See Cinema Comics Herald)

CRASH RYAN (Also see Dark Horse Presents #44)
Oct, 1984 - No. 4, Jan, 1985 (Baxter paper, limited series)
Epic Comics (Marvel)

1-4 .30 .75 1.50

CRAZY (Also see This Magazine is Crazy)
Dec, 1953 - No. 7, July, 1954
Atlas Comics (CSI)

1-Everett-c/a 11.50 34.00 80.00
2 10.00 30.00 60.00
3-7: 4-I Love Lucy satire. 5-Satire on censorship 8.35 25.00 50.00
NOTE: ***Ayers** a-5. **Berg** a-1, 2. **Burgos** c-5, 6. **Drucker** a-6. **Everett** a-1-4. **Al Hartley** a-4. **Heath** a-3, 7; c-7. **Maneely** a-1-7, c-3, 4. **Post** a-3-6.*

CRAZY (Satire)
Feb, 1973 - No. 3, June, 1973
Marvel Comics Group

1-3-Not Brand Echh-r. 1-Beatles cameo (r) .50 1.00

CRAZY MAGAZINE (Satire)
Oct, 1973 - No. 94, Apr, 1983 (40-90 cents, B&W magazine)
(#1, 44pgs; #2-90, reg. issues, 52pgs; #92-95, 68pgs)'
Marvel Comics Group

1-Wolverton(1 pg.), Bode-a; 3 pg. photo story of Neal Adams & Dick Giordano .40 1.00 2.00
2-Kurtzman's "Hey Look" 2 pg. reprint .60 1.20
3-16: 8-Casper parody. 9-Has 1st 8-c on-c .50 1.00
17-29,31-36,38-41,43, 48,50,51,53,54,56,57,59.60,62,63,65,66,68,69,71,72, 74,75,77,78,80,81,83,84,86,87,89,90: 20-Superheroes song sheet. 41-Kiss-c. 43-E.C. swipe from Mad #131. 60,92-Star Trek parodies. 62-Kiss-c & 2 pg. story. 63-Obnoxio app. 69-Richie Rich. 80-X-men. 81-Wolverine/Hulk. 87-Obnoxio origin .50 1.00
30,37,42,49,52,55,61,64,67,70,73,76,85,88: Super Specials ($1.00) all 84pgs. 85-Flintstones. 88-X-Men .60 1.20
58-Super Special ($1.25); contains free Crazy #1 (2/73) comic reprint .60 1.25
79-Super Special ($1.25)-Full color looney labels .60 1.25
82-Super Special ($1.25); X-Men on-c .60 1.25

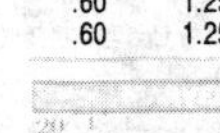

91-94: ($1.25) 91-Super Special; Black Knight by Maneely. 93-E.T.-c, & parody. 94-Avengers parody .60 1.25
Super Special 1(Summer, 1975, 100 pgs.)-Ploog, Neal Adams-r .35 .80 1.60
NOTE: ***N. Adams** a-2, 61r, 94p. **Austin** a-82i. **Buscema** a-2, 82. **Byrne** c-82p. **Nick Cardy** c-7, 8, 10, 12-16, Super Special 1. **Crandall** a-76r. **Ditko** a-68r, 79r, 82r. **Drucker** a-3. **Eisner** a-9-16. **Kelly Freas** c-1-6, 9, 11; a-7. **Ploog** a-1, 4, 7, 67r, 73r. **Rogers** a-82. **Sparling** a-92. **Wood** a-65r. Howard the Duck in 36, 50, 51, 53, 54, 59, 63, 65, 66, 68, 69, 71, 72, 74, 75, 77. Hulk in 46, c-42, 46, 57, 73. Star Wars in 32, 66; c-37.*

CRAZYMAN
Apr, 1992 - Present ($2.50, color, high quality paper)
Continuity Comics

1-($3.95, 52 pgs.)-Embossed-c; N. Adams part-i .80 2.00 4.00
2-5 ($2.50): 2-N. Adams/Bolland-c .50 1.25 2.50

CRAZY, MAN, CRAZY (Magazine) (Becomes This Magazine is...?)
V2#2, June, 1956
Humor Magazines (Charlton)

V2#2-Satire; Wolverton-a, 3 pgs. 8.35 25.00 50.00

CREATURE, THE (See Movie Classics)

CREATURES ON THE LOOSE (Formerly Tower of Shadows No. 1-9)
No. 10, March, 1971 - No. 37, Sept, 1975 (New-a & reprints)
Marvel Comics Group

10-First King Kull story; Wrightson-a; 15 cents 4.70 14.00 28.00
11-37: 16-Origin Warrior of Mars (begins? ends #21). 21,22-Steranko-c. 22-29-Thongor-c/stories. 30-Manwolf begins .60 1.50 3.00
NOTE: ***Crandall** a-13. **Ditko** r-15, 17, 18, 20, 22, 24, 27, 28. **Everett** a-16i(new). **Matt Fox** r-21i. **Howard** a-26i. **Gil Kane** a-16p, 17p; c-16, 20, 25, 29, 33p, 35p, 36p. **Kirby** r-16(2). **Morrow** a-20, 21. **Perez** a-33-37; c-34p. **Sinnott** r-21. **Tuska** a-31p, 32p.*

CREEPER, THE (See Beware... & 1st Issue Special)

CREEPY (Magazine)(See Warren Presents)
1964 - No. 145, Feb, 1983; No. 146, 1985 (B&W)
Warren Publishing Co./Harris Publ. #146

1-Frazetta-a; Jack Davis-c; 1st Warren all comics mag. 5.00 15.00 30.00
2 3.60 9.00 18.00
3-13: 10-Wrightson sketch; Brunner sketch (1st published work?) 1.80 4.50 9.00
14-Neal Adams 1st Warren work 2.40 6.00 12.00
15-25 1.40 3.50 7.00
26-40: 32-Harlan Ellison story 1.20 3.00 6.00
41-47,49-54,56-61: 61-Wertham parody 1.00 2.50 5.00
48,55,65-(1973, 1974, 1975 Annuals) 1.40 3.50 7.00
62-64,66-145: 113-All Wrightson-r issue. 139-All Toth-r issue. 144-Giant, $2.25; Frazetta-c 1.00 2.50 5.00
146 ($2.95) 1.40 3.50 7.00
Year Book 1968, 1969 1.40 3.50 7.00
Year Book 1970-Neal Adams, Ditko-a(r) 1.40 3.50 7.00
Annual 1971,1972 1.40 3.50 7.00
NOTE: *All issues contain many good artists works: **Neal Adams, Brunner, Corben, Craig (Taycee), Crandall, Ditko, Evans, Frazetta, Heath, Jeff Jones, Krenkel, McWilliams, Morrow, Nino, Orlando, Ploog, Severin, Torres, Toth, Williamson, Wood, & Wrightson**; covers by **Crandall, Davis, Frazetta, Morrow, San Julian, Todd/Bode**; Otto Binder's "Adam Link" stories in No. 2, 4, 6, 8, 9, 12, 13, 15 with **Orlando** art. **Frazetta** c-2-7, 9-11, 15-17, 27, 32, 83r, 89r. **E.A. Poe** adaptations in 66, 69, 70.*

CREEPY THINGS
July, 1975 - No. 6, June, 1976
Charlton Comics

1 .30 .75 1.50
2-6: Ditko-a in 3,5. Sutton c-3,4 .50 1.00
Modern Comics Reprint 2-6(1977) .50 1.00

CRIME AND JUSTICE (Rookie Cop? No. 27 on)
March, 1951 - No. 26, Sept, 1955
Capitol Stories/Charlton Comics

Crack Western #69, © QUA

Crazy #1(2/73), © MEG

Creepy #1, © WP

Crime and Justice #18, © CC

Crime and Punishment #8, © LEV

Crime Does Not Pay #27, © LEV

	GD25	FN65	NM94
1	14.00	43.00	100.00
2	4.20	12.50	25.00
3-8,10-13: 6-Negligee panels	4.00	11.00	22.00
9-Classic story "Comics Vs. Crime"	10.00	30.00	60.00
14-Color illos in **POP**; gory story of man who beheads women	6.35	19.00	38.00
15-17,19-26	3.20	8.00	16.00
18-Ditko-a	11.00	32.00	75.00

NOTE: ***Alascia*** *c-20.* ***Ayers*** *a-17.* ***Shuster*** *a-19-21; c-19. Bondage c-11, 12.*

CRIME AND PUNISHMENT (Title inspired by 1935 film)
April, 1948 - No. 74, Aug, 1955
Lev Gleason Publications

	GD25	FN65	NM94
1-Mr. Crime app. on-c	11.50	34.00	80.00
2	5.85	17.50	35.00
3-Used in **SOTI**, pg. 112; injury-to-eye panel; Fuje-a	7.00	21.00	42.00
4,5	4.70	14.00	28.00
6-10	4.00	11.00	22.00
11-20	4.00	10.00	20.00
21-30	3.20	8.00	16.00
31-38,40-44,46: 46-One page Frazetta-a	2.80	7.00	14.00
39-Drug mention story "The 5 Dopes"	4.20	12.50	25.00
45-"Hophead Killer" drug story	4.20	12.50	25.00
47-58,60-65,70-74: 58-Used in **POP**, pg. 79	2.40	6.00	12.00
59-Used in **SOTI**, illo-"What comic-book America stands for"	12.00	36.00	85.00
66-Toth-c/a(4); 3-D effect issue(3/54); 1st "Deep Dimension" process	18.00	54.00	125.00
67-"Monkey on His Back"-heroin story; 3-D effect issue	14.00	43.00	100.00
68-3-D effect issue; Toth-c (7/54)	12.00	36.00	85.00
69-"The Hot Rod Gang"-dope crazy kids	4.35	13.00	26.00

NOTE: ***Biro*** *c-most.* ***Everett*** *a-31.* ***Fuje*** *a-3, 4, 12, 13, 17, 18, 20, 26, 27.* ***Guardineer*** *a-2-4, 10, 14, 17, 18, 20, 26-28, 32, 38-44.* ***Kinstler*** *c-69.* ***McWilliams*** *a-41, 48, 49.* ***Tuska*** *a-28, 30, 51, 64, 70.*

CRIME AND PUNISHMENT: MARSHALL LAW TAKES MANHATTAN
1989 ($4.95, color, 52 pgs., direct sale only, mature readers)
Epic Comics (Marvel)

	GD25	FN65	NM94
nn-Graphic album featuring Marshall Law	1.00	2.50	5.00

CRIME CAN'T WIN (Formerly Cindy Smith)
No. 41, 9/50 - No. 43, 2/51; No. 4, 4/51 - No. 12, 9/53
Marvel/Atlas Comics (TCI 41/CCC 42,43,4-12)

	GD25	FN65	NM94
41(#1)	10.00	30.00	70.00
42(#2)	5.85	17.50	35.00
43(#3)-Horror story	7.00	21.00	42.00
4(4/51),5-12: 10-Possible use in **SOTI**, pg. 161	4.70	14.00	28.00

NOTE: ***Robinson*** *a-9-11.* ***Tuska*** *a-43.*

CRIME CASES COMICS (Formerly Willie Comics)
No. 24, 8/50 - No. 27, 3/51; No. 5, 5/51 - No. 12, 7/52
Marvel/Atlas Comics(CnPC No.24-8/MJMC No.9-12)

	GD25	FN65	NM94
24 (#1, 52 pgs.)	7.00	21.00	42.00
25-27(#2-4): 27-Morisi-a	4.35	13.00	26.00
5-12: 11-Robinson-a, 12-Tuska-a	4.00	11.00	22.00

CRIME CLINIC
No. 10, July-Aug, 1951 - No. 5, Summer, 1952
Ziff-Davis Publishing Co.

	GD25	FN65	NM94
10(#1)-Painted-c; origin Dr. Tom Rogers	11.50	34.00	80.00
11,3-5: 3-Used in **SOTI**, pg. 18. 4,5-Painted-c	9.15	27.50	55.00

NOTE: *Painted covers by* ***Saunders.*** ***Starr*** *a-10.*

CRIME DETECTIVE COMICS
Mar-Apr, 1948 - V3#8, May-June, 1953
Hillman Periodicals

	GD25	FN65	NM94
V1#1-The Invisible 6, costumed villains app; Fuje-c	11.00	32.00	75.00
2	4.70	14.00	28.00
3,4,6,7,10-12: 6-McWilliams-a	4.00	12.00	24.00
5-Krigstein-a	5.35	16.00	32.00
8-Kirbyish-a by McCann	4.00	12.00	24.00
9-Used in **SOTI**, pg. 16 & "Caricature of the author in a position comic book publishers wish he were in permanently" illo.	14.00	43.00	100.00
V2#1,4,7-Krigstein-a	4.35	13.00	26.00
2,3,5,6,8-12 (1-2/52)	3.60	9.00	18.00
V3#1-Drug use-c	3.60	9.00	18.00
2-8	3.20	8.00	16.00

NOTE: ***Briefer*** *a-V3#1.* ***Kinstlerish****-a by* ***McCann****-V2#7, V3#2.* ***Powell*** *a-11.*

CRIME DETECTOR
Jan, 1954 - No. 5, Sept, 1954
Timor Publications

	GD25	FN65	NM94
1	9.15	27.50	55.00
2	4.70	14.00	28.00
3,4	4.00	11.00	22.00
5-Disbrow-a (classic)	10.00	30.00	60.00

CRIME DOES NOT PAY (Formerly Silver Streak Comics No. 1-21)
No. 22, June, 1942 - No. 147, July, 1955 (1st crime comic)
Comic House/Lev Gleason/Golfing (Title inspired by film)

	GD25	FN65	NM94
22(23 on cover, 22 on indicia)-Origin The War Eagle & only app.; Chip Gardner begins; #22 was rebound in Complete Book of True Crime (Scarce)	125.00	375.00	750.00
23 (Scarce)	67.00	200.00	400.00
24-Intro. & 1st app. Mr. Crime (Scarce)	58.00	175.00	350.00
25-30	33.00	100.00	200.00
31-40	17.50	52.00	105.00
41-Origin & 1st app. Officer Common Sense	13.00	40.00	80.00
42-Electrocution-c	15.00	45.00	90.00
43-46,48-50: 44,45,50 are 68 pg. issues	10.00	30.00	60.00
47-Electric chair-c	15.00	45.00	90.00
51-70: 63,64-Possible use in **SOTI**, pg. 306. #63-Contains Biro & Gleason's self censorship code of 12 listed restrictions (5/48)	7.00	21.00	42.00
71-99: 87-Chip Gardner begins, ends #99	5.00	15.00	30.00
100	5.85	17.50	35.00
101-105,107-110: 102-Chip Gardner app. 105-Used in **POP**, pg. 84	4.00	10.00	20.00
106,114-Frazetta-a, 1 pg.	4.00	10.00	20.00
111-Used in **POP**, pgs. 80 & 81; injury-to-eye story illo	4.00	10.00	20.00
112,113,115-130	3.00	7.50	15.00
131-140	2.40	6.00	12.00
141,142-Last pre-code issue; Kubert-a(1)	4.00	12.00	24.00
143,147-Kubert-a, one story each	4.00	12.00	24.00
144-146	2.40	6.00	12.00
1(Golfing-1945)	3.20	8.00	16.00
The Best of...(1944, 128 pgs.)-Series contains 4 rebound issues	50.00	150.00	350.00
...1945 issue	39.00	118.00	275.00
...1946-48 issues	29.00	85.00	200.00
...1949-50 issues	24.00	70.00	165.00
...1951-53 issues	22.00	65.00	150.00

NOTE: *Many issues contain violent covers and stories. Who Dunnit by* ***Guardineer****-39-42, 44-105, 108-110; Chip Gardner by* ***Bob Fujitani (Fuje)****-88-103.* ***Alderman*** *a-29, 41-44, 49.* ***Dan Barry*** *a-75.* ***Biro*** *c-1-76, 122, 142.* ***Briefer*** *a-29(2), 30, 31, 33, 37, 39.* ***G. Colan*** *a-105.* ***Fuje*** *c-88, 89, 91-94, 96, 98, 99, 102, 103.* ***Guardineer*** *a-57, 71.* ***Kubert*** *c-143.* ***Landau*** *a-118.* ***Maurer*** *a-29, 39, 41, 42.* ***McWilliams*** *a-91, 93, 95, 100-103.* ***Palais*** *a-30, 33, 37, 39, 41-43, 44(2), 46, 49.* ***Powell*** *a-146, 147.* ***Tuska*** *a-48, 50(2), 51, 52, 56, 57(2), 60-64, 66, 67, 71. Painted c-87-102. Bondage c-43, 62, 98.*

CRIME EXPOSED
June, 1948; Dec, 1950 - No. 14, June, 1952
Marvel Comics (PPI)/Marvel Atlas Comics (PrPI)

	GD25	FN65	NM94
1(6/48)	13.00	40.00	90.00
1(12/50)	9.15	27.50	55.00
2	5.85	17.50	35.00
3-11,14: 10-Used in **POP**, pg. 81	4.20	12.50	25.00
12-Krigstein & Robinson-a	4.70	14.00	28.00
13-Used in **POP**, pg. 81; Krigstein-a	5.35	16.00	32.00

NOTE: ***Maneely** c-8. **Robinson** a-11, 12. **Tuska** a-3, 4.*

CRIMEFIGHTERS
April, 1948 - No. 10, Nov, 1949
Marvel Comics (CmPS 1-3/CCC 4-10)

	GD25	FN65	NM94
1-Some copies are undated & could be reprints	11.00	32.00	75.00
2,3: 3-Morphine addict story	5.85	17.50	35.00
4-10: 6-Anti-Wertham editorial. 9,10-Photo-c	4.70	14.00	28.00

CRIME FIGHTERS (...Always Win)
No. 11, Sept, 1954 - No. 13, Jan, 1955
Atlas Comics (CnPC)

	GD25	FN65	NM94
11,12: 11-Maneely-a	5.35	16.00	32.00
13-Pakula, Reinman, Severin-a	5.85	17.50	35.00

CRIME FIGHTING DETECTIVE (Shock Detective Cases No. 20 on; formerly Criminals on the Run)
No. 11, Apr-May, 1950 - No. 19, June, 1952
Star Publications

	GD25	FN65	NM94
11-L. B. Cole-c/a (2 pgs.)	5.85	17.50	35.00
12,13,15-19: 17-Young King Cole & Dr. Doom app.; L. B. Cole-c on all	4.20	12.50	25.00
14-L. B. Cole-c/a, r/Law-Crime #2	5.35	16.00	32.00

CRIME FILES
No. 5, Sept, 1952 - No. 6, Nov, 1952
Standard Comics

	GD25	FN65	NM94
5-Alex Toth-a; used in **SOTI**, pg. 4 (text)	13.00	40.00	90.00
6-Sekowsky-a	7.50	22.50	45.00

CRIME ILLUSTRATED (Magazine, 25 cents)
Nov-Dec, 1955 - No. 2, Spring, 1956 (Adult Suspense Stories on-c)
E. C. Comics

	GD25	FN65	NM94
1-Ingels & Crandall-a	9.15	27.50	55.00
2-Ingels & Crandall-a	7.50	22.50	45.00

NOTE: ***Craig** a-2. **Crandall** a-1, 2; c-2. **Evans** a-1. **Davis** a-2. **Ingels** a-1, 2. **Krigstein/Crandall** a-1. **Orlando** a-1, 2; c-1.*

CRIME INCORPORATED (Formerly Crimes Incorporated)
No. 2, Aug, 1950; No. 3, Aug, 1951
Fox Features Syndicate

	GD25	FN65	NM94
2	11.00	32.00	75.00
3(1951)-Hollingsworth-a	9.15	27.50	55.00

CRIME MACHINE (Magazine)
Feb, 1971 - No. 2, May, 1971 (B&W)
Skywald Publications

	GD25	FN65	NM94
1-Kubert-a(2)(r)(Avon)	3.00	7.50	15.00
2-Torres, Wildey-a; violent-c/a	2.40	6.00	12.00

CRIME MUST LOSE! (Formerly Sports Action?)
No. 4, Oct, 1950 - No. 12, April, 1952
Sports Action (Atlas Comics)

	GD25	FN65	NM94
4-Ann Brewster-a in all; c-used in N.Y. Legis. Comm. documents	9.15	27.50	55.00
5-12: 9-Robinson-a. 11-Used in **POP**, pg. 89	4.70	14.00	28.00

CRIME MUST PAY THE PENALTY (Formerly Four Favorites; Penalty No. 47, 48)
No. 33, Feb, 1948; No. 2, June, 1948 - No. 48, Jan, 1956
Ace Magazines (Current Books)

	GD25	FN65	NM94
33(#1, 2/48)-Becomes Four Teeners #34?	13.00	40.00	90.00
2(6/48)-Extreme violence; Palais-a?	10.00	30.00	60.00
3-"Frisco Mary" story used in Senate Investigation report, pg. 7	5.35	16.00	32.00
4,8-Transvestism stories	7.00	21.00	42.00
5-7,9,10	4.00	12.00	24.00
11-20	3.60	9.00	18.00
21-32,34-40,42-48	3.20	8.00	16.00
33(7/53)-"Dell Fabry-Junk King"-drug story; mentioned in Love and Death	4.70	14.00	28.00
41-Drug story-"Dealers in White Death"	4.70	14.00	28.00

NOTE: ***Cameron** a-29-31, 34, 35, 39-41. **Colan** a-20, 31. **Kremer** a-3, 37r. **Larsen** a-32. **Palais** a-5?,37.*

CRIME MUST STOP
October, 1952 (52 pgs.)
Hillman Periodicals

	GD25	FN65	NM94
V1#1(Scarce)-Similar to Monster Crime; Mort Lawrence, Krigstein-a	32.00	95.00	225.00

CRIME MYSTERIES (Secret Mysteries No. 16 on; combined with Crime Smashers No. 7 on)
May, 1952 - No. 15, Sept, 1954
Ribage Publishing Corp. (Trojan Magazines)

	GD25	FN65	NM94
1-Transvestism story	24.00	70.00	165.00
2-Marijuana story (7/52)	14.00	43.00	100.00
3-One pg. Frazetta-a	11.50	34.00	80.00
4-Cover shows girl in bondage having her blood drained; 1 pg. Frazetta-a	22.00	65.00	150.00
5-10	10.00	30.00	70.00
11,12,14	10.00	30.00	60.00
13-(5/54)-Angelo Torres 1st comic work (inks over Check's pencils); Check-a	12.00	36.00	85.00
15-Acid in face-c	14.00	43.00	100.00

NOTE: ***Fass** a-13; c-4, 10. **Hollingsworth** a-10-13, 15; c-2, 12, 13, 15. **Kiefer** a-4. **Woodbridge** a-13? Bondage-c-1, 8, 12.*

CRIME ON THE RUN (See Approved Comics #8)

CRIME ON THE WATERFRONT (Formerly Famous Gangsters)
No. 4, May, 1952 (Painted cover)
Realistic Publications

	GD25	FN65	NM94
4	14.00	43.00	100.00

CRIME PATROL (Formerly International #1-5; International Crime Patrol #6; becomes Crypt of Terror #17 on)
No. 7, Summer, 1948 - No. 16, Feb-Mar, 1950
E. C. Comics

	GD25	FN65	NM94
7-Intro. Captain Crime	40.00	120.00	280.00
8-14: 12-Ingels-a	36.00	107.00	250.00
15-Intro. of Crypt Keeper (inspired by Witches Tales radio show) & Crypt of Terror; used by N.Y. Legis. Comm.-last pg. Feldstein-a	129.00	385.00	900.00
16-2nd Crypt Keeper app.	93.00	280.00	650.00

NOTE: ***Craig** c/a in most issues. **Feldstein** a-9-16. **Kiefer** a-8, 10, 11. **Moldoff** a-7. **Roussos** a-16.*

CRIME PHOTOGRAPHER (See Casey...)

CRIME REPORTER
Aug, 1948 - No. 3, Dec, 1948 (Shows Oct.)
St. John Publ. Co.

	GD25	FN65	NM94
1-Drug club story	22.00	65.00	150.00
2-Used in **SOTI**: illo-"Children told me what the man was going to do with the red-hot poker;" r/Dynamic #17 with editing; Baker-c; Tuska-a	37.00	110.00	260.00
3-Baker-c; Tuska-a	17.00	50.00	115.00

CRIMES BY WOMEN

Crime Fighters #7, © MEG

Crime Must Stop V1/#1, © HILL

Crime Reporter #1, © STJ

Crimes By Women #4, © FOX

Crime SuspenStories #2, © WMG

Criminals On The Run V5/#1, © NOVP

	GD25	FN65	NM94

June, 1948 - No. 15, Aug, 1951; 1954
Fox Features Syndicate

1	57.00	170.00	400.00
2,3: 3-Used in **SOTI**, pg. 234	30.00	90.00	210.00
4,5,7-9,11-15: 8-Used in **POP**. 14-Spanking scene	27.00	81.00	190.00
6-Classic girl fight-c; acid-in-face panel	31.00	92.00	215.00
10-Used in **SOTI**, pg. 72	27.00	81.00	190.00
54(M.S. Publ.-'54)-Reprint; (formerly My Love Secret)	11.50	34.00	80.00

CRIMES INCORPORATED (Formerly My Past)
No. 12, June, 1950 (Crime Incorporated No. 2 on)
Fox Features Syndicate

12	7.00	21.00	42.00

CRIMES INCORPORATED (See Fox Giants)

CRIME SMASHER
Summer, 1948 (One Shot)
Fawcett Publications

1-Formerly Spy Smasher; see Whiz #76	24.00	72.00	165.00

CRIME SMASHERS (Becomes Secret Mysteries No. 16 on)
Oct, 1950 - No. 15, Mar, 1953
Ribage Publishing Corp.(Trojan Magazines)

1-Used in **SOTI**, pg. 19,20, & illo-"A girl raped and murdered;" Sally the Sleuth begins	36.00	107.00	250.00
2-Kubert-c	17.00	52.00	120.00
3,4	13.00	40.00	90.00
5-Wood-a	20.00	60.00	140.00
6,8-11	11.00	32.00	75.00
7-Female heroin junkie story	11.50	34.00	80.00
12-Injury to eye panel; 1 pg. Frazetta-a	12.00	36.00	85.00
13-Used in **POP**, pgs. 79,80; 1 pg. Frazetta-a	11.00	32.00	75.00
14,15	11.00	32.00	75.00

NOTE: ***Hollingsworth** a-14. **Kiefer** a-15. Bondage c-7, 9.*

CRIME SUSPENSTORIES (Formerly Vault of Horror No. 12-14)
No. 15, Oct-Nov, 1950 - No. 27, Feb-Mar, 1955
E. C. Comics

15-Identical to #1 in content: #1 printed on outside front cover. #15 (formerly "The Vault of Horror") printed and blackened out on inside front cover with Vol. 1, No. 1 printed over it. Evidently, several of No. 15 were printed before a decision was made not to drop the Vault of Horror and Haunt of Fear series. The print run was stopped on No. 15 and continued on No. 1. All of No. 15 were changed as described above.	96.00	290.00	675.00
1	72.00	215.00	500.00
2	43.00	130.00	300.00
3-5	29.00	85.00	200.00
6-10	23.00	70.00	160.00
11,12,14,15: 15-The Old Witch guest stars	17.00	50.00	115.00
13,16-Williamson-a	19.00	58.00	135.00
17-Williamson/Frazetta-a (6 pgs.)	22.00	65.00	150.00
18,19: 19-Used in **SOTI**, pg. 235	14.00	43.00	100.00
20-Cover used in **SOTI**, illo-"Cover of a children's comic book"	18.00	54.00	125.00
21,24-27: 24-"Food For Thought" similar to "Cave In" in Amazing Detective Cases #13 (1952)	10.00	30.00	70.00
22,23-Used in Senate investigation on juvenile delinquency. 22-Ax decapitation-c	14.00	43.00	100.00

NOTE: ***Craig** a-1-21; c-1-18, 20-22. **Crandall** a-18-26. **Davis** a-4, 5, 7, 9-12, 20. **Elder** a-17,18. **Evans** a-15, 19, 21, 23, 25, 27; c-23, 24. **Feldstein** c-19. **Ingels** a-1-12, 14, 15, 27.**Kamen** a-2, 4-18, 20-27; c-25-27. **Krigstein** a-22, 24, 25, 27. **Kurtzman** a-1, 3. **Orlando** a-16, 22, 24, 26. **Wood** a-1, 3. Issues No. 11-15 have E. C. "quickie" stories. No. 25 contains the famous "Are You a Red Dupe?" editorial. Ray Bradbury adaptations-15, 17.*

CRIME SUSPENSTORIES
Nov, 1992 - Present ($1.50, color)
Russ Cochran

1,2-r/Crime SuspenStories #1,2	.30	.75	1.50

CRIMINALS ON THE RUN (Formerly Young King Cole)
(Crime Fighting Detective No. 11 on)
V4#1, Aug-Sept, 1948 - #10, Dec-Jan, 1949-50
Premium Group (Novelty Press)

V4#1-Young King Cole continues	10.00	30.00	65.00
2-6: 6-Dr. Doom app.	8.35	25.00	50.00
7-Classic "Fish in the Face" cover by L. B. Cole	17.00	52.00	120.00
V5#1,2 (#8,9): 9-L. B. Cole-c	8.35	25.00	50.00
10-L. B. Cole-c	8.35	25.00	50.00

NOTE: *Most issues have **L. B. Cole** covers. **McWilliams** a-V4#6, 7, V5#2; c-V4#5.*

CRIMSON AVENGER, THE (See Detective Comics #20 for 1st app.)
(Also see Leading Comics #1 & World's Best/Finest Comics)
June, 1988 - No. 4, Sept, 1988 ($1.00, color, limited series)
DC Comics

1-4		.50	1.00

CRISIS ON INFINITE EARTHS (Also see Official...Index)
Apr, 1985 - No. 12, Mar, 1986 (12 issue maxi-series)
DC Comics

1-1st DC app. Blue Beetle & Detective Karp from Charlton; Perez-c on all	1.00	2.50	5.00
2-6: 6-Intro Charlton's Capt. Atom, Nightshade, Question, Judomaster, Peacemaker & Thunderbolt	.60	1.50	3.00
7-Double size; death of Supergirl	1.00	2.50	5.00
8-Death of Flash	1.20	3.00	6.00
9-11: 9-Intro. Charlton's Ghost. 10-Intro. Charlton's Banshee, Dr. Spectro, Image, Punch & Jewellee	.50	1.25	2.50
12-(52 pgs.)-Deaths of Dove, Kole, Lori Lemaris, Sunburst, G.A. Robin & Huntress; Kid Flash becomes new Flash	1.00	2.50	5.00

CRITICAL ERROR (Dark Horse) (Value: cover or less)

CRITICAL MASS (See A Shadowline Saga: Critical Mass)

CRITTERS (Also see Usagi Yojimbo Summer Special)
1986 - No. 50, 1990 ($1.70/$2.00, B&W)
Fantagraphics Books

1-Cutey Bunny, Usagi Yojimbo app.	.80	2.00	4.00
2-11: 3,10,11-Usagi Yojimbo app. 11-Christmas Special (68 pgs.); Usagi Yojimbo	.40	1.00	2.00
12-22,24-49: 14,38-Usagi Yojimbo app. 22-Watchmen parody; two diff. covers exist	.35	.85	1.70
23-With Alan Moore Flexi-disc ($3.95)	.80	2.00	4.00
50 ($4.95, 84 pgs.)-Neil the Horse, Capt. Jack, Sam & Max & Usagi Yojimbo app.; Quagmire, Shaw-a	1.00	2.50	5.00
Special 1 (1/88, $2.00)	.40	1.00	2.00

CROMWELL STONE (Dark Horse) (Value: cover or less)

CROSLEY'S HOUSE OF FUN (Also see Tee and Vee Crosley...)
1950 (32 pgs.; full color; paper cover)
Crosley Div. AVCO Mfg. Corp. (Giveaway)

nn-Strips revolve around Crosley appliances	3.60	9.00	18.00

CROSS AND THE SWITCHBLADE, THE (Spire Christian) (Value: cover or less)

CROSSFIRE (Spire Christian) (Value: cover or less)

CROSSFIRE (Eclipse) (Value: cover or less)

CROSSFIRE AND RAINBOW (Eclipse) (Value: cover or less)

CROSSING THE ROCKIES (See Classics Illustrated Special Issue)

CROSSROADS (First) (Value: cover or less)

CROW, THE (Also see Caliber Presents)
Feb, 1989 - No. 4, 1989 ($1.95, B&W, mini-series)

Caliber Press

	GD25	FN65	NM94
1	4.20	12.50	25.00
1-3-2nd printings	.40	1.00	2.00
2,4	2.40	6.00	12.00
2-3rd printing	.40	1.00	2.00
3-(Scarcer)	3.20	8.00	16.00

CROW, THE (Tundra)(Value: cover or less)

CROWN COMICS
Winter, 1944-45 - No. 19, July, 1949
Golfing/McCombs Publ.

	GD25	FN65	NM94
1-"The Oblong Box" E.A. Poe adaptation	20.00	60.00	140.00
2,3-Baker-a	11.00	32.00	75.00
4-6-Baker-c/a; Voodah app. #4,5	11.50	34.00	80.00
7-Feldstein, Baker, Kamen-a; Baker-c	11.00	32.00	75.00
8-Baker-a; Voodah app.	10.00	30.00	70.00
9-11,13-19: Voodah in #10-19	5.85	17.50	35.00
12-Feldstein?, Starr-a	7.00	21.00	42.00

NOTE: ***Bolle** a-11, 13-16, 18, 19; c-11p, 15. **Powell** a-19. **Starr** a-11-13; c-11i.*

CRUSADER FROM MARS (See Tops in Adventure)
Jan-Mar, 1952 - No. 2, Fall, 1952
Ziff-Davis Publ. Co.

	GD25	FN65	NM94
1	41.00	122.00	285.00
2-Bondage-c	32.00	96.00	225.00

CRUSADER RABBIT (See 4-Color No. 735,805)

CRUSADERS, THE (Chick)(Value: cover or less)

CRUSADERS (Southern Knights No. 2 on)
1982 (Magazine size, B&W)
Guild Publications

	GD25	FN65	NM94
1-1st app. Southern Knights	1.00	2.50	5.00

CRUSADERS, THE (Also see Black Hood, The Jaguar, The Comet, The Fly, Legend of the Shield, The Mighty... & The Webb)
May, 1992 - No. 8, Dec, 1992 ($1.00/$1.25, color)
Impact Comics (DC Comics)

	GD25	FN65	NM94
1-Contains 3 Impact trading cards		.60	1.25
2-8		.50	1.00

CRY FOR DAWN
1989-Present ($2.25-c, B&W, mature readers)
Cry For Dawn Pub.

	GD25	FN65	NM94
1	5.85	17.50	35.00
1-2nd, 3rd printing	.60	1.50	3.00
2	3.00	7.50	15.00
2-2nd printing	.45	1.15	2.25
3	1.60	4.00	8.00
4-9	.50	1.25	2.50

CRYING FREEMAN (Viz)(Value: cover or less)

CRYIN' LION COMICS
Fall, 1944 - No. 3, Spring, 1945
William H. Wise Co.

	GD25	FN65	NM94
1-Funny animal	10.00	30.00	65.00
2,3	6.35	19.00	38.00

CRYPT OF SHADOWS
Jan, 1973 - No. 21, Nov, 1975 (#1 & 2 are 20 cents)
Marvel Comics Group

	GD25	FN65	NM94
1-Wolverton-r/Advs. Into Terror #7	.80	2.00	4.00
2-21: 2-Starlin/Everett-c	.40	1.00	2.00

NOTE: ***Briefer** a-2r. **Ditko** a-13r, 18-20r. **Everett** a-6, 14r; c-2i. **Heath** a-1r. **Mort Lawrence** a-1r, 8r. **Maneely** a-2r. **Moldoff** a-8. **Powell** a-12r, 14r.*

CRYPT OF TERROR (Formerly Crime Patrol; becomes Tales From the Crypt No. 20 on.
No. 17, Apr-May, 1950 - No. 19, Aug-Sept, 1950
E. C. Comics

	GD25	FN65	NM94
17-1st New Trend to hit stands	171.00	515.00	1200.00
18,19	115.00	342.00	800.00

NOTE: ***Craig** c/a-17-19. **Feldstein** a-17-19. **Ingels** a-19. **Kurtzman** a-18. **Wood** a-18. Canadian reprints known; see Table of Contents.*

CUPID
Dec, 1949 - No. 2, Mar, 1950
Marvel Comics (U.S.A.)

	GD25	FN65	NM94
1-Photo-c	8.35	25.00	50.00
2-Betty Page ('50s pin-up queen) photo-c; Powell-a (see My Love #4)	30.00	40.00	90.00

CURIO
1930's(?) (Tabloid size, 16-20 pages)
Harry 'A' Chesler

	GD25	FN65	NM94
nn	11.00	32.00	75.00

CURLY KAYOE COMICS (Boxing)
1946 - No. 8, 1950; Jan, 1958
United Features Syndicate/Dell Publ. Co.

	GD25	FN65	NM94
1 (1946)-Strip-r (Fritzi Ritz); biography of Sam Leff, Kayoe's artist	10.00	30.00	65.00
2	5.35	16.00	32.00
3-8	4.00	11.00	22.00
United Presents...(Fall, 1948)	4.00	11.00	22.00
4-Color 871 (Dell, 1/58)	3.60	9.00	18.00

CUSTER'S LAST FIGHT
1950
Avon Periodicals

	GD25	FN65	NM94
nn-Partial reprint of Cowpuncher #1	11.00	32.00	75.00

CUTEY BUNNY (See Army Surplus Komikz Featuring...)

CUTIE PIE
May, 1955 - No. 3, Dec, 1955; No. 4, Feb, 1956; No. 5, Aug, 1956
Junior Reader's Guild (Lev Gleason)

	GD25	FN65	NM94
1	4.00	10.00	20.00
2-5: 4-Misdated 2/55	2.40	6.00	12.00

CYBER CRUSH (Fleetway/Quality)(Value: cover or less)

CYBERFORCE
Oct, 1992 - No. 4, 1993 ($1.95, color, mini-series)
Image Comics

	GD25	FN65	NM94
1-4: Silvestri-c/a. 1-Coupon for Image Comics #0	.40	1.00	2.00

CYBERPUNK (Innovation)(Value: cover or less)

CYBERPUNK: THE SERAPHIM FILES (Innovation)(Value: cover or less)

CYBERRAD
1991 - No. 7, 1992 ($2.00, color)(Direct sale & newsstand-c variations)
V2#1 - Present ($2.00, color)
Continuity Comics

	GD25	FN65	NM94
1-7: 5-Glow-in-the-dark-c by N. Adams (direct sale only). 6-Contains 4 pg. fold-out poster; N. Adams layouts	.40	1.00	2.00
V2#1-($2.95, direct sale ed.)-Die-cut-c w/B&W hologram on-c; Neal Adams sketches	.60	1.50	3.00
V2#1-($2.50, newsstand ed.)-Without sketches	.50	1.25	2.50
V2#2-5: 2-N. Adams-c	.40	1.00	2.00

CYBER 7 (Eclipse)(Value: cover or less)

CYCLONE COMICS (Also see Whirlwind Comics)
June, 1940 - No. 5, Nov, 1940
Bilbara Publishing Co.

	GD25	FN65	NM94
1-Origin Tornado Tom; Volton begins, Mister Q app.	63.00	186.00	375.00
2	33.00	100.00	200.00
3-5: 4,5-Mr. Q app.	27.00	82.00	165.00

The Crow #1, © Jim O'Barr

Crypt of Terror #18, © WMG

Cutie Pie #1, © LEV

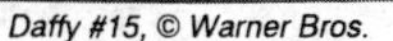
Daffy #15, © Warner Bros.

Dagar #14, © FOX

Daisy Handbook #2, © Daisy

CYNTHIA DOYLE, NURSE IN LOVE (Formerly Sweetheart Diary)
No. 66, Oct, 1962 - No. 74, Feb, 1964
Charlton Publications

	GD25	FN65	NM94
66-74	.80	2.00	4.00

DAFFY (Daffy Duck No. 18 on)(See Looney Tunes)
#457, 3/53 - #30, 7-9/62; #31, 10-12/62 - #145, 1983 (No #132,133)
Dell Publishing Co./Gold Key No. 31-127/Whitman No. 128 on

	GD25	FN65	NM94
4-Color 457(#1)-Elmer Fudd x-overs begin	7.50	22.50	45.00
4-Color 536,615('55)	4.00	11.00	22.00
4(1-3/56)-11('57)	2.80	7.00	14.00
12-19(1958-59)	2.00	5.00	10.00
20-40(1960-64)	1.20	3.00	6.00
41-60(1964-68)	.70	1.75	3.50
61-90(1969-74)-Road Runner in most	.50	1.25	2.50
91-131,134-145(1974-83)	.30	.75	1.50
Mini-Comic 1 (1976; 3-1/4x6-1/2")		.50	1.00

NOTE: *Reprint issues-No.41-46, 48, 50, 53-55, 58, 59, 65, 67, 69, 73, 81, 96, 103-108; 136-142, 144, 145(1/3-2/3-r). (See March of Comics No. 277, 288, 303, 313, 331, 347, 357,375, 387, 397, 402, 413, 425, 437, 460).*

DAFFYDILS
1911 (52 pgs.; 6x8"; B&W; hardcover)
Cupples & Leon Co.

	GD25	FN65	NM94
nn-By Tad	15.00	45.00	90.00

DAFFY TUNES COMICS
June, 1947; No. 12, Aug, 1947
Four-Star Publications

	GD25	FN65	NM94
nn	5.35	16.00	32.00
12-Al Fago-c/a	4.70	14.00	28.00

DAGAR, DESERT HAWK (Captain Kidd No. 24 on; formerly All Great)
No. 14, Feb, 1948 - No. 23, Apr, 1949 (No #17,18)
Fox Features Syndicate

	GD25	FN65	NM94
14-Tangi & Safari Cary begin; Edmond Good bondage-c/a	32.00	95.00	225.00
15,16-E. Good-a; 15-Bondage-c	19.00	58.00	135.00
19,20,22: 19-Used in SOTI, pg. 180 (Tangi)	17.00	52.00	120.00
21-'Bombs & Bums Away' panel in 'Flood of Death' story used in **SOTI**	22.00	65.00	150.00
23-Bondage-c	19.00	58.00	135.00

NOTE: *Tangi by* ***Kamen****-14-16, 19, 20; c-20, 21.*

DAGAR THE INVINCIBLE (Tales of Sword & Sorcery...) (Also see Dan Curtis Giveaways & Gold Key Spotlight)
Oct, 1972 - No. 18, Dec, 1976; No. 19, Apr, 1982
Gold Key

	GD25	FN65	NM94
1-Origin; intro. Villains Olstellon & Scor	2.40	6.00	12.00
2-5: 3-Intro. Graylin, Dagar's woman; Jarn x-over	1.20	3.00	6.00
6-1st Dark Gods story	1.00	2.50	5.00
7-10: 9-Intro. Torgus. 10-1st Three Witches story	.80	2.00	4.00
11-18: 13-Durak & Torgus x-over; story continues in Dr. Spektor #15. 14-Dagar's origin retold. 18-Origin retold	.50	1.25	2.50
19-Origin-r/#18		.60	1.20

NOTE: *Durak app. in 7, 12, 13. Tragg app. in 5, 11.*

DAGWOOD (Chic Young's) (Also see Blondie Comics)
Sept, 1950 - No. 140, Nov, 1965
Harvey Publications

	GD25	FN65	NM94
1	9.15	27.50	55.00
2	4.70	14.00	28.00
3-10	4.00	10.50	21.00
11-30	2.80	7.00	14.00
31-70	1.40	3.50	7.00
71-100	1.20	3.00	6.00
101-128,130,135	1.00	2.50	5.00
129,131-134,136-140-All are 68-pg. issues	1.40	3.50	7.00

NOTE: *Popeye and other one page strips appeared in early issues.*

DAGWOOD SPLITS THE ATOM (Also see Topix V8#4)
1949 (Science comic with King Features characters) (Giveaway)
King Features Syndicate

	GD25	FN65	NM94
nn- comic, text; Popeye, Olive Oyl, Henry, Mandrake, Little King, Katzenjammer Kids app.	4.00	12.00	24.00

DAI KAMIKAZE! (Now)(Value: cover or less)

DAISY AND DONALD (See Walt Disney Showcase No. 8)
May, 1973 - No. 59, 1984 (no No. 48)
Gold Key/Whitman No. 42 on

	GD25	FN65	NM94
1-Barks-r/WDC&S #280,308	1.20	3.00	6.00
2-5: 4-Barks-r/WDC&S #224	.70	1.75	3.50
6-10	.50	1.25	2.50
11-20	.40	1.00	2.00
21-47,49,50: 32-r/WDC&S #308. 50-r/#3	.30	.75	1.50
51-Barks-r/4-Color #1150	.35	.90	1.75
52-59: 52-r/#2. 55-r/#5		.60	1.20

DAISY & HER PUPS (Blondie's Dogs)
No. 21, 7/51 - No. 27, 7/52; No. 8, 9/52 - No. 25, 7/55
Harvey Publications

	GD25	FN65	NM94
21-27 (#1-7): 26,27 have No. 6 & 7 on cover but No. 26 & 27 on inside	1.60	4.00	8.00
8-25: 19-25-Exist?	1.20	3.00	6.00

DAISY COMICS
Dec, 1936 (Small size: 5-1/4x7-1/2")
Eastern Color Printing Co.

	GD25	FN65	NM94
nn-Joe Palooka, Buck Rogers (2 pgs. from Famous Funnies No. 18), Napoleon Flying to Fame, Butty & Fally	25.00	75.00	175.00

DAISY DUCK & UNCLE SCROOGE PICNIC TIME (See Dell Giant #33)

DAISY DUCK & UNCLE SCROOGE SHOW BOAT (See Dell Giant #55)

DAISY DUCK'S DIARY (See Dynabrite Comics, Four Color No. 600, 659, 743, 858, 948, 1055, 1150, 1247 & Walt Disney's Comics & Stories #298)

DAISY HANDBOOK
1946; No. 2, 1948 (132 pgs.)(10 cents)(Pocket-size)
Daisy Manufacturing Co.

	GD25	FN65	NM94
1-Buck Rogers, Red Ryder; Wolverton-a(2 pgs.)	24.00	73.00	170.00
2-Captain Marvel & Ibis the Invincible, Red Ryder, Boy Commandos & Robotman; Wolverton-a (2 pgs.); contains 8 pg. color catalog	24.00	73.00	170.00

DAISY LOW OF THE GIRL SCOUTS
1954, 1965 (16 pgs.; paper cover)
Girl Scouts of America

	GD25	FN65	NM94
1954-Story of Juliette Gordon Low	3.60	9.00	18.00
1965	1.20	3.00	6.00

DAISY MAE (See Oxydol-Dreft)

DAISY'S RED RYDER GUN BOOK
1955 (25 cents, 132 pages)(Pocket-size)
Daisy Manufacturing Co.

	GD25	FN65	NM94
nn-Boy Commandos, Red Ryder, 1 pg. Wolverton-a	15.00	45.00	105.00

DAKOTA LIL (See Fawcett Movie Comics)

DAKOTA NORTH
June, 1986 - No. 5, Feb, 1987
Marvel Comics Group

	GD25	FN65	NM94
1-5		.50	1.00

DAKTARI (Ivan Tors) (TV)

July, 1967 - No. 3, Oct, 1968; No. 4, Sept, 1969 (All have photo-c)
Dell Publishing Co.

	GD25	FN65	NM94
1	3.60	9.00	18.00
2-4	2.40	6.00	12.00

DALE EVANS COMICS (Also see Queen of the West...)
Sept-Oct, 1948 - No. 24, July-Aug, 1952 (No. 1-19: 52 pgs.)
National Periodical Publications

	GD25	FN65	NM94
1-Dale Evans & her horse Buttermilk begin; Sierra Smith begins by Alex Toth	45.00	135.00	315.00
2-Alex Toth-a	24.00	70.00	165.00
3-11-Alex Toth-a	19.00	58.00	135.00
12-24	10.00	30.00	65.00

NOTE: *Photo-c-1, 2, 4-14.*

DALGODA (Fantagraphics)(Value: cover or less)

DALTON BOYS, THE
1951
Avon Periodicals

	GD25	FN65	NM94
1-(No. on spine)-Kinstler-c	9.30	28.00	65.00

DAMAGE CONTROL (See Marvel Comics Presents #19)
5/89 - No. 4, 8/89; V2#1, 12/89 - No. 4, 2/90 ($1.00, color)
V3#1, 6/91 - No. 4, 9/91 ($1.25, all are mini-series)
Marvel Comics

	GD25	FN65	NM94
V1#1-3		.50	1.00
4-Wolverine app.	.30	.75	1.50
V2#1,3		.60	1.20
2,4-Punisher app.	.35	.90	1.80
V3#1-4 ($1.25): 1-Spider-Man app. 2-New Warriors app. 3,4-Silver Surfer app. 4-Infinity Guantlet parody		.60	1.25

DAN CURTIS GIVEAWAYS
1974 (24 pages) (3x6") (in color, all reprints)
Western Publishing Co.

	GD25	FN65	NM94
1-Dark Shadows, 2-Star Trek, 3-The Twilight Zone, 4-Ripley's Believe It or Not!, 5-Turok, Son of Stone, 6-Star Trek, 7-The Occult Files of Dr. Spektor, 8-Dagar the Invincible, 9-Grimm's Ghost Stories Set...	.60	1.50	3.00

DANDEE
1947
Four Star Publications

	GD25	FN65	NM94
nn	4.00	11.00	22.00

DAN DUNN (See Crackajack Funnies, Detective Dan, Famous Feature Stories & Red Ryder)

DANDY COMICS (Also see Happy Jack Howard)
Spring, 1947 - No. 7, Spring, 1948
E. C. Comics

	GD25	FN65	NM94
1-Vince Fago-a in all	22.00	65.00	150.00
2	15.00	45.00	105.00
3-7	11.50	34.00	80.00

DANGER
January, 1953 - No. 11, Aug, 1954
Comic Media/Allen Hardy Assoc.

	GD25	FN65	NM94
1-Heck-c/a	8.35	25.00	50.00
2,3,5-7,9-11: 6-``Narcotics" story	4.00	11.00	22.00
4-Marijuana cover/story	5.85	17.50	35.00
8-Bondage/torture/headlights panels	7.00	21.00	42.00

NOTE: ***Morisi** a-2, 5, 6(3), 10; c-2. Contains some-r from Danger & Dynamite.*

DANGER (Jim Bowie No. 15 on; formerly Comic Media title)
No. 12, June, 1955 - No. 14, Oct, 1955
Charlton Comics Group

	GD25	FN65	NM94
12(#1)	5.00	15.00	30.00
13,14: 14-r/#12	4.00	11.00	22.00

DANGER
1964
Super Comics

	GD25	FN65	NM94
Super Reprint #10-12 (Black Dwarf; #10-r/Great Comics #1 by Novack. #11-r/Johnny Danger #1. #12-r/Red Seal #?), #15-r/Spy Cases #26. #16-Unpublished Chesler material (Yankee Girl), #17-r/Scoop #8 (Capt. Courage & Enchanted Dagger), #18(nd)-r/Guns Against Gangsters #5 (Gun-Master, Annie Oakley, The Chameleon; L.B. Cole-r)	1.00	2.50	5.00

DANGER AND ADVENTURE (Formerly This Magazine Is Haunted; Robin Hood and His Merry Men No. 28 on)
No. 22, Feb, 1955 - No. 27, Feb, 1956
Charlton Comics

	GD25	FN65	NM94
22-Ibis the Invincible, Nyoka app.	6.70	20.00	40.00
23-Nyoka, Lance O'Casey app.	6.70	20.00	40.00
24-27: 24-Mike Danger & Johnny Adventure begin	4.20	12.50	25.00

DANGER IS OUR BUSINESS!
1953(Dec.) - No. 10, June, 1955
Toby Press

	GD25	FN65	NM94
1-Captain Comet by Williamson/Frazetta-a, 6 pgs. (science fiction)	30.00	90.00	210.00
2	6.35	19.00	38.00
3-10	4.70	14.00	28.00
I.W. Reprint #9('64)-Williamson/Frazetta-a r-/#1; Kinstler-c	7.50	22.50	45.00

DANGER IS THEIR BUSINESS (See A-1 Comics No. 50)

DANGER MAN (See 4-Color No. 1231)

DANGER TRAIL (Also see Showcase #50, 51)
July-Aug, 1950 - No. 5, Mar-Apr, 1951 (52 pgs.)
National Periodical Publications

	GD25	FN65	NM94
1-King Farrady begins, ends #4; Toth-a	64.00	192.00	450.00
2-Toth-a	47.00	149.00	325.00
3-Toth-a (rare; considered the rarest early '50s DC comic)	79.00	235.00	550.00
4,5-Toth-a in both. 5-Johnny Peril app.	41.00	122.00	285.00

DANIEL BOONE (See The Exploits of..., Fighting..., 4-Color No. 1163, Frontier Scout..., The Legends of... & March of Comics No. 306)

DAN'L BOONE
Sept, 1955 - No. 8, Sept, 1957
Magazine Enterprises/Sussex Publ. Co. No. 2 on

	GD25	FN65	NM94
1	8.35	25.00	50.00
2	5.35	16.00	32.00
3-8	4.20	12.50	25.00

DANIEL BOONE (TV) (See March of Comics No. 306)
Jan, 1965 - No. 15, Apr, 1969 (All photo-c?)
Gold Key

	GD25	FN65	NM94
1	9.15	27.50	55.00
2	4.70	14.00	28.00
3-5: 4,5-Fess Parker photo-c	3.00	7.50	15.00
6-15: 6,7,10,14-Fess Parker photo-c	1.80	4.50	9.00

DANNY BLAZE (Nature Boy No. 3 on)
Aug, 1955 - No. 2, Oct, 1955
Charlton Comics

	GD25	FN65	NM94
1,2	4.70	14.00	28.00

DANNY DINGLE (See Single Series #17 & Sparkler Comics)

DANNY KAYE'S BAND FUN BOOK
1959
H & A Selmer (Giveaway)

	GD25	FN65	NM94
nn	4.00	11.00	22.00

DANNY THOMAS SHOW, THE (See 4-Color No. 1180,1249)

DARBY O'GILL & THE LITTLE PEOPLE (See 4-Color No. 1024 & Movie Comics)

Dale Evans #1, © DC

Danger Is Our Business #3, © TOBY

Danger Trail #4, © DC

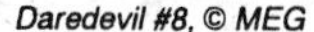
Daredevil #8, © MEG

Daredevil #238, © MEG

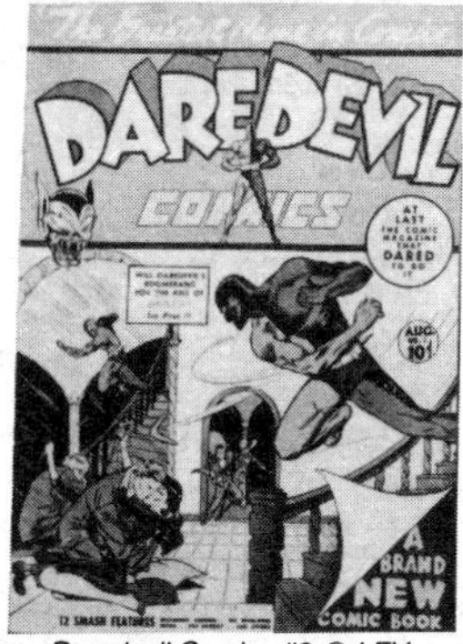

Daredevil Comics #2, © LEV

DARE (Fantagraphics) (Value: cover or less)

DAREDEVIL (...& the Black Widow #92-107 on-c only; see Giant-Size..., Marvel Advs., Marvel Graphic Novel #24, Marvel Super Heroes, '66 & Spider-Man and...)
April, 1964 - Present
Marvel Comics Group

	GD25	FN65	NM94
1-Origin & 1st app. Daredevil; reprinted in Marvel Super Heroes #1 (1966); death of Battling Murdock; intro Foggy Nelson & Karen Page	157.00	470.00	1100.00
2-Fantastic Four cameo; 2nd app. Electro (Spidey villain)	47.00	140.00	325.00
3-Origin & 1st app. The Owl	32.00	95.00	225.00
4	20.00	60.00	140.00
5-New Costume; Wood-a begins	19.00	57.00	130.00
6,8-10: 8-Origin/1st app. Stilt-Man	13.00	40.00	90.00
7-Daredevil battles Sub-Mariner & dons new red costume	17.00	50.00	115.00
11-15: 12-Romita's 1st work at Marvel; 1st app. Plunderer. 13-Facts about Ka-Zar's origin; Kirby-a	9.15	27.50	55.00
16,17-Spider-Man x-over	10.00	30.00	70.00
18-20: 18-Origin & 1st app. Gladiator	6.70	20.00	40.00
21-30: 24-Ka-Zar app. 27-Spider-Man x-over	4.20	12.50	25.00
31-40: 38-Fantastic Four x-over; cont'd in F.F. #73. 39-1st Exterminator (later becomes Death-Stalker)	4.00	10.00	20.00
41-49: 41-Death Mike Murdock. 42-1st app. Jester. 43-Vs. Captain America. 45-Statue of Liberty photo-c	3.00	7.50	15.00
50-52-B. Smith-a.	3.60	9.00	18.00
53-Origin retold; last 12 cent issue	4.00	10.00	20.00
54-60: 54-Spider-Man cameo. 56-1st app. Death's Head (9/69); story cont'd in #57 (not same as newer Death's Head)	1.80	4.50	9.00
57-Reveals i.d. to Karen Page; Death's Head app.	2.00	5.00	10.00
61-99: 62-1st app. Nighthawk. 81-Oversize issue; Black Widow begins	1.60	4.00	8.00
100-Origin retold	4.00	10.00	20.00
101-104,106,108-113,115-120	1.20	3.00	6.00
105-Origin Moondragon by Starlin (12/73); Thanos cameo in flashback (early app.)	2.40	6.00	12.00
107-Starlin-c	1.40	3.50	7.00
114-1st app. Deathstalker	1.60	4.00	8.00
121-130,133-137: 124-1st app. Copperhead; Black Widow leaves. 126-1st new Torpedo	.70	1.75	3.50
131-Origin Bullseye (1st app. in Nick Fury #15)	4.00	10.00	20.00
132-Bullseye app.	1.00	2.50	5.00
138-Ghost Rider-c/story; Death's Head is reincarnated; Byrne-a	2.20	5.50	11.00
139-157: 142-Nova cameo. 146-Bullseye app. 148-30 & 35 cent issues exist. 150-1st app. Paladin. 151-Reveals i.d. to Heather Glenn. 155-Black Widow returns. 156-1960s Daredevil app.	.70	1.75	3.50
158-Frank Miller art begins (5/79); origin/death of Deathstalker (see Captain America #235 & Spectacular Spider-Man #27	5.85	17.50	35.00
159	3.20	8.00	16.00
160,161	1.40	3.50	7.00
162-Ditko-a, no Miller-a	.50	1.25	2.50
163,164: 163-Hulk cameo. 164-Origin retold	1.20	3.00	6.00
165-167,170	1.00	2.50	5.00
168-Origin/1st app. Elektra	3.60	9.00	18.00
169-Elektra app.	1.40	3.50	7.00
171-175: 174,175-Elektra app.	.80	2.00	4.00
176-180-Elektra app. 179-Anti-smoking issue mentioned in the Congressional Record	.60	1.50	3.00
181-Double size; death of Elektra; Punisher cameo out of costume	1.40	3.50	7.00
182-184-Punisher app. by Miller (drug issues)	2.00	5.00	10.00
185-191: 187-New Black Widow. 189-Death of Stick. 190-(52 pgs.)-Elektra returns, part origin. 191-Last Miller Daredevil	.40	1.00	2.00
192-195,197-210: 208-Harlan Ellison scripts	.30	.75	1.50
196-Wolverine app.	2.40	6.00	12.00
211-225: 219-Miller scripts		.50	1.00
226-Frank Miller plots begin	.30	.75	1.50
227-Miller scripts begin	.60	1.50	3.00
228-233-Last Miller scripts	.40	1.00	2.00
234-237,239,240,242-247		.50	1.00
238-Mutant Massacre; Sabretooth app.	1.20	3.00	6.00
241-Todd McFarlane-a(p)	.60	1.50	3.00
248,249-Wolverine app.	1.20	3.00	6.00
250,251,253,258: 250-1st app. Bullet. 258-Intro The Bengal (a villain)		.50	1.00
252-(52 pgs.); Fall of the Mutants	.60	1.50	3.00
254-Origin & 1st app. Typhoid Mary	2.80	7.00	14.00
255-2nd app. Typhoid Mary	1.20	3.00	6.00
256-3rd app. Typhoid Mary	1.00	2.50	5.00
257-Punisher app. (x-over w/Punisher #10)	3.60	9.00	18.00
259,260-Typhoid Mary app. 260-Double size	.60	1.50	3.00
261-291,294,296-299: 272-Intro Shotgun (villain). 282-Silver Surfer app. (cameo in #281). 283-Capt. America app. 297-Typhoid Mary app.; Kingpin storyline begins. 299-Last $1.00-c		.50	1.00
292,293-Punisher app.	.40	1.00	2.00
295-Ghost Rider app.	.50	1.25	2.50
300-($2.00, 52 pgs.)-Kingpin story ends	.60	1.50	3.00
301-316: 305,306-Spider-Man-c/story. 309-Punisher-c/story; Terror app. 310-Calypso-c/story; Infinity War x-over		.60	1.25
Special 1(9/67, 25 cents, 68 pgs.)-new art	4.20	12.50	25.00
Special 2,3: 2(2/71, 25 cents, 52 pgs.)-Entire book has Powell/Wood-r; Wood-c. 3(1/72)-reprints	2.00	5.00	10.00
Annual 4(10/76)	1.00	2.50	5.00
Annual 4(#5)('89, $2.00, 68 pgs.)-Atlantis Attacks	.50	1.25	2.50
Annual 6(1990, $2.00, 68 pgs.)-Sutton-a	.40	1.00	2.00
Annual 7(1991, $2.00, 68 pgs.)-Guice-a (7 pgs.)	.40	1.00	2.00
Annual 8(1992, $2.25, 68 pgs.)-Deathlok-c/story	.40	1.15	2.25

NOTE: ***Art Adams*** *c-238p, 239.* ***Austin*** *a-191i; c-151i, 200i.* ***John Buscema*** *a-136, 137p, 234p, 235p; c-86p, 136i, 137p, 142, 219.* ***Byrne*** *c-200p, 201, 203, 223.* ***Colan*** *a(p)-20-49, 53-82, 84-98, 100, 110, 112, 124, 153, 154, 156, 157, Spec. 1p; c(p)-20-42, 44-49, 53-60, 71, 92, 98, 138, 153, 154, 156, 157, Annual 1.* ***Craig*** *a-50i, 52i.* ***Ditko*** *a-162, 234p, 235p, 264p; c-162.* ***Everett*** *c/a-1; inks-21, 83.* ***Gil Kane*** *a-141p, 146-148p, 151p; c(p)-85, 90, 91, 93, 94, 115, 116, 119, 120, 125-128, 133, 139, 147, 152.* ***Kirby*** *c-2-4, 5p, 12p, 13p, 136p.* ***Layton*** *c-202.* ***Miller*** *scripts-168-182, 183(part), 184-191, 219, 227-233; a-158-161p, 163-184p, 191p; c-158-161p, 163-184p, 185-189, 190p, 191.* ***Orlando*** *a-2-4p.* ***Powell*** *a-9p, 11p, Special 1r, 2r.* ***Simonson*** *c-199, 236p.* ***B. Smith*** *a-83p, 236p; c-51p, 52p.* ***Starlin*** *a-105p.* ***Steranko*** *c-44i.* ***Tuska*** *a-39i, 145p.* ***Williamson*** *a(i)-237, 239, 240, 243, 248-257, 259-282, 283(part), 284, 285, 287, 288(part), 289(part), 293-301; c(i)-237, 243, 244, 248-257, 259-263, 265-278, 280-289, Annual 8.* ***Wood*** *a-5-9i, 10, 11i, Spec. 2i; c-5i, 6-11, 164i.*

DAREDEVIL AND THE PUNISHER (Child's Play trade paperback)
1988 ($4.95, color, squarebound, one-shot)
Marvel Comics

	GD25	FN65	NM94
1-r/Daredevil #182-184 by Miller	1.60	4.00	8.00
1-2nd & 3rd printings	1.00	2.50	5.00

DAREDEVIL COMICS (See Silver Streak Comics)
July, 1941 - No. 134, Sept, 1956 (Charles Biro stories)
Lev Gleason Publications (Funnies, Inc. No. 1)

	GD25	FN65	VF82	NM94
1-No. 1 titled "Daredevil Battles Hitler;" The Silver Streak, Lance Hale, Cloud Curtis, Dickey Dean, Pirate Prince team up w/Daredevil and battle Hitler; Daredevil battles the Claw; Origin of Hitler feature story. Hitler photo app. on-c	400.00	1200.00	2200.00	3200.00

(Estimated up to 215 total copies exist, 12 in NM/Mint)

	GD25	FN65	NM94
2-London, Pat Patriot, Nightro, Real American No. 1, Dickie Dean, Pirate Prince, & Times Square begin; intro. & only app. The Pioneer, Champion of America	200.00	600.00	1200.00

	GD25	FN65	NM94
3-Origin of 13	117.00	350.00	700.00
4	100.00	300.00	600.00
5-Intro. Sniffer & Jinx; Ghost vs. Claw begins by Bob Wood, ends #20	92.00	275.00	550.00
6-(#7 in indicia)	78.00	232.00	465.00
7-10: 8-Nightro ends	64.00	192.00	385.00
11-London, Pat Patriot end; bondage/torture-c	58.00	175.00	350.00
12-Origin of The Claw; Scoop Scuttle by Wolverton begins (2-4 pgs.), ends #22, not in #21	92.00	275.00	550.00
13-Intro. of Little Wise Guys	92.00	275.00	550.00
14	46.00	138.00	275.00
15-Death of Meatball	67.00	200.00	400.00
16,17	42.00	125.00	250.00
18-New origin of Daredevil-Not same as Silver Streak #6	88.00	262.00	525.00
19,20	35.00	105.00	210.00
21-Reprints cover of Silver Streak #6(on inside) plus intro. of The Claw from Silver Streak #1	58.00	175.00	350.00
22-30: 27-Bondage/torture-c	23.00	68.00	135.00
31-Death of The Claw	50.00	150.00	300.00
32-37,39,40: 35-Two Daredevil stories begin, end #68 (35-40 are 64 pgs.)	16.00	48.00	95.00
38-Origin Daredevil retold from #18	29.00	86.00	175.00
41-50: 42-Intro. Kilroy in Daredevil	12.00	35.00	70.00
51-69-Last Daredevil issue (12/50)	9.15	27.50	55.00
70-Little Wise Guys take over book; McWilliams-a; Hot Rock Flanagan begins, ends #80	6.70	20.00	40.00
71-79,81: 79-Daredevil returns	5.00	15.00	30.00
80-Daredevil x-over	5.85	17.50	35.00
82,90-One page Frazetta ad in both	5.00	15.00	30.00
83-89,91-99,101-134	4.20	12.50	25.00
100	5.85	17.50	35.00

NOTE: ***Wolverton's*** *Scoop Scuttle-12-20, 22.* ***Biro*** *c/a-all?.* ***Bolle*** *a-125.* ***Maurer*** *a-75.* ***McWilliams*** *a-73, 75, 79, 80.*

DARE THE IMPOSSIBLE (Fleetway/Quality) (Value: cover or less)

DARING ADVENTURES (Also see Approved Comics)
Nov, 1953 (3-D)
St. John Publishing Co.

	GD25	FN65	NM94
1 (3-D)-Reprints lead story/Son of Sinbad #1 by Kubert	25.00	75.00	175.00

DARING ADVENTURES
1963 - 1964
I.W. Enterprises/Super Comics

	GD25	FN65	NM94
I.W. Reprint #9-r/Blue Bolt #115; Disbrow-a(3)	3.60	9.00	18.00
Super Reprint #10,11('63)-r/Dynamic #24,16; 11-Marijuana story; Yankee Boy app.	2.00	5.00	10.00
Super Reprint #12('64)-Phantom Lady from Fox(r/#14 only? w/splash page omitted)	10.00	30.00	70.00
Super Reprint #15('64)-r/Hooded Menace #1	7.00	21.00	42.00
Super Reprint #16('64)-r/Dynamic #12	2.00	5.00	10.00
Super Reprint #17('64)-r/Green Lama #3 by Raboy	3.60	9.00	18.00
Super Reprint #18-Origin Atlas from unpublished Atlas Comics #1	2.00	5.00	10.00

DARING COMICS (Formerly Daring Mystery) (Jeanie No. 13 on)
No. 9, Fall, 1944 - No. 12, Fall, 1945
Timely Comics (HPC)

	GD25	FN65	NM94
9-Human Torch & Sub-Mariner begin	57.00	170.00	340.00
10-The Angel only app.	50.00	150.00	300.00
11,12-The Destroyer app.	50.00	150.00	300.00

NOTE: ***Schomburg*** *c-9-11.* ***Sekowsky*** *c-12?*

DARING CONFESSIONS (Formerly Youthful Hearts)
No. 4, 11/52 - No. 7, 5/53; No. 8, 10/53
Youthful Magazines

	GD25	FN65	NM94
4-Doug Wildey-a	7.00	21.00	42.00
5-8: 6,8-Wildey-a	5.00	15.00	30.00

DARING LOVE (Radiant Love No. 2 on)
Sept-Oct, 1953
Gilmor Magazines

	GD25	FN65	NM94
1	5.35	16.00	32.00

DARING LOVE (Formerly Youthful Romances)
No. 15, 12/52; No. 16, 2/53-c, 4/53-Indicia; No. 17-4/53-c & indicia
Ribage/

	GD25	FN65	NM94
15	5.35	16.00	35.00
16,17: 17-Photo-c	4.70	14.00	28.00

NOTE: ***Colletta*** *a-15.* ***Wildey*** *a-17.*

DARING LOVE STORIES (See Fox Giants)

DARING MYSTERY COMICS (Comedy Comics No. 9 on; title changed to Daring Comics with No. 9)
1/40 - No. 5, 6/40; No. 6, 9/40; No. 7, 4/41 - No. 8, 1/42
Timely Comics (TPI 1-6/TCI 7,8)

	GD25	FN65	VF82	NM94
1-Origin The Fiery Mask by Joe Simon; Monako, Prince of Magic, John Steele, Soldier of Fortune, Doc Doyle begin; Flash Foster & Barney Mullen, Sea Rover only app; bondage-c	875.00	2625.00	4800.00	7000.00

(Estimated up to 60 total copies exist, 5 in NM/Mint)

	GD25	FN65	NM94
2-(Rare)-Origin The Phantom Bullet & only app.; The Laughing Mask & Mr. E only app.; Trojak the Tiger Man begins, ends #6; Zephyr Jones & K-4 & His Sky Devils app., also #4	400.00	1200.00	2400.00
3-The Phantom Reporter, Dale of FBI, Breeze Barton, Captain Strong & Marvex the Super-Robot only app.; The Purple Mask begins	267.00	800.00	1600.00
4-Last Purple Mask; Whirlwind Carter begins; Dan Gorman, G-Man app.	167.00	500.00	1000.00
5-The Falcon begins; The Fiery Mask, Little Hercules app. by Sagendorf in the Segar style; bondage-c	167.00	500.00	1000.00
6-Origin & only app. Marvel Boy by S&K; Flying Flame, Dynaman, & Stuporman only app.; The Fiery Mask by S&K; S&K-c	208.00	625.00	1250.00
7-Origin The Blue Diamond, Captain Daring by S&K, The Fin by Everett, The Challenger, The Silver Scorn & The Thunderer by Burgos; Mr. Millions app	192.00	575.00	1150.00
8-Origin Citizen V; Last Fin, Silver Scorn, Capt. Daring by Borth, Blue Diamond & The Thunderer; S&K-c; Rudy the Robot only app.	158.00	475.00	950.00

NOTE: ***Schomburg*** *c-1-4, 7.* ***Simon*** *a-2, 3, 5.*

DARING NEW ADVENTURES OF SUPERGIRL, THE
Nov, 1982 - No. 13, Nov, 1983 (Supergirl No. 14-on)
DC Comics

	GD25	FN65	NM94
1-Origin retold; Lois Lane back-ups in #2-12	.30	.75	1.50
2-13: 8,9-Doom Patrol app. 13-New costume; flag-c		.50	1.00

NOTE: ***Buckler*** *c-1p, 2p.* ***Giffen*** *c-3p, 4p.* ***Gil Kane*** *c-6, ,8, 9, 11-13.*

DARK ANGEL (Formerly Hell's Angel)
No. 6, Dec, 1992 - Present ($1.75, color)
Marvel Comics UK, Ltd.

	GD25	FN65	NM94
6-10; 6-Excalibur-c/story. 8-Psylocke app.	.35	.90	1.75

DARK CRYSTAL, THE
April, 1983 - No. 2, May, 1983
Marvel Comics Group

	GD25	FN65	NM94
1,2-Movie adaptation, part 1&2		.50	1.00

DARKEWOOD (Aircel) (Value: cover or less)

DARKHAWK
Mar, 1991 - Present ($1.00,/$1.25 color)
Marvel Comics

Daredevil Comics #26, © LEV

Daring Adventures #11, © Super Comics

Daring Mystery Comics #5, © MEG

Darkhawk #2, © MEG

Dark Horse Presents #51, © Dark Horse

Dark Mysteries #4, © Merit Publ.

	GD25	FN65	NM94
1-Origin/1st app. Darkhawk; Hobgoblin cameo	3.60	9.00	18.00
2,3-Spider-Man & Hobgoblin app.	2.20	5.50	11.00
4	1.60	4.00	8.00
5	1.40	3.50	7.00
6-Capt. America & Daredevil x-over	1.20	3.00	6.00
7,8	1.00	2.50	5.00
9-Punisher app.	1.40	3.50	7.00
10-12: 11-Last $1.00-c. 11,12-Tombstone app.	.60	1.50	3.00
13,14-Venom-c/story	1.20	3.00	6.00
15-24,26-28: 19-Spider-Man & Brotherhood of Evil Mutants-c/story. 20-Spider-Man app. 22-Ghost Rider-c/story		.60	1.25
25-($2.95, 52 pgs.)-Red holo-grafx foil-c w/double gatefold poster; origin of Darkhawk armor revealed	.60	1.50	3.00
Annual 1 (1992, $2.25, 68 pgs.)-Vs. Iron Man	.60	1.50	3.00

DARKHOLD: PAGES FROM THE BOOK OF SINS
Oct, 1992 - Present ($1.75, color)
Marvel Comics

	GD25	FN65	NM94
1-($2.75, 52 pgs.)-Polybagged w/poster by Andy & Adam Kubert; part 4 of Rise of the Midnight Sons storyline	.55	1.40	2.75
2-8: 3-Reintro Modred the Mystic (see Marvel Chillers #1). 5-Punisher & Ghost Rider app.	.35	.90	1.75

DARK HORSE CLASSICS
1992 - Present ($3.95, B&W, 52 pgs.)
Dark Horse Comics

	GD25	FN65	NM94
nn's: The Last of the Mohicans. 20,000 Leagues Under the Sea	.80	2.00	4.00

DARK HORSE COMICS
Aug, 1992 - Present ($2.50, color)
Dark Horse Comics

	GD25	FN65	NM94
1-Dorman double gategold painted-c; Predator, Robocop, Timecop & Renegade stories begin	.60	1.50	3.00
2-7: 2-Mignola-c. 3-Begin 3 part Aliens story; Aliens-c. 4-Predator-c. 6-Begin 4 part Robocop story	.50	1.25	2.50

DARK HORSE PRESENTS
July, 1986 - Present ($1.50/$1.75/$1.95/$2.25, B&W)
Dark Horse Comics

	GD25	FN65	NM94
1-1st app. Concrete by Paul Chadwick	2.40	6.00	12.00
1-2nd printing (1988, $1.50)	.50	1.25	2.50
1-Silver ink 3rd printing (1992, $2.25)-Says 2nd printing inside	.45	1.15	2.25
2-Concrete app.	1.40	3.50	7.00
3-Concrete app.	1.00	2.50	5.00
4,5-Concrete app.	.80	2.00	4.00
6-10: 6,8,10-Concrete app.	.60	1.50	3.00
11-19,21-23: 12,14,16,18,22-Concrete app.	.40	1.00	2.00
20-($2.95, 68 pgs.)-Concrete & Flaming Carrot	.60	1.50	3.00
24-Origin Aliens (11/88); Mr. Monster app.	5.85	17.50	35.00
25-31,33: 28-($2.95, 52 pgs.)-Concrete app. 33-($2.25, 44 pgs.)	.60	1.50	3.00
32-($3.50, 68 pgs.)-Annual; Concrete, American	.80	2.00	4.00
34-Aliens-c/story	1.40	3.50	7.00
35-Predator-c/story; begin $1.95-c	1.40	3.50	7.00
36-1st Aliens Vs. Predator story; painted-c	2.40	6.00	12.00
36-Same as above, but line drawn-c	2.00	5.00	10.00
37-39,41,44,45,47-50: 38-Concrete. 44-Crash Ryan. 48-50-Contain 2 trading cards. 50-S/F story by Perez	.40	1.00	2.00
40-($2.95, 52 pgs.)-1st Argosy story	.60	1.50	3.00
42,43-Aliens-c/stories	1.00	2.50	5.00
46-Prequel to new Predator II mini-series	.80	2.00	4.00
51-53-Sin City by Frank Miller, parts 2-4; 51,53-Miller-c	.50	1.25	2.50
54-The Next Men begins(1st app.) by Byrne(9/91)	1.60	4.00	8.00
55-2nd app. The Next Men; parts 5 & 6 of Sin City by Miller; Homocide by Morrow in both. 54-Morrow-c; begin $2.25-c. 55-Miller-c	.80	2.00	4.00
56-($3.95, 68 pg. annual)-2 part prologue to Aliens: Genocide; part 7 of Sin City by Miller; Next Men by Byrne	.80	2.00	4.00
57-($3.50, 52 pgs.)-Part 8 of Sin City by Miller; Next Men by Byrne; Byrne & Miller-c; Alien Fire story; swipes cover to Daredevil #1	.70	1.75	3.50
58-66,68-74: 58,59-Part 9,10 Sin City by Miller; Alien Fire stories. 60,61-Part 11,12 Sin City by Miller. 62-Last Sin City (entire book by Miller, c/a; 52pgs.). 64-Dr. Giggles begins (1st app.), ends #66; Boris the Bear story. 66-New Concrete story by Chadwick	.45	1.15	2.25
67-($3.95, 68 pgs.)-Begin 3 part prelude to Predator: Race War mini-series; Oscar Wilde adapt. by Russell	.80	2.00	4.00
... Fifth Anniversary Special nn (4/91, $9.95)-Part 1 of Sin City by Frank Miller (c/a); Aliens, Aliens vs. Predator, Concrete, Roachmill, Give Me Liberty & The American stories	2.00	5.00	10.00

NOTE: ***Geary*** *a-59, 60.* ***Miller*** *a-Special, 51-53, 55-62; c-59-62.* ***Moebius*** *a-63; c-63, 70.*

DARK KNIGHT (See Batman: The Dark Knight Returns)

DARKLON THE MYSTIC (Pacific)(Value: cover or less)

DARKMAN
Sept, 1990; Oct, 1990 - No. 3, Nov, 1990 ($1.50, color, movie adapt.)
Marvel Comics

	GD25	FN65	NM94
1 (9/90, $2.25, B&W mag., 68 pgs.)	.45	1.15	2.25
1-3: Reprints B&W magazine	.30	.75	1.50

DARK MANSION OF FORBIDDEN LOVE, THE (Becomes Forbidden Tales of Dark Mansion No. 5 on)
Sept-Oct, 1971 - No. 4, Mar-Apr, 1972
National Periodical Publications

	GD25	FN65	NM94
1	1.60	4.00	8.00
2-4: 2-Adams-c. 3-Jeff Jones-c	.80	2.00	4.00

DARK MYSTERIES
June-July, 1951 - No. 25?, 1955
"Master"-"Merit" Publications

	GD25	FN65	NM94
1-Wood-c/a (8 pgs.)	36.00	107.00	250.00
2-Wood/Harrison-c/a (8 pgs.)	27.00	81.00	190.00
3-9: 7-Dismemberment, hypo blood drainage stories	11.50	34.00	80.00
10-Cannibalism story	12.00	36.00	85.00
11-13,15-18: 11-Severed head panels. 13-Dismemberment-c/story. 17-The Old Gravedigger host	10.00	30.00	60.00
14-Several E.C. Craig swipes	10.00	30.00	65.00
19-Injury-to-eye panel; E.C. swipe	12.00	36.00	80.00
20-Female bondage, blood drainage story	10.00	30.00	70.00
21,22-Last pre-code issue, mis-dated 3/54 instead of 3/55	7.50	22.50	45.00
23-25 (#25-Exist?)	5.85	17.50	35.00

NOTE: ***Cameron*** *a-1, 2.* ***Myron Fass*** *c/a-21.* ***Harrison*** *a-3, 7; c-3.* ***Hollingsworth*** *a-7-17, 20, 21, 23.* ***Wildey*** *a-5. Woodish art by* ***Fleishman****-9; c-10. Bondage c-10, 18, 19.*

DARK SHADOWS
October, 1957 - No. 3, May, 1958
Steinway Comic Publications (Ajax)(America's Best)

	GD25	FN65	NM94
1	8.35	25.00	50.00
2,3	5.85	17.50	35.00

DARK SHADOWS (TV) (See Dan Curtis Giveaways)
March, 1969 - No. 35, Feb, 1976 (Photo-c: 1-7)
Gold Key

	GD25	FN65	NM94
1(30039-903)-With pull-out poster (25 cents)	22.00	65.00	150.00
1-Without poster	10.00	30.00	60.00
2	9.15	27.50	55.00
3-With pull-out poster	12.00	36.00	85.00

	GD25	FN65	NM94
3-Without poster	7.50	22.50	45.00
4-7: Last photo-c	9.15	27.50	55.00
8-10	6.35	19.00	38.00
11-20	4.70	14.00	28.00
21-35: 30-last painted-c	4.00	10.00	20.00
Story Digest 1 (6/70)-Photo-c	6.70	20.00	40.00

DARK SHADOWS (TV) (See Nightmare on Elm Street)
June, 1992 - No. 4, Dec, 1992 ($2.50, color, mini-series, coated stock)
Innovation Publications

	GD25	FN65	NM94
1-Based on '91 NBC TV mini-series; painted-c	.60	1.50	3.00
2-4	.50	1.25	2.50

DARKSTARS, THE
Oct, 1992 - Present ($1.75, color)
DC Comics

	GD25	FN65	NM94
1-1st app. The Darkstars	.60	1.50	3.00
2-8: 5-Hawkman & Hawkwoman app.	.35	.90	1.75

NOTE: ***Travis Charest*** *a(p)-4-on; c-2p, 3p.* ***Stroman*** *a-1-3; c-1.*

DARKWING DUCK (TV cartoon) (Also see Cartoon Tales)
Nov, 1991 - No. 4, Feb, 1992 ($1.50, color, limited series)
Disney Comics

	GD25	FN65	NM94
1-4: Adapts hour-long premiere TV episode	.30	.75	1.50

DARLING LOVE
Oct-Nov, 1949 - No. 11, 1952 (no month) (52 pgs.)
Close Up/Archie Publ. (A Darling Magazine)

	GD25	FN65	NM94
1-Photo-c	7.50	22.50	45.00
2	4.35	13.00	26.00
3-8,10,11: 5,6-photo-c	4.00	11.00	22.00
9-Krigstein-a	4.70	14.00	28.00

DARLING ROMANCE
Sept-Oct, 1949 - No. 7, 1951 (All photo-c)
Close Up (MLJ Publications)

	GD25	FN65	NM94
1-(52 pgs.)-Betty Page photo-c?	8.35	25.00	50.00
2	4.70	14.00	28.00
3-7	4.00	11.00	22.00

DASTARDLY & MUTTLEY (See Fun-In No. 1-4, 6 and Kite Fun Book)

DATE WITH DANGER
No. 5, Dec, 1952 - No. 6, Feb, 1953
Standard Comics

	GD25	FN65	NM94
5,6	4.35	13.00	26.00

DATE WITH DEBBI (Also see Debbi's Dates)
Jan-Feb, 1969 - No. 17, Sept-Oct, 1971; No. 18, Oct-Nov, 1972
National Periodical Publications

	GD25	FN65	NM94
1	2.00	5.00	10.00
2-5	1.20	3.00	6.00
6-18	.80	2.00	4.00

DATE WITH JUDY, A (Radio/TV, and 1948 movie)
Oct-Nov, 1947 - No. 79, Oct-Nov, 1960 (No. 1-25: 52 pgs.)
National Periodical Publications

	GD25	FN65	NM94
1-Teenage	18.00	54.00	125.00
2	9.15	27.50	55.00
3-10	6.70	20.00	40.00
11-20	4.35	13.00	26.00
21-40	4.00	10.00	20.00
41-45: 45-Last pre-code (2-3/55)	3.20	8.00	16.00
46-79: 79-Drucker-c/a	2.40	6.00	12.00

DATE WITH MILLIE, A (Life With Millie No. 8 on)
Oct, 1956 - No. 7, Aug, 1957; Oct, 1959 - No. 7, Oct, 1960
Atlas/Marvel Comics (MPC)

	GD25	FN65	NM94
1(10/56)-(1st Series)-Dan DeCarlo-a in #1-7	12.00	36.00	85.00
2	7.50	22.50	45.00
3-7	5.35	16.00	32.00
1(10/59)-(2nd Series)	8.35	25.00	50.00
2-7	4.70	14.00	28.00

DATE WITH PATSY, A (Also see Patsy Walker)
September, 1957
Atlas Comics

	GD25	FN65	NM94
1-Starring Patsy Walker	5.85	17.50	35.00

DAVID AND GOLIATH (See 4-Color No. 1205)

DAVID CASSIDY (TV?)(See Swing With Scooter #33)
Feb, 1972 - No. 14, Sept, 1973
Charlton Comics

	GD25	FN65	NM94
1	2.00	5.00	10.00
2-14: 5,7,9,14-Photo-c	1.40	3.50	7.00

DAVID LADD'S LIFE STORY (See Movie Classics)

DAVY CROCKETT (See Dell Giants, Fightin..., Frontier Fighters, It's Game Time, Power Record Comics, Western Tales & Wild Frontier)

DAVY CROCKETT
1951
Avon Periodicals

	GD25	FN65	NM94
nn-Tuska?, Reinman-a; Fawcette-c	10.00	30.00	70.00

DAVY CROCKETT (...King of the Wild Frontier No. 1,2)(TV)
5/55 - No. 671, 12/55; No. 1, 12/63; No. 2, 11/69 (Walt Disney)
Dell Publishing Co./Gold Key

	GD25	FN65	NM94
4-Color 631(#1)-Fess Parker photo-c	8.35	25.00	50.00
4-Color 639-Photo-c	5.85	17.50	35.00
4-Color 664,671(Marsh-a)-Photo-c	6.70	20.00	40.00
1(12/63-Gold Key)-Fess Parker photo-c; reprints	4.20	12.50	25.00
2(11/69)-Fess Parker photo-c; reprints	3.00	7.50	15.00
..Christmas Book (no date, 16pgs, paper-c)-Sears giveaway	4.00	10.00	20.00
..In the Raid at Piney Creek (1955, 16pgs, 5x7-1/4")-American Motors giveaway; slick, photo-c	4.70	28.00	28.00
..Safety Trails (1955, 16pgs, 3-1/4x7")-Cities Service giveaway	4.35	13.00	26.00

DAVY CROCKETT (...Frontier Fighter #1,2; Kid Montana #9 on)
Aug, 1955 - No. 8, Jan, 1957
Charlton Comics

	GD25	FN65	NM94
1	5.00	15.00	30.00
2	3.60	9.00	18.00
3-8	2.40	6.00	12.00
Hunting With...('55, 16 pgs.)-Ben Franklin Store giveaway (Publ.-S. Rose)	2.80	7.00	14.00

DAYS OF THE MOB (See In the Days of the Mob)

DAYTONA SPECIAL (Vortex)(Value: cover or less)

DAZEY'S DIARY
June-Aug, 1962
Dell Publishing Co.

	GD25	FN65	NM94
01-174-208: Bill Woggon-c/a	4.00	10.00	20.00

DAZZLER, THE (Also see Marvel Graphic Novel & X-Men #130)
March, 1981 - No. 42, Mar, 1986
Marvel Comics Group

	GD25	FN65	NM94
1,2-X-Men app.	.40	1.00	2.00
3-37,39-42: 10,11-Galactus app. 21-Double size; photo-c. 42-The Beast app.		.50	1.00
38-Wolverine-c/app.; X-Men app.	1.20	3.00	6.00

NOTE: *No. 1 distributed only through comic shops.* ***Alcala*** *a-1i, 2i.* ***Chadwick*** *a-38-42p; c(p)-39, 41, 42.* ***Guice*** *a-38i, 42i; c-38, 40.*

DC CHALLENGE
Nov, 1985 - No. 12, Oct, 1986 ($1.25, 12 issue maxi-series)
DC Comics

Date With Danger #5, © STD

Davy Crockett #1, © CC

Dazzler #38, © MEG

DC Comics Presents #15, © DC

DC 100 Page Super Spectacular #21, © DC

DC Special Series #17, © DC

GD25 FN65 NM94

1-11: 1-Colan-a. 4-Gil Kane-c/a .60 1.25
12-($2.00)-Perez/Austin-c .40 1.00 2.00
NOTE: *Batman app. in 1-4, 6-12. Joker app. in 7.* ***Giffen*** *c/a-11.* ***Swan/Austin*** *c-10.*

DC COMICS PRESENTS
July-Aug, 1978 - No. 97, Sept, 1986 (Superman team-ups in all)
DC Comics

1-12,14-25: 19-Batgirl .50 1.00
13-Legion of Super Heroes (also in #43 & 80) .40 1.00 2.00
26-(10/80)-Green Lantern; intro Cyborg, Starfire, Raven (New Teen Titans); Starlin-c/a; Sargon the Sorcerer back-up; 16 pg. preview of the New Teen Titans 1.40 3.50 7.00
27-40,42-71,73-76,79-84,86-97: 31,58-Robin. 35-Man-Bat. 42,47-Sandman. 52-Doom Patrol. 82-Adam Strange. 83-Batman & Outsiders. 86-88-Crisis x-over. 88-Creeper .50 1.00
41-Superman/Joker-c/story .50 1.25 2.50
72-Joker/Phantom Stranger-c/story .50 1.25 2.50
77,78-Animal Man app. (77-cover app. also) .60 1.50 3.00
85-Swamp Thing; Alan Moore scripts .60 1.50 3.00
Annual 1-4: 1(9/82)-G.A. Superman. 2(7/83)-Intro/origin Superwoman. 3(9/84)-Shazam. 4(10/85)-Superwoman .60 1.20
NOTE: ***Adkins*** *a-2, 54; c-2.* ***Gil Kane*** *a-28, 35, Annual 3; c-48p, 56, 58, 60, 62, 64, 68, Annual 2, 3.* ***Kirby*** *c/a-84.* ***Kubert*** *c/a-66.* ***Morrow*** *c/a-65.* ***Newton*** *c/a-54p.* ***Orlando*** *c-53i.* ***Perez*** *a-26p, 61p; c-38, 61, 94.* ***Starlin*** *a-26-29p, 36p, 37p; c-26-29, 36, 37, 93.* ***Toth*** *a-84.* ***Williamson*** *i-79, 85, 87.*

DC GRAPHIC NOVEL (Also see DC Science Fiction...)
Nov, 1983 - No. 7, 1986 ($5.95, 68 pgs.)
DC Comics

1-5,7: 1-Star Raiders. 2-Warlords; not from regular Warlord series. 3-The Medusa Chain; Ernie Colon story/a. 4-The Hunger Dogs; Kirby-c/a(p). 5-Me and Joe Priest; Chaykin-c. 7-Space Clusters; Nino-c/a 1.20 3.00 6.00
6-Metalzoic; Sienkiewicz-c ($6.95) 1.40 3.50 7.00

DC 100 PAGE SUPER SPECTACULAR
(Title is 100 Page...No. 14 on)(Square bound) (Reprints, 50 cents)
No. 4, Summer, 1971 - No. 13, 6/72; No. 14, 2/73 - No. 22, 11/73 (No #1-3)
National Periodical Publications

4,5: 4-Weird Mystery Tales; Johnny Peril & Phantom Stranger; cover & splashes by Wrightson; origin Jungle Boy of Jupiter. 5-Love Stories; Wood inks, 7pgs. .60 1.50 3.00
6-"World's Greatest Super-Heroes"-JLA, JSA, Spectre, Johnny Quick, Vigilante & Hawkman; contains unpublished Wildcat story; N. Adams wrap-around-c .70 1.75 3.50
7-13: 7-(See Superman #245). 8-(See Batman #238). 9-(See Our Army at War #242). 10-(See Adventure #416). 11-(See Flash #214).12-(See Superboy #185). 13-(See Superman #252)
14-Batman-r/Detective #31,32,156; Atom-r/Showcase #34 1.20 3.00 6.00
15-22: 15-r/2nd Boy Commandos/Det. #65. 17-JSA-r/All Star #37(38 pgs.); Sandman-r/Adv. #66. 20-Batman-r/Det. #66,68, others; origin Two-Face. 21-r/Brave & the Bold #54. 22-r/All-Flash #13 .40 1.00 2.00
NOTE: ***Anderson*** *r-11, 14, 18i, 22.* ***B. Baily*** *r-18, 20.* ***Burnley*** *r-18, 20.* ***Crandall*** *r-14p, 20.* ***Drucker*** *r-4.* ***Infantino*** *r-17, 20, 22.* ***G. Kane*** *r-18.* ***Kubert*** *r-6, 7, 16, 17; c-16, 19.* ***Meskin*** *r-4, 22.* ***Mooney*** *r-15, 21.* ***Toth*** *r-17, 20.*

DC SCIENCE FICTION GRAPHIC NOVEL
1985 - No. 7, 1987 ($5.95)
DC Comics

SF1-SF7: SF1-Hell on Earth by Robert Bloch; Giffen-p. SF2-Nightwings by Robert Silverberg; G. Colan-p. SF3-Frost & Fire by Bradbury. SF4-Merchants of Venus. SF5-Demon With A Glass Hand by Ellison; M. Rogers-a. SF6-The Magic Goes Away by Niven. SF7-Sandkings by George R.R. Martin 1.20 3.00 6.00

DC SILVER AGE CLASSICS
1992 - Present ($1.00, color, all reprints)
DC Comics

...Action Comics #252; r/1st Supergirl .50 1.00
...Adventure Comics #247; r/1st Legion of S.H. .50 1.00
...The Brave and the Bold #28; r/1st JLA .50 1.00
...Detective Comics #225; r/1st Martian Manhunter .50 1.00
...Detective Comics #327; r/1st new look Batman .50 1.00
...Green Lantern #76; r/Green Lantern/Gr. Arrow .50 1.00
...House of Secrets #92; r/1st Swamp Thing .50 1.00
...Showcase #4; r/1st S.A. Flash .50 1.00
...Showcase #22; r/1st S.A. Green Lantern .50 1.00
...Sugar and Spike #99; 2 unpublished stories .50 1.00

DC SPECIAL (Also see Super DC...)
10-12/68 - No. 15, 11-12/71; No. 16, Spr/75 - No. 29, 8-9/77
National Periodical Publications

1-All Infantino issue; Flash, Batman, Adam Strange-r; begin 68 pg., 25 cent issues, end #15 1.60 4.00 8.00
2-15: 5-All Kubert issue; Viking Prince, Sgt. Rock-r. 12-Viking Prince; Kubert-c/a(r/B&B almost entirely). 15-G.A. Plastic Man origin-r/Police #1; origin Woozy by Cole; last 68 pg. issue 1.00 2.50 5.00
16-29: 16-Super Heroes Battle Super Gorillas; r/Capt. Storm #1, 1st Johnny Cloud/All-Amer. Men of War #82. 17-Early S.A. Green Lantern-r. 22-Origin Robin Hood. 28-Earth Shattering Disaster Stories; Legion of Super-Heroes story. 27-Untold Origin of the Justice Society. 29-Secret Origin of the Justice Society .60 1.50 3.00
NOTE: ***N. Adams*** *c-3, 4, 6, 11, 29.* ***Grell*** *a-20; c-17.* ***Heath*** *a-12r.* ***G. Kane*** *a-6p, 13r, 17r, 19-21r.* ***Kubert*** *a-6r, 12r, 22.* ***Meskin*** *a-10.* ***Moreira*** *a-10.* ***Staton*** *a-29p.* ***Toth*** *a-13, 20r. #1-15: 25 cents; 16-27: 50 cent; 28, 29: 60 cents. #1-13, 16-21: 68 pgs.; 14, 15: 52 pgs.*

DC SPECIAL BLUE-RIBBON DIGEST
Mar-Apr, 1980 - No. 24, Aug, 1982
DC Comics

1-24: All reprints? .50 1.00
NOTE: ***N. Adams*** *a-16(6)r, 17r, 23r; c-16.* ***Aparo*** *a-6r, 24r; c-23.* ***Grell*** *a-8, 10; c-10.* ***Heath*** *a-14.* ***Kaluta*** *a-17r.* ***Gil Kane*** *a-22r.* ***Kirby*** *a-23r.* ***Kubert*** *a-3, 18r, 21r; c-7, 12, 14, 17, 18, 21, 24.* ***Morrow*** *a-24r.* ***Orlando*** *a-17r, 22r; c-1, 20.* ***Perez*** *c-19p.* ***Toth*** *a-21r, 24r.* ***Wood*** *a-3, 17r, 24r.* ***Wrightson*** *a-16r, 17r, 24r.*

DC SPECIAL SERIES
9/77 - No. 16, Fall, 1978; No. 17, 8/79 - No. 27, Fall, 1981
(No. 19,23,24 - digest size, 100 pgs.; No. 25-27 - over-sized)
National Periodical Publications/DC Comics

1-Five-Star Super-Hero Spectacular; Atom, Flash, Green Lantern, Aquaman, Batman, Kobra app.; N. Adams-c .60 1.50 3.00
2(#1)-The Original Swamp Thing Saga (1977)-r/Swamp Thing #1&2 by Wrightson; Wrightson wraparound-c .60 1.50 3.00
3-20,22-24: 6-Jones-a. 7-Ghosts Special. 10-Origin Dr. Fate, Lightray & Black Canary. 14,17,20-Original Swamp Thing Saga; r/Swamp Thing #3-10 by Wrightson (52-68 pgs.). 15-Batman Spectacular. 19-Secret Origins of Super-Heroes; origins Wonder Woman (new-a), Robin, & Batman-Superman team. 22-G.I. Combat .40 1.00 2.00
21-Miller-a (1st on Batman) 2.40 6.00 12.00
V5#25-($2.95, Sum/81)-Superman II the Adventure Continues; photos from movie & photo-c (see All-New Coll. Ed. C-62) .60 1.50 3.00
26-($2.95, Sum/81)-Superman and His Incredible Fortress of Solitude .60 1.50 3.00
27-($2.50)-Batman vs. The Incredible Hulk 1.00 2.50 5.00
NOTE: ***Golden*** *a-15.* ***Heath*** *a-12i, 16.* ***Kubert*** *c-13.* ***Nasser*** *a-1.* ***Rogers*** *c/a-15.* ***Starlin*** *c-12.* ***Staton*** *a-1. #25 & 26 were advertised as All-New Collectors' Edition C-63, C-64. #26 was originally planned as All-New Coll. Ed. C-30?; has C-630 & A.N.C.E. on cover.*

DC SPOTLIGHT
1985 (50th anniversary special)
DC Comics (giveaway)

1 .60 1.20

DC SUPER-STARS
March, 1976 - No. 18, Winter, 1978 (No.3-18: 52 pgs.)

National Periodical Publications/DC Comics

1-(68 pgs.)-Re-intro Teen Titans plus T. Titans-r .70 1.75 3.50

2-7,9,11-14,16,18: 2-6,8-Adam Strange; 2-(68 pgs.)-r/1st Adam Strange/Hawkman team-up from Mystery in Space #90 plus Atomic Knights origin-r. 13-Sergio Aragones Special .50 1.00

8-r/1st Space Ranger from Showcase #15, Adam Strange-r/Mystery in Space #89 & Star Rovers-r/M.I.S. #80 .70 1.75 3.50

10-Strange Sports Stories; Batman/Joker-c/story .80 2.00 4.00

15-Batman Spectacular; Golden & Rogers-a .50 1.25 2.50

17-Secret Origins of Super-Heroes(origin of The Huntress); origin Green Arrow by Grell; Legion app.; Earth II Batman & Catwoman marry (1st revealed; also see B&B #197) .40 1.00 2.00

NOTE: ***M. Anderson*** *r-2, 4, 6.* ***Aparo*** *c-7, 14, 17, 18.* ***Austin*** *a-11i.* ***Buckler*** *a-14p; c-10.* ***Grell*** *a-17.* ***G. Kane*** *a-1r, 10r.* ***Kubert*** *c-15.* ***Layton*** *c/a-16i, 17i.* ***Mooney*** *a-4r, 6r.* ***Morrow*** *c/a-11r.* ***Nasser*** *a-11.* ***Newton*** *c/a-16p.* ***Staton*** *a-17; c-17. No. 10, 12-18 contain all new material; the rest are reprints. #1 contains new and reprint material.*

D-DAY (Also see Special War Series)
Sum/63; No. 2, Fall/64; No. 4, 9/66; No. 5, 10/67; No. 6, 11/68
Charlton Comics (no No. 3)

1(1963)-Montes/Bache-c 2.40 6.00 12.00
2(Fall,'64)-Wood-a(3) 3.00 7.50 15.00
4-6('66-'68)-Montes/Bache-a #5 1.80 4.50 9.00

DEAD END CRIME STORIES
April, 1949 (52 pages)
Kirby Publishing Co.

nn-(Scarce)-Powell, Roussos-a 29.00 85.00 200.00

DEAD-EYE WESTERN COMICS
Nov-Dec, 1948 - V3#1, Apr-May, 1953
Hillman Periodicals

V1#1-(52 pgs.)-Krigstein, Roussos-a 10.00 30.00 60.00
V1#2,3-(52 pgs.) 5.00 15.00 30.00
V1#4-12-(52 pgs.) 4.00 10.00 20.00
V2#1,2,5-8,10-12: 1-7-(52 pgs.) 3.20 8.00 16.00
3,4-Krigstein-a (52 pgs.) 5.00 15.00 30.00
9-One pg. Frazetta ad 3.20 8.00 16.00
V3#1 2.80 7.00 14.00

NOTE: ***Briefer*** *a-V1#8. Kinstleresque stories by* ***McCann****-12, V2#1, 2, V3#1.* ***McWilliams*** *a-V1#5.* ***Ed Moore*** *a-V1#4.*

DEADFACE: DOING THE ISLANDS WITH BACCHUS
July, 1991 - No. 3, Sept, 1991 ($2.95, B&W, mini-series, 52 pgs.)
Dark Horse Comics

1-3: By Eddie Campbell .60 1.50 3.00

DEADFACE: EARTH, WATER, AIR, AND FIRE
July, 1992 - No. 4, Oct, 1992 ($2.50, B&W, mini-series; British-r)
Dark Horse Comics

1-4: By Eddie Campbell .50 1.25 2.50

DEADLIEST HEROES OF KUNG FU
Summer, 1975 (Magazine)
Marvel Comics Group

1 .35 .90 1.80

DEADLINE USA
Apr, 1992 - Present ($3.95, B&W, 52 pgs.)
Dark Horse Comics

1-10: Johnny Nemo w/Milligan scripts in all .80 2.00 4.00

DEADLY FOES OF SPIDER-MAN (Marvel)(Value: cover or less)

DEADLY HANDS OF KUNG FU, THE (See Master of Kung Fu)
April, 1974 - No. 33, Feb, 1977 (75 cents) (B&W - Magazine)
Marvel Comics Group

1(V1#4 listed in error)-Origin Sons of the Tiger; Shang-Chi, Master of Kung Fu begins; Bruce Lee photo pin-up .70 1.75 3.50
2,3,5 .40 1.00 2.00
4-Bruce Lee painted-c by Neal Adams; 8 pg. biog of Bruce Lee .70 1.75 3.50
6-14 .40 1.00 2.00
15-(Annual 1, Summer '75)-Origin Iron Fist retold (predates Iron Fist #1) .40 1.00 2.00
16-19,21-27,29-33: 17-1st Giffen-a (1 pg.; 11/75). 19-1st White Tiger. 22-1st app. Jack of Hearts; 1st Giffen story-a .30 .75 1.50
20-Origin The White Tiger; Perez-a .40 1.00 2.00
28-Origin Jack of Hearts; Bruce Lee life story .60 1.50 3.00
Special Album Edition 1(Summer, '74)-Adams-i .40 1.00 2.00

NOTE: ***N. Adams*** *a-1i(part), 27i; c-1, 2-4, 11, 12, 14, 17.* ***Giffen*** *a-22p, 24p.* ***G. Kane*** *a-23p.* ***Kirby*** *a-5r.* ***Nasser*** *a-27p, 28.* ***Perez*** *a(p)-6-14, 16, 17, 19, 21.* ***Rogers*** *a-26, 32, 33.* ***Starlin*** *a-1, 2r, 15r.* ***Staton*** *a-28p, 31, 32. Iron Fist in #10, 15, 18-24. Shang Chi, Master of Kung Fu in #1-9, 11-18, 33. Sons of the Tiger in #1, 3, 4, 6-14, 16-19 (White Tiger #20-24, 26, 27, 29-31).*

DEADMAN (See The Brave and the Bold & Phantom Stranger #39)
May, 1985 - No. 7, Nov, 1985 ($1.75, Baxter paper)
DC Comics

1-Deadman-r by Infantino, N. Adams in all .35 .90 1.75
2-7: 5-Batman-c/story-r/Str. Advs. 7-Batman-r .35 .90 1.75

DEADMAN
Mar, 1986 - No. 4, June, 1986 (75 cents, mini-series)
DC Comics

1-4: Lopez-c/a. 4-Byrne-c(p) .50 1.00

DEADMAN: EXORCISM
1992 - No. 2, 1992 ($4.95, color, mini-series, 52 pgs.)
DC Comics

1,2-Kelley Jones-c/a 1.00 2.50 5.00

DEADMAN: LOVE AFTER DEATH
1989 - No. 2, 1990 ($3.95, 2 issue series, mature readers, 52 pgs.)
DC Comics

Book One, Two: 1-Contains nudity .80 2.00 4.00

DEAD OF NIGHT
Dec, 1973 - No. 11, Aug, 1975
Marvel Comics Group

1-Horror reprints .40 1.00 2.00
2-11: 11-Intro Scarecrow; Kane/Wrightson-c .50 1.00

NOTE: ***Ditko*** *r-7, 10.* ***Everett*** *c-2.* ***Sinnott*** *r-1.*

DEADSHOT (See Batman #59 & Detective Comics #474)
Nov, 1988 - No. 4, Feb, 1989 ($1.00, color, mini-series)
DC Comics

1-4: Deadshot is a Batman villain .50 1.00

DEAD WHO WALK, THE (See Strange Mysteries, Super Reprint #15, 16)
1952 (One Shot)
Realistic Comics

nn 29.00 85.00 200.00

DEADWOOD GULCH
1931 (52 pages) (B&W)
Dell Publishing Co.

nn-By Charles "Boody" Rogers 11.50 34.00 80.00

DEADWORLD (Also see The Realm)
Dec, 1986 - Present ($1.50-$1.95, B&W, adults)($2.50 #15 on)
Arrow Comics/Caliber Comics

1 1.20 3.00 6.00
2 .80 2.00 4.00
3,4 .60 1.50 3.00
5-11: Graphic covers .60 1.50 3.00
5-11: Tame covers .40 1.00 2.00
12-28: Graphic covers .50 1.25 2.50
12-28: Tame covers .50 1.25 2.50

DC Super-Stars #2, © DC

D-Day #1, © CC

Dead-Eye Western V2#4, © HILL

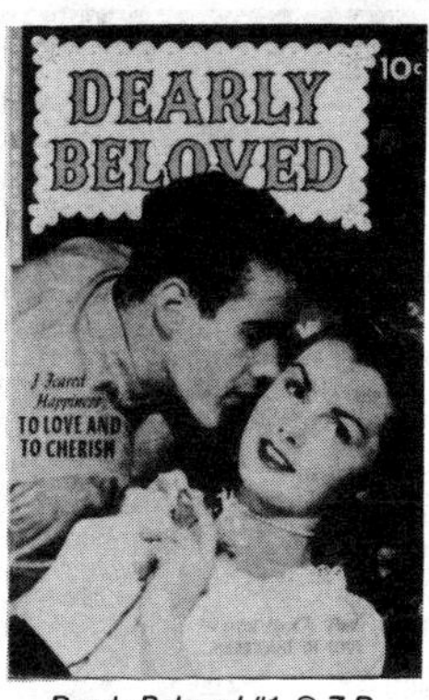

Dearly Beloved #1, © Z-D

Deathlok #2 (8/91), © MEG

Deathstroke: The Terminator #3, © DC

	GD25	FN65	NM94
DEAN MARTIN & JERRY LEWIS (See Adventures of...)			
DEAR BEATRICE FAIRFAX No. 5, Nov, 1950 - No. 9, Sept, 1951 (Vern Greene art) Best/Standard Comics(King Features)			
5	4.70	14.00	28.00
6-9	3.20	8.00	16.00
NOTE: ***Schomburg** air brush c-5-9.*			
DEAR HEART (Formerly Lonely Heart) No. 15, July, 1956 - No. 16, Sept, 1956 Ajax			
15,16	3.00	7.50	15.00
DEAR LONELY HEART (...Illustrated No. 1-6) Mar, 1951; No. 2, Oct, 1951 - No. 8, Oct, 1952 Artful Publications			
1	10.00	30.00	65.00
2	5.00	15.00	30.00
3-Matt Baker Jungle Girl story	10.00	30.00	65.00
4-8	4.35	13.00	26.00
DEAR LONELY HEARTS (Lonely Heart #9 on) Aug, 1953 - No. 8, Oct, 1954 Harwell Publ./Mystery Publ. Co. (Comic Media)			
1	5.00	15.00	30.00
2-8	3.20	8.00	16.00
DEARLY BELOVED Fall, 1952 Ziff-Davis Publishing Co.			
1-Photo-c	10.00	30.00	65.00
DEAR NANCY PARKER June, 1963 - No. 2, Sept, 1963 Gold Key			
1,2-Painted-c	3.00	7.50	15.00
DEATHLOK (Also see Astonishing Tales #25) July, 1990 - No. 4, Oct, 1990 ($3.95, limited series, 52 pgs.) Marvel Comics			
1-Guice-a(p)	2.40	6.00	12.00
2-4: 2-Guice-a(p). 3,4-Denys Cowan-a, c-4	1.60	4.00	8.00
DEATHLOK July, 1991 - Present ($1.75, color) Marvel Comics			
1-Silver ink cover; Denys Cowan-c/a(p) begins	.80	2.00	4.00
2-5: 2-Forge (X-Men) app. 3-Vs. Dr. Doom. 5-X-Men & F.F. x-over	.60	1.50	3.00
6-10: 6,7-Punisher x-over. 9,10-Ghost Rider-c/sty	.40	1.00	2.00
11-24: 16-Infinity War x-over. 17-Jae Lee-c	.35	.90	1.80
Annual 1 (1992, $2.25, 68 pgs.)-Guice & Cowan-p	.50	1.25	2.50
NOTE: ***Denys Cowan** a(p)-9-13, 15; c-9-12, 13p, 14. **Guice/Cowan** c-8.*			
DEATHLOK SPECIAL May, 1991 - No. 4, Late-June, 1991 ($2.00, bi-weekly mini-series) Marvel Comics			
1-4: r/1-4('90) w/new Guice-c #1,2; Cowan c-3,4	.55	1.40	2.80
1-2nd printing w/white-c	.45	1.15	2.30
DEATH OF CAPTAIN MARVEL (See Marvel Graphic Novel #1)			
DEATH OF MR. MONSTER, THE (See Mr. Monster #8)			
DEATH RATTLE (Kitchen Sink)(Value: cover or less)			
DEATH'S HEAD (See Daredevil #56 & Dragon's Claws #5) Dec, 1988 - No. 10, Sept, 1989 ($1.75, color)(Dragon's Claws spin-off) Marvel Comics			
1-Dragon's Claws spin-off	3.00	7.50	15.00
2-Fantastic Four app.	1.50	3.75	7.50
3,4	1.00	2.50	5.00
5-10: 9-Simonson-c(p)	.70	1.75	3.50
DEATH'S HEAD II (Also see Battletide) Mar, 1992 - No. 4, June (May inside), 1992 ($1.75, color, mini-series) Marvel Comics UK, Ltd.			
1	2.00	5.00	10.00
1,2-Silver ink 2nd printiings	.40	1.00	2.00
2-Fantastic Four app.	1.50	3.75	7.50
3,4: 4-Punisher, Spider-Man , Daredevil, Dr. Strange, Capt. America & Wolverine in the year 2020	.80	2.00	4.00
DEATH'S HEAD II Dec, 1992 - Present ($1.75, color) Marvel Comics UK, Ltd.			
1-6: 1-Gatefold-c; X-Men app. 4-X-Men app.	.35	.90	1.75
DEATHSTROKE: THE TERMINATOR (Also see Marvel & DC Present, New Teen Titans #2, New Titans & Tales of the Teen Titans #42-44) Aug, 1991 - Present ($1.75, color) DC Comics			
1-New Titans spin-off	1.60	4.00	8.00
1-Gold ink 2nd printing ($1.75)	.40	1.00	2.00
2	1.00	2.50	5.00
3-5	.60	1.50	3.00
6-22: 6,8-Batman cameo. 7,9-Batman-c/story. 9-1st app. new Vigilante (female) in cameo. 10-1st full app. new Vigilante; Perez-i. 13-Vs. Justice League; Team Titans cameo on last pg. 14-Total Chaos, part 1; Team Titans-c/story cont'd in New Titans #90. 15-Total Chaos, part 4	.35	.90	1.75
Annual 1 (1992 $3.50, 68 pgs.)-Nightwing & Vigilante app.; minor Eclipso app.	.70	1.75	3.50
DEATH VALLEY Oct, 1953 - No. 6, Aug, 1954? Comic Media			
1-Billy the Kid; Morisi-a; Andru/Esposito-c/a	6.35	19.00	38.00
2	4.00	11.00	22.00
3-6: 3,5-Morisi-a. 5-Discount-a	3.60	9.00	18.00
DEATH VALLEY (Becomes Frontier Scout, Daniel Boone No.10-13) No. 7, 6/55 - No. 9, 10/55 (Continued from Comic Media series) Charlton Comics			
7-9: 8-Wolverton-a (half pg.)	3.60	9.00	18.00
DEBBIE DEAN, CAREER GIRL April, 1945 - No. 2, July, 1945 Civil Service Publ.			
1,2-Newspaper reprints by Bert Whitman	10.00	30.00	65.00
DEBBI'S DATES (Also see Date With Debbi) Apr-May, 1969 - No. 11, Dec-Jan, 1970-71 National Periodical Publications			
1	2.00	5.00	10.00
2-11: 4-Neal Adams text illo. 6-Superman cameo	1.00	2.50	5.00
DEEP, THE (Movie) November, 1977 Marvel Comics Group			
1-Infantino-c/a	.30	.75	1.50
DEFENDERS, THE (TV) Sept-Nov, 1962 - No. 2, Feb-Apr, 1963 Dell Publishing Co.			
12-176-211(#1), 12-176-304(#2)	3.20	8.00	16.00

DEFENDERS, THE (Also see Giant-Size..., Marvel Feature, Marvel Treasury Edition, Secret Defenders & Sub-Mariner #34, 35; The New...#140-on)
Aug, 1972 - No. 152, Feb, 1986
Marvel Comics Group

	GD25	FN65	NM94
1-The Hulk, Doctor Strange, Sub-Mariner begin	9.15	27.50	55.00
2	4.70	14.00	28.00
3-5: 4-Valkyrie joins	4.00	10.00	20.00
6-9: 9-Avengers app.	3.60	9.00	18.00
10-Hulk vs. Thor; Avengers app.	4.20	12.50	25.00
11-14: 12-Last 20 cent issue	1.80	4.50	9.00
15,16-Magneto & Brotherhood of Evil Mutants app. from X-Men	2.40	6.00	12.00
17-20: 17-Power Man x-over (11/74)	1.40	3.50	7.00
21-25: 24,25-Son of Satan app.	1.10	2.75	5.50
26-29-Guardians of the Galaxy app. (#26 is 8/75; pre-dates Marvel Presents #3). 28-1st full app. Starhawk (cameo #27). 29-Starhawk joins Guardians	2.20	5.50	11.00
30-50: 31,32-Origin Nighthawk. 35-Intro New Red Guardian. 44-Hellcat joins. 45-Dr. Strange leaves	.90	2.25	4.50
51-60: 53-1st app. Lunatik in cameo (Lobo lookalike). 55-Origin Red Guardian; Lunatik cameo. 56-1st full Lunatik story	.80	2.00	4.00
61-72: 61-Lunatik & Spider-Man app. 70-73-Lunatik (origin #71)	.70	1.75	3.50
73-75-Foolkiller II app. (Greg Salinger). 74-Nighthawk resigns	.70	1.75	3.50
76-95,97-151: 77-Origin Omega. 78-Original Defenders return thru #101. 94-1st Gargoyle. 100-(52 pgs.)-Hellcat (Patsy Walker) revealed as Satan's daughter. 104-The Beast joins. 105-Son of Satan joins. 106-Death of Nighthawk. 120,121-Son of Satan-c/stories. 122-Final app. Son of Satan (2 pgs.). 129-New Mutants cameo (3/84, early x-over). 150-Double size; origin Cloud	.45	1.10	2.20
96-Ghost Rider app.	.90	2.20	4.40
125-Double size; intro new Defenders	.60	1.50	3.00
152-Double size; ties in with X-Factor & Secret Wars II	.55	1.40	2.80
Annual 1 (1976, 52 pgs.)-New book-length story	.80	2.00	4.00

NOTE: ***Art Adams*** *c-142p.* ***Austin*** *a-53i; c-65i, 119i, 145i.* ***Frank Bolle*** *a-7i, 10i, 11i.* ***Buckler*** *c(p)-34, 38, 76, 77, 79-86, 90, 91.* ***J. Buscema*** *c-66.* ***Giffen*** *a-42-49p, 50, 51-54p.* ***Golden*** *a-53p, 54p; c-94, 96.* ***Guice*** *c-129.* ***G. Kane*** *c(p)-13, 16, 18, 19, 21-26, 31-33, 35-37, 40, 41, 52, 55.* ***Kirby*** *c-42-45.* ***Mooney*** *a-3i, 31-34i, 62i, 63i, 85i.* ***Nasser*** *c-88p.* ***Perez*** *c(p)-51, 53, 54.* ***Rogers*** *c-98.* ***Starlin*** *c-110.* ***Tuska*** *a-57p. Silver Surfer in No. 2, 3, 6, 8-11, 92, 98-101, 107, 112-115, 122-125.*

DEFENDERS OF DYNATRON CITY
Feb, 1992 - No. 6, July, 1992 ($1.25, color, limited series)
Marvel Comics

	GD25	FN65	NM94
1-6-Lucasarts characters. 2-Origin		.60	1.25

DEFENDERS OF THE EARTH (TV)
Jan, 1987 - No. 5, Sept, 1987
Star Comics (Marvel)

	GD25	FN65	NM94
1-5: The Phantom, Mandrake The Magician, Flash Gordon begin		.50	1.00

THE DEFINITIVE DIRECTORY OF THE DC UNIVERSE (See Who's Who...)

DELECTA OF THE PLANETS (See Don Fortune & Fawcett Miniatures)

DELLA VISION (Patty Powers #4 on)
April, 1955 - No. 3, Aug, 1955
Atlas Comics

	GD25	FN65	NM94
1	10.00	30.00	60.00
2,3	6.70	20.00	40.00

DELL GIANT COMICS
No. 21, Sept, 1959 - No. 55, Sept, 1961 (Most 84 pages, 25 cents)
Dell Publishing Co.

	GD25	FN65	VF82	NM94
21-(#1)-M.G.M.'s Tom & Jerry Picnic Time (84pp, stapled binding)	9.00	27.00	55.00	110.00
22-Huey, Dewey & Louie Back to School(10/59, 84pp, square binding begins)	6.25	19.00	38.00	75.00
23-Marge's Little Lulu & Tubby Halloween Fun (10/59)-Tripp-a	11.00	32.00	65.00	130.00
24-Woody Woodpecker's Family Fun (11/59)	6.25	19.00	38.00	75.00
25-Tarzan's Jungle World(11/59)-Marsh-a	10.00	30.00	60.00	120.00
26-Christmas Parade-Barks-a, 16pgs.(Disney; 12/59)-Barks draws himself on wanted poster pg. 13	18.00	55.00	110.00	220.00
27-Man in Space r-/4-Color 716,866, & 954 (100 pages, 35 cents) (Disney)(TV)	9.00	27.00	55.00	110.00
28-Bugs Bunny's Winter Fun (2/60)	8.00	25.00	50.00	100.00
29-Marge's Little Lulu & Tubby in Hawaii (4/60)-Tripp-a	11.00	32.00	65.00	130.00
30-Disneyland USA(6/60)-Reprinted in Vacation in Disneyland	8.00	25.00	50.00	100.00
31-Huckleberry Hound Summer Fun (7/60)(TV)	11.00	32.00	65.00	130.00
32-Bugs Bunny Beach Party	4.60	14.00	28.00	55.00
33-Daisy Duck & Uncle Scrooge Picnic Time (9/60)	8.00	25.00	50.00	100.00
34-Nancy & Sluggo Summer Camp (8/60)	5.50	16.00	32.00	65.00
35-Huey, Dewey & Louie Back to School (10/60)	6.25	19.00	38.00	75.00
36-Marge's Little Lulu & Witch Hazel Halloween Fun(10/60)-Tripp-a	11.00	32.00	65.00	130.00
37-Tarzan, King of the Jungle(11/60)-Marsh-a	9.00	27.00	55.00	110.00
38-Uncle Donald & His Nephews Family Fun (11/60)	5.50	16.00	32.00	65.00
39-Walt Disney's Merry Christmas(12/60)	6.25	19.00	38.00	75.00
40-Woody Woodpecker Christmas Parade(12/60)	4.60	14.00	28.00	55.00
41-Yogi Bear's Winter Sports (12/60)(TV)	11.00	32.00	65.00	130.00
42-Marge's Little Lulu & Tubby in Australia (4/61)	11.00	32.00	65.00	130.00
43-Mighty Mouse in Outer Space (5/61)	18.00	55.00	110.00	220.00
44-Around the World with Huckleberry & His Friends (7/61)(TV)	11.00	32.00	65.00	130.00
45-Nancy & Sluggo Summer Camp (8/61)	4.60	14.00	28.00	55.00
46-Bugs Bunny Beach Party (8/61)	4.60	14.00	28.00	55.00
47-Mickey & Donald in Vacationland (8/61)	6.25	19.00	38.00	75.00
48-The Flintstones (No. 1)(Bedrock Bedlam)(7/61)(TV)	13.00	40.00	80.00	160.00
49-Huey, Dewey & Louie Back to School (9/61)	4.60	14.00	28.00	55.00
50-Marge's Little Lulu & Witch Hazel Trick 'N' Treat (10/61)	11.00	32.00	65.00	130.00
51-Tarzan, King of the Jungle by Jesse Marsh (11/61)	7.00	21.00	42.00	85.00
52-Uncle Donald & His Nephews Dude Ranch (11/61)	4.60	14.00	28.00	55.00
53-Donald Duck Merry Christmas(12/61)-Not by Barks	4.60	14.00	28.00	55.00
54-Woody Woodpecker Christmas Party(12/61)-issued after No. 55	5.50	16.00	32.00	65.00

The Defenders #6, © MEG

Dell Giant #30, © WDC

Dell Giant #51, © ERB

Bugs Bunny Christmas Funnies #5, © Warner Bros.

Donald Duck Beach Party #1, © WDC

Mickey Mouse Birthday Party #1, © WDC

	GD25	FN65	NM94
55-Daisy Duck & Uncle Scrooge Showboat (9/61)-1st app. Daisy Duck's nieces, April, May & June	14.00	41.00	82.00	165.00

NOTE: *All issues printed with & without ad on back cover.*

(OTHER DELL GIANT EDITIONS)

Title	GD25	FN65	NM94
Abraham Lincoln Life Story 1(3/58, 100p)	5.50	16.00	32.00	65.00
Bugs Bunny Christmas Funnies 1(11/50, 116p)	14.00	41.00	82.00	165.00
...**Christmas Funnies** 2(11/51, 116p)	9.00	27.00	55.00	110.00
...**Christmas Funnies** 3-5(11/52-11/54, 100p)-Becomes Christmas Party #6	8.00	25.00	50.00	100.00
...**Christmas Funnies** 7-9(12/56-12/58, 100p)	7.00	20.00	40.00	80.00
...**Christmas Party** 6(11/55, 100p)-Formerly Bugs Bunny Christmas Funnies	6.25	19.00	38.00	75.00
...**County Fair** 1(9/57, 100p	9.00	27.00	55.00	110.00
...**Halloween Parade** 1(10/53, 100p)	8.00	25.00	50.00	100.00
...**Halloween Parade** 2(10/54, 100p)-Trick 'N' Treat Halloween Fun No. 3 on	7.00	20.00	40.00	80.00
...**Trick 'N' Treat Halloween Fun** 3,4(10/55-10/56, 100p)-Formerly Halloween Parade #2	7.50	22.50	45.00	90.00
...**Vacation Funnies** 1(7/51, 112p)	14.00	41.00	82.00	165.00
...**Vacation Funnies** 2('52, 100p)	11.00	32.00	65.00	130.00
...**Vacation Funnies** 3-5('53-'55, 100p)	8.00	25.00	50.00	100.00
...**Vacation Funnies** 6-9('54-6/59, 100p)	7.00	20.00	40.00	80.00
Cadet Gray of West Point 1(4/58, 100p)-Williamson-a, 10pgs.; Buscema-a; photo-c	4.60	14.00	28.00	55.00
Christmas In Disneyland 1(12/57, 100p)-Barks-a, 18pgs.	11.00	32.00	65.00	130.00
Christmas Parade 1(11/49)-Barks-a, 25pgs; r-in G.K. Christmas Parade #5	39.00	120.00	235.00	470.00
Christmas Parade 2('50)-Barks-a, 25pgs; r-in G.K. Christmas Parade #6	27.00	81.00	162.00	325.00
Christmas Parade 3-7('51-'55, 116-100p)	5.50	16.00	32.00	65.00
Christmas Parade 8(12/56, 100p)-Barks-a, 8pgs.	11.00	32.00	65.00	130.00
Christmas Parade 9(12/58, 100p)-Barks-a, 20pgs.	13.00	40.00	80.00	160.00
Christmas Treasury, A 1(11/54, 100p)	7.00	20.00	40.00	80.00
Davy Crockett, King Of The Wild Frontier 1(9/55, 100p)-Photo-c; Marsh-a	14.00	41.00	82.00	165.00
Disneyland Birthday Party 1(10/58, 100p)-Barks-a, 16pgs.	11.00	32.00	65.00	130.00
Donald and Mickey In Disneyland 1(5/58, 100p)	6.25	19.00	38.00	75.00
Donald Duck Beach Party 1(7/54, 100p)	7.00	20.00	40.00	80.00
...**Beach Party** 2('55, 100p)	5.00	15.00	30.00	60.00
...**Beach Party** 3-5('56-'58, 100p)	4.60	14.00	28.00	55.00
...**Beach Party** 6(8/59, 84p)-Stapled	4.60	14.00	28.00	55.00
Donald Duck Fun Book 1,2('53-10/54, 100p)-Games, puzzles, comics & cut-outs (Rare)	21.00	62.00	125.00	250.00
Donald Duck In Disneyland 1(9/55, 100p)	4.60	14.00	28.00	55.00
Golden West Rodeo Treasury 1(10/57, 100p)	6.25	19.00	38.00	75.00
Huey, Dewey and Louie Back To School 1(9/58, 100p)	5.50	16.00	32.00	65.00
Lady and The Tramp 1(6/55, 100p)	7.00	20.00	40.00	80.00
Life Stories of American Presidents 1(11/57, 100p)-Buscema-a	4.00	12.00	25.00	50.00
Lone Ranger Golden West 3(8/55, 100p)-Formerly Lone Ranger Western Treasury	14.00	41.00	82.00	165.00
Lone Ranger Movie Story nn(3/56, 100p)-Origin Lone Ranger in text; Clayton Moore photo-c	27.00	81.00	162.00	325.00
...**Western Treasury** 1(9/53, 100p)-Origin Lone Ranger, Silver, &Tonto	16.00	48.00	95.00	190.00
...**Western Treasury** 2(8/54, 100p)-Becomes Lone Ranger Golden West #3	9.00	27.00	55.00	110.00
Marge's Little Lulu & Alvin Story Telling Time 1(3/59)-r/#2,5,3,11,30,10, 21,17,8,14,16; Stanley-a	11.00	32.00	65.00	130.00
...**& Her Friends** 4(3/56, 100p)-Tripp-a	8.00	25.00	50.00	100.00
...**& Her Special Friends** 3(3/55, 100p)-Tripp-a	8.00	25.00	50.00	100.00
...**& Tubby At Summer Camp** 5(10/57, 100p)-Tripp-a	8.00	25.00	50.00	100.00
...**& Tubby At Summer Camp** 2(10/58, 100p)-Tripp-a	8.00	25.00	50.00	100.00
...**& Tubby Halloween Fun** 6(10/57, 100p)-Tripp-a	8.00	25.00	50.00	100.00
...**& Tubby Halloween Fun** 2(10/58, 100p)-Tripp-a	8.00	25.00	50.00	100.00
...**& Tubby In Alaska** 1(7/59, 100p)-Tripp-a	8.00	25.00	50.00	100.00
...**On Vacation** 1(7/54, 100p)-r/4C-110,14,4C-146,5,4C-97,4,4C-158,3,1; Stanley-a	14.00	41.00	82.00	165.00
...**& Tubby Annual** 1(3/53, 100p)-r/4C-165,4C-74,4C-146,4C-97,4C-158, 4C-139,4C-131; Stanley-a	27.00	81.00	162.00	325.00
...**& Tubby Annual** 2('54, 100p)-r/4C-139,6,4C-115,4C-74,5,4C-97,3,4C-146, 18; Stanley-a	27.00	81.00	162.00	325.00
Marge's Tubby & His Clubhouse Pals 1(10/56, 100p)-1st app. Gran'pa Feeb, written by Stanley; 1st app. Janie; Tripp-a	11.00	32.00	65.00	130.00
Mickey Mouse Almanac 1(12/57, 100p)-Barks-a, 8pgs.	23.00	70.00	138.00	275.00
...**Birthday Party** 1(9/53, 100p)-r/entire 48pgs. of Gottfredson's "Mickey Mouse in Love Trouble" from WDC&S 36-39. Quality equal to original. Also reprints one story each from 4-Color 27, 29, & 181 plus 6 panels of high-lights in the career of Mickey Mouse	21.00	62.00	125.00	250.00
...**Club Parade** 1(12/55, 100p)-r/4-Color 16 with some art redrawn by Paul Murry & recolored with night scenes turned into day; quality much poorer than original	18.00	55.00	110.00	220.00
...**In Fantasy Land** 1(5/57, 100p)	8.00	25.00	50.00	100.00
...**In Frontier Land** 1(5/56, 100p)-Mickey Mouse Club issue	8.00	25.00	50.00	100.00
...**Summer Fun** 1(8/58, 100p)-Mobile cut-outs on back-c; becomes Summer Fun #2	7.50	22.50	45.00	90.00
Moses & The Ten Commandments 1(8/57, 100p)-Not based on movie; Dell's adaptation; Sekowsky-a	4.60	14.00	28.00	55.00
Nancy & Sluggo Travel Time 1(9/58, 100p)	6.25	19.00	38.00	75.00
Peter Pan Treasure Chest 1(1/53, 212p)-Disney; contains movie adaptation plus other stories	54.00	162.00	325.00	650.00

	GD25	FN65	VF82	NM94

Picnic Party 6,7(7/55-6/56, 100p)(Formerly Vacation Parade)-Uncle Scrooge, Mickey & Donald 6.25 19.00 38.00 75.00

Picnic Party 8(7/57, 100p)-Barks-a, 6pgs.
9.00 27.00 55.00 110.00

Pogo Parade 1(9/53, 100p)-Kelly-a(r-/Pogo from Animal Comics in this order: #11,13,21,14,27,16,23,9,18,15,17)
19.00 56.00 112.50 225.00

Raggedy Ann & Andy 1(2/55, 100p)
14.00 41.00 82.00 165.00

Santa Claus Funnies 1(11/52, 100p)-Dan Noonan -A Christmas Carol adaptation 7.00 20.00 40.00 80.00

Silly Symphonies 1(9/52, 100p)-r/Chicken Little, M. Mouse "The Brave Little Tailor," Mother Pluto, Three Little Pigs, Lady, Bucky Bug, Wise Little Hen, Little Hiawatha, Pedro, The Grasshopper & The Ants
14.00 41.00 82.00 165.00

Silly Symphonies 2(9/53, 100p)-r/M. Mouse-"The Sorcerer's Apprentice," Little Hiawatha, Peculiar Penguins, Lambert The Sheepish Lion, Pluto, Spotty Pig, The Golden Touch, Elmer Elephant, The Pelican & The Snipe
11.00 32.00 65.00 130.00

Silly Symphonies 3(2/54, 100p)-r/Mickey & The Beanstalk (4-Color #157), Little Minnehaha, Pablo, The Flying Gauchito, Pluto, & Bongo
10.50 31.00 62.00 125.00

Silly Symphonies 4(8/54, 100p)-r/Dumbo (4-Color 234), Morris The Midget Moose, The Country Cousin, Bongo, & Clara Cluck
10.00 30.00 60.00 120.00

Silly Symphonies 5(2/55, 100p)-r/Cinderella (4-Color 272), Bucky Bug, Pluto, Little Hiawatha, The 7 Dwarfs & Dumbo, Pinocchio
10.00 30.00 60.00 120.00

Silly Symphonies 6(8/55, 100p)-r/Pinocchio(WDC&S 63), The 7 Dwarfs & Thumper (WDC&S 45), M. Mouse-"Adventures With Robin Hood," Johnny Appleseed, Pluto & Peter Pan, & Bucky Bug; Cut-out on back-c
10.00 30.00 60.00 120.00

Silly Symphonies 7(2/57, 100p)-r/Reluctant Dragon (4-Color 13), Ugly Duckling, M. Mouse & Peter Pan, Jiminy Cricket, Peter & The Wolf, Brer Rabbit, Bucky Bug; Cut-out on back-c
14.00 41.00 82.00 165.00

Silly Symphonies 8(2/58, 100p)-r/Thumper Meets The 7 Dwarfs (4-Color 19), Jiminy Cricket, Niok, Brer Rabbit; Cut-out on back-c
8.00 25.00 50.00 100.00

Silly Symphonies 9(2/59, 100p)-r/Paul Bunyan, Humphrey Bear, Jiminy Cricket, The Social Lion, Goliath II; Cut-out on back-c
8.00 25.00 50.00 100.00

Sleeping Beauty 1(4/59, 100p)
17.00 50.00 100.00 200.00

Summer Fun 2(8/59, 100p)(Formerly Mickey Mouse...)-Barks-a(2), 24 pgs.
14.00 41.00 82.00 165.00

Tales From The Tomb 1(02-810-210)(10/62, 25 cent giant)-All stories written by John Stanley 8.00 25.00 50.00 100.00

Tarzan's Jungle Annual 1(8/52, 100p)
7.50 22.50 45.00 90.00

...Annual 2(8/53, 100p) 6.25 19.00 38.00 75.00

...Annual 3-7('54-9/58, 100p)(two No. 5s)-Manning-a-No. 3,5-7; Marsh-a in No. 1-7 5.50 16.00 32.00 65.00

Tom And Jerry Back To School 1(9/56, 100p)
11.00 32.00 65.00 130.00

...Picnic Time 1(7/58, 100p) 8.00 25.00 50.00 100.00

...Summer Fun 1(7/54, 100p)-Droopy written by Barks
11.00 32.00 65.00 130.00

...Summer Fun 2-4(7/55-7/57, 100p)
4.60 14.00 28.00 55.00

...Toy Fair 1(6/58, 100p) 6.25 19.00 38.00 75.00

...Winter Carnival 1(12/52, 100p)-Droopy written by Barks
20.00 60.00 120.00 240.00

...Winter Carnival 2(12/53, 100p)-Droopy written by Barks
14.00 41.00 82.00 165.00

...Winter Fun 3(12/54, 100p) 5.50 16.00 32.00 65.00

...Winter Fun 4-7(12/55-11/58, 100p)
4.60 14.00 28.00 55.00

Treasury of Dogs, A 1(10/56, 100p)
4.60 14.00 28.00 55.00

Treasury of Horses, A 1(9/55, 100p)
4.60 14.00 28.00 55.00

Uncle Scrooge Goes To Disneyland 1(8/57, 100p)-Barks-a, 20pgs.
14.00 41.00 82.00 165.00

Universal Presents-Dracula-The Mummy & Other Stories 02-530-311 (9-11/63, 84p)-r/Dracula 12-231-212, The Mummy 12-437-211 &part of Ghost Stories No. 1 8.00 25.00 50.00 100.00

Vacation In Disneyland 1(8/58, 100p)
5.50 16.00 32.00 65.00

Vacation Parade 1(7/50, 130p)-Donald Duck & Mickey Mouse; Barks-a, 55 pgs. 62.00 188.00 375.00 750.00

Vacation Parade 2(7/51, 100p)
11.00 32.00 65.00 130.00

Vacation Parade 3-5(7/52-7/54, 100p)-Becomes Picnic Party No. 6 on
5.50 16.00 32.00 65.00

Western Roundup 1(6/52, 100p)-Photo-c; Gene Autry, Roy Rogers, Johnny Mack Brown, Rex Allen, & Bill Elliott begin; photo back-c begin, end No. 14, 16,18 18.00 55.00 110.00 220.00

Western Roundup 2(2/53, 100p)-Photo-c
11.00 32.00 65.00 130.00

Western Roundup 3-5(7-9/53 - 1-3/54)-Photo-c
9.00 27.00 55.00 110.00

Western Roundup 6-10(4-6/54 - 4-6/55)-Photo-c
8.00 25.00 50.00 100.00

Western Roundup 11-13,16,17(100p)-Photo-c; Manning-a. 11-Flying A's Range Rider, Dale Evans begin
7.00 21.00 42.00 85.00

Western Roundup 14,15,25(1-3/59; 100p)-Photo-c
7.00 21.00 42.00 85.00

Western Roundup 18(100p)-Toth-a; last photo-c; Gene Autry ends
7.50 22.50 45.00 90.00

Western Roundup 19-24(100p)-Manning-a; 19-Buffalo Bill Jr. begins. 21-Rex Allen, Johnny Mack Brown end. 22-Jace Pearson's Texas Rangers, Rin Tin Tin, Tales of Wells Fargo & Wagon Train begin
6.25 19.00 38.00 75.00

Woody Woodpecker Back To School 1(10/52, 100p)
7.00 20.00 40.00 80.00

...Back To School 2-4,6('53-10/57, 100p)-County Fair No. 5
5.50 16.00 32.00 65.00

...County Fair 5(9/56, 100p)-Formerly Back To School
5.50 16.00 32.00 65.00

...County Fair 2(11/58, 100p) 4.60 14.00 28.00 55.00

DELL JUNIOR TREASURY (15 cents)
June, 1955 - No. 10, Oct, 1957 (All painted-c)
Dell Publishing Co.

	GD25	FN65	NM94
1-Alice in Wonderland; reprints 4-Color #331 (52 pgs.)	10.00	30.00	60.00
2-Aladdin & the Wonderful Lamp	7.50	22.50	45.00
3-Gulliver's Travels (1/56)	5.85	17.50	35.00
4-Adventures of Mr. Frog & Miss Mouse	6.70	20.00	40.00
5-The Wizard of Oz (7/56)	7.50	22.50	45.00
6-Heidi (10/56)	5.85	17.50	35.00
7-Santa and the Angel	5.85	17.50	35.00
8-Raggedy Ann and the Camel with the Wrinkled Knees	5.85	17.50	35.00
9-Clementina the Flying Pig	5.85	17.50	35.00
10-Adventures of Tom Sawyer	5.85	17.50	35.00

DEMON, THE (See Detective Comics No. 482-485)
Aug-Sept, 1972 - V3#16, Jan, 1974
National Periodical Publications

1-Origin; Kirby-c/a in 1-16 3.60 9.00 18.00

Sleeping Beauty #1, © WDC

Tom And Jerry's Winter Fun #4, © M.G.M.

Western Roundup #3, © DELL

The Demon #1 (7/90), © DC

Dennis the Menace #4, © FAW

Dennis the Menace Giant #35, © FAW

	GD25	FN65	VF82	NM94
2		1.80	4.50	9.00
6-16		1.40	3.50	7.00

DEMON, THE (2nd series)
Jan, 1987 - No. 4, Apr, 1987 (75 cents, mini-series)(#2 has #4 of 4 on-c)
DC Comics

1-4: Matt Wagner-a(p) & scripts .50 1.00

DEMON, THE (3rd series)
July, 1990 - Present ($1.50, color)
DC Comics

1: 1-4-Painted-c .35 .90 1.80
2-18,20-27: 3,8-Batman app. (cameo #4). 12-15-Lobo app. (1 pg. cameo #11). 23-Robin app. .30 .75 1.50
19-($2.50, 44 pgs.)-Lobo poster stapled inside .60 1.50 3.00
28-36: 28-Superman-c/story; begin $1.75-c. 32-Lobo app. .35 .90 1.75
Annual 1 (1992, $3.00, 68 pgs.)-Eclipso-c/story .60 1.50 3.00
NOTE: ***Alan Grant** scripts in #1-16, 20, 21, 23-25, Annual 1. **Wagner** a/scripts-22.*

DEMON DREAMS (Pacific) (Value: cover or less)

DEMON-HUNTER
September, 1975
Seaboard Periodicals (Atlas)

1-Origin; Buckler-c/a .50 1.00

DEMONIC TOYS (Eternity) (Value: cover or less)

DEMON KNIGHT: A GRIMJACK GRAPHIC NOVEL (First) (Value: cover or less)

DEN (Fantagor) (Value: cover or less)

DENNIS THE MENACE (Becomes ...Fun Fest Series; See The Best of... & The Very Best of...)(... Fun Fest on-c only to #156-166)
8/53 - #14, 1/56; #15, 3/56 - #31, 11/58; #32, 1/59 - #166, 11/79
Standard Comics/Pines No.15-31/Hallden (Fawcett) No.32 on

1-1st app. Mr. & Mrs. Wilson, Ruff & Dennis' mom & dad; Wiseman-a, written by Fred Toole-most issues 29.00 85.00 200.00
2 14.00 43.00 100.00
3-10 10.00 30.00 60.00
11-20 6.70 20.00 40.00
21-30: 22-1st app. Margaret w/blonde hair 4.20 12.50 25.00
31-40: 31-1st app. Joey. 37-A-Bomb blast panel 3.60 9.00 18.00
41-60 2.40 6.00 12.00
61-90 1.60 4.00 8.00
91-166 .80 2.00 4.00
...& Dirt('59,'68)-Soil Conservation giveaway; r-No. 36; Wiseman-c/a .80 2.00 4.00
...Away We Go('70)-Caladayl giveaway .80 2.00 4.00
...Coping with Family Stress-giveaway .60 1.50 3.00
...Takes a Poke at Poison('61)-Food & Drug Assn. giveaway; Wiseman-c/a .80 2.00 4.00
...Takes a Poke at Poison-Revised 1/66, 11/70, 1972, 1974, 1977, 1981 .60 1.50 3.00
NOTE: ***Wiseman** c/a-1-46, 53, 68, 69.*

DENNIS THE MENACE (Giants) (No. 1 titled Giant Vacation Special; becomes Dennis the Menace Bonus Magazine No. 76 on)
(#1-8,18,23,25,30,38: 100 pgs.; rest to #41: 84 pgs.; #42-75: 68 pgs.)
Summer, 1955 - No. 75, Dec, 1969
Standard/Pines/Hallden(Fawcett)

nn-Giant Vacation Special(Summ/55-Standard) 10.00 30.00 65.00
nn-Christmas issue (Winter '55) 9.15 27.50 55.00
2-Giant Vacation Special (Summer '56-Pines)
3-Giant Christmas issue (Winter '56-Pines)
4-Giant Vacation Special (Summer '57-Pines)
5-Giant Christmas issue (Winter '57-Pines)
6-In Hawaii (Giant Vacation Special)(Summer '58-Pines)
6-In Hawaii (Summer '59-Hallden)-2nd printing; says 3rd large printing on-c
6-In Hawaii (Summer '60)-3rd printing; says 4th large printing on-c
6-In Hawaii (Summer '62)-4th printing; says 5th large printing on-c
6-Giant Christmas issue (Winter '58)
each.... 6.70 20.00 40.00
7-In Hollywood (Winter '59-Hallden)
7-In Hollywood (Summer '61)-2nd printing
8-In Mexico (Winter '60, 100 pgs.-Hallden/Fawcett)
8-In Mexico (Summer '62, 2nd printing)
9-Goes to Camp (Summer '61, 84 pgs.)-1st CCA approved issue
9-Goes to Camp (Summer '62)-2nd printing
10-X-Mas issue (Winter '61)
11-Giant Christmas issue (Winter '62)
12-Triple Feature (Winter '62)
each.... 5.85 17.50 35.00
13-Best of Dennis the Menace (Spring '63)-Reprints
14-And His Dog Ruff (Summer '63)
15-In Washington, D.C. (Summer '63)
16-Goes to Camp (Summer '63)-Reprints No. 9
17-& His Pal Joey (Winter '63)
18-In Hawaii (Reprints No. 6)
19-Giant Christmas issue (Winter '63)
20-Spring Special (Spring '64)
each.... 3.60 9.00 18.00
21-40: 30-r/#6 1.80 4.50 9.00
41-75: 68-Partial-r/#6 1.20 3.00 6.00
NOTE: ***Wiseman** c/a-1-8, 12, 14, 15, 17, 20, 22, 27, 28, 31, 35, 36, 41, 49.*

DENNIS THE MENACE
Nov, 1981 - No. 13, Nov, 1982
Marvel Comics Group

1-13: 1,2-New art. 3-Part-r. 4,5-r. 5-X-Mas-c .50 1.00
NOTE: ***Hank Ketcham** c-most; a-3, 12. **Wiseman** a-4, 5.*

DENNIS THE MENACE AND HIS DOG RUFF
Summer, 1961
Hallden/Fawcett

1-Wiseman-c/a 4.70 14.00 28.00

DENNIS THE MENACE AND HIS FRIENDS
1969; No. 5, Jan, 1970 - No. 46, April, 1980 (All reprints)
Fawcett Publications

Dennis the Menace & Joey No. 2 (7/69) 2.00 5.00 10.00
Dennis the Menace & Ruff No. 2 (9/69) 1.60 4.00 8.00
Dennis the Menace & Mr. Wilson No. 1 (10/69) 2.00 5.00 10.00
Dennis & Margaret No. 1 (Winter '69) 1.00 2.50 5.00
5-20: 5-Dennis the Menace & Margaret. 6-...& Joey. 7-...& Ruff. 8-...& Mr. Wilson .60 1.50 3.00
21-37 .40 1.00 2.00
38-46 (Digest size, 148 pgs., 4/78, 95 cents) .60 1.50 3.00
NOTE: *Titles rotate every four issues, beginning with No. 5.*

DENNIS THE MENACE AND HIS PAL JOEY
Summer, 1961 (10 cents) (See Dennis the Menace Giants No. 45)
Fawcett Publications

1-Wiseman-c/a 5.00 15.00 30.00

DENNIS THE MENACE AND THE BIBLE KIDS
1977 (36 pages)
Word Books

1-10: 1-Jesus. 2-Joseph. 3-David. 4-The Bible Girls. 5-Moses. 6-More About Jesus. 7-The Lord's Prayer. 8-Stories Jesus told. 9-Paul, God's Traveller. 10-In the Beginning .50 1.00
NOTE: ***Ketcham** c/a in all.*

DENNIS THE MENACE BIG BONUS SERIES
No. 10, Feb, 1980 - No. 11, Apr, 1980

	GD25	FN65	VF82	NM94

Fawcett Publications

10,11	.30	.75	1.50

DENNIS THE MENACE BONUS MAGAZINE (Formerly Dennis the Menace Giants Nos. 1-75)
No. 76, 1/70 - No. 194, 10/79; (No. 76-124: 68 pgs.; No. 125-163: 52 pgs.; No. 164 on: 36 pgs.)
Fawcett Publications

76-90	.60	1.50	3.00
91-110	.40	1.00	2.00
111-194: 166-Indicia printed backwards		.50	1.00

DENNIS THE MENACE COMICS DIGEST
April, 1982 - No. 3, Aug, 1982 (Digest Size, $1.25)
Marvel Comics Group

1-3-Reprints	.40	1.00	2.00

NOTE: ***Hank Ketcham** c-all. **Wiseman** a-all. A few thousand No. 1's were published with a DC emblem on cover.*

DENNIS THE MENACE FUN BOOK
1960 (100 pages)
Fawcett Publications/Standard Comics

1-Part Wiseman-a	5.85	17.50	35.00

DENNIS THE MENACE FUN FEST SERIES (Formerly Dennis The Menace #166)
No. 16, Jan, 1980 - No. 17, Mar, 1980 (40 cents)
Hallden (Fawcett)

16,17-By Hank Ketcham		.50	1.00

DENNIS THE MENACE POCKET FULL OF FUN!
Spring, 1969 - No. 50, March, 1980 (196 pages) (Digest size)
Fawcett Publications (Hallden)

1-Reprints in all issues	2.00	5.00	10.00
2-10	1.00	2.50	5.00
11-28	.60	1.50	3.00
29-50: 35,40,46-Sunday strip-r	.30	.75	1.50

NOTE: *No. 1-28 are 196 pgs.; No. 29-36: 164 pgs.; No. 37: 148 pgs.; No. 38 on: 132 pgs. No. 8, 11, 15, 21, 25, 29 all contain strip reprints.*

DENNIS THE MENACE TELEVISION SPECIAL
Summer, 1961 - No. 2, Spring, 1962 (Giant)
Fawcett Publications (Hallden Div.)

1	5.35	16.00	32.00
2	3.60	9.00	18.00

DENNIS THE MENACE TRIPLE FEATURE
Winter, 1961 (Giant)
Fawcett Publications

1-Wiseman-c/a	5.35	16.00	32.00

DEPUTY, THE (See 4-Color No. 1077, 1130, 1225)

DEPUTY DAWG (TV) (Also see New Terrytoons)
Oct-Dec, 1961 - No. 1299, 1962; No. 1, Aug, 1965
Dell Publishing Co./Gold Key

4-Color 1238,1299	10.00	30.00	60.00
1(10164-508)(8/65)	8.35	25.00	50.00

DEPUTY DAWG PRESENTS DINKY DUCK AND HASHIMOTO-SAN
August, 1965 (TV)
Gold Key

1(10159-508)	8.35	25.00	50.00

DESIGN FOR SURVIVAL (Gen. Thomas S. Power's...)
1968 (36 pages in color) (25 cents)
American Security Council Press

nn-Propaganda against the Threat of Communism-Aircraft cover	4.00	10.00	20.00
Twin Circle Edition-Cover shows panels from inside	2.40	6.00	12.00

DESPERADO (Black Diamond Western No. 9 on)
June, 1948 - No. 8, Feb, 1949 (All 52 pgs.)
Lev Gleason Publications

1-Biro-c on all; contains inside photo-c of Charles Biro, Lev Gleason & Bob Wood	9.15	27.50	55.00
2	4.70	14.00	28.00
3-Story with over 20 killings	4.20	12.50	25.00
4-8	4.00	10.00	20.00

NOTE: ***Barry** a-2. **Fuje** a-4, 8. **Guardineer** a-5-7. **Kida** a-3-7. **Ed Moore** a-4, 6.*

DESTINATION MOON (See Fawcett Movie Comics, Space Adventures #20, 23, & Strange Adventures #1)

DESTROY!! (Eclipse) (Value: cover or less)

DESTROYER, THE
Nov, 1989 - No. 9, June, 1990 ($2.25, B&W, magazine, 52 pgs.)
Marvel Comics

1-Based on Remo Williams movie, paperbacks	.45	1.15	2.25
2-9: 2-Williamson part inks. 4-Ditko-a	.45	1.15	2.25

DESTROYER, THE
V2#1, March, 1991 ($1.95, color, 52 pgs.)
V3#1, Dec, 1991 - No. 4, Mar, 1992 ($1.95, color, mini-series)
Marvel Comics

V2#1-Based on Remo Williams paperbacks	.40	1.00	2.00
V3#1-4: 1-4-Simonson-c. 3-Morrow-a	.40	1.00	2.00

DESTROYER DUCK
1982 (no month) - No. 7, 5/84 (#2-7: Baxter paper) ($1.50)
Eclipse Comics

1-Origin Destroyer Duck; 1st app. Groo	.60	1.50	3.00
2-7: 2-Starling back-up begins		.50	1.00

NOTE: ***Neal Adams** c-1i. **Kirby** c/a-1-5p. **Miller** c-7.*

DESTRUCTOR, THE
February, 1975 - No. 4, Aug, 1975
Atlas/Seaboard

1-Origin; Ditko/Wood-a; Wood-c(i)	.30	.75	1.50
2-4: 2-Ditko/Wood-a. 3,4-Ditko-a(p)		.50	1.00

DETECTIVE COMICS (Also see Special Edition)
March, 1937 - Present
National Periodical Publications/DC Comics

	GD25	FN65	VF82
1-(Scarce)-Slam Bradley & Spy by Siegel & Shuster, Speed Saunders by Guardineer, Flat Foot Flannigan by Gustavson, Cosmo, the Phantom of Disguise, Buck Marshall, Bruce Nelson begin; Chin Lung-c from 'Claws of the Red Dragon' serial; Vincent Sullivan-c	4,000.00	10,000.00	20,000.00
(Estimated up to 30 total copies exist, 1 in NM/Mint)			
2 (Rare)-Craig Flessel-c begin, end #18	833.00	2500.00	5000.00
3 (Rare)	667.00	2000.00	4000.00

	GD25	FN65	NM94
4,5: 5-Larry Steele begins	350.00	1050.00	2100.00
6,7,9,10	233.00	700.00	1400.00
8-Mister Chang-c	300.00	900.00	1800.00
11-17,19: 17-1st app. Fu Manchu in Det.	200.00	600.00	1200.00
18-Fu Manchu-c	267.00	800.00	1600.00
20-The Crimson Avenger begins (1st app.)	316.00	950.00	1900.00
21,23-25	150.00	450.00	900.00
22-1st Crimson Avenger-c (12/38)	217.00	650.00	1300.00
26	167.00	500.00	1000.00

	GD25	FN65	VF82	NM94
27-The Batman & Commissioner Gordon begin (1st app.) by Bob Kane (5/39); Batman-c (1st)	12,100.00	36,000.00	61,000.00	85,000.00
(Estimated up to 50+ total copies exist, 3 in NM/Mint)				

27-Reprint, Oversize 13"x10." **WARNING**: This comic is an exact duplicate reprint of

Deputy Dawg Presents...#1, © Terrytoons

The Destroyer V2 #1 (3/91), © MEG

Detective Comics #1, © DC

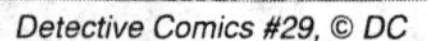
Detective Comics #29, © DC

Detective #122, © DC

Detective Comics #239, © DC

GD25 FN65 NM94

the original except for its size. DC published it in 1974 with a second cover titling it as Famous First Edition. There have been many reported cases of the outer cover being removed and the interior sold as the original edition. The reprint with the new outer cover removed is practically worthless.

	GD25	FN65		NM94
27(1984)-Oreo Cookies giveaway (32 pgs., paper-c, r-/Det. 27, 38 & Batman No. 1 (1st Joker)	4.35	13.00		26.00
28-2nd app. The Batman (6 pg. story)	900.00	2700.00		5400.00
	GD25	FN65	VF82	NM94
29-Batman-c; Doctor Death-c/story; Batman story now 10 pgs.	1100.00	3300.00	6600.00	11,000.00
(Estimated up to 75+ total copies exist, 6 in NM/Mint)				
	GD25	FN65		NM94
30,32: 30-Dr. Death app. 32-Batman uses gun	450.00	1350.00		2700.00
	GD25	FN65	VF82	NM94
31-Classic Batman-c; 1st Julie Madison, Bat Plane (Bat-Gyro) & Batarang; 31,32-1st 2 part Batman story	1100.00	3300.00	6600.00	11,000.00
(Estimated up to 75+ total copies exist, 6 in NM/Mint)				
33-Origin The Batman (1st told origin); Batman gunholster-c; Batman story now 12 pgs.	1700.00	5100.00	10,200.00	17,000.00
(Estimated up to 75+ total copies exist, 7 in NM/Mint)				
	GD25	FN65		NM94
34-Steve Malone begins; 2nd Crimson Avenger-c	350.00	1050.00		2100.00
35-Batman-c begin; hypo-c	585.00	1750.00		3500.00
36,37: 36-Origin Hugo Strange. 37-Cliff Crosby begins; last Batman solo story	417.00	1250.00		2500.00
	GD25	FN65	VF82	NM94
38-Origin/1st app. Robin the Boy Wonder (4/40)	1600.00	4800.00	9600.00	16,000.00
(Estimated up to 85+ total copies exist, 9 in NM/Mint)				
	GD25	FN65		NM94
39	367.00	1100.00		2200.00
40-Origin & 1st app. Clay Face (Basil Karlo); 1st Joker cover app. (6/40); Joker story intended for this issue was used in Batman #1 instead	433.00	1300.00		2600.00
41-Robin's 1st solo	233.00	700.00		1400.00
42-44: 44-Crimson Avenger-new costume	150.00	450.00		900.00
45-1st Joker story in Det. (4th in all, 11/40)	242.00	725.00		1450.00
46-50: 48-1st time car called Batmobile; Gotham City 1st mention. 49-Last Clay Face	135.00	405.00		810.00
51-57	108.00	325.00		650.00
58-1st Penguin app.; last Speed Saunders	267.00	800.00		1600.00
59-Last Steve Malone; 2nd Penguin; Wing becomes Crimson Avenger's aide	117.00	350.00		700.00
60-Intro. Air Wave; Joker app. (2nd in Det.)	117.00	350.00		700.00
61,63: 63-Last Cliff Crosby; 1st app. Mr. Baffle	100.00	300.00		600.00
62-Joker-c/story (2nd Joker-c, 4/42)	150.00	450.00		900.00
64-Origin & 1st app. Boy Commandos by Simon & Kirby (6/42); Joker app.	267.00	800.00		1600.00
65-Boy Commandos-c	133.00	400.00		800.00
66-Origin & 1st app. Two-Face	200.00	600.00		1200.00
67-1st Penguin-c (9/42)	133.00	400.00		800.00
68-Two-Face-c/story	100.00	300.00		600.00
69-Joker-c/story	117.00	350.00		700.00
70	87.00	260.00		520.00
71-Joker-c/story	105.00	312.00		625.00
72-75: 73-Scarecrow-c/story (1st Scarecrow-c). 74-1st Tweedledum & Tweedledee; S&K-a	80.00	240.00		480.00
76-Newsboy Legion & The Sandman x-over in Boy Commandos; S&K-a; Joker-c/story	121.00	362.00		725.00
77-79: All S&K-a	80.00	240.00		480.00
80-Two-Face app.; S&K-a	92.00	275.00		550.00
81,82,84,86-90: 81-1st Cavalier-c & app. 89-Last Crimson Avenger	71.00	212.00		425.00

GD25 FN65 NM94

	GD25	FN65	NM94
83-1st "skinny" Alfred (2/44)(see Batman #21; last S&K Boy Commandos. (also #92,128); most issues #84 on signed S&K are not by them	80.00	240.00	480.00
85-Joker-c/story; Last Spy; Kirby/Klech Boy Commandos	93.00	280.00	560.00
91,102-Joker-c/story	87.00	260.00	520.00
92-98: 96-Alfred's last name 'Beagle' revealed, later changed to 'Pennyworth' in #214	64.00	192.00	385.00
99-Penguin-c	88.00	262.00	525.00
100 (6/45)	96.00	288.00	575.00
101,103-108,110-113,115-117,119: 114-1st small logo (8/46)	58.00	175.00	350.00
109,114,118-Joker-c/stories	80.00	240.00	480.00
120-Penguin-c	92.00	275.00	550.00
121,123,125,127,129,130	56.00	168.00	335.00
122,126: 122-1st Catwoman-c(4/47). 126-Penguin-c	79.00	238.00	475.00
124,128-Joker-c/stories	73.00	220.00	440.00
131-136,139	48.00	142.00	285.00
137-Joker-c/story; last Air Wave	64.00	192.00	385.00
138-Origin Robotman (see Star Spangled #7 for 1st app.); series ends #202	83.00	250.00	500.00
140-The Riddler-c/story (1st app., 10/48)	200.00	600.00	1200.00
141,143-148,150: 150-Last Boy Commandos	50.00	150.00	300.00
142-2nd Riddler-c/story	80.00	238.00	475.00
149-Joker-c/story	67.00	200.00	400.00
151-Origin & 1st app. Pow Wow Smith	55.00	162.00	325.00
152,154,155,157-160: 152-Last Slam Bradley	50.00	150.00	300.00
153-1st Roy Raymond app.; origin The Human Fly	55.00	162.00	325.00
156(2/50)-The new classic Batmobile	62.00	188.00	375.00
161-167,169,170,172-176: Last 52 pgs.	55.00	162.00	325.00
168-Origin the Joker	235.00	585.00	1400.00
171-Penguin-c	75.00	225.00	450.00
177-179,181-186,188,189,191,192,194-199,201,202,204,206-210,212,214-216: 185-Secret of Batman's utility belt. 187-Two-Face app. 202-Last Robotman & Pow Wow Smith. 216-Last precode (2/55)	39.00	118.00	235.00
180,193-Joker-c/story	41.00	122.00	245.00
187-Two-Face-c	41.00	122.00	245.00
190-Origin Batman retold	55.00	162.00	325.00
200	50.00	150.00	300.00
203,211-Catwoman-c	41.00	102.00	245.00
205-Origin Batcave	55.00	135.00	325.00
213-Origin Mirror Man	48.00	120.00	290.00
217-224	33.00	85.00	200.00
225-(11/55)-1st app. Martian Manhunter-John Jones, later changed to J'onn J'onzz; origin begins; also see Batman #78	357.00	1070.00	2500.00
226-Origin Martian Manhunter continued	77.00	230.00	540.00
227-229	40.00	122.00	285.00
230-1st app. Mad Hatter; brief recap origin of Martian Manhunter	47.00	140.00	325.00
231-Brief origin recap Martian Manhunter	27.00	80.00	190.00
232,234,237-240: 239-Painted-c	27.00	80.00	190.00
233-Origin & 1st app. Batwoman	107.00	320.00	750.00
235-Origin Batman & his costume	47.00	140.00	325.00
236-J'onn J'onzz talks to parents and Mars-1st since being stranded on earth	30.00	90.00	210.00
241-260: 246-Intro. Diane Meade, J. Jones' girl. 249-4th app. Batwoman. 254-Bat-Hound-c/story. 257-Intro. & 1st app. Whirly Bats	19.00	58.00	135.00
261-J. Jones tie-in to sci/fi movie "Incredible Shrinking Man"	15.00	45.00	105.00

GD25 FN65 NM94

262-264,266,269,270: 261-1st app. Dr. Double X. 262-Origin Jackal. 267-Origin &1st app. Bat-Mite 15.00 45.00 105.00
265-Batman's origin retold with new facts 25.00 75.00 175.00
267-Origin & 1st app. Bat-Mite 18.00 54.00 125.00
268,271-Manhunter origin recap 15.00 45.00 105.00
272,274-280: 276-2nd Bat-Mite 11.00 32.00 75.00
273-J'onn J'onzz i.d. revealed for 1st time 12.00 36.00 85.00
281-297: 287-Origin J'onn J'onzz retold. 292-Last Roy Raymond. 293-Aquaman begins, ends #300. 297-Last 10 cent issue (11/61) 10.00 30.00 60.00
298-1st modern Clayface (Matt Hagen) 13.00 40.00 90.00
299,300(2/62) 5.85 17.50 35.00
301(3/62)-J'onn J'onzz returns to Mars (1st since stranded on earth 6 years before) 6.70 20.00 40.00
302-326,329,330: 311-Intro. Zook in John Jones; 1st app. Cat-Man. 318,325-Cat-Man-c/story (2nd & 3rd app.); also 1st & 2nd app. Batwoman as the Cat-Woman. 322-Bat-Girl's 1st/only app. in Det. 326-Last J'onn J'onzz, story cont'd in H.O.M. #143; intro. Idol-Head of Diabolu 5.00 15.00 30.00
327(5/64)-Elongated Man begins, ends #383; 1st new look Batman with new costume; Infantino/Giella new look-a begins 5.85 17.50 35.00
328-Death of Alfred; Bob Kane biog, 2pg. 9.15 27.50 55.00
331,333-340,342-358,360-364,366-368,370: 334-1st app. The Outsider. 345-Intro Block Buster. 351-Elongated Man new costume. 355-Zatanna x-over in Elongated Man. 356-Alfred brought back in Batman. 363-2nd app. new Batgirl. 370-1st Neal Adams-a on Batman (cover only, 12/67) 4.00 10.00 20.00
332,341,365-Joker-c/stories 4.35 13.00 26.00
359-Intro/origin new Batgirl-c/story (1/67) 4.35 13.00 26.00
369(11/67)-N. Adams-a (Elongated Man); 3rd app. S.A. Catwoman (cameo; leads into Batman #197); 3rd app. new Batgirl 5.00 15.00 30.00
371-1st new Batmobile from TV show (1/68) 3.00 7.50 15.00
372-386,389,390: 375-New Batmobile-c 2.40 6.00 12.00
387-r/1st Batman story from #27; Joker-c; last 12 cent issue 5.00 15.00 30.00
388-Joker-c/story 3.60 9.00 18.00
391-394,396,398,399,401,403,405,406,409: 392-1st app. Jason Bard. 401-2nd Batgirl/Robin team-up 1.80 4.50 9.00
395,397,402,404,407,408,410-Neal Adams-a 3.00 7.50 15.00
400-(6/70)-Origin & 1st app. Man-Bat; 1st Batgirl/Robin team-up; Neal Adams-a 4.00 11.00 22.00
411-420: 413-Last 15 cent issue. 414-25 cent, 52 pgs. begin, end #424. 418-Creeper x-over 1.80 4.50 9.00
421-436: 424-Last Batgirl; 1st She-Bat. 426,430,436-Elongated Man app. 428,434-Hawkman begins, ends #467 1.60 4.00 8.00
437-New Manhunter begins by Simonson, ends #443 2.40 6.00 12.00
438-445 (All 100 pgs.): 439-Origin Manhunter. 440-G.A. Manhunter, Hawkman, Dollman, Gr. Lantern; Toth-a. 441-G.A. Plastic Man, Batman, Ibis-r. 442-G.A. Newsboy Legion, Bl. Canary, Elongated Man, Dr. Fate-r. 443-Origin The Creeper-r; death of Manhunter; G.A. Green Lantern, Spectre-r; Batman-r/Batman #18. 444-G.A. Kid Eternity-r. 445-G.A. Dr. Midnite-r 2.00 5.00 10.00
446-460: 457-Origin retold & updated 1.40 3.50 7.00
461-465,469,470,480: 480-(44 pgs.). 463,464-1st app. Black Spider 1.00 2.50 5.00
466-468,471-474,478,479-Rogers-a in all. 466-1st app. Signalman since Batman #139. 469-Intro/origin Dr. Phosphorous. 470,471-1st modern app. Hugo Strange. 474-1st app. new Deadshot. 478-1st app. 3rd Clayface (Preston Payne). 479-(44 pgs.) 2.40 6.00 12.00
475,476-Joker-c/stories; Rogers-a 4.00 10.00 20.00
477-Neal Adams-a(r); Rogers-a, 3pgs. 3.00 7.50 15.00
481-(Combined with Batman Family, 12/78-1/79, begin $1.00, 68 pg. issues, ends #495); 481-495-Batgirl, Robin solo stories 2.00 5.00 10.00
482-Starlin/Russell, Golden-a; The Demon begins (origin-r), ends #485 (by Ditko #483-485) 1.40 3.50 7.00
483-40th Anniversary issue; origin retold; Newton Batman begins 1.60 4.00 8.00
484-499: 484-Origin Robin. 485-Death of Batwoman. 487-The Odd Man by Ditko. 489-Robin/Batgirl team-up. 490-Black Lightningbegins. 491-(#492 on inside). .80 2.00 4.00
500-($1.50)-Batman/Deadman team-up 1.40 3.50 7.00
501-503,505-523: 512-2nd app. new Dr. Death. 519-Last Batgirl. 521-Green Arrow series begins. 523-Solomon Grundy app. .70 1.75 3.50
504-Joker-c/story 1.30 3.25 6.50
524-2nd app. Jason Todd (cameo)(3/83) .90 2.25 4.50
525-3rd app. Jason Todd (See Batman #357) .70 1.75 3.50
526-Batman's 500th app. in Detective Comics ($1.50, 68pgs.); contains 55 pg. Joker story; Bob Kane pin-up 2.20 5.50 11.00
527-531,533,534,536-568,571,573: 542-Jason Todd quits as Robin (becomes Robin again #547). 549,550-Alan Moore scripts (Gr. Arrow). 554-1st new Black Canary. 566-Batman villains profiled. 567-Harlan Ellison scripts .50 1.25 2.50
532,569,570-Joker-c/stories 1.00 2.50 5.00
535-Intro new Robin (Jason Todd)-1st appeared in Batman 1.10 2.75 5.50
572 (60 pgs., $1.25)-50th Anniversary of Det. .70 1.75 3.50
574-Origin Batman & Jason Todd retold 1.00 2.50 5.00
575-Year 2 begins, ends #578 2.80 7.00 14.00
576-578: McFarlane-c/a 2.40 6.00 12.00
579-597,601-610: 579-New bat wing logo. 589-595-(52 pgs.)-Each contain free 16 pg. Batman stories. 604-607-Mudpack storyline; 604,607-Contain Batman mini-posters. 610-Faked death of Penguin; artists names app. on tombstone on-c .30 .75 1.50
598-($2.95, 84 pgs.)-"Blind Justice" storyline begins by Batman movie writer Sam Hamm, ends #600 1.20 3.00 6.00
599 .80 2.00 4.00
600-($2.95, 84 pgs.)-50th Anniversary of Batman in Det.; 1 pg. Neal Adams pin-up, among other artists 1.20 3.00 6.00
611-626,628-660: 612-1st new look Cat-Man. 615-"The Penguin Affair" part 2 (See Batman #448,449). 617-Joker-c/story. 624-1st new Catwoman (w/death) & 1st new Batwoman. 642-Return of Scarface, part 2. 644-Last $1.00-c. 652,653-Huntress-c/story w/new costume .60 1.25
627-($2.95, 84 pgs.)-Batman's 600th app. in Det.; reprints 1st story/#27 plus 3 versions (2 new) of same story .70 1.75 3.50
Annual 1(1988, $1.50) 1.00 2.50 5.00
Annual 2(1989, $2.00, 68 pgs.) .80 2.00 4.00
Annual 3(1990, $2.00, 68 pgs.) .40 1.00 2.00
Annual 4(1991, $2.00, 68 pgs.)-Painted-c .40 1.00 2.00
Annual 5(1992, $2.50, 68 pgs.)-Joker-c/story (54 pgs.) continued in Robin Annual #1; Sam Kieth-c; Eclipso app. .50 1.25 2.50

NOTE: ***Neal Adams*** *c-370, 372, 383, 385, 389, 391, 392, 394-422, 439.* ***Aparo*** *a-437, 438, 444-446, 500; c-430, 437, 440-446, 448, 468-470, 480, 484(back), 492-502,508, 509, 515, 518-522.* ***Austin*** *a(i)-450, 451, 463-468, 471-476; c(i)-474-476, 478.* ***Baily*** *a-443r.* ***Buckler*** *a-434, 446p, 479p; c(p)-467, 482, 505, 506, 511, 513-516, 518.* ***Burnley*** *a(Batman)-65, 75, 83, 100, 103, 125; c-62i, 63i, 64, 73i, 78, 83p, 96p, 103p, 105p, 108, 121p, 123p, 125p.* ***Colan*** *a(p)-510, 512, 517, 523, 528-538, 540-546, 555-567; c(p)-510, 512, 528, 530-535, 537, 538, 540, 541, 543-545, 556-558, 560-564.* ***J. Craig*** *a-488.* ***Ditko*** *a-443r, 483-485, 487.* ***Golden*** *a-482p.* ***Alan Grant*** *scripts-584-597, 601-621, 641, 642, Annual 5.* ***Grell*** *a-445, 455, 463p, 464p; c-455.* ***Guardineer*** *c-23, 24, 26, 28, 30, 32.* ***Gustavson*** *a-441r.* ***Infantino/Anderson*** *c-333, 337-340, 343, 344, 347, 351, 352, 359, 361-368, 371.* ***Kaluta*** *c-423, 424, 426-428, 431, 434, 438, 484, 486, 572.* ***Bob Kane*** *a-Most early issues #27 on, 297r, 356r, 438-440r, 442r, 443r.* ***Gil Kane*** *a(p)-368, 370-374, 384, 385, 388-407, 438r, 439r, 520.* ***Kane/Anderson*** *c-369.* ***Sam Kieth*** *c-654, Annual #5.* ***Kubert*** *a-438r, 439r, 500; c-348, 350.* ***McFarlane*** *c/a(p)-576-578.* ***Meskin*** *a-420r.* ***Moldoff/Giella*** *a-328, 330, 332, 334, 336, 338, 340, 342, 344, 346, 348, 350, 352, 354, 356.* ***Mooney*** *a-444r.* ***Moreira*** *a-153-300, 419r, 444r, 445r.* ***Newton*** *a(p)-480, 481, 483-499, 501-509, 511, 513-516, 518-520, 524, 526, 539; c-526p.* ***Irv Novick*** *c-375-377.* ***Robbins*** *a-426p, 429p.* ***Robinson*** *a-part: 66, 68, 71-73; all: 74-76, 79, 80; c-62, 64, 66, 68-74, 76, 79, 82, 86, 88, 442r, 443r.* ***Rogers*** *a-467, 478p, 479p, 481p; c-471p, 472p, 473, 474-479p.* ***Roussos*** *Airwave-76-105(most); c(i)-71, 72, 74-76, 79, 107.* ***Russell*** *a-481i, 482i.* ***Simon/Kirby*** *a-440r, 442r.* ***Simonson*** *a-437-443, 450, 469, 470, 500.* ***Dick Sprang*** *c-77, 82, 84, 85, 87, 89-93, 95-100, 102, 103i. 104i, 106, 108, 114, 117, 118, 122, 123, 128, 129, 131, 133, 135, 141, 148, 149, 168, 622-624.* ***Starlin*** *a-481p, 482p; c-503, 504, 567p.* ***Starr*** *a-444r.* ***Toth*** *r-414, 416, 418, 424, 440-444.* ***Tuska*** *a-486p, 490p.* ***Wrightson*** *c-425.*

Detective Comics #270, © DC

Detective #369, © DC

Detective #627, © DC

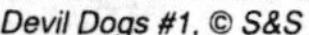
Devil Dogs #1, © S&S

Devil Kids #12, © HARV

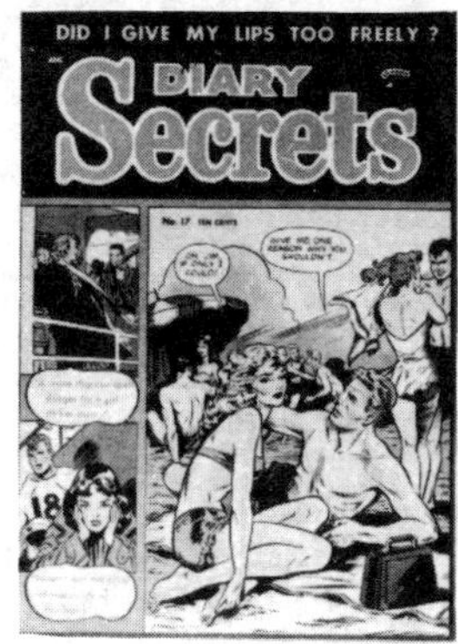

Diary Secrets #17, © STJ

GD25 FN65 NM94

DETECTIVE DAN, SECRET OP. 48
1933 (36 pgs.; 9x12") (B&W; Softcover)
Humor Publ. Co.
nn-By Norman Marsh; forerunner of Dan Dunn 11.50 34.00 80.00

DETECTIVE EYE (See Keen Detective Funnies)
Nov, 1940 - No. 2, Dec, 1940
Centaur Publications
1-Air Man & The Eye Sees begins; The Masked Marvel app. 125.00 375.00 750.00
2-Origin Don Rance and the Mysticape; Binder-a; Frank Thomas-c 87.00 262.00 525.00

DETECTIVE PICTURE STORIES (Keen Detective Funnies No. 8 on?)
Dec, 1936 - No. 7, 1937 (1st comic of a single theme)
Comics Magazine Company
1 183.00 550.00 1100.00
2-The Clock app. 78.00 232.00 465.00
3,4: 4-Eisner-a 73.00 216.00 435.00
5-7: 5-Kane-a; 6,7 (Exist)? 67.00 200.00 400.00

DETECTIVES, THE (See 4-Color No. 1168,1219,1240)

DETECTIVES, INC. (Eclipse)(Value: cover or less)

DETECTIVES, INC.: A TERROR OF DYING DREAMS (Eclipse)(Value: cover or less)

DEVIL DINOSAUR
April, 1978 - No. 9, Dec, 1978
Marvel Comics Group
1-9: Kirby/Royer-a in all; all have Kirby-c .30 .75 1.50

DEVIL-DOG DUGAN (Tales of the Marines No. 4 on)
July, 1956 - No. 3, Nov, 1956
Atlas Comics (OPI)
1-Severin-c 5.00 15.00 30.00
2-Iron Mike McGraw x-over; Severin-c 4.00 11.00 22.00
3 3.20 8.00 16.00

DEVIL DOGS
1942
Street & Smith Publishers
1-Boy Rangers, U.S. Marines 17.00 50.00 100.00

DEVILINA
Feb, 1975 - No. 2, May, 1975 (Magazine) (B&W)
Atlas/Seaboard
1,2: 1-Reese-a .60 1.50 3.00

DEVIL KIDS STARRING HOT STUFF
July, 1962 - No. 107, Oct, 1981 (Giant-Size #41-55)
Harvey Publications (Illustrated Humor)
1 10.00 30.00 65.00
2 5.35 16.00 32.00
3-10 (1/64) 3.20 8.00 16.00
11-20 1.30 4.00 9.00
21-30 1.40 3.50 7.00
31-40 ('71) 1.20 3.00 6.00
41-50: All 68 pg. Giants 1.40 3.50 7.00
51-55: All 52 pg. Giants 1.20 3.00 6.00
56-70 .80 2.00 4.00
71-90 .50 1.25 2.50
91-107 .30 .75 1.50

DEXTER COMICS
Summer, 1948 - No. 5, July, 1949
Dearfield Publ.
1-Teen-age humor 4.70 14.00 28.00
2-Junie Prom app. 4.00 11.00 22.00
3-5 2.80 7.00 14.00

DEXTER THE DEMON (Formerly Melvin The Monster)
No. 7, Sept, 1957 (Also see Cartoon Kids & Peter the Little Pest)
Atlas Comics (HPC)
7 3.20 8.00 16.00

DIARY CONFESSIONS (Formerly Ideal Romance)
No. 9, May, 1955 - No. 14, April, 1955
Stanmor/Key Publ.(Medal Comics)
9 4.00 10.00 20.00
10-14 2.40 6.00 12.00

DIARY LOVES (Formerly Love Diary #1; G. I. Sweethearts #32 on)
No. 2, Nov, 1949 - No. 31, April, 1953
Quality Comics Group
2-Ward-c/a, 9 pgs. 10.00 30.00 60.00
3 (1/50) 4.00 10.50 21.00
4-Crandall-a 5.70 17.00 34.00
5-7,10 3.00 7.50 15.00
8,9-Ward-a 6,8 pgs. plus Gustavson-#8 6.70 20.00 40.00
11,13,14,17-20 2.40 6.00 12.00
12,15,16-Ward-a 9,7,8 pgs. 5.70 17.00 34.00
21-Ward-a, 7 pgs. 4.70 14.00 28.00
22-31: 31-Whitney-a 1.80 4.50 9.00
NOTE: *Photo c-3-5, 8, 12-27.*

DIARY OF HORROR
December, 1952
Avon Periodicals
1-Hollingsworth-c/a; bondage-c 19.00 58.00 135.00

DIARY SECRETS (Formerly Teen-Age Diary Secrets)
No. 10, Feb, 1952 - No. 30, Sept, 1955
St. John Publishing Co.
10-Baker-c/a most issues 8.35 25.00 50.00
11-16,18,19: 11-Spanking panel 6.35 19.00 38.00
17,20-Kubert-a 7.00 21.00 42.00
21-30: 28-Last precode (3/55) 4.00 12.00 24.00
(See Giant Comics Edition for Annual)

DICK COLE (Sport Thrills No. 11 on)(See Blue Bolt & Four Most #1)
Dec-Jan, 1948-49 - No. 10, June-July, 1950
Curtis Publ./Star Publications
1-Sgt. Spook; L. B. Cole-c; McWilliams-a; Curt Swan's 1st work 10.00 30.00 65.00
2 6.35 19.00 38.00
3-10: 10-Joe Louis story 5.35 16.00 32.00
Accepted Reprint #7(V1#6 on-c)(1950's)-Reprints #7; L.B. Cole-c 4.00 10.00 20.00
Accepted Reprint #9(nd)-(Reprints #9 & #8-c) 4.00 10.00 20.00
NOTE: ***L. B. Cole*** *c-1, 3, 4, 6-10.* ***Al McWilliams*** *a-6. Dick Cole in 1-9. Baseball c-10. Basketball c-9. Football c-8.*

DICKIE DARE
1941 - No. 4, 1942 (#3 on sale 6/15/42)
Eastern Color Printing Co.
1-Caniff-a, Everett-c 27.00 82.00 165.00
2 16.00 48.00 95.00
3,4-Half Scorchy Smith by Noel Sickles who was very influential in Milton Caniff's development 17.00 50.00 100.00

DICK POWELL (See A-1 Comics No. 22)

DICK QUICK, ACE REPORTER (See Picture News #10)

DICK'S ADVENTURES IN DREAMLAND (See 4-Color No. 245)

DICK TRACY (See Famous Feature Stories, Harvey Comics Library, Limited Collectors'

GD25 FN65 NM94 | GD25 FN65 NM94

Ed., Mammoth Comics, Merry Christmas, The Original..., Popular Comics, Super Book No. 1, 7, 13, 25, Super Comics & Tastee-Freez)

DICK TRACY
May, 1937 - Jan, 1938
David McKay Publications

Feature Books nn - 100 pgs., partially reprinted as 4-Color No. 1 (appeared before Large Feature Comics, 1st Dick Tracy comic book)
(Very Rare-three known copies)
Estimated Value.... 535.00 1500.00 3200.00
Feature Books 4 - Reprints nn issue but with new cover added
90.00 270.00 630.00
Feature Books 6,9 72.00 215.00 500.00

DICK TRACY (...Monthly #1-24)
1939 - No. 24, Dec, 1949
Dell Publishing Co.

	GD25	FN65	NM94
Large Feature Comic 1(1939)	107.00	320.00	750.00
Large Feature Comic 4	57.00	170.00	400.00
Large Feature Comic 8,11,13,15	54.00	160.00	375.00

	GD25	FN65	VF82	NM94
4-Color 1(1939)('35-r)	280.00	700.00	1700.00	2800.00

(Estimated up to 75+ total copies exist, 5 in NM/Mint)

	GD25	FN65	NM94
4-Color 6(1940)('37-r)-(Scarce)	121.00	365.00	850.00
4-Color 8(1940)('38-'39-r)	68.00	205.00	475.00
Large Feature Comic 3(1941, Series II)	50.00	150.00	350.00
4-Color 21('41)('38-r)	57.00	170.00	400.00
4-Color 34('43)('39-'40-r)	40.00	120.00	280.00
4-Color 56('44)('40-r)	32.00	95.00	220.00
4-Color 96('46)('40-r)	24.00	70.00	165.00
4-Color 133('47)('40-'41-r)	19.00	57.00	135.00
4-Color 163('47)('41-r)	16.00	48.00	110.00
4-Color 215('48)-Titled "Sparkle Plenty," Tracy-r	9.30	28.00	65.00
1(1/48)('34-r)	43.00	130.00	300.00
2,3	24.00	73.00	150.00
4-10	22.00	65.00	150.00
11-18: 13-Bondage-c	14.00	43.00	100.00
19-1st app. Sparkle Plenty, B.O. Plenty & Gravel Gertie in a 3-pg. strip not by Gould	16.00	48.00	110.00
20-1st app. Sam Catchem; c/a not by Gould	12.00	36.00	85.00
21-24-Only 2 pg. Gould-a in each	12.00	36.00	85.00

NOTE: *No. 19-24 have a 2 pg. biography of a famous villain illustrated by **Gould**: 19-Little Face; 20-Flattop; 21-Breathless Mahoney; 22-Measles; 23-Itchy; 24-The Brow.*

DICK TRACY (Continued from Dell series)(...Comics Monthly #25-140)
No. 25, Mar, 1950 - No. 145, April, 1961
Harvey Publications

	GD25	FN65	NM94
25	17.00	52.00	120.00
26-28,30: 28-Bondage-c	12.00	36.00	85.00
29-1st app. Gravel Gertie in a Gould-r	16.00	48.00	110.00
31,32,34,35,37-40: 40-Intro/origin 2-way wrist radio	11.00	32.00	75.00
33-"Measles the Teen-Age Dope Pusher"	12.00	36.00	85.00
36-1st app. B.O. Plenty in a Gould-r	12.00	36.00	85.00
41-50	9.30	28.00	65.00
51-56,58-80: 51-2pgs Powell-a	8.50	25.50	60.00
57-1st app. Sam Catchem in a Gould-r	11.00	32.00	75.00
81-99,101-140	7.50	22.50	45.00
100	8.35	25.00	50.00
141-145 (25 cents)(titled "Dick Tracy")	7.00	21.00	42.00

NOTE: ***Powell** a(1-2pgs.)-43, 44, 104, 108, 109, 145. No. 110-120, 141-145 are all reprints from earlier issues.*

DICK TRACY (Blackthorne)(Value: cover or less)

DICK TRACY (Disney)(Value: cover or less)

DICK TRACY ADVENTURES (Gladstone)(Value: cover or less)

DICK TRACY & DICK TRACY JR. CAUGHT THE RACKETEERS, HOW
1933 (88 pages) (7x8") (Hardcover)
Cupples & Leon Co.

	GD25	FN65	NM94
2-(numbered on pg. 84)-Continuation of Stooge Viller book (daily strip reprints from 8/3/33 thru 11/8/33) (Rarer than No. 1)	43.00	130.00	300.00
with dust jacket....	60.00	180.00	420.00
Book 2 (32 pgs.; soft-c; has strips 9/18/33-11/8/33)	19.00	57.00	132.00

DICK TRACY & DICK TRACY JR. AND HOW THEY CAPTURED "STOOGE" VILLER (See Treasure Box of Famous Comics)
1933 (7x8-1/2") (Hard cover; One Shot; 100 pgs.)
Reprints 1932 & 1933 Dick Tracy daily strips
Cupples & Leon Co.

	GD25	FN65	NM94
nn(No.1)-1st app. of "Stooge" Viller	30.00	90.00	210.00
with dust jacket....	42.00	125.00	295.00

DICK TRACY, EXPLOITS OF
1946 (Strip reprints) (Hardcover) ($1.00)
Rosdon Books, Inc.

	GD25	FN65	NM94
1-Reprints the near complete case of "The Brow" from 6/12/44 to 9/24/44 (story starts a few weeks late)	22.00	65.00	150.00
with dust jacket....	36.00	107.00	250.00

DICK TRACY GIVEAWAYS
1939 - 1958; 1990

	GD25	FN65	NM94
Buster Brown Shoes Giveaway (1940s?, 36 pgs. in color); 1938-39-r by Gould	25.00	75.00	175.00
Gillmore Giveaway (See Superbook)			
...Hatful of Fun (No date, 1950-52)-32 pgs.; 8-1/2x10;" Dick Tracy hat promotion; Dick Tracy games, magic tricks. Miller Bros. premium	8.35	25.00	50.00
Motorola Giveaway (1953)-Reprints Harvey Comics Library #2	4.00	12.00	24.00
Original Dick Tracy by Chester Gould, The (Aug, 1990, 16 pgs., 5x8-1/2")-Gladstone Publ.; Bread Giveaway	4.00	10.00	20.00
Popped Wheat Giveaway (1947, 16 pgs. in color)-'40-r; Sig Feuchtwanger Publ.; Gould-a	2.00	5.00	10.00
...Presents the Family Fun Book; Tip Top Bread Giveaway, no date or number (1940, Fawcett Publ., 16 pgs. in color)-Spy Smasher, Ibis, Lance O'Casey app.	54.00	160.00	375.00
Same as above but without app. of heroes & Dick Tracy on cover only	10.00	30.00	60.00
Service Station Giveaway (1958, 16 pgs. in color)(regular size, slick cover)-Harvey Info. Press	3.20	8.00	16.00
Shoe Store Giveaway (Weatherbird)(1939, 16 pgs.)-Gould-a	11.00	32.00	75.00

DICK TRACY MONTHLY/WEEKLY
May, 1986 - No. 99, 1989 ($2.00, B&W) (Becomes Weekly #26 on)
Blackthorne Publishing

1-99: Gould-r. 30,31-Mr. Crime app. .40 1.00 2.00
NOTE: *#1-10 reprint strips 3/10/40-7/13/41; #10(pg.8)-51 reprint strips 4/6/49-12/31/55; #52-99 reprint strips 12/26/56-4/26/64.*

DICK TRACY SHEDS LIGHT ON THE MOLE
1949 (16 pgs.) (Ray-O-Vac Flashlights giveaway)
Western Printing Co.

nn-Not by Gould 5.85 17.50 35.00

DICK TRACY SPECIA (Blackthorne)(Value: cover or less)

DICK TRACY: THE EARLY YEARS (Blackthorne)(Value: cover or less)

DICK TRACY UNPRINTED STORIES (Blackthorne)(Value: cover or less)

DICK TURPIN (See Legend of Young...)

DICK WINGATE OF THE U.S. NAVY
1951; 1953 (no month)
Superior Publ./Toby Press

Dick Tracy Monthly #4, © Chicago Tribune

Dick Tracy Monthly #67, © Chicago Tribune

D. Tracy Tip Top Bread Giveaway (1940), © Chicago Tribune

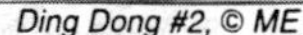
Ding Dong #2, © ME

Dirty Pair II #2, © Haruka Takachiho

Disney's Ducktales #13, WDC

	GD25	FN65	NM94
nn-U.S. Navy giveaway	1.80	4.50	9.00
1(1953, Toby)	2.80	7.00	14.00

DIE, MONSTER, DIE (See Movie Classics)

DIG 'EM
1973 (16 pgs.) (2-3/8x6")
Kellogg's Sugar Smacks Giveaway

	GD25	FN65	NM94
nn-4 different issues	.60	1.50	3.00

DIGITEK
Dec, 1992 - No. 4, Mar, 1993 ($1.95/$2.25, color, mini-series)
Marvel Comics UK, Ltd

	GD25	FN65	NM94
1,2 ($1.95)-	.40	1.00	2.00
3,4 ($2.25)	.45	1.15	2.25

DILLY (Dilly Duncan from Daredevil Comics; see Boy Comics #57)
May, 1953 - No. 3, Sept, 1953
Lev Gleason Publications

	GD25	FN65	NM94
1-Biro-c	4.00	10.00	20.00
2,3-Biro-c	2.40	6.00	12.00

DILTON'S STRANGE SCIENCE
May, 1989 - No. 5, May, 1990 (.75-$1.00, color)
Archie Comics

	GD25	FN65	NM94
1-5		.50	1.00

DIME COMICS
1945; 1951
Newsbook Publ. Corp.

	GD25	FN65	NM94
1-Silver Streak app.; L. B. Cole-c	13.00	40.00	90.00
1(1951), 5	2.80	7.00	14.00

DINGBATS (See 1st Issue Special)

DING DONG
Summer?, 1946 - No. 5, 1947 (52 pgs.)
Compix/Magazine Enterprises

	GD25	FN65	NM94
1-Funny animal	10.00	30.00	60.00
2 (11/46)	5.00	15.00	30.00
3 (Wint '46-'47) - 5	4.00	12.00	24.00

DINKY DUCK (Paul Terry's...) (See Blue Ribbon & New Terrytoons)
Nov, 1951 - No. 16, Sept, 1955; No. 16, Fall, 1956; No. 17, May, 1957 - No. 19, Summer, 1958
St. John Publishing Co./Pines No. 16 on

	GD25	FN65	NM94
1	5.85	17.50	35.00
2	3.60	9.00	18.00
3-10	2.00	5.00	10.00
11-16(9/55)	1.60	4.00	8.00
16(Fall,'56) - 19	1.20	3.00	6.00

DINKY DUCK & HASHIMOTO-SAN (See Deputy Dawg Presents...)

DINO (TV)(The Flintstones)
Aug, 1973 - No. 20, Jan, 1977
Charlton Publications

	GD25	FN65	NM94
1	1.20	3.00	6.00
2-20	.60	1.50	3.00

DINO RIDERS
Feb, 1989 - No. 3, 1989 ($1.00, color)
Marvel Comics

	GD25	FN65	NM94
1-3: Based on toys		.50	1.00

DINOSAUR REX (Fantagraphics)(Value: cover or less)

DINOSAURUS (See 4-Color No. 1120)

DINOSAURS ATTACK! THE GRAPHIC NOVEL
1991 - Book 3, 1992 ($3.95, color, mini-series, coated stock, stiff-c)
Eclipse Comics

	GD25	FN65	NM94
Book One - Three: Based on Topps trading cards	.70	2.00	4.00

DINOSAURS GRAPHIC NOVEL (TV)
1992 - No. 2, 1993 ($2.95, color, 52 pgs.)
Disney Comics

	GD25	FN65	NM94
1,2-Staton-a; based on Dinosaurs TV show	.60	1.50	3.00

DIPPY DUCK
October, 1957
Atlas Comics (OPI)

	GD25	FN65	NM94
1-Maneely-a	4.00	12.00	24.00

DIRECTORY TO A NONEXISTENT UNIVERSE (Eclipse)(Value: cover or less)

DIRTY DOZEN (See Movie Classics)

DIRTY PAIR
Dec, 1988 - No. 4, April, 1989 ($2.00, B&W, mini-series)
Eclipse Comics

	GD25	FN65	NM94
1-4: Japanese manga with original stories	.40	1.00	2.00

DIRTY PAIR II
June, 1989 - No. 5, Mar, 1990 ($2.00, B&W, mini-series)
Eclipse Comics

	GD25	FN65	NM94
1-5: 3-Cover is misnumbered as #1	.40	1.00	2.00

DIRTY PAIR III, THE
Aug, 1990 - No. 5, Aug, 1991 ($2.00, B&W, mini-series)
Eclipse Comics

	GD25	FN65	NM94
1,2	.40	1.00	2.00
3-5: ($2.25-c)	.45	1.15	2.25

DISHMAN (Eclipse)(Value: cover or less)

DISNEY COMIC ALBUM
1990(no month, year) - No. 9?, 1991 ($6.95-$7.95, color)
Disney Comics

	GD25	FN65	NM94
1,2 ($6.95): 1-Donald Duck and Gyro Gearloose by Barks(r). 2-Uncle Scrooge by Barks(r); Jr. Woodchucks app.	1.40	3.50	7.00
3-9: 3-Donald Duck-r/F.C. 308 by Barks; begin $7.95-c. 4-Mickey Mouse Meets the Phantom Blot; strip-r. 5-Chip 'n' Dale Rescue Rangers; new-a. 6-Uncle Scrooge. 7-Donald Duck in Too Many Pets; Barks-r(4). 8-Super Goof; r/S.G. #1, D.D. #102. 9-Mickey Mouse	1.60	4.00	8.00

DISNEYLAND BIRTHDAY PARTY (Also see Dell Giants)
Aug, 1985 ($2.50)
Gladstone Publishing Co.

	GD25	FN65	NM94
1-Reprints Dell Giant with new-photo-c	1.00	2.50	5.00
...Comics Digest #1-(Digest)	.50	1.25	2.50

DISNEYLAND, USA (See Dell Giant No. 30)

DISNEY'S COLOSSAL COMICS COLLECTION
1991 - Present ($1.95, color, digest-size, 96-132 pgs.)
Disney Comics

	GD25	FN65	NM94
1-10: Ducktales, Talespin, Chip 'n Dale's Rescue Rangers. 4-r/Darkwing Duck #1-4. 6-Goofy begins. 8-Little Mermaid	.40	1.00	2.00

DISNEY'S COMICS IN 3-D
1992 ($2.95, w/glasses, polybagged)
Disney Comics

	GD25	FN65	NM94
1-Infinity-c; Barks, Rosa, Gottfredson-r	.60	1.50	3.00

DISNEY'S DUCKTALES (TV) (Also see Ducktales)
Oct, 1988 - No. 13, May, 1990 (1,2,9-11: $1.50; 3-8: 95 cents, color)
Gladstone Publishing

	GD25	FN65	NM94
1-Barks-r	.70	1.75	3.50
2-11: 2,4-6,9-11-Barks-r. 7-Barks-r(1 pg.)	.40	1.00	2.00
12,13 ($1.95, 68 pgs.)-Barks-r; 12-r/F.C. #495	.45	1.10	2.20

DISNEY'S NEW ADVENTURES OF BEAUTY AND THE BEAST (Also see Beauty and the Beast)
1992 - No. 2, 1992 ($1.50, color, mini-series)
Disney Comics

	GD25	FN65	NM94
1,2-New stories based on movie	.30	.75	1.50

DISNEY'S TALESPIN LIMITED SERIES: "TAKE OFF" (See Talespin)
Jan, 1991 - No. 4, Apr, 1991 ($1.50, color, mini-series, 52 pgs.)
W. D. Publications (Disney Comics)

	GD25	FN65	NM94
1-4: Based on animated series; 4 part origin	.30	.75	1.50

DISNEY'S THE LITTLE MERMAID LIMITED SERIES
Feb, 1992 - No. 4, May, 1992 ($1.50, color, limited series)
Disney Comics

	GD25	FN65	NM94
1-4-All new adventures	.30	.75	1.50

DIVER DAN (TV)
Feb-Apr, 1962 - No. 2, June-Aug, 1962
Dell Publishing Co.

	GD25	FN65	NM94
4-Color 1254(#1), 2	5.35	16.00	32.00

DIXIE DUGAN (See Big Shot, Columbia Comics & Feature Funnies)
July, 1942 - No. 13, 1949 (Strip reprints in all)
McNaught Syndicate/Columbia/Publication Ent.

	GD25	FN65	NM94
1-Joe Palooka x-over by Ham Fisher	20.00	60.00	120.00
2	10.00	30.00	60.00
3	8.35	25.00	50.00
4,5(1945-46)-Bo strip-r	5.00	15.00	30.00
6-13(1/47-49): 6-Paperdoll cut-outs	4.00	12.00	24.00

DIXIE DUGAN
V3#1, Nov, 1951 - V4#4, Feb, 1954
Prize Publications (Headline)

	GD25	FN65	NM94
V3#1	5.00	15.00	30.00
2-4	4.00	10.00	20.00
V4#1-4(#5-8)	3.20	8.00	16.00

DIZZY DAMES
Sept-Oct, 1952 - No. 6, July-Aug, 1953
American Comics Group (B&M Distr. Co.)

	GD25	FN65	NM94
1-Whitney-c	5.35	16.00	32.00
2	4.00	11.00	22.00
3-6	3.00	7.50	15.00

DIZZY DON COMICS
1942 - No. 22, Oct, 1946; No. 3, Apr, 1947 (B&W)
F. E. Howard Publications/Dizzy Don Ent. Ltd (Canada)

	GD25	FN65	NM94
1	4.70	14.00	28.00
2	2.80	7.00	14.00
4-21	2.40	6.00	12.00
22-Full color, 52 pgs.	4.70	14.00	28.00
3 (4/47)-Full color, 52 pgs.	4.00	11.00	22.00

DIZZY DUCK (Formerly Barnyard Comics)
No. 32, Nov, 1950 - No. 39, Mar, 1952
Standard Comics

	GD25	FN65	NM94
32	5.00	15.00	30.00
33-39	3.20	8.00	16.00

DNAGENTS (Eclipse) (Value: cover or less)

DOBERMAN (See Sgt. Bilko's Private...)

DOBIE GILLIS (See The Many Loves of...)

DOC CARTER VD COMICS
1949 (16 pages in color) (Paper cover)
Health Publications Institute, Raleigh, N. C. (Giveaway)

	GD25	FN65	NM94
nn	14.00	43.00	100.00

DOC CHAOS: THE STRANGE ATTRACTOR (Vortex) (Value: cover or less)

DOC SAVAGE
November, 1966
Gold Key

	GD25	FN65	NM94
1-Adaptation of the Thousand-Headed Man; James Bama-c r-/'64 Doc Savage paperback	8.35	25.00	50.00

DOC SAVAGE (Also see Giant-Size...)
Oct, 1972 - No. 8, Jan, 1974
Marvel Comics Group

	GD25	FN65	NM94
1	1.40	3.50	7.00
2-8: 2,3-Steranko-c	.80	2.00	4.00

NOTE: *Gil Kane c-5, 6. Mooney a-1i. No. 1, 2 adapts pulp story "The Man of Bronze," No. 3, 4 adapts "Death in Silver," No. 5, 6 adapts "The Monsters," No. 7, 8 adapts "The Brand of The Werewolf."*

DOC SAVAGE (Magazine)
Aug, 1975 - No. 8, Spr, 1977 ($1.00, Black & White)
Marvel Comics Group

	GD25	FN65	NM94
1-Cover from movie poster; Ron Ely photo-c	.80	2.00	4.00
2-8: 1,3-Buscema-a	.50	1.25	2.50

DOC SAVAGE (DC, 1987 & 1988-90) (Value: cover or less)

DOC SAVAGE COMICS (Also see Shadow Comics)
May, 1940 - No. 20, Oct, 1943 (1st app. in Doc Savage pulp, 3/33)
Street & Smith Publications

	GD25	FN65	NM94
1-Doc Savage, Cap Fury, Danny Garrett, Mark Mallory, The Whisperer, Captain Death, Billy the Kid, Sheriff Pete & Treasure Island begin; Norgil, the Magician app.	200.00	600.00	1200.00
2-Origin & 1st app. Ajax, the Sun Man; Danny Garrett, The Whisperer end	92.00	275.00	550.00
3	75.00	225.00	450.00
4-Treasure Island ends; Tuska-a	58.00	175.00	350.00
5-Origin & 1st app. Astron, the Crocodile Queen, not in #9 & 11; Norgi the Magician app.	46.00	137.00	275.00
6-10: 6-Cap Fury ends; origin & only app. Red Falcon in Astron story. 8-Mark Mallory ends; Charlie McCarthy app. on cover. 9-Supersnipe app. 10-Origin & only app. The Thunderbolt	39.00	116.00	235.00
11,12	31.00	92.00	185.00
V2#1-8(#13-20): 16-The Pulp Hero, The Avenger app. 17-Sun Man ends; Nick Carter begins	31.00	92.00	185.00

DOC SAVAGE: THE DEVIL'S THOUGHTS
1992 (Says 1991) - No. 2, 1992 ($2.50, color, mini-series)
Millennium Publications

	GD25	FN65	NM94
1,2	.50	1.25	2.50

DOC SAVAGE: THE MAN OF BRONZE
1991 - No. 4, 1991 ($2.50, color, mini-series)
Millennium Publications

	GD25	FN65	NM94
1-4: 1-Bronze logo	.50	1.25	2.50
...: The Manual of Bronze 1 ($2.50, B&W, color, one-shot)-Unpublished proposed Doc Savage strip in color, B&W strip-r	.50	1.25	2.50

DOC SAVAGE: THE MAN OF BRONZE, DOOM DYNASTY
1992 (Says 1991) - No. 2, 1992 ($2.50, color, mini-series)
Millennium Publications

	GD25	FN65	NM94
1,2	.50	1.25	2.50

DOC STEARN...MR. MONSTER (See Mr. Monster)

DR. ANTHONY KING, HOLLYWOOD LOVE DOCTOR
1952(Jan.) - No. 3, May, 1953; No. 4, May, 1954
Minoan Publishing Corp./Harvey Publications No. 4

	GD25	FN65	NM94
1	6.35	19.00	38.00
2-4: 4-Powell-a	4.35	13.00	26.00

DR. ANTHONY'S LOVE CLINIC (See Mr. Anthony's...)

DR. BOBBS (See 4-Color No. 212)

DOCTOR BOOGIE (Media) (Value: cover or less)

Dixie Dugan #9, © McNaught Synd.

Doc Savage #1 (1972), © MEG

Doc Savage Comics #4, © S&S

Doctor Solar #11, © WEST

Doctor Strange #13 (1974), © MEG

Dr. Strange, Sorcerer Supreme #33, © MEG

GD25 FN65 NM94

DR. FATE (See 1st Issue Special, The Immortal..., Justice League, More Fun #55, & Showcase)

DOCTOR FATE
July, 1987 - No. 4, Oct, 1987 ($1.50, mini-series, Baxter)
DC Comics

1-4: Giffen-c/a in all .30 .75 1.50

DOCTOR FATE
Winter, 1988-'89 - No. 41, June, 1992 ($1.25-$1.50 #5 on, color)
DC Comics

1-31: 15-Justice League app. 25-1st new Dr. .30 .75 1.50
32-41: 32-Begin $1.75-c. 36-Original Dr. returns .35 .90 1.75
Annual 1(1989, $2.95, 68 pgs.)-Sutton-a .60 1.50 3.00

DR. FU MANCHU (See The Mask of...)
1964
I.W. Enterprises

1-Reprints Avon's "Mask of Dr. Fu Manchu;" Wood-a
5.70 17.00 40.00

DR. GIGGLES (See Dark Horse Presents #64-66)
Oct, 1992 - No. 2, Oct, 1992 ($2.50, color, mini-series)
Dark Horse Comics

1,2-Based on horror movie .50 1.25 2.50

DOCTOR GRAVES (Formerly The Many Ghosts of...)
No. 73, Sept, 1985 - No. 75, Jan, 1986
Charlton Comics

73-75 .50 1.00

DR. JEKYLL AND MR. HYDE (See A Star Presentation & Supernatural Thrillers #4)

DR. KILDARE (TV)
No. 1337, 4-6/62 - No. 9, 4-6/65 (All Richard Chamberlain photo-c)
Dell Publishing Co.

4-Color 1337(#1, 1962) 5.85 17.50 35.00
2-9 4.20 12.50 25.00

DR. MASTERS (See The Adventures of Young...)

DOCTOR SOLAR, MAN OF THE ATOM (Also see Solar)
10/62 - No. 27, 4/69; No. 28, 4/81 - No. 31, 3/82 (1-27 have painted-c)
Gold Key/Whitman No. 28 on

1-Origin/1st app. Dr. Solar (1st Gold Key comic-No. 10000-210)
32.00 95.00 225.00
2-Prof. Harbinger begins 11.50 34.00 80.00
3-5: 5-Intro. Man of the Atom in costume 8.35 25.00 50.00
6-10 5.35 16.00 32.00
11-14,16-20 4.70 14.00 28.00
15-Origin retold 5.85 17.50 35.00
21-27 4.00 10.00 20.00
28-31: 29-Magnus Robot Fighter begins. 31-The Sentinel app.
1.40 3.50 7.00
NOTE: ***Frank Bolle** a-6-19, 29-31; c-29i, 30i. **Bob Fugitani** a-1-5. **Spiegle** a-29-31. **Al McWilliams** a-20-23.*

DOCTOR SOLAR, MAN OF THE ATOM
1990 - No. 2?, 1991 ($7.95, color, card stock-c, high quality, 96 pgs.)
Valiant Comics

1,2: Reprints Gold Key series 1.60 4.00 8.00

DOCTOR SPEKTOR (See The Occult Files of...)

DOCTOR STRANGE (Formerly Strange Tales #1-168) (Also see The Defenders, Giant-Size..., Marvel Fanfare, Marvel Graphic Novel, Marvel Premiere, Marvel Treasury Ed. & Strange Tales, 2nd Series)
No. 169, 6/68 - No. 183, 11/69; 6/74 - No. 81, 2/87
Marvel Comics Group

169(#1)-Origin retold; panel swipe/M.D. #1-c 13.00 40.00 90.00
170-176 5.85 17.50 35.00
177-New costume. 5.35 16.00 32.00
178-183: 178-Black Knight app. 179-Spider-Man story-r. 180-Photo montage-c. 181-Brunner-c(part-i) 5.00 15.00 30.00
1(6/74)-Brunner-c/a 5.00 15.00 30.00
2 3.00 7.50 15.00
3-5 1.60 4.00 8.00
6-10 1.20 3.00 6.00
11-20 .90 2.25 4.50
21-26: 21-Origin-r/Doctor Strange #169 .70 1.75 3.50
27-77,79-81: 56-Origin retold .30 .75 1.50
78-New costume .50 1.25 2.50
Annual 1(1976, 52 pgs.)-New Russell-a (35 pgs.) .80 2.00 4.00
NOTE: ***Adkins** a-169, 170, 171i; c-169-171, 172i, 173. **Adams** a-4i. **Austin** a(i)-48-60, 66, 68, 70, 73; c(i)-38, 47-53, 55, 58-60, 70. **Brunner** a-1-5p; c-1-6, 22, 28-30, 33. **Colan** a(p)-172-178, 180-183, 6-18, 36-45, 47; c(p)-172, 174-183, 11-21, 23, 27, 35, 36, 47. **Ditko** a-179r, 3r. **Everett** c-183i. **Golden** a-46p, 55p; c-42-44, 46, 55p. **G. Kane** c(p)-8-10. **Miller** c-46p. **Nebres** a-20, 22, 23, 24i, 26i, 32i; c-32i, 34. **Rogers** a-48-53p; c-47p-53p. **Russell** a-34i, 46i, Annual 1. **B. Smith** c-179. **Paul Smith** a-54p, 56p, 65, 66p, 68p, 69, 71-73; c-56, 65, 66, 68, 71. **Starlin** a-23p, 26; c-25, 26. **Sutton** a-27-29p, 34p. Painted c-62, 63.*

DOCTOR STRANGE CLASSICS
Mar, 1984 - No. 4, June, 1984 ($1.50 cover price; Baxter paper)
Marvel Comics Group

1-4: Ditko-r; Byrne-c. 4-New Golden pin-up .40 1.00 2.00

DOCTOR STRANGE/GHOST RIDER SPECIAL
April, 1991 ($1.50, color)
Marvel Comics

1-Same-c & contents as Dr. Strange S.S. #28 1.00 2.50 5.00

DOCTOR STRANGE/SILVER DAGGER (Special Edition)
Mar, 1983 ($2.50, Baxter paper)
Marvel Comics

1-r/Dr. Strange #1,2,4,5; Wrightson-c .60 1.50 3.00

DOCTOR STRANGE, SORCERER SUPREME
Nov, 1988 - Present (Mando paper, $1.25-1.50, direct sales only)
Marvel Comics

1 ($1.25) 1.00 2.50 5.00
2-10,12-14,16-27,29,30 ($1.50): 3-New Defenders app. 5-Guice-c/a begins. 26-Werewolf by Night app. .30 .75 1.50
11-Hobgoblin app. 1.00 2.50 5.00
15-Unauthorized Amy Grant photo-c 1.40 3.50 7.00
28-Ghost Rider story cont'd from G.R. #12; same cover & contents as Doctor Strange/Ghost Rider Special #1 1.00 2.50 5.00
31-36-Infinity Gauntlet x-overs 31-Silver Surfer app. 33-Thanos-c & cameo. 36-Warlock app. .60 1.50 3.00
37-49,51-54: 37-Silver Surfer app. 38-Begin $1.75-c. 40-Daredevil x-over. 41-Wolverine-c/story. 42-47-Infinity War x-overs. 47-Gamora app.
.35 .90 1.75
50-($2.95, 52 pgs.)-Holo-grafx foil-c; Hulk, Ghost Rider & Silver Surfer app.; leads into new Secret Defenders series .60 1.50 3.00
Annual 2('92, $2.25, 68 pgs.)-Return of Defenders .45 1.15 2.25
NOTE: ***Colan** c/a-19. **Guice** a-5-16, 18, 20-24; c-5-12, 20-24. See 1st series for Annual #1.*

DR. TOM BRENT, YOUNG INTERN
Feb, 1963 - No. 5, Oct, 1963
Charlton Publications

1 1.60 4.00 8.00
2-5 1.00 2.50 5.00

DR. VOLTZ (See Mighty Midget Comics)

DOCTOR WHO (Also see Marvel Premiere #57-60)
Oct, 1984 - No. 23, Aug, 1986 ($1.50, Direct sales, Baxter paper)
Marvel Comics Group

1-23-British-r .50 1.00

DR. WHO & THE DALEKS (See Movie Classics)

DOCTOR ZERO
April, 1988 - No. 8, Aug, 1989 ($1.25/$1.50, color)
Epic Comics (Marvel)

	GD25	FN65	NM94
1-8: 1-Sienkiewicz-c (a-3i,4i). 6,7-Spiegle-a	.30	.75	1.50

DO-DO
1950 - No. 7, 1951 (5x7-1/4" Miniature) (5 cents)
Nation Wide Publishers

	GD25	FN65	NM94
1 (52 pgs.); funny animal	10.00	30.00	65.00
2-7	5.00	15.00	30.00

DODO & THE FROG, THE (Formerly Funny Stuff)
No. 80, 9-10/54 - No. 88, 1-2/56; No. 89, 8-9/56; No. 90, 10-11/56; No. 91, 9/57; No. 92, 11/57 (See Comic Cavalcade)
National Periodical Publications

	GD25	FN65	NM94
80-1st app. Doodles Duck by Sheldon Mayer	11.50	34.00	80.00
81-91: Doodles Duck by Sheldon Mayer in #81,83-90	8.35	25.00	50.00
92-(Scarce)-Doodles Duck by S. Mayer	10.00	30.00	70.00

DOGFACE DOOLEY
1951 - No. 5, 1953
Magazine Enterprises

	GD25	FN65	NM94
1(A-1 40)	4.00	12.00	24.00
2(A-1 43), 3(A-1 49), 4(A-1 53), 5(A-1 64)	3.20	8.00	16.00
I.W. Reprint #1('64), Super Reprint #17	1.20	3.00	6.00

DOG OF FLANDERS, A (See 4-Color No. 1088)

DOGPATCH (See Al Capp's... & Mammy Yokum)

DOINGS OF THE DOO DADS, THE
1922 (34 pgs.; 7-3/4x7-3/4"; B&W) (50 cents)
(Red & White cover; square binding)
Detroit News (Universal Feat. & Specialty Co.)

	GD25	FN65	NM94
nn-Reprints 1921 newspaper strip "Text & Pictures" given away as prize in the Detroit News Doo Dads contest; by Arch Dale	11.00	32.00	75.00

DOLLFACE & HER GANG (See 4-Color No. 309)

DOLLMAN
Sept, 1991 - No. 4, Dec, 1991 ($2.50, color, mini-series)
Eternity Comics

	GD25	FN65	NM94
1-4: Based on new movie	.50	1.25	2.50

DOLL MAN QUARTERLY, THE (Doll Man #17 on; also see Feature Comics #27 & Freedom Fighters)
Fall, 1941 - No. 7, Fall, '43; No. 8, Spring, '46 - No. 47, Oct, 1953
Quality Comics Group

	GD25	FN65	NM94
1-Dollman (by Cassone), Justin Wright begin	142.00	425.00	850.00
2-The Dragon begins; Crandall-a(5)	72.00	215.00	430.00
3,4	54.00	162.00	325.00
5-Crandall-a	42.00	125.00	250.00
6,7(1943)	30.00	90.00	180.00
8(1946)-1st app. Torchy by Bill Ward	33.00	100.00	200.00
9	25.00	75.00	150.00
10-20	20.00	60.00	120.00
21-30	17.00	50.00	100.00
31-36,38,40: 32-34-Jeb Rivers app.; 34 by Crandall(p)	14.00	42.00	85.00
37-Origin Dollgirl; Dollgirl bondage-c	20.00	60.00	120.00
39-"Narcotics...the Death Drug"-c-/story	14.00	42.00	85.00
41-47	10.00	30.00	60.00
Super Reprint #11('64, r-#20),15(r-#23),17(r-#28): 15,17-Torchy app.; Andru/Esposito-c	2.40	6.00	12.00

NOTE: ***Ward*** *Torchy in 8, 9, 11, 12, 14-24, 27; by Fox-#30, 35-47.* ***Crandall*** *a-2, 5, 10, 13 & Super #11, 17, 18.* ***Crandall/Cuidera*** *c-40-42.* ***Guardineer*** *a-3. Bondage c-27, 37, 38, 39.*

DOLLY
No. 10, July-Aug, 1951 (Funny animal)
Ziff-Davis Publ. Co.

	GD25	FN65	NM94
10-Painted-c	3.60	9.00	18.00

DOLLY DILL
1945
Marvel Comics/Newsstand Publ.

	GD25	FN65	NM94
1	10.00	30.00	65.00

DOLLY DIMPLES & BOBBY BOONCE'
1933
Cupples & Leon Co.

	GD25	FN65	NM94
nn	10.00	30.00	70.00

DOMINION (Eclipse)(Value: cover or less)

DOMINO CHANCE (Chance)(Value: cover or less)

DONALD AND MICKEY IN DISNEYLAND (See Dell Giants)

DONALD AND MICKEY MERRY CHRISTMAS (Formerly Famous Gang Book Of Comics)
1943 - 1949 (20 pgs.)(Giveaway) Put out each Christmas; 1943 issue titled "Firestone Presents Comics" (Disney)
K. K. Publ./Firestone Tire & Rubber Co.

	GD25	FN65	NM94
1943-Donald Duck reprint from WDC&S #32 by Carl Barks	50.00	150.00	400.00
1944-Donald Duck reprint from WDC&S #35 by Barks	48.00	145.00	385.00
1945-"Donald Duck's Best Christmas," 8 pgs. Carl Barks; intro. & 1st app. Grandma Duck in comic books	62.00	185.00	490.00
1946-Donald Duck in "Santa's Stormy Visit," 8 pgs. Carl Barks	47.00	140.00	370.00
1947-Donald Duck in "Three Good Little Ducks," 8 pgs. Carl Barks	38.00	115.00	305.00
1948-Donald Duck in "Toyland," 8 pgs. Carl Barks	37.00	110.00	290.00
1949-Donald Duck in "New Toys," 8 pgs. Carl Barks	43.00	130.00	345.00

DONALD AND SCROOGE
1992 ($8.95, color, squarebound, 100 pgs.)
Disney Comics

	GD25	FN65	NM94
nn-Don Rosa reprint special; r/U.S., D.D. Advs.	1.80	4.50	9.00

DONALD AND THE WHEEL (See 4-Color No. 1190)

DONALD DUCK (See Cheerios, Disney's Ducktales, Ducktales, Dynabrite Comics, Gladstone Comic Album, Mickey & Donald, Mickey Mouse Mag., Story Hour Series, Uncle Scrooge, Walt Disney's Comics & Stories, Wheaties & Whitman Comic Books)

DONALD DUCK
1935, 1936 (Linen-like text & color pictures; 1st book ever devoted to Donald Duck; see The Wise Little Hen for earlier app.) (9x13")
Whitman Publishing Co./Grosset & Dunlap/K.K.

	GD25	FN65	NM94
978(1935)-16 pgs.; story book	107.00	320.00	750.00
nn(1936)-36 pgs.; reprints '35 edition with expanded ill. & text	65.00	195.00	450.00
with dust jacket....	93.00	280.00	650.00

DONALD DUCK (Walt Disney's) (10 cents)
1938 (B&W) (8x11") (Cardboard covers)
Whitman/K.K. Publications
(Has Donald Duck with bubble pipe on front cover)

	GD25	FN65	VF82
nn-The first Donald Duck & Walt Disney comic book; 1936 & 1937 Sunday strip-r(in B&W); same format as the Feature Books; 1st strips with Huey, Dewey & Louie from 10/17/37	157.00	470.00	1100.00

(Prices vary widely on this book)

DONALD DUCK (Walt Disney's...#262 on; see 4-Color listings for titles &

Dodo and the Frog #89, © DC

The Doll Man Quarterly #1, © QUA

Donald and Mickey Merry Christmas 1949, © WDC

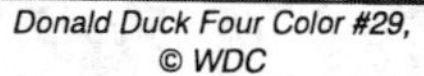
Donald Duck Four Color #29, © WDC

Donald Duck #26, © WDC

Donald Duck #246, © WDC

GD25 FN65 NM94

4-Color No. 1109 for origin story)
1940 - #84, 9-11/62; #85, 12/62 - #245, 1984; #246, 10/86 - #279, 5/90
Dell Publishing Co./Gold Key No. 85-216/Whitman No. 217-245/
Gladstone Publishing No. 246 on

	GD25	FN65	VF82	NM94
4-Color 4(1940)-Daily 1939 strip-r by Al Taliaferro	500.00	1250.00	3000.00	5000.00

(Estimated up to 175 total copies exist, 9 in NM/Mint)

	GD25	FN65	NM94
Large Feature Comic 16(1/41?)-1940 Sunday strips-r in B&W	185.00	557.00	1300.00
Large Feature Comic 20('41)-Comic Paint Book, r-single panels from Large Feature #16 at top of each page to color; daily strip-r across bottom of each page	285.00	857.00	2000.00

	GD25	FN65	VF82	NM94
4-Color 9('42)-"Finds Pirate Gold;"-64 pgs. by Carl Barks & Jack Hannah (pgs. 1,2,5,12-40 are by Barks, his 1st comic book work; © 8/17/42)	420.00	1050.00	2520.00	4200.00

(Estimated up to 270 total copies exist, 18 in NM/Mint)

	GD25	FN65	VF82	NM94
4-Color 29(9/43)-"Mummy's Ring" by Barks; reprinted in Uncle Scrooge & Donald Duck #1('65), W. D. Comics Digest #44('73) & Donald Duck Advs. #14	340.00	850.00	2040.00	3400.00

(Estimated up to 300 total copies exist, 14 in NM/Mint)

	GD25	FN65	NM94
4-Color 62(1/45)-"Frozen Gold;" 52 pgs. by Barks, reprinted in The Best of W.D. Comics & Donald Duck Advs. #4	120.00	360.00	960.00
4-Color 108(1946)-"Terror of the River;" 52 pgs. by Carl Barks; reprinted in Gladstone Comic Album #2	90.00	270.00	720.00
4-Color 147(5/47)-in "Volcano Valley" by Barks	60.00	180.00	480.00
4-Color 159(8/47)-in "The Ghost of the Grotto;" 52 pgs. by Carl Barks; reprinted in Best of Uncle Scrooge & Donald Duck #1 ('66) & The Best of W.D. Comics & D.D. Advs. #9; two Barks stories	54.00	160.00	430.00
4-Color 178(12/47)-1st Uncle Scrooge by Carl Barks; reprinted in Gold Key Christmas Parade No. 3 & The Best of W.D. Comics	64.00	192.00	510.00
4-Color 189(6/48)-by Carl Barks; reprinted in Best of Donald Duck & Uncle Scrooge #1('64) & D.D. Advs. #19	54.00	160.00	430.00
4-Color 199(10/48)-by Carl Barks; mentioned in Love and Death; r/in Gladstone Comic Album #5	54.00	160.00	430.00
4-Color 203(12/48)-by Barks; reprinted as Gold Key Christmas Parade #4	36.00	108.00	290.00
4-Color 223(4/49)-by Barks; reprinted as Best of Donald Duck #1 & Donald Duck Advs. #3	50.00	150.00	400.00
4-Color 238(8/49)-in "Voodoo Hoodoo" by Barks; on Disney's reprint banned list	38.00	112.00	300.00
256(12/49)-by Barks; reprinted in Best of Donald Duck & Uncle Scrooge #2('67), Gladstone Comic Album #16 & W.D. Comics Digest #44('73)	27.00	81.00	215.00
4-Color 263(2/50)-Two Barks stories; r-in D.D. #278	27.00	81.00	215.00
4-Color 275(5/50), 282(7/50), 291(9/50), 300(11/50)-All by Carl Barks; 275, 282 reprinted in W.D. Comics Digest #44('73). #275 r/in Gladstone Comic Album #10. #291 r/in D. Duck Advs. #16	25.00	75.00	200.00
4-Color 308(1/51), 318(3/51)-by Barks; #318-reprinted in W.D. Comics Digest #34 & D.D. Advs. #2,19	21.00	63.00	170.00
4-Color 328(5/51)-by Carl Barks	23.00	70.00	185.00
4-Color 339(7-8/51), 379-not by Barks	5.35	16.00	32.00
4-Color 348(9-10/51), 356,394-Barks-c only	8.35	25.00	50.00
4-Color 367(1-2/52)-by Barks; reprinted as Gold Key Christmas Parade #2 & #8	20.00	60.00	160.00
4-Color 408(7-8/52), 422(9-10/52)-All by Carl Barks. #408-r-in Best of Donald Duck & Uncle Scrooge #1('64) & Gladstone Comic Album #13	20.00	60.00	160.00
26(11-12/52)-In "Trick or Treat" (Barks-a, 36pgs.) 1st story r-in Walt Disney Digest #16 & Gladstone C.A. #23	26.00	78.00	180.00
27-30-Barks-c only	5.85	17.50	35.00
31-40	4.00	11.00	22.00
41-44,47-50	3.20	8.00	16.00
45-Barks-a, 6 pgs.	9.15	27.50	55.00
46-"Secret of Hondorica" by Barks, 24 pgs.; reprinted in Donald Duck #98 & 154	10.00	30.00	60.00
51-Barks, pg.	2.80	7.00	14.00
52-"Lost Peg-Leg Mine" by Barks, 10 pgs.	8.35	25.00	50.00
53,55-59	2.40	6.00	12.00
54-"Forbidden Valley" by Barks, 26 pgs.	9.75	29.00	58.00
60-"Donald Duck & the Titanic Ants" by Barks, 20 pgs. plus 6 more pages	8.35	25.00	50.00
61-67,69,70	2.00	5.00	10.00
68-Barks-a, 5 pgs.	4.35	13.00	26.00
71-Barks-r, pg.	2.40	6.00	12.00
72-78,80,82-97,99,100: 96-Donald Duck Album	2.00	5.00	10.00
79,81-Barks-a, 1pg.	2.00	5.00	10.00
98-Reprints #46 (Barks)	3.00	7.50	15.00
101-133: 102-Super Goof. 112-1st Moby Duck	1.20	3.00	6.00
134-Barks-r/#52 & WDC&S 194	1.40	3.50	7.00
135-Barks-r/WDC&S 198, 19 pgs.	1.00	2.50	5.00
136-153,155,156,158	.60	1.50	3.00
154-Barks-r(#46)	1.00	2.00	5.00
157,159,160,164: 157-Barks-r(#45). 159-Reprints/WDC&S #192 (10 pgs.). 160-Barks-r(#26). 164-Barks-r(#79)	.60	1.50	3.00
161-163,165-173,175-187,189-191	.40	1.00	2.00
174,188: 174-r/4-Color #394. 188-Barks-r/#68	.40	1.00	2.00
192-Barks-r(40 pgs.) from Donald Duck #60 & WDC&S #226,234 (52 pgs.)	.50	1.25	2.50
193-200,202-207,209-211,213-218: 217 has 216 on-c	.30	.75	1.50
201,208,212: 201-Barks-r/Christmas Parade #26, 16pgs. 208-Barks-r/#60 (6 pgs.). 212-Barks-r/WDC&S #130	.40	1.00	2.00
219-Barks-r/WDC&S #106,107, 10 pgs. ea.	.30	.75	1.50
220-227,231-245		.50	1.00
228-230: 228-Barks-r/F.C. #275. 229-Barks-r/F.C. #282. 230-Barks-r/ #52 & WDC&S #194	.30	.75	1.50
246-(1st Gladstone issue)-Barks-r/FC #422	1.80	4.50	9.00
247-249: 248,249-Barks-r/DD #54 & 26	.80	2.00	4.00
250-($1.50, 68 pgs.)-Barks-r/4-Color #9	3.00	7.50	15.00
251-256: 251-Barks-r/1945 Firestone. 254-Barks-r/FC #328. 256-Barks-r/FC #147	.60	1.50	3.00
257-($1.50, 52 pgs.)-Barks-r/Vac. Parade #1	.80	2.00	4.00
258-260	.50	1.25	2.50
261-277: 261-Barks-r/FC #300. 275-Kelly-r/FC #92	.30	.75	1.50
278-($1.95, 68 pgs.)-Rosa-a; Barks-r/FC #263	.50	1.25	2.50
279-($1.95, 68 pgs.)-Rosa-c; Barks-r/MOC #4	.50	1.25	2.50
Mini-Comic #1(1976)-(3-1/4x6-1/2"); r/D.D. #150			.10

NOTE: ***Carl Barks** wrote all issues he illustrated, but #117, 126, 138 contain his script only. Issues 4-Color #189, 199, 203, 223, 238, 256, 263, 275, 282, 308, 348, 356, 367, 394, 408, 422, 26-30, 35, 44, 46, 52, 55, 57, 60, 65, 70-73, 77-80, 83, 101, 103, 105, 106, 111, 126, 246r, 266r, 268r, 271r, 275r, 278r(F.C. 263) all have **Barks** covers. **Barks** r-263- 267, 269-278. #96 titled "Comic Album," #99-"Christmas Album." New art issues (notreprints)-106-46, 148-63, 167, 169, 170, 172, 173, 175, 178, 179, 196, 209, 223, 225, 236.*

DONALD DUCK
1944 (16 pg. Christmas giveaway)(paper cover)(2 versions)
K. K. Publications

	GD25	FN65	NM94
nn-Kelly cover reprint	39.00	115.00	270.00

DONALD DUCK ADVENTURES (Walt Disney's...#4 on)
Nov, 1987 - No. 20, Apr, 1990
Gladstone Publishing

	GD25	FN65	NM94
1	.55	1.65	3.30
2-r/F.C. #308	.35	1.10	2.20

3,4,6,7,9-11,13,15-18: 3-r/F.C. #223. 4-r/F.C. #62. 9-r/F.C. #159. 16-r/F.C. #291; Rosa-c. 18-r/F.C. #318; Rosa-c .30 .85 1.70
5,8-Don Rosa-a .35 1.10 2.20
12($1.50, 52pgs)-Rosa-c/a w/Barks poster .35 1.10 2.20
14-r/F.C. #29, "Mummy's Ring" .40 1.25 2.50
19 ($1.95, 68 pgs.)-Barks-r/F.C. #199 .35 1.00 2.00
20 ($1.95, 68 pgs.)-Barks-r/F.C. #189 & cover-r .35 1.00 2.00
NOTE: *Barks a-1-19r; c-10r, 14r. Rosa a-5, 8, 12; c-13, 16-18.*

DONALD DUCK ADVENTURES (2nd series)(Walt Disney's... #? on)
June, 1990 - Present ($1.50, color)
Disney Comics

1-Rosa-a & scripts .50 1.25 2.50
2-38: 2,3-Barks-r & new-a. 4,5-New-a? 9-r/F.C. #178 by Barks. 11-Mad #1 cover parody. 14-Barks-r. 21-r/FC #203 by Barks. 22-Rosa-a (10 pgs.). 24-Rosa-a & scripts. 34-Rosa-c/a .30 .75 1.50

DONALD DUCK ALBUM (See Comic Album No. 1,3 & Duck Album)
5-7/59 - F.C. No. 1239, 10-12/61; 1962; 8/63 - No. 2, Oct, 1963
Dell Publishing Co./Gold Key

4-Color 995,1182, 01204-207 (1962-Dell) 3.20 8.00 16.00
4-Color 1099,1140,1239-Barks-c 3.60 9.00 18.00
1(8/63-Gold Key)-Barks-c 3.20 8.00 16.00
2(10/63) 2.00 5.00 10.00

DONALD DUCK AND THE BOYS (Also see Story Hour Series)
1948 (Hardcover book; 5-1/4x5-1/2") 100pgs., art, text
Whitman Publishing Co.

845-Partial-r/WDC&S #74 by Barks 35.00 105.00 250.00
(Prices vary widely on this book)

DONALD DUCK AND THE RED FEATHER
1948 (4 pages) (8-1/2x11") (Black & White)
Red Feather Giveaway

nn 10.00 30.00 60.00

DONALD DUCK BEACH PARTY (Also see Dell Giants)
Sept, 1965 (12 cents)
Gold Key

1(#10158-509)-Barks-r/WDC&S #45; painted-c 4.00 12.00 28.00

DONALD DUCK BOOK (See Story Hour Series)

DONALD DUCK COMIC PAINT BOOK (See Large Feature Comic No. 20)

DONALD DUCK COMICS DIGEST
Nov, 1986 - No. 5, July, 1987 ($1.25-$1.50, 96 pgs.)
Gladstone Publishing

1-5: 1-Barks-c/a-r. 4,5-$1.50-c .40 1.00 2.00

DONALD DUCK FUN BOOK (See Dell Giants)

DONALD DUCK IN DISNEYLAND (See Dell Giants)

DONALD DUCK IN "THE LITTERBUG"
1963 (16 pgs., 5x7-1/4", soft-c) (Disney giveaway)
Keep America Beautiful

nn 4.00 12.00 24.00

DONALD DUCK MARCH OF COMICS
No. 4, 1947 - No. 69, 1951; No. 263, 1964 (Giveaway) (Disney)
K. K. Publications

nn(No.4)-"Maharajah Donald;" 30 pgs. by Carl Barks-(1947) 715.00 2150.00 5000.00
20-"Darkest Africa" by Carl Barks-(1948); 22 pgs.; on Disney's reprint banned list 357.00 1070.00 2500.00
41-"Race to South Seas" by Carl Barks-(1949); 22 pgs. 230.00 685.00 1600.00
56-(1950)-Barks-a on back-c 23.00 70.00 160.00
69-(1951)-Not by Barks; Barks-a on back-c 20.00 60.00 140.00
263-Not by Barks 7.00 21.00 42.00

DONALD DUCK MERRY CHRISTMAS (See Dell Giant No. 53)

DONALD DUCK PICNIC PARTY (See Picnic Party listed under Dell Giants)

DONALD DUCK "PLOTTING PICNICKERS"
1962 (16 pgs., 3-1/4x7", soft-c) (Disney)(Also see Ludwig Von Drake & Mickey Mouse)
Fritos Giveaway

nn 4.20 12.50 25.00

DONALD DUCK'S SURPRISE PARTY
1948 (16 pgs.) (Giveaway for Icy Frost Twins Ice Cream Bars)
Walt Disney Productions

nn-(Rare)-Kelly-c/a 215.00 650.00 1500.00

DONALD DUCK TELLS ABOUT KITES (See Kite Fun Book)

DONALD DUCK, THIS IS YOUR LIFE (See 4-Color No. 1109)

DONALD DUCK XMAS ALBUM (See regular Donald Duck No. 99)

DONALD IN MATHMAGIC LAND (See 4-Color No. 1051, 1198)

DONATELLO, TEENAGE MUTANT NINJA TURTLE
Aug, 1986 ($1.50, one-shot, B&W, 44 pgs.)
Mirage Studios

1 2.00 5.00 10.00

DONDI (See 4-Color No. 1176,1276)

DON FORTUNE MAGAZINE
Aug, 1946 - No. 6, Feb, 1947
Don Fortune Publishing Co.

1-Delecta of the Planets by C. C. Beck in all 11.00 32.00 75.00
2 8.35 25.00 50.00
3-6: 3-Bondage-c 5.35 16.00 32.00

DON NEWCOMBE
1950 (Baseball)
Fawcett Publications

nn 26.00 78.00 180.00

DON'T GIVE UP THE SHIP (See 4-Color #1049)

DON WINSLOW OF THE NAVY (See Crackajack Funnies, Famous FeatureStories, Four Color #2, 22, Popular Comics & Super Book #5,6)

DON WINSLOW OF THE NAVY (See TV Teens; Movie, Radio, TV)
2/43 - #64, 12/48; #65, 1/51 - #69, 9/51; #70, 3/55 - #73, 9/55
(Fightin' Navy No. 74 on)
Fawcett Publications/Charlton No. 70 on

1-(68 pgs.)-Captain Marvel on cover 64.00 192.00 385.00
2 33.00 100.00 200.00
3 23.00 70.00 140.00
4-6: 6-Flag-c 17.00 52.00 105.00
7-10: 8-Last 68 pg. issue? 13.00 40.00 80.00
11-20 9.15 27.50 55.00
21-40 6.70 20.00 40.00
41-63: 51,60-Singapore Sal (villain) app. 5.00 15.00 30.00
64(12/48)-Matt Baker-a 5.85 17.50 35.00
65(1/51) - 69(9/51): All photo-c. 65-Flying Saucer attack 6.70 20.00 40.00
70(3/55)-73: 70-73 r-/#26,58 & 59 4.35 13.00 26.00

DOOM FORCE SPECIAL
July, 1992 ($2.95, color, mature readers, 68 pgs.)
DC Comics

1-X-Force parody; Morrison scripts; Simonson, Steacy, others-a; Giffen/Mignola-c .60 1.50 3.00

DOOM PATROL, THE (Formerly My Greatest Adventure No. 1-85; see Brave and the Bold, DC Special Blue Ribbon Digest 19, Official...Index & Showcase No. 94-96)
No. 86, 3/64 - No. 121, 9-10/68; No. 122, 2/73 - No. 124, 6-7/73

Donald Duck Adventures #5, © WDC

Don Fortune Magazine #1, © Don Fortune

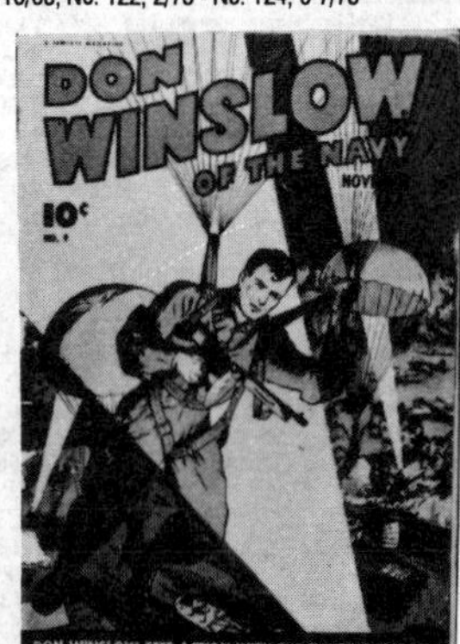

Don Winslow of the Navy #9, © FAW

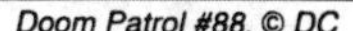
Doom Patrol #88, © DC

Dopey Duck #1, © MCG

Dorothy Lamour #2, © FOX

GD25 FN65 NM94

National Periodical Publications

	GD25	FN65	NM94
86-1 pg. origin (#86-121 are 12 cent issues)	10.00	30.00	70.00
87-99: 88-Origin The Chief. 91-Intro. Mento. 99-Intro. Beast Boy (later became the Changeling in New Teen Titans	7.50	22.50	45.00
100-Origin Beast Boy; Robot-Maniac series begins (12/65)	9.15	27.50	55.00
101-110: 102-Challengers of the Unknown app. 105-Robot-Maniac series ends. 106-Negative Man begins (origin)	4.20	12.50	25.00
111-120	4.00	10.00	20.00
121-Death of Doom Patrol; Orlando-c	10.00	30.00	60.00
122-124: All reprints	.50	1.25	2.50

DOOM PATROL
Oct, 1987 - Present (New format, direct sale, $1.50 #19 on)
DC Comics

	GD25	FN65	NM94
1	.40	1.00	2.00
2-18: 3-1st app. Lodestone. 4-1st app. Karma. 8,15,16-Art Adams-c(i). 18-Invasion		.50	1.00
19-New format & Grant Morrison scripts begin	3.00	7.50	15.00
20-25	1.80	4.50	9.00
26-30: 29-Superman app.	1.00	2.50	5.00
31-40: 39-Preview of World Without End	.40	1.00	2.00
41-49,51-56,58-60: 53-Steacy-a. 60-Last $1.50-c	.30	.75	1.50
50,57-($2.50, 52 pgs.)	.50	1.25	2.50
61-66: 61-Photo-c. 63-Last Morrison scripts	.35	.90	1.75
...And Suicide Squad Special 1(3/88, $1.50)	.30	.75	1.50
Annual 1('88, $1.50, 52pgs.)-No Morrison scripts	.30	.75	1.50

DOOMSDAY + 1
July, 1975 - No. 6, June, 1976; No. 7, June, 1978 - No. 12, May, 1979
Charlton Comics

	GD25	FN65	NM94
1: #1-5 are 25 cent issues	1.20	3.00	6.00
2	.90	2.25	4.50
3-6: 4-Intro Lor. 6-Begin 30 cent issues	.80	2.00	4.00
V3#7-12 (reprints #1-6)	.35	.80	1.60
5 (Modern Comics reprint, 1977)		.50	1.00

NOTE: ***Byrne** c/a-1-12; Painted covers-2-7.*

DOOMSDAY SQUAD, THE (Fantagraphics) (Value: cover or less)

DOOM 2099 (See Marvel Comics Presents #118)
Jan, 1993 - Present ($1.25, color)
Marvel Comics

	GD25	FN65	NM94
1-($1.75)-Metallic foil stamped-c	.40	1.00	2.00
2-6		.60	1.25

DOORWAY TO NIGHTMARE (See Cancelled Comic Cavalcade)
Jan-Feb, 1978 - No. 5, Sept-Oct, 1978
DC Comics

	GD25	FN65	NM94
1-5-Madame Xanadu in all. 4-Craig-a		.50	1.00

NOTE: ***Kaluta** covers on all. Merged into The Unexpected with No. 190.*

DOPEY DUCK COMICS (Wacky Duck No. 3) (See Super Funnies)
Fall, 1945 - No. 2, April, 1946
Timely Comics (NPP)

	GD25	FN65	NM94
1,2-Casper Cat, Krazy Krow	10.00	30.00	70.00

DOROTHY LAMOUR (Formerly Jungle Lil) (Stage, screen, radio)
No. 2, June, 1950 - No. 3, Aug, 1950
Fox Features Syndicate

	GD25	FN65	NM94
2,3-Wood-a(3) each, photo-c	12.00	36.00	85.00

DOT AND DASH AND THE LUCKY JINGLE PIGGIE
1942 (12 pages)
Sears Roebuck Christmas giveaway

	GD25	FN65	NM94
nn-Contains a war stamp album and a punch out Jingle Piggie bank	5.35	16.00	32.00

GD25 FN65 NM94

DOT DOTLAND (Formerly Little Dot Dotland)
No. 62, Sept, 1974 - No. 63, November, 1974
Harvey Publications

	GD25	FN65	NM94
62,63	.40	1.00	2.00

DOTTY (...& Her Boy Friends) (Formerly Four Teeners; Glamorous Romances No. 41 on)
No. 35, July, 1948 - No. 40, May, 1949
Ace Magazines (A. A. Wyn)

	GD25	FN65	NM94
35	4.35	13.00	26.00
36,38-40	2.80	7.00	14.00
37-Transvestism story	3.20	8.00	16.00

DOTTY DRIPPLE (Horace & Dotty Dripple No. 25 on)
1946 - No. 24, June, 1952 (See A-1 No. 1-8, 10)
Magazine Ent.(Life's Romances)/Harvey No. 3 on

	GD25	FN65	NM94
nn (nd) (10 cent)	4.00	10.50	21.00
2	2.00	5.00	10.00
3-10: 3,4-Powell-a	1.40	3.50	7.00
11-24	1.00	2.50	5.00

DOTTY DRIPPLE AND TAFFY
No. 646, Sept, 1955 - No. 903, May, 1958
Dell Publishing Co.

	GD25	FN65	NM94
4-Color 646 (#1)	3.60	9.00	18.00
4-Color 691,718,746,801,903	2.40	6.00	12.00

DOUBLE ACTION COMICS
No. 2, Jan, 1940 (Regular size; 68 pgs.; B&W, color cover)
National Periodical Publications

	GD25	FN65	NM94
2-Contains original stories(?); pre-hero DC contents; same cover as Adventure No. 37. (Five known copies) (not an ashcan) Estimated value....			7500.00

NOTE: *The cover to this book was probably reprinted from Adventure #37. #1 exists as an ash can copy with B&W cover; contains a coverless comic on inside with 1st & last page missing.*

DOUBLE COMICS
1940 - 1944 (132 pages)
Elliot Publications

	GD25	FN65	NM94
1940 issues; Masked Marvel-c & The Mad Mong vs. The White Flash covers known	150.00	450.00	900.00
1941 issues; Tornado Tim-c, Nordac-c, & Green Light covers known	108.00	325.00	650.00
1942 issues	92.00	275.00	550.00
1943,1944 issues	67.00	200.00	400.00

NOTE: *Double Comics consisted of an almost endless combination of pairs of remaindered, unsold issues of comics representing most publishers and usually mixed publishers in the same book; e.g., a Captain America with a Silver Streak, or a Feature with a Detective, etc., could appear inside the same cover. The actual contents would have to determine its price. Prices listed are for average contents. Any containing rare origin or first issues are worth much more. Covers also vary in same year. Value would be approximately 50 percent of contents.*

DOUBLE-CROSS (See The Crusaders)

DOUBLE-DARE ADVENTURES
Dec, 1966 - No. 2, March, 1967 (35-25 cents, 68 pgs.)
Harvey Publications

	GD25	FN65	NM94
1-Origin Bee-Man, Glowing Gladiator, & Magic-Master; Simon/Kirby-a (last S&K art as a team?)	4.70	14.00	28.00
2-Williamson/Crandall-a; r/Alarming Adv. #3('63)	4.00	10.00	20.00

NOTE: ***Powell** a-1. **Simon/Sparling** c-1, 2.*

DOUBLE DRAGON
July, 1991 - No. 6, Dec, 1991 (1.00, color, mini-series)
Marvel Comics

	GD25	FN65	NM94
1-6: Based on video game. 2-Arthur Adams-c		.50	1.00

DOUBLE LIFE OF PRIVATE STRONG, THE
June, 1959 - No. 2, Aug, 1959

Archie Publications/Radio Comics

	GD25	FN65	NM94
1-Origin The Shield; Simon & Kirby-c/a; intro./1st app. The Fly	47.00	140.00	325.00
2-S&K-c/a; Tuska-a; The Fly app.	32.00	95.00	225.00

DOUBLE TALK (Also see Two-Faces)
No date (1962?) (32 pgs.; full color; slick cover)
Christian Anti-Communism Crusade (Giveaway)
Feature Publications

	GD25	FN65	NM94
nn	10.00	30.00	60.00

DOUBLE TROUBLE
Nov, 1957 - No. 2, Jan-Feb, 1958
St. John Publishing Co.

	GD25	FN65	NM94
1,2	3.60	9.00	18.00

DOUBLE TROUBLE WITH GOOBER
No. 417, Aug, 1952 - No. 556, May, 1954
Dell Publishing Co.

	GD25	FN65	NM94
4-Color 417	2.80	7.00	14.00
4-Color 471,516,556	2.00	5.00	10.00

DOUBLE UP
1941 (200 pages) (Pocket size)
Elliott Publications

	GD25	FN65	NM94
1-Contains rebound copies of digest sized issues of Pocket Comics, Speed Comics, & Spitfire Comics	62.00	188.00	375.00

DOVER BOYS (See Adventures of the...)

DOVER THE BIRD
Spring, 1955
Famous Funnies Publishing Co.

	GD25	FN65	NM94
1	3.20	8.00	16.00

DOWN WITH CRIME
Nov, 1952 - No. 7, Nov, 1953
Fawcett Publications

	GD25	FN65	NM94
1	11.50	34.00	80.00
2-5: 2,4-Powell-a in each. 3-Used in **POP**, pg. 106; "H is for Heroin" drug story. 5-Bondage-c	7.50	22.50	45.00
6,7: 6-Used in **POP**, pg. 80	5.35	16.00	32.00

DO YOU BELIEVE IN NIGHTMARES?
Nov, 1957 - No. 2, Jan, 1958
St. John Publishing Co.

	GD25	FN65	NM94
1-Mostly Ditko-c/a	18.00	54.00	125.00
2-Ayers-a	10.00	30.00	65.00

D.P. 7
Nov, 1986 - No. 32, June, 1989 (26 on: $1.50)
Marvel Comics Group

	GD25	FN65	NM94
1-32		.60	1.25
Annual #1 (11/87)-Intro. The Witness		.65	1.25

NOTE: ***Williamson** a-9i, 11i; c-9i.*

DRACULA (See Giant-Size..., Marvel Graphic Novel & Tomb of...; also see Movie Classics under Universal Presents as well as Dracula)

DRACULA (See Movie Classics for No. 1)
No. 2, 11/66 - No. 4, 3/67; No. 6, 7/72 - No. 8, 7/73 (No #5)
Dell Publishing Co.

	GD25	FN65	NM94
2-Origin Dracula (11/66)	2.40	6.00	12.00
3,4-Intro. Fleeta #4('67)	1.40	3.50	7.00
6-('72)-r/#2 w/origin	1.00	2.50	5.00
7,8: 7-r/#3, 8-r/#4	.80	2.00	4.00

DRACULA (Magazine)
1979 (120 pages, full color)
Warren Publishing Co.

	GD25	FN65	NM94
Book 1-Maroto art; Spanish material translated into English	1.20	3.00	6.00

DRACULA (Bram Stoker's)
1992 - No. 4, 1993 ($2.95, color, mini-series, polybagged, adapts movie)
Topps Comics

	GD25	FN65	NM94
1-4 trading cards in all; photo scenes of movie	1.00	2.50	5.00
2-Bound-in poster; Mignola-c/a in all	.70	1.75	3.50
3,4: 3-Contains coupon to win 1 of 500 crimson foil-c edition of #1. 4-Contains coupon to win 1 of 500 uncut sheets of all 16 trading cards	.60	1.50	3.00

DRACULA LIVES! (Magazine)
1973(no month) - No. 13, July, 1975 (B&W) (75 cents)
Marvel Comics Group

	GD25	FN65	NM94
1	1.40	3.50	7.00
2,3: 2-Origin; Starlin-a	1.00	2.50	5.00
4-Ploog-a	.60	1.50	3.00
5(V2#1)-13: 5-Dracula series begins	.60	1.50	3.00
Annual 1(Summer '75, $1.25)-Morrow painted-c	.60	1.50	3.00

NOTE: ***N. Adams** a-2, 3i, 10i, Annual 1r(2, 3i). **Alcala** a-9. **Buscema** a-3p, 6p, Annual 1p. **Colan** a(p)-1, 2, 5, 6, 8. **Evans** a-7. **Heath** a-1r, 13. **Pakula** a-6r. **Weiss** r-Annual 1p.*

DRACULA 3-D (3-D Zone) (Value: cover or less)

DRAFT, THE
1988 (One shot, $3.50, color, squarebound)
Marvel Comics

	GD25	FN65	NM94
1-Sequel to "The Pitt"	.70	1.75	3.50

DRAG 'N' WHEELS (Formerly Top Eliminator)
No. 30, Sept, 1968 - No. 59, May, 1973
Charlton Comics

	GD25	FN65	NM94
30-40-Scot Jackson begins	1.20	3.00	6.00
41-50	.80	2.00	4.00
51-59: Scot Jackson	.60	1.50	3.00
Modern Comics Reprint 58('78)	.30	.75	1.50

DRAGON CHIANG (Eclipse) (Value: cover or less)

DRAGONFLIGHT (Eclipse) (Value: cover or less)

DRAGONFLY (Americomics) (Value: cover or less) (See Americomics #4)

DRAGONFORCE
1988 - No. 13, 1989 ($2.00, color)
Aircel Publishing

	GD25	FN65	NM94
1-Dale Keown-c/a/scripts in 1-12	1.40	3.50	7.00
2,3	1.00	2.50	5.00
4-6	.80	2.00	4.00
7-12	.70	1.75	3.50
13-No Keown-a	.40	1.00	2.00
...Chronicles Book 1-5 ($2.95, B&W, 60 pgs.): Dale Keown-r/Dragonring & Dragonforce	.50	1.50	3.00

DRAGONLANCE (DC) (Value: cover or less) (Also see TSR Worlds)

DRAGONQUEST
Dec, 1986 - No. 3, 1987 ($1.50, B&W, 28 pgs.)
Silverwolf Comics

	GD25	FN65	NM94
1-Tim Vigil-c/a in all	2.00	5.00	10.00
2,3	1.20	3.00	6.00

DRAGONRING (Aircel) (Value: cover or less)

DRAGON'S CLAWS
July, 1988 - No. 12, June?, 1989 ($1.25-$1.75, color, British)
Marvel Comics Ltd.

	GD25	FN65	NM94
1-4: 2-Begin $1.50-c	.25	.75	1.50
5-1st app. new Death's Head; begin $1.75-c	2.00	5.00	10.00
6-12	.35	.90	1.75

DRAGONSLAYER
October, 1981 - No. 2, Nov, 1981

Do You Believe in Nightmares? #1, © STJ

Dracula #2 (11/66), © DELL

Dragonforce #1, © Aircel Publ.

Dreadstar #6, © First Comics

Duck Album #353, © WDC

Dumbo Weekly #5, © WDC

Marvel Comics Group

	GD25	FN65	NM94
1,2-Paramount Disney movie adaptation		.50	1.00

DRAGOON WELLS MASSACRE (See 4-Color No. 815)

DRAGSTRIP HOTRODDERS (World of Wheels No. 17 on)
Sum, 1963; No. 2, Jan, 1965 - No. 16, Aug, 1967
Charlton Comics

	GD25	FN65	NM94
1	2.80	7.00	14.00
2-5	1.80	4.50	9.00
6-16	1.40	3.50	7.00

DRAMA OF AMERICA, THE
1973 (224 pages) ($1.95)
Action Text

	GD25	FN65	NM94
1-"Students' Supplement to History"	.60	1.50	3.00

DREAD (Eclipse) (Value: cover or less) (Clive Barker) (Graphic album)

DREADLANDS (Also see Epic)
1992 - No. 4, 1992 ($3.95, color, mini-series, coated stock, 52 pgs.)
Epic Comics (Marvel)

	GD25	FN65	NM94
1-4: Stiff-c	.80	2.00	4.00

DREAD OF NIGHT (Hamilton) (Value: cover or less)

DREADSTAR (Epic/First) (Value: Cover or less)

DREADSTAR AND COMPANY (Epic) (Value: cover or less)

DREAM BOOK OF LOVE (See A-1 Comics No. 106, 114, 123)

DREAM BOOK OF ROMANCE (See A-1 No. 92, 101, 109, 110, 124)

DREAMERY, THE (Eclipse) (Value: cover or less)

DREAM OF LOVE
1958 (Reprints)
I. W. Enterprises

	GD25	FN65	NM94
1,2,8: 1-Powell-a. 8-Kinstler-c	.80	2.00	4.00
9-Kinstler-c; 1pg. John Wayne interview & illo	.60	1.50	3.00

DREAMS OF THE RAREBIT FIEND
1905
Doffield & Co.?

nn-By Winsor McCay (Very Rare) (Three copies known to exist)
Estimated value.... $900.00–$1600.00

DREDD RULES (Fleetway/Quality) (Value: cover or less)

DRIFT MARLO
May-July, 1962 - No. 2, Oct-Dec, 1962
Dell Publishing Co.

	GD25	FN65	NM94
01-232-207(#1), 2(12-232-212)	2.80	7.00	14.00

DRISCOLL'S BOOK OF PIRATES
1934 (124 pgs.) (B&W; hardcover; 7x9")
David McKay Publ. (Not reprints)

	GD25	FN65	NM94
nn-By Montford Amory	12.00	36.00	85.00

DROIDS
April, 1986 - No. 8, June, 1987 (Based on Saturday morning cartoon)
Star Comics (Marvel)

	GD25	FN65	NM94
1-8: R2D2, C-3PO from Star Wars app.		.50	1.00

NOTE: ***Romita** a-3p. **Williamson** a-2i, 5i, 7i, 8i. **Sinnott** a-3i.*

DROWNED GIRL, THE
1990 ($5.95, color, mature readers, 52 pgs.)
Piranha Press (DC)

	GD25	FN65	NM94
nn	1.20	3.00	6.00

DRUG WARS (Pioneer) (Value: cover or less)

DRUM BEAT (See 4-Color No. 610)

DRUNKEN FIST (Jademan) (Value: cover or less)

DUCK ALBUM (See Donald Duck Album)
No. 353, Oct, 1951 - No. 840, Sept, 1957
Dell Publishing Co.

	GD25	FN65	NM94
4-Color 353-Barks-c	4.70	14.00	28.00
4-Color 450-Barks-c	4.20	12.50	25.00
4-Color 492,531,560,586,611,649,686	3.60	9.00	18.00
4-Color 726,782,840	3.20	8.00	16.00

DUCKTALES (Also see Disney's Ducktales)
June, 1990 - No. 18, Nov, 1991 ($1.50, color)
Disney Comics

	GD25	FN65	NM94
1-18: All new stories	.30	.75	1.50
...: The Movie nn (1990, 7.95, 68 pgs.)-Graphic novel adapting animated movie	1.60	4.00	8.00

DUDLEY (Teen-age)
Nov-Dec, 1949 - No. 3, Mar-Apr, 1950
Feature/Prize Publications

	GD25	FN65	NM94
1-By Boody Rogers	10.00	30.00	60.00
2,3	5.85	17.50	35.00

DUDLEY DO-RIGHT (TV)
Aug, 1970 - No. 7, Aug, 1971 (Jay Ward)
Charlton Comics

	GD25	FN65	NM94
1	5.85	17.50	35.00
2-7	4.20	12.50	25.00

DUKE OF THE K-9 PATROL
April, 1963
Gold Key

	GD25	FN65	NM94
1 (10052-304)	2.80	7.00	14.00

DUMBO (See 4-Color #17,234,668, Movie Comics, & Walt Disney Showcase #12)

DUMBO (Walt Disney's...)
1941 (K.K. Publ. Giveaway)
Weatherbird Shoes/Ernest Kern Co.(Detroit)

	GD25	FN65	NM94
nn-16 pgs., 9x10" (Rare)	25.00	75.00	175.00
nn-52 pgs., 5x8", slick cover in color; B&W interior; half text, half reprints/ 4-Color No. 17	14.00	43.00	100.00

DUMBO COMIC PAINT BOOK (See Large Feature Comic No. 19)

DUMBO WEEKLY
1942 (Premium supplied by Diamond D-X Gas Stations)
Walt Disney Productions

	GD25	FN65	NM94
1	20.00	60.00	140.00
2-16	10.00	30.00	60.00

NOTE: *A cover and binder came separate at gas stations. Came with membership card.*

DUNC AND LOO (1-3 titled "Around the Block with Dunc and Loo")
Oct-Dec, 1961 - No. 8, Oct-Dec, 1963
Dell Publishing Co.

	GD25	FN65	NM94
1	10.00	30.00	60.00
2	5.85	17.50	35.00
3-8	4.20	12.50	25.00

NOTE: *Written by **John Stanley**; **Bill Williams** art.*

DUNE
April, 1985 - No. 3, June, 1985
Marvel Comics

	GD25	FN65	NM94
1-3-r/Marvel Super Special; movie adaptation		.50	1.00

DURANGO KID, THE (Also see Best of the West, Great Western & White Indian) (Charles Starrett starred in Columbia's Durango Kid movies)
Oct-Nov, 1949 - No. 41, Oct-Nov, 1955 (All 36 pgs.)
Magazine Enterprises

	GD25	FN65	NM94
1-Charles Starrett photo-c; Durango Kid & his horse Raider begin; Dan Brand & Tipi (origin) begin by Frazetta & continue through #16	43.00	130.00	300.00
2(Starrett photo-c)	23.00	70.00	160.00
3-5(All-Starrett photo-c)	20.00	60.00	140.00
6-10: 7-Atomic weapon-c/story	10.00	30.00	70.00
11-16-Last Frazetta issue	8.35	25.00	50.00
17-Origin Durango Kid	10.00	30.00	70.00
18-Fred Meagher-a on Dan Brand begins	6.70	20.00	40.00
19-30: 19-Guardineer-c/a(3) begin, end #41. 23-Intro. The Red Scorpion	6.70	20.00	40.00
31-Red Scorpion returns	5.85	17.50	35.00
32-41-Bolle/Frazetta-a (Dan Brand)	7.50	22.50	45.00

NOTE: *#6, 8, 14, 15 contain **Frazetta** art not reprinted in White Indian. **Ayers** c-18. **Guardineer** a(3)-19-41; c-19-41. **Fred Meagher** a-18-29 at least.*

DURANGO KID, THE (AC)(Value: cover or less)

DWIGHT D. EISENHOWER
December, 1969
Dell Publishing Co.

	GD25	FN65	NM94
01-237-912 - Life story	2.80	7.00	14.00

DYNABRITE COMICS
1978 - 1979 (69 cents; 48 pgs.)(10x7-1/8"; cardboard covers)
(Blank inside covers)
Whitman Publishing Co.

11350 - Walt Disney's Mickey Mouse & the Beanstalk (4-C 157). 11350-1 - Mickey Mouse Album (4-C 1057,1151,1246). 11351 - Mickey Mouse & His Sky Adventure (4-C 214, 343). 11352 - Donald Duck (4-C 408, Donald Duck 45,52)-Barks-a. 11352-1 - Donald Duck (4-C 318, 10 pg. Barks/WDC&S 125,128)-Barks-c(r). 11353 - Daisy Duck's Diary (4-C 1055,1150) Barks-a. 11354 - Goofy: A Gaggle of Giggles. 11354-1 - Super Goof Meets Super Thief. 11355 - Uncle Scrooge (Barks-a/U.S. 12,33). 11355-1 - Uncle Scrooge (Barks-a/U.S. 13,16) - Barks-c(r). 11356 - (?). 11357 - Star Trek (r/-Star Trek 33,41). 11358 - Star Trek (r/-Star Trek 34,36). 11359 - Bugs Bunny-r. 11360 - Winnie the Pooh Fun and Fantasy (Disney-r). 11361 - Gyro Gearloose & the Disney Ducks (r/4-C 1047,1184)-Barks-c(r)

	GD25	FN65	NM94
	each....	.50	1.00

DYNAMIC ADVENTURES
No. 8, 1964 - No. 9, 1964
I. W. Enterprises

	GD25	FN65	NM94
8-Kayo Kirby-r by Baker?/Fight Comics #?	1.60	4.00	8.00
9-Reprints Avon's "Escape From Devil's Island"-Kinstler-c	1.80	4.50	9.00
nn(no date)-Reprints Risks Unlimited with Rip Carson, Senorita Rio	1.60	4.00	8.00

DYNAMIC CLASSICS (See Cancelled Comic Cavalcade)
Sept-Oct, 1978 (44 pgs.)
DC Comics

	GD25	FN65	NM94
1-Neal Adams Batman, Simonson Manhunter-r	.50	1.25	2.50

DYNAMIC COMICS (No #4-7)
Oct, 1941 - No. 3, Feb, 1942; No. 8, 1944 - No. 25, May, 1948
Harry 'A' Chesler

	GD25	FN65	NM94
1-Origin Major Victory by Charles Sultan (reprinted in Major Victory #1), Dynamic Man & Hale the Magician; The Black Cobra only app.	87.00	262.00	525.00
2-Origin Dynamic Boy & Lady Satan; intro. The Green Knight & sidekick Lance Cooper	45.00	135.00	270.00
3	35.00	105.00	210.00
8-Dan Hastings, The Echo, The Master Key, Yankee Boy begin; Yankee Doodle Jones app.; hypo story	35.00	105.00	210.00
9-Mr. E begins; Mac Raboy-c	37.00	110.00	220.00
10	29.00	86.00	175.00
11-15: 15-The Sky Chief app.	22.00	68.00	135.00
16-Marijuana story	24.00	72.00	145.00
17(1/46)-Illustrated in **SOTI**, "The children told me what the man was going to do with the hot poker," but Wertham saw this in Crime Reporter #2	33.00	100.00	200.00
18,19,21,22,24,25	14.00	42.00	85.00
20-Bare-breasted woman-c	20.00	60.00	120.00
23-Yankee Girl app.	14.00	42.00	85.00
I.W. Reprint #1,8('64): 1-r/#23. 8-Exist?	2.00	5.00	10.00

NOTE: ***Kinstler** c-IW #1. **Tuska** art in many issues, #3, 9, 11, 12, 16, 19. Bondage c-16.*

DYNAMITE (Becomes Johnny Dynamite No. 10 on)
May, 1953 - No. 9, Sept, 1954
Comic Media/Allen Hardy Publ.

	GD25	FN65	NM94
1-Pete Morisi-a; r-as Danger #6	10.00	30.00	70.00
2	6.35	19.00	38.00
3-Marijuana story; Johnny Dynamite begins by Pete Morisi(c/a); Heck text-a; man shot in face at close range	7.50	22.50	45.00
4-Injury-to-eye, prostitution; Morisi-a	9.15	27.50	55.00
5-9-Morisi-a in all. 6-Morisi-c	5.35	16.00	32.00

DYNAMO (Also see Tales of Thunder & T.H.U.N.D.E.R. Agents)
Aug, 1966 - No. 4, June, 1967 (25 cents)
Tower Comics

	GD25	FN65	NM94
1-Crandall/Wood, Ditko/Wood-a; Weed series begins; NoMan & Lightning cameos; Wood-c/a	5.00	15.00	30.00
2-4: Wood-c/a in all	4.00	10.00	20.00

NOTE: ***Adkins/Wood** a-2. **Ditko** a-4?. **Tuska** a-2, 3.*

DYNAMO JOE (Also see First Adventures & Mars)
May, 1986 - No. 15, Jan, 1988 (#12-15: $1.75)
First Comics

	GD25	FN65	NM94
1-15: 4-Cargonauts begin	.30	.75	1.50
Special 1(1/87)-Mostly-r/Mars	.30	.75	1.50

DYNOMUTT (TV)(See Scooby-Doo, 3rd series)
Nov, 1977 - No. 6, Sept, 1978 (Hanna-Barbera)
Marvel Comics Group

	GD25	FN65	NM94
1	.50	1.25	2.50
2-6: 3-Scooby Doo story	.30	.75	1.50

EAGLE, THE (1st Series) (See Science Comics & Weird Comics #8)
July, 1941 - No. 4, Jan, 1942
Fox Features Syndicate

	GD25	FN65	NM94
1-The Eagle begins; Rex Dexter of Mars app. by Briefer	96.00	290.00	575.00
2-The Spider Queen begins (origin)	54.00	162.00	325.00
3,4: 3-Joe Spook begins (origin)	42.00	125.00	250.00

EAGLE (2nd Series)
Feb-Mar, 1945 - No. 2, Apr-May, 1945
Rural Home Publ.

	GD25	FN65	NM94
1-Aviation stories	11.00	32.00	75.00
2-Lucky Aces	10.00	30.00	65.00

NOTE: ***L. B. Cole** c/a in each.*

EAGLE
Sept, 1986 - No. 26?, 1989 ($1.50/1.75/1.95, B&W)
Crystal Comics/Apple Comics #17 on

	GD25	FN65	NM94
1	.40	1.00	2.00
1-Signed and limited	.60	1.50	3.00
2-26: 12-Double size origin issue ($2.50)	.30	.75	1.50

EARTH MAN ON VENUS (An...) (Also see Strange Planets)
1951
Avon Periodicals

	GD25	FN65	NM94
nn-Wood-a (26 pgs.); Fawcette-c	74.00	225.00	520.00

EASTER BONNET SHOP (See March of Comics No. 29)

EASTER WITH MOTHER GOOSE (See 4-Color No. 103, 140, 185, 220)

EAST MEETS WEST (Innovation)(Value: cover or less)

EAT RIGHT TO WORK AND WIN
1942 (16 pages) (Giveaway)
Swift & Company

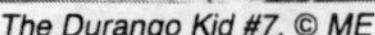
The Durango Kid #7, © ME

Dynamic Comics #8, © CHES

Dynamo #3, © TC

Eclipse Graphic Album Series #14, © Eclipse

Edgar Bergen Presents Charlie McCarthy #764, © E. Bergen

Eerie #8 ('50s), © AVON

GD25 FN65 NM94

Blondie, Henry, Flash Gordon by Alex Raymond, Toots & Casper, Thimble Theatre(Popeye), Tillie the Toiler, The Phantom, The Little King, & Bringing up Father - original strips just for this book -(in daily strip form which shows what foods we should eat and why) 20.00 60.00 140.00

E. C. CLASSIC REPRINTS
May, 1973 - No. 12, 1976 (E. C. Comics reprinted in color minus ads)
East Coast Comix Co.

1-The Crypt of Terror #1 (Tales From the Crypt #46) 1.20 3.00 6.00
2-Weird Science #15('52) .80 2.00 4.00
3-12: 3-Shock SuspenStories #12. 4-Haunt of Fear #12. 5-Weird Fantasy #13('52). 6-Crime SuspenStories #25. 7-Vault of Horror #26. 8-Shock SuspenStories #6. 9-Two-Fisted Tales #34. 10-Haunt of Fear #23. 11-Weird Science #12(#1). 12-Shock SuspenStories #2 .60 1.50 3.00

EC CLASSICS
Aug, 1985 - No. 12, 1986? (High quality paper; each-r 8 stories in color)
Russ Cochran (#2-12 were resolicited in 1990)($4.95, 56 pgs., 8X11")

1-12: 1-Tales From the Crypt. 2-Weird Science. 3-Two-Fisted Tales. 4-Shock SuspenStories. 5-Weird Fantasy. 6-Vault of Horror. 7-Weird Science-Fantasy (r/23,24). 8-Crime SuspensStories. 9-Haunt of Fear. 10-Panic (r/1,2). 11-Tales From the Crypt (r/23,24). 12-Weird Science (r/20,22) 1.00 2.50 5.00

ECHO OF FUTUREPAST (Pacific) (Value: cover or less)

ECLIPSE GRAPHIC ALBUM SERIES
Oct, 1978 - Present (8-1/2x11") (B&W #1-5)
Eclipse Comics

1-Sabre (10/78, B&W, 1st print.); Gulacy-a; 1st direct sale graphic novel 1.60 4.00 8.00
1-Sabre (2nd printing, 1/79) 1.60 4.00 8.00
1-Sabre (3rd printing, $5.95) 1.20 3.00 6.00
2-Night Music (11/79, B&W)-Russell-a 1.00 2.50 5.00
3-Detectives, Inc. (5/80, B&W)-Rogers-a 1.40 3.50 7.00
4-Stewart The Rat ('80, B&W)-G. Colan-a 1.40 3.50 7.00
5-The Price (10/81, B&W)-Starlin-a 2.40 6.00 12.00
6-I Am Coyote (11/84, color)-Rogers-c/a 1.60 4.00 8.00
7-The Rocketeer (9/85, color)-Dave Stevens-a (reprints chapters 1-5) (see Pacific Presents & Starslayer) 1.60 4.00 8.00
7-The Rocketeer (2nd print, $7.95) 1.60 4.00 8.00
7-The Rocketeer (3rd print, 1991, $8.95) 1.80 4.50 9.00
7-The Rocketeer, signed & limited hardcover 10.00 30.00 60.00
7-The Rocketeer, unsigned hard-c (3rd, $32.95) 5.50 16.50 33.00
8-Zorro In Old California ('86, color) 1.60 4.00 8.00
8-Hard cover 2.40 6.00 12.00
9-Sacred And The Profane ('86)-Steacy-a 3.20 8.00 16.00
9-Hard cover ($24.95) 4.20 12.50 25.00
10-Somerset Holmes ('86, $15.95)-Adults, soft-c 3.20 8.00 16.00
10-Hard cover ($24.95) 4.20 12.50 25.00
11-Floyd Farland, Citizen of the Future ('87, $3.95, B&W) .80 2.00 4.00
12-Silverheels ('87, $8.95, color) 1.80 4.50 9.00
12-Hard cover ($14.95) 3.00 7.50 15.00
12-Hard cover, signed & #'d ($24.95) 4.20 12.50 25.00
13-The Sisterhood of Steel ('87, $9.95, color) 2.00 5.00 10.00
14-Samurai, Son of Death ('87, $4.95, B&W) 1.00 2.50 5.00
14-Samurai, Son of Death ($3.95, 2nd print.) .80 2.00 4.00
15-Twisted Tales (11/87, color)-Dave Stevens-c .80 2.00 4.00
16-See Airfighters Classics #1
17-Valkyrie, Prisoner of the Past ('88, $3.95, color) .80 2.00 4.00
18-See Airfighters Classics #2
19-Scout: The Four Monsters ('88, $14.95, color)-r/Scout #1-7; soft-c 3.00 7.50 15.00
20-See Airfighters Classics #3

GD25 FN65 NM94

21-XYR-Multiple ending comic ('88, $3.95, B&W) .80 2.00 4.00
22-Alien Worlds #1 (5/88, $3.95, 52 pgs.)-Nudity .80 2.00 4.00
23-See Airfighters Classics #4
24-Heartbreak ($4.95, B&W) 1.00 2.50 5.00
25-Alex Toth's Zorro Vol. 1 ($10.95, B&W) 2.20 5.50 11.00
26-Alex Toth's Zorro Vol. 2 ($10.95, B&W) 2.20 5.50 11.00
27-Fast Fiction (She) ($5.95, B&W) 1.20 3.00 6.00
28-Miracleman Book I ($5.95) 1.20 3.00 6.00
29-Real Love: The Best of the Simon and Kirby Romance Comics (10/88, $12.95) 2.60 6.50 13.00
30-Brought To Light; Alan Moore scripts (1989) 2.20 5.50 11.00
30-Limited hardcover ed. ($29.95) 5.00 15.00 30.00
31-Pigeons From Hell by R. E. Howard (11/88) 1.60 4.00 8.00
31-Signed & Limited Edition ($29.95) 5.00 15.00 30.00

ECLIPSE MAGAZINE (Eclipse) (Value: cover or less)

ECLIPSE MONTHLY (Eclipse) (Value: cover or less)

ECLIPSO (See Brave and the Bold #64, House of Secrets #61 & Phantom Stranger, 1987)
Nov, 1992 - Present ($1.25, color)
DC Comics

1-8: 1-Giffen plots/Breakdowns begin .60 1.25

ECLIPSO: THE DARKNESS WITHIN
July, 1992 - No. 2, Oct, 1992 ($2.50, color, 68 pgs.)
DC Comics

1-With purple gem attached to-c .80 2.00 4.00
1-Without gem; Superman, Creeper app. .50 1.25 2.50
2-Concludes Eclipso storyline from annuals .50 1.25 2.50

E. C. 3-D CLASSICS (See Three Dimensional...)

EDDIE STANKY (Baseball Hero)
1951 (New York Giants)
Fawcett Publications

nn-Photo-c 17.00 52.00 120.00

EDGAR BERGEN PRESENTS CHARLIE McCARTHY
No. 764, 1938 (36 pgs.; 15x10"; in color)
Whitman Publishing Co. (Charlie McCarthy Co.)

764 (Scarce) 64.00 192.00 450.00

EDGE OF CHAOS (Pacific) (Value: cover or less)

EDWARD'S SHOES GIVEAWAY
1954 (Has clown on cover)
Edward's Shoe Store

Contains comic with new cover. Many combinations possible. Contents determines price, 50-60 percent of original. (Similar to Comics From Weatherbird & Free Comics to You)

ED WHEELAN'S JOKE BOOK STARRING FAT & SLAT (See Fat & Slat)

EERIE (Strange Worlds No. 18 on)
No. 1, Jan, 1947; No. 1, May-June, 1951 - No. 17, Aug-Sept, 1954
Avon Periodicals

1(1947)-1st horror comic; Kubert, Fugitani-a; bondage-c 61.00 182.00 425.00
1(1951)-Reprints story from 1947 #1 27.00 81.00 190.00
2-Wood-c/a; bondage-c 30.00 90.00 210.00
3-Wood-c; Kubert, Wood/Orlando-a 30.00 90.00 210.00
4,5-Wood-c 27.00 81.00 190.00
6,8,13,14: 8-Kinstler-a; bondage-c; Phantom Witch Doctor story 11.00 32.00 75.00
7-Wood/Orlando-c; Kubert-a 19.00 57.00 130.00
9-Kubert-a; Check-c 11.50 34.00 80.00
10,11: 10-Kinstler-a. 11-Kinstlerish-a by McCann 10.00 30.00 65.00
12-Dracula story from novel, 25 pgs. 12.00 36.00 85.00
15-Reprints No. 1('51)minus-c(bondage) 7.50 22.50 45.00

16-Wood-a r-/No. 2 9.15 2.50 55.00
17-Wood/Orlando & Kubert-a; reprints #3 minus inside & outside Wood-c
10.00 30.00 70.00

NOTE: ***Hollingsworth** a-9-11; c-10, 11.*

EERIE
1964
I. W. Enterprises

I.W. Reprint #1('64)-Wood-c(r); r-story/Spook #1 2.80 7.00 14.00
I.W. Reprint #2,6,8: 8-Dr. Drew by Grandenetti from Ghost #9
2.00 5.00 10.00
I.W. Reprint #9-r/Tales of Terror #1(Toby); Wood-c
2.80 7.00 14.00

EERIE (Magazine)(See Warren Presents)
No. 1, Sept, 1965; No. 2, Mar, 1966 - No. 139, Feb, 1983
Warren Publishing Co.

1-24 pgs., black & white, small size (5-1/4x7-1/4"), low distribution; cover from inside back cover of Creepy No. 2; stories reprinted from Creepy No. 7, 8. At least three different versions exist.

First Printing - B&W, 5-1/4" wide x 7-1/4" high, evenly trimmed. On page 18, panel 5, in the upper left-hand corner, the large rear view of a bald headed man blends into solid black and is unrecognizable. Overall printing quality is poor. 22.00 65.00 150.00

Second Printing - B&W, 5-1/4x7-1/4", with uneven, untrimmed edges (if one of these were trimmed evenly, the size would be less than as indicated). The figure of the bald headed man on page 18, panel 5 is clear and discernible. The staples have a 1/4" blue stripe.
10.00 30.00 65.00

Other unauthorized reproductions for comparison's sake would be practically worthless. One known version was probably shot off a first printing copy with some loss of detail; the finer lines tend to disappear in this version which can be determined by looking at the lower right-hand corner of page one, first story. The roof of the house is shaded with straight lines. These lines are sharp and distinct on original, but broken on this version.

NOTE: ***The Overstreet Comic Book Price Guide** recommends that, before buying a 1st issue, you consult an expert.*

2-Frazetta-c 4.00 10.00 20.00
3-Frazetta-c, 1 pg. art 3.00 7.50 15.00
4-10: 4-Frazetta-a (pg.). 9-Headlight-c 2.00 5.00 10.00
11-25: 23-Frazetta-c. 25-Steranko-c 1.60 4.00 8.00
26-41,43-45 1.00 2.50 5.00
42,51-(1973 & 1974 Annuals) 1.40 3.50 7.00
46-50,52,53,56-59,61-78: 78-The Mummy-r .80 2.00 4.00
54,55-Color Spirit story by Eisner, reprints sections 12/21/47 & 6/16/46
1.00 2.50 5.00
60-Summer Giant ($1.25) 1.20 3.00 6.00
79,80-Origin Darklon the Mystic by Starlin .80 2.00 4.00
81-139: 82-1st app. The Rook .50 1.25 2.50
Year Book 1970, 1971-Reprints in both 2.00 5.00 10.00
Year Book 1972-Reprints 1.40 3.50 7.00

NOTE: *The above books contain art by many good artists: **N. Adams, Brunner, Corben, Craig (Taycee), Crandall, Ditko, Eisner, Evans, Jeff Jones, Kinstler, Krenkel, McWilliams, Morrow, Orlando, Ploog, Severin, Starlin, Torres, Toth, Williamson, Wood,** and **Wrightson**; covers by **Bode', Corben, Davis, Frazetta, Morrow,** and **Orlando**. Annuals from 1973-on are included in regular numbering. 1970-74 Annuals are complete reprints. Annuals from 1975-on are in the format of the regular issues.*

EERIE ADVENTURES (Also see Weird Adventures)
Winter, 1951
Ziff-Davis Publ. Co.

1-Powell-a(2), McCann-a; used in **SOTI**; bondage-c; Krigstein back-c
14.00 43.00 100.00

NOTE: *Title dropped due to similarity to Avon's Eerie & legal action.*

EERIE TALES (Magazine)
1959 (Black & White)
Hastings Associates

1-Williamson, Torres, Tuska-a, Powell(2), & Morrow(2)-a
5.85 17.50 35.00

EERIE TALES
1963-1964
Super Comics

Super Reprint No. 10,11,12,18: 10('63)-r/Spook #27. Purple Claw in #11,12 ('63); #12-r/Avon's Eerie #1('51)-Kida-r 1.40 3.50 7.00
15-Wolverton-a, Spacehawk-r/Blue Bolt Weird Tales #113; Disbrow-a
4.00 10.50 21.00

EGBERT
Spring, 1946 - No. 20, 1950
Arnold Publications/Quality Comics Group

1-Funny animal; intro Egbert & The Count 11.50 34.00 80.00
2 7.50 22.50 45.00
3-10 4.35 13.00 26.00
11-20 3.60 9.00 18.00

EH! (...Dig This Crazy Comic) (From Here to Insanity No. 8 on)
Dec, 1953 - No. 7, Nov-Dec, 1954 (Satire)
Charlton Comics

1-Davisish-c/a by Ayers, Woodish-a by Giordano; Atomic Mouse app.
13.00 40.00 90.00
2-Ayers-c/a 10.00 30.00 65.00
3-7: 4,6-Sexual innuendo-c. 6-Ayers-a 10.00 30.00 60.00

EIGHT IS ENOUGH KITE FUN BOOK (See Kite Fun Book)

80 PAGE GIANT (...Magazine No. 2-15) (25 cents)
8/64 - No. 15, 10/65; No. 16, 11/65 - No. 89, 7/71 (All reprints)
National Periodical Publications (#1-56: 84 pgs.; #57-89: 68 pages)

1-Superman Annual; originally planned as Superman Annual #9 (8/64)
20.00 60.00 140.00
2-Jimmy Olsen 9.15 27.50 55.00
3,4: 3-Lois Lane. 4-Flash-G.A.-r; Infantino-a 5.85 17.50 35.00
5-Batman; has Sunday newspaper strip; Catwoman-r; Batman's Life Story-r (25th anniversary special) 7.50 22.50 45.00
6-Superman 5.85 17.50 35.00
7-Sgt. Rock's Prize Battle Tales; Kubert-c/a 5.85 17.50 35.00
8-More Secret Origins-origins of JLA, Aquaman, Robin, Atom, & Superman; Infantino-a 18.00 54.00 125.00
9-11: 9-Flash (r/Flash #106,117,123 & Showcase #14); Infantino-a. 10-Superboy. 11-Superman; all Luthor issue 5.85 17.50 35.00
12-Batman; has Sunday newspaper strip 6.70 20.00 40.00
13,14: 13-Jimmy Olsen. 14-Lois Lane 5.85 17.50 35.00
15-Superman and Batman; Joker-c/story 7.50 22.50 45.00

Continued as part of regular series under each title in which that particular book came out, a Giant being published instead of the regular size. Issues No. 16 to No. 89 are listed for your information. See individual titles for prices.

16-JLA #39 (11/65), 17-Batman #176, 18-Superman #183, 19-Our Army at War #164, 20-Action #334, 21-Flash #160, 22-Superboy #129, 23-Superman #187, 24-Batman #182, 25-Jimmy Olsen #95, 26-Lois Lane #68, 27-Batman #185, 28-World's Finest #161, 29-JLA #48, 30-Batman #187, 31-Superman #193, 32-Our Army at War #177, 33-Action #347, 34-Flash #169, 35-Superboy #138, 36-Superman #197, 37-Batman #193, 38-Jimmy Olsen #104, 39-Lois Lane #77, 40-World's Finest #170, 41-JLA #58, 42-Superman #202, 43-Batman #198, 44-Our Army at War #190, 45-Action #360, 46-Flash #178, 47-Superboy #147, 48-Superman #207, 49-Batman #203, 50-Jimmy Olsen #113, 51-Lois Lane #86, 52-World's Finest #179, 53-JLA #67, 54-Superman #212, 55-Batman #208, 56-Our Army at War #203, 57-Action #373, 58-Flash #187, 59-Superboy #156, 60-Superman #217, 61-Batman #213, 62-Jimmy Olsen #122, 63-Lois Lane #95, 64-World's Finest #188, 65-JLA #76, 66-Superman #222, 67-Batman #218, 68-Our Army at War #216, 69-Adventure #390, 70-Flash #196, 71-Superboy #165, 72-Superman #227, 73-Batman #223, 74-Jimmy Olsen #131, 75-Lois Lane #104, 76-World's Finest #197, 77-JLA #85, 78-Superman #232, 79-Batman #228, 80-Our Army at War #229, 81-Adventure #403, 82-Flash #205, 83-Superboy #174, 84-Superman #239, 85-Batman #233, 86-Jimmy Olsen #140, 87-Lois Lane #113, 88-World's Finest #206, 89-JLA #93.

87TH PRECINCT (TV)
Apr-June, 1962 - No. 2, July-Sept, 1962
Dell Publishing Co.

4-Color 1309(#1); Krigstein-a 8.35 25.00 50.00
2 6.70 20.00 40.00

EL BOMBO COMICS

Eerie Tales #12, © Super Comics

Eh! #5, © CC

80 Page Giant #14, © DC

Elementals #7, © Comico

Elfquest: Siege at Blue Mountain #4, © Apple Comics

Ellery Queen #2, © SUPR

1946
Standard Comics/Frances M. McQueeny

	GD25	FN65	NM94
nn(1946)	7.50	22.50	45.00
1(no date)	7.50	22.50	45.00

EL CID (See 4-Color No. 1259)

EL DIABLO (DC)(Value: cover or less)

EL DORADO (See Movie Classics)

ELECTRIC UNDERTOW (See Strikeforce Morituri: Electric Undertow)

ELECTRIC WARRIOR (DC)(Value: cover or less)

ELEKTRA: ASSASSIN
Aug, 1986 - No. 8, Mar, 1987 (Limited series, adults)
Epic Comics (Marvel)

	GD25	FN65	NM94
1-Miller scripts in all	1.00	2.50	5.00
2	.80	2.00	4.00
3-7	.60	1.50	3.00
8	1.20	3.00	6.00
Signed & numbered hardcover (Graphitti Designs, $39.95, 2000 print run)-reprints 1-8	6.75	20.00	40.00

ELEKTRA SAGA, THE
Feb, 1984 - No. 4, June, 1984 ($2.00, Baxter paper)
Marvel Comics Group

	GD25	FN65	NM94
1-4-r/Daredevil 168-190; Miller-c/a	.80	2.00	4.00

ELEMENTALS, THE (See The Justice Machine & Morningstar Spec.)
June, 1984 - No. 29, Sept, 1988; V2#1, Mar, 1989 - Present
Comico The Comic Co. ($1.50/$2.50, Baxter paper)

	GD25	FN65	NM94
1-Willingham-c/a, 1-8	1.00	2.50	5.00
2	.60	1.50	3.00
3-10: 9-Bissette-a(p). 10-Photo-c	.40	1.00	2.00
11-29	.30	.75	1.50
V2#1-25: 1-3-$1.95-c. 4-Begin $2.50-c. 16-1st app. Strike Force America. 18-Prelude to Avalon mini-series. 37-Prequel to Strike Force America series	.50	1.25	2.50
Special 1 (3/86)-Willingham-a(p)	.35	.90	1.75
Special 2 (1/89, $1.95)	.40	1.00	2.00

ELFLORD (Aircel)(Value: cover or less)

ELFQUEST (Also see Fantasy Quarterly & Warp Graphics Annual)
No. 2, Aug, 1978 - No. 21, Feb, 1985 (All magazine size)
No. 1, April, 1979
WaRP Graphics, Inc.

NOTE: *Elfquest* was originally published as one of the stories in **Fantasy Quarterly** #1. When the publisher went out of business, the creative team, Wendy and Richard Pini, formed WaRP Graphics and continued the series, beginning with **Elfquest** #2. **Elfquest** #1, which reprinted the story from **Fantasy Quarterly**, was published about the same time **Elfquest** #4 was released. Thereafter, most issues were reprinted as demand warranted, until Marvel announced it would reprint the entire series under its Epic imprint (Aug., 1985).

	GD25	FN65	NM94
1(4/79)-Reprints Elfquest story from Fantasy Quarterly No. 1			
1st printing ($1.00-c)	5.50	16.50	33.00
2nd printing ($1.25-c)	2.00	5.00	10.00
3rd printings ($1.50-c)	1.00	2.50	5.00
4th printing; different-c ($1.50-c)	.30	.75	1.50
2(8/78)-5: 1st printings ($1.00-c)	4.00	10.00	20.00
2nd printings ($1.25-c)	1.00	2.50	5.00
3rd & 4th printings ($1.50-c)(all 4th prints 1989)	.50	1.50	3.00
6-9: 1st printings ($1.25-c)	1.80	4.50	9.00
2nd printings ($1.50-c)	.80	2.00	4.00
3rd printings ($1.50-c)	.40	1.00	2.00
10-21: ($1.50 cover); 16-8pg. preview of A Distant Soil	1.20	3.00	6.00
10-14: 2nd printings ($1.50)	.30	.75	1.50
15-21 (only one printing)	1.20	3.00	6.00

ELFQUEST
Aug, 1985 - No. 32, Mar, 1988
Epic Comics (Marvel)

	GD25	FN65	NM94
1-Reprints in color the Elfquest epic by WaRP Graphics	1.00	2.50	5.00
2-5	.60	1.50	3.00
6-10	.45	1.15	2.25
11-20	.35	.90	1.80
21-32	.30	.75	1.50

ELFQUEST
1989 - No. 4, 1989 ($1.50, B&W)
WaRP Graphics

	GD25	FN65	NM94
1-4: Reprints original Elfquest series	.30	.75	1.50

ELFQUEST: KINGS OF THE BROKEN WHEEL
June, 1990 - No. 9, Feb, 1992 ($2.00, B&W) (3rd Elfquest saga)
WaRP Graphics

	GD25	FN65	NM94
1-9: By Richard & Wendy Pini; 1-Color insert	.40	1.00	2.00
1-2nd printing	.40	1.00	2.00

ELFQUEST: NEW BLOOD (...Summer Special on-c #1 only)
Aug, 1992 - Present ($2.00, color, bi-monthly)
WaRP Graphics

	GD25	FN65	NM94
1-($3.95, 68 pgs.)-Byrne-a/scripts (16 pgs.)	.80	2.00	4.00
2-4: Barry Blair-a in all	.40	1.00	2.00

ELFQUEST: SIEGE AT BLUE MOUNTAIN
Mar, 1987 - No. 8, Dec, 1988 ($1.75/$1.95, B&W, mini-series)
WaRP Graphics/Apple Comics

	GD25	FN65	NM94
1-Staton-a(i) in all; 2nd Elfquest saga	1.20	3.00	6.00
1-2nd printing	.40	1.00	2.00
2	.80	2.00	4.00
2,3-2nd printings	.35	.90	1.75
3-8	.50	1.25	2.50

ELF-THING (Eclipse)(Value: cover or less)

ELIMINATOR FULL COLOR SPECIAL (Eternity)(Value: cover or less)

ELLA CINDERS (See Comics On Parade, Comics Revue #1,4, Famous Comics Cartoon Book, Sparkler Comics, Tip Top & Treasury of Comics)

ELLA CINDERS
1938 - 1940
United Features Syndicate

	GD25	FN65	NM94
Single Series 3(1938)	27.00	80.00	190.00
Single Series 21(#2 on-c, #21 on inside), 28('40)	24.00	72.00	165.00

ELLA CINDERS
March, 1948 - No. 5, March, 1949
United Features Syndicate

	GD25	FN65	NM94
1-(#2 on cover)	10.00	30.00	65.00
2	5.85	17.50	35.00
3-5	4.35	13.00	26.00

ELLERY QUEEN
May, 1949 - No. 4, Nov, 1949
Superior Comics Ltd.

	GD25	FN65	NM94
1-Kamen-c; L.B. Cole-a; r-in Haunted Thrills	25.00	75.00	175.00
2-4: 3-Drug use stories(2)	17.00	50.00	115.00

NOTE: *Iger shop art in all issues.*

ELLERY QUEEN (TV)
1-3/52 - No. 2, Summer/52 (Saunders painted covers)
Ziff-Davis Publishing Co.

	GD25	FN65	NM94
1-Saunders-c	25.00	75.00	175.00
2-Saunders bondage, torture-c	22.00	65.00	150.00

ELLERY QUEEN (See Crackajack Funnies #23 & 4-Color No. 1165, 1243, 1289)

ELMER FUDD (Also see Camp Comics, Daffy & Super Book #10, 22)
No. 470, May, 1953 - No. 1293, Mar-May, 1962
Dell Publishing Co.
4-Color 470,558,628,689('56) 2.40 6.00 12.00
4-Color 725,783,841,888,938,977,1032,1081,1131,1171,1222,1293('62) 2.00 5.00 10.00

ELMO COMICS
January, 1948 (Daily strip-r)
St. John Publishing Co.
1-By Cecil Jensen 8.35 25.00 50.00

ELONGATED MAN (See Flash #112)
Jan, 1992 - No. 4, Apr, 1992 ($1.00, color, mini-series)
DC Comics
1-4: 3-The Flash app. .50 1.00

ELRIC (Pacific/First, all titles) (Value; cover or less)

EL SALVADOR - A HOUSE DIVIDED (Eclipse) (Value: cover or less)

ELSEWHERE PRINCE, THE (Moebius' Airtight Garage)
May, 1990 - No. 6, Oct, 1990 ($1.95, color, limited series)
Epic Comics (Marvel)
1-6: Moebius scripts & back-up-a in all .40 1.00 2.00

ELSIE THE COW
Oct-Nov, 1949 - No. 3, July-Aug, 1950
D. S. Publishing Co.
1-(36 pages) 14.00 43.00 100.00
2,3 11.00 32.00 75.00
Borden Milk Giveaway-(16 pgs., nn) (3 issues, 1957) 5.85 17.50 35.00
Elsie's Fun Book(1950; Borden Milk) 6.70 20.00 40.00
Everyday Birthday Fun With...(1957; 20 pgs.)(100th Anniversary); Kubert-a 5.85 17.50 35.00

ELSON'S PRESENTS
1981 (100 pgs., no cover price)
DC Comics
Series 1-6: Repackaged 1981 DC comics; Superman, Action, Flash, DC Comics Presents & Batman known. Series I has a Batman/Joker-c. Series 3-New Teen Titans #3('81) 1.00 2.50 5.00

ELVIRA'S HOUSE OF MYSTERY (DC) (Value: cover or less)

ELVIRA'S MISTRESS OF THE DARK (Marvel) (Value: cover or less)

ELVIS MANDIBLE, THE
1990 ($3.50, B&W, mature readers, 52 pgs.)
Piranha Press (DC)
nn .70 1.75 3.50

ELVIS PRESLEY (See Career Girl Romances #32, Go-Go, Howard Chaykin's American Flagg #10, Humbug #8, I Love You #60 & Young Lovers #18)

E-MAN
Oct, 1973 - No. 10, Sept, 1975 (Painted-c No. 7-10)
Charlton Comics
1-Origin E-Man; Staton c/a in all 3.00 7.50 15.00
2-4: 2,4-Ditko-a. 3-Howard-a 1.50 3.75 7.50
5-Miss Liberty Belle app. by Ditko 1.20 3.00 6.00
6,7,9,10-Early Byrne-a in all (#6 is 1/75) 1.50 3.75 7.50
8-Full-length story; Nova begins as E-Man's partner 1.80 4.50 9.00
1-4,9,10(Modern Comics reprints, '77) .50 1.00
NOTE: *Killjoy app.-No. 2, 4. Liberty Belle app.-No. 5. Rog 2000 app.-No. 6, 7, 9, 10. Travis app.-No. 3.* ***Tom Sutton*** *a-1.*

E-MAN (First & Comico) (Value: cover or less)

EMERALD DAWN
1991 ($4.95, color, squarebound)
DC Comics
nn-Reprints Green Lantern: Emerald Dawn #1-6 1.00 2.50 5.00

EMERALD DAWN II (See Green Lantern...)

EMERGENCY (Magazine)
June, 1976 - No. 4, Jan, 1977 (B&W)
Charlton Comics
1-Neal Adams-c/a; Heath, Austin-a .60 1.50 3.00
2,4: 2-N. Adams-c. 4-Alcala-a .30 .80 1.60
3-N. Adams-a .40 1.00 2.00

EMERGENCY (TV)
June, 1976 - No. 4, Dec, 1976
Charlton Comics
1-Staton-c; Byrne-a .60 1.50 3.00
2-4: 2-Staton-c .30 .75 1.50

EMERGENCY DOCTOR
Summer, 1963 (One Shot)
Charlton Comics
1 1.00 2.50 5.00

EMIL & THE DETECTIVES (See Movie Comics)

EMMA PEEL & JOHN STEED (See The Avengers)

EMPIRE STRIKES BACK, THE (See Marvel Comics Super Special #16 & Marvel Special Edition)

ENCHANTED APPLES OF OZ, THE (See First Comics Graphic Novel #5)

ENCHANTER (Eclipse) (Value: cover or less)

ENCHANTING LOVE
Oct, 1949 - No. 6, July, 1950 (All, 52 pgs.)
Kirby Publishing Co.
1-Photo-c 6.70 20.00 40.00
2-Photo-c; Powell-a 4.20 12.50 25.00
3,4,6: 3-Jimmy Stewart photo-c 3.60 9.00 18.00
5-Ingels-a, 9 pgs.; photo-c 10.00 30.00 62.00

ENCHANTMENT VISUALETTES (Magazine)
Dec, 1949 - No. 5, April, 1950 (Painted c-1)
World Editions
1-Contains two romance comic strips each 10.00 30.00 60.00
2 8.35 25.00 50.00
3-5 6.70 20.00 40.00

ENEMY ACE SPECIAL (Also see Our Army at War #151, Showcase #57, 58 & Star Spangled War Stories #138)
1990 ($1.00, color, one-shot)
DC Comics
1-Kubert-r/Our Army #151,153; c-r/Showcase 57 .30 .75 1.50

ENSIGN O'TOOLE (TV)
Aug-Oct, 1963 - No. 2, 1964
Dell Publishing Co.
1,2 2.40 6.00 12.00

ENSIGN PULVER (See Movie Classics)

EPIC
1992 - Book 4, 1992 ($4.95, color, mini-series, 52 pgs.)
Epic Comics (Marvel)
Book One-Four: 2-Dorman painted-c 1.00 2.50 5.00
NOTE: *Alien Legion in #3. Cholly & Flytrap by* ***Burden****(scripts) &* ***Suydam****(art) in 3, 4. Dinosaurs in #4. Dreadlands in #1. Hellraiser in #1. Nightbreed in #2. Sleeze Brothers in #2. Stalkers in #1-4. Wild Cards in #1-4.*

EPIC ILLUSTRATED (Magazine)
Spring, 1980 - No. 36, Feb, 1986 ($2.00-$2.50, B&W/Color, adults)
Marvel Comics Group
1-Frazetta-c .40 1.00 2.00

Elsie the Cow nn, © Borden Milk

Elvira's House of Mystery #3, © DC

E-Man #6 (1st series), © CC

Escape From Fear nn, © Planned Parenthood

The Eternals #6 (1976), © MEG

Etta Kett #13, © KING

GD25 FN65 NM94

2-26: 12-Wolverton Spacehawk-r edited & recolored w/article on him. 13-Bladerunner preview by Williamson. 14-Elric of Melnibone by Russell; Revenge of the Jedi preview. 15-Vallejo-c & interview; 1st Dreadstar story (cont'd in Dreadstar #1). 16-B. Smith-c/a(2). 20-The Sacred & the Profane begins by Ken Steacy. 26-Galactus series begins, ends #34; Cerebus the Aardvark story by Dave Sim .30 .75 1.50
27-36: ($2.50): 27-Groo. 28-Cerebus app. .50 1.25 2.50
NOTE: ***N. Adams** a-7; c-6. **Austin** a-15-20i. **Bode** a-19, 23, 27r. **Bolton** a-7, 10-12, 15, 18, 22-25; c-10, 18, 22, 23. **Boris** c/a-15. **Brunner** c-12. **Buscema** a-1p, 9p, 11-13p. **Byrne/Austin** a-26-34. **Chaykin** a-2; c-8. **Conrad** a-2-5, 7-9, 25-34; c-17. **Corben** a-15; c-2. **Frazetta** c-1. **Golden** a-3r. **Gulacy** c/a-3. **Jeff Jones** c-25. **Kaluta** a-17r, 21, 24r, 26; c-4, 28. **Nebres** a-1. **Reese** a-12. **Russell** a-2-4, 9, 14, 33; c-14. **Simonson** a-17. **B. Smith** c/a-7, 16. **Starlin** a-1-9, 14, 15, 34. **Steranko** c-19. **Williamson** a-13, 27, 34. **Wrightson** a-13p, 22, 25, 27, 34; c-30.*

EPIC LITE
Sept, 1991 ($3.95, color, one-shot, 52 pgs.)
Epic Comics (Marvel)
1-Bob the Alien, Normalman by Valentino .80 2.00 4.00

EPICURUS THE SAGE
1991 - Vol. 2, 1991 ($9.95, color, 8-1/8x10-7/8")
Piranha Press (DC Comics)
Volume 1,2-Sam Kieth-c/a 2.00 5.00 10.00

EPSILON WAVE (Independent/Elite) (Value: cover or less)

ERNIE COMICS (Formerly Andy Comics #21; All Love Romances #26 on)
No. 22, Sept, 1948 - No. 25, Mar, 1949
Current Books/Ace Periodicals
nn(9/48,11/48; #22,23) 4.35 13.00 26.00
24,25 3.20 8.00 16.00

ESCAPADE IN FLORENCE (See Movie Comics)

ESCAPE FROM DEVIL'S ISLAND
1952
Avon Periodicals
1-Kinstler-c; r/as Dynamic Adventures #9 20.00 60.00 140.00

ESCAPE FROM FEAR
1956, 1962, 1969 (8 pages full color) (On birth control)
Planned Parenthood of America (Giveaway)
1956 edition 10.00 30.00 60.00
1962 edition 6.70 20.00 40.00
1969 edition 4.00 10.00 20.00

ESCAPE FROM THE PLANET OF THE APES (See Power Record Comics)

ESCAPE TO WITCH MOUNTAIN (See Walt Disney Showcase No. 29)

ESPERS (Eclipse) (Value: cover or less)

ESPIONAGE (TV)
May-July, 1964 - No. 2, Aug-Oct, 1964
Dell Publishing Co.
1,2 2.80 7.00 14.00

ETC
1989 - No. 5, 1990 ($4.50, color, mini-series, adults, 60 pgs.)
Piranha Press (DC Comics)
Book 1-5: Conrad scripts/layouts in all .90 2.25 4.50

ETERNAL BIBLE, THE
1946 (Large size) (16 pages in color)
Authentic Publications
1 9.15 27.50 55.00

ETERNALS, THE
July, 1976 - No. 19, Jan, 1978
Marvel Comics Group
1-Origin .80 2.00 4.00
2-19: 2-1st app. Ajak & The Celestials. 14,15-Cosmic powered Hulk-c/story .50 1.25 2.50
Annual 1(10/77) .50 1.25 2.50
*NOTE: **Kirby** c/a(p) in all. Price changed from 25 cents to 30 cents during run of #1.*

ETERNALS, THE
Oct, 1985 - No. 12, Sept, 1986 (Maxi-series, mando paper)
Marvel Comics Group
1,12 ($1.25, 52 pgs.): 12-Williamson-a(i) .60 1.25
2-11-(75 cents) .50 1.00

ETERNALS: THE HEROD FACTOR
Nov, 1991 ($2.50, color, 68 pgs.)
Marvel Comics
1 .50 1.25 2.50

ETERNAL WARRIOR (See Solar #10 & 11)
Aug, 1992 - Present ($2.25, color)
Valiant
1-Miller-c; B. Smith/Layton-a(Unity x-over) 2.40 6.00 12.00
1-Gold logo 14.00 43.00 100.00
1-Gold foil logo 20.00 60.00 140.00
2-Unity x-over; Simonson-c 1.60 4.00 8.00
3-Archer & Armstrong x-over 1.20 3.00 6.00
4-2nd app. Bloodshot (last pg. cameo); see Rai #0 for 1st app.; Cowan-c 1.40 3.50 7.00
5-2nd full app. Bloodshot (12/92; see Rai #0); 1st app. Rising Spirit (new Rai) 2.40 6.00 12.00
6,7 .60 1.50 3.00
8-See Archer & Armstrong #8 for value; combined with Eternal Warrior #8
9-12 .45 1.10 2.25

ETERNITY SMITH (Renegade & Hero) (Value: cover or less)

ETTA KETT
No. 11, Dec, 1948 - No. 14, Sept, 1949
King Features Syndicate/Standard
11 6.70 20.00 40.00
12-14 4.35 13.00 26.00

EVANGELINE (Comico/First) (Value: cover or less)

EVA THE IMP
1957 - No. 2, Nov, 1957
Red Top Comic/Decker
1,2 2.40 6.00 12.00

EVEL KNIEVEL
1974 (20 pages) (Giveaway)
Marvel Comics Group (Ideal Toy Corp.)
nn-Contains photo on inside back-c .50 1.00

EVERYBODY'S COMICS (See Fox Giants)

EVERYMAN, THE
Nov, 1991 ($4.50, color, one-shot, 52 pgs.)
Epic Comics (Marvel)
1 .90 2.25 4.50

EVERYTHING HAPPENS TO HARVEY
Sept-Oct, 1953 - No. 7, Sept-Oct, 1954
National Periodical Publications
1 16.00 48.00 110.00
2 10.00 30.00 65.00
3-7 8.35 25.00 50.00

EVERYTHING'S ARCHIE
May, 1969 - No. 158?, 1991 (Giant issues No. 1-20)
Archie Publications
1 6.70 20.00 40.00

	GD25	FN65	NM94
2	4.00	10.00	20.00
3-5	2.00	5.00	10.00
6-10	1.20	3.00	6.00
11-20	.60	1.50	3.00
21-50	.30	.75	1.50
51-158: 142,148-Gene Colan-a		.50	1.00

EVERYTHING'S DUCKY (See 4-Color No. 1251)

EWOKS (TV) (See Star Comics Magazine)
June, 1985 - No. 15, Sept, 1987 (75 cents; $1.00 #14 on)
Star Comics (Marvel)

	GD25	FN65	NM94
1-15 (From Star Wars): 10-Williamson-a		.50	1.00

EXCALIBUR (Also see Marvel Comics Presents #31)
1987; Oct, 1988 - Present ($1.50, Baxter)($1.75 #24 on)
Marvel Comics

	GD25	FN65	NM94
Special Edition nn (The Sword is Drawn)(1987, $3.25)-This is the 1st Excalibur comic	2.40	6.00	12.00
Special Edition nn (2nd print, 10/88, $3.50)	.90	2.25	4.50
Special Edition nn (3rd print, 12/89, 4.50)	.90	2.25	4.50
...The Sword is Drawn (Apr, '92, 4.95-c)	1.00	2.50	5.00
1($1.50, 10/88)-X-Men spin-off; Nightcrawler, Shadowcat(Kitty Pryde), Capt. Britain, Phoenix & Meggan begin	2.00	5.00	10.00
2	1.00	2.50	5.00
3,4	.70	1.75	3.50
5-10	.60	1.50	3.00
11-15: 10,11-Rogers/Austin-a	.40	1.00	2.00
16-23: 19-Austin-i. 21-Intro Crusader X. 22-Iron Man x-over	.30	.75	1.50
24-40,42-49,51-66: 32-($1.50). 24-John Byrne app. in story; begin $1.75-c. 27-B. Smith-a(p). 37-Dr. Doom & Iron Man app. 49-Neal Adams c-swipe. 52,57-X-Men (Cyclops, Wolverine) app. 53-Spider-Man-c/story. 58-X-Men (Wolverine, Gambit, Cyclops, etc.)-c/story	.35	.90	1.75
41-X-Men (Wolverine) app.; Cable cameo	.40	1.00	2.00
50-($2.75, 56 pgs.)-New logo	.55	1.40	2.75
...Air Apparent nn (12/91, $4.95)-Simonson-c	1.00	2.50	5.00
...Mojo Mayhem nn ($4.50, 12/89)-Art Adams/Austin-c/a	1.00	2.50	5.00
Special...The Possession nn (7/91, $2.95, 52 pgs.)	.60	1.50	3.00
Special...XX Crossing (May, '92, 2.50-c)	.50	1.25	2.50

EXCITING COMICS
April, 1940 - No. 69, Sept, 1949
Nedor/Better Publications/Standard Comics

	GD25	FN65	NM94
1-Origin The Mask, Jim Hatfield, Sgt. Bill King, Dan Williams begin	92.00	275.00	550.00
2-The Sphinx begins; The Masked Rider app.; Son of the Gods begins, ends #8	42.00	125.00	250.00
3-5	33.00	100.00	200.00
6-8	22.00	68.00	135.00
9-Origin/1st app. of The Black Terror & sidekick Tim, begin series	117.00	350.00	700.00
10-13	39.00	116.00	235.00
14-Last Sphinx, Dan Williams	27.00	82.00	165.00
15-The Liberator begins (origin)	32.00	85.00	190.00
16-20: 20-The Mask ends	18.00	55.00	110.00
21,23-30: 28-Crime Crusader begins, ends #58	17.00	50.00	100.00
22-Origin The Eaglet; The American Eagle begins	18.00	55.00	110.00
31-38: 35-Liberator ends, not in 31-33	15.00	45.00	90.00
39-Origin Kara, Jungle Princess	22.00	66.00	135.00
40-50: 42-The Scarab begins. 49-Last Kara, Jungle Princess. 50-Last American Eagle	20.00	60.00	120.00
51-Miss Masque begins	25.00	75.00	150.00
52-54: Miss Masque ends	20.00	60.00	120.00
55-Judy of the Jungle begins(origin), ends #69; 1 pg. Ingels-a	25.00	75.00	150.00
56-58: All airbrush-c	23.00	70.00	140.00
59-Frazetta art in Caniff style; signed Frank Frazeta (one t), 9 pgs.	28.00	85.00	170.00
60-66: 60-Rick Howard, the Mystery Rider begins. 66-Robinson/Meskin-a	18.00	55.00	110.00
67-69	12.00	35.00	70.00

*NOTE: **Schomburg** (Xela) c-28-68; airbrush c-57-66. Black Terror by **R. Moreira**-#65. **Roussos** a-62. Bondage-c 9, 12, 13, 20, 23, 25, 30, 59.*

EXCITING ROMANCES
1949 (nd); No. 2, Spring, 1950 - No. 5, 10/50; No. 6 (1951, nd); No. 7, 9/51 - No. 14, 1/53
Fawcett Publications

	GD25	FN65	NM94
1(1949)	7.50	22.50	45.00
2-5-(1950)	4.70	14.00	28.00
6-14	4.00	10.00	20.00

*NOTE: **Powell** a-8-10. **Marcus Swayze** a-5, 6, 9. Photo c-1-7, 11, 12.*

EXCITING ROMANCE STORIES (See Fox Giants)

EXCITING WAR (Korean war)
No. 5, Sept, 1952 - No. 8, May, 1953; No. 9, Nov, 1953
Standard Comics (Better Publ.)

	GD25	FN65	NM94
5	4.20	12.50	25.00
6,7,9	2.80	7.00	14.00
8-Toth-a	4.70	14.00	28.00

EX-MUTANTS (Malibu) (Value: cover or less)

EXORCISTS (See The Crusaders)

EXOTIC ROMANCES (Formerly True War Romances)
No. 22, Oct, 1955 - No. 31, Nov, 1956
Quality Comics Group (Comic Magazines)

	GD25	FN65	NM94
22	5.00	15.00	30.00
23-26,29	3.20	8.00	16.00
27,31-Baker-c/a	5.00	15.00	30.00
28,30-Baker-a	4.70	14.00	28.00

EXPLOITS OF DANIEL BOONE
Nov, 1955 - No. 6, Sept, 1956
Quality Comics Group

	GD25	FN65	NM94
1-All have Cuidera-c(i)	12.00	36.00	85.00
2	7.50	22.50	45.00
3-6	5.85	17.50	35.00

EXPLOITS OF DICK TRACY (See Dick Tracy)

EXPLORER JOE
Winter, 1951 - No. 2, Oct-Nov, 1952
Ziff-Davis Comic Group (Approved Comics)

	GD25	FN65	NM94
1-Saunders painted-c	7.50	22.50	45.00
2-Krigstein-a	8.35	25.00	50.00

EXPLORERS OF THE UNKNOWN (See Archie Giant Series #587, 599)
June, 1990 - No. 6, Apr, 1991 ($1.00, color)
Archie Comics

	GD25	FN65	NM94
1-6: Featuring Archie and the gang		.50	1.00

EXPOSED (...True Crime Cases)
Mar-Apr, 1948 - No. 9, July-Aug, 1949
D. S. Publishing Co.

	GD25	FN65	NM94
1	10.00	30.00	65.00
2-Giggling killer story with excessive blood; two eye injury panels	10.00	30.00	70.00
3,8,9	5.35	16.00	32.00
4-Orlando-a	5.85	17.50	35.00
5-Breeze Lawson, Sky Sheriff by E. Good	5.85	17.50	35.00
6-Ingels-a; used in **SOTI**, illo.-"How to prepare an alibi"	18.00	54.00	125.00
7-Illo. in **SOTI**, "Diagram for housebreakers"; used by N.Y. Legis.			

Excalibur Special Edition #1 (3rd printing), © MEG

Exciting Comics #1, © STD

Exploits of Daniel Boone #1, © QUA

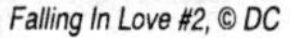
Falling In Love #2, © DC

Family Funnies #1, © HARV

Famous Comics #3, © KFS

	GD25	FN65	NM94
Committee	18.00	54.00	125.00

EXTRA!
Mar-Apr, 1955 - No. 5, Nov-Dec, 1955
E. C. Comics

	GD25	FN65	NM94
1-Not code approved	10.00	30.00	70.00
2-5	8.35	25.00	50.00

*NOTE: **Craig, Crandall, Severin** art in all.*

EXTRA COMICS
1948
Magazine Enterprises

	GD25	FN65	NM94
1-Giant; consisting of rebound ME comics. Two versions known; (1)-Funnyman by Siegel & Shuster, Space Ace, Undercover Girl, Red Fox by L.B. Cole, Trail Colt & (2)-All Funnyman	32.00	95.00	225.00

EYEBALL KID, THE (Dark Horse) (Value; cover or less)

FACE, THE (Tony Trent, the Face No. 3 on)
1941 - No. 2, 1941? (See Big Shot Comics)
Columbia Comics Group

	GD25	FN65	NM94
1-The Face; Mart Bailey-c	50.00	150.00	300.00
2-Bailey-c	33.00	95.00	200.00

FACULTY FUNNIES
June, 1989 - No. 5, May, 1990 (75 cents, color; 95 cents #2 on)
Archie Comics

	GD25	FN65	NM94
1-5: 1,2-The Awesome Four app.		.50	1.00

FAFHRD AND THE GREY MOUSER (Also see Sword of Sorcery & Wonder Woman #202)
Oct, 1990 - No. 4, 1991 ($4.50, color, 52 pgs.)
Marvel Comics

	GD25	FN65	NM94
1-4: Mignola/Williamson-a; Chaykin scripts	.90	2.25	4.50

FAIRY TALE PARADE (See Famous Fairy Tales)
June-July, 1942 - No. 121, Oct, 1946 (Most all by Walt Kelly)
Dell Publishing Co.

	GD25	FN65	NM94
1-Kelly-a begins	86.00	257.00	600.00
2(8-9/42)	48.00	145.00	335.00
3-5 (10-11/42 - 2-4/43)	31.00	92.00	215.00
6-9 (5-7/43 - 11-1/43-44)	24.00	72.00	170.00
4-Color 50('44)	23.00	70.00	160.00
4-Color 69('45)	20.00	60.00	140.00
4-Color 87('45)	17.00	51.00	120.00
4-Color 104,114('46)-Last Kelly issue	15.00	45.00	105.00
4-Color 121('46)-Not by Kelly	10.00	30.00	65.00

*NOTE: #1-9, 4-Color #50, 69 have **Kelly** c/a; 4-Color #87, 104, 114-**Kelly** art only. #9 has a redrawn version of The Reluctant Dragon. This series contains all the classic fairy tales from Jack In The Beanstalk to Cinderella.*

FAIRY TALES
No. 10, 1951 - No. 11, June-July, 1951
Ziff-Davis Publ. Co. (Approved Comics)

	GD25	FN65	NM94
10,11-Painted-c	10.00	30.00	70.00

FAITHFUL
November, 1949 - No. 2, Feb, 1950 (52 pgs.)
Marvel Comics/Lovers' Magazine

	GD25	FN65	NM94
1,2-Photo-c	5.00	15.00	30.00

FALCON (Also see Avengers #181 & Captain America #117 & 133)
Nov, 1983 - No. 4, Feb, 1984 (Mini-series) (See Marvel Premiere #49)
Marvel Comics Group

	GD25	FN65	NM94
1-4: 1-Paul Smith-c/a(p). 2-P. Smith-c		.50	1.00

FALLEN ANGELS
April, 1987 - No. 8, Nov, 1987 (Mini-series)
Marvel Comics Group

	GD25	FN65	NM94
1	.40	1.00	2.00
2-8	.25	.70	1.40

FALLING IN LOVE
Sept-Oct, 1955 - No. 143, Oct-Nov, 1973
Arleigh Publ. Co./National Periodical Publications

	GD25	FN65	NM94
1	19.00	58.00	135.00
2	10.00	30.00	65.00
3-10	6.35	19.0	38.00
11-20	4.35	13.00	26.00
21-40	3.60	9.00	18.00
41-46: 46-Last 10 cent issue	2.80	7.00	14.00
47-100,108: 108-Wood-a (4 pgs., 7/69)	1.40	3.50	7.00
101-107,109-143	1.00	2.50	5.00

*NOTE: **Colan** c/a-75, 81. 52 pgs.-#125-133.*

FALL OF THE HOUSE OF USHER, THE (See A Corben Special & Spirit section 8/22/48)

FALL OF THE ROMAN EMPIRE (See Movie Comics)

FAMILY AFFAIR (TV)
Feb, 1970 - No. 4, Oct, 1970 (25 cents)
Gold Key

	GD25	FN65	NM94
1-With pull-out poster; photo-c	4.20	12.50	25.00
2-4: 3,4-Photo-c	3.20	8.00	16.00

FAMILY FUNNIES
No. 9, Aug-Sept, 1946
Parents' Magazine Institute

	GD25	FN65	NM94
9	3.60	9.00	18.00

FAMILY FUNNIES (Tiny Tot Funnies No. 9 on)
Sept, 1950 - No. 8, April?, 1951
Harvey Publications

	GD25	FN65	NM94
1-Mandrake (has over 30 King Feature strips)	5.00	15.00	30.00
2-Flash Gordon, 1 pg.	4.00	10.00	20.00
3-8: 4,5,7-Flash Gordon, 1 pg.	3.60	9.00	18.00
1(black & white)	2.00	5.00	10.00

FAMOUS AUTHORS ILLUSTRATED (See Stories by...)

FAMOUS COMICS (Also see Favorite Comics)
No date; Mid 1930's (24 pages) (paper cover)
Zain-Eppy/United Features Syndicate

	GD25	FN65	NM94
nn-Reprinted from 1933 & 1934 newspaper strips in color; Joe Palooka, Hairbreadth Harry, Napoleon, The Nebbs, etc. (Nine different versions known)	25.00	75.00	175.00

FAMOUS COMICS
1934 (100 pgs., daily newspaper reprints)
(3-1/2x8-1/2"; paper cover) (came in a box)
King Features Syndicate (Whitman Publ. Co.)

	GD25	FN65	NM94
684(#1)-Little Jimmy, Katzenjammer Kids, & Barney Google	22.00	68.00	135.00
684(#2)-Polly, Little Jimmy, Katzenjammer Kids	22.00	68.00	135.00
684(#3)-Little Annie Rooney, Polly, Katzenjammer Kids	22.00	68.00	135.00
....Box price....	15.00	45.00	90.00

FAMOUS COMICS CARTOON BOOKS
1934 (72 pgs.; 8x7-1/4"; daily strip reprints)
Whitman Publishing Co. (B&W; hardbacks)

	GD25	FN65	NM94
1200-The Captain & the Kids (1st app?); Dirks reprints credited to Bernard Dibble	20.00	60.00	120.00
1202-Captain Easy (1st app?) & Wash Tubbs by Roy Crane	25.00	75.00	150.00
1203-Ella Cinders (1st app?)	20.00	60.00	120.00
1204-Freckles & His Friends (1st app?)	17.00	50.00	100.00

NOTE: Called Famous Funnies Cartoon Books inside.

FAMOUS CRIMES
June, 1948 - No. 19, Sept, 1950; No. 20, Aug, 1951; No. 51, 52, 1953
Fox Features Syndicate/M.S. Dist. No. 51,52

	GD25	FN65	NM94
1-Blue Beetle app. & crime story-r/Phantom Lady #16	19.00	57.00	130.00
2-Shows woman dissolved in acid; lingerie-c/panels	16.00	48.00	110.00
3-Injury-to-eye story used in **SOTI**, pg. 112; has two electrocution stories	19.00	57.00	130.00
4-6	9.15	27.50	55.00
7-"Tarzan, the Wyoming Killer" used in **SOTI**, pg. 44; drug trial/ possession story	16.00	48.00	110.00
8-20: 17-Morisi-a	6.70	20.00	40.00
51(nd, 1953)	6.70	20.00	40.00
52	4.00	12.00	24.00

FAMOUS FAIRY TALES
1943 (32 pgs.); 1944 (16 pgs.) (Soft covers)
K. K. Publ. Co. (Giveaway)

	GD25	FN65	NM94
1943-Reprints from Fairy Tale Parade No. 2,3; Kelly inside art	40.00	120.00	260.00
1944-Kelly inside art	28.00	85.00	180.00

FAMOUS FEATURE STORIES
1938 (68 pgs., 7-1/2x11")
Dell Publishing Co.

	GD25	FN65	NM94
1-Tarzan, Terry & the Pirates, King of the Royal Mtd., Buck Jones, Dick Tracy, Smilin' Jack, Dan Dunn, Don Winslow, G-Man, Tailspin Tommy, Mutt & Jeff, & Little Orphan Annie reprints - all illustrated text	62.00	188.00	375.00

FAMOUS FIRST EDITION (See Limited Collectors' Edition)
($1.00; 10x13-1/2"-Giant Size)(72pgs.; No.6-8, 68 pgs.)
1974 - No. 8, Aug-Sept, 1975; C-61, 1979
National Periodical Publications/DC Comics

	GD25	FN65	NM94
C-26-Action Comics #1; gold ink outer cover	1.40	3.50	7.00
C-28-Detective #27; silver ink outer cover	4.20	12.50	25.00
C-28-Hardbound edition	8.35	25.00	50.00
C-30-Sensation #1(1974); bronze ink outer cover	1.40	3.50	7.00
F-4-Whiz Comics #2(#1)(10-11/74)-Cover not identical to original (dropped "Gangway for Captain Marvel" from cover); gold ink on outer cover	1.40	3.50	7.00
F-5-Batman #1(F-6 inside); silver ink on outer-c	3.60	9.00	18.00
V2#F-6-Wonder Woman #1	1.00	2.50	5.00
F-7-All-Star Comics #3	1.20	3.00	6.00
F-8-Flash Comics #1(8-9/75)	1.20	3.00	6.00
V8#C-61-Superman #1(1979, $2.00)	1.60	4.00	8.00
Hardbound editions (w/dust jackets $5.00 extra) (Lyle Stuart, Inc.) C-26,C-30,F-4,F-6 known	2.40	6.00	12.00

Warning: The above books are almost **exact** reprints of the originals that they represent except for the Giant-Size format. None of the originals are Giant-Size. The first five issues and C-61 were printed with two covers. Reprint information can be found on the outside cover, but not on the inside cover which was reprinted exactly like the original (inside and out).

FAMOUS FUNNIES
1933 - No. 218, July, 1955
Eastern Color

	GD25	FN65	VF82	NM94
A Carnival of Comics (probably the second comic book), 36 pgs., no date given, no publisher, no number; contains strip reprints of The Bungle Family, Dixie Dugan, Hairbreadth Harry, Joe Palooka, Keeping Up With the Jones, Mutt & Jeff, Reg'lar Fellers, S'Matter Pop, Strange As It Seems, and others. This book was sold by M. C. Gaines to Wheatena, Milk-O-Malt, John Wanamaker, Kinney Shoe Stores, & others to be given away as premiums and radio giveaways (1933).	530.00	1590.00	3180.00	5300.00

(Estimated up to 50 total copies exist, 2 in NM/Mint)

	GD25	FN65	VF82	NM94
Series 1-(Very rare)(nd-early 1934)(68 pgs.) No publisher given (Eastern Color PrintingCo.); sold in chain stores for 10 cents. 35,000 print run. Contains Sunday strip reprints of Mutt & Jeff, Reg'lar Fellers, Nipper, Hairbreadth Harry, Strange As It Seems, Joe Palooka, Dixie Dugan, The Nebbs, Keeping Up With the Jones, and others. Inside front and back covers and pages 1-16 of Famous Funnies Series 1, #s 49-64 reprinted from **Famous Funnies, A Carnival of Comics**, and most of pages 17-48 reprinted from **Funnies on Parade**. This was the first comic book sold.	1700.00	4300.00	8500.00	12000.00

(Estimated up to 12 copies exist, 1 in NM/Mint)

	GD25	FN65	VF82	NM94
No. 1 (Rare)(7/34-on stands 5/34) - Eastern Color Printing Co. First monthly newsstand comic book. Contains Sunday strip reprints of Toonerville Folks, Mutt & Jeff, Hairbreadth Harry, S'Matter Pop, Nipper, Dixie Dugan, The Bungle Family, Connie, Ben Webster, Tailspin Tommy, The Nebbs, Joe Palooka, & others.	1285.00	3800.00	6400.00	9000.00

(Estimated up to 30 total copies exist, 2 in NM/Mint)

	GD25	FN65	VF82
2 (Rare)	283.00	850.00	1700.00
3-Buck Rogers Sunday strip reprints by Rick Yager begins, ends #218; not in #191-208; the number of the 1st strip reprinted is pg. 190, Series No. 1	333.00	1000.00	2000.00
4	108.00	325.00	650.00
5-1st Christmas-c on a newsstand comic	92.00	275.00	550.00
6-10	71.00	212.00	425.00

	GD25	FN65	NM94
11,12,18-Four pgs. of Buck Rogers in each issue, completes stories in Buck Rogers #1 which lacks these pages; #18-Two pgs. of Buck Rogers reprinted in Daisy Comics #1	62.00	188.00	375.00
13-17,19,20: 14-Has two Buck Rogers panels missing. 17-2nd Christmas-c on a newsstand comic	46.00	138.00	275.00
21,23-30: 27-(10/36)-War on Crime begins (4 pgs.); 1st true crime in comics (reprints); part photo-c. 29-X-Mas-c	33.00	100.00	200.00
22-Four pgs. of Buck Rogers needed to complete stories in Buck Rogers #1	37.00	112.00	225.00
31-34,36,37,39,40: 33-Careers of Baby Face Nelson & John Dillinger traced	25.00	75.00	150.00
35-Two pgs. Buck Rogers omitted in Buck Rogers #2	27.00	80.00	160.00
38-Full color portrait of Buck Rogers	25.00	75.00	150.00
41-60: 41,53-X-Mas-c. 55-Last bottom panel, pg. 4 in Buck Rogers redrawn in Buck Rogers #3	17.00	50.00	100.00
61,63,64,66,67,69,70	13.00	40.00	80.00
62,65,68-Two pgs. Kirby-a-"Lightnin' & the Lone Rider"	14.00	42.00	85.00
71,73,77-80: 80-Buck Rogers story continues from Buck Rogers #5	12.00	35.00	70.00
72-Speed Spaulding begins by Marvin Bradley (artist), ends #88. This series was written by Edwin Balmer & Philip Wylie (later appeared as film & book "When Worlds Collide")	12.50	37.50	75.00
74-76-Two pgs. Kirby-a in all	10.00	30.00	65.00
81-Origin & 1st app. Invisible Scarlet O'Neil (4/42); strip begins #82, ends #167	9.15	27.50	55.00
82-Buck Rogers-c	10.00	30.00	65.00
83-87,90: 87 has last Buck Rogers full page-r. 90-Bondage-c	9.15	27.50	55.00
88-Buck Rogers in "Moon's End" by Calkins, 2 pgs.(not reprints). Beginning with #88, all Buck Rogers pages have rearranged panels	10.00	30.00	60.00
89-Origin Fearless Flint, the Flint Man	10.00	30.00	60.00
91-93,95,96,98-99,101-110: 105-Series 2 begins (Strip Page #1)	7.00	21.00	42.00
94-Buck Rogers in "Solar Holocaust" by Calkins, 3 pgs.(not reprints)	8.35	25.00	50.00
97-War Bond promotion, Buck Rogers by Calkins, 2 pgs.(not reprints)	8.35	25.00	50.00
100	8.35	25.00	50.00
111-130	5.35	16.00	32.00
131-150: 137-Strip page No. 110 omitted	4.00	12.00	24.00
151-162,164-168	4.00	10.00	20.00
163-St. Valentine's Day-c	4.00	12.00	24.00

169,170-Two text illos. by Williamson, his 1st comic book work

Famous Crimes #15, © FOX

Famous Funnies #20, © EAS

Famous Funnies #212, © EAS

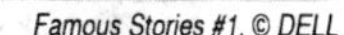

Famous Stories #1, © DELL

Fantastic #8, © YM

Fantastic Comics #17, © FOX

GD25 FN65 NM94

7.50 22.50 45.00
171-180: 171-Strip pgs. 227,229,230, Series 2 omitted. 172-Strip Pg. 232 omitted 4.00 10.00 20.00
181-190: Buck Rogers ends with start of strip pg. 302, Series 2 3.20 8.00 16.00
191-197,199,201,203,206-208: No Buck Rogers 2.80 7.00 14.00
198,202,205-One pg. Frazetta ads; no B. Rogers 3.60 9.00 18.00
200-Frazetta 1 pg. ad 3.60 9.00 18.00
204-Used in **POP**, pgs. 79,99 3.60 9.00 18.00
209-Buck Rogers begins with strip pg. 480, Series 2; Frazetta-c 37.00 110.00 220.00
210-216: Frazetta-c. 211-Buck Rogers ads by Anderson begins, ends #217. #215-Contains B. Rogers strip pg. 515-518, series 2 followed by pgs. 179-181, Series 3 37.00 110.00 220.00
217,218-B. Rogers ends with pg. 199, Series 3 4.00 10.00 20.00
*NOTE: **Rick Yager** did the Buck Rogers Sunday strips reprinted in Famous Funnies. The Sundays were formerly done by Russ Keaton and Lt. Dick Calkins did the dailies, but would sometimes assist Yager on a panel or two from time to time. Strip No. 169 is Yager's first full Buck Rogers page. Yager did the strip until 1958 when **Murphy Anderson** took over. **Tuska** art from 4/26/59 - 1965. Virtually every panel was rewritten for Famous Funnies. Not iden#tical to the original Sunday page. The Buck Rogers reprints run continuously through Famous Funnies issue No. 190 (Strip No. 302) with no break in story line. The story line has no continuity after No. 190. The Buck Rogers newspaper strips came out in four series: Series 1, 3/30/30 - 9/21/41 (No. 1 - 600); Series 2, 9/28/41 -10/21/51 (No. 1 -525)(Strip No. 110 (pg.) published in only a few newspapers); Series 3, 10/28/51 -2/9/58 (No. 100-428)(No No.1-99); Series 4, 2/16/58 - 6/13/65 (No numbers, dates only). **Everett** c-85, 86. **Moulton** a-100.*

FAMOUS FUNNIES
1964
Super Comics

Super Reprint Nos. 15-18 1.20 3.00 6.00

FAMOUS GANG BOOK OF COMICS (Becomes Donald & Mickey Merry Christmas 1943 on)
Dec, 1942 (32 pgs.; paper cover) (Christmas giveaway)
Firestone Tire & Rubber Co.

nn-(Rare)-Porky Pig, Bugs Bunny, Sniffles; r/Looney Tunes 67.00 200.00 500.00

FAMOUS GANGSTERS (Crime on the Waterfront No. 4)
April, 1951 - No. 3, Feb, 1952
Avon Periodicals/Realistic

1-Capone, Dillinger; c-/Avon paperback #329 17.00 51.00 120.00
2-Wood-c/a (1 pg.); r/Saint #7 & retitled "Mike Strong" 18.00 54.00 125.00
3-Lucky Luciano & Murder, Inc; c-/Avon paperback #66 18.00 54.00 125.00

FAMOUS INDIAN TRIBES
July-Sept, 1962; No. 2, July, 1972
Dell Publishing Co.

12-264-209(#1) (The Sioux) 1.80 4.50 9.00
2(7/72)-Reprints above .40 1.00 2.00

FAMOUS STARS
Nov-Dec, 1950 - No. 6, Spring, 1952 (All have photo covers)
Ziff-Davis Publ. Co.

1-Shelley Winters, Susan Peters, Ava Gardner, Shirley Temple; Whitney-a 17.00 51.00 120.00
2-Betty Hutton, Bing Crosby, Colleen Townsend, Gloria Swanson; Everett-a(2) 11.50 34.00 80.00
3-Farley Granger, Judy Garland's ordeal, Alan Ladd; Whitney-a 11.00 32.00 75.00
4-Al Jolson, Bob Mitchum, Ella Raines, Richard Conte, Vic Damone; Crandall-a, 6pgs. 10.00 30.00 70.00
5-Liz Taylor, Betty Grable, Esther Williams, George Brent; Krigstein-a 13.00 40.00 90.00
6-Gene Kelly, Hedy Lamarr, June Allyson, William Boyd, Janet Leigh, Gary Cooper 10.00 30.00 65.00

FAMOUS STORIES (...Book No. 2)
1942 - No. 2, 1942
Dell Publishing Co.

1,2: 1-Treasure Island. 2-Tom Sawyer 19.00 57.00 135.00

FAMOUS TV FUNDAY FUNNIES
Sept, 1961
Harvey Publications

1-Casper the Ghost 4.20 12.50 25.00

FAMOUS WESTERN BADMEN (Formerly Redskin)
No. 13, Dec, 1952 - No. 15, 1953
Youthful Magazines

13 6.70 20.00 40.00
14,15 4.70 14.00 28.00

FANTASTIC (Formerly Captain Science; Beware No. 10 on)
No. 8, Feb, 1952 - No. 9, April, 1952
Youthful Magazines

8-Capt. Science by Harrison; decapitation, shrunken head panels 17.00 51.00 115.00
9-Harrison-a 10.00 30.00 70.00

FANTASTIC ADVENTURES
1963 - 1964 (Reprints)
Super Comics

9,10,12,15,16,18: 9-r/? 10-r/He-Man #2(Toby). 12-Unpublished Chesler material? 15-r/Spook #23. 16-r/Dark Shadows #2(Steinway); Briefer-a. 18-r/Superior Stories #1 1.30 4.00 9.00
11-Wood-a; r/Blue Bolt #118 3.20 8.00 16.00
17-Baker-a(2) r/Seven Seas #6; 2.80 7.00 14.00

FANTASTIC COMICS
Dec, 1939 - No. 23, Nov, 1941
Fox Features Syndicate

1-Intro/origin Samson; Stardust, The Super Wizard, Sub Saunders (by Kiefer), Space Smith, Capt. Kidd begin 200.00 600.00 1200.00
2-Powell text illos 92.00 275.00 550.00
3-5: 3-Powell text illos 71.00 212.00 425.00
6-9: 6,7-Simon-c 58.00 175.00 350.00
10-Intro/origin David, Samson's aide 46.00 138.00 275.00
11-17,19,20,22: 16-Stardust ends 37.00 112.00 225.00
18-1st app. Black Fury & sidekick Chuck; ends #23 42.00 125.00 250.00
21,23: 21-The Banshee begins(origin); ends #23; Hitler-c. 23-Origin The Gladiator 42.00 125.00 250.00
*NOTE: **Lou Fine** c-1-5. **Tuska** a-3-5, 8. Bondage c-6, 8, 9.*

FANTASTIC COMICS (Fantastic Fears #1-9; Becomes Samson #12)
No. 10, Nov-Dec, 1954 - No. 11, Jan-Feb, 1955
Ajax/Farrell Publ.

10,11 7.50 22.50 45.00

FANTASTIC FABLES
Feb, 1987 ($1.50, B&W, 28 pgs.)
Silverwolf Comics

1-Tim Vigil-a (6 pgs.) .60 1.50 3.00

FANTASTIC FEARS (Formerly Captain Jet) (Fantastic Comics #10 on)
No. 7, May, 1953 - No. 9, Sept-Oct, 1954
Ajax/Farrell Publ.

7(#1, 5/53) 14.00 43.00 100.00
8(#2, 7/53) 10.00 30.00 60.00
3,4 8.35 25.00 50.00
5-(1-2/54)-Ditko story (1st in book) is written by Bruce Hamilton; r-in Weird V2#8 (Ditko's 3rd-a; see Black Magic #27) 36.00 108.00 250.00

	GD25	FN65	NM94
6-Decapitation of girl's head with paper cutter (classic)	18.00	54.00	125.00
7(5-6/54), 9(9-10/54)	7.50	22.50	45.00
8(7-8/54)-Contains story intended for Jo-Jo; name changed to Kaza; decapitation story	10.00	30.00	60.00

FANTASTIC FOUR (See America's Best TV..., Giant- Size..., Giant Size Super- Stars, Marvel Collectors Item Classics, Marvel Milestone Edition, Marvel's Greatest,Marvel Treasury Edition, Marvel Triple Action, Official Marvel Index to... & Power Record Comics)

FANTASTIC FOUR
Nov, 1961 - Present
Marvel Comics Group

	GD25	FN65	NM94
1-Origin/1st app. The Fantastic Four (Reed Richards: Mr. Fantastic, Johnny Storm: The Human Torch, Sue Storm: The Invisible Girl, & Ben Grimm: The Thing); origin/1st app. The Mole Man (Marvel's 1st super-hero group since the G.A.)	900.00	2700.00	7200.00
1-Golden Record Comic Set Reprint (mid-'60s)-cover not identical to original	14.00	43.00	100.00
with record (still sealed)	25.00	75.00	175.00
2-Vs. The Skrulls (last 10 cent issue)	230.00	685.00	1600.00
3-Fantastic Four don costumes & establish Headquarters; brief 1pg. origin; intro The Fantasti-Car; Human Torch drawn w/two left hands on-c	143.00	430.00	1000.00
4-1st Silver Age Sub-Mariner app. (5/62)	172.00	515.00	1200.00
5-Origin & 1st app. Doctor Doom	180.00	535.00	1250.00
6-Sub-Mariner, Dr. Doom team up; 1st Marvel villain team-up	93.00	280.00	650.00
7-10: 7-1st app. Kurrgo. 8-1st app. Puppet-Master & Alicia Masters. 9-Sub-Mariner app. 10-Stan Lee (1st app. in comics?) & Jack Kirby app. in story	68.00	205.00	475.00
11-Origin/1st app. The Impossible Man	50.00	150.00	350.00
12-Fantastic Four Vs. The Hulk (1st x-over)	64.00	192.00	450.00
13-Intro. The Watcher; 1st app. The Red Ghost	39.00	120.00	275.00
14-19: 14-Sub-Mariner x-over. 15-1st app. Mad Thinker. 16-1st Ant-Man x-over (7/63); Wasp cameo. 18-Origin/1st app. The Super Skrull. 19-Intro. Rama-Tut; Stan Lee & Jack Kirby cameo	26.00	78.00	180.00
20-Origin/1st app. The Molecule Man	30.00	90.00	210.00
21-Intro. The Hate Monger; 1st Sgt. Fury x-over (12/63)	17.00	52.00	120.00
22-24: 22-Sue Storm gains more powers	12.00	36.00	85.00
25,26-The Hulk vs. The Thing (their 1st battle). 25-1st Avengers x-over w/ Capt. America)(cameo, 4/64); 2nd S.A. app. Cap (takes place between Avengers #4 & 5. 26-Avengers x-over	36.00	107.00	250.00
27-1st Doctor Strange x-over (6/64)	13.00	40.00	90.00
28-Early X-Men x-over (7/64)	18.00	54.00	125.00
29,30: 30-Intro. Diablo	10.00	30.00	70.00
31-40: 31-Early Avengers x-over. 33-1st app. Attuma; part photo-c. 35-Intro/1st app. Dragon Man. 36-Intro/1st app. Madam Medusa & the Frightful Four (Sandman, Wizard, Paste Pot Pete). 39-Wood inks on Daredevil (early x-over)	9.00	27.00	54.00
41-47: 41-43-Frightful Four app. 44-Intro. Gorgan. 45-Last pg. cameo Black Bolt of Inhumans (12/65). 46-1st full app. Black Bolt (1/66)	6.35	19.00	38.00
48-Partial origin/1st app. The Silver Surfer & Galactus (3/66); Galactus cameo in last panel; 1st of 3 part story	72.00	215.00	500.00
49-2nd app. Silver Surfer & Galactus	14.00	43.00	100.00
50-Silver Surfer battles Galactus	18.00	54.00	125.00
51,54: 54-Inhumans cameo	5.00	15.00	30.00
52-1st app. The Black Panther (7/66)	9.15	27.50	55.00
53-Origin & 2nd app. The Black Panther	6.70	20.00	40.00
55-Thing battles Silver Surfer	6.70	20.00	40.00
56-60: Silver Surfer x-over. 59,60-Inhumans cameo	5.85	17.50	35.00
61-65,68-70: 61-Silver Surfer cameo	4.20	12.50	25.00
66-Begin 2 part origin of Him (Warlock); does not app. (9/67)	11.00	32.00	75.00
67-Origin/1st app. Him (Warlock); 1 pg. cameo; see Thor #165,166 for next app.	12.00	36.00	85.00
71,73,78-80: 73-Spider-Man, D.D., Thor x-over; cont'd from Daredevil #38	4.00	10.00	20.00
72,74-77: Silver Surfer app. in all	4.00	11.00	22.00
81-88: 81-Crystal joins & dons costume. 82,83-Inhumans app. 84-87-Dr. Doom app. 88-Last 12 cent issue	3.00	7.50	15.00
89-99,101,102: 94-Intro. Agatha Harkness. 102,103-Fantastic Four vs. Sub-Mariner	2.40	6.00	12.00
100 (7/70)	8.35	25.00	50.00
103-111: 108-Last Kirby issue (not in #103-107)	2.00	5.00	10.00
112-Hulk Vs. Thing (7/71)	4.20	12.50	25.00
113-115: 115-Last 15 cent issue	1.80	4.50	9.00
116-120: 116-(52 pgs.)	1.60	4.00	8.00
121-123-Silver Surfer x-over. 122,123-Galactus	2.00	5.00	10.00
124,125,127,129-149: 129-Intro. Thundra. 130-Sue leaves F.F. 131-Quicksilver app. 132-Medusa joins. 133-Thundra Vs. Thing. 142-Kirbyish-a by Buckler begins. 143-Dr. Doom app.	1.20	3.00	6.00
126-Origin F.F. retold; cover swipe of F.F. #1	1.40	3.50	7.00
128-Four pg. insert of F.F. Friends & Foes	1.40	3.50	7.00
150-Crystal & Quicksilver's wedding	1.40	3.50	7.00
151-154,158-160: Origin Thundra. 159-Medusa leaves; Sue rejoins	1.00	2.50	5.00
155-157: Silver Surfer in all	1.20	3.00	6.00
161-180: 164-The Crusader (old Marvel Boy) revived (origin #165). 176-Re-intro Impossible Man; Marvel artists app. 180-r/#101 by Kirby	.60	1.50	3.00
181-199: 189-G.A. Human Torch app. & origin retold. 190,191-Fantastic Four break up	.40	1.00	2.00
200-(11/78, 52 pgs.)-F.F. re-united vs. Dr. Doom	.80	2.00	4.00
201-208,219,222-231: 211-1st Terrax	.30	.75	1.50
209-216,218,220,221-Byrne-a. 209-1st Herbie the Robot. 220-Brief origin	.40	1.00	2.00
217-Dazzler app. by Byrne	.60	1.50	3.00
232-Byrne-a begins	.70	1.75	3.50
233-235,237-249,251-260: All Byrne-a. 238-Origin Frankie Raye. 244-Frankie Raye becomes Nova, Herald of Galactus. 252-Reads sideways; Annihilus app.; contains skin "Tattooz" decals	.50	1.25	2.50
236-20th Anniversary issue(11/81, 64 pgs., $1.00)-Brief origin F.F. Byrne-c/a(p); new Kirby-a(p)	.60	1.75	3.50
250-(52 pgs)-Spider-Man x-over; Byrne-a; Skrulls impersonate New X-Men	.60	1.75	3.50
261-285: 261-Silver Surfer. 262-Origin Galactus; Byrne writes & draws himself into story. 264-Swipes-c of F.F. #1	.50	1.25	2.50
286-2nd app. X-Factor continued from Avengers #263; story continues in X-Factor #1	.80	2.00	4.00
287-295: 292-Nick Fury app.		.50	1.00
296-($1.50)-Barry Smith-c/a; Thing rejoins	.40	1.05	2.10
297-305,307-318,320-330: 300-Johnny Storm & Alicia Masters wed. 312-X-Factor x-over. 327-Mr. Fantastic & Invisible Girl return		.50	1.00
306-New team begins	.30	.75	1.50
319-Double size	.40	1.00	2.00
331-346,351-357,359,360: 334-Simonson-c/scripts begin. 337-Simonson-a begins. 342-Spider-Man cameo. 356-F.F. vs. The New Warriors; Paul Ryan-c/a begins. 360-Last $1.00-c		.50	1.00
347-Ghost Rider, Wolverine, Spider-Man, Hulk-c/stories thru #349; Arthur Adams-c/a(p) in each	1.00	2.50	5.00
347-Gold 2nd printing	.40	1.00	2.00
348,349	.60	1.50	3.00
348-Gold 2nd printing		.50	1.00
350-($1.50, 52 pgs.)-Dr. Doom app.	.50	1.25	2.50
358-(11/91, $2.25, 88 pgs.)-30th anniversary issue; gives history of F.F.; die cut-c; Art Adams back-up story-a	.50	1.25	2.50
361-368,370,372-374,376: 362-Spider-Man app. 367-Wolverine app. (brief). 370-Infinity War x-over; Thanos & Magus app. 374-Secret Defenders (Ghost Rider, Hulk, Wolverine) x-over		.60	1.25

Fantastic Four #9, © MEG

Fantastic Four #67, © MEG

Fantastic Four #312, © MEG

Fantastic Four King Size Special #4, © MEG

Fantastic Worlds #5, © STD

Fantasy Masterpieces #7, © MEG

GD25 FN65 NM94

369-Infinity War x-over; Thanos app. .50 1.00 2.00
371-All white embossed-c .50 1.25 2.50
375-($2.95, 52 pgs.)-Holo-grafx foil-c .60 1.50 3.00
Annual 1('63)-Origin F.F.; Ditko-i 50.00 150.00 350.00
Annual 2('64)-Dr. Doom origin & c/story 29.00 85.00 200.00
Annual 3('65)-Reed & Sue wed; r/#6,11 1 12.00 36.00 85.00
Special 4(11/66)-G.A. Torch x-over & origin retold; r/#25,26 (Hulk vs. Thing) 7.50 22.50 45.00
Special 5(11/67)-New art; Intro. Psycho-Man; early Black Panther, Inhumans & Silver Surfer (1st solo story) app. 9.15 27.50 55.00
Special 6(11/68)-Intro. Annihilus; birth of Franklin Richards; new 48 pg. movie length epic; no reprints 5.00 15.00 30.00
Special 7(11/69)-All reprints 3.60 9.00 18.00
Special 8(12/70). 9(12/71). 10('73)-All reprints 1.80 4.50 9.00
Annual 11-14: 11(1976). 12(1978). 13(1978)-New-a. 14(1979)-New-a 1.00 2.50 5.00
Annual 15-20: 15(1980). 16(1981). 17(1983)-New Byrne-c/a. 18(1984). 19(1985). 20(1987) .60 1.50 3.00
Annual 21(1988)-Evolutionary War x-over .70 1.70 3.40
Annual 22-24 (1989-91, $2.00, 68 pgs.): 22-Atlantis Attacks x-over; Sub-Mariner & The Avengers app.; Buckler-a. 23-Byrne-c; Guice-p. 24-2 pg. origin recap of Fantastic Four; Guardians of the Galaxy x-over .40 1.00 2.00
Annual 25(1992, $2.25, 68 pgs.)-Moondragon story .45 1.15 2.25
Special Edition 1(5/84)-r/Annual #1; Byrne-c/a .40 1.00 2.00
...: Monsters Unleashed nn(1992, $5.95)-r/F.F. #347-349 w/new Arthur Adams-c 1.20 3.00 6.00
Giveaway (nn, 1981, 32pgs., Young Model Builders Club) .30 .80 1.60

NOTE: ***Arthur Adams*** *c/a-347-349p.* ***Austin*** *c(i)-232-236, 238, 240-242, 250i, 286i.* ***John Buscema*** *a(p)-107, 108(w/****Kirby & Romita****),109-130, 132, 134-141, 160, 173-175, 202, 296-309p, Annual 11, 13; c(p)-107-122, 124-129, 133-139, 202, Annual 12p, Special 10.* ***Byrne*** *a-209-218p, 220p, 221p, 232-265, 266i, 267-273, 274-293p, Annual 17, 19; c-211-214p, 220p, 232-236p, 237, 238p, 239, 240-242p, 243-249, 250p, 251-267, 269-277, 278-281p, 283p, 284, 285, 286p, 288-293, Annual, 17.* ***Ditko*** *a-13i, Annual 16.* ***G. Kane*** *c-150p, 160p.* ***Kirby*** *a-1-102p, 108, 180r, 189r, 236p, Special 1-10; c-1-101, 164, 167, 171-177, 180, 181, 190, 200, Annual 11, Special 1-7, 9.* ***Marcos*** *a-Annual 14i.* ***Mooney*** *a-118i, 152i.* ***Perez*** *a-164-167, 170-172, 176-178, 184-188, 191p, 192p. Annual 14p, 15p; c(p)-183-188, 191, 192, 194-197.* ***Simonson*** *a-337-341, 343, 344p, 345p, 346, 350p, 353, 354; c-212, 334-341, 342p, 343-346, 350, 353, 354.* ***Steranko*** *c-130-132p.* ***Williamson*** *c-357i.*

FANTASTIC FOUR INDEX (See Official...)

FANTASTIC FOUR ROAST
May, 1982 (75 cents, one shot, direct sale only)
Marvel Comics Group

1-Celebrates 20th anniversary of F.F.#1; X-Men, Ghost Rider & many others cameo; Golden, Miller, Buscema, Rogers, Byrne, Anderson art; Hembeck/Austin-c .80 2.00 4.00

FANTASTIC FOUR VS. X-MEN
Feb, 1987 - No. 4, June, 1987 (Mini-series)
Marvel Comics

1 .70 1.75 3.50
2-4: 4-Austin-a(i) .50 1.25 2.50

FANTASTIC GIANTS (Formerly Konga #1-23)
V2#24, September, 1966 (25 cents, 68 pgs.)
Charlton Comics

V2#24-Special Ditko issue; origin Konga & Gorgo reprinted plus two new Ditko stories 5.00 15.00 30.00

FANTASTIC TALES
1958 (no date) (Reprint)
I. W. Enterprises

1-Reprints Avon's "City of the Living Dead" 2.40 6.00 12.00

FANTASTIC VOYAGE (See Movie Comics)
Aug, 1969 - No. 2, Dec, 1969
Gold Key

1,2 (TV) 2.80 7.00 14.00

FANTASTIC VOYAGES OF SINDBAD, THE
Oct, 1965 - No. 2, June, 1967
Gold Key

1,2-Painted-c 4.00 12.00 22.00

FANTASTIC WORLDS
No. 5, Sept, 1952 - No. 7, Jan, 1953
Standard Comics

5-Toth, Anderson-a 16.00 48.00 110.00
6-Toth-c/a 14.00 43.00 100.00
7 9.15 27.50 55.00

FANTASY FEATURES (Americomics) (Value: cover or less)

FANTASY MASTERPIECES (Marvel Super Heroes No. 12 on)
Feb, 1966 - No. 11, Oct, 1967; Dec, 1979 - No. 14, Jan, 1981
Marvel Comics Group

1-Photo of Stan Lee (12 cent-c #1,2) 4.70 14.00 28.00
2-r/1st Fin Fang Foom from Strange Tales #89 1.80 4.50 9.00
3-8: 3-G.A. Capt. America-r begin, end #11; 1st 25 cent Giant; Colan-r. 7-Begin G.A. Sub-Mariner, Torch-r/M. Mystery. 8-Torch battles the Sub-Mariner-r/Marvel Mystery #9 2.20 5.50 11.00
9-Origin Human Torch-r/Marvel Comics #1 2.80 7.00 14.00
10,11: 10-r/origin & 1st app. All Winners Squad from All Winners #19. 11-r/origin of Toro (H.T. #1) & Black Knight #1 1.80 4.50 9.00
V2#1(12/79)-52 pgs.; 75 cents; r/origin Silver Surfer from Silver Surfer #1 with editing plus reprints cover; J. Buscema-a .90 2.25 4.50
2-14-Reprints Silver Surfer #2-14 w/covers .60 1.50 3.00

NOTE: ***Buscema*** *c-V2#7-9(in part).* ***Ditko*** *r-1-3, 7, 9.* ***Everett*** *r-1,7-9.* ***Matt Fox*** *r-9i.* ***Kirby*** *r-1-11.* ***Starlin*** *r-8-13. Some direct sale V2#14's had a 50 cent cover price. #3-11 contain Capt. America-r/Capt. America #3-10. #7-11 contain G.A.Human Torch & Sub-Mariner-r.*

FANTASY QUARTERLY (Also see Elfquest)
Spring, 1978 (B&W)
Independent Publishers Syndicate

1-1st app. Elfquest (2nd printing exist?) 6.70 20.00 40.00

FANTOMAN (Formerly Amazing Adventure Funnies)
No. 2, Aug, 1940 - No. 4, Dec, 1940
Centaur Publications

2-The Fantom of the Fair, The Arrow, Little Dynamite-r begin; origin The Ermine by Filchock; Fantoman app. in 2-4; Burgos, J. Cole, Ernst, Gustavson-a 100.00 300.00 600.00
3,4: Gustavson-r. 4-Red Blaze app. 80.00 238.00 475.00

FARGO KID (Formerly Justice Traps the Guilty)
V11#3(#1), June-July, 1958 - V11#5, Oct-Nov, 1958
Prize Publications

V11#3(#1)-Origin Fargo Kid, Severin-c/a; Williamson-a(2); Heath-a 10.00 30.00 70.00
V11#4,5-Severin-c/a 7.50 22.50 45.00

FARMER'S DAUGHTER, THE
Feb-Mar, 1954 - No. 3, June-July, 1954; No. 4, Oct, 1954
Stanhall Publ./Trojan Magazines

1-Lingerie, nudity panel 10.00 30.00 70.00
2-4(Stanhall) 7.50 22.50 45.00

FASHION IN ACTION (Eclipse) (Value: cover or less)

FASTEST GUN ALIVE, THE (See 4-Color No. 741)

FAST FICTION (...Action) (Stories by Famous Authors Ill. #6 on)
Oct, 1949 - No. 5, Mar, 1950 (All have Kiefer-c) (48 pgs.)
Seaboard Publ./Famous Authors Ill.

1-Scarlet Pimpernel; Jim Lavery-a 25.00 75.00 175.00

	GD25	FN65	NM94
2-Captain Blood; H. C. Kiefer-a	24.00	71.00	165.00
3-She, by Rider Haggard; Vincent Napoli-a	30.00	90.00	210.00
4-(1/50, 52 pgs.)-The 39 Steps; Lavery-a	19.00	57.00	130.00
5-Beau Geste; Kiefer-a	19.00	57.00	130.00

NOTE: ***Kiefer** a-2, 5; c-2, 3,5. **Lavery** c/a-1, 4. **Napoli** a-3.*

FAST WILLIE JACKSON
October, 1976 - No. 7, 1977
Fitzgerald Periodicals, Inc.

	GD25	FN65	NM94
1-7		.50	1.00

FAT ALBERT (..& the Cosby Kids) (TV)
March, 1974 - No. 29, Feb, 1979
Gold Key

	GD25	FN65	NM94
1	.60	.50	3.00
2-29		.50	1.00

FAT AND SLAT (Ed Wheelan) (Becomes Gunfighter No. 5 on)
Summer, 1947 - No. 4, Spring, 1948
E. C. Comics

	GD25	FN65	NM94
1-Intro/origin Voltage, Man of Lightning	20.00	60.00	140.00
2-4	14.00	43.00	100.00

FAT AND SLAT JOKE BOOK
Summer, 1944 (One Shot, 52 pages)
All-American Comics (William H. Wise)

	GD25	FN65	NM94
nn-by Ed Wheelan	16.00	48.00	110.00

FATE (See Hand of Fate & Thrill-O-Rama)

FATHER OF CHARITY
No date (32 pgs.; paper cover)
Catechetical Guild Giveaway

	GD25	FN65	NM94
nn	2.50	5.00	10.00

FATHOM (Comico) (Value: cover or less)

FATIMA...CHALLENGE TO THE WORLD
1951, 36 pgs. (15 cent cover)
Catechetical Guild

	GD25	FN65	NM94
nn (not same as 'Challenge to the World')	2.40	6.00	12.00

FATMAN, THE HUMAN FLYING SAUCER
April, 1967 - No. 3, Aug-Sept, 1967 (68 pgs.)
Lightning Comics(Milson Publ. Co.) (Written by Otto Binder)

	GD25	FN65	NM94
1-Origin Fatman & Tinman by C. C. Beck	5.85	17.50	35.00
2-Beck-a	4.00	11.00	22.00
3-(Scarce)-Beck-a	6.35	19.00	38.00

FAUNTLEROY COMICS (Superduck Presents...)
1950 - No. 3, 1952
Close-Up/Archie Publications

	GD25	FN65	NM94
1	5.85	17.50	35.00
2,3	4.00	12.00	22.00

FAUST
1989?(nd) - Present (B&W; 1,2: $2.00, 3-on: $2.25; adults, violent)
Northstar Publishing/Rebel Studios #7 on

	GD25	FN65	NM94
1-Decapitation-c; Tim Vigil-c/a in all	5.85	17.50	35.00
1-2nd printing	2.00	5.00	10.00
1-3rd printing	.50	1.25	2.50
2	4.20	12.50	25.00
2-2nd & 3rd printings	.50	1.25	2.50
3-Begin $2.25-c	3.00	7.50	15.00
3-2nd printing	.50	1.25	2.50
4	1.50	3.75	7.50
5-8	.60	1.50	3.00

FAVORITE COMICS (Also see Famous Comics)
1934 (36 pgs.)
Grocery Store Giveaway (Diff. Corp.) (detergent)

	GD25	FN65	NM94
Book #1-The Nebbs, Strange As It Seems, Napoleon, Dixie Dugan, Joe Palooka, S'Matter Pop, Hairbreadth Harry, etc. reprints	36.00	17.00	250.00
Book #2,3	29.00	85.00	200.00

FAWCETT MINIATURES (See Mighty Midget)
1946 (12-24 pgs.; 3-3/4x5") (Wheaties giveaways)
Fawcett Publications

	GD25	FN65	NM94
Captain Marvel-"And the Horn of Plenty;" Bulletman story	7.00	20.00	40.00
Captain Marvel-"& the Raiders From Space;" Golden Arrow story	7.00	20.00	40.00
Captain Marvel Jr.-"The Case of the Poison Press!" Bulletman story	7.00	20.00	40.00
Delecta of the Planets-C. C. Beck art; B&W inside; 12 pgs.; 3 printing variations (coloring) exist	17.00	50.00	100.00

FAWCETT MOTION PICTURE COMICS (See Motion Picture Comics)

FAWCETT MOVIE COMIC
1949 - No. 20, Dec, 1952 (All photo-c)
Fawcett Publications

	GD25	FN65	NM94
nn-"Dakota Lil"-George Montgomery & Rod Cameron(1949)	23.00	70.00	160.00
nn-"Copper Canyon"-Ray Milland & Hedy Lamarr(1950)	17.00	51.00	120.00
nn-"Destination Moon"-(1950)	50.00	150.00	350.00
nn-"Montana"-Errol Flynn & Alexis Smith('50)	17.00	51.00	120.00
nn-"Pioneer Marshal"-Monte Hale(1950)	17.00	51.00	120.00
nn-"Powder River Rustlers"-Rocky Lane(1950)	20.00	60.00	140.00
nn-"Singing Guns"-Vaughn Monroe & Ella Raines(1950)	16.00	48.00	110.00
7-"Gunmen of Abilene"-Rocky Lane; Bob Powell-a(1950)	20.00	60.00	140.00
8-"King of the Bullwhip"-Lash LaRue; Bob Powell-a(1950)	34.00	100.00	235.00
9-"The Old Frontier"-Monte Hale; Bob Powell-a(2/51; mis-dated 2/50)	17.00	51.00	120.00
10-"The Missourians"-Monte Hale(4/51)	17.00	51.00	120.00
11-"The Thundering Trail"-Lash LaRue(6/51)	26.00	78.00	180.00
12-"Rustlers on Horseback"-Rocky Lane(8/51)	20.00	60.00	140.00
13-"Warpath"-Edmond O'Brien & Forrest Tucker(10/51)	13.00	40.00	90.00
14-"Last Outpost"-Ronald Reagan(12/51)	35.00	105.00	245.00
15-(Scarce)-"The Man From Planet X"-Robert Clark; Shaffenberger-a (2/52)	150.00	450.00	1050.00
16-"10 Tall Men"-Burt Lancaster	10.00	30.00	70.00
17-"Rose of Cimarron"-Jack Buetel & Mala Powers	7.50	22.50	45.00
18-"The Brigand"-Anthony Dexter; Shaffenberger-a	8.35	25.00	50.00
19-"Carbine Williams"-James Stewart; Costanza-a	9.00	27.00	62.00
20-"Ivanhoe"-Liz Taylor	13.00	40.00	90.00

FAWCETT'S FUNNY ANIMALS (No. 1-26, 80-on titled "Funny Animals;" becomes Li'l Tomboy No. 92 on?)
12/42 - #79, 4/53; #80, 6/53 - #83, 12?/53; #84, 4/54 - #91, 2/56
Fawcett Publications/Charlton Comics No. 84 on

	GD25	FN65	NM94
1-Capt. Marvel on cover; intro. Hoppy The Captain Marvel Bunny, cloned from Capt. Marvel; Billy the Kid & Willie the Worm begin	39.00	118.00	275.00
2-Xmas-c	19.00	58.00	135.00
3-5	12.00	36.00	85.00
6,7,9,10	9.15	27.50	55.00
8-Flag-c	10.00	30.00	60.00
11-20	6.35	19.00	38.00
21-40: 25-Xmas-c. 26-St. Valentines Day-c	4.20	12.50	25.00

Fatman The Human Flying Saucer #2, © Lightning

Fawcett Miniature, © FAW

Fawcett's Funny Animals #11, © FAW

Fear #19, © MEG

Feature Book #1, © Zane Grey

Feature Comics #27, © QUA

GD25 FN65 NM94

41-88,90,91 3.60 9.00 18.00
89-(2/55)-Merry Mailman ish (TV)-part photo-c 4.20 12.50 25.00
NOTE: *Marvel Bunny in all issues to at least No. 68 (not in 49-54).*

FAZE ONE FAZERS (Americomics) (Value: cover or less)

F.B.I., THE
April-June, 1965
Dell Publishing Co.

1-Sinnott-a 2.40 6.00 12.00

F.B.I. STORY, THE (See 4-Color No. 1069)

FEAR (Adventure into...)
Nov, 1970 - No. 31, Dec, 1975 (No.1-6: Giant Size)
Marvel Comics Group

1-Fantasy & Sci-Fi reprints in early issues 1.60 4.00 8.00
2-6 .90 2.25 4.50
7-9 .60 1.50 3.00
10-Man-Thing begins, ends #19; Morrow/Chaykin-c/a
1.60 4.00 8.00
11,12: 11-N. Adams-c. 12-Starlin/Buckler-a .80 2.00 4.00
13,14,16-18: 17-Origin/1st app. Wundarr .50 1.25 2.50
15-1st full-length Man-Thing story .80 2.00 4.00
19-Intro. Howard the Duck; Val Mayerik-a 3.00 7.50 15.00
20-Morbius, the Living Vampire begins, ends #31 3.60 9.00 18.00
21-25 2.00 5.00 10.00
26-31 1.60 4.00 8.00
NOTE: ***Bolle** a-13i. **Brunner** c-15-17. **Buckler** a-11p, 12i. **Chaykin** a-10i. **Colan** a-23r. **Craig** a-10p. **Ditko** a-6-8r. **Evans** a-30. **Everett** a-9, 10i, 21r. **Gulacy** a-20p. **Gil Kane** a-21p; c(p)-20, 21, 23-28, 31. **Kirby** a-8r, 9r. **Maneely** a-24r. **Mooney** a-11i, 26r. **Morrow** a-11i. **Paul Reinman** a-14r. **Robbins** a(p)-25-27, 31. **Russell** a-23p, 24p. **Severin** c-8. **Starlin** c-12p.*

FEARBOOK (Eclipse) (Value: cover or less)

FEAR IN THE NIGHT (See Complete Mystery No. 3)

FEARLESS FAGAN (See 4-Color No. 441)

FEATURE BOOK (Dell) (See Large Feature Comic)

FEATURE BOOKS (Newspaper-r, early issues)
May, 1937 - No. 57, 1948 (B&W; Full color, 68 pgs. begin #26 on)
David McKay Publications

GD25 FN65 VF82

nn-Popeye & the Jeep (#1, 100 pgs.); reprinted as Feature Books #3
(Very Rare; only 3 known copies, 1-vf, 2-in low grade)
Estimated value.... 535.00 1500.00 3200.00
nn-Dick Tracy (#1)-Reprinted as Feature Book #4 (100 pgs.) & in part as 4-Color #1 (Rare, less than 10 known copies)
Estimated value.... 535.00 1500.00 3200.00
NOTE: *Above books were advertised together with different covers from Feat. Books #3 & 4.*

GD25 FN65 NM94

1-King of the Royal Mtd. (#1) 57.00 170.00 400.00
2-Popeye(6/37) by Segar 61.00 182.00 425.00
3-Popeye(7/37) by Segar; same as nn issue but a new cover added
54.00 190.00 375.00
4-Dick Tracy(8/37)-Same as nn issue but a new cover added
90.00 270.00 630.00
5-Popeye(9/37) by Segar 47.00 140.00 325.00
6-Dick Tracy(10/37) 72.00 215.00 500.00
7-Little Orphan Annie (#1) (Rare)-Reprints strips from 12/31/34 to 7/17/35
75.00 225.00 525.00
8-Secret Agent X-9-Not by Raymond 30.00 90.00 210.00
9-Dick Tracy(1/38) 72.00 215.00 500.00
10-Popeye(2/38) 47.00 140.00 325.00
11-Little Annie Rooney (#1) 24.00 73.00 170.00
12-Blondie (#1) (4/38) (Rare) 47.00 140.00 325.00
13-Inspector Wade 14.00 43.00 100.00
14-Popeye(6/38) by Segar (Scarce) 61.00 182.00 425.00
15-Barney Baxter (#1) (7/38) 22.00 65.00 150.00

GD25 FN65 NM94

16-Red Eagle 14.00 43.00 100.00
17-Gangbusters (#1) 34.00 103.00 240.00
18,19-Mandrake 29.00 85.00 200.00
20-Phantom (#1) 54.00 160.00 375.00
21-Lone Ranger 54.00 160.00 375.00
22-Phantom 43.00 130.00 300.00
23-Mandrake 29.00 85.00 200.00
24-Lone Ranger(1941) 54.00 160.00 375.00
25-Flash Gordon (#1)-Reprints not by Raymond 54.00 163.00 380.00
26-Prince Valiant(1941)-Harold Foster-a; newspaper strips reprinted, pgs. 1-28,30-63. Color & 68 pg. issues begin 73.00 218.00 510.00
27-29,31,34-Blondie 11.00 32.00 75.00
30-Katzenjammer Kids (#1) 11.50 34.00 80.00
32,35,41,44-Katzenjammer Kids 10.00 30.00 70.00
33(nn)-Romance of Flying-World War II photos 10.00 30.00 65.00
36('43),38,40('44),42,43,45,47-Blondie 10.00 30.00 70.00
37-Katzenjammer Kids; has photo & biog. of Harold H. Knerr(1883-1949) who took over strip from Rudolph Dirks in 1914 10.00 30.00 70.00
39-Phantom 36.00 110.00 250.00
46-Mandrake in the Fire World-(58 pgs.) 24.00 70.00 165.00
48-Maltese Falcon by Dashiell Hammett('46) 50.00 150.00 350.00
49,50-Perry Mason 16.00 48.00 110.00
51,54-Rip Kirby c/a by Raymond; origin-#51 24.00 70.00 165.00
52,55-Mandrake 21.00 62.00 145.00
53,56,57-Phantom 26.00 77.00 180.00
NOTE: *All Feature Books through #25 are over-sized 8x11-3/8" comics with color covers and black and white interiors. The covers are rough, heavy stock. The page counts, including covers, are as follows: nn, #3, 4-100 pgs.; #1, 2-52 pgs.; #5-25 are all 76 pgs. #33 was found in bound set from publisher.*

FEATURE COMICS (Formerly Feature Funnies)
No. 21, June, 1939 - No. 144, May, 1950
Quality Comics Group

21-Strips continue from Feature Funnies 37.00 110.00 220.00
22-26: 23-Charlie Chan begins 27.00 82.00 165.00
26-(nn, nd)-Cover in one color, (10 cents, 36pgs.; issue No. blanked out. 2 variations exist, each contain half of the regular #26)
7.50 22.50 45.00
27-(Rare)-Origin/1st app. Dollman by Eisner 208.00 625.00 1250.00
28-1st Lou Fine Dollman 90.00 270.00 540.00
29,30 57.00 170.00 340.00
31-Last Clock & Charlie Chan issue 48.00 145.00 290.00
32-37: 32-Rusty Ryan & Samar begin. 34-Captain Fortune app. 37-Last Fine Dollman 35.00 105.00 210.00
38-41: 38-Origin the Ace of Space. 39-Origin The Destroying Demon, ends #40. 40-Bruce Blackburn in costume 27.00 80.00 160.00
42,43,45-50: 42-USA, the Spirit of Old Glory begins. 46-Intro. Boyville Brigadiers in Rusty Ryan. 48-USA ends 17.00 52.00 105.00
44-Dollman by Crandall begins, ends #63; Crandall-a(2)
26.00 78.00 155.00
51-60: 56-Marijuana story in Swing Sisson strip. 57-Spider Widow begins. 60-Raven begins, ends #71 14.00 42.00 85.00
61-68 (5/43) 13.00 40.00 80.00
69,70-Phantom Lady x-over in Spider Widow 14.00 42.00 85.00
71-80,100: 71-Phantom Lady x-over. 72-Spider Widow ends
10.00 30.00 60.00
81-99 8.35 25.00 50.00
101-144: 139-Last Dollman. 140-Intro. Stuntman Stetson
6.35 19.00 38.00
NOTE: ***Celardo** a-37-43. **Crandall** a-44-60, 62, 63-on(most). **Gustavson** a-(Rusty Ryan)- 32-134. **Powell** a-34, 64-73.*

FEATURE FILMS
Mar-Apr, 1950 - No. 4, Sept-Oct, 1950 (1-3: photo-c)
National Periodical Publications

1-"Captain China" with John Payne, Gail Russell, Lon Chaney & Edgar

GD25 FN65 NM94

Bergen 43.00 130.00 300.00
2-"Riding High" with Bing Crosby 39.00 118.00 275.00
3-"The Eagle & the Hawk" with John Payne, Rhonda Fleming & D. O'Keefe 39.00 118.00 275.00
4-"Fancy Pants"-Bob Hope & Lucille Ball 50.00 150.00 300.00

FEATURE FUNNIES (Feature Comics No. 21 on)
Oct, 1937 - No. 20, May, 1939
Harry 'A' Chesler

1(V9#1-indicia)-Joe Palooka, Mickey Finn, The Bungles, Jane Arden, Dixie Dugan, Big Top, Ned Brant, Strange As It Seems, & Off the Record strip reprints begin 183.00 550.00 1100.00
2-The Hawk app. (11/37); Goldberg-c 87.00 262.00 525.00
3-Hawks of Seas begins by Eisner, ends #12; The Clock begins; Christmas-c 62.00 188.00 375.00
4,5 46.00 138.00 275.00
6-12: 11-Archie O'Toole by Bud Thomas begins, ends #22 37.00 112.00 225.00
13-Espionage, Starring Black X begins by Eisner, ends #20 41.00 122.00 245.00
14-20 32.00 95.00 190.00

FEATURE PRESENTATION, A (Feature Presentations Magazine #6) (Formerly Women in Love) (Also see Startling Terror Tales #11)
No. 5, April, 1950
Fox Features Syndicate

5(#1)-Black Tarantula 22.00 65.00 150.00

FEATURE PRESENTATIONS MAGAZINE (Formerly A Feature Presentation #5; becomes Feature Stories Magazine #3 on)
No. 6, July, 1950
Fox Features Syndicate

6(#2)-Moby Dick; Wood-c 17.00 52.00 120.00

FEATURE STORIES MAGAZINE (Formerly Feature Presentations Mag. #6)
No. 3, Aug, 1950 - No. 4, Oct, 1950
Fox Features Syndicate

3-Jungle Lil, Zegra stories; bondage-c 14.00 43.00 100.00
4 11.00 32.00 75.00

FEDERAL MEN COMICS (See Adventure Comics #32, The Comics Magazine, New Adventure Comics, New Book of Comics & New Comics)
No. 2, 1945 (DC reprints from 1930's)
Gerard Publ. Co.

2-Siegel & Shuster-a; cover redrawn from Detective #9; spanking panel 17.00 50.00 115.00

FELIX'S NEPHEWS INKY & DINKY
Sept, 1957 - No. 7, Oct, 1958
Harvey Publications

1-Cover shows Inky's left eye with 2 pupils 6.35 19.00 38.00
2-7 3.60 9.00 18.00
*NOTE: **Messmer** art in 1-6. **Oriolo** a-1-7.*

FELIX THE CAT
1931 (24 pgs.; 8x10-1/4")(1926, '27 color strip reprints)
McLoughlin Bros.

260-(Rare)-by Otto Messmer 92.00 275.00 550.00

FELIX THE CAT (See Cat Tales 3-D, The Funnies, March of Comics #24,36, 51, New Funnies & Popular Comics)
1943 - No. 118, Nov, 1961; Sept-Nov, 1962 - No. 12, July-Sept, 1965
Dell Publ. No. 1-19/Toby No. 20-61/Harvey No. 62-118/Dell

4-Color 15 54.00 160.00 375.00
4-Color 46('44) 34.00 100.00 240.00
4-Color 77('45) 32.00 95.00 225.00
4-Color 119('46) 25.00 75.00 175.00
4-Color 135('46) 19.00 57.00 130.00
4-Color 162(9/47) 14.00 43.00 100.00
1(2-3/48)(Dell) 20.00 60.00 140.00
2 10.00 30.00 70.00
3-5 9.15 27.50 55.00
6-19(2-3/51-Dell) 5.58 17.50 35.00
20-30(Toby): 28-(2/52)-Some copies have #29 on cover, #28 on inside 10.00 30.00 60.00
31,34,35-No Messmer-a 4.00 12.00 22.00
32,33,36-61(6/55-Toby)-Last Messmer issue 8.35 25.00 50.00
62(8/55)-100 (Harvey) 2.40 6.00 12.00
101-118(11/61): 101-117-Reprints. 118-All new-a 2.00 5.00 10.00
12-269-211(#1, 9-11/62)(Dell) 3.60 9.00 18.00
2-12(7-9/65)(Dell, TV) 2.00 5.00 10.00
3-D Comic Book 1(1953-One Shot) 26.00 77.00 180.00
Summer Annual 2('52)-Early 1930s Sunday strip-r (Exist?) 24.00 72.00 165.00
Summer Annual nn('53, 100 pgs., Toby)-1930s daily & Sunday-r 24.00 72.00 165.00
Winter Annual 2('54, 100 pgs., Toby)-1930s daily & Sunday-r 17.00 52.00 120.00
Summer Annual 3('55) (Exist?) 16.00 48.00 110.00
*NOTE: 4-Color No. 15, 46, 77 and the Toby Annuals are all daily or Sunday newspaper reprints from the 1930's drawn by **Otto Messmer**, who created Felix in 1915 for the Sullivan animation studio. He drew Felix from the beginning under contract to Pat Sullivan. In 1946 he went to work for Dell and wrote and pencilled most of the stories and inked some of them through the Toby Press issues. 101-r/#64; 102-r/#65; 103-r/#67; 104-117-r/#68-81. **Messmer**-a in all Dell/Toby/Harvey issues except #31, 34, 35, 97, 98, 100, 118. **Oriolo** a-20, 31-on.*

FELIX THE CAT (Also see The Nine Lives of...)
Sept, 1991 - Present ($1.25/$1.50, color, bi-monthly)
Harvey Comics

1-5: Reprints 1950s Toby issues by Messmer. 1-Inky and Dinky back-up story .60 1.25
6,7-($1.50-c) .30 .75 1.50
...Big Book V2#1 (9/92, $1.95, 52 pgs.) .40 1.00 2.00

FELIX THE CAT AND FRIENDS
1992 - Present ($1.95, color)
Felix Comics

1-4: 1-Contains Felix trading cards .40 1.00 2.00

FELIX THE CAT & HIS FRIENDS
Dec, 1953 - No. 3, 1954
Toby Press

1 7.50 22.50 45.00
2-3 5.85 17.50 35.00

FELIX THE CAT DIGEST MAGAZINE
July, 1992 - Present ($1.75, color, digest-size, 98 pgs.)
Harvey Comics

1-Felix, Richie Rich stories .35 .90 1.75

FEM FANTASTIQUE (AC)(Value: cover or less)

FEMFORCE (Also see Untold Origin of the Femforce)
Apr, 1985 - Present ($1.75/1.95/2.25; in color; B&W #16-56)
Americomics

1-Black-a in most; Nightveil, Ms. Victory begin 1.20 4.00 6.00
2 .80 2.00 4.00
3-30: 12-15-$1.95-c. 16-19-$2.25-c. 20-Begin $2.50-c, 44 pgs. 25-Origin/1st app. new Ms. Victory. 28-Colt leaves. 29,30-Camilla-r by Mayo from Jungle Comics .70 1.75 3.50
31-35,37-49,51-58: 31-Begin $2.75-c. 44-Contains mini-comic insert, Catman & Kitten #0. 51-Photo-c from movie. 57-Begin color issues .55 1.40 2.75
36-($2.95, 52 pgs.) .60 1.50 3.00
50-($2.95, color, 52 pgs.)-Contains flexi-disc; origin retold; most AC characters app. .60 1.50 3.00
Special 1 (Fall, '84)(B&W, 52pgs.)-1st app. Ms. Victory, She-Cat, Blue

Federal Men Comics #2, © Gerard Publ.

Felix The Cat Winter Annual #2, © KING

Femforce #31, © Americomics

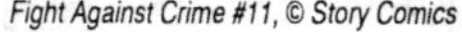
Fight Against Crime #11, © Story Comics — *Fight Comics #20, © FH* — *Fightin' Air Force #9, © CC*

	GD25	FN65	NM94
Bulleteer, Rio Rita & Lady Luger	.40	1.00	2.00
Frightbook 1 ('92, $2.95, B&W)-Halloween special	.60	1.50	3.00
In the House of Horror 1 ('89, $2.50, B&W)	.50	1.25	2.50
Night of the Demon 1 ('90, $2.75, B&W)	.55	1.40	2.75
Out of the Asylum Special 1 ('87, B&W, $1.95)	.40	1.00	2.00
Pin-Up Portfolio	.40	1.00	2.00

FEMFORCE UP CLOSE
Apr, 1992 - Present ($2.75, color, quarterly)
AC Comics

	GD25	FN65	NM94
1-4: 1-Stars Nightveil; inside f/c photo from Femforce movie. 2-Stars Stardust. 3-Stars Dragonfly. 4-Stars She-Cat	.55	1.40	2.75

FERDINAND THE BULL (See Mickey Mouse Magazine V4#3)
1938 (10 cents)(Large size; some color, rest B&W)
Dell Publishing Co.

	GD25	FN65	NM94
nn	11.00	32.00	75.00

FERRET (Malibu)(Value: cover or less)

FIBBER McGEE & MOLLY (See A-1 Comics No. 25)

55 DAYS AT PEKING (See Movie Comics)

FIGHT AGAINST CRIME (Fight Against the Guilty #22, 23)
May, 1951 - No. 21, Sept, 1954
Story Comics

	GD25	FN65	NM94
1	14.00	43.00	100.00
2	7.00	21.00	42.00
3,5: 5-Frazetta-a, 1 pg.	5.35	16.00	32.00
4-Drug story-"Hopped Up Killers"	7.50	22.50	45.00
6,7: 6-Used in **POP**, pgs. 83,84	5.00	15.00	30.00
8-Last crime format issue	5.00	15.00	30.00

NOTE: *No. 9-21 contain violent, gruesome stories with blood, dismemberment, decapitation, E.C. style plot twists and several E.C. swipes. Bondage c-4, 6, 18, 19.*

	GD25	FN65	NM94
9-11,13	10.00	30.00	70.00
12-Morphine drug story-"The Big Dope"	11.50	34.00	80.00
14-Tothish art by Ross Andru; electrocution-c	10.00	30.00	70.00
15-B&W & color illos in **POP**	10.00	30.00	65.00
16-E.C. story swipe/Haunt of Fear #19; Tothish-a by Ross Andru; bondage-c	11.50	34.00	80.00
17-Wildey E.C. swipe/Shock SuspenStories #9; knife through neck-c (1/54)	11.50	34.00	80.00
18,19: 19-Bondage/torture-c	10.00	30.00	65.00
20-Decapitation cover; contains hanging, ax murder, blood & violence	19.00	57.00	130.00
21-E.C. swipe	10.00	30.00	65.00

NOTE: ***Cameron** a-4, 5, 8. **Hollingsworth** a-3-7, 9, 10, 13. **Wildey** a-6, 15, 16.*

FIGHT AGAINST THE GUILTY (Formerly Fight Against Crime)
No. 22, Dec, 1954 - No. 23, Mar, 1955
Story Comics

	GD25	FN65	NM94
22-Tothish-a by Ross Andru; Ditko-a; E.C. story swipe; electrocution-c	10.00	30.00	65.00
23 (Last pre-code)-Hollingsworth-a	7.00	21.00	42.00

FIGHT COMICS
Jan, 1940 - No. 83, 11/52; No. 84, Wint, 1952-53; No. 85, Spring, 1953; No. 86, Summer, 1954
Fiction House Magazines

	GD25	FN65	NM94
1-Origin Spy Fighter, Starring Saber; Fine/Eisner-c; Eisner-a	133.00	400.00	800.00
2-Joe Louis life story	58.00	175.00	350.00
3-Rip Regan, the Power Man begins	50.00	150.00	300.00
4,5: 4-Fine-c	42.00	125.00	250.00
6-10: 6,7-Powell-c	33.00	100.00	200.0
11-14: Rip Regan ends	29.00	88.00	175.00
15-1st Super American	42.00	125.00	250.00
16-Captain Fight begins; Spy Fighter ends	42.00	125.00	250.00
17,18: Super American ends	33.00	100.00	200.00
19-Captain Fight ends; Senorita Rio begins (origin & 1st app.); Rip Carson, Chute Trooper begins	33.00	100.00	200.00
20	27.00	80.00	160.00
21-30	17.00	50.00	100.00
31,33-50: 31-Decapitation-c. 44-Capt. Flight returns. 48-Used in Love and Death by Legman	14.00	42.00	85.00
32-Tiger Girl begins	15.00	45.00	90.00
51-Origin Tiger Girl; Patsy Pin-Up app.	23.00	70.00	140.00
52-60,62-65-Last Baker issue	12.00	35.00	70.00
61-Origin Tiger Girl retold	14.00	42.00	85.00
66-78: 78-Used in POP, pg. 99	10.00	30.00	65.00
79-The Space Rangers app.	10.00	30.00	65.00
80-85	9.15	27.50	55.00
86-Two Tigerman stories by Evans-r/Rangers Comics #40,41; Moreira-r/Rangers Comics #45	10.00	30.00	65.00

NOTE: *Bondage covers, Lingerie, headlights panels are common. Tiger Girl by **Baker**- #36-60, 62-65; Kayo Kirby by **Baker**-#52-64, 67(not by Baker). **Eisner** c-1-3, 5, 10, 11. **Kamen** a-54?, 57? **Tuska** a-1, 5, 8, 10, 21, 29. **Whitman** c-73-84.*

FIGHT FOR FREEDOM
1949, 1951 (16 pgs.) (Giveaway)
National Association of Mfgrs./General Comics

	GD25	FN65	NM94
nn-Dan Barry-c/a; used in **POP**, pg. 102	5.00	15.00	30.00

FIGHT FOR LOVE
1952 (no month)
United Features Syndicate

	GD25	FN65	NM94
nn-Abbie & Slats newspaper-r	8.75	26.00	52.00

FIGHTING AIR FORCE (See United States Fighting Air Force)

FIGHTIN' AIR FORCE (Formerly Sherlock Holmes?; Never Again? War and Attack #54 on)
No. 3, Feb, 1956 - No. 53, Feb-Mar, 1966
Charlton Comics

	GD25	FN65	NM94
V1#3	3.60	9.00	18.00
4-10	2.00	5.00	10.00
11(3/58, 68 pgs.)	2.40	6.00	12.00
12 (100 pgs.)	3.20	8.00	16.00
13-30: 13,24-Glanzman-a. 24-Glanzman-c	1.60	4.00	8.00
31-50: 50-American Eagle begins	1.00	2.50	5.00
51-53	.60	1.50	3.00

FIGHTING AMERICAN
Apr-May, 1954 - No. 7, Apr-May, 1955
Headline Publications/Prize

	GD25	FN65	NM94
1-Origin Fighting American & Speedboy; S&K-c/a(3)	93.00	280.00	650.00
2-S&K-a(3)	47.00	140.00	325.00
3,4-S&K-a(3)	46.00	138.00	275.00
5-S&K-a(2); Kirby/?-a	46.00	138.00	275.00
6-Origin-r (4 pgs.) plus 2 pgs. by S&K	42.00	125.00	250.00
7-Kirby-a	37.00	112.00	225.00

NOTE: ***Simon & Kirby** covers on all. 6 is last pre-code issue.*

FIGHTING AMERICAN
October, 1966 (25 cents)
Harvey Publications

	GD25	FN65	NM94
1-Origin Fighting American & Speedboy by S&K-r; S&K-c/a(3); 1 pg. Neal Adams ad	3.00	7.50	15.00

FIGHTIN' ARMY (Formerly Soldier and Marine Comics; see Captain Willy Schultz)
No. 16, 1/56 - No. 127, 12/76; No. 128, 9/77 - No. 172, 11/84
Charlton Comics

	GD25	FN65	NM94
16	3.60	9.00	18.00
17-19,21-23,25-30	2.00	5.00	10.00

	GD25	FN65	NM94
20-Ditko-a	3.20	8.00	16.00
24 (68 pgs., 3/58)	2.40	6.00	12.00
31-45	1.60	4.00	8.00
46-60	1.00	2.50	5.00
61-80: 75-92-The Lonely War of Willy Schultz	.80	2.00	4.00
81-172: 89,90,92-Ditko-a; Devil Brigade in #79,82,83	.40	1.00	2.00
108(Modern Comics-1977)-Reprint	.30	.75	1.50

NOTE: ***Aparo** c-154.* ***Montes/Bache** a-48, 49, 51, 69, 75, 76, 170r.*

FIGHTING DANIEL BOONE
1953
Avon Periodicals

	GD25	FN65	NM94
nn-Kinstler-c/a, 22 pgs.	10.00	30.00	70.00
I.W. Reprint #1-Reprints #1 above; Kinstler-c/a; Lawrence/Alascia-a	1.60	4.00	8.00

FIGHTING DAVY CROCKETT (Formerly Kit Carson)
No. 9, Oct-Nov, 1955
Avon Periodicals

	GD25	FN65	NM94
9-Kinstler-c	5.00	15.00	30.00

FIGHTIN' FIVE, THE (Fightin' 5 #40 on?; formerly Space War; also see The Peacemaker)
July, 1964 - No. 41, Jan, 1967; No. 42, Oct, 1981 - No. 49, Dec, 1982
Charlton Comics

	GD25	FN65	NM94
V2#28-Origin Fightin' Five	3.60	8.00	18.00
29-39,41	2.00	5.00	10.00
40-Peacemaker begins	3.60	8.00	18.00
42-49: Reprints		.60	1.25

FIGHTING FRONTS!
Aug, 1952 - No. 5, Jan, 1953
Harvey Publications

	GD25	FN65	NM94
1	4.00	12.00	22.00
2-Extreme violence; Nostrand/Powell-a	4.20	12.50	25.00
3-5: 3-Powell-a	2.40	6.00	12.00

FIGHTING INDIAN STORIES (See Midget Comics)

FIGHTING INDIANS OF THE WILD WEST!
Mar, 1952 - No. 2, Nov, 1952
Avon Periodicals

	GD25	FN65	NM94
1-Larsen-a; McCann-a(2)	9.15	27.50	55.00
2-Kinstler-c & inside-c only; Larsen, McCann-a	5.85	17.50	35.00
100 Pg. Annual(1952, 25 cents)-Contains three comics rebound; Kinstler-c	17.00	50.00	115.00

FIGHTING LEATHERNECKS
Feb, 1952 - No. 6, Dec, 1952
Toby Press

	GD25	FN65	NM94
1-"Duke's Diary"-full pg. pin-ups by Sparling	9.15	27.50	55.00
2-"Duke's Diary"	6.35	19.00	38.00
3-5-"Gil's Gals"-full pg. pin-ups	6.35	19.00	38.00
6-(Same as No. 3-5?)	4.00	12.00	24.00

FIGHTING MAN, THE (War)
May, 1952 - No. 8, July, 1953
Ajax/Farrell Publications(Excellent Publ.)

	GD25	FN65	NM94
1	5.35	16.00	32.00
2	3.20	8.00	16.00
3-8	2.80	7.00	14.00
Annual 1 (100 pgs, 1952)	13.00	40.00	90.00

FIGHTIN' MARINES (Formerly The Texan; also see Approved Comics)
No. 15, 8/51 - No. 12, 3/53; No. 14, 5/55 - No. 132, 11/76;
No. 133, 10/77 - No. 176, 9/84 (No #13?)
St. John(Approved Comics)/Charlton Comics No. 14 on

	GD25	FN65	NM94
15(#1)-Matt Baker c/a "Leatherneck Jack;" slightly large size; Fightin' Texan No. 16 & 17?	14.00	43.00	100.00
2-1st Canteen Kate by Baker; slightly large size	16.00	48.00	110.00
3-9-Canteen Kate by Matt Baker; Baker c-#2,3,5-11	10.00	30.00	60.00
10-Baker-c	3.60	9.00	18.00
11,12-No Baker-a. 12-Last St. John issue?	2.40	6.00	12.00
14 (5/55; 1st Charlton issue; formerly?)-Canteen Kate by Baker	9.15	27.50	55.00
15-Baker-c	3.60	9.00	18.00
16,18-20-Not Baker-c	2.00	5.00	10.00
17-Canteen Kate by Baker	6.70	20.00	40.00
21-24	2.00	5.00	10.00
25-(68 pgs.)(3/58)-Check-a?	3.60	9.00	18.00
26-(100 pgs.)(8/58)-Check-a(5)	4.70	14.00	28.00
27-50	1.60	4.00	8.00
51-81,83-100: 78-Shotgun Harker & the Chicken series begin	.80	2.00	4.00
82-(100 pgs.)	1.40	3.50	7.00
101-122: 122-Pilot issue for "War" title (Fightin' Marines Presents War)	.60	1.50	3.00
123-176	.30	.75	1.50
120(Modern Comics reprint, 1977)	.30	.75	1.50

NOTE: *No. 14 & 16 (CC) reprint St. John issues; No. 16 reprints St. John insignia on cover.* ***Colan** a-3, 7.* ***Glanzman** c/a-92, 94.* ***Montes/Bache** a-48, 53, 55, 64, 65, 72-74, 77-83, 176r.*

FIGHTING MARSHAL OF THE WILD WEST (See The Hawk)

FIGHTIN' NAVY (Formerly Don Winslow)
No. 74, 1/56 - No. 125, 4-5/66; No. 126, 8/83 - No. 133, 10/84
Charlton Comics

	GD25	FN65	NM94
74	3.60	9.00	18.00
75-81	2.00	5.00	10.00
82-Sam Glanzman-a	1.40	3.50	7.00
83-99,101-105,106-125('66)	1.00	2.50	5.00
100	1.20	3.00	6.00
126-133 (1984)	.30	.75	1.50

NOTE: ***Montes/Bache** a-109.* ***Glanzman** a-131r.*

FIGHTING PRINCE OF DONEGAL, THE (See Movie Comics)

FIGHTIN' TEXAN (Formerly The Texan & Fightin' Marines?)
No. 16, Oct, 1952 - No. 17, Dec, 1952
St. John Publishing Co.

	GD25	FN65	NM94
16,17-Tuska-a each. 17-Cameron-c/a	4.35	13.00	26.00

FIGHTING UNDERSEA COMMANDOS (See Undersea Fighting...)
1952 - No. 5, April, 1953
Avon Periodicals

	GD25	FN65	NM94
1	6.35	19.00	38.00
2	4.35	13.00	26.00
3-5: 3-Ravielli-c. 4-Kinstler-c	4.00	12.00	22.00

FIGHTING WAR STORIES
Aug, 1952 - No. 5, 1953
Men's Publications/Story Comics

	GD25	FN65	NM94
1	4.70	14.00	28.00
2-5	3.00	7.50	15.00

FIGHTING YANK (See America's Best Comics & Startling Comics)
Sept, 1942 - No. 29, Aug, 1949
Nedor/Better Publ./Standard

	GD25	FN65	NM94
1-The Fighting Yank begins; Mystico, the Wonder Man app; bondage-c	100.00	300.00	600.00
2	46.00	138.00	275.00
3	31.00	92.00	185.00
4	24.00	72.00	145.00
5-10: 7-The Grim Reaper app.	18.00	55.00	110.00
11-20: 11-The Oracle app. 12-Hirohito bondage-c. 15-Bondage/torture-c. 18-The American Eagle app.	17.00	50.00	100.00
21,23,24: 21-Kara, Jungle Princess app. 24-Miss Masque app.			

Fighting Fronts! #1, © HARV

Fighting Leathernecks #4, © TOBY

The Fighting Yank #1, © STD

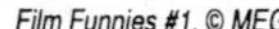
Film Funnies #1, © MEG

Firestorm #5, © DC

1st Issue Special #13, © DC

	GD25	FN65	NM94
	18.00	55.00	110.00
22-Miss Masque-c/story	22.00	68.00	135.00
25-Robinson/Meskin-a; strangulation, lingerie panel; The Cavalier app.	22.00	68.00	135.00
26-29: All-Robinson/Meskin-a. 28-One pg. Williamson-a	18.00	55.00	110.00

NOTE: *Schomburg (Xela) c-4-29; airbrush-c 28, 29. Bondage c-4, 8, 11, 15, 17.*

FIGHT THE ENEMY
Aug, 1966 - No. 3, Mar, 1967 (25 cents, 68 pgs.)
Tower Comics

	GD25	FN65	NM94
1-Lucky 7 & Mike Manly begin	4.00	10.00	20.00
2-Boris Vallejo, McWilliams-a	4.00	10.00	20.00
3-Wood-a pg; McWilliams, Bolle-a	3.20	8.00	16.00

FILM FUNNIES
Nov, 1949 - No. 2, Feb, 1950 (52 pgs.)
Marvel Comics (CPC)

	GD25	FN65	NM94
1-Krazy Krow	11.00	32.00	75.00
2	9.15	27.50	55.00

FILM STARS ROMANCES
Jan-Feb, 1950 - No. 3, May-June, 1950
Star Publications

	GD25	FN65	NM94
1-Rudy Valentino story; L. B. Cole-c; lingerie panels	17.00	51.00	120.00
2-Liz Taylor/Robert Taylor photo-c	19.00	57.00	130.00
3-Photo-c	14.00	43.00	100.00

FINAL CYCLE, THE (Dragon's Teeth) (Value: cover or less)

FIRE AND BLAST
1952 (16 pgs.; paper cover) (Giveaway)
National Fire Protection Assoc.

	GD25	FN65	NM94
nn-Mart Baily A-Bomb-c; about fire prevention	12.00	36.00	85.00

FIRE BALL XL5 (See Steve Zodiac & The ...)

FIRE CHIEF AND THE SAFE OL' FIREFLY, THE
1952 (16 pgs.) (Safety brochure given away at schools)
National Board of Fire Underwriters (produced by American Visuals Corp.) (Eisner)

	GD25	FN65	NM94
nn-(Rare) Eisner-c/a	50.00	150.00	350.00

FIREHAIR COMICS (Formerly Pioneer West Romances #3-6; also see Rangers Comics)
Winter/48-49 - No. 2, Wint/49-50; No. 7, Spr/51 - No. 11, Spr/52
Fiction House Magazines (Flying Stories)

	GD25	FN65	NM94
1	26.00	78.00	180.00
2	12.00	36.00	85.00
7-11	10.00	30.00	70.00
I.W. Reprint 8-Kinstler-c; reprints Rangers #57; Dr. Drew story by Grandenetti (nd)	2.00	5.00	10.00

FIRESTAR
March, 1986 - No. 4, June, 1986 (From Spider-Man TV series)
Marvel Comics Group

	GD25	FN65	NM94
1-X-Men & New Mutants app.	.60	1.50	3.00
2-Wolverine-c by Art Adams (p)	1.20	3.00	6.00
3,4	.40	1.00	2.00

FIRESTONE (See Donald And Mickey Merry Christmas)

FIRESTORM (See Cancelled Comic Cavalcade, DC Comics Presents, Flash #289, The Fury of... & Justice League of America #179)
March, 1978 - No. 5, Oct-Nov, 1978
DC Comics

	GD25	FN65	NM94
1-Origin & 1st app.	.60	1.50	3.00
2-5: 2-Origin Multiplex. 3-Origin Killer Frost. 4-1st app. Hyena	.40	1.00	2.00

FIRESTORM, THE NUCLEAR MAN (Formerly Fury of Firestorm)
No. 65, Nov, 1987 - No. 100, Aug, 1990
DC Comics

	GD25	FN65	NM94
65-99: 66-1st app. Zuggernaut; Firestorm vs. Green Lantern. 71-Death of Capt. X. 67,68-Millennium tie-ins. 83-1st new look		.50	1.00
100-($2.95, 68 pgs.)	.60	1.50	3.00
Annual 5 (10/87)-1st app. new Firestorm		.60	1.25

FIRST ADVENTURES (First) (Value: cover or less)

FIRST AMERICANS, THE (See 4-Color No. 843)

FIRST CHRISTMAS, THE (3-D)
1953 (25 cents) (Oversized - 8-1/4x10-1/4")
Fiction House Magazines (Real Adv. Publ. Co.)

	GD25	FN65	NM94
nn-(Scarce)-Kelly Freas-c; Biblical theme, birth of Christ; Nativity-c	34.00	102.00	240.00

FIRST COMICS GRAPHIC NOVEL
Jan, 1984 - No. 20? (52-176 pgs, high quality paper)
First Comics

	GD25	FN65	NM94
1-Beowulf ($5.95)	1.20	3.00	6.00
1-2nd printing ($6.95)	1.40	3.50	7.00
2-Time Beavers ($5.95)	1.20	3.00	6.00
3($11.95, 100 pgs.)-American Flagg! Hard Times. (2 printings)	2.40	6.00	12.00
4-Nexus ($6.95)-r/B&W 1-3	1.60	4.00	8.00
5-The Enchanted Apples of Oz ($7.95, 52pp)-Intro by Harlan Ellison (1986)	1.60	4.00	8.00
6-Elric of Melnibone ($14.95, 176pp)-Reprints with new color	3.00	7.50	15.00
7-The Secret Island Of Oz ($7.95)	1.60	4.00	8.00
8-Teenage Mutant Ninja Turtles Book I (132 pgs., r/TMNT #1-3 in color w/12 pgs. new-a ($9.95)-Origin	2.00	5.00	10.00
9-Time 2: The Epiphany by Chaykin, 52 pgs. ($7.95)	1.60	4.00	8.00
10-Teenage Mutant Ninja Turtles Book II ($9.95)-r/TMNT #4-6 in color	2.00	5.00	10.00
11-Sailor On The Sea of Fate ($14.95)	3.00	7.50	15.00
12-American Flagg! Southern Comfort ($11.95)	2.40	6.00	12.00
13-The Ice King Of Oz ($7.95)	1.60	4.00	8.00
14-Teenage Mutant Ninja Turtles Book III ($9.95)-r/TMNT #7,8 in color plus new 12 pg. story	2.00	5.00	10.00
15-Hex Breaker: Badger ($7.95, 64 pgs.)	1.60	4.00	8.00
16-The Forgotten Forest of Oz ($8.95)	1.80	4.50	9.00
17-Mazinger (64 pgs., $8.95)	1.80	4.50	9.00
18-Teenage Mutant Ninja Turtles Book IV ($9.95)-r/TMNT #10,11 plus 3 pg. fold-out	2.00	5.00	10.00
19-The Original Nexus Graphic Novel ($7.95, 104pgs)-Reprints First Comics Graphic Novel #4 ($7.95)	1.60	4.00	8.00
20-American Flagg!: State of the Union; r/A.F. 7-9 ($11.95, 96 pgs.)	2.40	6.00	12.00

NOTE: *Most or all issues have been reprinted.*

1ST FOLIO (The Joe Kubert School Presents...)
March, 1984 ($1.50, color)
Pacific Comics

	GD25	FN65	NM94
1-Kubert-c/a(2pgs.); Adam & Andy Kubert-a	.25	.75	1.50

1ST ISSUE SPECIAL
April, 1975 - No. 13, April, 1976
National Periodical Publications

1-7,9-13: 1-Intro. Atlas; Kirby-c/a. 2-Green Team (see Cancelled Comic Cavalcade). 3-Metamorpho by Ramona Fraden. 4-Lady Cop. 5-Manhunter; Kirby-c/a. 6-Dingbats; Kirby-c/a. 7-The Creeper by Ditko(c/a). 9-Dr. Fate; Kubert-c; Simonson-a. 10-The Outsiders. 11-Code Name:

GD25 FN65 NM94

Assassin; Grell-c. 12-Origin/1st app. new Starman; Kubert-c. 13-Return of the New Gods; Darkseid app.; 1st new costume Orion; predates New Gods #12 by more than a year (try out issue) .40 1.00 2.00
8-Origin/1st app. The Warlord; Grell-c/a 3.00 7.50 15.00

FIRST KISS
Dec, 1957 - No. 40, Jan, 1965
Charlton Comics

V1#1 2.40 6.00 12.00
V1#2-10 1.20 3.00 6.00
11-40 .70 1.75 3.50

FIRST LOVE ILLUSTRATED
2/49 - No. 9, 6/50; No. 10, 1/51 - No. 86, 3/58; No. 87, 9/58 - No. 88, 11/58; No. 89, 11/62, No. 90, 2/63
Harvey Publications(Home Comics)(True Love)

1-Powell-a(2) 7.50 22.50 45.00
2-Powell-a 4.00 12.00 24.00
3-"Was I Too Fat To Be Loved" story 4.00 12.00 24.00
4-10 3.60 9.00 18.00
11-30: 30-Lingerie panel 2.00 5.00 10.00
31-34,37,39-49: 49-Last pre-code (2/55) 1.80 4.50 9.00
35-Used in **SOTI**, illo-"The title of this comic book is First Love" 7.50 22.50 45.00
36-Communism story, "Love Slaves" 2.80 7.00 14.00
38-Nostrand-a 4.00 11.00 21.00
50-90 1.40 3.50 7.00
NOTE: ***Disbrow** a-13. **Orlando** c-87. **Powell** a-1, 3-5, 7, 10, 11, 13-17, 19-24, 26-29, 33,35-41, 43, 45, 46, 50, 54, 55, 57, 58, 61-63, 65, 71-73, 76, 79r, 82, 84, 88.*

FIRST MEN IN THE MOON (See Movie Comics)

FIRST ROMANCE MAGAZINE
8/49 - #6, 6/50; #7, 6/51 - #50, 2/58; #51, 9/58 - #52, 11/58
Home Comics(Harvey Publ.)/True Love

1 7.50 22.50 45.00
2 4.00 12.00 24.00
3-5 4.00 10.00 20.00
6-10 3.20 8.00 16.00
11-20 2.40 6.00 12.00
21-27,29-32: 32-Last pre-code issue (2/55) 1.80 4.50 9.00
28-Nostrand-a(Powell swipe) 3.60 9.00 18.00
33-52 1.40 3.50 7.00
NOTE: ***Powell** a-1-5, 8-10, 14, 18, 20-22, 24, 25, 28, 36, 46, 48, 51.*

FIRST TRIP TO THE MOON (See Space Adventures No. 20)

FISH POLICE (Fishwrap/Apple) (Value: cover or less)

FISH POLICE
V2#1, Oct, 1992 - Present ($1.25, color)
Marvel Comics

V2#1-8: 1-Hairballs Saga begins; r/#1 ('85) .60 1.25

5-STAR SUPER-HERO SPECTACULAR (See DC Special Series No. 1)

FLAME, THE (See Big 3 & Wonderworld Comics)
Summer, 1940 - No. 8, Jan, 1942 (#1,2: 68 pgs; #3-8: 44 pgs.)
Fox Features Syndicate

1-Flame stories from Wonderworld #5-9; origin The Flame; Lou Fine-a (36 pgs.), r/Wonderworld #3,10 167.00 500.00 1000.00
2-Fine-a(2). Wing Turner by Tuska 83.00 250.00 500.00
3-8: 3-Powell-a 50.00 150.00 300.00

FLAME, THE (Formerly Lone Eagle)
No. 5, Dec-Jan, 1954-55 - No. 3, April-May, 1955
Ajax/Farrell Publications (Excellent Publ.)

5(#1) 19.00 57.00 115.00
2,3 14.00 42.00 85.00

FLAMING CARROT (...Comics #6? on; also see Anything Goes, Cerebus & Visions)
5/84 - No. 5, 1/85; No. 6, 3/85 - Present ($1.70-$2.00, B&W)
Aardvark-Vanaheim/Renegade Press #6-17/Dark Horse #18 on

1-Bob Burden story/art 6.35 19.00 38.00
2 4.20 12.50 25.00
3 3.60 9.00 18.00
4-6 2.40 6.00 12.00
7-9 1.60 4.00 8.00
10-12 .80 2.00 4.00
13-15 .60 1.50 3.00
15-Variant without cover price 1.60 4.00 8.00
16-20: 18-1st Dark Horse issue .60 1.50 3.00
21-23,25: 25-Contains trading cards; TMNT app. .40 1.00 2.00
24-($2.50, 52 pgs.)-10th anniversary issue .50 1.25 2.50
26-28: 26-Begin $2.25-c. 26,27-Teenage Mutant Ninja Turtles x-over. 27-Todd McFarlane-c .45 1.15 2.25
29,30-($2.50-c) .50 1.25 2.50

FLAMING CARROT COMICS (Also see Junior Carrot Patrol)
Summer-Fall, 1981 ($1.95, One Shot) (Large size, 8x11)
Killian Barracks Press

1-By Bob Burden 11.00 32.00 75.00

FLAMING LOVE
Dec, 1949 - No. 6, Oct, 1950 (Photo covers #2-6)
Quality Comics Group (Comic Magazines)

1-Ward-c/a (9 pgs.) 19.00 58.00 135.00
2 10.00 30.00 60.00
3-Ward-a (9 pgs.); Crandall-a 13.00 40.00 90.00
4-6: 4-Gustavson-a 9.15 27.50 55.00

FLAMING WESTERN ROMANCES (Formerly Target Western Romances)
No. 3, Mar-Apr, 1950
Star Publications

3-Robert Taylor, Arlene Dahl photo on-c with biographies inside; L. B. Cole-c 20.00 60.00 140.00

FLARE (Also see Champions for 1st app. & League of Champions)
Nov, 1988 - No. 3?, 1989 ($2.75, color, 52 pgs)
V2#1, Nov, 1990 - No. 7, 1991 ($2.95, color, mature readers, 52 pgs.)
Hero Comics/Hero Graphics Vol. 2 on

1-3 .55 1.40 2.75
V2#1-3 ($2.95) .60 1.50 3.00
V2#4-6,8-10: 4-Begin $3.50-c. 5-Eternity Smith returns. 6-Intro The Tigress .70 1.75 3.50
V2#7 ($3.95) .80 2.00 4.00
Annual 1(1992, $4.50, B&W, 52 pgs.)-Champions-r .90 2.25 4.50

FLARE ADVENTURES
Feb, 1992 (90 cents, color, 20 pgs.)
Hero Graphics

1 .50 1.00

FLASH, THE (See Adventure, The Brave and the Bold, Crisis On Infinite Earths, DC Comics Presents, DC Special, DC Special Series, DC Super-Stars, Green Lantern; Justice League of America, Showcase, Super Team Family, & World's Finest)

FLASH, THE (Formerly Flash Comics)
No. 105, Feb-Mar, 1959 - No. 350, Oct, 1985
National Periodical Publ./DC Comics

Showcase #4 (9-10/56)-Origin/1st app. The Flash (1st DC S.A. superhero) & The Turtle; Kubert-a 1175.00 3525.00 9400.00
Showcase #8 (5-6/57)-2nd app. The Flash; origin & 1st app. Capt. Cold 543.00 1630.00 3800.00
Showcase #13 (3-4/58)-Origin Mr. Element 230.00 685.00 1600.00
Showcase #14 (5-6/58)-Origin Dr. Alchemy, formerly Mr. Element 230.00 685.00 1600.00
105-(2-3/59)-Origin Flash(retold), & Mirror Master 285.00 860.00 2000.00
106-Origin Grodd & Pied Piper; Flash's 1st visit to Gorilla City; begin Grodd

The Flame #1, © FOX

Flaming Western Romances #3, © STAR

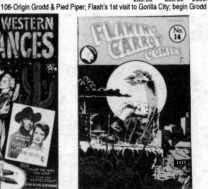

Flaming Carrot #14, © Bob Burden

The Flash #113, © DC

The Flash #229 © DC

The Flash #6, DC

	GD25	FN65	NM94
the Super Gorilla trilogy, ends #108 (Scarce)	93.00	280.00	650.00
107,108-Grodd trilogy ends	47.00	140.00	325.00
109	43.00	130.00	300.00
110-Intro/origin The Weather Wizard & Kid Flash who later becomes Flash in Crisis On Infinite Earths #12; begin Kid Flash trilogy, ends #112 (also in #114,116,118)	82.00	245.00	575.00
111	25.00	75.00	175.00
112-Origin & 1st app. Elongated Man (4-5/60); also apps. in #115,119,130	29.00	85.00	200.00
113-Origin & 1st app. Trickster	29.00	85.00	200.00
114-Captain Cold app. (see Showcase #8)	22.00	65.00	150.00
115,116,118-120: 119-Elongated Man marries Sue Dearborn. 120-Flash & Kid Flash team-up for 1st time	16.00	48.00	110.00
117-Origin & 1st app. Capt. Boomerang	22.00	65.00	150.00
121,122: 122-Origin & 1st app. The Top	11.50	34.00	80.00
123-Re-intro. Golden Age Flash; origins of both Flashes; 1st mention of an Earth II where DC G. A. heroes live	85.00	260.00	600.00
124-Last 10 cent issue	11.00	32.00	75.00
125-128,130: 128-Origin Abra Kadabra	10.00	30.00	65.00
129-2nd G.A. Flash x-over; J.S.A. cameo in flashback	25.00	75.00	175.00
131-136,138,140: 131-Early Green Lantern x-over (9/62). 136-1st Dexter Miles. 140-Origin & 1st app. Heat Wave	10.00	30.00	65.00
137-G.A. Flash x-over; J.S.A. cameo (1st S.A. app.)(1st real app. since 2-3/51); 1st S.A. app. Vandall Savage; JSA team decides to re-form	39.00	120.00	275.00
139-Origin & 1st app. Prof. Zoom	12.00	36.00	85.00
141-150: 142-Trickster app.	7.50	22.50	45.00
151-G.A. Flash vs. The Shade	10.00	30.00	60.00
152-159	5.00	15.00	30.00
160-(80-Pg. Giant G-21); G.A. Flash & Johnny Quick-r	6.70	20.00	40.00
161-168,170: 165-Silver Age Flash weds Iris West. 167-New facts about Flash's origin. 168-Green Lantern-c/story. 170-Dr. Mid-Nite, Dr. Fate, G.A. Flash x-over	4.20	12.50	25.00
169-(80-Pg. Giant G-34)-New facts about origin	6.70	20.00	40.00
171-174,176,177,179,180: 171-JLA, Green Lantern, Atom flashbacks. 173-G.A. Flash x-over. 174-Barry Allen reveals I.D. to wife	4.00	10.00	20.00
175-2nd Superman/Flash race (12/67; see Superman #199 & World's Finest #198,199); JLA cameo	11.50	34.00	80.00
178-(80-Pg. Giant G-46)	4.70	14.00	28.00
181-186,188-195,197-200: 186-Re-intro. Sargon	2.00	5.00	10.00
187,196: (68-Pg. Giants G-58, G-70)	3.60	9.00	18.00
201-204,206-210: 201-New G.A. Flash story. 208-52 pg. begin, end #213, 215,216. 206-Elongated Man begins	1.20	3.00	6.00
205-(68-Pg. Giant G-82)	2.00	5.00	10.00
211-213,216,220: 211-G.A. Flash origin-r/#104. 213-Reprints #137	1.20	3.00	6.00
214-DC 100 Page Super Spectacluar DC-11; origin Metal Men-r/Showcase #37; never before pubbed G.A. Flash story	1.60	4.00	8.00
215 (52 pgs.)-Flash-r/Showcase #4; G.A. Flash x-over, reprinted in #216	2.40	6.00	12.00
217-219: Neal Adams-a in all. 217-Green Lantern/Green Arrow series begins. 219-Last Green Arrow	2.00	5.00	10.00
221-225,227,228,230,231	1.20	3.00	6.00
226-Neal Adams-a	1.60	4.00	8.00
229,232,233-(All 100pgs.)-G.A. Flash-r & new-a	1.40	3.50	7.00
234-274,277-288,290: 243-Death of The Top. 245-Origin The Floronic Man in Green Lantern back-up, ends #246. 246-Last Green Lantern. 256-Death of The Top retold. 250-Intro Golden Glider. 265-267-(44 pgs.). 267-Origin of Flash's uniform. 270-Intro The Clown. 286-Intro/origin Rainbow Raider	.60	1.50	3.00
275,276-Iris West Allen dies	.60	1.50	3.00

	GD25	FN65	NM94
289-Perez 1st DC art; new Firestorm series begins, ends #304	1.00	2.50	5.00
291-299,301-305: 291-Intro/origin Colonel Computron. 298-Intro/origin new Shade. 301-Atomic Bomb-c. 303-The Top returns. 305-G.A. Flash x-over	.50	1.25	2.50
300-(52pgs.)-Origin Flash retold; 25th ann. issue	.80	2.00	4.00
306-Dr. Fate by Giffen begins, ends #313	.50	1.25	2.50
307-313-Giffen-a. 309-Origin Flash retold	.40	1.00	2.00
314-349: 318-323-Creeper back-ups. 323,324-Two part Flash vs. Flash story. 324-Death of Reverse Flash (Prof. Zoom). 328-Iris West Allen's death retold. 344-Origin Kid Flash	.40	1.00	2.00
350-Double size ($1.25)	1.00	2.50	5.00
Annual 1(10-12/63, 84pgs.)-Origin Elongated Man & Kid Flash-r; origin Grodd; G.A. Flash-r	35.00	107.00	250.00

NOTE: ***N. Adams*** *c-194, 195, 203, 204, 206-208, 211, 213, 215, 246.* ***M. Anderson*** *a-202i.* ***Austin*** *a-233i, 234i, 246i.* ***Buckler*** *a-271p, 272p; c(p)-247-250, 252, 253p, 255, 256p, 258, 262, 265-267, 269-271.* ***Giffen*** *a-306-313p; c-310p, 315.* ***Sid Greene*** *a-167-174i, 229i(r).* ***Grell*** *a-237p, 238p, 240-243p; c-236.* ***Infantino/Giella*** *c-105-112.* ***G. Kane*** *a-195p, 197-199p, 229r, 232r; c-197-199, 312p.* ***Kubert*** *a-108p, 215i(r); c-189-191.* ***Lopez*** *c-272.* ***Meskin*** *a-229r, 232r.* ***Perez*** *a-289-293p; c-293.* ***Starlin*** *a-294-296p.* ***Staton*** *c-263p, 264p. Green Lantern x-over-131, 143, 168, 171, 191.*

FLASH
June, 1987 - Present (75 cents, $1.00 #17 on)
DC Comics

	GD25	FN65	NM94
1-Guice-c/a begins; New Teen Titans app.	1.00	2.50	5.00
2,3: 3-Intro. Kilgore	.60	1.50	3.00
4-10: 4-Intro. Speed McGee. 7-1st app. Blue Trinity. 8,9-Millennium tie-ins. 9-1st app. The Chunk	.50	1.25	2.50
11-20: 12-Free extra 16 pg. Dr. Light story. 19-Free extra 16 pg. Flash story	.40	1.00	2.00
21-30: 28-Capt. Cold app. 29-New Phantom Lady app.	.30	.75	1.50
31-49,51-65: 40-Dr. Alchemy app. 62-Flash: Year One begins, ends #65. 65-Last $1.00-c		.50	1.00
50-($1.75, 52 pgs.)	.35	.90	1.75
66-75: 66-Aquaman app. 69-Green Lantern app. 70-Gorilla Grodd story ends		.60	1.25
Annual 1 (1987, $1.25)	.40	1.00	2.00
Annual 2 (1988, $1.50)	.35	.90	1.75
Annual 3 (1989, $1.75, 68 pgs.)-Gives history of G.A., Silver Age, & new Flash in text	.35	.90	1.75
Annual 4 (1991, $2.00, 68 pgs.)-Armaggedon 2001	.40	1.00	2.00
Annual 5 (1992, $2.50, 68 pgsd.)-Eclipso-c/story	.50	1.25	2.50
Special 1 (1990, $2.95, 84 pgs.)-50th anniversary issue; Kubert-c	.60	1.50	3.00
...TV Special 1 (1991, $3.95, 76 pgs.)-Photo-c plus behind the scenes photos of TV show; Saltares-a, Byrne scripts	.80	2.00	4.00

NOTE: ***Guice*** *a-1-9p, 11p, Annual 1p; c-1-9p, Annual 1p.* ***Perez*** *c-15-17, Annual 2i.*

FLASH COMICS (Whiz Comics No. 2 on)
Jan, 1940 (12 pgs., B&W, regular size)
(Not distributed to newsstands; printed for in-house use)
Fawcett Publications

NOTE: ***Whiz Comics*** *#2 was preceded by two books,* ***Flash Comics*** *and* ***Thrill Comics****, both dated Jan, 1940, (12 pgs, B&W, regular size) and were not distributed. These two books are identical except for the title, and were sent out to major distributors as ad copies to promote sales. It is believed that the complete 68 page issue of Fawcett's* ***Flash*** *and* ***Thrill Comics*** *#1 was finished and ready for publication with the January date. Since D.C. Comics was also about to publish a book with the same date and title, Fawcett hurriedly printed up the black and white version of* ***Flash Comics*** *to secure copyright before D.C. The inside covers are blank, with the covers and inside pages printed on a high quality uncoated paper stock.The eight page origin story of Captain Thunder is composed of pages 1-7 and 13 of the Captain Marvel story essentially as they appeared in the first issue of* ***Whiz Comics****. The balloon dialogue on page thirteen was relettered to tie the story into the end of page seven in* ***Flash*** *and* ***Thrill Comics*** *to produce a shorter version of the origin story for copyright purposes. Obviously, D.C. acquired the copyright and Fawcett dropped* ***Flash*** *as well as* ***Thrill*** *and came out with* ***Whiz Comics*** *a month later. Fawcett never used the cover to* ***Flash*** *and* ***Thrill*** *#1, designing a new cover for* ***Whiz Comics****. Fawcett also must have discovered that Captain*

*Thunder had already been used by another publisher (Captain Terry Thunder by Fiction House). All references to Captain Thunder were relettered to Captain Marvel before appearing in **Whiz**.*

1 (nn on-c, #1 on inside)-Origin & 1st app. Captain Thunder. Eight copies of Flash and three copies of Thrill exist. All 3 copies of Thrill sold in 1986 for between $4,000-$10,000 each. A NM copy of Thrill sold in 1987 for $12,000. A vg copy of Thrill sold in 1987 for $9000 cash; another copy sold in 1987 for $2000 cash, $10,000 trade; cover by Leo O'Mealia

FLASH COMICS (The Flash No. 105 on) (Also see All-Flash)
Jan, 1940 - No. 104, Feb, 1949
National Periodical Publications/All-American

	GD25	FN65	VF82	NM94
1-The Flash (origin/1st app.) by Harry Lampert, Hawkman (origin/1st app.) by Gardner Fox, The Whip, & Johnny Thunder (origin/1st app.) by Stan Asch; Cliff Cornwall by Moldoff, Flash Picture Novelets (later Minute Movies) begin; Moldoff (Shelly) cover; 1st app. Shiera Sanders who later becomes Hawkgirl, #24; reprinted in Famous First Edition (on sale 11/10/39)	2000.00	6000.00	12,000.00	20,000.00

(Estimated up to 75+ total copies exist, 7 in NM/Mint)

	GD25	FN65	NM94
2-Rod Rian begins, ends #11	400.00	1200.00	2400.00
3-King Standish begins, ends #41 (called The King #16-37,39-41); E.E. Hibbard-a begins on Flash	333.00	1000.00	2000.00
4-Moldoff (Shelly) Hawkman begins	275.00	825.00	1650.00
5, 6: 6-2nd Flash-	250.00	750.00	1500.00
7-10: 8-Male bondage-c	150.00	450.00	900.00
11-20: 12-Les Watts begins; "Sparks" #16 on. 17-Last Cliff Cornwall	108.00	325.00	650.00
21-23	92.00	275.00	550.00
24-Shiera becomes Hawkgirl (12/41)	125.00	375.00	750.00
25-30: 28-Last Les Sparks. 29-Ghost Patrol begins(origin, 1st app.), ends #104	75.00	225.00	450.00
31-40: 33-Origin Shade	67.00	200.00	400.00
41-50	62.00	188.00	375.00
51-61: 59-Last Minute Movies. 61-Last Moldoff Hawkman	50.00	150.00	300.00
62-Hawkman by Kubert begins	67.00	20.00	400.00
63-70: 66-68-Hop Harrigan in all. 70-Mutt & Jeff app.	50.00	150.00	300.00
71-85: 80-Atom begins, ends #104	50.00	150.00	300.00
86-Intro. The Black Canary in Johnny Thunder; rare in Mint due to black ink smearing on white cover	150.00	450.00	900.00
87-90: 88-Origin Ghost. 89-Intro villain Thorn	71.00	212.00	425.00
91,93-99: 98-Atom dons new costume	79.00	238.00	475.00
92-1st solo Black Canary	125.00	375.00	750.00
100 (10/48),103(Scarce)-52 pgs. each	150.00	450.00	900.00
101,102(Scarce)	117.00	350.00	700.00
104-Origin The Flash retold (Scarce)	283.00	850.00	1700.00
Wheaties Giveaway (1946, 32 pgs., 6-1/2x8-1/4")-Johnny Thunder, Ghost Patrol, The Flash & Kubert Hawkman app. NOTE: All known copies were taped to Wheaties boxes and are never found in mint condition. Copies with light tape residue bring the listed prices in all grades	170.00	500.00	–

NOTE: ***E.E. Hibbard** c-6, 12, 20, 24, 26, 28, 30, 44, 46, 48, 50, 62, 66, 68, 69, 72, 74, 76, 78, 80, 82. **Infantino** a-86p, 90, 93-95, 99-104; c-90, 92, 93, 97, 99, 101, 103. **Kinstler** a-87, 89(Hawkman); c-87. **Chet Kozlak** c-77, 79, 81. **Krigstein** a-94. **Kubert** a-62-76, 83, 85, 86, 88-104; c-63, 65, 67, 70, 71, 73, 75, 83, 85, 86, 88, 89, 91, 94, 96, 98, 100, 104. **Moldoff** a-3; c-3, 7-11, 13-17, plus odd #'s 19-61. **Martin Naydell** c-52, 54, 56, 58, 60, 64, 84.*

FLASH DIGEST, THE (See DC Special Series #24)

FLASH GORDON (See Defenders Of The Earth, Eat Right to Work..., Feature Book #25, Giant Comic Album, King Classics, King Comics, March of Comics #118, 133, 142, The Phantom #18, Street Comix & Wow Comics, 1st series)

FLASH GORDON
No. 10, 1943 - No. 512, Nov, 1953
Dell Publishing Co.

4-Color 10(1943)-by Alex Raymond; reprints "The Ice Kingdom"

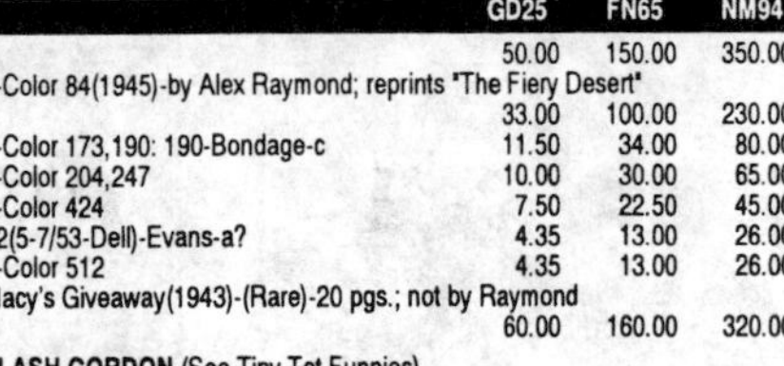

	GD25	FN65	NM94
	50.00	150.00	350.00
4-Color 84(1945)-by Alex Raymond; reprints "The Fiery Desert"	33.00	100.00	230.00
4-Color 173,190: 190-Bondage-c	11.50	34.00	80.00
4-Color 204,247	10.00	30.00	65.00
4-Color 424	7.50	22.50	45.00
2(5-7/53-Dell)-Evans-a?	4.35	13.00	26.00
4-Color 512	4.35	13.00	26.00
Macy's Giveaway(1943)-(Rare)-20 pgs.; not by Raymond	60.00	160.00	320.00

FLASH GORDON (See Tiny Tot Funnies)
Oct, 1950 - No. 4, April, 1951
Harvey Publications

	GD25	FN65	NM94
1-Alex Raymond-a; bondage-c; reprints strips from 7/14/40 to 12/8/40	17.00	51.00	120.00
2-Alex Raymond-a; r/strips 12/15/40-4/27/41	13.00	40.00	90.00
3,4-Alex Raymond-a; 3-bondage-c; r/strips 5/4/41-9/21/41. 4-r/strips 10/24/37-3/27/38	12.00	36.00	80.00

5-(Rare)-Small size-5-1/2x8-1/2"; B&W; 32 pgs.; Distributed to some mail subscribers only. Estimated value $200.00-$300.00

(Also see All-New No. 15, Boy Explorers No. 2, and Stuntman No. 3)

FLASH GORDON
1951 (Paper cover; 16 pgs. in color; regular size)
Harvey Comics (Gordon Bread giveaway)

	GD25	FN65	NM94
1,2: 1-r/strips 10/24/37 - 2/6/38. 2-r/strips 7/14/40 - 10/6/40; Reprints by Raymond each....	1.50	4.50	10.00

NOTE: *Most copies have brittle edges.*

FLASH GORDON
June, 1965
Gold Key

	GD25	FN65	NM94
1 (1947 reprint)-Painted-c	2.30	7.00	16.00

FLASH GORDON (Also see Comics Reading Libraries)
9/66 - #11, 12/67; #12, 2/69 - #18, 1/70; #19, 10-11/78 - #37, 3/82
(Painted covers No. 19-30, 34)
King #1-11/Charlton #12-18/Gold Key #19-23/Whitman #28 on

	GD25	FN65	NM94
1-Army giveaway(1968)("Complimentary" on cover)(Same as regular #1 minus Mandrake story & back-c)	2.40	6.00	12.00
1-Williamson c/a(2); E.C. swipe/Incredible S.F. #32. Mandrake story	3.60	9.00	18.00
2-Bolle, Gil Kane-c; Mandrake story	2.40	6.00	12.00
3-Williamson-c	2.80	7.00	14.00
4-Secret Agent X-9 begins, Williamson-c/a(3)	2.80	7.00	14.00
5-Williamson-c/a(2)	2.80	7.00	14.00
6,8-Crandall-a. 8-Secret Agent X-9-r	3.60	9.00	18.00
7-Raboy-a	2.80	7.00	14.00
9,10-Raymond-r. 10-Buckler's 1st pro work (11/67); Briggs-c	3.20	8.00	16.00
11-Crandall-a	2.40	6.00	12.00
12-Crandall-c/a	2.80	7.00	14.00
13-Jeff Jones-a (15 pgs.)	2.80	7.00	14.00
14-17: 17-Brick Bradford story	1.40	3.50	7.00
18-Kaluta-a (3rd pro work?)(see Teen Confess.)	1.60	4.00	8.00
19(9/78, G.K.), 20-30(10/80)	.60	1.50	3.00
30 (7/81; re-issue)	.30	.75	1.50
31-33: Movie adaptation; Williamson-a	.30	.75	1.50
34-37: Movie adaptation		.60	1.25

NOTE: ***Aparo** a-8. **Bolle** a-21, 22. **Boyette** a-14-18. **Buckler** a-10. **Crandall** c-6. **Estrada** a-3. **Gene Fawcette** a-29, 30, 34, 37. **McWilliams** a-31-33, 36.*

FLASH GORDON
June, 1988 - No. 9, Holiday, 1988-'89 ($1.25, color, mini-series)
DC Comics

	GD25	FN65	NM94
1-Painted-c	.25	.75	1.50
2-9: 5-Painted-c		.60	1.25

Flash Comics #20, © DC

Flash Comics #89, © DC

Flash Gordon #3 (HARV), © KING

The Flintstones #5 (Gold Key), © Hanna-Barbera

Flip #1, © HARV

Flying Aces #2, © Key Publ.

FLASH GORDON THE MOVIE
1980 ($1.95. color, 68 pgs., 8-1/4 x 11")
Western Publishing Co.

	GD25	FN65	NM94
11294-Williamson-c/a; adapts movie	.35	1.00	2.00
13743-Hardback edition	.85	2.50	5.00

FLASH SPECTACULAR, THE (See DC Special Series No. 11)

FLAT-TOP
11/53 - No. 3, 5/54; No. 4, 3/55 - No. 6, 7/55
Mazie Comics/Harvey Publ.(Magazine Publ.) No. 4 on

	GD25	FN65	NM94
1-Teenage	3.60	9.00	18.00
2,3	2.00	5.00	10.00
4-6	1.60	4.00	8.00

FLAXEN (Dark Horse)(Value: cover or less)

FLESH AND BONES (Fantagraphics)(Value: cover or less)

FLINTSTONE KIDS, THE (TV; See Star Comics Digest)
Aug, 1987 - No. 11, April, 1989
Star Comics/Marvel Comics #5 on

	GD25	FN65	NM94
1-11		.50	1.00

FLINTSTONES, THE (TV)(See Dell Giant #48 for No. 1)
No. 2, Nov-Dec, 1961 - No. 60, Sept, 1970 (Hanna-Barbera)
Dell Publ. Co./Gold Key No. 7 (10/62) on

	GD25	FN65	NM94
2	9.15	27.50	55.00
3-6(7-8/62)	6.35	19.00	38.00
7 (10/62; 1st GK)	6.35	19.00	38.00
8-10: Mr. & Mrs. J. Evil Scientist begin?	5.35	16.00	32.00
11-1st app. Pebbles (6/63)	7.50	22.50	45.00
12-15,17-20	4.70	14.00	28.00
16-1st app. Bamm-Bamm (1/64)	5.85	17.50	35.00
21-30: 24-1st app. The Grusomes app.	4.00	11.00	22.00
31-33,35-40: 31-Xmas-c. 33-Meet Frankenstein & Dracula. 39-Reprints	4.00	10.00	20.00
34-1st app. The Great Gazoo	4.70	14.00	28.00
41-60: 45-Last 12 cent issue	3.60	9.00	18.00
At N. Y. World's Fair('64)-J.W. Books(25 cents)-1st printing; no date on-c (29 cent version exists, 2nd print?)	4.70	14.00	28.00
At N. Y. World's Fair (1965 on-c; re-issue). NOTE: Warehouse find in 1984	1.00	2.50	5.00
Bigger & Boulder 1(#30013-211) (Gold Key Giant, 11/62, 25 cents, 84 pgs.)	9.15	27.50	55.00
Bigger & Boulder 2-(25 cents)(1966)-reprints B&B No. 1	7.50	22.50	45.00
...With Pebbles & Bamm Bamm(100 pgs., G.K.)-30028-511 (paper-c, 25 cents)(11/65)	7.50	22.50	45.00

NOTE: *(See Comic Album #16, Bamm-Bamm & Pebbles Flintstone, Dell Giant 48, Marchof Comics #229, 243, 271, 289, 299, 317, 327, 341, Pebbles Flintstone, Top Comics #2-4, and Whitman Comic Books.)*

FLINTSTONES, THE (TV)(...& Pebbles)
Nov, 1970 - No. 50, Feb, 1977 (Hanna-Barbera)
Charlton Comics

	GD25	FN65	NM94
1	5.85	17.50	35.00
2	3.60	9.00	18.00
3-7,9,10	2.40	6.00	12.00
8-"Flintstones Summer Vacation," 52 pgs. (Summer, 1971)	2.80	7.00	14.00
11-20	2.00	5.00	10.00
21-50: 37-Byrne text illos (early work; see Nightmare #20). 36-Mike Zeck illos (early work). 42-Byrne-a (2 pgs.)	1.60	5.00	10.00

(Also see Barney & Betty Rubble, Dino, The Great Gazoo, & Pebbles & Bamm-Bamm)

FLINTSTONES, THE (TV)(See Yogi Bear, 3rd series)
October, 1977 - No. 9, Feb, 1979 (Hanna-Barbera)
Marvel Comics Group

	GD25	FN65	NM94
1-9: Yogi Bear app. 4-The Jetsons app	.40	1.00	2.00

FLINTSTONES, THE
Sept, 1992 - Present ($1.25, color) (Hanna-Barbera)
Harvey Comics

	GD25	FN65	NM94
V2#1-4		.60	1.25
...Big Book 1 (11/92, $1.95, 52 pgs.), 2	.40	1.00	2.00
...Giant Size 1 (10/92, $2.25, 68 pgs.)	.45	1.15	2.25

FLINTSTONES CHRISTMAS PARTY, THE (See The Funtastic World of Hanna-Barbera No. 1)

FLIP
April, 1954 - No. 2, June, 1954 (Satire)
Harvey Publications

	GD25	FN65	NM94
1,2-Nostrand-a each. 2-Powell-a	13.00	40.00	90.00

FLIPPER (TV)
April, 1966 - No. 3, Nov, 1967 (All have photo-c)
Gold Key

	GD25	FN65	NM94
1	5.00	15.00	30.00
2,3	4.00	10.00	20.00

FLIPPITY & FLOP
12-1/51-52 - No. 46, 8-10/59; No. 47, 9-11/60
National Periodical Publ. (Signal Publ. Co.)

	GD25	FN65	NM94
1	14.00	43.00	110.00
2	10.00	30.00	65.00
3-5	7.50	22.50	45.00
6-10	6.70	20.00	40.00
11-20: 20-Last precode (3/55)	4.70	14.00	28.00
21-47	3.60	9.00	18.00

FLOYD FARLAND (See Eclipse Graphic Album Series #11)

FLY, THE (Also see Adventures of..., Blue Ribbon Comics & Flyman)
May, 1983 - No. 9, Oct, 1984
Archie Enterprises, Inc.

	GD25	FN65	NM94
1-9: 1-Mr. Justice app; origin Shield. 2-Flygirl app.		.50	1.00

NOTE: ***Buckler*** *a-1, 2.* ***Ditko*** *a-2-9; c-4-8p.* ***Nebres*** *c-3, 4, 5i, 6, 7i.* ***Steranko*** *c-1, 2.*

FLY, THE
Aug, 1991 - No. 17, Dec, 1992 ($1.00, color)
Impact Comics (DC)

	GD25	FN65	NM94
1-17: 4-Vs. The Black Hood. 9-Trading card inside		.50	1.00
Annual 1 ('92, $2.50, 68 pgs.)-Impact trading card	.50	1.25	2.50

FLY BOY (Also see Approved Comics)
Spring, 1952 - No. 4, 1953
Ziff-Davis Publ. Co. (Approved)

	GD25	FN65	NM94
1-Saunders painted-c	10.00	30.00	60.00
2-Saunders painted-c	6.70	20.00	40.00
3,4-Saunders painted-c	5.00	15.00	30.00

FLYING ACES
July, 1955 - No. 5, March, 1956
Key Publications

	GD25	FN65	NM94
1	3.20	8.00	16.00
2-5: 2-Trapani-a	1.80	4.50	9.00

FLYING A'S RANGE RIDER, THE (TV) (See Western Roundup under Dell Giants)
#404, 6-7/52; #2, June-Aug, 1953 - #24, Aug, 1959 (All photo-c)
Dell Publishing Co.

	GD25	FN65	NM94
4-Color 404(#1)-Titled "The Range Rider"	10.00	30.00	60.00
2	5.85	17.50	35.00
3-10	5.00	15.00	30.00
11-16,18-24	4.70	14.00	28.00
17-Toth-a	5.85	17.50	35.00

	GD25	FN65	NM94

FLYING CADET (WW II Plane Photos)
Jan, 1943 - V2#8, 1947 (Photos, comics)
Flying Cadet Publishing Co.

	GD25	FN65	NM94
V1#1	9.15	27.50	55.00
2	4.70	14.00	28.00
3-9 (Two #6's, Sept. & Oct.)	4.00	12.00	24.00
V2#1-7(#10-16)	3.60	9.00	18.00
8(#17)-Bare-breasted woman-c	10.00	30.00	60.00

FLYIN' JENNY
1946 - No. 2, 1947 (1945 strip reprints)
Pentagon Publ. Co./Leader Enterprises #2

	GD25	FN65	NM94
nn-Marcus Swayze strip-r (entire insides)	8.35	25.00	50.00
2-Baker-c; Swayze strip reprints	9.15	27.50	55.00

FLYING MODELS
V61#3, May, 1954 (16 pgs.) (5 cents)
H-K Publ. (Health-Knowledge Publs.)

	GD25	FN65	NM94
V61#3 (Rare)	5.00	15.00	30.00

FLYING NUN (TV)
Feb, 1968 - No. 4, Nov, 1968
Dell Publishing Co.

	GD25	FN65	NM94
1-Sally Field photo-c	4.00	11.00	21.00
2-4: 2-Sally Field photo-c	2.00	5.00	10.00

FLYING NURSES (See Sue & Sally Smith...)

FLYING SAUCERS
1950; 1952; 1953
Avon Periodicals/Realistic

	GD25	FN65	NM94
1(1950)-Wood-a, 21 pgs.; Fawcette-c	40.00	120.00	280.00
nn(1952)-Cover altered plus 2 pgs. of Wood-a not in original	38.00	115.00	265.00
nn(1953)-Reprints above	23.00	70.00	160.00

FLYING SAUCERS (Comics)
April, 1967 - No. 4, Nov, 1967; No. 5, Oct, 1969
Dell Publishing Co.

	GD25	FN65	NM94
1	2.00	5.00	10.00
2-5	1.20	3.00	6.00

FLY IN MY EYE: EXPOSED (Eclipse)(Value: cover or less) (Graphic Album)

FLY MAN (Formerly Adventures of The Fly; Mighty Comics #40 on)
No. 32, July, 1965 - No. 39, Sept, 1966 (Also see Mighty Crusaders)
Mighty Comics Group (Radio Comics) (Archie)

	GD25	FN65	NM94
32,33-Comet, Shield, Black Hood, The Fly & Flygirl x-over. 33-Re-intro Wizard, Hangman	4.00	12.00	24.00
34-36: 34-Shield begins. 35-Origin Black Hood. 36-Hangman x-over in Shield; re-intro. & origin of Web	3.00	7.50	15.00
37-39: 37-Hangman, Wizard x-over in Flyman; last Shield issue. 38-Web story. 39-Steel Sterling story	3.00	7.50	15.00

FOES (Ram)(Value: cover or less)

FOLLOW THE SUN (TV)
May-July, 1962 - No. 2, Sept-Nov, 1962 (Photo-c)
Dell Publishing Co.

	GD25	FN65	NM94
01-280-207(No.1), 12-280-211(No.2)	4.00	11.00	22.00

FOODINI (TV)(The Great...; see Jingle Dingle & Pinhead &...)
March, 1950 - No. 5, 1950
Continental Publications (Holyoke)

	GD25	FN65	NM94
1 (52 pgs.)	10.00	30.00	65.00
2	5.85	17.50	35.00
3-5	4.70	14.00	28.00

FOOEY (Magazine) (Satire)
Feb, 1961 - No. 4, May, 1961
Scoff Publishing Co.

	GD25	FN65	NM94
1	4.00	11.00	22.00
2-4	3.00	7.50	15.00

FOOFUR (TV)
Aug, 1987 - No. 6, June, 1988
Star Comics/Marvel Comics No. 5 on

	GD25	FN65	NM94
1-6		.50	1.00

FOOLKILLER (Also see The Amazing Spider-Man #225, The Defenders #73, Man-Thing #3 & Omega the Unknown #8)
Oct, 1990 - No. 10, Oct, 1991 ($1.75, color, limited series)
Marvel Comics

	GD25	FN65	NM94
1-Origin 3rd Foolkiller; Greg Salinger app.	.40	1.00	2.00
2-7,9,10: DeZuniga-a(i) in 1-4	.35	.90	1.75
8-Spider-Man x-over	.50	1.25	2.50

FOOTBALL THRILLS (See Tops In Adventure)
Fall-Winter, 1951-52 - No. 2, Fall, 1952
Ziff-Davis Publ. Co.

	GD25	FN65	NM94
1-Powell a(2); Saunders painted-c. Red Grange, Jim Thorpe app.	17.00	52.00	105.00
2-Saunders painted-c	10.00	30.00	70.00

FOR A NIGHT OF LOVE
1951
Avon Periodicals

	GD25	FN65	NM94
nn-Two stories adapted from the works of Emile Zola; Astarita, Ravielli-a; Kinstler-c	17.00	52.00	120.00

FORBIDDEN LOVE
Mar, 1950 - No. 4, Sept, 1950
Quality Comics Group

	GD25	FN65	NM94
1-(Scarce)-Classic photo-c; Crandall-a	50.00	150.00	350.00
2,3-(Scarce)-Photo-c	22.00	65.00	150.00
4-(Scarce)-Ward/Cuidera-a; photo-c	24.00	72.00	170.00

FORBIDDEN LOVE (See Dark Mansion of...)

FORBIDDEN PLANET
May, 1992 - No. 4, 1992 ($2.50, color, mini-series)
Innovation Publishing

	GD25	FN65	NM94
1-4: Adapts movie; painted covers	.50	1.25	2.50

FORBIDDEN TALES OF DARK MANSION (Formerly Dark Mansion of Forbidden Love #1-4)
No. 5, May-June, 1972 - No. 15, Feb-Mar, 1974
National Periodical Publications

	GD25	FN65	NM94
5-15: 13-Kane/Howard-a	.60	1.50	3.00

NOTE: ***N. Adams*** *c-9.* ***Alcala*** *a-9-11, 13.* ***Chaykin*** *a-7,15.* ***Evans*** *a-14.* ***Kaluta*** *c-7, 8, 13.* ***G. Kane*** *a-13.* ***Kirby*** *a-6.* ***Nino*** *a-8, 12, 15.* ***Redondo*** *a-14.*

FORBIDDEN WORLDS
7-8/51 - No. 34, 10-11/54; No. 35, 8/55 - No. 145, 8/67
(No. 1-5: 52 pgs.; No. 6-8: 44 pgs.)
American Comics Group

	GD25	FN65	NM94
1-Williamson/Frazetta-a (10 pgs.)	75.00	225.00	525.00
2	38.00	115.00	265.00
3-Williamson/Wood/Orlando-a (7 pgs.)	39.00	118.00	275.00
4	19.00	57.00	135.00
5-Krenkel/Williamson-a (8 pgs.)	32.00	95.00	225.00
6-Harrison/Williamson-a (8 pgs.)	27.00	81.00	190.00
7,8,10	13.50	41.00	95.00
9-A-Bomb explosion story	16.00	48.00	110.00
11-20	10.00	30.00	65.00
21-33: 24-E.C. swipe by Landau	7.50	22.50	45.00
34(10-11/54)(Scarce)(Becomes Young Heroes #35 on)-Last pre-code issue; A-Bomb explosion story	7.50	22.50	45.00
35(8/55)-Scarce	6.35	19.00	38.00
36-62	4.70	14.00	28.00
63,69,76,78-Williamson-a in all; w/Krenkel #69	.85	17.50	35.00

Fly Man #37, © AP

Foolkiller #8, © MEG

Forbidden Worlds #48, © ACG

Forever People #10 (1972), © DC

40 Big Pages of Mickey Mouse #945, © WDC

Four Color #1 (1st), © Chicago Tribune

	GD25	FN65	NM94
64,66-68,70-72,74,75,77,79-85,87-90	4.20	12.50	25.00
65-"There's a New Moon Tonight" listed in #114 as holding 1st record fan mail response	5.00	15.00	30.00
73-1st app. Herbie by Ogden Whitney	22.00	65.00	150.00
86-Flying saucer-c	5.00	15.00	30.00
91-93,95-100	3.60	9.00	18.00
94-Herbie app.	6.70	20.00	40.00
101-109,111-113,115,117-120	3.00	7.50	15.00
110,114,116-Herbie app. 114-1st Herbie-c; contains list of editor's top 20 ACG stories. 116-Herbie goes to Hell	4.20	12.50	25.00
121-124: 124-Magic Agent app.	3.00	7.50	15.00
125-Magic Agent app.; intro. & origin Magicman series, ends #141	3.60	9.00	18.00
126-130	3.00	7.50	15.00
131-139: 133-Origin/1st app. Dragonia in Magicman (1-2/66); returns in #138. 136-Nemesis x-over in Magicman.	2.40	6.00	12.00
140-Mark Midnight app. by Ditko	3.00	7.50	15.00
141-145	2.00	5.00	10.00

NOTE: ***Buscema** a-75, 79, 81, 82, 140r. **Cameron** a-5. **Disbrow** a-10. **Ditko** a-137p, 138, 140. **Landau** a-24, 27-29, 31-34, 48, 86r, 96, 143-45. **Lazarus** a-18, 23, 24, 57. **Moldoff** a-27, 31, 139r. **Reinman** a-93. **Whitney** a-115, 116, 137; c-40, 46, 57, 60, 68, 78, 79, 90, 93, 94, 100, 102, 103, 106-108, 114, 129.*

FORCE, THE (See The Crusaders)

FORCE OF BUDDHA'S PALM THE (Jademan) (Value: cover or less)

FORD ROTUNDA CHRISTMAS BOOK (See Christmas at the Rotunda)

FOREIGN INTRIGUES (Formerly Johnny Dynamite; becomes Battlefield Action #16 on)
No. 13, 1956 - No. 15, Aug, 1956
Charlton Comics

	GD25	FN65	NM94
13-15-Johnny Dynamite continues	4.00	12.00	22.00

FOREMOST BOYS (See 4Most)

FOREST FIRE (Also see Smokey The Bear)
1949 (dated-1950) (16 pgs., paper-c)
American Forestry Assn. (Commerical Comics)

	GD25	FN65	NM94
nn-Intro/1st app. Smokey The Forest Fire Preventing Bear; created by Rudy Wendelein; Wendelein/Sparling-a; 'Carter Oil Co.' on back-c of original	13.00	40.00	90.00

FOREVER, DARLING (See 4-Color No. 681)

FOREVER PEOPLE, THE
Feb-Mar, 1971 - No. 11, Oct-Nov, 1972
National Periodical Publications

	GD25	FN65	NM94
1-Superman x-over; Kirby-c/a begins; 1st full app. Darkseid (3rd anywhere, ties w/New Gods #1); Darkseid storyline begins, ends #8 (apps. in 1-4,6, 8; cameos in #5,11)	4.70	14.00	28.00
2-5: 4-G.A. reprints begin, end #9	3.60	9.00	18.00
6-11: 9,10-Deadman app.	1.60	4.00	8.00

NOTE: ***Kirby** c/a(p)-1-11; #4-9 contain Sandman reprints from Adventure #85, 84, 75, 80, 77, 74 in that order. #1-3, 10-11 are 36pgs; #4-9 are 52pgs.*

FOREVER PEOPLE
Feb, 1988 - No. 6, July, 1988 ($1.25, mini-series)
DC Comics

	GD25	FN65	NM94
1-6		.60	1.25

FOR GIRLS ONLY
Nov, 1953 (Digest size, 100 pgs.)
Bernard Bailey Enterprises

	GD25	FN65	NM94
1-Half comic book, half magazine	8.35	25.00	50.00

FORGOTTEN FOREST OF OZ, THE (See First Comics Graphic Novel #16)

FORGOTTEN REALMS (DC) (Value: cover or less)

FORGOTTEN STORY BEHIND NORTH BEACH, THE
No date (8 pgs.; paper cover)
Catechetical Guild

	GD25	FN65	NM94
nn	2.00	5.00	10.00

FOR LOVERS ONLY (Formerly Hollywood Romances)
No. 60, Aug, 1971 - No. 87, Nov, 1976
Charlton Comics

	GD25	FN65	NM94
60-87: 73-Spanking scene-c/story		.50	1.00

40 BIG PAGES OF MICKEY MOUSE
No. 945, 1936 (44 pgs.; 10-1/4x12"; cardboard cover)
Whitman Publishing Co.

	GD25	FN65	NM94
945-Reprints Mickey Mouse Magazine #1, but with a different cover; ads were eliminated and some illustrated stories had expanded text. The book is 3/4" shorter than Mickey Mouse Mag. #1, but the reprints are the same size (Rare)	100.00	300.00	600.00

48 FAMOUS AMERICANS
1947 (Giveaway) (Half-size in color)
J. C. Penney Co. (Cpr. Edwin H. Stroh)

	GD25	FN65	NM94
nn-Simon & Kirby-a	7.50	22.50	45.00

FOR YOUR EYES ONLY (See James Bond...)

FOUR COLOR
Sept?, 1939 - No. 1354, Apr-June, 1962
Dell Publishing Co.

NOTE: *Four Color only appears on issues #19-25, 1-99,101. Dell Publishing Co. filed these as Series I, #1-25, and Series II, #1-1354. Issues beginning with #710? were printed with and without ads on back cover. Issues without ads are worth more.*

SERIES I:	GD25	FN65	VF82	NM94
1(nn)-Dick Tracy	280.00	840.00	1700.00	2800.00

(Estimated up to 115 total copies exist, 5 in NM/Mint)

	GD25	FN65	NM94
2(nn)-Don Winslow of the Navy (#1) (Rare) (11/39?)	100.00	300.00	700.00
3(nn)-Myra North (1/40?)	64.00	193.00	450.00

	GD25	FN65	VF82	NM94
4-Donald Duck by Al Taliaferro (1940) (Disney) (3/40?)	500.00	1250.00	3000.00	5000.00

(Prices vary widely on this book)

	GD25	FN65	NM94
5-Smilin' Jack (#1) (5/40?)	54.00	160.00	375.00
6-Dick Tracy (Scarce)	121.00	365.00	850.00
7-Gang Busters	30.00	90.00	210.00
8-Dick Tracy	68.00	205.00	475.00
9-Terry and the Pirates-r/Super #9-29	54.00	160.00	375.00
10-Smilin' Jack	50.00	150.00	350.00
11-Smitty (#1)	32.00	95.00	220.00
12-Little Orphan Annie; reprints strips from 12/19/37 to 6/4/38	43.00	130.00	300.00
13-Walt Disney's Reluctant Dragon('41)-Contains 2 pages of photos from film; 2 pg. foreword to Fantasia by Leopold Stokowski; Donald Duck, Goofy, Baby Weems & Mickey Mouse (as the Sorcerer's Apprentice) app. (Disney)	107.00	320.00	750.00
14-Moon Mullins (#1)	29.00	85.00	200.00
15-Tillie the Toiler (#1)	29.00	85.00	200.00

	GD25	FN65	VF82
16-Mickey Mouse (#1) (Disney) by Gottfredson	445.00	1335.00	4000.00

(Prices vary widely on this book)

	GD25	FN65	NM94
17-Walt Disney's Dumbo, the Flying Elephant (#1) (1941)-Mickey Mouse, Donald Duck, & Pluto app. (Disney)	115.00	345.00	800.00
18-Jiggs and Maggie (#1) (1936-'38-r)	32.00	95.00	220.00
19-Barney Google and Snuffy Smith (#1)-(1st issue with Four Color on the cover)	32.00	95.00	220.00

	GD25	FN65	NM94
20-Tiny Tim	27.00	80.00	185.00
21-Dick Tracy	57.00	170.00	400.00
22-Don Winslow	24.00	70.00	165.00
23-Gang Busters	22.00	65.00	150.00
24-Captain Easy	29.00	86.00	200.00
25-Popeye (1942)	50.00	150.00	350.00
SERIES II:			
1-Little Joe (1942)	39.00	120.00	275.00
2-Harold Teen	22.00	65.00	150.00
3-Alley Oop (#1)	43.00	130.00	300.00
4-Smilin' Jack	39.00	120.00	275.00
5-Raggedy Ann and Andy (#1)	42.00	125.00	290.00
6-Smitty	17.00	51.00	120.00
7-Smokey Stover (#1)	29.00	85.00	200.00
8-Tillie the Toiler	17.00	51.00	120.00

	GD25	FN65	VF82	NM94
9-Donald Duck Finds Pirate Gold, by Carl Barks & Jack Hannah (Disney) (© 8/17/42)	420.00	1260.00	2520.00	4200.00

(Prices vary widely on this book)

	GD25	FN65	NM94
10-Flash Gordon by Alex Raymond; r-/from "The Ice Kingdom"	50.00	150.00	350.00
11-Wash Tubbs	26.00	77.00	180.00
12-Walt Disney's Bambi (#1); reprinted in Gladstone Comic Album #9	43.00	130.00	300.00
13-Mr. District Attorney (#1)-See The Funnies #35 for 1st app.	24.00	70.00	165.00
14-Smilin' Jack	32.00	95.00	220.00
15-Felix the Cat (#1)	54.00	160.00	375.00
16-Porky Pig (#1)(1942)-"Secret of the Haunted House"	47.00	140.00	325.00
17-Popeye	42.00	125.00	290.00
18-Little Orphan Annie's Junior Commandos; Flag-c; reprints strips from 6/14/42 to 11/21/42	34.00	105.00	240.00
19-Walt Disney's Thumper Meets the Seven Dwarfs (Disney); r-in Silly Symphonies	43.00	130.00	300.00
20-Barney Baxter	20.00	60.00	140.00
21-Oswald the Rabbit (#1)(1943)	30.00	90.00	210.00
22-Tillie the Toiler	14.00	43.00	100.00
23-Raggedy Ann and Andy	32.00	95.00	220.00
24-Gang Busters	22.00	65.00	150.00
25-Andy Panda (#1) (Walter Lantz)	34.00	100.00	240.00
26-Popeye	38.00	115.00	265.00
27-Walt Disney's Mickey Mouse and the Seven Colored Terror	57.00	171.00	400.00
28-Wash Tubbs	19.00	57.00	130.00

	GD25	FN65	VF82	NM94
29-Donald Duck and the Mummy's Ring, by Carl Barks (Disney) (9/43)	340.00	1020.00	2040.00	3400.00

(Prices vary widely on this book)

	GD25	FN65	NM94
30-Bambi's Children(1943)-Disney	42.00	125.00	290.00
31-Moon Mullins	16.00	48.00	110.00
32-Smitty	14.00	43.00	100.00
33-Bugs Bunny "Public Nuisance #1"	47.00	140.00	325.00
34-Dick Tracy	40.00	120.00	280.00
35-Smokey Stover	14.00	43.00	100.00
36-Smilin' Jack	19.00	57.00	130.00
37-Bringing Up Father	16.00	48.00	110.00
38-Roy Rogers (#1, © 4/44)-1st western comic with photo-c	72.00	215.00	500.00
39-Oswald the Rabbit('44)	2.00	60.00	140.00
40-Barney Google and Snuffy Smith	17.00	51.00	120.00
41-Mother Goose and Nursery Rhyme Comics (#1)-All by Walt Kelly	19.00	57.00	135.00
42-Tiny Tim (1934-r)	14.00	43.00	100.00

	GD25	FN65	NM94
43-Popeye (1938-'42-r)	27.00	81.00	190.00
44-Terry and the Pirates ('38-r)	36.00	107.00	250.00
45-Raggedy Ann	26.00	77.00	180.00
46-Felix the Cat and the Haunted Castle	34.00	100.00	240.00
47-Gene Autry (copyright 6/16/44)	39.00	118.00	275.00
48-Porky Pig of the Mounties by Carl Barks (7/44)	72.00	215.00	500.00
49-Snow White and the Seven Dwarfs (Disney)	37.00	110.00	260.00
50-Fairy Tale Parade-Walt Kelly art (1944)	23.00	70.00	160.00
51-Bugs Bunny Finds the Lost Treasure	25.00	75.00	175.00
52-Little Orphan Annie; reprints strips from 6/18/38 to 11/19/38	25.00	75.00	175.00
53-Wash Tubbs	14.00	43.00	100.00
54-Andy Panda	22.00	65.00	150.00
55-Tillie the Toiler	10.00	30.00	70.00
56-Dick Tracy	32.00	95.00	220.00
57-Gene Autry	34.00	103.00	240.00
58-Smilin' Jack	19.00	57.00	130.00
59-Mother Goose and Nursery Rhyme Comics-Kelly-c/a	17.00	51.00	120.00
60-Tiny Folks Funnies	11.50	34.00	80.00
61-Santa Claus Funnies(11/44)-Kelly art	22.00	65.00	150.00
62-Donald Duck in Frozen Gold, by Carl Barks (Disney) (1/45)	120.00	360.00	960.00
63-Roy Rogers; color photo-all 4-c	43.00	128.00	300.00
64-Smokey Stover	11.00	32.00	75.00
65-Smitty	11.00	32.00	75.00
66-Gene Autry	34.00	103.00	240.00
67-Oswald the Rabbit	14.00	43.00	100.00
68-Mother Goose and Nursery Rhyme Comics, by Walt Kelly	17.00	51.00	120.00
69-Fairy Tale Parade, by Walt Kelly	20.00	60.00	140.00
70-Popeye and Wimpy	23.00	70.00	160.00
71-Walt Disney's Three Caballeros, by Walt Kelly (© 4/45)-(Disney)	67.00	200.00	470.00
72-Raggedy Ann	22.00	65.00	150.00
73-The Gumps (#1)	10.00	30.00	60.00
74-Marge's Little Lulu (#1)	100.00	300.00	700.00
75-Gene Autry and the Wildcat	29.00	86.00	200.00
76-Little Orphan Annie; reprints strips from 2/28/40 to 6/24/40	21.00	62.00	145.00
77-Felix the Cat	32.00	95.00	225.00
78-Porky Pig and the Bandit Twins	19.00	56.00	130.00
79-Walt Disney's Mickey Mouse in The Riddle of the Red Hat by Carl Barks (8/45)	68.00	205.00	475.00
80-Smilin' Jack	14.00	43.00	100.00
81-Moon Mullins	10.00	30.00	60.00
82-Lone Ranger	36.00	107.00	250.00
83-Gene Autry in Outlaw Trail	29.00	86.00	200.00
84-Flash Gordon by Alex Raymond-Reprints from "The Fiery Desert"	33.00	100.00	230.00
85-Andy Panda and the Mad Dog Mystery	13.00	40.00	90.00
86-Roy Rogers; photo-c	31.00	92.00	215.00
87-Fairy Tale Parade by Walt Kelly; Dan Noonan cover	17.00	51.00	120.00
88-Bugs Bunny's Great Adventure	16.00	48.00	110.00
89-Tillie the Toiler	10.00	30.00	70.00
90-Christmas with Mother Goose by Walt Kelly (11/45)	16.50	50.00	115.00
91-Santa Claus Funnies by Walt Kelly (11/45)	17.00	51.00	120.00
92-Walt Disney's The Wonderful Adventures Of Pinocchio (1945); Donald Duck by Kelly, 16 pgs. (Disney)	3.00	90.00	210.00
93-Gene Autry in The Bandit of Black Rock	23.00	70.00	160.00
94-Winnie Winkle (1945)	11.00	32.00	75.00
95-Roy Rogers Comics; photo-c	31.00	92.00	215.00
96-Dick Tracy	24.00	70.00	165.00

Four Color #15, © KING

Four Color #51, © Warner Bros,

Four Color #107, © News Synd.

Four Color #130, © Walter Lantz Prod.

Four Color # 147, © WDC

Four Color #166, © Roy Rogers

	GD25	FN65	NM94
97-Marge's Little Lulu (1946)	47.00	140.00	330.00
98-Lone Ranger, The	27.00	81.00	190.00
99-Smitty	10.00	30.00	70.00
100-Gene Autry Comics; photo-c	23.00	70.00	160.00
101-Terry and the Pirates	23.00	70.00	160.00

NOTE: *No. 101 is last issue to carry "Four Color" logo on cover; all issues beginning with No. 100 are marked "...O. S." (One Shot) which can be found in the bottom left-hand panel on the first page; the numbers following "O. S." relate to the year/month issued.*

	GD25	FN65	NM94
102-Oswald the Rabbit-Walt Kelly art, 1 pg.	12.00	36.00	85.00
103-Easter with Mother Goose by Walt Kelly	16.00	48.00	110.00
104-Fairy Tale Parade by Walt Kelly	15.00	45.00	105.00
105-Albert the Alligator and Pogo Possum (#1) by Kelly (4/46)	65.00	195.00	450.00
106-Tillie the Toiler	9.15	27.50	55.00
107-Little Orphan Annie; reprints strips from 11/16/42 to 3/24/43	17.00	52.00	120.00
108-Donald Duck in The Terror of the River, by Carl Barks (Disney) (© 4/16/46)	90.00	270.00	720.00
109-Roy Rogers Comics; photo-c	24.00	71.00	165.00
110-Marge's Little Lulu	33.00	100.00	230.00
111-Captain Easy; spanking panels	11.00	32.00	75.00
112-Porky Pig's Adventure in Gopher Gulch	11.00	32.00	75.00
113-Popeye	12.00	36.00	85.00
115-Marge's Little Lulu	33.00	100.00	230.00
116-Mickey Mouse and the House of Many Mysteries (Disney)	19.00	56.00	130.00
117-Roy Rogers Comics; photo-c	17.00	51.00	120.00
118-Lone Ranger, The	27.00	81.00	190.00
119-Felix the Cat	25.00	75.00	175.00
120-Marge's Little Lulu	30.00	90.00	210.00
121-Fairy Tale Parade-(not Kelly)	10.00	30.00	65.00
122-Henry (#1) (10/46)	10.00	30.00	60.00
123-Bugs Bunny's Dangerous Venture	10.00	30.00	65.00
124-Roy Rogers Comics; photo-c	17.00	51.00	120.00
125-Lone Ranger, The	20.00	60.00	140.00
126-Christmas with Mother Goose by Walt Kelly (1946)	13.00	40.00	90.00
127-Popeye	12.00	36.00	85.00
128-Santa Claus Funnies-"Santa & the Angel" by Gollub; "A Mouse in the House" by Kelly	13.00	40.00	90.00
129-Walt Disney's Uncle Remus and His Tales of Brer Rabbit (#1) (1946)	16.00	48.00	110.00
130-Andy Panda (Walter Lantz)	8.35	25.00	50.00
131-Marge's Little Lulu	30.00	90.00	210.00
132-Tillie the Toiler (1947)	9.15	27.50	55.00
133-Dick Tracy	19.00	57.00	135.00
134-Tarzan and the Devil Ogre; Marsh-c/a	50.00	150.00	350.00
135-Felix the Cat	19.00	57.00	130.00
136-Lone Ranger, The	20.00	60.00	140.00
137-Roy Rogers Comics; photo-c	17.00	51.00	120.00
138-Smitty	9.15	27.50	55.00
139-Marge's Little Lulu (1947)	27.00	81.00	190.00
140-Easter with Mother Goose by Walt Kelly	13.00	40.00	90.00
141-Mickey Mouse and the Submarine Pirates (Disney)	17.00	51.00	120.00
142-Bugs Bunny and the Haunted Mountain	10.00	30.00	65.00
143-Oswald the Rabbit & the Prehistoric Egg	7.50	22.50	45.00
144-Roy Rogers Comics (1947)-Photo-c	17.00	51.00	120.00
145-Popeye	12.00	36.00	85.00
146-Marge's Little Lulu	27.00	81.00	190.00
147-Donald Duck in Volcano Valley, by Carl Barks (Disney) (5/47)	60.00	180.00	480.00
148-Albert the Alligator and Pogo Possum by Walt Kelly (5/47)	54.00	160.00	375.00
149-Smilin' Jack	10.00	30.00	70.00

	GD25	FN65	NM94
150-Tillie the Toiler (6/47)	7.50	22.50	45.00
151-Lone Ranger, The	17.00	51.00	120.00
152-Little Orphan Annie; reprints strips from 1/2/44 to 5/6/44	11.50	34.00	80.00
153-Roy Rogers Comics; photo-c	14.00	43.00	100.00
154-Walter Lantz Andy Panda	8.35	25.00	50.00
155-Henry (7/47)	7.50	22.50	45.00
156-Porky Pig and the Phantom	9.15	27.50	55.00
157-Mickey Mouse & the Beanstalk (Disney)	17.00	51.00	120.00
158-Marge's Little Lulu	27.00	81.00	190.00
159-Donald Duck in the Ghost of the Grotto, by Carl Barks (Disney) (8/47)	54.00	160.00	430.00
160-Roy Rogers Comics; photo-c	14.00	43.00	100.00
161-Tarzan and the Fires Of Tohr; Marsh-c/a	43.00	130.00	300.00
162-Felix the Cat (9/47)	14.00	43.00	100.00
163-Dick Tracy	16.00	48.00	110.00
164-Bugs Bunny Finds the Frozen Kingdom	10.00	30.00	65.00
165-Marge's Little Lulu	27.00	81.00	190.00
166-Roy Rogers Comics (52 pgs.)-Photo-c	14.00	43.00	100.00
167-Lone Ranger, The	17.00	51.00	120.00
168-Popeye (10/47)	12.00	36.00	85.00
169-Woody Woodpecker (#1)-"Manhunter in the North"; drug use story	11.50	34.00	80.00
170-Mickey Mouse on Spook's Island (11/47)(Disney)-reprinted in Mickey Mouse #103	14.00	43.00	100.00
171-Charlie McCarthy (#1) and the Twenty Thieves	13.00	40.00	90.00
172-Christmas with Mother Goose by Walt Kelly (11/47)	13.00	40.00	90.00
173-Flash Gordon	11.50	34.00	80.00
174-Winnie Winkle	6.70	20.00	40.00
175-Santa Claus Funnies by Walt Kelly (1947)	13.00	40.00	90.00
176-Tillie the Toiler (12/47)	7.50	22.50	45.00
177-Roy Rogers Comics-(36 pgs.); Photo-c	14.00	43.00	100.00
178-Donald Duck "Christmas on Bear Mountain" by Carl Barks; 1st app. Uncle Scrooge (Disney)(12/47)	64.00	192.00	510.00
179-Uncle Wiggily (#1)-Walt Kelly-c	13.00	40.00	90.00
180-Ozark Ike (#1)	9.15	27.50	55.00
181-Walt Disney's Mickey Mouse in Jungle Magic	14.00	43.00	100.00
182-Porky Pig in Never-Never Land (2/48)	9.15	27.50	55.00
183-Oswald the Rabbit (Lantz)	7.50	22.50	45.00
184-Tillie the Toiler	7.50	22.50	45.00
185-Easter with Mother Goose by Walt Kelly (1948)	12.00	36.00	85.00
186-Walt Disney's Bambi (4/48)-Reprinted as Movie Classic Bambi #3 (1956)	10.00	30.00	70.00
187-Bugs Bunny and the Dreadful Dragon	9.15	27.50	55.00
188-Woody Woodpecker (Lantz, 5/48)	10.00	30.00	60.00
189-Donald Duck in The Old Castle's Secret, by Carl Barks (Disney) (6/48)	54.00	160.00	430.00
190-Flash Gordon ('48)	11.50	34.00	80.00
191-Porky Pig to the Rescue	9.15	27.50	55.00
192-The Brownies (#1)-by Walt Kelly (7/48)	12.00	36.00	85.00
193-M.G.M. Presents Tom and Jerry (#1)(1948)	11.00	32.00	75.00
194-Mickey Mouse in The World Under the Sea (Disney)-Reprinted in Mickey Mouse #101	14.00	43.00	100.00
195-Tillie the Toiler	5.00	15.00	30.00
196-Charlie McCarthy in The Haunted Hide-Out; part photo-c	11.50	34.00	80.00
197-Spirit of the Border (#1) (Zane Grey) (1948)	9.15	27.50	55.00
198-Andy Panda	8.35	25.00	50.00
199-Donald Duck in Sheriff of Bullet Valley, by Carl Barks; Barks draws himself on wanted poster, last page; used in Love & Death (Disney) (10/48)	54.00	160.00	430.00

	GD25	FN65	NM94
200-Bugs Bunny, Super Sleuth (10/48)	9.15	27.50	55.00
201-Christmas with Mother Goose by W. Kelly	11.50	34.00	80.00
202-Woody Woodpecker	5.75	17.50	35.00
203-Donald Duck in the Golden Christmas Tree, by Carl Barks (Disney) (12/48)	36.00	108.00	290.00
204-Flash Gordon (12/48)	10.00	30.00	65.00
205-Santa Claus Funnies by Walt Kelly	11.50	34.00	80.00
206-Little Orphan Annie; reprints strips from 11/10/40 to 1/11/41	6.70	20.00	40.00
207-King of the Royal Mounted (#1) (12/48)	11.50	34.00	80.00
208-Brer Rabbit Does It Again (Disney) (1/49)	11.00	30.00	65.00
209-Harold Teen	4.00	11.00	22.00
210-Tippie and Cap Stubbs	4.00	11.00	22.00
211-Little Beaver (#1)	6.70	20.00	40.00
212-Dr. Bobbs	4.00	11.00	22.00
213-Tillie the Toiler	5.00	15.00	30.00
214-Mickey Mouse and His Sky Adventure (2/49)(Disney)-Reprinted in Mickey Mouse #105	11.00	32.00	75.00
215-Sparkle Plenty (Dick Tracy-r by Gould)	10.00	30.00	65.00
216-Andy Panda and the Police Pup (Lantz)	5.00	15.00	30.00
217-Bugs Bunny in Court Jester	9.15	27.50	55.00
218-3 Little Pigs and the Wonderful Magic Lamp (Disney) (3/49)	9.15	27.50	55.00
219-Swee'pea	9.15	27.50	55.00
220-Easter with Mother Goose by Walt Kelly	11.50	34.00	80.00
221-Uncle Wiggily-Walt Kelly cover in part	10.00	30.00	60.00
222-West of the Pecos (Zane Grey)	6.70	20.00	40.00
223-Donald Duck "Lost in the Andes" by Carl Barks (Disney-4/49) (square egg story)	50.00	150.00	400.00
224-Little Iodine (#1), by Hatlo (4/49)	10.00	30.00	60.00
225-Oswald the Rabbit (Lantz)	5.00	15.00	30.00
226-Porky Pig and Spoofy, the Spook	6.70	20.00	40.00
227-Seven Dwarfs (Disney)	10.00	30.00	65.00
228-Mark of Zorro, The (#1) (1949)	19.00	57.00	135.00
229-Smokey Stover	4.35	13.00	26.00
230-Sunset Pass (Zane Grey)	6.70	20.00	40.00
231-Mickey Mouse and the Rajah's Treasure (Disney)	11.00	32.00	75.00
232-Woody Woodpecker (Lantz, 6/49)	5.85	17.50	35.00
233-Bugs Bunny, Sleepwalking Sleuth	9.15	27.50	55.00
234-Dumbo in Sky Voyage (Disney)	8.35	25.00	50.00
235-Tiny Tim	5.00	15.00	30.00
236-Heritage of the Desert (Zane Grey) (1949)	6.70	20.00	40.00
237-Tillie the Toiler	5.00	15.00	30.00
238-Donald Duck in Voodoo Hoodoo, by Carl Barks (Disney) (8/49); this is on Disney's reprint banned list	38.00	112.00	300.00
239-Adventure Bound (8/49)	4.20	12.50	25.00
240-Andy Panda (Lantz)	5.00	15.00	30.00
241-Porky Pig, Mighty Hunter	6.70	20.00	40.00
242-Tippie and Cap Stubbs	4.00	11.00	22.00
243-Thumper Follows His Nose (Disney)	8.35	25.00	50.00
244-The Brownies by Walt Kelly	11.00	32.00	75.00
245-Dick's Adventures in Dreamland (9/49)	4.70	14.00	28.00
246-Thunder Mountain (Zane Grey)	4.70	14.00	28.00
247-Flash Gordon	10.00	30.00	65.00
248-Mickey Mouse and the Black Sorcerer (Disney)	11.00	32.00	75.00
249-Woody Woodpecker in the "Globetrotter" (10/49)	5.85	17.50	35.00
250-Bugs Bunny in Diamond Daze; used in **SOTI**, pg. 309	9.15	27.50	55.00
251-Hubert at Camp Moonbeam	4.20	12.50	25.00
252-Pinocchio (Disney)-not by Kelly; origin	10.00	30.00	60.00
253-Christmas with Mother Goose by W. Kelly	10.00	30.00	70.00
254-Santa Claus Funnies by Walt Kelly; Pogo & Albert story by Kelly (11/49)	11.50	34.00	80.00

	GD25	FN65	NM94
255-The Ranger (Zane Grey) (1949)	4.70	14.00	28.00
256-Donald Duck in "Luck of the North" by Carl Barks (Disney) (12/49)-Shows #257 on inside	27.00	81.00	215.00
257-Little Iodine	6.70	20.00	40.00
258-Andy Panda and the Balloon Race (Lantz)	5.00	15.00	30.00
259-Santa and the Angel (Gollub art-condensed from #128) & Santa at the Zoo (12/49)-two books in one	4.70	14.00	28.00
260-Porky Pig, Hero of the Wild West (12/49)	6.70	20.00	40.00
261-Mickey Mouse and the Missing Key (Disney)	11.00	32.00	75.00
262-Raggedy Ann and Andy	5.85	17.50	35.00
263-Donald Duck in "Land of the Totem Poles" by Carl Barks (Disney) (2/50)-has two Barks stories	27.00	81.00	215.00
264-Woody Woodpecker in the Magic Lantern (Lantz)	5.85	17.50	35.00
265-King of the Royal Mounted (Zane Grey)	9.35	28.00	56.00
266-Bugs Bunny on the "Isle of Hercules" (2/50)-Reprinted in Best of Bugs Bunny #1	7.50	22.50	45.00
267-Little Beaver-Harmon-c/a	4.00	10.00	20.00
268-Mickey Mouse's Surprise Visitor (1950) (Disney)	11.00	32.00	75.00
269-Johnny Mack Brown (#1)-Photo-c	16.00	48.00	110.00
270-Drift Fence (Zane Grey) (3/50)	4.70	14.00	28.00
271-Porky Pig in Phantom of the Plains	6.70	20.00	40.00
272-Cinderella (Disney) (4/50)	8.35	25.00	50.00
273-Oswald the Rabbit (Lantz)	5.00	15.00	30.00
274-Bugs Bunny, Hare-brained Reporter	7.50	22.50	45.00
275-Donald Duck in "Ancient Persia" by Carl Barks (Disney) (5/50)	25.00	75.00	200.00
276-Uncle Wiggily	6.70	20.00	40.00
277-Porky Pig in Desert Adventure (5/50)	6.70	20.00	40.00
278-Bill Elliott Comics (#1)-Photo-c	11.50	34.00	80.00
279-Mickey Mouse and Pluto Battle the Giant Ants (Disney); reprinted in Mickey Mouse #102 & 245	10.00	30.00	65.00
280-Andy Panda in The Isle Of Mechanical Men (Lantz)	5.00	15.00	30.00
281-Bugs Bunny in The Great Circus Mystery	7.50	22.50	45.00
282-Donald Duck and the Pixilated Parrot by Carl Barks (Disney) (© 5/23/50)	25.00	75.00	200.00
283-King of the Royal Mounted (7/50)	9.35	28.00	56.00
284-Porky Pig in The Kingdom of Nowhere	6.70	20.00	40.00
285-Bozo the Clown and His Minikin Circus (#1) (TV)	11.50	34.00	80.00
286-Mickey Mouse in The Uninvited Guest (Disney)	10.00	30.00	65.00
287-Gene Autry's Champion in The Ghost Of Black Mountain	9.15	27.50	55.00
288-Woody Woodpecker in Klondike Gold (Lantz)	5.85	17.50	35.00
289-Bugs Bunny in "Indian Trouble"	7.50	22.50	45.00
290-The Chief (#1) (8/50)	4.70	14.00	28.00
291-Donald Duck in "The Magic Hourglass" by Carl Barks (Disney) (9/50)	25.00	75.00	200.00
292-The Cisco Kid Comics (#1)	16.00	48.00	110.00
293-The Brownies-Kelly-c/a	10.00	30.00	70.00
294-Little Beaver	4.00	10.00	20.00
295-Porky Pig in President Porky (9/50)	6.70	20.00	40.00
296-Mickey Mouse in Private Eye for Hire (Disney)	10.00	30.00	65.00
297-Andy Panda in The Haunted Inn (Lantz, 10/50)	5.00	15.00	30.00
298-Bugs Bunny in Sheik for a Day	7.50	22.50	45.00
299-Buck Jones & the Iron Horse Trail (#1)	11.50	34.00	80.00
300-Donald Duck in "Big-Top Bedlam" by Carl Barks (Disney) (11/50)	25.00	75.00	200.00
301-The Mysterious Rider (Zane Grey)	4.70	14.00	28.00
302-Santa Claus Funnies (11/50)	4.00	10.00	20.00
303-Porky Pig in The Land of the Monstrous Flies	4.70	14.00	28.00

Four Color #228, © Johnston McCulley

Four Color #268, © WDC

Four Color #300, © WDC

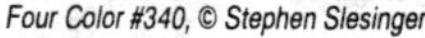
Four Color #340, © Stephen Slesinger

Four Color #351, © Warner Bros.

Four Color #389, © WEST

	GD25	FN65	NM94
304-Mickey Mouse in Tom-Tom Island (Disney) (12/50)	7.50	22.50	45.00
305-Woody Woodpecker (Lantz)	4.00	10.00	20.00
306-Raggedy Ann	4.60	14.00	28.00
307-Bugs Bunny in Lumber Jack Rabbit	6.35	19.00	38.00
308-Donald Duck in "Dangerous Disguise" by Carl Barks (Disney) (1/51)	21.00	63.00	170.00
309-Betty Betz' Dollface and Her Gang (1951)	4.20	12.50	25.00
310-King of the Royal Mounted (1/51)	5.85	17.50	35.00
311-Porky Pig in Midget Horses of Hidden Valley	4.70	14.00	28.00
312-Tonto (#1)	11.50	34.00	80.00
313-Mickey Mouse in The Mystery of the Double-Cross Ranch (#1) (Disney) (2/51)	7.50	22.50	45.00
314-Ambush (Zane Grey)	4.70	14.00	28.00
315-Oswald the Rabbit (Lantz)	3.60	9.00	18.00
316-Rex Allen (#1)-Photo-c; Marsh-a	14.00	43.00	100.00
317-Bugs Bunny in Hair Today Gone Tomorrow (#1)	6.35	19.00	38.00
318-Donald Duck in "No Such Varmint" by Carl Barks (#1)-Indicia shows #317 (Disney, © 1/23/51)	21.00	63.00	170.00
319-Gene Autry's Champion	4.20	12.50	25.00
320-Uncle Wiggily (#1)	5.85	17.50	35.00
321-Little Scouts (#1) (3/51)	3.00	7.50	15.00
322-Porky Pig in Roaring Rockets (#1 on-c)	4.70	14.00	28.00
323-Susie Q. Smith (#1) (3/51)	4.00	11.00	22.00
324-I Met a Handsome Cowboy (3/51)	7.50	22.50	45.00
325-Mickey Mouse in The Haunted Castle (#2) (Disney) (4/51)	7.50	22.50	45.00
326-Andy Panda (#1) (Lantz)	3.60	9.00	18.00
327-Bugs Bunny and the Rajah's Treasure (#2)	6.35	19.00	38.00
328-Donald Duck in Old California (#2) by Carl Barks-Peyote drug use issue (Disney) (5/51)	23.00	70.00	185.00
329-Roy Roger's Trigger (#1)(5/51)-Photo-c	10.00	30.00	65.00
330-Porky Pig Meets the Bristled Bruiser (#2)	4.70	14.00	28.00
331-Alice in Wonderland (Disney) (1951)	10.00	30.00	60.00
332-Little Beaver	4.00	10.00	20.00
333-Wilderness Trek (Zane Grey) (5/51)	4.70	14.00	28.00
334-Mickey Mouse and Yukon Gold (Disney) (6/51)	7.50	22.50	45.00
335-Francis the Famous Talking Mule (#1)-1st Dell non animated movie comic (all issues based on movie)	8.35	25.00	50.00
336-Woody Woodpecker (Lantz)	4.00	10.00	20.00
337-The Brownies-not by Walt Kelly	4.00	10.50	21.00
338-Bugs Bunny and the Rocking Horse Thieves	6.35	19.00	38.00
339-Donald Duck and the Magic Fountain-not by Carl Barks (Disney) (7-8/51)	5.35	16.00	32.00
340-King of the Royal Mounted (7/51)	5.85	17.50	35.00
341-Unbirthday Party with Alice in Wonderland (Disney) (7/51)	10.00	30.00	70.00
342-Porky Pig the Lucky Peppermint Mine	4.00	10.00	20.00
343-Mickey Mouse in The Ruby Eye of Homar-Guy-Am (Disney)-Reprinted in Mickey Mouse #104	5.85	17.50	35.00
344-Sergeant Preston from Challenge of The Yukon (#1) (TV)	10.00	30.00	65.00
345-Andy Panda in Scotland Yard (8-10/51) (Lantz)	3.60	9.00	18.00
346-Hideout (Zane Grey)	4.70	14.00	28.00
347-Bugs Bunny the Frigid Hare (8-9/51)	6.35	19.00	38.00
348-Donald Duck "The Crocodile Collector"-Barks-c only (Disney) (9-10/51)	8.35	25.00	50.00
349-Uncle Wiggily	5.85	17.50	35.00
350-Woody Woodpecker (Lantz)	4.00	10.00	20.00
351-Porky Pig and the Grand Canyon Giant (9-10/51)	4.00	10.00	20.00

	GD25	FN65	NM94
352-Mickey Mouse in The Mystery of Painted Valley (Disney)	5.85	17.50	35.00
353-Duck Album (#1)-Barks-c (Disney)	4.70	14.00	28.00
354-Raggedy Ann & Andy	4.70	14.00	28.00
355-Bugs Bunny Hot-Rod Hare	6.35	19.00	38.00
356-Donald Duck in "Rags to Riches"-Barks-c only	8.35	25.00	50.00
357-Comeback (Zane Grey)	4.00	12.00	24.00
358-Andy Panda (Lantz) (11-1/52)	3.60	9.00	18.00
359-Frosty the Snowman (#1)	6.70	20.00	40.00
360-Porky Pig in Tree of Fortune (11-12/51)	4.00	10.00	20.00
361-Santa Claus Funnies	4.00	10.00	20.00
362-Mickey Mouse and the Smuggled Diamonds (Disney)	5.85	17.50	35.00
363-King of the Royal Mounted	5.00	15.00	30.00
364-Woody Woodpecker (Lantz)	3.20	8.00	16.00
365-The Brownies-not by Kelly	4.00	10.50	21.00
366-Bugs Bunny Uncle Buckskin Comes to Town (12-1/52)	6.35	19.00	38.00
367-Donald Duck in "A Christmas for Shacktown" by Carl Barks (Disney) (1-2/52)	20.00	60.00	160.00
368-Bob Clampett's Beany and Cecil (#1)	17.00	51.00	120.00
369-The Lone Ranger's Famous Horse Hi-Yo Silver (#1); Silver's origin	8.35	25.00	50.00
370-Porky Pig in Trouble in the Big Trees	4.00	10.00	20.00
371-Mickey Mouse in The Inca Idol Case (1952) (Disney)	5.85	17.50	35.00
372-Riders of the Purple Sage (Zane Grey)	4.00	12.00	24.00
373-Sergeant Preston (TV)	5.85	17.50	35.00
374-Woody Woodpecker (Lantz)	3.20	8.00	16.00
375-John Carter of Mars (E. R. Burroughs)-Jesse Marsh-a; origin	20.00	60.00	140.00
376-Bugs Bunny, "The Magic Sneeze"	6.35	19.00	38.00
377-Susie Q. Smith	3.20	8.00	16.00
378-Tom Corbett, Space Cadet (#1) (TV)-McWilliams-a	14.00	43.00	100.00
379-Donald Duck in "Southern Hospitality"-not by Barks (Disney)	4.50	14.00	32.00
380-Raggedy Ann & Andy	4.70	14.00	28.00
381-Marge's Tubby (#1)	13.00	40.00	90.00
382-Snow White and the Seven Dwarfs (Disney)-origin; partial reprint of 4-Color #49 (Movie)	7.50	22.50	45.00
383-Andy Panda (Lantz)	2.80	7.00	14.00
384-King of the Royal Mounted (3/52)(Zane Grey)	5.00	15.00	30.00
385-Porky Pig inThe Isle of Missing Ships (3-4/52)	4.00	10.00	20.00
386-Uncle Scrooge (#1)-by Carl Barks (Disney) in "Only a Poor Old Man" (3/52)	75.00	225.00	525.00
387-Mickey Mouse in High Tibet (Disney) (4-5/52)	5.85	17.50	35.00
388-Oswald the Rabbit (Lantz)	3.60	9.00	18.00
389-Andy Hardy Comics (#1)	3.60	9.00	18.00
390-Woody Woodpecker (Lantz)	3.20	8.00	16.00
391-Uncle Wiggily	4.70	14.00	28.00
392-Hi-Yo Silver	4.00	12.00	24.00
393-Bugs Bunny	6.35	19.00	38.00
394-Donald Duck in Malayalaya-Barks-c only (Disney)	8.35	25.00	50.00
395-Forlorn River(Zane Grey)-First Nevada (5/52)	4.00	12.00	24.00
396-Tales of the Texas Rangers(#1)(TV)-Photo-c	10.00	30.00	65.00
397-Sergeant Preston of the Yukon (TV) (5/52)	5.85	17.50	35.00
398-The Brownies-not by Kelly	4.00	10.50	21.00
399-Porky Pig in The Lost Gold Mine	4.00	10.00	20.00
400-Tom Corbett, Space Cadet (TV)-McWilliams-c/a	9.15	27.50	55.00
401-Mickey Mouse and Goofy's Mechanical Wizard (Disney) (6-7/52)			

	GD25	FN65	NM94
	4.70	14.00	28.00
402-Mary Jane and Sniffles	9.15	27.50	55.00
403-Li'l Bad Wolf (Disney) (6/52)	4.00	11.00	22.00
404-The Range Rider (#1) (TV)-Photo-c	10.00	30.00	60.00
405-Woody Woodpecker (Lantz) (6-7/52)	3.20	8.00	16.00
406-Tweety and Sylvester (#1)	5.85	17.50	35.00
407-Bugs Bunny, Foreign-Legion Hare	4.70	14.00	28.00
408-Donald Duck and the Golden Helmet by Carl Barks (Disney) (7-8/52)	20.00	60.00	160.00
409-Andy Panda (7-9/52)	2.80	7.00	14.00
410-Porky Pig in The Water Wizard (7/52)	4.00	10.00	20.00
411-Mickey Mouse and the Old Sea Dog (Disney) (8-9/52)	4.70	14.00	28.00
412-Nevada (Zane Grey)	4.00	12.00	24.00
413-Robin Hood (Disney-Movie) (8/52)-Photo-c	5.00	15.00	30.00
414-Bob Clampett's Beany and Cecil (TV)	14.00	43.00	100.00
415-Rootie Kazootie (#1) (TV)	10.00	30.00	60.00
416-Woody Woodpecker (Lantz)	3.20	8.00	16.00
417-Double Trouble with Goober (#1) (8/52)	2.80	7.00	14.00
418-Rusty Riley, a Boy, a Horse, and a Dog (#1)-Frank Godwin-a (strip reprints) (8/52)	4.00	11.00	22.00
419-Sergeant Preston (TV)	5.85	17.50	35.00
420-Bugs Bunny in The Mysterious Buckaroo (8-9/52)	4.70	14.00	28.00
421-Tom Corbett, Space Cadet(TV)-McWilliams-a	9.15	27.50	55.00
422-Donald Duck and the Gilded Man, by Carl Barks (Disney) (9-10/52) (#423 on inside)	20.00	60.00	160.00
423-Rhubarb, Owner of the Brooklyn Ball Club (The Millionaire Cat) (#1)	4.00	11.00	22.00
424-Flash Gordon-Test Flight in Space (9/52)	7.50	22.50	45.00
425-Zorro, the Return of	11.50	34.00	80.00
426-Porky Pig in The Scalawag Leprechaun	4.00	10.00	20.00
427-Mickey Mouse and the Wonderful Whizzix (Disney) (10-11/52)-Reprinted in Mickey Mouse #100	4.70	14.00	28.00
428-Uncle Wiggily	4.20	12.50	25.00
429-Pluto in "Why Dogs Leave Home" (Disney) (10/52)	4.70	14.00	28.00
430-Marge's Tubby, the Shadow of a Man-Eater	8.35	25.00	50.00
431-Woody Woodpecker (10/52) (Lantz)	3.20	8.00	16.00
432-Bugs Bunny and the Rabbit Olympics	4.70	14.00	28.00
433-Wildfire (Zane Grey) (11-1/52-53)	4.00	12.00	24.00
434-Rin Tin Tin-"In Dark Danger" (#1) (TV) (11/52)-Photo-c	16.00	48.00	110.00
435-Frosty the Snowman (11/52)	4.00	10.50	21.00
436-The Brownies-not by Kelly (11/52)	3.60	9.00	18.00
437-John Carter of Mars (E. R. Burroughs)-Marsh-a	14.00	43.00	100.00
438-Annie Oakley (#1) (TV)	11.00	32.00	75.00
439-Little Hiawatha (Disney) (12/52)	4.20	12.50	25.00
440-Black Beauty (12/52)	3.20	8.00	16.00
441-Fearless Fagan	3.20	8.00	16.00
442-Peter Pan (Disney) (Movie)	6.70	20.00	40.00
443-Ben Bowie and His Mountain Men (#1)	6.70	20.00	40.00
444-Marge's Tubby	8.35	25.00	50.00
445-Charlie McCarthy	4.20	12.50	25.00
446-Captain Hook and Peter Pan (Disney) (Movie) (1/53)	7.50	22.50	45.00
447-Andy Hardy Comics	2.40	6.00	12.00
448-Bob Clampett's Beany and Cecil (TV)	14.00	43.00	100.00
449-Tappan's Burro (Zane Grey) (2-4/53)	4.00	12.00	24.00
450-Duck Album; Barks-c (Disney)	4.20	12.50	25.00
451-Rusty Riley-Frank Godwin-a (strip reprints) (2/53)	3.20	8.00	16.00
452-Raggedy Ann & Andy (1953)	4.70	14.00	28.00
453-Susie Q. Smith (2/53)	3.20	8.00	16.00
454-Krazy Kat Comics; not by Herriman	4.00	10.50	21.00
455-Johnny Mack Brown Comics(3/53)-Photo-c	4.70	14.00	28.00
456-Uncle Scrooge Back to the Klondike (#2) by Barks (3/53) (Disney)	38.00	115.00	265.00
457-Daffy (#1)	7.50	22.50	45.00
458-Oswald the Rabbit (Lantz)	2.80	7.00	14.00
459-Rootie Kazootie (TV)	6.70	20.00	40.00
460-Buck Jones (4/53)	4.70	14.00	28.00
461-Marge's Tubby	7.50	22.50	45.00
462-Little Scouts	1.80	4.50	9.00
463-Petunia (4/53)	3.20	8.00	16.00
464-Bozo (4/53)	9.15	27.50	55.00
465-Francis the Famous Talking Mule	4.20	12.50	25.00
466-Rhubarb, the Millionaire Cat	3.00	7.50	15.00
467-Desert Gold (Zane Grey) (5-7/53)	4.00	12.00	24.00
468-Goofy (#1) (Disney)	8.35	25.00	50.00
469-Beetle Bailey (#1) (5/53	8.35	25.00	50.00
470-Elmer Fudd	2.70	6.00	12.00
471-Double Trouble with Goober	2.00	5.00	10.00
472-Wild Bill Elliott (6/53)-Photo-c	5.35	16.00	32.00
473-Li'l Bad Wolf (Disney) (6/53)	3.60	9.00	18.00
474-Mary Jane and Sniffles	8.35	25.00	50.00
475-M.G.M.'s The Two Mouseketeers (#1)	5.85	17.50	35.00
476-Rin Tin Tin (TV)-Photo-c	9.15	27.50	55.00
477-Bob Clampett's Beany and Cecil (TV)	14.00	43.00	100.00
478-Charlie McCarthy	4.20	12.50	25.00
479-Queen of the West Dale Evans (#1)	11.50	34.00	80.00
480-Andy Hardy Comics	2.40	6.00	12.00
481-Annie Oakley And Tagg (TV)	7.50	22.50	45.00
482-Brownies-not by Kelly	3.60	9.00	18.00
483-Little Beaver (7/53)	3.60	9.00	18.00
484-River Feud (Zane Grey) (8-10/53)	4.00	12.00	24.00
485-The Little People-Walt Scott (#1)	5.85	17.50	35.00
486-Rusty Riley-Frank Godwin strip-r	3.20	8.00	16.00
487-Mowgli, the Jungle Book (Rudyard Kipling's)	4.20	12.50	25.00
488-John Carter of Mars (Burroughs)-Marsh-a	14.00	43.00	100.00
489-Tweety and Sylvester	3.60	9.00	18.00
490-Jungle Jim (#1)	5.85	17.50	35.00
491-Silvertip (#1) (Max Brand)-Kinstler-a (8/53)	9.15	27.50	55.00
492-Duck Album (Disney)	3.60	9.00	18.00
493-Johnny Mack Brown; photo-c	4.70	14.00	28.00
494-The Little King (#1)	8.35	25.00	50.00
495-Uncle Scrooge (#3) (Disney)-by Carl Barks (9/53)	32.00	95.00	220.00
496-The Green Hornet	19.00	58.00	135.00
497-Zorro (Sword of...)	11.50	34.00	80.00
498-Bugs Bunny's Album (9/53)	4.00	10.00	20.00
499-M.G.M.'s Spike and Tyke (#1) (9/53)	2.80	7.00	14.00
500-Buck Jones	4.70	14.00	28.00
501-Francis the Famous Talking Mule	4.20	12.50	25.00
502-Rootie Kazootie (TV)	6.70	20.00	40.00
503-Uncle Wiggily (10/53)	4.20	12.50	25.00
504-Krazy Kat; not by Herriman	4.00	10.50	21.00
505-The Sword and the Rose (Disney) (10/53) (TV)-Photo-c	4.70	14.00	28.00
506-The Little Scouts	1.80	4.50	9.00
507-Oswald the Rabbit (Lantz)	2.80	7.00	14.00
508-Bozo (10/53)	9.15	27.50	55.00
509-Pluto (Disney) (10/53)	4.70	14.00	28.00
510-Son of Black Beauty	3.20	8.00	16.00
511-Outlaw Trail (Zane Grey)-Kinstler-a	4.35	13.00	26.00
512-Flash Gordon (11/53)	4.35	13.00	26.00
513-Ben Bowie and His Mountain Men	4.00	10.50	21.00
514-Frosty the Snowman (11/53)	3.60	9.00	18.00
515-Andy Hardy	2.40	6.00	12.00
516-Double Trouble With Goober	2.00	5.00	10.00
517-Chip 'N' Dale (#1) (Disney)	4.00	10.50	21.00

Four Color #428, © Howard Garis

Four Color #459, © Rootie Kazootie, Inc.

Four Color #481, © Annie Oakley Ent.

Four Color #534, © Jill Marie Haycox

Four Color #577, © M.G.M.

Four Color #584, © Johnny Mack Brown

	GD25	FN65	NM94
518-Rivets (11/53)	2.40	6.00	12.00
519-Steve Canyon (#1)-Not by Milton Caniff	6.70	20.00	40.00
520-Wild Bill Elliott-Photo-c	5.35	16.00	32.00
521-Beetle Bailey (12/53)	4.20	12.50	25.00
522-The Brownies	3.60	9.00	18.00
523-Rin Tin Tin (TV)-Photo-c (12/53)	9.15	27.50	55.00
524-Tweety and Sylvester	3.60	9.00	18.00
525-Santa Claus Funnies	2.40	6.00	12.00
526-Napoleon	1.50	4.50	10.00
527-Charlie McCarthy	4.20	12.50	25.00
528-Queen of the West Dale Evans; photo-c	8.35	25.00	50.00
529-Little Beaver	3.60	9.00	18.00
530-Bob Clampett's Beany and Cecil (TV) (1/54)	14.00	43.00	100.00
531-Duck Album (Disney)	3.60	9.00	18.00
532-The Rustlers (Zane Grey) (2-4/54)	3.50	10.50	24.00
533-Raggedy Ann and Andy	4.70	14.00	28.00
534-Western Marshal(Ernest Haycox's)-Kinstler-a	5.00	15.00	30.00
535-I Love Lucy (#1) (TV) (2/54)-photo-c	32.00	95.00	225.00
536-Daffy (3/54)	4.00	11.00	22.00
537-Stormy, the Thoroughbred... (Disney-Movie) on top 2/3 of each page; Pluto story on bottom 1/3 of each page (2/54)	4.00	10.00	20.00
538-The Mask of Zorro; Kinstler-a	12.00	36.00	85.00
539-Ben and Me (Disney) (3/54)	3.00	7.50	15.00
540-Knights of the Round Table (3/54) (Movie)-Photo-c	5.85	17.50	35.00
541-Johnny Mack Brown; photo-c	4.70	14.00	28.00
542-Super Circus Featuring Mary Hartline (TV) (3/54)	4.70	14.00	28.00
543-Uncle Wiggily (3/54)	4.20	12.50	25.00
544-Rob Roy (Disney-Movie)-Manning-a; photo-c	9.15	27.50	55.00
545-The Wonderful Adventures of Pinocchio-Partial reprint of 4-Color #92 (Disney-Movie)	4.70	14.00	28.00
546-Buck Jones	4.70	14.00	28.00
547-Francis the Famous Talking Mule	4.20	12.50	25.00
548-Krazy Kat; not by Herriman (4/54)	3.60	9.00	18.00
549-Oswald the Rabbit (Lantz)	2.80	7.00	14.00
550-The Little Scouts	1.80	4.50	9.00
551-Bozo (4/54)	9.15	27.50	55.00
552-Beetle Bailey	4.20	12.50	25.00
553-Susie Q. Smith	3.20	8.00	16.00
554-Rusty Riley (Frank Godwin strip-r)	3.20	8.00	16.00
555-Range War (Zane Grey)	4.00	12.00	24.00
556-Double Trouble With Goober (5/54)	2.00	5.00	10.00
557-Ben Bowie and His Mountain Men	4.00	10.50	21.00
558-Elmer Fudd (5/54)	2.40	6.00	12.00
559-I Love Lucy (#2) (TV)-Photo-c	22.00	65.00	150.00
560-Duck Album (Disney) (5/54)	3.60	9.00	18.00
561-Mr. Magoo (5/54)	9.15	27.50	55.00
562-Goofy (Disney)	4.20	12.50	25.00
563-Rhubarb, the Millionaire Cat (6/54)	3.00	7.50	15.00
564-Li'l Bad Wolf (Disney)	3.60	9.00	18.00
565-Jungle Jim	3.60	9.00	18.00
566-Son of Black Beauty	3.20	8.00	16.00
567-Prince Valiant (#1)-By Bob Fuje (Movie)-Photo-c	8.35	25.00	50.00
568-Gypsy Colt (Movie) (6/54)	4.20	12.50	25.00
569-Priscilla's Pop	2.80	7.00	14.00
570-Bob Clampett's Beany and Cecil (TV)	14.00	43.00	100.00
571-Charlie McCarthy	4.20	12.50	25.00
572-Silvertip (Max Brand) (7/54); Kinstler-a	4.70	14.00	28.00
573-The Little People by Walt Scott	3.60	9.00	18.00
574-The Hand of Zorro	11.50	34.00	80.00
575-Annie Oakley and Tagg (TV)-Photo-c	7.50	22.50	45.00
576-Angel (#1) (8/54)	2.40	6.00	12.00

	GD25	FN65	NM94
577-M.G.M.'s Spike and Tyke	2.00	5.00	10.00
578-Steve Canyon (8/54)	4.35	13.00	26.00
579-Francis the Famous Talking Mule	4.20	12.50	25.00
580-Six Gun Ranch (Luke Short-8/54)	4.00	10.00	20.00
581-Chip 'N' Dale (#2) (Disney)	2.40	6.00	12.00
582-Mowgli Jungle Book (Kipling) (8/54)	4.00	10.00	20.00
583-The Lost Wagon Train (Zane Grey)	4.00	12.00	24.00
584-Johnny Mack Brown-Photo-c	4.70	14.00	28.00
585-Bugs Bunny's Album	4.00	10.00	20.00
586-Duck Album (Disney)	3.60	9.00	18.00
587-The Little Scouts	1.80	4.50	9.00
588-King Richard and the Crusaders (Movie) (10/54) Matt Baker-a; photo-c	10.00	30.00	60.00
589-Buck Jones	4.70	14.00	28.00
590-Hansel and Gretel; partial photo-c	5.00	15.00	30.00
591-Western Marshal(Ernest Haycox's)-Kinstler-a	5.00	15.00	30.00
592-Super Circus (TV)	4.70	14.00	28.00
593-Oswald the Rabbit (Lantz)	2.80	7.00	14.00
594-Bozo (10/54)	9.15	27.50	55.00
595-Pluto (Disney)	4.00	10.00	20.00
596-Turok, Son of Stone (#1)	43.00	130.00	300.00
597-The Little King	5.85	17.50	35.00
598-Captain Davy Jones	3.20	8.00	16.00
599-Ben Bowie and His Mountain Men	4.00	10.50	21.00
600-Daisy Duck's Diary (#1) (Disney) (11/54)	4.70	14.00	28.00
601-Frosty the Snowman	3.60	9.00	18.00
602-Mr. Magoo and Gerald McBoing-Boing	9.15	27.50	55.00
603-M.G.M.'s The Two Mouseketeers	3.60	9.00	18.00
604-Shadow on the Trail (Zane Grey)	4.00	12.00	24.00
605-The Brownies-not by Kelly (12/54)	3.60	9.00	18.00
606-Sir Lancelot (not TV)	7.50	22.50	45.00
607-Santa Claus Funnies	3.60	9.00	18.00
608-Silvertip-"Valley of Vanishing Men" (Max Brand)-Kinstler-a	4.70	14.00	28.00
609-The Littlest Outlaw (Disney-Movie) (1/55)-Photo-c	4.70	14.00	28.00
610-Drum Beat (Movie); Alan Ladd photo-c	10.00	30.00	65.00
611-Duck Album (Disney)	3.60	9.00	18.00
612-Little Beaver (1/55)	3.00	7.50	15.00
613-Western Marshal (Ernest Haycox's) (2/55)-Kinstler-a	5.00	15.00	30.00
614-20,000 Leagues Under the Sea (Disney) (Movie) (2/55)	5.00	15.00	30.00
615-Daffy	4.00	11.00	22.00
616-To the Last Man (Zane Grey)	4.00	12.00	24.00
617-The Quest of Zorro	11.50	34.00	80.00
618-Johnny Mack Brown; photo-c	4.70	14.00	28.00
619-Krazy Kat; not by Herriman	3.60	9.00	18.00
620-Mowgli Jungle Book (Kipling)	4.00	10.00	20.00
621-Francis the Famous Talking Mule (4/55)	4.00	10.50	21.00
622-Beetle Bailey	4.20	12.50	25.00
623-Oswald the Rabbit (Lantz)	2.00	5.00	10.00
624-Treasure Island(Disney-Movie)(4/55)-Photo-c	4.20	12.50	25.00
625-Beaver Valley (Disney-Movie)	4.00	10.00	20.00
626-Ben Bowie and His Mountain Men	4.00	10.50	21.00
627-Goofy (Disney) (5/55)	4.20	12.50	25.00
628-Elmer Fudd	2.40	6.00	12.00
629-Lady and the Tramp with Jock (Disney)	3.60	9.00	18.00
630-Priscilla's Pop	2.80	7.00	14.00
631-Davy Crockett, Indian Fighter (#1) (Disney) (5/55) (TV)-Fess Parker photo-c	8.35	25.00	50.00
632-Fighting Caravans (Zane Grey)	4.00	12.00	24.00
633-The Little People by Walt Scott (6/55)	3.60	8.00	18.00
634-Lady and the Tramp Album (Disney) (6/55)	3.20	8.00	16.00

	GD25	FN65	NM94
635-Bob Clampett's Beany and Cecil (TV)	14.00	43.00	100.00
636-Chip 'N' Dale (Disney)	2.40	6.00	12.00
637-Silvertip (Max Brand)-Kinstler-a	4.70	14.00	28.00
638-M.G.M.'s Spike and Tyke (8/55)	2.00	5.00	10.00
639-Davy Crockett at the Alamo (Disney) (7/55) (TV)-Fess Parker photo-c	5.85	17.50	35.00
640-Western Marshal(Ernest Haycox's)-Kinstler-a	5.00	15.00	30.00
641-Steve Canyon (1955)-by Caniff	4.35	13.00	26.00
642-M.G.M.'s The Two Mouseketeers	3.60	9.00	18.00
643-Wild Bill Elliott; photo-c	4.35	13.00	26.00
644-Sir Walter Raleigh (5/55)-Based on movie "The Virgin Queen;" photo-c	6.70	20.00	40.00
645-Johnny Mack Brown; photo-c	4.70	14.00	28.00
646-Dotty Dripple and Taffy (#1)	3.60	9.00	18.00
647-Bugs Bunny's Album (9/55)	4.00	10.00	20.00
648-Jace Pearson of the Texas Rangers (TV)-Photo-c	5.35	16.00	32.00
649-Duck Album (Disney)	3.60	9.00	18.00
650-Prince Valiant; by Bob Fuje	4.70	14.00	28.00
651-King Colt (Luke Short) (9/55)-Kinstler-a	4.00	12.00	24.00
652-Buck Jones	3.60	9.00	18.00
653-Smokey the Bear (#1) (10/55)	8.35	25.00	50.00
654-Pluto (Disney)	4.00	10.00	20.00
655-Francis the Famous Talking Mule	4.00	10.50	21.00
656-Turok, Son of Stone (#2) (10/55)	29.00	85.00	200.00
657-Ben Bowie and His Mountain Men	4.00	10.50	21.00
658-Goofy (Disney)	4.20	12.50	25.00
659-Daisy Duck's Diary (Disney)	3.20	8.00	16.00
660-Little Beaver	3.00	7.50	15.00
661-Frosty the Snowman	3.60	9.00	18.00
662-Zoo Parade (TV)-Marlin Perkins (11/55)	4.70	14.00	28.00
663-Winky Dink (TV)	7.50	22.50	45.00
664-Davy Crockett in the Great Keelboat Race (TV) (Disney) (11/55)-Fess Parker photo-c	6.70	20.00	40.00
665-The African Lion (Disney-Movie) (11/55)	4.20	12.50	25.00
666-Santa Claus Funnies	3.60	9.00	18.00
667-Silvertip and the Stolen Stallion (Max Brand) (12/55)-Kinstler-a	4.70	14.00	28.00
668-Dumbo (Disney) (12/55)	5.00	15.00	30.00
668-Dumbo (Disney) (1/58) different cover, same contents as above	5.00	15.00	30.00
669-Robin Hood (Disney-Movie) (12/55)-reprint of #413; photo-c	4.00	10.00	20.00
670-M.G.M's Mouse Musketeers (#1) (1/56)-Formerly the Two Mouseketeers	2.80	7.00	14.00
671-Davy Crockett and the River Pirates (TV) (Disney) (12/55)-Jesse Marsh-a; Fess Parker photo-c	6.70	20.00	40.00
672-Quentin Durward (1/56) (Movie)-Photo-c	5.85	17.50	35.00
673-Buffalo Bill, Jr. (#1) (TV)-Photo-c	5.85	17.50	35.00
674-The Little Rascals (#1) (TV)	5.85	17.50	35.00
675-Steve Donovan, Western Marshal (#1) (TV)-Kinstler-a; photo-c	6.70	20.00	40.00
676-Will-Yum!	2.80	7.00	14.00
677-Little King	5.85	17.50	35.00
678-The Last Hunt (Movie)-Photo-c	5.85	17.50	35.00
679-Gunsmoke (#1) (TV)	11.00	32.00	75.00
680-Out Our Way with the Worry Wart (2/56)	2.80	7.00	14.00
681-Forever, Darling (Movie) with Lucille Ball & Desi Arnaz (2/56)-; photo-c	10.00	30.00	65.00
682-When Knighthood Was in Flower (Disney-Movie)-Reprint of #505; photo-c	4.20	12.50	25.00
683-Hi and Lois (3/56)	2.40	6.00	12.00
684-Helen of Troy (Movie)-Buscema-a; photo-c	10.00	30.00	70.00
685-Johnny Mack Brown; photo-c	4.70	14.00	28.00
686-Duck Album (Disney)	3.60	9.00	18.00
687-The Indian Fighter (Movie)-Kirk Douglas photo-c	5.00	15.00	30.00
688-Alexander the Great (Movie) (5/56) Buscema-a; photo-c	5.85	17.50	35.00
689-Elmer Fudd (3/56)	2.40	6.00	12.00
690-The Conqueror (Movie) - John Wayne photo-c	14.00	43.00	100.00
691-Dotty Dripple and Taffy	2.40	6.00	12.00
692-The Little People-Walt Scott	3.20	8.00	16.00
693-Song of the South (Disney) (1956)-Partial reprint of #129	3.20	8.00	16.00
694-Super Circus (TV)-Photo-c	4.70	14.00	28.00
695-Little Beaver	3.00	7.50	15.00
696-Krazy Kat; not by Herriman (4/56)	3.60	9.00	18.00
697-Oswald the Rabbit (Lantz)	2.00	5.00	10.00
698-Francis the Famous Talking Mule (4/56)	4.00	10.50	21.00
699-Prince Valiant-by Bob Fuje	4.70	14.00	28.00
700-Water Birds and the Olympic Elk (Disney-Movie) (4/56)	4.20	12.50	25.00
701-Jiminy Cricket (#1) (Disney) (5/56)	5.00	15.00	30.00
702-The Goofy Success Story (Disney)	4.20	12.50	25.00
703-Scamp (#1) (Disney)	4.70	14.00	28.00
704-Priscilla's Pop (5/56)	2.80	7.00	14.00
705-Brave Eagle (#1) (TV)-Photo-c	4.70	14.00	28.00
706-Bongo and Lumpjaw (Disney) (6/56)	2.80	7.00	14.00
707-Corky and White Shadow (Disney) (5/56)-Mickey Mouse Club (TV); photo-c	4.00	11.00	22.00
708-Smokey the Bear	4.20	12.50	25.00
709-The Searchers (Movie) - John Wayne photo-c	29.00	85.00	200.00
710-Francis the Famous Talking Mule	4.00	10.50	21.00
711-M.G.M's Mouse Musketeers	2.00	5.00	10.00
712-The Great Locomotive Chase (Disney-Movie) (9/56)-Photo-c	4.70	14.00	28.00
713-The Animal World (Movie) (8/56)	4.70	14.00	28.00
714-Spin and Marty (#1) (TV) (Disney)-Mickey Mouse Club (6/56)-Photo-c	10.00	3.00	60.00
715-Timmy (8/56)	2.80	7.00	14.00
716-Man in Space (Disney-Movie)	4.20	12.50	25.00
717-Moby Dick (Movie)-Photo-c	7.50	22.50	45.00
718-Dotty Dripple and Taffy	2.40	6.00	12.00
719-Prince Valiant; by Bob Fuje (8/56)	4.70	14.00	28.00
720-Gunsmoke (TV)-Photo-c	5.85	17.50	35.00
721-Captain Kangaroo (TV)-Photo-c	13.00	40.00	90.00
722-Johnny Mack Brown-Photo-c	4.70	14.00	28.00
723-Santiago (Movie)-Kinstler-a (9/56); Alan Ladd photo-c	10.00	30.00	70.00
724-Bugs Bunny's Album	4.00	10.00	20.00
725-Elmer Fudd (9/56)	2.00	5.00	10.00
726-Duck Album (Disney) (9/56)	3.20	8.00	16.00
727-The Nature of Things (TV) (Disney)-Jesse Marsh-a	4.70	14.00	28.00
728-M.G.M's Mouse Musketeers	2.00	5.00	10.00
729-Bob Son of Battle (11/56)	3.20	8.00	16.00
730-Smokey Stover	3.20	8.00	16.00
731-Silvertip and The Fighting Four (Max Brand)-Kinstler-a	4.70	14.00	28.00
732-Zorro, the Challenge of (10/56)	11.50	34.00	80.00
733-Buck Jones	3.60	9.00	18.00
734-Cheyenne (#1) (TV) (10/56)-Clint Walker photo-c	11.50	34.00	80.00
735-Crusader Rabbit (#1) (TV)	24.00	70.00	165.00
736-Pluto (Disney)	3.20	8.00	16.00
737-Steve Canyon-Caniff-a	4.35	13.00	26.00
738-Westward Ho, the Wagons (Disney-Movie)-Fess Parker photo-c	4.70	14.00	28.00
739-Bounty Guns (Luke Short)-Drucker-a	4.00	10.00	20.00

DELL
Walt Disney's
Lady and the Tramp
ALBUM

Four Color #634, © WDC

Four Color #676, © John F. Dille

Four Color #713, © Warner Bros.

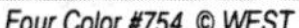
Four Color #754, © WEST

Four Color #789, © Dodd, Mead, & Co.

Four Color #808, © WDC

	GD25	FN65	NM94
740-Chilly Willy (#1) (Walter Lantz)	4.00	10.00	20.00
741-The Fastest Gun Alive (Movie)(9/56)-Photo-c	6.70	20.00	40.00
742-Buffalo Bill, Jr. (TV)-Photo-c	4.00	12.00	24.00
743-Daisy Duck's Diary (Disney) (11/56)	3.20	8.00	16.00
744-Little Beaver	3.00	7.50	15.00
745-Francis the Famous Talking Mule	4.00	10.50	21.00
746-Dotty Dripple and Taffy	2.40	6.00	12.00
747-Goofy (Disney)	4.00	12.50	25.00
748-Frosty the Snowman (11/56)	3.20	8.00	16.00
749-Secrets of Life (Disney-Movie)-Photo-c	4.70	14.00	28.00
750-The Great Cat Family (Disney-Movie)	4.70	14.00	28.00
751-Our Miss Brooks (TV)-Photo-c	6.70	20.00	40.00
752-Mandrake, the Magician	8.35	25.00	50.00
753-Walt Scott's Little People (11/56)	3.20	8.00	16.00
754-Smokey the Bear	4.20	12.50	25.00
755-The Littlest Snowman (12/56)	4.00	10.00	20.00
756-Santa Claus Funnies	3.60	9.00	18.00
757-The True Story of Jesse James (Movie)-Photo-c	9.15	27.50	55.00
758-Bear Country (Disney-Movie)	4.20	12.50	25.00
759-Circus Boy (TV)-The Monkees' Mickey Dolenz photo-c (12/56)	10.00	30.00	65.00
760-The Hardy Boys (#1) (TV) (Disney)-Mickey Mouse Club; photo-c	9.15	27.50	55.00
761-Howdy Doody (TV) (1/57)	9.15	27.50	55.00
762-The Sharkfighters (Movie) (1/57); Buscema-a; photo-c	10.00	30.00	70.00
763-Grandma Duck's Farm Friends (#1) (Disney)	5.85	17.50	35.00
764-M.G.M's Mouse Musketeers	2.00	5.00	10.00
765-Will-Yum!	2.80	7.00	14.00
766-Buffalo Bill, Jr. (TV)-Photo-c	4.00	12.00	24.00
767-Spin and Marty (TV) (Disney)-Mickey Mouse Club (2/57)	5.85	17.50	35.00
768-Steve Donovan, Western Marshal (TV)-Kinstler-a; photo-c	5.35	16.00	32.00
769-Gunsmoke (TV)	5.85	17.50	35.00
770-Brave Eagle (TV)-Photo-c	3.20	8.00	16.00
771-Brand of Empire (Luke Short)(3/57)-Drucker-a	4.00	10.00	20.00
772-Cheyenne (TV)-Clint Walker photo-c	6.70	20.00	40.00
773-The Brave One (Movie)-Photo-c	4.20	12.50	25.00
774-Hi and Lois (3/57)	2.40	6.00	12.00
775-Sir Lancelot and Brian (TV)-Buscema-a; photo-c	9.15	27.50	55.00
776-Johnny Mack Brown; photo-c	4.70	14.00	28.00
777-Scamp (Disney) (3/57)	3.00	7.50	15.00
778-The Little Rascals (TV)	3.60	9.00	18.00
779-Lee Hunter, Indian Fighter (3/57)	4.70	14.00	28.00
780-Captain Kangaroo (TV)-Photo-c	11.50	34.00	80.00
781-Fury (#1) (TV) (3/57)-Photo-c	9.15	27.50	55.00
782-Duck Album (Disney)	3.20	8.00	16.00
783-Elmer Fudd	2.00	5.00	10.00
784-Around the World in 80 Days (Movie) (2/57)-Photo-c	5.85	17.50	35.00
785-Circus Boy (TV) (4/57)-The Monkees' Mickey Dolenz photo-c	10.00	30.00	65.00
786-Cinderella (Disney) (3/57)-Partial-r of #272	3.60	9.00	18.00
787-Little Hiawatha (Disney) (4/57)	3.20	8.00	16.00
788-Prince Valiant; by Bob Fuje	4.70	14.00	28.00
789-Silvertip-Valley Thieves (Max Brand) (4/57)-Kinstler-a	4.70	14.00	28.00
790-The Wings of Eagles (Movie) (John Wayne)-Toth-a; John Wayne photo-c; 10 & 15 cent editions exist	15.00	45.00	105.00
791-The 77th Bengal Lancers (TV)-Photo-c	5.85	17.50	35.00
792-Oswald the Rabbit (Lantz)	2.00	5.00	10.00
793-Morty Meekle	2.80	7.00	14.00
794-The Count of Monte Cristo (5/57) (Movie)-Buscema-a	9.15	27.50	55.00
795-Jiminy Cricket (Disney)	3.60	9.00	18.00
796-Ludwig Bemelman's Madeleine and Genevieve	4.00	10.00	20.00
797-Gunsmoke (TV)-Photo-c	5.85	17.50	35.00
798-Buffalo Bill, Jr. (TV)-Photo-c	4.00	12.00	24.00
799-Priscilla's Pop	2.80	7.00	14.00
800-The Buccaneers (TV)-Photo-c	5.85	17.50	35.00
801-Dotty Dripple and Taffy	2.40	6.00	12.00
802-Goofy (Disney) (5/57)	4.20	12.50	25.00
803-Cheyenne (TV)-Clint Walker photo-c	6.70	20.00	40.00
804-Steve Canyon-Caniff-a (1957)	4.35	13.00	26.00
805-Crusader Rabbit (TV)	20.00	60.00	140.00
806-Scamp (Disney) (6/57)	3.00	7.50	15.00
807-Savage Range (Luke Short)-Drucker-a	4.00	10.00	20.00
808-Spin and Marty (TV)(Disney)-Mickey Mouse Club; photo-c	5.85	17.50	35.00
809-The Little People (Walt Scott)	3.20	8.00	16.00
810-Francis the Famous Talking Mule	3.60	9.00	18.00
811-Howdy Doody (TV) (7/57)	9.15	27.50	55.00
812-The Big Land(Movie); Alan Ladd photo-c	10.00	30.00	60.00
813-Circus Boy (TV)-The Monkees' Mickey Dolenz photo-c	10.00	30.00	65.00
814-Covered Wagons, Ho! (Disney)-Donald Duck (TV) (6/57); Mickey Mouse app.	3.60	9.00	18.00
815-Dragoon Wells Massacre (Movie)-photo-c	7.50	22.50	45.00
816-Brave Eagle (TV)-photo-c	3.20	8.00	16.00
817-Little Beaver	3.00	7.50	15.00
818-Smokey the Bear (6/57)	4.20	12.50	25.00
819-Mickey Mouse in Magicland (Disney) (7/57)	4.00	10.00	20.00
820-The Oklahoman (Movie)-Photo-c	8.35	25.00	50.00
821-Wringle Wrangle (Disney)-Based on movie "Westward Ho, the Wagons"-Marsh-a; Fess Parker photo-c	6.70	20.00	40.00
822-Paul Revere's Ride with Johnny Tremain (TV) (Disney)-Toth-a	10.00	30.00	60.00
823-Timmy	2.40	6.00	12.00
824-The Pride and the Passion (Movie) (8/57)-Frank Sinatra & Cary Grant photo-c	8.35	25.00	50.00
825-The Little Rascals (TV)	3.20	8.00	16.00
826-Spin and Marty and Annette (TV) (Disney)-Mickey Mouse Club; Annette Funicello photo-c	12.00	36.00	85.00
827-Smokey Stover (8/57)	3.20	8.00	16.00
828-Buffalo Bill, Jr. (TV)-Photo-c	4.00	12.00	24.00
829-Tales of the Pony Express (TV) (8/57)-Painted-c	4.00	11.00	22.00
830-The Hardy Boys (TV) (Disney)-Mickey Mouse Club (8/57); photo-c	7.50	22.50	45.00
831-No Sleep 'Til Dawn (Movie)-Carl Malden photo-c	5.85	17.50	35.00
832-Lolly and Pepper (#1)	3.20	8.00	16.00
833-Scamp (Disney) (9/57)	3.00	7.50	15.00
834-Johnny Mack Brown; photo-c	4.70	14.00	28.00
835-Silvertip-The False Rider (Max Brand)	4.00	12.00	24.00
836-Man in Flight (Disney) (TV) (9/57)	4.70	14.00	28.00
837-All-American Athlete Cotton Woods	4.70	14.00	28.00
838-Bugs Bunny's Life Story Album (9/57)	4.00	10.00	20.00
839-The Vigilantes (Movie)	6.70	20.00	40.00
840-Duck Album (Disney) (9/57)	3.20	8.00	16.00
841-Elmer Fudd	2.00	5.00	10.00
842-The Nature of Things (Disney-Movie) ('57)-Jesse Marsh-a (TV series)	4.70	14.00	28.00

	GD25	FN65	NM94
843-The First Americans (Disney) (TV)-Marsh-a	4.70	14.00	28.00
844-Gunsmoke (TV)-Photo-c	5.85	17.50	35.00
845-The Land Unknown (Movie)-Alex Toth-a	13.00	40.00	90.00
846-Gun Glory (Movie)-by Alex Toth; photo-c	12.00	36.00	85.00
847-Perri (squirrels) (Disney-Movie)-Two different covers published	3.20	8.00	16.00
848-Marauder's Moon	5.00	15.00	30.00
849-Prince Valiant; by Bob Fuje	4.70	14.00	28.00
850-Buck Jones	3.60	9.00	18.00
851-The Story of Mankind (Movie) (1/58)-Hedy Lamarr & Vincent Price photo-c	5.85	17.50	35.00
852-Chilly Willy (2/58) (Lantz)	2.40	6.00	12.00
853-Pluto (Disney) (10/57)	3.20	8.00	16.00
854-The Hunchback of Notre Dame (Movie)-Photo-c	11.50	34.00	80.00
855-Broken Arrow (TV)-Photo-c	4.70	14.00	28.00
856-Buffalo Bill, Jr. (TV)-Photo-c	4.00	12.00	24.00
857-The Goofy Adventure Story (Disney) (11/57)	3.60	9.00	18.00
858-Daisy Duck's Diary (Disney) (11/57)	3.20	8.00	16.00
859-Topper and Neil (TV) (11/57)	2.80	7.00	14.00
860-Wyatt Earp (#1) (TV)-Manning-a; photo-c	10.00	30.00	70.00
861-Frosty the Snowman	3.20	8.00	16.00
862-The Truth About Mother Goose (Disney-Movie) (11/57)	5.00	15.00	30.00
863-Francis the Famous Talking Mule	3.60	9.00	18.00
864-The Littlest Snowman	4.00	10.00	20.00
865-Andy Burnett (TV) (Disney) (12/57)-Photo-c	7.50	22.50	45.00
866-Mars and Beyond (Disney-Movie)	4.70	14.00	28.00
867-Santa Claus Funnies	3.60	9.00	18.00
868-The Little People (12/57)	3.20	8.00	16.00
869-Old Yeller (Disney-Movie)-Photo-c	4.00	12.00	24.00
870-Little Beaver (1/58)	3.00	7.50	15.00
871-Curly Kayoe	3.60	9.00	18.00
872-Captain Kangaroo (TV)-Photo-c	11.50	34.00	80.00
873-Grandma Duck's Farm Friends (Disney)	3.60	9.00	18.00
874-Old Ironsides (Disney-Movie with Johnny Tremain) (1/58)	4.00	12.00	24.00
875-Trumpets West (Luke Short) (2/58)	4.00	10.00	20.00
876-Tales of Wells Fargo (#1)(TV)(2/58)-Photo-c	10.00	30.00	60.00
877-Frontier Doctor with Rex Allen (TV)-Alex Toth-a; photo-c	10.00	30.00	70.00
878-Peanuts (#1)-Schulz-c only (2/58)	11.50	34.00	80.00
879-Brave Eagle (TV) (2/58)-Photo-c	3.20	8.00	16.00
880-Steve Donovan, Western Marshal-Drucker-a (TV)-Photo-c	4.00	10.50	21.00
881-The Captain and the Kids (2/58)	3.20	8.00	16.00
882-Zorro (Disney)-1st Disney issue; by Alex Toth (TV) (2/58); photo-c	10.00	30.00	70.00
883-The Little Rascals (TV)	3.20	8.00	16.00
884-Hawkeye and the Last of the Mohicans (TV) (3/58); photo-c	5.85	17.50	35.00
885-Fury (TV) (3/58)-Photo-c	5.85	17.50	35.00
886-Bongo and Lumpjaw (Disney) (3/58)	2.80	7.00	14.00
887-The Hardy Boys (Disney) (TV)-Mickey Mouse Club (1/58)-Photo-c	7.50	22.50	45.00
888-Elmer Fudd (3/58)	2.00	5.00	10.00
889-Clint and Mac (Disney) (TV) (3/58)-Alex Toth-a; photo-c	10.00	30.00	60.00
890-Wyatt Earp (TV)-by Russ Manning; photo-c	6.70	20.00	40.00
891-Light in the Forest (Disney-Movie) (3/58)-Fess Parker photo-c	4.70	14.00	28.00
892-Maverick (#1) (TV) (4/58)-James Garner/Jack Kelly photo-c	13.00	40.00	90.00
893-Jim Bowie (TV)-Photo-c	5.00	15.00	30.00
894-Oswald the Rabbit (Lantz)	2.00	5.00	10.00
895-Wagon Train (#1) (TV) (3/58)-Photo-c	9.15	27.50	55.00
896-The Adventures of Tinker Bell (Disney)	4.70	14.00	28.00
897-Jiminy Cricket (Disney)	3.60	9.00	18.00
898-Silvertip (Max Brand)-Kinstler-a (5/58)	4.70	14.00	28.00
899-Goofy (Disney) (5/58)	3.60	9.00	18.00
900-Prince Valiant; by Bob Fuje	4.70	14.00	28.00
901-Little Hiawatha (Disney)	3.20	8.00	16.00
902-Will-Yum!	2.80	7.00	14.00
903-Dotty Dripple and Taffy	2.40	6.00	12.00
904-Lee Hunter, Indian Fighter	4.00	10.00	20.00
905-Annette (Disney) (TV) (5/58)-Mickey Mouse Club; Annette Funicello photo-c	16.00	48.00	110.00
906-Francis the Famous Talking Mule	3.60	9.00	18.00
907-Sugarfoot (#1) (TV)Toth-a; photo-c	11.50	34.00	80.00
908-The Little People and the Giant-Walt Scott (5/58)	3.20	8.00	16.00
909-Smitty	3.00	7.50	15.00
910-The Vikings (Movie)-Buscema-a; Kirk Douglas photo-c	10.00	30.00	60.00
911-The Gray Ghost (TV) (Movie)-Photo-c	7.50	22.50	45.00
912-Leave It to Beaver (#1) (TV)-Photo-c	19.00	56.00	130.00
913-The Left-Handed Gun (Movie) (7/58); Paul Newman photo-c	10.00	30.00	65.00
914-No Time for Sergeants (Movie)-Photo-c; Toth-a	9.15	27.50	55.00
915-Casey Jones (TV)-Alan Hale photo-c	5.85	17.50	35.00
916-Red Ryder Ranch Comics (7/58)	2.80	7.00	14.00
917-The Life of Riley (TV)-Photo-c	11.00	32.00	75.00
918-Beep Beep, the Roadrunner (#1) (7/58)-Two different back covers were published	7.50	22.50	45.00
919-Boots and Saddles (#1) (TV)-Photo-c	7.50	22.50	45.00
920-Zorro (Disney) (TV) (6/58)Toth-a; photo-c	10.00	30.00	70.00
921-Wyatt Earp (TV)-Manning-a; photo-c	6.70	20.00	40.00
922-Johnny Mack Brown by Russ Manning; photo-c	5.35	16.00	32.00
923-Timmy	2.40	6.00	12.00
924-Colt .45 (#1) (TV) (8/58)-Photo-c	9.15	27.50	55.00
925-Last of the Fast Guns (Movie) (8/58)-Photo-c	5.85	17.50	35.00
926-Peter Pan (Disney)-Reprint of #442	3.60	9.00	18.00
927-Top Gun (Luke Short) Buscema-a	4.00	10.00	20.00
928-Sea Hunt (#1) (9/58) (TV)-Lloyd Bridges photo-c	10.00	30.00	70.00
929-Brave Eagle (TV)-Photo-c	3.20	8.00	16.00
930-Maverick (TV) (7/58)-James Garner/Jack Kelly photo-c	8.35	25.00	50.00
931-Have Gun, Will Travel (#1) (TV)-Photo-c	10.00	30.00	65.00
932-Smokey the Bear (His Life Story)	4.20	12.50	25.00
933-Zorro (Disney)-by Alex Toth (TV) (9/58)	10.00	30.00	70.00
934-Restless Gun (#1) (TV)-Photo-c	10.00	30.00	60.00
935-King of the Royal Mounted	4.00	10.50	21.00
936-The Little Rascals (TV)	3.20	8.00	16.00
937-Ruff and Reddy (#1) (9/58) (TV) (1st Hanna-Barbera comic book)	8.35	25.00	50.00
938-Elmer Fudd (9/58)	2.00	5.00	10.00
939-Steve Canyon - not by Caniff	4.00	12.00	24.00
940-Lolly and Pepper (10/58)	2.40	6.00	12.00
941-Pluto (Disney) (10/58)	3.20	8.00	16.00
942-Pony Express (TV)	4.00	11.00	22.00
943-White Wilderness (Disney-Movie) (10/58)	4.70	14.00	28.00
944-The 7th Voyage of Sindbad (Movie) (9/58)-Buscema-a	11.50	34.00	80.00
945-Maverick (TV)-James Garner/Jack Kelly photo-c	8.35	25.00	50.00
946-The Big Country (Movie)-Photo-c	5.85	17.50	35.00
947-Broken Arrow (TV)-Photo-c (11/58)	4.70	14.00	28.00
948-Daisy Duck's Diary (Disney) (11/58)	3.20	8.00	16.00
949-High Adventure(Lowell Thomas')(TV)-Photo-c	4.70	14.00	28.00

Four Color #863, © UFS

Four Color #871, © UFS

Four Color #919, © California National Products

WE'RE SAVING THE BEST FOR LAUGHS!
CLICK!
CLICK!
YEEOWW!
Archie AMERICANA SERIES
BEST OF THE Fifties
BAM!
TM & © 1992 Archie Comic Publications, Inc
YOWIE-E!
EE-EE!

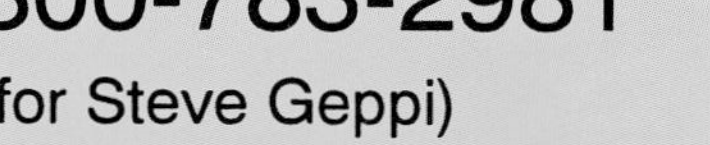

Flash #113, 1960, © DC
Origin/1st app. The Trickster

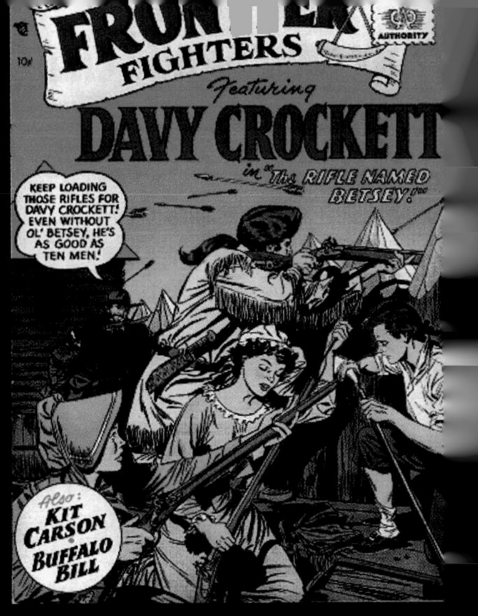

Frontier Fighters #2, 1955, © DC

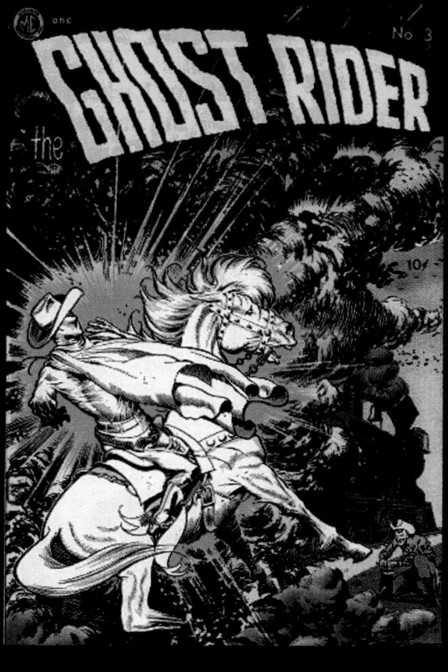

Ghost Rider #3, 1951, © Magazine Ent.

G. I. Combat #87, 1961, © DC
1st Haunted Tank

Green Lantern #59, 1968, © DC.
1st app. Guy Gardner.

Gunsmoke #4, 1949, © Western

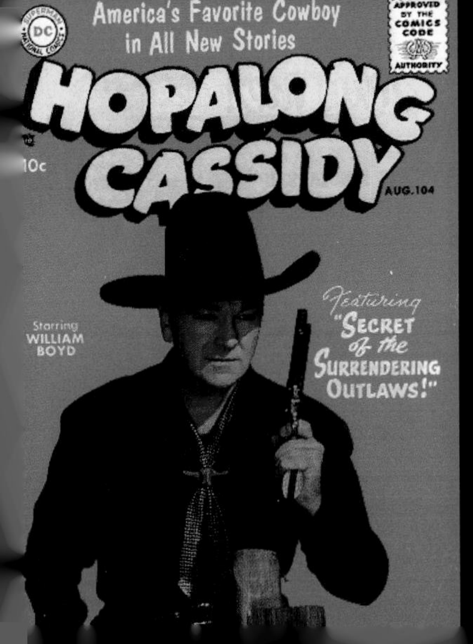

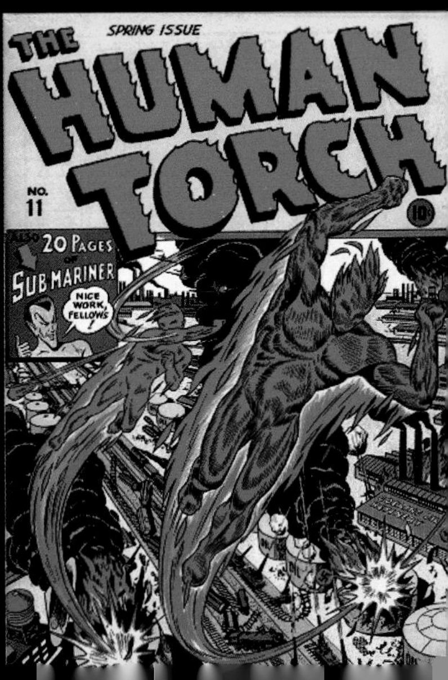

John Wayne Adventure Comics #5, 1950, © Toby

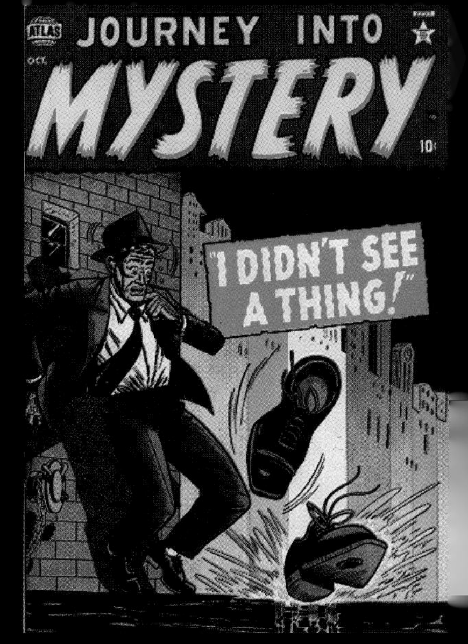

Journey Into Mystery #3, 1952, © Marvel

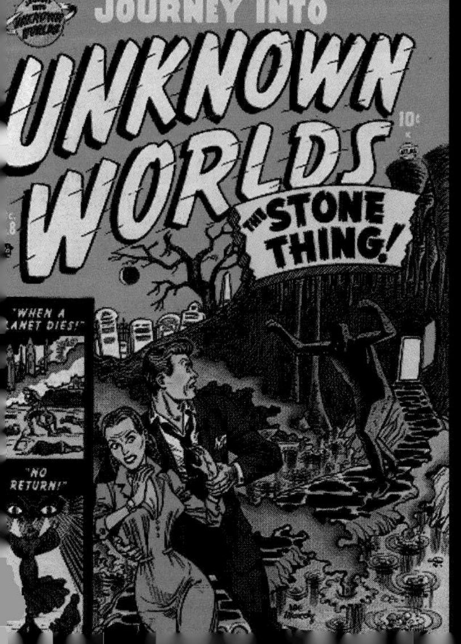

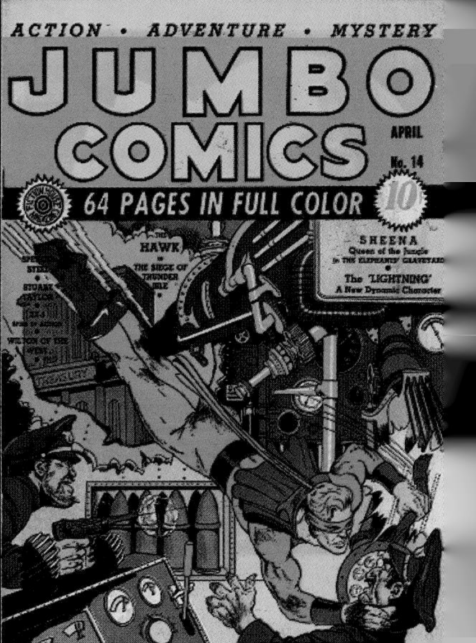

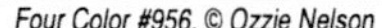
Four Color #956, © Ozzie Nelson

Four Color #1028, © CBS

Four Color #1030, © Hal Roach Studios

	GD25	FN65	NM94
950-Frosty the Snowman	3.20	8.00	16.00
951-The Lennon Sisters Life Story (TV)-Toth-a, 32 pgs.; photo-c	13.00	40.00	90.00
952-Goofy (Disney) (11/58)	3.60	9.00	18.00
953-Francis the Famous Talking Mule	3.60	9.00	18.00
954-Man in Space-Satellites (Disney-Movie)	4.70	14.00	28.00
955-Hi and Lois (11/58)	2.40	6.00	12.00
956-Ricky Nelson (#1) (TV)-Photo-c	23.00	70.00	160.00
957-Buffalo Bee (#1) (TV)	8.35	25.00	50.00
958-Santa Claus Funnies	3.00	7.50	15.00
959-Christmas Stories-(Walt Scott's Little People) (1951-56 strip reprints)	3.20	8.00	16.00
960-Zorro (Disney) (TV) (12/58)-Toth art	10.00	30.00	70.00
961-Jace Pearson's Tales of the Texas Rangers (TV)-Spiegle-a; photo-c	4.70	14.00	28.00
962-Maverick (TV) (1/59)-James Garner/Jack Kelly photo-c	8.35	25.00	50.00
963-Johnny Mack Brown; photo-c	4.70	14.00	28.00
964-The Hardy Boys (TV) (Disney) 91/59)-Mickey Mouse Club; photo-c	7.50	22.50	45.00
965-Grandma Duck's Farm Friends (Disney)(1/59)	3.60	9.00	18.00
966-Tonka (starring Sal Mineo; Disney-Movie)-Photo-c	5.85	17.50	35.00
967-Chilly Willy (2/59) (Lantz)	2.40	6.00	12.00
968-Tales of Wells Fargo (TV)-Photo-c	7.50	22.50	45.00
969-Peanuts (2/59)	10.00	30.00	60.00
970-Lawman (#1) (TV)-Photo-c	10.00	30.00	60.00
971-Wagon Train (TV)-Photo-c	5.00	15.00	30.00
972-Tom Thumb (Movie)-George Pal (1/59)	10.00	30.00	70.00
973-Sleeping Beauty and the Prince(Disney)(5/59)	5.85	17.50	35.00
974-The Little Rascals (TV) (3/59)	3.20	8.00	16.00
975-Fury (TV)-Photo-c	5.85	17.50	35.00
976-Zorro (Disney) (TV)-Toth-a; photo-c	10.00	30.00	70.00
977-Elmer Fudd (3/59)	2.00	5.00	10.00
978-Lolly and Pepper	2.40	6.00	12.00
979-Oswald the Rabbit (Lantz)	2.00	5.00	10.00
980-Maverick (TV) (4-6/59)-James Garner/Jack Kelly photo-c	8.35	25.00	50.00
981-Ruff and Reddy (TV) (Hanna-Barbera)	5.85	17.50	35.00
982-The New Adventures of Tinker Bell (TV) (Disney)	4.70	14.00	28.00
983-Have Gun, Will Travel (TV) (4-6/59)-Photo-c	6.70	20.00	40.00
984-Sleeping Beauty's Fairy Godmothers (Disney)	5.85	17.50	35.00
985-Shaggy Dog (Disney-Movie)-Photo-c	4.70	14.00	28.00
986-Restless Gun (TV)-Photo-c	6.70	20.00	40.00
987-Goofy (Disney) (7/59)	3.60	9.00	18.00
988-Little Hiawatha (Disney)	3.20	8.00	16.00
989-Jiminy Cricket (Disney) (5-7/59)	3.60	9.00	18.00
990-Huckleberry Hound (#1)(TV)(Hanna-Barbera)	6.70	20.00	40.00
991-Francis the Famous Talking Mule	3.60	9.00	18.00
992-Sugarfoot (TV)-Toth-a; photo-c	11.50	34.00	80.00
993-Jim Bowie (TV)-Photo-c	5.00	15.00	30.00
994-Sea Hunt (TV)-Lloyd Bridges photo-c	7.50	22.50	45.00
995-Donald Duck Album (Disney) (5-7/59)	3.20	8.00	16.00
996-Nevada (Zane Grey)	3.60	9.00	18.00
997-Walt Disney Presents-Tales of Texas John Slaughter (#1) (TV) (Disney)-Photo-c	5.00	15.00	30.00
998-Ricky Nelson (TV)-Photo-c	23.00	70.00	160.00
999-Leave It to Beaver (TV)-Photo-c	17.00	50.00	115.00
1000-The Gray Ghost (Movie) (6-8/59)-Photo-c	7.50	22.50	45.00
1001-Lowell Thomas' High Adventure (TV) (8-10/59)-Photo-c	4.70	14.00	28.00
1002-Buffalo Bee (TV)	5.85	17.50	35.00

	GD25	FN65	NM94
1003-Zorro (TV) (Disney)-Toth-a; photo-c	10.00	30.00	60.00
1004-Colt .45 (TV) (6-8/59)-Photo-c	6.70	20.00	40.00
1005-Maverick (TV)-James Garner/Jack Kelly photo-c	8.35	25.00	50.00
1006-Hercules (Movie)-Buscema-a	10.00	30.00	65.00
1007-John Paul Jones (Movie)-Robert Stack photo-c	4.70	14.00	28.00
1008-Beep Beep, the Road Runner (7-9/59)	4.20	12.50	25.00
1009-The Rifleman (#1) (TV)-Photo-c	14.00	43.00	100.00
1010-Grandma Duck's Farm Friends (Disney)-by Carl Barks	8.35	25.00	50.00
1011-Buckskin (#1) (TV)-Photo-c	9.15	27.50	55.00
1012-Last Train from Gun Hill (Movie) (7/59)-Photo-c	7.50	22.50	45.00
1013-Bat Masterson (#1) (TV) (8/59)-Gene Barry photo-c	8.35	25.00	50.00
1014-The Lennon Sisters (TV)-Toth-a; photo-c	13.00	40.00	90.00
1015-Peanuts-Schulz-c	10.00	30.00	60.00
1016-Smokey the Bear Nature Stories	3.60	9.00	18.00
1017-Chilly Willy (Lantz)	2.40	6.00	12.00
1018-Rio Bravo (Movie)(6/59)-John Wayne; Toth-a; John Wayne, Dean Martin & Ricky Nelson photo-c	22.00	65.00	150.00
1019-Wagon Train (TV)-Photo-c	5.00	15.00	30.00
1020-Jungle Jim-McWilliams-a	2.80	7.00	14.00
1021-Jace Pearson's Tales of the Texas Rangers (TV)-Photo-c	4.35	13.00	26.00
1022-Timmy	2.40	6.00	12.00
1023-Tales of Wells Fargo (TV)-Photo-c	7.50	22.50	45.00
1024-Darby O'Gill and the Little People (Disney-Movie)-Toth-a; photo-c	8.35	25.00	50.00
1025-Vacation in Disneyland (8-10/59)-Carl Barks-a (Disney)	8.35	25.00	50.00
1026-Spin and Marty (TV) (Disney) (9-11/59)-Mickey Mouse Club; photo-c	5.85	17.50	35.00
1027-The Texan (#1)(TV)-Photo-c	6.70	20.00	40.00
1028-Rawhide (#1) (TV) (9-11/59)-Clint Eastwood photo-c; Tufts-a	24.00	70.00	165.00
1029-Boots and Saddles (TV) (9/59)-Photo-c	5.00	15.00	30.00
1030-Spanky and Alfalfa, the Little Rascals (TV)	2.80	7.00	14.00
1031-Fury (TV)-Photo-c	5.85	17.50	35.00
1032-Elmer Fudd	2.00	5.00	10.00
1033-Steve Canyon-not by Caniff; photo-c	4.00	12.00	24.00
1034-Nancy and Sluggo Summer Camp (9-11/59)	2.80	7.00	14.00
1035-Lawman (TV)-Photo-c	5.35	16.00	32.00
1036-The Big Circus (Movie)-Photo-c	4.70	14.00	28.00
1037-Zorro (Disney) (TV)-Tufts-a; Annette Funicello photo-c	11.00	32.00	75.00
1038-Ruff and Reddy (TV)(Hanna-Barbera)(1959)	5.85	17.50	35.00
1039-Pluto (Disney) (11-1/60)	3.20	8.00	16.00
1040-Quick Draw McGraw (#1) (TV) (Hanna-Barbera) (12-2/60)	8.35	25.00	50.00
1041-Sea Hunt (TV) (10-12/59)-Toth-a; Lloyd Bridges photo-c	9.15	27.50	55.00
1042-The Three Chipmunks (Alvin, Simon & Theodore) (#1) (TV) (10-12/59)	3.60	9.00	18.00
1043-The Three Stooges (#1)-Photo-c	14.00	43.00	100.00
1044-Have Gun, Will Travel (TV)-Photo-c	6.70	20.00	40.00
1045-Restless Gun (TV)-Photo-c	6.70	20.00	40.00
1046-Beep Beep, the Road Runner (11-1/60)	4.20	12.50	25.00
1047-Gyro Gearloose (#1) (Disney)-Barks-c/a	10.00	30.00	60.00
1048-The Horse Soldiers (Movie) (John Wayne)-Sekowsky-a	17.00	52.00	120.00
1049-Don't Give Up the Ship (Movie) (8/59)-Jerry Lewis photo-c	5.85	17.50	35.00

	GD25	FN65	NM94
1050-Huckleberry Hound (TV) (Hanna-Barbera) (10-12/59)	5.00	15.00	30.00
1051-Donald in Mathmagic Land (Disney-Movie)	5.85	17.50	35.00
1052-Ben-Hur (Movie) (11/59)-Manning-a	9.15	27.50	55.00
1053-Goofy (Disney) (11-1/60)	3.60	9.00	18.00
1054-Huckleberry Hound Winter Fun (TV) (Hanna-Barbera) (12/59)	5.00	15.00	30.00
1055-Daisy Duck's Diary (Disney)-by Carl Barks (11-1/60)	6.70	20.00	40.00
1056-Yellowstone Kelly (Movie)-Clint Walker photo-c	4.70	14.00	28.00
1057-Mickey Mouse Album (Disney)	3.20	8.00	16.00
1058-Colt .45 (TV)-Photo-c	6.70	20.00	40.00
1059-Sugarfoot (TV)-Photo-c	7.50	22.50	45.00
1060-Journey to the Center of the Earth (Movie)-Pat Boone & James Mason photo-c	11.00	32.00	75.00
1061-Buffalo Bee (TV)	5.85	17.50	35.00
1062-Christmas Stories (Walt Scott's Little People strip-r)	3.20	8.00	16.00
1063-Santa Claus Funnies	3.00	7.50	15.00
1064-Bugs Bunny's Merry Christmas (12/59)	4.00	10.00	20.00
1065-Frosty the Snowman	3.20	8.00	16.00
1066-77 Sunset Strip (#1) (TV)-Toth-a (1-3/60)-Photo-c	11.00	32.00	75.00
1067-Yogi Bear (#1) (TV) (Hanna-Barbera)	10.00	30.00	60.00
1068-Francis the Famous Talking Mule	3.60	9.00	18.00
1069-The FBI Story (Movie)-Toth-a; James Stewart photo-c	10.00	30.00	65.00
1070-Solomon and Sheba (Movie)-Sekowsky-a; photo-c	9.15	27.50	55.00
1071-The Real McCoys (#1) (TV) (1-3/60)-Toth-a; photo-c	10.00	30.00	70.00
1072-Blythe (Marge's)	4.20	12.50	25.00
1073-Grandma Duck's Farm Friends-Barks-c/a (Disney)	8.35	25.00	50.00
1074-Chilly Willy (Lantz)	2.40	6.00	12.00
1075-Tales of Wells Fargo (TV)-Photo-c	7.50	22.50	45.00
1076-The Rebel (#1) (TV)-Sekowsky-a; photo-c	10.00	30.00	65.00
1077-The Deputy (#1) (TV)-Buscema-a; Henry Fonda photo-c	11.00	32.00	75.00
1078-The Three Stooges (2-4/60)-Photo-c	8.35	25.00	50.00
1079-The Little Rascals (TV) (Spanky & Alfalfa)	2.80	7.00	14.00
1080-Fury (TV) (2-4/60)-Photo-c	5.85	17.50	35.00
1081-Elmer Fudd	2.00	5.00	10.00
1082-Spin and Marty (Disney) (TV)-Photo-c	5.85	17.50	35.00
1083-Men into Space (TV)-Anderson-a; photo-c	5.00	15.00	30.00
1084-Speedy Gonzales	2.80	7.00	14.00
1085-The Time Machine (H.G. Wells) (Movie) (3/60)-Alex Toth-a	13.00	40.00	90.00
1086-Lolly and Pepper	2.40	6.00	12.00
1087-Peter Gunn (TV)-Photo-c	9.15	27.50	55.00
1088-A Dog of Flanders (Movie)-Photo-c	4.20	12.50	25.00
1089-Restless Gun (TV)-Photo-c	6.70	20.00	40.00
1090-Francis the Famous Talking Mule	3.60	9.00	18.00
1091-Jacky's Diary (4-6/60)	4.70	14.00	28.00
1092-Toby Tyler (Disney-Movie)-Photo-c	4.20	12.50	25.00
1093-MacKenzie's Raiders (Movie)-Photo-c	5.85	17.50	35.00
1094-Goofy (Disney)	3.60	9.00	18.00
1095-Gyro Gearloose (Disney)-Barks-c/a	6.70	20.00	40.00
1096-The Texan (TV)-Rory Calhoun photo-c	6.70	20.00	40.00
1097-Rawhide (TV)-Manning-a; Clint Eastwood photo-c	16.00	48.00	110.00
1098-Sugarfoot (TV)-Photo-c	7.50	22.50	45.00
1099-Donald Duck Album (Disney) (5-7/60) - Barks-c	3.60	9.00	18.00
1100-Annette's Life Story (Disney-Movie) (5/60)-Annette Funicello photo-c	17.00	52.00	120.00
1101-Robert Louis Stevenson's Kidnapped (Disney-Movie) (5/60); photo-c	5.00	15.00	30.00
1102-Wanted: Dead or Alive (#1) (TV) (5-7/60); Steve McQueen photo-c	11.50	34.00	80.00
1103-Leave It to Beaver (TV)-Photo-c	17.00	50.00	115.00
1104-Yogi Bear Goes to College (TV) (Hanna-Barbera) (6-8/60)	6.70	20.00	40.00
1105-Gale Storm (Oh! Susanna) (TV)-Toth-a; photo-c	12.00	36.00	85.00
1106-77 Sunset Strip(TV)(6-8/60)-Toth-a; photo-c	9.15	27.50	55.00
1107-Buckskin (TV)-Photo-c	6.70	20.00	40.00
1108-The Troubleshooters (TV)-Keenan Wynn photo-c	5.00	15.00	30.00
1109-This Is Your Life, Donald Duck (Disney) (TV) (8-10/60)-Gyro flashback to WDC&S #141; origin Donald Duck(1st told)	16.00	48.00	110.00
1110-Bonanza (#1) (TV) (6-8/60)-Photo-c	29.00	85.00	200.00
1111-Shotgun Slade (TV)-Photo-c	5.00	15.00	30.00
1112-Pixie and Dixie and Mr. Jinks (#1) (TV) (Hanna-Barbera) (7-9/60)	5.85	17.50	35.00
1113-Tales of Wells Fargo (TV)-Photo-c	7.50	22.50	45.00
1114-Huckleberry Finn (Movie) (7/60)-Photo-c	4.70	14.00	28.00
1115-Ricky Nelson (TV)-Manning-a; photo-c	18.00	54.00	125.00
1116-Boots and Saddles (TV) (8/60)-Photo-c	5.00	15.00	30.00
1117-Boy and the Pirates (Movie)-Photo-c	5.85	17.50	35.00
1118-The Sword and the Dragon (Movie) (6/60)-Photo-c	7.50	22.50	45.00
1119-Smokey the Bear Nature Stories	3.60	9.00	18.00
1120-Dinosaurus (Movie)-Painted-c	5.85	17.50	35.00
1121-Hercules Unchained (Movie) (8/60)-Crandall/Evans-a	9.15	27.50	55.00
1122-Chilly Willy (Lantz)	2.40	6.00	12.00
1123-Tombstone Territory (TV)-Photo-c	9.15	27.50	55.00
1124-Whirlybirds (#1) (TV)-Photo-c	9.15	27.50	55.00
1125-Laramie (#1) (TV)-Photo-c; G. Kane/Heath-a	8.35	25.00	50.00
1126-Sundance (TV) (8-10/60)-Earl Holliman photo-c	9.15	27.50	55.00
1127-The Three Stooges-Photo-c (8-10/60)	8.35	25.00	50.00
1128-Rocky and His Friends (#1) (TV) (Jay Ward) (8-10/60)	24.00	70.00	165.00
1129-Pollyanna (Disney-Movie)-Hayley Mills photo-c	10.00	30.00	60.00
1130-The Deputy (TV)-Buscema-a; Henry Fonda photo-c	9.15	27.50	55.00
1131-Elmer Fudd (9-11/60)	2.00	5.00	10.00
1132-Space Mouse (Lantz) (8-10/60)	4.00	12.00	24.00
1133-Fury (TV)-Photo-c	5.85	17.50	35.00
1134-Real McCoys (TV)-Toth-a; photo-c	10.00	30.00	70.00
1135-M.G.M.'s Mouse Musketeers (9-11/60)	2.00	5.00	10.00
1136-Jungle Cat (Disney-Movie)-Photo-c	5.00	15.00	30.00
1137-The Little Rascals (TV)	2.80	7.00	14.00
1138-The Rebel (TV)-Photo-c	9.15	27.50	55.00
1139-Spartacus (Movie) (11/60)-Buscema-a; photo-c	11.00	32.00	75.00
1140-Donald Duck Album (Disney)	3.60	9.00	18.00
1141-Huckleberry Hound for President (TV) (Hanna-Barbera) (10/60)	5.00	15.00	30.00
1142-Johnny Ringo (TV)-Photo-c	7.50	22.50	45.00
1143-Pluto (Disney) (11-1/61)	3.20	8.00	16.00
1144-The Story of Ruth (Movie)-Photo-c	10.00	30.00	70.00
1145-The Lost World (Movie)-Gil Kane-a; photo-c	10.00	30.00	70.00
1146-Restless Gun (TV)-Photo-c; Wildey-a	6.70	20.00	40.00
1147-Sugarfoot (TV)-Photo-c	7.50	22.50	45.00
1148-I Aim at the Stars-the Wernher Von Braun Story (Movie) (11-1/61)-			

Four Color #1044, © CBS

Four Color #1091, © KING

Four Color #1111, © Shotgun Prod., Inc.

Four Color #1167, © Overland Prod.

Four Color #1200, © Emcee S.A. Coire

Four Color #1234, © Four Crown Prod.

	GD25	FN65	NM94
Photo-c	5.85	17.50	35.00
1149-Goofy (Disney) (11-1/61)	3.60	9.00	18.00
1150-Daisy Duck's Diary (Disney) (12-1/61) by Carl Barks	6.70	20.00	40.00
1151-Mickey Mouse Album (Disney) (11-1/61)	3.20	8.00	16.00
1152-Rocky and His Friends (TV) (Jay Ward) (12-2/61)	20.00	60.00	140.00
1153-Frosty the Snowman	3.20	8.00	16.00
1154-Santa Claus Funnies	3.00	7.50	15.00
1155-North to Alaska (Movie) - John Wayne; photo-c	14.00	43.00	100.00
1156-Walt Disney Swiss Family Robinson (Movie) (12/60)-Photo-c	5.00	15.00	30.00
1157-Master of the World (Movie) (7/61)	5.00	15.00	30.00
1158-Three Worlds of Gulliver (2 issues exist with different covers) (Movie)-Photo-c	4.70	14.00	28.00
1159-77 Sunset Strip (TV)-Toth-a; photo-c	9.15	27.50	55.00
1160-Rawhide (TV)-Clint Eastwood photo-c	16.00	48.00	110.00
1161-Grandma Duck's Farm Friends (Disney) by Carl Barks (2-4/61)	8.35	25.00	50.00
1162-Yogi Bear Joins the Marines (TV) (Hanna-Barbera) (5-7/61)	6.70	20.00	40.00
1163-Daniel Boone (3-5/61); Marsh-a	5.00	15.00	30.00
1164-Wanted: Dead or Alive (TV)-Steve McQueen photo-c	10.00	30.00	70.00
1165-Ellery Queen (#1) (3-5/61)	10.00	30.00	70.00
1166-Rocky and His Friends (TV) (Jay Ward)	20.00	60.00	140.00
1167-Tales of Wells Fargo (TV)-Photo-c	6.70	20.00	40.00
1168-The Detectives (TV)-Robert Taylor photo-c	8.35	25.00	50.00
1169-New Adventures of Sherlock Holmes	14.00	43.00	100.00
1170-The Three Stooges (3-5/61)-Photo-c	8.35	25.00	50.00
1171-Elmer Fudd	2.00	5.00	10.00
1172-Fury (TV)-Photo-c	5.85	17.50	35.00
1173-The Twilight Zone (#1) (TV) (5/61)-Crandall/Evans-c/a	14.00	43.00	100.00
1174-The Little Rascals (TV)	2.80	7.00	14.00
1175-M.G.M.'s Mouse Musketeers (3-5/61)	2.00	5.00	10.00
1176-Dondi (Movie)-Origin; photo-c	4.20	12.50	25.00
1177-Chilly Willy (Lantz) (4-6/61)	2.40	6.00	12.00
1178-Ten Who Dared (Disney-Movie) (12/60)-Painted-c	4.70	14.00	28.00
1179-The Swamp Fox (TV) (Disney)-Leslie Nielson photo-c	5.85	17.50	35.00
1180-The Danny Thomas Show (TV)-Toth-a; photo-c	14.00	43.00	100.00
1181-Texas John Slaughter (TV) (Disney) (4-6/61)-Photo-c	4.20	12.50	25.00
1182-Donald Duck Album (Disney) (5-7/61)	3.20	8.00	16.00
1183-101 Dalmatians (Disney-Movie) (3/61)	5.00	15.00	30.00
1184-Gyro Gearloose; Barks-c/a (Disney) (5-7/61) Two variations exist	6.70	20.00	40.00
1185-Sweetie Pie	3.60	9.00	18.00
1186-Yak Yak (#1) by Jack Davis (2 versions - one minus 3-pg. Davis-c/a)	8.35	25.00	50.00
1187-The Three Stooges (6-8/61)-Photo-c	8.35	25.00	50.00
1188-Atlantis, the Lost Continent (Movie) (5/61)-Photo-c	10.00	30.00	65.00
1189-Greyfriars Bobby (Disney-Movie) (11/61)-Photo-c	5.00	15.00	30.00
1190-Donald and the Wheel (Disney-Movie) (11/61); Barks-c	5.85	17.50	35.00
1191-Leave It to Beaver (TV)-Photo-c	17.00	50.00	115.00
1192-Ricky Nelson (TV)-Manning-a; photo-c	18.00	54.00	125.00
1193-The Real McCoys (TV) (6-8/61)-Photo-c	9.15	27.50	55.00

	GD25	FN65	NM94
1194-Pepe (Movie) (4/61)-Photo-c	4.00	10.00	20.00
1195-National Velvet (#1) (TV)-Photo-c	5.85	17.50	35.00
1196-Pixie and Dixie and Mr. Jinks (TV) (Hanna-Barbera) (7-9/61)	4.20	12.50	25.00
1197-The Aquanauts (TV) (5-7/61)-Photo-c	5.85	17.50	35.00
1198-Donald in Mathmagic Land (Disney-Movie)-Reprint of #1051	5.85	17.50	35.00
1199-The Absent-Minded Professor (Disney-Movie) (4/61)-Photo-c	5.00	15.00	30.00
1200-Hennessey (TV) (8-10/61)-Gil Kane-a; photo-c	5.85	17.50	35.00
1201-Goofy (Disney) (8-10/61)	3.60	9.00	18.00
1202-Rawhide (TV)-Clint Eastwood photo-c	16.00	48.00	110.00
1203-Pinocchio (Disney) (3/62)	4.00	10.00	20.00
1204-Scamp (Disney)	2.00	5.00	10.00
1205-David and Goliath (Movie) (7/61)-Photo-c	5.00	15.00	30.00
1206-Lolly and Pepper (9-11/61)	2.40	6.00	12.00
1207-The Rebel (TV)-Sekowsky-a; photo-c	9.15	27.50	55.00
1208-Rocky and His Friends (Jay Ward) (TV)	20.00	60.00	140.00
1209-Sugarfoot (TV)-Photo-c (10-12/61)	7.50	22.50	45.00
1210-The Parent Trap (Disney-Movie) (8/61)-Hayley Mills photo-c	10.00	30.00	65.00
1211-77 Sunset Strip (TV)-Manning-a; photo-c	8.35	25.00	50.00
1212-Chilly Willy (Lantz) (7-9/61)	2.40	6.00	12.00
1213-Mysterious Island (Movie)-Photo-c	7.50	22.50	45.00
1214-Smokey the Bear	3.60	9.00	18.00
1215-Tales of Wells Fargo(TV)(10-12/61)-Photo-c	6.70	20.00	40.00
1216-Whirlybirds (TV)-Photo-c	7.50	22.50	45.00
1218-Fury (TV)-Photo-c	5.85	17.50	35.00
1219-The Detectives (TV)-Robert Taylor & Adam West photo-c	6.70	20.00	40.00
1220-Gunslinger (TV)-Photo-c	7.50	22.50	45.00
1221-Bonanza (TV) (9-11/61)-Photo-c	14.00	43.00	100.00
1222-Elmer Fudd (9-11/61)	2.00	5.00	10.00
1223-Laramie (TV)-Gil Kane-a; photo-c	5.35	16.00	32.00
1224-The Little Rascals (TV) (10-12/61)	2.80	7.00	14.00
1225-The Deputy (TV)-Henry Fonda photo-c	9.15	27.50	55.00
1226-Nikki, Wild Dog of the North (Disney-Movie) (9/61)-Photo-c	3.60	9.00	18.00
1227-Morgan the Pirate (Movie)-Photo-c	9.15	27.50	55.00
1229-Thief of Baghdad (Movie)-Evans-a; photo-c	10.00	30.00	65.00
1230-Voyage to the Bottom of the Sea (#1) (Movie)-Photo insert on-c	8.35	25.00	50.00
1231-Danger Man (TV) (9-11/61)-Patrick McGoohan photo-c	8.35	25.00	50.00
1232-On the Double (Movie)	4.20	12.50	25.00
1233-Tammy Tell Me True (Movie) (1961)	5.85	17.50	35.00
1234-The Phantom Planet (Movie) (1961)	5.00	15.00	30.00
1235-Mister Magoo (#1) (12-2/62)	7.50	22.50	45.00
1235-Mister Magoo (3-5/65) 2nd printing; reprint of 12-2/62 issue	4.20	12.50	25.00
1236-King of Kings (Movie)-Photo-c	7.50	22.50	45.00
1237-The Untouchables (#1) (TV)-Not by Toth; photo-c	14.00	43.00	100.00
1238-Deputy Dawg (TV)	10.00	30.00	60.00
1239-Donald Duck Album (Disney) (10-12/61)-Barks-c	3.60	9.00	18.00
1240-The Detectives (TV)-Tufts-a; Robert Taylor photo-c	6.70	20.00	40.00
1241-Sweetie Pie	3.60	9.00	18.00
1242-King Leonardo and His Short Subjects (#1) (TV) (11-1/62)	11.50	34.00	80.00
1243-Ellery Queen	7.50	22.50	45.00
1244-Space Mouse (Lantz) (11-1/62)	4.00	12.00	24.00

	GD25	FN65	NM94
1245-New Adventures of Sherlock Holmes	14.00	43.00	100.00
1246-Mickey Mouse Album (Disney)	3.20	8.00	16.00
1247-Daisy Duck's Diary (Disney) (12-2/62)	3.20	8.00	16.00
1248-Pluto (Disney)	3.20	8.00	16.00
1249-The Danny Thomas Show (TV)-Manning-a; photo-c	14.00	43.00	100.00
1250-The Four Horsemen of the Apocalypse (Movie)-Photo-c	5.85	17.50	35.00
1251-Everything's Ducky (Movie) (1961)	4.70	14.00	28.00
1252-The Andy Griffith Show (TV)-Photo-c; 1st show aired 10/3/60	22.00	65.00	150.00
1253-Space Man (#1) (1-3/62)	6.70	20.00	40.00
1254-"Diver Dan" (#1) (TV) (2-4/62)-Photo-c	5.35	16.00	32.00
1255-The Wonders of Aladdin (Movie) (1961)	5.85	17.50	35.00
1256-Kona, Monarch of Monster Isle (#1) (2-4/62)-Glanzman-a	5.85	17.50	35.00
1257-Car 54, Where Are You? (#1) (TV) (3-5/62)-Photo-c	6.35	19.00	38.00
1258-The Frogmen (#1)-Evans-a	6.70	20.00	40.00
1259-El Cid (Movie) (1961)-Photo-c	5.85	17.50	35.00
1260-The Horsemasters (TV, Movie) (Disney) (12-2/62)-Annette Funicello photo-c	8.35	25.00	50.00
1261-Rawhide (TV)-Clint Eastwood photo-c	16.00	48.00	110.00
1262-The Rebel (TV)-Photo-c	9.15	27.50	55.00
1263-77 Sunset Strip (TV) (12-2/62)-Manning-a; photo-c	8.35	25.00	50.00
1264-Pixie and Dixie and Mr. Jinks (TV) (Hanna-Barbera)	4.20	12.50	25.00
1265-The Real McCoys (TV)-Photo-c	9.15	27.50	55.00
1266-M.G.M.'s Spike and Tyke (12-2/62)	1.60	4.00	8.00
1267-Gyro Gearloose; Barks-c/a, 4 pgs. (Disney) (12-2/62)	5.35	16.00	32.00
1268-Oswald the Rabbit (Lantz)	2.00	5.00	10.00
1269-Rawhide (TV)-Clint Eastwood photo-c	16.00	48.00	110.00
1270-Bullwinkle and Rocky (#1) (TV) (Jay Ward) (3-5/62)	12.00	36.00	85.00
1271-Yogi Bear Birthday Party (TV) (Hanna-Barbera) (11/61)	5.00	15.00	30.00
1272-Frosty the Snowman	3.20	8.00	16.00
1273-Hans Brinker (Disney-Movie)-Photo-c	5.00	15.00	30.00
1274-Santa Claus Funnies (12/61)	3.00	7.50	15.00
1275-Rocky and His Friends (TV) (Jay Ward)	20.00	60.00	140.00
1276-Dondi	3.60	9.00	18.00
1278-King Leonardo and His Short Subjects (TV)	11.50	34.00	80.00
1279-Grandma Duck's Farm Friends (Disney)	3.60	9.00	18.00
1280-Hennessey (TV)-Photo-c	5.85	17.50	35.00
1281-Chilly Willy (Lantz) (4-6/62)	2.40	6.00	12.00
1282-Babes in Toyland (Disney-Movie) (1/62); Annette Funicello photo-c	10.00	30.00	60.00
1283-Bonanza (TV) (2-4/62)-Photo-c	14.00	43.00	100.00
1284-Laramie (TV)-Heath-a; photo-c	5.35	16.00	32.00
1285-Leave It to Beaver (TV)-Photo-c	17.00	50.00	115.00
1286-The Untouchables (TV)-Photo-c	14.00	43.00	100.00
1287-Man from Wells Fargo (TV)-Photo-c	4.70	14.00	28.00
1288-The Twilight Zone (TV) (4/62)-Crandall/Evans-c/a	10.00	30.00	65.00
1289-Ellery Queen	7.50	22.50	45.00
1290-M.G.M.'s Mouse Musketeers	2.00	5.00	10.00
1291-77 Sunset Strip (TV)-Manning-a; photo-c	8.35	25.00	50.00
1293-Elmer Fudd (3-5/62)	2.00	5.00	10.00
1294-Ripcord (TV)	5.85	17.50	35.00
1295-Mister Ed, the Talking Horse (#1) (TV) (3-5/62)-Photo-c	10.00	30.00	70.00
1296-Fury (TV) (3-5/62)-Photo-c	5.85	17.50	35.00
1297-Spanky, Alfalfa and the Little Rascals (TV)	2.80	7.00	14.00
1298-The Hathaways (TV)-Photo-c	4.70	14.00	28.00

	GD25	FN65	NM94
1299-Deputy Dawg (TV)	10.00	30.00	60.00
1300-The Comancheros (Movie) (1961)-John Wayne	15.00	45.00	105.00
1301-Adventures in Paradise (TV) (2-4/62)	4.20	12.50	25.00
1302-Johnny Jason, Teen Reporter (2-4/62)	2.80	7.00	14.00
1303-Lad: A Dog (Movie)-Photo-c	4.00	11.00	21.00
1304-Nellie the Nurse (3-5/62)-Stanley-a	9.15	27.50	55.00
1305-Mister Magoo (3-5/62)	7.50	22.50	45.00
1306-Target: The Corruptors (#1) (TV) (3-5/62)-Photo-c	4.20	12.50	25.00
1307-Margie (TV) (3-5/62)	4.00	11.00	22.00
1308-Tales of the Wizard of Oz (TV) (3-5/62)	10.00	30.00	70.00
1309-87th Precinct (#1) (TV) (4-6/62)-Krigstein-a; photo-c	8.35	25.00	50.00
1310-Huck and Yogi Winter Sports (TV) (Hanna-Barbera) (3/62)	5.85	17.50	35.00
1311-Rocky and His Friends (TV) (Jay Ward)	20.00	60.00	140.00
1312-National Velvet (TV)-Photo-c	4.00	10.00	20.00
1313-Moon Pilot (Disney-Movie)-Photo-c	4.70	14.00	28.00
1328-The Underwater City (Movie) (1961)-Evans-a; photo-c	6.70	20.00	40.00
1330-Brain Boy (#1)-Gil Kane-a	6.70	20.00	40.00
1332-Bachelor Father (TV)	7.50	22.50	45.00
1333-Short Ribs (4-6/62)	4.70	14.00	28.00
1335-Aggie Mack (4-6/62)	4.00	10.00	20.00
1336-On Stage; not by Leonard Starr	4.70	14.00	28.00
1337-Dr. Kildare (#1) (TV) (4-6/62)-Photo-c	5.85	17.50	35.00
1341-The Andy Griffith Show (TV) (4-6/62)-Photo-c	22.00	65.00	150.00
1348-Yak Yak (#2)-Jack Davis-c/a	7.50	22.50	45.00
1349-Yogi Bear Visits the U.N. (TV) (Hanna-Barbera) (1/62)-Photo-c	10.00	30.00	60.00
1350-Comanche (Disney-Movie)(1962)-Reprints 4-Color #966 (title change from "Tonka" to "Comanche") (4-6/62)-Sal Mineo photo-c	4.20	12.50	25.00
1354-Calvin & the Colonel (#1) (TV) (4-6/62)	6.70	20.00	40.00

NOTE: *Missing numbers probably do not exist.*

4-D MONKEY, THE (Leung's)(Value: cover or less)

FOUR FAVORITES (Crime Must Pay the Penalty No. 33 on)
Sept, 1941 - No. 32, Dec, 1947
Ace Magazines

	GD25	FN65	NM94
1-Vulcan, Lash Lightning, Magno the Magnetic Man & The Raven begin; flag-c	71.00	210.00	425.00
2-The Black Ace only app.	35.00	105.00	210.00
3-Last Vulcan	27.00	82.00	165.00
4,5: 4-The Raven & Vulcan end; Unknown Soldier begins, ends #28. 5-Captain Courageous begins, ends #28; not in #6	27.00	80.00	160.00
6-8: 6-The Flag app.; Mr. Risk begins	22.00	68.00	135.00
9,11-Kurtzman-a; 11-Hitler, Mussolini, Hirohito-c; L.B. Cole-a	29.00	88.00	175.00
10-Classic Kurtzman-c/a	33.00	100.00	200.00
12-L.B. Cole-a	16.00	48.00	95.00
13-20: 18,20-Palais-c/a	14.00	42.00	85.00
21-No Unknown Soldier; The Unknown app.	10.00	30.00	60.00
22-26: 22-Captain Courageous drops costume. 23-Unknown Soldier drops costume. 26-Last Magno	10.00	30.00	60.00
27-32: 29-Hap Hazard app.	8.35	25.00	50.00

NOTE: ***Jim Mooney** c-3. **Palais** c-18, 20, 24, 25.*

FOUR HORSEMEN, THE (See The Crusaders)

FOUR HORSEMEN OF THE APOCALYPSE, THE (See 4-Color No. 1250)

4MOST (Foremost Boys No. 32-40; becomes Thrilling Crime Cases #41 on)
Winter, 1941-42 - V8#5(#36), 9-10/49; #37, 11-12/49 - #40, 4-5/50
Novelty Publications/Star Publications No. 37-on

Four Color #1266, © M.G.M.

Four Color #1348, © WEST

Four Favorites #1, © ACE

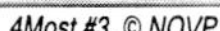
4Most #3, © NOVP

Fox Giants (March of Crime), © FOX

Fox Giants (Teen-Age Love), © FOX

	GD25	FN65	NM94
V1#1-The Target by Sid Greene, The Cadet & Dick Cole begin with origins retold; produced by Funnies Inc.	71.00	210.00	425.00
2-Last Target	33.00	100.00	200.00
3-Flag-c	28.00	85.00	170.00
4-1pg. Dr. Seuss(signed)	23.00	68.00	135.00
V2#1-4, V3#1-4	5.35	16.00	32.00
V4#1-4	4.20	12.50	25.00
V5#1-5: 1-The Target & Targeteers app.	3.70	11.00	22.00
V6#1-4,6: 1-White Rider & Super Horse begin	3.70	11.00	22.00
5-L. B. Cole-c	5.35	16.00	32.00
V7#1,3,5, V8#1	3.70	11.00	22.00
2,4,6-L. B. Cole-c. 6-Last Dick Cole	5.35	16.00	32.00
V8#2,3,5-L. B. Cole-c/a	7.50	22.50	45.00
4-L. B. Cole-a	4.70	14.00	28.00
37-40: 38-Johnny Weismuller life story. 38-40-L.B. Cole-c	4.70	14.00	28.00
Accepted Reprint 38-40 (nd): 40-r/Johnny Weismuller life story; all have L.B. Cole-c	4.00	10.50	21.00

FOUR-STAR BATTLE TALES
Feb-Mar, 1973 - No. 5, Nov-Dec, 1973
National Periodical Publications

	GD25	FN65	NM94
1-5: All reprints		.50	1.00

NOTE: ***Drucker** r-1, 3-5. **Heath** r-2, 5; c-1. **Krigstein** r-5. **Kubert** r-4; c-2.*

FOUR STAR SPECTACULAR
Mar-Apr, 1976 - No. 6, Jan-Feb, 1977
National Periodical Publications

	GD25	FN65	NM94
1-6: Reprints in all. 2-Infinity cover		.50	1.00

NOTE: *All contain DC Superhero reprints. #1 has 68 pages; #2-6, 52 pages. #1, 4-Hawkman app.; #2-Kid Flash app.; #3-Green Lantern app; #2, 4, 5-Wonder Woman, Superboy app; #5-Green Arrow, Vigilante app; #6-Blackhawk G.A.-r.*

FOUR TEENERS (Formerly Crime Must Pay The Penalty; Dotty No. 35 on)
No. 34, April, 1948 (52 pgs.)
A. A. Wyn

	GD25	FN65	NM94
34-Teen-age comic	3.60	9.00	18.00

FOX AND THE CROW (Stanley & His Monster No. 109 on) (See Comic Cavalcade & Real Screen Comics)
Dec-Jan, 1951-52 - No. 108, Feb-Mar, 1968
National Periodical Publications

	GD25	FN65	NM94
1	68.00	205.00	475.00
2(Scarce)	34.00	102.00	240.00
3-5	22.00	65.00	150.00
6-10	14.00	43.00	100.00
11-20	10.00	30.00	70.00
21-40: 22-Last precode issue (2/55)	7.00	21.00	42.00
41-60	5.00	15.00	30.00
61-80	4.00	10.50	21.00
81-94	2.80	7.00	14.00
95-Stanley & His Monster begins(origin)(1st app?)	3.60	9.00	18.00
96-99,101-108	1.60	4.00	8.00
100	2.00	5.00	10.00

NOTE: *Many covers by **Mort Drucker.***

FOX AND THE HOUND, THE (Disney)
Aug, 1981 - No. 3, Oct, 1981
Whitman Publishing Co.

	GD25	FN65	NM94
11292(#1),2,3-Based on animated movie		.50	1.00

FOX GIANTS
1944 - 1950 (132 - 196 pgs.)
Fox Features Syndicate

	GD25	FN65	NM94
Album of Crime nn(1949, 132p)	30.00	90.00	210.00
Album of Love nn(1949, 132p)	26.00	79.00	185.00
All Famous Crime Stories nn('49, 132p)	30.00	90.00	210.00
All Good Comics 1(1944, 132p)(R.W. Voigt)-The Bouncer, Purple Tigress, Puppeteer, Green Mask; Infinity-c	23.00	70.00	160.00
All Great nn(1944, 132p)-Capt. Jack Terry, Rick Evans, Jaguar Man	23.00	70.00	160.00
All Great nn(Chicago Nite Life News)(1945, 132p)-Green Mask, Bouncer, Puppeteer, Rick Evans, Rocket Kelly	26.00	79.00	185.00
All-Great Confessions nn(1949, 132p)	24.00	73.00	170.00
All Great Crime Stories nn('49, 132p)	28.00	85.00	200.00
All Great Jungle Adventures nn('49, 132p)	34.00	100.00	235.00
All Real Confession Magazine 3 (3/49, 132p)	24.00	73.00	170.00
All Real Confession Magazine 4 (4/49, 132p)	24.00	73.00	170.00
All Your Comics 1(1944, 132p)-The Puppeteer, Red Robbins, & Merciless the Sorcerer	26.00	78.00	180.00
Almanac Of Crime nn(1948, 148p)	30.00	90.00	210.00
Almanac Of Crime 1(1950, 132p)	28.00	85.00	200.00
Book Of Love nn(1950, 132p)	24.00	72.00	165.00
Burning Romances 1(1949, 132p)	28.00	85.00	200.00
Crimes Incorporated nn(1950, 132p)	26.00	79.00	185.00
Daring Love Stories nn(1950, 132p)	24.00	72.00	165.00
Everybody's Comics 1(1944, 196p)-The Green Mask, The Puppeteer, The Bouncer; (50 cents)	26.00	79.00	185.00
Everybody's Comics 1(1946, 196p)-Green Lama, The Puppeteer	21.00	62.00	145.00
Everybody's Comics 1(1946, 196p)-Same as 1945 Ribtickler	17.00	52.00	120.00
Everybody's Comics nn(1947, 132p)-Jo-Jo, Purple Tigress, Cosmo Cat, Bronze Man	21.00	62.00	145.00
Exciting Romance Stories nn('49, 132p)	24.00	70.00	165.00
Intimate Confessions nn(1950, 132p)	24.00	70.00	165.00
Journal Of Crime nn(1949, 132p)	28.00	85.00	200.00
Love Problems nn(1949, 132p)	25.00	75.00	175.00
Love Thrills nn(1950, 132p)	25.00	75.00	175.00
March of Crime nn('48, 132p)-Female w/rifle-c	26.00	79.00	185.00
March of Crime nn('49, 132p)-Cop w/pistol-c	26.00	79.00	185.00
March of Crime nn(1949, 132p)-Coffin & man w/machine-gun-c	26.00	79.00	185.00
Revealing Love Stories nn(1950, 132p)	24.00	70.00	165.00
Ribtickler nn(1945, 196p, 50¢)-Chicago Nite Life News; Marvel Mutt, Cosmo Cat, Flash Rabbit, The Nebbs app.	21.00	62.00	145.00
Romantic Thrills nn(1950, 132p)	24.00	70.00	165.00
Secret Love nn(1949, 132p)	24.00	70.00	165.00
Secret Love Stories nn(1949, 132p)	24.00	70.00	165.00
Strange Love nn(1950, 132p)-Photo-c	28.00	85.00	200.00
Sweetheart Scandals nn(1950, 132p)	24.00	70.00	165.00
Teen-Age Love nn(1950, 132p)	24.00	70.00	165.00
Throbbing Love nn(1950, 132p)-Photo-c; used in **POP**, pg. 107	28.00	85.00	200.00
Truth About Crime nn(1949, 132p)	28.00	85.00	200.00
Variety Comics 1(1946, 132p)-Blue Beetle, Jungle Jo	22.00	65.00	155.00
Variety Comics nn(1950, 132p)-Jungle Jo, My Secret Affair(w/Harrison/Wood-a), Crimes by Women & My Story	21.00	62.00	145.00
Western Roundup nn('50, 132p)-Hoot Gibson	25.00	75.00	175.00

NOTE: *Each of the above usually contain four remaindered Fox books minus covers. Since these missing covers often had the first page of the first story, most Giants therefore are incomplete. Approximate values are listed. Books with appearances of Phantom Lady, Rulah, Jo-Jo, etc. could bring more.*

FOXHOLE (Becomes Never Again #8?)
9-10/54 - No. 4, 3-4/55; No. 5, 7/55 - No. 7, 3/56
Mainline/Charlton Comics No. 5 on

	GD25	FN65	NM94
1-Classic Kirby-c	11.00	32.00	75.00
2-Kirby-c/a(2)	10.00	30.00	60.00
3-5-Kirby-c only	5.85	17.50	35.00
6-Kirby-c/a(2)	10.00	30.00	60.00

	GD25	FN65	NM94
7	2.40	6.00	12.00
Super Reprints #10-12,15-18: 10-r/? 11,12,18-r/Foxhole #1,2,3. 15,16-r/ United States Marines #5,8. 17-r/Monty Hall #?	.80	2.00	4.00

NOTE: ***Kirby** a(r)-Super #11, 12. **Powell** a(r)-Super #15, 16.*

FOXY FAGAN COMICS
Dec, 1946 - No. 7, Summer, 1948
Dearfield Publishing Co.

	GD25	FN65	NM94
1-Foxy Fagan & Little Buck begin	9.15	27.50	55.00
2	4.70	14.00	28.00
3-7	4.00	10.50	21.00

FOXY GRANDPA (Also see The Funnies, 1st series)
1901 - 1916 (Hardcover; strip reprints)
N. Y. Herald/Frederick A. Stokes Co./M. A. Donahue & Co./Bunny Publ.
(L. R. Hammersly Co.)

	GD25	FN65	VF82
1901-9x15" in color-N. Y. Herald	58.00	175.00	350.00
1902-"Latest Larks of...," 32 pgs. in color, 9x15"	50.00	150.00	300.00
1902-"The Many Advs. of...," 9-1/2x15-1/2", 148 pgs. in color (Hammersly)	58.00	175.00	350.00
1903-"Latest Advs.," 9x15", 24 pgs. in color, Hammersly Co.	50.00	150.00	300.00
1903-"...'s New Advs.," 10x15, 32 pgs. in color, Stokes	50.00	150.00	300.00
1904-"Up to Date," 10x15", 28 pgs. in color, Stokes	50.00	150.00	300.00
1905-"& Flip Flaps," 9-1/2x15-1/2", 52 pgs., in color	50.00	150.00	300.00
1905-"The Latest Advs. of," 9x15", 28, 52, & 66 pgs, in color, M.A. Donohue Co.; re-issue of 1902 issue	33.00	100.00	200.00
1905-"Merry Pranks of," 9-1/2x15-1/2", 52 pgs. in color, Donahue	33.00	100.00	200.00
1905-"Latest Larks of," 9-1/2x15-1/2", 52 pgs. in color, Donahue; re-issue of 1902 issue	33.00	100.00	200.00
1905-"Latest Larks of," 9-1/2x15-1/2", 24 pg. edition in color, Donahue; re-issue of 1902 issue	33.00	100.00	200.00
1906-"Frolics," 10x15", 30 pgs. in color, Stokes	33.00	100.00	200.00
1907	33.00	100.00	200.00
1908?-"Triumphs," 10x15"	33.00	100.00	200.00
1908?-"& Little Brother," 10x15"	33.00	100.00	200.00
1911-"Latest Tricks," r-1910,1911 Sundays in color-Stokes Co.	33.00	100.00	200.00
1914-9-1/2x15-1/2", 24 pgs., 6 color cartoons/page, Bunny Publ.	29.00	88.00	175.00
1916-"Merry Book," 10x15", 30 pgs. in color, Stokes	29.00	88.00	175.00

FOXY GRANDPA SPARKLETS SERIES
1908 (6-1/2x7-3/4"; 24 pgs. in color)
M. A. Donahue & Co.

	GD25	FN65	VF82
"... Rides the Goat," "...& His Boys," "...Playing Ball," "...Fun on the Farm," "...Fancy Shooting," "...Show the Boys Up Sports," "Plays Santa Claus" each....	33.00	100.00	200.00
900-...Playing Ball; Bunny illos; 8 pgs., linen like pgs., no date	25.00	75.00	150.00

FRACTURED FAIRY TALES (TV)
October, 1962 (Jay Ward)
Gold Key

	GD25	FN65	NM94
1 (10022-210)-From Bullwinkle TV show	10.00	30.00	65.00

FRAGGLE ROCK (TV)
Apr, 1985 - No. 8, Sept, 1986; V2#1, Apr, 1988 - No. 6, Sept, 1988
Star Comics (Marvel)/Marvel V2#1 on

	GD25	FN65	NM94
1-8 (75 cents)		.50	1.00
V2#1-6($1.00): Reprints 1st series		.50	1.00

FRANCIS, BROTHER OF THE UNIVERSE
1980 (75 cents) (52 pgs.) (One Shot)
Marvel Comics Group

	GD25	FN65	NM94
nn-Buscema/Marie Severin-a; story of Francis Bernadone celebrating his 800th birthday in 1982		.50	1.00

FRANCIS THE FAMOUS TALKING MULE (All based on movie) (See 4-Color #335, 465, 501, 547, 579, 621, 655, 698, 710, 745, 810, 863, 906, 953, 991, 1068, 1090)

FRANK BUCK (Formerly My True Love)
No. 70, May, 1950 - No. 3, Sept, 1950
Fox Features Syndicate

	GD25	FN65	NM94
70-Wood a(p)(3 stories)-Photo-c	12.00	36.00	85.00
71-Wood a? (9 pgs.), 3-Painted-c	9.15	27.50	55.00

FRANKENSTEIN (See Movie Classics)
Aug-Oct, 1964; No. 2, Sept, 1966 - No. 4, Mar, 1967
Dell Publishing Co.

	GD25	FN65	NM94
1(12-283-410)(1964)	2.80	7.00	14.00
2-Intro. & origin super-hero character (9/66)	1.60	4.00	8.00
3,4	1.20	3.00	6.00

FRANKENSTEIN (The Monster of...; also see Monsters Unleashed #2, Power Record Comics, Psycho & Silver Surfer #7)
Jan, 1973 - No. 18, Sept, 1975
Marvel Comics Group

	GD25	FN65	NM94
1-Ploog-c/a begins, ends #6	3.00	7.50	15.00
2-5,8,9: 8,9-Dracula app.	1.60	4.00	8.00
6,7,10	1.00	2.50	5.00
11-18	.60	1.50	3.00

NOTE: ***Adkins** c-17i. **Buscema** a-7-10p. **Ditko** a-12r. **G. Kane** c-15p. **Orlando** a-8r. **Ploog** a-1-3, 4p, 5p, 6; c-1-6. **Wrightson** c-18i.*

FRANKENSTEIN COMICS (Also See Prize Comics)
Sum, 1945 - V5#5(#33), Oct-Nov, 1954
Prize Publications (Crestwood/Feature)

	GD25	FN65	NM94
1-Frankenstein begins by Dick Briefer (origin); Frank Sinatra parody	50.00	150.00	350.00
2	25.00	75.00	175.00
3-5	18.00	54.00	125.00
6-10: 7-S&K a(r)/Headline Comics. 8(7-8/47)-Superman satire	16.00	48.00	110.00
11-17(1-2/49)-11-Boris Karloff parody-c/story. 17-Last humor issue	12.00	36.00	85.00
18(3/52)-New origin, horror series begins	16.00	48.00	110.00
19,20(V3#4, 8-9/52)	10.00	30.00	65.00
21(V3#5), 22(V3#6)	10.00	30.00	65.00
23(V4#1) - #28(V4#6)	10.00	30.00	65.00
29(V5#1) - #33(V5#5)	10.00	30.00	65.00

NOTE: ***Briefer** c/a-all. **Meskin** a-21, 29.*

FRANKENSTEIN, JR. (...& the Impossibles) (TV)
January, 1967 (Hanna-Barbera)
Gold Key

	GD25	FN65	NM94
1	2.80	7.00	14.00

FRANK FRAZETTA'S THUN'DA TALES (Fantagrahics) (Value: cover or less)

FRANK FRAZETTA'S UNTAMED LOVE (Fantagraphics) (Value: cover or less)

FRANKIE COMICS (...& Lana No. 13-15) (Formerly Movie Tunes; becomes Frankie Fuddle No. 16 on)
No. 4, Wint, 1946-47 - No. 15, June, 1949
Marvel Comics (MgPC)

	GD25	FN65	NM94
4-Mitzi, Margie, Daisy app.	8.35	25.00	50.00
5-9	4.35	13.00	26.00
10-15: 13-Anti-Wertham editorial	4.00	11.00	22.00

FRANKIE DOODLE (See Single Series #7 and Sparkler, both series)

FRANKIE FUDDLE (Formerly Frankie & Lana)
No. 16, Aug, 1949 - No. 17, Nov, 1949
Marvel Comics

The Latest Adventures of Foxy Grandpa (1905), © M.A. Donahue & Co.

Frank Buck #71, © FOX

Frankenstein Comics #14, © PRIZE

Freedom Agent #1, © WEST

Freedom Fighters #3, © DC

Frisky Animals #44, © STAR

	GD25	FN65	NM94
16,17	4.00	12.00	24.00

FRANK LUTHER'S SILLY PILLY COMICS (See Jingle Dingle...)
1950 (10 cents)
Children's Comics

	GD25	FN65	NM94
1-Characters from radio, records, & TV	4.00	12.00	24.00

FRANK MERRIWELL AT YALE (Speed Demons No. 5 on?)
June, 1955 - No. 4, Jan, 1956 (Also see Shadow Comics)
Charlton Comics

	GD25	FN65	NM94
1	3.60	9.00	18.00
2-4	2.40	6.00	12.00

FRANTIC (Magazine) (See Ratfink & Zany)
Oct, 1958 - V2#2, April, 1959 (Satire)
Pierce Publishing Co.

	GD25	FN65	NM94
V1#1,2	3.60	9.00	18.00
V2#1,2: 1-Burgos-a, Severin-c/a; Powell-a?	2.40	6.00	12.00

FREAKS' ARMOUR (Dark Horse) (Value: cover or less)

FRECKLES AND HIS FRIENDS (See Crackajack Funnies, Famous Comics Cartoon Book, Honeybee Birdwhistle... & Red Ryder)

FRECKLES AND HIS FRIENDS
No. 5, 11/47 - No. 12, 8/49; 11/55 - No. 4, 6/56
Standard Comics/Argo

	GD25	FN65	NM94
5-Reprints	5.00	15.00	30.00
6-12-Reprints; 11-Lingerie panels	3.60	9.00	18.00

NOTE: Some copies of No. 8 & 9 contain a printing oddity. The negatives were elongated in the engraving process, probably to conform to page dimensions on the filler pages. Those pages only look normal when viewed at a 45 degree angle.

	GD25	FN65	NM94
1(Argo,'55)-Reprints (NEA Service)	4.00	10.00	20.00
2-4	2.80	7.00	14.00

FREDDY (Formerly My Little Margie's Boy Friends) (Also see Blue Bird)
V2#12, June, 1958 - No. 47, Feb, 1965
Charlton Comics

	GD25	FN65	NM94
V2#12	2.00	5.00	10.00
13-15	1.00	2.50	5.00
16-47	.80	2.00	4.00
Schiff's Shoes Presents... #1 (1959)-Giveaway	.80	2.00	4.00

FREDDY
May-July, 1963 - No. 3, Oct-Dec, 1964
Dell Publishing Co.

	GD25	FN65	NM94
1-3	1.20	3.00	6.00

FREDDY KRUEGER'S A NIGHTMARE ON ELM STREET (Marvel) (Value: cover or less)

FREDDY'S DEAD: THE FINAL NIGHTMARE (Innovation) (Value: cover or less)

FRED HEMBECK DESTROYS THE MARVEL UNIVERSE
July, 1989 ($1.50, one-shot)
Marvel Comics

	GD25	FN65	NM94
1-Punisher app.; Staton-i (5 pgs.)	.30	.75	1.50

FRED HEMBECK SELLS THE MARVEL UNIVERSE
Oct, 1990 ($1.25, color, one-shot)
Marvel Comics

	GD25	FN65	NM94
1-Punisher, Wolverine parodies; Hembeck/Austin-c		.60	1.25

FREE COMICS TO YOU FROM... (name of shoe store) (Has clown on cover & another with a rabbit) (Like comics from Weather Bird & Edward's Shoes)
Circa 1956, 1960-61
Shoe Store Giveaway

Contains a comic bound with new cover - several combinations possible; some Harvey titles known. Contents determines price.

FREEDOM AGENT (Also see John Steele)
April, 1963
Gold Key

	GD25	FN65	NM94
1 (10054-304)-Painted-c	1.80	4.50	9.00

FREEDOM FIGHTERS (See Justice League of America #107,108)
Mar-Apr, 1976 - No. 15, July-Aug, 1978
National Periodical Publications/DC Comics

	GD25	FN65	NM94
1-Uncle Sam, The Ray, Black Condor, Doll Man, Human Bomb, & Phantom Lady begin	.40	1.00	2.00
2-15: 7-1st app. Crusaders. 10-Origin Doll Man; Cat-Man-c/story (4th app; 1st revival since Det. #325). 11-Origin The Ray. 12-Origin Firebrand. 13-Origin Black Condor. 14,15-Batgirl & Batwoman app. 15-Origin Phantom Lady		.50	1.00

NOTE: ***Buckler*** *c-5-11p, 13p, 14p.*

FREEDOM TRAIN
1948 (Giveaway)
Street & Smith Publications

	GD25	FN65	NM94
nn-Powell-c	3.00	7.50	15.00

FREEJACK (Now) (Value: cover or less)

FRENZY (Magazine) (Satire)
April, 1958 - No. 6, March, 1959
Picture Magazine

	GD25	FN65	NM94
1	3.60	9.00	18.00
2-6	2.40	6.00	12.00

FRIDAY FOSTER
October, 1972
Dell Publishing Co.

	GD25	FN65	NM94
1	2.40	6.00	12.00

FRIENDLY GHOST, CASPER, THE (Becomes Casper... #254 on)
Aug, 1958 - No. 224, Oct, 1982; No. 225, Oct, 1986 - No. 253, 1989
Harvey Publications

	GD25	FN65	NM94
1-Infinity-c	18.00	54.00	125.00
2	10.00	30.00	60.00
3-10: 6-X-Mas-c	5.00	15.00	30.00
11-20: 18-X-Mas-c	4.00	10.00	20.00
21-30	2.00	5.00	10.00
31-50	1.40	3.50	7.00
51-100: 54-X-Mas-c	1.00	2.50	5.00
101-159	.60	1.50	3.00
160-163: All 52 pg. Giants	.70	1.75	3.50
164-237: 173,179,185-Cub Scout Specials. 230-X-mas-c. 232-Valentine's-c	.30	.75	1.50
238-253: 238-Begin $1.00-c. 238,244-Halloween-c. 243-Last new material		.50	1.00
American Dental Assoc. giveaway-Small size (1967, 16 pgs.)	.80	2.00	4.00

FRIGHT
June, 1975 (August on inside)
Atlas/Seaboard Periodicals

	GD25	FN65	NM94
1-Origin The Son of Dracula; Frank Thorne-c/a		.50	1.00

FRIGHT NIGHT (Now) (Value: cover or less)

FRIGHT NIGHT II (Now) (Value: cover or less)

FRISKY ANIMALS (Formerly Frisky Fables; Super Cat #56 on)
No. 44, Jan, 1951 - No. 55, Sept, 1953
Star Publications

	GD25	FN65	NM94
44-Super Cat	10.00	30.00	60.00
45-Classic L. B. Cole-c	12.00	36.00	85.00
46-51,53-55-Super Cat	8.35	25.00	50.00
52-L. B. Cole-c/a, 3 pgs.	10.00	30.00	60.00

NOTE: *All have* ***L. B. Cole****-c. No. 47-No Super Cat.* ***Disbrow*** *a-49, 52.* ***Fago*** *a-51.*

	GD25	FN65	NM94

FRISKY ANIMALS ON PARADE (Formerly Parade Comics; becomes Superspook)
Sept, 1957 - No. 3, Dec-Jan, 1957-1958
Ajax-Farrell Publ. (Four Star Comic Corp.)

	GD25	FN65	NM94
1-L. B. Cole-c	7.50	22.50	45.00
2-No L. B. Cole-c	4.00	11.00	22.00
3-L. B. Cole-c	5.00	15.00	30.00

FRISKY FABLES (Frisky Animals No. 44 on)
Spring, 1945 - No. 44, Oct-Nov, 1949
Premium Group/Novelty Publ.

	GD25	FN65	NM94
V1#1-Al Fago-c/a	10.00	30.00	60.00
2,3(1945)	5.00	15.00	30.00
4-7(1946)	4.00	11.00	22.00
V2#1-9,11,12(1947)	3.20	8.00	16.00
10-Christmas-c	3.60	9.00	18.00
V3#1-12(1948): 4-Flag-c. 9-Infinity-c	2.80	7.00	14.00
V4#1-7	2.80	7.00	14.00
36-44(V4#8-12,V5#1-4)-L. B. Cole-c; 40-X-mas-c	7.50	22.50	45.00
Accepted Reprint No. 43 (nd); L.B. Cole-c	4.00	10.50	21.00

FRITZI RITZ (See Comics On Parade, Single Series #5, 1(reprint), Tip Top & United Comics)

FRITZI RITZ (United Comics No. 8-26)
Fall/48 - No. 7, 1949; No. 27, 3-4/53 - No. 36, 9-10/54; No. 42, 1/55; No. 43, 6/56 - No. 55, 9-11/57; No. 56, 12-2/57-58 - No. 59, 9-11/58
United Features Synd./St. John No. 37?-55/Dell No. 56 on

	GD25	FN65	NM94
nn(1948)-Special Fall issue	9.15	27.50	55.00
2	4.70	14.00	28.00
3-7(1949): 6-Abbie & Slats app.	4.00	10.50	21.00
27-29(1953): 29-Five pg. Abbie & Slats; 1 pg. Mamie by Russell Patterson	2.80	7.00	14.00
30-59: 36-1 pg. Mamie by Patterson. 43-Peanuts by Schulz	2.40	6.00	12.00

NOTE: Abbie & Slats in #6,7, 27-31. Li'l Abner in #33, 35, 36. Peanuts in #31, 43, 58, 59.

FROGMAN COMICS
Jan-Feb, 1952 - No. 11, May, 1953
Hillman Periodicals

	GD25	FN65	NM94
1	7.50	22.50	45.00
2	4.00	11.00	22.00
3,4,6-11: 4-Meskin-a	3.60	9.00	18.00
5-Krigstein-a	5.00	15.00	30.00

FROGMEN, THE
No. 1258, Feb-Apr, 1962 - No. 11, Nov-Jan, 1964-65 (Painted-c)
Dell Publishing Co.

	GD25	FN65	NM94
4-Color 1258(#1)-Evans-a	6.70	20.00	40.00
2,3-Evans-a; part Frazetta inks in #2,3	5.85	17.50	35.00
4,6-11	2.80	7.00	14.00
5-Toth-a	4.00	12.00	24.00

FROM BEYOND THE UNKNOWN
10-11/69 - No. 25, 11-12/73 (No. 7-11: 64 pgs.; No. 12-17: 52 pgs.)
National Periodical Publications

	GD25	FN65	NM94
1	1.20	3.00	6.00
2-10: 7-Intro. Col. Glenn Merrit	.80	2.00	4.00
11-25: Star Rovers-r begin #18,19. Space Museum in #23-25	.50	1.25	2.50

*NOTE: **N. Adams** c-3, 6, 8, 9. **Anderson** c-2, 4, 5, 10, 11i, 15-17, 22; reprints-3, 4, 6-8, 10, 11, 13-16, 24, 25. **Infantino** r-1-5, 7-19, 23-25; c-11p. **Kaluta** c-18, 19. **Kubert** c-1, 7, 12-14. **Toth** a-2r. **Wood** a-13i. Photo c-22.*

FROM HERE TO INSANITY (Satire) (Formerly Eh! No. 1-7)
(See Frantic & Frenzy)
No. 8, Feb, 1955 - V3#1, 1956
Charlton Comics

	GD25	FN65	NM94
8	8.35	25.00	50.00
9	6.70	20.00	40.00
10-Ditko-c/a (3 pgs.)	10.00	30.00	60.00
11,12-All Kirby except 4 pgs.	11.00	32.00	75.00
V3#1(1956)-Ward-c/a(2) (signed McCartney); 5 pgs. Wolverton; 3 pgs. Ditko; magazine format	20.00	60.00	140.00

FRONTIER DAYS
1956 (Giveaway)
Robin Hood Shoe Store (Brown Shoe)

	GD25	FN65	NM94
1	2.00	5.00	10.00

FRONTIER DOCTOR (See 4-Color No. 877)

FRONTIER FIGHTERS
Sept-Oct, 1955 - No. 8, Nov-Dec, 1956
National Periodical Publications

	GD25	FN65	NM94
1-Davy Crockett, Buffalo Bill by Kubert, Kit Carson begin (Scarce)	36.00	107.00	250.00
2	25.00	75.00	175.00
3-8	22.00	65.00	150.00

*NOTE: Buffalo Bill by **Kubert** in all.*

FRONTIER ROMANCES
Nov-Dec, 1949 - No. 2, Feb-Mar, 1950 (Painted-c)
Avon Periodicals/I. W.

	GD25	FN65	NM94
1-Used in **SOTI**, pg. 180(General reference) & illo. "Erotic spanking in a western comic book"	34.00	100.00	235.00
2 (Scarce)-Woodish-a by Stallman	20.00	60.00	140.00
I.W. Reprint #1-Reprints Avon's #1	4.00	10.50	21.00
I.W. Reprint #9-Reprints ?	2.40	6.00	12.00

FRONTIER SCOUT: DAN'L BOONE (Formerly Death Valley; The Masked Raider No. 14 on)
No. 10, Jan, 1956 - No. 13, Aug, 1956; V2#14, March, 1965
Charlton Comics

	GD25	FN65	NM94
10	5.00	15.00	30.00
11-13(1956)	3.60	9.00	18.00
V2#14(3/65)	1.60	4.00	8.00

FRONTIER TRAIL (The Rider No. 1-5)
No. 6, May, 1958
Ajax/Farrell Publ.

	GD25	FN65	NM94
6	3.20	8.00	16.00

FRONTIER WESTERN
Feb, 1956 - No. 10, Aug, 1957
Atlas Comics (PrPI)

	GD25	FN65	NM94
1	10.00	30.00	65.00
2,3,6-Williamson-a, 4 pgs. each	8.35	25.00	50.00
4,7,9,10: 10-Check-a	4.70	14.00	28.00
5-Crandall, Baker, Wildey, Davis-a; Williamson text illos	5.85	17.50	35.00
8-Crandall, Morrow, & Wildey-a	4.20	12.50	25.00

*NOTE: **Colan** a-2. **Drucker** a-3, 4. **Heath** c-5. **Maneely** c/a-2, 7. **Romita** a-7. **Severin** c-6, 8, 10. **Tuska** a-2. Ringo Kid in No. 4.*

FRONTLINE COMBAT
July-Aug, 1951 - No. 15, Jan, 1954
E. C. Comics

	GD25	FN65	NM94
1-Severin/Kurtzman-a	42.00	125.00	290.00
2	29.00	85.00	200.00
3	22.00	65.00	150.00
4-Used in **SOTI**, pg. 257; contains "Airburst" by Kurtzman which is his personal all-time favorite story	18.00	54.00	125.00
5	16.00	48.00	110.00
6-10	13.00	40.00	90.00
11-15	10.00	30.00	70.00

*NOTE: **Davis** a-in all; c-11, 12. **Evans** a-10-15. **Heath** a-1. **Kubert** a-14. **Kurtzman** a-1-5; c-1-9. **Severin** a-5-7, 9, 13, 15. **Severin/Elder** a-2-11; c-10. **Toth** a-8, 12. **Wood** a-1-4, 6-10, 12-15; c-13-15. Special issues: No. 7 (Iwo Jima), No. 9 (Civil War), No. 12 (Air Force).*

Frogman Comics #1, © HILL

Frontier Fighters #2, © DC

Frontline Combat #3, © WMG

Fugitives From Justice #1, © STJ

Fun Comics #10, © STAR

The Funnies #10, © DELL

	GD25	FN65	NM94

(Canadian reprints known; see Table of Contents.)

FRONT PAGE COMIC BOOK
1945
Front Page Comics (Harvey)

1-Kubert-a; intro. & 1st app. Man in Black by Powell; Fuje-c	22.00	65.00	150.00

FROST AND FIRE (See DC Science Fiction Graphic Novel)

FROSTY THE SNOWMAN
No. 359, Nov, 1951 - No. 1272, Dec-Feb?/1961-62
Dell Publishing Co.

4-Color 359 (#1)	6.70	20.00	40.00
4-Color 435	4.00	10.50	21.00
4-Color 514,601,661	3.60	9.00	18.00
4-Color 748,861,950,1065,1153,1272	3.20	8.00	16.00

FRUITMAN SPECIAL
Dec, 1969 (68 pages)
Harvey Publications

1-Funny super hero	2.40	6.00	12.00

F-TROOP (TV)
Aug, 1966 - No. 7, Aug, 1967 (All have photo-c)
Dell Publishing Co.

1	6.35	19.00	38.00
2-7	4.00	10.00	20.00

FUGITIVES FROM JUSTICE
Feb, 1952 - No. 5, Oct, 1952
St. John Publishing Co.

1	10.00	30.00	60.00
2-Matt Baker-a; Vic Flint strip reprints begin	10.00	30.00	60.00
3-Reprints panel from Authentic Police Cases that was used in **SOTI** with changes; Tuska-a	10.00	30.00	60.00
4	4.70	14.00	28.00
5-Last Vic Flint-r; bondage-c	5.85	17.50	35.00

FUGITOID
1985 (One shot, B&W, magazine size)
Mirage Studios

1-Ties into Teenage Mutant Ninja Turtles #5	2.20	5.50	11.00

FULL COLOR COMICS
1946
Fox Features Syndicate

nn	8.35	25.00	50.00

FULL OF FUN
Aug, 1957 - No. 2, Nov, 1957; 1964
Red Top (Decker Publ.)(Farrell)/I. W. Enterprises

1(1957)-Dave Berg-a	4.00	11.00	22.00
2-Reprints Bingo, the Monkey Doodle Boy	2.80	7.00	14.00
8-I.W. Reprint('64)	.80	2.00	4.00

FUN AT CHRISTMAS (See March of Comics No. 138)

FUN CLUB COMICS (See Interstate Theatres...)

FUN COMICS (Formerly Holiday Comics #1-8; Mighty Bear #13 on)
No. 9, Jan, 1953 - No. 12, Oct, 1953
Star Publications

9(Giant)-L. B. Cole-c	10.00	30.00	60.00
10-12-L. B. Cole-c	6.35	19.00	38.00

FUNDAY FUNNIES (See Famous TV..., and Harvey Hits No. 35,40)

FUN-IN (TV)(Hanna-Barbera)
Feb, 1970 - No. 10, Jan, 1972; No. 11, 4/74 - No. 15, 12/74
Gold Key

	GD25	FN65	NM94
1-Dastardly & Muttley in Their Flying Machines; Perils of Penelope Pitstop in #1-4; It's the Wolf in all	3.00	7.50	15.00
2-4,6-Cattanooga Cats in 2-4	1.40	3.50	7.00
5,7-Motormouse & Autocat, Dastardly & Muttley in both; It's the Wolf in #7	1.80	4.50	9.00
8,10-The Harlem Globetrotters, Dastardly & Muttley in #10	1.40	3.50	7.00
9-Where's Huddles?, Dastardly & Muttley, Motormouse & Autocat app.	1.80	4.50	9.00
11-15: 11-Butch Cassidy. 12,15-Speed Buggy. 13-Hair Bear Bunch. 14-Inch High Private Eye	1.00	2.50	5.00

FUNKY PHANTOM, THE (TV)
Mar, 1972 - No. 13, Mar, 1975 (Hanna-Barbera)
Gold Key

1	2.40	6.00	12.00
2-5	1.20	3.00	6.00
6-13	.70	1.75	3.50

FUNLAND
No date (25 cents)
Ziff-Davis (Approved Comics)

nn-Contains games, puzzles, etc.	10.00	30.00	65.00

FUNLAND COMICS
1945
Croyden Publishers

1	10.00	30.00	65.00

FUNNIES, THE (Also see Comic Cuts)
1929 - No. 36, 10/18/30 (10 cents; 5 cents No. 22 on) (16 pgs.)
Full tabloid size in color; not reprints; published every Saturday
Dell Publishing Co.

1-My Big Brudder, Johnathan, Jazzbo & Jim, Foxy Grandpa, Sniffy, Jimmy Jams & other strips begin; first four-color comic newsstand publication; also contains magic, puzzles & stories	37.00	112.00	225.00
2-21 (1930, 30 cents)	13.00	40.00	80.00
22(nn-7/12/30-5 cents)	10.00	30.00	60.00
23(nn-7/19/30-5 cents), 24(nn-7/26/30-5 cents), 25(nn-8/2/30), 26(nn-8/9/30), 27(nn-8/16/30), 28(nn-8/23/30), 29(nn-8/30/30), 30(nn-9/6/30), 31(nn-9/13/30), 32(nn-9/20/30), 33(nn-9/27/30), 34(nn-10/4/30), 35(nn-10/11/30), 36(nn, no date-10/18/30) each....	10.00	30.00	60.00

FUNNIES, THE (New Funnies No. 65 on)
Oct, 1936 - No. 64, May, 1942
Dell Publishing Co.

1-Tailspin Tommy, Mutt & Jeff, Alley Oop (1st app?), Capt. Easy, Don Dixon begin	133.00	400.00	800.00
2-Scribbly by Mayer begins (1st app.)	62.00	188.00	375.00
3	56.00	168.00	335.00
4,5: 4-Christmas-c	46.00	138.00	275.00
6-10	37.00	112.00	225.00
11-20: 16-Christmas-c	32.00	95.00	190.00
21-29: 25-Crime Busters by McWilliams(4pgs.)	25.00	75.00	150.00
30-John Carter of Mars (origin) begins by Edgar Rice Burroughs	71.00	212.00	425.00
31-44: 33-John Coleman Burroughs art begins on John Carter. 35-(9/39)-Mr. District Attorney begins; based on radio show	46.00	138.00	275.00
45-Origin/1st app. Phantasmo, the Master of the World (Dell's 1st super-hero) & his sidekick Whizzer McGee	32.00	95.00	190.00
46-50: 46-The Black Knight begins, ends #62	28.00	85.00	170.00
51-56-Last ERB John Carter of Mars	28.00	85.00	170.00
57-Intro. & origin Captain Midnight	75.00	225.00	450.00
58-60	29.00	88.00	175.00

	GD25	FN65	NM94
61-Andy Panda begins by Walter Lantz	32.00	95.00	190.00
62,63: 63-Last Captain Midnight-c; bondage-c	29.00	88.00	175.00
64-Format change; Oswald the Rabbit, Felix the Cat, Li'l Eight Ball app.; origin & 1st app. Woody Woodpecker in Oswald; last Capt. Midnight	62.00	188.00	375.00

NOTE: ***Mayer** c-26, 48. **McWilliams** art in many issues on "Rex King of the Deep."*

FUNNIES ANNUAL, THE
1959 ($1.00)(B&W; tabloid-size, approx. 7x10")
Avon Periodicals

1-(Rare)-Features the best newspaper comic strips of the year: Archie, Snuffy Smith, Beetle Bailey, Henry, Blondie, Steve Canyon, Buz Sawyer, The Little King, Hi & Lois, Popeye, & others. Also has a chronological history of the comics from 2000 B.C. to 1959.

	GD25	FN65	NM94
	30.00	90.00	210.00

FUNNIES ON PARADE (Premium)
1933 (Probably the 1st comic book) (36 pgs.; slick cover)
No date or publisher listed
Eastern Color Printing Co.

nn-Contains Sunday page reprints of Mutt & Jeff, Joe Palooka, Hairbreadth Harry, Reg'lar Fellers, Skippy, & others (10,000 print run). This book was printed for Proctor & Gamble to be given away & came out before Famous Funnies or Century of Comics.

GD25	FN65	VF82	NM94
600.00	1800.00	3600.00	6000.00

(Estimated up to 50 total copies exist, 3 in NM/Mint)

FUNNY ANIMALS (See Fawcett's Funny Animals)
Sept, 1984 - No. 2, Nov, 1984
Charlton Comics

	GD25	FN65	NM94
1,2-Atomic Mouse-r		.50	1.00

FUNNYBONE
1944 (132 pages)
La Salle Publishing Co.

	GD25	FN65	NM94
nn	17.00	52.00	120.00

FUNNY BOOK (...Magazine) (Hocus Pocus No. 9)
Dec, 1942 - No. 9, Aug-Sept, 1946
Parents' Magazine Press (Funny Book Publishing Corp.)

	GD25	FN65	NM94
1-Funny animal; Alice In Wonderland app.	10.00	30.00	65.00
2	5.35	16.00	32.00
3-9: 9-Hocus-Pocus strip	4.00	10.50	21.00

FUNNY COMICS (7 cents)
1955 (36 pgs.; 5x7"; in color)
Modern Store Publ.

	GD25	FN65	NM94
1-Funny animal	1.00	2.50	5.00

FUNNY COMIC TUNES (See Funny Tunes)

FUNNY FABLES
Aug, 1957 - V2#2, Nov, 1957
Decker Publications (Red Top Comics)

	GD25	FN65	NM94
V1#1	3.20	8.00	16.00
V2#1,2	2.00	5.00	10.00

FUNNY FILMS
Sept-Oct, 1949 - No. 29, May-June, 1954 (No. 1-4: 52 pgs.)
American Comics Group(Michel Publ./Titan Publ.)

	GD25	FN65	NM94
1-Puss An' Boots, Blunderbunny begin	11.00	32.00	75.00
2	6.35	19.00	38.00
3-10	4.35	13.00	26.00
11-20	3.60	9.00	18.00
21-29	2.80	7.00	14.00

FUNNY FOLKS (Hollywood... on cover only No. 16-26; becomes Hollywood Funny Folks No. 27 on)
April-May, 1946 - No. 26, June-July, 1950 (52 pgs., #16 on)
National Periodical Publications

	GD25	FN65	NM94
1-Nutsy Squirrel begins (1st app.) by Rube Grossman	26.00	78.00	180.00
2	13.00	40.00	90.00
3-5	10.00	30.00	60.00
6-10	7.50	22.50	45.00
11-26: 16-Begin 52 pg. issues (10-11/48)	5.35	16.00	32.00

NOTE: ***Sheldon Mayer** a-in some issues. **Post** a-18.*

FUNNY FROLICS
Summer, 1945 - No. 5, Dec, 1946
Timely/Marvel Comics (SPI)

	GD25	FN65	NM94
1-Sharpy Fox, Puffy Pig, Krazy Krow	11.50	34.00	80.00
2	6.70	20.00	40.00
3,4	5.35	16.00	32.00
5-Kurtzman-a	6.70	20.00	40.00

FUNNY FUNNIES
April, 1943 (68 pages)
Nedor Publishing Co.

	GD25	FN65	NM94
1 (Funny animals)	12.00	36.00	85.00

FUNNYMAN (Also see Extra Comics)
Dec, 1947; No. 1, Jan, 1948 - No. 6, Aug, 1948
Magazine Enterprises

nn(12/47)-Prepublication B&W undistributed copy by Siegel & Shuster-(5-3/4x8"), 16 pgs.; Sold in San Francisco in 1976 for $300.00

	GD25	FN65	NM94
1-Siegel & Shuster-a in all	19.00	58.00	135.00
2	14.00	43.00	100.00
3-6	11.50	34.00	80.00

FUNNY MOVIES (See 3-D Funny Movies)

FUNNY PAGES (Formerly The Comics Magazine)
No. 6, Nov, 1936 - No. 42, Oct, 1940
Comics Magazine Co./Ultem Publ.(Chesler)/Centaur Publications

	GD25	FN65	NM94
V1#6 (nn, nd)-The Clock begins (2 pgs., 1st app.), ends #11	67.00	200.00	400.00
7-11	44.00	132.00	265.00
V2#1 (9/37)(V2#2 on-c; V2#1 in indicia)	33.00	100.00	200.00
V2#2 (10/37)(V2#3 on-c; V2#2 in indicia)	33.0	100.00	200.00
3(11/37)-5	33.00	100.00	200.00
6(1st Centaur, 3/38)	58.00	175.00	350.00
7-9	40.00	120.00	240.00
10(Scarce)-1st app. of The Arrow by Gustavson (Blue costume)	142.00	425.00	850.00
11,12	71.00	212.00	425.00
V3#1-6	71.00	212.00	425.00
7-1st Arrow-c (9/39)	88.00	262.00	525.00
8,9: 9-Tarpe Mills jungle-c	71.00	212.00	425.00
10-2nd Arrow-c	79.00	238.00	475.00
V4#1(1/40, Arrow-c)-(Rare)-The Owl & The Phantom Rider app.; origin Mantoka, Maker of Magic by Jack Cole. Mad Ming begins, ends #42. Tarpe Mills-a	83.00	250.00	500.00
35-38: 35-Arrow-c. 36-38-Mad Ming-c	61.00	182.00	365.00
39-42-Arrow-c. 42-Last Arrow	61.00	182.00	365.00

NOTE: ***Burgos** c-V3#10. **Jack Cole** a-V2#3, 7, 8, 10, 11, V3#2, 6, 9, 10, V4#1, 37. **Eisner** a-V1#7, 8?, 10. **Ken Ernst** a-V1#7, 8. **Everett** a-V2#11 (illos). **Gill Fox** a-V2#11. **Sid Greene** a-39. **Guardineer** a-V2#2, 3, 5. **Gustavson** a-V2#5, 11, 12, V3#1-10, 35, 38-42; c-V3#7, 35, 39-42. **Bob Kane** a-V3#1. **McWilliams** a-V2#12, V3#1, 3-6. **Tarpe Mills** a-V3#8-10, V4#1; c-V3#9. **Ed Moore Jr.** a-V2#12. **Bob Wood** a-V2#2, 3, 8, 11, V3#6, 9, 10; c- V2#6, 7.*

FUNNY PICTURE STORIES (Comic Pages V3#4 on)
Nov, 1936 - V3#3, May, 1939
Comics Magazine Co./Centaur Publications

	GD25	FN65	NM94
V1#1-The Clock begins (c-feature)(see Funny Pages for 1st app.)	133.00	400.00	800.00
2	62.00	188.00	375.00
3-9: 4-Eisner-a; Christmas-c	44.00	132.00	265.00
V2#1 (9/37; V1#10 on-c; V2#1 in indicia)-Jack Strand begins	33.00	100.00	200.00
2 (10/37; V1#11 on-c; V2#2 in indicia)	33.00	100.00	200.00
3-5: 4-Xmas-c	29.00	87.00	175.00

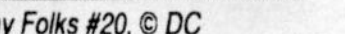

Funny Folks #20, © DC

Funnyman #3, © ME

Funny Pages V3#10, © CEN

Funny Stuff #36, © DC

Funny World #1, © Marbak Press

Future Comics #2, © DMP

	GD25	FN65	NM94
6-(1st Centaur, 3/38)	54.00	162.00	325.00
7-11	31.00	92.00	185.00
V3#1-3	27.00	82.00	165.00
Laundry giveaway (16-20 pgs., 1930s)-slick-c	18.00	55.00	110.00

NOTE: ***Biro*** *c-V2#1.* ***Guardineer*** *a-V1#11.* ***Bob Wood*** *c/a-V1#11, V2#2.*

FUNNY STUFF (Becomes The Dodo & the Frog No. 80)
Summer, 1944 - No. 79, July-Aug, 1954 (#1-7 are quarterly)
All-American/National Periodical Publications No. 7 on

	GD25	FN65	NM94
1-The Three Mouseketeers (ends #28) & The "Terrific Whatzit" begin; Sheldon Mayer-a	68.00	205.00	475.00
2-Sheldon Mayer-a	34.00	103.00	240.00
3-5: 3-Flash parody. 5-All Mayer-a/scripts issue	22.00	65.00	150.00
6-10 (6/46)	14.00	43.00	100.00
11-17,19,20: 20-1st Dodo and the Frog-c	10.00	30.00	70.00
18-The Dodo & the Frog (1st app?) begin?; X-Mas-c	17.00	52.00	120.00
21,23-30: 24-Infinity-c	7.50	22.50	45.00
22-Superman cameo	24.00	72.00	165.00
31-79: 70-1st Bo Bunny by Mayer & begins	5.35	16.00	32.00
Wheaties Giveaway(1946, 6-1/2x8-1/4") (Scarce)-Dodo & the Frog, Three Mouseketeers, etc.; came taped to Wheaties box; never found in better than fine	16.00	110.00	–

NOTE: ***Mayer*** *a-1-8, 55, ,57, 58, 61, 62, 64, 65, 68, 70, 72, 74-79; c-2, 5, 6, 8.*

FUNNY STUFF STOCKING STUFFER
March, 1985 ($1.25, 52 pgs.)
DC Comics

	GD25	FN65	NM94
1-Almost every DC funny animal featured		.60	1.25

FUNNY 3-D
December, 1953
Harvey Publications

	GD25	FN65	NM94
1	9.15	27.50	55.00

FUNNY TUNES (Animated Funny Comic Tunes No. 16-22; Funny Comic Tunes No. 23, on covers only; formerly Krazy Komics #15; Oscar No. 24 on)
No. 16, Summer, 1944 - No. 23, Fall, 1946
U.S.A. Comics Magazine Corp. (Timely)

	GD25	FN65	NM94
16-Silly, Ziggy, Krazy Krow begin	8.35	25.00	50.00
17 (Fall/'44)-Becomes Gay Comics #18 on?	5.35	16.00	32.00
18-22: 21-Super Rabbit app.	4.70	14.00	28.00
23-Kurtzman-a	6.35	19.00	38.00

FUNNY TUNES (Becomes Space Comics #4 on)
July, 1953 - No. 3, Dec-Jan, 1953-54
Avon Periodicals

	GD25	FN65	NM94
1-Space Mouse begins	5.35	16.00	32.00
2,3	4.00	10.50	21.00

FUNNY WORLD
1947 - No. 3, 1948
Marbak Press

	GD25	FN65	NM94
1-The Berrys, The Toodles & other strip reprints begin	5.85	17.50	35.00
2,3	4.35	13.00	26.00

FUNTASTIC WORLD OF HANNA-BARBERA, THE (TV)
Dec, 1977 - No. 3, June, 1978 ($1.25) (Oversized)
Marvel Comics Group

	GD25	FN65	NM94
1-3: 1-The Flintstones Christmas Party(12/77). 2-Yogi Bear's Easter Parade(3/78). 3-Laff-a-lympics(6/78)	1.00	2.50	5.00

FUN TIME
1953; No. 2, Spr, 1953; No. 3(nn), Sum, 1953; No. 4, Wint, 1953-54
Ace Periodicals

	GD25	FN65	NM94
1	3.20	8.00	16.00
2-4 (100 pgs. each)	6.70	20.00	40.00

FUN WITH SANTA CLAUS (See March of Comics No. 11, 108, 325)

FURTHER ADVENTURES OF INDIANA JONES, THE (Also see Indiana Jones and the Last Crusade & Indiana Jones and the Temple of Doom)
Jan, 1983 - No. 34, Mar, 1986
Marvel Comics Group

	GD25	FN65	NM94
1-34: 1-Byrne/Austin-a. 2-Byrne/Austin-c/a		.55	1.10

NOTE: ***Austin*** *a-6i, 9i; c-1i, 2i, 6i, 9i.* ***Chaykin*** *a-6p; c-6p, 8p-10p.* ***Ditko*** *a-21p, 25-28, 34.* ***Golden*** *c-24, 25.* ***Simonson*** *c-9. Painted c-14.*

FURTHER ADVENTURES OF NYOKA, THE JUNGLE GIRL, THE (AC)(Value: cover or less)

FURY (Straight Arrow's Horse...) (See A-1 No. 119)

FURY (TV) (See March Of Comics #200)
No. 781, Mar, 1957 - Nov, 1962 (All photo-c)
Dell Publishing Co./Gold Key

	GD25	FN65	NM94
4-Color 781	9.15	27.50	55.00
4-Color 885,975,1031,1080,1133,1172,1218,1296, 01292-208(#1-'62)	5.85	17.50	35.00
10020-211(11/62-G.K.)-Crandall-a	5.85	17.50	35.00

FURY OF FIRESTORM, THE (Becomes Firestorm The Nuclear Man #65 on; also see Firestorm)
June, 1982 - No. 64, Oct, 1987 (#19-on: 75 cents)
DC Comics

	GD25	FN65	NM94
1-Intro The Black Bison; brief origin	.40	1.00	2.00
2-64: 4-JLA x-over. 17-1st app. Firehaw. 21-Death of Killer Frost. 22-Origin. 23-Intro. Byte. 24-1st app. Blue Devil & Bug (origin); origin Byte. 34-1st app./origin Killer Frost II. 39-Weasel's i.d. revealed 41,42-Crisis x-over. 48-Intro. Moonbow. 53-Origin/1st app. Silver Shade. 55,56-Legends x-over. 58-1st app./origin Parasite		.50	1.00
61-Test cover variant; Superman logo	8.35	25.00	50.00
Annual 1(11/83)-1st app. new Firehawk		.60	1.25
Annual 2-4: 2(11/84), 3(11/85), 4(10/86)		.60	1.25

NOTE: ***Colan*** *a-19p, Annual 4p.* ***Giffen*** *a-Annual 4p.* ***Gil Kane*** *c-30.* ***Nino*** *a-37.* ***Tuska*** *a-(p)-17, 18, 32, 45.*

FUSION (Eclipse)(Value: cover or less)

FUTURE COMICS
June, 1940 - No. 4, Sept, 1940
David McKay Publications

	GD25	FN65	NM94
1-Origin The Phantom; The Lone Ranger, & Saturn Against the Earth begin	150.00	450.00	900.00
2	83.00	250.00	500.00
3,4	67.00	200.00	400.00

FUTURE WORLD COMICS
Summer, 1946 - No. 2, Fall, 1946
George W. Dougherty

	GD25	FN65	NM94
1,2	14.00	43.00	100.00

FUTURE WORLD COMIX (Warren Presents... on cover)
September, 1978
Warren Publications

	GD25	FN65	NM94
1	.30	.75	1.50

FUTURIANS, THE (Lodestone)(Value: cover or less)

G-8 (See G-Eight)

GABBY (Formerly Ken Shannon) (Teen humor)
No. 11, July, 1953; No. 2, Sept, 1953 - No. 9, Sept, 1954
Quality Comics Group

	GD25	FN65	NM94
11(#1)(7/53)	4.20	12.50	25.00
2	3.20	8.00	16.00
3-9	2.00	5.00	10.00

	GD25	FN65	NM94

GABBY GOB (See Harvey Hits No. 85, 90, 94, 97, 100, 103, 106, 109)

GABBY HAYES ADVENTURE COMICS
Dec, 1953
Toby Press

	GD25	FN65	NM94
1-Photo-c	10.00	30.00	65.00

GABBY HAYES WESTERN (Movie star) (See Monte Hale, Real Western Hero & Western Hero)
Nov, 1948 - No. 50, Jan, 1953; No. 51, Dec, 1954 - No. 59, Jan, 1957
Fawcett Publications/Charlton Comics No. 51 on

	GD25	FN65	NM94
1-Gabby & his horse Corker begin; photo front/back-c begin	30.00	90.00	210.00
2	14.00	43.00	100.00
3-5	10.00	30.00	70.00
6-10: 9-Young Falcon begins	10.00	30.00	60.00
11-20: 19-Last photo back-c	7.50	22.50	45.00
21-49: 20,22,24,26,28,29-(52 pgs.)	5.00	15.00	30.00
50-(1/53)-Last Fawcett issue; last photo-c?	5.85	17.50	35.00
51-(12/54)-1st Charlton issue; photo-c	5.85	17.50	35.00
52-59(1955-57): 53,55-Photo-c. 58-Swayze-a	3.60	9.00	18.00
Quaker Oats Giveaway nn's(#1-5, 1951, 2-1/2x7") (Kagran Corp.)-...In Tracks of Guilt, ...In the Fence Post Mystery, ...In the "Accidental Sherlock," ... In the Frame-Up known	8.35	25.00	50.00

GAGS
July, 1937 - V3#10, Oct, 1944 (13-3/4x10-3/4")
United Features Synd./Triangle Publ. No. 9 on

	GD25	FN65	NM94
1(7/37)-52 pgs.; 20 pgs. Grin & Bear It, Fellow Citizen	5.00	15.00	30.00
V1#9 (36 pgs.) (7/42)	3.60	9.00	18.00
V3#10	2.40	7.00	14.00

GALACTIC WAR COMIX (Warren Presents... on cover)
December, 1978
Warren Publications

	GD25	FN65	NM94
nn-Wood, Williamson-r	.30	.75	1.50

GALLANT MEN, THE (TV)
October, 1963 (Photo-c)
Gold Key

	GD25	FN65	NM94
1(10085-310)-Manning-a	2.00	5.00	10.00

GALLEGHER, BOY REPORTER (TV)
May, 1965 (Disney)
Gold Key

	GD25	FN65	NM94
1(10149-505)-Photo-c	1.80	4.50	9.00

GAMEBOY
1990 - No. 6? ($1.95, color, coated-c)
Valiant Comics

	GD25	FN65	NM94
1-6: 3,4,6-Layton-c. 4-Morrow-a. 5-Layton-c(i)	.40	1.00	2.00

GAMMARAUDERS (DC) (Value: cover or less)

GANDY GOOSE (See All Surprise, Paul Terry's & Terry-Toons)
Mar, 1953 - No. 5, Nov, 1953; No. 5, Fall, 1956 - No. 6, Sum/58
St. John Publ. Co./Pines No. 5,6

	GD25	FN65	NM94
1	5.35	16.00	32.00
2	3.20	8.00	16.00
3-5(1953)(St. John)	2.80	7.00	14.00
5,6(1956-58)(Pines)	2.00	5.00	10.00

GANG BUSTERS (See Popular Comics #38)
1938 - 1943
David McKay/Dell Publishing Co.

	GD25	FN65	NM94
Feature Books 17(McKay)('38)	34.00	103.00	240.00
Large Feature Comic 10('39)-(Scarce)	40.00	120.00	275.00
Large Feature Comic 17('41)	25.00	75.00	175.00
4-Color 7(1940)	30.00	90.00	210.00
4-Color 23,24('42-43)	22.00	65.00	150.00

GANG BUSTERS (Radio/TV)(Gangbusters #14 on)
Dec-Jan, 1947-48 - No. 67, Dec-Jan, 1958-59 (No. 1-23: 52 pgs.)
National Periodical Publications

	GD25	FN65	NM94
1	47.00	140.00	325.00
2	20.00	60.00	140.00
3-10: 9,10-Photo-c	13.00	40.00	90.00
11-13-Photo-c	11.00	32.00	75.00
14,17-Frazetta-a, 8 pgs. each. 14-Photo-c	20.00	60.00	140.00
15,16,18-20	8.35	25.00	50.00
21-30: 26-Kirby-a	6.70	20.00	40.00
31-44: 44-Last Pre-code (2-3/55)	5.85	17.50	35.00
45-67	4.70	14.00	28.00

NOTE: ***Barry** a-6, 8, 10. **Drucker** a-51. **Moreira** a-48, 50, 59. **Roussos** a-8.*

GANGSTERS AND GUN MOLLS
Sept, 1951 - No. 4, June, 1952 (Painted-c)
Avon Periodical/Realistic Comics

	GD25	FN65	NM94
1-Wood-a, 1 pg; c-/Avon paperback #292	25.00	75.00	175.00
2-Check-a, 8 pgs.; Kamen-a	19.00	57.00	130.00
3-Marijuana mention story; used in **POP**, pg. 84-85	17.00	52.00	120.00
4	13.00	40.00	90.00

GANGSTERS CAN'T WIN
Feb-Mar, 1948 - No. 9, June-July, 1949
D. S. Publishing Co.

	GD25	FN65	NM94
1	14.00	43.00	100.00
2	8.35	25.00	50.00
3-6: 4-Acid in face story	6.70	20.00	40.00
7-9	5.00	15.00	30.00

NOTE: ***Ingles** a-5, 6. **McWilliams** a-5, 7. **Reinman** c-6.*

GANG WORLD
No. 5, Nov, 1952 - No. 6, Jan, 1953
Standard Comics

	GD25	FN65	NM94
5-Bondage-c	10.00	30.00	60.00
6	6.70	20.00	40.00

GARGOYLE (See The Defenders #94)
June, 1985 - No. 4, Sept, 1985 (75 cents, limited series)
Marvel Comics Group

	GD25	FN65	NM94
1-4: 1-Wrightson-c; character from Defenders		.50	1.00

GARRISON'S GORILLAS (TV)
Jan, 1968 - No. 4, Oct, 1968; No. 5, Oct, 1969 (Photo-c)
Dell Publishing Co.

	GD25	FN65	NM94
1	4.00	11.00	22.00
2-5: 5-Reprints #1	3.00	7.50	15.00

GASOLINE ALLEY (Also see Popular Comics & Super Comics)
1929 (B&W daily strip reprints)(7x8-3/4"; hardcover)
Reilly & Lee Publishers

	GD25	FN65	NM94
nn-By King (96 pgs.)	14.00	43.00	100.00

GASOLINE ALLEY (Top Love Stories No. 3 on?)
Sept-Oct, 1950 - No. 2, Dec, 1950 (Newspaper reprints)
Star Publications

	GD25	FN65	NM94
1-Contains 1 pg. intro. history of the strip (The Life of Skeezix); reprints 15 scenes of highlights from 1921-1935, plus an adventure from 1935 and 1936 strips; a 2-pg. filler is included on the life of the creator Frank King, with photo of the cartoonist.	12.00	36.00	85.00
2-(1936-37 reprints)-L. B. Cole-c	13.00	40.00	90.00

(See Super Book No. 21)

GASP!
March, 1967 - No. 4, Aug, 1967 (12 cents)
American Comics Group

	GD25	FN65	NM94
1	4.00	10.00	20.00

Gabby Hayes Western #13, © FAW

Gang Busters #10, © DC

Gangsters Can't Win #6, © DS

Gay #27, © MEG

G-8 And His Battle Aces #1, © WEST

Gene Autry Comics #6 (Dell) © Gene Autry

	GD25	FN65	NM94
2-4	2.40	6.00	12.00

GAY COMICS (Honeymoon No. 41)
Mar, 1944 (no month); No. 18, Fall, 1944 - No. 40, Oct, 1949
Timely Comics/USA Comic Mag. Co. No. 18-24

	GD25	FN65	NM94
1-Wolverton's Powerhouse Pepper; Tessie the Typist begins; Millie the Model & Willie app. (One Shot)	27.00	81.00	190.00
18-(Formerly Funny Tunes #17?)-Wolverton-a	13.50	41.00	95.00
19-29-Wolverton-a in all. 24,29-Kurtzman-a	11.50	34.00	80.00
30,33,36,37-Kurtzman's "Hey Look"	5.00	15.00	30.00
31-Kurtzman's "Hey Look"(1), Giggles 'N' Grins (1)	5.00	15.00	30.00
32,35,38-40: 35-Nellie The Nurse begins?	4.00	11.00	22.00
34-Three Kurtzman's "Hey Look"	5.85	17.50	35.00

GAY COMICS (Also see Smile, Tickle, & Whee Comics)
1955 (52 pgs.; 5x7-1/4"; 7 cents)
Modern Store Publ.

	GD25	FN65	NM94
1	.80	2.00	4.00

GAY PURR-EE (See Movie Comics)

GEEK, THE (See Brother Power...)

G-8 AND HIS BATTLE ACES
October, 1966
Gold Key

	GD25	FN65	NM94
1 (10184-610)-Painted-c	3.20	8.00	16.00

G-8 AND HIS BATTLE ACES
1991 ($1.50, color, one-shot)
Blazing Comics

	GD25	FN65	NM94
1-Glanzman-a; Truman-c	.30	.75	1.50

NOTE: *Flip book format with "The Spider's Web" #1 on other side w/* ***Glanzman****-a,* ***Truman****-c.*

GEM COMICS
April, 1945 (52 pgs.) (Bondage-c)
Spotlight Publishers

	GD25	FN65	NM94
1-Little Mohee, Steve Strong app.	13.00	40.00	90.00

GENE AUTRY (See March of Comics No. 25, 28, 39, 54, 78, 90, 104, 120, 135, 150 & Western Roundup under Dell Giants)

GENE AUTRY COMICS (Movie, Radio star; singing cowboy)
(Dell takes over with No. 11)
1941 (On sale 12/31/41) - No. 10, 1943 (68 pgs.)
Fawcett Publications

	GD25	FN65	NM94
1 (Rare)-Gene Autry & his horse Champion begin	257.00	770.00	1800.00
2	72.00	215.00	500.00
3-5	50.00	150.00	350.00
6-10	43.00	130.00	300.00

GENE AUTRY COMICS (...& Champion No. 102 on)
No. 11, 1943 - No. 121, Jan-Mar, 1959 (TV - later issues)
Dell Publishing Co.

	GD25	FN65	NM94
11 (1943, 60 pgs.)-Continuation of Fawcett series; photo back-c	50.00	150.00	350.00
12 (2/44, 60 pgs.)	47.00	140.00	325.00
4-Color 47(1944, 60 pgs.)	39.00	118.00	275.00
4-Color 57(11/44),66('45)(52 pgs. each)	34.00	103.00	240.00
4-Color 75,83('45, 36 pgs. each)	29.00	85.00	200.00
4-Color 93,100('45-46, 36 pgs. each)	23.00	70.00	160.00
1(5-6/46, 52 pgs.)	39.00	118.00	275.00
2(7-8/46)-Photo-c begin, end #111	20.00	60.00	140.00
3-5: 4-Intro Flapjack Hobbs	16.00	48.00	110.00
6-10	11.50	34.00	80.00
11-20: 20-Panhandle Pete begins	10.00	30.00	60.00
21-29(36pgs.)	7.50	22.50	45.00
30-40(52pgs.)	7.50	22.50	45.00
41-56(52pgs.)	5.85	17.50	35.00
57-66(36pgs.): 58-X-mas-c	4.00	11.00	22.00
67-80(52pgs.)	4.35	13.00	26.00
81-90(52pgs.): 82-X-mas-c. 87-Blank inside-c	4.00	10.00	20.00
91-99(36pgs. No. 91-on). 94-X-mas-c	2.80	7.00	14.00
100	4.00	10.00	20.00
101-111-Last Gene Autry photo-c	2.80	7.00	14.00
112-121-All Champion painted-c	2.00	5.00	10.00
...Adventure Comics And Play-Fun Book ('40s)-36 pgs., 8x6-1/2"; games, comics, magic	36.00	107.00	250.00
Pillsbury Premium('47)-36 pgs., 6-1/2x7-1/2"; games, comics, puzzles	24.00	73.00	170.00
Quaker Oats Giveaway(1950)-2-1/2x6-3/4"; 5 different versions; "Death Card Gang," "Phantoms of the Cave," "Riddle of Laughing Mtn.," "Secret of Lost Valley," "Bond of the Broken Arrow" (came in wrapper) each...	10.00	30.00	70.00
3-D Giveaway(1953)-Pocket-size; 5 different	12.00	36.00	85.00

NOTE: *Photo back covers 4-18, 20-45, 48-65.* ***Manning*** *a-118.* ***Jesse Marsh*** *art: 4-Color No. 66, 75, 93, 100, No. 1-25, 27-37, 39, 40.*

GENE AUTRY'S CHAMPION (TV)
No. 287, 8/50; No. 319, 2/51; No. 3, 8-10/51 - No. 19, 8-10/55
Dell Publishing Co.

	GD25	FN65	NM94
4-Color 287(#1)('50, 52pgs.)-Photo-c	10.00	30.00	65.00
4-Color 319(#2, '51), 3-(Painted-c begin)	4.20	12.50	25.00
4-19: 19-Last painted-c	2.00	5.00	10.00

GENE AUTRY TIM (Formerly Tim) (Becomes Tim in Space)
1950 (Half-size) (Black & White Giveaway)
Tim Stores

	GD25	FN65	NM94
nn-Several issues (All Scarce)	7.50	22.50	45.00

GENERAL DOUGLAS MACARTHUR
1951
Fox Features Syndicate

	GD25	FN65	NM94
nn	12.00	36.00	85.00

GENERIC COMIC, THE
April, 1984 (One-shot)
Marvel Comics Group

	GD25	FN65	NM94
1		.50	1.00

GENTLE BEN (TV)
Feb, 1968 - No. 5, Oct, 1969 (All photo-c)
Dell Publishing Co.

	GD25	FN65	NM94
1	3.60	9.00	18.00
2-5: 5-Reprints #1	2.00	5.00	10.00

GEORGE OF THE JUNGLE (TV)(See America's Best TV Comics)
Feb, 1969 - No. 2, Oct, 1969 (Jay Ward)
Gold Key

	GD25	FN65	NM94
1,2	6.70	20.00	40.00

GEORGE PAL'S PUPPETOONS
Dec, 1945 - No. 18, Dec, 1947; No. 19, 1950
Fawcett Publications

	GD25	FN65	NM94
1-Captain Marvel app. on cover	29.00	85.00	200.00
2	14.00	43.00	100.00
3-10	10.00	30.00	65.00
11-19	8.35	25.00	50.00

GEORGIE COMICS (...& Judy Comics #20-35?; see All Teen & Teen Comics)
Spring, 1945 - No. 39, Oct, 1952
Timely Comics/GPI No. 1-34

	GD25	FN65	NM94
1-Dave Berg-a	12.00	36.00	85.00
2	6.70	20.00	40.00

	GD25	FN65	NM94
3-5,7,8	4.70	14.00	28.00
6-Georgie visits Timely Comics	6.35	19.00	38.00
9,10-Kurtzman's "Hey Look" (1 & ?); Margie app.	6.35	19.00	38.00
11,12: 11-Margie, Millie app.	4.00	11.00	22.00
13-Kurtzman's "Hey Look," 3 pgs.	5.35	16.00	32.00
14-Wolverton-a(1 pg.); Kurtzman's "Hey Look"	6.35	19.00	38.00
15,16,18-20	3.60	9.00	18.00
17,29-Kurtzman's "Hey Look," 1 pg.	4.70	14.00	28.00
21-24,27,28,30-39: 21-Anti-Wertham editorial	2.80	7.00	14.00
25-Painted cover by classic pin-up artist Peter Driben	5.00	15.00	30.00
26-Logo design swipe from Archie Comics	2.80	7.00	14.00

GERALD McBOING-BOING AND THE NEARSIGHTED MR. MAGOO (TV)
(Mr. Magoo No. 6 on)
Aug-Oct, 1952 - No. 5, Aug-Oct, 1953
Dell Publishing Co.

	GD25	FN65	NM94
1	7.50	22.50	45.00
2-5	6.70	20.00	40.00

GERONIMO
1950 - No. 4, Feb, 1952
Avon Periodicals

	GD25	FN65	NM94
1-Indian Fighter; Maneely-a; Texas Rangers-r/Cowpuncher #1; Fawcette-c	10.00	30.00	70.00
2-On the Warpath; Kit West app.; Kinstler-c/a	6.70	20.00	40.00
3-And His Apache Murderers; Kinstler-c/a(2); Kit West-r/Cowpuncher #6	6.70	20.00	40.00
4-Savage Raids of; Kinstler-c & inside front-c; Kinstlerish-a by McCann(3)	5.35	16.00	32.00

GERONIMO JONES
Sept, 1971 - No. 9, Jan, 1973
Charlton Comics

	GD25	FN65	NM94
1	.80	2.00	4.00
2-9	.40	1.00	2.00
Modern Comics Reprint #7('78)	.30	.75	1.50

GETALONG GANG, THE (TV)
May, 1985 - No. 6, March, 1986
Star Comics (Marvel)

	GD25	FN65	NM94
1-6: Saturday morning TV stars		.50	1.00

GET LOST
Feb-Mar, 1954 - No. 3, June-July, 1954 (Satire)
Mikeross Publications/New Comics

	GD25	FN65	NM94
1	12.00	36.00	85.00
2-Has 4 pg. E.C. parody featuring "The Sewer Keeper"	10.00	30.00	60.00
3-John Wayne 'Hondo' parody	8.35	25.00	50.00
1,2 (10,12/87-New Comics)-B&W r-original		.50	1.00

GET SMART (TV)
June, 1966 - No. 8, Sept, 1967 (All have Don Adams photo-c)
Dell Publishing Co.

	GD25	FN65	NM94
1	9.15	27.50	55.00
2-Ditko-a	6.70	20.00	40.00
3-8: 3-Ditko-a(p)	5.85	17.50	35.00

GHOST (...Comics #9)
1951(Winter) - No. 11, Summer, 1954
Fiction House Magazines

	GD25	FN65	NM94
1-Most covers by Whitman	37.00	110.00	260.00
2-Ghost Gallery & Werewolf Hunter stories	17.00	52.00	120.00
3-9: 3,6,7,9-Bondage-c. 9-Abel, Discount-a	14.00	43.00	100.00
10,11-Dr. Drew by Grandenetti in each, reprinted from Rangers; 11-Evans-r/Rangers #39; Grandenetti-r/Rangers #49	17.00	52.00	120.00

GHOST BREAKERS (Also see Racket Squad in Action, Red Dragon & (CC) Sherlock Holmes Comics)
Sept, 1948 - No. 2, Dec, 1948 (52 pages)
Street & Smith Publications

	GD25	FN65	NM94
1-Powell-c/a(3); Dr. Neff (magician) app.	20.00	60.00	140.00
2-Powell-c/a(2); Maneely-a	16.00	48.00	110.00

GHOSTBUSTERS (TV) (First) (Value: cover or less)

GHOSTBUSTERS II (Now) (Value: cover or less)

GHOST CASTLE (See Tales of...)

GHOSTLY HAUNTS (Formerly Ghost Manor)
#20, 9/71 - #53, 12/76; #54, 9/77 - #55, 10/77; #56, 1/78 - #58, 4/78
Charlton Comics

	GD25	FN65	NM94
20-58: 27-Dr. Graves x-over. 32-New logo. 33-Back to old logo. 39-Origin & 1st app. Destiny Fox	.60	1.50	3.00
40,41(Modern Comics-r, 1977, 1978)	.30	.75	1.50

NOTE: ***Ditko*** *a-22-25, 27, 28, 31-34, 36-41, 43-48, 50, 52, 54, 56r; c-22-27, 30, 33-37, 47, 54, 56.* ***Glanzman*** *a-20.* ***Howard*** *a-27, 30, 35, 42.* ***Newton*** *c/a-42.* ***Staton*** *a-35; c-28, 46.* ***Sutton*** *c-33, 37, 39, 41.*

GHOSTLY TALES (Formerly Blue Beetle No. 50-54)
No. 55, 4-5/66 - No. 124, 12/76; No. 125, 9/77 - No. 169, 10/84
Charlton Comics

	GD25	FN65	NM94
55-Intro. & origin Dr. Graves	1.60	4.00	8.00
56-70-Dr. Graves ends	.80	2.00	4.00
71-169: 107-Sutton, Wood-a. 114-Newton-a	.60	1.50	3.00

NOTE: ***Ditko*** *a-55-58, 60, 61, 67, 69-73, 75-90, 92-95, 97, 99-118, 120-122, 125r, 126r, 131-133r, 136-141r, 143r, 144r, 152, 155, 161, 163; c-67, 69, 73, 77, 78, 83, 84, 86-90, 92-97, 99, 102, 109, 111, 118, 120-122, 125, 131-133, 163.* ***Glanzman*** *a-167.* ***Howard*** *a-95, 98, 99, 117; c-98, 107, 120, 121, 161.* ***Morisi*** *a-83, 84, 86.* ***Newton*** *a-114; c-115.* ***Palais*** *a-61.* ***Staton*** *a-161; c-117.* ***Sutton*** *a-107, 112-114; c-100, 106, 110, 113(painted).* ***Wood*** *a-107.*

GHOSTLY WEIRD STORIES (Formerly Blue Bolt Weird)
No. 120, Sept, 1953 - No. 124, Sept, 1954
Star Publications

	GD25	FN65	NM94
120-Jo-Jo-r	14.00	43.00	100.00
121-Jo-Jo-r	10.00	30.00	70.00
122-The Mask-r/Capt. Flight #5; Rulah-r; has 1pg. story 'Death and the Devil Pills'-r/Western Outlaws #17	10.00	30.00	70.00
123-Jo-Jo; Disbrow-a(2)	10.00	30.00	70.00
124-Torpedo Man	10.00	30.00	70.00

NOTE: ***Disbrow*** *a-120-124.* ***L. B. Cole*** *covers-all issues (#122 is a sci-fi cover).*

GHOST MANOR (Ghostly Haunts No. 20 on)
July, 1968 - No. 19, July, 1971
Charlton Comics

	GD25	FN65	NM94
1	1.60	4.00	8.00
2-5	.80	2.00	4.00
6-12,17: 17-Morisi-a	.60	1.50	3.00
13-16,18,19-Ditko-a; c-15,18,19	.80	2.00	4.00

GHOST MANOR (2nd Series)
Oct, 1971 - No. 32, Dec, 1976; No. 33, Sept, 1977 - No. 77, 11/84
Charlton Comics

	GD25	FN65	NM94
1	1.60	4.00	8.00
2-7,9,10	.80	2.00	4.00
8-Wood-a	1.00	2.50	5.00
11-56,58-77: 18-20-Newton-a. 22-Newton-c/a. 21-E-Man, Blue Beetle, Capt. Atom cameos. 28-Nudity panels. 40-Torture & drug use	.60	1.50	3.00
57-Wood, Ditko, Howard-a	.80	2.00	4.00
19(Modern Comics reprint, 1977)		.50	1.00

NOTE: ***Ditko*** *a-4, 8, 10, 11(2), 13, 14, 18, 20-22, 24-26, 28, 29, 31, 37r, 38r, 40r, 42-44r, 46r, 47, 51r, 52r, 54r, 57, 60, 62(4), 64r, 71; c-2-7, 9-11, 14-16, 28, 31, 37, 38, 42, 43, 46, 47, 51, 52, 60, 62, 64.* ***Howard*** *a-4, 8, 19-21, 57.* ***Newton*** *a-18-20, 22, 64.* ***Sutton*** *a-19;c-8, 18.*

GHOST RIDER (See A-1 Comics, Best of the West, Black Phantom, Bobby Benson, Great Western, Red Mask & Tim Holt)
1950 - No. 14, 1954
Magazine Enterprises

Gerald McBoing Boing #3, © UPA

Ghost Comics #2, © FH

Ghost Manor #20 (2nd series), © CC

Ghost Rider #7(1952), © ME

Ghost Rider #4 (2/74), © MEG

Ghost Stories #4, © DELL

	GD25	FN65	NM94

NOTE: The character was inspired by Vaughn Monroe's "Ghost Riders in the Sky," and Disney's movie "The Headless Horseman."

	GD25	FN65	NM94
1(A-1 #27)-Origin Ghost Rider	43.00	130.00	300.00
2-5: 2(A-1 #29), 3(A-1 #31), 4(A-1 #34), 5(A-1 #37)-All Frazetta-c only	40.00	120.00	285.00
6,7: 6(A-1 #44)-Loco weed story, 7(A-1 #51)	16.00	48.00	110.00
8,9: 8(A-1 #57)-Drug use story, 9(A-1 #69)	13.50	41.00	95.00
10(A-1 #71)-Vs. Frankenstein	13.50	41.00	95.00
11-14: 11(A-1 #75), 12(A-1 #80)-Bondage-c, 13(A-1 #84), 14(A-1 #112)	11.50	34.00	80.00

NOTE: ***Dick Ayers** art in all; c-1, 6-14.*

GHOST RIDER, THE (See Night Rider & Western Gunfighters)
Feb, 1967 - No. 7, Nov, 1967 (Western hero)(All 12 cent-c)
Marvel Comics Group

	GD25	FN65	NM94
1-Origin Ghost Rider; Kid Colt-r begin	5.00	15.00	30.00
2-7: 6-Last Kid Colt-r; All Ayers-c/a(p)	2.80	7.00	14.00

GHOST RIDER (See The Champions, Marvel Spotlight #5, Marvel Team-Up #15, 58, Marvel Treasury Edition #18, Marvel Two-In-One #8, The Original Ghost Rider & The Original Ghost Rider Rides Again)
Sept, 1973 - No. 81, June, 1983 (Super-hero)
Marvel Comics Group

	GD25	FN65	NM94
1-Johnny Blaze, the Ghost Rider begins; 1st app. Daimon Hellstrom (Son of Satan) in cameo	12.00	36.00	85.00
2-1st full app. Daimon Hellstrom; gives glimpse of costume (1 panel); story continues in Marvel Spotlight #12	5.85	17.50	35.00
3-5: 3-Ghost Rider gets new cycle; Son of Satan app.	5.00	15.00	30.00
6-10: 10-Reprints origin/1st app. from Marvel Spotlight #5; Ploog-a	3.60	9.00	18.00
11-19	3.00	7.50	15.00
20-Daredevil x-over; ties into D.D. #138; Byrne-a	4.00	10.00	20.00
21-30: 22-1st app. Enforcer. 29,30-Vs. Dr. Strange	1.80	4.50	9.00
31-49	1.40	3.50	7.00
50-Double size	1.60	4.00	8.00
51-67,69-76,78-80: 80-Brief origin recap	.90	2.20	4.40
68,77-Origin retold	1.40	3.50	7.00
81-Death of Ghost Rider (Demon leaves Blaze)	2.00	5.00	10.00

NOTE: ***Anderson** c-64p. **Infantino** a(p)-43, 44, 51. **G. Kane** a-21p; c(p)-1, 2, 4, 5, 8, 9, 11-13, 19, 20, 24, 25. **Kirby** c-21-23. **Mooney** a-2-9p, 30i. **Nebres** c-26i. **Newton** a-23i. **Perez** c-26p. **Shores** a-2i. J. **Sparling** a-62p, 64p, 65p. **Starlin** a(p)-35. **Sutton** a-1p, 44i, 64i, 65i, 66, 67i. **Tuska** a-13p, 14p, 16p.*

GHOST RIDER (Also see Doctor Strange/Ghost Rider Special & Marvel Comics Presents)
V2#1, May, 1990 - Present ($1.50/$1.75, color)
Marvel Comics

	GD25	FN65	NM94
V2#1-($1.95, 52 pgs.)-Origin/1st app. new Ghost Rider; Kingpin app.	4.20	12.50	25.00
1-2nd printing	1.40	3.50	7.00
2	3.60	9.00	18.00
3-Kingpin app.	2.40	6.00	12.00
4-Scarcer	4.00	10.00	20.00
5-Punisher app.; Jim Lee-c	4.00	10.00	20.00
5-Gold background 2nd printing	2.00	5.00	10.00
6-Punisher app.	2.00	5.00	10.00
7-10: 9-X-Factor app. 10-Reintro Johnny Blaze on last pg.	1.00	2.50	5.00
11-14: 11-Stroman-c/a(p). 12,13-Dr. Strange/cont'd in D.S. #28. 13-Painted-c. 14-Johnny Blaze vs. Ghost Rider; origin recap 1st Ghost Rider (Blaze)	.60	1.50	3.00
15-Glow in the dark-c; begin $1.75-c	1.60	4.00	8.00
15-Gold background 2nd printing	.60	1.50	3.00
16,17-Spider-Man/Hobgoblin-c/story	.70	1.75	3.50
18-24,29,30,32-38: 18-Painted-c by Nelson. 29-Wolverine-c/story. 32-Dr. Strange x-over; Johnny Blaze app.	.35	.90	1.75
25-($2.75)-Contains pop-up scene	.60	1.50	3.00
26,27-X-Men x-over; Lee/Williams-c on both	.60	1.50	3.00
28-($2.50, 52 pgs.)-Polybagged w/poster; part 1 of Rise of the Midnight Sons storyline (see Ghost Rider/Blaze #1)	.80	2.00	4.00
31-($2.50, 52 pgs.)-Polybagged w/poster; part 6 of Rise of the Midnight Sons	.50	1.25	2.50
...And Cable 1 (9/92, $3.95, color, stiff-c, 68 pgs.)-Reprints Marvel Comics Presents #90-98 w/new Kieth-c	.80	2.00	4.00

NOTE: ***Andy & Joe Kubert** c/a-28-31.*

GHOST RIDER/BLAZE: SPIRITS OF VENGEANCE
Aug, 1992 - Present ($1.75, color)
Marvel Comics

	GD25	FN65	NM94
1-($2.75, 52 pgs.)-Polybagged w/poster; part 2 of Rise of the Midnight Sons storyline; Adam Kubert-c/a begins	.80	2.00	4.00
2-10: 4-Art Adams & Joe Kubert-p. 5,6-Spirits of Venom parts 2 & 4 cont'd from Web of Spider-Man #95,96 w/Demogoblin	.35	.90	1.75

GHOST RIDER/CAPTAIN AMERICA: FEAR
Oct, 1992 ($5.95, color, 52 pgs.)
Marvel Comics

	GD25	FN65	NM94
nn-Wraparound gatefold-c; Williamson inks	1.20	3.00	6.00

GHOST RIDER; WOLVERINE; PUNISHER: HEARTS OF DARKNESS
Dec, 1991 ($4.95, color, one-shot, 52 pgs.)
Marvel Comics

	GD25	FN65	NM94
1-Double gatefold-c; John Romita, Jr.-c/a(p)	1.00	2.50	5.00

GHOSTS (Ghost No. 1)
Sept-Oct, 1971 - No. 112, May, 1982 (No. 1-5: 52 pgs.)
National Periodical Publications/DC Comics

	GD25	FN65	NM94
1	1.20	3.00	6.00
2-Wood-a(i)	.80	2.00	4.00
3-5	.50	1.50	3.00
6-20	.40	1.00	2.00
21-96	.30	.75	1.50
97-99-The Spectre app. 97,98-Spectre-c	.40	1.00	2.00
100-112: 100-Infinity-c		.50	1.00

NOTE: ***B. Baily** a-77. **J. Craig** a-108. **Ditko** a-77, 111. **Giffen** a-104p, 106p, 111p. **Golden** a-88. **Kaluta** c-7, 93, 101. **Kubert** c-89, 105-108, 111. **Mayer** a-111. **McWilliams** a-99. **Win Mortimer** a-89, 91, 94. **Newton** a-92p, 94p. **Nino** a-35, 37, 57. **Orlando** a-74i; c-80. **Redondo** a-8, 13, 45. **Sparling** a(p)-90, 93, 94. **Spiegle** a-103, 105.*

GHOSTS SPECIAL (See DC Special Series No. 7)

GHOST STORIES (See Amazing Ghost Stories)

GHOST STORIES
Sept-Nov, 1962; No. 2, Apr-June, 1963 - No. 37, Oct, 1973
Dell Publishing Co.

	GD25	FN65	NM94
12-295-211(#1)-Written by John Stanley	4.35	13.00	26.00
2	2.80	7.00	14.00
3-10: Two No. 6's exist with different c/a(12-295-406 & 12-295-503) #12-295-503 is actually #9 with indicia to #6	2.00	5.00	10.00
11-20	1.20	3.00	6.00
21-37	1.00	2.50	5.00

NOTE: *#21-34, 36, 37 all reprint earlier issues.*

GHOUL TALES (Magazine)
Nov, 1970 - No. 5, July, 1971 (52 pages) (B&W)
Stanley Publications

	GD25	FN65	NM94
1-Aragon pre-code reprints; Mr. Mystery as host; bondage-c	3.60	9.00	18.00
2,3: 2-(1/71)Reprint/Climax #1. 3-(3/71)	1.60	4.00	8.00
4-(5/71)Reprints story "The Way to a Man's Heart" used in **SOTI**	3.60	9.00	18.00
5-ACG reprints	1.60	4.00	8.00

GD25 FN65 NM94

NOTE: *No. 1-4 contain pre-code Aragon reprints.*

GIANT BOY BOOK OF COMICS (See Boy)
1945 (Hardcover) (240 pages)
Newsbook Publications (Gleason)

1-Crimebuster & Young Robin Hood 67.00 200.00 400.00

GIANT COMIC ALBUM
1972 (52 pgs., 11x14", B&W, 59 cents, cardboard-c)
King Features Syndicate

Newspaper reprints: Little Iodine, Katzenjammer Kids, Henry, Mandrake the Magician ('59 Falk), Popeye, Beetle Bailey, Barney Google, Blondie, Flash Gordon ('68-69 Dan Barry), & Snuffy Smith
each... 2.00 5.00 10.00

GIANT COMICS
Summer, 1957 - No. 3, Winter, 1957 (100 pgs.) (25 cents)
Charlton Comics

1-Atomic Mouse, Hoppy app. 11.50 34.00 80.00
2,3-Atomic Mouse, Rabbit, Christmas Book, Romance stories known
10.00 30.00 65.00

NOTE: *The above may be rebound comics; contents could vary.*

GIANT COMICS (See Wham-O Giant Comics)

GIANT COMICS EDITION (See Terry-Toons)
1947 - No. 17, 1950 (All 100-164 pgs.) (25 cents)
St. John Publishing Co.

1-Mighty Mouse 32.00 95.00 225.00
2-Abbie & Slats 14.00 43.00 100.00
3-Terry-Toons Album; 100 pgs. 24.00 70.00 165.00
4-Crime comics; contains Red Seal No. 16, used & illo. in **SOTI**
35.00 105.00 245.00
5-Police Case Book(4/49)-Contents varies; contains remaindered St. John books - some volumes contain 5 copies rather than 4, with 160 pages; Matt Baker-c 34.00 100.00 235.00
5A-Terry-Toons Album, 132 pgs. 24.00 70.00 165.00
6-Western Picture Stories; Baker-c/a(3); Tuska-a; The Sky Chief, Blue Monk, Ventrilo app., 132 pgs. 32.00 95.00 225.00
7-Contains a teen-age romance plus 3 Mopsy comics
20.00 60.00 140.00
8-The Adventures of Mighty Mouse (10/49) 24.00 70.00 165.00
9-Romance and Confession Stories; Kubert-a(4); Baker-a; photo-c
32.00 95.00 225.00
10-Terry-Toons 24.00 70.00 165.00
11-Western Picture Stories-Baker-c/a(4); The Sky Chief, Desperado, & Blue Monk app.; another version with Son of Sinbad by Kubert
32.00 95.00 190.00
12-Diary Secrets; Baker prostitute-c; 4 St. John romance comics; Baker-a
50.00 150.00 350.00
13-Romances; Baker, Kubert-a 27.00 80.00 185.00
14-Mighty Mouse Album 24.00 70.00 165.00
15-Romances (4 love comics)-Baker-c 29.00 85.00 200.00
16-Little Audrey, Abbott & Costello, Casper 24.00 70.00 165.00
17(nn)-Mighty Mouse Album (nn, no date, but did follow No. 16); 100 pgs. on cover but has 148 pgs. 24.00 70.00 165.00

NOTE: *The above books contain remaindered comics and contents could vary with each issue. No. 11, 12 have part photo magazine insides.*

GIANT COMICS EDITIONS
1940's (132 pages)
United Features Syndicate

1-Abbie & Slats, Abbott & Costello, Jim Hardy, Ella Cinders, Iron Vic
25.00 75.00 175.00
2-Jim Hardy & Gordo 19.00 57.00 130.00

NOTE: *Above books contain rebound copies; contents can vary.*

GIANT GRAB BAG OF COMICS (See Archie All-Star Specials under Archie Comics)

GIANTS (See Thrilling True Story of the Baseball...)

GIANT-SIZE...
May, 1974 - Dec, 1975 (35-50 cents, 52-68 pgs.)(Some titles quarterly)
Marvel Comics Group

Avengers 1(8/74)-New-a plus G.A. H. Torch-r; 1st modern app. The Whizzer; 1st & only modern app. Miss America 1.20 3.00 6.00
Avengers 2,3: 2(11/74)-Death of the Swordsman. 3(2/75)
.80 2.00 4.00
Avengers 4,5: 4(6/75)-Vision marries Scarlet Witch. 5(12/75)-Reprints Avengers Special #1 .60 1.50 3.00
Captain America 1(12/75)-r/stories T.O.S. 59-63 by Kirby (#63 reprints origin) 1.60 4.00 8.00
Captain Marvel 1(12/75)-r/Capt. Marvel #17, 20 by Gil Kane (p)
1.40 3.50 7.00
Chillers 1(6/74, 52 pgs)-Curse of Dracula; origin/1st app. Lilith, Dracula's daughter; Heath-r, Colan-c/a(p); becomes Giant-Size Dracula #2 on
.60 1.50 3.00
Chillers 1(2/75, 50 cents, 68 pgs.)-Alacala-a .50 1.25 2.50
Chillers 2(5/75)-All-r; Everett-r from Advs. into Weird Worlds
.40 1.00 2.00
Chillers 3(8/75)-Wrightson-c(new)/a(r); Colan, Kirby, Smith-r
.60 1.50 3.00
Conan 1(9/74)-B. Smith-r/#3; start adaptation of Howard's "Hour of the Dragon;" 1st app. Belit; new-a begins 1.20 3.00 6.00
Conan 2(12/74)-B. Smith-r/#5; Sutton-a(i)(#1 also); Buscema-c
1.00 2.50 5.00
Conan 3-5: 3(4/75)-B. Smith-r/#6; Sutton-a(i). 4(6/75)-B. Smith-r/#7. 5(1975)-B. Smith-r/#14,15; Kirby-c .60 1.50 3.00
Creatures 1(5/74, 52 pgs.)-Werewolf app; 1st app. Tigra (formerly Cat); Crandall-r; becomes Giant-Size Werewolf w/#2 .40 1.00 2.00
Daredevil 1(1975) 1.20 3.00 6.00
Defenders 1(7/74)-Silver Surfer app.; Starlin-a; Ditko, Everett & Kirby reprints
1.80 4.50 9.00
Defenders 2(10/74, 68 pgs.)-New G. Kane-c/a(p); Son of Satan app.; Sub-Mariner-r by Everett; Ditko-r/Strange Tales #119 (Dr. Strange)
1.00 2.50 5.00
Defenders 3-5: 3(1/75)-Newton, Starlin-a; Ditko, Everett-r. 4(4/75)-Ditko, Everett-r; G. Kane-c. 5-(7/75)-Guardians app. .80 2.00 4.00
Doc Savage 1(1975, 68 pgs.)-r/#1,2; Mooney-r .60 1.50 3.00
Doctor Strange 1(11/75)-Reprints stories from Strange Tales #164-168; Lawrence, Tuska-r 1.00 2.50 5.00
Dracula 2(9/74, 50 cents)-Formerly Giant-Size Chillers
.80 2.00 4.00
Dracula 3(12/74)-Fox-r/Uncanny Tales #6 .60 1.50 3.00
Dracula 4(3/75)-Ditko-r(2) .40 1.00 2.00
Dracula 5(6/75)-1st Byrne art at Marvel 1.00 2.50 5.00
Fantastic Four 2-4: 2(8/74)-Formerly Giant-Size Super-Stars; Ditko-r. 3(11/74). 4(2/75)-1st Madrox; 2-4-All have Buscema-a
1.60 4.00 8.00
Fantastic Four 5,6: 5(5/75)-All-r; Kirby, G. Kane-r. 6(10/75)-All-r; Kirby-r
1.20 3.00 6.00
Hulk 1(1975) 2.00 5.00 10.00
Invaders 1(6/75, 50 cents, 68 pgs.)-Origin; G.A. Sub-Mariner-r/Sub-Mariner #1; intro Master Man 1.00 2.50 5.00
Iron Man 1(1975)-Ditko reprint 1.60 4.00 8.00
Kid Colt 1-3: 1(1/75). 2(4/75). 3(7/75) .60 1.50 3.00
Man-Thing 1(8/74)-New Ploog-c/a; Ditko, Kirby-r (#1-5 all have new Man-Thing stories, pre-hero-r & are 68 pgs.) 1.00 2.50 5.00
Man-Thing 2,3: 2(11/74)-Buscema-c/a(p); Kirby, Powell-r. 3(2/75)-Alcala-a; Ditko, Kirby, Sutton-r; Gil Kane-c .60 1.50 3.00
Man-Thing 4,5: 4(5/75)-Howard the Duck by Brunner-c/a; Ditko-r. 5(8/75)-Howard the Duck by Brunner (p); Buscema-a(p); Sutton-a(i); G. Kane-c
1.00 2.50 5.00
Marvel Triple Action 1,2: 1(5/75). 2(7/75) .35 1.00 2.00
Master of Kung Fu 1(9/74)-Russell-a; Yellow Claw-r in #1-4; Gulacy-a in #1,2 1.20 3.00 6.00
Master of Kung Fu 2(12/74)-r/Yellow Claw #1 .70 1.75 3.50
Master of Kung Fu 3(3/75)-Gulacy-a .60 1.50 3.00

Giant Comics Edition #8, © Viacom

Giant-Size Conan #1, © MEG

Giant-Size Defenders #2, © MEG

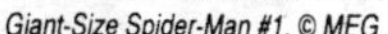

Giant-Size Spider-Man #1, © MEG

G.I. Combat #246, © DC

G-I In Battle #2, © AJAX

	GD25	FN65	NM94
Master of Kung Fu 4(6/75)	.60	1.50	3.00
Power Man 1(1975)	1.00	2.50	5.00
Spider-Man 1(7/74)-Kirby/Ditko, Byrne-r plus new-a (Dracula-c/story)	4.00	10.00	20.00
Spider-Man 2,3: 2(10/74). 3(1/75)-Byrne-r	1.60	4.00	8.00
Spider-Man 4(4/75)-3rd Punisher app.; Byrne, Ditko-r	10.00	30.00	70.00
Spider-Man 5,6: 5(7/75)-Byrne-r. 6(9/75)	1.40	3.50	7.00
Super-Heroes Featuring Spider-Man 1(6/74, 35 cents, 52 pgs.)-Spider-Man vs. Man-Wolf; Morbius, the Living Vampire app.; Ditko-r; G. Kane-a(p); Spidey villains app.	7.50	22.50	45.00
Super-Stars 1(5/74, 35 cents, 52 pgs.)-Fantastic Four; Thing vs. Hulk; Kirbyish-c/a by Buckler/Sinnott; F.F. villains profiled; becomes Giant-Size Fantastic Four #2 on	2.40	6.00	12.00
Super-Villain Team-Up 1(3/75, 68 pgs.)-Craig-r(i) (Also see Fantastic Four #6 for 1st super-villain team-up)	1.20	3.00	6.00
Super-Villain Team-Up 2(6/75, 68 pgs.)-Dr. Doom, Sub-Mariner app.; Spider-Man-r/Amazing Spider-Man #8 by Ditko; Sekowsky-a(p)	.80	2.00	4.00
Thor 1(7/75)	1.00	2.50	5.00
Werewolf 2(10/74, 68 pgs.)-Formerly Giant-Size Creatures; Ditko-r; Frankenstein app	.60	1.50	3.00
Werewolf 3-5: 3(1/75, 68 pgs.). 4(4/75, 68 pgs.)-Morbius the Living Vampire app. 5(7/75, 68 pgs.)	.60	1.50	3.00
X-Men 1(Summer, 1975, 50 cents, 68 pgs.)-1st app. new X-Men; intro Nightcrawler, Storm, Colossus & Thunderbird; 2nd full app. Wolverine after Incredible Hulk #181	29.00	85.00	200.00
X-Men 2(11/75)-N. Adams-r(51 pgs)	4.20	12.50	25.00

GIANT SPECTACULAR COMICS (See Archie All-Star Special under Archie Comics)

GIANT SUMMER FUN BOOK (See Terry-Toons...)

G. I. COMBAT
Oct, 1952 - No. 43, Dec, 1956
Quality Comics Group

	GD25	FN65	NM94
1-Crandall-c; Cuidera a-1-43i	30.00	90.00	210.00
2	14.00	43.00	100.00
3-5,10-Crandall-c/a	13.00	40.00	90.00
6-Crandall-a	11.50	34.00	80.00
7-9	10.00	30.00	60.00
11-20	8.35	25.00	50.00
21-31,33,35-43	6.70	20.00	40.00
32-Nuclear attack-c	8.35	25.00	50.00
34-Crandall-a	7.50	22.50	45.00

G. I. COMBAT (See DC Special Series #22)
No. 44, Jan, 1957 - No. 288, Mar, 1987
National Periodical Publications/DC Comics

	GD25	FN65	NM94
44-Grandenetti c-44-48	27.00	80.00	190.00
45	14.00	43.00	100.00
46-50	10.00	30.00	65.00
51-60	7.50	22.50	45.00
61-66,68-80	5.00	15.00	30.00
67-1st Tank Killer	9.15	27.50	55.00
81,82,84-86	4.20	12.50	25.00
83-1st Big Al, Little Al, & Charlie Cigar	5.00	15.00	30.00
87-1st Haunted Tank	10.00	30.00	60.00
88-90: Last 10 cent issue	2.80	7.00	14.00
91-113,115-120	2.00	5.00	10.00
114-Origin Haunted Tank	4.20	12.50	25.00
121-137,139,140: 136-Last 12 cent issue	1.60	4.00	8.00
138-Intro. The Losers (Capt. Storm, Gunner/Sarge, Johnny Cloud) in Haunted Tank (10-11/69)	1.80	4.50	9.00
141-200: 146-148-(25 cent, 68 pgs.). 149-154-(52 pgs.). 150-Ice Cream Soldier story (tells how he got his name). 151-Capt. Storm story. 151,153-Medal of Honor series by Maurer	.80	2.00	4.00
201-281: 201-245,247-259 are $1.00 size. 232-Origin Kana the Ninja. 244-Death of Slim Stryker; 1st app. The Mercenaries. 246-(76 pgs., $1.50)-30th Anniversary issue. 257-Intro. Stuart's Raiders. 260-Begin $1.25, 52 pg. issues, end #281. 264-Intro Sgt. Bullet; origin Kana. 269-Intro. The Bravos of Vietnam	.40	1.00	2.00
282-288 (75 cents): 282-New advs. begin	.40	1.00	2.00

NOTE: ***N. Adams** c-168, 201, 202. **Check** a-168, 173. **Drucker** a-48, 61, 63, 66, 71, 72, 76, 134, 140, 141, 144, 147, 148, 153. **Evans** a-135, 138, 158, 164, 166, 201, 202, 204, 205, 215, 256. Giffen a-267. **Glanzman** a-most issues. **Kubert/Heath** a-most issues; **Kubert** covers most issues. **Morrow** a-159-161(2 pgs.). **Redondo** a-189, 240i, 243i. **Sekowsky** a-162p. **Severin** a-147, 152, 154. **Simonson** c-169. **Thorne** a-152, 156. **Wildey** a-153. Johnny Cloud app.-No. 112, 115, 120. Mlle. Marie app.-No. 123, 132, 200. Sgt. Rock app.-#111-113, 115, 120, 125, 141, 146, 147, 149, 200. USS Stevens by **Glanzman**-#145, 150-153, 157.*

G. I. COMICS (Also see Jeep & Overseas Comics)
1945 (Distributed to U. S. armed forces)
Giveaways

	GD25	FN65	NM94
1-49-Contains Prince Valiant by Foster, Blondie, Smilin' Jack, Mickey Finn, Terry & the Pirates, Donald Duck, Alley Oop, Moon Mullins & Capt. Easy strip reprints	4.00	12.00	28.00

GIDGET (TV)
April, 1966 - No. 2, Dec, 1966
Dell Publishing Co.

	GD25	FN65	NM94
1,2: 1-Sally Field photo-c	5.85	17.50	35.00

GIFT (See The Crusaders)

GIFT COMICS (50 cents)
1942 - No. 4, 1949 (No. 1-3: 324 pgs.; No. 4: 152 pgs.)
Fawcett Publications

	GD25	FN65	NM94
1-Captain Marvel, Bulletman, Golden Arrow, Ibis the Invincible, Mr. Scarlet, & Spy Smasher app. Not rebound, remaindered comics, printed at same time as originals	175.00	525.00	1050.00
2	123.00	370.00	735.00
3	87.00	262.00	525.00
4-The Marvel Family, Captain Marvel, etc.; each issue can vary in contents	61.00	182.00	365.00

GIFTS FROM SANTA (See March of Comics No. 137)

GIGGLE COMICS (Spencer Spook No. 100) (Also see Ha Ha Comics)
Oct, 1943 - No. 99, Jan-Feb, 1955
Creston No.1-63/American Comics Group No. 64 on

	GD25	FN65	NM94
1	20.00	60.00	140.00
2	10.00	30.00	65.00
3-5: Ken Hultgren-a begins?	7.00	21.00	42.00
6-10: 9-1st Superkatt	5.85	17.50	35.00
11-20	4.20	12.50	25.00
21-40: 32-Patriotic-c. 39-St. Valentine's Day-c	4.00	10.00	20.00
41-54,56-59,61-99: 95-Spencer Spook app.	3.20	8.00	16.00
55,60-Milt Gross-a	4.00	11.00	22.00

G-I IN BATTLE (G-I No. 1 only)
Aug, 1952 - No. 9, July, 1953; Mar, 1957 - No. 6, May, 1958
Ajax-Farrell Publ./Four Star

	GD25	FN65	NM94
1	5.00	15.00	30.00
2	3.20	8.00	16.00
3-9	2.40	6.00	12.00
Annual 1(1952, 100 pgs.)	14.00	43.00	100.00
1(1957-Ajax)	4.00	10.00	20.00
2-6	2.00	5.00	10.00

G. I. JANE
May, 1953 - No. 11, Mar, 1955 (Misdated 3/54)
Stanhall/Merit No. 11

	GD25	FN65	NM94
1	6.70	20.00	40.00
2-7(5/54)	4.00	10.00	20.00

	GD25	FN65	NM94
8-10(12/54, Stanhall)	3.20	8.00	16.00
11 (3/55, Merit)	3.00	7.50	15.00

G. I. JOE (Also see Advs. of..., Showcase #53, 54 & The Yardbirds)
No. 10, 1950; No. 11, 4-5/51 - No. 51, 6/57 (52pgs.: 10-14,6-17?)
Ziff-Davis Publ. Co. (Korean War)

	GD25	FN65	NM94
10(#1, 1950)-Saunders painted-c begin	7.50	22.50	45.00
11-14(#2-5, 10/51)	4.70	14.00	28.00
V2#6(12/51)-17-(Last 52pgs.?)	4.20	12.50	25.00
18-(100 pg. Giant-'52)	10.00	30.00	70.00
19-30: 20-22,24,28-31-The Yardbirds app.	4.00	10.00	20.00
31-47,49-51	3.60	9.00	18.00
48-Atom bomb story	4.00	10.00	20.00

NOTE: ***Powell** a-V2#7, 8, 11. **Norman Saunders** painted c-10-14, V2#6-14, 26, 30, 31, 35, 38, 39. **Tuska** a-7. Bondage c-29, 35, 38.*

G. I. JOE (America's Movable Fighting Man)
1967 (36 pages) (5-1/8x8-3/8")
Custom Comics

	GD25	FN65	NM94
nn-Schaffenberger-a		.50	1.00

G. I. JOE AND THE TRANSFORMERS
Jan, 1987 - No. 4, Apr, 1987 (Mini-series)
Marvel Comics Group

	GD25	FN65	NM94
1-4		.50	1.00

G. I. JOE, A REAL AMERICAN HERO
June, 1982 - Present
Marvel Comics Group

	GD25	FN65	NM94
1-Printed on Baxter paper	1.20	3.00	6.00
2-Printed on reg. paper	1.40	3.50	7.00
3-10	.80	2.00	4.00
11-20: 11-Intro Airborne	.40	1.00	2.00
21,22	.60	1.50	3.00
23-25,28-30	.40	1.00	2.00
26,27-Origin Snake-Eyes parts 1 & 2	.60	1.50	3.00
31-136: 33-New headquarters. 60-Todd McFarlane-a. 94-96,103-Snake-Eyes app.		.50	1.00
All 2nd printings		.50	1.00
Special Treasury Edition (1982)-r/#1	.80	2.00	4.00
...Yearbook 1 (3/85)-r/#1; Golden-c	.60	1.50	3.00
...Yearbook 2 (3/86)-Golden-c/a , 3(3/87, 68 pgs.)	.40	1.00	2.00
...Yearbook 4 (2/88)	.30	.75	1.50

NOTE: ***Golden** c-23, 29, 34, 36. **Heath** a-24. **Rogers** a-75p, 77-82p, 84p, 86p; c-77.*

G. I. JOE COMICS MAGAZINE
Dec, 1986 - No. 13, 1988 ($1.50, digest-size)
Marvel Comics Group

	GD25	FN65	NM94
1-13: G.I. Joe-r	.30	.75	1.50

G.I. JOE EUROPEAN MISSIONS (Action Force in indicia)
June, 1988 - No. 15, Dec, 1989 ($1.50/$1.75 #12 on, color)
Marvel Comics Ltd. (British)

	GD25	FN65	NM94
1-15: Reprints Action Force	.30	.75	1.50

G. I. JOE ORDER OF BATTLE, THE
Dec, 1986 - No. 4, Mar, 1987 (Mini-series)
Marvel Comics Group

	GD25	FN65	NM94
1-4		.50	1.00

G. I. JOE SPECIAL MISSIONS (Indicia title: Special Missions)
Oct, 1986 - No. 28, Dec, 1989 ($1.00, color)
Marvel Comics Group

	GD25	FN65	NM94
1-28		.50	1.00

G. I. JUNIORS (See Harvey Hits No. 86, 91, 95, 98, 101, 104, 107, 110, 112, 114, 116, 118, 120, 122)

GILGAMESH II
1989 - No. 4, 1989 ($3.95, mini-series, prestige format)
DC Comics

	GD25	FN65	NM94
1-4: Starlin-c/a, scripts; mature readers	.80	2.00	4.00

GIL THORP
May-July, 1963
Dell Publishing Co.

	GD25	FN65	NM94
1-Caniffish-a	2.80	7.00	14.00

GINGER (Li'l Jinx No. 11 on?)
1951 - No. 10, Summer, 1954
Archie Publications

	GD25	FN65	NM94
1	10.00	30.00	65.00
2	5.85	17.50	35.00
3-6	4.20	12.50	25.00
7-10-Katy Keene app.	6.35	19.00	38.00

GINGER FOX (Also see The World of Ginger Fox)
Sept, 1988 - No. 4, Dec, 1988 ($1.75, color, mini-series)
Comico

	GD25	FN65	NM94
1-4: 1-4-part photo-c	.35	.90	1.75

G.I. R.A.M.B.O.T.
April, 1987 - No. 2? ($1.95, color)
Wonder Color Comics/Pied Piper #2

	GD25	FN65	NM94
1,2: 2-Exist?	.40	1.00	2.00

GIRL COMICS (Becomes Girl Confessions No. 13 on)
Nov, 1949 - No. 12, Jan, 1952 (Photo-c 1-4)
Marvel/Atlas Comics(CnPC)

	GD25	FN65	NM94
1 (52 pgs.)	10.00	30.00	70.00
2-Kubert-a	6.70	20.00	40.00
3-Everett-a; Liz Taylor photo-c	8.35	25.00	50.00
4-11: 10-12-Sol Brodsky-c	4.70	14.00	28.00
12-Krigstein-a	5.85	17.50	35.00

GIRL CONFESSIONS (Formerly Girl Comics)
No. 13, Mar, 1952 - No. 35, Aug, 1954
Atlas Comics (CnPC/ZPC)

	GD25	FN65	NM94
13-Everett-a	6.35	19.00	38.00
14,15,19,20	4.20	12.50	25.00
16-18-Everett-a	5.00	15.00	30.00
21-35	3.00	7.50	15.00

GIRL FROM U.N.C.L.E., THE (TV) (Also see The Man From...)
Jan, 1967 - No. 5, Oct, 1967
Gold Key

	GD25	FN65	NM94
1-McWilliams-a; Stephanie Powers photo front/back-c & pin-ups (no ads, 12 cents)	6.35	19.00	38.00
2-5-Leonard Swift-Courier No. 5	4.20	12.50	25.00

GIRLS' FUN & FASHION MAGAZINE (Formerly Polly Pigtails)
V5#44, Jan, 1950 - V5#47, July, 1950
Parents' Magazine Institute

	GD25	FN65	NM94
V5#44	3.20	8.00	16.00
45-47	1.80	4.50	9.00

GIRLS IN LOVE
May, 1950 - No. 2, July, 1950
Fawcett Publications

	GD25	FN65	NM94
1,2-Photo-c	5.85	17.50	35.00

GIRLS IN LOVE (Formerly G. I. Sweethearts No. 45)
No. 46, Sept, 1955 - No. 57, Dec, 1956
Quality Comics Group

	GD25	FN65	NM94
46	4.20	12.50	25.00
47-56: 54-'Commie' story	3.00	7.50	15.00
57-Matt Baker-c/a	4.70	14.00	28.00

GIRLS IN WHITE (See Harvey Comics Hits No. 58)

GIRLS' LIFE
Jan, 1954 - No. 6, Nov, 1954

G.I. Joe V2#10, © Z-D

Girl Confessions #25, © MEG

Girls In Love #46, © QUA

Girls' Love Stories #3, © DC

Girls' Romances #8, © DC

Gizmo #6, © Mirage Studios

	GD25	FN65	NM94
Atlas Comics (BFP)			
1-Patsy Walker	6.35	19.00	38.00
2	3.60	9.00	18.00
3-6	3.00	7.50	15.00

GIRLS' LOVE STORIES
Aug-Sept, 1949 - No. 180, Nov-Dec, 1973 (No. 1-13: 52 pgs.)
National Comics(Signal Publ. No. 9-65/Arleigh No. 83-117)

	GD25	FN65	NM94
1-Toth, Kinstler-a, 8 pgs. each; photo-c	33.00	100.00	225.00
2-Kinstler-a?	16.00	48.00	110.00
3-10: 1-9-Photo-c. 7-Infantino-c(p)	10.00	30.00	70.00
11-20	8.35	25.00	50.00
21-33: 21-Kinstler-a. 33-Last pre-code (1-2/55)	5.00	15.00	30.00
34-50	4.20	12.50	25.00
51-99: 83-Last 10 cent issue	3.00	7.50	15.00
100	3.60	9.00	18.00
101-146: 113-117-April O'Day app.	1.40	3.50	7.00
147-151-"Confessions" serial	1.00	2.50	5.00
152-180: 161-170, 52 pgs.	.80	2.00	4.00

GIRLS' ROMANCES
Feb-Mar, 1950 - No. 160, Oct, 1971 (No. 1-11: 52 pgs.)
National Periodical Publ.(Signal Publ. No. 7-79/Arleigh No. 84)

	GD25	FN65	NM94
1-Photo-c	33.00	100.00	225.00
2-Photo-c; Toth-a	16.00	48.00	110.00
3-10: 3-6-Photo-c	10.00	30.00	70.00
11,12,14-20	8.35	25.00	50.00
13-Toth-c	10.00	30.00	60.00
21-31: 31-Last pre-code (2-3/55)	5.00	15.00	30.00
32-50	4.20	12.50	25.00
51-99: 80-Last 10 cent issue	3.00	7.50	15.00
100	3.60	9.00	18.00
101-108,110-120	2.00	5.00	10.00
109-Beatles-c/story	5.85	17.50	35.00
121-133,135-140	1.40	3.50	7.00
134-Neal Adams-c	1.80	4.50	9.00
141-160: 159,160-52 pgs.	.80	2.00	4.00

G. I. SWEETHEARTS (Formerly Diary Loves; Girls In Love #46 on)
No. 32, June, 1953 - No. 45, May, 1955
Quality Comics Group

	GD25	FN65	NM94
32	4.00	10.50	21.00
33-45: 44-Last pre-code (3/55)	2.40	6.00	12.00

G.I. TALES (Formerly Sgt. Barney Barker No. 1-3)
No. 4, Feb, 1957 - No. 6, July, 1957
Atlas Comics (MCI)

	GD25	FN65	NM94
4-Severin-a(4)	4.20	12.50	25.00
5	3.20	8.00	16.00
6-Orlando, Powell, & Woodbridge-a	3.60	9.00	18.00

GIVE ME LIBERTY (Dark Horse) (Value: cover or less)

G. I. WAR BRIDES
April, 1954 - No. 8, June, 1955
Superior Publishers Ltd.

	GD25	FN65	NM94
1	4.00	10.50	21.00
2	2.00	5.00	10.00
3-8: 4-Kamenesque-a; lingerie panels	1.60	4.00	8.00

G. I. WAR TALES
Mar-Apr, 1973 - No. 4, Oct-Nov, 1973
National Periodical Publications

	GD25	FN65	NM94
1-4: Reprints. 2-N. Adams-a(r), 4-Krigstein-a(r)		.50	1.00

NOTE: ***Drucker** a-3r, 4r. **Heath** a-4r. **Kubert** a-2, 3; c-4r.*

GIZMO (Also see Domino Chance)
May-June, 1985 (B&W, one shot)
Chance Ent.

	GD25	FN65	NM94
1	1.00	2.50	5.00

GIZMO
1986 - No. 6, July, 1987 ($1.50, B&W)
Mirage Studios

	GD25	FN65	NM94
1	.60	1.50	3.00
2-6	.30	.75	1.50

GLADSTONE COMIC ALBUM (Also see The Original Dick Tracy Comic...)
1987 - No. 28, 1990 (8-1/2x11")($5.95)(#26-28: $9.95)
Gladstone Publishing

	GD25	FN65	NM94
1-10: 1-Uncle Scrooge; Barks-r; Beck-c. 2-Donald Duck; r/F.C. #108 by Barks. 3-Mickey Mouse-r by Gottfredson. 4-Uncle Scrooge; r/F.C. #456 by Barks. 5-Donald Duck Advs.; r/F.C. #199. 6-Uncle Scrooge-r by Barks. 7-Donald Duck-r by Barks. 8-Mickey Mouse-r. 9-Bambi; r/F.C. #12. 10-Donald Duck Advs.; r/F.C. #275	1.20	3.00	6.00
11-20: 11-Uncle Scrooge; r/U.S. #4. 12-Donald And Daisy; r/F.C. #1055, WDC&S. 13-Donald Duck Advs.; r/F.C. #408. 14-Uncle Scrooge; Barks-r/U.S #21. 15-Donald And Gladstone; Barks-r. 16-Donald Duck Advs.; r/F.C. #238. 17-Mickey Mouse strip-r (The World of Tomorrow, The Pirate Ghost Ship). 18-Donald Duck and the Junior Woodchucks; Barks-r. 19-Uncle Scrooge; r/U.S. #12; Rosa-c. 20-Uncle Scrooge; r/F.C. #386; Barks-c/a(r)	1.20	3.00	6.00
21-25: 21-Donald Duck Family; Barks-c/a(r). 22-Mickey Mouse strip-r. 23-Donald Duck; Barks-r/D.D. #26. 24-Uncle Scrooge; Barks-r; Rosa-c. 25-D. Duck; Barks-c/a-r/F.C. #367	1.20	3.00	6.00
26-28: 26-Mickey and Donald; Gottfredson-c/a(r). 27-Donald Duck; r/WDC&S by Barks; Barks painted-c. 28-Uncle Scrooge & Donald Duck; Rosa-c/a (4 stories)	2.00	5.00	10.00
Special 1 (1989, $9.95)-Donald Duck Finds Pirate Gold; r/F.C. #9	2.00	5.00	10.00
Special 2 (1989, $8.95)-Uncle Scrooge and Donald Duck; Barks-r/Uncle Scrooge #5; Rosa-c	1.80	4.50	9.00
Special 3 (1989, $8.95)-Mickey Mouse strip-r	1.80	4.50	9.00
Special 4 (1989, $11.95)-Uncle Scrooge; Rosa-c/a-r/Son of the Sun from U.S. #219 plus Barks-r/U.S.	2.40	6.00	12.00
Special 5 (1990, $11.95)-Donald Duck Advs.; Barks-r/F.C. #282 & 422 plus Barks painted-c	2.40	6.00	12.00
Special 6 (1990, $12.95)-Uncle Scrooge; Barks-c/a-r/Uncle Scrooge	2.60	6.50	13.00
Special 7 (1990, $13.95)-Mickey Mouse; Gottfredson strip-r	2.80	7.00	14.00

GLAMOROUS ROMANCES (Formerly Dotty)
No. 41, Sept, 1949 - No. 90, Oct, 1956 (Photo-c 68-90)
Ace Magazines (A. A. Wyn)

	GD25	FN65	NM94
41-Dotty app.	4.35	13.00	26.00
42-72,74-80: 50-61-Painted-c. 80-Last pre-code (2/55)	2.40	6.00	12.00
73-L.B. Cole-a(r)-/All Love #27	3.00	7.50	15.00
81-90	2.00	5.00	10.00

GLOBAL FORCE (Silverline) (Value: cover or less)

GNOME MOBILE, THE (See Movie Comics)

GOBBLEDYGOOK
1984 - No. 2, 1984 (B&W)(1st Mirage comic, both published at same time)
Mirage Studios

	GD25	FN65	NM94
1,2-24 pgs., early TMNT	32.00	95.00	220.00

GOBBLEDYGOOK
Dec, 1986 (One shot, $3.50, B&W, 100 pgs.)
Mirage Studios

	GD25	FN65	NM94
1-New 8 pg. TMNT story plus a Donatello/Michaelangelo 7 pg. story & a Gizmo story; Corben-i(r)/TMNT #7	1.00	4.00	5.00

GOBLIN, THE
June, 1982 - No. 4, Dec, 1982 (Magazine, $2.25)
Warren Publishing Co.

1-The Gremlin app; Golden-a(p) .45 1.15 2.25
2-4: 2-1st Hobgoblin .45 1.15 2.25

GODFATHERS, THE (See The Crusaders)

GOD IS (Spire Christian)(Value: cover or less)

GODS FOR HIRE (Hot Comics)(Value; cover or less)

GOD'S HEROES IN AMERICA
1956 (nn) (68 pgs.) (25-35 cents)
Catechetical Guild Educational Society

307 1.60 4.00 8.00

GOD'S SMUGGLER (Spire Christian)(Value: cover or less)

GODZILLA
August, 1977 - No. 24, July, 1979 (Based on movie series)
Marvel Comics Group

1-Mooney-i 1.20 3.00 6.00
2-10: 2-Tuska-i. 3-Champions app.(w/o Ghost Rider). 4,5-Sutton-a .80 2.00 4.00
11-24: 20-F.F. app. 21,22-Devil Dinosaur app. .50 1.25 2.50

GODZILLA
May, 1988 - No. 6, 1988 ($1.95, B&W, mini-series)
Dark Horse Comics

1 1.20 3.00 6.00
2-6 .60 1.50 3.00
...Collection (1990, $10.95)-r/1-6 with new-c 2.20 5.50 11.00
...Color Special 1 (Sum, 1992, #3.50, color, 44 pgs.)-Arthur Adams wrap-around-c/a & part scripts .70 1.75 3.50
King Of The Monsters Special (8/87, $1.50)-Origin; Bissette-c/a .60 1.50 3.00

GO-GO
June, 1966 - No. 9, Oct, 1967
Charlton Comics

1-Miss Bikini Luv begins; Rolling Stones, Beatles, Elvis, Sonny & Cher, Bob Dylan, Sinatra, parody; Herman's Hermits pin-ups 4.00 12.00 24.00
2-Ringo Starr, David McCallum & Beatles photos on cover; Beatles story and photos 4.00 12.00 24.00
3,4: 3-Blooperman begins, ends #6 2.80 7.00 14.00
5-9: 5-Super Hero & TV satire by Jim Aparo & Grass Green begins. 6-8-Aparo-a. 6-Petula Clark photo-c. 7-Photo of Brian Wilson of Beach Boys on-c & Beach Boys photo inside f/b-c. 8-Monkees photo on-c & photo inside f/b-c 2.80 7.00 14.00

GO-GO AND ANIMAL (See Tippy's Friends...)

GOING STEADY (Formerly Teen-Age Temptations)
No. 10, Dec, 1954 - No. 13, June, 1955; No. 14, Oct, 1955
St. John Publishing Co.

10(1954)-Matt Baker-c/a 9.15 27.50 55.00
11(2/55, last precode), 12(4/55)-Baker-c 4.70 14.00 28.00
13(6/55)-Baker-c/a 5.85 17.50 35.00
14(10/55)-Matt Baker-c/a, 25 pgs. 6.35 19.00 38.00

GOING STEADY (Formerly Personal Love)
V3#3, Feb, 1960 - V3#6, Aug, 1960; V4#1, Sept-Oct, 1960
Prize Publications/Headline

V3#3-6, V4#1 1.60 4.00 8.00

GOING STEADY WITH BETTY (Becomes Betty & Her Steady No. 2)
Nov-Dec, 1949
Avon Periodicals

1 9.15 27.50 55.00

GOLDEN ARROW (See Fawcett Miniatures, Mighty Midget & Whiz Comics)

GOLDEN ARROW (...Western No. 6)
Wint, 1942-43 - No. 6, Spring, 1947
Fawcett Publications

1-Golden Arrow begins 22.00 65.00 150.00
2 10.00 30.00 65.00
3-5 8.35 25.00 50.00
6-Krigstein-a 9.15 27.50 55.00
...Well Known Comics (1944; 12 pgs.; 8x10"; paper-c; glued binding)-Bestmaid/Samuel Lowe giveaway; printed in green 6.00 18.00 42.00

GOLDEN COMICS DIGEST
May, 1969 - No. 48, Jan, 1976
Gold Key

NOTE: *Whitman editions exist of many titles and are generally valued less.*

1-Tom & Jerry, Woody Woodpecker, Bugs Bunny 2.40 6.00 12.00
2-Hanna-Barbera TV Fun Favorites; Space Ghost, Flintstones, Atom Ant, Jetsons, Yogi Bear, Banana Splits, others app. 2.00 5.00 10.00
3-Tom & Jerry, Woody Woodpecker 1.00 2.50 5.00
4-Tarzan; Manning & Marsh-a 2.40 6.00 12.00
5,8-Tom & Jerry, W. Woodpecker, Bugs Bunny .80 2.00 4.00
6-Bugs Bunny .80 2.00 4.00
7-Hanna-Barbera TV Fun Favorites 1.20 3.00 6.00
9-Tarzan 2.00 5.00 10.00
10-17: 10-Bugs Bunny. 11-Hanna-Barbera TV Fun Favorites. 12-Tom & Jerry, Bugs Bunny, W. Woodpecker Journey to the Sun. 13-Tom & Jerry. 14-Bugs Bunny Fun Packed Funnies. 15-Tom & Jerry, Woody Woodpecker, Bugs Bunny. 16-Woody Woodpecker Cartoon Special. 17-Bugs Bunny .80 2.00 4.00
18-Tom & Jerry; Barney Bear-r by Barks 1.00 2.50 5.00
19-Little Lulu 2.40 6.00 12.00
20-22: 20-Woody Woodpecker Falltime Funtime. 21-Bugs Bunny Showtime. 22-Tom & Jerry Winter Wingding .80 2.00 4.00
23-Little Lulu & Tubby Fun Fling 2.40 6.00 12.00
24-26,28: 24-Woody Woodpecker Fun Festival. 25-Tom & Jerry. 26-Bugs Bunny Halloween Hulla-Boo-Loo; Dr. Spektor article, also #25. 28-Tom & Jerry .80 2.00 4.00
27-Little Lulu & Tubby in Hawaii 2.00 5.00 10.00
29-Little Lulu & Tubby 2.00 5.00 10.00
30-Bugs Bunny Vacation Funnies .80 2.00 4.00
31-Turok, Son of Stone; r/4-Color #596,656 1.60 4.00 8.00
32-Woody Woodpecker Summer Fun .80 2.00 4.00
33,36: 33-Little Lulu & Tubby Halloween Fun; Dr. Spektor app. 36-Little Lulu & Her Friends 2.40 6.00 12.00
34,35,37-39: 34-Bugs Bunny Winter Funnies. 35-Tom & Jerry Snowtime Funtime. 37-Woody Woodpecker County Fair. 38-The Pink Panther. 39-Bugs Bunny Summer Fun .80 2.00 4.00
40,43: 40-Little Lulu & Tubby Trick or Treat; all by Stanley. 43-Little Lulu in Paris 2.40 6.00 12.00
41,42,44,45,47: 41-Tom & Jerry Winter Carnival. 42-Bugs Bunny. 44-Woody Woodpecker Family Fun Festival. 45-The Pink Panther. 47-Bugs Bunny .60 1.50 3.00
46-Little Lulu & Tubby 2.00 5.00 10.00
48-The Lone Ranger 1.00 2.50 5.00
NOTE: *#1-30, 164 pages; #31 on, 132 pages.*

GOLDEN LAD
July, 1945 - No. 5, June, 1946
Spark Publications

1-Origin Golden Lad & Swift Arrow 46.00 138.00 275.00
2-Mort Meskin-c/a 22.00 68.00 135.00
3,4-Mort Meskin-c/a 18.00 55.00 110.00
5-Origin Golden Girl; Shaman & Flame app. 22.00 68.00 135.00
NOTE: *All have* **Robinson**, *and* **Roussos** *art plus* **Meskin** *covers and art. #5 is 52pgs.*

Godzilla #9, © MEG

Going Steady With Betty #1, © AVON

Golden Comics Digest #2, © Hanna-Barbera

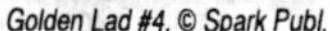

Golden Lad #4, © Spark Publ.

Golden West Love #1, © Kirby Publ.

Goofy Comics #29, © STD

GD25 FN65 NM94

GOLDEN LEGACY
1966 - 1972 (Black History) (25 cents)
Fitzgerald Publishing Co.

1-Toussaint L'Ouverture (1966), 2-Harriet Tubman (1967), 3-Crispus Attucks & the Minutemen (1967), 4-Benjamin Banneker (1968), 5-Matthew Henson (1969), 6-Alexander Dumas & Family (1969), 7-Frederick Douglass, Part 1 (1969), 8-Frederick Douglass, Part 2 (1970), 9-Robert Smalls (1970), 10-J. Cinque & the Amistad Mutiny (1970), 11-Men in Action: White, Marshall J. Wilkins (1970), 12-Black Cowboys (1972), 13-The Life of Martin Luther King, Jr. (1972), 14-The Life of Alexander Pushkin (1971), 15-Ancient African Kingdoms (1972), 16-Black Inventors (1972)
each.... .30 .75 1.50
1-10,12,13,15,16(1976)-Reprints .50 1.00

GOLDEN LOVE STORIES (Formerly Golden West Love)
No. 4, April, 1950
Kirby Publishing Co.

4-Powell-a; Glenn Ford/Janet Leigh photo-c 10.00 30.00 60.00

GOLDEN PICTURE CLASSIC, A
1956-1957 (Text stories w/illustrations in color; 100 pgs. each)
Western Printing Co. (Simon & Shuster)

CL-401: Treasure Island 8.35 25.00 50.00
CL-402: Tom Sawyer 7.00 21.00 42.00
CL-403: Black Beauty 7.00 21.00 42.00
CL-404: Little Women 7.00 21.00 42.00
CL-405: Heidi 7.00 21.00 42.00
CL-406: Ben Hur 4.70 14.00 28.00
CL-407: Around the World in 80 Days 4.70 14.00 28.00
CL-408: Sherlock Holmes 5.85 17.50 35.00
CL-409: The Three Musketeers 4.70 14.00 28.00
CL-410: The Merry Advs. of Robin Hood 4.70 14.00 28.00
CL-411: Hans Brinker 5.85 17.50 35.00
CL-412: The Count of Monte Cristo 5.85 17.50 35.00
(Both soft & hardcover editions are valued the same)

NOTE: *Recent research has uncovered new information. Apparently #s 1-6 were issued in 1956 and #7-12 in 1957. But they can be found in five different series listings: CL-1 to CL-12 (softbound); CL-401 to CL-412 (also softbound); CL-101 to CL-112 (hardbound); plus two new series discoveries: A Golden Reading Adventure, publ. by Golden Press; edited down to 60 pages and reduced in size to 6x9"; only #s discovered so far are #381 (CL-4), #382 (CL-6) & #387 (CL-3). They have no reorder list and some have covers different from GPC. There have also been found British hardbound editions of GPC with dust jackets. Copies of all five listed series vary from scarce to very rare. Some editions of some series have not yet been found at all.*

GOLDEN PICTURE STORY BOOK
Dec, 1961 (52 pgs.; 50 cents; large size) (All are scarce)
Racine Press (Western)

ST-1-Huckleberry Hound (TV) 13.00 40.00 90.00
ST-2-Yogi Bear (TV) 13.00 40.00 90.00
ST-3-Babes in Toyland (Walt Disney's...)-Annette Funicello photo-c 11.50 34.00 80.00
ST-4-(...of Disney Ducks)-Walt Disney's Wonderful World of Ducks (Donald Duck, Uncle Scrooge, Donald's Nephews, Grandma Duck, Ludwig Von Drake, & Gyro Gearloose stories) 11.50 34.00 80.00

GOLDEN RECORD COMIC (See Amazing Spider-Man #1, Avengers #4, Fantastic Four #1, Journey Into Mystery #83)

GOLDEN WEST LOVE (Golden Love Stories No. 4)
Sept-Oct, 1949 - No. 3, Feb, 1950 (All 52 pgs.)
Kirby Publishing Co.

1-Powell-a in all; Roussos-a; painted-c 10.00 30.00 70.00
2,3: Photo-c 8.35 25.00 50.00

GOLDEN WEST RODEO TREASURY (See Dell Giants)

GOLDILOCKS (See March of Comics No. 1)

GOLDILOCKS & THE THREE BEARS
1943 (Giveaway)
K. K. Publications

GD25 FN65 NM94

nn 8.35 25.00 50.00

GOLD KEY CHAMPION
Mar, 1978 - No. 2, May, 1978 (52 pages) (50 cents)
Gold Key

1-Space Family Robinson; -r .50 1.00
2-Mighty Samson; -r .50 1.00

GOLD KEY SPOTLIGHT
May, 1976 - No. 11, Feb, 1978
Gold Key

1-Tom, Dick & Harriet .80 2.00 4.00
2-5,710,11: 2-Wacky Advs. of Cracky. 3-Wacky Witch. 4-Tom, Dick & Harriet. 5-Wacky Advs. of Cracky. 7-Wacky Witch & Greta Ghost 10-O. G. Whiz. 11-Tom, Dick & Harriet .60 1.50 3.00
6,8,9: 6-Dagar the Invincible; Santos-a; origin Demonomicon. 8-The Occult Files of Dr. Spektor, Simbar, Lu-sai; Santos-a. 9-Tragg .80 2.00 4.00

GOLD MEDAL COMICS
1945 (132 pages) (One shot)
Cambridge House

nn-Captain Truth by Fugitani, Crime Detector, The Witch of Salem, Luckyman, others app. 14.00 43.00 100.00

GOMER PYLE (TV)
July, 1966 - No. 3, Jan, 1967
Gold Key

1-Photo front/back-c 6.70 20.00 40.00
2,3 5.85 17.50 35.00

GOODBYE, MR. CHIPS (See Movie Comics)

GOOD GIRL ART QUARTERLY (AC) (Value: cover or less)

GOOFY (Disney) (See Dynabrite Comics, Mickey Mouse Magazine V4#7, Walt Disney Showcase #35 & Wheaties)
No. 468, May, 1953 - Sept-Nov, 1962
Dell Publishing Co.

4-Color 468 (#1) 8.35 25.00 50.00
4-Color 562,627,658,747,802 4.20 12.50 25.00
4-Color 899,952,987,1053,1094,1149,1201 3.60 9.00 18.00
12-308-211 (Dell, 9-11/62) 3.60 9.00 18.00

GOOFY ADVENTURES
June, 1990 - No. 17, 1991 ($1.50, color)
Disney Comics

1-17: All new stories. 2-Joshua Quagmire-a w/free poster. 7-WDC&S-r plus new-a. 9-Gottfredson-r. 14-Super Goof story. 15-All Super Goof issue. 17-Gene Colan-a(p) .30 .75 1.50

GOOFY ADVENTURE STORY (See 4-Color No. 857)

GOOFY COMICS (Companion to Happy Comics)
June, 1943 - No. 48, 1953
Nedor Publ. Co. No. 1-14/Standard No. 14-48 (Animated Cartoons)

1 16.00 48.00 110.00
2 9.15 27.50 55.00
3-10 5.85 17.50 35.00
11-19 4.35 13.00 26.00
20-35-Frazetta text illos in all 5.85 17.50 35.00
36-48 4.00 10.00 20.00

GOOFY SUCCESS STORY (See 4-Color No. 702)

GOOSE (Humor magazine)
Sept, 1976 - No. 3, 1976 (52 pgs.) (75 cents)
Cousins Publ. (Fawcett)

1-3 .50 1.00

GORDO (See Comics Revue No. 5)

GORGO (Based on movie) (See Return of...)
May, 1961 - No. 23, Sept, 1965
Charlton Comics

	GD25	FN65	NM94
1-Ditko-a, 22 pgs.	22.00	65.00	150.00
2,3-Ditko-c/a	11.00	32.00	75.00
4-10: 4-Ditko-c	7.50	22.50	45.00
11,13-16-Ditko-a	5.85	17.50	35.00
12,17-23: 12-Reptisaurus x-over; Montes/Bache-a-No. 17-23. 20-Giordano-c	3.20	8.00	16.00
Gorgo's Revenge('62)-Becomes Return of...	4.70	14.00	28.00

GOSPEL BLIMP, THE (Spire Christian)(Value: cover or less)

GOTHAM BY GASLIGHT (A Tale of the Batman)(See Batman: Master of...)
1989 ($3.95, one-shot, squarebound, 52 pgs.)
DC Comics

	GD25	FN65	NM94
nn-Mignola/Russell-a; intro by Robert Bloch	.80	2.00	4.00

GOTHAM NIGHTS
Mar, 1992 - No. 4, June, 1992 ($1.25, color, mini-series)
DC Comics

	GD25	FN65	NM94
1-4: Featuring Batman		.60	1.25

GOTHIC ROMANCES
January, 1975 (B&W Magazine) (75 cents)
Atlas/Seaboard Publ.

	GD25	FN65	NM94
1-Neal Adams-a	.35	.90	1.80

GOVERNOR & J. J., THE (TV)
Feb, 1970 - No. 3, Aug, 1970 (Photo-c)
Gold Key

	GD25	FN65	NM94
1	4.20	12.50	25.00
2,3	3.60	9.00	18.00

GRAFIK MUZIK (Caliber)(Value: cover or less)

GRANDMA DUCK'S FARM FRIENDS (See 4-Color #763, 873, 965, 1010, 1073, 1161, 1279, Walt Disney's Comics & Stories #293 & Wheaties)

GRAND PRIX (Formerly Hot Rod Racers)
No. 16, Sept, 1967 - No. 31, May, 1970
Charlton Comics

	GD25	FN65	NM94
16: Features Rick Roberts	2.00	5.00	10.00
17-20	1.60	4.00	8.00
21-31	1.00	2.50	5.00

GRAVE TALES (Also see Maggots)
Oct, 1991 - No. 3, Feb, 1992 ($3.95, B&W, magazine, 52 pgs.)
Hamilton Comics

	GD25	FN65	NM94
1-3: 1-Staton-c/a. 2-Staton-a; Morrow-c	.80	2.00	4.00

GRAY GHOST, THE (See 4-Color No. 911, 1000)

GREAT ACTION COMICS
1958 (Reprints)
I. W. Enterprises

	GD25	FN65	NM94
1-Captain Truth reprinted from Gold Medal #1	1.80	4.50	9.00
8,9-Reprints Phantom Lady #15 & 23	9.15	27.50	55.00

GREAT AMERICAN COMICS PRESENTS - THE SECRET VOICE
1945 (10 cents)
Peter George 4-Star Publ./American Features Syndicate

	GD25	FN65	NM94
1-Anti-Nazi; 'What Really Happened to Hitler'	10.00	30.00	70.00

GREAT AMERICAN WESTERN, THE (AC)(Value: cover or less)

GREAT CAT FAMILY, THE (See 4-Color No. 750)

GREAT COMICS
Nov, 1941 - No. 3, Jan, 1942
Great Comics Publications

	GD25	FN65	NM94
1-Origin The Great Zarro; Madame Strange begins	71.00	210.00	425.00
2	42.00	125.00	250.00
3-Futuro Takes Hitler to Hell; "The Lost City" movie story (starring William Boyd); continues in Choice Comics #3	75.00	225.00	450.00

GREAT COMICS
1945
Novack Publishing Co./Jubilee Comics/Barrel O' Fun

	GD25	FN65	NM94
1-(Novack)-The Defenders, Capt. Power app.; L. B. Cole-c	13.00	40.00	80.00
1-(Jubilee)-Same cover; Boogey Man, Satanas, & The Sorcerer & His Apprentice	10.00	30.00	65.00
1-(Barrel O' Fun)-L. B. Cole-c; Barrel O' Fun overprinted in indicia; Li'l Cactus, Cuckoo Sheriff (humorous)	4.70	14.00	28.00

GREAT DOGPATCH MYSTERY (See Mammy Yokum & the...)

GREATEST BATMAN STORIES EVER TOLD, THE
1988 (Color reprints) (Greatest Stories Vol. 2)
DC Comics

	GD25	FN65	NM94
Softcover ($15.95)-Simonson-c	3.60	9.00	18.00
Hardcover ($24.95) with dust jacket	8.35	25.00	50.00
Softcover (1992, $16.95, Vol. 2)-Catwoman & Penguin stories	3.40	8.50	17.00

GREATEST JOKER STORIES EVER TOLD, THE
1988 (Color reprints) (Greatest Stories Vol. 3)
DC Comics

	GD25	FN65	NM94
Softcover ($14.95)-Brian Bolland Joker-c	3.20	8.00	16.00
Hardcover ($19.95) with dust jacket	6.70	20.00	40.00
Stacked Deck ...Expanded Edition (1990, $29.95)-Longmeadow Press Publ.	5.00	15.00	30.00

GREAT EXPLOITS
October, 1957
Decker Publ./Red Top

	GD25	FN65	NM94
1-Krigstein-a(2) (re-issue on cover); reprints Daring Advs. #6 by Approved Comics	5.00	15.00	30.00

GREAT FOODINI, THE (See Foodini)

GREAT GAZOO, THE (The Flintstones)(TV)
Aug, 1973 - No. 20, Jan, 1977 (Hanna-Barbera)
Charlton Comics

	GD25	FN65	NM94
1	1.20	3.00	6.00
2-20	.60	1.50	3.00

GREAT GRAPE APE, THE (TV)(See TV Stars #1)
Sept, 1976 - No. 2, Nov, 1976 (Hanna-Barbera)
Charlton Comics

	GD25	FN65	NM94
1,2	1.00	2.50	5.00

GREAT LOCOMOTIVE CHASE, THE (See 4-Color No. 712)

GREAT LOVER ROMANCES (Young Lover Romances #4,5)
3/51; #2, 1951(nd); #3, 1952 (nd); #6, Oct?, 1952 - No. 22, May, 1955
Toby Press (Photo-c #1-3,13,17)

	GD25	FN65	NM94
1-Jon Juan story-r/J.J. #1 by Schomburg; Dr. Anthony King app.	9.15	27.50	55.00
2-Jon Juan, Dr. Anthony King app.	4.70	14.00	28.00
3,7,9-14,16-22 (no #4,5)	2.80	7.00	14.00
6-Kurtzman-a (10/52)	5.00	15.00	30.00
8-Five pgs. of "Pin-Up Pete" by Sparling	5.00	15.00	30.00
15-Liz Taylor photo-c	5.85	17.50	35.00

GREAT MOUSE DETECTIVE, THE
1991 ($4.95, color)
Disney Comics

	GD25	FN65	NM94
nn-Graphic novel adapting new movie	1.00	2.50	5.00

GREAT PEOPLE OF GENESIS, THE
No date (64 pgs.) (Religious giveaway)

Gorgo #17, © M.G.M.

Great Comics #2, © GP

Great Lover Romances #8, © TOBY

Great Western #11, © ME

Green Arrow #10, © DC

Green Hornet Comics #4, © The Green Hornet

GD25 FN65 NM94

David C. Cook Publ. Co.
nn-Reprint/Sunday Pix Weekly 2.00 5.00 10.00

GREAT RACE, THE (See Movie Classics)

GREAT SACRAMENT, THE
1953 (36 pages, giveaway)
Catechetical Guild
nn 200 5.00 10.00

GREAT SCOTT SHOE STORE (See Bulls-Eye)

GREAT WEST (Magazine)
1969 (52 pages) (Black & White)
M. F. Enterprises
V1#1 .40 1.00 2.00

GREAT WESTERN
No. 8, Jan-Mar, 1954 - No. 11, Oct-Dec, 1954
Magazine Enterprises
8(A-1 93)-Trail Colt by Guardineer; Powell Red Hawk-r/Straight Arrow begins, ends #11; Durango Kid story 13.00 40.00 90.00
9(A-1 105), 11(A-1 127)-Ghost Rider, Durango Kid app. in each. 9-Red Mask-c, but no app. 7.50 22.50 45.00
10(A-1 113)-The Calico Kid by Guardineer-r/Tim Holt #8; Straight Arrow, Durango Kid app. 7.50 22.50 45.00
I.W. Reprint #1,2 9: 1,2-r/Straight Arrow #36,42. 9-r/Straight Arrow #? 1.60 4.00 8.00
I.W. Reprint #8-Origin Ghost Rider(r/Tim Holt #11); Tim Holt app.; Bolle-a 2.40 6.00 12.00
NOTE: ***Guardineer*** *c-8.* ***Powell*** *a(r)-8-11 (from Straight Arrow).*

GREEN ARROW (See Action #440, Adventure, Brave & the Bold, DC Super Stars #17, Detective #521, Flash #217, Green Lantern #76, Justice League of America #4, Leading, More Fun #73 (1st app.) and World's Finest Comics)

GREEN ARROW
May, 1983 - No. 4, Aug, 1983 (Mini-series)
DC Comics
1-Origin; Speedy cameo .80 2.00 4.00
2-4 .60 1.50 3.00

GREEN ARROW
Feb, 1988 - Present ($1.00, mature readers)(Painted-c #1-3)
DC Comics
1-Mike Grell scripts in all 1.40 3.50 7.00
2 .60 1.50 3.00
3-49,51-74: 27,28-Warlord app. 35-38-Co-stars Black Canary; Bill Wray-i. 40-Grell-a. 47-Begin $1.50-c. 63-No longer has mature readers on-c. 63-66-Shado app. 68-Last $1.50-c .35 .90 1.75
50-($2.50, 52 pgs.) .50 1.25 2.50
Annual 1('88, $2.00)-No Grell scripts .40 1.00 2.00
Annual 2('89, $2.50, 68pgs.)-No Grell scripts; recaps origin Green Arrow, Speedy, Black Canary & others .50 1.25 2.50
Annual 3('90, $2.50, 68pgs.)-Bill Wray-a .60 1.50 3.00
Annual 4('91, $2.95, 68pgs.)-50th anniversary issue .40 1.00 2.00
Annual 5('92, $3.00, 68pgs.)-Batman, Eclipso app. .60 1.50 3.00
NOTE: ***Denys Cowan*** *a(p)-39, 41-43, 47, 48; c(p)-41-43.* ***Mike Grell*** *c-1-4, 10p, 39, 40, 44, 45, 47-71, Annual 4, 5.* ***Springer*** *a-67, 68.*

GREEN ARROW: THE LONG BOW HUNTERS
Aug, 1987 - No. 3, Oct, 1987 ($2.95, color, mature readers)
DC Comics
1-Grell-c/a in all 1.60 4.00 8.00
1,2-2nd printings .40 1.00 2.00
2 .80 2.00 4.00
3 .60 1.50 3.00
Trade paperback (1989, $12.95) reprints #1-3 2.60 6.50 13.00

GD25 FN65 NM94

GREEN ARROW: THE WONDER YEAR
Feb, 1993 - No. 4, May, 1993 ($1.75, color, mini-series)
DC Comics
1-4: By Grell (scripts & pencils) & Morrow (inks) .35 .90 1.75

GREEN BERET, THE (See Tales of...)

GREEN GIANT COMICS (Also see Colossus Comics)
1940 (no price on cover)
Pelican Publ. (Funnies, Inc.)
GD25 FN65 VF82 NM94
1-Dr. Nerod, Green Giant, Black Arrow, Mundoo & Master Mystic app.; origin Colossus (Rare) 575.00 1725.00 3160.00 4600.00
(Estimated up to 17 copies exist, 3 in NM/Mint)
NOTE: The idea for this book came about during a stroll through a grocery store. Printed by Moreau Publ. of Orange, N.J. as an experiment to see if they could profitably use the idle time of their 40-page Hoe color press. The experiment failed due to the difficulty of obtaining good quality color registration and Mr. Moreau believes the book never reached the stands. The book has no price or date which lends credence to this. Contains five pages reprinted from Motion Picture Funnies Weekly.

GREEN-GREY SPONGE-SUIT SUSHI TURTLES (Mirage)(Value: cover or less)

GREENHAVEN (Aircel)(Value: cover or less)

GREEN HORNET, THE (TV)(See Four Color #496)
Feb, 1967 - No. 3, Aug, 1967
Gold Key
1-All have Bruce Lee photo-c 16.00 48.00 110.00
2,3 12.00 36.00 85.00

GREEN HORNET, THE (Also see Kato of the... & Tales of the...)
Nov, 1989 - No. 14, Feb, 1991 ($1.75, color)
V2#1, Sept, 1991 - Present ($1.95, color)
Now Comics
1 ($2.95, double-size)-Steranko painted-c; G.A. Green Hornet 4.00 10.00 20.00
1-2nd printing ('90, $3.95)-New Butler-c .80 2.00 4.00
2 2.00 5.00 10.00
3-5: 5-Death of original (1930s) Green Hornet 1.20 3.00 6.00
6-8: 6-Dave Dorman painted-c .60 1.50 3.00
9-18 .40 1.00 2.00
V2#1-11,13,14-16: 1-Butler painted-c. 9-Mayerik-c .40 1.00 2.00
12-Color Green Hornet button polybagged inside (2.50-c) .70 1.75 3.50
Annual 1 ('92, 2.50-c) .50 1.25 2.50

GREEN HORNET COMICS (...Racket Buster #44) (Radio, movies)
Dec, 1940 - No. 47, Sept, 1949 (See All New #13,14)
Helnit Publ. Co.(Holyoke) No. 1-6/Family Comics(Harvey) No. 7-on
1-Green Hornet begins(1st app.); painted-c 210.00 625.00 1250.00
2 92.00 275.00 550.00
3 75.00 225.00 450.00
4-6 (8/41) 57.00 170.00 340.00
7 (6/42)-Origin The Zebra; Robin Hood & Spirit of 76 begin 54.00 162.00 325.00
8-10 46.00 138.00 275.00
11,12-Mr. Q in both 37.00 112.00 225.00
13-20 31.00 92.00 185.00
21-30: 24-Sci-Fi-c 27.00 82.00 165.00
31-The Man in Black Called Fate begins 29.00 87.00 175.00
32-36: 36-Spanking panel 25.00 75.00 150.00
37-Shock Gibson app. by Powell; S&K Kid Adonis reprinted from Stuntman #3 27.00 80.00 160.00
38-Shock Gibson, Kid Adonis app. 25.00 75.00 150.00
39-Stuntman story by S&K 30.00 90.00 180.00
40,41 18.00 55.00 110.00
42-47-Kerry Drake in all. 45-Boy Explorers on-c only. 46-"Case of the Marijuana Racket" cover/story; Kerry Drake app. 116.00 48.00 110.00

NOTE: ***Fuje** a-23, 24, 26. **Henkle** c-7-9. **Kubert** a-20, 30. **Powell** a-7-10, 12, 14, 16-21, 30, 31(2), 32(3), 33, 34(3), 35, 36, 37(2), 38. **Robinson** a-27. **Schomburg** c-15, 17-23. Kirbyish c-7, 9, 15. Bondage c-8, 14, 18, 26, 36.*

GREEN JET COMICS, THE (See Comic Books, Series 1)

GREEN LAMA (Also see Comic Books, Series 1, Daring Adventures #17 & Prize Comics #7)
Dec, 1944 - No. 8, March, 1946
Spark Publications/Prize No. 7 on

	GD25	FN65	NM94
1-Intro. The Green Lama, Lt. Hercules & The Boy Champions; Mac Raboy-c/a #1-8	87.00	262.00	525.00
2-Lt. Hercules borrows the Human Torch's powers for one panel	58.00	175.00	350.00
3,6-8: 7-X-mas-c; Raboy craft tint art	46.00	138.00	275.00
4-Dick Tracy take-off in Lt. Hercules story by H. L. Gold (sci-fiction writer)	46.00	138.00	275.00
5-Lt. Hercules story; Little Orphan Annie, Smilin' Jack & Snuffy Smith take-off (5/45)	46.00	138.00	275.00

NOTE: ***Robinson** a-3-5. Formerly a pulp hero who began in 1940.*

GREEN LANTERN (1st Series) (See All-American, All Flash Quarterly, All Star Comics, The Big All-American & Comic Cavalcade)
Fall, 1941 - No. 38, May-June, 1949
National Periodical Publications/All-American

	GD25	FN65	VF82	NM94
1-Origin retold	1,000.00	3,000.00	6,000.00	10,000.00

(Estimated up to 200 total copies exist, 8 in NM/Mint)

	GD25	FN65	NM94
2-1st book-length story	433.00	1300.00	2600.00
3	291.00	875.00	1750.00
4-Classic war-c	242.00	725.00	1450.00
5	150.00	450.00	900.00
6-8: 8-Hop Harrigan begins	125.00	375.00	750.00
9,10: 10-Origin Vandal Savage	112.00	338.00	675.00
11-17,19,20: 12-Origin Gambler	96.00	288.00	575.00
18-Christmas-c	108.00	325.00	650.00
21-30: 27-Origin Sky Pirate. 30-Origin/1st app. Streak the Wonder Dog by Toth	83.00	250.00	500.00
31-35: 35-Kubert-c. 35-38-New logo	71.00	210.00	425.00
36-38: 37-Sargon the Sorcerer app.	100.00	300.00	600.00

*NOTE: Book-length stories #2-7. **Mayer/Moldoff** c-9. **Mayer/Purcell** c-8. **Purcell** c-1. **Mart Nodell** c-2, 3, 7. **Paul Reinman** c-11, 12, 15-22. **Toth** a-28, 30, 31, 34-38; c-28, 30, 34p, 36-38p. Cover to #8 says Fall while the indicia says Summer Issue.*

GREEN LANTERN (See Action Comics Weekly, Adventure Comics, Brave & the Bold, DC Special, DC Special Series, Flash, Guy Gardner, Guy Gardner Reborn, Justice League of America, Showcase & Tales of The...Corps)

GREEN LANTERN (2nd series)(Green Lantern Corps #206 on)
7-8/60 - No. 89, 4-5/72; No. 90, 8-9/76 - No. 205, 10/86
National Periodical Publications/DC Comics

	GD25	FN65	NM94
Showcase #22 (9-10/59)-Origin & 1st app. Silver Age Green Lantern by Gil Kane	320.00	960.00	2250.00
Showcase #23,24 (11-12/59, 1-2/60)	115.00	345.00	800.00
1-(7-8/60)-Origin retold; Gil Kane-a begins	200.00	600.00	1400.00
2-1st Pieface	72.00	215.00	500.00
3-Contains readers poll	43.00	130.00	300.00
4,5: 5-Origin & 1st app. Hector Hammond	33.00	100.00	230.00
6-10: 6-Intro Tomar-re the alien G.L. 7-Origin/1st app. Sinestro. 8-1st 5700 A.D. story; painted-c. 9-1st Jordan Brothers; last 10 cent issue	22.00	65.00	150.00
11,12	15.00	45.00	105.00
13-Flash x-over	19.00	58.00	135.00
14-20: 14-Origin/1st app. Sonar. 16-Origin Star Sapphire. 20-Flash x-over	13.50	41.00	95.00
21-30: 21-Origin Dr. Polaris. 23-1st Tattooed Man. 24-Origin Shark. 29-JLA cameo; 1st Blackhand	11.50	34.00	80.00
31-39	10.00	30.00	60.00
40-1st app. Crisis (10/65); 2nd solo G.A. Green Lantern in Silver Age (see Showcase #55); origin The Guardians; Doiby Dickles app.	47.00	140.00	325.00
41-44,46-50: 42-Zatanna x-over. 43-Flash x-over	6.70	20.00	40.00
45-G.A. Green Lantern x-over	9.15	27.50	55.00
51,53-58	4.20	12.50	25.00
52-G.A. Green Lantern x-over	5.50	16.50	33.00
59-1st app. Guy Gardner (3/68)	18.00	54.00	125.00
60,62-69: 69-Wood inks; last 12 cent issue	3.20	8.00	16.00
61-G.A. Green Lantern x-over	4.20	12.50	25.00
70-75	2.60	6.50	13.00
76-Begin Green Lantern/Green Arrow series (by Neal Adams #76-89) ends #122	14.00	43.00	100.00
77	6.00	18.00	36.00
78-80	4.35	13.00	26.00
81-84: 82-Wrightson-i(1 pg.). 83-G.L. reveals i.d. to Carol Ferris. 84-Neal Adams/Wrightson-a(22 pgs.); last 15 cent-c; partial photo-c	4.00	11.00	22.00
85,86(52 pgs.)-Drug propaganda books. 86-G.A. Green Lantern-r; Toth-a	5.35	16.00	32.00
87(52 pgs.): 2nd app. Guy Gardner (cameo); 1st app. John Stewart (becomes Green Lantern in #182)	4.00	10.00	20.00
88(2-3/72, 52 pgs.)-Unpubbed G.A. Green Lantern story; Green Lantern-r/ Showcase #23. N. Adams-a (1 pg.)	1.00	2.50	5.00
89(4-5/72, 52 pgs.)-G.A. Green Lantern-r	2.00	5.00	10.00
90(8-9/76)-99	.60	1.50	3.00
100-(Giant)-1st app. Air Wave II	1.00	2.50	5.00
101-111,113-115,117-119: 107-1st Tales of the G.L. Corps story. 108-110-(44pgs)-G.A. Green Lantern. 111-Origin retold; G.A. Green Lantern app.	.50	1.25	2.50
112-G.A. Green Lantern origin retold	1.20	3.00	6.00
116-1st app. Guy Gardner as a Green Lantern	4.00	10.00	20.00
120,121,124-135,138-140,142-149: 130-132-Tales of the G.L. Corps. 132-Adam Strange series begins, ends 147. 142,143-Omega Men app.; Perez-c. 144-Omega Men cameo. 148-Tales of the G.L. Corps begins, ends #173	.30	.75	1.50
122-Last Green Lantern/Green Arrow team-up	.40	1.00	2.00
123-Green Lantern back to solo action; 2nd app. Guy Gardner as Green Lantern	1.00	2.50	5.00
136,137-1st app. Citadel; Space Ranger app.	.50	1.25	2.50
141-1st app. Omega Men	.50	1.25	2.50
150-Anniversary issue, 52 pgs.; no G.L. Corps	.50	1.25	2.50
151-170: 159-Origin Evil Star. 160,161-Omega Men app. 181-Hal Jordan resigns as G.L. 182-John Stewart becomes new G.L.; origin recap of Hal Jordan as G.L.	.30	.75	1.50
171-193,196-199,201-205: (75 cent cover). 185-Origin new G.L. (John Stewart). 188-I.D. revealed; Alan Moore back-up scripts. 191-1st app. Star Sapphire. 194,198-Crisis x-over. 199-Hal Jorda returns as a member of G.L. Corps (3 G.L.s now). 201-Green Lantern Corps begins (is cover title & says premiere issue)	.30	.75	1.50
194-Hal Jordan/Guy Gardner battle; Guardians choose Guy Gardner to become new G.L.	.50	1.25	2.50
195-Guy Gardner becomes Green Lantern; Crisis x-over	2.20	5.50	11.00
200-Double-size	.50	1.25	2.50
Annual 1 (See Tales Of The...)			
Annual 3 (See Green Lantern Corps Annual #3)			
Special 1 (1988), 2 (1989)-(Both $1.50, 52 pgs.)	.50	1.25	2.50

NOTE: ***N. Adams** a-76, 77-87p, 89; c-63, 76-89. **M. Anderson** a-137i. **Austin** a-93i, 94i, 171i. **Greene** a-39-49i, 58-63i; c-54-58i. **Grell** a-90, 91, 92-100p, 106p, 108-110p; c-90, 93-100, 101p, 102-106, 108-112. **Gil Kane** a-1-49p, 50-57, 58-61p, 68-75p, 85p(r), 87p(r), 88p(r), 156, 177, 184p; c-1-52, 54-61p, 67-75, 123, 154, 156, 165-171, 177, 184. **Newton** a-148p, 149p, 181. **Perez** c-132p, 141-144. **Sekowsky** a-65p, 170p. **Sparling** a-63p. **Starlin** c-129, 133. **Staton** a-117p, 123-127p, 128, 129-131p, 132-139, 140p, 141-146, 147p, 148-150, 151-155p; c-107p, 117p, 135(i), 136p, 145p, 146, 147, 148-152p, 155p. **Toth** a-86r, 171p. **Tuska** a-166-168p, 170p.*

GREEN LANTERN (3rd series)
June, 1990 - Present ($1.00/$1.25, color)

Green Lama #3, © PRIZE

Green Lantern #13 (1st series), © DC

Green Lantern #14 (2nd series), © DC

Green Lantern: Emerald Dawn #6, © DC

The Green Mask #3, © FOX

Grendel #3 (color series), © Comico

	GD25	FN65	NM94
DC Comics			
1-Hal Jordan, John Stewart & Guy Gardner return; Batman app.	.60	1.75	3.50
2,3	.40	1.00	2.00
4-8		.60	1.20
9-12-Guy Gardner solo story	.50	1.25	2.50
13-($1.75, 52 pgs.)	.40	1.00	2.00
14-18,20-24,26: 18-Guy Gardner solo story. 26-Last $1.00-c		.50	1.00
19-($1.75, 52 pgs.)-50th anniversary issue; Mart Nodell (original G.A. artist) part-p on G.A. Gr. Lantern; G. Kane-c	.35	.90	1.75
25-($1.75, 52 pgs.)-Hal Jordan/Guy Gardner battle	.40	1.00	2.00
27-40: 30,31-Gorilla Grodd-c/story(see Flash #69)		.60	1.25
Annual 1 (1992, $2.50, 68 pgs.)-Eclipso app.	.50	1.25	2.50
...The Road Back nn (1992, $8.95)-r/1-8 w/covers	1.80	4.50	9.00

NOTE: ***Staton** a(p)-9-12; c-9-12.*

GREEN LANTERN CORPS, THE (Formerly Green Lantern; see Tales of...)
No. 206, Nov, 1986 - No. 224, May, 1988
DC Comics

206-223: 220,221-Millennium tie-ins		.50	1.00
224-Double size last issue	.30	.75	1.50
..Corps Annual 2 (12/86)-Formerly Tales of ...Annual #1; Alan Moore scripts	.30	.75	1.50
..Corps Annual 3 (8/87)-Indicia says Green Lantern Annual #3; Moore scripts; Byrne-a	.30	.75	1.50

NOTE: ***Austin** a-Annual 3i. **Gil Kane** a-223, 224p; c-223, 224. **Russell** a-Annual 3i. **Staton** a-207-213p, 217p, 221p, 222p, Annual 3; c-207-213p, 217p, 221p, 222p. **Willingham** a-213p, 219p, 220p, 218p, 219p, Annual 2, 3p; c-218p, 219p.*

GREEN LANTERN CORPS QUARTERLY
Summer, 1992 - Present ($2.50, color, 68 pgs.)
DC Comics

1-4: 1-G.A. Green Lantern story; Staton-a(p). 2-G.A. G.L.-c/story; Austin-c(i); Gulacy-a(p). 3-G.A. G.L. story. 4-Austin-i	.50	1.25	2.50

GREEN LANTERN: EMERALD DAWN (Also see Emerald Dawn)
Dec, 1989 - No. 6, May, 1990 ($1.00, color, mini-series)
DC Comics

1-Origin retold; Giffen plots in all	1.60	4.00	8.00
2	1.20	3.00	6.00
3,4	.80	2.00	4.00
5,6	.40	1.00	2.00

GREEN LANTERN: EMERALD DAWN II (Emerald Dawn II #1 & 2)
Apr, 1991 - No. 6, Sept, 1991 ($1.00, color, mini-series)
DC Comics

1	.30	.75	1.50
2-6		.50	1.00

GREEN LANTERN: GANTHET'S TALE
1992 ($5.95, color, one-shot, 68 pgs.)
DC Comics

nn-Silver foil stamped logo; Byrne-c/a	1.20	3.00	6.00

GREEN LANTERN/GREEN ARROW (Also see The Flash #217)
Oct, 1983 - No. 7, April, 1984 (52-60 pgs.)
DC Comics

1-7: Reprints Green Lantern #76-89	.50	1.50	3.00

NOTE: ***Neal Adams** r-1-7; c-1-4. **Wrightson** r-4, 5.*

GREEN LANTERN: MOSAIC
June, 1992 - Present ($1.25, color)
DC Comics

1-12: Featuring John Stewart. 1-Painted-c		.60	1.25

GREEN MASK, THE (See Mystery Men)
Summer, 1940 - No. 9, 2/42; No. 10, 8/44 - No. 11, 11/44;
V2#1, Spring, 1945 - No. 6, 10-11/46
Fox Features Syndicate

	GD25	FN65	NM94
V1#1-Origin The Green Mask & Domino; reprints/Mystery Men #1-3,5-7; Lou Fine-c	133.00	400.00	800.00
2-Zanzibar The Magician by Tuska	67.00	200.00	400.00
3-Powell-a; Marijuana story	42.00	125.00	250.00
4-Navy Jones begins, ends #6	33.00	100.00	200.00
5	29.00	88.00	175.00
6-The Nightbird begins, ends #9; bondage/torture-c	25.00	75.00	150.00
7-9: 9(2/42)-Becomes The Bouncer #10(nn) on? & Green Mask #10 on	20.00	60.00	120.00
10,11: 10-Origin One Round Hogan & Rocket Kelly	17.00	50.00	100.00
V2#1	12.50	38.00	75.00
2-6	10.00	30.00	65.00

GREEN PLANET, THE
1962 (One Shot)
Charlton Comics

nn-Giordano-c	5.00	15.00	30.00

GREEN TEAM (See Cancelled Comic Cavalcade & 1st Issue Special)

GREETINGS FROM SANTA (See March of Comics No. 48)

GRENDEL (Also see Primer No. 2 and Mage)
Mar, 1983 - No. 3, Feb, 1984 ($1.50, B&W)(#1 has indicia to Skrog #1)
Comico

1-Origin Hunter Rose	8.35	25.00	50.00
2,3: 2-Origin Argent	6.35	19.00	38.00

GRENDEL
Oct, 1986 - No. 40, Feb, 1991 ($1.50-$1.95-$2.50, color) (Mature readers)
Comico

1	.80	2.00	4.00
1,2-2nd printings	.30	.75	1.50
2	.45	1.30	2.60
3-10: 4-Dave Stevens-c(i)	.40	1.00	2.00
11-15: 13-15-Ken Steacy-c	.35	.90	1.75
16-Re-intro Mage (series begins, ends #19)	.80	2.00	4.00
17-32: 18-26-$1.75-c; 27-32-$1.95-c	.40	1.00	2.00
33-($2.75, 44 pgs.)	.55	1.40	2.75
34-40: 34-Begin $2.50 cover price	.50	1.25	2.50
Devil by the Deed (Graphic Novel, 10/86, $5.95, 52 pgs.)-r/Grendel back-ups/ Mage 6-14; Alan Moore intro.	1.40	3.50	7.00
Devil's Legacy ($14.95, 1988, Graphic Novel)	3.00	7.50	15.00
Devil's Vagary (10/87, B&W & red)-No price; included in Comico Collection	2.40	6.00	12.00

GRENDEL: WAR CHILD
Aug, 1992 - No. 10, 1993 ($2.50, color, limited series, mature readers)
Dark Horse Comics

1-10: Bisley painted-c; Wagner-i & scripts	.50	1.25	2.50

GREYFRIARS BOBBY (See 4-Color No. 1189)

GREYLORE (Sirius)(Value: cover or less)

GRIFFIN, THE (DC)(Value: cover or less)

GRIM GHOST, THE
Jan, 1975 - No. 3, July, 1975
Atlas/Seaboard Publ.

1-3: 1-Origin. 3-Heath-c		.50	1.00

GRIMJACK (Also see Demon Knight & Starslayer)
Aug, 1984 - No. 81, Apr, 1991
First Comics

	GD25	FN65	NM94
1	.40	1.00	2.00
2-25: 20-Sutton-c/a begins. 22-Bolland-a	.30	.75	1.50
26-2nd color Teenage Mutant Ninja Turtles	1.00	2.50	5.00
27-38: 30-Dynamo Joe x-over; 31-Mandrake-c/a begins		.60	1.25
39-74,76-81 (Later issues $1.95, $2.25-c)		.60	1.25
75-($5.95, 52 pgs.)-Fold-out map; coated stock	1.20	3.00	6.00

GRIMJACK CASEFILES (First)(Value: cover or less)

GRIMM'S GHOST STORIES (See Dan Curtis)
Jan, 1972 - No. 60, June, 1982 (Painted-c #1-42,44,46-56)
Gold Key/Whitman No. 55 on

	GD25	FN65	NM94
1	1.20	3.00	6.00
2-4,6,7,9,10	.60	1.50	3.00
5,8-Williamson-a	.80	2.00	4.00
11-16,18-35: 32,34-Reprints	.40	1.00	2.00
17-Crandall-a	.60	1.50	3.00
36-55,57-60: 43,44-(52 pgs.). 43,45-Photo-c	.30	.75	1.50
56-Williamson-a(r)	.40	1.00	2.00
Mini-Comic No. 1 (3-1/4x6-1/2", 1976)		.50	1.00

NOTE: *Reprints-#32?, 34?, 39, 43, 44, 47?, 53; 56-60(1/3).* ***Bolle*** *a-17, 22-25, 27, 29(2), 33, 35, 43r, 45(2), 48(2), 50, 52.* ***Celardo*** *a-26, 28p, 30, 31, 43(2), 45.* ***Lopez*** *a-24, 25.* ***McWilliams*** *a-33, 44r, 48, 58.* ***Win Mortimer*** *a-31, 33, 49, 51, 55, 56, 58(2), 59, 60.* ***Roussos*** *a-25, 30.* ***Sparling*** *a-23, 24, 28, 30, 31, 33, 43r, 44, 45, 51(2), 52, 56, 58, 59(2), 60.* ***Spiegle*** *a-44.*

GRIN (The American Funny Book) (Magazine)
Nov, 1972 - No. 3, April, 1973 (52 pgs.) (Satire)
APAG House Pubs

	GD25	FN65	NM94
1	.40	1.00	2.00
2,3		.50	1.00

GRIN & BEAR IT (See Gags & Large Feature Comic No. 28)

GRIPS (Extreme violence)
Sept, 1986 - No. 4, Dec, 1986 ($1.50, B&W, adults)
Silverwolf Comics

	GD25	FN65	NM94
1-Tim Vigil-c/a in all	3.60	9.00	18.00
2	2.60	6.50	13.00
3	2.20	5.50	11.00
4	2.00	5.00	10.00

GRIT GRADY (See Holyoke One-Shot No. 1)

GROO CARNIVAL, THE
Dec, 1991 ($8.95, color, trade paperback)
Epic Comics (Marvel)

	GD25	FN65	NM94
nn-Reprints Groo #9-12 by Aragones	1.50	4.50	9.00

GROO CHRONICLES, THE (Marvel)(Value: cover or less)

GROO SPECIAL
Oct, 1984 ($2.00, 52 pgs., Baxter paper)
Eclipse Comics

	GD25	FN65	NM94
1-Aragones-c/a	5.85	17.50	35.00

GROO THE WANDERER (See Destroyer Duck, Marvel Graphic Novel #32 & & Starslayer)
Dec, 1982 - No. 8, Apr, 1984
Pacific Comics

	GD25	FN65	NM94
1-Aragones-c/a(p) in all; Aragones biog., photo	4.20	12.50	25.00
2	3.00	7.50	15.00
3-7: 5-Deluxe paper (1.00-c)	2.40	6.00	12.00
8	1.80	4.50	9.00

GROO THE WANDERER (Sergio Aragones'...)
March, 1985 - Present
Epic Comics (Marvel)

	GD25	FN65	NM94
1-Aragones-c/a in all	1.80	4.50	9.00
2	1.00	2.50	5.00
3-10	.70	1.75	3.50
11-20	.50	1.25	2.50
21-30	.40	1.00	2.00
31-86: 50-($1.50, double size)		.60	1.25
87-99: 87-Begin $2.25, direct sale only, high quality paper issues	.45	1.10	2.25
100-($2.95, 52 pgs.)	.60	1.50	3.00

GROOVY (Cartoon Comics - not CCA approved)
March, 1968 - No. 3, July, 1968
Marvel Comics Group

	GD25	FN65	NM94
1-Monkees, Ringo Starr photos	4.00	11.00	22.00
2,3	3.20	8.00	16.00

GROUP LARUE, THE (Innovation)(Value: cover or less)

GUADALCANAL DIARY (Also see American Library)
1945 (One Shot) (See Thirty Seconds Over Tokyo)
David McKay Publishing Co.

	GD25	FN65	NM94
nn-B&W text & pictures; painted-c	22.00	65.00	130.00

GUARDIANS OF JUSTICE & THE O-FORCE (Shadow)(Value: cover or less)

GUARDIANS OF THE GALAXY (Also see The Defenders #26, Marvel Presents #3, Marvel Super-Heroes #18, Marvel Two-In-One #5)
June, 1990 - Present ($1.00, color)
Marvel Comics

	GD25	FN65	NM94
1-Valentino-c/a(p) begin; painted-c	1.60	4.00	8.00
2,3: 2-Zeck-c(i)	1.00	2.50	5.00
4-6: 5-McFarlane-c(i)	.70	1.75	3.50
7-10: 7-Intro Malevolence (Mephisto's daughter); Perez-c(i). 8-Intro Rancor (descendant of Wolverine) in cameo. 9-1st full app. Rancor; Rob Liefeld-c(i). 10-Jim Lee-c(i)	.60	1.50	3.00
11,12,15: 15-Starlin-c(i)	.40	1.00	2.00
13,14-1st app. Spirit of Vengeance (futuristic Ghost Rider). 14-Spirit of Vengeance vs. The Guardians	1.20	3.00	6.00
16-($1.50, 52 pgs.)-Starlin-c(i)	.40	1.00	2.00
17-23,26-36: 17-20-31st century Punishers storyline. 20-Last $1.00-c. 21-Rancor app. 22-Reintro Starhawk. 26-Origin retold. 27-28-Infinity War x-over; 27-Inhumans app.		.60	1.25
24-Silver Surfer-c/story; Ron Lim-c	.60	1.50	3.00
25-($2.50)-Prism foil-c; Silver Surfer/Galactus-c/s	.70	1.75	3.50
25-($2.50)-Without foil-c; newsstand edition	.40	1.00	2.00
Annual 1 (1991, $2.00, 68 pgs.)-2 pg. origin	.50	1.25	2.50
Annual 2 (1992, $2.25, 68 pgs.)-Spirit of Vengeance-c/story	.45	1.15	2.25

GUERRILLA WAR (Formerly Jungle War Stories)
No. 12, July-Sept, 1965 - No. 14, Mar, 1966
Dell Publishing Co.

	GD25	FN65	NM94
12-14	1.60	4.00	8.00

GUILTY (See Justice Traps the Guilty)

GULF FUNNY WEEKLY (Gulf Comic Weekly No. 1-4)
1933 - No. 422, 5/23/41 (in full color; 4 pgs.; tabloid size to 2/3/39; 2/10/39 on, regular comic book size)(early issues undated)
Gulf Oil Company (Giveaway)

	GD25	FN65	NM94
1	11.00	32.00	75.00
2-30	4.00	12.00	24.00
31-100	3.60	9.00	18.00
101-196	2.80	7.00	14.00
197-Wings Winfair begins(1/29/37); by Fred Meagher beginning in 1938	15.00	45.00	90.00
198-300 (Last tabloid size)	6.70	20.00	40.00
301-350 (Regular size)	4.00	10.00	20.00
351-422	2.80	7.00	14.00

GULLIVER'S TRAVELS (See Dell Jr. Treasury No. 3)
Sept-Nov, 1965 - No. 3, May, 1966
Dell Publishing Co.

	GD25	FN65	NM94
1	3.60	9.00	18.00
2,3	2.40	6.00	12.00

Grimjack #4, © First Comics

Guadalcanal Diary nn, © DMP

Guardians of the Galaxy #12, © MEG

The Gumps nn (1924), © Sidney Smith

Gunfighter #10, © WMG

Guns Against Gangsters #2, © NOVP

	GD25	FN65	NM94

GUMBY'S SUMMER FUN SPECIAL
July, 1987 ($2.50, color)
Comico

	GD25	FN65	NM94
1-Art Adams-c/a, B. Burden story	.90	2.25	4.50

GUMBY'S WINTER FUN SPECIAL
Dec, 1988 ($2.50, color, 44 pgs.)
Comico

	GD25	FN65	NM94
1-Art Adams-c/a	.50	1.25	2.50

GUMPS, THE
No. 2, 1918; 1924 - No. 8, 1931 (10x10")(52 pgs.; black & white)
Landfield-Kupfer/Cupples & Leon No. 2

	GD25	FN65	NM94
Book No.2(1918)-(Rare); 5-1/4x13-1/3"; paper cover; 36 pgs. daily strip reprints by Sidney Smith	28.00	85.00	170.00
nn(1924)-By Sidney Smith	17.00	50.00	100.00
2,3	14.00	42.00	85.00
4-7	12.50	37.50	75.00
8-(10x14"); 36 pgs.; B&W; National Arts Co.	12.50	37.50	75.00

GUMPS, THE (See Merry Christmas..., Popular & Super Comics)
No. 73, 1945; Mar-Apr, 1947 - No. 5, Nov-Dec, 1947
Dell Publ. Co./Bridgeport Herald Corp.

	GD25	FN65	NM94
4-Color 73 (Dell)(1945)	10.00	30.00	60.00
1 (3-4/47)	10.00	30.00	60.00
2-5	5.85	17.50	35.00

GUNFIGHTER (Fat & Slat #1-4) (Becomes Haunt of Fear #15 on)
No. 5, Summer, 1948 - No. 14, Mar-Apr, 1950
E. C. Comics (Fables Publ. Co.)

	GD25	FN65	NM94
5,6-Moon Girl in each	38.00	115.00	265.00
7-14: 14-Bondage-c	25.00	75.00	175.00

NOTE: ***Craig & H. C. Kiefer** art in most issues. **Craig** c-5, 6, 13, 14. **Feldstein/Craig** a-10. **Feldstein** a-7-11. **Harrison/Wood** a-13, 14. **Ingels** a-5-14; c-7-12.*

GUNFIGHTERS, THE
1963 - 1964
Super Comics (Reprints)

	GD25	FN65	NM94
10-12,15,16,18: 10,11-r/Billy the Kid #s? 12-r/The Rider #5(Swift Arrow). 15-r/Straight Arrow #42; Powell-r. 16-r/Billy the Kid #?(Toby). 18-r/ The Rider #3; Severin-c	1.00	2.50	5.00

GUNFIGHTERS, THE (Formerly Kid Montana)
No. 51, 10/66 - No. 52, 10/67; No. 53, 6/79 - No. 85, 7/84
Charlton Comics

	GD25	FN65	NM94
51,52	1.20	3.00	6.00
53-85: 53,54-Williamson/Torres-r/Six Gun Heroes #47,49. 56-Williamson/ Severin-c; Severin-r/Sheriff of Tombstone #1. 85-S&K-r/1955 Bullseye	.60	1.50	3.00

GUN GLORY (See 4-Color No. 846)

GUNHAWK, THE (Formerly Whip Wilson)(See Wild Western)
No. 12, Nov, 1950 - No. 18, Dec, 1951
Marvel Comics/Atlas (MCI)

	GD25	FN65	NM94
12	10.00	30.00	60.00
13-18: 13-Tuska-a. 16-Colan-a. 18-Maneely-c	8.35	25.00	50.00

GUNHAWKS (Gunhawk No. 7)
October, 1972 - No. 7, October, 1973
Marvel Comics Group

	GD25	FN65	NM94
1-Reno Jones, Kid Cassidy; Shores-c/a(p)	.80	2.00	4.00
2-7: 6-Kid Cassidy dies. 7-Reno Jones solo	.60	1.50	3.00

GUNHED (Viz)(Value: cover or less)

GUNMASTER (Becomes Judo Master #89 on; formerly Six-Gun Heroes)
9/64 - No. 4, 1965; No. 84, 7/65 - No. 88, 3-4/66; No. 89, 10/67
Charlton Comics

	GD25	FN65	NM94
V1#1	2.40	6.00	12.00
2-4,V5#84-86: 4-Blank inside-c	1.40	3.50	7.00
V5#87-89	1.00	2.50	5.00

NOTE: *Vol. 5 was originally cancelled with #88 (3-4/66). #89 on, became Judo Master, then later in 1967, Charlton issued #89 as a Gunmaster one-shot.*

GUNS AGAINST GANGSTERS (True-To-Life Romances #8 on)
Sept-Oct, 1948 - V2#1, Sept-Oct, 1949
Curtis Publications/Novelty Press

	GD25	FN65	NM94
1-Toni Gayle begins by Schomburg	13.00	40.00	90.00
2	10.00	30.00	60.00
3-6, V2#1,2: 6-Toni Gayle-c	9.15	27.50	55.00

NOTE: ***L. B. Cole** c-1-6, V2#1, 2; a-1, 2, 3(2), 4-6.*

GUNSLINGER (See 4-Color No. 1220)

GUNSLINGER (Formerly Tex Dawson...)
No. 2, April, 1973 - No. 3, June, 1973
Marvel Comics Group

	GD25	FN65	NM94
2,3		.50	1.00

GUNSMOKE
Apr-May, 1949 - No. 16, Jan, 1952
Western Comics (Youthful Magazines)

	GD25	FN65	NM94
1-Gunsmoke & Masked Marvel begin by Ingels; Ingels bondage-c	24.00	73.00	170.00
2-Ingels-c/a(2)	13.50	41.00	95.00
3-Ingels bondage-c/a	11.50	34.00	80.00
4-6: Ingels-c	10.00	30.00	65.00
7-10	6.35	19.00	38.00
11-16: 15,16-Western/horror stories	4.70	14.00	28.00

NOTE: ***Stallman** a-11, 14. **Wildey** a-15, 16.*

GUNSMOKE (TV)
No. 679, 2/56 - No. 27, 6-7/61; 2/69 - No. 6, 2/70
Dell Publishing Co./Gold Key (All have James Arness photo-c)

	GD25	FN65	NM94
4-Color 679(#1)	11.00	32.00	75.00
4-Color 720,769,797,844	5.85	17.50	35.00
6(11-1/57-58), 7	5.85	17.50	35.00
8,9,11,12-Williamson-a in all, 4 pgs. each	7.00	21.00	42.00
10-Williamson/Crandall-a, 4 pgs.	7.00	21.00	42.00
13-27	5.35	16.00	32.00
Gunsmoke Film Story (11/62-G.K. Giant) No. 30008-211	6.70	20.00	40.00
1 (Gold Key)	4.00	11.00	22.00
2-6('69-70)	2.40	6.00	12.00

GUNSMOKE TRAIL
June, 1957 - No. 4, Dec, 1957
Ajax-Farrell Publ./Four Star Comic Corp.

	GD25	FN65	NM94
1	6.70	20.00	40.00
2-4	4.00	11.00	22.00

GUNSMOKE WESTERN (Formerly Western Tales of Black Rider)
No. 32, Dec, 1955 - No. 77, July, 1963
Atlas Comics No. 32-35(CPS/NPI); Marvel No. 36 on

	GD25	FN65	NM94
32	10.00	30.00	60.00
33,35,36-Williamson-a in each: 5,6 & 4 pgs. plus Drucker-a #33. 33-Kinstler-a?	8.35	25.00	50.00
34-Baker-a, 4 pgs.	4.20	12.50	25.00
37-Davis-a(2); Williamson text illo	4.70	14.00	28.00
38,39: 39-Williamson text illo (unsigned)	4.00	11.00	22.00
40-Williamson/Mayo-a, 4 pgs.	5.00	15.00	30.00
41,42,45-49,51-55,57-60: 49,52-Kid from Texas story. 57-1st Two Gun Kid by Severin. 60-Sam Hawk app. in Kid Colt	2.80	7.00	14.00
43,44-Torres-a	3.60	9.00	18.00
50,61-Crandall-a	4.00	11.00	22.00
56-Matt Baker-a	3.60	9.00	18.00

	GD25	FN65	NM94
62-71,73-77	2.40	6.00	12.00
72-Origin Kid Colt	3.60	9.00	18.00

NOTE: ***Colan** a-36, 37, 39, 72, 76. **Davis** a-37, 52, 54, 55; c-50, 54. **Ditko** a-66. **Drucker** a-34. **Heath** c-33. **Jack Keller** a-40, 60, 72; c-72. **Kirby** a-47, 50, 51, 59, 62(3), 63-67, 69, 71, 73, 77; c-56(w/**Ditko**),57, 58, 60, 61(w/**Ayers**), 62, 63, 66, 68, 69, 71-77. **Severin** a-59-61; c-34, 39, 42, 43. **Tuska** a-34. **Wildey** a-10, 37, 42, 56, 57. Kid Colt in all. Two-Gun Kid in No. 57, 59, 60-63. Wyatt Earp in No. 45, 48, 49, 52, 54, 55, 58.*

GUNS OF FACT & FICTION (See A-1 Comics No. 13)

GUN THAT WON THE WEST, THE
1956 (24 pgs.; regular size) (Giveaway)
Winchester-Western Division & Olin Mathieson Chemical Corp.

	GD25	FN65	NM94
nn-Painted-c	4.20	12.50	25.00

GUY GARDNER (Also see Green Lantern #59)
Oct, 1992 - Present ($1.25, color)
DC Comics

	GD25	FN65	NM94
1-8: 1-Staton-c/a(p) begin		.60	1.25

GUY GARDNER REBORN
1992 - Book 3, 1992 ($4.95, color, mini-series)
DC Comics

	GD25	FN65	NM94
1-3: Staton-c/a(p). 1-Lobo-c/cameo. 2,3-Lobo-c/s	1.00	2.50	5.00

GYPSY COLT (See 4-Color No. 568)

GYRO GEARLOOSE (See Dynabrite Comics, Walt Disney's C&S #140 & Walt Disney Showcase #18)
No. 1047, Nov-Jan/1959-60 - May-July, 1962 (Disney)
Dell Publishing Co.

	GD25	FN65	NM94
4-Color 1047 (No. 1)-Barks-c/a	10.00	30.00	60.00
4-Color 1095,1184-All by Carl Barks	6.70	20.00	40.00
4-Color 1267-Barks c/a, 4 pgs.	5.35	16.00	32.00
No. 01-329-207 (5-7/62)-Barks-c only	4.00	10.50	21.00

HACKER FILES, THE
Aug, 1992 - No. 12, 1993 ($1.95, color)
DC Comics

	GD25	FN65	NM94
1-12: 1-Sutton-a(p) begins; computer generated-c	.40	1.00	2.00

HAGAR THE HORRIBLE (See Comics Reading Libraries)

HA HA COMICS (Teepee Tim No. 100 on; also see Giggle Comics)
Oct, 1943 - No. 99, Jan, 1955
Scope Mag.(Creston Publ.) No. 1-80/American Comics Group

	GD25	FN65	NM94
1	20.00	60.00	140.00
2	10.00	30.00	65.00
3-5: Ken Hultgren-a begins?	7.00	21.00	42.00
6-10	5.85	17.50	35.00
11-20: 14-Infinity-c	4.20	12.50	25.00
21-40	4.00	10.00	20.00
41-94,96-99: 49-XMas-c	3.20	8.00	16.00
95-3-D effect-c	10.00	30.00	60.00

HAIR BEAR BUNCH, THE (TV) (See Fun-In No. 13)
Feb, 1972 - No. 9, Feb, 1974 (Hanna-Barbera)
Gold Key

	GD25	FN65	NM94
1	1.60	4.00	8.00
2-9	1.00	2.50	5.00

HALLELUJAH TRAIL, THE (See Movie Classics)

HALL OF FAME FEATURING THE T.H.U.N.D.E.R. AGENTS
May, 1983 - No. 3, Dec, 1983
JC Productions(Archie Comics Group)

	GD25	FN65	NM94
1-3: Thunder Agents-r(Crandall, Tuska, Wood-a)		.50	1.00

HALLOWEEN HORROR (Eclipse) (Value: cover or less)

HALO JONES (See The Ballad of...)

HAMMERLOCKE
Sept, 1992 - No. 9, May, 1993 ($1.75, color, mini-series)
DC Comics

	GD25	FN65	NM94
1-($2.50, 52 pgs.)	.50	1.25	2.50
2-9	.35	.90	1.75

HAMMER OF GOD (First) (Value: cover or less)

HAMMER OF GOD: SWORD OF JUSTICE (First) (Value: cover or less)

HANDBOOK OF THE CONAN UNIVERSE, THE
June, 1985 ($1.25, color, one-shot)
Marvel Comics

	GD25	FN65	NM94
1		.60	1.25

HAND OF FATE (Formerly Men Against Crime)
No. 8, Dec, 1951 - No. 26, March, 1955
Ace Magazines

	GD25	FN65	NM94
8: Surrealistic text story	16.00	48.00	110.00
9,10	10.00	30.00	60.00
11-18,20,22,23	7.50	22.50	45.00
19-Bondage, hypo needle scenes	9.15	27.50	55.00
21-Necronomicon story; drug belladonna used	10.00	30.00	60.00
24-Electric chair-c	10.00	30.00	70.00
25(11/54), 25(12/54)	6.35	19.00	38.00
26-Nostrand-a	8.35	25.00	50.00

NOTE: ***Cameron** a-9, 10, 19-25; c-13. **Sekowsky** a-8, 9, 13, 14.*

HAND OF FATE (Eclipse) (Value: cover or less)

HANDS OF THE DRAGON
June, 1975
Seaboard Periodicals (Atlas)

	GD25	FN65	NM94
1-Origin; Mooney inks		.50	1.00

HANGMAN COMICS (Special Comics No. 1; Black Hood No. 9 on)
(Also see Flyman, Mighty Comics, Mighty Crusaders & Pep Comics)
No. 2, Spring, 1942 - No. 8, Fall, 1943
MLJ Magazines

	GD25	FN65	NM94
2-The Hangman, Boy Buddies begin	108.00	325.00	650.00
3-8: 3-Beheading splash pg. 8-2nd app. Super Duck (ties w/Jolly Jingles #11)	56.00	168.00	335.00

NOTE: ***Fuje** a-7(3), 8(3); c-3. **Reinman** c/a-3. Bondage c-3.*

HANK
1946
Pentagon Publishing Co.

	GD25	FN65	NM94
nn-Coulton Waugh's newspaper reprint	5.85	17.50	35.00

HANNA-BARBERA (See Golden Comics Digest No. 2, 7, 11)

HANNA-BARBERA BAND WAGON (TV)
Oct, 1962 - No. 3, April, 1963
Gold Key

	GD25	FN65	NM94
1,2-Giants, 84 pgs.	5.65	17.00	45.00
3-Regular size	5.00	15.00	30.00

HANNA-BARBERA GIANT SIZE
Oct, 1992 - Present ($2.25, color, 68 pgs.)
Harvey Comics

	GD25	FN65	NM94
V2#1-Flintstones, Yogi Bear, Magilla Gorilla, Huckleberry Hound, Quick Draw McGraw, Yakky Doodle & Chopper, Jetsons & other stories	.45	1.15	2.25

HANNA-BARBERA HI-ADVENTURE HEROES (See Hi-Adventure...)

HANNA-BARBERA PARADE (TV)
Sept, 1971 - No. 10, Dec, 1972
Charlton Comics

	GD25	FN65	NM94
1	4.70	14.00	28.00
2-10: 7-"Summer Picnic"-52 pgs.	3.00	7.50	15.00

NOTE: *No. 4 (1/72) went on sale late in 1972 with the January 1973 issues.*

HANNA-BARBERA SPOTLIGHT (See Spotlight)

HANNA-BARBERA SUPER TV HEROES (TV)

Ha Ha Comics #12, © ACG

The Hand of Fate #10, © ACE

Hangman Comics #7, © AP

Hanna-Barbera Super TV Heroes #1, © Hanna-Barbera

Hap Hazard Comics #1, © ACE

Happy Comics #19, © STD

	GD25	FN65	NM94

April, 1968 - No. 7, Oct, 1969 (Hanna-Barbera)
Gold Key

	GD25	FN65	NM94
1-The Birdman, The Herculoids(ends #6; not in #2), Moby Dick, Young Samson & Goliath(ends #2,4), and The Mighty Mightor begin; Spiegle-a in all	11.50	34.00	80.00
2-The Galaxy Trio app.; Shazzan begins; 12 & 15 cent versions exist	9.15	27.50	55.00
3-7: The Space Ghost app. in #3,6,7	7.50	22.50	45.00

HANNA-BARBERA TV FUN FAVORITES (See Golden Comics Digest #2,7,11)

HANNA-BARBERA (TV STARS) (See TV Stars)

HANS BRINKER (See 4-Color No. 1273)

HANS CHRISTIAN ANDERSEN
1953 (100 pgs. - Special Issue)
Ziff-Davis Publ. Co.

	GD25	FN65	NM94
nn-Danny Kaye (movie)-Photo-c	11.00	32.00	75.00

HANSEL & GRETEL (See 4-Color No. 590)

HANSI, THE GIRL WHO LOVED THE SWASTIKA (Spire Christian) (Value: cover or less)

HANS UND FRITZ
1917 (10x13'/2"; 1916 strip-r in B&W); 1929 (28 pgs.; 10x13-1/2")
The Saalfield Publishing Co.

	GD25	FN65	NM94
nn-By R. Dirks	46.00	138.00	275.00
193-(Very Rare)-By R. Dirks; contains B&W Sunday strip reprints of Katzenjammer Kids & Hawkshaw the Detective from 1916	46.00	138.00	275.00
...The Funny Larks Of 2(1929)	46.00	138.00	275.00

HAP HAZARD COMICS (Real Love No. 25 on)
1944 - No. 24, Feb, 1949
Ace Magazines (Readers' Research)

	GD25	FN65	NM94
1	8.35	25.00	50.00
2	4.20	12.50	25.00
3-10	3.20	8.00	16.00
11-13,15-24	2.40	6.00	12.00
14-Feldstein-c (4/47)	5.00	15.00	30.00

HAP HOPPER (See Comics Revue No. 2)

HAPPIEST MILLIONAIRE, THE (See Movie Comics)

HAPPINESS AND HEALING FOR YOU (Also see Oral Roberts'...)
1955 (36 pgs.; slick cover) (Oral Roberts Giveaway)
Commercial Comics

	GD25	FN65	NM94
nn	8.35	25.00	50.00

NOTE: *The success of this book prompted Oral Roberts to go into the publishing business himself to produce his own material.*

HAPPI TIM (See March of Comics No. 182)

HAPPY COMICS (Happy Rabbit No. 41 on)
Aug, 1943 - No. 40, Dec, 1950 (Companion to Goofy Comics)
Nedor Publ./Standard Comics (Animated Cartoons)

	GD25	FN65	NM94
1	16.00	48.00	110.00
2	9.15	27.50	55.00
3-10	5.85	17.50	35.00
11-19	4.00	12.00	24.00
20-31,34-37-Frazetta text illos in all (2 in #34&35, 3 in #27,28,30). 27-Al Fago-a	4.70	14.00	28.00
32-Frazetta-a, 7 pgs. plus two text illos; Roussos-a	10.00	30.00	70.00
33-Frazetta-a(2), 6 pgs. each (Scarce)	16.00	48.00	110.00
38-40	3.00	7.50	15.00

HAPPY DAYS (TV)(See Kite Fun Book)
March, 1979 - No. 6, Feb, 1980
Gold Key

	GD25	FN65	NM94
1	1.00	2.50	5.00
2-6	.60	1.50	3.00

HAPPY HOLIDAY (See March of Comics No. 181)

HAPPY HOOLIGAN (See Alphonse...)
1903 (18 pgs.) (Sunday strip reprints in color)
Hearst's New York American-Journal

	GD25	FN65	NM94
Book 1-by Fred Opper	50.00	150.00	300.00
50 Pg. Edition(1903)-10x15" in color	54.00	162.00	325.00

HAPPY HOOLIGAN (Handy...) (See The Travels of...)
1908 (32 pgs. in color) (10x15"; cardboard covers)
Frederick A. Stokes Co.

	GD25	FN65	NM94
nn	46.00	138.00	275.00

HAPPY HOOLIGAN (Story of...)
No. 281, 1932 (16 pgs.; 9-1/2x12"; softcover)
McLoughlin Bros.

	GD25	FN65	NM94
281-Three-color text, pictures on heavy paper	14.00	42.00	85.00

HAPPY HOULIHANS (Saddle Justice No. 3 on; see Blackstone, The Magician Detective)
Fall, 1947 - No. 2, Winter, 1947-48
E. C. Comics

	GD25	FN65	NM94
1-Origin Moon Girl	32.00	95.00	225.00
2	17.00	50.00	115.00

HAPPY JACK
August, 1957 - No. 2, Nov, 1957
Red Top (Decker)

	GD25	FN65	NM94
V1#1,2	3.00	7.50	15.00

HAPPY JACK HOWARD
1957
Red Top (Farrell)/Decker

	GD25	FN65	NM94
nn-Reprints Handy Andy story from E. C. Dandy Comics #5, renamed "Happy Jack"	4.00	10.00	20.00

HAPPY RABBIT (Formerly Happy Comics)
No. 41, Feb, 1951 - No. 48, April, 1952
Standard Comics (Animated Cartoons)

	GD25	FN65	NM94
41	4.00	10.00	20.00
42-48	2.00	5.00	10.00

HARBINGER
Jan, 1992 - Present ($1.95, color)
Valiant

	GD25	FN65	NM94
0-(Advance)	22.00	65.00	150.00
1-1st app.	14.00	43.00	100.00
2	7.50	22.50	45.00
3	4.00	10.00	20.00
4	5.85	17.50	35.00
5,6	2.40	6.00	12.00
7-9: 8,9-Unity x-overs. 8-Miller-c. 9-Simonson-c	1.40	3.50	7.00
10-1st app. H.A.R.D Corps (10/92)	1.60	4.00	8.00
11-18	.50	1.25	2.50
Trade paperback nn (1992, $9.95)-Reprints #1-4 & comes polybagged with a copy of Harbinger #0 w/new-c	6.70	20.00	40.00

HARD BOILED (Dark Horse) (Value: cover or less)

H.A.R.D. CORPS, THE (See Harbinger #10)
Dec, 1992 - Present ($2.25, color)
Valiant

	GD25	FN65	NM94
1-(Advance)	14.00	43.00	100.00
1-($2.50)-Gatefold-c by Jim Lee & Bob Layton	1.00	2.50	5.00

	GD25	FN65	NM94
2-6	.50	1.25	2.50

HARD LOOKS (Dark Horse)(Value: cover or less)

HARDY BOYS, THE (Disney)(See 4-Color No. 760, 830, 887, 964)

HARDY BOYS, THE (TV)
April, 1970 - No. 4, Jan, 1971
Gold Key

	GD25	FN65	NM94
1	2.00	5.00	10.00
2-4	1.20	3.00	6.00

HARLEM GLOBETROTTERS (TV) (See Fun-In No. 8, 10)
April, 1972 - No. 12, Jan, 1975 (Hanna-Barbera)
Gold Key

	GD25	FN65	NM94
1	1.20	3.00	6.00
2-12	.60	1.50	3.00

NOTE: #4, 8, and 12 contain 16 extra pages of advertising.

HAROLD TEEN (See 4-Color #2, 209, Popular Comics, Super Comics & Treasure Box of Famous Comics)

HAROLD TEEN (Adv. of...)
1929-31 (36-52 pgs.) (Paper covers)
Cupples & Leon Co.

	GD25	FN65	NM94
nn-B&W daily strip reprints by Carl Ed	14.00	42.00	85.00

HARVEY
Oct, 1970; No. 2, 12/70; No. 3, 6/72 - No. 6, 12/72
Marvel Comics Group

	GD25	FN65	NM94
1	1.20	3.00	6.00
2-6	.80	2.00	4.00

HARVEY COLLECTORS COMICS (Richie Rich Collectors Comics #10 on, cover title only)
Sept, 1975 - No. 15, Jan, 1978; No. 16, Oct, 1979 (52 pgs.)
Harvey Publications

	GD25	FN65	NM94
1-Reprints Richie Rich #1,2	1.00	2.50	5.00
2-10	.60	1.50	3.00
11-16: 16-Sad Sack-r		.60	1.25

NOTE: *All reprints: Casper-#2, 7, Richie Rich-#1, 3, 5, 6, 8-15, Sad Sack-#16. Wendy-#4. #6 titled 'Richie Rich...'on inside.*

HARVEY COMICS HITS
No. 51, Oct, 1951 - No. 62, Dec, 1952
Harvey Publications

	GD25	FN65	NM94
51-The Phantom	13.50	41.00	95.00
52-Steve Canyon	8.35	25.00	50.00
53-Mandrake the Magician	11.50	34.00	80.00
54-Tim Tyler's Tales of Jungle Terror	7.50	22.50	45.00
55-Mary Worth	4.00	12.00	24.00
56-The Phantom; bondage-c	11.50	34.00	80.00
57-Rip Kirby-"Kidnap Racket;" entire book by Alex Raymond	10.00	30.00	65.00
58-Girls in White	4.00	11.00	22.00
59-Tales of the Invisible Scarlet O'Neil	7.50	22.50	45.00
60-Paramount Animated Comics #1 (2nd app. Baby Huey); 1st Harvey app. Baby Huey	20.00	60.00	140.00
61-Casper the Friendly Ghost; 1st Harvey Casper	24.00	72.00	165.00
62-Paramount Animated Comics	8.35	25.00	50.00

HARVEY COMICS LIBRARY
April, 1952 - No. 2, 1952
Harvey Publications

	GD25	FN65	NM94
1-Teen-Age Dope Slaves as exposed by Rex Morgan, M.D.; drug propaganda story; used in **SOTI**, pg. 27	47.00	140.00	325.00
(Prices vary widely on this book)			
2-Sparkle Plenty (Dick Tracy in "Blackmail Terror")	12.00	36.00	85.00

HARVEY COMICS SPOTLIGHT
Sept, 1987 - No. 4, Mar, 1988 (#1-3: 75 cents, #4: $1.00)
Harvey Comics

	GD25	FN65	NM94
1-4: 1,2-new material. 1-Sad Sack, 2-Baby Huey, 3-Little Dot. 4-Little Audrey		.50	1.00

HARVEY HITS
Sept, 1957 - No. 122, Nov, 1967
Harvey Publications

	GD25	FN65	NM94
1-The Phantom	16.00	48.00	110.00
2-Rags Rabbit (10/57)	2.40	6.00	12.00
3-Richie Rich (11/57)-r/Little Dot; 1st book devoted to Richie Rich; see Little Dot for 1st app.; X-mas-c	54.00	160.00	375.00
4-Little Dot's Uncles (12/57)	10.00	30.00	65.00
5-Stevie Mazie's Boy Friend	1.80	4.50	9.00
6-The Phantom (2/58); Kirby-c; 2pg. Powell-a	10.00	30.00	70.00
7-Wendy the Witch	10.00	30.00	65.00
8-Sad Sack's Army Life	4.00	10.50	21.00
9-Richie Rich's Golden Deeds-r (2nd book devoted to Richie Rich)	32.00	95.00	225.00
10-Little Lotta	7.50	22.50	45.00
11-Little Audrey Summer Fun (7/58)	5.35	16.00	32.00
12-The Phantom; Kirby-c; 2pg. Powell-a (8/58)	8.35	25.00	50.00
13-Little Dot's Uncles (9/58); Richie Rich 1pg.	7.50	22.50	45.00
14-Herman & Katnip (10/58)	2.40	6.00	12.00
15-The Phantom (12/58)-1 pg. origin	8.00	24.00	48.00
16-Wendy the Witch (1/59)	5.85	17.50	35.00
17-Sad Sack's Army Life (2/59)	3.20	8.00	16.00
18-Buzzy & the Crow	3.00	7.50	15.00
19-Little Audrey (4/59)	4.00	10.50	21.00
20-Casper & Spooky	4.35	13.00	26.00
21-Wendy the Witch	4.00	10.00	20.00
22-Sad Sack's Army Life	2.40	6.00	12.00
23-Wendy the Witch (8/59)	4.00	10.00	20.00
24-Little Dot's Uncles (9/59); Richie Rich 1pg.	5.85	17.50	35.00
25-Herman & Katnip (10/59)	2.00	5.00	10.00
26-The Phantom (11/59)	7.50	22.50	45.00
27-Wendy the Good Little Witch	4.00	10.00	20.00
28-Sad Sack's Army Life	1.20	3.00	6.00
29-Harvey-Toon (No.1)('60); Casper, Buzzy	3.60	9.00	18.00
30-Wendy the Witch (3/60)	4.00	11.00	22.00
31-Herman & Katnip (4/60)	1.00	2.50	5.00
32-Sad Sack's Army Life (5/60)	1.20	3.00	6.00
33-Wendy the Witch (6/60)	4.00	11.00	22.00
34-Harvey-Toon (7/60)	2.00	5.00	10.00
35-Funday Funnies (8/60)	1.00	2.50	5.00
36-The Phantom (1960)	5.85	17.50	35.00
37-Casper & Nightmare	3.20	8.00	16.00
38-Harvey-Toon	2.40	6.00	12.00
39-Sad Sack's Army Life (12/60)	1.20	3.00	6.00
40-Funday Funnies	.80	2.00	4.00
41-Herman & Katnip	.80	2.00	4.00
42-Harvey-Toon (3/61)	1.20	3.00	6.00
43-Sad Sack's Army Life (4/61)	1.20	3.00	6.00
44-The Phantom (5/61)	5.85	17.50	35.00
45-Casper & Nightmare	2.40	6.00	12.00
46-Harvey-Toon (7/61)	1.20	3.00	6.00
47-Sad Sack's Army Life (8/61)	1.20	3.00	6.00
48-The Phantom (9/61)	5.00	15.00	30.00
49-Stumbo the Giant (1st app. in Hot Stuff)	7.50	22.50	45.00
50-Harvey-Toon (11/61)	1.20	3.00	6.00
51-Sad Sack's Army Life (12/61)	1.20	3.00	6.00
52-Casper & Nightmare	2.40	6.00	12.00
53-Harvey-Toons (2/62)	1.00	2.50	5.00
54-Stumbo the Giant	4.00	12.00	24.00
55-Sad Sack's Army Life (4/62)	1.20	3.00	6.00
56-Casper & Nightmare	2.40	6.00	12.00

Harvey Comics Hits #57, © HARV

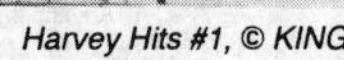
Harvey Hits #1, © KING

Harvey Hits #3, © HARV

Haunted Library #21, © CC

Haunted Thrills #14, © AJAX

The Haunt of Fear #11, © WMG

	GD25	FN65	NM94
57-Stumbo the Giant	4.00	12.00	24.00
58-Sad Sack's Army Life	1.20	3.00	6.00
59-Casper & Nightmare (7/62)	2.40	6.00	12.00
60-Stumbo the Giant (9/62)	4.00	12.00	24.00
61-Sad Sack's Army Life	1.20	3.00	6.00
62-Casper & Nightmare	2.00	5.00	10.00
63-Stumbo the Giant	4.00	12.00	24.00
64-Sad Sack's Army Life (1/63)	1.20	3.00	6.00
65-Casper & Nightmare	2.00	5.00	10.00
66-Stumbo The Giant	4.00	12.00	24.00
67-Sad Sack's Army Life (4/63)	1.20	3.00	6.00
68-Casper & Nightmare	2.00	5.00	10.00
69-Stumbo the Giant (6/63)	4.00	12.00	24.00
70-Sad Sack's Army Life (7/63)	1.20	3.00	6.00
71-Casper & Nightmare (8/63)	.80	2.00	4.00
72-Stumbo the Giant	4.00	12.00	24.00
73-Little Sad Sack (10/63)	1.20	3.00	6.00
74-Sad Sack's Muttsy... (11/63)	1.20	3.00	6.00
75-Casper & Nightmare	1.60	4.00	8.00
76-Little Sad Sack	1.20	3.00	6.00
77-Sad Sack's Muttsy...	1.20	3.00	6.00
78-Stumbo the Giant	4.00	12.00	24.00
79-87: 79-Little Sad Sack (4/64). 80-Sad Sack's Muttsy... (5/64). 81-Little Sad Sack. 82-Sad Sack's Muttsy... 83-Little Sad Sack(8/64). 84-Sad Sack's Muttsy... 85-Gabby Gob (No.1)(10/64). 86-G. I. Juniors (No.1). 87-Sad Sack's Muttsy... (12/64)	1.20	3.00	6.00
88-Stumbo the Giant (1/65)	4.00	12.00	24.00
89-122: 89-Sad Sack's Muttsy... 90-Gabby Gob. 91-G. I. Juniors. 92-Sad Sack's Muttsy... (5/65). 93-Sadie Sack (6/65). 94-Gabby Gob. 95-G. I. Juniors. 96-Sad Sack's Muttsy... (9/65). 97-Gabby Gob. 98-G. I. Juniors (11/65). 99-Sad Sack's Muttsy... (12/65). 100-Gabby Gob. 101-G. I. Juniors (2/66). 102-Sad Sack's Muttsy... (3/66). 103-Gabby Gob. 104-G. I. Juniors. 105-Sad Sack's Muttsy... 106-Gabby Gob (7/66). 107-G. I. Juniors (8/66). 108-Sad Sack's Muttsy... 109-Gabby Gob. 110-G. I. Juniors (11/66). 111-Sad Sack's Muttsy... (12/66). 112-G. I. Juniors. 113-Sad Sack's Muttsy... 114-G. I. Juniors. 115-Sad Sack's Muttsy... 116-G. I. Juniors. 117-Sad Sack's Muttsy... 118-G. I. Juniors. 119-Sad Sack's Muttsy... (8/67). 120-G. I. Juniors (9/67). 121-Sad Sack's Muttsy... (10/67). 122-G. I. Juniors	1.00	2.50	5.00

HARVEY HITS COMICS
Nov, 1986 - No. 6, Oct, 1987
Harvey Publications

	GD25	FN65	NM94
1-6: Little Lotta, Little Dot, Wendy & Baby Huey		.50	1.00

HARVEY POP COMICS (Teen Humor)
Oct, 1968 - No. 2, Nov, 1969 (Both are 68 pg. Giants)
Harvey Publications

	GD25	FN65	NM94
1,2-The Cowsills	2.00	5.00	10.00

HARVEY 3-D HITS (See Sad Sack)

HARVEY-TOON (...S) (See Harvey Hits No. 29, 34, 38, 42, 46, 50, 53)

HARVEY WISEGUYS (...Digest #? on)
Nov, 1987; #2, Nov, 1988; #3, Apr, 1989 - No. 4, Nov, 1989 (98 pgs., digest-size, $1.25-$1.75)
Harvey Comics

	GD25	FN65	NM94
1,2: 1-Hot Stuff, Spooky, etc. 2 (68 pgs.)		.60	1.25
3,4	.35	.90	1.75

HATARI (See Movie Classics)

HATHAWAYS, THE (See 4-Color No. 1298)

HAUNTED (See This Magazine Is Haunted)

HAUNTED (Baron Weirwulf's Haunted Library #21 on)
9/71 - No. 30, 11/76; No. 31, 9/77 - No. 75, 9/84
Charlton Comics

	GD25	FN65	NM94
1	1.60	4.00	8.00
2-5	.80	2.00	4.00
6-21	.60	1.50	3.00
22-75: 64,75-r	.30	.75	1.50

NOTE: ***Aparo** c-45. **Ditko** a-1-8, 11-16, 18, 23, 24, 28, 30, 34r, 36r, 39-42r, 47r, 49-51r, 57, 60, 74. c-1-7, 11, 13, 14, 16, 30, 41, 47, 49-51, 74. **Howard** a-18, 22, 32. **Morisi** a-13. **Newton** a-17, 21, 59r; c-21, 22(painted). **Staton** a-18, 21, 22, 30, 33; c-18, 33. **Sutton** a-21, 22, 38; c-15, 17, 18, 23(painted), 24(painted), 64r. #51 reprints #1; #49 reprints Tales of the Mysterious Traveler #4.*

HAUNTED LOVE
April, 1973 - No. 11, Sept, 1975
Charlton Comics

	GD25	FN65	NM94
1-Tom Sutton-a (16 pgs.)	1.00	2.50	5.00
2,3,6-11	.40	1.00	2.00
4,5-Ditko-a	.50	1.25	2.50
Modern Comics #1(1978)		.50	1.00

NOTE: ***Howard** a-8i. **Newton** c-8, 9. **Staton** a-5.*

HAUNTED THRILLS
June, 1952 - No. 18, Nov-Dec, 1954
Ajax/Farrell Publications

	GD25	FN65	NM94
1-r/Ellery Queen #1	16.00	48.00	110.00
2-L. B. Cole-a r-/Ellery Queen #1	10.00	30.00	65.00
3-5: 3-Drug use story	9.15	27.50	55.00
6-12: 7-Hitler story. 11-Nazi death camp story	7.50	22.50	45.00
13,16-18: 18-Lingerie panels	5.85	17.50	35.00
14-Jesus Christ apps. in story by Webb	5.85	17.50	35.00
15-Jo-Jo-r	6.35	19.00	38.00

NOTE: ***Kamenish** art in most issues. **Webb** a-12.*

HAUNT OF FEAR (Formerly Gunfighter)
No. 15, May-June, 1950 - No. 28, Nov-Dec, 1954
E. C. Comics

	GD25	FN65	NM94
15(#1, 1950)(Scarce)	157.00	470.00	1100.00
16	80.00	240.00	550.00
17-Origin of Crypt of Terror, Vault of Horror, & Haunt of Fear; used in **SOTI**, pg. 43; last pg. Ingels-a used by N.Y. Legis. Comm.; story "Monster Maker" based on Frankenstein	80.00	240.00	550.00
4	57.00	170.00	400.00
5-Injury-to-eye panel, pg. 4	43.00	130.00	300.00
6-10: 8-Shrunken head cover. 10-Ingels biog.	31.00	92.00	215.00
11-13,15-18: 11-Kamen biog. 12-Feldstein biog. 16,18-Ray Bradbury adaptations. 18-Ray Bradbury biog.	22.00	65.00	150.00
14-Origin Old Witch by Ingels	34.00	100.00	235.00
19-Used in **SOTI**, ill.-"A comic book baseball game" & Senate investigation on juvenile delinq. bondage/decapitation-c	28.00	85.00	200.00
20-Feldstein-r/Vault of Horror #12	20.00	60.00	140.00
21,22,25,27: 27-Cannibalism story; Wertham cameo	13.00	40.00	90.00
23-Used in **SOTI**, pg. 241	14.00	43.00	100.00
24-Used in Senate Investigative Report, pg.8	13.00	40.00	90.00
26-Contains anti-censorship editorial, 'Are you a Red Dupe?'	13.00	40.00	90.00
28-Low distribution	14.00	43.00	100.00

NOTE: *(Canadian reprints known; see Table of Contents). **Craig** a-15-17, 5, 7, 10, 12, 13; c-15-17, 5-7. **Crandall** a-20, 21, 26, 27. **Davis** a-4-26, 28. **Evans** a-15-19, 22-25, 27. **Feldstein** a-15-17, 20; c-4, 8-10. **Ingels** a-16, 17, 4-28; c-11-28. **Kamen** a-16, 4, 6, 7, 9-11, 13-19, 21-28. **Krigstein** a-28. **Kurtzman** a-15(#1), 17(#3). **Orlando** a-9, 12. **Wood** a-15, 16, 4-6.*

HAUNT OF FEAR, THE
May, 1991 - No. 2, July, 1991 ($2.00, color, 68 pgs.)
Gladstone Publishing

	GD25	FN65	NM94
1,2: 1-Ghastly Ingels-c(r); 2-Craig-c(r)	.50	1.25	2.50

HAUNT OF FEAR
Sept, 1991 - No. 5, 1992 ($2.00, color, 68 pgs.)

Nov, 1992 - Present ($1.50, color)
Russ Cochran

	GD25	FN65	NM94
1-Ingels-c(r)	.50	1.25	2.50
2-5	.40	1.00	2.00
1,2-r/HOF #15,16 with original-c	.30	.75	1.50

HAUNT OF HORROR, THE (Magazine)
May, 1974 - No. 5, Jan, 1975 (75 cents) (B&W)
Cadence Comics Publ. (Marvel)

	GD25	FN65	NM94
1	1.20	3.00	6.00
2,4: 2-Origin & 1st app. Gabriel the Devil Hunter; Satana begins. 4-Neal Adams-a	1.00	2.50	5.00
3,5: 5-Evans-a(2)	.80	2.00	4.00

NOTE: ***Alcala*** *a-2.* ***Colan*** *a-2p.* ***Heath*** *r-1.* ***Krigstein*** *r-3.* ***Reese*** *a-1.* ***Simonson*** *a-1.*

HAVE GUN, WILL TRAVEL (TV)
No. 931, 8/58 - No. 14, 7-9/62 (All Richard Boone photo-c)
Dell Publishing Co.

	GD25	FN65	NM94
4-Color 931 (#1)	10.00	30.00	65.00
4-Color 983,1044 (#2,3)	6.70	20.00	40.00
4 (1-3/60) - 14	5.00	15.00	30.00

HAVOK & WOLVERINE - MELTDOWN (See Marvel Comics Presents #24)
Mar, 1989 - No. 4, Oct, 1989 ($3.50, mini-series, squarebound)
Epic Comics (Marvel)

	GD25	FN65	NM94
1-Mature readers, violent	.80	2.00	4.00
2-4	.70	1.75	3.50

HAWAIIAN EYE (TV)
July, 1963 (Troy Donahue, Connie Stevens photo-c)
Gold Key

	GD25	FN65	NM94
1 (10073-307)	4.20	12.50	25.00

HAWAIIAN ILLUSTRATED LEGENDS SERIES
1975 (B&W)(Cover printed w/blue, yellow, and green)
Hogarth Press

	GD25	FN65	NM94
1-Kalelealuaka, the Mysterious Warrior		.60	1.20
2,3(Exist?)		.50	1.00

HAWK, THE (Also see Approved Comics #1, 7 & Tops In Adventure)
Wint/51 - No. 3, 11-12/52; No. 4, 1953 - No. 12, 5/55
Ziff-Davis/St. John Publ. Co. No. 4 on

	GD25	FN65	NM94
1-Anderson-a	11.00	32.00	75.00
2 (Sum, '52)-Kubert, Infantino-a; painted-c	7.50	22.50	45.00
3-8,11: 8-Reprints #3 with diff.-c. 11-Buckskin Belle & The Texan app.	5.35	16.00	32.00
9-Baker-c/a; Kubert-a(r)/#2	6.35	19.00	38.00
10-Baker-c/a; r/one story from #2	6.35	19.00	38.00
12-Baker-c/a; Buckskin Belle app.	6.35	19.00	38.00
3-D 1(11/53)-Baker-c	22.00	65.00	150.00

NOTE: ***Baker*** *c-8-12.* ***Larsen*** *a-10.* ***Tuska*** *a-1, 9, 12. Painted c-1, 7.*

HAWK AND DOVE (2nd series)
Oct, 1988 - No. 5, Holiday, 1988-89 ($1.00, color, mini-series)
DC Comics

	GD25	FN65	NM94
1-Rob Liefeld-c/a(p) in all	1.00	2.50	5.00
2-5	.60	1.50	3.00

HAWK AND DOVE (DC, 1989-91, 3rd series)(Value: cover or less)

HAWK AND THE DOVE, THE (See Showcase #75 & Teen Titans)
Aug-Sept, 1968 - No. 6, June-July, 1969 (1st series)
National Periodical Publications

	GD25	FN65	NM94
Showcase #75 (7-8/67)-Origin & 1st app. Hawk and the Dove; Ditko-c/a	10.00	30.00	60.00
1-Ditko-c/a	5.85	17.50	35.00
2-6: 5-Teen Titans cameo	4.20	12.50	25.00

NOTE: ***Ditko*** *c/a-1, 2.* ***Gil Kane*** *a-3p, 4p, 5, 6p; c-3-6.*

HAWKEYE (See The Avengers #16 & Tales Of Suspense #57)
Sept, 1983 - No. 4, Dec, 1983 (Mini-series)
Marvel Comics Group

	GD25	FN65	NM94
1-4: 1-Origin Hawkeye. 3-Origin Mockingbird		.50	1.00

HAWKEYE & THE LAST OF THE MOHICANS (See 4-Color No. 884)

HAWKMAN (See Atom & Hawkman, The Brave & the Bold, DC Comics Presents, Detective, Flash Comics, Hawkworld, Justice League of America #31, Mystery in Space, Shadow War Of..., Showcase, & World's Finest)

HAWKMAN (1st series) (Also see The Atom #7)
Apr-May, 1964 - No. 27, Aug-Sept, 1968
National Periodical Publications

	GD25	FN65	NM94
Brave and the Bold #34 (2-3/61)-Origin & 1st app. S.A. Hawkman & Byth by Kubert; 1st S.A. Hawkman tryout	115.00	345.00	800.00
Brave and the Bold #35,36 (4-5/61, 6-7/61): Hawkman by Kubert. 36-Origin Shadow Thief	32.00	95.00	225.00
Brave and the Bold #42,44 (6-7/62, 10-11/62)-Hawkman by Kubert; 2nd Hawkman tryout series	16.00	48.00	110.00
Brave and the Bold #43 (8-9/62)-Hawkman origin retold by Kubert (see Mystery in Space for 3rd tryout series)	19.00	57.00	130.00
1-(4-5/64)-Anderson-c/a begins, ends #21	50.00	150.00	350.00
2	18.00	54.00	125.00
3,5	11.00	32.00	75.00
4-Origin & 1st app. Zatanna	12.00	36.00	85.00
6-10: 9-Atom cameo; Hawkman & Atom learn each other's I.D.; 2nd app. Shadow Thief	8.35	25.00	50.00
11-15	5.85	17.50	35.00
16-27: 18-Adam Strange x-over (cameo #19). 25-G.A. Hawkman-r by Moldoff. 27-Kubert-c	4.00	12.00	24.00

HAWKMAN (2nd series)
Aug, 1986 - No. 17, Dec, 1987
DC Comics

	GD25	FN65	NM94
1-17: 10-Byrne-c		.50	1.00
Special #1 (1986, $1.25)	.30	.75	1.50
Trade paperback (1989, $19.95)-r/Brave and the Bold #34-36,42-44 by Kubert; Kubert-c	4.00	10.00	20.00

HAWKMOON: (First, all titles)(Value: cover or less)

HAWKSHAW THE DETECTIVE (See Advs. of..., Hans Und Fritz & Okay)
1917 (24 pgs.; B&W; 10½x13½") (Sunday strip reprints)
The Saalfield Publishing Co.

	GD25	FN65	NM94
nn-By Gus Mager	14.00	42.00	85.00

HAWKWORLD
1989 - No. 3, 1989 ($3.95, prestige format, mini-series)
DC Comics

	GD25	FN65	NM94
Book 1-Hawkman dons new costume	.90	2.25	4.50
Book 2,3-Truman-c/a/scripts in #1-3	.80	2.00	4.00

HAWKWORLD
June, 1990 - No. 32, Mar, 1993 ($1.50/$1.75, on-going series)
DC Comics

	GD25	FN65	NM94
1-Hawkman spin-off	.50	1.25	2.50
2-32: 15,16-War of the Gods x-over. 22-J'onn J'onzz app.	.35	.90	1.75
Annual 1 (1990, $2.95, 68 pgs.)-Flash app.	.60	1.50	3.00
Annual 2 (1991, $2.95, 68 pgs.)-2nd print exists with silver ink-c	.60	1.50	3.00
Annual 3 (1992, $2.95, 68 pgs.)-Eclipso app.	.60	1.50	3.00

HAWTHORN-MELODY FARMS DAIRY COMICS
No date (1950's) (Giveaway)
Everybody's Publishing Co.

	GD25	FN65	NM94
nn-Cheerie Chick, Tuffy Turtle, Robin Koo Koo, Donald & Longhorn Legends	1.60	4.00	8.00

HAYWIRE (DC)(Value: cover or less)

Have Gun, Will Travel #6, © CBS

Hawk and the Dove #2 (10-11/68), © DC

Hawkman #25 (1st series), © DC

Headline Comics #47, © PRIZE

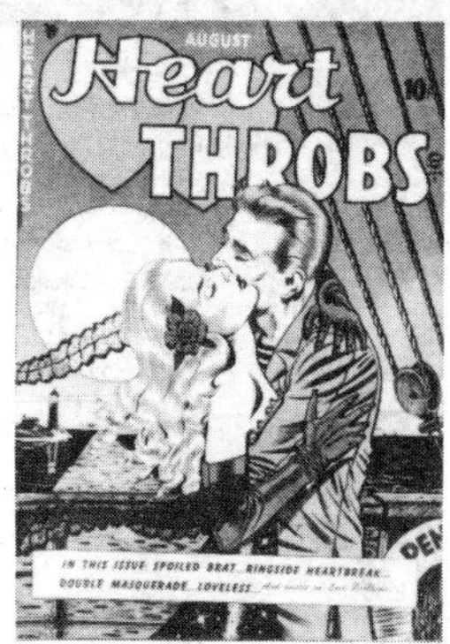

Heart Throbs #1, © DC

Heckle and Jeckle #2 (2/63), © CBS

HEADLINE COMICS (...Crime No. 32-39)
Feb, 1943 - No. 22, Nov-Dec, 1946; No. 23, 1947 - No. 77, Oct, 1956
Prize Publications

	GD25	FN65	NM94
1-Yank & Doodle x-over in Junior Rangers	24.00	73.00	170.00
2	10.00	30.00	70.00
3-Used in **POP**, pg. 84	9.15	27.50	55.00
4-7,9,10: 4,9,10-Hitler stories in each	9.15	27.50	55.00
8-Classic Hitler-c	14.00	43.00	100.00
11,12	5.85	17.50	35.00
13-15-Blue Streak in all	6.35	19.00	38.00
16-Origin Atomic Man	12.00	36.00	85.00
17,18,20,21: 21-Atomic Man ends (9-10/46)	6.70	20.00	40.00
19-S&K-a	13.00	40.00	90.00
22-Kiefer-c	4.00	10.50	21.00
23,24: (All S&K-a). 24-Dope-crazy killer story	11.00	32.00	75.00
25-35-S&K-c/a. 25-Powell-a	10.00	30.00	60.00
36-S&K-a	8.35	25.00	50.00
37-One pg. S&K, Severin-a; Jack Kirby photo-c	4.20	12.50	25.00
38,40-Meskin-a	3.20	8.00	16.00
39,41,42,45-48,50-55: 51-Kirby-c. 45-Kirby-a	2.00	5.00	10.00
43,49-Meskin-a	2.40	6.00	12.00
44-S&K-c; Severin/Elder, Meskin-a	4.70	14.00	28.00
56-S&K-a	4.20	12.50	25.00
57-77: 72-Meskin-c/a(i)	2.00	5.00	10.00

NOTE: ***Hollingsworth** a-30. Photo c-38, 42, 43.*

HEADMAN (Innovation) (Value: cover or less)

HEAP, THE
Sept, 1971 (52 pages)
Skywald Publications

	GD25	FN65	NM94
1-Kinstler-r/Strange Worlds #8	.60	1.50	3.00

HEART AND SOUL
April-May, 1954 - No. 2, June-July, 1954
Mikeross Publications

	GD25	FN65	NM94
1,2	4.20	12.50	25.00

HEARTS OF DARKNESS (See Ghost Rider; Wolverine; Punisher: Hearts of...)
Dec, 1992 (Color, $4.95)
Marvel Comics

	GD25	FN65	NM94
1-Ghost Rider, Punisher, Wolverine app; double gatefold-c	1.00	2.50	5.00

HEART THROBS (Love Stories No. 147 on)
8/49 - No. 8, 10/50; No. 9, 3/52 - No. 146, Oct, 1972
Quality Comics/National Periodical #47(4-5/57) on (Arleigh #48-101)

	GD25	FN65	NM94
1-Classic Ward-c, Gustavson-a, 9 pgs.	23.00	70.00	160.00
2-Ward-c/a (9 pgs); Gustavson-a	11.50	34.00	80.00
3-Gustavson-a	5.00	15.00	30.00
4,6,8-Ward-a, 8-9 pgs.	7.50	22.50	45.00
5,7	3.60	9.00	18.00
9-Robert Mitchum, Jane Russell photo-c	5.85	17.50	35.00
10,15-Ward-a	5.85	17.50	35.00
11-14,16-20: 12 (7/52)	2.80	7.00	14.00
21-Ward-c	4.70	14.00	28.00
22,23-Ward-a(p)	4.00	10.00	20.00
24-33: 33-Last pre-code (3/55)	2.40	6.00	12.00
34-39,41-46 (12/56; last Quality issue)	2.00	5.00	10.00
40-Ward-a; r-7 pgs./#21	3.60	9.00	18.00
47-(4-5/57; 1st DC issue)	13.00	40.00	90.00
48-60	5.85	17.50	35.00
61-70	4.20	12.50	25.00
71-100: 74-Last 10 cent issue	3.60	9.00	18.00
101-The Beatles app. on-c	7.50	22.50	45.00
102-120: 102-123-(Serial)-Three Girls, Their Lives, Their Loves. 120-Neal Adams-c	1.60	4.00	8.00
121-146: #133-142, 52 pgs.	1.20	3.00	6.00

NOTE: ***Gustavson** a-8. **Tuska** a-128. Photo c-4, 8-10, 15, 17.*

HEATHCLIFF (See Star Comics Magazine)
Apr, 1985 - No. 56, Feb, 1991 (#16-on, $1.00)
Star Comics/Marvel Comics No. 23 on

	GD25	FN65	NM94
1-49,51-56: Post-a most issues. 43-X-Mas issue. 47-Batman parody (Catman vs. the Soaker)		.50	1.00
50-($1.50, 52 pgs.)	.30	.75	1.50
Annual 1 ('87)		.60	1.20

HEATHCLIFF'S FUNHOUSE
May, 1987 - No. 10, 1988
Star Comics/Marvel Comics No. 6 on

	GD25	FN65	NM94
1-10		.50	1.00

HECKLE AND JECKLE (See Blue Ribbon, Paul Terry's & Terry-Toons Comics)
10/51 - No. 24, 10/55; No. 25, Fall/56 - No. 34, 6/59
St. John Publ. Co. No. 1-24/Pines No. 25 on

	GD25	FN65	NM94
1	22.00	65.00	150.00
2	11.00	32.00	75.00
3-5	9.15	27.50	55.00
6-10	6.35	19.00	38.00
11-20	4.70	14.00	28.00
21-34	4.00	10.00	20.00

HECKLE AND JECKLE (TV) (See New Terrytoons)
11/62 - No. 4, 8/63; 5/66; No. 2, 10/66; No. 3, 8/67
Gold Key/Dell Publishing Co.

	GD25	FN65	NM94
1 (11/62; Gold Key)	4.70	14.00	28.00
2-4	2.80	7.00	14.00
1 (5/66; Dell)	3.60	9.00	18.00
2,3	2.80	7.00	14.00

(See March of Comics No. 379, 472, 484)

HECKLE AND JECKLE 3-D (Spotlight) (Value: cover or less)

HECKLER, THE
Sept, 1992 - Present ($1.25, color)
DC Comics

	GD25	FN65	NM94
1-10: 1-Giffen-c/a(p) begin		.60	1.25

HECTOR COMICS
Nov, 1953 - No. 3, 1954
Key Publications

	GD25	FN65	NM94
1	3.20	8.00	16.00
2,3	2.00	5.00	10.00

HECTOR HEATHCOTE (TV)
March, 1964
Gold Key

	GD25	FN65	NM94
1 (10111-403)	4.20	12.50	25.00

HEDY DEVINE COMICS (Formerly All Winners #21? or Teen #22?(6/47); Hedy of Hollywood #36 on; also see Annie Oakley, Comedy & Venus)
No. 22, Aug, 1947 - No. 50, Sept, 1952
Marvel Comics (RCM)/Atlas #50

	GD25	FN65	NM94
22-1st app. Hedy Devine	8.35	25.00	50.00
23,24,27-30: 23-Wolverton-a, 1 pg; Kurtzman's "Hey Look," 2 pgs. 24,27-30-"Hey Look" by Kurtzman, 1-3 pgs.	9.15	27.50	55.00
25-Classic "Hey Look" by Kurtzman-"Optical Illusion"	10.00	30.00	60.00
26-"Giggles & Grins" by Kurtzman	6.70	20.00	40.00
31-34,36-50: 32-Anti-Wertham editorial	4.20	12.50	25.00
35-Four pgs. "Rusty" by Kurtzman	7.50	22.50	45.00

HEDY-MILLIE-TESSIE COMEDY (See Comedy Comics)

HEDY WOLFE (Also see Patsy & Hedy)
August, 1957
Atlas Publishing Co. (Emgee)

	GD25	FN65	NM94
1-Al Hartley-c	5.85	17.50	35.00

HEE HAW (TV)
July, 1970 - No. 7, Aug, 1971
Charlton Press

	GD25	FN65	NM94
1	2.00	5.00	10.00
2-7	1.60	4.00	8.00

HEIDI (See Dell Jr. Treasury No. 6)

HELEN OF TROY (See 4-Color No. 684)

HELLBLAZER (John Constantine) (See Saga of Swamp Thing #37)
Jan, 1988 - Present ($1.25-1.50, adults)
DC Comics

	GD25	FN65	NM94
1-(44 pgs.)	3.40	8.50	17.00
2-5	2.00	5.00	10.00
6-10: 9-X-over w/Swamp Thing #76. 10-Swamp Thing cameo	1.00	2.50	5.00
11-20	.70	1.75	3.50
21-30: 25,26-Grant Morrison scripts. 27-Neil Gaiman scripts; Dave McKean-a	.60	1.50	3.00
31-39,41-49: 36-Preview of World Without End. 44-Begin $1.75-c	.50	1.25	2.50
40-($2.25, 52 pgs.)-Dave McKean-a & colors; preview of Kid Eternity	.60	1.50	3.00
50-($3.00, 52 pgs.)	.60	1.50	3.00
51-65: 63-Metallic ink on-c	.35	.90	1.75
Annual 1 (1989, $2.95, 68 pgs.)	.90	2.25	4.50

NOTE: ***Sutton** a-44i, 45i.*

HELLO, I'M JOHNNY CASH (Spire Christian) (Value: cover or less)

HELL ON EARTH (See DC Science Fiction Graphic Novel)

HELLO PAL COMICS (Short Story Comics)
Jan, 1943 - No. 3, May, 1943 (Photo-c)
Harvey Publications

	GD25	FN65	NM94
1-Rocketman & Rocketgirl begin; Yankee Doodle Jones app.; Mickey Rooney photo-c	46.00	138.00	275.00
2-Charlie McCarthy photo-c	32.00	95.00	190.00
3-Bob Hope photo-c	37.00	110.00	225.00

HELLRAISER NIGHTBREED – JIHAD (Epic) (Value: cover or less)

HELLRAISER III: HELL ON EARTH (Epic) (Value: cover or less) (Movie Special)

HELL-RIDER (Magazine)
Aug, 1971 - No. 2, Oct, 1971 (B&W)
Skywald Publications

	GD25	FN65	NM94
1,2: 1-Origin & 1st app.; Butterfly & Wildbunch begins	1.00	2.50	5.00

NOTE: *#3 advertised in Psycho #5 but did not come out. **Buckler** a-1, 2. **Morrow** c-3.*

HELL'S ANGEL (Becomes Dark Angel #6 on)
July, 1992 - No. 5, Nov, 1993 ($1.75, color)
Marvel Comics UK

	GD25	FN65	NM94
1-5: X-Men (Wolverine, Cyclops)-c/stories. 1-Origin. 3-Jim Lee cover swipe	.35	.90	1.75

HE-MAN (See Masters Of The Universe)

HE-MAN (Also see Tops In Adventure)
Fall, 1952
Ziff-Davis Publ. Co. (Approved Comics)

	GD25	FN65	NM94
1-Kinstler-c; Powell-a	9.15	27.50	55.00

HE-MAN
May, 1954 - No. 2, July, 1954 (Painted-c)
Toby Press

	GD25	FN65	NM94
1	8.35	25.00	50.00
2	6.70	20.00	40.00

HENNESSEY (See 4-Color No. 1200, 1280)

HENRY
1935 (52 pages) (Daily B&W strip reprints)
David McKay Publications

	GD25	FN65	NM94
1-By Carl Anderson	11.00	32.00	75.00

HENRY (See King Comics & Magic Comics)
No. 122, Oct, 1946 - No. 65, Apr-June, 1961
Dell Publishing Co.

	GD25	FN65	NM94
4-Color 122	10.00	30.00	60.00
4-Color 155 (7/47)	7.50	22.50	45.00
1 (1-3/48)	8.35	25.00	50.00
2	4.00	10.00	20.00
3-10	3.00	7.50	15.00
11-20: 20-Infinity-c	2.40	6.00	12.00
21-30	1.80	4.50	9.00
31-40	1.40	3.50	7.00
41-65	1.20	3.00	6.00

HENRY (See Giant Comic Album and March of Comics No. 43, 58, 84, 101, 112, 129, 147, 162, 178, 189)

HENRY ALDRICH COMICS (TV)
Aug-Sept, 1950 - No. 22, Sept-Nov, 1954
Dell Publishing Co.

	GD25	FN65	NM94
1-Part series written by John Stanley; Bill Williams-a	7.50	22.50	45.00
2	4.20	12.50	25.00
3-5	4.00	10.00	20.00
6-10	3.60	9.00	18.00
11-22	2.80	7.00	14.00
Giveaway (16 pgs., soft-c, 1951)-Capehart radio	4.00	10.00	20.00

HENRY BREWSTER
Feb, 1966 - V2#7, Sept, 1967 (All Giants)
Country Wide (M.F. Ent.)

	GD25	FN65	NM94
1	1.20	3.00	6.00
2-6(12/66)-Powell-a in most	.80	2.00	4.00
V2#7	.60	1.50	3.00

HERBIE (See Forbidden Worlds & Unknown Worlds)
April-May, 1964 - No. 23, Feb, 1967 (All 12 cents)
American Comics Group

	GD25	FN65	NM94
1-Whitney-c/a in most issues	14.00	43.00	100.00
2-4	8.35	25.00	50.00
5-Beatles, Dean Martin, F. Sinatra app.	10.00	30.00	65.00
6,7,9,10	6.70	20.00	40.00
8-Origin The Fat Fury	8.35	25.00	50.00
11-23: 14-Nemesis & Magicman app. 17-r/2nd Herbie from Forbidden Worlds #94. 23-r/1st Herbie from F.W. #73	4.70	14.00	28.00

HERBIE
Oct, 1992 - No. 12, 1993 ($2.50, color, limited series)
Dark Horse Comics

	GD25	FN65	NM94
1-6: Whitney-r plus new-c/a. 1-Byrne-c/a/scripts. 3-Bob Burden-c/a. 4-Art Adams-c	.50	1.25	2.50

HERBIE GOES TO MONTE CARLO, HERBIE RIDES AGAIN (See Walt Disney Showcase No. 24, 41)

HERCULES (See Hit Comics #1-21, Journey Into Mystery Annual, Marvel Graphic Novel #37, Marvel Premiere #26 & The Mighty...)

HERCULES
Oct, 1967 - No. 13, Sept, 1969; Dec, 1968
Charlton Comics

	GD25	FN65	NM94
1-Thane of Bagarth series begins; Glanzman	1.80	4.50	9.00

Hellblazer #4, © DC

He-Man #1 (1952), © Z-D

Herbie #6 (ACG), © Sword in Stone Prod.

Hercules Unbound #7, © DC

Hero For Hire #1, © MEG

Heroic Comics #16, © FF

	GD25	FN65	NM94
2-13: 1,3-5,7,9,10-Aparo-a	1.20	3.00	6.00
8-(Low distribution)(12/68, 35 cents, B&W); magazine format; new Hercules story plus-r story/#1; Thane-r/#1-3	3.60	9.00	18.00
Modern Comics reprint 10('77), 11('78)		.50	1.00

HERCULES (Prince of Power) (Also see The Champions)
Sept, 1982 - No. 4, Dec, 1982; Mar, 1984 - No. 4, June, 1984
Marvel Comics Group

1-4	.30	.75	1.50
V2#1-4 (Mini-series)		.50	1.00

NOTE: ***Layton*** *a-1, 2, 3p, 4p, V2#1-4; c-1-4, V2#1-4.*

HERCULES UNBOUND
Oct-Nov, 1975 - No. 12, Aug-Sept, 1977
National Periodical Publications

1-Wood inks begin		.60	1.20
2-12: 10-Atomic Knights x-over		.50	1.00

NOTE: ***Buckler*** *c-7p.* ***Layton*** *inks-No. 9, 10.* ***Simonson*** *a-7-10p, 11, 12; c- 8p, 9-12.* ***Wood*** *a-1-8i; c-7i, 8i.*

HERCULES UNCHAINED (See 4-Color No. 1006, 1121)

HERE COMES SANTA (See March of Comics No. 30, 213, 340)

HERE IS SANTA CLAUS
1930s (16 pgs., 8 in color) (stiff paper covers)
Goldsmith Publishing Co. (Kann's in Washington, D.C.)

nn	5.00	15.00	30.00

HERE'S HOW AMERICA'S CARTOONISTS HELP TO SELL U.S. SAVINGS BONDS
1950? (16 pgs.; paper cover)
Harvey Comics giveaway

Contains: Joe Palooka, Donald Duck, Archie, Kerry Drake, Red Ryder, Blondie & Steve Canyon	11.00	32.00	75.00

HERE'S HOWIE COMICS
Jan-Feb, 1952 - No. 18, Nov-Dec, 1954
National Periodical Publications

1	14.00	43.00	100.00
2	8.35	25.00	50.00
3-5	6.35	19.00	38.00
6-10	4.70	14.00	28.00
11-18	4.00	11.00	22.00

HERMAN & KATNIP (See Harvey Hits #14,25,31,41 & Paramount Animated Comics#1)

HERO (Marvel) (Value: cover or less)

HERO ALLIANCE, THE (Sirius) (Value: cover or less)

HERO ALLIANCE (Wonder) (Value: cover or less)

HERO ALLIANCE (Innovation, all titles) (Value: cover or less)

HEROES AGAINST HUNGER
1986 (One shot) ($1.50) (For famine relief)
DC Comics

1-Superman, Batman app.; Neal Adams-c(p); includes many artists work; Jeff Jones assist(2pg.) on B. Smith-a	.30	.75	1.50

HEROES ALL CATHOLIC ACTION ILLUSTRATED
1943 - V6#5, March 10, 1948 (paper covers)
Heroes All Co.

V1#1,2-(16 pgs., 8x11")	8.35	25.00	50.00
V2#1(1/44)-3(3/44)-(16 pgs., 8x11")	5.00	15.00	30.00
V3#1(1/45)-10(10/45)-(16 pgs., 8x11")	4.20	12.50	25.00
V4#1-35 (12/20/46)-(16 pgs.)	3.60	9.00	18.00
V5#1(1/10/47)-8(2/28/47)-(16 pgs.)	2.80	7.00	14.00
V5#9(3/7/47)-20(11/25/47)-(32 pgs.)	2.80	7.00	14.00
V6#1(1/10/48)-5(3/10/48)-(32 pgs.)	2.80	7.00	14.00

HEROES FOR HOPE STARRING THE X-MEN
Dec, 1985 ($1.50, one-shot, 52pgs., proceeds donated to famine relief)
Marvel Comics Group

	GD25	FN65	NM94
1-Stephen King scripts; Byrne, Miller, Corben-a; Wrightson/J. Jones-a (3 pgs.); Art Adams-c; Starlin back-c	.80	2.00	4.00

HEROES, INC. PRESENTS CANNON
1969 - No. 2, 1976 (Sold at Army PX's)
Wally Wood/CPL/Gang Publ. No. 2

nn-Ditko, Wood-a; Wood-c; Reese-a(p)	1.60	4.00	8.00
2-Wood-c; Ditko, Byrne, Wood-a; 8-1/2x10-1/2"; B&W; $2.00	.80	2.00	4.00

NOTE: *First issue not distributed by publisher; 1,800 copies were stored and 900 copies were stolen from warehouse. Many copies have surfaced in recent years.*

HEROES OF THE WILD FRONTIER (Formerly Baffling Mysteries)
No. 27, Jan, 1956 - No. 2, Apr, 1956
Ace Periodicals

27(#1),2	3.20	8.00	16.00

HERO FOR HIRE (Power Man No. 17 on; also see Cage)
June, 1972 - No. 16, Dec, 1973
Marvel Comics Group

1-Origin & 1st app. Luke Cage; Tuska-a(p)	5.85	17.50	35.00
2-5: 2,3-Tuska-a(p). 3-1st app. Mace. 4-1st app. Phil Fox of the Bugle	3.00	7.50	15.00
6-10: 8,9-Dr. Doom app. 9-F.F. app.	1.40	3.50	7.00
11-16: 14-Origin retold. 15-Everett Subby-r('53). 16-Origin Stilletto; death of Rackham	1.20	3.00	6.00

HERO-GRAPHICS SUPER-SAMPLER (Hero) (Value: cover or less)

HERO HOTLINE (DC) (Value: cover or less)

HEROIC ADVENTURES (See Adventures)

HEROIC COMICS (Reg'lar Fellers...#1-15; New Heroic #41 on)
Aug, 1940 - No. 97, June, 1955
Eastern Color Printing Co./Famous Funnies(Funnies, Inc. No. 1)

1-Hydroman(origin) by Bill Everett, The Purple Zombie (origin) & Mann of India by Tarpe Mills begins	83.00	250.00	500.00
2	42.00	125.00	250.00
3,4	33.00	100.00	200.00
5,6	25.00	75.00	150.00
7-Origin Man O'Metal, 1 pg.	29.00	88.00	175.00
8-10: 10-Lingerie panels	17.00	50.00	100.00
11,13: 13-Crandall/Fine-a	15.00	45.00	90.00
12-Music Master(origin) begins by Everett, ends No. 31; last Purple Zombie & Mann of India	17.00	50.00	100.00
14,15-Hydroman x-over in Rainbow Boy. 14-Origin Rainbow Boy. 15-1st app. Downbeat	17.00	50.00	100.00
16-20: 17-Rainbow Boy x-over in Hydroman. 19-Rainbow Boy x-over in Hydroman & vice versa	12.50	38.00	75.00
21-30:25-Rainbow Boy x-over in Hydroman. 28-Last Man O'Metal. 29-Last Hydroman	8.35	25.00	50.00
31,34,38	2.80	7.00	14.00
32,36,37-Toth-a, 3-4 pgs.	4.35	13.00	26.00
33,35-Toth-a, 8 & 9 pgs.	4.70	14.00	28.00
39-42-Toth, Ingels-a	4.70	14.00	28.00
43,46,47,49-Toth-a, 2-4 pgs. 47-Ingels-a	4.00	10.00	20.00
44,45,50-Toth-a, 6-9 pgs.	4.00	12.00	24.00
48,53,54	2.40	6.00	12.00
51-Williamson-a	4.35	13.00	26.00
52-Williamson-a (3 pg. story)	3.60	9.00	18.00
55-Toth-c/a	4.00	11.00	22.00
56-60-Toth-c. 60-Everett-a	3.60	9.00	18.00
61-Everett-a	2.40	6.00	12.00
62,64-Everett-c/a	2.80	7.00	14.00
63-Everett-c	2.00	5.00	10.00

	GD25	FN65	NM94
65-Williamson/Frazetta-a; Evans-a, 2 pgs.	5.85	17.50	35.00
66,75,94-Frazetta-a, 2 pgs. each	2.80	7.00	14.00
67,73-Frazetta-a, 4 pgs. each	4.00	10.00	20.00
68,74,76-80,84,85,88-93,95-97: 95-Last pre-code	2.00	5.00	10.00
69,72-Frazetta-a (6 & 8 pgs. each)	5.85	17.50	35.00
70,71,86,87-Frazetta, 3-4 pgs. each; 1 pg. ad by Frazetta in #70	3.60	9.00	18.00
81,82-One pg. Frazetta art	2.40	6.00	12.00
83-Frazetta-a, 1/2 pg.	2.40	6.00	12.00

NOTE: ***Evans** a-64, 65. **Everett** a-(Hydroman-c/a-No. 1-9), 44, 60-64; c-1-9, 62-64. **Sid Greene** a-38-43, 46. **Guardineer** a-42(3), 43, 44, 45(2), 49(3), 50, 60, 61(2), 65, 67(2) 70-72. **Ingels** c-41. **Kiefer** a-46, 48; c-19-22, 24, 44, 46, 48, 51-53, 65, 67-69, 71-74, 76, 77, 79, 80, 82, 85, 88, 89. **Mort Lawrence** a-45. **Tarpe Mills** a-2(2), 3(2), 10. **Ed Moore** a-49, 52-54, 56-63, 65-69, 72-74, 76, 77. **H.G. Peter** a-58-74, 76, 77, 87. **Paul Reinman** a-49. **Rico** a-31. Captain Tootsie by **Beck**-31, 32. Painted-c #16 on.*

HEX (Replaces Jonah Hex)
Sept, 1985 - No. 18, Feb, 1987 (Story continues from Jonah Hex 92)
DC Comics

	GD25	FN65	NM94
1-10,14-18: 1-Hex in post-atomic war world; origin. 6-Origin Stiletta		.50	1.00
11-13: All contain future Batman storyline. 13-Intro The Dogs of War (origin #15)	.40	1.00	2.00

NOTE: ***Giffen** a-15-18; c-15, 17, 18.*

HEXBREAKER (See First Comics Graphic Novel #15)

HEY THERE, IT'S YOGI BEAR (See Movie Comics)

HI-ADVENTURE HEROES (TV)
May, 1969 - No. 2, Aug, 1969 (Hanna-Barbera)
Gold Key

	GD25	FN65	NM94
1-Three Musketeers, Gulliver, Arabian Knights stories	3.60	9.00	18.00
2-Three Musketeers, Micro-Venture, Arabian Knights	3.00	7.50	15.00

HI AND LOIS (See 4-Color No. 683, 774, 955)

HI AND LOIS
Nov, 1969 - No. 11, July, 1971
Charlton Comics

	GD25	FN65	NM94
1	2.00	5.00	10.00
2-11	1.00	2.50	5.00

HICKORY (See All Humor Comics)
Oct, 1949 - No. 6, Aug, 1950
Quality Comics Group

	GD25	FN65	NM94
1-Sahl-c/a in all; Feldstein?-a	10.00	30.00	60.00
2	4.70	14.00	28.00
3-6	4.00	11.00	22.00

HIDDEN CREW, THE (See The United States Air Force Presents:...)

HIDE-OUT (See 4-Color No. 346)

HIDING PLACE, THE (Spire Christian) (Value: cover or less)

HIGH ADVENTURE
October, 1957
Red Top(Decker) Comics (Farrell)

	GD25	FN65	NM94
1-Krigstein-r from Explorer Joe (re-issue on-c)	3.60	9.00	18.00

HIGH ADVENTURE (See 4-Color No. 949, 1001)

HIGH CHAPPARAL (TV)
August, 1968 (Photo-c)
Gold Key

	GD25	FN65	NM94
1 (10226-808)-Tufts-a	4.70	14.00	28.00

HIGH SCHOOL CONFIDENTIAL DIARY (Confidential Diary #12 on)
June, 1960 - No. 11, March, 1962
Charlton Comics

	GD25	FN65	NM94
1	2.80	7.00	14.00
2-11	1.20	3.00	6.00

HI-HO COMICS
nd (2/46?) - No. 3, 1946
Four Star Publications

	GD25	FN65	NM94
1-Funny Animal; L. B. Cole-c	11.50	34.00	80.00
2,3: 2-L. B. Cole-c	8.35	25.00	50.00

HI-JINX (See Teen-age Animal Funnies)
July-Aug, 1947 - No. 7, July-Aug, 1948
B&I Publ. Co.(American Comics Group)/Creston/La Salle Publ. Co.

	GD25	FN65	NM94
1-Teen-age, funny animal	10.00	30.00	60.00
2,3	5.85	17.50	35.00
4-7-Milt Gross	6.35	19.00	38.00
nn-(© 1945, 25 cents, 132 Pgs.)(La Salle)	10.00	30.00	70.00

HI-LITE COMICS
Fall, 1945
E. R. Ross Publishing Co.

	GD25	FN65	NM94
1-Miss Shady	9.15	27.50	55.00

HILLBILLY COMICS
Aug, 1955 - No. 4, July, 1956 (Satire)
Charlton Comics

	GD25	FN65	NM94
1	4.70	14.00	28.00
2-4	3.20	8.00	16.00

HIP-IT-TY HOP (See March of Comics No. 15)

HI-SCHOOL ROMANCE (...Romances No. 41 on)
Oct, 1949 - No. 5, June, 1950; No. 6, Dec, 1950 - No. 73, Mar, 1958; No. 74, Sept, 1958 - No. 75, Nov, 1958
Harvey Publications/True Love(Home Comics)

	GD25	FN65	NM94
1-Photo-c	6.70	20.00	40.00
2	4.00	10.50	21.00
3-9: 5-Photo-c	3.00	7.50	15.00
10-Rape story	4.00	10.50	21.00
11-20	2.00	5.00	10.00
21-31	1.80	4.50	9.00
32-"Unholy passion" story	3.20	8.00	16.00
33-36: 36-Last pre-code (2/55)	1.40	3.50	7.00
37-75	1.20	3.00	6.00

NOTE: ***Powell** a-1-3, 5, 8, 12-16, 18, 21-23, 25-27, 30-34, 36, 37, 39, 45-48, 50-52, 57, 58, 60, 64, 65, 67, 69.*

HI-SCHOOL ROMANCE DATE BOOK
Nov, 1962 - No. 3, Mar, 1963 (25 cent Giant)
Harvey Publications

	GD25	FN65	NM94
1-Powell, Baker-a	3.20	8.00	16.00
2,3	1.40	3.50	7.00

HIS NAME IS SAVAGE (Magazine format)
June, 1968 (35 cents, one shot, 52 pgs.)
Adventure House Press

	GD25	FN65	NM94
1-Gil Kane-a	4.00	10.50	21.00

HI-SPOT COMICS (Red Ryder No. 1 & No. 3 on)
No. 2, Nov, 1940
Hawley Publications

	GD25	FN65	NM94
2-David Innes of Pellucidar; art by J. C. Burroughs; written by Edgar Rice Burroughs	83.00	250.00	500.00

HISTORY OF THE DC UNIVERSE
Sept, 1986 - No. 2, Nov, 1986 ($2.95)
DC Comics

	GD25	FN65	NM94
1,2: 1-Perez-c/a	.60	1.50	3.00
Limited Edition hardcover	7.50	22.50	45.00

HIT COMICS
July, 1940 - No. 65, July, 1950
Quality Comics Group

Hex #6, © DC

Hi Ho Comics #1, © Four Star

Hi-School Romance #12, © HARV

Hit Comics #29, © QUA

Hogan's Heroes #9, © Bing Crosby Prod.

Hollywood Confessions #1, © STJ

	GD25	FN65	NM94
1-Origin Neon, the Unknown & Hercules; intro. The Red Bee; Bob & Swab, Blaze Barton, the Strange Twins, X-5 Super Agent, Casey Jones & Jack & Jill (ends #7) begin	283.00	850.00	1700.00
2-The Old Witch begins, ends #14	122.00	368.00	735.00
3-Casey Jones ends; transvestism story-'Jack & Jill'	96.00	288.00	575.00
4-Super Agent (ends #17), & Betty Bates (ends #65) begin; X-5 ends	83.00	250.00	500.00
5-Classic cover	125.00	375.00	750.00
6-10: 10-Old Witch by Crandall (4 pgs.); 1st work in comics	67.00	200.00	400.00
11-17: 13-Blaze Barton ends. 17-Last Neon; Crandall Hercules in all	61.00	182.00	365.00
18-Origin Stormy Foster, the Great Defender; The Ghost of Flanders begins; Crandall-c	70.00	210.00	420.00
19,20	61.00	182.00	365.00
21-24: 21-Last Hercules. 24-Last Red Bee & Strange Twins	52.00	158.00	315.00
25-Origin Kid Eternity and begins by Moldoff	70.00	210.00	420.00
26-Blackhawk x-over in Kid Eternity	56.00	168.00	335.00
27-29	32.00	95.00	190.00
30,31-"Bill the Magnificent" by Kurtzman, 11 pgs. in each	27.00	82.00	165.00
32-40: 32-Plastic Man x-over. 34-Last Stormy Foster	14.00	42.00	85.00
41-50	10.00	30.00	60.00
51-60-Last Kid Eternity	9.15	27.50	55.00
61-63-Crandall-c/a; 61-Jeb Rivers begins	10.00	30.00	60.00
64,65-Crandall-a	9.15	27.50	55.00

NOTE: ***Crandall** a-11-17(Hercules), 23, 24(Stormy Foster); c-18-20, 23, 24. **Fine** c-1-14, 16, 17(most). **Ward** c-33. Bondage c-7, 64.*

HI-YO SILVER (See Lone Ranger's Famous Horse... and also see The Lone Ranger and March of Comics No. 215)

HOBBIT, THE (Eclipse) (Value: cover or less)

HOCUS POCUS (Formerly Funny Book)
No. 9, Aug-Sept, 1946
Parents' Magazine Press

	GD25	FN65	NM94
9	3.60	9.00	18.00

HOGAN'S HEROES (TV)
June, 1966 - No. 8, Sept, 1967; No. 9, Oct, 1969
Dell Publishing Co.

	GD25	FN65	NM94
1: #1-7 photo-c	5.85	17.50	35.00
2,3-Ditko-a(p)	4.00	11.00	22.00
4-9: 9-Reprints #1	3.00	7.50	15.00

HOLIDAY COMICS
1942 (196 pages) (25 cents)
Fawcett Publications

	GD25	FN65	NM94
1-Contains three Fawcett comics; Capt. Marvel, Nyoka #1, & Whiz. Not rebound, remaindered comics printed at the same time as originals	112.00	338.00	675.00

HOLIDAY COMICS (Becomes Fun Comics #9-12)
January, 1951 - No. 8, Oct, 1952
Star Publications

	GD25	FN65	NM94
1-Funny animal contents (Frisky Fables) in all; L. B. Cole-c	14.00	43.00	100.00
2-Classic L. B. Cole-c	16.00	48.00	110.00
3-8: 5,8-X-Mas-c; all L.B. Cole-c	10.00	30.00	65.00
Accepted Reprint 4 (nd)-L.B. Cole-c	5.35	16.00	32.00

HOLIDAY DIGEST
1988 ($1.25, digest-size)
Harvey Comics

	GD25	FN65	NM94
1		.60	1.25

HOLIDAY PARADE (Walt Disney's...)
Winter, 1990-91 (no yr. given) - Present ($2.95, color, annual, 68 pgs.)
W. D. Publications (Disney)

	GD25	FN65	NM94
1-Reprints 1947 Firestone by Barks plus new-a	.60	1.50	3.00
2-(Win/90-91)-Barks-r plus other stories	.60	1.50	3.00

HOLI-DAY SURPRISE (Formerly Summer Fun)
V2#55, Mar, 1967 (25 cents)
Charlton Comics

	GD25	FN65	NM94
V2#55-Giant	1.00	2.50	5.00

HOLLYWOOD COMICS
Winter, 1944 (52 pgs.)
New Age Publishers

	GD25	FN65	NM94
1-Funny animals	11.00	32.00	75.00

HOLLYWOOD CONFESSIONS
Oct, 1949 - No. 2, Dec, 1949
St. John Publishing Co.

	GD25	FN65	NM94
1-Kubert-c/a (entire book)	14.00	43.00	100.00
2-Kubert-c/a (entire book) (Scarce)	22.00	65.00	150.00

HOLLYWOOD DIARY
Dec, 1949 - No. 5, July-Aug, 1950
Quality Comics Group

	GD25	FN65	NM94
1	10.00	30.00	70.00
2-Photo-c	7.00	21.00	42.00
3-5: 3,5-Photo-c	5.85	17.50	35.00

HOLLYWOOD FILM STORIES
April, 1950 - No. 4, Oct, 1950
Feature Publications/Prize

	GD25	FN65	NM94
1-"Fumetti" type movie comic	10.00	30.00	70.00
2-4	8.35	25.00	50.00

HOLLYWOOD FUNNY FOLKS (Formerly Funny Folks; Becomes Nutsy Squirrel #61 on)
No. 27, Aug-Sept, 1950 - No. 60, July-Aug, 1954
National Periodical Publications

	GD25	FN65	NM94
27	8.35	25.00	50.00
28-40	5.00	15.00	30.00
41-60	4.20	12.50	25.00

NOTE: ***Sheldon Mayer** a-27-35, 37-40, 43-46, 48-51, 53, 56, 57, 60.*

HOLLYWOOD LOVE DOCTOR (See Doctor Anthony King...)

HOLLYWOOD PICTORIAL (...Romances on cover)
No. 3, January, 1950
St. John Publishing Co.

	GD25	FN65	NM94
3-Matt Baker-a; photo-c	11.00	32.00	75.00

(Becomes a movie magazine - Hollywood Pictorial Western with No. 4.)

HOLLYWOOD ROMANCES (Formerly Brides In Love; becomes For Lovers Only #60 on)
V2#46, 11/66; #47, 10/67; #48, 11/68; V3#49, 11/69 - V3#59, 6/71
Charlton Comics

	GD25	FN65	NM94
V2#46-Rolling Stones-c/story	4.20	12.50	25.00
V2#47-V3#59: 56-"Born to Heart Break" begins	1.00	2.50	5.00

HOLLYWOOD SECRETS
Nov, 1949 - No. 6, Sept, 1950
Quality Comics Group

	GD25	FN65	NM94
1-Ward-c/a, 9pgs.	19.00	58.00	135.00
2-Crandall-a, Ward-c/a, 9 pgs.	11.50	34.00	80.00
3-6: All photo-c; 5-Lex Barker (Tarzan)-c	6.70	20.00	40.00
...of Romance, I.W. Reprint #9; Kinstler-c; Ward, Crandall-a	1.20	3.00	6.00

GD25 FN65 NM94 | GD25 FN65 NM94

HOLLYWOOD SUPERSTARS
Nov, 1990 - No. 5, Apr, 1991 ($2.25, color)
Epic Comics (Marvel)

1-($2.95, 52 pgs.)-Spiegle-c/a in all .60 1.50 3.00
2-5 ($2.25) .45 1.15 2.25

HOLO-MAN (See Power Record Comics)

HOLYOKE ONE-SHOT
1944 - No. 10, 1945 (All reprints)
Holyoke Publishing Co. (Tem Publ.)

1-Grit Grady (on cover only), Miss Victory, Alias X (origin)-All reprints from Captain Fearless 7.00 21.00 42.00
2-Rusty Dugan (Corporal); Capt. Fearless (origin), Mr. Miracle (origin) app. 7.00 21.00 42.00
3-Miss Victory-Crash #4-r; Cat Man (origin), Solar Legion by Kirby app.; Miss Victory on cover only (1945) 13.00 40.00 90.00
4-Mr. Miracle-The Blue Streak app. 6.35 19.00 38.00
5-U.S. Border Patrol Comics (Sgt. Dick Carter of the...), Miss Victory (story matches cover to #3), Citizen Smith, & Mr. Miracle app. 7.00 21.00 42.00
6-Capt. Fearless, Alias X, Capt. Stone (splash used as-c to #10); Diamond Jim & Rusty Dugan (splash from cover of #2) 6.35 19.00 38.00
7-Z-2, Strong Man, Blue Streak (story matches cover to #8)-Reprints from Crash #2 7.50 22.50 45.00
8-Blue Streak, Strong Man (story matches cover to #7)-Crash reprints 6.35 19.00 38.00
9-Citizen Smith, The Blue Streak, Solar Legion by Kirby & Strongman, the Perfect Human app.; reprints from Crash #4 & 5; Citizen Smith on cover only-from story in #5 (1944-before #3) 10.00 30.00 60.00
10-Captain Stone (Crash reprints); Solar Legion by S&K 10.00 30.00 60.00

HOMER COBB (See Adventures of...)

HOMER HOOPER
July, 1953 - No. 4, Dec., 1953
Atlas Comics

1 5.85 17.50 35.00
2-4 4.00 11.00 22.00

HOMER, THE HAPPY GHOST (See Adventures of...)
3/55 - No. 22, 11/58; V2#1, 11/69 - V2#5, 7/70
Atlas(ACI/PPI/WPI)/Marvel Comics

V1#1-Dan DeCarlo-a begins, ends #22 8.35 25.00 50.00
2 4.20 12.50 25.00
3-10 3.60 9.00 18.00
11-22 2.80 7.00 14.00
V2#1 - V2#5 (1969-70) 1.20 3.00 6.00

HOME RUN (See A-1 Comics No. 89)

HOME, SWEET HOME
1925 (10-1/4x10")
M.S. Publishing Co.

nn-By Tuthill 17.00 50.00 100.00

HOMICIDE (Dark Horse) (Value: cover or less)

HONEYBEE BIRDWHISTLE AND HER PET PEPI (Introducing...)
1969 (24 pgs.; B&W; slick cover)
Newspaper Enterprise Association (Giveaway)

nn-Contains Freckles newspaper strips with a short biography of Henry Fornhals (artist) & Fred Fox (writer) of the strip 4.30 13.00 30.00

HONEYMOON (Formerly Gay Comics)
No. 41, January, 1950
A Lover's Magazine(USA) (Marvel)

41-Photo-c; article by Betty Grable 5.35 16.00 32.00

HONEYMOONERS, THE (TV) (Lodestone) (Value: cover or less)

HONEYMOONERS, THE (TV) (Triad) (Value: cover or less)

HONEYMOON ROMANCE
April, 1950 - No. 2, July, 1950 (25 cents) (digest size)
Artful Publications(Canadian)

1,2-(Rare) 22.00 65.00 150.00

HONEY WEST (TV)
September, 1966 (Photo-c)
Gold Key

1 (10186-609) 10.00 30.00 65.00

HONG KONG PHOOEY (TV)
June, 1975 - No. 9, Nov, 1976 (Hanna-Barbera)
Charlton Comics

1 2.00 5.00 10.00
2 1.00 2.50 5.00
3-9 .60 1.50 3.00

HOODED HORSEMAN, THE (Also see Blazing West)
No. 21, 1-2/52 - No. 27, 1-2/53; No. 18, 12-1/54-55 - No. 27, 6-7/56
American Comics Group (Michel Publ.)

21(1-2/52)-Hooded Horseman, Injun Jones continue 10.00 30.00 65.00
22 6.35 19.00 38.00
23-25,27(1-2/53) 5.00 15.00 30.00
26-Origin/1st app. Cowboy Sahib by L. Starr 7.50 22.50 45.00
18(11-12/54)(Formerly Out of the Night) 5.00 15.00 30.00
19-Last precode (1-2/55) 9.15 27.50 55.00
20-Origin Johnny Injun 5.00 15.00 30.00
21-24,26,27(6-7/56) 4.35 13.00 26.00
25-Cowboy Sahib on cover only; Hooded Horseman i.d. revealed 5.00 15.00 30.00

NOTE: *Whitney c/a-21('52), 20-22.*

HOODED MENACE, THE (Also see Daring Adventures)
1951 (One Shot)
Realistic/Avon Periodicals

nn-Based on a band of hooded outlaws in the Pacific Northwest, 1900-1906; reprinted in Daring Advs. #15 32.00 95.00 225.00

HOODS UP
1953 (16 pgs.; 15 cents) (Eisner-c/a in all)
Fram Corp. (Dist. to service station owners)

1-(Very Rare; only 2 known) 50.00 150.00 350.00
2-6-(Very Rare; only 1 known of 3-4, 2 known of #2) 50.00 150.00 350.00

NOTE: *Convertible Connie gives tips for service stations, selling Fram oil filters.*

HOOK
Early Feb, 1992 - No. 4, Late Mar, 1992 ($1.00, color, mini-series)
Marvel Comics

1-4: Adapts movie; Vess-c; 1-Morrow-a(p) .50 1.00
nn (1991, $5.95, 84 pgs.)-Contains #1-4; Vess-c 1.20 3.00 6.00
1 (1991, $2.95, color, magazine, 84 pgs.)-Contains #1-4; Vess-c (same cover as nn issue) .60 1.50 3.00

HOOT GIBSON'S WESTERN ROUNDUP (See Western Roundup under Fox Giants)

HOOT GIBSON WESTERN (Formerly My Love Story)
No. 5, May, 1950 - No. 3, Sept, 1950
Fox Features Syndicate

5,6(#1,2): 5-Photo-c 14.00 43.00 100.00
3-Wood-a 17.00 52.00 100.00

HOPALONG CASSIDY (Also see Bill Boyd Western, Master Comics, Real Western Hero, Six Gun Heroes & Western Hero; Bill Boyd starred as H. Cassidy in the movies; H. Cassidy in movies, radio & TV)
Feb, 1943; No. 2, Summer, 1946 - No. 85, Jan, 1954
Fawcett Publications

Homer, the Happy Ghost #16, © MEG

Honeybee Birdwhistle nn, © Newspaper Enterprise

The Hooded Menace #1, © AVON

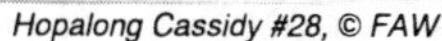

Hopalong Cassidy #28, © FAW

Horrific #9, © Comic Media

Hot Dog #1, © ME

	GD25	FN65	NM94
1 (1943, 68pgs.)-H. Cassidy & his horse Topper begin (on sale 1/8/43)-Captain Marvel app. on-c	257.00	770.00	1800.00
2-(Sum, '46)	50.00	150.00	350.00
3,4: 3-(Fall, '46, 52pgs. begin)	24.00	70.00	165.00
5-"Mad Barber" story mentioned in **SOTI**, pgs. 308,309	22.00	65.00	150.00
6-10	17.00	51.00	120.00
11-19: 11,13-19-Photo-c	12.00	36.00	85.00
20-29 (52pgs.)-Painted/photo-c	10.00	30.00	65.00
30,31,33,34,37-39,41 (52pgs.)-Painted-c	6.70	20.00	40.00
32,40 (36pgs.)-Painted-c	5.85	17.50	35.00
35,42,43,45 (52pgs.)-Photo-c	7.00	21.00	42.00
36,44,48 (36pgs.)-Photo-c	5.85	17.50	35.00
46,47,49-51,53,54,56 (52pgs.)-Photo-c	6.35	19.00	38.00
52,55,57-70 (36pgs.)-Photo-c	4.70	14.00	28.00
71-84-Photo-c	4.00	12.00	24.00
85-Last Fawcett issue; photo-c	5.00	15.00	30.00

NOTE: *Line-drawn c-1-10, 12.*

	GD25	FN65	NM94
Grape Nuts Flakes giveaway (1950,9x6")	10.00	30.00	60.00
...& the Mad Barber (1951 Bond Bread giveaway)-7x5"; used in **SOTI**, pgs. 308,309	17.00	51.00	120.00
...Meets the Brend Brothers Bandits (1951 Bond Bread giveaway, color, paper-c, 16pgs. 3-1/2x7")-Fawcett Publ.	8.35	25.00	50.00
...Strange Legacy ('51 Bond Bread giveaway)	8.35	25.00	50.00
White Tower Giveaway ('46, 16pgs., paper-c)	8.35	25.00	50.00

HOPALONG CASSIDY (TV)
No. 86, Feb, 1954 - No. 135, May-June, 1959 (All-36pgs.)
National Periodical Publications

	GD25	FN65	NM94
86-Photo covers continue	22.00	65.00	150.00
87	13.00	40.00	90.00
88-90	10.00	30.00	65.00
91-99 (98 has #93 on-c; last precode issue, 2/55)	8.35	25.00	50.00
100	10.00	30.00	60.00
101-108-Last photo-c	6.70	20.00	40.00
109-135: 124-Painted-c	5.85	17.50	35.00

NOTE: ***Gil Kane** art-1956 up. **Kubert** a-123.*

HOPE SHIP
June-Aug, 1963
Dell Publishing Co.

	GD25	FN65	NM94
1	1.80	4.50	9.00

HOPPY THE MARVEL BUNNY (See Fawcett's Funny Animals)
Dec, 1945 - No. 15, Sept, 1947
Fawcett Publications

	GD25	FN65	NM94
1	19.00	57.00	130.00
2	10.00	30.00	65.00
3-15: 7-Xmas-c	8.35	25.00	50.00
...Well Known Comics (1944,8-1/2x10-1/2", paper-c) Bestmaid/Samuel Lowe (printed in red or blue)	6.70	20.00	40.00

HORACE & DOTTY DRIPPLE (Dotty Dripple No. 1-24)
No. 25, Aug, 1952 - No. 43, Oct, 1955
Harvey Publications

	GD25	FN65	NM94
25-43	1.20	3.00	6.00

HORIZONTAL LIEUTENANT, THE (See Movie Classics)

HOROBI (Viz) (Value: cover or less)

HORRIFIC (Terrific No. 14 on)
Sept, 1952 - No. 13, Sept, 1954
Artful/Comic Media/Harwell/Mystery

	GD25	FN65	NM94
1	14.00	43.00	100.00
2	8.35	25.00	50.00
3-Bullet in head-c	11.50	34.00	80.00
4,5,7,9,10	5.85	17.50	35.00
6-Jack The Ripper story	6.70	20.00	40.00
8-Origin & 1st app. The Teller(E.C. parody)	8.35	25.00	50.00
11-13: 11-Swipe/Witches Tales #6,27	4.70	14.00	28.00

NOTE: ***Don Heck** a-8; c-3-13. **Hollingsworth** a-4. **Morisi** a-8. **Palais** a-5, 7-12.*

HORROR FROM THE TOMB (Mysterious Stories No. 2 on)
Sept, 1954
Premier Magazine Co.

	GD25	FN65	NM94
1-Woodbridge/Torres, Check-a	14.00	43.00	100.00

HORRORS, THE (Formerly Startling Terror Tales #10)
No. 11, Jan, 1953 - No. 15, Apr, 1954
Star Publications

	GD25	FN65	NM94
11-Horrors of War; Disbrow-a(2)	10.00	30.00	65.00
12-Horrors of War; color illo in **POP**	10.00	30.00	60.00
13-Horrors of Mystery; crime stories	9.15	27.50	55.00
14,15-Horrors of the Underworld	10.00	30.00	60.00

NOTE: *All have **L. B. Cole** covers; a-12. **Hollingsworth** a-13. **Palais** a-13r.*

HORROR TALES (Magazine)
V1#7, 6/69 - V6#6, 12/74; V7#1, 2/75; V7#2, 5/76 - V8#5, 1977; V9#3, 8/78; (V1-V6: 52 pgs.; V7, V8#2: 112 pgs.; V8#4 on: 68 pgs.) (No V5#3, V8#1,3)
Eerie Publications

	GD25	FN65	NM94
V1#7	2.40	6.00	12.00
V1#8,9	1.60	4.00	8.00
V2#1-6('70), V3#1-6('71)	1.20	3.00	6.00
V4#1-3,5-7('72)	1.20	3.00	6.00
V4#4-LSD story reprint/Weird V3#5	2.40	6.00	12.00
V5#1,2,4,5(6/73),5(10/73),6(12/73),V6#1-6('74),V7#1,2,4('76),V7#3('76)-Giant issue,V8#2,4,5('77),V9#3(8/78, $1.50)	1.20	3.00	6.00

NOTE: *Bondage-c-V6#1, 3, V7#2.*

HORSE FEATHERS COMICS
Nov, 1945 - No. 4, July, 1948 (52 pgs.)
Lev Gleason Publications

	GD25	FN65	NM94
1-Wolverton's Scoop Scuttle, 2 pgs.	12.00	36.00	85.00
2	5.85	17.50	35.00
3,4: 3-(5/48)	4.35	13.00	26.00

HORSEMASTERS, THE (See 4-Color No. 1260)

HORSE SOLDIERS, THE (See 4-Color No. 1048)

HORSE WITHOUT A HEAD, THE (See Movie Comics)

HOT DOG
June-July, 1954 - No. 4, Dec-Jan, 1954-55
Magazine Enterprises

	GD25	FN65	NM94
1(A-1 #107)	4.20	12.50	25.00
2,3(A-1 #115),4(A-1 #136)	3.20	8.00	16.00

HOT DOG (See Jughead's Pal, Hotdog)

HOTEL DEPAREE - SUNDANCE (See 4-Color No. 1126)

HOT ROD AND SPEEDWAY COMICS
Feb-Mar, 1952 - No. 5, Apr-May, 1953
Hillman Periodicals

	GD25	FN65	NM94
1	11.00	32.00	75.00
2-Krigstein-a	10.00	30.00	60.00
3-5	4.20	12.50	25.00

HOT ROD COMICS (See XMas Comics)
Nov, 1951 (no month given) - V2#7, Feb, 1953
Fawcett Publications

	GD25	FN65	NM94
nn (V1#1)-Powell-c/a in all	14.00	43.00	100.00
2 (4/52)	10.00	30.00	60.00
3-6, V2#7	5.85	17.50	35.00

HOT ROD KING

	GD25	FN65	NM94

Fall, 1952
Ziff-Davis Publ. Co.

	GD25	FN65	NM94
1-Giacoia-a; painted-c	13.00	40.00	90.00

HOT ROD RACERS (Grand Prix No. 16 on)
Dec, 1964 - No. 15, July, 1967
Charlton Comics

	GD25	FN65	NM94
1	4.20	12.50	25.00
2-5	2.40	6.00	12.00
6-15	1.60	4.00	8.00

HOT RODS AND RACING CARS
Nov, 1951 - No. 120, June, 1973
Charlton Comics (Motor Mag. No. 1)

	GD25	FN65	NM94
1	10.00	30.00	70.00
2	6.70	20.00	40.00
3-10	4.20	12.50	25.00
11-20	3.60	9.00	18.00
21-34,36-40	2.40	6.00	12.00
35 (68 pgs., 6/58)	3.60	9.00	18.00
41-60	2.00	5.00	10.00
61-80	1.20	3.00	6.00
81-100	1.00	2.50	5.00
101-120	.80	2.00	4.00

HOT SHOT CHARLIE
1947 (Lee Elias)
Hillman Periodicals

	GD25	FN65	NM94
1	4.70	14.00	28.00

HOTSPUR (Eclipse)(Value: cover or less)

HOT STUFF
V2#1, Sept, 1991 - No. 4? ($1.00, color)
Harvey Comics

	GD25	FN65	NM94
V2#1-4: 1-Stumbo back-up story		.50	1.00

HOT STUFF CREEPY CAVES
Nov, 1974 - No. 7, Nov, 1975
Harvey Publications

	GD25	FN65	NM94
1	1.00	2.50	5.00
2-5	.60	1.50	3.00
6,7	.30	.75	1.50

HOT STUFF DIGEST
July, 1992 - Present ($1.75, color, digest size)
Harvey Comics

	GD25	FN65	NM94
V2#1-4: Hot Stuff, Stumbo, Richie Rich stories	.35	.90	1.75

HOT STUFF GIANT SIZE
Oct, 1992 - Present ($2.25, color, 68 pgs.)
Harvey Comics

	GD25	FN65	NM94
V2#1-Hot Stuff & Stumbo stories	.45	1.15	2.25

HOT STUFF SIZZLERS
July, 1960 - No. 59, Mar, 1974; V2#1, Aug, 1992
Harvey Publications

	GD25	FN65	NM94
1: 68 pgs. begin	8.35	25.00	50.00
2-5	3.60	9.00	18.00
6-10	2.40	6.00	12.00
11-20	1.60	4.00	8.00
21-45: Last 68 pgs.	1.00	2.50	5.00
46-52: All 52 pgs.	.70	1.75	3.50
53-59	.60	1.50	3.00
V2#1-($1.25)-Stumbo back-up		.60	1.25

HOT STUFF, THE LITTLE DEVIL (Also see Devil Kids & Harvey Hits)
10/57 - No. 141, 7/77; No. 142, 2/78 - No. 164, 8/82; No. 165, 10/86 - No. 171, 11/87; No. 172, 11/88; No. 173, Sept, 1990 - No. 177, 1/91
Harvey Publications (Illustrated Humor)

	GD25	FN65	NM94
1	20.00	60.00	140.00
2-1st app. Stumbo the Giant	11.50	34.00	80.00
3-5	10.00	30.00	60.00
6-10	5.00	15.00	30.00
11-20	3.60	9.00	18.00
21-40	2.00	5.00	10.00
41-60	1.00	2.50	5.00
61-105	.60	1.50	3.00
106-112: All 52 pg. Giants	.80	2.00	4.00
113-177-Later issues $1.00-c		.50	1.00
Shoestore Giveaway('63)	1.00	2.50	5.00

HOT WHEELS (TV)
Mar-Apr, 1970 - No. 6, Jan-Feb, 1971
National Periodical Publications

	GD25	FN65	NM94
1	5.85	17.50	35.00
2,4,5	3.20	8.00	16.00
3-Neal Adams-c	4.00	12.00	24.00
6-Neal Adams-c/a	4.70	14.00	28.00

NOTE: *Toth a-1p, 2-5; c-1p, 5.*

HOUSE OF MYSTERY (See Brave and the Bold #93, Elvira's House of Mystery, Limited Collectors' Edition & Super DC Giant)

HOUSE OF MYSTERY, THE
Dec-Jan, 1951-52 - No. 321, Oct, 1983 (No. 199-203: 52 pgs.)
National Periodical Publications/DC Comics

	GD25	FN65	NM94
1	85.00	260.00	600.00
2	35.00	107.00	250.00
3	29.00	85.00	200.00
4,5	25.00	75.00	175.00
6-10	19.00	58.00	135.00
11-15	16.00	48.00	110.00
16(7/53)-25	11.00	32.00	75.00
26-35(2/55)-Last pre-code issue; 30-Woodish-a	10.00	30.00	60.00
36-49	7.50	22.50	45.00
50-Text story of Orson Welles' War of the Worlds broadcast	6.70	20.00	40.00
51-60	5.00	15.00	30.00
61,63,65,66,70,72,76,84,85-Kirby-a	4.70	14.00	28.00
62,64,67-69,71,73-75,77-83,86-99	3.60	9.00	18.00
100 (7/60)	4.00	12.00	24.00
101-116: Last 10 cent issue. 109-Toth, Kubert-a	3.60	9.00	18.00
117-119,121-130: 117-Swipes-c to HOS #20	2.40	6.00	12.00
120-Toth-a	3.20	8.00	16.00
131-142	2.00	5.00	10.00
143-J'onn J'onzz, Manhunter begins (6/64), ends #173; story continues from Detective #326	17.00	52.00	120.00
144	9.15	27.50	55.00
145-155,157-159: 149-Toth-a. 158-Origin/1st app. Diabolu Idol-Head in J'onn J'onzz	6.70	20.00	40.00
156-Robby Reed begins (origin), ends #173	7.50	22.50	45.00
160-(7/66)-Robby Reed becomes Plastic Man in this issue only; 1st S.A. app. Plastic Man; intro Marco Xavier (Martin Manhunter) & Vulture Crime Organization; ends #173	9.15	27.50	55.00
161-173: 169-Origin/1st app. Gem Girl	4.70	14.00	28.00
174-177,182: 174-Mystery format begins. 182-Toth-a	1.60	4.00	8.00
178-Neal Adams-a; last 12 cent issue (2/68)	2.40	6.00	12.00
179-N. Adams/Orlando, Wrightson-a (1st pro work, 3 pgs.)	4.00	10.00	20.00
180,181,183: Wrightson-a (3, 10, & 3 pgs.). 180-Kane-Wood-a(2). 183-Wood-a	1.40	3.50	7.00
184-Kane/Wood, Toth-a	1.00	2.50	5.00
185-Williamson/Kaluta-a; 3 pgs. Howard-a	1.60	4.00	8.00
186-N. Adams-a; Wrightson-a, 10 pgs.	1.60	4.00	8.00
187,190: 187-Toth-a. 190-Toth-a(r)	.60	1.50	3.00

188,191,195-Wrightson-a (8, 3 & 10 pgs.). 195-Swamp creature story by

Hot Rods and Racing Cars #5, © CC

The House of Mystery #2, © DC

House of Mystery #74, © DC

House of Secrets #10, © DC

House of Secrets #66, © DC

Howard the Duck #4, © MEG

	GD25	FN65	NM94
Wrightson similar to Swamp Thing (10/71)	1.60	4.00	8.00
189-Wood-a	.60	1.50	3.00
192-194,196-198,200-203,205-223,225-227: 194-Toth, Kirby-a; 48 pgs. begin, end #198. 207-Wrightson-a. 221-Wrightson/Kaluta-a (8 pgs.). 226-Wrightson-r; Phantom Stranger-r	.60	1.50	3.00
199-Wood, Kirby-a; 52pgs. begin, end 203	.80	2.00	4.00
204-Wrightson-a, 9 pgs.	.80	2.00	4.00
224-N. Adams/Wrightson-a(r); begin 100 pg. issues; Phantom Stranger-r	1.00	2.50	5.00
228-N. Adams inks; Wrightson-r	.80	2.00	4.00
229-321: 229-Wrightson-a(r); Toth-r; last 100 pg. issue. 230-(68 pgs.) 251-259-(84 pgs.). 251-Wood-a	.60	1.50	3.00

NOTE: ***Neal Adams*** *a-236i; c-175-192, 197, 199, 251-254.* ***M. Anderson*** *c/a-37.* ***Aragones*** *a-186, 251.* ***Baily*** *a-279p.* ***Cameron*** *a-76, 79.* ***Colan*** *a-202r.* ***Craig*** *a-263, 275, 295, 300.* ***Ditko*** *a-236p, 247, 254, 258, 276; c-277.* ***Drucker*** *a-37.* ***Evans*** *c-218.* ***Fraden*** *a-251.* ***Giunta*** *a-199.* ***Golden*** *a-257, 259.* ***Heath*** *a-194r; c-203.* ***Howard*** *a-182, 185, 187, 196, 229r, 247i, 254, 279i.* ***Kaluta*** *a-195, 200, 250r; c-200-202, 210, 212, 233, 260, 261, 263, 265, 267, 268, 273, 276, 284, 287, 288, 293-295, 300, 302, 304, 305, 309-319, 321.* ***Bob Kane*** *a-84.* ***Gil Kane*** *a-196p, 253p, 300p.* ***Kirby*** *a-194r, 199r; c-65, 76, 78, 79, 85.* ***Kubert*** *c-282, 283, 285, 286, 289-292, 297-299, 301, 303, 306-308.* ***Maneely*** *a-68.* ***Mayer*** *a-317p.* ***Meskin*** *a-52-144 (most), 224r, 229r; c-63, 66, 124, 127.* ***Mooney*** *a-24, 159, 160.* ***Moreira*** *a-3, 4, 20-50, 58, 59, 62, 68, 77, 79, 90, 108, 113, 123, 201r, 228; c-4-28, 44, 47, 50, 54, 59, 62, 64, 68, 70, 73.* ***Morrow*** *a-192, 196, 255, 320i.* ***Mortimer*** *a-204(3 pgs.).* ***Nasser*** *a-276.* ***Newton*** *a-259, 272.* ***Nino*** *a-204, 212, 213, 220, 224, 225, 245, 250, 252-256, 283.* ***Orlando*** *a-175(2 pgs.), 178, 240i; c-240, 258p, 262, 264p, 270p, 271, 272, 274, 275, 278, 296i.* ***Redondo*** *a-194, 195, 197, 202, 203, 207, 211, 214, 217, 219, 226, 227, 229, 235, 241, 287(layout), 302p, 303i, 308; c-229.* ***Reese*** *a-195, 200, 205i.* ***Rogers*** *a-254, 274, 277.* ***Roussos*** *a-65, 84, 224i.* ***Sekowsky*** *a-282p.* ***Sparling*** *a-203.* ***Starlin*** *a-207(2 pgs.), 282p; c-281.* ***Leonard Starr*** *a-9.* ***Staton*** *a-300p.* ***Sutton*** *a-271, 290, 291, 293, 295, 297-299, 302, 303, 306-309, 310-313i, 314.* ***Tuska*** *a-293p, 294p, 316p.* ***Wrightson*** *c-193-195, 204, 207, 209, 211, 213, 214, 217, 221, 231, 236, 255, 256.*

HOUSE OF SECRETS (Combined with The Unexpected after #154)
11-12/56 - No. 80, 9-10/66; No. 81, 8-9/69 - No. 140, 2-3/76;
No. 141, 8-9/76 - No. 154, 10-11/78
National Periodical Publications/DC Comics

	GD25	FN65	NM94
1-Drucker-a; Moreira-c	60.00	180.00	425.00
2-Moreira-a	27.00	80.00	190.00
3-Kirby-c/a	22.00	65.00	150.00
4,8-Kirby-a	12.00	36.00	85.00
5-7,9-11: 11-Lou Cameron-a(unsigned)	10.00	30.00	65.00
12-Kirby-c/a	11.00	32.00	75.00
13-15	8.35	25.00	50.00
16-20	6.70	20.00	40.00
21,22,24-30	5.35	16.00	32.00
23-Origin/1st app. Mark Merlin & begin series	6.70	20.00	40.00
31-50: 48-Toth-a. 50-Last 10 cent issue	4.00	11.00	22.00
51-60: 58-Origin Mark Merlin retold	3.00	7.50	15.00
61-First Eclipso (7-8/63) and begin series	16.00	48.00	110.00
62	7.50	22.50	45.00
63-65,67-Toth-a on Eclipso (see Brave and the Bold #64)	5.85	17.50	35.00
66-1st Eclipso-c (also #67,70,78,79); Toth-a	9.15	27.50	55.00
68-80: 73-Mark Merlin ends, Prince Ra-Man begins. 76-Prine Ra-Man vs. Eclipso. 80-Eclipso, Prince Ra-Man end	4.20	12.50	25.00
81-91: 81-Mystery format begins. 82-Neal Adams-c(i). 85-N. Adams-a(i). 87-Wrightson & Kaluta-a. 90-Buckler (early work)/N. Adams-a	1.00	2.50	5.00
92-1st app. Swamp Thing-c/story (8 pgs.)(6-7/71) by Berni Wrightson(p) w/JeffJones/Kaluta/Weiss ink assists	32.00	95.00	225.00
93-100: 94-Wrightson inks. 96-Wood-a	.70	1.75	3.50
101-154: 140-Origin The Patchworkman		.50	1.00

NOTE: ***Neal Adams*** *c-81, 82, 84-88, 90, 91.* ***Cameron*** *a-15.* ***Colan*** *a-63.* ***Ditko*** *a-139p, 148.* ***Elias*** *a-58.* ***Evans*** *a-118.* ***Finlay*** *a-7r(Real Fact?).* ***Glanzman*** *a-91.* ***Golden*** *a-151.* ***Heath*** *a-31.* ***Kaluta*** *a-87, 98, 99; c-98, 99, 101, 102, 149, 151, 154.* ***Bob Kane*** *a-18, 21.* ***G. Kane*** *a-85p.* ***Kirby*** *c-3, 11, 12.* ***Kubert*** *a-39.* ***Meskin*** *a-2-68 (most); c-55-60.* ***Moreira*** *a-7, 8, 51, 54, 102-104, 106, 108, 113, 116, 118, 121, 123, 127; c-1, 2, 4-10, 13-20.* ***Morrow*** *a-86, 89, 90; c-89, 146-148.* ***Nino*** *a-101, 103, 106, 109, 115, 117, 126, 128, 131, 147, 153.* ***Redondo*** *a-95, 99, 102, 104p, 113, 116, 134, 139, 140.* ***Reese*** *a-85.* ***Starlin*** *c-150.* ***Sutton*** *a-154.* ***Toth*** *a-63-67, 83, 93r, 94r, 96r, 98r, 123.* ***Tuska*** *a-90, 104.* ***Wrightson*** *c-92-94, 96, 100, 103, 106, 107, 135, 139.*

HOUSE OF TERROR (3-D)
October, 1953 (1st 3-D horror comic)
St. John Publishing Co.

	GD25	FN65	NM94
1-Kubert, Baker-a	19.00	58.00	135.00

HOUSE OF YANG, THE (See Yang)
July, 1975 - No. 6, June, 1976; 1978
Charlton Comics

	GD25	FN65	NM94
1	.30	.75	1.50
2-6		.50	1.00
Modern Comics #1,2(1978)		.50	1.00

HOUSE II: THE SECOND STORY
Oct, 1987 (One-shot)
Marvel Comics

	GD25	FN65	NM94
1-Adapts movie	.40	1.00	2.00

HOWARD CHAYKIN'S AMERICAN FLAGG! (First)(Value: cover or less)

HOWARD THE DUCK (See Bizarre Adventures #34, Fear, Man-Thing & Marvel Treasury Edition)
Jan, 1976 - No. 31, May, 1979; No. 32, Jan, 1986; No. 33, Sept, 1986
Marvel Comics Group

	GD25	FN65	NM94
1-Brunner-c/a; Spider-Man x-over (low distr.)	2.00	5.00	10.00
2-11: 2-Brunner-c/a (low distr.). 3-Buscema-a(p)	.40	1.00	2.00
12-1st app. Kiss (cameo, 3/77)	.80	2.00	4.00
13-Kiss app. (1st full story)	1.00	2.50	5.00
14-33: 16-Album issue; 3 pgs. comics		.50	1.00
Annual 1(1977, 52 pgs.)-Mayerik-a		.50	1.00

NOTE: ***Austin*** *c-29i.* ***Bolland*** *c-33.* ***Brunner*** *a-1p, 2p; c-1, 2.* ***Buckler*** *c-3p.* ***Buscema*** *a-3p.* ***Colan*** *a(p)-4-15, 17-20, 24-27, 30, 31; c(p)-4-31, Annual 1p.* ***Leialoha*** *a-1-13i; c(i)-3-5, 8-11.* ***Mayerik*** *a-22, 23, 33.* ***P. Smith*** *a-30p. Man-Thing app. in #22, 23.*

HOWARD THE DUCK (Magazine)
October, 1979 - No. 9, March, 1981 (B&W, 68 pgs.)
Marvel Comics Group

	GD25	FN65	NM94
1	.30	.75	1.50
2,3,5-9: 3-Xmas issue. 7-Has poster by Byrne		.50	1.00
4-Beatles, John Lennon, Elvis, Kiss & Devo cameos; Hitler app.		.60	1.20

NOTE: ***Buscema*** *a-4p.* ***Colan*** *a-1-5p, 7-9p.* ***Jack Davis*** *c-3.* ***Golden*** *a(p)-1, 5, 6(51pgs.).* ***Rogers*** *a-7, 8.* ***Simonson*** *a-7.*

HOWARD THE DUCK: THE MOVIE
Dec, 1986 - No. 3, Feb, 1987 (Mini-series)
Marvel Comics Group

	GD25	FN65	NM94
1-3: Movie adaptation; r/Marvel Super Special		.50	1.00

HOW BOYS AND GIRLS CAN HELP WIN THE WAR
1942 (One Shot) (10 cents)
The Parents' Magazine Institute

	GD25	FN65	NM94
1-All proceeds used to buy war bonds	16.00	48.00	110.00

HOWDY DOODY (TV)(See Poll Parrot)
1/50 - No. 38, 7-9/56; No. 761, 1/57; No. 811, 7/57
Dell Publishing Co.

	GD25	FN65	NM94
1-(Scarce)-Photo-c; 1st TV comic	54.00	160.00	375.00
2-Photo-c	16.00	48.00	110.00
3-5: All photo-c	10.00	30.00	70.00
6-Used in **SOTI**, pg. 309; painted-c begin	10.00	30.00	65.00
7-10	10.00	30.00	60.00
11-20	7.50	22.50	45.00
21-38	6.70	20.00	40.00
4-Color 761,811	9.15	27.50	55.00

HOW IT BEGAN (See Single Series No. 15)

HOW SANTA GOT HIS RED SUIT (See March of Comics No. 2)

HOW STALIN HOPES WE WILL DESTROY AMERICA
1951 (16 pgs.) (Giveaway)
Joe Lowe Co. (Pictorial News)

	GD25	FN65	NM94
nn	39.00	118.00	275.00

(Prices vary widely on this book)

HOW THE WEST WAS WON (See Movie Comics)

HOW TO DRAW FOR THE COMICS
No date (1942?) (64 pgs.; B&W & color) (10 Cents) (No ads)
Street and Smith

	GD25	FN65	NM94
nn-Art by Winsor McCay, George Marcoux(Supersnipe artist), Vernon Greene (The Shadow artist), Jack Binder(with biog.), Thorton Fisher, Jon Small, & Jack Farr; has biographies of each artist	14.00	43.00	100.00

H. P. LOVECRAFT'S CTHULHU
Dec, 1991 - No. 3, Feb?, 1992 ($2.50, color, mini-series)
Millennium Publications

	GD25	FN65	NM94
1-3: 1-Contains trading cards on thin stock	.50	1.25	2.50

H. R. PUFNSTUF (TV) (See March of Comics 360)
Oct, 1970 - No. 8, July, 1972
Gold Key

	GD25	FN65	NM94
1-Photo-c (all have photo-c?)	11.00	32.00	75.00
2-8	5.00	15.00	30.00

HUBERT (See 4-Color No. 251)

HUCK & YOGI JAMBOREE (TV)
March, 1961 (116 pgs.; $1.00) (B&W original material)
(6-1/4x9"; cardboard cover; high quality paper)
Dell Publishing Co.

	GD25	FN65	NM94
nn	6.70	20.00	40.00

HUCK & YOGI WINTER SPORTS (See 4-Color No. 1310)

HUCK FINN (See The New Adventures of... & Power Record Comics)

HUCKLEBERRY FINN (See 4-Color No. 1114)

HUCKLEBERRY HOUND (See Dell Giant #31,44, Golden Picture Story Book, Kite Fun Book, March of Comics #199, 214, 235, Spotlight #1 & Whitman Comic Books)

HUCKLEBERRY HOUND (TV)
No. 990, 5-7/59 - No. 43, 10/70 (Hanna-Barbera)
Dell/Gold Key No. 18 (10/62) on

	GD25	FN65	NM94
4-Color 990(#1)	6.70	20.00	40.00
4-Color 1050,1054 (12/59)	5.00	15.00	30.00
3(1-2/60) - 7 (9-10/60)	5.00	15.00	30.00
4-Color 1141 (10/60)	5.00	15.00	30.00
8-10	4.00	11.00	22.00
11-17 (6-8/62)	3.20	8.00	16.00
18,19 (84pgs.; 18-20 titled ...Chuckleberry Tales)	5.00	15.00	40.00
20-30: 20-Titled Chuckleberry Tales	2.80	7.00	14.00
31-43: 37-reprints	2.40	6.00	12.00

HUCKLEBERRY HOUND (TV)
Nov, 1970 - No. 8, Jan, 1972 (Hanna-Barbera)
Charlton Comics

	GD25	FN65	NM94
1	3.00	7.50	15.00
2-8	2.00	5.00	10.00

HUEY, DEWEY, & LOUIE (See Donald Duck, 1938 for 1st app. Also see Mickey Mouse Magazine V4#2, V5#7 & Walt Disney's Junior Woodchucks Limited Series)

HUEY, DEWEY, & LOUIE BACK TO SCHOOL (See Dell Giant #22, 35, 49 & Dell Giants)

HUEY, DEWEY AND LOUIE JUNIOR WOODCHUCKS (Disney)
Aug, 1966 - No. 81, 1984 (See Walt Disney's C&S #125)
Gold Key No. 1-61/Whitman No. 62 on

	GD25	FN65	NM94
1	4.00	10.50	21.00
2,3(12/68)	2.80	7.00	14.00
4,5(4/70)-Barks-r	2.80	7.00	14.00
6-17-Written by Barks	1.80	4.50	9.00
18,27-30	1.00	2.50	5.00
19-23,25-Written by Barks. 22,23,25-Barks-r	1.20	3.00	6.00
24,26-Barks-r	1.20	3.00	6.00
31-57,60-81: 41,70,80-Reprints	.40	1.00	2.00
58,59-Barks-r	.60	1.50	3.00

NOTE: ***Barks** story reprints-No. 22-26, 35, 42, 45, 51.*

HUGGA BUNCH (TV) (Marvel)(Value: cover or less)

HULK (Formerly The Rampaging Hulk; also see The Incredible Hulk)
No. 10, Aug, 1978 - No. 27, June, 1981 (Magazine)($1.50, color)
Marvel Comics Group

	GD25	FN65	NM94
10	.30	.75	1.50
11-Moon Knight begins, ends 20	.80	2.00	4.00
12-15: Moon Knight stories	.50	1.25	2.50
16,19,21,22,24-27: 24-Part color. 25-27 are B&W	.30	.75	1.50
17,18,20: Moon Knight stories	.40	1.00	2.00
23-Last full color issue; Banner is attacked	.40	1.00	2.00

NOTE: ***Alcala** a(i)-15, 17-20, 22, 24-27. **Buscema** a-23; c-26. **Chaykin** a-21-25. **Colan** a(p)-11, 19, 24-27. **Jusko** painted c-12. **Nebres** a-16. **Sienkiewicz** a-13, 17, 20. **Simonson** a-27; c-23. Dominic Fortune appears in #21-24.*

HUMAN FLY
1963 - 1964 (Reprints)
I.W. Enterprises/Super

	GD25	FN65	NM94
I.W. Reprint #1-Reprints Blue Beetle #44('46)	1.20	3.00	6.00
Super Reprint #10-R/Blue Beetle #46('47)	1.20	3.00	6.00

HUMAN FLY, THE
Sept, 1977 - No. 19, Mar, 1979
Marvel Comics Group

	GD25	FN65	NM94
1-Origin; Spider-Man x-over	.80	2.00	4.00
2-Ghost Rider app.	1.20	3.00	6.00
3-19: 9-Daredevil x-over; Byrne-c(p)	.30	.75	1.50

NOTE: ***Austin** c-4i, 9i. **Elias** a-1, 3p, 4p, 7p, 10-12p, 15p, 18p, 19p. **Layton** c-19.*

HUMAN TARGET SPECIAL (TV)
Nov, 1991 ($2.00, color, 52 pgs.)
DC Comics

	GD25	FN65	NM94
1	.40	1.00	2.00

HUMAN TORCH, THE (Red Raven #1)(See All-Select, All Winners, Marvel Mystery, Men's Adventures, Mystic Comics (2nd series), Sub-Mariner, USA & Young Men)
No. 2, Fall, 1940 - No. 15, Spring, 1944;
No. 16, Fall, 1944 - No. 35, Mar, 1949 (Becomes Love Tales);
No. 36, April, 1954 - No. 38, Aug, 1954
Timely/Marvel Comics (TP 2,3/TCI 4-9/SePI 10/SnPC 11-25/CnPC 26-35/Atlas Comics (CPC 36-38))

	GD25	FN65	VF82	NM94
2(#1)-Intro & Origin Toro; The Falcon, The Fiery Mask, Mantor the Magician, & Microman only app.; Human Torch by Burgos, Sub-Mariner by Everett begin (origin of each in text)	780.00	2340.00	4700.00	7800.00

(Estimated up to 190 total copies exist, 10 in NM/Mint)

	GD25	FN65	NM94
3(#2)-40pg. H.T. story; H.T. & S.M. battle over who is best artist in text-Everett or Burgos	300.00	900.00	1800.00
4(#3)-Origin The Patriot in text; last Everett Sub-Mariner; Sid Greene-a	233.00	700.00	1400.00
5(#4)-The Patriot app; Angel x-over in Sub-Mariner (Summer, 1941)	167.00	500.00	1000.00
5-Human Torch battles Sub-Mariner (Fall,'41)	250.00	750.00	1500.00
6,7,9	108.00	325.00	650.00
8-Human Torch battles Sub-Mariner; Wolverton-a, 1 pg.	167.00	500.00	1000.00
10-Human Torch battles Sub-Mariner; Wolverton-a, 1 pg.			

Huckleberry Hound #12, © Hanna-Barbera

Human Fly #8, © MEG

Human Torch #6, © MEG

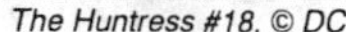
The Huntress #18, © DC

Ibis the Invincible #4, © FAW

Ideal #3, © MCG

	GD25	FN65	NM94
	125.00	375.00	750.00
11-15: 14-1st Atlas Globe logo	83.00	250.00	500.00
16-20: 20-Last War issue	63.00	190.00	380.00
21-30: 23(Sum/46)-Becomes Junior Miss 24?	57.00	170.00	340.00
31-Namora x-over in Sub-Mariner (also #30); last Toro	47.00	142.00	285.00
32-Sungirl, Namora app.; Sungirl-c	47.00	142.00	285.00
33-Capt. America x-over	52.00	155.00	310.00
34-Sungirl solo	48.00	145.00	290.00
35-Captain America & Sungirl app. (1949)	52.00	155.00	310.00
36-38(1954)-Sub-Mariner in all	44.00	132.00	265.00

NOTE: ***Ayers*** *Human Torch in 36(3).* ***Brodsky*** *c-25, 31-33?, 37, 38,* ***Burgos*** *c-36.* ***Everett*** *a-1-3, 27, 28, 30, 37, 38.* ***Powell*** *a-36(Sub-Mariner).* ***Schomburg*** *c-1-3, 5-8, 10-23.* ***Sekowsky*** *c-28, 34?, 35?* ***Shores*** *c-24, 26, 27, 29, 30.* ***Mickey Spillane*** *text 4-6. Bondage c-2, 12, 19.*

HUMAN TORCH, THE (Also see Avengers West Coast, Fantastic Four, The Invaders, Saga of the Original... & Strange Tales #101)
Sept, 1974 - No. 8, Nov, 1975
Marvel Comics Group

	GD25	FN65	NM94
1: 1-8-r/stories from Strange Tales #101-108	1.00	2.50	5.00
2-8: 1st H.T. title since G.A. 7-vs. Sub-Mariner	.60	1.50	3.00

NOTE: *Golden Age & Silver Age Human Torch-r #1-8.* ***Ayers*** *r-6, 7.* ***Kirby/Ayers*** *r-1-5, 8.*

HUMBUG (Satire by Harvey Kurtzman)
Aug, 1957 - No. 9, May, 1958; No. 10, June, 1958; No. 11, Oct, 1958
Humbug Publications

	GD25	FN65	NM94
1	12.00	36.00	85.00
2	7.50	22.50	45.00
3-9: 8-Elvis in Jailbreak Rock	5.00	15.00	30.00
10,11-Magazine format. 10-Photo-c	7.50	22.50	45.00
Bound Volume(#1-6)-Sold by publisher	23.00	70.00	160.00
Bound Volume(#1-9)	26.00	77.00	180.00

NOTE: ***Davis*** *a-1-11.* ***Elder*** *a-2-4, 6-9, 11.* ***Heath*** *a-2, 4-8, 10.* ***Jaffee*** *a-2, 4-9.* ***Kurtzman*** *a-11.* ***Wood*** *a-1.*

HUMDINGER (Becomes White Rider and Super Horse #3 on?)
May-June, 1946 - V2#2, July-Aug, 1947
Novelty Press/Premium Group

	GD25	FN65	NM94
1-Jerkwater Line, Mickey Starlight by Don Rico, Dink begin	10.00	30.00	65.00
2	5.35	16.00	32.00
3-6, V2#1,2	4.00	11.00	22.00

HUMOR (See All Humor Comics)

HUMPHREY COMICS (Also see Joe Palooka)
October, 1948 - No. 22, April, 1952
Harvey Publications

	GD25	FN65	NM94
1-Joe Palooka's pal (r); (52 pgs.)-Powell-a	9.15	27.50	55.00
2,3: Powell-a	4.20	12.50	25.00
4-Boy Heroes app.; Powell-a	5.00	15.00	30.00
5-8,10: 5,6-Powell-a. 7-Little Dot app.	3.60	9.00	18.00
9-Origin Humphrey	4.20	12.50	25.00
11-22	2.40	6.00	12.00

HUNCHBACK OF NOTRE DAME, THE (See 4-Color No. 854)

HUNK
August, 1961 - No. 11, 1963
Charlton Comics

	GD25	FN65	NM94
1	1.40	3.50	7.00
2-11	.70	1.75	3.50

HUNTED (Formerly My Love Memoirs)
No. 13, July, 1950 - No. 2, Sept, 1950
Fox Features Syndicate

	GD25	FN65	NM94
13(#1)-Used in **SOTI**, pg. 42 & illo.-"Treating police contemptuously" (lower left); Hollingsworth bondage-c	17.00	50.00	115.00
2	7.50	22.50	45.00

HUNTRESS, THE (See All-Star Comics #69, DC Super Stars #17, Detective #652, Infinity, Inc. #1, Sensation Comics #68 & Wonder Woman #271)
April, 1989 - No. 19, Oct, 1990 ($1.00, color, mature readers)
DC Comics

	GD25	FN65	NM94
1-19: Staton-c/a(p) in all. 17-19-Batman-c/stories		.50	1.00

HURRICANE COMICS
1945 (52 pgs.)
Cambridge House

	GD25	FN65	NM94
1-(Humor, funny animal)	11.00	32.00	75.00

HYBRIDS (See Revengers Special)

HYPER MYSTERY COMICS
May, 1940 - No. 2, June, 1940 (68 pgs.)
Hyper Publications

	GD25	FN65	NM94
1-Hyper, the Phenomenal begins	92.00	275.00	550.00
2	67.00	200.00	400.00

I AIM AT THE STARS (See 4-Color No. 1148)

I AM COYOTE (See Eclipse Graphic Album Series & Eclipse Magazine #2)

I AM LEGEND (Eclipse)(Value: cover or less)

IBIS, THE INVINCIBLE (See Fawcett Min., Mighty Midget & Whiz)
1943 (Feb) - #2, 1943; #3, Wint, 1945 - #5, Fall, 1946; #6, Spring, 1948
Fawcett Publications

	GD25	FN65	NM94
1-Origin Ibis; Raboy-c; on sale 1/2/43	108.00	325.00	650.00
2-Bondage-c	58.00	175.00	350.00
3-Wolverton-a #3-6 (4 pgs. each)	47.00	140.00	280.00
4-6: 5-Bondage-c	37.00	110.00	225.00

NOTE: ***Mac Raboy*** *c(p)-3-5.* ***Shaffenberger*** *c-6.*

ICE KING OF OZ, THE (See First Comics Graphic Novel #13)

ICEMAN (Also see The Champions & X-Men #94)
Dec, 1984 - No. 4, June, 1985 (Limited series)
Marvel Comics Group

	GD25	FN65	NM94
1	.40	1.00	2.00
2,4	.30	.75	1.50
3-The Defenders, Champions (Ghost Rider) & the original X-Men x-over	.50	1.25	2.50

ICICLE (Hero)(Value: cover or less)

I COME IN PEACE (Greater Mercury)(Value: cover or less)

IDAHO
June-Aug, 1963 - No. 8, July-Sept, 1965
Dell Publishing Co.

	GD25	FN65	NM94
1	2.00	5.00	10.00
2-8: 5-7-Painted-c	1.20	3.00	6.00

IDEAL (... a Classical Comic) (2nd Series) (Love Romances No. 6?)
July, 1948 - No. 5, March, 1949 (Feature length stories)
Timely Comics

	GD25	FN65	NM94
1-Antony & Cleopatra	20.00	60.00	140.00
2-The Corpses of Dr. Sacotti	17.00	52.00	120.00
3-Joan of Arc; used in **SOTI**, pg. 308-'Boer War'	15.00	45.00	105.00
4-Richard the Lion-hearted; titled "...the World's Greatest Comics;" The Witness app.	24.00	72.00	165.00
5-Ideal Love & Romance; photo-c	10.00	30.00	60.00

IDEAL COMICS (1st Series) (Willie Comics No. 5 on)
Fall, 1944 - No. 4, Spring, 1946
Timely Comics (MgPC)

	GD25	FN65	NM94
1-Super Rabbit in all	11.00	32.00	75.00
2	8.35	25.00	50.00
3,4	7.50	22.50	45.00

	GD25	FN65	NM94

IDEAL LOVE & ROMANCE (See Ideal, A Classical Comic)

IDEAL ROMANCE (Formerly Tender Romance)
No. 3, April, 1954 - No. 8, Feb, 1955 (Diary Confessions No. 9 on)
Key Publications

	GD25	FN65	NM94
3-Bernard Baily-c	4.35	13.00	26.00
4-8: 4,5-B. Baily-c	2.80	7.00	14.00

IDOL
1992 - No. 3, 1992 ($2.95, color, mini-series, 52 pgs.)
Epic Comics (Marvel)

	GD25	FN65	NM94
Book 1-3	.60	1.50	3.00

I DREAM OF JEANNIE (TV)
April, 1965 - No. 2, Dec, 1966 (Photo-c)
Dell Publishing Co.

	GD25	FN65	NM94
1,2-Barbara Eden photo-c	8.35	25.00	50.00

IF THE DEVIL WOULD TALK
1950; 1958 (32 pgs.; paper cover; in full color)
Roman Catholic Catechetical Guild/Impact Publ.

	GD25	FN65	NM94
nn-(Scarce)-About secularism (20-30 copies known to exist); very low distribution	50.00	150.00	350.00
1958 Edition-(Impact Publ.); art & script changed to meet church criticism of earlier edition; 80 plus copies known to exist	36.00	107.00	250.00
Black & White version of nn edition; small size; only 4 known copies exist	30.00	90.00	200.00

NOTE: The original edition of this book was printed and killed by the Guild's board of directors. It is believed that a very limited number of copies were distributed. The 1958 version was a complete bomb with very limited, if any, circulation. In 1979, 11 original, 4 1958 reprints, and 4 B&W's surfaced from the Guild's old files in St. Paul, Minnesota.

ILLUSTRATED GAGS (See Single Series No. 16)

ILLUSTRATED LIBRARY OF..., AN (See Classics Illustrated Giants)

ILLUSTRATED STORIES OF THE OPERAS
1943 (16 pgs.; B&W) (25 cents) (cover-B&W & red)
Baily (Bernard) Publ. Co.

	GD25	FN65	NM94
nn-(Rare)-Faust (part-r in Cisco Kid #1)	39.00	120.00	275.00
nn-(Rare)-Aida	39.00	120.00	275.00
nn-(Rare)-Carmen; Baily-a	39.00	120.00	275.00
nn-(Rare)-Rigoleito	39.00	120.00	275.00

ILLUSTRATED STORY OF ROBIN HOOD & HIS MERRY MEN, THE (See Classics Giveaways, 12/44)

ILLUSTRATED TARZAN BOOK, THE (See Tarzan Book)

I LOVED (Formerly Rulah; Colossal Features Magazine No. 33 on)
No. 28, July, 1949 - No. 32, Mar, 1950
Fox Features Syndicate

	GD25	FN65	NM94
28	5.00	15.00	30.00
29-32	3.60	9.00	18.00

I LOVE LUCY (Eternity) (Value: cover or less)

I LOVE LUCY COMICS (TV) (Also see The Lucy Show)
No. 535, Feb, 1954 - No. 35, Apr-June, 1962 (All photo-c)
Dell Publishing Co.

	GD25	FN65	NM94
4-Color 535(#1)	32.00	95.00	225.00
4-Color 559(#2, 5/54)	22.00	65.00	150.00
3 (8-10/54) - 5	13.00	40.00	90.00
6-10	10.00	30.00	70.00
11-20	10.00	30.00	60.00
21-35	8.35	25.00	50.00

I LOVE YOU
June, 1950 (One shot)
Fawcett Publications

	GD25	FN65	NM94
1-Photo-c	9.15	27.50	55.00

I LOVE YOU (Formerly In Love)
No. 7, 9/55 - No. 121, 12/76; No. 122, 3/79 - No. 130, 5/80
Charlton Comics

	GD25	FN65	NM94
7-Kirby-c, Powell-a	5.85	17.50	35.00
8-10	2.00	5.00	10.00
11-16,18-20	1.40	3.50	7.00
17-68 pg. Giant	1.80	4.50	9.00
21-25,27-50	1.00	2.50	5.00
26-Torres-a	1.40	3.50	7.00
51-59	.80	2.00	4.00
60(1/66)-Elvis Presley line drawn c/story	10.00	30.00	70.00
61-85	.60	1.50	3.00
86-130		.50	1.00

I'M A COP
1954 - No. 3, 1954?
Magazine Enterprises

	GD25	FN65	NM94
1(A-1 #111)-Powell-c/a in all	8.35	25.00	50.00
2(A-1 #126), 3(A-1 #128)	4.70	14.00	28.00

IMAGE GRAPHIC NOVEL (Image International) (Value: cover or less)

I'M DICKENS - HE'S FENSTER (TV)
May-July, 1963 - No. 2, Aug-Oct, 1963 (Photo-c)
Dell Publishing Co.

	GD25	FN65	NM94
1,2	4.00	11.00	22.00

I MET A HANDSOME COWBOY (See 4-Color No. 324)

IMMORTAL DOCTOR FATE, THE (DC) (Value: cover or less)

IMPACT
Mar-Apr, 1955 - No. 5, Nov-Dec, 1955
E. C. Comics

	GD25	FN65	NM94
1-Not code approved	11.00	32.00	75.00
2	8.35	25.00	50.00
3-5: 4-Crandall-a	7.00	21.00	42.00

*NOTE: **Crandall** a-1-4. **Davis** a-2-4; c-1-5. **Evans** a-1, 4, 5. **Ingels** a-in all. **Kamen** a-3. **Krigstein** a-1, 5. **Orlando** a-2, 5.*

IMPACT CHRISTMAS SPECIAL
1991 ($2.50, color, 68 pgs.)
Impact Comics (DC Comics)

	GD25	FN65	NM94
1-Gift of the Magi by Infantino/Rogers; The Black Hood, The Fly, The Jaguar, & The Shield stories	.50	1.25	2.50

IMPOSSIBLE MAN SUMMER VACATION SPECTACULAR, THE (Marvel) (Value: cover or less)

INCAL, THE
Nov, 1988 - No. 3, Jan, 1989 ($10.95/$12.95, adults)
Epic Comics (Marvel)

	GD25	FN65	NM94
1,3: Moebius-c/a in all; sexual content	2.20	5.50	11.00
2-($12.95)	2.60	6.50	13.00

INCREDIBLE HULK, THE (See Aurora, The Avengers #1, The Defenders #1, Giant-Size..., Hulk, Marvel Collectors Item Classics, Marvel Comics Presents #26, Marvel Fanfare, Marvel Treasury Edition, Power Record Comics, Rampaging Hulk & She-Hulk)

INCREDIBLE HULK, THE
May, 1962 - No. 6, Mar, 1963; No. 102, Apr, 1968 - Present
Marvel Comics Group

	GD25	FN65	NM94
1-Origin & 1st app. (skin is grey colored)	500.00	1500.00	4000.00
2-1st green skinned Hulk; Ditko-a(i)	170.00	515.00	1200.00
3-Origin retold; 1st app. Ringmaster & Hercules (9/62)	107.00	320.00	750.00
4,5: 4-Brief origin retold	87.00	260.00	600.00
6-Intro. Teen Brigade; all Ditko-a	143.00	430.00	1000.00
102-(Formerly Tales to Astonish)-Origin retold; story continued from Tales to Astonish #101	22.00	65.00	150.00
103	10.00	30.00	60.00
104-Rhino app.	9.15	27.50	55.00
105-108: 105-1st Missing Link	6.70	20.00	40.00
109,110: 109-Ka-Zar app.	4.70	14.00	28.00

If the Devil Would Talk #1, © CG

I Love Lucy #18, © Lucille Ball & Desi Arnaz

The Incredible Hulk #3, © MEG

The Incredible Hulk #278, © MEG

The Incredible Hulk #340, © MEG

The Incredible Hulk and Wolverine #1, © MEG

	GD25	FN65	NM94
111-117: 117-Last 12 cent issue	4.00	10.00	20.00
118-121,123-125: 118-Hulk vs. Sub-Mariner	2.00	5.00	10.00
122-Hulk battles Thing (12/69)	2.60	6.50	13.00
126-140: 126-1st Barbara Norriss (Valkyrie). 131-Hulk vs. Iron Man; 1st Jim Wilson, Hulk's new sidekick. 136-1st Xeron, The Star-Slayer. 140-Written by Harlan Ellison; 1st Jarella, Hulk's love	1.55	3.85	7.70
141-1st app. Doc Samson	1.30	3.30	6.60
142-144,146-161,163-171,173-175: 149-1st app. The Inheritor. 155-1st app. Shaper. 158-Warlock cameo(12/72); pre-dates Strange Tales #178. 161-The Mimic dies; Beast app. 163-1st app. The Gremlin. 164-1st Capt. Omen & Colonel John D. Armbruster. 166-1st Zzzax. 168-1st The Harpy; nudity panels of Betty Brant. 169-1st app. Bi-Beast	1.10	2.75	5.50
145-(52 pgs.)-Origin retold	1.55	3.85	7.70
162-1st app. The Wendigo; Beast app.	1.30	3.30	6.60
172-X-Men cameo; origin Juggernaut retold	1.30	3.30	6.60
176-Warlock cameo (2 panels only); same date as Strange Tales #178 (6/74)	1.40	3.50	7.00
177-1st actual death of Warlock (last panel only)	2.00	5.00	10.00
178-Rebirth of Warlock	4.00	10.00	20.00
179-No Warlock	1.00	2.50	5.00
180-(10/74)-1st app. Wolverine (cameo last pg.)	10.00	30.00	60.00
181-(11/74)-1st full Wolverine story	43.00	130.00	300.00
182-Wolverine cameo; 1st Crackajack Jackson	7.50	22.50	45.00
183-199: 185-Death of Col. Armbruster	.70	1.75	3.50
200-Silver Surfer app.; anniversary issue	4.20	12.50	25.00
201-240: 212-1st The Constrictor. 227-Original Avengers app. 232-Capt. America x-over from C.A. #230. 233-Marvel Man app. 234-(4/79)-1st app. Quasar (formerly Marvel Man & changes name to Quasar)	.60	1.50	3.00
241-249,251-299: 271-Rocket Raccoon app. 272-Sasquatch & Wendigo app.; Wolverine & Alpha Flight cameo in flashback. 278,279-Most Marvel characters app. (Wolverine in both). 279-X-Men & Alpha Flight cameos. 282-284-She-Hulk app. 293-F.F. app.	.40	1.00	2.00
250-Giant size; Silver Surfer app.	1.60	4.00	8.00
300-(10/84, 52 pgs.)-Spider-Man app in new black costume on-c & 2 pg. cameo	.80	2.00	4.00
301-313: 312-Origin Hulk retold	.50	1.25	2.50
314-Byrne-c/a begins, ends #319	1.00	2.50	5.00
315-319: 319-Bruce Banner & Betty Talbot wed	.50	1.25	2.50
320-323,325,327-329	.40	1.00	2.00
324-1st app. Grey Hulk since #1 (c-swipe of #1)	2.00	5.00	10.00
326-Grey vs. Green Hulk	1.00	2.50	5.00
330-1st McFarlane issue (4/87)	4.20	12.50	25.00
331-Grey Hulk series begins	3.20	8.00	16.00
332-334,336-339: 336,337-X-Factor app.	2.20	5.50	11.00
335-No McFarlane-a	.60	1.50	3.00
340-Hulk battles Wolverine by McFarlane	7.50	22.50	45.00
341-344	1.40	3.50	7.00
345-($1.50, 52 pgs.)	1.60	4.00	8.00
346-Last McFarlane issue	1.20	3.00	6.00
347-349,351-358,360-366	.60	1.50	3.00
350-Double size	.80	2.00	4.00
359-Wolverine app. (illusion only)	.90	2.25	4.50
367-1st Dale Keown-a on Hulk (3/90)	4.00	10.00	20.00
368-Sam Kieth-c/a	3.00	7.50	15.00
369,370-Dale Keown-c/a. 370,371-Original Defenders app.	2.00	5.00	10.00
371,373-376: Keown-c/a. 376-Green vs. Grey Hulk	1.20	3.00	6.00
372-Green Hulk app.; Keown-c/a	3.60	9.00	18.00
377-1st all new Hulk; fluorescent-c; Keown-c/a	4.00	10.00	20.00
377-Gold logo 2nd printing	1.40	3.50	7.00
378,380,389: No Keown-a. 380-Doc Samson app.	.60	1.50	3.00
379-Keown-a	1.60	4.00	8.00
381-388,390-392-Keown-a. 385-Infinity Gauntlet x-over. 389-Last $1.00-c. 392-X-Factor app.	.80	2.00	4.00
393-($2.50, 72 pgs.)-30th anniversary issue; green foil stamped-c; swipes-c to #1; has pin-ups of classic battles	1.60	4.00	8.00
393-2nd printing	.60	1.50	3.00
394-No Keown-c/a; intro Trauma	.30	.75	1.50
395,396-Punisher-c/stories; Keown-c/a	.40	1.00	2.00
397-Begin "Ghost of the Past" 4-part sty; Keown c/a	.40	1.00	2.00
398,399: 398-Last Keown-c/a	.30	.75	1.50
400-($2.50, 68 pgs.)-Holo-grafx foil-c & r/TTA #63	.50	1.25	2.50
401-406		.60	1.25
Special 1(10/68, 25 cents, 68pg.)-New 51 pg. story, Hulk battles The Inhumans; Steranko-c	8.35	25.00	50.00
Special 2(10/69, 25 cents, 68pg.)-Origin retold	5.00	15.00	30.00
Special 3(1/71, 25 cents, 68pg.)	1.60	4.00	8.00
Special 4 (1/72)	1.20	3.00	6.00
Annual 5(1976)	.80	2.00	4.00
Annual 6 (1977)	.40	1.00	2.00
Annual 7(1978)-Byrne/Layton-c/a; Iceman & Angel app. in book-length story	.60	1.50	3.00
Annual 8-16: 8('79)-Book-length Sasquatch-c/story. 9('80). 10('81). 11('82)-Doc Samson back-up by Miller(p)(5 pgs.); Spider-Man & Avengers app. Buckler-a(p). 12('83). 13('84). 14('85). 15('86). 16('90, $2.00, 68 pgs.)-She-Hulk app.	.40	1.00	2.00
Annual 17(1991, $2.00, 68 pgs.)-Origin retold	.40	1.00	2.00
Annual 18 (1992 ($2.25, 68 pgs.)-Return of the Defenders, part I; no Keown-c/a	.40	1.15	2.25
...Versus Quasimodo 1 (3/83, one-shot)-Based on Saturday morning cartoon	.30	.75	1.50

NOTE: ***Adkins** a-111-116i. **Austin** a(i)-350, 351, 353, 354; c-302i, 350i. **Ayers** a-3-5i. **John Buscema** c-202p. **Byrne** a-314-319p; c-314-316, 318, 319, 359. **Colan** c-363. **Ditko** a-2i, 6, 249, Annual 2r(5), 3r, 9p; c-2i, 6, 235, 249. **Everett** c-133i. **Golden** c-248, 251. **Kane** c(p)-193, 194, 196, 198. **Dale Keown** a(p)-367, 369-377, 379, 381-388, 390-393, 395-398; c-369-377p, 381, 382p, 384, 385, 386, 387p, 388, 390p, 391-393, 395p, 396, 397p, 398. **Kirby** a-1-5p, Special 2, 3p, Annual 5p; c-1-5, Annual 5. **McFarlane** a-330-334p, 336-339p, 340-343, 344-346p; c-330p, 340p, 341-343, 344p, 345, 346p. **Miller** c-258p, 261, 264, 268. **Mooney** a-230p, 287i, 288i. **Powell** a-Special 3r(2). **Romita** a-Annual 17p. **Severin** a(i)-108-110, 131-133, 141-151, 153-155; c(i)-109, 110, 132, 142, 144-155. **Simonson** c-283, 364-367. **Starlin** a-222p; c-217. **Staton** a(i)-187-189, 191-209. **Tuska** a-102i, 105i, 106i, 218p. **Williamson** a-310i; c-310i, 311i. **Wrightson** c-197.*

INCREDIBLE HULK AND WOLVERINE, THE
Oct, 1986 (One shot, $2.50, color)
Marvel Comics Group

	GD25	FN65	NM94
1-r-/1st app. Wolverine from Incred. Hulk #180,181; Wolverine back-up by Austin(i); Byrne-c	2.80	7.00	14.00

INCREDIBLE HULK: FUTURE IMPERFECT
1992 - No. 2, 1993 ($5.95, color, 52 pgs.)
Marvel Comics

	GD25	FN65	NM94
1,2-Embossed-c; Perez-c/a	1.20	3.00	6.00

INCREDIBLE MR. LIMPET, THE (See Movie Classics)

INCREDIBLE SCIENCE FICTION (Formerly Weird Science-Fantasy)
No. 30, July-Aug, 1955 - No. 33, Jan-Feb, 1956
E. C. Comics

	GD25	FN65	NM94
30,33: 33-Story-r/Weird Fantasy #18	25.00	75.00	175.00
31-Williamson/Krenkel-a, Wood-a(2)	28.00	85.00	200.00
32-Williamson/Krenkel-a	28.00	85.00	200.00

NOTE: ***Davis** a-30, 32, 33; c-30-32. **Krigstein** a-in all. **Orlando** a-30, 32, 33("Judgement Day" reprint). **Wood** a-30, 31, 33; c-33.*

INDIANA JONES (See Dark Horse Comics & Further Adventures of...)

INDIANA JONES AND THE FATE OF ATLANTIS
March, 1991 - No. 4, Sept, 1991 ($2.50, color, mini-series)
Dark Horse Comics

1-4: Dorman painted-c on all; 1,2-Contain trading cards (#1 has a 2nd

	GD25	FN65	NM94
printing, 10/91)	.50	1.25	2.50

INDIANA JONES AND THE LAST CRUSADE
1989 - No. 4, 1989 ($1.00, color, limited series, movie adaptation)
Marvel Comics

	GD25	FN65	NM94
1-4: Dan Barry-a(p); Williamson-i assist		.50	1.00
1 (1989, $2.95, B&W mag., 80 pgs.)	.50	1.50	3.00

INDIANA JONES AND THE TEMPLE OF DOOM
Sept, 1984 - No. 3, Nov, 1984 (Movie adaptation)
Marvel Comics Group

	GD25	FN65	NM94
1-3-r/Marvel Super Special; Guice-a		.50	1.00

INDIAN BRAVES (Baffling Mysteries No. 5 on)
March, 1951 - No. 4, Sept, 1951
Ace Magazines

	GD25	FN65	NM94
1-Green Arrowhead begins, ends #3	5.85	17.50	35.00
2	3.60	9.00	18.00
3,4	2.80	7.00	14.00
I.W. Reprint #1 (nd)-r/Indian Braves #4	1.00	2.50	5.00

INDIAN CHIEF (White Eagle...) (Formerly The Chief)
No. 3, July-Sept, 1951 - No. 33, Jan-Mar, 1959 (All painted-c)
Dell Publishing Co.

	GD25	FN65	NM94
3	3.60	9.00	18.00
4-11: 6-White Eagle app.	2.40	6.00	12.00
12-1st White Eagle(10-12/53)-Not same as earlier character	3.60	9.00	18.00
13-29	1.80	4.50	9.00
30-33-Buscema-a	2.00	5.00	10.00

INDIAN CHIEF (See March of Comics No. 94, 110, 127, 140, 159, 170, 187)

INDIAN FIGHTER, THE (See 4-Color No. 687)

INDIAN FIGHTER
May, 1950 - No. 11, Jan, 1952
Youthful Magazines

	GD25	FN65	NM94
1	6.70	20.00	40.00
2-Wildey-a/c(bondage)	4.00	11.00	22.00
3-11: 3,4-Wildey-a	2.80	7.00	14.00

NOTE: ***Walter Johnson*** *c-1, 3, 4, 6.* ***Palais*** *a-10.* ***Stallman*** *a-7.* ***Wildey*** *a-2-4; c-2, 5.*

INDIAN LEGENDS OF THE NIAGARA (See American Graphics)

INDIANS
Spring, 1950 - No. 17, Spring, 1953 (1-8: 52 pgs.)
Fiction House Magazines (Wings Publ. Co.)

	GD25	FN65	NM94
1-Manzar The White Indian, Long Bow & Orphan of the Storm begin	14.00	43.00	100.00
2-Starlight begins	8.35	25.00	50.00
3-5: 5-17-Most-c by Whitman	6.70	20.00	40.00
6-10	5.35	16.00	32.00
11-17	4.35	13.00	26.00

INDIANS OF THE WILD WEST
Circa 1958? (no date) (Reprints)
I. W. Enterprises

	GD25	FN65	NM94
9-Kinstler-c; Whitman-a; r/Indians #?	1.20	3.00	6.00

INDIANS ON THE WARPATH
No date (Late 40s, early 50s) (132 pages)
St. John Publishing Co.

	GD25	FN65	NM94
nn-Matt Baker-c; contains St. John comics rebound. Many combinations possible	19.00	57.00	130.00

INDIAN TRIBES (See Famous Indian Tribes)

INDIAN WARRIORS (Formerly White Rider and Super Horse; becomes Western Crime Cases #9)
No. 7, June, 1951 - No. 8, Sept, 1951
Star Publications

	GD25	FN65	NM94
7-White Rider & Superhorse continue; L.B. Cole-c	6.35	19.00	38.00
8-L. B. Cole-c	4.70	14.00	28.00
3-D 1(12/53)-L. B. Cole-c	24.00	72.00	165.00
Accepted Reprint(nn)(inside cover shows White Rider & Superhorse #11)-r/cover/#7; origin White Rider &..;. L. B. Cole-c	3.60	9.00	18.00
Accepted Reprint #8 (nd); L.B. Cole-c	3.60	9.00	18.00

INDOORS-OUTDOORS (See Wisco)

INDOOR SPORTS
nd (64 pgs.; 6x9"; B&W reprints; hardcover)
National Specials Co.

	GD25	FN65	NM94
nn-By Tad	4.35	13.00	26.00

INFERIOR FIVE, THE (Inferior 5 #11, 12) (See Showcase #62, 63, 65)
3-4/67 - No. 10, 9-10/68; No. 11, 8-9/72 - No. 12, 10-11/72
National Periodical Publications (#1-10: 12 cents)

	GD25	FN65	NM94
Showcase #62 (5-6/66)-Origin & 1st app.	7.50	22.50	45.00
Showcase #63,65 (7-8/66, 11-12/66)-2nd & 3rd app.	4.00	11.00	22.00
1-(3-4/67)-Sekowsky-a(p)	5.00	15.00	30.00
2-Plastic Man, F.F. app.; Sekowsky-a(p)	3.00	7.50	15.00
3-10: 4-Thor app. 6-Stars DC staff. 10-Superman x-over; F.F., Spider-Man & Sub-Mariner app.	2.00	5.00	10.00
11,12-Orlando-c/a; both r/Showcase #62,63	2.00	5.00	10.00

INFINITY GAUNTLET (The... #2 on; see The Infinity War & Warlock & the Infinity Watch)
July, 1991 - No. 6, Dec, 1991 ($2.50, color, limited series)
Marvel Comics

	GD25	FN65	NM94
1-Thanos-c/stories in all; Starlin scripts in all	1.20	3.00	6.00
2	.80	2.00	4.00
3-6: 5,6-Ron Lim-c/a	.60	1.50	3.00

NOTE: ***Lim*** *a-3p(part), 5p, 6p; c-5i, 6i.* ***Perez*** *a-1-3p, 4p(part); c-1(painted), 2-4, 5i, 6i.*

INFINITY, INC. (See All-Star Squadron #25)
Mar, 1984 - No. 53, Aug, 1988 ($1.25, Baxter paper, 36 pgs.)
DC Comics

	GD25	FN65	NM94
1-Brainwave, Jr., Fury, The Huntress, Jade, Northwind, Nuklon, Obsidian, Power Girl, Silver Scarab & Star Spangled Kid begin	.35	.85	1.75
2-5: 2-Dr. Midnite, G.A. Flash, W. Woman, Dr. Fate, Hourman, Green Lantern, Wildcat app. 5-Nudity panels		.50	1.00
6-13,38-49,51-53: 46,47-Millennium tie-ins		.50	1.00
14-Todd McFarlane-a (5/85, 2nd full story)	.60	1.50	3.00
15-37-McFarlane-a (20,23,24: 5 pgs. only; 33: 2 pgs.); 18-24-Crisis x-over. 21-Intro new Hourman & Dr. Midnight. 26-New Wildcat app. 31-Star Spangled Kid becomes Skyman. 32-Green Fury becomes Green Flame. 33-Origin Obsidian	.40	1.00	2.00
50 ($2.50, 52 pgs.)	.50	1.25	2.50
Annual 1,2: 1(12/85)-Crisis x-over. 2('88, $2.00)	.40	1.00	2.00
Special 1 (1987, $1.50)	.30	.75	1.50

NOTE: ***Kubert*** *r-4.* ***McFarlane*** *a-14-37p, Annual 1p; c(p)-14-19, 22, 25, 26, 31-33, 37, Annual 1.* ***Newton*** *a-12p, 13p(last work 4/85).* ***Tuska*** *a-11p. JSA app. 3-10.*

INFINITY WAR, THE (Also see Infinity Gauntlet & Warlock and the Infinity...)
June, 1992 - No. 6, Nov, 1992 ($2.50, color, mini-series)
Marvel Comics

	GD25	FN65	NM94
1-Starlin scripts, Lim-c/a(p), Thanos app. in all	1.00	2.50	5.00
2-6: All have wraparound gatefold covers	.40	1.25	2.50

INFORMER, THE
April, 1954 - No. 5, Dec, 1954
Feature Television Productions

	GD25	FN65	NM94
1-Sekowsky-a begins	5.85	17.50	35.00
2	4.00	12.00	24.00
3-5	4.00	10.00	20.00

IN HIS STEPS (Spire Christiain)(Value: cover or less)

Indian Chief #27, © DELL

Indian Fighter #3, © YM

Infinity, Inc.#9, © DC

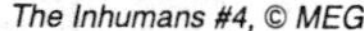
The Inhumans #4, © MEG

Intimate Love #15, © STD

Intimate Secrets of Romace #2, © STAR

INHUMANOIDS, THE (TV) (Marvel)(Value: cover or less)

INHUMANS, THE (See Amazing Adventures, Fantastic Four #45, Marvel Graphic Novel & Thor #146)
Oct, 1975 - No. 12, Aug, 1977
Marvel Comics Group

	GD25	FN65	NM94
1: #1-4 are 25 cent issues	.60	1.50	3.00
2-12: 9-Reprints Amazing Adventures #1,2('70)	.30	.75	1.50
Special 1(4/90, $1.50, 52 pgs.)-F.F. cameo	.30	.75	1.50

NOTE: ***Buckler** c-2-4p, 5. **Gil Kane** a-5-7p; c-1p, 7p, 8p. **Kirby** a-9r. **Mooney** a-11i. **Perez** a-1-4p, 8p.*

INKY & DINKY (See Felix's Nephews...)

IN LOVE (I Love You No. 7 on)
Aug-Sept, 1954 - No. 6, July, 1955 ('Adult Reading' on-c)
Mainline/Charlton No. 5 (5/55)-on

	GD25	FN65	NM94
1-Simon & Kirby-a	11.50	34.00	80.00
2-S&K-a; book-length novel	7.50	22.50	45.00
3,4-S&K-a. 3-Last pre-code (12-1/54-55)	6.35	19.00	38.00
5-S&K-c only	4.00	11.00	22.00
6-No S&K-a	2.80	7.00	14.00

IN LOVE WITH JESUS
1952 (36 pages) (Giveaway)
Catechetical Educational Society

	GD25	FN65	NM94
nn	2.80	7.00	14.00

INNOVATION SPECTACULAR (Innovation)(Value: cover or less)

INNOVATION SUMMER FUN SPECIAL (Innovation)(Value: cover or less)

INSANE (Dark Horse)(Value: cover or less)

IN SEARCH OF THE CASTAWAYS (See Movie Comics)

INSIDE CRIME (Formerly My Intimate Affair)
No. 3, July, 1950 - No. 2, Sept, 1950
Fox Features Syndicate (Hero Books)

	GD25	FN65	NM94
3-Wood-a, 10 pgs.; L. B. Cole-c	12.00	36.00	85.00
2-Used in SOTI, pg. 182,183; r/Spook #24	10.00	30.00	70.00
nn(no publ. listed, nd)	4.70	14.00	28.00

INSPECTOR, THE (Also see The Pink Panther)
July, 1974 - No. 19, Feb, 1978
Gold Key

	GD25	FN65	NM94
1	1.40	3.50	7.00
2-5	.70	1.75	3.50
6-19: 11-Reprints	.35	.90	1.75

INSPECTOR GILL OF THE FISH POLICE (See Fish Police)

INSPECTOR WADE (See Feature Books #13)

INTERFACE (Epic)(Value: cover or less)

INTERNATIONAL COMICS (...Crime Patrol No. 6)
Spring, 1947 - No. 5, Nov-Dec, 1947
E. C. Comics

	GD25	FN65	NM94
1-Schaffenberger-a begins, ends #4	47.00	140.00	325.00
2	34.00	100.00	235.00
3-5	27.00	80.00	190.00

INTERNATIONAL CRIME PATROL (Formerly International Comics #1-5; becomes Crime Patrol No. 7 on)
No. 6, Spring, 1948
E. C. Comics

	GD25	FN65	NM94
6-Moon Girl app.	50.00	150.00	350.00

INTERSTATE THEATRES' FUN CLUB COMICS
Mid 1940's (10 cents on cover) (B&W cover) (Premium)
Interstate Theatres

	GD25	FN65	NM94
Cover features MLJ characters looking at a copy of Top-Notch Comics, but contains an early Detective Comic on inside; many combinations possible	4.70	14.00	28.00

IN THE DAYS OF THE MOB (Magazine)
Fall, 1971 (Black & White)
Hampshire Dist. Ltd. (National)

	GD25	FN65	NM94
1-Kirby-a; John Dillinger wanted poster inside	1.20	3.00	6.00

IN THE PRESENCE OF MINE ENEMIES (Spire Christian)(Value: cover or less)

INTIMATE (Teen-Age Love No. 4 on)
December, 1957 - No. 3, May, 1958
Charlton Comics

	GD25	FN65	NM94
1-3	1.40	3.50	7.00

INTIMATE CONFESSIONS (See Fox Giants)

INTIMATE CONFESSIONS
July-Aug, 1951 - No. 7, Aug, 1952; No. 8, Mar, 1953 (All painted-c)
Realistic Comics

	GD25	FN65	NM94
1-Kinstler-c/a; c/Avon paperback #222	50.00	150.00	350.00
2	10.00	30.00	60.00
3-c/Avon paperback #250; Kinstler-c/a	12.00	36.00	80.00
4-6,8: 4-c/Avon paperback #304; Kinstler-c. 6-c/Avon paperback #120. 8-c/Avon paperback #375; Kinstler-a	10.00	30.00	60.00
7-Spanking panel	10.00	30.00	70.00

INTIMATE CONFESSIONS
1964
I. W. Enterprises/Super Comics

	GD25	FN65	NM94
I.W. Reprint #9,10	.80	2.00	4.00
Super Reprint #12,18	.80	2.00	4.00

INTIMATE LOVE
No. 5, 1950 - No. 28, Aug, 1954
Standard Comics

	GD25	FN65	NM94
5	4.00	11.00	22.00
6-8-Severin/Elder-a	4.35	13.00	26.00
9	2.00	5.00	10.00
10-Jane Russell, Robert Mitchum photo-c	4.35	13.00	26.00
11-18,20,23,25,27,28	1.60	4.00	8.00
19,21,22,24,26-Toth-a	4.70	14.00	28.00

NOTE: ***Celardo** a-8, 10. **Colletta** a-23. **Moreira** a-13(2). Photo-c-6, 7, 10, 12, 14, 15, 18-20, 24, 26, 27.*

INTIMATE SECRETS OF ROMANCE
Sept, 1953 - No. 2, April, 1954
Star Publications

	GD25	FN65	NM94
1,2-L. B. Cole-c	6.35	19.00	38.00

INTRIGUE
January, 1955
Quality Comics Group

	GD25	FN65	NM94
1-Horror; Jack Cole reprint/Web of Evil	13.00	40.00	90.00

INTRUDER (TSR)(Value; cover or less)

INVADERS, THE (TV)
Oct, 1967 - No. 4, Oct, 1968 (All have photo-c)
Gold Key

	GD25	FN65	NM94
1-Spiegle-a in all	5.85	17.50	35.00
2-4	4.20	12.50	25.00

INVADERS, THE (Also see The Avengers #71 & Giant-Size Invaders)
August, 1975 - No. 40, May, 1979; No. 41, Sept, 1979
Marvel Comics Group

	GD25	FN65	NM94
1-Captain America & Bucky, Human Torch & Toro, & Sub-Mariner begin; #1-7 are 25 cent issues	1.60	4.00	8.00

2-10: 2-1st app. Mailbag & Brain-Drain. 3-Battle issue; intro U-Man. 6-Liberty Legion app; intro/1st app. Union Jack; two cover prices, 25 & 30 cents. 7-Intro Baron Blood; Human Torch origin retold. 9-Origin Baron

Blood. 10-G.A. Capt. America-r/C.A #22 1.10 2.75 5.50
11-19: 11-Origin Spitfire; intro The Blue Bullet. 14-1st app. The Crusaders. 16-Re-intro The Destroyer. 17-Intro Warrior Woman. 18-Re-intro The Destroyer w/new origin. 19-Hitler-c/story .80 2.00 4.00
20-Reprints origin/1st app. Sub-Mariner from Motion Picture Funnies Weekly with color added & brief write-up about MPFW; 1st app. new Union Jack II 1.00 2.50 5.00
21-Reprints Marvel Mystery #10 (battle issue) .70 1.75 3.50
22,23,25-40: 22-New origin Toro. 25-All new-a begins. 28-Intro new Human Top & Golden Girl. 29-Intro Teutonic Knight. 31-Frankenstein-c/story. 32,33-Thor app. 34-Mighty Destroyer joins. 35-The Whizzer app. .50 1.25 2.50
24-r/Marvel Mystery #17 (team-up issue; all-r) .60 1.50 3.00
41-Double size last issue .60 1.50 3.00
Annual 1(9/77)-Schomburg, Rico stories (new); Schomburg-c/a (1st for Marvel in 30 years); Avengers app.; re-intro The Shark & The Hyena .60 1.50 3.00

NOTE: ***Buckler** a-5. **Everett** r-20('39), 21(1940), 24, Annual 1. **Gil Kane** c(p)-13, 17, 18, 20-27. **Kirby** c(p)-3-12, 14-16, 32, 33. **Mooney** a-5i, 16, 22. **Robbins** a-1-4, 6-9, 10(3 pg.), 11-15, 17-21, 23, 25-28; c-28.*

INVADERS FROM HOME (DC) (Value: cover or less)

INVASION
Holiday, 1988-'89 - No. 3, Jan, 1989 ($2.95, mini-series, 84 pgs.)
DC Comics

1-McFarlane/Russell-a .70 1.75 3.50
2,3: 2-McFarlane/Russell-a .60 1.50 3.00

INVINCIBLE FOUR OF KUNGFU & NINJA (Leung) (Value: cover or less)

INVISIBLE BOY (See Approved Comics)

INVISIBLE MAN, THE (See Superior Stories #1 & Supernatural Thrillers #2)

INVISIBLE SCARLET O'NEIL (Also see Famous Funnies #81 & Harvey Comics Hits 59)
Dec, 1950 - No. 3, April, 1951
Famous Funnies (Harvey)

1 10.00 30.00 65.00
2,3 7.50 22.50 45.00

IRON CORPORAL, THE (See Army War Heroes #22)
No. 23, Oct, 1985 - No. 25, Feb, 1986
Charlton Comics

23-25: Glanzman-a(r) .50 1.00

IRON FIST (See Deadly Hands of Kung Fu, Marvel Premiere & Power Man)
Nov, 1975 - No. 15, Sept, 1977
Marvel Comics Group

1-Iron Fist battles Iron Man (#1-6: 25 cent-c) 4.20 12.50 25.00
2 2.40 6.00 12.00
3-5 1.80 4.50 9.00
6-10: 8-Origin retold 1.40 3.50 7.00
11-13: 12-Capt. America app. 1.20 3.00 6.00
14-1st app. Sabretooth (see Power Man #66) 13.00 40.00 90.00
15-X-Men app., Byrne-a (30 & 35 cents) 4.00 11.00 22.00

NOTE: ***Adkins** a-8p, 10i, 13i; c-8i. **Byrne** a-1-15p; c-8p, 15p. **G. Kane** c-4-6p. **McWilliams** a-1i.*

IRONHAND OF ALMURIC (Dark Horse) (Value: cover or less)

IRON HORSE (TV)
March, 1967 - No. 2, June, 1967
Dell Publishing Co.

1,2 2.40 6.00 12.00

IRONJAW (Also see The Barbarians)
Jan, 1975 - No. 4, July, 1975
Atlas/Seaboard Publ.

1-Neal Adams-c; Sekowsky-a(p) .30 .75 1.50
2-4: 2-Neal Adams-c. 4-Origin .50 1.00

IRON MAN (Also see The Avengers #1, Giant-Size..., Marvel Collectors Item Classics, Marvel Double Feature, Marvel Fanfare & Tales of Suspense #39)
May, 1968 - Present
Marvel Comics Group

1-Origin; Colan-c/a(p); story continued from Iron Man & Sub-Mariner #1 50.00 150.00 350.00
2 16.00 48.00 110.00
3 11.00 32.00 75.00
4,5 9.15 27.50 55.00
6-10: 9-Iron Man battles green Hulk-like android 6.70 20.00 40.00
11-15: 15-Last 12 cent issue 5.35 16.00 32.00
16-20 4.00 10.00 20.00
21-24,26-42: 22-Death of Janice Cord. 27-Intro Fire Brand. 33-1st app. Spymaster. 35-Nick Fury & Daredevil x-over. 42-Last 15 cent issue 3.00 7.50 15.00
25-Iron Man battles Sub-Mariner 3.60 9.00 18.00
43-Intro The Guardsman; 25 cent giant 3.00 7.50 15.00
44-46,48-50: 46-The Guardsman dies. 50-Princess Python app. 2.00 5.00 10.00
47-Origin retold; Smith-a(p) 3.20 8.00 16.00
51-53: 53-Starlin part pencils 1.60 4.00 8.00
54-Iron Man battles Sub-Mariner; 1st app. Moondragon (1/73) as Madame MacEvil; Everett part-c 2.80 7.00 14.00
55-1st app. Thanos, Drax the Destroyer, Mentor, Starfox & Kronos (2/73); Starlin-c/a 14.00 43.00 100.00
56-Starlin-a 4.00 10.00 20.00
57-67,69,70: 59-Firebrand returns. 65-Origin Dr. Spectrum. 66-Iron Man vs. Thor. 67-Last 20 cent issue 1.50 3.75 7.50
68-Starlin-c; origin retold 2.00 5.00 10.00
71-99: 72-Cameo portraits of N. Adams, Brunner. 76-r/#9. 86-1st app. Blizzard. 87-Origin Blizzard. 89-Last 25 cent issue. 96-1st app. new Guardsman 1.00 2.50 5.00
100-(7/77)-Starlin-c 2.00 5.00 10.00
101-117: 101-Intro DreadKnight. 109-1st app. new Crimson Dynamo; 1st app. Vanguard. 110-Origin Jack of Hearts retold 1.00 2.50 5.00
118-Byrne-a(p) 1.20 3.00 6.00
119,120,123-128-Tony Stark recovers from alcohol problem. 120,121-Sub-Mariner x-over. 125-Ant-Man app. .90 2.20 4.40
121,122,129-149: 122-Origin. 131,132-Hulk x-over .50 1.20 2.40
150-Double size .65 1.65 3.30
151-168: 152-New armor. 161-Moon Knight app. 167-Tony Stark alcohol problem starts again .40 1.00 2.00
169-New Iron Man (Jim Rhodes replaces Tony Stark) 1.75 4.40 8.80
170 1.00 2.50 5.00
171 .60 1.50 3.00
172-199: 172-Captain America x-over. 186-Intro Vibro. 190-Scarlet Witch app. 191-198-Tony Stark returns as original Iron Man. 192-Both Iron Men battle .40 1.00 2.00
200-(11/85, $1.25, 52 pgs.)-Tony Stark returns as new Iron Man (red & white armor) thru #230 .90 2.20 4.40
201-224: 213-Intro new Dominic Fortune. 214-Spider-Woman apps. in new black costume (1/87) .30 .75 1.50
225-Double size ($1.25) 1.10 2.75 5.50
226-243,245-249: 228-Vs. Capt. America. 231-Intro new Iron Man. 233-Antman app. 234-Spider-Man x-over. 243-Tony Stark looses use of legs. 247-Hulk x-over .30 .75 1.50
244-($1.50, 52 pgs.)-New Armor makes him walk .90 2.20 4.40
250-($1.50, 52 pgs.)-Dr. Doom-c/story .35 .85 1.70
251-274,276-283,285-287,289,291,292: 258-277-Byrne scripts. 271-Fin Fang Foom app. 276-Black Widow-c/story; last $1.00-c .60 1.25
275-($1.50, 52 pgs.) .30 .75 1.50
284-Death of Iron Man 1.00 2.50 5.00
288-($2.50, 52pg.)-Foil stamped-c; Iron Man's 350th app. in comics .50 1.25 2.50
290-($2.95, 52pg.)-Gold foil stamped-c; 30th ann. .60 1.50 3.00

The Invaders #28, © MEG

Iron Fist #5, © MEG

Iron Man #25, © MEG

Iron Man & Sub-Mariner #1, © MEG

I Spy #2, © Three F Prod.

Is This Tomorrow #1, © CG

GD25 FN65 NM94

Special 1(8/70)-Sub-Mariner x-over; Everett-c 3.60 9.00 18.00
Special 2(11/71)-r/TOS #81,82,91 (all-r) 1.60 4.00 8.00
Annual 3(1976)-Man-Thing app. .80 2.00 4.00
King Size 4(8/77)-The Champions (w/Ghost Rider) app.; Newton-a(i)
.60 1.50 3.00
Annual 5-9: 5(1982)-New-a. 6(1983)-New Iron Man(J. Rhodes) app. 7(1984). 8(1986)-X-Factor app. 9(1987) .40 1.00 2.00
Annual 10(1989, $2.00, 68 pgs.)-Atlantis Attacks x-over; P. Smith-a; Layton/Guice-a; Sub-Mariner app. .50 1.25 2.50
Annual 11,12 ($2.00, 68 pgs.): 11-(1990)-Origin of Mrs. Arbogast by Ditko (p&i). 12-(1991)-1 pg. origin recap; Ant-Man back-up story
.40 1.00 2.00
Annual 13 (1992, $2.25, 68 pgs.)-Darkhawk & Avengers West Coast app.; Colan/Williamson-a .50 1.25 2.50
Graphic Novel: Crash (1988, $12.95, Adults, 72 pgs?)-Computer generated art & color; violence & nudity 2.60 6.50 13.00

NOTE: ***Austin*** *c-105i, 109-111i, 151i.* ***Byrne*** *a-118p; c-109p, 253.* ***Colan*** *a-1p, 253, Special 1p(3); c-1p.* ***Craig*** *a-1i, 2-4, 5-13i, 14, 15-19i, 24p, 25p, 26-28i; c-2-4.* ***Ditko*** *a-160p.* ***Everett*** *c-29.* ***Guice*** *a-233-241p.* ***G. Kane*** *c(p)-52-54, 63, 67, 72-75, 77, 78, 88, 98.* ***Kirby*** *a-Special 1p; c-13, 80p, 90, 92-95.* ***Mooney*** *a-40i, 43i, 47i.* ***Perez*** *c-103p.* ***Simonson*** *c-Annual 8.* ***B. Smith*** *a-229, 232p, 243i; c-229, 232.* ***P. Smith*** *a-159p, 245p, Annual 10p; c-159.* ***Starlin*** *a-53p(part), 55p, 56p; c-55p, 160, 163.* ***Tuska*** *a-5-13p, 15-23p, 24i, 32p, 38-46p, 48-54p, 57-61p, 63-69p, 70-72p, 78p, 86-92p, 95-106p, Annual 4p.* ***Wood*** *a-Special 1i.*

IRON MAN & SUB-MARINER
April, 1968 (One Shot) (Pre-dates Iron Man #1 & Sub-Mariner #1)
Marvel Comics Group

1-Iron Man story by Colan/Craig continued from Tales of suspense #99 & continued in Iron Man #1; Sub-Mariner story by Colan continued from Tales to Astonish #101 & continued in Sub-Mariner #1; Colan/Everett-c
22.00 65.00 150.00

IRON MARSHALL (Jademan) (Value: cover or less)

IRON VIC (See Comics Revue No. 3)
1940; Aug, 1947 - No. 3, 1947
United Features Syndicate/St. John Publ. Co.

Single Series 22 19.00 57.00 130.00
2,3(St. John) 4.35 13.00 26.00

IRONWOLF (DC) (Value: cover or less)

ISIS (TV) (Also see Shazam)
Oct-Nov, 1976 - No. 8, Dec-Jan, 1977-78
National Periodical Publications/DC Comics

1-Wood inks .30 .75 1.50
2-8: 5-Isis new look. 7-Origin .50 1.00

ISLAND AT THE TOP OF THE WORLD (See Walt Disney Showcase #27)

ISLAND OF DR. MOREAU, THE (Movie)
October, 1977 (52 pgs.)
Marvel Comics Group

1-Gil Kane-c .50 1.00

I SPY (TV)
Aug, 1966 - No. 6, Sept, 1968 (All have photo-c)
Gold Key

1-Bill Cosby, Robert Culp photo covers 16.00 48.00 110.00
2-6: 3,4-McWilliams-a 10.00 30.00 65.00

IS THIS TOMORROW?
1947 (One Shot) (3 editions) (52 pages)
Catechetical Guild

1-Theme of communists taking over the USA; (no price on cover) Used in **POP**, pg. 102 10.00 30.00 70.00
1-(10 cents on cover) 14.00 42.00 100.00
1-Has blank circle with no price on cover 14.00 42.00 100.00
Black & White advance copy titled "Confidential"-(52 pgs.)-Contains script and art edited out of the color edition, including one page of extreme violence showing mob nailing a Cardinal to a door; (only two known copies) 43.00 130.00 300.00

NOTE: *The original color version first sold for 10 cents. Since sales were good, it was later printed as a giveaway. Approximately four million in total were printed. The two black and white copies listed plus two other versions as well as a full color untrimmed version surfaced in 1979 from the Guild's old files in St. Paul, Minnesota.*

IT! (See Astonishing Tales No. 21-24 & Supernatural Thrillers No. 1)

IT HAPPENS IN THE BEST FAMILIES
1920 (52 pages) (B&W Sundays)
Powers Photo Engraving Co.

nn-By Briggs 12.50 37.50 75.00
Special Railroad Edition(30 cents)-r-/strips from 1914-1920
10.00 30.00 65.00

IT REALLY HAPPENED
1944 - No. 11, Oct, 1947
William H. Wise No. 1,2/Standard (Visual Editions)

1-Kit Carson story 10.00 30.00 65.00
2 5.35 16.00 32.00
3,4,6,9 4.20 12.50 25.00
5-Lou Gehrig story 8.35 25.00 50.00
7-Teddy Roosevelt story 4.70 14.00 28.00
8-Story of Roy Rogers 10.00 30.00 65.00
10-Honus Wagner story 7.50 22.50 45.00
11-Baker-a 6.70 20.00 40.00

NOTE: ***Guardineer*** *a-7(2), 8(2), 11.* ***Schomburg*** *c-1-7, 9-11.*

IT RHYMES WITH LUST (Also see Bold Stories & Candid Tales)
1950 (Digest size) (128 pages)
St. John Publishing Co.

nn (Rare)-Matt Baker & Ray Osrin-a 28.00 85.00 200.00

IT'S ABOUT TIME (TV)
January, 1967
Gold Key

1 (10195-701)-Photo-c 4.00 11.00 22.00

IT'S A DUCK'S LIFE
Feb, 1950 - No. 11, Feb, 1952
Marvel Comics/Atlas(MMC)

1-Buck Duck, Super Rabbit begin 9.15 27.50 55.00
2 4.70 14.00 28.00
3-11 3.60 9.00 18.00

IT'S FUN TO STAY ALIVE (Giveaway)
1948 (16 pgs.) (heavy stock paper)
National Automobile Dealers Association

Featuring: Bugs Bunny, The Berrys, Dixie Dugan, Elmer, Henry, Tim Tyler, Bruce Gentry, Abbie & Slats, Joe Jinks, The Toodles, & Cokey; all art copyright 1946-48 drawn especially for this book. 13.00 40.00 90.00

IT'S GAMETIME
Sept-Oct, 1955 - No. 4, Mar-Apr, 1956
National Periodical Publications

1-(Scarce)-Infinity-c; Davy Crockett app. in puzzle
46.00 140.00 325.00
2-4(Scarce): 2-Dodo & The Frog 39.00 118.00 275.00

IT'S LOVE, LOVE, LOVE
November, 1957 - No. 2, Jan, 1958 (10 cents)
St. John Publishing Co.

1,2 3.00 7.50 15.00

IVANHOE (See Fawcett Movie Comics No. 20)

IVANHOE
July-Sept, 1963

	GD25	FN65	NM94
Dell Publishing Co.			
1 (12-373-309)	4.00	10.00	20.00

IWO JIMA (See Spectacular Features Magazine)

JACE PEARSON OF THE TEXAS RANGERS (4-Color #396 is titled Tales of the Texas Rangers; ...'s Tales of ... #11-on)(See Western Roundup under Dell Giants)(Radio/TV)
No. 396, 5/52 - No. 1021, 8-10/59 (No #10) (All-Photo-c)
Dell Publishing Co.

	GD25	FN65	NM94
4-Color 396 (#1)	10.00	30.00	65.00
2(5-7/53) - 9(2-4/55)	5.35	16.00	32.00
4-Color 648(#10, 9/55)	5.35	16.00	32.00
11(11-2/55-56) - 14,17-20(6-8/58)	4.35	13.00	26.00
15,16-Toth-a	5.85	17.50	35.00
4-Color 961-Spiegle-a	4.70	14.00	28.00
4-Color 1021	4.35	13.00	26.00

NOTE: *Joel McCrea photo c-1-9, F.C. 648 (starred on radio show only); Willard Parker photo c-11-on (starred on TV series).*

JACK & JILL VISIT TOYTOWN WITH ELMER THE ELF
1949 (16 pgs.) (paper cover)
Butler Brothers (Toytown Stores Giveaway)

	GD25	FN65	NM94
nn	2.00	5.00	10.00

JACK ARMSTRONG (Radio)(See True Comics)
Nov, 1947 - No. 9, Sept, 1948; No. 10, Mar, 1949 - No. 13, Sept, 1949
Parents' Institute

	GD25	FN65	NM94
1	14.00	43.00	100.00
2	10.00	30.00	60.00
3-5	8.35	25.00	50.00
6-13	6.70	20.00	40.00
12-Premium version(distr. in Chicago only); Free printed on upper right-c; no price (Rare)	10.00	30.00	70.00

JACK HUNTER (Blackthorne)(Value: cover or less)

JACKIE GLEASON (TV) (Also see The Honeymooners)
1948 - No. 2, 1948; Sept, 1955 - No. 4, Dec, 1955?
St. John Publishing Co.

	GD25	FN65	NM94
1(1948)	50.00	150.00	350.00
2(1948)	39.00	118.00	275.00
1(1955)(TV)-Photo-c	43.00	130.00	300.00
2-4	29.00	85.00	200.00

JACKIE GLEASON AND THE HONEYMOONERS (TV)
June-July, 1956 - No. 12, Apr-May, 1958
National Periodical Publications

	GD25	FN65	NM94
1	64.00	193.00	450.00
2	50.00	150.00	350.00
3-11	36.00	107.00	250.00
12 (Scarce)	54.00	160.00	375.00

JACKIE JOKERS (Also see Richie Rich &...)
March, 1973 - No. 4, Sept, 1973
Harvey Publications

	GD25	FN65	NM94
1-4: 2-President Nixon app.		.50	1.00

JACKIE ROBINSON (Famous Plays of...) (Also see Negro Heroes #2 & Picture News #4)
May, 1950 - No. 6, 1952 (Baseball hero) (All photo-c)
Fawcett Publications

	GD25	FN65	NM94
nn	54.00	160.00	375.00
2	34.00	103.00	240.00
3-6	29.00	85.00	200.00

JACK IN THE BOX (Formerly Yellowjacket Comics #1-10; becomes Cowboy Western Comics #17 on)
Feb, 1946; No. 11, Oct, 1946 - No. 16, Nov-Dec, 1947
Frank Comunale/Charlton Comics No. 11 on

	GD25	FN65	NM94
1-Stitches, Marty Mouse & Nutsy McKrow	8.35	25.00	50.00
11-Yellowjacket	9.15	27.50	55.00
12,14,15	4.00	11.00	22.00
13-Wolverton-a	11.50	34.00	80.00
16-12pg. adapt. of Silas Marner; Kiefer-a	5.85	17.50	35.00

JACK OF HEARTS (Also see The Deadly Hands of Kung Fu #22 & Marvel Premiere #44)
Jan, 1984 - No. 4, April, 1984 (60 cents, mini-series)
Marvel Comics Group

	GD25	FN65	NM94
1-4		.50	1.00

JACKPOT COMICS (Jolly Jingles #10 on)
Spring, 1941 - No. 9, Spring, 1943
MLJ Magazines

	GD25	FN65	NM94
1-The Black Hood, Mr. Justice, Steel Sterling & Sgt. Boyle begin; Biro-c	150.00	450.00	900.00
2-S. Cooper-c	73.00	218.00	435.00
3-Hubbell-c	58.00	175.00	350.00
4-Archie begins (on sale 12/41)-(also see Pep Comics #22); Novick-c	150.00	450.00	900.00
5-Hitler-c by Montana	73.00	218.00	435.00
6-9: 6,7-Bondage-c by Novick. 8,9-Sahle-c	63.00	128.00	375.00

JACK Q FROST (See Unearthly Spectaculars)

JACK THE GIANT KILLER (See Movie Classics)

JACK THE GIANT KILLER (New Adventures of...)
Aug-Sept, 1953
Bimfort & Co.

	GD25	FN65	NM94
V1#1-H. C. Kiefer-c/a	11.50	34.00	80.00

JACKY'S DIARY (See 4-Color No. 1091)

JADEMAN COLLECTION (Jademan)(Value: cover or less)

JADEMAN KUNG FU SPECIAL (Jademan)(Value: cover or less)

JAGUAR, THE (Also see The Adventures of...)
Aug, 1991 - No. 14, Oct, 1992 ($1.00, color)
Impact Comics (DC)

	GD25	FN65	NM94
1-14: 4-The Black Hood x-over; 7-Sienkiewicz-c. 9-Contains Crusaders trading card		.50	1.00
Annual 1 (1992, $2.50, 68 pgs.)-W/trading card	.50	1.25	2.50

JAKE THRASH (Aircel)(Value: cover or less)

JAMBOREE
Feb, 1946(no mo. given) - No. 3, April, 1946
Round Publishing Co.

	GD25	FN65	NM94
1-Funny animal	10.00	30.00	60.00
2,3	7.50	22.50	45.00

JAMES BOND FOR YOUR EYES ONLY
Oct, 1981 - No. 2, Nov, 1981
Marvel Comics Group

	GD25	FN65	NM94
1,2-Movie adapt.; r-/Marvel Super Spec. #19		.50	1.00

JAMES BOND JR. (TV)
Jan, 1992 - No. 12, Dec, 1992 (#1: $1.00, #2-on: $1.25, color)
Marvel Comics

	GD25	FN65	NM94
1-12: Based on animated TV show		.60	1.25

JAMES BOND: LICENCE TO KILL (See Licence To Kill)

JAMES BOND: PERMISSION TO DIE
1989 - No. 3, 1991 ($3.95, color, mini-series, squarebound, 52 pgs.)
Eclipse Comics/ACME Press

	GD25	FN65	NM94
1-3: Mike Grell-c/a/scripts in all. 3-($4.95)	1.00	2.50	5.00

JAMES BOND 007: SERPENT'S TOOTH
July, 1992 - No. 3, Sept, 1992 ($4.95, color, mini-series)
Acme Comics/Dark Horse Comics

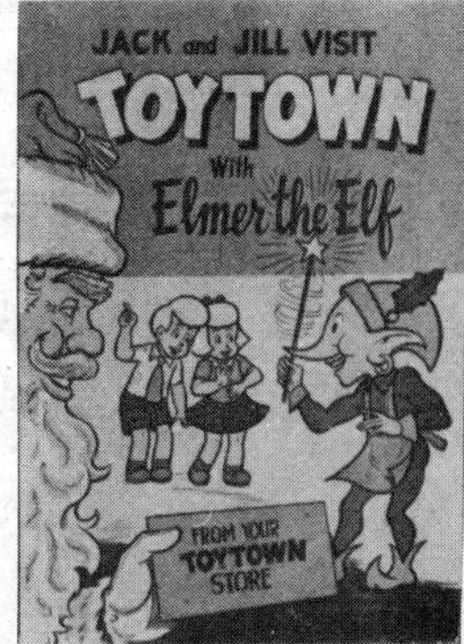

Jack and Jill Visit Toytown (1949), © Butler Bros.

Jackie Robinson #1, © FAW

Jackpot Comics #4, © AP

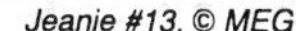
Jeanie #13, © MEG

Jeep Comics #3, © R.B. Leffingwell

Jerry Drummer V2/#10, © CC

	GD25	FN65	NM94
1-3: Paul Gulacy-c/a	1.00	2.50	5.00

JAM: SUPER COOL COLOR INJECTED TURBO ADVENTURE #1 FROM HELL!, THE (Comico) (Value: cover or less)

JANE ARDEN (See Feature Funnies & Pageant of Comics)
March, 1948 - No. 2, June, 1948
St. John (United Features Syndicate)

	GD25	FN65	NM94
1-Newspaper reprints	11.50	34.00	80.00
2	8.35	25.00	50.00

JANN OF THE JUNGLE (Jungle Tales No. 1-7)
No. 8, Nov, 1955 - No. 17, June, 1957
Atlas Comics (CSI)

	GD25	FN65	NM94
8(#1)	13.00	40.00	90.00
9,11-15	7.50	22.50	45.00
10-Williamson/Colletta-c	8.35	25.00	50.00
16,17-Williamson/Mayo-a(3), 5 pgs. each	10.00	30.00	65.00

NOTE: ***Everett** c-15-17. **Heck** a-8, 15, 17. **Maneely** c-11. **Shores** a-8.*

JASON & THE ARGONAUTS (See Movie Classics)

JAWS 2 (See Marvel Comics Super Special, A)

JCP FEATURES
Feb, 1982-c; Dec, 1981-indicia ($2.00, one-shot, B&W)
J.C. Productions (Archie)

	GD25	FN65	NM94
1-T.H.U.N.D.E.R. Agents; Black Hood by Morrow & Neal Adams	.40	1.00	2.00

JEANIE COMICS (Formerly All Surprise; Cowgirl Romances #28)
No. 13, April, 1947 - No. 27, Oct, 1949
Marvel Comics/Atlas(CPC)

	GD25	FN65	NM94
13-Mitzi, Willie begin	10.00	30.00	60.00
14,15	6.70	20.00	40.00
16-Used in Love and Death by Legman; Kurtzman's "Hey Look"	9.15	27.50	55.00
17-19,22-Kurtzman's "Hey Look," 1-3 pgs. each	5.85	17.50	35.00
20,21,23-27	4.70	14.00	28.00

JEEP COMICS (Also see G.I. Comics and Overseas Comics)
Winter, 1944 - No. 3, Mar-Apr, 1948
R. B. Leffingwell & Co.

	GD25	FN65	NM94
1-Capt. Power, Criss Cross & Jeep & Peep (costumed) begin	13.00	40.00	90.00
2	10.00	30.00	60.00
3-L. B. Cole-c	10.00	30.00	65.00
1-29(Giveaways)-Strip reprints in all; Tarzan, Flash Gordon, Blondie, The Nebbs, Little Iodine, Red Ryder, Don Winslow, The Phantom, Johnny Hazard, Katzenjammer Kids; distr. to U.S. Armed Forces in mid 1940's	4.00	10.00	20.00

JEFF JORDAN, U.S. AGENT
Dec, 1947 - Jan, 1948
D. S. Publishing Co.

	GD25	FN65	NM94
1	7.50	22.50	45.00

JEMM, SON OF SATURN
Sept, 1984 - No. 12, Aug, 1985 (12 part maxi-series; mando paper)
DC Comics

	GD25	FN65	NM94
1-12: Colan p-all; c-1-5p, 7-12p. 3-Origin		.50	1.00

JERRY DRUMMER (Formerly Soldier & Marine V2#9)
V2#10, Apr, 1957 - V3#12, Oct, 1957
Charlton Comics

	GD25	FN65	NM94
V2#10, V3#11,12: 11-Whitman-c/a	3.00	7.50	15.00

JERRY IGER'S... (All titles, Blackthorne/First) (Value: cover or less)

JERRY LEWIS (See The Adventures of...)

JESSE JAMES (See 4-Color No. 757 & The Legend of...)

JESSE JAMES (See Badmen of the West & Blazing Sixguns)
8/50 - No. 9, 11/52; No. 15, 10/53 - No. 29, 8-9/56
Avon Periodicals

	GD25	FN65	NM94
1-Kubert Alabam-r/Cowpuncher #1	11.50	34.00	80.00
2-Kubert-a(3)	10.00	30.00	65.00
3-Kubert Alabam-r/Cowpuncher #2	9.15	27.50	55.00
4,9-No Kubert	4.00	11.00	22.00
5,6-Kubert Jesse James-a(3); 5-Wood-a(1pg.)	9.15	27.50	55.00
7-Kubert Jesse James-a(2)	7.50	22.50	45.00
8-Kinstler-a(3)	5.00	15.00	30.00
15-Kinstler-r/#3	3.60	9.00	18.00
16-Kinstler-r/#3 & story-r/Butch Cassidy #1	4.00	10.00	20.00
17-19,21: 17-Jesse James-r/#4; Kinstler-c idea from Kubert splash in #6. 18-Kubert Jesse James-r/#5. 19-Kubert Jesse James-r/#6. 21-Two Jesse James-r/#4, Kinstler-r/#4	3.00	7.50	15.00
20-Williamson/Frazetta-a; r/Chief Vic. Apache Massacre; Kubert Jesse James-r/#6; Kit West story by Larsen	10.00	30.00	60.00
22,23-No Kubert	3.00	7.50	15.00
24-New McCarty strip by Kinstler; Kinstler-r	3.00	7.50	15.00
25-New McCarty Jesse James strip by Kinstler; Jesse James-r/#7,9	3.00	7.50	15.00
26,27-New McCarty Jesse James strip plus a Kinstler/McCann Jesse James-r	3.00	7.50	15.00
28,29: 28-Reprints most of Red Mountain, Featuring Quantrells Raiders	3.00	7.50	15.00
Annual(nn; 1952; 25 cents)-"...Brings Six-Gun Justice to the West" (100pgs.)-3 earlier issues rebound; Kubert, Kinstler-a(3)	19.00	57.00	130.00

NOTE: *Mostly reprints #10 on. **Fawcette** c-1, 2. **Kida** a-5. **Kinstler** a-3, 4, 7-9, 15r, 16r(2), 21-27; c-3, 4, 9, 17-27. Painted c-5, 6. 22 has 2 stories r/Sheriff Bob Dixon's Chuck Wagon #1 with name changed to Sheriff Bob Trent.*

JESSE JAMES
July, 1953
Realistic Publications

	GD25	FN65	NM94
nn-Reprints Avon's #1; same-c, colors different	6.70	20.00	40.00

JEST (Formerly Snap; becomes Kayo #12)
No. 10, 1944; No. 11, 1944
Harry 'A' Chesler

	GD25	FN65	NM94
10-Johnny Rebel & Yankee Boy app. in text	8.35	25.00	50.00
11-Little Nemo in Adventure Land	9.15	27.50	55.00

JESTER
No. 10, 1945
Harry 'A' Chesler

	GD25	FN65	NM94
10	7.50	22.50	45.00

JESUS (Spire Christian) (Value: cover or less)

JET (See Jet Powers)

JET ACES
1952 - No. 4, 1953
Fiction House Magazines

	GD25	FN65	NM94
1	8.35	25.00	50.00
2-4	4.70	14.00	28.00

JET DREAM (...& Her Stuntgirl Counterspies)
June, 1968
Gold Key

	GD25	FN65	NM94
1	3.20	8.00	16.00

JET FIGHTERS (Korean War)
No. 5, Nov, 1952 - No. 7, Mar, 1953
Standard Magazines

	GD25	FN65	NM94
5,7-Toth-a. 5-Toth-c	7.50	22.50	45.00
6-Celardo-a	3.60	9.00	18.00

JET POWER
1963
I.W. Enterprises

	GD25	FN65	NM94
I.W. Reprint 1,2-r/Jet Powers #1,2	3.20	8.00	16.00

JET POWERS (American Air Forces No. 5 on)
1950 - No. 4, 1951
Magazine Enterprises

	GD25	FN65	NM94
1(A-1 #30)-Powell-c/a begins	20.00	60.00	140.00
2(A-1 #32)	14.00	43.00	100.00
3(A-1 #35)-Williamson/Evans-a	24.00	72.00	165.00
4(A-1 #38)-Williamson/Wood-a; "The Rain of Sleep" drug story	24.00	72.00	165.00

JET PUP (See 3-D Features)

JETSONS, THE (TV)(See March of Comics #276, 330, 348 & Spotlight #3)
Jan, 1963 - No. 36, Oct, 1970 (Hanna-Barbera)
Gold Key

	GD25	FN65	NM94
1	21.00	63.00	145.00
2	11.50	34.00	80.00
3-10	10.00	30.00	60.00
11-20	6.70	20.00	40.00
21-36	5.00	15.00	30.00

JETSONS, THE (TV)
Nov, 1970 - No. 20, Dec, 1973 (Hanna-Barbera)
Charlton Comics

	GD25	FN65	NM94
1	8.00	28.00	48.00
2	4.20	12.50	25.00
3-10	3.60	9.00	18.00
11-20	2.40	6.00	12.00

JETSONS, THE (TV)
V2#1, Sept, 1992 - Present ($1.25, color) (Hanna-Barbera)
Harvey Comics

	GD25	FN65	NM94
V2#1,2		.60	1.25
...Big Book V2#1,2 ($1.95, 52 pgs.): 1-(11/92)	.40	1.00	2.00
...Giant Size 1,2 ($2.25, 68 pgs): 1-(10/92)	.45	1.15	2.25

JETTA OF THE 21ST CENTURY
No. 5, Dec, 1952 - No. 7, Apr, 1953 (Teen-age Archie type)
Standard Comics

	GD25	FN65	NM94
5	11.00	32.00	75.00
6,7	7.50	22.50	45.00

JEZEBEL JADE (Comico)(Value: cover or less)

JIGGS & MAGGIE (See 4-Color No. 18)

JIGGS & MAGGIE
No. 11, 1949(June) - No. 21, 2/53; No. 22, 4/53 - No. 27, 2-3/54
Standard Comics/Harvey Publications No. 22 on

	GD25	FN65	NM94
11	8.35	25.00	50.00
12-15,17-21	4.35	13.00	26.00
16-Wood text illos.	5.85	17.50	35.00
22-25,27: 22-24-Little Dot app.	4.00	10.00	20.00
26-Four pgs. partially in 3-D	11.00	32.00	75.00

NOTE: *Sunday page reprints by McManus loosely blended into story continuity. Based on Bringing Up Father strip. Advertised on covers as "All New."*

JIGSAW (Big Hero Adventures)
Sept, 1966 - No. 2, Dec, 1966 (36 pgs.)
Harvey Publications (Funday Funnies)

	GD25	FN65	NM94
1-Origin; Crandall-a, 5pgs.	1.40	3.00	7.00
2-Man From S.R.A.M.	1.00	2.50	5.00

JIGSAW OF DOOM (See Complete Mystery No. 2)

JIM BOWIE (Formerly Danger; Black Jack No. 20 on)
No. 15, 1955? - No. 19, April, 1957
Charlton Comics

	GD25	FN65	NM94
15	4.35	13.00	26.00
16-19	3.20	8.00	16.00

JIM BOWIE (See 4-Color No. 893,993, & Western Tales)

JIM DANDY
May, 1956 - No. 3, Sept, 1956 (Charles Biro)
Dandy Magazine (Lev Gleason)

	GD25	FN65	NM94
1	4.35	13.00	26.00
2,3	3.00	7.50	15.00

JIM HARDY (Also see Sparkler & Treasury of Comics #2&5)
1939; 1942; 1947 - No. 2, 1947
United Features Syndicate/Spotlight Publ.

	GD25	FN65	NM94
Single Series 6 ('39)	26.00	77.00	180.00
Single Series 27('42)	20.00	60.00	140.00
1('47)-Spotlight Publ.	8.35	25.00	50.00
2	4.70	14.00	28.00

JIM HARDY
1944 (132 pages, 25 cents) (Tip Top, Sparkler-r)
Spotlight/United Features Syndicate

	GD25	FN65	NM94
(1944)-Origin Mirror Man; Triple Terror app.	33.00	100.00	200.00

JIMINY CRICKET (See 4-Color No. 701, 795, 897, 989, Mickey Mouse Mag. V5#3 & Walt Disney Showcase #37)

JIMMY (James Swinnerton)
1905 (10x15") (40 pages in color)
N. Y. American & Journal

	GD25	FN65	NM94
nn	33.00	100.00	200.00

JIMMY DURANTE (See A-1 Comics No. 18, 20)

JIMMY OLSEN (See Superman's Pal...)

JIMMY WAKELY (Cowboy movie star)
Sept-Oct, 1949 - No. 18, July-Aug, 1952 (1-13: 52pgs.)
National Periodical Publications

	GD25	FN65	NM94
1-Photo-c, 52 pgs. begin; Alex Toth-a; Kit Colby Girl Sheriff begins	52.00	158.00	365.00
2-Toth-a	32.00	95.00	225.00
3,6,7-Frazetta-a in all, 3 pgs. each; Toth-a in all. 7-Last photo-c?	36.00	107.00	250.00
4-Frazetta-a, 3 pgs.; Kurtzman "Pot-Shot Pete," 1 pg; Toth-a	36.00	107.00	250.00
5,8-15,18-Toth-a; 12,14-Kubert-a, 3 & 2 pgs.	25.00	75.00	175.00
16,17	21.00	62.00	145.00

NOTE: ***Gil Kane** c-10-19p.*

JIM RAY'S AVIATION SKETCH BOOK
Mar-Apr, 1946 - No. 2, May-June, 1946
Vital Publishers

	GD25	FN65	NM94
1,2-Picture stories about planes and pilots	18.00	55.00	110.00

JIM SOLAR (See Wisco/Klarer)

JINGLE BELLS (See March of Comics No. 65)

JINGLE BELLS CHRISTMAS BOOK
1971 (20 pgs.; B&W inside; slick cover)
Montgomery Ward (Giveaway)

	GD25	FN65	NM94
nn	.40	1.00	2.00

JINGLE DINGLE CHRISTMAS STOCKING COMICS
V2#1, 1951 (no date listed) (100 pgs.; giant-size)(25 cents)
Stanhall Publications (Publ.-annually)

	GD25	FN65	NM94
V2#1-Foodini & Pinhead, Silly Pilly plus games & puzzles	10.00	30.00	70.00

JINGLE JANGLE COMICS (Also see Puzzle Fun Comics)
Feb, 1942 - No. 42, Dec, 1949
Eastern Color Printing Co.

Jet Fighters #6, © STD

The Jetsons #3, © Hanna-Barbera

Jimmy Wakely #3, © DC

Jingle Jangle Comics #15, © EAS

Joe Palooka #26, © Ham Fisher

John Carter of Mars #2, © ERB

	GD25	FN65	NM94
1-Pie-Face Prince of Old Pretzleburg, Jingle Jangle Tales by George Carlson, Hortense, & Benny Bear begin	29.00	85.00	200.00
2,3-No Pie-Face Prince	13.00	40.00	90.00
4-Pie-Face Prince cover	13.00	40.00	90.00
5	11.50	34.00	80.00
6-10: 8-No Pie-Face Prince	10.00	30.00	70.00
11-15	7.50	22.50	45.00
16-30: 17,18-No Pie-Face Prince. 30-XMas-c	5.85	17.50	35.00
31-42: 36,42-Xmas-c	4.35	13.00	26.00

NOTE: ***George Carlson** a-(2) in all except No. 2, 3, 8; c-1-6. **Carlson** 1 pg. puzzles in 9, 10, 12-15, 18, 20. **Carlson** illustrated a series of Uncle Wiggily books in 1930's.*

JING PALS
Feb, 1946 - No. 4, Aug?, 1946 (Funny animal)
Victory Publishing Corporation

	GD25	FN65	NM94
1-Wishing Willie, Puggy Panda & Johnny Rabbit begin	8.35	25.00	50.00
2-4	4.70	14.00	28.00

JINKS, PIXIE, AND DIXIE (See Kite Fun Book & Whitman Comic Books)

JOAN OF ARC (See A-1 Comics No. 21 & Ideal a Classical Comic)

JOAN OF ARC
No date (28 pages)
Catechetical Guild (Topix) (Giveaway)

	GD25	FN65	NM94
nn	9.15	27.50	55.00

NOTE: *Unpublished version exists which came from the Guild's files.*

JOE COLLEGE
Fall, 1949 - No. 2, Winter, 1950 (Teen-age humor)
Hillman Periodicals

	GD25	FN65	NM94
1,2-Powell-a; 1-Briefer-a	6.00	18.00	36.00

JOE JINKS (See Single Series No. 12)

JOE LOUIS (See Fight Comics #2, Picture News #6 & True Comics #5)
Sept, 1950 - No. 2, Nov, 1950 (Photo-c) (Boxing champ) (See Dick Cole #10)
Fawcett Publications

	GD25	FN65	NM94
1-Photo-c; life story	39.00	118.00	275.00
2-Photo-c	26.00	77.00	180.00

JOE PALOOKA
1933 (B&W daily strip reprints) (52 pages)
Cupples & Leon Co.

	GD25	FN65	NM94
nn-(Scarce)-by Fisher	70.00	210.00	420.00

JOE PALOOKA (1st Series) (Also see Big Shot Comics, Columbia Comics & Feature Funnies)
1942 - No. 4, 1944
Columbia Comic Corp. (Publication Enterprises)

	GD25	FN65	NM94
1-1st to portray American president; gov't permission required	50.00	150.00	300.00
2 (1943)-Hitler-c	29.00	88.00	175.00
3,4	20.00	60.00	120.00

JOE PALOOKA (2nd Series) (Battle Adv. #68-74; ...Advs. #75, 77-81, 83-85, 87; Champ of the Comics #76, 82, 86, 89-93) (See All-New)
Nov, 1945 - No. 118, Mar, 1961
Harvey Publications

	GD25	FN65	NM94
1	36.00	107.00	250.00
2	16.00	48.00	110.00
3,4,6,7-1st Flyin' Fool, ends #25	10.00	30.00	65.00
5-Boy Explorers by S&K (7-8/46)	13.00	40.00	90.00
8-10	8.35	25.00	50.00
11-14,16-20: 19-Freedom Train-c	6.35	19.00	38.00
15-Origin Humphrey; Super heroine Atoma app. by Powell	10.00	30.00	60.00
21-30: 27-1st app. Little Max? (12/48). 30-Nude female painting	5.00	15.00	30.00
31-61: 44-Joe Palooka marries Ann Howe	4.00	11.00	22.00
62-S&K Boy Explorers-r	4.70	14.00	28.00
63-80: 66,67-'Commie' torture story	3.60	9.00	18.00
81-99,101-115	2.80	7.00	14.00
100	3.60	9.00	18.00
116-S&K Boy Explorers-r (Giant, '60)	4.20	12.50	25.00
117,118-Giants	4.00	11.00	22.00
...Body Building Instruction Book (1958 Sports Toy giveaway, 16pgs., 5-1/4x7")-Origin	8.35	25.00	50.00
...Fights His Way Back (1945 Giveaway, 24 pgs.) Family Comics	16.00	48.00	110.00
...in Hi There! (1949 Red Cross giveaway, 12 pgs., 4-3/4x6")	7.50	22.50	45.00
...in It's All in the Family (1945 Red Cross giveaway, 16 pgs., regular size)	10.00	30.00	60.00
...**Visits the Lost City** nn (1945) (One Shot) (50 cents)-164 page continuous story strip reprint. Has biography & photo of Ham Fisher; possibly the single longest comic book story published (159 pgs.?)	79.00	235.00	550.00

NOTE: ***Nostrand/Powell** a-73. **Powell** a-7, 8, 10, 12, 14, 17, 19, 26-45, 47-53, 70, 73 at least. Black Cat text stories #8, 12, 13, 19.*

JOE YANK
No. 5, March, 1952 - No. 16, 1954
Standard Comics (Visual Editions)

	GD25	FN65	NM94
5-Celardo, Tuska-a	4.00	12.00	24.00
6-Toth, Severin/Elder-a	5.85	17.50	35.00
7	3.20	8.00	16.00
8-Toth-c	4.20	12.50	25.00
9-16: 9-Andru-c. 12-Andru-a	2.80	7.00	14.00

JOHN BOLTON'S HALLS OF HORROR (Eclipse) (Value: cover or less)

JOHN BYRNE'S NEXT MEN (See Dark Horse Presents #54)
Jan, 1992 - Present ($2.50, color)
Dark Horse Comics

	GD25	FN65	NM94
1-Silver foil embossed-c; Byrne-c/a/scripts in all	1.40	3.50	7.00
1-2nd printing with gold ink logo	.70	1.75	3.50
0-(2/92)-r/chapters 1-4 from DHP w/new Byrne-c	1.00	2.50	5.00
2	.70	1.75	3.50
3,4	.60	1.50	3.00
5-14	.50	1.25	2.50

NOTE: *Issues 1 through 6 contain certificates redeemable for an exclusive Next Men trading card set by Byrne.*

JOHN CARTER OF MARS (See 4-Color #375, 437, 488, The Funnies & Tarzan #207)

JOHN CARTER OF MARS
April, 1964 - No. 3, Oct, 1964
Gold Key

	GD25	FN65	NM94
1(10104-404)-r/4-Color 375; Jesse Marsh-a	4.00	10.00	20.00
2(407), 3(410)-r/4-Color 437 & 488; Marsh-a	3.20	8.00	16.00

JOHN CARTER OF MARS
1970 (72 pgs.; paper cover; 10-1/2x16-1/2"; B&W)
House of Greystroke

	GD25	FN65	NM94
1941-42 Sunday strip reprints; John Coleman Burroughs-a	4.00	10.00	20.00

JOHN CARTER, WARLORD OF MARS (Also see Weird Worlds)
June, 1977 - No. 28, Oct, 1979
Marvel Comics Group

	GD25	FN65	NM94
1-17,19-28: 1-Origin. 11-Origin Dejah Thoris		.50	1.00
18-Miller-a(p)	.30	.75	1.50
Annuals 1-3: 1(1977). 2(1978). 3(1979)-All 52 pgs. with new book-length stories		.50	1.00

NOTE: ***Austin** c-24i. **Gil Kane** a-1-10p; c-1p, 2p, 3, 4-9p, 10, 15p, Annual 1p. **Layton** a-17i.*

GD25 FN65 NM94

***Miller** c-25, 26p. **Nebres** a-2-4i, 8-16i; c(i)-6-9, 11-22, 25, Annual 1. **Perez** c-24p. **Simonson** a-15p. **Sutton** a-7i.*

JOHN F. KENNEDY, CHAMPION OF FREEDOM
1964 (no month) (25 cents)
Worden & Childs

	GD25	FN65	NM94
nn-Photo-c	6.70	20.00	40.00

JOHN F. KENNEDY LIFE STORY
Aug-Oct, 1964; Nov, 1965; June, 1966 (12 cents)
Dell Publishing Co.

	GD25	FN65	NM94
12-378-410	5.00	15.00	30.00
12-378-511 (reprint, 11/65)	4.00	10.00	20.00
12-378-606 (reprint, 6/66)	3.60	9.00	18.00

JOHN FORCE (See Magic Agent)

JOHN HIX SCRAP BOOK, THE
Late 1930's (no date) (68 pgs.; reg. size; 10 cents)
Eastern Color Printing Co. (McNaught Synd.)

	GD25	FN65	NM94
1-Strange As It Seems (resembles Single Series books)	19.00	58.00	135.00
2-Strange As It Seems	16.00	48.00	110.00

JOHN LAW DETECTIVE (Eclipse)(Value: cover or less)

JOHNNY APPLESEED (See Story Hour Series)

JOHNNY CASH (See Hello, I'm...)

JOHNNY DANGER
1950
Toby Press

	GD25	FN65	NM94
1-Photo-c; Sparling-a	10.00	30.00	70.00

JOHNNY DANGER PRIVATE DETECTIVE
1954 (Reprinted in Danger #11 by Super)
Toby Press

	GD25	FN65	NM94
1-Opium den story	8.35	25.00	50.00

JOHNNY DYNAMITE (Formerly Dynamite #1-9; Foreign Intrigues #13 on)
No. 10, June, 1955 - No. 12, Oct, 1955
Charlton Comics

	GD25	FN65	NM94
10-12	4.20	12.50	25.00

JOHNNY HAZARD
No. 5, Aug, 1948 - No. 8, May, 1949; No. 35, date?
Best Books (Standard Comics) (King Features)

	GD25	FN65	NM94
5-Strip reprints by Frank Robbins	10.00	30.00	60.00
6,8-Strip reprints by Frank Robbins	6.70	20.00	40.00
7-New art, not Robbins	5.00	15.00	30.00
35	5.00	15.00	30.00

JOHNNY JASON (...Teen Reporter)
Feb-Apr, 1962 - No. 2, June-Aug, 1962
Dell Publishing Co.

	GD25	FN65	NM94
4-Color 1302, 2(01380-208)	2.00	5.00	10.00

JOHNNY JINGLE'S LUCKY DAY
1956 (16 pgs.; 7-1/4x5-1/8") (Giveaway) (Disney)
American Dairy Association

	GD25	FN65	NM94
nn	3.60	9.00	18.00

JOHNNY LAW, SKY RANGER
Apr, 1955 - No. 3, Aug, 1955; No. 4, Nov, 1955
Good Comics (Lev Gleason)

	GD25	FN65	NM94
1-Edmond Good-c/a	4.70	14.00	28.00
2-4	3.60	9.00	18.00

JOHNNY MACK BROWN (TV western star; see Western Roundup under Dell Giants)
No. 269, Mar, 1950 - No. 963, Feb, 1959 (All Photo-c)
Dell Publishing Co.

	GD25	FN65	NM94
4-Color 269(#1)(3/50, 52pgs.)-Johnny Mack Brown & his horse Rebel begin; photo front/back-c begin; Marsh-a begins, ends #9	16.00	48.00	110.00
2(10-12/50, 52pgs.)	9.15	27.50	55.00
3(1-3/51, 52pgs.)	6.35	19.00	38.00
4-10 (9-11/52)(36pgs.)	4.70	14.00	28.00
4-Color 455,493,541,584,618	4.70	14.00	28.00
4-Color 645,685,722,776,834,963	4.70	14.00	28.00
4-Color 922-Manning-a	5.35	16.00	32.00

JOHNNY NEMO
Sept, 1985 - No. 3, Feb, 1986 (Mini-series)
Eclipse Comics

	GD25	FN65	NM94
1,2 ($1.75 cover)	.35	.90	1.80
3 ($2.00 cover)	.40	1.00	2.00

JOHNNY RINGO (See 4-Color No. 1142)

JOHNNY STARBOARD (See Wisco)

JOHNNY THUNDER
Feb-Mar, 1973 - No. 3, July-Aug, 1973
National Periodical Publications

	GD25	FN65	NM94
1-Johnny Thunder & Nighthawk-r begin	.30	.75	1.50
2,3: 2-Trigger Twins app.		.50	1.00

NOTE: *All contain 1950s DC reprints from All-American Western. **Drucker** r-2, 3. **G. Kane** r-2, 3. **Moriera** r-1. **Toth** r-1, 3; c-1r, 3r. Also see All-American, All-Star Western, Flash Comics, Western Comics, World's Best & World's Finest.*

JOHN PAUL JONES (See Four Color No. 1007)

JOHN STEED & EMMA PEEL (See The Avengers, Gold Key series)

JOHN STEELE SECRET AGENT (Also see Freedom Agent)
December, 1964 (Freedom Agent)
Gold Key

	GD25	FN65	NM94
1	10.00	30.00	60.00

JOHN WAYNE ADVENTURE COMICS (Movie star; See Big Tex, Oxydol-Dreft, Tim McCoy & With The Marines...#1)
Winter, 1949-50 - No. 31, May, 1955 (Photo-c: 1-12,17,25-on)
Toby Press

	GD25	FN65	NM94
1 (36pgs.)-Photo-c begin	57.00	170.00	400.00
2 (36pgs.)-Williamson/Frazetta-a(2) 6 & 2 pgs. (one story-r/Billy the Kid #1); photo back-c	45.00	135.00	310.00
3 (36pgs.)-Williamson/Frazetta-a(2), 16 pgs. total; photo back-c	45.00	135.00	310.00
4 (52pgs.)-Williamson/Frazetta-a(2), 16 pgs. total	45.00	135.00	310.00
5 (52pgs.)-Kurtzman-a-(Alfred "L" Newman in Potshot Pete)	32.00	95.00	220.00
6 (52pgs.)-Williamson/Frazetta-a, 10 pgs; Kurtzman a-`Pot-Shot Pete,' 5pgs.; & "Genius Jones," 1 pg.	43.00	130.00	300.00
7 (52pgs.)-Williamson/Frazetta-a, 10 pgs.	34.00	100.00	240.00
8 (36pgs.)-Williamson/Frazetta-a(2), 12 & 9 pgs.	43.00	130.00	300.00
9-11: Photo western-c	23.00	70.00	160.00
12-Photo war-c; Kurtzman-a, 2 pgs. "Genius"	23.00	70.00	160.00
13-15: 13-Line-drawn-c begin, end #24	20.00	60.00	140.00
16-Williamson/Frazetta-r/Billy the Kid #1	22.00	65.00	150.00
17-Photo-c	23.00	70.00	160.00
18-Williamson/Frazetta-a (r/#4 & 8, 19 pgs.)	25.00	75.00	175.00
19-24: 23-Evans-a?	18.00	54.00	125.00
25-Photo-c resume; end #31; Williamson/Frazetta-r/Billy the Kid #3	25.00	75.00	175.00
26-28,30-Photo-c	22.00	65.00	150.00
29,31-Williamson/Frazetta-a in each (r/#4, 2)	23.00	70.00	160.00

NOTE: *Williamsonish art in later issues by **Gerald McCann**.*

JO-JO COMICS (...Congo King #7-29; My Desire #30 on)
(Also see Fantastic Fears and Jungle Jo)

John Carter, Warlord of Mars #1, © MEG

Johnny Mack Brown #2, © Johnny Mack Brown

John Wayne Adventure Comics #26, © TOBY

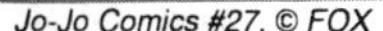
Jo-Jo Comics #27, © FOX

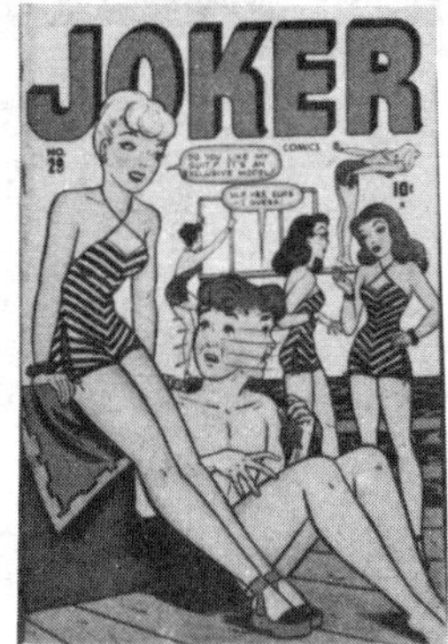

Joker Comics #29, © MEG

Jonah Hex #16, © DC

GD25 FN65 NM94

1945 - No. 29, July, 1949 (two No.7's; no No. 13)
Fox Feature Syndicate

nn(1945)-Funny animal, humor 9.15 27.50 55.00
2(Sum,'46)-6: Funny animal; 2-Ten pg. Electro story 4.70 14.00 28.00
7(7/47)-Jo-Jo, Congo King begins (1st app.); Bronze Man & Purlpe Tigress app. 36.00 107.00 250.00
7(#8) (9/47) 26.00 77.00 180.00
8-10(#9-11): 8-Tanee begins 22.00 65.00 150.00
11,12(#12,13),14,16: 11,16-Kamen bondage-c 19.00 57.00 130.00
15-Cited by Dr. Wertham in 5/47 Saturday Review of Literature 20.00 60.00 140.00
17-Kamen bondage-c 20.00 60.00 140.00
18-20 19.00 57.00 130.00
21-29: 21-Hollingsworth-a(4 pgs.; 23-1 pg.) 17.00 52.00 120.00

NOTE: *Many bondage-c/a by **Baker/Kamen/Feldstein/Good.** No. 7's have Princesses Gwenna, Geesa, Yolda, & Safra before settling down on Tanee.*

JO-JOY (The Adventures of...)
1945 - 1953 (Christmas gift comic, 16 pgs., 7-1/16x10-1/4")
W. T. Grant Dept. Stores

1945-53 issues 3.60 9.00 18.00

JOKEBOOK COMICS DIGEST ANNUAL (...Magazine No. 5 on)
Oct, 1977 - No. 13, Oct, 1983 (Digest Size)
Archie Publications

1(10/77)-Reprints; Neal Adams-a .60 1.50 3.00
2(4/78)-13 .60 1.50 3.00

JOKER, THE (See Batman #1, Batman: The Killing Joke, Brave & the Bold, Detective, Greatest Joker Stories & Justice League Annual #2)
May, 1975 - No. 9, Sept-Oct, 1976
National Periodical Publications

1-Two-Face app. 3.00 7.50 15.00
2,3: 3-The Creeper app. 1.60 4.00 8.00
4-6: 4-Green Arrow-c/s. 6-Sherlock Holmes-c/s 1.20 3.00 6.00
7-9: 7-Lex Luthor-c/story. 8-Scarecrow-c/story. 9-Catwoman-c/story 1.00 2.50 5.00

JOKER COMICS (Adventures Into Terror No. 43 on)
April, 1942 - No. 42, August, 1950
Timely/Marvel Comics No. 36 on (TCI/CDS)

1-(Rare)-Powerhouse Pepper (1st app.) begins by Wolverton; Stuporman app. from Daring 107.00 320.00 750.00
2-Wolverton-a; 1st app. Tessie the Typist 43.00 130.00 300.00
3-5-Wolverton-a 30.00 90.00 210.00
6-10-Wolverton-a 21.00 62.00 145.00
11-20-Wolverton-a 17.00 52.00 120.00
21,22,24-27,29,30-Wolverton cont'd. & Kurtzman's "Hey Look" in #24-27 14.00 43.00 100.00
23-1st "Hey Look" by Kurtzman; Wolverton-a 16.00 48.00 110.00
28,32,34,37-41 4.20 12.50 25.00
31-Last Powerhouse Pepper; not in #28 10.00 30.00 70.00
33,35,36-Kurtzman's "Hey Look" 5.85 17.50 35.00
42-Only app. 'Patty Pinup,' a clone of Millie the Model 5.00 15.00 30.00

JOLLY CHRISTMAS, A (See March of Comics No. 269)

JOLLY CHRISTMAS BOOK (See Christmas Journey Through Space)
1951; 1954; 1955 (36 pgs.; 24 pgs.)
Promotional Publ. Co.

1951-(Woolworth giveaway)-slightly oversized; no slick cover; Marv Levy-c/a 4.20 12.50 25.00
1954-(Hot Shoppes giveaway)-regular size-reprints 1951 issue; slick cover added; 24 pgs.; no ads 4.20 12.50 25.00
1955-(J. M. McDonald Co. giveaway)-reg. size 3.60 9.00 18.00

GD25 FN65 NM94

JOLLY COMICS
1947
Four Star Publishing Co.

1 5.00 15.00 30.00

JOLLY JINGLES (Formerly Jackpot Comics)
No. 10, Sum, 1943 - No. 16, Wint, 1944/45
MLJ Magazines

10-Super Duck begins (origin & 1st app.); Woody The Woodpecker begins (not same as Lantz character) 23.00 70.00 160.00
11 (Fall, '43)-2nd Super Duck(see Hangman #8) 11.00 32.00 75.00
12-Hitler-c 10.00 30.00 60.00
13-16 7.50 22.50 45.00

JONAH HEX (See All-Star Western, Hex and Weird Western Tales)
Mar-Apr, 1977 - No. 92, Aug, 1985
National Periodical Publications/DC Comics

1 3.00 7.50 15.00
2-6,8-10: 9-Wrightson-c 1.00 2.50 5.00
7-Explains Hex's face disfigurement 1.20 3.00 6.00
11-20: 12-Starlin-c .60 1.50 3.00
21-50: 31,32-Origin retold .40 1.00 2.00
51-92: 92-Story continued in Hex #1 .50 1.00

NOTE: ***Aparo** c-76p. **Ayers** a(p)-35-37, 40, 41, 44-53, 56, 58-82. **Kubert** c-43-46. **Morrow** a-90-92; c-10. **Spiegle(Tothish)** a-34, 38, 40, 49, 52. Batlash back-ups in 49, 52. El Diablo back-ups in 48, 56-60, 73-75. Scalphunter back-ups in 40, 41, 45-47.*

JONAH HEX AND OTHER WESTERN TALES (Blue Ribbon Digest)
Sept-Oct, 1979 - No. 3, Jan-Feb, 1980 (100 pgs.)
DC Comics

1-3: 1-Origin Scalphunter-r; painted-c. 2-Weird Western Tales-r; Neal Adams, Toth, Aragones, Gil Kane-a .50 1.00

JONAH HEX SPECTACULAR (See DC Special Series No. 16)

JONESY (Formerly Crack Western)
No. 85, Aug, 1953; No. 2, Oct, 1953 - No. 8, Oct, 1954
Comic Favorite/Quality Comics Group

85(#1)-Teen-age humor 4.00 11.00 22.00
2 2.80 7.00 14.00
3-8 1.80 4.50 9.00

JON JUAN (Also see Great Lover Romances)
Spring, 1950
Toby Press

1-All Schomburg-a (signed Al Reid on-c); written by Siegel; used in **SOTI**, pg. 38 13.50 41.00 9.00

JONNI THUNDER (...A.K.A. Thunderbolt)
Feb, 1985 - No. 4, Aug, 1985 (75 cents, mini-series)
DC Comics

1-4: 1-Origin .50 1.00

JONNY QUEST (TV)
December, 1964 (Hanna-Barbera)
Gold Key

1 (10139-412) 25.00 75.00 175.00

JONNY QUEST (TV) (Comico) (Value: cover or less)

JONNY QUEST CLASSICS (TV) (First) (Value: cover or less)

JON SABLE, FREELANCE (First) (Value: cover or less)

JOSEPH & HIS BRETHREN (See The Living Bible)

JOSIE (She's... #1-16) (...& the Pussycats #45 on) (See Archie Giant Series Magazine #528, 540, 551, 562, 571, 584, 597, 610, 622)
Feb, 1963 - No. 106, Oct, 1982
Archie Publications/Radio Comics

1 11.50 34.00 80.00

	GD25	FN65	NM94
2	6.70	20.00	40.00
3-5	4.00	11.00	22.00
6-10	3.20	8.00	16.00
11-20	2.40	6.00	12.00
21-30: 22-Mighty Man & Mighty (Josie Girl) app.	1.40	3.50	7.00
31-54	1.00	2.50	5.00
55-74(52pg. issues)	.40	1.00	2.00
75-106	.30	.75	1.50

JOURNAL OF CRIME (See Fox Giants)

JOURNEY (Also see Journey: Wardrums)
1983 - No. 14, 9/84; No. 15, 4/85 - No. 27, 7/86 (B&W)
Aardvark-Vanaheim #1-14/Fantagraphics Books #15-on

	GD25	FN65	NM94
1	1.00	2.50	5.00
2	.60	1.50	3.00
3-27: 20-Sam Kieth-a		.60	1.25

JOURNEY INTO FEAR
May, 1951 - No. 21, Sept, 1954
Superior-Dynamic Publications

	GD25	FN65	NM94
1-Baker-r(2)	24.00	72.00	165.00
2	13.50	41.00	95.00
3,4	11.00	32.00	75.00
5-10,15: 15-Used in **SOTI**, pg. 389	10.00	30.00	60.00
11-14,16-21	8.35	25.00	50.00

NOTE: *Kamenish 'headlight'-a most issues.* ***Robinson*** *a-10.*

JOURNEY INTO MYSTERY (1st Series) (Thor No. 126 on)
6/52 - No. 48, 8/57; No. 49, 11/58 - No. 125, 2/66
Atlas(CPS No. 1-48/AMI No. 49-68/Marvel No. 69 (6/61) on)

	GD25	FN65	NM94
1	130.00	385.00	900.00
2	57.00	170.00	400.00
3,4	43.00	130.00	300.00
5-11	25.00	75.00	175.00
12-20,22: 22-Davisesque-a; last pre-code issue (2/55)	21.00	63.00	145.00
21-Kubert-a; Tothish-a by Andru	22.00	65.00	155.00
23-32,35-38,40: 24-Torres?-a	12.00	36.00	85.00
33-Williamson-a	15.00	45.00	105.00
34,39: 34-Krigstein-a. 39-Wood-a	13.50	41.00	95.00
41-Crandall-a; Frazettaesque-a by Morrow	10.00	30.00	70.00
42,48-Torres-a	10.00	30.00	70.00
43,44-Williamson/Mayo-a in both	11.00	32.00	75.00
45,47,52,53	10.00	30.00	65.00
46-Torres & Krigstein-a	11.00	32.00	75.00
49-Matt Fox, Check-a	12.00	36.00	85.00
50,54: 50-Davis-a. 54-Williamson-a	10.00	30.00	65.00
51-Kirby/Wood-a	10.00	30.00	70.00
55-61,63-75: 66-Return of Xemnu. 74-Contents change to Fantasy. 75-Last 10 cent issue	10.00	30.00	65.00
62-1st app. Xemnu (Titan) called "The Hulk"	14.00	43.00	100.00
76,77,79-82: 80-Anti-communist propaganda story	9.15	27.50	55.00
78-The Sorceror (Dr. Strange prototype) app. (3/62)	11.50	34.00	80.00
83-Origin & 1st app. The Mighty Thor by Kirby (8/62) and begin series; Thor-c also begin	275.00	825.00	2200.00
83-Reprint from the Golden Record Comic Set	10.00	30.00	65.00
with the record (1966) (still sealed)	19.00	57.00	130.00
84-2nd app. Thor	85.00	260.00	600.00
85-1st app. Loki & Heimdall; Odin cameo (1 panel)	47.00	140.00	325.00
86-1st full app. Odin	32.00	95.00	225.00
87-89: 89-Reprints origin Thor from #83	22.00	65.00	150.00
90-No Kirby-a	13.00	40.00	90.00
91,92,94-96-Sinnott-a	11.50	34.00	80.00
93,97-Kirby-a; Tales of Asgard series begins #97 (origin which concludes in #99)	16.00	48.00	110.00
98-100-Kirby/Heck-a. 98-Origin/1st app. The Human Cobra. 99-1st app. Surtur & Mr. Hyde	11.00	32.00	75.00
101-108,110: 102-Intro Sif. 103-1st app. Enchantress. 105-109-Ten extra pgs. Kirby-a in each. 107-1st app. Grey Gargoyle. 108-(9/64)-Early Dr. Strange & Avengers x-over.	8.35	25.00	50.00
109-Magneto-c & app.	10.00	30.00	70.00
111,113,114,116-125: 118-1st app. Destroyer. 119-Intro Hogun, Fandrall, Volstagg. 124-Hercules-c/story	7.50	22.50	45.00
112-Thor Vs. Hulk (1/65). 112,113-Origin Loki	14.00	43.00	100.00
115-Detailed origin Loki	8.35	25.00	50.00
Annual 1('65, 25 cents, 72 pgs.)-New Thor vs. Hercules-c/story (see The Incredible Hulk #3); Kirby-c/a; r/#85,93,95,97	13.50	41.00	95.00

NOTE: ***Ayers*** *a-14, 39, 64i, 71i, 74i, 80i.* ***Bailey*** *a-43.* ***Briefer*** *a-5, 12.* ***Cameron*** *a-35.* ***Check*** *a-17.* ***Colan*** *a-23, 81; c-14.* ***Ditko*** *a-33, 38, 50-96; c-71, 88i.* ***Ditko/Kirby*** *a-50-83.* ***Everett*** *a-20, 48; c-4-7, 9, 36, 37, 39-42, 44, 45, 47.* ***Forte*** *a-19, 35, 40, 53.* ***Heath*** *a-4-6, 11, 14; c-1, 8, 11, 15, 51.* ***Heck*** *a-53, 73.* ***Kirby*** *a(p)-51, 52, 56, 57, 60, 62, 64, 66, 69, 71-74, 76, 79, 80-89, 93, 97, 98, 100(w/****Heck****), 101-125; c-50-82(w/****Ditko****), 83 & 84(w/****Sinnott****), 85-96(w/****Ayers****), 97-152p.* ***Leiber/Fox*** *a-93, 98-102.* ***Maneely*** *c-20-22.* ***Morisi*** *a-42.* ***Morrow*** *a-41, 42.* ***Orlando*** *a-30, 45, 57.* ***Mac Pakula*** *(Tothish) a-9, 35, 41.* ***Powell*** *a-20, 27, 34.* ***Reinman*** *a-39, 87, 92, 96i.* ***Robinson*** *a-9.* ***Roussos*** *a-39.* ***Robert Sale*** *a-14.* ***Severin*** *a-27; c-30.* ***Sinnott*** *a-41; c-50.* ***Tuska*** *a-11.* ***Wildey*** *a-16.*

JOURNEY INTO MYSTERY (2nd Series)
Oct, 1972 - No. 19, Oct, 1975
Marvel Comics Group

	GD25	FN65	NM94
1-Robert Howard adaptation; Starlin/Ploog-a	1.20	3.00	6.00
2,3,5-Bloch adaptation; 5-Last new story	.60	1.50	3.00
4,6-19: 4-H. P. Lovecraft adaptation	.40	1.00	2.00

NOTE: ***N. Adams*** *a-2i.* ***Ditko*** *r-7, 10, 12, 14, 15, 19; c-10.* ***Everett*** *r-9, 14.* ***G. Kane*** *a-1p, 2p; c-1-3p.* ***Kirby*** *r-7, 13, 18, 19; c-7.* ***Mort Lawrence*** *r-2.* ***Maneely*** *r-3.* ***Orlando*** *r-16.* ***Reese*** *a-1, 2i.* ***Starlin*** *a-1p, 3p.* ***Torres*** *r-16.* ***Wildey*** *r-9, 14.*

JOURNEY INTO UNKNOWN WORLDS (Formerly Teen)
No. 36, 9/50 - No. 38, 2/51; No. 4, 4/51 - No. 59, 8/57
Atlas Comics (WFP)

	GD25	FN65	NM94
36(#1)-Science fiction/weird; "End Of The Earth" c/story	93.00	280.00	650.00
37(#2)-Science fiction; "When Worlds Collide" c/story; Everett-c/a; Hitler story	47.00	140.00	325.00
38(#3)-Science fiction	39.00	118.00	275.00
4-6,8,10-Science fiction/weird	25.00	75.00	175.00
7-Wolverton-a-"Planet of Terror," 6 pgs; electric chair c-inset/story	41.00	122.00	285.00
9-Giant eyeball story	29.00	85.00	200.00
11,12-Krigstein-a	19.00	58.00	135.00
13,16,17,20	13.00	40.00	90.00
14-Wolverton-a-"One of Our Graveyards Is Missing," 4 pgs; Tuska-a	32.00	95.00	225.00
15-Wolverton-a-"They Crawl by Night," 5 pgs.; 2 pg. Maneely s/f story	32.00	95.00	225.00
18,19-Matt Fox-a	15.00	45.00	105.00
21-33: 21-Decapitation-c. 24-Sci/fic story. 26-Atom bomb panel. 27-Sid Check-a. 33-Last pre-code (2/55)	10.00	30.00	65.00
34-Kubert, Torres-a	9.15	27.50	55.00
35-Torres-a	8.35	25.00	50.00
36-42	7.50	22.50	45.00
43,44: 43-Krigstein-a. 44-Davis-a	8.35	25.00	50.00
45,55,59-Williamson-a in all; with Mayo #55,59. 55-Crandall-a	8.35	25.00	50.00
46,47,49,52,56-58	6.70	20.00	40.00
48,53-Crandall-a; Check-a, #48	8.35	25.00	50.00
50-Davis, Crandall-a	8.35	25.00	50.00
51-Ditko, Wood-a	9.15	27.50	55.00
54-Torres-a	6.70	20.00	40.00

NOTE: ***Ayers*** *a-24, 43,* ***Berg*** *a-38(#3), 43.* ***Lou Cameron*** *a-33.* ***Colan*** *a-37(#2), 6, 17, 19, 20, 23, 39.* ***Ditko*** *a-45, 51.* ***Drucker*** *a-35, 58.* ***Everett*** *a-37(#2), 11, 14, 41, 55, 56; c-37(#2), 11, 13, 14, 17, 22, 47, 48, 50, 53-55, 59.* ***Forte*** *a-49.* ***Fox*** *a-21i.* ***Heath*** *a-36(#1), 4, 6-8, 17, 20, 22, 36i; c-18.* ***Keller*** *a-15.* ***Mort Lawrence*** *a-38, 39.* ***Maneely*** *a-7, 8, 15, 16, 22, 49, 58; c-*

Journey Into Fear #14, © SUPR

Journey Into Mystery #5, © MEG

Journey Into Unknown Worlds #36, © MEG

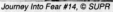

Judge Dredd #26, © Quality Comics

Judy Canova #24, © FOX

Jughead's Fantasy #2, © AP

	GD25	FN65	NM94

*25, 52. **Morrow** a-48. **Orlando** a-44, 57. **Pakula** a-36. **Powell** a-42, 53, 54. **Reinman** a-8. **Rico** a-21. **Robert Sale** a-24, 49. **Sekowsky** a-4, 5, 9. **Severin** a-38, 51; c-38, 48i, 56. **Sinnott** a-9, 21, 24. **Tuska** a-38(#3), 14. **Wildey** a-25, 43, 44.*

JOURNEY OF DISCOVERY WITH MARK STEEL (See Mark Steel)

JOURNEY TO THE CENTER OF THE EARTH (See 4-Color No. 1060)

JUDE, THE FORGOTTEN SAINT
1954 (16 pgs.; 8x11"; full color; paper cover)
Catechetical Guild Education Society

	GD25	FN65	NM94
nn	2.00	5.00	10.00

JUDGE COLT
Oct, 1969 - No. 4, Sept, 1970
Gold Key

	GD25	FN65	NM94
1	1.60	4.00	8.00
2-4	1.00	2.50	5.00

JUDGE DREDD (...Classics #62 on; also see Batman - Judge Dredd, Dredd Rules, The Law of Dredd & 2000 A.D. Monthly)
Nov, 1983 - No. 35, 1986; V2#1, Oct, 1986 - No. 60?, 1991
Eagle Comics/IPC Magazines Ltd./Quality Comics #34-35, V2#1-37/ Fleetway #38 on

	GD25	FN65	NM94
1-Bolland-c/a begins, ends #?	1.80	4.50	9.00
2-35	.60	1.50	3.00
V2#1-('86)-New look begins	.40	1.00	2.00
V2#2-6	.30	.75	1.50
V2#7-21/22: 14-Bolland-a. 20-Begin $1.50-c		.65	1.30
V2#23/24-Two issue numbers in one	.30	.75	1.50
25-38: 28-1st app. Megaman (super-hero)	.30	.75	1.50
39-50: 39-Begin $1.75-c	.35	.90	1.75
51-78: 51-Begin $1.95-c. 53-Bolland-a. 57-Reprints 1st published Judge Dredd story	.40	1.00	2.00
Special 1		.70	1.40

NOTE: ***Guice** c-V2#23/24, 26, 27.*

JUDGE DREDD (Definitive Editions) (Fleetway/Quality) (Value: cover or less)

JUDGE DREDD'S CRIME FILE (Eagle & Quality) (Value: cover or less)

JUDGE DREDD'S HARDCASE PAPERS (Fleetway/Quality) (Value: cover or less)

JUDGE DREDD: THE EARLY CASES (Eagle) (Value: cover or less)

JUDGE DREDD: THE JUDGE CHILD QUEST (Eagle) (Value: cover or less)

JUDGE DREDD: THE MEGAZINE (Fleetway/Quality) (Value: cover or less)

JUDGE PARKER
Feb, 1956 - No. 2, 1956
Argo

	GD25	FN65	NM94
1	4.00	12.00	24.00
2	2.80	7.00	14.00

JUDO JOE
Aug, 1953 - No. 3, Dec, 1953
Jay-Jay Corp.

	GD25	FN65	NM94
1-Drug ring story	4.70	14.00	28.00
2,3: 3-Hypo needle story	4.00	10.00	20.00

JUDOMASTER (Gun Master #84-89) (Also see Crisis on Infinite Earths, Sarge Steel #6 & Special War Series)
No. 89, May-June, 1966 - No. 98, Dec, 1967 (Two No. 89's)
Charlton Comics

	GD25	FN65	NM94
89-98: 91-Sarge Steel begins. 93-Intro. Tiger	2.40	6.00	12.00
93,94,96,98(Modern Comics reprint, 1977)		.50	1.00

NOTE: ***Morisi** Thunderbolt #90. #91 has 1 pg. biography on writer/artist Frank McLoughlin.*

JUDY CANOVA (Formerly My Experience) (Stage, screen, radio)
No. 23, May, 1950 - No. 3, Sept, 1950
Fox Features Syndicate

	GD25	FN65	NM94
23(#1)-Wood-c,a(p)?	11.50	34.00	80.00
24-Wood-a(p)	11.50	34.00	80.00
3-Wood-c; Wood/Orlando-a	13.50	41.00	95.00

JUDY GARLAND (See Famous Stars)

JUDY JOINS THE WAVES
1951 (For U.S. Navy)
Toby Press

	GD25	FN65	NM94
nn	4.00	12.00	24.00

JUGHEAD (Formerly Archie's Pal...)
No. 127, Dec, 1965 - No. 352, June, 1987
Archie Publications

	GD25	FN65	NM94
127-130	2.00	5.00	10.00
131,133,135-160	1.40	3.50	7.00
132,134: 132-Shield-c; The Fly & Black Hood app.; Shield cameo. 134-Shield-c	1.60	4.00	8.00
161-200	.80	2.00	4.00
201-240	.40	1.00	2.00
241-352: 300-Anniversary issue; infinity-c	.30	.75	1.50

JUGHEAD (2nd series)
Aug, 1987 - Present (.75/$1.00/$1.25)
Archie Enterprises

	GD25	FN65	NM94
1-46: 4-X-Mas issue. 17-Colan-c/a		.60	1.25

JUGHEAD AS CAPTAIN HERO
Oct, 1966 - No. 7, Nov, 1967
Archie Publications

	GD25	FN65	NM94
1	4.35	13.00	26.00
2	3.20	8.00	16.00
3-7	2.00	5.00	10.00

JUGHEAD JONES COMICS DIGEST, THE (...Magazine No. 10-64; Jughead Jones Digest Magazine #65)
June, 1977 - Present ($1.35-$1.50, digest-size, 128 pgs.)
Archie Publications

	GD25	FN65	NM94
1-Neal Adams-a; Capt. Hero-r	1.20	3.00	6.00
2(9/77)-Neal Adams-a	.80	2.00	4.00
3-50: 7-Origin Jaguar-r; N. Adams-a. 13-r/1957 Jughead's Folly	.40	1.00	2.00
51-82	.30	.75	1.50

JUGHEAD'S DINER
Apr, 1990 - No. 7, Apr, 1991 ($1.00, color)
Archie Comics

	GD25	FN65	NM94
1-7		.50	1.00

JUGHEAD'S DOUBLE DIGEST (...Magazine #5)
Oct, 1989 - Present ($2.25/$2.50, quarterly, 256 pgs.)
Archie Comics

	GD25	FN65	NM94
1-18: 2,5-Capt. Hero stories	.50	1.25	2.50

JUGHEAD'S EAT-OUT COMIC BOOK MAGAZINE (See Archie Giant Series Magazine No. 170)

JUGHEAD'S FANTASY
Aug, 1960 - No. 3, Dec, 1960
Archie Publications

	GD25	FN65	NM94
1	14.00	43.00	100.00
2	10.00	30.00	70.00
3	10.00	30.00	60.00

JUGHEAD'S FOLLY
1957
Archie Publications (Close-Up)

	GD25	FN65	NM94
1-Jughead a la Elvis (Rare)	32.00	95.00	220.00

JUGHEAD'S JOKES
Aug, 1967 - No. 78, Sept, 1982

(No. 1-8, 38 on: reg. size; No. 9-23: 68 pgs.; No. 24-37: 52 pgs.)
Archie Publications

	GD25	FN65	NM94
1	5.85	17.50	35.00
2	3.60	9.00	18.00
3-5	2.00	5.00	10.00
6-10	1.00	2.50	5.00
11-30	.60	1.50	3.00
31-50	.40	1.00	2.00
51-78	.30	.75	1.50

JUGHEAD'S PAL HOT DOG (See Laugh #14 for 1st app.)
Jan, 1990 - No. 5, Oct, 1990 ($1.00, color)
Archie Comics

	GD25	FN65	NM94
1-5		.50	1.00

JUGHEAD'S SOUL FOOD (Spire Christian) (Value: cover or less)

JUGHEAD'S TIME POLICE
July, 1990 - No. 6, May, 1991 ($1.00, color, bi-monthly)
Archie Comics

	GD25	FN65	NM94
1-6: Colan a-3-6p; c-3-6		.50	1.00

JUGHEAD WITH ARCHIE DIGEST (...Plus Betty & Veronica & Reggie Too No. 1,2; ...Magazine #33-?, 101-on; ...Comics Digest Mag.)
March, 1974 - Present (Digest Size; $1.00-$1.25-$1.35-$1.50)
Archie Publications

	GD25	FN65	NM94
1	3.00	7.50	15.00
2	1.40	3.50	7.00
3-10	.80	2.00	4.00
11-20: Capt. Hero-r in #14-16; Pureheart the Powerful #18,21,22; Capt. Pureheart #17,19	.60	1.50	3.00
21-50: 29-The Shield-r. 30-The Fly-r	.40	1.00	2.00
51-116	.30	.75	1.50

JUKE BOX COMICS
March, 1948 - No. 6, Jan, 1949
Famous Funnies

	GD25	FN65	NM94
1-Toth-c/a; Hollingsworth-a	32.00	95.00	225.00
2-Transvestism story	18.00	54.00	125.00
3-6: 4-Jimmy Durante line drawn-c. 6-Features Desi Arnaz plus Arnaz line drawn-c	13.00	40.00	90.00

JUMBO COMICS (Created by S.M. Iger)
Sept, 1938 - No. 167, Mar, 1953 (No. 1-3: 68 pgs.; No. 4-8: 52 pgs.)
(No. 1-8 oversized-10x14"; black & white)
Fiction House Magazines (Real Adv. Publ. Co.)

	GD25	FN65	VF82	NM94
1-(Rare)-Sheena Queen of the Jungle by Meskin, The Hawk by Eisner, The Hunchback by Dick Briefer(ends #8) begin; 1st comic art by Jack Kirby (Count of Monte Cristo & Wilton of the West); Mickey Mouse appears (1 panel) with brief biography of Walt Disney; 1st app. Peter Pupp by Bob Kane. Note: Sheena was created by Iger for publication in England as a newspaper strip. The early issues of Jumbo contain Sheena strip-r	750.00	2250.00	4500.00	7500.00

(Estimated up to 45 total copies exist, 1 in NM/Mint)

	GD25	FN65	VF82
2-(Rare)-Origin Sheena. Diary of Dr. Hayward by Kirby (also #3) plus 2 other stories; contains strip from Universal Film featuring Edgar Bergen & Charlie McCarthy plus-c (preview of film)	400.00	1200.00	2400.00
3-Last Kirby issue	300.00	900.00	1800.00
4-(Scarce)-Origin The Hawk by Eisner; Wilton of the West by Fine (ends #14)(1st comic work); Count of Monte Cristo by Fine (ends #15); The Diary of Dr. Hayward by Fine (cont'd #8,9)	285.00	855.00	1700.00
5-Christmas-c	200.00	600.00	1200.00
6-8-Last B&W issue. #8 was a N. Y. World's Fair Special Edition; Frank Buck's Jungleland story	158.00	475.00	950.00
9-Stuart Taylor begins by Fine; Fine-c; 1st color issue (8-9/39)-1st Sheena (jungle) cover; 8-1/4x10-1/4"(oversized in width only)	167.00	500.00	1000.00

	GD25	FN65	NM94
10-13: 10-Regular size 68 pg. issues begin; Sheena dons new costume w/ origin costume. 12-The Hawk-c	83.00	250.00	500.00
14-Intro. Lightning (super-hero) on-c only	95.00	290.00	575.00
15,17-20: 17-Lightning part-c	54.00	162.00	325.00
16-Lightning-c	67.00	200.00	400.00
21-30: 22-1st Tom, Dick & Harry; origin The Hawk retold	42.00	125.00	250.00
31-40: 31-(9/41)-1st app. Mars God of War in Stuart Taylor story (see Planet Comics #15. 35-Shows V2#11 (correct number does not appear)	37.00	112.00	225.00
41-50	29.00	88.00	175.00
51-60: 52-Last Tom, Dick & Harry	26.00	78.00	155.00
61-70: 68-Sky Girl begins, ends #130; not in #79	18.00	55.00	110.00
71-99: 89-ZX5 becomes a private eye. 94-Used in Love and Death by Legman	15.00	45.00	90.00
100	18.00	55.00	110.00
101-110	13.00	40.00	80.00
111-140,150-158: 155-Used in **POP**, pg. 98	12.00	35.00	70.00
141-149-Two Sheena stories. 141-Long Bow, Indian Boy begins, ends #160	14.00	42.00	85.00
159-163: Space Scouts serial in all; 163-Suicide Smith app.	11.00	32.00	65.00
164-The Star Pirate begins, ends #165	11.00	32.00	65.00
165-167: 165,167-Space Rangers app.	11.00	32.00	65.00

NOTE: *Bondage covers, negligee panels, torture, etc. are common in this series. Hawks of the Seas, Inspector Dayton, Spies in Action, Sports Shorts, & Uncle Otto by Eisner, #1-7. Hawk by* ***Eisner****-#10-15.* ***Eisner*** *c-1-7, 11-13, 15. 1pg. Patsy pin-ups in 92-97, 99-101. Sheena by* ***Meskin****-#1, 4; by* ***Powell****-#2, 3, 5-28;* ***Powell*** *c-14, 16, 17, 19. Sky Girl by* ***Matt Baker****-#69-78, 80-124.* ***Bailey*** *a-3-8.* ***Briefer*** *a-1-8, 10.* ***Fine*** *a-14; c-8-10.* ***Kamen*** *a-101, 105, 123, 132; c-105, 121-145.* ***Bob Kane*** *a-1-8.* ***Whitman*** *c-146-167(most). Jungle c-9, 13, 15, 17 on.*

JUMPING JACKS PRESENTS THE WHIZ KIDS
1978 (In 3-D) with glasses (4 pages)
Jumping Jacks Stores giveaway

	GD25	FN65	NM94
nn		.50	1.00

JUNGLE ACTION
Oct, 1954 - No. 6, Aug, 1955
Atlas Comics (IPC)

	GD25	FN65	NM94
1-Leopard Girl begins by Al Hartley (#1,3); Jungle Boy by Forte; Maneely-a in all	16.00	48.00	110.00
2-(3-D effect cover)	20.00	60.00	140.00
3-6: 3-Last precode (2/55)	10.00	30.00	70.00

NOTE: ***Maneely*** *c-1, 2, 5, 6.* ***Romita*** *a-3, 6.* ***Shores*** *a-3, 6; c-3, 4?.*

JUNGLE ACTION (...& Black Panther #18-21?)
Oct, 1972 - No. 24, Nov, 1976
Marvel Comics Group

	GD25	FN65	NM94
1-Lorna, Jann-r (All reprints in 1-4)	1.40	3.50	7.00
2-4	.70	1.75	3.50
5-Black Panther begins; new stories begin	1.40	3.50	7.00
6-18: 8-Origin Black Panther. 9-Contains pull-out ad by Mark Jewelers	.70	1.75	3.50
19-24: 19-23-KKK x-over. 23-r/#22. 24-1st Wind Eagle	.50	1.25	2.50

NOTE: ***Buckler*** *a-6-9p, 22; c-8p, 12p.* ***Buscema*** *a-5p; c-22.* ***Byrne*** *c-23.* ***Gil Kane*** *a-8p; c-2, 4, 10p, 11p, 13-17, 19, 24.* ***Kirby*** *c-18.* ***Maneely*** *r-1.* ***Russell*** *a-13i.* ***Starlin*** *c-3p.*

JUNGLE ADVENTURES
1963 - 1964 (Reprints)
Super Comics

	GD25	FN65	NM94
10,12,15: 10-r/Terrors of the Jungle #10(Rulah). 12-r/Zoot #14(Rulah).15-r/Jungle Comics #152(Kaanga/Jungle #152)	3.20	8.00	16.00
17-r/Jo-Jo #?	3.20	8.00	16.00
18-Reprints/White Princess of the Jungle #1; no Kinstler-a; origin of both White Princess & Cap'n Courage	4.00	10.00	20.00

Juke Box Comics #1, © FF

Jumbo Comics #14, © FH

Jumbo Comics #73, © FH

Jungle Comics #22, © FH — *Jungle Jim #15 (Dell) © KING* — *Jungle Lil #1, © FOX*

GD25 FN65 NM94

JUNGLE ADVENTURES
March, 1971 - No. 3, June, 1971 (25 cents, 52 pgs.)
Skywald Comics

1-Zangar origin; reprints of Jo-Jo, Blue Gorilla(origin)/White Princess #3, Kinstler-r/White Princess #2 — 1.60 4.00 8.00
2-Zangar, Sheena-r/Sheena #17 & Jumbo #162, Jo-Jo, origin Slave Girl Princess-r — 1.60 4.00 8.00
3-Zangar, Jo-Jo, White Princess-r — 1.60 4.00 8.00

JUNGLE BOOK (See King Louie and Mowgli, Movie Comics, Walt Disney Showcase #45 & Walt Disney's The Jungle Book)

JUNGLE CAT (See 4-Color No. 1136)

JUNGLE COMICS
1/40 - No. 157, 3/53; No. 158, Spr, 1953 - No. 163, Summer, 1954
Fiction House Magazines

1-Origin The White Panther, Kaanga, Lord of the Jungle, Tabu, Wizard of the Jungle; Wambi, the Jungle Boy, Camilla & Capt. Terry Thunder begin — 200.00 600.00 1200.00
2-Fantomah, Mystery Woman of the Jungle begins, ends #51; The Red Panther begins, ends #26 — 92.00 275.00 550.00
3,4 — 79.00 238.00 475.00
5 — 62.00 188.00 375.00
6-10: 7,8-Powell-c — 50.00 150.00 300.00
11-20: 13-Tuska-c — 37.00 112.00 225.00
21-30: 25-Shows V2#1 (correct number does not appear). #27-New origin Fantomah, Daughter of the Pharoahs; Camilla dons new costume — 31.00 92.00 185.00
31-40 — 25.00 75.00 150.00
41,43-50 — 20.00 60.00 120.00
42-Kaanga by Crandall, 12 pgs. — 23.00 70.00 140.00
51-60 — 18.00 55.00 110.00
61-70 — 15.00 45.00 90.00
71-80: 79-New origin Tabu — 13.00 40.00 80.00
81-97,99,101-110 — 12.50 37.50 75.00
98-Used in **SOTI**, pg. 185 & illo-"In ordinary comic books, there are pictures within pictures for children who know how to look"; used by N.Y. Legis. Comm. — 21.00 62.00 125.00
100 — 15.00 45.00 90.00
111-163: 104-In Camilla story villain is Dr. Wertham. 118-Clyde Beatty app. 135-Desert Panther begins in Terry Thunder (origin), not in #137; ends (dies) #138. 143,145-Used in **POP**, pg. 99. 152-Tiger Girl begins. 158-Sheena app. — 12.50 37.50 75.00
I.W. Reprint #1,9: 1-r/? 9-r/#151 — 2.40 6.00 12.00

NOTE: *Bondage covers, negligee panels, torture, etc. are common to this series. Camilla by* ***Fran Hopper****-#70-91; by* ***Baker****-#100-113, 115, 116; by* ***Lubbers****-#98, 99 by* ***Tuska****-#63. Kaanga by* ***John Celardo****-#80-113; by* ***Larsen****-#71, 75, 76, 79; by* ***Moreira****-#68-70, 72-74; by* ***Maurice Whitman****-#114, 115, 117, 118, 124-163. Kaanga by* ***Moriera****-#58, 63, 64, 66, 67; by* ***Tuska****-#37. Tabu by* ***Larsen****-#63, 64, 67-75, 84, 85, 90, 91; by* ***Whitman****-#93-110, 114. Terry Thunder by* ***Celardo****-#79; by* ***Lubbers****-#80, 85. Tiger Girl-r by* ***Baker****-#152, 156, 157, 159.* ***Astarita*** *c-46.* ***Baker*** *c-114-131(most).* ***Celardo*** *a-78; c-59-113(most).* ***Eisner*** *c-2, 5, 6.* ***Fine*** *c-1.* ***Larsen*** *a-65, 66, 71, 72, 74, 75, 79, 83, 84, 87-90.* ***Lubbers*** *a-84(Terry Thunder).* ***Moriera*** *c-43, 44.* ***Morisi*** *a-51.* ***Powell*** *c-7, 8.* ***Sultan*** *c-3, 4.* ***Tuska*** *c-13.* ***Whitman*** *c-132-163(most).* ***Zolnerwich*** *c-11, 12, 18-41.*

JUNGLE COMICS (Blackthorne) (Value: cover or less)

JUNGLE GIRL (See Lorna,...)

JUNGLE GIRL (Nyoka, Jungle Girl No. 2 on)
Fall, 1942 (One shot)(No month listed)
Fawcett Publications

1-Bondage-c; photo of Kay Aldridge who played Nyoka in movie serial app. on-c. Adaptation of the classic Republic movie serial Perils of Nyoka. 1st comic to devote entire contents to a movie adaptation — 70.00 210.00 420.00

JUNGLE JIM (Also see Ace Comics)
No. 11, Jan, 1949 - No. 20, Apr, 1951
Standard Comics (Best Books)

11 — 4.70 14.00 28.00
12-20 — 3.20 8.00 16.00

JUNGLE JIM
No. 490, 8/53 - No. 1020, 8-10/59 (Painted-c)
Dell Publishing Co.

4-Color 490(#1) — 5.85 17.50 35.00
4-Color 565(#2, 6/54) — 3.60 9.00 18.00
3(10-12/54)-5 — 3.20 8.00 16.00
6-19(1-3/59) — 2.80 7.00 14.00
4-Color 1020(#20) — 2.80 7.00 14.00

JUNGLE JIM
No. 5, December, 1967
King Features Syndicate

5-Reprints Dell #5; Wood-c — 2.40 6.00 12.00

JUNGLE JIM (Continued from Dell series)
No. 22, Feb, 1969 - No. 28, Feb, 1970 (#21 was an overseas edition only)
Charlton Comics

22-Dan Flagg begins; Ditko/Wood-a — 4.00 10.00 20.00
23-26: 23-Last Dan Flagg; Howard-c. 24-Jungle People begin — 2.40 6.00 12.00
27,28: 27-Ditko/Howard-a. 28-Ditko-a — 3.00 7.50 15.00

JUNGLE JO
Mar, 1950 - No. 6, Mar, 1951
Fox Feature Syndicate (Hero Books)

nn-Jo-Jo blanked out, leaving Congo King; came out after Jo-Jo #29 (intended as Jo-Jo #30?) — 17.00 52.00 120.00
1-Tangi begins; part Wood-a — 20.00 60.00 140.00
2 — 14.00 43.00 100.00
3-6 — 13.00 40.00 90.00

JUNGLE LIL (Dorothy Lamour #2 on; also see Feature Stories Magazine)
April, 1950
Fox Feature Syndicate (Hero Books)

1 — 16.00 48.00 110.00

JUNGLE TALES (Jann of the Jungle No. 8 on)
Sept, 1954 - No. 7, Sept, 1955
Atlas Comics (CSI)

1-Jann of the Jungle — 16.00 48.00 110.00
2-7: 3-Last precode (1/55) — 11.00 32.00 75.00

NOTE: ***Heath*** *c-5.* ***Heck*** *a-6, 7.* ***Maneely*** *a-2; c-1, 3.* ***Shores*** *a-5-7; c-4, 6.* ***Tuska*** *a-2.*

JUNGLE TALES OF TARZAN
Dec, 1964 - No. 4, July, 1965
Charlton Comics

1 — 4.00 10.00 20.00
2-4 — 3.20 8.00 16.00

NOTE: ***Giordano*** *c-3p.* ***Glanzman*** *a-1-3.* ***Montes/Bache*** *a-4.*

JUNGLE TERROR (See Harvey Comics Hits No. 54)

JUNGLE THRILLS (Formerly Sports Thrills; Terrors of the Jungle #17 on)
No. 16, Feb, 1952; Dec, 1953; No. 7, 1954
Star Publications

16-Phantom Lady & Rulah story-reprint/All Top No. 15; used in **POP**, pg. 98,99; L. B. Cole-c — 20.00 60.00 140.00
3-D 1(12/53)-Jungle Lil & Jungle Jo appear; L. B. Cole-c — 25.00 75.00 175.00
7-Titled 'Picture Scope Jungle Adventures;' (1954, 36 pgs, 15 cents)-3-D effect c/stories; story & coloring book; Disbrow-a/script; L.B. Cole-c — 21.00 62.00 145.00

JUNGLE TWINS, THE (Tono & Kono)

Apr, 1972 - No. 17, Nov, 1975; No. 18, May, 1982
Gold Key/Whitman No. 18

	GD25	FN65	NM94
1	1.20	3.00	6.00
2-5	.70	1.75	3.50
6-18: 18-Reprints	.40	1.00	2.00

NOTE: *UFO c/story No. 13. Painted-c No. 1-17.* ***Spiegle*** *c-18.*

JUNGLE WAR STORIES (Guerrilla War No. 12 on)
July-Sept, 1962 - No. 11, Apr-June, 1965 (Painted-c)
Dell Publishing Co.

	GD25	FN65	NM94
01-384-209 (#1)	2.40	6.00	12.00
2-11	1.60	4.00	8.00

JUNIE PROM (Also see Dexter Comics)
Winter, 1947-48 - No. 7, Aug, 1949
Dearfield Publishing Co.

	GD25	FN65	NM94
1-Teen-age	7.50	22.50	45.00
2	4.20	12.50	25.00
3-7	3.20	8.00	16.00

JUNIOR CARROT PATROL (Dark Horse)(Value: cover or less)

JUNIOR COMICS (Formerly Li'l Pan; becomes Western Outlaws with #17)
No. 9, Sept, 1947 - No. 16, July, 1948
Fox Feature Syndicate

	GD25	FN65	NM94
9-Feldstein-c/a; headlights-c	41.00	122.00	285.00
10-16-Feldstein-c/a; headlights-c on all	37.00	112.00	260.00

JUNIOR FUNNIES (Formerly Tiny Tot Funnies No. 9)
No. 10, Aug, 1951 - No. 13, Feb, 1952
Harvey Publications (King Features Synd.)

	GD25	FN65	NM94
10-Partial reprints in all; Blondie, Dagwood, Daisy, Henry, Popeye, Felix, Katzenjammer Kids	2.80	7.00	14.00
11-13	2.40	6.00	12.00

JUNIOR HOPP COMICS
Feb, 1952 - No. 3, July, 1952
Stanmor Publ.

	GD25	FN65	NM94
1	5.85	17.50	35.00
2,3: 3-Dave Berg-a	3.60	9.00	18.00

JUNIOR MEDICS OF AMERICA, THE
No. 1359, 1957 (15 cents)
E. R. Squire & Sons

	GD25	FN65	NM94
1359	2.40	6.00	12.00

JUNIOR MISS
Winter, 1944; No. 24, April, 1947 - No. 39, Aug, 1950
Timely/Marvel Comics (CnPC)

	GD25	FN65	NM94
1-Frank Sinatra & June Allyson life story	14.00	43.00	100.00
24-Formerly The Human Torch #23?	6.35	19.00	38.00
25-38	4.00	11.00	22.00
39-Kurtzman-a	4.70	14.00	28.00

NOTE: *Painted-c 35-37. 37-all romance. 35, 36, 38-mostly teen humor.*

JUNIOR PARTNERS (Formerly Oral Roberts' True Stories)
No. 120, Aug, 1959 - V3#12, Dec, 1961
Oral Roberts Evangelistic Assn.

	GD25	FN65	NM94
120(#1)	4.00	10.00	20.00
2(9/59)	2.80	7.00	14.00
3-12(7/60)	1.80	4.50	9.00
V2#1(8/60)-5(12/60)	1.20	3.00	6.00
V3#1(1/61)-12	1.00	2.50	5.00

JUNIOR TREASURY (See Dell Junior...)

JUNIOR WOODCHUCKS (See Huey, Dewey & Louie... & Walt Disney's...)

JUSTICE
Nov, 1986 - No. 32, June, 1989
Marvel Comics Group

	GD25	FN65	NM94
1-31: 26-32-$1.50-c		.50	1.00
32-Unauthorized Joker app. (1 panel only)	.60	1.50	3.00

JUSTICE COMICS (Formerly Wacky Duck; Tales of Justice #53 on)
No. 7, Fall/47 - No. 9, 6/48; No. 4, 8/48 - No. 52, 3/55
Marvel/Atlas comics (NPP 7-9,4-19/CnPC 20-23/MjMC 24-38/Male 39-52

	GD25	FN65	NM94
7(#1, 1947)	11.50	34.00	80.00
8(#2)-Kurtzman-a-"Giggles 'N' Grins," (3)	9.15	27.50	55.00
9(#3, 6/48)	8.35	25.00	50.00
4	7.50	22.50	45.00
5-9: 8-Anti-Wertham editorial	5.85	17.50	35.00
10-15-Photo-c	5.00	15.00	30.00
16-30	4.20	12.50	25.00
31-40,42-47,49-52-Last precode	4.00	11.00	22.00
41-Electrocution-c	8.00	24.00	48.00
48-Pakula & Tuska-a	4.00	11.00	22.00

NOTE: ***Heath*** *a-24.* ***Maneely*** *c-44, 52.* ***Pakula*** *a-43, 45, 48.* ***Louis Ravielli*** *a-39.* ***Robinson*** *a-22, 25, 41.* ***Shores*** *c-7(#1), 8(#2)?* ***Tuska*** *a-48.* ***Wildey*** *a-52.*

JUSTICE, INC. (The Avenger)
May-June, 1975 - No. 4, Nov-Dec, 1975
National Periodical Publications

	GD25	FN65	NM94
1-McWilliams-a, Kubert-c; origin		.60	1.25
2-4: 2-4-Kirby-a(p), c-2,3p. 4-Kubert-c		.50	1.00

NOTE: *Adapted from Kenneth Robeson novel, creator of Doc Savage.*

JUSTICE, INC. (DC)(Value: cover or less)

JUSTICE LEAGUE (...International #7-25; ...America #26 on)
May, 1987 - Present (Also see Legends #6)
DC Comics

	GD25	FN65	NM94
1-Batman, Green Lantern(Guy Gardner), Blue Beetle, Mr. Miracle, Capt. Marvel & Martian Manhunter begin	1.40	3.50	7.00
2	.80	2.00	4.00
3-Regular cover (white background)	.60	1.50	3.00
3-Limited cover (yellow background, Superman logo)	14.00	43.00	100.00
4-Booster Gold joins	.50	1.25	2.50
5,6: 5-Origin Gray Man; Batman vs. Guy Gardner; Creeper app.	.50	1.25	2.50
7-($1.25, 52 pgs.)-Capt. Marvel & Dr. Fate resign; Capt. Atom, Rocket Red join	.50	1.50	3.00
8-10: 9,10-Millennium x-over	.30	.75	1.50
11-23: 16-Bruce Wayne-c/story. 18-21-Lobo app.		.60	1.20
24-($1.50)-1st app. Justice League Europe	.30	.75	1.50
25-49,51-62: 31,32-Justice League Europe x-over. 58-Lobo app. 61-New team begins; swipes-c to JLA #1(10-11/60). 62-Last $1.00-c		.50	1.00
50-($1.75, 52 pgs.)	.35	.85	1.75
63-68,71-74		.60	1.25
69-Doomsday tie-in; takes place between Superman: The Man of Steel #18 & Superman #74	1.40	3.50	7.00
69,70-2nd printings		.60	1.25
70-Funeral for a Friend part 1	1.00	2.50	5.00
Annual 1 (1987)	.40	1.00	2.00
Annual 2 (1988)-Joker-c/story; Batman cameo	.40	1.00	2.00
Annual 3 (1989, $1.75, 68 pgs.)	.40	1.00	2.00
Annual 4 (1990, $2.00, 68 pgs.)	.40	1.00	2.00
Annual 5 (1991, $2.00, 68 pgs.)-Armageddon 2001 x-over; 2nd printing exists with silver ink-c	.40	1.00	2.00
Annual 6 (1992, $2.50, 68 pgs.)	.50	1.25	2.50
Special 1 (1990, $1.50, 52 pgs.)-Giffen plots	.30	.75	1.50
Special 2 (1991, $2.95, 52 pgs.)-Staton-a(p)	.60	1.50	3.00
Spectacular 1 (1992, $1.50, 52 pgs.)-Intro new JLI & JLE teams; ties into JLI #61 & JLE #37	.30	.75	1.50
A New Beginning Trade Paperback ($12.95, 1989)-r/1-7	2.60	6.50	13.00

NOTE: ***Austin*** *a-1i, 60i; c-1i.* ***Giffen*** *a-8-10; c-21p.* ***Guice*** *a-62i.* ***Russell*** *c-54i.* ***Willingham***

Junior Comics #13, © FOX

Justice Comics #5, © MEG

Justice League America #26, © DC

Justice League of America #23, © DC

Justice League of America #108, © DC

Justice League of America #154, © DC

GD25 FN65 NM94

a-30p, Annual 2.

JUSTICE LEAGUE EUROPE
April, 1989 - Present (75 cents; $1.00 #5 on)
DC Comics

1-Giffen plots in all; breakdowns in 1-8,13-30 .40 1.00 2.00
2-49: 7-9-Batman app. 7,8-JLA x-over. 8,9-Superman app. 12-Metal Men app. 20,21-Rogers-c/a(p). 33,34-Lobo vs. Despero. 37-New team begins; swipes-c to JLA #9; see JLA Spectacular. 38-Last $1.00-c .60 1.25
Annual 1 (1990, $2.00, 68 pgs.)-Return of the Global Guardians; Giffen plots/breakdowns .40 1.00 2.00
Annual 2 (1991, $2.00, 68pgs.)-Armageddon 2001; Giffen-p; Golden-i; Rogers-p .40 1.00 2.00
Annual 3 (1992, $2.50, 68 pgs.)-Eclipso app. .50 1.25 2.50

JUSTICE LEAGUE OF AMERICA (See Brave & the Bold #28-30, Mystery In Space #75 & Official...Index)
Oct-Nov, 1960 - No. 261, Apr, 1987 (91-99,139-157: 52 pgs.)
National Periodical Publications/DC Comics

Brave and the Bold #28 (2-3/60)-Intro/1st app. Justice League of America; origin Snapper Carr 325.00 975.00 2600.00
Brave and the Bold #29,30 (4-5/60, 6-7/60) 143.00 430.00 1000.00
1-(10-11/60)-Origin Despero; Aquaman, Batman, Flash, Green Lantern, J'onn J'onzz, Superman & Wonder Woman continue from Brave and the Bold 250.00 750.00 1750.00
2 65.00 200.00 460.00
3-Origin/1st app. Kanjar Ro 50.00 150.00 350.00
4-Green Arrow joins JLA 38.00 115.00 265.00
5-Origin Dr. Destiny 29.00 85.00 200.00
6-8,10: 6-Origin Prof. Amos Fortune. 7-Last 10 cent issue. 10-Origin Felix Faust; 1st app. Time Lord 24.00 72.00 165.00
9-Origin J.L.A. (1st origin) 34.00 103.00 240.00
11-15: 12-Origin & 1st app. Dr. Light. 13-Speedy app. 14-Atom joins JLA 17.00 50.00 115.00
16-20: 17-Adam Strange flashback 13.00 40.00 90.00
21-"Crisis on Earth-One;" re-intro. of JSA (1st S.A. app. Hourman & Dr. Fate) 25.00 75.00 175.00
22-"Crisis on Earth-Two;" JSA x-over (story continued from #21) 23.00 70.00 160.00
23-28: 24-Adam Strange app. 28-Robin app. 6.70 23.00 46.00
29,30-JSA x-over. 29-1st Silver Age app. Starman; "Crisis on Earth-Three" 8.70 26.00 52.00
31-Hawkman joins JLA, Hawkgirl cameo 6.35 15.50 31.00
32-Intro & Origin Brain Storm 4.35 13.00 26.00
33,35,36,40,41: 41-Intro & origin The Key 4.00 11.50 23.00
34-Joker-c/story 5.00 15.00 30.00
37,38-JSA x-over (1st S.A. app. Mr. Terrific #38). 37-Batman cameo. 38-"Crisis on Earth-A" 6.86 20.50 41.00
39-Giant G-16; r/B&B #28,30 & JLA #5 4.35 13.00 26.00
42-45: 42-Metamorpho app. 43-Intro. Royal Flush Gang 2.80 7.00 14.00
46-JSA x-over; 1st S.A. app. Sandman 7.50 22.50 45.00
47-JSA x-over 4.00 10.50 21.00
48-Giant G-29; r/JLA #2,3 & B&B #29 4.00 10.50 21.00
49-54,57,59,60 2.40 6.00 12.00
55-Intro. Earth 2 Robin (1st G.A. Robin in S.A.) 4.70 14.00 28.00
56-JLA vs. JSA 3.00 7.50 15.00
58-Giant G-41; r/JLA #6,8,1 2.40 6.00 12.00
61-63,66,68-72: 69-Wonder Woman quits. 71-Manhunter leaves. 72-Last 12 cent issue 1.60 4.00 8.00
64,65-JSA story. 64-Origin/1st app. S.A. Red Tornado 1.80 4.50 9.00
67-Giant G-53; r/JLA #4,14,31 1.80 4.50 9.00
73,74,77-80: 74-Black Canary joins. 78-Re-intro Vigilante (1st S.A. app?) 1.00 2.50 5.00
75-2nd app. Green Arrow in new costume 1.20 3.00 6.00
76-Giant G-65 1.20 3.00 6.00
81-84,86-92: 83-Death of Spectre .80 2.00 4.00
85,93-(Giant G-77,G-89; 68 pgs.) 1.20 3.00 6.00
94-Reprints 1st Sandman story (Adv. #40) & origin/1st app. Starman (Adv. #61); Deadman x-over; N. Adams-a(4 pgs.); begin 25 cent, 52 pg. issues, ends #99 3.60 9.00 18.00
95-Origin Dr. Fate & Dr. Midnight reprint (from More Fun #67, All-American #25) 1.40 3.50 7.00
96-Origin Hourman (Adv. #48); Wildcat-r 1.40 3.50 7.00
97-Origin JLA retold; Sargon, Starman-r 1.00 2.50 5.00
98,99: 98-G.A. Sargon, Starman-r. 99-G.A. Sandman, Starman, Atom-r; last 52 pg. issue 1.00 2.50 5.00
100-(8/72) 1.20 3.00 6.00
101,102: JSA x-overs. 102-Red Tornado dies 1.20 3.00 6.00
103-106,109: 103-Phantom Stranger joins. 105-Elongated Man joins. 106-New Red Tornado joins. 109-Hawkman resigns .60 1.50 3.00
107,108-G.A. Uncle Sam, Black Condor, The Ray, Dollman, Phantom Lady & The Human Bomb (JSA) x-over 1.20 3.00 6.00
110-116: All 100 pgs. 111-Shining Knight, Green Arrow-r. 112-Crimson Avenger, Vigilante-r; origin Starman-r/Adv. #81 .80 2.00 4.00
117-190: 117-Hawkman rejoins. 120,121,138-Adam Strange app. 128-Wonder Woman rejoins. 129-Death of Red Tornado. 135-137-G.A. Bulletman, Bulletgirl, Spy Smasher, Mr. Scarlet, Pinky & Ibis x-over. 137-Superman battles G.A. Capt. Marvel. 139-157-(52 pgs.). 144-Origin retold; origin J'onn J'onnz. 145-Red Tornado resurrected. 158-160-(44 pgs.). 161-Zatanna joins & new costume. 171-Mr. Terrific murdered. 178-Cover similar to #1; J'onn J'onzz app. 179-Firestorm joins. 181-Green Arrow leaves .40 1.00 2.00
191-199: 192,193-Real origin Red Tornado. 193-1st app. All-Star Squadron as free 16 pg. insert .30 .75 1.50
200-Anniversary issue (76pgs., $1.50); origin retold; Green Arrow rejoins .60 1.50 3.00
201-220: 203-Intro/origin new Royal Flush Gang. 207,208-JSA, JLA, & All-Star Squadron team-up. 219,220-True origin Black Canary .30 .75 1.50
221-250 (75 cents): 228-Re-intro Martian Manhunter. 233-New JLA begins. 243-Aquaman leaves. 244,245-Crisis x-over. 250-Batman rejoins .30 .75 1.50
251-260: 253-1st told origin Despero. 258-Death of Vibe. 258-261-Legends x-over. 260-Death of Steel .50 1.00
261-Last issue .60 1.25 2.50
Annual 1(1983) .60 1.25 2.50
Annual 2(1984)-Intro new J.L.A. .30 .75 1.50
Annual 3(1985)-Crisis x-over .30 .75 1.50

NOTE: ***Neal Adams*** *c-63, 66, 67, 70, 74, 79, 81, 82, 86-89, 91, 92, 94, 96-98, 138, 139.* ***M. Anderson*** *c-1-4, 6, 7, 10, 12-14.* ***Aparo*** *a-200.* ***Austin*** *a-200i.* ***Baily*** *a-96r.* ***Burnley*** *r-94, 98, 99.* ***Greene*** *a-46-61i, 64-73i, 110i(r).* ***Grell*** *c-117, 122.* ***Kaluta*** *c-154p.* ***Gil Kane*** *a-200.* ***Krigstein*** *a-96(r/Sensation #84).* ***Kubert*** *a-200; c-72, 73.* ***Nino*** *a-228i, 230i.* ***Orlando*** *c-151i.* ***Perez*** *a-184-186p, 192-197p, 200p; c-184p, 186, 192-195, 196p, 197p, 199, 200, 201p, 202, 203-205p, 207-209, 212-215, 217, 219, 220.* ***Reinman*** *r-97.* ***Roussos*** *a-62i.* ***Sekowsky*** *a-37, 38, 44-63p, 110-112p(r); c-46-48p, 51p.* ***Sekowsky/Anderson*** *c-5, 8, 9, 11, 15.* ***B. Smith*** *c-185i.* ***Starlin*** *c-178-180, 183, 185p.* ***Staton*** *a-244p; c-157p, 244p.* ***Toth*** *r-110.* ***Tuska*** *a-153, 228p, 241-243p. JSA x-overs-21, 22, 29, 30, 37, 38, 46, 47, 55, 56, 64, 65, 73, 74, 82, 83, 91, 92, 100, 101, 102, 107, 108, 110, 113, 115, 123, 124, 135-137, 147, 148, 159, 160, 171, 172, 183-185, 195-197, 207-209, 219, 220, 231, 232, 244.*

JUSTICE LEAGUE QUARTERLY (DC)(Value: cover or less)

JUSTICE MACHINE, THE
June, 1981 - No. 5, Nov, 1983 ($2.00, No. 1-3, Magazine size)
Noble Comics

1-Byrne-c(p) 1.60 4.00 8.00
2-Austin-c(i) 1.00 2.50 5.00
3 .80 2.00 4.00
4,5 .60 1.50 3.00

	GD25	FN65	NM94
Annual 1 (1/84, 68 pgs.)(published by Texas Comics); 1st app. The Elementals; Golden-c(p)	1.20	3.00	6.00

JUSTICE MACHINE (Comico) (Value: cover or less)

JUSTICE MACHINE, THE (Innovation) (Value: cover or less)

JUSTICE MACHINE FEATURING THE ELEMENTALS (Comico) (Value: cover or less)

JUSTICE SOCIETY OF AMERICA (See Adventure #461 & All-Star #3)
April, 1991 - No. 8, Nov, 1991 ($1.00, color, limited series)
DC Comics

	GD25	FN65	NM94
1-Flash	.35	.90	1.75
2,3: 2-Black Canary. 3-Green Lantern		.60	1.25
4-8: 4-Hawkman. 5-Flash/Hawkman. 6-Green Lantern/Black Canary. 7-JSA		.50	1.00

JUSTICE SOCIETY OF AMERICA (Also see Last Days of the... Special)
Aug, 1992 - Present ($1.25, color)
DC Comics

	GD25	FN65	NM94
1	.30	.75	1.50
2-10		.60	1.25

JUSTICE TRAPS THE GUILTY (Fargo Kid V11#3 on)
Oct-Nov, 1947 - V11#2(#92), Apr-May, 1958
Prize/Headline Publications

	GD25	FN65	NM94
V2#1-S&K-c/a; electrocution-c	26.00	78.00	180.00
2-S&K-c/a	13.00	40.00	90.00
3-5-S&K-c/a	11.50	34.00	80.00
6-S&K-c/a; Feldstein-a	12.00	36.00	85.00
7,9-S&K-c/a. 7-V2#1 in indicia; #7 on-c	10.00	30.00	70.00
8,10-Krigstein-a; S&K-c. 10-S&K-a	11.50	34.00	80.00
11,19-S&K-c	6.70	20.00	40.00
12,14-17,20-No S&K. 14-Severin/Elder-a(8pg.)	4.00	10.00	20.00
13-Used in **SOTI**, pg. 110-111	5.00	15.00	30.00
18-S&K-c, Elder-a	4.20	12.50	25.00
21,30-S&K-c/a	4.70	14.00	28.00
22,23,27-S&K-c	4.00	11.00	22.00
24-26,28,29,31-50	2.80	7.00	14.00
51-57,59-70: 56-Ben Oda, Mort Meskin, Simon & Kirby app. on-c	2.40	6.00	12.00
58-Illo. in **SOTI**, "Treating police contemptuously" (top left); text on heroin	13.00	40.00	90.00
71-92: 76-Orlando-a	2.40	6.00	12.00

NOTE: ***Bailey** a-12, 13. **Elder** a-8. **Kirby** a-19p. **Meskin** a-22, 27, 63, 64; c-45, 46. **Robinson/Meskin** a-5, 19. **Severin** a-8, 11p. Photo c-12, 15, 16.*

JUST KIDS
No. 283, 1932 (16 pages; 9-1/2x12"; paper cover)
McLoughlin Bros.

	GD25	FN65	NM94
283-Three-color text, pictures on heavy paper	10.00	30.00	70.00

JUST MARRIED
January, 1958 - No. 114, Dec, 1976
Charlton Comics

	GD25	FN65	NM94
1	4.00	10.00	20.00
2	2.00	5.00	10.00
3-10	1.40	3.50	7.00
11-30	.80	2.00	4.00
31-50	.40	1.00	2.00
51-114		.50	1.00

JUSTY (Viz) (Value: cover or less)

KA'A'NGA COMICS (...Jungle King)(See Jungle Comics)
Spring, 1949 - No. 20, Summer, 1954
Fiction House Magazines (Glen-Kel Publ. Co.)

	GD25	FN65	NM94
1-Ka'a'nga, Lord of the Jungle begins	32.00	95.00	225.00
2 (Wint., '49-'50)	16.00	48.00	110.00
3,4	12.00	36.00	85.00
5-Camilla app.	10.00	30.00	60.00
6-10: 7-Tuska-a. 9-Tabu, Wizard of the Jungle app. 10-Used in **POP**, pg. 99	8.35	25.00	50.00
11-15: 15-Camilla-r by Baker/Jungle #106	6.70	20.00	40.00
16-Sheena app.	7.50	22.50	45.00
17-20	5.85	17.50	35.00
I.W. Reprint #1,8: 1-r/#18; Kinstler-c. 8-r/#10	1.60	4.00	8.00

NOTE: ***Celardo** c-1. **Whitman** c-8-20(most).*

KAMANDI, THE LAST BOY ON EARTH (Also see Brave and the Bold #57 & 120 & Cancelled Comic Cavalcade)
Oct-Nov, 1972 - V7#59, Sept-Oct, 1978
National Periodical Publications/DC Comics

	GD25	FN65	NM94
1-Origin	4.20	12.50	25.00
2	3.00	7.50	15.00
3-5: 4-Intro. Prince Tuftan of the Tigers	1.80	4.50	9.00
6-10	1.20	3.00	6.00
11-20	.80	2.00	4.00
21-40: 24-Last 20 cent issue. 29-Superman x-over. 31-Intro Pyra. 32-(68 pgs.)-r/origin from #1 plus one new story; 4 pg. biog. of Jack Kirby with B&W photos	.60	1.50	3.00
41-59: 58-Karate Kid x-over from LSH. 59-(44 pgs.)-The Return of Omac back-up by Starlin-c/a(p)	.50	1.25	2.50

NOTE: ***Ayers** a(p)-48-59 (most). **Giffen** a-44p, 45p. **Kirby** a-1-40p; c-1-33. **Kubert** c-34-41. **Nasser** a-45p, 46p. **Starlin** a-59p; c-57, 59p.*

KAMUI (Eclipse) (Value: cover or less)

KARATE KID (See Action, Adventure, Legion of Super-Heroes, & Superboy)
Mar-Apr, 1976 - No. 15, July-Aug, 1978 (Legion spin-off)
National Periodical Publications/DC Comics

	GD25	FN65	NM94
1-Meets Iris Jacobs; Estrada/Staton-a		.60	1.20
2-15: 2-Major Disaster app. 15-Continued into Kamandi #58		.50	1.00

NOTE: ***Grell** c-1-4, 5p, 6p, 7, 8. **Staton** a-1-9i. Legion x-over-No. 1, 2, 4, 6, 10, 12, 13. Princess Projectra x-over-#8, 9.*

KASCO KOMICS
1945; No. 2, 1949 (regular size; paper cover)
Kasko Grainfeed (Giveaway)

	GD25	FN65	NM94
1(1945)-Similar to Katy Keene; Bill Woggon-a; 28 pgs.; 6-7/8x9-7/8"	11.50	34.00	80.00
2(1949)-Woggon-a	10.00	30.00	70.00

KATHY
September, 1949 - No. 17, Sept, 1955
Standard Comics

	GD25	FN65	NM94
1-Teen-age	5.85	17.50	35.00
2-Schomburg-c	3.60	9.00	18.00
3-5	2.80	7.00	14.00
6-17: 17-Code approved	2.00	5.00	10.00

KATHY
Oct, 1959 - No. 27, Feb, 1964
Atlas Comics/Marvel (ZPC)

	GD25	FN65	NM94
1-Teen-age	5.00	15.00	30.00
2	3.00	7.50	15.00
3-15	1.60	4.00	8.00
16-27	1.20	3.00	6.00

KAT KARSON
No date (Reprint)
I. W. Enterprises

	GD25	FN65	NM94
1-Funny animals	1.00	2.50	5.00

KATO OF THE GREEN HORNET (Now) (Value: cover or less)

KATY AND KEN VISIT SANTA WITH MISTER WISH
1948 (16 pgs.; paper cover)
S. S. Kresge Co. (Giveaway)

Justice Traps the Guilty V2#20, © PRIZE

Kamandi #8, © DC

Kasco Komics #2, © Kasco

Katy Keene #48, © AP

The Katzenjammer Kids #2, © KING

Keen Detective Funnies #19, © CEN

	GD25	FN65	NM94
nn	3.60	9.00	18.00

KATY KEENE (Also see Kasco Komics, Laugh, Pep, Suzie, & Wilbur)
1949 - No. 4, 1951; No. 5, 3/52 - No. 62, Oct, 1961
Archie Publ./Close-Up/Radio Comics

	GD25	FN65	NM94
1-Bill Woggon-a begins	72.00	215.00	500.00
2	36.00	108.00	250.00
3-5	30.00	90.00	210.00
6-10	25.00	75.00	175.00
11,13-20	22.00	65.00	150.00
12-(Scarce)	24.00	73.00	170.00
21-40	16.00	48.00	110.00
41-62	11.50	34.00	80.00
Annual 1('54)	40.00	120.00	280.00
Annual 2-6('55-59)	22.00	65.00	150.00
3-D 1(1953-Large size)	32.00	95.00	225.00
Charm 1(9/58)	19.00	58.00	135.00
Glamour 1(1957)	19.00	58.00	135.00
Spectacular 1('56)	19.00	58.00	135.00

KATY KEENE COMICS DIGEST MAGAZINE
1987 - No. 10, July, 1990 ($1.25-$1.35-$1.50, digest size)
Close-Up, Inc. (Archie Ent.)

	GD25	FN65	NM94
1-10	.30	.75	1.50

KATY KEENE FASHION BOOK MAGAZINE
1955 - No. 13, Sum, '56 - N. 23, Wint, '58-59 (nn 3-10)
Radio Comics/Archie Publications

	GD25	FN65	NM94
1	36.00	108.00	250.00
2	22.00	65.00	150.00
11-18: 18-Photo Bill Woggon	16.00	48.00	110.00
19-23	12.00	36.00	85.00

KATY KEENE HOLIDAY FUN (See Archie Giant Series Magazine No. 7, 12)

KATY KEENE PINUP PARADE
1955 - No. 15, Summer, 1961 (25 cents)
Radio Comics/Archie Publications

	GD25	FN65	NM94
1	36.00	108.00	250.00
2	22.00	65.00	150.00
3-5	18.00	54.00	125.00
6-10,12-14: 8-Mad parody. 10-Photo of Bill Woggon	14.00	43.00	100.00
11-Story of how comics get CCA approved, narrated by Katy	18.00	54.00	125.00
15(Rare)-Photo artist & family	36.00	108.00	250.00

KATY KEENE SPECIAL (Katy Keene #7 on; see Laugh Comics Digest)
Sept, 1983 - No. 33, 1990 (Later issues published quarterly)
Archie Enterprises

	GD25	FN65	NM94
1-33: 1-Woggon-r; new Woggon-c. 3-Woggon-r		.50	1.00

KATZENJAMMER KIDS, THE (Also see Hans Und Fritz)
1903 (50 pgs.; 10x15-1/4"; in color)
New York American & Journal
(By Rudolph Dirks; strip 1st appeared in 1898)

	GD25	FN65	NM94
1903 (Rare)	67.00	200.00	400.00
1905-Tricks of...(10x15)	46.00	138.00	275.00
1906-Stokes-10x16", 32 pgs. in color	46.00	138.00	275.00
1910-The Komical...(10x15)	42.00	125.00	250.00
1921-Embee Dist. Co., 10x16", 20 pgs. in color	33.00	100.00	200.00

KATZENJAMMER KIDS, THE (See Giant Comic Album)
1945-1946; Summer, 1947 - No. 27, Feb-Mar, 1954
David McKay Publ./Standard No. 12-21(Spring/'50 - 53)/Harvey
No. 22, 4/53 on

	GD25	FN65	NM94
Feature Books 30	11.50	34.00	80.00
Feature Books 32,35('45),41,44('46)	10.00	30.00	65.00
Feature Book 37-Has photos & biography of Harold Knerr	11.00	32.00	75.00
1(1947)	11.00	32.00	75.00
2	6.35	19.00	38.00
3-11	4.35	13.00	26.00
12-14(Standard)	4.00	10.00	20.00
15-21(Standard)	3.20	8.00	16.00
22-25,27(Harvey): 22-24-Henry app.	2.40	6.00	12.00
26-Half in 3-D	14.00	43.00	100.00

KAYO (Formerly Bullseye & Jest; becomes Carnival Comics)
No. 12, March, 1945
Harry 'A' Chesler

	GD25	FN65	NM94
12-Green Knight, Capt. Glory, Little Nemo (not by McCay)	9.15	27.50	55.00

KA-ZAR (Also see Marvel Comics #1, Savage Tales #6 & X-Men #10)
Aug, 1970 - No. 3, Mar, 1971 (Giant-Size, 68 pgs.)
Marvel Comics Group

	GD25	FN65	NM94
1-Reprints earlier Ka-Zar stories; Avengers x-over in Hercules; Daredevil, X-Men app; hidden profanity-c	2.40	6.00	12.00
2,3-Daredevil-r. 2-Ka-Zar origin, X-Men-r	1.60	4.00	8.00

NOTE: ***Kirby** c/a-all. **Colan** a-1p(r). #1-Reprints X-Men #10? & Daredevil #13?*

KA-ZAR
Jan, 1974 - No. 20, Feb, 1977 (Regular Size)
Marvel Comics Group

	GD25	FN65	NM94
1	.50	1.25	2.50
2-20	.30	.75	1.50

NOTE: ***Alcala** a-6i, 8i. **Brunner** c-4. J. **Buscema** a-6-10p; c-1, 5, 7. **Heath** a-12. **G. Kane** c(p)-3, 5, 8-11, 15, 20. **Kirby** c-12p. **Reinman** a-1p.*

KA-ZAR THE SAVAGE (See Marvel Fanfare)
Apr, 1981 - No. 34, Oct, 1984 (Regular size) (Mando paper #10 on)
Marvel Comics Group

	GD25	FN65	NM94
1-34: 11-Origin Zabu. 12-Two versions: With & without panel missing (1600 printed with panel). 20-Kraven the Hunter-c/story (also apps. in #21). 21-23,25,26-Spider-Man app. 26-Photo-c. 29-Double size; Ka-Zar & Shanna wed		.50	1.00

NOTE: ***B. Anderson** a-1-15p, 18, 19; c-1-17, 18p, 20(back). **G. Kane** a(back-up)-11, 12, 14.*

KEEN DETECTIVE FUNNIES (Formerly Detective Picture Stories?)
No. 8, July, 1938 - No. 24, Sept, 1940
Centaur Publications

	GD25	FN65	NM94
V1#8-The Clock continues-r/Funny Picture Stories #1	100.00	300.00	600.00
9-Tex Martin by Eisner	58.00	175.00	350.00
10,11: 11-Dean Denton story (begins?)	50.00	150.00	300.00
V2#1,2-The Eye Sees by Frank Thomas begins; ends #23(Not in V2#3&5). 2-Jack Cole-a	44.00	132.00	265.00
3-6,9-11: 3-TNT Todd begins. 4-Gabby Flynn begins. 5,6-Dean Denton story	44.00	132.00	265.00
7-The Masked Marvel by Ben Thompson begins	83.00	250.00	500.00
8-Nudist ranch panel w/four girls	50.00	150.00	300.00
12(12/39)-Origin The Eye Sees by Frank Thomas; death of Masked Marvel's sidekick ZL	58.00	175.00	350.00
V3#1,2	50.00	150.00	300.00
18,19,21,22: 18-Bondage/torture-c	50.00	150.00	300.00
20-Classic Eye Sees-c by Thomas	62.00	188.00	375.00
23,24: 23-Air Man begins (intro). 24-Air Man-c	58.00	175.00	350.00

NOTE: ***Burgos** a-V2#2. **Jack Cole** a-V2#2. **Eisner** a-10, V2#6r. **Ken Ernst** a-V2#4-7, 9, 10, 19, 21. **Everett** a-V2#6, 7, 9, 11, 12, 20. **Guardineer** a-V2#5, 66. **Gustavson** a-V2#4-6. **Simon** c-V3#1.*

KEEN KOMICS
V2#1, May, 1939 - V2#3, Nov, 1939

Centaur Publications

V2#1(Large size)-Dan Hastings (s/f), The Big Top, Bob Phantom the Magician, The Mad Goddess app. 66.00 200.00 400.00
V2#2(Reg. size)-The Forbidden Idol of Machu Picchu; Cut Carson by Burgos begins 42.00 125.00 250.00
V2#3-Saddle Sniffl by Jack Cole, Circus Pays, Kings Revenge app. 42.00 125.00 250.00
NOTE: ***Binder** a-V2#2. **Burgos** a-V2#2, 3. **Ken Ernst** a-V2#3. **Gustavson** a-V2#2. **Jack Cole** a-V2#3.*

KEEN TEENS
1945 - No. 6, Sept, 1947
Life's Romances Publ./Leader/Magazine Enterprises

nn-14 pgs. Claire Voyant (cont'd. in other nn issue) movie photos, Dotty Dripple, Gertie O'Grady & Sissy; Van Johnson, Frank Sinatra photo-c 14.00 43.00 100.00
nn-16 pgs. Claire Voyant & 16 pgs. movie photos 14.00 43.00 100.00
3-6: 4-Glenn Ford-c. 5-Perry Como-c 5.00 15.00 30.00

KEEPING UP WITH THE JONESES
1920 - No. 2, 1921 (52 pgs.; 9-1/4x9-1/4"; B&W daily strip reprints)
Cupples & Leon Co.

1,2-By Pop Momand 16.00 48.00 110.00

KELLYS, THE (Formerly Rusty Comics; Spy Cases No. 26 on)
No. 23, Jan, 1950 - No. 25, June, 1950
Marvel Comics (HPC)

23 8.35 25.00 50.00
24,25: 24-Margie app. 5.00 15.00 30.00

KELVIN MACE (Vortex) (Value: cover or less)

KEN MAYNARD WESTERN (Movie star) (See Wow Comics, 1936)
Sept, 1950 - No. 8, Feb, 1952 (All-36pgs; photo front/back-c)
Fawcett Publications

1-Ken Maynard & his horse Tarzan begin 39.00 118.00 275.00
2 25.00 75.00 175.00
3-8: 6-Atomic bomb explosion panel 19.00 58.00 135.00

KEN SHANNON (Becomes Gabby #11 on) (Also see Police Comics #103)
Oct, 1951 - No. 10, Apr, 1953 (A private eye)
Quality Comics Group

1-Crandall-a 16.00 48.00 110.00
2-Crandall c/a(2) 12.00 36.00 85.00
3-5-Crandall-a 10.00 30.00 60.00
6-Crandall-c/a 10.00 30.00 65.00
7,9-Crandall-a 9.15 27.50 55.00
8-Opium den drug use story 7.50 22.50 45.00
10-Crandall-c 8.35 25.00 50.00
NOTE: ***Crandall/Cuidera** c-1-10. **Jack Cole** a-1-9. No. 11-15 published after title change to Gabby.*

KEN STUART
Jan, 1949 (Sea Adventures)
Publication Enterprises

1-Frank Borth-c/a 5.85 17.50 35.00

KENT BLAKE OF THE SECRET SERVICE (Spy)
May, 1951 - No. 14, July, 1953
Marvel/Atlas Comics(20CC)

1-Injury to eye, bondage, torture; Brodsky-c 10.00 30.00 60.00
2-Drug use w/hypo scenes; Brodsky-c 6.70 20.00 40.00
3-14: 8-R.Q. Sale-a (2 pgs.) 4.20 12.50 25.00
NOTE: ***Heath** c-5, 7, 8. **Infantino** c-12. **Maneely** c-3. **Sinnott** a-2(3). **Tuska** a-8(3pg.)*

KERRY DRAKE
Jan, 1956 - No. 2, March, 1956
Argo

1,2-Newspaper-r 4.70 14.00 28.00

KERRY DRAKE DETECTIVE CASES (...Racket Buster No. 32,33)
(Also see Chamber of Clues & Green Hornet Comics #42-47)
1944 - No. 5, 1944; No. 6, Jan, 1948 - No. 33, Aug, 1952
Life's Romances/Com/Magazine Ent. No.1-5/Harvey No.6 on

nn(1944)(A-1 Comics)(slightly over-size) 14.00 43.00 100.00
2 10.00 30.00 65.00
3-5(1944) 8.35 25.00 50.00
6,8(1948): Lady Crime by Powell. 8-Bondage-c 5.00 15.00 30.00
7-Kubert-a; biog of Andriola (artist) 5.85 17.50 35.00
9,10-Two-part marijuana story; Kerry smokes marijuana in #10 9.15 27.50 55.00
11-15 4.35 13.00 26.00
16-33 4.00 10.00 20.00
...in the Case of the Sleeping City-(1951-Publishers Synd.)-16 pg. giveaway for armed forces; paper cover 3.60 9.00 18.00
NOTE: ***Andiola** c-6-9. **Berg** a-5. **Powell** a-10-23, 28, 29.*

KEWPIES
Spring, 1949
Will Eisner Publications

1-Feiffer-a; Kewpie Doll ad on back cover 32.00 95.00 225.00

KEY COMICS
Jan, 1944 - No. 5, Aug, 1946
Consolidated Magazines

1-The Key, Will-O-The-Wisp begin 21.00 62.00 125.00
2 (3/44) 10.00 30.00 60.00
3,4: 4-(5/46)-Origin John Quincy The Atom (begins) 7.50 22.50 45.00
5-4pg. Faust Opera adapt; Kiefer-a; back-c advertises "Masterpieces Illustrated" by Lloyd Jacquet after he left Classic Comics (no copies of Masterpieces Illustrated known) 10.00 30.00 65.00

KEY COMICS
1951 - 1956 (32 pages) (Giveaway)
Key Clothing Co./Peterson Clothing
Contains a comic from different publishers bound with new cover. Cover changed each year. Many combinations possible. Distributed in Nebraska, Iowa, & Kansas. Contents would determine price, 40-60 percent of original.

KEY RING COMICS
1941 (16 pgs.; two colors) (sold 5 for 10 cents)
Dell Publishing Co.

1-Sky Hawk 3.00 7.50 15.00
1-Viking Carter 3.00 7.50 15.00
1-Features Sleepy Samson 3.20 8.00 16.00
1-Origin Greg Gilday-r/War Comics #2 3.20 8.00 16.00
1-Radior(Super hero) 2.80 7.00 14.00
NOTE: *Each book has two holes in spine to put in binder.*

KICKERS, INC. (Marvel) (Value: cover or less)

KID CARROTS
September, 1953
St. John Publishing Co.

1-Funny animal 4.00 10.00 20.00

KID COLT OUTLAW (Kid Colt #1-4; ...Outlaw #5-on) (Also see All Western Winners, Best Western, Black Rider, Giant-Size..., Two-Gun Kid, Two-Gun Western, Western Winners, Wild Western, Wisco)
8/48 - No. 139, 3/68; No. 140, 11/69 - No. 229, 4/79
Marvel Comics(LCC) 1-16; Atlas(LMC) 17-102; Marvel 103-on

1-Kid Colt & his horse Steel begin; Two-Gun Kid app. 50.00 150.00 350.00
2 25.00 75.00 175.00
3-5: 4-Anti-Wertham editorial; Tex Taylor app. 5-Blaze Carson app. 18.00 54.00 125.00
6-8: 6-Tex Taylor app; 7-Nimo the Lion begins, ends #10 12.00 36.00 85.00
9,10 (52 pgs.) 13.00 40.00 90.00

Ken Maynard Western #4, © FAW

Kerry Drake Detective Cases #11, © HARV

Key Comics #3, © Consolidated Mag.

Kid Colt Outlaw #44, © MEG

Kiddie Kapers #1 (10/57), © AJAX

Kid Eternity #10, © QUA

	GD25	FN65	NM94
11-Origin	16.00	48.00	110.00
12-20	10.00	30.00	60.00
21-32	8.35	25.00	50.00
33-45: Black Rider in all	6.70	20.00	40.00
46,47,49,50	5.85	17.50	35.00
48-Kubert-a	6.70	20.00	40.00
51-53,55,56	5.00	15.00	30.00
54-Williamson/Maneely-c	5.85	17.50	35.00
57-60,66: 4-pg. Williamson-a in all. 59-Reprints Rawhide Kid #79; Colan text illo	6.70	20.00	40.00
61-63,67-78,80-86: 86-Kirby-a(r)	4.00	10.00	20.00
64,65-Crandall-a	4.70	14.00	28.00
79,87: 79-Origin retold. 87-Davis-a(r)	4.20	12.50	25.00
88,89-Williamson-a in both (4 pgs.). 89-Redrawn Matt Slade #2	4.70	14.00	28.00
90-99,101-Last 10 cent issues	2.40	6.00	12.00
100	3.60	9.00	18.00
101-120	2.00	5.00	10.00
121-140: 121-Rawhide Kid x-over. 125-Two-Gun Kid x-over. 130-132-68 pg. issues with one new story each; 130-Origin. 140-Reprints begin	1.40	3.50	7.00
141-160: 156-Giant; reprints (later issues all-r)	.80	2.00	4.00
161-229: 170-Origin retold. 229-Rawhide Kid-r	.40	1.00	2.00
...Album (no date; 1950's; Atlas Comics)-132 pgs.; random binding, cardboard cover, B&W stories; contents can vary (Rare)	54.00	160.00	375.00

NOTE: ***Ayers*** *a-many.* ***Colan*** *a-52, 53; c(p)-223, 228, 229.* ***Crandall*** *a-140r, 167r.* ***Everett*** *a-90, 137i, 225i(r).* ***Heath*** *a-8(2); c-34, 35, 39, 44, 46, 48, 49, 57, 64.* ***Jack Keller*** *a-25(2), 26-68(3-4), 78, 94p, 98, 99, 108, 110, 132.* ***Kirby*** *a-86r, 93, 96, 119, 176(part); c-87, 92-95, 97, 99-112, 114-117, 121-123, 197r.* ***Maneely*** *a-12, 68, 81; c-17, 19, 40-43, 47, 52, 53, 62, 65, 68, 78, 81.* ***Morrow*** *a-173r, 216r.* ***Rico*** *a-13, 18.* ***Severin*** *c-58, 59.* ***Shores*** *a-39, 41-43; c-1-10(most), 24.* ***Sutton*** *a-137p, 225p(r).* ***Wildey*** *a-47, 54, 82.* ***Williamson*** *r-147, 170, 172, 216.* ***Woodbridge*** *a-64, 81. Black Rider in #33-45, 74, 86. Iron Mask in #110, 114, 121, 127. Sam Hawk in #84, 101, 111, 121, 146, 174, 181, 188.*

KID COWBOY (Also see Approved Comics #4 & Boy Cowboy)
1950 - No. 14, 1954 (painted covers)
Ziff-Davis Publ./St. John (Approved Comics)

	GD25	FN65	NM94
1-Lucy Belle & Red Feather begin	8.35	25.00	50.00
2-Maneely-c	4.70	14.00	28.00
3-14: 5-Berg-a	4.00	11.00	22.00

KIDDIE KAPERS
1945?(nd); Oct, 1957; 1963 - 1964
Kiddie Kapers Co., 1945/Decker Publ. (Red Top-Farrell)

	GD25	FN65	NM94
1(nd, 1945-46?, 36 pgs.)-Infinity-c; funny animal	5.00	15.00	30.00
1(10/57)(Decker)-Little Bit reprints from Kiddie Karnival	2.80	7.00	14.00
Super Reprint #7, 10('63), 12, 14('63), 15,17('64), 18('64)	.80	2.00	4.00

KIDDIE KARNIVAL
1952 (100 pgs., 25 cents) (One Shot)
Ziff-Davis Publ. Co. (Approved Comics)

	GD25	FN65	NM94
nn-Rebound Little Bit #1,2	19.00	57.00	135.00

KID ETERNITY (Becomes Buccaneers) (See Hit Comics)
Spring, 1946 - No. 18, Nov, 1949
Quality Comics Group

	GD25	FN65	NM94
1	47.00	140.00	280.00
2	24.00	72.00	145.00
3-Mac Raboy-a	26.00	78.00	155.00
4-10	13.00	40.00	80.00
11-18	9.15	27.50	55.00

KID ETERNITY (DC)(Value: cover or less)

KID FROM DODGE CITY, THE
July, 1957 - No. 2, Sept, 1957
Atlas Comics (MMC)

	GD25	FN65	NM94
1-Don Heck-c	5.35	16.00	32.00
2-Everett-c	3.60	9.00	18.00

KID FROM TEXAS, THE (A Texas Ranger)
June, 1957 - No. 2, Aug, 1957
Atlas Comics (CSI)

	GD25	FN65	NM94
1-Powell-a; Severin-c	5.85	17.50	35.00
2	4.00	10.00	20.00

KID KOKO
1958
I. W. Enterprises

	GD25	FN65	NM94
Reprint #1,2-(r/M.E.'s Koko & Kola #4, 1947)	1.00	2.50	5.00

KID KOMICS (Kid Movie Komics No. 11)
Feb, 1943 - No. 10, Spring, 1946
Timely Comics (USA 1,2/FCI 3-10)

	GD25	FN65	NM94
1-Origin Captain Wonder & sidekick Tim Mullrooney, & Subbie; intro the Sea-Going Lad, Pinto Pete, & Trixie Trouble; Knuckles & Whitewash Jones only app.; Wolverton art, 7 pgs.	200.00	600.00	1200.00
2-The Young Allies, Red Hawk, & Tommy Tyme begin; last Captain Wonder & Subbie	92.00	275.00	550.00
3-The Vision & Daredevils app.	62.00	188.00	375.00
4-The Destroyer begins; Sub-Mariner app.; Red Hawk & Tommy Tyme end	58.00	175.00	350.00
5,6	45.00	135.00	270.00
7-10: The Whizzer app. 7; Destroyer not in #7,8; 10-Last Destroyer, Young Allies & Whizzer	42.00	125.00	250.00

NOTE: ***Brodsky*** *c-5.* ***Schomburg*** *c-2-4, 6-10.* ***Shores*** *c-1.*

KID MONTANA (Formerly Davy Crockett Frontier Fighter; The Gunfighters No. 51 on)
V2#9, Nov, 1957 - No. 50, Mar, 1965
Charlton Comics

	GD25	FN65	NM94
V2#9	5.00	15.00	30.00
10	3.00	7.50	15.00
11,12,14-20	2.00	5.00	10.00
13-Williamson-a	3.60	9.00	18.00
21-35	1.20	3.00	6.00
36-50	.80	2.00	4.00

NOTE: *Title change to Montana Kid on cover only on #44; remained Kid Montana on inside.*

KID MOVIE KOMICS (Formerly Kid Komics; Rusty Comics #12 on)
No. 11, Summer, 1946
Timely Comics

	GD25	FN65	NM94
11-Silly Seal & Ziggy Pig; 2 pgs. Kurtzman "Hey Look" plus 6 pg. "Pigtales" story	16.00	48.00	110.00

KIDNAPPED (See 4-Color No. 1101 & Movie Comics)

KIDNAP RACKET (See Harvey Comics Hits No. 57)

KID 'N PLAY
Feb, 1992 - Present ($1.25, color)
Marvel Comics

	GD25	FN65	NM94
1-12: 1-Infinity-c. 9-Hulk, X-Men, Punisher, Ghost Rider & Venom app. in Play's dream & on cover		.60	1.25

KID SLADE GUNFIGHTER (Formerly Matt Slade...)
No. 5, Jan, 1957 - No. 8, July, 1957
Atlas Comics (SPI)

	GD25	FN65	NM94
5-Maneely, Roth, Severin-a in all; Maneely-c	6.35	19.00	38.00
6,8-Severin-c	4.00	10.00	20.00
7-Williamson/Mayo-a, 4 pgs.	5.85	17.50	35.00

KID ZOO COMICS
July, 1948 (52 pgs.)
Street & Smith Publications

	GD25	FN65	NM94
1-Funny Animal	14.00	43.00	100.00

KILLER (...Tales By Timothy Truman)
March, 1985 ($1.75, one-shot, color, Baxter paper)
Eclipse Comics

1-Timothy Truman-c/a	.35	.90	1.75

KILLERS, THE
1947 - No. 2, 1948 (No month)
Magazine Enterprises

1-Mr. Zin, the Hatchet Killer; mentioned in **SOTI**, pgs. 179,180; used by N.Y. Legis. Comm.; L. B. Cole-c	46.00	137.00	320.00
2-(Scarce)-Hashish smoking story; "Dying, Dying, Dead" drug story; Whitney, Ingels-a; Whitney hanging-c	46.00	137.00	320.00

KILLING JOKE, THE (See Batman: The Killing Joke)

KILROYS, THE
June-July, 1947 - No. 54, June-July, 1955
B&I Publ. Co. No. 1-19/American Comics Group

1	14.00	43.00	100.00
2	8.35	25.00	50.00
3-5: 5-Gross-a	5.85	17.50	35.00
6-10: 8-Milt Gross's Moronica	4.70	14.00	28.00
11-20: 14-Gross-a	4.20	12.50	25.00
21-30	3.60	9.00	18.00
31-47,50-54	3.20	8.00	16.00
48,49-(3-D effect)	12.00	36.00	85.00

KING CLASSICS
1977 (85 cents each) (36 pages, cardboard covers)
King Features (Printed in Spain for U.S. distr.)

1-Connecticut Yankee, 2-Last of the Mohicans, 3-Moby Dick, 4-Robin Hood, 5-Swiss Family Robinson, 6-Robinson Crusoe, 7-Treasure Island, 8-20,000 Leagues, 9-Christmas Carol, 10-Huck Finn, 11-Around the World in 80 Days, 12-Davy Crockett, 13-Don Quixote, 14-Gold Bug, 15-Ivanhoe, 16-Three Musketeers, 17-Baron Munchausen, 18-Alice in Wonderland, 19-Black Arrow, 20-Five Weeks in a Balloon, 21-Great Expectations, 22-Gulliver's Travels, 23-Prince & Pauper, 24-Lawrence of Arabia (Originals, 1977-78)

each....	1.60	4.00	8.00
Reprints, 1979; HRN-24)	1.20	3.00	6.00

NOTE: *The first eight issues were not numbered. Issues No. 25-32 were advertised but not published. The 1977 originals have HRN 32a; the 1978 originals have HRN 32b.*

KING COLT (See 4-Color No. 651)

KING COMICS (Strip reprints)
Apr, 1936 - No. 159, Feb, 1952 (Winter on cover)
David McKay Publications/Standard #156-on

	GD25	FN65	VF82
1-Flash Gordon by Alex Raymond; Brick Bradford, Popeye, Henry & Mandrake the Magician begin	585.00	1750.00	3500.00

(Estimated up to 25 total copies exist, none in NM/Mint)

	GD25	FN65	NM94
2	192.00	575.00	1150.00
3	133.00	400.00	800.00
4	96.00	288.00	575.00
5	75.00	225.00	450.00
6-10: 9-X-Mas-c	50.00	150.00	300.00
11-20	40.00	120.00	240.00
21-30: 21-X-Mas-c	32.00	95.00	190.00
31-40: 33-Last Segar Popeye	27.00	80.00	160.00
41-50: 46-Little Lulu, Alvin & Tubby app. as text illos by Marge Buell. 50-The Lone Ranger begins	24.00	72.00	145.00
51-60: 52-Barney Baxter begins?	17.00	52.00	105.00
61-The Phantom begins	15.00	45.00	90.00
62-80: 76-Flag-c	12.50	37.50	75.00
81-99: 82-Blondie begins?	10.00	30.00	65.00
100	13.00	40.00	80.00
101-114: 114-Last Raymond issue (1 pg.); Flash Gordon by Austin Briggs begins, ends #155	10.00	30.00	60.00
115-145: 117-Phantom origin retold	7.50	22.50	45.00
146,147-Prince Valiant in both	5.35	16.00	32.00
148-155-Flash Gordon ends	5.35	16.00	32.00
156-159	4.70	14.00	28.00

NOTE: *Marge Buell text illos in No. 24-46 at least.*

KING CONAN (Conan The King No. 20 on)
March, 1980 - No. 19, Nov, 1983 (52 pgs.)
Marvel Comics Group

1	.50	1.25	2.50
2-6: 4-Death of Thoth Amon	.35	.90	1.75
7-19: 7-1st Paul Smith-a, 1 pg. pin-up (9/81)	.35	.90	1.75

NOTE: ***J. Buscema** a-1-9p, 17p; c(p)-1-5, 7-9, 14, 17. **Kaluta** c-19. **Nebres** a-17i, 18, 19i. **Severin** c-18. **Simonson** c-6.*

KING KONG (See Movie Comics)

KING LEONARDO & HIS SHORT SUBJECTS (TV)
Nov-Jan, 1961-62 - No. 4, Sept, 1963
Dell Publishing Co./Gold Key

4-Color 1242,1278	11.50	34.00	80.00
01390-207(5-7/62)(Dell)	10.00	30.00	60.00
1 (10/62)	10.00	30.00	60.00
2-4	7.50	22.50	45.00

KING LOUIE & MOWGLI
May, 1968 (Disney)
Gold Key

1 (#10223-805)-Characters from Jungle Book	3.00	7.50	15.00

KING OF DIAMONDS (TV)
July-Sept, 1962
Dell Publishing Co.

01-391-209-Photo-c	4.20	12.50	25.00

KING OF KINGS (See 4-Color No. 1236)

KING OF THE BAD MEN OF DEADWOOD
1950 (See Wild Bill Hickok #16)
Avon Periodicals

nn-Kinstler-c; Kamen/Feldstein-r/Cowpuncher #2	11.00	32.00	75.00

KING OF THE ROYAL MOUNTED (See Famous Feature Stories, Feature Books #1, Large Feature Comic #9, King Comics, Red Ryder #3 & Super Book #2, 6)

KING OF THE ROYAL MOUNTED (Zane Grey's)
No. 207, Dec, 1948 - No. 935, Sept-Nov, 1958
Dell Publishing Co.

4-Color 207(#1, 12/48)	11.50	34.00	80.00
4-Color 265,283	9.35	28.00	56.00
4-Color 310,340	5.85	17.50	35.00
4-Color 363,384	5.00	15.00	30.00
8(6-8/52)-10	5.00	15.00	30.00
11-20	4.35	13.00	26.00
21-28(3-5/58)	4.00	10.50	21.00
4-Color 935(9-11/58)	4.00	10.50	21.00

NOTE: *4-Color No. 207, 265, 283, 310, 340, 363, 384 are all newspaper reprints with **Jim Gary** art. No. 8 on are all Dell originals. Painted c-No. 9-on.*

KING RICHARD & THE CRUSADERS (See 4-Color No. 588)

KINGS OF THE NIGHT (Dark Horse)(Value: cover or less)

KING SOLOMON'S MINES
1951 (Movie)
Avon Periodicals

nn(#1 on 1st page)	23.00	70.00	160.00

KISS (See Crazy Magazine, Howard the Duck #12, 13, Marvel Comics Super Special #1, 5, Rock Fantasy Comics #10 & Rock N' Roll Comics #9)

KISSYFUR (TV) (DC)(Value: cover or less)

KIT CARSON (Formerly All True Detective Cases No. 4; Fighting Davy Crockett No. 9; see Blazing Sixguns & Frontier Fighters)
1950; No. 2, 8/51 - No. 3, 12/51; No. 5, 11-12/54 - No. 8, 9/55

King Comics #6, © KING

King Leonardo #4, © Leonardo TV Prod.

King of the Royal Mounted #12, © Stephen Slesinger

Kit Carson #6, © AVON

Knights of the Roundtable #1, © DELL

Kobra #2, © DC

	GD25	FN65	NM94
Avon Periodicals			
nn(#1) (1950)	9.15	27.50	55.00
2(8/51)	5.35	16.00	32.00
3(12/51)	4.70	14.00	28.00
5-6,8(11-12/54-9/55)-Formerly All True Detective Cases (last pre-code)	4.20	12.50	25.00
7-McCann-a?	4.70	14.00	28.00
I.W. Reprint #10('63)-r/Kit Carson #1; Severin-c	1.40	3.50	7.00

NOTE: ***Kinstler*** *c-1-3, 5-8.*

KIT CARSON & THE BLACKFEET WARRIORS
1953
Realistic

	GD25	FN65	NM94
nn-Reprint; Kinstler-c	7.50	22.50	45.00

KITE FUN BOOK
1954 - 1981 (16pgs, 5x7-1/4", soft-c)
Pacific, Gas & Electric/Sou. California Edison/Florida Power & Light

	GD25	FN65	NM94
1954-Donald Duck Tells About Kites-Fla. Power, S.C.E. & version with label issues-Barks pencils-8 pgs.; inks-7 pgs. (Rare)	285.00	850.00	1800.00
1954-Donald Duck Tells About Kites-P.G.&E. issue -7th page redrawn changing middle 3 panels to show P.G.&E. in story line; (All barks; last page Barks pencils only) Scarce	250.00	750.00	1600.00
1954-Pinocchio Learns About Kites	29.00	85.00	200.00
1955-Brer Rabbit in "A Kite Tail" (Disney)	25.00	75.00	175.00
1956-Woody Woodpecker	10.00	30.00	70.00
1957-?			
1958-Tom And Jerry	6.70	20.00	40.00
1960-Porky Pig	5.00	15.00	30.00
1960-Bugs Bunny	5.00	15.00	30.00
1961-Huckleberry Hound (Hanna-Barbera)	5.85	17.50	35.00
1962-Yogi Bear (Hanna-Barbera)	4.20	12.50	25.00
1963-Rocky and Bullwinkle (Jay Ward)	12.00	35.00	70.00
1963-Top Cat (Hanna-Barbera)	3.20	8.00	16.00
1964-Magilla Gorilla (Hanna-Barbera)	4.00	10.00	20.00
1965-Jinks, Pixie and Dixie (Hanna-Barbera)	2.80	7.00	14.00
1965-Tweety and Sylvester (Warner); S.C.E. version with Reddy Kilowatt app.	1.60	4.00	8.00
1966-Secret Squirrel (Hanna-Barbera); S.C.E. version with Reddy Kilowatt app.	6.70	20.00	40.00
1967-Beep! Beep! The Road Runner (TV)	2.00	5.00	10.00
1968-Bugs Bunny	2.40	6.00	12.00
1969-Dastardly and Muttley (Hanna-Barbera)	3.00	7.50	15.00
1970-Rocky and Bullwinkle (Jay Ward)	9.15	27.50	55.00
1971-Beep! Beep! The Road Runner (TV)	1.60	4.00	8.00
1972-The Pink Panther (TV)	1.20	3.00	6.00
1973-Lassie (TV)	4.00	10.00	20.00
1974-Underdog (TV)	1.60	4.00	8.00
1975-Ben Franklin	.80	2.00	4.00
1976-The Brady Bunch (TV)	2.00	5.00	10.00
1977-Ben Franklin	.80	2.00	4.00
1977-Popeye	2.40	6.00	12.00
1978-Happy Days (TV)	1.20	3.00	6.00
1979-Eight is Enough (TV)	1.00	2.50	5.00
1980-The Waltons (TV, released in 1981)	1.20	3.00	6.00

KIT KARTER
May-July, 1962
Dell Publishing Co.

	GD25	FN65	NM94
1	2.40	6.00	12.00

KITTY
October, 1948
St. John Publishing Co.

	GD25	FN65	NM94
1-Lily Renee-a	4.70	14.00	28.00

KITTY PRYDE AND WOLVERINE
Nov, 1984 - No. 6, April, 1985 (Mini-series)
Marvel Comics Group

	GD25	FN65	NM94
1 (From X-Men)	1.20	3.00	6.00
2-6	.60	1.50	3.00

KLARER GIVEAWAYS (See Wisco)

KNIGHTS OF PENDRAGON, THE (Also see Pendragon)
July, 1990 - No. 18, Dec, 1991 ($1.95, color)
Marvel Comics Ltd.

	GD25	FN65	NM94
1-18: 1-Capt. Britain app. 2,8-Free poster inside. 9,10-Bolton-c. 11,18-Iron Man app.	.40	1.00	2.00

KNIGHTS OF THE ROUND TABLE (See 4-Color No. 540)

KNIGHTS OF THE ROUND TABLE
No. 10, April, 1957
Pines Comics

	GD25	FN65	NM94
10	3.20	8.00	16.00

KNIGHTS OF THE ROUND TABLE
Nov-Jan, 1963-64
Dell Publishing Co.

	GD25	FN65	NM94
1 (12-397-401)-Painted-c	4.00	10.00	20.00

KNOCK KNOCK (...Who's There?)
No. 801, 1936 (52 pages) (8x9", B&W)
Whitman Publ./Gerona Publications

	GD25	FN65	NM94
801-Joke book; Bob Dunn-a	5.00	15.00	30.00

KNOCKOUT ADVENTURES
Winter, 1953-54
Fiction House Magazines

	GD25	FN65	NM94
1-Reprints Fight Comics #53	10.00	30.00	60.00

KNOW YOUR MASS
No. 303, 1958 (100 Pg. Giant) (35 cents) (square binding)
Catechetical Guild

	GD25	FN65	NM94
303-In color	3.20	8.00	16.00

KOBRA (See DC Special Series No. 1)
Feb-Mar, 1976 - No. 7, Mar-Apr, 1977
National Periodical Publications

	GD25	FN65	NM94
1-Art plotted by Kirby; only 25 cent issue	.30	.75	1.50
2-7: (30 cent-c) 3-Giffen-a		.50	1.00

NOTE: ***Austin*** *a-3i.* ***Buckler*** *a-5p; c-5p.* ***Kubert*** *c-4.* ***Nasser*** *a-6p, 7; c-7.*

KOKEY KOALA
May, 1952
Toby Press

	GD25	FN65	NM94
1	5.85	17.50	35.00

KOKO AND KOLA (Also see Tick Tock Tales)
Fall, 1946 - No. 5, May, 1947; No. 6, 1950
Com/Magazine Enterprises

	GD25	FN65	NM94
1-Funny animal	6.35	19.00	38.00
2	4.00	10.00	20.00
3-5,6(A-1 28)	3.60	9.00	18.00

KO KOMICS
October, 1945
Gerona Publications

	GD25	FN65	NM94
1-The Duke of Darkness & The Menace (hero); Kirby-c	33.00	100.00	200.00

KOMIC KARTOONS
Fall, 1945 - No. 2, Winter, 1945
Timely Comics (EPC)

	GD25	FN65	NM94
1,2-Andy Wolf, Bertie Mouse	11.50	34.00	80.00

KOMIK PAGES (Formerly Snap; becomes Bullseye #11)
April, 1945 (All reprints)
Harry 'A' Chesler, Jr. (Our Army, Inc.)

	GD25	FN65	NM94
10(#1 on inside)-Land O' Nod by Rick Yager (2 pgs.), Animal Crackers, Foxy GrandPa, Tom, Dick & Mary, Cheerio Minstrels, Red Starr plus other 1-2 pg. strips; Cole-a	10.00	30.00	70.00

KONA (...Monarch of Monster Isle)
Feb-Apr, 1962 - No. 21, Jan-Mar, 1967 (Painted-c)
Dell Publishing Co.

	GD25	FN65	NM94
4-Color 1256 (#1)	5.85	17.50	35.00
2-10: 4-Anak begins	3.20	8.00	16.00
11-21	2.00	5.00	10.00

NOTE: ***Glanzman** a-all issues.*

KONGA (Fantastic Giants No. 24) (See Return of...)
1960; No. 2, Aug, 1961 - No. 23, Nov, 1965
Charlton Comics

	GD25	FN65	NM94
1(1960)-Based on movie; Giordano-c	23.00	70.00	160.00
2-Giordano-c	11.50	34.00	80.00
3-5	10.00	30.00	65.00
6-15	6.70	20.00	40.00
16-23	5.00	15.00	30.00

NOTE: ***Ditko** a-1, 3-15; c-4, 6-9. **Glanzman** a-12. **Montes & Bache** a-16-23.*

KONGA'S REVENGE (Formerly Return of...)
No. 2, Summer, 1963 - No. 3, Fall, 1964; Dec, 1968
Charlton Comics

	GD25	FN65	NM94
2,3: 2-Ditko-c/a	5.00	15.00	30.00
1(12/68)-Reprints Konga's Revenge #3	3.00	7.50	15.00

KONG THE UNTAMED
June-July, 1975 - V2#5, Feb-Mar, 1976
National Periodical Publications

	GD25	FN65	NM94
1-Wrightson-c; Alcala-a	.30	.75	1.50
2-5: 2-Wrightson-c; 2,3-Alcala-a		.50	1.00

KOOKIE
Feb-Apr, 1962 - No. 2, May-July, 1962 (15 cents)
Dell Publishing Co.

	GD25	FN65	NM94
1,2-Written by John Stanley; Bill Williams-a	7.50	22.50	45.00

KOOSH KINS
Oct, 1991 - No. 4, Apr, 1992 ($1.00, color, bi-monthly, mini-series)
Archie Comics

	GD25	FN65	NM94
1-4		.50	1.00

K. O. PUNCH, THE (Also see Lucky Fights It Through)
1948 (Educational giveaway)
E. C. Comics

	GD25	FN65	NM94
nn-Feldstein-splash; Kamen-a	125.00	375.00	750.00

KORAK, SON OF TARZAN (Edgar Rice Burroughs)
Jan, 1964 - No. 45, Jan, 1972 (Painted-c No. 1-?)
Gold Key

	GD25	FN65	NM94
1-Russ Manning-a	5.85	17.50	35.00
2-11-Russ Manning-a	3.60	9.00	18.00
12-21: 12,13-Warren Tufts-a. 14-Jon of the Kalahari ends. 15-Mabu, Jungle Boy begins. 21-Manning-a	2.80	7.00	14.00
22-30	1.80	4.50	9.00
31-45	1.40	3.50	7.00

KORAK, SON OF TARZAN (Tarzan Family #60 on; see Tarzan #230)
V9#46, May-June, 1972 - V12#56, Feb-Mar, 1974; No. 57, May-June, 1975 - No. 59, Sept-Oct, 1975 (Edgar Rice Burroughs)
National Periodical Publications

	GD25	FN65	NM94
46-(52 pgs.)-Carson of Venus begins (origin), ends #56; Pellucidar feature; Weiss-a	.60	1.50	3.00
47-59: 49-Origin Korak retold	.30	.75	1.50

NOTE: ***Kaluta** a-46-56. All have covers by **Joe Kubert. Manning** strip reprints-No. 57-59. **Frank Thorn** a-46-51.*

KOREA MY HOME (Also see Yalta to Korea)
nd (1950s)
Johnstone and Cushing

	GD25	FN65	NM94
nn-Anti-communist; Korean War	20.00	60.00	140.00

KORG: 70,000 B. C. (TV)
May, 1975 - No. 9, Nov, 1976 (Hanna-Barbera)
Charlton Publications

	GD25	FN65	NM94
1	.80	2.00	4.00
2-9: 2-Painted-c; Byrne text illos	.40	1.00	2.00

KORNER KID COMICS
1947
Four Star Publications

	GD25	FN65	NM94
1	4.70	14.00	28.00

KRAZY KAT
1946 (Hardcover)
Holt

	GD25	FN65	NM94
Reprints daily & Sunday strips by Herriman	26.00	78.00	180.00
with dust jacket (Rare)....	64.00	192.00	450.00

KRAZY KAT (See Ace Comics & March of Comics No. 72, 87)

KRAZY KAT COMICS (...& Ignatz the Mouse early issues)
May-June, 1951 - F.C. #696, Apr, 1956; Jan, 1964 (None by Herriman)
Dell Publishing Co./Gold Key

	GD25	FN65	NM94
1(1951)	6.70	20.00	40.00
2-5 (#5, 8-10/52)	4.70	14.00	28.00
4-Color 454,504	4.00	10.50	21.00
4-Color 548,619,696 (4/56)	3.60	9.00	18.00
1(10098-401)(1/64-Gold Key)(TV)	3.60	9.00	18.00

KRAZY KOMICS (1st Series) (Cindy Comics No. 27 on)
July, 1942 - No. 26, Spr, 1947 (Also see Ziggy Pig)
Timely Comics (USA No. 1-21/JPC No. 22-26)

	GD25	FN65	NM94
1-Ziggy Pig & Silly Seal begins	29.00	85.00	200.00
2	13.00	40.00	90.00
3-10: 9-Hitler parody	10.00	30.00	60.00
11,13,14	7.50	22.50	45.00
12-Timely's entire art staff drew themselves into a Creeper story	11.00	32.00	75.00
15-(8-9/44)-Becomes Funny Tunes #16; has "Super Soldier" by Pfc. Stan Lee	7.50	22.50	45.00
16-24,26: 16-(10-11/44)	5.00	15.00	30.00
25-Kurtzman-a, 6 pgs.	7.50	22.50	45.00

KRAZY KOMICS (2nd Series)
Aug, 1948 - No. 2, Nov, 1948
Timely/Marvel Comics

	GD25	FN65	NM94
1-Wolverton (10 pgs.) & Kurtzman (8 pgs.)-a; Eustice Hayseed begins (Li'l Abner swipe)	25.00	75.00	175.00
2-Wolverton-a, 10 pgs.; Powerhouse Pepper cameo	18.00	54.00	125.00

KRAZY KROW (Also see Dopey Duck, Film Funnies, Funny Frolics & Movie Tunes)
Summer, 1945 - No. 3, Wint, 1945/46
Marvel Comics (ZPC)

	GD25	FN65	NM94
1	11.00	32.00	75.00
2,3	7.50	22.50	45.00
I.W. Reprint #1('57), 2('58), 7	1.20	3.00	6.00

KRAZYLIFE (Becomes Nutty Life #2)
1945 (no month)
Fox Feature Syndicate

Kona #10, © DELL

Konga #14, © American International

Korak, Son of Tarzan #49, © ERB

Krazylife #1, © FOX

Kull the Conqueror #3 (7/72), © MEG

Lady Luck #87, © QUA

	GD25	FN65	NM94
1-Funny animal	9.15	27.50	55.00

KREE/SKRULL WAR STARRING THE AVENGERS, THE
Sept, 1983 - No. 2, Oct, 1983 ($2.50, 68 pgs.; Baxter paper)
Marvel Comics Group

	GD25	FN65	NM94
1,2	.60	1.50	3.00

NOTE: *Neal Adams p-1r, 2. Buscema a-1r, 2r. Simonson a-1p; c-1p.*

KRIM-KO KOMICS
5/18/35 - No. 6, 6/22/35; 1936 - 1939 (Giveaway) (weekly)
Krim-ko Chocolate Drink

	GD25	FN65	NM94
1-(16 pgs., soft-c, Dairy giveaways)-Tom, Mary & Sparky Advs. by Russell Keaton, Jim Hawkins by Dick Moores, Mystery Island! by Rick Yager begin	10.00	30.00	60.00
2-6 (6/22/35)	6.70	20.00	40.00
Lola, Secret Agent; 184 issues, 4 pg. giveaways - all original stories each....	4.20	12.50	25.00

KROFFT SUPERSHOW (TV)
April, 1978 - No. 6, Jan, 1979
Gold Key

	GD25	FN65	NM94
1-Photo-c	.60	1.50	3.00
2-6: 6-Photo-c	.30	.75	1.50

KRULL
Nov, 1983 - No. 2, Dec, 1983 (Movie adaptation)
Marvel Comics Group

	GD25	FN65	NM94
1,2-r/Marvel Super Special. 1-Photo-c from movie		.50	1.00

KRYPTON CHRONICLES
Sept, 1981 - No. 3, Nov, 1981
DC Comics

	GD25	FN65	NM94
1-Buckler-c(p)	.30	.75	1.50
2,3		.50	1.00

KULL AND THE BARBARIANS (Magazine)
May, 1975 - No. 3, Sept, 1975 ($1.00, B&W, 84 pgs.)
Marvel Comics Group

	GD25	FN65	NM94
1-Andru/Wood-r/Kull #1; 2 pgs. Neal Adams; Gil Kane(p), Marie & John Severin-a(r); Krenkel text illo	.50	1.25	2.50
2,3: 2-Red Sonja by Chaykin begins; Soloman Kane by Weiss/N. Adams; Gil Kane-a. 3-Origin Red Sonja by Chaykin; N. Adams-a; Solomon Kane app.	.35	.90	1.80

KULL THE CONQUEROR (...the Destroyer #11 on; see Marvel Preview)
June, 1971 - No. 2, Sept, 1971; No. 3, July, 1972 - No. 15, Aug, 1974; No. 16, Aug, 1976 - No. 29, Oct, 1978
Marvel Comics Group

	GD25	FN65	NM94
1-Andru/Wood-a; origin Kull; 15 cent-c	1.60	4.00	8.00
2-5: 2-Last 15 cent issue. 3-13: 20 cent-c	.80	2.00	4.00
6-10	.60	1.50	3.00
11-29: 11-15-Ploog-a. 14-16: 25 cent-c	.40	1.00	2.00

NOTE: *No. 1, 2, 7-9, 11 are based on Robert E. Howard stories. Alcala a-17p, 18-20i; c-24. Ditko a-12r, 15r. Gil Kane c-15p, 21. Nebres a-22i-27i; c-25i, 27i. Ploog c-11, 12p, 13. Severin a-2-9i; c-2-10i, 19. Starlin c-14.*

KULL THE CONQUEROR (Marvel, 1982) (Value: cover or less)

KULL THE CONQUEROR (Marvel, 1983) (Value: cover or less)

KUNG FU (See Deadly Hands of..., & Master of...)

KUNG FU FIGHTER (See Richard Dragon...)

LABOR IS A PARTNER
1949 (32 pgs. in color; paper cover)
Catechetical Guild Educational Society

	GD25	FN65	NM94
nn-Anti-communism	17.00	51.00	120.00
Confidential Preview-(B&W, 8-1/2x11", saddle stitched)-only one known copy; text varies from color version, advertises next book on secularism (If the Devil Would Talk)	35.00	100.00	200.00

LABYRINTH (Marvel) (Value: cover or less)

LAD: A DOG
1961 - No. 2, July-Sept, 1962
Dell Publishing Co.

	GD25	FN65	NM94
4-Color 1303 (movie), 2	4.00	10.50	21.00

LADY AND THE TRAMP (See Dell Giants, 4-Color No. 629, 634, & Movie Comics)

LADY AND THE TRAMP IN "BUTTER LATE THAN NEVER"
1955 (16 pgs., 5x7-1/4", soft-c) (Walt Disney)
American Dairy Association (Premium)

	GD25	FN65	NM94
nn	4.70	14.00	28.00

LADY ARCANE (Hero) (Value: cover or less)

LADY BOUNTIFUL
1917 (10-1/4x13-1/2"; 24 pgs.; B&W; cardboard cover)
Saalfield Publ. Co./Press Publ. Co.

	GD25	FN65	NM94
nn-By Gene Carr; 2 panels per page	13.00	40.00	80.00

LADY COP (See 1st Issue Special)

LADY FOR A NIGHT (See Cinema Comics Herald)

LADY LUCK (Formerly Smash #1-85) (Also see Spirit Sections #1)
No. 86, Dec, 1949 - No. 90, Aug, 1950
Quality Comics Group

	GD25	FN65	NM94
86(#1)	43.00	130.00	300.00
87-90	32.00	95.00	225.00

LAFF-A-LYMPICS (TV) (See The Funtastic World of Hanna-Barbera)
Mar, 1978 - No. 13, Mar, 1979 (Hanna-Barbera)
Marvel Comics Group

	GD25	FN65	NM94
1-13: Yogi Bear, Scooby Doo, Pixie & Dixie, etc.		.50	1.00

LAFFY-DAFFY COMICS
Feb, 1945 - No. 2, March, 1945
Rural Home Publ. Co.

	GD25	FN65	NM94
1,2	4.70	14.00	28.00

LANA (Little Lana No. 8 on)
Aug, 1948 - No. 7, Aug, 1949 (Also see Annie Oakley)
Marvel Comics (MjMC)

	GD25	FN65	NM94
1-Rusty, Millie begin	10.00	30.00	65.00
2-Kurtzman's "Hey Look" (1); last Rusty	7.50	22.50	45.00
3-7: 3-Nellie begins	4.70	14.00	28.00

LANCELOT & GUINEVERE (See Movie Classics)

LANCELOT LINK, SECRET CHIMP (TV)
April, 1971 - No. 8, Feb, 1973
Gold Key

	GD25	FN65	NM94
1-Photo-c	2.80	7.00	14.00
2-8: 2-Photo-c	1.60	4.00	8.00

LANCELOT STRONG (See The Shield)

LANCE O'CASEY (See Mighty Midget & Whiz Comics)
Spring, 1946 - No. 3, Fall, 1946; No. 4, Summer, 1948
Fawcett Publications

	GD25	FN65	NM94
1-Captain Marvel app. on-c	13.00	40.00	900.00
2	8.35	25.00	50.00
3,4	6.70	20.00	40.00

NOTE: *The cover for the 1st issue was done in 1942 but was not published until 1946. The cover shows 68 pages but actually has only 36 pages.*

LANCER (TV) (Western)
Feb, 1969 - No. 3, Sept, 1969 (All photo-c)
Gold Key

	GD25	FN65	NM94
1	4.00	10.00	20.00

GD25 FN65 NM94

2,3 3.00 7.50 15.00

LAND OF THE GIANTS (TV)
Nov, 1968 - No. 5, Sept, 1969 (All have photo-c)
Gold Key

1 4.70 14.00 28.00
2-5 3.20 8.00 16.00

LAND OF THE LOST COMICS (Radio)
July-Aug, 1946 - No. 9, Spring, 1948
E. C. Comics

1 22.00 65.00 150.00
2 14.00 43.00 100.00
3-9 11.50 34.00 80.00

LAND UNKNOWN, THE (See 4-Color No. 845)

LARAMIE (TV)
Aug, 1960 - July, 1962 (All photo-c)
Dell Publishing Co.

4-Color 1125-Gil Kane/Heath-a 8.35 25.00 50.00
4-Color 1223,1284 5.35 16.00 32.00
01-418-207 (7/62) 5.35 16.00 32.00

LAREDO (TV)
June, 1966
Gold Key

1 (10179-606)-Photo-c 3.20 8.00 16.00

LARGE FEATURE COMIC (Formerly called Black & White)
1939 - No. 13, 1943
Dell Publishing Co.

1 (**Series I**)-Dick Tracy Meets the Blank 107.00 320.00 750.00
2-Terry & the Pirates (#1) 54.00 160.00 375.00
3-Heigh-Yo Silver! The Lone Ranger (text & ill.)(76 pgs.); also exists as a Whitman #710 57.00 170.00 400.00
4-Dick Tracy Gets His Man 57.00 170.00 400.00
5-Tarzan (#1) by Harold Foster (origin); reprints 1st dailies from 1929 93.00 280.00 650.00
6-Terry & the Pirates & The Dragon Lady; reprints dailies from 1936 49.00 145.00 340.00
7-(Scarce)-52 pgs.; The Lone Ranger-Hi-Yo Silver the Lone Ranger to the Rescue; also exists as a Whitman #715 64.00 195.00 450.00
8-Dick Tracy Racket Buster 54.00 160.00 375.00
9-King of the Royal Mounted 27.00 80.00 185.00
10-(Scarce)-Gang Busters (No. appears on inside front cover); first slick cover 40.00 120.00 275.00
11-Dick Tracy Foils the Mad Doc Hump 54.00 160.00 375.00
12-Smilin' Jack 37.00 110.00 260.00
13-Dick Tracy & Scotty 54.00 160.00 375.00
14-Smilin' Jack 37.00 110.00 260.00
15-Dick Tracy & the Kidnapped Princes 54.00 160.00 375.00
16-Donald Duck-1st app. Daisy Duck on back cover (6/41-Disney) 185.00 560.00 1300.00
(Prices vary widely on this book)
17-Gang Busters (1941) 25.00 75.00 175.00
18-Phantasmo 20.00 60.00 140.00
19-Dumbo Comic Paint Book (Disney); partial-r from 4-Color #17 170.00 515.00 1200.00
20-Donald Duck Comic Paint Book (rarer than #16) (Disney) 285.00 860.00 2000.00
(Prices vary widely on this book)
21,22: 21-Private Buck. 22-Nuts & Jolts 10.00 30.00 65.00
23-The Nebbs 12.00 36.00 85.00
24-Popeye (Thimble Theatre) by Segar 47.00 140.00 325.00
25-Smilin' Jack-1st issue to show title on-c 37.00 110.00 260.00
26-Smitty 22.00 65.00 150.00
27-Terry & the Pirates; Caniff-c/a 39.00 120.00 275.00
28-Grin & Bear It 10.00 30.00 60.00
29-Moon Mullins 19.00 58.00 135.00
30-Tillie the Toiler 17.00 51.00 120.00
1 (**Series II**)-Peter Rabbit by Cady; arrival date-3/27/42 38.00 115.00 265.00
2-Winnie Winkle (#1) 13.00 40.00 90.00
3-Dick Tracy 50.00 150.00 350.00
4-Tiny Tim (#1) 27.00 80.00 185.00
5-Toots & Casper 10.00 30.00 60.00
6-Terry & the Pirates; Caniff-a 39.00 120.00 275.00
7-Pluto Saves the Ship (#1)(Disney) written by Carl Barks, Jack Hannah, & Nick George (Barks' 1st comic book work) 65.00 195.00 455.00
8-Bugs Bunny (#1)('42) 72.00 215.00 500.00
9-Bringing Up Father 13.00 40.00 90.00
10-Popeye (Thimble Theatre) 38.00 115.00 265.00
11-Barney Google & Snuffy Smith 17.00 51.00 120.00
12-Private Buck 10.00 30.00 60.00
13-(nn)-1001 Hours Of Fun; puzzles & games; by A. W. Nugent. This book was bound as #13 with Large Feature Comics in publisher's files 10.00 30.00 60.00

NOTE: *The Black & White Feature Books are oversized 8x11-3/8" comics with color covers and black and white interiors. The first nine issues all have rough, heavy stock covers and, except for #7, all have 76 pages, including covers. #7 and #10-on all have 52 pages. Beginning with #10 the covers are slick and thin and, because of their size, are difficult to handle without damaging. For this reason, they are seldom found in fine to mint condition. The paper stock, unlike Wow #1 and Capt. Marvel #1, is itself not unstable ...just thin.*

LARRY DOBY, BASEBALL HERO
1950 (Cleveland Indians)
Fawcett Publications

nn-Bill Ward-a; photo-c 47.00 140.00 325.00

LARRY HARMON'S LAUREL AND HARDY (...Comics)
July-Aug, 1972 (Regular size)
National Periodical Publications

1 .60 1.50 3.00

LARS OF MARS
No. 10, Apr-May, 1951 - No. 11, July-Aug, 1951 (Painted-c)
Ziff-Davis Publishing Co.

10-Origin; Anderson-a(3) in each 37.00 110.00 260.00
11-Gene Colan-a 32.00 95.00 220.00

LARS OF MARS 3-D (Eclipse)(Value: cover or less)

LASER ERASER & PRESSBUTTON (Eclipse)(Value: cover or less)

LASH LARUE WESTERN (Movie star; king of the bullwhip)(See Fawcett Movie Comic, Motion Picture Comics & Six-Gun Heroes)
Sum, 1949 - No. 46, Jan, 1954 (36pgs., 1-7,9,13,16-on)
Fawcett Publications

1-Lash & his horse Black Diamond begin; photo front/back-c begin 79.00 235.00 550.00
2(11/49) 34.00 100.00 235.00
3-5 29.00 85.00 200.00
6,7,9: 6-Last photo back-c; intro. Frontier Phantom (Lash's twin brother) 22.00 65.00 150.00
8,10 (52pgs.) 23.00 70.00 160.00
11,12,14,15 (52pgs.) 14.00 43.00 100.00
13,16-20 (36pgs.) 13.00 40.00 90.00
21-30: 21-The Frontier Phantom app. 11.00 32.00 75.00
31-45 10.00 30.00 65.00
46-Last Fawcett issue & photo-c 10.00 30.00 70.00

LASH LARUE WESTERN (Continues from Fawcett series)
No. 47, Mar-Apr, 1954 - No. 84, June, 1961
Charlton Comics

47-Photo-c 11.00 32.00 75.00
48 9.15 27.50 55.00
49-60 7.00 21.00 42.00
61-66,69,70: 52-r/#8; 53-r/#22 5.85 17.50 35.00

Land of the Lost Comics #2, © WMG

Large Feature Comics #10, © DELL

Lash LaRue Western #37, © FAW

Lassie #2, © M.G.M.

Last Days of the Justice Society Special #1, © DC

Laugh Comics #57, © AP

	GD25	FN65	NM94
67,68-(68 pgs.). 68-Check-a	6.70	20.00	40.00
71-83	4.20	12.50	25.00
84-Last issue	5.00	15.00	30.00

LASH LARUE WESTERN (AC)(Value: cover or less)

LASSIE (TV)(M-G-M's... #1-36; see Kite Fun Book)
June, 1950 - No. 70, July, 1969
Dell Publishing Co./Gold Key No. 59 (10/62) on

	GD25	FN65	NM94
1 (52 pgs.)-Photo-c; inside lists One Shot #282 in error	10.00	30.00	70.00
2-Painted-c begin	5.35	16.00	32.00
3-10	4.00	11.00	22.00
11-19: 12-Rocky Langford (Lassie's master) marries Gerry Lawrence. 15-1st app. Timbu	3.20	8.00	16.00
20-22-Matt Baker-a	4.00	11.00	22.00
23-40: 33-Robinson-a. 39-1st app. Timmy as Lassie picks up her TV family	2.40	6.00	12.00
41-70: 63-Last Timmy (10/63). 64-r/#19. 65-Forest Ranger Corey Stuart begins, ends #69. 70-Forest Rangers Bob Ericson & Scott Turner app. (Lassie's new masters)	1.60	4.00	8.00
11193(1978, $1.95, 224 pgs., Golden Press)-Baker-r (92 pgs.)	1.00	2.50	5.00
The Adventures of...(Red Heart Dog Food giveaway, 1949)-16 pgs, soft-c; 1st app. Lassie in comics	11.00	32.00	75.00

NOTE: *Photo c-57, 63. (See March of Comics #210, 217, 230, 254, 266, 278, 296, 308, 324, 334, 346, 358, 370, 381, 394, 411, 432)*

LAST AMERICAN, THE
Dec, 1990 - No. 4, March, 1991 ($2.25, color, mini-series)
Epic Comics (Marvel)

	GD25	FN65	NM94
1-4: Alan Grant scripts	.45	1.15	2.25

LAST DAYS OF THE JUSTICE SOCIETY SPECIAL
1986 ($2.50, one shot, 68 pgs.)
DC Comics

	GD25	FN65	NM94
1-62 pg. JSA story plus unpubbed G.A. pg.	.50	1.25	2.50

LAST GENERATION, THE (Black Tie)(Value: cover or less)

LAST HUNT, THE (See 4-Color No. 678)

LAST KISS (Acme)(Value: cover or less)

LAST OF THE COMANCHES (See Wild Bill Hickok #28)
1953 (Movie)
Avon Periodicals

	GD25	FN65	NM94
nn-Kinstler-c/a, 21pgs.; Ravielli-a	10.00	30.00	70.00

LAST OF THE ERIES, THE (See American Graphics)

LAST OF THE FAST GUNS, THE (See 4-Color No. 925)

LAST OF THE MOHICANS (See King Classics & White Rider and...)

LAST OF THE VIKING HEROES, THE (Also see Silver Star #1)
Mar, 1987 - Present ($1.50-$1.95, color)
Genesis West Comics

	GD25	FN65	NM94
1-4: 4-Intro The Phantom Force	.50	1.25	2.50
1-Signed edition ($1.50)	.30	.75	1.50
5A-Kirby/Stevens-c	.60	1.50	3.00
5B,6 ($1.95)	.40	1.00	2.00
7-Art Adams-c	.60	1.50	3.00
8-12: 8-Kirby back-c	.50	1.25	2.50
Summer Special 1-3: 1-(1988)-Frazetta-c & illos. 2(1990, $2.50)-A TMNT app. 3 (1991, $2.50)-Teenage Mutant Ninja Turtles	.60	1.50	3.00
Summer Special 1-Signed edition (sold for $1.95)	.40	1.00	2.00

NOTE: *Art Adams c-7. Byrne c-3. Kirby c-1p, 5p. Perez c-2i. Stevens c-5Ai.*

LAST STARFIGHTER, THE
Oct, 1984 - No. 3, Dec, 1984 (75 cents, movie adaptation)
Marvel Comics Group

	GD25	FN65	NM94
1-3: r/Marvel Super Special; Guice-c		.50	1.00

LAST TRAIN FROM GUN HILL (See 4-Color No. 1012)

LATEST ADVENTURES OF FOXY GRANDPA (See Foxy Grandpa)

LATEST COMICS (Super Duper No. 3?)
March, 1945 - No. 2, 1945?
Spotlight Publ./Palace Promotions (Jubilee)

	GD25	FN65	NM94
1-Super Duper	8.35	25.00	50.00
2-Bee-29 (nd)	6.70	20.00	40.00

LAUGH
June, 1987 - No. 30, 1991 (.75-$1.00, color)
Archie Enterprises

	GD25	FN65	NM94
V2#1-30: 5,19-X-Mas issues. 14-1st app. Hot Dog. 24-Re-intro Super Duck		.50	1.00

LAUGH COMICS (Formerly Black Hood #1-19) (Laugh #226 on)
No. 20, Fall, 1946 - No. 400, Apr, 1987
Archie Publications (Close-Up)

	GD25	FN65	NM94
20-Archie begins; Katy Keene & Taffy begin by Woggon; Suzie & Wilbur also begin	43.00	130.00	300.00
21-25: 24-"Pipsy" by Kirby, 6 pgs.	22.00	65.00	150.00
26-30	11.50	34.00	80.00
31-40	10.00	30.00	60.00
41-60: 41,54-Debbi by Woggon	5.85	17.50	35.00
61-80: 67-Debbi by Woggon	4.00	11.00	22.00
81-99	3.60	9.00	18.00
100	4.20	12.50	25.00
101-126: 125-Debbi app.	2.40	6.00	12.00
127-144: Super-hero app. in all (see note)	3.20	8.00	16.00
145-160: 157-Josie app.	1.40	3.50	7.00
161-165,167-200	1.00	2.50	5.00
166-Beatles-c	2.80	7.00	14.00
201-240	.50	1.25	2.50
241-280	.30	.75	1.50
281-400: 381-384-Katy Keene app.; by Woggon-381,382		.50	1.00

NOTE: *The Fly app. in 128, 129, 132, 134, 138, 139. Flygirl app. in 136, 137, 143. Flyman app. in 137. The Jaguar app. in 127, 130, 131, 133, 135, 140-142, 144. Josie app. in 145, 160, 164. Katy Keene app. in 20-125, 129, 130, 133. Many issues contain paper dolls.*

LAUGH COMICS DIGEST (...Magazine #23-89; Laugh Digest Mag. #90 on)
8/74; No. 2, 9/75; No. 3, 3/76 - Present (Digest-size)
Archie Publications (Close-Up No. 1, 3 on)

	GD25	FN65	NM94
1-Neal Adams-a	1.20	3.00	6.00
2,7,8,19-Neal Adams-a	.60	1.50	3.00
3-6,9-18,20-50	.40	1.00	2.00
51-108: Later issues $1.35,$1.50-c	.30	.75	1.50

NOTE: *Katy Keene in 23, 25, 27, 32-38, 40, 45-48, 50. The Fly-r in 19, 20. The Jaguar-r in 25, 27. Mr. Justice-r in 21. The Web-r in 23.*

LAUGH COMIX (Formerly Top Notch Laugh; Suzie Comics No. 49 on)
No. 46, Summer, 1944 - No. 48, Winter, 1944-45
MLJ Magazines

	GD25	FN65	NM94
46-Wilbur & Suzie in all; Harry Sahle-c	11.50	34.00	80.00
47,48: 47-Sahle-c	10.00	30.00	60.00

LAUGH-IN MAGAZINE (TV)(Magazine)
Oct, 1968 - No. 12, Oct, 1969 (50 cents) (Satire)
Laufer Publ. Co.

	GD25	FN65	NM94
V1#1	3.00	7.50	15.00
2-12	1.40	3.50	7.00

LAUREL & HARDY (See Larry Harmon's... & March of Comics No. 302, 314)

LAUREL AND HARDY (...Comics)
3/49 - No. 3, 9/49; No. 26, 11/55 - No. 28, 3/56 (No #4-25)
St. John Publishing Co.

Issue	GD25	FN65	NM94
1	43.00	130.00	300.00
2	24.00	73.00	170.00
3	18.00	54.00	125.00
26-28 (Reprints)	11.50	34.00	80.00

LAUREL AND HARDY (TV)
Oct, 1962 - No. 4, Sept-Nov, 1963
Dell Publishing Co.

Issue	GD25	FN65	NM94
12-423-210 (8-10/62)	4.70	14.00	28.00
2-4 (Dell)	4.00	11.00	22.00

LAUREL AND HARDY (Larry Harmon's...)
Jan, 1967 - No. 2, Oct, 1967
Gold Key

Issue	GD25	FN65	NM94
1,2: 1-Photo back-c	4.00	11.00	22.00

LAW AGAINST CRIME (Law-Crime on cover)
April, 1948 - No. 3, Aug, 1948
Essenkay Publishing Co.

Issue	GD25	FN65	NM94
1-(#1-3: Half funny animal, half crime stories)-L. B. Cole electrocution-c/a	32.00	95.00	220.00
2-L. B. Cole-c/a	23.00	70.00	160.00
3-L. B. Cole-c/a; used in **SOTI**, pg. 180,181 & illo-"The wish to hurt or kill couples in lovers' lanes;" reprinted in All-Famous Crime #9	30.00	90.00	210.00

LAWBREAKERS (...Suspense Stories No. 10 on)
Mar, 1951 - No. 9, Oct-Nov, 1952
Law and Order Magazines (Charlton Comics)

Issue	GD25	FN65	NM94
1	14.00	43.00	100.00
2	7.50	22.50	45.00
3,5,6,8,9: 5-Drug story	5.85	17.50	35.00
4-"White Death" junkie story	7.50	22.50	45.00
7-"The Deadly Dopesters" drug story	7.50	22.50	45.00

LAWBREAKERS ALWAYS LOSE!
Spring, 1948 - No. 10, Oct, 1949
Marvel Comics (CBS)

Issue	GD25	FN65	NM94
1-2pg. Kurtzman-a, 'Giggles 'n Grins'	14.00	43.00	100.00
2	8.35	25.00	50.00
3-5: 4-Vampire story	6.70	20.00	40.00
6(2/49)-Has editorial defense against charges of Dr. Wertham	7.50	22.50	45.00
7-Used in **SOTI**, illo-"Comic-book philosophy"	14.00	43.00	100.00
8-10: 9,10-Photo-c	5.35	16.00	32.00

NOTE: ***Brodsky*** *c-4, 5.* ***Shores*** *c-1-3, 6-8.*

LAWBREAKERS SUSPENSE STORIES (Formerly Lawbreakers; Strange Suspense Stories No. 16 on)
No. 10, Jan, 1953 - No. 15, Nov, 1953
Capitol Stories/Charlton Comics

Issue	GD25	FN65	NM94
10	10.00	30.00	65.00
11 (3/53)-Severed tongues-c/story & woman negligee scene	29.00	85.00	200.00
12-14	5.85	17.50	35.00
15-Acid-in-face-c/story; hands dissolved in acid story	14.00	43.00	100.00

LAW-CRIME (See Law Against Crime)

LAWMAN (TV)
No. 970, Feb, 1959 - No. 11, Apr-June, 1962 (All photo-c)
Dell Publishing Co.

Issue	GD25	FN65	NM94
4-Color 970(#1)	10.00	30.00	60.00
4-Color 1035('60)	5.35	16.00	32.00
3(2-4/60)-Toth-a	5.85	17.50	35.00
4-11	4.35	13.00	26.00

LAW OF DREDD, THE (Quality)(Value: cover or less)

LAWRENCE (See Movie Classics)

LAZARUS CHURCHYARD
June, 1992 - No. 3, 1992 ($3.95, color, coated stock, 44 pgs.)
Tundra Publishing

Issue	GD25	FN65	NM94
1-3	.70	2.00	4.00

LEADING COMICS (...Screen Comics No. 42 on)
Winter, 1941-42 - No. 41, Feb-Mar, 1950
National Periodical Publications

Issue	GD25	FN65	NM94
1-Origin The Seven Soldiers of Victory; Crimson Avenger, Green Arrow & Speedy, Shining Knight, The Vigilante, Star Spangled Kid & Stripesy begin. The Dummy (Vigilante villain) app.	250.00	750.00	1500.00
2-Meskin-a	72.00	275.00	550.00
3	57.00	225.00	450.00
4,5	50.00	188.00	375.00
6-10	43.00	170.00	340.00
11-14(Spring, 1945)	32.00	125.00	250.00
15-(Sum,'45)-Contents change to funny animal	13.00	50.00	100.00
16-22,24-30	7.50	22.50	45.00
23-1st app. Peter Porkchops by Otto Feur	14.00	55.00	110.00
31,32,34-41	5.85	17.50	35.00
33-(Scarce)	9.15	27.50	55.00

NOTE: ***Rube Grossman****-a(Peter Porkchops)-most #15-on; c-15-41.* ***Post*** *a-23-37, 39, 41.*

LEADING SCREEN COMICS (Formerly Leading Comics)
No. 42, Apr-May, 1950 - No. 77, Aug-Sept, 1955
National Periodical Publications

Issue	GD25	FN65	NM94
42	7.50	22.50	45.00
43-77	5.85	17.50	35.00

NOTE: ***Grossman*** *a-most.* ***Mayer*** *a-45-48, 50, 54-57, 60, 62-74, 75(3), 76, 77.*

LEAGUE OF CHAMPIONS, THE (Hero)(Value: cover or less)

LEATHERFACE (Arpad)(Value: cover or less)

LEATHERNECK THE MARINE (See Mighty Midget Comics)

LEAVE IT TO BEAVER (TV)
No. 912, June, 1958 - May-July, 1962 (All photo-c)
Dell Publishing Co.

Issue	GD25	FN65	NM94
4-Color 912	19.00	56.00	130.00
4-Color 999,1103,1191,1285, 01-428-207	17.00	50.00	115.00

LEAVE IT TO BINKY (Binky No. 72 on) (See Showcase #70 & Super DC Giant) (No. 1-22: 52 pgs.)
2-3/48 - #60, 10/58; #61, 6-7/68 - #71, 2-3/70 (Teen-age humor)
National Periodical Publications

Issue	GD25	FN65	NM94
1-Lucy wears Superman costume	22.00	65.00	150.00
2	11.00	32.00	75.00
3,4	6.70	20.00	40.00
5-Superman cameo	10.00	30.00	60.00
6-10	5.85	17.50	35.00
11-14,16-20	4.70	14.00	28.00
15-Scribbly story by Mayer	7.50	22.50	45.00
21-28,30-45: 45-Last pre-code (2/55)	3.60	9.00	18.00
29-Used in **POP**, pg. 78	3.60	9.00	18.00
46-60: 60-(10/58)	2.40	6.00	12.00
Showcase #70 (9-10/67)-Tryout issue	1.70	4.25	8.50
61-71: 61-(6-7/68)	1.40	3.50	7.00

NOTE: ***Drucker*** *a-28.* ***Mayer*** *a-1, 2, 15. Created by* ***Mayer.***

LEE HUNTER, INDIAN FIGHTER (See 4-Color No. 779, 904)

LEFT-HANDED GUN, THE (See 4-Color No. 913)

LEGEND OF CUSTER, THE (TV)
January, 1968
Dell Publishing Co.

Issue	GD25	FN65	NM94
1-Wayne Maunder photo-c	2.00	5.00	10.00

LEGEND OF JESSE JAMES, THE (TV)

Law-Breakers #9, © CC

Lawman #6, © Warner Bros.

Leading Comics #12, © DC

Legends of Daniel Boone #2, © DC

Legends of the Dark Knight #5, © DC

L.E.G.I.O.N. #6, © DC

	GD25	FN65	NM94
February, 1966			
Gold Key			
10172-602-Photo-c	3.00	7.50	15.00

LEGEND OF KAMUI, THE (See Kamui)

LEGEND OF LOBO, THE (See Movie Comics)

LEGEND OF THE SHIELD, THE
July, 1991 - No. 16, Oct, 1992 ($1.00, color)
Impact Comics (DC)

	GD25	FN65	NM94
1-16: 6,7-The Fly x-over. 12-Contains trading card		.50	1.00
Annual 1 (1992, $2.50, 68 pgs.)-W/trading card	.50	1.25	2.50

LEGEND OF WONDER WOMAN, THE (DC)(Value: cover or less)

LEGEND OF YOUNG DICK TURPIN, THE (TV)
May, 1966 (Disney TV episode)
Gold Key

	GD25	FN65	NM94
1 (10176-605)-Photo/painted-c	1.80	4.50	9.00

LEGEND OF ZELDA, THE (Link: The Legend... in indicia)
1990 - No. 4, 1990 ($1.95, color, coated stiff-c)
V2#1, 1991 - No. 5, 1991 ($1.50, color)
Valiant Comics

	GD25	FN65	NM94
1-4: 4-Layton-c(i)	.40	1.00	2.00
V2#1-5	.30	.75	1.50

LEGENDS
Nov, 1986 - No. 6, Apr, 1987 (75 cents, mini-series)
DC Comics

	GD25	FN65	NM94
1-Byrne-c/a(p) in all; 1st app. new Capt. Marvel	.40	1.10	2.20
2-5: 3-1st app. new Suicide Squad; death of Blockbuster	.30	.70	1.40
6-1st app. new Justice League	1.00	2.50	5.00

LEGENDS OF DANIEL BOONE, THE
Oct-Nov, 1955 - No. 8, Dec-Jan, 1956-57
National Periodical Publications

	GD25	FN65	NM94
1 (Scarce)-Nick Cardy c-1-8	39.00	118.00	275.00
2 (Scarce)	29.00	85.00	200.00
3-8 (Scarce)	25.00	75.00	175.00

LEGENDS OF NASCAR, THE
1990 - Present (Color)(#1 3rd printing (1/91) says 2nd printing inside)
Vortex Comics

	GD25	FN65	NM94
1-Bill Elliott biog.; Trimpe-a ($1.50-c)	2.00	5.00	10.00
1-2nd printing (11/90, $2.00-c)	.80	2.00	4.00
1-3rd print; contains Maxx racecards ($3.00-c)	1.00	2.50	5.00
2-Richard Petty	.60	1.50	3.00
3-14: 3-Ken Schrader (7/91). 4-Bobby Allison; Spiegle-a(p); Adkins part-i. 5-Sterling Marlin. 6-Bill Elliott	.40	1.00	2.00
1-13-Hologram cover versions. 2-Hologram shows Bill Elliott's car by mistake (all are numbered & limited)	1.00	2.50	5.00
2-Hologram corrected version	1.00	2.50	5.00

LEGENDS OF THE DARK KNIGHT (Batman: ... #37 on)
Nov, 1989 - Present ($1.50/$1.75, color)
DC Comics

	GD25	FN65	NM94
1-"Shaman" begins, ends #5; outer cover has four different color variations, all worth same	1.20	3.00	6.00
2	.60	1.50	3.00
3-5	.40	1.10	2.20
6-10-"Gothic" by Grant Morrison (scripts)	.60	1.50	3.00
11-18: 11-15-Gulacy/Austin-a. 14-Catwoman app.	.40	1.00	2.00
19-44: 19-Begin $1.75-c. 38-Bat-Mite-c/story	.35	.90	1.75
Annual 1 (1991, $3.95, 68 pgs.)-Joker app.	.80	2.00	4.00
Annual 2 (1992, $3.50, 68 pgs.)-Netzer-c/a	.70	1.75	3.50

NOTE: ***Chaykin** scripts-24-26. **Alan Grant** scripts-38. **Gil Kane** c/a-24-26. **Russell** a-42.*

LEGENDS OF THE STARGRAZERS (Innovation)(Value: cover or less)

L.E.G.I.O.N. (The # to right of title represents year of print; also see Lobo)
Feb, 1989 - Present ($1.50, color)
DC Comics

	GD25	FN65	NM94
1-Giffen plots/breakdowns in #1-12	.35	1.00	2.00
2-22,24-47: 3-Lobo app. #3 on. 4-1st Lobo-c this title. 5-Lobo joins Legion. 28-Giffen-c(p). 31-Capt. Marvel app.	.25	.75	1.50
23-($2.50, 52 pgs.)	.40	1.25	2.50
48,49,51,52: 48-Begin $1.75-c	.35	.90	1.75
50-($3.50, 68 pgs.)	.70	1.75	3.50
Annual 1-3 (1990-1992, $2.95, 68 pgs.): 1-Lobo, Superman app. 2-Alan Grant scripts	.50	1.50	3.00

NOTE: ***Alan Grant** scripts in #1-39, Annual 1, 2.*

LEGIONNAIRES THREE
Jan, 1986 - No. 4, May, 1986 (75 cents, mini-series)
DC comics

	GD25	FN65	NM94
1-4		.50	1.00

LEGION OF MONSTERS (Magazine)(Also see Marvel Premiere #28 & Marvel Preview #8)
September, 1975 ($1.00, B&W, 76 pgs.)
Marvel Comics Group

	GD25	FN65	NM94
1-Origin & 1st app. Legion of Monsters; Neal Adams-c; Morrow-a; origin & only app. The Manphibian	.40	1.00	2.00

LEGION OF NIGHT, THE
Oct, 1991 - No. 2, Oct, 1991 ($4.95, color, 52 pgs.)
Marvel Comics

	GD25	FN65	NM94
1,2-Whilce Portacio-c/a(p)	1.00	2.50	5.00

LEGION OF SUBSTITUTE HEROES SPECIAL (DC)(Value: cover or less)

LEGION OF SUPER-HEROES (See Action, Adventure, All New Collectors Edition, Limited Collectors Ed., Secrets of the..., Superboy & Superman)
Feb, 1973 - No. 4, July-Aug, 1973
National Periodical Publications

	GD25	FN65	NM94
1-Legion & Tommy Tomorrow reprints begin	1.60	4.00	8.00
2-4: 2-Forte-r. 3-r/Adv. #340. Action #240. 4-r/Adv. #341, Action #233; Mooney-r	1.00	2.50	5.00

LEGION OF SUPER-HEROES, THE (Formerly Superboy and...; Tales of The Legion No. 314 on)
No. 259, Jan, 1980 - No. 313, July, 1984
DC Comics

	GD25	FN65	NM94
259(#1)-Superboy leaves Legion	.60	1.50	3.00
260-270: 265-Contains 28pg. insert 'Superman & the TR5-80 Computer;' Origin Tyroc; Tyroc leaves Legion	.40	1.00	2.00
271-284: 272-Blok joins; origin; 20pg. insert-Dial 'H' For Hero. 277-Intro Reflecto. 280-Superboy re-joins legion. 282-Origin Reflecto. 283-Origin Wildfire	.30	.75	1.50
285,286-Giffen back up story	.40	1.00	2.00
287-Giffen-a on Legion begins	.55	1.40	2.80
288-290: 290-294-Great Darkness saga	.40	1.00	2.00
291-293	.30	.75	1.50
294-Double size (52 pgs.); Giffen-a(p)	.35	.90	1.80
295-299,301-305: 297-Origin retold. 298-Free 16pg. Amethyst preview		.60	1.20
300-Double size, 64 pgs., Mando paper; c/a by almost everyone at DC	.40	1.00	2.00
306-313 (75 cent-c): 306-Brief origin Star Boy		.50	1.00
Annual 1(1982, 52 pgs.)-Giffen-c/a; 1st app./origin new Invisible Kid who joins Legion	.40	1.00	2.00
Annual 2,3: 2(1983, 52 pgs.)-Giffen-c; Karate Kid & Princess Projectra wed & resign. 3(1984, 52 pgs.)	.30	.75	1.50

...The Great Darkness Saga (1989, $17.95, 196 pgs.)-r/LSH #287,290-294 &

Annual #3; Giffen-c/a 3.60 9.00 18.00

NOTE: **Aparo** *c-282, 283.* **Austin** *c-268i.* **Buckler** *c-273p, 274p, 276p.* **Colan** *a-311p.* **Ditko** *a(p)-267, 268, 272, 274, 276, 281.* **Giffen** *a-285-313p, Annual 1p; c-287p, 288p, 289, 290p, 291p, 292, 293, 294-299p, 300, 301-313p, Annual 1p, 2p.* **Perez** *c-268p, 277-280, 281p.* **Starlin** *a-265.* **Staton** *a-259p, 260p, 280.* **Tuska** *a-308p.*

LEGION OF SUPER-HEROES (Reprinted in Tales of the Legion)
Aug, 1984 - No. 63, Aug, 1989 ($1.25-$1.75, deluxe format)
DC Comics

1-Silver ink logo .40 1.00 2.00
2-10: 4-Death of Karate Kid. 5-Death of Nemesis Kid .30 .80 1.60
11-14: 12-Cosmic Boy, Lightning Lad, & Saturn Girl resign. 14-Intro new members: Tellus, Sensor Girl, Quislet .60 1.20
15-18: 15-17-Crisis tie-ins. 18-Crisis x-over .30 .80 1.60
19-25: 25-Sensor Girl i.d. revealed as Princess Projectra .60 1.20
26-36,39-44: 35-Saturn Girl rejoins. 40-$1.75 cover price begins. 42,43-Millennium tie-ins. 44-Origin Quislet .55 1.10
37,38-Death of Superboy 2.00 5.00 10.00
45 ($2.95, 68 pgs.) .60 1.50 3.00
46-49,51-62 .55 1.10
50-Double size, $2.50 .50 1.25 2.50
63-Final issue .25 .70 1.40
Annual 1 (10/85, 52 pgs.)-Crisis tie-in .35 .90 1.80
Annual 2 (1986, 52 pgs.). 3 (1987, 52 pgs.) .30 .80 1.60
Annual 4 (1988, $2.50, 52 pgs.) .40 1.00 2.00

NOTE: **Byrne** *c-36p.* **Giffen** *a(p)-1, 2, 50-55, 57-63, Annual 1p, 2; c-1-5p, 54p, Annual 1.* **Orlando** *a-6p.* **Steacy** *c-45-50, Annual 3.*

LEGION OF SUPER-HEROES
Nov, 1989 - Present ($1.75, color)
DC Comics

1-Giffen-c/a(p) & scripts begin (4 pg.-a only #18) .35 .90 1.75
2-44: 8-Origin. 13-Free poster by Giffen showing new costumes. 21-24-Lobo & Darkseid storyline. 26-New map of headquarters. 34-Six pg. preview of Timber Wolf mini-series. 40-Legionnaires app. .35 .90 1.75
Annual 1,2 (1990, 1991, $3.50, 68 pgs.) .70 1.75 3.50

NOTE: **Giffen** *a-1-24; breakdowns-26-32, 34-36; c-1-7, 8(part), 9-24.* **Brandon Peterson** *a(p)-15(1st for DC), 16, 18, Annual 2(54 pgs.); c-Annual 2p.* **Swan/Anderson** *c-8(part).*

LEMONADE KID, THE (See Bobby Benson's B-Bar-B Riders)
1990 ($2.50, color, 28 pgs.)
AC Comics

1-Powell-c(r); Red Hawk-r by Powell; Lemonade Kid-r/Bobby Benson by Powell (2 stories) .50 1.25 2.50

LENNON SISTERS LIFE STORY, THE (See 4-Color No. 951, 1014)

LEONARDO (Also see Teenage Mutant Ninja Turtles)
Dec, 1986 ($1.50, B&W, One shot)
Mirage Studios

1 1.60 4.00 8.00

LEO THE LION
No date (10 cents)
I. W. Enterprises

1-Reprint .80 2.00 4.00

LEROY (Teen-age)
Nov, 1949 - No. 6, Nov, 1950
Standard Comics

1 4.70 14.00 28.00
2-Frazetta text illo. 4.00 11.00 22.00
3-6: 3-Lubbers-a 3.00 7.50 15.00

LET'S PRETEND (CBS radio)
May-June, 1950 - No. 3, Sept-Oct, 1950
D. S. Publishing Co.

1 10.00 30.00 60.00

2,3 7.50 22.50 45.00

LET'S READ THE NEWSPAPER
1974
Charlton Press

nn-Features Quincy by Ted Sheares .50 1.00

LET'S TAKE A TRIP (TV) (CBS TV Presents)
Spring, 1958
Pines Comics

1-Marv Levy-c/a 2.80 7.00 14.00

LETTERS TO SANTA (See March of Comics No. 228)

LEX LUTHOR: THE UNAUTHORIZED BIOGRAPHY (DC)(Value: cover or less)

LIBERTY COMICS (Miss Liberty No. 1)
No. 4, 1945 - No. 15, 1946 (MLJ & other reprints)
Green Publishing Co.

4 10.00 30.00 70.00
5 (5/46)-The Prankster app; Starr-a 9.15 27.50 55.00
10-Hangman & Boy Buddies app.; Suzie & Wilbur begin; reprint of Hangman #8 11.50 34.00 80.00
11(V2#2, 1/46)-Wilbur in women's clothes 10.00 30.00 65.00
12-Black Hood & Suzie app. 10.00 30.00 65.00
14,15-Patty of Airliner; Starr-a in both 6.35 19.00 38.00

LIBERTY GUARDS
No date (1946?)
Chicago Mail Order

nn-Reprints Man of War #1 with cover of Liberty Scouts #1; Gustavson-c 23.00 70.00 140.00

LIBERTY PROJECT, THE (Eclipse)(Value: cover or less)

LIBERTY SCOUTS (See Liberty Guards & Man of War)
No. 2, June, 1941 - No. 3, Aug, 1941
Centaur Publications

2(#1)-Origin The Fire-Man, Man of War; Vapo-Man & Liberty Scouts begin; Gustavson-c/a in both 100.00 300.00 600.00
3(#2)-Origin & 1st app. The Sentinel 75.00 225.00 450.00

LICENCE TO KILL (Eclipse)(Value: cover or less)

LIDSVILLE (TV)
Oct, 1972 - No. 5, Oct, 1973
Gold Key

1 2.40 6.00 12.00
2-5 1.20 3.00 6.00

LIEUTENANT, THE (TV)
April-June, 1964
Dell Publishing Co.

1-Photo-c 2.00 5.00 10.00

LIEUTENANT BLUEBERRY (Also see Blueberry)
1991 - No. 3, 1991 (Color, graphic novel)
Epic Comics (Marvel)

1,2 ($8.95)-Moebius-a in all 1.80 4.50 9.00
3 ($14.95) 3.00 7.50 15.00

LT. ROBIN CRUSOE, U.S.N. (See Movie Comics & Walt Disney Showcase #26)

LIFE OF CAPTAIN MARVEL, THE
Aug, 1985 - No. 5, Dec, 1985 ($2.00 cover; Baxter paper)
Marvel Comics Group

1-All reprint Starlin issues of Iron Man #55, Capt. Marvel #25-34 plus Marvel Feature #12 (all with Thanos) 1.30 3.25 6.50
2-5: 4-New Thanos back-c by Starlin .80 2.00 4.00

LIFE OF CHRIST, THE
No. 301, 1949 (100 pages) (35 cents)
Catechetical Guild Educational Society

Legion of Super-Heroes #2 (1973), © DC

Leroy #5, © STD

Liberty Comics #10, © Green Publ.

Life Story #1, © FAW

Life With Archie #15, © AP

Lightning Comics #6, © ACE

	GD25	FN65	NM94
301-Reprints from Topix(1949)-V5#11,12	3.20	8.00	16.00

LIFE OF CHRIST VISUALIZED
1942 - No. 3, 1943
Standard Publishers

	GD25	FN65	NM94
1-3: All came in cardboard case	3.20	8.00	16.00
With case.....	5.85	17.50	35.00

LIFE OF CHRIST VISUALIZED
1946? (48 pgs. in color)
The Standard Publ. Co.

	GD25	FN65	NM94
nn	1.20	3.00	6.00

LIFE OF ESTHER VISUALIZED
No. 2062, 1947 (48 pgs. in color)
The Standard Publ. Co.

	GD25	FN65	NM94
2062	1.20	3.00	6.00

LIFE OF JOSEPH VISUALIZED
No. 1054, 1946 (48 pgs. in color)
The Standard Publ. Co.

	GD25	FN65	NM94
1054	1.20	3.00	6.00

LIFE OF PAUL (See The Living Bible)

LIFE OF POPE JOHN PAUL II, THE
Jan, 1983
Marvel Comics Group

	GD25	FN65	NM94
1	.30	.75	1.50

LIFE OF RILEY, THE (See 4-Color No. 917)

LIFE OF THE BLESSED VIRGIN
1950 (68 pages) (square binding)
Catechetical Guild (Giveaway)

	GD25	FN65	NM94
nn-Contains "The Woman of the Promise" & "Mother of Us All" rebound	3.20	8.00	16.00

LIFE'S LIKE THAT
1945 (68 pgs.; B&W; 25 cents)
Croyden Publ. Co.

	GD25	FN65	NM94
nn-Newspaper Sunday strip-r by Neher	4.70	14.00	28.00

LIFE'S LITTLE JOKES
No date (1924) (52 pgs.; B&W)
M.S. Publ. Co.

	GD25	FN65	NM94
nn-By Rube Goldberg	22.00	65.00	150.00

LIFE STORIES OF AMERICAN PRESIDENTS (See Dell Giants)

LIFE STORY
Apr, 1949 - V8#46, Jan, 1953; V8#47, Apr, 1953 (All have photo-c?)
Fawcett Publications

	GD25	FN65	NM94
V1#1	7.50	22.50	45.00
2	3.60	9.00	18.00
3-6	3.20	8.00	16.00
V2#7-12	2.40	7.00	14.00
V3#13-Wood-a	9.15	27.50	55.00
V3#14-18, V4#19-21,23,24	2.40	7.00	14.00
V4#22-Drug use story	3.20	8.00	16.00
V5#25-30, V6#31-35	2.40	7.00	14.00
V6#36-"I sold drugs" on-c	3.20	8.00	16.00
V7#37,40-42, V8#44,45	1.80	4.50	9.00
V7#38, V8#43-Evans-a	3.60	9.00	18.00
V7#39-Drug Smuggling & Junkie story	2.80	7.00	14.00
V8#46,47 (Scarce)	2.80	7.00	14.00

NOTE: ***Powell** a-13, 23, 24, 26, 28, 30, 32, 39. **Marcus Swayze** a-1-3, 10-12, 15, 16, 20, 21, 23-25, 31, 35, 37, 40, 44, 46.*

LIFE WITH ARCHIE
Sept, 1958 - No. 290?, 1991
Archie Publications

	GD25	FN65	NM94
1	27.00	81.00	190.00
2	13.00	40.00	90.00
3-5	10.00	30.00	65.00
6-10	5.35	16.00	32.00
11-20	4.00	10.00	20.00
21-30	3.00	7.50	15.00
31-41	1.80	4.50	9.00
42-45: 42-Pureheart begins, ends #59	1.40	3.50	7.00
46-Origin Pureheart	2.00	5.00	10.00
47-59: 50-United Three begin: Pureheart (Archie), Superteen (Betty), Capt. Hero (Jughead). 59-Pureheart ends	1.00	2.50	5.00
60-100: 60-Archie band begins	.60	1.50	3.00
101-290: 279-Intro Mustang Sally ($1.00)		.60	1.25

NOTE: ***Gene Colan** a-272-279, 285, 286.*

LIFE WITH MILLIE (Formerly A Date With Millie) (Modeling With Millie No. 21 on)
No. 8, Dec, 1960 - No. 20, Dec, 1962
Atlas/Marvel Comics Group

	GD25	FN65	NM94
8	5.00	15.00	30.00
9-11	4.00	11.00	22.00
12-20	3.20	8.00	16.00

LIFE WITH SNARKY PARKER (TV)
August, 1950
Fox Feature Syndicate

	GD25	FN65	NM94
1	15.00	45.00	105.00

LIGHT AND DARKNESS WAR, THE
Oct, 1988 - No. 6, Dec, 1989 ($1.95, color, limited series)
Epic Comics (Marvel)

	GD25	FN65	NM94
1-6	.40	1.00	2.00

LIGHT FANTASTIC, THE (Terry Pratchett's)
June, 1992 - No. 4, Sept, 1992 ($2.50, color, mini-series)
Innovation Publishing

	GD25	FN65	NM94
1-4: Adapts 2nd novel in Discworld series	.50	1.25	2.50

LIGHT IN THE FOREST (See 4-Color No. 891)

LIGHTNING COMICS (Formerly Sure-Fire No. 1-3)
No. 4, Dec, 1940 - No. 13(V3#1), June, 1942
Ace Magazines

	GD25	FN65	NM94
4-Characters continue from Sure-Fire	54.00	162.00	325.00
5,6: 6-Dr. Nemesis begins	37.00	110.00	225.00
V2#1-6: 2-"Flash Lightning" becomes "Lash..."	32.00	95.00	190.00
V3#1-Intro. Lightning Girl & The Sword	32.00	95.00	190.00

NOTE: ***Anderson** a-V2#6. **Mooney** c-V1#6, V2#2. Bondage c-V2#6.*

LI'L (See Little)

LILY OF THE ALLEY IN THE FUNNIES
No date (1920's?) (10-1/4x15-1/2"; 28 pgs. in color)
Whitman Publishers

	GD25	FN65	NM94
W936 - By T. Burke	13.00	40.00	80.00

LIMITED COLLECTORS' EDITION (See Famous First Edition & Rudolph the Red Nosed Reindeer; becomes All-New Collectors' Edition)
(#21-34,51-59: 84 pgs.; #35-41: 68 pgs.; #42-50: 60 pgs.)
C-21, Summer, 1973 - No. C-59, 1978 ($1.00) (10x13-1/2")
National Periodical Publications/DC Comics

	GD25	FN65	NM94
nn(C-20)-Rudolph (date?)	.80	2.00	4.00
C-21: Shazam (TV); r/Captain Marvel Jr. #11 by Raboy; C.C. Beck-c, biog. & photo	.60	1.50	3.00
C-22: Tarzan; complete origin reprinted from #207-210; all Kubert-c/a; Joe Kubert biography & photo inside	.60	1.50	3.00

	GD25	FN65	NM94
C-23: House of Mystery; Wrightson, N. Adams/Orlando, G. Kane/Wood, Toth, Aragones, Sparling reprints	.30	1.00	2.00
C-24: Rudolph The Red-nosed Reindeer	.40	1.00	2.00
C-25: Batman; Neal Adams-c/a(r); G.A. Joker-r; Batman/Enemy Ace-r; has photos from TV show	1.20	3.00	6.00
C-26: See Famous First Edition C-26 (same contents)			
C-27: Shazam (TV); G.A. Capt. Marvel & Mary Marvel-r; Beck-r	.40	1.00	2.00
C-29: Tarzan; reprints "Return of Tarzan" from #219-223 by Kubert; Kubert-c	.60	1.50	3.00
C-31: Superman; origin-r; N. Adams-a; photos of George Reeves from 1950s TV show on inside b/c; Burnley, Boring-r	.60	1.50	3.00
C-32: Ghosts (new-a)	.40	1.00	2.00
C-33: Rudolph The Red-nosed Reindeer(new-a)	.40	1.00	2.00
C-34: Christmas with the Super-Heroes; unpublished Angel & Ape story by Oksner & Wood; Batman & Teen Titans-r	.60	1.50	3.00
C-35: Shazam (TV); photo cover features TV's Captain Marvel, Jackson Bostwick; Beck-r; TV photos inside b/c	.40	1.00	2.00
C-36: The Bible; all new adaptation beginning with Genesis by Kubert, Redondo & Mayer; Kubert-c	.60	1.50	3.00
C-37: Batman; r-1946 Sundays; inside b/c photos of Batman TV show villains (all villain issue; r/G.A. Joker, Catwoman, Penguin, Two-Face, & Scarecrow stories plus 1946 Sundays-r)	1.20	3.00	6.00
C-38: Superman; 1 pg. N. Adams; part photo-c; photos from TV show on inside back-c	.40	1.00	2.00
C-39: Secret Origins of Super-Villains; N. Adams-i(r); G.A. Batman-r; Beck-r	.40	1.00	2.00
C-40: Dick Tracy by Gould featuring Flattop; newspaper-r from 12/21/43 - 5/17/44; biog. of Chester Gould	.80	2.00	4.00
C-41: Super Friends (TV); JLA-r(1965); Toth-c/a	.40	1.00	2.00
C-42: Rudolph	.40	1.00	2.00
C-43: Christmas with the Super-Heroes; Wrightson, S&K, Neal Adams-a	.60	1.50	3.00
C-44: Batman; N. Adams-p(r) & G.A.-r; painted-c	1.20	3.00	6.00
C-45: More Secret Origins of Super-Villains; Flash-r/#105; G.A. Wonder Woman & Batman/Catwoman-r	.40	1.00	2.00
C-46: Justice League of America(1963-r); 3 pgs. Toth-a	.60	1.50	3.00
C-47: Superman Salutes the Bicentennial (Tomahawk interior); 2 pgs. new-a	.30	.75	1.50
C-48: Superman Vs. The Flash (Superman/Flash race); swipes-c to Superman #199; r/Superman #199 & Flash #175; 6 pgs. Neal Adams-a	.60	1.50	3.00
C-49: Superboy & the Legion of Super-Heroes	.40	1.00	2.00
C-50: Rudolph The Red-nosed Reindeer	.30	.75	1.50
C-51: Batman; Neal Adams-c/a	1.20	3.00	6.00
C-52: The Best of DC; Neal Adams-c/a; Toth, Kubert-a	.60	1.50	3.00
C-57: Welcome Back, Kotter-r(TV)(5/78)	.30	.75	1.50
C-59: Batman's Strangest Cases; N. Adams-r; Wrightson-r/Swamp Thing #7; N. Adams/Wrightson-c	1.20	3.00	6.00

NOTE: *All-r with exception of some special features and covers.* ***Aparo*** *a-52r; c-37.* ***Grell*** *c-49.* ***Infantino*** *a-25, 39, 44, 45, 52.* ***Bob Kane*** *r-25.* ***Robinson*** *r-25, 44.* ***Sprang*** *r-44. Issues #21-31, 35-39, 45, 48 have back cover cut-outs.*

LINDA (Phantom Lady No. 5 on)
Apr-May, 1954 - No. 4, Oct-Nov, 1954
Ajax-Farrell Publ. Co.

	GD25	FN65	NM94
1-Kamenish-a	10.00	30.00	60.00
2-Lingerie panel	7.00	21.00	42.00
3,4	5.85	17.50	35.00

LINDA CARTER, STUDENT NURSE
Sept, 1961 - No. 9, Jan, 1963
Atlas Comics (AMI)

	GD25	FN65	NM94
1-Al Hartley-c	4.00	10.00	20.00
2-9	2.80	7.00	14.00

LINDA LARK
Oct-Dec, 1961 - No. 8, Aug-Oct, 1963
Dell Publishing Co.

	GD25	FN65	NM94
1	2.40	6.00	12.00
2-8	1.20	3.00	6.00

LINUS, THE LIONHEARTED (TV)
September, 1965
Gold Key

	GD25	FN65	NM94
1 (10155-509)	6.70	20.00	40.00

LION, THE (See Movie Comics)

LION OF SPARTA (See Movie Classics)

LIPPY THE LION AND HARDY HAR HAR (TV)
March, 1963 (Hanna-Barbera)
Gold Key

	GD25	FN65	NM94
1 (10049-303)	6.70	20.00	40.00

LI'L ABNER (See Comics on Parade, Sparkle, Sparkler Comics, Tip Top Comics & Tip Topper)
1939 - 1940
United Features Syndicate

	GD25	FN65	NM94
Single Series 4 ('39)	43.00	130.00	300.00
Single Series 18 ('40) (#18 on inside, #2 on-c)	36.00	110.00	250.00

LI'L ABNER (Al Capp's) (See Oxydol-Dreft)
No. 61, Dec, 1947 - No. 97, Jan, 1955
Harvey Publ. No. 61-69 (2/49)/Toby Press No. 70 on

	GD25	FN65	NM94
61(#1)-Wolverton & Powell-a	20.00	60.00	140.00
62-65: 65-Powell-a	13.00	40.00	90.00
66,67,69,70	11.00	32.00	75.00
68-Full length Fearless Fosdick story	11.50	34.00	80.00
71-74,76,80	10.00	30.00	60.00
75,77-79,86,91-All with Kurtzman art; 91-r/#77	11.00	32.00	75.00
81-85,87-90,92-94,96,97: 93-reprints #71	8.35	25.00	50.00
95-Full length Fearless Fosdick story	10.00	30.00	70.00
...& the Creatures from Drop-Outer Space-nn (Job Corps giveaway; 36 pgs., in color)	10.00	30.00	65.00
...Joins the Navy (1950) (Toby Press Premium)	8.35	25.00	50.00
...by Al Capp Giveaway (Circa 1955, nd)	8.35	25.00	50.00

LI'L ABNER
1951
Toby Press

	GD25	FN65	NM94
1	13.00	40.00	90.00

LI'L ABNER'S DOGPATCH (See Al Capp's...)

LITTLE AL OF THE F.B.I.
No. 10, 1950 (no month) - No. 11, Apr-May, 1951
Ziff-Davis Publications (Saunders painted-c)

	GD25	FN65	NM94
10(1950)	8.35	25.00	50.00
11(1951)	6.70	20.00	40.00

LITTLE AL OF THE SECRET SERVICE
No. 10, 7-8/51; No, 2, 9-10/51; No. 3, Winter, 1951
Ziff-Davis Publications (Saunders painted-c)

	GD25	FN65	NM94
10(#1)-Spanking panel	10.00	30.00	65.00
2,3	6.70	20.00	40.00

LITTLE ALONZO
1938 (B&W, 5-1/2x8-1/2")(Christmas giveaway)
Macy's Dept. Store

	GD25	FN65	NM94
nn-By Ferdinand the Bull's Munro Leaf	5.85	17.50	35.00

LITTLE AMBROSE
September, 1958
Archie Publications

	GD25	FN65	NM94
1-Bob Bolling-c	10.00	30.00	60.00

Limited Collector's Edition C-38, © DC

Linda Carter, Student Nurse #5, © MEG

Li'l Abner #83, © UFS

Little Archie #1, © AP

Little Audrey Yearbook (1950), © STJ

Little Beaver #7, © Stephen Slesinger

LITTLE ANGEL
No. 5, Sept, 1954; No. 6, Sept, 1955 - No. 16, Sept, 1959
Standard (Visual Editions)/Pines

	GD25	FN65	NM94
5	4.00	11.00	22.00
6-16	2.40	6.00	12.00

LITTLE ANNIE ROONEY
1935 (48 pgs.; B&W dailies) (25 cents)
David McKay Publications

	GD25	FN65	NM94
Book 1-Daily strip-r by Darrell McClure	10.00	30.00	70.00

LITTLE ANNIE ROONEY (See King Comics & Treasury of Comics)
1938; Aug, 1948 - No. 3, Oct, 1948
David McKay/St. John/Standard

	GD25	FN65	NM94
Feature Books 11 (McKay, 1938)	24.00	73.00	170.00
1 (St. John)	10.00	30.00	60.00
2,3	5.35	16.00	32.00

LITTLE ARCHIE (The Adventures of... #13-on) (See Archie Giant Series Mag. #527, 534, 538, 545, 549, 556, 560, 566, 570, 583, 594, 596, 607, 609, 619)
1956 - No. 180, Feb, 1983 (Giants No. 3-84)
Archie Publications

	GD25	FN65	NM94
1-(Scarce)	32.00	95.00	220.00
2	16.00	48.00	110.00
3-5	11.00	32.00	75.00
6-10	9.15	27.50	55.00
11-20	5.35	16.00	32.00
21-30	4.00	10.00	20.00
31-40: Little Pureheart apps. #40-42,44	2.00	5.00	10.00
41-60: 42-Intro. The Little Archies. 59-Little Sabrina begins	1.20	3.00	6.00
61-84: 84-Last Giant-Size	.80	2.00	4.00
85-100	.50	1.25	2.50
101-180	.30	.75	1.50
...In Animal Land 1(1957)	11.00	32.00	75.00
...In Animal Land 17(Winter, 1957-58)-19(Summer,1958)-Formerly Li'l Jinx	5.85	17.50	35.00

LITTLE ARCHIE
Apr, 1991 ($1.00, color)
Archie Comics

	GD25	FN65	NM94
1		.50	1.00

LITTLE ARCHIE CHRISTMAS SPECIAL (See Archie Giant Series #581)

LITTLE ARCHIE COMICS DIGEST ANNUAL (...Magazine #5 on)
10/77 - No. 48, 5/91 (Digest-size, 128 pgs., later issues $1.35-$1.50)
Archie Publications

	GD25	FN65	NM94
1(10/77)-Reprints	.40	1.00	2.00
2(4/78)-Neal Adams-a	.30	.70	1.40
3(11/78)-The Fly-r by S&K; Neal Adams-a	.30	.70	1.40
4(4/79) - 48: 28,40,46-Christmas-c	.30	.70	1.40

NOTE: *Little Archie, Little Jinx, Little Jughead & Little Sabrina in most issues.*

LITTLE ARCHIE DIGEST MAGAZINE
July, 1991 - Present ($1.50, digest size)
Archie Comics

	GD25	FN65	NM94
V2#1-7	.30	.75	1.50

LITTLE ARCHIE MYSTERY
Aug, 1963 - No. 2, Oct, 1963
Archie Publications

	GD25	FN65	NM94
1	10.00	30.00	60.00
2	5.00	15.00	30.00

LITTLE ASPIRIN (See Little Lenny & Wisco)
July, 1949 - No. 3, Dec, 1949 (52 pages)
Marvel Comics (CnPC)

	GD25	FN65	NM94
1-Oscar app.; Kurtzman-a, 4 pgs.	10.00	30.00	65.00
2-Kurtzman-a, 4 pgs.	5.85	17.50	35.00
3-No Kurtzman	3.60	9.00	18.00

LITTLE AUDREY (Also see Playful...)
April, 1948 - No. 24, May, 1952
St. John Publ.

	GD25	FN65	NM94
1-1st app. Little Audrey	22.00	65.00	150.00
2	10.00	30.00	70.00
3-5	9.15	27.50	55.00
6-10	5.35	16.00	32.00
11-20	4.00	10.00	20.00
21-24	3.00	7.50	15.00

LITTLE AUDREY (See Harvey Hits #11, 19)
No. 25, Aug, 1952 - No. 53, April, 1957
Harvey Publications

	GD25	FN65	NM94
25 (Paramount Pictures Famous Star)	6.70	20.00	40.00
26-30: 26-28-Casper app.	4.00	10.00	20.00
31-40: 32-35-Casper app.	2.80	7.00	14.00
41-53	2.00	5.00	10.00
...Clubhouse 1 (9/61, 68 pg. Giant) w/reprints	5.00	15.00	30.00

LITTLE AUDREY
Aug, 1992 - Present ($1.25, color)
Harvey Comics

	GD25	FN65	NM94
V2#1-3		.60	1.25

LITTLE AUDREY (...Yearbook)
1950 (260 pages) (50 cents)
St. John Publishing Co.

	GD25	FN65	NM94
Contains 8 complete 1949 comics rebound; Casper, Alice in Wonderland, Little Audrey, Abbott & Costello, Pinocchio, Moon Mullins, Three Stooges (from Jubilee), Little Annie Rooney app. (Rare)	52.00	155.00	360.00

(Also see All Good & Treasury of Comics)

NOTE: *This book contains remaindered St. John comics; many variations possible.*

LITTLE AUDREY & MELVIN (Audrey & Melvin No. 62)
May, 1962 - No. 61, Dec, 1973
Harvey Publications

	GD25	FN65	NM94
1	6.70	20.00	40.00
2-5	4.00	10.00	20.00
6-10	2.40	6.00	12.00
11-20	1.60	4.00	8.00
21-40	1.00	2.50	5.00
41-50,54-61	.80	2.00	4.00
51-53: All 52 pg. Giants	1.00	2.50	5.00

LITTLE AUDREY TV FUNTIME
Sept, 1962 - No. 33, Oct, 1971 (#1-31: 68 pgs.; #32,33: 52 pgs.)
Harvey Publications

	GD25	FN65	NM94
1-Richie Rich app.	4.70	14.00	28.00
2,3: Richie Rich app.	3.00	7.50	15.00
4,5: 5-25 & 35 cent issues exist	2.40	6.00	12.00
6-10	1.20	3.00	6.00
11-20	1.00	2.50	5.00
21-33	.80	2.00	4.00

LITTLE BAD WOLF (See 4-Color #403, 473, 564, Walt Disney's C&S #52, Walt Disney Showcase #21 & Wheaties)

LITTLE BEAVER
No. 211, Jan, 1949 - No. 870, Jan, 1958 (All painted-c)
Dell Publishing Co.

	GD25	FN65	NM94
4-Color 211('49)-All Harman-a	6.70	20.00	40.00
4-Color 267,294,332(5/51)	4.00	10.00	20.00
3(10-12/51)-8(1-3/53)	3.60	9.00	18.00
4-Color 483(8-10/53),529	3.60	9.00	18.00

	GD25	FN65	NM94
4-Color 612,660,695,744,817,870	3.00	7.50	15.00

LITTLE BIT
March, 1949 - No. 2, 1949
Jubilee/St. John Publishing Co.

	GD25	FN65	NM94
1,2	3.60	9.00	18.00

LITTLE DOT (See Humphrey, Li'l Max, Sad Sack, and Tastee-Freez Comics)
Sept, 1953 - No. 164, April, 1976
Harvey Publications

	GD25	FN65	NM94
1-Intro./1st app. Richie Rich & Little Lotta	54.00	160.00	375.00
2-1st app. Freckles & Pee Wee (Richie Rich's poor friends)	27.00	81.00	190.00
3	17.00	50.00	120.00
4	12.00	36.00	85.00
5-Origin dots on Little Dot's dress	19.00	57.00	130.00
6-Richie Rich, Little Lotta, & Little Dot all on cover; 1st Richie Rich cover featured	16.00	48.00	110.00
7-10	8.35	25.00	50.00
11-20	6.35	19.00	38.00
21-40	3.60	9.00	18.00
41-60	1.80	4.50	9.00
61-80	1.00	2.50	5.00
81-100	.80	2.00	4.00
101-141	.60	1.50	3.00
142-145: All 52 pg. Giants	.70	1.75	3.50
146-164	.30	.75	1.50
Shoe store giveaway 2	4.70	14.00	28.00

NOTE: *Richie Rich & Little Lotta in all.*

LITTLE DOT
Sept, 1992 - Present ($1.25, color)
Harvey Comics

	GD25	FN65	NM94
V2#1,2: Little Dot, Little Lotta, Richie Rich in all		.60	1.25

LITTLE DOT DOTLAND (Dot Dotland No. 62, 63)
July, 1962 - No. 61, Dec, 1973
Harvey Publications

	GD25	FN65	NM94
1-Richie Rich begins	6.70	20.00	40.00
2,3	4.00	10.00	20.00
4,5	2.80	7.00	14.00
6-10	1.80	4.50	9.00
11-20	1.40	3.50	7.00
21-30	.80	2.00	4.00
31-50,55-61	.60	1.50	3.00
51-54: All 52 pg. Giants	1.00	2.50	5.00

LITTLE DOT'S UNCLES & AUNTS (See Harvey Hits No. 4, 13, 24)
Oct, 1961; No. 2, Aug, 1962 - No. 52, April, 1974
Harvey Enterprises

	GD25	FN65	NM94
1-Richie Rich begins; 68 pgs. begin	7.50	22.50	45.00
2,3	4.00	11.00	22.00
4,5	2.40	6.00	12.00
6-10	1.80	4.50	9.00
11-20	1.40	3.50	7.00
21-37: Last 68 pg. issue	1.00	2.50	5.00
38-52: All 52 pg. Giants	.80	2.00	4.00

LITTLE DRACULA
Jan, 1992 - No. 3, July?, 1992 ($1.25, color, quarterly, mini-series)
Harvey Comics

	GD25	FN65	NM94
1-3		.60	1.25

LITTLE EVA
May, 1952 - No. 31, Nov, 1956
St. John Publishing Co.

	GD25	FN65	NM94
1	8.35	25.00	50.00
2	4.20	12.50	25.00
3-5	3.20	8.00	16.00
6-10	2.00	5.00	10.00
11-31	1.80	4.50	9.00
3-D 1,2(10/53-11/53); 1-Infinity-c	12.00	36.00	84.00
I.W. Reprint #1-3,6-8	.40	1.00	2.00
Super Reprint #10,12('63),14,16,18('64)	.40	1.00	2.00

LITTLE FIR TREE, THE
nd (1942) (8-1/2x11") (12 pgs. with cover, color & B&W, heavy paper)
W. T. Grant Co. (Christmas giveaway)

nn-Story by Hans Christian Anderson; 8 pg. Kelly-r/Santa Claus Funnies; not signed.
(One copy in Mint sold for $1750.00 in 1986 & another copy in VF sold for $1000.00 in 1991)

LI'L GENIUS (Summer Fun No. 54) (See Blue Bird)
1954 - No. 52, 1/65; No. 53, 10/65; No. 54, 10/85 - No. 55, 1/86
Charlton Comics

	GD25	FN65	NM94
1	5.85	17.50	35.00
2	3.60	9.00	18.00
3-15,19,20	2.40	6.00	12.00
16,17-(68 pgs.)	3.00	7.50	15.00
18-(100 pgs., 10/58)	4.00	11.00	22.00
21-35	1.80	4.50	9.00
36-53	1.00	2.50	5.00
54,55	.30	.75	1.50

LI'L GHOST
Feb, 1958 - No. 3, Mar, 1959
St. John Publishing Co./Fago No. 1 on

	GD25	FN65	NM94
1(St. John)	5.00	15.00	30.00
1(Fago)	4.00	10.00	20.00
2,3	3.00	7.50	15.00

LITTLE GIANT COMICS
7/38 - No. 3, 10/38; No. 4, 2/39 (132 pgs.) (6-3/4x4-1/2")
Centaur Publications

	GD25	FN65	NM94
1-B&W with color-c	37.00	110.00	220.00
2,3-B&W with color-c	30.00	90.00	180.00
4 (6-5/8x9-3/8")(68 pgs., B&W inside)	32.00	95.00	190.00

NOTE: ***Gustavson** a-1. **Pinajian** a-4. **Bob Wood** a-1.*

LITTLE GIANT DETECTIVE FUNNIES
Oct, 1938 - No. 4, Jan, 1939 (132 pgs., B&W) (6-3/4x4-1/2")
Centaur Publications

	GD25	FN65	NM94
1-B&W with color-c	37.00	110.00	220.00
2,3	30.00	90.00	180.00
4(1/39)-B&W; color-c; 68 pgs., 6x9"; Eisner-r	32.00	95.00	190.00

LITTLE GIANT MOVIE FUNNIES
Aug, 1938 - No. 2, Oct, 1938 (132 pgs., B&W) (6-3/4x4-1/2")
Centaur Publications

	GD25	FN65	NM94
1-Ed Wheelan's "Minute Movies"-r	37.00	110.00	220.00
2-Ed Wheelan's "Minute Movies"-r	27.00	82.00	165.00

LITTLE GROUCHO (...Grouchy No. 2) (See Tippy Terry)
No. 16; Feb-Mar, 1955 - No. 2, June-July, 1955
Reston Publ. Co.

	GD25	FN65	NM94
16, 1 (2-3/55)	4.70	14.00	28.00
2(6-7/55)	3.60	9.00	18.00

LITTLE HIAWATHA (See 4-Color #439, 787, 901, 988 & Walt Disney's C&S #143)

LITTLE IKE
April, 1953 - No. 4, Oct, 1953
St. John Publishing Co.

	GD25	FN65	NM94
1	5.85	17.50	35.00
2	3.60	9.00	18.00
3,4	2.80	7.00	14.00

LITTLE IODINE (See Giant Comic Album)

Little Dot #19, © HARV

Little Eva 3-D #1, © STJ

Little Giant Detective Funnies #1, © CEN

Little Lizzie #5, © MEG

Little Lotta #3, © HARV

Little Max #1, © HARV

No. 224, 4/49 - No. 257, 1949: 3-5/50 - No. 56, 4-6/62 (1-4: 52pgs.)
Dell Publishing Co.

	GD25	FN65	NM94
4-Color 224-By Jimmy Hatlo	10.00	30.00	60.00
4-Color 257	6.70	20.00	40.00
1(3-5/50)	8.35	25.00	50.00
2-5	4.00	10.00	20.00
6-10	2.40	6.00	12.00
11-20	2.00	5.00	10.00
21-30: 27-Xmas-c	1.80	4.50	9.00
31-40	1.40	3.50	7.00
41-56	1.00	2.50	5.00

LITTLE JACK FROST
1951
Avon Periodicals

	GD25	FN65	NM94
1	4.70	14.00	28.00

LI'L JINX (Formerly Ginger?) (Little Archie in Animal Land #17) (Also see Pep Comics #62)
No. 11(#1), Nov, 1956 - No. 16, Sept, 1957
Archie Publications

	GD25	FN65	NM94
11 (#1)	7.00	21.00	42.00
12-16	4.70	14.00	28.00

LI'L JINX (See Archie Giant Series Magazine No. 223)

LI'L JINX CHRISTMAS BAG (See Archie Giant Series Mag. No. 195, 206, 219)

LI'L JINX GIANT LAUGH-OUT (See Archie Giant Series Mag. No. 176, 185)
No. 33, Sept, 1971 - No. 43, Nov, 1973 (52 pgs.)
Archie Publications

	GD25	FN65	NM94
33-43	.60	1.50	3.00

LITTLE JOE (See 4-Color #1, Popular Comics & Super Comics)

LITTLE JOE
April, 1953
St. John Publishing Co.

	GD25	FN65	NM94
1	2.80	7.00	14.00

LITTLE JOHNNY & THE TEDDY BEARS
1907 (10x14") (32 pgs. in color)
Reilly & Britton Co.

	GD25	FN65	NM94
nn-By J. R. Bray	20.00	60.00	140.00

LI'L KIDS (Also see Li'l Pals)
8/70 - No. 2, 10/70; No. 3, 11/71 - No. 12, 6/73
Marvel Comics Group

	GD25	FN65	NM94
1	1.60	4.00	8.00
2-12: 10,11-Calvin app.	.80	2.00	4.00

LITTLE KING (See 4-Color No. 494, 597, 677)

LITTLE KLINKER
Nov, 1960 (20 pgs.) (slick cover)
Little Klinker Ventures (Montgomery Ward Giveaway)

	GD25	FN65	NM94
nn	1.60	4.00	8.00

LITTLE LANA (Formerly Lana)
No. 8, Nov, 1949; No. 9, Mar, 1950
Marvel Comics (MjMC)

	GD25	FN65	NM94
8,9	4.00	12.00	24.00

LITTLE LENNY
June, 1949 - No. 3, Nov, 1949
Marvel Comics (CDS)

	GD25	FN65	NM94
1-Little Aspirin app.	6.35	19.00	38.00
2 3	3.60	9.00	18.00

LITTLE LIZZIE
6/49 - No. 5, 4/50; 9/53 - No. 3, Jan, 1954
Marvel Comics (PrPI)/Atlas (OMC)

	GD25	FN65	NM94
1	7.00	21.00	42.00
2-5	4.00	11.00	22.00
1 (1953, 2nd series)	4.70	14.00	28.00
2,3	3.60	9.00	18.00

LITTLE LOTTA (See Harvey Hits No. 10)
11/55 - No. 110, 11/73; No. 111, 9/74 - No. 121, 5/76
V2#1, Oct, 1992 - Present ($1.25, color)
Harvey Publications

	GD25	FN65	NM94
1-Richie Rich (r) & Little Dot begin	25.00	75.00	175.00
2,3	11.00	32.00	75.00
4,5	7.50	22.50	45.00
6-10	5.85	17.50	35.00
11-20	4.00	10.00	20.00
21-40	2.40	6.00	12.00
41-60	1.80	4.50	9.00
61-80	1.00	2.50	5.00
81-99	.60	1.50	3.00
100-103: All 52 pg. Giants	.80	2.00	4.00
104-121	.40	1.00	2.00
V2#1-3 (1992)		.60	1.25

LITTLE LOTTA FOODLAND
9/63 - No. 14, 10/67; No. 15, 10/68 - No. 29, Oct, 1972
Harvey Publications

	GD25	FN65	NM94
1: 68 pgs. begin, end #26	9.15	27.50	55.00
2,3	4.70	14.00	28.00
4,5	3.60	9.00	18.00
6-10	2.40	6.00	12.00
11-20	1.80	4.50	9.00
21-26	1.40	3.50	7.00
27,28: Both 52 pgs.	1.00	2.50	5.00
29: 36 pgs.	.80	2.00	4.00

LITTLE LULU (Formerly Marge's...)
No. 207, Sept, 1972 - No. 268, April, 1984
Gold Key 207-257/Whitman 258 on

	GD25	FN65	NM94
207,209,220-Stanley-r. 207-1st app. Henrietta	1.20	3.00	6.00
208,210-219: 208-1st app. Snobbly, Wilbur's brother	1.00	2.50	5.00
221-240,242-249, 250(r/#166), 251-254(r/#206)	.80	2.00	4.00
241,263,268-Stanley-r	.80	2.00	4.00
255-262,264-267: 256-r/#212	.40	1.00	2.00

LITTLE MARY MIXUP (See Comics On Parade & Single Series #10, 26)

LITTLE MAX COMICS (Joe Palooka's Pal; see Joe Palooka)
Oct, 1949 - No. 73, Nov, 1961
Harvey Publications

	GD25	FN65	NM94
1-Infinity-c; Little Dot begins	10.00	30.00	70.00
2-Little Dot app.	5.85	17.50	35.00
3-Little Dot app.	4.20	12.50	25.00
4-10: 5-Little Dot app., 1pg.	2.80	7.00	14.00
11-20	2.00	5.00	10.00
21-73: 23-Little Dot app. 38-r/#20. 70-73-Little Lotta, Richie Rich app.	1.40	3.50	7.00

LI'L MENACE
Dec, 1958 - No. 3, May, 1959
Fago Magazine Co.

	GD25	FN65	NM94
1-Peter Rabbit app.	4.35	13.00	26.00
2-Peter Rabbit (Vincent Fago's)	3.60	9.00	18.00
3	2.80	7.00	14.00

LITTLE MERMAID, THE (Walt Disney's...; also see Disney's...)

	GD25	FN65	NM94

1990 (no date given)($5.95, color, no ads, 52 pgs.)
W. D. Publications (Disney)

	GD25	FN65	NM94
nn-Adapts animated movie	1.20	3.00	6.00
nn-Comic version ($2.50)	.50	1.25	2.50

LITTLE MERMAID, THE
1992 - No. 4, 1992 ($1.50, color, mini-series)
Disney Comics

	GD25	FN65	NM94
1-4: Based on movie	.30	.75	1.50

LITTLE MISS MUFFET
No. 11, Dec, 1948 - No. 13, March, 1949
Best Books (Standard Comics)/King Features Synd.

	GD25	FN65	NM94
11-Strip reprints; Fanny Cory-a	6.35	19.00	38.00
12,13-Strip reprints; Fanny Cory-a	4.20	12.50	25.00

LITTLE MISS SUNBEAM COMICS
June-July, 1950 - No. 4, Dec-Jan, 1950-51
Magazine Enterprises/Quality Bakers of America

	GD25	FN65	NM94
1	8.35	25.00	50.00
2-4	4.35	13.00	26.00
...Advs. In Space ('55)	3.60	9.00	18.00
Bread Giveaway 1-4(Quality Bakers, 1949-50)-14 pgs. each	3.20	8.00	16.00
Bread Giveaway (1957,61; 16pgs, reg. size)	2.80	7.00	14.00

LITTLE MONSTERS, THE (See March of Comics #423, Three Stooges #17)
Nov, 1964 - No. 44, Feb, 1978
Gold Key

	GD25	FN65	NM94
1	3.00	7.50	15.00
2	1.60	4.00	8.00
3-10	1.20	3.00	6.00
11-20	.60	1.50	3.00
21-44: 20,34-39,43-reprints	.30	.75	1.50

LITTLE MONSTERS (Now)(Value: cover or less)

LITTLE NEMO (See Cocomalt, Future Comics, Help, Jest, Kayo, Punch, Red Seal, & Superworld; most by Winsor McCay Jr., son of famous artist) (Other McCay books: see Little Sammy Sneeze & Dreams of the Rarebit Fiend)

LITTLE NEMO (...in Slumberland)
1906, 1909 (Sunday strip reprints in color) (cardboard covers)
Doffield & Co.(1906)/Cupples & Leon Co.(1909)

	GD25	FN65	NM94
1906-11x16-1/2" in color by Winsor McCay; 30 pgs. (Very Rare)	250.00	750.00	1500.00
1909-10x14" in color by Winsor McCay (Very Rare)	200.00	600.00	1200.00

LITTLE NEMO (...in Slumberland)
1945 (28 pgs.; 11x7-1/4"; B&W)
McCay Features/Nostalgia Press('69)

	GD25	FN65	NM94
1905 & 1911 reprints by Winsor McCay	5.00	15.00	35.00
1969-70 (Exact reprint)	1.30	4.00	8.00

LITTLE ORPHAN ANNIE (See Annie, Famous Feature Stories, Feature Books #7, Marvel Super Special, Merry Christmas..., Popular Comics, Super Book #7, 11, 23 & Super Comics)

LITTLE ORPHAN ANNIE (See Treasure Box of Famous Comics)
1926 - 1934 (Daily strip reprints) (7x8-3/4") (B&W)
Cupples & Leon Co.
(Hardcover Editions, 100 pages)

	GD25	FN65	NM94
1(1926)-Little Orphan Annie	23.00	70.00	140.00
2('27)-In the Circus	17.00	50.00	100.00
3('28)-The Haunted House	17.00	50.00	100.00
4('29)-Bucking the World	17.00	50.00	100.00
5('30)-Never Say Die	17.00	50.00	100.00
6('31)-Shipwrecked	17.00	50.00	100.00
7('32)-A Willing Helper	12.50	37.50	75.00
8('33)-In Cosmic City	12.50	37.50	75.00
9('34)-Uncle Dan	17.00	50.00	100.00

NOTE: Hardcovers with dust jackets are worth 20-50 percent more; the earlier the book, the higher the percentage. Each book reprints dailies from the previous year.

LITTLE ORPHAN ANNIE
No. 7, 1937 - No. 3, Sept-Nov, 1948; No. 206, Dec, 1948
David McKay Publ./Dell Publishing Co.

	GD25	FN65	NM94
Feature Books(McKay) 7-(1937) (Rare)	75.00	225.00	525.00
4-Color 12(1941)	43.00	130.00	300.00
4-Color 18(1943)-Flag-c	34.00	105.00	240.00
4-Color 52(1944)	25.00	75.00	175.00
4-Color 76(1945)	21.00	62.00	145.00
4-Color 107(1946)	17.00	52.00	120.00
4-Color 152(1947)	11.50	34.00	80.00
1(3-5/48)-r/strips from 5/7/44 to 7/30/44	12.00	36.00	84.00
2-r/strips from 7/21/40 to 9/9/40	8.35	25.00	50.00
3-r/strips from 9/10/40 to 11/9/40	8.35	25.00	50.00
4-Color 206(12/48)	6.70	20.00	40.00
Junior Commandos Giveaway(same-c as 4-Color #18, K.K. Publ.)(Big Shoe Store); same back cover as '47 Popped Wheat giveaway; 16 pgs; flag-c; r/strips 9/7/42-10/10/42	17.00	52.00	120.00
Popped Wheat Giveaway('47)-16 pgs. full color; reprints strips from 5/3/40 to 6/20/40	1.20	3.00	6.00
Quaker Sparkies Giveaway(1940)	9.15	27.50	55.00
Quaker Sparkies Giveaway(1941, Full color, 20 pgs.); :LOA and the Rescue;" r/strips 4/13/39-6/21/39 & 7/6/39-7/17/39. "LOA and the Kidnappers;" r/strips 11/28/38-1/28/39	8.35	25.00	50.00
Quaker Sparkies Giveaway(1942, Full color, 20 pgs.); "LOA and Mr. Gudge;" r/strips 2/13/38-3/21/38 & 4/18/37-5/30/37. "LOA and the Great Am"	6.70	20.00	40.00

LI'L PALS (Also see Li'l Kids)
Sept, 1972 - No. 5, May, 1973
Marvel Comics Group

	GD25	FN65	NM94
1-5	.60	1.50	3.00

LI'L PAN (Formerly Rocket Kelly; becomes Junior Comics with #9)
No. 6, Dec-Jan, 1947 - No. 8, Apr-May, 1947
Fox Features Syndicate

	GD25	FN65	NM94
6	5.00	15.00	30.00
7,8: 7-Atomic bomb story	4.00	10.00	20.00

LITTLE PEOPLE (See 4-Color #485, 573, 633, 692, 753, 809, 868, 908, 959, 1024, 1062)

LITTLE RASCALS (See 4-Color #674, 778, 825, 883, 936, 974, 1030, 1079, 1137, 1174, 1224, 1297)

LI'L RASCAL TWINS (Formerly Nature Boy)
No. 6, 1957 - No. 18, Jan, 1960
Charlton Comics

	GD25	FN65	NM94
6-Li'l Genius & Tomboy in all	4.00	10.00	20.00
7-18	2.00	5.00	10.00

LITTLE ROQUEFORT COMICS
June, 1952 - No. 9, Oct, 1953; No. 10, Summer, 1958
St. John Publishing Co./Pines No. 10

	GD25	FN65	NM94
1	6.35	19.00	38.00
2	3.60	9.00	18.00
3-10	2.80	7.00	14.00

LITTLE SAD SACK (See Harvey Hits No. 73, 76, 79, 81, 83)
Oct, 1964 - No. 19, Nov, 1967
Harvey Publications

	GD25	FN65	NM94
1-Richie Rich app. on cover only	3.00	7.50	15.00
2-19	1.00	2.50	5.00

LITTLE SAMMY SNEEZE
1905 (28 pgs. in color; 11x16-1/2")
New York Herald Co.

Little Miss Sunbeam (1957), © Quality Bakers

Little Orphan Annie #2 (1927), © News Synd.

Little Orphan Annie Popped Wheat Giveaway, © News Synd.

Little Scouts #2, © Roland Coe

The Living Bible #1, © Living Bible Corp.

Lobo #4, © DC

	GD25	FN65	NM94
nn-By Winsor McCay (Rare)	267.00	800.00	1600.00

NOTE: *Rarely found in fine to mint condition.*

LITTLE SCOUTS
No. 321, Mar, 1951 - No. 587, Oct, 1954
Dell Publishing Co.

	GD25	FN65	NM94
4-Color #321 (#1, 3/51)	3.00	7.50	15.00
2(10-12/51) - 6(10-12/52)	1.80	4.50	9.00
4-Color #462,506,550,587	1.80	4.50	9.00

LITTLE SHOP OF HORRORS SPECIAL (DC)(Value: cover or less)

LITTLE SPUNKY
No date (1963?) (10 cents)
I. W. Enterprises

	GD25	FN65	NM94
1-Reprint	.60	1.50	3.00

LITTLE STOOGES, THE (The Three Stooges' Sons)
Sept, 1972 - No. 7, Mar, 1974
Gold Key

	GD25	FN65	NM94
1-Norman Maurer cover/stories in all	1.60	4.00	8.00
2-7	.80	2.00	4.00

LITTLEST OUTLAW (See 4-Color #609)

LITTLEST SNOWMAN, THE
No. 755, 12/56; No. 864, 12/57; 12-2/1963-64
Dell Publishing Co.

	GD25	FN65	NM94
4-Color #755,864, 1(1964)	4.00	10.00	20.00

LI'L TOMBOY (Formerly Fawcett's Funny Animals)
V14#92, Oct, 1956; No. 93, Mar, 1957 - No. 107, Feb, 1960
Charlton Comics

	GD25	FN65	NM94
V14#92	3.20	8.00	16.00
93-107: 97-Atomic Bunny app.	2.40	6.00	12.00

LITTLE TREE THAT WASN'T WANTED, THE
1960, (Color, 28 pgs.)
W. T. Grant Co. (Giveaway)

	GD25	FN65	NM94
nn-Christmas giveaway	1.20	3.00	6.00

LI'L WILLIE COMICS (Formerly & becomes Willie Comics #22 on)
No. 20, July, 1949 - No. 21, Sept, 1949
Marvel Comics (MgPC)

	GD25	FN65	NM94
20,21: 20-Little Aspirin app.	4.20	12.50	25.00

LITTLE WOMEN (See Power Record Comics)

LIVE IT UP (Spire Christian)(Value: cover or less)

LIVING BIBLE, THE
Fall, 1945 - No. 3, Spring, 1946
Living Bible Corp.

	GD25	FN65	NM94
1-Life of Paul	14.00	43.00	100.00
2-Joseph & His Brethren	10.00	30.00	60.00
3-Chaplains At War (classic-c)	16.00	48.00	110.00

NOTE: *All have **L. B. Cole** -c.*

LOBO
Dec, 1965; No. 2, Oct, 1966
Dell Publishing Co.

	GD25	FN65	NM94
1,2	1.60	4.00	8.00

LOBO (Also see Action #650, Adventures of Superman, Justice League, L.E.G.I.O.N., Mister Miracle, Omega Men #3 & Superman #41)
Nov, 1990 - No. 4, Feb, 1991 ($1.50, color, mini-series)

	GD25	FN65	NM94
1-(99 cents)-Giffen plots/Breakdowns in all	1.20	3.00	6.00
2-Legion '89 spin-off	.50	1.25	2.50
3,4: 1-4 have Bisley painted covers	.50	1.20	2.40
...: Blazing Chain of Love 1 (9/92, $1.50)-Denys Cowan-c/a; Alan Grant scripts	.30	.75	1.50
...Paramilitary Christmas Special 1 (1991, $2.39, 52 pgs.)	.45	1.20	2.40

LOBO: INFANTICIDE
Oct, 1992 - No. 4, Jan, 1993 ($1.50, color, mini-series, mature readers)
DC Comics

	GD25	FN65	NM94
1-4: Giffen-c/a; Alan Grant scripts	.30	.75	1.50

LOBO'S BACK
May, 1992 - No. 4, Nov, 1992 ($1.50, color, mini-series, mature readers)
DC Comics

	GD25	FN65	NM94
1-4: 1-Has 3 outer covers. Bisley painted-c 1,2; a-1-4. 3-Sam Kieth-c; all have Giffen plots/breakdown & Grant scripts	.40	1.00	2.00

LOCKE! (Blackthorne)(Value: cover or less)

LOCO (Magazine) (Satire)
Aug, 1958 - V1#3, Jan, 1959
Satire Publications

	GD25	FN65	NM94
V1#1-Chic Stone-a	4.00	10.00	20.00
V1#2,3-Severin-a, 2 pgs. Davis; 3-Heath-a	3.00	7.50	15.00

LOGAN'S RUN
Jan, 1977 - No. 7, July, 1977
Marvel Comics Group

	GD25	FN65	NM94
1: 1-5-Based on novel & movie	.70	1.75	3.50
2-5,7: 6,7-New stories adapted from novel	.35	1.00	2.00
6-1st Thanos solo story (back-up story)	4.00	10.00	20.00

NOTE: ***Austin** a-6i. **Gulacy** c-6. **Kane** c-7p. **Perez** a-1-5p; c-1-5p. **Sutton** a-6p, 7p.*

LOIS LANE (DC)(Value: cover or less)(Also see Daring New Adventures of Supergirl and Showcase)

LOLLY AND PEPPER
No. 832, Sept, 1957 - July, 1962
Dell Publishing Co.

	GD25	FN65	NM94
4-Color 832(#1)	3.20	8.00	16.00
4-Color 940,978,1086,1206	2.40	6.00	12.00
01-459-207 (7/62)	2.40	6.00	12.00

LOMAX (See Police Action)

LONE EAGLE (The Flame No. 5 on)
Apr-May, 1954 - No. 4, Oct-Nov, 1954
Ajax/Farrell Publications

	GD25	FN65	NM94
1	7.50	22.50	45.00
2-4: 3-Bondage-c	4.70	14.00	28.00

LONELY HEART (Formerly Dear Lonely Hearts; Dear Heart #15 on)
No. 9, March, 1955 - No. 14, Feb, 1956
Ajax/Farrell Publ. (Excellent Publ.)

	GD25	FN65	NM94
9-Kamenesque-a; (Last precode)	5.00	15.00	30.00
10-14	3.20	8.00	16.00

LONE RANGER, THE (See Ace Comics, Aurora, Dell Giants, Feature Books #21, 24, Future Comics, Golden Comics Digest #48, King Comics, Magic Comics & March of Comics #165, 174, 193, 208, 225, 238, 310, 322, 338, 350)

LONE RANGER, THE
No. 3, 1939 - No. 167, Feb, 1947
Dell Publishing Co.

	GD25	FN65	NM94
Large Feature Comic 3(1939)-Heigh-Yo Silver; text with illus. by Robert Weisman; also exists as a Whitman #710	57.00	170.00	400.00
Large Feature Comic 7(1939)-Ill. by Henry Vallely; Hi-Yo Silver the Lone Ranger to the Rescue; also exists as a Whitman #715	64.00	195.00	450.00
Feature Book 21('40), 24('41)	54.00	160.00	375.00
4-Color 82('45)	36.00	102.00	250.00
4-Color 98('45),118('46)	27.00	81.00	190.00
4-Color 125('46),136('47)	20.00	60.00	140.00

	GD25	FN65	NM94
4-Color 151,167('47)	17.00	51.00	120.00

LONE RANGER, THE (Movie, radio & TV; Clayton Moore starred as Lone Ranger in the movies; No. 1-37: strip reprints)(See Dell Giants)
Jan-Feb, 1948 - No. 145, May-July, 1962
Dell Publishing Co.

	GD25	FN65	NM94
1 (36pgs.)-The Lone Ranger, his horse Silver, companion Tonto & his horse Scout begin	57.00	170.00	400.00
2 (52pgs. begin, end #41)	27.00	80.00	190.00
3-5	22.00	65.00	150.00
6,7,9,10	17.00	51.00	120.00
8-Origin retold; Indian back-c begin, end #35	22.00	65.00	155.00
11-20: 11-"Young Hawk" Indian boy serial begins, ends #145	11.50	34.00	80.00
21,22,24-31: 51-Reprint. 31-1st Mask logo	10.00	30.00	65.00
23-Origin retold	13.00	40.00	90.00
32-37: 32-Painted-c begin. 36-Animal photo back-c begin, end #49. 37-Last newspaper-r issue; new outfit	8.35	25.00	50.00
38-41 (All 52pgs.)	7.00	21.00	42.00
42-50 (36pgs.)	5.85	17.50	35.00
51-74 (52pgs.): 71-Blank inside-c	5.85	17.50	35.00
75-99: 76-Flag-c. 79-X-mas-c	4.70	14.00	28.00
100	6.70	20.00	40.00
101-111: Last painted-c	5.00	15.00	30.00
112-Clayton Moore photo-c begin, end #145	16.00	48.00	110.00
113-117	9.15	27.50	55.00
118-Origin Lone Ranger, Tonto, & Silver retold; Special anniversary issue	14.00	43.00	100.00
119-145: 139-Last issue by Fran Striker	8.35	25.00	50.00
Cheerios Giveaways (1954, 16 pgs., 2-1/2x7", soft-c) #1-"The Lone Ranger, His Mask & How He Met Tonto." #2-"The Lone Ranger & the Story of Silver" each....	13.00	40.00	90.00
Doll Giveaways (Gabriel Ind.)(1973, 3-1/4x5")-"The Story of The L.R." & The Carson City Bank Robbery"	1.60	4.00	8.00
How the Lone Ranger Captured Silver Book(1936)-Silvercup Bread giveaway	47.00	140.00	320.00
...In Milk for Big Mike (1955, Dairy Association giveaway), soft-c; 5x7-1/4", 16 pgs.	11.00	32.00	75.00
Merita Bread giveaway (1954, 16 pgs., 5x7-1/4")-"How to Be a Lone Ranger Health & Safety Scout"	11.00	32.00	75.00

NOTE: ***Hank Hartman*** *painted c(signed)-65, 66, 70, 75, 82; unsigned-64?, 67-69?, 71, 72, 73?, 74?, 76-78, 80, 81, 83-91, 92?, 93-111.* ***Ernest Nordli*** *painted c(signed)-42, 50, 52, 53, 56, 59, 60; unsigned-39-41, 44-49, 51, 54, 55, 57, 58, 61-63?*

LONE RANGER, THE
9/64 - No. 16, 12/69; No. 17, 11/72; No. 18, 9/74 - No. 28, 3/77
Gold Key (Reprints in #13-20)

	GD25	FN65	NM94
1-Retells origin	4.00	10.00	20.00
2	2.00	5.00	10.00
3-10: Small Bear-r in #6-12	1.40	3.50	7.00
11-17	1.20	3.00	6.00
18-28	1.00	2.50	5.00
Golden West 1(30029-610, 10/66)-Giant-r/most Golden West #3-including Clayton Moore photo front/back-c	6.50	19.00	45.00

LONE RANGER COMICS, THE
1939(inside) (shows 1938 on-c) (52 pgs. in color; regular size)
Lone Ranger, Inc. (Ice cream mail order)

	GD25	FN65	VF82
nn-(Scarce)-The first western comic devoted to a single character; not by Vallely	250.00	750.00	1500.00

(Estimated up to 20 total copies exist, none in NM/Mint)

LONE RANGER'S COMPANION TONTO, THE (TV)
No. 312, Jan, 1951 - No. 33, Nov-Jan/58-59 (All painted-c)
Dell Publishing Co.

	GD25	FN65	NM94
4-Color 312(#1, 1951)	11.50	34.00	80.00
2(8-10/51),3: (#2 titled 'Tonto')	6.70	20.00	40.00
4-10	4.00	11.00	22.00
11-20	3.60	9.00	18.00
21-33	2.40	6.00	12.00

NOTE: ***Ernest Nordli*** *painted c(signed)-2, 7; unsigned-3-6, 8-11, 12?, 13, 14, 18?, 22-24? See Aurora Comic Booklets.*

LONE RANGER'S FAMOUS HORSE HI-YO SILVER, THE (TV)
No. 369, Jan, 1952 - No. 36, Oct-Dec, 1960 (All painted-c)
Dell Publishing Co.

	GD25	FN65	NM94
4-Color 369(#1)-Silver's origin as told by The Lone Ranger	8.35	25.00	50.00
4-Color 392(#2, 4/52)	4.00	12.00	24.00
3(7-9/52)-10(4-6/52)	2.40	7.00	14.00
11-36	2.00	5.00	10.00

LONE RIDER (Also see The Rider)
April, 1951 - No. 26, July, 1955 (36pgs., 3-on)
Superior Comics(Farrell Publications)

	GD25	FN65	NM94
1 (52pgs.)-The Lone Rider & his horse Lightnin' begin; Kamenish-a begins	10.00	30.00	70.00
2 (52pgs.)-The Golden Arrow begins (origin)	6.35	19.00	38.00
3-6: 6-Last Golden Arrow	5.00	15.00	30.00
7-Golden Arrow becomes Swift Arrow; origin of his shield	6.35	19.00	38.00
8-Origin Swift Arrow	7.50	22.50	45.00
9,10	4.20	12.50	25.00
11-14	4.00	10.00	20.00
15-Golden Arrow origin-r from #2, changing name to Swift Arrow	4.20	12.50	25.00
16-20,22-26: 23-Apache Kid app.	3.60	9.00	18.00
21-3-D effect-c	9.15	27.50	55.00

LONE WOLF AND CUB (First)(Value: cover or less)

LONG BOW (...Indian Boy)(See Indians & Jumbo Comics #141)
1951 - No. 9, Wint, 1952/53
Fiction House Magazines (Real Adventures Publ.)

	GD25	FN65	NM94
1-Most covers by Maurice Whitman	10.00	30.00	60.00
2	6.70	20.00	40.00
3-9	5.00	15.00	30.00

LONG JOHN SILVER & THE PIRATES (Formerly Terry & the Pirates)
No. 30, Aug, 1956 - No. 32, March, 1957 (TV)
Charlton Comics

	GD25	FN65	NM94
30-32: Whitman-c	5.00	15.00	30.00

LONGSHOT (Also see X-Men #10, 1992)
Sept, 1985 - No. 6, Feb, 1986 (Limited series)
Marvel Comics Group

	GD25	FN65	NM94
1-Arthur Adams/Whilce Portacio-c/a in all	2.40	6.00	12.00
2	2.00	5.00	10.00
3-5: 4-Spider-Man app.	1.60	4.00	8.00
6-Double size	1.80	4.50	9.00
Trade Paperback (1989, $16.95)-r/1-6	2.85	8.50	17.00

LOONEY TUNES (2nd Series)
April, 1975 - No. 47, July, 1984
Gold Key/Whitman

	GD25	FN65	NM94
1	.40	1.00	2.00
2-47: Reprints: #1-4,16; 38-46(1/3-r)		.50	1.00

LOONEY TUNES AND MERRIE MELODIES COMICS ("Looney Tunes" #166 (8/55) on)
1941 - No. 246, July-Sept, 1962
Dell Publishing Co.

	GD25	FN65	VF82	NM94
1-Porky Pig, Bugs Bunny, Daffy Duck, Elmer Fudd, Mary Jane & Sniffles, Pat, Patsy and Pete begin (1st comic book app. of each). Bugs Bunny story by Win Smith (early Mickey Mouse artist)	260.00	780.00	1560.00	2600.00

(Estimated up to 170 total copies exist, 8 in NM/Mint)

The Lone Ranger #54, © Lone Ranger

The Lone Ranger's Companion Tonto #27, © Lone Ranger

The Lone Rider #13, © SUPR

Looney Tunes and Merrie Melodies #38, © Warner Bros.

Lorna, The Jungle Girl #23, © MEG

Lost Worlds #6, © STD

	GD25	FN65	NM94
2 (11/41)	82.00	245.00	575.00
3-Kandi the Cave Kid begins by Walt Kelly; also in #4-6,8,11,15	68.00	205.00	475.00
4-Kelly-a	61.00	182.00	425.00
5-Bugs Bunny The Super-Duper Rabbit story (1st funny animal super hero, 3/42; also see Coo Coo); Kelly-a	49.00	145.00	340.00
6,8-Kelly-a	38.00	115.00	265.00
7,9,10: 9-Painted-c. 10-Flag-c	30.00	90.00	210.00
11,15-Kelly-a; 15-X-Mas-c	30.00	90.00	210.00
12-14,16-19	27.00	82.00	190.00
20-25: Pat, Patsy & Pete by Walt Kelly in all	27.00	82.00	190.00
26-30	19.00	57.00	130.00
31-40	14.00	43.00	100.00
41-50	11.00	32.00	75.00
51-60	7.50	22.50	45.00
61-80	4.70	14.00	28.00
81-99: 87-X-Mas-c	4.00	10.00	20.00
100	4.00	11.00	22.00
101-120	3.60	9.00	18.00
121-150	2.80	7.00	14.00
151-200: 159-X-Mas-c	2.00	5.00	10.00
201-246	1.40	3.50	7.00

LOONY SPORTS (Magazine)
Spring, 1975 (68 pages)
3-Strikes Publishing Co.

	GD25	FN65	NM94
1-Sports satire	.40	1.00	2.00

LOOY DOT DOPE (See Single Series No. 13)

LORD JIM (See Movie Comics)

LORDS OF THE ULTRA-REALM (DC)(Value: cover or less)

LORNA THE JUNGLE GIRL (...Jungle Queen #1-5)
July, 1953 - No. 26, Aug, 1957
Atlas Comics (NPI 1/OMC 2-11/NPI 12-26)

	GD25	FN65	NM94
1-Origin	16.00	48.00	110.00
2-Intro. & 1st app. Greg Knight	9.15	27.50	55.00
3-5	7.50	22.50	45.00
6-11: 11-Last pre-code (1/55)	5.85	17.50	35.00
12-17,19-26: 14-Colletta & Maneely-c	4.20	12.50	25.00
18-Williamson/Colleta-c	5.35	16.00	32.00

NOTE: ***Brodsky** c-1-3, 5, 9. **Everett** c-21, 23-26. **Heath** c-6, 7. **Maneely** c-12, 15. **Romita** a-20, 22, 24, 26. **Shores** a-14-16, 24, 26; c-11, 13, 16. **Tuska** a-6.*

LOSERS SPECIAL (DC)(Value: cover or less)

LOST CONTINENT (Eclipse)(Value: cover or less)

LOST IN SPACE (TV) (Space Family Robinson..., on Space Station One)
(Formerly Space Family Robinson; see Gold Key Champion)
No. 37, 10/73 - No. 54, 11/78; No. 55, 3/81 - No. 59, 5/82
Gold Key

	GD25	FN65	NM94
37-48	.70	1.75	3.50
49-59: Reprints-#49,50,55-59	.40	1.00	2.00

NOTE: ***Spiegle** a-37-59. All have painted-c.*

LOST IN SPACE
Aug, 1991 - No. 12, Jan, 1993 ($2.50, color, limited series)
Innovation Publishing

	GD25	FN65	NM94
1-12: Bill Mumy (Will Robinson) scripts in #1-9. 9-Perez-c	.50	1.25	2.50
1,2-Special Ed.; r/#1,2 plus new art & new-c	.50	1.25	2.50
Annual 1,2 (1991, 1992, $2.95, 48 pgs.)	.60	1.50	3.00

LOST PLANET (Eclipse)(Value: cover or less)

LOST WORLD, THE (See 4-Color #1145)

LOST WORLDS
No. 5, Oct, 1952 - No. 6, Dec, 1952
Standard Comics

	GD25	FN65	NM94
5-"Alice in Terrorland" by Toth; J. Katz-a	19.00	57.00	135.00
6-Toth-a	16.00	48.00	110.00

LOTS 'O' FUN COMICS
1940's? (5 cents) (heavy stock; blue covers)
Robert Allen Co.

nn-Contents can vary; Felix, Planet Comics known; contents would determine value. Similar to Up-To-Date Comics. Remainders - re-packaged.

LOU GEHRIG (See The Pride of the Yankees)

LOVE ADVENTURES (Actual Confessions #13)
Oct, 1949; No. 2, Jan, 1950; No. 3, Feb, 1951 - No. 12, Aug, 1952
Marvel (IPS)/Atlas Comics (MPI)

	GD25	FN65	NM94
1-Photo-c	8.35	25.00	50.00
2-Powell-a; Tyrone Power, Gene Tierney photo-c	8.35	25.00	50.00
3-8,10-12: 8-Robinson-a	4.00	11.00	22.00
9-Everett-a	4.35	13.00	26.00

LOVE AND MARRIAGE
March, 1952 - No. 16, Sept, 1954
Superior Comics Ltd.

	GD25	FN65	NM94
1	6.70	20.00	40.00
2	4.00	10.00	20.00
3-10	2.80	7.00	14.00
11-16	2.00	5.00	10.00
I.W. Reprint #1,2,8,11,14	.60	1.50	3.00
Super Reprint #10('63),15,17('64)	.60	1.50	3.00

NOTE: *All issues have **Kamenish** art.*

LOVE AND ROCKETS
July, 1982 - No. 34? (B&W, adults only)
Fantagraphics Books

	GD25	FN65	NM94
1-B&W-c ($2.95; small size, publ. by Hernandez Bros.)(800 printed)	7.50	22.50	45.00
1 (Fall, '82; color-c)	4.00	10.00	20.00
1-2nd & 3rd printing	.50	1.25	2.50
2	2.40	6.00	10.00
2-11,29-31: 2nd printings ($2.50)	.40	1.25	2.50
3-5	1.40	3.50	7.00
6-10	.80	2.00	4.00
11-39: 30($2.95, 52 pgs.). 31-on: $2.50-c	.50	1.25	2.50

LOVE AND ROMANCE
Sept, 1971 - No. 24, Sept, 1975
Charlton Comics

	GD25	FN65	NM94
1	.60	1.50	3.00
2-24		.50	1.00

LOVE AT FIRST SIGHT
Oct, 1949 - No. 42, Aug, 1956 (Photo-c: 21-42)
Ace Magazines (RAR Publ. Co./Periodical House)

	GD25	FN65	NM94
1-Painted-c	7.50	22.50	45.00
2-Painted-c	4.00	10.00	20.00
3-10: 4-Painted-c	2.80	7.00	14.00
11-20	2.00	5.00	10.00
21-33: 33-Last pre-code	1.60	4.00	8.00
34-42	1.20	3.00	6.00

LOVE BUG, THE (See Movie Comics)

LOVE CLASSICS
Nov, 1949 - No. 2, Feb, 1950 (Photo-c)
A Lover's Magazine/Marvel Comics

	GD25	FN65	NM94
1,2: 2-Virginia Mayo photo-c; 30 pg. story "I Was a Small Town Flirt"	7.50	22.50	45.00

LOVE CONFESSIONS
Oct, 1949 - No. 54, Dec, 1956 (Photo-c: 3,4,6,11-18,21)
Quality Comics Group

	GD25	FN65	NM94
1-Ward-c/a, 9 pgs; Gustavson-a	14.00	43.00	100.00
2-Gustavson-a	5.85	17.50	35.00
3	4.00	12.00	24.00
4-Crandall-a	5.35	16.00	32.00
5-Ward-a, 7 pgs.	6.35	19.00	38.00
6,7,9,11-13,15,16,18	2.00	6.00	12.00
8,10-Ward-a(2 stories in #10)	5.35	16.00	32.00
14,17,19,22-Ward-a; 17-Faith Domerque photo-c	4.70	14.00	28.00
20-Baker-a?, Ward-a(2)	5.35	16.00	32.00
21,23-28,30-38,40-42: Last precode, 4/55	1.60	4.00	8.00
29-Ward-a	4.20	12.50	25.00
39-Matt Baker-a	2.40	6.00	12.00
43,44,46-48,50-54: 47-Ward-c?	1.40	3.50	7.00
45-Ward-a	3.00	7.50	15.00
49-Baker-c/a	3.60	9.00	18.00

LOVE DIARY
July, 1949 - No. 48, Oct, 1955 (Photo-c: 1-24,27,29) (52 pgs. #1-11?)
Our Publishing Co./Toytown/Patches

	GD25	FN65	NM94
1-Krigstein-a	10.00	30.00	60.00
2,3-Krigstein & Mort Leav-a in each	6.70	20.00	40.00
4-8	3.20	8.00	16.00
9,10-Everett-a	4.00	10.00	20.00
11-20: 16,20-Mort Leav-a	2.40	6.00	12.00
21-30,32-48: 45-Leav-a. 47-Last precode(12/54)	1.80	4.50	9.00
31-John Buscema headlights-c	2.40	6.00	12.00

LOVE DIARY (Diary Loves #2 on)
September, 1949
Quality Comics Group

	GD25	FN65	NM94
1-Ward-c/a, 9 pgs.	13.00	40.00	90.00

LOVE DIARY
July, 1958 - No. 102, Dec, 1976
Charlton Comics

	GD25	FN65	NM94
1	4.20	12.50	25.00
2	2.40	6.00	12.00
3-5,7-10: 10-Photo-c	1.60	4.00	8.00
6-Torres-a	2.40	6.00	12.00
11-20: 20-Photo-c	1.00	2.50	5.00
21-40	.60	1.50	3.00
41-60	.40	1.00	2.00
61-102		.50	1.00

LOVE DOCTOR (See Dr. Anthony King...)

LOVE DRAMAS (True Secrets No. 3 on?)
Oct, 1949 - No. 2, Jan, 1950
Marvel Comics (IPS)

	GD25	FN65	NM94
1-Jack Kamen-a; photo-c	10.00	30.00	65.00
2	6.70	20.00	40.00

LOVE EXPERIENCES (Challenge of the Unknown No. 6)
Oct, 1949 - No. 5, June, 1950; No. 6, Apr, 1951 - No. 38, June, 1956
Ace Periodicals (A.A. Wyn/Periodical House)

	GD25	FN65	NM94
1-Painted-c	5.85	17.50	35.00
2	3.60	9.00	18.00
3-5: 5-Painted-c	2.40	6.00	12.00
6-10	2.00	5.00	10.00
11-30: 30-Last pre-code (2/55)	1.60	4.00	8.00
31-38: 38-Indicia date-6/56; c-date-8/56	1.40	3.50	7.00

NOTE: *Anne Brewster a-15. Photo c-4, 15-35, 38.*

LOVE JOURNAL
No. 10, Oct, 1951 - No. 25, July, 1954
Our Publishing Co.

	GD25	FN65	NM94
10	5.00	15.00	30.00
11-25: 19-Mort Leav-a	3.20	8.00	16.00

LOVELAND
Nov, 1949 - No. 2, Feb, 1950 (52 pgs.)
Mutual Mag./Eye Publ. (Marvel)

	GD25	FN65	NM94
1,2-Photo-c	5.35	16.00	32.00

LOVE LESSONS
Oct, 1949 - No. 5, June, 1950
Harvey Comics/Key Publ. No. 5

	GD25	FN65	NM94
1-Metallic silver-c printed over the cancelled covers of Love Letters #1; indicia title is "Love Letters"	6.70	20.00	40.00
2-Powell-a; photo-c	3.20	8.00	16.00
3-5: 3-Photo-c	2.80	7.00	14.00

LOVE LETTERS (10/49, Harvey; advertised but never published; covers were printed before cancellation and were used as the cover to Love Lessions #1)

LOVE LETTERS (Love Secrets No. 32 on)
11/49 - #6, 9/50; #7, 3/51 - #31, 6/53; #32, 2/54 - #51, 12/56
Quality Comics Group

	GD25	FN65	NM94
1-Ward-c, Gustavson-a	11.00	32.00	75.00
2-Ward-c, Gustavson-a	10.00	30.00	60.00
3-Gustavson-a	6.70	20.00	40.00
4-Ward-a, 9 pgs.	10.00	30.00	60.00
5-8,10	2.80	7.00	14.00
9-One pg. Ward-"Be Popular with the Opposite Sex"; Robert Mitchum photo-c	4.00	12.00	24.00
11-Ward-r/Broadway Romances #2 & retitled	4.00	12.00	24.00
12-15,18-20	2.00	5.00	10.00
16,17-Ward-a; 16-Anthony Quinn photo-c. 17-Jane Russell photo-c	5.85	17.50	35.00
21-29	1.80	4.50	9.00
30,31(6/53)-Ward-a	4.00	10.00	20.00
32(2/54) - 39: 39-Last precode (4/55)	1.60	4.00	8.00
40-48	1.20	3.00	6.00
49,50-Baker-a	3.60	9.00	18.00
51-Baker-c	3.00	7.50	15.00

NOTE: *Photo-c on most 3-28.*

LOVE LIFE
Nov, 1951
P. L. Publishing Co.

	GD25	FN65	NM94
1	4.70	14.00	28.00

LOVELORN (Confessions of the Lovelorn #52 on)
Aug-Sept, 1949 - No. 51, July, 1954 (No. 1-26, 52 pgs.)
American Comics Group (Michel Publ./Regis Publ.)

	GD25	FN65	NM94
1	8.35	25.00	50.00
2	4.20	12.50	25.00
3-10	3.60	9.00	18.00
11-20,22-48: 18-Drucker-a(2pgs.). 46-Lazarus-a	2.40	6.00	12.00
21-Prostitution story	4.00	11.00	22.00
49-51-Has 3-D effect	10.00	30.00	65.00

LOVE MEMORIES
1949 (no month) - No. 4, July, 1950 (All photo-c)
Fawcett Publications

	GD25	FN65	NM94
1	6.35	19.00	38.00
2-4	4.00	11.00	22.00

LOVE MYSTERY
June, 1950 - No. 3, Oct, 1950 (All photo-c)
Fawcett Publications

	GD25	FN65	NM94
1-George Evans-a	12.00	36.00	85.00
2,3-Evans-a. 3-Powell-a	10.00	30.00	65.00

LOVE PROBLEMS (See Fox Giants)

LOVE PROBLEMS AND ADVICE ILLUSTRATED (Becomes Romance

Love Diary #21, © Our Publ.

Love Letters #22, © QUA

Lovelorn #26, © ACG

Love Romances #36, © MEG

Love Scandals #4, © QUA

Love Tales #36, © MEG

Stories of True Love No. 45 on)
June, 1949 - No. 6, Apr, 1950; No. 7, Jan, 1951 - No. 44, Mar, 1957
McCombs/Harvey Publ./Home Comics

	GD25	FN65	NM94
V1#1	7.50	22.50	45.00
2	4.00	11.00	22.00
3-10: 9-Elias-c	3.20	8.00	16.00
11-13,15-23,25-31: 31-Last pre-code (1/55)	2.00	5.00	10.00
14,24-Rape scene	2.40	6.00	12.00
32-37,39-44	1.60	4.00	8.00
38-S&K-c	4.00	10.00	20.00

NOTE: ***Powell** a-1, 2, 7-14, 17-25, 28, 29, 33, 40, 41. #3 has True Love... on inside.*

LOVE ROMANCES (Formerly Ideal #5?)
No. 6, May, 1949 - No. 106, July, 1963
Timely/Marvel/Atlas(TCI No. 7-71/Male No. 72-106)

	GD25	FN65	NM94
6-Photo-c	6.70	20.00	40.00
7-Photo-c; Kamen-a	4.70	14.00	28.00
8-Kubert-a; photo-c	5.00	15.00	30.00
9-20: 9-12-Photo-c	3.60	9.00	18.00
21,24-Krigstein-a	5.00	15.00	30.00
22,23,25-35,37,39,40	2.80	7.00	14.00
36,38-Krigstein-a	4.35	13.00	26.00
41-44,46,47: Last precode (2/55)	2.80	7.00	14.00
45,57-Matt Baker-a	3.20	8.00	16.00
48,50-52,54-56,58-74	2.00	5.00	10.00
49,53-Toth-a, 6 & ? pgs.	4.70	14.00	28.00
75,77,82-Matt Baker-a	2.80	7.00	14.00
76,78-81,84,86-95: Last 10 cent issue?	2.00	5.00	10.00
83-Kirby-c, Severin-a	3.60	9.00	18.00
85,96-Kirby-c/a	4.00	10.00	20.00
97,100-104	1.80	4.50	9.00
98-Kirby-a(4)	5.00	15.00	30.00
99,105,106-Kirby-a	3.60	9.00	18.00

NOTE: ***Anne Brewster** a-67, 72. **Colletta** a-37, 40, 42, 44, 67(2); c-42, 44, 49, 80. **Everett** c-70. **Heath** a-87. **Kirby** c-80, 85, 88. **Robinson** a-29.*

LOVERS (Formerly Blonde Phantom)
No. 23, May, 1949 - No. 86, Aug?, 1957
Marvel Comics No. 23,24/Atlas No. 25 on (ANC)

	GD25	FN65	NM94
23-Photo-c	6.70	20.00	40.00
24-Tothish plus Robinson-a; photo-c	4.00	10.00	20.00
25,30-Kubert-a; 7, 10 pgs.	4.35	13.00	26.00
26-29,31-36,39,40: 26-28-Photo-c	2.80	7.00	14.00
37,38-Krigstein-a	5.00	15.00	30.00
41-Everett-a(2)	4.00	10.00	20.00
42,44-65: 65-Last pre-code (1/55)	2.40	6.00	12.00
43-Frazetta 1 pg. ad	2.40	6.00	12.00
66,68-86	2.00	5.00	10.00
67-Toth-a	4.20	12.50	25.00

NOTE: ***Anne Brewster** a-86. **Colletta** a-54, 59, 62, 64, 65, 69, 85; c-61, 64, 65, 75. **Heath** a-61. **Powell** a-27, 30. **Robinson** a-54, 56.*

LOVERS' LANE
Oct, 1949 - No. 41, June, 1954 (No. 1-18: 52 pgs.)
Lev Gleason Publications

	GD25	FN65	NM94
1-Biro-c	5.85	17.50	35.00
2	3.60	9.00	18.00
3-20: 20-Frazetta 1 pg. ad	2.40	6.00	12.00
21-38,40,41	1.40	3.50	7.00
39-Story narrated by Frank Sinatra	3.60	9.00	18.00

NOTE: ***Briefer** a-6, 21. **Fuje** a-4, 16; c-many. **Guardineer** a-1. **Kinstler** c-41. **Tuska** a-6. Painted c-2-18. Photo c-19-22, 26-28.*

LOVE SCANDALS
Feb, 1950 - No. 5, Oct, 1950 (Photo-c #2-5) (All 52 pgs.)
Quality Comics Group

	GD25	FN65	NM94
1-Ward-c/a, 9 pgs.	12.00	36.00	85.00
2,3: 2-Gustavson-a	5.00	15.00	30.00
4-Ward-a, 18 pgs; Gil Fox-a	10.00	30.00	70.00
5-C. Cuidera-a; tomboy story 'I Hated Being a Woman'	4.70	14.00	28.00

LOVE SECRETS (Formerly Love Letters #31)
No. 32, Aug, 1953 - No. 56, Dec, 1956
Quality Comics Group

	GD25	FN65	NM94
32	4.70	14.00	28.00
33,35-39	2.80	7.00	14.00
34-Ward-a	4.70	14.00	28.00
40-Matt Baker-c	4.00	10.00	20.00
41-43: 43-Last precode (3/55)	2.00	5.00	10.00
44,47-50,53,54	1.60	4.00	8.00
45,46-Ward-a. 46-Baker-a	4.00	11.00	22.00
51,52-Ward(r). 52-r/Love Confessions #17	2.80	7.00	14.00
55,56-Baker-a. 56-Baker-c	2.80	7.00	14.00

LOVE SECRETS
Oct, 1949 - No. 2, Jan, 1950 (52 pgs., photo-c)
Marvel Comics(IPC)

	GD25	FN65	NM94
1	6.70	20.00	40.00
2	5.00	15.00	30.00

LOVE STORIES (Formerly My Love Affair #5)
No. 6, 1950 - No. 12, 1951
Fox Feature Syndicate

	GD25	FN65	NM94
6,8-Wood-a	11.00	32.00	75.00
7,9-12	5.00	15.00	30.00

LOVE STORIES (Formerly Heart Throbs)
No. 147, Nov, 1972 - No. 152, Oct-Nov, 1973
National Periodical Publications

	GD25	FN65	NM94
147-152	.80	2.00	4.00

LOVE STORIES OF MARY WORTH (See Harvey Comics Hits #55 & Mary Worth)
Sept, 1949 - No. 5, May, 1950
Harvey Publications

	GD25	FN65	NM94
1-1940's newspaper reprints-#1-4	4.00	12.00	24.00
2	3.60	9.00	18.00
3-5: 3-Kamen/Baker-a?	3.20	8.00	16.00

LOVE TALES (Formerly The Human Torch #35)
No. 36, 5/49 - No. 58, 8/52; No. 59, date? - No. 75, Sept, 1957
Marvel/Atlas Comics (ZPC No. 36-50/MMC No. 67-75)

	GD25	FN65	NM94
36-Photo-c	6.70	20.00	40.00
37	4.20	12.50	25.00
38-44,46-50: 39-41-Photo-c	3.00	7.50	15.00
45-Powell-a	3.20	8.00	16.00
51,69-Everett-a	4.00	10.00	20.00
52-Krigstein-a	4.00	11.00	22.00
53-60: 60-Last pre-code (2/55)	1.80	4.50	9.00
61-68,70-75	1.40	3.50	7.00

LOVE THRILLS (See Fox Giants)

LOVE TRAILS
Dec, 1949 - No. 2, Mar, 1950 (52 pgs.)
A Lover's Magazine (CDS)(Marvel)

	GD25	FN65	NM94
1,2: 1-Photo-c	5.85	17.50	35.00

LOWELL THOMAS' HIGH ADVENTURE (See 4-Color #949, 1001)

LT. (See Lieutenant)

LUCKY COMICS
Jan, 1944; No. 2, Summer, 1945 - No. 5, Summer, 1946
Consolidated Magazines

	GD25	FN65	NM94
1-Lucky Starr, Bobbie	10.00	30.00	65.00
2-5	5.85	17.50	35.00

LUCKY DUCK
No. 5, Jan, 1953 - No. 8, Sept, 1953
Standard Comics (Literary Ent.)

	GD25	FN65	NM94
5-Irving Spector-a	5.85	17.50	35.00
6-8-Irving Spector-a	4.20	12.50	25.00

LUCKY FIGHTS IT THROUGH (Also see The K. O. Punch)
1949 (16 pgs. in color; paper cover) (Giveaway)
Educational Comics

	GD25	FN65	NM94
nn-(Very Rare)-1st Kurtzman work for E. C.; V.D. prevention	142.00	425.00	1000.00

(Prices vary widely on this book)

NOTE: *Subtitled "The Story of That Ignorant, Ignorant Cowboy." Prepared for Communications Materials Center, Columbia University.*

LUCKY "7" COMICS
1944 (No date listed)
Howard Publishers Ltd.

	GD25	FN65	NM94
1-Congo Raider, Punch Powers; bondage-c	18.00	55.00	110.00

LUCKY STAR (Western)
1950 - No. 7, 1951; No. 8, 1953 - No. 14, 1955 (5x7-1/4"; full color, 5 cents)
Nation Wide Publ. Co.

	GD25	FN65	NM94
nn (#1)-(52 pgs.)-Davis-a	8.35	25.00	50.00
2,3-(52 pgs.)-Davis-a	5.85	17.50	35.00
4-7-(52 pgs.)-Davis-a	4.70	14.00	28.00
8-14-(36 pgs.)	3.60	9.00	18.00
Given away with Lucky Star Western Wear by the Juvenile Mfg. Co.	3.60	9.00	18.00

LUCY SHOW, THE (TV) (Also see I Love Lucy)
June, 1963 - No. 5, June, 1964 (Photo-c: 1,2)
Gold Key

	GD25	FN65	NM94
1	10.00	30.00	65.00
2	7.50	22.50	45.00
3-5: Photo back c-1,2,4,5	6.70	20.00	40.00

LUCY, THE REAL GONE GAL (Meet Miss Pepper #5 on)
June, 1953 - No. 4, Dec, 1953
St. John Publishing Co.

	GD25	FN65	NM94
1-Negligee panels	7.50	22.50	45.00
2	4.20	12.50	25.00
3,4: 3-Drucker-a	4.00	10.00	20.00

LUDWIG BEMELMAN'S MADELEINE & GENEVIEVE (See 4-Color #796)

LUDWIG VON DRAKE (TV)(Disney)(See Walt Disney's C&S #256)
Nov-Dec, 1961 - No. 4, June-Aug, 1962
Dell Publishing Co.

	GD25	FN65	NM94
1	4.00	10.00	20.00
2-4	2.40	6.00	12.00
...Fish Stampede (1962, Fritos giveaway)-16 pgs., 3-1/4x7", soft-c; also see Donald Duck & Mickey Mouse	3.60	9.00	18.00

LUGER (Eclipse)(Value: cover or less)

LUKE CAGE (See Cage & Hero for Hire)

LUKE SHORT'S WESTERN STORIES
No. 580, Aug, 1954 - No. 927, Aug, 1958
Dell Publishing Co.

	GD25	FN65	NM94
4-Color 580(8/54)	4.00	10.00	20.00
4-Color 651(9/55)-Kinstler-a	4.00	12.00	24.00
4-Color 739,771,807,875,927	4.00	10.00	20.00
4-Color 848	5.00	15.00	30.00

LUNATIC FRINGE, THE (Innovation)(Value: cover or less)

LUNATICKLE (Magazine) (Satire)
Feb, 1956 - No. 2, Apr, 1956
Whitstone Publ.

	GD25	FN65	NM94
1,2-Kubert-a	2.40	6.00	12.00

LYNDON B. JOHNSON
March, 1965
Dell Publishing Co.

	GD25	FN65	NM94
12-445-503-Photo-c	2.40	6.00	12.00

M (Eclipse)(Value: cover or less)

MACHINE MAN (Also see 2001, A Space Odyssey)
Apr, 1978 - No. 9, Dec, 1978; No. 10, Aug, 1979 - No. 19, Feb, 1981
Marvel Comics Group

	GD25	FN65	NM94
1	.60	1.50	3.00
2-17	.30	.75	1.50
18-Wendigo, Alpha Flight-ties into X-Men #140	1.00	2.50	5.00
19-1st app. Jack O'Lantern (Macendale, who later becomes 2nd Hobgoblin)	3.00	7.50	15.00

NOTE: ***Austin** c-7i, 19i. **Buckler** c-17p, 18p. **Byrne** c-14p. **Ditko** a-10-19; c-10-13, 14i, 15, 16. **Kirby** a-1-9p; c-1-5, 7-9p. **Layton** c-7i. **Miller** c-19p. **Simonson** c-6.*

MACHINE MAN
Oct, 1984 - No. 4, Jan, 1985 (Limited-series)
Marvel Comics Group

	GD25	FN65	NM94
1-Barry Smith-c/a(p) in all	.30	.75	1.50
2-4		.60	1.20

MACKENZIE'S RAIDERS (See 4-Color #1093)

MACO TOYS COMIC
1959 (36 pages; full color) (Giveaway)
Maco Toys/Charlton Comics

	GD25	FN65	NM94
1-All military stories featuring Maco Toys	1.20	3.00	6.00

MACROSS (Becomes Robotech: The Macross Saga #2 on)
Dec, 1984 ($1.50)
Comico

	GD25	FN65	NM94
1	1.60	4.00	8.00

MACROSS II
1992 - No. 10, 1993 ($2.75, B&W, limited series)
Viz Select Comics

	GD25	FN65	NM94
1-10: Based on video series	.55	1.40	2.75

MAD
Oct-Nov, 1952 - Present (No. 24 on are magazine format)
(Kurtzman editor No. 1-28, Feldstein No. 29 - No. ?)
E. C. Comics

	GD25	FN65	NM94
1-Wood, Davis, Elder start as regulars	285.00	860.00	2000.00
2-Dick Tracy cameo	75.00	225.00	525.00
3,4: 3-Stan Lee mentioned. 4-Reefer mention story "Flob Was a Slob" by Davis; Superman parody	48.00	145.00	335.00
5-Low distr.; W.M. Gaines biog.	82.00	245.00	575.00
6-11: 6-Popeye cameo. 11-Wolverton-a	34.00	103.00	240.00
12-15	29.00	85.00	200.00
16-23(5/55): 18-Alice in Wonderland by Jack Davis. 21-1st app. Alfred E. Neuman on-c in fake ad. 22-All by Elder. 23-Special cancel announcement	22.00	65.00	150.00
24(7/55)-1st magazine issue (25 cents); Kurtzman logo & border on-c; 1st "What? Me Worry?" on-c; 2nd printing exists	50.00	150.00	350.00
25-Jaffee starts as regular writer	22.00	65.00	150.00
26,27: 27-Jaffee starts as story artist; new logo	18.00	54.00	125.00
28-Last issue edited by Kurtzman; (three cover variations exist with different wording on contents banner on lower right of cover; value of each the same)	17.00	50.00	115.00
29-Kamen-a; Don Martin starts as regular; Feldstein editing begins	17.00	50.00	115.00
30-1st A. E. Neuman cover by Mingo; last Elder-a; Bob Clarke starts as regular; Disneyland spoof	23.00	70.00	160.00
31-Freas starts as regular; last Davis-a until #99	13.00	40.00	90.00

The Lucy Show #2, © Desilu

Lucy The Real Gone Gal #1, © STJ

Mad #15, © WMG

Mad #289, © WMG

Madballs #1, © MEG

Madhouse #4 (1954), © AJAX

	GD25	FN65	NM94
32,33: 32-Orlando, Drucker, Woodbridge start as regulars; Wood back-c. 33-Orlando back-c	11.50	34.00	80.00
34-Berg starts as regular	10.00	30.00	70.00
35-Mingo wraparound-c; Crandall-a	10.00	30.00	70.00
36-40	8.35	25.00	50.00
41-50	5.85	17.50	35.00
51-60: 60-Two Clarke-c; Prohias starts as reg.	5.00	15.00	30.00
61-70: 64-Rickard starts as regular. 68-Martin-c	4.00	11.00	22.00
71-80: 76-Aragones starts as regular	3.60	9.00	18.00
81-90: 86-1st Fold-in. 89-One strip by Walt Kelly. 90-Frazetta back-c; Beatles app.	3.20	8.00	16.00
91-100: 91-Jaffee starts as story artist. 99-Davis-a resumes	2.80	7.00	14.00
101-120: 101-Infinity-c. 105-Batman TV show take-off. 106-Frazetta back-c	2.40	6.00	12.00
121-140: 121-Beatles app. 122-Ronald Reagan photo inside; Drucker & Mingo-c. 128-Last Orlando. 130-Torres begins as reg. 131-Reagan photo back-c. 135,139-Davis-c	1.60	4.00	8.00
141-170: 165-Martin-c. 169-Drucker-c	1.20	3.00	6.00
171-200: 182-Bob Jones starts as regular. 186-Star Trek take-off. 187-Harry North starts as regular. 196-Star Wars take-off	1.00	2.50	5.00
201-320: 203-Star Wars take-off. 204-Hulk TV show take-off. 208-Superman movie take-off. 245- Last Rikard-a. 274-Last Martin-a. 284-Roger Rabbit-c/story. 289-Batman movie parody. 291-TMNT-c only. 299-Simpson's-c/story. 306-TMNT III movie parody. 308-Terminator parody. 311-Addams Family-c/story. 314-Batman Returns-c/story	.35	.90	1.75
300-303 (1/91-6/91)-Special Hussein Asylum Editions; only distributed to the troops in the Middle East	.50	1.25	2.50

NOTE: ***Aragones*** *c-210, 293.* ***Davis*** *c-2, 27, 135, 139, 173, 178, 212, 213, 219, 246, 260, 296, 308.* ***Drucker*** *c-122, 169, 176, 225, 234, 264, 266, 274, 280, 285, 297, 299, 303, 314, 315.* ***Elder*** *c-5, 259, 261, 268.* ***Jules Feiffer*** *a(r)-42.* ***Freas*** *c-39-59, 62-67, 69-70, 72, 74.* ***Heath*** *a-14, 27.* ***Jaffee*** *c-199, 217, 224, 258.* ***Kamen*** *a-29.* ***Krigstein*** *a-12, 17, 24, 26.* ***Kurtzman*** *c-1, 3, 4, 6-10, 13, 16, 18.* ***Martin*** *c-68, 165, 229.* ***Mingo*** *c-30-37, 61, 71, 75-80, 82-114, 117-124, 126, 129, 131, 133, 134, 136, 140, 143-148, 150-162, 164, 166-168, 171, 172, 174, 175, 177, 179, 181, 183, 185, 198, 206, 209, 211, 214, 218, 221, 222, 300.* ***John Severin*** *a-1-6, 9, 10.* ***Wolverton*** *c-11; a-11, 17, 29, 31, 36, 40, 82, 137.* ***Wood*** *a-24-45, 59; c-26, 28, 29.* ***Woodbridge*** *a-43.*

MAD (See ...Follies, ...Special, More Trash from..., and The Worst from...)

MAD ABOUT MILLIE (Also see Millie the Model)
April, 1969 - No. 17, Dec, 1970
Marvel Comics Group

	GD25	FN65	NM94
1-Giant issue	4.20	12.50	25.00
2-17: 16,17-r	2.40	6.00	12.00
Annual 1(11/71)	1.80	4.50	9.00

MADAME XANADU (DC)(Value: cover or less)

MADBALLS
Sept, 1986 - No. 3, Nov, 1986; No. 4, June, 1987 - No. 10, June, 1988
Star Comics/Marvel Comics #9 on

	GD25	FN65	NM94
1-10: Based on toys. 9-Post-a		.50	1.00

MAD DISCO
1980 (One shot)(36 pgs.)
E.C. Comics

	GD25	FN65	NM94
1-Includes 30 minute flexi-disc of Mad disco music	.40	1.00	2.00

MAD DOGS
Feb, 1992 - No. 3, July, 1992 ($2.50, B&W, mini-series)
Eclipse Comics

	GD25	FN65	NM94
1-3	.50	1.25	2.50

MAD 84 (Mad Extra)
1984 (84 pgs.)
E.C. Comics

	GD25	FN65	NM94
1	.40	1.00	2.00

MAD FOLLIES (Special)
1963 - No. 7, 1969
E. C. Comics

	GD25	FN65	NM94
nn(1963)-Paperback book covers	16.00	48.00	110.00
2(1964)-Calendar	10.00	30.00	70.00
3(1965)-Mischief Stickers	8.35	25.00	50.00
4(1966)-Mobile; Frazetta-r/back-c Mad #90	10.00	30.00	60.00
5(1967)-Stencils	6.70	20.00	40.00
6(1968)-Mischief Stickers	5.00	15.00	30.00
7(1969)-Nasty Cards	5.00	15.00	30.00

NOTE: ***Clarke*** *c-4.* ***Frazetta*** *r-4, 6 (1 pg. ea.).* ***Mingo*** *c-1-3.* ***Orlando*** *a-5.*

MAD HATTER, THE (Costume Hero)
Jan-Feb, 1946; No. 2, Sept-Oct, 1946
O. W. Comics Corp.

	GD25	FN65	NM94
1-Freddy the Firefly begins; Giunta-c/a	35.00	105.00	210.00
2-Has ad for E.C.'s Animal Fables #1	23.00	70.00	140.00

MADHOUSE
3-4/54 - No. 4, 9-10/54; 6/57 - No. 4, Dec?, 1957
Ajax/Farrell Publ. (Excellent Publ./4-Star)

	GD25	FN65	NM94
1(1954)	14.00	43.00	100.00
2,3	8.35	25.00	50.00
4-Surrealistic-c	12.00	36.00	85.00
1(1957, 2nd series)	5.85	17.50	35.00
2-4	4.70	14.00	28.00

MAD HOUSE (Formerly Madhouse Glads; ...Comics #104? on)
No. 95, 9/74 - No. 97, 1/75; No. 98, 8/75 - No. 130, 10/82
Red Circle Productions/Archie Publications

	GD25	FN65	NM94
95,96-Horror stories through #97	.40	1.00	2.00
97-Intro. Henry Hobson; Morrow, Thorne-a		.50	1.00
98-130-Satire/humor stories		.50	1.00
Annual 8(1970-71)- 12(1974-75)-Formerly Madhouse Ma-ad Annual. 11-Wood-a(r)	.30	.75	1.50
...Comics Digest 1('75-76)- 8(8/82)(...Mag. #5 on)	.40	1.00	2.00

NOTE: ***B. Jones*** *a-96.* ***McWilliams*** *a-97.* ***Morrow*** *a-96; c-95-97.* ***Wildey*** *a-95, 96. See Archie Comics Digest #1, 13.*

MADHOUSE GLADS (Formerly ...Ma-ad; Madhouse #95 on)
No. 73, May, 1970 - No. 94, Aug, 1974 (No. 78-92: 52 pgs.)
Archie Publications

	GD25	FN65	NM94
73	.80	2.00	4.00
74-94	.60	1.50	3.00

MADHOUSE MA-AD(...Jokes #67-70; ...Freak-Out #71-74)
(Formerly Archie's Madhouse) (Becomes Madhouse Glads #75 on)
No. 67, April, 1969 - No. 72, Jan, 1970
Archie Publications

	GD25	FN65	NM94
67-72	.80	2.00	4.00
...Annual 7(1969-70)-Formerly Archie's Madhouse Annual; becomes Madhouse Annual	.80	2.00	4.00

MADMAN
Mar, 1992 - No. 3, 1992 ($3.95, duotone, high quality, 52 pgs.)
Tundra Publishing

	GD25	FN65	NM94
1-3	.80	2.00	4.00

MAD MONSTER PARTY (See Movie Classics)

MAD SPECIAL (...Super Special)
Fall, 1970 - Present (84 - 116 pages)
E. C. Publications, Inc.

	GD25	FN65	NM94
Fall 1970(#1)-Bonus-Voodoo Doll; contains 17 pgs. new material	6.70	20.00	40.00
Spring 1971(#2)-Wall Nuts; 17 pgs. new material	4.20	12.50	25.00
3-Protest Stickers	4.20	12.50	25.00

4-8: 4-Mini Posters. 5-Mad Flag. 6-Mad Mischief Stickers. 7-Presidential

candidate posters, Wild Shocking Message posters. 8-TV Guise
 3.60 9.00 18.00
9(1972)-Contains Nostalgic Mad #1 (28pp) 3.00 7.50 15.00
10,11,13: 10-Nonsense Stickers (Don Martin). 11-33-1/3 RPM record. 13-Sickie Stickers; 3 pgs. new Wolverton 3.00 7.50 15.00
12-Contains Nostalgic Mad #2 (36 pgs.); Davis, Wolverton-a
 3.00 7.50 15.00
14-Vital Message posters & Art Depreciation paintings
 2.00 5.00 10.00
15-Contains Nostalgic Mad #3 (28 pgs.) 2.40 6.00 12.00
16,17,19,20: 16-Mad-hesive Stickers. 17-Don Martin posters. 20-Martin Stickers 1.80 4.50 9.00
18-Contains Nostalgic Mad #4 (36 pgs.) 2.00 5.00 10.00
21,24-Contains Nostalgic Mad #5 (28 pgs.) & #6 (28 pgs.)
 2.00 5.00 10.00
22,23,25-27,29,30: 22-Diplomas. 23-Martin Stickers. 25-Martin Posters. 26-33-1/3 RPM record. 27-Mad Shock-Sticks. 29-Mad Collectable-Correctables Posters. 30-The Movies 1.00 2.50 5.00
28-Contains Nostalgic Mad #7 (36 pgs.) 1.20 3.00 6.00
31,33-60: 36-Has 96 pgs. of comic book & comic strip spoofs: titles "The Comics" on-c 1.00 2.50 5.00
32-Contains Nostalgic Mad #8 1.40 3.50 7.00
61-90: 71-Batman parodies-r by Wood, Drucker. 83-All Star Trek spoof issue
 .70 1.75 3.50
76-(Fall, 1991)-Special Hussein Asylum Edition; distributed only to the troops in the Middle East 1.00 2.50 5.00

NOTE: *#28-30 have no number on cover.* ***Freas*** *c-76.* ***Mingo*** *c-9, 11, 15, 19, 23.*

MAGE (The Hero Discovered...; also see Grendel #16)
Feb, 1984 (no month) - #15, Dec, 1986 ($1.50, Mando paper)
Comico

1-Violence; Comico's 1st color comic 1.40 3.50 7.00
2 1.00 2.50 5.00
3-5: 3-Intro Edsel .60 1.50 3.00
6-Grendel begins (1st in color) 2.80 7.00 14.00
7-1st new Grendel story 1.60 4.00 8.00
8-14: 13-Grendel dies. 14-Grendel ends .50 1.25 2.50
15-$2.95, Double size w/pullout poster .60 1.50 3.00

MAGGOTS (Hamilton) (Value: cover or less)

MAGIC AGENT (See Forbidden Worlds & Unknown Worlds)
Jan-Feb, 1962 - No. 3, May-June, 1962
American Comics Group

1-Origin & 1st app. John Force 3.20 8.00 16.00
2,3 2.00 5.00 10.00

MAGIC COMICS
Aug, 1939 - No. 123, Nov-Dec, 1949
David McKay Publications

1-Mandrake the Magician, Henry, Popeye (not by Segar), Blondie, Barney Baxter, Secret Agent X-9 (not by Raymond), Bunky by Billy DeBeck & Thornton Burgess text stories illustrated by Harrison Cady begin
 133.00 400.00 800.00
2 63.00 188.00 375.00
3 47.00 140.00 280.00
4 40.00 120.00 240.00
5 33.00 100.00 200.00
6-10 27.00 80.00 160.00
11-16,18-20 22.00 65.00 130.00
17-The Lone Ranger begins 23.00 70.00 140.00
21-30 15.00 45.00 90.00
31-40 12.00 35.00 70.00
41-50 9.15 27.50 55.00
51-60 7.50 22.50 45.00
61-70 5.35 16.00 32.00
71-99 4.35 13.00 26.00
100 5.35 16.00 32.00
101-106,109-123 4.00 11.00 22.00
107,108-Flash Gordon app; not by Raymond 4.70 14.00 28.00

MAGICA DE SPELL (See Walt Disney Showcase #30)

MAGIC FLUTE, THE (See Night Music #9-11)

MAGIC OF CHRISTMAS AT NEWBERRYS, THE
1967 (20 pgs.; slick cover; B&W inside)
E. S. London (Giveaway)

nn .60 1.50 3.00

MAGIC SWORD, THE (See Movie Classics)

MAGIK (Illyana and Storm Limited Series)
Dec, 1983 - No. 4, Mar, 1984 (60 cents, mini-series)
Marvel Comics Group

1-Characters from X-Men; Inferno begins; X-Men cameo (Buscema pencils 1,2; c-1p .50 1.25 2.50
2-4: 2-Nightcrawler app. & X-Men cameo .40 1.00 2.00

MAGILLA GORILLA (TV) (See Kite Fun Book)
May, 1964 - No. 10, Dec, 1968 (Hanna-Barbera)
Gold Key

1 5.85 17.50 35.00
2-10: 3-Vs. Yogi Bear for President 4.00 10.00 20.00

MAGILLA GORILLA (TV) (See Spotlight #4)
Nov, 1970 - No. 5, July, 1971 (Hanna-Barbera)
Charlton Comics

1 3.60 9.00 18.00
2-5 2.40 6.00 12.00

MAGNUS (...Robot Fighter) (Also see Vintage Magnus)
May, 1991 - Present ($1.75/$1.95/$2.25, color, high quality paper)
Valiant Comics

1-Nichols/Layton-c/a; 1-8 have trading cards 5.85 17.50 35.00
2 3.60 9.00 18.00
3,4 2.40 6.00 12.00
5-1st app. Rai (10/91); 5-8 are in flip book format and back-c & half of book are Rai #1-4 mini-series 3.60 9.00 18.00
6-Rai is Valiant's 1st original character 1.40 3.50 7.00
7,8: Rai #2-4 on flip side. 8-Begin $1.95-c 2.00 5.00 10.00
0-Origin issue; Layton-a; ordered through mail w/coupons from 1st 8 issues plus 50 cents; B. Smith trading card 14.00 43.00 100.00
0-Sold thru comic shops without trading card 8.35 25.00 50.00
9-11: 11-Last $1.95-c 1.00 2.50 5.00
12-($3.25, 44pgs.)-Turok-c/story (1st app. in Valiant universe, 5/92); has 8 pg. Magnus story insert 8.35 25.00 50.00
13-20,22-24,26: 15,16-Unity x-overs. 15-Miller-c. 16-Birth of Magnus; 24-Story cont'd in Rai & the Future Force #9 .45 1.15 2.25
21-New direction & new logo; Reese inks 1.00 2.50 5.00
21-(Gold) 6.70 20.00 40.00
25-($2.95)-Embossed silver foil-c; new costume .60 1.50 3.00

NOTE: ***Ditko/Reese*** *a-18.* ***Layton*** *a(i)-5; c(i)-6-9; back(i)-5-8.* ***Simonson*** *c-16.*

MAGNUS, ROBOT FIGHTER (...4000 A.D.) (See Doctor Solar)
Feb, 1963 - No. 46, Jan, 1977 (Painted covers)
Gold Key

1-Origin & 1st app. Magnus; Aliens (1st app.) series begins
 29.00 85.00 200.00
2,3 13.50 41.00 95.00
4-10: 10-Simonson fan club illo (5/65, 1st-a?) 10.00 30.00 60.00
11-20 6.70 20.00 40.00
21,24-28: 22-Origin-r/#1. 28-Aliens ends 4.20 12.50 25.00
22,23-12 cent and 15 cent editions exist 4.20 12.50 25.00
29-46-Reprints 2.40 6.00 12.00

NOTE: ***Manning*** *a-1-22, 29-43(r).* ***Spiegle*** *a-23, 44r.*

MAID OF THE MIST (See American Graphics)

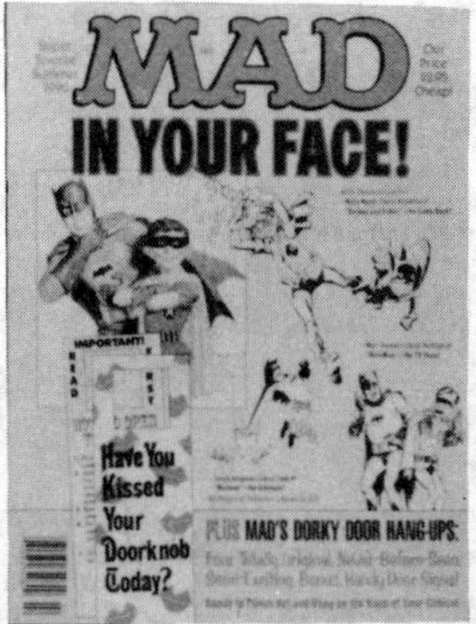

Mad Super Special #71, © WMG

Magic Comics #103, © DMP

Magnus #1 (Valiant), © WEST

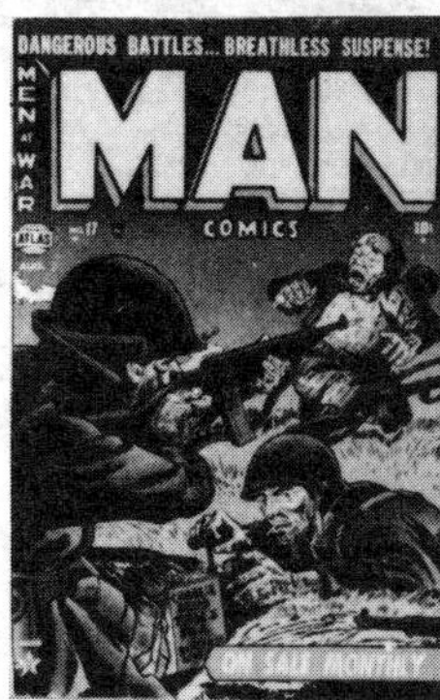

Man Comics #17, © MEG

The Man From U.N.C.L.E. #18, © M.G.M.

Man in Black #2, © HARV

	GD25	FN65	NM94

MAI, THE PSYCHIC GIRL (Eclipse) (Value: cover or less)

MAJOR HOOPLE COMICS (See Crackajack Funnies)
nd (Jan, 1943)
Nedor Publications

	GD25	FN65	NM94
1-Mary Worth, Phantom Soldier app. by Moldoff	25.00	75.00	150.00

MAJOR INAPAK THE SPACE ACE
1951 (20 pages) (Giveaway)
Magazine Enterprises (Inapac Foods)

	GD25	FN65	NM94
1-Bob Powell-c/a		.50	1.00

NOTE: *Many warehouse copies surfaced in 1973.*

MAJOR VICTORY COMICS (Also see Dynamic Comics)
1944 - No. 3, Summer, 1945
H. Clay Glover/Service Publ./Harry 'A' Chesler

	GD25	FN65	NM94
1-Origin Major Victory by C. Sultan (reprint from Dynamic #1); 1st app. Spider Woman	38.00	115.00	230.00
2-Dynamic Boy app.	25.00	75.00	150.00
3-Rocket Boy app.	19.00	58.00	115.00

MALTESE FALCON (See Feature Books No. 48)

MALU IN THE LAND OF ADVENTURE
1964 (See White Princess of Jungle #2)
I. W. Enterprises

	GD25	FN65	NM94
1-r/Avon's Slave Girl Comics #1; Severin-c	4.70	14.00	28.00

MAMMOTH COMICS
1938 (84 pages) (Black & White, 8-1/2x11-1/2")
Whitman Publishing Co. (K. K. Publications)

	GD25	FN65	NM94
1-Alley Oop, Terry & the Pirates, Dick Tracy, Little Orphan Annie, Wash Tubbs, Moon Mullins, Smilin' Jack, Tailspin Tommy & other reprints	96.00	288.00	575.00

MAMMY YOKUM & THE GREAT DOGPATCH MYSTERY
1951 (Giveaway)
Toby Press

	GD25	FN65	NM94
nn-Li'l Abner	16.00	48.00	110.00

MAN-BAT (See Batman Family, Brave & the Bold, & Detective #400)
Dec-Jan, 1975-76 - No. 2, Feb-Mar, 1976; Dec, 1984
National Periodical Publications/DC Comics

	GD25	FN65	NM94
1-Ditko-a(p); Aparo-c; Batman, She-Bat app.	.90	2.25	4.50
2-Aparo-c	.60	1.50	3.00
1 (12/84)-N. Adams-r(3)/Det. (Vs. Batman on-c)	.80	2.00	4.00

MAN COMICS
Dec, 1949 - No. 28, Sept, 1953 (#1-6: 52 pgs.)
Marvel/Atlas Comics (NPI)

	GD25	FN65	NM94
1-Tuska-a	10.00	30.00	65.00
2-Tuska-a	5.85	17.50	35.00
3-5	4.70	14.00	28.00
6-8	4.00	11.00	22.00
9-13,15: 9-Format changes to war	3.60	9.00	18.00
14-Henkel (3 pgs.); Pakula-a	4.20	12.50	25.00
16-21,23-28: 28-Crime issue	3.00	7.50	15.00
22-Krigstein-a, 5 pgs.	5.85	17.50	35.00

NOTE: ***Berg** a-14, 15, 19. **Colan** a-9, 21. **Everett** a-8, 22; c-22, 25. **Heath** a-11, 17, 21. Kubertish a-by **Bob Brown**-3. **Maneely** a-11; c-10, 11. **Reinman** a-11. **Robinson** a-7, 10, 14. **Robert Sale** a-9, 11. **Sinnott** a-22, 23. **Tuska** a-14, 23.*

MANDRAKE THE MAGICIAN (See Defenders Of The Earth, Feature Books #18, 19, 123, 46, 52, 55, Giant Comic Album, King Comics, Magic Comics, The Phantom #21, Tiny Tot Funnies & Wow Comics, '36)

MANDRAKE THE MAGICIAN (See Harvey Comics Hits #53)
Sept, 1966 - No. 10, Nov, 1967 (Also see Four Color #752)
King Comics (All 12 cents)

	GD25	FN65	NM94
1-Begin S.O.S. Phantom, ends #3	4.00	11.00	22.00
2-7,9: 4-Girl Phantom app. 5-Flying Saucer-c/story. 5,6-Brick Bradford app. 7-Origin Lothar. 9-Brick Bradford app.	2.40	6.00	12.00
8-Jeff Jones-a (4 pgs.)	3.60	9.00	18.00
10-Rip Kirby app.; Raymond-a (14 pgs.)	4.00	11.00	22.00

MAN FROM ATLANTIS (TV)
Feb, 1978 - No. 7, Aug, 1978
Marvel Comics Group

	GD25	FN65	NM94
1-($1.00, 84 pgs.)-Sutton-a(p), Buscema-c; origin		.60	1.20
2-7 (#1: cast photos & origin Mark Harris inside)		.50	1.00

MAN FROM PLANET X, THE (Planet X Productions) (Value: cover or less)

MAN FROM U.N.C.L.E., THE (TV) (Also see The Girl From...)
Feb, 1965 - No. 22, April, 1969 (All photo covers)
Gold Key

	GD25	FN65	NM94
1	11.50	34.00	80.00
2-Photo back c-2-8	9.15	27.50	55.00
3-10: 7-Jet Dream begins (all new stories)	5.00	15.00	35.00
11-22: 21,22-Reprint #10 & 7	4.70	14.00	28.00

MAN FROM U.N.C.L.E., THE (Entertainment) (Value: cover or less)

MAN FROM WELLS FARGO (TV)
No. 1287, Feb-Apr, 1962 - May-July, 1962 (Photo-c)
Dell Publishing Co.

	GD25	FN65	NM94
4-Color 1287, #01-495-207	4.70	14.00	28.00

MANGLE TANGLE TALES (Innovation) (Value: cover or less)

MANHUNT! (Becomes Red Fox #15 on)
Oct, 1947 - No. 14, 1953
Magazine Enterprises

	GD25	FN65	NM94
1-Red Fox by L. B. Cole, Undercover Girl by Whitney, Space Ace begin; negligee panels	24.00	70.00	165.00
2-Electrocution-c	18.00	54.00	125.00
3-6	16.00	48.00	110.00
7-10: 7-Space Ace ends. 8-Trail Colt begins (intro/1st app.) by Guardineer. 10-G. Ingels-a	13.00	40.00	90.00
11(8/48)-Frazetta-a, 7 pgs.; The Duke, Scotland Yard begin	20.00	60.00	140.00
12	10.00	30.00	70.00
13(A-1 #63)-Frazetta, r-/Trail Colt #1, 7 pgs.	19.00	57.00	130.00
14(A-1 #77)-Bondage/hypo-c; last L. B. Cole Red Fox; Ingels-a	13.00	40.00	90.00

NOTE: ***Guardineer** a-1-5; c-8. **Whitney** a-2-14; c-1-6, 10. Red Fox by **L. B. Cole**-#1-14. #15 was advertised but came out as Red Fox #15. Bondage c-6.*

MANHUNTER (See Brave & the Bold, Detective Comics, 1st Issue Special, House of Mystery #143 and Justice League of America)
1984 ($2.50, 76 pgs; high quality paper)
DC Comics

	GD25	FN65	NM94
1-Simonson-c/a(r)/Detective; Batman app.	.50	1.25	2.50

MANHUNTER (DC Comics, 1988-90) (Value: cover or less)

MAN IN BLACK (See Thrill-O-Rama) (Also see All New Comics, Front Page, Green Hornet #31, Strange Story & Tally-Ho Comics)
Sept, 1957 - No. 4, Mar, 1958
Harvey Publications

	GD25	FN65	NM94
1-Bob Powell-c/a	10.00	30.00	60.00
2-4: Powell-c/a	6.70	20.00	40.00

MAN IN FLIGHT (See 4-Color #836)

MAN IN SPACE (See Dell Giant #27 & 4-Color #716, 954)

MAN OF PEACE, POPE PIUS XII
1950 (See Pope Pius XII... & To V2#8)
Catechetical Guild

	GD25	FN65	NM94
nn-All Powell-a	4.00	10.50	21.00

MAN OF STEEL, THE (Also see Superman: The Man of Steel)
1986 (June release) - No. 6, 1986 (75 cents, mini-series)
DC Comics

	GD25	FN65	NM94
1-Silver logo; Byrne-c/a/scripts in all; origin		.50	1.00
1-Alternate-c for newsstand sales		.50	1.00
1-Distr. to toy stores by So Much Fun		.50	1.00
2-6: 2-Intro. Lois Lane, Jimmy Olsen. 3-Intro/origin Magpie; Batman-c/story. 4-Intro. new Lex Luthor		.50	1.00
...The Complete Saga nn-Contains #1-6, given away in contest	.40	1.00	2.00
Limited Edition, softcover	5.00	15.00	30.00

NOTE: *Issues 1-6 were released between Action #583 (9/86) & Action #584 (1/87) plus Superman #423 (9/86) & Superman #424 (1/87).*

MAN OF WAR (See Liberty Guards & Liberty Scouts)
Nov, 1941 - No. 2, Jan, 1942
Centaur Publications

	GD25	FN65	NM94
1-The Fire-Man, Man of War, The Sentinel, Liberty Guards, & Vapo-Man begin; Gustavson-c/a; Flag-c	108.00	325.00	650.00
2-Intro The Ferret; Gustavson-c/a	92.00	275.00	550.00

MAN OF WAR (Eclipse Comics) (Value: cover or less)

MAN O' MARS
1953; 1964
Fiction House Magazines

	GD25	FN65	NM94
1-Space Rangers; Whitman-c	24.00	70.00	165.00
I.W. Reprint #1-r/Man O'Mars #1; Murphy Anderson-a	4.00	12.00	24.00

MANTECH ROBOT WARRIORS (Archie) (Value: cover or less)

MAN-THING (See Fear, Giant-Size..., Marvel Comics Presents, Marvel Fanfare, Monsters Unleashed, Power Record Comics & Savage Tales)
Jan, 1974 - No. 22, Oct, 1975; V2#1, Nov, 1979 - V2#11, July, 1981
Marvel Comics Group

	GD25	FN65	NM94
1-Howard the Duck(2nd app.) cont'd/Fear #19	3.20	8.00	16.00
2	1.40	3.50	7.00
3-1st app. original Foolkiller	1.20	3.00	6.00
4-Origin Foolkiller; last app. 1st Foolkiller	.70	1.75	3.50
5-11-Ploog-a. 11-Foolkiller cameo (flashback)	.50	1.25	2.50
12-22: 19-1st app. Scavenger. 20-Spidey cameo. 21-Origin Scavenger, Man-Thing. 22-Howard the Duck cameo	.40	1.00	2.00
V2#1(1979) - 11: 6-Golden-c		.50	1.00

NOTE: ***Alcala** a-14. **Brunner** c-1. J. **Buscema** a-12p, 13p, 16p. **Gil Kane** c-4p, 10p, 12-20p, 21. **Mooney** a-17, 18, 19p, 20-22, V2#1-3p. **Ploog** Man-Thing-5p, 6p, 7, 8, 9-11p; c-5, 6, 8, 9, 11. **Sutton** a-13i. No. 19 says #10 in indicia.*

MAN WITH THE X-RAY EYES, THE (See X,... under Movie Comics)

MANY GHOSTS OF DR. GRAVES, THE (Doctor Graves #73 on)
5/67 - No. 60, 12/76; No. 61, 9/77 - No. 62, 10/77; No. 63, 2/78 - No. 65, 4/78; No. 66, 6/81 - No. 72, 5/82
Charlton Comics

	GD25	FN65	NM94
1-Palais-a; early issues 12 cent-c	1.60	4.00	8.00
2-10	.80	2.00	4.00
11-20	.50	1.25	2.50
21-44,46-72: 47,49-Newton-a	.30	.75	1.50
45-1st Newton comic work (8 pgs.); new logo	.60	1.50	3.00
Modern Comics Reprint 12,25 ('78)		.50	1.00

NOTE: ***Aparo** a-66r, 69r; c-66, 67. **Byrne** c-54. **Ditko** a-1, 7, 9, 11-13, 15-18, 20-22, 24, 26, 27, 35, 37, 38, 40-44, 47, 48, 51-54, 58, 60r-65r, 70, 72; c-11-13, 16-18, 22, 24, 26-35, 38, 40, 55, 58, 62-65. **Howard** a-45i; c-48. **Morisi** a-13, 14, 23, 26. **Newton** a-45, 47p, 49p; c-49, 52. **Sutton** a-42, 49; c-42, 44, 45; painted c-53.*

MANY LOVES OF DOBIE GILLIS (TV)
May-June, 1960 - No. 26, Oct, 1964
National Periodical Publications

	GD25	FN65	NM94
1-Most covers by Bob Oskner	22.00	65.00	150.00
2-5	11.00	32.00	75.00
6-10	10.00	30.00	60.00
11-26: 20-Drucker-a	8.35	25.00	50.00

MARAUDER'S MOON (See 4-Color #848)

MARCH OF COMICS (Boys' and Girls'...#3-353)
1946 - No. 488, April, 1982 (#1-4 are not numbered)
(K.K. Giveaway) (Founded by Sig Feuchtwanger)
K. K. Publications/Western Publishing Co.

Early issues were full size, 32 pages, and were printed with and without an extra cover of slick stock, just for the advertiser. The binding was stapled if the slick cover was added; otherwise, the pages were glued together at the spine. Most 1948 - 1951 issues were full size,24 pages, pulp covers. Starting in 1952 they were half-size and 32 pages with slick covers.1959 and later issues had only 16 pages plus covers. 1952 -1959 issues read oblong; 1960 and later issues read upright.

	GD25	FN65	NM94
nn (#1, 1946)-Goldilocks; Kelly back-c; 16pgs., stapled	29.00	86.00	200.00
nn (#2, 1946)-How Santa Got His Red Suit; Kelly-a (11 pgs., r/4-Color #61) ('44); 16pgs., stapled	29.00	86.00	200.00
nn (#3, 1947)-Our Gang (Walt Kelly)	40.00	120.00	280.00
nn (#4)-Donald Duck by Carl Barks, "Maharajah Donald," 28 pgs.; Kelly-c? (Disney)	715.00	2150.00	5000.00
5-Andy Panda	16.00	48.00	110.00
6-Popular Fairy Tales; Kelly-c; Noonan-a(2)	19.00	57.00	135.00
7-Oswald the Rabbit	19.00	57.00	135.00
8-Mickey Mouse, 32 pgs. (Disney)	50.00	150.00	350.00
9(nn)-The Story of the Gloomy Bunny	10.00	30.00	60.00
10-Out of Santa's Bag	8.35	25.00	50.00
11-Fun With Santa Claus	6.70	20.00	40.00
12-Santa's Toys	6.70	20.00	40.00
13-Santa's Surprise	6.70	20.00	40.00
14-Santa's Candy Kitchen	6.70	20.00	40.00
15-Hip-It-Ty Hop & the Big Bass Viol	6.70	20.00	40.00
16-Woody Woodpecker (1947)	11.00	32.00	75.00
17-Roy Rogers (1948)	22.00	65.00	150.00
18-Popular Fairy Tales	11.00	32.00	75.00
19-Uncle Wiggily	10.00	30.00	60.00
20-Donald Duck by Carl Barks, "Darkest Africa," 22 pgs.; Kelly-c (Disney) (on Disney's reprint banned list)	357.00	1070.00	2500.00
21-Tom and Jerry	10.00	30.00	70.00
22-Andy Panda	10.00	30.00	60.00
23-Raggedy Ann; Kerr-a	13.00	40.00	90.00
24-Felix the Cat, 1932 daily strip reprints by Otto Messmer	22.00	65.00	150.00
25-Gene Autry	22.00	65.00	150.00
26-Our Gang; Walt Kelly	22.00	65.00	150.00
27-Mickey Mouse; r/in M. M. #240 (Disney)	36.00	108.00	250.00
28-Gene Autry	22.00	65.00	150.00
29-Easter Bonnet Shop	5.00	15.00	30.00
30-Here Comes Santa	4.00	12.00	24.00
31-Santa's Busy Corner	4.00	12.00	24.00
32-No book produced			
33-A Christmas Carol	4.00	12.00	24.00
34-Woody Woodpecker	10.00	30.00	60.00
35-Roy Rogers (1948)	22.00	65.00	150.00
36-Felix the Cat(1949); by Messmer; 1934 daily strip-r	17.00	51.00	120.00
37-Popeye	14.00	43.00	100.00
38-Oswald the Rabbit	7.50	22.50	45.00
39-Gene Autry	22.00	65.00	150.00
40-Andy and Woody	7.50	22.50	45.00
41-Donald Duck by Carl Barks, "Race to the South Seas," 22 pgs.; Kelly-c	230.00	685.00	1600.00
42-Porky Pig	7.50	22.50	45.00
43-Henry	5.85	17.50	35.00
44-Bugs Bunny	10.00	30.00	60.00
45-Mickey Mouse (Disney)	31.00	92.00	215.00
46-Tom and Jerry	10.00	30.00	60.00
47-Roy Rogers	19.00	57.00	130.00

Man of Steel #2, © DC

Man-Thing #10, © MEG

March of Comics #20, © WDC

March of Comics #44, © Warner Bros.

March of Comics #66, © KING

March of Comics #77, © Roy Rogers

	GD25	FN65	NM94
48-Greetings from Santa	4.00	10.50	21.00
49-Santa Is Here	4.00	10.50	21.00
50-Santa Claus' Workshop (1949)	4.00	10.50	21.00
51-Felix the Cat (1950) by Messmer	14.00	43.00	100.00
52-Popeye	11.50	34.00	80.00
53-Oswald the Rabbit	7.50	22.50	45.00
54-Gene Autry	17.00	52.00	120.00
55-Andy and Woody	6.70	20.00	40.00
56-Donald Duck-not by Barks; Barks art on back-c (Disney)	23.00	70.00	160.00
57-Porky Pig	6.70	20.00	40.00
58-Henry	4.20	12.50	25.00
59-Bugs Bunny	8.35	25.00	50.00
60-Mickey Mouse (Disney)	19.00	58.00	135.00
61-Tom and Jerry	6.70	20.00	40.00
62-Roy Rogers	17.00	51.00	120.00
63-Welcome Santa; 1/2-size, oblong	4.00	10.50	21.00
64(nn)-Santa's Helpers; 1/2-size, oblong	4.00	10.50	21.00
65(nn)-Jingle Bells (1950)–1/2-size, oblong	4.00	10.50	21.00
66-Popeye (1951)	10.00	30.00	70.00
67-Oswald the Rabbit	5.85	17.50	35.00
68-Roy Rogers	16.00	48.00	110.00
69-Donald Duck; Barks-a on back-c (Disney)	20.00	60.00	140.00
70-Tom and Jerry	5.85	17.50	35.00
71-Porky Pig	5.85	17.50	35.00
72-Krazy Kat	8.35	25.00	50.00
73-Roy Rogers	13.00	40.00	90.00
74-Mickey Mouse (1951)(Disney)	16.00	48.00	110.00
75-Bugs Bunny	6.70	20.00	40.00
76-Andy and Woody	5.85	17.50	35.00
77-Roy Rogers	14.00	42.00	85.00
78-Gene Autry (1951); last regular size issue	14.00	42.00	85.00
79-Andy Panda (1952, 5x7" size)	4.00	10.50	21.00
80-Popeye	10.00	30.00	60.00
81-Oswald the Rabbit	4.00	12.00	24.00
82-Tarzan; Lex Barker photo-c	16.00	48.00	110.00
83-Bugs Bunny	5.00	15.00	30.00
84-Henry	3.60	9.00	18.00
85-Woody Woodpecker	3.60	9.00	18.00
86-Roy Rogers	11.00	32.00	75.00
87-Krazy Kat	6.70	20.00	40.00
88-Tom and Jerry	4.00	10.50	21.00
89-Porky Pig	3.60	9.00	18.00
90-Gene Autry	11.00	32.00	75.00
91-Roy Rogers & Santa	11.00	32.00	75.00
92-Christmas with Santa	3.20	8.00	16.00
93-Woody Woodpecker (1953)	3.60	9.00	18.00
94-Indian Chief	8.35	25.00	50.00
95-Oswald the Rabbit	3.60	9.00	18.00
96-Popeye	9.15	27.50	55.00
97-Bugs Bunny	4.20	12.50	25.00
98-Tarzan; Lex Barker photo-c	16.00	48.00	110.00
99-Porky Pig	3.60	9.00	18.00
100-Roy Rogers	10.00	30.00	60.00
101-Henry	3.20	8.00	16.00
102-Tom Corbett (TV); painted-c	13.00	40.00	90.00
103-Tom and Jerry	3.20	8.00	16.00
104-Gene Autry	10.00	30.00	60.00
105-Roy Rogers	10.00	30.00	60.00
106-Santa's Helpers	3.20	8.00	16.00
107-Santa's Christmas Book - not published			
108-Fun with Santa (1953)	3.20	8.00	16.00
109-Woody Woodpecker (1954)	3.20	8.00	16.00
110-Indian Chief	4.70	14.00	28.00
111-Oswald the Rabbit	3.20	8.00	16.00
112-Henry	2.80	7.00	14.00
113-Porky Pig	3.20	8.00	16.00
114-Tarzan; Russ Manning-a	16.00	48.00	110.00
115-Bugs Bunny	4.00	10.50	21.00
116-Roy Rogers	10.00	30.00	60.00
117-Popeye	9.15	27.50	55.00
118-Flash Gordon; painted-c	11.00	32.00	75.00
119-Tom and Jerry	3.20	8.00	16.00
120-Gene Autry	10.00	30.00	60.00
121-Roy Rogers	10.00	30.00	60.00
122-Santa's Surprise (1954)	2.40	6.00	12.00
123-Santa's Christmas Book	2.40	6.00	12.00
124-Woody Woodpecker (1955)	2.80	7.00	14.00
125-Tarzan; Lex Barker photo-c	14.00	43.00	100.00
126-Oswald the Rabbit	2.80	7.00	14.00
127-Indian Chief	4.00	12.00	24.00
128-Tom and Jerry	2.80	7.00	14.00
129-Henry	2.40	6.00	12.00
130-Porky Pig	2.80	7.00	14.00
131-Roy Rogers	10.00	30.00	60.00
132-Bugs Bunny	3.20	8.00	16.00
133-Flash Gordon; painted-c	10.00	30.00	65.00
134-Popeye	5.85	17.50	35.00
135-Gene Autry	9.15	27.50	55.00
136-Roy Rogers	9.15	27.50	55.00
137-Gifts from Santa	2.00	5.00	10.00
138-Fun at Christmas (1955)	2.00	5.00	10.00
139-Woody Woodpecker (1956)	2.80	7.00	14.00
140-Indian Chief	4.00	12.00	24.00
141-Oswald the Rabbit	2.80	7.00	14.00
142-Flash Gordon	10.00	30.00	65.00
143-Porky Pig	2.80	7.00	14.00
144-Tarzan; Russ Manning-a; painted-c	13.00	40.00	90.00
145-Tom and Jerry	2.80	7.00	14.00
146-Roy Rogers; photo-c	10.00	30.00	60.00
147-Henry	2.00	5.00	10.00
148-Popeye	5.85	17.50	35.00
149-Bugs Bunny	3.20	8.00	16.00
150-Gene Autry	9.15	27.50	55.00
151-Roy Rogers	9.15	27.50	55.00
152-The Night Before Christmas	2.00	5.00	10.00
153-Merry Christmas (1956)	2.00	5.00	10.00
154-Tom and Jerry (1957)	2.80	7.00	14.00
155-Tarzan; photo-c	13.00	40.00	90.00
156-Oswald the Rabbit	2.80	7.00	14.00
157-Popeye	5.00	15.00	30.00
158-Woody Woodpecker	2.80	7.00	14.00
159-Indian Chief	4.00	12.00	24.00
160-Bugs Bunny	3.20	8.00	16.00
161-Roy Rogers	7.50	22.50	45.00
162-Henry	2.00	5.00	10.00
163-Rin Tin Tin (TV)	5.00	15.00	30.00
164-Porky Pig	2.80	7.00	14.00
165-The Lone Ranger	8.35	25.00	50.00
166-Santa and His Reindeer	2.00	5.00	10.00
167-Roy Rogers and Santa	7.50	22.50	45.00
168-Santa Claus' Workshop (1957)	2.00	5.00	10.00
169-Popeye (1958)	5.00	15.00	30.00
170-Indian Chief	4.00	12.00	24.00
171-Oswald the Rabbit	2.40	6.00	12.00
172-Tarzan	11.00	32.00	75.00
173-Tom and Jerry	2.40	6.00	12.00
174-The Lone Ranger	8.35	25.00	50.00

	GD25	FN65	NM94
175-Porky Pig	2.40	6.00	12.00
176-Roy Rogers	7.00	21.00	42.00
177-Woody Woodpecker	2.40	6.00	12.00
178-Henry	2.00	5.00	10.00
179-Bugs Bunny	2.40	6.00	12.00
180-Rin Tin Tin (TV)	4.70	14.00	28.00
181-Happy Holiday	1.80	4.50	9.00
182-Happi Tim	2.40	6.00	12.00
183-Welcome Santa (1958)	1.80	4.50	9.00
184-Woody Woodpecker (1959)	2.40	6.00	12.00
185-Tarzan; photo-c	11.00	32.00	75.00
186-Oswald the Rabbit	2.40	6.00	12.00
187-Indian Chief	4.00	12.00	24.00
188-Bugs Bunny	2.40	6.00	12.00
189-Henry	1.80	4.50	9.00
190-Tom and Jerry	2.40	6.00	12.00
191-Roy Rogers	7.00	21.00	42.00
192-Porky Pig	2.40	6.00	12.00
193-The Lone Ranger	8.35	25.00	50.00
194-Popeye	5.00	15.00	30.00
195-Rin Tin Tin (TV)	4.70	14.00	28.00
196-Sears Special - not published			
197-Santa Is Coming	1.80	4.50	9.00
198-Santa's Helpers (1959)	1.80	4.50	9.00
199-Huckleberry Hound (TV)(1960)	5.00	15.00	30.00
200-Fury (TV)	4.70	14.00	28.00
201-Bugs Bunny	2.40	6.00	12.00
202-Space Explorer	6.70	20.00	40.00
203-Woody Woodpecker	2.00	5.00	10.00
204-Tarzan	9.15	27.50	55.00
205-Mighty Mouse	5.00	15.00	30.00
206-Roy Rogers; photo-c	7.00	21.00	42.00
207-Tom and Jerry	2.00	5.00	10.00
208-The Lone Ranger; Clayton Moore photo-c	11.00	32.00	75.00
209-Porky Pig	2.00	5.00	10.00
210-Lassie (TV)	4.70	14.00	28.00
211-Sears Special - not published			
212-Christmas Eve	1.80	4.50	9.00
213-Here Comes Santa (1960)	1.80	4.50	9.00
214-Huckleberry Hound (TV)(1961)	4.70	14.00	28.00
215-Hi Yo Silver	5.00	15.00	30.00
216-Rocky & His Friends (TV)(1961); 1st solo book; predates Rocky and His Fiendish Friends #1	8.35	25.00	50.00
217-Lassie (TV)	4.00	10.50	21.00
218-Porky Pig	2.00	5.00	10.00
219-Journey to the Sun	4.20	12.50	25.00
220-Bugs Bunny	2.40	6.00	12.00
221-Roy and Dale; photo-c	6.35	19.00	38.00
222-Woody Woodpecker	2.00	5.00	10.00
223-Tarzan	9.15	27.50	55.00
224-Tom and Jerry	2.00	5.00	10.00
225-The Lone Ranger	6.35	19.00	38.00
226-Christmas Treasury (1961)	1.80	4.50	9.00
227-Sears Special - not published?			
228-Letters to Santa (1961)	1.80	4.50	9.00
229-The Flintstones (TV)(1962); early app.; predates 1st Flintstones Gold Key issue (#7)	8.35	25.00	50.00
230-Lassie (TV)	4.00	10.50	21.00
231-Bugs Bunny	2.40	6.00	12.00
232-The Three Stooges	8.35	25.00	50.00
233-Bullwinkle (TV)	10.00	30.00	65.00
234-Smokey the Bear	3.00	7.50	15.00
235-Huckleberry Hound (TV)	4.70	14.00	28.00
236-Roy and Dale	5.00	15.00	30.00
237-Mighty Mouse	4.00	12.00	24.00
238-The Lone Ranger	6.35	19.00	38.00

	GD25	FN65	NM94
239-Woody Woodpecker	2.00	5.00	10.00
240-Tarzan	7.00	21.00	42.00
241-Santa Claus Around the World	1.80	4.50	9.00
242-Santa's Toyland (1962)	1.80	4.50	9.00
243-The Flintstones (TV)(1963)	7.50	22.50	45.00
244-Mister Ed (TV); photo-c	5.00	15.00	30.00
245-Bugs Bunny	2.40	6.00	12.00
246-Popeye	4.00	10.50	21.00
247-Mighty Mouse	4.00	12.00	24.00
248-The Three Stooges	8.35	25.00	50.00
249-Woody Woodpecker	2.00	5.00	10.00
250-Roy and Dale	5.00	15.00	30.00
251-Little Lulu & Witch Hazel	13.50	41.00	95.00
252-Tarzan; painted-c	7.00	21.00	42.00
253-Yogi Bear (TV)	5.00	15.00	30.00
254-Lassie (TV)	4.00	10.50	21.00
255-Santa's Christmas List	1.80	4.50	9.00
256-Christmas Party (1963)	1.80	4.50	9.00
257-Mighty Mouse	4.00	12.00	24.00
258-The Sword in the Stone (Disney)	7.50	22.50	45.00
259-Bugs Bunny	2.40	6.00	12.00
260-Mister Ed (TV)	4.00	12.00	24.00
261-Woody Woodpecker	2.00	5.00	10.00
262-Tarzan	7.00	21.00	42.00
263-Donald Duck; not by Barks (Disney)	7.00	21.00	42.00
264-Popeye	4.00	10.50	21.00
265-Yogi Bear (TV)	4.00	12.00	24.00
266-Lassie (TV)	3.60	9.00	18.00
267-Little Lulu; Irving Tripp-a	11.00	32.00	75.00
268-The Three Stooges	7.50	22.50	45.00
269-A Jolly Christmas	1.80	4.50	9.00
270-Santa's Little Helpers	1.80	4.50	9.00
271-The Flintstones (TV)(1965)	7.50	22.50	45.00
272-Tarzan	7.00	21.00	42.00
273-Bugs Bunny	2.40	6.00	12.00
274-Popeye	4.00	10.50	21.00
275-Little Lulu; Irving Tripp-a	10.00	30.00	62.00
276-The Jetsons (TV)	11.00	32.00	75.00
277-Daffy Duck	2.40	6.00	12.00
278-Lassie (TV)	3.60	9.00	18.00
279-Yogi Bear (TV)	4.00	12.00	24.00
280-The Three Stooges; photo-c	7.50	22.50	45.00
281-Tom and Jerry	1.60	4.00	8.00
282-Mister Ed (TV)	4.00	12.00	24.00
283-Santa's Visit	1.80	4.50	9.00
284-Christmas Parade (1965)	1.80	4.50	9.00
285-Astro Boy (TV)	24.50	73.00	170.00
286-Tarzan	6.35	19.00	38.00
287-Bugs Bunny	2.40	6.00	12.00
288-Daffy Duck	2.00	5.00	10.00
289-The Flintstones (TV)	6.70	20.00	40.00
290-Mister Ed (TV); photo-c	4.00	10.00	20.00
291-Yogi Bear (TV)	4.00	10.00	20.00
292-The Three Stooges; photo-c	7.50	22.50	45.00
293-Little Lulu; Irving Tripp-a	8.35	25.00	50.00
294-Popeye	4.00	10.50	21.00
295-Tom and Jerry	1.60	4.00	8.00
296-Lassie (TV); photo-c	3.20	8.00	16.00
297-Christmas Bells	1.80	4.50	9.00
298-Santa's Sleigh (1966)	1.80	4.50	9.00
299-The Flintstones (TV)(1967)	6.70	20.00	40.00
300-Tarzan	6.35	19.00	38.00
301-Bugs Bunny	2.00	5.00	10.00
302-Laurel and Hardy (TV); photo-c	4.35	13.00	26.00
303-Daffy Duck	1.20	3.00	6.00
304-The Three Stooges; photo-c	6.70	20.00	40.00

March of Comics #185, © ERB

March of Comics #203, © W. Lantz Prod.

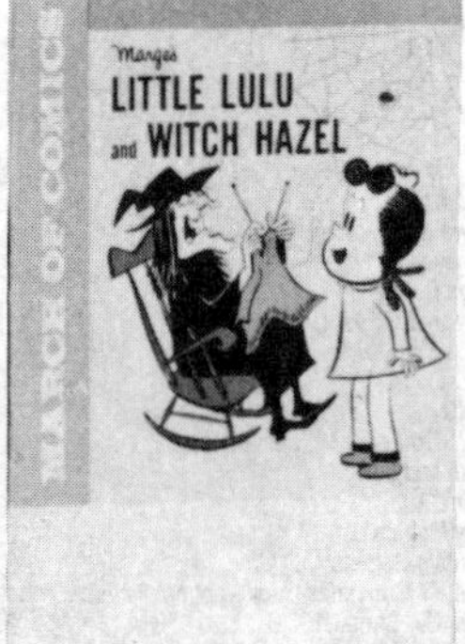

March of Comics #251, © WEST

March of Comics #299, © Hanna-Barbera

March of Comics #354, © ERB

March of Comics #405, © WEST

	GD25	FN65	NM94
305-Tom and Jerry	1.20	3.00	6.00
306-Daniel Boone (TV); Fess Parker photo-c	4.20	12.50	25.00
307-Little Lulu; Irving Tripp-a	6.70	20.00	40.00
308-Lassie (TV); photo-c	2.80	7.00	14.00
309-Yogi Bear (TV)	3.60	9.00	18.00
310-The Lone Ranger; Clayton Moore photo-c	11.00	32.00	75.00
311-Santa's Show	1.60	4.00	8.00
312-Christmas Album (1967)	1.60	4.00	8.00
313-Daffy Duck (1968)	1.20	3.00	6.00
314-Laurel and Hardy (TV)	4.00	12.00	24.00
315-Bugs Bunny	2.00	5.00	10.00
316-The Three Stooges	5.85	17.50	35.00
317-The Flintstones (TV)	5.85	17.50	35.00
318-Tarzan	5.85	17.50	35.00
319-Yogi Bear (TV)	3.60	9.00	18.00
320-Space Family Robinson (TV); Spiegle-a	10.00	30.00	70.00
321-Tom and Jerry	1.20	3.00	6.00
322-The Lone Ranger	5.35	16.00	32.00
323-Little Lulu; not by Stanley	4.00	12.00	24.00
324-Lassie (TV); photo-c	2.80	7.00	14.00
325-Fun with Santa	1.60	4.00	8.00
326-Christmas Story (1968)	1.60	4.00	8.00
327-The Flintstones (TV)(1969)	5.85	17.50	35.00
328-Space Family Robinson (TV); Spiegle-a	10.00	30.00	70.00
329-Bugs Bunny	2.00	5.00	10.00
330-The Jetsons (TV)	10.00	30.00	60.00
331-Daffy Duck	1.20	3.00	6.00
332-Tarzan	4.70	14.00	28.00
333-Tom and Jerry	1.20	3.00	6.00
334-Lassie (TV)	2.40	6.00	12.00
335-Little Lulu	4.00	12.00	24.00
336-The Three Stooges	5.85	17.50	35.00
337-Yogi Bear (TV)	3.60	9.00	18.00
338-The Lone Ranger	5.35	16.00	32.00
339-(Was not published)			
340-Here Comes Santa (1969)	1.60	4.00	8.00
341-The Flintstones (TV)	5.85	17.50	35.00
342-Tarzan	4.70	14.00	28.00
343-Bugs Bunny	1.60	4.00	8.00
344-Yogi Bear (TV)	3.20	8.00	16.00
345-Tom and Jerry	1.20	3.00	6.00
346-Lassie (TV)	2.40	6.00	12.00
347-Daffy Duck	1.20	3.00	6.00
348-The Jetsons (TV)	8.35	25.00	50.00
349-Little Lulu; not by Stanley	4.00	10.50	21.00
350-The Lone Ranger	4.70	14.00	28.00
351-Beep-Beep, the Road Runner (TV)	2.00	5.00	10.00
352-Space Family Robinson (TV); Spiegle-a	10.00	30.00	70.00
353-Beep-Beep, the Road Runner (1971) (TV)	2.00	5.00	10.00
354-Tarzan (1971)	4.00	12.00	24.00
355-Little Lulu; not by Stanley	4.00	10.50	21.00
356-Scooby Doo, Where Are You? (TV)	3.60	9.00	18.00
357-Daffy Duck & Porky Pig	1.20	3.00	6.00
358-Lassie (TV)	2.40	6.00	12.00
359-Baby Snoots	2.00	5.00	10.00
360-H. R. Pufnstuf (TV); photo-c	2.00	5.00	10.00
361-Tom and Jerry	1.20	3.00	6.00
362-Smokey the Bear (TV)	1.20	3.00	6.00
363-Bugs Bunny & Yosemite Sam	1.60	4.00	8.00
364-The Banana Splits (TV); photo-c	1.40	3.50	7.00
365-Tom and Jerry (1972)	1.20	3.00	6.00
366-Tarzan	4.00	11.00	22.00
367-Bugs Bunny & Porky Pig	1.60	4.00	8.00
368-Scooby Doo (TV)(4/72)	3.20	8.00	16.00
369-Little Lulu; not by Stanley	3.20	8.00	16.00
370-Lassie (TV); photo-c	2.40	6.00	12.00
371-Baby Snoots	1.60	4.00	8.00
372-Smokey the Bear (TV)	1.20	3.00	6.00
373-The Three Stooges	5.00	15.00	30.00
374-Wacky Witch	1.20	3.00	6.00
375-Beep-Beep & Daffy Duck (TV)	1.20	3.00	6.00
376-The Pink Panther (1972) (TV)	2.00	5.00	10.00
377-Baby Snoots (1973)	1.60	4.00	8.00
378-Turok, Son of Stone	10.00	30.00	70.00
379-Heckle & Jeckle New Terrytoons (TV)	1.00	2.50	5.00
380-Bugs Bunny & Yosemite Sam	1.00	2.50	5.00
381-Lassie (TV)	2.00	5.00	10.00
382-Scooby Doo, Where Are You? (TV)	2.80	7.00	14.00
383-Smokey the Bear (TV)	1.00	2.50	5.00
384-Pink Panther (TV)	1.60	4.00	8.00
385-Little Lulu	2.80	7.00	14.00
386-Wacky Witch	1.00	2.50	5.00
387-Beep-Beep & Daffy Duck (TV)	1.00	2.50	5.00
388-Tom and Jerry (1973)	1.00	2.50	5.00
389-Little Lulu; not by Stanley	2.80	7.00	14.00
390-Pink Panther (TV)	1.20	3.00	6.00
391-Scooby Doo (TV)	2.80	7.00	14.00
392-Bugs Bunny & Yosemite Sam	1.00	2.50	5.00
393-New Terrytoons (Heckle & Jeckle) (TV)	1.00	2.50	5.00
394-Lassie (TV)	1.60	4.00	8.00
395-Woodsy Owl	1.00	2.50	5.00
396-Baby Snoots	1.20	3.00	6.00
397-Beep-Beep & Daffy Duck (TV)	1.00	2.50	5.00
398-Wacky Witch	1.00	2.50	5.00
399-Turok, Son of Stone	10.00	30.00	60.00
400-Tom and Jerry	1.00	2.50	5.00
401-Baby Snoots (1975) (r/#371)	1.20	3.00	6.00
402-Daffy Duck (r/#313)	.80	2.00	4.00
403-Bugs Bunny (r/#343)	1.00	2.50	5.00
404-Space Family Robinson (TV)(r/#328)	10.00	30.00	60.00
405-Cracky	.80	2.00	4.00
406-Little Lulu (r/#355)	2.40	6.00	12.00
407-Smokey the Bear (TV)(r/#362)	1.00	2.50	5.00
408-Turok, Son of Stone	8.35	25.00	50.00
409-Pink Panther (TV)	.80	2.00	4.00
410-Wacky Witch	.60	1.50	3.00
411-Lassie (TV)(r/#324)	1.60	4.00	8.00
412-New Terrytoons (1975) (TV)	.60	1.50	3.00
413-Daffy Duck (1976)(r/#331)	.60	1.50	3.00
414-Space Family Robinson (r/#328)	8.35	25.00	50.00
415-Bugs Bunny (r/#329)	.60	1.50	3.00
416-Beep-Beep, the Road Runner (r/#353)(TV)	.60	1.50	3.00
417-Little Lulu (r/#323)	2.40	6.00	12.00
418-Pink Panther (r/#384) (TV)	.60	1.50	3.00
419-Baby Snoots (r/#377)	.80	2.00	4.00
420-Woody Woodpecker	.60	1.50	3.00
421-Tweety & Sylvester	.60	1.50	3.00
422-Wacky Witch (r/#386)	.60	1.50	3.00
423-Little Monsters	.80	2.00	4.00
424-Cracky (12/76)	.60	1.50	3.00
425-Daffy Duck	.60	1.50	3.00
426-Underdog (TV)	3.00	7.50	15.00
427-Little Lulu (r/#335)	1.60	4.00	8.00
428-Bugs Bunny	.60	1.50	3.00
429-The Pink Panther (TV)	.60	1.50	3.00
430-Beep-Beep, the Road Runner (TV)	.60	1.50	3.00
431-Baby Snoots	.80	2.00	4.00
432-Lassie (TV)	1.00	2.50	5.00

	GD25	FN65	NM94
433-437: 433-Tweety & Sylvester. 434-Wacky Witch. 435-New Terrytoons(TV). 436-Wacky Advs. of Cracky. 437-Daffy Duck	.60	1.50	3.00
438-Underdog (TV)	3.00	7.50	15.00
439-Little Lulu (r/#349)	1.60	4.00	8.00
440-442,444-446: 440-Bugs Bunny. 441-The Pink Panther (TV). 442-Beep-Beep, the Road Runner (TV). 444-Tom and Jerry. 445-Tweety and Sylvester. 446-Wacky Witch	.60	1.50	3.00
443-Baby Snoots	.80	2.00	4.00
447-Mighty Mouse	1.20	3.00	6.00
448-455,457,458: 448-Cracky. 449-Pink Panther (TV). 450-Baby Snoots 451-Tom and Jerry. 452-Bugs Bunny. 453-Popeye. 454-Woody Woodpecker. 455-Beep-Beep, the Road Runner (TV). 457-Tweety & Sylvester. 458-Wacky Witch	.60	1.50	3.00
456-Little Lulu (r/#369)	1.20	3.00	6.00
459-Mighty Mouse	1.20	3.00	6.00
460-466: 460-Daffy Duck. 461-The Pink Panther (TV). 462-Baby Snoots. 463-Tom and Jerry. 464-Bugs Bunny. 465-Popeye. 466-Woody Woodpecker	.60	1.50	3.00
467-Underdog (TV)	2.40	6.00	12.00
468-Little Lulu (r/#385)	.80	2.00	4.00
469-Tweety & Sylvester	.60	1.50	3.00
470-Wacky Witch	.60	1.50	3.00
471-Mighty Mouse	.80	2.50	5.00
472-474,476-478: 472-Heckle & Jeckle(12/80). 473-Pink Panther(1/81)(TV). 474-Baby Snoots. 476-Bugs Bunny. 477-Popeye. 478-Woody Woodpecker	.60	1.50	3.00
475-Little Lulu (r/#323)	.80	2.00	4.00
479-Underdog (TV)	2.00	5.00	10.00
480-482: 480-Tom and Jerry. 481-Tweety and Sylvester. 482-Wacky Witch	.60	1.50	3.00
483-Mighty Mouse	.80	2.00	5.00
484-487: 484-Heckle & Jeckle. 485-Baby Snoots. 486-The Pink Panther (TV). 487-Bugs Bunny	.60	1.50	3.00
488-Little Lulu (r/#335)	.80	2.00	4.00

MARCH OF CRIME (Formerly My Love Affair #1-6) (See Fox Giants)
No. 7, July, 1950 - No. 2, Sept, 1950; No. 3, Sept, 1951
Fox Features Syndicate

	GD25	FN65	NM94
7(#1)(7/50)-Wood-a	19.00	57.00	130.00
2(9/50)-Wood-a (exceptional)	19.00	57.00	130.00
3(9/51)	9.15	27.50	55.00

MARCO POLO
1962 (Movie classic)
Charlton Comics Group

	GD25	FN65	NM94
nn (Scarce)-Glanzman-c/a, 25pgs.	10.00	30.00	70.00

MARC SPECTOR: MOON KNIGHT (Also see Moon Knight)
June, 1989 - Present ($1.50/$1.75, color, direct sale only)
Marvel Comics

	GD25	FN65	NM94
1	.60	1.50	3.00
2-7: 4-Intro new Midnight	.40	1.00	2.00
8,9-Punisher app.	1.40	3.50	7.00
10-18: 20-Guice-c. 21-23-Cowan-c(p)	.40	1.00	2.00
19-21-Spider-Man & Punisher app.	1.20	3.00	6.00
22-24,26-31,34: 34-Last $1.50-c	.30	.75	1.50
25-($2.50, 52 pgs.)-Ghost Rider app.	.60	1.50	3.00
32,33-Hobgoblin II (Macendale) & Spider-Man (in black costume) app.	.60	1.50	3.00
35-38-Punisher story	.40	1.00	2.00
39-49: 42-44-Infinity War x-over	.35	.90	1.75
50-($2.95)-Special die-cut cover	.60	1.50	3.00

MARGARET O'BRIEN (See The Adventures of...)

MARGE'S LITTLE LULU (Little Lulu #207 on)
No. 74, 6/45 - No. 164, 7-9/62; No. 165, 10/62 - No. 206, 8/72
Dell Publishing Co./Gold Key #165-206

Marjorie Henderson Buell, born in Philadelphia, Pa., in 1904, created Little Lulu, a cartoon character that appeared weekly in the Saturday Evening Post from Feb. 23, 1935 through Dec. 30, 1944. She was not responsible for any of the comic books. **John Stanley** did pencils only on all Little Lulu comics through at least #135 (1959). He did pencils and inks on Four Color #74 & 97. **Irving Tripp** began inking stories from #1 on, and remained the comic's illustrator throughout its entire run. **Stanley** did storyboards (layouts), pencils, and scripts in all cases and inking only on covers. His word balloons were written in cursive. **Tripp** and occasionally other artists at Western Publ. in Poughkeepsie, N.Y. blew up the pencilled pages, inked the blowups, and lettered them. **Arnold Drake** did storyboards, pencils and scripts starting with #197 (1970) on, amidst reprinted issues. **Buell** sold her rights exclusively to Western Publ. in Dec., 1971. The earlier issues had to be approved by **Buell** prior to publication.

	GD25	FN65	NM94
4-Color 74('45)-Intro Lulu, Tubby & Alvin	100.00	300.00	700.00
4-Color 97(2/46)	47.00	140.00	330.00
(Above two books are all John Stanley - cover, pencils, and inks.)			
4-Color 110('46)-1st Alvin Story Telling Time; 1st app. Willy	33.00	100.00	230.00
4-Color 115-1st app. Boys' Clubhouse	33.00	100.00	230.00
4-Color 120, 131: 120-1st app. Eddie	30.00	90.00	210.00
4-Color 139('47),146,158	27.00	81.00	190.00
4-Color 165 (10/47)-Smokes doll hair & has wild hallucinations. 1st Tubby detective story	27.00	81.00	190.00
1(1-2/48)-Lulu's Diary feature begins	56.00	168.00	390.00
2-1st app. Gloria; 1st Tubby story in a L.L. comic; 1st app. Miss Feeny	29.00	87.00	200.00
3-5	25.00	75.00	175.00
6-10: 7-1st app. Annie; Xmas-c	18.00	54.00	125.00
11-20: 19-1st app. Wilbur. 20-1st app. Mr. McNabbem	15.00	45.00	105.00
21-30: 26-r/F.C. 110. 30-Xmas-c	11.50	34.00	80.00
31-38,40: 35-1st Mumday story	10.00	30.00	60.00
39-Intro. Witch Hazel in "That Awful Witch Hazel"	10.00	30.00	70.00
41-60: 42-Xmas-c. 45-2nd Witch Hazel app. 49-Gives Stanley & others credit	9.15	27.50	55.00
61-80: 63-1st app. Chubby (Tubby's cousin). 68-1st app. Prof. Cleff. 78-Xmas-c. 80-Intro. Little Itch (2/55)	6.70	20.00	40.00
81-99: 90-Xmas-c	5.00	15.00	30.00
100	5.85	17.50	35.00
101-130: 123-1st app. Fifi	4.20	12.50	25.00
131-164: 135-Last Stanley-p	4.00	10.50	21.00
165-Giant; ...In Paris ('62)	5.85	17.50	35.00
166-Giant; ...Christmas Diary ('62-'63)	5.85	17.50	35.00
167-169	3.00	7.50	15.00
170,172,175,176,178-196,198-200-Stanley-r. 182-1st app. Little Scarecrow Boy	2.40	6.00	12.00
171,173,174,177,197	1.40	3.50	7.00
201,203,206-Last issue to carry Marge's name	1.00	2.50	5.00
202,204,205-Stanley-r	1.60	4.00	8.00
...& Tubby in Japan (12¢)(5-7/62) 01476-207	8.35	25.00	50.00
...Summer Camp 1(8/67-G.K.-Giant) '57-58-r	5.85	17.50	35.00
...Trick 'N' Treat 1(12¢)(12/62-Gold Key)	6.70	20.00	40.00

NOTE: *See Dell Giant Comics #23, 29, 36, 42, 50, & Dell Giants for annuals. All Giants not by Stanley from L.L. on Vacation (7/54) on. Irving Tripp a-#1-on. Christmas c-7, 18, 30, 42, 78, 90, 126, 166, 250. Summer Camp issues #173, 177, 181, 189, 197, 201, 206.*

MARGE'S LITTLE LULU (See Golden Comics Digest #19, 23, 27, 29, 33, 36, 40, 43, 46, & March of Comics #251, 267, 275, 293, 307, 323, 335, 349, 355, 369, 385, 406, 417, 427, 439, 456, 468, 475, 488)

MARGE'S TUBBY (Little Lulu)(See Dell Giants)
No. 381, Aug, 1952 - No. 49, Dec-Feb, 1961-62
Dell Publishing Co./Gold Key

	GD25	FN65	NM94
4-Color 381(#1)-Stanley script; Irving Tripp-a	13.00	40.00	90.00
4-Color 430,444-Stanley-a	8.35	25.00	50.00
4-Color 461 (4/53)-1st Tubby & Men From Mars story; Stanley-a	7.50	22.50	45.00
5 (7-9/53)-Stanley-a	5.85	17.50	35.00
6-10	4.00	12.00	24.00
11-20	4.00	10.50	21.00

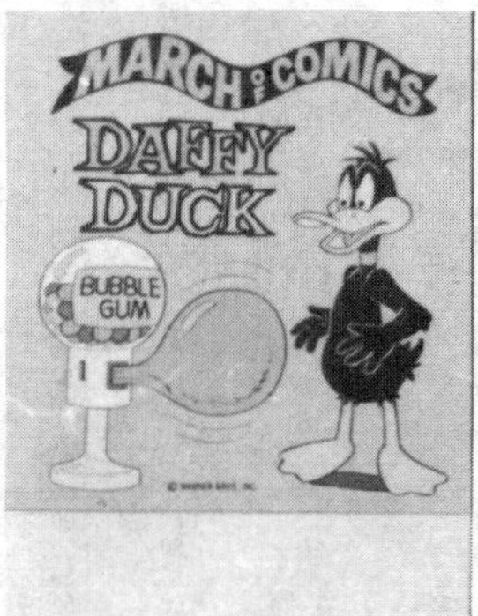

March of Comics #460, © Warner Bros.

Marc Spector: Moon Knight #10, © MEG

Marge's Little Lulu #23, © WEST

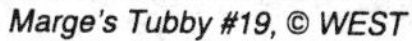
Marge's Tubby #19, © WEST

Margie #39, © MEG

Marmaduke Mouse #45, © QUA

	GD25	FN65	NM94
21-30	3.60	9.00	18.00
31-49	3.20	8.00	16.00
...& the Little Men From Mars No. 30020-410(10/64-G.K.)-25 cents, 68 pgs.	6.70	20.00	40.00

NOTE: ***John Stanley*** *did all storyboards & scripts through at least #35 (1959).* ***Lloyd White*** *did all art except F.C. 381, 430, 444, 461 & #5.*

MARGIE (See My Little...)

MARGIE (TV)
No. 1307, Mar-May, 1962 - No. 2, July-Sept, 1962 (Photo-c)
Dell Publishing Co.

	GD25	FN65	NM94
4-Color 1307(#1), 2	4.00	11.00	22.00

MARGIE COMICS (Formerly Comedy Comics; Reno Browne #50 on)
(Also see Cindy Comics & Teen Comics)
No. 35, Winter, 1946-47 - No. 49, Dec, 1949
Marvel Comics (ACI)

	GD25	FN65	NM94
35	7.50	22.50	45.00
36-38,42,45,47-49	4.20	12.50	25.00
39,41,43(2),44,46-Kurtzman's "Hey Look"	5.85	17.50	35.00
40-Three "Hey Looks," three "Giggles & Grins" by Kurtzman	7.00	21.00	42.00

MARINES (See Tell It to the...)

MARINES ATTACK
Aug, 1964 - No. 9, Feb-Mar, 1966
Charlton Comics

	GD25	FN65	NM94
1	1.60	4.00	8.00
2-9	.80	2.00	4.00

MARINES AT WAR (Formerly Tales of the Marines #4)
No. 5, April, 1957 - No. 7, Aug, 1957
Atlas Comics (OPI)

	GD25	FN65	NM94
5-7	3.00	7.50	15.00

NOTE: ***Colan*** *a-5.* ***Drucker*** *a-5.* ***Everett*** *a-5.* ***Maneely*** *a-5.* ***Orlando*** *a-7.* ***Severin*** *c-5.*

MARINES IN ACTION
June, 1955 - No. 14, Sept, 1957
Atlas News Co.

	GD25	FN65	NM94
1-Rock Murdock, Boot Camp Brady begin	5.00	15.00	30.00
2-14	3.00	7.50	15.00

NOTE: ***Berg*** *a-2, 8, 9, 11, 14.* ***Heath*** *c-2, 9.* ***Maneely*** *c-1.* ***Severin*** *a-4; c-7-11, 14.*

MARINES IN BATTLE
Aug, 1954 - No. 25, Sept, 1958
Atlas Comics (ACI No. 1-12/WPI No. 13-25)

	GD25	FN65	NM94
1-Heath-c; Iron Mike McGraw by Heath; history of U.S. Marine Corps. begins	8.35	25.00	50.00
2-Heath-c	4.20	12.50	25.00
3-6,8-10: 4-Last precode (2/55)	4.00	10.00	20.00
7-Kubert/Moskowitz-a (6 pgs.)	4.70	14.00	28.00
11-16,18-21,24	3.00	7.50	15.00
17-Williamson-a (3 pgs.)	5.85	17.50	35.00
22,25-Torres-a	4.00	10.00	20.00
23-Crandall-a; Mark Murdock app.	4.20	12.50	25.00

NOTE: ***Berg*** *a-22.* ***G. Colan*** *a-22, 23.* ***Drucker*** *a-6.* ***Everett*** *a-4, 15; c-21.* ***Heath*** *c-1, 2, 4.* ***Maneely*** *c-24.* ***Orlando*** *a-14.* ***Pakula*** *a-6, 23.* ***Powell*** *a-16.* ***Severin*** *a-22; c-12.* ***Sinnott*** *a-23.* ***Tuska*** *a-15.*

MARINE WAR HEROES (Charlton Premiere #19 on)
Jan, 1964 - No. 18, Mar, 1967
Charlton Comics

	GD25	FN65	NM94
1-Montes/Bache-c/a	1.60	4.00	8.00
2-18: 14,18-Montes/Bache-a	1.00	2.50	5.00

MARK, THE (Dark Horse) (Value: cover or less) (Also see Mayhem)

MARK HAZZARD: MERC (Marvel) (Value: cover or less)

MARK OF ZORRO (See 4-Color #228)

MARKSMAN, THE (Hero Comics) (Value: cover or less) (Also see Champions)

MARK STEEL
1967, 1968, 1972 (24 pgs.) (Color)
American Iron & Steel Institute (Giveaway)

	GD25	FN65	NM94
1967,1968-"Journey of Discovery with..."; Neal Adams art	3.60	9.00	18.00
1972-"...Fights Pollution"; N. Adams-a	1.80	4.50	9.00

MARK TRAIL
Oct, 1955; No. 5, Summer, 1959
Standard Magazines (Hall Syndicate)/Fawcett Publ. No. 5

	GD25	FN65	NM94
1(1955)-Sunday strip-r	5.00	15.00	30.00
5(1959)	3.60	9.00	18.00
...Adventure Book of Nature 1(Summer, 1958; Pines)-100 pg. Giant; contains 78 Sunday strip-r	7.50	22.50	45.00

MARMADUKE MONK
No date; 1963 (10 cents)
I. W. Enterprises/Super Comics

	GD25	FN65	NM94
1-I.W. Reprint(nd), 14-(Super Reprint)(1963)	.80	2.00	4.00

MARMADUKE MOUSE
Spring, 1946 - No. 65, Dec, 1956 (All 52 pgs.?)
Quality Comics Group (Arnold Publ.)

	GD25	FN65	NM94
1-Funny animal	10.00	30.00	65.00
2	5.35	16.00	32.00
3-10	4.20	12.50	25.00
11-30	3.60	9.00	18.00
31-65	2.40	6.00	12.00
Super Reprint #14(1963)	1.20	3.00	6.00

MARRIED ... WITH CHILDREN (TV)
June, 1990 - No. 7, Feb, 1991(12/90 inside) ($1.75, color)
V2#1, Sept, 1991 - Present? ($1.95, color)
Now Comics

	GD25	FN65	NM94
1-Based on Fox TV show	1.40	3.50	7.00
1-2nd printing ($1.75)	.60	1.50	3.00
2-Photo-c	1.00	2.50	5.00
2-2nd printing ($1.75)	.35	.90	1.75
3	.45	1.10	2.20
4-7	.35	.90	1.75
V2#1-8: 1,4,5-Photo-c	.40	1.00	2.00
Special 1 (7/92, $1.95)-Kelly Bundy photo-c/poster	.40	1.00	2.00

MARS (First Comics) (Value: cover or less)

MARS & BEYOND (See 4-Color #866)

MARSHAL BLUEBERRY (See Blueberry)
1991 ($14.95, color, graphic novel)
Epic Comics (Marvel)

	GD25	FN65	NM94
1-Moebius-a	3.00	7.50	15.00

MARSHAL LAW (Also see Crime And Punishment: Marshall Law...)
Oct, 1987 - No. 6, May, 1989 ($1.95, color, adults)
Epic Comics (Marvel)

	GD25	FN65	NM94
1	.70	1.75	3.50
2-6	.40	1.00	2.00

MARSHALL LAW - KINGDOM OF THE BLIND (Apocalypse Publishing) (Value: cover or less)

MARSHALL LAW: SUPER BABYLON (Dark Horse) (Value: cover or less)

M.A.R.S. PATROL TOTAL WAR (Formerly Total War #1,2)
No. 3, Sept, 1966 - No. 10, Aug, 1969 (All-Painted-c)
Gold Key

	GD25	FN65	NM94
3-Wood-a	4.00	11.00	22.00

4-10 2.40 6.00 12.00

MARTHA WAYNE (See The Story of...)

MARTIAN MANHUNTER (DC, 1988) (Value: cover or less)

MARTIAN MANHUNTER: AMERICAN SECRETS (DC Comics) (Value: cover or less)

MARTIN KANE (Formerly My Secret Affair) (Radio-TV) (Private Eye)
No. 4, June, 1950 - No. 2, Aug, 1950
Fox Features Syndicate (Hero Books)

4(#1)-Wood-c/a(2); used in **SOTI**, pg. 160; photo back cover
20.00 60.00 120.00
2-Orlando-a, 5pgs; Wood-a(2) 12.00 36.00 85.00

MARTY MOUSE
No date (1958?) (10 cents)
I. W. Enterprises

1-Reprint .80 2.00 4.00

MARVEL ACTION UNIVERSE (TV)
Jan, 1989 ($1.00, color, one-shot)
Marvel Comics

1-r/Spider-Man And His Amazing Friends .50 1.00

MARVEL ADVENTURES STARRING DAREDEVIL (Marvel) (Value: cover or less)

MARVEL AND DC PRESENT FEATURING THE UNCANNY X-MEN AND THE NEW TEEN TITANS
1982 ($2.00, one shot, 68 pgs., printed on Baxter paper)
Marvel Comics Group/DC Comics

1-Deathstroke the Terminator & Darkseid app.; Simonson/Austin-c/a
3.00 7.50 15.00

MARVEL BOY (Astonishing #3 on; see Marvel Super Action #4)
Dec, 1950 - No. 2, Feb, 1951
Marvel Comics (MPC)

1-Origin Marvel Boy by Russ Heath 47.00 140.00 325.00
2-Everett-a 40.00 120.00 275.00

MARVEL CHILLERS (Also see Giant-Size Chillers)
Oct, 1975 - No. 7, Oct, 1976 (All 25 cent issues)
Marvel Comics Group

1-Intro. Modred the Mystic, ends #2; Kane-c(p) .60 1.50 3.00
2-7: 3-Tigra, the Were-Woman begins (origin), ends #7. Chaykin/Wrightson-c. 4-Kraven app. 5,6-Red Wolf app. 6-Byrne-a(p); Buckler-c(p). 7-Kirby-c; Tuska-p .30 .75 1.50

MARVEL CLASSICS COMICS SERIES FEATURING... (Also see Pendulum Illustrated Classics)
1976 - No. 36, Dec, 1978 (52 pgs., no ads)
Marvel Comics Group

1-Dr. Jekyll and Mr. Hyde .60 1.50 3.00
2-27,29-36 .40 1.00 2.00
28-1st Golden-c/a; The Pit and the Pendulum 1.00 2.50 5.00

NOTE: ***Adkins*** *c-1i, 4i, 12i.* ***Alcala*** *a-34i; c-34.* ***Bolle*** *a-35.* ***Buscema*** *c-17p, 19p, 26p.* ***Golden*** *c/a-28.* ***Gil Kane*** *c-1-16p, 21p, 22p, 24p, 32p.* ***Nebres*** *a-5; c-24i.* ***Nino*** *a-2, 8, 12.* ***Redondo*** *a-1, 9. No. 1-12 were reprinted from Pendulum Illustrated Classics.*

MARVEL COLLECTORS ITEM CLASSICS (Marvel's Greatest #23 on)
Feb, 1965 - No. 22, Aug, 1969 (68 pgs.)
Marvel Comics Group(ATF)

1-Fantastic Four, Spider-Man, Thor, Hulk, Iron Man-r begin; all are 25 cent cover price 6.70 20.00 40.00
2 (4/66) - 4 4.00 10.00 20.00
5-22: 22-r/The Man in the Ant Hill/TTA #27 1.80 4.50 9.00

NOTE: *All reprints;* ***Ditko, Kirby*** *art in all.*

MARVEL COMICS (Marvel Mystery Comics #2 on)
October, November, 1939
Timely Comics (Funnies, Inc.)

NOTE: The first issue was originally dated October 1939. Most copies have a black circle stamped over the date (on cover and inside) with "November" printed over it. However, some copies do not have the November overprint and could have a higher value. Most No. 1's have printing defects, i.e., tilted pages which caused trimming into the panels usually on right side and bottom. Covers exist with and without gloss finish.

GD25 FN65 VF82 NM94

1-Origin Sub-Mariner by Bill Everett(1st newsstand app.); 1st 8 pgs. were produced for Motion Picture Funnies Weekly #1 which was probably not distributed outside of advance copies; intro Human Torch by Carl Burgos, Kazar the Great (1st Tarzan clone), & Jungle Terror(only app.); intro. The Angel by Gustavson, The Masked Raider & his horse Lightning(ends #12); cover by sci/fi pulp illustrator Frank R. Paul; interview with Burgos & Everett 7,900.00 23,600.00 47,250.00 63,000.00
(Estimated up to 50 total copies exist, 4 in NM/Mint)

MARVEL COMICS PRESENTS
Early Sept, 1988 - Present ($1.25/$1.50, color, bi-weekly)
Marvel Comics

GD25 FN65 NM94

1-Wolverine by Buscema in #1-10 2.00 5.00 10.00
2-5 1.00 2.50 5.00
6-10: 6-Sub-Mariner app. 10-Colossus begins .80 2.00 4.00
11-32,34-37: 17-Cyclops begins. 19-1st app. Damage Control. 24-Havok begins. 25-Origin/1st app. Nth Man. 26-Hulk begins by Rogers. 29-Quasar app. 31-Excalibur begins by Austin (i). 33-Capt. America. 37-Devil-Slayer app. .40 1.00 2.00
33-Jim Lee-a .60 1.50 3.00
38-Wolverine begins by Buscema; Hulk app. 1.00 2.50 5.00
39-47,51-53: 39-Spider-Man app. 46-Liefeld Wolverine-c. 51-53-Wolverine by Rob Liefeld .60 1.50 3.00
48-50-Wolverine & Spider-Man team-up by Erik Larsen. 48-Wasp app. 50-Silver Surfer. 50-53-Comet Man; Bill Mumy scripts
1.00 2.50 5.00
54-61-Wolverine/Hulk; 54-Werewolf by Night begins; The Shroud by Ditko. 58-Iron Man by Ditko. 59-Punisher 1.20 3.00 6.00
62-Deathlok & Wolverine stories 1.60 4.00 8.00
63-Wolverine .80 2.00 4.00
64-71-Wolverine/Ghost Rider 8 part story. 70-Liefeld Ghost Rider/Wolverine-c .90 2.25 4.50
72-Begin 13 part Weapon-X story(Wolverine origin) by B. Windsor-Smith (prologue) 1.60 4.00 8.00
73-Weapon-X part 1; Black Knight, Sub-Mariner 1.00 2.50 5.00
74-Weapon-X part 2; Black Knight, Sub-Mariner .80 2.00 4.00
75-80: 77-Mr. Fantastic story. 78-Iron Man by Steacy. 80,81-Capt. America by Ditko/Austin .60 1.50 3.00
81-84: 81-Daredevil by Rogers/Williamson. 82-Power Man. 83-Human Torch by Ditko(a&scripts); $1.00-c direct, $1.25 newsstand. 84-Last Weapon-X (24 pg. conclusion) .50 1.25 2.50
85-Begin 8 part Wolverine story by Sam Kieth (c/a); 1st Kieth-a on Wolverine; begin 8 part Beast story by Jae Lee(p) with Liefeld part pencils #85,86
1.20 3.00 6.00
86-89 .80 2.00 4.00
90-Begin 8 part Ghost Rider & Cable story, ends #97; begin flip book format with two covers 1.00 2.50 5.00
91-94: 93-Begin 6 part Wolverine story, ends #98 .60 1.50 3.00
95-98: 95-Begin $1.50-c. 98-Begin 2 part Ghost Rider story
.40 1.00 2.00
99,101-107,112-116: 99-Spider-Man story. 101-Begin 6 part Ghost Rider/Strange story & begin 8 part Wolverine/Nightcrawler story by Colan/Williamson; Punisher story. 107-Begin 6 part Ghost Rider/Werewolf by Night story. 112-Demogoblin story by Colan/Williamson; Pip the Troll story w/Starlin scripts & Gamora cameo. 113-Begin 6 part Giant-Man & begin 6 part Ghost Rider/Iron Fist stories .30 .75 1.50
100-Full-length Ghost Rider/Wolverine story by Sam Kieth w/Tim Vigil assists; anniversary issue, non flip-book .50 1.25 2.50
108-111: 108-Begin 4 part Thanos story; Starlin scripts. 109-Begin 8 part Wolverine/Typhoid Mary story. 111-Iron Fist .40 1.00 2.00
117-Preview of Ravage 2099 (1st app.); begin 6 part Wolverine/Venom story w/Kieth-a .50 1.25 2.50

Marvel Chillers #4, © MEG

Marvel Comics #1, © MEG

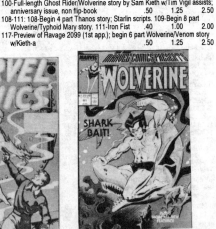

Marvel Comics Presents #41, © MEG

Marvel Double Feature #15, © MEG

Marvel Family #34, © FAW

Marvel Feature #2 (3/72), © MEG

GD25 FN65 NM94

118-Preview of Doom 2099 (1st app.) .50 1.25 2.50
119-130: 119-Begin Ghost Rider/Cloak & Dagger story by Colan. 123-Begin 8 part Ghost Rider/Typhoid Mary story; begin 4 part She Hulk story; begin 8 partWolverine/Lynx story .30 .75 1.50

NOTE: ***Austin** a-31-37i; c-48i, 50i, 99i. **Buscema** a-1-10, 38-47; c-6. **Byrne** a-79; c-71. **Colan** a(p)-36, 37. **Colan/Williamson** a-101-108. **Ditko** a-7p, 56p, 58, 80, 81, 83. **Guice** a-62. **Sam Kieth** a-85-92, 117-122; c-85-98, 99p, 100-108, 118; back c-109-113, 117. **Liefeld** a-51, 52, 53p(2), 85p; c-46, 70. **McFarlane** c-32. **Mooney** a-73. **Rogers** a-26, 38, 46i, 81p. **Russell** c-4i. **Saltares** a-8p(early), 38-45p. **Simonson** c-1. **B. Smith** a-72-84; c-72-84. **P. Smith** c-34. **Sparling** a-33. **Starlin** a-89i. **Staton** a-74. **Steacy** a-78. **Sutton** a-101-105. **Williamson** c-62i. Two Gun Kid by **Gil Kane** in #116, 122.*

MARVEL COMICS SUPER SPECIAL, A (Marvel Super Special #5 on)
1977 - No. 41(?), Nov, 1986 (nn 7) (Magazine; $1.50)
Marvel Comics Group

1-Kiss, 40 pgs. comics plus photos & features; Simonson-a(p); also see Howard the Duck #12 10.00 30.00 60.00
2-Conan (1978) .60 1.50 3.00
3-Close Encounters of the Third Kind (1978); Simonson-a .40 1.00 2.00
4-The Beatles Story (1978)-Perez/Janson-a; has photos & articles 1.60 4.00 8.00
5-Kiss (1978)-Includes poster 5.85 17.50 35.00
6-Jaws II (1978) .30 .75 1.50
7-Sgt. Pepper; Beatles movie adaptation; withdrawn from U.S. distribution
8-Battlestar Galactica; tabloid size ($1.50, 1978); adapts TV show .40 1.00 2.00
8-Battlestar Galactica; publ. in reg. magazine format; low distribution ($1.50, 8-1/2x11") 1.00 2.50 5.00
9,10: 9-Conan. 10-Star-Lord .40 1.00 2.00
11-13-Weirdworld begins #11; 25 copy special press run of each with gold seal and signed by artists (Proof quality), Spring-June, 1979 10.00 30.00 60.00
11-13-Weirdworld (regular issues): 11-Fold-out centerfold .50 1.25 2.50
14-Miller-c(p); adapts movie "Meteor" .60 1.20
15-Star Trek with photos & pin-ups($1.50) .60 1.20
15-With $2.00 price (scarce); the price was changed at tail end of a 200,000 press run .80 2.00 4.00
16-20 (Movie adaptations): 16-Empire Strikes Back; Williamson-a. 17-Xanadu. 18-Raiders of the Lost Ark. 19-For Your Eyes Only (James Bond). 20-Dragonslayer .35 .90 1.75
21-41 (Movie adaptations): 21-Conan. 22-Bladerunner; Williamson-a; Steranko-c. 23-Annie. 24-The Dark Crystal. 25-Rock and Rule-w/photos; artwork is from movie. 26-Octopussy (James Bond). 27-Return of the Jedi. 28-Krull; photo-c. 29-Tarzan of the Apes (Greystoke movie). 30-Indiana Jones and the Temple of Doom. 31-The Last Star Fighter. 32-The Muppets Take Manhattan. 33-Buckaroo Bonzai. 34-Sheena. 35-Conan The Destroyer. 36-Dune. 37-2010. 38-Red Sonja. 39-Santa Claus: The Movie. 40-Labyrinth. 41-Howard The Duck .35 .90 1.75

NOTE: ***J. Buscema** a-1, 2, 9, 11-13, 18p, 21, 35, 40; c-11(part), 12. **Chaykin** a-9, 19p; c-18, 19. **Colan** a(p)-6, 10, 14. **Morrow** a-34; c-1i, 34. **Nebres** a-11. **Spiegle** a-29. **Stevens** a-27. **Williamson** a-27. #22-28 contain photos from movies.*

MARVEL DOUBLE FEATURE
Dec, 1973 - No. 21, Mar, 1977
Marvel Comics Group

1-Capt. America, Iron Man-r/T.O.S. begin .80 2.00 4.00
2-16,20,21 .40 1.00 2.00
17-Reprints story/Iron Man & Sub-Mariner #1 .60 1.50 3.00
18,19-Colan/Craig-r from Iron Man #1 in both .80 2.00 4.00

NOTE: ***Colan** r-1-19p. **Craig** r-17-19i. **G. Kane** r-15p; c-15p. **Kirby** r-1-16p, 20, 21; c-17-20.*

MARVEL FAMILY (Also see Captain Marvel Adventures No. 18)
Dec, 1945 - No. 89, Jan, 1954
Fawcett Publications

1-Origin Captain Marvel, Captain Marvel Jr., Mary Marvel, & Uncle Marvel retold; origin/1st app. Black Adam 100.00 300.00 600.00
2-The 3 Lt. Marvels & Uncle Marvel app. 50.00 150.00 300.00
3 37.00 110.00 225.00
4,5 32.00 95.00 190.00
6-10: 7-Shazam app. 25.00 75.00 150.00
11-20 18.00 55.00 110.00
21-30 13.00 40.00 80.00
31-40 12.00 35.00 70.00
41-46,48-50 10.00 30.00 60.00
47-Flying Saucer-c/story 12.50 37.50 75.00
51-76,79,80,82-89: 78,81-Used in **POP**, pgs. 92,93 9.15 27.50 55.00
77-Communist Threat-c 12.50 37.50 75.00

MARVEL FANFARE
March, 1982 - No. 60, Jan, 1992 ($1.25-$2.25, slick paper, direct sale)
Marvel Comics Group

1-Spider-Man/Angel team-up; 1st Paul Smith-a; Daredevil app. 1.60 4.00 8.00
2-Spider-Man, Ka-Zar, The Angel. F.F. origin retold 1.20 3.00 6.00
3,4-X-Men & Ka-Zar. 4-Deathlok, Spidey app. 1.00 2.50 5.00
5-Dr. Strange, Capt. America .60 1.50 3.00
6-15: 6-Spider-Man, Scarlet Witch. 7-Incredible Hulk; D.D. back-up(also 15). 8-Dr. Strange; Wolf Boy begins. 9-Man-Thing. 10-13-Black Widow. 14-The Vision. 15-The Thing by Barry Smith, c/a .50 1.25 2.50
16-32,34-50: 16,17-Skywolf. 16-Sub-Mariner back-up. 17-Hulk back-up. 18-Capt. America by Miller. 19-Cloak and Dagger. 20-Thing/Dr. Strange. 21-Thing/Dr. Strange/Hulk. 22,23-Iron Man vs. Dr. Octopus. 24-26-Weirdworld. 24-Wolverine back-up. 27-Daredevil/Spider-Man. 28-Alpha Flight. 29-Hulk. 30-Moon Knight. 31,32-Captain America. 34-37-Warriors Three. 38-Moon Knight/Dazzler. 39-Moon Knight/Hawkeye. 40-Angel/Rogue & Storm. 41-Dr. Strange. 42-Spider-Man. 43-Sub-Mariner/Human Torch. 44-Iron Man vs. Dr. Doom by Ken Steacy. 45-All pin-up issue by Steacy, Art Adams & others. 46-Fantastic Four. 47-Hulk. 48-She-Hulk/Vision. 49-Dr. Strange/Nick Fury. 50-X-Factor; begin $2.25-c .50 1.25 2.50
33-X-Men, Wolverine app.; Punisher pin-up 1.20 3.00 6.00
51-($2.95, 52 pgs.)-Silver Surfer; Fantastic Four & Capt. Marvel app.; 51,52-Colan/Williamson back-up (Dr. Strange) .60 1.50 3.00
52,53: 52-54-Black Knight; 53-Iron Man back up .50 1.25 2.50
54,55-Wolverine back-ups. 55-Power Pack .60 1.50 3.00
56-60: 56-59-Shanna the She-Devil. 58-Vision & Scarlet Witch back-up. 60-Black Panther/Rogue/Daredevil stories .50 1.25 2.50

NOTE: ***Art Adams** c-13. **Austin** a-1i, 4i, 33i, 38i; c-8i, 33i. **Buscema** a-51p. **Byrne** a-1p, 29, 48; c-29. **Chiodo** painted c-56-59. **Colan** a-51p. **Cowan/Simonson** c/a-60. **Golden** a-1, 2, 4p, 47; c-1, 2, 47. **Infantino** c/a(p)-8. **Gil Kane** a-8-11p. **Miller** a-18; c-1(Back-c), 18. **Perez** a-10, 11p, 12, 13p; c-10-13p. **Rogers** a-5p; c-5p. **Russell** a-5i, 6i, 8-11i, 43i; c-5i, 6. **Paul Smith** a-1p, 4p, 32, 60; c-4p. Staton c/a-50(p). **Williamson** a-30i, 51i.*

MARVEL FEATURE (See Marvel Two-In-One)
Dec, 1971 - No. 12, Nov, 1973 (1,2: 25 cent giants)(1-3: Quarterly)
Marvel Comics Group

1-Origin/1st app. The Defenders (Sub-Mariner, Hulk & Dr. Strange); see Sub-Mariner #34,35 for prequel; Dr. Strange solo story (predates D.S. #1) plus 1950s Sub-Mariner-r; Neal Adams-c 10.00 30.00 65.00
2-2nd app. Defenders; 1950s Sub-Mariner-r 4.70 14.00 28.00
3-Defenders ends 4.70 14.00 28.00
4-Re-intro Antman(1st app. since 1960s), begin series; brief origin; Spider-Man app. 2.40 6.00 12.00
5-10: 6-Wasp app. & begins team-ups. 8-Origin Antman & Wasp-r/TTA #44. 9-Iron Man app. 10-Last Antman 1.00 2.50 5.00
11-Thing vs. Hulk; 1st Thing solo book (9/73); origin Fantastic Four retold 1.40 3.50 7.00
12-Thing/Iron Man; early Thanos app.; occurs after Capt. Marvel #33; Starlin-a(p) 1.80 4.50 9.00

NOTE: ***Bolle** a-9i. **Everett** a-1i, 3i. **Hartley** r-10. **Kane** c-3p, 7p. **Russell** a-7-10p. **Starlin** a-8,*

11, 12; c-8.

MARVEL FEATURE (Also see Red Sonja)
Nov, 1975 - No. 7, Nov, 1976 (Story continues in Conan #68)
Marvel Comics Group

1-Red Sonja begins (pre-dates Red Sonja #1); adapts Howard short story; Adams-r/Savage Sword of Conan #1 .70 1.75 3.50
2-7: Thorne-c/a in #2-7. 7-Battles Conan .40 1.00 2.00

MARVEL FUMETTI BOOK
April, 1984 (One shot) ($1.00 cover price)
Marvel Comics Group

1-All photos; Stan Lee photo-c; A. Adams touch-ups .50 1.00

MARVEL GRAPHIC NOVEL
1982 - Present ($5.95-$6.95)
Marvel Comics Group (Epic Comics)

1-Death of Captain Marvel (1st Marvel graphic novel); Capt. Marvel battles Thanos 4.20 12.50 25.00
1 (2nd & 3rd printings) 1.20 3.00 6.00
2-Elric: The Dreaming City 1.60 4.00 8.00
3-Dreadstar; Starlin-c/a, 48pgs. 1.40 3.50 7.00
4-Origin/1st app. The New Mutants 3.00 6.50 15.00
4,5-2nd printings 1.20 3.00 6.00
5-X-Men; book-length story (1982) 2.40 6.00 12.00
6-18: 6-The Star Slammers. 7-Killraven. 8-Super Boxers; Byrne scripts. 9-The Futurians. 10-Heartburst. 11-Void Indigo. 12-The Dazzler. 13-Starstruck. 14-The Swords Of The Swashbucklers. 15-The Raven Banner (Asgard). 16-The Aladdin Effect. 17-Revenge Of The Living Monolith. 18-She Hulk 1.20 3.00 6.00
19-32: 19-The Witch Queen of Acheron (Conan). 20-Greenberg the Vampire. 21-Marada the She-Wolf. 22-Amaz. Spider-Man in Hooky by Wrightson. 23-Dr. Strange. 24-Love and War (Daredevil); Miller scripts. 25-Alien Legion. 26-Dracula. 27-Avengers (Emperor Doom). 28-Conan the Reaver. 29-The Big Chance (Thing vs. Hulk). 30-A Sailor's Story. 31-Wolfpack. 32-Death of Groo 1.40 3.50 7.00
32-2nd printing ($5.95) 1.20 3.00 6.00
33,34,36,37: 33-Thor. 34-Predator & Prey (Cloak & Dagger). 36-Willow (movie adapt.). 37-Hercules 1.40 3.50 7.00
35-Hitler's Astrologer (Shadow, $12.95, hard-c) 2.60 6.50 13.00
35-Soft cover reprint (1990, $10.95) 2.20 5.50 11.00
38-Silver Surfer (Judgement Day)($14.95) 3.00 7.50 15.00
nn-Inhumans (1988, $7.95)-Williamson-i 1.60 4.00 8.00
nn-Last of the Dragons (1988, $6.95) 1.40 3.50 7.00
nn-Who Framed Roger Rabbit (1989, $6.95) 1.40 3.50 7.00
nn-Roger Rabbit In The Resurrection Of Doom (1989, $8.95) 1.80 4.50 9.00
nn-Arena by Bruce Jones ($5.95) 1.20 3.00 6.00
NOTE: *Aragones a-27, 32. Byrne c/a-18. Kaluta a-13, 35p; c-13. Miller a-24p. Simonson a-6; c-6. Starlin c/a-1,3. Williamson a-34. Wrightson c-29i.*

MARVEL HOLIDAY SPECIAL
1991 ($2.25, color, 84 pgs.)
Marvel Comics

1-X-Men, Fantastic Four, Punisher, Thor, Capt. America, Ghost Rider, Capt. Ultra, Spidey stories; Art Adams-c/a .45 1.15 2.25

MARVEL ILLUSTRATED: SWIMSUIT ISSUE (See Marvel Swimsuit Spec.)
1991 ($3.95, color, magazine, 52 pgs.)
Marvel Comics

V1#1-Parody of Sports Illustrated swimsuit issue; Mary Jane Parker centerfold pin-up by Jusko; 2nd print exists .80 2.00 4.00

MARVEL MILESTONE EDITION
1991 - Present ($2.95, color, coated stock)(r/originals with original ads)
Marvel Comics

...: X-Men #1-Reprints X-Men #1 .60 1.50 3.00
...: Giant Size X-Men #1-($3.95, 68 pgs.) .80 2.00 4.00
...: Fantastic Four #1 (11/91) .60 1.50 3.00
...: Amazing Fantasy #15 (3/92) .60 1.50 3.00
...: Incredible Hulk #1 (3/92, says 3/91 by error) .60 1.50 3.00
...: Amazing Spider-Man #1 (1/93) .60 1.50 3.00
...: Amazing Spider-Man #129 (1/93) .60 1.50 3.00
...: Fantastic Four #5 (1/93) .60 1.50 3.00
...: Iron Fist #14 (1/93) .60 1.50 3.00
...: Iron Man #55 (1/93) .60 1.50 3.00
...: Tales of Suspense #39 (3/93) .60 1.50 3.00

MARVEL MINI-BOOKS
1966 (50 pgs., B&W; 5/8"x7/8") (6 different issues)
Marvel Comics Group (Smallest comics ever published)

Captain America, Spider-Man, Sgt. Fury, Hulk, Thor 2.40 6.00 12.00
Millie the Model 2.40 6.00 12.00
NOTE: *Each came in six different color covers, usually one color: Pink, yellow, green, etc.*

MARVEL MOVIE PREMIERE (Magazine)
Sept, 1975 (One Shot) (Black & White)
Marvel Comics Group

1-Burroughs' "The Land That Time Forgot" adaptation .40 1.00 2.00

MARVEL MOVIE SHOWCASE FEATURING STAR WARS
Nov, 1982 - No. 2, Dec, 1982 ($1.25, 68 pgs.)
Marvel Comics Group

1,2-Star Wars movie adaptation; reprints Star Wars #1-6 by Chaykin; 1-Reprints-c to Star Wars #1. 2-Stevens-r .60 1.25

MARVEL MOVIE SPOTLIGHT FEATURING RAIDERS OF THE LOST ARK
Nov, 1982 ($1.25, 68 pgs.)
Marvel Comics Group

1-Edited-r/Raiders of the Lost Ark #1-3; Buscema-c/a(p); movie adaptation .60 1.25

MARVEL MYSTERY COMICS (Formerly Marvel Comics) (Becomes Marvel Tales No. 93 on)
No. 2, Dec, 1939 - No. 92, June, 1949
Timely /Marvel Comics (TP #2-17/TCI #18-54/MCI #55-92)

GD25 FN65 VF82 NM94
2-American Ace begins, ends #3; Human Torch (blue costume) by Burgos, Sub-Mariner by Everett continue; 2 pg. origin recap of Human Torch 1060.00 3200.00 5800.00 8500.00
(Estimated up to 50 total copies exist, 5 in NM/Mint)
GD25 FN65 NM94
3-New logo from Marvel pulp begins 533.00 1600.00 3200.00
4-Intro. Electro, the Marvel of the Age (ends #19), The Ferret, Mystery Detective (ends #9) 433.00 1300.00 2600.00
GD25 FN65 VF82 NM94
5 (Scarce) 800.00 2400.00 4400.00 6500.00
(Estimated up to 75 total copies exist, 3 in NM/Mint)
GD25 FN65 NM94
6,7: 6-Gustavson Angel story 285.00 850.00 1700.00
8-Human Torch & Sub-Mariner battle 350.00 1050.00 2100.00
GD25 FN65 VF82 NM94
9-(Scarce)-Human Torch & Sub-Mariner battle 690.00 2060.00 3800.00 5500.00
(Estimated up to 75 total copies exist, 6 in NM/Mint)
GD25 FN65 NM94
10-Human Torch & Sub-Mariner battle, conclusion; Terry Vance, the Schoolboy Sleuth begins, ends #57 267.00 800.00 1600.00
11 200.00 600.00 1200.00
12-Classic Kirby-c 183.00 550.00 1100.00
13-Intro. & 1st app. The Vision by S&K; Sub-Mariner dons new costume, ends #15 225.00 675.00 1350.00
14-16: 15-S&K Vision, Gustavson Angel story 125.00 375.00 750.00
17-Human Torch/Sub-Mariner team-up by Burgos/Everett; pin-up on back-c 142.00 425.00 850.00

Marvel Feature #4 (2nd series),
© MEG

Marvel Milestone Edition #1,
© MEG

Marvel Mystery Comics #3,
© MEG

Marvel Mystery Comics #32, © MEG

Marvel Mystery Comics #81, © MEG

Marvel Premiere #6, © MEG

	GD25	FN65	NM94
18	117.00	350.00	700.00
19-Origin Toro in text	125.00	375.00	750.00
20-Origin The Angel in text	125.00	375.00	750.00
21-Intro. & 1st app. The Patriot; not in #46-48; pin-up on back-c	108.00	325.00	650.00
22-25: 23-Last Gustavson Angel; origin The Vision in text. 24-Injury-to-eye story	92.00	275.00	550.00
26-30: 27-Ka-Zar ends; last S&K Vision who battles Satan. 28-Jimmy Jupiter in the Land of Nowhere begins, ends #48; Sub-Mariner vs. The Flying Dutchman	87.00	262.00	525.00
31-Sub-Mariner by Everett ends, begins again #84	83.00	250.00	500.00
32-1st app. The Boboes	83.00	250.00	500.00
33,35-40: 40-Zeppelin-c	83.00	250.00	500.00
34-Everett, Burgos, Martin Goodman, Funnies, Inc. office appear in story & battles Hitler; last Burgos Human Torch	96.00	288.00	575.00
41-43,45-48: 46-Hitler-c. 48-Last Vision; flag-c	75.00	225.00	450.00
44-Classic Super Plane-c	75.00	225.00	450.00
49-Origin Miss America	96.00	288.00	575.00
50-Mary becomes Miss Patriot (origin)	75.00	225.00	450.00
51-60: 53-Bondage-c	67.00	200.00	400.00
61,62,64-Last German War-c	62.00	188.00	375.00
63-Classic Hitler War-c; The Villainess Cat-Woman only app.	67.00	200.00	400.00
65,66-Last Japanese War-c	62.00	188.00	375.00
67-75: 74-Last Patriot. 75-Young Allies begin	58.00	175.00	350.00
76-78: 76-Ten Chapter Miss America serial begins, ends #85	58.00	175.00	350.00
79-New cover format; Super Villains begin on cover; last Angel	58.00	175.00	350.00
80-1st app. Capt. America in Marvel Comics	72.00	218.00	435.00
81-Captain America app.	62.00	188.00	375.00
82-Origin Namora; 1st Sub-Mariner/Namora team-up; Captain America app.	108.00	325.00	650.00
83,85: 83-Last Young Allies. 85-Last Miss America; Blonde Phantom app.	54.00	162.00	325.00
84-Blonde Phantom, Sub-Mariner by Everett begins; Captain America app.	75.00	225.00	450.00
86-Blonde Phantom i.d. revealed; Captain America app.; last Bucky app.	62.00	188.00	375.00
87-1st Capt. America/Golden Girl team-up	67.00	200.00	400.00
88-Golden Girl, Namora, & Sun Girl (1st in Marvel Comics) x-over; Captain America, Blonde Phantom app.; last Toro	62.00	188.00	375.00
89-1st Human Torch/Sun Girl team-up; 1st Captain America solo; Blonde Phantom app.	64.00	192.00	385.00
90-Blonde Phantom un-masked; Captain America app.	67.00	200.00	400.00
91-Capt. America app.; intro Venus; Blonde Phantom & Sub-Mariner end	67.00	200.00	400.00
92-Feature story on the birth of the Human Torch and the death of Professor Horton (his creator); 1st app. The Witness in Marvel Comics; Captain America app.	100.00	300.00	600.00
132 Pg. issue, B&W, 25 cents (1943-44)-printed in N. Y.; square binding, blank inside covers; has Marvel No. 33-c in color; contains Capt. America #18 & Marvel Mystery Comics #33; same contents as Captain America Annual (only three copies known to exist)	500.00	1500.00	3000.00

NOTE: ***Brodsky*** *c-49, 72, 86, 88-92.* ***Crandall*** *a-26i.* ***Everett*** *c-7-9, 27, 84.* ***Gabrielle*** *c-30-32.* ***Schomburg*** *c-3-11, 13-29, 33-36, 39-48, 50-59, 63-69, 74, 76, 132 pg. issue.* ***Shores*** *c-37, 38, 75p, 77, 78p, 79p, 80, 81p, 82-84, 85p, 87p.* ***Sekowsky*** *c-73. Bondage covers-3, 4, 7, 12, 28, 29, 49, 50, 52, 56, 57, 58, 59, 65. Remember Pearl Harbor issues-#30-32.*

MARVEL NO-PRIZE BOOK, THE (The Official... on-c)
Jan, 1983 (One Shot, Direct Sale only)
Marvel Comics Group

	GD25	FN65	NM94
1-Golden-c		.50	1.00

MARVEL PREMIERE
April, 1972 - No. 61, Aug, 1981 (A tryout book for new characters)
Marvel Comics Group

	GD25	FN65	NM94
1-Origin Warlock (pre #1) by Gil Kane/Adkins; origin Counter-Earth; Hulk & Thor cameo (#1-14 are 25 cent-c)	7.50	22.50	45.00
2-Warlock ends; Kirby Yellow Claw-r	4.70	14.00	28.00
3-Dr. Strange series begins (pre #1, 7/72), B. Smith-a(p); Smith-c?	5.00	15.00	30.00
4-Smith/Brunner-a	2.40	6.00	12.00
5-9	1.40	3.50	7.00
10-Death of the Ancient One	2.00	5.00	10.00
11-14: 11-Dr. Strange origin-r by Ditko. 14-Last Dr. Strange (3/74), gets own title 3 months later	1.00	2.50	5.00
15-Origin/1st app. Iron Fist (5/74), ends #25	7.50	22.50	45.00
16-24: Iron Fist in all. 16-Hama's 1st Marvel-a	2.40	6.00	12.00
25-1st Byrne Iron Fist (moves to own title next)	3.00	7.50	15.00
26,27: 26-Hercules. 27-Satana	1.00	2.50	5.00
28-Legion of Monsters (Ghost Rider, Man-Thing, Morbius, Werewolf)	2.40	6.00	12.00
29-49,51-56,61: 29,30-The Liberty Legion. 29-1st modern app. Patriot. 31-1st app. Woodgod; last 25 cent issue. 32-1st app. Monark Starstalker. 33,34-1st color app. Solomon Kane. 35-Origin/1st app. 3-D Man. 36,37-3-D Man. 38-1st Weirdworld. 39,40-Torpedo. 41-1st Seeker 3001! 42-Tigra. 43-Paladin. 44-Jack of Hearts (1st solo book, 10/78). 45,46-Man-Wolf. 47-Origin/1st app. new Ant-Man. 48-Ant-Man. 49-The Falcon (1st solo book, 8/79). 51-53-Black Panther. 54-1st Caleb Hammer. 55-Wonder Man. 56-1st color app. Dominic Fortune. 61-Star Lord	.30	.75	1.50
50-1st app. Alice Cooper; co-plotted by Alice	1.20	3.00	6.00
57-Dr. Who (1st U.S. app.)	.60	1.50	3.00
58-60-Dr. Who	.40	1.00	2.00

NOTE: ***N. Adams*** *(Crusty Bunkers) part inks-10, 12, 13.* ***Austin*** *a-50i, 56i; c-46i, 50i, 56i, 58.* ***Brunner*** *a-4i, 6p, 9-14p; c-9-14.* ***Byrne*** *a-47p, 48p.* ***Chaykin*** *a-32-34; c-32, 33, 56.* ***Giffen*** *a-31p, 44p; c-44.* ***Gil Kane*** *a(p)-1, 2, 15; c(p)-1, 2, 15, 16, 22-24, 27, 36, 37.* ***Kirby*** *c-26, 29-31, 35.* ***Layton*** *a-47i, 48i; c-47.* ***McWilliams*** *a-25i.* ***Miller*** *c-49p, 53p, 58p.* ***Nebres*** *a-44i; c-38i.* ***Nino*** *a-38i.* ***Perez*** *c/a-38p, 45p, 46p.* ***Ploog*** *a-38; c-5-7.* ***Russell*** *a-7p.* ***Simonson*** *a-60(2pgs.); c-57.* ***Starlin*** *a-8p; c-8.* ***Sutton*** *a-41, 43, 50p, 61; c-50p, 61. #57-60 published w/two different prices on-c.*

MARVEL PRESENTS
October, 1975 - No. 12, Aug, 1977 (#1-5 are 25 cent-c)
Marvel Comics Group

	GD25	FN65	NM94
1-Origin & 1st app. Bloodstone	1.10	2.75	5.50
2-Origin Bloodstone continued; Kirby-c	.80	2.00	4.00
3-Guardians of the Galaxy (1st solo book, 2/76) begins, ends #12	4.20	12.50	25.00
4-7,9-12: 9,10-Origin Starhawk	3.00	7.50	15.00
8-r/story from Silver Surfer #2 plus 4 pgs. new-a	3.20	8.00	16.00

NOTE: ***Austin*** *a-6i.* ***Buscema*** *r-8p.* ***Chaykin*** *a-5i.* ***Kane*** *c-1p.* ***Starlin*** *layouts-10.*

MARVEL PREVIEW (Magazine) (Bizarre Adventures #25 on)
Feb, 1975 - No. 24, Winter, 1980 (B&W) ($1.00)
Marvel Comics Group

	GD25	FN65	NM94
1-Man-Gods From Beyond the Stars; Crusty Bunkers (Neal Adams)-a(i) & cover; Nino-a	.40	1.00	2.00
2-Origin The Punisher (see Amaz. Spider-Man #129 & Classic Punisher); 1st app. Dominic Fortune; Morrow-c	26.00	78.00	180.00
3-7,9,10: 3-Blade the Vampire Slayer. 4-Star-Lord & Sword in the Star (origins & 1st app.). 5,6-Sherlock Holmes. 6-N. Adams frontispiece. 7-Satana, Sword in the Star app. 9-Man-God; origin Star Hawk, ends #20. 10-Thor the Mighty. 10,11-Starlin frontispiece in each	.40	1.00	2.00
8-Legion of Monsters; Morbius app.	1.60	4.00	8.00
11-20,22-24: 11-Star-Lord; Byrne-a. 12-Haunt of Horror. 14,15-Star-Lord; 14-Starlin painted-c. 16-Masters of Terror. 17-Blackmark by G. Kane (see SSOC #1-3). 18-Star-Lord. 19-Kull. 20-Bizarre Advs. 22-King Arthur. 23-Bizarre Advs.; Miller-a. 24-Debut Paradox	.40	1.00	2.00

21-Moon Knight (Spr/80)-Predates Moon Knight #1; The Shroud by Ditko .80 2.00 4.00

NOTE: ***N. Adams*** *(C. Bunkers) r-20i.* ***Buscema*** *a-22, 23.* ***Byrne*** *a-11.* ***Chaykin*** *a-20r; c-20 (new).* ***Colan*** *a-8, 16p(3), 18p, 23p; c-16p.* ***Elias*** *a-18.* ***Giffen*** *a-7.* ***Infantino*** *a-14p.* ***Kaluta*** *a-12; c-15.* ***Miller*** *a-23.* ***Morrow*** *a-8i; c-2-4.* ***Perez*** *a-20p.* ***Ploog*** *a-8.* ***Starlin*** *c-13, 14. Nudity in some issues*

MARVEL SAGA, THE
Dec, 1985 - No. 25, Dec, 1987
Marvel Comics Group

1 .30 .75 1.50
2-25 .50 1.00

NOTE: ***Williamson*** *a(i)-9, 10; c(i)-7, 10-12, 14, 16.*

MARVEL'S GREATEST COMICS (Marvel Collectors Item Classics #1-22)
No. 23, Oct, 1969 - No. 96, Jan, 1981
Marvel Comics Group

23-30: Begin Fantastic Four-r/#30s?-116 .60 1.50 3.00
31-34,38-96: 42-Silver Surfer-r/F.F.(others?) .40 1.00 2.00
35-37-Silver Surfer-r/Fantastic Four #48-50 .40 1.00 2.00

NOTE: *Dr. Strange, Fantastic Four, Iron Man, Watcher-#23, 24. Capt. America, Dr. Strange, Iron Man, Fantastic Four-#25-28. Fantastic Four-#38-96.* ***Buscema*** *r-85-92; c-87-92r.* ***Ditko*** *r-23-28.* ***Kirby*** *r-23-82; c-75, 77p, 80p. #81 reprints Fantastic Four #100.*

MARVELS OF SCIENCE
March, 1946 - No. 4, June, 1946
Charlton Comics

1-A-Bomb story 11.00 32.00 75.00
2-4 8.35 25.00 50.00

MARVEL SPECIAL EDITION FEATURING... (Also see Special Collectors' Edition)
1975 - 1978 (84 pgs.) (Oversized)
Marvel Comics Group

1-The Spectacular Spider-Man ($1.50); r/Amazing Spider-Man #6,35, Annual 1; Ditko-a(r) .40 1.00 2.00
1-Star Wars (1977, $1.00); r/Star Wars #1-3 .40 1.00 2.00
2-Star Wars (1978, $1.00); r/Star Wars #4-6 .30 .75 1.50
3-Star Wars ('78, $2.50, 116pgs.); r/S. Wars #1-6 .50 1.25 2.50
3-Close Encounters of the Third Kind (1978, $1.50, 56 pgs.)-Movie adaptation; Simonson-a(p) .30 .75 1.50
V2#2(Spring, 1980, $2.00, oversized)-"Star Wars: The Empire Strikes Back;" r/Marvel Comics Super Special #16 .30 .75 1.50

NOTE: ***Chaykin*** *c/a(r)-1(1977), 2, 3.* ***Stevens*** *a(r)-2i, 3i.* ***Williamson*** *a(r)-V2#2.*

MARVEL SPECTACULAR
Aug, 1973 - No. 19, Nov, 1975
Marvel Comics Group

1-Thor-r from mid-sixties begin by Kirby .40 1.00 2.00
2-19 .30 .75 1.50

MARVEL SPOTLIGHT (...& Son of Satan #19, 20, 23, 24)
Nov, 1971 - No. 33, Apr, 1977; V2#1, July, 1979 - V2#11, Mar, 1981
Marvel Comics Group (A try-out book for new characters)

1-Origin Red Wolf (western hero)(1st solo book, pre #1); Wood inks, Neal Adams-c; only 15 cent issue 4.00 12.00 24.00
2-(25 cents, 52 pgs.)-Venus-r by Everett; origin/1st app. Werewolf By Night (begins) by Ploog; N. Adams-c 5.00 15.00 30.00
3,4: 4-Werewolf By Night ends (2/72) 2.80 7.00 14.00
5-Origin/1st app. Ghost Rider (8/72) & begins 18.00 54.00 125.00
6-8: 6-Origin G.R. retold. 8-Last Ploog issue 9.15 27.50 55.00
9-11-Last Ghost Rider (gets own title next mo.) 7.50 22.50 45.00
12-Origin & 2nd full app. The Son of Satan (10/73); story cont'd from Ghost Rider #2 & into #3; series begins, ends #24 1.80 4.50 9.00
13-21,23,24: 14-Last 20 cent issue. 24-Last Son of Satan (10/75); gets own title 12/75 .90 2.25 4.50
22-Ghost Rider-c & cameo (5 panels) 2.00 5.00 10.00
25-27,30,31: 25-Sinbad; contains pull-out Mark Jewelers ad. 26-Scarecrow. 27-Sub-Mariner. 30-The Warriors Three. 31-Nick Fury .70 1.75 3.50

28,29: Moon Knight (28-1st solo app., 6/76). 29-Last 25 cent issue 2.00 5.00 10.00
32-1st app./partial origin Spider-Woman (2/77); Nick Fury app. 1.60 4.00 8.00
33-Deathlok; 1st app. Devil-Slayer 1.60 4.00 8.00
V2#1-11: 1-4,8-Capt. Marvel. 5-Dragon Lord. 6,7-StarLord; origin #6. 9-11-Capt. Universe (see Micronauts #8) .50 1.00

NOTE: ***Austin*** *c-V2#2i, 8.* ***J. Buscema*** *c/a-30p.* ***Chaykin*** *a-31; c-26, 31.* ***Colan*** *a-18p, 19p.* ***Ditko*** *a-V2#4, 5, 9-11; c-V2#4, 9-11.* ***Kane*** *c-21p, 32p.* ***Kirby*** *c-29p.* ***McWilliams*** *a-20i.* ***Miller*** *a-V2#8p; c(p)-V2#2, 5, 7-9.* ***Mooney*** *a-8i, 10i, 14p, 15, 16p, 17p, 24p, 27, 32i.* ***Nasser*** *a-33p.* ***Ploog*** *a-2-5, 6-8p; c-3-9.* ***Romita*** *c-13.* ***Sutton*** *a-9-11p, V2#6, 7. #29-25 cent & 30 cent issues exist.*

MARVEL SUPER ACTION (Magazine)
January, 1976 (One Shot) (76 pgs.; black & white)
Marvel Comics Group

1-Origin & 2nd app. Dominic Fortune; Early Punisher app.; Weird World & The Huntress; Evans & Ploog-a 13.00 40.00 90.00

MARVEL SUPER ACTION
May, 1977 - No. 37, Nov, 1981
Marvel Comics Group

1-Reprints Capt. America #100 by Kirby .50 1.25 2.50
2,3,5-13: r/Capt. America #101,102,103-111. 11-Origin-r. 12,13-Classic Steranko-c/a(r) .30 .75 1.50
4-Marvel Boy-r(origin)/M. Boy #1 .30 .75 1.50
14-37: r/Avengers #55,56, Annual 2, others .50 1.00

NOTE: ***Buscema*** *a(r)-14p, 15p; c-18-20, 22, 35r-37.* ***Everett*** *a-4.* ***Heath*** *a-4r.* ***Kirby*** *r-1-3, 5-11.* ***B. Smith*** *a-27r, 28r.* ***Steranko*** *a(r)-12p, 13p; c-12r, 13r.*

MARVEL SUPER HERO CONTEST OF CHAMPIONS
June, 1982 - No. 3, Aug, 1982 (Mini-Series)
Marvel Comics Group

1-3: Features nearly all Marvel characters currently appearing in their comics; 1st Marvel limited series .80 2.00 4.00

MARVEL SUPER HEROES
October, 1966 (25 cents, 68 pgs.) (1st Marvel One-shot)
Marvel Comics Group

1-r/origin Daredevil from D.D. #1; r/Avengers #2; G.A. Sub-Mariner-r/ Marvel Mystery #8 (Human Torch app.) 1.00 30.00 65.00

MARVEL SUPER-HEROES (Formerly Fantasy Masterpieces #1-11)
(Also see Giant-Size Super Heroes) (#12-20: 25 cents, 68 pgs.)
No. 12, 12/67 - No. 31, 11/71; No. 32, 9/72 - No. 105, 1/82
Marvel Comics Group

12-Origin & 1st app. Capt. Marvel of the Kree; G.A. Human Torch, Destroyer, Capt. America, Black Knight, Sub-Mariner-r (#12-20 all contain new stories and reprints) 14.00 43.00 100.00
13-2nd app. Capt. Marvel; G.A. Black Knight, Torch, Vision, Capt. America, Sub-Mariner-r 7.50 22.5 45.00
14-Amazing Spider-Man (5/68, new-a by Andru/Everett); G.A. Sub-Mariner, Torch, Mercury (1st Kirby-a at Marvel), Black Knight, Capt. America reprints 13.00 40.00 90.00
15-Black Bolt cameo in Medusa (new-a); Black Knight, Sub-Mariner, Black Marvel, Capt. America-r 2.40 6.00 12.00
16-Origin & 1st app. S. A. Phantom Eagle; G.A. Torch, Capt. America, Black Knight, Patriot, Sub-Mariner-r 2.40 6.00 12.00
17-Origin Black Knight (new-a); G.A. Torch, Sub-Mariner-r; reprint from All-Winners Squad #21 (cover & story) 2.40 6.00 12.00
18-Origin/1st app. Guardians of the Galaxy (1/69); G.A. Sub-Mariner, All-Winners Squad-r 10.00 30.00 60.00
19-Ka-Zar (new-a); G.A. Torch, Marvel Boy, Black Knight, Sub-Mariner reprints; Smith-c(p); Tuska-a(r) 2.40 6.00 12.00
20-Doctor Doom (5/69); r/Young Men #24 w/-c 2.40 6.00 12.00
21-31: All-r issues. 21-X-Men-r begin? 31-Last Giant issue 1.20 3.00 6.00
32-105: 32-Hulk/Sub-Mariner-r begin from TTA. 56-r/origin Hulk/Inc. Hulk #102; Hulk-r begin .50 1.00

Marvel's Greatest Comics #35, © MEG

Marvel Spotlight #10, © MEG

Marvel Super-Heroes #20, © MEG

Marvel Tales #127 (1st Series), © MEG

Marvel Tales #10 (1967), © MEG

Marvel Tales #114, © MEG

GD25 FN65 NM94

NOTE: ***Austin** a-104. **Colan** a(p)-12, 13, 15, 18; c-12, 13, 15, 18. **Everett** a-14i(new); r-14, 15i, 18, 19, 33; c-85(r). New **Kirby** c-22, 27. **Maneely** r-14, 15, 19. **Severin** r-83-85i, 100-102; c-100-102r. **Starlin** c-47. **Tuska** a-19p. Black Knight-r by **Maneely** in 12-16, 19. Sub-Mariner-r by **Everett** in 12-20.*

MARVEL SUPER-HEROES
May, 1990 - Present ($2.95-$2.25/$2.50, quarterly, 68-84 pgs.)
Marvel Comics

1-Moon Knight, Hercules, Black Panther, Magik, Brother Voodoo, Speedball (by Ditko) & Hellcat; Hembeck-a .70 1.75 3.50
2,4-5: 2-Rogue, Speedball (by Ditko), Iron Man, Falcon, Tigra & Daredevil. 4-Spider-Man/Nick Fury, Daredevil, Speedball, Wonder Man, Spitfire & Black Knight; Byrne-c. 5-Thor, Dr. Strange, Thing & She-Hulk; Speedball by Ditko(p) .60 1.50 3.00
V2#3-Retells origin Capt. America w/new facts; Blue Shield, Capt. Marvel, Speedball, Wasp; Hulk by Ditko/Rogers .80 2.00 4.00
V2#6-9: 6-8-$2.25-c. 6,7-X-Men, Cloak & Dagger, The Shroud (by Ditko) & Marvel Boy in each. 8-X-Men, Namor & Iron Man (by Ditko). 9-W.C. Avengers, Iron Man app.; Kieth-c(p); begin $2.50-c .60 1.50 3.00
V2#10-Ms. Marvel/Sabretooth-c/story (intended for Ms. Marvel #24; shows-c to #24); Namor, Vision, Scarlet Witch stories .60 1.50 3.00
V2#11,12: 11-Ghost Rider-c/story (origin); Giant-Man, Ms. Marvel stories. 12-Dr. Strange, Falcon, Iron Man .50 1.25 2.50
V2#13-($2.75)-All Iron Man issue; 30th anniversary .55 1.40 2.75

MARVEL SUPER HEROES SECRET WARS (See Secret Wars II)
May, 1984 - No. 12, Apr, 1985 (Limited series)
Marvel Comics Group

1 .70 1.75 3.50
1-3-2nd printings (sold in multi-packs) .50 1.00
2-7,9-12: 6-The Wasp dies. 7-Intro. new Spider-Woman. 12-($1.00, 52 pgs.) .40 1.00 2.00
8-Spider-Man's new costume explained as Alien costume (later becomes Venom) 3.00 7.50 15.00

MARVEL SUPER SPECIAL A (See Marvel Comics Super...)

MARVEL SWIMSUIT SPECIAL (Also see Marvel Illustrated...)
1992 ($3.95, color, magazine, 52 pgs.)
Marvel Comics

1-Silvestri-c; pin-ups by many good artists .80 2.00 4.00

MARVEL TAILS STARRING PETER PORKER THE SPECTACULAR SPIDER-HAM
Nov, 1983 (One Shot)
Marvel Comics Group

1-Peter Porker, the Spectacular Spider-Ham, Captain Americat, Goose Rider, Hulk Bunny app. .30 .75 1.50

MARVEL TALES (Formerly Marvel Mystery Comics #1-92)
No. 93, Aug, 1949 - No. 159, Aug, 1957
Marvel/Atlas Comics (MCI)

93 57.00 171.00 400.00
94-Everett-a 42.00 125.00 290.00
95,96,99,101,103,105 27.00 81.00 190.00
97-Sun Girl, 2 pgs; Kirbyish-a; one story used in N.Y. State Legislative document 34.00 103.00 240.00
98-Krigstein-a 27.00 81.00 190.00
100 27.00 81.00 190.00
102-Wolverton-a "The End of the World," 6 pgs. 39.00 118.00 275.00
104-Wolverton-a "Gateway to Horror," 6 pgs. 36.00 107.00 250.00
106,107-Krigstein-a. 106-Decapitation story 23.00 70.00 160.00
108-120: 118-Hypo-c/panels in End of World story. 120-Jack Katz-a 14.00 43.00 100.00
121,123-131: 128-Flying Saucer-c. 131-Last precode (2/55) 11.50 34.00 80.00
122-Kubert-a 12.00 36.00 85.00
132,133,135-141,143,145 8.35 25.00 50.00
134-Krigstein, Kubert-a; flying saucer-c 10.00 30.00 60.00
142-Krigstein-a 8.35 25.00 50.00
144-Williamson/Krenkel-a, 3 pgs. 9.15 27.50 55.00
146,148-151,154,155,158 6.70 20.00 40.00
147-Ditko-a 8.35 25.00 50.00
152-Wood, Morrow-a 8.35 25.00 50.00
153-Everett End of World c/story 9.15 27.50 55.00
156-Torres-a 6.70 20.00 40.00
157,159-Krigstein-a 8.35 25.00 50.00

NOTE: ***Andru** a-103. **Briefer** a-118. **Check** a-147. **Colan** a-105, 107, 118, 120, 121, 127, 131. **Drucker** a-127, 135, 141, 146, 150. **Everett** a-98, 104, 106(2), 108(2), 131, 148, 151, 153, 155; c-107, 109, 111, 112, 114, 117, 127, 143, 147-151, 153, 155, 156. **Forte** a-119, 125, 130. **Heath** a-110, 113, 118, 119; c-104-106, 110, 130. **Gil Kane** a-117. **Lawrence** a-130. **Maneely** a-111, 126, 129; c-108, 116, 120, 129, 152. **Mooney** a-114. **Morisi** a-153. **Morrow** a-150, 152, 156. **Orlando** a-149, 151, 157. **Pakula** a-119, 121, 135, 144, 150, 152, 156. **Powell** a-136, 137, 150, 154. **Ravielli** a-117. **Rico** a-97, 99. **Romita** a-108. **Sekowsky** a-96-98. **Shores** a-110; c-96. **Sinnott** a-105, 116. **Tuska** a-114. **Whitney** a-107. **Wildey** a-126, 138.*

MARVEL TALES (...Annual #1,2; ...Starring Spider-Man #123 on)
1964 - Present (No. 1-32: 72 pgs.)
Marvel Comics Group (NPP earlier issues)

1-Reprints origins of Spider-Man/Amazing Fantasy #15, Hulk/Inc. Hulk#1, Ant-Man/T.T.A. #35, Giant Man/T.T.A. #49, Iron Man/T.O.S. #39,48, Thor/J.I.M. #83 & r/Sgt. Fury #1 30.00 9.00 210.00
2 ('65)-r/X-Men #1(origin), Avengers #1(origin), origin Dr. Strange-r/Strange Tales #115 & origin Hulk(Hulk #3) 10.00 30.00 65.00
3 (7/66)-Spider-Man, Strange Tales, Journey into Mystery, Tales to Astonish-r begin (r/Strange Tales #101) 5.00 15.00 30.00
4,5 2.80 7.00 14.00
6-8,10: 10-Reprints 1st Kraven/Amaz. S-M #15 1.80 4.50 9.00
9-r/Amazing Spider-Man #14 w/cover 2.20 5.50 11.00
11-32: 11-Spider-Man battles Daredevil-r/Amaz. Spider-Man #16. 13-Origin Marvel Boy-r/M. Boy #1. 22-Green Goblin-c/story-r/Amaz. Spider-Man #27. 30-New Angel story. 32-Last 72 pg. issue 1.20 3.00 6.00
33-105: 33-Kraven-r; 52 pgs. 34-Begin reg. size issues. 75-Origin Spider-Man-r. 77-79-Drug issues-r/A. Spider-Man #96-98. 98-Death of Gwen Stacy-r/A. Spider-Man #121 (Green Goblin). 99-Death Green Goblin-r/A. Spider-Man #122. 100-(52 pgs.)-New Hawkeye/Two Gun Kid story. 101-105-All Spider-Man-r .30 .75 1.50
106-1st Punisher-r/Amazing Spider-Man #129 1.80 4.50 9.00
107-133-All Spider-Man-r. 111,112-r/Spider-Man #134,135 (Punisher). 113, 114-r/Spider-Man #136,137(Green Goblin) .50 1.00
134-136-Dr. Strange-r begin; SpM stories continue. 134-Dr. Strange-r/Strange Tales #110 .50 1.00
137-Origin-r Dr. Strange; shows original unprinted-c & origin Spider-Man/Amazing Fantasy #15 1.00 2.50 5.00
137-Nabisco giveaway .50 1.00
138-Reprints all Amazing Spider-Man #1; begin reprints of Spider-Man with covers similar to originals 1.00 2.50 5.00
139-144: r/Amazing Spider-Man #2-7 .40 1.00 2.00
145-191,193-199: Spider-Man-r continue w/#8 on. 149-Contains skin "Tattooz." 150-($1.00, 52pgs.)-r/Spider-Man Annual 1(Kraven app.). 153-r/1st Kraven/Spider-Man #15. 155-r/2nd Gr. Goblin/Spider-Man #17. 161,164,165-Gr. Goblin-c/stories-r/Spider-Man #23,26,27. 178,179-Green Goblin-c/story-r/Spider-Man #39,40. 187,189-Kraven-r. 191-($1.50, 68pgs.)-r/Spider-Man #96-98. 193-Byrne-r/Marvel Team-Up begin w/scripts .60 1.20
192-($1.25, 52 pgs.)-r/Spider-Man #121,122 .40 1.00 2.00
200-Double size ($1.25)-Miller-c & r/Annual #14 .30 .75 1.50
201-208,210-222: 208-Last Byrne-r. 210,211-r/Spidey 134,135. 212,213-r/Gnt. Size Spidey 4. 213-r/1st solo Silver Surfer story/F.F. Annual #5. 214, 215-r/Spidey 161,162. 222-Reprints origin Punisher/Spectacular Spider-Man #83; last Punisher reprint .50 1.00
209-Reprints 1st app. The Punisher/Amazing Spider-Man #129; Punisher

reprints begin, end #222 .50 1.25 2.50
223-McFarlane-c begin, end #239 .30 .75 1.50
224-249,251,252,254-257: 233-Spider-Man/X-Men team-ups begin; r/X-Men #35. 234-r/Marvel Team-Up #4. 235,236-r/M. Team-Up Annual #1. 237, 238-r/M. Team-Up #150. 239,240-r/M. Team-Up #38,90(Beast). 242-r/M. Team-Up #89. 243-r/M. Team-Up #117(Wolverine). 251-r/Spider-Man #100(Gr. Goblin-c/story). 252-r/1st app. Morbius/Amaz. Spider-Man #101. 254-r/M. Team-Up #15(Ghost Rider); new painted-c. 255,256-Spider-Man & Ghost Rider-r/Marvel Team-Up #58,91. 257-Hobgoblin-r begin(r/A. Spider-Man #238); last $1.00-c .50 1.00
250-($1.50, 52pgs.)-r/1st Karma/M. Team-Up #100 .30 .75 1.50
253-($1.50, 52 pgs.)-r/Amaz. S-M #102 .30 .75 1.50
258-274: 258-261-r/A. Spider-Man #239,249-251(Hobgoblin). 262,263-r/Marv. Team-Up #53,54. 262-New X-Men vs. Sunstroke story. 263-New Wood-god origin story. 264,265-r/A. Spider-Man Annual 5. 266-Begins alien costume-r/A. S-M 252. 267-270-r/A. S-M #253-256 .60 1.25

NOTE: *All contain reprints; some have new art. #89-97-r/Amazing Spider-Man #110-118; #98-136-r/#121-159; #137-150-r/Amazing Fantasy #15, #1-12 & Annual 1; #151-167-r/#13-28 & Annual 2; #168-186-r/#29-46.* ***Austin*** *a-100i.* ***Byrne*** *a(r)-193-198p, 201-208p.* ***Ditko*** *a-1-30, 83, 100, 137-155.* ***G. Kane*** *a-71, 81, 98-101p, 249r; c-125-127p, 130p, 137-155.* ***Sam Kieth*** *c-255, 262, 263.* ***Ron Lim*** *c-266p, 267p.* ***McFarlane*** *c-223-239.* ***Mooney*** *a-63, 95-97i, 103(i).* ***Nasser*** *a-100p.* ***Nebres*** *a-242i.* ***Perez*** *c-259-261.* ***Rogers*** *c-240, 241, 243-251.*

MARVEL TEAM-UP (See Marvel Treasury Edition #18 & Official Marvel Index To...)
March, 1972 - No. 150, Feb, 1985
Marvel Comics Group
NOTE: *Spider-Man team-ups in all but Nos. 18, 23, 26, 29, 32, 35, 97, 104, 105, 137.*

1-Human Torch 9.15 27.50 55.00
2-Human Torch 4.00 11.00 22.00
3-Spider-Man/Human Torch vs. Morbius (part 1) 5.85 17.50 35.00
4-Spider-Man/X-Men vs. Morbius (part 2 of sty.) 7.50 22.50 45.00
5-10: 5-Vision. 6-Thing. 7-Thor. 8-The Cat. 9-Iron Man. 10-H-T 2.00 5.00 10.00
11-14,16-20: 11-Inhumans. 12-Werewolf. 13-Capt. America. 14-Sub-Mariner. 16-Capt. Marvel. 17-Mr. Fantastic. 18-H-T/Hulk. 19-Ka-Zar. 20-Black Panther; last 20 cent issue 1.60 4.00 8.00
15-1st Spider-Man/Ghost Rider team-up (11/73) 3.00 7.50 15.00
21-30: 21-Dr. Strange. 22-Hawkeye. 23-H-T/Iceman (X-Men cameo). 24-Brother Voodoo. 25-Daredevil. 26-H-T/Thor. 27-Hulk. 28-Hercules. 29-H-T/Iron Man. 30-Falcon 1.20 3.00 6.00
31-45,47-50: 31-Iron Fist. 32-H-T/Son of Satan. 33-Nighthawk. 34-Valkyrie. 35-H-T/Dr. Strange. 36-Frankenstein. 37-Man-Wolf. 38-Beast. 39-H-T. 40-Sons of the Tiger/H-T. 41-Scarlet Witch. 42-The Vision. 43-Dr. Doom; retells origin. 44-Moondragon. 45-Killraven. 47-Thing. 48-Iron Man; last 25 cent issue. 49-Dr. Strange; Iron Man app. 50-Iron Man; Dr. Strange app. 1.00 2.50 5.00
46-Spider-Man/Deathlok team-up 2.20 5.50 11.00
51,52,56,57: 51-Iron Man; Dr. Strange app. 52-Capt. America. 56-Daredevil. 57-Black Widow .70 1.75 3.50
53-Hulk; Woodgod & X-Men app., 1st Byrne-a on X-Men (1/77) 2.40 6.00 12.00
54,59,60: 54-Hulk; Woodgod app. 59-Yellowjacket/The Wasp. 60-The Wasp (Byrne-a in all) 1.20 3.00 6.00
55-Warlock-c/story; Byrne-a 1.60 4.00 8.00
58-Ghost Rider 1.20 3.00 6.00
61-70: All Byrne-a; 61-H-T. 62-Ms. Marvel; last 30 cent issue. . 63-Iron Fist. 64-Daughters of the Dragon. 65-Capt. Britain (1st U.S. app.). 66-Capt. Britain; 1st app. Arcade. 67-Tigra; Kraven the Hunter app. 68-Man-Thing. 69-Havok (from X-Men). 70-Thor .65 1.65 3.30
71-74,76-78,80: 71-Falcon. 72-Iron Man. 73-Daredevil. 74-Not Ready for Prime Time Players (Belushi). 76-Dr. Strange. 77-Ms. Marvel. 78-Wonder Man. 80-Dr. Strange/Clea; last 35 cent issue .60 1.50 3.00
75,79: 75-Power Man. 79-Mary Jane Watson as Red Sonja. Both have Byrne-a(p) .65 1.65 3.30
81-85,87,88,90,92-99: 81-Satana. 82-Black Widow. 83-Nick Fury. 84-Shang-Chi. 92-Hawkeye. 93-Werewolf by Night. 94-SpM vs. The Shroud. 95-Mockingbird (intro.); Nick Fury app. 96-Howard the Duck; last 40 cent issue. 97-Spider-Woman/Hulk. 98-Black Widow. 99-Machine Man. 85-Shang-Chi/Black Widow/Nick Fury. 87-Black Panther. 88-Invisible Girl. 90-Beast .40 1.00 2.00
86-Guardians of the Galaxy .80 2.00 4.00
89-Nightcrawler (from X-Men) .60 1.50 3.00
91-Ghost Rider 1.00 2.50 5.00
100-(Double-size)-Fantastic Four/Storm/Black Panther; origin/1st app. Karma, one of the New Mutants; origin Storm; X-Men x-over; Miller-c/a(p); Byrne-a (on X-Men app. only) 1.40 3.50 7.00
101-116: 101-Nighthawk(Ditko-a). 102-Doc Samson. 103-Ant-Man. 104-Hulk/Ka-Zar. 105-Hulk/Powerman/Iron Fist. 106-Capt. America. 107-She-Hulk. 108-Paladin; Dazzler cameo. 109-Dazzler; Paladin app. 110-Iron Man. 111-Devil-Slayer. 112-King Kull; last 50 cent issue. 113-Quasar. 114-Falcon. 115-Thor. 116-Valkyrie .30 .75 1.50
117-Wolverine-c/story 2.40 6.00 12.00
118-140,142-149: 118-Professor X; Wolverine app. (4 pgs.); X-Men cameo. 119-Gargoyle. 120-Dominic Fortune. 121-Human Torch. 122-Man-Thing. 123-Daredevil. 124-The Beast. 125-Tigra. 126-Hulk & Powerman/Son of Satan. 127-The Watcher. 128-Capt. America; Spider-Man/Capt. America photo-c. 129-The Vision. 130-Scarlet Witch. 131-Frogman. 132-Mr. Fantastic. 133-Fantastic Four. 134-Jack of Hearts. 135-Kitty Pryde; X-Men cameo. 136-Wonder Man. 137-Aunt May/Franklin Richards. 138-Sandman. 139-Nick Fury. 140-Black Widow. 142-Capt. Marvel. 143-Starfox. 144-Moon Knight. 145-Iron Man. 146-Nomad. 147-Human Torch; SpM back to old costume. 148-Thor. 149-Cannonball .30 .75 1.50
141-Daredevil; SpM/Black Widow app. (Spidey in new black costume #141-146; #141 ties w/Amaz. S-M #252 for 1st black costume) .60 1.50 3.00
150-X-Men ($1.00, double-size); B. Smith-c .70 1.75 3.50
Annual 1(1976)-SpM/X-Men (early app.) 2.80 7.00 14.00
Annuals 2-7: 2(1979)-SpM/Hulk. 3(1980)-Hulk/Power Man/Machine Man/Iron Fist; Miller-c(p). 4(1981)-SpM/Daredevil/Moon Knight/Power Man/Iron Fist; brief origins of each; Miller-c; Miller scripts on Daredevil. 5(1982)-SpM/The Thing/Scarlet Witch/Dr. Strange/Quasar. 6(1983)-SpM/New Mutants (early app.), Cloak & Dagger. 7(1984)-Alpha Flight; Byrne-c(i) .40 1.00 2.00

NOTE: ***Art Adams*** *c-141p.* ***Austin*** *a-79i; c-76i, 79i, 96i, 101i, 112i, 130i.* ***Bolle*** *a-9i.* ***Byrne*** *a(p)-53-55, 59-70, 75, 79, 100; c-68p, 70p, 72p, 75, 76p, 79p, 129i, 133i.* ***Colan*** *a-87p.* ***Ditko*** *a-101.* ***Kane*** *a(p)-4-6, 13, 14, 16-19, 23; c(p)-4, 13, 14, 17-19, 23, 25, 26, 32-35, 37, 41, 44, 45, 47, 53, 54.* ***Miller*** *a-100p; c-95p, 99p, 100p, 102p, 106.* ***Mooney*** *a-2i, 7i, 8, 10p, 11p, 16i, 24-31p, 72, 93i, Annual 5i.* ***Nasser*** *a-89p; c-101p.* ***Simonson*** *c-99i, 148.* ***Paul Smith*** *c-131, 132.* ***Starlin*** *c-27.* ***Sutton*** *a-93p. "H-T" means Human Torch; "SpM" means Spider-Man; "S-M" means Sub-Mariner.*

MARVEL TREASURY EDITION ($1.50-$2.50)
1974; No 2, Dec, 1974 - No. 28, 1981 (100 pgs.; oversized, new &-r)
Marvel Comics Group

1-Spectacular Spider-Man; story-r/Marvel Super-Heroes #14; Romita-c/a(r); G. Kane, Ditko-r; Green Goblin/Hulk-r 1.00 2.50 5.00
1-1,000 numbered copies signed by Stan Lee & John Romita on front-c & sold thru mail for $5.00; 1st 1,000 copies off the press 2.40 6.00 12.00
2-4: 2-Fantastic Four-r/F.F. 6,11,48-50(Silver Surfer). 3-The Mighty Thor-r/Thor #125-130. 4-Conan the Barbarian; Barry Smith-c/a(r)/Conan #11 .50 1.25 2.50
5-14,16,17: 5-The Hulk (origin-r/Hulk #3). 6-Dr. Strange. 7-Mighty Avengers. 8-Giant Superhero Holidy Grab-Bag; Spider-Man, Hulk, Nick Fury. 9-Giant; Super-hero Team-up. 10-Thor; r/Thor #154-157. 11-Fantastic Four. 12-Howard the Duck(r/#H. the Duck #1 & G.S. Man-Thing #4,5) plus new Defenders story. 13-Giant Super-Hero Holiday Grab-Bag. 14-Spider-Man. 16-The Defenders (origin) & Valkyrie; r/Defenders #1,4,13,14. 17-The Hulk .40 1.00 2.00
15-Conan; Barry Smith, Neal Adams-i .50 1.25 2.50
18-The Astonishing Spider-Man; r/Spider-Man's 1st team-ups with Iron Fist, The X-Men, Ghost Rider & Werewolf by Night .40 1.00 2.00
19-28: 19-Conan the Barbarian. 20-Hulk. 21-Fantastic Four. 22-Spider-Man. 23-Conan. 24-Rampaging Hulk. 25-Spider-Man vs. The Hulk. 26-The

Marvel Team-Up #5, © MEG

Marvel Team-Up #32, © MEG

Marvel Treasury Edition #2, © MEG

Marvel Triple Action #13, © MEG

Marvel Two-In-One #39, © MEG

Mary Marvel #23, © FAW

GD25 FN65 NM94

Hulk; Wolverine app. 27-Spider-Man. 28-Spider-Man/Superman; (origin of each) .80 2.00 4.00

NOTE: *Reprints-2, 3, 5, 7-9, 13, 14, 16, 17.* ***Neal Adams*** *a(i)-6, 15.* ***Brunner*** *a-6, 12; c-6.* ***Buscema*** *a-15, 19, 28; c-28.* ***Colan*** *a-6r; c-12p.* ***Ditko*** *a-1, 6.* ***Gil Kane*** *c-16p.* ***Kirby*** *a-2, 10, 11; c-7.* ***Romita*** *c-1, 5.* ***B. Smith*** *a-4, 15, 19; c-4, 19.*

MARVEL TREASURY OF OZ FEATURING THE MARVELOUS LAND OF OZ
1975 (oversized) ($1.50)(See MGM's Marvelous...)
Marvel Comics Group

1-Buscema-a; Romita-c .40 1.00 2.00

MARVEL TREASURY SPECIAL (Also see 2001: A Space Odyssey)
1974; 1976 (84 pgs.; oversized) ($1.50)
Marvel Comics Group

Vol. 1-Spider-Man, Torch, Sub-Mariner, Avengers "Giant Superhero Holiday Grab-Bag;" Wood, Colan/Everett, plus 2 Kirby-r; reprints Hulk vs. Thing from Fantastic Four #25,26 .30 .75 1.50
Vol. 1-... Featuring Captain America's Bicentennial Battles (6/76)-Kirby-a; B. Smith inks, 11 pgs. .30 .75 1.50

MARVEL TRIPLE ACTION (See Giant-Size...)
Feb, 1972 - No. 24, Mar, 1975; No. 25, Aug, 1975 - No. 47, Apr, 1979
Marvel Comics Group

1-(25 cent giant, 52pgs.)-Dr. Doom, Silver Surfer, The Thing begin, end #4 ('66 reprints from Fantastic Four) .60 1.50 3.00
2-47: 45-r/X-Men #45. 46-r/Avengers #53(X-Men) .50 1.00

NOTE: *#5-44, 46, 47 reprint Avengers #11 thru ?. #40-r/Avengers #48(1st Black Knight).* ***Buscema*** *a(r)-35p, 36p, 38p, 39p, 41, 42, 43p, 44p, 46p, 47p.* ***Ditko*** *a-2r; c-47.* ***Kirby*** *a(r)-1-4p.* ***Starlin*** *c-7.* ***Tuska*** *a(r)-40p, 43i, 46i, 47i. #2 through at least #17 are 20 cent-c.*

MARVEL TWO-IN-ONE (...Featuring ... #82? on; see The Thing)
January, 1974 - No. 100, June, 1983
Marvel Comics Group

1-Thing team-ups begin; Man-Thing 3.60 9.00 18.00
2-4: 2-Sub-Mariner; last 20 cent issue. 3-Daredevil. 4-Capt. America 1.60 4.00 8.00
5-Guardians of the Galaxy 3.20 8.00 16.00
6-Dr. Strange (11/74) 2.80 7.00 14.00
7,9,10 1.20 3.00 6.00
8-Early Ghost Rider app. (3/75) 2.00 5.00 10.00
11-20: 13-Power Man. 14-Son of Satan (early app.). 17-Spider-Man. 18-Last 25 cent issue .80 2.00 4.00
21-26,28,29,31-40: 29-Master of Kung Fu; Spider-Woman cameo. 39-Vision .60 1.50 3.00
27-Deathlok 1.40 3.50 7.00
30-2nd full app. Spider-Woman (see Marvel Spotlight #32 for 1st app.) 1.00 2.50 5.00
41,42,44-49: 42-Capt. America. 45-Capt. Marvel. 46-Thing battles Hulk-c/story .30 .75 1.50
43,50,53,55-Byrne-a(p). 53-Quasar .50 1.25 2.50
51-The Beast, Nick Fury, Ms. Marvel; Miller-p .60 1.50 3.00
52-Moon Knight app. .60 1.50 3.00
54-Death of Deathlok; Byrne-a 3.20 8.00 16.00
56-60,64-68,70-79,81,82: 60-Intro. Impossible Woman. 68-Angel. 71-1st app. Maelstrom. 75-Avengers (52 pgs.). 76-Iceman .50 1.00
61-63: 61-Starhawk (from Guardians); "The Coming of Her" storyline begins, ends #63; cover similar to F.F. #67 (Him-c). 62-Moondragon; Thanos & Warlock cameo in flashback; Starhawk app. 63-Warlock?; Warlock revived shortly; Starhawk & Moondragon app. .50 1.25 2.50
69-Guardians of the Galaxy .80 2.00 4.00
80-Ghost Rider 1.00 3.00 6.00
83,84: 83-Sasquatch. 84-Alpha Flight app. .40 1.00 2.00
85-99: 90-Spider-Man. 93-Jocasta dies. 96-X-Men-c & cameo .50 1.00
100-Double size, Byrne scripts .30 .75 1.50
Annual 1 (1976, 52 pgs.)-Thing/Liberty Legion .40 1.00 2.00
Annual 2(1977, 52 pgs.)-Thing/Spider-Man; 2nd death of Thanos; end of Thanos saga; Warlock app.; Starlin-c/a 4.20 12.50 25.00
Annual 3 (1978, 52 pgs.)-Nova .30 .75 1.50
Annual 4 (1979, 52 pgs.)-Black Bolt .30 .75 1.50
Annual 5-7: 5(1980, 52 pgs.)-Hulk. 6(1981, 52 pgs.)-1st app. American Eagle. 7(1982, 52 pgs.)-The Thing/Champion; Sasquatch, Colossus app. .50 1.00

NOTE: ***Austin*** *c(i)-42, 54, 56, 58, 61, 63, 66.* ***John Buscema*** *a-30p, 45; c-30p.* ***Byrne*** *(p)-43, 50, 53-55; c-43, 53p, 56p, 98i, 99i.* ***Gil Kane*** *a-1p, 2p; c(p)-1-3, 9, 11, 14, 28.* ***Kirby*** *c-10, 12, 19p, 20, 25, 27.* ***Mooney*** *a-18i, 38i, 90i.* ***Nasser*** *a-70p.* ***Perez*** *a(p)-56-58, 60, 64, 65; c(p)-32, 33, 42, 50-52, 54, 55, 57, 58, 61-66, 70.* ***Roussos*** *a-Annual 1i.* ***Simonson*** *c-43i, 97p, Annual 6i.* ***Starlin*** *c-6, Annual 1.* ***Tuska*** *a-6p.*

MARVEL UNIVERSE (See Official Handbook Of The...)

MARVIN MOUSE
September, 1957
Atlas Comics (BPC)

1-Everett-c/a; Maneely-a 5.85 17.50 35.00

MARY JANE & SNIFFLES (See 4-Color #402, 474 & Looney Tunes)

MARY MARVEL COMICS (Monte Hale #29 on) (Also see Captain Marvel #18, Marvel Family, Shazam, & Wow Comics)
Dec, 1945 - No. 28, Sept, 1948
Fawcett Publications

1-Captain Marvel introduces Mary on-c; intro/origin Georgia Sivana 83.00 250.00 500.00
2 42.00 125.00 250.00
3,4 30.00 90.00 180.00
5-8: 8-Bulletgirl x-over in Mary Marvel 20.00 60.00 120.00
9,10 17.00 50.00 100.00
11-20 12.50 37.50 75.00
21-28 10.00 30.00 65.00

MARY POPPINS (See Movie Comics & Walt Disney Showcase No. 17)

MARY'S GREATEST APOSTLE (St. Louis Grignion de Montfort)
No date (16 pages; paper cover)
Catechetical Guild (Topix) (Giveaway)

nn 2.40 6.00 12.00

MARY WORTH (See Harvey Comics Hits #55 & Love Stories of...)
March, 1956 (Also see Romantic Picture Novelettes)
Argo

1 4.70 14.00 28.00

MASK (TV)(DC Comics, 1985 & 1987)(Value: cover or less)

MASK, THE (Dark Horse)Value: cover or less)

MASK RETURNS, THE (Dark Horse)(Value: cover or less)

MASK COMICS
Feb-Mar, 1945 - No. 2, Apr-May, 1945; No. 2, Fall, 1945
Rural Home Publications

1-Classic L. B. Cole Satan-c/a; Palais-a 86.00 270.00 600.00
2-(Scarce)Classic L. B. Cole Satan-c; Black Rider, The Boy Magician, & The Collector app. 50.00 150.00 350.00
2(Fall, 1945)-No publ.-same as regular #2; L. B. Cole-c 34.00 103.00 240.00

MASKED BANDIT, THE
1952
Avon Periodicals

nn-Kinstler-a 10.00 30.00 70.00

MASKED MAN, THE (Eclipse)(Value: cover or less)

MASKED MARVEL (See Keen Detective Funnies)
Sept, 1940 - No. 3, Dec, 1940
Centaur Publications

1-The Masked Marvel begins 117.00 350.00 700.00

2,3: 2-Gustavson, Tarpe Mills-a 83.00 250.00 500.00

MASKED RAIDER, THE (Billy The Kid #9 on; Frontier Scout, Daniel Boone #10-13; also see Blue Bird)
June, 1955 - No. 8, July, 1957; No. 14, Aug, 1958 - No. 30, June, 1961
Charlton Comics

1-Painted-c 7.50 22.50 45.00
2 4.00 11.00 22.00
3-8: 8-Billy The Kid app. 3.60 9.00 18.00
14,16-30: 22-Rocky Lane app. 2.40 6.00 12.00
15-Williamson-a, 7 pgs. 3.60 9.00 18.00

MASKED RANGER
April, 1954 - No. 9, Aug, 1955
Premier Magazines

1-The M. Ranger, his horse Streak, & The Crimson Avenger (origin) begin, end #9; Woodbridge/Frazetta-a 22.00 65.00 150.00
2,3 6.70 20.00 40.00
4-8-All Woodbridge-a. 5-Jesse James by Woodbridge. 6-Billy The Kid by Woodbridge. 7-Wild Bill Hickok by Woodbridge. 8-Jim Bowie's Life Story 8.35 25.00 50.00
9-Torres-a; Wyatt Earp by Woodbridge 9.15 27.50 55.00
NOTE: ***Check** a-1. **Woodbridge** c/a-1, 4-9.*

MASK OF DR. FU MANCHU, THE (See Dr. Fu Manchu)
1951
Avon Periodicals

1-Sax Rohmer adapt.; Wood-c/a (26 pgs.); Hollingsworth-a 59.00 175.00 410.00

MASQUE OF THE RED DEATH (See Movie Classics)

MASQUES (J. N. Williamson's...)(Innovation)(Value: cover or less)

MASTER COMICS (Combined with Slam Bang Comics #7 on)
Mar, 1940 - No. 133, Apr, 1953 (No. 1-6: oversized issues)
(#1-3: 15 cents, 52pgs.; #4-6: 10 cents, 36pgs.)
Fawcett Publications

GD25 FN65 VF82 NM94

1-Origin Master Man; The Devil's Dagger, El Carim, Master of Magic, Rick O'Say, Morton Murch, White Rajah, Shipwreck Roberts, Frontier Marshal, Streak Sloan, Mr. Clue begin (all features end #6) 280.00 840.00 1700.00 2800.00
(Estimated up to 100 total copies exist, 4 in NM/Mint)

GD25 FN65 NM94

2 142.00 425.00 850.00
3-5 100.00 300.00 600.00
6-Last Master Man 100.00 250.00 600.00
NOTE: *#1-6 rarely found in near mint to mint condition due to large-size format.*
7-(10/40)-Bulletman, Zoro, the Mystery Man (ends #22), Lee Granger, Jungle King, & Buck Jones begin; only app. The War Bird & Mark Swift & the Time Retarder; Zoro, Lee Granger, Jungle King & Mark Swift all continue from Slam Bang 167.00 500.00 1000.00
8-The Red Gaucho (ends #13), Captain Venture (ends #22) & The Planet Princess begin 92.00 275.00 550.00
9,10: 10-Lee Granger ends 75.00 225.00 450.00
11-Origin Minute-Man 167.00 500.00 1000.00
12 92.00 275.00 550.00
13-Origin Bulletgirl; Hitler-c 129.00 388.00 775.00
14-16: 14-Companions Three begins, ends #31 75.00 225.00 450.00
17-20: 17-Raboy-a on Bulletman begins. 20-Captain Marvel cameo app. in Bulletman 72.00 218.00 435.00

GD25 FN65 VF82 NM94

21-(12/41; Scarce)-Captain Marvel & Bulletman team up against Capt. Nazi; origin Capt. Marvel Jr's most famous nemesis Captain Nazi who will cause creation of Capt. Marvel Jr. in Whiz #25. Part I of trilogy origin of Capt. Marvel Jr.; 1st Mac Raboy-c for Fawcett 220.00 660.00 1320.00 2200.00
(Estimated up to 110 total copies exist, 6 in NM/Mint)
22-(1/42)-Captain Marvel Jr. moves over from Whiz #25 & teams up with Bulletman against Captain Nazi; part III of trilogy origin of Capt. Marvel Jr. & his 1st cover and adventure 200.00 600.00 1200.00 2000.00
(Estimated up to 135 total copies exist, 7 in NM/Mint)

GD25 FN65 NM94

23-Capt. Marvel Jr. c/stories begins (1st solo story); fights Capt. Nazi by himself 167.00 500.00 1000.00
24,25,29: 29-Hitler & Hirohito-c 67.00 200.00 400.00
26-28,30-Captain Marvel Jr. vs. Capt. Nazi. 30-Flag-c 67.00 200.00 400.00
31,32: 32-Last El Carim & Buck Jones; intro Balbo, the Boy Magician in El Carim story 48.00 145.00 290.00
33-Balbo, the Boy Magician (ends #47), Hopalong Cassidy (ends #49) begins 48.00 145.00 290.00
34-Capt. Marvel Jr. vs. Capt. Nazi 48.00 145.00 290.00
35 47.00 140.00 280.00
36-40: 40-Flag-c 42.00 125.00 250.00
41-Bulletman, Capt. Marvel Jr. & Bulletgirl x-over in Minute-Man; only app. Crime Crusaders Club (Capt. Marvel Jr., Minute-Man, Bulletman & Bulletgirl); only team in Fawcett Comics 46.00 138.00 275.00
42-47,49: 47-Hitler becomes Corpl. Hitler Jr. 49-Last Minute-Man 27.00 80.00 160.00
48-Intro. Bulletboy; Capt. Marvel cameo in Minute-Man 32.00 95.00 190.00
50-Radar, Nyoka the Jungle Girl begin; Capt. Marvel x-over in Radar; origin Radar 20.00 60.00 120.00
51-58 13.00 40.00 80.00
59-62: Nyoka serial "Terrible Tiara" in all; 61-Capt. Marvel Jr. 1st meets Uncle Marvel 15.00 45.00 90.00
63-80 10.00 30.00 65.00
81,83-87,89-91,95-99: 88-Hopalong Cassidy begins (ends #94). 95-Tom Mix begins (ends #133) 9.15 27.50 55.00
82,88,92-94-Krigstein-a 10.00 30.00 60.00
100 10.00 30.00 60.00
101-106-Last Bulletman 7.50 22.50 45.00
107-132: 132-B&W and color illos in **POP** 6.70 20.00 40.00
133-Bill Battle app. 8.35 25.00 50.00
NOTE: ***Mac Raboy** a-15-39, 40 in part, 42, 58; c-21-49, 51, 52, 54, 56, 58, 59.*

MASTER DETECTIVE
1964 (Reprints)
Super Comics

10,17,18: 10,18-Exist? 17-r/Young King Cole #?; McWilliams-r .80 2.00 4.00

MASTER OF KUNG FU (Formerly Special Marvel Edition; see Deadly Hands of Kung Fu & Giant-Size...)
No. 17, April, 1974 - No. 125, June, 1983
Marvel Comics Group

17-Starlin-a; intro Black Jack Tarr 3.00 7.50 15.00
18-20: 19-Man-Thing app. 1.60 4.00 8.00
21-23,25-30 1.00 2.50 5.00
24-Starlin, Simonson-a 1.20 3.00 6.00
31-99: 33-1st Leiko Wu. 43-Last 25 cent issue .50 1.25 2.50
100-Double size .60 1.50 3.00
101-117,119-124 .40 1.00 2.00
118,125-Double size issues .50 1.25 2.50
Annual 1(4/76)-Iron Fist .80 2.00 4.00
NOTE: ***Austin** c-63i, 74i. **Buscema** c-44p. **Gulacy** a(p)-18-20, 22, 25, 29-31, 33-35, 38, 39, 40(p&i), 42-50, 53r(#20); c-51, 55, 64, 67. **Gil Kane** c(p)-20, 38, 39, 42, 45, 59, 63. **Nebres** c-73i. **Starlin** a-17p, 24; c-54. **Sutton** a-42i. #53 reprints #20.*

MASTER OF KUNG-FU: BLEEDING BLACK (Marvel)(Value: cover or less)

MASTER OF RAMPLING GATE (Anne Rice's...)(Innovation)(Value: cover or less)

MASTER OF THE WORLD (See 4-Color #1157)

MASTERS OF TERROR (Magazine)
July, 1975 - No. 2, Sept, 1975 (Black & White) (All reprints)

Masked Ranger #3, © PG

Master Comics #31, © FAW

Master of Kung Fu #17, MEG

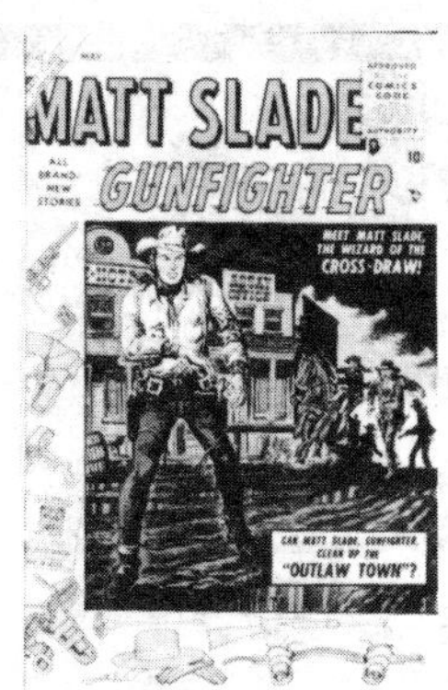

Matt Slade, Gunfighter #1, © MEG

Medal of Honor #1, © A.S. Curtis

Meet Corliss Archer #2, © FOX

GD25 FN65 NM94

Marvel Comics Group
1-Brunner, Barry Smith-a; Morrow-c; Neal Adams-r(i); Starlin-a(p); Gil Kane-a .35 .90 1.80
2-Reese, Kane, Mayerik-a; Steranko-c .60 1.20

MASTERS OF THE UNIVERSE (DC, 1982 & 1986-88) (Value: cover or less)

MASTERS OF THE UNIVERSE (Comic Album)
1984 (8x11"; $2.95; 64 pgs.)
Western Publishing Co.
11362-Based on Mattel toy & cartoon .60 1.50 3.00

MASTERWORKS SERIES OF GREAT COMIC BOOK ARTISTS, THE (Sea Gate/DC) (Value: cover or less)

MATT SLADE GUNFIGHTER (Kid Slade Gunfighter #5 on?; See Western Gunfighters)
May, 1956 - No. 4, Nov, 1956
Atlas Comics (SPI)
1-Matt & his horse Eagle; Williamson/Torres-a 10.00 30.00 70.00
2-Williamson-a 6.70 20.00 40.00
3,4 5.00 15.00 30.00
NOTE: ***Maneely** a-1, 3, 4; c-1, 2, 4. **Roth** a-2-4. **Severin** a-1, 3, 4. **Maneely** c/a-1.*

MAUD
1906 (32 pgs. in color; 10x15") (cardboard covers)
Frederick A. Stokes Co.
nn-By Fred Opper 25.00 75.00 150.00

MAVERICK (TV)
No. 892, 4/58 - No. 19, 4-6/62 (All have photo-c)
Dell Publishing Co.
4-Color 892 (#1): James Garner/Jack Kelly photo-c begin 13.00 40.00 90.00
4-Color 930,945,962,980,1005 (6-8/59) 8.35 25.00 50.00
7 (10-12/59) - 14: Last Garner/Kelly-c 6.70 20.00 40.00
15-18: Jack Kelly/Roger Moore photo-c 6.70 20.00 40.00
19-Jack Kelly photo-c 6.70 20.00 40.00

MAVERICK MARSHAL
Nov, 1958 - No. 7, May, 1960
Charlton Comics
1 3.20 8.00 16.00
2-7 1.80 4.50 9.00

MAX BRAND (See Silvertip)

MAXIMORTAL, THE (King Hell/Tundra) (Value: cover or less)

MAYA (See Movie Classics)
March, 1968
Gold Key
1 (10218-803)(TV) 2.00 5.00 10.00

MAYHEM (Dark Horse) (Value: cover or less)

MAZE AGENCY, THE (Comico/Innovation) (Value: cover or less)

MAZIE (...& Her Friends) (See Mortie, Stevie & Tastee-Freez)
1953 - #12, 1954; #13, 12/54 - #22, 9/56; #23, 9/57 - #28, 8/58
Mazie Comics(Magazine Publ.)/Harvey Publ. No. 13-on
1-(Teen-age)-Stevie's girl friend 4.20 12.50 25.00
2 2.40 6.00 12.00
3-10 1.80 4.50 9.00
11-28 1.20 3.00 6.00

MAZIE
1950 - No. 7, 1951 (5 cents) (5x7-1/4"-miniature) (52 pgs.)
Nation Wide Publishers
1-Teen-age 8.35 25.00 50.00
2-7 4.20 12.50 25.00

GD25 FN65 NM94

MAZINGER (See First Comics Graphic Novel #17)

'MAZING MAN (DC) (Value: cover or less)

McCRORY'S CHRISTMAS BOOK
1955 (36 pgs.; slick cover)
Western Printing Co. (McCrory Stores Corp. giveaway)
nn-Painted-c 2.80 7.00 14.00

McCRORY'S TOYLAND BRINGS YOU SANTA'S PRIVATE EYES
1956 (16 pgs.)
Promotional Publ. Co. (Giveaway)
nn-Has 9 pg. story plus 7 pg. toy ads 2.00 5.00 10.00

McCRORY'S WONDERFUL CHRISTMAS
1954 (20 pgs.; slick cover)
Promotional Publ. Co. (Giveaway)
nn 2.80 7.00 14.00

McHALE'S NAVY (TV) (See Movie Classics)
May-July, 1963 - No. 3, Nov-Jan, 1963-64 (All have photo-c)
Dell Publishing Co.
1 4.20 12.50 25.00
2,3 4.00 10.00 20.00

McKEEVER & THE COLONEL (TV)
Feb-Apr, 1963 - No. 3, Aug-Oct, 1963
Dell Publishing Co.
1-Photo-c 4.70 14.00 28.00
2,3 4.00 11.00 22.00

McLINTOCK (See Movie Comics)

MD
Apr-May, 1955 - No. 5, Dec-Jan, 1955-56
E. C. Comics
1-Not approved by code 10.00 30.00 60.00
2-5 7.50 22.50 45.00
NOTE: ***Crandall, Evans, Ingels, Orlando** art in all issues; **Craig** c-1-5.*

MECHA (Dark Horse) (Value: cover or less)

MEDAL FOR BOWZER, A
No date (1948-50?)
Will Eisner Giveaway
nn-Eisner-c/script 24.00 73.00 170.00

MEDAL OF HONOR COMICS
Spring, 1946
A. S. Curtis
1-War stories 6.00 18.00 42.00

MEDIA STARR (Innovation) (Value: cover or less)

MEET ANGEL (Formerly Angel & the Ape)
No. 7, Nov-Dec, 1969
National Periodical Publications
7-Wood-a(i) 1.80 4.50 9.00

MEET CORLISS ARCHER (Radio/Movie) (My Life #4 on)
March, 1948 - No. 3, July, 1948
Fox Features Syndicate
1-(Teen-age)-Feldstein-c/a 34.00 103.00 240.00
2-Feldstein-c only 26.00 77.00 180.00
3-Part Feldstein-c only 20.00 60.00 140.00
NOTE: *No. 1-3 used in Seduction of the Innocent, pg. 39.*

MEET HERCULES (See Three Stooges)

MEET HIYA A FRIEND OF SANTA CLAUS
1949 (18 pgs.?) (paper cover)
Julian J. Proskauer/Sundial Shoe Stores, etc. (Giveaway)

	GD25	FN65	NM94
nn	4.70	14.00	28.00

MEET MERTON
Dec, 1953 - No. 4, June, 1954
Toby Press

	GD25	FN65	NM94
1-(Teen-age)-Dave Berg-a	4.70	14.00	28.00
2-Dave Berg-a	3.20	8.00	16.00
3,4-Dave Berg-a. 3-Berg-c	2.80	7.00	14.00
I.W. Reprint #9	.40	1.00	2.00
Super Reprint #11('63), 18	.40	1.00	2.00

MEET MISS BLISS (Becomes Stories Of Romance #5 on)
May, 1955 - No. 4, Nov, 1955
Atlas Comics (LMC)

	GD25	FN65	NM94
1-Al Hartley-a	6.35	19.00	38.00
2-4	4.20	12.50	25.00

MEET MISS PEPPER (Formerly Lucy, The Real Gone Gal)
No. 5, April, 1954 - No. 6, June, 1954
St. John Publishing Co.

	GD25	FN65	NM94
5-Kubert/Maurer-a	13.00	40.00	90.00
6-Kubert/Maurer-a; Kubert-c	11.00	32.00	75.00

MEET THE NEW POST GAZETTE SUNDAY FUNNIES
3/12/49 (16 pgs.; paper covers) (7-1/4x10-1/4")
Commercial Comics (insert in newspaper)
Pittsburgh Post Gazette

Dick Tracy by Gould, Gasoline Alley, Terry & the Pirates, Brenda Starr, Buck Rogers by Yager, The Gumps, Peter Rabbit by Fago, Superman, Funnyman by Siegel & Shuster, The Saint, Archie, & others done especially for this book. A fine copy sold at auction in 1985 for $276.00.
Estimated value.... $150 – $300

MEGALITH (Continuity)(Value: cover or less)

MEGATON (A super hero)
Nov, 1983; No. 2, Oct, 1985 - V2#3 (B&W, color V2#1 on)
Megaton Publ. (#3: 44 pgs.; #4: 52 pgs.)

	GD25	FN65	NM94
1-($2.00, 68 pgs.)-Erik Larsen's 1st pro work; Vanguard by Larsen begins, ends #4; Guice-c/a(p); Gustovich-a(p) in #1,2	1.60	4.00	8.00
2 ($2.00, 68 pgs.)-Larsen-a; Guice-c/a(p)	1.00	2.50	5.00
3-1st app. Savage Dragon-c/story by Larsen	1.60	4.00	8.00
4-2nd app. Savage Dragon by Larsen; 4,5-Wildman by Grass Green	1.20	3.00	6.00
5-1st Liefeld published-a (inside f/c, 6/86)	.60	1.50	3.00
6-8: 8-Liefeld-a (1 pg. ad)	.30	.75	1.50
...Explosion (1987, 16 pg. color giveaway)-1st app. Youngblood by Rob Liefeld (2 pg. spread); shows Megaton heroes	4.00	10.00	20.00
V2#1-3 ($1.50, color)	.30	.75	1.50
Special 1 (1987, $2.00)	.40	1.00	2.00
X-Mas 2 (1987)	.40	1.00	2.00

NOTE: *Copies of Megaton Explosion were also released in early 1992 all signed by Rob Liefeldand were made available to retailers.*

MEGATON MAN (Kitchen Sink)(Value: cover or less)

MEL ALLEN SPORTS COMICS
No. 5, Nov, 1949; No. 6, June, 1950
Standard Comics

	GD25	FN65	NM94
5(#1 on inside)-Tuska-a	11.50	34.00	80.00
6(#2)	8.35	25.00	50.00

MELVIN MONSTER (See Peter, the Little Pest)
Apr-June, 1965 - No. 10, Oct, 1969
Dell Publishing Co.

	GD25	FN65	NM94
1-By John Stanley	11.50	34.00	80.00
2-10-All by Stanley. #10 r-/#1	10.00	30.00	60.00

MELVIN THE MONSTER (Dexter The Demon #7)
July, 1956 - No. 6, July, 1957
Atlas Comics (HPC)

	GD25	FN65	NM94
1-Maneely-c/a	7.50	22.50	45.00
2-6: 4-Maneely-c/a	5.35	16.00	32.00

MEMORIES (Epic Comics)(Value: cover or less)

MENACE
March, 1953 - No. 11, May, 1954
Atlas Comics (HPC)

	GD25	FN65	NM94
1-Everett-c/a	24.00	70.00	165.00
2-Post-atom bomb disaster by Everett; anti-Communist propaganda/torture scenes; Sinnott s/f story	14.00	43.00	100.00
3,4,6-Everett-a. 6-Romita s/f story	11.50	34.00	80.00
5-Origin & 1st app. The Zombie by Everett (reprinted in Tales of the Zombie #1)(7/53)	17.00	52.00	120.00
7,8,10,11: 7-Frankenstein story. 8-End of world story; Heath 3-D art(3 pgs.). 10-H-Bomb panels	10.00	30.00	65.00
9-Everett-a r-in Vampire Tales #1	10.00	30.00	70.00

NOTE: ***Brodsky** c-7, 8, 11. **Colan** a-6; c-9. **Everett** a-1-6, 9; c-1-6. **Heath** a-1-8; c-10. **Katz** a-11. **Maneely** a-3, 5, 7-9. **Powell** a-11. **Romita** a-3, 6, 8, 11. **Shelly** a-10. **Shores** a-7. **Sinnott** a-2, 7. **Tuska** a-1, 2, 5.*

MEN AGAINST CRIME (Formerly Mr. Risk; Hand of Fate #8 on)
No. 3, Feb, 1951 - No. 7, Oct, 1951
Ace Magazines

	GD25	FN65	NM94
3-Mr. Risk app.	5.35	16.00	32.00
4-7: 4-Colan-a; entire book reprinted as Trapped! #4	3.60	9.00	18.00

MEN, GUNS, & CATTLE (See Classics Illustrated Special Issue)

MEN IN ACTION (Battle Brady #10 on)
April, 1952 - No. 9, Dec, 1952
Atlas Comics (IPS)

	GD25	FN65	NM94
1-Berg, Reinman-a	6.70	20.00	40.00
2	4.00	10.00	20.00
3-6,8,9: 3-Heath-c/a	3.20	8.00	16.00
7-Krigstein-a; Heath-c	5.00	15.00	30.00

NOTE: ***Brodsky** c-1,4-6. **Maneely** c-5. **Pakula** a-1, 6. **Robinson** c-8. **Shores** c-9.*

MEN IN ACTION
April, 1957 - No. 9, 1958
Ajax/Farrell Publications

	GD25	FN65	NM94
1	4.70	14.00	28.00
2	3.20	8.00	16.00
3-9	2.40	6.00	12.00

MEN INTO SPACE (See 4-Color No. 1083)

MEN OF BATTLE (Also see New Men of Battle)
V1#5, March, 1943 (Hardcover)
Catechetical Guild

	GD25	FN65	NM94
V1#5-Topix reprints	3.00	7.50	15.00

MEN OF COURAGE
1949
Catechetical Guild

	GD25	FN65	NM94
Bound Topix comics-V7#2,4,6,8,10,16,18,20	3.00	7.50	15.00

MEN OF WAR
August, 1977 - No. 26, March, 1980 (#9,10: 44 pgs.)
DC Comics, Inc.

	GD25	FN65	NM94
1-Enemy Ace, Gravedigger (origin #1,2) begin	.40	1.00	2.00
2-26: 9-Unknown Soldier app.		.50	1.00

NOTE: ***Chaykin** a-9, 10, 12-14, 19, 20. **Evans** c-25. **Kubert** c-2-23, 24p, 26.*

MEN'S ADVENTURES (Formerly True Adventures)
No. 4, Aug, 1950 - No. 28, July, 1954
Marvel/Atlas Comics (CCC)

	GD25	FN65	NM94
4(#1)(52 pgs.)	12.00	36.00	85.00
5-Flying Saucer story	7.50	22.50	45.00
6-8: 8-Sci/fic story	5.85	17.50	35.00
9-20: All war format	4.00	11.00	22.00

Megaton #1, © Megaton Publ.

Menace #6, © MEG

Men of War #9, © DC

Men's Adventures #24, © MEG

Metal Men #50, © DC

Metamorpho #4, © DC

	GD25	FN65	NM94
21,22,24-26: All horror format	5.00	15.00	30.00
23-Crandall-a; Fox-a(i)	6.70	20.00	40.00
27,28-Captain America, Human Torch, & Sub-Mariner app. in each	43.00	130.00	300.00

NOTE: ***Ayers*** *a-27(H. Torch).* ***Berg*** *a-15, 16.* ***Brodsky*** *c-4-9, 11, 12, 16-18, 24.* ***Burgos*** *c-27, 28(H. Torch).* ***Colan*** *a-14, 19.* ***Everett*** *a-10, 14, 22, 25, 28; c-14, 21-23.* ***Heath*** *a-8, 11, 24; c-13, 20, 26.* ***Lawrence*** *a-23; 27(C. America).* ***Maneely*** *a-24; c-10, 15.* ***Mac Pakula*** *a-15, 25.* ***Post*** *a-23.* ***Powell*** *a-27(Sub-Mariner).* ***Reinman*** *a-11, 12.* ***Robinson*** *c-19.* ***Romita*** *a-22.* ***Shores*** *c-25.* ***Sinnott*** *a-21.* ***Tuska*** *a-24. Adventure-#4-8; War-#9-20; Horror-#21-26.*

MEN WHO MOVE THE NATION
(Giveaway) (Black & White)
Publisher unknown

nn-Neal Adams-a — 4.00 | 10.00 | 20.00

MEPHISTO VS... (See Silver Surfer #3)
Apr, 1987 - No. 4, July, 1987 ($1.50, mini-series)
Marvel Comics Group

1-Fantastic Four; Austin-i — .40 | 1.00 | 2.00
2-4: 2-X-Factor. 3-X-Men. 4-Avengers — .30 | .80 | 1.60

MERC (See Mark Hazzard: Merc)

MERCHANTS OF DEATH (Acme Press (Eclipse)) (Value: cover or less)

MERLIN JONES AS THE MONKEY'S UNCLE (See Movie Comics and The Misadventures of... under Movie Comics)

MERRILL'S MARAUDERS (See Movie Classics)

MERRY CHRISTMAS (See A Christmas Adv., Donald Duck..., Dell Giant #39, & March of Comics #153)

MERRY CHRISTMAS, A
1948 (nn) (Giveaway)
K. K. Publications (Child Life Shoes)

nn — 4.00 | 12.00 | 24.00

MERRY CHRISTMAS
1956 (7-1/4x5-1/4")
K. K. Publications (Blue Bird Shoes Giveaway)

nn — 1.80 | 4.50 | 9.00

MERRY CHRISTMAS FROM MICKEY MOUSE
1939 (16 pgs.) (Color & B&W)
K. K. Publications (Shoe store giveaway)

nn-Donald Duck & Pluto app.; text with art (Rare); c-reprint/Mickey Mouse Mag. V3#3 (12/37) — 83.00 | 210.00 | 500.00

MERRY CHRISTMAS FROM SEARS TOYLAND
1939 (16 pgs.) (In color)
Sears Roebuck Giveaway

nn-Dick Tracy, Little Orphan Annie, The Gumps, Terry & the Pirates — 20.00 | 60.00 | 140.00

MERRY COMICS
December, 1945 (No cover price)
Carlton Publishing Co.

nn-Boogeyman app. — 10.00 | 30.00 | 70.00

MERRY COMICS
1947
Four Star Publications

1 — 7.50 | 22.50 | 45.00

MERRY-GO-ROUND COMICS
1944 (132 pgs.; 25 cents); 1946; 9-10/47 - No. 2, 1948
LaSalle Publ. Co./Croyden Publ./Rotary Litho.

nn(1944)(LaSalle) — 11.00 | 32.00 | 75.00
21 — 4.00 | 12.00 | 24.00
1(1946)(Croyden) — 6.35 | 19.00 | 38.00
V1#1,2(1947-48; 52 pgs.)(Rotary Litho. Co. Ltd., Canada);Ken Hultgren-a — 4.35 | 13.00 | 26.00

MERRY MAILMAN (See Fawcett's Funny Animals #89)

MERRY MOUSE (Also see Space Comics)
June, 1953 - No. 4, Jan-Feb, 1954
Avon Periodicals

1 — 5.00 | 15.00 | 30.00
2-4 — 3.20 | 8.00 | 16.00

META-4 (First) (Value: cover or less)

METAL MEN (See Brave & the Bold, DC Comics Presents, and Showcase)
4-5/63 - No. 41, 12-1/69-70; No. 42, 2-3/73 - No. 44, 7-8/73;
No. 45, 4-5/76 - No. 56, 2-3/78
National Periodical Publications/DC Comics

	GD25	FN65	NM94
Showcase #37 (3-4/62)-1st app. Metal Men	50.00	150.00	350.00
Showcase #38-40 (5-6/62 - 9-10/62)-Metal Men	29.00	85.00	200.00
1-(4-5/63)	35.00	107.00	250.00
2	14.00	43.00	100.00
3-5	10.00	30.00	65.00
6-10	6.70	2.00	40.00
11-20	4.70	14.00	28.00
21-26,28-30	3.60	9.00	18.00
27-Origin Metal Men	6.70	20.00	40.00
31-41(1968-70): 38-Last 12 cent issue. 41-Last 15 cent issue	3.00	7.50	15.00
42-44(1973)-Reprints	1.40	3.50	7.00
45('76)-49-Simonson-a in all	1.40	3.50	7.00
50-56: 50-Part-r. 54,55-Green Lantern x-over	1.40	3.50	7.00

NOTE: ***Andru/Esposito*** *c-1-29.* ***Aparo*** *c-53-56.* ***Giordano*** *c-45, 46.* ***Kane*** *a-30, 31p; c-31.* ***Simonson*** *a-45-49; c-47-52.* ***Staton*** *a-50-56.*

METAMORPHO (See Action Comics, Brave & the Bold, 1st Issue Special, & World's Finest)
July-Aug, 1965 - No. 17, Mar-Apr, 1968 (All 12 cent issues)
National Periodical Publications

	GD25	FN65	NM94
Brave and the Bold #57 (12-1/64-65)-Origin & 1st app. Metamorpho by Ramona Fraden	13.00	45.00	90.00
Brave and the Bold #58 (2-3/65)-2nd app.	6.70	20.00	40.00
1-(7-8/65)	10.00	30.00	65.00
2,3	6.00	18.00	36.00
4-6	4.00	10.00	20.00
7-9	3.20	8.00	16.00
10-Origin & 1st app. Element Girl (1-2/67)	4.00	11.00	22.00
11-17	2.40	6.00	12.00

NOTE: ***Ramona Fraden*** *a-B&B 57, 58, 1-4.* ***Orlando*** *a-5, 6; c-5-9, 11.* ***Sal Trapani*** *a-7-16.*

METAPHYSIQUE (Norm Breyfogle's...) (Eclipse) (Value: cover or less)

METEOR COMICS
November, 1945
L. L. Baird (Croyden)

1-Captain Wizard, Impossible Man, Race Wilkins app.; origin Baldy Bean, Capt. Wizard's sidekick; bare-breasted mermaids story — 20.00 | 60.00 | 120.00

METROPOL (See Ted McKeever's...)

MGM'S MARVELOUS WIZARD OF OZ (See Marvel Treasury of Oz)
1975 ($1.50, 84 pgs.; oversize)
Marvel Comics Group/National Periodical Publications

1-Adaptation of MGM's movie; J. Buscema-a — .80 | 2.00 | 4.00

M.G.M'S MOUSE MUSKETEERS (Formerly M.G.M.'s The Two Mouseketeers)
No. 670, Jan, 1956 - No. 1290, Mar-May, 1962
Dell Publishing Co.

4-Color 670 (#4) — 2.80 | 7.00 | 14.00
4-Color 711,728,764 — 2.00 | 5.00 | 10.00

GD25 FN65 NM94

8 (4-6/57) - 21 (3-5/60) 1.60 4.00 8.00
4-Color 1135,1175,1290 2.00 5.00 10.00

M.G.M.'S SPIKE AND TYKE
No. 499, Sept, 1953 - No. 1266, Dec-Feb, 1961-62
Dell Publishing Co.

4-Color 499 (#1) 2.80 7.00 14.00
4-Color 577,638 2.00 5.00 10.00
4(12-2/55-56)-10 1.60 4.00 8.00
11-24(12-2/60-61) 1.40 3.50 7.00
4-Color 1266 1.60 4.00 8.00

M.G.M.'S THE TWO MOUSKETEERS (See 4-Color 475, 603, 642)

MICHAELANGELO CHRISTMAS SPECIAL (See Teenage Mutant Ninja Turtles Christmas Special)

MICHAELANGELO, TEENAGE MUTANT NINJA TURTLE
1986 (One shot) ($1.50, B&W)
Mirage Studios

1 2.40 6.00 12.00
1-2nd printing ('89, $1.75)-Reprint plus new-a .60 1.50 3.00

MICKEY AND DONALD (Walt Disney's...#3 on)
Mar, 1988 - No. 18, May, 1990 (95 cents, color)
Gladstone Publishing

1-Don Rosa-a; r/1949 Firestone giveaway .80 2.00 4.00
2 .50 1.25 2.50
3-Infinity-c .40 1.00 2.00
4-8: Barks-r .60 1.20
9-15: 9-r/1948 Firestone giveaway; X-Mas-c .50 1.00
16 ($1.50, 52 pgs.)-r/FC #157 .30 .75 1.50
17,18 ($1.95, 68 pgs.): 17-Barks M.M.-r/FC #79 plus Barks D.D.-r; Rosa-a; X-Mas-c. 18-Kelly-c(r); Barks-r .40 1.00 2.00
NOTE: ***Barks** reprints in 1-15, 17, 18. **Kelly** c-13r, 14 (r/Walt Disney's C&S #58), 18r.*

MICKEY AND DONALD IN VACATIONLAND (See Dell Giant No. 47)

MICKEY & THE BEANSTALK (See Story Hour Series)

MICKEY & THE SLEUTH (See Walt Disney Showcase #38, 39, 42)

MICKEY FINN (Also see Big Shot Comics #74 & Feature Funnies)
Nov?, 1942 - V3#2, May, 1952
Eastern Color 1-4/McNaught Synd. #5 on (Columbia)/Headline V3#2

1 19.00 57.00 135.00
2 10.00 30.00 70.00
3-Charlie Chan app. 8.35 25.00 50.00
4 5.85 17.50 35.00
5-10 4.20 12.50 25.00
11-15(1949): 12-Sparky Watts app. 3.60 9.00 18.00
V3#1,2(1952) 2.40 6.00 12.00

MICKEY MANTLE (See Baseball's Greatest Heroes #1)

MICKEY MOUSE
1931 - No. 4, 1934 (52 pgs.; 10x9-3/4"; cardboard covers)
David McKay Publications

1(1931) 100.00 300.00 700.00
2(1932) 75.00 225.00 525.00
3(1933)-All color Sunday reprints; page #'s 5-17, 32-48 reissued in Whitman #948 115.00 345.00 800.00
4(1934) 64.00 193.00 450.00
NOTE: *Each book reprints strips from previous year - dailies in black and white in #1, 2, 4; Sundays in color in No. 3. Later reprints exist; i.e., #2 (1934).*

MICKEY MOUSE
1933 (Copyright date, printing date unknown)
(30 pages; 10x8-3/4"; cardboard covers)
Whitman Publishing Co.

948-(1932 Sunday strips in color) 105.00 310.00 725.00
NOTE: *Some copies were bound with a second front cover upside-down instead of the regular back cover; both covers have the same art, but different right and left margins. The above book is an exact, but abbreviated reissue of David McKay No. 3 but with -inch of border trimmed from the top and bottom.*

GD25 FN65 NM94

MICKEY MOUSE (See The Best of Walt Disney Comics, Cheerios giveaways, Donald Donald and ..., Dynabrite Comics, 40 Big Pages..., Gladstone Comic Album, Merry Christmas From..., Mickey and Donald, Walt Disney's Comics & Stories & Wheaties)

MICKEY MOUSE (...Secret Agent #107-109; Walt Disney's... #148-205?)
(See Dell Giants for annuals)
#16, 1941 - #84, 7-9/62; #85, 11/62 - #218, 7/84; #219, 10/86 - #256, 4/90
Dell Publ. Co./Gold Key #85-204/Whitman #205-218/Gladstone #219 on

GD25 FN65 VF82
4-Color 16(1941)-1st M.M. comic book-"vs. the Phantom Blot" by Gottfredson 445.00 1335.00 4000.00
(Estimated up to 200 total copies exist, 5 in VF-NM)

GD25 FN65 NM94
4-Color 27(1943)-"7 Colored Terror" 57.00 171.00 400.00
4-Color 79(1945)-By Carl Barks (1 story) 68.00 205.00 475.00
4-Color 116(1946) 19.00 56.00 130.00
4-Color 141,157(1947) 17.00 51.00 120.00
4-Color 170,181,194('48) 14.00 43.00 100.00
4-Color 214('49),231,248,261 11.00 32.00 75.00
4-Color 268-Reprints/WDC&S #22-24 by Gottfredson ("SurpriseVisitor") 11.00 32.00 75.00
4-Color 279,286,296 10.00 30.00 65.00
4-Color 304,313(#1),325(#2),334 7.50 22.50 45.00
4-Color 343,352,362,371,387 5.85 17.50 35.00
4-Color 401,411,427(10-11/52) 4.70 14.00 28.00
4-Color 819-Mickey Mouse in Magicland 4.00 10.00 20.00
4-Color 1057,1151,1246(1959-61)-Album 3.20 8.00 16.00
28(12-1/52-53)-32,34 2.80 7.00 14.00
33-(Exists with 2 dates, 10-11/53 & 12-1/54) 2.80 7.00 14.00
35-50 1.80 4.50 9.00
51-73,75-80 1.40 3.50 7.00
74-Story swipe-"The Rare Stamp Search" from 4-Color #422-"The Gilded Man" 1.80 4.50 9.00
81-99: 93,95-titled "Mickey Mouse Club Album" 1.40 3.50 7.00
100-105: Reprints 4-Color #427,194,279,170,343,214 in that order 1.60 4.00 8.00
106-120 1.40 3.50 7.00
121-130 1.00 2.50 5.00
131-146 .80 2.00 4.00
147,148: 147-Reprints "The Phantom Fires" from WDC&S #200-202.148-Reprints "The Mystery of Lonely Valley" from WDC&S #208-210 1.00 2.50 5.00
149-158 .60 1.50 3.00
159-Reprints "The Sunken City" from WDC&S #205-207 .80 2.00 4.00
160-170: 162-170-r .60 1.50 3.00
171-178,180-218: 200-r/Four Color #371 .30 .75 1.50
179-(52 pgs.) .30 .75 1.50
219-1st Gladstone issue; The Seven Ghosts serial-r begins by Gottfredson 1.00 2.50 5.00
220,221 .60 1.50 3.00
222-225: 222-Editor-in Grief strip-r .50 1.25 2.50
226-230 .30 .75 1.50
231-243,245-254: 240-r/March of Comics #27. 245-r/F.C. #279. 250-r/F.C. #248 .50 1.00
244 (1/89, $2.95, 100 pgs.)-Squarebound 60th anniversary issue; gives history of Mickey .70 1.75 3.50
255,256 ($1.95, 68 pgs.) .40 1.00 2.00
NOTE: *Reprints #195-197, 198(2/3), 199(1/3), 200-208, 211(1/2), 212, 213, 215(1/3), 216-on.*
Album 01-518-210(Dell), 1(10082-309)(9/63-Gold Key) 1.40 3.50 7.00
...& Goofy "Bicep Bungle"(1952, 16 pgs., 3-1/4x7") Fritos giveaway, soft-c (also see Donald Duck & Ludwig Von Drake) 4.00 10.50 21.00
...& Goofy Explore Business(1978) .50 1.00

Mickey And Donald #13, © WDC

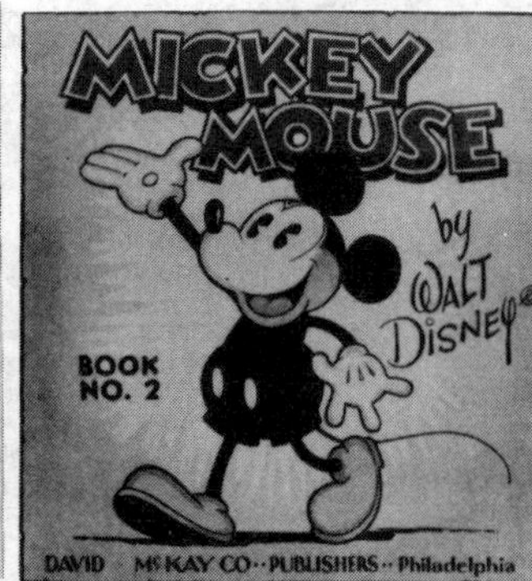

Mickey Mouse #2 (McKay 1934), © WDC

Mickey Mouse #219, © WDC

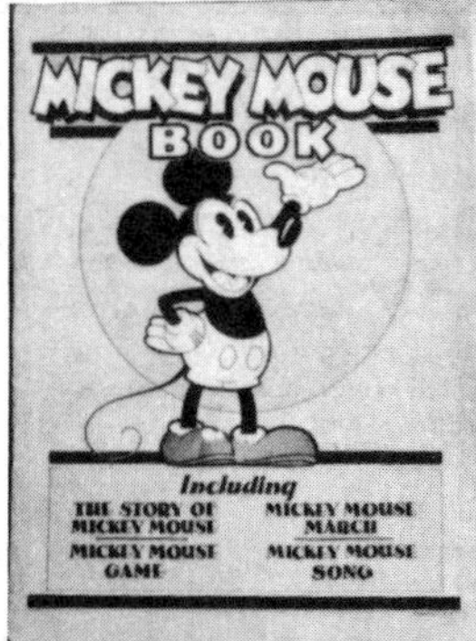

Mickey Mouse Book (1930), © WDC

Mickey Mouse Magazine V1#3 (1935) © WDC

Mickey Mouse Magazine V2#5, © WDC

GD25 FN65 NM94

...& Goofy Explore Energy(1976-1978) 36 pgs.; Exxon giveaway in color; regular size .50 1.00
...& Goofy Explore Energy Conservation(1976-1978)-Exxon .50 1.00
...& Goofy Explore The Universe of Energy(1985) 20pgs.; Exxon giveaway in color; regular size .50 1.00
Club 1(1/64-Gold Key)(TV) 3.00 7.50 15.00
Mini Comic 1(1976)(3-1/4x6-1/2")-Reprints 158 .50 1.00
New Mickey Mouse Club Fun Book 11190 (Golden Press, 1977, $1.95, 224 pgs.) .45 1.20 2.40
Surprise Party 1(30037-901, G.K.)(1/69)-40th Anniversary (see Walt Disney Showcase #47) 3.20 8.00 16.00
Surprise Party 1(1979)-r/1969 issue .40 1.00 2.00

MICKEY MOUSE ADVENTURES
June, 1990 - No. 18, Nov, 1991 ($1.50, color)
Disney Comics

1-18: 1-Bradbury, Murry-r/M.M. #45,73 plus new-a. 2-Begin all new stories. 8-Byrne-c. 9-Fantasia 50th ann. issue w/new adapt. of movie. 10-Gottfredson-r .30 .75 1.50

MICKEY MOUSE BOOK
1930 (4 printings, 20pgs., magazine size, paperbound)
Bibo & Lang

nn-Very first Disney book with games, cartoons & songs; only Disney book to offer the origin of Mickey (based on a story originated by 11 yr. old Bobette Bibo). First app. Mickey & Minnie Mouse. Clarabelle Cow & Horace Horsecollar app. on back cover. Walt Disney, so the story goes, named him 'Mickey Mouse' after the green color of Ireland because he ate old green cheese. The book was printed in black & green to reinforce the Irish theme.

NOTE: One of the printings has a daily Win Smith M. Mouse strip at bottom of back cover; another printing is blank in this area. It has not been definitely proven how to identify each printing. Most copies are missing pages 9 & 10 which contain a puzzle to be cut out. Ublwerks-c

	GD25	FN65	VF82	NM94
1st-4th Prints (complete)	750.00	1800.00	3800.00	5000.00

(Estimated up to 75 total copies exist, 4 in NM/Mint)

	GD25	FN65	VF82
1st-4th Printings (pgs. 9&10 cut out, but not missing)	400.00	900.00	2000.00
1st-4th Printings (pgs. 9&10 missing)	350.00	800.00	1800.00

MICKEY MOUSE CLUB MAGAZINE (See Walt Disney...)

MICKEY MOUSE CLUB SPECIAL (See The New Mickey Mouse...)

MICKEY MOUSE COMICS DIGEST
1986 - No. 5, 1987 (96 pgs.)
Gladstone Publishing

	GD25	FN65	NM94
1-3 ($1.25)		.60	1.25
4,5 ($1.50)	.30	.75	1.50

MICKEY MOUSE MAGAZINE
V1#1, Jan, 1933 - V1#9, Sept, 1933 (5-1/4x7-1/4")
No. 1-3 published by Kamen-Blair (Kay Kamen, Inc.)
Walt Disney Productions

(Scarce)-Distributed by dairies and leading stores through their local theatres. First few issues had 5 cents listed on cover, later ones had no price.

	GD25	FN65	VF82
V1#1	400.00	800.00	2200.00
2-9	117.00	350.00	700.00

MICKEY MOUSE MAGAZINE
V1#1, Nov, 1933 - V2#12, Oct, 1935
Mills giveaways issued by different dairies
Walt Disney Productions

	GD25	FN65	NM94
V1#1	72.00	215.00	500.00
2-12: 2-X-Mas issue	25.00	75.00	175.00
V2#1-12: 2-X-Mas issue. 4-St. Valentine-c	16.50	50.00	115.00

MICKEY MOUSE MAGAZINE (Becomes Walt Disney's Comics & Stories) (No V3#1, V4#6)
Summer, 1935 (June-Aug, indicia) - V5#12, Sept, 1940
V1#1-5, V3#11,12, V4#1-3 are 44 pgs; V2#3-100 pgs; V5#12-68 pgs; rest are 36 pgs.
K. K. Publications/Western Publishing Co.

	GD25	FN65	VF82	NM94
V1#1 (Large size, 13-1/4x10-1/4"; 25 cents)-Contains puzzles, games, cels, stories and comics of Disney characters. Promotional magazine for Disney cartoon movies and paraphernalia	800.00	3000.00	5000.00	8000.00

(Estimated up to 100 total copies exist, 3 in NM/Mint)

Note: *Some copies were autographed by the editors & given away with all early one year subscriptions.*

	GD25	FN65	VF82
2 (Size change, 11-1/2x8-1/2"; 10/35; 10 cents)-High quality paper begins; Messmer-a	121.00	365.00	850.00
3,4: 3-Messmer-a	68.00	205.00	475.00
5-1st Donald Duck solo-c; last 44pg. & high quality paper issue	72.00	215.00	500.00
6-9: 6-36 pg. issues begin; Donald becomes editor. 8-2nd Donald solo-c. 9-1st Mickey/Minnie-c	64.00	193.00	450.00
10-12, V2#1,2: 11-1st Pluto/Mickey-c; Donald fires himself and appoints Mickey as editor	61.00	182.00	425.00
V2#3-Special 100 pg. Christmas issue (25 cents); Messmer-a; Donald becomes editor of Wise Quacks	171.00	515.00	1200.00
4-Mickey Mouse Comics & Roy Ranger (adventure strip) begin; both end V2#9; Messmer-a	54.00	160.00	375.00

	GD25	FN65	NM94
5-Ted True (adventure strip, ends V2#9) & Silly Symphony Comics (ends V3#3) begin	43.00	130.00	300.00
6-9: 6-1st solo Minnie-c. 6-9-Mickey Mouse Movies cut-out in each	43.00	130.00	300.00
10-1st full color issue; Mickey Mouse (by Gottfredson; ends V3#12) & Silly Symphony (ends V3#3) full color Sunday-r, Peter The Farm Detective (ends V5#8) & Ole Of The North (ends V3#3) begins	57.00	170.00	400.00
11-13: 12-Hiawatha-c & feature story	43.00	130.00	300.00
V3#2-Big Bad Wolf Halloween-c	43.00	130.00	300.00
3 (12/37)-1st app. Snow White & The Seven Dwarfs (before release of movie)(possibly 1st in print); Mickey Christmas-c	86.00	260.00	600.00
4 (1/38)-Snow White & The Seven Dwarfs serial begins (on stands before release of movie); Ducky Symphony (ends V3#11) begins	72.00	215.00	500.00
5-1st Snow White & Seven Dwarfs-c (St. Valentine's Day)	86.00	260.00	600.00
6-Snow White serial ends; Lonesome Ghosts app. (2 pp.)	50.00	150.00	350.00
7-Seven Dwarfs Easter-c	43.00	130.00	300.00
8-10: 9-Dopey-c. 10-1st solo Goofy-c	40.00	120.00	280.00
11,12 (44 pgs; 8 more pgs. color added). 11-Mickey the Sheriff serial (ends V4#3) & Donald Duck strip-r (ends V3#12) begin. Color feature on Snow White's Forest Friends	43.00	130.00	300.00
V4#1 (10/38; 44 pgs.)-Brave Little Tailor-c/feature story, nominated for Academy Award; Bobby & Chip by Otto Messmer (ends V4#2) & The Practical Pig (ends V4#2) begin	43.00	130.00	300.00
2 (44 pgs.)-1st Huey, Dewey & Louie-c	40.00	120.00	280.00
3 (12/38, 44 pgs.)-Ferdinand The Bull-c/feature story, Academy Award winner; Mickey Mouse & The Whalers serial begins, ends V4#12	43.00	130.00	300.00
4-Spotty, Mother Pluto strip-r begin, end V4#8	40.00	120.00	280.00

5-St. Valentine's day-c. 1st Pluto solo-c 43.00 130.00 300.00
7 (3/39)-The Ugly Duckling-c/feature story, Academy Award winner
43.00 130.00 300.00
7 (4/39)-Goofy & Wilbur The Grasshopper classic-c/feature story from 1st Goofy cartoon movie; Timid Elmer begins, ends V5#5
43.00 130.00 300.00
8-Big Bad Wolf-c from Practical Pig movie poster; Practical Pig feature story 43.00 130.00 300.00
9-Donald Duck & Mickey Mouse Sunday-r begin; The Pointer feature story, nominated for Academy Award 43.00 130.00 300.00
10-Classic July 4th drum & fife-c; last Donald Sunday-r
50.00 150.00 350.00
11-1st slick-c; last over-sized issue 40.00 120.00 280.00
12 (9/39; format change, 10-1/4x8-1/4")-1st full color, cover to cover issue; Donald's Penguin-c/feature story 48.00 145.00 335.00
V5#1-Black Pete-c; Officer Duck-c/feature story; Autograph Hound feature story; Robinson Crusoe serial begins 48.00 145.00 335.00
2-Goofy-c; 1st app. Pinocchio (cameo) 64.00 195.00 450.00
3 (12/39)-Pinocchio Christmas-c (Before movie release). 1st app. Jiminy Crickett; Pinocchio serial begins 72.00 215.00 500.00
4,5: 5-Jiminy Crickett-c; Pinocchio serial ends; Donald's Dog Laundry feature story 48.00 145.00 335.00
6-Tugboat Mickey feature story; Rip Van Winkle feature begins, ends V5#8 47.00 140.00 325.00
7-2nd Huey, Dewey & Louie-c 47.00 140.00 325.00
8-Last magazine size issue; 2nd solo Pluto-c; Figaro & Cleo feature story
47.00 140.00 325.00
9 (6/40; change to comic book size)-Jiminy Crickett feature story; Donald-c & Sunday-r begin 52.00 155.00 360.00
10-Special Independence Day issue 52.00 155.00 360.00
11-Hawaiian Holiday & Mickey's Trailor feature stories; last 36 pg. issue
52.00 155.00 360.00
12 (Format change)-The transition issue (68 pgs.) becoming a comic book. With only a title change to follow, becomes Walt Disney's Comics & Stories #1 with the next issue 357.00 1070.00 2500.00
V4#1 (Giveaway) 36.00 107.00 250.00

NOTE: *Otto Messmer-a is in many issues of the first two-three years. The following story titles and issues have gags created by* ***Carl Barks:*** *V4#3(12/38)-'Donald's Better Self' & 'Donald's Golf Game;' V4#4(1/39)-'Donald's Lucky Day;' V4#7(3/39)-'Hockey Champ;' V4#7(4/39)-'Donald's Cousin Gus;' V4#9(6/39)-'Sea Scouts;' V4#12(9/39)-'Donald's Penguin;' V5#9 (6/40)-'Donald's Vacation;' V5#10(7/40)-'Bone Trouble;' V5#12(9/40)-'Window Cleaners.'*

MICKEY MOUSE MARCH OF COMICS
1947 - 1951 (Giveaway)
K. K. Publications

8(1947)-32 pgs. 50.00 150.00 350.00
27(1948) 36.00 107.00 250.00
45(1949) 31.00 92.00 215.00
60(1950) 19.00 58.00 135.00
74(1951) 16.00 48.00 110.00

MICKEY MOUSE SUMMER FUN (See Dell Giants)

MICKEY MOUSE'S SUMMER VACATION (See Story Hour Series)

MICROBOTS, THE
December, 1971 (One Shot)
Gold Key

1 (10271-112) 1.40 3.50 7.00

MICRONAUTS
Jan, 1979 - No. 59, Aug, 1984 (Mando paper #53 on)
Marvel Comics Group

1-Intro/1st app. Baron Karza .45 1.10 2.20
2-5 .60 1.20
6-36,39-59: 7-Man-Thing app. 8-1st app. Capt. Universe (8/79). 9-1st app. Cilicia. 13-1st app. Jasmine. 15-Death of Microtron. 15-17-Fantastic Four app. 17-Death of Jasmine. 20-Ant-Man app. 21-Microverse series begins. 25-Origin Baron Karza. 25-29-Nick Fury app. 27-Death of Biotron. 34,35-Dr. Strange app. 35-Double size; origin Microverse; intro Death Squad. 40-Fantastic Four app. 57-Double size. 59-Golden painted-c
.50 1.00
37-Nightcrawler app.; X-Men cameo (2 pgs.) .40 1.00 2.00
38-First direct sale .30 .80 1.60
nn-Reprints #1-3; blank UPC; diamond on top .40
Annual 1(12/79)-Ditko-c/a .50 1.25 2.50
Annual 2(10/80)-Ditko-c/a .40 1.00 2.00

NOTE: *#38-on distributed only through comic shops.* ***N. Adams*** *c-7i.* ***Chaykin*** *a-13-18p.* ***Ditko*** *a-39p.* ***Giffen*** *a-36p, 37p(part).* ***Golden*** *a-1-12p; c-2-7p, 8-23, 24p, 38, 39, 59.* ***Guice*** *a-48-58p; c-49-58.* ***Gil Kane*** *a-38, 40-45p; c-40-45.* ***Layton*** *c-33-37.* ***Miller*** *c-31.*

MICRONAUTS (Marvel, 1984-86) (Value: cover or less)

MICRONAUTS SPECIAL EDITION (Marvel) (Value: cover or less)

MIDGET COMICS (Fighting Indian Stories)
Feb, 1950 - No. 2, Apr, 1950 (5-3/8"x7-3/8," 68 pgs.)
St. John Publishng Co.

1-Matt Baker-c 8.35 25.00 50.00
2-Tex West, Cowboy Marshal 5.00 15.00 30.00

MIDNIGHT
April, 1957 - No. 6, June, 1958
Ajax/Farrell Publ. (Four Star Comic Corp.)

1-Reprints from Voodoo & Strange Fantasy with some changes
7.50 22.50 45.00
2-6 4.20 12.50 25.00

MIDNIGHT EYE
1991 - No. 6, 1992 ($4.95, color, adults, 44 pgs.)
Viz Premiere Comics

1-6: Japenese stories translated into English 1.00 2.50 5.00

MIDNIGHT MYSTERY
Jan-Feb, 1961 - No. 7, Oct, 1961
American Comics Group

1-Sci/Fi story 6.70 20.00 40.00
2-7: 7-Gustavson-a 4.00 10.00 20.00

NOTE: ***Reinman*** *a-1, 3.* ***Whitney*** *a-1, 4-6; c-1-3, 5, 7.*

MIDNIGHT TALES
Dec, 1972 - No. 18, May, 1976
Charlton Press

V1#1 .80 2.00 4.00
2-18: 11-14-Newton-a(p) .60 1.50 3.00
12,17(Modern Comics reprint, 1977) .50 1.00

NOTE: ***Adkins*** *a-12i, 13i.* ***Ditko*** *a-12.* ***Howard*** *(Wood imitator) a-1-15, 17, 18; c-1-18.* ***Don Newton*** *a-11-14p.* ***Staton*** *a-1, 3-11, 13.* ***Sutton*** *a-3-5, 7-10.*

MIGHTY ATOM, THE (...& the Pixies #6) (Formerly The Pixies #1-5)
No. 6, 1949; Nov, 1957 - No. 6, Aug-Sept, 1958
Magazine Enterprises

6(1949-M.E.)-no month (1st Series) 4.00 12.00 24.00
1-6(2nd Series)-Pixies-r 2.40 6.00 12.00
I.W. Reprint #1(nd) .40 1.00 2.00
Giveaway(1959, '63, Whitman)-Evans-a 1.60 4.00 8.00
Giveaway ('65r, '67r, '68r, '73r, '76r) .50 1.00

MIGHTY BEAR (Formerly Fun Comics; becomes Unsane #15)
No. 13, Jan, 1954 - No. 14, Mar, 1954; 9/57 - No. 3, 2/58
Star Publ. No. 13,14/Ajax-Farrell (Four Star)

13,14-L. B. Cole-c 5.85 17.50 35.00
1-3('57-58)Four Star; becomes Mighty Ghost #4 3.00 7.50 15.00

MIGHTY COMICS (...Presents) (Formerly Flyman)
No. 40, Nov, 1966 - No. 50, Oct, 1967 (All 12 cent issues)
Radio Comics (Archie)

40-Web 2.40 6.00 12.00
41-50: 41-Shield, Black Hood. 42-Black Hood. 43-Shield, Web & Black Hood. 44-Black Hood, Steel Sterling & The Shield. 45-Shield & Hangman; origin

Micronauts #1, © MEG

Midnight Mystery #7, © ACG

The Mighty Atom #6, © ME

Mighty Comics #43, © AP

The Mighty Heroes #1, © CBS

Mighty Mouse #64, © Viacom

Web retold. 46-Steel Sterling, Web & Black Hood. 47-Black Hood & Mr. Justice. 48-Shield & Hangman; Wizard x-over in Shield. 49-Steel Sterling & Fox; Black Hood x-over in Steel Sterling. 50-Black Hood & Web; Inferno x-over in Web — 2.00 | 5.00 | 10.00

NOTE: ***Paul Reinman a-40-50.***

MIGHTY CRUSADERS, THE (Also see Adventures of the Fly, The Crusaders & Fly Man)
Nov, 1965 - No. 7, Oct, 1966 (All 12 cent issues)
Mighty Comics Group (Radio Comics)

	GD25	FN65	NM94
1-Origin The Shield	4.20	12.50	25.00
2-Origin Comet	2.80	7.00	14.00
3-Origin Fly-Man	2.40	6.00	12.00
4-Fireball, Inferno (1st S.A. app.), Firefly, Web, Fox, Bob Phantom, Blackjack, Hangman, Zambini, Kardak, Steel Sterling, Mr. Justice, Wizard, Capt. Flag, Jaguar x-over	3.00	7.50	15.00
5-Intro. Ultra-Men (Fox, Web, Capt. Flag) & Terrific Three (Jaguar, Mr. Justice, Steel Sterling)	2.40	6.00	12.00
6,7: 7-Steel Sterling feature; origin Fly-Girl	2.40	6.00	12.00

NOTE: ***Reinman a-6.***

MIGHTY CRUSADERS, THE (All New Advs. of...#2)
Mar, 1983 - No. 13, Sept, 1985 ($1.00, 36 pgs, Mando paper)
Red Circle Prod./Archie Ent. No. 6 on

	GD25	FN65	NM94
1-13: 1-Origin Black Hood, The Fly, Fly Girl, The Shield, The Wizard, The Jaguar, Pvt. Strong & The Web. 2-Mister Midnight begins. 4-Darkling replaces Shield. 5-Origin Jaguar, Shield begins. 7-Untold origin Jaguar		.50	1.00

NOTE: ***Buckler a-1-3, 4i, 5p, 7p, 8i, 9i; c-1-10p.***

MIGHTY GHOST (Formerly Mighty Bear #1-3)
No. 4, June, 1958
Ajax/Farrell Publ.

	GD25	FN65	NM94
4	2.40	6.00	12.00

MIGHTY HERCULES, THE (TV)
July, 1963 - No. 2, Nov, 1963
Gold Key

	GD25	FN65	NM94
1,2(10072-307, 10072-311)	11.00	32.00	75.00

MIGHTY HEROES, THE (TV) (Funny)
Mar, 1967 - No. 4, July, 1967
Dell Publishing Co.

	GD25	FN65	NM94
1-Also has a 1957 Heckle & Jeckle-r	11.00	32.00	75.00
2-4: 4-Has two 1958 Mighty Mouse-r	8.35	25.00	50.00

MIGHTY MARVEL WESTERN, THE
Oct, 1968 - No. 46, Sept, 1976 (#1-14: 68 pgs.; #15,16: 52 pgs.)
Marvel Comics Group (LMC earlier issues)

	GD25	FN65	NM94
1-Begin Kid Colt, Rawhide Kid, Two-Gun Kid-r	1.20	3.00	6.00
2-10	.60	1.50	3.00
11-20	.40	1.00	2.00
21-46: 24-Kid Colt-r end. 25-Matt Slade-r begin. 31-Baker-r. 32-Origin-r/Rawhide Kid #23; Williamson-r/Kid Slade #7. 37-Williamson, Kirby-r/Two-Gun Kid 51		.60	1.20

NOTE: ***Jack Davis** a(r)-21-24. **Keller** r-1, 22. **Kirby** a(r)-1-3, 6, 9, 12, 14, 16, 26, 29, 32, 36, 41, 43, 44; c-29. **Maneely** a(r)-22. No Matt Slade-#43.*

MIGHTY MIDGET COMICS, THE (Miniature)
No date; circa 1942-1943 (36 pages) (Approx. 5x4")
(Black & White & Red) (Sold 2 for 5 cents)
Samuel E. Lowe & Co.

	GD25	FN65	NM94
Bulletman #11(1943)-r/cover/Bulletman #3	6.70	20.00	40.00
Captain Marvel #11	6.70	20.00	40.00

	GD25	FN65	–
Captain Marvel #11 (Same as above except for full color ad on back cover; this issue was glued to cover of Captain Marvel #20 and is not found in fine-mint condition)	200.00	625.00	–

	GD25	FN65	NM94
Captain Marvel Jr. #11	6.70	20.00	40.00

	GD25	FN65	–
Captain Marvel Jr. #11 (Same as above except for full color ad on back-c; this issue was glued to cover of Captain Marvel #21 and is not found in fine-mint condition)	200.00	625.00	–

	GD25	FN65	NM94
Golden Arrow #11	4.20	12.50	25.00
Ibis the Invincible #11(1942)-Origin; reprints cover to Ibis #1	6.70	20.00	40.00
Spy Smasher #11(1942)	6.70	20.00	40.00

NOTE: *The above books came in a box called "box full of books" and was distributed with other Samuel Lowe puzzles, paper dolls, coloring books, etc. They are not titled Mighty Midget Comics. All have a war bond seal on back cover which is otherwise blank. These books came in a "Mighty Midget" flat cardboard counter display rack.*

	GD25	FN65	NM94
Balbo, the Boy Magician #12	3.20	8.00	16.00
Bulletman #12	5.85	17.50	35.00
Commando Yank #12	4.20	12.50	25.00
Dr. Voltz the Human Generator	3.20	8.00	16.00
Lance O'Casey #12	3.20	8.00	16.00
Leatherneck the Marine	3.20	8.00	16.00
Minute Man #12	5.85	17.50	35.00
Mister Q	3.20	8.00	16.00
Mr. Scarlet & Pinky #12	4.70	14.00	28.00
Pat Wilton & His Flying Fortress	3.20	8.00	16.00
The Phantom Eagle #12	4.00	10.50	21.00
State Trooper Stops Crime	3.20	8.00	16.00
Tornado Tom; r-/from Cyclone #1-3; origin	3.60	9.00	18.00

MIGHTY MOUSE (See Adventures of..., Dell Giant #43, Giant Comics Edition, March of Comics #205, 237, 247, 257, 447, 459, 471, 483, Oxydol-Dreft, Paul Terry's, & Terry-Toons Comics)

MIGHTY MOUSE (1st Series)
Fall, 1946 - No. 4, Summer, 1947
Timely/Marvel Comics (20th Century Fox)

	GD25	FN65	NM94
1	68.00	205.00	475.00
2	34.00	103.00	240.00
3,4	23.00	70.00	160.00

MIGHTY MOUSE (2nd Series) (Paul Terry's... #62-71)
Aug, 1947 - No. 67, 11/55; No. 68, 3/56 - No. 83, 6/59
St. John Publishing Co./Pines No. 68 (3/56) on (TV issues #72 on)

	GD25	FN65	NM94
5(#1)	24.00	70.00	165.00
6-10	12.00	34.00	85.00
11-19	8.35	25.00	50.00
20 (11/50) - 25-(52 pgs.)	6.36	19.00	38.00
20-25-(36 pg. editions)	5.85	17.50	35.00
26-37: 35-Flying saucer-c	4.70	14.00	28.00
38-45-(100 pgs.)	10.00	30.00	70.00
46-83: 62-64,67-Painted-c. 82-Infinity-c	4.20	12.50	25.00
Album 1(10/52)-100 pgs.	19.00	57.00	130.00
Album 2(11/52-St. John) - 3(12/52) (100 pgs.)	14.00	43.00	100.00
Fun Club Magazine 1(Fall, 1957-Pines, 100 pgs.) (CBS TV-Tom Terrific)	10.00	30.00	70.00
Fun Club Magazine 2-6(Winter, 1958-Pines)	6.70	20.00	40.00
3-D 1-(1st printing-9/53)(St. John)-stiff covers	22.00	65.00	150.00
3-D 1-(2nd printing-10/53)-slick, glossy covers, slightly smaller	19.00	57.00	130.00
3-D 2(11/53), 3(12/53)-(St. John)	17.00	51.00	120.00

MIGHTY MOUSE (TV)(3rd Series)(Formerly Adventures of Mighty Mouse)
No. 161, Oct, 1964 - No. 172, Oct, 1968
Gold Key/Dell Publishing Co. No. 166-on

	GD25	FN65	NM94
161(10/64)-165(9/65)-(Becomes Advs. of... No. 166 on)	4.00	10.00	20.00
166(3/66), 167(6/66)-172	3.00	7.50	15.00

MIGHTY MOUSE (TV)(Spotlight, 1987)(Value: cover or less)

MIGHTY MOUSE (TV)
Oct, 1990 - No. 10, July, 1991 ($1.00, color)(Based on Sat. cartoon)
Marvel Comics

	GD25	FN65	NM94
1-10: 1-Dark Knight-c parody. 2-10: 3-Intro Bat-Bat; Byrne-c. 4,5-Crisis-c/story parodies w/Perez-c. 6-Spider-Man-c parody. 7-Origin Bat-Bat		.50	1.00

MIGHTY MOUSE ADVENTURES (Adventures of... #2 on)
November, 1951
St. John Publishing Co.

	GD25	FN65	NM94
1	22.00	65.00	150.00

MIGHTY MOUSE ADVENTURE STORIES (Paul Terry's... on-c only)
1953 (384 pgs.) (50 Cents)
St. John Publishing Co.

	GD25	FN65	NM94
nn-Rebound issues	34.00	100.00	235.00

MIGHTY MUTANIMALS (See Teenage Mutant Ninja Turtles Advs. #19)
May, 1991 - No. 3, July, 1991 ($1.00, color, mini-series)
Apr, 1992 - Present ($1.25, color)
Archie Comics

	GD25	FN65	NM94
1-3: 1-Story cont'd from TMNT Advs. #19		.50	1.00
1-8 (1992)		.60	1.25

MIGHTY SAMSON (Also see Gold Key Champion)
7/64 - #20, 11/69; #21, 8/72; #22, 12/73 - #31, 3/76; #32, 8/82
Gold Key

	GD25	FN65	NM94
1-Origin; Thorne-a begins; painted c-1-31	4.00	11.00	22.00
2-5	2.20	5.50	11.00
6-10: 7-Tom Morrow begins, ends #20	1.70	4.25	8.50
11-20	1.50	3.75	7.50
21-32: 21,22,32-r	.80	2.00	4.00

MIGHTY THOR (See Thor)

MIKE BARNETT, MAN AGAINST CRIME (TV)
Dec, 1951 - No. 6, 1952
Fawcett Publications

	GD25	FN65	NM94
1	10.00	30.00	60.00
2	5.85	17.50	35.00
3,4,6	4.70	14.00	28.00
5-"Market for Morphine" cover/story	6.35	19.00	38.00

MIKE GRELL'S SABLE (First)(Value: cover or less)

MIKE MIST MINUTE MIST-ERIES (See Ms. Tree/Mike Mist in 3-D)
April, 1981 ($1.25, B&W, one-shot)
Eclipse Comics

	GD25	FN65	NM94
1		.60	1.25

MIKE SHAYNE PRIVATE EYE
Nov-Jan, 1962 - No. 3, Sept-Nov, 1962
Dell Publishing Co.

	GD25	FN65	NM94
1	2.80	7.00	14.00
2,3	1.80	4.50	9.00

MILITARY COMICS (Becomes Modern Comics #44 on)
Aug, 1941 - No. 43, Oct, 1945
Quality Comics Group

	GD25	FN65	VF82	NM94
1-Origin/1st app. Blackhawk by C. Cuidera (Eisner scripts); Miss America, The Death Patrol by Jack Cole (also #2-7,27-30), & The Blue Tracer by Guardineer; X of the Underground, The Yankee Eagle, Q-Boat & Shot & Shell, Archie Atkins, Loops & Banks by Bud Ernest (Bob Powell)(ends #13) begin	350.00	1050.00	2100.00	3500.00

(Estimated up to 160 total copies exist, 9 in NM/Mint)

	GD25	FN65	NM94
2-Secret War News begins (by McWilliams #2-16); Cole-a	183.00	550.00	1100.00
3-Origin/1st app. Chop Chop	150.00	450.00	900.00
4	125.00	375.00	750.00
5-The Sniper begins; Miss America in costume #4-7	100.00	300.00	600.00
6-9: 8-X of the Underground begins (ends #13). 9-The Phantom Clipper begins (ends #16)	83.00	250.00	500.00
10-Classic Eisner-c	92.00	275.00	550.00
11-Flag-c	67.00	200.00	400.00
12-Blackhawk by Crandall begins, ends #22	92.00	275.00	550.00
13-15: 14-Private Dogtag begins (ends #83)	62.00	188.00	375.00
16-20: 16-Blue Tracer ends. 17-P.T. Boat begins	54.00	162.00	325.00
21-31: 22-Last Crandall Blackhawk. 23-Shrunken head-c. 27-Death Patrol revived	48.00	145.00	290.00
32-43	42.00	125.00	250.00

NOTE: ***Berg** a-6. **Al Bryant** c-31-34, 38, 40-43. **J. Cole** a-1-3, 27-32. **Crandall** a-12-22; c-13-20. **Cuidera** c-2-9. **Eisner** c-1, 2(part), 9, 10. **Kotsky** c-21-29, 35, 37, 39. **McWilliams** a-2-16. **Powell** a-1-13. **Ward** Blackhawk-30, 31(15 pgs. each); c-30.*

MILITARY WILLY
1907 (14 pgs.; in color (every other page))
(regular comic book format)(7x9-1/2")(stapled)
J. I. Austen Co.

	GD25	FN65	NM94
nn-By F. R. Morgan	21.00	62.00	125.00

MILLENNIUM (DC)(Value: cover or less)

MILLENNIUM INDEX (Independent)(Value: cover or less)

MILLIE, THE LOVABLE MONSTER
Sept-Nov, 1962 - No. 6, Jan, 1973
Dell Publishing Co.

	GD25	FN65	NM94
12-523-211, 2(8-10/63)	4.00	10.00	20.00
3(8-10/64)	3.00	7.50	15.00
4(7/72), 5(10/72), 6(1/73)	1.60	4.00	8.00

NOTE: ***Woggon** a-3-6; c-3-6. 4 reprints 1; 5 reprints 2; 6 reprints 3.*

MILLIE THE MODEL (See Comedy Comics, A Date With..., Gay Comics, Life With..., Mad About... & Modeling With...)
1945 - No. 207, December, 1973
Marvel/Atlas/Marvel Comics (CnPC #1)(SPI/Male/VPI)

	GD25	FN65	NM94
1-Origin	36.00	107.00	250.00
2 (10/46)-Millie becomes The Blonde Phantom to sell Blonde Phantom perfume; a pre-Blonde Phantom app. (see All-Select #11, Fall, '46)	20.00	60.00	140.00
3-7: 4,5- Willie app. 7-Willie smokes extra strong tobacco	12.00	36.00	85.00
8,10-Kurtzman's "Hey Look." 8-Willie & Rusty app.	12.00	36.00	85.00
9-Powerhouse Pepper by Wolverton, 4 pgs.	15.00	45.00	105.00
11-Kurtzman-a, "Giggles 'n Grins"	9.15	27.50	55.00
12,15,17-20: 12-Rusty & Hedy Devine app.	6.35	19.00	38.00
13,14,16-Kurtzman's "Hey Look." 13-Hedy Devine app.	8.35	25.00	50.00
21-30	4.70	14.00	28.00
31-60	3.60	9.00	18.00
61-99	2.40	6.00	12.00
100	3.60	9.00	18.00
101-153,155-190: 107-Jack Kirby app. in story	1.60	4.00	8.00
154-New Millie begins (10/67)	2.40	6.00	12.00
191-207: 192-(52 pgs.)	1.00	2.50	5.00
Annual 1(1962)-Early Marvel annual (2nd?)	8.35	25.00	50.00
Annual 2-10(1963-11/71)	4.70	14.00	28.00
Queen-Size 11(9/74), 12(1975)	3.00	7.50	15.00

NOTE: ***Dan DeCarlo** a-18-93.*

MILLION DOLLAR DIGEST (Richie Rich... #23 on; also see Richie Rich...)
11/86 - No. 7, 11/87; No. 8, 4/88 - Present ($1.25-$1.75, digest size)
Harvey Publications

Mighty Samson #1, © WEST

Military Comics #31, © QUA

Millie the Model #38, © MEG

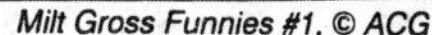
Milt Gross Funnies #1, © ACG

Miss Beverly Hills #2, © DC

Miss Fury #2, © MEG

	GD25	FN65	NM94
1-8		.60	1.25
9-30 (1992)	.35	.90	1.75

MILT GROSS FUNNIES (Also see Picture News #1)
Aug, 1947 - No. 2, Sept, 1947
Milt Gross, Inc. (ACG?)

	GD25	FN65	NM94
1,2	7.50	22.50	45.00

MILTON THE MONSTER & FEARLESS FLY (TV)
May, 1966
Gold Key

	GD25	FN65	NM94
1 (10175-605)	6.70	20.00	40.00

MINUTE MAN (See Master Comics & Mighty Midget Comics)
Summer, 1941 - No. 3, Spring, 1942
Fawcett Publications

	GD25	FN65	NM94
1	100.00	300.00	600.00
2,3	79.00	238.00	475.00

MINUTE MAN
No date (B&W; 16 pgs.; paper cover blue & red)
Sovereign Service Station giveaway

	GD25	FN65	NM94
nn-American history	1.20	3.00	6.00

MINUTE MAN ANSWERS THE CALL, THE
1942 (4 pages)
By M. C. Gaines (War Bonds giveaway)

	GD25	FN65	NM94
nn-Sheldon Moldoff-a	8.35	25.00	50.00

MIRACLE COMICS
Feb, 1940 - No. 4, March, 1941
Hillman Periodicals

	GD25	FN65	NM94
1-Sky Wizard, Master of Space, Dash Dixon, Man of Might, Pinkie Parker, Dusty Doyle, The Kid Cop, K-7, Secret Agent, The Scorpion, & Blandu, Jungle Queen begin; Masked Angel only app.	108.00	325.00	650.00
2	57.00	170.00	340.00
3,4: 3-Bill Colt, the Ghost Rider begins. 4-The Veiled Prophet & Bullet Bob app.	50.00	150.00	300.00

MIRACLEMAN (Eclipse) (Value: cover or less)

MIRACLEMAN: APOCRYPHA (Eclipse) (Value: cover or less)

MIRACLEMAN FAMILY (Eclipse) (Value: cover or less)

MIRACLE OF THE WHITE STALLIONS, THE (See Movie Comics)

MIRACLE SQUAD, THE (Fantagraphics) (Value: cover or less)

MIRACLE SQUAD: BLOOD AND DUST, THE (Apple) (Value: cover or less)

MIRRORWALKER (Now) (Value: cover or less)

MISADVENTURES OF MERLIN JONES, THE (See Movie Comics & Merlin Jones as the Monkey's Uncle under Movie Comics)

MISCHIEVOUS MONKS OF CROCODILE ISLE, THE
1908 (8-1/2x11-1/2"; 4 pgs. in color; 12 pgs.)
J. I. Austen Co., Chicago

	GD25	FN65	NM94
nn-By F. R. Morgan; reads longwise	15.00	45.00	90.00

MISS AMERICA COMICS (Miss America Magazine #2 on; also see Blonde Phantom & Marvel Mystery Comics)
1944 (One Shot)
Marvel Comics (20CC)

	GD25	FN65	NM94
1-2 pgs. pin-ups	75.00	225.00	450.00

MISS AMERICA MAGAZINE (Formerly Miss America; Miss America #51 on)
V1#2, Nov, 1944 - No. 93, Nov, 1958
Miss America Publ. Corp./Marvel/Atlas (MAP)

	GD25	FN65	NM94
V1#2-Photo-c of teenage girl in Miss America costume; Miss America, Patsy Walker (intro.) comic stories plus movie reviews & stories; intro. Buzz Baxter & Hedy Wolfe	62.00	188.00	375.00
3-5-Miss America & Patsy Walker stories	25.00	75.00	150.00
6-Patsy Walker only	6.35	19.00	38.00
V2#1(4/45)-6(9/45)-Patsy Walker continues	4.00	10.00	20.00
V3#1(10/45)-6(4/46)	4.00	10.00	20.00
V4#1(5/46),2,5(9/46)	3.60	9.00	18.00
V4#3(7/46)-Liz Taylor photo-c	5.85	17.50	35.00
V4#4 (8/46; 68pgs.)	3.20	8.00	16.00
V4#6 (10/46; 92pgs.)	3.20	8.00	16.00
V5#1(11/46)-6(4/47), V6#1(5/47)-3(7/47)	3.20	8.00	16.00
V7#1(8/47)-14,16-23(#56, 6/49)	2.80	7.00	14.00
V7#15-All comics	3.20	8.00	16.00
V7#24(#57, 7/49)-Kamen-a (becomes Best Western #58 on?)	2.80	7.00	14.00
V7#25(8/49), 27-44(3/52), VII,nn(5/52)	2.40	6.00	12.00
V7#26(9/49)-All comics	3.20	8.00	16.00
V1,nn(7/52)-V1,nn(1/53)(#46-49)	2.40	6.00	12.00
V7#50(Spring '53), V1#51-V7?#54(7/53)	2.40	6.00	12.00
55-93	2.40	6.00	12.00

NOTE: *Photo-c #1, 4, V2#4, 5, V3#5, V4#3, 4, 6, V7#15, 16, 24, 26, 34, 37, 38.* ***Powell*** *a-V7#31.*

MISS BEVERLY HILLS OF HOLLYWOOD (See Adventures of Bob Hope)
Mar-Apr, 1949 - No. 9, July-Aug, 1950 (52 pgs.)
National Periodical Publications

	GD25	FN65	NM94
1 (Meets Alan Ladd)	36.00	107.00	250.00
2-William Holden photo-c	25.00	75.00	175.00
3-5: 3,4-Part photo-c	22.00	65.00	150.00
6,7,9	19.00	58.00	135.00
8-Reagan photo on-c	25.00	75.00	175.00

MISS CAIRO JONES
1945
Croyden Publishers

	GD25	FN65	NM94
1-Bob Oksner daily newspaper-r (1st strip story); lingerie panels	14.00	43.00	100.00

MISS FURY COMICS (Newspaper strip reprints)
Winter, 1942-43 - No. 8, Winter, 1946
Timely Comics (NPI 1/CmPI 2/MPC 3-8)

	GD25	FN65	NM94
1-Origin Miss Fury by Tarpe' Mills (68 pgs.) in costume w/pin-ups	200.00	600.00	1200.00
2-(60 pgs.)-In costume w/pin-ups	96.00	288.00	575.00
3-(60 pgs.)-In costume w/pin-ups; Hitler-c	79.00	238.00	475.00
4-(52 pgs.)-In costume, 2 pgs. w/pin-ups	63.00	188.00	375.00
5-(52 pgs.)-In costume w/pin-ups	58.00	175.00	350.00
6-(52 pgs.)-Not in costume in inside stories, w/pin-ups	54.00	162.00	325.00
7,8-(36 pgs.)-In costume 1 pg. each; no pin-ups	54.00	162.00	325.00

NOTE: ***Schomburg*** *c-1, 5, 6.*

MISS FURY
1991 - No. 4, 1991 ($2.50, color, mini-series)
Adventure Comics

	GD25	FN65	NM94
1-4: 1-Origin; granddaughter of original Miss Fury	.40	1.25	2.50
1-Limited ed. ($4.95)	.85	2.50	5.00

MISSION IMPOSSIBLE (TV)
May, 1967 - No. 4, Oct, 1968; No. 5, Oct, 1969 (All have photo-c)
Dell Publishing Co.

	GD25	FN65	NM94
1	6.70	20.00	40.00
2-5: 5-reprints #1	4.70	14.00	28.00

MISS LIBERTY (Becomes Liberty Comics)
1945 (MLJ reprints)
Burten Publishing Co.

1-The Shield & Dusty, The Wizard, & Roy, the Super Boy app.;

	GD25	FN65	NM94
r/Shield-Wizard #13	23.00	68.00	135.00

MISS MELODY LANE OF BROADWAY (See The Adventures of Bob Hope)
Feb-Mar, 1950 - No. 3, June-July, 1950 (52 pgs.)
National Periodical Publications

	GD25	FN65	NM94
1	34.00	103.00	240.00
2,3	25.00	75.00	175.00

MISS PEACH
Oct-Dec, 1963; 1969
Dell Publishing Co.

	GD25	FN65	NM94
1-Jack Mendelsohn-a/script	8.35	25.00	50.00
...Tells You How to Grow(1969; 25 cents)-Mel Lazarus-a; also given away (36 pgs.)	5.00	15.00	30.00

MISS PEPPER (See Meet Miss Pepper)

MISS SUNBEAM (See Little Miss...)

MISS VICTORY (See Captain Fearless #1,2, Holyoke One-Shot #3, Veri Best Sure Fire & Veri Best Sure Shot Comics)

MISS VICTORY GOLDEN ANNIVERSARY SPECIA (AC)(Value: cover or less)

MR. & MRS.
1922 (52 & 28 pgs.) (9x9-1/2", cardboard-c)
Whitman Publishing Co.

	GD25	FN65	NM94
nn-By Briggs (B&W, 52pgs.)	15.00	45.00	90.00
nn-28 pgs.-(9x9-1/2")-Sunday strips-r in color	18.00	55.00	110.00

MR. & MRS. BEANS (See Single Series #11)

MR. & MRS. J. EVIL SCIENTIST (TV)(See The Flintstones)
Nov, 1963 - No. 4, Sept, 1966 (Hanna-Barbera)
Gold Key

	GD25	FN65	NM94
1-From The Flintstones	5.00	15.00	30.00
2-4	3.60	9.00	18.00

MR. ANTHONY'S LOVE CLINIC (Based on radio show)
Nov, 1949 - No. 5, Apr-May, 1950 (52 pgs.)
Hillman Periodicals

	GD25	FN65	NM94
1-Photo-c	7.50	22.50	45.00
2	4.70	14.00	28.00
3-5: 5-Photo-c	4.00	12.00	24.00

MR. BUG GOES TO TOWN (See Cinema Comics Herald)
1941 (52 pgs.)(Giveaway)
K.K. Publications

	GD25	FN65	NM94
nn-Cartoon movie	37.00	110.00	260.00

MR. DISTRICT ATTORNEY (Radio/TV)
Jan-Feb, 1948 - No. 67, Jan-Feb, 1959 (1-23: 52 pgs.)
National Periodical Publications

	GD25	FN65	NM94
1-Howard Purcell c-5-23 (most)	57.00	171.00	400.00
2	23.00	70.00	160.00
3-5	17.00	54.00	120.00
6-10	13.00	40.00	90.00
11-20	11.00	32.00	75.00
21-43: 43-Last pre-code (1-2/55)	8.35	25.00	50.00
44-67	6.70	20.00	40.00

MR. DISTRICT ATTORNEY (See 4-Color #13 & The Funnies #35)

MISTER E (DC)(Value: cover or less)

MISTER ED, THE TALKING HORSE (TV)
Mar-May, 1962 - No. 6, Feb, 1964 (All photo-c; photo back-c: 1-6)
Dell Publishing Co./Gold Key

	GD25	FN65	NM94
4-Color 1295	10.00	30.00	70.00
1(11/62) (Gold Key)-Photo-c	7.50	22.50	45.00
2-6-Photo-c	4.20	12.50	25.00

(See March of Comics #244, 260, 282, 290)

MR. MAGOO (TV) (The Nearsighted..., ...& Gerald McBoing Boing 1954 issues; formerly Gerald McBoing-Boing And ...)
No. 6, Nov-Jan, 1953-54; 5/54 - 3-5/62; 9-11/63 - 3-5/65
Dell Publishing Co.

	GD25	FN65	NM94
6	9.15	27.50	55.00
4-Color 561(5/54),602(11/54)	9.15	27.50	55.00
4-Color 1235(#1, 12-2/62),1305(#2, 3-5/62)	7.50	22.50	45.00
3(9-11/63) - 5	6.70	20.00	40.00
4-Color 1235(12-536-505)(3-5/65)-2nd Printing	4.20	12.50	25.00

MISTER MIRACLE (See Cancelled Comic Cavalcade)
3-4/71 - V4#18, 2-3/74; V5#19, 9/77 - V6#25, 8-9/78; 1987
National Periodical Publications/DC Comics

	GD25	FN65	NM94
1-(#1-3 are 15 cents)	2.80	7.00	14.00
2,3	1.80	4.50	9.00
4-8: 4-Boy Commandos-r begin; all 52 pgs.	1.60	4.00	8.00
9,10: 9-Origin Mr. Miracle; Darkseid cameo	1.20	3.00	6.00
11-18: 15-Intro/1st app. Shilo Norman. 18-Barda & Scott Free wed; New Gods app. & Darkseid cameo	1.00	2.50	5.00
19-25 (1977-1978)	.60	1.50	3.00
Special 1(1987, $1.25, 52 pgs.)	.40	1.00	2.00

NOTE: ***Austin** a-19i. **Ditko** a-6r. **Golden** a-23-25p; c-25p. **Heath** a-24i, 25i; c-25i. **Kirby** a(p)/c-1-18. **Nasser** a-19i. **Rogers** a-19-22p; c-19, 20p, 21p, 22-24. **Wolverton** a-6r. 4-8 contain **Simon & Kirby** Boy Commandos reprints from Detective 82,76, Boy Commandos 1, 3 & Detective 64 in that order.*

MISTER MIRACLE (DC, 1989-91)(Value: cover or less)

MR. MIRACLE (See Capt. Fearless #1 & Holyoke One-Shot #4)

MR. MONSTER (Doc Stearn... #7 on; See Airboy-Mr. Monster Special, Dark Horse Presents, Super Duper Comics & Vanguard Illustrated #7)
Jan, 1985 - No. 10, June, 1987 ($1.75, color, Baxter paper)
Eclipse Comics

	GD25	FN65	NM94
1-1st story-r from Vanguard Ill. #7(1st app.)	1.00	2.50	5.00
2-Dave Stevens-c	.50	1.25	2.50
3-10: 3-Alan Moore scripts; Wolverton-r/Weird Mysteries #5. 6-Ditko-r/Fantastic Fears #5 plus new Giffen-a 10 6-D issue	.35	.85	1.75

MR. MONSTER (Dark Horse, 1988)(Value: cover or less)

MR. MONSTER ATTACKS! (Tundra)(Value: cover or less)

MR. MONSTER'S SUPER-DUPER SPECIAL (Eclipse)(Value: cover or less)

MR. MUSCLES (Formerly Blue Beetle #18-21)
No. 22, Mar, 1956; No. 23, Aug, 1956
Charlton Comics

	GD25	FN65	NM94
22,23	4.00	10.00	20.00

MISTER MYSTERY
Sept, 1951 - No. 19, Oct, 1954
Mr. Publ. (Media Publ.) No. 1-3/SPM Publ./Stanmore (Aragon)

	GD25	FN65	NM94
1-Kurtzmanesque horror story	27.00	80.00	190.00
2,3-Kurtzmanesque story. 3-Anti-Wertham edit.	19.00	58.00	135.00
4,6: Bondage-c; 6-Torture	19.00	58.00	135.00
5,8,10	15.00	45.00	105.00
7-"The Brain Bats of Venus" by Wolverton; partially re-used in Weird Tales of the Future #7	49.00	150.00	345.00
9-Nostrand-a	16.00	48.00	110.00
11-Wolverton "Robot Woman" story/Weird Mysteries #2, cut up, rewritten & partially redrawn	27.00	80.00	190.00
12-Classic injury to eye-c	43.00	130.00	300.00
13,14,17,19: 17-Severed heads-c	11.50	34.00	80.00
15-"Living Dead" junkie story	13.00	40.00	90.00
16-Bondage-c	13.00	40.00	90.00
18-"Robot Woman" by Wolverton reprinted from Weird Mysteries #2; decapitation, bondage-c	24.00	72.00	165.00

NOTE: ***Andru** a-1, 2p, 3p. **Andru/Esposito** c-1-3. **Baily** c-10-18(most). Bondage c-7. Some issues have graphic dismemberment scenes.*

MR. MYSTIC (See Will Eisner Presents)

MISTER Q (See Mighty Midget Comics & Our Flag Comics #5)

Mr. District Attorney #17, © DC

Mister Miracle #13 (1970s), © DC

Mister Mystery #4, © Media Publ.

Mitzi's Boyfriend #7, © MEG

Modern Comics #70, © QUA

Modern Love #4, © WMG

MR. RISK (Formerly All Romances; Men Against Crime #3 on)
No. 7, Oct, 1950 - No. 2, Dec, 1950
Ace Magazines

	GD25	FN65	NM94
7,2	4.20	12.50	25.00

MR. SCARLET & PINKY (See Mighty Midget Comics)

MISTER UNIVERSE (Professional wrestler)
July, 1951; No. 2, Oct, 1951 - No. 5, April, 1952
Mr. Publications Media Publ. (Stanmor, Aragon)

	GD25	FN65	NM94
1	11.00	32.00	75.00
2-"Jungle That Time Forgot," (24 pg. story)	8.35	25.00	50.00
3-Marijuana story	8.35	25.00	50.00
4,5-"Goes to War"	4.70	14.00	28.00

MISTER X (See Vortex)
6/84 - No. 14, 8/88 ($1.50-$2.25, direct sales, color, coated paper)
V2#1, Apr, 1989 - V2#12, Mar, 1990 ($2.00-$2.50, B&W, newsprint)
Mr. Publications/Vortex Comics

	GD25	FN65	NM94
1	1.00	2.50	5.00
2	.60	1.50	3.00
3-18: 14-Last color issue	.40	1.00	2.00
V2#1-11 (Second Coming, $2.00, B&W): 1-Four different covers. 10-Photo-c	.40	1.00	2.00
V2#12,13 9$2.50)	.50	1.25	2.50
Graphic Novel, Return of... ($11.95)-r/1-4	2.40	6.00	12.00
Hardcover Limited Edition ($34.95)	5.85	17.50	35.00

MISTY (Marvel) (Value: cover or less)

MITZI COMICS (...Boy Friend #2 on)(See All Teen)
Spring, 1948 (One Shot)
Timely Comics

	GD25	FN65	NM94
1-Kurtzman's "Hey Look" plus 3 pgs. "Giggles 'n' Grins"	10.00	30.00	70.00

MITZI'S BOY FRIEND (Formerly Mitzi; becomes Mitzi's Romances)
No. 2, June, 1948 - No. 7, April, 1949
Marvel Comics (TCI)

	GD25	FN65	NM94
2	5.35	16.00	32.00
3-7	4.20	12.50	25.00

MITZI'S ROMANCES (Formerly Mitzi's Boy Friend)
No. 8, June, 1949 - No. 10, Dec, 1949
Timely/Marvel Comics (TCI)

	GD25	FN65	NM94
8-Becomes True Life Tales #8 (10/49) on?	5.35	16.00	32.00
9,10: 10-Painted-c	4.20	12.50	25.00

MOBY DICK (See Feature Presentations #6, Four Color #717, and King Classics)

MOBY DUCK (See Donald Duck #112 & Walt Disney Showcase #2,11)
Oct, 1967 - No. 11, Oct, 1970; No. 12, Jan, 1974 - No. 30, Feb, 1978
Gold Key (Disney)

	GD25	FN65	NM94
1	1.60	4.00	8.00
2-5	1.00	2.50	5.00
6-11	.60	1.50	3.00
12-30: 21,30-r	.40	1.00	2.00

MODEL FUN (With Bobby Benson)
No. 3, Winter, 1954-55 - No. 5, July, 1955
Harle Publications

	GD25	FN65	NM94
3-Bobby Benson	5.00	15.00	30.00
4,5-Bobby Benson	3.60	9.00	18.00

MODELING WITH MILLIE (Formerly Life With Millie)
No. 21, Feb, 1963 - No. 54, June, 1967
Atlas/Marvel Comics Group (Male Publ.)

	GD25	FN65	NM94
21	5.00	15.00	30.00
22-30	3.60	9.00	18.00
31-54	3.00	7.50	15.00

MODERN COMICS (Formerly Military Comics #1-43)
No. 44, Nov, 1945 - No. 102, Oct, 1950
Quality Comics Group

	GD25	FN65	NM94
44-Blackhawk continues	42.00	125.00	250.00
45-52: 49-1st app. Fear, Lady Adventuress	25.00	75.00	150.00
53-Torchy by Ward begins (9/46)	32.00	95.00	190.00
54-60: 55-J. Cole-a	22.00	65.00	130.00
61-77,79,80: 73-J. Cole-a	20.00	60.00	120.00
78-1st app. Madame Butterfly	22.00	65.00	130.00
81-99,101: 82,83-One pg. J. Cole-a. 83-The Spirit app.; last 52 pg. issue?	20.00	60.00	120.00
100	20.00	60.00	120.00
102-(Scarce)-J. Cole-a; Spirit by Eisner app.	23.00	70.00	140.00

NOTE: ***Al Bryant*** *c-44-51, 54, 55, 66, 69.* ***Jack Cole*** *a-55, 73.* ***Crandall*** *Blackhawk-#46-51, 54, 56, 58-60, 64, 67-70, 73, 76-78, 80-83; c-60-65, 67, 68, 70-95.* ***Crandall/Cuidera*** *c-56-59, 96-102.* ***Gustavson*** *a-47.* ***Ward*** *Blackhawk-#52, 53, 55 (15 pgs. each). Torchy in #53-102; by* ***Ward*** *only in #53-89(9/49); by* ***Gil Fox*** *#93, 102.*

MODERN LOVE
June-July, 1949 - No. 8, Aug-Sept, 1950
E. C. Comics

	GD25	FN65	NM94
1	44.00	133.00	310.00
2-Craig/Feldstein-c	36.00	107.00	250.00
3-Spanking panels	30.00	90.00	210.00
4-6 (Scarce): 4-Bra/panties panels	42.00	126.00	295.00
7,8	32.00	95.00	225.00

NOTE: ***Craig*** *a-3.* ***Feldstein*** *a-in most issues; c-1, 2i, 3-8.* ***Harrison*** *a-4.* ***Iger*** *a-6-8.* ***Ingels*** *a-1, 2, 4-7.* ***Palais*** *a-5.* ***Wood*** *a-7.* ***Wood/Harrison*** *a-5-7. (Canadian reprints known; see Table of Contents.)*

MOD LOVE
1967 (36 pages) (50 cents)
Western Publishing Co.

	GD25	FN65	NM94
1	4.00	10.00	20.00

MODNIKS, THE
Aug, 1967 - No. 2, Aug, 1970
Gold Key

	GD25	FN65	NM94
10206-708(#1), 2	1.60	4.00	8.00

MOD SQUAD (TV)
Jan, 1969 - No. 3, Oct, 1969 - No. 8, April, 1971
Dell Publishing Co.

	GD25	FN65	NM94
1-Photo-c	4.00	10.00	20.00
2-8: 2-4-Photo-c. 8-Reprints #2	2.40	6.00	12.00

MOD WHEELS
March, 1971 - No. 19, Jan, 1976
Gold Key

	GD25	FN65	NM94
1	2.00	5.00	10.00
2-19: 11,15-Extra 16pgs. ads	1.00	2.50	5.00

MOE & SHMOE COMICS
Spring, 1948 - No. 2, Summer, 1948
O. S. Publ. Co.

	GD25	FN65	NM94
1	5.35	16.00	32.00
2	4.00	12.00	24.00

MOEBIUS
Oct, 1987 - No. 6, 1988; No. 7, 1990 ($9.95, graphic novel, adults, 8x11")
Epic Comics (Marvel)

	GD25	FN65	NM94
1,2,4-6: (#2, 2nd printing, $9.95)	2.00	5.00	10.00
3,7: 3-(1st & 2nd printings, $12.95)	2.60	6.50	13.00
0 (1990, $12.95)	2.60	6.50	13.00
Moebius I-Signed & numbered hard-c ($45.95, Graphitti Designs, 1,500 copies)-r/#1-3	7.70	23.00	46.00

	GD25	FN65	NM94

MOLLY MANTON'S ROMANCES (Romantic Affairs #3)
Sept, 1949 - No. 2, Dec, 1949 (52 pgs.)
Marvel Comics (SePI)

Issue	GD25	FN65	NM94
1-Photo-c (becomes Blaze the Wonder Collie #2 (10/49) on? & Molly Manton's Romances #2	7.50	22.50	45.00
2-Titled "Romances of...;" photo-c	5.00	15.00	30.00

MOLLY O'DAY (Super Sleuth)
February, 1945 (1st Avon comic)
Avon Periodicals

Issue	GD25	FN65	NM94
1-Molly O'Day, The Enchanted Dagger by Tuska (r/Yankee #1), Capt'n Courage, Corporal Grant app.	32.00	95.00	220.00

MONKEES, THE (TV)(Also see Circus Boy, Groovy, Not Brand Echh #3, Teen-Age Talk, Teen Beam & Teen Beat)
March, 1967 - No. 17, Oct, 1969 (#1-4,6,7,10 have photo-c)
Dell Publishing Co.

Issue	GD25	FN65	NM94
1	10.00	30.00	65.00
2-4,6,7,10: All photo-c	5.85	17.50	35.00
5,8,9,11-17: 17 reprints #1	4.20	12.50	25.00

MONKEY & THE BEAR, THE
Sept, 1953 - No. 3, Jan, 1954
Atlas Comics (ZPC)

Issue	GD25	FN65	NM94
1-Howie Post-a	4.20	12.50	25.00
2,3	3.00	7.50	15.00

MONKEYSHINES COMICS
Summer, 1944 - No. 27, July, 1949
Ace Periodicals/Publishers Specialists/Current Books/Unity Publ.

Issue	GD25	FN65	NM94
1	6.70	20.00	40.00
2	4.00	10.00	20.00
3-10	3.20	8.00	16.00
11-27: 23,24-Fago-c/a	2.80	7.00	14.00

MONKEY SHINES OF MARSELEEN
1909 (11-1/2x17") (28 pages in two colors)
Cupples & Leon Co.

Issue	GD25	FN65	NM94
nn-By Norman E. Jennett	18.00	55.00	110.00

MONKEY'S UNCLE, THE (See Merlin Jones As... under Movie Comics)

MONOLITH (Comico)(Value: cover or less)

MONROES, THE (TV)
April, 1967
Dell Publishing Co.

Issue	GD25	FN65	NM94
1-Photo-c	3.00	7.50	15.00

MONSTER
1953 - No. 2, 1953
Fiction House Magazines

Issue	GD25	FN65	NM94
1-Dr. Drew by Grandenetti; reprint from Rangers Comics #48; Whitman-c	24.00	70.00	165.00
2 -Whitman-c	20.00	60.00	140.00

MONSTER CRIME COMICS (Also see Crime Must Stop)
October, 1952 (15 cents, 52 pgs.)
Hillman Periodicals

Issue	GD25	FN65	NM94
1 (Scarce)	55.00	165.00	330.00

MONSTER HOWLS (Magazine)
December, 1966 (Satire) (35 cents) (68 pgs.)
Humor-Vision

Issue	GD25	FN65	NM94
1	3.60	9.00	18.00

MONSTER HUNTERS
Aug, 1975 - No. 9, Jan, 1977; No. 10, Oct, 1977 - No. 18, Feb, 1979
Charlton Comics

Issue	GD25	FN65	NM94
1,2: 1-Howard-a; Newton-c. 2-Ditko-a	.80	2.00	4.00
3-13,15-18	.40	1.00	2.00
14-Special all-Ditko issue	.60	1.50	3.00
1,2(Modern Comics reprints, 1977)		.50	1.00

NOTE: ***Ditko** a-2, 6, 8, 10, 13-15r, 18r; c-13-15, 18. **Howard** r-13. **Morisi** a-1. **Staton** a-1, 13. **Sutton** a-2, 4; c-2, 4. Reprints in #12-18.*

MONSTER IN MY POCKET (Harvey)(Value: cover or less)

MONSTER OF FRANKENSTEIN (See Frankenstein)

MONSTERS ON THE PROWL (Chamber of Darkness #1-8)
No. 9, 2/71 - No. 27, 11/73; No. 28, 6/74 - No. 30, 10/74
Marvel Comics Group (No. 13,14: 52 pgs.)

Issue	GD25	FN65	NM94
9-Barry Smith inks	.80	2.00	4.00
10-30: 16-King Kull app.; Severin-c	.40	1.00	2.00

NOTE: ***Ditko** r-5, 9, 14, 16. **Kirby** r-10-17, 21, 23, 25, 27, 28, 30; c-9, 25. **Kirby/Ditko** r-14, 17-20, 22, 24, 26, 29. **Reinman** r-5. **Marie/John Severin** a-16(Kull). 9-13, 15 contain one new story. Woodish art by **Reese**-11. King Kull created by Robert E. Howard.*

MONSTERS UNLEASHED (Magazine)
July, 1973 - No. 11, April, 1975; Summer, 1975 (B&W)
Marvel Comics Group

Issue	GD25	FN65	NM94
1	1.00	2.50	5.00
2-11: 2-The Frankenstein Monster begins. 3-Neal Adams-c; The Man-Thing begins (origin-r)-N. Adams-a. 4-Intro. Satana, the Devil's daughter; Krigstein-r. 7-Williamson-a(r). 8-N. Adams-r. 9-Wendigo app. 10-Origin Tigra	.60	1.50	3.00
Annual 1(Summer,1975)-Kane-a	.40	1.00	2.00

NOTE: ***Boris** c-2, 6. **Brunner** a-2; c-11. **J. Buscema** a-2p, 4p, 5p. **Colan** a-1, 4r. **Davis** a-3r. **Everett** a-2r. **G. Kane** a-3. **Morrow** a-3; c-1. **Perez** a-8. **Ploog** a-6. **Reese** a-1, 2. **Tuska** a-3p. **Wildey** a-1r.*

MONTANA KID, THE (See Kid Montana)

MONTE HALE WESTERN (Movie star; Formerly Mary Marvel #1-28; also see Fawcett Movie Comic, Motion Picture Comics, Picture News #8, Real Western Hero, Six-Gun Heroes, Western Hero & XMas Comics)
No. 29, Oct, 1948 - No. 88, Jan, 1956
Fawcett Publications/Charlton No. 83 on

Issue	GD25	FN65	NM94
29-(#1, 52pgs.)-Photo-c begin, end #82; Monte Hale & his horse Pardner begin	32.00	95.00	225.00
30-(52 pgs.)-Big Bow and Little Arrow begin, end #34; Captain Tootsie by Beck	16.00	48.00	110.00
31-36,38-40-(52 pgs.): 34-Gabby Hayes begins, ends #80. 39-Captain Tootsie by Beck	13.00	40.00	90.00
37,41,45,49-(36 pgs.)	9.15	27.50	55.00
42-44,46-48,50-(52 pgs.): 47-Big Bow & Little Arrow app.	10.00	30.00	60.00
51,52,54-56,58,59-(52 pgs.)	7.50	22.50	45.00
53,57-(36 pgs.): 53-Slim Pickens app.	6.35	19.00	38.00
60-81: 36pgs. #60-on. 80-Gabby Hayes ends	6.35	19.00	38.00
82-Last Fawcett issue (6/53)	8.35	25.00	50.00
83-1st Charlton issue (2/55); B&W photo back-c begin. Gabby Hayes returns, ends #86	8.35	25.00	50.00
84 (4/55)	6.35	19.00	38.00
85-86	5.85	17.50	35.00
87-Wolverton-r, pg.	6.35	19.00	38.00
88-Last issue	6.35	19.00	38.00

NOTE: ***Gil Kane** a-33?, 34? Rocky Lane -1 pg. (Carnation ad)-38, 40, 41, 43, 44, 46, 55.*

MONTY HALL OF THE U.S. MARINES (See With the Marines...)
Aug, 1951 - No. 11, 1953
Toby Press

Issue	GD25	FN65	NM94
1	6.35	19.00	38.00
2	4.00	12.00	24.00
3-5	4.00	10.00	20.00
6-11	3.00	7.50	15.00

NOTE: *3-7 have full page pin-ups (Pin-Up Pete) by **Jack Sparling** in all.*

MOON, A GIRL...ROMANCE, A (Becomes Weird Fantasy #13 on; formerly Moon Girl #1-8)
No. 9, Sept-Oct, 1949 - No. 12, Mar-Apr, 1950

Monkeyshines Comics #24, © ACE

Monster Crime #1, © HILL

Monte Hale Western #51, © FAW

Moon Knight V2#3, © MEG

Mopsy #5, © STJ

More Fun Comics #17 (1/37), © DC

	GD25	FN65	NM94
E. C. Comics			
9-Moon Girl cameo; spanking panels	57.00	171.00	400.00
10,11	43.00	130.00	300.00
12-(Scarce)	60.00	180.00	420.00

NOTE: ***Feldstein, Ingels*** *art in all.* ***Wood/Harrison*** *a-10-12. Canadian reprints known; see Table of Contents.*

MOON GIRL AND THE PRINCE (#1) (Moon Girl #2-6; Moon Girl Fights Crime #7, 8; becomes A Moon, A Girl, Romance #9 on)(Also see Animal Fables #7 and Happy Houlihans)
Fall, 1947 - No. 8, Summer, 1949
E. C. Comics

	GD25	FN65	NM94
1-Origin Moon Girl	72.00	215.00	500.00
2	39.00	115.00	270.00
3,4: 4-Moon Girl vs. a vampire	33.00	100.00	230.00
5-E.C.'s 1st horror story, "Zombie Terror"	72.00	215.00	500.00
6-8 (Scarce): 7-Origin Star (Moongirl's sidekick)	39.00	120.00	275.00

NOTE: ***Craig*** *a-2, 5.* ***Moldoff*** *a-1-8.* ***Wheelan's*** *Fat and Slat app. in #3, 4, 6. #2 & #3 are 52 pgs., #4 on, 36 pgs. Canadian reprints known; (see Table of Contents.)*

MOON KNIGHT (Also see The Hulk, Marc Spector..., Marvel Preview #21, Marvel Spotlight & Werewolf by Night #32)
November, 1980 - No. 38, July, 1984 (Mando paper No. 33 on)
Marvel Comics Group

	GD25	FN65	NM94
1-Origin resumed in #4; begin Sienkiewicz-c/a	.80	2.00	4.00
2-34,36-38: 4-Intro Midnight Man. 16-The Thing app. 25-Double size	.30	.75	1.50
35-($1.00, 52 pgs.)-X-men app.; F.F. cameo	.40	1.00	2.00

NOTE: ***Austin*** *c-27i, 31i.* ***Kaluta*** *c-36-38; back c-35.* ***Miller*** *c-9, 12p, 13p, 15?, 27p.* ***Ploog*** *back c-35.* ***Sienkiewicz*** *a-1-15, 17-20, 22-26, 28-30, 37; c-1-5, 7, 8, 10, 11, 14-26, 28-30, 31p, 33, 34.*

MOON KNIGHT
June, 1985 - No. 6, Dec, 1985
Marvel Comics Group

	GD25	FN65	NM94
V2#1-6: 1-Double size; new costume. 6-Painted-c		.50	1.00

MOON KNIGHT: DIVIDED WE FALL
1992 ($4.95, color, 52 pgs.)
Marvel Comics

	GD25	FN65	NM94
nn-Denys Cowan-c/a(p)	1.00	2.50	5.00

MOON KNIGHT SPECIAL
Oct, 1992 ($2.50, color, 52 pgs.)
Marvel Comics

	GD25	FN65	NM94
1-Shang Chi, Master of Kung Fu-c/story	.50	1.25	2.50

MOON KNIGHT SPECIAL EDITION
Nov, 1983 - No. 3, Jan, 1984 ($2.00, mini-series, Baxter paper)
Marvel Comics Group

	GD25	FN65	NM94
1-3: Reprints from Hulk mag. by Sienkiewicz	.30	.75	1.50

MOON MULLINS
1927 - 1933 (52 pgs.) (daily B&W strip reprints)
Cupples & Leon Co.

	GD25	FN65	NM94
Series 1('27)-By Willard	18.00	55.00	110.00
Series 2('28), Series 3('29), Series 4('30)	15.00	45.00	90.00
Series 5('31), 6('32), 7('33)	12.00	35.00	70.00
Big Book 1('30)-B&W	22.00	65.00	130.00

MOON MULLINS (See Popular Comics, Super Book #3 & Super Comics)
1941 - 1945
Dell Publishing Co.

	GD25	FN65	NM94
4-Color 14(1941)	29.00	85.00	200.00
Large Feature Comic 29(1941)	19.00	58.00	135.00
4-Color 31(1943)	16.00	48.00	110.00
4-Color 81(1945)	10.00	30.00	60.00

MOON MULLINS
Dec-Jan, 1947-48 - No. 8, 1949 (52 pgs.)
Michel Publ. (American Comics Group)

	GD25	FN65	NM94
1-Alternating Sunday & daily strip-r	11.00	32.00	75.00
2	7.50	22.50	45.00
3-8	5.85	17.50	35.00

NOTE: ***Milt Gross*** *a-2-6, 8.* ***Willard*** *r-all.*

MOON PILOT (See 4-Color #1313)

MOONSHADOW
May, 1985 - No. 12, Feb, 1987 ($1.50-$1.75)(Adults only)
Epic Comics (Marvel)

	GD25	FN65	NM94
1-Origin	.80	2.00	4.00
2-12: 11-Origin	.50	1.25	2.50
Trade paperback (1987?)-reprints	2.80	7.00	14.00
Signed & #'d hard-c ($39.95, 1,200 copies)-r/1-12	6.70	20.00	40.00

MOON-SPINNERS, THE (See Movie Comics)

MOPSY (See Pageant of Comics & TV Teens)
Feb, 1948 - No. 19, Sept, 1953
St. John Publ. Co.

	GD25	FN65	NM94
1-Part-r; r-/"Some Punkins" by Neher	12.00	36.00	85.00
2	7.50	22.50	45.00
3-10(1953): 8-Lingerie panels	5.85	17.50	35.00
11-19: 19-Lingerie-c	4.70	14.00	28.00

NOTE: *#1, 3-6, 13, 18, 19 have paper dolls.*

MORBIUS: THE LIVING VAMPIRE (Also see Amazing Spider-Man #101, 102, Fear #20, Marvel Team-Up #3, 4 & Vampire Tales)
Sept, 1992 - Present ($1.75, color)
Marvel Comics

	GD25	FN65	NM94
1-($2.75, 52 pgs.)-Polybagged w/poster; Ghost Rider & Johnny Blaze x-over (part 3 of Rise of the Midnight Sons)	.80	2.00	4.00
2	.50	1.25	2.50
3-5: 3,4-Vs. Spider-Man-c/story	.40	1.00	2.00
6-10	.35	.90	1.75

MORE FUN COMICS (Formerly New Fun Comics #1-6)
No. 7, Jan, 1936 - No. 127, Nov-Dec, 1947 (No. 7,9-11: paper-c)
National Periodical Publications

	GD25	FN65	VF82
7(1/36)-Oversized, paper-c; 1 pg. Kelly-a (Estimated up to 15 total copies exist, none in NM/Mint)	550.00	1375.00	2200.00
8(2/36)-Oversized (10x12"), slick-c; 1 pg. Kelly-a	370.00	1100.00	2200.00
9(3-4/36)(Very rare, 1st comic-sized issue)-Last Henri Duval by Siegel & Shuster	370.00	1100.00	2200.00
10,11(7/36): 11-1st 'Calling All Cars' by Siegel & Shuster	233.00	700.00	1400.00
12(8/36)-Slick-c begin	200.00	600.00	1200.00
V2#1(9/36, #13)	192.00	575.00	1150.00
2(10/36, #14)-Dr. Occult in costume (1st in color)(Superman proto-type-1st DC appearance) continues from The Comics Magazine, ends #17 (Estimated up to 10 total copies exist, none in NM/Mint)	833.00	2500.00	5000.00
V2#3(11/36, #15), 16(V2#4), 17(V2#5)-Cover numbering begins #16. 16-Xmas-c. Last Superman tryout issue	367.00	1100.00	2200.00
18-20(V2#8, 5/37)	117.00	350.00	700.00

	GD25	FN65	NM94
21(V2#9)-24(V2#12, 9/37)	92.00	275.00	550.00
25(V3#1, 10/37)-27(V3#3, 12/37): 27-Xmas-c	92.00	275.00	550.00
28-30: 30-1st non-funny cover	92.00	275.00	550.00
31-35: 32-Last Dr. Occult	83.00	250.00	500.00
36-40: 36-The Masked Ranger & sidekick Pedro begins, ends #41. 39-Xmas-c	79.00	238.00	475.00
41-50	67.00	200.00	400.00
51-The Spectre app. (in costume) in one panel ad at end of Buccaneer story			

267.00 800.00 1600.00

GD25 FN65 VF82 NM94

52-(2/40)-Origin/1st app. The Spectre (in costume splash panel only), part 1 by Bernard Baily (parts 1 & 2 written by Jerry Siegel; last Wing Brady 2500.00 7500.00 15,000.00 25,000.00
(Estimated up to 60 total copies exist, 3 in NM/Mint)
53-Origin The Spectre (in costume at end of story), part 2; Capt. Desmo begins 1550.00 4650.00 9300.00 15,500.00
(Estimated up to 60 total copies exist, 3 in NM/Mint)
54-The Spectre in costume; last King Carter
550.00 1650.00 3025.00 4400.00
55-(Scarce)-Dr. Fate begins (Intro & 1st app.); last Bulldog Martin
750.00 2250.00 4125.00 6000.00
(Estimated up to 100 total copies exist, 6 in NM/Mint)

GD25 FN65 NM94

56-60: 56-Congo Bill begins; 1st Dr. Fate-c (classic). 58-Classic Spectre-c
240.00 725.00 1450.00
61-66: 61-Classic Dr. Fate-c. 63-Last St. Bob Neal. 64-Lance Larkin begins. 65-Classic Spectre-c 185.00 550.00 1100.00

GD25 FN65 VF82 NM94

67-Origin (1st) Dr. Fate; last Congo Bill & Biff Bronson
375.00 1125.00 2060.00 3000.00
(Estimated up to 105 total copies exist, 6 in NM/Mint)

GD25 FN65 NM94

68-70: 68-Clip Carson begins. 70-Last Lance Larkin
150.00 450.00 900.00

GD25 FN65 VF82 NM94

71-Origin & 1st app. Johnny Quick by Mort Wysinger
340.00 1000.00 2000.00 2700.00
(Estimated up to 90 total copies exist, 6 in NM/Mint)

GD25 FN65 NM94

72-Dr. Fate's new helmet; last Sgt. Carey, Sgt. O'Malley & Captain Desmo
125.00 375.00 750.00

GD25 FN65 VF82 NM94

73-Origin & 1st app. Aquaman (11/41); intro. Green Arrow & Speedy
560.00 1700.00 3100.00 4500.00
(Estimated up to 85 total copies exist, 5 in NM/Mint)

GD25 FN65 NM94

74-2nd Aquaman 150.00 450.00 900.00
75-80: 76-Last Clip Carson; Johnny Quick by Meskin begins, ends #97. 80-Last large logo 133.00 400.00 800.00
81-88: 81-1st small logo. 87-Last Radio Squad 92.00 275.00 550.00
89-Origin Green Arrow & Speedy Team-up 108.00 325.00 650.00
90-99: 93-Dover & Clover begin. 97-Kubert-a. 98-Last Dr. Fate
62.00 188.00 375.00
100 92.00 275.00 550.00

GD25 FN65 VF82 NM94

101-Origin & 1st app. Superboy (3/44) (not by Siegel & Shuster); last Spectre issue 420.00 1260.00 2500.00 4200.00
(Estimated up to 200 total copies exist, 9 in NM/Mint)

GD25 FN65 NM94

102-2nd Superboy 108.00 325.00 650.00
103-3rd Superboy 75.00 225.00 450.00
104-107: 104-1st Superboy-c. 105-Superboy-c. 107-Last Johnny Quick & Superboy 62.00 188.00 375.00
108-120: 108-Genius Jones begins 12.00 38.00 75.00
121-124,126: 121-123,126-Post-c 10.00 30.00 60.00
125-Superman on cover 58.00 175.00 350.00
127-(Scarce)-Post-c/a 22.00 65.00 130.00

NOTE: *All issues are scarce to rare. Cover features: The Spectre-#52-55, 57-60, 62-67. Dr. Fate-#56, 61, 68-76. The Green Arrow & Speedy-#77-85, 88-97, 99, 101; w/Dover & Clover-#98. Johnny Quick-#86, 87, 100. Genius Jones-#108-127.* ***Baily*** *a-45, 52-on; c-52-55, 57-60, 62-67.* ***Al Capp*** *a-45(signed Koppy).* ***Ellsworth*** *c-7.* ***Craig Flessel*** *c-30, 31, 35-48(most).* ***Guardineer*** *c-47, 49, 50.* ***Kiefer*** *a-20.* ***Meskin*** *c-86, 87, 100?* ***Moldoff*** *c-51.* ***George Papp*** *c-77-85.* ***Post*** *c-121-127.* ***Vincent Sullivan*** *c-8-28, 32-34.*

MORE SEYMOUR (See Seymour My Son)
October, 1963

Archie Publications
1 2.40 6.00 12.00

MORE TRASH FROM MAD (Annual)
1958 - No. 12, 1969
E. C. Comics

nn(1958)-8 pgs. color Mad reprint from #20 16.00 48.00 110.00
2(1959)-Market Product Labels 11.00 32.00 75.00
3(1960)-Text book covers 10.00 30.00 65.00
4(1961)-Sing Along with Mad booklet 10.00 30.00 65.00
5(1962)-Window Stickers; r/from Mad #39 6.70 20.00 40.00
6(1963)-TV Guise booklet 8.35 25.00 50.00
7(1964)-Alfred E. Neuman commemorative stamps
4.70 14.00 28.00
8(1965)-Life size poster-Alfred E. Neuman 3.15 9.50 22.00
9,10(1966-67)-Mischief Sticker 3.60 9.00 18.00
11(1968)-Campaign poster & bumper sticker 3.60 9.00 18.00
12(1969)-Pocket medals 3.60 9.00 18.00

NOTE: ***Kelly Freas*** *c-1, 2, 4.* ***Mingo*** *c-3, 5-9, 12.*

MORGAN THE PIRATE (See 4-Color #1227)

MORLOCK 2001
Feb, 1975 - No. 3, July, 1975
Atlas/Seaboard Publ.

1,2: 1-(Super-hero)-Origin & 1st app. .50 1.00
3-Ditko/Wrightson-a; origin The Midnight Man & The Midnight Men
.60 1.20

MORNINGSTAR SPECIAL (Comico) (Value: cover or less)

MORTIE (Mazie's Friend)
Dec, 1952 - No. 4, June, 1953?
Magazine Publishers

1 4.00 12.00 24.00
2-4 2.80 7.00 14.00

MORTY MEEKLE (See 4-Color #793)

MOSES & THE TEN COMMANDMENTS (See Dell Giants)

MOTHER GOOSE (See Christmas With Mother Goose & 4-Color #41, 59, 68, 862)

MOTHER OF US ALL
1950? (32 pgs.)
Catechetical Guild Giveaway

nn 1.60 4.00 8.00

MOTHER TERESA OF CALCUTTA
1984
Marvel Comics Group

1 .60 1.25

MOTION PICTURE COMICS (See Fawcett Movie Comics)
No. 101, 1950 - No. 114, Jan, 1953 (All-photo-c)
Fawcett Publications

101-"Vanishing Westerner"-Monte Hale (1950) 25.00 75.00 175.00
102-"Code of the Silver Sage"-Rocky Lane (1/51) 24.00 72.00 165.00
103-"Covered Wagon Raid"-Rocky Lane (3/51) 24.00 72.00 165.00
104-"Vigilante Hideout"-Rocky Lane (5/51)-Book length Powell-a
24.00 72.00 165.00
105-"Red Badge of Courage"-Audie Murphy; Bob Powell-a (7/51)
29.00 85.00 200.00
106-"The Texas Rangers"-George Montgomery (9/51)
24.00 72.00 165.00
107-"Frisco Tornado"-Rocky Lane (11/51) 22.00 65.00 150.00
108-"Mask of the Avenger"-John Derek 14.00 43.00 100.00
109-"Rough Rider of Durango"-Rocky Lane 22.00 65.00 150.00
110-"When Worlds Collide"-George Evans-a (1951); Williamson & Evans drew themselves in story; (also see Famous Funnies No. 72-88)
69.00 208.00 485.00

More Fun Comics #48, © DC

More Fun Comics #62, © DC

Motion Picture Comics #110, © Paramount Pictures

Movie Classics (The Creature), © Universal

Movie Classics (The Hallelujah Trail), © Mirish-Kappa

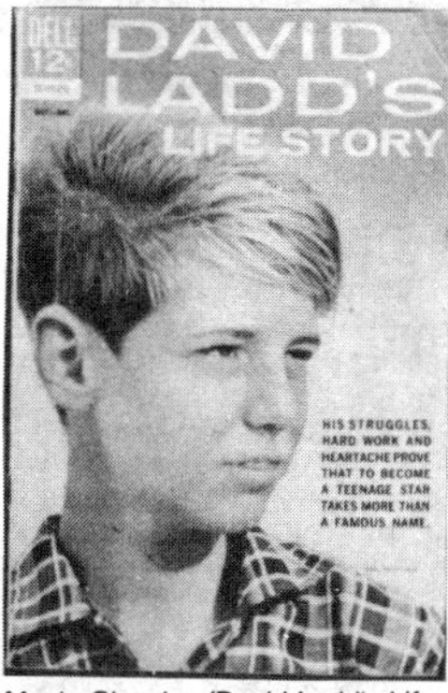

Movie Classics (David Ladd's Life Story), © David Ladd

GD25 FN65 NM94

111-"The Vanishing Outpost"-Lash LaRue 26.00 78.00 180.00
112-"Brave Warrior"-Jon Hall & Jay Silverheels 13.00 40.00 90.00
113-"Walk East on Beacon"-George Murphy; Shaffenberger-a
10.00 30.00 65.00
114-"Cripple Creek"-George Montgomery (1/53) 11.00 32.00 75.00

MOTION PICTURE FUNNIES WEEKLY (Amazing Man #5 on?)
1939 (36 pgs.)(Giveaway)(Black & White)
No month given; last panel in Sub-Mariner story dated 4/39
(Also see Colossus, Green Giant & Invaders No. 20)
First Funnies, Inc.

1-Origin & 1st printed app. Sub-Mariner by Bill Everett (8 pgs.); Fred Schwab-c; reprinted in Marvel Mystery #1 with color added over the craft tint which was used to shade the black & white version; Spy Ring, American Ace (reprinted in Marvel Mystery #3) app. (Rare)-only eight (8) known copies, one near mint with white pages, the rest with brown pages.
2600.00 5500.00 -----
Covers only to #2-4 (set) 600.00

NOTE: The only eight known copies (with a ninth suspected) were discovered in 1974 in the estate of the deceased publisher. Covers only to issues No. 2-4 were also found which evidently were printed in advance along with #1. #1 was to be distributed only through motion picture movie houses. However, it is believed that only advanced copies were sent out and the motion picture houses not going for the idea. Possible distribution at local theaters in Boston suspected. The last panel of Sub-Mariner contains a rectangular box with "Continued Next Week" printed in it. When reprinted in Marvel Mystery, the box was left in with lettering omitted.

MOTORBIKE PUPPIES, THE (Dark Zulu Lies)(Value: cover or less)

MOTORMOUTH
June, 1992 - Present ($1.75, color)
Marvel Comics UK

1-12: 1,2-Nick Fury app. 3-Punisher-c/story. 5,6-Nick Fury & Punisher app. 6-Cable cameo. 7-Cable-c/story .30 .90 1.80

MOUNTAIN MEN (See Ben Bowie)

MOUSE MUSKETEERS (See M.G.M.'s...)

MOUSE ON THE MOON, THE (See Movie Classics)

MOVIE CLASSICS
Jan, 1963 - Dec, 1969
Dell Publishing Co.

(Before 1963, most movie adaptations were part of the 4-Color series)

Around the World Under the Sea 12-030-612 (12/66)
2.80 7.00 14.00
Bambi 3(4/56)-Disney; r/4-Color #186 2.80 7.00 14.00
Battle of the Bulge 12-056-606 (6/66) 3.60 9.00 18.00
Beach Blanket Bingo 12-058-509 6.70 20.00 40.00
Bon Voyage 01-068-212 (12/62)-Disney; photo-c 2.80 7.00 14.00
Castilian, The 12-110-401 4.00 10.00 20.00
Cat, The 12-109-612 (12/66) 2.40 6.00 12.00
Cheyenne Autumn 12-112-506 (4-6/65) 6.70 20.00 40.00
Circus World, Samuel Bronston's 12-115-411; John Wayne app.; John Wayne photo-c 11.00 32.00 75.00
Countdown 12-150-710 (10/67); James Caan photo-c
3.20 8.00 16.00
Creature, The 1 (12-142-302) (12-2/62-63) 4.70 14.00 28.00
Creature, The 12-142-410 (10/64) 3.20 8.00 16.00
David Ladd's Life Story 12-173-212 (10-12/62)-Photo-c
8.35 25.00 50.00
Die, Monster, Die 12-175-603 (3/66)-Photo-c 4.20 12.50 25.00
Dirty Dozen 12-180-710 (10/67) 4.70 14.00 28.00
Dr. Who & the Daleks 12-190-612 (12/66)-Peter Cushing photo-c
12.00 36.00 85.00
Dracula 12-231-212 (10-12/62) 4.00 10.00 20.00
El Dorado 12-240-710 (10/67)-John Wayne; photo-c
12.00 36.00 85.00

GD25 FN65 NM94

Ensign Pulver 12-257-410 (8-10/64) 3.20 8.00 16.00
Frankenstein 12-283-305 (3-5/63) 4.00 11.00 22.00
Great Race, The 12-299-603 (3/66)-Natallie Wood, Tony Curtis photo-c
4.20 12.50 25.00
Hallelujah Trail, The 12-307-602 (2/66) (Shows 1/66 inside); Burt Lancaster, Lee Remick photo-c 5.00 15.00 30.00
Hatari 12-340-301 (1/63)-John Wayne 9.15 27.50 55.00
Horizontal Lieutenant, The 01-348-210 (10/62) 2.80 7.00 14.00
Incredible Mr. Limpet, The 12-370-408; Don Knotts photo-c
4.00 11.00 22.00
Jack the Giant Killer 12-374-301 (1/63) 8.35 25.00 50.00
Jason & the Argonauts 12-376-310 (8-10/63)-Photo-c
10.00 30.00 60.00
Lancelot & Guinevere 12-416-310 (10/63) 7.50 22.50 45.00
Lawrence 12-426-308 (8/63)-Story of Lawrence of Arabia; movie ad on back-c; not exactly like movie 5.85 17.50 35.00
Lion of Sparta 12-439-301 (1/63) 3.20 8.00 16.00
Mad Monster Party 12-460-801 (9/67) 6.70 20.00 40.00
Magic Sword, The 01-496-209 (9/62) 5.85 17.50 35.00
Masque of the Red Death 12-490-410 (8-10/64)-Vincent Price photo-c
5.00 15.00 30.00
Maya 12-495-612 (12/66)-Clint Walker & Jay North part photo-c
5.00 15.00 30.00
McHale's Navy 12-500-412 (10-12/64) 3.60 9.00 18.00
Merrill's Marauders 12-510-301 (1/63)-Photo-c 3.20 8.00 16.00
Mouse on the Moon, The 12-530-312 (10/12/63)-Photo-c
3.60 9.00 18.00
Mummy, The 12-537-211 (9-11/62) 2 versions with different back-c
4.20 12.50 25.00
Music Man, The 12-538-301 (1/63) 3.20 8.00 16.00
Naked Prey, The 12-545-612 (12/66)-Photo-c 7.50 22.50 45.00
Night of the Grizzly, The 12-558-612 (12/66)-Photo-c
4.20 12.50 25.00
None But the Brave 12-565-506 (4-6/65) 6.70 20.00 40.00
Operation Bikini 12-597-310 (10/63)-Photo-c 4.00 10.00 20.00
Operation Crossbow 12-590-512 (10-12/65) 4.00 10.00 20.00
Prince & the Pauper, The 01-654-207 (5-7/62)-Disney
4.00 10.00 20.00
Raven, The 12-680-309 (9/63)-Vincent Price photo-c
5.00 15.00 30.00
Ring of Bright Water 01-701-910 (10/69) (inside shows #12-701-909)
4.20 12.50 25.00
Runaway, The 12-707-412 (10-12/64) 2.80 7.00 14.00
Santa Claus Conquers the Martians #? (1964)-Photo-c
8.35 25.00 50.00
Santa Claus Conquers the Martians 12-725-603 (3/66, 12 cents)-Reprints 1964 issue; photo-c 6.70 20.00 40.00
Another version given away with a Golden Record, SLP 170, nn, no price (3/66)-Complete with record 14.00 43.00 100.00
Six Black Horses 12-750-301 (1/63)-Photo-c 4.00 10.00 20.00
Ski Party 12-743-511 (9-11/65)-Frankie Avalon photo-c
5.00 15.00 30.00
Smoky 12-746-702 (2/67) 2.80 7.00 14.00
Sons of Katie Elder 12-748-511 (9-11/65); John Wayne app.; photo-c
14.00 43.00 100.00
Tales of Terror 12-793-302 (2/63)-Evans-a 3.00 7.50 15.00
Three Stooges Meet Hercules 01-828-208 (8/62)-Photo-c
9.15 27.50 55.00
Tomb of Ligeia 12-830-506 (4-6/65) 3.20 8.00 16.00
Treasure Island 01-845-211 (7-9/62)-Disney; r/4-Color #624
2.40 6.00 12.00
Twice Told Tales (Nathaniel Hawthorne) 12-840-401 (11-1/63-64); Vincent Price photo-c 4.00 11.00 22.00
Two on a Guillotine 12-850-506 (4-6/65) 3.20 8.00 16.00

GD25 FN65 NM94

Valley of Gwangi 01-880-912 (12/69) 8.35 25.00 50.00
War Gods of the Deep 12-900-509 (7-9/65) 3.20 8.00 16.00
War Wagon, The 12-533-709 (9/67); John Wayne app.
10.00 30.00 70.00
Who's Minding the Mint? 12-924-708 (8/67)-Jerry Lewis photo-c
2.80 7.00 14.00
Wolfman, The 12-922-308 (6-8/63) 3.20 8.00 16.00
Wolfman, The 1(12-922-410)(8-10/64)-2nd printing; r/#12-922-308
3.20 8.00 16.00
Zulu 12-950-410 (8-10/64)-Photo-c 10.00 30.00 60.00

MOVIE COMICS (See Cinema Comics Herald & Fawcett Movie Comics)

MOVIE COMICS
April, 1939 - No. 6, Sept, 1939 (Most all photo-c)
National Periodical Publications/Picture Comics

1-"Gunga Din," "Son of Frankenstein," "The Great Man Votes," "Fisherman's Wharf," & "Scouts to the Rescue" part 1; Wheelan "Minute Movies" begin 233.00 700.00 1400.00
2-"Stagecoach," "The Saint Strikes Back," "King of the Turf," "Scouts to the Rescue" part 2, "Arizona Legion" 150.00 450.00 900.00
3-"East Side of Heaven," "Mystery in the White Room," "Four Feathers," "Mexican Rose" with Gene Autry, "Spirit of Culver," "Many Secrets," "The Mikado" 123.00 370.00 740.00
4-"Captain Fury," Gene Autry in "Blue Montana Skies," "Streets of N.Y." with Jackie Cooper, "Oregon Trail" part 1 with Johnny Mack Brown, "Big Town Czar" with Barton MacLane, & "Star Reporter" with Warren Hull
105.00 315.00 625.00
5-"Man in the Iron Mask," "Five Came Back," "Wolf Call," "The Girl & the Gambler," "The House of Fear," "The Family Next Door," "Oregon Trail" part 2 105.00 315.00 625.00
6-"The Phantom Creeps," "Chumps at Oxford," & "The Oregon Trail" part 3 130.00 390.00 775.00

NOTE: *Above books contain many original movie stills with dialogue from movie scripts. All issues are scarce.*

MOVIE COMICS
Dec, 1946 - No. 4, 1947
Fiction House Magazines

1-Big Town & Johnny Danger begin; Celardo-a 37.00 110.00 225.00
2-(2/47)-"White Tie & Tails" with William Bendix; Mitzi of the Movies begins by Matt Baker, ends #4 27.00 80.00 160.00
3-(6/47)-Andy Hardy 27.00 80.00 160.00
4-Mitzi In Hollywood by Matt Baker 32.00 95.00 190.00

MOVIE COMICS
Oct, 1962 - March, 1972
Gold Key/Whitman

Alice in Wonderland 10144-503 (3/65)-Disney; partial reprint of 4-Color #331
2.80 7.00 14.00
Aristocats, The 1 (30045-103)(3/71)-Disney; with pull-out poster (25 cents)
5.85 17.50 35.00
Bambi 1 (10087-309)(9/63)-Disney; r/4-C #186 3.20 8.00 16.00
Bambi 2 (10087-607)(7/66)-Disney; r4-C #186 2.80 7.00 14.00
Beneath the Planet of the Apes 30044-012 (12/70)-with pull-out poster; photo-c 4.35 13.00 26.00
Big Red 10026-211 (11/62)-Disney; photo-c 2.00 5.00 10.00
Big Red 10026-503 (3/65)-Disney; reprints 10026-211; photo-c
2.00 5.00 10.00
Blackbeard's Ghost 10222-806 (6/68)-Disney 2.40 6.00 12.00
Bullwhip Griffin 10181-706 (6/67)-Disney; Manning-a; photo-c
4.00 10.00 20.00
Captain Sindbad 10077-309 (9/63)-Manning-a; photo-c
5.85 17.50 35.00
Chitty Chitty Bang Bang 1 (30038-902)(2/69)-with pull-out poster; Disney; photo-c 4.35 13.00 26.00
Cinderella 10152-508 (8/65)-Disney; r/4-C #786 2.40 6.00 12.00
Darby O'Gill & the Little People 10251-001(1/70)-Disney; reprints 4-Color #1024 (Toth-a); photo-c 4.20 12.50 25.00
Dumbo 1 (10090-310)(10/63)-Disney; r/4-C #668 2.40 6.00 12.00
Emil & the Detectives 10120-502 (2/65)-Disney; photo-c
3.60 9.00 18.00
Escapade in Florence 1 (10043-301)(1/63)-Disney; starring Annette Funicello
6.70 20.00 40.00
Fall of the Roman Empire 10118-407 (7/64); Sophia Loren photo-c
4.00 10.00 20.00
Fantastic Voyage 10178-702 (2/67)-Wood/Adkins-a; photo-c
4.70 14.00 28.00
55 Days at Peking 10081-309 (9/63)-Photo-c 4.00 10.00 20.00
Fighting Prince of Donegal, The 10193-701 (1/67)-Disney
2.80 7.00 14.00
First Men in the Moon 10132-503 (3/65)-Fred Fredericks-a; photo-c
3.60 9.00 18.00
Gay Purr-ee 30017-301(1/63, 84pgs.) 4.35 13.00 26.00
Gnome Mobile, The 10207-710 (10/67)-Disney 3.60 9.00 18.00
Goodbye, Mr. Chips 10246-006 (6/70)-Peter O'Toole photo-c
3.20 8.00 16.00
Happiest Millionaire, The 10221-804 (4/68)-Disney
2.00 5.00 10.00
Hey There, It's Yogi Bear 10122-409 (9/64)-Hanna-Barbera
4.20 12.50 25.00
Horse Without a Head, The 10109-401 (1/64)-Disney
2.40 6.00 12.00
How the West Was Won 10074-307 (7/63)-Tufts-a
4.35 13.00 26.00
In Search of the Castaways 10048-303 (3/63)-Disney; Hayley Mills photo-c
5.85 17.50 35.00
Jungle Book, The 1 (6022-801)(1/68-Whitman)-Disney; large size (10x13-1/2"); 59 cents 3.60 9.00 18.00
Jungle Book, The 1 (30033-803)(3/68, 68 pgs.)-Disney; same contents as Whitman #1 1.80 4.50 9.00
Jungle Book, The 1 (6/78, $1.00 tabloid) .60 1.20
Jungle Book (1984)-r/Giant .50 1.00
Kidnapped 10080-306 (6/63)-Disney; reprints 4-Color #1101; photo-c
2.00 5.00 10.00
King Kong 30036-809(9/68-68 pgs.)-painted-c 3.20 8.00 16.00
King Kong nn-Whitman Treasury($1.00,68pgs.,1968), same cover as Gold Key issue 1.00 2.50 5.00
King Kong 11299(#1-786, 10x13-1/4", 68pgs., $1.00, 1978)
.50 1.00
Lady and the Tramp 10042-301 (1/63)-Disney; r/4-Color #629
2.40 6.00 12.00
Lady and the Tramp 1 (1967-Giant; 25 cents)-Disney; reprints part of Dell #1
4.00 11.00 22.00
Lady and the Tramp 2 (10042-203)(3/72)-Disney; r/4-Color #629
1.60 4.00 8.00
Legend of Lobo, The 1 (10059-303)(3/63)-Disney; photo-c
2.00 5.00 10.00
Lt. Robin Crusoe, U.S.N. 10191-610 (10/66)-Disney; Dick Van Dyke photo-c
2.40 6.00 12.00
Lion, The 10035-301 (1/63)-Photo-c 2.00 5.00 10.00
Lord Jim 10156-509 (9/65)-Photo-c 2.80 7.00 14.00
Love Bug, The 10237-906 (6/69)-Disney; Buddy Hackett photo-c
2.40 6.00 12.00
Mary Poppins 10136-501 (1/65)-Disney; photo-c 4.20 12.50 25.00
Mary Poppins 30023-501 (1/65-68 pgs.)-Disney; photo-c
6.70 20.00 40.00
McLintock 10110-403 (3/64); John Wayne app.; John Wayne & Maureen O'Hara photo-c; spanking panel 13.00 40.00 90.00
Merlin Jones as the Monkey's Uncle 10115-510 (10/65)-Disney; Annette Funicello front/back photo-c 4.20 12.50 25.00
Miracle of the White Stallions, The 10065-306 (6/63)-Disney
2.80 7.00 14.00
Misadventures of Merlin Jones, The 10115-405 (5/64)-Disney; Annette

Movie Classic (Valley of Gwangi), © Warner Bros. Seven Arts Int'l

Movie Classic (The Werewolf) (2nd Printing), © Universal Pictures

Movie Comics (Lady and the Tramp), © WDC

Movie Comics (Swiss Family, Robinson), © WDC

Ms. Marvel #19, © MEG

Muggsy Mouse #1, © ME

	GD25	FN65	NM94
Funicello photo front/back-c	4.20	12.50	25.00
Moon-Spinners, The 10124-410 (10/64)-Disney; Haley Mills photo-c	5.85	17.50	35.00
Mutiny on the Bounty 1 (10040-302)(2/63)-Marlon Brando photo-c	4.00	10.00	20.00
Nikki, Wild Dog of the North 10141-412 (12/64)-Disney; reprints 4-Color #1226	1.80	4.50	9.00
Old Yeller 10168-601 (1/66)-Disney; reprints 4-Color #869; photo-c	2.00	5.00	10.00
One Hundred & One Dalmations 1 (10247-002) (2/70)-Disney; reprints 4-Color #1183	2.40	6.00	12.00
Peter Pan 1 (10086-309)(9/63)-Disney; reprints 4-Color #442	2.80	7.00	14.00
Peter Pan 2 (10086-909)(9/69)-Disney; reprints 4-Color #442	1.80	4.50	9.00
Peter Pan 1 ('83)-r/4-Color #442		.50	1.00
P.T. 109 10123-409 (9/64)-John F. Kennedy	4.70	14.00	28.00
Rio Conchos 10143-503(3/65)	4.35	13.00	26.00
Robin Hood 10163-506 (6/65)-Disney; reprints 4-Color #413	2.40	6.00	12.00
Shaggy Dog & the Absent-Minded Professor 30032-708 (8/67-Giant, 68 pgs.) Disney; reprints 4-Color #985,1199	4.35	13.00	26.00
Sleeping Beauty 1 (30042-009)(9/70)-Disney; reprints 4-Color #973; with pull-out poster	4.35	13.00	26.00
Snow White & the Seven Dwarfs 1 (10091-310)(10/63)-Disney; reprints 4-Color #382	2.80	7.00	14.00
Snow White & the Seven Dwarfs 10091-709 (9/67)-Disney; reprints 4-Color #382	2.40	6.00	12.00
Snow White & the Seven Dwarfs 90091-204 (2/84)-Reprints 4-Color #382		.50	1.00
Son of Flubber 1 (10057-304)(4/63)-Disney; sequel to "The Absent-Minded Professor"	2.80	7.00	14.00
Summer Magic 10076-309 (9/63)-Disney; Hayley Mills photo-c; Manning-a	6.35	19.00	38.00
Swiss Family Robinson 10236-904 (4/69)-Disney; reprints 4-Color #1156; photo-c	2.80	7.00	14.00
Sword in the Stone, The 30019-402 (2/64-Giant, 84 pgs.)-Disney	4.35	13.00	26.00
That Darn Cat 10171-602 (2/66)-Disney; Hayley Mills photo-c	5.85	17.50	35.00
Those Magnificent Men in Their Flying Machines 10162-510 (10/65); photo-c	2.80	7.00	14.00
Three Stooges in Orbit 30016-211 (11/62-Giant, 32 pgs.)-All photos from movie; stiff-photo-c	10.00	30.00	65.00
Tiger Walks, A 10117-406 (6/64)-Disney; Torres, Tufts-a; photo-c	4.70	14.00	28.00
Toby Tyler 10142-502 (2/65)-Disney; reprints 4-Color #1092; photo-c	2.40	6.00	12.00
Treasure Island 1 (10200-703)(3/67)-Disney; reprints 4-Color #624; photo-c	2.00	5.00	10.00
20,000 Leagues Under the Sea 1 (10095-312)(12/63)-Disney; reprints 4-Color #614	2.00	5.00	10.00
Wonderful Adventures of Pinocchio, The 1 (10089-310)(10/63)-Disney; reprints 4-Color #545	2.00	5.00	10.00
Wonderful Adventures of Pinocchio, The 10089-109 (9/71)-Disney; reprints 4-Color #545	2.00	5.00	10.00
Wonderful World of the Brothers Grimm 1 (10008-210)(10/62)	4.00	10.00	20.00
X, the Man with the X-Ray Eyes 10083-309 (9/63)-Ray Milland photo on-c	6.70	20.00	40.00
Yellow Submarine 35000-902 (2/69-Giant, 68 pgs.)-with pull-out poster; The Beatles cartoon movie	17.00	52.00	120.00
Without poster	8.35	25.00	50.00

MOVIE LOVE (Also see Personal Love)
Feb, 1950 - No. 22, Aug, 1953
Famous Funnies

	GD25	FN65	NM94
1-Dick Powell photo-c	8.35	25.00	50.00
2	4.35	13.00	26.00
3-7,9	4.00	10.00	20.00
8-Williamson/Frazetta-a, 6 pgs.	23.00	70.00	160.00
10-Frazetta-a, 6 pgs.	28.00	85.00	200.00
11,12,14-16	3.20	8.00	16.00
13-Ronald Reagan photo-c with 1 pg. biog.	15.00	45.00	105.00
17-One pg. Frazetta ad	3.60	9.00	18.00
18-22	3.20	8.00	16.00

NOTE: *Each issue has a full-length movie adaptation with photo covers.*

MOVIE THRILLERS
1949 (Movie adaptation; photo-c)
Magazine Enterprises

	GD25	FN65	NM94
1-"Rope of Sand" with Burt Lancaster	22.00	65.00	150.00

MOVIE TOWN ANIMAL ANTICS (Formerly Animal Antics; becomes Raccoon Kids #52 on)
No. 24, Jan-Feb, 1950 - No. 51, July-Aug, 1954
National Periodical Publications

	GD25	FN65	NM94
24-Raccoon Kids continue	8.35	25.00	50.00
25-51	6.70	20.00	40.00

NOTE: ***Sheldon Mayer** a-28-33, 35, 37-41, 43, 44, 47, 49-51.*

MOVIE TUNES COMICS (Formerly Animated...; Frankie No. 4 on)
No. 3, Fall, 1946
Marvel Comics (MgPC)

	GD25	FN65	NM94
3-Super Rabbit, Krazy Krow, Silly Seal & Ziggy Pig	7.50	22.50	45.00

MOWGLI JUNGLE BOOK (See 4-Color #487, 582, 620)

MR. (See Mister)

MS. MARVEL (Also see The Avengers #183)
Jan, 1977 - No. 23, Apr, 1979
Marvel Comics Group

	GD25	FN65	NM94
1-1st app. Ms. Marvel; Scorpion app. in #1,2	.80	2.00	4.00
2-Origin	.60	1.50	3.00
3-10: 5-Vision app. 10-Last 30 cent issue	.40	1.00	2.00
11-23: 18-Avengers x-over. 19-Capt. Marvel app. 20-New costume. 23-Vance Astro (leader of the Guardians) app.	.30	.75	1.50

NOTE: ***Austin** c-14i, 16i, 17i, 22i. **Buscema** a-1-3p; c(p)-2, 4, 6, 7, 15. **Infantino** a-14p, 19p. **Gil Kane** c-8. **Mooney** a-4-8p, 13p, 15-18p. **Starlin** c-12.*

MS. MYSTIC (Pacific & Continuity)(Value; cover or less)

MS. TREE QUARTERLY (DC)(Value: cover or less)

MS. TREE'S THRILLING DETECTIVE ADVS (Eclipse)(Value: cover or less)

MS. VICTORY SPECIAL (Americomics)(Value: cover or less)

MUGGSY MOUSE (Also see Tick Tock Tales)
1951 - No. 3, 1951; No. 4, 1954 - No. 5, 1954; 1963
Magazine Enterprises

	GD25	FN65	NM94
1(A-1 #33)	4.20	12.50	25.00
2(A-1 #36)-Racist-c	5.85	17.50	35.00
3(A-1 #39), 4(A-1 #95), 5(A-1 #99)	2.40	6.00	12.00
Super Reprint #14(1963)	.60	1.50	3.00
I.W. Reprint #1,2 (nd)	.60	1.50	3.00

MUGGY-DOO, BOY CAT
July, 1953 - No. 4, Jan, 1954
Stanhall Publ.

	GD25	FN65	NM94
1-Irving Spector-a	5.00	15.00	30.00
2-4	4.00	10.00	20.00
Super Reprint #12('63), 16('64)	.60	1.50	3.00

MUMMY, THE (See Universal Presents... under Dell Giants & Movie Classics)

MUMMY ARCHIVES, THE (Millennium) (Value: cover or less)

MUNDEN'S BAR ANNUAL (First) (Value: cover or less)

MUNSTERS, THE (TV)
Jan, 1965 - No. 16, Jan, 1968 (All photo-c?)
Gold Key

	GD25	FN65	NM94
1 (10134-501)-Photo-c	17.00	52.00	120.00
2	10.00	30.00	60.00
3-5: 4,6-Photo-c	8.35	25.00	50.00
6-16: 16-Photo-c	7.50	22.50	45.00

MUPPET BABIES, THE (TV) (Marvel & Harvey) (Value; cover or less)

MUPPETS TAKE MANHATTAN, THE (Marvel) (Value: cover or less)

MURDER, INCORPORATED (My Private Life #16 on)
1/48 - No. 15, 12/49; (2 No.9's); 6/50 - No. 3, 8/51
Fox Feature Syndicate

	GD25	FN65	NM94
1 (1st Series)	22.00	65.00	150.00
2-Electrocution story; #1,2 have 'For Adults Only' on-c	16.00	48.00	110.00
3-7,9(4/49),10(5/49),11-15	9.15	27.50	55.00
8-Used in **SOTI**, pg. 160	11.00	32.00	75.00
9(3/49)-Possible use in **SOTI**, pg. 145; r/Blue Beetle #56('48)	10.00	30.00	60.00
5(#1, 6/50)(2nd Series)-Formerly My Desire #4	7.50	22.50	45.00
2(8/50)-Morisi-a	5.85	17.50	35.00
3(8/51)-Used in **POP**, pg. 81; Rico-a; lingerie-c/panels	7.50	22.50	45.00

MURDEROUS GANGSTERS
July, 1951; No. 2, Dec, 1951 - No. 4, June, 1952
Avon Periodicals/Realistic No. 3 on

	GD25	FN65	NM94
1-Pretty Boy Floyd, Leggs Diamond; 1 pg. Wood-a	23.00	70.00	160.00
2-Baby-Face Nelson; 1 pg. Wood-a	14.00	43.00	100.00
3-Painted-c	11.50	34.00	80.00
4-"Murder by Needle" drug story; Mort Lawrence-a; Kinstler-c	14.00	43.00	100.00

MURDER TALES (Magazine)
V1#10, Nov, 1970 - V1#11, Jan, 1971 (52 pages)
World Famous Publications

	GD25	FN65	NM94
V1#10-One pg. Frazetta ad	2.40	6.00	12.00
11-Guardineer-r; bondage-c	1.20	3.00	6.00

MUSHMOUSE AND PUNKIN PUSS (TV)
September, 1965 (Hanna-Barbera)
Gold Key

	GD25	FN65	NM94
1 (10153-509)	6.70	20.00	40.00

MUSIC MAN, THE (See Movie Classics)

MUTANT MISADVENTURES OF CLOAK AND DAGGER, THE (Becomes Cloak and Dagger #14 on)
Oct, 1988 - No. 19, Aug, 1991 (#1: $1.25; #2-on: $1.50, color)
Marvel Comics

	GD25	FN65	NM94
1-8,10-18: 1-X-Factor app. 9,10-Painted-c. 12-Dr. Doom app. 14-Begin new direction. 16-18-Spider-Man x-over. 18-Infinity Gauntlet x-over; Thanos cameo; Ghost Rider app.	.30	.75	1.50
9-($2.50, 52 pgs.)-The Avengers x-over	.50	1.25	2.50
19-($2.50, 52 pgs.)-Origin Cloak & Dagger	.50	1.25	2.50

NOTE: ***Austin** a-12i; c(i)-4, 12, 13; scripts-all. **Russell** a-2i. **Williamson** a-14i-16i; c-15i.*

MUTANTS & MISFITS (Silverline) (Value: cover or less)

MUTATIS
1992 - No. 3, 1992 ($2.25, color, mini-series)
Epic Comics (Marvel)

	GD25	FN65	NM94
1-3: Painted-c	.45	1.15	2.25

MUTINY (Stormy Tales of Seven Seas)
Oct, 1954 - No. 3, Feb, 1955
Aragon Magazines

	GD25	FN65	NM94
1	10.00	30.00	60.00
2,3: 2-Capt. Mutiny. 3-Bondage-c	6.70	20.00	40.00

MUTINY ON THE BOUNTY (See Classics Illustrated #100 & Movie Comics)

MUTT & JEFF (...Cartoon, The)
1910 - No. 5, 1916 (5-3/4x15-1/2") (Hardcover-B&W)
Ball Publications

	GD25	FN65	VF82
1(1910)(68 pgs., 50 cents)	58.00	175.00	350.00
2,3: 2(1911, 68 pgs.)-Opium den panels; Jeff smokes opium (pipe dreams). 3(1912, 68 pgs.)	50.00	150.00	300.00
4(1915)(68 pgs., 50 cents)(Rare)	54.00	162.00	325.00
5(1916)(68 pgs.)(Rare)-Photos of Fisher, 1st pg.	63.00	188.00	375.00

NOTE: *Mutt & Jeff first appeared in newspapers in 1908. Cover variations exist showing Mutt & Jeff reading various newspapers; i.e., The Oregon Journal, The American, and The Detroit News. Reprinting of each issue began soon after publication. No. 5 may not have been reprinted. Values listed include the reprints.*

MUTT & JEFF
No. 6, 1916 - No. 22, 1933? (B&W dailies) (9-1/2x9-1/2"; stiff-c; 52 pgs.)
Cupples & Leon Co.

	GD25	FN65	VF82
6-22-By Bud Fisher	29.00	88.00	175.00

NOTE: *Later issues are somewhat rarer.*

	GD25	FN65	VF82
nn(1920)-(Advs. of...) 16x11"; 20 pgs.; reprints 1919 Sunday strips	50.00	150.00	300.00
Big Book nn(1926, 144pgs., hardcovers)	33.00	100.00	200.00
w/dust jacket....	58.00	175.00	350.00
Big Book 1(1928)-Thick book (hardcovers)	33.00	100.00	200.00
w/dust jacket....	58.00	175.00	350.00
Big Book 2(1929)-Thick book (hardcovers)	33.00	100.00	200.00
w/dust jacket....	58.00	175.00	350.00

NOTE: *The Big Books contain three previous issues rebound.*

MUTT & JEFF
1921 (9x15")
Embee Publ. Co.

	GD25	FN65	VF82
nn-Sunday strips in color (Rare)	75.00	225.00	450.00

MUTT AND JEFF (See All-American, All-Flash #18, Cicero's Cat, Comic Cavalcade, Famous Feature Stories, The Funnies, Popular & Xmas Comics)
Summer, 1939 (nd) - No. 148, Nov, 1965
All American/National 1-103(6/58)/Dell 104(10/58)-115 (10-12/59)/
Harvey 116(2/60)-148

	GD25	FN65	NM94
1(nn)-Lost Wheels	108.00	325.00	650.00
2(nn)-Charging Bull (Summer, 1940, nd; on sale 6/20/40)	58.00	175.00	350.00
3(nn)-Bucking Broncos (Summer, 1941, nd)	42.00	125.00	250.00
4(Winter, '41), 5(Summer, '42)	31.00	92.00	185.00
6-10	18.00	55.00	110.00
11-20	12.50	37.50	75.00
21-30	8.35	25.00	50.00
31-50	5.35	16.00	32.00
51-75-Last Fisher issue. 53-Last 52pgs.	4.20	12.50	25.00
76-99,101-103: 76-Last precode issue(1/55)	3.60	9.00	18.00
100	4.00	10.00	20.00
104-148: 117,118,120-131-Richie Rich app.	2.40	6.00	12.00
...Jokes 1-3(8/60-61, Harvey)-84 pgs.; Richie Rich in all; Little Dot in #2,3	3.60	9.00	18.00
...New Jokes 1-4(10/63-11/65, Harvey)-68 pgs.; Richie Rich in #1-3; Stumbo in #1	1.60	4.00	8.00

NOTE: *Issues 1-74 by **Bud Fisher**. 86 on by **Al Smith**. Issues from 1963 on have **Fisher** reprints. Clarification: early issues signed by Fisher are mostly drawn by Smith.*

MY BROTHERS' KEEPER (Spire Christian) (Value: cover or less)

MY CONFESSIONS (My Confession #7&8; formerly Western True Crime; A Spectacular Feature Magazine #11)

The Munsters #1, © Kayro-Vue Prod.

Murder Incorporated #8 (2nd series), © FOX

Mutt and Jeff #8, © Ball Syndicate

My Experience #20, © FOX

My Favorite Martian #2, © Jack Cherton TV

My Greatest Adventure #22, © DC

No. 7, Aug, 1949 - No. 10, Jan-Feb, 1950
Fox Feature Syndicate

	GD25	FN65	NM94
7-Wood-a (10 pgs.)	12.00	36.00	85.00
8-Wood-a (19 pgs.)	10.00	30.00	70.00
9,10	5.00	15.00	30.00

MY DATE COMICS
July, 1947 - V1No.4, Jan, 1948 (1st Romance comic)
Hillman Periodicals

	GD25	FN65	NM94
1-S&K-c/a	17.00	52.00	120.00
2-4-S&K, Dan Barry-a	11.50	34.00	80.00

MY DESIRE (Formerly Jo-Jo Comics; becomes Murder, Inc. #5 on)
No. 30, Aug, 1949 - No. 4, April, 1950
Fox Feature Syndicate

	GD25	FN65	NM94
30(#1)	7.50	22.50	45.00
31 (#2),3,4	5.00	15.00	30.00
31 (Canadian edition)	4.00	10.00	20.00
32(12/49)-Wood-a	10.00	30.00	70.00

MY DIARY (Becomes My Friend Irma #3 on?)
Dec, 1949 - No. 2, Mar, 1950
Marvel Comics (A Lovers Mag.)

	GD25	FN65	NM94
1,2: 1-Photo-c	7.50	22.50	45.00

MY DOG TIGE (Buster Brown's Dog)
1957 (Giveaway)
Buster Brown Shoes

	GD25	FN65	NM94
nn	3.20	8.00	16.00

MY EXPERIENCE (Formerly All Top; becomes Judy Canova #23 on)
No. 19, Sept, 1949 - No. 22, Mar, 1950
Fox Feature Syndicate

	GD25	FN65	NM94
19-Wood-a	12.00	36.00	85.00
20	5.00	15.00	30.00
21-Wood-a(2)	13.00	40.00	90.00
22-Wood-a, 9 pgs.	10.00	30.00	70.00

MY FAVORITE MARTIAN (TV)
1/64; No.2, 7/64 - No. 9, 10/66 (No. 1,3-9 have photo-c)
Gold Key

	GD25	FN65	NM94
1-Russ Manning-a	10.00	30.00	65.00
2	5.00	15.00	30.00
3-9	5.85	17.50	35.00

MY FRIEND IRMA (Radio/TV) (Formerly My Diary? and/or Western Life Romances?)
No. 3, June, 1950 - No. 47, Dec, 1954; No. 48, Feb, 1955
Marvel/Atlas Comics (BFP)

	GD25	FN65	NM94
3-(52 pgs.)-Dan DeCarlo-a in all	8.35	25.00	50.00
4-Kurtzman-a, 10 pgs.	10.00	30.00	60.00
5-"Egghead Doodle" by Kurtzman, 4 pgs.	7.50	22.50	45.00
6,8-10: 9-paper dolls, 1pg; Millie app.	4.70	14.00	28.00
7-One pg. Kurtzman-a	5.00	15.00	30.00
11-23: 23-One pg. Frazetta-a	3.60	9.00	18.00
24-48	2.40	6.00	12.00

MY GIRL PEARL
4/55 - #4, 10/55; #5, 7/57 - #6, 9/57; #7, 8/60 - #11, ?/61
Atlas Comics

	GD25	FN65	NM94
1-Dan DeCarlo-a in #1-6	7.50	22.50	45.00
2	4.20	12.50	25.00
3-6	2.40	6.00	12.00
7-11	2.00	5.00	10.00

MY GREATEST ADVENTURE (Doom Patrol #86 on)
Jan-Feb, 1955 - No. 85, Feb, 1964
National Periodical Publications

	GD25	FN65	NM94
1-Before CCA	82.00	250.00	575.00
2	39.00	120.00	275.00
3-5	25.00	75.00	175.00
6-10: 6-Science fiction format begins	19.00	57.00	130.00
11-14,19	13.00	40.00	90.00
15-18,20,21,28-Kirby-a. 18-Kirby-c	14.00	43.00	100.00
22-27,29,30	9.15	27.50	55.00
31-40	6.70	20.00	40.00
41-57,59	4.20	12.50	25.00
58,60,61-Toth-a; Last 10 cent issue	4.70	14.00	28.00
62-79: 77-Toth-a	2.80	7.00	14.00
80-(6/63)-Intro/origin Doom Patrol and begin series; origin Robotman, Negative Man, & Elasti-Girl	32.00	95.00	225.00
81-85: 81,85-Toth-a	12.00	36.00	85.00

NOTE: ***Anderson** a-42. **Cameron** a-24. **Colan** a-77. **Meskin** a-25, 26, 32, 39, 45, 50, 56, 57, 61, 64, 70, 73, 74, 76, 79; c-76. **Moreira** a-11, 12, 15, 17, 20, 23, 25, 27, 37, 40-43, 46, 48, 55-57, 59, 60, 62-65, 67, 69, 70; c-1-4, 7-10. **Roussos** c/a-71-73. **Wildey** a-32.*

MY GREATEST THRILLS IN BASEBALL
Date? (16 pg. Giveaway)
Mission of California

	GD25	FN65	NM94
nn-By Mickey Mantle	39.00	118.00	275.00

MY GREAT LOVE (Becomes Will Rogers Western #5)
Oct, 1949 - No. 4, Apr, 1950
Fox Feature Syndicate

	GD25	FN65	NM94
1	8.35	25.00	50.00
2-4	4.70	14.00	28.00

MY INTIMATE AFFAIR (Inside Crime #3)
Mar, 1950 - No. 2, May, 1950
Fox Feature Syndicate

	GD25	FN65	NM94
1	8.35	25.00	50.00
2	4.70	14.00	28.00

MY LIFE (Formerly Meet Corliss Archer)
No. 4, Sept, 1948 - No. 15, July, 1950
Fox Feature Syndicate

	GD25	FN65	NM94
4-Used in **SOTI**, pg. 39; Kamen/Feldstein-a	22.00	65.00	150.00
5-Kamen-a	10.00	30.00	65.00
6-Kamen/Feldstein-a	10.00	30.00	70.00
7-Wash cover	7.50	22.50	45.00
8,9,11-15	4.70	14.00	28.00
10-Wood-a	10.00	30.00	70.00

MY LITTLE MARGIE (TV)
July, 1954 - No. 54, Nov, 1964
Charlton Comics

	GD25	FN65	NM94
1-Photo front/back-c	14.00	43.00	100.00
2-Photo front/back-c	8.35	25.00	50.00
3-7,10	4.70	14.00	28.00
8,9-Infinity-c	5.35	16.00	32.00
11-13: part-photo-c (#13, 8/56)	4.20	12.50	25.00
14-19	3.60	9.00	18.00
20-(100 page issue)	6.70	20.00	40.00
21-35-Last 10 cent issue?	2.40	6.00	12.00
36-53	1.60	4.00	8.00
54-Beatles on cover; lead story spoofs the Beatle haircut craze of the 1960's	11.00	32.00	75.00

NOTE: *Doll cut-outs in 32, 33, 40, 45, 50.*

MY LITTLE MARGIE'S BOY FRIENDS (TV) (Freddy V2#12 on)
Aug, 1955 - No. 11, Apr?, 1958
Charlton Comics

	GD25	FN65	NM94
1-Has several Archie swipes	7.50	22.50	45.00
2	4.70	14.00	28.00

	GD25	FN65	NM94
3-11	3.60	9.00	18.00

MY LITTLE MARGIE'S FASHIONS (TV)
Feb, 1959 - No. 5, Nov, 1959
Charlton Comics

	GD25	FN65	NM94
1	7.50	22.50	45.00
2-5	4.70	14.00	28.00

MY LOVE (Becomes Two Gun Western #5 (11/50) on?)
July, 1949 - No. 4, Apr, 1950 (All photo-c)
Marvel Comics (CLDS)

	GD25	FN65	NM94
1	6.70	20.00	40.00
2,3	4.20	12.50	25.00
4-Betty Page photo-c (see Cupid #2)	16.00	48.00	110.00

MY LOVE
Sept, 1969 - No. 39, Mar, 1976
Marvel Comics Group

	GD25	FN65	NM94
1	1.60	4.00	8.00
2-9	.80	2.00	4.00
10-Williamson-r/My Own Romance #71; Kirby-a	1.20	3.00	6.00
11-20: 14-Morrow-c/a; Kirby/Colletta-r	.60	1.50	3.00
21,22,24-39: 38,39-Reprints	.60	1.50	3.00
23-Steranko-r/Our Love Story #5	.80	2.00	4.00
Special(12/71)	.60	1.50	3.00

NOTE: ***John Buscema** a-2-7, 10. **Colan** a-4-6. **Colan/Everett** a-27r.*

MY LOVE AFFAIR (March of Crime #7 on)
July, 1949 - No. 6, May, 1950
Fox Feature Syndicate

	GD25	FN65	NM94
1	8.35	25.00	50.00
2	5.00	15.00	30.00
3-6-Wood-a. 5-(3/50)-Becomes Love Stories #6	10.00	30.00	70.00

MY LOVE LIFE (Formerly Zegra)
No. 6, June, 1949 - No. 13, Aug, 1950; No. 13, Sept, 1951
Fox Feature Syndicate

	GD25	FN65	NM94
6-Kamenish-a	10.00	30.00	60.00
7-13	5.00	15.00	30.00
13 (9/51)	4.20	12.50	25.00

MY LOVE MEMOIRS (Formerly Women Outlaws; Hunted #13 on)
No. 9, Nov, 1949 - No. 12, May, 1950
Fox Feature Syndicate

	GD25	FN65	NM94
9,11,12-Wood-a	10.00	30.00	70.00
10	5.00	15.00	30.00

MY LOVE SECRET (Formerly Phantom Lady; Animal Crackers #31)
No. 24, June, 1949 - No. 30, June, 1950; No. 53, 1954
Fox Feature Syndicate/M. S. Distr.

	GD25	FN65	NM94
24-Kamen/Feldstein-a	10.00	30.00	65.00
25-Possible caricature of Wood on-c?	5.85	17.50	35.00
26,28-Wood-a	10.00	30.00	70.00
27,29,30: 30-Photo-c	4.70	14.00	28.00
53-(Reprint, M.S. Distr.) 1954? nd given; formerly Western Thrillers; becomes Crimes by Women #54; photo-c	3.60	9.00	18.00

MY LOVE STORY (Hoot Gibson Western #5 on)
Sept, 1949 - No. 4, Mar, 1950
Fox Feature Syndicate

	GD25	FN65	NM94
1	8.35	25.00	50.00
2	4.70	14.00	28.00
3,4-Wood-a	10.00	30.00	70.00

MY LOVE STORY
April, 1956 - No. 9, Aug, 1957
Atlas Comics (GPS)

	GD25	FN65	NM94
1	5.85	17.50	35.00
2	3.60	9.00	18.00
3-Matt Baker-a	4.00	12.00	24.00
4-6,8,9	3.00	7.50	15.00
7-Matt Baker, Toth-a	4.35	13.00	26.00

NOTE: ***Brewster** a-3. **Colletta** a-1(2), 3, 4(2), 5; c-3.*

MY NAME IS CHAOS
1992 - No. 4, 1992 ($4.95, color, mini-series, 52 pgs.)
DC Comics

	GD25	FN65	NM94
Book 1-4: Tom Veitch scripts; painted-c	1.00	2.50	5.00

MY ONLY LOVE
July, 1975 - No. 9, Nov, 1976
Charlton Comics

	GD25	FN65	NM94
1,2,4-9	.60	1.50	3.00
3-Toth-a	.80	2.00	4.00

MY OWN ROMANCE (Formerly My Romance; Teen-Age Romance #77 on)
No. 4, Mar, 1949 - No. 76, July, 1960
Marvel/Atlas (MjPC/RCM No. 4-59/ZPC No. 60-76)

	GD25	FN65	NM94
4-Photo-c	7.50	22.50	45.00
5-10: 5,6,8-10-Photo-c	4.00	10.00	20.00
11-20: 14-Powell-a	3.20	8.00	16.00
21-42: 42-Last precode (2/55)	2.80	7.00	14.00
43-54,56-60	2.00	5.00	10.00
55-Toth-a	4.00	12.00	24.00
61-70,72-76	1.60	4.00	8.00
71-Williamson-a	4.35	13.00	26.00

NOTE: ***Brewster** a-59. **Colletta** a-45(2), 48, 50, 55, 57(2), 59; c-58i, 59, 61. **Everett** a-25; c-58p. **Morisi** a-18. **Orlando** a-61. **Romita** a-36. **Tuska** a-10.*

MY PAL DIZZY (See Comic Books, Series I)

MY PAST (...Confessions) (Formerly Western Thrillers)
No. 7, Aug, 1949 - No. 11, April, 1950 (Crimes Inc. #12)
Fox Feature Syndicate

	GD25	FN65	NM94
7	8.35	25.00	50.00
8-10	5.00	15.00	30.00
11-Wood-a	10.00	30.00	70.00

MY PERSONAL PROBLEM
11/55; No. 2, 2/56; No. 3, 9/56 - No. 4, 11/56; 10/57 - No. 3, 5/58
Ajax/Farrell/Steinway Comic

	GD25	FN65	NM94
1	5.00	15.00	30.00
2-4	3.60	9.00	18.00
1-3('57-'58)-Steinway	2.80	7.00	14.00

MY PRIVATE LIFE (Formerly Murder, Inc.; becomes Pedro #18)
No. 16, Feb, 1950 - No. 17, April, 1950
Fox Feature Syndicate

	GD25	FN65	NM94
16,17	6.70	20.00	40.00

MYRA NORTH (See The Comics, Crackajack Funnies, 4-Color #3 & Red Ryder)

MY REAL LOVE
No. 5, June, 1952
Standard Comics

	GD25	FN65	NM94
5-Toth-a, 3 pgs.; Tuska, Cardy, Vern Greene-a; photo-c	7.00	21.00	42.00

MY ROMANCE (Becomes My Own Romance #4 on)
Sept, 1948 - No. 3, Jan, 1949
Marvel Comics (RCM)

	GD25	FN65	NM94
1	7.50	22.50	45.00
2,3: 2-Anti-Wertham editorial (11/48)	4.35	13.00	26.00

MY ROMANTIC ADVENTURES (Formerly Romantic Adventures)
No. 68, 8/56 - No. 115, 12/60; No. 116, 7/61 - No. 138, 3/64
American Comics Group

	GD25	FN65	NM94
68	4.35	13.00	26.00
69-85	2.80	7.00	14.00
86-Three pg. Williamson-a (2/58)	4.00	12.00	24.00

My Love Memoirs #11, © FOX

My Love Story #2, © FOX

My Romance #1, © MEG

My Secret Life #24, © FOX

My Secret Marriage #16, © SUPR

Mysteries of Unexplored Worlds #25, © CC

	GD25	FN65	NM94
87-100	2.00	5.00	10.00
101-138	1.20	3.00	6.00

NOTE: *Whitney art in most issues.*

MY SECRET (Becomes Our Secret #4 on)
Aug, 1949 - No. 3, Oct, 1949
Superior Comics, Ltd.

	GD25	FN65	NM94
1	7.50	22.50	45.00
2,3	5.00	15.00	30.00

MY SECRET AFFAIR (Becomes Martin Kane #4)
Dec, 1949 - No. 3, April, 1950
Hero Book (Fox Feature Syndicate)

	GD25	FN65	NM94
1-Harrison/Wood-a, 10 pgs.	11.50	34.00	80.00
2-Wood-a (poor)	8.35	25.00	50.00
3-Wood-a	10.00	30.00	70.00

MY SECRET CONFESSION
September, 1955
Sterling Comics

	GD25	FN65	NM94
1-Sekowsky-a	4.20	12.50	25.00

MY SECRET LIFE (Formerly Western Outlaws; Romeo Tubbs #26 on)
No. 22, July, 1949 - No. 27, May, 1950
Fox Feature Syndicate

	GD25	FN65	NM94
22	6.70	20.00	40.00
23,26-Wood-a, 6 pgs.	10.00	30.00	70.00
24,25,27	4.35	13.00	26.00

NOTE: *The title was changed to Romeo Tubbs after #25 even though #26 & 27 did come out.*

MY SECRET LIFE (Formerly Young Lovers; Sue & Sally Smith #48)
No. 19, Aug, 1957 - No. 47, Sept, 1962
Charlton Comics

	GD25	FN65	NM94
19	2.80	7.00	14.00
20-35	1.40	3.50	7.00
36-47: 44-Last 10 cent issue	1.00	2.50	5.00

MY SECRET MARRIAGE
May, 1953 - No. 24, July, 1956
Superior Comics, Ltd.

	GD25	FN65	NM94
1	6.70	20.00	40.00
2	4.00	10.00	20.00
3-24	2.80	7.00	14.00
I.W. Reprint #9	.40	1.00	2.00

NOTE: *Many issues contain **Kamenish** art.*

MY SECRET ROMANCE (Becomes A Star Presentation #3)
Jan, 1950 - No. 2, March, 1950
Hero Book (Fox Feature Syndicate)

	GD25	FN65	NM94
1-Wood-a	11.00	32.00	75.00
2-Wood-a	10.00	30.00	70.00

MY SECRET STORY (Formerly Captain Kidd #25; Sabu #30 on)
No. 26, Oct, 1949 - No. 29, April, 1950
Fox Feature Syndicate

	GD25	FN65	NM94
26	7.50	22.50	45.00
27-29	5.00	15.00	30.00

MYSTERIES (...Weird & Strange)
May, 1953 - No. 11, Jan, 1955
Superior/Dynamic Publ. (Randall Publ. Ltd.)

	GD25	FN65	NM94
1	14.00	43.00	100.00
2-A-Bomb blast story	8.35	25.00	50.00
3-9,11	5.85	17.50	35.00
10-Kamenish-c/a reprinted from Strange Mysteries #2; cover is from a panel in Strange Mysteries #2	7.00	21.00	42.00

MYSTERIES OF SCOTLAND YARD (See A-1 Comics #121)

MYSTERIES OF UNEXPLORED WORLDS (See Blue Bird) (Becomes Son of Vulcan V2#49 on)
Aug, 1956; No. 2, Jan, 1957 - No. 48, Sept, 1965
Charlton Comics

	GD25	FN65	NM94
1	19.00	58.00	135.00
2-No Ditko	8.35	25.00	50.00
3,4,8,9-Ditko-a	11.50	34.00	80.00
5,6-Ditko-c/a (all)	13.00	40.00	90.00
7-(2/58, 68 pgs.); Ditko-a(4)	13.00	40.00	90.00
10-Ditko-c/a(4)	13.00	40.00	90.00
11-Ditko-c/a(3)-signed J. Kotdi	13.00	40.00	90.00
12,19,21-24,26-Ditko-a	10.00	30.00	60.00
13-18,20	3.60	9.00	18.00
25,27-30	3.00	7.50	15.00
31-45	1.60	4.00	8.00
46(5/65)-Son of Vulcan begins (origin/1st app.)	3.00	7.50	15.00
47,48	1.80	4.50	9.00

NOTE: ***Ditko** c-3-6, 10, 11, 19, 21-24. Covers to #23 & 24 reprint story panels.*

MYSTERIOUS ADVENTURES
March, 1951 - No. 24, Mar, 1955; No. 25, Aug, 1955
Story Comics

	GD25	FN65	NM94
1	20.00	60.00	140.00
2	10.00	30.00	70.00
3,4,6,10	9.15	27.50	55.00
5-Bondage-c	11.00	32.00	75.00
7-Daggar in eye panel	15.00	45.00	105.00
8-Eyeball story	13.00	40.00	90.00
9-Extreme violence	11.00	32.00	75.00
11-13: 11(12/52)-Used in **SOTI**, pg. 84	11.50	34.00	80.00
14-E.C. Old Witch swipe	10.00	30.00	60.00
15-21: 18-Used in Senate Investigative report, pgs. 5,6; E.C. swipe/TFTC #35; The Coffin-Keeper & Corpse (hosts). 20-Used by Wertham in the Senate hearings. 21-Bondage/beheading-c	14.00	43.00	100.00
22-'Cinderella' parody	10.00	30.00	65.00
23-Disbrow-a (6 pgs.); E.C. swipe "The Mystery Keeper's Tale" (host) and "Mother Ghoul's Nursery Tale"	10.00	30.00	60.00
24,25	8.35	25.00	50.00

NOTE: ***Tothish** art by **Ross Andru**-#22, 23. **Bache** a-8. **Cameron** a-5-7. **Harrison** a-12. **Hollingsworth** a-3-8, 12. **Schaffenberger** a-24, 25. **Wildey** a-15, 17.*

MYSTERIOUS ISLAND (See 4-Color #1213)

MYSTERIOUS ISLE
Nov-Jan, 1963/64 (Jules Verne)
Dell Publishing Co.

	GD25	FN65	NM94
1	2.00	5.00	10.00

MYSTERIOUS STORIES (Formerly Horror From the Tomb #1)
No. 2, Dec-Jan, 1954-1955 - No. 7, Dec, 1955
Premier Magazines

	GD25	FN65	NM94
2-Woodbridge-c; last pre-code issue	13.00	40.00	90.00
3-Woodbridge-c/a	10.00	30.00	60.00
4-7: 5-Cinderella parody. 6-Woodbridge-c	9.15	27.50	55.00

NOTE: ***Hollingsworth** a-2, 4.*

MYSTERIOUS SUSPENSE
October, 1968 (12 cents)
Charlton Comics

	GD25	FN65	NM94
1-Return of the Question by Ditko (c/a)	4.00	10.00	20.00

MYSTERIOUS TRAVELER (See Tales of the...)

MYSTERIOUS TRAVELER COMICS (Radio)
Nov, 1948
Trans-World Publications

	GD25	FN65	NM94
1-Powell-c/a(2); Poe adaptation, "Tell Tale Heart"	33.00	100.00	200.00

MYSTERY COMICS
1944 - No. 4, 1944 (No months given)
William H. Wise & Co.

1-The Magnet, The Silver Knight, Brad Spencer, Wonderman, Dick Devins, King of Futuria, & Zudo the Jungle Boy begin; Schomburg-c on all 50.00 150.00 300.00
2-Bondage-c 32.00 95.00 190.00
3-Lance Lewis, Space Detective begins 27.00 82.00 165.00
4(V2#1 inside) 27.00 82.00 165.00

MYSTERY COMICS DIGEST
March, 1972 - No. 26, Oct, 1975
Gold Key

1-Ripley's Believe It or Not; reprint of Ripley's #1 origin Ra-Ka-Tep the Mummy; Wood-a 1.00 2.50 5.00
2-Boris Karloff Tales of Mystery; Wood-a; 1st app. Werewolf Count Wulfstein .50 1.25 2.50
3-Twilight Zone (TV); Crandall, Toth & George Evans-a; 1st app. Tragg & Simbar the Lion Lord; 2 Crandall/Frazetta-a r-Twilight Zone #1 .50 1.25 2.50
4-Ripley's Believe It or Not; 1st app. Baron Tibor, the Vampire .40 1.00 2.00
5-Boris Karloff Tales of Mystery; 1st app. Dr. Spektor .40 1.00 2.00
6-Twilight Zone (TV); 1st app. U.S. Marshal Reid & Sir Duane .40 1.00 2.00
7-Ripley's Believe It or Not; origin The Lurker in the Swamp; 1st app. Duroc .60 1.20
8-Boris Karloff Tales of Mystery; McWilliams-r .60 1.20
9-Twilight Zone (TV); Williamson, Crandall, McWilliams-a; 2nd Tragg app. .50 1.25 2.50
10,13-Ripley's Believe It or Not .50 1.00
11,14-Boris Karloff Tales of Mystery. 14-1st app. Xorkon .50 1.00
12,15-Twilight Zone (TV) .50 1.00
16,19,22,25-Ripley's Believe It or Not .50 1.00
17-Boris Karloff Tales of Mystery; Williamson-r .30 .75 1.50
18,21,24-Twilight Zone (TV) .50 1.00
20,23,26-Boris Karloff Tales of Mystery .50 1.00
NOTE: *Dr. Spektor app.-#5, 10-12, 21. Durak app.-#15. Duroc app.-#14 (later called Durak). King George 1st app.-#8.*

MYSTERY IN SPACE
4-5/51 - No. 110, 9/66; No. 111, 9/80 - No. 117, 3/81 (#1-3: 52 pgs.)
National Periodical Publications

1-Frazetta-a, 8 pgs.; Knights of the Galaxy begins, ends #8 207.00 621.00 1450.00
2 79.00 235.00 550.00
3 64.00 195.00 450.00
4,5 50.00 150.00 350.00
6-10: 7-Toth-a 43.00 130.00 300.00
11-15: 13-Toth-a 29.00 85.00 200.00
16-18,20-25: Interplanetary Insurance feature by Infantino in all. 24-Last pre-code issue 25.00 75.00 175.00
19-Virgil Finlay-a 29.00 85.00 200.00
26-40: 26-Space Cabbie begins 18.00 54.00 125.00
41-52: 47-Space Cabbie feature ends 14.00 43.00 100.00
53-Adam Strange begins (8/59, 10 pg. story) (1st app. in Showcase) 97.00 290.00 675.00
54 37.900 110.00 250.00
55 22.00 65.00 150.00
56-60: 59-Kane/Anderson-a 15.00 45.00 105.00
61-71: 61-1st app. Adam Strange foe Ulthoon. 62-1st app. A.S. foe Mortan. 63-Origin Vandor. 66-Star Rovers begin. 68-Dust Devils app. 71-Last 10 cent issue 10.00 30.00 70.00
72-74,76-80 8.35 25.00 50.00
75-JLA x-over in Adam Strange (5/62) 20.00 60.00 140.00
81-86 5.00 15.00 30.00
87-(11/63)-Adam Strange/Hawkman double feat. 13.00 40.00 90.00
88-90: 88-89-Adam Strange & Hawkman stories. 90-Adam Strange & Hawkman team-up for 1st time (3/64); Hawkman moves to own title next month (Hawkman's 3rd tryout title) 8.35 25.00 50.00
91-103: 91-End Infantino art on Adam Strange; double-length Adam Strange story. 92-Space Ranger begins (6/64), ends #103. 92-94,96,98-Space Ranger-c. 94,98-Adam Strange/Space Ranger team-up. 102-Adam Strange ends (no Space Ranger). 103-Origin Ultra, the Multi-Alien; last Space Ranger 2.80 7.00 14.00
104-110: 110-(9/66)-Last 10 cent issue 1.00 2.50 5.00
V17#111(9/80)-117: 117-Newton-a(3 pgs.) .40 1.00 2.00
NOTE: ***Anderson** a-2, 4, 8-10, 12-17, 19, 45-48, 51, 57, 59i, 61-64, 70, 76, 87-91; c-9, 10, 15-25, 87, 89, 105-108, 110. **Aparo** a-111. **Austin** a-112i. **Bolland** a-115. **Craig** a-114, 116. **Ditko** a-111, 114-116. **Drucker** a-13, 14. **Elias** a-98, 102, 103. **Golden** a-113p. **Sid Greene** a-78, 91. **Infantino** a-1-8, 11, 14-25, 27-46, 48, 49, 51, 53-91, 103, 117; c-60-86, 88, 90, 91, 105, 107. **Gil Kane** a-14p, 15p, 18p, 19p, 26p, 29-59p(most), 100-102; c-52, 101. **Kubert** a-113; c-111-115. **Moriera** c-27, 28. **Rogers** a-111. **Sekowsky** a-52. **Simon & Kirby** a-4(2 pgs.). **Spiegle** a-111, 114. **Starlin** c-116. **Sutton** a-112. **Tuska** a-115p, 117p.*

MYSTERY MEN COMICS
Aug, 1939 - No. 31, Feb, 1942
Fox Features Syndicate

1-Intro. & 1st app. The Blue Beetle, The Green Mask, Rex Dexter of Mars by Briefer, Zanzibar by Tuska, Lt. Drake, D-13-Secret Agent by Powell, Chen Chang, Wing Turner, & Captain Denny Scott 208.00 625.00 1250.00
2 100.00 300.00 600.00
3 (10/39) 88.00 262.00 525.00
4-Capt. Savage begins 75.00 225.00 450.00
5 58.00 175.00 350.00
6-8 53.00 160.00 320.00
9-The Moth begins 44.00 132.00 265.00
10-Wing Turner by Kirby 44.00 132.00 265.00
11-Intro. Domino 33.00 100.00 200.00
12,14-18 30.00 90.00 180.00
13-Intro. Lynx & sidekick Blackie 35.00 105.00 210.00
19-Intro. & 1st app. Miss X (ends #21) 35.00 105.00 210.00
20-31: 26-The Wraith begins 28.00 85.00 170.00
NOTE: ***Briefer** a-1-15, 20, 24; c-9. **Cuidera** a-22. **Lou Fine** c-1-8. **Powell** a-1-15, 24. **Simon** c-10-12. **Tuska** a-1-16, 22, 24, 27. Bondage-c 1, 3, 7, 8, 25, 27-29, 31.*

MYSTERY TALES
March, 1952 - No. 54, Aug, 1957
Atlas Comics (20CC)

1 30.00 90.00 210.00
2-Krigstein-a 16.00 48.00 110.00
3-10: 6-A-Bomb panel. 10-Story similar to 'The Assassin' from Shock SuspenStories 11.50 34.00 80.00
11,13-21: 14-Maneely s/f story. 20-Electric chair issue. 21-Matt Fox-a; decapitation story 10.00 30.00 60.00
12-Matt Fox-a 10.00 30.00 70.00
22-Forte/Matt Fox c; a(i) 10.00 30.00 70.00
23-26 (2/55)-Last precode issue 8.35 25.00 50.00
27,29-34,35,37,38,41-43,48,49: 43-Morisi story contains Frazetta art swipes from Untamed Love 6.70 20.00 40.00
28-Jack Katz-a 7.50 22.50 45.00
36,39-Krigstein-a 7.50 22.50 45.00
40,45-Ditko-a (#45 is 3 pgs. only) 7.50 22.50 45.00
44,51-Williamson/Krenkel-a 8.35 25.00 50.00
46-Williamson/Krenkel-a; Crandall text illos 8.35 25.00 50.00
47-Crandall, Ditko, Powell-a 8.35 25.00 50.00
50-Torres, Morrow-a 7.50 22.50 45.00
52,53 5.00 15.00 30.00
54-Crandall, Check-a 6.70 20.00 40.00
NOTE: ***Ayers** a-18, 49, 52. **Berg** a-17, 51. **Colan** a-1, 3, 18, 35, 43. **Colletta** a-18. **Drucker** a-41. **Everett** a-2, 29, 33, 35, 41; c-8-11, 14, 38, 39, 41, 43, 44, 46, 48-51, 53. **Fass** a-16. **Forte** a-21, 22, 45, 46. **Matt Fox** a-12?, 21, 22; c-22. **Heath** a-3; c-3, 15, 17, 26. **Heck** a-25. **Kinstler** a-15. **Mort Lawrence** a-26, 32, 34. **Maneely** a-1, 9, 14, 22; c-12, 23, 24, 27. **Mooney***

Mysterious Adventures #9, © Story Comics

Mystery in Space #39, © DC

Mystery Men #16, © FOX

Mystic #19, © MEG

Mystical Tales #2, © MEG

Mystic Comics #6 (1st Series), © MEG

GD25 FN65 NM94

*a-3, 40. **Morisi** a-43, 49, 52. **Morrow** a-50. **Orlando** a-51. **Pakula** a-16. **Powell** a-21, 29, 37, 38, 47. **Reinman** a-1, 14, 17. **Robinson** a-7p, 42. **Romita** a-37. **Roussos** a-4, 44. **R.Q. Sale** a-45, 46, 49. **Severin** c-52. **Shores** a-17, 45. **Tuska** a-10, 12, 14. **Whitney** a-2. **Wildey** a-37.*

MYSTERY TALES
1964
Super Comics

Super Reprint #16,17('64): 16-r/Tales of Horror #2. 17-r/Eerie #14(Avon) 1.00 2.50 5.00
Super Reprint #18-Kubert-r/Strange Terrors #4 1.00 2.50 5.00

MYSTIC (3rd Series)
March, 1951 - No. 61, Aug, 1957
Marvel/Atlas Comics (CLDS 1/CSI 2-21/OMC 22-35/CSI 35-61)

1-Atom bomb panels 30.00 90.00 210.00
2 16.00 48.00 110.00
3-Eyes torn out 14.00 43.00 100.00
4-"The Devil Birds" by Wolverton, 6 pgs. 29.00 85.00 200.00
5,7-10 10.00 30.00 70.00
6-"The Eye of Doom" by Wolverton, 7 pgs. 29.00 85.00 200.00
11-20: 16-Bondage/torture c/story 10.00 30.00 65.00
21-25,27-36-Last precode (3/55). 25-E.C. swipe 8.35 25.00 50.00
26-Atomic War, severed head stories 10.00 30.00 60.00
37-51,53-57,61: 57-Story "Trapped in the Ant-Hill" (1957) is very similar to "The Man in the Ant Hill" in TTA #27 6.70 20.00 40.00
52-Wood-a; Crandall-a? 9.15 27.50 55.00
58,59-Krigstein-a 7.50 22.50 45.00
60-Williamson/Mayo-a, 4 pgs. 7.50 22.50 45.00

NOTE: ***Andru** a-23, 25. **Ayers** a-35, 53; c-8. **Berg** a-49. **Cameron** a-49, 51. **Check** a-31, 60. **Colan** a-3, 7, 12, 21, 37, 60. **Colletta** a-29. **Drucker** a-46, 52, 56. **Everett** a-8, 9, 17, 40, 44, 57; c-13, 18, 21, 42, 47, 49, 51-55, 57-59, 61. **Forte** a-35, 52, 58. **Fox** a-24i. **Al Hartley** a-35. **Heath** a-10; c-10, 20, 22, 23, 25, 30. **Infantino** a-12. **Kane** a-8, 24p. **Jack Katz** a-31, 33. **Mort Lawrence** a-19, 37. **Maneely** a-22, 24, 58; c-7, 15, 28, 29, 31. **Moldoff** a-29. **Morisi** a-48, 49, 52. **Morrow** a-51. **Orlando** a-57, 61. **Pakula** a-52, 57, 59. **Powell** a-52, 54-56. **Robinson** a-5. **Romita** a-11, 15. **R.Q. Sale** a-35, 53, 58. **Sekowsky** a-1, 2, 4, 5. **Severin** c-56, 60. **Tuska** a-15. **Whitney** a-33. **Wildey** a-28, 30. **Ed Win** a-17, 20. Canadian reprints known-title 'Startling.'*

MYSTICAL TALES
June, 1956 - No. 8, Aug, 1957
Atlas Comics (CCC 1/EPI 2-8)

1-Everett-c/a 17.00 52.00 120.00
2,4: 2-Berg-a 10.00 30.00 60.00
3,5: 3-Crandall-a. 5-Williamson-a, 4 pgs. 10.00 30.00 65.00
6-Torres, Krigstein-a 9.15 27.50 55.00
7-Bolle, Forte, Torres, Orlando-a 8.35 25.00 50.00
8-Krigstein, Check-a 9.15 27.50 55.00

NOTE: ***Everett** a-1; c-1-4, 6, 7. **Orlando** a-1, 2, 7. **Pakula** a-3. **Powell** a-1, 4.*

MYSTIC COMICS (1st Series)
March, 1940 - No. 10, Aug, 1942
Timely Comics (TPI 1-5/TCI 8-10)

GD25 FN65 VF82 NM94

1-Origin The Blue Blaze, The Dynamic Man, & Flexo the Rubber Man; Zephyr Jones, 3X's & Deep Sea Demon app.; The Magician begins; c-from Spider pulp V18#1, 6/39
690.00 2060.00 3800.00 5500.00
(Estimated up to 110 total copies exist, 4 in NM/Mint)

GD25 FN65 NM94

2-The Invisible Man & Master Mind Excello begin; Space Rangers, Zara of the Jungle, Taxi Taylor app. 233.00 700.00 1400.00
3-Origin Hercules, who last appears in #4 183.00 550.00 1100.00
4-Origin The Thin Man & The Black Widow; Merzak the Mystic app.; last Flexo, Dynamic Man, Invisible Man & Blue Blaze (some issues have date sticker on cover; others have July w/August overprint in silver color); Roosevelt assassination-c 208.00 625.00 1250.00
5-Origin The Black Marvel, The Blazing Skull, The Sub-Earth Man, Super Slave & The Terror; The Moon Man & Black Widow app.
200.00 600.00 1200.00

GD25 FN65 NM94

6-Origin The Challenger & The Destroyer 183.00 550.00 1100.00
7-The Witness begins (origin); origin Davey & the Demon; last Black Widow; Hitler opening Pandora's Box-c by Simon & Kirby
158.00 475.00 950.00
8,9: 9-Gary Gaunt app.; last Black Marvel, Mystic & Blazing Skull; Hitler-c
117.00 350.00 700.00
10-Father Time, World of Wonder, & Red Skeleton app.; last Challenger & Terror 117.00 350.00 700.00

NOTE: ***Gabrielle** c-8-10. **Kirby/Schomburg** c-6. **Rico** a-9(2). **Schomburg** a-1-4; c-1-5. **Sekowsky** a-9. **Sekowsky/Klein** a-8(Challenger). Bondage c-1, 2, 9.*

MYSTIC COMICS (2nd Series)
Oct, 1944 - No. 4, Winter, 1944-45
Timely Comics (ANC)

1-The Angel, The Destroyer, The Human Torch, Terry Vance the Schoolboy Sleuth, & Tommy Tyme begin 105.00 318.00 635.00
2-Last Human Torch & Terry Vance; bondage-hypo-c
63.00 188.00 375.00
3-Last Angel (two stories) & Tommy Tyme 58.00 175.00 350.00
4-The Young Allies app.; Schomburg-a? 53.00 160.00 320.00

MY STORY (...True Romances in Pictures #5,6) (Formerly Zago)
No. 5, May, 1949 - No. 12, Aug, 1950
Hero Books (Fox Features Syndicate)

5-Kamen/Feldstein-a 10.00 30.00 65.00
6-8,11,12: 12-Photo-c 4.70 14.00 28.00
9,10-Wood-a 10.00 30.00 70.00

MY TRUE LOVE (Formerly Western Killers #64; Frank Buck #70 on)
No. 65, July, 1949 - No. 69, March, 1950
Fox Features Syndicate

65 7.00 21.00 42.00
66-69: 69-Morisi-a 5.00 15.00 30.00

NAIVE INTER-DIMENSIONAL COMMANDO KOALAS (Eclipse) (Value: cover or less)

NAKED PREY, THE (See Movie Classics)

'NAM, THE (See Savage Tales #1, 2nd series)
Dec, 1986 - Present
Marvel Comics Group

1-Golden a(p)/c begins, ends #13 1.00 2.50 5.00
1 (2nd printing) .50 1.00
2 .60 1.50 3.00
3-7: 7 Golden-a, 2pgs. .40 1.00 2.00
8-64: 32-Death R. Kennedy. 58-Silver logo .30 .75 1.50
52-Frank Castle (The Punisher) app. .80 2.00 4.00
53-Frank Castle (The Punisher) app. .60 1.50 3.00
52,53-Gold 2nd printings .60 1.25
54-74,76-80: 65-Heath-c/a; begin $1.75-c. 67-69-Punisher 3 part story. 70-Lomax scripts begin .35 .85 1.75
75-($2.25, 52 pgs.) .45 1.10 2.25
Trade Paperback 1-r/#1-4 .90 2.25 4.50
Trade Paperback 2-r/#5-8 1.30 3.25 6.50

'NAM MAGAZINE, THE (Marvel) (Value: value: cover or less)

NAMORA (See Marvel Mystery Comics & Sub-Mariner Comics)
Fall, 1948 - No. 3, Dec, 1948
Marvel Comics (PrPI)

1-Sub-Mariner x-over in Namora; Namora by Everett(2), Sub-Mariner by Rico (10 pgs.) 96.00 288.00 575.00
2-The Blonde Phantom & Sub-Mariner story; Everett-a
83.00 250.00 500.00
3-(Scarce)-Sub-Mariner app.; Everett-a 75.00 225.00 450.00

NAMOR, THE SUB-MARINER (See Prince Namor & Sub-Mariner)
Apr, 1990 - Present ($1.00/$1.25, color)

Marvel Comics

	GD25	FN65	NM94
1-Byrne-c/a/scripts in 1-25 (scripts only #26-32)	.70	1.75	3.50
2-5: 5-Iron Man app.	.40	1.00	2.00
6-11: 8,10,16-Re-intro Iron Fist (8-cameo only)	.30	.75	1.50
12-($1.50, 52 pgs.)-Re-intro. The Invaders	.40	1.00	2.00
13-22: 18-Punisher cameo (1 panel); 21-Wolverine cameo. 22-Last $1.00-c. 23-Wolverine cameo		.50	1.00
23-25: 24-Namor vs. Wolverine		.60	1.25
26-New look for Namor w/new costume; 1st Jae Lee-c/a this title (5/92) & begins	1.60	4.00	8.00
27	1.00	2.50	5.00
28	.80	2.00	4.00
29,30	.50	1.25	2.50
31-36,38: 28-Iron Fist app.		.60	1.25
37-($2.00)-Holo-grafx foil-c	.40	1.00	2.00
Annual 1(1991, $2.00, 68pgs.)-3 pg. origin recap	.40	1.00	2.00
Annual 2(1992, $2.25, 68pgs.)-Return/Defenders	.45	1.15	2.25

NANCY AND SLUGGO (See Comics On Parade & Sparkle Comics)
No. 16, 1949 - No. 23, 1954
United Features Syndicate

	GD25	FN65	NM94
16(#1)	5.85	17.50	35.00
17-23	4.00	10.00	20.00

NANCY & SLUGGO (Nancy #146-173; formerly Sparkler Comics)
No. 121, Apr, 1955 - No. 192, Oct, 1963
St. John/Dell #146-187/Gold Key #188 on

	GD25	FN65	NM94
121(4/55)(St. John)	4.20	12.50	25.00
122-145(7/57)(St. John)	3.60	9.00	18.00
146(9/57)-Peanuts begins, ends #192 (Dell)	4.00	10.00	20.00
147-161 (Dell)	2.80	7.00	14.00
162-165,177-180-John Stanley-a	5.85	17.50	35.00
166-176-Oona & Her Haunted House series; Stanley-a	6.70	20.00	40.00
181-187(3-5/62)(Dell)	2.40	6.00	12.00
188(10/62)-192 (Gold Key)	2.40	6.00	12.00
4-Color 1034(9-11/59)-Summer Camp	2.80	7.00	14.00

(See Dell Giant #34, 45 & Dell Giants)

NANNY AND THE PROFESSOR (TV)
Aug, 1970 - No. 2, Oct, 1970 (Photo-c)
Dell Publishing Co.

	GD25	FN65	NM94
1(01-546-008), 2	4.20	12.50	25.00

NAPOLEON (See 4-Color No. 526)

NAPOLEON & SAMANTHA (See Walt Disney Showcase No. 10)

NAPOLEON & UNCLE ELBY (See Clifford McBride's...)
July, 1942 (68 pages) (One Shot)
Eastern Color Printing Co.

	GD25	FN65	NM94
1	23.00	70.00	140.00
1945-American Book-Strafford Press (128 pgs.) (8x10-1/2"-B&W reprints; hardcover)	12.00	35.00	70.00

NASCUB ADVENTURES, THE (New Image) (Value: cover or less)

NATHANIEL DUSK (DC) (Value: cover or less)

NATHANIEL DUSK II (DC) (Value: cover or less)

NATIONAL COMICS
July, 1940 - No. 75, Nov, 1949
Quality Comics Group

	GD25	FN65	NM94
1-Uncle Sam begins; Origin sidekick Buddy by Eisner; origin Wonder Boy & Kid Dixon; Merlin the Magician (ends #45); Cyclone, Kid Patrol, Sally O'Neil Policewoman, Pen Miller (ends #22), Prop Powers (ends #26), & Paul Bunyan (ends #22) begin	250.00	750.00	1500.00
2	117.00	350.00	700.00
3-Last Eisner Uncle Sam	92.00	275.00	550.00
4-Last Cyclone	67.00	200.00	400.00
5-(11/40)-Quicksilver begins (3rd w/lightning speed?); origin Uncle Sam; bondage-c	83.00	250.00	500.00
6-11: 8-Jack & Jill begins (ends #22). 9-Flag-c	63.00	188.00	375.00
12	46.00	138.00	275.00
13-16-Lou Fine-a	54.00	162.00	325.00
17,19-22	43.00	130.00	260.00
18-(12/41)-Shows orientals attacking Pearl Harbor; on stands one month before actual event	54.00	162.00	325.00
23-The Unknown & Destroyer 171 begin	46.00	138.00	275.00
24-26,28,30: 26-Wonder Boy ends	32.00	95.00	190.00
27-G-2 the Unknown begins (ends #46)	32.00	95.00	190.00
29-Origin The Unknown	32.00	95.00	190.00
31-33: 33-Chic Carter begins (ends #47)	29.00	88.00	175.00
34-40: 35-Last Kid Patrol. 39-Hitler-c	18.00	55.00	110.00
41-50: 42-The Barker begins (1st app?); The Barker covers begin. 48-Origin The Whistler	13.00	40.00	80.00
51-Sally O'Neil by Ward, 8 pgs. (12/45)	18.00	55.00	110.00
52-60	10.00	30.00	60.00
61-67: 67-Format change; Quicksilver app.	7.50	22.50	45.00
68-75: The Barker ends	5.00	15.00	30.00

NOTE: ***Cole*** *Quicksilver-13; Barker-43; c-43, 46, 47, 49, 50, 51.* ***Crandall*** *Uncle Sam-11-13 (with Fine), 25, 26; c-24-26, 30-33, 43.* ***Crandall*** *Paul Bunyan-10-13.* ***Fine*** *Uncle Sam-13 (w/Crandall), 17, 18; c-1-14, 16, 18, 21.* ***Guardineer*** *Quicksilver-27, 35.* ***Gustavson*** *Quicksilver -14-26.* ***McWilliams*** *a-23-28, 55, 57. Uncle Sam c-1-41. The Barker c-42-75.*

NATIONAL CRUMB, THE (Magazine-Size)
August, 1975 (52 pages) (Satire)
Mayfair Publications

	GD25	FN65	NM94
1	1.20	3.00	6.00

NATIONAL VELVET (TV)
May-July, 1961 - No. 2, March, 1963 (All photo-c)
Dell Publishing Co./Gold Key

	GD25	FN65	NM94
4-Color 1195 (#1)	5.85	17.50	35.00
4-Color 1312	4.00	10.00	20.00
01-556-207, 12-556-210 (Dell)	3.60	9.00	18.00
1(12/62), 2(3/63) (Gold Key)	3.60	9.00	18.00

NATION OF SNITCHES
1990 ($4.95, color, 52 pgs.)
Piranha Press (DC)

	GD25	FN65	NM94
nn	1.00	2.50	5.00

NATURE BOY (Formerly Danny Blaze; Li'l Rascal Twins #6 on)
No. 3, March, 1956 - No. 5, Feb, 1957
Charlton Comics

	GD25	FN65	NM94
3-Origin; Blue Beetle story; Buscema-c/a	16.00	48.00	110.00
4,5	12.00	36.00	85.00

NOTE: ***John Buscema*** *a-3, 4p, 5; c-3.* ***Powell*** *a-4.*

NATURE OF THINGS (See 4-Color No. 727, 842)

NAUSICAA OF THE VALLEY OF WIND (Viz) (Value: cover or less)

NAVY ACTION (Sailor Sweeney #12-14)
Aug, 1954 - No. 11, Apr, 1956; No. 15, 1/57 - No. 18, 8/57
Atlas Comics (CDS)

	GD25	FN65	NM94
1-Powell-a	8.35	25.00	50.00
2-Lawrence-a	4.20	12.50	25.00
3-11: 4-Last precode (2/55)	3.00	7.50	15.00
15-18	2.40	6.00	12.00

NOTE: ***Berg*** *a-7, 9.* ***Colan*** *a-8.* ***Drucker*** *a-7, 17.* ***Everett*** *a-3, 7, 16; c-16, 17.* ***Heath*** *c-1, 2, 6.* ***Maneely*** *a-7, 8, 18; c-1, 9, 11.* ***Pakula*** *a-2, 3, 9.* ***Reinman*** *a-17.*

NAVY COMBAT
June, 1955 - No. 20, Oct, 1958
Atlas Comics (MPI)

	GD25	FN65	NM94
1-Torpedo Taylor begins by Don Heck	8.35	25.00	50.00
2	4.20	12.50	25.00
3-10	3.60	9.00	18.00

Nancy and Sluggo #131, © STJ

National Comics #34, © QUA

National Velvet #2, © M.G.M.

Naza #6, © DELL

Negro Romance #1, © FAW

Nellie the Nurse #14, © MEG

	GD25	FN65	NM94
11,13,15,16,18-20	3.00	7.50	15.00
12-Crandall-a	5.00	15.00	30.00
14-Torres-a	4.00	11.00	22.00
17-Williamson-a, 4 pgs.; Torres-a	4.20	12.50	25.00

NOTE: ***Berg** a-10, 11. **Colan** a-11. **Drucker** a-7. **Everett** a-3, 20; c-8 & 9 w/**Tuska**, 10, 13-16. **Heck** a-11(2). **Maneely** c-1, 6, 11, 17. **Morisi** a-8. **Pakula** a-7. **Powell** a-20.*

NAVY HEROES
1945
Almanac Publishing Co.

	GD25	FN65	NM94
1-Heavy in propaganda	6.70	20.00	40.00

NAVY: HISTORY & TRADITION
1958 - 1961 (nn) (Giveaway)
Stokes Walesby Co./Dept. of Navy

	GD25	FN65	NM94
1772-1778, 1778-1782, 1782-1817, 1817-1865, 1865-1936, 1940-1945	4.00	12.00	24.00
1861: Naval Actions of the Civil War: 1865	4.00	12.00	24.00

NAVY PATROL
May, 1955 - No. 4, Nov, 1955
Key Publications

	GD25	FN65	NM94
1	4.00	10.00	20.00
2-4	2.00	5.00	10.00

NAVY TALES
Jan, 1957 - No. 4, July, 1957
Atlas Comics (CDS)

	GD25	FN65	NM94
1-Everett-c; Berg, Powell-a	6.70	20.00	40.00
2-Williamson/Mayo-a(5 pgs); Crandall-a	6.70	20.00	40.00
3,4-Reinman-a; Severin-c. 4-Crandall-a	5.35	16.00	32.00

NOTE: ***Colan** a-4. **Maneely** c-2. **Sinnott** a-4.*

NAVY TASK FORCE
Feb, 1954 - No. 8, April, 1956
Stanmor Publications/Aragon Mag. No. 4-8

	GD25	FN65	NM94
1	4.20	12.50	25.00
2	2.40	6.00	12.00
3-8: #8-r/Navy Patrol #1	1.60	4.00	8.00

NAVY WAR HEROES
Jan, 1964 - No. 7, Mar-Apr, 1965
Charlton Comics

	GD25	FN65	NM94
1	1.20	3.00	6.00
2-7	.60	1.50	2.00

NAZA (Stone Age Warrior)
Nov-Jan, 1963/64 - No. 9, March, 1966
Dell Publishing Co.

	GD25	FN65	NM94
1 (12-555-401)-Painted-c	2.40	6.00	12.00
2-9: 2-4-Painted-c	1.60	4.00	8.00

NAZZ, THE (DC)(Value: cover or less)

NEBBS, THE
1928 (Daily B&W strip reprints; 52 pages)
Cupples & Leon Co.

	GD25	FN65	NM94
nn-By Sol Hess; Carlson-a	11.50	34.00	80.00

NEBBS, THE (Also see Crackajack Funnies)
1941; 1945
Dell Publishing Co./Croydon Publishing Co.

	GD25	FN65	NM94
Large Feature Comic 23(1941)	12.00	36.00	85.00
1(1945, 36 pgs.)-Reprints	8.35	25.00	50.00

NECROMANCER: THE GRAPHIC NOVEL
1989 ($8.95, color)
Epic Comics (Marvel)

	GD25	FN65	NM94
nn	1.80	4.50	9.00

NECROPOLIS (Fleetway/Quality)(Value: cover or less)

NECROSCOPE (Malibu)(Value: cover or less)

NEGRO (See All-Negro)

NEGRO HEROES (Calling All Girls, Real Heroes, & True Comics reprints)
Spring, 1947 - No. 2, Summer, 1948
Parents' Magazine Institute

	GD25	FN65	NM94
1	38.00	115.00	265.00
2-Jackie Robinson story	47.00	140.00	325.00

NEGRO ROMANCE (Negro Romances #4)
June, 1950 - No. 3, Oct, 1950 (All photo-c)
Fawcett Publications

	GD25	FN65	NM94
1-Evans-a	79.00	235.00	550.00
2,3	64.00	195.00	450.00

NEGRO ROMANCES (Formerly Negro Romance; Romantic Secrets #5 on)
No. 4, May, 1955
Charlton Comics

	GD25	FN65	NM94
4-Reprints Fawcett #2	50.00	150.00	350.00

NEIL THE HORSE (Aardvark-Vanaheim/Renegade)(Value: cover or less)

NELLIE THE NURSE (Also see Gay Comics)
1945 - No. 36, Oct, 1952; 1957
Marvel/Atlas Comics (SPI/LMC)

	GD25	FN65	NM94
1	18.00	54.00	125.00
2	10.00	30.00	60.00
3,4	7.50	22.50	45.00
5-Kurtzman's "Hey Look"(3); Georgie app.	9.15	27.50	55.00
6-8,10: 7,8-Georgie app. 10-Millie app.	5.85	17.50	35.00
9-Wolverton-a (1 pg.); Mille the Model app.	6.70	20.00	40.00
11,14-16,18-Kurtzman's "Hey Look"	7.50	22.50	45.00
12-"Giggles 'n' Grins" by Kurtzman	5.85	17.50	35.00
13,17,19,20: 17-Annie Oakley app.	5.00	15.00	30.00
21-27,29,30	4.20	12.50	25.00
28-Kurtzman's Rusty reprint	5.00	15.00	30.00
31-36: 36-Post-c	4.00	10.00	20.00
1('57)-Leading Mag. (Atlas)-Everett-a, 20 pgs	4.35	13.00	26.00

NELLIE THE NURSE (See 4-Color No. 1304)

NEMESIS THE WARLOCK (Eagle)(Value: cover or less)

NEMESIS THE WARLOCK (Fleetway/Quality)(Value: cover or less)

NEUTRO
January, 1967
Dell Publishing Co.

	GD25	FN65	NM94
1-Jack Sparling-c/a (super hero)	3.00	7.50	15.00

NEVADA (See Zane Grey's Stories of the West #1)

NEVER AGAIN (War stories; becomes Soldier & Marine V2#9)
Aug, 1955 - No. 2, Oct?, 1955; No. 8, July, 1956 (No #3-7)
Charlton Comics

	GD25	FN65	NM94
1	5.00	15.00	30.00
2 (Becomes Fightin' Air Force #3), 8(Formerly Foxhole?)	3.00	7.50	15.00

NEW ADVENTURE COMICS (Formerly New Comics; becomes Adventure Comics #32 on)
V1#12, Jan, 1937 - No. 31, Oct, 1938
National Periodical Publications

	GD25	FN65	VF82
V1#12-Federal Men by Siegel & Shuster continues; Jor-L mentioned; Whitney Ellsworth-c begin, end #14	200.00	600.00	1200.00
V2#1(2/37, #13), V2#2 (#14)	142.00	425.00	850.00

	GD25	FN65	NM94
15(V2#3)-20(V2#8): 15-1st Adventure logo; Craig Flessel-c begin, end			

#31. 16-1st Shuster-c; 1st non-funny cover. 17-Nadir, Master of Magic begins, ends #30 142.00 425.00 850.00
21(V2#9),22(V2#10, 2/37): 22-X-Mas-c 117.00 350.00 700.00
23-31 92.00 275.00 550.00

NEW ADVENTURE OF WALT DISNEY'S SNOW WHITE AND THE SEVEN DWARFS, A (See Snow White Bendix Giveaway)

NEW ADVENTURES OF CHARLIE CHAN, THE (TV)
May-June, 1958 - No. 6, Mar-Apr, 1959
National Periodical Publications

1 (Scarce)-Gil Kane/Sid Greene-a in all 50.00 150.00 350.00
2 (Scarce) 32.00 95.00 225.00
3-6 (Scarce)-Greene/Giella-a 25.00 75.00 175.00

NEW ADVENTURES OF CHOLLY AND FLYTRAP: TILL DEATH DO US PART, THE (Epic) (Value: cover or less)

NEW ADVENTURES OF HUCK FINN, THE (TV)
December, 1968 (Hanna-Barbera)
Gold Key

1-"The Curse of Thut;" part photo-c 2.80 7.00 14.00

NEW ADVENTURES OF PETER PAN (Disney)
1953 (36 pgs.; 5x7-1/4") (Admiral giveaway)
Western Publishing Co.

nn 5.85 17.50 35.00

NEW ADVENTURES OF PINOCCHIO (TV)
Oct-Dec, 1962 - No. 3, Sept-Nov, 1963
Dell Publishing Co.

12-562-212(#1) 8.35 25.00 50.00
2,3 6.70 20.00 40.00

NEW ADVENTURES OF ROBIN HOOD (See Robin Hood)

NEW ADVENTURES OF SHERLOCK HOLMES (See 4-Color #1169, 1245)

NEW ADVENTURES OF SUPERBOY, THE (Also see Superboy)
Jan, 1980 - No. 54, June, 1984
DC Comics

1-54: 7-Has extra story "The Computers That Saved Metropolis" by Starlin (Radio Shack giveaway w/indicia) 11-Superboy gets new power. 14-Lex Luthor app. 15-Superboy gets new parents. 28-Dial "H" For Hero begins, ends #49. 45-47-1st app. Sunburst. 48-Begin 75 cent-c. 50-Legion app. .50 1.00

NOTE: ***Buckler** a-9p; c-36p. **Giffen** a-50; c-50. 40i. **Gil Kane** c-32p, 33p, 35, 39, 41-49. **Miller** c-51. **Starlin** a-7. Krypto back-ups in 17, 22. Superbaby in 11, 14, 19, 24.*

NEW ADVENTURES OF THE PHANTOM BLOT, THE (See The Phantom Blot)

NEW AMERICA (Eclipse) (Value: cover or less)

NEW ARCHIES, THE (TV)
Oct, 1987 - No. 22, May, 1990 (75 cents)
Archie Comic Publications

1-16: 3-Xmas issue .50 1.00
17-22 (.95-$1.00): 21-Xmas issue .50 1.00

NEW ARCHIES DIGEST (TV) (...Comics Digest Magazine #4?-10; ... Digest Magazine #11 on)
1988 - No. 14, July, 1991 ($1.35-$1.50, digest size, quarterly)
Archie Comics

1-14: 6-Begin $1.50-c .25 .75 1.50

NEW BOOK OF COMICS (Also see Big Book Of Fun)
1937; No. 2, Spring, 1938 (100 pgs. each) (Reprints)
National Periodical Publ.

GD25 FN65 VF82

1(Rare)-1st regular size comic annual; 2nd DC annual; contains r/New Comics #1-4 & More Fun #9; r/Federal Men (8 pgs.), Henri Duval (1 pg.), & Dr. Occult in costume (1pg.) by Siegel & Shuster; Moldoff, Sheldon Mayer (15 pgs.)-a 700.00 2100.00 3500.00
(Estimated up to 50 total copies exist, none in NM/Mint)

GD25 FN65 NM94

2-Contains-r/More Fun #15 & 16; r/Dr. Occult in costume (a Superman proto-type), & Calling All Cars (4 pgs.) by Siegel & Shuster 370.00 1100.00 2200.00

NEW COMICS (New Adventure #12 on)
12/35 - No. 11, 12/36 (No. 1-6: paper cover) (No. 1-5: 84 pgs.)
National Periodical Publ.

GD25 FN65 VF82

V1#1-Billy the Kid, Sagebrush 'n' Cactus, Jibby Jones, Needles, The Vikings, Sir Loin of Beef, Now-When I Was a Boy, & other 1-2 pg. strips; 2 pgs. Kelly art(1st)-(Gulliver's Travels); Sheldon Mayer-a(1st)(2 2pg. strips); Vincent Sullivan-c 1000.00 3000.00 5000.00
(Estimated up to 50 total copies exist, none in NM/Mint)
2-Federal Men by Siegel & Shuster begins (Also see The Comics Magazine #2); Sheldon Mayer, Kelly-a (Rare) 385.00 1150.00 2300.00
3-6: 3,4-Sheldon Mayer-a which continues in The Comics Magazine #1. 3-Vincent Sullivan-c. 4-Dickens' "A Tale of Two Cities" adaptation begins. 5-Junior Federal Men Club; Kiefer-a. 6-"She" adaptation begins 225.00 675.00 1350.00
7-11: 11-Christmas-c 190.00 575.00 1150.00

NOTE: *#1-6 rarely occur in mint condition. **Whitney Ellsworth** c-4-11.*

NEW DEFENDERS (See Defenders)

NEW DNAGENTS, THE (Eclipse) (Value: cover or less) (Formerly DNAgents)

NEW FUN COMICS (More Fun #7 on; see Big Book of Fun Comics)
Feb, 1935 - No. 6, Oct, 1935 (10x15", No. 1-4,: slick covers)
(No. 1-5: 36 pgs; 40 pgs. No. 6)
National Periodical Publications

GD25 FN65 VF82

V1#1 (1st DC comic); 1st app. Oswald The Rabbit; Jack Woods (cowboy) begins 3400.00 10,200.00 17,000.00
(Estimated up to 10 total copies exist, 1 in VF/NM)
2(3/35)-(Very Rare) 1250.00 3750.00 7500.00
(Estimated up to 5 total copies exist)
3-5(8/35): 3-Don Drake on the Planet Soro-c/story (sci/fi, 4/35). 5-Soft-c 585.00 1750.00 3500.00
6(10/35)-1st Dr. Occult by Siegel & Shuster (Leger & Reuths); last "New Fun" title. "New Comics" #1 begins in Dec. which is reason for title change to More Fun; Henri Duval (ends #9) by Siegel & Shuster begins; paper-c 670.00 2000.00 4000.00
(Estimated up to 10 total copies exist of #3-6)

NEW FUNNIES (The Funnies #1-64; Walter Lantz...#109 on; New TV... #259, 260, 272, 273; TV Funnies #261-271)
No. 65, July, 1942 - No. 288, Mar-Apr, 1962
Dell Publishing Co.

GD25 FN65 NM94

65(#1)-Andy Panda in a world of real people, Raggedy Ann & Andy, Oswald the Rabbit (with Woody Woodpecker x-overs), Li'l Eight Ball & Peter Rabbit begin 47.00 140.00 325.00
66-70: 66-Felix the Cat begins. 67-Billy & Bonnie Bee by Frank Thomas begins. 69-Kelly-a (2 pgs.); The Brownies begin (not by Kelly) 24.00 70.00 165.00
71-75: 72-Kelly illos. 75-Brownies by Kelly? 15.00 45.00 105.00
76-Andy Panda (Carl Barks & Pabian-a); Woody Woodpecker x-over in Oswald ends 57.00 171.00 400.00
77,78: 78-Andy Panda in a world with real people ends 15.00 45.00 105.00
79-81 10.00 30.00 70.00
82-Brownies by Kelly begins; Homer Pigeon begins 11.50 34.00 80.00
83-85-Brownies by Kelly in ea. 83-X-mas-c. 85-Woody Woodpecker, 1pg. strip begins 11.50 34.00 80.00
86-90: 87-Woody Woodpecker stories begin 7.50 22.50 45.00
91-99 4.70 14.00 28.00
100 (6/45) 5.85 17.50 35.00
101-110 4.00 10.00 20.00
111-120: 119-X-mas-c 3.00 7.50 15.00

New Adventure Comics #26, © DC

New Adventures of Superboy #15, © DC

New Fun Comics #5, © DC

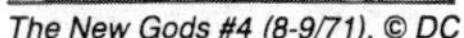
The New Gods #4 (8-9/71), © DC

New Mutants #99, © MEG

New Romances #8, © STD

	GD25	FN65	NM94
121-150: 131,143-X-mas-c	2.40	6.00	12.00
151-200: 155-X-mas-c. 168-X-mas-c. 182-Origin & 1st app. Knothead & Splinter. 191-X-mas-c	1.40	3.50	7.00
201-240	1.20	3.00	6.00
241-288: 270,271-Walter Lantz c-app. 281-1st story swipes/WDC&S #100	1.00	2.50	5.00

NOTE: *Early issues written by* ***John Stanley.***

NEW GODS, THE (New Gods #12 on)(See Adventure #459, 1st Issue Special #13 & Super-Team Family)
2-3/71 - V2#11, 10-11/72; V3#12, 7/77 - V3#19, 7-8/78
National Periodical Publications/DC Comics

	GD25	FN65	NM94
1-Intro/1st app. Orion; 3rd app. Darkseid (cameo; ties w/Forever People #1 as 3rd app.) (#1-3 are 15 cent issues)	4.70	14.00	28.00
2-Darkseid-c/story (2nd full app., 4-5/71)	3.00	7.50	15.00
3-1st app. Black Racer	2.60	6.50	13.00
4-9: (25 cent, 52 pg. giants): 4-Darkseid cameo; origin Manhunter-r. 5,7,8-Young Gods feature. 7-Darkseid app. (2-3/72); origin Orion. 9-1st app. Bug	2.00	5.00	10.00
10,11	1.60	4.00	8.00
12-19: Darkseid storyline w/minor apps. 12-New costume Orion (see 1st Issue Special #13 for 1st new costume)	.60	1.50	3.00

NOTE: *#4-9(25 cents, 52 pgs.) contain Manhunter-r by* ***Simon & Kirby*** *from Adventure #73, 74, 75, 76, 77, 78 with covers in that order.* ***Adkins*** *i-12-14, 17-19.* ***Kirby*** *c/a-1-11p.* ***Newton*** *a(p)-12-14, 16-19.* ***Starlin*** *c-17.* ***Staton*** *c-19p.*

NEW GODS, THE (DC, 1984 & 1989 series)(Value: cover or less)

NEW GUARDIANS, THE (DC)(Value: cover or less)

NEW HEROIC (See Heroic)

NEW JUSTICE MACHINE, THE (Innovation)(Value: cover or less)

NEW KIDS ON THE BLOCK, THE (Harvey)(Value: cover or less)

NEWLYWEDS
1907; 1917 (cardboard covers)
Saalfield Publ. Co.

	GD25	FN65	NM94
...& Their Baby' by McManus; Saalfield, (1907, 13x10," 52 pgs.); daily strips in full color	44.00	132.00	265.00
...& Their Baby's Comic Pictures, The, by McManus, Saalfield, (1917, 14x10," 22 pgs, oblong, cardboard-c); reprints `Newlyweds' (Baby Snookums stips) mainly from 1916; blue cover; says for painting & crayoning, but some pages in color. (Scarce)	37.00	110.00	225.00

NEW MEN OF BATTLE, THE
1949 (nn) (Carboard covers)
Catechetical Guild

	GD25	FN65	NM94
nn(V8#1-3,5,6)-192 pgs.; contains 5 issues of Topix rebound	4.00	10.00	20.00
nn(V8#7-V8#11)-160 pgs.; contains 5 issues of Topix	4.00	10.00	20.00

NEW MUTANTS, THE (See Marvel Graphic Novel #4 for 1st app.)
March, 1983 - No. 100, April, 1991
Marvel Comics Group

	GD25	FN65	NM94
1	1.40	3.50	7.00
2,3: 3,4-Ties into X-Men #167	.80	2.00	4.00
4-10: 10-1st app. Magma	.60	1.50	3.00
11-17,19,20: 13-Kitty Pryde app. 16-1st app. Warpath (w/out costume); see X-Men #193	.50	1.25	2.50
18-Intro. new Warlock	1.60	4.00	8.00
21-Double size; origin new Warlock; newsstand version has cover price written in by Sienkiewicz	1.20	3.00	6.00
22-30: 23-25-Cloak & Dagger app.	.50	1.25	2.50
31-58: 35-Magneto introduced as new headmaster. 50-Double size. 58-Contains pull-out mutant registration form	.40	1.00	2.00
59-Fall of The Mutants begins, ends #61	.70	1.75	3.50
60-($1.25, 52 pgs.)	.50	1.25	2.50
61-Fall of The Mutants ends	.40	1.00	2.00
62,64-72,74-85: 68-Intro Spyder. 76-X-Factor & X-Terminator app. 85-Liefeld-c begin		.60	1.25
63-X-Men & Wolverine clones app.; begin $1.00-c	.70	1.75	3.50
73-($1.50, 52 pgs.)	.40	1.00	2.00
86-Rob Liefeld-a begins; McFarlane-c(i) swiped from Ditko splash pg.; Cable cameo (last page teaser)	3.00	7.50	15.00
87-1st full app. Cable (3/90)	8.35	25.00	50.00
87-2nd printing; gold metallic ink-c ($1.00)	.30	.75	1.50
88-2nd app. Cable	4.00	10.00	20.00
89-3rd app. Cable	3.00	7.50	15.00
90,91: 90-New costumes. 90,91-Sabretooth app.	2.40	6.00	12.00
92-No Liefeld-a; Liefeld-c	1.00	2.50	5.00
93,94-Cable vs. Wolverine	2.40	6.00	15.00
95-97-X-Tinction Agenda x-over. 95-Death of new Warlock. 97-Wolverine & Cable-c, but no app.	2.40	6.00	12.00
95-Gold 2nd printing	.50	1.25	2.50
98-1st app. Deadpool, Gideon & Domino; 2nd Shatterstar (cameo)	2.40	6.00	12.00
99-1st app. of Feral (of X-Force)	1.60	4.00	8.00
100-($1.50, 52 pgs.)-1st app. X-Force (cameo)	1.60	4.00	8.00
100-Gold 2nd printing	.60	1.50	3.00
100-Silver ink 3rd printing	.30	.75	1.50
Annual 1 (1984)	.80	2.00	4.00
Annual 2 (1986, $1.25)	.50	1.25	2.50
Annual 3 (1987, $1.25)	.40	1.00	2.00
Annual 4(1988, $1.75)-Evolutionary War x-over	.50	1.25	2.50
Annual 5(1989, $2.00, 68 pgs.)-Atlantis Attacks; 1st Liefeld-a on New Mutants	3.60	9.00	18.00
Annual 6(1990, $2.00, 68 pgs.)-1st new costumes by Liefeld (3 pgs.); 1st app. (cameo) Shatterstar (of X-Force)	.40	1.00	2.00
Annual 7(1991, $2.00, 68 pgs.)-Liefeld pin-up only; X-Terminators back-up story; 2nd app. X-Force (continued in New Warriors Annual #1)	.40	1.00	2.00
Special 1-Special Edition ('85, 68 pgs.)-ties in with X-Men Alpha Flight mini-series; cont'd in X-Men Annual #9; Art Adams/Austin-a	1.00	2.50	5.00
Summer Special 1(Sum/90, $2.95, 84 pgs.)	.60	1.50	3.00

NOTE: ***Art Adams*** *c-38, 39.* ***Austin*** *c-57i.* ***Byrne*** *c/a-75p.* ***Liefeld*** *a-86-91p, 93-96p, 98-100, Annual 5p, 6(3 pgs.); c-85-91p, 92, 93p, 94, 95, 96p, 97-100, Annual 5, 6p.* ***McFarlane*** *c-85-89i, 93i.* ***Russell*** *a-48i.* ***Sienkiewicz*** *a-18-31, 35-38i; c-18-31, 35, 37.* ***Simonson*** *c-11p.* ***B. Smith*** *c-36, 40-48.* ***Williamson*** *a(i)-69, 71-73, 78-80, 82, 83; c(i)-69, 72, 73, 78i.*

NEW PEOPLE, THE (TV)
Jan, 1970 - No. 2, May, 1970
Dell Publishing Co.

	GD25	FN65	NM94
1,2	2.40	6.00	12.00

NEW ROMANCES
No. 5, May, 1951 - No. 21, Apr?, 1954
Standard Comics

	GD25	FN65	NM94
5	6.70	20.00	40.00
6-9: 6-Barbara Bel Geddes, Richard Basehart "Fourteen Hours." 9-Photo-c from '50s movie	4.00	10.00	20.00
10,14,16,17-Toth-a	7.50	22.50	45.00
11-Toth-a; Liz Taylor, Montgomery Cliff photo-c	9.15	27.50	55.00
12,13,15,18-21	2.80	7.00	14.00

NOTE: ***Celardo*** *a-9.* ***Moreira*** *a-6.* ***Tuska*** *a-7, 20. Photo c-6-16.*

NEW STATESMEN, THE (Fleetway/Quality)(Value: cover or less)

NEWSTRALIA (Innovation)(Value: cover or less)

NEW TALENT SHOWCASE (DC)(Value: cover or less)

NEW TEEN TITANS, THE (See DC Comics Presents 26, Marvel and DC Present & Teen Titans; Tales of the Teen Titans #41 on)
November, 1980 - No. 40, March, 1984
DC Comics

1-Robin, Kid Flash, Wonder Girl, The Changeling, Starfire, The Raven, Cyborg begin; partial origin 2.00 5.00 10.00
2-1st app. Deathstroke the Terminator 2.80 7.00 14.00
3-9: 3-Origin Starfire; Intro The Fearsome. 4-Origin continues; J.L.A. app. 6-Origin Raven. 7-Cyborg origin. 8-Origin Kid Flash retold. 9-Minor cameo Deathstroke on last pg. .80 2.00 4.00
10-2nd app. Deathstroke the Terminator; origin Changeling retold 2.00 5.00 10.00
11-20: 13-Return of Madame Rouge & Capt. Zahl; Robotman revived. 14-Return of Mento; origin Doom Patrol. 15-Death of Madame Rouge & Capt. Zahl; intro. new Brotherhood of Evil 16-1st app. Capt. Carrot (free 16 pg. preview). 18-Return of Starfire. 19-Hawkman teams-up .30 .75 1.50
21-30: 21-Intro Night Force in free 16 pg. insert; intro Brother Blood. 23-1st app. Vigilante (not in costume), & Blackfire. 24-Omega Men app. 25-Omega Men cameo; free 16 pg. preview Masters of the Universe. 26-1st Terra. 27-Free 16 pg. preview Atari Force. 29-The New Brotherhood of Evil & Speedy app. 30-Terra joins the Titans .60 1.20
31-33,35-38,40: 38-Origin Wonder Girl .50 1.00
34-3rd app. Deathstroke the Terminator 1.00 2.50 5.00
39-Last Dick Grayson as Robin; Kid Flash quits .40 1.00 2.00
Annual 1(11/82)-Omega Men app. .25 .70 1.40
Annual V2#2(9/83)-1st app. Vigilante in costume .35 .90 1.75
Annual 3 (See Tales of the Teen Titans Annual #3)
nn(11/83-Keebler Co. Giveaway)-In cooperation with "The President's Drug Awareness Campaign" .60 1.20
nn-(re-issue of above on Mando paper for direct sales market); American Soft Drink Ind. version; I.B.M. Corp. version .50 1.00

NOTE: ***Perez** a-1-4p, 6-34p, 37-40p, Annual 1p, 2p; c-1-12, 13-17p, 18-21, 22p, 23p, 24-37, 38, 39(painted), 40, Annual 1, 2.*

NEW TEEN TITANS, THE (Becomes The New Titans #50 on)
Aug, 1984 - No. 49, Nov, 1988 ($1.25-$1.75; deluxe format)
DC Comics

1-New storyline; Perez-c/a begins .80 2.00 4.00
2,3: 2-Re-intro Lilith .55 1.40 2.80
4-10: 5-Death of Trigon. 7-9-Origin Lilith. 8-Intro Kole. 10-Kole joins .35 .90 1.80
11-19: 13,14-Crisis x-over .60 1.20
20-Robin (Jason Todd) joins; original Teen Titans return .40 1.00 2.00
21-49: 37-Begin $1.75-c. 38-Infinity, Inc. x-over. 47-Origin all Titans .30 .70 1.40
Annual 1 (9/85)-Intro. Vanguard .40 1.00 2.00
Annual 2 (8/86; $2.50): Byrne c/a(p); origin Brother Blood; intro new Dr. Light .50 1.25 2.50
Annual 3 (11/87)-Intro. Danny Chase .30 1.00 2.00
Annual 4 ('88, $2.50)-Perez-c .45 1.15 2.25

NOTE: ***Orlando** c-33p. **Perez** a-1-5; c-1-6, 19-23, 43. **Steacy** c-47.*

NEW TERRYTOONS (TV)
6-8/60 - No. 8, 3-5/62; 10/62 - No. 54, 1/79
Dell Publishing Co./Gold Key

1(1960-Dell)-Deputy Dawg, Dinky Duck & Hashimoto San begin 4.20 12.50 25.00
2-8(1962) 2.80 7.00 14.00
1(30010-210)(10/62-Gold Key, 84 pgs.)-Heckle & Jeckle begins 6.70 20.00 40.00
2(30010-301)-84 pgs. 5.85 17.50 35.00
3-10 2.00 5.00 10.00
11-20 1.00 2.50 5.00
21-30 .60 1.50 3.00
31-54 .40 1.00 2.00

NOTE: *Reprints: #4-12, 38, 40, 47. (See March of Comics #379, 393, 412, 435)*

NEW TESTAMENT STORIES VISUALIZED
1946 - 1947
Standard Publishing Co.

"New Testament Heroes–Acts of Apostles Visualized, Book I"
"New Testament Heroes–Acts of Apostles Visualized, Book II"
"Parables Jesus Told" Set.... 10.00 30.00 60.00

NOTE: *All three are contained in a cardboard case, illustrated on front and info about the set.*

NEW TITANS, THE (Formerly The New Teen Titans)
No. 50, Dec, 1988 - Present ($1.75, color)
DC Comics

50-Perez-c/a begins; new origin Wonder Girl .90 2.25 4.50
51-59: 50-55-Painted-c. 55-Nightwing (Dick Grayson) forces Danny Chase to resign; Batman app. in flashback .50 1.25 2.50
60-A Lonely Place of Dying Part 2 continues from Batman #440; new Robin tie-in; Timothy Drake app. 1.30 3.25 6.50
61-A Lonely Place of Dying Part 4 .80 2.00 4.00
62-65: Deathstroke the Terminator app. 65-Timothy Drake (Robin) app. 1.00 2.50 5.00
66-69,71: 71-(44 pgs.)-10th anniversary issue; Deathstroke cameo .60 1.50 3.00
70-1st Deathstroke solo cover/story .70 1.75 3.50
72-79: Deathstroke in all. 74-Intro. Pantha. 79-Terra brought back to life .60 1.50 3.00
80-98: Deathstroke in #80-84,86. 80-2nd app. Team Titans. 83,84-Deathstroke kills his son, Jericho. 85-Team Titans app. 86-Deathstroke vs. Nightwing-c/story; last Deathstroke app. 87-New costume Nightwing. 90-92-Parts 2,5,8 Total Chaos (Team Titans) .35 .90 1.75
Annual 5,6 (1989, 1990, $3.50, 68 pgs.) .70 1.75 3.50
Annual 7 (1991, $3.50, 68 pgs.)-Armaggedon 2001 x-over; 1st app. Teen (Team) Titans (new group) .70 1.75 3.50
Annual 8 (1992, $3.50, 68 pgs.)-Deathstroke app.; Eclipso app. (minor) .70 1.75 3.50

NOTE: ***Perez** a-50-55p, 57-60p, 61(layouts); c-50-61, 62-67i, Annual 5i; co-plots-66.*

NEW TV FUNNIES (See New Funnies)

NEW WARRIORS, THE (See Thor #411,412)
July, 1990 - Present ($1.00/$1.25, color)
Marvel Comics

1-Williamson-i; Bagley-c/a(p) in 1-13, Annual 1 4.00 10.00 20.00
1-Gold 2nd printing (7/91) .60 1.50 3.00
2-Williamson-c/a(i) 2.40 6.00 12.00
3: 1,3-Guice-c(i) 1.60 4.00 8.00
4,5 1.30 3.25 6.50
6,7,10: 7-Punisher cameo (last pg.) .80 2.00 4.00
8,9-Punisher app. 1.20 3.00 6.00
11-14: 14-Darkhawk & Namor x-over .50 1.25 2.50
15-19: 17-Fantastic Four & Silver Surfer x-over. 19-Gideon (of X-Force) app.; last $1.00-c .30 .75 1.50
20-24,26-36: 28-Intro Turbo & Cardinal .60 1.25
25-($2.50, 52 pgs.)-Die-cut cover .50 1.25 2.50
Annual 1 (1991, $2.00, 68 pgs.)-Origins all members; 3rd app. X-Force (cont'd from New Mutants Annual #7 & cont'd in X-Men Annual #15); x-over before X-Force #1 .90 2.25 4.50
Annual 2 (1992, $2.25, 68 pgs.) .45 1.15 2.25

NEW WAVE, THE (Eclipse)(Value: cover or less)

NEW WORLD (See Comic Books, series I)

NEW YORK GIANTS (See Thrilling True Story of the Baseball Giants)

NEW YORK STATE JOINT LEGISLATIVE COMMITTEE TO STUDY THE PUBLICATION OF COMICS, THE
1951, 1955
N.Y. State Legislative Document

This document was referenced by Wertham for **Seduction of the Innocent.** Contains numerous repros from comics showing violence, sadism, torture, and sex.
1955 version (196p, No. 37, 2/23/55)-Sold for $180 in 1986.

NEW YORK WORLD'S FAIR (Also see Big Book of Fun & New Book of Fun)
1939, 1940 (100pgs.; cardboard covers) (DC's 4th & 5th annuals)
National Periodical Publ. GD25 FN65 VF82 NM94

New Teen Titans #21, (1st series) © DC

The New Titans #56, © DC

The New Warriors #6, © MEG

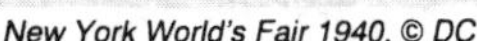

New York World's Fair 1940, © DC

Nickel Comics #7, © FAW

Nick Fury, Agent of Shield #7 (12/68), © MEG

	GD25	FN65	NM94
1939-Scoop Scanlon, Superman (blonde haired Superman on-c), Sandman, Zatara, Slam Bradley, Ginger Snap by Bob Kane begin; 1st published app. The Sandman (see Adventure #40 for his 1st drawn story)	1060.00 3190.00	5830.00	8500.00
(Estimated up to 110 total copies exist, 4 in NM/Mint)			
1940-Batman, Hourman, Johnny Thunderbolt, Red, White & Blue & Hanko (by Craig Flessel) app.; Superman, Batman & Robin-c (1st time they all appear together); early Robin app.; 1st Burnley-c/a (per Burnley)	625.00 1900.00	3400.00	5000.00

NOTE: *The 1939 edition was published 4/30/39, the day the fair opened, at 25 cents, and was first sold only at the fair. Since all other comics were 10 cents, it didn't sell. Remaining copies were advertised beginning in the August issues of most DC comics for 25 cents, but soon the price was dropped to 15 cents. Everyone that sent a quarter through the mail for it received a free Superman #1 or a #2 to make up the dime difference. 15 cent stickers were placed over the 25 cent price. Four variations on the 15 cent stickers are known. The 1940 edition was priced at 15 cents.*

NEW YORK: YEAR ZERO (Eclipse)(Value: cover or less)

NEXT MAN (Comico)(Value: cover or less)

NEXT MEN (See John Byrne's...)

NEXT NEXUS, THE (First)(Value: cover or less)

NEXUS (See First Comics Graphic Novel #4, 19 & The Next Nexus)
June, 1981 - No. 6, Mar, 1984; No. 7, Apr, 1985 - No. 80?, May, 1991
(Direct sale only, 36 pgs.; V2#1('83)-printed on Baxter paper
Capital Comics/First Comics No. 7 on

	GD25	FN65	NM94
1-B&W version; mag. size; w/double size poster	2.40	6.00	12.00
1-B&W 1981 limited edition; 500 copies printed and signed; same as above except this version has a 2-pg. poster & a pencil sketch on paperboard by Rude	3.60	9.00	18.00
2-B&W, magazine size	1.40	3.50	7.00
3-B&W, magazine size; contains 33-1/3 rpm record ($2.95 price)	.80	2.00	4.00
V2#1-Color version	.60	1.50	3.00
2-80: 2-Nexus' origin begins. 50-($3.50, 52 pgs.). 73-Begin $2.25-c	.40	1.00	2.00

NOTE: ***Bissette** c-29. **Rude** c-3(B&W), V2#1-22, 24-27, 33-36, 39-42, 45-48, 50, 58-60; a-1-3, V2#1-7, 8-16p, 18-22p, 24-27p, 33-36p, 39-42p, 45-48p, 50, 58, 59p, 60. **Paul Smith** a-37, 38, 43, 44, 51-55p; c-37, 38, 43, 44, 51-55.*

NEXUS FILES (First)(Value: cover or less)

NEXUS LEGENDS (First)(Value: cover or less)

NEXUS THE LIBERATOR (Dark Horse)(Value: cover or less)

NEXUS: THE ORIGIN (Dark Horse)(Value: cover or less)

NFL SUPERPRO (Marvel)(Value: cover or less)

NICKEL COMICS
1938 (Pocket size - 7-1/2x5-1/2")(132 pgs.)
Dell Publishing Co.

	GD25	FN65	NM94
1-"Bobby & Chip" by Otto Messmer, Felix the Cat artist. Contains some English reprints	47.00	140.00	275.00

NICKEL COMICS
May, 1940 - No. 8, Aug, 1940 (36 pgs.; Bi-Weekly; 5 cents)
Fawcett Publications

	GD25	FN65	NM94
1-Origin/1st app. Bulletman	150.00	450.00	900.00
2	70.00	210.00	425.00
3	58.00	175.00	350.00
4-The Red Gaucho begins	54.00	162.00	325.00
5-8: 8-World's Fair-c; Bulletman moved to Master Comics #7 in Oct.	50.00	150.00	300.00

NOTE: ***Beck** c-5-8. **Jack Binder** c-1-4. Bondage c-5.*

NICK FURY, AGENT OF SHIELD (See Marvel Spotlight #31 & Shield)
6/68 - No. 15, 11/69; No. 16, 11/70 - No. 18, 3/71
Marvel Comics Group

	GD25	FN65	NM94
1	6.70	20.00	40.00
2-4: 4-Origin retold	4.00	10.00	20.00
5-Classic-c	4.00	12.00	24.00
6,7	1.10	5.50	11.00
8-11,13: 9-Hate Monger begins (ends #11). 11-Smith-c. 13-1st app. Super-Patriot; last 12 cent issue	1.20	3.00	6.00
12-Smith-c/a	1.60	4.00	8.00
14-Begin 15 cent-c	.70	1.75	3.50
15-1st app. & death of Bullseye-c/story(11/69)	4.20	12.50	25.00
16-18-(25 cents, 52 pgs.)-r/Str. Tales #135-143	.40	1.00	2.00

NOTE: ***Adkins** a-3i. **Craig** a-10i. **Sid Greene** a-12i. **Kirby** a-16-18r. **Springer** a-4, 6, 7, 8p, 9, 10p, 11; c-8, 9. **Steranko** a(p)-1-3, 5; c-1-7.*

NICK FURY AGENT OF SHIELD (Also see Strange Tales #135)
Dec, 1983 - No. 2, Jan, 1984 ($2.00, Baxter paper, 52 pgs.)
Marvel Comics Group

	GD25	FN65	NM94
1,2-r/Nick Fury #1-4; new Steranko-c	.40	1.00	2.00

NICK FURY, AGENT OF S.H.I.E.L.D.
Sept, 1989 - Present ($1.50/$1.75, color)
Marvel Comics

	GD25	FN65	NM94
V2#1-26: 10-Capt. America app. 13-Return of The Yellow Claw. 15-Fantastic Four app.	.30	.75	1.50
27-29-Wolverine-c/stories	.40	1.00	2.00
30-42: 30,31-Deathlok app. 32-Begin $1.75-c. 36-Cage app. 37-Woodgod c/story. 38-41-Flashes back to pre-Shield days after WWII	.35	.90	1.75

NOTE: ***Alan Grant** scripts-11. **Guice** a(p)-20-23, 25, 26; c-20-28.*

NICK FURY VS. S.H.I.E.L.D.
June, 1988 - No. 6, Nov, 1988 ($3.50, 52pgs, color, deluxe format)
Marvel Comics

	GD25	FN65	NM94
1-Steranko-c	1.40	3.50	7.00
2-(Low print run) Sienkiewicz-c	1.60	4.00	8.00
3-6	.70	1.75	3.50

NICK HALIDAY
May, 1956
Argo

	GD25	FN65	NM94
1-Daily & Sunday strip-r by Petree	5.35	16.00	32.00

NIGHT AND THE ENEMY (Graphic Novel)
1988 (8-1/2x11") ($11.95, color, 80pgs.)
Comico

	GD25	FN65	NM94
1-Harlan Ellison scripts/Ken Steacy-c/a; r/Epic Illustrated & new-a (1st and 2nd printings)	2.40	6.00	12.00
1-Limited edition ($39.95)	6.70	20.00	40.00

NIGHT BEFORE CHRISTMAS, THE (See March of Comics No. 152)

NIGHTBREED (See Clive Barker's Nightbreed)

NIGHTCAT (Marvel)(Value: cover or less)

NIGHTCRAWLER
Nov, 1985 - No. 4, Feb, 1986 (Mini-series from X-Men)
Marvel Comics Group

	GD25	FN65	NM94
1-Cockrum-c/a	.50	1.25	2.50
2-4	.35	.90	1.75

NIGHT FORCE, THE (See New Teen Titans #21)
Aug, 1982, No. 14, Sept, 1983 (60 cents)
DC Comics

	GD25	FN65	NM94
1-14: 13-Origin The Baron. 14-Nudity panels		.50	1.00

NOTE: ***Colan** c/a-1-14p. **Giordano** c-1i, 2i, 4i, 5i, 7i, 12i.*

NIGHTINGALE, THE
1948 (14 pgs., 7¹/4x10¹/4", B&W) (10 cents)
Henry H. Stansbury Once-Upon-A-Time Press, Inc.

(Very Rare)-Low distribution; distributed to Westchester County & Bronx, N.Y. only; used in **Seduction of the Innocent**, pg. 312,313 as the 1st and only "good" comic book ever published. Ill. by Dong Kingman; 1,500 words of text, printed on high quality paper & no word balloons. Copyright registered 10/22/48, distributed week of 12/5/48. (By Hans Christian Andersen) Estimated value. $200

NIGHTMARE
Summer, 1952 - No. 2, Fall, 1952; No. 3,4, 1953 (Painted-c)
Ziff-Davis (Approved Comics)/St. John No. 3,4

	GD25	FN65	NM94
1-1pg. Kinstler-a; Tuska-a(2)	24.00	70.00	165.00
2-Kinstler-a-Poe's "Pit & the Pendulum"	17.00	52.00	120.00
3-Kinstler-a	13.00	40.00	90.00
4-Exist?	11.00	32.00	75.00

NIGHTMARE (Weird Horrors #1-9) (Amazing Ghost Stories #14 on)
No. 10, Dec, 1953 - No. 13, Aug, 1954
St. John Publishing Co.

	GD25	FN65	NM94
10-Reprints Ziff-Davis Weird Thrillers #2 w/new Kubert-c plus 2 pgs. Kinstler-a; Anderson, Colan & Toth-a	24.00	73.00	170.00
11-Krigstein-a; Poe adapt., "Hop Frog"	17.00	52.00	120.00
12-Kubert bondage-c; adaptation of Poe's "The Black Cat;" Cannibalism story	14.00	43.00	100.00
13-Reprints Z-D Weird Thrillers #3 with new cover; Powell-a(2), Tuska-a; Baker-c	10.00	30.00	60.00

NIGHTMARE (Magazine)
Dec, 1970 - No. 23, Feb, 1975 (B&W, 68 pages)
Skywald Publishing Corp.

	GD25	FN65	NM94
1-Everett-a	3.00	7.50	15.00
2-5: 4-Decapitation story	1.40	3.50	7.00
6-Kaluta-a; Jeff Jones photo & interview	1.60	4.00	8.00
7,9,10	1.20	3.00	6.00
8-Features E. C. movie "Tales From the Crypt;" reprints some E.C. comics panels	2.00	5.00	10.00
11-23: 12-Excessive gore, severed heads. 20-Byrne's 1st artwork (8/74); severed head-c. 21-(1974 Summer Special)-Kaluta-a. 22-Tomb of Horror issue. 23-(1975 Winter Special)	.70	1.75	3.50
Annual 1(1972)-B. Jones-a	1.00	2.50	5.00
Winter Special 1(1973)	1.00	2.50	5.00
Yearbook-nn(1974)	1.00	2.50	5.00

NOTE: ***Adkins** a-5. **Boris** c-2, 3, 5 (#4 is not by Boris). **Byrne** a-20p. **Everett** a-4, 5. **Jeff Jones** a-6, 21r(Psycho #6); c-6. **Katz** a-5. **Reese** a-4, 5. **Wildey** a-5, 6, 21, '74 Yearbook. **Wrightson** a-9.*

NIGHTMARE (Alex Nino's...) (Innovation) (Value: cover or less)

NIGHTMARE & CASPER (See Harvey Hits #71) (Casper & Nightmare #6 on) (See Casper The Friendly Ghost #19)
Aug, 1963 - No. 5, Aug, 1964 (25 cents)
Harvey Publications

	GD25	FN65	NM94
1-All reprints?	5.35	16.00	32.00
2-5: All reprints?	2.80	7.00	14.00

NIGHTMARE ON ELM STREET, A (See Freddy Krueger's...)

NIGHTMARE ON ELM STREET: THE BEGINNING, A (Innovation) (Value: cover or less)

NIGHTMARES (See Do You Believe in Nightmares)

NIGHTMARES (Eclipse) (Value: cover or less)

NIGHTMARES ON ELM STREET (Innovation) (Value: cover or less)

NIGHTMASK (Marvel) (Value: cover or less)

NIGHT MASTER (Silverwolf) (Value: cover or less)

NIGHT MUSIC (Eclipse) (Value: cover or less)

NIGHT NURSE
Nov, 1972 - No. 4, May, 1973
Marvel Comics Group

	GD25	FN65	NM94
1-4	.40	1.00	2.00

NIGHT OF MYSTERY
1953 (no month) (One Shot)
Avon Periodicals

	GD25	FN65	NM94
nn-1pg. Kinstler-a, Hollingsworth-c	19.00	57.00	130.00

NIGHT OF THE GRIZZLY, THE (See Movie Classics)

NIGHTRAVEN: THE COLLECTED STORIES
1990 ($9.95, color, graphic novel)
Marvel Comics UK, Ltd.

	GD25	FN65	NM94
nn-Bolton-a; David Lloyd-c/a	2.00	5.00	10.00

NIGHT RIDER
Oct, 1974 - No. 6, Aug, 1975 (Western)
Marvel Comics Group

	GD25	FN65	NM94
1: 1-6 reprint Ghost Rider #1-6 (#1-origin)	.40	1.00	2.00
2-6		.60	1.25

NIGHTSTALKERS
Nov, 1992 - Present ($1.75, color)
Marvel Comics

	GD25	FN65	NM94
1-($2.75, 52 pgs.)-Polybagged w/poster; part 5 of Rise of the Midnight Sons storyline; Garney/Palmer-c/a begins	.60	1.50	3.00
2-8: 5-Punisher app.	.35	.90	1.75

NIGHT THRASHER: FOUR CONTROL (See The New Warriors)
Oct, 1992 - No. 4, Jan, 1993 ($2.00, color, mini-series)
Marvel Comics

	GD25	FN65	NM94
1-Hero from New Warriors	.50	1.25	2.50
2-4: 2-Intro Tantrum. 3-Gideon (of X-Force) app.	.40	1.00	2.00

NIGHTVEIL (Americomics) (Value: cover or less)

NIGHTWINGS (See DC Science Fiction Graphic Novel)

NIKKI, WILD DOG OF THE NORTH (See 4-Color 1226 & Movie Comics)

NINE LIVES OF FELIX THE CAT, THE (Harvey) (Value: cover or less)

1984 (Magazine) (1994 #11 on)
June, 1978 - No. 10, Jan, 1980 ($1.50)
Warren Publishing Co.

	GD25	FN65	NM94
1-Nino-a in all	.60	1.50	3.00
2-10	.35	.90	1.80

NOTE: ***Alacla** a-1-3, 5i. **Corben** a-1-8; c-1, 2. **Thorne** a-7-10. **Wood** a-1, 2, 5i.*

1994 (Formerly 1984) (Magazine)
No. 11, Feb, 1980 - No. 29, Feb, 1983
Warren Publishing Co.

	GD25	FN65	NM94
11-29: 27-The Warhawks return	.40	1.00	2.00

NOTE: ***Corben** c-26. **Nino** a-11-19, 20(2), 21, 25, 26, 28; c-21. **Redondo** c-20. **Thorne** a-11-14, 17-21, 25, 26, 28, 29.*

NINJA HIGH SCHOOL IN COLOR (Eternity) (Value: cover or less)

NINJA HIGH SCHOOL: THE PROM FORMULA (Eternity) (Value: cover or less)

NINTENDO COMICS SYSTEM (Valiant) (Value: cover or less)

NIPPY'S POP
1917 (Sunday strip reprints-B&W) (10-1/2x13-1/2")
The Saalfield Publishing Co.

	GD25	FN65	NM94
nn-32 pages	11.00	32.00	75.00

NOAH'S ARK (Spire Christian) (Value: cover or less)

NOMAD (See Captain America #180)
Nov, 1990 - No. 4, Feb, 1991 ($1.50, color)
Marvel Comics

	GD25	FN65	NM94
1: 1,4-Captain America app.	.50	1.25	2.50
2-4	.40	1.00	2.00

NOMAD
V2#1, May, 1992 - Present ($1.75, color)
Marvel Comics

	GD25	FN65	NM94
V2#1-($2.00)-Has gatefold-c w/map/wanted poster	.60	1.50	3.00
2-5: 5-Punisher vs. Nomad-c/story.	.40	1.00	2.00

6-14: 6-Punisher & Daredevil-c/story cont'd in Punisher War Journal #48.

Nightmare #2, © Z-D

Night Rider #2, © MEG

Nomad #2 (12/90), © MEG

Noman #1, © Tower Comics

Nova #22, © MEG

Nuts! #1, © PG

	GD25	FN65	NM94
7-Gambit-c/story. 10-Red Wolf app.	.35	.90	1.75

NOMAN (See Thunder Agents)
Nov, 1966 - No. 2, March, 1967 (25 cents, 68 pgs.)
Tower Comics

1-Wood/Williamson-c; Lightning begins; Dynamo cameo; Kane-a(p) & Whitney-a	5.85	17.50	35.00
2-Wood-c only; Dynamo x-over; Whitney-a	4.00	12.00	24.00

NONE BUT THE BRAVE (See Movie Classics)

NOODNIK COMICS (See Pinky the Egghead)
1953; No. 2, Feb, 1954 - No. 5, Aug, 1954
Comic Media/Mystery/Biltmore

3-D(1953-Comic Media)(#1)	27.00	80.00	185.00
2-5	4.70	14.00	28.00

NORMALMAN (Renegade)(Value: cover or less)

NORTH AVENUE IRREGULARS (See Walt Disney Showcase #49)

NORTH TO ALASKA (See 4-Color No. 1155)

NORTHWEST MOUNTIES (Also see Approved Comics #12)
Oct, 1948 - No. 4, July, 1949
Jubilee Publications/St. John

1-Rose of the Yukon by Matt Baker; Walter Johnson-a; Lubbers-c	19.00	57.00	135.00
2-Baker-a; Lubbers-c. Ventrilo app.	13.50	41.00	95.00
3-Bondage-c, Baker-a; Sky Chief, K-9 app.	14.00	43.00	100.00
4-Baker-c, 2 pgs.; Blue Monk & The Desperado app.	14.00	43.00	100.00

NOSFERATU (Dark Horse)(Value: cover or less)

NOSFERATU, PLAGUE OF TERROR (Millennium)(Value: cover or less)

NO SLEEP 'TIL DAWN (See 4-Color #831)

NOT BRAND ECHH (Brand Echh #1-4; See Crazy, 1973)
Aug, 1967 - No. 13, May, 1969 (No. 9-13: 25 cents, 68 pages)
Marvel Comics Group (LMC)

1: 1-8 are 12 cent issues	4.20	12.50	25.00
2-4: 3-Origin Thor, Hulk & Capt. America; Monkees, Alfred E. Neuman cameo. 4-X-Men app.	2.40	6.00	12.00
5-8: 5-Origin/intro. Forbush Man. 7-Origin Fantastical-4 & Stuporman. 8-Beatles cameo; X-Men satire	2.40	6.00	12.00
9-13-All Giants. 9-Beatles cameo. 10-All-r; The Old Witch, Crypt Keeper & Vault Keeper cameos. 12,13-Beatles cameo	2.80	7.00	14.00

NOTE: ***Colan** a-4p, 5p, 8p. **Everett** a-1i. **Kirby** a(p)-1, 3, 5-7, 10; c-1. **Severin** a-1; c-3, 7, 8. **Sutton** a-4, 5i, 7i, 8; c-5. Archie satire in #9. Avengers satire in #8, 12.*

NOTHING CAN STOP THE JUGGERNAUT (Marvel)(Value: cover or less)

NO TIME FOR SERGEANTS (TV)
No. 914, July, 1958; Feb-Apr, 1965 - No. 3, Aug-Oct, 1965
Dell Publishing Co.

4-Color 914 (Movie)-Toth-a	9.15	27.50	55.00
1(2-4/65)-3 (TV): Photo-c	4.00	11.00	22.00

NOVA (The Man Called... No. 22-25)
Sept, 1976 - No. 25, May, 1979
Marvel Comics Group

1-Origin/1st app. Nova	1.40	3.50	7.00
2-11: 4-Thor x-over	.70	1.75	3.50
12-Spider-Man x-over	1.00	2.50	5.00
13-25: 13-Intro Crime-Buster. 14-Last 30 cent issue. 18-Yellow Claw app.	.40	1.00	2.00

NOTE: ***Austin** c-21i, 23i. **John Buscema** a(p)-1-3, 8, 21; c-1p, 2, 15. **Infantino** a(p)-15-20, 22-25; c-17-20, 21p, 23p, 24p. **Kirby** c-4p, 5, 7. **Nebres** c-25i. **Simonson** a-23i.*

NOW AGE ILLUSTRATED (See Pendulum Illustrated Classics)

NTH MAN THE ULTIMATE NINJA (See Marvel Comics Presents 25)
Aug, 1989 - No. 16, Sept, 1990 ($1.00, color)
Marvel Comics

	GD25	FN65	NM94
1-7,9-16-Ninja mercenary		.50	1.00
8-Dale Keown's 1st Marvel work (1/90, pencils)	1.00	2.50	5.00

NUCLEUS (Also see Cerebus)
May, 1979 ($1.50, B&W, adult fanzine)
Heiro-Graphic Publications

1-Contains "Demonhorn" by Dave Sim; early app. of Cerebus The Aardvark (4 pg. story)	4.20	12.50	25.00

NUKLA
Oct-Dec, 1965 - No. 4, Sept, 1966
Dell Publishing Co.

1-Origin Nukla (super hero)	3.60	9.00	18.00
2,3	2.00	5.00	10.00
4-Ditko-a, c(p)	4.00	10.00	20.00

NURSE BETSY CRANE (Formerly Teen Secret Diary)
V2#12, Aug, 1961 - V2#27, Mar, 1964 (See Soap Opera Romances)
Charlton Comics

V2#12-27	.80	2.00	4.00

NURSE HELEN GRANT (See The Romances of...)

NURSE LINDA LARK (See Linda Lark)

NURSERY RHYMES
No. 2, 1950 - No. 10, July-Aug, 1951 (Painted-c)
Ziff-Davis Publ. Co. (Approved Comics)

2	10.00	30.00	65.00
3-10: 10-Howie Post-a	7.50	22.50	45.00

NURSES, THE (TV)
April, 1963 - No. 3, Oct, 1963 (Photo-c: #1,2)
Gold Key

1	3.00	7.50	15.00
2,3	2.00	5.00	10.00

NUTS! (Satire)
March, 1954 - No. 5, Nov, 1954
Premiere Comics Group

1-Hollingsworth-a	14.00	43.00	100.00
2,4,5: 5-Capt. Marvel parody	10.00	30.00	70.00
3-Drug "reefers" mentioned	11.00	32.00	75.00

NUTS (Magazine) (Satire)
Feb, 1958 - No. 2, April, 1958
Health Knowledge

1	4.70	14.00	28.00
2	4.00	11.00	22.00

NUTS & JOLTS (See Large Feature Comic #22)

NUTSY SQUIRREL (Formerly Hollywood Funny Folks)(Also see Comic Cavalcade)
#61, 9-10/54 - #69, 1-2/56; #70, 8-9/56 - #71, 10-11/56; #72, 11/57
National Periodical Publications

61-Mayer-a; Grossman-a in all	9.15	27.50	55.00
62-72: Mayer a-62,65,67-72	5.85	17.50	35.00

NUTTY COMICS
Winter, 1946 (Funny animal)
Fawcett Publications

1-Capt. Kidd story; 1 pg. Wolverton-a	10.00	30.00	60.00

NUTTY COMICS
1945 - No. 8, June-July, 1947
Home Comics (Harvey Publications)

	GD25	FN65	NM94
nn-Helpful Hank, Bozo Bear & others	4.35	13.00	26.00
2-4	3.60	9.00	18.00
5-8: 5-Rags Rabbit begins(1st app.); infinity-c	2.80	7.00	14.00

NUTTY LIFE (Formerly Krazy Life #1; becomes Wotalife Comics #3 on)
No. 2, Summer, 1946
Fox Features Syndicate

	GD25	FN65	NM94
2	5.85	17.50	35.00

NYOKA, THE JUNGLE GIRL (Formerly Jungle Girl; see The Further Adventures of..., Master Comics #50 & XMas Comics)
No. 2, Winter, 1945 - No. 77, June, 1953 (Movie serial)
Fawcett Publications

	GD25	FN65	NM94
2	38.00	115.00	265.00
3	21.00	62.00	145.00
4,5	17.00	51.00	120.00
6-10	12.00	36.00	85.00
11,13,14,16-18-Krigstein-a	12.00	36.00	85.00
12,15,19,20	10.00	30.00	70.00
21-30: 25-Clayton Moore photo-c?	7.00	21.00	42.00
31-40	5.35	16.00	32.00
41-50	4.20	12.50	25.00
51-60	4.00	10.00	20.00
61-77	3.20	8.00	16.00

NOTE: *Photo-c from movies 25, 27, 28, 30-70, 72, 76. Bondage c-4, 5, 7, 8, 14, 24.*

NYOKA, THE JUNGLE GIRL (Formerly Zoo Funnies; Space Adventures #23 on)
No. 14, Nov, 1955 - No. 22, Nov, 1957
Charlton Comics

	GD25	FN65	NM94
14	5.00	15.00	30.00
15-22	4.00	10.00	20.00

OAK ISLAND ADVENTURE (Disney) (Value: cover or less)

OAKLAND PRESS FUNNYBOOK, THE
9/17/78 - 4/13/80 (16 pgs.) (Weekly)
Full color in comic book form; changes to tabloid size 4/20/80-on
The Oakland Press

	GD25	FN65	NM94
Contains Tarzan by Manning, Marmaduke, Bugs Bunny, etc. (low distribution); 9/23/79 - 4/13/80 contain Buck Rogers by Gray Morrow & Jim Lawrence	.30	.80	1.60

OAKY DOAKS
July, 1942 (One Shot)
Eastern Color Printing Co.

	GD25	FN65	NM94
1	23.00	68.00	135.00

OBIE
1953 (6 cents)
Store Comics

	GD25	FN65	NM94
1	.80	2.00	4.00

OBNOXIO THE CLOWN
April, 1983 (One Shot) (Character from Crazy Magazine)
Marvel Comics Group

	GD25	FN65	NM94
1-Vs. the X-Men		.50	1.00

OCCULT FILES OF DR. SPEKTOR, THE
Apr, 1973 - No. 24, Feb, 1977; No. 25, May, 1982 (Painted-c #1-24)
Gold Key/Whitman No. 25

	GD25	FN65	NM94
1-1st app. Lakota; Baron Tibor begins	1.60	4.00	8.00
2-5	.80	2.00	4.00
6-10	.60	1.50	3.00
11-13,15-25: 11-1st app. Spektor as Werewolf. 25-Reprints	.40	1.00	2.00
14-Dr. Solar app.	1.00	2.50	5.00
9(Modern Comics reprint, 1977)	.30	.75	1.50

NOTE: *Also see Dan Curtis, Golden Comics Digest 33, Gold Key Spotlight, Mystery Comics Digest 5, & Spine Tingling Tales.*

ODELL'S ADVENTURES IN 3-D (See Adventures in 3-D)

OFFICIAL CRISIS ON INFINITE EARTHS INDEX, THE (Eclipse) (Value: cover or less)

OFFICIAL CRISIS ON INFINITE EARTHS CROSSOVER INDEX, THE (Eclipse) (Value: cover or less)

OFFICIAL DOOM PATROL INDEX, THE (Eclipse) (Value: cover or less)

OFFICIAL HANDBOOK OF THE CONAN UNIVERSE (See Handbook of...)

OFFICIAL HANDBOOK OF THE MARVEL UNIVERSE, THE
Jan, 1983 - No. 15, May, 1984
Marvel Comics Group

	GD25	FN65	NM94
1-Lists Marvel heroes & villains (letter A)	1.20	3.00	6.00
2 (B-C)	1.00	2.50	5.00
3-5: 3-(C-D). 4-(D-G). 5-(H-J)	.80	2.00	4.00
6-9: 6-(K-L). 7-(M). 8-(N-P); Punisher-c. 9-(Q-S)	.60	1.50	3.00
10-15: 10-(S). 11-(S-U). 12-(V-Z); Wolverine-c. 13,14-Book of the Dead. 15-Weaponry catalogue	.50	1.25	2.50

NOTE: ***Byrne** c/a(p)-1-14; c-15p. **Grell** a-9. **Layton** a-2, 5, 7. **Miller** a-2, 3. **Nebres** a-3, 4, 8. **Simonson** a-11. **Paul Smith** a-1-3, 6, 7, 9, 10, 12. **Starlin** a-7. **Steranko** a-8p.*

OFFICIAL HANDBOOK OF THE MARVEL UNIVERSE, THE
Dec, 1985 - No. 20, Feb, 1988 ($1.50 cover; maxi-series)
Marvel Comics Group

	GD25	FN65	NM94
V2#1-Byrne-c	.80	2.00	4.00
2-5: 2,3-Byrne-c	.60	1.50	3.00
6-10	.50	1.25	2.50
11-20	.40	1.00	2.00
Trade paperback Vol. 1-10	1.40	3.50	7.00

OFFICIAL HANDBOOK OF THE MARVEL UNIVERSE, THE
July, 1989 - No. 8, Mid-Dec, 1990 ($1.50, color, mini-series, 52 pgs.)
Marvel Comics

	GD25	FN65	NM94
V3#1-8: 1-McFarlane-a(2 pgs.)	.30	.75	1.50

OFFICIAL HAWKMAN INDEX, THE (Independent) (Value: cover or less)

OFFICIAL JUSTICE LEAGUE OF AMERICA INDEX, THE (Independent) (Value: cover or less)

OFFICIAL LEGION OF SUPER-HEROES INDEX, THE (Independent) (Value: cover or less)

OFFICIAL MARVEL INDEX TO MARVEL TEAM-UP (Marvel) (Value: cover or less)

OFFICIAL MARVEL INDEX TO THE AMAZING SPIDER-MAN (Marvel) (Value: cover or less)

OFFICIAL MARVEL INDEX TO THE AVENGERS, THE (Marvel) (Value: cover or less)

OFFICIAL MARVEL INDEX TO THE FANTASTIC FOUR (Marvel) (Value: cover or less)

OFFICIAL MARVEL INDEX TO THE X-MEN, THE (Marvel) (Value: cover or less)

OFFICIAL SOUPY SALES COMIC (See Soupy Sales)

OFFICIAL TEEN TITANS INDEX, THE (Eclipse) (Value: cover or less)

OFFICIAL TRUE CRIME CASES (Formerly Sub-Mariner #23; All-True Crime Cases #26 on)
No. 24, Fall, 1947 - No. 25, Winter, 1947-48
Marvel Comics (OCI)

	GD25	FN65	NM94
24(#1)-Burgos-a; Syd Shores-c	11.00	32.00	75.00
25-Syd Shores-c; Kurtzman's 'Hey Look'	10.00	30.00	60.00

OF SUCH IS THE KINGDOM
1955 (36 pgs., 15 cents)
George A. Pflaum

	GD25	FN65	NM94
nn-Reprints from 1951 Treasure Chest	2.00	5.00	10.00

O.G. WHIZ (See Gold Key Spotlight #10)
2/71 - No. 6, 5/72; No. 7, 5/78 - No. 11, 1/79 (No. 7: 52 pgs.)
Gold Key

	GD25	FN65	NM94
1,2-John Stanley scripts	7.50	22.50	45.00

Nyoka, the Jungle Girl #43, © FAW

Oaky Doaks #1, © EAS

Occult Files of Dr. Spektor #23, © WEST

OK Comics #2, © UFS

Omac #4 (3-4/75), © DC

Omega the Unknown #1, © MEG

	GD25	FN65	NM94
3-6(1972)	4.00	11.00	22.00
7-11(1978-79)-Part-r: 9-Tubby app.	1.40	3.50	7.00

OH, BROTHER! (Teen Comedy)
Jan, 1953 - No. 5, Oct, 1953
Stanhall Publ.

	GD25	FN65	NM94
1-By Bill Williams	4.00	12.00	24.00
2-5	2.80	7.00	14.00

OH SKIN-NAY!
1913 (8-1/2x13")
P.F. Volland & Co.

	GD25	FN65	NM94
nn-The Days Of Real Sport by Briggs	17.00	50.00	100.00

OH SUSANNA (See 4-Color #1105)

OKAY COMICS
July, 1940
United Features Syndicate

	GD25	FN65	NM94
1-Captain & the Kids & Hawkshaw the Detective reprints	30.00	90.00	180.00

OK COMICS
July, 1940 - No. 2, Oct, 1940
United Features Syndicate

	GD25	FN65	NM94
1-Little Giant, Phantom Knight, Sunset Smith, & The Teller Twins begin	47.00	140.00	280.00
2 (Rare)-Origin Mister Mist	45.00	135.00	270.00

OKLAHOMA KID
June, 1957 - No. 4, 1958
Ajax/Farrell Publ.

	GD25	FN65	NM94
1	5.85	17.50	35.00
2-4	4.00	10.00	20.00

OKLAHOMAN, THE (See 4-Color #820)

OLD GLORY COMICS
1944 (Giveaway)
Chesapeake & Ohio Railway

	GD25	FN65	NM94
nn-Capt. Fearless reprint	4.00	10.00	20.00

OLD IRONSIDES (See 4-Color #874)

OLD YELLER (See 4-Color #869, Movie Comics, and Walt Disney Showcase #25)

OLYMPIANS, THE (Epic)(Value: cover or less)

OMAC (One Man Army, ...Corps. #4 on; also see Kamandi #59 & Warlord)
Sept-Oct, 1974 - No. 8, Nov-Dec, 1975
National Periodical Publications

	GD25	FN65	NM94
1-Origin	1.00	2.50	5.00
2-8: 8-2pg. Neal Adams ad	.60	1.50	3.00

NOTE: ***Kirby** a-1-8p; c-1-7p. **Kubert** c-8. See Cancelled Comic Cavalcade.*

OMAC: ONE MAN ARMY CORPS
1991 - No. 4, 1991 ($3.95, B&W, mini-series, mature readers, 52 pgs.)
DC Comics

	GD25	FN65	NM94
Book One - Four: John Byrne-c/a & scripts	.80	2.00	4.00

OMAHA THE CAT DANCER
1984 (no month) - No. 2, 1984 ($1.60-$1.75, B&W, adults)
SteelDragon Press

	GD25	FN65	NM94
1-Preview ($1.60)	1.60	4.00	8.00
1-Regular #1	1.25	3.20	6.40
1-2nd print	.35	.85	1.70
2-($1.75-c)	.90	2.30	4.60

OMAHA THE CAT DANCER
1984 - No. 17, 1992 ($2.00, B&W, adults)
Kitchen Sink Press

	GD25	FN65	NM94
1-Reprints SteelDragon #1	1.25	3.20	6.40
1-2nd printing ($2.50)	.60	1.50	3.00
2-Reprints SteelDragon #2	.55	1.35	2.70
2-2nd printing	.35	.90	1.75
3,4	.55	1.35	2.70
3,4-2nd printings	.35	.90	1.75
5-17: 15-17-($2.50)	.35	.90	1.75
0-(3/90, $2.00)-r/1st app./Bizarre Sex #9(1981)	.40	1.00	2.00

NOTE: *Issues 1 thru 13 have been reprinted with $2.50 cover price. 3rd prints exist?*

O'MALLEY AND THE ALLEY CATS
April, 1971 - No. 9, Jan, 1974 (Disney)
Gold Key

	GD25	FN65	NM94
1	2.40	6.00	12.00
2-9	1.60	4.00	8.00

OMEGA ELITE (Blackthorne)(Value: cover or less)

OMEGA MEN, THE (See Green Lantern #141)
Dec, 1982 - No. 38, May, 1986 ($1.00-$1.50; Baxter paper)
DC Comics

	GD25	FN65	NM94
1	.30	.75	1.50
2,4,6-8,11-18,21-36,38: 2-Origin Broot. 7-Origin The Citadel; Lobo app? 26,27-Alan Moore scripts. 30-Intro new Primus. 31-Crisis x-over. 34,35-Teen Titans x-over		.50	1.00
3-1st app. Lobo (5 pgs.)(6/83); Lobo-c	2.00	5.00	10.00
5,9-2nd & 3rd app. Lobo (cameo, 2 pgs. each)	.80	2.00	4.00
10-1st full Lobo story	2.00	5.00	10.00
19-Lobo cameo	.30	.75	1.50
20-2nd full Lobo story	1.20	3.00	6.00
37-1st solo Lobo story (8 pg. back-up by Giffen)	.60	1.50	3.00
Annual 1(11/84, 52 pgs.), 2(11/85)	.30	.75	1.50

NOTE: ***Giffen** c/a-1-6p. **Morrow** a-24r. **Nino** c/a-16, 21.*

OMEGA THE UNKNOWN
March, 1976 - No. 10, Oct, 1977
Marvel Comics Group

	GD25	FN65	NM94
1-1st app. Omega	.80	2.00	4.00
2-7,10: 2-Hulk app. 3-Electro app.	.40	1.00	2.00
8-1st app. 2nd Foolkiller (Greg Salinger), 1 panel only (cameo)	.80	2.00	4.00
9-1st full app. Foolkiller	1.00	2.50	5.00

NOTE: ***Kane** c(p)-3, 5, 8, 9. **Mooney** a-1-3, 4p, 5, 6p, 7, 8i, 9, 10.*

OMEN
1989 - No. 3? ($2.00, B&W, adults)
Northstar Publishing

	GD25	FN65	NM94
1-Tim Vigil-c/a in all	1.60	4.00	8.00
1-2nd printing	.50	1.25	2.50
2,3	.60	1.50	3.00

OMNI MEN (Blackthorne)(Value: cover or less)

ONE (Pacific)(Value: cover or less)

ONE, THE (Epic)(Value: cover or less)

ONE-ARM SWORDSMAN, THE (Victory)(Value: cover or less)

ONE HUNDRED AND ONE DALMATIANS (See 4-Color #1183, Cartoon Tales, Movie Comics, and Walt Disney Showcase #9, 51)

101 DALMATIONS
1991 (Color, graphic novel, 52 pgs.)
Disney Comics

	GD25	FN65	NM94
nn-($4.95, direct sale)-r/movie adaptation & more	1.00	2.50	5.00
1-($2.95, newsstand edition)	.60	1.50	3.00

100 PAGES OF COMICS
1937 (Stiff covers; square binding)
Dell Publishing Co.

101(Found on back cover)-Alley Oop, Wash Tubbs, Capt. Easy, Og Son of Fire, Apple Mary, Tom Mix, Dan Dunn, Tailspin Tommy, Doctor Doom 88.00 262.00 525.00

100 PAGE SUPER SPECTACULAR (See DC 100 Page ...)

ONE MILE UP (Eclipse)(Value: cover or less)

$1,000,000 DUCK (See Walt Disney Showcase #5)

ONE MILLION YEARS AGO (Tor #2 on)
September, 1953
St. John Publishing Co.

1-Origin; Kubert-c/a 13.00 40.00 90.00

ONE SHOT (See 4-Color...)

1001 HOURS OF FUN (See Large Feature Comic #13)

ON STAGE (See 4-Color #1336)

ON THE AIR
1947 (Giveaway) (paper cover)
NBC Network Comic

nn-(Rare) 14.00 43.00 100.00

ON THE DOUBLE (See 4-Color #1232)

ON THE LINKS
December, 1926 (48 pages) (9x10")
Associated Feature Service

nn-Daily strip-r 11.50 34.00 80.00

ON THE ROAD WITH ANDRAE CROUCH (Spire Christian)(Value: cover or less)

ON THE SPOT (Pretty Boy Floyd...)
Fall, 1948
Fawcett Publications

nn-Pretty Boy Floyd photo on-c; bondage-c 20.00 60.00 120.00

ONYX OVERLORD (Marvel)(Value: cover or less)

OPEN SPACE (Marvel)(Value: cover or less)

OPERATION BIKINI (See Movie Classics)

OPERATION BUCHAREST (See The Crusaders)

OPERATION CROSSBOW (See Movie Classics)

OPERATION PERIL
Oct-Nov, 1950 - No. 16, Apr-May, 1953 (#1-5: 52 pgs.)
American Comics Group (Michel Publ.)

1-Time Travelers, Danny Danger (by Leonard Starr) & Typhoon Tyler (by Ogden Whitney) begin 18.00 54.00 125.00
2 11.00 32.00 75.00
3-5: 3-Horror story. 5-Sci/fi story 10.00 30.00 65.00
6-12-Last Time Travelers 9.15 27.50 55.00
13-16: All war format 4.20 12.50 25.00
NOTE: ***Starr** a-2, 5. **Whitney** a-1, 2, 5-10, 12; c-1, 3, 5, 8, 9.*

ORAL ROBERTS' TRUE STORIES (Junior Partners #120 on)
1956 (no month) - No. 119, 7/59 (15 cents)(No #102: 25 cents)
TelePix Publ. (Oral Roberts' Evangelistic Assoc./Healing Waters)

V1#1(1956)-(Not code approved)-"The Miracle Touch" 11.00 32.00 75.00
102-(Only issue approved by code, 10/56) 7.50 22.50 45.00
103-119: 115-(114 on inside) 4.20 12.50 25.00
NOTE: *Also see Happiness & Healing For You.*

ORANGE BIRD, THE
No date (1980) (36 pgs.; in color; slick cover)
Walt Disney Educational Media Co.

nn-Included with educational kit on foods .50 1.00
...in Nutrition Adventures nn (1980) .30 .60
...and the Nutrition Know-How Revue nn (1983) .30 .60

ORBIT (Eclipse)(Value: cover or less)

ORIENTAL HEROES (Jademan)(Value: cover or less)

ORIGINAL ASTRO BOY, THE (Now)(Value: cover or less)(Also see Astro Boy)

ORIGINAL BLACK CAT, THE (Recollections)(Value: cover or less)

ORIGINAL DICK TRACY, THE (Gladstone)(Value: cover or less)

ORIGINAL E-MAN AND MICHAEL MAUSER, THE (First)(Value: cover or less)

ORIGINAL GHOST RIDER, THE
July, 1992 - Present ($1.75, color)
Marvel Comics

1-12: 1-7-r/Marvel Spotlight #5-11 by Ploog w/new-c. 3-New Phantom Rider (former Night Rider) back-ups begin by Ayers. 4-Quesada-c(p). 8,9-r/Ghost Rider #1,2. 10-r/Marvel Spotlight #12 .35 .90 1.75

ORIGINAL GHOST RIDER RIDES AGAIN, THE
July, 1991 - No. 7, Jan, 1992, ($1.50, color, mini-series, 52 pgs.)
Marvel Comics

1-Reprints Ghost Rider #68(origin),69 w/covers .30 .75 1.50
2-7: Reprints G.R. #70-81 w/covers .30 .75 1.50

ORIGINAL NEXUS GRAPHIC NOVEL (See First Comics Graphic Novel #19)

ORIGINAL SHIELD, THE
April, 1984 - No. 4, Oct, 1984
Archie Enterprises, Inc.

1-4: 1,2-Origin Shield; Ayers p-1-4, Nebres c-1,2 .50 1.00

ORIGINAL SWAMP THING SAGA, THE (See DC Special Series #2, 14, 17, 20)

OSCAR COMICS (Formerly Funny Tunes; Awful...#11 & 12)
(Also see Cindy Comics)
No. 24, Spring, 1947 - No. 10, Apr, 1949; No. 13, Oct, 1949
Marvel Comics

24(#1, Spring, 1947) 8.35 25.00 50.00
25(#2, Sum, 1947)-Wolverton-a plus Kurtzman's "Hey Look" 10.00 30.00 65.00
3-9,13: 8-Margie app. 5.35 16.00 32.00
10-Kurtzman's "Hey Look" 7.50 22.50 45.00

OSWALD THE RABBIT (Also see New Fun Comics #1)
No. 21, 1943 - No. 1268, 12-2/61-62 (Walter Lantz)
Dell Publishing Co.

4-Color 21(1943) 30.00 90.00 210.00
4-Color 39(1943) 20.00 60.00 140.00
4-Color 67(1944) 14.00 43.00 100.00
4-Color 102(1946)-Kelly-a, 1 pg. 12.00 36.00 85.00
4-Color 143,183 7.50 22.50 45.00
4-Color 225,273 5.00 15.00 30.00
4-Color 315,388 3.60 9.00 18.00
4-Color 458,507,549,593 2.80 7.00 14.00
4-Color 623,697,792,894,979,1268 2.00 5.00 10.00

OSWALD THE RABBIT (See The Funnies, March of Comics #7, 38, 53, 67, 81, 95, 111, 126, 141, 156, 171, 186, New Funnies & Super Book #8, 20)

OUR ARMY AT WAR (Becomes Sgt. Rock #302 on; also see Army At War)
Aug, 1952 - No. 301, Feb, 1977
National Periodical Publications

1 86.00 260.00 600.00
2 43.00 130.00 300.00
3,4: 4-Krigstein-a 36.00 107.00 250.00
5-7 25.00 75.00 175.00
8-11,14-Krigstein-a 25.00 75.00 175.00
12,15-20 18.00 54.00 125.00
13-Krigstein-c/a; flag-c 23.00 70.00 160.00
21-31: Last precode (2/55) 12.00 36.00 85.00
32-40 11.00 32.00 75.00
41-60 10.00 30.00 60.00
61-70 8.35 25.00 50.00
71-80 6.70 20.00 40.00

On the Spot nn, © FAW

Operation Peril #3, © ACG

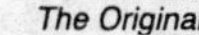

The Original Shield #2, © AP

Our Army at War #94, © DC

Our Fighting Forces #71, © DC

Our Gang Comics #16, © M.G.M.

	GD25	FN65	NM94
81-1st Sgt. Rock app. (4/59) by Andru & Esposito in Easy Co. story	110.00	332.00	775.00
82-Sgt. Rock cameo in Easy Co. story (6 panels)	29.00	86.00	200.00
83-1st Kubert Sgt. Rock (6/59)	39.00	120.00	275.00
84,86-90	14.00	43.00	100.00
85-Origin & 1st app. Ice Cream Soldier	16.00	48.00	110.00
91-All Sgt. Rock issue	39.00	120.00	275.00
92-100: 92-1st app. Bulldozer. 95-1st app. Zack	9.15	27.50	55.00
101-120: 101-1st app. Buster. 111-1st app. Wee Willie & Sunny. 113-1st app. Wildman & Jackie Johnson. 118-Sunny dies	4.70	14.00	28.00
121-127,129-150: 126-1st app. Canary. 139-1st app. Little Sure Shot. 140-All Sgt. Rock issue	3.00	7.50	15.00
128-Training & origin Sgt. Rock	14.00	43.00	100.00
151-Intro. Enemy Ace by Kubert (2/65)	12.00	36.00	85.00
152,154,156,157,159-163,165-170: 157-2 pg. pin-up. 162,163-Viking Prince x-over in Sgt. Rock	2.80	7.00	14.00
153-2nd app. Enemy Ace (4/65)	8.35	25.00	50.00
155-3rd app. Enemy Ace (6/65)(see Showcase)	4.00	10.00	20.00
158-Origin & 1st app. Iron Major(9/65), formerly Iron Captain	3.20	8.00	16.00
164-Giant G-19	3.20	8.00	16.00
171-176,178-181	2.00	5.00	10.00
177-(80 pg. Giant G-32)	2.20	5.50	11.00
182,183,186-Neal Adams-a. 186-Origin retold	2.00	5.00	10.00
184,185,187-189,191-199: 184-Wee Willie dies. 189-Intro. The Teen-age Underground Fighters of Unit 3	1.60	4.00	8.00
190-(80 pg. Giant G-44)	1.80	4.50	9.00
200-12 pg. Rock story told in verse; Evans-a	2.20	5.50	11.00
201-Krigstein-r/#14	1.30	3.25	6.50
202,204-215: 204,205-All reprints; no Sgt. Rock	.90	2.20	4.40
203-(80 pg. Giant G-56)-All-r, no Sgt. Rock	1.30	3.25	6.50
216,229-(80 pg. Giants G-68, G-80): 216-Has G-58 on-c by mistake	1.10	2.75	5.50
217-228,230-239,241,243-301: 244-N. Adams-a? 280-200th app. Sgt. Rock; reprints Our Army at War #81,83	.90	2.20	4.40
240-Neal Adams-a	1.10	2.75	5.50
242-(50 cent issue DC-9)-Kubert-c	1.10	2.75	5.50

NOTE ***Alcala** a-251. **Drucker** a-27, 67, 68, 79, 82, 83, 96, 164, 177, 203, 212, 243r, 244, 269r, 275r, 280r. **Evans** a-165-175, 200, 266, 269, 270, 274, 276, 278, 280. **Glanzman** a-218, 220, 222, 223, 225, 227, 230-232, 238, 240, 241, 244, 247, 248, 256-259, 261, 265-267, 271, 282, 283, 298. **Grell** a-287. **Heath** a-50, 164, & most 176-281. **Kubert** a-38, 59, 67, 68 & most issues from 83-165, 233, 267, 275, 300. **Maurer** a-233, 237, 239, 240, 45, 280, 284, 288, 290, 291, 295. **Severin** a-236, 252, 265, 267, 269r, 272. **Toth** a-235, 241, 254. **Wildey** a-283-285, 287p. **Wood** a-249.*

OUR FIGHTING FORCES
Oct-Nov, 1954 - No. 181, Sept-Oct, 1978
National Periodical Publications/DC Comics

	GD25	FN65	NM94
1-Grandenetti-c/a	57.00	170.00	400.00
2	29.00	85.00	200.00
3-Kubert-c; last precode issue (3/55)	25.00	75.00	175.00
4,5	18.00	54.00	125.00
6-9	14.00	43.00	100.00
10-Wood-a	16.00	48.00	110.00
11-20	12.00	36.00	85.00
21-30	8.35	25.00	50.00
31-40	7.50	22.50	45.00
41-Unknown Soldier tryout	10.00	30.00	60.00
42-44	6.35	19.00	38.00
45-Gunner & Sarge begin (ends #94)	22.00	65.00	150.00
46	10.00	30.00	65.00
47	7.50	22.50	45.00
48-50	5.00	15.00	30.00
51-64: 64-Last 10 cent issue	3.60	9.00	18.00
65-70	2.40	6.00	12.00
71-90	1.20	3.00	6.00
91-100: 95-Devil-Dog begins, ends 98. 99-Capt. Hunter begins, ends #106	.80	2.00	4.00
101-122: 106-Hunters Hellcats begin. 116-Mlle. Marie app. 121-Intro. Heller	.60	1.50	3.00
123-181: 123-Losers (Capt. Storm, Gunner & Sarge, Johnny Cloud) begin. 134,146-Toth-a	.60	1.50	3.00

NOTE: ***N. Adams** c-147. **Drucker** a-28, 37, 39, 42-44, 49, 53, 133r. **Evans** a-149, 164-174, 177-181. **Glanzman** a-125-128, 132, 134, 138-141, 143, 144. **Heath** a-2, 16, 18, 28, 41, 44, 49, 114, 135-138r; c-51. **Kirby** a-151-162p; c-152-159. **Kubert** c/a in many issues. **Maurer** a-135. **Redondo** a-166. **Severin** a-123-130, 131i, 132-150.*

OUR FIGHTING MEN IN ACTION (See Men In Action)

OUR FLAG COMICS
Aug, 1941 - No. 5, April, 1942
Ace Magazines

	GD25	FN65	NM94
1-Captain Victory, The Unknown Soldier (intro.) & The Three Cheers begin	133.00	400.00	800.00
2-Origin The Flag (patriotic hero); 1st app?	72.00	215.00	430.00
3-5: 5-Intro & 1st app. Mr. Risk	63.00	188.00	375.00

NOTE: ***Anderson** a-1, 4. **Mooney** a-1, 2; c-2.*

OUR GANG COMICS (With Tom & Jerry #39-59; becomes Tom & Jerry #60 on; based on film characters)
Sept-Oct, 1942 - No. 59, June, 1949
Dell Publishing Co.

	GD25	FN65	NM94
1-Our Gang & Barney Bear by Kelly, Tom & Jerry, Pete Smith, Flip & Dip, The Milky Way begin	63.00	190.00	440.00
2	30.00	90.00	210.00
3-5: 3-Benny Burro begins	19.00	58.00	135.00
6-Bumbazine & Albert only app. by Kelly	33.00	100.00	230.00
7-No Kelly story	15.00	45.00	105.00
8-Benny Burro begins by Barks	32.00	95.00	225.00
9-Barks-a(2): Benny Burro & Happy Hound; no Kelly story	26.50	79.00	185.00
10-Benny Burro by Barks	22.00	65.00	150.00
11-1st Barney Bear & Benny Burro by Barks; Happy Hound by Barks	22.00	65.00	150.00
12-20	13.00	40.00	90.00
21-30: 30-X-Mas-c	10.00	30.00	70.00
31-36-Last Barks issue	8.35	25.00	50.00
37-40	4.00	11.00	22.00
41-50	3.00	7.50	15.00
51-57	2.60	6.50	13.00
58,59-No Kelly art or Our Gang stories	2.20	5.50	11.00

NOTE: ***Barks** art in part only. **Barks** did not write Barney Bear stories #30-34. (See March of Comics #3,26). Early issues have photo back-c.*

OUR LADY OF FATIMA
3/11/55 (15 cents) (36 pages)
Catechetical Guild Educational Society

	GD25	FN65	NM94
395	3.00	7.50	15.00

OUR LOVE (True Secrets #3 on?)
Sept, 1949 - No. 2, Jan, 1950
Marvel Comics (SPC)

	GD25	FN65	NM94
1-Photo-c	7.50	22.50	45.00
2-Photo-c	4.20	12.50	25.00

OUR LOVE STORY
Oct, 1969 - No. 38, Feb, 1976
Marvel Comics Group

	GD25	FN65	NM94
1	1.20	3.00	6.00
2-4,6-13	.70	1.75	3.50
5-Steranko-a	2.40	6.00	12.00
14-New story by Gary Fredrich & Tarpe' Mills	1.00	2.50	5.00
15-38: 27-Colan/Everett-a(r?); Kirby/Colletta-r	.40	1.00	2.00

NOTE: *J. Buscema a-1-3, 5-7, 9, 35r; c-24, 27, 35. Colan a-3-6, 24r(#4), 26.*

OUR MISS BROOKS (See 4-Color #751)

OUR SECRET (Formerly My Secret)
No. 4, Dec, 1949 - No. 8, Jun, 1950
Superior Comics Ltd.

	GD25	FN65	NM94
4-Kamen-a; spanking scene	8.35	25.00	50.00
5,6,8	5.35	16.00	32.00
7-Contains 9 pg. story intended for unpublished Ellery Queen #5	5.85	17.50	35.00

OUTBURSTS OF EVERETT TRUE
1921 (32 pages) (B&W)
Saalfield Publ. Co.

	GD25	FN65	NM94
1907 (2-panel strips reprint)	14.00	42.50	85.00

OUTCASTS (DC)(Value: cover or less)

OUTER LIMITS, THE (TV)
Jan-Mar, 1964 - No. 18, Oct, 1969 (All painted-c)
Dell Publishing Co.

	GD25	FN65	NM94
1	6.70	20.00	40.00
2	4.00	10.00	20.00
3-10	2.80	7.00	14.00
11-18: 17-Reprints #1. 18-r/#2	2.40	6.00	12.00

OUTER SPACE (Formerly This Magazine Is Haunted, 2nd Series)
No. 17, May, 1958 - No. 25, Dec, 1959; Nov, 1968
Charlton Comics

	GD25	FN65	NM94
17-Williamson/Wood style art; not by them (Sid Check?)	8.35	25.00	50.00
18-20-Ditko-a	10.00	30.00	65.00
21-25: 21-Ditko-c	5.85	17.50	35.00
V2#1(11/68)-Ditko-a, Boyette-c	3.00	7.50	15.00

OUTLANDERS (Dark Horse)(Value: cover or less)

OUTLAW (See Return of the...)

OUTLAW FIGHTERS
Aug, 1954 - No. 5, April, 1955
Atlas Comics (IPC)

	GD25	FN65	NM94
1-Tuska-a	7.50	22.50	45.00
2-5: 5-Heath-c/a, 7pgs.	5.00	15.00	30.00

NOTE: *Heath c/a-5. Maneely c-2. Pakula a-2. Reinman a-2. Tuska a-1, 2.*

OUTLAW KID, THE (1st Series; see Wild Western)
Sept, 1954 - No. 19, Sept, 1957
Atlas Comics (CCC No. 1-11/EPI No. 12-29)

	GD25	FN65	NM94
1-Origin; The Outlaw Kid & his horse Thunder begin; Black Rider app.	13.00	40.00	90.00
2-Black Rider app.	7.50	22.50	45.00
3-7,9: 3-Wildey-a(3)	6.70	20.00	40.00
8-Williamson/Woodbridge-a, 4 pgs.	5.35	16.00	32.00
10-Williamson-a	5.85	17.50	35.00
11-17,19: 15-Williamson text illo (unsigned)	4.00	11.00	22.00
18-Williamson-a	5.00	15.00	30.00

NOTE: *Berg a-4, 7, 13. Maneely c-1-3, 5-8, 11, 12, 18. Pakula a-3. Severin c-10, 17. Shores a-1. Wildey a-1(3), 2-8, 10-18, 19(4); c-4.*

OUTLAW KID, THE (2nd Series)
Aug, 1970 - No. 30, Oct, 1975
Marvel Comics Group

	GD25	FN65	NM94
1,2-Reprints; 1-Orlando-r, Wildey-r(3)	1.00	2.50	5.00
3,9-Williamson-a(r)	.60	1.50	3.00
4-8: 8-Crandall-r	.40	1.00	2.00
10-30: 10-Origin; new-a in #10-16. 27-Origin-r/#10	.30	.75	1.50

NOTE: *Ayers a-10, 27r. Berg a-7, 25r. Gil Kane c-10, 11, 15, 27r, 28. Roussos a-10i, 27i(r). Severin c-1, 9, 20, 25. Wildey r-1-4, 6-9, 19-22, 25, 26. Williamson a-28r. Woodbridge/Williamson a-9r.*

OUTLAWS
Feb-Mar, 1948 - No. 9, June-July, 1949
D. S. Publishing Co.

	GD25	FN65	NM94
1-Violent & suggestive stories	14.00	43.00	100.00
2-Ingels-a	14.00	43.00	100.00
3,5,6: 3-Not Frazetta. 5-Sky Sheriff by Good app. 6-McWilliams-a	6.70	20.00	40.00
4-Orlando-a	8.35	25.00	50.00
7,8-Ingels-a in each	11.00	32.00	75.00
9-(Scarce)-Frazetta-a, 7 pgs.	27.00	81.00	190.00

NOTE: *Another #3 was printed in Canada with Frazetta art "Prairie Jinx," 7 pgs.*

OUTLAWS, THE (Formerly Western Crime Cases)
No. 10, May, 1952 - No. 13, Sept, 1953; No. 14, April, 1954
Star Publishing Co.

	GD25	FN65	NM94
10-L. B. Cole-c	5.00	15.00	30.00
11-14-L. B. Cole-c. 14-Reprints Western Thrillers #4 (Fox) w/new L.B. Cole-c; Kamen, Feldstein-r	4.20	12.50	25.00

OUTLAWS, THE (DC)(Value: cover or less)

OUTLAWS OF THE WEST (Formerly Cody of the Pony Express #10)
No. 11, 7/57 - No. 81, 5/70; No. 82, 7/79 - No. 88, 4/80
Charlton Comics

	GD25	FN65	NM94
11	5.35	16.00	32.00
12,13,15-17,19,20	3.20	8.00	16.00
14-(68 pgs., 2/58)	4.00	10.00	20.00
18-Ditko-a	7.00	21.00	42.00
21-30	2.00	5.00	10.00
31-50	1.20	3.00	6.00
51-70: 54-Kid Montana app. 64-Captain Doom begins (1st app.)	.70	1.75	3.50
71-81: 73-Origin & 1st app. The Sharp Shooter, last app. #74. 75-Last Capt. Doom. 80,81-Ditko-a	.40	1.00	2.00
82-88	.30	.75	1.50
64,79(Modern Comics-r, 1977, '78)		.50	1.00

OUTLAWS OF THE WILD WEST
1952 (132 pages) (25 cents)
Avon Periodicals

	GD25	FN65	NM94
1-Wood back-c; Kubert-a (3 Jesse James-r)	19.00	58.00	135.00

OUT OF SANTA'S BAG (See March of Comics #10)

OUT OF THE NIGHT (The Hooded Horseman #18 on)
Feb-Mar, 1952 - No. 17, Oct-Nov, 1954
American Comics Group (Creston/Scope)

	GD25	FN65	NM94
1-Williamson/LeDoux-a, 9 pgs.	30.00	90.00	210.00
2-Williamson-a, 5 pgs.	25.00	75.00	175.00
3,5-10: 9-Sci/Fic story	10.00	30.00	70.00
4-Williamson-a, 7 pgs.	23.00	70.00	160.00
11-17: 13-Nostrand-a? 17-E.C. Wood swipe	9.15	27.50	55.00

NOTE: *Landau a-14, 16, 17. Shelly a-12.*

OUT OF THE PAST A CLUE TO THE FUTURE
1946? (16 pages) (paper cover)
E. C. Comics (Public Affairs Comm.)

	GD25	FN65	NM94
nn-Based on public affairs pamphlet-"What Foreign Trade Means to You"	16.00	48.00	110.00

OUT OF THE SHADOWS
No. 5, July, 1952 - No. 14, Aug, 1954
Standard Comics/Visual Editions

	GD25	FN65	NM94
5-Toth-p; Moreira, Tuska-a; Roussos-c	16.00	48.00	110.00
6-Toth/Celardo-a; Katz-a(2)	12.00	36.00	85.00
7-Jack Katz-c/a(2)	10.00	30.00	60.00
8,10: 8-Katz-c10-Sekowsky-a	6.70	20.00	40.00
9-Crandall-a(2)	10.00	30.00	60.00
11-Toth-a, 2 pgs.; Katz-a; Andru-c	10.00	30.00	60.00
12-Toth/Peppe-a(2); Katz-a	12.00	36.00	85.00

Outer Space #18, © CC

Outlaws #4, © DS

Out of the Night #7, © ACG

Ozark Ike #B11, © STD

Panhandle Pete and Jennifer #2, © J. Charles Laue

Panic #3 (1954), © WMG

	GD25	FN65	NM94
13-Cannabalism story; Sekowsky-a; Roussos-c	10.00	30.00	60.00
14-Toth-a	10.00	30.00	65.00

OUT OF THIS WORLD
June, 1950 (One Shot)
Avon Periodicals

	GD25	FN65	NM94
1-Kubert-a(2) (one reprinted/Eerie #1, 1947) plus Crom the Barbarian by Giunta (origin); Fawcette-c	42.00	125.00	290.00

OUT OF THIS WORLD
Aug, 1956 - No. 16, Dec, 1959
Charlton Comics

	GD25	FN65	NM94
1	10.00	30.00	70.00
2	5.85	17.50	35.00
3-6-Ditko-a(4) each	13.00	40.00	90.00
7-(2/58, 15 cents, 68 pgs.)-Ditko-c/a(4)	13.00	40.00	90.00
8-(5/58, 15 cents, 68 pgs.)-Ditko-a(2)	11.00	32.00	75.00
9-12,16-Ditko-a	10.00	30.00	65.00
13-15	4.00	10.00	20.00

NOTE: ***Ditko** c-3-7, 11, 12, 16. **Reinman** a-10.*

OUT OUR WAY WITH WORRY WART (See 4-Color No. 680)

OUTPOSTS (Blackthorne)(Value: cover or less)

OUTSIDERS, THE (DC)(Value: cover or less)

OUTSTANDING AMERICAN WAR HEROES
1944 (16 pgs.) (paper cover)
The Parents' Institute

	GD25	FN65	NM94
nn-Reprints from True Comics	3.60	9.00	18.00

OVERSEAS COMICS (Also see G.I. Comics & Jeep Comics)
1944 (7-1/4x10-1/4"; 16 pgs. in color)
Giveaway (Distributed to U.S. armed forces)

	GD25	FN65	NM94
23-65-Bringing Up Father, Popeye, Joe Palooka, Dick Tracy, Superman, Gasoline Alley, Buz Sawyer, Li'l Abner, Blondie, Terry & the Pirates, Out Our Way	4.00	10.50	21.00

OWL, THE
April, 1967; No. 2, April, 1968
Gold Key

	GD25	FN65	NM94
1,2-Written by Jerry Siegel	3.60	9.00	18.00

OXYDOL-DREFT
1950 (Set of 6 pocket-size giveaways; distributed through the mail as a set)
Oxydol-Dreft (Scarce)

	GD25	FN65	NM94
1-3: 1-Li'l Abner. 2-Daisy Mae. 3-Shmoo	10.00	30.00	60.00
4-John Wayne; Williamson/Frazetta-c from John Wayne #3	13.00	40.00	90.00
5-Archie	8.35	25.00	50.00
6-Terrytoons Mighty Mouse	10.00	30.00	60.00

NOTE: *Set is worth more with original envelope.*

OZ (See First Comics Graphic Novel, Marvel Treaury Of Oz & MGM's Marvelous...)

OZARK IKE
Feb, 1948; Nov, 1948 - No. 24, Dec, 1951; No. 25, Sept, 1952
Dell Publishing Co./Standard Comics B11 on

	GD25	FN65	NM94
4-Color 180(1948-Dell)	9.15	27.50	55.00
B11, B12, 13-15	6.70	20.00	40.00
16-25	5.00	15.00	30.00

OZ-WONDERLAND WARS, THE
Jan, 1986 - No. 3, March, 1986 (Mini-series)
DC Comics

	GD25	FN65	NM94
1-3	.40	1.00	2.00

OZZIE & BABS (TV Teens #14 on)
Dec, 1947 - No. 13, Fall, 1949
Fawcett Publications

	GD25	FN65	NM94
1-Teen-age	5.85	17.50	35.00
2	3.60	9.00	18.00
3-13	2.60	6.50	13.00

OZZIE & HARRIET (See The Adventures of...)

PACIFIC COMICS GRAPHIC NOVEL (See Image Graphic Novel)

PACIFIC PRESENTS (Also see Starslayer #2, 3)
Oct, 1982 - No. 2, Apr, 1983; No. 3, Mar, 1984 - No. 4, June, 1984
Pacific Comics

	GD25	FN65	NM94
1-Chapter 3 of The Rocketeer; Stevens-c/a	1.20	3.00	6.00
2-Chapter 4 of The Rocketeer (4th app.); nudity; Stevens-c/a	.80	2.00	4.00
3,4: 3-1st app. Vanity	.40	1.00	2.00

NOTE: ***Conrad** a-3, 4; c-3. **Ditko** a-1-3; c-1(1/2). **Dave Stevens** a-1, 2; c-1(1/2), 2.*

PADRE OF THE POOR
nd (Giveaway) (16 pgs.; paper cover)
Catechetical Guild

	GD25	FN65	NM94
nn	2.00	5.00	10.00

PAGEANT OF COMICS (See Jane Arden & Mopsy)
Sept, 1947 - No. 2, Oct, 1947
Archer St. John

	GD25	FN65	NM94
1-Mopsy strip-r	6.35	19.00	38.00
2-Jane Arden strip-r	6.35	19.00	38.00

PANCHO VILLA
1950
Avon Periodicals

	GD25	FN65	NM94
nn-Kinstler-c	13.50	41.00	95.00

PANHANDLE PETE AND JENNIFER (TV)
July, 1951 - No. 3, Nov, 1951
J. Charles Laue Publishing Co.

	GD25	FN65	NM94
1	5.85	17.50	35.00
2,3	4.20	12.50	25.00

PANIC (Companion to Mad)
Feb-Mar, 1954 - No. 12, Dec-Jan, 1955-56
E. C. Comics (Tiny Tot Comics)

	GD25	FN65	NM94
1-Used in Senate Investigation hearings; Elder draws entire E. C. staff	14.00	43.00	100.00
2	9.15	27.50	55.00
3,4: 3-Senate Subcommittee parody; Davis draws Gaines, Feldstein & Kelly, 1 pg.; Old King Cole smokes marijuana. 4-Infinity-c	6.70	20.00	40.00
5-11: 8-Last pre-code issue	5.85	17.50	35.00
12 (Low distribution; many thousands were destroyed)	8.35	25.00	50.00

NOTE: ***Davis** a-1-12; c-12. **Elder** a-1-12. **Feldstein** c-1-3, 5. **Kamen** a-1. **Orlando** a-1-9. **Wolverton** c-4, panel-3. **Wood** a-2-9, 11, 12.*

PANIC (Magazine) (Satire)
July, 1958 - No. 6, July, 1959; V2#10, Dec, 1965 - V2#12, 1966
Panic Publications

	GD25	FN65	NM94
1	5.85	17.50	35.00
2-6	4.00	10.00	20.00
V2#10-12: Reprints earlier issues	2.00	5.00	10.00

NOTE: ***Davis** a-3(2 pgs.), 4, 5, 10; c-10. **Elder** a-5. **Powell** a-V2#10, 11. **Torres** a-1-5. **Tuska** a-V2#11.*

PARADAX (Eclipse & Vortex)(Value: cover or less)

PARADE (See Hanna-Barbera...)

PARADE COMICS (Frisky Animals on Parade #2 on)
Sept, 1957
Ajax/Farrell Publ. (World Famous Publ.)

	GD25	FN65	NM94
1	3.60	9.00	18.00

NOTE: *Cover title: Frisky Animals on Parade.*

PARADE OF PLEASURE
1954 (192 pgs.) (Hardback book)
Derric Verschoyle Ltd., London, England

By Geoffrey Wagner. Contains section devoted to the censorship of American comic books with illustrations in color and black and white. (Also see **Seduction of the Innocent**). Distributed in USA by Library Publishers, N. Y.

	GD25	FN65	NM94
N. Y.	30.00	90.00	210.00
with dust jacket....	55.00	165.00	385.00

PARAMOUNT ANIMATED COMICS (See Harvey Comics Hits #60,62)
Feb, 1953 - No. 22, July, 1956
Harvey Publications

	GD25	FN65	NM94
1-Baby Huey, Herman & Katnip, Buzzy the Crow begin	13.00	40.00	90.00
2	8.35	25.00	50.00
3-6	6.35	19.00	38.00
7-Baby Huey becomes permanent cover feature; cover title becomes Baby Huey with #9	13.00	40.00	90.00
8-10: 9-Infinity-c	5.85	17.50	35.00
11-22	4.20	12.50	25.00

PARANOIA (Adventure)(Value: cover or less)

PARENT TRAP, THE (See 4-Color #1210)

PARODY
Mar, 1977 (B&W humor magazine)
Armour Publishing

	GD25	FN65	NM94
1	.40	1.00	2.00

PAROLE BREAKERS
Dec, 1951 - No. 3, July, 1952
Avon Periodicals/Realistic #2 on

	GD25	FN65	NM94
1(#2 on inside)-r-c/Avon paperback #283	22.00	65.00	150.00
2-Kubert-a; r-c/Avon paperback #114	15.00	45.00	105.00
3-Kinstler-c	14.00	43.00	100.00

PARTRIDGE FAMILY, THE (TV)
March, 1971 - No. 21, Dec, 1973
Charlton Comics

	GD25	FN65	NM94
1	3.00	7.50	15.00
2-4,6-21	1.60	4.00	8.00
5-Partridge Family Summer Special (52 pgs.); The Shadow, Lone Ranger, Charlie McCarthy, Flash Gordon, Hopalong Cassidy, Gene Autry & others app.	3.60	9.00	18.00

PARTS UNKNOWN
July, 1992 - No. 4, Oct, 1992 ($2.50, B&W, mini-series, mature readers)
Eclipse Comics/FX

	GD25	FN65	NM94
1-4: All contain FX gaming cards	.50	1.25	2.50

PASSION, THE
No. 394, 1955
Catechetical Guild

	GD25	FN65	NM94
394	2.80	7.00	14.00

PAT BOONE (TV)(Also see Superman's Girlfriend Lois Lane #9)
Sept-Oct, 1959 - No. 5, May-Jun, 1960 (All have photo-c)
National Periodical Publications

	GD25	FN65	NM94
1	29.00	85.00	200.00
2-5: 4-Previews "Journey To The Center Of The Earth"	20.00	60.00	140.00

PATCHES
Mar-Apr, 1945 - No. 11, Nov, 1947
Rural Home/Patches Publ. (Orbit)

	GD25	FN65	NM94
1-L. B. Cole-c	13.00	40.00	90.00
2	7.50	22.50	45.00
3-11: 5-Danny Kaye-c/story; L.B. Cole-c. 7-Hopalong Cassidy-c/story. 9-Leav/Keigstein-a (16 pgs.). 10-Jack Carson (radio) c/story; Leav-c. 11-Red Skelton story	6.70	20.00	40.00

PATHWAYS TO FANTASY
July, 1984
Pacific Comics

	GD25	FN65	NM94
1-Barry Smith-c/a; Jeff Jones-a (4 pgs.)	.30	.75	1.50

PATORUZU (See Adventures of...)

PATSY & HEDY (Also see Hedy Wolfe)
Feb, 1952 - No. 110, Feb, 1967
Atlas Comics/Marvel (GPI/Male)

	GD25	FN65	NM94
1-Patsy Walker & Hedy Wolfe	10.00	30.00	70.00
2	5.85	17.50	35.00
3-10	4.70	14.00	28.00
11-20	3.60	9.00	18.00
21-40	2.80	7.00	14.00
41-60	1.80	4.50	9.00
61-110: 88-Lingerie panel	1.20	3.00	6.00
Annual 1(1963)	4.20	12.50	25.00

PATSY & HER PALS
May, 1953 - No. 29, Aug, 1957
Atlas Comics (PPI)

	GD25	FN65	NM94
1-Patsy Walker	9.15	27.50	55.00
2	4.70	14.00	28.00
3-10	4.00	10.00	20.00
11-29: 24-Everett-c	2.80	7.00	14.00

PATSY WALKER (See All Teen, A Date With Patsy, Girls' Life, Miss America Magazine, Patsy & Hedy, Patsy & Her Pals & Teen Comics)
1945 (no month) - No. 124, Dec, 1965
Marvel/Atlas Comics (BPC)

	GD25	FN65	NM94
1	29.00	85.00	200.00
2	14.00	43.00	100.00
3-10: 5-Injury-to-eye-c	10.00	30.00	60.00
11,12,15,16,18	7.50	22.50	45.00
13,14,17,19-22-Kurtzman's "Hey Look"	9.15	27.50	55.00
23,24	5.00	15.00	30.00
25-Rusty by Kurtzman; painted-c	9.15	27.50	55.00
26-29,31: 26-31: 52 pgs.	4.20	12.50	25.00
30(52 pgs.)-Egghead Doodle by Kurtzman, 1pg.	6.70	20.00	40.00
32-57: Last precode (3/55)	3.20	8.00	16.00
58-80	2.40	6.00	12.00
81-99: 92,98-Millie x-over	1.60	4.00	8.00
100	2.00	5.00	10.00
101-124	1.20	3.00	6.00
Fashion Parade 1(1966)-68 pgs.	4.20	12.50	25.00

NOTE: *Painted c-25-28. Anti-Wertham editorial in #21. Georgie app. in #8, 11. Millie app. in #10, 92, 98. Mitzi app. in #11. Rusty app. in #12, 25. Willie app. in #12.* ***Al Jaffee*** *c-57, 58.*

PAT THE BRAT (Adventures of Pipsqueak #34 on)
June, 1953; Summer, 1955 - No. 4, 5/56; No. 15, 7/56 - No. 33, 7/59
Archie Publications (Radio)

	GD25	FN65	NM94
nn(6/53)	9.15	27.50	55.00
1(Summer, 1955)	5.85	17.50	35.00
2-4-(5/56) (#5-14 not published)	4.00	10.00	20.00
15-(7/56)-33	2.00	5.00	10.00

PAT THE BRAT COMICS DIGEST MAGAZINE
October, 1980
Archie Publications

	GD25	FN65	NM94
1	.30	.75	1.50

PATTY POWERS (Formerly Della Vision #3)
No. 4, Oct, 1955 - No. 7, Oct, 1956
Atlas Comics

	GD25	FN65	NM94
4	4.70	14.00	28.00

Parole Breakers #1, © AVON

Patsy & Hedy #18, © MEG

Patsy Walker #7, © MEG

Paul Terry's Comics #89, © Viacom Int.

Pawnee Bill #1, © Story Comics

Peanuts #6, © UFS

	GD25	FN65	NM94
5-7	3.20	8.00	16.00

PAT WILTON (See Mighty Midget Comics)

PAUL (Spire Christian) (Value: cover or less)

PAULINE PERIL (See The Close Shaves of...)

PAUL REVERE'S RIDE (See 4-Color #822 & Walt Disney Showcase #34)

PAUL TERRY'S ADVENTURES OF MIGHTY MOUSE (See Adventures of...)

PAUL TERRY'S COMICS (Formerly Terry-Toons Comics; becomes Adventures of Mighty Mouse No. 126 on)
No. 85, Mar, 1951 - No. 125, May, 1955
St. John Publishing Co.

	GD25	FN65	NM94
85,86-Same as Terry-Toons #85, & 86 with only a title change; published at same time?	7.50	22.50	45.00
87-99: 89-Mighty Mouse begins, ends #125	4.70	14.00	28.00
100	5.85	17.50	35.00
101-104,107-125: 121,122,125-Painted-c	4.20	12.50	25.00
105,106-Giant Comics Edition, 100pgs. (9/53 & ?)	10.00	30.00	70.00

PAUL TERRY'S HOW TO DRAW FUNNY CARTOONS
1940's (14 pages) (Black & White)
Terrytoons, Inc. (Giveaway)

	GD25	FN65	NM94
nn-Heckle & Jeckle, Mighty Mouse, etc.	10.00	30.00	65.00

PAUL TERRY'S MIGHTY MOUSE (See Mighty Mouse)

PAUL TERRY'S MIGHTY MOUSE ADVENTURE STORIES (See Mighty Mouse Adventure Stories)

PAWNEE BILL
Feb, 1951 - No. 3, July, 1951
Story Comics (Youthful Magazines?)

	GD25	FN65	NM94
1-Bat Masterson, Wyatt Earp app.	7.50	22.50	45.00
2,3: 3-Origin Golden Warrior; Cameron-a	4.70	14.00	28.00

PAY-OFF (This Is the..., ...Crime, ...Detective Stories)
July-Aug, 1948 - No. 5, Mar-Apr, 1949 (52 pages)
D. S. Publishing Co.

	GD25	FN65	NM94
1	10.00	30.00	70.00
2	6.70	20.00	40.00
3-5	5.85	17.50	35.00

PEACEMAKER, THE (Also see Fightin' Five)
V3#1, Mar, 1967 - No. 5, Nov, 1967 (All 12 cent cover price)
Charlton Comics

	GD25	FN65	NM94
1-Fightin' Five begins	3.00	7.50	15.00
2,3,5	1.60	4.00	8.00
4-Origin The Peacemaker	3.00	7.50	15.00
1,2(Modern Comics reprint, 1978)		.50	1.00

PEACEMAKER (DC) (Value: cover or less) (Also see Crisis On Infinite Earths)

PEANUTS (Charlie Brown) (See Fritzi Ritz, Nancy & Sluggo, Tip Top, Tip Topper & United Comics)
No. 878, 2/58 - No. 13, 5-7/62; 5/63 - No. 4, 2/64
Dell Publishing Co./Gold Key

	GD25	FN65	NM94
4-Color 878(#1)	11.50	34.00	80.00
4-Color 969,1015('59)	10.00	30.00	60.00
4(2-4/60)	6.70	20.00	40.00
5-13	4.70	14.00	28.00
1(Gold Key, 5/63)	6.70	20.00	40.00
2-4	4.70	14.00	28.00
1(1953-54)-Reprints United Features' Strange As It Seems, Willie, Ferdnand	10.00	30.00	60.00

PEBBLES & BAMM BAMM (TV)
Jan, 1972 - No. 36, Dec, 1976 (Hanna-Barbera)
Charlton Comics

	GD25	FN65	NM94
1	4.20	12.50	25.00
2-10	2.40	6.00	12.00
11-36	1.60	4.00	8.00

PEBBLES FLINTSTONE (TV)
Sept, 1963 (Hanna-Barbera)
Gold Key

	GD25	FN65	NM94
1 (10088-309)	7.50	22.50	45.00

PECKS BAD BOY
1906 - 1908 (Strip reprints) (11-1/4x15-3/4")
Thompson of Chicago (by Walt McDougal)

	GD25	FN65	NM94
...& Cousin Cynthia(1907)-In color	30.00	90.00	180.00
...& His Chums(1908)-Hardcover; in full color; 16 pgs.	30.00	90.00	180.00
Advs. of...And His Country Cousins (1906)-In color, 18 pgs., oblong	30.00	90.00	180.00
Advs. of...in Pictures(1908)-In color; Stanton & Van V. Liet Co.	30.00	90.00	180.00

PEDRO (Formerly My Private Life #17; also see Romeo Tubbs)
No. 18, June, 1950 - No. 2, Aug, 1950?
Fox Features Syndicate

	GD25	FN65	NM94
18(#1)-Wood-c/a(p)	14.00	43.00	100.00
2-Wood-a?	11.00	32.00	75.00

PEE-WEE PIXIES (See The Pixies)

PELLEAS AND MELISANDE (See Night Music #4, 5)

PENALTY (See Crime Must Pay the...)

PENDRAGON (Knights of... #5 on; also see Knights of...)
July, 1992 - Present ($1.75, color)
Marvel Comics UK, Ltd.

	GD25	FN65	NM94
1-12: 1-4-Iron Man app. 6-8-Spider-Man app.	.35	.90	1.75

PENDULUM ILLUSTRATED BIOGRAPHIES
1979 (B&W)
Pendulum Press

19-355x-George Washington/Thomas Jefferson, 19-3495-Charles Lindbergh/Amelia Earhart, 19-3509-Harry Houdini/Walt Disney, 19-3517-Davy Crockett/Daniel Boone-Redondo-a, 19-3525-Elvis Presley/Beatles, 19-3533-Benjamin Franklin/Martin Luther King Jr, 19-3541-Abraham Lincoln/Franklin D. Roosevelt, 19-3568-Marie Curie/Albert Einstein-Redondo-a, 19-3576-Thomas Edison/Alexander Graham Bell-Redondo-a, 19-3584-Vince Lombardi/Pele, 19-3592-Babe Ruth/Jackie Robinson, 19-3606-Jim Thorpe/Althea Gibson

	GD25	FN65	NM94
Softback		1.50	
Hardback		4.50	

NOTE: *Above books still available from publisher.*

PENDULUM ILLUSTRATED CLASSICS (Now Age Illustrated)
1973 - 1978 (75 cents, 62pp, B&W, 5-3/8x8") (Also see Marvel Classics)
Pendulum Press

64-100x(1973)-Dracula-Redondo art, 64-131x-The Invisible Man-Nino art, 64-0968-Dr. Jekyll and Mr. Hyde-Redondo art, 64-1005-Black Beauty, 64-1010-Call of the Wild, 64-1020-Frankenstein, 64-1025-Huckleburry Finn, 64-1030-Moby Dick-Nino-a, 64-1040-Red Badge of Courage, 64-1045-The Time Machine-Nino-a, 64-1050-Tom Sawyer, 64-1055-Twenty Thousand Leagues Under the Sea, 64-1069-Treasure Island, 64-1328(1974)-Kidnapped, 64-1336-Three Musketeers-Nino art, 64-1344-A Tale of Two Cities, 64-1352-Journey to the Center of the Earth, 64-1360-The War of the Worlds-Nino-a, 64-1379-The Greatest Advs. of Sherlock Holmes-Redondo art, 64-1387-Mysterious Island, 64-1395-Hunchback of Notre Dame, 64-1409-Helen Keller-story of my life, 64-1417-Scarlet Letter, 64-1425-Gulliver's Travels, 64-2618(1977)-Around the World in Eighty Days, 64-2626-Captains Courageous, 64-2634-Connecticut Yankee, 64-2642-The Hound of the Baskervilles, 64-2650-The House of Seven Gables, 64-2669-Jane Eyre, 64-2677-The Last of the Mohicans, 64-2685-The Best of O'Henry, 64-2693-The Best of Poe-Redondo-a, 64-2707-Two Years Before the Mast, 64-2715-White Fang, 64-2723-Wuthering Heights, 64-3126(1978)-Ben Hur-Redondo art, 64-3134-A Christmas Carol, 64-3142-The Food of the Gods, 64-3150-Ivanhoe, 64-3169-The Man in the Iron Mask, 64-3177-The Prince and the Pauper, 64-3185-The Prisoner of Zenda, 64-3193-The Return of the Native, 64-3207-Robinson Crusoe, 64-3215-The Scarlet Pimpernel, 64-3223-The Sea Wolf, 64-3231-The Swiss Family Robinson, 64-3851-Billy Budd, 64-386x-Crime and Punishment, 64-3878-Don Quixote, 64-3886-Great Expectations, 64-3894-Heidi, 64-3908-The Iliad, 64-3916-Lord Jim, 64-3924-The Mutiny on Board H.M.S.

Bounty, 64-3932-The Odyssey, 64-3940-Oliver Twist, 64-3959-Pride and Prejudice, 64-3967-The Turn of the Screw

Softback — 1.45
Hardback — 4.50

NOTE: *All of the above books can be ordered from the publisher; some were reprinted as Marvel Classic Comics #1-12. In 1972 there was another brief series of 12 titles which contained Classics Ill. artwork. They were entitled* ***Now Age Books*** *Illustrated, but can be easily distinguished from later series by the small Classics Illustrated logo at the top of the front cover. The format is the same as the later series. The 48 pg. C.I. art was stretched out to make 62 pgs. After Twin Circle Publ. terminated the Classics Ill. series in 1971, they made a one year contract with Pendulum Press to print these twelve titles of C.I. art. Pendulum was unhappy with the contract, and at the end of 1972 began their own art series, utilizing the talents of the Filipino artist group. One detail which makes this rather confusing is that when they redid the art in 1973, they gave it the same identifying no. as the 1972 series. All 12 of the 1972 C.I. editions have new covers, taken from internal art panels. In spite of their recent age, all of the 1972 C.I. series are very rare. Mint copies would fetch at least $50. Here is a list of the 1972 series, with C.I. title no. counterpart:*

64-1005 (Cl#60-A2) 64-1010 (Cl#91) 64-1015 (Cl-Jr #503) 64-1020 (Cl#26)
64-1025 (Cl#19-A2) 64-1030 (Cl#5-A2) 64-1035 (Cl#169) 64-1040 (Cl#98)
64-1045 (Cl#133) 64-1050 (Cl#50-A2) 64-1055 (Cl#47) 64-1060 (Cl-Jr#535)

PENDULUM ILLUSTRATED ORIGINALS
1979 (in color)
Pendulum Press

94-4254-Solarman: The Beginning — .30 — .80 — 1.60

PENDULUM'S ILLUSTRATED STORIES
1990 - No. 72, 1990? (No cover price ($4.95), color, squarebound, 68 pgs.)
Pendulum Press

1-72: Reprints Pendulum Ill. Classics series — 1.00 — 2.50 — 5.00

PENNY
1947 - No. 6, Sept-Oct, 1949 (Newspaper reprints)
Avon Comics

1-Photo & biography of creator — 7.50 — 22.50 — 45.00
2-5 — 4.20 — 12.50 — 25.00
6-Perry Como photo on-c — 5.00 — 15.00 — 30.00

PEP COMICS (See Archie Giant Series #576, 589, 601, 614, 624)
Jan, 1940 - No. 411?, 1987
MLJ Magazines/Archie Publications No. 56 (3/46) on

GD25 FN65 VF82 NM94

1-Intro. The Shield by Irving Novick (1st patriotic hero); origin The Comet by Jack Cole, The Queen of Diamonds & Kayo Ward; The Rocket, The Press Guardian (The Falcon #1 only), Sergeant Boyle, Fu Chang, & Bentley of of Scotland Yard — 375.00 — 1125.00 — 2060.00 — 3000.00
(Estimated up to 150 total copies exist, 7 in NM/Mint)

GD25 FN65 NM94

2-Origin The Rocket — 117.00 — 350.00 — 700.00
3 — 92.00 — 275.00 — 550.00
4-Wizard cameo — 73.00 — 220.00 — 440.00
5-Wizard cameo in Shield story — 73.00 — 220.00 — 440.00
6-10: 8-Last Cole Comet; no Cole-a in #6,7 — 55.00 — 165.00 — 330.00
11-Dusty, Shield's sidekick begins; last Press Guardian, Fu Chang — 62.00 — 188.00 — 375.00
12-Origin Fireball; last Rocket & Queen of Diamonds; Danny in Wonderland begins — 75.00 — 225.00 — 450.00
13-15 — 50.00 — 150.00 — 300.00
16-Origin Madam Satan; blood drainage-c — 75.00 — 225.00 — 450.00
17-Origin The Hangman; death of The Comet; Comet is revealed as Hangman's brother — 158.00 — 475.00 — 950.00
18-21: 20-Last Fireball. 21-Last Madam Satan — 48.00 — 145.00 — 290.00

GD25 FN65 VF82 NM94

22-Intro. & 1st app. Archie, Betty, & Jughead(12/41); (also see Jackpot) — 425.00 — 1275.00 — 2300.00 — 3400.00
(Estimated up to 150 total copies exist, 7 in NM/Mint)

GD25 FN65 NM94

23 — 80.00 — 240.00 — 480.00
24,25 — 70.00 — 210.00 — 420.00
26-1st app. Veronica Lodge — 92.00 — 275.00 — 550.00
27-30: 30-Capt. Commando begins — 57.00 — 170.00 — 340.00
31-35: 31-MLJ offices & artists are visited in Sgt. Boyle story. 34-Bondage/Hypo-c — 47.00 — 140.00 — 280.00
36-1st Archie-c — 79.00 — 238.00 — 475.00
37-40 — 35.00 — 105.00 — 210.00
41-50: 41-Archie-c begin. 47-Last Hangman issue; infinity-c. 48-Black Hood begins (5/44); ends #51,59,60 — 25.00 — 75.00 — 150.00
51-60: 52-Suzie begins. 56-Last Capt. Commando. 59-Black Hood not in costume; spanking & lingerie panels; Archie dresses as his aunt; Suzie ends. 60-Katy Keene begins, ends #154 — 17.00 — 52.00 — 105.00
61-65-Last Shield. 62-1st app. Li'l Jinx — 13.00 — 40.00 — 80.00
66-80: 66-G-Man Club becomes Archie Club (2/48); Nevada Jones by Bill Woggon — 8.75 — 26.00 — 52.00
81-99 — 6.35 — 19.00 — 38.00
100 — 8.35 — 25.00 — 50.00
101-130 — 3.60 — 9.00 — 18.00
131-149 — 2.00 — 5.00 — 10.00
150-160-Super-heroes app. in each (see note). 150 (10/61?)-2nd or 3rd app. The Jaguar? 157-Li'l Jinx story — 2.40 — 6.00 — 12.00
161-167,169-200 — 1.00 — 2.50 — 5.00
168-Jaguar app. — 1.40 — 3.50 — 7.00
201-260 — .60 — 1.50 — 3.00
261-411: 383-Marvelous Maureen begins (Sci/fi). 393-Thunderbunny begins — .50 — 1.00

NOTE: ***Biro*** *a-2, 4, 5.* ***Jack Cole*** *a-1-5, 8.* ***Al Fagaly*** *c-55-72(most).* ***Fuje*** *a-39, 45, 47; c-34.* ***Meskin*** *a-2, 4, 5, 11(2).* ***Montana*** *c-30, 32, 33, 36, 73-87(most).* ***Novick*** *c-1-28, 29(w/ Schomburg), 31i.* ***Harry Sahle*** *c-35, 39-50.* ***Schomburg*** *c-38.* ***Bob Wood*** *a-2, 4-6, 11. The Fly app. in 151, 154, 160. Flygirl app. in 153, 155, 156, 158. Jaguar app. in 150, 152, 157, 159, 168. Katy Keene by* ***Bill Woggon*** *in many later issues. Bondage c-7, 12, 13, 15, 18, 21, 31, 32.*

PEPE (See 4-Color #1194)

PERCY & FERDIE
1921 (52 pages) (B&W dailies, 10x10", cardboard-c)
Cupples & Leon Co.

nn-By H. A. MacGill — 11.00 — 32.00 — 75.00

PERFECT CRIME, THE
Oct, 1949 - No. 33, May, 1953 (#2-12, 52 pgs.)
Cross Publications

1-Powell-a(2) — 11.50 — 34.00 — 80.00
2 (4/50) — 8.35 — 25.00 — 50.00
3-10: 7-Steve Duncan begins, ends #30 — 6.70 — 20.00 — 40.00
11-Used in **SOTI**, pg. 159 — 8.35 — 25.00 — 50.00
12-14 — 5.00 — 15.00 — 30.00
15-"The Most Terrible Menace"-2 pg. drug editorial — 5.85 — 17.50 — 35.00
16,17,19-25,27-29,31-33 — 4.00 — 11.00 — 22.00
18-Drug cover, heroin drug propaganda story, plus 2 pg. drug editorial — 11.00 — 32.00 — 75.00
26-Drug-c with hypodermic; drug propaganda story — 11.50 — 34.00 — 80.00
30-Strangulation cover — 10.00 — 30.00 — 70.00

NOTE: ***Powell*** *a-No. 1, 2, 4.* ***Wildey*** *a-1, 5. Bondage c-11.*

PERFECT LOVE
#10, 8-9/51 (cover date; 5-6/51 indicia date); #2, 10-11/51 - #10, 12/53
Ziff-Davis(Approved Comics)/St. John No. 9 on

10(#1)(8-9/51) — 10.00 — 30.00 — 60.00
2(10-11/51) — 6.70 — 20.00 — 40.00
3,5-7: 3-Painted-c. 5-Photo-c — 4.70 — 14.00 — 28.00
4,8 (Fall, 1952)-Kinstler-a; last Z-D issue — 5.00 — 15.00 — 30.00
9,10 (10/53, 12/53, St. John): 9-Painted-c. 10-Photo-c — 4.35 — 13.00 — 26.00

PERRI (See 4-Color #847)

PERRY MASON (See Feature Books #49, 50)

PERRY MASON MYSTERY MAGAZINE (TV)

Pep Comics #15, © AP

Pep Comics #71, © AP

The Perfect Crime #12, © Cross Publ.

Personal Love #30, © FF

Peter Panda #5, © DC

Peter Porkchops #1, © DC

	GD25	FN65	NM94
June-Aug, 1964 - No. 2, Oct-Dec, 1964			
Dell Publishing Co.			
1,2: 2-Raymond Burr photo-c	4.00	10.00	20.00

PERSONAL LOVE (Also see Movie Love)
Jan, 1950 - No. 33, June, 1955
Famous Funnies

	GD25	FN65	NM94
1	10.00	30.00	60.00
2	5.00	15.00	30.00
3-7,10	4.00	12.00	24.00
8,9-Kinstler-a	4.70	14.00	28.00
11-Toth-a	7.50	22.50	45.00
12,16,17-One pg. Frazetta each	4.35	13.00	26.00
13-15,18-23	4.00	10.00	20.00
24,27,28-Frazetta-a in all-8,8&6 pgs.	23.00	70.00	160.00
25-Frazetta-a (tribute to Betty Page, 7 pg. story); Tyrone Power/Terry Moore photo-c from "King of the Khyber Rifles"	23.00	70.00	160.00
26,29-31,33: 31-Last pre-code (2/55)	3.20	8.00	16.00
32-Classic Frazetta-a, 8 pgs.; Kirk Douglas/Bella Darvi photo-c	39.00	116.00	270.00

NOTE: *All have photo-c.* ***Everett*** *a-5, 9, 10, 24.*

PERSONAL LOVE (Going Steady V3#3 on)
V1#1, Sept, 1957 - V3#2, Nov-Dec, 1959
Prize Publ. (Headline)

	GD25	FN65	NM94
V1#1	4.20	12.50	25.00
2	2.80	7.00	14.00
3-6(7-8/58)	2.40	6.00	12.00
V2#1(9-10/58)-V2#6(7-8/59)	1.80	4.50	9.00
V3#1-Wood/Orlando-a	3.20	8.00	16.00
2	1.60	4.00	8.00

PETER CANNON - THUNDERBOLT (Also see Thunderbolt)
Sept, 1992 - Present ($1.25, color)(See Crisis on Infinite Earths)
DC Comics

	GD25	FN65	NM94
1-10		.60	1.25

PETER COTTONTAIL
Jan, 1954; Feb, 1954 - No. 2, Mar, 1954
Key Publications

	GD25	FN65	NM94
1(1/54)-Not 3-D	5.35	16.00	32.00
1(2/54)-(3-D); Written by Bruce Hamilton	17.00	52.00	120.00
2-Reprints 3-D #1 but not in 3-D	4.35	13.00	26.00

PETER GUNN (See 4-Color #1087)

PETER PAN (See 4-Color #442, 446, 926, Hook, Movie Classics & Comics, New Adventures of... & Walt Disney Showcase #36)

PETER PAN
1991 ($5.95, color, graphic novel, 68 pgs.)(Celebrates release of video)
Disney Comics

	GD25	FN65	NM94
nn-r/Peter Pan Treasure Chest from 1953	1.00	3.00	6.00

PETER PANDA
Aug-Sept, 1953 - No. 31, Aug-Sept, 1958
National Periodical Publications

	GD25	FN65	NM94
1-Grossman-c/a in all	25.00	75.00	175.00
2	11.50	34.00	80.00
3-10	10.00	30.00	60.00
11-31	5.85	17.50	35.00

PETER PAN: THE RETURN TO NEVER-NEVER LAND (Adventure)(Value: cover or less)

PETER PAN TREASURE CHEST (See Dell Giants)

PETER PARKER (See The Spectacular Spider-Man)

PETER PAT (See Single Series #8)

PETER PAUL'S 4 IN 1 JUMBO COMIC BOOK
No date (1953)
Capitol Stories

	GD25	FN65	NM94
1-Contains 4 comics bound; Space Adventures, Space Western, Crime & Justice, Racket Squad in Action	29.00	88.00	175.00

PETER PENNY AND HIS MAGIC DOLLAR
1947 (16 pgs.; paper cover; regular size)
American Bankers Association, N. Y. (Giveaway)

	GD25	FN65	NM94
nn-(Scarce)-Used in **SOTI**, pg. 310, 311	11.50	34.00	80.00
Another version (7-1/2x11")-redrawn, 16 pgs., paper-c	7.50	22.50	45.00

PETER PIG
No. 5, May, 1953 - No. 6, Aug, 1953
Standard Comics

	GD25	FN65	NM94
5,6	3.00	7.50	15.00

PETER PORKCHOPS (See Leading Comics #23)
11-12/49 - No. 61, 9-11/59; No. 62, 10-12/60 (1-5: 52 pgs.)
National Periodical Publications

	GD25	FN65	NM94
1	25.00	75.00	175.00
2	11.50	34.00	80.00
3-10	10.00	30.00	60.00
11-30	6.70	20.00	40.00
31-62	5.00	15.00	30.00

NOTE: ***Otto Feur*** *a-all.* ***Sheldon Mayer*** *a-30-38, 40-44, 46-52, 61.*

PETER PORKER, THE SPECTACULAR SPIDER-HAM
May, 1985 - No. 17, Sept, 1987 (Also see Marvel Tails)
Star Comics (Marvel)

	GD25	FN65	NM94
1-Michael Golden-c	.40	1.00	2.00
2-17: 13-Halloween issue		.50	1.00

NOTE: *Back-up features: 2-X-Bugs. 3-Iron Mouse. 4-Croctor Strange. 5-Thrr, Dog of Thunder.*

PETER POTAMUS (TV)
January, 1965 (Hanna-Barbera)
Gold Key

	GD25	FN65	NM94
1	5.00	15.00	30.00

PETER RABBIT (See Large Feature Comic #1, New Funnies #65 & Space Comics)

PETER RABBIT
1922 - 1923 (9¼x6¼") (paper cover)
John H. Eggers Co. The House of Little Books Publishers

	GD25	FN65	NM94
B1-B4-(Rare)-(Set of 4 books which came in a cardboard box)-Each book reprints of a Sunday page per page and contains 8 B&W and 2 color pages; by Harrison Cady each....	23.00	70.00	160.00

PETER RABBIT (Adventures of...; New Advs. of... later issues)
1947 - No. 34, Aug-Sept, 1956
Avon Periodicals

	GD25	FN65	NM94
1(1947)-Reprints 1943-44 Sunday strips; contains a biography & drawing of Cady	23.00	70.00	160.00
2 (4/48)	18.00	54.00	125.00
3 ('48) - 6(7/49)-Last Cady issue	16.50	50.00	115.00
7-10(1950-8/51)	4.00	10.50	21.00
11(11/51)-34('56)-Avon's character	2.60	6.50	13.00
...Easter Parade (132 pgs.; 1952)	10.00	30.00	70.00
...Jumbo Book (1954-Giant Size, 25 cents)-6 pgs. Jesse James by Kinstler	15.00	45.00	105.00

PETER RABBIT
1958
Fago Magazine Co.

	GD25	FN65	NM94
1	4.00	12.00	24.00

PETER RABBIT 3-D (Eternity) (Value: cover or less)

PETER, THE LITTLE PEST (#4 titled Petey)
Nov, 1969 - No. 4, May, 1970
Marvel Comics Group

	GD25	FN65	NM94
1	1.00	2.50	5.00
2-4-Reprints Dexter the Demon & Melvin the Monster	.80	2.00	4.00

PETER WHEAT (The Adventures of...)
1948 - 1956? (16 pgs. in color) (paper covers)
Bakers Associates Giveaway

	GD25	FN65	NM94
nn(No.1)-States on last page, end of 1st Adventure of...; Kelly-a	22.00	65.00	150.00
nn(4 issues)-Kelly-a	14.00	43.00	100.00
6-10-All Kelly-a	11.00	32.00	75.00
11-20-All Kelly-a	10.00	30.00	65.00
21-35-All Kelly-a	8.35	25.00	50.00
36-66	5.35	16.00	32.00
...Artist's Workbook ('54, digest size)	4.70	14.00	28.00
...Four-In-One Fun Pack (Vol. 2, '54), oblong, comics w/puzzles	5.00	15.00	30.00
...Fun Book ('52, 32pgs., paper-c, B&W & color, 8-1/2x10-3/4"), contains cut-outs, puzzles, games, magic & pages to color	8.35	25.00	50.00

NOTE: ***Al Hubbard** art #36 on; written by **Del Connell**.*

PETER WHEAT NEWS
1948 - No. 30, 1950 (4 pgs. in color)
Bakers Associates

	GD25	FN65	NM94
Vol. 1-All have 2 pgs. Peter Wheat by Kelly	22.00	65.00	150.00
2-10	13.00	40.00	90.00
11-20	7.50	22.50	45.00
21-30	5.00	15.00	30.00

NOTE: *Early issues have no date & **Kelly** art.*

PETE'S DRAGON (See Walt Disney Showcase #43)

PETE THE PANIC
November, 1955
Stanmor Publications

	GD25	FN65	NM94
nn-Code approved	2.40	6.00	12.00

PETEY (See Peter, the Little Pest)

PETTICOAT JUNCTION (TV)
Oct-Dec, 1964 - No. 5, Oct-Dec, 1965 (#1-3, 5 have photo-c)
Dell Publishing Co.

	GD25	FN65	NM94
1	6.70	20.00	40.00
2-5	4.20	12.50	25.00

PETUNIA (See 4-Color #463)

PHANTASMO (See Large Feature Comic #18)

PHANTOM, THE
1939 - 1949
David McKay Publishing Co.

	GD25	FN65	NM94
Feature Books 20	54.00	160.00	375.00
Feature Books 22	43.00	130.00	300.00
Feature Books 39	36.00	110.00	250.00
Feature Books 53,56,57	26.00	77.00	180.00

PHANTOM, THE (See Ace Comics, Defenders Of The Earth, Eat Right to Work and Win, Future Comics, Harvey Comics Hits #51,56, Harvey Hits #1, 6, 12, 15, 26, 36, 44, 48, & King Comics)

PHANTOM, THE (nn 29-Published overseas only) (Also see Comics Reading Library)
Nov, 1962 - No. 17, July, 1966; No. 18, Sept, 1966 - No. 28, Dec, 1967; No. 30, Feb, 1969 - No. 74, Jan, 1977
Gold Key (#1-17)/King (#18-28)/Charlton (#30 on)

	GD25	FN65	NM94
1-Manning-a	10.00	30.00	60.00
2-King, Queen & Jack begins, ends #11	5.00	15.00	30.00
3-10	4.20	12.50	25.00
11-17: 12-Track Hunter begins	4.00	10.00	20.00
18-Flash Gordon begins; Wood-a	4.00	11.00	22.00
19,20-Flash Gordon ends (both by Gil Kane)	3.00	7.50	15.00
21-24,26,27: 21-Mandrake begins. 20,24-Girl Phantom app. 26-Brick Bradford app.	3.00	7.50	15.00
25-Jeff Jones-a(4 pgs.); 1 pg. Williamson ad	3.00	7.50	15.00
28(nn)-Brick Bradford app.	2.40	6.00	12.00
30-40: 36,39-Ditko-a	2.00	5.00	10.00
41-66: 46-Intro. The Piranha. 62-Bolle-c	1.60	4.00	8.00
67-71,73-Newton-c/a; 67-Origin retold	1.00	2.50	5.00
72,74: 74-Newton Flag-c; Newton-a	1.00	2.50	5.00

NOTE: ***Aparo** a-31-34, 36-38; c-31-38, 60, 61. Painted c-1-17.*

PHANTOM, THE
May, 1988 - No. 4, Aug, 1988 ($1.25, color, mini-series)
DC Comics

	GD25	FN65	NM94
1-4: Orlando-c/a in all		.60	1.25

PHANTOM, THE
Mar, 1989 - No. 13, Mar, 1990 ($1.50, color)
DC Comics

	GD25	FN65	NM94
1-13: 1-Brief origin	.30	.75	1.50

PHANTOM, THE
1992 - Present ($2.25, color)
Wolf Publishing

	GD25	FN65	NM94
1-8	.45	1.15	2.25

PHANTOM BLOT, THE (#1 titled New Adventures of...)
Oct, 1964 - No. 7, Nov, 1966 (Disney)
Gold Key

	GD25	FN65	NM94
1 (Meets The Beagle Boys)	4.00	11.00	22.00
2-1st Super Goof	3.00	7.50	15.00
3-7	2.40	6.00	12.00

PHANTOM EAGLE (See Mighty Midget, Marvel Super Heroes #16 & Wow #6)

PHANTOM LADY (1st Series) (My Love Secret #24 on) (Also see All Top, Daring Adventures, Freedom Fighters, Jungle Thrills, & Wonder Boy)
No. 13, Aug, 1947 - No. 23 April, 1949
Fox Features Syndicate

	GD25	FN65	NM94
13(#1)-Phantom Lady by Matt Baker begins; The Blue Beetle app.	135.00	407.00	950.00
14(#2)	93.00	280.00	650.00
15-P.L. injected with experimental drug	72.00	215.00	500.00
16-Negligee-c, panels	72.00	215.00	500.00
17-Classic bondage cover; used in **SOTI**, illo-"Sexual stimulation by combining 'headlights' with the sadist's dream of tying up a woman"	165.00	495.00	1150.00
18,19	64.00	195.00	450.00
20-23: 23-Bondage-c	57.00	170.00	400.00

NOTE: ***Matt Baker** a-in all; c-13, 15-21. **Kamen** a-22, 23.*

PHANTOM LADY (2nd Series) (See Terrific Comics) (Formerly Linda)
V1#5, Dec-Jan, 1954/1955 - No. 4, June, 1955
Ajax/Farrell Publ.

	GD25	FN65	NM94
V1#5(#1)-By Matt Baker	39.00	120.00	275.00
V1#2-Last pre-code	32.00	95.00	225.00
3,4-Red Rocket	26.00	77.00	180.00

PHANTOM PLANET, THE (See 4-Color No. 1234)

PHANTOM STRANGER, THE (1st Series) (See Saga of Swamp Thing)
Aug-Sept, 1952 - No. 6, June-July, 1953
National Periodical Publications

	GD25	FN65	NM94
1 (Scarce)	100.00	300.00	700.00
2 (Scarce)	72.00	215.00	500.00
3-6 (Scarce)	57.00	171.00	400.00

Peter Wheat #42, © Bakers Assoc.

The Phantom #9 (Gold Key), © KING

Phantom Lady #21, © FOX

The Phantom Stranger #29, © DC

Pictorial Romances #5, © STJ

Picture News #1, © Lafayette Street Corp.

	GD25	FN65	NM94

PHANTOM STRANGER, THE (2nd Series) (See Showcase #80)
May-June, 1969 - No. 41, Feb-Mar, 1976
National Periodical Publications

	GD25	FN65	NM94
1-1st S.A. app. P. Stranger; only 12 cent issue	6.70	20.00	40.00
2,3	2.80	7.00	14.00
4-Neal Adams-a	3.20	8.00	16.00
5-7	2.00	5.00	10.00
8-14: 14-Last 15 cent issue	1.50	3.75	7.50
15-19: All 25 cent giants (52 pgs.)	.90	2.25	4.50
20-41: 22-Dark Circle begins. 23-Spawn of Frankenstein begins by Kaluta; series ends #30. 31-The Black Orchid begins. 34-Last 20 cent issue (#35 on are 25 cents). 39-41-Deadman app.	.70	1.75	3.50

NOTE: ***N. Adams** a-4; c-3-19. **Aparo** a-7-26; c-20-24, 33-41. **B. Bailey** a-27-30. **DeZuniga** a-14-16, 19-22, 31, 34. **Grell** a-33. **Kaluta** a-23-25; c-26. **Meskin** r-15, 16, 18. **Redondo** a-32, 35, 36. **Sparling** a-20. **Starr** a-17r. **Toth** a-15r. Black Orchid by **Carrilo**-38-41. Dr. 13 solo in-13, 18, 20. Frankenstein by **Kaluta**-23-25; by **Baily**-27-30. No Black Orchid-33, 34, 37.*

PHANTOM STRANGER (See Justice League of America #103)
Oct, 1987 - No. 4, Jan, 1988 (75 cents, color, mini-series)
DC Comics

	GD25	FN65	NM94
1-Mignola/Russell-c/a & Eclipso app. in all	.30	.75	1.50
2-4: 3,4-Eclipso-c		.50	1.00

PHANTOM WITCH DOCTOR (Also see Durango Kid #8 & Eerie #8)
1952
Avon Periodicals

	GD25	FN65	NM94
1-Kinstler-c/a (7 pgs.)	24.00	73.00	170.00

PHANTOM ZONE, THE (See Adventure #283 & Superboy #100, 104)
January, 1982 - No. 4, April, 1982
DC Comics

	GD25	FN65	NM94
1-Superman app. in all		.50	1.00
2-4: Batman, Green Lantern app.		.60	1.25

NOTE: ***Colan** a-1-4p; c-1-4p. **Giordano** c-1-4i.*

PHAZE (Eclipse)(Value: cover or less)

PHIL RIZZUTO (Baseball Hero)(See Sport Thrills, Accepted reprint)
1951 (New York Yankees)
Fawcett Publications

	GD25	FN65	NM94
nn-Photo-c	40.00	120.00	275.00

PHOENIX
Jan, 1975 - No. 4, Oct, 1975
Atlas/Seaboard Publ.

	GD25	FN65	NM94
1-Origin		.60	1.20
2-4: 3-Origin & only app. The Dark Avenger. 4-New origin/costume The Protector (formerly Phoenix)		.50	1.00

NOTE: ***Infantino** appears in #1, 2. **Austin** a-3i. **Thorne** c-3.*

PHOENIX (...The Untold Story)
April, 1984 ($2.00, One shot)
Marvel Comics Group

	GD25	FN65	NM94
1-Byrne/Austin-r/X-Men #137 with original unpublished ending	1.20	3.00	6.00

PICNIC PARTY (See Dell Giants)

PICTORIAL CONFESSIONS (Pictorial Romances #4 on)
Sept, 1949 - No. 3, Dec, 1949
St. John Publishing Co.

	GD25	FN65	NM94
1-Baker-c/a(3)	12.00	36.00	84.00
2-Baker-a; photo-c	7.00	21.00	42.00
3-Kubert, Baker-a; part Kubert-c	10.00	30.00	60.00

PICTORIAL LOVE STORIES (Formerly Tim McCoy)
No. 22, Oct, 1949 - No. 26, July, 1950
Charlton Comics

	GD25	FN65	NM94
22-26-"Me-Dan Cupid" in all	10.00	30.00	60.00

PICTORIAL LOVE STORIES
October, 1952
St. John Publishing Co.

	GD25	FN65	NM94
1-Baker-c/a	11.50	34.00	80.00

PICTORIAL ROMANCES (Formerly Pictorial Confessions)
No. 4, Jan, 1950; No. 5, Jan, 1951 - No. 24, Mar, 1954
St. John Publishing Co.

	GD25	FN65	NM94
4-All Baker	11.50	34.00	80.00
5,10-All Matt Baker issues	10.00	30.00	60.00
6-9,12,13,15,16-Baker-c, 2-3 stories	6.70	20.00	40.00
11-Baker-c/a(3); Kubert-a	7.50	22.50	45.00
14,21-24-Baker-c/a each	5.35	16.00	32.00
17-20(7/53)-100 pgs. each; Baker-c/a	12.00	36.00	85.00

NOTE: ***Matt Baker** art in most issues. **Estrada** a-19(2).*

PICTURE NEWS
Jan, 1946 - No. 10, Jan-Feb, 1947
Lafayette Street Corp.

	GD25	FN65	NM94
1-Milt Gross begins, ends No. 6; 4 pg. Kirby-a; A-Bomb-c/story	23.00	68.00	135.00
2-Atomic explosion panels; Frank Sinatra, Perry Como stories	10.00	30.00	60.00
3-Atomic explosion panels; Frank Sinatra, June Allyson stories	9.15	27.50	55.00
4-Atomic explosion panels; "Caesar and Cleopatra" movie adaptation; Jackie Robinson story	10.00	30.00	60.00
5-7: 5-Hank Greenberg story. 6-Joe Louis c/story	6.70	20.00	40.00
8-Monte Hale story(9-10/46; 1st?)	8.35	25.00	50.00
9-A-Bomb story; "Crooked Mile" movie adaptation; Joe DiMaggio story	10.00	30.00	60.00
10-A-Bomb story; Krigstein, Gross-a	8.35	25.00	50.00

PICTURE PARADE (Picture Progress #5 on)
Sept, 1953 - V1#4, Dec, 1953 (28 pages)
Gilberton Company (Also see A Christmas Adventure)

	GD25	FN65	NM94
V1#1-Andy's Atomic Adventures-A-bomb blast-c; (Teachers version distributed to schools exists)	10.00	30.00	70.00
2-Around the World with the United Nations	7.50	22.50	45.00
3-Adventures of the Lost One(The American Indian), 4-A Christmas Adventure (r-under same title in '69)	7.50	22.50	45.00

PICTURE PROGRESS (Formerly Picture Parade)
V1#5, Jan, 1954 - V3#2, Oct, 1955 (28-36 pgs.)
Gilberton Corp.

	GD25	FN65	NM94
V1#5-9,V2#1-9: 5-News in Review 1953, 6-The Birth of America, 7-The Four Seasons, 8-Paul Revere's Ride, 9-The Hawaiian Islands(5/54), V2#1-The Story of Flight(9/54), 2-Vote for Crazy River(The Meaning of Elections), 3-Louis Pasteur, 4-The Star Spangled Banner, 5-News in Review 1954, 6-Alaska: The Great Land, 7-Life in the Circus, 8-The Time of the Cave Man, 9-Summer Fun(5/55)	3.60	9.00	18.00
V3#1,2: 1-The Man Who Discovered America, 2-The Lewis & Clark Expedition	3.60	9.00	18.00

PICTURE SCOPE JUNGLE ADVENTURES (See Jungle Thrills)

PICTURE STORIES FROM AMERICAN HISTORY
1945 - No. 4, Sum, 1947 (#1,2: 10 cents, 56pgs.; #3: 15 cents, 52pgs.)
National/All-American/E. C. Comics

	GD25	FN65	NM94
1	14.00	43.00	100.00
2-4	10.00	30.00	65.00

PICTURE STORIES FROM SCIENCE
Spring, 1947 - No. 2, Fall, 1947
E.C. Comics

	GD25	FN65	NM94
1,2	14.00	43.00	100.00

PICTURE STORIES FROM THE BIBLE

Fall, 1942-3 & 1944-46
National/All-American/E.C. Comics

	GD25	FN65	NM94
1-4('42-Fall,'43)-Old Testament (DC)	14.00	43.00	100.00
Complete Old Testament Edition, 232pgs.(12/43-DC);-1st printing; contains #1-4; 2nd - 8th (1/47) printings exist; later printings by E.C.	17.00	52.00	120.00
Complete Old Testament Edition (1945-publ. by Bible Pictures Ltd.)-232 pgs., hardbound, in color with dust jacket	17.00	52.00	120.00

NOTE: *Both Old and New Testaments published in England by Bible Pictures Ltd. in hardback, 1943, in color, 376 pages, and were also published by Scarf Press in 1979 (Old Test., $9.95) and in 1980 (New Test., $7.95)*

	GD25	FN65	NM94
1-3(New Test.; 1944-46, DC)-52pgs. ea.	10.00	30.00	70.00
The Complete Life of Christ Edition (1945)-96pgs.; contains #1&2 of the New Testament Edition	14.00	43.00	100.00
1,2(Old Testament-r in comic book form)(E.C., 1946; 52pgs.)	10.00	30.00	70.00
1-3(New Testament-r in comic book form)(E.C., 1946; 52pgs.)	10.00	30.00	70.00
Complete New Testament Edition (1946-E.C.)-144 pgs.; contains #1-3	14.00	43.00	100.00

NOTE: *Another British series entitled **The Bible Illustrated** from 1947 has recently been discovered, with the same internal artwork. This eight edition series (5-OT, 3-NT) is of particular interest to Classics Ill. collectors because it exactly copied the C.I. logo format. The British publisher was Thorpe & Porter, who in 1951 began publishing the British Classics Ill. series. All editions of The Bible Ill. have new British painted covers. While this market is still new, and not all editions have as yet been found, current market value is about the same as the first U.S. editions of Picture Stories From The Bible.*

PICTURE STORIES FROM WORLD HISTORY
Spring, 1947 - No. 2, Summer, 1947 (52,48 pgs.)
E.C. Comics

	GD25	FN65	NM94
1,2	14.00	43.00	100.00

PINHEAD & FOODINI (TV)(Also see Foodini & Jingle Dingle Christmas...)
July, 1951 - No. 4, Jan, 1952
Fawcett Publications

	GD25	FN65	NM94
1-(52 pgs.)-Photo-c; based on TV puppet show	19.00	58.00	135.00
2-Photo-c	10.00	30.00	65.00
3,4: 3-Photo-c	7.50	22.50	45.00

PINK LAFFIN
1922 (9x12")(Strip-r)
Whitman Publishing Co.

	GD25	FN65	NM94
...the Lighter Side of Life, ...He Tells 'Em, ...and His Family, ...Knockouts; Ray Gleason-a (All rare) each...	11.50	34.00	80.00

PINK PANTHER, THE (TV)(See Kite Fun Book)
April, 1971 - No. 87, 1984
Gold Key

	GD25	FN65	NM94
1-The Inspector begins	3.00	7.50	15.00
2-10	1.40	3.00	7.00
11-30: Warren Tufts-a #16-on	1.00	2.50	5.00
31-60	.60	1.50	3.00
61-87	.50	1.25	2.50
Mini-comic No. 1(1976)(3-1/4x6-1/2")	.40	1.00	2.00

NOTE: *Pink Panther began as a movie cartoon. (See Golden Comics Digest #38, 45 and March of Comics #376, 384, 390, 409, 418, 429, 441, 449, 461, 473, 486); #37, 72, 80-85 contain reprints.*

PINKY LEE (See Adventures of...)

PINKY THE EGGHEAD
1963 (Reprints from Noodnik)
I.W./Super Comics

	GD25	FN65	NM94
I.W. Reprint #1,2(nd)	.60	1.50	3.00
Super Reprint #14	.60	1.50	3.00

PINOCCHIO (See 4-Color #92, 252, 545, 1203, Mickey Mouse Mag. V5#3, Movie Comics under Wonderful Advs. of..., New Advs. of..., Thrilling Comics #2, Walt Disney Showcase, Walt Disney's..., Wonderful Advs. of..., & World's Greatest Stories #2)

PINOCCHIO
1940 (10 pages; linen-like paper)
Montgomery Ward Co. (Giveaway)

	GD25	FN65	NM94
nn	14.00	43.00	100.00

PINOCCHIO AND THE EMPEROR OF THE NIGHT (Marvel)(Value: cover or less)

PINOCCHIO LEARNS ABOUT KITES (See Kite Fun Book)

PIN-UP PETE (Also see Great Lover Romances & Monty Hall...)
1952
Toby Press

	GD25	FN65	NM94
1-Jack Sparling pin-ups	11.00	32.00	75.00

PIONEER MARSHAL (See Fawcett Movie Comics)

PIONEER PICTURE STORIES
Dec, 1941 - No. 9, Dec, 1943
Street & Smith Publications

	GD25	FN65	NM94
1	16.00	48.00	110.00
2	10.00	30.00	60.00
3-9	7.50	22.50	45.00

PIONEER WEST ROMANCES (Firehair #1,2,7-11)
No. 3, Spring, 1950 - No. 6, Winter, 1950-51
Fiction House Magazines

	GD25	FN65	NM94
3-(52 pgs.)-Firehair continues	11.00	32.00	75.00
4-6	10.00	30.00	60.00

PIPSQUEAK (See The Adventures of...)

PIRACY
Oct-Nov, 1954 - No. 7, Oct-Nov, 1955
E. C. Comics

	GD25	FN65	NM94
1-Williamson/Torres-a	18.00	54.00	125.00
2-Williamson/Torres-a	12.00	36.00	85.00
3-7	10.00	30.00	70.00

NOTE: ***Crandall** a-in all; c-2-4. **Davis** a-1, 2, 6. **Evans** a-3-7; c-7. **Ingels** a-3-7. **Krigstein** a-3-5, 7; c-5, 6. **Wood** a-1, 2; c-1.*

PIRANA (See Thrill-O-Rama #2, 3)

PIRATE CORPS, THE (Eternity)(Value: cover or less)

PIRATE OF THE GULF, THE (See Superior Stories #2)

PIRATES COMICS
Feb-Mar, 1950 - No. 4, Aug-Sept, 1950 (All 52 pgs.)
Hillman Periodicals

	GD25	FN65	NM94
1	13.00	40.00	90.00
2-Dave Berg-a	10.00	30.00	60.00
3,4-Berg-a	9.15	27.50	55.00

PIRATES OF DARK WATER, THE (TV)(Marvel)(Value: cover or less)

P.I.'S: MICHAEL MAUSER AND MS. TREE, THE (First)(Value: cover or less)

PITT, THE (Marvel)(Value: cover or less)(Also see The Draft & The War)

PIUS XII MAN OF PEACE
No date (12 pgs.; 5-1/2x8-1/2") (B&W)
Catechetical Guild Giveaway

	GD25	FN65	NM94
nn	4.00	10.50	21.00

PIXIE & DIXIE & MR. JINKS (TV)(See Jinks, Pixie, and Dixie & Whitman Comic Books)
July-Sept, 1960 - Feb, 1963 (Hanna-Barbera)
Dell Publishing Co./Gold Key

	GD25	FN65	NM94
4-Color 1112	5.85	17.50	35.00
4-Color 1196,1264	4.20	12.50	25.00
01-631-207 (Dell), 1(2/63-Gold Key)	4.20	12.50	25.00

PIXIE PUZZLE ROCKET TO ADVENTURELAND
November, 1952
Avon Periodicals

Picture Stories From World History #1, © WMG

Pirates Comics #3, © HILL

Pixie & Dixie & Mr. Jinks #01-631-207, © Hanna-Barbera

Planet Comics #58, © FH

Plastic Man #18 ('40s), © QUA

Plastic Man #2 (1-2/67), © DC

	GD25	FN65	NM94
1	9.15	27.50	55.00

PIXIES, THE (Advs. of...) (The Mighty Atom and ...#6 on)
Winter, 1946 - No. 4, Fall?, 1947; No. 5, 1948
Magazine Enterprises

	GD25	FN65	NM94
1-Mighty Atom	4.35	13.00	26.00
2-5-Mighty Atom	2.80	7.00	14.00
I.W. Reprint #1(1958), 8-(Pee-Wee Pixies), 10-I.W. on cover, Super on inside	.80	2.00	4.00

PLANET COMICS
1/40 - No. 62, 9/49; No. 63, Wint, 1949-50; No. 64, Spring, 1950; No. 65, 1951(nd); No. 66-68, 1952(nd); No. 69, Wint, 1952-53; No. 70-72, 1953(nd); No. 73, Winter, 1953-54
Fiction House Magazines

	GD25	FN65	VF82	NM94
1-Origin Auro, Lord of Jupiter by Briefer; Flint Baker & The Red Comet begin; Eisner/Fine-c	625.00	1875.00	3450.00	5000.00

(Estimated up to 160 total copies exist, 10 in NM/Mint)

	GD25	FN65	NM94
2-Lou Fine-c (Scarce)	283.00	850.00	1700.00
3-Eisner-c	217.00	650.00	1300.00
4-Gale Allen and the Girl Squadron begins	192.00	575.00	1150.00
5,6-(Scarce): 5-Eisner/Fine-c	175.00	525.00	1050.00
7-12: 12-The Star Pirate begins	140.00	420.00	840.00
13-14: 13-Reff Ryan begins	112.00	338.00	675.00
15-(Scarce)-Mars, God of War begins (11/42); see Jumbo Comics #31 for 1st app.	217.00	650.00	1300.00
16-20,22	104.00	310.00	625.00
21-The Lost World & Hunt Bowman begin	107.00	320.00	640.00
23-26: 26-The Space Rangers begin	96.00	288.00	575.00
27-30	77.00	230.00	460.00
31-35: 33-Origin Star Pirates Wonder Boots, reprinted in #52. 35-Mysta of the Moon begins	64.00	192.00	385.00
36-45: 41-New origin of "Auro, Lord of Jupiter." 42-Last Gale Allen. 43-Futura begins	58.00	175.00	350.00
46-60: 53-Used in **SOTI**, pg. 32	44.00	132.00	265.00
61-68,70: 65-70-All partial-r of earlier issues	32.00	95.00	190.00
69-Used in **POP**, pgs. 101,102	32.00	95.00	190.00
71-73-No series stories	23.00	70.00	140.00
I.W. Reprint #1(nd)-r/#70; cover-r from Attack on Planet Mars	4.70	14.00	28.00
I.W. Reprint #8 (r/#72), 9-r/#73	4.70	14.00	28.00

NOTE: ***Anderson*** *a-33-38, 40-51 (Star Pirate).* ***Matt Baker*** *a-53-59 (Mysta of the Moon).* ***Celardo*** *c-12.* ***Elias*** *c-70.* ***Evans*** *a-50-64 (Lost World).* ***Fine*** *c-2, 5.* ***Hopper*** *a-31, 35 (Gale Allen), 48, 49 (Mysta of the Moon).* ***Ingels*** *a-24-31 (Lost World), 56-61 (Auro, Lord of Jupiter).* ***Lubbers*** *a-44, 46 (Space Rangers); c-40, 41.* ***Renee*** *a-40 (Lost World); c-33, 35, 39.* ***Tuska*** *a-30 (Star Pirate).* ***M. Whitman*** *a-50-52 (Mysta of the Moon), 53-56 (Star Pirate); c-71-73.* ***Starr*** *a-59.* ***Zolnerwich*** *c-10. 13-25. Bondage c-53.*

PLANET COMICS
Apr, 1988 - No. 3? (2.00, color; B&W #3)
Blackthorne Publishing

	GD25	FN65	NM94
1-3: New stories. 1-Dave Stevens-c	.40	1.00	2.00

PLANET OF THE APES (Magazine) (Also see Adventures on the... & Power Record Comics)
Aug, 1974 - No. 29, Feb, 1977 (B&W) (Based on movies)
Marvel Comics Group

	GD25	FN65	NM94
1-Ploog-a	1.00	2.50	5.00
2-Ploog-a	.60	1.50	3.00
3-10	.40	1.00	2.00
11-20	.30	.75	1.50
21-29		.50	1.00

NOTE: ***Alcala*** *a-7-11, 17-22, 24.* ***Ploog*** *a-1-8, 11, 13, 14, 19.* ***Sutton*** *a-11, 12, 15, 17, 19, 20, 23, 24, 29.* ***Tuska*** *a-1-6.*

PLANET OF THE APES
Apr, 1990 - No. 24, 1992 ($2.50, B&W)
Adventure Comics

	GD25	FN65	NM94
1-New movie tie-in; comes w/outer-c(3 colors)	1.00	2.50	5.00
1-Limited serial numbered edition ($5.00)	1.60	4.00	8.00
1-2nd printing (no outer-c)	.50	1.25	2.50
2-24	.50	1.25	2.50
Annual 1 ($3.50)	.70	1.75	3.50

PLANET OF VAMPIRES
Feb, 1975 - No. 3, July, 1975
Seaboard Publications (Atlas)

	GD25	FN65	NM94
1-Neal Adams-c(i); 1st Broderick c/a(p)	.30	.75	1.50
2,3: 2-Neal Adams-c. 3-Heath-c/a		.50	1.00

PLANET TERRY (Marvel)(Value: cover or less)

PLASTIC FORKS (Marvel)(Value: cover or less)

PLASTIC MAN (Also see Police Comics & Smash Comics #17)
Sum, 1943 - No. 64, Nov, 1956
Vital Publ. No. 1,2/Quality Comics No. 3 on

	GD25	FN65	NM94
nn(#1)-'In The Game of Death;' Jack Cole-c/a begins; ends-#64?	193.00	580.00	1350.00
nn(#2, 2/44)-'The Gay Nineties Nightmare'	117.00	350.00	700.00
3 (Spr, '46)	75.00	225.00	450.00
4 (Sum, '46)	62.00	188.00	375.00
5 (Aut, '46)	54.00	162.00	325.00
6-10	42.00	125.00	250.00
11-20	37.00	110.00	225.00
21-30: 26-Last non-r issue?	30.00	90.00	180.00
31-40: 40-Used in POP, pg. 91	23.00	70.00	140.00
41-64: 53-Last precode issue	18.00	55.00	110.00
Super Reprint 11,16,18: 11('63)-r/#16. 16-r/#18; Cole-a. 18('64)-Spirit-r by Eisner from Police #95	4.00	12.00	24.00

NOTE: ***Cole*** *r-44, 49, 56, 58, 59 at least.* ***Cuidera*** *c-32-64i.*

PLASTIC MAN (See DC Special #15 & House of Mystery #160)
11-12/66 - No. 10, 5-6/68; V4#11, 2-3/76 - No. 20, 10-11/77
National Periodical Publications/DC Comics

	GD25	FN65	NM94
1-Real 1st app. Silver Age Plastic Man (House of Mystery #160 is actually tryout); Gil Kane-c/a; 12 cent issues begin	6.70	20.00	40.00
2-5: 4-Infantino-c; Mortimer-a	4.00	10.00	20.00
6-10('68): 10-Sparling-a; last 12 cent issue	2.00	5.00	10.00
V4#11('76)-20: 11-20-Fraden-p. 17-Origin retold	.50	1.25	2.50

PLASTIC MAN (DC)(Value: cover or less)

PLAYFUL LITTLE AUDREY (TV)(Also see Little Audrey #25)
6/57 - No. 110, 11/73; No. 111, 8/74 - No. 121, 4/76
Harvey Publications

	GD25	FN65	NM94
1	14.00	43.00	100.00
2	8.35	25.00	50.00
3-5	6.35	19.00	38.00
6-10	4.20	12.50	25.00
11-20	2.40	6.00	12.00
21-40	1.80	4.50	9.00
41-60	1.40	3.50	7.00
61-80	1.00	2.50	5.00
81-99	.80	2.00	4.00
100: 52 pg. Giant	1.20	3.00	6.00
101-103: 52 pg. Giants	1.00	2.50	5.00
104-121	.60	1.50	3.00

PLAYFUL LITTLE AUDREY IN 3-D (See Blackthorne 3-D Series #66)

PLOP! (Also see The Best of DC #60)
Sept-Oct, 1973 - No. 24, Nov-Dec, 1976
National Periodical Publications

	GD25	FN65	NM94
1-20: Sergio Aragones-a. 1,5-Wrightson-a	.70	1.75	3.50
21,22,24 (52 pgs.)	.80	2.00	4.00

	GD25	FN65	NM94
23-No Aragones-a (52 pgs.)	.30	.75	1.50

NOTE: ***Alcala*** *a-1-3.* ***Anderson*** *a-5.* ***Aragones*** *a-1-22, 24.* ***Ditko*** *a-16p.* ***Evans*** *a-1.* ***Mayer*** *a-1.* ***Orlando*** *a-21, 22; c-21.* ***Sekowsky*** *a-5, 6p.* ***Toth*** *a-11.* ***Wolverton*** *r-4, 22, 23(1 pg.); c(r)-1-12, 14, 17, 18.* ***Wood*** *a-14, 16i, 18-24; c-13, 15, 16, 19.*

PLUTO (See Cheerios Premiums, Four Color #537, Mickey Mouse Magazine, Walt Disney Showcase #4, 7, 13, 20, 23, 33 & Wheaties)
No. 7, 1942; No. 429, 10/52 - No. 1248, 11-1/61-62 (Walt Disney)
Dell Publishing Co.

	GD25	FN65	NM94
Large Feature Comic 7(1942)	65.00	195.00	455.00
4-Color 429,509	4.70	14.00	28.00
4-Color 595,654	4.00	10.00	20.00
4-Color 736,853,941,1039,1143,1248	3.20	8.00	16.00

POCAHONTAS
1941 - No. 2, 1942
Pocahontas Fuel Company

	GD25	FN65	NM94
nn(#1), 2	8.35	25.00	50.00

POCKET COMICS (Also see Double Up)
Aug, 1941 - No. 4, Jan, 1942 (Pocket size; 100 pgs.)
Harvey Publications (1st Harvey comic)

	GD25	FN65	NM94
1-Origin The Black Cat, Cadet Blakey the Spirit of '76, The Red Blazer, The Phantom, Sphinx, & The Zebra; Phantom Ranger, British Agent #99, Spin Hawkins, Satan, Lord of Evil begin	61.00	182.00	365.00
2: Simon-c/a in #1-3	40.00	120.00	240.00
3,4	30.00	90.00	180.00

POGO PARADE (See Dell Giants)

POGO POSSUM (Also see Animal Comics & Special Delivery)
No. 105, 4/46 - No. 148, 5/47; 10-12/49 - No. 16, 4-6/54
Dell Publishing Co.

	GD25	FN65	NM94
4-Color 105(1946)-Kelly-c/a	65.00	195.00	450.00
4-Color 148-Kelly-c/a	54.00	160.00	375.00
1-(10-12/49)-Kelly-c/a in all	50.00	150.00	350.00
2	26.00	80.00	185.00
3-5	19.00	58.00	135.00
6-10: 10-Infinity-c	16.50	50.00	115.00
11-16: 11-X-mas-c	13.50	41.00	95.00

NOTE: *#1-4, 9-13: 52 pgs.; #5-8, 14-16: 36 pgs.*

POINT BLANK (Eclipse) (Value: cover or less)

POLICE ACADEMY (TV) (Marvel) (Value: cover or less)

POLICE ACTION
Jan, 1954 - No. 7, Nov, 1954
Atlas News Co.

	GD25	FN65	NM94
1-Violent-a by Robert Q. Sale	10.00	30.00	60.00
2	5.00	15.00	30.00
3-7: 7-Powell-a	4.20	12.50	25.00

NOTE: ***Ayers*** *a-4, 5.* ***Colan*** *a-1.* ***Forte*** *a-1, 2.* ***Mort Lawrence*** *a-5.* ***Maneely*** *a-3; c-1, 5.* ***Reinman*** *a-6, 7.*

POLICE ACTION
Feb, 1975 - No. 3, June, 1975
Atlas/Seaboard Publ.

	GD25	FN65	NM94
1-3: 1-Lomax, N.Y.P.D., Luke Malone begin; McWilliams-a. 2-Origin Luke Malone, Manhunter		.50	1.00

NOTE: ***Ploog*** *art in all.* ***Sekowsky/McWilliams*** *a-1-3.* ***Thorne*** *c-3.*

POLICE AGAINST CRIME
April, 1954 - No. 9, Aug, 1955
Premiere Magazines

	GD25	FN65	NM94
1-Disbrow-a; extreme violence (man's face slashed with knife); Hollingsworth-a	10.00	30.00	70.00
2-Hollingsworth-a	6.70	20.00	40.00
3-9	5.00	15.00	30.00

POLICE BADGE #479 (Formerly Spy Thrillers #1-4)
No. 5, Sept, 1955
Atlas Comics (PrPI)

	GD25	FN65	NM94
5-Maneely-c	5.00	15.00	30.00

POLICE CASE BOOK (See Giant Comics Editions)

POLICE CASES (See Authentic... & Record Book of...)

POLICE COMICS
Aug, 1941 - No. 127, Oct, 1953
Quality Comics Group (Comic Magazines)

	GD25	FN65	NM94
1-Origin/1st app. Plastic Man by Jack Cole (r-in DC Special #15), The Human Bomb by Gustavson, & No. 711; intro. Chic Carter by Eisner, The Firebrand by Reed Crandall, The Mouthpiece by Guardineer, Phantom Lady, & The Sword; Firebrand-c 1-4	417.00	1250.00	2500.00
2-Plastic Man smuggles opium	200.00	600.00	1200.00
3	142.00	425.00	850.00
4	133.00	400.00	800.00
5-Plastic Man-c begin; Plastic Man forced to smoke marijuana	125.00	375.00	750.00
6,7	100.00	300.00	700.00
8-Manhunter begins (origin)	142.00	425.00	850.00
9,10	108.00	325.00	650.00
11-The Spirit strip reprints begin by Eisner (origin-strip #1); 1st comic book app. The Spirit	167.00	500.00	1000.00
12-Intro. Ebony	104.00	312.00	625.00
13-Intro. Woozy Winks; last Firebrand	104.00	312.00	625.00
14-19: 15-Last No. 711; Destiny begins	69.00	208.00	415.00
20-The Raven x-over in Phantom Lady; features Jack Cole himself	69.00	208.00	415.00
21,22: 21-Raven & Spider Widow x-over in Phantom Lady (cameo in #22)	54.00	162.00	325.00
23-30: 23-Last Phantom Lady. 24-26-Flatfoot Burns by Kurtzman in all	47.00	140.00	280.00
31-41: 37-1st app. Candy by Sahle & begins. 41-Last Spirit-r by Eisner	33.00	100.00	200.00
42,43-Spirit-r by Eisner/Fine	29.00	88.00	175.00
44-Fine Spirit-r begin, end #88,90,92	25.00	75.00	150.00
45-50: 50-(#50 on-c, #49 on inside, 1/46)	25.00	75.00	150.00
51-60: 58-Last Human Bomb	20.00	60.00	120.00
61-88: 63-(Some issues have #65 printed on cover, but #63 on inside) Kurtzman-a, 6pgs.	17.00	50.00	100.00
89,91,93-No Spirit	15.00	45.00	90.00
90,92-Spirit by Fine	18.00	55.00	110.00
94-99,101,102: Spirit by Eisner in all; 101-Last Manhunter. 102-Last Spirit & Plastic Man by Jack Cole	23.00	70.00	140.00
100	27.00	80.00	160.00
103-Content change to crime; Ken Shannon & T-Man begin (1st app. of each)	13.00	40.00	80.00
104-111,114-127: Crandall-a most issues (not in 104,122,125-127). 109-Atomic bomb story	9.15	27.50	55.00
112-Crandall-a	9.15	27.50	55.00
113-Crandall-c/a(2), 9 pgs. each	10.00	30.00	60.00

NOTE: *Most Spirit stories signed by Eisner are not by him; all are reprints.* ***Cole*** *c-17, 19-21, 24-26, 28-31, 36-38, 40-42, 45-48, 65-68, 69, 73, 75.* ***Crandall*** *Firebrand-1-8. Spirit by* ***Eisner*** *1-41, 94-102; by* ***Eisner/Fine****-42, 43; by* ***Fine****-44-88, 90, 92. 103, 109.* ***Al Bryant*** *c-33, 34.* ***Cole*** *c-17-32, 35-102(most).* ***Crandall*** *c-13, 14.* ***Crandall/Cuidera*** *c-105-127.* ***Eisner*** *c-4i.* ***Gill Fox*** *c-1-3, 4p, 5-12, 15. Bondage c-103, 109, 125.*

POLICE LINE-UP
Aug, 1951 - No. 4, July, 1952 (Painted-c)
Realistic Comics/Avon Periodicals

	GD25	FN65	NM94
1-Wood-a, 1 pg. plus part-c; spanking panel-r/Saint #5	18.00	54.00	125.00
2-Classic story "The Religious Murder Cult," drugs, perversion; r/Saint #5; c-r/Avon paperback #329	14.00	43.00	100.00
3-Kubert-a(r)/part-c, Kinstler-a	10.00	30.00	65.00
4-Kinstler-a	10.00	30.00	65.00

POLICE THRILLS

Pogo Possum #2, © Walt Kelly

Police Action #1 (1/54), © MEG

Police Comics #42, © QUA

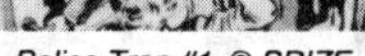
Police Trap #1, © PRIZE

Polly Pigtails #7, © PMI

Popeye #70, © KING

	GD25	FN65	NM94

1954
Ajax/Farrell Publications

	GD25	FN65	NM94
1-Exist?	5.85	17.50	35.00

POLICE TRAP (Public Defender In Action #7 on)
8-9/54 - No. 4, 2-3/55; No. 5, 7/55 - No. 6, 9/55
Mainline (Prize) No. 1-4/Charlton No. 5,6

	GD25	FN65	NM94
1-S&K covers-all issues	11.00	32.00	75.00
2-4	7.00	21.00	42.00
5,6-S&K-c/a	10.00	30.00	70.00

POLICE TRAP
No. 11, 1963; No. 16-18, 1964
Super Comics

	GD25	FN65	NM94
Reprint #11,16-18: 11-r/Police Trap #3. 16-r/Justice Traps the Guilty #? 17-r/Inside Crime #3	1.00	2.50	5.00

POLL PARROT
Poll Parrot Shoe Store/International Shoe
1950 - No. 4, 1951; No. 2, 1959 - No. 16, 1962
K. K. Publications (Giveaway)

	GD25	FN65	NM94
1 ('50)-Howdy Doody; small size	11.50	34.00	80.00
2-4('51)-Howdy Doody	10.00	30.00	60.00
2('59)-16('62): 2-The Secret of Crumbley Castle. 5-Bandit Busters. 7-The Make-Believe Mummy. 8-Mixed Up Mission('60). 10-The Frightful Flight. 11-Showdown at Sunup. 12-Maniac at Mubu Island. 13-...and the Runaway Genie. 14-Bully for You. 15-Trapped In Tall Timber. 16-...& the Rajah's Ruby('62)	3.00	7.50	15.00

POLLY & HER PALS (See Comic Monthly #1)

POLLYANNA (See 4-Color #1129)

POLLY PIGTAILS (Girls' Fun & Fashion Magazine #44 on)
Jan, 1946 - V4#43, Oct-Nov, 1949
Parents' Magazine Institute/Polly Pigtails

	GD25	FN65	NM94
1-Infinity-c; photo-c	7.50	22.50	45.00
2	4.00	11.00	22.00
3-5	3.00	7.50	15.00
6-10: 7-Photo-c	2.40	6.00	12.00
11-30: 22-Photo-c	1.80	4.50	9.00
31-43	1.60	4.00	8.00

PONY EXPRESS (See Four Color #942)

PONYTAIL
7-9/62 - No. 12, 10-12/65; No. 13, 11/69 - No. 20, 1/71
Dell Publishing Co./Charlton No. 13 on

	GD25	FN65	NM94
12-641-209(#1)	2.00	5.00	10.00
2-12	1.20	3.00	6.00
13-20	.80	2.00	4.00

POP COMICS (7 cents)
1955 (36 pgs.; 5x7"; in color)
Modern Store Publ.

	GD25	FN65	NM94
1-Funny animal	.80	2.00	4.00

POPEYE (See Comic Album #7, 11, 15, Comics Reading Libraries, Eat Right to Work and Win, Giant Comic Album, King Comics, Kite Fun Book, Magic Comics, March of Comics #37, 52, 66, 80, 96, 117, 134, 148, 157, 169, 194, 246, 264, 274, 294, 453, 465, 477 & Wow Comics, 1st series)

POPEYE (See Thimble Theatre)
1935 (25 cents; 52 pgs.; B&W) (By Segar)
David McKay Publications

	GD25	FN65	NM94
1-Daily strip serial reprints-"The Gold Mine Thieves"	54.00	160.00	375.00
2-Daily strip-r	45.00	135.00	315.00

NOTE: *Popeye first entered Thimble Theatre in 1929.*

POPEYE
1937 - 1939 (All by Segar)
David McKay Publications

	GD25	FN65	NM94
Feature Books nn (100 pgs.) (Very Rare)	535.00	1400.00	3200.00
Feature Books 2 (52 pgs.)	61.00	182.00	425.00
Feature Books 3 (100 pgs.)-r/nn issue with a new-c	54.00	160.00	375.00
Feature Books 5,10 (76 pgs.)	47.00	140.00	325.00
Feature Books 14 (76 pgs.) (Scarce)	61.00	182.00	425.00

POPEYE (Strip reprints through 4-Color #70)
1941 - 1947; #1, 2-4/48 - #65, 7-9/62; #66, 10/62 - #80, 5/66; #81, 8/66 - #92, 12/67; #94, 2/69 - #138, 1/77; #139, 5/78 - #171, 7/84 (no #93,160,161)
Dell #1-65/Gold Key #66-80/King #81-92/Charlton #94-138/Gold Key #139-155/Whitman #156 on

	GD25	FN65	NM94
Large Feature Comic 24('41)- by Segar	47.00	140.00	325.00
4-Color 25('41)-by Segar	50.00	150.00	350.00
Large Feature Comic 10('43)	38.00	115.00	265.00
4-Color 17('43)-by Segar	42.00	125.00	290.00
4-Color 26('43)-by Segar	38.00	115.00	265.00
4-Color 43('44)	27.00	81.00	190.00
4-Color 70('45)-Title: ...& Wimpy	23.00	70.00	160.00
4-Color 113('46-original strips begin),127,145('47),168	12.00	36.00	85.00
1(2-4/48)(Dell)	27.00	81.00	190.00
2	14.00	43.00	100.00
3-10	11.50	34.00	80.00
11-20	10.00	30.00	65.00
21-40	8.35	25.00	50.00
41-45,47-50	5.85	17.50	35.00
46-Origin Swee' Pee	8.35	25.00	50.00
51-60	4.70	14.00	28.00
61-65 (Last Dell issue)	4.00	11.00	22.00
66,67-Both 84 pgs. (Gold Key)	6.70	20.00	40.00
68-80	3.60	9.00	18.00
81-92,94-100	2.40	6.00	12.00
101-130	1.60	4.00	8.00
131-159,162-171: 144-50th Anniversary issue	1.20	3.00	6.00
Bold Detergent giveaway (Same as regular issue #94)	.80	2.00	4.00

NOTE: *Reprints-#145, 147, 149, 151, 153, 155, 157, 163-68(1/3), 170.*

POPEYE
1972 - 1974 (36 pgs. in color)
Charlton (King Features) (Giveaway)

	GD25	FN65	NM94
E-1 to E-15 (Educational comics)	.40	1.00	2.00
nn-Popeye Gettin' Better Grades-4 pgs. used as intro. to above giveaways (in color)	.40	1.00	2.00

POPEYE CARTOON BOOK
1934 (40 pgs. with cover)(8x13")(cardboard covers)
The Saalfield Publ. Co.

	GD25	FN65	NM94
2095-(Rare)-1933 strip reprints in color by Segar; each page contains a vertical half of a Sunday strip, so the continuity reads row by row completely across each double page spread. If each page is read by itself, the continuity makes no sense. Each double page spread reprints one complete Sunday page (from 1933)	108.00	325.00	650.00
12 Page Version	63.00	188.00	375.00

POPEYE SPECIAL (Ocean)(Value: cover or less)

POPPLES (TV, movie)(Marvel)(Value: cover or less)

POPPO OF THE POPCORN THEATRE
10/29/55 - No. 13, 1956 (Published weekly)
Fuller Publishing Co. (Publishers Weekly)

	GD25	FN65	NM94
1	5.00	15.00	30.00

	GD25	FN65	NM94
2-5	4.00	10.00	20.00
6-13	3.00	7.50	15.00

NOTE: *By **Charles Biro.** 10 cent cover, given away by supermarkets such as IGA.*

POP-POP COMICS
No date (Circa 1945) (52 pgs.)
R. B. Leffingwell Co.

	GD25	FN65	NM94
1-Funny animal	6.45	19.00	38.00

POPSICLE PETE FUN BOOK (See All-American Comics #6)
1947, 1948
Joe Lowe Corp.

	GD25	FN65	NM94
nn-36 pgs. in color; Sammy 'n' Claras, The King Who Couldn't Sleep & Popsicle Pete stories, games, cut-outs; has ad, pg. 20, to order Classics Ill. by sending wrappers	8.35	25.00	50.00
Adventure Book ('48)	6.70	20.00	40.00

POPULAR COMICS
Feb, 1936 - No. 145, July-Sept, 1948
Dell Publishing Co.

	GD25	FN65	VF82
1-Dick Tracy (1st comic book app.), Little Orphan Annie, Terry & the Pirates, Gasoline Alley, Don Winslow, Harold Teen, Little Joe, Skippy, Moon Mullins, Mutt & Jeff, Tailspin Tommy, Smitty, Smokey Stover, Winnie Winkle & The Gumps begin (all strip-r)	320.00	960.00	1600.00
(Estimated up to 90 total copies exist, 4 in NM/Mint)			
2	105.00	315.00	630.00
3	88.00	262.00	525.00
4,5: 5-Tom Mix begins	67.00	200.00	400.00
6-10: 8,9-Scribbly, Reglar Fellers app.	54.00	162.00	325.00

	GD25	FN65	NM94
11-20: 12-Xmas-c	44.00	132.00	265.00
21-27: 27-Last Terry & the Pirates, Little Orphan Annie, & Dick Tracy	32.00	95.00	190.00
28-37: 28-Gene Autry app. 31,32-Tim McCoy app. 35-Christmas-c; Tex Ritter app.	27.00	80.00	160.00
38-43-Tarzan in text only. 38-Gang Busters (radio) & Zane Grey's Tex Thorne begins? 43-1st non-funny-c?	30.00	90.00	180.00
44,45: 45-Hurricane Kid-c	22.00	65.00	130.00
46-Origin Martan, the Marvel Man	23.00	85.00	170.00
47-50	20.00	60.00	120.00
51-Origin The Voice (The Invisible Detective) strip begins	21.00	62.00	125.00
52-59: 55-End of World story	17.00	50.00	100.00
60-Origin Professor Supermind and Son	17.50	52.00	105.00
61-71: 63-Smilin' Jack begins	14.00	42.00	85.00
72-The Owl & Terry & the Pirates begin; Smokey Stover reprints begin	24.00	72.00	145.00
73-75	17.50	52.00	105.00
76-78-Capt. Midnight in all	22.00	65.00	130.00
79-85-Last Owl	15.00	45.00	90.00
86-99: 98-Felix the Cat, Smokey Stover-r begin	12.00	35.00	70.00
100	13.00	40.00	80.00
101-130	7.50	22.50	45.00
131-145: 142-Last Terry & the Pirates	6.70	20.00	40.00

POPULAR FAIRY TALES (See March of Comics #6, 18)

POPULAR ROMANCE
No. 5, Dec, 1949 - No. 29, July, 1954
Better-Standard Publications

	GD25	FN65	NM94
5	4.70	14.00	28.00
6-9: 7-Palais-a; lingerie panels	3.60	9.00	18.00
10-Wood-a, 2 pgs.	4.70	14.00	28.00
11,12,14-16,18-21,28,29	2.80	7.00	14.00
13,17-Severin/Elder-a, 3&8 pgs.	3.60	9.00	18.00
22-27-Toth-a	6.35	19.00	38.00

NOTE: *All have photo-c. **Tuska** art in most issues.*

POPULAR TEEN-AGERS (Secrets of Love) (School Day Romances #1-4)
No. 5, Sept, 1950 - No. 23, Nov, 1954
Star Publications

	GD25	FN65	NM94
5-Toni Gay, Honey Bunn, etc.; L. B. Cole-c	13.00	40.00	90.00
6-8 (7/51)-Toni Gay, Honey Bunn, etc.; all have L. B. Cole-c; 6-Negligee panels	11.00	32.00	75.00
9-(...Romances; 1st romance issue, 10/51)	6.35	19.00	38.00
10-(...Secrets of Love)	6.35	19.00	38.00
11,16,18,19,22,23	5.00	15.00	30.00
12,13,17,20,21-Disbrow-a	5.35	16.00	32.00
14-Harrison/Wood-a; 2 spanking scenes	12.00	36.00	85.00
15-Wood?, Disbrow-a	10.00	30.00	65.00
Accepted Reprint 5,6 (nd); L.B. Cole-c	3.60	9.00	18.00

NOTE: *All have **L. B. Cole** covers.*

PORE LI'L MOSE
1902 (30 pgs.; 10-1/2x15"; in full color)
New York Herald Publ. by Grand Union Tea
Cupples & Leon Co.

	GD25	FN65	NM94
nn-By R. F. Outcault; 1 pg. strips about early Negroes	50.00	150.00	350.00

PORKY PIG (See Bugs Bunny &..., Kite Fun Book, March of Comics #42, 57, 71, 89, 99, 113, 130, 143, 164, 175, 192, 209, 218, 367, and Super Book #6, 18, 30)

PORKY PIG (...& Bugs Bunny #40-69)
No. 16, 1942 - No. 81, Mar-Apr, 1962; Jan, 1965 - No. 109, July, 1984
Dell Publishing Co./Gold Key No. 1-93/Whitman No. 94 on

	GD25	FN65	NM94
4-Color 16(#1, 1942)	47.00	140.00	325.00
4-Color 48(1944)-Carl Barks-a	72.00	215.00	500.00
4-Color 78(1945)	19.00	56.00	130.00
4-Color 112(7/46)	11.00	32.00	75.00
4-Color 156,182,191('49)	9.15	27.50	55.00
4-Color 226,241('49),260,271,277,284,295	6.70	20.00	40.00
4-Color 303,311,322,330	4.70	14.00	28.00
4-Color 342,351,360,370,385,399,410,426	4.00	10.00	20.00
25 (11-12/52)-30	2.40	6.00	12.00
31-50	1.20	3.00	6.00
51-81(3-4/62)	.80	2.00	4.00
1(1/65-Gold Key)(2nd Series)	1.60	4.00	8.00
2,4,5-r/4-Color 226,284 & 271 in that order	.80	2.00	4.00
3,6-10	.60	1.50	3.00
11-50	.30	.75	1.50
51-109		.50	1.00

NOTE: *Reprints-#1-8, 9-35(2/3); 36-46, 58, 67, 69-74, 76, 78, 102-109(1/3-1/2).*

PORKY'S BOOK OF TRICKS
1942 (48 pages) (8-1/2x5-1/2")
K. K. Publications (Giveaway)

	GD25	FN65	NM94
nn-7 pg. comic story, text stories, plus games & puzzles	29.00	85.00	200.00

PORTIA PRINZ OF THE GLAMAZONS (Eclipse)(Value: cover or less)

POST GAZETTE (See Meet the New...)

POWDER RIVER RUSTLERS (See Fawcett Movie Comics)

POWER COMICS
1944 - No. 4, 1945
Holyoke Publ. Co./Narrative Publ.

	GD25	FN65	NM94
1-L. B. Cole-c	50.00	150.00	300.00
2-Hitler, Hirohito-c	50.00	150.00	300.00
3-Classic L.B. Cole-c; Dr. Mephisto begins?	50.00	150.00	300.00
4: L.B. Cole-c; Miss Espionage app. #3,4	42.00	125.00	250.00

POWER COMICS
1977 - No. 5, Dec, 1977 (B&W)
Power Comics Co.

	GD25	FN65	NM94
1-"A Boy And His Aardvark" by Dave Sim; first Dave Sim aardvark (not Cerebus)	1.40	3.50	7.00

Pop-Pop Comics #1, © R. B. Leffingwell

Popular Comics #45, © DELL

Popular Teen-Agers #19, © STAR

Powerhouse Pepper #5, © MEG

Power Man #17, © MEG

Prez #1, © DC

	GD25	FN65	NM94
1-Reprint (3/77, black-c)	.80	2.00	4.00
2-Cobalt Blue by Gustovich	.40	1.00	2.00
3-5: 3-Nightwitch. 4-Northern Light. 5-Bluebird	.40	1.00	2.00

POWER COMICS (Eclipse) (Value: cover or less)

POWER FACTOR (Wonder & Innovation) (Value: cover or less)

POWER GIRL (DC) (Value: cover or less) (See Infinity, Inc. & Showcase #97-99)

POWERHOUSE PEPPER COMICS (See Gay Comics, Joker Comics & Tessie the Typist)
No. 1, 1943; No. 2, May, 1948 - No. 5, Nov, 1948
Marvel Comics (20CC)

	GD25	FN65	NM94
1-(60 pgs.)-Wolverton-c/a in all	79.00	235.00	550.00
2	47.00	140.00	325.00
3,4	43.00	130.00	300.00
5-(Scarce)	50.00	150.00	350.00

POWER LINE (Marvel) (Value: cover or less)

POWER LORDS (DC) (Value: cover or less)

POWER MAN (Formerly Hero for Hire; ...& Iron Fist #68 on; see Cage & Giant-Size...)
No. 17, Feb, 1974 - No. 125, Sept, 1986
Marvel Comics Group

	GD25	FN65	NM94
17-Luke Cage continues; Iron Man app.	2.40	6.00	12.00
18-20: 18-Last 20 cent issue	1.40	3.50	7.00
21-31: 31-Part Neal Adams-i. 34-Last 25 cents	.90	2.25	4.50
32-48: 36-r/Hero For Hire #12. 41-1st app. Thunderbolt. 45-Starlin-c. 48-Byrne-a; Power Man/Iron Fist 1st meet	.60	1.50	3.00
49,50-Byrne-a(p); 50-Iron Fist joins Cage	.60	1.50	3.00
51-56,58-60: 58-Intro El Aguila	.30	.75	1.50
57-New X-Men app. (6/79)	1.00	2.50	5.00
61-65,67-77,79-83,85-124: 75-Double size. 77-Daredevil app. 87-Moon Knight app. 90-Unus app. 109-The Reaper app. 100-Double size; origin K'un L'un		.50	1.00
66-2nd app. Sabretooth (see Iron Fist #14)	5.00	15.00	30.00
78-3rd app. Sabretooth (cameo under cloak)	2.40	6.00	12.00
84-4th app. Sabretooth	2.40	6.00	12.00
125-Double size; death of Iron Fist	.40	1.00	2.00
Annual 1(1976)-Punisher cameo in flashback	.80	2.00	4.00

NOTE: ***Austin*** *c-102i.* ***Byrne*** *a-48-50; c-102, 104, 106, 107, 112-116.* ***Kane*** *c(p)-24, 25, 28, 48.* ***Miller*** *a-68, 76(2pgs.); c-66-68, 70-74, 80i.* ***Mooney*** *a-38i, 53i, 55i.* ***Nebres*** *a-76p.* ***Nino*** *a-42i, 43i.* ***Perez*** *a-27.* ***B. Smith*** *a-47i.* ***Tuska*** *a(p)-17, 20, 24, 26, 28, 29, 36, 47. Painted c-75, 100.*

POWER OF STRONGMAN, THE (AC) (Value: cover or less)

POWER OF THE ATOM (DC) (Value: cover or less) (See Secret Origins #29)

POWER PACHYDERMS (Marvel) (Value: cover or less)

POWER PACK
Aug, 1984 - No. 62, Feb, 1991
Marvel Comics Group

	GD25	FN65	NM94
1-($1.00, 52 pgs.)-Origin & 1st app. Power Pack	.40	1.00	2.00
2-18,20-26,28,30-45,47-62		.50	1.00
19-Dbl. size; Cloak & Dagger, Wolverine app.	1.40	3.50	7.00
27-Mutant massacre; Wolverine & Sabretooth app.	1.60	4.00	8.00
29-Spider-Man & Hobgoblin app.	.40	1.00	2.00
46-Punisher app.	.60	1.50	3.00
...Holiday Special 1 (2/92, $2.25, 68 pgs.)		.50	1.00

NOTE: ***Austin*** *scripts-53.* ***Morrow*** *a-51.* ***Spiegle*** *a-55i.* ***Williamson*** *a(i)-43, 50, 52.*

POWER RECORD COMICS
1974 - 1978 ($1.49, 7X10" comics, 20 pgs. with 45 R.P.M. record)
Marvel Comics/Power Records

PR10-Spider-Man-r/from #124,125; Man-Wolf app. PR11-Hulk-r. PR12-Captain America-r/#168. PR13-Fantastic Four-r/#126. PR14-Frankenstein-Ploog-r/#1. PR15-Tomb of Dracula-Colan-r/#2. PR16-Man-Thing-Ploog-r/#5. PR17-Werewolf By Night-Ploog-r/Marvel Spotlight #2. PR18-Planet of the Apes-r. PR19-Escape From the Planet of the Apes-r. PR20-Beneath the Planet of the Apes-r. PR21-Battle for the Planet of the Apes-r. PR24-Spider-Man II-New-a begins. PR25-Star Trek "Passage to Moauv." PR26-Star Trek "Crier in Emptiness." PR27-Batman "Stacked Cards;" N. Adams-a(p). PR28-Superman "Alien Creatures." PR29-Space: 1999 "Breakaway." PR30-Batman; N. Adams-r/Det.(7 pgs.). PR31-Conan-N. Adams-a; reprinted in Conan #116. PR32-Space: 1999 "Return to the Beginning." PR33-Superman-G.A. origin, Buckler-a(p). PR34-Superman. PR35-Wonder Woman-Buckler-a(p). PR36-Holo-Man. PR37-Robin Hood. PR39-Huckleberry Finn. PR40-Davy Crockett. PR41-Robinson Crusoe. PR42-20,000 Leagues Under the Sea. PR47-Little Women

	GD25	FN65	NM94
With record; each...	1.70	5.00	10.00

POW MAGAZINE (Bob Sproul's) (Satire Magazine)
Aug, 1966 - No. 3, Feb, 1967 (30 cents)
Humor-Vision

	GD25	FN65	NM94
1-3: 2-Jones-a. 3-Wrightson-a	4.00	10.00	20.00

PRAIRIE MOON AND OTHER STORIES (Dark Horse) (Value: cover or less)

PREDATOR (Also see Aliens Vs. Predator, Batman vs. ... & Dark Horse Presents)
June, 1989 - No. 4, Mar, 1990 ($2.25, color, mini-series)
Dark Horse Comics

	GD25	FN65	NM94
1-Based on movie; 1st app. Predator	5.50	16.50	33.00
1-2nd printing	1.40	3.50	7.00
2	3.20	8.00	16.00
3	2.00	5.00	10.00
4	1.40	3.50	7.00
Trade paperback (1990, $12.95)-r/#1-4	2.60	6.50	13.00

PREDATOR: BIG GAME
Mar, 1991 - No. 4, June, 1991 ($2.50, color, mini-series)
Dark Horse Comics

	GD25	FN65	NM94
1: 1-3-Contain 2 Dark Horse trading cards	.80	2.00	4.00
2-4	.60	1.50	3.00

PREDATOR BLOODY SANDS OF TIME
Feb, 1992 - No. 2, Feb, 1992 ($2.50, color, mini-series)
Dark Horse Comics

	GD25	FN65	NM94
1,2-Dan Barry-c/a(p)/scripts	.50	1.25	2.50

PREDATOR COLD WAR
Sept, 1991 - No. 4, Dec, 1991 ($2.50, color, mini-series)
Dark Horse Comics

	GD25	FN65	NM94
1-All have painted-c	.80	2.00	4.00
2-4	.60	1.50	3.00

PREDATOR 2
Feb, 1991 - No. 2, June, 1991 ($2.50, color, mini-series)
Dark Horse Comics

	GD25	FN65	NM94
1-Adapts movie; trading cards inside; photo-c	.70	1.75	3.50
2-Trading cards inside; photo-c	.50	1.25	2.50

PREDATOR VS. MAGNUS ROBOT FIGHTER
Nov, 1992 - No. 2, Dec, 1992 ($2.95, color)
Dark Horse/Valiant

	GD25	FN65	NM94
1 (Platinum edition)-Barry Smith-c	11.50	34.00	80.00
1 (Regular)-Barry Smith-c; Lee Weeks-a in both	1.00	2.50	5.00
2-Barry Smith-c	.70	1.75	3.50

PREHISTORIC WORLD (See Classics Illustrated Special Issue)

PREMIERE (See Charlton Premiere)

PRESTO KID, THE (See Red Mask)

PRETTY BOY FLOYD (See On the Spot)

PREZ (See Cancelled Comic Cavalcade & Supergirl #10)
Aug-Sept, 1973 - No. 4, Feb-Mar, 1974
National Periodical Publications

	GD25	FN65	NM94
1-4: 1-Origin; Joe Simon scripts		.50	1.00

PRICE, THE (See Eclipse Graphic Album Series)

PRIDE AND THE PASSION, THE (See 4-Color #824)

PRIDE OF THE YANKEES, THE (See Real Heroes & Sport Comics)
1949 (The Life of Lou Gehrig)
Magazine Enterprises

	GD25	FN65	NM94
nn-Photo-c; Ogden Whitney-a	50.00	150.00	350.00

PRIMAL (Dark Horse) (Value: cover or less)

PRIMAL MAN (See The Crusaders)

PRIMER (Comico...)
Oct, 1982 - No. 6, Feb, 1984 (B&W)
Comico

	GD25	FN65	NM94
1 (52 pgs.)	.80	2.00	4.00
2-1st app. Grendel & Argent by Wagner	4.20	12.50	25.00
3,5	.50	1.25	2.50
4-1st Sam Kieth art in comics	.80	2.00	4.00
6-Intro & 1st app. Evangeline	.80	2.00	4.00

PRIMUS (TV)
Feb, 1972 - No. 7, Oct, 1972
Charlton Comics

	GD25	FN65	NM94
1-Staton-a in all	1.60	4.00	8.00
6-Drug propaganda story	1.00	2.50	5.00

PRINCE: ALTER EGO (Piranha) (Value: cover or less)

PRINCE AND THE PAUPER, THE (Disney) (Value: cover or less)

PRINCE NAMOR, THE SUB-MARINER (Marvel) (Value: cover or less) (Also see Namor ...)

PRINCE NIGHTMARE (Aaaargh) (Value: cover or less)

PRINCE VALIANT (See Ace Comics, Comics Reading Libraries, Feature Books #26, Four Color #567, 650, 699, 719, 788, 849, 900 & King Comics #146, 147)

PRIORITY: WHITE HEAT (AC) (Value: cover or less)

PRISCILLA'S POP (See 4-Color #569, 630, 704, 799)

PRISON BARS (See Behind...)

PRISON BREAK!
1951 (Sept) - No. 5, Sept, 1952
Avon Periodicals/Realistic No. 3 on

	GD25	FN65	NM94
1-Wood-c & 1 pg.; has-r/Saint #7 retitled Michael Strong Private Eye	22.00	65.00	150.00
2-Wood-c; Kubert-a; Kinstler inside front-c	15.00	45.00	105.00
3-Orlando, Check-a; c-/Avon paperback 179	12.00	36.00	85.00
4,5: 4-Kinstler-c & inside f/c; Lawrence, Lazarus-a. 5-Kinstler-c; Infantino-a	11.50	34.00	80.00

PRISONER, THE (TV) (DC) (Value: cover or less)

PRISON RIOT
1952
Avon Periodicals

	GD25	FN65	NM94
1-Marijuana Murders-1 pg. text; Kinstler-c	15.00	45.00	105.00

PRISON TO PRAISE
1974 (35 cents)
Logos International

	GD25	FN65	NM94
nn-True Story of Merlin R. Carothers		.50	1.00

PRIVATE BUCK (See Large Feature Comic #12 & 21)

PRIVATEERS (Vanguard) (Value: cover or less)

PRIVATE EYE (Cover title: Rocky Jordan...#6-8)
Jan, 1951 - No. 8, March, 1952
Atlas Comics (MCI)

	GD25	FN65	NM94
1-Cover title: Crime Cases... #1-5	10.00	30.00	65.00
2,3-Tuska c/a(3)	6.70	20.00	40.00
4-8	5.00	15.00	30.00

NOTE: *Henkel a-6(3), 7; c-7. **Sinnott** a-6.*

PRIVATE EYE (See Mike Shayne...)

PRIVATE SECRETARY
Dec-Feb, 1962-63 - No. 2, Mar-May, 1963
Dell Publishing Co.

	GD25	FN65	NM94
1,2	2.00	5.00	10.00

PRIVATE STRONG (See The Double Life of...)

PRIZE COMICS (...Western #69 on) (Also see Treasure Comics)
March, 1940 - No. 68, Feb-Mar, 1948
Prize Publications

	GD25	FN65	NM94
1-Origin Power Nelson, The Futureman & Jupiter, Master Magician; Ted O'Neil, Secret Agent M-11, Jaxon of the Jungle, Bucky Brady & Storm Curtis begin	133.00	400.00	800.00
2-The Black Owl begins	58.00	175.00	350.00
3,4	48.00	145.00	290.00
5,6: Dr. Dekkar, Master of Monsters app. in each	46.00	138.00	275.00
7-(Scarce)-Black Owl by S&K; origin/1st app. Dr. Frost & Frankenstein; The Green Lama, Capt. Gallant, The Great Voodini & Twist Turner begin	100.00	300.00	600.00
8,9-Black Owl & Ted O'Neil by S&K	54.00	162.00	325.00
10-12,14-20: 11-Origin Bulldog Denny. 16-Spike Mason begins	46.00	138.00	275.00
13-Yank & Doodle begin (origin)	50.00	150.00	300.00
21-24	32.00	95.00	190.00
25-30	18.00	55.00	110.00
31-33	14.00	42.50	85.00
34-Origin Airmale, Yank & Doodle; The Black Owl joins army, Yank & Doodle's father assumes Black Owl's role	17.00	50.00	100.00
35-36,38-40: 35-Flying Fist & Bingo begin	12.50	37.50	75.00
37-Intro. Stampy, Airmale's sidekick; Hitler-c	13.00	40.00	80.00
41-50: 45-Yank & Doodle learn Black Owl's I.D. (their father). 48-Prince Ra begins	9.15	27.50	55.00
51-62,64,67,68: 53-Transvestism story. 55-No Frankenstein. 57-X-Mas-c 64-Black Owl retires	6.50	25.00	50.00
65,66-Frankenstein-c by Briefer	9.15	27.50	55.00
63-Simon & Kirby c/a	10.00	30.00	65.00

NOTE: ***Briefer** a 7-on; c-65, 66. **J. Binder** a-16; c-21-29. **Guardineer** a-62. **Kiefer** c-62. **Palais** c-68. **Simon & Kirby** c-63, 75, 83.*

PRIZE COMICS WESTERN (Formerly Prize Comics #1-68)
No. 69(V7#2), Apr-May, 1948 - No. 119, Nov-Dec, 1956
Prize Publications (Feature) (No. 69-84: 52 pgs.)

	GD25	FN65	NM94
69(V7#2)	10.00	30.00	65.00
70-75	8.35	25.00	50.00
76-Randolph Scott photo-c; "Canadian Pacific" movie adaptation	10.00	30.00	65.00
77-Photo-c; Severin/Elder, Mart Bailey-a; "Streets of Laredo" movie adapt.	9.15	27.50	55.00
78-Photo-c; Kurtzman-a, 10 pgs.; Severin, Mart Bailey-a; "Bullet Code," & "Roughshod" movie adapt.	11.00	32.00	75.00
79-Photo-c; Kurtzman-a, 8 pgs.; Severin/Elder, Severin, Mart Bailey-a; "Stage To Chino" movie adapt.	11.00	32.00	75.00
80,81-Photo-c; Severin/Elder-a(2)	9.15	27.50	55.00
82-Photo-c; 1st app. The Preacher by Mart Bailey; Severin/Elder-a(3)	9.15	27.50	55.00
83,84	7.50	22.50	45.00
85-1st app. American Eagle by John Severin & begins (V9#6, 1-2/51)	16.00	48.00	110.00
86,92,101-105	8.35	25.00	50.00
87-91,93-99,110,111-Severin/Elder a(2-3) each	9.15	27.50	55.00
100	10.00	30.00	65.00
106-108,112	5.85	17.50	35.00
109-Severin/Williamson-a	9.15	27.50	55.00
113-Williamson/Severin-a(2)/Frazetta?	10.00	30.00	60.00

Prison Break! #1, © AVON

Prize Comics #22, © PRIZE

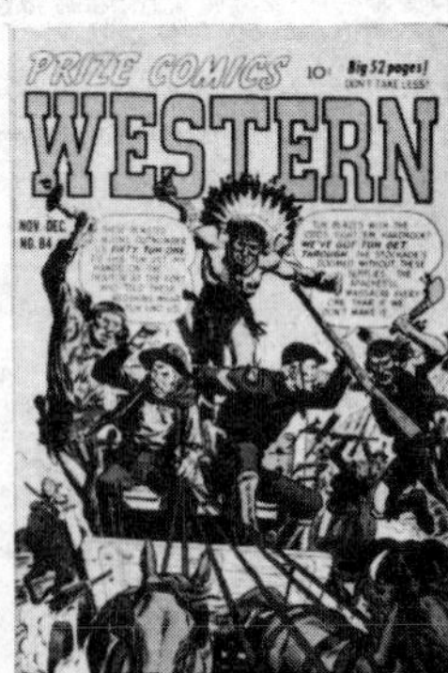

Prize Comics Western #84, © PRIZE

Prize Mystery #1, © Key Publ.

Public Enemies #7, © DS

Punch Comics #21, © CHES

	GD25	FN65	NM94
114-119: Drifter series in all; by Mort Meskin #114-118	4.70	14.00	28.00

NOTE: ***Fass*** *a-81.* ***Severin & Elder*** *c-84-99.* ***Severin*** *a-72, 75, 77-79, 83-86, 96, 97, 100-105; c-100-109(most), 110-119.* ***Simon & Kirby*** *c-75, 83.*

PRIZE MYSTERY
May, 1955 - No. 3, Sept, 1955
Key Publications

	GD25	FN65	NM94
1	4.70	14.00	28.00
2,3	4.00	10.00	20.00

PROFESSIONAL FOOTBALL (See Charlton Sport Library)

PROFESSOR COFFIN
No. 19, Oct, 1985 - No. 21, Feb, 1986
Charlton Comics

	GD25	FN65	NM94
19-21: Wayne Howard-a(r)		.50	1.00

PROFESSOR OM (Innovation) (Value: cover or less)

PROJECT: HERO (Vanguard) (Value: cover or less)

PROTECTORS (Also see The Ferret)
Sept, 1992 - Present ($1.95/$2.50, color)
Malibu Comics

	GD25	FN65	NM94
1-4 ($2.50, direct sale)-With poster. 1-Origin	.50	1.25	2.50
1-4 ($1.95, newsstand)-Without poster	.40	1.00	2.00

PROWLER (Eclipse) (Value: cover or less) (Also see Revenge of the...)

PROWLER IN "WHITE ZOMBIE", THE (Eclipse) (Value: cover or less)

PSI-FORCE (Marvel) (Value: cover or less)

PSI-JUDGE ANDERSON (Fleetway/Quality) (Value: cover or less)

PSYCHO (Magazine)
Jan, 1971 - No. 24, Mar, 1975 (68 pgs.; B&W) (No #22?)
Skywald Publishing Corp.

	GD25	FN65	NM94
1-All reprints	1.60	4.00	8.00
2-Origin & 1st app. The Heap, & Frankenstein series by Adkins	1.20	3.00	6.00
3-24: 13-Cannabalism. 18-Injury to eye-c. 20-Severed Head-c. 24-1975 Winter Special	.60	1.50	3.00
Annual 1 (1972)	1.00	2.50	5.00
Fall Special(1974)-Reese, Wildey-a(r)	.60	1.50	3.00
Yearbook(1974-nn)	.60	1.50	3.00

NOTE: ***Boris*** *c-3, 5.* ***Buckler*** *a-4, 5.* ***Everett*** *a-3-6.* ***Jeff Jones*** *a-6, 7, 9; c-12.* ***Kaluta*** *a-13.* ***Katz/Buckler*** *a-3.* ***Morrow*** *a-1.* ***Reese*** *a-5.* ***Sutton*** *a-3.* ***Wildey*** *a-5.*

PSYCHO, THE (DC) (Value: cover or less)

PSYCHO (Alfred Hitchcock's...) (Innovation) (Value: cover or less) (Adapts movie)

PSYCHOANALYSIS
Mar-Apr, 1955 - No. 4, Sept-Oct, 1955
E. C. Comics

	GD25	FN65	NM94
1-All Kamen-c/a; not approved by code	11.00	32.00	75.00
2-4-Kamen-c/a in all	10.00	30.00	60.00

PSYCHOBLAST (First) (Value: cover or less)

P.T. 109 (See Movie Comics)

PUBLIC DEFENDER IN ACTION (Formerly Police Trap)
No. 7, Mar, 1956 - No. 12, Oct, 1957
Charlton Comics

	GD25	FN65	NM94
7	5.85	17.50	35.00
8-12	4.00	10.00	20.00

PUBLIC ENEMIES
1948 - No. 9, June-July, 1949
D. S. Publishing Co.

	GD25	FN65	NM94
1	10.00	30.00	70.00
2-Used in **SOTI**, pg. 95	11.00	32.00	75.00
3-5: 5-Arrival date of 10/1/48	7.50	22.50	45.00
6,8,9	5.85	17.50	35.00
7-McWilliams-a; injury to eye panel	7.50	22.50	45.00

PUDGY PIG
Sept, 1958 - No. 2, Nov, 1958
Charlton Comics

	GD25	FN65	NM94
1,2	2.40	6.00	12.00

PUMA BLUES (Aardvark-Vanaheim) (Value: cover or less)

PUNCH & JUDY COMICS
1944; No. 2, Fall, 1944 - V3#2, 12/47; V3#3, 6/51 - V3#9, 12/51
Hillman Periodicals

	GD25	FN65	NM94
V1#1-(60 pgs.)	11.00	32.00	75.00
2	6.35	19.00	38.00
3-12(7/46)	4.70	14.00	28.00
V2#1,3-9	3.60	9.00	18.00
V2#2,10-12, V3#1-Kirby-a(2) each	11.00	32.00	75.00
V3#2-Kirby-a	10.00	30.00	65.00
3-9	3.20	8.00	16.00

PUNCH COMICS
12/41; #2, 2/42; #9, 7/44 - #19, 10/46; #20, 7/47 - #23, 1/48
Harry 'A' Chesler

	GD25	FN65	NM94
1-Mr. E, The Sky Chief, Hale the Magician, Kitty Kelly begin	67.00	200.00	400.00
2-Captain Glory app.	37.00	110.00	225.00
9-Rocketman & Rocket Girl & The Master Key begin	23.00	70.00	140.00
10-Sky Chief app.; J. Cole-a; Master Key-r/Scoop #3	18.00	55.00	110.00
11-Origin Master Key-r/Scoop #1; Sky Chief, Little Nemo app.; Jack Cole-a; Fineish art by Sultan	18.00	55.00	110.00
12-Rocket Boy & Capt. Glory app; Skull-c	17.00	50.00	100.00
13-17,19: 13-Cover has list of 4 Chesler artists' names on tombstone	16.00	48.00	95.00
18-Bondage-c; hypodermic panels	18.00	55.00	110.00
20-Unique cover with bare-breasted women	33.00	100.00	200.00
21-Hypo needle story	17.00	50.00	100.00
22,23-Little Nemo-not by McCay	14.00	42.00	85.00

PUNCHY AND THE BLACK CROW
No. 10, Oct, 1985 - No. 12, Feb, 1986
Charlton Comics

	GD25	FN65	NM94
10-12: Al Fago funny animal-r		.50	1.00

PUNISHER (See Amazing Spider-Man #129, Blood and Glory, Captain America #241, Classic Punisher, Daredevil #182-184, 257, Daredevil and the..., Ghost Rider V2#5, 6, Marc Spector #8 & 9, Marvel Preview #2, Marvel Super Action, Marvel Tales, Power Pack #46, Spectacular Spider-Man #81-83, 140, 141, 143 & new Strange Tales #13 & 14)

PUNISHER
Jan, 1986 - No. 5, May, 1986 (Mini-series)
Marvel Comics Group

	GD25	FN65	NM94
1-Double size	8.35	25.00	50.00
2	4.20	12.50	25.00
3-Has 2 cover prices, 75 & 95(w/UPC) cents	3.00	7.50	15.00
4,5	2.40	6.00	12.00
Trade Paperback-r/#1-5 (1988)	2.20	5.50	11.00

PUNISHER
July, 1987 - Present
Marvel Comics Group

	GD25	FN65	NM94
V2#1	5.00	15.00	30.00
2	3.00	7.50	15.00
3-5	1.80	4.50	9.00
6,7: 7-Last 75 cent issue	1.60	4.00	8.00

	GD25	FN65	NM94
8-Portacio/Williams-c/a begins, ends #18	2.00	5.00	10.00
9-Scarcer, low distribution	2.20	5.50	11.00
10-Daredevil app.; ties in w/Daredevil #257	4.50	13.50	27.00
11-15: 13-18-Kingpin app.	1.40	3.50	7.00
16-20: 19-Stroman-c/a. 20-Portacio-c(p)	1.00	2.50	5.00
21-24,26-30: 24-1st app. Shadowmasters	.60	1.50	3.00
25-Double size ($1.50)-Shadowmasters app.	.80	2.00	4.00
31-40	.40	1.00	2.00
41-49		.60	1.25
50-($1.50, 52 pgs.)	.30	.75	1.50
51-59: 57-Photo-c; came with outer-c. 59-Punisher is severely cut & has skin grafts (has black skin); last $1.00-c		.50	1.00
60-74,76-78: 60-Begin $1.25-c. 60,61-Luke Cage app. 62-Punisher back to white skin. 68-Tarantula-c/story		.60	1.25
75-($2.75, 52 pgs.)-Embossed silver ink-c	.55	1.40	2.75
Annual 1 (1988)-Evolutionary War x-over	2.40	6.00	12.00
Annual 2 (1989, $2.00, 68 pgs.)-Atlantis Attacks x-over; Jim Lee-a(p) (back-up story, 6 pgs.); Moon Knight app.	1.40	3.50	7.00
Annual 3 (1990, $2.00, 68 pgs.)	.40	1.00	2.00
Annual 4 (1991, $2.00, 68 pgs.)-Golden-c(p)	.40	1.00	2.00
Annual 5 (1992, $2.25, 68 pgs.)	.45	1.15	2.25
Back to School Special 1 (11/92, $2.95, 68 pgs.)	.60	1.50	3.00
Summer Special 1 (8/91, $2.95, 52 pgs.)-No ads	.60	1.50	3.00
Summer Special 2 (8/92, $2.50, 52 pgs.)-Bisley painted-c; Austin-a(i)	.50	1.25	2.50
...and Wolverine in African Saga nn (1989, $5.95, 52 pgs.)-Reprints Punisher War Journal #6 & 7; Jim Lee-c/a(r)	1.20	3.00	6.00
...Bloodlines nn (1991, $5.95, 68 pgs.)	1.20	3.00	6.00
...: Die Hard in the Big Easy nn (1992, $4.95, 52 pgs.)	1.00	2.50	5.00
...G-Force nn (1992, $4.95, 52 pgs.)-Painted-c	1.00	2.50	5.00
...Holiday Special nn (1992, $2.95)	.60	1.50	3.00
...Movie Special 1 (6/90, $5.95, 68 pgs.)	1.20	3.00	6.00
...: No Escape nn (1990, $4.95, 52pgs.)-New-a	1.20	3.00	6.00
...The Prize nn (1990, $4.95, 68 pgs.)-New-a	1.00	2.50	5.00

NOTE: ***Austin*** *c(i)-47, 48.* ***Cowan*** *c-39.* ***Heath*** *a-26, 27; c-25, 26.* ***Quesada*** *c-56p.* ***Sienkiewicz*** *c-Back to School 1.* ***Williamson*** *a(i)-25, 61, 62, 64-70, Annual 5; c(i)-62, 65-68.*

PUNISHER ARMORY, THE
7/90 ($1.50); No. 2, 6/91; No. 3, 4/92 - Present ($1.75/$2.00)
Marvel Comics

	GD25	FN65	NM94
1-r/weapons pgs. from War Journal; Jim Lee-c	1.00	2.50	5.00
2-Jim Lee-c	.45	1.15	2.25
3-5-($2.00-c): All new material. 3-Jusko painted-c	.50	1.25	2.50

PUNISHER MAGAZINE, THE
Oct, 1989 - No. 16, Nov, 1990 ($2.25, B&W, Magazine, 52 pgs.)
Marvel Comics

	GD25	FN65	NM94
1-3: 1-r/Punisher #1('86). 2,3-r/Punisher 2-5	.45	1.15	2.25
4-16: 4-7-r/Punisher V2#1-8. 4-Chiodo-c. 8-r/Punisher #10 & Daredevil #257; Portacio & Lee-r. 14-r/Punisher War Journal #1,2 w/new Lee-c. 16-r/Punisher W. J. #3,8	.45	1.15	2.25

NOTE: ***Chiodo*** *painted c-4, 7, 16.* ***Jusko*** *painted c-6, 8.* ***Jim Lee*** *r-8, 14-16; c-14.* ***Portacio/Williams*** *r-7-12.*

PUNISHER MOVIE COMIC
Nov, 1989 - No. 3, Dec, 1989 ($1.00, color, mini-series)
Marvel Comics

	GD25	FN65	NM94
1-3: Movie adaptation	.30	.75	1.50
1 (1989, $4.95, squarebound)-contains #1-3	1.00	2.50	5.00

PUNISHER: P.O.V.
1991 - No. 4, 1991 ($4.95, color, mini-series, 52 pgs.)
Marvel Comics

	GD25	FN65	NM94
1-4: Starlin scripts & Wrightson painted-c/a in all. 2-Nick Fury app.	1.00	2.50	5.00

PUNISHER: THE GHOSTS OF INNOCENTS
1993 - No. 2, 1993 ($5.95, color)
Marvel Comics

	GD25	FN65	NM94
1,2-Starlin scripts	1.20	3.00	6.00

PUNISHER 2099 (See Punisher War Journal #50)
Feb, 1993 - Present ($1.25, color)
Marvel Comics

	GD25	FN65	NM94
1-($1.75)-Foil stamped-c	.50	1.25	2.50
2-4		.60	1.25

PUNISHER WAR JOURNAL, THE
Nov, 1988 - Present ($1.50/$1.75, color)
Marvel Comics

	GD25	FN65	NM94
1-Origin The Punisher; Jim Lee-c/a begins; Matt Murdock cameo; 1st Lee-a on Punisher	4.00	10.00	20.00
2-Daredevil x-over	2.40	7.00	14.00
3-5: 3-Daredevil x-over	2.00	5.00	10.00
6-Two part Wolverine story begins	4.00	10.00	20.00
7-Wolverine story ends	2.00	5.00	10.00
8-10	1.40	3.50	7.00
11-13,17-19: 19-Last Jim Lee-c/a	1.00	2.50	5.00
14-16,20-22: No Jim Lee-a. 13-15-Heath-i. 14,15-Spider-Man x-over	2.50	1.25	2.50
23-28,31-49,51-54: 23-Begin $1.75-c. 31-Andy & Joe Kubert art. 36-Photo-c. 47,48-Nomad/Daredevil-c/stories; see Nomad	.35	.90	1.75
29,30-Ghost Rider app.	.50	1.25	2.50
50-($2.50, 52 pgs.)-Preview of Punisher 2099 (1st app.); embossed-c	.50	1.25	2.50

NOTE: ***Jusko*** *painted c-31, 32.* ***Jim Lee*** *a(p)-1-13, 17-19; c-1-15, 17, 18, 19p. Painted c-40.*

PUNISHER: WAR ZONE, THE
Mar, 1992 - Present ($1.75, color)
Marvel Comics

	GD25	FN65	NM94
1-($2.25, 40pgs.)-Die-cut-c; Romita, Jr.-c/a begins	.70	1.75	3.50
2	.50	1.25	2.50
3-16: 8-Last Romita, Jr.-c/a	.35	.90	1.75

PUPPET COMICS
Spring, 1946 - No. 2, Summer, 1946
George W. Dougherty Co.

	GD25	FN65	NM94
1,2-Funny animal	5.85	17.50	35.00

PUPPET MASTER 2: CHILDREN OF THE PUPPET MASTER (Eternity)(Value: cover or less)

PUPPETOONS (See George Pal's...)

PURE OIL COMICS (Also see Salerno Carnival of Comics, 24 Pages of Comics, & Vicks Comics)
Late 1930's (24 pgs.; regular size) (paper cover)
Pure Oil Giveaway

	GD25	FN65	NM94
nn-Contains 1-2 pg. strips; i.e., Hairbreadth Harry, Skyroads, Buck Rogers by Calkins & Yager, Olly of the Movies, Napoleon, S'Matter Pop, etc.	29.00	85.00	200.00
Also a 16 pg. 1938 giveaway w/Buck Rogers	23.00	70.00	160.00

PURPLE CLAW, THE (Also see Tales of Horror)
Jan, 1953 - No. 3, May, 1953
Minoan Publishing Co./Toby Press

	GD25	FN65	NM94
1-Origin	14.00	43.00	100.00
2,3: 1-3 r-in Tales of Horror #9-11	10.00	30.00	65.00
I.W. Reprint #8-Reprints #1	1.60	4.00	8.00

PUSSYCAT (Magazine)
Oct, 1968 (B&W reprints from Men's magazines)
Marvel Comics Group

	GD25	FN65	NM94
1-(Scarce)-Ward, Everett, Wood-a; Everett-c	16.00	48.00	110.00

PUZZLE FUN COMICS (Also see Jingle Jangle)
Spring, 1946 - No. 2, Summer, 1946 (52 pgs.)
George W. Dougherty Co.

Punisher V2#44, © MEG

The Punisher War Journal #12, © MEG

Pussycat #1, © MEG

Quasar #14, © MEG

Queen of the West, Dale Evans #11, © Roy Rogers

Quick Draw McGraw #5 (Dell), © Hanna-Barbera

	GD25	FN65	NM94
1(1946)-Gustavson-a	12.00	36.00	85.00
2	10.00	30.00	65.00

*NOTE: #1 & 2('46) each contain a **George Carlson** cover plus a 6 pg. story "Alec in Fumbleland;" also many puzzles in each.*

QUACK!
July, 1976 - No. 6, 1977? ($1.25, B&W)
Star Reach Productions

	GD25	FN65	NM94
1-Brunner-c/a on Duckaneer (Howard the Duck clone); Stevens, Gilbert, Shaw-a	1.00	2.50	5.00
2,4-6: 2-Newton the Rabbit Wonder by Aragones/Leialoha; Gilbert, Shaw-a; Leialoha-c. 6-Brunner-a (Duckeneer); Gilbert-a	.40	1.00	2.00
3-The Beavers by Dave Sim; Gilbert, Shaw-a; Sim/Leialoha-c	1.00	2.50	5.00

QUADRANT
1983 - No. 7, 1986 (B&W, nudity, adults)
Quadrant Publications

	GD25	FN65	NM94
1-Peter Hsu-c/a in all	2.40	6.00	12.00
2	.80	2.00	4.00
3-7	.40	1.00	2.00

QUAKER OATS (Also see Cap'n Crunch)
1965 (Giveaway) (2x5") (16 pages)
Quaker Oats Co.

	GD25	FN65	NM94
"Plenty of Glutton," "Lava Come-Back," "Kite Tale," "A Witch in Time"	.60	1.50	3.00

QUANTUM LEAP (TV) (See A Nightmare on Elm Street)
Sept, 1991 - Present ($2.50, color, painted-c)
Innovation Publishing

	GD25	FN65	NM94
1-10: Based on TV show; all have painted-c. 8-Has photo gallery	.50	1.25	2.50
Special Edition 1 (10/92)-r/#1 w/8 extra pgs. of photos & articles	.50	1.25	2.50

QUASAR (See Avengers #302, Captain America #217, Incredible Hulk #234 & Marvel Team-Up #113)
Oct, 1989 - Present ($1.00/$1.25, color) (Direct sale #17 on)
Marvel Comics

	GD25	FN65	NM94
1-Origin; formerly Marvel Boy/Marvel Man	.40	1.00	2.00
2-5: 3-Human Torch app.	.30	.75	1.50
6-Venom cameo (2 pgs.)	.40	1.00	2.00
7-Cosmic Spidey app.	.50	1.25	2.50
8-15,18-24: 11-Excalibur x-over. 14-McFarlane-c. 20-Fantastic Four app. 23-Ghost Rider x-over		.60	1.20
16-($1.50, 52 pgs.)	.30	.75	1.50
17-Flash parody (Buried Alien)	.40	1.00	2.00
25-($1.50, 52 pgs.)-New costume Quasar	.30	.75	1.50
26-Infinity Guantlet x-over; Thanos-c/story	.40	1.00	2.00
27-Infinity Guantlet x-over	.30	.75	1.50
28-30: 30-Thanos cameo in flashback; last $1.00-c		.50	1.00
31-46: 31-D.P. 7 guest stars. 38-40-Infinity War x-overs. 38-Battles Warlock. 39-Thanos-c & cameo. 40-Thanos app.		.60	1.25

NOTE: #32-34 also have newsstand versions which are renumbered on the cover #1-3 with the actual issue number appearing in the indicia.

QUEEN OF THE DAMNED, THE (Anne Rice's...) (Innovation) (Value: cover or less)

QUEEN OF THE WEST, DALE EVANS (TV) (See Dale Evans Comics & Western Roundup under Dell Giants)
No. 479, 7/53 - No. 22, 1-3/59 (All photo-c; photo back c-4-8, 15)
Dell Publishing Co.

	GD25	FN65	NM94
4-Color 479(#1, '53)	11.50	34.00	80.00
4-Color 528(#2, '54)	8.35	25.00	50.00
3(4-6/54)-Toth-a	9.15	27.50	55.00
4-Toth, Manning-a	9.15	27.50	55.00
5-10-Manning-a. 5-Marsh-a	6.35	19.00	38.00
11,19,21-No Manning 21-Tufts-a	4.70	14.00	28.00
12-18,20,22-Manning-a	5.85	17.50	35.00

QUENTIN DURWARD (See 4-Color #672)

QUESTAR ILLUSTRATED SCIENCE FICTION CLASSICS
1977 (224 pgs.) ($1.95)
Golden Press

	GD25	FN65	NM94
11197-Stories by Asimov, Sturgeon, Silverberg & Niven; Starstream-r	.60	1.50	3.00

QUEST FOR DREAMS LOST
1987 ($2.00, B&W, 52 pgs.) (Proceeds donated to help illiteracy)
Literacy Volunteers of Chicago

	GD25	FN65	NM94
1-Teenage Mutant Ninja Turtles, Trollords, Silent Invasion, The Realm, Wordsmith, Reacto Man, Eb'nn, the Aniverse	.50	1.25	2.50

QUESTION, THE (See Americomics, Blue Beetle (1967), Charlton Bullseye & Mysterious Suspense)

QUESTION, THE (DC) (Value: cover or less)

QUESTION QUARTERLY, THE (DC) (Value: cover or less)

QUESTPROBE
8/84; No. 2, 1/85; No. 3, 11/85 - No. 4, 12/85 (Limited series)
Marvel Comics Group

	GD25	FN65	NM94
1-4: 1-The Hulk app. by Romita. 2-Spider-Man; Mooney-a(i). 3-Human Torch & Thing		.50	1.00

QUICK-DRAW McGRAW (TV) (Hanna-Barbera)
No. 1040, 12-2/59-60 - No. 11, 7-9/62; No. 12, 11/62; No. 13, 2/63; No. 14, 4/63; No. 15, 6/69
Dell Publishing Co./Gold Key No. 12 on

	GD25	FN65	NM94
4-Color 1040(#1)	8.35	25.00	50.00
2(4-6/60)-6	5.85	17.50	35.00
7-11	4.20	12.50	25.00
12,13-Title change to ...Fun-Type Roundup (84 pgs.)	5.65	17.00	45.00
14,15	3.60	9.00	18.00

(See Whitman Comic Books)

QUICK-DRAW McGRAW (TV) (See Spotlight #2)
Nov, 1970 - No. 8, Jan, 1972 (Hanna-Barbera)
Charlton Comics

	GD25	FN65	NM94
1	4.00	10.00	20.00
2-8	2.40	6.00	12.00

QUICK-TRIGGER WESTERN (...Action #12; Cowboy Action #5-11)
No. 12, May, 1956 - No. 19, Sept, 1957
Atlas Comics (ACI No. 12/WPI No. 13-19)

	GD25	FN65	NM94
12-Baker-a	7.50	22.50	45.00
13-Williamson-a, 5 pgs.	8.35	25.00	50.00
14-Everett, Crandall, Torres-a; Heath-c	7.00	21.00	42.00
15-Torres, Crandall-a	5.85	17.50	35.00
16-Orlando, Kirby-a	5.00	15.00	30.00
17,18: 18-Baker-a	5.00	15.00	30.00
19	4.00	11.00	22.00

*NOTE: **Ayers** a-17. **Colan** a-16. **Maneely** a-15, 17; c-15, 18. **Morrow** a-18. **Powell** a-14. **Severin** a-19; c-12, 13, 16, 17, 19. **Shores** a-16. **Tuska** a-17.*

QUINCY (See Comics Reading Libraries)

RACCOON KIDS, THE (Formerly Movietown Animal Antics)
No. 52, Sept-Oct, 1954 - No. 64, Nov, 1957
National Periodical Publications (Arleigh No. 63,64)

	GD25	FN65	NM94
52-Doodles Duck by Mayer	10.00	30.00	60.00
53-64: 53-62-Doodles Duck by Mayer	7.50	22.50	45.00

RACE FOR THE MOON
March, 1958 - No. 3, Nov, 1958

Harvey Publications

	GD25	FN65	NM94
1-Powell-a(5); -pg. S&K-a; cover redrawn from Galaxy Science Fiction pulp (5/53)	9.15	27.50	55.00
2-Kirby/Williamson-c(r)/a(3)	16.00	48.00	110.00
3-Kirby/Williamson-c/a(4)	16.50	50.00	115.00

RACE OF SCORPIONS (Dark Horse)(Value: cover or less)

RACER-X (Now)(Value: cover or less)

RACKET SQUAD IN ACTION
May-June, 1952 - No. 29, March, 1958
Capitol Stories/Charlton Comics

	GD25	FN65	NM94
1	13.00	40.00	90.00
2-4	6.70	20.00	40.00
5-Dr. Neff, Ghost Breaker app; headlights-c	9.15	27.50	55.00
6-Dr. Neff, Ghost Breaker app.	6.70	20.00	40.00
7-10: 10-Explosion-c	5.00	15.00	30.00
11-Ditko-c/a	13.00	40.00	90.00
12-Ditko explosion-c (classic); Shuster-a(2)	24.00	72.00	165.00
13-Shuster-c(p)/a; acid in woman's face	7.50	22.50	45.00
14-"Shakedown" marijuana story	7.50	22.50	45.00
15-28	4.20	12.50	25.00
29-(68 pgs.)(15 cents)	4.70	14.00	28.00

RADIANT LOVE (Formerly Daring Love #1)
No. 2, Dec, 1953 - No. 6, Aug, 1954
Gilmor Magazines

	GD25	FN65	NM94
2	4.00	11.00	22.00
3-6	2.80	7.00	14.00

RAGAMUFFINS (Eclipse)(Value: cover or less)

RAGGEDY ANN AND ANDY (See Dell Giants, March of Comics #23 & New Funnies)
No. 5, 1942 - No. 533, 2/54; 10-12/64 - No. 4, 3/66
Dell Publishing Co.

	GD25	FN65	NM94
4-Color 5(1942)	42.00	125.00	290.00
4-Color 23(1943)	32.00	95.00	220.00
4-Color 45(1943)	26.00	77.00	180.00
4-Color 72(1945)	22.00	65.00	150.00
1(6/46)-Billy & Bonnie Bee by Frank Thomas	22.00	65.00	150.00
2,3: 3-Egbert Elephant by Dan Noonan begins	11.00	32.00	75.00
4-Kelly-a, 16 pgs.	11.50	34.00	80.00
5-10: 7-Little Black Sambo, Black Mumbo & Black Jumbo only app; Christmas-c	10.00	30.00	60.00
11-20	8.35	25.00	50.00
21-Alice In Wonderland cover/story	8.35	25.00	50.00
22-27,29-39(8/49), 4-Color 262(1/50)	5.85	17.50	35.00
28-Kelly-c	6.70	20.00	40.00
4-Color 306,354,380,452,533	4.70	14.00	28.00
1(10-12/64-Dell)	3.00	7.50	15.00
2,3(10-12/65), 4(3/66)	1.60	4.00	8.00

NOTE: ***Kelly** art ("Animal Mother Goose")-#1-34, 36, 37; c-28. Peterkin Pottle by **John Stanley** in 32-38.*

RAGGEDY ANN AND ANDY
Dec, 1971 - No. 6, Sept, 1973
Gold Key

	GD25	FN65	NM94
1	1.60	4.00	8.00
2-6	.80	2.00	4.00

RAGGEDY ANN & THE CAMEL WITH THE WRINKLED KNEES (See Dell Jr. Treasury #8)

RAGMAN (See Batman Family #20, The Brave & The Bold #196 & Cancelled Comic Cavalcade)
Aug-Sept, 1976 - No. 5, June-July, 1977
National Periodical Publications/DC Comics No. 5

	GD25	FN65	NM94
1-Origin	.60	1.50	3.00
2-5: 2-Origin ends; Kubert-c. 4-Drug use story	.30	.75	1.50

NOTE: ***Kubert** a-4, 5; c-1-5. **Redondo** studios a-1-4.*

RAGMAN (2nd series)
Oct, 1991 - No. 8, May, 1992 ($1.50, color, mini-series)
DC Comics

	GD25	FN65	NM94
1-Giffen plots/breakdowns	.60	1.50	3.00
2-8: 3-Origin. 8-Batman-c/story	.30	.75	1.50

RAGS RABBIT (See Harvey Hits #2, Harvey Wiseguys & Tastee Freez)
No. 11, June, 1951 - No. 18, March, 1954
Harvey Publications

	GD25	FN65	NM94
11-(See Nutty Comics #5 for 1st app.)	2.80	7.00	14.00
12-18	2.40	6.00	12.00

RAI (Rai and the Future Force #9 on; see Magnus #5-8)
Mar, 1991 - No. 0, Nov, 1992; No. 9, May, 1993 - Present ($1.95/$2.25, color)
Valiant

	GD25	FN65	NM94
1-Valiant's 1st original character	3.00	7.50	15.00
2,3	1.60	4.00	8.00
4-Low printing; last $1.95-c	5.00	15.00	30.00
5,6,8: 6,7-Unity x-overs	.70	1.75	3.50
7-Death of Rai	1.60	4.00	8.00
0-(11/92)-Origin/1st app. new Rai & 1st app. Bloodshot (2 pgs.); tells future of all characters; also see Eternal Warrior #4	4.20	12.50	25.00
9,10: 9-Story cont'd from Magnus #24; Magnus, Eternal Warrior & X-O app.	.45	1.10	2.25

NOTE: ***Layton** c-2i. **Miller** c-6. **Simonson** c-7.*

RAIDERS OF THE LOST ARK
Sept, 1981 - No. 3, Nov, 1981 (Movie adaptation)
Marvel Comics Group

	GD25	FN65	NM94
1-r/Marvel Comics Super Special #18	.30	.75	1.50
2,3		.50	1.00

NOTE: ***Buscema** a(p)-1-3; c(p)-1. **Simonson** a-3i; scripts-1-3.*

RAINBOW BRITE AND THE STAR STEALER (DC)(Value: cover or less)

RALPH KINER, HOME RUN KING
1950 (Pittsburgh Pirates)
Fawcett Publications

	GD25	FN65	NM94
nn-Photo-c	35.00	105.00	245.00

RALPH SNART ADVENTURES (Now)(Value: cover or less)

RAMAR OF THE JUNGLE (TV)
1954 (no month); No. 2, Sept, 1955 - No. 5, Sept, 1956
Toby Press No. 1/Charlton No. 2 on

	GD25	FN65	NM94
1-Jon Hall photo-c	10.00	30.00	60.00
2-5	7.50	22.50	45.00

RAMPAGING HULK (The Hulk #10 on; see Marvel Treasury Edition)
Jan, 1977 - No. 9, June, 1978 ($1.00, B&W magazine)
Marvel Comics Group

	GD25	FN65	NM94
1-Bloodstone featured	.80	2.00	4.00
2-Old X-Men app; origin old & new X-Men in text w/Cockrum illos	1.60	4.00	8.00
3-9: 9-Thor vs. Hulk battle; Shanna the She-Devil story	.40	1.00	2.00

NOTE: ***Alcala** a-1-3i, 5i, 8i. **Buscema** a-1. **Giffen** a-4. **Nino** a-4i. **Simonson** a-1-3p. **Starlin** a-4(w/Nino), 7; c-4, 5, 7.*

RANDOLPH SCOTT (Movie star)(See Crack Western #67, Prize Comics Western #76, Western Hearts #8, Western Love #1 & Western Winners #7)

RANGE BUSTERS
Sept, 1950 - No. 8, 1951
Fox Features Syndicate

	GD25	FN65	NM94
1	10.00	30.00	60.00
2	6.70	20.00	40.00
3-8	5.85	17.50	35.00

RANGE BUSTERS (Formerly Cowboy Love?; Wyatt Earp, Frontier Marshall

Racket Squad in Action #5, © CC

Raggedy Ann and Andy #39, © DELL

Ragman #2 (10-11/76), © DC

Range Romances #3, © QUA

Rangers Comics #14, © FH

The Rat Patrol #5, © Mirisch-Rich T.V. Prod.

#11 on)
No. 8, May, 1955 - No. 10, Sept, 1955
Charlton Comics

	GD25	FN65	NM94
8	5.00	15.00	30.00
9,10	3.60	9.00	18.00

RANGELAND LOVE
Dec, 1949 - No. 2, Mar, 1950 (52 pgs.)
Atlas Comics (CDS)

	GD25	FN65	NM94
1-Robert Taylor & Arlene Dahl photo-c	9.15	27.50	55.00
2-Photo-c	8.35	25.00	50.00

RANGER, THE (See 4-Color #255)

RANGE RIDER (See The Flying A's...)

RANGE RIDER, THE (See 4-Color #404)

RANGE ROMANCES
Dec, 1949 - No. 5, Aug, 1950 (#5: 52 pgs.)
Comic Magazines (Quality Comics)

	GD25	FN65	NM94
1-Gustavson-c/a	14.00	43.00	100.00
2-Crandall-c/a; "spanking" scene	17.00	52.00	120.00
3-Crandall, Gustavson-a; photo-c	11.50	34.00	80.00
4-Crandall-a; photo-c	10.00	30.00	65.00
5-Gustavson-a; Crandall-a(p); photo-c	10.00	30.00	70.00

RANGERS COMICS (...of Freedom #1-7)
10/41 - No. 67, 10/52; No. 68, Fall, 1952; No. 69, Winter, 1952-53
Fiction House Magazines (Flying stories)

	GD25	FN65	NM94
1-Intro. Ranger Girl & The Rangers of Freedom; ends #7, cover app. only-#5	117.00	350.00	700.00
2	54.00	162.00	325.00
3	46.00	138.00	275.00
4,5	42.00	125.00	250.00
6-10: 8-U.S. Rangers begin	33.00	100.00	200.00
11,12-Commando Rangers app.	30.00	90.00	180.00
13-Commando Ranger begins-not same as Commando Rangers	30.00	90.00	180.00
14-20	22.00	118.00	135.00
21-Intro/origin Firehair (begins)	27.00	80.00	160.00
22-30: 23-Kazanda begins, ends #28. 28-Tiger Man begins (origin). 30-Crusoe Island begins, ends #40	18.00	55.00	110.00
31-40: 33-Hypodermic panels	15.00	45.00	90.00
41-46	12.00	35.00	70.00
47-56-"Eisnerish" Dr. Drew by Grandenetti	12.50	37.50	75.00
57-60-Straight Dr. Drew by Grandenetti	10.00	30.00	60.00
61,62,64-66: 64-Suicide Smith begins	9.15	27.50	55.00
63-Used in **POP**, pgs. 85, 99	9.15	27.50	55.00
67-69: 67-Space Rangers begin, end #69	9.15	27.50	55.00

NOTE: *Bondage, discipline covers, lingerie panels are common.* ***M. Anderson*** *a-30?* ***Baker*** *a-36-38, 42, 44.* ***John Celardo*** *a-34, 36-39.* ***Lee Elias*** *a-21-28.* ***Evans*** *a-19, 38-46, 48, 51, 52.* ***Hopper*** *a-25, 26.* ***Ingels*** *a-13-16.* ***Larsen*** *a-34.* ***Bob Lubbers*** *a-30-38, 40-44; c-40-45.* ***Moreira*** *a-41-47.* ***Tuska*** *a-16, 17, 19, 22.* ***M. Whitman*** *c-61-66.* ***Zolnerwich*** *c-1-17.*

RANGO (TV)
August, 1967
Dell Publishing Co.

	GD25	FN65	NM94
1-Tim Conway photo-c	3.20	8.00	16.00

RANMA 1/2 (Viz)(Value: cover or less)

RAPHAEL (See Teenage Mutant Ninja Turtles)
1985 (One shot, $1.50, B&W w/2 color cover, 7-1/2x11")
Mirage Studios

	GD25	FN65	NM94
1-1st Turtles one-shot spin-off; contains 1st drawing of the Turtles as a group from 1983	2.00	5.00	10.00
1-2nd print. (11/87)-New-c & 8pgs.-a	.80	2.00	4.00

RATFINK (See Frantic & Zany)
October, 1964
Canrom, Inc.

	GD25	FN65	NM94
1-Woodbridge-a	4.00	11.00	22.00

RAT PATROL, THE (TV)
March, 1967 - No. 5, Nov, 1967; No. 6, Oct, 1969
Dell Publishing Co.

	GD25	FN65	NM94
1-Christopher George photo-c	5.85	17.50	35.00
2	4.20	12.50	25.00
3-6: 3-6-Photo-c	3.60	9.00	18.00

RAVAGE 2099 (See Marvel Comics Presents #117)
Dec, 1992 - Present ($1.25, color)
Marvel Comics

	GD25	FN65	NM94
1-($1.75)-Gold foil stamped-c; Paul Ryan-c/a & Stan Lee scripts begin	.50	1.25	2.50
2,3	.40	1.00	2.00
4-6	.35	.85	1.75

RAVEN, THE (See Movie Classics)

RAVENS AND RAINBOWS (Pacific)(Value: cover or less)

RAWHIDE (TV)
Sept-Nov, 1959 - June-Aug, 1962; July, 1963 - No. 2, Jan, 1964
Dell Publishing Co./Gold Key

	GD25	FN65	NM94
4-Color 1028 (#1)	24.00	70.00	165.00
4-Color 1097,1160,1202,1261,1269	16.00	48.00	110.00
01-684-208(8/62-Dell)	14.00	43.00	100.00
1(10071-307, G.K.), 2-(12 cents)	12.00	36.00	85.00

NOTE: *All have Clint Eastwood photo-c.* ***Tufts*** *a-1028.*

RAWHIDE KID
3/55 - No. 16, 9/57; No. 17, 8/60 - No. 151, 5/79
Atlas/Marvel Comics (CnPC No. 1-16/AMI No. 17-30)

	GD25	FN65	NM94
1-Rawhide Kid, his horse Apache & sidekick Randy begin; Wyatt Earp app.; #1 was not code approved	43.00	130.00	300.00
2	17.00	52.00	120.00
3-5	11.50	34.00	80.00
6-10: 7-Williamson-a (4 pgs.)	10.00	30.00	60.00
11-16: 16-Torres-a	7.50	22.50	45.00
17-Origin by Jack Kirby	11.00	32.00	75.00
18-22,24-30	5.85	17.50	35.00
23-Origin retold by Jack Kirby	10.00	30.00	65.00
31,32,36-44,46: 40-Two-Gun Kid x-over. 42-1st Larry Lieber issue. 46-Toth-a	5.00	15.00	30.00
33-35-Davis-a. 35-Intro & death of The Raven	5.85	17.50	35.00
45-Origin retold	5.85	17.50	35.00
47-70: 50-Kid Colt x-over. 64-Kid Colt story. 66-Two-Gun Kid story. 67-Kid Colt story	2.80	7.00	14.00
71-86: 79-Williamson-a(r). 86-Origin-r; Williamson-r/Ringo Kid #13 (4 pgs.)	1.60	4.00	8.00
87-99,101-151: 115-Last new story	1.20	3.00	6.00
100-Origin retold & expanded	2.00	5.00	10.00
Special 1(9/71, 25 cents, 68pgs.)-All Kirby/Ayers-r	1.20	3.00	6.00

NOTE: ***Ayers*** *a-13, 14, 16.* ***Colan*** *a-5, 35, 37; c-145p, 148p, 149p.* ***Davis*** *a-125r.* ***Everett*** *a-54i, 65, 66, 88, 96i, 148i(r).* ***Gulacy*** *c-147.* ***Heath*** *c-4.* ***G. Kane*** *c-101, 144.* ***Keller*** *a-5, 144r.* ***Kirby*** *a-17-32, 34, 42, 43, 84, 86, 92, 109r, 112r, 137r, Spec. 1; c-17-35, 37, 40, 41, 43-47, 137r.* ***Maneely*** *c-1, 2, 5, 6, 14.* ***Morisi*** *a-13.* ***Roussos*** *r-146i, 147i, 149-151i.* ***Severin*** *a-16; c-8, 13.* ***Torres*** *a-99r.* ***Tuska*** *a-14.* ***Wildey*** *r-146-151(Outlaw Kid).* ***Williamson*** *a-79r, 86r, 95r, 111r.*

RAWHIDE KID (Marvel)(Value: cover or less)

RAY, THE (See Smash Comics #14)
Feb, 1992 - No. 6, July, 1992 ($1.00, color, mini-series)
DC Comics

	GD25	FN65	NM94
1-Sienkiewicz-c; Joe Quesada-a(p) in 1-5	1.20	3.00	6.00
2	.70	1.75	3.50

	GD25	FN65	NM94
3: 3-6-Quesada-c(p)	.60	1.50	3.00
4-6: 6-Quesada layouts only	.40	1.00	2.00

REAL ADVENTURE COMICS (Action Adventure #2 on)
April, 1955
Gillmor Magazines

1	3.20	8.00	16.00

REAL CLUE CRIME STORIES (Formerly Clue Comics)
V2#4, June, 1947 - V8#3, May, 1953
Hillman Periodicals

V2#4(#1)-S&K c/a(3); Dan Barry-a	19.00	58.00	135.00
5-7-S&K c/a(3-4); 7-Iron Lady app.	16.00	48.00	110.00
8-12	4.70	14.00	28.00
V3#1-8,10-12, V4#1-3,5-8,11,12	4.00	10.00	20.00
V3#9-Used in **SOTI**, pg. 102	6.70	20.00	40.00
V4#4-S&K-a	5.85	17.50	35.00
V4#9,10-Krigstein-a	5.85	17.50	35.00
V5#1-5,7,8,10,12	3.60	9.00	18.00
6,9,11-Krigstein-a	5.85	17.50	35.00
V6#1-5,8,9,11	2.80	7.00	14.00
6,7,10,12-Krigstein-a. 10-Bondage-c	5.85	17.50	35.00
V7#1-3,5-11, V8#1-3: V7#6-1 pg. Frazetta ad	2.80	7.00	14.00
4,12-Krigstein-a	5.85	17.50	35.00

NOTE: ***Barry** a-9, 10; c-V2#8. **Briefer** a-V6#6. **Fuje** a- V2#7(2), 8, 11. **Infantino** a-V2#8; c-V2#11. **Lawrence** a-V3#8, V5#7. **Powell** a-V4#11, 12. V5#4, 5, 7 are 68 pgs.*

REAL EXPERIENCES (Formerly Tiny Tessie)
No. 25, January, 1950
Atlas Comics (20CC)

25	4.00	10.00	20.00

REAL FACT COMICS
Mar-Apr, 1946 - No. 21, July-Aug, 1949
National Periodical Publications

1-S&K-c/a; Harry Houdini story; Just Imagine begins (not by Finlay)	37.00	110.00	225.00
2-S&K-a; Rin-Tin-Tin story	24.00	122.00	145.00
3-H.G. Wells, Lon Chaney story	14.00	42.00	85.00
4-Virgil Finlay-a on 'Just Imagine' begins, ends #12 (2 pgs. each); Jimmy Stewart story	22.00	65.00	130.00
5-Batman/Robin-c; 5 pg. story about creation of Batman & Robin; Tom Mix story	125.00	375.00	750.00
6-Origin & 1st app. Tommy Tomorrow by Finlay; Flag-c; 1st writing by Harlan Ellison (letter column, non-professional); "First Man to Reach Mars" epic-c/story	83.00	250.00	500.00
7-(No. 6 on inside)-Roussos-a	10.00	30.00	65.00
8-2nd app. Tommy Tomorrow by Finlay	42.00	125.00	250.00
9-S&K-a; Glenn Miller story	18.00	55.00	110.00
10-Vigilante by Meskin; 4 pg. Finlay s/f story	17.00	52.00	105.00
11,12: 11-Kinstler-a	10.00	30.00	65.00
13-Dale Evans and Tommy Tomorrow-c/stories	39.00	118.00	235.00
14,17,18: 14-Will Rogers story	9.15	27.50	55.00
15-Nuclear Explosion part-c	10.00	30.00	65.00
16-Tommy Tomorrow app.; 1st Planeteers?	33.00	100.00	200.00
19-Sir Arthur Conan Doyle story	9.15	27.50	55.00
20-Kubert-a, 4 pgs; Daniel Boone story	13.00	40.00	80.00
21-Kubert-a, 2 pgs; Kit Carson story	9.15	27.50	55.00

NOTE: ***Barry** c-16. **Virgil Finlay** c-6, 8. **Meskin** c-10. **Roussos** a-1-4.*

REAL FUN OF DRIVING!!, THE
1965, 1967 (Regular size)
Chrysler Corp.

nn-Shaffenberger-a, 12pgs.	1.00	2.50	5.00

REAL FUNNIES
Jan, 1943 - No. 3, June, 1943
Nedor Publishing Co.

1-Funny animal, humor; Black Terrier app. (clone of The Black Terror)

	GD25	FN65	NM94
	17.00	52.00	120.00
2,3	10.00	30.00	60.00

REAL GHOSTBUSTERS, THE (Now)(Value: cover or less)(Also see Slimer)

REAL HEROES COMICS
Sept, 1941 - No. 16, Oct, 1946
Parents' Magazine Institute

1-Roosevelt-c/story	20.00	60.00	120.00
2	8.35	25.00	50.00
3-5,7-10	6.70	20.00	40.00
6-Lou Gehrig-c/story	12.00	35.00	70.00
11-16: 13-Kiefer-a	4.20	12.50	25.00

REAL HIT
1944 (Savings Bond premium)
Fox Features Publications

1-Blue Beetle-r	12.00	35.00	70.00

NOTE: *Two versions exist, with and without covers. The coverless version has the title, No. 1 and price printed at top of splash page.*

REALISTIC ROMANCES
July-Aug, 1951 - No. 17, Aug-Sept, 1954 (no No. 9-14)
Realistic Comics/Avon Periodicals

1-Kinstler-a; c-/Avon paperback #211	11.00	32.00	75.00
2	6.35	19.00	38.00
3,4	4.70	14.00	28.00
5,8-Kinstler-a	5.00	15.00	30.00
6-c-/Diversey Prize Novels #6; Kinstler-a	5.85	17.50	35.00
7-Evans-a?; c-/Avon paperback #360	5.85	17.50	35.00
15,17	4.20	12.50	25.00
16-Kinstler marijuana story-r/Romantic Love #6	5.85	17.50	35.00
I.W. Reprint #1,8,9	.35	.90	1.80

NOTE: ***Astarita** a-2-4, 7, 8.*

REAL LIFE COMICS
Sept, 1941 - No. 59, Sept, 1952
Nedor/Better/Standard Publ./Pictorial Magazine No. 13

1-Uncle Sam c/story	25.00	75.00	150.00
2	12.50	37.50	75.00
3-Hitler cover	18.00	55.00	110.00
4,5: 4-Story of American flag "Old Glory"	8.35	25.00	50.00
6-10	7.50	22.50	45.00
11-20: 17-Albert Einstein story	5.35	16.00	32.00
21-23,25,26,28-30: 29-A-Bomb story	4.20	12.50	25.00
24-Story of Baseball	8.35	25.00	50.00
27-Schomburg A-Bomb-c; story of A-Bomb	8.35	25.00	50.00
31-33,35,36,42-44,48,49	4.00	10.00	20.00
34,37-41,45-47: 34-Jimmy Stewart story. 37-Story of motion pictures; Bing Crosby story. 38-Jane Froman story. 39-"1,000,000 A.D." story. 40-Bob Feller story. 41-Jimmie Foxx story; "Home Run" Baker story. 45-Story of Olympic games; Burl Ives story. 46-Douglas Fairbanks Jr. & Sr. story. 47-George Gershwin story	4.20	12.50	25.00
50-Frazetta-a (5 pgs.)	17.00	50.00	100.00
51-Jules Verne "Journey to the Moon" by Evans	10.00	30.00	60.00
52-Frazetta-a (4 pgs.); Severin/Elder-a(2); Evans-a	17.00	50.00	100.00
53-57-Severin/Elder-a	6.70	20.00	40.00
58-Severin/Elder-a(2)	7.50	22.50	45.00
59-1pg. Frazetta; Severin/Elder-a	6.70	20.00	40.00

NOTE: *Some issues had two titles. **Guardineer** a-40(2), 44. **Schomburg** c-1, 2, 4, 5, 7, 11, 13-21, 23, 24, 26, 28, 30-32, 34-40, 42, 44-47, 55. Photo-c 5, 6.*

REAL LIFE SECRETS (Real Secrets #2 on)
Sept, 1949 (One shot)
Ace Periodicals

1-Painted-c	5.35	16.00	32.00

REAL LIFE STORY OF FESS PARKER (Magazine)
1955

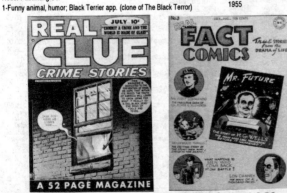

Real Clue Crime Stories V3#5, © HILL

Real Fact Comics #3, © DC

Realistic Romances #8, © REAL

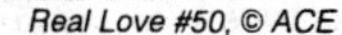
Real Love #50, © ACE

Real Screen Comics 8, © DC

Real Western Hero #71, © FAW

	GD25	FN65	NM94
Dell Publishing Co.			
1	10.00	30.00	60.00

REAL LIFE TALES OF SUSPENSE (See Suspense)

REAL LOVE (Formerly Hap Hazard)
No. 25, April, 1949 - No. 76, Nov, 1956
Ace Periodicals (A. A. Wyn)

	GD25	FN65	NM94
25	5.85	17.50	35.00
26	3.60	9.00	18.00
27-L. B. Cole-a	4.70	14.00	28.00
28-35	2.40	6.00	12.00
36-66: 66-Last pre-code (2/55)	2.0	5.00	10.00
67-76	1.40	3.50	7.00

NOTE: *Photo c-50-76. Painted c-46.*

REALM, THE
Feb, 1986 - No. 20? ($1.50-$1.95, B&W)
Arrow Comics/WeeBee Comics #13/Caliber Press #14 on

	GD25	FN65	NM94
1	.80	2.00	4.00
2	.40	1.00	2.00
3,5-16: 13-Begin $1.95-c		.60	1.25
4-1st app. Deadworld	4.00	10.00	20.00
17-20: 17-Begin $2.50-c	.50	1.25	2.50
Book 1 ($4.95, B&W)	1.00	2.50	5.00

REAL McCOYS, THE (TV)
No. 1071, 1-3/60 - 5-7/1962 (Photo-c)
Dell Publishing Co.

	GD25	FN65	NM94
4-Color 1071,1134-Toth-a in both	10.00	30.00	70.00
4-Color 1193,1265	9.15	27.50	55.00
01-689-207 (5-7/62)	8.35	25.00	50.00

REAL SCREEN COMICS (#1 titled Real Screen Funnies; TV Screen Cartoons #129-138)
Spring, 1945 - No. 128, May-June, 1959 (#1-40: 52 pgs.)
National Periodical Publications

	GD25	FN65	NM94
1-The Fox & the Crow, Flippity & Flop, Tito & His Burro begin	79.00	235.00	550.00
2	39.00	120.00	275.00
3-5	24.00	72.00	165.00
6-10 (2-3/47)	16.00	48.00	110.00
11-20 (10-11/48): 13-The Crow x-over in Flippity & Flop	11.50	34.00	80.00
21-30 (6-7/50)	10.00	30.00	60.00
31-50	8.35	25.00	50.00
51-99	5.85	17.50	35.00
100	6.70	20.00	40.00
101-128	4.20	12.50	25.00

REAL SECRETS (Formerly Real Life Secrets)
No. 2, Nov, 1950 - No. 5, May, 1950
Ace Periodicals

	GD25	FN65	NM94
2	5.35	16.00	32.00
3-5: 3-Photo-c	3.20	8.00	16.00

REAL SPORTS COMICS (All Sports Comics #2 on)
Oct-Nov, 1948 (52 pgs.)
Hillman Periodicals

	GD25	FN65	NM94
1-Powell-a (12 pgs.)	25.00	75.00	150.00

REAL WAR STORIES
July, 1987; No. 2, Jan, 1991 ($2.00, color, 52 pgs.)
Eclipse Comics

	GD25	FN65	NM94
1-Bolland-a(p), Bissette-a, Totleben-a(i); Alan Moore scripts (2nd printing exists, 2/88)	.40	1.00	2.00
2-($4.95)	1.00	2.50	5.00

REAL WESTERN HERO (Formerly Wow #1-69; Western Hero #76 on)
No. 70, Sept, 1948 - No. 75, Feb, 1949 (All 52 pgs.)
Fawcett Publications

	GD25	FN65	NM94
70(#1)-Tom Mix, Monte Hale, Hopalong Cassidy, Young Falcon begin	23.00	70.00	160.00
71-75: 71-Gabby Hayes begins. 71,72-Captain Tootsie by Beck. 75-Big Bow and Little Arrow app.	14.00	43.00	100.00

NOTE: *Painted/photo c-70-73; painted c-74, 75.*

REAL WEST ROMANCES
4-5/49 - V1#6, 3/50; V2#1, Apr-May, 1950 (All 52 pgs. & photo-c)
Crestwood Publishing Co./Prize Publ.

	GD25	FN65	NM94
V1#1-S&K-a(p)	11.50	34.00	80.00
2-Spanking panel	10.00	30.00	70.00
3-Kirby-a(p) only	6.70	20.00	40.00
4-S&K-a; Whip Wilson, Reno Browne photo-c	11.00	32.00	75.00
5-Audie Murphy, Gale Storm photo-c; S&K-a	10.00	30.00	60.00
6-Produced by S&K, no S&K-a	8.35	25.00	50.00
V2#1-Kirby-a(p)	5.85	17.50	35.00

NOTE: ***Meskin** a-V1#5, 6. **Severin/Elder** a-V1#3-6, V2#1. **Meskin** a-V1#6. **Leonard Starr** a-1-3. Photo-c V1#1-5, V2#1.*

RE-ANIMATOR IN FULL COLOR
Oct, 1991 - No. 3, 1992 ($2.95, color, mini-series)
Adventure Comics

	GD25	FN65	NM94
1-3: Adapts horror movie. 1-Dorman painted-c	.60	1.50	3.00

REAP THE WILD WIND (See Cinema Comics Herald)

REBEL, THE (See 4-Color #1076, 1138, 1207, 1262)

RECORD BOOK OF FAMOUS POLICE CASES
1949 (25 cents, 132 pgs.)
St. John Publishing Co.

	GD25	FN65	NM94
nn-Kubert-a(3); r/Son of Sinbad; Baker-c	24.00	72.00	165.00

RED ARROW
May-June, 1951 - No. 3, Oct, 1951
P. L. Publishing Co.

	GD25	FN65	NM94
1	6.70	20.00	40.00
2,3	5.00	15.00	30.00

RED BALL COMIC BOOK
1947 (Red Ball Shoes giveaway)
Parents' Magazine Institute

	GD25	FN65	NM94
nn-Reprints from True Comics	2.40	6.00	12.00

RED BAND COMICS
Feb, 1945 - No. 4, May, 1945
Enwil Associates

	GD25	FN65	NM94
1	17.00	50.00	100.00
2-Origin Bogeyman & Santanas	14.00	42.00	85.00
3,4-Captain Wizard app. in both; each has identical contents/cover	12.50	37.50	75.00

RED CIRCLE COMICS
Jan, 1945 - No. 4, April, 1945
Rural Home Publications (Enwil)

	GD25	FN65	NM94
1-The Prankster & Red Riot begin	17.00	50.00	100.00
2-Starr-a; The Judge (costumed hero) app.	13.00	40.00	80.00
3,4-Starr-c/a. 3-The Prankster not in costume	10.00	30.00	60.00
4-(Dated 4/45)-Leftover covers to #4 were later restapled over early 1950s coverless comics; variations in the coverless comics used are endless; Woman Outlaws, Dorothy Lamour, Crime Does Not Pay, Sabu, Diary Loves, Love Confessions & Young Love V3#3 known	7.50	22.50	45.00

RED CIRCLE SORCERY (Chilling Adventures in Sorcery #1-5)
No. 6, Apr, 1974 - No. 11, Feb, 1975

Red Circle Productions (Archie)

6-11: 8-Only app. The Cobra. 10-Wood-a(i) .30 .75 1.50

NOTE: *Chaykin a-6, 10. B. Jones a-7(w/Wrightson, Kaluta, J. Jones). McWilliams a-10(2 & 3 pgs.). Mooney a-11p. Morrow a-6-8, 9(text illos), 10, 11i; c-6-11. Thorne a-8, 10. Toth a-8, 9.*

REDDEVIL (AC)(Value: cover or less)

RED DOG (See Night Music #7)

RED DRAGON COMICS (1st Series) (Formerly Trail Blazers; see Super Magician V5#7, 8)
No. 5, Jan, 1943 - No. 9, Jan, 1944
Street & Smith Publications

5-Origin Red Rover, the Crimson Crimebuster; Rex King, Man of Adventure, Captain Jack Commando, & The Minute Man begin; text origin Red Dragon; Binder-c 54.00 162.00 325.00
6-Origin The Black Crusader & Red Dragon (3/43) 47.00 142.00 285.00
7,8: 8-The Red Knight app. 32.00 95.00 190.00
9-Origin Chuck Magnon, Immortal Man 32.00 95.00 190.00

RED DRAGON COMICS (2nd Series)(See Super Magician V2#8)
Nov, 1947 - No. 6, Jan, 1949; No. 7, July, 1949
Street & Smith Publications

1-Red Dragon begins; Elliman, Nigel app.; Edd Cartier-c/a 58.00 175.00 350.00
2-Cartier-c 47.00 142.00 285.00
3-1st app. Dr. Neff by Powell; Elliman, Nigel app. 37.00 110.00 225.00
4-Cartier c/a 52.00 162.00 315.00
5-7 29.00 88.00 175.00

NOTE: *Maneely a-5, 7. Powell a-2-7; c-3, 5, 7.*

REDDY GOOSE
No #, 1958?; No. 2, Jan, 1959 - No. 16, July, 1962 (Giveaway)
International Shoe Co. (Western Printing)

nn (#1) 6.70 20.00 40.00
2-16 4.00 10.50 21.00

REDDY KILOWATT (5 cents) (Also see Story of Edison)
1946 - No. 2, 1947; 1956 - 1960 (no month) (16 pgs.; paper cover)
Educational Comics (E. C.)

nn-Reddy Made Magic (1946, 5 cents) 12.00 35.00 70.00
nn-Reddy Made Magic (1958) 5.35 16.00 32.00
2-Edison, the Man Who Changed the World (3/4" smaller than #1) (1947, 5 cents) 12.00 35.00 70.00
...Comic Book 2 (1954)-"Light's Diamond Jubilee" 6.70 20.00 40.00
...Comic Book 2 (1958)-"Wizard of Light," 16 pgs. 5.35 16.00 32.00
...Comic Book 3 (1956)-"The Space Kite," 8 pgs.; Orlando story; regular size 5.35 16.00 32.00
...Comic Book 3 (1960)-"The Space Kite," 8 pgs.; Orlando story; regular size 4.70 14.00 28.00

NOTE: *Several copies surfaced in 1979.*

REDDY MADE MAGIC
1956, 1958 (16 pages) (paper cover)
Educational Comics (E. C.)

1-Reddy Kilowatt-r (splash panel changed) 8.00 24.00 48.00
1 (1958 edition) 5.00 15.00 30.00

RED EAGLE (See Feature Books #16)

REDEYE (See Comics Reading Libraries)

RED FOX (Formerly Manhunt! #1-14; also see Extra Comics)
No. 15, 1954
Magazine Enterprises

15(A-1 #108)-Undercover Girl story; L.B. Cole-c/a (Red Fox); r-from Manhunt; Powell-a 10.00 30.00 70.00

RED GOOSE COMIC SELECTIONS (See Comic Selections)

RED HAWK (See A-1 Comics #90, Bobby Benson's... #14-16 & Straight Arrow #2)

RED ICEBERG, THE
1960 (10 cents) (16 pgs.) (Communist propaganda)
Impact Publ. (Catechetical Guild)

nn-(Rare)-'We The People'-back-c 37.00 110.00 240.00
2nd version-'Impact Press'-back-c 43.00 130.00 280.00

NOTE: *This book was the Guild's last anti-communist propaganda book and had very limited circulation. 3 - 4 copies surfaced in 1979 from the defunct publisher's files. Other copies do turn up.*

RED MASK (Formerly Tim Holt; see Best Comics, Blazing Six-Guns)
No. 42, 6-7/1954 - No. 53, 5/56; No. 54, 9/57
Magazine Enterprises No. 42-53/Sussex No. 54 (M.E. on-c)

42-Ghost Rider by Ayers continues, ends #50; Black Phantom continues; 3-D effect c/stories begin 13.50 41.00 95.00
43-3-D effect-c/stories 11.50 34.00 80.00
44-50: 3-D effect stories only. 47-Last pre-code issue. 50-Last Ghost Rider 11.00 32.00 75.00
51-The Presto Kid begins by Ayers (1st app.); Presto Kid-c begins, ends #54; last 3-D effect story 11.00 32.00 75.00
52-Origin The Presto Kid 11.00 32.00 75.00
53,54-Last Black Phantom 9.15 27.50 55.00
I.W. Reprint #1 (r-/#52). 2 (nd, r/#51 w/diff.-c). 3, 8 (nd; Kinstler-c); 8-r/Red Mask #52 1.60 4.00 8.00

NOTE: *Ayers art on Ghost Rider & Presto Kid. Bolle art in all (Red Mask); c-43, 44, 49. Guardineer a-52. Black Phantom in #42-44, 47-50, 53, 54.*

REDMASK OF THE RIO GRANDE (AC)(Value: cover or less)

RED MOUNTAIN FEATURING QUANTRELL'S RAIDERS
1952 (Movie) (Also see Jesse James #28)
Avon Periodicals

nn-Alan Ladd; Kinstler-c/a 16.00 48.00 110.00

"RED" RABBIT COMICS
Jan, 1947 - No. 22, Aug-Sept, 1951
Dearfield Comic/J. Charles Laue Publ. Co.

1 8.35 25.00 50.00
2 4.70 14.00 28.00
3-10 4.00 10.00 20.00
11-17,19-22 3.20 8.00 16.00
18-Flying Saucer-c (1/51) 4.00 10.00 20.00

RED RAVEN COMICS (Human Torch #2 on; also see X-Men #44)
August, 1940 (Also see Sub-Mariner #26, 2nd series)
Timely Comics

GD25 FN65 VF82 NM94

1-Origin Red Raven; Comet Pierce & Mercury by Kirby, The Human Top & The Eternal Brain; intro. Magar, the Mystic & only app.; Kirby-c (his 1st signed work) 750.00 2250.00 4100.00 6000.00
(Estimated up to 135 total copies exist, 6 in NM/Mint)

RED RYDER COMICS (Hi Spot #2)(Movies, radio)(See Crackajack Funnies)
9/40; No. 3, 8/41 - No. 5, 12/41; No. 6, 4/42 - No. 151, 4-6/57
Hawley Publ. No. 1-5/Dell Publishing Co.(K.K.) No. 6 on

GD25 FN65 NM94

1-Red Ryder, his horse Thunder, Little Beaver & his horse Papoose strip reprints begin by Fred Harman; 1st meeting of Red & Little Beaver; Harman line-drawn-c #1-85 100.00 300.00 700.00
3-(Scarce)-Alley Oop, King of the Royal Mtd., Capt. Easy, Freckles & His Friends, Myra North, Dan Dunn strip-r begin 64.00 195.00 250.00
4,5 36.00 107.00 250.00
6-1st Dell issue 36.00 107.00 250.00
7-10 29.00 85.00 200.00
11-20 22.00 65.00 150.00
21-32-Last Alley Oop, Dan Dunn, Capt. Easy, Freckles 14.00 43.00 100.00
33-40 (52 pgs.) 10.00 30.00 60.00
41 (52 pgs.)-Rocky Lane photo back-c; photo back-c begin, end #57 10.00 30.00 65.00

Red Dragon Comics #7 (7/43), © S&S

Red Mask #51, © ME

Red Ryder Comics #19, © DELL

Red Seal Comics #22, © SUPR

Redskin #1, © YM

Red Wolf #1, © MEG

	GD25	FN65	NM94
42-46 (52 pgs.): 46-Last Red Ryder strip-r	8.35	25.00	50.00
47-53 (52 pgs.): 47-New stories on Red Ryder begin	6.70	20.00	40.00
54-57 (36 pgs.)	5.35	16.00	32.00
58-73 (36 pgs.): 73-Last King of the Royal Mtd; strip-r by Jim Gary	5.00	15.00	30.00
74-85,93 (52 pgs.)-Harman line-drawn-c	5.35	16.00	32.00
86-92 (52 pgs.)-Harman painted-c	5.35	16.00	32.00
94-96 (36 pgs.)-Harman painted-c	4.20	12.50	25.00
97,98,107,108 (36 pgs.)-Harman line-drawn-c	4.20	12.50	25.00
99,101-106 (36 pgs.)-Jim Bannon Photo-c	4.20	12.50	25.00
100 (36 pgs.)-Bannon photo-c	4.70	14.00	28.00
109-118 (52 pgs.)-Harman line-drawn-c	3.60	9.00	18.00
119-129 (52 pgs.): 119-Painted-c begin, not by Harman, end #151	3.20	8.00	16.00
130-144 (#130 on have 36 pgs.)	2.80	7.00	14.00
145-148: 145-Title change to Red Ryder Ranch Magazine with photos	2.40	6.00	12.00
149-151: 149-Title changed to Red Ryder Ranch Comics	2.40	6.00	12.00
4-Color 916 (7/58)	2.80	7.00	14.00
Buster Brown Shoes Giveaway (1941, 32pgs., color, soft-c)	19.00	57.00	132.00
Red Ryder Super Book Of Comics 10 (1944; paper-c; 32 pgs.; blank back-c)-Magic Morro app.	19.00	57.00	132.00
Red Ryder Victory Patrol-nn(1944, 32 pgs.)-r-/#43,44; comic has a paper-c & is stapled inside a triple cardboard fold-out-c; contains membership card, decoder, map of R.R. home range, etc. Herky app. (Langendorf Bread giveaway; sub-titled 'Super Book of Comics') (Rare)	215.00	645.00	1500.00
Wells Lamont Corp. giveaway (1950)-16 pgs. in color; regular size; paper-c; 1941-r	19.00	56.00	130.00

NOTE: ***Fred Harman** a-1-99; c-1-98, 107-118. Don Red Barry, Allan Rocky Lane, Wild Bill Elliott & Jim Bannon starred as Red Ryder in the movies. Robert Blake starred as Little Beaver.*

RED RYDER PAINT BOOK
1941 (148 pages) (8-1/2x11-1/2")
Whitman Publishing Co.

	GD25	FN65	NM94
nn-Reprints 1940 daily strips	19.00	56.00	130.00

RED SEAL COMICS (Formerly Carnival Comics, and/or Spotlight Comics?)
No. 14, 10/45 - No. 18, 10/46; No. 19, 6/47 - No. 22, 12/47
Harry 'A' Chesler/Superior Publ. No. 19 on

	GD25	FN65	NM94
14-The Black Dwarf begins (continued from Spotlight?); Little Nemo app; bondage/hypo-c; Tuska-a	32.00	95.00	190.00
15-Torture story	24.00	122.00	145.00
16-Used in **SOTI**, pg. 181, illo-"Outside the forbidden pages of de Sade, you find draining a girl's blood only in children's comics;" drug club story r-later in Crime Reporter #1; Veiled Avenger & Barry Kuda app; Tuska-a	33.00	100.00	200.00
17-Lady Satan, Yankee Girl & Sky Chief app; Tuska-a	21.00	62.00	125.00
18,20-Lady Satan & Sky Chief app.	21.00	62.00	125.00
19-No Black Dwarf (on cover only); Zor, El Tigre app.	17.00	50.00	100.00
21-Lady Satan & Black Dwarf app.	17.00	50.00	100.00
22-Zor, Rocketman app. (68 pgs.)	17.00	50.00	100.00

REDSKIN (Famous Western Badmen #13 on)
Sept, 1950 - No. 12, Oct, 1952
Youthful Magazines

	GD25	FN65	NM94
1-Walter Johnson-a (7 pgs.)	8.35	25.00	50.00
2	5.85	17.50	35.00
3-12: 6,12-Bondage-c	4.20	12.50	25.00

NOTE: ***Palais** a-11. **Wildey** a-5, 11.*

RED SONJA (Also see Conan #23, Kull & The Barbarians, Marvel Feature & Savage Sword Of Conan #1)
1/77 - No. 15, 5/79; V1#1, 2/83 - V2#2, 3/83; V3#1, 8/83 - V3#4, 2/84; V3#5, 1/85 - V3#13, 1986
Marvel Comics Group

	GD25	FN65	NM94
1-Created by Robert E. Howard	.60	1.50	3.00
2-5: 5-Last 30 cent issue	.40	1.00	2.00
6-15, V1#1,V2#2: 14-Last 35 cent issue		.50	1.00
V3#1-4 ($1.00, 52 pgs.)		.60	1.20
5-13 (65-75 cents)		.50	1.00

NOTE: ***Brunner** c-12-14. **J. Buscema** a(p)-12, 13, 15; c-V#1. **Nebres** a-V3#3i(part). **N. Redondo** a-8i, V3#2i, 3i. **Simonson** a-V3#1. **Thorne** c/a-1-11.*

RED SONJA: THE MOVIE (Marvel) (Value: cover or less)

RED TORNADO (DC) (Value: cover or less) (See All-American #20 & Justice League of America #64)

RED WARRIOR
Jan, 1951 - No. 6, Dec, 1951
Marvel/Atlas Comics (TCI)

	GD25	FN65	NM94
1-Red Warrior & his horse White Wing; Tuska-a	10.00	30.00	60.00
2-Tuska-c	6.70	20.00	40.00
3-6: 4-Origin White Wing. 6-Maneely-c	5.00	15.00	30.00

RED WOLF (See Avengers #80 & Marvel Spotlight #1)
May, 1972 - No. 9, Sept, 1973
Marvel Comics Group

	GD25	FN65	NM94
1-(Western hero); Gil Kane/Severin-c; Shores-a	.80	2.00	4.00
2-9: 2-Kane-c; Shores-a. 6-Tuska-r in back-up. 7-Red Wolf as super hero begins. 9-Origin sidekick, Lobo (wolf)	.40	1.00	2.00

REESE'S PIECES (Eclipse) (Value: cover or less)

REFORM SCHOOL GIRL!
1951
Realistic Comics

	GD25	FN65	NM94
nn-Used in **SOTI**, pg. 358, & cover ill. with caption "Comic books are supposed to be like fairy tales"	71.00	215.00	500.00

(Prices vary widely on this book)

NOTE: *The cover and title originated from a digest-sized book published by Diversey Publishing Co. of Chicago in 1948. The original book "House of Fury," Doubleday, came out in 1941. The girl's real name which appears on the cover of the digest and comic is Marty Collins, Canadian model and ice skating star who posed for this special color photograph for the Diversey novel.*

REGENTS ILLUSTRATED CLASSICS
1981 (Plus more recent reprintings)
(48 pgs., b&w-a with 14 pages of teaching helps)
Prentice Hall Regents, Englewood Cliffs, NJ 07632
NOTE: *This series contains Classics Ill. art, and was produced from the same illegal source as **Cassette Books.** But when Twin Circle sued to stop the sale of the Cassette Books, they decided to permit this series to continue. This series was produced as a teaching aid. The 20 title series is divided into four levels based upon number of basic words used therein. There is also a teacher's manual for each level. All of the titles are still available from the publisher for about $5 each retail. The number to call for mail order purchases is (201)767-5937. Almost all of the issues have new covers taken from some interior art panel. Here is a list of the series by Regents ident. no. and the Classics Ill. counterpart.*

16770(CI#24-A2)18333(CI#3-A2)21668(CI#13-A2)32224(CI#21)33051(CI#26)
35788(CI#84)37153(CI#16)44460(CI#19-A2)44808(CI#18-A2)52395(CI#4-A2)
58627(CI#5-A2)60067(CI#30)68405(CI#23-A1)70302(CI#29)78192(CI#7-A2)
78193(CI#10-A2)79679(CI#85)92046(CI#1-A2)93062(CI#64)93512(CI#25)

REGGIE (Formerly Archie's Rival...; Reggie & Me #19 on)
No. 15, Sept, 1963 - No. 18, Nov, 1965
Archie Publications

	GD25	FN65	NM94
15(9/63), 16(10/64)	5.85	17.50	35.00
17(8/65), 18(11/65)	5.85	17.50	35.00

NOTE: *Cover title No. 15 & 16 is Archie's Rival Reggie.*

REGGIE AND ME (Formerly Reggie)
No. 19, Aug, 1966 - No. 126, Sept, 1980 (No. 50-68: 52 pgs.)

Archie Publications

	GD25	FN65	NM94
19-Evilheart app.	3.20	8.00	16.00
20-23-Evilheart app.; with Pureheart #22	1.60	4.00	8.00
24-40	.50	1.25	2.50
41-60	.30	.75	1.50
61-126		.50	1.00

REGGIE'S JOKES (See Reggie's Wise Guy Jokes)

REGGIE'S WISE GUY JOKES
Aug, 1968 - No. 60, Jan, 1982 (#5 on are Giants)
Archie Publications

	GD25	FN65	NM94
1	2.80	7.00	14.00
2-4	1.20	3.00	6.00
5-10	.60	1.50	3.00
11-28	.30	.75	1.50
29-60		.50	1.00

REGISTERED NURSE
Summer, 1963
Charlton Comics

	GD25	FN65	NM94
1-r/Nurse Betsy Crane & Cynthia Doyle	1.00	2.50	5.00

REG'LAR FELLERS (See All-American Comics, Popular Comics & Treasure Box of Famous Comics)
1921 - 1929
Cupples & Leon Co./MS Publishng Co.

	GD25	FN65	NM94
1(1921)-52 pgs. B&W dailies (Cupples & Leon, 10x10")	15.00	45.00	90.00
1925, 48 pgs. B&W dailies (MS Publ.)	15.00	45.00	90.00
Softcover (1929, nn, 36 pgs.)	15.00	45.00	90.00
Hardcover (1929)-B&W reprints, 96 pgs.	17.00	50.00	100.00

REG'LAR FELLERS
No. 5, Nov, 1947 - No. 6, Mar, 1948
Visual Editions (Standard)

	GD25	FN65	NM94
5,6	5.85	17.50	35.00

REG'LAR FELLERS HEROIC (See Heroic Comics)

REID FLEMING, WORLD'S TOUGHEST MILKMAN (Eclipse)(Value: cover or less)

RELUCTANT DRAGON, THE (See 4-Color #13)

REMEMBER PEARL HARBOR
1942 (68 pages) (Illustrated story of the battle)
Street & Smith Publications

	GD25	FN65	NM94
nn-Uncle Sam-c; Jack Binder-a	30.00	90.00	210.00

REN & STIMPY SHOW, THE (TV)
Dec, 1992 - Present ($1.75, color)
Marvel Comics

	GD25	FN65	NM94
1-($2.25)-Polybagged w/scratch & sniff Ren or Stimpy air fowler (equal amounts of each were made)	1.20	3.00	6.00
1-2nd printing	.45	1.10	2.25
2	.60	1.50	3.00
3	.55	1.40	2.75
4-6: 6-Spider-Man x-over	.35	.90	1.75

RENO BROWNE, HOLLYWOOD'S GREATEST COWGIRL (Formerly Margie Comics; Apache Kid #53 on); also see Western Hearts, Western Life Romances & Western Love)
No. 50, April, 1950 - No. 52, Sept, 1950 (52 pgs.)
Marvel Comics (MPC)

	GD25	FN65	NM94
50-Photo-c	18.00	54.00	125.00
51,52: 51-Photo-c	17.00	50.00	115.00

REPTILICUS (Becomes Reptisaurus #3 on)
Aug, 1961 - No. 2, Oct, 1961
Charlton Comics

	GD25	FN65	NM94
1 (Movie)	10.00	30.00	70.00
2	8.35	25.00	50.00

REPTISAURUS (Reptilicus #1,2)
V2#3, Jan, 1962 - No. 8, Dec, 1962; Summer, 1963
Charlton Comics

	GD25	FN65	NM94
V2#3-8: 8-Montes/Bache-c/a	4.20	12.50	25.00
Special Edition 1 (Summer, 1963)	4.20	12.50	25.00

REQUIEM FOR DRACULA
1993 ($2.00, color)
Marvel Comics

	GD25	FN65	NM94
nn-r/Tomb of Dracula #69,70	.40	1.00	2.00

RESCUERS, THE (See Walt Disney Showcase #40)

RESCUERS DOWN UNDER (Disney)(Value: cover or less)

RESTLESS GUN (See 4-Color #934, 986, 1045, 1089, 1146)

RETURN FROM WITCH MOUNTAIN (See Walt Disney Showcase #44)

RETURN OF GORGO, THE (Formerly Gorgo's Revenge)
No. 2, Aug, 1963 - No. 3, Fall, 1964 (#2 is last 10 cent issue; #3 is 12 cents)
Charlton Comics

	GD25	FN65	NM94
2,3-Ditko-c/a; based on M.G.M. movie	6.70	20.00	40.00

RETURN OF KONGA, THE (Konga's Revenge #2 on)
1962
Charlton Comics

	GD25	FN65	NM94
nn	6.70	20.00	40.00

RETURN OF MEGATON MAN (Kitchen Sink)(Value: cover or less)

RETURN OF THE OUTLAW
Feb, 1953 - No. 11, 1955
Toby Press (Minoan)

	GD25	FN65	NM94
1-Billy the Kid	5.35	17.50	35.00
2	4.00	10.00	20.00
3-11	3.20	8.00	16.00

REVEALING LOVE STORIES (See Fox Giants)

REVEALING ROMANCES
Sept, 1949 - No. 6, Aug, 1950
Ace Magazines

	GD25	FN65	NM94
1	5.00	15.00	30.00
2	3.20	8.00	16.00
3-6	2.40	6.00	12.00

REVELATIONS (Eclipse)(Value: cover or less)

REVENGE OF THE PROWLER (Eclipse)(Value: cover or less)

REVENGERS FEATURING ARMOR AND SILVER STREAK, THE (Continuity)(Value: cover or less)(Becomes Armor #4 on)

REVENGERS FEATURING MEGALITH (Continuity)(Value: cover or less)

REVENGERS SPECIAL (Continuity)(Value: cover or less)

REX ALLEN COMICS (Movie star)(Also see 4-Color #877 & Western Roundup under Dell Giants)
No. 316, Feb, 1951 - No. 31, Dec-Feb, 1958-59 (All-photo-c)
Dell Publishing Co.

	GD25	FN65	NM94
4-Color 316(#1)(52 pgs.)-Rex Allen & his horse Koko begin; Marsh-a	14.00	43.00	100.00
2 (9-11/51, 36 pgs.)	8.35	25.00	50.00
3-10	6.35	19.00	38.00
11-20	5.00	15.00	30.00
21-23,25-31	4.70	14.00	28.00
24-Toth-a	5.85	17.50	35.00

NOTE: ***Manning** a-20, 27-30. Photo back-c F.C. #316, 2-12, 20, 21.*

REX DEXTER OF MARS (See Mystery Men Comics)
Fall, 1940
Fox Features Syndicate

1-Rex Dexter, Patty O'Day, & Zanzibar (Tuska-a) app.; Briefer-c/a

Reno Browne, Hollywood's Greatest Cowgirl #51, © MEG

Reptisaurus V2#5, © CC

Rex Allen Comics #16, © DELL

Ribtickler #1, © FOX

Richard Dragon, Kung-Fu Fighter #2, © DC

Richie Rich #2, © HARV

	GD25	FN65	NM94
	125.00	375.00	750.00

REX HART (Formerly Blaze Carson; Whip Wilson #9 on)
No. 6, Aug, 1949 - No. 8, Feb, 1950 (All photo-c)
Timely/Marvel Comics (USA)

	GD25	FN65	NM94
6-Rex Hart & his horse Warrior begin; Black Rider app; Captain Tootsie by Beck	16.00	48.00	110.00
7,8: 18pg. Thriller in each. 8-Blaze the Wonder Collie app. in text	11.50	34.00	80.00

REX MORGAN, M.D. (Also see Harvey Comics Library)
Dec, 1955 - No. 3, 1956
Argo Publ.

	GD25	FN65	NM94
1-Reprints Rex Morgan daily newspaper strips & daily panel-r of "These Women" by D'Alessio & "Timeout" by Jeff Keate	7.50	22.50	45.00
2,3	5.00	15.00	30.00

REX THE WONDER DOG (See The Adventures of...)

RHUBARB, THE MILLIONAIRE CAT (See 4-Color #423, 466, 563)

RIBIT! (Comico) (Value: cover or less)

RIBTICKLER (Also see Fox Giants)
1945 - No. 9, Aug, 1947; 1957; 1959
Fox Feature Synd./Green Publ. (1957)/Norlen (1959)

	GD25	FN65	NM94
1	8.35	25.00	50.00
2	4.20	12.50	25.00
3-9: 3,7-Cosmo Cat app.	3.60	9.00	18.00
3,7,8 (Green Publ.-1957)	2.00	5.00	10.00
3,7,8 (Norlen Mag.-1959)	2.00	5.00	10.00

RICHARD DRAGON, KUNG-FU FIGHTER (See Brave & the Bold)
Apr-May, 1975 - No. 18, Nov-Dec, 1977 (1-4 are based on novel)
National Periodical Publications/DC Comics

	GD25	FN65	NM94
1,2: 2-Starlin-a(p)	.30	.75	1.50
3-18: 3-Kirby-c/a(p). 4-8-Wood inks		.50	1.00

RICHARD THE LION-HEARTED (See Ideal a Classical Comic)

RICHIE RICH (See Harvey Collectors Comics, Harvey Hits, Little Dot, Little Lotta, Little Sad Sack, Million Dollar Digest, Mutt & Jeff, Super Richie, and 3-D Dolly)

RICHIE RICH (...the Poor Little Rich Boy) (See Harvey Hits #3, 9)
Nov, 1960 - #218, Oct, 1982; #219, Oct, 1986 - #254, Jan, 1991
Harvey Publications

	GD25	FN65	NM94
1-(See Little Dot for 1st app.)	72.00	215.00	500.00
2	36.00	107.00	250.00
3-5	20.00	60.00	140.00
6-10: 8-Christmas-c	12.00	36.00	85.00
11-20	6.70	20.00	40.00
21-40	4.20	12.50	25.00
41-60	3.20	8.00	16.00
61-80: 65-1st app. Dollar the Dog	2.00	5.00	10.00
81-99	1.20	3.00	6.00
100(12/70)-1st app. Irona The robot maid	2.00	5.00	10.00
101-111,117-120	1.00	2.50	5.00
112-116: All 52 pg. Giants	1.20	3.00	6.00
121-140	.70	1.75	3.50
141-160: 145-Infinity-c	.60	1.50	3.00
161-180	.40	1.00	2.00
181-254: 237-Last original material	.30	.75	1.50

RICHIE RICH (2nd series) (Harvey) (Value: cover or less)

RICHIE RICH ADVENTURE DIGEST MAGAZINE (Harvey) (Value: cover or less)

RICHIE RICH AND... (Harvey) (Value: cover or less)

RICHIE RICH AND BILLY BELLHOPS
October, 1977 (One Shot) (52pgs.)
Harvey Publications

	GD25	FN65	NM94
1	.60	1.50	3.00

RICHIE RICH AND CADBURY
10/77; #2, 9/78 - #23, 7/82; #24, 7/90 - #29, 1/91 (1-10: 52pgs.)
Harvey Publications

	GD25	FN65	NM94
1	1.00	2.50	5.00
2-5	.40	1.00	2.00
6-29: 24-Begin $1.00-c		.50	1.00

RICHIE RICH AND CASPER
Aug, 1974 - No. 45, Sept, 1982
Harvey Publications

	GD25	FN65	NM94
1	1.60	4.00	8.00
2-5	.80	2.00	4.00
6-10: 10-Xmas-c	.40	1.00	2.00
11-20	.30	.75	1.50
21-40: 22-Xmas-c		.60	1.20
41-45		.50	1.00

RICHIE RICH AND DOLLAR THE DOG (See Richie Rich #65)
Sept, 1977 - No. 24, Aug, 1982 (#1-10: 52pgs.)
Harvey Publications

	GD25	FN65	NM94
1	.80	2.00	4.00
2-10	.40	1.00	2.00
11-24		.50	1.00

RICHIE RICH AND DOT
October, 1974 (One Shot)
Harvey Publications

	GD25	FN65	NM94
1	1.20	3.00	6.00

RICHIE RICH AND GLORIA
Sept, 1977 - No. 25, Sept, 1982 (#1-11: 52pgs.)
Harvey Publications

	GD25	FN65	NM94
1	.80	2.00	4.00
2-5	.40	1.00	2.00
6-25		.50	1.00

RICHIE RICH AND HIS GIRLFRIENDS
April, 1979 - No. 16, Dec, 1982
Harvey Publications

	GD25	FN65	NM94
1: 52 pg. Giant	.60	1.50	3.00
2: 52 pg. Giant	.50	1.20	2.40
3-10	.40	1.00	2.00
11-16		.50	1.00

RICHIE RICH AND HIS MEAN COUSIN REGGIE
April, 1979 - No. 3, 1980 (50 cents) (#1,2: 52pgs.)
Harvey Publications

	GD25	FN65	NM94
1	.40	1.00	2.00
2-3: (#4 was advertised, but never released)	.30	.75	1.50

RICHIE RICH AND JACKIE JOKERS
Nov, 1973 - No. 48, Dec, 1982
Harvey Publications

	GD25	FN65	NM94
1: 52 pg. Giant	3.60	9.00	18.00
2,3: 52 pg. Giants	1.80	4.50	9.00
4,5	1.20	3.00	6.00
6-10	.80	2.00	4.00
11-20: 11-1st app. Kool Katz	.60	1.50	3.00
21-40: 26-Star Wars parody	.30	.75	1.50
41-48		.50	1.00

RICHIE RICH AND PROFESSOR KEENBEAN
Sept, 1990 - No. 2, Nov, 1990 ($1.00, color)
Harvey Comics

	GD25	FN65	NM94
1,2		.50	1.00

RICHIE RICH AND THE NEW KIDS ON THE BLOCK (Harvey)(Value: cover or less)

RICHIE RICH AND TIMMY TIME
Sept, 1977 (50 Cents) (One Shot) (52 pages)
Harvey Publications

	GD25	FN65	NM94
1	.60	1.50	3.00

RICHIE RICH BANK BOOKS
Oct, 1972 - No. 59, Sept, 1982
Harvey Publications

	GD25	FN65	NM94
1	4.00	10.00	20.00
2-5	2.00	5.00	10.00
6-10	1.20	3.00	6.00
11-20	.80	2.00	4.00
21-30	.60	1.50	3.00
31-40	.40	1.00	2.00
41-59		.50	1.00

RICHIE RICH BEST OF THE YEARS
Oct, 1977 - No. 6, June, 1980 (Digest) (128 pages)
Harvey Publications

	GD25	FN65	NM94
1(10/77)-Reprints, #2(10/78)-Reprints, #3(6/79-75 cents)	.40	1.00	2.00
4-6(11/79-6/80-95 cents)		.50	1.00

RICHIE RICH BIG BUCKS (Harvey)(Value: cover or less)

RICHIE RICH BILLIONS
Oct, 1974 - No. 48, Oct, 1982 (#1-33: 52pgs.)
Harvey Publications

	GD25	FN65	NM94
1	2.80	7.00	14.00
2-5	1.40	3.50	7.00
6-10	1.00	2.50	5.00
11-20	.60	1.50	3.00
21-33 (Last 52 pgs.)	.40	1.00	2.00
34-48		.50	1.00

RICHIE RICH CASH
Sept, 1974 - No. 47, Aug, 1982
Harvey Publications

	GD25	FN65	NM94
1-1st app. Dr. N-R-Gee	2.80	7.00	14.00
2-5	1.40	3.50	7.00
6-10	.80	2.00	4.00
11-20	.60	1.50	3.00
21-30	.40	1.00	2.00
31-47		.50	1.00

RICHIE RICH CASH MONEY
May, 1992 - No. 2?, 1992 ($1.25, color)
Harvey Comics

	GD25	FN65	NM94
1,2		.60	1.25

RICHIE RICH, CASPER & WENDY NATIONAL LEAGUE
June, 1976 (52 pages)
Harvey Publications

	GD25	FN65	NM94
1 (Released-3/76 with 6/76 date)	.60	1.50	3.00
1 (6/76)-2nd version w/San Francisco Giants & KTVU 2 logos; has "Compliments of Giants and Straw Hat Pizza" on-c	.60	1.50	3.00

RICHIE RICH COLLECTORS COMICS (See Harvey Collectors Comics)

RICHIE RICH DIAMONDS
Aug, 1972 - No. 59, Aug, 1982 (#1, 23-45: 52pgs.)
Harvey Publications

	GD25	FN65	NM94
1: 52 pg. Giant	4.20	12.50	25.00
2-5	2.00	5.00	10.00
6-10	1.20	3.00	6.00
11-22	.80	2.00	4.00
23-30	.60	1.50	3.00
31-45: 39-Origin Little Dot	.30	.75	1.50
46-50		.60	1.20
51-59		.50	1.00

RICHIE RICH DIGEST (Harvey)(Value: cover or less)

RICHIE RICH DIGEST STORIES (Harvey)(Value: cover or less)

RICHIE RICH DIGEST WINNERS (Harvey)(Value: cover or less)

RICHIE RICH DOLLARS & CENTS
Aug, 1963 - No. 109, Aug, 1982 (#1-43: 68 pgs.; 44-60, 71-94: 52pgs.)
Harvey Publications

	GD25	FN65	NM94
1: (#1-64 are all reprint issues)	11.50	34.00	80.00
2	5.85	17.50	35.00
3-5: 5-r/1st app. of R.R. from Little Dot #1	4.00	10.00	20.00
6-10	2.80	7.00	14.00
11-20	2.40	6.00	12.00
21-30	1.40	3.50	7.00
31-43: Last 68 pg. issue	.80	2.00	4.00
44-60: All 52 pgs.	.60	1.50	3.00
61-70	.50	1.25	2.50
71-94: All 52 pgs.	.30	.75	1.50
95-109: 100-Anniversary issue		.50	1.00

RICHIE RICH FORTUNES
Sept, 1971 - No. 63, July, 1982 (#1-15: 52pgs.)
Harvey Publications

	GD25	FN65	NM94
1	4.20	12.50	25.00
2-5	2.00	5.00	10.00
6-10	1.20	3.00	6.00
11-15: Last 52 pg. Giant	1.00	2.50	5.00
16-30	.60	1.50	3.00
31-40	.30	.75	1.50
41-63		.50	1.00

RICHIE RICH GEMS
Sept, 1974 - No. 43, Sept, 1982
Harvey Publications

	GD25	FN65	NM94
1	2.80	7.00	14.00
2-5	1.40	3.50	7.00
6-10	.80	2.00	4.00
11-20	.50	1.25	2.50
21-30	.30	.75	1.50
31-43: 38-1st app. Stone-Age Riches		.50	1.00

RICHIE RICH GIANT SIZE
Oct, 1992 - Present ($2.25, color, 68 pgs.)
Harvey Comics

	GD25	FN65	NM94
V2#1,2-Richie Rich, Little Audrey & Melvin, Little Dot & Little Lotta stories	.45	1.15	2.25

RICHIE RICH GOLD AND SILVER
Sept, 1975 - No. 42, Oct, 1982 (#1-27: 52pgs.)
Harvey Publications

	GD25	FN65	NM94
1	2.00	5.00	10.00
2-5	1.00	2.50	5.00
6-10	.40	1.00	2.00
11-27	.30	.75	1.50
28-42		.50	1.00

RICHIE RICH GOLD NUGGETS DIGEST (Harvey)(Value: cover or less)

RICHIE RICH HOLIDAY DIGEST MAGAZINE (...Digest #4)
Jan, 1980 - #3, Jan, 1982; #4, 3/88; #5, 2/89 (Published annually)
Harvey Publications

	GD25	FN65	NM94
1-3: All X-Mas-c		.50	1.00
4-(3/88, $1.25), 5-(2/89, $1.75)		.60	1.25

RICHIE RICH INVENTIONS
Oct, 1977 - No. 26, Oct, 1982 (#1-11: 52pgs.)
Harvey Publications

	GD25	FN65	NM94
1	1.00	2.50	5.00
2-5	.50	1.25	2.50
6-11	.30	.75	1.50
12-26		.50	1.00

RICHIE RICH JACKPOTS
Oct, 1972 - No. 58, Aug, 1982 (#41-43: 52pgs.)
Harvey Publications

	GD25	FN65	NM94
1	4.20	12.50	25.00
2-5	2.40	6.00	12.00
6-10	1.40	3.50	7.00
11-20	.80	2.00	4.00
21-30	.60	1.50	3.00
31-40,44-50	.40	1.00	2.00
41-43 (52 pgs.)	.60	1.50	3.00
51-58	.30	.75	1.50

RICHIE RICH MILLION DOLLAR DIGEST (...Magazine #?-on)(Also see Million Dollar Digest)
October, 1980 - No. 9, Oct, 1982 ($1.50)
Harvey Publications

	GD25	FN65	NM94
1-9	.30	.75	1.50

RICHIE RICH MILLIONS
9/61; #2, 9/62 - #113, 10/82 (#1-48: 68 pgs.; 49-64, 85-97: 52 pgs.)
Harvey Publications

	GD25	FN65	NM94
1: (#1-5 are all reprint issues)	13.00	40.00	90.00
2	7.50	22.50	45.00
3-10: (All other giants are new & reprints)	5.85	17.50	35.00
11-20	3.60	9.00	18.00
21-30	2.00	5.00	10.00
31-48: Last 68 pg. Giant	1.40	3.50	7.00
49-64: 52 pg. Giants	.80	2.00	4.00
65-74: 68-1st app. Super Richie (11/74)	.60	1.50	3.00
75-94: 52 pg. Giants	.70	1.75	3.50
95-100	.30	.75	1.50
101-113		.50	1.00

RICHIE RICH MONEY WORLD
Sept, 1972 - No. 59, Sept, 1982
Harvey Publications

	GD25	FN65	NM94
1: 52 pg. Giant	4.20	12.50	25.00
2-5	2.00	5.00	10.00
6-10: 9,10-Richie Rich mistakenly named Little Lotta on covers	1.00	2.50	5.00
11-20	.60	1.50	3.00
21-30	.40	1.00	2.00
31-50	.30	.75	1.50
51-59		.50	1.00

The Rifleman #14, © Four Star

Rima, the Jungle Girl #5, © DC

Ringo Kid Western #6, © MEG

	GD25	FN65	NM94
...Digest 1 (2/91, $1.75) - 6 (1993)	.35	.90	1.75

RICHIE RICH PROFITS
Oct, 1974 - No. 47, Sept, 1982
Harvey Publications

	GD25	FN65	NM94
1	3.20	8.00	16.00
2-5	1.60	4.00	8.00
6-10	.80	2.00	4.00
11-20: 15-Christmas-c	.60	1.50	3.00
21-30	.30	.75	1.50
31-47		.50	1.00

RICHIE RICH RELICS (Harvey) (Value: cover or less)

RICHIE RICH RICHES
July, 1972 - No. 59, Aug, 1982 (#1, 2, 41-45: 52pgs.)
Harvey Publications

	GD25	FN65	NM94
1: 52 pg. Giant	3.60	9.00	18.00
2: 52 pg. Giant	1.80	4.50	9.00
3-5	1.40	3.50	7.00
6-10	.80	2.00	4.00
11-20: 17-Super Richie app. (3/75)	.60	1.50	3.00
21-40	.30	.75	1.50
41-45: 52 pg. Giants	.40	1.00	2.00
46-59		.50	1.00

RICHIE RICH SUCCESS STORIES
Nov, 1964 - No. 105, Sept, 1982 (#1-38: 68pgs., 39-55, 67-90: 52pgs.)
Harvey Publications

	GD25	FN65	NM94
1	11.50	34.00	80.00
2-5	5.85	17.50	35.00
6-10	3.60	9.00	18.00
11-30: 27-1st Penny Van Dough (8/69)	2.00	5.00	10.00
31-38: Last 68 pg. Giant	1.40	3.50	7.00
39-55: 52 pgs.	1.00	2.50	5.00
56-66	.70	1.75	3.50
67-90: 52 pgs. (Early issues are reprints)	.40	1.00	2.00
91-105	.30	.75	1.50

RICHIE RICH TREASURE CHEST DIGEST (...Magazine #3)
Apr, 1982 - No. 3, Aug, 1982 (95 Cents, Digest Magazine)
Harvey Publications

	GD25	FN65	NM94
1-3	.30	.75	1.50

RICHIE RICH VACATION DIGEST
Oct, 1992 - Present ($1.75, color, digest size)
Harvey Comics

	GD25	FN65	NM94
1	.35	.90	1.75

RICHIE RICH VACATIONS DIGEST
11/77; No. 2, 10/78 - No. 7, 10/81; No. 8, 8/82 (Digest, 132 pgs.)
Harvey Publications

	GD25	FN65	NM94
1-Reprints	.40	1.00	2.00
2-8	.30	.75	1.50

RICHIE RICH VAULT OF MYSTERY
Nov, 1974 - No. 47, Sept, 1982
Harvey Publications

	GD25	FN65	NM94
1	2.00	5.00	10.00
2-10	1.00	2.50	5.00
11-20	.60	1.50	3.00
21-30	.40	1.00	2.00
31-47		.50	1.00

RICHIE RICH ZILLIONZ
Oct, 1976 - No. 33, Sept, 1982 (#1-4: 68pgs.; #5-18: 52pgs.)
Harvey Publications

	GD25	FN65	NM94
1	2.00	5.00	10.00
2-4: Last 68 pg. Giant	1.00	2.50	5.00
5-10	.60	1.50	3.00
11-18: Last 52 pg. Giant	.30	.75	1.50
19-33		.50	1.00

RICK GEARY'S WONDERS AND ODDITIES (Dark Horse) (Value: cover or less)

RICKY
No. 5, September, 1953
Standard Comics (Visual Editions)

	GD25	FN65	NM94
5	3.20	8.00	16.00

RICKY NELSON (TV)(See Sweethearts V2#42)
No. 956, Dec, 1958 - No. 1192, June, 1961 (All photo-c)
Dell Publishing Co.

	GD25	FN65	NM94
4-Color 956,998	23.00	70.00	160.00
4-Color 1115,1192-Manning-a	18.00	54.00	125.00

RIDER, THE (Frontier Trail #6; also see Blazing Sixguns I.W. #10, 11)
March, 1957 - No. 5, 1958
Ajax/Farrell Publ. (Four Star Comic Corp.)

	GD25	FN65	NM94
1-Swift Arrow, Lone Rider begin	6.35	19.00	38.00
2-5	4.00	11.00	22.00

RIFLEMAN, THE (TV)
No. 1009, 7-9/59 - No. 12, 7-9/62; No. 13, 11/62 - No. 20, 10/64
Dell Publ. Co./Gold Key No. 13 on

	GD25	FN65	NM94
4-Color 1009 (#1)	14.00	43.00	100.00
2 (1-3/60)	10.00	30.00	60.00
3-Toth-a, 4 pgs.	10.00	30.00	70.00
4,5,7-10	8.35	25.00	50.00
6-Toth-a, 4pgs.	10.00	30.00	60.00
11-20	6.70	20.00	40.00

NOTE: ***Warren Tufts** a-2-9. All have Chuck Connors photo-c. Photo back c-13-15.*

RIMA, THE JUNGLE GIRL
Apr-May, 1974 - No. 7, Apr-May, 1975
National Periodical Publications

	GD25	FN65	NM94
1-Origin, part 1 (#1-5: 20 cent-c, 6,7: 25 cents)	.60	1.50	3.00
2-4-Origin, part 2,3,&4	.30	.75	1.50
5-7: 7-Origin & only app. Space Marshal		.50	1.00

NOTE: ***Kubert** c-1-7. **Nino** a-1-5. **Redondo** a-1-6.*

RING OF BRIGHT WATER (See Movie Classics)

RING OF THE NIBELUNG, THE (DC) (Value: cover or less)

RINGO KID, THE (2nd Series)
Jan, 1970 - No. 23, Nov, 1973; No. 24, Nov, 1975 - No. 30, Nov, 1976
Marvel Comics Group

	GD25	FN65	NM94
1-Williamson-a r-from #10, 1956	.60	1.50	3.00
2-30: 13-Wildey-r. 20-Williamson-r/#1	.30	.75	1.50

RINGO KID WESTERN, THE (See Wild Western & Western Trails)
Aug, 1954 - No. 21, Sept, 1957 (1st series)
Atlas Comics (HPC)/Marvel Comics

	GD25	FN65	NM94
1-Origin; The Ringo Kid begins	14.00	43.00	100.00
2-Black Rider app.; origin/1st app. Ringo's Horse Arab	9.15	27.50	55.00
3-5	5.85	17.50	35.00
6-8-Severin-a(3) each	6.70	20.00	40.00
9,11,12,14-21: 12-Orlando-a, 4pgs.	4.20	12.50	25.00
10,13-Williamson-a, 4 pgs.	5.85	17.50	35.00

NOTE: ***Berg** a-8. **Maneely** a-1-5, 15, 16(text illos only), 17(4), 18, 20, 21; c-1-6, 8, 13, 15-18, 20. **J. Severin** c-10, 11. **Sinnott** a-1. **Wildey** a-16-18.*

RIN TIN TIN (See March of Comics #163,180,195)

RIN TIN TIN (TV) (...& Rusty #21 on; see Western Roundup under Dell Giants)
Nov, 1952 - No. 38, May-July, 1961; Nov, 1963 (All Photo-c)

	GD25	FN65	NM94
Dell Publishing Co./Gold Key			
4-Color 434 (#1)	16.00	48.00	110.00
4-Color 476,523	9.15	27.50	55.00
4(3-5/54)-10	6.70	20.00	40.00
11-20	5.85	17.50	35.00
21-38	5.00	15.00	30.00
... & Rusty 1 (11/63-Gold Key)	6.70	20.00	40.00

RIO (Comico) (Value: cover or less) (Also see Eclipse Monthly)

RIO AT BAY (Dark Horse) (Value: cover or less)

RIO BRAVO (See 4-Color #1018)

RIO CONCHOS (See Movie Comics)

RIOT (Satire)
Apr, 1954 - No. 3, Aug, 1954; No. 4, Feb, 1956 - No. 6, June, 1956
Atlas Comics (ACI No. 1-5/WPI No. 6)

	GD25	FN65	NM94
1-Russ Heath-a	13.00	40.00	90.00
2-Li'l Abner satire by Post	10.00	30.00	70.00
3-Last precode (8/54)	10.00	30.00	60.00
4-Infinity-c; Marilyn Monroe "7 Year Itch" movie satire; Mad Rip-off ads	12.00	36.00	85.00
5-Marilyn Monroe, John Wayne parody; part photo-c	13.00	40.00	90.00
6-Lorna of the Jungle satire by Everett; Dennis the Menace satire-c/story	10.00	30.00	60.00

NOTE: ***Berg*** *a-3.* ***Burgos*** *c-1, 2.* ***Colan*** *a-1.* ***Everett*** *a-1, 4, 6.* ***Heath*** *a-1.* ***Maneely*** *a-1, 2, 4-6; c-3, 4, 6.* ***Post*** *a-1-4.* ***Reinman*** *a-2.* ***Severin*** *a-4-6.*

R.I.P. (TSR) (Value: cover or less)

RIPCORD (See 4-Color #1294)

RIP HUNTER TIME MASTER (See Showcase #20, 21, 25, 26)
Mar-Apr, 1961 - No. 29, Nov-Dec, 1965 (Also see Time Masters)
National Periodical Publications

	GD25	FN65	NM94
Showcase #20 (5-6/59)-Origin & 1st app. Rip Hunter; Moriera-a	65.00	195.00	450.00
Showcase #21 (7-8/59)-2nd app. Rip Hunter; Sekowsky-c/a	29.00	85.00	200.00
Showcase #25,26 (3-4/60, 5-6/60)-3rd & 4th app. Rip Hunter by Kubert	22.00	65.00	150.00
1-(3-4/61)	43.00	130.00	300.00
2	22.00	65.00	150.00
3-5: 5-Last 10 cent issue	12.00	36.00	85.00
6,7-Toth-a in each	10.00	30.00	65.00
8-15	7.50	22.50	45.00
16-20	6.35	19.00	38.00
21-29: 29-G. Kane-c	5.00	15.00	30.00

RIP IN TIME (Fantagor) (Value: cover or less)

RIP KIRBY (See Feature Books #51, 54, Harvey Comics Hits #57, & Street Comix)

RIPLEY'S BELIEVE IT OR NOT!
Sept, 1953 - No. 4, March, 1954
Harvey Publications

	GD25	FN65	NM94
1-Powell-a	8.35	25.00	50.00
2-4	5.35	16.00	32.00
J. C. Penney giveaway (1948)	5.85	17.50	35.00

RIPLEY'S BELIEVE IT OR NOT! (Formerly ...True War Stories)
No. 4, April, 1967 - No. 94, Feb, 1980
Gold Key

	GD25	FN65	NM94
4-Photo-c; McWilliams-a	4.00	10.00	20.00
5-Subtitled "True War Stories;" Evans-a	2.40	6.00	12.00
6-10: 6-McWilliams-a. 10-Evans-a(2)	2.40	6.00	12.00
11-20: 15-Evans-a	1.80	4.50	9.00
21-30	1.20	3.00	6.00
31-38,40-60	.80	2.00	4.00
39-Crandall-a	1.00	2.50	5.00
61-94: 74,77-83 (52 pgs.)	.60	1.50	3.00
Story Digest Mag. 1(6/70)-4-3/4x6-1/2"	1.40	3.50	7.00

NOTE: ***Evanish*** *art by* ***Luiz Dominguez*** *#22-25, 27, 30, 31, 40.* ***Jeff Jones*** *a-5(2 pgs.).* ***McWilliams*** *a-65, 70, 89.* ***Orlando*** *a-8.* ***Sparling*** *c-68. Reprints-74, 77-84, 87 (part); 91, 93 (all).* ***Williamson, Wood*** *a-80r/#1.*

RIPLEY'S BELIEVE IT OR NOT! (See Ace Comics, All-American Comics, Mystery Comics Digest #1, 4, 7, 10, 13, 16, 19, 22, 25)

RIPLEY'S BELIEVE IT OR NOT TRUE GHOST STORIES (Becomes ...True War Stories) (See Dan Curtis)
June, 1965 - No. 2, Oct, 1966
Gold Key

	GD25	FN65	NM94
1-Williamson, Wood & Evans-a; photo-c	5.00	15.00	30.00
2-Orlando, McWilliams-a; photo-c	3.60	9.00	18.00
Mini-Comic 1(1976-3-1/4x6-1/2")	.30	.75	1.50
11186(1977)-Golden Press; ($1.95, 224 pgs.)-All-r	.60	1.50	3.00
11401(3/79)-Golden Press; ($1.00, 96 pgs.)-All-r	.30	.75	1.50

RIPLEY'S BELIEVE IT OR NOT TRUE WAR STORIES (Formerly ...True Ghost Stories; becomes Ripley's Believe It or Not #4 on)
Nov, 1966
Gold Key

	GD25	FN65	NM94
1(#3)-Williamson-a	4.00	10.00	20.00

RIPLEY'S BELIEVE IT OR NOT! TRUE WEIRD
June, 1966 - No. 2, Aug, 1966 (B&W Magazine)
Ripley Enterprises

	GD25	FN65	NM94
1,2-Comic stories & text	1.20	3.00	6.00

RIVERDALE HIGH
Aug, 1990 - No. 5, Apr, 1991 ($1.00, color, bi-monthly)
Archie Comics

	GD25	FN65	NM94
1-5		.50	1.00

RIVETS (See 4-Color #518)

RIVETS (A dog)
Jan, 1956 - No. 3, May, 1956
Argo Publ.

	GD25	FN65	NM94
1-Reprints Sunday & daily newspaper strips	4.00	11.00	22.00
2,3	2.80	7.00	14.00

ROACHMILL (Blackthorne & Dark Horse, 1986 & '88) (Value: cover or less)

ROAD RUNNER (See Beep Beep, the...)

ROBERT E. HOWARD'S CONAN THE BARBARIAN (Marvel) (Value: cover or less)

ROBIN (See Aurora, Detective Comics #38, New Teen Titans, Robin II, Robin III, Robin 3000, Star Spangled Comics #65 & Teen Titans)

ROBIN (See Batman #457)
Jan, 1991 - No. 5, May, 1991 ($1.00, color, mini-series)
DC Comics

	GD25	FN65	NM94
1-Free poster by N. Adams; Bolland-c on all	1.20	3.00	6.00
1-2nd printing, 3rd printing (without poster)	.30	.75	1.50
2	.50	1.25	2.50
2-2nd printing		.50	1.00
3-5	.30	.75	1.50
Annual 1 (1992, $2.50, 68 pgs.)-Grant/Wagner scripts; Sam Kieth-c	.50	1.25	2.50

ROBIN: A HERO REBORN
1991 ($4.95, squarebound, trade paperback)
DC Comics

	GD25	FN65	NM94
nn-r/Batman #455-457 & Robin #1-5; Bolland-c	1.00	2.50	5.00

ROBIN HOOD (See The Advs. of..., Brave and the Bold, Four Color #413, 669, King Classics, Movie Comics & Power Record Comics)

ROBIN HOOD (...& His Merry Men, The Illustrated Story of...) (See Classic Comics #7 & Classics Giveaways, 12/44)

ROBIN HOOD (New Adventures of...)

Riot #3, © MEG

Rip Hunter Time Master #9, © DC

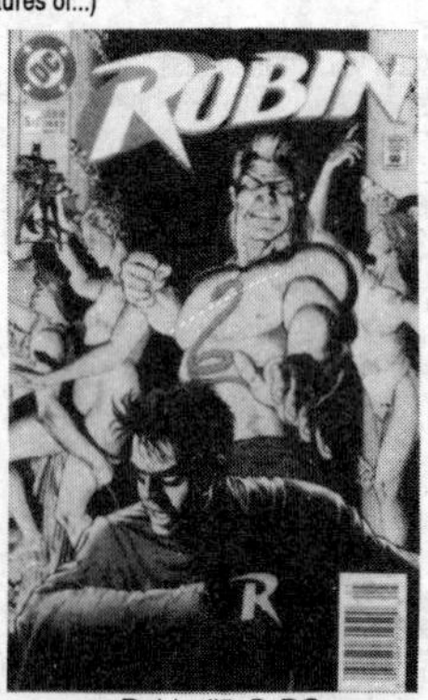

Robin #5, © DC

Robin Hood and His Merry Men #30, © CC

Robin Hood Tales #12, © DC

Robocop #8, © Orion Pictures

1952 (36 pages) (5x7-1/4")
Walt Disney Productions (Flour giveaways)

	GD25	FN65	NM94
"New Adventures of Robin Hood," "Ghosts of Waylea Castle," & "The Miller's Ransom" each....	3.20	8.00	16.00

ROBIN HOOD (Adventures of... #7, 8)
No. 52, Nov, 1955 - No. 6, June, 1957
Magazine Enterprises (Sussex Publ. Co.)

	GD25	FN65	NM94
52 (#1)-Origin Robin Hood & Sir Gallant of the Round Table	9.15	27.50	55.00
53, 3-6	6.70	20.00	40.00
I.W. Reprint #1,2,9: 1-r/#3. 2-r/#4. 9-r/#52 (1963)	1.20	3.00	6.00
Super Reprint #10,15: 10-r/#53. 15-r/#5	1.20	3.00	6.00
Super Reprint #11,17(1964)-Both exist?	1.20	3.00	6.00

NOTE: *Bolle a-in all; c-52. Powell a-6.*

ROBIN HOOD (Not Disney)
May-July, 1963 (One shot)
Dell Publishing Co.

	GD25	FN65	NM94
1	2.40	6.00	12.00

ROBIN HOOD
1973 (Disney) (8-1/2x11"; cardboard covers) ($1.50, 52 pages)
Western Publishing Co.

	GD25	FN65	NM94
96151-"Robin Hood," based on movie, 96152-"The Mystery of Sherwood Forest," 96153-"In King Richard's Service," 96154-"The Wizard's Ring" each....	.80	2.00	4.00

ROBIN HOOD
July, 1991 - No. 3, 1991 ($2.50, color, mini-series)
Eclipse Comics

	GD25	FN65	NM94
1-3: Timothy Truman layouts	.50	1.25	2.50

ROBIN HOOD AND HIS MERRY MEN (Formerly Danger & Adventure)
No. 28, April, 1956 - No. 38, Aug, 1958
Charlton Comics

	GD25	FN65	NM94
28	5.00	15.00	30.00
29-37	4.00	10.00	20.00
38-Ditko-a (5 pgs.)	8.35	25.00	50.00

ROBIN HOOD'S FRONTIER DAYS (...Western Tales)
No date (Circa 1955) 20 pages, slick-c (Seven issues?)
Shoe Store Giveaway (Robin Hood Stores)

	GD25	FN65	NM94
nn	4.20	12.50	25.00
nn-Issues with Crandall-a	6.70	20.00	40.00

ROBIN HOOD TALES (Published by National Periodical #7 on)
Feb, 1956 - No. 6, Nov-Dec, 1956
Quality Comics Group (Comic Magazines)

	GD25	FN65	NM94
1-All have Baker/Cuidera-c	13.00	40.00	90.00
2-5-Matt Baker-a	13.00	40.00	90.00
6	10.00	30.00	60.00
Frontier Days giveaway (1956)	4.70	14.00	28.00

ROBIN HOOD TALES (Continued from Quality series)
No. 7, Jan-Feb, 1957 - No. 14, Mar-Apr, 1958
National Periodical Publications

	GD25	FN65	NM94
7-All have Andru/Esposito-c	22.00	65.00	150.00
8-14	18.00	54.00	125.00

ROBINSON CRUSOE (See King Classics & Power Record Comics)
Nov-Jan, 1963-64
Dell Publishing Co.

	GD25	FN65	NM94
1	1.60	4.00	8.00

ROBIN II (The Joker's Wild)
Oct, 1991 - No. 4, Dec, 1991 ($1.50, color, mini-series)
DC Comics

	GD25	FN65	NM94
1-(Direct sale, $1.50)-With 4 different-c; same hologram on each	.30	.75	1.50
1-(Newsstand, $1.00)-No hologram; 1 version		.50	1.00
1-Collector's set ($10.00)-Contains all 5 versions bagged with hologram trading card inside	2.00	5.00	10.00
2-(Direct sale, $1.50)-With 3 different-c	.30	.75	1.50
2-4-(Newsstand, $1.00)-1 version of each		.50	1.00
2-Collector's set ($8.00)-Contains all 4 versions bagged with hologram trading card inside	1.60	4.00	8.00
3-(Direct sale, $1.50)-With 2 different-c	.30	.75	1.50
3-Collector's set ($6.00)-Contains all 3 versions bagged with hologram trading card inside	1.20	3.00	6.00
4-(Direct sale, $1.50)-Only one version	.30	.75	1.50
4-Collector's set ($4.00)-Contains both versions bagged with Bat-Signal hologram trading card	.80	2.00	4.00
Multi-pack (All four issues w/hologram sticker)	.80	2.00	4.00
Deluxe Complete Set ($30.00)-Contains all 14 versions of #1-4 plus a new hologram trading card; numbered & limited to 25,000; comes with slipcase & 2 acid free backing boards	5.00	15.00	30.00

ROBIN III: CRY OF THE HUNTRESS
Dec, 1992 - No. 6, Mar, 1993 (Color, mini-series)
DC Comics

	GD25	FN65	NM94
1-6 ($2.50, collector's ed.)-Polybagged w/movement enhanced-c plus mini-poster of newsstand-c by Zeck	.50	1.25	2.50
1-6 ($1.25, newsstand ed.): All have Zeck-c		.60	1.25

ROBIN 3000
1993 - No. 2, 1993 ($4.95, color, mini-series, 52 pgs.)
DC Comics

	GD25	FN65	NM94
1,2-Elseworlds storyline; Russell-c/a	1.00	2.50	5.00

ROBOCOP
Oct, 1987 ($2.00, B&W, magazine, one-shot)
Marvel Comics

	GD25	FN65	NM94
1-Movie adaptation	.40	1.00	2.00

ROBOCOP
March, 1990 - No. 23, Jan, 1992 ($1.50, color)
Marvel Comics

	GD25	FN65	NM94
1-Based on movie	1.40	3.50	7.00
2	1.00	2.50	5.00
3-6	.60	1.50	3.00
7-23	.30	.75	1.50
nn (7/90, $4.95, color, 52 pgs.)-r/B&W magazine in color; adapts 1st movie	1.00	2.50	5.00

ROBOCOP: PRIME SUSPECT
Oct, 1992 - No. 4, Jan, 1993 ($2.50, color, mini-series)
Dark Horse Comics

	GD25	FN65	NM94
1-4: Nelson painted-c	.50	1.25	2.50

ROBOCOP 2
Aug, 1990 ($2.25, B&W, magazine, 68 pgs.)
Marvel Comics

	GD25	FN65	NM94
1-Adapts movie sequel	.45	1.15	2.25

ROBOCOP 2
Aug, 1990; Late Aug, 1990 - #3, Late Sept, 1990 ($1.00, mini-series)
Marvel Comics

	GD25	FN65	NM94
nn-(8/90, $4.95, color, 68 pgs.)-Same contents as B&W magazine	1.00	2.50	5.00
1: #1-3 reprint no number issue	.60	1.50	3.00
2,3: 2-Guice-c(i)	.30	.75	1.50

ROBOCOP 3
Aug, 1992 - No. 3, 1992

Dark Horse Comics

	GD25	FN65	NM94
1-3	.50	1.25	2.50

ROBOCOP VERSUS THE TERMINATOR
Sept, 1992 - No. 4, Dec, 1992 ($2.50, color, mini-series)
Dark Horse Comics

	GD25	FN65	NM94
1-4: Miller scripts & Simonson-c/a in all	.50	1.25	2.50

NOTE: *All contain a different Robocop cardboard cut-out stand-up.*

ROBO-HUNTER (Eagle)(Value: cover or less)(Also see Sam Slade...)

R.O.B.O.T. BATTALION 2050 (Eclipse)(Value: cover or less)

ROBOT COMICS (Renegade)(Value: cover or less)

ROBOTECH DEFENDERS
Mar, 1985 - No. 2, Apr, 1985 (Mini-series)
DC Comics

	GD25	FN65	NM94
1,2		.50	1.00

ROBOTECH IN 3-D (Comico)(Value: cover or less)

ROBOTECH MASTERS (TV)
July, 1985 - No. 23, Apr, 1988 ($1.50, color)
Comico

	GD25	FN65	NM94
1	.60	1.50	3.00
2-23	.40	1.00	2.00

ROBOTECH SPECIAL (Comico)(Value: cover or less)

ROBOTECH THE GRAPHIC NOVEL (Comico)(Value: cover or less)

ROBOTECH: THE MACROSS SAGA (TV)(Formerly Macross)
No. 2, Feb, 1985 - No. 36, Feb, 1989 ($1.50, color)
Comico

	GD25	FN65	NM94
2	.60	1.50	3.00
3-10	.40	1.00	2.00
11-36: 12,17-Ken Steacy painted-c	.35	.85	1.75

ROBOTECH: THE NEW GENERATION (TV)(Comico)(Value: cover or less)

ROBOTECH II: THE SENTINELS SWIMSUIT SPECTACULAR (Eternity)(Value: cover or less)

ROBOTIX (Marvel)(Value: cover or less)

ROBOTMEN OF THE LOST PLANET (Also see Space Thrillers)
1952 (Also see Strange Worlds #19)
Avon Periodicals

	GD25	FN65	NM94
1-Kinstler-a (3 pgs.); Fawcette-a	64.00	190.00	445.00

ROB ROY (See 4-Color #544)

ROCK AND ROLLO (Formerly TV Teens)
V2#14, Oct, 1957 - No. 19, Sept, 1958
Charlton Comics

	GD25	FN65	NM94
V2#14-19	3.00	7.50	15.00

ROCKET COMICS
Mar, 1940 - No. 3, May, 1940
Hillman Periodicals

	GD25	FN65	NM94
1-Rocket Riley, Red Roberts the Electro Man (origin), The Phantom Ranger, The Steel Shark, The Defender, Buzzard Barnes, Lefty Larson, & The Defender, the Man with a Thousand Faces begin	142.00	425.00	850.00
2,3	75.00	225.00	450.00

ROCKETEER, THE (See Eclipse Graphic Album Series, Pacific Presents & Starslayer)

ROCKETEER ADVENTURE MAGAZINE, THE
July, 1988; No. 2, July, 1989 ($2.00/$2.75, color)
Comico

	GD25	FN65	NM94
1-Dave Stevens-c/a in all; Kaluta back-up-a	1.20	3.00	6.00
2 (7/89, $2.75)-Stevens/Dorman painted-c	.80	2.00	4.00

ROCKETEER SPECIAL EDITION, THE
Nov, 1984 ($1.50, color, Baxter paper)(Chapter 5 of Rocketeer serial)
Eclipse Comics

	GD25	FN65	NM94
1-Stevens-c/a; Kaluta back-c; pin-ups inside	2.00	5.00	10.00

ROCKETEER THE OFFICIAL MOVIE ADAPT. THE (Disney)(Value: cover or less)

ROCKET KELLY (See The Bouncer, Green Mask #10); becomes Li'l Pan #6)
1944; Fall, 1945 - No. 5, Oct-Nov, 1946
Fox Feature Syndicate

	GD25	FN65	NM94
nn (1944)	17.00	50.00	100.00
1	17.00	50.00	100.00
2-The Puppeteer app. (costumed hero)	12.00	35.00	70.00
3-5: 5-(#5 on cover, #4 inside)	10.00	30.00	60.00

ROCKETMAN (Strange Fantasy #2 on)
June, 1952 (Also see Hello Pal & Scoop Comics)
Ajax/Farrell Publications

	GD25	FN65	NM94
1-Rocketman & Cosmo	20.00	60.00	140.00

ROCKET MAN: KING OF THE ROCKET MEN (Innovation)(Value: cover or less)

ROCKET RACCOON (Marvel)(Value: cover or less)

ROCKET RANGER (Adventure)(Value: cover or less)

ROCKETS AND RANGE RIDERS
May, 1957 (16 pages, soft-c) (Giveaway)
Richfield Oil Corp.

	GD25	FN65	NM94
nn-Toth-a	13.00	40.00	90.00

ROCKET SHIP X
September, 1951; 1952
Fox Features Syndicate

	GD25	FN65	NM94
1	40.00	120.00	280.00
1952 (nn, nd, no publ.)-Edited 1951-c	27.00	81.00	190.00

ROCKET TO ADVENTURE LAND (See Pixie Puzzle...)

ROCKET TO THE MOON
1951
Avon Periodicals

	GD25	FN65	NM94
nn-Orlando-c/a; adapts Otis Aldebert Kline's "Maza of the Moon"	67.00	200.00	465.00

ROCK FANTASY COMICS
Dec, 1989 - No. 16?, 1991 ($2.25-$3.00, B&W)(No cover price)
Rock Fantasy Comics

	GD25	FN65	NM94
1-Pink Floyd part I	.80	2.00	4.00
1-2nd printing ($3.00-c)	.60	1.50	3.00
2,3: 2-Rolling Stones #1. 4-Led Zeppelin #1	.60	1.50	3.00
2,3: 2nd printings ($3.00-c, 1/90 & 2/90)	.60	1.50	3.00
4-Stevie Nicks Not published			
5-Monstrosities of Rock #1; photo back-c	.60	1.50	3.00
5-2nd printing ($3.00, 3/90 indicia, 2/90-c)	.60	1.50	3.00
6-15: 6-Guns n' Roses #1 (1st & 2nd prints, 3/90)-Begin $3.00-c. 7-Sex Pistols #1. 8-Alice Cooper Not published. 9-Van Halen #1; photo back-c. 10-Kiss #1; photo back-c. 11-Jimi Hendrix #1; wraparound-c	.60	1.50	3.00
16-($5.00, 68 pgs.)-The Great Gig in the Sky	1.00	2.50	5.00

ROCK HAPPENING (Harvey Pop Comics:...)(See Bunny)
Sept, 1969 - No. 2, Nov, 1969
Harvey Publications

	GD25	FN65	NM94
1,2: Featuring Bunny	3.00	7.50	15.00

ROCK N' ROLL COMICS
June, 1989 - Present ($1.50-$1.95, B&W; color #15 on)
Revolutionary Comics

	GD25	FN65	NM94
1-Guns N' Roses	2.00	5.00	10.00
1-2nd thru 6th printings	.30	.75	1.50
1-7th printing (Full color w/new-c/a; $1.95)	.40	1.00	2.00
2-Metallica	1.00	2.50	5.00
2-2nd thru 6th printings (6th in color)	.30	.75	1.50

Robotmen of the Lost Planet #1, © AVON

Rocket Kelly #3, © FOX

Rock Happening #2, © HARV

Rocky and His Fiendish Friends #4, © Ward Prod.

Rocky Lane Western #9, © FAW

Roly Poly Comic Book #1, © Green Publishing

	GD25	FN65	NM94
3-Bon Jovi (no reprints)	.50	1.25	2.50
4-8,10-60: 4-Motley Crue(2nd printing only, 1st destroyed). 5-Def Leppard (2 printings). 6-Rolling Stones(4 printings). 7-The Who(3 printings). 8-Skid Row; not published. 10-Warrant/Whitesnake(2 printings; 1st has 2 diff.-c) 11-Aerosmith (2 printings?). 12-New Kids on the Block(2 printings). 12-3rd printing; rewritten & titled NKOTB Hate Book. 13-Led Zeppelin. 14-Sex Pistols. 15-Poison; 1st color issue. 16-Van Halen. 17-Madonna. 18-Alice Cooper. 19-Public Enemy/2 Live Crew. 20-Queensryche/Tesla. 21-Prince? 22-AC/DC; begin $2.50-c. 23-Living Colour. 24-Anthrax	.50	1.25	2.50
9-Kiss	.80	2.00	4.00
9-2nd & 3rd printings	.40	1.00	2.00

NOTE: *Most issues were reprinted except for #3. Later reprints are in color. #8 was not released.*

ROCKY AND HIS FIENDISH FRIENDS (TV)(Bullwinkle)
Oct, 1962 - No. 5, Sept, 1963 (Jay Ward)
Gold Key

	GD25	FN65	NM94
1 (84 pgs., 25 cents)	20.00	60.00	140.00
2,3 (84 pgs., 25 cents)	11.50	34.00	80.00
4,5 (Regular size, 12 cents)	10.00	30.00	60.00

ROCKY AND HIS FRIENDS (See 4-Color #1128, 1152, 1166, 1208, 1275, 1311, Kite Fun Book and March of Comics #216)

ROCKY HORROR PICTURE SHOW THE COMIC BOOK, THE
July, 1990 - No. 3, 1990 ($2.95, color, mini-series, 52 pgs.)(Photo-c #1)
Caliber Press

	GD25	FN65	NM94
1-Adapts cult film plus photos, etc.	1.00	2.50	5.00
1-2nd printing	.60	1.50	3.00
2,3	.70	1.75	3.50
...Collection ($4.95)	1.00	2.50	5.00

ROCKY JONES SPACE RANGER (See Space Adventures #15-18)

ROCKY JORDAN PRIVATE EYE (See Private Eye)

ROCKY LANE WESTERN (Allan Rocky Lane starred in Republic movies & TV (for a short time as Allan Lane, Red Ryder & Rocky Lane) (See Black Jack Fawcett Movie Comics, Motion Picture Comics & Six Gun Heroes)
May, 1949 - No. 87, Nov, 1959
Fawcett Publications/Charlton No. 56 on

	GD25	FN65	NM94
1 (36 pgs.)-Rocky, his stallion Black Jack, & Slim Pickens begin; photo-c begin, end #57; photo back-c	57.00	171.00	400.00
2 (36 pgs.)-Last photo back-c	25.00	75.00	175.00
3-5 (52 pgs.): 4-Captain Tootsie by Beck	17.00	52.00	120.00
6,10 (36 pgs.)	13.50	41.00	95.00
7-9 (52 pgs.)	14.00	43.00	100.00
11-13,15-17 (52 pgs.): 15-Black Jack's Hitching Post begins, ends #25	11.00	32.00	75.00
14,18 (36 pgs.)	10.00	30.00	65.00
19-21,23,24 (52 pgs.): 20-Last Slim Pickens. 21-Dee Dickens begins, ends #55,57,65-68	10.00	30.00	65.00
22,25-28,30 (36 pgs. begin)	10.00	30.00	60.00
29-Classic complete novel "The Land of Missing Men,"-hidden land of ancient temple ruins (r-in #65)	11.00	32.00	75.00
31-40	9.15	27.50	55.00
41-54	7.50	22.50	45.00
55-Last Fawcett issue (1/54)	8.35	25.00	50.00
56-1st Charlton issue (2/54)-Photo-c	10.00	30.00	70.00
57,60-Photo-c	7.50	22.50	45.00
58,59,61-64: 59-61-Young Falcon app. 64-Slim Pickens app.	5.35	16.00	32.00
65-r/#29, "The Land of Missing Men"	5.85	17.50	35.00
66-68: Reprints #30,31,32	5.00	15.00	30.00
69-78,80-86	5.00	15.00	30.00
79-Giant Edition, 68 pgs.	6.35	19.00	38.00
87-Last issue	5.85	17.50	35.00

NOTE: *Complete novels in #10, 14, 18, 22, 25, 30-32, 36, 38, 39, 49. Captain Tootsie in #4, 12, 20. Big Bow and Little Arrow in #11, 28, 63. Black Jack's Hitching Post in #15-25, 64, 73.*

ROCKY LANE WESTERN (AC)(Value: cover or less)

ROD CAMERON WESTERN (Movie star)
Feb, 1950 - No. 20, April, 1953
Fawcett Publications

	GD25	FN65	NM94
1-Rod Cameron, his horse War Paint, & Sam The Sheriff begin; photo front/back-c begin	42.00	125.00	290.00
2	19.00	57.00	130.00
3-Novel length story "The Mystery of the Seven Cities of Cibola"	16.00	48.00	110.00
4-10: 9-Last photo back-c	12.00	36.00	85.00
11-19	11.00	32.00	75.00
20-Last issue & photo-c	11.50	34.00	80.00

NOTE: *Novel length stories in No. 1-8, 12-14.*

RODEO RYAN (See A-1 Comics #8)

ROGER BEAN, R. G. (Regular Guy)
1915 - No. 5, 1917 (34 pgs.; B&W; 4-3/4x16"; cardboard covers)
(No. 1 & 4 bound on side, No. 3 bound at top)
The Indiana News Co.

	GD25	FN65	NM94
1-By Chic Jackson (48 pgs.)	11.00	32.00	75.00
2-5	9.15	27.50	55.00

ROGER DODGER (Also in Exciting Comics #57 on)
No. 5, Aug, 1952
Standard Comics

	GD25	FN65	NM94
5-Teen-age	3.20	8.00	16.00

ROGER RABBIT (Also see Marvel Graphic Novel)
June, 1990 - No. 18, Nov, 1991 ($1.50, color)
Disney Comics

	GD25	FN65	NM94
1-All new stories	.60	1.50	3.00
2,3	.40	1.00	2.00
4-18	.30	.75	1.50

ROGER RABBIT'S TOONTOWN
Aug, 1991 - No. 5, Dec, 1991 ($1.50, color)
Disney Comics

	GD25	FN65	NM94
1-5	.30	.75	1.50

ROG 2000 (Pacific & Fantagraphics)(Value: cover or less)

ROGUE TROOPER (Fleetway/Quality)(Value: cover or less)

ROGUE TROOPER: THE FINAL WARRIOR (Quality)(Value: cover or less)

ROLY POLY COMIC BOOK
1944 - No. 15, 1946 (MLJ reprints)
Green Publishing Co.

	GD25	FN65	NM94
1-Red Rube & Steel Sterling begin; Sahle-c	17.00	52.00	120.00
6-The Blue Circle & The Steel Fist app.	10.00	30.00	60.00
10-Origin Red Rube retold; Steel Sterling story (Zip #41)	9.15	27.50	55.00
11,12,14: The Black Hood app. in each. 14-Decapitation-c	10.00	30.00	60.00
15-The Blue Circle & The Steel Fist app.; cover exact swipe from Fox Blue Beetle #1	20.00	60.00	140.00

ROM
December, 1979 - No. 75, Feb, 1986
Marvel Comics Group

	GD25	FN65	NM94
1-Based on a Parker Bros. toy; origin/1st app.	.50	1.25	2.50
2-5		.60	1.20
6-16: 13-Saga of the Space Knights begins		.50	1.00
17,18-X-Men app.	.50	1.25	2.50
19-24,26-30: 19-X-Men cameo. 24-F.F. cameo; Skrulls, Nova & The New Champions app. 26,27-Galactus app.		.50	1.00

GD25 FN65 NM94

25-Double size .60 1.20
31-75: 31,32-Brother of Evil Mutants app. 32-X-Men cameo. 34,35-Sub-Mariner app. 41,42-Dr. Strange app. 50-Skrulls app. (52 pgs.). 56,57-Alpha Flight app. 58,59-Ant-Man app. 65-West Coast Avengers & Beta Ray Bill app. 65,66-X-Men app. .50 1.00
Annual 1,4: 1(1982, 52 pgs.). 4(1985, 52 pgs.) .60 1.20
Annual 2,3: 2(1983, 52 pgs.). 3(1984, 52 pgs.) .50 1.00
NOTE: ***Austin** c-3i, 18i, 61i. **Byrne** a-74i; c-56, 57, 74. **Ditko** a-59-75p. **Golden** c-7-12, 19. **Guice** a-61i; c-55, 58, 60p, 70p. **Layton** a-59i, 72i; c-15, 59i, 69. **Miller** c-2p?, 3p, 17p, 18p. **Russell** a(i)-64, 65, 67, 69, 71, 75; c-64, 65i, 66, 71i, 75. **Severin** c-41p. **Sienkiewicz** a-53i; c-46, 47, 52-54, 68, 71p, Annual 2. **P. Smith** c-59p. **Starlin** c-67.*

ROMANCE (See True Stories of...)

ROMANCE AND CONFESSION STORIES (See Giant Comics Edition)
No date (1949) (100pgs.)
St. John Publishing Co.
1-Baker-c/a; remaindered St. John love comics 25.00 75.00 175.00

ROMANCE DIARY
December, 1949 - No. 2, March, 1950
Marvel Comics (CDS)(CLDS)
1,2 7.50 22.50 45.00

ROMANCE OF FLYING, THE (See Feature Books #33)

ROMANCES OF MOLLY MANTON (See Molly Manton)

ROMANCES OF NURSE HELEN GRANT, THE
August, 1957
Atlas Comics (VPI)
1 3.60 9.00 18.00

ROMANCES OF THE WEST (Becomes Romantic Affairs #3?)
Nov, 1949 - No. 2, Mar, 1950 (52 pgs.)
Marvel Comics (SPC)
1-Movie photo-c of Yvonne DeCarlo & Howard Duff (Calamity Jane & Sam Bass) 12.00 36.00 85.00
2-Photo-c 9.15 27.50 55.00

ROMANCE STORIES OF TRUE LOVE (Formerly Love Problems & Advice)
No. 45, 5/57 - No. 50, 3/58; No. 51, 9/58 - No. 52, 11/58
Harvey Publications
45-51: 45,46,48-50-Powell-a 2.40 6.00 12.00
52-Matt Baker-a 4.00 10.50 21.00

ROMANCE TALES (Formerly Western Winners #6?)
No. 7, Oct, 1949 - No. 9, March, 1950 (7,8: photo-c)
Marvel Comics (CDS)
7 6.70 20.00 40.00
8,9: 8-Everett-a 5.00 15.00 30.00

ROMANCE TRAIL
July-Aug, 1949 - No. 6, May-June, 1950
National Periodical Publications
1-Kinstler, Toth-a; Jimmy Wakely photo-c 36.00 107.00 250.00
2-Kinstler-a; photo-c 17.00 52.00 120.00
3-Photo-c; Kinstler, Toth-a 19.00 58.00 135.00
4-Photo-c; Toth-a 14.00 43.00 100.00
5,6: 5-Photo-c 11.50 34.00 80.00

ROMAN HOLIDAYS, THE (TV)
Feb, 1973 - No. 4, Nov, 1973 (Hanna-Barbera)
Gold Key
1 2.40 6.00 12.00
2-4 1.80 4.50 9.00

ROMANTIC ADVENTURES (My... #49-67, covers only)
Mar-Apr, 1949 - No. 67, July, 1956 (Becomes My... No. 68 on)
American Comics Group (B&I Publ. Co.)
1 9.15 27.50 55.00
2 5.00 15.00 30.00
3-10 3.60 9.00 18.00
11-20 (4/52) 2.80 7.00 14.00
21-46,49,51,52: 52-Last Pre-code (2/55) 2.00 5.00 10.00
47,48-3-D effect 5.85 17.50 35.00
50-Classic cover/story "Love of A Lunatic" 5.00 15.00 30.00
53-67 1.60 4.00 8.00
NOTE: *#1-23, 52 pgs. **Shelly** a-40. Whitney c/art in many issues.*

ROMANTIC AFFAIRS (Formerly Molly Manton's Romances #2 and/or Romances of the West #2?)
No. 3, March, 1950
Marvel Comics (SPC)
3-Photo-c from Molly Manton's Romances #2 4.20 12.50 25.00

ROMANTIC CONFESSIONS
Oct, 1949 - V3#1, April-May, 1953
Hillman Periodicals
V1#1-McWilliams-a 8.35 25.00 50.00
2-Briefer-a; negligee panels 5.00 15.00 30.00
3-12 3.60 9.00 18.00
V2#1,2,4-8,10-12: 2-McWilliams-a 2.80 7.00 14.00
3-Krigstein-a 5.85 17.50 35.00
9-One pg. Frazetta ad 2.80 7.00 14.00
V3#1 2.80 7.00 14.00

ROMANTIC HEARTS
Mar, 1951 - No. 10, Oct, 1952; July, 1953 - No. 12, July, 1955
Story Comics/Master/Merit Pubs.
1(3/51) (1st Series) 7.50 22.50 45.00
2 4.00 11.00 22.00
3-10 3.60 9.00 18.00
1(7/53) (2nd Series) 4.70 14.00 28.00
2 3.20 8.00 16.00
3-12 2.40 6.00 12.00

ROMANTIC LOVE
9-10/49 - #3, 1-2/50; #4, 2-3/51 - #13, 10/52; #20, 3-4/54 - #23, 9-10/54
Avon Periodicals/Realistic (No #14-19)
1-c-/Avon paperback #252 13.00 40.00 90.00
2-5: 3-c-/paperback Novel Library #12. 4-c-/paperback Diversey Prize Novel #5. 5-c-/paperback Novel Library #34 8.35 25.00 50.00
6-"Thrill Crazy"-marijuana story; c-/Avon paperback #207; Kinstler-a 10.00 30.00 65.00
7,8: 8-Astarita-a(2) 7.50 22.50 45.00
9-12: 9-c-/paperback Novel Library #41; Kinstler-a. 10-c-/Avon paperback #212. 11-c-/paperback Novel Library #17; Kinstler-a. 12-c-/paperback Novel Library #13 8.35 25.00 50.00
13,21,22: 22-Kinstler-c 7.50 22.50 45.00
20-Kinstler-c/a 7.50 22.50 45.00
23-Kinstler-c 5.85 17.50 35.00
nn(1-3/53)(Realistic-r) 5.00 15.00 30.00
NOTE: ***Astarita** a-7, 10, 11, 21. Painted c-7, 9, 10, 11.*

ROMANTIC LOVE
No. 4, June, 1950
Quality Comics Group
4 (6/50)(Exist?) 4.20 12.50 25.00
I.W. Reprint #2,3,8 .40 1.00 2.00

ROMANTIC MARRIAGE (Cinderella Love #25 on)
#1-3 (1950, no months); #4, 5-6/51 - #17, 9/52; #18, 9/53 - #24, 9/54
Ziff-Davis/St. John No. 18 on (#1-8: 52 pgs.)
1-Photo-c 10.00 30.00 70.00
2-Painted-c; Anderson-a (also #15) 6.70 20.00 40.00
3-9: 3,4,8,9-Painted-c; 5-7-Photo-c 5.00 15.00 30.00
10-Unusual format; front-c is a painted-c; back-c is a photo-c complete with logo, price, etc. 10.00 30.00 60.00
11-17 (9/52; last Z-D issue): 13-Photo-c 4.20 12.50 25.00

Romantic Adventures #23, © ACG

Romantic Hearts #4 (1st series), © Story Comics

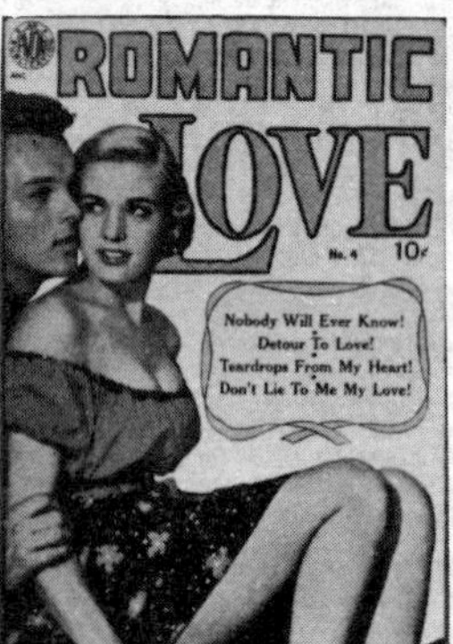

Romantic Love #4, © AVON

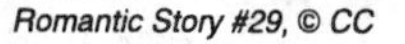
Romantic Story #29, © CC

Rootie Kazootie #5, © Rootie Kazootie, Inc.

Roundup #1, © DS

	GD25	FN65	NM94
18-22,24: 20-Photo-c	4.20	12.50	25.00
23-Baker-c	4.70	14.00	28.00

ROMANTIC PICTURE NOVELETTES
1946
Magazine Enterprises

	GD25	FN65	NM94
1-Mary Worth-r	10.00	30.00	65.00

ROMANTIC SECRETS (Becomes Time For Love)
Sept, 1949 - No. 39, 4/53; No. 5, 10/55 - No. 52, 11/64 (#1-5: photo-c)
Fawcett/Charlton Comics No. 5 (10/55) on

	GD25	FN65	NM94
1	9.15	27.50	55.00
2,3	5.00	15.00	30.00
4,9-Evans-a	5.85	17.50	35.00
5-8,10	3.60	9.00	18.00
11-23	3.20	8.00	16.00
24-Evans-a	4.70	14.00	28.00
25-39	2.40	6.00	12.00
5 (Charlton, 2nd series)(10/55, formerly Negro Romances #4)	4.70	14.00	28.00
6-10	2.80	7.00	14.00
11-20	1.20	3.00	6.00
21-35: Last 10 cent issue?	1.00	2.50	5.00
36-52('64)	.60	1.50	3.00

NOTE: ***Bailey*** *a-20.* ***Powell*** *a(1st series)-5, 7, 10, 12, 16, 17, 20, 26, 29, 33, 34, 36, 37.* ***Sekowsky*** *a-26. Photo c(1st series)-1-5, 16, 25, 27, 33.* ***Swayze*** *a(1st series)-16, 18, 19, 23, 26-28, 31, 32, 39.*

ROMANTIC STORY (Cowboy Love #28 on)
11/49 - #22, Sum, 1953; #23, 5/54 - #27, 12/54; #28, 8/55 - #130, 11/73
Fawcett/Charlton Comics No. 23 on

	GD25	FN65	NM94
1-Photo-c begin, end #22,24	10.00	30.00	60.00
2	5.00	15.00	30.00
3-5	4.20	12.50	25.00
6-14	3.60	9.00	18.00
15-Evans-a	4.70	14.00	28.00
16-22(Sum, '53; last Fawcett issue). 21-Toth-a?	2.80	7.00	14.00
23-39: 26,29-Wood swipes	2.80	7.00	14.00
40-(100 pgs.)	4.35	13.00	26.00
41-50	2.00	5.00	10.00
51-80: 57-Hypo needle story	1.00	2.50	5.00
81-100	.60	1.50	3.00
101-130	.40	1.00	2.00

NOTE: ***Powell*** *a-7, 8, 16, 20, 30.* ***Marcus Swayze*** *a-2, 12, 20, 32.*

ROMANTIC THRILLS (See Fox Giants)

ROMANTIC WESTERN
Winter, 1949 - No. 3, June, 1950 (All Photo-c)
Fawcett Publications

	GD25	FN65	NM94
1	11.00	32.00	75.00
2-Williamson, McWilliams-a	12.00	36.00	85.00
3	9.15	27.50	55.00

ROMEO TUBBS (Formerly My Secret Life)
No. 26, 5/50 - No. 28, 7/50; No. 1, 1950; No. 27, 12/52
Fox Feature Syndicate/Green Publ. Co. No. 27

	GD25	FN65	NM94
26-Teen-age	8.35	25.00	50.00
27-Contains Pedro on inside; Wood-a	11.00	32.00	75.00
28, 1	6.70	20.00	40.00

RONALD McDONALD (TV)
Sept, 1970 - No. 4, March, 1971
Charlton Press (King Features Synd.)

	GD25	FN65	NM94
1	1.00	2.50	5.00
2-4	.60	1.50	3.00

RONIN
July, 1983 - No. 6, Apr, 1984 ($2.50, mini-series, 52 pgs.)
DC Comics

	GD25	FN65	NM94
1-Miller script, c/a in all	.80	2.00	4.00
2-5	.60	1.50	3.00
6-Scarcer	1.20	3.00	6.00
Trade paperback (1987, $12.95)-Reprints #1-6	2.60	6.50	13.00

ROOK (See Eerie Magazine & Warren Presents: The Rook)
November, 1979 - No. 14, April, 1982
Warren Publications

	GD25	FN65	NM94
1-Nino-a	.30	.75	1.50
2-14: 3,4-Toth-a		.50	1.00

ROOKIE COP (Formerly Crime and Justice?)
No. 27, Nov, 1955 - No. 33, Aug, 1957
Charlton Comics

	GD25	FN65	NM94
27	5.35	16.00	32.00
28-33	3.60	9.00	18.00

ROOM 222 (TV)
Jan, 1970; No. 2, May, 1970 - No. 4, Jan, 1971
Dell Publishing Co.

	GD25	FN65	NM94
1	6.70	20.00	40.00
2-4: 2,4-Photo-c. 3-Marijuana story. 4 r/#1	4.20	12.50	25.00

ROOTIE KAZOOTIE (TV)(See 3-D-ell)
No. 415, Aug, 1952 - No. 6, Oct-Dec, 1954
Dell Publishing Co.

	GD25	FN65	NM94
4-Color 415 (#1)	10.00	30.00	60.00
4-Color 459,502(#2,3)	6.70	20.00	40.00
4(4-6/54)-6	6.70	20.00	40.00

ROOTS OF THE SWAMPTHING (DC)(Value: cover or less)

ROUND THE WORLD GIFT
No date (mid 1940's) (4 pages)
National War Fund (Giveaway)

	GD25	FN65	NM94
nn	11.50	34.00	80.00

ROUNDUP (Western Crime)
July-Aug, 1948 - No. 5, Mar-Apr, 1949 (52 pgs.)
D. S. Publishing Co.

	GD25	FN65	NM94
1-Kiefer-a	10.00	30.00	70.00
2-Marijuana drug mention story	10.00	30.00	60.00
3-5	7.00	21.00	42.00

ROYAL ROY (Marvel)(Value: cover or less)

ROY CAMPANELLA, BASEBALL HERO
1950
Fawcett Publications

	GD25	FN65	NM94
nn-Photo-c	46.00	138.00	275.00

ROY ROGERS (See March of Comics #17, 35, 47, 62, 68, 73, 77, 86, 91, 100, 105, 116, 121, 131, 136, 146, 151, 161, 167, 176, 191, 206, 221, 236, 250)

ROY ROGERS AND TRIGGER
April, 1967
Gold Key

	GD25	FN65	NM94
1-Photo-c; reprints	4.20	12.50	25.00

ROY ROGERS COMICS (See Western Roundup under Dell Giants)
No. 38, 4/44 - No. 177, 12/47 (#38-166: 52 pgs.)
Dell Publishing Co.

	GD25	FN65	NM94
4-Color 38 (1944)-49pg. story; photo front/back-c on all 4-Color issues (1st western comic with photo-c)	72.00	215.00	500.00
4-Color 63 (1945)-Color photos on all four-c	43.00	128.00	300.00
4-Color 86,95 (1945)	31.00	92.00	215.00
4-Color 109 (1946)	24.00	71.00	165.00

GD25 FN65 NM94

4-Color 117,124,137,144 17.00 51.00 120.00
4-Color 153,160,166: 166-48pg. story 14.00 43.00 100.00
4-Color 177 (36 pgs.)-32pg. story 14.00 43.00 100.00

ROY ROGERS COMICS (...& Trigger #92(8/55)-on)(Roy starred in Republic movies, radio & TV) (Singing cowboy) (Also see Dale Evans, It Really Happened #8, Queen of the West..., & Roy Rogers' Trigger)
Jan, 1948 - No. 145, Sept-Oct, 1961 (#1-19: 36 pgs.)
Dell Publishing Co.

1-Roy, his horse Trigger, & Chuck Wagon Charley's Tales begin; photo-c begin, end #145 50.00 150.00 350.00
2 23.00 70.00 160.00
3-5 18.00 54.00 125.00
6-10 13.00 40.00 90.00
11-19: 19-...Charley's Tales ends 10.00 30.00 65.00
20 (52 pgs.)-Trigger feature begins, ends #46 10.00 30.00 65.00
21-30 (52 pgs.) 9.15 27.50 55.00
31-46 (52 pgs.): 37-X-mas-c 7.00 21.00 42.00
47-56 (36 pgs.): 47-Chuck Wagon Charley's Tales returns, ends #133. 49-X-mas-c. 55-Last photo back-c 5.35 16.00 32.00
57 (52 pgs.)-Heroin drug propaganda story 6.35 19.00 38.00
58-70 (52 pgs.): 61-X-mas-c 5.00 15.00 30.00
71-80 (52 pgs.): 73-X-mas-c 4.20 12.50 25.00
81-91 (36 pgs. #81-on): 85-X-mas-c 4.00 10.00 20.00
92-99,101-110,112-118: 92-Title changed to Roy Rogers and Trigger (8/55) 4.00 10.00 20.00
100-Trigger feature returns, ends #133? 5.35 16.00 32.00
111,119-124-Toth-a 5.85 17.50 35.00
125-131: 125-Toth-a (1 pg.) 4.20 12.50 25.00
132-144-Manning-a. 144-Dale Evans featured 4.70 14.00 28.00
145-Last issue 5.85 17.50 35.00
...& the Man From Dodge City (Dodge giveaway, 16 pgs., 1954)-Frontier, Inc. (5x7-1/4") 11.00 32.00 75.00
Official Roy Rogers Riders Club Comics (1952; 16 pgs., reg. size, paper-c) 11.50 34.00 80.00

NOTE: ***Buscema** a-74-108(2 stories each). **Manning** a-123, 124, 132-144. **Marsh** a-110. Photo back-c No. 1-9, 11-35, 38-55.*

ROY ROGERS' TRIGGER (TV)
No. 329, May, 1951 - No. 17, June-Aug, 1955
Dell Publishing Co.

4-Color 329 (#1)-Painted-c 10.00 30.00 65.00
2 (9-11/51)-Photo-c 10.00 30.00 60.00
3-5: 3-Painted-c begin, end #17 2.80 7.00 14.00
6-17: Title merges with Roy Rogers after #17 1.50 4.50 9.00

ROY ROGERS WESTERN CLASSICS (AC) (Value: cover or less)

RUDOLPH, THE RED NOSED REINDEER (See Limited Collectors' Edition #20, 24, 33, 42, 50)

RUDOLPH, THE RED NOSED REINDEER
1939 (2,400,000 copies printed); Dec, 1951
Montgomery Ward (Giveaway)

Paper cover - 1st app. in print; written by Robert May; ill. by Denver Gillen 10.00 30.00 70.00
Hardcover version 14.00 43.00 100.00
1951 version (Has 1939 date)-36 pgs., illos in three colors; red-c 4.70 14.00 28.00

RUDOLPH, THE RED-NOSED REINDEER
1950 - No. 13?, Winter, 1962-63 (Issues are not numbered)
National Periodical Publications

1950 issue; Grossman-c/a begins 10.00 30.00 65.00
1951-54 issues (4 total) 6.70 20.00 40.00
1955-62 issues (8 total) 4.00 11.00 22.00

NOTE: *The 1962-63 issue is 84 pages. 13 total issues published.*

RUFF AND REDDY (TV)
No. 937, 9/58 - No. 12, 1-3/62 (Hanna-Barbera)(#9 on: 15 cents)
Dell Publishing Co.

4-Color 937(#1)(1st Hanna-Barbera comic book) 8.35 25.00 50.00
4-Color 981,1038 5.85 17.50 35.00
4(1-3/60)-12: 8-Last 10 cent issue 4.20 12.50 25.00

RUGGED ACTION (Strange Stories of Suspense #5 on)
Dec, 1954 - No. 4, June, 1955
Atlas Comics (CSI)

1-Brodsky-c 6.70 20.00 40.00
2-4: 2-Last precode (2/55) 4.20 12.50 25.00

NOTE: ***Ayers** a-2, 3. **Maneely** c-2, 3. **Severin** a-2.*

RULAH JUNGLE GODDESS (Formerly Zoot; I Loved #28 on) (Also see All Top Comics & Terrors of the Jungle)
No. 17, Aug, 1948 - No. 27, June, 1949
Fox Features Syndicate

17 43.00 130.00 300.00
18-Classic girl-fight interior splash 34.00 100.00 235.00
19,20 32.00 95.00 220.00
21-Used in **SOTI**, pg. 388,389 34.00 100.00 235.00
22-Used in **SOTI**, pg. 22,23 32.00 95.00 220.00
23-27 22.00 65.00 155.00

NOTE: ***Kamen** c-17-19, 21, 22.*

RUNAWAY, THE (See Movie Classics)

RUN BABY RUN
1974 (39 cents)
Logos International

nn-By Tony Tallarico from Nicky Cruz's book .50 1.00

RUN, BUDDY, RUN (TV)
June, 1967 (Photo-c)
Gold Key

1 (10204-706) 2.40 6.00 12.00

RUST
7/87 - No. 15, 11/88; V2#1, 2/89 - No. 7, 1989 ($1.50-$1.75, color)
Now Comics

1-3 ($1.50) .30 .75 1.50
4-11,13-15, V2#1-7 ($1.75) .35 .90 1.75
12-(8/88, $1.75)-5 pg. preview of The Terminator (1st app.) 1.60 4.00 8.00

RUST (Adventure, '92) (Value: cover or less)

RUSTY, BOY DETECTIVE
Mar-April, 1955 - No. 5, Nov, 1955
Good Comics/Lev Gleason

1-Bob Wood, Carl Hubbell-a begins 5.00 15.00 30.00
2-5 3.60 9.00 18.00

RUSTY COMICS (Formerly Kid Movie Comics; Rusty and Her Family #21, 22; The Kelleys #23 on; see Millie The Model)
No. 12, Apr, 1947 - No. 22, Sept, 1949
Marvel Comics (HPC)

12-Mitzi app. 10.00 30.00 65.00
13 6.70 20.00 40.00
14-Wolverton's Powerhouse Pepper (4 pgs.) plus Kurtzman's "Hey Look" 10.00 30.00 70.00
15-17-Kurtzman's "Hey Look" 9.15 27.50 55.00
18,19 4.70 14.00 28.00
20-Kurtzman, 5 pgs. 9.15 27.50 55.00
21,22-Kurtzman, 17 & 22 pgs. 11.50 34.00 80.00

RUSTY DUGAN (See Holyoke One-Shot #2)

RUSTY RILEY (See 4-Color #418, 451, 486, 554)

SAARI (The Jungle Goddess)
November, 1951
P. L. Publishing Co.

Roy Rogers Comics #100, © Roy Rogers

Rudolph, the Red-Nosed Reindeer, 1950 issue, © DC

Rulah Jungle Goddess #20, © FOX

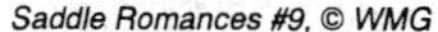
Saddle Romances #9, © WMG

Sad Sack Comics #3, © HARV

Sad Sack Laugh Special #6, © HARV

	GD25	FN65	NM94
1	23.00	70.00	160.00

SABLE (First)(Value: cover or less)(Formerly Jon Sable, Freelance; also see Mike Grell's...)

SABRE (Eclipse)(Value: cover or less)(Also see Eclipse Graphic Album Series)

SABRINA'S CHRISTMAS MAGIC (See Archie Giant Series Magazine #196, 207, 220, 231, 243, 455, 467, 479, 491, 503, 515)

SABRINA, THE TEEN-AGE WITCH (TV)(See Archie Giant Series 544, Archie's Madhouse 22, Archie's TV..., Chilling Advs. In Sorcery)
April, 1971 - No. 77, Jan, 1983 (Giants No. 1-17)
Archie Publications

	GD25	FN65	NM94
1	5.00	15.00	30.00
2	2.80	7.00	14.00
3-5: 3,4-Archie's Group x-over	1.40	3.50	7.00
6-10	1.00	2.50	5.00
11-20	.60	1.50	3.00
21-77	.40	1.00	2.00

SABU, "ELEPHANT BOY" (Movie; formerly My Secret Story)
No. 30, June, 1950 - No. 2, Aug, 1950
Fox Features Syndicate

	GD25	FN65	NM94
30(#1)-Wood-a; photo-c	12.00	36.00	85.00
2-Photo-c; Kamen-a	10.00	30.00	60.00

SACRAMENTS, THE
October, 1955 (25 cents)
Catechetical Guild Educational Society

	GD25	FN65	NM94
304	2.40	6.00	12.00

SACRED AND THE PROFANE, THE (See Eclipse Graphic Album Series #9 & Epic Illustrated #20)

SAD CASE OF WAITING ROOM WILLIE, THE
1950? (nd) (14 pgs. in color; paper covers; regular size)
American Visuals Corp. (For Baltimore Medical Society)

	GD25	FN65	NM94
nn-By Will Eisner (Rare)	43.00	130.00	300.00

SADDLE JUSTICE (Happy Houlihans #1,2; Saddle Romances #9 on)
No. 3, Spring, 1948 - No. 8, Sept-Oct, 1949
E. C. Comics

	GD25	FN65	NM94
3-The 1st E.C. by Bill Gaines to break away from M. C. Gaines' old Educational Comics format. Craig, Feldstein, H. C. Kiefer, & Stan Asch-a. Mentioned in Love and Death	34.00	100.00	235.00
4-1st Graham Ingels-a for E.C.	34.00	100.00	235.00
5-8-Ingels-a in all	30.00	90.00	210.00

NOTE: *Craig and Feldstein art in most issues. Canadian reprints known; see Table of Contents. Craig c-3, 4. Ingels c-5-8. #4 contains a biography of Craig.*

SADDLE ROMANCES (Saddle Justice #3-8; Weird Science #12 on)
No. 9, Nov-Dec, 1949 - No. 11, Mar-Apr, 1950
E. C. Comics

	GD25	FN65	NM94
9-Ingels-c/a	36.00	107.00	250.00
10-Wood's 1st work at E. C.; Ingels-a	38.00	115.00	265.00
11-Ingels-a	36.00	107.00	250.00

NOTE: *Canadian reprints known; see Table of Contents. Feldstein c-10. Wood/Harrison a-10, 11.*

SADIE SACK (See Harvey Hits #93)

SAD SACK AND THE SARGE
Sept, 1957 - No. 155, June, 1982
Harvey Publications

	GD25	FN65	NM94
1	10.00	30.00	65.00
2	4.20	12.50	25.00
3-10	4.00	10.00	20.00
11-20	2.40	6.00	12.00
21-30	1.40	3.50	7.00
31-50	1.20	3.00	6.00
51-90,97-100	.60	1.50	3.00
91-96: All 52 pg. Giants	.80	2.00	4.00
101-155	.40	1.00	2.00

SAD SACK COMICS (See Harvey Collector's Comics #16, Little Sad Sack, Tastee Freez Comics #4 & True Comics #55)
Sept, 1949 - No. 287, Oct, 1982; No. 288, 1992 - Present
Harvey Publications

	GD25	FN65	NM94
1-Infinity-c; Little Dot begins (1st app.); civilian issues begin, end #21	32.00	95.00	225.00
2-Flying Fool by Powell	14.00	43.00	100.00
3	10.00	30.00	60.00
4-10	6.70	20.00	40.00
11-21	4.70	14.00	28.00
22-("Back In The Army Again" on covers #22-36). : "The Specialist" story about Sad Sack's return to Army	3.00	7.50	15.00
23-50	2.00	5.00	10.00
51-100	1.20	3.00	6.00
101-150	.60	1.50	3.00
151-222	.40	1.00	2.00
223-228 (25 cent Giants, 52 pgs.)	.60	1.50	3.00
229-287: 286,287 had limited distribution	.40	1.00	2.00
288,289 ($2.75, 1992): 289-50th anniversary issue	.55	1.40	2.75
3-D 1 (1/54-titled "Harvey 3-D Hits")	16.00	48.00	110.00
Armed Forces Complimentary copies, HD #1-40 ('57-'62)	1.00	2.50	5.00

NOTE: *The Sad Sack Comics comic book was a spin-off from a Sunday Newspaper strip launched through John Wheeler's Bell Syndicate. The previous Sunday page and the first 21 comics depicted the Sad Sack in civvies. Unpopularity caused the Sunday page to be discontinued in the early '50s. Meanwhile Sad Sack returned to the Army, by popular demand, in issue No. 22, remaining there ever since. Incidentally, relatively few of the first 21 issues were ever collected and remain scarce due to this.*

SAD SACK FUN AROUND THE WORLD
1974 (no month)
Harvey Publications

	GD25	FN65	NM94
1-About Great Britain	.60	1.50	3.00

SAD SACK GOES HOME
1951 (16 pgs. in color)
Harvey Publications

	GD25	FN65	NM94
nn-by George Baker	5.00	15.00	30.00

SAD SACK LAUGH SPECIAL
Winter, 1958-59 - No. 93, Feb, 1977 (#1-60: 68 pgs.; #61-76: 52 pgs.)
Harvey Publications

	GD25	FN65	NM94
1	6.70	20.00	40.00
2	4.00	10.00	20.00
3-10	3.00	7.50	15.00
11-30	1.60	4.00	8.00
31-60: Last 68 pg. Giant	1.00	2.50	5.00
61-76: 52 pg. issues	.80	2.00	4.00
77-93	.60	1.50	3.00

SAD SACK NAVY, GOBS 'N' GALS
Aug, 1972 - No. 8, Oct, 1973
Harvey Publications

	GD25	FN65	NM94
1: 52 pg. Giant	1.00	2.50	5.00
2-8	.60	1.50	3.00

SAD SACK'S ARMY LIFE (See Harvey Hits #8, 17, 22, 28, 32, 39, 43, 47, 51, 55, 58, 61, 64, 67, 70)

SAD SACK'S ARMY LIFE (...Parade #1-57, ...Today #58 on)
Oct, 1963 - No. 60, Nov, 1975; No. 61, May, 1976
Harvey Publications

	GD25	FN65	NM94
1: 68 pg. issues begin	4.20	12.50	25.00
2-10	2.40	6.00	12.00
11-20	1.20	3.00	6.00

GD25 FN65 NM94

21-34: Last 68 pg. issue .80 2.00 4.00
35-51: All 52 pgs. .50 1.25 2.50
52-61 .40 1.00 2.00

SAD SACK'S FUNNY FRIENDS (See Harvey Hits #75)
Dec, 1955 - No. 75, Oct, 1969
Harvey Publications

1 7.50 22.50 45.00
2-10 4.00 11.00 22.00
11-20 2.00 5.00 10.00
21-30 1.00 2.50 5.00
31-75 .60 1.50 3.00

SAD SACK'S MUTTSY (See Harvey Hits #74, 77, 80, 82, 84, 87, 89, 92, 96, 99, 102, 105, 108, 111, 113, 115, 117, 119, 121)

SAD SACK USA (...Vacation #8)
Nov, 1972 - No. 7, Nov, 1973; No. 8, Oct, 1974
Harvey Publications

1 .80 2.00 4.00
2-8 .40 1.00 2.00

SAD SACK WITH SARGE & SADIE
Sept, 1972 - No. 8, Nov, 1973
Harvey Publications

1: 52 pg. Giant .80 2.00 4.00
2-8 .40 1.00 2.00

SAD SAD SACK WORLD
Oct, 1964 - No. 46, Dec, 1973 (#1-31: 68 pgs.; #32-38: 52 pgs.)
Harvey Publications

1 2.80 7.00 14.00
2-10 1.20 3.00 6.00
11-31: Last 68 pg. issue 1.00 2.50 5.00
32-38: All 52 pgs. .60 1.50 3.00
39-46 .40 1.00 2.00

SAGA OF BIG RED, THE
Sept, 1976 ($1.25) (In color)
Omaha World-Herald

nn-by Win Mumma; story of the Nebraska Cornhuskers (sports)
.40 1.00 2.00

SAGA OF CRYSTAR, CRYSTAL WARRIOR, THE (Marvel) (Value: cover or less)

SAGA OF RA'S AL GHUL, THE (DC) (Value: cover or less)

SAGA OF SWAMP THING, THE (Swamp Thing #39-41, 46 on)
May, 1982 - Present (Later issues for mature readers; #86 on: $1.50)
DC Comics

1-Origin retold; Phantom Stranger series begins; ends #13; Yeates-c/a begins .30 .75 1.50
2-15: 2-Photo-c from movie .50 1.00
16-19: Bissette-a. 13-Last Yeates-a .40 1.00 2.00
20-1st Alan Moore issue 3.60 9.00 18.00
21-New origin 3.00 7.50 15.00
22-25: 24-JLA x-over; Last Yeates-c 1.20 3.00 6.00
26-30 .80 2.00 4.00
31-33: 33-r/1st app. from House of Secrets #92 .50 1.25 2.50
34 1.80 4.50 9.00
35,36 .45 1.10 2.25
37-1st app. John Constantine, apps. thru #40 2.00 5.00 10.00
38-40: John Constantine app. .80 2.00 4.00
41-45: 44-Batman cameo .35 .90 1.75
46-51: 46-Crisis x-over; Batman cameo & John Constantine app. 50-($1.25, 52 pgs.)-Deadman, Dr. Fate, Demon .30 .75 1.50
52-Arkham Asylum-c/story; Joker-c/cameo .60 1.50 3.00
53-($1.25, 52 pgs.)-Arkham Asylum; Batman-c/story
.80 2.00 4.00
54-64: 58-Spectre preview. 64-Last Moore issue .60 1.25
65-99,101-109: 65-Direct only begins. 66-Batman & Arkham Asylum story 70,76-John Constantine x-over; 76-X-over w/Hellblazer #9. 79-Superman-c/story. 84-Sandman cameo. 85-Jonah Hex app. 102-Preview of World Without End .35 .90 1.75
100 ($2.50, 52 pgs.) .50 1.25 2.50
110-124,126-132: 110-Begin $1.75-c. 129-Metallic ink on-c
.35 .90 1.75
125-($2.95, 52 pgs.)-20th anniversary issue .60 1.50 3.00
Annual 1(1982, $1.00)-Movie Adapt.; painted-c .50 1.00
Annual 2(1985)-Alan Moore scripts, Bissette-a(p) .60 1.50 3.00
Annual 3(1987, $2.00)-New format; Bolland-c .40 1.00 2.00
Annual 4(1988, $2.00)-Batman-c/story .60 1.50 3.00
Annual 5(1989, $2.95, 68 pgs.)-Batman cameo; re-intro Brother Power, 1st app. since 1968 .60 1.50 3.00
Annual 6(1991, $2.95, 68 pgs.) .60 1.50 3.00
Saga of the Swamp Thing ('87, $10.95)-r/#21-27 2.00 5.50 11.00
2nd printing (1989, $12.95) 2.60 6.50 13.00
...Love and Death (1990, $17.95)-r/#28-34 & Annual #2; Totleben painted-c
3.60 9.00 18.00

NOTE: ***Bissette*** *a(p)-16-19, 21-27, 29, 30, 34-36, 39-42, 44, 46, 50, 64; c-17i, 24-32p, 35-37p, 40p, 44p, 46-50p, 51-58, 61, 62, 63p.* ***Kaluta*** *c/a-74.* ***Spiegle*** *a-1-3, 6.* ***Sutton*** *a-98p.* ***Totleben*** *a(i)-10, 16-27, 29, 31, 34-40, 42, 44, 46, 48, 50, 53, 55i; c-25-32i, 33, 35-40i, 42i, 44i, 46-50i, 53, 55i, 59p, 64, 65, 68, 73, 76, 80, 82, 84, 89, 91-100, Annual 4, 5.* ***Vess*** *c-121.* ***Williamson*** *86i.* ***Wrightson*** *a-18i(r), 33r. John Constantine appears in #44-51, 65-67, 70-74, 76, 77, 114, 115.*

SAGA OF THE ORIGINAL HUMAN TORCH (Marvel) (Value: cover or less)

SAGA OF THE SUB-MARINER, THE (Marvel) (Value: cover or less)

SAILOR ON THE SEA OF FATE (See First Comics Graphic Novel #11)

SAILOR SWEENEY (Navy Action #1-11, 15 on)
No. 12, July, 1956 - No. 14, Nov, 1956
Atlas Comics (CDS)

12-14: 12-Shores-a. 13-Severin-c 5.00 15.00 30.00

SAINT, THE (Also see Movie Comics(DC) #2 & Silver Streak #18)
Aug, 1947 - No. 12, Mar, 1952
Avon Periodicals

1-Kamen bondage-c/a 39.00 120.00 275.00
2 20.00 60.00 140.00
3,4: 4-Lingerie panels 16.00 48.00 110.00
5-Spanking panel 24.00 72.00 165.00
6-Miss Fury app., 14 pgs. 26.00 77.00 180.00
7-c-/Avon paperback #118 14.00 43.00 100.00
8,9(12/50): Saint strip-r in #8-12; 9-Kinstler-c 11.50 34.00 80.00
10-Wood-a, 1 pg; c-/Avon paperback #289 11.50 34.00 80.00
11 10.00 30.00 60.00
12-c-/Avon paperback #123 11.00 32.00 75.00

NOTE: *Lucky Dale, Girl Detective in #1,2,4,6.* ***Hollingsworth*** *a-4, 6. Painted-c 8,10,11.*

ST. GEORGE (Marvel) (Value: cover or less)

ST. SWITHIN'S DAY (Trident) (Value: cover or less)

SALERNO CARNIVAL OF COMICS (Also see Pure Oil Comics, 24 Pages of Comics, & Vicks Comics)
Late 1930s (16 pgs.) (paper cover) (Giveaway)
Salerno Cookie Co.

nn-Color reprints of Calkins' Buck Rogers & Skyroads, plus other strips from Famous Funnies 42.00 125.00 250.00

SALOME' (See Night Music #6)

SAM & MAX FREELANCE POLICE (Marvel) (Value: cover or less)

SAM AND MAX, FREELANCE POLICE SPECIAL (Comico) (Value: cover or less)

SAM & MAX FREELANCE POLICE SPECIAL COLOR COLLECTION (Marvel) (Value: cover or less)

SAM HILL PRIVATE EYE
1950 - No. 7, 1951
Close-Up (Archie)

Sad Sack's Funny Friends #4, © HARV

The Saga of Swamp Thing #5, © DC

The Saint #10, © AVON

Samson #5, © FOX

The Sandman #5 (10-11/75), © DC

Sandman #9, © DC

	GD25	FN65	NM94
1	10.00	30.00	60.00
2	5.85	17.50	35.00
3-7	4.70	14.00	28.00

SAM SLADE ROBOHUNTER (Quality) (Value: cover or less)

SAMSON (1st Series) (Capt. Aero #7 on; see Big 3 Comics)
Fall, 1940 - No. 6, Sept, 1941 (See Fantastic Comics)
Fox Features Syndicate

	GD25	FN65	NM94
1-Samson begins, ends #6; Powell-a, signed 'Rensie;' Wing Turner by Tuska app; Fine-c?	87.00	262.00	525.00
2-Dr. Fung by Powell; Fine-c?	44.00	132.00	265.00
3-Navy Jones app.; Simon-c	35.00	105.00	210.00
4-Yarko the Great, Master Magician begins	30.00	90.00	180.00
5,6: 6-Origin The Topper	27.00	82.00	165.00

SAMSON (2nd Series) (Formerly Fantastic Comics #10, 11)
No. 12, April, 1955 - No. 14, Aug, 1955
Ajax/Farrell Publications (Four Star)

	GD25	FN65	NM94
12-Wonder Boy	14.00	43.00	100.00
13,14: 13-Wonder Boy, Rocket Man	10.00	30.00	70.00

SAMSON (See Mighty Samson)

SAMSON & DELILAH (See A Spectacular Feature Magazine)

SAMUEL BRONSTON'S CIRCUS WORLD (See Circus World under Movie Comics)

SAMURAI (Also see Eclipse Graphic Album Series #14)
1985 - No. 22 ($1.70, B&W)
Aircel Publications

	GD25	FN65	NM94
1	.80	2.00	4.00
1-2nd & 3rd printing	.35	.85	1.70
2-12	.40	1.00	2.00
2-2nd printing	.35	.85	1.70
13-Dale Keown's 1st published artwork	1.20	3.00	6.00
14-16-Dale Keown-a	.80	2.00	4.00
17-22	.35	.85	1.70

SAMURAI CAT (Marvel) (Value: cover or less)

SAMUREE (Continuity) (Value: cover or less)

SANCTUARY (Viz) (Value: cover or less)

SANDMAN, THE (See Adventure Comics #40 & World's Finest #3)
Winter, 1974; No. 2, Apr-May, 1975 - No. 6, Dec-Jan, 1975-76
National Periodical Publications

	GD25	FN65	NM94
1-Kirby-a; Joe Simon scripts	1.50	3.75	7.50
2-6: 6-Kirby/Wood-c/a	.80	2.00	4.00

NOTE: *Kirby a-1p, 4-6p; c-1-5, 6p.*

SANDMAN
Jan, 1989 - Present ($1.50/$1.75, color, mature readers)
DC Comics

	GD25	FN65	NM94
1 ($2.00, 52 pgs.): Neil Gaiman scripts begin; Sam Kieth-a(p) in #1-5	6.70	20.00	40.00
2	4.70	14.00	28.00
3-5: 3-John Constantine app.	4.00	11.00	22.00
6-8: 8-Regular ed. has Jeanette Kahn publishorial & American Cancer Society ad w/no indicia on inside front-c	3.00	7.50	15.00
8-Limited ed. (600+ copies?); has Karen Berger editorial and next issue teaser (has indicia)	22.00	65.00	150.00
9-13: 10-Has explaination about #8 mixup	1.80	4.50	9.00
14-($2.50, 52 pgs.)	2.20	5.50	11.00
15-20: 16-Photo-c. 19-Vess-a	1.00	2.50	5.00
21-27: Seasons of Mist storyline. 22-World Without End preview. 24-Russell-i	.90	2.25	4.50
28-30	.60	1.50	3.00
31-35,37-44: 38-40-Photo-c. 41-Bronze ink logo. 43-Neil Gaiman scripts	.35	.85	1.75
36-($2.50, 52 pgs.)	.60	1.50	3.00
45-49: 45-Begin $1.75-c. 47-Metallic ink on-c	.35	.85	1.75
Special 1(1991, $3.50, 68 pgs.)-Glow-in-the-dark-c	1.10	2.75	5.50
Trade paperback (1990, $12.95, 296 pgs.)-r/#8-16	2.60	6.50	13.00

SANDS OF THE SOUTH PACIFIC
January, 1953
Toby Press

	GD25	FN65	NM94
1	11.50	34.00	80.00

SANTA AND HIS REINDEER (See March of Comics #166)

SANTA AND POLLYANNA PLAY THE GLAD GAME
Aug, 1960 (16 pages) (Disney giveaway)
Sales Promotion

	GD25	FN65	NM94
nn	2.00	5.00	10.00

SANTA AND THE ANGEL (See Dell Junior Treasury #7 & Four Color #259)

SANTA & THE BUCCANEERS
1959
Promotional Publ. Co. (Giveaway)

	GD25	FN65	NM94
nn-Reprints 1952 Santa & the Pirates	1.60	4.00	8.00

SANTA & THE CHRISTMAS CHICKADEE
1974 (20 pgs.)
Murphy's (Giveaway)

	GD25	FN65	NM94
nn	1.00	2.50	5.00

SANTA & THE PIRATES
1952
Promotional Publ. Co. (Giveaway)

	GD25	FN65	NM94
nn-Marv Levy-c/a	1.40	3.50	7.00

SANTA AT THE ZOO (See 4-Color #259)

SANTA CLAUS AROUND THE WORLD (See March of Comics #241)

SANTA CLAUS CONQUERS THE MARTIANS (See Movie Classics)

SANTA CLAUS FUNNIES (Also see The Little Fir Tree)
nd; 1940 (Color & B&W; 8x10"; 12pgs., heavy paper)
W. T. Grant Co./Whitman Publishing (Giveaway)

	GD25	FN65	NM94
nn-(2 versions)	10.00	30.00	60.00

SANTA CLAUS FUNNIES (Also see Dell Giants)
Dec?, 1942 - No. 1274, Dec, 1961
Dell Publishing Co.

	GD25	FN65	NM94
nn(#1)(1942)-Kelly-a	36.00	107.00	250.00
2(12/43)-Kelly-a	23.00	70.00	160.00
4-Color 61(1944)-Kelly-a	22.00	65.00	150.00
4-Color 91(1945)-Kelly-a	17.00	51.00	120.00
4-Color 128('46),175('47)-Kelly-a	13.00	40.00	90.00
4-Color 205,254-Kelly-a	11.50	34.00	80.00
4-Color 302,361	4.00	10.00	20.00
4-Color 525,607,666,756,867	3.60	9.00	18.00
4-Color 958,1063,1154,1274	3.00	7.50	15.00

NOTE: *Most issues contain only one Kelly story.*

SANTA CLAUS PARADE
1951; No. 2, Dec, 1952; No. 3, Jan, 1955 (25 cents)
Ziff-Davis (Approved Comics)/St. John Publishing Co.

	GD25	FN65	NM94
nn(1951-Ziff-Davis)-116 pgs. (Xmas Special 1,2)	14.00	43.00	100.00
2(12/52-Ziff-Davis)-100 pgs.; Dave Berg-a	11.00	32.00	75.00
V1#3(1/55-St. John)-100 pgs.	10.00	30.00	70.00

SANTA CLAUS' WORKSHOP (See March of Comics #50, 168)

SANTA IS COMING (See March of Comics #197)

SANTA IS HERE (See March of Comics #49)

SANTA ON THE JOLLY ROGER

1965
Promotional Publ. Co. (Giveaway)

	GD25	FN65	NM94
nn-Marv Levy-c/a	.80	2.00	4.00

SANTA! SANTA!
1974 (20 pgs.)
R. Jackson (Montgomery Ward giveaway)

	GD25	FN65	NM94
nn	.60	1.50	3.00

SANTA'S BUSY CORNER (See March of Comics #31)
SANTA'S CANDY KITCHEN (See March of Comics #14)
SANTA'S CHRISTMAS BOOK (See March of Comics #123)
SANTA'S CHRISTMAS COMICS
December, 1952 (100 pages)
Standard Comics (Best Books)

	GD25	FN65	NM94
nn-Supermouse, Dizzy Duck, Happy Rabbit, etc.	10.00	30.00	70.00

SANTA'S CHRISTMAS COMIC VARIETY SHOW
1943 (24 pages)
Sears Roebuck & Co.

	GD25	FN65	NM94
Contains puzzles & new comics of Dick Tracy, Little Orphan Annie, Moon Mullins, Terry & the Pirates, etc.	13.00	40.00	90.00

SANTA'S CHRISTMAS LIST (See March of Comics #255)
SANTA'S CHRISTMAS TIME STORIES
nd (late 1940s) (16 pgs.; paper cover)
Premium Sales, Inc. (Giveaway)

	GD25	FN65	NM94
nn	3.60	9.00	18.00

SANTA'S CIRCUS
1964 (half-size)
Promotional Publ. Co. (Giveaway)

	GD25	FN65	NM94
nn-Marv Levy-c/a	1.20	3.00	6.00

SANTA'S FUN BOOK
1951, 1952 (regular size, 16 pages, paper-c)
Promotional Publ. Co. (Murphy's giveaway)

	GD25	FN65	NM94
nn	2.40	6.00	12.00

SANTA'S GIFT BOOK
No date (16 pgs.)
No Publisher

	GD25	FN65	NM94
nn-Puzzles, games only	1.60	4.00	8.00

SANTA'S HELPERS (See March of Comics #64, 106, 198)
SANTA'S LITTLE HELPERS (See March of Comics #270)
SANTA'S NEW STORY BOOK
1949 (16 pgs.; paper cover)
Wallace Hamilton Campbell (Giveaway)

	GD25	FN65	NM94
nn	4.00	11.00	22.00

SANTA'S REAL STORY BOOK
1948, 1952 (16 pgs.)
Wallace Hamilton Campbell/W. W. Orris (Giveaway)

	GD25	FN65	NM94
nn	4.00	11.00	22.00

SANTA'S RIDE
1959
W. T. Grant Co. (Giveaway)

	GD25	FN65	NM94
nn	2.40	6.00	12.00

SANTA'S RODEO
1964 (half-size)
Promotional Publ. Co. (Giveaway)

	GD25	FN65	NM94
nn-Marv Levy-a	1.00	2.50	5.00

SANTA'S SECRETS
1951, 1952? (16 pgs.; paper cover)
Sam B. Anson Christmas giveaway

	GD25	FN65	NM94
nn	2.80	7.00	14.00

SANTA'S SHOW (See March of Comics #311)
SANTA'S SLEIGH (See March of Comics #298)
SANTA'S STORIES
1953 (Regular size; paper cover)
K. K. Publications (Klines Dept. Store)

	GD25	FN65	NM94
nn-Kelly-a	13.00	40.00	90.00
nn-Another version (1953, glossy-c, half-size, 7-1/4x5-1/4")-Kelly-a	10.00	30.00	65.00

SANTA'S SURPRISE (See March of Comics #13)
SANTA'S SURPRISE
1947 (36 pgs.; slick cover)
K. K. Publications (Giveaway)

	GD25	FN65	NM94
nn	4.20	12.50	25.00

SANTA'S TINKER TOTS
1958
Charlton Comics

	GD25	FN65	NM94
1-Based on "The Tinker Tots Keep Christmas"	2.40	6.00	12.00

SANTA'S TOYLAND (See March of Comics #242)
SANTA'S TOYS (See March of Comics #12)
SANTA'S TOYTOWN FUN BOOK
1952, 1953?
Promotional Publ. Co. (Giveaway)

	GD25	FN65	NM94
nn-Marv Levy-c	1.40	3.50	7.00

SANTA'S VISIT (See March of Comics #283)
SANTIAGO (See 4-Color #723)
SARGE SNORKEL (Beetle Bailey)
Oct, 1973 - No. 17, Dec, 1976
Charlton Comics

	GD25	FN65	NM94
1	1.00	2.50	5.00
2-17	.40	1.00	2.00

SARGE STEEL (Becomes Secret Agent #9 on; also see Judomaster)
Dec, 1964 - No. 8, Mar-Apr, 1966
Charlton Comics

	GD25	FN65	NM94
1-Origin	2.00	5.00	10.00
2-5,7,8:	1.00	2.50	5.00
6-Judomaster app. (2nd app?)	1.40	3.50	7.00

SAVAGE COMBAT TALES
Feb, 1975 - No. 3, July, 1975
Atlas/Seaboard Publ.

	GD25	FN65	NM94
1-3: 1-Sgt. Stryker's Death Squad begins (origin). 2-Only app. Warhawk		.50	1.00

NOTE: ***McWilliams** a-1-3; c-1. **Sparling** a-1, 3. **Toth** a-2.*

SAVAGE DRAGON, THE (See Megaton #3 & 4)
July, 1992 - No. 3, Dec, 1992 ($1.95, color, mini-series)
Image Comics

	GD25	FN65	NM94
1-Erik Larsen-c/a/scripts & bound-in poster in all	1.20	3.00	6.00
2	.80	2.00	4.00
3-Contains coupon for Image Comics #0	.60	1.50	3.00
3-With coupon missing	.40	1.00	2.00

SAVAGE HENRY (Vortex) (Value: cover or less)
SAVAGE RAIDS OF GERONIMO (See Geronimo #4)
SAVAGE RANGE (See 4-Color #807)
SAVAGE SHE-HULK, THE (See The Avengers, Marvel Graphic Novel #18 & The Sensational She-Hulk)
Feb, 1980 - No. 25, Feb, 1982

Santa's Gift Book nn, © Unknown

Santa's New Story Book nn, © W. H. Campbell

Sarge Steel #1, © CC

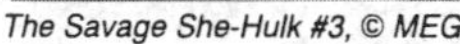

The Savage She-Hulk #3, © MEG

Savage Tales #3, © MEG

The Scarecrow of Romney Marsh #1, © WDC

Marvel Comics Group

	GD25	FN65	NM94
1-Origin & 1st app. She-Hulk	1.00	2.50	5.00
2-10	.50	1.25	2.50
11-25: 25-(52 pgs.)	.40	1.00	2.00

NOTE: ***Austin*** *a-25i; c-23i-25i.* ***J. Buscema*** *a-1p; c-1, 2p.* ***Golden*** *c-8-11.*

SAVAGE SWORD OF CONAN (The... #41 on; ...The Barbarian #175 on)
Aug, 1974 - Present ($1.00, B&W magazine)(Mature readers)
Marvel Comics Group

	GD25	FN65	NM94
1-Smith-r; J. Buscema/N. Adams/Krenkel-a; origin Blackmark by Gil Kane (part 1, ends #3); Blackmark's 1st app. in magazine form-r/from paper-back) & Red Sonja (3rd app.)	10.00	30.00	70.00
2-Neal Adams-c; Chaykin/N. Adams-a	5.00	15.00	30.00
3-Severin/B. Smith-a; N. Adams-a	3.00	7.50	15.00
4-N. Adams/Kane-a(r)	2.40	6.00	12.00
5-10: 5-Jeff Jones frontispiece (r)	2.00	5.00	10.00
11-20	1.60	4.00	8.00
21-50: 34-3 pg. preview of Conan newspaper strip. 35-Cover similar to Savage Tales #1. 45-Red Sonja returns; begin $1.25-c	1.40	3.50	7.00
51-100: 63-Toth frontispiece. 70-Article on movie. 83-Red Sonja-r by Neal Adams from #1	.80	2.00	4.00
101-176: 163-Begin $2.25-c. 169-King Kull story. 171-Soloman Kane by Williamson (i). 172-Red Sonja story	.60	1.50	3.00
177-210: 179,187,192-Red Sonja app. 190-193-4 part King Kull story. 196, 202-King Kull story. 200-New Buscema-a; Robert E. Howard app. with Conan in story. 204-60th anniversary (1932-92)	.45	1.15	2.25
Special 1(1975, B&W)-B. Smith-r/Conan #10,13	1.60	4.00	8.00

NOTE: ***N. Adams*** *a-14p, 60, 83p(r).* ***Alcala*** *a-2 ,4, 7, 12, 15-20, 23, 24, 28, 59, 67, 69, 75, 76i, 80i, 82i, 83i, 89, 180i, 184i, 187i, 189i.* ***Austin*** *a-78i.* ***Boris*** *painted c-1, 4, 5, 7, 9, 10, 12, 15.* ***Brunner*** *a-30; c-8, 30.* ***Buscema*** *a-1-5, 7, 10-12, 15-24, 26-28, 31, 32, 36-43, 45, 47-58p, 60-67p, 70, 71-74p, 76-81p, 87-96p, 98, 99-101p, 190-203p; painted c-40.* ***Chaykin*** *c-31.* ***Chiodo*** *painted c-71, 76, 79, 81, 84, 85, 178.* ***Corben*** *a-4, 16, 29.* ***Finlay*** *a-16.* ***Golden*** *a-98, 101; c-98, 101, 105, 106, 117, 124, 150.* ***Kaluta*** *a-11, 18; c-3, 91, 93.* ***Gil Kane*** *a-2, 3, 8, 13r, 29, 47, 64, 65, 67, 85p, 86p.* ***Krenkel*** *a-9, 11, 14, 16, 24.* ***Morrow*** *a-7.* ***Nebres*** *a-93i, 101i, 107, 114.* ***Newton*** *a-6.* ***Nino*** *c/a-6.* ***Redondo*** *painted c-48-50, 52, 56, 57, 85i, 90, 96i.* ***Marie & John Severin*** *a-Special 1.* ***Simonson*** *a-7, 8, 12, 15-17.* ***Barry Smith*** *a-7, 16, 24, 82r, Special 1r.* ***Starlin*** *c-26.* ***Toth*** *a-64.* ***Williamson*** *a(i)-162, 171, 186. No. 8 & 10 contain a Robert E. Howard Conan adaptation.*

SAVAGE TALES (...Featuring Conan #4 on)(Magazine)
May, 1971; No. 2, 10/73; No. 3, 2/74 - No. 12, Summer, 1975 (B&W)
Marvel Comics Group

	GD25	FN65	NM94
1-Origin/1st app. The Man-Thing by Morrow; Conan the Barbarian by Barry Smith (1st Conan x-over outside his own title); Femizons by Romita begin; Ka-Zar story by Buscema	14.00	43.00	100.00
2-B. Smith, Brunner, Morrow, Williamson-a; Wrightson King Kull reprint/ Creatures on the Loose #10	6.70	20.00	40.00
3-B. Smith, Brunner, Steranko, Williamson-a	4.20	12.50	25.00
4,5-N. Adams-c; last Conan (Smith-r/#4) plus Kane/N. Adams-a. 5-Brak the Barbarian begins, ends #8	3.20	8.00	16.00
6-Ka-Zar begins; Williamson-r; N. Adams-c	1.00	2.50	5.00
7-N. Adams-i	.90	2.25	4.50
8-Shanna, the She-Devil app. thru #10; Williamson-r	.80	2.00	4.00
9,11	.60	1.50	3.00
10-Neal Adams-a(i), Williamson-r	.80	2.00	4.00
...Featuring Ka-Zar Annual 1 (Summer '75, B&W)(#12 on inside)-Ka-Zar origin by G. Kane; B. Smith-r/Astonish. Tales	1.00	2.50	5.00

NOTE: ***Boris*** *c-7, 10.* ***Buscema*** *a-5r, 6p, 8p; c-2.* ***Colan*** *a-1p.* ***Fabian*** *c-8.* ***Golden*** *a-1, 4; c-1.* ***Heath*** *a-10p, 11p.* ***Kaluta*** *c-9.* ***Maneely*** *r-2, 4(The Crusader in both).* ***Morrow*** *a-1, 2, Annual 1.* ***Reese*** *a-2.* ***Severin*** *a-1-7.* ***Starlin*** *a-5. Robert E. Howard adaptations-1-4.*

SAVAGE TALES (Magazine size)
Nov, 1985 - No. 9, Mar, 1987 ($1.50, B&W, mature readers)
Marvel Comics Group

	GD25	FN65	NM94
1-1st app. The Nam; Golden, Morrow-a	1.00	2.50	5.00
2-9: 2,7-Morrow-a. 4-2nd Nam story; Golden-a	.30	.75	1.50

SAVED BY THE BELL (Harvey)(Value: cover or less)

SCAMP (Walt Disney)(See Walt Disney's Comics & Stories #204)
No. 703, 5/56 - No. 1204, 8-10/61; 11/67 - No. 45, 1/79
Dell Publishing Co./Gold Key

	GD25	FN65	NM94
4-Color 703(#1)	4.70	14.00	28.00
4-Color 777,806('57),833	3.00	7.50	15.00
5(3-5/58)-10(6-8/59)	2.40	6.00	12.00
11-16(12-2/60-61)	2.00	5.00	10.00
4-Color 1204(1961)	2.00	5.00	10.00
1(12/67-Gold Key)-Reprints begin	1.60	4.00	8.00
2(3/69)-10	.80	2.00	4.00
11-20	.60	1.50	3.00
21-45	.30	.75	1.50

NOTE: *New stories-#20(in part), 22-25, 27, 29-31, 34, 36-40, 42-45. New covers-#11, 12, 14, 15, 17-25, 27, 29-31, 34, 36-38.*

SCAR FACE (See The Crusaders)

SCARECROW OF ROMNEY MARSH, THE (See W. Disney Showcase #53)
April, 1964 - No. 3, Oct, 1965 (Disney TV Show)
Gold Key

	GD25	FN65	NM94
10112-404 (#1)	4.00	10.00	20.00
2,3	3.00	7.50	15.00

SCARLET O'NEIL (See Harvey Comics Hits #59 & Invisible...)

SCARLETT
1992 - Present ($1.75, color)
DC Comics

	GD25	FN65	NM94
1-($2.95)-Cont'd from Batman #488	.60	1.50	3.00
2-4	.35	.90	1.75

SCARY TALES
8/75 - #9, 1/77; #10, 9/77 - #20, 6/79; #21, 8/80 - #46, 10/84
Charlton Comics

	GD25	FN65	NM94
1-Origin/1st app. Countess Von Bludd, not in #2	.60	1.50	3.00
2-11: 3-Sutton painted-c	.30	.75	1.50
12-36,39,46-All reprints	.30	.75	1.50
37,38,40-45-New-a. 38-Mr. Jigsaw app.	.30	.75	1.50
1(Modern Comics reprint, 1977)		.50	1.00

NOTE: ***Adkins*** *a-31i; c-31i.* ***Ditko*** *a-3, 5, 7, 8(2), 11, 12, 14-16r, 18(3)r, 19r, 21r, 30r, 32, 39r; c-5, 11, 14, 18, 30, 32.* ***Newton*** *a-31p; c-31p.* ***Powell*** *a-18r.* ***Staton*** *a-1(2 pgs.), 4, 20r; c-1, 20.* ***Sutton*** *a-9; c-4, 9.*

SCAVENGERS (Quality)(Value: cover or less)

SCHOOL DAY ROMANCES (...of Teen-Agers #4; Popular Teen-Agers #5 on)
Nov-Dec, 1949 - No. 4, May-June, 1950
Star Publications

	GD25	FN65	NM94
1-Tony Gayle (later Gay), Gingersnapp	11.00	32.00	75.00
2,3: 3-Photo-c	7.50	22.50	45.00
4-Ronald Reagan photo-c/L.B. Cole-c	14.00	43.00	100.00

NOTE: *All have* ***L. B. Cole*** *covers.*

SCHWINN BICYCLE BOOK (...Bike Thrills, 1959)
1949; 1952; 1959 (10 cents)
Schwinn Bicycle Co.

	GD25	FN65	NM94
1949	4.00	10.50	21.00
1952-Believe It or Not type facts; comic format; 36 pgs.	2.00	5.00	10.00
1959	1.60	4.00	8.00

SCIENCE COMICS (1st Series)
Feb, 1940 - No. 8, Sept, 1940
Fox Features Syndicate

	GD25	FN65	NM94
1-Origin Dynamo (called Electro in #1), The Eagle (1st app.), & Navy Jones; Marga, The Panther Woman (1st app.), Cosmic Carson & Perisphere Payne, Dr. Doom begin; bondage/hypo-c	200.00	600.00	1200.00
2	100.00	300.00	600.00

	GD25	FN65	NM94
3,4: 4-Kirby-a	83.00	250.00	500.00
5-8	58.00	175.00	350.00

NOTE: *Cosmic Carson by **Tuska**-#1-3; by **Kirby**-#4. **Lou Fine** c-1-3 only.*

SCIENCE COMICS (2nd Series)
January, 1946 - No. 5, 1946
Humor Publications (Ace Magazines?)

	GD25	FN65	NM94
1-Palais-c/a in No. 1-3; A-Bomb-c	7.50	22.50	45.00
2	4.00	11.00	22.00
3-Feldstein-a, 6 pgs.	9.15	27.50	55.00
4,5	4.00	10.00	20.00

SCIENCE COMICS
May, 1947 (8 pgs. in color)
Ziff-Davis Publ. Co.

	GD25	FN65	NM94
nn-Could be ordered by mail for 10 cents; like the nn Amazing Advs. & Boy Cowboy; (1950)-used to test the market	27.00	80.00	185.00

SCIENCE COMICS
March, 1951
Export Publication Ent., Toronto, Canada
Distr. in U.S. by Kable News Co.

	GD25	FN65	NM94
1-Science Adventure stories plus some true science features	5.00	15.00	30.00

SCIENCE FICTION SPACE ADVENTURES (See Space Adventures)

SCOOBY DOO (TV)(...Where are you? #1-16,26; ...Mystery Comics #17-25, 27 on)(See March Of Comics #356, 368, 382, 391)
March, 1970 - No. 30, Feb, 1975 (Hanna-Barbera)
Gold Key

	GD25	FN65	NM94
1	4.70	14.00	28.00
2-5	3.20	8.00	16.00
6-10	2.40	6.00	12.00
11-20: 11-Tufts-a	1.60	4.00	8.00
21-30	1.00	2.50	5.00

SCOOBY DOO (TV)
April, 1975 - No. 11, Dec, 1976 (Hanna-Barbera)
Charlton Comics

	GD25	FN65	NM94
1	3.00	7.50	15.00
2-5	1.20	3.00	6.00
6-11	1.00	2.50	5.00

SCOOBY-DOO (TV)
Oct, 1977 - No. 9, Feb, 1979 (Hanna-Barbera)
Marvel Comics Group

	GD25	FN65	NM94
1-Dyno-Mutt begins	.60	1.50	3.00
2-9	.30	.75	1.50

SCOOBY-DOO (TV)
Sept, 1992 - Present ($1.25, color)
Harvey Comics

	GD25	FN65	NM94
V2#1,2		.60	1.25
...Giant Size 1 (10/92, $2.25, 68 pgs.) - 2	.45	1.15	2.25

SCOOP COMICS (Becomes Yankee Comics #4-7, a digest sized cartoon book not listed in this guide; becomes Snap #9)
November, 1941 - No. 3, Mar, 1943; No. 8, 1944
Harry 'A' Chesler (Holyoke)

	GD25	FN65	NM94
1-Intro. Rocketman & Rocketgirl; origin The Master Key; Dan Hastings begins; Charles Sultan-c/a	58.00	175.00	350.00
2-Rocket Boy app; Injury to eye story (same as Spotlight #3)	35.00	105.00	210.00
3-Injury to eye story-r from #2; Rocket Boy	29.00	88.00	175.00
8-Formerly Yankee Comics; becomes Snap	20.00	60.00	120.00

SCOOTER (See Swing With...)

SCOOTER COMICS
April, 1946
Rucker Publ. Ltd. (Canadian)

	GD25	FN65	NM94
1-Teen-age/funny animal	5.85	17.50	35.00

SCORCHED EARTH (Tundra) (Value: cover or less)

SCORE, THE (Piranha) (Value: cover or less)

SCORPION
Feb, 1975 - No. 3, July, 1975
Atlas/Seaboard Publ.

	GD25	FN65	NM94
1-Intro.; bondage-c by Chaykin		.60	1.20
2,3: 2-Wrightson-a; Kaluta, Simonson assists(p)		.50	1.00

NOTE: ***Chaykin** a-1, 2; c-1. **Mooney** a-3i.*

SCORPIO ROSE (Eclipse) (Value: cover or less)

SCOTLAND YARD (Inspector Farnsworth of...) (Texas Rangers in Action #5 on?)
June, 1955 - No. 4, March, 1956
Charlton Comics Group

	GD25	FN65	NM94
1-Tothish-a	9.15	27.50	55.00
2-4: 2-Tothish-a	5.85	17.50	35.00

SCOUT (Eclipse) (Value: cover or less)

SCOUT: WAR SHAMAN (Eclipse) (Value: cover or less) (Formerly Scout)

SCREAM (...Comics) (Andy Comics #20 on)
Fall, 1944 - No. 19, April, 1948
Humor Publications/Current Books(Ace Magazines)

	GD25	FN65	NM94
1	10.00	30.00	60.00
2	5.00	15.00	30.00
3-15: 11-Racist humor (Indians)	4.20	12.50	25.00
16-Intro. Lily-Belle	4.20	12.50	25.00
17,19	4.00	10.00	20.00
18-Hypo needle story	4.70	14.00	28.00

SCREAM (Magazine)
Aug, 1973 - No. 11, Feb, 1975 (68 pgs.) (B&W)
Skywald Publishing Corp.

	GD25	FN65	NM94
1	1.60	4.00	8.00
2-5: 2-Origin Lady Satan. 3 (12/73)-#3 found on pg. 22	.80	2.00	4.00
6-11: 6-Origin The Victims. 9-Severed head-c. 11-"Mr. Poe and the Raven" story	.60	1.50	3.00

SCRIBBLY (See All-American Comics, Buzzy, The Funnies, Leave It To Binky & Popular Comics)
8-9/48 - No. 13, 8-9/50; No. 14, 10-11/51 - No. 15, 12-1/51-52
National Periodical Publications

	GD25	FN65	NM94
1-Sheldon Mayer-a in all; 52pgs. begin	75.00	225.00	525.00
2	50.00	150.00	350.00
3-5	39.00	120.00	275.00
6-10	29.00	85.00	200.00
11-15: 13-Last 52 pgs.	24.00	70.00	165.00

SEA DEVILS (See Limited Collectors' Edition #39,45, & Showcase #27-29)
Sept-Oct, 1961 - No. 35, May-June, 1967
National Periodical Publications

	GD25	FN65	NM94
Showcase #27 (7-8/60)-1st app. Sea Devils	60.00	182.00	425.00
Showcase #28,29 (9-10/60, 11-12/60)-2nd & 3rd app. Sea Devils	32.00	95.00	220.00
1-(9-10/61)	39.00	120.00	275.00
2-Last 10 cent issue	17.00	52.00	120.00
3-5: 3-Begin 12 cent issues thru #35	11.00	32.00	75.00
6-10	6.70	20.00	40.00
11,12,14-20	4.70	14.00	28.00
13-Kubert, Colan-a	5.35	16.00	32.00
21-35: 22-Intro. International Sea Devils; origin & 1st app. Capt. X & Man Fish	4.00	10.00	20.00

NOTE: ***Heath** a-B&B 27-29, 1-10; c-B&B 27-29, 1-10, 14-16. **Moldoff** a-16i.*

Science Comics #5, © FOX

Scribbly #6, © DC

Sea Devils #5, © DC

The Sea Hound nn, © AVON

Secret Love #1 (4/57), © AJAX

Secret Missions #1, © AVON

	GD25	FN65	NM94

SEADRAGON (Elite)(Value: cover or less)

SEA HOUND, THE (Capt. Silver's Log Of The...)
1945 (no month) - No. 4, Jan-Feb, 1946
Avon Periodicals

	GD25	FN65	NM94
nn	9.15	27.50	55.00
2-4 (#2, 9-10/45)	6.70	20.00	40.00

SEA HOUND, THE (Radio)
No. 3, July, 1949 - No. 4, Sept, 1949
Capt. Silver Syndicate

	GD25	FN65	NM94
3,4	5.85	17.50	35.00

SEA HUNT (TV)
No. 928, 8/58 - No. 1041, 10-12/59; No. 4, 1-3/60 - No. 13, 4-6/62
Dell Publishing Co. (All have Lloyd Bridges photo-c)

	GD25	FN65	NM94
4-Color 928(#1)	10.00	30.00	70.00
4-Color 994(#2), 4-13: Manning-a #4-6,8-11,13	7.50	22.50	45.00
4-Color 1041(#3)-Toth-a	9.15	27.50	55.00

SEARCH FOR LOVE
Feb-Mar, 1950 - No. 2, Apr-May, 1950 (52 pgs.)
American Comics Group

	GD25	FN65	NM94
1	7.50	22.50	45.00
2,3(6-7/50): 3-Exist?	4.20	12.50	25.00

SEARCHERS (See 4-Color #709)

SEARS (See Merry Christmas From...)

SEASON'S GREETINGS
1935 (6-1/4x5-1/4") (32 pgs. in color)
Hallmark (King Features)

nn-Cover features Mickey Mouse, Popeye, Jiggs & Skippy. "The Night Before Christmas" told one panel per page, each panel by a famous artist featuring their character. Art by Alex Raymond, Gottfredson, Swinnerton, Segar, Chic Young, Milt Gross, Sullivan (Messmer), Herriman, McManus, Percy Crosby & others (22 artists in all)
Estimated value.... $300.00– $500.00

SECRET AGENT (Formerly Sarge Steel)
V2#9, Oct, 1966; V2#10, Oct, 1967
Charlton Comics

	GD25	FN65	NM94
V2#9-Sarge Steel part-r begins	1.60	4.00	8.00
10-Tiffany Sinn, CIA app. (from Career Girl Romances #39); Aparo-a	.80	2.00	4.00

SECRET AGENT (TV)
Nov, 1966 - No. 2, Jan, 1968
Gold Key

	GD25	FN65	NM94
1-Photo-c	10.00	30.00	60.00
2-Photo-c	6.70	20.00	40.00

SECRET AGENT X-9 (See Flash Gordon #4 by King)
1934 (Book 1: 84 pgs.; Book 2: 124 pgs.) (8x7-1/2")
David McKay Publications

	GD25	FN65	NM94
Book 1-Contains reprints of the first 13 weeks of the strip by Alex Raymond; complete except for 2 dailies	38.00	115.00	265.00
Book 2-Contains reprints immediately following contents of Book 1, for 20 weeks by Alex Raymond; complete except for two dailies. Note: Raymond mis-dated the last five strips from 6/34, and while the dating sequence is confusing, the continuity is correct	32.00	95.00	225.00

SECRET AGENT X-9 (See Feature Books #8 & Magic Comics)

SECRET AGENT Z-2 (See Holyoke One-Shot No. 7)

SECRET DEFENDERS (Also see The Defenders & Fantastic Four #374)
Mar, 1993 - Present ($1.75, color)
Marvel Comics

	GD25	FN65	NM94
1-($2.50)-Foil stamped-c; Dr. Strange, Nomad, Wolverine, Spider Woman & Darkhawk begin	.55	1.40	2.75
2-4	.35	.90	1.75

SECRET DIARY OF EERIE ADVENTURES
1953 (One Shot) (25 cent giant; 100 pgs.)
Avon Periodicals

	GD25	FN65	NM94
nn-(Rare) Kubert-a; Hollingsworth-c; Sid Check back-c	86.00	257.00	600.00

SECRET HEARTS
9-10/49 - No. 6, 7-8/50; No. 7, 12-1/51-52 - No. 153, 7/71
(No. 1-6: photo-c; all 52 pgs.)
National Periodical Publications (Beverly)(Arleigh No. 50-113)

	GD25	FN65	NM94
1-Photo-c begin, end #6	29.00	85.00	200.00
2-Toth-a	14.00	43.00	100.00
3,6 (1950)	13.00	40.00	90.00
4,5-Toth-a	13.50	41.00	95.00
7(12-1/51-52) (Rare)	13.50	41.00	95.00
8-10 (1952)	10.00	30.00	60.00
11-20	8.35	25.00	50.00
21-26: 26-Last precode (2-3/55)	6.70	20.00	40.00
27-40	5.00	15.00	30.00
41-50	4.00	10.00	20.00
51-60	3.00	7.50	15.00
61-75: Last 10 cent issue	2.40	6.00	12.00
76-109	1.60	4.00	8.00
110-"Reach for Happiness" serial begins, ends #138	1.20	3.00	6.00
111-119,121-126,128-133,135-138	.80	2.00	4.00
120,134-Neal Adams-c	1.00	2.50	5.00
127 (4/68)-Beatles cameo	1.00	2.50	5.00
139,140	.80	2.00	4.00
141,142-"20 Miles to Heartbreak," Chapter 2 & 3 (See Young Love for Chapters 1 & 4); Toth, Colletta-a	.60	1.50	3.00
143-148,150-153: 144-Morrow-a. 153-Kirby-i	.60	1.50	3.00
149-Toth-a	.80	2.00	4.00

SECRET ISLAND OF OZ, THE (See First Comics Graphic Novel)

SECRET LOVE (See Fox Giants & Sinister House of...)

SECRET LOVE
12/55 - No. 3, 8/56; 4/57 - No. 5, 2/58; No. 6, 6/58
Ajax-Farrell/Four Star Comic Corp. No. 2 on

	GD25	FN65	NM94
1(12/55-Ajax, 1st series)	5.00	15.00	30.00
2,3	3.60	9.00	18.00
1(4/57-Ajax, 2nd series)	4.00	11.00	22.00
2-6: 5-Bakerish-a	2.80	7.00	14.00

SECRET LOVES
Nov, 1949 - No. 6, Sept, 1950 (#5: photo-c)
Comic Magazines/Quality Comics Group

	GD25	FN65	NM94
1-Ward-c	11.50	34.00	80.00
2-Ward-c	10.00	30.00	70.00
3-Crandall-a	8.35	25.00	50.00
4,6	5.00	15.00	30.00
5-Suggestive art "Boom Town Babe"	7.00	21.00	42.00

SECRET LOVE STORIES (See Fox Giants)

SECRET MISSIONS
February, 1950
St. John Publishing Co.

	GD25	FN65	NM94
1-Kubert-c	11.00	32.00	75.00

SECRET MYSTERIES (Formerly Crime Mysteries & Crime Smashers)
No. 16, Nov, 1954 - No. 19, July, 1955
Ribage/Merit Publications No. 17 on

	GD25	FN65	NM94
16-Horror, Palais-a	10.00	30.00	65.00
17-19-Horror; #17-mis-dated 3/54?	6.70	20.00	40.00

SECRET ORIGINS (See 80 Page Giant #8)
Aug-Oct, 1961 (Annual) (Reprints)
National Periodical Publications

	GD25	FN65	NM94
1-Origin Adam Strange (Showcase #17), Green Lantern (Gr. Lantern #1), Challengers (partial-r/Showcase #6, 6 pgs. Kirby-a). J'onn J'onzz (Det. #225), The Flash (Showcase #4). Green Arrow (1pg. text). Superman-Batman team (W. Finest #94). Wonder Woman (Wonder Woman #105)	25.00	75.00	200.00

SECRET ORIGINS
Feb-Mar, 1973 - No. 6, Jan-Feb, 1974; No. 7, Oct-Nov, 1974
National Periodical Publications (All origin reprints)

	GD25	FN65	NM94
1-Superman(r/1 pg. origin/Action #1, 1st time since G.A.), Batman(Det. #33), Ghost(Flash #88), The Flash(Showcase #4)	1.80	4.50	9.00
2-4: 2-Green Lantern(Showcase #22), The Atom(Showcase #34), Supergirl (Action #252). 3-Wonder Woman(W.W. #1), Wildcat(Sensation #1). 4-Vigilante(Action #42) by Meskin, Kid Eternity(Hit #25)	.80	2.00	4.00
5-7: 5-The Spectre by Baily(More Fun #52,53). 6-Blackhawk(Military #1) & Legion of Super-Heroes(Superboy #147). 7-Robin(Detective #38), Aquaman (More Fun #73)	.60	1.50	3.00

NOTE: ***Infantino** a-1. **Kane** a-2. **Kubert** a-1.*

SECRET ORIGINS
4/86 - No. 50, 8/90 (All origins)(52 pgs. #6 on)(#27 on: $1.50)
DC Comics

	GD25	FN65	NM94
1-Origin Superman	.70	1.75	3.50
2-Blue Beetle	.50	1.25	2.50
3-5: 3-Shazam. 4-Firestorm. 5-Crimson Avenger	.40	1.00	2.00
6-Halo/G.A. Batman	.80	2.00	4.00
7-10: 7-Green Lantern(Guy Gardner)/G.A. Sandman. 8-Shadow Lass/Doll Man. 9-G.A. Flash/Skyman. 10-Phantom Stranger w/Alan Moore scripts; Legends spin-off	.40	1.00	2.00
11,12,14-26: 11-G.A. Hawkman/Power Girl. 12-Challs of Unknown/G.A. Fury. 14-Suicide Squad; Legends spin-off. 15-Spectre/Deadman. 16-G.A. Hourman/Warlord. 17-Adam Strange/Dr. Occult. 18-G.A. Gr. Lantern/The Creeper. 19-Uncle Sam/The Guardian. 20-Batgirl/G.A. Dr. Mid-Nite. 21-Jonah Hex/Black Condor. 22-Manhunters. 23-Floronic Man/Guardians of the Universe. 24-Blue Devil/Dr. Fate. 25-LSH/Atom. 26-Black Lightning/ Miss America	.40	1.00	2.00
13-Origin Nightwing; Johnny Thunder app.	.80	2.00	4.00
27-38,40-44: 27-Zatara/Zatanna. 28-Midnight/Nightshade. 29-Power of the Atom/Mr. America; new 3 pg. Red Tornado story by Mayer (last app. of Scribbly, 8/88). 30-Plastic Man/Elongated Man. 31-JSA. 32-JLA. 33-35-JLI. 36-Green Lantern/Poison Ivy. 37-Legion Of Substitute Heroes/Doctor Light. 38-Green Arrow/Speedy; Grell scripts. 40-All Ape issue. 41-Rogues Gallery of Flash. 42-Phantom Girl/Grim Ghost. 43-Original Hawk & Dove/ Cave Carson/Chris KL-99. 44-Batman app.; story based on Det. #40	.35	.90	1.75
39-Animal Man-c/story continued in Animal Man #10; Grant Morrison scripts; Batman app.	.80	2.00	4.00
45-49: 45-Blackhawk/El Diablo. 46-JLA/LSH/New Titans. 47-LSH. 48-Ambush Bug/Stanley & His Monster/Rex the Wonder Dog/Trigger Twins. 49-Newsboy Legion/Silent Knight/brief origin Bouncing Boy	.30	.75	1.50
50-($3.95, 100 pgs.)-Batman & Robin in text, Flash of Two Worlds, Johnny Thunder, Dolphin, Black Canary & Space Museum	.80	2.00	4.00
Annual 1 (8/87)-Capt. Comet/Doom Patrol	.40	1.00	2.00
Annual 2 ('88, $2.00)-Origin Flash II & Flash III	.40	1.00	2.00
Annual 3 ('89, $2.95, 84 pgs.)-Teen Titans; 1st app. new Flamebird who replaces original Bat-Girl	.60	1.50	3.00
Special 1 (10/89, $2.00)-Batman villains: Penguin, Riddler, & Two-Face; Bolland-c	.50	1.25	2.50

NOTE: ***Art Adams** a-33i(part). **M. Anderson** 8, 19, 21; c-19(part). **Bolland** c-7. **Byrne** c/a-Annual 1. **Colan** c/a-5p. **Forte** a-37. **Giffen** a-18p, 44p, 48. **Kaluta** c-39. **Gil Kane** a-2, 28; c-2p. **Kirby** c-19(part). **Mayer** a-29. **Morrow** a-21. **Orlando** a-10. **Perez** a-50i; c- Annual 3. **Rogers** a-6p. **Russell** a-27i. **Staton** a-36, 50p. **Steacy** a-35. **Tuska** a-4p, 9p.*

SECRET ORIGINS OF SUPER-HEROES (See DC Special Series #10, 19)

SECRET ORIGINS OF THE WORLD'S GREATEST SUPER-HEROES
(DC)(Value: cover or less)

SECRET ROMANCE
Oct, 1968 - No. 41, Nov, 1976; No. 42, Mar, 1979 - No. 48, Feb, 1980
Charlton Comics

	GD25	FN65	NM94
1-Begin 12 cent issues, ends ?	1.40	3.50	7.00
2-10: 9-Reese-a	.80	2.00	4.00
11-48	.40	1.00	2.00

NOTE: *Beyond the Stars app.-No. 9, 11, 12, 14.*

SECRET ROMANCES
April 1951 - No. 27, July, 1955
Superior Publications Ltd.

	GD25	FN65	NM94
1	8.35	25.00	50.00
2	4.70	14.00	28.00
3-10	4.00	11.00	22.00
11-13,15-18,20-27	3.20	8.00	16.00
14,19-Lingerie panels	4.00	11.00	22.00

SECRET SERVICE (See Kent Blake of the...)

SECRET SIX (See Action Comics Weekly)
Apr-May, 1968 - No. 7, Apr-May, 1969 (12 cents)
National Periodical Publications

	GD25	FN65	NM94
1-Origin/1st app.	5.00	15.00	30.00
2-7	3.60	9.00	18.00

SECRET SOCIETY OF SUPER-VILLAINS
May-June, 1976 - No. 15, June-July, 1978
National Periodical Publications/DC Comics

	GD25	FN65	NM94
1-Origin; JLA cameo & Capt. Cold app.	.40	1.00	2.00
2-5: 2-Re-intro/origin Capt. Comet; Green Lantern x-over. 5-Green Lantern, Hawkman x-over; Darkseid app.	.30	.75	1.50
6-15: 9,10-Creeper x-over. 11-Capt. Comet; Orlando-i. 15-G.A. Atom, Dr. Midnite, & JSA app.		.60	1.20

SECRET SOCIETY OF SUPER-VILLAINS SPECIAL (See DC Special Series #6)

SECRETS OF HAUNTED HOUSE
4-5/75 - #5, 12-1/75-76; #6, 6-7/77 - #14, 10-11/78; #15, 8/79 - #46, 3/82
National Periodical Publications/DC Comics

	GD25	FN65	NM94
1	.60	1.50	3.00
2-10	.40	1.00	2.00
11-46: 31-Mr. E series begins, ends #41		.60	1.25

NOTE: ***Bissette** a-46. **Buckler** c-32-40p. **Ditko** a-9, 12, 41, 45. **Golden** a-10. **Howard** a-13i. **Kaluta** c-8, 10, 11, 14, 16, 29. **Kubert** c-41, 42. **Sheldon Mayer** a-43p. **McWilliams** a-35. **Nasser** a-24. **Newton** a-30p. **Nino** a-1, 13, 19. **Orlando** c-13, 30, 43, 45i. **N. Redondo** a-4, 5, 29. **Rogers** c-26. **Spiegle** a-31-41. **Wrightson** c-5, 44.*

SECRETS OF HAUNTED HOUSE SPECIAL (See DC Special Series #12)

SECRETS OF LIFE (See 4-Color #749)

SECRETS OF LOVE (See Popular Teen-Agers...)

SECRETS OF LOVE AND MARRIAGE
V2#1, Aug, 1956 - V2#25, June, 1961
Charlton Comics

	GD25	FN65	NM94
V2#1	3.20	8.00	16.00
V2#2-6	2.00	5.00	10.00
V2#7-9(All 68 pgs.)	1.40	3.50	7.00
10-25	1.20	3.00	6.00

SECRETS OF MAGIC (See Wisco)

SECRETS OF SINISTER HOUSE (Sinister House of Secret Love #1-4)
No. 5, June-July, 1972 - No. 18, June-July, 1974
National Periodical Publications

Secret Mysteries #18, © Merit Publ.

Secret Origins #1 (1961), © DC

Secret Romance #1, © CC

Select Detective #1, © DS

The Sensational She-Hulk #10, © MEG

Sensation Comics #8, © DC

	GD25	FN65	NM94
5-9: 7-Redondo-a	.40	1.00	2.00
10-Neal Adams-a(i)	1.00	2.50	5.00
11-18: 17-Barry-a; early Chaykin 1 pg. strip	.30	.75	1.50

NOTE: ***Alcala** a-6, 13, 14. **Kaluta** c-6, 7. **Nino** a-8, 11-13. Ambrose Bierce adapt.-#14.*

SECRETS OF THE LEGION OF SUPER-HEROES
Jan, 1981 - No. 3, March, 1981 (Mini-series)
DC Comics

1-3: 1-Origin of the Legion. 2-Retells origins of Brainiac 5, Shrinking Violet, Sun-Boy, Bouncing Boy, Ultra-Boy, Matter-Eater Lad, Mon-El, Karate Kid, & Dream Girl .50 1.00

SECRETS OF TRUE LOVE
February, 1958
St. John Publishing Co.

	GD25	FN65	NM94
1	3.20	8.00	16.00

SECRETS OF YOUNG BRIDES
No. 5, Sept, 1957 - No. 44, Oct, 1964; July, 1975 - No. 9, Nov, 1976
Charlton Comics

	GD25	FN65	NM94
5	3.60	9.00	18.00
6-10: 8-Negligee panel	1.80	4.50	9.00
11-20	1.40	3.50	7.00
21-30: Last 10 cent issue?	1.00	2.50	5.00
31-44	.60	1.50	3.00
1-9 (2nd series)	.30	.75	1.50

SECRET SQUIRREL (TV)(See Kite Fun Book)
October, 1966 (Hanna-Barbera)
Gold Key

	GD25	FN65	NM94
1	5.85	17.50	35.00

SECRET STORY ROMANCES (Becomes True Tales of Love)
Nov, 1953 - No. 21, Mar, 1956
Atlas Comics (TCI)

	GD25	FN65	NM94
1-Everett-a	7.50	22.50	45.00
2	4.00	11.00	22.00
3-11: 11-Last pre-code (2/55)	3.60	9.00	18.00
12-21	3.00	7.50	15.00

NOTE: ***Colletta** a-10, 14, 15, 17, 21; c-10, 14, 17.*

SECRET VOICE, THE (See Great American Comics Presents...)

SECRET WARS II (Also see Marvel Super Heroes...)
July, 1985 - No. 9, Mar, 1986 (Maxi-series)
Marvel Comics Group

1-9: 2,8,9-X-Men app. 5,8,9-Spider-Man app. 9-Double sized (75 cents) .50 1.00

SECTAURS (Marvel)(Value: cover or less)

SEDUCTION OF THE INNOCENT (Also see N. Y. State Joint Legis. Committee to Study...)
1953, 1954 (399 pages) (Hardback)
Rinehart & Co., Inc., N. Y. (Also printed in Canada by Clarke, Irwin & Co. Ltd., Toronto)
Written by Dr. Fredric Wertham

(1st Version)-with bibliographical note intact (several copies got out before the comic publishers forced the removal of this page) 70.00 150.00
with dust jacket.... 175.00 350.00
(2nd Version)-without bibliographical note 42.00 90.00
with dust jacket.... 80.00 160.00
(3rd Version)-Published in England by Kennikat Press, 1954, 399 pgs. has bibliographical page 30.00 60.00
1972 r-/of 3rd version; 400 pgs. w/bibliography page; Kennikat Press 12.00 24.00

NOTE: *Material from this book appeared in the November, 1953(Vol.70, pp50-53,214) issue of the **Ladies' Home Journal** under the title "What Parents Don't Know About Comic Books." With the release of this book, Dr. Wertham reveals seven years of research attempting to link juvenile delinquency to comic books. Many illustrations showing excessive violence, sex, sadism, and torture are shown. This book was used at the Kefauver Senate hearings which led to the Comics Code Authority. Because of the influence this book had on the comic in dustry and the collector's interest in it, we feel this listing is justified. Also see **Parade of Pleasure.***

SEDUCTION OF THE INNOCENT! (Eclipse)(Value: cover or less)

SELECT DETECTIVE
Aug-Sept, 1948 - No. 3, Dec-Jan, 1948-49
D. S. Publishing Co.

	GD25	FN65	NM94
1-Matt Baker-a	11.00	32.00	75.00
2-Baker, McWilliams-a	9.15	27.50	55.00
3	7.50	22.50	45.00

SEMPER FI (Marvel)(Value: cover or less)

SENSATIONAL POLICE CASES (Becomes Captain Steve Savage, 2nd series)
1952; 1954 - No. 4, 1954
Avon Periodicals

	GD25	FN65	NM94
nn-100 pg. issue (1952, 25 cents)-Kubert & Kinstler-a	23.00	70.00	160.00
1 (1954)	9.15	27.50	55.00
2-4: 2-Kirbyish-a. 4-Reprint/Saint #5	6.35	19.00	38.00
I.W. Reprint #5-(1963?, nd)-Reprints Prison Break #5(1952-Realistic); Infantino-a	2.00	5.00	10.00

SENSATIONAL SHE-HULK, THE (Also see Savage She-Hulk)
V2#1, 5/89 - Present ($1.50/$1.75, color, deluxe format) (She-Hulk #21 on)
Marvel Comics

	GD25	FN65	NM94
V2#1-Byrne-c/a(p)/scripts begin, end #8	.60	1.50	3.00
2-8: 3-Spidey. 4-Reintro G.A. Blonde Phantom	.45	1.10	2.20
9-49,51,52: 14-17-Howard the Duck app. 21-23-Return of the Blonde Phantom. 22-All Winners Squad app. 25-Thor app. 26-Excalibur app.; Guice-c. 29-Wolverine app. (3 pgs.). 30-Hobgoblin-c & cameo. 31-Byrne-c/a/scripts begin again. 35-Last $1.50-c. 37-Wolverine/Punisher/Spidey-c, but no app. 39-Thing app.	.35	.90	1.75
50-($2.95, 52 pgs.)-Green & silver foil stamped-c; anniversary issue; last Byrne-a; Austin, Chaykin, Simonson-a	.60	1.50	3.00

SENSATIONAL SHE-HULK IN CEREMONY, THE (Marvel)(Value: cover or less)

SENSATIONAL SPIDER-MAN (Marvel)(Value: cover or less)

SENSATION COMICS (Sensation Mystery #110 on)
Jan, 1942 - No. 109, May-June, 1952
National Periodical Publ./All-American

	GD25	FN65	VF82	NM94
1-Origin Mr. Terrific(1st app.), Wildcat(1st app.), The Gay Ghost, & Little Boy Blue; Wonder Woman(cont'd from All Star #8), The Black Pirate begin; intro. Justice & Fair Play Club	520.00	1560.00	3120.00	5200.00

(Estimated up to 150 total copies exist, 7 in NM/Mint)

1-Reprint, Oversize 13-1/2x10." **WARNING**: This comic is an exact duplicate reprint of the original except for its size. DC published it in 1974 with a second cover titling it as a Famous First Edition. There have been many reported cases of the outer cover being removed and the interior sold as the original edition. The reprint with the new outer cover removed is practically worthless.

	GD25	FN65	NM94
2-Etta Candy begins	233.00	700.00	1400.00
3-W. Woman gets secretary's job	125.00	375.00	750.00
4-1st app. Stretch Skinner in Wildcat	108.00	325.00	650.00
5-Intro. Justin, Black Pirate's son	83.00	250.00	500.00
6-Origin/1st app. Wonder Woman's magic lasso	83.00	250.00	500.00
7-10	68.00	205.00	410.00
11,12,14-20	58.00	175.00	350.00
13-Hitler, Tojo, Mussolini-c	67.00	200.00	400.00
21-30	44.00	132.00	265.00
31-33	35.00	105.00	210.00

34-Sargon, the Sorcerer begins, ends #36; begins again #52

	GD25	FN65	NM94
	35.00	105.00	210.00
35-40: 38-Xmas-c	28.00	85.00	170.00
41-50: 43-The Whip app.	24.00	72.00	145.00
51-60: 51-Last Black Pirate. 56,57-Sargon by Kubert	21.00	62.00	125.00
61-80: 63-Last Mr. Terrific. 65,66-Wildcat by Kubert. 68-Origin Huntress	21.00	62.00	125.00
81-Used in **SOTI**, pg. 33,34; Krigstein-a	23.00	68.00	135.00
82-90: 83-Last Sargon. 86-The Atom app. 90-Last Wildcat	17.00	50.00	100.00
91-Streak begins by Alex Toth	17.00	50.00	100.00
92,93: 92-Toth-a, 2 pgs.	16.00	48.00	95.00
94-1st all girl issue	19.00	57.00	115.00
95-99,101-106: Wonder Woman ends. 99-1st app. Astra, Girl of the Future, ends #106. 105-Last 52 pgs.	19.00	57.00	115.00
100	27.00	82.00	165.00
107-(Scarce)-1st mystery issue; Johnny Peril by Toth(p), 8 pgs.	33.00	100.00	200.00
108-(Scarce)-Johnny Peril by Toth(p)	29.00	88.00	175.00
109-(Scarce)-Johnny Peril by Toth(p)	33.00	100.00	200.00

NOTE: ***Krigstein** a-(Wildcat)-81, 83, 84. **Moldoff** Black Pirate-1-25; Black Pirate not in 34-36, 43-48. **Oskner** c(i)-89-91, 94-106. Wonder Woman by **H. G. Peter**, all issues except #8, 17-19, 21; c-4-7, 9-18, 20-88, 92, 93. **Toth** a-91, 98; c-107.*

SENSATION MYSTERY (Formerly Sensation #1-109)
No. 110, July-Aug, 1952 - No. 116, July-Aug, 1953
National Periodical Publications

	GD25	FN65	NM94
110-Johnny Peril continues	18.00	54.00	125.00
111-116-Johnny Peril in all. 116-M. Anderson-a	18.00	54.00	125.00

NOTE: ***M. Anderson** c-110. **Colan** a-114p. **Giunta** a-112. **G. Kane** c(p)-108, 109, 111-115.*

SENTINELS OF JUSTICE, THE (See Americomics & Captain Paragon &...)

SENTRY SPECIAL
1991 ($2.75, color)(Hero Alliance spin-off)
Innovation Publishing

	GD25	FN65	NM94
1-Lost in Space preview (3 pgs.)	.55	1.40	2.75

SERAPHIM (Innovation)(Value: cover or less)

SERGEANT BARNEY BARKER (Becomes G. I. Tales #4 on)
Aug, 1956 - No. 3, Dec, 1956
Atlas Comics (MCI)

	GD25	FN65	NM94
1-Severin-a(4)	10.00	30.00	70.00
2,3-Severin-a(4). 3-Severin-c	8.35	25.00	50.00

SERGEANT BILKO (Phil Silvers) (TV)
May-June, 1957 - No. 18, Mar-Apr, 1960
National Periodical Publications

	GD25	FN65	NM94
1-All have Bob Oskner-c	47.00	140.00	325.00
2	26.00	77.00	180.00
3-5	19.00	57.00	135.00
6-18: 11,12,15,17-Photo-c	16.00	48.00	110.00

SGT. BILKO'S PVT. DOBERMAN (TV)
June-July, 1958 - No. 11, Feb-Mar, 1960
National Periodical Publications

	GD25	FN65	NM94
1-Bob Oskner c-1-4,7,11	25.00	75.00	175.00
2	16.00	48.00	110.00
3-5: 5-Photo-c	12.00	36.00	85.00
6-11: 6,9-Photo-c	10.00	30.00	60.00

SGT. DICK CARTER OF THE U.S. BORDER PATROL (See Holyoke One-Shot)

SGT. FURY (& His Howling Commandos)(See Special Marvel Edition)
May, 1963 - No. 167, Dec, 1981
Marvel Comics Group (BPC earlier issues)

	GD25	FN65	NM94
1-1st app. Sgt. Nick Fury (becomes agent of Shield in Strange Tales #135; Kirby/Ayers-c/a; 1st Dum-Dum Dugan & the Howlers	57.00	170.00	400.00
2-Kirby-a	25.00	75.00	175.00
3-5: 3-Reed Richards x-over. 4-Death of Junior Juniper. 5-1st Baron Strucker app.; Kirby-a	13.00	40.00	90.00
6-10: 8-Baron Zemo, 1st Percival Pinkerton app. 9-Hitler-c & app. 10-1st app. Capt. Savage (the Skipper)	10.00	30.00	65.00
11,12,14-20: 14-1st Blitz Squad. 18-Death of Pamela Hawley	5.85	17.50	35.00
13-Captain America & Bucky app.(12/64); 1st Capt. America x-over outside The Avengers; Kirby-a	16.00	48.00	110.00
21-30: 25-Red Skull app. 27-1st app. Eric Koenig; origin Fury's eye patch	4.00	11.00	22.00
31-50: 34-Origin Howling Commandos. 35-Eric Koenig joins Howlers. 43-Bob Hope, Glen Miller app. 44-Flashback-Howlers 1st mission	2.80	7.00	14.00
51-60	2.40	6.00	12.00
61-80: 64-Capt. Savage & Raiders x-over. 76-Fury's Father app. in WWI story.	2.00	5.00	10.00
81-100: 98-Deadly Dozen x-over. 100-Capt. America, Fantastic 4 cameos; Stan Lee, Martin Goodman & others app.	1.60	4.00	8.00
101-120: 101-Origin retold.	1.00	2.50	5.00
121-130	.90	2.25	4.50
131-150	.60	1.50	3.00
151-167: 167-Reprints	.50	1.25	2.50
Annual 1(1965, 25 cents, 72pgs.)-r/#4,5 & new-a	10.00	30.00	60.00
Special 2(1966)	4.20	12.50	25.00
Special 3(1967)	3.00	7.50	15.00
Special 4(1968)	2.00	5.00	10.00
Special 5-7(1969-11/71)	1.20	2.60	6.00

NOTE: ***Ayers** a-8. **Ditko** a-15i. **Gil Kane** c-37, 96. **Kirby** a-1-7, 13p, 167p(r). Special 5; c-1-20, 25, 167p. **Severin** a-44-46, 48, 162, 164; inks-49-79, Special 4, 6; c-4i, 5, 6, 44, 46, 110, 149i, 155i, 162-166. **Sutton** a-57p. Reprints in #80, 82, 85, 87, 89, 91, 93, 95, 99, 101, 103, 105, 107, 109, 111, 145.*

SGT. FURY AND HIS HOWLING DEFENDERS (See The Defenders #147)

SERGEANT PRESTON OF THE YUKON (TV)
No. 344, Aug, 1951 - No. 29, Nov-Jan, 1958-59
Dell Publishing Co.

	GD25	FN65	NM94
4-Color 344(#1)-Sergeant Preston & his dog Yukon King begin; painted-c begin, end #18	10.00	30.00	65.00
4-Color 373,397,419('52)	5.85	17.50	35.00
5(11-1/52-53)-10(2-4/54)	4.35	13.00	26.00
11,12,14-17	4.00	10.00	20.00
13-Origin Sgt. Preston	4.35	13.00	26.00
18-Origin Yukon King; last painted-c	4.35	13.00	26.00
19-29: All photo-c	5.00	15.00	30.00

SERGEANT PRESTON OF THE YUKON
1956 (4 comic booklets) (Soft-c, 16pgs., 7x2-1/2" & 5x2-1/2")
Giveaways with Quaker Cereals

	GD25	FN65	NM94
"How He Found Yukon King," "The Case That Made Him A Sergeant," "How Yukon King Saved Him From The Wolves," "How He Became A Mountie" each...	4.70	14.00	28.00

SGT. ROCK (Formerly Our Army at War; see Brave & the Bold #52)
No. 302, March, 1977 - No. 422, July, 1988
National Periodical Publications/DC Comics

	GD25	FN65	NM94
302	1.60	4.00	8.00
303-310	1.20	3.00	6.00
311-320: 318-Reprints	.80	2.00	4.00
321-350	.60	1.50	3.00
351-422: 422-1st Joe, Adam, Andy Kubert-a team	.30	.75	1.50
Annual 2-4: 2(1982)-Formerly Sgt. Rock's Prize Battle Tales #1. 3(1983). 4(1984)	.50	1.25	2.50

NOTE: ***Estrada** a-322, 327, 331, 336, 337, 341, 342i. **Glanzman** a-384, 421. **Kubert** a-302, 303, 305r, 306, 328, 351, 356, 368, 373, 422; c-317, 318r, 319-323, 325-333-on, Annual 2, 3. **Severin** a-347. **Spiegle** a-382, Annual 2, 3. **Thorne** a-384. **Toth** a-385r. **Wildey** a-307, 311, 313, 314.*

SGT. ROCK SPECIAL (Sgt. Rock #14 on; see DC Special Series #3)
Oct, 1988 - No. 21, Feb, 1992; No. 1, 1992 ($2.00, color, quarterly, 52 pgs.)

Sergeant Bilko #11, © CBS

Sgt. Fury #13, © MEG

Sergeant Preston of the Yukon #7, © Sgt. Preston

Seven Seas Comics #4, © Universal Phoenix Feat.

The Shadow #3 (Archie), © Conde Nast

Shadow Comics V2#7, © Conde Nast

	GD25	FN65	NM94
DC Comics			
1	.50	1.25	2.50
2-8,10-21: All reprints; 5-r/1st Sgt. Rock/Our Army At War #81. 7-Tomahawk-r by Thorne. 10-All Rock issue. 11-r/1st Haunted Tank story. 12-All Kubert issue; begins monthly. 13-Dinosaur story by Heath(r). 14-Enemy Ace-r (22 pgs.) by Adams/Kubert. 15-Enemy Ace (22 pgs.) by Kubert. 16-Iron Major-c/story. 16,17-Enemy Ace-r. 19-r/Batman/Sgt. Rock team-up/B&B #108	.40	1.00	2.00
9-Enemy Ace-r by Kubert	.50	1.25	2.50
1 (1992, $2.95, 68 pgs.)-Simonson-c; unpubbed Kubert-a; Glanzman, Russell, Pratt, & Wagner-a	.60	1.50	3.00

NOTE: ***Neal Adams** r-1, 8, 14p. **Chaykin** r-3, 9(2pg.); c-3. **Drucker** r-6. **Glanzman** r-20. **Heath** r-5, 9-13, 16, 19, 21. **Krigstein** r-4, 8. **Kubert** r-1-17, 20, 21; c-1p, 2, 8, 14-21. **Miller** r-6p. **Severin** r-3, 6, 10. **Simonson** r-2, 4; c-4. **Thorne** r-7. **Toth** r-2, 8, 11. **Wood** r-4.*

SGT. ROCK SPECTACULAR (See DC Special Series #13)

SGT. ROCK'S PRIZE BATTLE TALES (Becomes Sgt. Rock Annual #2 on; see DC Special Series #18 & 80 Page Giant #7)
Winter, 1964 (One Shot) (Giant - 80 pgs.)
National Periodical Publications

	GD25	FN65	NM94
1-Kubert, Heath-r; new Kubert-c	10.00	30.00	60.00

SGT. STRYKER'S DEATH SQUAD (See Savage Combat Tales)

SERGIO ARAGONES' GROO THE WANDERER (See Groo...)

SEVEN BLOCK (Marvel) (Value: cover or less)

SEVEN DEAD MEN (See Complete Mystery #1)

SEVEN DWARFS (See 4-Color #227, 382)

SEVEN SAMUROID, THE (See Image Graphic Novel)

SEVEN SEAS COMICS
Apr, 1946 - No. 6, 1947 (no month)
Universal Phoenix Features/Leader No. 6

	GD25	FN65	NM94
1-South Sea Girl by Matt Baker, Capt. Cutlass begin; Tugboat Tessie by Baker app.	38.00	115.00	265.00
2	34.00	100.00	235.00
3-6: 3-Six pg. Feldstein-a	29.00	85.00	200.00

NOTE: ***Baker** a-1-6; c-3-6.*

1776 (See Charlton Classic Library)

7TH VOYAGE OF SINBAD, THE (See 4-Color #944)

77 SUNSET STRIP (TV)
No. 1066, 1-3/60 - No. 2, 2/63 (All photo-c)
Dell Publ. Co./Gold Key

	GD25	FN65	NM94
4-Color 1066-Toth-a	11.00	32.00	75.00
4-Color 1106,1159-Toth-a	9.15	27.50	55.00
4-Color 1211,1263,1291, 01-742-209(7-9/62)-Manning-a in all	8.35	25.00	50.00
1(11/62-G.K.), 2-Manning-a in each	8.35	25.00	50.00

77TH BENGAL LANCERS, THE (See 4-Color #791)

SEX, LIES AND MUTUAL FUNDS OF THE YUPPIES FROM HELL (Marvel) (Value: cover or less) (Also see Yuppies From Hell)

SEYMOUR, MY SON (See More Seymour)
September, 1963
Archie Publications (Radio Comics)

	GD25	FN65	NM94
1	4.00	11.00	22.00

SHADE, THE CHANGING MAN (See Cancelled Comic Cavalcade)
June-July, 1977 - No. 8, Aug-Sept, 1978 (Also see Suicide Squad #16)
National Periodical Publications/DC Comics

	GD25	FN65	NM94
1-Ditko-c/a in all	.80	2.00	4.00
2-8	.50	1.25	2.50

SHADE, THE CHANGING MAN (2nd series)
July, 1990 - Present ($1.50/$1.75, color, mature readers)
DC Comics

	GD25	FN65	NM94
1-($2.50, 52 pgs.)	.50	1.25	2.50
2-16: 6-Preview of World Without End	.35	.90	1.75
17-36: 17-Begin $1.75-c. 33-Metallic ink on-c	.35	.90	1.75

SHADO: SONG OF THE DRAGON (See Green Arrow #63-66)
1992 - No. 4, 1992 ($4.95, color, mini-series, 52 pgs.)
DC Comics

	GD25	FN65	NM94
Book One - Four: Grell scripts; Morrow-a(i)	1.00	2.50	5.00

SHADOW, THE
Aug, 1964 - No. 8, Sept, 1965 (All 12 cents)
Archie Comics (Radio Comics)

	GD25	FN65	NM94
1	4.20	12.50	25.00
2-8: 3,4,6,7-The Fly 1 pg. strips. 7-Shield app.	3.20	8.00	16.00

SHADOW, THE
Oct-Nov, 1973 - No. 12, Aug-Sept, 1975
National Periodical Publications

	GD25	FN65	NM94
1-Kaluta-a begins	4.00	12.00	24.00
2	2.80	7.00	14.00
3-Kaluta/Wrightson-a	3.80	9.50	19.00
4,6-Kaluta-a ends. 4-Chaykin, Wrightson part-i	2.40	6.00	12.00
5,7-12: 11-The Avenger (pulp character) x-over	1.60	4.00	8.00

NOTE: ***Craig** a-10. **Cruz** a-10-12. **Kaluta** a-1, 2, 3p, 4, 6; c-1-4, 6, 10-12. **Kubert** c-9. **Robbins** a-5, 7-9; c-5, 7, 8.*

SHADOW, THE (DC, 1986 & 1987 editions) (Value: cover or less)

SHADOW COMICS (Pulp, radio)
March, 1940 - V9#5, Aug, 1949
Street & Smith Publications
NOTE: *The Shadow first appeared on radio in 1929 and was featured in pulps beginning in 1931. The early covers of this series were reprinted from the pulp covers.*

	GD25	FN65	NM94
V1#1-Shadow, Doc Savage, Bill Barnes, Nick Carter, Frank Merriwell, Iron Munro, the Astonishing Man begin	267.00	800.00	1600.00
2-The Avenger begins, ends #6; Capt. Fury only app.	100.00	300.00	600.00
3(nn-5/40)-Norgil the Magician app.; cover is exact swipe of Shadow pulp from 1/33	83.00	250.00	500.00
4,5: 4-The Three Musketeers begins, ends #8. 5-Doc Savage ends	67.00	200.00	400.00
6,8,9: 9-Norgil the Magician app.	55.00	165.00	330.00
7-Origin & 1st app. The Hooded Wasp & Wasplet; series ends V3#8	62.00	188.00	375.00
10-Origin The Iron Ghost, ends #11; The Dead End Kids begins, ends #14	55.00	165.00	330.00
11-Origin Hooded Wasp & Wasplet retold	55.00	165.00	330.00
12-Dead End Kids app.	47.00	140.00	280.00
V2#1,2(11/41): 2-Dead End Kids story	36.00	125.00	250.00
3-Origin & 1st app. Supersnipe; series begins; Little Nemo story	55.00	165.00	330.00
4,5: 4-Little Nemo story	40.00	120.00	240.00
6-9: 6-Blackstone the Magician app.	37.00	110.00	220.00
10-12: 10-Supersnipe app.	37.00	110.00	220.00
V3#1-12: 10-Doc Savage begins, not in V5#5, V6#10-12, V8#4	33.00	100.00	200.00
V4#1-12	30.00	90.00	180.00
V5#1-12	27.00	82.00	165.00
V6#1-11: 9-Intro. Shadow, Jr.	25.00	75.00	150.00
12-Powell-c/a; atom bomb panels	27.00	82.00	165.00
V7#1,2,5,7-9,12: 2,5-Shadow, Jr. app.; Powell-a	27.00	82.00	165.00
3,6,11-Powell-c/a	29.00	88.00	175.00
4-Powell-c/a; Atom bomb panels	33.00	100.00	200.00
10(1/48)-Flying Saucer issue; Powell-c/a (2nd of this theme; see The Spirit 9/28/47)	37.00	110.00	220.00
V8#1-12-Powell-a. 8-Powell Spider-c/a	29.00	88.00	175.00

V9#1,5-Powell-a 27.00 82.00 165.00
2-4-Powell-c/a 29.00 88.00 175.00
NOTE: ***Powell** art in most issues beginning V6#12.*

SHADOWHAWK (See Youngblood #2)
Aug, 1992 - No. 4, 1992 ($1.95, color, mini-series)
Image Comics

1-($2.50)-Embossed silver foil stamped-c; Valentino/Liefeld-c; Valentino-c/a/ scripts in all; has coupon for Image #0 3.00 7.50 15.00
1-With coupon missing .80 2.00 4.00
1-($1.95)-Newsstand version w/o foil stamp .80 2.00 4.00
2-Shadowhawk poster w/McFarlane-i; brief Spawn app.; wraparound-c w/silver ink highlights .70 1.75 3.50
3,4: 4-Savage Dragon app. .40 1.00 2.00

SHADOWLINE SAGA: CRITICAL MASS, A (Marvel) (Value: cover or less)

SHADOWMAN
May, 1992 - Present ($2.50, color)
Valiant

1 4.00 11.00 22.00
2 1.60 4.00 8.00
3 1.20 3.00 6.00
4,5 1.00 2.50 5.00
6-10 .60 1.50 3.00
11-14 .50 1.25 2.50

SHADOWMASTERS (Marvel) (Value: cover or less)

SHADOW OF THE BATMAN
Dec, 1985 - No. 5, Apr, 1986 ($1.75, mini-series)
DC Comics

1-Detective-r (all have wraparound-c) 1.20 3.00 6.00
2,3,5: 3-Penguin-c & cameo. 5-Clayface app. .70 1.75 3.50
4-Joker-c/story 1.00 2.50 5.00
NOTE: ***Austin** a(new)-2i, 3i; r-2-4i. **Rogers** a(new)-1, 2p, 3p, 4, 5; r-1-5p; c-1-5.*

SHADOW OF THE TORTURER, THE (Innovation) (Value: cover or less)

SHADOW PLAY (Whitman) (Value: cover or less)

SHADOW RIDERS
Feb, 1993 - No. 4, May, 1993 ($1.75, color, mini-series)
Marvel Comics UK, Ltd.

1-4: 1-Cable & Ghost Rider app. .35 .90 1.75

SHADOWS FROM BEYOND (Formerly Unusual Tales)
V2#50, October, 1966
Charlton Comics

V2#50-Ditko-c 1.20 3.00 6.00

SHADOW STRIKES!, THE (DC) (Value: cover or less)

SHADOW WAR OF HAWKMAN (DC) (Value: cover or less)

SHAGGY DOG & THE ABSENT-MINDED PROFESSOR (See 4-Color #985, Movie Comics & Walt Disney Showcase #46)

SHANNA, THE SHE-DEVIL (See Savage Tales #8)
Dec, 1972 - No. 5, Aug, 1973 (All are 20 cent issues)
Marvel Comics Group

1-1st app. Shanna; Steranko-c; Tuska-a(p) 1.20 3.00 6.00
2-Steranko-c; heroin drug story .80 2.00 4.00
3-5 .40 1.00 2.00

SHARK FIGHTERS, THE (See 4-Color No. 762)

SHARP COMICS (Slightly large size)
Winter, 1945-46 - V1#2, Spring, 1946 (52 pgs.)
H. C. Blackerby

V1#1-Origin Dick Royce Planetarian 26.00 78.00 155.00
2-Origin The Pioneer; Michael Morgan, Dick Royce, Sir Gallagher, Planetarian, Steve Hagen, Weeny and Pop app. 22.00 65.00 130.00

SHARPY FOX (See Comic Capers & Funny Frolics)
1958; 1963
I. W. Enterprises/Super Comics

1,2-I.W. Reprint (1958) .80 2.00 4.00
14-Super Reprint (1963) .80 2.00 4.00

SHATTER (First, all issues) (Value: cover or less)

SHAZAM (See Giant Comics to Color & Limited Collectors' Edition)

SHAZAM! (TV) (See World's Finest #253)
Feb, 1973 - No. 35, May-June, 1978
National Periodical Publications/DC Comics

1-1st revival of original Captain Marvel since G.A. (origin retold), by Beck; Capt. Marvel Jr. & Mary Marvel x-over .60 1.50 3.00
2-35: 2,6-Infinity photo-c; re-intro Mr. Mind & Tawney. 4-Origin retold. 5-Capt. Marvel Jr. origin retold. 8-(100 pgs.)-r/Capt. Marvel Jr. by Raboy; origin/C.M. #80; origin Mary Marvel/C.M. #18; origin Mr. Tawny/C.M. #79. 10-Last C.C. Beck issue. 11-Shaffenberger-a begins. 12-17-(All 100 pgs.). 15-Lex Luthor x-over. 25-1st app. Isis. 30-1st DC app. 3 Lt. Marvels. 31-1st DC app. Minuteman. 34-Origin Capt. Nazi & Capt. Marvel Jr. retold .30 .75 1.50
NOTE: *Reprints in #1-8, 10, 12-17, 21-24. **Beck** a-1-10, 12-17r, 21-24r; c-1, 3-9. **Nasser** c-35p. **Newton** a-35p. **Raboy** a-5r, 8r, 17r. **Shaffenberger** a-11, 14-20, 25, 26, 27p, 28, 29-31p, 33i, 35i; c-20, 22, 23, 25, 26i, 27i, 28-33.*

SHAZAM: THE NEW BEGINNING
Apr, 1987 - No. 4, July, 1987 (Mini-series; Legends spin-off)
DC Comics

1-New origin Captain Marvel; Marvel Family cameo .50 1.00
2-4: Sivana & Black Adam app. .50 1.00

SHEA THEATRE COMICS (Also see Theatre Comics)
No date (1940's) (32 pgs.)
Shea Theatre

nn-Contains Rocket Comics; MLJ cover in mono color 5.70 17.00 40.00

SHEENA (Marvel) (Value: cover or less)

SHEENA, QUEEN OF THE JUNGLE (See Jerry Iger's Classic..., Jumbo Comics, & 3-D Sheena)
Spring, 1942; No. 2, Wint, 1942-43; No. 3, Spring, 1943; No. 4, Fall, 1948; No. 5, Sum, 1949; No. 6, Spring, 1950; No. 7-10, 1950(nd); No. 11, Spring, 1951 - No. 18, Winter, 1952-53 (#1,2: 68 pgs.)
Fiction House Magazines

1-Sheena begins 150.00 450.00 900.00
2 (Winter, 1942/43) 79.00 238.00 475.00
3 (Spring, 1943) 54.00 162.00 325.00
4, 5 (Fall, 1948 - Sum., '49) 33.00 100.00 200.00
6,7 (Spring, 50 - 1950, 52 pgs.) 29.00 88.00 175.00
8-10('50, 36 pgs.) 25.00 75.00 150.00
11-18: 18-Used in **POP**, pg. 98 22.00 65.00 130.00
I.W. Reprint #9-r/#18; c-r/White Princess #3 4.00 12.00 24.00
NOTE: ***Baker** c-5-10? **Whitman** c-11-18(most).*

SHEENA 3-D (Eclipse) (Value: cover or less)

SHE-HULK (See The Savage She-Hulk & The Sensational She-Hulk)

SHERIFF BOB DIXON'S CHUCK WAGON (TV)
November, 1950 (See Wild Bill Hickok #22)
Avon Periodicals

1-Kinstler-c/a(3) 9.15 27.50 55.00

SHERIFF OF COCHISE, THE
1957 (16 pages) (TV Show)
Mobil Giveaway

nn-Shaffenberger-a 2.40 6.00 12.00

SHERIFF OF TOMBSTONE
Nov, 1958 - No. 17, Sept, 1961

Shadow of the Batman #4, © DC

Shazam! #1, © DC

Sheena, Queen of the Jungle #9, © FH

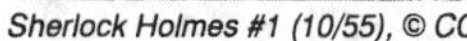
Sherlock Holmes #1 (10/55), © CC

Shield Wizard Comics #1, © AP

Shock SuspenStories #11, © WMG

GD25 FN65 NM94

Charlton Comics
V1#1-Williamson/Severin-c; Severin-a 6.70 20.00 40.00
2 4.00 11.00 22.00
3-17 2.80 7.00 14.00

SHERLOCK HOLMES (See 4-Color #1169,1245, Marvel Preview & Spectacular Stories)

SHERLOCK HOLMES (All New Baffling Adventures of...)
Oct, 1955 - No. 2, Mar, 1956 (Young Eagle #3 on?)
Charlton Comics
1-Dr. Neff, Ghost Breaker app. 29.00 85.00 200.00
2 25.00 75.00 175.00

SHERLOCK HOLMES (Also see The Joker)
Sept-Oct, 1975
National Periodical Publications
1-Cruz-a; Simonson-c .30 .75 1.50

SHERRY THE SHOWGIRL (Showgirls #4)
July, 1956 - No. 3, Dec, 1956; No. 5, Apr, 1957 - No. 7, Aug, 1957
Atlas Comics
1-Dan DeCarlo-a in all 7.50 22.50 45.00
2 5.00 15.00 30.00
3,5-7 4.00 11.00 22.00

SHIELD (Nick Fury & His Agents of...) (Also see Nick Fury)
Feb, 1973 - No. 5, Oct, 1973 (All 20 cents)
Marvel Comics Group
1-Steranko-c .90 2.25 4.50
2-5: 2-Steranko flag-c. 1-5 all contain-r from Str. Tales #146-155. 3-5-are cover-r; 3-Kirby/Steranko-c(r). 4-Steranko-c(r) .40 1.00 2.00
NOTE: ***Buscema** a-3p(r). **Kirby** layouts 1-5; c-3 (w/**Steranko**). **Steranko** a-3r, 4r(2).*

SHIELD, THE (Becomes Shield-Steel Sterling #3; #1 titled Lancelot Strong; also see Advs. of the Fly, Double Life of Private Strong, Fly Man, Mighty Comics, The Mighty Crusaders & The Original...)
June, 1983 - No. 2, Aug, 1983
Archie Enterprises, Inc.
1,2: Steel Sterling app. .50 1.00

SHIELD-STEEL STERLING (Formerly The Shield)
No. 3, Dec, 1983 (Becomes Steel Sterling No. 4)
Archie Enterprises, Inc.
3-Nino-a .50 1.00

SHIELD WIZARD COMICS (Also see Pep Comics & Top-Notch Comics)
Summer, 1940 - No. 13, Spring, 1944
MLJ Magazines
1-(V1#5 on inside)-Origin The Shield by Irving Novick & The Wizard by Ed Ashe, Jr; Flag-c 171.00 515.00 1200.00
2-Origin The Shield retold; intro. Wizard's sidekick, Roy 87.00 262.00 525.00
3,4 62.00 188.00 375.00
5-Dusty, the Boy Detective begins 58.00 175.00 350.00
6-8: 6-Roy the Super Boy begins 50.00 150.00 300.00
9-13: 13-Bondage-c 46.00 138.00 275.00
NOTE: ***Bob Montana** c-13. **Novick** c-1-11. **Harry Sahle** c-12.*

SHIP AHOY
November, 1944 (52 pgs.)
Spotlight Publishers
1-L. B. Cole-c 8.35 25.00 50.00

SHIPWRECKED! (Disney) (Value: cover or less)

SHMOO (See Al Capp's... & Washable Jones &...)

SHOCK (Magazine)
(Reprints from horror comics) (Black & White)
May, 1969 - V3#4, Sept, 1971

GD25 FN65 NM94

Stanley Publications
V1#1-Cover-r/Weird Tales of the Future #7 by Bernard Baily 4.00 10.00 20.00
2-Wolverton-r/Weird Mysteries 5; r-Weird Mysteries #7 used in **SOTI**; cover r/Weird Chills #1 3.00 7.50 15.00
3,5,6 2.00 5.00 10.00
4-Harrison/Williamson-r/Forbid. Worlds #6 2.40 6.00 12.00
V2#2, V1#8, V2#4-6, V3#1-4 2.00 5.00 10.00
NOTE: ***Disbrow** r-V2#4; Bondage c-V1#4, V2#6, V3#1.*

SHOCK DETECTIVE CASES (Formerly Crime Fighting Detective)
(Becomes Spook Detective Cases No. 22)
No. 20, Sept, 1952 - No. 21, Nov, 1952
Star Publications
20,21-L.B. Cole-c 7.50 22.50 45.00
NOTE: ***Palais** a-20. No. 21-Fox-r.*

SHOCK ILLUSTRATED (Magazine format)
Sept-Oct, 1955 - No. 3, Spring, 1956 (Adult Entertainment on-c #1,2)
E. C. Comics
1-All by Kamen; drugs, prostitution, wife swapping 3.50 10.50 24.00
2-Williamson-a redrawn from Crime SuspenStories #13 plus Ingels, Crandall, & Evans 4.00 12.00 28.00
3-Only 100 known copies bound & given away at E.C. office; Crandall, Evans-a 100.00 300.00 700.00
(Prices vary widely on this book)

SHOCKING MYSTERY CASES (Formerly Thrilling Crime Cases)
No. 50, Sept, 1952 - No. 60, Oct, 1954
Star Publications
50-Disbrow "Frankenstein" story 16.00 48.00 110.00
51-Disbrow-a 9.15 27.50 55.00
52-55,57-60 7.50 22.50 45.00
56-Drug use story 8.35 25.00 50.00
NOTE: ***L. B. Cole** covers on all; a-60(2 pgs.). **Hollingsworth** a-52. **Morisi** a-55.*

SHOCKING TALES DIGEST MAGAZINE
Oct, 1981 (95 cents)
Harvey Publications
1-1957-58-r; Powell, Kirby, Nostrand-a .40 1.00 2.00

SHOCK SUSPENSTORIES
Feb-Mar, 1952 - No. 18, Dec-Jan, 1954-55
E. C. Comics
1-Classic Feldstein electrocution-c; Ray Bradbury adaptation 57.00 170.00 400.00
2 34.00 100.00 235.00
3 23.00 70.00 160.00
4-Used in **SOTI**, pg. 387,388 23.00 70.00 160.00
5-Hanging-c 22.00 65.00 150.00
6,7: 6-Classic bondage-c. 7-Classic face melting-c 27.00 81.00 190.00
8-Williamson-a 23.00 70.00 160.00
9-11: 9-Injury to eye panel. 10-Junkie story 19.00 57.00 130.00
12-"The Monkey"-classic junkie cover/story; anti-drug propaganda issue 22.00 65.00 155.00
13-Frazetta's only solo story for E.C., 7 pgs. 27.00 81.00 190.00
14-Used in Senate Investigation hearings 14.00 43.00 100.00
15-Used in 1954 Reader's Digest article, "For the Kiddies to Read;" Bill Gaines stars in prose story "The EC Caper" 14.00 43.00 100.00
16-"Red Dupe" editorial; rape story 13.00 40.00 90.00
17,18 13.00 40.00 90.00
NOTE: ***Ray Bradbury** adaptations-1, 7, 9. **Craig** a-11; c-11. **Crandall** a-9-13, 15-18. **Davis** a-1-5. **Evans** a-7, 8, 14-18; c-16-18. **Feldstein** c-1, 7-9, 12. **Ingels** a-1, 2, 6. **Kamen** a-in all; c-10. **Krigstein** a-14, 18. **Orlando** a-1, 3-7, 9, 10, 12, 16, 17. **Wood** a-2-15; c-2-6, 14.*

SHOCK SUSPENSTORIES

	GD25	FN65	NM94
Sept, 1992 - Present ($1.50, color, quarterly)			
Russ Cochran			
1,2-r/#1,2 above. 1-Feldstein-c. 2-Wood-c	.30	.75	1.50

SHOGUN WARRIORS
Feb, 1979 - No. 20, Sept, 1980 (Based on Mattel toys)
Marvel Comics Group

	GD25	FN65	NM94
1-Raydeen, Combatra, & Dangard Ace begin	.60	1.50	3.00
2-10	.40	1.00	2.00
11-20: 11-Austin-c. 12-Simonson-c	.30	.75	1.50

SHOOK UP (Magazine) (Satire)
November, 1958
Dodsworth Publ. Co.

	GD25	FN65	NM94
V1#1	2.80	7.00	14.00

SHORT RIBS (See 4-Color #1333)

SHORT STORY COMICS (See Hello Pal,...)

SHORTY SHINER
June, 1956 - No. 3, Oct, 1956
Dandy Magazine (Charles Biro)

	GD25	FN65	NM94
1	4.00	10.00	20.00
2,3	2.80	7.00	14.00

SHOTGUN SLADE (See 4-Color #1111)

SHOWCASE (See Cancelled Comic Cavalcade & New Talent...)
3-4/56 - No. 93, 9/70; No. 94, 8-9/77 - No. 104, 9/78
National Periodical Publications/DC Comics

	GD25	FN65	NM94
1-Fire Fighters	215.00	645.00	1500.00
2-King of the Wild; Kubert-a (animal stories)	72.00	215.00	500.00
3-The Frogmen by Russ Heath	68.00	205.00	475.00
4-Origin/1st app. The Flash (1st DC Silver Age hero, Sept-Oct, 1956) & The Turtle; Kubert-a; r/in Secret Origins #1 ('61 & '73); Flash shown reading G.A. Flash #13	1175.00	3525.00	9400.00
5-Manhunters	85.00	260.00	600.00
6-Origin/1st app. Challengers of the Unknown by Kirby, partly r/in Secret Origins #1 & Challengers #64,65 (1st Silver Age super-hero team & 1st original concept S.A. series)	215.00	645.00	1500.00
7-Challengers of the Unknown by Kirby reprinted in Challengers of the Unknown #75	107.00	320.00	750.00
8-The Flash; (2nd app.) origin & 1st app. Capt. Cold	475.00	1425.00	3800.00
9-Lois Lane (Pre-#1, 7-8/57) (1st Showcase character to win own series)	200.00	600.00	1400.00
10-Lois Lane; Jor-el cameo	143.00	430.00	1000.00
11,12-Challengers of the Unknown by Kirby	90.00	270.00	625.00
13-The Flash; origin Mr. Element	230.00	685.00	1600.00
14-The Flash; origin Dr. Alchemy, former Mr. Element	230.00	685.00	1600.00
15-Space Ranger (1st app., 7-8/58)	93.00	280.00	650.00
16-Space Ranger	54.00	160.00	375.00
17-Adventures on Other Worlds; origin/1st app. Adam Strange (11-12/58)	135.00	407.00	950.00
18-Adventures on Other Worlds (A. Strange)	68.00	205.00	475.00
19-Adam Strange; 1st Adam Strange logo	68.00	205.00	475.00
20-Origin & 1st app. Rip Hunter (5-6/59); Moriera-a	64.00	195.00	450.00
21-Rip Hunter; Sekowsky-c/a	29.00	85.00	200.00
22-Origin & 1st app. Silver Age Green Lantern by Gil Kane (9-10/59); reprinted in Secret Origins #2	320.00	960.00	2250.00
23,24-Green Lantern. 23-Nuclear explosion-c	115.00	345.00	800.00
25,26-Rip Hunter by Kubert	22.00	65.00	150.00
27-1st app. Sea Devils (7-8/60); Heath-c/a	61.00	182.00	425.00
28,29-Sea Devils; Heath-c/a	32.00	95.00	220.00
30-Origin Silver Age Aquaman (1-2/61) (see Adventure #260 for 1st S.A. origin)	54.00	160.00	375.00
31-33-Aquaman	26.00	78.00	180.00
34-Origin & 1st app. Silver Age Atom by Kane & Anderson (9-10/61); reprinted in Secret Origins #2	122.00	365.00	850.00
35-The Atom by Gil Kane; last 10 cent issue	68.00	205.00	475.00
36-The Atom by Gil Kane (1-2/62)	50.00	150.00	350.00
37-1st app. Metal Men (3-4/62)	50.00	150.00	350.00
38-40-Metal Men	29.00	85.00	200.00
41,42-Tommy Tomorrow (parts 1&2). 42-Origin	10.00	30.00	65.00
43-Dr. No (James Bond); Nodel-a; originally published as British Classics Illustrated #158A, and as #6 in a European Detective series, all with a diff. painted-c. This Showcase #43 version is actually censored, deleting all racial skin color, and dialogue thought to be racially demeaning (1st DC Silver Age movie adaptation)(based on Ian Fleming novel & movie)	43.00	130.00	300.00
44-Tommy Tomorrow	7.50	22.50	45.00
45-Sgt. Rock; origin retold; Heath-c	13.50	41.00	95.00
46,47-Tommy Tomorrow	5.35	16.00	32.00
48,49-Cave Carson	4.00	11.00	22.00
50,51-I Spy (Danger Trail-r by Infantino), King Farady story (#50 has new 4 pg. story)	4.70	14.00	28.00
52-Cave Carson	4.00	11.00	22.00
53,54-G.I. Joe; Heath-a	5.00	15.00	30.00
55-Dr. Fate & Hourman. (3-4/65)-Origin of each in text; 1st solo app. G.A. Green Lantern in Silver Age (pre-dates Gr. Lantern #40); 1st S.A. app. Solomon Grundy	18.00	54.00	125.00
56-Dr. Fate & Hourman	6.70	20.00	40.00
57-Enemy Ace by Kubert (4th app. after Our Army at War #155)	8.35	25.00	50.00
58-Enemy Ace by Kubert (5th app.)	8.35	25.00	50.00
59-Teen Titans (3rd app., 11-12/65)	10.00	30.00	65.00
60-1st Silver Age app. The Spectre; Anderson-a (1-2/66); origin in text	18.00	54.00	125.00
61,64-The Spectre by Anderson	10.00	30.00	60.00
62-Origin & 1st app. Inferior Five (5-6/66)	7.50	22.50	45.00
63,65-Inferior Five	4.00	11.00	22.00
66,67-B'wana Beast	2.00	5.00	10.00
68,69,71-Maniaks	2.00	5.00	10.00
70-Binky (9-10/67)-Tryout issue	2.00	5.00	10.00
72-Top Gun (Johnny Thunder-r)-Toth-a	2.00	5.00	10.00
73-Origin/1st app. Creeper; Ditko-c/a (3-4/67)	9.15	27.50	55.00
74-Intro/1st app. Anthro; Post-c/a (5-6/67)	7.00	21.00	42.00
75-Origin/1st app. Hawk & the Dove; Ditko-c/a	10.00	30.00	60.00
76-1st app. Bat Lash (9-10/67)	4.70	14.00	28.00
77-1st app. Angel & The Ape	5.00	15.00	30.00
78-Jonny Double	2.60	6.50	13.00
79-Dolphin; Aqualad origin-r	4.00	11.00	22.00
80-Phantom Stranger-r; Neal Adams-c	2.00	5.00	10.00
81-Windy & Willy	1.40	3.50	7.00
82-1st app. Nightmaster by Grandenetti & Giordano; Kubert-c	5.85	17.50	35.00
83,84-Nightmaster by Wrightson w/Jones/Kaluta ink assist in each; Kubert-c. 84-Origin retold; last 12 cent-c?	5.85	17.50	35.00
85-87-Firehair; Kubert-a	1.80	4.50	9.00
88-90-Jason's Quest: 90-Manhunter 2070 app.	.90	2.25	4.50
91-93-Manhunter 2070; origin-92	.90	2.25	4.50
94-Intro/origin new Doom Patrol & Robotman	1.30	3.25	6.50
95,96-The Doom Patrol. 95-Origin Celsius	.70	1.75	3.50
97-99-Power Girl; origin-97,98; JSA cameos	.70	1.75	3.50
100-(52 pgs.)-Most Showcase characters featured	.70	1.75	3.50
101-103-Hawkman; Adam Strange x-over	.70	1.75	3.50
104-(52 pgs.)-O.S.S. Spies at War	.70	1.75	3.50

NOTE: ***Anderson** a-22-24i, 34-36i, 55, 56, 60, 61, 64, 101-103i; c-50i, 51i, 55, 56, 60, 61, 64. **Aparo** c-94-96. **Boring** c-10. **Estrada** a-104. **Fraden** c(p)-30, 31, 33. **Heath** c-3, 27-29. **Infantino** c/a(p)-4, 8, 13, 14; c-50p, 51p. **Gil Kane** a-22-24p, 34-36p; c-17-19, 22-24p(w/**Giella**), 31. **Kane/Anderson** c-34-36. **Kirby** c-11, 12. **Kirby/Stein** c-6, 7. **Kubert** a-2, 4i, 25, 26, 45, 53, 54, 72; c-25, 26, 53, 54, 57, 58, 82-87, 101-104; c-2, 4i. **Moriera** c-5. **Orlando** a-62p, 63p, 97i; c-62, 63, 97i. **Sekowsky** a-65p. **Sparling** a-78. **Staton** a-94, 95-*

Showcase #1, © DC

Showcase #19, © DC

Showcase #23, © DC

Silly Tunes #1, © MEG

Silver Streak Comics #2, © LEV

Silver Streak Comics #16, © LEV

	GD25	FN65	NM94

99p, 100; c-97-100p.

SHOWCASE '93
Jan, 1993 - No. 12, 1993 ($1.95, color, limited series)
DC Comics

1-4: 1-Begin 4 part Catwoman story & 6 part Blue Devil story; begin Cyborg story; Art Adams/Austin-c. 2-Maguire/Austin-c. Flash by Travis Charest (p) begins; Bolland-c .40 1.00 2.00

SHOWGIRLS (Formerly Sherry the Showgirl #3)
No. 4, 2/57; June, 1957 - No. 2, Aug, 1957
Atlas Comics (MPC No. 2)

4-Dan DeCarlo-a 5.00 15.00 30.00
1-Millie, Sherry, Chili, Pearl & Hazel begin 7.00 21.00 42.00
2 5.00 15.00 30.00

SHROUD OF MYSTERY (Whitman) (Value: cover or less)

SICK (Sick Special #131) (Magazine) (Satire)
Aug, 1960 - No. 131, Feb, 1980
Feature Publ./Headline Publ./Crestwood Publ. Co./Hewfred Publ./
Pyramid Comm./Charlton Publ. No. 109 (4/76) on

V1#1-Jack Paar photo on-c; Torres-a 12.00 36.00 85.00
2-5-Torres-a in all 7.50 22.50 45.00
6 5.00 15.00 30.00
V2#1-8(#7-14) 4.20 12.50 25.00
V3#1-8(#15-22) 3.60 9.00 18.00
V4#1-5(#23-27) 3.00 7.50 15.00
28-32,34-40 2.00 5.00 10.00
33-Ringo Starr photo-c & spoof on "A Hard Day's Night;" inside-c has Beatles photos 3.60 9.00 18.00
41-131: 45 has #44 on-c & #45 on inside. 70-John & Yoko-c. 128-Superman-c/movie parody. 131-Superman parody 1.20 3.00 6.00
Annual 1969, 1970, 1971 3.00 7.50 15.00
Annual 2-4(1980) 1.40 3.50 7.00
Big Sick Laff-in (1968)-w/psychedelic posters 3.60 9.00 18.00
Birthday Annual (1967)-3pg. Huckleberry Fink fold out 3.60 9.00 18.00
7th Annual Yearbook (1967)-Davis-c, 2pg. glossy poster insert 3.60 9.00 18.00
Special 2 (1978) 1.00 2.50 5.00
Yearbook 14(1974), 15(1975)-84pgs. 1.20 3.00 6.00

*NOTE: **Davis** a-42, 87; c-31, 32. **Powell** a-7, 31, 57. **Simon** a-1-3, 10, 41, 42, 87, 99; c-1, 47, 57, 59, 69, 91, 95-97, 99, 100, 102, 107, 112. **Torres** a-1-3, 31, 47, 49. **Tuska** a-14, 41-43. Civil War Blackouts-23, 24. #42 has biography of Bob Powell.*

SIDESHOW
1949 (One Shot)
Avon Periodicals

1-(Rare)-Similar to Bachelor's Diary 18.00 54.00 125.00

SIEGEL AND SHUSTER: DATELINE 1930s (Eclipse) (Value: cover or less)

SILENT INVASION, THE (Renegade) (Value: cover or less)

SILENT MOBIUS (Viz) (Value: cover or less)

SILK HAT HARRY'S DIVORCE SUIT
1912 (5-3/4x15-1/2") (B&W)
M. A. Donoghue & Co.

Newspaper reprints by Tad (Thomas Dorgan) 12.00 36.00 85.00

SILLY PILLY (See Frank Luther's...)

SILLY SYMPHONIES (See Dell Giants)

SILLY TUNES
Fall, 1945 - No. 7, June, 1947
Timely Comics

1-Silly Seal, Ziggy Pig begin 11.00 32.00 75.00
2 6.70 20.00 40.00

	GD25	FN65	NM94

3-7 5.00 15.00 30.00

SILVER (See Lone Ranger's Famous Horse...)

SILVERBACK (Comico) (Value: cover or less)

SILVERBLADE (DC) (Value: cover or less)

SILVERHAWKS (Marvel) (Value: cover or less)

SILVERHEELS (Pacific) (Value: cover or less)

SILVER KID WESTERN
Oct, 1954 - No. 5, 1955
Key/Stanmor Publications

1 5.85 17.50 35.00
2 3.60 9.00 18.00
3-5 3.20 8.00 16.00
I.W. Reprint #1,2-Severin-c: 1-r/#? 2-r/#1 .80 2.00 4.00

SILVER SABLE AND THE WILD PACK (See Amazing Spider-Man #265)
June, 1992 - Present ($1.25, color)
Marvel Comics

1-($2.00)-Silver embossed & foil stamped-c; Spider-Man app. .60 1.50 3.00
2-4: 4,5-Dr. Doom c/story .40 1.00 2.00
5-12: 6,7-Deathlok-c/story. 9-Origin Silver Sable .60 1.25

SILVER STAR (Pacific) (Value: cover or less)

SILVER STREAK COMICS (Crime Does Not Pay #22 on)
Dec, 1939 - No. 21, May, 1942; No. 22-24, 1946 (Silver logo-#1-5)
Your Guide Publs. No. 1-7/New Friday Publs. No. 8-17/Comic House Publ./Newsbook Publ.

GD25 FN65 VF82 NM94

1-(Scarce)-Intro The Claw by Cole (r-/in Daredevil #21), Red Reeves, Boy Magician, & Captain Fearless; The Wasp, Mister Midnight begin; Spirit Man app. Silver metallic-c begin, end #5 500.00 1500.00 2750.00 4000.00
(Estimated up to 100 total copies exist, 6 in NM/Mint)

GD25 FN65 NM94

2-The Claw by Cole; Simon-c/a 217.00 650.00 1300.00
3-1st app. & origin Silver Streak (2nd with lightning speed); Dickie Dean the Boy Inventor, Lance Hale, Ace Powers, Bill Wayne, & The Planet Patrol begin 183.00 550.00 1100.00
4-Sky Wolf begins; Silver Streak by Jack Cole (new costume); 1st app. Jackie, Lance Hale's sidekick 96.00 285.00 575.00
5-Jack Cole c/a(2) 117.00 350.00 700.00

GD25 FN65 VF82 NM94

6-(Scarce)-Origin & 1st app. Daredevil (blue & yellow costume) by Jack Binder; The Claw returns; classic Cole Claw-c 425.00 1275.00 2340.00 3400.00
7-Claw vs. Daredevil (new costume-blue & red) by Jack Cole & 3 other Cole stories (38 pgs.) 357.00 1070.00 1960.00 2500.00
(#6, 7-Estimated up to 120 total copies of each exist, 7-10 in NM/Mint)

GD25 FN65 NM94

8-Claw vs. Daredevil by Cole; last Cole Silver Streak 146.00 438.00 875.00
9-Claw vs. Daredevil by Cole 112.00 335.00 6750.00
10-Origin Captain Battle; Claw vs. Daredevil by Cole 100.00 300.00 600.00
11-Intro. Mercury by Bob Wood, Silver Streak's sidekick; conclusion Claw vs. Daredevil by Rico; in 'Presto Martin,' 2nd pg., newspaper says 'Roussos does it again' 71.00 210.00 425.00
12-14: 13-Origin Thun-Dohr 58.00 175.00 350.00
15-17-Last Daredevil issue. 16-Hitler-c 54.00 162.00 325.00
18-The Saint begins; by Leslie Charteris (see Movie Comics #2 by DC) 44.00 132.00 265.00
19-21(1942): 20,21 have Wolverton's Scoop Scuttle 30.00 90.00 180.00

22,24(1946)-Reprints 18.00 55.00 110.00
23-Reprints?; bondage-c 18.00 55.00 110.00
nn(11/46)(Newsbook Publ.)-R-/S.S. story from #4-7 plus 2 Captain Fearless stories, all in color; bondage/torture-c 27.00 80.00 185.00

NOTE: **Binder** c-3, 4, 13-15, 17. **Jack Cole** a-(Daredevil)-#6-10, (Dickie Dean)-#3-10, (Pirate Prince)-#7, (Silver Streak)-#4-8, nn; c-5 (Silver Streak), 6-8 (Daredevil). **Everett** Red Reed begins #20. **Guardineer** a-#8-13. **Don Rico** a-11-17 (Daredevil); c-11, 12, 16. **Simon** a-3 (Silver Streak). **Bob Wood** a-9 (Silver Streak); c-9, 10. Claw c-#1, 2, 6-8.

SILVER SURFER (See Fantastic Four, Fantasy Masterpieces V2#1, Marvel Graphic Novel, Marvel Presents #8, Marvel's Greatest Comics & Tales To Astonish #92)

SILVER SURFER, THE
Aug, 1968 - No. 18, Sept, 1970; June, 1982 (No. 1-7: 25 cents, 68 pgs.)
Marvel Comics Group

1-More detailed origin by John Buscema (p); The Watcher back-up stories begin (origin), end #7 43.00 130.00 300.00
2 14.00 43.00 100.00
3-1st app. Mephisto 13.00 40.00 90.00
4-Low distribution; Thor & Loki app. 43.00 130.00 300.00
5-7-Last giant size. 5-The Stranger app. 6-Brunner inks. 7-1st app. Frankenstein's monster (cameo); Brunner-c 10.00 30.00 60.00
8-10: 8-18-(15 cent issues) 7.50 22.50 45.00
11-13,15-18: 15-Spider-Man vs. Human Torch; Fantastic Four app. 17-Nick Fury app. 18-Vs. The Inhumans; Kirby-c/a 5.85 17.50 35.00
14-Spider-Man x-over 9.15 27.50 55.00
V2#1 (6/82, 52 pgs.)-Byrne-c/a 1.60 4.00 8.00

NOTE: **Adkins** a-8-15i. **Brunner** a-6i; c-7. **J. Buscema** a-1-17p. **Colan** a-1-3p. **Reinman** a-1-4i. #1-14 were reprinted in Fantasy Masterpieces V2#1-14.

SILVER SURFER (See Marvel Graphic Novel #38)
V3#1, July, 1987 - Present
Marvel Comics Group

V3#1-Double size ($1.25) 2.00 5.00 10.00
2 .80 2.00 4.00
3-10 .50 1.25 2.50
11-14 .40 1.00 2.00
15-Ron Lim-c/a begins (9/88) 2.00 5.00 10.00
16,17 1.20 3.00 6.00
18-20 .80 2.00 4.00
21-24,26-30,33,40-43,48: 37-Drax-c & 1st full app. 39-Alan Grant scripts. 48,50-Last Starlin scripts .40 1.00 2.00
25,31 ($1.50, 52 pgs.): 25-Skrulls app. .50 1.25 2.50
32,39-No Ron Lim-c/a .30 .75 1.50
34-Thanos returns (cameo); Starlin scripts begin 2.40 6.00 12.00
35-1st full Thanos app. in Silver Surfer; reintro Drax the Destroyer on last pg. (cameo) 2.80 7.00 14.00
36-Recaps history of Thanos; Capt. Marvel & Warlock app. in recap 1.40 3.50 7.00
37-1st full app. Drax the Destroyer; Drax-c 1.00 2.50 5.00
38-Silver Surfer battles Thanos 1.35 4.00 8.00
44,45,49-Thanos stories (c-44,45) .50 1.50 3.00
46,47-Return of Adam Warlock. 46-Reintro Gamora & Pip the Troll. 47-Warlock battles Drax 1.60 4.00 8.00
50-($1.50, 52 pgs.)-Silver Surfer battles Thanos; story cont'd in Infinity Gauntlet #1; embossed & silver foil stamped-c; thick cover stock 1.80 4.50 9.00
50-2nd printing .60 1.50 3.00
51-53: Infinity Gauntlet x-over .60 1.50 3.00
54-57: Infinity Gauntlet x-overs. 54-Rhino app. 55,56-Thanos-c & app. 57-Thanos-c & cameo .50 1.25 2.50
58,59-Infinity Guantlet x-overs; 58-Ron Lim-c only. 59-Thanos battles Silver Surfer-c/story; Thanos joins .80 2.00 4.00
60-66: 61-Last $1.00-c. 63-Capt. Marvel app. .30 .75 1.50
67-69-Infinity War x-overs .40 1.00 2.00
70-74,76-80 .60 1.25
75-($2.50, 52 pgs.)-Foil embossed-c; Lim-c/a .70 1.75 3.50
Annual 1 (1988, $1.75)-Evolutionary War app.; 1st Ron Lim-a on Silver Surfer (20 pg. back-up story & pin-ups) 1.40 3.50 7.00
Annual 2 (1989, $2.00, 68 pgs.)-Atlantis Attacks .50 1.25 2.50
Annual 3 (1990, $2.00, 68 pgs.) .50 1.25 2.50
Annual 4 (1991, $2.00, 68 pgs.)-3 pg. origin story; Silver Surfer battles the Guardians of the Galaxy .50 1.25 2.50
Annual 5 (1992, $2.25, 68 pgs.)-Return of the Defenders, part 3; Lim-c/a (3 pgs. of pin-ups only) .50 1.25 2.50
...: The First Coming of Galactus nn (1993, $5.95, 68 pgs.)-Reprints Fantastic Four #48-50 with new Lim-c 1.20 3.00 6.00

NOTE: **Austin** c(i)-71, 73, 74. **Ron Lim** a(p)-15-31, 33-38, 40-55, (56, 57-part-p), 60-65, 73-75; c(p)-15-31, 32-38, 40-75, Annual 5. **Marshall Rogers** a-1-10, 12, 19, 21; c-1-12, 21.

SILVER SURFER, THE
Dec, 1988 - No. 2, Jan, 1989 ($1.00, limited series)
Epic Comics (Marvel)

1,2: By Stan Lee (scripts) & Moebius (art) .50 1.25 2.50

SILVERTIP (Max Brand)
No. 491, Aug, 1953 - No. 898, May, 1958
Dell Publishing Co.

4-Color 491 (#1) 9.15 27.50 55.00
4-Color 572,608,637,667,731,789,898-Kinstler-a; all painted-c 4.70 14.00 28.00
4-Color 835 4.00 12.00 24.00

SIMULATORS, THE (Neatly Chiseled Features)(Value: cover or less)

SINBAD, JR (TV Cartoon)
Sept-Nov, 1965 - No. 3, May, 1966
Dell Publishing Co.

1 3.00 7.50 15.00
2,3 2.00 5.00 10.00

SINDBAD (See Capt. Sindbad under Movie Comics, and Fantastic Voyages of Sindbad)

SINGING GUNS (See Fawcett Movie Comics)

SINGLE SERIES (Comics on Parade #30 on)(Also see John Hix...)
1938 - No. 28, 1942 (All 68 pgs.)
United Features Syndicate

1-Captain and the Kids (#1) 54.00 160.00 375.00
2-Broncho Bill (1939) (#1) 32.00 95.00 200.00
3-Ella Cinders (1939) 27.00 80.00 190.00
4-Li'l Abner (1939) (#1) 43.00 130.00 300.00
5-Fritzi Ritz (#1) 19.00 57.00 135.00
6-Jim Hardy by Dick Moores (#1) 26.00 77.00 180.00
7-Frankie Doodle 19.00 57.00 135.00
8-Peter Pat (On sale 7/14/39) 19.00 57.00 135.00
9-Strange As It Seems 19.00 57.00 135.00
10-Little Mary Mixup 19.00 57.00 135.00
11-Mr. and Mrs. Beans 19.00 57.00 135.00
12-Joe Jinks 17.00 52.00 120.00
13-Looy Dot Dope 17.00 52.00 120.00
14-Billy Make Believe 17.00 52.00 120.00
15-How It Began (1939) 19.00 57.00 135.00
16-Illustrated Gags (1940)-Has ad for Captain and the Kids #1 reprint listed below 11.00 32.00 75.00
17-Danny Dingle 14.00 43.00 100.00
18-Li'l Abner (#2 on-c) 36.00 110.00 250.00
19-Broncho Bill (#2 on-c) 26.00 77.00 180.00
20-Tarzan by Hal Foster 86.00 260.00 600.00
21-Ella Cinders (#2 on-c; on sale 3/19/40) 24.00 72.00 165.00
22-Iron Vic 19.00 57.00 130.00
23-Tailspin Tommy by Hal Forrest (#1) 22.00 65.00 150.00
24-Alice in Wonderland (#1) 29.00 85.00 200.00
25-Abbie and Slats 23.00 70.00 160.00
26-Little Mary Mixup (#2 on-c, 1940) 19.00 57.00 135.00
27-Jim Hardy by Dick Moores (1942) 20.00 60.00 140.00
28-Ella Cinders and Abbie and Slats (1942) 20.00 60.00 140.00
1-Captain and the Kids (1939 reprint)-2nd Edition

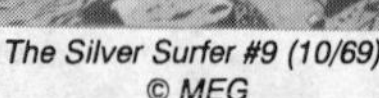

The Silver Surfer #9 (10/69), © MEG

The Silver Surfer V3#47, © MEG

Single Series #1 (1938), © UFS

Six-Gun Heroes #21, © FAW

Skeleton Hand #1, © ACG

Skippy's Own Book of Comics nn, © Percy Crosby

	GD25	FN65	NM94
	30.00	90.00	210.00
1-Fritzi Ritz (1939 reprint)-2nd edition	16.00	48.00	110.00

NOTE: *Some issues given away at the 1939-40 New York World's Fair (#6).*

SINISTER HOUSE OF SECRET LOVE, THE (Becomes Secrets of Sinister House No. 5 on)
Oct-Nov, 1971 - No. 4, Apr-May, 1972
National Periodical Publications

	GD25	FN65	NM94
1	.60	1.50	3.00
2-4: 2-Jeff Jones-c. 3-Toth-a, 36 pgs.	.40	1.00	2.00

SIR LANCELOT (See 4-Color #606, 775)

SIR WALTER RALEIGH (See 4-Color #644)

SISTERHOOD OF STEEL (Marvel)(Value: cover or less)

6 BLACK HORSES (See Movie Classics)

SIX FROM SIRIUS (Marvel, series I & II)(Value: cover or less)

SIX-GUN HEROES
March, 1950 - No. 23, Nov, 1953 (Photo-c #1-23)
Fawcett Publications

	GD25	FN65	NM94
1-Rocky Lane, Hopalong Cassidy, Smiley Burnette begin	36.00	107.00	250.00
2	18.00	54.00	125.00
3-5	12.00	36.00	85.00
6-15: 6-Lash LaRue begins	10.00	30.00	70.00
16-22: 17-Last Smiley Burnette. 18-Monte Hale begins	10.00	30.00	60.00
23-Last Fawcett issue	10.00	30.00	65.00

NOTE: *Hopalong Cassidy photo c-1-3. Monte Hale photo c-18. Rocky Lane photo c-4, 5, 7, 9, 11, 13, 15, 17, 20, 21, 23. Lash LaRue photo c-6, 8, 10, 12, 14, 16, 19, 22.*

SIX-GUN HEROES (Continued from Fawcett; Gunmasters #84 on)
No. 24, Jan, 1954 - No. 83, Mar-Apr, 1965 (All Vol. 4)(See Blue Bird)
Charlton Comics

	GD25	FN65	NM94
24-Lash LaRue, Hopalong Cassidy, Rocky Lane & Tex Ritter begin; photo-c	11.00	32.00	75.00
25	6.70	20.00	40.00
26-30: 26-Rod Cameron story. 28-Tom Mix begins?	5.85	17.50	35.00
31-40	4.70	14.00	28.00
41-46,48,50	4.20	12.50	25.00
47-Williamson-a, 2 pgs; Torres-a	5.00	15.00	30.00
49-Williamson-a, 5 pgs	5.00	15.00	30.00
51-60: 58-Gunmaster app.	3.20	8.00	16.00
61-70: 62-Origin Gunmaster	2.40	6.00	12.00
71-83: 76-Gunmaster begins	2.00	5.00	10.00

SIXGUN RANCH (See 4-Color #580)

SIX-GUN WESTERN
Jan, 1957 - No. 4, July, 1957
Atlas Comics (CDS)

	GD25	FN65	NM94
1-Crandall-a; two Williamson text illos	10.00	30.00	70.00
2,3-Williamson-a in both	9.15	27.50	55.00
4-Woodbridge-a	5.00	15.00	30.00

NOTE: *Ayers a-2, 3. Maneely a-1; c-2, 3. Orlando a-2. Pakula a-2. Powell a-3. Romita a-1, 4. Severin c-1, 4. Shores a-2.*

SIX MILLION DOLLAR MAN, THE (TV)
6/76 - No. 4, 12/76; No. 5, 10/77; No. 6, 2/78 - No. 9, 6/78
Charlton Comics

	GD25	FN65	NM94
1-Staton-c/a; Lee Majors photo on-c	.40	1.00	2.00
2-Neal Adams-c; Staton-a		.60	1.20
3-9		.50	1.00

SIX MILLION DOLLAR MAN, THE (TV)(Magazine)
July, 1976 - No. 7, Nov, 1977 (B&W)
Charlton Comics

	GD25	FN65	NM94
1-Neal Adams-c/a	.60	1.50	3.00
2-N. Adams-c	.30	.80	1.60
3-7: 3-N. Adams part inks; Chaykin-a		.60	1.20

666 THE MARK OF THE BEAST (Fleetway/Quality)(Value: cover or less)

SKATEMAN (Pacific)(Value: cover or less)

SKATING SKILLS
1957 (36 & 12 pages; 5x7", two versions) (10 cents)
Custom Comics, Inc./Chicago Roller Skates

	GD25	FN65	NM94
nn-Resembles old ACG cover plus interior art	1.00	2.50	5.00

SKEEZIX (Also see Gasoline Alley)
1925 - 1928 (Strip reprints) (soft covers) (pictures & text)
Reilly & Lee Co.

	GD25	FN65	NM94
...and Uncle Walt (1924)-Origin	14.00	42.00	85.00
...and Pal (1925)	11.00	32.00	65.00
...at the Circus (1926)	11.00	32.00	65.00
...& Uncle Walt (1927)	11.00	32.00	65.00
...Out West (1928)	11.00	32.00	65.00
Hardback Editions...	15.00	45.00	90.00

SKELETON HAND (...In Secrets of the Supernatural)
Sept-Oct, 1952 - No. 6, July-Aug, 1953
American Comics Group (B&M Dist. Co.)

	GD25	FN65	NM94
1	19.00	58.00	135.00
2	12.00	36.00	85.00
3-6	11.00	32.00	75.00

SKI PARTY (See Movie Classics)

SKIPPY
Circa 1920s (10x8", 16 pgs., color/B&W cartoons)
No publisher listed

	GD25	FN65	NM94
nn-By Percy Crosby	67.00	200.00	465.00

SKIPPY'S OWN BOOK OF COMICS (See Popular Comics)
1934 (52 pages) (Giveaway)(Strip reprints)
No publisher listed

	GD25	FN65	VF82	NM94
nn-(Rare)-By Percy Crosby	417.00	1040.00	2500.00	4500.00

(Estimated up to 40 total copies exist, 2 in NM/Mint)

Published by Max C. Gaines for Phillip's Dental Magnesia to be advertised on the Skippy Radio Show and given away with the purchase of a tube of Phillip's Tooth Paste. This is the first four-color comic book of reprints about one character.

SKREEMER (DC)(Value: cover or less)

SKULL & BONES
1992 - No. 3, 1992 ($4.95, color, mini-series, 52 pgs.)
DC Comics

	GD25	FN65	NM94
Book 1-3: 1-1st app.	1.00	2.50	5.00

SKULL, THE SLAYER
August, 1975 - No. 8, Nov, 1976
Marvel Comics Group

	GD25	FN65	NM94
1-Origin & 1st app.; Gil Kane-c	.30	.75	1.50
2-8: 2-Gil Kane-c. 8-Kirby-c		.50	1.00

SKY BLAZERS (Radio)
Sept, 1940 - No. 2, Nov, 1940
Hawley Publications

	GD25	FN65	NM94
1-Sky Pirates, Ace Archer, Flying Aces begin	30.00	90.00	180.00
2	25.00	75.00	150.00

SKY KING "RUNAWAY TRAIN" (TV)
1964 (16 pages) (regular size)
National Biscuit Co.

	GD25	FN65	NM94
nn	3.00	7.50	15.00

SKYMAN (See Big Shot Comics & Sparky Watts)

Fall?, 1941 - No. 2, 1941; No. 3, 1948 - No. 4, 1948
Columbia Comics Group

	GD25	FN65	NM94
1-Origin Skyman, The Face, Sparky Watts app.; Whitney-a; 3rd story-r from Big Shot #1; Whitney c-1-4	57.00	170.00	340.00
2 (1941)-Yankee Doodle	31.00	92.00	185.00
3,4 (1948)	20.00	60.00	120.00

SKY PILOT
No. 10, 1950(nd) - No. 11, Apr-May, 1951 (Saunders painted-c)
Ziff-Davis Publ. Co.

	GD25	FN65	NM94
10,11-Frank Borth-a	7.50	22.50	45.00

SKY RANGER (See Johnny Law...)

SKYROCKET
1944
Harry 'A' Chesler

	GD25	FN65	NM94
nn-Alias the Dragon, Dr. Vampire, Skyrocket & The Desperado app.	17.00	50.00	100.00

SKY SHERIFF (Breeze Lawson...) (Also see Exposed & Outlaws)
Summer, 1948
D. S. Publishing Co.

	GD25	FN65	NM94
1-Edmond Good-c/a	7.50	22.50	45.00

SKY WOLF (Also see Airboy)
Mar, 1988 - No. 3, Oct, 1988 ($1.75-$1.95, color, mini series)
Eclipse Comics

	GD25	FN65	NM94
1,2 ($1.75)	.35	.90	1.75
3 ($1.95)	.40	1.00	2.00

SLAINE, THE BERSERKER (Quality) (Value: cover or less)

SLAM BANG COMICS (Western Desperado #8)
March, 1940 - No. 7, Sept, 1940 (Combined with Master Comics #7)
Fawcett Publications

	GD25	FN65	NM94
1-Diamond Jack, Mark Swift & The Time Retarder, Lee Granger, Jungle King begin & continue in Master	92.00	275.00	550.00
2	42.00	125.00	250.00
3-Classic-c	55.00	165.00	330.00
4-7: 6,7-Zoro, the Mystery Man. 7-Bondage-c	37.00	110.00	220.00

SLAM BANG COMICS
No. 9, No date
Post Cereal Giveaway

	GD25	FN65	NM94
9-Dynamic Man, Echo, Mr. E, Yankee Boy app.	3.60	9.00	18.00

SLAPSTICK
Nov, 1992 - No. 4, Feb, 1993 ($1.25, color, mini-series)
Marvel Comics

	GD25	FN65	NM94
1-4: Fry/Austin-c/a. 4-Ghost Rider, D.D., F.F. app.		.60	1.25

SLAPSTICK COMICS
nd (1946?) (36 pages)
Comic Magazines Distributors

	GD25	FN65	NM94
nn-Firetop feature; Post-a(2)	11.00	32.00	75.00

SLASH-D DOUBLECROSS
1950 (132 pgs.) (pocket size)
St. John Publishing Co.

	GD25	FN65	NM94
nn-Western comics	11.50	34.00	80.00

SLASH MARAUD (DC) (Value: cover or less)

SLAUGHTERMAN (Comico) (Value: cover or less)

SLAVE GIRL COMICS (See Malu... & White Princess of the Jungle #2)
Feb, 1949 - No. 2, Apr, 1949 (52 pgs.)
Avon Periodicals/Eternity Comics

	GD25	FN65	NM94
1-Larsen-c/a	50.00	150.00	350.00
2-Larsen-a	39.00	120.00	275.00
1 (3/89, $2.25, B&W, 44 pgs., Eternity)-r/#1	.45	1.15	2.25

SLEDGE HAMMER (TV) (Marvel) (Value: cover or less)

SLEEPING BEAUTY (See Dell Giants, 4-Color #973, 984 & Movie Comics)

SLEEPWALKER
June, 1991 - Present ($1.00/$1.25, color)
Marvel Comics

	GD25	FN65	NM94
1-1st app.	.60	1.50	3.00
2-5: 4-Williamson-i. 5-Spider-Man-c/story	.40	1.00	2.00
6-10: 7-Infinity Gauntlet x-over. 8-Vs. Deathlok-c/story; last $1.00-c	.30	.75	1.50
11-18,20-24: 11-Ghost Rider-c/story. 12-Quesada-c/a(p) 14-Intro Spectra. 15-F.F.-c/story. 17-Darkhawk & Spider-Man x-over. 18-Infinity War x-over; Quesada/Williamson-c. 20,21-Sam Kieth-c. 21,22-Hobgoblin app.		.60	1.25
19-($2.00)-Die-cut Sleepwalker mask cover	.40	1.00	2.00
Holiday Special nn (1992, $2.00)	.40	1.00	2.00

SLEEZE BROTHERS, THE (Marvel) (Value: cover or less)

SLICK CHICK COMICS
1947(nd) - No. 3, 1947(nd)
Leader Enterprises

	GD25	FN65	NM94
1	7.50	22.50	45.00
2,3	5.85	17.50	35.00

SLIMER! (TV) (Now) (Value: cover or less)

SLIM MORGAN (See Wisco)

SLUGGER (Of the Little Wise Guys)
April, 1956
Lev Gleason Publications

	GD25	FN65	NM94
1-Biro-c	4.00	10.00	20.00

SMASH COMICS (Becomes Lady Luck #86 on)
Aug, 1939 - No. 85, Oct, 1949
Quality Comics Group

	GD25	FN65	NM94
1-Origin Hugh Hazard & His Iron Man, Bozo the Robot, Espionage, Starring Black X by Eisner, & Hooded Justice (Invisible Justice #2 on); Chic Carter & Wings Wendall begin	117.00	350.00	700.00
2-The Lone Star Rider app; Invisible Hood gains power of invisibility	48.00	145.00	290.00
3-Captain Cook & Eisner's John Law begin	33.00	100.00	200.00
4,5: 4-Flash Fulton begins	30.00	90.00	180.00
6-12: 12-One pg. Fine-a	25.00	75.00	150.00
13-Magno begins; last Eisner issue; The Ray app. in full page ad; The Purple Trio begins	25.00	75.00	150.00
14-Intro. The Ray by Lou Fine & others	145.00	438.00	875.00
15,16: 16-The Scarlet Seal begins	70.00	210.00	420.00
17-Wun Cloo becomes plastic super-hero by Jack Cole (9-months before Plastic Man)	70.00	210.00	420.00
18-Midnight by Jack Cole begins (origin)	83.00	250.00	500.00
19-22: Last Fine Ray; The Jester begins-#22	50.00	150.00	300.00
23,24: 24-The Sword app.; last Chic Carter; Wings Wendall dons new costume #24,25	43.00	130.00	260.00
25-Origin Wildfire; Rookie Rankin begins	50.00	150.00	300.00
26-30: 28-Midnight-c begin	40.00	120.00	240.00
31,32,34: Ray by Rudy Palais; also #33	29.00	88.00	175.00
33-Origin The Marksman	37.00	110.00	220.00
35-37	29.00	88.00	175.00
38-The Yankee Eagle begins; last Midnight by Jack Cole	29.00	88.00	175.00
39,40-Last Ray issue	24.00	72.00	145.00
41,43-50	12.00	35.00	70.00
42-Lady Luck begins by Klaus Nordling	13.00	40.00	80.00
51-60	10.00	30.00	60.00
61-70	8.35	25.00	50.00
71-85	7.50	22.50	45.00

NOTE: *Al Bryant c-54, 63-68. **Cole** a-17-38, 68, 69, 72, 73, 78, 80, 83, 85; c-38, 60-62, 69-*

Skyman #2, © CCG

Sleepwalker #1, © MEG

Smash Comics #16, © QUA

Smiley Burnette Western #4, © FAW

Smilin' Jack #4, © N.Y. News Syndicate

Smitty #3 (8-10/48), © N.Y. News Syndicate

*84. **Crandall** a-(Ray)-23-29, 35-38; c-36, 39, 40, 42-44, 46. **Fine** a(Ray)-14, 15, 16(w/**Tuska**), 17-22. **Fox** c-24-35. **Fuje** Ray-30. **Gil Fox** a-6-7, 9, 11-13. **Guardineer** a-(The Marksman)-39-?, 49, 52. **Gustavson** a-4-7, 9, 11-13 (The Jester)-22-46; (Magno)-13-21; (Midnight)-39(Cole inks), 49, 52, 63-65. **Kotzky** a-(Espionage)-33-38; c-45, 47-53. **Nordling** a-49, 52, 63-65. **Powell** a-11, 12, (Abdul the Arab)-13-24.*

SMASH HIT SPORTS COMICS
V2#1, Jan, 1949
Essankay Publications

	GD25	FN65	NM94
V2#1-L.B. Cole-c/a	13.00	40.00	80.00

S'MATTER POP?
1917 (44 pgs.; B&W; 10x14"; cardboard covers)
Saalfield Publ. Co.

	GD25	FN65	NM94
nn-By Charlie Payne; in full color; pages printed on one side	25.00	75.00	150.00

SMILE COMICS (Also see Gay Comics, Tickle, & Whee)
1955 (52 pages; 5x7-1/4") (7 cents)
Modern Store Publ.

	GD25	FN65	NM94
1	.60	1.50	3.00

SMILEY BURNETTE WESTERN (Also see Six-Gun Heroes)
March, 1950 - No. 4, Oct, 1950 (All photo front & back-c)
Fawcett Publications

	GD25	FN65	NM94
1-Red Eagle begins	34.00	102.00	240.00
2-4	23.00	70.00	160.00

SMILIN' JACK (See Famous Feature Stories, Popular Comics, Super Book #1, 2, 7, 19 & Super Comics)
No. 5, 1940 - No. 8, Oct-Dec, 1949
Dell Publishing Co.

	GD25	FN65	NM94
4-Color 5	54.00	160.00	375.00
4-Color 10 (1940)	50.00	150.00	350.00
Large Feature Comic 12,14,25 (1941)	37.00	110.00	260.00
4-Color 4 (1942)	39.00	120.00	275.00
4-Color 14 (1943)	32.00	95.00	220.00
4-Color 36,58 (1943-44)	19.00	57.00	130.00
4-Color 80 (1945)	14.00	43.00	100.00
4-Color 149 (1947)	10.00	30.00	70.00
1 (1-3/48)	10.00	30.00	70.00
2	5.85	17.50	35.00
3-8 (10-12/49)	4.35	13.00	26.00
Popped Wheat Giveaway(1947)-1938 strip reprints; 16 pgs. in full color	.95	2.40	4.80
Shoe Store Giveaway-1938 strip reprints; 16 pgs.	4.00	10.00	20.00
Sparked Wheat Giveaway(1942)-16 pgs. in full color	4.00	10.00	20.00

SMILING SPOOK SPUNKY (See Spunky)

SMITTY (See Treasure Box of Famous Comics)
1928 - 1933 (B&W newspaper strip reprints)
(cardboard covers; 9-1/2x9-1/2", 52 pgs.; 7x8-1/4", 36 pgs.)
Cupples & Leon Co.

	GD25	FN65	NM94
1928-(96pgs. 7x8-3/4")	17.00	50.00	100.00
1928-(Softcover, 36pgs., nn)	17.50	52.00	105.00
1929-At the Ball Game, 1930-The Flying Office Boy, 1931-The Jockey, 1932-In the North Woods....each....	12.50	37.50	75.00
1933-At Military School	12.50	37.50	75.00
Mid-1930s issue (reprint of 1928 Treasure Box issue)-36 pgs.; 7x8-3/4"	10.00	30.00	65.00
Hardback Editions (100 pgs., 7x8-1/4") with dust jacket each....	23.00	70.00	140.00

SMITTY (See Popular Comics, Super Book #2, 4 & Super Comics)
No. 11, 1940 - No. 7, Aug-Oct, 1949; Apr, 1958
Dell Publishing Co.

	GD25	FN65	NM94
4-Color 11 (1940)	32.00	95.00	2200.00
Large Feature Comic 26 (1941)	22.00	65.00	150.00
4-Color 6 (1942)	17.00	51.00	120.00
4-Color 32 (1943)	14.00	43.00	100.00
4-Color 65 (1945)	11.00	32.00	75.00
4-Color 99 (1946)	10.00	30.00	65.00
4-Color 138 (1947)	9.15	27.50	55.00
1 (11-1/47-48)	9.15	27.50	55.00
2	4.70	14.00	28.00
3 (8-10/48), 4 (1949)	3.60	9.00	18.00
5-7, 4-Color 909 (4/58)	3.00	7.50	15.00

SMOKEY BEAR (TV) (See March Of Comics #234, 362, 372, 383, 407)
Feb, 1970 - No. 13, Mar, 1973
Gold Key

	GD25	FN65	NM94
1	1.20	3.00	6.00
2-13	.60	1.50	3.00

SMOKEY STOVER (See Popular Comics, Super Book #5, 17, 29 & Super Comics)
No. 7, 1942 - No. 827, Aug, 1957
Dell Publishing Co.

	GD25	FN65	NM94
4-Color 7 (1942)-Reprints	29.00	85.00	200.00
4-Color 35 (1943)	14.00	43.00	100.00
4-Color 64 (1944)	11.00	32.00	75.00
4-Color 229 (1949)	4.35	13.00	26.00
4-Color 730,827	3.20	8.00	16.00
General Motors giveaway (1953)	4.00	12.00	24.00
National Fire Protection giveaway(1953 & 1954)-16 pgs., paper-c	4.00	12.00	24.00

SMOKEY THE BEAR (See Forest Fire for 1st app.)
No. 653, 10/55 - No. 1214, 8/61 (See March of Comics #234)
Dell Publishing Co.

	GD25	FN65	NM94
4-Color 653 (#1)	8.35	25.00	50.00
4-Color 708,754,818,932	4.20	12.50	25.00
4-Color 1016,1119,1214	3.60	9.00	18.00
True Story of..., The('59)-U.S. Forest Service giveaway-Publ. by Western Printing Co. (reprinted in 1964 & 1969)-Reprints 1st 16 pgs. of 4-Color 932	2.40	6.00	12.00

SMOKY (See Movie Classics)

SMURFS (TV)(Marvel)(Value: cover or less)

SNAFU (Magazine)
Nov, 1955 - V2#2, Mar, 1956 (B&W)
Atlas Comics (RCM)

	GD25	FN65	NM94
V1#1-Heath/Severin-a; Everett, Maneely-a	8.35	25.00	50.00
V2#1,2-Severin-a	6.70	20.00	40.00

SNAGGLEPUSS (TV)(See Spotlight #4)
Oct, 1962 - No. 4, Sept, 1963 (Hanna-Barbera)
Gold Key

	GD25	FN65	NM94
1	6.70	20.00	40.00
2-4	4.20	12.50	25.00

SNAP (Formerly Scoop #8; becomes Jest #10,11 & Komik Pages #10)
No. 9, 1944
Harry 'A' Chesler

	GD25	FN65	NM94
9-Manhunter, The Voice	10.00	30.00	60.00

SNAPPY COMICS
1945
Cima Publ. Co. (Prize Publ.)

	GD25	FN65	NM94
1-Airmale app; 9 pg. Sorcerer's Apprentice adapt; Kiefer-a	13.00	40.00	80.00

SNARKY PARKER (See Life With...)

SNIFFY THE PUP
No. 5, Nov, 1949 - No. 18, Sept, 1953
Standard Publications (Animated Cartoons)

	GD25	FN65	NM94
5-Two Frazetta text illos	6.70	20.00	40.00
6-10	2.80	7.00	14.00
11-18	2.00	5.00	10.00

SNOOPER AND BLABBER DETECTIVES (TV)
Nov, 1962 - No. 3, May, 1963 (Hanna-Barbera)
Gold Key

	GD25	FN65	NM94
1 (See Whitman Comic Books)	6.70	20.00	40.00
2,3	5.00	15.00	30.00

SNOW FOR CHRISTMAS
1957 (16 pages) (Giveaway)
W. T. Grant Co.

	GD25	FN65	NM94
nn	3.00	7.50	15.00

SNOW WHITE (See Christmas With..., 4-Color #49,227,382, Mickey Mouse Magazine, & Movie Comics)

SNOW WHITE AND THE SEVEN DWARFS
1952 (32 pgs.; 5x7-1/4", soft-c) (Disney)
Bendix Washing Machines

	GD25	FN65	NM94
nn	6.70	20.00	40.00

SNOW WHITE AND THE SEVEN DWARFS
1957 (small size)
Promotional Publ. Co.

	GD25	FN65	NM94
nn	4.00	10.50	21.00

SNOW WHITE AND THE SEVEN DWARFS
1958 (16 pgs, 5x7-1/4", soft-c) (Disney premium)
Western Printing Co.

	GD25	FN65	NM94
nn-"Mystery of the Missing Magic"	4.35	13.00	26.00

SNOW WHITE AND THE SEVEN DWARFS
April, 1982 (60 cent cover price)
Whitman Publications

	GD25	FN65	NM94
nn-r/Four Color #49		.50	1.00

SNOW WHITE AND THE SEVEN DWARFS GOLDEN ANNIVERSARY
Fall, 1987 ($2.95, color, magazine size, 52 pgs.)
Gladstone Publishing

	GD25	FN65	NM94
1-Contains poster	.60	1.50	3.00

SNOW WHITE AND THE 7 DWARFS IN "MILKY WAY"
1955 (16 pgs., soft-c, 5x7-1/4") (Disney premium)
American Dairy Association

	GD25	FN65	NM94
nn	6.70	20.00	40.00

SOAP OPERA LOVE
Feb, 1983 - No. 3, June, 1983
Charlton Comics

	GD25	FN65	NM94
1-3		.50	1.00

SOAP OPERA ROMANCES
July, 1982 - No. 5, March, 1983
Charlton Comics

	GD25	FN65	NM94
1-5-Nurse Betsy Crane-r		.50	1.00

SOJOURN ($1.50)
Sept, 1977 - No. 2, 1978 (Full tabloid size) (Color & B&W)
White Cliffs Publ. Co.

	GD25	FN65	NM94
1-Tor by Kubert, Eagle by Severin, E. V. Race, Private Investigator by Doug Wildey, T. C. Mars by S. Aragones begin plus other strips	.30	.80	1.60
2	.30	.80	1.60

SOLAR (Man of the Atom; also see Doctor Solar)
Sept, 1991 - Present ($1.75/$1.95, color, 44 pgs.)
Valiant

	GD25	FN65	NM94
1-Layton-i on Solar; Barry Windsor-Smith-c/a	5.00	15.00	30.00
2-Layton-i on Solar, Smith-a	3.00	7.50	15.00
3-1st app. Harada	3.00	7.50	15.00
4	1.80	4.50	9.00
5-7-($1.95-c): 7-vs. X-O Armor	1.50	3.75	7.50
8,9: 8-Begin $2.25-c	1.20	3.00	6.00
10-($3.95)-1st app. Eternal Warrior (6 pgs.); black embossed-c; last chapter in origin of Solar	8.35	25.00	50.00
10-2nd printing ($3.95)	.80	2.00	4.00
11-1st full app. Eternal Warrior	3.00	7.50	15.00
12-15: 12,13-Unity x-overs	1.00	2.50	5.00
16-22	.45	1.15	2.25

NOTE: *#1-10 all have free 8 pg. insert "Alpha and Omega" which is a 10 chapter Solar origin story. All 10 centerfolds can pieced together to show climax of story.* ***Ditko*** *a-11p, 14p.* ***Layton*** *a-1-3i; c-2i, 11i.* ***Miller*** *c-12.* ***Simonson*** *c-13.* ***B. Smith*** *a-1-10; c-1, 3, 5, 7.*

SOLARMAN (Marvel) (Value: cover or less)

SOLDIER & MARINE COMICS (Fightin' Army #16 on)
No. 11, Dec, 1954 - No. 15, Aug, 1955; V2#9, Dec, 1956
Charlton Comics (Toby Press of Conn. V1#11)

	GD25	FN65	NM94
V1#11 (12/54)-Bob Powell-a	3.00	7.50	15.00
V1#12(2/55)-15	2.00	5.00	10.00
V2#9(Formerly Never Again; Jerry Drummer V2#10 on)	2.00	5.00	10.00

SOLDIER COMICS
Jan, 1952 - No. 11, Sept, 1953
Fawcett Publications

	GD25	FN65	NM94
1	6.70	20.00	40.00
2	4.00	10.00	20.00
3-5	3.20	8.00	16.00
6-11: 8-Illo. in **POP**	2.40	6.00	12.00

SOLDIERS OF FORTUNE
Mar-Apr, 1951 - No. 13, Feb-Mar, 1953
American Comics Group (Creston Publ. Corp.)

	GD25	FN65	NM94
1-Capt. Crossbones by Shelly, Ace Carter, Lance Larson begin	13.00	40.00	90.00
2	9.15	27.50	55.00
3-10: 6-Bondage-c	7.50	22.50	45.00
11-13 (War format)	3.60	9.00	18.00

NOTE: ***Shelly*** *a-1-3, 5.* ***Whitney*** *a-6, 8-11, 13; c-1-3, 5, 6.*

SOLDIERS OF FREEDOM (Americomics) (Value: cover or less)

SOLO AVENGERS (Marvel) (Value: cover or less)

SOLOMON AND SHEBA (See 4-Color #1070)

SOLOMON KANE (Marvel) (Value: cover or less)

SOMERSET HOLMES (Pacific/Eclipse) (Value: cover or less)

SONG OF THE SOUTH (See Brer Rabbit & 4-Color #693)

SONIC DISRUPTORS (DC) (Value: cover or less)

SONIC HEDGEHOG
Feb, 1993 - No. 3, May, 1993 ($1.25, color, mini-series)
Archie Comics

	GD25	FN65	NM94
0(2/93),1-3: Shaw-a(p) & covers		.60	1.25

SON OF AMBUSH BUG (DC) (Value: cover or less)

SON OF BLACK BEAUTY (See 4-Color #510, 566)

SON OF CELLULOID (Eclipse) (Value: cover or less)

SON OF FLUBBER (See Movie Comics)

SON OF MUTANT WORLD (Fantagor) (Value: cover or less)

SON OF SATAN (Also see Ghost Rider #1 & Marvel Spotlight #12)
Dec, 1975 - No. 8, Feb, 1977
Marvel Comics Group

Snooper and Blabber Detectives #2, © Hanna-Barbera

Solar #1, © West

Soldier Comics #3, © FAW

Son of Satan #3, © MEG

Space Adventures #13, © CC

Space Busters #2, © Z-D

	GD25	FN65	NM94
1-Mooney-a; Kane-c(p), Starlin splash(p)	.80	2.00	4.00
2-8: 2-Origin The Possessor. 8-Heath-a	.50	1.25	2.50

SON OF SINBAD (Also see Abbott & Costello & Daring Adventures)
February, 1950
St. John Publishing Co.

	GD25	FN65	NM94
1-Kubert-c/a	27.00	81.00	190.00

SON OF TOMAHAWK (See Tomahawk)

SON OF VULCAN (Formerly Mysteries of Unexplored Worlds #1-48; Thunderbolt V3#51 on)
V2#49, Nov, 1965 - V2#50, Jan, 1966
Charlton Comics

	GD25	FN65	NM94
V2#49,50: 50-Roy Thomas scripts (1st pro work)	2.00	5.00	10.00

SON OF YUPPIES FROM HELL (Marvel)(Value: cover or less)(Also see Yuppies From Hell)

SONS OF KATIE ELDER (See Movie Classics)

SORCERY (See Chilling Adventures in... & Red Circle...)

SORORITY SECRETS
July, 1954
Toby Press

	GD25	FN65	NM94
1	4.70	14.00	28.00

SOULQUEST (Innovation)(Value: cover or less)

SOUPY SALES COMIC BOOK (TV)(The Official...)
1965
Archie Publications

	GD25	FN65	NM94
1	10.00	30.00	60.00

SOUTHERN KNIGHTS, THE (Guild Publ./Fictioneer Books)(Formerly Crusaders #1)(Value: cover or less)

SOVIET SUPER SOLDIERS (Marvel)(Value: cover or less)

SPACE ACE (Also see Manhunt!)
No. 5, 1952
Magazine Enterprises

	GD25	FN65	NM94
5(A-1 #61)-Guardineer-a	29.00	86.00	200.00

SPACE ACTION
June, 1952 - No. 3, Oct, 1952
Ace Magazines (Junior Books)

	GD25	FN65	NM94
1	39.00	115.00	270.00
2,3	30.00	90.00	210.00

SPACE ADVENTURES (War At Sea #22 on)
7/52 - No. 21, 8/56; No. 23, 5/58 - No. 59, 11/64; V3#60, 10/67; V1#2, 7/68 - V1#8, 7/69; No. 9, 5/78 - No. 13, 3/79
Capitol Stories/Charlton Comics

	GD25	FN65	NM94
1	25.00	75.00	175.00
2	11.00	32.00	75.00
3-5	10.00	30.00	60.00
6-9: 7-Sex change story	9.15	27.50	55.00
10,11-Ditko-c/a; 11-Two Ditko stories	22.00	65.00	150.00
12-Ditko-c (classic)	27.00	80.00	185.00
13-(Fox-r, 10-11/54); Blue Beetle story	10.00	30.00	60.00
14-Blue Beetle story (Fox-r, 12-1/54-55, last pre-code)	9.15	27.50	55.00
15,17,18-Rocky Jones app.(TV); 15-Part photo-c	10.00	30.00	60.00
16-Krigstein-a; Rockey Jones app.	11.50	34.00	80.00
19	7.50	22.50	45.00
20-Reprints Fawcett's "Destination Moon"	15.00	45.00	105.00
21-(8/56) (no #22)(Becomes War At Sea)	8.35	25.00	50.00
23-(5/58; formerly Nyoka, The Jungle Girl)-Reprints Fawcett's "Destination Moon"	12.00	36.00	85.00
24,25,31,32-Ditko-a	10.00	30.00	65.00
26,27-Ditko-a(4) each	11.00	32.00	75.00
28-30	4.20	12.50	25.00
33-Origin/1st app. Capt. Atom by Ditko (3/60)	24.00	70.00	165.00
34-40,42-All Captain Atom by Ditko	10.00	30.00	70.00
41,43-59: 44-1st app. Mercury Man; also in #45	2.00	5.00	10.00
V3#60(#1, 10/67)-Origin Paul Mann & The Saucers From the Future	3.00	7.50	15.00
2-8('68-'69)-2,5,6,8-Ditko-a; 2,4-Aparo-c/a	1.60	4.00	8.00
9-13('78-'79)-Capt. Atom-r/Space Adventures by Ditko; 9-Reprints origin/1st app. Capt. Atom from #33	.30	.75	1.50

NOTE: ***Aparo** a-V3#60. c-V3#8. **Ditko** c-12, 31-42. **Krigstein** c-15. **Shuster** a-11.*

SPACE ARK (AC)(Value: cover or less)

SPACE BUSTERS
Spring/52 - No. 3, Fall/52 (Painted covers by Norman Saunders)
Ziff-Davis Publ. Co.

	GD25	FN65	NM94
1-Krigstein-a(3)	43.00	130.00	300.00
2,3: 2-Kinstler-a(2pgs.); Krigstein-a(3)	36.00	107.00	250.00

NOTE: ***Anderson** a-2. Bondage c-2.*

SPACE CADET (See Tom Corbett,...)

SPACE COMICS (Formerly Funny Tunes)
No. 4, Mar-Apr, 1954 - No. 5, May-June, 1954
Avon Periodicals

	GD25	FN65	NM94
4,5-Space Mouse, Peter Rabbit, Super Pup, & Merry Mouse app.	4.00	10.00	20.00
I.W. Reprint #8 (nd)-Space Mouse-r	.80	2.00	4.00

SPACED
1982 - No. 13, 1988 ($1.25/$1.50, B&W, quarterly)
Anthony Smith Publ. #1,2/Unbridled Ambition/Eclipse Comics #10 on

	GD25	FN65	NM94
1-($1.25-c)	4.20	12.50	25.00
2 -($1.25-c)	3.00	7.50	15.00
3,4: 3-Begin $1.50-c	1.40	3.50	7.00
5,6	.60	1.50	3.00
7-13	.30	.75	1.50
Special Edition (1983, Mimeo)	1.20	3.00	6.00

SPACE DETECTIVE
July, 1951 - No. 4, July, 1952
Avon Periodicals

	GD25	FN65	NM94
1-Rod Hathway, Space Det. begins, ends #4; Wood-c/a(3)-23 pgs.; "Opium Smugglers of Venus" drug story; Lucky Dale-r/Saint #4	68.00	205.00	475.00
2-Tales from the Shadow Squad story; Wood/Orlando-c; Wood inside layouts	34.00	103.00	240.00
3-Kinstler-c	22.00	65.00	150.00
4-Kinstlerish-a by McCann	22.00	65.00	150.00
I.W. Reprint #1(Reprints #2), 8(Reprints cover #1 & part Famous Funnies #191)	3.00	7.50	15.00
I.W. Reprint #9-Exist?	3.00	7.50	15.00

SPACE EXPLORER (See March of Comics #202)

SPACE FAMILY ROBINSON (TV)(...Lost in Space #15-36)(Becomes Lost in Space #37 on)
Dec, 1962 - No. 36, Oct, 1969 (All painted covers)
Gold Key

	GD25	FN65	NM94
1-(Low distribution); Spiegle-a in all	22.00	65.00	150.00
2(3/63)-Family becomes lost in space	10.00	30.00	60.00
3-10: 6-Captain Venture begins	5.85	17.50	35.00
11-20	4.00	11.00	22.00
21-36	2.80	7.00	14.00

SPACE FAMILY ROBINSON (See March of Comics #320, 328, 352, 404, 414)

SPACE GHOST (TV) (Also see Golden Comics Digest #2 & Hanna-Barbera Super TV Heroes #3-7)

March, 1967 (Hanna-Barbera) (TV debut was 9/10/66)
Gold Key

	GD25	FN65	NM94
1 (10199-703)-Spiegle-a	22.00	65.00	150.00

SPACE GHOST (TV)(Comico)(Value: cover or less)

SPACE GIANTS, THE
1979 (One shot, $1.00, B&W, TV)
FBN Publications

	GD25	FN65	NM94
1-Based on Japanese TV series	1.00	2.50	5.00

SPACEHAWK (Dark Horse)(Value: cover or less)

SPACE KAT-ETS (in 3-D)
Dec, 1953 (25 cents)
Power Publishing Co.

	GD25	FN65	NM94
1	25.00	75.00	175.00

SPACEMAN (Speed Carter...)
Sept, 1953 - No. 6, July, 1954
Atlas Comics (CnPC)

	GD25	FN65	NM94
1	34.00	102.00	240.00
2	23.00	70.00	160.00
3-6: 4-A-Bomb-c	9.00	57.00	135.00

NOTE: ***Everett** c-1, 3. **Heath** a-1. **Maneely** a-1(3), 2(4), 3(3), 4-6; c-5, 6. **Romita** a-1. **Sekowsky** c-4. **Sekowsky/Abel** a-4(3). **Tuska** a-5(3).*

SPACE MAN
No. 1253, 1-3/62 - No. 8, 3-5/64; No. 9, 7/72 - No. 10, 10/72
Dell Publishing Co.

	GD25	FN65	NM94
4-Color 1253 (#1)(1-3/62)	6.70	20.00	40.00
2,3	4.00	10.00	20.00
4-8	3.00	7.50	15.00
9,10: 9-Reprints #1253. 10-Reprints #2	1.00	2.50	5.00

SPACE MOUSE (Also see Space Comics)
April, 1953 - No. 5, Apr-May, 1954
Avon Periodicals

	GD25	FN65	NM94
1	5.85	17.50	35.00
2	4.00	12.00	24.00
3-5	3.20	8.00	16.00

SPACE MOUSE (Walter Lantz...#1; see Comic Album #17)
No. 1132, Aug-Oct, 1960 - No. 5, Nov, 1963 (Walter Lantz)
Dell Publishing Co./Gold Key

	GD25	FN65	NM94
4-Color 1132,1244	4.00	12.00	24.00
1(11/62)(G.K.)	4.00	10.00	20.00
2-5	3.00	7.50	15.00

SPACE MYSTERIES
1964 (Reprints)
I.W. Enterprises

	GD25	FN65	NM94
1-r/Journey Into Unknown Worlds #4 w/new-c	1.00	2.50	5.00
8,9: 9-r/Planet Comics #73	1.00	2.50	5.00

SPACE: 1999 (TV) (Also see Power Record Comics)
Nov, 1975 - No. 7, Nov, 1976
Charlton Comics

	GD25	FN65	NM94
1-Staton-c/a; origin Moonbase Alpha	.60	1.50	3.00
2,7: 2-Staton-a	.40	1.00	2.00
3-6: All Byrne-a; c-3,5,6	.80	2.00	4.00

SPACE: 1999 (TV)(Magazine)
Nov, 1975 - No. 8, Nov, 1976 (B&W) (#7 shows #6 on inside)
Charlton Comics

	GD25	FN65	NM94
1-Origin Moonbase Alpha; Morrow-c/a	.60	1.50	3.00
2,3-Morrow-c/a	.35	.90	1.80
4-8: 4-6-Morrow-c. 5,8-Morrow-a	.30	.80	1.60

SPACE PATROL (TV)
Summer/52 - No. 2, Oct-Nov/52 (Painted-c by Norman Saunders)
Ziff-Davis Publishing Co. (Approved Comics)

	GD25	FN65	NM94
1-Krigstein-a	49.00	145.00	340.00
2-Krigstein-a(3)	40.00	120.00	280.00
...'s Special Mission (8 pgs., B&W, Giveaway)	50.00	150.00	350.00

SPACE PIRATES (See Archie Giant Series #533)

SPACE SQUADRON (Becomes Space Worlds #6)
June, 1951 - No. 5, Feb, 1952
Marvel/Atlas Comics (ACI)

	GD25	FN65	NM94
1: Brodsky c-1,5	37.00	110.00	260.00
2: Tuska c-2-4	32.00	95.00	220.00
3-5: 3-Capt. Jet Dixon by Tuska(3)	24.00	73.00	170.00

SPACE THRILLERS
1954 (Giant) (25 cents)
Avon Periodicals

	GD25	FN65	NM94
nn-(Scarce)-Robotmen of the Lost Planet; contains 3 rebound comics of The Saint & Strange Worlds. Contents could vary	70.00	210.00	490.00

SPACE TRIP TO THE MOON (See Space Adventures #23)

SPACE USAGI
June, 1992 - No. 3, 1992 ($2.00, B&W, mini-series)
Mirage Studios

	GD25	FN65	NM94
1-3: Usagi Yojimbo by Stan Sakai	.40	1.00	2.00

SPACE WAR (Fightin' Five #28 on)
Oct, 1959 - No. 27, Mar, 1964; No. 28, Mar, 1978 - No. 34, 3/79
Charlton Comics

	GD25	FN65	NM94
V1#1-Giordano-c begin, end #3	11.00	32.00	75.00
2,3	5.85	17.50	35.00
4-6,8,10-Ditko-c/a	11.00	32.00	75.00
7,9,11-15: Last 10 cent issue?	3.60	9.00	18.00
16-27	3.00	7.50	15.00
28,29,33,34-Ditko-c/a(r)	5.00	15.00	30.00
30-Ditko-c/a(r); Staton, Sutton/Wood-a	5.35	16.00	32.00
31-Ditko-c/a; atom-blast-c	5.35	16.00	32.00
32-r/Charlton Premiere V2#2; Sutton-a	.40	1.00	2.00

SPACE WESTERN (Formerly Cowboy Western Comics; becomes Cowboy Western Comics #46 on)
No. 40, Oct, 1952 - No. 45, Aug, 1953
Charlton Comics (Capitol Stories)

	GD25	FN65	NM94
40-Intro Spurs Jackson & His Space Vigilantes; flying saucer story	30.00	90.00	210.00
41,43-45: 41-Flying saucer-c	23.00	70.00	160.00
42-Atom bomb explosion-c	24.00	73.00	170.00

SPACE WORLDS (Formerly Space Squadron #1-5)
No. 6, April, 1952
Atlas Comics (Male)

	GD25	FN65	NM94
6-Sol Brodsky-c	20.00	60.00	140.00

SPANKY & ALFALFA & THE LITTLE RASCALS (See The Little Rascals)

SPANNER'S GALAXY (DC)(Value: cover or less)

SPARKIE, RADIO PIXIE (Radio)(Becomes Big Jon & Sparkie #4)
Winter, 1951 - No. 3, July-Aug, 1952 (Painted-c)(Sparkie #2,3; #1?)
Ziff-Davis Publ. Co.

	GD25	FN65	NM94
1-Based on children's radio program	13.00	40.00	90.00
2,3: 3-Big Jon and Sparkie on-c only	10.00	30.00	70.00

SPARKLE COMICS
Oct-Nov, 1948 - No. 33, Dec-Jan, 1953-54
United Features Syndicate

	GD25	FN65	NM94
1-Li'l Abner, Nancy, Captain & the Kids, Ella Cinders (52 pgs.)	9.15	27.50	55.00
2	4.70	14.00	28.00
3-10	4.00	10.00	20.00

Space Man #6, © DELL

Space Squadron #1, © MEG

Space War #24, © CC

Sparkler Comics #20, © UFS

Sparky Watts #2, © CCG

Special Comics #1, © AP

	GD25	FN65	NM94
11-20	3.20	8.00	16.00
21-33	2.40	6.00	12.00

SPARKLE PLENTY (See 4-Color #215 & Harvey Comics Library #2)

SPARKLER COMICS (1st Series)
July, 1940 - No. 2, 1940
United Feature Comic Group

	GD25	FN65	NM94
1-Jim Hardy	27.00	82.00	165.00
2-Frankie Doodle	18.00	55.00	110.00

SPARKLER COMICS (2nd Series)(Nancy & Sluggo #121 on)(Cover title becomes Nancy and Sluggo #101? on)
July, 1941 - No. 120, Jan, 1955
United Features Syndicate

	GD25	FN65	NM94
1-Origin Sparkman; Tarzan (by Hogarth in all issues), Captain & the Kids, Ella Cinders, Danny Dingle, Dynamite Dunn, Nancy, Abbie & Slats, Broncho Bill, Frankie Doodle, begin; Sparkman c-#1-12	117.00	350.00	700.00
2	50.00	150.00	300.00
3,4	42.00	125.00	250.00
5-10: 9-Sparkman's new costume	37.00	110.00	220.00
11-13,15-20: 12-Sparkman new costume (color change). 19-1st Race Riley	28.00	85.00	170.00
14-Tarzan-c by Hogarth	32.00	95.00	190.00
21-24,26,27,29,30: 22-Race Riley & the Commandos strips begin, ends #44	22.00	68.00	135.00
25,28,31,34,37,39-Tarzan-c by Hogarth	27.00	82.00	165.00
32,33,35,36,38,40	12.50	37.50	75.00
41,43,45,46,48,49	9.15	27.50	55.00
42,44,47,50-Tarzan-c	17.00	50.00	100.00
51,52,54-70: 57-Li'l Abner begins (not in #58); Fearless Fosdick app. in #58	6.70	20.00	40.00
53-Tarzan-c by Hogarth	14.00	42.50	85.00
71-80	5.00	15.00	30.00
81,82,84-90: 85-Li'l Abner ends. 86-Lingerie panels	4.20	12.50	25.00
83-Tarzan-c	7.50	22.50	45.00
91-96,98-99	4.20	12.50	25.00
97-Origin Casey Ruggles by Warren Tufts	9.15	27.50	55.00
100	5.35	16.00	32.00
101-107,109-112,114-120	3.60	9.00	18.00
108,113-Toth-a	7.50	22.50	45.00

SPARKLING LOVE
June, 1950; 1953
Avon Periodicals/Realistic (1953)

	GD25	FN65	NM94
1(Avon)-Kubert-a; photo-c	12.00	36.00	85.00
nn(1953)-Reprint; Kubert-a	5.85	17.50	35.00

SPARKLING STARS
June, 1944 - No. 33, March, 1948
Holyoke Publishing Co.

	GD25	FN65	NM94
1-Hell's Angels, FBI, Boxie Weaver & Ali Baba begin	10.00	30.00	65.00
2-Speed Spaulding story	6.70	20.00	40.00
3-Actual FBI case photos & war photos	4.70	14.00	28.00
4-10: 7-X-mas-c	4.00	12.00	24.00
11-19: 13-Origin/1st app. Jungo the Man-Beast	4.00	10.00	20.00
20-Intro Fangs the Wolf Boy	4.00	12.00	24.00
21-29,32,33: 29-Bondage-c	4.00	10.00	20.00
31-Sid Greene-a	4.00	12.00	24.00

SPARK MAN (See Sparkler Comics)
1945 (One Shot) (36 pages)
Frances M. McQueeny

	GD25	FN65	NM94
1-Origin Spark Man; female torture story; cover redrawn from Sparkler #1	18.00	54.00	125.00

SPARKY WATTS (Also see Big Shot Comics & Columbia Comics)
Nov?, 1942 - No. 10, 1949
Columbia Comic Corp.

	GD25	FN65	NM94
1(1942)-Skyman & The Face app; Hitler-c	25.00	75.00	150.00
2(1943)	12.00	35.00	70.00
3(1944)	10.00	30.00	60.00
4(1944)-Origin	9.15	27.50	55.00
5(1947)-Skyman app.	7.00	21.00	42.00
6,7,9,10: 6(1947),10(1949)	4.35	13.00	26.00
8(1948)-Surrealistic-c	5.85	17.50	35.00

NOTE: ***Boody Rogers** c-1-8.*

SPARTACUS (See 4-Color #1139)

SPAWN
May, 1992 - Present ($1.95, color, mature readers)
Image Comics

	GD25	FN65	NM94
1-McFarlane-c/a begins; McFarlane/Steacy-c	1.20	3.00	6.00
1-2nd printing	.40	1.00	2.00
2-McFarlane/Steacy-c	.80	2.00	4.00
3,5-10: 9-Neil Gaiman scripts. 10-Cerebus app.; contains Bloodwulf poster by Liefeld	.40	1.00	2.00
4-Has coupon for Image Comics #0-Alan Moore scripts w/Miller poster	1.20	3.00	6.00
4-With coupon missing	.40	1.00	2.00

SPECIAL AGENT (Steve Saunders...)(Also see True Comics #68)
Dec, 1947 - No. 8, Sept, 1949
Parents' Magazine Institute (Commended Comics No. 2)

	GD25	FN65	NM94
1-J. Edgar Hoover photo on-c	7.50	22.50	45.00
2	4.00	11.00	22.00
3-8	3.60	9.00	18.00

SPECIAL COLLECTORS' EDITION
Dec, 1975 (No month given) (10-1/4x13-1/2")
Marvel Comics Group

	GD25	FN65	NM94
1-Kung Fu, Iron Fist & Sons of the Tiger	.60	1.50	3.00

SPECIAL COMICS (Becomes Hangman #2 on)
Winter, 1941-42
MLJ Magazines

	GD25	FN65	NM94
1-Origin The Boy Buddies (Shield & Wizard x-over); death of The Comet; origin The Hangman retold	133.00	400.00	800.00

SPECIAL DELIVERY
1951 (32 pgs.; B&W)
Post Hall Synd. (Giveaway)

nn-Origin of Pogo, Swamp, etc.; 2 pg. biog. on Walt Kelly
(One copy sold in 1980 for $150.00)

SPECIAL EDITION (See Gorgo and Reptisaurus)

SPECIAL EDITION (U. S. Navy Giveaways)
1944 - 1945 (Regular comic format with wording simplified, 52pgs.)
National Periodical Publications

	GD25	FN65	NM94
1-Action (1944)-reprints Action #80	82.00	245.00	490.00
2-Action (1944)-reprints Action #81	82.00	245.00	490.00
3-Superman (1944)-reprints Superman #33	82.00	245.00	490.00
4-Detective (1944)-reprints Detective #97	87.00	262.00	525.00
5-Superman (1945)-reprints Superman #34	82.00	245.00	490.00
6-Action (1945)-reprints Action #84	82.00	245.00	490.00

NOTE: ***Wayne Boring** c-1, 2, 6. **Dick Sprang** c-4.*

SPECIAL EDITION COMICS
1940 (August) (One Shot, 68pgs.)
Fawcett Publications

GD25 FN65 VF82 NM94

1-1st book devoted entirely to Captain Marvel; C.C. Beck-c/a; only app. of Capt. Marvel with belt buckle; Capt. Marvel appears with button-down flap; 1st story (came out before Captain Marvel #1)
500.00 1500.00 3000.00 5000.00
(Estimated up to 150 total copies exist, 7 in NM/Mint)

NOTE: *Prices vary widely on this book. Since this book is all Captain Marvel stories, it is actually a pre-Captain Marvel #1. There is speculation that this book almost became* ***Captain Marvel*** *#1. After* ***Special Edition*** *was published, there was an editor change at Fawcett. The new editor commissioned Kirby to do a nn* ***Captain Marvel*** *book early in 1941. This book was followed by a 2nd book several months later. This 2nd book was advertised as a #3 (making Special Edition the #1, & the nn issue the #2). However, the 2nd book did come out as a #2.*

SPECIAL EDITION: SPIDER-MAN VS. THE HULK (See listing under The Amazing Spider-Man)

SPECIAL EDITION X-MEN
Feb, 1983 (One Shot) (Baxter paper, $2.00)
Marvel Comics Group

	GD25	FN65	NM94
1-r/Giant-Size X-Men #1 plus one new story	2.40	6.00	12.00

SPECIAL MARVEL EDITION (Master of Kung Fu #17 on)
Jan, 1971 - No. 16, Feb, 1974
Marvel Comics Group

	GD25	FN65	NM94
1-Thor-r by Kirby; 68 pgs.	1.00	2.50	5.00
2-4: Thor-r by Kirby; 68 pg. Giant	.80	2.00	4.00
5-14: Sgt. Fury-r; 11-Reprints Sgt. Fury #13 (Captain America app.)	.70	1.75	3.50
15-Master of Kung Fu (Shang-Chi) begins (1st app., 12/73); Starlin-a; origin/1st app. Nayland Smith & Dr. Petric	5.70	17.00	34.00
16-1st app. Midnight; Starlin-a (2nd Shang-Chi)	4.00	12.00	24.00

SPECIAL MISSIONS (See G.I. Joe...)

SPECIAL WAR SERIES (Attack V4#3 on?)
Aug, 1965 - No. 4, Nov, 1965
Charlton Comics

	GD25	FN65	NM94
V4#1-D-Day (also see D-Day listing)	1.60	4.00	8.00
2-Attack!	1.00	2.50	5.00
3-War & Attack (also see War & Attack)	1.00	2.50	5.00
4-Judomaster (intro/1st app.)	4.00	10.00	20.00

SPECTACULAR ADVENTURES (See Adventures)

SPECTACULAR FEATURE MAGAZINE, A (Formerly My Confessions) (Spectacular Features Magazine #12)
No. 11, April, 1950
Fox Feature Syndicate

	GD25	FN65	NM94
11 (#1)-Samson & Delilah	1600	48.00	110.00

SPECTACULAR FEATURES MAGAZINE (Formerly A Spectacular Feature Magazine)
No. 12, June, 1950 - No. 3, Aug, 1950
Fox Feature Syndicate

	GD25	FN65	NM94
12 (#2)-Iwo Jima; photo flag-c	16.00	48.00	110.00
3-True Crime Cases	11.00	32.00	75.00

SPECTACULAR SPIDER-MAN, THE (See Marvel Special Edition and Marvel Treasury Edition)

SPECTACULAR SPIDER-MAN, THE (Magazine)
July, 1968 - No. 2, Nov, 1968 (35 cents)
Marvel Comics Group

	GD25	FN65	NM94
1-(B&W)-Romita/Mooney 52 pg. story plus updated origin story with Everett-a(i)	9.15	27.50	55.00
2-(Color)-Green Goblin-c & 58 pg. story; Romita painted-c (story reprinted in King Size Spider-Man #9); Romita/Mooney-a	11.00	32.00	75.00

SPECTACULAR SPIDER-MAN, THE (Peter Parker...#54-132,134)
Dec, 1976 - Present
Marvel Comics Group

	GD25	FN65	NM94
1-Origin retold; return of Tarantula	7.35	22.00	44.00
2-Kraven the Hunter app.	3.60	9.00	18.00
3-5: 3-Intro Lightmaster. 4-Vulture app.	2.40	6.00	12.00
6-8-Morbius app.; 6-r/Marvel Team-Up #3 w/Morbius	3.60	9.00	18.00
9-20: 9,10-White Tiger app. 17,18-Champions cameo (Ghost Rider)	1.20	3.00	6.00
21,24-26: 21-Scorpion app. 26-Daredevil app.	1.00	2.50	5.00
22,23-Moon Knight app.	1.60	4.00	8.00
27-Miller's 1st art on Daredevil (2/79); also see Captain America #235	2.40	6.00	12.00
28-Miller Daredevil (p)	1.80	4.50	9.00
29-55,57,59: 33-Origin Iguana. 38-Morbius app.	.80	2.00	4.00
56-2nd app. Jack O'Lantern (Macendale) & 1st Spidey/Jack O'Lantern battle (7/81)	1.60	4.00	8.00
58-Byrne-a(p)	1.00	2.50	5.00
60-Double size; origin retold with new facts revealed	.80	2.00	4.00
61-63,65-68,71-74: 65-Kraven the Hunter app.	.60	1.50	3.00
64-1st app. Cloak & Dagger (3/82)	2.40	6.00	12.00
69,70-Cloak & Dagger app.	1.80	4.50	9.00
75-Double size	.80	2.00	4.00
76-80: 79-Punisher cameo	.60	1.50	3.00
81,82-Punisher, Cloak & Dagger app.	2.80	7.00	14.00
83-Origin Punisher retold	3.60	9.00	18.00
84,86-99: 90-Spider-man's new black costume, last panel(ties w/Amazing Spider-Man #252 & Marvel Team-Up #141). 94-96-Cloak & Dagger app. 98-Intro The Spot	.60	1.50	3.00
85-Hobgoblin (Ned Leeds) app. (12/83); gains powers of original Green Goblin (see Amazing Spider-Man #238)	4.20	12.50	25.00
100-(3/85)-Double size	.80	2.00	4.00
101-115,117,118,120-129: 107-110-Death of Jean DeWolff. 111-Secret Wars II tie-in. 128-Black Cat new costume	.50	1.25	2.50
116,119-Sabretooth-c/story	1.00	2.50	5.00
130-Hobgoblin app.	.80	2.00	4.00
131-Six part Kraven tie-in	1.20	3.00	6.00
132-Kraven tie-in	1.00	2.50	5.00
133-139: 139-Origin Tombstone	.40	1.00	2.00
140-Punisher cameo app.	.60	1.50	3.00
141-Punisher app.	1.60	4.00	8.00
142,143-Punisher app.	1.00	2.50	5.00
144-146,148-157: 151-Tombstone returns	.40	1.00	2.00
147-1st app. new Hobgoblin (Macendale).	4.00	10.00	20.00
158-Spider-Man gets new powers (1st Cosmic Spidey, continued in Web of Spider-Man #59)	2.40	6.00	12.00
159-Cosmic Spider-Man app.	1.60	4.00	8.00
160-170: 161-163-Hobgoblin app. 168-170-Avengers x-over. 169-1st app. The Outlaws	.30	.75	1.50
171-184: 180,181,183,184-Green Goblin app. 184-Last $1.00-c		.50	1.00
185-188,190-199: 197-Original X-Men app		.60	1.25
189-($2.95, 52 pgs.)-Hologram-c; battles Green Goblin; origin Spidey retold; Vess poster w/Spidey & Hobgoblin	1.60	4.00	8.00
189 (2nd printing)	.60	1.50	3.00
195-(Deluxe ed.)-Polybagged w/audio cassette	.50	1.25	2.50
200-($2.95)-Holo-grafx foil-c	.60	1.50	3.00
Annual 1 (1979)	1.00	2.50	5.00
Annual 2 (1980)-Origin/1st app. Rapier	.80	2.00	4.00
Annual 3-7: 3(1981)-Last Man-Wolf. 4(1984). 5(1985). 6(10/86). 7(1987)	.60	1.50	3.00
Annual 8 (1988, $1.75)-Evolutionary War x-over	.80	2.00	4.00
Annual 9 (1989, $2.00, 68 pgs.)-Atlantis Attacks	.60	1.50	3.00
Annual 10 (1990, $2.00, 68 pgs.)-McFarlane-a	.50	1.25	2.50
Annual 11 (1991, $2.00, 68 pgs.)-Iron Man app.	.40	1.00	2.00
Annual 12 (1992, $2.25, 68 pgs.)-Venom solo story cont'd from Amazing Spider-Man Annual #26	.45	1.15	2.25

NOTE: ***Austin*** *c-21i, Annual 11i.* ***Byrne*** *c(p)-17, 43, 58, 101, 102.* ***Giffen*** *a-120p.* *Hembeck*

Special Edition X-Men #1, © MEG

Spectacular Features Magazine #12, © FOX

The Spectacular Spider-Man #17, © MEG

The Spectre #6 (9-10/68), © DC

Speed Comics #42, © HARV

Spellbound #18, © MEG

c/a-86p. ***Miller*** *c-46p, 48p, 50, 51p, 52p, 54p, 55, 56p, 57, 60.* ***Mooney*** *a-7i, 11i, 21p, 23p, 25p, 26p, 29-34p, 36p, 37p, 39i, 41, 42i, 49p, 50i, 51i, 53p, 54-57i, 59-66i, 68i, 71i, 73-79i, 81-83i, 85i, 87-99i, 102i, 125p, Annual 1i, 2p.* ***Nasser*** *c-37p.* ***Perez*** *c-10.* ***Simonson*** *c-54i.*

SPECTACULAR STORIES MAGAZINE (Formerly A Star Presentation)
No. 4, July, 1950 - No. 3, Sept, 1950
Fox Feature Sydicate (Hero Books)

	GD25	FN65	NM94
4-Sherlock Holmes	23.00	70.00	160.00
3-The St. Valentine's Day Massacre	14.00	43.00	100.00

SPECTRE, THE (See Adventure Comics 431, More Fun & Showcase)
Nov-Dec, 1967 - No. 10, May-June, 1969 (All 12 cents)
National Periodical Publications

	GD25	FN65	NM94
Showcase #60 (1-2/66)-1st Silver Age app. The Spectre; Murphy Anderson-a; origin in text	18.00	54.00	125.00
Showcase #61,64 (3-4/66, 9-10/66)-2nd & 3rd app. The Spectre by Murphy Anderson	10.00	30.00	60.00
1-(11-12/67)-Anderson-c/a	10.00	30.00	60.00
2-5-Neal Adams-c/a; 3-Wildcat x-over	6.35	19.00	38.00
6-8,10: 6-8-Anderson inks. 7-Hourman app.	3.00	7.50	15.00
9-Wrightson-a	3.60	9.00	18.00

SPECTRE, THE (DC 1987-'89) (Value: cover or less)

SPECTRE, THE
Dec, 1992 - Present ($175, color)
DC Comics

	GD25	FN65	NM94
1-($1.95)-Glow-in-the-dark-c; Mandrake-c/a	.50	1.50	3.00
2-6: Mandrake-c/a	.35	.90	1.75

SPEEDBALL (See Amazing Spider-Man Annual #12, Marvel Super-Heroes & The New Warriors)
Sept, 1988(10/88-inside) - No. 11, July, 1989 (75 cents, color)
Marvel Comics

	GD25	FN65	NM94
1-11: Ditko/Guice a-1-4, c-1; Ditko c-1-11p		.50	1.00

SPEED BUGGY (TV)(Also see Fun-In #12, 15)
July, 1975 - No. 9, Nov, 1976 (Hanna-Barbera)
Charlton Comics

	GD25	FN65	NM94
1	.60	1.50	3.00
2-9	.30	.75	1.50

SPEED CARTER SPACEMAN (See Spaceman)

SPEED COMICS (New Speed)(Also see Double Up)
10/39 - #11, 8/40; #12, 3/41 - #44, 1-2/47 (#14-16: pocket size, 100 pgs.)
Brookwood Publ./Speed Publ./Harvey Publications No. 14 on

	GD25	FN65	NM94
1-Origin Shock Gibson; Ted Parrish, the Man with 1000 Faces begins; Powell-a	117.00	350.00	700.00
2-Powell-a	58.00	175.00	350.00
3	37.00	110.00	220.00
4,5: 4-Powell-a?	31.00	92.00	185.00
6-11: 7-Mars Mason begins, ends #11	26.00	78.00	155.00
12 (3/41; shows #11 in indicia)-The Wasp begins; Major Colt app. (Capt. Colt #12)	31.00	92.00	185.00
13-Intro. Captain Freedom & Young Defenders; Girl Commandos, Pat Parker, War Nurse begins; Major Colt app.	37.00	110.00	220.00
14-16 (100 pg. pocket size, 1941): 14-2nd Harvey comic (See Pocket). 15-Pat Parker dons costume, last in costume #23; no Girl Commandos	29.00	88.00	175.00
17-Black Cat begins; origin Black Cat-r/Pocket #1; not in #40,41	46.00	138.00	275.00
18-20	25.00	75.00	150.00
21,22,25-30: 26-Flag-c	22.00	65.00	130.00
23-Origin Girl Commandos	31.00	92.00	185.00
24-Pat Parker team-up with Girl Commandos	22.00	65.00	130.00
31-44: 38-Flag-c	18.0	55.00	110.00

NOTE: ***Al Avison*** *c-14-16, 30, 43.* ***Briefer*** *a-6, 7.* ***Jon Henri*** *(Kirbyesque) c-17-20.* ***Kubert*** *a-7-11(Mars Mason), 37, 38, 42-44.* ***Kirby/Caseneuve*** *c-21-23.* ***Palais*** *c-37, 39-42.* ***Powell*** *a-1, 2, 4-7, 28, 31, 44.* ***Schomburg*** *c-31-36.* ***Tuska*** *a-3, 6, 7. Bondage c-18, 35.*

SPEED DEMONS (Formerly Frank Merriwell at Yale #1-4?; Submarine Attack #11 on)
No. 5, Feb, 1957 - No. 10, 1958
Charlton Comics

	GD25	FN65	NM94
5-10	2.00	5.00	10.00

SPEED RACER (Now) (Value: cover or less)

SPEED SMITH THE HOT ROD KING
Spring, 1952
Ziff-Davis Publishing Co.

	GD25	FN65	NM94
1-Saunders painted-c	11.50	34.00	80.00

SPEEDY GONZALES (See 4-Color #1084)

SPEEDY RABBIT (See Television Puppet Show)
nd (1953); 1963
Realistic/I. W. Enterprises/Super Comics

	GD25	FN65	NM94
nn (1953)-Realistic Reprint?	1.60	4.00	8.00
I.W. Reprint #1 (2 versions w/diff. c/stories exist)	.40	1.00	2.00
Super Reprint #14(1963)	.40	1.00	2.00

SPELLBINDERS (Quality) (Value: cover or less)

SPELLBOUND (See The Crusaders)

SPELLBOUND (Tales to Hold You... #1, Stories to Hold You...)
Mar, 1952 - #23, June, 1954; #24, Oct, 1955 - #34, June, 1957
Atlas Comics (ACI 1-15/Male 16-23/BPC 24-34)

	GD25	FN65	NM94
1	29.00	85.00	200.00
2-Edgar A. Poe app.	14.00	43.00	100.00
3-5: 3-Whitney-a; cannibalism story	12.00	36.00	85.00
6-Krigstein-a	12.00	36.00	85.00
7-10: 8-Ayers-a	10.00	30.00	65.00
11-16,18-20: 14-Ed Win-a	8.35	25.00	50.00
17-Krigstein-a	10.00	3.00	60.00
21-23-Last precode (6/54)	7.50	22.50	45.00
24-28,30,31,34: 25-Orlando-a	5.85	17.50	35.00
29-Ditko-a (4 pgs.)	7.50	22.50	45.00
32,33-Torres-a	7.50	22.50	45.00

NOTE: ***Brodsky*** *a-5; c-1, 5-7, 10, 11, 13, 15, 25-27, 32.* ***Colan*** *a-17.* ***Everett*** *a-2, 5, 7, 10, 16, 28, 31; c-2, 8, 9, 14, 17-19, 28, 30.* ***Forgione/Abel*** *a-29.* ***Forte/Fox*** *a-16.* ***Al Hartley*** *a-2.* ***Heath*** *a-2, 4, 8, 9, 12, 14, 16; c-3, 4, 12, 16, 20, 21.* ***Infantino*** *a-15.* ***Keller*** *a-5.* ***Kida*** *a-2, 14.* ***Maneely*** *a-7, 14, 27; c-24, 29, 31.* ***Mooney*** *a-5, 13, 18.* ***Mac Pakula*** *a-22, 32.* ***Post*** *a-8.* ***Powell*** *a-19, 20, 32.* ***Robinson*** *a-1.* ***Romita*** *a-24, 26, 27.* ***R.Q. Sale*** *a-29.* ***Sekowsky*** *a-5.* ***Severin*** *c-29.* ***Sinnott*** *a-8, 16, 17.*

SPELLBOUND (Marvel, 1988) (Value: cover or less)

SPELLJAMMER (DC) (Value: cover or less)

SPENCER SPOOK (Formerly Giggle Comics; see Advs. of...)
No. 100, Mar-Apr, 1955 - No. 101, May-June, 1955
American Comics Group

	GD25	FN65	NM94
100,101	4.00	10.00	20.00

SPIDER, THE (Eclipse) (Value: cover or less)

SPIDER-MAN (See Amazing..., Giant-Size..., Marvel Tales, Marvel Team-Up, Spectacular..., Spidey Super Stories, & Web Of...)

SPIDER-MAN
Aug, 1990 - Present ($1.75, color)
Marvel Comics

	GD25	FN65	NM94
1-Silver edition, direct sale only (unbagged)	1.60	4.00	8.00
1-Silver bagged edition; direct sale, no price on comic, but $2.00 on plastic bag (still sealed)(125,000 print run)	4.20	12.50	25.00
1-Regular edition w/Spidey face in UPC area (unbagged); green-c	1.00	2.50	5.00
1-Regular bagged edition w/Spidey face in UPC area (price is for still sealed only); green cover (125,000)	3.00	7.50	15.00

1-Newsstand bagged w/UPC code (sealed) 1.40 3.50 7.00
1-Gold edition, 2nd printing (unbagged) with Spider-Man in box (400,000-450,000) 1.00 2.50 5.00
1-Gold 2nd printing w/UPC code; sold in Wal-Mart; not scarce .80 2.00 4.00
1-Platinum ed. mailed to retailers only (10,000 print run); has new McFarlane-a & editorial material instead of ads; stiff-c, no cover price 50.00 150.00 350.00
2-McFarlane-c/a/scripts continue 1.20 3.00 6.00
3-5 .80 2.00 4.00
6,7-Ghost Rider & Hobgoblin app. 1.20 3.00 6.00
8-Wolverine cameo; Wolverine storyline begins .60 1.50 3.00
9-12: 12-Wolverine storyline ends .60 1.50 3.00
13-Spidey's black costume returns 1.00 2.50 5.00
14,15,18-25: 13,14-Spidey in black costume. 15-Eric Larsen-c/a; Beast-c/story. 18-Ghost Rider-c/story. 18-23-Sinister Six storyline. 19-Hulk & Hobgoblin-c & app. 20-22-Deathlok app. & Larsen-c/a. 22-Ghost Rider, Hulk, Hobgoblin app. 23-Gatefold-c. 24-Infinity War x-over w/Demogoblin & Hobgoblin-c/story .35 .90 1.75
16-X-Force-c/story w/Liefeld assists; continues in X-Force #4; reads sideways; Last McFarlane issue .50 1.25 2.50
17-Thanos-c/story; Williamson-c/a(i) .50 1.25 2.50
26-($3.50, 52 pgs.)-Hologram-c w/gatefold poster; Spidey retells his origin .70 1.75 3.50
27-34: 27,28-Marshall Rogers/Keith Williams-c/a .35 .90 1.75

SPIDER-MAN AND DAREDEVIL
March, 1984 ($2.00, one-shot, deluxe paper)
Marvel Comics Group

1-r/Spectacular Spider-Man #26-28 by Miller .60 1.50 3.00

SPIDER-MAN AND HIS AMAZING FRIENDS
Dec, 1981 (One shot) (See Marvel Action Universe)
Marvel Comics Group

1-Adapted from NBC TV cartoon show; Green Goblin-c/story; 1st Spidey, Firestar, Iceman team-up; Spiegle-p .60 1.50 3.00

SPIDER-MAN AND THE INCREDIBLE HULK (See listing under Amazing...)

SPIDER-MAN COMICS MAGAZINE
Jan, 1987 - No. 13, 1988 ($1.50, Digest-size)
Marvel Comics Group

1-13-Reprints .30 .75 1.50

SPIDER-MAN/DR. STRANGE: THE WAY TO DUSTY DEATH
1993 ($6.95, 68 pgs.)
Marvel Comics

nn 1.40 3.50 7.00

SPIDER-MAN SAGA (Marvel)(Value: cover or less)

SPIDER-MAN 2099 (See Amazing Spider-Man #365)
Nov, 1992 - Present ($1.25, color)
Marvel Comics

1-($1.75, stiff-c)-Red foil stamped-c; begins origin of Miguel O'Hara (Spider-Man 2099); Leonardi/Williamson-c/a .60 1.50 3.00
2-Origin continued .30 .75 1.50
3-8: 4-Doom 2099 app. .60 1.25

SPIDER-MAN VS. VENOM
1990 ($8.95, trade paperback)
Marvel Comics

nn-r/Amazing Spider-Man #300,315-317 w/new McFarlane-c 1.80 4.50 9.00

SPIDER-MAN VS. WOLVERINE
Feb, 1987 (One-shot); V2#1, 1990 (Both have 68 pgs.)
Marvel Comics Group

1-Williamson-c/a(i); intro Charlemagne; death of Ned Leeds (old Hobgoblin) 4.00 10.00 20.00
V2#1 (1990, $4.95)-Reprints #1 (2/87) 1.00 2.50 5.00

SPIDER REIGN OF THE VAMPIRE KING, THE (Also see The Spider)
1992 - No. 3, 1992 ($4.95, color, coated stock, mini-series, 52 pgs.)
Eclipse Books

Book One - Three: Truman scripts & painted-c 1.00 2.50 5.00

SPIDER'S WEB, THE (See G-8 and His Battle Aces)

SPIDER-WOMAN (Also see The Avengers #240, Marvel Spotlight #32, Marvel Super Heroes Secret Wars #7 & Marvel Two-In-One #29)
April, 1978 - No. 50, June, 1983 (New logo #47 on)
Marvel Comics Group

1-New complete origin & mask added 1.00 2.50 5.00
2-36,39-49: 6,19-Werewolf by Night app. 20,28,29-Spider-Man app. 46-Kingpin app. 49-Tigra app. .30 .75 1.50
37,38-X-Men x-over; 37-1st Siryn; origin retold; photo-c .60 1.50 3.00
50-(52 pgs.)-Death of Spider-Woman; photo-c .60 1.50 3.00
NOTE: ***Austin*** *a-37i.* ***Byrne*** *c-26p.* ***Layton*** *c-19.* ***Miller*** *c-32p.*

SPIDEY SUPER STORIES (Spider-Man)
Oct, 1974 - No. 57, Mar, 1982 (35 cents) (no ads)
Marvel/Children's TV Workshop

1-Origin (stories simplified) .80 2.00 4.00
2-12: 2-Kraven. 6-Iceman .60 1.50 3.00
13-38,40-44,46-57: 31-Moondragon-c/story; Dr. Doom app. 33-Hulk. 34-Sub-Mariner. 38-F.F. 44-Vision. 56-Battles Jack O'Lantern-c/story (exactly one year after 1st app. in Machine Man #19) .40 1.00 2.00
39-Thanos-c/story .80 2.00 4.00
45-Silver Surfer & Dr. Doom app. .80 2.00 4.00

SPIKE AND TYKE (See M.G.M.'s...)

SPIN & MARTY (TV) (Walt Disney's)(See Walt Disney Showcase #32)
No. 714, June, 1956 - No. 1082, Mar-May, 1960 (All photo-c)
Dell Publishing Co. (Mickey Mouse Club)

4-Color 714 (#1) 10.00 30.00 60.00
4-Color 767,808 5.85 17.50 35.00
4-Color 826-Annette Funicello photo-c 12.00 36.00 85.00
5(3-5/58) - 9(6-8/59) 5.85 17.50 35.00
4-Color 1026,1082 5.85 17.50 35.00

SPINE-TINGLING TALES (Doctor Spektor Presents...)
May, 1975 - No. 4, Jan, 1976 (All 25 cent issues)
Gold Key

1-4: 1-1st Tragg-r/Mystery Comics Digest #3. 2-Origin Ra-Ka-Tep-r/Mystery Comics Digest #1; Dr. Spektor #12. 3-All Durak-r issue; 4-Baron Tibor's 1st app.-r/Mystery Comics Digest #4 .50 1.00

SPIRAL PATH, THE (Eclipse)(Value: cover or less)

SPIRAL ZONE
Feb, 1988 - No. 4, May, 1988 ($1.00, mini-series)
DC Comics

1-4-Based on Tonka toys .50 1.00

SPIRIT, THE (Weekly Comic Book)
6/2/40 - 10/5/52 (16 pgs.; 8 pgs.) (no cover) (in color)
(Distributed through various newspapers and other sources)
Will Eisner
NOTE: **Eisner** script, pencils/inks for the most part from 6/2/40-4/26/42; a few stories assisted by Jack Cole, Fine, Powell and Kotsky.

6/2/40(#1)-Origin/1st app. The Spirit; reprinted in Police #11; Lady Luck (Brenda Banks)(1st app.) by Chuck Mazoujian & Mr. Mystic (1st. app.) by S. R. (Bob) Powell begin 60.00 180.00 420.00
6/9/40(#2) 26.00 78.00 180.00
6/16/40(#3)-Black Queen app. in Spirit 17.00 51.00 110.00
6/23/40(#4)-Mr. Mystic receives magical necklace 13.00 40.00 90.00
6/30/40(#5) 13.00 40.00 90.00

Spider-Man #11, © MEG

Spider-Woman #4, © MEG

Spin & Marty #6, © WDC

The Spirit 1/5/41, © Will Eisner

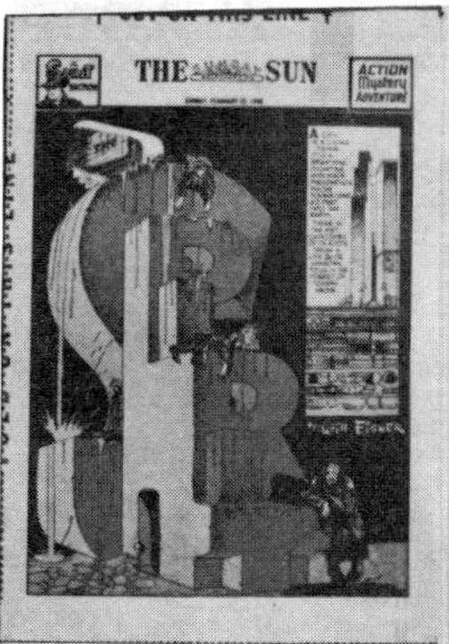

The Spirit 2/22/48, © Will Eisner

The Spirit 6/18/50, © Will Eisner

	GD25	FN65	NM94
7/7/40(#6)-Black Queen app. in Spirit	13.00	40.00	90.00
7/14/40(#7)-8/4/40(#10)	10.00	30.50	70.00
8/11/40-9/22/40	9.00	27.00	62.00
9/29/40-Ellen drops engagement with Homer Creep	8.00	24.00	56.00
10/6/40-11/3/40	8.00	24.00	56.00
11/10/40-The Black Queen app.	8.00	24.00	56.00
11/17/40, 11/24/40	8.00	24.00	56.00
12/1/40-Ellen spanking by Spirit on cover & inside; Eisner-1st 3 pgs., J. Cole rest	11.50	34.00	80.00
12/8/40-3/9/41	5.70	17.00	40.00
3/16/41-Intro. & 1st app. Silk Satin	10.00	30.00	70.00
3/23/41-6/1/41: 5/11/41-Last Lady Luck by Mazoujian; 5/18/41-Lady Luck by Nick Viscardi begins, ends 2/22/42	5.70	17.00	40.00
6/8/41-2nd app. Satin; Spirit learns Satin is also a British agent	8.50	25.50	60.00
6/15/41-1st app. Twilight	7.00	21.00	50.00
6/22/41-Hitler app. in Spirit	5.00	15.00	35.00
6/29/41-1/25/42,2/8/42	5.00	15.00	35.00
2/1/42-1st app. Duchess	7.00	21.00	50.00
2/15/42-4/26/42-Lady Luck by Klaus Nordling begins 3/1/42	5.00	15.00	35.00
5/3/42-8/16/42-Eisner/Fine/Quality staff assists on Spirit	4.00	12.00	24.00
8/23/42-Satin cover splash; Spirit by Eisner/Fine although signed by Fine	8.00	24.00	56.00
8/30/42,9/27/42-10/11/42,10/25/42-11/8/42-Eisner/Fine/Quality staff assists on Spirit	4.00	12.00	24.00
9/6/42-9/20/42,10/18/42-Fine/Belfi art on Spirit; scripts by Manly Wade Wellman	2.75	8.00	16.00
11/15/42-12/6/42,12/20/42,12/27/42,1/17/43-4/18/43,5/9/43-8/8/43-Wellman/Woolfolk scripts, Fine pencils, Quality staff inks	2.75	8.00	16.00
12/13/42,1/3/43,1/10/43,4/25/43,5/2/43-Eisner scripts/layouts; Fine pencils, Quality staff inks	3.35	10.00	20.00
8/15/43-Eisner script/layout; pencils/inks by Quality staff; Jack Cole-a	2.00	6.00	12.00
8/22/43-12/12/43-Wellman/Woolfolk scripts, Fine pencils, Quality staff inks; Mr. Mystic by Guardineer-10/10/43-10/24/43	2.00	6.00	12.00
12/19/43-8/13/44-Wellman/Woolfolk/Jack Cole scripts; Cole, Fine & Robin King-a; Last Mr. Mystic-5/14/44	1.70	5.00	10.00
8/20/44-12/16/45-Wellman/Woolfolk scripts; Fine art with unknown staff assists	1.70	5.00	10.00

NOTE: *Scripts/layouts by Eisner, or Eisner/Nordling, Eisner/Mercer or Spranger/Eisner; inks by Eisner or Eisner/Spranger in issues 12/23/45-2/2/47.*

	GD25	FN65	NM94
12/23/45-1/6/46: 12/23/45-Christmas-c	3.50	10.50	24.00
1/13/46-Origin Spirit retold	5.00	15.00	35.00
1/20/46-1st postwar Satin app.	4.50	14.00	32.00
1/27/46-3/10/46: 3/3/46-Last Lady Luck by Nordling	3.50	10.50	24.00
3/17/46-Intro. & 1st app. Nylon	4.50	14.00	32.00
3/24/46,3/31/46,4/14/46	3.50	10.50	24.00
4/7/46-2nd app. Nylon	4.00	12.00	28.00
4/21/46-Intro. & 1st app. Mr. Carrion & His Pet Buzzard Julia	5.00	15.00	35.00
4/28/46-5/12/46,5/26/46-6/30/46: Lady Luck by Fred Schwab in issues 5/5/46-11/3/46	3.50	10.50	24.00
5/19/46-2nd app. Mr. Carrion	4.00	12.00	28.00
7/7/46-Intro. & 1st app. Dulcet Tone & Skinny	5.00	15.00	35.00
7/14/46-9/29/46	3.50	10.50	24.00
10/6/46-Intro. & 1st app. P'Gell	5.70	17.00	40.00
10/13/46-11/3/46,11/16/46-11/24/46	3.50	10.50	24.00
11/10/46-2nd app. P'Gell	4.00	12.00	28.00
12/1/46-3rd app. P'Gell	3.70	11.00	26.00

	GD25	FN65	NM94
12/8/46-2/2/47	3.00	9.00	21.00

NOTE: *Scripts, pencils/inks by Eisner except where noted in issues 2/9/47-12/19/48.*

	GD25	FN65	NM94
2/9/47-7/6/47: 6/8/47-Eisner self satire	3.00	9.00	21.00
7/13/47-"Hansel & Gretel" fairy tales	4.50	14.00	32.00
7/20/47-Li'L Abner, Daddy Warbucks, Dick Tracy, Fearless Fosdick parody; A-Bomb blast-c	4.50	14.00	32.00
7/27/47-9/14/47	3.00	9.00	21.00
9/21/47-Pearl Harbor flashback	3.00	9.00	21.00
9/28/47-1st mention of Flying Saucers in comics-3 months after 1st sighting in Idaho on 6/25/47	6.50	19.00	45.00
10/5/47-"Cinderella" fairy tales	4.50	14.00	32.00
10/12/47-11/30/47	3.00	9.00	21.00
12/7/47-Intro. & 1st app. Powder Pouf	5.00	15.00	35.00
12/14/47-12/28/47	3.00	9.00	21.00
1/4/48-2nd app. Powder Pouf	4.00	12.00	28.00
1/11/48-1st app. Sparrow Fallon; Powder Pouf app.	4.00	12.00	28.00
1/18/48-He-Man ad cover; satire issue	4.00	12.00	28.00
1/25/48-Intro. & 1st app. Castanet	4.50	14.00	32.00
2/1/48-2nd app. Castanet	3.50	10.50	24.00
2/8/48-3/7/48	3.00	9.00	21.00
3/14/48-Only app. Kretchma	3.50	10.50	24.00
3/21/48,3/28/48,4/11/48-4/25/48	3.00	9.00	21.00
4/4/48-Only app. Wild Rice	3.50	10.50	24.00
5/2/48-2nd app. Sparrow	3.00	9.00	21.00
5/9/48-6/27/48,7/11/48,7/18/48: 6/13/48-Television issue	3.00	9.00	21.00
7/4/48-Spirit by Andre Le Blanc	2.00	6.00	14.00
7/25/48-Ambrose Bierce's "The Thing" adaptation classic by Eisner/Grandenetti	6.50	19.00	45.00
8/1/48-8/15/48,8/29/48-9/12/48	3.00	9.00	21.00
8/22/48-Poe's "Fall of the House of Usher" classic by Eisner/Grandenetti	6.50	19.00	45.00
9/19/48-Only app. Lorelei	3.70	11.00	26.00
9/26/48-10/31/48	3.00	9.00	21.00
11/7/48-Only app. Plaster of Paris	4.00	12.00	28.00
11/14/48-12/19/48	3.00	9.00	21.00

NOTE: *Scripts by Eisner or Feiffer or Eisner/Feiffer or Nordling. Art by Eisner with backgrounds by Eisner, Grandenetti, Le Blanc, Stallman, Nordling, Dixon and/or others in issues 12/26/48-4/1/51 except where noted.*

	GD25	FN65	NM94
12/26/48-Reprints some covers of 1948 with flashbacks	3.00	9.00	21.00
1/2/49-1/16/49	3.00	9.00	21.00
1/23/49,1/30/49-1st & 2nd app. Thorne	4.00	12.00	28.00
2/6/49-8/14/49	3.00	9.00	21.00
8/21/49,8/28/49-1st & 2nd app. Monica Veto	4.00	12.00	28.00
9/4/49,9/11/49	3.00	9.00	21.00
9/18/49-Love comic cover; has gag love comic ads on inside	4.30	13.00	30.00
9/25/49-Only app. Ice	3.70	11.00	26.00
10/2/49,10/9/49-Autumn News appears & dies in 10/9 issue	3.70	11.00	26.00
10/16/49-11/27/49,12/18/49,12/25/49	3.00	9.00	21.00
12/4/49,12/11/49-1st & 2nd app. Flaxen	4.00	12.00	24.00
1/1/50-Flashbacks to all of the Spirit girls-Thorne, Ellen, Satin, & Monica	5.00	15.00	35.00
1/8/50-Intro. & 1st app. Sand Saref	7.00	21.00	50.00
1/15/50-2nd app. Saref	5.00	15.00	35.00
1/22/50-2/5/50	3.00	9.00	21.00
2/12/50-Roller Derby issue	3.50	10.50	24.00
2/19/50-Half Dead Mr. Lox - Classic horror	3.70	11.00	26.00
2/26/50-4/23/50,5/14/50,5/28/50,7/23/50-9/3/50	3.00	9.00	21.00
4/30/50-Script/art by Le Blanc with Eisner framing	1.70	5.00	10.00
5/7/50,6/4/50-7/16/50-Abe Kanegson-a	1.70	5.00	10.00

	GD25	FN65	NM94
5/21/50-Script by Feiffer/Eisner, art by Blaisdell, Eisner framing	1.70	5.00	10.00
9/10/50-P'Gell returns	4.00	12.00	28.00
9/17/50-1/7/51	3.00	9.00	21.00
1/14/51-Life Magazine cover; brief biography of Comm. Dolan, Sand Saref, Silk Satin, P'Gell, Sammy & Willum, Darling O'Shea, & Mr. Carrion & His Pet Buzzard Julia, with pin-ups by Eisner	3.70	11.00	26.00
1/21/51,2/4/51-4/1/51	3.00	9.00	21.00
1/28/51-"The Meanest Man in the World" classic by Eisner	3.70	11.00	26.00
4/8/51-7/29/51,8/12/51-Last Eisner issue	3.00	9.00	21.00
8/5/51,8/19/51-7/20/52-Not Eisner	1.70	5.00	10.00
7/27/52-(Rare)-Denny Colt in Outer Space by Wally Wood; 7 pg. S/F story of E.C. vintage	32.00	95.00	225.00
8/3/52-(Rare)-"Mission...The Moon" by Wood	32.00	95.00	225.00
8/10/52-(Rare)-"A DP On The Moon" by Wood	32.00	95.00	225.00
8/17/52-(Rare)-"Heart" by Wood/Eisner	27.00	81.00	190.00
8/24/52-(Rare)-"Rescue" by Wood	32.00	95.00	225.00
8/31/52-(Rare)-"The Last Man" by Wood	32.00	95.00	225.00
9/7/52-(Rare)-"The Man in The Moon" by Wood	32.00	95.00	225.00
9/14/52-(Rare)-Eisner/Wenzel-a	6.50	19.00	45.00
9/21/52-(Rare)-"Denny Colt, Alias The Spirit/Space Report" by Eisner/Wenzel	11.50	34.00	80.00
9/28/52-(Rare)-"Return From The Moon" by Wood	32.00	95.00	225.00
10/5/52-(Rare)-"The Last Story" by Eisner	11.50	34.00	80.00

Large Tabloid pages from 1946 on (Eisner) - Price 30 percent over listed prices.

NOTE: *Spirit sections came out in both large and small format. Some newspapers went to the 8-pg. format months before others. Some printed the pages so they cannot be folded into a small comic book section; these are worth less. (Also see Three Comics & Spiritman).*

SPIRIT, THE (1st Series)(Also see Police Comics #11)
1944 - No. 22, Aug, 1950
Quality Comics Group (Vital)

	GD25	FN65	NM94
nn(#1)-"Wanted Dead or Alive"	50.00	150.00	350.00
nn(#2)-"Crime Doesn't Pay"	32.00	95.00	220.00
nn(#3)-"Murder Runs Wild"	24.00	73.00	170.00
4,5: 4-Flatfoot Burns begins, ends #22	18.00	54.00	125.00
6-10	16.00	48.00	110.00
11	14.00	43.00	100.00
12-17-Eisner-c. 19-Honeybun app.	23.00	70.00	160.00
18-21-Strip-r by Eisner; Eisner-c	32.00	95.00	220.00
22-Used by N.Y. Legis. Comm; classic Eisner-c	46.00	137.00	320.00
Super Reprint #11-r/Quality Spirit #19 by Eisner	2.40	6.00	12.00
Super Reprint #12-r/Spirit #17 by Fine; Simon-c	2.00	5.00	10.00

SPIRIT, THE (2nd Series)
Spring, 1952 - No. 5, 1954
Fiction House Magazines

	GD25	FN65	NM94
1-Not Eisner	24.00	73.00	170.00
2-Eisner-c/a(2)	27.00	80.00	185.00
3-Eisner/Grandenetti-c	17.00	52.00	120.00
4-Eisner/Grandenetti-c; Eisner-a	20.00	60.00	140.00
5-Eisner-c/a(4)	26.00	77.00	180.00

SPIRIT, THE
Oct, 1966 - No. 2, Mar, 1967 (Giant Size, 25 cents, 68 pgs.)
Harvey Publications

	GD25	FN65	NM94
1-Eisner-r plus 9 new pgs.(Origin Denny Colt, Take 3, plus 2 filler pages)	4.70	14.00	28.00
2-Eisner-r plus 9 new pgs.(origin of the Octopus)	4.70	14.00	28.00

SPIRIT, THE (Underground)
Jan, 1973 - No. 2, Sept, 1973 (Black & White)
Kitchen Sink Enterprises (Krupp Comics)

	GD25	FN65	NM94
1-New Eisner-c, 4 pgs. new Eisner-a plus-r (titled Crime Convention)	1.60	4.00	8.00
2-New Eisner-c, 4 pgs. new Eisner-a plus-r (titled Meets P'Gell)	2.00	5.00	10.00

SPIRIT, THE (Magazine)
4/74 - No. 16, 10/76; No. 17, Winter, 1977 - No. 41, 6/83 (B&W w/color)
Warren Publ. Co./Krupp Comic Works No. 17 on

	GD25	FN65	NM94
1-Eisner-r begin	1.00	2.50	5.00
2-5	.60	1.50	3.00
6-9,11-16: 7-All Ebony issue. 8-Female Foes issue. 12-X-Mas issue. 16-Giant Summer Special ($1.50)	.50	1.20	2.40
10-Giant Summer Special ($1.50)-Origin	.55	1.40	2.80
17,18(8/78): 17-Lady Luck-r. 20-Outer Space-r		.60	1.20
19-21-New Eisner-a. 20,21-Wood-r (#21-r/A DP on the Moon by Wood)		.60	1.20
22,23-Wood-r (#22-r/Mission the Moon by Wood)		.60	1.20
24-29,31-35: 28-r/last story (10/5/52)		.60	1.20
30-(7/81)-Special Spirit Jam issue w/Caniff, Corben, Bolland, Byrne, Miller, Kurtzman, Rogers, Sienkiewicz-a & 40 others	.30	.75	1.50
36-Begin Spirit Section-r; r/1st story (6/2/40) in color; new Eisner-c/a (18 pgs.)($2.95)	.60	1.50	3.00
37-41: 37-r/2nd story in color plus 18 pgs. new Eisner-a. 38-41: r/3rd - 6th stories in color. 41-Lady Luck Mr. Mystic in color	.60	1.50	3.00
Special 1(1975)-All Eisner-a	.35	.90	1.80

NOTE: *Covers pencilled/inked by* ***Eisner*** *only #1-9,12-16; painted by Eisner & Ken Kelly #10 & 11; painted by Eisner #17-up; one color story reprinted in #1-10.* ***Austin*** *a-30i.* ***Byrne*** *a-30p.* ***Miller*** *a-30p.*

SPIRIT, THE (See Will Eisner's 3-D Classics Featuring...)
Oct, 1983 - No. 87, Jan, 1992 (Baxter paper) ($2.00)
Kitchen Sink Enterprises

	GD25	FN65	NM94
1-4: 1-Origin-r/12/23/45 Spirit Section. 2-r/sections 1/20/46-2/10/46. 3-r/2/17/46-3/10/46. 4-r/3/17/46-4/7/46	.40	1.00	2.00
5-11 ($2.95 cover): 11-Last color issue	.40	1.00	2.00
12-87 ($1.95-$2.00, B&W): 54-r/section 2/19/50. 85-87-Reprint the Outer Space Spirit stories by Wood. 86-r/A DP on the Moon by Wood from 1952	.40	1.00	2.00

SPIRIT: THE ORIGIN YEARS
May, 1992 - Present ($2.95, B&W, high quality paper)
Kitchen Sink Press

	GD25	FN65	NM94
1-4: 1-r/sections 6/2/40(origin)-6/23/40 (all 1940s)	.60	1.50	3.00

SPIRITMAN (Also see Three Comics)
No date (1944) (10 cents)
(Triangle Sales Co. ad on back cover)
No publisher listed

	GD25	FN65	NM94
1-Three 16pg. Spirit sections bound together, (1944, 10 cents, 48 pgs.)	15.00	45.00	105.00
2-Two Spirit sections (3/26/44, 4/2/44) bound together; by Lou Fine	12.00	36.00	85.00

SPIRIT WORLD (Magazine)
Fall, 1971 (Black & White)
National Periodical Publications

	GD25	FN65	NM94
1-Kirby-a; Neal Adams-c	1.20	3.00	6.00

SPITFIRE
No. 132, 1944 (Aug) - No. 133, 1945 (Female undercover agent)
Malverne Herald (Elliot)(J. R. Mahon)

	GD25	FN65	NM94
132,133: Both have Classics Gift Box ads on b/c with checklist to #20	11.50	34.00	80.00

SPITFIRE AND THE TROUBLESHOOTERS (Marvel)(Value: cover or less)

SPITFIRE COMICS (Also see Double Up)
Aug, 1941 - No. 2, Oct, 1941 (Pocket size; 100 pgs.)
Harvey Publications

	GD25	FN65	NM94
1-Origin The Clown, The Fly-Man, The Spitfire & The Magician From Bagdad	40.00	120.00	240.00

The Spirit 8/3/52, © Will Eisner

The Spirit #19 (Quality), © Will Eisner

Spitfire #132, © EP

Spook #25, © STAR

Sports Action #4, © MEG

Sport Thrills #13, © STAR

	GD25	FN65	NM94
2	35.00	105.00	210.00

SPOOF
Oct, 1970; No. 2, Nov, 1972 - No. 5, May, 1973
Marvel Comics Group

1-Infinity-c; Dark Shadows-c & parody	.80	2.00	4.00
2-5: 3-Beatles, Osmond's, Jackson 5, David Cassidy, Nixon & Agnew-c. 5-Rod Serling, Woody Allen, Ted Kennedy-c	.40	1.00	2.00

SPOOK (Formerly Shock Detective Cases)
No. 22, Jan, 1953 - No. 30, Oct, 1954
Star Publications

22-Sgt. Spook-r; acid in face story; hanging-c	12.00	36.00	85.00
23,25,27: 27-Two Sgt. Spook-r	9.15	27.50	55.00
24-Used in **SOTI**, pg. 182,183-r/Inside Crime #2; Transvestism story	10.00	30.00	70.00
26-Disbrow-a	10.00	30.00	60.00
28,29-Rulah app. 29-Jo-Jo app.	10.00	30.00	60.00
30-Disbrow-c/a(2); only Star-c	10.00	30.00	60.00

NOTE: *L. B. Cole covers-all issues; a-28(1pg.). Disbrow a-26(2), 28, 29(2), 30(2); No. 30 r/Blue Bolt Weird Tales #114.*

SPOOK COMICS
1946
Baily Publications/Star

1-Mr. Lucifer story	14.00	43.00	100.00

SPOOKY (The Tuff Little Ghost; see Casper The Friendly Ghost)
11/55 - 139, 11/73; No. 140, 7/74 - No. 155, 3/77; No. 156, 12/77 - No. 158, 4/78; No. 159, 9/78; No. 160, 10/79; No. 161, 9/80
Harvey Publications

1-Nightmare begins (see Casper #19)	22.00	65.00	150.00
2	10.00	30.00	70.00
3-10(1956-57)	5.00	15.00	30.00
11-20(1957-58)	3.00	7.50	15.00
21-40(1958-59)	1.80	4.50	9.00
41-60	1.20	3.00	6.00
61-80	1.00	2.50	5.00
81-120	.60	1.50	3.00
121-126,133-140	.40	1.00	2.00
127-132: All 52 pg. Giants	.60	1.50	3.00
141-161	.30	.75	1.50

SPOOKY
1991 - No. 4, 1992 ($1.00/$1.25, color)
Harvey Comics

1-4: 3-Begin $1.25-c		.60	1.25
...Digest 1 (10/92, $1.75)-Casper, Wendy, etc.	.35	.90	1.75

SPOOKY HAUNTED HOUSE
Oct, 1972 - No. 15, Feb, 1975
Harvey Publications

1	2.00	5.00	10.00
2-5	1.00	2.50	5.00
6-10	.50	1.25	2.50
11-15	.30	.75	1.50

SPOOKY MYSTERIES
No date (1946) (10 cents)
Your Guide Publ. Co.

1-Mr. Spooky, Super Snooper, Pinky, Girl Detective app.	10.00	30.00	60.00

SPOOKY SPOOKTOWN
9/61; No. 2, 9/62 - No. 52, 12/73; No. 53, 10/74 - No. 66, Dec, 1976
Harvey Publications

1-Casper, Spooky; 68 pgs. begin	10.00	30.00	60.00

	GD25	FN65	NM94
2	5.00	15.00	30.00
3-5	4.00	10.00	20.00
6-10	2.40	6.00	12.00
11-20	1.60	4.00	8.00
21-39: Last 68 pg. issue	.80	2.00	4.00
40-45: All 52 pgs.	.60	1.50	3.00
46-66	.40	1.00	2.00

SPORT COMICS (Becomes True Sport Picture Stories #5 on)
Oct, 1940(No mo.) - No. 4, Nov, 1941
Street & Smith Publications

1-Life story of Lou Gehrig	37.00	110.00	225.00
2	18.00	55.00	110.00
3,4	17.00	50.00	100.00

SPORT LIBRARY (See Charlton Sport Library)

SPORTS ACTION (Formerly Sport Stars)
No. 2, Feb, 1950 - No. 14, Sept, 1952
Marvel/Atlas Comics (ACI No. 2,3/SAI No. 4-14)

2-Powell painted-c; George Gipp life story	20.00	60.00	120.00
3-Everett-a	13.00	40.00	80.00
4-11,14: Weiss-a	12.00	35.00	70.00
12,13: 12-Everett-c. 13-Krigstein-a	13.00	40.00	80.00

NOTE: *Title may have changed after No. 3, to Crime Must Lose No. 4 on, due to publisher change. **Sol Brodsky** c-4-7, 13, 14. **Maneely** c-3, 8-11.*

SPORT STARS
Feb-Mar, 1946 - No. 4, Aug-Sept, 1946 (Half comic, half photo magazine)
Parents' Magazine Institute (Sport Stars)

1-"How Tarzan Got That Way" story of Johnny Weissmuller	25.00	75.00	150.00
2-Baseball greats	17.00	50.00	100.00
3,4	13.00	40.00	80.00

SPORT STARS (Becomes Sports Action #2 on)
Nov, 1949 (52 pgs.)
Marvel Comics (ACI)

1-Knute Rockne; painted-c	25.00	75.00	150.00

SPORT THRILLS (Formerly Dick Cole; becomes Jungle thrills #16)
No. 11, Nov, 1950 - No. 15, Nov, 1951
Star Publications

11-Dick Cole app; Ted Williams & Ty Cobb life stories	12.00	35.00	70.00
12-L. B. Cole c/a	8.35	25.00	50.00
13-15-All L. B. Cole-c; 13-Dick Cole app. 14-Johnny Weissmuler life story	8.35	25.00	50.00
Accepted Reprint #11 (#15 on-c, nd); L.B. Cole-c	3.60	9.00	18.00
Accepted Reprint #12 (nd); L.B. Cole-c; Joe DiMaggio & Phil Rizzuto life stories	3.60	9.00	18.00

SPOTLIGHT (TV)
Sept, 1978 - No. 4, Mar, 1979 (Hanna-Barbera)
Marvel Comics Group

1-Huckleberry Hound, Yogi Bear; Shaw-a. 2-Quick Draw McGraw. Augie Doggie, Snooper & Blabber. 3-The Jetsons, Yakky Doodle. 4-Magilla Gorilla, Snagglepuss	.40	1.00	2.00

SPOTLIGHT COMICS (Becomes Red Seal Comics #14 on?)
Nov, 1944 - No. 3, 1945
Harry 'A' Chesler (Our Army, Inc.)

1-The Black Dwarf (cont'd in Red Seal?), The Veiled Avenger, & Barry Kuda begin; Tuska-c	35.00	105.00	210.00
2	28.00	85.00	170.00
3-Injury to eye story (same as Scoop #3)	31.00	92.00	185.00

SPOTTY THE PUP (Becomes Super Pup #4, see Television Puppet Show)

	GD25	FN65	NM94

No. 2, Oct-Nov, 1953 - No. 3, Dec-Jan, 1953-54
Avon Periodicals/Realistic Comics

	GD25	FN65	NM94
2,3	3.20	8.00	16.00
nn (1953, Realistic-r)	2.00	5.00	10.00

SPUNKY (...Junior Cowboy)(...Comics #2 on)
April, 1949 - No. 7, Nov, 1951
Standard Comics

	GD25	FN65	NM94
1,2-Text illos by Frazetta	5.00	15.00	30.00
3-7	3.20	8.00	16.00

SPUNKY THE SMILING SPOOK
Aug, 1957 - No. 4, May, 1958
Ajax/Farrell (World Famous Comics/Four Star Comic Corp.)

	GD25	FN65	NM94
1-Reprints from Frisky Fables	4.20	12.50	25.00
2-4	3.20	8.00	16.00

SPY AND COUNTERSPY (Becomes Spy Hunters #3 on)
Aug-Sept, 1949 - No. 2, Oct-Nov, 1949 (52 pgs.)
American Comics Group

	GD25	FN65	NM94
1-Origin, 1st app. Jonathan Kent, Counterspy	11.00	32.00	75.00
2	9.15	27.50	55.00

SPY CASES (Formerly The Kellys)
No. 26, Sept, 1950 - No. 19, Oct, 1953
Marvel/Atlas Comics (Hercules Publ.)

	GD25	FN65	NM94
26 (#1)	10.00	30.00	70.00
27(#2),28(#3, 2/51): 27-Everett-a; bondage-c	7.50	22.50	45.00
4(4/51) - 7,9,10	5.35	16.00	32.00
8-A-Bomb-c/story	6.70	20.00	40.00
11-19: 11-14-War format	4.20	12.50	25.00

NOTE: ***Sol Brodsky** c-1-5, 8, 9, 11-14, 17, 18. **Maneely** a-8; c-7, 10. **Tuska** a-7.*

SPY FIGHTERS
March, 1951 - No. 15, July, 1953
Marvel/Atlas Comics (CSI)

	GD25	FN65	NM94
1-Tuska-a; Brodsky-c	11.00	32.00	75.00
2-Tuska-a	6.35	19.00	38.00
3-13: 3-5-Brodsky-c. 7-Heath-c	5.00	15.00	30.00
14,15-Pakula-a(3), Ed Win-a. 15-Brodsky-c	5.35	16.00	32.00

SPY-HUNTERS (Formerly Spy & Counterspy)
No. 3, Dec-Jan, 1949-50 - No. 24, June-July, 1953 (#3-11: 52 pgs.)
American Comics Group

	GD25	FN65	NM94
3-Jonathan Kent continues, ends #10	11.00	32.00	75.00
4-10: 4,8,10-Starr-a	7.50	22.50	45.00
11-15,17-22,24: 18-War-c begin. 21-War-c/stories begin	5.00	15.00	30.00
16-Williamson-a (9 pgs.)	9.15	27.50	55.00
23-Graphic torture, injury to eye panel	10.00	30.00	65.00

NOTE: ***Drucker** a-12. **Whitney** a-many issues; c-7, 8, 10-12, 16.*

SPYMAN (Top Secret Adventures on cover)
Sept, 1966 - No. 3, Feb, 1967 (12 cents)
Harvey Publications (Illustrated Humor)

	GD25	FN65	NM94
1-Steranko-a(p)-1st pro work; 1pg. Neal Adams ad; Tuska-c/a, Crandall-a(i)	4.00	11.00	22.00
2,3: Simon-c. 2-Steranko-a(p)	3.00	7.50	15.00

SPY SMASHER (See Mighty Midget, Whiz & XMas Comics)
Fall, 1941 - No. 11, Feb, 1943 (Also see Crime Smasher)
Fawcett Publications

	GD25	FN65	NM94
1-Spy Smasher begins; silver metallic-c	183.00	550.00	1100.00
2-Raboy-c	92.00	275.00	550.00
3,4: 3-Bondage-c	75.00	225.00	450.00
5-7: Raboy-a; 6-Raboy-c/a. 7-Part photo-c	67.00	200.00	400.00
8-11: 9-Hitler, Tojo, Mussolini-c. 10-Hitler-c	58.00	175.00	350.00
Well Known Comics (1944, 12 pgs., 8-1/2x10-1/2"), paper-c, glued binding, printed in green; Bestmaid/Samuel Lowe giveaway	17.00	50.00	100.00

SPY THRILLERS (Police Badge No. 479 #5)
Nov, 1954 - No. 4, May, 1955
Atlas Comics (PrPI)

	GD25	FN65	NM94
1-Brodsky c-1,2	10.00	30.00	60.00
2-Last precode (1/55)	5.85	17.50	35.00
3,4	4.20	12.50	25.00

SQUADRON SUPREME (Marvel)(Value: cover or less)

SQUALOR (First)(Value: cover or less)

SQUEEKS
Oct, 1953 - No. 5, June, 1954
Lev Gleason Publications

	GD25	FN65	NM94
1-Funny animal; Biro-c	4.70	14.00	28.00
2-Biro-c	2.80	7.00	14.00
3-5: 3-Biro-c	2.40	6.00	12.00

STAINLESS STEEL RAT (Eagle)(Value: cover or less)

STALKER
June-July, 1975 - No. 4, Dec-Jan, 1975-76
National Periodical Publications

	GD25	FN65	NM94
1-Origin & 1st app; Ditko/Wood-c/a	.60	1.50	3.00
2-4-Ditko/Wood-c/a	.40	1.00	2.00

STALKERS (Marvel)(Value: cover or less)(Also see Epic)

STAMP COMICS (Stamps... on-c; Thrilling Advs. In...#8)
Oct, 1951 - No. 7, Oct, 1952 (No. 1: 15 cents)
Youthful Magazines/Stamp Comics, Inc.

	GD25	FN65	NM94
1('Stamps' on indicia No. 1)	19.00	57.00	135.00
2	10.00	30.00	70.00
3-6: 3,4-Kiefer, Wildey-a	10.00	30.00	60.00
7-Roy Krenkel, 4 pgs.	12.00	36.00	85.00

NOTE: *Promotes stamp collecting; gives stories behind various commemorative stamps. No. 2, 10 cents printed over 15 cents c-price. **Kiefer** a-1-7. **Kirkel** a-1-6. **Napoli** a-2-7. **Palais** a-2-4, 7.*

STANLEY & HIS MONSTER (Formerly The Fox & the Crow)
No. 109, Apr-May, 1968 - No. 112, Oct-Nov, 1968
National Periodical Publications

	GD25	FN65	NM94
109-112	2.00	5.00	10.00

STANLEY & HIS MONSTER
Feb, 1993 - Present ($1.50, color)
DC Comics

	GD25	FN65	NM94
1-4	.30	.75	1.50

STAR BLAZERS (Comico, 1987 & 1989)(Value: cover or less)

STAR BRAND (Marvel)(Value: cover or less)

STAR COMICS
Feb, 1937 - V2#7 (No. 23), Aug, 1939 (#1-6: large size)
Ultem Publ. (Harry `A' Chesler)/Centaur Publications

	GD25	FN65	NM94
V1#1-Dan Hastings (s/f) begins	100.00	300.00	600.00
2	50.00	150.00	300.00
3-6 (#6, 9/37): 5-Little Nemo	46.00	138.00	275.00
7-9: 8-Severed head centerspread; Impy & Little Nemo by Winsor McCay Jr, Popeye app. by Bob Wood; Mickey Mouse-c app.	38.00	115.00	230.00
10 (1st Centaur; 3/38)-Impy by Winsor McCay Jr; Don Marlow by Guardineer begins	58.00	175.00	350.00
11-1st Jack Cole comic-a, 1 pg. (4/38)	38.00	115.00	230.00
12-15: 12-Riders of the Golden West begins; Little Nemo app. 15-Speed Silvers by Gustavson & The Last Pirate by Burgos begins	37.00	110.00	225.00
16 (12/38)-The Phantom Rider & his horse Thunder begins, ends V2#6	37.00	110.00	225.00
V2#1(#17, 2/39)	37.00	110.00	225.00

Spy-Hunters #14, © ACG

Squeeks #1, © LEV

Star Comics V1#5, © CEN

Star-Lord the Special Edition #1, © MEG

Star Ranger #6, © CEN

Stars and Stripes Comics #5, © CEN

GD25 FN65 NM94

2-7(#18-23): 2-Diana Deane by Tarpe Mills app. 3-Drama of Hollywood by Mills begins. 7-Jungle Queen app. 35.00 105.00 210.00
NOTE: *Biro c-9, 10. Burgos a-15, 16, V2#1-7. Ken Ernst a-10, 12, 14. Filchock c-15, 18, 22. Gill Fox c-14, V2#2, 3. Guardineer a-6, 8-14. Gustavson a-13-16, V2#1-7. Winsor McCay c-4, 5. Tarpe Mills a-15, V2#1-7. Schwab c-20, 23. Bob Wood a-10, 12, 13; c-7, 8.*

STAR COMICS MAGAZINE (Marvel) (Value: cover or less)

STAR FEATURE COMICS
1963
I. W. Enterprises

Reprint #9-Stunt-Man Stetson-r/Feat. Comics #141 .60 1.50 3.00

STARFIRE (See New Teen Titans & Teen Titans #18)
Aug-Sept, 1976 - No. 8, Oct-Nov, 1977
National Periodical Publications/DC Comics

1-Origin (CCA stamp fell off cover art; so it was approved by code) .30 .75 1.50
2-8 .50 1.00

STAR HUNTERS (See DC Super Stars #16)
Oct-Nov, 1977 - No. 7, Oct-Nov, 1978
National Periodical Publications/DC Comics

1-7: 1-Newton-a(p). 7-Giant .50 1.00
NOTE: *Buckler a-4-7p; c-1-7p. Layton a-1-5i; c-1-6i. Nasser a-3p. Sutton a-6i.*

STARK TERROR (Magazine)
Dec, 1970 - No. 5, Aug, 1971 (52 pages) (B&W)
Stanley Publications

1-Bondage, torture-c 3.00 7.50 15.00
2-4 (Gillmor/Aragon-r) 1.60 4.00 8.00
5 (ACG-r) 1.40 3.50 7.00

STARLET O'HARA IN HOLLYWOOD (Teen-age) (Also see Cookie)
Dec, 1948 - No. 4, Sept, 1949
Standard Comics

1-Owen Fitzgerald-a in all 11.00 32.00 75.00
2 9.15 27.50 55.00
3,4 7.50 22.50 45.00

STAR-LORD THE SPECIAL EDITION (Also see Marvel Comics Super Special #10, Marvel Premiere & Preview & Marvel Spotlight V2#6,7)
Feb, 1982 (One Shot) (Direct sale, 1st Baxter paper comic)
Marvel Comics Group

1-Byrne/Austin-a; Austin-c, Golden-a(p); 8 pgs. of new-a; Dr. Who story 1.00 2.50 5.00

STARMAN (See Adventure #467, Brave & the Bold, 1st Issue Special, Justice League & Showcase)
Oct, 1988 - No. 45, Apr, 1992 ($1.00, color)
DC Comics

1-27,29-45: 1-Origin. 4-Intro The Power Elite. 9,10,34-Batman app. 14-Superman app. 17-Power Girl app. 26,27-G.A. Starman app. 38-War of the Gods x-over. 42-Lobo cameo. 42-45-Eclipso-c/stories (#43,44 with Lobo) .50 1.00
28-Starman disguised as Superman; leads into Superman #50 .40 1.00 2.00

STARMASTERS (Americomics) (Value: cover or less)

STAR PRESENTATION, A (Formerly My Secret Romance #1,2; Spectacular Stories #4 on) (Also see This Is Suspense)
No. 3, May, 1950
Fox Features Syndicate (Hero Books)

3-Dr. Jekyll & Mr. Hyde by Wood & Harrison (reprinted in Startling Terror Tales #10); "The Repulsing Dwarf" by Wood; Wood-c 36.00 107.00 250.00

STAR QUEST COMIX (Warren Presents... on cover)
October, 1978
Warren Publications

1 .50 1.00

STAR RAIDERS (See DC Graphic Novel #1)

STAR RANGER (Cowboy Comics #13 on)
Feb, 1937 - No. 12, May, 1938 (Large size: No. 1-6)
Ultem Publ./Centaur Publications

1-(1st Western comic)-Ace & Deuce, Air Plunder; Flessel-a 108.00 325.00 650.00
2 50.00 150.00 300.00
3-6 47.00 130.00 260.00
7-9: 8-Christmas-c 37.00 110.00 225.00
V2#10 (1st Centaur; 3/38) 58.00 175.00 350.00
11,12 46.00 138.00 275.00
NOTE: *J. Cole a-10, 12; c-12. Ken Ernst a-11. Gill Fox a-8(illo), 9, 10. Guardineer a-1, 3, 6, 7, 8(illos), 9, 10, 12. Gustavson a-8-10, 12. Fred Schwab c-2-11. Bob Wood a-8-10.*

STAR RANGER FUNNIES (Formerly Cowboy Comics)
V1#15, Oct, 1938 - V2#5, Oct, 1939
Centaur Publications

V1#15-Eisner, Gustavson-a 70.00 200.00 400.00
V2#1 (1/39) 50.00 150.00 300.00
2-5: 2-Night Hawk by Gustavson. 4-Kit Carson app. 42.00 125.00 250.00
NOTE: *Jack Cole a-V2#1, 3; c-V2#1. Filchock c-V2#2, 3. Guardineer a-V2#3. Gustavson a-V2#2. Pinajian c/a-V2#5.*

STAR REACH CLASSICS (Eclipse) (Value: cover or less)

STARR FLAGG, UNDERCOVER GIRL (See Undercover...)

STARRIORS (Marvel) (Value: cover or less)

STARS AND STRIPES COMICS
No. 2, May, 1941 - No. 6, Dec, 1941
Centaur Publications

2(#1)-The Shark, The Iron Skull, Aman, The Amazing Man, Mighty Man, Minimidget begin; The Voice & Dash Dartwell, the Human Meteor, Reef Kinkaid app.; Gustavson Flag-c 133.00 400.00 800.00
3-Origin Dr. Synthe; The Black Panther app. 92.00 275.00 550.00
4-Origin/1st app. The Stars and Stripes; injury to eye-c 77.00 230.00 460.00
5(#5 on cover & inside) 58.00 175.00 350.00
5(#6)-(#5 on cover, #6 on inside) 58.00 175.00 350.00
NOTE: *Gustavson c/a-3. Myron Strauss c-4, 5(#5), 5(#6).*

STARSLAYER
Feb, 1982 - No. 6, Apr, 1983; No. 7, Aug, 1983 - No. 34, Nov, 1985
Pacific Comics/First Comics No. 7 on

1-Origin; excessive blood & gore; 1 pg. Rocketeer cameo which continues in #2 .60 1.50 3.00
2-Origin/1st full app. the Rocketeer by Dave Stevens (Chapter 1 of Rocketeer saga; see Pacific Presents #1,2) 2.40 6.00 12.00
3-Chapter 2 of Rocketeer saga by Stevens 1.40 3.50 7.00
4 .40 1.00 2.00
5-2nd app. Groo the Wanderer by Aragones 1.20 3.00 6.00
6,7: 7-Grell-a ends .40 1.00 2.00
8-34: 10-1st app. Grimjack (11/83, ends #17). 18-Starslayer meets Grimjack. 20-The Black Flame begins(1st app.), ends #33. 27-Book length Black Flame story .50 1.00
NOTE: *Grell a-1-7; c-1-8. Stevens back c-2, 3. Sutton a-17p, 20-22p, 24-27p, 29-33p.*

STAR SPANGLED COMICS (...War Stories #131 on)
Oct, 1941 - No. 130, July, 1952
National Periodical Publications

1-Origin Tarantula; Captain X of the R.A.F., Star Spangled Kid (see Action #40) & Armstrong of the Army begin 250.00 750.00 1500.00
2 96.00 288.00 575.00

	GD25	FN65	NM94
3-5	63.00	188.00	375.00
6-Last Armstrong of the Army	42.00	125.00	250.00

	GD25	FN65	VF82	NM94
7-Origin/1st app. The Guardian by S&K, & Robotman by Paul Cassidy; The Newsboy Legion & TNT begin; last Captain X	350.00	1050.00	1900.00	2800.00

(Estimated up to 100 total copies exist, 5 in NM/Mint)

	GD25	FN65	NM94
8-Origin TNT & Dan the Dyna-Mite	142.00	425.00	850.00
9,10	117.00	350.00	700.00
11-17	96.00	288.00	575.00
18-Origin Star Spangled Kid	121.00	362.00	725.00
19-Last Tarantula	96.00	288.00	575.00
20-Liberty Belle begins	96.00	288.00	575.00
21-29-Last S&K issue; 23-Last TNT. 25-Robotman by Jimmy Thompson begins	75.00	225.00	450.00
30-40: 31-S&K-c	33.00	100.00	200.00
41-50	29.00	88.00	175.00
51-64: Last Newsboy Legion & The Guardian; last Liberty Belle? #53 by S&K	29.00	88.00	175.00
65-Robin begins with cover app. (2/47); Batman cameo in 1 panel; Robin-c begin, end #95	100.00	300.00	600.00
66-Batman cameo in Robin story	62.00	188.00	375.00
67,68,70-80: 72-Burnley Robin-c	50.00	150.00	300.00
69-Origin/1st app. Tomahawk by F. Ray	75.00	225.00	450.00
81-Origin Merry, Girl of 1000 Gimmicks in Star Spangled Kid story	40.00	120.00	240.00
82,85: 82-Last Robotman?	40.00	120.00	240.00
83-Tomahawk enters the lost valley, a land of dinosaurs; Capt. Compass begins, ends #130	40.00	120.00	240.00
84,87 (Rare): 87-Batman cameo in Robin	58.00	175.00	350.00
86-Batman cameo in Robin story; last Star Spangled Kid	44.00	132.00	265.00
88(1/49)-94: Batman-c/stories in all. 91-Federal Men begin, end #93. 94-Manhunters Around the World begin, end #121	50.00	150.00	300.00
95-Batman story; last Robin-c	44.00	132.00	265.00
96,98-Batman cameo in Robin stories. 96-1st Tomahawk-c	32.00	95.00	190.00
97,99	25.00	75.00	150.00
100	32.00	95.00	190.00
101-109,118,119,121: 121-Last Tomahawk-c	23.00	70.00	140.00
110,111,120-Batman cameo in Robin stories. 120-Last 52 pg. issue	25.00	75.00	150.00
112-Batman & Robin story	27.00	82.00	165.00
113-Frazetta-a (10 pgs.)	37.00	110.00	220.00
114-Retells Robin's origin (3/51); Batman & Robin story	33.00	100.00	200.00
115,117-Batman app. in Robin stories	25.00	75.00	150.00
116-Flag-c	23.00	70.00	140.00
122-(11/51)-Ghost Breaker-c/stories begin (origin), ends #130	23.00	70.00	140.00
123-126,128,129	17.00	50.00	100.00
127-Batman cameo	18.00	55.00	110.00
130-Batman cameo in Robin story	20.00	60.00	120.00

NOTE: *Most all issues after #29 signed by Simon & Kirby are not by them.* ***Bill Ely*** *c-122-130.* ***Mortimer*** *c-65-74(most), 76-95(most).* ***Fred Ray*** *c-96-121.* ***S&K*** *c-7-31, 33, 34, 36, 37, 39, 40, 48, 49, 50-54, 56-58.* ***Hal Sherman*** *c-1-6.* ***Dick Sprang*** *c-75.*

STAR SPANGLED WAR STORIES (Formerly Star Spangled Comics #1-130; The Unknown Soldier #205 on) (See Showcase)
No. 131, 8/52 - No. 133, 10/52; No. 3, 11/52 - No. 204, 2-3/77
National Periodical Publications

	GD25	FN65	NM94
131(#1)	57.00	170.00	400.00
132	37.00	110.00	250.00
133-Used in **POP**, Pg. 94	29.00	85.00	200.00
3-6: 4-Devil Dog Dugan app. 6-Evans-a	24.00	70.00	165.00
7-10	17.00	52.00	120.00
11-20	14.00	43.00	100.00
21-30: Last precode (2/55)	11.50	34.00	80.00
31-33,35-40	9.15	27.50	55.00
34-Krigstein-a	10.00	30.00	60.00
41-50	7.50	22.50	45.00
51-83: 67-Easy Co. story without Sgt. Rock	6.00	18.00	36.00
84-Origin Mlle. Marie	11.00	32.00	75.00
85-89-Mlle. Marie in all	7.00	21.00	42.00
90-1st dinosaur issue-c/story (4-5/60)	25.00	75.00	175.00
91,93-No dinosaur stories	5.00	15.00	30.00
92,94-99: All dinosaur-c/stories	11.00	34.00	78.00
100-Dinosaur-c/story	13.50	41.00	95.00
101-133,135-137-Last dinosaur story; Heath Birdman-#129,131	9.15	27.50	55.00
134-Dinosaur story; Neal Adams-a	10.00	30.00	60.00
138-New Enemy Ace-c/stories begin by Joe Kubert (4-5/68), end #150 (also see Our Army at War #151 & Showcase #57)	6.70	20.00	40.00
139-143,145: 145-Last 12 cent issue (6-7/69)	3.60	9.00	18.00
144-Neal Adams/Kubert-a	4.00	10.00	20.00
146-Enemy Ace-c only	2.00	5.00	10.00
147,148-New Enemy Ace sty	2.80	7.00	14.00
149,150-Last new Enemy ace by Kubert. Viking Prince by Kubert	2.40	6.00	12.00
151-1st Unknown Soldier (6-7/70); Enemy Ace-r begin; end #161	4.20	12.50	25.00
152,153,155-Enemy Ace reprints	2.00	5.00	10.00
154-Origin Unknown Soldier	4.00	10.00	20.00
156-1st Battle Album	1.40	3.50	7.00
157-161-Last Enemy Ace	1.00	2.50	5.00
162-204: 181-183-Enemy Ace vs. Balloon Buster serial app.	.40	1.00	2.00

NOTE: ***Chaykin*** *a-167.* ***Drucker*** *a-59, 61, 64, 66, 67, 73-84.* ***Estrada*** *a-149.* ***John Giunta*** *a-72.* ***Glanzman*** *a-167, 171, 172, 174.* ***Heath*** *a-122, 132, 133; c-67, 122, 132-134.* ***Kaluta*** *a-197i; c-167.* ***G. Kane*** *a-169.* ***Kubert*** *a-6-163(most later issues), 200.* ***Maurer*** *a-160, 165.* ***Severin*** *a-65, 162.* ***S&K*** *c-7-31, 33, 34, 37, 40.* ***Simonson*** *a-170, 172, 174, 180.* ***Sutton*** *a-168.* ***Thorne*** *a-183.* ***Toth*** *a-164.* ***Wildey*** *a-161. Suicide Squad in 110, 116-118, 120, 121, 127.*

STARSTREAM (Whitman)(Value: cover or less)

STARSTRUCK (Marvel & Dark Horse)(Value: cover or less)

STAR STUDDED
1945 (25 cents; 132 pgs.); 1945 (196 pgs.)
Cambridge House/Superior Publishers

	GD25	FN65	NM94
nn-Captain Combat by Giunta, Ghost Woman, Commandette, & Red Rogue app.; Infantino-a	16.00	48.00	110.00
nn-The Cadet, Edison Bell, Hoot Gibson, Jungle Lil (196 pgs.); copies vary - Blue Beetle in some	12.00	36.00	85.00

STAR TEAM
1977 (20 pgs.) (6-1/2x5")
Marvel Comics Group (Ideal Toy Giveaway)

	GD25	FN65	NM94
nn		.50	1.00

STARTLING COMICS
June, 1940 - No. 53, May, 1948
Better Publications (Nedor)

	GD25	FN65	NM94
1-Origin Captain Future-Man Of Tomorrow, Mystico (By Eisner/Fine), The Wonder Man; The Masked Rider & his horse Pinto begins; Masked Rider formerly in pulps; drug use story	105.00	310.00	625.00
2-Don Davis, Espionage Ace begins	46.00	138.00	275.00
3	35.00	105.00	210.00
4	27.00	82.00	165.00
5-9	20.00	60.00	120.00
10-The Fighting Yank begins (origin/1st app.)	108.00	325.00	650.00
11-15: 12-Hitler, Hirohito, Mussolini-c	26.00	78.00	155.00
16-Origin The Four Comrades; not in #32,35	29.00	88.00	175.00

Star Spangled Comics #36, © DC

Star Spangled War Stories #138, © DC

Startling Comics #13, © BP

Startling Terror Tales #8, © STAR

Star Trek #8 (Gold Key), © Paramount

Star Trek: The Next Generation #7 (4/90), © Paramount

	GD25	FN65	NM94
17-Last Masked Rider & Mystico	18.00	55.00	110.00
18-Pyroman begins (origin)	50.00	150.00	300.00
19	20.00	60.00	120.00
20-The Oracle begins; not in #26,28,33,34	20.00	60.00	120.00
21-Origin The Ape, Oracle's enemy	18.00	55.00	110.00
22-33	17.00	50.00	100.00
34-Origin The Scarab & only app.	18.00	55.00	110.00
35-Hypodermic syringe attacks Fighting Yank in drug story	18.00	55.00	110.00
36-43: 36-Last Four Comrades. 38-Bondage/torture-c. 40-Last Capt. Future & Oracle. 41-Front Page Peggy begins; A-Bomb-c. 43-Last Pyroman	17.00	50.00	100.00
44-Lance Lewis, Space Detective begins; Ingels-c	27.00	82.00	165.00
45-Tygra begins (Intro/origin); Ingels-c/a	27.00	82.00	165.00
46-Ingels-c/a	27.00	82.00	165.00
47,48,50-53: 50.51-Sea-Eagle app.	20.00	60.00	120.00
49-Robot-c; last Fighting Yank	23.00	70.00	140.00

NOTE: ***Ingels** a-45; c-44, 45, 46(wash). **Schomburg** (Xela) c-21-43; 47-53 (airbrush). **Tuska** c-45? Bondage c-16, 21, 37, 46-49.*

STARTLING TERROR TALES
No. 10, May, 1952 - No. 14, Feb, 1953; No. 4, Apr, 1953 - No. 11, 1954
Star Publications

	GD25	FN65	NM94
10-(1st Series)-Wood/Harrison-a (r/A Star Presentation #3) Disbrow/Cole-c; becomes 4 different titles after #10; becomes Confessions of Love #11 on, The Horrors #11 on, Terrifying Tales #11 on, Terrors of the Jungle #11 on & continues w/Startling Terror #11	27.00	81.00	190.00
11-(#1a, 8/52)-L. B. Cole Spider-c; r-Fox's "A Feature Presentation" #5	15.00	45.00	105.00
12(#1b),14(#3)	7.50	22.50	45.00
13(#2)-Jo-Jo-r; Disbrow-a	8.35	25.00	50.00
4-7,9,11(1953-54) (2nd Series)	6.70	20.00	40.00
8-Spanking scene-r/Crimes By Women #14	7.50	22.50	45.00
10-Disbrow-a	7.50	22.50	45.00

NOTE: ***L. B. Cole** covers-all issues. **Palais** a-V2#8r, V2#11r.*

STAR TREK (TV) (See Dan Curtis Giveaways, Dynabrite Comics & Power Record Comics)
7/67; No. 2, 6/68; No. 3, 12/68; No. 4, 6/69 - No. 61, 3/79
Gold Key

	GD25	FN65	NM94
1-Photo-c begin, end #9	50.00	150.00	350.00
2	25.00	75.00	175.00
3-5	21.00	63.00	145.00
6-9	16.00	48.00	110.00
10-20	10.00	30.00	60.00
21-30	7.50	22.50	45.00
31-40	4.70	14.00	28.00
41-61: 52-Drug propaganda story	3.60	9.00	18.00
...the Enterprise Logs nn(8/76)-Golden Press, ($1.95, 224 pgs.)-r/#1-8 plus 7 pgs. by McWilliams (#11185)-Photo-c	1.80	4.50	9.00
...the Enterprise Logs Vol.2('76)-r/#9-17 (#11187)-Photo-c	1.60	4.00	8.00
...the Enterprise Logs Vol.3('77)-r/#18-26 (#11188); McWilliams-a (4 pgs.)-Photo-c	1.40	3.50	7.00
Star Trek Vol.4(Winter'77)-Reprints #27,28,30-34,36,38 (#11189) plus 3 pgs. new art	1.40	3.50	7.00

NOTE: ***McWilliams** a-38, 40-44, 46-61. #29 reprints #1; #35 reprints #4; #37 reprints #5; #45 reprints #7. The tabloids all have photo covers and blank inside covers. Painted covers #10-44, 46-59.*

STAR TREK
April, 1980 - No. 18, Feb, 1982
Marvel Comics Group

	GD25	FN65	NM94
1-r/Marvel Super Special; movie adapt.	.90	2.25	4.50
2-18: 5-Miller-c	.60	1.50	3.00

NOTE: ***Austin** c-18i. **Buscema** a-13. **Gil Kane** a-15. **Nasser** c/a-7. **Simonson** c-17.*

STAR TREK (Also see Who's Who In Star Trek)
Feb, 1984 - No. 56, Nov, 1988 (Mando paper, 75 cents)
DC Comics

	GD25	FN65	NM94
1-Sutton-a(p) begin	1.80	4.50	9.00
2-5	1.10	2.75	5.50
6-10: 7-Origin Saavik	.90	2.25	4.50
11-20	.60	1.50	3.00
21-32	.45	1.10	2.20
33-($1.25, 52 pgs.)-20th anniversary issue	.70	1.75	3.50
34-49: 37-Painted-c. 49-Begin $1.00-c	.30	.75	1.50
50-($1.50, 52 pgs.)	.50	1.25	2.50
51-56		.50	1.00
Annual 1-3: 1(1985). 2(1986). 3(1988, $1.50)	.50	1.25	2.50

NOTE: ***Morrow** a-28, 35, 36, 56. **Orlando** c-8i. **Perez** c-1-3. **Spiegle** a-19. **Starlin** c-24, 25. **Sutton** a-1-6p, 8-18p, 20-27p, 29p, 31-34p, 39-52p, 55p; c-4-6p, 8-22p, 46p.*

STAR TREK
Oct, 1989 - Present ($1.50/$1.75, color)
DC Comics

	GD25	FN65	NM94
1-Capt. Kirk and crew	1.40	3.50	7.00
2,3	.60	1.50	3.00
4-23,25-30: 10-12-The Trial of James T. Kirk. 21-Begin $1.75-c	.40	1.00	2.00
24-($2.95, 68 pgs.)-40 pg. epic w/pin-ups	.60	1.50	3.00
31-46	.35	.90	1.75
Annual 1,2('90, '91, $2.95, 68pgs.): 1-Morrow-a	.60	1.50	3.00
Annual 3 (1992, $3.50, 68 pgs.)-Painted-c	.70	1.75	3.50

STAR TREK VI: THE UNDISCOVERED COUNTRY
1992 (Movie adaptation)
DC Comics

	GD25	FN65	NM94
1-($2.95, regular edition, 68 pgs.)	.60	1.50	3.00
nn-($5.95, prestige edition)-Has photos of movie not included in regular edition; painted-c by Palmer; photo back-c	1.20	3.00	6.00

STAR TREK MOVIE SPECIAL
June, 1984 - No. 2, 1987 ($1.50, 68pgs); 1989 ($2.00, 52 pgs.)
DC Comics

	GD25	FN65	NM94
1-Adapts Star Trek III; Sutton-p (64 pgs.)	.30	.75	1.50
2-Adapts Star Trek IV; Sutton-a (64 pgs.)	.30	.75	1.50
1 (1989)-Adapts Star Trek V; painted-c	.40	1.00	2.00

STAR TREK - THE MODALA IMPERATIVE
Late July, 1991 - No. 4, Late Sept, 1991 ($1.75, color, mini-series)
DC Comics

	GD25	FN65	NM94
1	.50	1.25	2.50
2-4	.40	1.00	2.00

STAR TREK: THE NEXT GENERATION (TV)
Feb, 1988 - No. 6, July, 1988 (Mini series, based on TV show)
DC Comics

	GD25	FN65	NM94
1 (52 pgs.)-Sienkiewicz painted-c	2.00	5.00	10.00
2-6 ($1.00)	1.20	3.00	6.00

STAR TREK: THE NEXT GENERATION (TV)
Oct, 1989 - Present ($1.50/$1.75, color)
DC Comics

	GD25	FN65	NM94
1-Capt. Picard and crew from TV show	1.80	4.50	9.00
2,3	1.20	3.00	6.00
4,5	.90	2.25	4.50
6-10	.60	1.50	3.00
11-23,25-30: 21-Begin $1.75-c	.40	1.00	2.00
24-($2.50, 52 pgs.)	.50	1.25	2.50
31-46	.35	.90	1.75
Annual 1 (1990, $2.95, 68 pgs.)	.70	1.75	3.50
Annual 2 (1991, $3.50, 68 pgs.)	.80	2.00	4.00

STAR TREK: THE NEXT GENERATION - THE MODALA IMPERATIVE
Early Sept, 1991 - No. 4, 1991 ($1.75, color, mini-series)
DC Comics

	GD25	FN65	NM94
1	.50	1.25	2.50
2-4	.40	1.00	2.00

STAR WARS (Movie) (See Classic..., Contemporary Motivators, The Droids, The Ewoks, Marvel Movie Showcase & Marvel Special Edition)
July, 1977 - No. 107, Sept, 1986
Marvel Comics Group

	GD25	FN65	NM94
1-(Regular 30 cent edition)-Price in square w/UPC code; #1-6 adapt first movie	3.60	9.00	18.00
1-(35 cent cover; limited distribution - 1500 copies?)- Price in square w/UPC code (see note below)	50.00	150.00	350.00
2-6: 4-Battle with Darth Vader 6-Dave Stevens-i	1.20	3.00	6.00
7-10	.60	1.50	3.00
11-20	.40	1.00	2.00
21-38	.30	.75	1.50
39-44-The Empire Strikes Back-r by Al Williamson in all	.40	1.00	2.00
45-107: 92,100-($1.00, 52 pgs.)		.50	1.00
1-9-Reprints; has "reprint" in upper lefthand corner of cover or on inside or price and number inside a diamond with no date or UPC on cover; 30 cents and 35 cents issues published		.50	1.00
Annual 1 (12/79)	.40	1.00	2.00
Annual 2 (11/82), 3(12/83)		.60	1.20

NOTE: *The rare 35 cent edition has the cover price in a square box, and the UPC box in the lower left hand corner has the UPC code lines running through it.* ***Austin*** *c-11-15i, 21i, 38; c-12-15i, 21i.* ***Byrne*** *c-13p.* ***Chaykin*** *a-1-10p; c-1.* ***Golden*** *c/a-38.* ***Miller*** *c-47p.* ***Nebres*** *c/a-Annual 2i.* ***Portacio*** *a-107i.* ***Sienkiewicz*** *c-92i, 98.* ***Simonson*** *a-16p, 49p, 51-63p, 65p, 66p; c-16, 49-51, 52p, 53-62, Annual 1.* ***Steacy*** *painted a-105i, 106i; c-105.* ***Williamson*** *a-39-44p, 50p, 98; c-39, 40, 41-44p. Painted c-81, 87, 92, 95, 98, 100, 105.*

STAR WARS: DARK EMPIRE
Dec, 1992 - No. 6, Oct, 1992 ($2.95, color, limited series)
Dark Horse Comics

	GD25	FN65	NM94
1-All have Dorman painted-c	4.00	10.00	20.00
1-2nd printing	.60	1.50	3.00
2-Low print run	4.20	12.50	25.00
2,3-2nd printings	.60	1.50	3.00
3	1.20	3.00	6.00
4	.80	2.00	4.00
5,6	.60	1.50	3.00

STAR WARS: RETURN OF THE JEDI
Oct, 1983 - No. 4, Jan, 1984 (Mini-series, movie adaptation)
Marvel Comics Group

	GD25	FN65	NM94
1-4-Williamson-p in all; r/Marvel Super Special #27		.50	1.00
Oversized issue (1983, $2.95, 10-3/4x8-1/4", 68 pgs., cardboard-c)-Reprints above 4 issues	.60	1.50	3.00

STATIC (Charlton)(Value: cover or less)

STEED AND MRS. PEEL (TV)(Eclipse)(Value: cover or less)

STEELGRIP STARKEY (Epic)(Value: cover or less)

STEEL STERLING (Formerly Shield-Steel Sterling; see Blue Ribbon, Jackpot, Mighty Comics, Mighty Crusaders, Roly Poly & Zip Comics)
No. 4, Jan, 1984 - No. 7, July, 1984
Archie Enterprises, Inc.

	GD25	FN65	NM94
4-7: 6-McWilliams-a		.50	1.00

STEEL, THE INDESTRUCTIBLE MAN (See All-Star Squadron #8)
March, 1978 - No. 5, Oct-Nov, 1978
DC Comics

	GD25	FN65	NM94
1		.60	1.20
2-5: 5-Giant		.50	1.00

STEELTOWN ROCKERS (Marvel)(Value: cover or less)

STEVE CANYON (See 4-Color #519, 578, 641, 737, 804, 939, 1033, and Harvey Comics Hits #52)

STEVE CANYON
1959 (96 pgs.; no text; 6-3/4x9"; hardcover)(B&W inside)
Grosset & Dunlap

	GD25	FN65	NM94
100100-Reprints 2 stories from strip (1953, 1957)	3.00	9.00	21.00
100100 (softcover edition)	2.50	7.50	17.00

STEVE CANYON COMICS
Feb, 1948 - No. 6, Dec, 1948 (Strip reprints) (No. 4,5: 52pgs.)
Harvey Publications

	GD25	FN65	NM94
1-Origin; has biog of Milton Caniff; Powell-a, 2 pgs.; Caniff-a	17.00	52.00	120.00
2-Caniff, Powell-a	11.50	34.00	80.00
3-6: Caniff, Powell-a in all. 6-Intro Madame Lynx	10.00	30.00	70.00
Dept. Store giveaway #3(6/48, 36pp)	10.00	30.00	65.00
...'s Secret Mission (1951, 16 pgs., Armed Forces giveaway); Caniff-a	10.00	30.00	60.00
Strictly for the Smart Birds-16 pgs., 1951; Information Comics Div. (Harvey) Premium	9.35	28.00	56.00

STEVE CANYON IN 3-D
June, 1986 (One shot, $2.25)
Kitchen Sink Press

	GD25	FN65	NM94
1-Contains unpublished story from 1954	.45	1.15	2.25

STEVE DONOVAN, WESTERN MARSHAL (TV)
No. 675, Feb, 1956 - No. 880, Feb, 1958 (All photo-c)
Dell Publishing Co.

	GD25	FN65	NM94
4-Color 675-Kinstler-a	6.70	20.00	40.00
4-Color 768-Kinstler-a	5.35	16.00	32.00
4-Color 880	4.00	10.50	21.00

STEVE ROPER
April, 1948 - No. 5, Dec, 1948
Famous Funnies

	GD25	FN65	NM94
1-Contains 1944 daily newspaper-r	8.35	25.00	50.00
2	4.70	14.00	28.00
3-5	4.00	11.00	22.00

STEVE SAUNDERS SPECIAL AGENT (See Special Agent)

STEVE SAVAGE (See Captain...)

STEVE ZODIAC & THE FIRE BALL XL-5 (TV)
January, 1964
Gold Key

	GD25	FN65	NM94
1 (10108-401	7.50	22.50	45.00

STEVIE (Also see Mazie & Mortie)
Nov, 1952 - No. 6, April, 1954
Mazie (Magazine Publ.)

	GD25	FN65	NM94
1	4.00	12.00	24.00
2-6	2.80	7.00	14.00

STEVIE MAZIE'S BOY FRIEND (See Harvey Hits #5)

STEWART THE RAT (See Eclipse Graphic Album Series)

ST. GEORGE (See listing under Saint...)

STIGG'S INFERNO (Vortex/Eclipse)(Value: cover or less)

STING OF THE GREEN HORNET (See The Green Hornet)
June, 1992 - No. 4, 1992 ($2.50, color, mini-series)
Now Comics

	GD25	FN65	NM94
1-4: Butler-c/a	.50	1.25	2.50
1-4 ($2.75)-Collectors Ed.; polybagged w/poster	.55	1.40	2.75

STONEY BURKE (TV)
June-Aug, 1963 - No. 2, Sept-Nov, 1963
Dell Publishing Co.

	GD25	FN65	NM94
1,2	2.00	5.00	10.00

Star Wars #2, © Lucasfilms

Steel, the Indestructible Man #3, © DC

Steve Canyon Strictly for the Smart Birds nn, © Milton Caniff

Stories By Famous Authors Illustrated #7, © FAI

The Story of the Commandos nn, © L.I. Independent

Straight Arrow #4, © ME

	GD25	FN65	NM94

STONY CRAIG
1946 (No #)
Pentagon Publishing Co.

nn-Reprints Bell Syndicate's "Sgt. Stony Craig" newspaper strips 5.00 15.00 30.00

STORIES BY FAMOUS AUTHORS ILLUSTRATED (Fast Fiction #1-5)
No. 6, Aug, 1950 - No. 13, March, 1951
Seaboard Publ./Famous Authors Ill.

1-Scarlet Pimpernel-Baroness Orczy 22.00 65.00 155.00
2-Capt. Blood-Raphael Sabatini 22.00 65.00 155.00
3-She, by Haggard 27.00 81.00 190.00
4-The 39 Steps-John Buchan 14.00 43.00 100.00
5-Beau Geste-P. C. Wren 15.00 45.00 105.00

NOTE: *The above five issues are exact reprints of Fast Fiction #1-5 except for the title change and new Kiefer covers on #1 and 2. The above 5 issues were released before Famous Authors #6.*

6-Macbeth, by Shakespeare; Kiefer art (8/50); used in **SOTI**, pg. 22,143; Kiefer-c; 36 pgs. 17.00 52.00 120.00
7-The Window; Kiefer-c/a; 52 pgs. 13.50 41.00 95.00
8-Hamlet, by Shakespeare; Kiefer-c/a; 36pgs. 17.00 52.00 120.00
9-Nicholas Nickleby, by Dickens; G. Schrotter-a; 52 pgs. 14.00 43.00 100.00
10-Romeo & Juliet, by Shakespeare; Kiefer-c/a; 36 pgs. 14.00 43.00 100.00
11-Ben-Hur; Schrotter-a; 52 pgs. 15.00 45.00 105.00
12-La Svengali; Schrotter-a; 36 pgs. 15.00 45.00 105.00
13-Scaramouche; Kiefer-c/a; 36 pgs. 15.00 45.00 105.00

NOTE: *Artwork was prepared/advertised for #14, The Red Badge Of Courage. Gilberton bought out Famous Authors, Ltd. and used that story as C.I. #98. Famous Authors, Ltd. then published the Classics Junior series. The Famous Authors titles were published as part of the regular Classics Ill. Series in Brazil starting in 1952.*

STORIES OF CHRISTMAS
1942 (32 pages; paper cover) (Giveaway)
K. K. Publications

nn-Adaptation of "A Christmas Carol;" Kelly story-"The Fir Tree;" Infinity-c 32.00 95.00 220.00

STORIES OF ROMANCE (Formerly Meet Miss Bliss)
No. 5, Mar, 1956 - No. 13, Aug, 1957
Atlas Comics (LMC)

5-Baker-a? 4.70 14.00 28.00
6-13 2.80 7.00 14.00

NOTE: *Ann **Brewster** a-13. **Colletta** a-9(2); c-5.*

STORMWATCHER (Eclipse)(Value: cover or less)

STORMY (See 4-Color #537)

STORY HOUR SERIES (Disney)
1948, 1949; 1951-1953 (36 pgs., paper-c) (4-1/2x6-1/4")
Given away with subscription to Walt Disney's Comics & Stories
Whitman Publishing Co.

nn(1948)-Mickey Mouse and Boy Thursday 8.35 25.00 50.00
nn(1948)-Mickey Mouse Miracle Maker 8.35 25.00 50.00
nn(1948)-Minnie Mouse and Antique Chair 8.35 25.00 50.00
nn(1949)-The Three Orphan Kittens(B&W & color) 4.20 12.50 25.00
nn(1949)-Danny-The Little Black Lamb 4.20 12.50 25.00
800-Donald Duck in "Bringing Up the Boys;" 1948 10.00 30.00 70.00
1953 edition 6.70 20.00 40.00
801-Mickey Mouse's Summer Vacation; 1948 6.70 20.00 40.00
1951, 1952 edition 4.00 10.00 20.00
802-Bugs Bunny's Adventures; 1948 5.00 15.00 30.00
803-Bongo; 1948 4.20 12.50 25.00
804 Mickey and the Beanstalk; 1948 5.35 16.00 32.00
805-15-Andy Panda and His Friends; 1949 4.70 14.00 28.00
806-15-Tom and Jerry; 1949 4.70 14.00 28.00
808-15-Johnny Appleseed; 1949 4.20 12.50 25.00
1948, 1949 Hard Cover Edition of each.... $2.00 - $3.00 more.

STORY OF EDISON, THE
1956 (16 pgs.) (Reddy Killowatt)
Educational Comics

nn-Reprint of Reddy Kilowatt #2(1947) 5.00 15.00 30.00

STORY OF HARRY S. TRUMAN, THE
1948 (16 pgs.) (In color, regular size)(Soft-c)
Democratic National Committee (Giveaway)

nn-Gives biography on career of Truman; used in **SOTI**, pg. 311 10.00 30.00 70.00

STORY OF JESUS (See Classics Illustrated Special Issue)

STORY OF MANKIND, THE (See 4-Color #851)

STORY OF MARTHA WAYNE, THE
April, 1956
Argo Publ.

1-Newspaper-r 3.60 9.00 18.00

STORY OF RUTH, THE (See 4-Color #1144)

STORY OF THE COMMANDOS, THE (Combined Operations)
1943 (68 pgs.; B&W) (15 cents)
Long Island Independent (Distr. by Gilberton)

nn-All text (no comics); photos & illustrations; ad for Classic Comics on back cover (Rare) 19.00 58.00 135.00

STORY OF THE GLOOMY BUNNY, THE (See March of Comics #9)

STRAIGHT ARROW (Radio)(See Best of the West & Great Western)
Feb-Mar, 1950 - No. 55, Mar, 1956 (All 36 pgs.)
Magazine Enterprises

1-Straight Arrow (alias Steve Adams) & his palomino Fury begin; 1st mention of Sundown Valley & the Secret Cave; Whitney-a 25.00 75.00 175.00
2-Red Hawk begins (1st app?) by Powell (Origin), ends #55 13.00 40.00 90.00
3-Frazetta-c 15.00 45.00 105.00
4,5: 4-Secret Cave-c 7.50 22.50 45.00
6-10 5.85 17.50 35.00
11-Classic story "The Valley of Time," with an ancient civilization made of gold 6.70 20.00 40.00
12-19 4.35 13.00 26.00
20-Origin Straight Arrow's Shield 7.50 22.50 45.00
21-Origin Fury 8.35 25.00 50.00
22-Frazetta-c 11.00 32.00 75.00
23,25-30: 25-Secret Cave-c. 28-Red Hawk meets The Vikings 4.35 13.00 26.00
24-Classic story "The Dragons of Doom!" with prehistoric pteradactyls 6.35 19.00 38.00
31-38: 36-Red Hawk drug story by Powell 4.00 12.00 24.00
39-Classic story "The Canyon Beast," with a dinosaur egg hatching a Tyranosaurus Rex 5.00 15.00 30.00
40-Classic story "Secret of The Spanish Specters," with Conquistadors' lost treasure 5.00 15.00 30.00
41,42,44-54: 45-Secret Cave-c 3.60 9.00 18.00
43-Intro & 1st app. Blaze, Straight Arrow's Warrior dog 4.20 12.50 25.00
55-Last issue 4.70 14.00 28.00

NOTE: *Fred **Meagher** a 1-55; c-1, 2, 4-21, 23-55. **Powell** a 2-55. Many issues advertise the radio premiums associated with Straight Arrow.*

STRAIGHT ARROW'S FURY (See A-1 Comics #119)

STRANGE
March, 1957 - No. 6, May, 1958

Ajax-Farrell Publ. (Four Star Comic Corp.)

	GD25	FN65	NM94
1	10.00	30.00	60.00
2	5.35	16.00	32.00
3-6	4.20	12.50	25.00

STRANGE ADVENTURES
Aug-Sept, 1950 - No. 244, Oct-Nov, 1973 (No. 1-12: 52 pgs.)
National Periodical Publications

	GD25	FN65	NM94
1-Adaptation of "Destination Moon;" preview of movie w/photo-c from movie; adapt. of Edmond Hamilton's "Chris KL-99" in #1-3; Darwin Jones begins	185.00	560.00	1300.00
2	87.00	260.00	600.00
3,4	54.00	160.00	375.00
5-8,10: 7-Origin Kris KL-99	47.00	140.00	325.00
9-Captain Comet begins (6/51, intro/origin)	107.00	320.00	750.00
11-20: 12,13,17,18-Toth-a	36.00	107.00	250.00
21-30: 28-Atomic explosion panel	25.00	75.00	175.00
31,34-38	23.00	70.00	160.00
32,33-Krigstein-a	24.00	72.00	165.00
39-Ill. in **SOTI**-"Treating police contemptuously" (top right)	30.00	90.00	210.00
40-49-Last Capt. Comet; not in 45,47,48	20.00	60.00	140.00
50-53-Last precode issue (2/55)	16.00	48.00	110.00
54-70	10.00	30.00	60.00
71-99	7.50	22.50	45.00
100	10.00	30.00	65.00
101-110: 104-Space Museum begins by Sekowsky	5.85	17.50	35.00
111-116,118,119: 114-Star Hawkins begins, ends #185; Heath-a in Wood E.C. style	5.00	15.00	30.00
117-Origin/1st app. Atomic Knights (6/60)	43.00	130.00	300.00
120-2nd app. Atomic Knights	17.00	52.00	120.00
121,122,124,125,127,128,130,131,133,134: 124-Origin Faceless Creature. 134-Last 10 cent issue	4.00	12.00	24.00
123,126-3rd & 4th app. Atomic Knights	10.00	30.00	60.00
129,132,135,138,141,144,147-Atomic Knights app.	5.70	17.00	34.00
136,137,139,140,142,143,145,146,148,149,151,152,154,155,157-159	4.00	10.00	20.00
150,153,156,160: Atomic Knights in each. 153-2nd app. Faceless Creature; atomic explosion-c (6/63). 159-Star Rovers app.; Gil Kane/Anderson-a. 160-Last Atomic Knights	4.20	12.50	25.00
161-179: 161-Last Space Museum. 163-Star Rovers app. 170-Infinity-c. 177-Origin Immortal Man	2.00	5.00	10.00
180-Origin/1st app. Animal Man	26.00	77.00	180.00
181-183,185-189: 187-Origin The Enchantress	1.40	3.50	7.00
184-2nd app. Animal Man by Gil Kane	14.00	43.00	100.00
190-1st app. Animal Man in costume	17.00	52.00	120.00
191-194,196-200,202-204	.85	2.50	5.00
195-1st full length Animal Man story	10.00	30.00	70.00
201-Last Animal Man; 2nd full length story	5.85	17.50	35.00
205-Intro/origin Deadman by Infantino (10/67) & begin series, ends #216	6.70	20.00	40.00
206-Neal Adams-a begins	5.00	15.00	30.00
207-210	4.00	10.00	20.00
211-216: 211-Space Museum-r	3.00	7.50	15.00
217-221,223-231: 217-Adam Strange & Atomic Knights-r begin. 218-Last 12 cent issue. 225-Last 15 cent issue. 226-New Adam Strange text story w/illos by Anderson (8 pgs.). 226-236-(68-52 pgs.). 231-Last Atomic Knights reprint	.80	2.00	4.00
222-New Adam Strange story; Kane/Anderson-a	1.60	4.00	8.00
232-244	.40	1.00	2.00

NOTE: ***Neal Adams*** *a-206-216; c-207-216, 228, 235.* ***Anderson*** *a-8-52, 94, 96, 99, 115, 117, 119-163, 217r, 218r, 222, 223-225r, 226, 242i(r); c-18, 19, 21, 23, 24, 27, 30, 32-44(most); c/r-157i, 190i, 217-224, 228-231, 233, 235-239, 241-243.* ***Ditko*** *a-188, 189.* ***Drucker*** *a-42, 43, 45.* ***Elias*** *a-212.* ***Finlay*** *a-2, 3, 6, 7, 210r, 229r.* ***Giunta*** *a-237r.* ***Heath*** *a-116.* ***Infantino*** *a-10-101, 106-151, 154, 157-163, 180, 190, 218-221r, 223-244p(r); c-50; c(r)-190p, 197, 199-211, 218-221, 223-244.* ***Kaluta*** *c-238, 240.* ***Gil Kane*** *a-8-116, 124, 125, 130, 138, 146-157, 173-186, 204r, 222r, 227-231r; c(p)-11-17, 25, 154, 157.* ***Kubert*** *a-55(2 pgs.), 226; c-219, 220, 225-227, 232, 234.* ***Moriera*** *c-26, 28, 29, 71.* ***Morrow*** *c-230.* ***Mortimer*** *c-8.* ***Powell*** *a-4.* ***Sekowsky*** *a-71p, 97-162p, 217p(r), 218p(r); c-206, 217-219r.* ***Simon & Kirby*** *a-2r (2 pg.)* ***Sparling*** *a-201.* ***Toth*** *a-8, 12, 13, 17-19.* ***Wood*** *a-154i. Atomic Knights in #117, 120, 123, 126, 129, 132, 135, 138, 141, 144, 147, 150, 153, 156, 160. Atomic Knights reprints by* ***Anderson*** *in 119-221. Chris KL99 in 1-3, 5, 7, 9, 11, 15. Capt. Comet covers-9-14, 17-19, 24, 26, 27, 32-44.*

STRANGE AS IT SEEMS (See Famous Funnies-A Carnival of Comics, Feature Funnies #1, The John Hix Scrap Book & Peanuts)

STRANGE AS IT SEEMS
1932 (64 pgs.; B&W; square binding)
Blue-Star Publishing Co.

	GD25	FN65	NM94
1-Newspaper-r	16.00	48.00	110.00

NOTE: *Published with and without No. 1 and price on cover.*

	GD25	FN65	NM94
Ex-Lax giveaway(1936, B&W, 24pgs., 5x7")-McNaught Synd.	3.20	8.00	16.00

STRANGE AS IT SEEMS
1939
United Features Syndicate

	GD25	FN65	NM94
Single Series 9, 1, 2	19.00	58.00	135.00

STRANGE CONFESSIONS
Jan-Mar, 1952 - No. 4, Fall, 1952
Ziff-Davis Publ. Co. (Approved)

	GD25	FN65	NM94
1(Scarce)-Photo-c; Kinstler-a	24.00	73.00	170.00
2(Scarce)	17.00	52.00	120.00
3(Scarce)-#3 on-c, #2 on inside; Reformatory girl story; photo-c	17.00	52.00	120.00
4(Scarce)-Reformatory girl story	17.00	52.00	120.00

STRANGE DAYS (Eclipse)(Value: cover or less)

STRANGE FANTASY (Formerly Rocketman)
Aug, 1952 - No. 14, Oct-Nov, 1954
Ajax-Farrell

	GD25	FN65	NM94
2(#1, 8/52)-Jungle Princess story; Kamenish-a; reprinted from Ellery Queen #1	14.00	43.00	100.00
2(10/52)-No Black Cat or Rulah; Bakerish, Kamenish-a; hypo/meathook-c	12.00	36.00	85.00
3-Rulah story, called Pulah	11.50	34.00	80.00
4-Rocket Man app.	10.00	30.00	70.00
5,6,8,10,12,14	8.35	25.00	50.00
7-Madam Satan/Slave story	10.00	30.00	70.00
9(w/Black Cat), 9(w/Boy's Ranch; S&K-a)(A rebinding of Harvey interiors; not publ. by Ajax)	10.00	30.00	65.00
9-Regular issue	8.35	25.00	50.00
11-Jungle story	9.15	27.50	55.00
13-Bondage-c; Rulah (Kolah) story	11.00	32.00	75.00

STRANGE GALAXY (Magazine)
V1#8, Feb, 1971 - No. 11, Aug, 1971 (B&W)
Eerie Publications

	GD25	FN65	NM94
V1#8-Reprints-c/Fantastic V19#3 (2/70) (a pulp)	2.40	6.00	12.00
9-11	1.60	4.00	8.00

STRANGE JOURNEY
Sept, 1957 - No. 4, June, 1958 (Farrell reprints)
America's Best (Steinway Publ.) (Ajax/Farrell)

	GD25	FN65	NM94
1	10.00	30.00	60.00
2-4	5.85	17.50	35.00

STRANGE LOVE (See Fox Giants)

STRANGE MYSTERIES
Sept, 1951 - No. 21, Jan, 1955
Superior/Dynamic Publications

	GD25	FN65	NM94
1-Kamenish-a begins	24.00	73.00	170.00
2	13.00	40.00	90.00

Strange Adventures #16, © DC

Strange Fantasy #7, © AJAX

Strange Journey #1, © AJAX

Strange Mysteries #13, © SUPR

Strange Suspense Stories #77, © CC

Strange Tales #2, © MEG

	GD25	FN65	NM94
3-5	10.00	30.00	65.00
6-8	10.00	30.00	60.00
9-Bondage 3-D effect-c	11.50	34.00	80.00
10-Used in **SOTI**, pg. 181	9.15	27.50	55.00
11-18	7.50	22.50	45.00
19-r/Journey Into Fear #1; cover is a splash from one story; Baker-r(2)	9.15	27.50	55.00
20,21-Reprints; 20-r/#1 with new-c	5.85	17.50	35.00

STRANGE MYSTERIES
1963 - 1964
I. W. Enterprises/Super Comics

	GD25	FN65	NM94
I.W. Reprint #9; Rulah-r/Spook #28	1.60	4.00	8.00
Super Reprint #10-12,15-17('63-'64): 10,11-r/Strange #2,1. 12-r/Tales of Horror #5 (3/53) less-c. 15-r/Dark Mysteries #23. 16-r/The Dead Who Walk. 17-r/Dark Mysteries #22	1.60	4.00	8.00
Super Reprint #18-r/Witchcraft #1; Kubert-a	1.60	4.00	8.00

STRANGE PLANETS
1958; 1963-64
I. W. Enterprises/Super Comics

	GD25	FN65	NM94
I.W. Reprint #1(nd)-Reprints E. C. Incredible S/F #30 plus-c/Strange Worlds #3	5.85	17.50	35.00
I.W. Reprint #8-r/? Exist?	3.20	8.00	16.00
I.W. Reprint #9-Orlando/Wood-r/Strange Worlds #4; cover-r from Flying Saucers #1	9.15	27.50	55.00
Super Reprint #10-Wood-r (22 pg.) from Space Detective #1; cover-r/Attack on Planet Mars	8.35	25.00	50.00
Super Reprint #11-Wood-r (25 pg.) from An Earthman on Venus	10.00	30.00	70.00
Super Reprint #12-Orlando-r/Rocket to the Moon	8.35	25.00	50.00
Super Reprint #15-Reprints Journey Into Unknown Worlds #8; Heath, Colan-r	3.00	7.50	15.00
Super Reprint #16-Reprints Avon's Strange Worlds #6; Kinstler, Check-a	4.00	10.00	20.00
Super Reprint #17-r/?	1.80	4.50	9.00
Super Reprint #18-Reprints Great Exploits #1 (Daring Adventures #6); Space Busters, Explorer Joe, The Son of Robin Hood; Krigstein-a	3.20	8.00	16.00

STRANGE SPORTS STORIES (See Brave & the Bold, DC Special, and DC Super Stars #10)
Sept-Oct, 1973 - No. 6, July-Aug, 1974
National Periodical Publications

	GD25	FN65	NM94
Brave and the Bold #45-49 (12-1/62-63 - 8-9/63)-Strange Sports Stories by Infantino	4.70	14.00	28.00
1	1.20	3.00	6.00
2-6: 3-Swan/Anderson-a	.60	1.50	3.00

STRANGE STORIES FROM ANOTHER WORLD (Unknown World #1)
No. 2, Aug, 1952 - No. 5, Feb, 1953
Fawcett Publications

	GD25	FN65	NM94
2-Saunders painted-c	23.00	70.00	160.00
3-5-Saunders painted-c	17.00	52.00	120.00

STRANGE STORIES OF SUSPENSE (Rugged Action #1-4)
No. 5, Oct, 1955 - No. 16, Aug, 1957
Atlas Comics (CSI)

	GD25	FN65	NM94
5(#1)	14.00	43.00	100.00
6,9	10.00	30.00	60.00
7-E. C. swipe cover/Vault of Horror #32	10.00	30.00	65.00
8-Williamson/Mayo-a; Pakula-a	10.00	30.00	65.00
10-Crandall, Torres, Meskin-a	10.00	30.00	65.00
11-13: 12-Torres, Pakula-a. 13-E.C. art swipes	6.70	20.00	40.00
14-16: 14-Williamson-a. 15-Krigstein-a. 16-Fox, Powell-a	7.50	22.50	45.00

NOTE: ***Everett** a-6, 7, 13; c-8, 9, 11-14. **Heath** a-5. **Maneely** c-5. **Morisi** a-11. **Morrow** a-13. **Powell** a-8. **Severin** c-7. **Wildey** a-14.*

STRANGE STORY (Also see Front Page)
June-July, 1946 (52 pages)
Harvey Publications

	GD25	FN65	NM94
1-The Man in Black Called Fate by Powell	13.50	41.00	95.00

STRANGE SUSPENSE STORIES (Lawbreakers Suspense Stories #10-15; This Is Suspense #23-26; Captain Atom V1#78 on)
6/52 - No. 5, 2/53; No. 16, 1/54 - No. 22, 11/54; No. 27, 10/55 - No. 77, 10/65; V3#1, 10/67 - V1#9, 9/69
Fawcett Publications/Charlton Comics No. 16 on

	GD25	FN65	NM94
1-(Fawcett)-Powell, Sekowsky-a	34.00	102.00	240.00
2-George Evans horror story	22.00	65.00	150.00
3-5 (2/53)-George Evans horror stories	18.00	54.00	125.00
16(1-2/54)	10.00	30.00	70.00
17,21	9.15	27.50	55.00
18-E.C. swipe/HOF 7; Ditko-c/a(2)	14.00	43.00	100.00
19-Ditko electric chair-c; Ditko-a	19.00	58.00	135.00
20-Ditko-c/a(2)	14.00	43.00	100.00
22(11/54)-Ditko-c, Shuster-a; last pre-code issue; becomes This Is Suspense	12.00	36.00	85.00
27(10/55)-(Formerly This Is Suspense #26)	5.00	15.00	30.00
28-30,38	4.00	11.00	22.00
31-33,35,37,40-Ditko-c/a(2-3 each)	10.00	30.00	60.00
34-Story of ruthless business man, Wm. B. Gaines; Ditko-c/a	17.00	52.00	120.00
36-(68 pgs.); Ditko-a(4)	10.00	30.00	65.00
39,41,52,53-Ditko-a	8.35	25.00	50.00
42-44,46,49,54-60	3.60	9.00	18.00
45,47,48,50,51-Ditko-c/a	6.70	20.00	40.00
61-74	1.20	3.00	6.00
75(6/65)-Reprints origin/1st app. Captain Atom by Ditko from Space Adventures #33 (75-77: 12 cent issues)	10.00	30.00	65.00
76,77-Captain Atom-r by Ditko/Space Advs.	4.20	12.50	25.00
V3#1(10/67)-4: All 12 cent issues	1.60	4.00	8.00
V1#2-9: 2-Ditko-a, atom bomb-c (all 12 cents)	1.00	2.50	5.00

NOTE: ***Alascia** a-19. **Aparo** a-V3#1, 2. **Baily** a-1-3; c-2, 5. **Evans** c-3, 4. **Montes/Bache** c-66. **Powell** a-4. **Shuster** a-19, 21. **Marcus Swayze** a-27.*

STRANGE TALES (... Featuring Warlock #178-181; becomes Doctor Strange #169 on)
June, 1951 - #168, May, 1968; #169, Sept, 1973 - #188, Nov, 1976
Atlas (CCPC #1-67/ZPC #68-79/VPI #80-85)/Marvel #86(7/61) on

	GD25	FN65	NM94
1	143.00	430.00	1000.00
2	57.00	170.00	400.00
3,5: 3-Atom bomb panels	43.00	130.00	300.00
4-"The Evil Eye," cosmic eyeball story	47.00	140.00	325.00
6-9	32.00	95.00	225.00
10-Krigstein-a	34.00	100.00	235.00
11-14,16-20	17.00	52.00	120.00
15-Krigstein-a	18.00	54.00	125.00
21,23-27,29-34: 27-Atom bomb panels. 33-Davis-a. 34-Last pre-code issue (2/55)	14.00	43.00	100.00
22-Krigstein, Forte/Fox-a	15.00	45.00	105.00
28-Jack Katz story used in Senate Investigation report, pgs. 7 & 169	15.00	45.00	105.00
35-41,43,44	11.00	32.00	75.00
42,45,59,61-Krigstein-a; #61 (2/58)	11.50	34.00	80.00
46-57,60: 53,56-Crandall-a. 60-(8/57)	10.00	30.00	60.00
58,64-Williamson-a in each, with Mayo-#58	10.00	30.00	65.00
62,63,65,66: 62-Torres-a. 66-Crandall-a	9.15	27.50	55.00
67-78,80: Ditko/Kirby-a in #67-80	10.00	30.00	70.00
79-Dr. Strange prototype story (12/60)	14.00	43.00	100.00

81-83,85-92: Ditko/Kirby-a in all. 89-1st app. Fin Fang Foom (10/61) by

Kirby. 92-Last 10 cent issue 10.00 30.00 60.00
84-Magneto prototype (5/61); has powers like Magneto of X-Men over two years later; Ditko/Kirby-a 12.00 36.00 85.00
93-96,98-100: Kirby-a 9.15 27.50 55.00
97-Aunt May & Uncle Ben prototype by Ditko, 3 months before Amazing Fantasy #15. Kirby-a 22.00 65.00 150.00
101-Human Torch begins by Kirby (10/62); origin recap Fantastic Four & Human Torch 72.00 215.00 500.00
102-1st app. Wizard 29.00 85.00 200.00
103-105: 104-1st app. Trapster 22.00 65.00 150.00
106,108,109: 106-Fantastic Four guests (3/63) 14.00 43.00 100.00
107-Human Torch/Sub-Mariner battle 17.00 52.00 120.00
110-(7/63)-Intro Doctor Strange, Ancient One & Wong by Ditko 82.00 245.00 575.00
111-2nd Dr. Strange 29.00 85.00 200.00
112,113 10.00 30.00 70.00
114-Acrobat disguised as Captain America, 1st app. since the G.A.; intro. & 1st app. Victoria Bentley; 3rd Dr. Strange app. & begin series (11/63) 29.00 85.00 200.00
115-Origin Dr. Strange; Human Torch vs. Sandman (Spidey villain; 2nd app. & brief origin); early Spider-Man x-over, 12/63 39.00 120.00 275.00
116-Human Torch battles The Thing; 1st Thing x-over 10.00 30.00 65.00
117,118,120: 120-1st Iceman x-over (from X-Men) 7.50 22.50 45.00
119-Spider-Man x-over (2 pg. cameo) 10.00 30.00 70.00
121,122,124-134: Thing/Torch team-up in 121-134. 125-Torch & Thing battle Sub-Mariner (10/64). 126-Intro Clea. 128-Quicksilver & Scarlet Witch app. (1/65). 130-The Beatles cameo. 134-Last Human Torch; The Watcher-c/story; Wood-a(i) 5.85 17.50 35.00
123-1st Thor x-over; Loki app. 6.70 20.00 40.00
135-Col. (formerly Sgt.) Nick Fury becomes Nick Fury Agent of Shield (origin/ 1st app.) by Kirby (8/65); series begins, ends #168 9.15 27.50 55.00
136-147,149: 138-Intro Eternity. 146-Last Ditko Dr. Strange who is in consecutive stories since #113. 147-Dr. Strange (by Everett #147-152) continues thru #168, then Dr. Strange #169 4.00 11.00 22.00
148-Origin Ancient One 4.70 14.00 28.00
150(11/66)-John Buscema's 1st work at Marvel 4.00 11.00 22.00
151-Kirby/Steranko-c/a: 1st Marvel work by Steranko 4.70 14.00 28.00
152,153-Kirby/Steranko-a 4.00 11.00 22.00
154-158-Steranko-a/script 4.00 11.00 22.00
159-Origin Nick Fury retold; Intro Val; Captain America-c/story; Steranko-a 4.20 12.50 25.00
160-162-Steranko-a/scripts; Capt. America app. 4.00 10.00 20.00
163-166,168-Steranko-a(p). 168-Last Nick Fury (gets own book next month) & last Dr. Strange who also gets own book 2.85 8.50 20.00
167-Steranko pen/script; classic flag-c 4.70 14.00 28.00
169-177: 169-1st app. Brother Voodoo(origin in 169,170) & begin series, ends 173. 174-Origin Golem. 177-Brunner-c .50 1.25 2.50
178-(6/74)-Warlock by Starlin begins; origin Warlock & Him retold; 1st app. Magus; Starlin-c/a & scripts in 178-181 (all before Warlock #9) 3.60 9.00 18.00
179-181-All Warlock. 179-Intro/1st app. Pip the Troll. 180-Intro Gamora. 181-Warlock story continued in Warlock #9 1.80 4.50 9.00
182-188 .50 1.25 2.50
Annual 1(1962)-Reprints from Strange Tales #73,76,78, Tales of Suspense #7,9, Tales to Astonish #1,6,7, & Journey Into Mystery #53,55,59 36.00 107.00 250.00
Annual 2(7/63)-Reprints from Strange Tales #67, Strange Worlds (Atlas) #1-3, World of Fantasy #16; new Human Torch vs. Spider-Man story by Kirby/ Ditko (1st Spidey x-over; tied for 6th app. with Amazing Spider-Man #5); Kirby-c 43.00 130.00 300.00

NOTE: ***Briefer** a-17. **Burgos** a-123p. **J. Buscema** a-174p. **Colan** a-11, 20, 53, 169-173p, 188p. **Davis** c-71. **Ditko** a-46, 50, 67-122, 123-125p, 126-146, 175r, 182-188r; c-51, 93, 115, 121, 146. **Everett** a-4, 21, 40-42, 73, 147-152, 164i; c-8, 10, 11, 13, 15, 24, 45, 49-54, 56, 58, 60, 61, 63, 148, 150, 152, 158i. **Forte** a-27, 43, 50, 53, 54, 60. **Heath** c-6, 18-20. **Kamen** a-45. **G. Kane** c-170-173, 182p. **Kirby** Human Torch-101-105, 108, 109, 114, 120; Nick Fury-135p, 141-143p; (Layouts)-135-153; other **Kirby** a-67-100p; c-68-70, 72-92, 94, 95, 101-114, 116-123, 125-130, 132-135, 136p, 138-145, 147, 149, 151p. **Kirby/Ayers** c-101-106, 108-110. **Lawrence** a-29. **Leiber/ Fox** a-110, 111, 113. **Maneely** a-3, 42; c-33, 40. **Moldoff** a-20. **Mooney** a-174i. **Morisi** a-53. **Morrow** a-54. **Orlando** a-41, 44, 46, 49, 52. **Powell** a-42, 44, 49, 54, 130-134p; c-131p. **Reinman** a-11, 50, 74, 88, 91, 95, 104, 106, 112i, 124-127i. **Robinson** a-17. **Roussos** c-201i. **R.Q. Sale** c-16. **Sekowski** a-3, 11. **Severin** a(i)-136-138; c-137. **Starlin** a-178, 179, 180p, 181p; c-178-180, 181p. **Steranko** a-151-161, 162-168p; c-151i, 153, 155, 157, 159, 161, 163, 165, 167. **Torres** a-53, 62. **Tuska** a-14, 166p. **Whitney** a-149. **Wildey** a-42. **Woodbridge** a-59. Fantastic Four cameos in #101-134. Jack Katz app.-26.*

STRANGE TALES (Marvel, 1987-'88)(Value: cover or less)

STRANGE TALES OF THE UNUSUAL
Dec, 1955 - No. 11, Aug, 1957
Atlas Comics (ACI No. 1-4/WPI No. 5-11)

1-Powell-a 19.00 58.00 135.00
2 10.00 30.00 65.00
3-Williamson-a, 4 pgs. 10.00 30.00 70.00
4,6,8,11 7.50 22.50 45.00
5-Crandall, Ditko-a 10.00 30.00 65.00
7,9: 7-Kirby, Orlando-a. 9-Krigstein-a 8.35 25.00 50.00
10-Torres, Morrow-a 7.50 22.50 45.00

NOTE: ***Baily** a-6. **Brodsky** c-2-4. **Everett** a-2, 6; c-6, 9, 11. **Heck** a-1. **Maneely** c-1. **Orlando** a-7. **Pakula** a-10. **Romita** a-1. **R.Q. Sale** a-3. **Wildey** a-3.*

STRANGE TERRORS
June, 1952 - No. 7, Mar, 1953
St. John Publishing Co.

1-Bondage-c; Zombies spelled Zoombies on-c; Fineesque-a 19.00 58.00 135.00
2 11.00 32.00 75.00
3-Kubert-a; painted-c 14.00 43.00 100.00
4-Kubert-a(reprinted in Mystery Tales #18); Ekgren-c; Fineesque-a; Jerry Iger caricature 19.00 58.00 135.00
5-Kubert-a; painted-c 14.00 43.00 100.00
6-Giant, 100 pgs.(1/53); bondage-c 19.00 58.00 135.00
7-Giant, 100 pgs.; Kubert-c/a 23.00 70.00 160.00

NOTE: ***Cameron** a-6, 7. **Morisi** a-6.*

STRANGE WORLD OF YOUR DREAMS
Aug, 1952 - No. 4, Jan-Feb, 1953
Prize Publications

1-Simon & Kirby-a 32.00 95.00 220.00
2,3-Simon & Kirby-a. 2-Meskin-a 24.00 72.00 165.00
4-S&K-c; Meskin-a 20.00 60.00 140.00

STRANGE WORLDS (#18 continued from Avon's Eerie #1-17)
11/50 - No. 9, 11/52; No. 18, 10-11/54 - No. 22, 9-10/55 (No #11-17)
Avon Periodicals

1-Kenton of the Star Patrol by Kubert (r-/Eerie #1-'47); Crom the Barbarian by John Giunta 478.00 140.00 320.00
2-Wood-a; Crom the Barbarian by Giunta; Dara of the Vikings app.; used in **SOTI**, pg. 112; injury to eye panel 40.00 120.00 280.00
3-Wood/Orlando-a (Kenton), Wood/Williamson/Frazetta/Krenkel/Orlando-a (7 pgs.); Malu Slave Girl Princess app.; Kinstler-c 73.00 220.00 510.00
4-Wood-c/a (Kenton); Orlando-a; origin The Enchanted Daggar; Sultan-a 39.00 115.00 270.00
5-Orlando/Wood-a (Kenton); Wood-c 32.00 95.00 220.00
6-Kinstler-a(2); Orlando/Wood-c; Check-a 22.00 65.00 150.00
7-Fawcette & Becker/Alascia-a 16.00 48.00 110.00
8-Kubert, Kinstler, Hollingsworth & Lazarus-a; Lazarus-c 17.00 52.00 120.00
9-Kinstler, Fawcette, Alascia-a 16.00 48.00 110.00
18-(Formerly Eerie #17)-r/"Attack on Planet Mars" by Kubert 16.00 48.00 110.00
19-r/Avon's "Robotmen of the Lost Planet;" last pre-code issue 16.00 48.00 110.00

Strange Tales #106, © MEG

Strange Terrors #2, © STJ

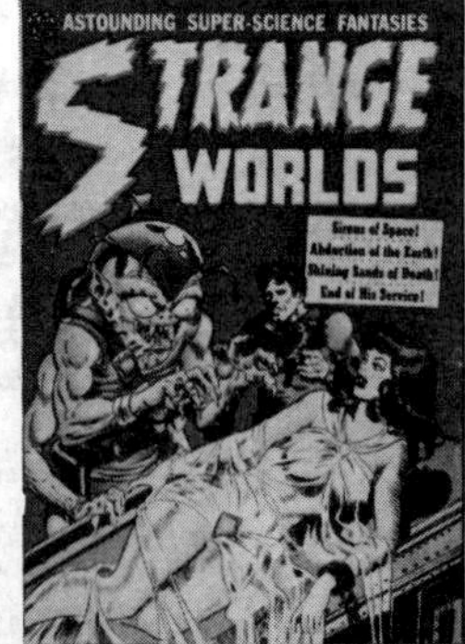

Strange Worlds #5, © AVON

Strange Worlds #1, © MEG

Stuntman Comics #1, © HARV

The Sub-Mariner #6, © MEG

GD25 FN65 NM94

20-War stories; Wood-c(r)/U.S. Paratroops #1 4.70 14.00 28.00
21,22-War stories 4.00 11.50 23.00
I.W. Reprint #5-Kinstler-a(r)/Avon's #9 1.60 4.00 8.00

STRANGE WORLDS
Dec, 1958 - No. 5, Aug, 1959
Marvel Comics (MPI No. 1,2/Male No. 3,5)

1-Kirby & Ditko-a; flying saucer issue 34.00 102.00 240.00
2-Ditko-c/a 20.00 60.00 140.00
3-Kirby-a(2) 17.00 50.00 115.00
4-Williamson-a 16.00 48.00 110.00
5-Ditko-a 13.00 40.00 90.00

NOTE: ***Buscema** a-3, 4. **Ditko** a-1-5; c-2. **Kirby** a-1, 3. **Kirby/Brodsky** c-1, 3-5.*

STRAWBERRY SHORTCAKE (Marvel) (Value: cover or less)

STRAY TOASTERS (Marvel) (Value: cover or less)

STREET COMIX (50 cents)
1973 (36 pgs.; B&W) (20,000 print run)
Street Enterprises/King Features

1-Rip Kirby .50 1.00
2-Flash Gordon .60 1.20

STREETFIGHTER (Ocean) (Value: cover or less)

STREET POET RAY (Blackthorne) (Value: cover or less)

STREETS (DC) (Value: cover or less)

STRICTLY PRIVATE
July, 1942 (#1 on sale 6/15/42)
Eastern Color Printing Co.

1,2 17.00 50.00 100.00

STRIKE! (Eclipse) (Value: cover or less)

STRIKE FORCE AMERICA (Comico) (Value: cover or less) (See The Elementals V2#16)

STRIKEFORCE: MORITURI (Marvel, 1986 & 1989 titles) (Value: cover or less)

STRIKER (Viz) (Value: cover or less)

STRONG MAN (Also see Complimentary Comics & Power of...)
Mar-Apr, 1955 - No. 4, Sept-Oct, 1955
Magazine Enterprises

1(A-1 #130)-Powell-c/a 12.00 36.00 85.00
2-4: (A-1 #132,134,139)-Powell-a. 2-Powell-c 11.00 32.00 75.00

STRONTIUM DOG (Eagle & Quality) (Value: cover or less)

STRYFE'S STRIKE FILE
Jan, 1993 ($1.75, color, no ads)
Marvel Comics

1-Stroman, Capullo, Andy Kubert, Brandon Peterson-a; metallic ink-c
.35 .90 1.75

STUMBO THE GIANT (See Harvey Hits #49, 54, 57, 60, 63, 66, 69, 72, 78, 88 & Hot Stuff #2)

STUMBO TINYTOWN
Oct, 1963 - No. 13, Nov, 1966
Harvey Publications

1 11.50 34.00 80.00
2 6.70 20.00 40.00
3-5 4.70 14.00 28.00
6-13 4.00 12.00 24.00

STUNTMAN COMICS (Also see Thrills Of Tomorrow)
Apr-May, 1946 - No. 2, June-July, 1946; No. 3, Oct-Nov, 1946
Harvey Publications

1-Origin Stuntman by S&K reprinted in Black Cat #9
75.00 225.00 450.00
2-S&K-a; The Duke of Broadway story 50.00 150.00 300.00
3-Small size (5-1/2x8-1/2"; B&W; 32 pgs.); distributed to mail subscribers only; S&K-a; Kid Adonis by S&K reprinted in Green Hornet #37
Estimated value... $250.00-$400.00
(Also see All-New #15, Boy Explorers #2, Flash Gordon #5 & Thrills of Tomorrow)

SUBMARINE ATTACK (Formerly Speed Demons)
No. 11, May, 1958 - No. 54, Feb-Mar, 1966
Charlton Comics

11 2.40 6.00 12.00
12-20 1.40 3.50 7.00
21-54 1.00 2.50 5.00

NOTE: ***Glanzman** c/a-25. **Montes/Bache** a-38, 40, 41.*

SUB-MARINER (See All-Select, All-Winners, Blonde Phantom, Daring, The Defenders, Fantastic Four #4, Human Torch, The Invaders, Iron Man &..., Marvel Mystery, Marvel Spotlight #27, Men's Adventures, Motion Picture Funnies Weekly, Namora, Namor, The..., Prince Namor, The Sub-Mariner, Saga Of The..., Tales to Astonish #70 & 2nd series, USA & Young Men)

SUB-MARINER, THE (2nd Series) (Sub-Mariner #31 on)
May, 1968 - No. 72, Sept, 1974 (No. 43: 52 pgs.)
Marvel Comics Group

1-Origin Sub-Mariner; story continued from Iron Man & Sub-Mariner #1
18.00 54.00 125.00
2-Triton app. 7.50 22.50 45.00
3-10: 5-1st Tiger Shark. 7-Photo-c. 8-Sub-Mariner vs. Thing. 9-1st app. Serpent Crown (origin in #10 & 12) 4.00 12.00 24.00
11-13,15: 15-Last 12 cent issue 3.00 7.50 15.00
14-Sub-Mariner vs. G.A. Human Torch; death of Toro (1st modern app. & only app. Toro) 5.00 15.00 30.00
16-20: 19-1st Sting Ray; Stan Lee, Romita, Heck, Thomas, Everett & Kirby cameos. 20-Dr. Doom app. 2.00 5.00 10.00
21-33,36-40: 22-Dr. Strange x-over. 25-Origin Atlantis. 30-Capt. Marvel x-over. 37-Death of Lady Dorma. 38-Origin. 40-Spider-Man x-over
1.40 3.50 7.00
34,35-Prelude to 1st Defenders story. 34-Hulk & Silver Surfer x-over. 35-Namor/Hulk/Silver Surfer team-up to battle The Avengers-c/story (3/71); hints at teaming up again 1.70 5.00 12.00
41-72: 42-Last 15 cent issue. 44,45-Sub-Mariner vs. H. Torch. 47,48-Dr. Doom app. 49-Cosmic Cube story. 50-1st app. Nita, Namor's niece (later Namorita in New Warriors). 59-1st battle with Thor. 61-Last artwork by Everett; 1st 4 pgs. completed by Mortimer; pgs. 5-20 by Mooney. 62-1st Tales of Atlantis, ends 66. 64-Hitler cameo. 67-New costume; F.F. x-over. 69-Spider-Man x-over (6 panels) .80 2.00 4.00
Special 1,2: 1(1/71)-r/Tales to Astonish #70-73. 2(1/72)-r/T.T.A. #74-76; Everett-a 1.20 3.00 6.00

NOTE: ***Bolle** a-67i. **Buscema** a(p)-1-8, 20, 24. **Colan** a(p)-10, 11, 40, 43, 46-49, Special 1, 2; c(p)-10, 11, 40. **Craig** a-17, 19-23i. **Everett** a-45r, 50-55, 57, 58, 59-61(plot), 63(plot); c-47, 48i, 55, 57-59i, 61, Spec. 2. **G. Kane** c(p)-42-52, 58, 66, 70, 71. **Mooney** a-24i, 25i, 32-35i, 39i, 42i, 44i, 45i, 60i, 61i, 65p, 66p, 68i. Severin c/a-38i. **Starlin** c-59p. **Tuska** a-41p, 42p, 69-71p. **Wrightson** a-36i. #53, 54-r/stories Sub-Mariner Comics #41 & 39.*

SUB-MARINER COMICS (1st Series) (The Sub-Mariner #1,2,33-42) (Official True Crime Cases #24 on; Amazing Mysteries #32 on; Best Love #33 on)
Spring, 1941 - No. 23, Sum, 1947; No. 24, Wint, 1947 - No. 31, 4/49; No. 32, 7/49; No. 33, 4/54 - No. 42, 10/55
Timely/Marvel Comics (TCI 1-7/SePI 8/MPI 9-32/Atlas Comics (CCC 33-42))

GD25 FN65 VF82 NM94

1-The Sub-Mariner by Everett & The Angel begin
600.00 1800.00 3600.00 6000.00
(Estimated up to 190 total copies exist, 8 in NM/Mint)

GD25 FN65 NM94

2-Everett-a 283.00 850.00 1700.00
3-Churchill assassination-c; 40 pg. Sub-Mariner story
217.00 650.00 1300.00
4-Everett-a, 40 pgs.; 1 pg. Wolverton-a 183.00 550.00 1100.00
5: 5,8-Gabrielle/Klein-c 133.00 400.00 800.00
6-10: 9-Wolverton-a, 3 pgs.; flag-c 100.00 300.00 600.00

	GD25	FN65	NM94
11-15	68.00	205.00	410.00
16-20	63.00	190.00	380.00
21-Last Angel; Everett-a	54.00	162.00	325.00
22-Young Allies app.	54.00	162.00	325.00
23-The Human Torch, Namora x-over	54.00	162.00	325.00
24-Namora x-over	54.00	162.00	325.00
25-The Blonde Phantom begins, ends No. 31; Kurtzman-a; Namora x-over	63.00	190.00	380.00
26-28: 28-Namora cover; Everett-a	54.00	162.00	325.00
29-31 (4/49): 29-The Human Torch app. 31-Capt. America app.	54.00	162.00	325.00
32 (7/49, Scarce)-Origin Sub-Mariner	104.00	312.00	625.00
33 (4/54)-Origin Sub-Mariner; The Human Torch app.; Namora x-over in Sub-Mariner #33-42	54.00	162.00	325.00
34,35-Human Torch in each	44.00	132.00	265.00
36,37,39-41: 36,39-41-Namora app.	44.00	132.00	265.00
38-Origin Sub-Mariner's wings; Namora app. Last pre-code (2/55)	54.00	162.00	325.00
42-Last issue	54.00	162.00	325.00

NOTE: *Angel by* ***Gustavson****-#1, 8.* ***Brodsky*** *c-34-36, 42.* ***Everett*** *a-1-4, 22-24, 26-42; c-32, 33, 40.* ***Maneely*** *a-38; c-37, 39-41.* ***Rico*** *c-27-31.* ***Schomburg*** *c-1-4, 6, 8-18, 20.* ***Sekowsky*** *c-24. 25, 26(w/Rico).* ***Shores*** *c-21-23, 38. Bondage c-13, 22, 24, 25, 34.*

SUBSPECIES
May, 1991 - No. 4, Aug, 1991 ($2.50, color, mini-series)
Eternity Comics

1-4: New stories based on horror movie	.50	1.25	2.50

SUBURBAN SHE-DEVILS (Marvel)(Value: cover or less)

SUE & SALLY SMITH (Formerly My Secret Life)
V2#48, Nov, 1962 - No. 54, Nov, 1963 (Flying Nurses)
Charlton Comics

V2#48	1.20	3.00	6.00
49-54	.80	2.00	4.00

SUGAR & SPIKE (Also see The Best of DC)
Apr-May, 1956 - No. 98, Oct-Nov, 1971
National Periodical Publications

1 (Scarce)	93.00	280.00	650.00
2	47.00	140.00	325.00
3-5	39.00	120.00	275.00
6-10	23.00	70.00	160.00
11-20	21.00	63.00	145.00
21-29,31-40: 26-X-Mas-c	11.00	32.00	75.00
30-Scribbly & Scribbly, Jr. x-over	12.00	36.00	85.00
41-60	7.35	22.00	44.00
61-80: 72-Origin & 1st app. Bernie the Brain	4.35	13.00	26.00
81-98: 84-Bernie the Brain apps. as Superman in 1 panel (9/69). 85-(68 pgs.); r-#72. #96-(68 pgs.). #97,98-(52 pgs.)	4.00	10.00	20.00

NOTE: *All written and drawn by* ***Sheldon Mayer.***

SUGAR BEAR
No date, circa 1975? (16 pages) (2-1/2x4-1/2")
Post Cereal Giveaway

"The Almost Take Over of the Post Office," "The Race Across the Atlantic," "The Zoo Goes Wild" each...		.50	1.00

SUGAR BOWL COMICS (Teen-age)
May, 1948 - No. 5, Jan, 1949
Famous Funnies

1-Toth-c/a	10.00	30.00	70.00
2,4,5	4.20	12.50	25.00
3-Toth-a	8.35	25.00	50.00

SUGARFOOT (See 4-Color #907, 992, 1059, 1098, 1147, 1209)

SUICIDE SQUAD (DC)(Value: cover or less)(See Brave & the Bold, Doom Patrol & Suicide Squad)

SUMMER FUN (See Dell Giants)

SUMMER FUN (Formerly Li'l Genius; Holiday Surprise #55)
No. 54, Oct, 1966 (Giant)
Charlton Comics

54	1.20	3.00	6.00

SUMMER FUN (Disney, 1991)(Value: cover or less)

SUMMER LOVE (Formerly Brides in Love?)
V2#46, Oct, 1965; V2#47, Oct, 1966; V2#48, Nov, 1968
Charlton Comics

V2#46-Beatles-c/story	6.70	20.00	40.00
47-Beatles story	6.70	20.00	40.00
48	.80	2.00	4.00

SUMMER MAGIC (See Movie Comics)

SUNDANCE (See 4-Color #1126)

SUNDANCE KID (Also see Blazing Six-Guns)
June, 1971 - No. 3, Sept, 1971 (52 pages)
Skywald Publications

1-Durango Kid; Two Kirby Bullseye-r	.60	1.50	3.00
2-Swift Arrow, Durango Kid, Bullseye by S&K; Meskin plus 1 pg. origin	.40	1.00	2.00
3-Durango Kid, Billy the Kid, Red Hawk-r	.30	.75	1.50

SUNDAY FUNNIES
1950
Harvey Publications

1	2.80	7.00	14.00

SUN DEVILS (DC)(Value: cover or less)

SUN FUN KOMIKS
1939 (15 cents; black, white & red)
Sun Publications

1-Satire on comics	17.00	51.00	120.00

SUN GIRL (See The Human Torch & Marvel Mystery Comics #88)
Aug, 1948 - No. 3, Dec, 1948
Marvel Comics (CCC)

1-Sun Girl begins; Miss America app.	79.00	238.00	475.00
2,3: 2-The Blonde Phantom begins	62.00	188.00	375.00

SUNNY, AMERICA'S SWEETHEART (Formerly Cosmo Cat #1-10)
No. 11, Dec, 1947 - No. 14, June, 1948
Fox Features Syndicate

11-Feldstein-c/a	39.00	120.00	275.00
12-14-Feldstein-c/a; 14-Lingerie panels	32.00	95.00	225.00
I.W. Reprint #8-Feldstein-a; r/Fox issue	10.00	30.00	60.00

SUN-RUNNERS (Pacific/Eclipse/Amazing)(Value: cover or less)

SUNSET CARSON (Also see Cowboy Western)
Feb, 1951 - No. 4, 1951 (No month)
Charlton Comics

1-Photo/retouched-c (Scarce, all issues)	64.00	195.00	450.00
2	50.00	150.00	350.00
3,4	39.00	118.00	275.00

SUPER ANIMALS PRESENTS PIDGY & THE MAGIC GLASSES
Dec, 1953
Star Publications

3-D 1-L. B. Cole-c	30.00	90.00	210.00

SUPER BOOK OF COMICS
nd (1943?) (32 pgs., soft-c) (Pan-Am/Gilmore Oil/Kelloggs premiums)
Western Publishing Co.

nn-Dick Tracy (Gilmore)-Magic Morro app.	36.00	107.00	250.00
1-Dick Tracy & The Smuggling Ring; Stratosphere Jim app. (Rare) (Pan-Am)	29.00	85.00	200.00
1-Smilin' Jack, Magic Morro (Pan-Am)	8.35	25.00	50.00

Sub-Mariner Comics #27, © MEG

Sun Girl #1, © MEG

Sunny, America's Sweetheart #14, © FOX

Super-Book of Comics #1 (Omar, 1944), © Chicago Tribune

Superboy #2, © DC

Superboy #50, © DC

	GD25	FN65	NM94
2-Smilin' Jack, Stratosphere Jim (Pan-Am)	8.35	25.00	50.00
2-Smitty, Magic Morro (Pan-Am)	8.35	25.00	50.00
3-Captain Midnight, Magic Morro (Pan-Am)	11.00	32.00	75.00
3-Moon Mullins?	6.70	20.00	40.00
4-Red Ryder, Magic Morro (Pan-Am)	6.70	20.00	40.00
4-Smitty, Stratosphere Jim (Pan-Am)	6.70	20.00	40.00
5-Don Winslow, Magic Morro (Gilmore)	6.70	20.00	40.00
5-Don Winslow, Stratosphere Jim (Pan-Am)	6.70	20.00	40.00
5-Terry & the Pirates	11.50	34.00	80.00
6-Don Winslow, Stratosphere Jim (Pan-Am)-McWilliams-a	8.35	25.00	50.00
6-King of the Royal Mounted, Magic Morro (Pan-Am)	8.35	25.00	50.00
7-Dick Tracy, Magic Morro (Pan-Am)	13.00	40.00	90.00
7-Little Orphan Annie	8.35	25.00	50.00
8-Dick Tracy, Stratosphere Jim (Pan-Am)	13.00	40.00	90.00
8-Dan Dunn, Magic Morro (Pan-Am)	8.35	25.00	50.00
9-Terry & the Pirates, Magic Morro (Pan-Am)	10.00	30.00	70.00
10-Red Ryder, Magic Morro (Pan-Am)	6.70	20.00	40.00

SUPER-BOOK OF COMICS
(Omar Bread & Hancock Oil Co. giveaways)
1944 - No. 30, 1947 (Omar); 1947 - 1948 (Hancock) (16 pgs.)
Western Publishing Co.

Note: The Hancock issues are all exact reprints of the earlier Omar issues. The issue numbers were removed in some of the reprints.

	GD25	FN65	NM94
1-Dick Tracy (Omar, 1944)	17.00	51.00	120.00
1-Dick Tracy (Hancock, 1947)	13.00	40.00	90.00
2-Bugs Bunny (Omar, 1944)	5.85	17.50	35.00
2-Bugs Bunny (Hancock, 1947)	4.70	14.00	28.00
3-Terry & the Pirates (Omar, 1944)	10.00	30.00	70.00
3-Terry & the Pirates (Hancock, 1947)	10.00	30.00	60.00
4-Andy Panda (Omar, 1944)	6.35	19.00	38.00
4-Andy Panda (Hancock, 1947)	4.70	14.00	28.00
5-Smokey Stover (Omar, 1945)	4.70	14.00	28.00
5-Smokey Stover (Hancock, 1947)	3.60	9.00	18.00
6-Porky Pig (Omar, 1945)	5.85	17.50	35.00
6-Porky Pig (Hancock, 1947)	4.70	14.00	28.00
7-Smilin' Jack (Omar, 1945)	5.85	17.50	35.00
7-Smilin' Jack (Hancock, 1947)	4.70	14.00	28.00
8-Oswald the Rabbit (Omar, 1945)	4.70	14.00	28.00
8-Oswald the Rabbit (Hancock, 1947)	3.60	9.00	18.00
9-Alley Oop (Omar, 1945)	11.00	32.00	75.00
9-Alley Oop (Hancock, 1947)	10.00	30.00	65.00
10-Elmer Fudd (Omar, 1945)	4.70	14.00	28.00
10-Elmer Fudd (Hancock, 1947)	3.60	9.00	18.00
11-Little Orphan Annie (Omar, 1945)	6.70	20.00	40.00
11-Little Orphan Annie (Hancock, 1947)	5.00	15.00	30.00
12-Woody Woodpecker (Omar, 1945)	4.70	14.00	28.00
12-Woody Woodpecker (Hancock, 1947)	3.60	9.00	18.00
13-Dick Tracy (Omar, 1945)	11.00	32.00	75.00
13-Dick Tracy (Hancock, 1947)	10.00	30.00	65.00
14-Bugs Bunny (Omar, 1945)	4.70	14.00	28.00
14-Bugs Bunny (Hancock, 1947)	3.60	9.00	18.00
15-Andy Panda (Omar, 1945)	4.00	12.00	24.00
15-Andy Panda (Hancock, 1947)	3.60	9.00	18.00
16-Terry & the Pirates (Omar, 1945)	10.00	30.00	65.00
16-Terry & the Pirates (Hancock, 1947)	8.35	25.00	50.00
17-Smokey Stover (Omar, 1946)	4.70	14.00	28.00
17-Smokey Stover (Hancock, 1948?)	3.60	9.00	18.00
18-Porky Pig (Omar, 1946)	4.00	12.00	24.00
18-Porky Pig (Hancock, 1948?)	3.60	9.00	18.00
19-Smilin' Jack (Omar, 1946)	4.70	14.00	28.00
nn-Smilin' Jack (Hancock, 1948)	3.60	9.00	18.00
20-Oswald the Rabbit (Omar, 1946)	4.00	12.00	24.00
nn-Oswald the Rabbit (Hancock, 1948)	3.60	9.00	18.00
21-Gasoline Alley (Omar, 1946)	6.70	20.00	40.00
nn-Gasoline Alley (Hancock, 1948)	5.00	15.00	30.00
22-Elmer Fudd (Omar, 1946)	4.00	12.00	24.00
nn-Elmer Fudd (Hancock, 1948)	3.60	9.00	18.00
23-Little Orphan Annie (Omar, 1946)	5.85	17.50	35.00
nn-Little Orphan Annie (Hancock, 1948)	4.70	14.00	28.00
24-Woody Woodpecker (Omar, 1946)	4.00	12.00	24.00
nn-Woody Woodpecker (Hancock, 1948)	3.60	9.00	18.00
25-Dick Tracy (Omar, 1946)	10.00	30.00	65.00
nn-Dick Tracy (Hancock, 1948)	8.35	25.00	50.00
26-Bugs Bunny (Omar, 1946))	4.00	12.00	24.00
nn-Bugs Bunny (Hancock, 1948)	3.60	9.00	18.00
27-Andy Panda (Omar, 1946)	4.00	12.00	24.00
27-Andy Panda (Hancock, 1948)	3.60	9.00	18.00
28-Terry & the Pirates (Omar, 1946)	10.00	30.00	65.00
28-Terry & the Pirates (Hancock, 1948)	8.35	25.00	50.00
29-Smokey Stover (Omar, 1947)	4.00	12.00	24.00
29-Smokey Stover (Hancock, 1948)	3.60	9.00	18.00
30-Porky Pig (Omar, 1947)	4.00	12.00	24.00
30-Porky Pig (Hancock, 1948)	3.60	9.00	18.00
nn-Bugs Bunny (Hancock, 1948)-Does not match any Omar book	3.60	9.00	18.00

SUPERBOY (See Adventure, Aurora, DC Comics Presents, DC 100 Page Super Spect. #15, DC Super Stars, 80 Page Giant #10, More Fun, The New Advs. of... & Superman Family #191)

SUPERBOY (...& the Legion of Super-Heroes with #231)(Becomes The Legion of Super-Heroes No. 259 on)
Mar-Apr, 1949 - No. 258, Dec, 1979 (#1-16: 52 pgs.)
National Periodical Publications/DC Comics

	GD25	FN65	VF82	NM94
1-Superman cover	350.00	1050.00	2100.00	3500.00

(Estimated up to 275 total copies exist, 15 in NM/Mint)

	GD25	FN65	NM94
2-Used in **SOTI**, pg. 35-36,226	121.00	365.00	850.00
3	90.00	270.00	625.00
4,5: 5-1st pre-Supergirl tryout	73.00	220.00	375.00
6-10: 8-1st Superbaby. 10-1st app. Lana Lang	54.00	160.00	375.00
11-15	39.00	120.00	275.00
16-20	29.00	85.00	200.00
21-26,28-30	22.00	65.00	150.00
27-Low distribution	24.00	72.00	165.00
31-38: 38-Last pre-code issue	16.00	48.00	110.00
39-48,50 (7/56)	12.00	36.00	85.00
49 (6/56)-1st app. Metallo (Jor-El's robot)	16.00	48.00	110.00
51-60	10.00	30.00	65.00
61-67	9.15	27.50	55.00
68-Origin/1st app. original Bizarro (10-11/58)	43.00	130.00	300.00
69-77,79: 75-Spanking-c. 76-1st Supermonkey. 77-Pre-Pete Ross tryout	7.50	22.50	45.00
78-Origin Mr. Mxyzptlk & Superboy's costume	11.50	34.00	80.00
80-1st meeting Superboy/Supergirl (4/60)	11.00	32.00	75.00
81,83-85,87,88: 83-Origin/1st app. Kryptonite Kid	5.35	16.00	32.00
82-1st Bizarro Krypto	6.35	19.00	38.00
86(1/61)-4th Legion app; Intro Pete Ross	11.50	34.00	80.00
89(6/61)-1st app. Mon-el; 2nd Phantom Zone	20.00	60.00	140.00
90-93: 90-Pete Ross learns Superboy's I.D. 92-Last 10 cent issue. 93-10th Legion app. (12/61); Chameleon Boy app.	5.35	16.00	32.00
94-97,99	4.00	10.00	20.00
98(7/62)-18th Legion app; origin & 1st app. Ultra Boy; Pete Ross joins Legion	5.00	15.00	30.00

100(10/62)-Ultra Boy app; 1st app. Phantom Zone villains, Dr. Xadu & Erndine. 2 pg. map of Krypton; origin Superboy retold; r-cover of

	GD25	FN65	NM94
Superman #1; Pete Ross joins Legion	17.00	52.00	120.00
101-120: 104-Origin Phantom Zone. 115-Atomic bomb-c. 117-Legion app.	2.00	5.00	10.00
121-128: 124(10/65)-1st app. Insect Queen (Lana Lang). 125-Legion cameo. 126-Origin Krypto the Super Dog retold with new facts	1.20	3.00	6.00
129 (80-pg. Giant G-22)-Reprints origin Mon-el	1.60	4.00	8.00
130-137,139,140: 131-Legion statues cameo in Dog Legionnaires story. 132-1st app. Supremo	.80	2.00	4.00
138 (80-pg. Giant G-35)	1.60	4.00	8.00
141-146,148-155,157-164,166-173,175,176: 145-Superboy's parents regain their youth. 171-1st app. Aquaboy? 172,173,176-Legion app.; 172-Origin Yango (Super Ape)	.60	1.50	3.00
147(6/68)-Giant G-47; origin Saturn Girl, Lightning Lad, Cosmic Boy; origin Legion of Super-Pets-r/Adv. #293?	1.60	4.00	8.00
156,165,174 (Giants G-59,71,83)	1.20	3.00	6.00
177-184,186,187 (All 52 pgs.): 184-Origin Dial H for Hero-r	.40	1.00	2.00
185-DC 100 Pg. Super Spectacular #12; Legion-c/story; Teen Titans, Kid Eternity(r/Hit #46), Star Spangled Kid-r(S.S. 55)	.50	1.25	2.50
188-196: 188-Origin Karkan. 191-Origin Sunboy retold; Legion app. 193-Chameleon Boy & Shrinking Violet get new costumes. 195-1st app. Erg/Wildfire; Phantom Girl gets new costume. 196-Last Superboy solo story	.30	.75	1.50
197-Legion series begins; Lightning Lad's new costume	1.00	2.50	5.00
198,199: 198-Element Lad & Princess Projectra get new costumes	.40	1.00	2.00
200-Bouncing Boy & Duo Damsel marry; Jonn' Jonzz' cameo	.90	2.25	4.50
201,204,206,207,209: 201-Re-intro Erg as Wildfire. 204-Supergirl resigns from Legion. 206-Ferro Lad & Invisible Kid app. 209-Karate Kid gets new costume	.40	1.00	2.00
202,205-(100 pgs.): 202-Light Lass gets new costume	.50	1.25	2.50
203-Invisible Kid dies	.60	1.50	3.00
208,210: 208-(68 pgs.). 210-Origin Karate Kid	.50	1.25	2.50
211-220: 212-Matter-Eater Lad resigns. 216-1st app. Tyroc who joins Legion in #218	.35	.90	1.80
221-249: 226-Intro. Dawnstar. 228-Death of Chemical King. 240-Origin Dawnstar. 242-(52 pgs.). 243-Legion of Substitute Heroes app. 243-245-(44 pgs.)		.60	1.20
250-258: 253-Intro Blok. 257-Return of Bouncing Boy & Duo Damsel by Ditko		.50	1.00
Annual 1(Sum/64, 84 pgs.)-Origin Krypto-r	10.00	30.00	70.00
...Spectacular 1(1980, Giant)-Distr. through comic stores; mostly-r		.50	1.00

NOTE: ***Neal Adams** c-143, 145, 146, 148-155, 157-161, 163, 164, 166-168, 172, 173, 175, 176, 178. **M. Anderson** a-245i. **Ditko** a-257p. **Grell** a-202i, 203-219, 220-224p, 235p; c-207-232, 235, 236p, 237, 239p, 240p, 243p, 246, 258. **Nasser** a(p)-222, 225, 226, 230, 231, 233, 236. **Simonson** a-237p. **Starlin** a(p)-239, 250, 251; c-238. **Staton** a-227p, 243-249p, 252-258p; c-247-251p. **Tuska** a-172, 173, 176, 183, 235p. **Wood** inks-152-155, 157-161. Legion app.-172, 173, 176, 177, 183, 184, 188, 190, 191, 193, 195.*

SUPERBOY (TV)(DC, 1990-'91) (Value: cover or less)

SUPER BRAT
January, 1954 - No. 4, July, 1954
Toby Press

	GD25	FN65	NM94
1 (1954)	3.60	9.00	18.00
2-4: 4-Li'l Teevy by Mel Lazarus	2.00	5.00	10.00
I.W. Reprint #1,2,3,7,8('58)	.30	.75	1.50
I.W. (Super) Reprint #10('63)	.30	.75	1.50

SUPERCAR (TV)
Nov, 1962 - No. 4, Aug, 1963 (All painted covers)
Gold Key

	GD25	FN65	NM94
1	22.00	65.00	150.00
2,3	11.00	32.00	75.00
4	16.00	48.00	110.00

SUPER CAT (Formerly Frisky Animals; also see Animal Crackers)
No. 56, Nov, 1953 - No. 58, May, 1954; Sept, 1957 - No. 4, May, 1958
Star Publications #56-58/Ajax/Farrell Publ. (Four Star Comic Corp.)

	GD25	FN65	NM94
56-58-L.B. Cole-c on all	8.35	25.00	50.00
1(1957-Ajax)	4.20	12.50	25.00
2-4	3.00	7.50	15.00

SUPER CIRCUS (TV)
January, 1951 - No. 5, 1951 (Mary Hartline)
Cross Publishing Co.

	GD25	FN65	NM94
1-Cast photos on-c	7.50	22.50	45.00
2-Cast photos on-c	5.85	17.50	35.00
3-5	4.20	12.50	25.00

SUPER CIRCUS (TV)
No. 542, March, 1954 - No. 694, Mar, 1956 (Feat. Mary Hartline)
Dell Publishing Co.

	GD25	FN65	NM94
4-Color 542,592,694: Mary Hartline photo-c	4.70	14.00	28.00

SUPER COMICS
May, 1938 - No. 121, Feb-Mar, 1949
Dell Publishing Co.

	GD25	FN65	NM94
1-Terry & The Pirates, The Gumps, Dick Tracy, Little Orphan Annie, Little Joe, Gasoline Alley, Smilin' Jack, Smokey Stover, Smitty, Tiny Tim, Moon Mullins, Harold Teen, Winnie Winkle begin	125.00	375.00	750.00
2	61.00	182.00	365.00
3	53.00	160.00	320.00
4,5	44.00	132.00	265.00
6-10	35.00	105.00	210.00
11-20	28.00	85.00	170.00
21-29: 21-Magic Morro begins (origin, 2/40). 22,27-Ken Ernst-c (also #25?)	24.00	72.00	145.00
30-"Sea Hawk" movie adaptation-c/story with Errol Flynn	24.00	72.00	145.00
31-40: 34-Ken Ernst-c. 35-Dick Tracy-c begin	20.00	60.00	120.00
41-50: 43-Terry & The Pirates ends	16.00	47.00	95.00
51-60	12.00	35.00	70.00
61-70: 65-Brenda Starr-r begin? 67-X-mas-c	10.00	30.00	60.00
71-80	9.15	27.50	55.00
81-99	6.70	20.00	40.00
100	9.15	27.50	55.00
101-115-Last Dick Tracy (moves to own title)	5.35	16.00	32.00
116,118-All Smokey Stover	4.70	14.00	28.00
117-All Gasoline Alley	4.70	14.00	28.00
119-121-Terry & The Pirates app. in all	4.70	14.00	28.00

SUPER COPS, THE (Red Circle) (Value: cover or less)

SUPER COPS (Now) (Value: cover or less)

SUPER CRACKED (See Cracked)

SUPER DC GIANT (25-50 cents, all 68-52 pg. Giants)
No. 13, 9-10/70 - No. 26, 7-8/71; V3#27, Summer, 1976 (No #1-12)
National Periodical Publications

	GD25	FN65	NM94
S-13-Binky	.60	1.50	3.00
S-14-Top Guns of the West; Kubert-c; Trigger Twins, Johnny Thunder, Wyoming Kid-r; Moreira-r (9-10/70)	.60	1.50	3.00
S-15-Western Comics; Kubert-c; Pow Wow Smith, Vigilante, Buffalo Bill-r; new Gil Kane-a (9-10/70)	.80	2.00	4.00
S-16-Best of the Brave & the Bold; Batman-r & Metamorpho origin-r from Brave & the Bold	.80	2.00	4.00
S-17-Love 1970	.50	1.25	2.50
S-18-Three Mouseketeers; Dizzy Dog, Doodles Duck, Bo Bunny-r; Sheldon Mayer-a	.60	1.50	3.00
S-19-Jerry Lewis; no Neal Adams-a	.60	1.50	3.00
S-20-House of Mystery; N. Adams-c; Kirby-r(3)	.60	1.50	3.00

Superboy #145, © DC

Super Cat #57, © STAR

Super Comics #49, © DELL

Super Duck #29, © AP

Super Friends #1, © DC

Super Fun #1, © Gillmor

	GD25	FN65	NM94
S-21-Love 1971	.40	1.00	2.00
S-22-Top Guns of the West	.50	1.25	2.50
S-23-The Unexpected	.40	1.00	2.00
S-24-Supergirl (1st solo book?)	.40	1.00	2.00
S-25-Challengers of the Unknown; all Kirby/Wood-r	.60	1.50	3.00
S-26-Aquaman (1971)	.60	1.50	3.00
27-Strange Flying Saucers Advs. (Sum, 1976)	.40	1.00	2.00

NOTE: ***Sid Greene** r-27p(2), **Heath** r-27. **G. Kane** a-14r(2), 15, 27r(p). **Kubert** r-16.*

SUPER-DOOPER COMICS
1946 - No. 8, 1946 (10 cents)(32 pages)(paper cover)
Able Manufacturing Co.

	GD25	FN65	NM94
1-The Clock, Gangbuster app.	11.00	32.00	65.00
2	6.35	19.00	38.00
3,4,6	4.70	14.00	28.00
5,7-Capt. Freedom & Shock Gibson	6.35	19.00	38.00
8-Shock Gibson, Sam Hill	6.35	19.00	38.00

SUPER DUCK COMICS (The Cockeyed Wonder) (See Jolly Jingles)
Fall, 1944 - No. 94, Dec, 1960 (Also see Laugh #24)
MLJ Mag. No. 1-4(9/45)/Close-Up No. 5 on (Archie)

	GD25	FN65	NM94
1-Origin	27.00	81.00	190.00
2-Bill Vigoda-c	12.00	36.00	85.00
3-5: 4-20-Al Fagaly-c(most)	10.00	30.00	60.00
6-10	7.50	22.50	45.00
11-20	4.70	14.00	28.00
21,23-40	4.00	12.00	24.00
22-Used in **SOTI**, pg. 35,307,308	5.00	15.00	30.00
41-60	3.20	8.00	16.00
61-94	2.40	6.00	12.00

SUPER DUPER
No. 5, 1941 - No. 11, 1941
Harvey Publications

	GD25	FN65	NM94
5-Captain Freedom & Shock Gibson app.	17.00	52.00	120.00
8,11	10.00	30.00	60.00

SUPER DUPER COMICS (Formerly Latest Comics?)
No. 3, May-June, 1947
F. E. Howard Publ.

	GD25	FN65	NM94
3-1st app. Mr. Monster	5.85	17.50	35.00

SUPER FRIENDS (TV) (Also see Best of DC & Limited Collectors' Edition)
Nov, 1976 - No. 47, Aug, 1981 (#14 is 44 pgs.)
National Periodical Publications/DC Comics

	GD25	FN65	NM94
1-Superman, Batman, Robin, Wonder Woman, Aquaman, Atom, Wendy, Marvin & Wonder Dog begin	.40	1.00	2.00
2-47: 7-1st app. Wonder Twins, & The Seraph. 8-1st app. Jack O'Lantern. 9-1st app. Icemaiden. 13-1st app. Dr. Mist. 14-Origin Wonder Twins. 25-1st app. Fire & Green Fury. 31-Black Orchid app. 36,43-Plastic Man app. 47-Origin Fire & Green Fury	.30	.75	1.50
...Special 1 (1981, giveaway, no ads, no code or price)-r/Super Friends #19 & 36		.50	1.00

NOTE: ***Estrada** a-1p, 2p. **Orlando** a-1p. **Staton** a-43, 45.*

SUPER FUN
January, 1956 (By A.W. Nugent)
Gillmor Magazines

	GD25	FN65	NM94
1-Comics, puzzles, cut-outs by A.W. Nugent	2.40	6.00	12.00

SUPER FUNNIES (...Western Funnies #3,4)
Dec, 1953 - No. 4, June, 1954
Superior Comics Publishers Ltd. (Canada)

	GD25	FN65	NM94
1-(3-D)-Dopey Duck; make your own 3-D glasses cut-out inside front-c; did not come w/glasses	29.00	85.00	200.00
2-Horror & crime satire	5.35	16.00	32.00
3-Geronimo, Billy The Kid app.	4.00	10.00	20.00
4-(Western-Phantom Ranger)	4.00	10.00	20.00

SUPERGEAR COMICS
1976 (4 pages in color) (slick paper)
Jacobs Corp. (Giveaway)

	GD25	FN65	NM94
nn-(Rare)-Superman, Lois Lane; Steve Lombard app. (500 copies printed, over half destroyed?)	1.20	3.00	6.00

SUPERGIRL (See Action, Adventure #281, Brave & the Bold, Crisis on Infinite Earths #7, Daring New Advs. of..., Super DC Giant, Superman Family, & Super-Team Family)

SUPERGIRL
Nov, 1972 - No. 9, Dec-Jan, 1973-74; No. 10, Sept-Oct, 1974
National Periodical Publications

	GD25	FN65	NM94
1-1st solo title; Zatanna begins, ends #5	.40	1.00	2.00
2-10: 5-Zatanna origin-r. 8-JLA x-over; Batman cameo		.50	1.00

NOTE: *Zatanna in #1-5, 7(Guest); Prez app. in #10. #1-8 are 20 cent issues.*

SUPERGIRL (Formerly Daring New Adventures of...)
No. 14, Dec, 1983 - No. 23, Sept, 1984
DC Comics

	GD25	FN65	NM94
14-23: 16-Ambush Bug app. 20-JLA & New Teen Titans app.		.50	1.00
... Movie Special (1985)-Adapts movie; Morrow-a; photo back-c		.60	1.20
Giveaway ('84, '86 Baxter, nn)(American Honda/U.S. Dept. Transportation)-Torres-c/a		.60	1.20

SUPER GOOF (Walt Disney) (See Dynabrite & The Phantom Blot)
Oct, 1965 - No. 74, 1982
Gold Key No. 1-57/Whitman No. 58 on

	GD25	FN65	NM94
1	3.00	7.50	15.00
2-10	1.40	3.50	7.00
11-20	1.00	2.50	5.00
21-30	.60	1.50	3.00
31-50	.40	1.00	2.00
51-74		.50	1.00

NOTE: *Reprints in #16, 24, 28, 29, 37, 38, 43, 45, 46, 54(1/2), 56-58, 65(1/2), 72(r-#2).*

SUPER GREEN BERET (Tod Holton...)
April, 1967 - No. 2, June, 1967 (25 cents, 68 pgs.)
Lightning Comics (Milson Publ. Co.)

	GD25	FN65	NM94
1,2	3.00	7.50	15.00

SUPER HEROES (See Giant-Size... & Marvel...)

SUPER HEROES
Jan, 1967 - No. 4, June, 1967
Dell Publishing Co.

	GD25	FN65	NM94
1-Origin & 1st app. Fab 4	3.60	9.00	18.00
2-4	2.00	5.00	10.00

SUPER-HEROES BATTLE SUPER-GORILLAS (See DC Special #16)
Winter, 1976 (One Shot, 52 pgs.; all reprints)
National Periodical Publications

	GD25	FN65	NM94
1-Superman, Batman, Flash stories; Infantino-a(p)		.50	1.00

SUPER HEROES PUZZLES AND GAMES
1979 (32 pgs.) (regular size)
General Mills Giveaway (Marvel Comics Group)

	GD25	FN65	NM94
nn-Four 2-pg. origin stories of Spider-Man, Captain America, The Hulk, & Spider-Woman	.80	2.00	4.00

SUPER HEROES VERSUS SUPER VILLAINS
July, 1966 (no month given)(68 pgs.)
Archie Publications (Radio Comics)

	GD25	FN65	NM94
1-Flyman, Black Hood, The Web, Shield-r; Reinman-a	4.70	14.00	28.00

SUPERICHIE (Formerly Super Richie)

	GD25	FN65	NM94
No. 5, Oct, 1976 - No. 18, Jan, 1979 (52 pgs. giants)			
Harvey Publications			
5-18: 5-Origin/1st app. new costumes for Rippy & Crashman		.50	1.00

SUPERIOR STORIES
May-June, 1955 - No. 4, Nov-Dec, 1955
Nesbit Publishing Co.

	GD25	FN65	NM94
1-H.G. Well's The Invisible Man	10.00	30.00	65.00
2-The Pirate of the Gulf by J.H. Ingrahams	5.85	17.50	35.00
3-Wreck of the Grosvenor	5.85	17.50	35.00
4-O'Henry's "The Texas Rangers"	6.35	19.00	38.00

NOTE: ***Morisi** c/a in all.*

SUPER MAGIC (Super Magician Comics #2 on)
May, 1941
Street & Smith Publications

	GD25	FN65	NM94
V1#1-Blackstone the Magician app.; origin & 1st app. Rex King (Black Fury); Charles Sultan-c	57.00	170.00	340.00

SUPER MAGICIAN COMICS (Super Magic #1)
No. 2, Sept, 1941 - V5#8, Feb-Mar, 1947
Street & Smith Publications

	GD25	FN65	NM94
V1#2-Rex King, Man of Adventure app.	23.00	70.00	140.00
3-Tao-Anwar, Boy Magician begins	14.00	42.00	85.00
4-Origin Transo	13.00	40.00	80.00
5-7,9-12: 8-Abbott & Costello story. 11-Supersnipe app.	13.00	40.00	80.00
8-Abbott & Costello story	15.00	45.00	90.00
V2#1-The Shadow app.	21.00	62.00	125.00
2-12: 5-Origin Tigerman. 8-Red Dragon begins	7.50	22.50	45.00
V3#1-12: 5-Origin Mr. Twilight	7.50	22.50	45.00
V4#1-12: 11-Nigel Elliman begins	5.85	17.50	35.00
V5#1-6	5.85	17.50	35.00
7,8-Red Dragon by Edd Cartier-c/a	18.00	55.00	110.00

NOTE: ***Jack Binder** c-1-14(most).*

SUPERMAN (See Action Comics, Advs. of..., All-New Coll. Ed., All-Star Comics, Best of DC, Brave & the Bold, Cosmic Odyssey, DC Comics Presents, Heroes Against Hunger, Krypton Chronicles, Limited Coll. Ed., Man of Steel, Phantom Zone, Power Record Comics, Special Edition, Super Friends, Superman: The Man of Steel, Taylor's Christmas Tabloid, Three-Dimension Advs., World Of Krypton, World Of Metropolis, World Of Smallville & World's Finest)

SUPERMAN (Becomes Adventures Of...#424 on)
Summer, 1939 - No. 423, Sept, 1986 (#1-5 are quarterly)
National Periodical Publications/DC Comics

	GD25	FN65	VF82	NM94
1(nn)-1st four Action stories reprinted; origin Superman by Siegel & Shuster; has a new 2 pg. origin plus 4 pgs. omitted in Action story; see The Comics Magazine #1 & More Fun #14-17 for Superman proto-type app.; 1st pin-up Superman on back-c	6,500.00	19,500.00	39,000.00	65,000.00

(Estimated up to 190 total copies exist, 3 in NM/Mint)

1-Reprint, Oversize 13-1/2x10". **WARNING**: This comic is an exact duplicate reprint of the original except for its size. DC published it in 1978 with a second cover titling it as a Famous First Edition. There have been many reported cases of the outer cover being removed and the interior sold as the original edition. The reprint with the new outer cover removed is practically worthless.

	GD25	FN65	NM94
2-All daily strip-r	750.00	2250.00	4500.00
3-2nd story-r from Action #5; 3rd story-r from Action #6	500.00	1500.00	3000.00
4-2nd mention of Daily Planet (Spr/40); also see Action #23; 2nd app. Luthor (red-headed; also see Action #23)	392.00	1175.00	2350.00
5	283.00	850.00	1700.00
6,7: 7-1st Perry White?	225.00	675.00	1350.00
8-10: 10-1st bald Luthor app.	183.00	550.00	1100.00
11-13,15: 13-Jimmy Olsen & Luthor app.	133.00	400.00	800.00
14-Patriotic Shield-c by Fred Ray	200.00	600.00	1200.00
16-20: 17-Hitler, Hirohito-c	117.00	350.00	700.00
21-23,25	92.00	275.00	550.00
24-Flag-c	108.00	325.00	650.00
26-29: 27-1st Lois Lane-c. 28-Lois Lane Girl Reporter series begins, ends #40,42	85.00	255.00	510.00
28-Overseas edition for Armed Forces; same as reg. #28	85.00	255.00	510.00
30-Origin & 1st app. Mr. Mxyztplk (pronounced "Mix-it-plk") in comic books; name later became Mxyzptlk ("Mix-yez-pit-l-ick"); the character was inspired by a combination of the name of Al Capp's Joe Blyfstyk (the little man with the black cloud over his head) & the devilish antics of Bugs Bunny; he 1st app. in newspaper 3/7/44	133.00	400.00	800.00
31-40: 33-(3-4/45)-3rd app. Mxyztplk. 38-Atomic bomb story (1-2/46); delayed because of gov't cencorship	72.00	218.00	435.00
41-50: 45-Lois Lane as Superwoman (see Action #60 for 1st app.)	54.00	162.00	325.00
51,52	44.00	132.00	265.00
53-Origin Superman retold; 10th anniversary	150.00	450.00	900.00
54,56-60	47.00	140.00	280.00
55-Used in **SOTI**, pg. 33	48.00	145.00	290.00
61-Origin Superman retold; origin Green Kryptonite (1st Kryptonite story); Superman returns to Krypton for 1st time & sees his parents for 1st time since infancy, discovers he's not earth man	83.00	250.00	500.00
62-65,67-70: 62-Orson Welles app. 65-1st Krypton Foes: Mala, K120, & U-Ban. 68-1st Luthor-c in Superman	46.00	138.00	275.00
66-2nd Superbaby story	46.00	138.00	275.00
71-75: 75-Some have #74 on-c	42.00	125.00	250.00
72-Giveaway(9-10/51)-(Rare)-Price blackened out; came with banner wrapped around book; without banner	53.00	160.00	320.00
72-Giveaway with banner	67.00	200.00	400.00
76-Batman x-over; Superman & Batman learn each other's I.D.	117.00	350.00	700.00
77-81: 78-Last 52 pg. issue. 81-Used in **POP**, pg. 88	34.00	102.00	235.00
82-87,89,90	31.00	92.00	215.00
88-Prankster, Toyman & Luthor app.	32.00	95.00	225.00
91-95: 95-Last precode issue	29.00	85.00	200.00
96-99	27.00	80.00	185.00
100 (9-10/55)	107.00	321.00	750.00
101-110	24.00	70.00	165.00
111-120	21.00	63.00	145.00
121-130: 123-Pre-Supergirl tryout. 127-Origin/1st app. Titano. 128-Red Kryptonite used (4/59). 129-Intro/origin Lori Lemaris, The Mermaid	17.00	50.00	115.00
131-139: 139-Lori Lemaris app.; "Untold Story of Red Kryptonite" back-up story	12.00	36.00	85.00
140-1st Blue Kryptonite & Bizarro Supergirl; origin Bizarro Jr. #1	13.50	41.00	95.00
141-145,148: 142-2nd Batman x-over	10.00	30.00	60.00
146-Superman's life story	11.50	34.00	80.00
147(8/61)-7th Legion app; 1st app. Legion of Super-Villains; 1st app. Adult Legion; swipes-c to Adv. #247	11.00	32.00	75.00
149(11/61)-9th Legion app. (cameo); last 10 cent issue	10.00	30.00	65.00
150-162: 152(4/62)-15th Legion app. 155(8/62)-19th Legion app; Lightning Man & Cosmic Man, & Adult Legion app. 156,162-Legion app. 157-Gold Kryptonite used (see Adv. 299); Mon-el app.; Lightning Lad cameo (11/62). 158-1st app. Flamebird & Nightwing & Nor-Kan of Kandor. 161-1st told death of Ma and Pa Kent	5.00	15.00	30.00
161-2nd printing (1987, $1.25-c)-New DC logo; sold thru So Much Fun Toy Stores (cover title: Superman Classic)	.30	.75	1.50
163-166,168-180: 166-XMas-c. 168-All Luthor issue. 169-Last Sally Selwyn. 170-Pres. Kennedy story is finally published after delay from #169 due to assassination. 172,173-Legion cameos. 174-Super-Mxyzptlk; Bizarro app.	4.00	11.00	22.00
167-New origin Brainiac & Brainiac 5; intro Tixarla (later Luthor's wife)	7.50	22.50	45.00

Superior Stories #1, © Nesbit Publ.

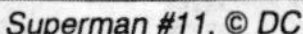
Superman #11, © DC

Superman #28, © DC

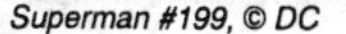

Superman #199, © DC

Superman Annual #2 (1960), © DC

Superman #3 (3/87), © DC

	GD25	FN65	NM94
181,182,184-186,188-192,194-196,198,200: 181-1st 2965 story/series. 189-Origin/destruction of Krypton II	2.80	7.00	14.00
183,187,193,197 (Giants G-18,G-23,G-31,G-36)	3.20	8.00	16.00
199-1st Superman/Flash race (8/67): also see Flash #175 & World's Finest #198,199	17.00	52.00	120.00
201,203-206,208-211,213-216,218-221,223-226,228-231,234-238: 213-Brainiac-5 app.	1.80	4.50	9.00
202 (80-pg. Giant G-42)-All Bizarro issue	2.40	6.00	12.00
207,212,217,222,239 (Giants G-48,G-54,G-60,G-66,G-84): 207-Legion app.; 30th anniversary Superman (6/68)	2.40	6.00	12.00
227,232(Giants, G-78,G-72)-All Krypton issues	2.40	6.00	12.00
233-2nd app. Morgan Edge, Clark Kent switch from newspaper reporter to TV newscaster	1.80	4.50	9.00
240-Kaluta-a	1.00	2.50	5.00
241-244 (All 52 pgs.): 243-G.A.-r/#38	.80	2.00	4.00
245-DC 100 Pg. Super Spectacular #7; Air Wave, Kid Eternity, Hawkman-r; Atom-r/Atom #3	1.00	2.50	5.00
246-248,250,251,253 (All 52 pgs.): 246-G.A.-r/#40. 248-World of Krypton story. 251-G.A.-r/#45. 253-Finlay-a, 2 pgs., G.A.-r/#13	.60	1.50	3.00
249,254-Neal Adams-a. 249-(52 pgs.); origin & 1st app. Terra-Man by Neal Adams (inks)	1.40	3.50	7.00
252-DC 100 Pg. Super Spectacular #13; Ray(r/Smash #17), Black Condor, (r/Crack #18), Hawkman(r/Flash #24); Starman-r/Adv. #67; Dr. Fate & Spectre-r/More Fun #57; N. Adams-c	1.20	3.00	6.00
255-271,273-277,279-283: 263-Photo-c. 264-1st app. Steve Lombard. 276-Intro Capt. Thunder. 279-Batman, Batgirl app.	.40	1.00	2.00
272,278,284-All 100 pgs. G.A.-r in all. 272-r/2nd app. Mr. Mxyztplk from Action #80	.60	1.50	3.00
285-299: 292-Origin Lex Luthor retold	.30	.75	1.50
300-Retells origin	1.00	2.50	5.00
301-399: 301,320-Solomon Grundy app. 323-Intro. Atomic Skull. 327-329-(44 pgs.). 330-More facts revealed about I. D. 338-The bottled city of Kandor enlarged. 344-Frankenstein & Dracula app. 353-Brief origin. 354, 355,357-Superman 2020 stories (354-Debut of Superman III). 356-World of Krypton story (also #360,367,375). 372-Superman 2021 story. 376-Free 16 pg. preview Daring New Advs. of Supergirl. 377-Free 16 pg. preview Masters of the Universe	.30	.75	1.50
400 (10/84, $1.50, 68 pgs.)-Many top artists featured; Chaykin painted cover, Miller back-c	.60	1.50	3.00
401-410,412-422: 405-Super-Batman story. 408-Nuclear Holocaust-c/story. 414,415-Crisis x-over. 422-Horror-c	.30	.75	1.50
411-Special Julius Schwartz tribute issue	.30	.75	1.50
423-Alan Moore scripts; Perez-a(i)	1.40	3.50	7.00
Annual 1(10/60, 84 pgs.)-Reprints 1st Supergirl story/Action #252; r/Lois Lane #1 (1st Silver Age DC annual)	47.00	140.00	320.00
Annual 2(1960)-Brainiac, Titano, Metallo, Bizarro origin-r	25.00	75.00	175.00
Annual 3(1961)	18.00	54.00	125.00
Annual 4(1961)-11th Legion app; 1st Legion origins (text & pictures)	14.00	43.00	100.00
Annual 5(Sum, 1962)-All Krypton issue	10.00	30.00	70.00
Annual 6(Wint, 1962-63)-Legion-r/Adv. #247	10.00	30.00	60.00
Annual 7(Sum, 1963)-Origin-r/Superman-Batman team/Adv. 275; r/1955 Superman dailies	7.50	22.50	45.00
Annual 8(Wint, 1963-64)-All origins issue	5.85	17.50	35.00
Annual 9(8/64)-Was advertised but came out as 80 Page Giant #1 instead			
Annual 9(1983)-Toth/Austin-a	.80	2.00	4.00
Annuals 10-12: 10(1984, $1.25)-M. Anderson inks. 11(1985)-Moore scripts. 12(1986)	.60	1.50	3.00
...IV Movie Special (1987, $2.00, one-shot)-Movie adaptation; Heck-a	.40	1.00	2.00
Special 1(1983)-G. Kane-c/a; contains German-r	.60	1.50	3.00
Special 2,3(1984, 1985, $1.25, 52 pgs.)	.60	1.50	3.00

	GD25	FN65	NM94
The Amazing World of Superman "Official Metropolis Edition" (1973, $2.00, 14x10-1/2")-Origin retold; Wood-r(i) from Superboy #153,161	1.60	4.00	8.00
Kelloggs Giveaway-(2/3 normal size, 1954)-r-two stories/Superman #55	30.00	90.00	200.00
...Meets the Quik Bunny (1987, Nestles Quik premium, 36 pgs.)		.50	1.00
...Movie Special-(9/83)-Adaptation of Superman III; other versions exist with store logos on bottom 1/3 of-c		.50	1.00
Pizza Hut Premium(12/77)-Exact-r of #97,113	.30	.75	1.50
Radio Shack Giveaway-36pgs. (7/80) "The Computers That Saved Metropolis;" Starlin/Giordano-a; advertising insert in Action 509, New Advs. of Superboy 7, Legion of Super-Heroes 265, & House of Mystery 282. (All comics were 64 pgs.) Cover of inserts printed on newsprint. Giveaway contains 4 extra pgs. of Radio Shack advertising that inserts do not	.30	.75	1.50
Radio Shack Giveaway-(7/81) "Victory by Computer"	.30	.75	1.50
Radio Shack Giveaway-(7/82) "Computer Masters of Metropolis"		.50	1.00
11195(2/79,224pp,$1.95)-Golden Press	.45	1.20	2.40

NOTE: ***N. Adams*** *a-249i, 254p; c-204-208, 210, 212-215, 219, 231, 233-237, 240-243, 249-252, 254, 263, 307, 308, 313, 314, 317.* ***Adkins*** *a-323i.* ***Austin*** *c-368i.* ***Wayne Boring*** *art-late 1940's to early 1960's.* ***Buckler*** *a(p)-352, 363, 364, 369; c(p)-324-327, 356, 363, 368, 369, 373, 376, 378.* ***Burnley*** *a-252r; c-19-25, 30, 33, 34, 35p, 38p, 39p, 45p.* ***Fine*** *a-252r.* ***Gil Kane*** *a-272r, 367, 372, 375, Special 2; c-374p, 375p, 377, 381, 382, 384-390, 392, Annual 9.* ***Kubert*** *c-216.* ***Morrow*** *a-238.* ***Perez*** *c-364p.* ***Starlin*** *c-355.* ***Staton*** *a-354i, 355i.* ***Williamson*** *a(i)-408-410, 412-416; c-408i, 409i.* ***Wrightson*** *a-400, 416.*

SUPERMAN (2nd series)
Jan, 1987 - Present (.75/$1.00/$1.25)
DC Comics

	GD25	FN65	NM94
1-Byrne-c/a begins; intro new Metallo	.40	1.00	2.00
2-8,10: 3-Legends x-over; Darkseid-c & app. 7-Origin/1st app. Rampage. 8-Legion app.		.60	1.20
9-Joker-c	.60	1.50	3.00
11-49,51,52,54-56,58-67: 11-1st new Mr. Mxyzptlk. 12-Lori Lemaris revived. 13-1st app. Toyman. 13,14-Millennium x-over. 20-Doom Patrol app.; Supergirl revived in cameo. 21-Supergirl-c/story. 31-Mr. Mxyzptlk app. 37-Newsboy Legion app. 41-Lobo app. 44-Batman storyline, part 1. 45-Free extra 8 pgs. 54-Newsboy Legion story. 63-Aquaman x-over. 67-Last $1.00-c		.50	1.00
50-($1.50, 52 pgs.)-Clark Kent proposes to Lois	.80	2.00	4.00
50-2nd printing		.50	1.00
53-Clark reveals i.d. to Lois cont'd from Action #662	.50	1.25	2.50
53-2nd printing		.50	1.00
57-($1.75, 52 pgs.)	.35	.90	1.75
68-72,76-80: 65,66,68-Deathstroke-c/stories. 70-Superman & Robin team-up. 76,77-Funeral for a Friend parts 4 & 8		.65	1.25
73-Doomsday cameo	.80	2.00	4.00
74-Doomsday battle issue, part2, cont'd from Justice League #69.	1.00	2.50	5.00
73,74-2nd printings	.30	.75	1.50
75-Doomsday, part 6; death of Superman; polybagged w/poster of funeral, obituary from Daily Planet, postage stamp & armband premiums ($2.50)	3.00	7.50	15.00
75-Newsstand copy (no upc code)	1.00	2.50	5.00
75-Newsstand copy (no upc code, 2nd print)	.30	.75	1.50
75-Newsstand copy (no upc code, 3rd, 4th prints)		.60	1.25
75-Newsstand copy w/upc code	.80	2.00	4.00
76,77-Funeral for a friend	.40	1.00	2.00
Annual 1 (1987)-No Byrne-a	.30	.75	1.50
Annual 2 (1988)-Byrne-a; Newsboy Legion; return of the Guardian	.30	.75	1.50
Annual 3 (1991, $2.00, 68 pgs.)-Armageddon 2001 x-over; Batman app.;			

GD25 FN65 NM94

Austin-c(i) & part inks .80 2.00 4.00
Annual 3-2nd & 3rd printings; 3rd has silver ink .40 1.00 2.00
Annual 3 (1992, $2.50, 68 pgs.)-Eclipso app. .50 1.25 2.50
Special 1 (1992, $3.50, 68 pgs.)-Simonson-c/a .70 1.75 3.50
NOTE: ***Austin** a(i)-1-3. **Byrne** a-1-16p, 17, 19-21p, 22; c-1-17, 20-22; scripts-1-22. **Gulce** c/a-64. **Kirby** c-37p. **Russell** c/a-23i. **Simonson** c-69i. #19-21 2nd printings sold in multi-packs.*

SUPERMAN & THE GREAT CLEVELAND FIRE (Giveaway)
1948 (4 pages, no cover)(Hospital Fund)
National Periodical Publications

nn-In full color 46.00 140.00 325.00

SUPERMAN FAMILY, THE (Formerly Superman's Pal Jimmy Olsen)
No. 164, Apr-May, 1974 - No. 222, Sept, 1982
National Periodical Publications/DC Comics

164-Jimmy Olsen, Supergirl, Lois Lane begin .30 .75 1.50
165-176 (100-68 pgs.) .60 1.20
177-181 (52 pgs.) .50 1.00
182,194: Marshall Rogers-a in each. 182-$1.00 issues begin; Krypto begins, ends #192 .40 1.00 2.00
183-193,195-222: 183-Nightwing-Flamebird begins, ends #194. 189-Brainiac 5, Mon-el app. 191-Superboy begins, ends #198. 200-Book length story. 211-Earth II Batman & Catwoman marry .50 1.00
NOTE: ***N. Adams** c-182-185. **Anderson** a-186i. **Buckler** c(p)-190, 191, 209, 210, 215, 217, 220. **Jones** a-191-193. **Gil Kane** c(p)-221, 222. **Mortimer** a(p)-191-193, 199, 201-222. **Orlando** a(i)-186, 187. **Rogers** a-182, 194. **Staton** a-191-194, 196p. **Tuska** a(p)-203, 207-209.*

SUPERMAN FOR EARTH
1991 ($4.95, color, 52 pgs.)(Printed on recycled paper)
DC Comics

nn-Ordway wraparound-c 1.00 2.50 5.00

SUPERMAN (Miniature)
1942; 1955 - 1956 (3 issues; no #'s; 32 pgs.)
The pages are numbered in the 1st issue: 1-32; 2nd: 1A-32A, and 3rd: 1B-32B
National Periodical Publications

No date-Py-Co-Pay Tooth Powder giveaway (8 pgs.; circa 1942) 72.00 215.00 500.00
1-The Superman Time Capsule (Kellogg's Sugar Smacks)(1955) 43.00 130.00 300.00
1A-Duel in Space (1955) 32.00 95.00 225.00
1B-The Super Show of Metropolis (also #1-32, no B)(1955) 32.00 95.00 225.00
NOTE: *Numbering variations exist. Each title could have any combination-#1, 1A, or 1B.*

SUPERMAN RECORD COMIC
1966 (Golden Records)
National Periodical Publications

(with record)-Record reads origin of Superman from comic; came with iron-on patch, decoder, membership card & button; comic-r/Superman #125,146 10.00 30.00 70.00
Comic only 3.60 11.00 25.00

SUPERMAN'S BUDDY (Costume Comic)
1954 (4 pgs.) (One Shot) (Came in box w/costume; slick-paper/c)
National Periodical Publications

1-(Rare)-w/box & costume 130.00 385.00 900.00
Comic only 57.00 171.00 400.00
1-(1958 edition)-Printed in 2 colors 14.00 43.00 100.00

SUPERMAN'S CHRISTMAS ADVENTURE
1940, 1944 (16 pgs.) (Giveaway)
Distr. by Nehi drinks, Bailey Store, Ivey-Keith Co., Kennedy's Boys Shop, Macy's Store, Boston Store
National Periodical Publications

1(1940)-Burnley-a; Fred Ray-c 267.00 800.00 1600.00
nn(1944) w/Santa Claus & X-mas tree-c 83.00 250.00 500.00
nn(1944) w/Candy cane & Superman-c 73.00 220.00 440.00

SUPERMAN SCRAPBOOK (Has blank pages; contains no comics)

SUPERMAN'S GIRLFRIEND LOIS LANE (See Action Comics #1, 80 Page Giant #3, 14, Lois Lane, Showcase #9, 10, Superman #28 & Superman Family)

SUPERMAN'S GIRLFRIEND LOIS LANE
Mar-Apr, 1958 - No. 136, Jan-Feb, 1974; No. 137, Sept-Oct, 1974
National Periodical Publications

Showcase #9 (7-8/57)-Lois Lane (pre #1); 1st Showcase character to win own series 200.00 600.00 1400.00
Showcase #10 (9-10/57)-Jor-el cameo 143.00 430.00 1000.00
1-(3-4/58) 130.00 385.00 900.00
2 57.00 170.00 400.00
3 39.00 120.00 275.00
4,5 27.00 80.00 185.00
6-10: 9-Pat Boone app. 18.00 54.00 125.00
11-20: 14-Supergirl x-over; Batman app? 10.00 30.00 65.00
21-29: 23-1st app. Lena Thorul, Lex Luthor's sister. 27-Bizarro-c/story. 29-Aquaman, Batman, Green Arrow cameo; last 10 cent issue 7.50 22.50 45.00
30-32,34-49: 47-Legion app. 4.00 11.00 22.00
33(5/62)-Mon-el app. 4.00 12.00 24.00
50(7/64)-Triplicate Girl, Phantom Girl & Shrinking Violet app. 3.60 9.00 18.00
51-55,57-67,69: 59-Jor-el app.; Batman back-up story 2.40 6.00 12.00
56-Saturn Girl app. 2.80 7.00 14.00
68-(Giant G-26) 3.60 9.00 18.00
70-Penguin & Catwoman app. (1st S.A. Catwoman, 11/66; also see Det. #369 for 3rd app.); Batman & Robin cameo 18.00 54.00 125.00
71-Catwoman story cont'd from #70 (2nd app.) 12.00 36.00 85.00
72,73,75,76,78 1.60 4.00 8.00
74-1st Bizarro Flash; JLA cameo 3.00 7.50 15.00
77-(Giant G-39) 1.80 4.50 9.00
79-Neal Adams-c begin, end #95,108 1.00 2.50 5.00
80-85,87-94: 89-Batman x-over; all N. Adams-c .80 2.00 4.00
86,95: (Giants G-51,G-63)-Both have Neal Adams-c. 95-Wonder Woman x-over 1.20 3.00 6.00
96-103,105-111: 105-Origin/1st app. The Rose & the Thorn. 108-Neal Adams-c. 111-Morrow-a .70 1.75 3.50
104,113-(Giants G-75,87) 1.20 3.00 6.00
112,114-123 (52 pgs.): 122-G.A.-r/Superman #30. 123-G.A. Batman-r/Batman #35 (w/Catwoman) .60 1.50 3.00
124-137: 130-Last Rose & the Thorn. 132-New Zatanna story. 136-Wonder Woman x-over .40 1.00 2.00
Annual 1(Sum, 1962) 10.00 30.00 65.00
Annual 2(Sum,1963) 6.70 20.00 40.00
NOTE: ***Buckler** a-117-121p. **Curt Swan** a-1-50(most); c(p)-1-15.*

SUPERMAN'S PAL JIMMY OLSEN (Superman Family #164 on)
(See Action Comics #6 for 1st app. & 80 Page Giant)
Sept-Oct, 1954 - No. 163, Feb-Mar, 1974
National Periodical Publications

1 171.00 515.00 1200.00
2 85.00 26.00 600.00
3-Last pre-code issue 54.00 160.00 375.00
4,5 36.00 107.00 250.00
6-10 25.00 75.00 175.00
11-20 16.00 48.00 110.00
21-30: 29-1st app. Krypto in Jimmy Olsen 10.00 30.00 65.00
31-40: 31-Origin Elastic Lad. 33-One pg. biography of Jack Larson (TV Jimmy Olsen). 36-Intro Lucy Lane. 37-2nd app. Elastic Lad; 1st cover app. 7.50 22.50 45.00
41-50: 41-1st J.O. Robot. 48-Intro/origin Superman Emergency Squad 5.00 15.00 30.00
51-56: 56-Last 10 cent issue 4.00 10.00 20.00
57-62,64-70: 57-Olsen marries Supergirl. 62-Mon-el & Elastic Lad app. but not as Legionnaires. 70-Element Lad app. 2.00 5.00 10.00

Superman's Christmas Adventure 1940, © DC

Superman's Girlfriend Lois Lane #51, © DC

Superman's Pal Jimmy Olsen #19, © DC

Superman's Pal Jimmy Olsen #87, © DC

Superman-Tim 3/50, © DC

Super-Mystery Comics V1#1, © ACE

	GD25	FN65	NM94
63(9/62)-Legion of Super-Villains app.	2.20	5.50	11.00
71,74,75,78,80-84,86,89,90: 86-Jimmy Olsen Robot becomes Congorilla	1.40	3.50	7.00
72(10/63)-Legion app; Elastic Lad (Olsen) joins	1.80	4.50	9.00
73-Ultra Boy app.	1.80	4.50	9.00
76,85-Legion app.	1.80	4.50	9.00
77,79: 77-Olsen with Colossal Boy's powers & costume; origin Titano retold. 79(9/64)-Titled The Red-headed Beatle of 1000 B.C.	1.40	3.50	7.00
87-Legion of Super-Villains app.	1.80	4.50	9.00
88-Star Boy app.	1.40	3.50	7.00
91-94,96-99: 99-Olsen w/powers & costumes of Lightning Lad, Sun Boy & Star Boy	.90	2.25	4.50
95,104 (Giants G-25,G-38)	2.20	5.50	11.00
100-Legion cameo	1.40	3.50	7.00
101-103,105-112,114-121,123-130,132: 106-Legion app. 110-Infinity-c. 117-Batman & Legion cameo	.70	1.75	3.50
113,122,131 (Giants G-50,G-62,G-74)	.70	1.75	3.50
133-Re-intro Newsboy Legion & begins by Kirby	.90	2.25	4.50
134-1st app. Darkseid (1 panel, 12/70)	1.00	2.50	5.00
135-163: 135-2nd app. Darkseid (1 pg. cameo; see New Gods & Forever People); G.A. Guardian app. 136-Origin new Guardian. 139-Last 15 cent issue. 140-(Giant G-86). 141-Newsboy Legion-r by S&K begin (52 pgs. begin); full pg. self-portrait Kirby. 149,150-G.A. Plastic Man-r in both; last 52 pg. issue. 150-Newsboy Legion app.	.60	1.50	3.00

NOTE: *Issues #141-148 contain **Simon & Kirby** Newsboy Legion reprints from Star Spangled #7, 8, 9, 10, 11, 12, 13, 14 in that order. **N. Adams** c-109-112, 115, 117, 118, 120, 121, 132, 134-136, 147, 148. **Kirby** a-133-139p, 141-148p; c-133, 139, 145p. **Kirby/N. Adams** c-137, 138, 141-144, 146. **Curt Swan** c-1-14(most).*

SUPERMAN SPECTACULAR (Also see DC Special Series #5)
1982 (Magazine size)(Square binding)
DC Comics

	GD25	FN65	NM94
1	.35	1.00	2.00

SUPERMAN: THE EARTH STEALERS
1988 ($2.95, one-shot, 52pgs, prestige format)
DC Comics

	GD25	FN65	NM94
1-Byrne scripts; painted-c	.70	1.75	3.50
1-2nd printing	.60	1.50	3.00

SUPERMAN: THE MAN OF STEEL (Also see The Man of Steel)
July, 1991 - Present ($1.00/$1.25, color)
DC Comics

	GD25	FN65	NM94
1-($1.75, 52 pgs.)	.35	.90	1.75
2-10: 3-War of the Gods x-over. 5-Reads sideways. 10-Last $1.00-c		.50	1.00
11-16: 14-Superman & Robin team-up		.60	1.25
17-1st app. Doomsday (cameo)	.80	2.00	4.00
18-1st full app. Doomsday	2.00	5.00	10.00
18-2nd & 3rd print.		.60	1.25
19-Doomsday battle issue (c/story)	.60	1.50	3.00
20,21-Funeral for a Friend	.40	1.00	2.00
Annual 1 (1992, $2.50, 68 pgs.)-Eclipso app.; Joe Quesada-c(p)	.40	1.25	2.50

SUPERMAN: THE SECRET YEARS
Feb, 1985 - No. 4, May, 1985 (Mini-series)
DC Comics

	GD25	FN65	NM94
1-Miller-c on all	.30	.75	1.50
2-4		.50	1.00

SUPERMAN 3-D (See Three-Dimension Adventures)

SUPERMAN-TIM (Becomes Tim)
Aug, 1942 - May, 1950 (-size) (B&W Giveaway w/2 color covers)
Superman-Tim Stores/National Periodical Publications

	GD25	FN65	NM94
8/42	67.00	200.00	400.00
2/43, 3/43, 6/43, 8/43, 9/43, 3/44, 2/45, 11/49 issues-Two pg. Superman illos in each	15.00	45.00	90.00
10/43, 12/43, 2/44, 4/44-1/45, 3/45, 4/45, 4/46, 5/46, 6/46, 7/46, 8/46 issues-no Superman	12.00	35.00	70.00
9/46-1st stamp album issue (worth more if complete with Superman stamps)	33.00	100.00	200.00
10/46-1st Superman story	22.00	68.00	135.00
11/46, 12/46, 1/47, 2/47, 3/47, 4/47, 5/47-8/47 issues-Superman story in each; 2/47-Infinity-c	22.00	68.00	135.00
9/47-Stamp album issue & Superman story	30.00	90.00	180.00
10/47, 11/47, 12/47-Superman stories	23.00	68.00	135.00
1/48, 2/48, 6/48, 8/48, 10/48, 11/48, 2/49-10/49 issues-no Superman	17.00	50.00	100.00
9/48-Stamp album issue	18.00	55.00	110.00
12/49-5/50 Superman stories	20.00	60.00	120.00

NOTE: *16 pgs. through 9/47; 8 pgs. 10/47 on? The stamp album issues (3) may contain Superman stamps that were made to glue in these books. Books with the stamps in cluded would be worth more, and the value would depend upon completeness of the album. There is no stamp album in the 9/49 issue.*

SUPERMAN VS. THE AMAZING SPIDER-MAN (Also see Marvel Treasury Edition No. 28)
1976 (100 pgs.) ($2.00) (Over-sized)
National Periodical Publications/Marvel Comics Group

	GD25	FN65	NM94
1-Andru/Giordano-a	1.20	3.00	6.00
1-2nd printing; 5000 numbered copies signed by Stan Lee & Carmine Infantino on front cover & sold through mail	2.40	6.00	12.00

SUPERMAN WORKBOOK
1945 (One Shot) (68 pgs; reprints) (B&W)
National Periodical Publ./Juvenile Group Foundation

	GD25	FN65	NM94
nn-Cover-r/Superman #14	108.00	325.00	650.00

SUPER MARIO BROS. (Also see Adventures of the...)
1990 - No. 5?, 1991 ($1.95, color, slick-c)
V2#1, 1991 - No. 5, 1991 ($1.50, color)
Valiant Comics

	GD25	FN65	NM94
1-5: 1-Wildman-a	.40	1.00	2.00
V2#1-5	.30	.75	1.50
Special Edition 1 (1990, $1.95)-Wildman-a	.40	1.00	2.00

SUPERMOUSE (...the Big Cheese; see Coo Coo Comics)
Dec, 1948 - No. 34, Sept, 1955; No. 35, Apr, 1956 - No. 45, Fall, 1958
Standard Comics/Pines No. 35 on (Literary Ent.)

	GD25	FN65	NM94
1-Frazetta text illos (3)	20.00	60.00	140.00
2-Frazetta text illos	10.00	30.00	70.00
3,5,6-Text illos by Frazetta in all	9.15	27.50	55.00
4-Two pg. text illos by Frazetta	10.00	30.00	60.00
7-10	4.00	11.00	22.00
11-20: 13-Racist humor (Indians)	3.60	9.00	18.00
21-45	2.40	6.00	12.00
1-Summer Holiday issue (Summer, 1957-Pines)-100 pgs.	9.15	27.50	55.00
2-Giant Summer issue (Summer, 1958-Pines)-100 pgs.	6.70	20.00	40.00

SUPER-MYSTERY COMICS
July, 1940 - V8#6, July, 1949
Ace Magazines (Periodical House)

	GD25	FN65	NM94
V1#1-Magno, the Magnetic Man & Vulcan begin	108.00	325.00	650.00
2	50.00	150.00	300.00
3-The Black Spider begins	42.00	125.00	250.00
4-Origin Davy	37.00	110.00	220.00
5-Intro. The Clown; begin series	37.00	110.00	220.00
6(2/41)	31.00	92.00	185.00
V2#1(4/41)-Origin Buckskin	31.00	92.00	185.00

2-6(2/42) 28.00 85.00 170.00
V3#1(4/42),2: 1-Vulcan & Black Ace begin 25.00 75.00 150.00
3-Intro. The Lancer; Dr. Nemesis & The Sword begin; Kurtzman-c/a(2) (Mr. Risk & Paul Revere Jr.) 35.00 105.00 210.00
4-Kurtzman-c/a 28.00 85.00 170.00
5-Kurtzman-a(2); L.B. Cole-a; Mr. Risk app. 29.00 88.00 175.00
6(10/43)-Mr. Risk app.; Kurtzman's Paul Revere Jr.; L.B. Cole-a 29.00 88.00 175.00
V4#1(1/44)-L.B. Cole-a 22.00 68.00 135.00
2-6(4/45): 2,5,6-Mr. Risk app. 17.00 52.00 105.00
V5#1(7/45)-6 14.00 42.00 85.00
V6#1-6: 3-Torture story. 4-Last Magno. Mr. Risk app. in #2,4-6 12.00 35.00 70.00
V7#1-6, V8#1-4,6 12.00 35.00 70.00
V8#5-Meskin, Tuska, Sid Greene-a 13.00 40.00 80.00

NOTE: ***Sid Greene** a-V7#4. **Mooney** c-V1#5, 6, V2#1-6. **Palais** a-V5#3, 4; c-V4#6-V5#4, V6#2, V8#4. Bondage c-V2#5, 6, V3#2, 5.*

SUPERNATURAL THRILLERS
Dec, 1972 - No. 6, Nov, 1973; No. 7, July, 1974 - No. 15, Oct, 1975
Marvel Comics Group

1-3: 1-It!-Sturgeon adaptation. 2-The Invisible Man. 3-The Valley of the Worm .60 1.20
4-15: 4-Dr. Jekyll & Mr. Hyde. 5-1st app. The Living Mummy. 6-The Headless Horseman. 7-The Living Mummy begins .50 1.00

NOTE: ***Brunner** c-11. **Buckler** a-5p. **Ditko** a-8r, 9r. **G. Kane** a-3p; c-3, 9p, 15p. **Mayerik** a-2p, 7, 8, 9p, 10p, 11. **McWilliams** a-14i. **Mortimer** a-4. **Steranko** c-1, 2. **Sutton** a-15. **Tuska** a-6p. Robert E. Howard story-#3.*

SUPER POWERS
7/84 - No. 5, 11/84; 9/85 - No. 6, 2/86; 9/86 - No. 4, 12/86
DC Comics

1 (7/84, 1st series)-Joker/Penguin-c/story; Batman app.; Kirby-c .60 1.20
2-5: 5-Kirby-c/a .50 1.00
1 (9/85, 2nd series)-Kirby-c/a in all; Capt. Marvel & Firestorm join; Batman cameo .50 1.00
2-6: 4-Batman cameo. 5,6-Batman app. .50 1.00
1-4 (1986, 3rd series): 1-Cyborg joins; 1st app. Samurai from Super Friends TV show. 1-4-Batman cameos .50 1.00

SUPER PUP (Formerly Spotty The Pup) (See Space Comics)
No. 4, Mar-Apr, 1954 - No. 5, 1954
Avon Periodicals

4,5 3.20 8.00 16.00

SUPER RABBIT (See All Surprise, Animated Movie Tunes, Comedy Comics, Comic Capers, Ideal Comics, It's A Duck's Life, Movie Tunes & Wisco)
Fall, 1944 - No. 14, Nov, 1948
Timely Comics (CmPI)

	GD25	FN65	NM94
1-Hitler-c	43.00	130.00	300.00
2	22.00	65.00	150.00
3-5	13.00	40.00	90.00
6-Origin	14.00	43.00	100.00
7-10; 9-Infinity-c	9.15	27.50	55.00
11-Kurtzman's "Hey Look"	10.00	30.00	65.00
12-14	8.35	25.00	50.00
I.W. Reprint #1,2('58),7,10('63)	1.20	3.00	6.00

SUPER RICHIE (Superichie #5 on) (See Richie Rich Millions #68)
Sept, 1975 - No. 4, Mar, 1976 (All 52 pg. Giants)
Harvey Publications

1 .60 1.50 3.00
2-4 .40 1.00 2.00

SUPERSNIPE COMICS (Formerly Army & Navy #1-5)
V1#6, Oct, 1942 - V5#1, Aug-Sept, 1949 (See Shadow Comics V2#3)
Street & Smith Publications

V1#6-Rex King Man of Adventure (costumed hero) by Jack Binder begins; Supersnipe by George Marcoux continues from Army & Navy #5; Bill Ward-a 58.00 175.00 350.00
7,8,10-12: 8-Hitler, Tojo, Mussolini-c. 11-Little Nemo app. 35.00 105.00 210.00
9-Doc Savage x-over in Supersnipe; Hitler-c 4600 138.00 275.00
V2#1-12: 1-Huck Finn by Clare Dwiggins begins, ends V3#5 23.00 70.00 140.00
V3#1-12: 8-Bobby Crusoe by Dwiggins begins, ends V3#12. 9-Xmas-c 20.00 60.00 120.00
V4#1-12, V5#1: V4#10-Xmas-c 14.00 42.00 85.00

NOTE: ***George Marcoux** c-V1#6-V3#4. Doc Savage app. in some issues.*

SUPERSPOOK (Formerly Frisky Animals on Parade)
No. 4, June, 1958
Ajax/Farrell Publications

4 3.60 9.00 18.00

SUPER SPY (See Wham Comics)
Oct, 1940 - No. 2, Nov, 1940 (Reprints)
Centaur Publications

1-Origin The Sparkler 100.00 300.00 600.00
2-The Inner Circle, Dean Denton, Tim Blain, The Drew Ghost, The Night Hawk by Gustavson, & S.S. Swanson by Glanz app. 70.00 210.00 425.00

SUPER STAR HOLIDAY SPECIAL (See DC Special Series #21)

SUPER-TEAM FAMILY
10-11/75 - No. 15, 3-4/78 (#1-4: 68 pgs.; #5 on: 52 pgs.)
National Periodical Publications/DC Comics

1-Reprints by Neal Adams & Kane/Wood .40 1.00 2.00
2,3-New stories .30 .75 1.50
4-7-Reprints; 4-G.A. JSA-r & Superman/Batman/Robin-r from World's Finest .50 1.00
8-10-New Challengers of the Unknown stories .40 1.00 2.00
11-15-New stories .60 1.20

NOTE: ***Neal Adams** r-1-3. **Brunner** c-3. **Buckler** c-8p. **Tuska** a-7r. **Wood** a-1i(r), 3.*

SUPER TV HEROES (See Hanna-Barbera...)

SUPER-VILLAIN CLASSICS (Marvel)(Value: cover or less)

SUPER-VILLAIN TEAM-UP (See Fantastic Four #6 & Giant-Size...)
8/75 - No. 14, 10/77; No. 15, 11/78; No. 16, 5/79; No. 17, 6/80
Marvel Comics Group

1-Sub-Mariner & Dr. Doom begin, end #10 1.00 2.50 5.00
2-17: 5-1st Shroud. 6-F.F., Shroud app. 7-Origin Shroud. 9-Avengers app. 11-15-Dr. Doom & Red Skull app. .50 1.25 2.50

NOTE: ***Buckler** c-4p, 5p, 7p. **Buscema** c-1. **Byrne/Austin** c-14. **Evans** a-1p, 3p. **Everett** a-1p. **Giffen** a-8p, 13p; c-13p. **Kane** c-2p, 9p. **Mooney** a-4i. **Starlin** c-6. **Tuska** a-1p, 15p(r). **Wood** a-15p(r).*

SUPER WESTERN COMICS (Also see Buffalo Bill)
Aug, 1950 - No. 4, Mar, 1951
Youthful Magazines

1-Buffalo Bill begins; Calamity Jane app; Powell-c/a 6.70 20.00 40.00
2-4 4.20 12.50 25.00

SUPER WESTERN FUNNIES (See Super Funnies)

SUPERWORLD COMICS
April, 1940 - No. 3, Aug, 1940 (All have 68 pgs.)
Hugo Gernsback (Komos Publ.)

1-Origin Hip Knox, Super Hypnotist; Mitey Powers & Buzz Allen, the Invisible Avenger, Little Nemo begin; cover by Frank R. Paul 200.00 600.00 1200.00
2-Marvo 1,2 Go+, the Super Boy of the Year 2680 125.00 375.00 750.00
3 100.00 300.00 600.00

SUPREME (See Youngblood #3)

Supersnipe Comics V2#9, © S&S

Super-Villain Team-Up #1, © MEG

Superworld Comics #3, © Hugo Gernsback

Suspense #3, © MEG

Suspense Comics #6, © Continental Magazines

Swamp Thing #1, © MEG

GD25 FN65 NM94

Nov, 1992 - Present ($1.95, color)
Image Comics

1-4: Rob Liefeld-a(i) & scripts .40 1.00 2.00

SURE-FIRE COMICS (Lightning Comics #4 on)
June, 1940 - No. 4, Oct, 1940 (Two No. 3's)
Ace Magazines

V1#1-Origin Flash Lightning; X-The Phantom Fed, Ace McCoy, Buck Steele, Marvo the Magician, The Raven, Whiz Wilson (Time Traveler) begin 92.00 275.00 550.00
2 55.00 165.00 330.00
3(9/40) 46.00 138.00 275.00
3(#4)(10/40)-nn on-c, #3 on inside 46.00 138.00 275.00

SURF 'N' WHEELS
Nov, 1969 - No. 6, Sept, 1970
Charlton Comics

1 1.20 3.00 6.00
2-6 1.00 2.50 5.00

SURGE (Eclipse)(Value: cover or less)

SURPRISE ADVENTURES (Formerly Tormented)
No. 3, Mar, 1955 - No. 5, July, 1955
Sterling Comic Group

3-5: 3,5-Sekowsky-a 4.00 10.00 20.00

SUSIE Q. SMITH (See Four Color #323, 377, 453, 553)

SUSPENSE (Radio/TV; Real Life Tales of... #1-4) (Amazing Detective Cases #3 on?)
Dec, 1949 - No. 29, Apr, 1953 (#1-8,17-23: 52 pgs.)
Marvel/Atlas Comics (CnPC No. 1-10/BFP No. 11-29)

1-Powell-a; Peter Lorre, Sidney Greenstreet photo-c from Hammett's "The Verdict" 30.00 90.00 210.00
2-Crime stories; Gale Storm & Dennis O'Keefe photo-c 14.00 43.00 100.00
3-Change to horror 16.00 48.00 110.00
4,7-10 10.00 30.00 70.00
5-Krigstein, Tuska, Everett-a 11.50 34.00 80.00
6-Tuska, Everett, Morisi-a 10.00 30.00 70.00
11-17,19,20: 14-Hypo-c; A-Bomb panels 10.00 30.00 60.00
18,22-Krigstein-a 10.00 30.00 70.00
21,23,26-29 7.50 22.50 45.00
24-Tuska-a 8.35 25.00 50.00
25-Electric chair-c/story 10.00 30.00 70.00

NOTE: ***Ayers** a-20. **Briefer** a-5, 7, 27. **Brodsky** c-4, 6-9, 11, 16, 17, 25. **Colan** a-8(2), 9. **Everett** a-5, 6(2), 19, 23, 28; c-21-23, 26. **Fuje** a-29. **Heath** a-5, 6, 8, 10, 12, 14; c-14, 19, 24. **Maneely** a-12, 23, 24, 28, 29; c-5, 6p, 10, 13, 15, 18. **Mooney** a-24, 28. **Morisi** a-6, 12. **Palais** a-10. **Rico** a-7-9. **Robinson** a-29. **Romita** a-20(2), 25. **Sekowsky** a-11, 13, 14. **Sinnott** a-23, 25. **Tuska** a-5, 6(2), 12; c-12. **Whitney** a-15, 16, 22. **Ed Win** a-27.*

SUSPENSE COMICS
Dec, 1943 - No. 12, Sept, 1946
Continental Magazines

1-The Grey Mask begins; bondage/torture-c; L. B. Cole-a (7 pgs.) 75.00 225.00 450.00
2-Intro. The Mask; Rico, Giunta, L. B. Cole-a (7 pgs.) 42.00 125.00 250.00
3-L.B. Cole-a; Schomburg-c 42.00 125.00 250.00
4-6: 5-L. B. Cole-c 39.00 118.00 235.00
7,9,10,12: 9-L.B. Cole eyeball-c 35.00 105.00 210.00
8-Classic L. B. Cole spider-c 83.00 250.00 500.00
11-Classic Devil-c 67.00 200.00 400.00

NOTE: ***L. B. Cole** c-5-12. **Larsen** a-11. **Palais** a-10, 11. Bondage c-1, 3, 4.*

SUSPENSE DETECTIVE
June, 1952 - No. 5, Mar, 1953
Fawcett Publications

GD25 FN65 NM94

1-Evans-a (11 pgs); Baily-c/a 19.00 57.00 135.00
2-Evans-a (10 pgs.) 11.50 34.00 80.00
3-5 10.00 30.00 60.00

NOTE: ***Baily** a-4, 5; c-1-3. **Sekowsky** a-2, 4, 5; c-5.*

SUSPENSE STORIES (See Strange Suspense Stories)

SUZIE COMICS (Formerly Laugh Comix; see Laugh Comics, Liberty Comics #10, Pep Comics & Top-Notch Comics #28)
No. 49, Spring, 1945 - No. 100, Aug, 1954
Close-Up No. 49,50/MLJ Mag./Archie No. 51 on

49-Ginger begins 16.00 48.00 110.00
50-55: 54-Transvestism story 10.00 30.00 70.00
56-Katy Keene begins by Woggon 10.00 30.00 65.00
57-65 7.50 22.50 45.00
66-80 6.70 20.00 40.00
81-100: 88-Used in **POP**, pgs. 76,77; Bill Woggon draws himself in story. 100-Last Katy Keene 5.85 17.50 35.00

NOTE: ***Al Fagaly** c-49-55, 57-67. Katy Keene app. in 53-82, 85-100.*

SWAMP FOX, THE (See 4-Color #1179 & Walt Disney Presents #2)

SWAMP FOX, THE
1960 (14 pgs, small size) (Canada Dry Premiums)
Walt Disney Productions

Titles: (A)-Tory Masquerade, (B)-Rindau Rampage, (C)-Turnabout Tactics; each came in paper sleeve, books 1,2 & 3;
Set with sleeves 4.00 12.00 24.00
Comic only 1.60 4.00 8.00

SWAMP THING (See Brave & the Bold, Challengers of the Unknown #82, DC Comics, Presents #8 & 85, DC Special Series #2, 14, 17, 20, House of Secrets #92, Limited Collectors' Edition C-59, Roots of the..., & The Saga of...)

SWAMP THING
Oct-Nov, 1972 - No. 24, Aug-Sept, 1976
National Periodical Publications/DC Comics

1-Wrightson-c/a begins 8.35 25.00 50.00
2 4.20 12.50 25.00
3-Intro. Patchworkman 2.80 7.00 14.00
4-6,8-10: 10-Last Wrightson issue 2.40 6.00 12.00
7-Batman-c/story 2.80 7.00 14.00
11-24-Redondo-a; 23-Swamp Thing reverts back to Dr. Holland. 23,24-New logo .60 1.50 3.00

NOTE: ***J. Jones** a-9i(assist). **Kaluta** a-9i. **Redondo** c-12-19, 21. **Wrightson** issues (#1-10) reprinted in DC Special Series #2, 14, 17, 20 & Roots of the Swampthing.*

SWAT MALONE
Sept, 1955
Swat Malone Enterprises

V1#1-Hy Fleishman-a 6.70 20.00 40.00

SWEENEY (Formerly Buz Sawyer)
No. 4, 6, 1949 - No. 5, 10, 1949
Standard Comics

4,5-Crane-a #5 5.85 17.50 35.00

SWEE'PEA (See 4-Color #219)

SWEETHEART DIARY (Cynthia Doyle #66-on)
Wint, 1949; #2, Spr, 1950; #3, 6/50 - #5, 10/50; #6, 1951(nd); #7, 9/51 - #14, 1/53; #32, 10/55; #33, 4/56 - #65, 8/62 (#1-14: photo-c)
Fawcett Publications/Charlton Comics No. 32 on

1 10.00 30.00 60.00
2 5.00 15.00 30.00
3,4-Wood-a 10.00 30.00 65.00
5-10: 8-Bailey-a 4.20 12.50 25.00
11-14: 13-Swayze-a. 14-Last Fawcett issue 2.80 7.00 14.00
32 (10/55; 1st Charlton issue)(Formerly Cowboy Love #31) 3.60 9.00 18.00

	GD25	FN65	NM94
33-40: 34-Swayze-a	1.60	4.00	8.00
41-60	1.00	2.50	5.00
61-65	.60	1.50	3.00

SWEETHEARTS (Formerly Captain Midnight)
#68, 10/48 - #121, 5/53; #122, 3/54; V2#23, 5/54 - #137, 12/73
Fawcett Publications/Charlton No. 122 on

	GD25	FN65	NM94
68-Robert Mitchum photo-c	10.00	30.00	65.00
69-80	4.00	10.50	21.00
81-84,86-93,95-99	3.00	7.50	15.00
85,94,103,105,110,117-George Evans-a	4.20	12.50	25.00
100	3.60	9.00	18.00
101,107-Powell-a	3.20	8.00	16.00
102,104,106,108,109,112-116,118,121	2.00	5.00	10.00
111-1 pg. Ronald Reagan biography	4.35	13.00	26.00
119-Marilyn Monroe photo-c; also appears in story; part Wood-a	23.00	70.00	160.00
120-Atom Bomb story	5.85	17.50	35.00
122-(1st Charlton? 3/54)-Marijuana story	5.00	15.00	30.00
V2#23 (5/54)-28: 28-Last precode issue (2/55)	2.00	5.00	10.00
29-39,41,43-45,47-50	1.40	3.50	7.00
40-Photo-c; Tommy Sands story	3.00	7.50	15.00
42-Ricky Nelson photo-c/story	5.85	17.50	35.00
46-Jimmy Rodgers photo-c/story	3.00	7.50	15.00
51-60	1.40	3.50	7.00
61-80	1.00	2.50	5.00
81-100	.60	1.50	3.00
101-110	.40	1.00	2.00
111-137	.30	.75	1.50

NOTE: *Photo c-68-121(Fawcett), 40, 42, 46(Charlton).* ***Swayze*** *a(Fawcett)-70-118(most).*

SWEETHEART SCANDALS (See Fox Giants)

SWEETIE PIE (See 4-Color #1185, 1241)

SWEETIE PIE
Dec, 1955 - No. 15, Fall, 1957
Ajax-Farrell/Pines (Literary Ent.)

	GD25	FN65	NM94
1-By Nadine Seltzer	4.00	10.50	21.00
2 (5/56; last Ajax?)	2.40	6.00	12.00
3-15 (#3-10, exist?)	1.60	4.00	8.00

SWEET LOVE
Sept, 1949 - No. 5, May, 1950
Home Comics (Harvey)

	GD25	FN65	NM94
1-Photo-c	5.00	15.00	30.00
2-Photo-c	3.60	9.00	18.00
3,4: 3-Powell-a; 4-Photo-c	2.80	7.00	14.00
5-Kamen, Powell-a; photo-c	4.20	12.50	25.00

SWEET ROMANCE
October, 1968
Charlton Comics

	GD25	FN65	NM94
1	.60	1.50	3.00

SWEET SIXTEEN
Aug-Sept, 1946 - No. 13, Jan, 1948
Parents' Magazine Institute

	GD25	FN65	NM94
1-Van Johnson's life story; Dorothy Dare, Queen of Hollywood Stunt Artists begins (in all issues); part photo-c	10.00	30.00	65.00
2-Jane Powell, Roddy McDowall "Holiday in Mexico" photo-c	6.70	20.00	40.00
3-6,8-11: 6-Dick Haymes story	5.00	15.00	30.00
7-Ronald Reagan's life story	11.00	32.00	75.00
12-Bob Cummings, Vic Damone story	5.00	15.00	30.00
13-Robert Mitchum's life story	5.85	17.50	35.00

SWEET XVI (Marvel) (Value: cover or less)

SWIFT ARROW (Also see Lone Rider & The Rider)
Feb-Mar, 1954 - No. 5, Oct-Nov, 1954; Apr, 1957 - No. 3, Sept, 1957
Ajax/Farrell Publications

	GD25	FN65	NM94
1(1954) (1st Series)	8.35	25.00	50.00
2	4.70	14.00	28.00
3-5: 5-Lone Rider story	4.00	11.00	22.00
1 (2nd Series) (Swift Arrow's Gunfighters #4)	4.00	11.00	22.00
2,3: 2-Lone Rider begins	3.60	9.00	18.00

SWIFT ARROW'S GUNFIGHTERS (Formerly Swift Arrow)
No. 4, Nov, 1957
Ajax/Farrell Publ. (Four Star Comic Corp.)

	GD25	FN65	NM94
4	4.00	10.00	20.00

SWIFTSURE (Harrier) (Value: cover or less)

SWING WITH SCOOTER
June-July, 1966 - No. 35, Aug-Sept, 1971; No. 36, Oct-Nov, 1972
National Periodical Publications

	GD25	FN65	NM94
1	3.00	7.50	15.00
2-10: 9-Alfred E. Newman swipe in last panel	1.40	3.50	7.00
11-20	1.20	3.00	6.00
21-36: 33-Interview with David Cassidy. 34-Interview with Ron Ely (Doc Savage)	1.00	2.50	5.00

NOTE: ***Orlando*** *a-1-11; c-1-11, 13. #20, 33, 34: 68 pgs.; #35: 52 pgs.*

SWISS FAMILY ROBINSON (See 4-Color #1156, King Classics & Movie Comics)

SWORD & THE DRAGON, THE (See 4-Color #1118)

SWORD & THE ROSE, THE (See 4-Color #505, 682)

SWORD IN THE STONE, THE (See March of Comics #258 & Movie Comics)

SWORD OF SORCERY
Feb-Mar, 1973 - No. 5, Nov-Dec, 1973
National Periodical Publications

	GD25	FN65	NM94
1-Leiber Fafhrd & The Grey Mouser; Chaykin/Neal Adams (Crusty Bunkers) art; Kaluta-c	.60	1.50	3.00
2-Wrightson-c(i); Neal Adams-a(i)	.40	1.00	2.00
3-5: 3-Wrightson-i(5pg.). 5-Starlin-a(p); Conan cameo	.30	.75	1.50

NOTE: ***Chaykin*** *a-1-4p; c-2p, 3-5.* ***Kaluta*** *a-3i.* ***Simonson*** *a-3i, 4i, 5p; c-5.*

SWORD OF THE ATOM (DC) (Value: cover or less)

SWORDS OF TEXAS (Eclipse) (Value: cover or less)

SWORDS OF THE SWASHBUCKLERS (Marvel) (Value: cover or less)

SYPHONS (Now) (Value: cover or less)

TAFFY COMICS
Mar-Apr, 1945 - No. 12, 1948
Rural Home/Orbit Publ.

	GD25	FN65	NM94
1-L.B. Cole-c; origin of Wiggles The Wonderworm plus 7 chapter WWII funny animal adventures	10.00	30.00	60.00
2-L.B. Cole-c	6.70	20.00	40.00
3,4,6-12: 6-Perry Como-c/story. 7-Duke Ellington, 2 pgs.	4.70	14.00	28.00
5-L.B. Cole-c; Van Johnson story	5.35	16.00	32.00

TAILGUNNER JO (DC) (Value: cover or less)

TAILSPIN
November, 1944
Spotlight Publishers

	GD25	FN65	NM94
nn-Firebird app.; L.B. Cole-c	10.00	30.00	65.00

TAILSPIN TOMMY STORY & PICTURE BOOK
No. 266, 1931? (nd) (Color stip reprints; 10x10")
McLoughlin Bros.

	GD25	FN65	NM94
266-By Forrest	20.00	60.00	120.00

TAILSPIN TOMMY (Also see Famous Feature Stories & The Funnies)
1932 (100 pages, hardcover)
Cupples & Leon Co.

Sweethearts #120 (1st series), © FAW

Swift Arrow #5 (10-11/54), © AJAX

Sword of Sorcery #3, © DC

Tales Calculated to Drive You Bats #2, © AP

Tales From the Crypt #46, © WMG

Tales of Horror #12, © TOBY

GD25 FN65 NM94

nn-(Rare)-B&W strip reprints from 1930 by Hal Forrest & Glenn Claffin 23.00 70.00 140.00

TAILSPIN TOMMY (Also see Popular Comics)
1940; 1946
United Features Syndicate/Service Publ. Co.

Single Series 23(1940) 22.00 65.00 150.00
Best Seller (nd, 1946)-Service Publ. Co. 10.00 30.00 70.00

TALENT SHOWCASE (See New Talent Showcase)

TALES CALCULATED TO DRIVE YOU BATS
Nov, 1961 - No. 7, Nov, 1962; 1966 (Satire)
Archie Publications

1-Only 10 cent issue; has cut-out Werewolf mask (price includes mask) 7.50 22.50 45.00
2-Begin 12 cent issues 4.20 12.50 25.00
3-6 3.60 9.00 18.00
7-Storyline change 3.00 7.50 15.00
1(1966)-25 cents 4.00 10.00 20.00

TALES FROM THE ANIVERSE (Arrow)(Value: cover or less)

TALES FROM THE CRYPT (Formerly The Crypt Of Terror; see Three Dimensional...)
No. 20, Oct-Nov, 1950 - No. 46, Feb-Mar, 1955
E.C. Comics

20 89.00 270.00 625.00
21-Kurtzman-r/Haunt of Fear #15(#1) 72.00 215.00 500.00
22-Moon Girl costume at costume party, one panel 57.00 170.00 400.00
23-25: 24-E. A. Poe adaptation 43.00 130.00 300.00
26-30 36.00 107.00 250.00
31-Williamson-a(1st at E.C.); B&W and color illos. in **POP**; Kamen draws himself, Gaines & Feldstein; Ingels, Craig & Davis draw themselves in his story 40.00 120.00 280.00
32,35-39 29.00 85.00 200.00
33-Origin The Crypt Keeper 49.00 145.00 340.00
34-Used in **POP**, pg. 83; lingerie panels 29.00 85.00 200.00
40-Used in Senate hearings & in Hartford Cournat anti-comics editorials-1954 29.00 85.00 200.00
41-45: 45-2pgs. showing E.C. staff 27.00 81.00 190.00
46-Low distribution; pre-advertised cover for unpublished 4th horror title 'Crypt of Terror' used on this book 33.00 100.00 230.00

NOTE: ***Ray Bradbury** adaptations-34, 36. **Craig** a-20, 22-24; c-20. **Crandall** a-38, 44. **Davis** a-24-46; c-29-46. **Elder** a-37, 38. **Evans** a-32-34, 36, 40, 41, 43, 46. **Feldstein** a-20-23; c-21-25, 28. Ingels a-in all. **Kamen** a-20, 22, 25, 27-31, 33-36, 39, 41-45. **Krigstein** a-40, 42, 45. **Kurtzman** a-21. **Orlando** a-27-30, 35, 37, 39, 41-45. **Wood** a-21, 24, 25; c-26, 27. Canadian reprints known; see Table of Contents.*

TALES FROM THE CRYPT (Magazine)
No. 10, July, 1968 (35 cents)(B&W)
Eerie Publications

10-Contains Farrell reprints from 1950s 2.40 6.00 12.00

TALES FROM THE CRYPT
July, 1990 - No. 6, May, 1991 ($1.95, color, 68 pgs.)(#4 on: $2.00)
Gladstone Publishing

1-r/TFTC #33 & Crime S.S. #17; Davis-c(r) .80 2.00 4.00
2-Davis-c(r) .60 1.50 3.00
3-6: 3,5,6-Davis-c(r). 4-Craig-c(r) .50 1.25 2.50

TALES FROM THE CRYPT (Cochran, large size)(Value: cover or less)

TALES FROM THE CRYPT
Sept, 1992 - Present ($1.50, color)
Russ Cochran

1-4: 1-r/Crypt of Terror #17; Craig-c(r) .30 .75 1.50

TALES FROM THE GREAT BOOK
Feb, 1955 - No. 4, Jan, 1956
Famous Funnies

1-Story of Samson 5.35 16.00 32.00
2-4-Lehti-a in all 3.60 9.00 18.00

TALES FROM THE HEART OF AFRICA (Marvel)(Value: cover or less)

TALES FROM THE TOMB (See Dell Giants)

TALES FROM THE TOMB (Magazine)
V1#6, July, 1969 - V7#1, Feb, 1975 (52 pgs.)
Eerie Publications

V1#6-8 3.60 9.00 18.00
V2#1-3,5,6: 6-Rulah-r 2.00 5.00 10.00
4-LSD story-r/Weird V3#5 2.00 5.00 10.00
V3#1-Rulah-r 2.00 5.00 10.00
2-6('70),V4#1-5('72),V5#1-6('73),V6#1-6('74),V7#1('75) 1.60 4.00 8.00

TALES OF ASGARD
Oct, 1968 (25 cents, 68 pages); Feb, 1984 ($1.25, 52 pgs.)
Marvel Comics Group

1-Reprints Tales of Asgard (Thor) back-up stories from Journey into Mystery #97-106; new Kirby-c 4.70 14.00 28.00
V2#1 (2/84)-Thor-r; Simonson-c .50 1.00

TALES OF DEMON DICK & BUNKER BILL
1934 (78 pgs; 5x10-1/2"; B&W)(hardcover)
Whitman Publishing Co.

793-By Dick Spencer 12.00 36.00 85.00

TALES OF EVIL
Feb, 1975 - No. 3, July, 1975
Atlas/Seaboard Publ.

1-3: 2-Intro. The Bog Beast; Sparling-a. 3-Origin The Man-Monster; Buckler-a(p) .50 1.00

NOTE: ***Grandenetti** a-1, 2. **Lieber** c-1. **Sekowsky** a-1. **Sutton** a-2. **Thorne** c-2.*

TALES OF GHOST CASTLE
May-June, 1975 - No. 3, Sept-Oct, 1975
National Periodical Publications

1-3: 1,3-Redondo-a. 2-Nino-a .50 1.00

TALES OF G.I. JOE (Marvel)(Value: cover or less)

TALES OF HORROR
June, 1952 - No. 13, Oct, 1954
Toby Press/Minoan Publ. Corp.

1 16.00 48.00 110.00
2-Torture scenes 12.00 36.00 85.00
3-8,13 8.35 25.00 50.00
9-11-Reprints Purple Claw #1-3 9.15 27.50 55.00
12-Myron Fass-c/a; torture scenes 10.00 30.00 60.00

NOTE: ***Andru** a-5. **Bally** a-5. **Myron Fass** a-2, 3, 12; c-1-3, 12. **Hollingsworth** a-2. **Sparling** a-6, 9; c-9.*

TALES OF JUSTICE
No. 53, May, 1955 - No. 67, Aug, 1957
Atlas Comics(MjMC No. 53-66/Male No. 67)

53 9.15 27.50 55.00
54-57: 54-Powell-a 5.85 17.50 35.00
58,59-Krigstein-a 7.50 22.50 45.00
60-63,65: 60-Powell-a 4.20 12.50 25.00
64,67-Crandall-a 5.85 17.50 35.00
66-Torres, Orlando-a 5.85 17.50 35.00

NOTE: ***Everett** a-53, 60. **Orlando** a-65, 66. **Severin** a-64; c-58, 60, 65. **Wildey** a-64, 67.*

TALES OF ORDINARY MADNESS (Dark Horse)(Value: cover or less)

TALES OF SUSPENSE (Becomes Captain America #100 on)

Jan, 1959 - No. 99, March, 1968
Atlas (WPI No. 1,2/Male No. 3-12/VPI No. 13-18)/Marvel No. 19 on

1-Williamson-a, 5 pgs. 93.00 280.00 650.00
2,3: 3-Flying saucer-c/story 36.00 107.00 250.00
4-Williamson-a, 4 pgs; Kirby/Everett c/a 39.00 120.00 275.00
5-10 23.00 70.00 160.00
11-15,17-20: 12-Crandall-a. 14-Intro. Colossus 17.00 52.00 120.00
16-1st Metallo (4/61, Iron Man prototype) 24.00 72.00 165.00
21-25: 25-Last 10 cent issue 12.00 36.00 85.00
26-38: 32-Sazzik The Sorcerer app.; "The Man and the Beehive;" story came out same year as "The Man in the Ant Hill" in TTA #27 (1st Antman)-characters were tested to see which got best fan response 11.00 32.00 75.00
39 (3/63)-Origin/1st app. Iron Man & begin series; 1st Iron Man story has Kirby layouts 250.00 750.00 2000.00
40-2nd app. Iron Man (in new armor) 115.00 345.00 800.00
41-3rd app. Iron Man; Dr. Strange (villain) app. 65.00 195.00 450.00
42-45: 45-Intro. & 1st app. Happy & Pepper 29.00 85.00 200.00
46,47: 46-1st app. Crimson Dynamo 17.00 52.00 120.00
48-New Iron Man armor 22.00 65.00 150.00
49-1st X-Men x-over (same date as X-Men #3, 1/64); 1st Tales of the Watcher back-up story 14.00 43.00 100.00
50-1st app. Mandarin 11.00 32.00 75.00
51-1st Scarecrow 10.00 30.00 65.00
52-1st app. The Black Widow (4/64) 13.00 40.00 90.00
53-Origin & 2nd app. The Watcher (5/64); 2nd Black Widow app. 11.00 32.00 75.00
54-56: 56-1st app. Unicorn 7.50 22.50 45.00
57-Origin/1st app. Hawkeye (9/64) 15.00 45.00 105.00
58-Captain America battles Iron Man (10/64)-Classic-c; 2nd Kraven app. (Cap's 1st app. in this title) 25.00 75.00 175.00
59-Iron Man plus Captain America double feature begins (11/64); 1st S.A. Captain America solo story; intro Jarvis, Avenger's butler; classic-c 25.00 75.00 175.00
60-2nd app. Hawkeye (#64 is 3rd app.) 11.50 34.00 80.00
61,62,64: 62-Origin Mandarin (2/65) 7.50 22.50 45.00
63-1st Silver Age origin Captain America (3/65) 17.00 52.00 120.00
65-1st Silver-Age Red Skull (6/65) 11.00 32.00 75.00
66-Origin Red Skull 11.00 32.00 75.00
67-78,81-98: 69-1st app. Titanium Man. 75-1st app. Agent 13 later named Sharon Carter. 76-Intro Batroc & Sharon Carter, Agent 13 of Shield. 78-Col. Nick Fury app. 92-1st Nick Fury x-over (cameo, as Agent of Shield, 8/67). 94-Intro Modok. 95-Capt. America's i.d. revealed. 98-1st app. Zemo in cameo (#99 is 1st full app.) 5.50 16.50 33.00
79-Begin 3 part Iron Man Sub-Mariner battle story; Sub-mariner-c & cameo; 1st app. Cosmic Cube 6.70 20.00 40.00
80-Iron Man battles Sub-Mariner story cont'd in Tales to Astonish #82 7.35 22.00 44.00
99-Captain America story cont'd in Captain America #100; Iron Man story cont'd in Iron Man & Sub-Mariner #1 8.35 25.00 50.00

NOTE: ***J. Buscema** a-1. **Colan** a-39, 73-99p; c(p)-73, 75, 77, 79, 81, 83, 85-87, 89, 91, 93, 95, 97, 99. **Craig** a-99i. **Crandall** a-12. **Davis** a-38. **Ditko** c(i)-2, 10, 13. **Ditko/Kirby** art in most issues #2-15, 17-49. **Everett** a-8. **Forte** a-5, 9. **Heath** a-10. **Gil Kane** a-88p, 89-91; c-88, 89-91p. **Kirby** a(p)-40, 41, 43, 59-75, 77-86, 92-99; layouts-69-75, 77; c(p)4-28(most), 29-56, 58-72, 74, 76, 78, 80, 82, 84, 86, 92, 94, 96, 98. **Leiber/Fox** a-42, 43, 45, 51. **Reinman** a-26, 44i, 49i, 52i, 53i. **Tuska** a-58, 70-74. **Wood** c/a-71i.*

TALES OF SWORD & SORCERY (See Dagar)

TALES OF TERROR
1952 (no month)
Toby Press Publications

1-Fawcette-c; Ravielli-a 10.00 30.00 60.00

NOTE: *This title was cancelled due to similarity to the E.C. title.*

TALES OF TERROR (See Movie Classics)

TALES OF TERROR (Magazine)
Summer, 1964
Eerie Publications

1 3.60 9.00 18.00

TALES OF TERROR (Eclipse) (Value: cover or less)

TALES OF TERROR ANNUAL
1951 - No. 3, 1953 (25 cents) (132 pgs.)
E.C. Comics

	GD25	FN65	VF82
nn(1951)(Scarce)-Feldstein infinity-c	367.00	1100.00	2200.00

(Estimated up to 35 total copies exist, 3 in NM/Mint)

	GD25	FN65	NM94
2(1952)-Feldstein-c	158.00	475.00	950.00
3(1953)	117.00	350.00	700.00

NOTE: *No. 1 contains three horror and one science fiction comic which came out in 1950. No. 2 contains a horror, crime, and science fiction book which generally had cover dates in 1951, and No. 3 had horror, crime, and shock books that generally appeared in 1952. All E.C. annuals contain four complete books that did not sell on the stands which were rebound in the annual format, minus the covers, and sold from the E.C. office and on the stands in key cities. The contents of each annual may vary in the same year.*

TALES OF TERROR ILLUSTRATED (See Terror Illustrated)

TALES OF TEXAS JOHN SLAUGHTER (See 4-Color #997)

TALES OF THE BEANWORLD
Feb, 1985 - No. 19, 1991 ($1.50/$2.00, B&W)
Beanworld Press/Eclipse Comics

1 .80 2.00 4.00
2-19 .40 1.00 2.00

TALES OF THE GREEN BERET
Jan, 1967 - No. 5, Oct, 1969
Dell Publishing Co.

1-Glanzman-a in 1-4,5r 3.00 7.50 15.00
2-5: 5 reprints #1 1.80 4.50 9.00

TALES OF THE GREEN HORNET (Now) (Value: cover or less)

TALES OF THE GREEN LANTERN CORPS (DC) (Value: cover or less) (See Green Lantern #107)

TALES OF THE INVISIBLE SCARLET O'NEIL (See Harvey Comics Hits 59)

TALES OF THE KILLERS (Magazine)
V1#10, Dec, 1970 - V1#11, Feb, 1971 (B&W, 52pgs.)
World Famous Periodicals

V1#10-One pg. Frazetta 2.40 6.00 12.00
11 1.60 4.00 8.00

TALES OF THE LEGION (DC) (Value: cover or less) (Formerly The Legion of Super-Heroes)

TALES OF THE MARINES (Formerly Devil-Dog Dugan #1-3)
No. 4, Feb, 1957 (Marines At War #5 on)
Atlas Comics (OPI)

4-Powell-a; Severin-c 3.20 8.00 16.00

TALES OF THE MYSTERIOUS TRAVELER (See Mysterious...)
Aug, 1956 - No. 13, June, 1959; V2#14, Oct, 1985 - No. 15, Dec, 1985
Charlton Comics

1-No Ditko-a 24.00 72.00 165.00
2-Ditko-a(1) 19.00 58.00 135.00
3-Ditko-c/a(1) 18.00 54.00 125.00
4-6-Ditko-c/a(3-4 stories each) 24.00 73.00 170.00
7-9-Ditko-a(1-2 each). 8-Rocke-c 18.00 54.00 125.00
10,11-Ditko-c/a(3-4 each) 20.00 60.00 140.00
12,13 8.35 25.00 50.00
V2#14,15 (1985)-Ditko-c/a .50 1.00

TALES OF THE NEW TEEN TITANS (DC) (Value: cover or less)

TALES OF THE PONY EXPRESS (See 4-Color #829, 942)

TALES OF THE SUN RUNNERS (Sirius) (Value: cover or less)

TALES OF THE TEENAGE MUTANT NINJA TURTLES

Tales of Suspense #3, © MEG

Tales of Suspense #66, © MEG

Tales of Terror Annual #2, © WMG

Tales of the Unexpected #80, © DC

Tales to Astonish #20, © MEG

Tales to Astonish #82, © MEG

GD25 FN65 NM94

May, 1987 - No. 7, Apr, 1989 (B&W, $1.50)(See Teenage Mutant...)
Mirage Studios

1 — 1.00 — 2.50 — 5.00
2-7: Title merges w/Teenage Mutant Ninja... — .60 — 1.50 — 3.00

TALES OF THE TEEN TITANS (Formerly The New Teen Titans)
No. 41, April, 1984 - No. 91, July, 1988 (75 cents)
DC Comics

41,45-59: 46-Aqualad & Aquagirl join. 50-Double size. 53-Intro Azreal. 56-Intro Jinx. 57-Neutron app. 59-r/DC Comics Presents #26 — .50 — 1.00
42-44: The Judas Contract part 1-3 with Deathstroke the Terminator in all; concludes in Annual #3. 44-Dick Grayson becomes Nightwing (3rd to be Nightwing) & joins Titans; Jericho (Deathstroke's son) joins; origin Deathstroke — 1.60 — 4.00 — 8.00
60-91-r/New Teen Titans Baxter series. 68-B. Smith-c. 70-Origin Kole. 83-91 are $1.00 cover — .50 — 1.00
Annual 3(1984, $1.25)-Part 4 of The Judas Contract; Deathstroke-c/story; Death of Terra; indicia says Teen Titans Annual; formerly New Teen Titans Annual #1,2 — .60 — 1.50 — 3.00
Annual 4,5: 4-(1986, $1.25)-Reprints. 5(1987) — .60 — 1.25

TALES OF THE TEXAS RANGERS (See Jace Pearson...)

TALES OF THE UNEXPECTED (The Unexpected #105 on)(See Super DC Giant)
Feb-Mar, 1956 - No. 104, Dec-Jan, 1967-68
National Periodical Publications

1 — 79.00 — 235.00 — 550.00
2 — 39.00 — 120.00 — 275.00
3-5 — 27.00 — 80.00 — 180.00
6-10 — 20.00 — 60.00 — 140.00
11,14,19,20 — 11.50 — 34.00 — 80.00
12,13,15-18,21-24: All have Kirby-a. 16-Character named 'Thor' with a magic hammer (not like later Thor) — 13.00 — 40.00 — 90.00
25-30 — 10.00 — 30.00 — 65.00
31-39 — 9.15 — 27.50 — 55.00
40-Space Ranger begins (8/59), ends #82 (1st app. in Showcase #15) — 60.00 — 182.00 — 425.00
41,42-Space Ranger stories — 22.00 — 65.00 — 150.00
43-1st Space Ranger-c this title, plus story — 39.00 — 120.00 — 275.00
44-46 — 17.00 — 52.00 — 120.00
47-50 — 12.00 — 36.00 — 85.00
51-60: 54-Dinosaur-c/story — 10.00 — 30.00 — 70.00
61-67: 67-Last 10 cent issue — 8.35 — 25.00 — 50.00
68-82: 82-Last Space Ranger — 4.20 — 12.50 — 25.00
83-100: 91-1st Automan (also in #94,97) — 2.80 — 7.00 — 14.00
101-104 — 2.40 — 6.00 — 12.00

NOTE: ***Neal Adams*** *c-104.* ***Anderson*** *a-50.* ***Brown*** *a-50-82(Space Ranger); c-19, 40, & many Space Ranger-c.* ***Cameron*** *a-24, 27, 29; c-24.* ***Heath*** *a-49.* ***Bob Kane*** *a-24, 48.* ***Kirby*** *a-12, 13, 15-18, 21-24; c-13, 18, 22.* ***Meskin*** *a-15, 18, 26, 27, 35, 66.* ***Moreira*** *a-16, 20, 29, 38, 44, 62, 71; c-38.* ***Roussos*** *c-10.* ***Wildey*** *a-31.*

TALES OF THE WEST (See 3-D...)

TALES OF THE WIZARD OF OZ (See 4-Color #1308)

TALES OF THE ZOMBIE (Magazine)
Aug, 1973 - No. 10, Mar, 1975 (75 cents)(B&W)
Marvel Comics Group

V1#1-Reprint/Menace #5; origin — 3.00 — 7.50 — 15.00
2,3: 2-Everett biography & memorial — 1.60 — 4.00 — 8.00
V2#1(#4)-Photos & text of James Bond movie "Live & Let Die" — 1.60 — 4.00 — 8.00
5-10: 8-Kaluta-a — 1.60 — 4.00 — 8.00
Annual 1(Summer,'75)(#11)-B&W; Everett, Buscema-a — 1.00 — 2.50 — 5.00

NOTE: ***Alcala*** *a-7-9.* ***Boris*** *c-1-4.* ***Colan*** *a-2r, 6.* ***Heath*** *a-5r.* ***Reese*** *a-2.* ***Tuska*** *a-2r.*

GD25 FN65 NM94

TALES OF THUNDER (Deluxe)(Value: cover or less)

TALES OF VOODOO (Magazine)
V1#11, Nov, 1968 - V7#6, Nov, 1974
Eerie Publications

V1#11 — 4.00 — 10.00 — 20.00
V2#1(3/69)-V2#4(9/69) — 2.40 — 6.00 — 12.00
V3#1-6('70): 4-'Claws of the Cat' redrawn from Climax #1 — 2.00 — 5.00 — 10.00
V4#1-6('71), V5#1-6('72), V6#1-6('73), V7#1-6('74) — 2.00 — 5.00 — 10.00
Annual 1 — 2.00 — 5.00 — 10.00

NOTE: *Bondage-c-V1#10, V2#4, V3#4.*

TALES OF WELLS FARGO (See 4-Color #876, 968, 1023,1075, 1113, 1167, 1215, & Western Roundup under Dell Giants)

TALESPIN (Also see Cartoon Tales & Disney's Talespin Limited Series)
June, 1992 - No. 7, Dec, 1992 ($1.50, color)
Disney Comics

1-7 — .30 — .75 — 1.50

TALES TO ASTONISH (Becomes The Incredible Hulk #102 on)
Jan, 1959 - No. 101, March, 1968
Atlas (MAP No. 1/ZPC No. 2-14/VPI No. 15-21/Marvel No. 22 on

1-Jack Davis-a — 87.00 — 260.00 — 600.00
2-Ditko-c — 43.00 — 130.00 — 300.00
3-5: 5-Williamson-a (4 pgs.) — 29.00 — 85.00 — 200.00
6-10 — 24.00 — 70.00 — 165.00
11-20: 13-Swipes story from Menace #8 — 17.00 — 52.00 — 120.00
21-26,28-34 — 12.00 — 36.00 — 85.00
27-1st Antman app. (1/62); last 10 cent issue — 190.00 — 565.00 — 1500.00
35-(9/62)-2nd app. Antman, 1st in costume; begin series — 115.00 — 345.00 — 800.00
36-3rd app. Antman — 54.00 — 160.00 — 375.00
37-40: 38-1st app. Egghead — 27.00 — 80.00 — 185.00
41-43 — 17.00 — 52.00 — 120.00
44-Origin & 1st app. The Wasp (6/63) — 22.00 — 65.00 — 150.00
45-48 — 12.00 — 36.00 — 85.00
49-Antman becomes Giant Man — 17.00 — 50.00 — 115.00
50-56,58: 50-Origin/1st app. Human Top; 1st app. Whirlwind. 52-Origin/1st app. Black Knight (2/64) — 10.00 — 30.00 — 60.00
57-Early Spider-Man app. (7/64) — 11.50 — 34.00 — 80.00
59-Giant Man vs. Hulk feature story — 13.50 — 41.00 — 95.00
60-Giant Man plus Hulk double feature begins — 17.00 — 50.00 — 115.00
61-69: 62-1st app./origin The Leader; new Wasp costume. 65-New Giant Man costume. 68-New Human Top costume. 69-Last Giant Man — 7.00 — 21.00 — 42.00
70-Sub-Mariner & Incredible Hulk begins — 10.00 — 30.00 — 65.00
71-81,83-91,94-99: 79-Hulk vs. Hercules-c/story. 81-1st app. Boomerang. 90-1st app. The Abomination. 97-X-Men cameo (brief) — 5.00 — 15.00 — 30.00
82-Iron Man battles Sub-Mariner (1st Iron Man x-over outside The Avengers); story cont'd from Tales of Suspense #80 — 7.00 — 21.00 — 42.00
92,93-1st Silver Surfer x-over (outside of F.F., 7/67 & 8/67). 93-Hulk battles Silver Surfer — 6.35 — 19.00 — 38.00
100-Hulk battles Sub-Mariner full-length story — 6.35 — 19.00 — 38.00
101-Hulk story cont'd in Incredible Hulk #102; Sub-Mariner story continued in Iron Man & Sub-Mariner #1 — 9.15 — 27.50 — 55.00

NOTE: ***Ayers*** *c(i)-9-12, 16, 18, 19.* ***Berg*** *a-1.* ***Burgos*** *a-62-64p.* ***Buscema*** *a-85-87p.* ***Colan*** *a(p)-70-76, 78-82, 84, 85, 101; c(p)-71-76, 78, 80, 82, 84, 86, 88, 90.* ***Ditko*** *a-most issues-1-48, 50i, 60-67; c-2, 7i, 8i, 14i, 17i.* ***Everett*** *a-78, 79i, 80-84, 85-90i, 94i, 95, 96; c(i)-79-81, 83, 86, 88.* ***Forte*** *a-6.* ***Kane*** *a-76, 88-91; c-89, 91.* ***Kirby*** *a(p)-1-34(most), 35-40, 44, 49-51, 68-70, 82, 83; layouts-71-84; c(p)-1, 3-48, 50-70, 72, 73, 75, 77, 78, 79, 81, 85, 90.* ***Leiber/Fox*** *a-47, 48, 50, 51.* ***Powell*** *a-65-69p, 73, 74.* ***Reinman*** *a-6, 36, 45, 46, 54i, 56-60i.*

TALES TO ASTONISH (2nd Series)
Dec, 1979 - No. 14, Jan, 1981

Marvel Comics Group

V1#1-Reprints Sub-Mariner #1 by Buscema .60 1.20
2-14: Reprints Sub-Mariner #2-14 .50 1.00

TALES TO HOLD YOU SPELLBOUND (See Spellbound)

TALKING KOMICS
1947 (20 pages) (Slick covers)
Belda Record & Publ. Co.

Each comic contained a record that followed the story - much like the Golden Record sets. Known titles: Chirpy Cricket, Lonesome Octopus, Sleepy Santa, Grumpy Shark, Flying Turtle, Happy Grasshopper with records... 1.60 4.00 8.00

TALLY-HO COMICS
December, 1944
Swappers Quarterly (Baily Publ. Co.)

nn-Frazetta's 1st work as Giunta's assistant; Man in Black horror story; violence; Giunta-c 23.00 70.00 160.00

TALOS OF THE WILDERNESS SEA (DC)(Value: cover or less)

TALULLAH (See Comic Books Series I)

TAMMY, TELL ME TRUE (See 4-Color #1233)

TANK GIRL (Dark Horse)(Value: cover or less)

TAPPING THE VEIN (Eclipse)(Value: cover or less)

TARANTULA (See Weird Suspense)

TARGET: AIRBOY (Eclipse)(Value: cover or less)

TARGET COMICS (...Western Romances #106 on)
Feb, 1940 - V10#3 (#105), Aug-Sept, 1949
Funnies, Inc./Novelty Publications/Star Publications

V1#1-Origin & 1st app. Manowar, The White Streak by Burgos, & Bulls-Eye Bill by Everett; City Editor (ends #5), High Grass Twins by Jack Cole (ends #4), T-Men by Joe Simon(ends #9), Rip Rory (ends #4), Fantastic Feature Films by Tarpe Mills (ends #39, & Calling 2-R(ends #14) begin; Marijuana use story 233.00 700.00 1400.00
2 117.00 350.00 700.00
3,4 83.00 250.00 500.00
5-Origin The White Streak in text; Space Hawk by Wolverton begins (see Blue Bolt & Circus) 191.00 575.00 1150.00
6-The Chameleon by Everett begins; White Streak origin cont'd. in text 108.00 325.00 650.00
7-Wolverton Spacehawk-c (Scarce) 250.00 750.00 1500.00
8,9,12 83.00 250.00 500.00
10-Intro. & 1st app. The Target; Kirby-c 117.00 350.00 700.00
11-Origin The Target & The Targeteers 108.00 325.00 650.00
V2#1-Target by Bob Wood; flag-c 58.00 175.00 350.00
2-Ten part Treasure Island serial begins; Harold Delay-a; reprinted in Catholic Comics V3#1-10 (see Key Comics #5) 55.00 165.00 330.00
3-5: 4-Kit Carter, The Cadet begins 42.00 125.00 250.00
6-9: Red Seal with White Streak in 6-10 42.00 125.00 250.00
10-Classic-c 50.00 150.00 300.00
11,12: 12-10-part Last of the Mohicans serial begins; Delay-a 42.00 125.00 250.00
V3#1-10-Last Wolverton issue. 8-Flag-c; 6-part Gulliver Travels serial begins; Delay-a 42.00 125.00 250.00
11,12 7.50 22.50 45.00
V4#1-12: 6-Targetoons by Wolverton, 1 pg. 4.70 14.00 28.00
V5#1-8 4.00 11.00 22.00
V6#1-10, V7#1-12 4.00 10.00 20.00
V8#1,3-5,8,9,11,12 3.60 9.00 18.00
2,6,7-Krigstein-a 4.00 11.00 22.00
10-L.B. Cole-c 7.50 22.50 45.00
V9#1,3,6,8,10,12, V10#2,3-L.B. Cole-c 7.50 22.50 45.00
V9#2,4,5,7,9,11, V10#1 3.60 9.00 18.00

NOTE: ***Jack Cole** a-1-8. **Everett** a-1-9; c(signed Blake)-1, 2. **Al Fago** c-V6#8. **Sid Greene** c-V2#9, 12, V3#3. **Tarpe Mills** a-1-4, 6, 8, 11, V3#1. **Rico** a-V7#4, 10, V8#5, 6, V9#3; c-V7#6, 8, 10, V8#2, 4, 6, 7. **Simon** a-1, 2. **Bob Wood** c-V2#2, 3, 5, 6.*

TARGET: THE CORRUPTORS (TV)
No. 1306, Mar-May, 1962 - No. 3, Oct-Dec, 1962 (All have photo-c)
Dell Publishing Co.

4-Color 1306(#1), #2,3 4.20 12.50 25.00

TARGET WESTERN ROMANCES (Formerly Target Comics; becomes Flaming Western Romances #3)
No. 106, Oct-Nov, 1949 - No. 107, Dec-Jan, 1949-50
Star Publications

106(#1)-Silhouette nudity panel; L.B. Cole-c 16.00 48.00 110.00
107(#2)-L.B. Cole-c; lingerie panels 12.00 36.00 85.00

TARGITT
March, 1975 - No. 3, July, 1975
Atlas/Seaboard Publ.

1-3: 1-Origin; Nostrand-a in all. 2-1st in costume .50 1.00

TARZAN (See Aurora, Comics on Parade, Crackajack, DC 100-Page Super Spec., Famous Feature Stories #1, Golden Comics Digest #4, 9, Jeep Comics #1-29, Jungle Tales of..., Limited Collectors' Edition, Popular, Sparkler, Sport Stars #1, Tip Top & Top Comics)

TARZAN
No. 5, 1939 - No. 161, Aug, 1947
Dell Publishing Co./United Features Syndicate

Large Feature Comic 5('39)-(Scarce)-By Hal Foster; reprints 1st dailies from 1929 93.00 280.00 650.00
Single Series 20(:40)-By Hal Foster 86.00 260.00 600.00
4-Color 134(2/47)-Marsh-c/a 50.00 150.00 350.00
4-Color 161(8/47)-Marsh-c/a 43.00 130.00 300.00

TARZAN (...of the Apes #138 on)
1-2/48 - No. 131, 7-8/62; No. 132, 11/62 - No. 206, 2/72
Dell Publishing Co./Gold Key No. 132 on

1-Jesse Marsh-a begins 79.00 235.00 550.00
2 47.00 140.00 325.00
3-5 34.00 103.00 240.00
6-10: 6-1st Tantor the Elephant. 7-1st Valley of the Monsters 27.00 81.00 190.00
11-15: 11-Two Against the Jungle begins, ends #24. 13-Lex Barker photo-c begin 23.00 70.00 160.00
16-20 17.00 51.00 120.00
21-24,26-30 13.00 40.00 90.00
25-1st "Brothers of the Spear" episode; series ends #156,160,161,196-206 16.00 48.00 110.00
31-40 8.00 24.00 55.00
41-54: Last Barker photo-c 6.50 19.00 45.00
55-60: 56-Eight pg. Boy story 5.00 15.00 35.00
61,62,64-70 4.00 12.00 28.00
63-Two Tarzan stories, 1 by Manning 4.30 13.00 30.00
71-79 3.15 9.50 22.00
80-99: 80-Gordon Scott photo-c begin 3.50 10.50 24.00
100 4.30 13.00 30.00
101-109 2.85 8.50 20.00
110 (Scarce)-Last photo-c 3.15 9.50 22.00
111-120 2.30 7.00 16.00
121-131: Last Dell issue 1.70 5.00 12.00
132-154: 132-1st Gold Key issue 1.50 4.50 10.00
155-Origin Tarzan 1.70 5.00 12.00
156-161: 157-Banlu, Dog of the Arande begins, ends #159, 195. 169-Leopard Girl app. 1.00 3.00 7.00
162,165,168,171 (TV)-Ron Ely photo covers 1.30 4.00 9.00
163,164,166-167,169-170: 169-Leopard Girl app. .85 2.60 6.00
172-199,201-206: 178-Tarzan origin r-/#155; Leopard Girl app, also in #179,190-193 .70 2.00 5.00
200 (Scarce) .85 2.60 6.00

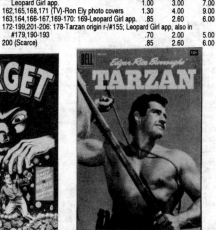

Target Comics V1#12, © NOVP

Target Comics V9#12, © NOVP

Tarzan #108, © ERB

Tarzan #208, © ERB

Tasmanian Devil & His Tasty Friends #1, © Warner Bros.

Tastee-Freez Comics #3, © Paramount

GD25 FN65 NM94

Story Digest 1(6/70)-G.K. .85 2.60 6.00

NOTE: #162, 165, 168, 171 are TV issues. #1-153 all have **Marsh** art on Tarzan. #154-161, 163, 164, 166, 167, 172-177 all have **Manning** art on Tarzan. #178, 202 have **Manning** Tarzan reprints. No "Brothers of the Spear" in #1-24, 157-159, 162-195. #39-126, 128-156 all have **Russ Manning** art on "Brothers of the Spear." #196-201, 203-205 all have **Manning** B.O.T.S. reprints; #25-38, 127 all have Jesse **Marsh** art on B.O.T.S. #206 has a Marsh B.O.T.S. reprint. **Gollub** c-8-12. **Marsh** c-1-7. **Doug Wildey** a-162, 179-187. Many issues have front and back photo covers.

TARZAN (Continuation of Gold Key series)
No. 207, April, 1972 - No. 258, Feb, 1977
National Periodical Publications

207-Origin Tarzan by Joe Kubert, part 1; John Carter begins (origin); 52 pg. issues thru #209 1.00 2.50 5.00
208,209: 208-210-Parts 2-4 of origin. 209-Last John Carter .60 1.50 3.00
210,211: 210-Kubert-a. 211-Hogarth, Kubert-a .40 1.00 2.00
212-214: Adaptations from "Jungle Tales of Tarzan." 213-Beyond the Farthest Star begins, ends #218 .40 1.00 2.00
215-218,224,225-All by Kubert. 215-part Foster-r .40 1.00 2.00
219-223: Adapts "The Return of Tarzan" by Kubert .40 1.00 2.00
226-229: 226-Manning-a .40 1.00 2.00
230-100 pgs.; Kubert, Kaluta-a(p); Korak begins, ends #234; Carson of Venus app. .50 1.25 2.50
231-234: Adapts "Tarzan and the Lion Man;" all 100 pgs.; Rex, the Wonder Dog r-#232, 233 .40 1.00 2.00
235-Last Kubert issue; 100 pgs. .40 1.00 2.00
236-258: 238-(68 pgs.). 240-243 adapts "Tarzan & the Castaways." 250-256-Adapts "Tarzan the Untamed." 252,253-r/#213 .40 1.00 2.00
Comic Digest 1(Fall, 1972)(DC)-50 cents; 160 pgs.; digest size; Kubert-c, Manning-a .60 1.50 3.00

NOTE: **Anderson** a-207, 209, 217, 218. **Chaykin** a-216. **Finlay** a(r)-212. **Foster** strip-r #207-209, 211, 212, 221. **Heath** a-230i. **G. Kane** a-232p, 233p. **Kubert** a-207-225, 227-235, 257r, 258r; c-207-249, 253. Lopez a-250-555p; c-250p, 251, 252, 254. **Manning** strip-r 230-235, 238. **Morrow** a-208. **Nino** a-231-234. **Sparling** a-230. **Starr** a-233r.

TARZAN
June, 1977 - No. 29, Oct, 1979
Marvel Comics Group

1 .30 .75 1.50
2-29: 2-Origin by John Buscema .50 1.00
Annual 1-3: 1-(1977). 2-(1978). 3-(1979) .50 1.00

NOTE: **N. Adams** c-11i, 12i. **Alcala** a-9i, 10i; c-8i, 9i. **Buckler** c-25-27p, Annual 3p. **John Buscema** a-1-3, 4-18p, Annual 1; c-1-7, 8p, 9p, 10, 11p, 12p, 13, 14-19p, 21p, 22, 23p, 24p, 28p, Annual 1. **Mooney** a-22i. **Nebres** a-22i. **Russell** a-29i.

TARZAN BOOK (The Illustrated...)
1929 (80 pages)(7x9")
Grosset & Dunlap

1(Rare)-Contains 1st B&W Tarzan newspaper comics from 1929. Cloth reinforced spine & dust jacket (50 cents); Foster-c
with dust jacket... 54.00 160.00 375.00
without dust jacket... 24.00 70.00 165.00
2nd Printing(1934)-76 pgs.; 25 cents; 4 Foster pages dropped; paper spine, circle in lower right cover with 25 cents price. The 25 cents is barely visible on some copies 15.00 45.00 105.00
1967-House of Greystoke reprint-7x10", using the complete 300 illustrations/text from the 1929 edition minus the original indicia, foreword, etc. Initial version bound in gold paper & sold for $5. Officially titled **Burroughs Biblophile #2**. A very few additional copies were bound in heavier blue paper.
Gold binding... 3.60 9.00 18.00
Blue binding... 4.00 12.00 24.00

TARZAN FAMILY, THE (Formerly Korak, Son of Tarzan)
No. 60, Nov-Dec, 1975 - No. 66, Nov-Dec, 1976
(No. 60-62: 68 pgs.; No. 63 on: 52 pgs.)
National Periodical Publications

GD25 FN65 NM94

60-66: 60-Korak begins; Kaluta-r .50 1.00

NOTE: Carson of Venus-r 60-65. New John Carter-62-64, 65r, 66r. New Korak-60-66. Pellucidar feature-66. Foster strip r-60(9/4/32-10/16/32), 62(6/29/32-7/31/32), 63(10/11/31-12/13/31). **Kaluta** Carson of Venus-60-65. **Kubert** a-61, 64; c-60-64. **Manning** strip-r 60-62, 64. **Morrow** a-66r.

TARZAN KING OF THE JUNGLE (See Dell Giant #37, 51)

TARZAN, LORD OF THE JUNGLE
Sept, 1965 (Giant)(soft paper cover)(25 cents)
Gold Key

1-Marsh-r 4.70 14.00 28.00

TARZAN: LOVE, LIES AND THE LOST CITY (See Tarzan the Warrior)
Aug. 10, 1992 - No. 3, Sept, 1992 ($2.50, color, mini-series)
Malibu Comics

1-($3.95, 68 pgs.)-Flip book format; Simonson & Wagner scripts .80 2.00 4.00
2,3-No Simonson or Wagner scripts .50 1.25 2.50

TARZAN MARCH OF COMICS (See March of Comics #82, 98, 114, 125, 144, 155, 172, 185, 204, 223, 240, 252, 262, 272, 286, 300, 332, 342, 354, 366)

TARZAN OF THE APES
1934? (Hardcover, 68 pgs., 4x12")
Metropolitan Newspaper Service

1-Strip reprints 14.00 43.00 100.00

TARZAN OF THE APES (Marvel)(Value: cover or less)

TARZAN OF THE APES TO COLOR
No. 988, 1933 (24 pages)(10-3/4x15-1/4")(Coloring book)
Saalfield Publishing Co.

988-(Very Rare)-Contains 1929 daily reprints with some new art by Hal Foster. Two panels blown up large on each page; 25 percent in color; believed to be the only time these panels ever appeared in color 93.00 280.00 650.00

TARZAN'S JUNGLE ANNUAL (See Dell Giants)

TARZAN'S JUNGLE WORLD (See Dell Giant #25)

TARZAN THE WARRIOR (Also see Tarzan: Love, Lies and the Lost City)
March 19, 1992 - No. 5, 1992 ($2.50, color, mini-series)
Malibu Comics

1-5: 1-Bisley painted pack-c (flip book format-c) .50 1.25 2.50
1-2nd printing w/o flip-c by Bisley .50 1.25 2.50

TASMANIAN DEVIL & HIS TASTY FRIENDS
November, 1962
Gold Key

1-Bugs Bunny & Elmer Fudd x-over 6.70 20.00 40.00

TASTEE-FREEZ COMICS
1957 (36 pages)(10 cents)(6 different issues)
Harvey Comics

1,3: 1-Little Dot. 3-Casper 4.70 14.00 28.00
2,4,5: 2-Rags Rabbit. 4-Sad Sack. 5-Mazie 3.20 8.00 16.00
6-Dick Tracy 5.00 15.00 30.00

TAYLOR'S CHRISTMAS TABLOID
Mid 1930s, Cleveland, Ohio
Dept. Store Giveaway (Tabloid size; in color)

nn-(Very Rare)-Among the earliest pro work of Siegel & Shuster; one full color page called "The Battle in the Stratosphere," with a pre-Superman look; Shuster art thoughout. (Only 1 known copy)
Estimated value... $1200.00

TEAM AMERICA (See Captain America #269)
June, 1982 - No. 12, May, 1983
Marvel Comics Group

1-Origin; Ideal Toy motorcycle characters .60 1.20

	GD25	FN65	NM94
2-10: 9-Iron man app.		.50	1.00
11-Ghost Rider app.	1.00	2.50	5.00
12-Double size	.40	1.00	2.00

TEAM HELIX
Jan, 1993 - No. 4, Apr, 1993 ($1.75, color, mini-series)
Marvel Comics

1-4: Teen Super Group. 1,2-Wolverine app.	.35	.90	1.75

TEAM TITANS (See Deathstroke & New Titans Annual #7)
Sept, 1992 - Present ($1.75, color)
DC Comics

1-Five different #1s exist w/origins in 1st half & the same 2nd story in each: Killowat, Mirage, Nightrider w/Netzer/Perez-a, Redwing, & Terra w/part Perez-p; part 3 of Total Chaos	.45	1.15	2.25
2-Total Chaos, part 6	.40	1.00	2.00
3-10	.35	.90	1.75

TEAM YANKEE (First) (Value: cover or less)

TEDDY ROOSEVELT & HIS ROUGH RIDERS (See Real Heroes #1)
1950
Avon Periodicals

1-Kinstler-c; Palais-a; Flag-c	11.50	34.00	80.00

TEDDY ROOSEVELT ROUGH RIDER (See Battlefield #22 & Classics Illustrated Special Issue)

TED MCKEEVER'S METROPOL (Epic, 1991 & 1992) (Value: cover or less)

TEE AND VEE CROSLEY IN TELEVISION LAND COMICS
(Also see Crosley's House of Fun)
1951 (52 pgs.; 8x11"; paper cover; in color)
Crosley Division, Avco Mfg. Corp. (Giveaway)

Many stories, puzzles, cut-outs, games, etc.	4.20	12.50	25.00

TEENA
No. 11, 1948 - No. 15, 1948; No. 20, Aug, 1949 - No. 22, Oct, 1950
Magazine Enterprises/Standard Comics No. 20 on

A-1 #11-Teen-age	5.00	15.00	30.00
A-1 #12, 15	4.20	12.50	25.00
20-22 (Standard)	3.00	7.50	15.00

TEEN-AGE BRIDES (True Bride's Experiences #8 on)
Aug, 1953 - No. 7, Aug, 1954
Harvey/Home Comics

1-Powell-a	4.70	14.00	28.00
2-Powell-a	4.00	10.00	20.00
3-7: 3,6-Powell-a	3.20	8.00	16.00

TEEN-AGE CONFESSIONS (See Teen Confessions)

TEEN-AGE CONFIDENTIAL CONFESSIONS
July, 1960 - No. 22, 1964
Charlton Comics

1	3.00	7.50	15.00
2-10	1.60	4.00	8.00
11-22	1.00	2.50	5.00

TEEN-AGE DIARY SECRETS (Formerly Blue Ribbon Comics; becomes Diary Secrets #10 on)
No. 4, 9/49; nn (#5), 9/49 - No. 7, 11/49; No. 8, 2/50; No. 9, 8/50
St. John Publishing Co.

4(9/49)-oversized; part mag., part comic	12.00	36.00	85.00
nn(#5),6,8: 8-Photo-c; Baker-a(2-3) in each	10.00	30.00	60.00
7,9-Digest size	10.00	30.00	70.00

TEEN-AGE DOPE SLAVES (See Harvey Comics Library #1)

TEENAGE HOTRODDERS (Top Eliminator #25 on; see Blue Bird)
April, 1963 - No. 24, July, 1967
Charlton Comics

1	3.00	7.50	15.00
2-10	1.60	4.00	8.00
11-24	1.20	3.00	6.00

TEEN-AGE LOVE (See Fox Giants)

TEEN-AGE LOVE (Formerly Intimate)
V2#4, July, 1958 - No. 96, Dec, 1973
Charlton Comics

V2#4	3.00	7.50	15.00
5-9	1.60	4.00	8.00
10(9/59)-20	1.20	3.00	6.00
21-35	1.00	2.50	5.00
36-70	.40	1.00	2.00
71-96: 61&62-Jonnie Love begins (origin)		.50	1.00

TEENAGE MUTANT NINJA TURTLES (Also see Anything Goes, Donatello, First Comics Graphic Novel, Gobbledygook, Grimjack #26, Leonardo, Michaelangelo, Raphael & Tales Of The...)
1984 - Present ($1.50-$1.75, B&W; all 44-52 pgs.)
Mirage Studios

1-1st printing (3000 copies)-Only printing to have ad for Gobbledygook #1 & 2; Shredder app. (#1-4: 7-1/2x11")	36.00	107.00	250.00
1-2nd printing (6/84)(15,000 copies)	5.85	17.50	35.00
1-3rd printing (2/85)(36,000 copies)	3.00	7.50	15.00
1-4th printing, new-c (50,000 copies)	2.00	5.00	10.00
1-5th printing, new-c (8/88-c, 11/88 inside)	.40	1.00	2.00
1-Counterfeit. **Note**: Most counterfeit copies have a inch wide white streak or scratch marks across the center of back cover. Black part of cover is a bluish black instead of a deep black. Inside paper is very white & inside cover is bright white. These counterfeit the 1st printings.			
2-1st printing (1984; 15,000 copies)	11.00	32.00	75.00
2-2nd printing	2.00	5.00	10.00
2-3rd printing; new Corben-c/a (2/85)	.60	1.50	3.00
2-Counterfeit with glossy cover stock.			
3-1st printing (1985, 44 pgs.)	5.00	15.00	30.00
3-Variant, 500 copies, given away in NYC. Has 'Laird's Photo' in white rather than light blue	12.00	36.00	85.00
3-2nd printing; contains new back-up story	.60	1.50	3.00
4-1st printing (1985, 44 pgs.)-	3.00	7.50	15.00
4-2nd printing (5/87)	.40	1.00	2.00
5-Fugitoid begins, ends #7; 1st full color-c ('85)	2.00	5.00	10.00
5-2nd printing (11/87)	.40	1.00	2.00
6-1st printing (1986)	1.60	4.00	8.00
6-2nd printing (4/88-c, 5/88 inside)	.40	1.00	2.00
7-4 pg. Eastman/Corben color insert; 1st color TMNT (1986, $1.75-c); Bade Biker back-up story	1.60	4.00	8.00
7-2nd printing (1/89) w/o color insert	.40	1.00	2.00
8-Cerebus-c/story with Dave Sim-a (1986)	1.20	3.00	6.00
9,10: 9 (9/86)-Rip In Time by Corben	1.00	2.50	5.00
11-15	.70	1.75	3.50
16-18: 18-Mark Bode'-a	.60	1.50	3.00
18-2nd printing ($2.25, color, 44 pgs.)-New-c	.40	1.00	2.00
19-51: 19-Begin $1.75-c. 24-26-Veitch-c/a. 35-Begin $2.00-c. 50-Features pin-ups by Larsen, McFarlane, Simonson, etc.	.40	1.00	2.00
32-2nd printing ($2.75, 52 pgs., full color)	.45	1.40	2.75
52-58: 52-Begin $2.25-c	.40	1.15	2.25
Book 1,2($1.50, B&W): 2-Corben-c	.25	.75	1.50
... Christmas Special 1 (12/90, $1.75, B&W, 52 pgs.)-Cover title: Michaelangelo Christmas Special; r/Michaelangelo one-shot plus new Raphael story	.30	.90	1.75
Special: "Times" Pipeline nn (9/92, $2.95, color, 44 pgs.)-Mark Bode-c/a	.50	1.50	3.00

TEENAGE MUTANT NINJA TURTLES (Archie) (Value: cover or less) (The Movie)

TEENAGE MUTANT NINJA TURTLES ADVENTURES (TV)
8/88 - No. 3, 12/88; 3/89 - Present ($1.00, color)
Archie Comics

Teen-Age Confindential Confessions #1, © CC

Teen-Age Diary Secrets #8, © STJ

Teenage Mutant Ninja Turtles #8, © MS

Teen-Age Romances #20, © STJ

Teen-Age Temptations #9, © STJ

Teen Comics #26, © MEG

	GD25	FN65	NM94
1-Adapts TV cartoon; not by Eastman/Laird	.60	1.50	3.00
2,3 (Mini-series)	.40	1.00	2.00
1 (2nd on going series)	.50	1.25	2.50
2-5: 5-Begins original stories not based on TV	.40	1.00	2.00
6-44: 14-Simpson-a(p). 19-1st Mighty Mutanimals (also in #20). 20-Begin $1.25-c. 22-Gene Colan-c/a		.60	1.25
1-11: 2nd printings		.50	1.00
nn (Spring, 1991, $2.50, 68 pgs.)-(Meet Archie)	.50	1.25	2.50
nn (Sum, 1991, $2.50, 68 pgs.)-(Movie II)-Adapts movie sequel	.50	1.25	2.50
...Meet the Conservation Corps 1 (1992, $2.50, 68 pgs.)	.50	1.25	2.50
...Special 1 (Sum/92, $2.50, 68 pgs.)-Bill Wray-c	.50	1.25	2.50

NOTE: *There are 2nd printings of #1-11 w/B&W inside covers. Originals are color.*

TEENAGE MUTANT NINJA TURTLES PRESENTS: APRIL O'NEIL
Jan, 1993 - No. 3, Mar, 1993 ($1.25, color, mini-series)
Archie Comics

	GD25	FN65	NM94
1-3		.60	1.25

TEEN-AGE ROMANCE (Formerly My Own Romance)
No. 77, Sept, 1960 - No. 86, March, 1962
Marvel Comics (ZPC)

	GD25	FN65	NM94
77-86	2.00	5.00	10.00

TEEN-AGE ROMANCES
Jan, 1949 - No. 45, Dec, 1955
St. John Publ. co. (Approved Comics)

	GD25	FN65	NM94
1-Baker-c/a(1)	17.00	51.00	120.00
2-Baker-c/a	10.00	30.00	65.00
3-Baker-c/a(3); spanking panel	10.00	30.00	70.00
4,5,7,8-Photo-c; Baker-a(2-3) each	8.35	25.00	50.00
6-Slightly large size; photo-c; part magazine; Baker-a (10/49)	8.35	25.00	50.00
9-Baker-c/a; Kubert-a	10.00	30.00	70.00
10-12,20-Baker-c/a(2-3) each	7.50	22.50	45.00
13-19,21,22-Complete issues by Baker	10.00	30.00	70.00
23-25-Baker-c/a(2-3) each	6.35	19.00	38.00
26,27,33,34,36-42-Last Precode, 3/55; Baker-a. 38-Suggestive-c	4.35	13.00	26.00
28-30-No Baker-a	2.80	7.00	14.00
31-Baker-c	3.20	8.00	16.00
32-Baker-c/a, 1pg.	3.20	8.00	16.00
35-Baker-c/a, 16pgs.	4.20	12.50	25.00
43-45-Baker-a	3.60	9.00	18.00

TEEN-AGE TALK
1964
I.W. Enterprises

	GD25	FN65	NM94
Reprint #1-Monkees photo-c	1.60	4.00	8.00
Reprint #5,8,9	.40	1.00	2.00

TEEN-AGE TEMPTATIONS (Going Steady #10 on)(See True Love Pictorial)
Oct, 1952 - No. 9, Aug, 1954
St. John Publishing co.

	GD25	FN65	NM94
1-Baker-c/a; has story "Reform School Girl" by Estrada	19.00	57.00	130.00
2-Baker-c	7.50	22.50	45.00
3-7,9-Baker-c/a	10.00	30.00	70.00
8-Teenagers smoke reefers; Baker-c/a	11.00	32.00	75.00

NOTE: ***Estrada** a-1, 3-5.*

TEEN BEAM (Formerly Teen Beat #1)
No. 2, Jan-Feb, 1968
National Periodical Publications

	GD25	FN65	NM94
2-Orlando, Drucker-a(r); Monkees photo-c	3.00	7.50	15.00

TEEN BEAT (Becomes Teen Beam #2)
Nov-Dec, 1967
National Periodical Publications

	GD25	FN65	NM94
1-Photos & text only; Monkees photo-c	4.00	10.00	20.00

TEEN COMICS (Formerly All Teen; Journey Into Unknown Worlds #36 on)
No. 21, April, 1947 - No. 35, May, 1950
Marvel comics (WFP)

	GD25	FN65	NM94
21-Kurtzman's "Hey Look;" Patsy Walker, Cindy, Georgie, Margie app.; Syd Shores-a begins, end #23	7.50	22.50	45.00
22,23,25,27,29,31-35: 22-(6/47)-Becomes Hedy Devine #22 (8/47) on?	4.70	14.00	28.00
24,26,28,30-Kurtzman's "Hey Look"	7.00	21.00	42.00

TEEN CONFESSIONS
Aug, 1959 - No. 97, Nov, 1976
Charlton Comics

	GD25	FN65	NM94
1	5.85	17.50	35.00
2	3.60	9.00	18.00
3-10	2.40	6.00	12.00
11-30	1.40	3.50	7.00
31-Beatles-c	6.70	20.00	40.00
32-36,38-55	.80	2.00	4.00
37 (1/66)-Beatles Fan Club story; Beatles-c	6.70	20.00	40.00
56-97: 89,90-Newton-c		.50	1.00
59-Kaluta's 1st pro work? (12/69)	.80	2.00	4.00

TEENIE WEENIES, THE
No. 10, 1950 - No. 11, 1951 (Newspaper reprints)
Ziff-Davis Publishing Co.

	GD25	FN65	NM94
10,11	10.00	30.00	70.00

TEEN-IN (Tippy Teen)
Summer, 1968 - No. 4, Fall, 1969
Tower Comics

	GD25	FN65	NM94
nn(#1, Summer, 1968), nn(#2, Spring, 1969),3,4	2.40	6.00	12.00

TEEN LIFE (Formerly Young Life)
No. 3, Winter, 1945 - No. 5, Fall, 1945
New Age/Quality Comics Group

	GD25	FN65	NM94
3-June Allyson photo-c	5.85	17.50	35.00
4-Duke Ellington story	5.00	15.00	30.00
5-Van Johnson, Woody Herman & Jackie Robinson articles	6.70	20.00	40.00

TEEN ROMANCES
1964
Super Comics

	GD25	FN65	NM94
10,11,15-17-Reprints	.40	1.00	2.00

TEEN SECRET DIARY (Nurse Betsy Crane #12 on)
Oct, 1959 - No. 11, June, 1961; No. 1, 1972
Charlton Comics

	GD25	FN65	NM94
1	3.60	9.00	18.00
2	1.60	4.00	8.00
3-11	1.00	2.50	5.00
1 (1972)	.40	1.00	2.00

TEEN TALK (See Teen)

TEEN TITANS (See Brave & the Bold, DC Super-Stars #1, Marvel & DC Present, New Teen Titans, Official...Index and Showcase)
1-2/66 - No. 43, 1-2/73; No. 44, 11/76 - No. 53, 2/78
National Periodical Publications/DC Comics

	GD25	FN65	NM94
Brave and the Bold #54 (6-7/64)-Origin & 1st app. Teen Titans; Kid Flash, Robin & Aqualad begin	25.00	75.00	175.00

Brave and the Bold #60 (6-7/65)-2nd app. Teen Titans; 1st app. new

	GD25	FN65	NM94
Wonder Girl (Donna Troy), who joins Titans	10.00	30.00	60.00
Showcase #59 (11-12/65)-3rd app. Teen Titans	10.00	30.00	65.00
1-(1-2/66)-Titans join Peace Corps; Batman, Flash, Aquaman, Wonder Woman cameos	20.00	60.00	140.00
2	10.00	30.00	65.00
3-5: 4-Speedy app. 6-Beast Boy x-over; readers polled on him joining Titans	5.70	17.00	34.00
6-10: 6-Doom Patrol app.	4.20	12.50	25.00
11-19: 11-Speedy app. 13-X-Mas-c. 18-1st app. Starfire (11-12/68). 19-Wood-i; Speedy begins as regular	3.20	8.00	16.00
20-22: All Neal Adams-a. 21-Hawk & Dove app.; last 12 cent issue. 22-Origin Wonder Girl	4.00	10.00	20.00
23-30: 23-Wonder Girl dons new costume. 25-Flash, Aquaman, Batman, Green Arrow, Green Lantern, Superman, & Hawk & Dove guests; 1st app. Lilith who joins T.T. West in #50. 29-Hawk & Dove & Ocean Master app. 30-Aquagirl app.	2.00	5.00	10.00
31-43: 31-Hawk & Dove app. 36,37-Superboy-r. 38-Green Arrow/Speedy-r; Aquaman/Aqualad story. 39-Hawk & Dove-r. (36-39: 52 pgs.)	1.40	3.50	7.00
44,45,47,49,51,52: 44-Mal becomes the Guardian	.80	2.00	4.00
46-Joker's daughter begins(see Batman Family)	1.80	4.50	9.00
48-Intro Bumblebee; Joker's daughter becomes Harlequin	1.80	4.50	9.00
50-1st revival original Bat-Girl; intro. Teen Titans West	1.60	4.00	8.00
53-Origin retold	1.00	2.50	5.00

NOTE: *Aparo a-36.* ***Buckler*** *c-46-53.* ***Cardy*** *c-1-16.* ***Kane*** *a(p)-19, 22-24, 39r.* ***Tuska*** *a(p)-31, 36, 38, 39.*

TEEN TITANS SPOTLIGHT (DC)(Value: cover or less)

TEEPEE TIM (Formerly Ha Ha Comics)
No. 100, Feb-Mar, 1955 - No. 102, June-July, 1955
American Comics Group

	GD25	FN65	NM94
100-102	2.40	6.00	12.00

TEGRA JUNGLE EMPRESS (Zegra Jungle Empress #2 on)
August, 1948
Fox Features Syndicate

	GD25	FN65	NM94
1-Blue Beetle, Rocket Kelly app.; used in **SOTI**, pg. 31	25.00	75.00	175.00

TEKWORLD (William Shatner's... on-c only)
Sept, 1992 - Present ($1.75, color)
Epic comics (Marvel)

	GD25	FN65	NM94
1-Based on Shatner's novel, TekWar, set in L.A. in the year 2120	.50	1.25	2.50
2-10	.35	.90	1.75

TELEVISION (See TV)

TELEVISION COMICS
No. 5, Feb, 1950 - No. 8, Nov, 1950
Standard Comics (Animated Cartoons)

	GD25	FN65	NM94
5-1st app. Willy Nilly	5.85	17.50	35.00
6-8: 6 has #2 on inside	4.00	11.00	22.00

TELEVISION PUPPET SHOW
1950 - No. 2, Nov, 1950
Avon Periodicals

	GD25	FN65	NM94
1,2: Speedy Rabbit, Spotty The Pup	10.00	30.00	70.00

TELEVISION TEENS MOPSY (See TV Teens)

TELL IT TO THE MARINES
Mar, 1952 - No. 15, July, 1955
Toby Press Publications

	GD25	FN65	NM94
1-Lover O'Leary and His Liberty Belles (with Pin-ups), ends #6	10.00	30.00	60.00
2-Madame Cobra-c/story	5.85	17.50	35.00
3-5	4.20	12.50	25.00
6-12,14,15: 7-9,14,15-Photo-c	3.20	8.00	16.00
13-John Wayne photo-c	6.70	20.00	40.00
I.W. Reprint #1,9: 1-Exist? 9-r/#1 above	.40	1.00	2.00
Super Reprint #16('64)-r/#4 above	.40	1.00	2.00

TEMPUS FUGITIVE (DC)(Value: cover or less)

TEN COMMANDMENTS (See Moses & the... and Classics Illustrated Special)

TENDER LOVE STORIES
Feb, 1971 - No. 4, July, 1971 (All 52pgs.)(25 cents)
Skywald Publ. Corp.

	GD25	FN65	NM94
1-4	.60	1.50	3.00

TENDER ROMANCE (Ideal Romance #3 on)
Dec, 1953 - No. 2, Feb, 1954
Key Publications (Gilmour Magazines)

	GD25	FN65	NM94
1-Headlight & lingerie panels; B. Baily-c	10.00	30.00	60.00
2-Bernard Baily-c	5.35	16.00	32.00

TENNESSEE JED (Radio)
nd (1945) (16 pgs.; paper cover; regular size; giveaway)
Fox Syndicate? (Wm. C. Popper & Co.)

	GD25	FN65	NM94
nn	10.00	30.00	70.00

TENNIS (...For Speed, Stamina, Strength, Skill)
1956 (16 pgs.; soft cover; 10 cents)
Tennis Educational Foundation

	GD25	FN65	NM94
Book 1-Endorsed by Gene Tunney, Ralph Kiner, etc. showing how tennis has helped them	4.00	10.50	21.00

TENSE SUSPENSE
Dec, 1958 - No. 2, Feb, 1959
Fago Publications

	GD25	FN65	NM94
1,2	4.20	12.50	25.00

TEN STORY LOVE (Formerly a pulp magazine with same title)
V29#3, June-July, 1951 - V36#5(#209), Sept, 1956 (#3-6: 52 pgs.)
Ace Periodicals

	GD25	FN65	NM94
V29#3(#177)-Part comic, part text	6.70	20.00	40.00
4-6(1/52)	3.60	9.00	18.00
V30#1(3/52)-6(1/53)	2.80	7.00	14.00
V31#1(2/53),V32#2(4/53)-6(12/53)	2.00	5.00	10.00
V33#1(1/54)-3(5#54, #195), V34#4(7/54, #196)-6(10/54, #198)	2.00	5.00	10.00
V35#1(12/54, #199)-3(4/55, #201)-Last precode	1.60	4.00	8.00
V35#4-6(9/55, #201-204), V36#1(11/55, #205)-3, 5(9/56, #209)	1.40	3.50	7.00
V36#4-L.B. Cole-a	2.80	7.00	14.00

TEN WHO DARED (See 4-Color #1178)

TERMINATOR, THE (See Robocop vs. ... & Rust #12 for 1st app.)
Sept, 1988 - No. 17, 1989 ($1.75, color, Baxter paper)
Now Comics

	GD25	FN65	NM94
1-Based on movie	4.20	12.50	25.00
2	2.40	6.00	12.00
3-5	1.40	3.50	7.00
6-10	1.00	2.50	5.00
11,13-17	.50	1.25	2.50
12 ($2.95, 52 pgs.)-Intro. John Connor	.60	1.50	3.00
Trade paperback (1989, $9.95)	2.00	5.00	10.00

TERMINATOR, THE
Aug, 1990 - No. 4, Nov, 1990 ($2.50, color, mini-series)
Dark Horse Comics

	GD25	FN65	NM94
1-Set 39 years later than the movie	1.20	3.00	6.00
2-4	.60	1.50	3.00

TERMINATOR: ALL MY FUTURES PAST, THE

Teen Titans #5, © DC

Tell It to the Marines #3, © TOBY

Tense Suspense #1, © Fago Publ.

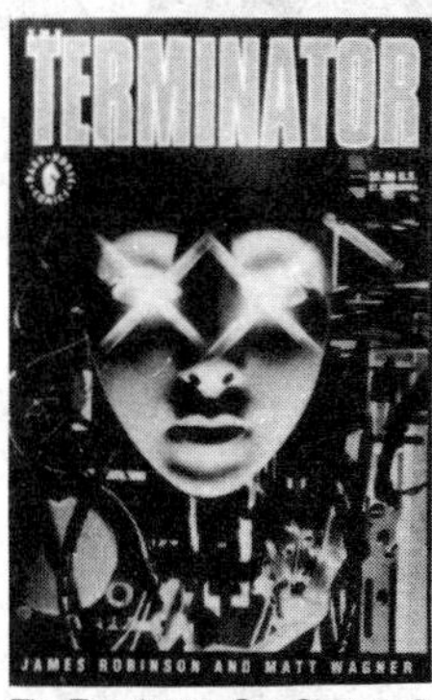

The Terminator: One Shot nn, © Cinema '84/Hemdale Film

Terrific Comics #5, © Continental Magazines

Terrifying Tales #12, © STAR

GD25 FN65 NM94

V3#1, Aug, 1990 - V3#2, Sept, 1990 ($1.75, color, mini-series)
Now Comics

V3#1,2 .50 1.25 2.50

TERMINATOR: ENDGAME, THE
Sept, 1992 - No. 3, Nov, 1992 ($2.50, color, mini-series)
Dark Horse Comics

1-3: Guice-a(p); painted-c .50 1.25 2.50

TERMINATOR: HUNTERS AND KILLERS, THE
Mar, 1992 - No. 3, May, 1992 ($2.50, color, mini-series)
Dark Horse Comics

1-3 .50 1.25 2.50

TERMINATOR: ONE SHOT, THE
July, 1991 ($5.95, color, 56 pgs.)
Dark Horse Comics

nn-Matt Wagner-a; contains stiff pop-up inside 1.20 3.00 6.00

TERMINATOR: SECONDARY OBJECTIVES, THE
July, 1991 - No. 4, Oct, 1991 ($2.50, color, mini-series)
Dark Horse Comics

1-Gulacy-c/a(p) in all .60 1.50 3.00
2-4 .50 1.25 2.50

TERMINATOR: THE BURNING EARTH, THE
V2#1, Mar, 1990 - V2#5, July, 1990 ($1.75, color, mini-series)
Now Comics

V2#1 .80 2.00 4.00
2 .60 1.50 3.00
3-5 .40 1.00 2.00
Trade paperback (1990, $9.95)-Reprints V2#1-5 2.00 5.00 10.00

TERMINATOR: THE ENEMY WITHIN, THE
Nov, 1991 - No. 4, Feb, 1992 ($2.50, color, mini-series)
Dark Horse Comics

1-4: All have Simon Bisley painted-c .50 1.25 2.50

TERMINATOR 2: JUDGEMENT DAY
Early Sept, 1991 - No. 3, Early Oct, 1991 ($1.00, color, mini-series)
Marvel Comics

1-Based on movie sequel; 1-3-Same as nn issues .60 1.20
2,3 .50 1.00
nn (1991, $4.95, squarebound, 68 pgs.)-Photo-c 1.00 2.50 5.00
nn (1991, $2.25, B&W, magazine, 68 pgs.) .45 1.15 2.25

TERRAFORMERS (Wonder) (Value: cover or less)

TERRANAUTS (Fantasy General) (Value: cover or less)

TERRIFIC COMICS
Jan, 1944 - No. 6, Nov, 1944
Continental Magazines

1-Kid Terrific; opium story 75.00 225.00 450.00
2-The Boomerang by L.B. Cole & Ed Wheelan's "Comics" McCormick, called the world's #1 comic book fan begins; Schomburg-c 62.00 188.00 375.00
3-Diana becomes Boomerang's costumed aide 50.00 150.00 300.00
4-Classic war-c 62.00 188.00 375.00
5-The Reckoner begins; Boomerang & Diana by L.B. Cole; Schomburg bondage-c 54.00 162.00 325.00
6-L.B. Cole-c/a 54.00 162.00 325.00
NOTE: ***L.B. Cole** a-1, 2(2), 3-6. **Fuje** a-5, 6. **Rico** a-2; c-1.*

TERRIFIC COMICS (Formerly Horrific; Wonder Boy #17 on)
No. 14, Dec, 1954; No. 16, Mar, 1955 (No #15)
Mystery Publ.(Comic Media)/(Ajax/Farrell)

14-Art swipe/Advs. into the Unknown #37; injury-to-eye-c; page-2, panel 5 swiped from Phantom Stranger #4; surrealistic Palais-a; Human Cross story 10.00 30.00 70.00
16-Wonder Boy app. (precode) 8.35 25.00 50.00

GD25 FN65 NM94

TERRIFYING TALES (Formerly Startling Terror Tales #10)
No. 11, Jan, 1953 - No. 15, Apr, 1954
Star Publications

11-Used in **POP**, pgs. 99,100; all Jo-Jo-r 22.00 65.00 150.00
12-All Jo-Jo-r; L.B. Cole splash 17.00 52.00 120.00
13-All Rulah-r; classic devil-c 23.00 70.00 160.00
14-All Rulah reprints 17.00 52.00 120.00
15-Rulah, Zago-r; used in **SOTI**-r/Rulah #22 17.00 52.00 120.00
NOTE: *All issues have **L.B. Cole** covers; bondage covers-No. 12-14.*

TERROR ILLUSTRATED (Adult Tales of...)
Nov-Dec, 1955 - No. 2, Spring, 1956 (Magazine, 25 cents)
E.C. Comics

1-Adult Entertainment on-c 10.00 30.00 60.00
2-Charles Sultan-a 8.35 25.00 50.00
NOTE: ***Craig, Evans, Ingels, Orlando** art in each. **Crandall** c-1, 2.*

TERROR INC. (See A Shadowline Saga #3)
July, 1992 - Present ($1.75, color)
Marvel Comics

1 .60 1.50 3.00
2-12: 9-Wolverine app. .35 .90 1.75

TERRORS OF THE JUNGLE (Formerly Jungle Thrills)
No. 17, 5/52 - No. 21, 2/53; No. 4, 4/53 - No. 10, 9/54
Star Publications

17-Reprints Rulah #21, used in **SOTI**; L.B. Cole bondage-c 20.00 60.00 140.00
18-Jo-Jo-r 13.00 40.00 90.00
19,20(1952)-Jo-Jo-r; Disbrow-a 11.50 34.00 80.00
21-Jungle Jo, Tangi-r; used in **POP**, pg. 100 & color illos.; shrunken heads on-c 14.00 43.00 100.00
4,6,7-Disbrow-a 11.50 34.00 80.00
5,8,10: All Disbrow-a. 5-Jo-Jo-r. 8-Rulah, Jo-Jo-r. 10-Rulah-r 11.50 34.00 80.00
9-Jo-Jo-r; Disbrow-a; Tangi by Orlando 11.50 34.00 80.00
NOTE: ***L.B. Cole** c-all; bondage c-17, 19, 21, 5, 7.*

TERROR TALES (See Beware Terror Tales)

TERROR TALES (Magazine)
V1#7, 1969 - V6#6, Dec, 1974; V7#1, Apr, 1976 - V10, 1979?
(V1-V6: 52 pgs.; V7 on: 68 pgs.)
Eerie Publications

V1#7 3.60 9.00 18.00
V1#8-11('69): 9-Bondage-c 2.00 5.00 10.00
V2#1-6('70), V3#1-6('71), V4#1-7('72), V5#1-6('73), V6#1-6('74) 1.60 4.00 8.00
V7#1,4(no V7#2), V8#1-3('77), V9, V10 1.60 4.00 8.00
V7#3-LSD story-r/Weird V3#5 1.60 4.00 8.00

TERRY AND THE PIRATES (See Famous Feature Stories, Merry Christmas From Sears Toyland, Popular Comics, Super Book #3,5,9,16,28, & Super Comics)

TERRY AND THE PIRATES
1939 - 1953 (By Milton Caniff)
Dell Publishing Co.

Large Feature Comic 2(1939) 54.00 160.00 375.00
Large Feature Comic 6(1939)-r/1936 dailies 49.00 145.00 340.00
4-Color 9(1940) 54.00 160.00 375.00
Large Feature Comic 27('41), 6('42) 39.00 120.00 275.00
4-Color 44('43) 36.00 107.00 250.00
4-Color 101('45) 23.00 70.00 160.00
Buster Brown Shoes giveaway(1938)-32 pgs.; in color 20.00 60.00 140.00

	GD25	FN65	NM94
Canada Dry Premiums-Books #1-3(1953-Harvey)-36 pgs.; 2x5"	6.70	20.00	40.00
Family Album(1942)	11.00	32.00	75.00
Gambles Giveaway (1938)-16 pgs.	4.70	14.00	28.00
Gillmore Giveaway(1938)-24 pgs.	5.35	16.00	32.00
Popped Wheat Giveaway(1938)-Strip reprints in full color; Caniff-a	1.00	2.50	5.00
Shoe Store giveaway (Weatherbird)(1938, 16 pgs., soft-c)(2-diff.)	5.85	17.50	35.00
Sparked Wheat Giveaway(1942)-16 pgs. in color	5.85	17.50	35.00

TERRY AND THE PIRATES
1941 (16 pgs.; regular size)
Libby's Radio Premium

	GD25	FN65	NM94
"Adventure of the Ruby of Genghis Khan" - Each pg. is a puzzle that must be completed to read the story	43.00	130.00	300.00

TERRY AND THE PIRATES (Formerly Boy Explorers; Long John Silver & the Pirates #30 on) (Daily strip-r) (Two #26's)
No. 3, 4/47 - No. 26, 4/51; No. 26, 6/55 - No. 28, 10/55
Harvey Publications/Charlton No. 26-28

	GD25	FN65	NM94
3(#1)-Boy Explorers by S&K; Terry & the Pirates begin by Caniff	22.00	65.00	150.00
4-S&K Boy Explorers	14.00	43.00	100.00
5-10	8.35	25.00	50.00
11-Man in Black app. by Powell	8.35	25.00	50.00
12-20: 16-Girl threatened with red hot poker	6.70	20.00	40.00
21-26(4/51)-Last Caniff issue	5.85	17.50	35.00
26-28('55)(Formerly This Is Suspense)-Not by Caniff	5.00	15.00	28.00

NOTE: ***Powell** a (Tommy Tween)-5-10, 12, 14; 15-17(-2 pgs.).*

TERRY BEARS COMICS (TerryToons, The... #4)
June, 1952 - No. 3, Oct, 1952
St. John Publishing Co.

	GD25	FN65	NM94
1	4.00	10.00	20.00
2,3	3.20	8.00	16.00

TERRY-TOONS COMICS (1st Series) (Becomes Paul Terry's Comics #85 on; later issues titled "Paul Terry's...") (See Giant Comics Edition)
Oct, 1942 - No. 86, May, 1951
Timely/Marvel No. 1-59 (8/47)(Becomes Best Western No. 58 on?, Marvel)/ St. John No. 60 (9/47) on

	GD25	FN65	NM94
1 (Scarce)-Features characters that 1st app. on movie screen; Gandy Goose begins	75.00	225.00	525.00
2	36.00	107.00	250.00
3-5	23.00	70.00	160.00
6-10: 7-Hitler, Hirohito, Mussolini-c	16.00	48.00	110.00
11-20	11.00	32.00	75.00
21-37	8.35	25.00	50.00
38-Mighty Mouse begins (1st app., 11/45)	68.00	205.00	475.00
39-2nd app. Mighty Mouse	19.00	57.00	130.00
40-49: 43-Infinity-c	10.00	30.00	60.00
50-1st app. Heckle & Jeckle	22.00	65.00	150.00
51-60: 55-Infinity-c. 60(9/47)-Atomic explosion panel; 1st St. John issue	7.50	22.50	45.00
61-84	5.00	15.00	30.00
85,86-Same book as Paul Terry's Comics #85,86 with only a title change; published at same time?	5.00	15.00	30.00

TERRY-TOONS COMICS (2nd Series)
June, 1952 - No. 9, Nov, 1953
St. John Publishing Co./Pines

	GD25	FN65	NM94
1	10.00	30.00	60.00
2	5.00	15.00	30.00
3-9	4.20	12.50	25.00
Giant Summer Fun Book 101,102(Summer, 1957, Summer, 1958)(TV; Tom Terrific app.)	6.70	20.00	40.00

TERRYTOONS, THE TERRY BEARS (Formerly Terry Bears)
No. 4, Summer, 1958
Pines Comics

	GD25	FN65	NM94
4	3.00	7.50	15.00

TESSIE THE TYPIST (Tiny Tessie #24; see Comedy Comics, Gay Comics & Joker Comics)
Summer, 1944 - No. 23, Aug, 1949
Timely/Marvel Comics (20CC)

	GD25	FN65	NM94
1-Doc Rockblock & others by Wolverton	32.00	95.00	225.00
2-Wolverton's Powerhouse Pepper	19.00	57.00	135.00
3-No Wolverton	6.70	20.00	40.00
4,5,7,8-Wolverton-a	11.50	34.00	80.00
6-Kurtzman's "Hey Look," 2 pgs. Wolverton	12.00	36.00	85.00
9-Wolverton's Powerhouse Pepper (8 pgs.) & 1 pg. Kurtzman's "Hey Look	15.00	45.00	105.00
10-Wolverton's Powerhouse Pepper (4 pgs.)	13.50	41.00	95.00
11-Wolverton's Powerhouse Pepper (8 pgs.)	15.00	45.00	105.00
12-Wolverton's Powerhouse Pepper (4 pgs.) & 1 pg. Kurtzman's "Hey Look"	13.50	41.00	95.00
13-Wolverton's Powerhouse Pepper (4 pgs.)	13.00	40.00	90.00
14-Wolverton's Dr. Whackyhack (1 pg.); 1 pgs. Kurtzman's "Hey Look"	10.00	30.00	65.00
15-Kurtzman's "Hey Look" (3 pgs.) & 3 pgs. Giggles 'n' Grins	10.00	30.00	70.00
16-18-Kurtzman's "Hey Look" (?, 2 & 1 pg.)	7.50	22.50	45.00
19-Annie Oakley story (8 pgs.)	5.85	17.50	35.00
20-23: 20-Anti-Wertham editorial (2/49)	5.00	15.00	30.00

NOTE: *Lana app.-21. Millie The Model app.-13, 15, 17, 21. Rusty app.-10, 11, 13, 15, 17.*

TEXAN, THE (Fightin' Marines #15 on; Fightin' Texan #16 on)
Aug, 1948 - No. 15, Oct, 1951
St. John Publishing Co.

	GD25	FN65	NM94
1-Buckskin Belle	10.00	30.00	65.00
2	5.35	16.00	32.00
3,10: 10-Oversized issue	4.70	14.00	28.00
4,5,7,15-Baker-c/a	8.35	25.00	50.00
6,9-Baker-c	5.35	16.00	32.00
8,11,13,14-Baker-c/a(2-3) each	8.35	25.00	50.00
12-All Matt Baker; Peyote story	10.00	30.00	65.00

NOTE: ***Matt Baker** c-4-15. **Larsen** a-4-6, 8-10. **Tuska** a-1, 2, 7-9.*

TEXAN, THE (See 4-Color #1027, 1096)

TEXAS JOHN SLAUGHTER (See 4-Color #997, 1181 & Walt Disney Presents #2)

TEXAS KID (See Two-Gun Western, Wild Western)
Jan, 1951 - No. 10, July, 1952
Marvel/Atlas Comics (LMC)

	GD25	FN65	NM94
1-Origin; Texas Kid (alias Lance Temple) & his horse Thunder begin; Tuska-a	11.00	32.00	75.00
2	6.35	19.00	38.00
3-10	5.00	15.00	30.00

NOTE: ***Maneely** a-1-4; c-1, 3, 5-10.*

TEXAS RANGERS, THE (See Jace Pearson of... and Superior Stories #4)

TEXAS RANGERS IN ACTION (Formerly Captain Gallant or Scotland Yard?)
No. 5, July, 1956 - No. 79, Aug, 1970 (See Blue Bird Comics)
Charlton Comics

	GD25	FN65	NM94
5	4.70	14.00	28.00
6-10	3.20	8.00	16.00
11-Williamson-a(5&8 pgs.); Torres/Williamson-a (5 pgs.)	5.00	15.00	30.00
12,14-20	2.00	5.00	10.00
13-Williamson-a (5 pgs); Torres, Morisi-a	4.00	12.00	24.00
21-30: 30-Last 10 cent issue?	1.60	4.00	8.00
31-59	1.20	3.00	6.00
60-Riley's Rangers begin	.80	2.00	4.00

Terry-Toons Comics #1, © Paul Terry

Tessie the Typist #18, © MEG

The Texan #8, © STJ

Tex Granger #21, © PMI

Tex Ritter Western #17, © FAW

The Thanos Quest #2, © MEG

GD25 FN65 NM94

61-70: 65-1st app. The Man Called Loco, origin in #67 .60 1.50 3.00
71-79 .40 1.00 2.00
76(Modern Comics-r, 1977) .50 1.00

TEXAS SLIM (See A-1 Comics #2-8,10)

TEX DAWSON, GUN-SLINGER (Gunslinger #2 on)
January, 1973 (20 cents)(Also see Western Kid, 1st series)
Marvel Comics Group

1-Steranko-c; Williamson-r(4 pgs.); Tex Dawson-r by Romita(3) from 1955 .30 .75 1.50

TEX FARNUM (See Wisco)

TEX FARRELL
Mar-Apr, 1948
D. S. Publishing Co.

1-Tex Farrell & his horse Lightning; Shelly-c 9.15 27.50 55.00

TEX GRANGER (Formerly Calling All Boys; see True Comics)
No. 18, June, 1948 - No. 24, Sept, 1949
Parents' Magazine Institute/Commended

18-Tex Granger & his horse Bullet begin 7.50 22.50 45.00
19 5.85 17.50 35.00
20-24: 22-Wild Bill Hickok story 5.00 15.00 30.00

TEX MORGAN (See Blaze Carson and Wild Western)
Aug, 1948 - No. 9, Feb, 1950
Marvel Comics (CCC)

1-Tex Morgan, his horse Lightning & sidekick Lobo begin 13.50 41.00 95.00
2 10.00 30.00 70.00
3-6: 3,4-Arizona Annie app. 8.35 25.00 50.00
7-9: All photo-c. 7-Captain Tootsie by Beck. 8-18pg. story "The Terror of Rimrock Valley;" Diablo app. 11.00 32.00 75.00

NOTE: *Tex Taylor app.-6, 7, 9.* ***Brodsky*** *c-6.* ***Syd Shores*** *c-2, 5.*

TEX RITTER WESTERN (Movie star; singing cowboy; see Six-Gun Heroes and Western Hero)
Oct, 1950 - No. 46, May, 1959 (Photo-c: 1-21)
Fawcett No. 1-20 (1/54)/Charlton No. 21 on

1-Tex Ritter, his stallion White Flash & dog Fury begin; photo front/back-c begin 43.00 130.00 300.00
2 19.00 58.00 135.00
3-5: 5-Last photo back-c 16.00 48.00 110.00
6-10 13.00 40.00 90.00
11-19 8.50 25.50 60.00
20-Last Fawcett issue (1/54) 10.00 30.00 70.00
21-1st Charlton issue; photo-c (3/54) 11.50 34.00 80.00
22-B&W photo back-c begin, end #32 7.00 21.00 42.00
23-30: 23-25-Young Falcon app. 5.85 17.50 35.00
31-38,40-45 5.00 15.00 30.00
39-Williamson-a; Whitman-c (1/58) 6.70 20.00 40.00
46-Last issue 5.85 17.50 35.00

TEX TAYLOR (See Blaze Carson, Kid Colt, Tex Morgan, Wild West, Wild Western, & Wisco)
Sept, 1948 - No. 9, March, 1950
Marvel Comics (HPC)

1-Tex Taylor & his horse Fury begin 14.00 43.00 100.00
2 10.00 30.00 65.00
3 10.00 30.00 60.00
4-6: All photo-c. 4-Anti-Wertham editorial. 5,6-Blaze Carson app. 10.00 30.00 65.00
7-Photo-c; 18pg. Movie-Length Thriller "Trapped in Time's Lost Land!" with sabre toothed tigers, dinosaurs; Diablo app. 11.00 32.00 75.00
8-Photo-c; 18pg. Movie-Length Thriller "The Mystery of Devil-Tree Plateau!" with dwarf horses, dwarf people & a lost miniature Inca type village; Diablo app. 11.00 32.00 75.00
9-Photo-c; 18pg. Movie-Length Thriller "Guns Along the Border!" Captain Tootsie by Schreiber; Nimo The Mountain Lion app. 11.00 32.00 75.00

NOTE: ***Syd Shores*** *c-1-3.*

THANE OF BAGARTH (Also see Hercules, 1967 series)
No. 24, Oct, 1985 - No. 25, Dec, 1985
Charlton Comics

24,25 .50 1.00

THANOS QUEST, THE (See Capt. Marvel #25, Infinity Gauntlet, Iron Man #55, Logan's Run, Marvel Feature #12, Silver Surfer #34 & Warlock #9)
1990 - No. 2, 1990 ($4.95, color, squarebound, 52 pgs.)
Marvel Comics

1-Both have Starlin scripts & covers 3.00 7.50 15.00
2 2.00 5.00 10.00
1,2-2nd printings ($4.95) 1.00 2.50 5.00

THAT DARN CAT (See Movie Comics & Walt Disney Showcase #19)

THAT'S MY POP! GOES NUTS FOR FAIR
1939 (76 pages) (B&W)
Bystander Press

nn-by Milt Gross 17.00 50.00 100.00

THAT THE WORLD MAY BELIEVE
No date (16 pgs.) (Graymoor Friars distr.)
Catechetical Guild Giveaway

nn 1.60 4.00 8.00

THAT WILKIN BOY (Meet Bingo...)
Jan, 1969 - No. 52, Oct, 1982
Archie Publications

1 2.40 6.00 12.00
2-10 1.20 3.00 6.00
11-26: 26-Last Giant issue .80 2.00 4.00
27-52 .40 1.00 2.00

T.H.E. CAT (TV)
Mar, 1967 - No. 4, Oct, 1967 (All have photo-c)
Dell Publishing Co.

1 3.60 9.00 18.00
2-4 2.40 6.00 12.00

THERE'S A NEW WORLD COMING (Spire Christian)(Value: cover or less)

THEY ALL KISSED THE BRIDE (See Cinema Comics Herald)

THEY RING THE BELL
1946
Fox Feature Syndicate

1 10.00 30.00 60.00

THIEF OF BAGHDAD (See 4-Color #1229)

THIMBLE THEATRE STARRING POPEYE
1931 - No. 2, 1932 (52 pgs.; 25 cents; B&W)
Sonnet Publishing Co.

1-Daily strip serial-r in both by Segar 72.00 215.00 500.00
2 57.00 170.00 400.00

NOTE: *Probably the first Popeye reprint book. Popeye first entered Thimble Theatre in 1929.*

THIMK (Magazine) (Satire)
May, 1958 - No. 6, May, 1959
Counterpoint

1 4.70 14.00 28.00
2-6 3.20 8.00 16.00

THING!, THE (Blue Beetle #18 on)

Feb, 1952 - No. 17, Nov, 1954
Song Hits No. 1,2/Capitol Stories/Charlton

	GD25	FN65	NM94
1	36.00	107.00	250.00
2,3	27.00	81.00	190.00
4-6,8,10: 5-Severed head-c; headlights	19.00	57.00	135.00
7-Injury to eye-c & inside panel. E.C. swipes from Vault of Horror #28	36.00	107.00	250.00
9-Used in **SOTI**, pg. 388 & illo-"Stomping on the face is a form of brutality which modern children learn early"	37.00	110.00	260.00
11-Necronomicon story; Hansel & Gretel parody; Injury-to-eye panel; Check-a	32.00	95.00	220.00
12-"Cinderella" parody; Ditko-c/a; lingerie panels	43.00	130.00	300.00
13,15-Ditko c/a(3 & 5); 13-Ditko E.C. swipe/Haunt of Fear #15(#1)-"House of Horror"	43.00	130.00	300.00
14-Extreme violence/torture; Rumpelstiltskin story; Ditko-c/a(4)	43.00	130.00	300.00
16-Injury to eye panel	24.00	73.00	170.00
17-Ditko-c; classic parody-"Through the Looking Glass;" Powell-a(r)	36.00	107.00	250.00

NOTE: *Excessive violence, severed heads, injury to eye are common No. 5 on.* ***Al Fago*** *c-4.* ***Forgione*** *c-1i, 2, 6, 8, 9.* ***Palais*** *c-16.*

THING, THE (See Fantastic Four, Marvel Fanfare, Marvel Feature #11, 12 & Marvel Two-In-One)
July, 1983 - No. 36, June, 1986
Marvel Comics Group

	GD25	FN65	NM94
1-Life story of Ben Grimm; Byrne scripts begin	.40	1.00	2.00
2-36: 5-Spider-Man, She-Hulk app.		.60	1.20

NOTE: ***Byrne*** *a-2i, 7; c-1, 7, 36i; scripts-1-13, 19-22.* ***Sienkiewicz*** *c-13i.*

THING, THE (From Another World)
1991 - No. 2, 1992 ($2.95, color, mini-series, stiff-c)
Dark Horse Comics

	GD25	FN65	NM94
1,2-Based on Universal movie; painted-c/a	.60	1.50	3.00

THING FROM ANOTHER WORLD: CLIMATE OF FEAR, THE
July, 1992 - No. 4, Dec, 1992 ($2.50, color, mini-series)
Dark Horse Comics

	GD25	FN65	NM94
1-4: Painted-c	.50	1.25	2.50

THIRD WORLD WAR (Fleetway)(Value: cover or less)

THIRTEEN (...Going on 18)
11-1/61-62 - No. 25, 12/67; No. 26, 7/69 - No. 29, 1/71
Dell Publishing Co.

	GD25	FN65	NM94
1	5.35	16.00	32.00
2-10	4.20	12.50	25.00
11-29: 26-29-r	3.60	9.00	18.00

NOTE: ***John Stanley*** *script-No. 3-29; art?*

13: ASSASSIN (TSR)(Value: cover or less)

THIRTY SECONDS OVER TOKYO (Also see Guadacanal Diary)
1943 (Movie) (Also see American Library)
David McKay Co.

	GD25	FN65	NM94
nn-(B&W, text & pictures)	27.00	80.00	185.00

THIS IS SUSPENSE! (Formerly Strange Suspense Stories; Strange Suspense Stories #27 on)
No. 23, Feb, 1955 - No. 26, Aug, 1955
Charlton Comics

	GD25	FN65	NM94
23-Wood-a(r)/A Star Presentation #3-"Dr. Jekyll & Mr. Hyde"	13.00	40.00	90.00
24-Evans-a	8.35	25.00	50.00
25,26: 26-Marcus Swayze-a	5.35	16.00	32.00

THIS IS THE PAYOFF (See Pay-Off)

THIS IS WAR
No. 5, July, 1952 - No. 9, May, 1953
Standard Comics

	GD25	FN65	NM94
5-Toth-a	9.15	27.50	55.00
6,9-Toth-a	7.50	22.50	45.00
7,8: 8-Ross Andru-c	3.00	7.50	15.00

THIS IS YOUR LIFE, DONALD DUCK (See 4-Color #1109)

THIS MAGAZINE IS CRAZY (Crazy #? on)
V3#2, July, 1957 - V4#8, Feb, 1959 (25 cents, magazine, 68 pgs.)
Charlton Publ. (Humor Magazines)

	GD25	FN65	NM94
V3#2-V4#7: V4#5-Russian Sputnik-c parody	3.60	9.00	18.00
V4#8-Davis-a (8 pgs.)	4.20	12.50	25.00

THIS MAGAZINE IS HAUNTED (Danger and Adventure #22 on)
Oct, 1951 - No. 14, 12/53; No. 15, 2/54 - V3#21, Nov, 1954
Fawcett Publications/Charlton No. 15(2/54) on

	GD25	FN65	NM94
1-Evans-a(i?)	27.00	81.00	190.00
2,5-Evans-a	19.00	57.00	130.00
3,4	10.00	30.00	65.00
6-9,11,12,14	8.35	25.00	50.00
10-Severed head-c	12.00	36.00	85.00
13-Severed head-c/story	11.50	34.00	80.00
15,20	7.50	22.50	45.00
16,19-Ditko-c. 19-Injury-to-eye panel; story-r/#1	13.50	41.00	95.00
17-Ditko-c/a(4); blood drainage story	19.00	57.00	130.00
18-Ditko-c/a(1 story); E.C. swipe/Haunt of Fear #5; injury-to-eye panel	16.00	48.00	110.00
21-Ditko-c, Evans-a	12.00	36.00	85.00

NOTE: ***Baily*** *a-1, 3, 4, 21r/#1.* ***Powell*** *a-3-5, 11, 12, 17.* ***Shuster*** *a-18-20.*

THIS MAGAZINE IS HAUNTED (2nd Series) (Formerly Zaza the Mystic; Outer Space #17 on)
V2#12, July, 1957 - V2#16, April, 1958
Charlton Comics

	GD25	FN65	NM94
V2#12-14-Ditko-c/a in all	16.00	48.00	110.00
15-No Ditko-c/a	3.60	9.00	18.00
16-Ditko-a	11.00	32.00	75.00

THIS MAGAZINE IS WILD (See Wild)

THIS WAS YOUR LIFE (Chick)(Value: cover or less)

THOR (See Avengers #1, Giant-Size..., Marvel Collectors Item Classics, Marvel Graphic Novel 33, Marvel Preview, Marvel Spectacular, Marvel Treasury Edition, Special Marvel Edition & Tales of Asgard)

THOR (Formerly Journey Into Mystery)(The Mighty Thor #413 on)
March, 1966 - Present
Marvel Comics Group

	GD25	FN65	NM94
126-Thor continues (125-130 Thor vs. Hercules)	12.00	36.00	85.00
127-133,135-140: 127-1st app. Pluto	6.35	19.00	38.00
134-Intro High Evolutionary	8.35	25.00	50.00
141-157,159,160: 146-Inhumans begin, end #151. 146,147-Origin The Inhumans. 148,149-Origin Black Bolt in each; 149-Origin Medusa, Crystal, Maximus, Gorgon, Kornak	4.20	12.50	25.00
158-Origin-r/#83; 158,159-Origin Dr. Blake (Thor)	9.15	27.50	55.00
161,163,167,170-179-Last Kirby issue	3.20	8.00	16.00
162,168,169-Origin Galactus	4.70	14.00	28.00
164-Brief cameo Warlock (Him) (5/69)	3.60	9.00	18.00
165-1st full app Warlock (Him) (6/69, 2nd since Fantastic Four #66,67); last 12 cent issue	6.70	20.00	40.00
166-2nd full app. Warlock (Him); battles Thor	5.85	17.50	35.00
180,181-Neal Adams-a	2.00	5.00	10.00
182-192,194-200	1.00	2.50	5.00
193-(25 cents, 52 pgs.); Silver Surfer x-over	5.00	15.00	30.00
201-250: 225-Intro. Firelord	.70	1.75	3.50
251-280: 271-Iron Man x-over. 274-Death of Balder the Brave	.50	1.25	2.50
281-299: 294-Origin Asgard & Odin	.40	1.00	2.00
300-(12/80)-End of Asgard; origin of Odin & The Destroyer	1.00	2.50	5.00

The Thing! #10, © CC

This Magazine Is Haunted #2, © FAW

Thor #131, © MEG

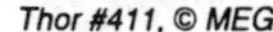
Thor #411, © MEG

3-D Circus #1, © FH

3-D Dolly #1, © HARV

	GD25	FN65	NM94
301-336: 316-Iron Man x-over	.30	.75	1.50
337-Simonson-c/a begins, ends #382; Beta Ray Bill becomes new Thor	1.00	2.50	5.00
338-Two variants exist, 60 & 75 cents	.50	1.25	2.50
339,340: 340-Donald Blake returns as Thor	.30	.75	1.50
341-373,375-381,383: 373-X-Factor tie-in		.50	1.00
374-Mutant Massacre; X-Factor app.	1.60	4.00	8.00
382-($1.25)-Anniversary issue; last Simonson-a	.40	1.00	2.00
384-Intro. new Thor	.40	1.00	2.00
385-399,401-410,413-428: 385-Hulk x-over. 391-Spider-Man x-over. 395-Intro Earth Force. 408-Eric Masterson becomes Thor. 427,428-Excalibur x-over		.50	1.00
400-($1.75, 68 pgs.)-Origin Loki	.50	1.25	2.50
411-Intro New Warriors (apps. in costume in last panel); Juggernaut-c/story	.60	1.50	3.00
412-1st full app. New Warriors (Marvel Boy, Kid Nova, Namorita, Night Thrasher, Firestar & Speedball)	3.60	9.00	18.00
429,430-Ghost Rider x-over	.60	1.50	3.00
431,434-443: 434-Capt. America x-over. 437-Thor vs. Quasar; Hercules app.; Tales of Asgard back-up stories begin. 443-Dr. Strange & Silver Surfer x-over; last $1.00-c		.60	1.25
432-($1.50, 52 pgs.)-Thor's 300th app. (vs. Loki); reprints origin & 1st app. from Journey into Mystery #83	.60	1.50	3.00
433-Intro new Thor	.60	1.50	3.00
444-449,451-462: 448-Spider-Man-c/story. 455-Dr. Strange back-up. 459-Intro Thunderstrike. 460-Starlin scripts begin; old Thor returns		.60	1.25
450-($2.50, 68 pgs.)-Flip-book format; r/story JIM #87 plus-c (1st Loki) & a gallery of past-c; gatefold-c	.60	1.50	3.00
Special 2(9/66)-See Journey Into Mystery for 1st annual	6.70	20.00	40.00
King Size Special 3(1/71)	1.60	4.00	8.00
Special 4(12/71)-r/Thor #131,132 & JIM #113	1.60	4.00	8.00
Annual 5,7,8: 5(11/76). 7(1978). 8(1979)	1.20	3.00	6.00
Annual 6 (10/77)-Guardians of the Galaxy app.	1.20	3.00	6.00
Annual 9-12: 9('81). 10('82). 11('83). 12('84)	.60	1.50	3.00
Annual 13-16: 13(1985). 14('89, $2.00, 68 pgs.)-Atlantis Attacks. 15('90, $2.00, 68 pgs.). 16('91, $2.00, 68 pgs.)-3 pg. origin; Guardians of the Galaxy x-over	.40	1.00	2.00
Annual 17 (1992, $2.25, 68 pgs.)	.45	1.15	2.25
...Alone Against the Celestials nn (6/92, $5.95)-r/Thor #387-389	1.20	3.00	6.00

NOTE: ***Neal Adams** a-180,181; c-179-181. **Austin** a-342i, 346i; c-312i. **Buscema** a(p)-178, 182-213, 215-226, 231-238, 241-253, 254r, 256-259, 272-278, 283-285, 370, Annual 6, 8, 11i; c(p)-175, 182-196, 198-200, 202-204, 206, 211, 212, 215, 219, 221, 226, 256, 259, 261, 262, 272-278, 283, 289, 370, Annual 6. **Everett** a(i)-143, 170-175; c(i)-171, 172, 174, 176, 241. **Gil Kane** a-318p; c(p)-201, 205, 207-210, 216, 220, 222, 223, 231, 233-240, 242, 243, 318. **Kirby** a(p)-126-177, 179, 194, 254r; c(p)-126-169, 171-174, 176-178, 249-253, 255, 257, 258, Annual 5, Special 1-4. **Mooney** a(i)-201, 204, 214-216, 218, 322i, 324i, 325i, 327i. **Sienkiewicz** c-332, 333, 335. **Simonson** a-260-271p, 337-354, 357-367, 380, Annual 7p; c-260, 263-271, 337-355, 357-369, 371, 373-382, Annual 7. **Starlin** c-213.*

THOSE MAGNIFICENT MEN IN THEIR FLYING MACHINES (See Movie Comics)

THREE CABALLEROS (See 4-Color #71)

THREE CHIPMUNKS, THE (See 4-Color #1042)

THREE COMICS (Also see Spiritman)
1944 (10 cents, 48pgs.) (2 different covers exist)
The Penny King Co.

	GD25	FN65	NM94
1,3,4-Lady Luck, Mr. Mystic, The Spirit app. (3 Spirit sections bound together)-Lou Fine-a	17.00	52.00	120.00

NOTE: *No. 1 contains Spirit Sections 4/9/44 - 4/23/44, and No. 4 is also from 4/44.*

3-D (NOTE: The prices of all the 3-D comics listed include glasses. Deduct 40-50 percent if glasses are missing, and reduce slightly if glasses are loose.)

3-D ACTION
Jan, 1954 (Oversized) (15 cents)(2 pairs of glasses included)
Atlas Comics (ACI)

	GD25	FN65	NM94
1-Battle Brady; Sol Brodsky-c	32.00	95.00	220.00

3-D ADVENTURE COMICS (Stats)(Value: cover or less)

3-D ALIEN TERROR (Eclipse)(Value: cover or less)

3-D ANIMAL FUN (See Animal Fun)

3-D BATMAN (Also see Batman 3-D)
1953, Reprinted in 1966
National Periodical Publications

	GD25	FN65	NM94
1953-Reprints Batman #42 & 48(Penguin-c/story); Tommy Tomorrow app. (25 cents)	92.00	275.00	635.00
1966-Tommy Tomorrow app.; Penguin-c/story(r); has inside-c photos of Batman & Robin from TV show (50 cents)	30.00	90.00	210.00

3-D CIRCUS
1953 (25 cents)
Fiction House Magazines (Real Adventures Publ.)

	GD25	FN65	NM94
1	32.00	95.00	220.00

3-D COMICS (See Mighty Mouse and Tor)

3-D DOLLY
December, 1953 (2 pairs glasses included)
Harvey Publications

	GD25	FN65	NM94
1-Richie Rich story redrawn from his 1st app. in Little Dot #1	19.00	57.00	130.00

3-D-ELL
1953 - No. 3, 1953 (3-D comics) (25 cents)
Dell Publishing Co.

	GD25	FN65	NM94
1,2-Rootie Kazootie	32.00	95.00	225.00
3-Flukey Luke	30.00	90.00	210.00

3-D EXOTIC BEAUTIES (3-D Zone)(Value: cover or less)

3-D FEATURES PRESENT JET PUP
Oct-Dec, 1953
Dimensions Public

	GD25	FN65	NM94
1-Irving Spector-a(2)	32.00	95.00	220.00

3-D FUNNY MOVIES
1953 (25 cents)
Comic Media

	GD25	FN65	NM94
1-Bugsey Bear & Paddy Pelican	32.00	95.00	220.00

THREE-DIMENSION ADVENTURES (Superman)
1953 (Large size)
National Periodical Publications

	GD25	FN65	NM94
nn-Origin Superman (new art)	90.00	270.00	630.00

THREE DIMENSIONAL ALIEN WORLDS (Pacific)(Value: cover or less)

THREE DIMENSIONAL DNAGENTS (See New DNAgents)

THREE DIMENSIONAL E. C. CLASSICS (Three Dimensional Tales From the Crypt No. 2)
Spring, 1954 (Prices include glasses; came with 2 pairs)
E. C. Comics

	GD25	FN65	NM94
1-Stories by Wood (Mad #3), Krigstein (W.S. #7), Evans (F.C. #13), & Ingels (CSS #5); Kurtzman-c	60.00	180.00	420.00

NOTE: *Stories redrawn to 3-D format. Original stories not necessarily by artists listed. CSS: Crime SuspenStories; F.C.: Frontline Combat; W.S.: Weird Science.*

THREE DIMENSIONAL TALES FROM THE CRYPT (Formerly Three Dimensional E. C. Classics)(Cover title: ...From the Crypt of Terror)
No. 2, Spring, 1954 (Prices include glasses; came with 2 pair)
E. C. Comics

2-Davis (TFTC #25), Elder (VOH #14), Craig (TFTC #24), & Orlando

	GD25	FN65	NM94
(TFTC #22) stories; Feldstein-c	60.00	180.00	420.00

NOTE: *Stories redrawn to 3-D format. Original stories not necessarily by artists listed. TFTC: Tales From the Crypt; VOH: Vault of Horror.*

3-D LOVE
December, 1953 (25 cents)
Steriographic Publ. (Mikeross Publ.)

	GD25	FN65	NM94
1	32.00	95.00	220.00

3-D NOODNICK (See Noodnick)

3-D ROMANCE
January, 1954 (25 cents)
Steriographic Publ. (Mikeross Publ.)

	GD25	FN65	NM94
1	32.00	95.00	220.00

3-D SHEENA, JUNGLE QUEEN (Also see Sheena 3-D)
1953
Fiction House Magazines

	GD25	FN65	NM94
1-Maurice Whitman-c	54.00	160.00	375.00

3-D SUBSTANCE (3-D Zone) (Value: cover or less)

3-D TALES OF THE WEST
Jan, 1954 (Oversized) (15 cents)(2 pair glasses included)
Atlas Comics (CPS)

	GD25	FN65	NM94
1 (3-D)-Sol Brodsky-c	32.00	95.00	220.00

3-D THREE STOOGES (Eclipse) (Value: cover or less)

3-D WHACK (See Whack)

3-D ZONE, THE (3-D Zone) (Value: cover or less)

3 FUNMAKERS, THE
1908 (64 pgs.) (10x15")
Stokes and Company

	GD25	FN65	NM94
nn-Maude, Katzenjammer Kids, Happy Hooligan (1904-06 Sunday strip reprints in color)	40.00	120.00	240.00

3 LITTLE PIGS (See 4-Color #218)

3 LITTLE PIGS, THE (See Walt Disney Showcase #15 & 21)
May, 1964; No. 2, Sept, 1968 (Walt Disney)
Gold Key

	GD25	FN65	NM94
1-Reprints 4-Color #218	2.40	6.00	12.00
2	1.60	4.00	8.00

THREE MOUSEKETEERS, THE (1st Series)
3-4/56 - No. 24, 9-10/59; No. 25, 8-9/60 - No. 26, 10-12/60
National Periodical Publications

	GD25	FN65	NM94
1	14.00	43.00	100.00
2	8.35	25.00	50.00
3-10	6.70	20.00	40.00
11-26: 24-Cover says 11/59, inside says 9-10/59	5.00	15.00	30.00

NOTE: ***Rube Grossman** a-1-26. **Sheldon Mayer** a-1-8; c-1, 3, 4, 6, 7.*

THREE MOUSEKETEERS, THE (2nd Series) (See Super DC Giant)
May-June, 1970 - No. 7, May-June, 1971 (#5-7: 68 pgs.)
National Periodical Publications

	GD25	FN65	NM94
1-Mayer-r in all	1.60	4.00	8.00
2-7: 5-Dodo & the Frog, Bo Bunny & Doodles Duck begin	.80	2.00	4.00

THREE NURSES (Confidential Diary #12-17; Career Girl Romances #24 on)
V3#18, May, 1963 - V3#23, Mar, 1964
Charlton Comics

	GD25	FN65	NM94
V3#18-23	.80	2.00	4.00

THREE RASCALS
1958; 1963
I. W. Enterprises

	GD25	FN65	NM94
I.W. Reprint #1,2,10: 1-(Says Super Comics on inside)-(M.E.'s Clubhouse Rascals). #2-(1958). 10-(1963)-r/#1	.40	1.00	2.00

THREE RING COMICS
March, 1945
Spotlight Publishers

	GD25	FN65	NM94
1	7.00	21.00	50.00

THREE ROCKETEERS (See Blast-Off)

THREE STOOGES (See Comic Album #18, The Little Stooges, March of Comics #232, 248, 268, 280, 292, 304, 316, 336, 373, Movie Classics & Comics & 3-D Three Stooges)

THREE STOOGES
Feb, 1949 - No. 2, May, 1949; Sept, 1953 - No. 7, Oct, 1954
Jubilee No. 1,2/St. John No. 1 (9/53) on

	GD25	FN65	NM94
1-(Scarce, 1949)-Kubert-a; infinity-c	64.00	193.00	450.00
2-(Scarce)-Kubert, Maurer-a	54.00	160.00	375.00
1(9/53)-Hollywood Stunt Girl by Kubert, 7 pgs.	47.00	140.00	325.00
2(3-D, 10/53)-Stunt Girl story by Kubert	32.00	95.00	225.00
3(3-D, 11/53)	32.00	95.00	225.00
4(3/54)-7(10/54): 7-Part photo-c	25.00	75.00	175.00

NOTE: *All issues have **Kubert-Maurer** art. **Maurer** c-1, 2('49), 1('53).*

THREE STOOGES
No. 1043, Oct-Dec, 1959 - No. 55, June, 1972
Dell Publishing Co./Gold Key No. 10 (10/62) on

	GD25	FN65	NM94
4-Color 1043 (#1)	14.00	43.00	100.00
4-Color 1078,1127,1170,1187	8.35	25.00	50.00
6(9-11/61) - 10: 6-Professor Putter begins; ends #16	6.70	20.00	40.00
11-14,16-20: 17-The Little Monsters begin (5/64)(1st app.?)	5.85	17.50	35.00
15-Go Around the World in a Daze (movie scenes)	6.70	20.00	40.00
21,23-30	5.00	15.00	30.00
22-Movie scenes/"The Outlaws Is Coming"	5.85	17.50	35.00
31-55	4.20	12.50	25.00

NOTE: *All Four Colors, 6-50, 52-55 have photo-c.*

THREE STOOGES IN 3-D, THE (Eternity) (Value: cover or less)

3 WORLDS OF GULLIVER (See 4-Color #1158)

THRILL COMICS (See Flash Comics, Fawcett)

THRILLER (DC) (Value: cover or less)

THRILLING ADVENTURES IN STAMPS COMICS
V1#8, Jan, 1953 (25 cents) (100 pages) (Formerly Stamp Comics)
Stamp Comics, Inc. (Very Rare)

	GD25	FN65	NM94
V1#8-Harrison, Wildey, Kiefer, Napoli-a	50.00	150.00	350.00

THRILLING ADVENTURE STORIES (See Tigerman)
Feb, 1975 - No. 2, Aug, 1975 (B&W, 68 pgs.)
Atlas/Seaboard Publ.

	GD25	FN65	NM94
1,2: 1-Tigerman, Kromag the Killer begin; Heath, Thorne-a. 2-Heath, Toth, Severin, Simonson-a; Neal Adams-c	.45	1.20	2.40

THRILLING COMICS
Feb, 1940 - No. 80, April, 1951
Better Publ./Nedor/Standard Comics

	GD25	FN65	NM94
1-Origin Dr. Strange (37 pgs.), ends #?; Nickie Norton of the Secret Service begins	100.00	300.00	600.00
2-The Rio Kid, The Woman in Red, Pinocchio begins	42.00	125.00	250.00
3-The Ghost & Lone Eagle begin	37.00	110.00	220.00
4-10: 5-Dr. Strange changed to Doc Strange	25.00	75.00	150.00
11-18,20	19.00	57.00	115.00
19-Origin The American Crusader (1st app?), ends #39,41	24.00	72.00	165.00
21-30: 24-Intro. Mike, Doc Strange's sidekick. 29-Last Rio Kid	16.00	48.00	110.00
31-40: 36-Commando Cubs begin	12.00	36.00	85.00
41,44-Hitler-c	12.00	36.00	85.00

The Three Mouseketeers #21, © DC

The Three Stooges #39, © Norman Maurer Prod.

Thrilling Comics #13, © STD

Thrilling Crime Cases #48, © STAR

Thrills of Tomorrow #20, © HARV

Thunder Agents #1, © TC

	GD25	FN65	NM94
42,43,45-52: 52-The Ghost ends	10.00	30.00	70.00
53-The Phantom Detective begins; The Cavalier app.; no Commando Cubs	10.00	30.00	70.00
54-The Cavalier app.; no Commando Cubs	10.00	30.00	70.00
55-Lone Eagle ends	10.00	30.00	70.00
56-Princess Pantha begins	19.00	57.00	130.00
57-66: 61-Ingels-a; The Lone Eagle app. 65-Last Phantom Detective & Commando Cubs. 66-Frazetta text illo	16.00	48.00	110.00
67,70-73: Frazetta-a(5-7 pgs.) in each. 72-Sea Eagle app.	19.00	58.00	135.00
68,69-Frazetta-a(2), 8 & 6 pgs.; 9 & 7 pgs.	20.00	60.00	140.00
74-Last Princess Pantha; Tara app. Buck Ranger, Cowboy Detective begins	10.00	30.00	65.00
75-78: 75-Western format begins	5.85	17.50	35.00
79-Krigstein-a	7.50	22.50	45.00
80-Severin & Elder, Celardo, Moreira-a	7.50	22.50	45.00

NOTE: *Bondage c-5, 9, 13, 20, 22, 27-30, 38, 41, 52, 54, 70.* ***Kinstler*** *a-45, 48.* ***Leo Morey*** *a-7.* ***Schomburg*** *(Xela) c-7, 9-19, 36-80 (airbrush 62-71).* ***Tuska*** *a-63. Woman in Red not in #19, 23, 31-33, 39-45. No. 72 exists as a Canadian reprint with no* ***Frazetta*** *story.*

THRILLING CRIME CASES (Formerly 4Most; becomes Shocking Mystery Cases #50 on)
No. 41, June-July, 1950 - No. 49, 1952
Star Publications

	GD25	FN65	NM94
41	9.15	27.50	55.00
42-44-Chameleon story-Fox-r	7.50	22.50	45.00
45-48: 47-Used in **POP**, pg. 84	6.70	20.00	40.00
49-Classic L. B. Cole-c	15.00	45.00	105.00

NOTE: ***L. B. Cole*** *c-all; a-43p, 45p, 46p, 49(2pgs.).* ***Disbrow*** *a-48.* ***Hollingsworth*** *a-48.*

THRILLING ROMANCES
No. 5, Dec, 1949 - No. 26, June, 1954
Standard Comics

	GD25	FN65	NM94
5	6.70	20.00	40.00
6,8	3.60	9.00	18.00
7-Severin/Elder-a, 7 pgs.	4.70	14.00	28.00
9,10-Severin/Elder-a	4.20	12.50	25.00
11,14-21,26: 15-Tony Martin/Janet Leigh photo-c	3.00	7.50	15.00
12-Wood-a, 2 pgs.; photo-c	6.70	20.00	40.00
13-Severin-a	4.00	11.00	22.00
22-25-Toth-a	5.35	16.00	32.00

NOTE: *All photo-c.* ***Celardo*** *a-9, 16.* ***Colletta*** *a-23, 24(2).* ***Tuska*** *a-9.*

THRILLING SCIENCE TALES (AC)(Value: cover or less)

THRILLING TRUE STORY OF THE BASEBALL....
1952 (Photo-c, each)
Fawcett Publications

	GD25	FN65	NM94
...Giants-photo-c; has Willie Mays rookie photo-biography	47.00	140.00	325.00
...Yankees-photo-c	42.00	125.00	290.00

THRILLOGY (Pacific)(Value: cover or less)

THRILL-O-RAMA
Oct, 1965 - No. 3, Dec, 1966
Harvey Publications (Fun Films)

	GD25	FN65	NM94
1-Fate (Man in Black) by Powell app.; Doug Wildey-a(2); Simon-c	1.60	4.00	8.00
2-Pirana begins; Williamson 2 pgs.; Fate (Man in Black) app.; Tuska/Simon-c	1.60	4.00	8.00
3-Fate (Man in Black) app.; Sparling-c	1.00	2.50	5.00

THRILLS OF TOMORROW (Formerly Tomb of Terror)
No. 17, Oct, 1954 - No. 20, April, 1955
Harvey Publications

	GD25	FN65	NM94
17-Powell-a (horror); r/Witches Tales #7	4.70	14.00	28.00
18-Powell-a (horror); r/Tomb of Terror #1	4.00	11.00	22.00
19,20-Stuntman by S&K (r/from Stuntman #1 & 2); 19 has origin & is last pre-code (2/55)	16.00	48.00	110.00

NOTE: ***Kirby*** *c-19, 20.* ***Palais*** *a-17.* ***Simon*** *c-18?*

THROBBING LOVE (See Fox Giants)

THROUGH GATES OF SPLENDOR (Spire Christian)(Value: cover or less)

THUMPER (See 4-Color #19 & 243)

THUN'DA (...King of the Congo)
1952 - No. 6, 1953
Magazine Enterprises

	GD25	FN65	NM94
1(A-1 #47)-Origin; Frazetta c/a; only comic done entirely by Frazetta; all Thun'da stories, no Cave Girl	83.00	250.00	580.00
2(A-1 #56)-Powell-c/a begins, ends #6; Intro/1st app. Cave Girl in filler strip (also app. in 3-6)	12.00	36.00	84.00
3(A-1 #73), 4(A-1 #78)	10.00	30.00	62.00
5(A-1 #83), 6(A-1 #86)	9.35	28.00	56.00

THUN'DA TALES (See Frank Frazetta's...)

THUNDER AGENTS (See Dynamo, Noman & Tales Of Thunder)
11/65 - No. 17, 12/67; No. 18, 9/68, No. 19, 11/68, No. 20, 11/69
(No. 1-16: 68 pgs.; No. 17 on: 52 pgs.)(All are 25 cents)
Tower Comics

	GD25	FN65	NM94
1-Origin & 1st app. Dynamo, Noman, Menthor, & The Thunder Squad; 1st app. The Iron Maiden	10.00	30.00	65.00
2-Death of Egghead	5.85	17.50	35.00
3-5: 4-Guy Gilbert becomes Lightning who joins Thunder Squad; Iron Maiden app.	4.00	12.00	24.00
6-10: 7-Death of Menthor. 8-Origin & 1st app. The Raven	3.00	7.50	15.00
11-15: 13-Undersea Agent app.; no Raven story	2.00	5.00	10.00
16-19	1.60	4.00	8.00
20-Special Collectors Edition; all reprints	.80	2.00	4.00

NOTE: ***Crandall*** *a-1, 4p, 5p, 18, 20r; c-18.* ***Ditko*** *a-6, 7p, 12p, 13?, 14p, 16, 18.* ***Giunta*** *a-6.* ***Kane*** *a-1, 5p, 6p?, 14, 16p; c-14, 15.* ***Reinman*** *a-13.* ***Sekowsky*** *a-6.* ***Tuska*** *a-1p, 7, 8, 10, 13-17, 19.* ***Whitney*** *a-9p, 10, 13, 15, 17, 18; c-17.* ***Wood*** *a-1-11, 15(w/****Ditko****-12, 18), (inks-#9, 13, 14, 16, 17), 19i, 20r; c-1-8, 9i, 10-13(#10 w/****Williamson****(p)), 16.*

T.H.U.N.D.E.R. AGENTS (See Blue Ribbon Comics, Hall of Fame Featuring the..., JCP Features & Wally Wood's...)
May, 1983 - No. 2, Jan, 1984
JC Comics (Archie Publications)

	GD25	FN65	NM94
1,2-New material	.40	1.00	2.00

THUNDER BIRDS (See Cinema Comics Herald)

THUNDERBOLT (See The Atomic...)

THUNDERBOLT (Peter Cannon...; see Crisis on Infinite Earths & Peter...)
Jan, 1966; No. 51, Mar-Apr, 1966 - No. 60, Nov, 1967
Charlton Comics

	GD25	FN65	NM94
1-Origin	2.00	5.00	10.00
51-(Formerly Son of Vulcan #50)	1.00	2.50	5.00
52-59: 54-Sentinels begin. 59-Last Thunderbolt & Sentinels (back-up story)	.80	2.00	4.00
60-Prankster app.	1.00	2.50	5.00
Modern Comics-r. 57,58('77)		.50	1.00

NOTE: ***Aparo*** *a-60.* ***Morisi*** *a-1, 51-56, 58; c-1, 51-56, 58, 59.*

THUNDERBUNNY (Red Circle)(Value: cover or less)(Also see Blue Ribbon Comics #13, Charlton Bullseye & Pep Comics #393)

THUNDER MOUNTAIN (See 4-Color #246)

TICK, THE (Also see The Chroma-Tick)
June, 1988 - Present ($1.75-$1.95-$2.25; B&W, over-sized)
New England Comics Press

	GD25	FN65	NM94
Special Edition 1-1st comic book app. serially numbered & limited to 5000 copies	5.85	17.50	30.00
Special Edition 2-Serially numbered and limited to 3000 copies			

4.20 12.50 25.00
1-Reprints Special Ed. 1 w/minor changes 4.20 12.50 25.00
1-2nd printing .60 1.50 3.00
1-3rd printing ($1.95, 6/89) .40 1.00 2.00
1-4th printing ($2.25) .45 1.15 2.25
1-5th printing ($2.75) .55 1.40 2.75
2-Reprints Special Ed. 2 w/minor changes 3.00 7.50 15.00
2-2nd printing ($1.95) .60 1.50 3.00
2-3rd & 4th printings ($2.25) .45 1.15 2.25
2-5th printing ($2.75) .55 1.40 2.75
3-5 ($1.95): 4-1st app. Paul the Samurai .80 2.00 4.00
3-2nd & 3rd printings ($2.25) .45 1.15 2.25
3-4th printing ($2.75) .55 1.40 2.75
4-2nd printing ($2.25) .45 1.15 2.25
4-3rd - 5th printings ($2.75) .55 1.40 2.75
6-8 ($2.25) .45 1.15 2.25
5-8-2nd printings ($2.75) .55 1.40 2.75
6-3rd printing ($2.75) .55 1.40 2.75
8-Variant with no logo, price, issue number or company logos
1.60 4.00 8.00
9-12 ($2.75) .55 1.40 2.75
The Tick's Giant Circus of the Mighty 1 (Summer, 1992, $2.75, B&W, magazine size) .55 1.40 2.75

TICKLE COMICS (Also see Gay, Smile, & Whee Comics)
1955 (52 pages) (5x7-1/4") (7 cents)
Modern Store Publ.
1 .50 1.25 2.50

TICK TOCK TALES
Jan, 1946 - V3#33, Jan-Feb, 1951
Magazine Enterprises
1-Koko & Kola begin 8.35 25.00 50.00
2 4.35 13.00 26.00
3-10 4.00 10.00 20.00
11-33: 19-Flag-c. 23-Muggsy Mouse, The Pixies & Tom-Tom The Jungle Boy app. 2.80 7.00 14.00

TIGER (Also see Comics Reading Libraries)
March, 1970 - No. 6, Jan, 1971 (15 cents)
Charlton Press (King Features)
1 1.00 2.50 5.00
2-6 .60 1.50 3.00

TIGER BOY (See Unearthly Spectaculars)

TIGER GIRL
September, 1968
Gold Key
1(10227-809)-Sparling-c/a; Jerry Siegel scripts 4.00 10.00 20.00

TIGERMAN (Also see Thrilling Adventure Stories)
April, 1975 - No. 3, Sept, 1975 (All 25 cent issues)
Seaboard Periodicals (Atlas)
1-3: 2,3-Ditko-p in each .50 1.00

TIGER WALKS, A (See Movie Comics)

TILLIE THE TOILER
1925 - No. 8, 1933 (52 pgs.) (B&W daily strip reprints)
Cupples & Leon Co.
nn (#1) 18.00 55.00 110.00
2-8 11.00 32.00 65.00
NOTE: *First strip appearance was January, 1921.*

TILLIE THE TOILER (See Comic Monthly)
No. 15, 1941 - No. 237, July, 1949
Dell Publishing Co.
4-Color 15(1941) 29.00 85.00 200.00
Large Feature Comic 30(1941) 17.00 51.00 120.00
4-Color 8(1942) 17.00 51.00 12.00
4-Color 22(1943) 14.00 43.00 100.00
4-Color 55(1944) 10.00 30.00 70.00
4-Color 89(1945) 10.00 30.00 70.00
4-Color 106('45),132('46) 9.15 27.50 55.00
4-Color 150,176,184 7.50 22.50 45.00
4-Color 195,213,237 5.00 15.00 30.00

TILLY AND TED-TINKERTOTLAND
1945 (Giveaway) (20 pgs.)
W. T. Grant Co.
nn-Christmas comic 4.20 12.50 25.00

TIM (Formerly Superman-Tim; becomes Gene Autry-Tim)
June, 1950 - Oct, 1950 (Half-size, B&W)
Tim Stores
4 issues; 6/50, 9/50, 10/50 known 5.00 15.00 30.00

TIMBER WOLF (See Adventure Comics #327 & Legion of Super-Heroes)
Nov, 1992 - No. 5, Mar, 1993 ($1.25, color, mini-series)
DC Comics
1-5 .60 1.25

TIME BANDITS (Marvel) (Value: cover or less)

TIME BEAVERS (See First Comics Graphic Novel #2)

TIME FOR LOVE (Formerly Romantic Secrets)
V2#53, Oct, 1966; Oct, 1967 - No. 47, May, 1976
Charlton Comics
V2#53(10/66), 1(10/67), 2(12/67)-20 .80 2.00 4.00
21-47 .40 1.00 2.00

TIME KILLERS (Fleetway/Quality) (Value: cover or less)

TIMELESS TOPIX (See Topix)

TIME MACHINE, THE (See 4-Color #1085)

TIME MASTERS (DC) (Value: cover or less)

TIMESPIRITS (Marvel) (Value: cover or less)

TIME TUNNEL, THE (TV)
Feb, 1967 - No. 2, July, 1967
Gold Key
1,2-Photo back-c 4.70 14.00 28.00

TIME TWISTERS (Quality) (Value: cover or less)

TIME 2: THE EPIPHANY (See First Comics Graphic Novel #9)

TIME WARP (DC) (Value: cover or less) (See The Unexpected #210)

TIME WARRIORS THE BEGINNING (Fantasy General) (Value: cover or less)

TIM HOLT (Movie star) (Becomes Red Mask #42 on; also see Crack Western #72, & Great Western)
1948 - No. 41, April-May, 1954 (All 36 pgs.)
Magazine Enterprises
1-(A-1 #14)-Photo-c begin, end No. 18, 29; Tim Holt, His horse Lightning & sidekick Chito begin 41.00 122.00 285.00
2-(A-1 #17)(9-10/48) 25.00 75.00 175.00
3-(A-1 #19)-Photo back-c 17.00 51.00 120.00
4(1-2/49),5: 5-Photo back-c 13.50 41.00 95.00
6-1st app. The Calico Kid (alias Rex Fury), his horse Ebony & Sidekick Sing-Song(begin series); photo back-c 15.00 45.00 105.00
7-10: 7-Calico Kid by Ayers. 8-Calico Kid by Guardineer (r-in/Great Western #10). 9-Map of Tim's Home Range 11.00 32.00 75.00
11-The Calico Kid becomes The Ghost Rider (Origin & 1st app.) by Dick Ayers (r-in/Great Western I.W. #8); his horse Spectre & sidekick Sing-Song begin series 29.00 85.00 200.00
12-16,18-Last photo-c 9.15 27.50 55.00
17-Frazetta Ghost Rider-c 25.00 75.00 175.00
19,22,24: 19-Last Tim Holt-c; Bolle line-drawn-c begin

Tick Tock Tales #19, © ME

Tillie the Toiler nn (#1, 1925), © KING

Tim Holt #16, © ME

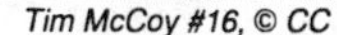
Tim McCoy #16, © CC

Tim Tyler Cowboy #13, © KING

Tip Top Comics #1, © UFS

GD25 FN65 NM94

7.50 22.50 45.00
20-Tim Holt becomes Redmask (Origin); begin series; Redmask-c #20-on 10.00 30.00 70.00
21-Frazetta Ghost Rider/Redmask-c 21.50 65.00 150.00
23-Frazetta Redmask-c 17.00 51.00 120.00
25-1st app. Black Phantom 11.50 34.00 80.00
26-30: 28-Wild Bill Hickok, Bat Masterson team up with Redmask. 29-B&W photo-c 6.35 19.00 38.00
31-33-Ghost Rider ends 5.85 17.50 35.00
34-Tales of the Ghost Rider begins (horror)-Classic "The Flower Women" & "Hard Boiled Harry!" 7.50 22.50 45.00
35-Last Tales of the Ghost Rider 6.70 20.00 40.00
36-The Ghost Rider returns, ends #41; liquid hallucinogenic drug story 7.50 22.50 45.00
37-Ghost Rider classic "To Touch Is to Die!," about Inca treasure 7.50 22.50 45.00
38-The Black Phantom begins (not in #39); classic Ghost Rider "The Phantom Guns of Feather Gap!" 7.50 22.50 45.00
39-41: All 3-D effect c/stories 10.00 30.00 65.00
NOTE: ***Dick Ayers** a-7, 9-41. **Bolle** a-1-41; c-19, 20, 22, 24-28, 30-41.*

TIM IN SPACE (Formerly Gene Autry Tim; becomes Tim Tomorrow)
1950 (1/2 size giveaway) (B&W)
Tim Stores
nn 3.60 9.00 18.00

TIM McCOY (Formerly Zoo Funnies; Pictorial Love Stories #22 on)
No. 16, Oct, 1948 - No. 21, Aug, 1949 (Western Movie Stories)
Charlton Comics
16-John Wayne, Montgomery Clift app. in "Red River;" photo back-c 29.00 85.00 200.00
17-21: 17-Allan "Rocky" Lane guest stars. 18-Rod Cameron guest stars. 20-Jimmy Wakely guest stars. 21-Johnny Mack Brown guest stars 24.00 73.00 170.00

TIM McCOY, POLICE CAR 17
No. 674, 1934 (32 pgs.) (11x14-3/4") (B&W) (Like Feature Books)
Whitman Publishing Co.
674-1933 movie ill. 18.00 54.00 125.00

TIMMY (See 4-Color #715, 823, 923, 1022)

TIMMY THE TIMID GHOST (Formerly Win-A-Prize?; see Blue Bird)
No. 3, 2/56 - No. 44, 10/64; No. 45, 9/66; 10/67 - No. 23, 7/71; V4#24, 9/85 - No. 26, 1/86
Charlton Comics
3(1956) (1st Series) 5.00 15.00 30.00
4,5 3.00 7.50 15.00
6-10 1.40 3.50 7.00
11,12(4/58,10/58)(100pgs.) 4.00 10.00 20.00
13-20 1.40 3.50 7.00
21-45(1966) .80 2.00 4.00
1(10/67, 2nd series) 1.00 2.50 5.00
2-23 .40 1.00 2.00
24-26 (1985-86): Fago-r .50 1.00

TIM TOMORROW (Formerly Tim In Space)
8/51, 9/51, 10/51, Christmas, 1951 (5x7-3/4")
Tim Stores
nn-Prof. Fumble & Captain Kit Comet in all 3.60 9.00 18.00

TIM TYLER (See Harvey Comics Hits #54)

TIM TYLER (Also see Comics Reading Libraries)
1942
Better Publications
1 9.15 27.50 55.00

TIM TYLER COWBOY
No. 11, Nov, 1948 - No. 18, 1950
Standard Comics (King Features Synd.)
11 5.35 16.00 32.00
12-18 4.00 11.00 22.00

TINKER BELL (See 4-Color #896, 982, & Walt Disney Showcase #37)

TINY FOLKS FUNNIES (See 4-Color #60)

TINY TESSIE (Tessie #1-23; Real Experiences #25)
No. 24, Oct, 1949
Marvel Comics (20CC)
24 5.00 15.00 30.00

TINY TIM (Also see Super Comics)
No. 4, 1941 - No. 235, July, 1949
Dell Publishing Co.
Large Feature Comic 4('41) 27.00 80.00 185.00
4-Color 20(1941) 27.00 80.00 185.00
4-Color 42(1943) 14.00 43.00 100.00
4-Color 235 5.00 15.00 30.00

TINY TOT COMICS
Mar, 1946 - No. 10, Nov-Dec, 1947 (For younger readers)
E. C. Comics
1(nn) (52 pgs.) 19.00 58.00 135.00
2 (5/46, 52 pgs.) 12.00 36.00 85.00
3-10: 10-Christmas-c 11.00 32.00 75.00

TINY TOT FUNNIES (Formerly Family Funnies; becomes Junior Funnies)
No. 9, June, 1951
Harvey Publ. (King Features Synd.)
9-Flash Gordon, Mandrake 4.20 12.50 25.00

TINY TOTS COMICS
1943 (Not reprints)
Dell Publishing Co.
1-Kelly-a(2); fairy tales 32.00 95.00 225.00

TIPPY & CAP STUBBS (See 4-Color #210, 242 & Popular Comics)

TIPPY'S FRIENDS GO-GO & ANIMAL
July, 1966 - No. 15, Oct, 1969 (25 cents)
Tower Comics
1 3.00 7.50 15.00
2-5,7,9-15: 12-15 titled "Tippy's Friend Go-Go" 2.00 5.00 10.00
6-The Monkees photo-c 4.70 14.00 28.00
8-Beatles app. on front/back-c 6.70 20.00 40.00

TIPPY TEEN (See Vicki)
Nov, 1965 - No. 27, Feb, 1970 (25 cents)
Tower Comics
1 2.40 6.00 12.00
2-27: 5-1pg. Beatles pin-up. 16-Twiggy photo-c 1.20 3.00 6.00
Special Collectors' Editions nn-(1969, 25 cents) 1.20 3.00 6.00

TIPPY TERRY
1963
Super/I. W. Enterprises
Super Reprint #14('63)-Little Grouchy reprints .60 1.20
I.W. Reprint #1 (nd) .60 1.20

TIP TOP COMICS
4/36 - No. 210, 1957; No. 211, 11-1/57-58 - No. 225, 5-7/61
United Features #1-187/St. John #188-210/Dell Publishing Co. #211 on
GD25 FN65 VF82 NM94
1-Tarzan by Hal Foster, Li'l Abner, Broncho Bill, Fritzi Ritz, Ella Cinders, Capt. & The Kids begin; strip-r (1st comic book app. of each) 500.00 1500.00 2250.00 3000.00

(Estimated up to 80 total copies exist, 4 in NM/Mint)

	GD25	FN65	VF88
2	108.00	325.00	650.00
3	83.00	250.00	500.00
4	62.00	188.00	375.00
5-10: 7-Photo & biography of Edgar Rice Burroughs. 8-Christmas-c	50.00	150.00	300.00
	GD25	**FN65**	**NM94**
11-20: 20-Christmas-c	42.00	125.00	250.00
21-40: 32-1st published Jack Davis-a (cartoon). 36-Kurtzman panel (1st published comic work)	32.00	95.00	190.00
41-Has 1st Tarzan Sunday	32.00	95.00	190.00
42-50: 43-Mort Walker panel	28.00	85.00	170.00
51-53	25.00	75.00	150.00
54-Origin Mirror Man & Triple Terror, also featured on cover	32.00	95.00	190.00
55,56,58,60: Last Tarzan by Foster	19.00	57.00	115.00
57,59,61,62-Tarzan by Hogarth	25.00	75.00	150.00
63-80: 65,67-70,72-74,77,78-No Tarzan	10.00	30.00	70.00
81-90	10.00	30.00	65.00
91-99	7.50	22.50	45.00
100	9.15	27.50	55.00
101-140: 110-Gordo story. 111-Li'l Abner app. 118, 132-No Tarzan. 137-Sadie Hawkins Day story	5.35	16.00	32.00
141-170: 145,151-Gordo stories. 157-Last Li'l Abner; lingerie panels	4.00	11.00	22.00
171-188-Tarzan reprints by B. Lubbers in all. #177?-Peanuts by Schulz begins; no Peanuts in #178,179,181-183	4.20	12.50	25.00
189-225	3.20	8.00	16.00
Bound Volumes (Very Rare) sold at 1939 World's Fair; bound by publisher in pictorial comic boards (also see Comics on Parade)			
Bound issues 1-12	200.00	600.00	1200.00
Bound issues 13-24	133.00	400.00	800.00
Bound issues 25-36	108.00	325.00	650.00

NOTE: *Tarzan covers-#3, 9, 11, 13, 16, 18, 21, 24, 27, 30, 32-34, 36, 37, 39, 41, 43, 45, 47, 50, 52 (all worth 10-20 percent more). Tarzan by **Foster**-#1-40, 44-50; by **Rex Maxon**-#41-43; by **Burne Hogarth**-#57, 59, 62.*

TIP TOPPER COMICS
Oct-Nov, 1949 - No. 28, 1954
United Features Syndicate

	GD25	FN65	NM94
1-Li'l Abner, Abbie & Slats	7.00	21.00	42.00
2	4.35	13.00	26.00
3-5: 5-Fearless Fosdick app.	4.00	11.00	22.00
6-10: 6-Fearless Fosdick app.	3.60	9.00	18.00
11-25: 17-22,24,26-Peanuts app. (2 pgs.)	2.80	7.00	14.00
26-28-Twin Earths	4.35	13.00	26.00

NOTE: *Many lingerie panels in Fritzi Ritz stories.*

T-MAN (Also see Police Comics #103)
Sept, 1951 - No. 38, Dec, 1956
Quality Comics Group

	GD25	FN65	NM94
1-Jack Cole-a	19.00	57.00	130.00
2-Crandall-c	10.00	30.00	70.00
3,6-8: All Crandall-c	10.00	30.00	60.00
4,5-Crandall-c/a each	10.00	30.00	65.00
9,10-Crandall-c	8.35	25.00	50.00
11-Used in **POP**, pg. 95 & color illo.	6.70	20.00	40.00
12-19,21,22,24,26: 24-Last pre-code (4/55)	5.00	15.00	30.00
20,23-H-Bomb explosion-c/stories	8.35	25.00	50.00
25-All Crandall-a	7.50	22.50	45.00
27-38	4.20	12.50	25.00

NOTE: *Anti-communist stories common.* ***Crandall** c-2-10p.* ***Cuidera** c(i)-1-38. Bondage c-15.*

TNT COMICS
Feb, 1946 (36 pgs.)
Charles Publishing Co.

	GD25	FN65	NM94
1-Yellowjacket app.	15.00	45.00	90.00

TOBY TYLER (See 4-Color #1092 and Movie Comics)

TODAY'S BRIDES
Nov, 1955; No. 2, Feb, 1956; No. 3, Sept, 1956; No. 4, Nov, 1956
Ajax/Farrell Publishing Co.

	GD25	FN65	NM94
1	4.35	13.00	26.00
2-4	2.80	7.00	14.00

TODAY'S ROMANCE
No. 5, March, 1952 - No. 8, Sept, 1952
Standard Comics

	GD25	FN65	NM94
5	4.20	12.50	25.00
6-Toth-a	5.00	15.00	30.00
7,8	2.40	6.00	12.00

TOKA (Jungle King)
Aug-Oct, 1964 - No. 10, Jan, 1967 (Painted-c #1,2)
Dell Publishing Co.

	GD25	FN65	NM94
1	2.40	6.00	12.00
2	1.20	3.00	6.00
3-10	1.00	2.50	5.00

TOMAHAWK (Son of... on-c of #131-140; see Star Spangled Comics #69 & World's Finest Comics #65)
Sept-Oct, 1950 - No. 140, May-June, 1972
National Periodical Publications

	GD25	FN65	NM94
1-Tomahawk begins by Fred Ray	82.00	245.00	575.00
2-Frazetta/Williamson-a (4 pgs.)	39.00	120.00	275.00
3-5	27.00	81.00	190.00
6-10: 7-Last 52 pg. issue	19.00	57.00	130.00
11-20	11.50	34.00	80.00
21-27,30: 30-Last precode (2/55)	10.00	30.00	65.00
28-1st app. Lord Shilling (arch-foe)	11.00	32.00	75.00
29-Frazetta-r/Jimmy Wakely #3 (3 pgs.)	15.00	45.00	105.00
31-40	10.00	30.00	60.00
41-50	7.50	22.50	45.00
51-56,58-60	5.35	16.00	32.00
57-Frazetta-r/Jimmy Wakely #6 (3 pgs.)	10.00	30.00	60.00
61-77: 77-Last 10 cent issue	4.00	11.00	22.00
78-85: 81-1st app. Miss Liberty. 83-Origin Tomahawk's Rangers	3.00	7.50	15.00
86-100: 96-Origin/1st app. The Hood, alias Lady Shilling	2.00	5.00	10.00
101-110: 107-Origin/1st app. Thunder-Man	1.60	4.00	8.00
111-130,132-138,140	.80	2.00	4.00
131-Frazetta-r/Jimmy Wakely #7 (3 pgs.); origin Firehair retold	1.00	2.50	5.00
139-Frazetta-r/Star Spangled #113	.80	2.00	4.00

NOTE: ***Neal Adams** c-116-119, 121, 123-130.* ***Fred Ray** c-1-4, 7-19, 21-25, 28. Firehair by **Kubert**-131-134, 136.* ***Maurer** a-138.* ***Severin** a-135.* ***Starr** a-5.*

TOM AND JERRY (See Comic Album #4, 8, 12, Dell Giant #21, Dell Giants, Four Color #193, Golden Comics Digest #1, 5, 8, 13, 15, 18, 22, 25, 28, 35, Kite fun Book & March of Comics #21, 46, 61, 70, 88, 103, 119, 128, 145, 154, 173, 190, 207, 224, 281, 295, 305, 321, 333, 345, 361, 365, 388, 400, 444, 451, 463, 480)

TOM AND JERRY (...Comics, early issues) (M.G.M.)
(Formerly Our Gang No. 1-59) (See Dell Giants for annuals)
No. 193, 6/48; No. 60, 7/49 - No. 212, 7-9/62; No. 213, 11/62 - No. 291, 2/75; No. 292, 3/77 - No. 342, 5/82 - No. 344, 1982?
Dell Publishing Co./Gold Key No. 213-327/Whitman No. 328 on

	GD25	FN65	NM94
4-Color 193 (#1)-Titled "M.G.M. Presents..."	11.00	32.00	75.00
60	6.35	19.00	38.00
61	5.35	16.00	32.00
62-70: 66-X-mas-c	4.20	12.50	25.00
71-80: 77-X-mas-c	4.00	10.00	20.00
81-99: 90-X-mas-c	3.60	9.00	18.00
100	4.00	10.00	20.00
101-120	2.80	7.00	14.00

T-Man #35, © QUA

Tomahawk #95, © DC

Tom and Jerry #92, © M.G.M.

Tomb of Terror #5, © HARV

Tom Corbett, Space Cadet #6, © DELL

Tom Mix Western #56, © FAW

	GD25	FN65	NM94
121-140: 126-X-mas-c	2.40	6.00	12.00
141-160	1.80	4.50	9.00
161-200	1.40	3.50	7.00
201-212(7-9/62)(Last Dell issue)	1.20	3.00	6.00
213,214-(84 pgs.)-Titled "...Funhouse"	4.00	10.00	20.00
215-240: 215-Titled "...Funhouse"	1.00	2.50	5.00
241-270	.80	2.00	4.00
271-300: 286 "Tom & Jerry"	.60	1.50	3.00
301-344	.30	.75	1.50
Mouse From T.R.A.P. 1(7/66)-Giant, G. K.	3.60	9.00	18.00
Summer Fun 1(7/67, 68pgs.)(Gold Key)-Reprints Barks' Droopy from Summer Fun #1	3.60	9.00	18.00

NOTE: *#60-87, 98-121, 268, 277, 289, 302 are 52 pages. Reprints-#225, 241, 245, 247, 252, 254, 266, 268, 270, 292-327, 329-342, 344.*

TOM & JERRY (Harvey)(Value: cover or less)

TOM & JERRY AND FRIENDS (Harvey)(Value: cover or less)

TOMB OF DARKNESS (Formerly Beware)
No. 9, July, 1974 - No. 23, Nov, 1976
Marvel Comics Group

	GD25	FN65	NM94
9-23: 15,19-Ditko-r. 17-Woodbridge-r/Astonishing #62; Powell-r. 20-Everett Venus-r/Venus #19. 23-Everett-r		.50	1.00

TOMB OF DRACULA (See Giant-Size Dracula, Dracula Lives, Power Record Comics & Requiem for Dracula)
April, 1972 - No. 70, Aug, 1979
Marvel Comics Group

	GD25	FN65	NM94
1-1st app. Dracula; Colan-p in all	8.35	25.00	50.00
2	4.70	14.00	28.00
3-5: 3-Intro. Dr. Rachel Van Helsing & Inspector Chelm	3.60	9.00	18.00
6-10: 10-1st app. Blade the Vampire Slayer	3.00	7.50	15.00
11-20: 12-Brunner-c(p). 13-Origin Blade	2.00	5.00	10.00
21-40	1.60	4.00	8.00
41-49,51-60	1.00	2.50	5.00
50-Silver Surfer app.	1.60	4.00	8.00
61-70: 70-Double size	.80	2.00	4.00

NOTE: ***N. Adams** c-1, 6. **Colan** a-1-70p; c(p)-8, 38-42, 44-56, 58-70. **Wrightson** c-43.*

TOMB OF DRACULA, THE (Magazine)
Oct, 1979 - No. 6, Aug, 1980 (B&W)
Marvel Comics Group

	GD25	FN65	NM94
1,4-6	.60	1.50	3.00
2,3: 2-Ditko-a (36 pgs.). 3-Miller-a(2 pg. sketch)	.80	2.00	4.00

NOTE: ***Buscema** a-4p, 5p. **Chaykin** c-5, 6. **Colan** a(p)-1, 3-6. **Miller** a-3. **Romita** a-2p.*

TOMB OF DRACULA
1991 - No. 4, 1992 ($4.95, color, squarebound, mini-series, 52 pgs.)
Epic Comics (Marvel)

	GD25	FN65	NM94
Book 1-4: Colan/Williamson-a; Colan painted-c	1.00	2.50	5.00

TOMB OF LEGEIA (See Movie Classics)

TOMB OF TERROR (Thrills of Tomorrow #17 on)
June, 1952 - No. 16, July, 1954
Harvey Publications

	GD25	FN65	NM94
1	11.00	32.00	75.00
2	7.50	22.50	45.00
3-Bondage-c; atomic disaster story	9.15	27.50	55.00
4-12: 4-Heart ripped out. 8-12-Nostrand-a	7.50	22.50	45.00
13,14-Special S/F issues. 14-Check-a	10.00	30.00	65.00
15-S/F issue; c-shows head exploding	11.50	34.00	80.00
16-Special S/F issue; Nostrand-a	10.00	30.00	65.00

NOTE: ***Edd Cartier** a-13? **Elias** c-2, 5-16. **Kremer** a-1, 7; c-1. **Nostrand** a-8-12, 15r 16. **Palais** a-2, 3, 5-7. **Powell** a-1, 3, 5, 9-16. **Sparling** a-12, 13, 15.*

TOMBSTONE TERRITORY (See 4-Color #1123)

TOM CAT (Formerly Bo; Atom The Cat #9 on)
No. 4, Apr, 1956 - No. 8, July, 1957
Charlton Comics

	GD25	FN65	NM94
4-Al Fago-c/a	4.00	10.00	20.00
5-8	2.80	7.00	14.00

TOM CORBETT, SPACE CADET (TV)
No. 378, Jan-Feb, 1952 - No. 11, Sept-Nov, 1954 (All painted covers)
Dell Publishing Co.

	GD25	FN65	NM94
4-Color 378 (#1)-McWilliams-a	14.00	43.00	100.00
4-Color 400,421-McWilliams-a	9.15	27.50	55.00
4(11-1/53) - 11	5.85	17.50	35.00

TOM CORBETT SPACE CADET (See March of Comics #102)

TOM CORBETT SPACE CADET (TV)
V2#1, May-June, 1955 - V2#3, Sept-Oct, 1955
Prize Publications

	GD25	FN65	NM94
V2#1	14.00	43.00	100.00
2,3-Meskin-c	13.00	40.00	90.00

TOM, DICK & HARRIET (See Gold Key Spotlight)

TOM LANDRY AND THE DALLAS COWBOYS (Spire Christian)(Value: cover or less)

TOM MIX (...Commandos Comics #10-12)
Sept, 1940 - No. 12, Nov, 1942 (36 pages); 1983 (One-shot)
Given away for two Ralston box-tops; in cereal box, 1983
Ralston-Purina Co.

	GD25	FN65	NM94
1-Origin (life) Tom Mix; Fred Meagher-a	142.00	430.00	1000.00
2	57.00	170.00	400.00
3-9	43.00	130.00	300.00
10-12: 10-Origin Tom Mix Commando Unit; Speed O'Dare begins. 12-Sci/fi-c	36.00	107.00	250.00
1983-"Taking of Grizzly Grebb," Toth-a; 16 pg. miniature	1.20	3.00	6.00

TOM MIX WESTERN (Movie, radio star) (Also see The Comics, Crackajack Funnies, Master Comics, 100 Pages Of Comics, Popular Comics, Real Western Hero, Six Gun Heroes, Western Hero & XMas Comics)
Jan, 1948 - No. 61, May, 1953 (1-17: 52 pgs.)
Fawcett Publications

	GD25	FN65	NM94
1 (Photo-c, 52 pgs.)-Tom Mix & his horse Tony begin; Tumbleweed Jr. begins, ends #52,54,55	68.00	205.00	475.00
2 (Photo-c)	29.00	85.00	200.00
3-5 (Painted/photo-c): 5-Billy the Kid & Oscar app.	23.00	70.00	160.00
6,7 (Painted/photo-c)	19.00	57.00	130.00
8-Kinstler tempera-c	19.00	57.00	130.00
9,10 (Painted/photo-c)-Used in **SOTI**, pgs. 323-325	16.50	50.00	115.00
11-Kinstler oil-c	16.00	48.00	110.00
12 (Painted/photo-c)	13.00	40.00	90.00
13-17 (Painted-c, 52 pgs.)	13.00	40.00	90.00
18,22 (Painted-c, 36 pgs.)	11.00	32.00	75.00
19 (Photo-c, 52 pgs.)	12.00	36.00	85.00
20,21,23 (Painted-c, 52 pgs.)	10.00	30.00	70.00
24,25,27-29 (52 pgs.): 24-Photo-c begin, end #61. 29-Slim Pickens app.	10.00	30.00	70.00
26,30 (36 pgs.)	10.00	30.00	65.00
31-33,35-37,39,40,42 (52 pgs.): 39-Red Eagle app.	10.00	30.00	60.00
34,38 (36 pgs. begin)	8.35	25.00	50.00
41,43-60	6.35	19.00	38.00
61-Last issue	7.50	22.50	45.00

NOTE: *Photo-c from 1930s Tom Mix movies (he died in 1940). Many issues contain ads for Tom Mix, Rocky Lane, Space Patrol and other premiums. **Captain Tootsie** by C.C. Beck in*

No. 6-11, 20.

TOM MIX WESTERN
1988 - No. 2, 1989? ($2.95, B&W w/16 pgs. color, 44 pgs.)
AC Comics

1-Tom Mix-r/Master #124,128,131,102 plus Billy the Kid-r by Severin;
photo front/back/inside-c .60 1.50 3.00
2-($2.50, B&W)-Gabby Hayes-r; photo covers .50 1.25 2.50
...Holiday Album 1 (1990, $3.50, B&W, one-shot, 44 pgs.)-Contains photos &
1950s Tom Mix-r; photo inside-c .70 1.75 3.50

TOMMY OF THE BIG TOP
No. 10, Sept, 1948 - No. 12, Mar, 1949
King Features Syndicate/Standard Comics

10-By John Lehti 4.20 12.50 25.00
11,12 3.00 7.50 15.00

TOMORROW KNIGHTS (Marvel)(Value: cover or less)

TOM SAWYER (See Adventures of... & Famous Stories)

TOM SAWYER & HUCK FINN
1925 (52 pgs.) (10-3/4x10") (stiff covers)
Stoll & Edwards Co.

nn-By Dwiggins; reprints 1923, 1924 Sunday strips in color
17.00 50.00 100.00

TOM SAWYER COMICS
1951? (paper cover)
Giveaway

nn-Contains a coverless Hopalong Cassidy from 1951; other combinations
possible 1.20 3.00 6.00

TOM SKINNER-UP FROM HARLEM (See Up From Harlem)

TOM TERRIFIC! (TV)(See Mighty Mouse Fun Club Magazine #1)
Summer, 1957 - No. 6, Fall, 1958
Pines Comics (Paul Terry)

1 12.00 36.00 85.00
2-6 10.00 30.00 65.00

TOM THUMB (See 4-Color #972)

TOM-TOM, THE JUNGLE BOY (See Tick Tock Tales)
1947 - No. 3, 1947; Nov, 1957 - No. 3, Mar, 1958
Magazine Enterprises

1-Funny animal 5.35 16.00 32.00
2,3(1947) 4.00 11.00 22.00
... & Itchi the Monk 1(11/57) - 3(3/58) 2.00 5.00 10.00
I.W. Reprint No. 1,2,8,10 .30 .75 1.50

TONKA (See 4-Color #966)

TONTO (See The Lone Ranger's Companion...)

TONY TRENT (The Face #1,2)
No. 3, 1948 - No. 4, 1949
Big Shot/Columbia Comics Group

3,4: 3-The Face app. by Mart Bailey 8.35 25.00 50.00

TOODLE TWINS, THE
Jan-Feb, 1951 - No. 10, July-Aug, 1951; Mar, 1956 (Newspaper-r)
Ziff-Davis (Approved Comics)/Argo

1 6.70 20.00 40.00
2 4.00 12.00 24.00
3-10: 10-Painted-c, some newspaper-r 4.00 10.00 20.00
1(Argo, 3/56) 4.00 10.00 20.00

TOONERVILLE TROLLEY
1921 (Daily strip reprints) (B&W) (52 pgs.)
Cupples & Leon Co.

1-By Fontaine Fox 22.00 65.00 130.00

TOOTS & CASPER (See Large Feature Comic #5)

TOP ADVENTURE COMICS
1964 (Reprints)
I. W. Enterprises

1-r/High Adv. (Explorer Joe #2); Krigstein-r 1.40 3.50 7.00
2-Black Dwarf-r/Red Seal #22; Kinstler-c 1.40 3.50 7.00

TOP CAT (TV) (Hanna-Barbera)(See Kite Fun Book)
12-2/61-62 - No. 3, 6-8/62; No. 4, 10/62 - No. 31, 9/70
Dell Publishing Co./Gold Key No. 4 on

1 11.50 34.00 80.00
2 6.70 20.00 40.00
3-5 4.20 12.50 25.00
6-10 3.60 9.00 18.00
11-20 2.40 6.00 12.00
21-31: 21,24,25,29-Reprints 1.60 4.00 8.00

TOP CAT (TV) (Hanna-Barbera)(See TV Stars #4)
Nov, 1970 - No. 20, Nov, 1973
Charlton Comics

1 3.60 9.00 18.00
2-10 2.00 5.00 10.00
11-20 1.20 3.00 6.00
NOTE: *#8 (1/72) went on sale late in 1972 between #14 and #15 with the 1/73 issues.*

TOP COMICS
July, 1967 (All reprints)
K. K. Publications/Gold Key

nn-The Gnome-Mobile (Disney-movie) 1.20 3.00 6.00
1-Beagle Boys (#7), Bugs Bunny, Chip 'n' Dale, Daffy Duck (#50), Flipper, Huckleberry Hound, Huey, Dewey & Louie, Junior Woodchucks, Lassie, The Little Monsters (#71), Moby Duck, Porky Pig (has Gold Key label - says Top Comics on inside), Scamp, Super Goof, Tarzan of the Apes (#169), Three Stooges (#35), Tom & Jerry Top Cat (#21), Tweety & Sylvester (#7), Walt Disney C&S (#322), Woody Woodpecker, Yogi Bear, Zorro (r/G.K. Zorro #7 w/Toth-a; says 2nd printing) known; each character
given own book 1.20 3.00 6.00
1-Uncle Scrooge (#70) 2.00 5.00 10.00
1-Donald Duck (not Barks), Mickey Mouse 1.60 4.00 8.00
1-Flintstones 4.00 10.00 20.00
1-The Jetsons 5.00 15.00 30.00
2-Bugs Bunny, Daffy Duck, Donald Duck (not Barks), Mickey Mouse (#114), Porky Pig, Super Goof, Three Stooges, Tom & Jerry, Tweety & Sylvester, Uncle Scrooge (#71)-Barks-c, Walt Disney's C&S (r/#325), Woody Woodpecker, Yogi Bear (#30), Zorro (r/#8; Toth-a) 1.20 3.00 6.00
2-Snow White & 7 Dwarfs(6/67)(1944-r) 1.60 4.00 8.00
3-Donald Duck 1.40 3.50 7.00
3-Uncle Scrooge (#72) 2.00 5.00 10.00
3,4-The Flintstones 4.00 10.00 20.00
3-Mickey Mouse (r/#115), Tom & Jerry, Woody Woodpecker, Yogi Bear
1.20 3.00 6.00
4-Mickey Mouse, Woody Woodpecker 1.20 3.00 6.00
NOTE: *Each book in this series is identical to its counterpart except for cover, and came out at same time. The number in parentheses is the original issue it contains.*

TOP DETECTIVE COMICS
1964 (Reprints)
I. W. Enterprises

9-r/Young King Cole #14; Dr. Drew (not Grandenetti)
1.00 2.50 5.00

TOP DOG (See Star Comics Magazine, 75 cents)
Apr, 1985 - No. 14, June, 1987 (Children's book)
Star Comics (Marvel)

1-14: 14-($1.00) .50 1.00

TOP ELIMINATOR (Teenage Hotrodders #1-24; Drag 'n' Wheels #30 on)
No. 25, Sept, 1967 - No. 29, July, 1968
Charlton Comics

Tommy of the Big Top #11, © KING

Tom Terrific! #1, © CBS

Tony Trent #3, © Z-D

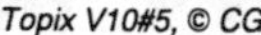
Topix V10#5, © CG

Top-Notch Laugh Comics #29, © AP

Top Secrets #1, © S&S

	GD25	FN65	NM94
25-29	.80	2.00	4.00

TOP FLIGHT COMICS
1947; July, 1949
Four Star Publications/St. John Publishing Co.

	GD25	FN65	NM94
1(1947)	5.85	17.50	35.00
1(7/49, St. John)-Hector the Inspector	4.20	12.50	25.00

TOP GUN (See 4-Color #927 & Showcase #72)

TOP GUNS OF THE WEST (See Super DC Giant)

TOPIX (...Comics) (Timeless Topix-early issues) (Also see Men of Battle, Men of Courage & Treasure Chest)(V1-V5#1,V7#1-20-paper-c)
11/42 - V10#15, 1/28/52 (Weekly - later issues)
Catechetical Guild Educational Society

	GD25	FN65	NM94
V1#1(8pgs.,8x11")	10.00	30.00	60.00
2,3(8pgs.,8x11")	5.85	17.50	35.00
4-8(16pgs.,8x11")	4.20	12.50	25.00
V2#1-10(16pgs.,8x11"): V2#8-Pope Pius XII	4.00	10.00	20.00
V3#1-10(16pgs.,8x11")	3.60	9.00	18.00
V4#1-10	3.60	9.00	18.00
V5#1(10/46,52pgs.)-9,12-15(12/47)-#13 shows V5#4	2.00	5.00	10.00
10,11-Life of Christ editions	4.00	10.00	20.00
V6#1-14	1.20	3.00	6.00
V7#1(9/1/48)-20(6/15/49), 32pgs.	1.20	3.00	6.00
V8#1(9/19/49)-3,5-11,13-30(5/15/50)	1.20	3.00	6.00
4-Dagwood Splits the Atom(10/10/49)-Magazine format	2.40	6.00	12.00
12-Ingels-a	4.20	12.50	25.00
V9#1(9/25/50)-11,13-30(5/14/51)	1.00	2.50	5.00
12-Special 36pg. Xmas issue, text illos format	1.40	3.50	7.00
V10#1(10/1/51)-15: 14-Hollingsworth-a	1.00	2.50	5.00

TOP JUNGLE COMICS
1964 (Reprint)
I. W. Enterprises

	GD25	FN65	NM94
1(nd)-Reprints White Princess of the Jungle #3, minus cover	1.40	3.50	7.00

TOP LOVE STORIES (Formerly Gasoline Alley #2)
No. 3, 5/51 - No. 19, 3/54
Star Publications

	GD25	FN65	NM94
3(#1)	7.50	22.50	45.00
4,5,7-9	5.85	17.50	35.00
6-Wood-a	10.00	30.00	65.00
10-16,18,19-Disbrow-a	5.85	17.50	35.00
17-Wood art (Fox-r)	7.50	22.50	45.00

NOTE: *All have **L. B. Cole** covers.*

TOP-NOTCH COMICS (...Laugh #28-45; Laugh Comix #46 on)
Dec, 1939 - No. 45, June, 1944
MLJ Magazines

	GD25	FN65	NM94
1-Origin The Wizard; Kardak the Mystic Magician, Swift of the Secret Service (ends #3), Air Patrol, The Westpointer, Manhunters (by J. Cole), Mystic (ends #2) & Scott Rand (ends #3) begin	250.00	750.00	1500.00
2-Dick Storm (ends #8), Stacy Knight M.D. (ends #4) begin; Jack Cole-a	100.00	300.00	600.00
3-Bob Phantom, Scott Rand on Mars begin; J. Cole-a	75.00	225.00	450.00
4-Origin/1st app. Streak Chandler on Mars; Moore of the Mounted only app.; J. Cole-a	63.00	190.00	380.00
5-Flag-c; origin/1st app. Galahad; Shanghai Sheridan begins (ends #8); Shield cameo; Novick-a	63.00	190.00	380.00
6-Meskin-a	50.00	150.00	300.00
7-The Shield x-over in Wizard; The Wizard dons new costume	58.00	175.00	350.00
8-Origin The Firefly & Roy, the Super Boy	67.00	200.00	400.00
9-Origin & 1st app. The Black Hood; Fran Frazier begins	217.00	650.00	1300.00
10	88.00	265.00	530.00
11-20	48.00	145.00	290.00
21-30: 23-26-Roy app. 24-No Wizard. 25-Last Bob Phantom. 27-Last Firefly. 28-Suzie begins. 29-Last Kardak	38.00	115.00	230.00
31-44: 33-Dotty & Ditto by Woggon begins. 44-Black Hood series ends	22.00	65.00	130.00
45-Last issue	25.00	75.00	150.00

NOTE: ***J. Binder** a-1-3. **Meskin** a-2, 3, 6, 15. **Bob Montana** a-30; c-28-31. **Harry Sahle** c-42-45. **Woggon** a-33-40, 42. Bondage c-17, 19. Black Hood also appeared on radio in 1944.*

TOPPER & NEIL (See 4-Color #859)

TOPPS COMICS
1947
Four Star Publications

	GD25	FN65	NM94
1-L. B. Cole-c	8.35	25.00	50.00

TOPS
July, 1949 - No. 2, Sept, 1949 (68 pgs, 25 cents) (10-1/4x13-1/4")
(Large size-magazine format; for the adult reader)
Tops Magazine, Inc. (Lev Gleason)

	GD25	FN65	NM94
1 (Rare)-Story by Dashiell Hammett; Crandall/Lubbers, Tuska, Dan Barry, Fuje-a; Biro painted-c	83.00	250.00	500.00
2 (Rare)-Crandall/Lubbers, Biro, Kida, Fuje, Guardineer-a	75.00	225.00	450.00

TOPS COMICS (See Tops in Humor)
1944 (Small size, 32 pgs.) (7-1/4x5")
Consolidated Book (Lev Gleason)

	GD25	FN65	NM94
2001-The Jack of Spades	11.00	32.00	75.00
2002-Rip Raider	6.70	20.00	40.00
2003-Red Birch (gag cartoons)	1.60	4.00	8.00

TOPS COMICS
1944 (132 pages) (10 cents)
Consolidated Book Publishers

	GD25	FN65	NM94
nn(Color-c, inside in red shade & some in full color)-Ace Kelly by Rick Yager, Black Orchid, Don on the Farm, Dinky Dinkerton (Rare)	22.00	65.00	130.00

NOTE: *This book is printed in such a way that when the staple is removed, the strips on the left side of the book correspond with the same strips on the right side. Therefore, if strips are removed from the book, each strip can be folded into a complete comic section of its own.*

TOP SECRET
January, 1952
Hillman Publ.

	GD25	FN65	NM94
1	11.00	32.00	75.00

TOP SECRET ADVENTURES (See Spyman)

TOP SECRETS (...of the F.B.I.)
Nov, 1947 - No. 10, July-Aug, 1949
Street & Smith Publications

	GD25	FN65	NM94
1-Powell-c/a	17.00	52.00	120.00
2-Powell-c/a	12.00	36.00	85.00
3-6,8-10-Powell-a	11.00	32.00	75.00
7-Used in SOTI, pg. 90 & illo.-"How to hurt people;" used by N.Y. Legis. Comm.; Powell-c/a	16.00	48.00	110.00

NOTE: ***Powell** c-1-3, 5-10.*

TOPS IN ADVENTURE
Fall, 1952 (25 cents, 132 pages)
Ziff-Davis Publishing Co.

	GD25	FN65	NM94
1-Crusader from Mars, The Hawk, Football Thrills, He-Man; Powell-a; painted-c	29.00	85.00	200.00

TOPS IN HUMOR (See Tops Comics?)

1944 (Small size) (7-1/4x5")
Consolidated Book Publ. (Lev Gleason)

2001(#1)-Origin The Jack of Spades, Ace Kelly by Rick Yager, Black Orchid (female crime fighter) app. 11.50 34.00 80.00
2 7.00 21.00 42.00

TOP SPOT COMICS
1945
Top Spot Publ. Co.

1-The Menace, Duke of Darkness app. 14.00 43.00 100.00

TOPSY-TURVY
April, 1945
R. B. Leffingwell Publ.

1-1st app. Cookie 5.35 16.00 32.00

TOR (Formerly One Million Years Ago)
No. 2, Oct, 1953; No. 3, May, 1954 - No. 5, Oct, 1954
St. John Publishing Co.

3-D 2(10/53)-Kubert-a 10.00 30.00 65.00
3-D 2(10/53)-Oversized, otherwise same contents 9.15 27.50 55.00
3-D 2(11/53)-Kubert-a 9.15 27.50 55.00
3-5-Kubert-a; 3-Danny Dreams by Toth 10.00 30.00 65.00
NOTE: *The two October 3-D's have same contents and* ***Powell*** *art; the November issue is titled 3-D Comics.*

TOR (See Sojourn)
May-June, 1975 - No. 6, Mar-Apr, 1976
National Periodical Publications

1-6: 1-New origin by Kubert. 2-Origin-r/St. John #1 .50 1.00
NOTE: ***Kubert*** *a-1, 2-6r; c-1-6.* ***Toth*** *a(p)-3r.*

TOR (3-D) (Eclipse) (Value: cover or less)

TORCHY (...Blonde Bombshell) (See Dollman, Military, & Modern)
Nov, 1949 - No. 6, Sept, 1950
Quality Comics Group

1-Bill Ward-c, Gil Fox-a 79.00 235.00 550.00
2,3-Fox-c/a 36.00 107.00 250.00
4-Fox-c/a(3), Ward-a, 9pgs. 47.00 140.00 325.00
5,6-Ward-c/a, 9 pgs; Fox-a(3) each 57.00 170.00 390.00
Super Reprint #16(1964)-r/#4 with new-c 6.70 20.00 40.00

TO RIVERDALE AND BACK AGAIN (Archie Comics Presents...)
1990 ($2.50, 68 pgs.)
Archie Comics

nn-Byrne-c, Colan-a(p); adapts NBC TV movie .50 1.25 2.50

TORMENTED, THE (Becomes Surprise Adventures #3 on)
July, 1954 - No. 2, Sept, 1954
Sterling Comics

1,2 10.00 30.00 60.00

TORNADO TOM (See Mighty Midget Comics)

TOTAL ECLIPSE (Eclipse) (Value: cover or less)

TOTAL ECLIPSE: THE SERAPHIM OBJECTIVE (Eclipse) (Value: cover or less)

TOTAL RECALL (DC) (Value: cover or less)

TOTAL WAR (M.A.R.S. Patrol #3 on)
July, 1965 - No. 2, Oct, 1965 (Painted covers)
Gold Key

1,2-Wood-a in each 4.00 11.00 22.00

TOUGH KID SQUAD COMICS
March, 1942
Timely Comics (TCI) GD25 FN65 VF82 NM94

1-(Scarce)-Origin The Human Top & The Tough Kid Squad; The Flying Flame app. 475.00 1425.00 2600.00 3800.00
(Estimated up to 100 total copies exist, 6 in NM/Mint)

TOWER OF SHADOWS (Creatures on the Loose #10 on)
Sept, 1969 - No. 9, Jan, 1971
Marvel Comics Group GD25 FN65 NM94

1-Steranko, Craig-a 3.60 9.00 18.00
2-Neal Adams-a 1.60 4.00 8.00
3-Barry Smith, Tuska-a 1.80 4.50 9.00
4-Kirby/Everett-c 1.20 3.00 6.00
5,7-B. Smith(p), Wood-a (Wood draws himself-1st pg., 1st panel-#5) 1.60 4.00 8.00
6,8: Wood-a; 8-Wrightson-c 1.20 3.00 6.00
9-Wrightson-c; Roy Thomas app. 1.00 2.50 5.00
Special 1(12/71)-Neal Adams-a 1.00 2.50 5.00
NOTE: ***J. Buscema*** *a-1p, 2p.* ***Colan*** *a-3p, 6p.* ***J. Craig*** *a-1.* ***Ditko*** *a-6, 8, 9r, Special 1.* ***Everett*** *a-9(i)r; c-5i.* ***Kirby*** *a-9(p)r.* ***Severin*** *c-5p, 6.* ***Steranko*** *a-1.* ***Tuska*** *a-3.* ***Wood*** *a-5-8. Issues 1-9 contain new stories with some pre-Marvel age reprints in 6-9.* ***H. P. Lovecraft*** *adaptation-9.*

TOWN & COUNTRY
May, 1940
Publisher?

nn-Origin The Falcon 30.00 90.00 210.00

TOWN THAT FORGOT SANTA, THE
1961 (24 pages) (Giveaway)
W. T. Grant Co.

nn 2.40 6.00 12.00

TOXIC AVENGER (Marvel) (Value: cover or less)

TOXIC CRUSADERS (TV)
May, 1992 - Present ($1.25, color)
Marvel Comics

1-3-Sam Kieth-c; based on USA network cartoon .25 .75 1.50
4-10 .60 1.25

TOYBOY (Continuity) (Value: cover or less)

TOYLAND COMICS
Jan, 1947 - No. 4, July?, 1947
Fiction House Magazines

1 14.00 43.00 100.00
2-4: 3-Tuska-a 10.00 30.00 60.00
148 pg. issue 16.00 48.00 110.00
NOTE: *All above contain strips by* ***Al Walker.***

TOY TOWN COMICS
1945 - No. 7, May, 1947
Toytown/Orbit Publ./B. Antin/Swapper Quarterly

1-Mertie Mouse; L. B. Cole-c/a 11.50 34.00 80.00
2-L. B. Cole-a 8.35 25.00 50.00
3-7-L. B. Cole-a 7.00 21.00 42.00

TRAGG AND THE SKY GODS (See Gold Key Spotlight, Mystery Comics Digest #3,9 & Spine Tingling Tales)
June, 1975 - No. 8, Feb, 1977; No. 9, May, 1982 (Painted-c #3-8)
Gold Key/Whitman No. 9

1-Origin .60 1.20
2-9: 4-Sabre-Fang app. 8-Ostellon app.; 9-r/#1 .50 1.00
NOTE: ***Santos*** *a-1, 2, 9r; c-3-7.* ***Spiegel*** *a-3-8.*

TRAIL BLAZERS (Red Dragon #5 on)
1941 - No. 4, 1942
Street & Smith Publications

1-True stories of American heroes 22.00 65.00 130.00
2 13.00 40.00 80.00
3,4 12.00 35.00 70.00

TRAIL COLT (Also see Extra Comics & Manhunt!)
1949 - No. 2, 1949
Magazine Enterprises

nn(A-1 #24)-7 pg. Frazetta-a r-in Manhunt #13; Undercover Girl app.; The

Tor #5 (10/54), © STJ

The Tormented #2, © Sterling Comics

Tower of Shadows #7, © MEG

Trapped! #3, © ACE

Treasure Chest V5#3, © George A. Pflaum

Treasure Comics #5, ©

GD25 FN65 NM94

Red Fox by L. B. Cole; Ingels-c; Whitney-a (Scarce)
29.00 85.00 200.00
2(A-1 #26)-Undercover Girl; Ingels-c; L. B. Cole-a, 6 pgs.
23.00 70.00 160.00

TRANCERS (Eternity) (Value: cover or less)

TRANSFORMERS, THE (TV) (Marvel, all titles) (Value: cover or less) (Also see G.I. Joe and...)

TRANSMUTATION OF IKE GARUDA, THE (Marvel) (Value: cover or less)

TRAPPED
1951 (Giveaway) (16 pages) (soft cover)
Harvey Publications (Columbia University Press)

nn-Drug education comic (30,000 printed?) distributed to schools.; mentioned in **SOTI**, pgs. 256,350 2.40 6.00 12.00

NOTE: *Many copies surfaced in 1979 causing a setback in price; beware of trimmed edges, because many copies have a brittle edge.*

TRAPPED!
Oct, 1954 - No. 5, June?, 1955
Periodical House Magazines (Ace)

1 (All reprints) 5.35 16.00 32.00
2-5: 4-r/Men Against Crime #4 in its entirety 4.00 10.00 20.00

NOTE: ***Colan** a-1, 4. **Sekowsky** a-1.*

TRASH (Trash) (Value: cover or less)

TRAVELS OF HAPPY HOOLIGAN, THE
1906 (10-1/4x15-3/4", 32 pgs., cardboard covers)
Frederick A. Stokes Co.

nn-Contains reprints from 1905 37.00 110.00 220.00

TRAVELS OF JAIMIE McPHEETERS, THE (TV)
December, 1963
Gold Key

1-Kurt Russell 4.00 10.00 20.00

TREASURE BOX OF FAMOUS COMICS
Mid 1930's (36 pgs.) (6-7/8x8-1/2") (paper covers)
Cupples & Leon Co.

Box plus 5 titles: Reg'lar Fellers(1928), Little Orphan Annie(1926), Smitty (1928), Harold Teen(1931), How D. Tracy & D. Tracy Jr. Caught The Racketeers (1933) (These are abbreviated versions of hardcover editions)
Softcovers (Set).... 93.00 280.00 650.00
Hardcovers (Set)... 107.00 320.00 750.00

NOTE: *Dates shown are copyright dates; all books actually came out in 1934 or later.*

TREASURE CHEST (Catholic Guild; also see Topix)
3/12/46 - V27#8, July, 1972 (Educational comics)
George A. Pflaum (not publ. during Summer)

V1#1 10.00 30.00 70.00
2-6 (5/21/46): 5-Dr. Styx app. by Baily 5.00 15.00 30.00
V2#1-20 (9/3/46-5/27/47) 3.60 9.00 18.00
V3#1-5,7-20 (1st slick cover) 3.60 9.00 18.00
V3#6-Jules Verne's "Voyage to the Moon" 5.00 15.00 30.00
V4#1-20 (9/9/48-5/31/49) 2.40 6.00 12.00
V5#1-20 (9/6/49-5/31/50) 2.00 5.00 10.00
V6#1-20 (9/14/50-5/31/51) 2.00 5.00 10.00
V7#1-20 (9/13/51-6/5/52) 1.20 3.00 6.00
V8#1-20 (9/11/52-6/4/53) 1.20 3.00 6.00
V9#1-20 ('53-'54) 1.20 3.00 6.00
V10#1-20 ('54-'55) 1.20 3.00 6.00
V11('55-'56), V12('56-'57) 1.00 2.50 5.00
V13#1,3-5,7,9-V17#1 ('57-'63) .80 2.00 4.00
V13#2,6,8-Ingels-a 4.20 12.50 25.00
V17#2-'This Godless Communism' series begins(not in odd #'d issues); cover shows hammer & sickle over Statue of Liberty; 8pg. Crandall-a of family life under communism 11.50 34.00 80.00

GD25 FN65 NM94

V17#3,5,7,9,11,13,15,17,19 .80 2.00 4.00
V17#4,6,14-'This Godless Communism' stories 9.15 27.50 55.00
V17#8-Shows red octopus encompassing Earth, firing squad; 8pg. Crandall-a
10.00 30.00 65.00
V17#10-'This Godless Communism' - how Stalin came to power, part I; Crandall-a 10.00 30.00 60.00
V17#12-Stalin in WWII, forced labor, death by exhaustion; Crandall-a
10.00 30.00 60.00
V17#16-Kruschev takes over; de-Stalinization 10.00 30.00 60.00
V17#18-Kruschev's control; murder of revolters, brainwash, space race by Crandall 10.00 30.00 60.00
V17#20-End of series; Kruschev-people are puppets, firing squads hammer & sickle over Statue of Liberty, snake around communist manifesto by Crandall 10.00 30.00 60.00
V18#1-20, V19#11-20, V20#1-20('64-'65): V18#11-Crandall draws himself & 13 other artists on cover .60 1.50 3.00
V18#5-'What About Red China?' - describes how communists took over China
4.20 12.50 25.00
V19#1-10-'Red Victim' anti-communist series in all 4.20 12.50 25.00
V21-V25('65-'70)-(two V24#5's 11/7/68 & 11/21/68) (no V24#6)
.40 1.00 2.00
V26, V27#1-8 (V26,27-68 pgs.) .40 1.00 2.00
Summer Edition V1#1-6('66), V2#1-6('67) .40 1.00 2.00

NOTE: ***Anderson** a-V18#13. **Borth** a-V7#10-19 (serial), V8#8-17 (serial), V9#1-10 (serial), V13#2, 6, 11, V14-V25 (except V22#1-3, 11-13), Summer Ed. V1#3-6. **Crandall** a-V16#7, 9, 12, 14, 16-18, 20; V17#1, 2, 4-6, 10, 12, 14, 16-18, 20; V18#1, 2, 3(2pg.), 7, 9-20; V19#4, 11, 13, 16, 19, 20; V20#1, 2, 4, 6, 8-10, 12, 14-16, 18, 20; V21#1-5, 8-11, 13, 16-18; V22#3, 7, 9-11, 14; V23#3, 6, 9, 16, 18; V24#7, 8, 10, 13, 16; V25#8, 16; V27#1-7r, 8r(2 pg.), Summer Ed. V1#3-5, V2#3; c-V16#7, V18#2(part), 7, 11, V19#4, 19, 20, V20#15, V21#5, 9, V22#3, 7, 9, 11, V23#9, 16, V24#13, 16, V25#8, Summer Ed. V1#2 (back c-V1#2-5). **Powell** a-V10#11. V19#11, 15, V10#13, V13#6, 8 all have wraparound covers. All the above Crandall issues should be priced by condition from **$4-8.00** in mint unless already priced.*

TREASURE CHEST OF THE WORLD'S BEST COMICS
1945 (500 pgs.) (hardcover)
Superior, Toronto, Canada

Contains Blue Beetle, Captain Combat, John Wayne, Dynamic Man, Nemo, Li'l Abner; contents can vary - represents random binding of extra books; Capt. America on-c 67.00 200.00 400.00

TREASURE COMICS
No date (1943) (324 pgs.; cardboard covers) (50 cents)
Prize Publications? (no publisher listed)

1-(Rare)-Contains rebound Prize Comics #7-11 from 1942 (blank inside-c)
167.00 500.00 1000.00

TREASURE COMICS
June-July, 1945 - No. 12, Fall, 1947
Prize Publications (American Boys' Comics)

1-Paul Bunyan & Marco Polo begin; Highwayman & Carrot Topp only app.; Kiefer-a 14.00 43.00 100.00
2-Arabian Knight, Gorilla King, Dr. Styx begin 8.35 25.00 50.00
3,4,9,12: 9-Kiefer-a 5.85 17.50 35.00
5-Marco Polo-c; Kirby-a(p)?; Krigstein-a 10.00 30.00 70.00
6,11-Krigstein-a; 11-Krigstein-c 10.00 30.00 60.00
7,8-Frazetta-a, 5 pgs. each 22.00 65.00 154.00
10-Kirby-c/a 13.00 40.00 90.00

NOTE: ***Barry** a-9, 11. **Roussos** a-11.*

TREASURE ISLAND (See Classics Illustrated #64, Doc Savage Comics #1, 4-Color #624, King Classics, Movie Classics & Movie Comics)

TREASURY OF COMICS
1947; No. 2, July, 1947 - No. 4, Sept, 1947; No. 5, Jan, 1948
St. John Publishing Co.

nn(#1)-Abbie 'n' Slats (nn on-c, #1 on inside) 11.00 32.00 75.00
2-Jim Hardy Comics 8.35 25.00 50.00
3-Bill Bumlin 5.85 17.50 35.00

4-Abbie 'n' Slats 8.35 25.00 50.00
5-Jim Hardy Comics #1 8.35 25.00 50.00

TREASURY OF COMICS
Mar, 1948 - No. 5, 1948 (Reg. size); 1948-1950 (Over 500 pgs., $1.00)
St. John Publishing Co.

1 13.50 41.00 95.00
2(#2 on-c, #1 on inside) 10.00 30.00 60.00
3-5 8.35 25.00 50.00
1-(1948, 500 pgs., hard-c)-Abbie & Slats, Abbott & Costello, Casper (1st comic book app?), Little Annie Rooney, Little Audrey, Jim Hardy, Ella Cinders (16 books bound together) (Rare) 100.00 300.00 700.00
1(1949, 500pgs.)-Same format as above 100.00 300.00 700.00
1(1950, 500pgs.)-Same format as above; different-c; (also see Little Audrey Yearbook) (Rare) 100.00 300.00 700.00

TREASURY OF DOGS, A (See Dell Giants)

TREASURY OF HORSES, A (See Dell Giants)

TREKKER (Dark Horse) (Value: cover or less)

TRIALS OF LULU AND LEANDER, THE
1906 (32 pgs. in color) (10x16")
William A. Stokes Co.

nn-By F. M. Howarth 19.00 57.00 130.00

TRIGGER (See Roy Rogers'...)

TRIGGER TWINS
Mar-Apr, 1973 (One Shot, 20 cent issue)
National Periodical Publications

1-Trigger Twins & Pow Wow Smith-r/All-Star Western #94,103 & Western Comics #81; Infantino-r(p) .60 1.50 3.00

TRIPLE GIANT COMICS (See Archie All-Star Specials under Archie Comics)

TRIPLE THREAT
Winter, 1945
Special Action/Holyoke/Gerona Publ.

1-Duke of Darkness, King O'Leary 9.15 27.50 55.00

TRIP WITH SANTA ON CHRISTMAS EVE, A
No date (early 1950s) (16 pgs.; full color; paper cover)
Rockford Dry Goods Co. (Giveaway)

nn 3.20 8.00 16.00

TROLLORDS (Comico & Apple) (Value: cover or less)

TROUBLE SHOOTERS, THE (See 4-Color #1108)

TROUBLE WITH GIRLS, THE (Malibu/Eternity) (Value: cover or less)

TRUE ADVENTURES (Formerly True Western) (Men's Adventures #4 on)
No. 3, May, 1950 (52 pgs.)
Marvel Comics (CCC)

3-Powell, Sekowsky-a; Brodsky-c 10.00 30.00 65.00

TRUE ANIMAL PICTURE STORIES
Winter, 1947 - No. 2, Spr-Summer, 1947
True Comics Press

1,2 5.35 16.00 32.00

TRUE AVIATION PICTURE STORIES (Becomes Aviation Adventures & Model Building #16 on)
1942 - No. 15, Sept-Oct, 1946
Parents' Magazine Institute

1-(#1 & 2 titled ...Aviation Comics Digest) (not digest size) 10.00 30.00 65.00
2 5.85 17.50 35.00
3-14 5.00 15.00 30.00
15-(titled "True Aviation Adventures & Model Building") 4.20 12.50 25.00

TRUE BRIDE'S EXPERIENCES (Formerly Teen-Age Brides)
(True Bride-To-Be Romances No. 17 on)
No. 8, Oct, 1954 - No. 16, Feb, 1956
True Love (Harvey Publications)

8 4.00 10.00 20.00
9,10: 10-Last pre-code (2/55) 2.40 6.00 12.00
11-15 1.80 4.50 9.00
16-Spanking panels (3) 4.00 12.00 24.00
NOTE: *Powell a-8-10, 12, 13.*

TRUE BRIDE-TO-BE ROMANCES (Formerly True Bride's Experiences)
No. 17, Apr, 1956 - No. 30, Nov, 1958
Home Comics/True Love (Harvey)

17-S&K-c, Powell-a 4.70 14.00 28.00
18-20,22,25-28,30 2.00 5.00 10.00
21,23,24,29-Powell-a. 29-Baker-a (1 pg.) 3.00 7.50 15.00

TRUE COMICS (Also see Outstanding American War Heroes)
April, 1941 - No. 84, Aug, 1950
True Comics/Parents' Magazine Press

1-Marathon run story; life story Winston Churchill 20.00 60.00 140.00
2-Everett-a 10.00 30.00 70.00
3-Basebasll Hall of Fame story 11.50 34.00 80.00
4,5: 4-Story of American flag "Old Glory." 5-Life story of Joe Louis 10.00 30.00 60.00
6-Baseball World Series story 11.00 32.00 75.00
7-10 6.70 20.00 40.00
11-17,18-20: 13-Harry Houdini story. 14-Charlie McCarthy story. 15-Flag-c; Bob Feller story. 18-Story of America begins, ends #26 5.85 17.50 35.00
17-Brooklyn Dodgers story 7.50 22.50 45.00
21-30 5.00 15.00 30.00
31-Red Grange story 4.20 12.50 25.00
32-46: 39-FDR story. 46-George Gershwin story 4.00 11.00 22.00
47-Atomic bomb issue 6.70 20.00 40.00
48-66: 55(12/46)-1st app. Sad Sack by Baker, pg. 58-Jim Jeffries (boxer) story; Harry Houdini story. 59-Bob Hope story. 66-Will Rogers story 4.00 10.00 20.00
67-1st oversized issue (12/47); Steve Saunders, Special Agent begins 4.20 12.50 25.00
68-72,74-79: 69-Jack Benny story. 71-Joe DiMaggio story. 78-Stan Musial story 3.00 7.50 15.00
73-Walt Disney's life story 4.20 12.50 25.00
80-84 (Scarce)-All distr. to subscribers through mail only; paper-c; 81-Red Grange story 16.00 48.00 110.00
(Prices vary widely on issues 80-84)
NOTE: *Bob Kane a-7. Palais a-80. Powell c/a-80. #80-84 have soft covers and combined with Tex Granger, Jack Armstrong, and Calling All Kids. #68-78 featured true FBI adventures.*

TRUE COMICS AND ADVENTURE STORIES
1965 (Giant) (25 cents)
Parents' Magazine Institute

1,2-Fighting Hero of Viet Nam; LBJ on-c 1.40 3.50 7.00

TRUE COMPLETE MYSTERY (Formerly Complete Mystery)
No. 5, April, 1949 - No. 8, Oct, 1949
Marvel Comics (PrPI)

5 13.00 40.00 90.00
6-8: 6-8-Photo-c 10.00 30.00 70.00

TRUE CONFIDENCES
1949 (Fall) - No. 4, June, 1950 (All photo-c)
Fawcett Publications

1-Has ad for Fawcett Love Adventures #1, but publ. as Love Memoirs #1 as Marvel published the title first; Swayze-a 10.00 30.00 60.00
2-4: 3-Swayze-a. 4-Powell-a 5.85 17.50 35.00

TRUE CRIME CASES

Triple Threat #1, © HOKE

True Aviation Picture Stories #5, © PMI

True Comics #1, © PMI

True Crime Comics V2#1, © Magazine Village

True Life Secrets #7, © CC

True Secrets #18, © MEG

	GD25	FN65	NM94

1944 (100 pgs.)
St. John Publishing Co.

1944	24.00	72.00	165.00

TRUE CRIME COMICS (Also see Complete Book of...)
No. 2, May, 1947; No. 3, July-Aug, 1948 - No. 6, June-July, 1949; V2#1, Aug-Sept, 1949 (52 pgs.)
Magazine Village

2-Jack Cole-c/a; used in **SOTI**, pg. 81,82 plus illo.-"A sample of the injury-to-eye motif" & illo.-"Dragging living people to death;" used in **POP**, pg. 105; "Murder, Morphine and Me" classic drug propaganda story used by N.Y. Legis. Comm.	82.00	245.00	575.00
3-Classic Cole-c/a; drug story with hypo, opium den & withdrawing addict	57.00	170.00	400.00
4-Jack Cole-c/a; c-taken from a story panel in #3; r-(2) **SOTI** & **POP** stories/#2	50.00	150.00	350.00
5-Jack Cole-c; Marijuana racket story	29.00	85.00	200.00
6	14.00	43.00	100.00
V2#1-Used in **SOTI**, pgs. 81,82 & illo.-"Dragging living people to death;" Toth, Wood (3 pgs.), Roussos-a; Cole-r from #2	42.00	125.00	290.00

NOTE: *V2#1 was reprinted in Canada as V2#9 (12/49); same-c & contents minus Wood-a.*

TRUE GHOST STORIES (See Ripley's...)

TRUE LIFE ROMANCES (...Romance on cover)
Dec, 1955 - No. 3, Aug, 1956
Ajax/Farrell Publications

1	5.85	17.50	35.00
2	3.60	9.00	18.00
3-Disbrow-a	4.00	11.00	22.00

TRUE LIFE SECRETS
Mar-April, 1951 - No. 28, Sept, 1955; No. 29, Jan, 1956
Romantic Love Stories/Charlton

1	7.50	22.50	45.00
2	4.00	11.00	22.00
3-19	3.60	9.00	18.00
20-29: 25-Last precode(3/55)	2.60	6.50	13.00

TRUE LIFE TALES Formerly Mitzi's Romances #8?)
No. 8, Oct, 1949 - No. 2, Jan, 1950
Marvel Comics (CCC)

8(10/49), 2(1/50)-Photo-c	5.85	17.50	35.00

TRUE LOVE (Eclipse) (Value: cover or less)

TRUE LOVE CONFESSIONS
May, 1954 - No. 11, Jan, 1956
Premier Magazines

1-Marijuana story	6.70	20.00	40.00
2	3.60	9.00	18.00
3-11	2.80	7.00	14.00

TRUE LOVE PICTORIAL
1952 - No. 11, Aug, 1954
St. John Publishing Co.

1	10.00	30.00	60.00
2	5.00	15.00	30.00
3-5(All 100 pgs.): 5-Formerly Teen-Age Temptations (4/53); Kubert-a in #3,5; Baker-a in #3-5	17.00	51.00	120.00
6,7-Baker-c/a	8.35	25.00	50.00
8,10,11-Baker-c/a	7.50	22.50	45.00
9-Baker-c	5.85	17.50	35.00

TRUE MOVIE AND TELEVISION (Part magazine)
Aug, 1950 - No. 3, Nov, 1950; No. 4, Mar, 1951 (52 pgs.) (10 cents)
Toby Press

1-Liz Taylor photo-c; Gene Autry, Shirley Temple, Li'l Abner app.	24.00	73.00	170.00
2-Janet Leigh/Liz Taylor photo-c; Frazetta John Wayne illo	18.00	54.00	125.00
3-June Allyson photo-c; Montgomery Cliff, Esther Williams, Andrews Sisters app; Li'l Abner featured	17.00	50.00	115.00
4	7.50	22.50	45.00

NOTE: *16 pages in color, rest movie material in black & white.*

TRUE SECRETS (Formerly Our Love?)
No. 3, Mar, 1950; No. 4, Feb, 1951 - No. 40, Sept, 1956
Marvel (IPS)/Atlas Comics (MPI) #4 on

3 (52 pgs.)(IPS one-shot)	7.50	22.50	45.00
4,5,7-10	4.00	11.00	22.00
6,22-Everett-a	5.00	15.00	30.00
11-20	3.60	9.00	18.00
21,23-28: 28-Last pre-code (2/55)	2.40	6.00	12.00
29-40: 24-Colletta-c. 34,36-Colletta-a	2.00	5.00	10.00

TRUE SPORT PICTURE STORIES (Formerly Sport Comics)
V1#5, Feb, 1942 - V5#2, July-Aug, 1949
Street & Smith Publications

V1#5	17.00	52.00	120.00
6-12 (1942-43)	10.00	30.00	65.00
V2#1-12 (1944-45)	9.15	27.50	55.00
V3#1-12 (1946-47)	7.50	22.50	45.00
V4#1-12 (1948-49), V5#1,2	6.70	20.00	40.00

NOTE: ***Powell** a-V3#10, V4#1-4, 6-8, 10-12; V5#1, 2; c-V4#5-7, 9, 10.*

TRUE STORIES OF ROMANCE
Jan, 1950 - No. 3, May, 1950 (All photo-c)
Fawcett Publications

1	7.50	22.50	45.00
2,3: 3-Marcus Swayze-a	5.00	15.00	30.00

TRUE STORY OF JESSE JAMES, THE (See 4-Color #757)

TRUE SWEETHEART SECRETS
5/50; No. 2, 7/50; No. 3, 1951(nd); No. 4, 9/51 - No. 11, 1/53
Fawcett Publications (All photo-c)

1-Photo-c; Debbie Reynolds?	8.35	25.00	50.00
2-Wood-a, 11 pgs.	11.00	32.00	75.00
3-11: 4,5-Powell-a. 8-Marcus Swayze-a	5.00	15.00	30.00

TRUE TALES OF LOVE (Formerly Secret Story Romances)
No. 22, April, 1956 - No. 31, Sept, 1957
Atlas Comics (TCI)

22	4.20	12.50	25.00
23-31-Colletta-a in most	2.40	6.00	12.00

TRUE TALES OF ROMANCE
No. 4, June, 1950
Fawcett Publications

4	4.70	14.00	28.00

TRUE 3-D
Dec, 1953 - No. 2, Feb, 1954
Harvey Publications

1-Nostrand, Powell-a	6.70	20.00	40.00
2-Powell-a	10.00	30.00	70.00

NOTE: *Many copies of #1 surfaced in 1984.*

TRUE-TO-LIFE ROMANCES (Formerly Guns Against Gangsters)
#8, 11-12/49; #9, 1-2/50; #3, 4/50 - #5, 9/50; #6, 1/51 - #23, 10/54
Star Publications

8(#1, 1949)	10.00	30.00	60.00
9(#2),4-10	7.00	21.00	42.00
3-Janet Leigh/Glenn Ford photo on-c	8.35	25.00	50.00
11,22,23	5.85	17.50	35.00

	GD25	FN65	NM94
12-14,17-21-Disbrow-a	7.50	22.50	45.00
15,16-Wood & Disbrow-a in each	10.00	30.00	70.00

NOTE: *Kamen a-13.* ***Kamen/Feldstein*** *a-14. All have* ***L.B. Cole*** *covers.*

TRUE WAR EXPERIENCES
Aug, 1952 - No. 4, Dec, 1952
Harvey Publications

	GD25	FN65	NM94
1	5.00	15.00	30.00
2-4	3.00	7.50	15.00

TRUE WAR ROMANCES
Sept, 1952 - No. 21, June, 1955
Quality Comics Group

	GD25	FN65	NM94
1-Photo-c	7.50	22.50	45.00
2	4.00	11.00	22.00
3-10: 9-Whitney-a	3.20	8.00	16.00
11-21: 20-Last precode (4/55). 14-Whitney-a	2.40	6.00	12.00

TRUE WAR STORIES (See Ripley's...)

TRUE WESTERN (True Adventures #3)
Dec, 1949 - No. 2, March, 1950
Marvel Comics (MMC)

	GD25	FN65	NM94
1-Photo-c; Billy The Kid story	10.00	30.00	70.00
2: Alan Ladd photo-c	12.00	36.00	85.00

TRUE WEST ROMANCE
No. 21, 1952
Quality Comics Group

	GD25	FN65	NM94
21 (Exist?)	3.60	9.00	18.00

TRUMP (Magazine format)
Jan, 1957 - No. 2, Mar, 1957 (50 cents)
HMH Publishing Co.

	GD25	FN65	NM94
1-Harvey Kurtzman satire	12.00	36.00	85.00
2-Harvey Kurtzman satire	11.00	32.00	75.00

NOTE: ***Davis, Elder, Heath, Jaffee*** *art-#1,2;* ***Wood*** *a-1. Article by Mel Brooks in #2.*

TRUMPETS WEST (See 4-Color #875)

TRUTH ABOUT CRIME (See Fox Giants)

TRUTH ABOUT MOTHER GOOSE (See 4-Color #862)

TRUTH BEHIND THE TRIAL OF CARDINAL MINDSZENTY, THE (See Cardinal Mindszenty)

TRUTHFUL LOVE (Formerly Youthful Love)
No. 2, July, 1950
Youthful Magazines

	GD25	FN65	NM94
2-Ingrid Bergman's true life story	5.00	15.00	30.00

TRY-OUT WINNER BOOK (Marvel) (Value: cover or less)

TSR WORLDS (DC) (Value: cover or less)

TUBBY (See Marge's...)

TUFF GHOSTS STARRING SPOOKY
July, 1962 - No. 39, Nov, 1970; No. 40, Sept, 1971 - No. 43, Oct, 1972
Harvey Publications

	GD25	FN65	NM94
1	5.85	17.50	35.00
2-5	4.00	10.00	20.00
6-10	2.40	6.00	12.00
11-20	1.20	3.00	6.00
21-30	1.00	2.50	5.00
31-39,43	.40	1.00	2.00
40-42: 52 pg. Giants	.60	1.50	3.00

TUFFY
No. 5, July, 1949 - No. 9, Oct, 1950
Standard Comics

	GD25	FN65	NM94
5-All by Sid Hoff	4.00	10.50	21.00
6-9	2.00	5.00	10.00

TUFFY TURTLE
No date
I. W. Enterprises

	GD25	FN65	NM94
1-Reprint	.40	1.00	2.00

TUROK, SON OF STONE (See Dan Curtis, Golden Comics Digest #31, Magnus #12 & March of Comics #378, 399, 408)
No. 596, 12/54 - No. 29, 9/62; No. 30, 12/62 - No. 91, 7/74; No. 92, 9/74 - No. 125, 1/80; No. 126, 3/81 - No. 130, 4/82
Dell Publ. Co. #1-29(9/62)/Gold Key #30(12/62)-89(3/74)/Gold Key or Whitman #90(5/74)-125(1/80)/Whitman #126(3/81) on

	GD25	FN65	NM94
4-Color 596 (12/54)(#1)-1st app./origin Turok & Andar	43.00	130.00	300.00
4-Color 656 (10/55)(#2)-1st mention of Lanok	29.00	85.00	200.00
3(3-5/56)-5: 3-Cave men	22.00	65.00	150.00
6-10: 8-Dinosaur of the deep	13.50	41.00	95.00
11-20: 17-Prehistoric Pygmies	10.00	30.00	60.00
21-30: 30-33-Painted back-c pin-ups	5.85	17.50	35.00
31-40	4.20	12.50	25.00
41-50	3.60	9.00	18.00
51-60: 58-Flying Saucer c/story	2.00	5.00	10.00
61-70: 62-12 & 15 cent-c. 63-Only line drawn-c	1.40	3.50	7.00
71-84: 84-Origin & 1st app. Hutec	1.00	2.50	5.00
85-130: 98-r/#58 w/o spaceship & spacemen on-c. 114,115-(52 pgs.)	.60	1.50	3.00
Giant 1(30031-611) (11/66)	10.00	30.00	60.00

NOTE: *Most painted-c; line-drawn #63 & 130.* ***Alberto Gioletti*** *a-24-27, 30-119, 123; painted-c No. 30-129.* ***Sparling*** *a-117, 120-130. Reprints-#36, 54, 57, 75, 112, 114(1/3), 115(1/3), 118, 121, 125, 127(1/3), 128, 129(1/3), 130(1/3), Giant 1. Cover r-93, 94, 97-99, 126(all different from original covers.*

TURTLE SOUP
Sept, 1987 ($2.00, B&W, one shot, 76 pgs.)
Mirage Studios

	GD25	FN65	NM94
1-Featuring Teenage Mutant Ninja Turtles	.80	2.00	4.00

TURTLE SOUP (Mirage, 1991-92) (Value: cover or less)

TV CASPER & COMPANY
Aug, 1963 - No. 46, April, 1974 (25 cent Giants)
Harvey Publications

	GD25	FN65	NM94
1: 68 pg. Giants begin	6.70	20.00	40.00
2-5	4.00	10.00	20.00
6-10	2.40	6.00	12.00
11-20	1.20	3.00	6.00
21-31: Last 68 pg. issue	1.00	2.50	5.00
32-46: All 52 pgs.	.60	1.50	3.00

NOTE: *Many issues contain reprints.*

TV FUNDAY FUNNIES (See Famous TV...)

TV FUNNIES (See New Funnies)

TV FUNTIME (See Little Audrey)

TV LAUGHOUT (See Archie's...)

TV SCREEN CARTOONS (Formerly Real Screen)
No. 129, July-Aug, 1959 - No. 138, Jan-Feb, 1961
National Periodical Publications

	GD25	FN65	NM94
129-138 (Scarce)	5.85	17.50	35.00

TV STARS (TV)
Aug, 1978 - No. 4, Feb, 1979 (Hanna-Barbera)
Marvel Comics Group

	GD25	FN65	NM94
1-Great Grape Ape app.	1.00	2.50	5.00
2,4: 4-Top Cat app.	.40	1.00	2.00
3-Toth-c/a; Dave Stevens inks	.80	2.00	4.00

TV TEENS (Formerly Ozzie & Babs; Rock and Rollo #14 on)
V1#14, Feb, 1954 - V2#13, July, 1956
Charlton Comics

True War Romances #1, © QUA

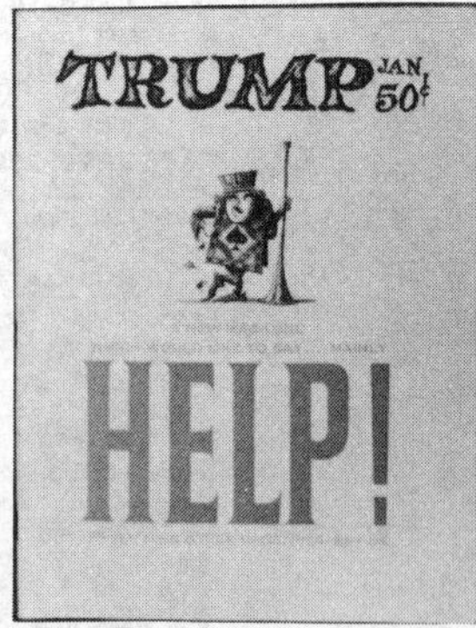

Trump #1, © Harvey Kurtzman

Turok, Son of Stone #22, © WEST

12 O'Clock High #1, © 20th Century-Fox

The Twilight Zone #26, © Cayuga Prod.

Two-Fisted Tales #21, © WMG

	GD25	FN65	NM94
V1#14-Ozzie & Babs	5.35	16.00	32.00
15	3.20	8.00	16.00
V2#3(6/54) - 7-Don Winslow	3.60	9.00	18.00
8(7/55)-13-Mopsy	3.20	8.00	16.00

TWEETY AND SYLVESTER (1st Series)
No. 406, June, 1952 - No. 37, June-Aug, 1962
Dell Publishing Co.

	GD25	FN65	NM94
4-Color 406 (#1)	5.85	17.50	35.00
4-Color 489,524	3.60	9.00	18.00
4 (3-5/54) - 20	1.80	4.50	9.00
21-37	1.00	2.50	5.00

(See March of Comics #421, 433, 445, 457, 469, 481)

TWEETY AND SYLVESTER (2nd Series)(See Kite Fun Book)
Nov, 1963; No. 2, Nov, 1965 - No. 121, July, 1984
Gold Key No. 1-102/Whitman No. 103 on

	GD25	FN65	NM94
1	2.00	5.00	10.00
2-10	1.00	2.50	5.00
11-30	.60	1.50	3.00
31-70	.30	.75	1.50
71-121: 99,119-r(1/3)		.50	1.00
Mini Comic No. 1(1976)-3-1/4x6-1/2"		.50	1.00

12 O'CLOCK HIGH (TV)
Jan-Mar, 1965 - No. 2, Apr-June, 1965 (Photo-c)
Dell Publishing Co.

	GD25	FN65	NM94
1,2	4.20	12.50	25.00

24 PAGES OF COMICS (No title) (Also see Pure Oil Comics, Salerno Carnival of Comics, & Vicks Comics)
Late 1930s
Giveaway by various outlets including Sears

	GD25	FN65	NM94
nn-Contains strip reprints-Buck Rogers, Napoleon, Sky Roads, War on Crime	23.00	70.00	160.00

20,000 LEAGUES UNDER THE SEA (See 4-Color #614, King Classics, Movie Comics & Power Record Comics)

TWICE TOLD TALES (See Movie Classics)

TWILIGHT (DC) (Value: cover or less)

TWILIGHT AVENGER, THE (Elite) (Value: cover or less)

TWILIGHT MAN (First) (Value: cover or less)

TWILIGHT ZONE, THE (TV) (See Dan Curtis)
No. 1173, 3-5/61 - No. 91, 4/79; No. 92, 5/82
Dell Publishing Co./Gold Key/Whitman No. 92

	GD25	FN65	NM94
4-Color 1173 (#1)-Crandall/Evans-c/a	14.00	43.00	100.00
4-Color 1288-Crandall/Evans-c/a	10.00	30.00	65.00
01-860-207 (5-7/62-Dell, 15 cents)	7.50	22.50	45.00
12-860-210 on-c; 01-860-210 on inside(8-10/62-Dell)-Evans-c/a; Crandall/Frazetta-a(2)	7.50	22.50	45.00
1(11/62-Gold Key)-Crandall/Frazetta-a(10 & 11 pgs.); Evans-a	9.15	27.50	55.00
2	5.85	17.50	35.00
3-11: 3,4,9-Toth-a, 11,10 & 15 pgs.	4.00	10.00	20.00
12,13,15: 12-Williamson-a. 13-Williamson/Crandall-a. 15-Crandall-a	3.60	9.00	18.00
14-Williamson/Orlando/Crandall/Torres-a	3.60	9.00	18.00
16-20	2.40	6.00	12.00
21-27: 21-Crandall-a(r). 25-Evans/Crandall-a(r); Toth-r/#4. 26-Flying Saucer-c/story; Crandall, Evans-a(r). 27-Evans-r(2)	1.60	4.00	8.00
28-32: 32-Evans-a(r)	.80	2.00	4.00
33-51: 43-Crandall-a. 51-Williamson-a	.60	1.50	3.00
52-70	.30	.75	1.50
71-92: 71-Reprint. 83,84-(52 pgs.)		.50	1.00
Mini Comic #1(1976-3-1/4x6-1/2")		.50	1.00

NOTE: **Bolle** *a-13(w/***McWilliams***), 50, 57, 59, 77, 78, 80, 83, 84.* **McWilliams** *a-59, 78, 80, 82, 84.* **Orlando** *a-15, 19, 20, 22, 23.* **Sekowsky** *a-3.* **Simonson** *a-50, 83r.* **Weiss** *a-39. (See Mystery Comics Digest 3, 6, 9, 12, 15, 18, 21, 24). Reprints-26(1/3), 71, 73, 79, 83, 84, 86, 92. Painted c-1-91.*

TWILIGHT ZONE, THE (TV)
Nov, 1990 ($2.95, color)
V2#1, Nov, 1991 - Present ($1.95, color)
Now Comics

	GD25	FN65	NM94
1-(11/90, $2.95, 52 pgs.)-Direct sale edition; Neal Adams-a, Sienkiewicz-c; Harlan Ellison scripts	1.00	2.50	5.00
1-(11/90, $1.75)-Newsstand ed. w/N. Adams-c	.35	.90	1.75
1-Prestige Format (10/91, $4.95)-Reprints above with extra Harlan Ellison short story	1.20	3.00	6.00
1-Collector's Edition (10/91, $2.50)-None-code approved and polybagged; reprints 11/90 issue; gold logo	2.00	5.00	10.00
1-Reprint ($2.50)-r/direct sale 11/90 version	.50	1.25	2.50
1-Reprint ($2.50)-r/newsstand 11/90 version	.50	1.25	2.50
V2#1-(Direct sale, non-code-c)-B. Jones scripts	.40	1.00	2.00
V2#1-(Newsstand, code approved-c)	.40	1.00	2.00
V2#2-8,10-16	.40	1.00	2.00
V2#9-($2.95)-3-D Special; polybagged w/glasses & hologram on-c	.60	1.50	3.00
V2#9-($4.95)-Prestige Edition; contains 2 extra stories & a different hologram on-c; polybagged w/glasses	1.00	2.50	5.00

TWINKLE COMICS
May, 1945
Spotlight Publishers

	GD25	FN65	NM94
1	11.00	32.00	75.00

TWIST, THE
July-September, 1962
Dell Publishing Co.

	GD25	FN65	NM94
01-864-209-Painted-c	4.20	12.50	25.00

TWISTED TALES (Pacific) (Value: cover or less)

TWO BIT THE WACKY WOODPECKER (See Wacky...)
1951 - No. 3, May, 1953
Toby Press

	GD25	FN65	NM94
1	4.20	12.50	25.00
2,3	2.40	6.00	12.00

TWO FACES OF COMMUNISM (Also see Double Talk)
1961 (36 pgs.; paper cover) (Giveaway)
Christian Anti-Communism Crusade, Houston, Texas

	GD25	FN65	NM94
nn	11.00	32.00	75.00

TWO-FISTED TALES (Formerly Haunt of Fear #15-17)
No. 18, Nov-Dec, 1950 - No. 41, Feb-Mar, 1955
E. C. Comics

	GD25	FN65	NM94
18(#1)-Kurtzman-c	72.00	215.00	500.00
19-Kurtzman-c	52.00	156.00	365.00
20-Kurtzman-c	32.00	95.00	220.00
21,22-Kurtzman-c	24.00	70.00	165.00
23-25-Kurtzman-c	18.00	54.00	125.00
26-35: 33-"Atom Bomb" by Wood	13.00	40.00	90.00
36-41	10.00	30.00	60.00
Two-Fisted Annual, 1952	64.00	193.00	450.00
Two-Fisted Annual, 1953	48.00	145.00	335.00

NOTE: **Berg** *a-29.* **Craig** *a-18, 19, 32.* **Crandall** *a-35, 36.* **Davis** *a-20-36, 40; c-30, 34, 35, 41, Annual 2.* **Evans** *a-34, 40, 41; c-40.* **Feldstein** *a-18.* **Krigstein** *a-41.* **Kubert** *a-32, 33.* **Kurtzman** *a-18-25; c-18-29, 31, Annual 1.* **Severin** *a-26, 28, 29, 31, 34-41 (No. 37-39 are all-***Severin** *issues); c-36-39.* **Severin/Elder** *a-19-29, 31, 33, 36.* **Wood** *a-18-28, 30-35, 41; c-32, 33. Special issues: #26 (ChanJin Reservoir), 31 (Civil War), 35 (Civil War). Canadian reprints known; see Table of Contents. #25-Davis biog. #27-Wood biog. #28-Kurtzman biog.*

TWO-FISTED TALES

Oct, 1992 - Present ($1.50, color)
Russ Cochran

1-4: 1-r/Two-Fisted #18(#1); Kurtzman-c .30 .75 1.50

TWO-GUN KID (Also see All Western Winners, Best Western, Black Rider, Blaze Carson, Kid Colt, Western Winners, Wild West, & Wild Western)
3/48(No mo.) - No. 10, 11/49; No. 11, 12/53 - No. 59, 4/61; No. 60, 11/62 - No. 92, 3/68; No. 93, 7/70 - No. 136, 4/77
Marvel/Atlas (MCI No. 1-10/HPC No. 11-59/Marvel No. 60 on)

1-Two-Gun Kid & his horse Cyclone begin; The Sheriff begins 54.00 160.00 375.00
2 24.00 70.00 165.00
3,4: 3-Annie Oakley app. 17.00 52.00 120.00
5-Pre-Black Rider app. (Wint. 48/49); Spanking panel. Anti-Wertham editorial (1st?) 20.00 60.00 140.00
6-10(11/49): 8-Blaze Carson app. 9-Black Rider app. 13.50 41.00 95.00
11(12/53)-Black Rider app.; explains how Kid Colt became an outlaw 11.00 32.00 75.00
12-Black Rider app. 11.00 32.00 75.00
13-20: 13-1st to have Atlas globe on-c 9.15 27.50 55.00
21-24,26-29 7.50 22.50 45.00
25,30: 25-Williamson-a(5 pgs.). 30-Williamson/Torres-a(4 pgs.) 8.35 25.00 50.00
31-33,35,37-40 5.35 16.00 32.00
34-Crandall-a 5.85 17.50 35.00
36,41,42,48-Origin in all 5.85 17.50 35.00
43,44,47 4.20 12.50 25.00
45,46-Davis-a 4.70 14.00 28.00
49,50,52,55,57-Severin-a(2) in each 4.00 11.00 22.00
51-Williamson-a, 5 pgs. 4.70 14.00 28.00
53,54-Severin-a(3) in each 4.20 12.50 25.00
56,59: 59-Last 10 cent issue (4/61) 2.40 6.00 12.00
58,60-New origin 2.40 6.00 12.00
61-80: 64-Intro. Boom-Boom 1.20 3.00 6.00
81-92: 92-Last new story; last 12 cent issue .70 1.75 3.50
93-100,102-136 .30 .75 1.50
101-Origin retold/#58 .40 1.00 2.00

NOTE: ***Ayers** a-26, 27. **Davis** c-45-47. **Drucker** a-23. **Everett** a-82, 91. **Fuje** a-13. **Heath** a-3(2), 4(3), 5(2), 7; c-13, 21, 23, 53. **Keller** a-16, 19, 28. **Kirby** a-54, 55, 57-62, 75-77, 90, 95, 101, 119, 120, 129; c-10, 52, 54-65, 67-72, 74-76, 116. **Maneely** a-20; c-11, 12, 16, 19, 20, 25-28, 35, 49. **Powell** a-38, 102, 104. **Severin** a-9, 29, 51, 55, 57, 99r(3); c-9, 51, 99. **Shores** c-1-8, 11. **Tuska** a-11, 12. **Whitney** a-87, 89-91, 98-113, 124, 129; c-87, 89, 91, 113. **Wildey** a-21. **Williamson** a-110r. Kid Colt in #13, 14, 16-21.*

TWO GUN WESTERN (1st Series) (Formerly Casey Crime Photographer #1-4? or My Love #1-4?)
No. 5, Nov, 1950 - No. 14, June, 1952
Marvel/Atlas Comics (MPC)

5-The Apache Kid (Intro & origin) & his horse Nightwind begin by Buscema 13.00 40.00 90.00
6-10: 8-Kid Colt, The Texas Kid & his horse Thunder begin? 10.00 30.00 60.00
11-14: 13-Black Rider app. 7.50 22.50 45.00

NOTE: ***Maneely** a-6, 7, 9; c-6, 11-13. **Morrow** a-9. **Romita** a-8. **Wildey** a-8.*

2-GUN WESTERN (2nd Series) (Formerly Billy Buckskin #1-3; Two-Gun Western #5 on)
No. 4, May, 1956
Atlas Comics (MgPC)

4-Apache Kid; Colan, Ditko, Severin, Sinnott-a; Maneely-c 10.00 30.00 60.00

TWO-GUN WESTERN (Formerly 2-Gun Western)
No. 5, July, 1956 - No. 12, Sept, 1957
Atlas Comics (MgPC)

5-Black Rider app. 8.35 25.00 50.00
6,7 5.00 15.00 30.00
8,10,12-Crandall-a 6.70 20.00 40.00
9,11-Williamson-a in both, 5 pgs. each 6.70 20.00 40.00

NOTE: ***Ayers** a-9. **Colan** a-5. **Everett** c-12. **Forgione** a-5, 6. **Kirby** a-12. **Maneely** a-6, 8, 12; c-5, 6, 8, 11. **Morrow** a-9, 10. **Powell** a-7, 11. **Severin** c-10. **Sinnott** a-5. **Wildey** a-9.*

TWO MOUSEKETEERS, THE (See 4-Color #475, 603, 642 under M.G.M.'s...; becomes M.G.M.'s Mouse Musketeers)

TWO ON A GUILLOTINE (See Movie Classics)

2000 A.D. MONTHLY/PRESENTS (Eagle/Quality) (Value: cover or less)

2000AD SHOWCASE (Quality) (Value: cover or less)

2001,A SPACE ODYSSEY (Marvel, Treasury Special & '76 series) (Value: cover or less)

2001 NIGHTS (Viz) (Value: cover or less)

2010 (Marvel) (Value: cover or less)

UFO & ALIEN COMIX
Jan, 1978 (One Shot)
Warren Publishing Co.

nn-Toth, Severin-a(r) .30 .80 1.60

UFO & OUTER SPACE (Formerly UFO Flying Saucers)
No. 14, June, 1978 - No. 25, Feb, 1980 (All painted covers)
Gold Key

14-Reprints UFO Flying Saucers #3 .40 1.00 2.00
15,16-Reprints .60 1.20
17-20-New material .30 .75 1.50
21-25: 23-McWilliams-a. 24-(3 pg.-r). 25-Reprints UFO Flying Saucers #2 w/cover .50 1.00

UFO ENCOUNTERS
May, 1978 (228 pages) ($1.95)
Western Publishing Co.

11192-Reprints UFO Flying Saucers .80 2.00 4.00
11404-Vol.1 (128 pgs.)-See UFO Mysteries for Vol.2 .40 1.00 2.00

UFO FLYING SAUCERS (UFO & Outer Space #14 on)
Oct, 1968 - No. 13, Jan, 1977 (No. 2 on, 36 pgs.)
Gold Key

1(30035-810) (68 pgs.) 3.00 7.50 15.00
2(11/70), 3(11/72), 4(11/74) 1.60 4.00 8.00
5(2/75)-13: Bolle-a #4 on 1.00 2.50 5.00

UFO MYSTERIES
1978 (96 pages) ($1.00) (Reprints)
Western Publishing Co.

11400($1.00, 96 pgs.) .40 1.00 2.00
11404(Vol.2)-Cont'd from UFO Encounters, pgs. 129-224 .40 1.00 2.00

ULTRA KLUTZ (Onward) (Value: cover or less)

UNBIRTHDAY PARTY WITH ALICE IN WONDERLAND (See 4-Color #341)

UNCANNY TALES
June, 1952 - No. 56, Sept, 1957
Atlas Comics (PrPI/PPI)

1-Heath-a 34.00 103.00 240.00
2 17.00 52.00 120.00
3-5 14.00 43.00 100.00
6-Wolvertonish-a by Matt Fox 14.00 43.00 100.00
7-10: 8-Tothish-a. 9-Crandall-a 13.00 40.00 90.00
11-20: 17-Atom bomb panels; anti-communist story; Hitler story. 19-Krenkel-a 11.00 32.00 75.00
21-27: 25-Nostrand-a? 10.00 30.00 60.00
28-Last precode issue (1/55); Kubert-a; #1-28 contain 2-3 sci/fi stories each 10.00 30.00 65.00
29-41,43-49,52 5.85 17.50 35.00
42,54,56-Krigstein-a 8.35 25.00 50.00

Two-Gun Kid #27, © MEG

Two Gun Western #10 (10/51), © MEG

Uncanny Tales #4, © MEG

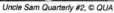

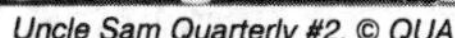
Uncle Sam Quarterly #2, © QUA

Uncle Scrooge #4, © WDC

Uncle Scrooge #41, © WDC

	GD25	FN65	NM94
50,53,55-Torres-a	6.70	20.00	40.00
51	7.50	22.50	45.00

NOTE: ***Andru** a-15, 27. **Ayers** a-22. **Bailey** a-51. **Briefer** a-19, 20. **Brodsky** c-1, 3, 4, 6, 8, 12-16, 19. **Brodsky/Everett** c-9. **Cameron** a-47. **Colan** a-11, 16, 17, 52. **Drucker** a-37, 42, 45. **Everett** a-2, 12, 32, 36, 39, 48; c-7, 11, 17, 39, 41, 50, 52, 53. **Fass** a-9, 10, 15, 24. Forte a-18, 27, 34, 52, 53. **Heath** a-13, 14; c-5, 10, 18. **Keller** a-3. **Lawrence** a-14, 17, 19, 23, 27, 28, 35. **Maneely** a-4, 8, 10, 16, 29, 35; c-2, 22, 26, 33, 38. **Moldoff** a-23. **Morisi** a-48, 52. **Morrow** a-46, 51. **Orlando** a-49, 50, 53. **Powell** a-12, 18, 34, 36, 38, 43, 50, 56. **Robinson** a-3, 13. **Reinman** a-12. **Romita** a-10. **Roussos** a-8. **Sale** a-47, 53; c-20. **Sekowsky** a-25. **Sinnott** a-15, 52. **Torres** a-53. **Tothish**-a by **Andru**-27. **Wildey** a-22, 48.*

UNCANNY TALES
Dec, 1973 - No. 12, Oct, 1975
Marvel Comics Group

	GD25	FN65	NM94
1-Crandall-r/Uncanny Tales #9('50s)	.40	1.00	2.00
2-12	.30	.75	1.50

NOTE: *Ditko reprints-#4, 6-8, 10-12.*

UNCANNY X-MEN, THE (See X-Men)

UNCANNY X-MEN AND THE NEW TEEN TITANS (See Marvel and DC Present...)

UNCANNY X-MEN AT THE STATE FAIR OF TEXAS, THE
1983 (36 pgs.)(One-Shot)
Marvel Comics Group

	GD25	FN65	NM94
nn	4.00	10.00	20.00

UNCANNY X-MEN IN DAYS OF FUTURE PAST, THE
1989 ($3.95, color, squarebound, 52 pgs.)
Marvel Comics

	GD25	FN65	NM94
nn-Byrne/Austin-r (2 stories); Guice-c(p)	.80	2.00	4.00

UNCENSORED MOUSE, THE
Apr, 1989 - No. 2, Apr, 1989 ($1.95, B&W)(Came sealed in plastic bag)
Eternity Comics

	GD25	FN65	NM94
1-Early Gottfredson strip-r in each	.80	2.00	4.00
2-Both contain racial stereotyping & violence	1.20	3.00	6.00

NOTE: *Both issues contain unauthorized reprints. Series was cancelled.*

UNCLE CHARLIE'S FABLES
Jan, 1952 - No. 5, Sept, 1952
Lev Gleason Publications

	GD25	FN65	NM94
1-Norman Maurer-a; has Biro's picture	7.50	22.50	45.00
2-Fuje-a; Biro photo; Biro painted-c	5.00	15.00	30.00
3-5: 4-Biro-c	4.20	12.50	25.00

UNCLE DONALD & HIS NEPHEWS DUDE RANCH (See Dell Giant #52)

UNCLE DONALD & HIS NEPHEWS FAMILY FUN (See Dell Giant #38)

UNCLE JOE'S FUNNIES
1938 (B&W)
Centaur Publications

	GD25	FN65	NM94
1-Games/puzzles, some interior art; Bill Everett-c	25.00	75.00	175.00

UNCLE MILTY (TV)
Dec, 1950 - No. 4, July, 1951 (52 pgs.)
Victoria Publications/True Cross

	GD25	FN65	NM94
1-Milton Berle	29.00	85.00	200.00
2	16.00	48.00	110.00
3,4	13.00	40.00	90.00

UNCLE REMUS & HIS TALES OF BRER RABBIT (See 4-Color #129, 208, 693)

UNCLE SAM QUARTERLY (Blackhawk #9 on)(See Freedom Fighters)
Autumn, 1941 - No. 8, Fall, 1943 (Also see National Comics)
Quality Comics Group

	GD25	FN65	NM94
1-Origin Uncle Sam; Fine/Eisner-c, chapter headings, 2 pgs. by Eisner. (2 versions: dark cover, no price; light cover with price sticker); Jack Cole-a	158.00	475.00	950.00
2-Cameos by The Ray, Black Condor, Quicksilver, The Red Bee, Alias the Spider, Hercules & Neon the Unknown; Eisner, Fine-c/a	79.00	238.00	475.00
3-Tuska-c/a	58.00	175.00	350.00
4	50.00	150.00	300.00
5-8	42.00	125.00	250.00

NOTE: ***Kotzky** (or **Tuska**) a-4-8.*

UNCLE SAM'S CHRISTMAS STORY
1958
Promotional Publ. Co. (Giveaway)

	GD25	FN65	NM94
nn-Reprints 1956 Christmas USA	2.00	5.00	10.00

UNCLE SCROOGE (Disney)(See Cartoon Tales, Dell Giants #33, 55, Donald and Scrooge, Dynabrite, Four Color #178, Gladstone Comic Album, Walt Disney's Comics & Stories #98)
No. 386, 3/52 - No. 39, 8-10/62; No. 40, 12/62 - No. 209, 1984; No. 210, 10/86 - No. 242, 4/90; No. 243, 6/90 - Present
Dell #1-39/Gold Key #40-173/Whitman #174-209/Gladstone #210-242/ Disney Comics #243 on

	GD25	FN65	NM94
4-Color 386(#1)-in "Only a Poor Old Man" by Carl Barks; r-in Uncle Scrooge & Donald Duck #1('65) & The Best of Walt Disney Comics (1974)	75.00	225.00	525.00
1-(1986)-Reprints F.C. #386; given away with lithograph "Dam Disaster at Money Lake" & as a subscription offer giveaway to Gladstone subscribers	.40	1.00	2.00
4-Color 456(#2)-in "Back to the Klondike" by Carl Barks; r-in Best of U.S. & D.D. #1('66) & Gladstone C.A. #4	38.00	115.00	265.00
4-Color 495(#3)-r-in #105	32.00	95.00	220.00
4(12-2/53-54)-r-in Gladstone Comic Album #11	24.00	73.00	170.00
5-r-in Gladstone Spec. #2 & W.D. Digest #1	20.00	60.00	140.00
6-r-in U.S. #106,165,233 & Best of U.S. & D.D. #1('66)	19.00	57.00	130.00
7-The Seven Cities of Cibola by Barks; r-in #217 & Best of D.D. & U.S. #2 ('67)	14.00	43.00	100.00
8-10: 8-r-in #111,222. 9-r-in #104,214. 10-r-in #67	11.50	34.00	80.00
11-20: 11-r-in #237. 17-r-in #215. 19-r-in Gladstone C.A. #1. 20-r-in #213	10.00	30.00	70.00
21-30: 26-r-in #211	10.00	30.00	60.00
31-40: 34-r-in #228	8.35	25.00	50.00
41-50	6.70	20.00	40.00
51-60	5.85	17.50	35.00
61-66,68-70: 70-Last Barks issue w/original story	5.00	15.00	30.00
67,72,73-Barks-r	4.00	10.00	20.00
71-Written by Barks only	4.00	10.00	20.00
74-One pg. Barks-r	2.40	6.00	12.00
75-81,83-Not by Barks	2.40	6.00	12.00
82,84-Barks-r begin	2.40	6.00	12.00
85-100	2.00	5.00	10.00
101-110	1.60	4.00	8.00
111-120	1.40	3.50	7.00
121-141,143-152,154-157	1.20	3.00	6.00
142-Reprints 4-Color #456 with-c	1.40	3.50	7.00
153,158,162-164,166,168-170,178,180: No Barks	.80	2.00	4.00
159-160,165,167,172-176-Barks-a	.80	2.00	4.00
161(r/#14), 171(r/#11), 177(r/#16), 179(r/#9), 183(r/#6)-Barks-r	.80	2.00	4.00
181(r/4-Color #495), 195(r/4-Color #386)	.40	1.00	2.00
182,186,191-194,197-202,204-206: No Barks	.30	.75	1.50
184,185,187,188-Barks-a	.30	.75	1.50
189(r/#5), 190(r/#4), 196(r/#13), 203(r/#12), 207(r/#93,92), 208(r/U.S. #18), 209(r/U.S. #21)-Barks-r	.30	.75	1.50
210-1st Gladstone issue; r/WDC&S #134 (1st Beagle Boys)	1.00	2.50	5.00
211-218: 217-r/U.S. #7(Seven Cities of Cibola)	.50	1.25	2.50

	GD25	FN65	NM94
219-Son Of The Sun by Rosa	2.00	5.00	10.00
220-Don Rosa story/a	.60	1.50	3.00
221-230: 224-Rosa-c/a. 226,227-Rosa-a	.30	.75	1.50
231-240: 235-Rosa story/art		.50	1.00
241-($1.95, 68 pgs.)-Rosa finishes over Barks-r	.40	1.00	2.00
242-($1.95, 68 pgs.)-Barks-r; Rosa-a(1 pg.)	.40	1.00	2.00
243-249,251-280($1.50): 243-1st by Disney Comics; new-a begins. 261-263-Don Rosa-c/a. 274-All Barks issue. 275-Contains poster by Rosa	.30	.75	1.50
250-($2.25, 52 pgs.)-Barks-r; wraparound-c	.45	1.15	2.25
Uncle Scrooge & Money(G.K.)-Barks-r/from WDC&S #130 (3/67)	4.35	13.00	26.00
Mini Comic #1(1976)(3-1/4x6-1/2")-r/U.S. #115; Barks-c		.50	1.00

NOTE: ***Barks** c-4-Color 386, 456, 495, #4-37, 39, 40, 43-71. **Barks** r-210-218, 220-223, 224 (2pg.), 225-234, 236-242, 250-253, 255, 256, 258, 265, 267, 268, 272-277; c(r)-210, 212, 221, 228, 229, 232, 233. **Rosa** a-219, 220, 224, 226, 227, 235, 261-263, 268, 276, 277; c-219, 224, 231, 261-263, 276; scripts-219, 220, 224, 235, 261, 276.*

UNCLE SCROOGE ADVENTURES (Walt Disney's...#4 on)
Nov, 1987 - No. 21, May, 1990
Gladstone Publishing

	GD25	FN65	NM94
1-Barks-r begin	.80	2.00	4.00
2-5: 5-Rosa-c/a	.30	.75	1.50
6-19: 9,14-Rosa-a. 10-r/U.S. #18(all Barks)		.50	1.00
20,21 ($1.95, 68 pgs.) 20-Rosa-c/a. 21-Rosa-a	.40	1.00	2.00

NOTE: ***Barks** r-1-4, 6-8, 10-13, 15-21; c(r)-15, 16, 17, 21. **Rosa** a-5, 9, 14, 20, 21; c-5, 13, 14, 17(finishes), 20; scripts-5, 9, 14.*

UNCLE SCROOGE & DONALD DUCK
June, 1965 (25 cents, paper cover)
Gold Key

	GD25	FN65	NM94
1-Reprint of 4-Color #386(#1) & lead story from 4-Color #29	8.35	25.00	50.00

UNCLE SCROOGE COMICS DIGEST
Dec, 1986 - No. 5, Aug, 1987 ($1.25, Digest-size)
Gladstone Publishing

	GD25	FN65	NM94
1-5		.60	1.25

UNCLE SCROOGE GOES TO DISNEYLAND (See Dell Giants)
Aug, 1985 ($2.50)
Gladstone Publishing Ltd.

	GD25	FN65	NM94
1-Reprints Dell Giant w/new-c by Mel Crawford, based on old cover	.50	1.25	2.50
...Comics Digest 1 ($1.50, digest size)	.30	.75	1.50

UNCLE WIGGILY (See 4-Color #179, 221, 276, 320, 349, 391, 428, 503, 543, & March of Comics #19)

UNDERCOVER GIRL (Starr Flagg) (See Extra Comics & Manhunt!)
No. 5, 1952 - No. 7, 1954
Magazine Enterprises

	GD25	FN65	NM94
5(#1)(A-1 #62)-Fallon of the F.B.I. in all	26.00	77.00	180.00
6(A-1 #98), 7(A-1 #118)-All have Starr Flagg	24.00	70.00	165.00

NOTE: ***Powell** c-6, 7. **Whitney** a-5-7.*

UNDERDOG (TV)(See Kite Fun Book & March of Comics #426, 438, 467, 479)
July, 1970 - No. 10, Jan, 1972; Mar, 1975 - No. 23, Feb, 1979
Charlton Comics/Gold Key

	GD25	FN65	NM94
1 (1st series, Charlton)	5.35	16.00	32.00
2-10	3.00	7.50	15.00
1 (2nd series, Gold Key)	4.00	10.00	20.00
2-10	1.80	4.50	9.00
11-23: 13-1st app. Shack of Solitude	1.20	3.00	6.00

UNDERDOG (Spotlight) (Value: cover or less)

UNDERSEA AGENT
Jan, 1966 - No. 6, Mar, 1967 (25 cents, 68 pages)
Tower Comics

	GD25	FN65	NM94
1-Davy Jones, Undersea Agent begins	5.85	17.50	35.00
2-6: 2-Jones gains magnetic powers. 5-Origin & 1st app. of Merman. 6-Kane?/Wood-c(r)	4.00	11.00	22.00

NOTE: ***Gil Kane** a-3-6; c-4, 5. **Moldoff** a-2i.*

UNDERSEA FIGHTING COMMANDOS (See Fighting Undersea...)
May, 1952 - No. 5, Jan, 1953; 1964
Avon Periodicals

	GD25	FN65	NM94
1-Ravielli-c	5.85	17.50	35.00
2	4.00	10.00	20.00
3-5	3.60	9.00	18.00
I.W. Reprint #1,2('64): 1-r/#? 2-r/#1; Severin-c	1.20	3.00	6.00

UNDERWATER CITY, THE (See 4-Color #1328)

UNDERWORLD (True Crime Stories)
Feb-Mar, 1948 - No. 9, June-July, 1949 (52 pgs.)
D. S. Publishing Co.

	GD25	FN65	NM94
1-Moldoff-c; excessive violence	20.00	60.00	140.00
2-Moldoff-c; Ma Barker story used in **SOTI**, pg. 95; female electrocution panel; lingerie art	22.00	65.00	150.00
3-McWilliams-c/a; extreme violence, mutilation	17.00	52.00	120.00
4-Used in Love and Death by Legman; Ingels-a	13.00	40.00	90.00
5-Ingels-a	10.00	30.00	65.00
6-9: 8-Ravielli-a	8.35	25.00	50.00

UNDERWORLD (DC) (Value: cover or less)

UNDERWORLD CRIME
June, 1952 - No. 9, Oct, 1953
Fawcett Publications

	GD25	FN65	NM94
1	16.00	48.00	110.00
2	10.00	30.00	60.00
3-6,8,9 (8,9-exist?)	9.15	27.50	55.00
7-Bondage/torture-c	13.00	40.00	90.00

UNDERWORLD STORY, THE
1950 (Movie)
Avon Periodicals

	GD25	FN65	NM94
nn-(Scarce)-Ravielli-c	16.00	48.00	110.00

UNEARTHLY SPECTACULARS
Oct, 1965 - No. 3, Mar, 1967 (#1: 12 cents; #2,3: 25 cent giants)
Harvey Publications

	GD25	FN65	NM94
1-Tiger Boy; Simon-c	2.00	5.00	10.00
2-Jack Q. Frost, Tiger Boy & Three Rocketeers app.; Williamson, Wood, Kane-a; r-1 story/Thrill-O-Rama #2	3.60	9.00	18.00
3-Jack Q. Frost app.; Williamson/Crandall-a; r-from Alarming Advs. #1, 1962	3.60	9.00	18.00

NOTE: ***Crandall** a-3r. **G. Kane** a-2. **Orlando** a-3. **Simon, Sparling, Wood** c-2. **Simon/Kirby** a-3r. **Torres** a-1?. **Wildey** a-1(3). **Williamson** a-2, 3r. **Wood** a-2(2).*

UNEXPECTED, THE (Formerly Tales of the...)
No. 105, Feb-Mar, 1968 - No. 222, May, 1982
National Periodical Publications/DC Comics

	GD25	FN65	NM94
105-Begin 12 cent cover price	2.40	6.00	12.00
106-113: 113-Last 12 cent issue (6-7/69)	1.60	4.00	8.00
114,115,117,118,120,122-127	1.00	2.50	5.00
116,119,121,128-Wrightson-a	1.40	3.50	7.00
129-162: 132-136-(52 pgs.). 157-162-(100 pgs.)	.50	1.25	2.50
163-188: 187,188-(44 pgs.)		.60	1.20
189,190,192-195 ($1.00, 68 pgs.): 189 on are combined with House of Secrets & The Witching Hour	.25	.70	1.40
191-Rogers-a(p) ($1.00, 68 pgs.)	.50	1.25	2.50
196-221: 200-Return of Johhny Peril by Tuska. 205-213-Johnny Peril app. 210-Time Warp story		.50	1.00

NOTE: ***Neal Adams** c-110, 112-118, 121, 124. **J. Craig** a-195. **Ditko** a-189, 221p, 222p; c-222. **Drucker** a-107r, 132r. **Giffen** a-219, 222. **Kaluta** c-203, 212. **Kirby** a-127r, 162. **Kubert** c-204, 214-216, 219-221. **Mayer** a-217p, 220, 221p. **Moldoff** a-136r. **Moreira** a-133. **Mortimer** a-212p. **Newton** a-204p. **Orlando** a-202; c-191. **Perez** a-217p. **Redondo** a-155, 166, 195. **Reese** a-145. **Sparling** a-107, 205-209p, 212p. **Spiegle** a-217. **Starlin** c-198. **Toth***

Undersea Agent #1, © TC

Underworld #4, © DS

The Unexpected #106, © DC

United States Fighting Air Force #1, © SUPR

Unknown World #1, © FAW

The Unseen #6, © STD

GD25 FN65 NM94

a-126r, 127r. ***Tuska*** *a-127, 132, 134, 136, 139, 152, 180, 200p.* ***Wildey*** *a-128r, 193.* ***Wood*** *a-122i, 133i, 137i, 138i.* ***Wrightson*** *a-161r(2 pgs.). Johnny Peril in #106-117, 200, 205-213.*

UNEXPECTED ANNUAL, THE (See DC Special Series #4)

UNIDENTIFIED FLYING ODDBALL (See Walt Disney Showcase #52)

UNITED COMICS (Formerly Fritzi Ritz #7)
Aug, 1940; No. 8, 1950 - No. 26, Jan-Feb, 1953
United Features Syndicate

1(68 pgs.)-Fritzi Ritz & Phil Fumble 14.00 43.00 100.00
8-Fritzi Ritz, Abbie & Slats 3.60 9.00 18.00
9-26: 20-Strange As It Seems; Russell Patterson Cheesecake-a. 22,25-Peanuts app. 3.20 8.00 16.00
NOTE: *Abbie & Slats reprinted from Tip Top.*

UNITED NATIONS, THE (See Classics Illustrated Special Issue)

UNITED STATES AIR FORCE PRESENTS: THE HIDDEN CREW
1964 (36 pages) (full color)
U.S. Air Force

nn-Shaffenberger-a .60 1.50 3.00

UNITED STATES FIGHTING AIR FORCE (Also see U.S. Fighting Air Force)
Sept, 1952 - No. 29, Oct, 1956
Superior Comics Ltd.

1 5.35 16.00 32.00
2 3.20 8.00 16.00
3-10 1.80 4.50 9.00
11-29 1.40 3.50 7.00

UNITED STATES MARINES
1943 - No. 4, 1944; No. 5, 1952 - No. 8, 1952; No. 7 - No. 11, 1953
William H. Wise/Life's Romances Publ. Co./Magazine Enterprises #5-8/Toby Press #7-11

nn-Mart Bailey-a 5.85 17.50 35.00
2-Bailey-a 4.35 13.00 26.00
3,4 4.00 11.00 22.00
5(A-1 #55), 6(A-1 #60), 7(A-1 #68), 8(A-1 #72) 4.00 10.00 20.00
7-11 (Toby) 1.80 4.50 9.00
NOTE: ***Powell*** *a-5-7.*

UNITY
Aug, 1992 - No. 1, 1992 (Color, free, both limited, 20 pgs.)
Valiant

0-(8/92)-Prequel to Unity x-overs in all Valiant titles; free to everone that bought all 8 titles that month; B. Smith-c/a 2.00 5.00 10.00
0-Red logo; sames above, but w/red logo (5,000) 14.00 43.00 100.00
1-(?/92)-Epilogue to unity x-overs; B. Smith-c/a 3.00 7.50 15.00
1(Gold) 14.00 43.00 100.00
1 (Platinum) 20.00 60.00 140.00

UNIVERSAL PRESENTS DRACULA (See Dell Giants)

UNIVERSAL SOLDIER
Sept, 1992 - No. 3, Nov, 1992 (Color, mini-series, based on movie)
Now Comics

1-3 ($2.50, direct sale ed.)-Polybagged, mature readers. 1-Hologram on-c; all direct sale editions have painted-c .50 1.25 2.50
1-3 ($1.95, newsstand ed.)-Rewritten & redrawn code approved version; all newsstand editions have photo-c .40 1.00 2.00

UNKEPT PROMISE
1949 (24 pages)
Legion of Truth (Giveaway)

nn-Anti-alcohol 6.70 20.00 40.00

UNKNOWN MAN, THE
1951 (Movie)
Avon Periodicals

nn-Kinstler-c 17.00 52.00 120.00

UNKNOWN SOLDIER (Formerly Star-Spangled War Stories)
No. 205, Apr-May, 1977 - No. 268, Oct, 1982
National Periodical Publications/DC Comics

205-268: 219-221-(44 pgs.). 248,249-Origin. 251-Enemy Ace begins. 268-Death of Unknown Soldier .30 .75 1.50
NOTE: ***Chaykin*** *a-234.* ***Evans*** *a-265-267; c-235.* ***Kubert*** *c-Most.* ***Miller*** *a-219p.* ***Severin*** *a-251-253, 260, 261, 265-267.* ***Simonson*** *a-254-256.* ***Spiegle*** *a-258, 259, 262-264.*

UNKNOWN SOLDIER, THE (DC)(Value: cover or less)(See Brave & the Bold #146)

UNKNOWN WORLD (Strange Stories From Another World #2 on)
June, 1952
Fawcett Publications

1-Norman Saunders painted-c 19.00 58.00 135.00

UNKNOWN WORLDS (See Journey Into...)

UNKNOWN WORLDS
Aug, 1960 - No. 57, Aug, 1967
American Comics Group/Best Synd. Features

1 11.50 34.00 80.00
2-5: 2-Dinosaur-c/story 6.70 20.00 40.00
6-11: 9-Dinosaur-c/story. 11-Last 10 cent issue 5.00 15.00 30.00
12-19: 12-Begin 12 cent issues?; ends #57 4.00 11.00 22.00
20-Herbie cameo (12-1/62-63) 4.70 14.00 28.00
21-35 3.60 9.00 18.00
36-"The People vs. Hendricks" by Craig; most popular ACG story ever 4.00 11.00 22.00
37-46 3.00 7.50 15.00
47-Williamson-a r-from Adventures Into the Unknown #96, 3 pgs.; Craig-a 3.60 9.00 18.00
48-57: 53-Frankenstein app. 2.40 6.00 12.00
NOTE: ***Ditko*** *a-49, 50p, 54.* ***Forte*** *a-3, 6, 11.* ***Landau*** *a-56(2).* ***Reinman*** *a-3, 9, 13, 20, 22, 23, 36, 38, 54.* ***Whitney*** *c/a-most issues. John Force, Magic Agent app.-No. 35, 36, 48, 50, 52, 54, 56.*

UNKNOWN WORLDS OF FRANK BRUNNER (Eclipse)(Value: cover or less)

UNKNOWN WORLDS OF SCIENCE FICTION
Jan, 1975 - No. 6, Nov, 1975; 1976 (B&W Magazine) ($1.00)
Marvel Comics Group

1-Williamson/Krenkel/Torres/Frazetta-r/Witzend #1, Neal Adams-r/Phase 1; Brunner & Kaluta-r; Freas/Romita-c .60 1.50 3.00
2-6: 5-Kaluta text illos .50 1.20 2.40
Special 1(1976,100 pgs.)-Newton painted-c .50 1.20 2.40
NOTE: ***Brunner*** *a-2; c-4, 6.* ***Buscema*** *a-Special 1p.* ***Chaykin*** *a-5.* ***Colan*** *a(p)-1, 3, 5, 6.* ***Corben*** *a-4.* ***Kaluta*** *a-2, Special 1(ext illos); c-2.* ***Morrow*** *a-3, 5.* ***Nino*** *a-3, 6, Special 1.* ***Perez*** *a-2, 3. Ray Bradbury interview in #1.*

UNSANE (Formerly Mighty Bear #13, 14? or The Outlaws #10-14?)
No. 15, June, 1954
Star Publications

15-Disbrow-a(2); L. B. Cole-c 16.00 48.00 110.00

UNSEEN, THE
No. 5, 1952 - No. 15, July, 1954
Visual Editions/Standard Comics

5-Toth-a 13.50 41.00 95.00
6,7,9,10-Jack Katz-a 10.00 30.00 60.00
8,11,13,14 7.50 22.50 45.00
12,15-Toth-a. 12-Tuska-a 10.00 30.00 65.00
NOTE: ***Nick Cardy*** *c-12.* ***Fawcette*** *a-13, 14.* ***Sekowsky*** *a-7, 8(2), 10, 13.*

UNTAMED LOVE (Also see Frank Frazetta's Untamed Love)
Jan, 1950 - No. 5, Sept, 1950
Quality Comics Group (Comic Magazines)

1-Ward-c, Gustavson-a 13.50 41.00 95.00
2,4: 2-Photo-c 9.15 27.50 55.00

3,5-Gustavson-a 10.00 30.00 60.00

UNTOLD LEGEND OF THE BATMAN, THE
July, 1980 - No. 3, Sept, 1980 (Mini-series)
DC Comics

1-Origin; Joker-c; Byrne's 1st work at DC .80 2.00 4.00
2,3 .60 1.50 3.00
1-3: Batman cereal premiums (28 pgs., 6X9"); 1st & 2nd printings known .50 1.00

NOTE: *Aparo a-1i, 2, 3. Byrne a-1p.*

UNTOLD ORIGIN OF THE FEMFORCE, THE (AC)(Value: cover or less)

UNTOUCHABLES, THE (TV)
No. 1237, 10-12/61 - No. 4, 8-10/62 (All have Robert Stack photo-c)
Dell Publishing Co.

4-Color 1237,1286 14.00 43.00 100.00
01-879-207, 12-879-210(01879-210 on inside) 10.00 30.00 60.00
Topps Bubblegum premiums-2x4", 8 pgs. (3 diff. issues) "The Organization, Jamaica Ginger, The Otto Frick Story (drug), 3000 Suspects, The Antidote, Mexican Stakeout, Little Egypt, Purple Gang, Bugs Moran Story, & Lily Dallas Story" 2.80 7.00 14.00

UNUSUAL TALES (Blue Beetle & Shadow From Beyond #50 on)
Nov, 1955 - No. 49, Mar-Apr, 1965
Charlton Comics

1 12.00 36.00 85.00
2 6.70 20.00 40.00
3-5 4.20 12.50 25.00
6-Ditko-c only 5.35 16.00 32.00
7,8-Ditko-c/a 12.00 36.00 85.00
9-Ditko-c/a, 20 pgs. 13.00 40.00 90.00
10-Ditko-c/a(4) 14.00 43.00 100.00
11-(3/58, 68 pgs.)-Ditko-a(4) 13.50 41.00 95.00
12,14-Ditko-a 10.00 30.00 65.00
13,16-20 4.00 10.00 20.00
15-Ditko-c/a 10.00 30.00 65.00
21,24,28 2.80 7.00 14.00
22,23,25-27,29-Ditko-a 6.70 20.00 40.00
30-49 2.40 6.00 12.00

NOTE: *Colan a-11. Ditko c-22, 23, 25-27, 31(part).*

UP FROM HARLEM (Spire Christian)(Value: cover or less)

UP-TO-DATE COMICS
No date (1938) (36 pgs.; B&W cover) (10 cents)
King Features Syndicate

nn-Popeye & Henry cover; The Phantom, Jungle Jim & Flash Gordon by Raymond, The Katzenjammer Kids, Curley Harper & others 19.00 56.00 130.00
(Variations to above contents exist.)

UP YOUR NOSE AND OUT YOUR EAR (Magazine)
April, 1972 - No. 2, June, 1972 (52 pgs.) (Satire)
Klevart Enterprises

V1#1,2 .60 1.50 3.00

URTH 4 (Continuity)(Value: cover or less)

USA COMICS
Aug, 1941 - No. 17, Fall, 1945
Timely Comics (USA) GD25 FN65 VF82 NM94

1-Origin Major Liberty (called Mr. Liberty #1), Rockman by Wolverton, & The Whizzer by Avison; The Defender with sidekick Rusty & Jack Frost begin; The Young Avenger only app.; S&K-c plus 1 pg. art 500.00 1500.00 2750.00 4000.00
(Estimated up to 145 total copies exist, 7 in NM/Mint)

GD2 FN65 NM94

2-Origin Captain Terror & The Vagabond; last Wolverton Rockman 225.00 675.00 1350.00
3-No Whizzer 175.00 525.00 1050.00
4-Last Rockman, Major Liberty, Defender, Jack Frost, & Capt. Terror; Corporal Dix app. 140.00 420.00 840.00
5-Origin American Avenger & Roko the Amazing; The Blue Blade, The Black Widow & Victory Boys, Gypo the Gypsy Giant & Hills of Horror only app.; Sergeant Dix begins; no Whizzer. Hitler-c 117.00 350.00 700.00
6-Captain America, The Destroyer, Jap Buster Johnson, Jeep Jones begin; Terror Squad only app. 140.00 420.00 840.00
7-Captain Daring, Disk-Eyes the Detective by Wolverton app.; origin & only app. Marvel Boy; Secret Stamp begins; no Whizzer, Sergeant Dix 122.00 365.00 730.00
8-10: 9-Last Secret Stamp. 10-The Thunderbird only app. 88.00 262.00 525.00
11,12: 11-No Jeep Jones 75.00 225.00 450.00
13-17: 13-No Whizzer; Jeep Jones ends. 15-No Destroyer; Jap Buster Johnson ends 55.00 165.00 330.00

NOTE: *Brodsky c-14. Gabrielle c-4, 8. Schomburg c-6-8, 10, 12, 13, 15-17. Shores a-1, 4; c-3, 9, 11. Ed Win a-4.*

U.S. AGENT (See Jeff Jordan...)

USAGI YOJIMBO (See Albedo, Doomsday Squad #3 & Space Usagi)
July, 1987 - Present ($2.00, B&W)
Fantagraphics Books

1 .70 1.75 3.50
1,8,10-2nd printings .40 1.00 2.00
2-9,11-28: 11-Aragones-a .40 1.00 2.00
10-Leonardo app. (TMNT) .80 2.00 4.00
29-34: 29-Begin $2.25-c .45 1.15 2.25
Color Special 1 (11/89, $2.95, 68 pgs.)-new & r .60 1.50 3.00
Summer Special 1 (1986, B&W, $2.75)-r/early Albedo issues 1.60 4.00 8.00

U.S. AIR FORCE COMICS (Army Attack #38 on)
Oct, 1958 - No. 37, Mar-Apr, 1965
Charlton Comics

1 3.60 9.00 18.00
2 1.80 4.50 9.00
3-10 1.00 2.50 5.00
11-20 .80 2.00 4.00
21-37 .60 1.50 3.00

NOTE: *Glanzman c/a-9, 10, 12. Montes/Bache a-33.*

USA IS READY
1941 (68 pgs.) (One Shot)
Dell Publishing Co.

1-War propaganda 29.00 90.00 175.00

U.S. BORDER PATROL COMICS (Sgt. Dick Carter of the...) (See Holyoke One Shot)

U.S. FIGHTING AIR FORCE (Also see United States Fighting Air Force)
No date (1960s?)
I. W. Enterprises

1,9(nd): 1-r/United States Fighting...#?. 9-r/#1 .45 1.15 2.25

U.S. FIGHTING MEN
1963 - 1964 (Reprints)
Super Comics

10-r/With the U.S. Paratroops #4(Avon) .80 2.00 4.00
11,12,15-18: 11-r/Monty Hall #10. 12,16,17,18-r/U.S. Fighting Air Force #10,3,?&? 15-r/Man Comics #11 .40 1.00 2.00

U.S. JONES (Also see Wonderworld Comics #28)
Nov, 1941 - No. 2, Jan, 1942
Fox Features Syndicate

1-U.S. Jones & The Topper begin 78.00 232.00 465.00
2 60.00 182.00 365.00

U.S. MARINES
Fall, 1964 (One shot, 12 cents)
Charlton Comics

Unusual Tales #5, © CC

USA Comics #15, © MEG

U.S. Jones #1, © FOX

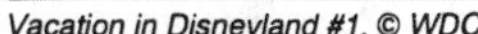
Vacation in Disneyland #1, © WDC

Valor #5, © WMG

Vampirella #7, © Harris Publ.

GD25 FN65 NM94

1 .80 2.00 4.00

U.S. MARINES IN ACTION!
Aug, 1952 - No. 3, Dec, 1952
Avon Periodicals

1-Louis Ravielli-c/a 4.70 14.00 28.00
2,3: 3-Kinstler-c 3.20 8.00 16.00

U.S. 1 (Marvel)(Value: cover or less)

U.S. PARATROOPS (See With the...)

U.S. PARATROOPS
1964?
I. W. Enterprises

1,8: 1-r/With the U.S. Paratroops #1; Wood-c. 8-r/With the U.S. Paratroops #6; Kinstler-c .80 2.00 4.00

U.S. TANK COMMANDOS
June, 1952 - No. 4, March, 1953
Avon Periodicals

1-Kinstler-c 4.70 14.00 28.00
2-4: 2-Kinstler-c 3.20 8.00 16.00
I.W. Reprint #1,8: 1-r/#1. 8-r/#3 .80 2.00 4.00
NOTE: ***Kinstler** a-3, 4, I.W. #1; c-1-4, I.W. #1, 8.*

"V" (TV)(DC)(Value: cover or less)

VACATION COMICS (See A-1 Comics #16)

VACATION DIGEST (Harvey)(Value: cover or less)

VACATION IN DISNEYLAND (Also see Dell Giants)
Aug-Oct, 1959; May, 1965 (Walt Disney)
Dell Publishing Co./Gold Key (1965)

4-Color 1025-Barks-a 8.35 25.00 50.00
1(30024-508)(G.K., 5/65, 25 cents)-r/Dell Giant #30 & cover to #1 ('58); celebrates Disneyland's 10th anniversary 2.40 6.00 12.00

VACATION PARADE (See Dell Giants)

VALKYRIE (Eclipse, 1987 & 1988)(Value: cover or less)

VALLEY OF THE DINOSAURS (TV)
April, 1975 - No. 11, Dec, 1976 (Hanna-Barbara)
Charlton Comics

1 .40 1.00 2.00
2-11: 3-Byrne text illos (early work) .30 .75 1.50

VALLEY OF GWANGI (See Movie Classics)

VALOR
Mar-Apr, 1955 - No. 5, Nov-Dec, 1955
E. C. Comics

1-Williamson/Torres-a; Wood-c/a 22.00 65.00 150.00
2-Williamson-c/a; Wood-a 19.00 57.00 130.00
3,4: 3-Williamson, Crandall-a. 4-Wood-c 13.00 40.00 90.00
5-Wood-c/a; Williamson/Evans-a 11.50 34.00 80.00
NOTE: ***Crandall** a-3, 4. **Ingels** a-1, 2, 4, 5. **Krigstein** a-1-5. **Orlando** a-3, 4; c-3. **Wood** a-1, 2, 5; c-1, 4, 5.*

VALOR
Nov, 1992 - Present ($1.25, color)
DC Comics

1-8: 1-Eclipso the Darkness Within aftermath. 2-Vs. Supergirl .60 1.25

VALOR THUNDERSTAR AND HIS FIREFLIES (Now)(Value: cover or less)

VAMPIRE LESTAT, THE
Jan, 1990 - No. 12, 1991 ($2.50, painted color, mini-series)
Innovation Publishing

1-Adapts novel; Bolton painted-c on all 4.20 12.50 25.00
1-2nd printing (has UPC code, 1st prints don't) .60 1.50 3.00

GD25 FN65 NM94

1-3rd & 4th printings .50 1.25 2.50
2-1st printing 2.00 5.00 10.00
2-2nd & 3rd printings .50 1.25 2.50
3-5 1.20 3.00 6.00
3-6,9-2nd printings .50 1.25 2.50
6-12 .80 2.00 4.00

VAMPIRELLA (Magazine)(See Warren Presents)
Sept, 1969 - No. 112, Feb, 1983; No. 113, Jan, 1988? (B&W)
Warren Publishing Co./Harris Publications #113

1-Intro. Vampirella 18.00 54.00 125.00
2-Amazonia series begins, ends #12 8.35 25.00 50.00
3 (Low distribution) 22.00 65.00 150.00
4-7 5.35 16.00 32.00
8-Vampi begins by Tom Sutton as serious strip (early issues-gag line) 5.00 15.00 30.00
9-Barry Smith-a; Boris-c 5.70 17.00 34.00
10-No Vampi story 3.60 9.00 18.00
11-15: 11-Origin, 1st app. Pendragon. 12-Vampi by Gonzales begins 4.00 11.00 22.00
16-18,20-25: 17-Tomb of the Gods begins, ends #22. 25-Begin partial color issues 2.60 6.50 13.00
19 (1973 Annual) 3.00 7.50 15.00
26,28-36,38-40: 30-Intro. Pantha. 31-Origin Luana, the Beast Girl. 33-Pantha ends 1.40 3.50 7.00
27 (1974 Annual) 1.80 4.50 9.00
37 (1975 Annual) 1.60 4.00 8.00
41-45,47-50: 50-Spirit cameo by Eisner .80 2.00 4.00
46-Origin retold (10/75) .90 2.50 4.50
51-99: 93-Cassandra St. Knight begins, ends #103; new Pantha series begins, ends 108 .50 1.25 2.50
100 (96 pg. r-special)-Origin retold .60 1.50 3.00
101-110,112: 108-Torpedo series by Toth begins .35 .90 1.80
111-Giant Collector's Edition ($2.50) .50 1.25 2.50
113 (1988) .30 .75 1.50
Annual 1(1972)-New origin Vampirella by Gonzales; reprints by Neal Adams (from #1), Wood (from #9) 11.00 32.00 75.00
Special 1 (1977; large-square bound) 1.40 3.50 7.00
NOTE: ***Neal Adams** a-1, 10p, 19p(r/#10). **Alcala** a-90, 93i. **Bode'/Todd** c-3. **Bode'/Jones** c-4. **Boris** c-9. **Brunner** a-10. **Corben** a-30, 31, 33, 54. **Crandall** a-1, 19(r/#1). **Frazetta** c-1, 5, 7, 11, 31. **Heath** a-76-78, 83. **Jones** a-5, 9, 12, 27, 32, 33(2pg.), 34, 50i, 83r. **Nino** a-59i, 61i, 67, 76, 85, 90. **Ploog** a-14. **Barry Smith** a-9. **Starlin** a-78. **Sutton** a-11. **Toth** a-90i, 108, 110. **Wood** a-9, 10, 12, 19(r/#12), 27; c-9. **Wrightson** a-33(w/Jones), 63. All reprint issues-37, 74, 83, 87, 91, 105, 107, 109, 111. Annuals from 1973 on are included in regular numbering. Later annuals are same format as regular issues.*

VAMPIRELLA
Oct, 1992 - Present ($2.95, color)
Harris Publications

1-4 .60 1.50 3.00

VAMPIRELLA: MORNING IN AMERICA
1991 - No. 4, 1992 ($3.95, B&W, mini-series, 52 pgs.)
Harris Publications/Dark Horse Comics

1: All have Kaluta painted covers .90 2.25 4.50
2-4 .80 2.00 4.00

VAMPIRE TALES (Magazine)
Aug, 1973 - No. 11, June, 1975 (B&W) (75 cents)
Marvel Comics Group

1-Morbius, the Living Vampire begins by Pablo Marcos (1st solo Morbius series) 4.20 12.50 25.00
2-Intro. Satana; Steranko-r 2.00 5.00 10.00
3,4,6-11: 3-Satana app. 6-1st Lilith app. 8-Blade app. (see Tomb of Dracula) .80 2.00 4.00
5-Origin Morbius 1.60 4.00 8.00
Annual 1(10/75)-Heath-r/#9 .40 1.00 2.00

NOTE: **Alcala** a-6, 8, 9i. **Boris** c-4, 6. **Chaykin** a-7. **Everett** a-1r. **Gulacy** a-7p. **Heath** a-9. **Infantino** a-3r. **Gil Kane** a-4, 5r.

VANGUARD (...Outpost: Earth) (See Megaton)
1987 ($1.50, color)
Megaton Comics

	GD25	FN65	NM94
1-Erik Larsen-c(p)	.60	1.50	3.00

VANGUARD ILLUSTRATED
Nov, 1983 - No. 7, May, 1984 (Color, Baxter paper)
Pacific Comics

	GD25	FN65	NM94
1-6: 1,7-Nudity scenes. 2-1st app. Stargrazers (see Legends of the Stargrazers; Dave Stevens-c	.30	.75	1.50
7-1st app. Mr. Monster (r-in Mr. Monster #1)	1.00	2.50	5.00

NOTE: **Evans** a-7. **Kaluta** c-5, 7p. **Perez** a-6; c-6. **Rude** a-1-4; c-4. **Williamson** c-3.

VANITY (Pacific) (Value: cover or less)

VARIETY COMICS
1944 - No. 2, 1945; No. 3, 1946 - No. 5, 1946?
Rural Home Publications/Croyden Publ. Co.

	GD25	FN65	NM94
1-Origin Captain Valiant	11.00	32.00	75.00
2-Captain Valiant	6.35	19.00	38.00
3(1946-Croyden)-Captain Valiant	5.35	16.00	32.00
4,5	4.70	14.00	28.00

VARIETY COMICS (See Fox Giants)

VARSITY
1945
Parents' Magazine Institute

	GD25	FN65	NM94
1	4.70	14.00	28.00

VAUDEVILLE AND OTHER THINGS
1900 (10x13-1/2") (in color) (18+ pgs.)
Isaac H. Blandiard Co.

	GD25	FN65	NM94
nn-By Bunny	33.00	100.00	200.00

VAULT OF EVIL
Feb, 1973 - No. 23, Nov, 1975
Marvel Comics Group

	GD25	FN65	NM94
1 (1950s reprints begin)	.40	1.00	2.00
2-23: 3,4-Brunner-c	.30	.75	1.50

NOTE: **Ditko** a-14r, 15r, 20-22r. **Drucker** a-10r(Mystic #52), 13r(Uncanny Tales #42). **Everett** a-11r(Menace #2), 13r(Menace #4); c-10. **Heath** a-5r. **Krigstein** a-20r(Uncanny Tales #54). **Reinman** r-1. **Tuska** a-6r.

VAULT OF HORROR (Formerly War Against Crime #1-11)
No. 12, Apr-May, 1950 - No. 40, Dec-Jan, 1954-55
E. C. Comics

	GD25	FN65	NM94
12 (Scarce)	315.00	945.00	2200.00
13-Morphine story	29.00	235.00	550.00
14	72.00	215.00	500.00
15	57.00	170.00	400.00
16	41.00	125.00	290.00
17-19	32.00	95.00	220.00
20-25: 22-Frankenstein adaptation. 23-Used in **POP**, pg. 84. 24-Craig biography	24.00	73.00	170.00
26-B&W & color illos in **POP**	24.00	73.00	170.00
27-35: 31-Ray Bradbury biog. 35-X-Mas-c	18.00	54.00	125.00
36-"Pipe Dream"-classic opium addict story by Krigstein; "Twin Bill" cited in articles by T.E. Murphy, Wertham	18.00	54.00	125.00
37-1st app. Drusilla, a Vampirella look alike; Williamson-a	18.00	54.00	125.00
38-39: 39-Bondage-c	15.00	45.00	105.00
40-Low distribution	18.00	54.00	125.00

NOTE: **Craig** art in all but No. 13 & 33; c-12-40. **Crandall** a-33, 34, 39. **Davis** a-17-38. **Evans** a-27, 28, 30, 32, 33. **Feldstein** a-12-16. **Ingels** a-13-20, 22-40. **Kamen** a-15-22, 25, 29, 35. **Krigstein** a-36, 38-40. **Kurtzman** a-12, 13. **Orlando** a-24, 31, 40. **Wood** a-12-14. #22, 29 & 31 have Ray Bradbury adaptations. #16 & 17 have H. P. Lovecraft adapts.

VAULT OF HORROR, THE
Aug, 1990 - No. 6, June, 1991 ($1.95, color, 68 pgs.)(#4 on: $2.00)
Gladstone Publishing

	GD25	FN65	NM94
1-Craig-c(r); all contain EC reprints	.80	2.00	4.00
2-Craig-c(r)	.60	1.50	3.00
3-6: 4-6-Craig-c(r). 3-Ingels-c(r)	.50	1.25	2.50

VAULT OF HORROR
1991 - No. 5, 1991 ($2.00, color)
Oct, 1992 - Present ($1.50, color)
Russ Cochran

	GD25	FN65	NM94
1-5: E.C reprints	.40	1.00	2.00
1-4: 1-r/VOH #12 (#1); Craig-c	.30	.75	1.50

V...-COMICS (Morse code for "V" - 3 dots, 1 dash)
Jan, 1942 - No. 2, Mar-Apr, 1942
Fox Features Syndicate

	GD25	FN65	NM94
1-Origin V-Man & the Boys; The Banshee & The Black Fury, The Queen of Evil, & V-Agents begin	79.00	238.00	475.00
2-Bondage/torture-c	65.00	195.00	390.00

VECTOR (Now) (Value: cover or less)

VEGAS KNIGHTS
1989 ($1.95, color)
Pioneer Comics

	GD25	FN65	NM94
1	.40	1.00	2.00

VENGEANCE SQUAD
July, 1975 - No. 6, May, 1976 (#1-3 are 25 cent issues)
Charlton Comics

	GD25	FN65	NM94
1-Mike Mauser, Private eye begins by Staton	.30	.75	1.50
2-6: Morisi-a in all		.60	1.20
5,6(Modern Comics-r, 1977)		.50	1.00

VENOM (Also see Amazing Spider-Man #298 & Marvel Comics Presents)
Feb, 1993 - No. 6, July, 1993 ($1.75, color, limited series)
Marvel Comics

	GD25	FN65	NM94
1-($2.95)-Black holo-grafx-c; Bagley-c/a begins	.60	1.50	3.00
2-6	.35	.90	1.75

VENTURE (AC) (Value: cover or less)

VENUS (See Marvel Spotlight #2 & Weird Wonder Tales)
August, 1948 - No. 19, April, 1952 (Also see Marvel Mystery #91)
Marvel/Atlas Comics (CMC 1-9/LCC 10-19)

	GD25	FN65	NM94
1-Venus & Hedy Devine begin; Kurtzman's "Hey Look"	61.00	182.00	425.00
2	36.00	107.00	250.00
3,5	30.00	90.00	210.00
4-Kurtzman's "Hey Look"	32.00	95.00	225.00
6-9: 6-Loki app. 7,8-Painted-c	29.00	85.00	200.00
10-S/F-horror issues begin (7/50)	30.00	90.00	210.00
11-S/F end of the world(11/50)	36.00	107.00	250.00
12-Colan-a	25.00	75.00	175.00
13-19-Venus by Everett, 2-3 stories each; covers-#13,15-19; 14-Everett part cover (Venus). 17-Bondage-c	39.00	118.00	275.00

NOTE: **Berg** s/f story-13. **Everett** c-13, 14(part; Venus only), 15-19. **Heath** s/f story-11. **Maneely** s/f story-10(3pg.), 16. **Morisi** a-19. **Syd Shores** c-6.

VENUS WARS, THE (Dark Horse) (Value: cover or less)

VENUS WARS II, THE (Dark Horse) (Value: cover or less)

VERI BEST SURE FIRE COMICS
No date (circa 1945) (Reprints Holyoke One-Shots)
Holyoke Publishing Co.

	GD25	FN65	NM94
1-Captain Aero, Alias X, Miss Victory, Commandos of the Devil Dogs, Red Cross, Hammerhead Hawley, Capt. Aero's Sky Scouts, Flagman app.	20.00	60.00	120.00

VERI BEST SURE SHOT COMICS
No date (circa 1945) (Reprints Holyoke One-Shots)

Variety Comics #1, © RH

Vault of Horror #29, © WMG

Venus #2, © MEG

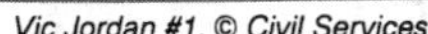

Vic Jordan #1, © Civil Services

Vicks Comics nn (1st), © EAS

Victory Comics #3, © HILL

GD25 FN65 NM94

Holyoke Publishing Co.

1-Capt. Aero, Miss Victory by Quinlan, Alias X, The Red Cross, Flagman, Commandos of the Devil Dogs, Hammerhead Hawley, Capt. Aero's Sky Scouts 20.00 60.00 120.00

VERONICA (Also see Archie's Girls, Betty &...)
April, 1989 - Present (75 & 95 cents, color)
Archie Comics

1-30: 1,2-(75 cents). 3-30 (.95-$1.00) .50 1.00
21-30: 21-Begin $1.25-c .60 1.25

VERONICA'S PASSPORT DIGEST MAGAZINE
Nov, 1992 - Present ($1.50, color, digest size)
Harvey Comics

1 .30 .75 1.50

VERONICA'S SUMMER SPECIAL (See Archie Giant Series Magazine #615, 625)

VERY BEST OF DENNIS THE MENACE, THE
July, 1979 - No. 2, Apr, 1980 (132 pgs., Digest, 95 cents, $1.00)
Fawcett Publications

1,2-Reprints .40 1.00 2.00

VERY BEST OF DENNIS THE MENACE, THE
April, 1982 - No. 3, Aug, 1982 ($1.25, digest size)
Marvel Comics Group

1-3-Reprints .60 1.25

NOTE: *Hank Ketcham c-all. A few thousand of #1 & 2 were printed with DC emblem.*

V FOR VENDETTA (DC)(Value: cover or less)

VIC BRIDGES FAZERS SKETCHBOOK AND FACT FILE (AC)(Value: cover or less)

VIC FLINT (Crime Buster...)(See Authentic Police Cases #10-14 & Fugitives From Justice #2)
August, 1948 - No. 5, April, 1949 (Newspaper reprints; NEA Service)
St. John Publishing Co.

1 8.35 25.00 50.00
2 5.00 15.00 30.00
3-5 4.20 12.50 25.00

VIC FLINT
Feb, 1956 - No. 2, May, 1956 (Newspaper reprints)
Argo Publ.

1,2 4.70 14.00 28.00

VIC JORDAN (Also see Big Shot Comics #32)
April, 1945
Civil Service Publ.

1-1944 daily newspaper-r 9.15 27.50 55.00

VICKI (Humor)
Feb, 1975 - No. 4, July, 1975 (No. 1,2: 68 pgs.)
Atlas/Seaboard Publ.

1-Reprints Tippy Teen .60 1.50 3.00
2-4 .30 .80 1.60

VICKI VALENTINE (Renegade)(Value: cover or less)

VICKS COMICS (Also see Pure Oil Comics, Salerno Carnival of Comics & 24 Pages of Comics)
nd (circa 1938) (68 pgs. in color) (Giveaway)
Eastern Color Printing Co. (Vicks Chemical Co.)

nn-Famous Funnies-r (before #40); contains 5 pgs. Buck Rogers (4 pgs. from F.F. #15, & 1 pg. from #16) Joe Palooka, Napoleon, etc. app. 55.00 165.00 385.00
nn-16 loose, untrimmed page giveaway; paper-c; r/Famous Funnies #14; Buck Rogers, Joe Palooka app. 20.00 60.00 140.00

VICKY
Oct, 1948 - No. 5, June, 1949
Ace Magazine

nn(10/48) 4.20 12.50 25.00
4(12/48), nn(2/49), 4(4/49), 5(6/49) 4.00 10.00 20.00

VIC TORRY & HIS FLYING SAUCER (Also see Mr. Monster's...#5)
1950 (One Shot)
Fawcett Publications

nn-Book-length saucer story by Powell; photo/painted-c 36.00 107.00 250.00

VICTORY COMICS
Aug, 1941 - No. 4, Dec, 1941
Hillman Periodicals

1-The Conqueror by Bill Everett, The Crusader, & Bomber Burns begin; Conqueror's origin in text; Everett-c; #1 by Funnies, Inc. 150.00 450.00 900.00
2-Everett-c/a 75.00 225.00 450.00
3,4 50.00 150.00 300.00

VIC VERITY MAGAZINE
1945 - No. 7, Sept, 1946 (A comic book)
Vic Verity Publications

1-C. C. Beck-c/a 10.00 30.00 70.00
2 5.85 17.50 35.00
3-7: 6-Beck-a. 7-Beck-c 5.00 15.00 30.00

VIDEO JACK (Marvel)(Value: cover or less)

VIETNAM JOURNAL
Nov, 1987 - No. 11, July, 1989 ($1.75/$1.95, B&W)
Apple Comics

1-Don Lomax-c/a/scripts in all .60 1.50 3.00
1-2nd print .40 1.00 2.00
2-11: 10,11-$2.00/$2.25-c .40 1.00 2.00
...: Indian Country Vol. 1 (1990, $12.95)-r/#1-4 plus one new story 2.60 6.50 13.00

VIGILANTE, THE (DC)(Value: cover or less)(Also see Action Comics #42, Justice League of America #78, Leading Comics, New Teen Titans #23 & World's Finest #244)

VIGILANTES, THE (See 4-Color #839)

VIKINGS, THE (See 4-Color #910)

VILLAINS AND VIGILANTES (Eclipse)(Value: cover or less)

VINTAGE MAGNUS (...Robot Fighter)
Jan, 1992 - No. 4, Apr, 1992 ($1.95, color, mini-series)
Valiant

1-Layton-c; r/origin from Magnus R.F. #22 1.00 2.50 5.00
2-4 .60 1.50 3.00

VIRGINIAN, THE (TV)
June, 1963
Gold Key

1(10060-306)-Part photo-c 4.20 12.50 25.00

VISION AND THE SCARLET WITCH, THE (Marvel, 1982 & 1985)(Value: cover or less)

VISIONARIES (Marvel)(Value: cover or less)

VISIONS
1979 - No. 5, 1983 (B&W, fanzine)
Vision Publications

1-Flaming Carrot begins(1st app?); N. Adams-c 11.50 34.00 80.00
2-N. Adams, Rogers-a; Gulacy back-c; signed & numbered to 2000 5.85 17.50 35.00
3-Williamson-c(p); Steranko back-c 3.00 7.50 15.00
4-Flaming Carrot-c & info. 4.00 10.00 20.00

5-1 pg. Flaming Carrot 2.00 5.00 10.00
NOTE: *After #4, Visions became an annual publication of The Atlanta Fantasy Fair.*

VOID INDIGO (Marvel) (Value: cover or less)

VOLTRON (TV) (Modern) (Value: cover or less)

VOODA (Jungle Princess) (Formerly Voodoo)
No. 20, April, 1955 - No. 22, Aug, 1955
Ajax-Farrell (Four Star Publications)

20-Baker-c/a (r/Seven Seas #6); last pre-code 13.00 40.00 900.00
21,22-Baker-a plus Kamen/Baker story, Kimbo Boy of Jungle, & Baker-c (p) in all. 22-Censored Jo-Jo-r (name Powaa) 11.50 34.00 80.00
NOTE: *#20-22 each contain one heavily censored-r of South Sea Girl by **Baker** from Seven Seas Comics with name changed to Vooda. #20-r/Seven Seas #6; #21-r/#4; #22-4/#3.*

VOODOO (Vooda #20 on)
May, 1952 - No. 19, Jan-Feb, 1955
Ajax-Farrell (Four Star Publ.)

1-South Sea Girl-r by Baker 23.00 70.00 160.00
2-Rulah story-r plus South Sea Girl from Seven Seas #2 by Baker (name changed from Alani to El'nee) 18.00 54.00 125.00
3-Bakerish-a; man stabbed in face 13.00 40.00 90.00
4,8-Baker-r. 8-Severed head panels 13.00 40.00 90.00
5-7,9,10: 5-Nazi death camp story (flaying alive). 6-Severed head panels 10.00 30.00 65.00
11-14,16-18: 14-Zombies take over America. 16-Post nuclear world story. 17-Electric chair panels 9.15 27.50 55.00
15-Opium drug story-r/Ellery Queen #3 10.00 30.00 60.00
19-Bondage-c; Baker-a(2)(r) 11.00 32.00 75.00
Annual 1(1952)(25 cents); Baker-a 30.00 90.00 210.00

VOODOO (See Tales of...)

VORTEX
Nov, 1982 - No. 15, 1988(No month) ($1.50-$1.75, B&W)
Vortex Publs.

1 ($1.95)-Peter Hsu-a; Ken Steacy-c; nudity 2.40 6.00 12.00
2-1st app. Mister X (on-c only) 1.00 2.50 5.00
3 .80 2.00 4.00
4-15: 12-Sam Kieth-a .40 1.00 2.00

VORTEX
1991 - No. 2? ($2.50, color, limited series)
Comico

1,2: Heroes from The Elementals .50 1.25 2.50

VOYAGE TO THE BOTTOM OF THE SEA (TV)
No. 1230, Sept-Nov, 1961; Dec, 1964 - #16, Apr, 1970 (Painted covers)
Dell Publishing Co./Gold Key

4-Color 1230(Movie-1961) 8.35 25.00 50.00
10133-412(#1, 12/64)(Gold Key) 5.00 15.00 30.00
2(7/65) - 5: Photo back-c, 1-5 4.00 10.00 20.00
6-14 3.00 7.50 15.00
15,16-Reprints 2.00 5.00 10.00

VOYAGE TO THE DEEP
Sept-Nov, 1962 - No. 4, Nov-Jan, 1964 (Painted-c)
Dell Publishing Co.

1 4.20 12.50 25.00
2-4 3.00 7.50 15.00

WACKO
Sept, 1980 - No. 3, Oct, 1981 (B&W magazine, 84 pgs.)
Ideal Publ. Corp.

1-3 .40 1.00 2.00

WACKY ADVENTURES OF CRACKY (Also see Gold Key Spotlight)
Dec, 1972 - No. 12, Sept, 1975
Gold Key

1 1.40 3.50 7.00
2 .80 2.00 4.00
3-12 .40 1.00 2.00
(See March of Comics #405, 424, 436, 448)

WACKY DUCK (Formerly Dopey Duck?; Justice Comics #7 on)
No. 3, Fall, 1946 - No. 6, Summer, 1947; 8/48 - No. 2, 10/48
Marvel Comics (NPP)

3 10.00 30.00 65.00
4-Infinity-c 12.00 36.00 85.00
5,6(1946-47) 9.15 27.50 55.00
1,2(1948) 6.35 19.00 38.00
I.W. Reprint #1,2,7('58) .60 1.50 3.00
Super Reprint #10(I.W. on-c, Super-inside) .60 1.50 3.00

WACKY QUACKY (See Wisco)

WACKY RACES (TV)
Aug, 1969 - No. 7, Apr, 1972 (Hanna-Barbera)
Gold Key

1 3.00 7.50 15.00
2-7 1.60 4.00 8.00

WACKY SQUIRREL (Also see Dark Horse Presents)
Oct, 1987 - No. 4, 1988 ($1.75, B&W)
Dark Horse Comics

1-4: 4-Superman parody .35 .90 1.75
Halloween Adventure Special 1 (1987, $2.00) .40 1.00 2.00
Summer Fun Special 1 (1988, $2.00) .40 1.00 2.00

WACKY WITCH (Also see Gold Key Spotlight)
March, 1971 - No. 21, Dec, 1975
Gold Key

1 2.40 6.00 12.00
2 1.20 3.00 6.00
3-21 .60 1.50 3.00
(See March of Comics #374, 398, 410, 422, 434, 446, 458, 470, 482)

WACKY WOODPECKER (See Two Bit...)
1958; 1963
I. W. Enterprises/Super Comics

I.W. Reprint #1,2,7(nd-r-/Two Bit...) .40 1.00 2.00
Super Reprint #10('63) .40 1.00 2.00

WAGON TRAIN (1st Series) (TV) (See Western Roundup under Dell Giants)
No. 895, Mar, 1958 - No. 13, Apr-June, 1962 (All photo-c)
Dell Publishing Co.

4-Color 895 (#1) 9.15 27.50 55.00
4-Color 971(#2),1019(#3) 5.00 15.00 30.00
4(1-3/60),6-13 4.35 13.00 26.00
5-Toth-a 5.35 16.00 32.00

WAGON TRAIN (2nd Series)(TV)
Jan, 1964 - No. 4, Oct, 1964 (All photo-c)
Gold Key

1-Tufts-a in all 4.20 12.50 25.00
2-4 3.60 9.00 18.00

WAITING ROOM WILLIE (See Sad Case of...)

WALLY (Teen-age)
Dec, 1962 - No. 4, Sept, 1963
Gold Key

1 3.00 7.50 15.00
2-4 1.60 4.00 8.00

WALLY THE WIZARD (Marvel) (Value: cover or less)

WALLY WOOD'S T.H.U.N.D.E.R. AGENTS (Deluxe) (Value: cover or less)

WALT DISNEY CHRISTMAS PARADE (Also see Christmas Parade)
Winter, 1977 (224 pgs.) (cardboard covers, $1.95)
Whitman Publishing Co. (Golden Press)

Vooda #21, © AJAX

Voyage to the Bottom of the Sea #6, © 20th Century-Fox

Wagon Train #5 (Dell), © Revue Prod.

Walt Disney Presents #2, © WDC

Walt Disney's Comics and Stories #4 (regular ed.), © WDC

Walt Disney's Comics and Stories #92, © WDC

GD25 FN65 NM94

11191-Barks-r/Christmas in Disneyland #1, Dell Christmas Parade #9 & Dell Giant #53 .50 1.20 2.40

WALT DISNEY COMICS DIGEST
June, 1968 - No. 57, Feb, 1976 (50 cents) (Digest size)
Gold Key

1-Reprints Uncle Scrooge #5; 192 pgs. 4.00 10.50 21.00
2-4-Barks-r 2.40 6.00 12.00
5-Daisy Duck by Barks (8 pgs.); last published story by Barks (art only) plus 21 pg. Scrooge-r by Barks 2.80 7.00 14.00
6-13-All Barks-r 1.20 3.00 6.00
14,15 .80 2.00 4.00
16-Reprints Donald Duck #26 by Barks 1.60 4.00 8.00
17-20-Barks-r .95 2.40 4.80
21-31,33,35-37-Barks-r; 24-Toth Zorro .80 2.00 4.00
32 .60 1.50 3.00
34-Reprints 4-Color #318 1.60 4.00 8.00
38-Reprints Christmas in Disneyland #1 1.20 3.00 6.00
39-Two Barks-r/WDC&S #272, 4-Color #1073 plus Toth Zorro-r .95 2.40 4.80
40-Mickey Mouse-r by Gottfredson .60 1.50 3.00
41,45,47-49 .35 .90 1.80
42,43-Barks-r .60 1.50 3.00
44-(Has Gold Key emblem, 50 cents)-Reprints 1st story of 4-Color #29,256, 275,282 2.80 7.00 14.00
44-Republished in 1976 by Whitman; not identical to original; a bit smaller, blank back-c, 69 cent-c 1.20 3.00 6.00
46,50,52-Barks-r. 52-Barks-r/WDC&S #161,132 .60 1.50 3.00
51-Reprints 4-Color #71 .95 2.40 4.80
53-55: 53-Reprints Dell Giant #30. 54-Reprints Donald Duck Beach Party #2. 55-Reprints Dell Giant #49 .30 .80 1.60
56-Reprint/Uncle Scrooge #32 (Barks) plus another Barks story .60 1.50 3.00
57-Reprint/Mickey Mouse Almanac('57) & two Barks stories .60 1.50 3.00

NOTE: *#1-10, 196 pgs.; #11-41, 164 pgs.; #42 on, 132 pgs. Old issues were being reprinted & distributed by Whitman in 1976.*

WALT DISNEY PRESENTS (TV)
No. 997, June-Aug, 1959 - No. 6, Dec-Feb, 1960-61 (All photo-c)
Dell Publishing Co.

4-Color 997 (#1) 5.00 15.00 30.00
2(12-2/60)-The Swamp Fox(origin), Elfego Baca, Texas John Slaughter (Disney TV show) begin 4.00 10.00 20.00
3-6: 5-Swamp Fox by Warren Tufts 4.00 10.00 20.00

WALT DISNEY'S CHRISTMAS PARADE (Also see Christmas Parade)
Winter, 1988; No. 2, Winter, 1989 ($2.95, 100 pgs.)
Gladstone Publishing

1,2: 1-Barks-r/painted-c. 2-Barks-r .60 1.50 3.00

WALT DISNEY'S COMICS AND STORIES (Cont. of Mickey Mouse Magazine) (#1-30 contain Donald Duck newspaper reprints)
(Titled 'Comics And Stories' #264 on)
10/40 - #263, 8/62; #264, 10/62 - #510, 1984; #511, 10/86 - Present
Dell Publishing Co./Gold Key #264-473/Whitman #474-510/Gladstone #511-547(4/90)/Disney Comics #548(6/90) on

NOTE: The whole number can always be found at the bottom of the title page in the lower left-hand or right hand panel.

GD25 FN65 VF82 NM94

1(V1#1-c; V2#1-indicia)-Donald Duck strip-r by Al Taliaferro & Gottfredson's Mickey Mouse begin 670.00 2000.00 4000.00 6700.00
(Estimated up to 245 total copies exist, 12 in NM/Mint)

GD25 FN65 NM94

2 360.00 1070.00 2500.00
3 115.00 345.00 800.00
4-X-mas-c 86.00 257.00 600.00
4-Special promotional, complimentary issue; cover same except one corner was blanked out & boxed in to identify the giveaway (not a paste-over). This special pressing was probably sent out to former subscribers to Mickey Mouse Mag. whose subscriptions had expired. (Very rare-5 known copies) 129.00 385.00 900.00
5 71.00 215.00 500.00
6-10 57.00 170.00 400.00
11-14 50.00 150.00 350.00
15-17: 15-The 3 Little Kittens (17 pgs.). 16-The 3 Little Pigs (29 pgs.); X-mas-c. 17-The Ugly Duckling (4 pgs.) 45.00 135.00 315.00
18-21 38.00 115.00 265.00
22-30: 22-Flag-c 32.00 95.00 225.00
31-New Donald Duck stories by Carl Barks begin; see Four Color #9 for first Barks Donald Duck 215.00 645.00 1500.00
32-Barks-a 100.00 300.00 700.00
33-Barks-a (infinity-c) 71.00 215.00 500.00
34-Gremlins by Walt Kelly begin, end #41; Barks-a 59.00 178.00 415.00
35,36-Barks-a 52.00 155.00 365.00
37-Donald Duck by Jack Hannah 26.00 77.00 180.00
38-40-Barks-a. 39-Christmas-c. 40-Gremlins by Kelly; no Barks-a 36.00 107.00 250.00
41-50-Barks-a; 41-Gremlins by Kelly 29.00 85.00 200.00
51-60-Barks-a; 51-Christmas-c. 52-Li'l Bad Wolf begins, ends #203 (not in #55). 58-Kelly flag-c 22.00 65.00 150.00
61-70: Barks-a. 61-Dumbo story. 63,64-Pinocchio stories. 63-Cover swipe from New Funnies #94. 64-X-mas-c. 65-Pluto story. 66-Infinity-c. 67,68-Mickey Mouse Sunday-r by Bill Wright 16.00 48.00 125.00
71-80: Barks-a. 75-77-Brer Rabbit stories, no Mickey Mouse. 76-X-Mas-c 11.50 34.00 90.00
81-87,89,90: Barks-a. 82-84-Bongo stories. 86-90-Goofy & Agnes app. 89-Chip 'n' Dale story 9.50 28.50 75.00
88-1st app. Gladstone Gander by Barks 11.50 34.00 90.00
91-97,99: Barks-a. 95-1st WDC&S Barks-c. 96-No Mickey Mouse; Little Toot begins, ends #97. 99-X-Mas-c 7.50 22.50 58.00
98-1st Uncle Scrooge app. in WDC&S 16.00 48.00 125.00
100-Barks-a 8.50 25.50 65.00
101-110-Barks-a. 107-Taliaferro-c; Donald acquires super powers 6.50 19.50 50.00
111,114,117-All Barks 5.00 15.00 40.00
112-Drug (ether) issue (Donald Duck) 5.00 15.00 40.00
113,115,116,118-123: No Barks. 116-Dumbo x-over. 121-Grandma Duck begins, ends #168; not in #135,142,146,155 2.25 6.75 18.00
124,126-130-All Barks. 124-X-Mas-c 4.35 13.00 35.00
125-1st app. Junior Woodchucks; Barks-a 7.00 21.00 55.00
131,133,135-139-All Barks 4.35 13.00 35.00
132-Barks-a(2) (D. Duck & Grandma Duck) 5.15 15.50 40.00
134-Intro. & 1st app. The Beagle Boys 8.50 25.50 65.00
140-1st app. Gyro Gearloose by Barks 8.50 25.50 65.00
141-150-All Barks. 143-Little Hiawatha begins, ends #151,159 2.65 8.00 21.00
151-170-All Barks 2.25 6.75 18.00
171-200-All Barks 2.00 6.00 16.00
201-240: All Barks. 204-Chip 'n' Dale & Scamp begin 1.70 5.00 14.00
241-283: Barks-a. 241-Dumbo x-over. 247-Gyro Gearloose begins, ends #274. 256-Ludwig Von Drake begins, ends #274 1.50 4.50 10.00
284,285,287,290,295,296,309-311-Not by Barks .85 2.50 6.00
286,288,289,291-294,297,298,308-All Barks stories; 293-Grandma Duck's Farm Friends. 297-Gyro Gearloose. 298-Daisy Duck's Diary-r 1.35 4.00 9.00
299-307-All contain early Barks-r (#43-117). 305-Gyro Gearloose 1.50 4.50 10.00

GD25 FN65 NM94

312-Last Barks issue with original story 1.35 4.00 9.00
313-315,317-327,329-334,336-341 .85 2.50 5.00
316-Last issue published during life of Walt Disney .85 2.50 5.00
328,335,342-350-Barks-r 1.00 3.00 6.00
351-360-With posters inside; Barks reprints (2 versions of each with & without posters)-without posters... .85 2.50 5.00
351-360-With posters 1.15 3.50 9.00
361-400-Barks-r .85 2.50 5.00
401-429-Barks-r .70 2.00 4.00
430,433,437,438,441,444,445,466,506-No Barks .35 1.00 2.00
431,432,434-436,439,440,442,443-Barks-r .35 1.00 2.00
446-465,467-505,507-510: All Barks-r. 494-r/WDC&S #98 (1st Uncle Scrooge) .25 .75 1.50
511-Wuzzles by Disney studio (1st by Gladstone) 1.00 2.50 5.00
512 .60 1.50 3.00
513-520: 518-Infinity-c .35 .90 1.80
521-540: 522-r/1st app. Huey, Dewey & Louie from D. Duck Sunday page. 535-546-Barks-r .30 .75 1.50
541-545: (All $1.50, 52 pgs.) .30 .75 1.50
546,547-($1.95, 68 pgs.): 546-Kelly-r. 547-Rosa-a .40 1.00 2.00
548,549,551-570,572,573,578,579,581 ($1.50): 548-New-a. 549-Barks-r begin. 556-r/Mickey Mouse Cheerios Premium by Dick Moores. 570-Valentine issue; has Mickey/Minnie centerfold .30 .75 1.50
550 ($2.25, 52 pgs.)-Donald Duck by Barks; previously only printed in The Netherlands (1st time in U.S.); also reprints 1st app. Chip 'n Dale & 1st app. Scamp .45 1.15 2.25
571,574-577,580,582,583 ($2.95, 68 pgs.): 571-r/Donald Duck's Atomic Bomb by Barks/Cheerios. 574-r/1st Pinocchio Sunday strip(1939-40). 580-r/Donald Duck's 1st app./Little Red Hen .60 1.50 3.00

NOTE: *(#1-38, 68 pgs.; #39-42, 60 pgs.; #43-57, 61-134, 143-168, 446, 447, 52 pgs.; #58-60, 135-142, 169-540, 36 pgs.)*

NOTE: ***Barks** art in all issues #31 on, except where noted; c-95, 96, 104, 108, 109, 130-172, 174-178, 183, 198-200, 204, 206-209, 212-216, 218, 220, 226, 228-233, 235-238, 240-243, 247, 250, 253, 256, 260, 261, 276-283, 288-292, 295-298, 301, 303, 304, 306, 307, 309, 310, 313-316, 319, 321, 322, 324, 326, 328, 329, 331, 332, 334, 341, 342, 350, 351, 540(never before published), 546r, 557-582r(most). **Kelly** r-546, 547; covers(most)-34-94, 97-103, 105, 106, 110-123, 537r, 538r, 541r, 543r, 544r. Walt Disney's Comics & Stories featured Mickey Mouse serials which were in practically every issue from #1 through #394. The titles of the serials, along with the issues they are in, are listed in previous editions of this price guide. **Floyd Gottfredson** Mickey Mouse serials in issues #1-61, 63-74, 77-92 plus "Mickey Mouse in a Warplant" (3 pgs.), and "Pluto Catches a Nazi Spy" (4 pgs.) in #62; "Mystery Next Door," #93; "Sunken Treasure," #94; "Aunt Marissa," #95; "Gangland," #98; "Thanksgiving Dinner," #99; and "The Talking Dog," #100. Mickey Mouse by **Paul Murry** #152 on except 155-57 (**Dick Moore**), 327-29 (**Tony Strobl**), 348-50 (**Jack Manning**). **Don Rosa** story/a-523, 524, 526, 528, 531, 547. **Al Taliaferro** Silly Symphonies in #5-"Three Little Pigs;" #13-"Birds of a Feather;" #14-"The Boarding School Mystery;" #15-"Cookieland" and "Three Little Kittens;" #16-"Three Little Pigs;" #17-"The Ugly Duckling" and "The Robber Kitten;" #19-"Penguin Isle;" and "Bucky Bug" in #20-23, 25, 26, 28 (one continuous story from 1932-34; first 2 pgs. not Taliaferro).*

WALT DISNEY'S COMICS & STORIES
1943 (36 pgs.) (Dept. store Xmas giveaway)
Walt Disney Productions

nn 45.00 135.00 300.00

WALT DISNEY'S COMICS & STORIES
Mid 1940's ('45-48), 1952 (4 pgs. in color) (slick paper)
Dell Publishing Co.(Special Xmas offer)

1940's version - subscription form for WDC&S - (Reprints two differrent WDC&S covers with subscription forms printed on inside covers) 10.00 30.00 60.00
1952 version 5.85 17.50 35.00

WALT DISNEY'S COMICS DIGEST
Dec, 1986 - No. 7, Sept, 1987
Gladstone Publishing

1-7 .60 1.25

WALT DISNEY SHOWCASE
Oct, 1970 - No. 54, Jan, 1980 (No. 44-48: 68pgs., 49-54: 52pgs.)
Gold Key

1-Boatniks (Movie)-Photo-c 3.00 7.50 15.00
2-Moby Duck 1.60 4.00 8.00
3,4,7: 3-Bongo & Lumpjaw-r. 4,7-Pluto-r 1.40 3.50 7.00
5-$1,000,000 Duck (Movie)-Photo-c 2.00 5.00 10.00
6-Bedknobs & Broomsticks (Movie) 2.00 5.00 10.00
8-Daisy & Donald 1.40 3.50 7.00
9-101 Dalmatians (cartoon feat.); r/F.C. #1183 1.60 4.00 8.00
10-Napoleon & Samantha (Movie)-Photo-c 2.00 5.00 10.00
11-Moby Duck-r 1.20 3.00 6.00
12-Dumbo-r/Four Color #668 1.40 3.50 7.00
13-Pluto-r 1.20 3.00 6.00
14-World's Greatest Athlete (Movie)-Photo-c 2.00 5.00 10.00
15-3 Little Pigs-r 1.40 3.50 7.00
16-Aristocats (cartoon feature); r/Aristocats #1 2.00 5.00 10.00
17-Mary Poppins; r/M.P. #10136-501-Photo-c 2.00 5.00 10.00
18-Gyro Gearloose; Barks-r/F.C. #1047,1184 2.00 5.00 10.00
19-That Darn Cat; r/That Darn Cat #10171-602-Hayley Mills photo-c 2.00 5.00 10.00
20,23-Pluto-r 1.40 3.50 7.00
21-Li'l Bad Wolf & The Three Little Pigs 1.20 3.00 6.00
22-Unbirthday Party with Alice in Wonderland; r/Four Color #341 1.60 4.00 8.00
24-26: 24-Herbie Rides Again (Movie); sequel to "The Love Bug;" photo-c. 25-Old Yeller (Movie); r/F.C. #869; Photo-c. 26-Lt. Robin Crusoe USN (Movie); r/Lt. Robin Crusoe USN #10191-601; photo-c 1.40 3.50 7.00
27-Island at the Top of the World (Movie)-Photo-c 1.60 4.00 8.00
28-Brer Rabbit, Bucky Bug-r/WDC&S #58 1.40 3.50 7.00
29-Escape to Witch Mountain (Movie)-Photo-c 1.60 4.00 8.00
30-Magica De Spell; Barks-r/Uncle Scrooge #36 & WDC&S #258 2.80 7.00 14.00
31-Bambi (cartoon feature); r/Four Color #186 1.60 4.00 8.00
32-Spin & Marty-r/F.C. #1026; Mickey Mouse Club (TV)-Photo-c 2.00 5.00 10.00
33-39: 33-Pluto-r/F.C. #1143. 34-Paul Revere's Ride with Johnny Tremain (TV); r/F.C. #822. 35-Goofy-r/F.C. #952. 36-Peter Pan-r/F.C. #442. 37-Tinker Bell & Jiminy Cricket-r/F.C. #982,989. 38,39-Mickey & the Sleuth, Parts 1 & 2 1.00 2.50 5.00
40-The Rescuers (cartoon feature) 1.20 3.00 6.00
41-Herbie Goes to Monte Carlo (Movie); sequel to "Herbie Rides Again;" photo-c 1.40 3.50 7.00
42-Mickey & the Sleuth 1.00 2.50 5.00
43-Pete's Dragon (Movie)-Photo-c 1.60 4.00 8.00
44-Return From Witch Mountain (new) & In Search of the Castaways-r (Movies)-Photo-c; 68 pg. giants begin 1.60 4.00 8.00
45-The Jungle Book (Movie); r/#30033-803 1.60 4.00 8.00
46-The Cat From Outer Space (Movie)(new), & The Shaggy Dog (Movie)-r/F.C. #985; photo-c 1.20 3.00 6.00
47-Mickey Mouse Surprise Party-r 1.20 3.00 6.00
48-The Wonderful Advs. of Pinocchio-r/F.C. #1203; last 68 pg. issue 1.20 3.00 6.00
49-54: 49-North Avenue Irregulars (Movie); Zorro-r/Zorro #11; 52 pgs. begin; photo-c. 50-Bedknobs & Broomsticks-r/#6; Mooncussers-r/World of Adv. #1; photo-c. 51-101 Dalmatians-r. 52-Unidentified Flying Oddball (Movie); r/Picnic Party #8; photo-c. 53-The Scarecrow-r (TV). 54-The Black Hole (Movie)-Photo-c .80 2.00 4.00

WALT DISNEY'S JUNIOR WOODCHUCKS LIMITED SERIES
July, 1991 - No. 4, Oct, 1991 ($1.50, color, limited series; new & reprint-a)
W. D. Publications (Disney)

1-4: 1-The Beagle Boys app.; Barks-r .30 .75 1.50

WALT DISNEY'S MAGAZINE (TV)(Formerly Walt Disney's Mickey Mouse Club Magazine) (50 cents) (Bi-monthly)
V2#4, June, 1957 - V4#6, Oct, 1959
Western Publishing Co.

V2#4-Stories & articles on the Mouseketeers, Zorro, & Goofy and other

Walt Disney's Comics and Stories #531, © WDC

Walt Disney's Comics & Stories nn (1943 XMas giveaway), © WDC

Walt Disney Showcase #30, © WDC

Wambi, Jungle Boy #8, © FH

Wanted Comics #30, © Toytown Publ.

War Action #1, © MEG

	GD25	FN65	NM94
Disney characters & people	5.85	17.50	35.00
V2#5, V2#6(10/57)	4.70	14.00	28.00
V3#1(12/57), V3#3-6(10/58)	4.00	10.50	21.00
V3#2-Annette Funicello photo-c	7.50	22.50	45.00
V4#1(12/58) - V4#2-4,6(10/59)	4.00	10.50	21.00
V4#5-Annette Funicello photo-c	6.70	20.00	40.00

NOTE: V2#4-V3#6 were 11-1/2x8-1/2", 48 pgs.; V4#1 on were 10x8", 52 pgs. (Peak circulation of 400,000).

WALT DISNEY'S MERRY CHRISTMAS (See Dell Giant #39)

WALT DISNEY'S MICKEY MOUSE CLUB MAGAZINE (TV)(Becomes Walt Disney's Magazine) (Quarterly)
Winter, 1956 - V2#3, April, 1957 (11x8") (48 pgs.)
Western Publishing Co.

	GD25	FN65	NM94
V1#1	11.00	32.00	75.00
2-4	6.70	20.00	40.00
V2#1-3	5.35	16.00	32.00
Annual(1956)-Two different issues; ($1.50-Whitman); 120 pgs., cardboard covers, 11-3/4x8-3/4"; reprints	12.00	36.00	85.00
Annual(1957)-Same as above	11.00	32.00	75.00

WALT DISNEY'S PINOCCHIO SPECIAL (Gladstone) (Value: cover or less)

WALT DISNEY'S SEBASTIAN (Disney) (Value: cover or less)

WALT DISNEY'S SPRING FEVER (Disney) (Value: cover or less)

WALT DISNEY'S THE JUNGLE BOOK (Disney) (Value: cover or less)

WALT DISNEY'S WHEATIES PREMIUMS (See Wheaties)

WALTER LANTZ ANDY PANDA (Also see Andy Panda)
Aug, 1973 - No. 23, Jan, 1978 (Walter Lantz)
Gold Key

	GD25	FN65	NM94
1-Reprints	1.00	2.50	5.00
2-10-All reprints	.40	1.00	2.00
11-23: 15,17-19,22-Reprints	.30	.75	1.50

WALT KELLY'S...
Dec, 1987; April, 1988 ($1.75-$2.50, color, Baxter)
Eclipse Comics

	GD25	FN65	NM94
...Christmas Classics 1 (1987, $1.75)-Kelly-r/Peter Wheat & Santa Claus Funnies	.35	.90	1.75
...Springtime Tales 1 (4/88, $2.50)-Kelly-r	.50	1.25	2.50

WALTONS, THE (See Kite Fun Book)

WALT SCOTT'S CHRISTMAS STORIES (See 4-Color #959, 1062)

WAMBI, JUNGLE BOY (See Jungle Comics)
Spring, 1942; No. 2, Wint, 1942-43; No. 3, Spring, 1943; No. 4, Fall, 1948; No. 5, Sum, 1949; No. 6, Spring, 1950; No. 7-10, 1950(nd); No. 11, Spring, 1951 - No. 18, Winter, 1952-53 (#1-3: 68 pgs.)
Fiction House Magazines

	GD25	FN65	NM94
1-Wambi, the Jungle Boy begins	46.00	138.00	275.00
2 (1942)-Kiefer-c	25.00	75.00	150.00
3 (1943)-Kiefer-c/a	17.50	52.50	105.00
4 (1948)-Origin in text	10.00	30.00	70.00
5 (Fall, 1949, 36 pgs.)-Kiefer-c/a	10.00	30.00	60.00
6-10: 7-(52 pgs.)	8.35	25.00	50.00
11-18	5.85	17.50	35.00
I.W. Reprint #8('64)-r/#12 with new-c	1.80	4.50	9.00

*NOTE: **Alex Blum** c-8. **Kiefer** c-1-5. **Whitman** c-11-18.*

WANDERERS (DC) (Value: cover or less) (See Adventure Comics #375, 376)

WANTED COMICS
No. 9, Sept-Oct, 1947 - No. 53, April, 1953 (#9-33: 52 pgs.)
Toytown Publications/Patches/Orbit Publ.

	GD25	FN65	NM94
9	10.00	30.00	60.00
10,11: 10-Giunta-a; radio's Mr. D. A. app.	5.85	17.50	35.00
12-Used in **SOTI**, pg. 277	6.70	20.00	40.00
13-Heroin drug propaganda story	5.85	17.50	35.00
14-Marijuana drug mention story, 2 pgs.	4.20	12.50	25.00
15-17,19,20	4.00	11.00	22.00
18-Marijuana story, "Satan's Cigarettes"; r-in #45 & retitled	11.50	34.00	80.00
21,22: 21-Krigstein-a. 22-Extreme violence	5.00	15.00	30.00
23,25-34,36-38,40-44,46-48,53	3.00	7.50	15.00
24-Krigstein-a; "The Dope King," marijuana mention story	5.85	17.50	35.00
35-Used in **SOTI**, pg. 160	5.00	15.00	30.00
39-Drug propaganda sty "The Horror Weed"	8.35	25.00	50.00
45-Marijuana story from #18	4.70	14.00	28.00
49-Has unstable pink-c that fades easily; rare in mint condition	3.60	9.00	18.00
50-Has unstable pink-c like #49; surrealist-c by Buscema; horror stories	7.50	22.50	45.00
51-"Holiday of Horror"-junkie story; drug-c	5.00	15.00	30.00
52-Classic "Cult of Killers" opium use story	5.00	15.00	30.00

*NOTE: **Buscema** c-50, 51. **Lawrence** and **Leav** c/a most issues. **Syd Shores** c/a-48.*

WANTED: DEAD OR ALIVE (See 4-Color #1102,1164)

WANTED, THE WORLD'S MOST DANGEROUS VILLAINS
July-Aug, 1972 - No. 9, Aug-Sept, 1973 (All reprints)
National Periodical Publications (See DC Special)

	GD25	FN65	NM94
1-Batman, Green Lantern (story r-from G.L. #1), & Green Arrow	.80	2.00	4.00
2-Batman/Joker/Penguin-c/story r-from Batman #25; plus Flash story (r-from Flash #121)	1.20	3.00	6.00
3-9: 3-Dr. Fate(r/More Fun #65), Hawkman(r/Flash #100), & Vigilante(r/Action #69). 4-Gr. Lantern(r/All-American #61) & Kid Eternity(r/Kid Eternity #15). 5-Dollman/Green Lantern. 6-Burnley Starman; Wildcat/Sargon. 7-Johnny Quick(r/More fun #76), Hawkman(r/Flash #90), Hourman by Baily(r/Adv. #72). 8-Dr. Fate/Flash(r/Flash #114). 9-S&K Sandman/Superman	.40	1.00	2.00

*NOTE: **Kane** r-1, 5. **Kubert** r-3i, 6, 7. **Meskin** r-3, 7. **Reinman** r-4, 6.*

WAR
July, 1975 - No. 9, Nov, 1976; No. 10, Sept, 1978 - No. 49?, 1984
Charlton Comics

	GD25	FN65	NM94
1-49: 47-Reprints		.50	1.00
7,9(Modern Comics-r, 1977)		.50	1.00

WAR, THE (Marvel) (Value: cover or less)

WAR ACTION
April, 1952 - No. 14, June, 1953
Atlas Comics (CPS)

	GD25	FN65	NM94
1	10.00	30.00	60.00
2	5.00	15.00	30.00
3-10,14: 7-Pakula-a	4.00	11.00	22.00
11-13-Krigstein-a	5.85	17.50	35.00

*NOTE: **Brodsky** c-1-4. **Heath** a-1; c-7, 14. **Keller** a-6. **Maneely** a-1. **Tuska** a-2, 8.*

WAR ADVENTURES
Jan, 1952 - No. 13, Feb, 1953
Atlas Comics (HPC)

	GD25	FN65	NM94
1-Tuska-a	8.35	25.00	50.00
2	4.20	12.50	25.00
3-7,9-13: 3-Pakula-a. 7-Maneely-c	3.60	9.00	18.00
8-Krigstein-a	5.85	17.50	35.00

*NOTE: **Brodsky** c-1-3, 6, 8, 11, 12. **Heath** a-5, 7, 10; c-4, 5, 9, 13. **Robinson** a-3; c-10.*

WAR ADVENTURES ON THE BATTLEFIELD (See Battlefield)

WAR AGAINST CRIME! (Becomes Vault of Horror #12 on)
Spring, 1948 - No. 11, Feb-Mar, 1950
E. C. Comics

	GD25	FN65	NM94
1	50.00	150.00	350.00
2,3	27.00	81.00	190.00
4-9	26.00	77.00	180.00
10-1st Vault Keeper app.	129.00	385.00	900.00
11-2nd Vault Keeper app.	79.00	235.00	550.00

NOTE: *All have **Johnny Craig** covers. **Feldstein** a-4, 7-9. **Harrison/Wood** a-11. **Ingels** a-1, 2, 8. **Palais** a-8.*

WAR AND ATTACK (Also see Special War Series #3)
Fall, 1964; V2#54, June, 1966 - V2#63, Dec, 1967
Charlton Comics

	GD25	FN65	NM94
1-Wood-a	2.00	5.00	10.00
V2#54(6/66)-#63 (Formerly Fightin' Air Force)	1.20	3.00	6.00

NOTE: ***Montes/Bache** a-55, 56, 60, 63.*

WAR AT SEA (Formerly Space Adventures)
No. 22, Nov, 1957 - No. 42, June, 1961
Charlton Comics

	GD25	FN65	NM94
22	3.00	7.50	15.00
23-30	1.40	3.50	7.00
31-42	1.00	2.50	5.00

WAR BATTLES
Feb, 1952 - No. 9, Dec, 1953
Harvey Publications

	GD25	FN65	NM94
1-Powell-a	5.85	17.50	35.00
2-Powell-a	4.00	10.00	20.00
3-5,7-9: 3,7-Powell-a	3.00	7.50	15.00
6-Nostrand-a	4.20	12.50	25.00

WAR BIRDS
1952(nd) - No. 3, Winter, 1952-53
Fiction House Magazines

	GD25	FN65	NM94
1	10.00	30.00	60.00
2,3	5.85	17.50	35.00

WAR COMBAT (Combat Casey #6 on)
March, 1952 - No. 5, Nov, 1952
Atlas Comics (LBI No. 1/SAI No. 2-5)

	GD25	FN65	NM94
1	6.70	20.00	40.00
2	4.20	12.50	25.00
3-5	3.60	9.00	18.00

NOTE: ***Berg** a-2, 4, 5. **Brodsky** c-1, 2, 4, 5. **Henkel** a-5. **Maneely** a-1, 4; c-3.*

WAR COMICS (War Stories #5 on)(See Key Ring Comics)
May, 1940 (No mo. given) - No. 4, 1941(nd)
Dell Publishing Co.

	GD25	FN65	NM94
1-Sikandur the Robot Master, Sky Hawk, Scoop Mason, War Correspondent begin; McWilliams-c	32.00	95.00	220.00
2-Origin Greg Gilday	16.00	48.00	110.00
3-Joan becomes Greg Gilday's aide	11.00	32.00	75.00
4-Origin Night Devils	13.00	40.00	90.00

WAR COMICS
Dec, 1950 - No. 49, Sept, 1957
Marvel/Atlas (USA No. 1-41/JPI No. 42-49)

	GD25	FN65	NM94
1	11.00	32.00	75.00
2	6.70	20.00	40.00
3-10	5.00	15.00	30.00
11-20	3.60	9.00	18.00
21,23-32: Last precode (2/55). 26-Valley Forge story	3.00	7.50	15.00
22-Krigstein-a	6.35	19.00	38.00
33-37,39-42,44,45,47,48	3.00	7.50	15.00
38-Kubert/Moskowitz-a	4.70	14.00	28.00
43,49-Torres-a. 43-Davis E.C. swipe	4.20	12.50	25.00
46-Crandall-a	4.70	14.00	28.00

NOTE: ***Colan** a-4, 36, 48, 49. **Drucker** a-37, 43, 48. **Everett** a-17. **Heath** a-7-9, 16, 19, 25, 36; c-11, 16, 19, 25, 26, 29-31, 36. **G. Kane** a-19. **Lawrence** a-36. **Maneely** a-7, 9; c-6, 27, 37. **Orlando** a-42, 48. **Pakula** a-26. **Ravielli** a-27. **Reinman** a-26. **Robinson** a-15; c-13. **Severin** a-26, 27; c-48.*

WAR DOGS OF THE U.S. ARMY
1952
Avon Periodicals

	GD25	FN65	NM94
1-Kinstler-c/a	9.15	27.50	55.00

WARFRONT
9/51 - #35, 11/58; #36, 10/65; #37, 9/66 - #38, 12/66; #39, 2/67
Harvey Publications

	GD25	FN65	NM94
1	6.70	20.00	40.00
2	4.00	10.00	20.00
3-10	2.80	7.00	14.00
11,12,14,16-20	2.00	5.00	10.00
13,15,22-Nostrand-a	5.00	15.00	30.00
21,23-27,29,31-33,35	1.80	4.50	9.00
28,30,34-Kirby-c	4.00	10.00	20.00
36-Dynamite Joe begins, ends #39; Williamson-a	2.40	6.00	12.00
37-Wood-a, 17pgs.	2.80	7.00	14.00
38,39-Wood-a, 2-3 pgs.; Lone Tiger app.	1.60	4.00	8.00

NOTE: ***Powell** a-1-6, 9-11, 14, 17, 20, 23, 25-28, 30, 31, 34, 36. **Powell/Nostrand** a-12, 13, 15. **Simon** c-36?, 38.*

WAR FURY
Sept, 1952 - No. 4, March, 1953
Comic Media/Harwell (Allen Hardy Associates)

	GD25	FN65	NM94
1-Heck-c/a in all; Palais-a; bullet hole in forehead-c; all issues are very violent	5.35	16.00	32.00
2-4: 4-Morisi-a	3.60	9.00	18.00

WAR GODS OF THE DEEP (See Movie Classics)

WARHAWKS (TSR)(Value: cover or less)

WARHEADS
June, 1992 - Present ($1.75, color)
Marvel Comics UK

	GD25	FN65	NM94
1-Wolverine-c/story; indicia says #2 by mistake	.60	1.50	3.00
2-12: 2-Nick Fury app. 3-Iron Man-c/story. 4,5-X-Force. 5-Liger vs. Cable. 6,7-Death's Head II app. (#6 is cameo)	.35	.90	1.75

WAR HEROES (See Marine War Heroes)

WAR HEROES
7-9/42 (no month); No. 2, 10-12/42 - No. 10, 10-12/44; No. 11, 3/45
Dell Publishing Co.

	GD25	FN65	NM94
1	14.00	43.00	100.00
2	8.35	25.00	50.00
3,5: 3-Pro-Russian back-c	5.85	17.50	35.00
4-Disney's Gremlins app.	11.50	34.00	80.00
6-11: 6-Tothish-a by Discount	5.00	15.00	30.00

NOTE: *No. 1 was to be released in July, but was delayed.*

WAR HEROES
May, 1952 - No. 8, April, 1953
Ace Magazines

	GD25	FN65	NM94
1	5.85	17.50	35.00
2-Lou Cameron-a	3.60	9.00	18.00
3-8: 6,7-Cameron-a	3.00	7.50	15.00

WAR HEROES (Also see Blue Bird Comics)
Feb, 1963 - No. 27, Nov, 1967
Charlton Comics

	GD25	FN65	NM94
1	2.00	5.00	10.00
2-10: 2-John F. Kennedy story	1.00	2.50	5.00
11-27: 27-1st Devils Brigade by Glanzman	.60	1.50	3.00

NOTE: ***Montes/Bache** a-3-7, 21, 25, 27; c-3-7.*

WAR IS HELL
Jan, 1973 - No. 15, Oct, 1975
Marvel Comics Group

War Against Crime #2, © WMG

War Comics #1 (5/40), © DELL

War Heroes #2 (7/52), © ACE

Warlock #2 (10/72), © MEG

Warlord #3, © DC

War Stories #8, © DELL

	GD25	FN65	NM94
1-Williamson-a(r), 5 pgs.; Ayers-a	.30	.75	1.50
2-15: 2-9-All reprints		.50	1.00

NOTE: ***Bolle** a-3r. **Powell** a-1. **Woodbridge** a-1. Sgt. Fury reprints-7, 8.*

WARLOCK (The Power of...) (Also see Fantastic Four #66, 67, Incredible Hulk #178, Infinity War, Marvel Premiere #1, Silver Surfer V3#46, Strange Tales #178-181 & Thor #165)
Aug, 1972 - No. 8, Oct, 1973; No. 9, Oct, 1975 - No. 15, Nov, 1976
Marvel Comics Group

	GD25	FN65	NM94
1-Origin by Kane	5.85	17.50	35.00
2,3	3.00	7.50	15.00
4-8: 4-Death of Eddie Roberts	2.00	5.00	10.00
9-Starlin's 2nd Thanos saga begins, ends #15; new costume Warlock; Thanos cameo only; story cont'd from Strange Tales #178-181; Starlin-c/a in #9-15	2.50	6.25	12.50
10-Origin Thanos & Gamora; recaps events from Capt. Marvel #25-34. Thanos vs. The Magus-c/story	6.70	20.00	40.00
11-Thanos app.	5.35	16.00	32.00
12-14: 14-Origin Star Thief; last 25 cent issue	2.80	7.00	14.00
15-Thanos-c/story	4.70	14.00	28.00

NOTE: ***Buscema** a-2p; c-8p. **G. Kane** a-1p, 3-5p; c-1p, 2, 3, 4p, 5p, 7p. **Starlin** a-9-14p, 15; c-11p, 12p, 13-15. **Sutton** a-1-8i.*

WARLOCK (...Special Edition on-c)
Dec, 1982 - No. 6, May, 1983 ($2.00, 52 pgs.) (slick paper)
Marvel Comics Group

	GD25	FN65	NM94
1-6: 1-Warlock-r/Strange Tales #178-180. 2-r/Str. Tales #180,181 & Warlock #9. 3-r/Warlock #10-12(Thanos origin recap). 4-r/Warlock #12-15. 5-r/Warlock #15, Marvel Team-Up #55 & Avengers Ann. #7. 6-r/2nd half Avengers Annual #7 & Marvel Two-in-One Annual #2	1.80	4.50	9.00
Special Edition #1(12/83)	.60	1.50	3.00

NOTE: ***Byrne** a-5r. **Starlin** a-1-6r; c-1-6(new). Direct sale only.*

WARLOCK
V2#1, May, 1992 - No. 6, Oct, 1992 ($2.50, color, limited series)
Marvel Comics

	GD25	FN65	NM94
V2#1-Reprints 1982 reprint series w/Thanos	.70	1.75	3.50
2-6	.60	1.50	3.00

WARLOCK AND THE INFINITY WATCH
Feb, 1992 - Present ($1.75, color) (Sequel to Infinity Gauntlet)
Marvel Comics

	GD25	FN65	NM94
1-Starlin scripts begin; brief origin recap Warlock	1.00	2.50	5.00
2-Reintro Moondragon	.80	2.00	4.00
3	.60	1.50	3.00
4-6	.45	1.15	2.25
7-16: 7-Reintro The Magus; Moondragon app.; Thanos cameo on last 2 pgs. 8,9-Thanos battles Gamora-c/story. 8-Magus & Moondragon app. 10-Thanos-c/story; Magus app.	.35	.90	1.75

NOTE: ***Austin** a-1-4i; c-1-4i.*

WARLOCK 5 (Aircel) (Value: cover or less)

WARLORD (See 1st Issue Special)
1-2/76; No.2, 3-4/76; No.3, 10-11/76 - No. 133, Wint, 1988-89
National Periodical Publications/DC Comics #123 on

	GD25	FN65	NM94
1-Story cont'd. from 1st Issue Special #8	3.00	7.50	15.00
2-Intro. Machiste	1.60	4.00	8.00
3-5	1.00	2.50	5.00
6-10: 6-Intro Mariah. 7-Origin Machiste. 9-Dons new costume	.80	2.00	4.00
11-20: 11-Origin-r. 12-Intro Aton. 15-Tara returns; Warlord has son	.60	1.50	3.00
21-40: 27-New facts about origin. 28-1st app. Wizard World. 32-Intro Shakira. 37,38-Origin Omac by Starlin. 38-Intro Jennifer Morgan, Warlord's daughter. 39-Omac ends. 40-Warlord gets new costume	.40	1.00	2.00
41-47,49-52: 42-47-Omac back-up series. 49-Claw The Unconquered app. 50-Death of Aton. 51-Reprints #1		.50	1.00
48-(52pgs.)-1st app. Arak; contains free 14 pg. Arak Son of Thunder; Claw The Unconquered app.	.40	1.00	2.00
53-130,132: 55-Arion Lord of Atlantis begins, ends #62. 63-The Barren Earth begins; free 16pg. Masters of the Universe preview. 91-Origin w/new facts. 114,115-Legends x-over. 100-($1.25, 52 pgs.). 125-Death of Tara		.50	1.00
131-1st DC work by Rob Liefeld (9/88)	.40	1.00	2.00
133-($1.50, 52 pgs.)	.30	.75	1.50
Remco Toy Giveaway (2-3/4x4")		.50	1.00
Annual 1(1982)-Grell-c, a(p)	.40	1.00	2.00
Annual 2-6: 2('83). 3('84). 4('85). 5('86). 6('87)		.50	1.00

NOTE: ***Grell** a-1-15, 16-50p, 51r, 52p, 59p, Annual 1p; c-1-70, 100-104, 112, 116, 117, Annual 1, 5. **Wayne Howard** a-64i. **Starlin** a-37-39p.*

WARLORD (DC) (Value: cover or less)

WARLORDS (See DC Graphic Novel #2)

WAR OF THE GODS (DC) (Value: cover or less)

WARP (First) (Value: cover or less)

WARPED (Empire) (Value: cover or less)

WARPATH
Nov, 1954 - No. 3, April, 1955
Key Publications/Stanmor

	GD25	FN65	NM94
1	6.70	20.00	40.00
2,3	4.00	11.00	22.00

WARP GRAPHICS ANNUAL (WaRP) (Value: cover or less)

WARREN PRESENTS
Jan, 1979 - No. 14, Nov, 1981
Warren Publications

	GD25	FN65	NM94
1-14-Eerie, Creepy, & Vampirella-r	.40	1.00	2.00
...The Rook 1 (5/79)-r/Eerie #82-85	.40	1.00	2.00

WAR REPORT
Sept, 1952 - No. 5, May, 1953
Ajax/Farrell Publications (Excellent Publ.)

	GD25	FN65	NM94
1	5.85	17.50	35.00
2	3.60	9.00	18.00
3-5: 4-Used in **POP**, pg. 94	3.00	7.50	15.00

WARRIOR COMICS
1945 (1930s DC reprints)
H.C. Blackerby

	GD25	FN65	NM94
1-Wing Brady, The Iron Man, Mark Markon	10.00	30.00	70.00

WAR ROMANCES (See True...)

WAR SHIPS
1942 (36 pgs.) (Similar to Large Feature Comics)
Dell Publishing Co.

	GD25	FN65	NM94
nn-Cover by McWilliams; contains photos & drawings of U.S. war ships	10.00	30.00	70.00

WAR STORIES (Formerly War Comics)
No. 5, 1942(nd) - No. 8, Feb-Apr, 1943
Dell Publishing Co.

	GD25	FN65	NM94
5-Origin The Whistler	14.00	43.00	100.00
6-8: 6-8-Night Devils app.	11.00	32.00	75.00

WAR STORIES (Korea)
Sept, 1952 - No. 5, May, 1953
Ajax/Farrell Publications (Excellent Publ.)

	GD25	FN65	NM94
1	5.35	16.00	32.00
2	3.20	8.00	16.00
3-5	2.80	7.00	14.00

WAR STORIES (See Star Spangled...)

WART AND THE WIZARD
Feb, 1964 (Walt Disney)
Gold Key

1 (10102-402) 3.00 7.50 15.00

WARTIME ROMANCES
July, 1951 - No. 18, Nov, 1953
St. John Publishing co.

1-All Baker-a 12.00 36.00 85.00
2-All Baker-a 8.35 25.00 50.00
3,4-All Baker-a 7.50 22.50 45.00
5-8-Baker-c/a(2-3) each 6.70 20.00 40.00
9-12,16,18-Baker-c/a each 5.00 15.00 30.00
13-15,17-Baker-c only 4.00 11.00 22.00

WAR VICTORY ADVENTURES (#1 titled War Victory Comics)
Summer, 1942 - No. 3, Winter, 1943-44 (5 cents)
U.S. Treasury Dept./War Victory/Harvey Publ.

1-(Promotion of Savings Bonds)-Featuring America's greatest comic art by top syndicated cartoonists; Blondie, Joe Palooka, Green Hornet, Dick Tracy, Superman, Gumps, etc.; (36 pgs.); All profits contributed to U.S.O. 23.00 70.00 160.00
2-Battle of Stalingrad story; Powell-a 11.50 34.00 80.00
3-Capt. Red Cross-c & text only; Powell-a 10.00 30.00 70.00

WAR WAGON, THE (See Movie Classics)

WAR WINGS
October, 1968
Charlton Comics

1 .80 2.00 4.00

WARWORLD! (Dark Horse)(Value: cover or less)

WASHABLE JONES & SHMOO
June, 1953
Harvey Publications

1 12.00 36.00 85.00

WASH TUBBS (See The Comics, Crackajack Funnies & 4-Color #11, 28, 53)

WASTELAND (DC)(Value: cover or less)

WATCHMEN
Sept, 1986 - No. 12, Oct, 1987 (12 issue maxi-series)
DC Comics

1-Alan Moore scripts in all .80 2.00 4.00
2-12 .60 1.50 3.00

WATCH OUT FOR BIG TALK
1950
Giveaway

nn-Dan Barry-a (about crooked politicians) 4.00 10.00 20.00

WATER BIRDS AND THE OLYMPIC ELK (See 4-Color #700)

WCW WORLD CHAMPIONSHIP WRESTLING (TV)
Apr, 1992 - Present ($1.25, color)
Marvel Comics

1-14: All have photo-c of wrestlers .60 1.25

WEASEL PATROL SPECIAL, THE (Eclipse)(Value: cover or less)

WEATHER-BIRD (See Comics From..., Dick Tracy, Free Comics to You... & Terry and the Pirates)
1958 - No. 16, July, 1962 (Shoe store giveaway)
International Shoe Co./Western Printing Co.

1 3.60 9.00 18.00
2-16 1.80 4.50 9.00

NOTE: *The numbers are located in the lower bottom panel, pg. 1. All feature a character called Weather-Bird.*

WEATHER BIRD COMICS (See Comics From Weather Bird)
1957 (Giveaway)
Weather Bird Shoes

nn-Contains a comic bound with new cover. Several combinations possible; contents determines price (40 - 60 percent of contents).

WEAVEWORLD (Epic)(Value: cover or less)

WEB, THE (Also see Mighty Comics & Mighty Crusaders)
Sept, 1991 - No. 14, Oct, 1992 ($1.00, color)
Impact Comics (DC)

1-14: 5-The Fly x-over 9-Trading card inside .50 1.00
Annual 1 (1992, $2.50, 68 pgs.)-W/Trading card .50 1.25 2.50

NOTE: ***Gil Kane** c-5, 9, 10, 12-14. **Bill Wray** a(i)-1-9, 10(part).*

WEB OF EVIL
Nov, 1952 - No. 21, Dec, 1954
Comic Magazines/Quality Comics Group

1-Used in **SOTI**, pg. 388. Jack Cole-a; morphine use story 25.00 75.00 175.00
2,3-Jack Cole-a 16.00 48.00 110.00
4,6,7-Jack Cole-c/a 16.00 48.00 110.00
5-Electrocution-c; Jack Cole-c/a 19.00 58.00 135.00
8-11-Jack Cole-a 12.00 36.00 85.00
12,13,15,16,19-21 7.50 22.50 45.00
14-Part Crandall-c; Old Witch swipe 8.35 25.00 50.00
17-Opium drug propaganda story 7.50 22.50 45.00
18-Acid-in-face story 10.00 30.00 60.00

NOTE: ***Jack Cole** a(2 each)-2, 6, 8, 9. **Cuidera** c-1-21i. **Ravielli** a-13.*

WEB OF HORROR (Magazine)
Dec, 1969 - No. 3, Apr, 1970
Major Magazines

1-Jeff Jones painted-c; Wrightson-a 4.20 12.50 25.00
2-Jones painted-c; Wrightson-a(2), Kaluta-a 3.60 9.00 18.00
3-Wrightson-c/a (1st published-c); Brunner, Kaluta, Bruce Jones-a 3.60 9.00 18.00

WEB OF MYSTERY
Feb, 1951 - No. 29, Sept, 1955
Ace Magazines (A. A. Wyn)

1 19.00 58.00 135.00
2-Bakerish-a 11.50 34.00 80.00
3-10: 4-Colan-a 10.00 30.00 70.00
11-18,20-26: 12-John Chilly's 1st cover art. 13-Surrealistic-c. 20-r/The Beyond #1 10.00 30.00 60.00
19-Reprints Challenge of the Unknown #6 used in N.Y. Legislative Committee 10.00 30.00 60.00
27-Bakerish-a(r/The Beyond #2); last pre-code issue 9.15 27.50 55.00
28,29: 28-All-r 6.70 20.00 40.00

NOTE: *This series was to appear as "Creepy Stories," but title was changed before publication. **Cameron** a-6, 8, 11-13, 17-20, 22, 24, 25, 27; c-8, 13, 17. **Palais** a-28r. **Sekowsky** a-1-3, 7, 8, 11, 14, 21, 29. **Tothish** a-by **Bill Discount** #16. 29-all-r, 19-28-partial-r.*

WEB OF SPIDER-MAN
Apr, 1985 - Present
Marvel Comics Group

1-Painted-c (4th app. black costume?) 4.20 12.50 25.00
2,3 1.40 3.50 7.00
4-8: 7-Hulk x-over; Wolverine splash 1.00 2.50 5.00
9-13: 10-Dominic Fortune guest stars; painted-c .90 2.25 4.50
14-28: 19-Intro Humbug & Solo .80 2.00 4.00
29-Wolverine, new Hobgoblin (Macendale) app. 2.60 6.50 13.00
30-Origin recap The Rose & Hobgoblin I (entire book is flashback story); Punisher & Wolverine cameo 2.40 6.00 12.00
31,32-Six part Kraven storyline begins 1.60 4.00 8.00
33,34 .30 .75 1.50
35-37,39-47,49: 35-1st app. Tombstone .60 1.20

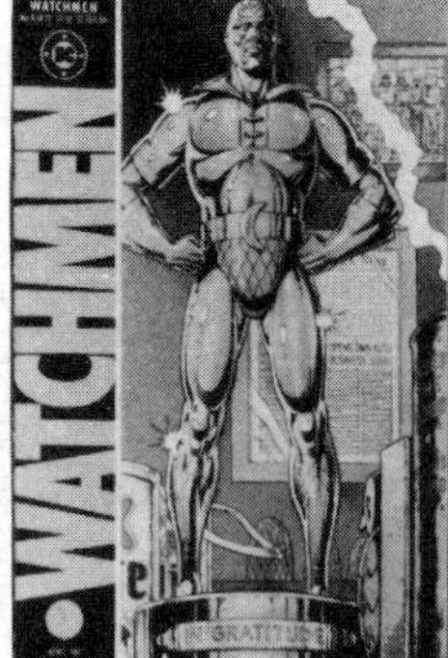

Watchmen #8, © DC

Web of Mystery #2, © ACE

The Web of Spider-Man #7, © MEG

The Web of Spider-Man Annual #5, © MEG

Weird Comics #5, © FOX

SCIENCE FICTION
NO. 16
NOV-DEC
WEIRD
10¢
FANTASY

Weird Fantasy #16 (#4), © WMG

GD25 FN65 NM94

38-Hobgoblin app.; begin $1.00-c 1.20 3.00 6.00
48-Origin Hobgoblin II(Demogoblin); Kingpin app. 2.80 7.00 14.00
50-($1.50, 52 pgs.) .40 1.00 2.00
51-58 .55 1.10
59-Cosmic Spidey cont'd from Spect. Spider-Man 1.80 4.50 9.00
60-65,68-89: 69,70-Hulk x-over. 74-76-Austin-c(i). 76-Fantastic Four x-over. 78-Cloak & Dagger app. 84-Begin 6 part Rose & Hobgoblin II storyline; last $1.00-c .60 1.25
66,67-Green Goblin (Norman Osborn) app. as a super-hero .40 1.00 2.00
90-($2.95, 52 pgs.)-Polybagged w/hologram-c, gatefold poster showing Spider-Man & Spider-Man 2099 1.20 3.00 6.00
90 (2nd printing) .60 1.50 3.00
91-99: 93,94-Hobgoblin (Macendale) Reborn-c/story, parts 1,2; Moon Knight app. 93-Gives brief history of Hobgoblin. 94-Venom cameo. 95,96-Spirits of Venom, part 1,3 w/Ghost Rider/Blaze/Spidey vs. Venom & Demogoblin (cont'd in Ghost Rider/Blaze #5,6) .60 1.25
100-($2.95, 52 pgs.)-Holo-grafx foil-c .60 1.50 3.00
Annual 1 (1985) .50 1.25 2.50
Annual 2 (1986)-New Mutants; Art Adams-a 1.40 3.50 7.00
Annual 3 (1987) .50 1.25 2.50
Annual 4 (1988, $1.75)-Evolutionary War x-over .60 1.50 3.00
Annual 5 (1989, $2.00, 68pgs.)-Atlantis Attacks; Captain Universe by Ditko (p) & Silver Sable stories; F.F. app. .50 1.25 2.50
Annual 6 ('90, $2.00, 68pgs.)-Punisher back-up plus Capt. Universe by Ditko; G. Kane-a .50 1.25 2.50
Annual 7 (1991, $2.00, 68 pgs.)-Origins of Hobgoblin I, Hobgoblin II, Green Goblin I & II & Venom; Austin-c(i) .50 1.25 2.50
Annual 8 (1992, $2.25, 68 pgs.)-Part 3 of Venom story; New Warriors x-over; Black Cat back-up story .50 1.25 2.50

WEDDING BELLS
Feb, 1954 - No. 19, Nov, 1956
Quality Comics Group

1-Whitney-a 9.15 27.50 55.00
2 5.00 15.00 30.00
3-9: 8-Last precode (4/55) 3.60 9.00 18.00
10-Ward-a, 9 pgs. 8.00 24.00 48.00
11-14,17 2.40 6.00 12.00
15-Baker-c 3.00 7.50 15.00
16-Baker-c/a 4.00 11.00 22.00
18,19-Baker-a each 3.60 9.00 18.00

WEEKENDER, THE
V1#4, 1945 - V2#1, 1946 (52 pages)
Rucker Publ. Co.

V1#4(1945) 11.00 32.00 75.00
V2#1-36 pgs. comics, 16 in newspaper format with photos; partial Dynamic Comics reprints; 4 pgs. of cels from the Disney film Pinocchio; Little Nemo story by Winsor McCay, Jr.; Jack Cole-a 13.00 40.00 90.00

WEEKLY COMIC MAGAZINE
May 12, 1940 (16 pgs.) (Full Color) (Others exist without super-heroes)
Fox Publications

(1st Version)-8 pg. Blue Beetle story, 7 pg. Patty O'Day story; two copies known to exist. Estimated value.... $500.00
(2nd Version)-7 two-pg. adventures of Blue Beetle, Patty O'Day, Yarko, Dr. Fung, Green Mask, Spark Stevens, & Rex Dexter; one copy known to exist. Estimated value.... $400.00
Discovered with business papers, letters and exploitation material promoting **Weekly Comic Magazine** for use by newspapers in the same manner of **The Spirit** weeklies. Interesting note: these are dated three weeks before the first Spirit comic. Letters indicate that samples may have been sent to a few newspapers. These sections were actually 15-1/2x22" pages which will fold down to an approximate 8x10" comic booklet. Other various comic sections were found with the above, but were more like the Sunday comic sections in format.

WEIRD (Magazine)
V1#10, 1/66 - V8#6, 12/74; V9#1, 1/75 - V10#3, 1977
(V1-V8: 52 pgs.; V9 on: 68 pgs.)
Eerie Publications

V1#10(#1)-Intro. Morris the Caretaker of Weird (ends V2#10); Burgos-a 3.60 9.00 18.00
11,12 2.00 5.00 10.00
V2#1-4(10/67), V3#1(1/68), V2#6(4/68)-V2#7,9,10(12/68), V3#1(2/69)-V3#4 2.00 5.00 10.00
V2#8-r/Ditko's 1st story/Fantastic Fears #5 2.40 6.00 12.00
5(12/69)-Rulah reprint; "Rulah" changed to "Pulah;" LSD story reprinted in Horror Tales V4#4, Tales From the Tomb V2#4, & Terror Tales V7#3 2.00 5.00 10.00
V4#1-6('70), V5#1-6('71), V6#1-7('72), V7#1-7('73), V8#1-6('74), V9#1-4 (1/75-'76)(no V9#1), V10#1-3('77) 2.00 5.00 10.00

WEIRD, THE (DC)(Value: cover or less)

WEIRD ADVENTURES
May-June, 1951 - No. 3, Sept-Oct, 1951
P. L. Publishing Co. (Canada)

1-"The She-Wolf Killer" by Matt Baker, 6 pgs. 19.00 58.00 135.00
2-Bondage/hypodermic panel 14.00 43.00 100.00
3-Male bondage/torture-c; severed head story 13.00 40.00 90.00

WEIRD ADVENTURES
No. 10, July-Aug, 1951
Ziff-Davis Publishing Co.

10-Painted-c 16.00 48.00 110.00

WEIRD CHILLS
July, 1954 - No. 3, Nov, 1954
Key Publications

1-Wolverton-r/Weird Mysteries No. 4; blood transfusion-c by Baily 30.00 90.00 210.00
2-Extremely violent injury to eye-c by Baily 29.00 85.00 200.00
3-Bondage E.C. swipe-c by Baily 16.00 48.00 110.00

WEIRD COMICS
April, 1940 - No. 20, Jan, 1942
Fox Features Syndicate

1-The Birdman, Thor, God of Thunder (ends #5), The Sorceress of Zoom, Blast Bennett, Typhon, Voodoo Man, & Dr. Mortal begin; Lou Fine bondage-c 167.00 500.00 1000.00
2-Lou Fine-c 79.00 238.00 475.00
3,4: 3-Simon-c. 4-Torture-c 54.00 162.00 325.00
5-Intro. Dart & sidekick Ace (ends #20); bondage/hypo-c 58.00 175.00 350.00
6,7-Dynamite Thor app. in each 54.00 162.00 325.00
8-Dynamo, the Eagle (1st app.) & sidekick Buddy & Marga, the Panther Woman begin 54.00 162.00 325.00
9,10: 10-Navy Jones app. 46.00 138.00 275.00
11-20: 16-Flag-c. 17-Origin The Black Rider. 20-Origin The Rapier; Swoop Curtis app; Churchill & Hitler-c 37.00 110.00 225.00

WEIRD FANTASY (Formerly A Moon, A Girl, Romance; becomes Weird Science-Fantasy #23 on)
No. 13, May-June, 1950 - No. 22, Nov-Dec, 1953
E. C. Comics

13(#1) (1950) 100.00 300.00 700.00
14-Necronomicon story; atomic explosion-c 55.00 165.00 385.00
15,16: 16-Used in **SOTI**, pg. 144 46.00 140.00 325.00
17 (1951) 39.00 118.00 275.00
6-10 29.00 86.00 200.00
11-13 (1952): 12-E.C. artists cameo. 13-Anti-Wertham "Cosmic Correspondence" 22.00 65.00 150.00
14-Frazetta/Williamson(1st team-up at E.C.)/Krenkel-a, 7 pgs.; Orlando draws

E.C. staff; "Cosmic Ray Bomb Explosion" by Feldstein stars Gaines & Feldstein 36.00 107.00 250.00
15-Williamson/Evans-a(3), 4,3,&7 pgs. 24.00 71.00 165.00
16-19-Williamson/Krenkel-a in all. 18-Williamson/Feldstein-c 22.00 65.00 150.00
20-Frazetta/Williamson-a, 7 pgs. 24.00 71.00 165.00
21-Frazetta/Williamson-c & Williamson/Krenkel-a 36.00 107.00 250.00
22-Bradbury adaptation 16.00 48.00 110.00

NOTE: ***Ray Bradbury*** *adaptations-13, 17-20, 22.* ***Crandall*** *a-22.* ***Elder*** *a-17.* ***Feldstein*** *a-13(#1)-8; c-13(#1)-18 (#18 w/****Williamson****), 20.* ***Harrison/Wood*** *a-13.* ***Kamen*** *a-13(#1)-16, 18-22.* ***Krigstein*** *a-22.* ***Kurtzman*** *a-13(#1)-17(#5), 6.* ***Orlando*** *a-9-22 (2 stories in #16); c-19, 22.* ***Severin/Elder*** *a-18-21.* ***Wood*** *a-13(#1)-14, 17(2 stories ea. in #10-13). Canadian reprints exist; see Table of Contents.*

WEIRD FANTASY
Oct, 1992 - Present ($1.50, color)
Russ Cochran

1,2-r/Weird Fantasy #13,14(#1,2); Feldstein-c .30 .75 1.50

WEIRD HORRORS (Nightmare #10 on)
June, 1952 - No. 9, Oct, 1953
St. John Publishing Co.

1-Tuska-a 19.00 57.00 130.00
2,3: 3-Hashish story 10.00 30.00 65.00
4,5 10.00 30.00 60.00
6-Ekgren-c; atomic bomb story 17.00 52.00 120.00
7-Ekgren-c; Kubert, Cameron-a 19.00 57.00 130.00
8,9-Kubert-c/a 13.00 40.00 90.00

NOTE: ***Cameron*** *a-7, 9.* ***Finesque*** *a-1-5.* ***Forgione*** *a-6.* ***Morisi*** *a-3. Bondage c-8.*

WEIRD MYSTERIES
Oct, 1952 - No. 12, Sept, 1954
Gillmore Publications

1-Partial Wolverton-c swiped from splash page "Flight to the Future" in Weird Tales of the Future #2; "Eternity" has an Ingels swipe 29.00 85.00 200.00
2-"Robot Woman" by Wolverton; Bernard Baily-c-reprinted in Mister Mystery #18; acid in face panel 48.00 145.00 335.00
3,6: Both have decapitation-c 19.00 58.00 135.00
4-"The Man Who Never Smiled" (3 pgs.) by Wolverton; B. Baily skull-c 39.00 120.00 275.00
5-Wolverton story "Swamp Monster," 6 pgs. 39.00 120.00 275.00
7-Used in **SOTI**, illo-"Indeed" & illo-"Sex and blood" 32.00 95.00 225.00
8-Wolverton-c panel reprint/#5; used in a 1954 Readers Digest anti-comics article by T. E. Murphy entitled "For the Kiddies to Read" 19.00 58.00 135.00
9-Excessive violence, gore & torture 18.00 54.00 125.00
10-Silhouetted nudity panel 16.00 48.00 110.00
11,12 13.00 40.00 90.00

NOTE: ***Baily*** *c-2-12.*

WEIRD MYSTERIES (Magazine)
Mar-Apr, 1959 (68 pages) (35 cents) (B&W)
Pastime Publications

1-Torres-a; E. C. swipe from Tales From the Crypt #46 by Tuska "The Ragman" 4.70 14.00 28.00

WEIRD MYSTERY TALES (See DC 100 Page Super Spectacular)

WEIRD MYSTERY TALES (See Cancelled Comic Cavalcade)
Jul-Aug, 1972 - No. 24, Nov, 1975
National Periodical Publications

1-Kirby-a; Wrightson splash pg. .60 1.50 3.00
2-24: 21-Wrightson-c .30 .75 1.50

NOTE: ***Alcala*** *a-5, 10, 13, 14.* ***Aparo*** *c-4.* ***Bolle*** *a-8.* ***Howard*** *a-4.* ***Kaluta*** *a-24; c-1.* ***G. Kane*** *a-10.* ***Kirby*** *a-1, 2p, 3p.* ***Nino*** *a-5, 6, 9, 13, 16, 21.* ***Redondo*** *a-9.* ***Starlin*** *a-3?, 4.* ***Wood*** *a-23.*

WEIRD ROMANCE (Eclipse)(Value: cover or less)

WEIRD SCIENCE (Formerly Saddle Romances) (Becomes Weird Science-Fantasy #23 on)
No. 12, May-June, 1950 - No. 22, Nov-Dec, 1953
E. C. Comics

12(#1) (1950) 105.00 310.00 725.00
13 59.00 175.00 410.00
14,15 (1950) 52.00 154.00 360.00
5-10: 5-Atomic explosion-c 33.00 100.00 230.00
11-14 (1952): 12-"Dream of Doom" star Gaines & E.C. artists 22.00 65.00 150.00
15-18-Williamson/Krenkel-a in each; 15-Williamson-a. 17-Used in **POP**, pgs. 81,82. 18-Bill Gaines doll app. in story 24.00 73.00 170.00
19,20-Williamson/Frazetta-a, 7 pgs each. 19-Used in **SOTI**, illo-"A young girl on her wedding night stabs her sleeping husband to death with a hatpin..." 33.00 100.00 230.00
21-Williamson/Frazetta-a, 6 pgs.; Wood draws E.C. staff; Gaines & Feldstein app. in story 33.00 100.00 230.00
22-Williamson/Frazetta/Krenkel/Krigstein-a, 8 pgs.; Wood draws himself in his story (last pg. & panel) 33.00 100.00 230.00

NOTE: ***Elder*** *a-14, 19.* ***Evans*** *a-22.* ***Feldstein*** *a-12(#1)-8; c-12(#1)-8, 11.* ***Ingels*** *a-15.* ***Kamen*** *a-12(#1)-13, 15-18, 20, 21.* ***Kurtzman*** *a-12(#1)-7.* ***Orlando*** *a-10-22.* ***Wood*** *a-12(#1), 13(#2), 5-22 (#9, 10, 12, 13 all have 2* ***Wood*** *stories); c-9, 10, 12-22. Canadian reprints exist; see Table of Contents.*

WEIRD SCIENCE
Sept, 1990 - No. 4, Mar, 1991 ($1.95, color, 68 pgs.)(#3 on: $2.00)
Gladstone Publishing

1-Wood-c(r); all reprints in each .60 1.50 3.00
2-4: 2-4-Wood-c(r) .50 1.25 2.50

WEIRD SCIENCE
Sept, 1992 - Present ($1.50, color)
Russ Cochran

1,2-r/Weird Science #12,13(#1,2); Feldstein-c .30 .75 1.50

WEIRD SCIENCE-FANTASY (Formerly Weird Science & Weird Fantasy) (Becomes Incredible Science Fiction #30)
No. 23 Mar, 1954 - No. 29, May-June, 1955 (#23,24: 15 cent-c)
E. C. Comics

23-Williamson, Wood-a; Bradbury adaptation 24.00 71.00 165.00
24-Williamson & Wood-a; Harlan Ellison's 1st professional story, 'Upheaval!,' later adapted into a short story as 'Mealtime,' and then into a TV episode of Voyage to the Bottom of the Sea as 'The Price of Doom' 24.00 71.00 165.00
25-Williamson-c; Williamson/Torres/Krenkel-a plus Wood-a; Bradbury adaptation; cover price back to 10 cents 27.00 81.00 190.00
26-Flying Saucer Report; Wood, Crandall, Orlando-a 22.00 65.00 155.00
27 24.00 71.00 165.00
28-Williamson/Krenkel/Torres-a; Wood-a 26.00 77.00 180.00
29-Frazetta-c; Williamson/Krenkel & Wood-a; last pre-code issue 45.00 135.00 315.00

NOTE: ***Crandall*** *a-26, 27, 29.* ***Evans*** *a-26.* ***Feldstein*** *c-24, 26, 28.* ***Kamen*** *a-27, 28.* ***Krigstein*** *a-23-25.* ***Orlando*** *a-in all.* ***Wood*** *a-in all; c-23, 27. The cover to #29 was originally intended for Famous Funnies #217, but was rejected.*

WEIRD SCIENCE-FANTASY
Nov, 1992 - Present ($1.50, color)
Russ Cochran

1,2-r/Weird Science-Fantasy #23,24 .30 .75 1.50

WEIRD SCIENCE-FANTASY ANNUAL
1952, 1953 (Sold thru the E. C. office & on the stands in some major cities) (25 cents, 132 pgs.)
E. C. Comics

1952-Feldstein-c 129.00 385.00 900.00
1953 79.00 235.00 550.00

NOTE: *The 1952 annual contains books cover-dated in 1951 & 1952, and the 1953 annual from 1952 & 1953. Contents of each annual may vary in same year.*

Weird Mysteries #11, © Gillmore Publ.

Weird Science #13 (#2), © WMG

Weird Science-Fantasy Annual (1952), © WMG

Weird Tales of the Future #2, © S.P.M. Publ.

GHOSTLY TALES OF SPINE-CHILLING HORROR
WEIRD
TERROR

Weird Terror #3, © Comic Media

Weird Worlds #10, © DC

WEIRD SUSPENSE
Feb, 1975 - No. 3, July, 1975
Atlas/Seaboard Publ.

	GD25	FN65	NM94
1-3: 1-Tarantula begins. 3-Buckler-c		.50	1.00

WEIRD SUSPENSE STORIES (Canadian reprint of Crime SuspenStories #1-3; see Table of Contents)

WEIRD TALES ILLUSTRATED
1992 - No. 2, 1992 ($2.95, color, high quality paper)
Millennium Publications

	GD25	FN65	NM94
1,2-Bolton painted-c. 1-Adapts E.A. Poe & Harlan Ellison stories. 2-E.A. Poe & H.P. Lovecraft adaptations	.60	1.50	3.00
1-($4.95, 52 pgs.)-Deluxe edition w/Tim Vigil-a not in regular #1; stiff-c; Bolton painted-c	1.00	2.50	5.00

WEIRD TALES OF THE FUTURE
March, 1952 - No. 8, July, 1953
S.P.M. Publ. No. 1-4/Aragon Publ. No. 5-8

	GD25	FN65	NM94
1-Andru-a(2); Wolverton partial-c	36.00	107.00	250.00
2,3-Wolverton-c/a(3) each. 2-"Jumpin Jupiter" satire by Wolverton begins, ends #5	61.00	182.00	425.00
4-"Jumpin Jupiter" satire by Wolverton; partial Wolverton-c	34.00	100.00	235.00
5-Wolverton-c/a(2)	61.00	182.00	425.00
6-Bernard Baily-c	20.00	60.00	140.00
7-"The Mind Movers" from the art to Wolverton's "Brain Bats of Venus" from Mr. Mystery #7 which was cut apart, pasted up, partially redrawn, and rewritten by Harry Kantor, the editor; Bernard Baily-c	32.00	95.00	225.00
8-Reprints Weird Mysteries #1(10/52) minus cover; gory cover showing heart ripped out by B. Baily	20.00	60.00	140.00

WEIRD TALES OF THE MACABRE (Magazine)
Jan, 1975 - No. 2, Mar, 1975 (B&W) (75 cents)
Atlas/Seaboard Publ.

	GD25	FN65	NM94
1-Jeff Jones painted-c	.40	1.00	2.00
2-Boris Vallejo painted-c, Severin-a	.30	.80	1.60

WEIRD TERROR (Also see Horrific)
Sept, 1952 - No. 13, Sept, 1954
Allen Hardy Associates (Comic Media)

	GD25	FN65	NM94
1-"Portrait of Death," adapted from Lovecraft's "Pickman's Model;" lingerie panels, Hitler story	19.00	57.00	130.00
2-Text on Marquis DeSade, Torture, Demonology, & St. Elmo's Fire	11.50	34.00	80.00
3-Extreme violence, whipping, torture; article on sin eating, dowsing	11.00	32.00	75.00
4-Dismemberment, decapitation, article on human flesh for sale, Devil, whipping	13.50	41.00	95.00
5-Article on body snatching, mutilation; cannibalism story	11.00	32.00	75.00
6-Dismemberment, decapitation, man hit by lightning	13.50	41.00	95.00
7,9,10	10.00	30.00	65.00
8-Decapitation story; Ambrose Bierce adapt.	12.00	36.00	85.00
11-End of the world story with atomic blast panels; Tothish-a by Bill Discount	12.00	36.00	85.00
12-Discount-a	9.15	27.50	55.00
13-Severed head panels	10.00	30.00	65.00

NOTE: *Don Heck c/a-most issues. Landau a-6. Morisi a-2-5, 7, 9, 12. Palais a-1, 5, 6, 8(2), 10, 12. Powell a-10. Ravielli a-11, 20.*

WEIRD THRILLERS
Sept-Oct, 1951 - No. 5, Oct-Nov, 1952 (#2-4: painted-c)
Ziff-Davis Publ. Co. (Approved Comics)

	GD25	FN65	NM94
1-Rondo Hatton photo-c	25.00	75.00	175.00
2-Toth, Anderson, Colan-a	19.00	57.00	130.00
3-Two Powell, Tuska-a; classic-c	17.00	52.00	120.00
4-Kubert, Tuska-a	16.00	48.00	110.00
5-Powell-a	14.00	43.00	100.00

NOTE: *M. Anderson a-2, 3. Roussos a-4. #2, 3 reprinted in Nightmare #10 & 13; #4, 5 r-/in Amazing Ghost Stories #16 & #15.*

WEIRD WAR TALES (DC)(Value: cover or less)

WEIRD WESTERN TALES (Formerly All-Star Western)
No. 12, June-July, 1972 - No. 70, Aug, 1980 (No. 12: 52 pgs.)
National Periodical Publications/DC Comics

	GD25	FN65	NM94
12-Bat Lash, Pow Wow Smith reprints; El Diablo by Neal Adams/Wrightson	1.20	3.00	6.00
13,15-Neal Adams-a. 15-N. Adams-c	1.20	3.00	6.00
14,29: 14-Toth-a. 29-Origin Jonah Hex	.60	1.50	3.00
16-28,30-70: 39-Origin/1st app. Scalphunter	.30	.75	1.50

NOTE: *Evans inks-39-48; c-39i, 40, 47. G. Kane a-15. Kubert c-12, 33. Starlin c-44, 45. Wildey a-26. 48 & 49 are 44 pages.*

WEIRD WONDER TALES
Dec, 1973 - No. 22, May, 1977
Marvel Comics Group

	GD25	FN65	NM94
1-Wolverton-r/Mystic #6 (Eye of Doom)	.40	1.00	2.00
2-22: 16-18-Venus-r by Everett/Venus #19,18 & 17. 19-22-Dr. Druid (Droom)-r	.30	.75	1.50

NOTE: *All 1950s & early 1960s reprints. Check r-1. Colan r-17. Ditko r-4, 5, 10-13, 19-21. Drucker r-12, 20. Everett r-3(Spellbound #16), 6(Astonishing #10), 9(Adv. Into Mystery #5). Kirby r-6, 11, 13, 16-22; c-17, 19, 20. Krigstein r-19. Kubert r-22. Maneely r-8. Mooney r-7p. Powell r-3, 7. Torres r-7. Wildey r-2, 7.*

WEIRD WORLDS (See Adventures Into...)

WEIRD WORLDS (Magazine)
V1#10(12/70), V2#1(2/71) - No. 4, Aug, 1971 (52 pgs.)
Eerie Publications

	GD25	FN65	NM94
V1#10	2.00	5.00	10.00
V2#1-4	1.60	4.00	8.00

WEIRD WORLDS
Aug-Sept, 1972 - No. 9, Jan-Feb, 1974; No. 10, Oct-Nov, 1974
National Periodical Publications

	GD25	FN65	NM94
1-Edgar Rice Burrough's John Carter Warlord of Mars & David Innes begin (1st DC app.); Kubert-c	.60	1.50	3.00
2-7: 7-Last John Carter	.30	.75	1.50
8-10: 8-Iron Wolf begins by Chaykin (1st app.)		.50	1.00

NOTE: *Neal Adams a-2i, 3i. John Carter by Andersonin #1-3. Chaykin c-7, 8. Kaluta a-4; c-4-6, 10. Orlando a-4i; c-2, 3. Wrightson a-2i.*

WELCOME BACK, KOTTER (TV) (See Limited Collectors' Edition #57)
Nov, 1976 - No. 10, Mar-Apr, 1978
National Periodical Publications/DC Comics

	GD25	FN65	NM94
1-Sparling-a(p)	.40	1.00	2.00
2-10: 3-Estrada-a		.50	1.00

WELCOME SANTA (See March of Comics #63,183)

WELLS FARGO (See Tales of...)

WENDY AND THE NEW KIDS ON THE BLOCK (Harvey)(Value: cover or less)

WENDY DIGEST (Harvey)(Value: cover or less)

WENDY PARKER COMICS
July, 1953 - No. 8, July, 1954
Atlas Comics (OMC)

	GD25	FN65	NM94
1	6.70	20.00	40.00
2	4.00	11.00	22.00
3-8	3.60	9.00	18.00

WENDY, THE GOOD LITTLE WITCH (TV)
8/60 - #82, 11/73; #83, 8/74 - #93, 4/76; #94, 9/90 - #97, 12/90
Harvey Publications

	GD25	FN65	NM94
1-Casper the Friendly Ghost begins	11.00	32.00	75.00
2	5.85	17.50	35.00
3-5	4.20	12.50	25.00
6-10	3.60	9.00	18.00
11-20	2.00	5.00	10.00
21-30	1.20	3.00	6.00
31-50	.80	2.00	4.00
51-69	.70	1.75	3.50
70-74: All 52 pg. Giants	.80	2.00	4.00
75-93	.40	1.00	2.00
94-97 (1990, $1.00-c)		.50	1.00

(See Casper the Friendly Ghost #20 & Harvey Hits #7, 16, 21, 23, 27, 30, 33)

WENDY THE GOOD LITTLE WITCH (2nd series)
Apr, 1991 - Present ($1.00/$1.25, color)
Harvey Comics

	GD25	FN65	NM94
1-10-Reprints Wendy & Casper stories. 6-Last $1.00-c		.50	1.00

WENDY WITCH WORLD
10/61; No. 2, 9/62 - No. 52, 12/73; No. 53, 9/74
Harvey Publications

	GD25	FN65	NM94
1: 68 pg. Giants begin	7.50	22.50	45.00
2-5	4.00	11.00	22.00
6-10	2.40	6.00	12.00
11-20	1.40	3.50	7.00
21-30	.80	2.00	4.00
31-39: Last 68 pg. issue	.60	1.50	3.00
40-45: 52 pg. issues	.50	1.25	2.50
46-53	.40	1.00	2.00

WEREWOLF (Super Hero)
Dec, 1966 - No. 3, April, 1967
Dell Publishing Co.

	GD25	FN65	NM94
1	1.00	2.50	5.00
2,3	.60	1.50	3.00

WEREWOLF BY NIGHT (See Giant-Size..., Marvel Spotlight #2-4 & Power Record Comics)
Sept, 1972 - No. 43, Mar, 1977
Marvel Comics Group

	GD25	FN65	NM94
1-Ploog-a-cont'd. from Marvel Spotlight #4	5.00	15.00	30.00
2	3.00	7.50	15.00
3-5	2.00	5.00	10.00
6-10	1.60	4.00	8.00
11-20: 15-New origin Werewolf; Dracula app.	1.40	3.50	7.00
21-31	1.00	2.50	5.00
32-Origin & 1st app. Moon Knight (4/75?)	7.50	22.50	45.00
33-2nd app. Moon Knight	4.20	12.50	25.00
34-36,38-43: 35-Starlin/Wrightson-c	.60	1.50	3.00
37-Moon Knight app; part Wrightson-c	1.40	3.50	7.00

NOTE: *Bolle a-6i. G. Kane a-11p, 12p; c-21, 22, 24-30, 34p. Mooney a-7i. Ploog 1-4p, 5, 6p, 7p, 13-16p; c-5-8, 13-16. Reinman a-8i. Sutton a(i)-9, 11, 16, 35.*

WEREWOLVES & VAMPIRES (Magazine)
1962 (One Shot)
Charlton Comics

	GD25	FN65	NM94
1	5.00	15.00	30.00

WEST COAST AVENGERS
Sept, 1984 - No. 4, Dec, 1984 (Mini-series; Mando paper)
Marvel Comics Group

	GD25	FN65	NM94
1-Origin & 1st app. W.C. Avengers; Hawkeye, Iron Man, Mockingbird & Tigra	.60	1.50	3.00
2-4	.30	.75	1.50

WEST COAST AVENGERS (Becomes Avengers West Coast #48 on)
Oct, 1985 - No. 47, Aug, 1989 (On-going series)
Marvel Comics Group

	GD25	FN65	NM94
V2#1	.60	1.50	3.00
2-10	.40	1.00	2.00
11-20	.30	.75	1.50
21-41		.50	1.00
42-Byrne-a(p)/scripts begin	.45	1.10	2.20
43-47: 46,46-Byrne-c. 46-1st app. Great Lakes Avengers		.55	1.10
Annual 1 (1986)	.45	1.10	2.20
Annual 2 (1987)	.40	1.00	2.00
Annual 3 (1988, $1.75)-Evolutionary War app.	.55	1.40	2.75
Annual V2#4 (1989, $2.00, 68 pgs.)-Atlantis Attacks; Byrne/Austin-a	.45	1.10	2.20
Annual V2#5 (1990, $2.00, 68 pgs.)	.40	1.00	2.00
Annual V2#6 (1991, $2.00, 68 pgs.)	.40	1.00	2.00
Annual V2#7 (1992, $2.25, 68 pgs.)-Darkhawk app.	.45	1.15	2.25

WESTERN ACTION
No. 7, 1964
I. W. Enterprises

	GD25	FN65	NM94
7-Reprints Cow Puncher #? by Avon	.40	1.00	2.00

WESTERN ACTION
February, 1975
Atlas/Seaboard Publ.

	GD25	FN65	NM94
1-Kid Cody by Wildey & The Comanche Kid stories; intro. The Renegade		.50	1.00

WESTERN ACTION THRILLERS
April, 1937 (100 pages)(Square binding)
Dell Publishers

	GD25	FN65	NM94
1-Buffalo Bill, The Texas Kid, Laramie Joe, Two-Gun Thompson, & Wild West Bill app.	58.00	175.00	350.00

WESTERN ADVENTURES COMICS (Western Love Trails #7 on)
Oct, 1948 - No. 6, Aug, 1949
Ace Magazines

	GD25	FN65	NM94
nn(#1)-Sheriff Sal, The Cross-Draw Kid, Sam Bass begin	12.00	36.00	85.00
nn(#2)(12/48)	7.50	22.50	45.00
nn(#3)(2/49)-Used in **SOTI**, pgs. 30,31	8.35	25.00	50.00
4-6	5.85	17.50	35.00

WESTERN BANDITS
1952 (Painted-c)
Avon Periodicals

	GD25	FN65	NM94
1-Butch Cassidy, The Daltons by Larsen; Kinstler-a; c-part-r/paperback Avon Western Novel #1	10.00	30.00	65.00

WESTERN BANDIT TRAILS (See Approved Comics)
Jan, 1949 - No. 3, July, 1949
St. John Publishing Co.

	GD25	FN65	NM94
1-Tuska-a; Baker-c; Blue Monk, Ventrilo app.	12.00	36.00	85.00
2-Baker-c	10.00	30.00	60.00
3-Baker-c/a; Tuska-a	10.00	30.00	70.00

WESTERN COMICS (See Super DC Giant #15)
Jan-Feb, 1948 - No. 85, Jan-Feb, 1961 (1-27: 52pgs.)
National Periodical Publications

	GD25	FN65	NM94
1-The Wyoming Kid & his horse Racer, The Vigilante (Meskin-a), The Cowboy Marshal, Rodeo Rick begin	54.00	160.00	375.00
2	26.00	77.00	180.00
3,4-Last Vigilante	22.00	65.00	150.00
5-Nighthawk & his horse Nightwind begin (not in #6); Captain Tootsie by Beck	19.00	57.00	130.00
6,7,9,10	14.00	43.00	100.00
8-Origin Wyoming Kid; 2 pg. pin-ups of rodeo queens	20.00	60.00	140.00
11-20	12.00	36.00	85.00
21-40: 24-Starr-a. 27-Last 52 pgs.	10.00	30.00	60.00
41-49: Last precode (2/55). 43-Pow Wow Smith begins, ends #85			

Werewolf By Night #3, © MEG

Western Action Thrillers #1, © DELL

Western Comics #1, © DC

Western Crime Busters #7, © TM

Western Fighters 3-D #1, © HILL

Western Hero #76, © FAW

GD25 FN65 NM94

9.15 27.50 55.00
50-60 8.35 25.00 50.00
61-85-Last Wyoming Kid. 77-Origin Matt Savage Trail Boss. 82-1st app. Fleetfoot, Pow Wow's girlfriend 5.85 17.50 35.00
NOTE: ***G. Kane, Infantino** art in most. **Meskin** a-1-4. **Moreira** a-28-39. **Post** a-3-5.*

WESTERN CRIME BUSTERS
Sept, 1950 - No. 10, Mar-Apr, 1952
Trojan Magazines

1-Six-Gun Smith, Wilma West, K-Bar-Kate, & Fighting Bob Dale begin; headlight-a 18.00 54.00 125.00
2 10.00 30.00 70.00
3-5: 3-Myron Fass-c 10.00 30.00 60.00
6-Wood-a 22.00 65.00 150.00
7-Six-Gun Smith by Wood 22.00 65.00 150.00
8 10.00 30.00 60.00
9-Tex Gordon & Wilma West by Wood; Lariat Lucy app. 22.00 65.00 150.00
10-Wood-a 20.00 60.00 140.00

WESTERN CRIME CASES (Formerly Indian Warriors #7,8; becomes The Outlaws #10 on)
No. 9, Dec, 1951
Star Publications

9-White Rider & Super Horse; L. B. Cole-c 5.85 17.50 35.00

WESTERN DESPERADO COMICS (Formerly Slam Bang Comics)
No. 8, 1940 (Oct.?)
Fawcett Publications

8-(Rare) 47.00 140.00 325.00

WESTERNER, THE (Wild Bill Pecos)
No. 14, June, 1948 - No. 41, Dec, 1951 (#14-31: 52 pgs.)
"Wanted" Comic Group/Toytown/Patches

14 8.35 25.00 50.00
15-17,19-21: 19-Meskin-a 4.00 11.00 22.00
18,22-25-Krigstein-a 6.70 20.00 40.00
26(4/50)-Origin & 1st app. Calamity Kate, series ends #32; Krigstein-a 8.35 25.00 50.00
27-Krigstein-a(2) 10.00 30.00 60.00
28-41: 33-Quest app. 37-Lobo, the Wolf Boy begins 3.20 8.00 16.00
NOTE: ***Mort Lawrence** a-20-27, 29, 37, 39; c-19, 22-24, 26, 27. **Leav** c-14, 31. **Syd Shores** a-39; c-34, 35, 37-41.*

WESTERNER, THE
1964
Super Comics

Super Reprint 15-17: 15-r/Oklahoma Kid #? 16-r/Crack Western #65; Severin, Crandall-r. 17-r/Blazing Western #2; Severin-r .40 1.00 2.00

WESTERN FIGHTERS
Apr-May, 1948 - V4#7, Mar-Apr, 1953 (#1-V3#2: 52 pgs.)
Hillman Periodicals/Star Publ.

V1#1-Simon & Kirby-c 18.00 54.00 125.00
2-Kirby-a(p)? 7.50 22.50 45.00
3-Fuje-c 5.85 17.50 35.00
4-Krigstein, Ingels, Fuje-a 7.50 22.50 45.00
5,6,8,9,12 4.70 14.00 28.00
7,10-Krigstein-a 7.50 22.50 45.00
11-Williamson/Frazetta-a 17.00 52.00 120.00
V2#1-Krigstein-a 7.50 22.50 45.00
2-12: 4-Berg-a 3.60 9.00 18.00
V3#1-11 3.20 8.00 16.00
12-Krigstein-a 6.70 20.00 40.00
V4#1,4-7 3.20 8.00 16.00
2,3-Krigstein-a 6.35 19.00 38.00

GD25 FN65 NM94

3-D 1(12/53, Star Publ.)- L. B. Cole -c 24.00 72.00 165.00
NOTE: ***Kinstlerish** a-V2#6, 8, 9, 12; V3#2, 5-7, 11, 12; V4#1(plus cover). **McWilliams** a-11. **Powell** a-V2#2. **Reinman** a-1-12, V4#3. **Rowich** c-5, 6i. **Starr** a-5.*

WESTERN FRONTIER
Apr-May, 1951 - No. 7, 1952
P. L. Publishers

1 7.50 22.50 45.00
2 4.35 13.00 26.00
3-7 3.60 9.00 18.00

WESTERN GUNFIGHTERS (1st Series) (Apache Kid #11-19)
No. 20, June, 1956 - No. 27, Aug, 1957
Atlas Comics (CPS)

20 7.50 22.50 45.00
21-Crandall-a 7.50 22.50 45.00
22-Wood & Powell-a 10.00 30.00 70.00
23,24: 23-Williamson-a. 24-Toth-a 7.50 22.50 45.00
25-27 5.00 15.00 30.00
NOTE: ***Berg** a-20. **Colan** a-20, 27. **Crandall** a-21. **Heath** a-25. **Maneely** a-24, 25; c-22, 23, 25. **Morisi** a-24. **Pakula** a-23. **Severin** c-20, 27. **Woodbridge** a-27.*

WESTERN GUNFIGHTERS (2nd Series)
Aug, 1970 - No. 33, Nov, 1975 (#1-6: 25 cents, 68 pgs.; #7: 52 pgs.)
Marvel Comics Group

1-Ghost Rider begins; Fort Rango, Renegades & Gunhawk app. 1.00 2.50 5.00
2-33: 2-Origin Nightwind (Apache Kid's horse). 7-Origin Ghost Rider retold. 10-Origin Black Rider. 12-Origin Matt Slade .60 1.50 3.00
NOTE: ***Baker** r-2, 3. **Colan** r-2. **Drucker** r-3. **Everett** a-6i. **G. Kane** c-29, 31. **Kirby** a-1p(r), 10, 11. **Kubert** r-2. **Maneely** r-2, 10. **Morrow** r-29. **Severin** c-10. **Barry Smith** a-4. **Steranko** c-14. **Sutton** a-1, 2i, 3, 4. **Torres** r-26('57). **Wildey** r-8, 9. **Williamson** r-2, 18. **Woodbridge** r-27('57). Renegades in #4, 5; Ghost Rider in #1-7.*

WESTERN HEARTS
Dec, 1949 - No. 10, Mar, 1952 (All photo-c)
Standard Comics

1-Severin-a; Whip Wilson & Reno Browne photo-c 11.00 32.00 75.00
2-Beverly Tyler & Jerome Courtland photo-c from movie "Palomino;" Williamson/Frazetta-a (2 pgs.) 13.00 40.00 90.00
3-Rex Allen photo-c 5.85 17.50 35.00
4-7,10-Severin & Elder, Al Carreno-a. 5-Ray Milland & Hedy Lamarr photo-c. 6-Fred MacMurray photo-c. 7-Jock Mahoney photo-c. 10-Bill Williams & Jane Nigh photo-c 5.85 17.50 35.00
8-Randolph Scott/Janis Carter photo-c from "Santa Fe;" Severin & Elder-a 6.70 20.00 40.00
9-Whip Wilson & Reno Browne photo-c; Severin & Elder-a 8.35 25.00 50.00

WESTERN HERO (Wow Comics #1-69; Real Western Hero #70-75)
No. 76, Mar, 1949 - No. 112, Mar, 1952
Fawcett Publications

76(#1, 52 pgs.)-Tom Mix, Hopalong Cassidy, Monte Hale, Gabby Hayes, Young Falcon (ends #78,80), & Big Bow and Little Arrow (ends #102,105) begin; painted-c begin 19.00 58.00 135.00
77 (52 pgs.) 11.50 34.00 80.00
78,80-82 (52 pgs.): 81-Capt. Tootsie by Beck 11.50 34.00 80.00
79,83 (36 pgs.): 83-Last painted-c 10.00 30.00 65.00
84-86,88-90 (52 pgs.): 84-Photo-c begin, end #112. 86-Last Hopalong Cassidy 10.00 30.00 70.00
87,91,95,99 (36 pgs.): 87-Bill Boyd begins, ends #95 10.00 30.00 60.00
92-94,96-98,101 (52 pgs.): 96-Tex Ritter begins. 101-Red Eagle app. 10.00 30.00 65.00
100 (52 pgs.) 10.00 30.00 70.00
102-111: 102-Begin 36 pg. issues 10.00 30.00 60.00

112-Last issue 10.00 30.00 65.00
NOTE: *1/2 to 1 pg. Rocky Lane (Carnation) in 80-83, 86, 88, 97.*

WESTERN KID (1st Series)
Dec, 1954 - No. 17, Aug, 1957
Atlas Comics (CPC)

1-Origin; The Western Kid (Tex Dawson), his stallion Whirlwind & dog Lightning begin 10.00 30.00 70.00
2 (2/55)-Last pre-code 5.85 17.50 35.00
3-8 5.00 15.00 30.00
9,10-Williamson-a in both, 4 pgs. each 5.85 17.50 35.00
11-17 4.00 11.00 22.00
NOTE: ***Ayers** a-6, 7. **Maneely** c-2-7, 10, 14. **Romita** a-1-17; c-1, 12. **Severin** c-17.*

WESTERN KID, THE (2nd Series)
Dec, 1971 - No. 5, Aug, 1972 (All 20 cent issues)
Marvel Comics Group

1-Reprints; Romita-c/a(3) .60 1.50 3.00
2-5: 2-Romita-a; Severin-c. 3-Williamson-r. 4-Everett-r .40 1.00 2.00

WESTERN KILLERS
nn, Aug?, 1948; No. 60, Sept, 1948 - No. 64, May, 1949; No. 6, July, 1949
Fox Features Syndicate

nn(#59?)(nd, F&J Trading Co.)-Range Busters; formerly Blue Beetle #57? 10.00 30.00 65.00
60 (#1, 9/48)-Extreme violence; lingerie panel 13.00 40.00 90.00
61-64, 6: 61-Jack Cole, Starr-a 10.00 30.00 60.00

WESTERN LIFE ROMANCES (My Friend Irma #3 on?)
Dec, 1949 - No. 2, Mar, 1950 (52 pgs.)
Marvel Comics (IPP)

1-Whip Wilson & Reno Browne photo-c 11.00 32.00 75.00
2-Audie Murphy photo-c; spanking scene 10.00 30.00 60.00

WESTERN LOVE
July-Aug, 1949 - No. 5, Mar-Apr, 1950 (All photo-c & 52 pgs.)
Prize Publications

1-S&K-a; Randolph Scott "Canadian Pacific" photo-c (see Prize Comics #76) 14.00 43.00 100.00
2,5-S&K-a: 2-Whip Wilson & Reno Browne photo-c. 5-Dale Robertson photo-c 11.50 34.00 80.00
3,4: 3-Reno Browne? photo-c 9.15 27.50 55.00
NOTE: ***Meskin & Severin/Elder** a-2-5.*

WESTERN LOVE TRAILS (Formerly Western Adventures)
No. 7, Nov, 1949 - No. 9, Mar, 1950
Ace Magazines (A. A. Wyn)

7 8.35 25.00 50.00
8,9 5.85 17.50 35.00

WESTERN MARSHAL (See Steve Donovan... & Ernest Haycox's 4-Color 534, 591, 613, 640 & [based on Haycox's "Trailtown"])

WESTERN OUTLAWS (Junior Comics #9-16; My Secret Life #22 on)
No. 17, Sept, 1948 - No. 21, May, 1949
Fox Features Syndicate

17-Kamen-a; Iger shop-a in all; 1 pg. 'Death and the Devil Pills' r-in Ghostly Weird #122 14.00 43.00 100.00
18-21 10.00 30.00 60.00

WESTERN OUTLAWS
Feb, 1954 - No. 21, Aug, 1957
Atlas Comics (ACI No. 1-14/WPI No. 15-21)

1-Heath, Powell-a; Maneely hanging-c 11.00 32.00 75.00
2 6.70 20.00 40.00
3-10: 7-Violent-a by R.Q. Sale 5.00 15.00 30.00
11,14-Williamson-a in both, 6 pgs. each 6.35 19.00 38.00
12,18,20,21: Severin covers 4.20 12.50 25.00
13-Baker-a 4.70 14.00 28.00
15-Torres-a 5.00 15.00 30.00
16-Williamson text illo 4.00 11.00 22.00
17,19-Crandall-a. 17-Williamson text illo 5.00 15.00 30.00
NOTE: ***Ayers** a-7, 10, 18, 20. **Bolle** a-21. **Colan** a-5, 10, 11, 17. **Drucker** a-11. **Everett** a-9, 10. **Heath** a-1; c-3, 4, 8, 16. **Kubert** a-9p. **Maneely** a-13, 16, 17, 19; c-5, 7, 9, 10, 12, 13. **Morisi** a-18. **Powell** a-3, 16. **Romita** a-7, 13. **Severin** a-8, 16, 19; c-17, 18, 20, 21. **Tuska** a-6, 15.*

WESTERN OUTLAWS & SHERIFFS (Formerly Best Western)
No. 60, Dec, 1949 - No. 73, June, 1952
Marvel/Atlas Comics (IPC)

60 (52 pgs.) 12.00 36.00 85.00
61-65: 61-Photo-c 10.00 30.00 70.00
66,68-72: 66-Story contains 5 hangings 7.50 22.50 45.00
67-Cannibalism story 10.00 30.00 65.00
73-Black Rider story; Everett-c 8.35 25.00 50.00
NOTE: ***Maneely** a-62, 67; c-62, 69-73. **Robinson** a-68. **Sinnott** a-70. **Tuska** a-69-71.*

WESTERN PICTURE STORIES (1st Western comic)
Feb, 1937 - No. 4, June, 1937
Comics Magazine Company

1-Will Eisner-a 117.00 350.00 700.00
2-Will Eisner-a 75.00 225.00 450.00
3,4: 3-Eisner-a 62.00 188.00 375.00

WESTERN PICTURE STORIES (See Giant Comics Edition #6, 11)

WESTERN ROMANCES (See Target...)

WESTERN ROUGH RIDERS
Nov, 1954 - No. 4, May, 1955
Gillmor Magazines No. 1,4 (Stanmor Publications)

1 5.00 15.00 30.00
2-4 3.60 9.00 18.00

WESTERN ROUNDUP (See Dell Giants & Fox Giants)

WESTERN TALES (Formerly Witches...)
No. 31, Oct, 1955 - No. 33, July-Sept, 1956
Harvey Publications

31,32-All S&K-a; Davy Crockett app. in each 10.00 30.00 60.00
33-S&K-a; Jim Bowie app. 10.00 30.00 60.00
NOTE: *#32 & 33 contain Boy's Ranch reprints. **Kirby** c-31.*

WESTERN TALES OF BLACK RIDER (Formerly Black Rider; Gunsmoke Western #32 on)
No. 28, May, 1955 - No. 31, Nov, 1955
Atlas Comics (CPS)

28 (#1): The Spider (a villain) dies 10.00 30.00 65.00
29-31 7.50 22.50 45.00
NOTE: ***Lawrence** a-30. **Maneely** c-28-30. **Severin** a-28. **Shores** c-31.*

WESTERN TEAM-UP
November, 1973 (20 cents)
Marvel Comics Group

1-Origin & 1st app. The Dakota Kid; Rawhide Kid-r; Gunsmoke Kid-r by Jack Davis .30 .75 1.50

WESTERN THRILLERS (My Past Confessions #7 on)
Aug, 1948 - No. 6, June, 1949; No. 52, 1954?
Fox Features Syndicate/M.S. Distr. No. 52

1-"Velvet Rose"-Kamenish-a; "Two-Gun Sal," "Striker Sisters" (all women outlaws issue); Brodsky-c 26.00 77.00 180.00
2 10.00 30.00 65.00
3,6 9.15 27.50 55.00
4,5-Bakerish-a; 5-Butch Cassidy app. 10.00 30.00 70.00
52-(Reprint, M.S. Dist.)-1954? No date given (becomes My Love Secret #53) 4.20 12.50 25.00

WESTERN THRILLERS (Cowboy Action #5 on)
Nov, 1954 - No. 4, Feb, 1955 (All-r/Western Outlaws & Sheriffs)
Atlas Comics (ACI)

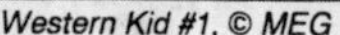
Western Kid #1, © MEG

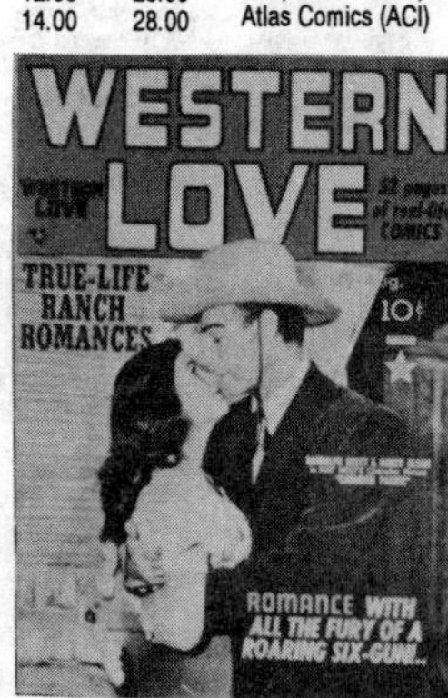

Western Love #1, © PRIZE

Western Thrillers #1, © FOX

Western Winners #5, © MEG

Whack #1, © STJ

What If...? V2#10, © MEG

GD25 FN65 NM94

1 10.00 30.00 60.00
2-4 5.35 16.00 32.00
NOTE: ***Heath** c-3. **Maneely** a-1; c-2. **Powell** a-4. **Robinson** a-4. **Romita** c-4. **Tuska** a-2.*

WESTERN TRAILS
May, 1957 - No. 2, July, 1957
Atlas Comics (SAI)

1-Ringo Kid app.; Severin-c 6.70 20.00 40.00
2-Severin-c 5.00 15.00 30.00
NOTE: ***Bolle** a-1, 2. **Maneely** a-1, 2. **Severin** c-1, 2.*

WESTERN TRUE CRIME (Becomes My Confessions)
No. 15, Aug, 1948 - No. 6, June, 1949
Fox Features Syndicate

15(#1)-Kamenish-a; formerly Zoot #14 (5/48)? 13.00 40.00 90.00
16(#2)-Kamenish-a; headlight panels, violence 10.00 30.00 65.00
3,5,6 6.70 20.00 40.00
4-Johnny Craig-a 11.50 34.00 80.00

WESTERN WINNERS (Formerly All-Western Winners; becomes Black Rider #8 on & Romance Tales #7 on?)
No. 5, June, 1949 - No. 7, Dec, 1949
Marvel Comics (CDS)

5-Two-Gun Kid, Kid Colt, Black Rider; Shores-c 19.00 58.00 135.00
6-Two-Gun Kid, Black Rider, Heath Kid Colt story; Captain Tootsie by C.C. Beck 17.00 50.00 115.00
7-Randolph Scott Photo-c w/true stories about the West 17.00 50.00 115.00

WEST OF THE PECOS (See 4-Color #222)

WESTWARD HO, THE WAGONS (See 4-Color #738)

WETWORKS (Also see WILDC.A.T.S: Covert Action Teams #3)
Oct, 1992 - No. 3, 1993 ($1.95, color, mini-series)
Image Comics

1-Whilce Portacio-c/a begins .60 1.50 3.00
2,3 .40 1.00 2.00

WHACK (Satire)
Oct, 1953 - No. 3, May, 1954
St. John Publishing Co. (Jubilee Publ.)

1-(3-D)-Kubert-a; Maurer-c 20.00 60.00 140.00
2,3-Kubert-a in each. 2-Bing Crosby on-c; Mighty Mouse & Steve Canyon parodies. 3-Maurer-c 10.00 30.00 70.00

WHACKY (See Wacky)

WHAM COMICS (See Super Spy)
Nov, 1940 - No. 2, Dec, 1940
Centaur Publications

1-The Sparkler, The Phantom Rider, Craig Carter and the Magic Ring Detector, Copper Slug, Speed Silvers by Gustavson, Speed Centaur & Jon Linton (s/f) begin 96.00 288.00 575.00
2-Origin Blue Fire & Solarman; The Buzzard app. 71.00 210.00 425.00

WHAM-O GIANT COMICS (98 cents)
April, 1967 (Newspaper size) (One Shot) (Full Color)
Wham-O Mfg. Co. (Six issue subscription was advertised)

1-Radian & Goody Bumpkin by Wood; 1 pg. Stanley-a; Fine, Tufts-a; flying saucer reports; wraparound-c 4.20 12.50 25.00

WHAT DO YOU KNOW ABOUT THIS COMICS SEAL OF APPROVAL?
nd (1955) (4pgs.; color; slick paper-c)
No publisher listed (DC Comics Giveaway)

nn-(Rare) 50.00 150.00 350.00

WHAT IF? (What If? Featuring... #13 & #?-33)(1st series)
Feb, 1977 - No. 47, Oct, 1984; June, 1988 (All 52 pgs.)
Marvel Comics Group

1-Brief origin Spider-Man, Fantastic Four 3.00 7.50 15.00
2-Origin The Hulk retold 1.80 4.50 9.00
3-5: 3-Avengers. 4-Invaders. 5-Capt. America 1.20 3.00 6.00
6-10: 8-Daredevil. 9-Origins Venus, Marvel Boy, Human Robot, 3-D Man. 11-Marvel Bullpen as Fantastic Four 1.00 2.50 5.00
11,12 .80 2.00 4.00
13-Conan app.; John Buscema-c/a(p) 1.20 3.00 6.00
14-16,18-26,29,30: 18-Dr. Strange. 19,30-Spider-Man. 22-Origin Dr. Doom retold .80 2.00 4.00
17-Ghost Rider & Son of Satan app. 1.40 3.50 7.00
27-X-Men app.; Miller-c 2.00 5.00 10.00
28-Daredevil by Miller; Ghost Rider app. 2.00 5.00 10.00
31-Featuring Wolverine & the Hulk; X-Men app.; death of Hulk, Wolverine & Magneto 2.80 7.00 14.00
32-47: 32,36-Byrne-a. 34-Marvel crew each draw themselves. 35-What if Elektra had lived?; Miller/Austin-a. 37-Old X-Men & Silver Surfer app. 39-Thor battles Conan .40 1.00 2.00
Special 1 ($1.50, 6088)-Iron Man, F.F., Thor app. .40 1.00 2.00
NOTE: ***Austin** a-27p, 32i, 34, 35i; c-35i, 36i. **J. Buscema** a-13p, 15p; c-10, 13p, 23p. **Byrne** a-32i, 36; c-36p. **Colan** a-21p; c-17p, 18p, 21p. **Ditko** a-35, Special 1. **Golden** c-29, 40-42. **Guice** a-40p. **Gil Kane** a-3p, 24p; c(p)-2-4, 7, 8. **Kirby** a-11p; c-9p, 11p. **Layton** a-32i, 33i; c-30, 32p, 33i, 34. **Miller** a-28p, 32i, 35p; c-27, 28p. **Mooney** a-8i, 30i. **Perez** a-15p. **Robbins** a-4p. **Simonson** a-15p, 32i. **Starlin** a-32i. **Stevens** a-16i(part). **Sutton** a-2i, 18p, 28. **Tuska** a-5p. **Weiss** a-37p.*

WHAT IF...? (2nd series)
V2#1, July, 1989 - Present ($1.25 color)
Marvel Comics

V2#1-...The Avengers Had Lost the Evol. War 1.00 2.50 5.00
2-5: 2-Daredevil, Punisher app. .60 1.50 3.00
6-X-Men app. .80 2.00 4.00
7-Wolverine app.; Liefeld-c/a(1st on Wolvie?) 1.20 3.00 6.00
8,11: 11-Fantastic Four app.; McFarlane-c(i) .40 1.00 2.00
9,12-X-Men .60 1.50 3.00
10-Punisher .70 1.75 3.50
13-15,17-21,23,27-29: 13-Prof. X; Jim Lee-c. 14-Capt. Marvel; Austin-c. 15-F.F. 17-Spider-Man/Kraven. 18-F.F. 19-Vision. 20,21-Spider-Man. 23-X-Men. 27-Namor/F.F. 28,29-Capt. America. 31-Cosmic Spider-Man & Venom app.; Hobgoblin cameo .30 .75 1.50
16-Conan battles Wolverine; Red Sonja app.; X-Men cameo .90 2.25 4.50
22-Silver Surfer by Lim/Austin-c/a .60 1.50 3.00
24-Wolverine; Punisher app. .60 1.50 3.00
25-($1.50, 52 pgs.)-Wolverine app. .60 1.50 3.00
26-Punisher app. .40 1.00 2.00
30-($1.75, 52 pgs.)-Sue Richards/F.F. .35 .90 1.75
31-40: 31-Cosmic Spider-Man & Venom app.; Hobgoblin cameo. 32,33-Phoenix; X-Men app. 35-Fantastic Five (w/Spidey). 36-Avengers vs. Guardians of the Galaxy. 37-Wolverine. 38-Thor; Rogers-p(part). 40-Storm; X-Men app. .30 .75 1.50
41-($1.75, 52 pgs.)-Avengers vs. Galactus .35 .90 1.75
42-48: 42-Spider-Man. 43-Wolverine. 44-Venom/Punisher. 45-Ghost Rider. 46,47-Cable 2 part story .60 1.25

WHAT'S BEHIND THESE HEADLINES
1948 (16 pgs.)
William C. Popper Co.

nn-Comic insert-"The Plot to Steal the World" 3.00 7.50 15.00

'WHAT'S NEW? - THE COLLECTED ADVENTURES OF PHIL & DIXIE'
Oct, 1991 - No. 2, 1991? ($5.95, mostly color, squarebound, 52 pgs.)
Palliard Press

1,2-By Phil Foglio 1.00 3.00 6.00

WHAT THE- -?!
Aug, 1988 - Present ($1.25-$1.50, semi-annually #5 on)

Marvel Comics

1-All contain parodies .50 1.25 2.50
2,4,5: 5-Punisher/Wolverine parody; Jim Lee-a .30 .75 1.50
3-X-Men parody; Todd McFarlane-a .60 1.50 3.00
6-24: 6-($1.00)-Acts of Vengeance (Punisher, Wolverine, Alpha Flight)-Byrne/Austin-a. 7-($1.25)-Avengers vs. Justice League parody; Patsy Walker story. 9-Wolverine. 10-Byrne-c/a. 11,13-Byrne-c. 13-Silver Surfer, Batman 2 movie parody. 16-Flip comic w/EC back-c parody. 17-Wolverine/Punisher parody. 18-Star Trek parody w/Wolverine, Thanos. 19-Flip comic w/Punisher, Wolverine, Ghost Rider. 20-Infinity War parody. 21-Weapon X parody. 22-Punisher/Wolverine parody. 23-New Warriors parody. 24-Infinity Guantlet parody w/Thanos .60 1.25

NOTE: *Austin a-6i. **Byrne** a-2, 6, 10; c-2, 6-8, 10, 12, 13. **Golden** a-22. **Dale Keown** a-8p(8 pgs.). **McFarlane** a-3. **Rogers** c-15i, 16p. **Severin** a-2. **Staton** a-21p. **Williamson** a-2i.*

WHEATIES (Premiums) (32 titles)
1950 & 1951 (32 pages) (pocket size)
Walt Disney Productions

(Set A-1 to A-8, 1950)
A-1-Mickey Mouse & the Disappearing Island, A-2-Grandma Duck, Homespun Detective, A-3-Donald Duck & the Haunted Jewels, A-4-Donald Duck & the Giant Ape, A-5-Mickey Mouse, Roving Reporter, A-6-Li'l Bad Wolf, Forest Ranger, A-7-Goofy, Tightrope Acrobat, A-8-Pluto & the Bogus Money each.... 4.00 10.00 20.00

(Set B-1 to B-8, 1950)
B-1-Mickey Mouse & the Pharoah's Curse, B-2-Pluto, Canine Cowpoke, B-3-Donald Duck & the Buccaneers, B-4-Mickey Mouse & the Mystery Sea Monster, B-5-Li'l Bad Wolf in the Hollow Tree Hideout, B-6-Donald Duck, Trail Blazer, B-7-Goofy & the Gangsters, B-8 Donald Duck, Klondike Kid each.... 3.60 9.00 18.00

(Set C-1 to C-8, 1951)
C-1-Donald Duck & the Inca Idol, C-2-Mickey Mouse & the Magic Mountain, C-3-Li'l Bad Wolf, Fire Fighter, C-4-Gus & Jaq Save the Ship, C-5-Donald Duck in the Lost Lakes, C-6-Mickey Mouse & the Stagecoach Bandits, C-7-Goofy, Big Game Hunter, C-8-Donald Duck Deep-Sea Diver each.... 3.60 9.00 18.00

(Set D-1 to D-8, 1951)
D-1-Donald Duck in Indian Country, D-2-Mickey Mouse and the Abandoned Mine, D-3-Pluto & the Mysterious Package, D-4-Bre'r Rabbit's Sunken Treasure, D-5-Donald Duck, Mighty Mystic, D-6-Mickey Mouse & the Medicine Man, D-7-Li'l Bad Wolf and the Secret of the Woods, D-8-Minnie Mouse, Girl Explorer each.... 3.60 9.00 18.00

NOTE: *Some copies lack the Wheaties ad.*

WHEE COMICS (Also see Gay, Smile & Tickle Comics)
1955 (52 pgs.) (5x7-1/4") (7 cents)
Modern Store Publications

1-Funny animal .80 2.00 4.00

WHEELIE AND THE CHOPPER BUNCH (TV)
July, 1975 - No. 7, July, 1976 (Hanna-Barbera)
Charlton Comics

1,2-Byrne text illos (see Nightmare for 1st art). 1-Staton-a. 2-Byrne-c 1.40 3.50 7.00
3-7-Staton-a. 3-Byrne-c & text illos .80 2.00 4.00

WHEN KNIGHTHOOD WAS IN FLOWER (See 4-Color #505, 682)

WHEN SCHOOL IS OUT (See Wisco)

WHERE CREATURES ROAM
July, 1970 - No. 8, Sept, 1971
Marvel Comics Group

1-Kirby/Ayers-r .80 2.00 4.00
2-8-Kirby-r .40 1.00 2.00

NOTE: ***Ditko** r-1, 2, 4, 6, 7. All contain pre super-hero reprints.*

WHERE MONSTERS DWELL
Jan, 1970 - No. 38, Oct, 1975
Marvel Comics Group

1-Kirby/Ditko-r; all contain pre super-hero-r .80 2.00 4.00
2-10,12: 4-Crandall-a(r). 12-Giant issue .40 1.00 2.00
11,13-37: 18,20-Starlin-c .30 .75 1.50
38-Williamson-r/World of Suspense #3 .40 1.00 2.00

NOTE: ***Ditko** a(r)-4, 8, 10, 12, 17-19, 23-25, 37. **Reinman** a-4r. **Severin** c-15.*

WHERE'S HUDDLES? (TV) (See Fun-In #9)
Jan, 1971 - No. 3, Dec, 1971 (Hanna-Barbera)
Gold Key

1 1.60 4.00 8.00
2,3: 3-r-most #1 1.00 2.50 5.00

WHIP WILSON (Movie star) (Formerly Rex Hart; Gunhawk #12 on; see Western Hearts, Western Life Romances, Western Love)
No. 9, April, 1950 - No. 11, Sept, 1950 (#9,10: 52pgs.; #11: 36pgs.)
Marvel Comics

9-Photo-c; Whip Wilson & his horse Bullet begin; origin Bullet; issue #23 listed on splash page; cover changed to #9 39.00 118.00 275.00
10,11-Photo-c 25.00 75.00 175.00
I.W. Reprint #1(1964)-Kinstler-c; r-Marvel #11 2.40 6.00 12.00

WHIRLWIND COMICS (Also see Cyclone Comics)
June, 1940 - No. 3, Sept, 1940
Nita Publication

1-Cyclone begins (origin) 54.00 160.00 375.00
2,3 38.00 115.00 265.00

WHIRLYBIRDS (See 4-Color #1124, 1216)

WHISPER (Capital & First) (Value: cover or less)

WHITE CHIEF OF THE PAWNEE INDIANS
1951
Avon Periodicals

nn-Kit West app.; Kinstler-c 10.00 30.00 65.00

WHITE EAGLE INDIAN CHIEF (See Indian Chief)

WHITE FANG (Disney, movie adapt.) (Value: cover or less)

WHITE INDIAN
No. 11, July, 1953 - No. 15, 1954
Magazine Enterprises

11(A-1 94), 12(A-1 101), 13(A-1 104)-Frazetta-r(Dan Brand) in all from Durango Kid. 11-Powell-c 16.00 48.00 110.00
14(A-1 117), 15(A-1 135)-Check-a; Torres-a-#15 8.35 25.00 50.00

NOTE: *#11 contains reprints from Durango Kid #1-4; #12 from #5, 9, 10, 11; #13 from #7, 12, 13, 16. #14 & 15 contain all new stories.*

WHITE PRINCESS OF THE JUNGLE (Also see Jungle Adventures & Top Jungle Comics)
July, 1951 - No. 5, Nov, 1952
Avon Periodicals

1-Origin of White Princess (Taanda) & Capt'n Courage (r); Kinstler-c 24.00 73.00 170.00
2-Reprints origin of Malu, Slave Girl Princess from Avon's Slave Girl Comics #1 w/Malu changed to Zora; Kinstler-c/a(2) 19.00 57.00 130.00
3-Origin Blue Gorilla; Kinstler-c/a 14.00 43.00 100.00
4-Jack Barnum, White Hunter app.; r/Sheena #9 12.00 36.00 85.00
5-Blue Gorilla by McCann?; Kinstler inside-c; Fawcette/Alascia-a(3) 12.00 36.00 85.00

WHITE RIDER AND SUPER HORSE (Formerly Humdinger V2#2; Indian Warriors #7 on; also see Blue Bolt #1, 4Most & Western Crime Cases)
1950 - No. 6, Mar, 1951
Novelty-Star Publications/Accepted Publ.

1: 1-3-Exist? 8.35 25.00 50.00
2,3 5.85 17.50 35.00
4-6-Adapts "The Last of the Mohicans." 4-(9/50)-Says #11 on inside

Where Creatures Roam #1, © MEG

Whip Wilson #11, © MEG

Whirlwind Comics #1, © Nita Publ.

Whiz Comics #19, © FAW

Whiz Comics #107, © FAW

Wilbur Comics #1, © AP

GD25 FN65 NM94

5.85 17.50 35.00
Accepted Reprint #5(r/#5),6 (nd); L.B. Cole-c 4.00 11.00 22.00
NOTE: *All have **L. B. Cole** covers.*

WHITE WILDERNESS (See 4-Color #943)

WHITMAN COMIC BOOKS
1962 (136 pgs.; 7-3/4x5-3/4; hardcover) (B&W)
Whitman Publishing Co.

1-7: 1-Yogi Bear. 2-Huckleberry Hound. 3-Mr. Jinks and Pixie & Dixie. 4-The Flintstones. 5-Augie Doggie & Loopy de Loop. 6-Snooper & Blabber Fearless Detectives/Quick Draw McGraw of the Wild West. 7-Bugs Bunny-r from #47,51,53,54 & 55 .80 2.00 4.00
8-Donald Duck-reprints most of WDC&S #209-213. Includes 5 Barks stories, 1 complete Mickey Mouse serial & 1 Mickey Mouse serial missing the 1st episode 7.75 22.00 44.00
NOTE: *Hanna-Barbera #1-6(TV), original stories. Dell reprints-#7, 8.*

WHIZ COMICS (Formerly Flash Comics & Thrill Comics #1)
No. 2, Feb, 1940 - No. 155, June, 1953
Fawcett Publications

GD25 FN65 VF82 NM94

1-(nn on cover, #2 inside)-Origin & 1st newsstand app. Captain Marvel (formerly Captain Thunder) by C. C. Beck (created by Bill Parker), Spy Smasher, Golden Arrow, Ibis the Invincible, Dan Dare, Scoop Smith, Sivana, & Lance O'Casey begin
4,200.00 12,600.00 25,200.00 42,000.00
(Estimated up to 100 total copies exist, 3 in NM/Mint)
(The only Mint copy sold in 1990 for $74,000 cash/trade)

1-Reprint, oversize 13-1/2"x10". **WARNING**: This comic is an exact duplicate reprint (except for dropping "Gangway for Captain Marvel" from-c) of the original except for its size. DC published it in 1974 with a second cover titling it as a Famous First Edition. There have been many reported cases of the outer cover being removed and the interior sold as the original edition. The reprint with the new outer cover removed is practically worthless.

GD25 FN65 NM94

2-(3/40, nn on cover, #3 inside); cover to Flash #1 redrawn, pg. 12, panel 4; Spy Smasher reveals I.D. to Eve 343.00 1030.00 2400.00
3-(4/40, #3 on-c, #4 inside)-1st app. Beautia 250.00 750.00 1500.00
4-(5/40, #4 on cover, #5 inside)-Brief origin Capt. Marvel retold 208.00 625.00 1250.00
5-Captain Marvel wears button-down flap on splash page only 158.00 475.00 950.00
6-10: 7-Dr. Voodoo begins (by Raboy-#9-22) 122.00 368.00 735.00
11-14: 12-Capt. Marvel does not wear cape 87.00 262.00 525.00
15-Origin Sivana; Dr. Voodoo by Raboy 105.00 315.00 630.00
16-18-Spy Smasher battles Captain Marvel 105.00 315.00 630.00
19,20 62.00 188.00 375.00
21-Origin & 1st app. Lt. Marvels 67.00 200.00 400.00
22-24: 23-Only Dr. Voodoo by Tuska 50.00 150.00 300.00
25-(12/41)-Captain Nazi jumps from Master Comics #21 to take on Capt. Marvel solo after being beaten by Capt. Marvel/Bulletman team, causing the creation of Capt. Marvel Jr.; 1st app./origin of Capt. Marvel Jr. (part II of trilogy origin); Captain Marvel sends Jr. back to Master #22 to aid Bulletman against Capt. Nazi; origin Old Shazam in text 150.00 450.00 900.00
26-30 44.00 132.00 265.00
31,32: 32-1st app. The Trolls; Hitler/Mussolini satire by Beck 37.00 110.00 220.00
33-Spy Smasher, Captain Marvel x-over on cover and inside 42.00 125.00 250.00
34,36-40: 37-The Trolls app. by Swayze 29.00 88.00 175.00
35-Captain Marvel & Spy Smasher-c 33.00 100.00 200.00
41-50: 43-Spy Smasher, Ibis, Golden Arrow x-over in Capt. Marvel. 44-Flag-c. 47-Origin recap (1 pg.) 20.00 60.00 120.00
51-60: 52-Capt. Marvel x-over in Ibis. 57-Spy Smasher, Golden Arrow, Ibis cameo 17.00 50.00 100.00
61-70 15.00 45.00 90.00

GD25 FN65 NM94

71,77-80 12.00 35.00 70.00
72-76-Two Captain Marvel stories in each; 76-Spy Smasher becomes Crime Smasher 12.50 37.50 75.00
81-99: 86-Captain Marvel battles Sivana Family. 91-Infinity-c 12.50 37.50 75.00
100 15.00 45.00 90.00
101-106: 102-Commando Yank app. 106-Bulletman app. 10.00 30.00 60.00
107-152: 107-White House photo-c. 108-Brooklyn Bridge photo-c. 112-Photo-c. 139-Infinity-c. 142-Used in **POP**, pg. 89 10.00 30.00 60.00
153-155-(Scarce): 155-Dr. Death story 14.00 42.50 85.00
Wheaties Giveaway(1946, Miniature)-6-1/2x8-1/4", 32 pgs.; all copies were taped at each corner to a box of Wheaties and are never found in fine or mint condition; "Capt. Marvel & the Water Thieves," plus Golden Arrow, Ibis stories 50.00 200.00 –
NOTE: ***Krigstein** Golden Arrow-No. 75, 78, 91, 95, 96, 98-100. **M.Swayze** a-37, 38, 59; c-38. **Schaffenberger** c-138-158(most). **Wolverton** 1/2 pg. "Culture Corner"-No. 65-68, 70-85, 87-96, 98-100, 102-109, 112-121, 123, 125, 126, 128-131, 133, 134, 136, 142, 143, 146.*

WHODUNIT
Aug-Sept, 1948 - No. 3, Dec-Jan, 1948-49 (#1: 52 pgs.)
D.S. Publishing Co.

1-Baker-a, 7pgs. 10.00 30.00 65.00
2,3 6.70 20.00 40.00

WHODUNNIT? (Eclipse) (Value: cover or less)

WHO FRAMED ROGER RABBIT (See Marvel Graphic Novel)

WHO IS NEXT?
No. 5, January, 1953
Standard Comics

5-Toth, Sekowsky, Andru-a 11.50 34.00 80.00

WHO'S MINDING THE MINT? (See Movie Classics)

WHO'S WHO IN STAR TREK (DC) (Value: cover or less)

WHO'S WHO IN THE LEGION OF SUPER-HEROES (DC) (Value: cover or less)

WHO'S WHO: THE DEFINITIVE DIRECTORY OF THE DC UNIVERSE (DC) (Value: cover or less)

WHO'S WHO UPDATE '87 (DC) (Value: cover or less)

WHO'S WHO UPDATE '88 (DC) Value: cover or less)

WILBUR COMICS (Teen-age) (Also see Laugh Comics, Laugh Comix, Liberty Comics #10 & Zip Comics)
Sum', 1944 - No. 87, 11/59; No. 88, 9/63; No. 89, 10/64; No. 90, 10/65 (No. 1-46: 52 pgs.)
MLJ Magazines/Archie Publ. No. 8, Spring, 1946 on

1 30.00 90.00 210.00
2(Fall, 1944) 15.00 45.00 105.00
3,4(Wint, '44-45; Spr, '45) 12.00 36.00 85.00
5-1st app. Katy Keene (Sum, 1945) & begin series; Wilbur story same as Archie story in Archie #1 except that Wilbur replaces Archie 43.00 130.00 300.00
6-10(Fall, 1946) 11.50 34.00 80.00
11-20 8.35 25.00 50.00
21-30(1949) 5.35 16.00 32.00
31-50 4.00 10.00 20.00
51-70 3.00 7.50 15.00
71-90: 88-Last 10 cent issue (9/63) 1.60 4.00 8.00
NOTE: *Katy Keene in No. 5-56, 58-69.*

WILD
Feb, 1954 - No. 5, Aug, 1954
Atlas Comics (IPC)

1 11.50 34.00 80.00
2 8.35 25.00 50.00

3-5 6.70 20.00 40.00
NOTE: *Berg a-5; c-4. Burgos c-3. Colan a-4. Everett a-1-3. Heath a-2, 3, 5. Maneely a-1-3, 5; c-1, 5. Post a-2, 5. Ed Win a-1, 3.*

WILD (This Magazine Is...) (Magazine)
Jan, 1968 - No. 3, 1968 (52 pgs.) (Satire)
Dell Publishing Co.
1-3 1.20 3.00 6.00

WILD ANIMALS (Pacific) (Value: cover or less)

WILD BILL ELLIOTT (Also see Western Roundup under Dell Giants)
No. 278, 5/50 - No. 643, 7/55 (No #11,12) (All photo-c)
Dell Publishing Co.
4-Color 278(#1, 52pgs.)-Titled "Bill Elliott;" Bill & his horse Stormy begin; photo front/back-c begin 11.50 34.00 80.00
2 (11/50), 3 (52 pgs.) 6.70 20.00 40.00
4-10(10-12/52) 5.35 16.00 32.00
4-Color 472(6/53),520(12/53)-Last photo back-c 5.35 16.00 32.00
13(4-6/54) - 17(4-6/55) 4.35 13.00 26.00
4-Color 643 (7/55) 4.35 13.00 26.00

WILD BILL HICKOK (Also see Blazing Sixguns)
Sept-Oct, 1949 - No. 28, May-June, 1956
Avon Periodicals
1-Ingels-c 11.50 34.00 80.00
2-Painted-c; Kit West app. 6.70 20.00 40.00
3-5-Painted-c (4-Cover by Howard Winfield) 4.00 11.00 22.00
6-10,12: 8-10-Painted-c 4.00 11.00 22.00
11,14-Kinstler-c/a 4.20 12.50 25.00
13,15,17,18,20: 20-Kit West by Larsen 3.00 7.50 15.00
16-Kamen-a; r-3 stories/King of the Badmen of Deadwood 4.00 10.50 21.00
19-Meskin-a 3.00 7.50 15.00
21-Reprints 2 stories/Chief Crazy Horse 3.00 7.50 15.00
22-McCann-a?; r-/Sheriff Bob Dixon's... 3.00 7.50 15.00
23-27-Kinstler-c/a(r) 4.00 10.00 20.00
28-Kinstler-c/a (new); r-/Last of the Comanches 4.00 10.00 20.00
I.W. Reprint #1-r/#2; Kinstler-c .80 2.00 4.00
Super Reprint #10-12: 10-r/#18. 11-r/#?. 12-r/#8 .80 2.00 4.00
NOTE: *#23, 25 contain numerous editing deletions in both art and script due to code. Kinstler c-6, 7, 11-14, 17, 18, 20-22, 24-28. Howard Larsen a-1, 2, 4, 5, 6(3), 7-9, 11, 12, 17, 18, 20-24, 26. Meskin a-7. Reinman a-6, 17.*

WILD BILL HICKOK AND JINGLES (TV)(Formerly Cowboy Western)
No. 68, March, 1958 - No. 75, Dec, 1959 (Also see Blue Bird)
Charlton Comics
68,69-Williamson-a (all are 10 cent issues) 6.35 19.00 38.00
70-Two pgs. Williamson-a 4.20 12.50 25.00
71-75 (#76, exist?) 2.80 7.00 14.00

WILD BILL PECOS WESTERN (AC) (Value: cover or less)

WILD BOY OF THE CONGO (Also see Approved Comics)
No. 10, 2-3/51 - No. 12, 8-9/51; No. 4, 10-11/51 - No. 15, 6/55
Ziff-Davis No. 10-12,4-6/St. John No. 7? on
10(#1)(2-3/51)-Origin; bondage-c by Saunders; used in **SOTI**, pg. 189 11.00 32.00 75.00
11(4-5/51),12(8-9/51)-Norman Saunders-c 7.00 21.00 42.00
4(10-11/51)-Saunders bondage-c 7.00 21.00 42.00
5(Winter,'51)-Saunders-c 5.85 17.50 35.00
6,8,9(10/53),10: 6-Saunders-c 5.85 17.50 35.00
7(8-9/52)-Baker-c; Kinstler-a 6.70 20.00 40.00
11-13-Baker-c. 11-Kinstler-a (2 pgs.) 6.70 20.00 40.00
14(4/55)-Baker-c; r-#12('51) 6.70 20.00 40.00
15(6/55) 4.70 14.00 28.00

WILD CARDS (Marvel) (Value: cover or less)

WILDC.A.T.S: COVERT ACTION TEAMS
Aug, 1992 - No. 3, 1992 ($1.95, color, mini-series)
Image Comics
1-1st app.; Jim Lee/Williams-c/a & Lee scripts begin; contains 2 trading cards .80 2.00 4.00
1-Gold signed edition 11.50 34.00 80.00
1-Gold unsigned edition 8.35 25.00 50.00
2-($2.50)-Prism foil stamped-c; contains coupon for Image Comics #0 & 4 pg. preview to Portacio's Wetworks (back-up) 1.20 3.00 6.00
2-Newsstand ed., no prism or coupon .40 1.00 2.00
3 .40 1.00 2.00

WILD DOG (DC) (Value: cover or less)

WILD FRONTIER (Cheyenne Kid #8 on)
Oct, 1955 - No. 7, April, 1957
Charlton Comics
1-Davy Crockett 5.35 16.00 32.00
2-6-Davy Crockett in all 3.60 9.00 18.00
7-Origin Cheyenne Kid 3.60 9.00 18.00

WILD KINGDOM (TV)
1965 (Giveaway) (regular size) (16 pgs., slick-c)
Western Printing Co.
nn-Mutual of Omaha's... 2.40 6.00 12.00

WILD WEST (Wild Western #3 on)
Spring, 1948 - No. 2, July, 1948
Marvel Comics (WFP)
1-Two-Gun Kid, Arizona Annie, & Tex Taylor begin; Shores-c 14.00 43.00 100.00
2-Captain Tootsie by Beck; Shores-c 13.00 40.00 90.00

WILD WEST (Black Fury #1-57)
V2#58, November, 1966
Charlton Comics
V2#58 .40 1.00 2.00

WILD WEST C.O.W.-BOYS OF MOO MESA (TV)
Dec, 1992 - No. 3, Feb, 1993; Mar, 1993 - Present ($1.25, color)
Archie Comics
1-3 (Mini-series) .60 1.25
1-4 .60 1.25

WILD WESTERN (Formerly Wild West #1,2)
No. 3, 9/48 - No. 57, 9/57 (3-11: 52 pgs; 12-on: 36 pgs)
Marvel/Atlas Comics (WFP)
3(#1)-Tex Morgan begins; Two-Gun Kid, Tex Taylor, & Arizona Annie continue from Wild West 16.00 48.00 110.00
4-Last Arizona Annie; Captain Tootsie by Beck; Kid Colt app. 11.00 32.00 75.00
5-2nd app. Black Rider (1/49); Blaze Carson, Captain Tootsie (by Beck) app. 12.00 36.00 85.00
6-8: 6-Blaze Carson app; anti-Wertham editorial 10.00 30.00 60.00
9-Photo-c; Black Rider begins, ends #19 11.00 32.00 75.00
10-Charles Starrett photo-c 12.00 36.00 85.00
11-(Last 52 pg. issue) 9.15 27.50 55.00
12-14,16-19: All Black Rider-c/stories. 12-14-The Prairie Kid & his horse Fury app. 7.50 22.50 45.00
15-Red Larabee, Gunhawk (origin), his horse Blaze, & Apache Kid begin, end #22; Black Rider-c/story 9.15 27.50 55.00
20-29: 20-Kid Colt-c begin. 24-Has 2 Kid Colt stories. 26-1st app. The Ringo Kid? (2/53); 4 pg. story 7.00 21.00 42.00
30-Katz-a 7.50 22.50 45.00
31-40 5.00 15.00 30.00
41-47,49-51,53,57 4.00 11.00 22.00
48-Williamson/Torres-a (4 pgs); Drucker-a 5.85 17.50 35.00
52-Crandall-a 5.85 17.50 35.00
54,55-Williamson-a in both (5 & 4 pgs.), #54 with Mayo plus 2 text illos 5.35 16.00 32.00

Wild Bill Elliott #10, © DELL

Wild Bill Hickok #1, © AVON

Wild Western #14, © MEG

Willie Comics #6, © MEG

Willie the Penguin #1, © STD

Wings Comics #10, © FH

	GD25	FN65	NM94
56-Baker-a?	4.00	11.00	22.00

NOTE: *Annie Oakley in #46, 47. Apache Kid in #15-22, 39. Arizona Kid in #21, 23. Arrowhead in #34-39. Black Rider in #5, 9-19, 33-44. Fighting Texan in #17. Kid Colt in #4-6, 9-11, 20-47, 52, 54-56. Outlaw Kid in #43. Red Hawkins in #13, 14. Ringo Kid in #26, 39, 41, 43, 44, 46, 47, 50, 52-56. Tex Morgan in #3, 4, 6, 9, 11. Tex Taylor in #3-6, 9, 11. Texas Kid in #23-25. Two-Gun Kid in #3-6, 9, 11, 12, 33-39, 41. Wyatt Earp in #47.* **Ayers** *a-41, 42.* **Berg** *a-26; c-24.* **Colan** *a-49.* **Forte** *a-28, 30.* **Al Hartley** *a-16.* **Heath** *a-4, 5, 8; c-34, 44.* **Keller** *a-24, 26(2), 29-40, 44-46, 48, 52.* **Maneely** *a-10, 12, 15, 16, 28, 35, 38, 40-45; c-18-22, 33, 35, 36, 38, 39, 41, 42, 45.* **Morisi** *a-23, 52.* **Pakula** *a-42, 52.* **Powell** *a-51.* **Romita** *a-24(2).* **Severin** *a-46, 47.* **Shores** *a-3, 5, 30, 31, 33, 35, 36, 38, 41; c-3-5.* **Sinnott** *a-34-39.* **Wildey** *a-43. Bondage c-19.*

WILD WESTERN ACTION (Also see The Bravados)
March, 1971 - No. 3, June, 1971 (Reprints, 25 cents, 52 pgs.)
Skywald Publishing Corp.

	GD25	FN65	NM94
1-Durango Kid, Straight Arrow; with all references to "Straight" in story relettered to "Swift;" Bravados begin; Shores-r	.40	1.00	2.00
2-Billy Nevada, Durango Kid	.30	.75	1.50
3-Red Mask, Durango Kid	.30	.75	1.50

WILD WESTERN ROUNDUP
Oct, 1957; 1960-'61
Red Top/Decker Publications/I. W. Enterprises

	GD25	FN65	NM94
1(1957)-Kid Cowboy-r	2.40	6.00	12.00
I.W. Reprint #1('60-61)-r/#1 by Red Top	.80	2.00	4.00

WILD WEST RODEO
1953 (15 cents)
Star Publications

	GD25	FN65	NM94
1-A comic book coloring book with regular full color cover & B&W inside	3.60	9.00	18.00

WILD WILD WEST, THE (TV)
June, 1966 - No. 7, Oct, 1969
Gold Key

	GD25	FN65	NM94
1,2-McWilliams-a	7.50	22.50	45.00
3-7	5.85	17.50	35.00

WILD, WILD WEST, THE (TV)(Millennium)(Value: cover or less)

WILKIN BOY (See That...)

WILL EISNER PRESENTS (Eclipse)(Value: cover or less)

WILL EISNER'S 3-D CLASSICS FEATURING THE SPIRIT (Kitchen Sink)(Value: cover or less)

WILLIE COMICS (Formerly Ideal #1-4; Crime Cases #24 on; Li'l Willie #20 & 21) (See Gay Comics, Laugh, Millie The Model & Wisco)
#5, Fall, 1946 - #19, 4/49; #22, 1/50 - #23, 5/50 (No #20 & 21)
Marvel Comics (MgPC)

	GD25	FN65	NM94
5(#1)-George, Margie, Nellie The Nurse & Willie begin	10.00	30.00	60.00
6,8,9	5.00	15.00	30.00
7(1),10,11-Kurtzman's "Hey Look"	6.70	20.00	40.00
12,14-18,22,23	4.20	12.50	25.00
13,19-Kurtzman's "Hey Look"	5.85	17.50	35.00

NOTE: *Cindy app. in #17. Jeanie app. in #17. Little Lizzie app. in #22.*

WILLIE MAYS (See The Amazing...)

WILLIE THE PENGUIN
April, 1951 - No. 6, April, 1952
Standard Comics

	GD25	FN65	NM94
1	4.35	13.00	26.00
2-6	3.00	7.50	15.00

WILLIE THE WISE-GUY (Also see Cartoon Kids)
Sept, 1957
Atlas Comics (NPP)

	GD25	FN65	NM94
1-Kida, Maneely-a	4.70	14.00	28.00

WILLIE WESTINGHOUSE EDISON SMITH THE BOY INVENTOR
1906 (36 pgs. in color) (10x16")
William A. Stokes Co.

	GD25	FN65	NM94
nn-By Frank Crane	24.00	71.00	165.00

WILLOW (Marvel)(Value: cover or less)

WILL ROGERS WESTERN (Formerly My Great Love #1-4; see Blazing & True Comics #66)
No. 5, June, 1950 - No. 2, Aug, 1950
Fox Features Syndicate

	GD25	FN65	NM94
5(#1),2: Photo-c	22.00	65.00	150.00

WILL-YUM (See 4-Color #676, 765, 902)

WIN A PRIZE COMICS (Timmy The Timid Ghost #3 on?)
Feb, 1955 - No. 2, Apr, 1955
Charlton Comics

	GD25	FN65	NM94
V1#1-S&K-a; Poe adapt; E.C. War swipe	39.00	120.00	275.00
2-S&K-a	25.00	75.00	175.00

WINDY & WILLY
May-June, 1969 - No. 4, Nov-Dec, 1969
National Periodical Publications

	GD25	FN65	NM94
1-4: r/Dobie Gillis with some art changes	.60	1.50	3.00

WINGS COMICS
9/40 - No. 109, 9/49; No. 110, Wint, 1949-50; No. 111, Spring, 1950; No. 112, 1950(nd); No. 113 - No. 115, 1950(nd); No. 116, 1952(nd); No. 117, Fall, 1952 - No. 122, Wint, 1953-54; No. 123 - No. 124, 1954(nd)
Fiction House Magazines

	GD25	FN65	NM94
1-Skull Squad, Clipper Kirk, Suicide Smith, Jane Martin, War Nurse, Phantom Falcons, Greasemonkey Griffin, Parachute Patrol & Powder Burns begin	117.00	350.00	700.00
2	54.00	162.00	325.00
3-5	41.00	122.00	245.00
6-10	35.00	105.00	210.00
11-15	30.00	90.00	180.00
16-Origin Captain Wings	33.00	100.00	200.00
17-20	22.00	68.00	135.00
21-30	20.00	60.00	120.00
31-40	15.00	45.00	90.00
41-50	12.50	37.50	75.00
51-60: 60-Last Skull Squad	10.00	30.00	65.00
61-67: 66-Ghost Patrol begins (becomes Ghost Squadron #71 on), ends #112?	10.00	30.00	65.00
68,69: 68-Clipper Kirk becomes The Phantom Falcon-origin, Part 1; part 2 in #69	10.00	30.00	65.00
70-72: 70-1st app. The Phantom Falcon in costume, origin-Part 3; Capt. Wings battles Col. Kamikaze in all	9.15	27.50	55.00
73-99: 80-Phantom Falcon by Larsen	9.15	27.50	55.00
100	10.00	30.00	60.00
101-124: 111-Last Jane Martin. 112-Flying Saucer-c/story (1950). 115-Used in **POP**, pg. 89	7.50	22.50	45.00

NOTE: *Bondage covers are common. Captain Wings battles Sky Hag-#75, 76; ...Mr. Atlantis-#85-92; ...Mr. Pupin(Red Agent)-#98-103. Capt. Wings by* **Elias**-*#52-64, 68; by* **Lubbers**-*#29-32, 70-103, 110; by* **Renee**-*#33-46.* **Evans** *a-85-103, 105, 106, 108-111(Jane Martin).* **Larsen** *a-52, 59, 64, 73-77. Jane Martin by* **Fran Hopper**-*#68-84; Suicide Smith by* **John Celardo**-*#76, 79-103; by* **Hollingsworth**-*#68, 105-109, 111; Ghost Squadron by* **Maurice Whitman**-*#68, 72-78, 80, 82-110; Skull Squad by* **M. Baker**-*#52-60; Clipper Kirk by* **Baker**-*#60, 61; by* **Colan**-*#53; by* **Ingels**-*(some issues?). Phantom Falcon by* **Larsen**-*#78, 80-83.* **Elias** *c-58-72.* **Fawcette** *c-3-12, 16, 17, 19, 22-33.* **Lubbers** *c-74-109.* **Tuska** *a-5.* **Whitman** *c-110-124.* **Zolnerwich** *c-15, 21.*

WINGS OF THE EAGLES, THE (See 4-Color #790)

WINKY DINK (Adventures of...)
No. 75, March, 1957 (One Shot)
Pines Comics

	GD25	FN65	NM94
75-Marv Levy-c/a	3.60	9.00	18.00

WINKY DINK (See 4-Color #663)

WINNIE-THE-POOH (Also see Dynabrite Comics)
January, 1977 - No. 33, 1984 (Walt Disney)
(Winnie-The-Pooh began as Edward Bear in 1926 by Milne)
Gold Key No. 1-17/Whitman No. 18 on

	GD25	FN65	NM94
1-New art	.30	.75	1.50
2-4,6-11		.50	1.00
5,12-33-New material		.50	1.00

WINNIE WINKLE
1930 - No. 4, 1933 (52 pgs.) (B&W daily strip reprints)
Cupples & Leon Co.

	GD25	FN65	NM94
1	13.00	40.00	80.00
2-4	10.00	30.00	60.00

WINNIE WINKLE (See Popular Comics & Super Comics)
1941 - No. 7, Sept-Nov, 1949
Dell Publishing Co.

	GD25	FN65	NM94
Large Feature Comic 2('41)	13.00	40.00	90.00
4-Color 94('45)	11.00	32.00	75.00
4-Color 174	6.70	20.00	40.00
1(3-5/48)-Contains daily & Sunday newspaper-r from 1939-1941	5.00	15.00	30.00
2 (6-8/48)	4.20	12.50	25.00
3-7	3.20	8.00	16.00

WINTERWORLD (Eclipse) (Value: cover or less)

WISCO/KLARER COMIC BOOK (Miniature)
1948 - 1964 (24 pgs.) (3x6-3/4")
Marvel Comics/Vital Publications/Fawcett Publications
Given away by Wisco "99" Service Stations, Carnation Malted Milk, Klarer Health Wieners, Fleers Dubble Bubble Gum, Rodeo All-Meat Wieners, Perfect Potato Chips, & others; see ad in Tom Mix #21

	GD25	FN65	NM94
Blackstone & the Gold Medal Mystery(1948)	4.00	11.00	22.00
Blackstone "Solves the Sealed Vault Mystery"(1950)	4.00	11.00	22.00
Blaze Carson in "The Sheriff Shoots It Out"(1950)	4.00	11.00	22.00
Captain Marvel & Billy's Big Game (r/Capt. Marvel Adv. #76)	26.00	80.00	185.00
(Prices vary widely on this book)			
China Boy in "A Trip to the Zoo" #10(1948)	1.20	3.00	6.00
Indoors-Outdoors Game Book	1.20	3.00	6.00
Jim Solar Space Sheriff in "Battle for Mars," "Between Two Worlds," "Conquers Outer Space," "The Creatures on the Comet," "Defeats the Moon Missile Men," "Encounter Creatures on Comet," "Meet the Jupiter Jumpers," "Meets the Man From Mars," "On Traffic Duty," "Outlaws of the Spaceways," "Pirates of the Planet X," "Protects Space Lanes," "Raiders From the Sun," "Ring Around Saturn," "Robots of Rhea," "The Sky Ruby," "Spacetts of the Sky," "Spidermen of Venus," "Trouble on Mercury"	3.60	9.00	18.00
Johnny Starboard & the Underseas Pirates('48)	1.20	3.00	6.00
Kid Colt in "He Lived by His Guns"(1950)	5.00	15.00	30.00
Little Aspirin as "Crook Catcher" #2(1950)	1.00	2.50	5.00
Little Aspirin in "Naughty But Nice" #6(1950)	1.00	2.50	5.00
Return of the Black Phantom (not M.E. character)(Roy Dare)(1948)	2.00	5.00	10.00
Secrets of Magic	2.00	5.00	10.00
Slim Morgan "Brings Justice to Mesa City" #3	2.00	5.00	10.00
Super Rabbit(1950)-Cuts Red Tape, Stops Crime Wave!	2.00	5.00	10.00
Tex Farnum, Frontiersman(1948)	2.40	6.00	12.00
Tex Taylor in "Draw or Die, Cowpoke!" (1950)	4.00	11.00	22.00
Tex Taylor in "An Exciting Adventure at the Gold Mine" (1950)	4.00	11.00	22.00
Wacky Quacky in "All-Aboard"	.80	2.00	4.00
When School Is Out	.80	2.00	4.00
Willie in a "Comic-Comic Book Fall" #1	1.00	2.50	5.00
Wonder Duck "An Adventure at the Rodeo of the Fearless Quacker!" (1950)	.80	2.00	4.00

Rare uncut version of three; includes Capt. Marvel, Tex Farnum, Black Phantom   Estimated value.... $300.00

GD25 FN65 NM94

WISE GUYS (See Harvey...)

WISE LITTLE HEN, THE
1934 (48 pgs.); 1935; 1937 (Story book)
David McKay Publ./Whitman

	GD25	FN65	NM94
nn-2nd book app. Donald Duck; Donald app. on cover with Wise Little Hen & Practical Pig; painted cover; same artist as the B&W's from Silly Symphony Cartoon, The Wise Little Hen (1934) (McKay)	58.00	175.00	350.00
1935 Edition with dust jacket; 44 pgs. with color, 8-3/4x9-3/4" (Whitman)	37.00	110.00	220.00
888(1937)-9-1/2x13", 12 pgs. (Whitman) Donald Duck app.	20.00	60.00	120.00

WITCHCRAFT (See Strange Mysteries, Super Reprint #18)
Mar-Apr, 1952 - No. 6, Mar, 1953
Avon Periodicals

	GD25	FN65	NM94
1-Kubert-a; 1 pg. Check-a	32.00	95.00	225.00
2-Kubert & Check-a	22.00	65.00	150.00
3,6: 3-Lawrence-a; Kinstler inside-c	14.00	43.00	100.00
4-People cooked alive c/story	17.00	52.00	120.00
5-Kelly Freas-c	22.00	65.00	150.00

NOTE: ***Hollingsworth** a-4-6; c-4, 6. **McCann** a-3?*

WITCHES TALES (Witches Western Tales #29,30)
Jan, 1951 - No. 28, Dec, 1954 (date misprinted as 4/55)
Witches Tales/Harvey Publications

	GD25	FN65	NM94
1-Powell-a (1 pg.)	17.00	52.00	120.00
2-Eye injury panel	9.15	27.50	55.00
3-7,9,10	6.35	19.00	38.00
8-Eye injury panels	7.50	22.50	45.00
11-13,15,16: 12-Acid in face story	5.35	16.00	32.00
14,17-Powell/Nostrand-a. 17-Atomic disaster story	7.50	22.50	45.00
18-Nostrand-a; E.C. swipe/Shock S.S.	7.50	22.50	45.00
19-Nostrand-a; E.C. swipe/"Glutton;" Devil-c	7.50	22.50	45.00
20-24-Nostrand-a. 21-E.C. swipe; rape story. 23-Wood E.C. swipes/Two-Fisted Tales #34	7.50	22.50	45.00
25-Nostrand-a; E.C. swipe/Mad Barber	7.50	22.50	45.00
26-28: 27-r/#6 with diff.-c. 28-r/#8 with diff.-c	4.20	12.50	25.00

NOTE: ***Check** a-24. **Elias** c-8, 10, 16-27. **Kremer** a-18; c-25. **Nostrand** a-17-25; 14, 17(w/Powell). **Palais** a-1, 2, 4(2), 5(2), 7-9, 12, 14, 15, 17. **Powell** a-3-7, 10, 11, 19-27. Bondage-c 1, 3, 5, 6, 8, 9.*

WITCHES TALES (Magazine)
V1#7, July, 1969 - V7#1, Feb, 1975 (52 pgs.) (B&W)
Eerie Publications

	GD25	FN65	NM94
V1#7(7/69) - 9(11/69)	2.80	7.00	14.00
V2#1-6('70), V3#1-6('71)	2.00	5.00	10.00
V4#1-6('72), V5#1-6('73), V6#1-6('74), V7#1	1.80	4.50	9.00

NOTE: *Ajax/Farrell reprints in early issues.*

WITCHES' WESTERN TALES (Formerly Witches Tales) (Western Tales #31 on)
No. 29, Feb, 1955 - No. 30, April, 1955
Harvey Publications

	GD25	FN65	NM94
29,30-S&K-r/from Boys' Ranch including-c. 29-Last pre-code	10.00	30.00	65.00

WITCHING HOUR (The ... later issues)
Feb-Mar, 1969 - No. 85, Oct, 1978
National Periodical Publications/DC Comics

	GD25	FN65	NM94
1-Toth-a, plus Neal Adams-a (2 pgs.)	3.00	7.50	15.00
2,6	1.60	4.00	8.00
3,5-Wrightson-a; Toth-p. 3-Last 12 cent issue	1.00	2.50	5.00

Winnie Winkle #6, © DELL

Witchcraft #5, © AVON

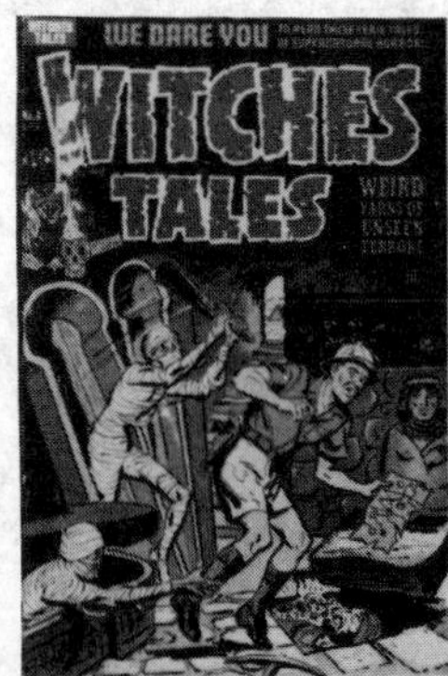

Witches Tales #4, © HARV

With the Marines on the Battlefronts of the World #1, © TOBY

The Witness #1, © MEG

Wolverine #46, © MEG

	GD25	FN65	NM94
4,7,9-12: Toth-a in all	.80	2.00	4.00
8-Toth, Neal Adams-a	1.00	2.50	5.00
13-Neal Adams-c/a, 2pgs.	.80	2.00	4.00
14-Williamson/Garzon, Jones-a; N. Adams-c	.80	2.00	4.00
15-20	.40	1.00	2.00
21-85: 38-(100 pgs.). 84-(44 pgs.)		.50	1.00

NOTE: *Combined with The Unexpected with #189.* ***Neal Adams*** *c-7-11, 13, 14.* ***Alcala*** *a-24, 27, 33, 41, 43.* ***Anderson*** *a-9, 38.* ***Cardy*** *c-4, 5.* ***Kaluta*** *a-7.* ***Kane*** *a-12p.* ***Morrow*** *a-10, 13, 15, 16.* ***Nino*** *a-31, 40, 45, 47.* ***Redondo*** *a-20, 23, 24, 34, 65; c-53.* ***Reese*** *a-23.* ***Sparling*** *a-1.* ***Toth*** *a-1, 3-5, 7-12, 38r.* ***Tuska*** *a-11, 12.* ***Wood*** *a-15.*

WITHIN OUR REACH (Star Reach)(Value: cover or less)

WITH THE MARINES ON THE BATTLEFRONTS OF THE WORLD
1953 (no month) - No. 2, March, 1954 (Photo covers)
Toby Press

	GD25	FN65	NM94
1-John Wayne story	17.00	52.00	120.00
2-Monty Hall in #1,2	4.20	12.50	25.00

WITH THE U.S. PARATROOPS BEHIND ENEMY LINES (Also see U.S. Paratroops...; #2-5 titled U.S. Paratroops...)
1951 - No. 6, Dec, 1952
Avon Periodicals

	GD25	FN65	NM94
1-Wood-c & inside f/c	10.00	30.00	70.00
2 -Kinstler-c & inside f/c only	5.85	17.50	35.00
3-6	4.70	14.00	28.00

NOTE: ***Kinstler*** *a-6; c-2, 4, 5.*

WITNESS, THE (Also see Amazing Mysteries, Captain America #71, Ideal #4, Marvel Mystery #92 & Mystic #7)
Sept, 1948
Marvel Comics (MjMe)

	GD25	FN65	NM94
1(Scarce)-Rico-c?	64.00	192.00	450.00

WITTY COMICS
1945 - No. 7, 1945
Irwin H. Rubin Publ./Chicago Nite Life News No. 2

	GD25	FN65	NM94
1-The Pioneer, Junior Patrol	9.15	27.50	55.00
2-The Pioneer, Junior Patrol	5.85	17.50	35.00
3-7-Skyhawk	5.00	15.00	30.00

WIZARD OF FOURTH STREET, THE (Dark Horse)(Value: cover or less)

WIZARD OF OZ (See Classics Illustrated Jr. 535, Dell Jr. Treasury No. 5, First Comics Graphic Novel, 4-Color No. 1308, Marvelous..., & Marvel Treasury of Oz)

WOLF GAL (See Al Capp's...)

WOLFMAN, THE (See Movie Classics)

WOLFPACK (Marvel)(Value: cover or less)

WOLVERINE (See Alpha Flight, Daredevil #196, 249, Ghost Rider; Wolverine; Punisher, Havok & ..., Incredible Hulk #180, Incredible Hulk &..., Kitty Pryde And..., Marvel Comics Presents, Power Pack, Punisher and..., Spider-Man vs... & X-Men #94)

WOLVERINE
Sept, 1982 - No. 4, Dec, 1982 (Mini-series)
Marvel Comics Group

	GD25	FN65	NM94
1-Frank Miller-c/a(p) in all	5.35	16.00	32.00
2,3	4.00	11.00	22.00
4	4.20	12.50	25.00
Trade Paperback #1 (7/87, $4.95)-Reprints #1-4 with new Miller-c	1.60	4.00	8.00
Trade Paperback nn-2nd printing ($9.95)-r/#1-4	2.00	5.00	10.00

WOLVERINE
Nov, 1988 - Present ($1.50-$1.75, color, Baxter paper)
Marvel Comics

	GD25	FN65	NM94
1-Buscema a-1-16, c-1-10; Williamson i-1,4-8	5.00	15.00	30.00
2	2.80	7.00	14.00
3-5	2.00	5.00	10.00
6-9: 6-McFarlane back-c. 7,8-Hulk app.	1.60	4.00	8.00
10-1st battle with Sabretooth (before Wolverine had his claws)	4.20	12.50	25.00
11-16: 11-New costume	1.20	3.00	6.00
17-20: 17-Byrne-c/a(p) begins, ends #23	.80	2.00	4.00
21-30	.60	1.50	3.00
31-40,44,47: 26-Begin $1.75-c	.40	1.00	2.00
41-Sabretooth claims to be Wolverine's father; Cable cameo	2.00	5.00	10.00
41-Gold 2nd printing ($1.75)	.40	1.00	2.00
42-Sabretooth, Cable & Nick Fury app.; Sabretooth proven not to be Wolverine's father	1.00	2.50	5.00
42-Gold ink 2nd printing ($1.75)	.30	.90	1.75
43-Sabretooth cameo (2 panels); saga ends	.80	2.00	4.00
45,46-Sabretooth-c/stories	.70	1.75	3.50
48,49-Sabretooth app. 48-Begin 3 part Weapon X sequel	.50	1.25	2.50
50-($2.50, 64 pgs.)-Die-cut-c; Wolverine back to old yellow costume; Forge, Cyclops, Jubilee, Jean Grey & Nick Fury app.	1.00	2.50	5.00
51-70: 51-Sabretooth-c & app. 54-Shatterstar(from X-Force) app. 55-Gambit, Jubilee, Sunfire-c/story. 58,59-Terror, Inc. x-over. 60-64-Sabretooth storyline (60,62,64-c also)	.35	.85	1.75
Annual nn (1990, $4.50, squarebound, 52 pgs.)-The Jungle Adventure; Simonson scripts; Mignola-c/a	.90	2.25	4.50
Annual 2 (12/90, $4.95, squarebound, 52 pgs.)-Bloodlust	1.00	2.50	5.00
Annual nn (#3, 8/91, $5.95, 68 pgs.)-Rahne of Terror; Cable & The New Mutants app.; Andy Kubert-c/a (2nd print exists)	1.20	3.00	6.00
...Battles the Incredible Hulk nn (1989, $4.95, squarebound, 52 pg.)-r/Incredible Hulk #180,181	1.60	4.00	8.00
...: Inner Fury nn (1992, $5.95, 52 pgs.)-Metallic ink-c; Sienkiewicz-c/a	1.20	3.00	6.00
...: Save the Tiger 1 (7/92, $2.95, 84 pgs.)-Reprints Wolverine stories from Marvel Comics Presents #1-10 w/new Kieth-c	.60	1.50	3.00

NOTE: ***Austin*** *c-3i.* ***Buscema*** *25, 27p.* ***Byrne*** *a-17-22p, 23; c-17-22, 23p.* ***Colan*** *a-24.* ***Andy Kubert*** *c/a-51.* ***Stroman*** *a-44p.* ***Williamson*** *a-3i; c(i)-1, 3-6.*

WOLVERINE SAGA
Sept, 1989 - No. 4, Mid-Dec, 1989 ($3.95, color, mini-series, 52 pgs.)
Marvel Comics

	GD25	FN65	NM94
1-Gives history; Liefeld/Austin-c (front & back)	1.00	2.50	5.00
2-4: 2-Romita, Jr./Austin-c. 4-Kaluta-c	.80	2.00	4.00

WOMAN OF THE PROMISE, THE
1950 (General Distr.) (32 pgs.) (paper cover)
Catechetical Guild

	GD25	FN65	NM94
nn	3.00	7.50	15.00

WOMEN IN LOVE (A Feature Presentation #5)
Aug, 1949 - No. 4, Feb, 1950
Fox Features Synd./Hero Books

	GD25	FN65	NM94
1	12.00	36.00	85.00
2-Kamen/Feldstein-c	10.00	30.00	65.00
3	7.50	22.50	45.00
4-Wood-a	10.00	30.00	65.00

WOMEN IN LOVE
Winter, 1952 (100 pgs.)
Ziff-Davis Publishing Co.

	GD25	FN65	NM94
nn-Kinstler-a (Scarce)	29.00	85.00	200.00

WOMEN OUTLAWS (My Love Memories #9 on)(Also see Red Circle)
July, 1948 - No. 8, Sept, 1949
Fox Features Syndicate

	GD25	FN65	NM94
1-Used in **SOTI**, illo "Giving children an image of American womanhood"; negligee panels	33.00	100.00	230.00

GD25 FN65 NM94

2-Spanking panel 27.00 81.00 190.00
3-Kamenish-a 25.00 75.00 175.00
4-8 19.00 57.00 130.00
nn(nd)-Contains Cody of the Pony Express; same cover as #7
13.50 41.00 95.00

WOMEN TO LOVE
No date (1953)
Realistic

nn-(Scarce)-Reprints Complete Romance #1; c-/Avon paperback #165
22.00 65.00 150.00

WONDER BOY (Formerly Terrific Comics) (See Blue Bolt, Bomber Comics & Samson)
No. 17, May, 1955 - No. 18, July, 1955
Ajax/Farrell Publ.

17-Phantom Lady app. Bakerish-c/a 16.00 48.00 110.00
18-Phantom Lady app. 14.00 43.00 100.00
NOTE: *Phantom Lady not by Matt Baker.*

WONDER COMICS (Wonderworld #3 on)
May, 1939 - No. 2, June, 1939
Fox Features Syndicate

GD25 FN65 VF82 NM94
1-(Scarce)-Wonder Man only app. by Will Eisner; Dr. Fung (by Powell), K-51 begins; Bob Kane-a; Eisner-c
525.00 1575.00 2900.00 4200.00
(Estimated up to 70 total copies exist, 3 in NM/Mint)
GD25 FN65 NM94
2-(Scarce)-Yarko the Great, Master Magician by Eisner begins; 'Spark' Stevens by Bob Kane, Patty O'Day, Tex Mason app. Lou Fine's 1st-c; Fine-a (2 pgs.) 250.00 750.00 1500.00

WONDER COMICS
May, 1944 - No. 20, Oct, 1948
Great/Nedor/Better Publications

1-The Grim Reaper & Spectro, the Mind Reader begin; Hitler/Hirohito bondage-c 47.00 142.00 285.00
2-Origin The Grim Reaper; Super Sleuths begin, end #8,17
28.00 85.00 170.00
3-5 25.00 75.00 150.00
6-10: 6-Flag-c. 8-Last Spectro. 9-Wonderman begins
22.00 65.00 130.00
11-14-Dick Devens, King of Futuria begins #11, ends #14
25.00 75.00 150.00
15-Tara begins (origin), ends #20 27.00 82.00 165.00
16,18: 16-Spectro app.; last Grim Reaper. 18-The Silver Knight begins
24.00 122.00 145.00
17-Wonderman with Frazetta panels; Jill Trent with all Frazetta inks
27.00 80.00 160.00
19-Frazetta panels 25.00 75.00 150.00
20-Most of Silver Knight by Frazetta 30.00 90.00 180.00
NOTE: ***Ingels** c-11, 12. **Schomburg (Xela)** c-1-10; (airbrush)-13-20. Bondage c-12, 13, 15.*

WONDER DUCK (See Wisco)
Sept, 1949 - No. 3, Mar, 1950
Marvel Comics (CDS)

1 8.35 25.00 50.00
2,3 5.85 17.50 35.00

WONDERFUL ADVENTURES OF PINOCCHIO, THE (See Movie Comics & Walt Disney Showcase #48)
No. 3, April, 1982 (Walt Disney)
Whitman Publishing Co.

3-(Continuation of Movie Comics?); r/FC #92 .50 1.00

WONDERFUL WORLD OF DUCKS (See Golden Picture Story Book)
1975
Colgate Palmolive Co.

1-Mostly-r .50 1.00

GD25 FN65 NM94

WONDERFUL WORLD OF THE BROTHERS GRIMM (See Movie Comics)

WONDERLAND COMICS
Summer, 1945 - No. 9, Feb-Mar, 1947
Feature Publications/Prize

1 5.85 17.50 35.00
2-Howard Post-c/a(2) 3.60 9.00 18.00
3-9: 4-Post-c 2.80 7.00 14.00

WONDER MAN (Marvel, 1986 & 1991)(Value: cover or less)(See The Avengers #9, 151)

WONDERS OF ALADDIN, THE (See 4-Color #1255)

WONDER WOMAN (See Adventure Comics #459, All-Star Comics, Brave & the Bold, DC Comics Presents, Justice League of America, Legend of..., Power Record Comics, Sensation Comics, Super Friends and World's Finest Comics #244)

WONDER WOMAN
Summer, 1942 - No. 329, Feb, 1986
National Periodical Publications/All-American Publ./DC Comics

GD25 FN65 VF82 NM94
1-Origin Wonder Woman retold (more detailed than All-Star #8); r-in Famous First Edition; H. G. Peter-c/a begins
625.00 1875.00 3440.00 5000.00
(Estimated up to 150 total copies exist, 8 in NM/Mint)
GD25 FN65 NM94
2-Origin & 1st app. Mars; Duke of Deception app.
167.00 500.00 1000.00
3 117.00 350.00 700.00
4,5: 5-1st Dr. Psycho app. 83.00 250.00 500.00
6-10: 6-1st Cheetah app. 67.00 200.00 400.00
11-20 50.00 150.00 300.00
21-30 42.00 125.00 250.00
31-40: 38-Last H.G. Peter-c 33.00 100.00 200.00
41-44,46-49: 49-Used in **SOTI**, pgs. 234,236; last 52 pg. issue
22.00 68.00 135.00
45-Origin retold 46.00 138.00 275.00
50-(44 pgs.)-Used in **POP**, pg. 97 21.00 62.00 125.00
51-60 16.00 48.00 95.00
61-72: 62-Origin of W.W. i.d. 64-Story about 3-D movies. 70-1st Angle Man app. 72-Last pre-code 14.00 42.00 85.00
73-90: 80-Origin The Invisible Plane. 89-Flying saucer-c/story
10.00 30.00 65.00
91-94,96-99 97-Last H. G. Peter-a. 98-Origin W.W. i.d. with new facts
7.00 22.50 45.00
95-A-Bomb-c 8.35 25.00 50.00
100 10.00 30.00 65.00
101-104,106-110: 107-1st advs. of Wonder Girl; 1st Merboy; tells how Wonder Woman won her costume 6.35 19.00 38.00
105-(Scarce)-Wonder Woman's secret origin; W. Woman appears as a girl (not Wonder Girl) 22.00 65.00 150.00
111-120 4.70 14.00 28.00
121-126: 122-1st app. Wonder Tot. 124-2nd app. Wonder Woman Family. 126-Last 10 cent issue 3.20 8.00 16.00
127-130: 128-Origin The Invisible Plane retold 2.00 5.00 10.00
131-150: 132-Flying saucer-c 1.40 3.50 7.00
151-155,157,158,160-170 (1967) 1.20 3.00 6.00
156-(8/65)-Early mention of a comic book shop & comic collecting; mentions DCs selling for $100 a copy 1.20 3.00 6.00
159-Origin retold (1/66); 1st S.A. origin? 1.40 3.50 7.00
171-178 .80 2.00 4.00
179-195: 179-Wears no costume to issue #203. 180-Death of Steve Trevor. 195-Wood inks? .60 1.50 3.00
196 (52 pgs.)-Origin-r/All-Star #8(6 out of 9 pgs.) .70 1.75 3.50
197,198 (52 pgs.)-Reprints .70 1.75 3.50
199,200 (5-6/72)-Jeff Jones-c; 52 pgs. 1.00 2.50 5.00
201-210: 204-Return to old costume; death of I Ching. 202-Fafhrd & The Grey Mouser debut .30 .75 1.50
211-240: 211,214-(100 pgs.), 217-(68 pgs.). 220-N. Adams assist. 223-Steve

Wonder Comics #2 (6/39), © FOX

Wonder Comics #3, © BP

Wonder Woman #2 (Fall, 1942), © DC

Wonder Woman #268, © DC

Wonderworld Comics #9, © FOX

The World Around Us #6, © GIL

GD25 FN65 NM94

Trevor revived as Steve Howard & learns W.W.'s I.D. 228-Both Wonder Women team up & new World War II stories begin, end #243. 237-Origin retold. 243-Both W. Women team-up again .50 1.00
241-266,269-280,284-286: 241-Intro Bouncer. 247-249-(44 pgs.). 248-Steve Trevor Howard dies. 249-Hawkgirl app. 250-Origin/1st app. Orana, the new W. Woman. 251-Orana dies. 269-Last Wood a(i) for DC? (7/80). 271-Huntress & 3rd Life of Steve Trevor begin .50 1.00
267,268-Re-intro Animal Man (5/80 & 6/80) 3.00 7.50 15.00
281-283: Joker covers & stories .60 1.50 3.00
287-New Teen Titans x-over .30 .75 1.50
288-299,301-328: 288-New costume & logo. 291-293-Three part epic with Super-Heroines .50 1.00
300-($1.50, 76 pgs.)-Anniversary issue; Giffen-a; New Teen Titans, JLA & G.A. Wonder Woman app. .30 .75 1.50
329-Double size .30 .75 1.50
Pizza Hut Giveaways (12/77)-Reprints #60,62 .50 1.00

NOTE: ***Andru/Esposito** c-66-160(most). **Colan** a-288-305p; c-288-290p. **Giffen** a-300p. **Grell** c-217. **Kaluta** c-297. **Gil Kane** c-294p, 303-305, 307, 312, 314. **Miller** c-298p. **Morrow** c-233. **Nasser** a-232p; c-231p, 232p. **Bob Oskner** c(i)-39-65(most). **Perez** c-283p, 284p. **Spiegle** a-312. **Staton** a(p)-241, 271-287, 289, 290, 294-299; c(p)-241, 245, 246. Huntress app. 271-290, 294-299, 301-321.*

WONDER WOMAN
Feb, 1987 - Present (.75/$1.00/$1.25)
DC Comics

1-New origin; Perez-c/a begins .60 1.50 3.00
2-20: 8-Origin Cheetah. 12,13-Millennium x-over. 18,26-Free 16 pg. story .60 1.25
21-49,51-62: 24-Last Perez-a; scripts continue thru #62. 60-Vs. Lobo; last Perez-c. 62-Last $1.00-c .50 1.00
50-($1.50, 52 pgs.)-New Titans, Justice League .30 .75 1.50
63-74: 63-New direction & Bolland-c begin; Deathstroke story continued from Wonder Woman Special #1 .60 1.25
Annual 1,2: 1 ('88, $1.50)-Art Adams-a(p&i). 2 ('89, $2.00, 68 pgs.)-All women artists issue; Perez-c(i) .40 1.00 2.00
Annual 3 (1992, $2.50, 68 pgs.)-Quesada-c(p) .50 1.25 2.50
Special 1 (1992, $1.75, 52 pgs.)-Deathstroke-c/story continued in Wonder Woman #63 .40 1.00 2.00

WONDER WOMAN SPECTACULAR (See DC Special Series #9)

WONDER WORKER OF PERU
No date (16 pgs.) (B&W) (5x7")
Catechetical Guild (Giveaway)

nn 3.00 7.50 15.00

WONDERWORLD COMICS (Formerly Wonder Comics)
No. 3, July, 1939 - No. 33, Jan, 1942
Fox Features Syndicate

3-Intro The Flame by Fine; Dr. Fung (Powell-a), K-51 (Powell-a?), & Yarko the Great, Master Magician (Eisner-a) continues; Eisner/Fine-c 200.00 600.00 1200.00
4 83.00 250.00 500.00
5-10 75.00 225.00 450.00
11-Origin The Flame 92.00 275.00 550.00
12-20: 13-Dr. Fung ends 47.00 140.00 280.00
21-Origin The Black Lion & Cub 42.00 125.00 250.00
22-27: 22,25-Dr. Fung app. 32.00 95.00 190.00
28-1st app/origin U.S. Jones; Lu-Nar, the Moon Man begins 42.00 125.00 250.00
29,31-33: 32-Hitler-c 25.00 75.00 150.00
30-Origin Flame Girl 52.00 155.00 310.00

NOTE: *Spies at War by **Eisner** in #13, 17. Yarko by **Eisner** in #3-11. **Eisner** text illos-3. **Lou Fine** a-3-11; c-3-13, 15; text illos-4. **Nordling** a-4-14. **Powell** a-3-12. **Tuska** a-5-9. Bondage-c 14, 15, 28, 31, 32.*

WONDERWORLDS
1992 ($3.50, color, squarebound, 100 pgs.)

GD25 FN65 NM94

Innovation Publishing

1-Rebound super-hero comics, contents may vary; Hero Alliance, Terraformers, etc. .70 1.75 3.50

WOODSY OWL (See March of Comics #395)
Nov, 1973 - No. 10, Feb, 1976
Gold Key

1 .60 1.50 3.00
2-10 .30 .75 1.50

WOODY WOODPECKER (Walter Lantz... #73 on?)(See Dell Giants for annuals) (Also see The Funnies, Jolly Jingles, Kite Fun Book, New Funnies)
No. 169, 10/47 - No. 72, 5-7/62; No. 73, 10/62 - No. 201, 4/84 (nn 192)
Dell Publishing Co./Gold Key No. 73-187/Whitman No. 188 on

4-Color 169-Drug turns Woody into a Mr. Hyde 11.50 34.00 85.00
4-Color 188 10.00 30.00 60.00
4-Color 202,232,249,264,288 5.85 17.50 35.00
4-Color 305,336,350 4.00 10.00 20.00
4-Color 364,374,390,405,416,431('52) 3.20 8.00 16.00
16 (12-1/52-53) - 30('55) 2.40 6.00 12.00
31-50 1.60 4.00 8.00
51-72 (Last Dell) 1.20 3.00 6.00
73-75 (Giants, 84 pgs., Gold Key) 2.25 6.75 18.00
76-80 1.00 2.50 5.00
81-100 .80 2.00 4.00
101-120 .60 1.50 3.00
121-191,193-201 (No #192) .40 1.00 2.00
Christmas Parade 1(11/68-Giant)(G.K.) 3.20 8.00 16.00
Clover Stamp-Newspaper Boy Contest('56)-9 pg. story-(Giveaway) 2.40 6.00 12.00
In Chevrolet Wonderland(1954-Giveaway)(Western Publ.)-20 pgs., full story line; Chilly Willy app. 6.70 20.00 40.00
...Meets Scotty McTape(1953-Scotch Tape giveaway)-16 pgs., full size 5.85 17.50 35.00
Summer Fun 1(6/66-G.K.)(84 pgs.) 2.75 8.25 22.00

NOTE: *15 cent editions exist. Reprints-No. 92, 102, 103, 105, 106, 124, 125, 152, 153, 157, 162, 165, 194(1/3)-200(1/3).*

WOODY WOODPECKER (See Comic Album #5,9,13, Dell Giant #24, 40, 54, Dell Giants, The Funnies, Golden Comics Digest #1, 3, 5, 8, 15, 16, 20, 24, 32, 37, 44, March of Comics #16, 34, 85, 93, 109, 124, 139, 158, 177, 184, 203, 222, 239, 249, 261, 420, 454, 466, 478, New Funnies & Super Book #12, 24)

WOODY WOODPECKER (Harvey)(Value: cover or less)

WOODY WOODPECKER AND FRIENDS (Harvey)(Value: cover or less)

WOOLWORTH'S CHRISTMAS STORY BOOK
1952 - 1954 (16 pgs., paper-c) (See Jolly Christmas Book)
Promotional Publ. Co.(Western Printing Co.)

nn 4.00 10.00 20.00

NOTE: *1952 issue-Marv Levy c/a.*

WOOLWORTH'S HAPPY TIME CHRISTMAS BOOK
1952 (Christmas giveaway, 36 pgs.)
F. W. Woolworth Co.(Whitman Publ. Co.)

nn 4.00 10.00 20.00

WORLD AROUND US, THE (Illustrated Story of...)
Sept, 1958 - No. 36, Oct, 1961 (25 cents)
Gilberton Publishers (Classics Illustrated)

1-Dogs; Evans-a 4.00 11.00 22.00
2-4: 2-Indians; Check-a. 3-Horses; L. B. Cole-c. 4-Railroads; L. B. Cole-a (5 pgs.) 4.00 11.00 22.00
5-Space; Ingels-a 5.00 15.00 30.00
6-The F.B.I.; Disbrow, Evans, Ingels-a 4.00 12.00 24.00
7-Pirates; Disbrow, Ingels-a 4.70 14.00 28.00
8-Flight; Evans, Ingels, Crandall-a 4.35 13.00 26.00
9-Army; Disbrow, Ingels, Orlando-a 4.00 12.00 24.00

10-13: 10-Navy; Disbrow, Kinstler-a. 11-Marine Corps. 12-Coast Guard; Ingels-a(9 pgs.). 13-Air Force; L.B. Cole-c 4.00 10.00 20.00
14-French Revolution; Crandall, Evans, Kinstler-a 5.35 16.00 32.00
15-Prehistoric Animals; Al Williamson-a, 6 & 10 pgs. plus Morrow-a 5.35 16.00 32.00
16-18: 16-Crusades; Kinstler-a. 17-Festivals; Evans, Crandall-a. 18-Great Scientists; Crandall, Evans, Torres, Williamson, Morrow-a 4.70 14.00 28.00
19-Jungle; Crandall, Williamson, Morrow-a 5.85 17.50 35.00
20-Communications; Crandall, Evans, Torres-a 6.35 19.00 38.00
21-American Presidents; Crandall/Evans, Morrow-a 4.70 14.00 28.00
22-Boating; Morrow-a 3.60 9.00 18.00
23-Great Explorers; Crandall, Evans-a 4.00 11.00 22.00
24-Ghosts; Morrow, Evans-a 4.70 14.00 28.00
25-Magic; Evans, Morrow-a 4.70 14.00 28.00
26-The Civil War 5.35 16.00 32.00
27-Mountains (High Advs.); Crandall/Evans, Morrow, Torres-a 4.70 14.00 28.00
28-Whaling; Crandall, Evans, Morrow, Torres, Wildey-a; L.B. Cole-c 4.20 12.50 25.00
29-Vikings; Crandall, Evans, Torres, Morrow-a 4.70 14.00 28.00
30-Undersea Adventure; Crandall/Evans, Kirby, Morrow, Torres-a 5.35 16.00 32.00
31-Hunting; Crandall/Evans, Ingels, Kinstler, Kirby-a 4.35 13.00 26.00
32,33: 32-For Gold & Glory; Morrow, Kirby, Crandall, Evans-a. 33-Famous Teens; Torres, Crandall, Evans-a 4.35 13.00 26.00
34-36: 34-Fishing; Crandall/Evans-a. 35-Spies; Kirby, Morrow?, Evans-a. 36-Fight for Life (Medicine); Kirby-a 4.00 11.00 22.00

NOTE: See Classics Illustrated Special Edition. Another *World Around Us* issue entitled *The Sea* had been prepared in 1962 but was never published in the U.S. It was published in the British/European *World Around Us* series. Those series then continued with seven additional WAU titles not in the U.S. series.

WORLD FAMOUS HEROES MAGAZINE
Oct, 1941 - No. 4, Apr, 1942 (a comic book)
Comic Corp. of America (Centaur)

1-Gustavson-c; Lubbers, Glanzman-a; Davy Crockett story; Flag-c 67.00 200.00 400.00
2-Lou Gehrig life story; Lubbers-a 33.00 100.00 200.00
3,4-Lubbers-a; 4-Wild Bill Hickok app. 29.00 88.00 175.00

WORLD FAMOUS STORIES
1945
Croyden Publishers

1-Ali Baba, Hansel & Gretel, Rip Van Winkle, Mid-Summer Night's Dream 8.35 25.00 50.00

WORLD IS HIS PARISH, THE
1953 (15 cents)
George A. Pflaum

nn-The story of Pope Pius XII 4.00 11.00 22.00

WORLD OF ADVENTURE (Walt Disney's...)(TV)
April, 1963 - No. 3, Oct, 1963 (All 12 cents)
Gold Key

1-3-Disney TV characters; Savage Sam, Johnny Shiloh, Capt. Nemo, The Mooncussers 1.00 2.50 5.00

WORLD OF ARCHIE, THE (See Archie Giant Series Mag. #148, 151, 156, 160, 165, 171, 177, 182, 188, 193, 200, 208, 213, 225, 232, 237, 244, 249, 456, 461, 468, 473, 480, 485, 492, 497, 504, 509, 516, 521, 532, 543, 554, 565, 574, 587, 599, 612, 627)

WORLD OF ARCHIE
Aug, 1992 - Present ($1.25, color)
Archie Comics

1-3 .60 1.25

WORLD OF FANTASY
May, 1956 - No. 19, Aug, 1959
Atlas Comics (CPC No. 1-15/ZPC No. 16-19)

1 17.00 52.00 120.00
2-Williamson-a, 4 pgs. 11.50 34.00 80.00
3-Sid Check, Roussos-a 9.15 27.50 55.00
4-7 7.50 22.50 45.00
8-Matt Fox, Orlando, Berg-a 10.00 30.00 60.00
9-Krigstein-a 8.35 25.00 50.00
10,12-15 6.70 20.00 40.00
11-Torres-a 7.50 22.50 45.00
16-Williamson-a, 4 pgs.; Ditko, Kirby-a 9.15 27.50 55.00
17-19-Ditko, Kirby-a 8.35 25.00 50.00

NOTE: ***Ayers*** *a-3.* ***B. Baily*** *a-4.* ***Berg*** *a-5, 6, 8.* ***Brodsky*** *c-3.* ***Check*** *a-3.* ***Ditko*** *a-17, 19.* ***Everett*** *a-2; c-4-7, 9, 12, 13.* ***Forte*** *a-4.* ***Infantino*** *a-14.* ***Kirby*** *c-15, 17-19.* ***Krigstein*** *a-9.* ***Maneely*** *c-2, 14.* ***Mooney*** *a-14.* ***Morrow*** *a-7.* ***Orlando*** *a-8, 13, 14.* ***Pakula*** *a-9.* ***Powell*** *a-4, 6.* ***R.Q. Sale*** *a-3, 9.* ***Severin*** *c-1.*

WORLD OF GIANT COMICS, THE (See Archie All-Star Specials under Archie Comics)

WORLD OF GINGER FOX, THE (Comico) (Value: cover or less)

WORLD OF JUGHEAD, THE (See Archie Giant Series Mag. #9, 14, 19, 24, 30, 136, 143, 149, 152, 157, 161, 166, 172, 178, 183, 189, 194, 202, 209, 215, 227, 233, 239, 245, 251, 457, 463, 469, 475, 481, 487, 493, 499, 505, 511, 517, 523, 531, 542, 553, 564, 577, 590, 602)

WORLD OF KRYPTON, THE (World of...#3; see Superman #248)
7/79 - No. 3, 9/79; 12/87 - No. 4, 3/88 (Both are mini-series)
DC Comics, Inc.

1-3 (1979, 40 cents): 1-Jor-El marries Lara. 3-Baby Superman sent to Earth; Krypton explodes; Mon-el app. .50 1.00
1-4 (75 cents)-Byrne scripts; Byrne/Simonson-c .50 1.00

WORLD OF METROPOLIS (DC) (Value: cover or less)

WORLD OF MYSTERY
June, 1956 - No. 7, July, 1957
Atlas Comics (GPI)

1-Torres, Orlando-a; Powell-a? 17.00 52.00 120.00
2-Woodish-a 6.70 20.00 40.00
3-Torres, Davis, Ditko-a 9.15 27.50 55.00
4-Pakula, Powell-a 10.00 30.00 60.00
5,7: 5-Orlando-a 6.70 20.00 40.00
6-Williamson/Mayo-a, 4 pgs.; Ditko-a; Crandall text illo 10.00 30.00 65.00

NOTE: ***Brodsky*** *c-2.* ***Colan*** *a-7.* ***Everett*** *c-1, 3.* ***Pakula*** *a-4, 6.* ***Romita*** *a-2.* ***Severin*** *c-7.*

WORLD OF SMALLVILLE (DC) (Value: cover or less)

WORLD OF SUSPENSE
April, 1956 - No. 8, July, 1957
Atlas News Co.

1 16.00 48.00 110.00
2-Ditko-a (4 pgs.) 9.15 27.50 55.00
3,7-Williamson-a in both, 4 pgs. each; #7-with Mayo 10.00 30.00 60.00
4-6,8 6.70 20.00 40.00

NOTE: ***Berg*** *a-6.* ***Cameron*** *a-2.* ***Ditko*** *a-2.* ***Drucker*** *a-1.* ***Everett*** *a-1, 5; c-6.* ***Heck*** *a-5.* ***Maneely*** *a-1; c-1-3.* ***Orlando*** *a-5.* ***Powell*** *a-6.* ***Reinman*** *a-4.* ***Roussos*** *a-6.* ***Shores*** *a-1.*

WORLD OF WHEELS (Formerly Dragstrip Hotrodders)
No. 17, Oct, 1967 - No. 32, June, 1970
Charlton Comics

17-20-Features Ken King .80 2.00 4.00
21-32-Features Ken King .60 1.50 3.00
Modern Comics Reprint 23(1978) .40 1.00 2.00

WORLD OF WOOD (Eclipse) (Value: cover or less)

WORLD'S BEST COMICS (World's Finest Comics #2 on)
Spring, 1941 (Cardboard-c)(DC's 6th annual format comic)
National Periodical Publications (100 pgs.)

World of Fantasy #3, © MEG

World of Mystery #6, © MEG

World of Suspense #4, © MEG

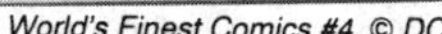

World's Finest Comics #4, © DC

World's Finest Comics #19, © DC

World's Finest Comics #121, © DC

GD25 FN65 NM94

	GD25	FN65	VF82	NM94
1-The Batman, Superman, Crimson Avenger, Johnny Thunder, The King, Young Dr. Davis, Zatara, Lando, Man of Magic, & Red, White & Blue begin; Superman, Batman & Robin covers begin (inside-c is blank); Fred Ray-c	750.00	2250.00	4100.00	6000.00

(Estimated up to 185 total copies exist, 6 in NM/Mint)

WORLDS BEYOND (Worlds of Fear #2 on)
Nov, 1951
Fawcett Publications

	GD25	FN65	NM94
1-Powell, Bailey-a	17.00	52.00	120.00

WORLD'S FAIR COMICS (See New York....)

WORLD'S FINEST (DC, 1990)(Value: cover or less)

WORLD'S FINEST COMICS (Formerly World's Best Comics #1)
No. 2, Sum, 1941 - No. 323, Jan, 1986 (early issues have 100 pgs.)
National Periodical Publ./DC Comics (#1-17 have cardboard covers)

	GD25	FN65	NM94
2 (100 pgs.)-Superman, Batman & Robin covers continue from World's Best	300.00	900.00	1800.00
3-The Sandman begins; last Johnny Thunder; origin & 1st app. The Scarecrow	233.00	700.00	1400.00
4-Hop Harrigan app.; last Young Dr. Davis	167.00	500.00	1000.00
5-Intro. TNT & Dan the Dyna-Mite; last King & Crimson Avenger	167.00	500.00	1000.00
6-Star Spangled Kid begins; Aquaman app.; S&K Sandman with Sandy in new costume begins, ends #7	125.00	375.00	750.00
7-Green Arrow begins; last Lando, King, & Red, White & Blue; S&K art	125.00	375.00	750.00
8-Boy Commandos begin (by Simon(p) #12)	117.00	350.00	700.00
9-Batman cameo in Star Spangled Kid; S&K-a; last 100 pg. issue; Hitler, Mussolini, Tojo-c	121.00	362.00	725.00
10-S&K-a	104.00	310.00	625.00
11-17-Last cardboard cover issue	96.00	288.00	575.00
18-20: 18-Paper covers begin; last Star Spangled Kid	83.00	250.00	500.00
21-30: 30-Johnny Peril app.	58.00	175.00	350.00
31-40: 33-35-Tomahawk app.	50.00	150.00	300.00
41-50: 41-Boy Commandos end. 42-Wyoming Kid begins, ends #63. 43-Full Steam Foley begins, ends #48. 48-Last square binding. 49-Tom Sparks, Boy Inventor begins	40.00	120.00	240.00
51-60: 51-Zatara ends. 59-Manhunters Around the World begins, ends #62	40.00	120.00	240.00
61-64: 61-Joker story. 63-Capt. Compass app.	17.00	50.00	100.00
65-Origin Superman; Tomahawk begins, ends #101	48.00	145.00	290.00
66-70-(15 cent issues, scarce)-Last 68pg. issue	37.00	110.00	225.00
71-(10 cent issue, scarce)-Superman & Batman begin as team	57.00	170.00	400.00
72,73-(10 cent issues, scarce)	35.00	107.00	250.00
74-80: 74-Last pre-code issue. 77-Superman loses powers & Batman obtains them this issue only	25.00	75.00	175.00
81-90: 88-1st Joker/Luthor team-up. 90-Batwoman's 1st app. in World's Finest (3rd app. anywhere)	17.00	52.00	120.00
91-93,95-99: 96-99-Kirby Green Arrow	11.50	34.00	80.00
94-Origin Superman/Batman team retold	43.00	130.00	300.00
100 (3/59)	24.00	73.00	170.00
101-110: 102-Tommy Tomorrow begins, ends #124	10.00	30.00	60.00
111-121: 111-1st app. The Clock King. 113-Intro. Miss Arrowette in Green Arrow; 1st Bat-Mite/Mr. Mxyzptlk team-up. 121-Last 10 cent issue	7.50	22.50	45.00
122-128,130-142: 123-2nd Bat-Mite/Mr. Mxyzptlk team-up. 125-Aquaman begins, ends #139. 135-Last Dick Sprang story. 140-Last Green Arrow. 142-Origin The Composite Superman (villain); Legion app.	4.00	10.00	20.00
129-Joker/Luthor team-up-c/story	5.00	15.00	30.00
143-150: 143-1st Mailbag	2.40	6.00	12.00
151-155,157-160	2.00	5.00	10.00
156-1st Bizarro Batman; Joker-c/story	8.35	25.00	50.00
161,170 (80-Pg. Giants G-28,G-40)	2.40	6.00	12.00
162-165,167-169,171-174: 168,172-Adult Legion app.	1.40	3.50	7.00
166-Joker-c/story	2.40	6.00	12.00
175,176-Neal Adams-a; both r-J'onn J'onzz origin/Detective #225,226	2.00	5.00	10.00
177-Joker/Luthor team-up-c/story	2.00	5.00	10.00
178,180-187: 182-Silent Knight-r/Brave & Bold #6. 186-Johnny Quick-r. 187-Green Arrow origin-r/Adv. #256	.80	2.00	4.00
179,188 (80-Pg. Giants G-52,G-64): 179-r/#94	1.00	2.50	5.00
189-196: 190-193-Robin-r	.60	1.50	3.00
197-(80 Pg. Giant G-76)	.80	2.00	4.00
198,199-3rd Surperman/Flash race (see Flash #175 & Superman #199)	7.50	22.50	45.00
200-205: 205-(52 pgs.)-6 pgs. Shining Knight by Frazetta/Adv. #153; Teen Titans x-over	.50	1.25	2.50
206 (80-Pg. Giant G-88)	.50	1.25	2.50
207-248: 207-212-(52 pgs.). 208-Origin Robotman-r/Det. #138. 215-Intro. Batman Jr. & Superman Jr. 217-Metamorpho begins, ends #220; Batman/ Superman team-ups begin. 223-228-(100 pgs.). 223-N. Adams-r. 223-Deadman origin. 226-N. Adams, S&K, Toth-r; Manhunter part origin-r/Det. #225,226. 229-r/origin Superman-Batman team. 244-Green Arrow, Black Canary, Wonder Woman, Vigilante begin; $1.00, 84 pg. issues begin. 246-Death of Stuff in Vigilante; origin Vigilante retold. 248-Last Vigilante	.40	1.00	2.00
249-The Creeper begins by Ditko, ends #255	.80	2.00	4.00
250-270,272-299: 250-The Creeper origin retold by Ditko. 252-Last 84 pg. issue. 253-Capt. Marvel begins; 68 pgs. begin, end #265. 255-Last Creeper. 256-Hawkman begins. 257-Black Lightning begins. 266-282-(52 pgs.). 267-Challengers of the Unknown app. 268-Capt. Marvel Jr. origin retold. 274-Zatanna begins. 279,280-Capt. Marvel Jr. & Kid Eternity learn they are brothers. 284-Legion app. 298-Begin 75 cent-c	.30	.75	1.50
271-Origin Superman/Batman team retold	.40	1.00	2.00
300-($1.25, 52pgs.)-Justice League of America, New Teen Titans & The Outsiders app.; Perez-a(3 pgs.)	.40	1.00	2.00
301-323: 304-Origin Null and Void. 309,319-Free 16 pg. story in each (309-Flash Force 2000, 319-Mask preview)	.30	.75	1.50
Giveaway (c. 1944-45, 8 pgs., in color, paper-c)-Johnny Everyman-r/World's Finest	11.50	34.00	80.00
Giveaway (c. 1949, 8 pgs., in color, paper-c)-"Make Way For Youth"-r/World's Finest; based on film of same name	7.00	21.00	50.00

NOTE: ***Neal Adams** a-230r; c-174-176, 178-180, 182, 183, 185, 186, 199-205, 208-211, 244-246, 258. **Austin** a-244-246i. **Burnley** a-8, 10; c-7-9, 11-14, 15p?, 16-18p, 20-31p. **Colan** a-274p, 297, 299. **Ditko** a-249-255. **Giffen** a-322; c-284p, 322. **G. Kane** a-38, 174r, 282, 283; c-281, 282, 289. **Kirby** a-187. **Kubert** Zatara-40-44. **Miller** c-285p. **Mooney** c-134. **Morrow** a-245-248. **Mortimer** c-16-21, 26-71. **Nasser** a(p)-244-246, 259, 260. **Newton** a-253-281p. **Orlando** a-224r. **Perez** a-300i; c-271, 276, 277p, 278p. **Fred Ray** c-2-6. **Robinson** a-2, 9, 13-15; c-13-16. **Rogers** a-259p. **Roussos** a-212r. **Simonson** c-291. **Spiegle** a-275-278, 284. **Staton** a-262p, 273p. **Swan/Mortimer** c-79-82. **Toth** a-228r. **Tuska** a-230r, 250p, 252p, 254p, 257p, 283p, 284p, 308p. Boy Commandos by **Infantino** #39-41.*

(Also see 80 Page Giant #15)

WORLD'S FINEST COMICS DIGEST (See DC Special Series #23)

WORLD'S GREATEST ATHLETE (See Walt Disney Showcase #14)

WORLD'S GREATEST SONGS
Sept, 1954
Atlas Comics (Male)

	GD25	FN65	NM94
1-(Scarce) Heath & Harry Anderson-a; Eddie Fisher life story	22.00	65.00	150.00

WORLD'S GREATEST STORIES
Jan, 1949 - No. 2, May, 1949
Jubilee Publications

	GD25	FN65	NM94
1-Alice in Wonderland	13.50	41.00	95.00
2-Pinocchio	12.00	36.00	85.00

WORLD'S GREATEST SUPER HEROES
1977 (3-3/4x3-3/4") (24 pgs. in color) (Giveaway)
DC Comics (Nutra Comics) (Child Vitamins, Inc.)

	GD25	FN65	NM94
nn-Batman & Robin app.; health tips	.40	1.00	2.00

WORLDS OF FEAR (Formerly Worlds Beyond #1)
V1#2, Jan, 1952 - V2#10, June, 1953
Fawcett Publications

	GD25	FN65	NM94
V1#2	16.00	48.00	110.00
3-Evans-a	13.00	40.00	90.00
4-6(9/52)	11.50	34.00	80.00
V2#7-9	10.00	30.00	70.00
10-Saunders Painted-c; man with no eyes surrounded by eyeballs-c	19.00	57.00	130.00

NOTE: *Powell a-2, 4, 5. Sekowsky a-4, 5.*

WORLDS UNKNOWN
May, 1973 - No. 8, Aug, 1974
Marvel Comics Group

	GD25	FN65	NM94
1-r/from Astonishing #54; Torres, Reese-a	.60	1.50	3.00
2-8	.40	1.00	2.00

NOTE: *Adkins/Mooney a-5. Buscema c/a-4p. W. Howard c/a-3i. Kane a(p)-1,2; c(p)-5, 6, 8. Sutton a-2. Tuska a(p)-7, 8; c-7p. No. 7, 8 has Golden Voyage of Sinbad movie adaptation.*

WORLD WAR STORIES
Apr-June, 1965 - No. 3, Dec, 1965
Dell Publishing Co.

	GD25	FN65	NM94
1-Glanzman-a in all	3.60	9.00	18.00
2,3	2.00	5.00	10.00

WORLD WAR II (See Classics Illustrated Special Issue)

WORLD WAR III
Mar, 1953 - No. 2, May, 1953
Ace Periodicals

	GD25	FN65	NM94
1-(Scarce)-Atomic bomb-c	38.00	115.00	265.00
2-Used in **POP**, pg. 78 & B&W & color illos; Cameron-a	32.00	95.00	225.00

WORLD WITHOUT END (DC) (Value: cover or less)

WORLD WRESTLING FEDERATION BATTLEMANIA
1991 - No. 5?, 1991 ($2.50, color, magazine size, 68 pgs.)
Valiant

	GD25	FN65	NM94
1-5: 5-Includes 2 free pull-out posters	.50	1.25	2.50

WORST FROM MAD, THE (Annual)
1958 - No. 12, 1969 (Each annual cover is reprinted from the cover of the Mad issues being reprinted)
E. C. Comics

	GD25	FN65	NM94
nn(1958)-Bonus; record labels & travel stickers; 1st Mad annual; r/Mad #29-34	18.00	54.00	125.00
2(1959)-Bonus is small 33⅓ rpm record entitled "Meet the Staff of Mad;" r/Mad #35-40	25.00	75.00	175.00
3(1960)-20x30" campaign poster "Alfred E. Neuman for President;" r/Mad #41-46	14.00	43.00	100.00
4(1961)-Sunday comics section; r/Mad #47-54	14.00	43.00	100.00
5(1962)-Has 33-1/3 record; r/Mad #55-62	20.00	60.00	140.00
6(1963)-Has 33-1/3 record; r/Mad #63-70	22.00	65.00	150.00
7(1964)-Mad protest signs; r/Mad #71-76	9.15	27.50	55.00
8(1965)-Build a Mad Zeppelin	10.00	30.00	65.00
9(1966)-33-1/3 rpm record	13.00	40.00	90.00
10(1967)-Mad bumper sticker	5.35	16.00	32.00
11(1968)-Mad cover window stickers	5.35	16.00	32.00
12(1969)-Mad picture postcards; Orlando-a	5.35	16.00	32.00

NOTE: *Covers: Bob Clarke-#8. Mingo-#7, 9-12.*

WOTALIFE COMICS (Formerly Nutty Life #2; Phantom Lady #13 on)
No. 3, Aug-Sept, 1946 - No. 12, July, 1947; 1959
Fox Features Syndicate/Norlen Mag.

	GD25	FN65	NM94
3-Cosmo Cat	6.70	20.00	40.00
4-12-Cosmo Cat	4.20	12.50	25.00
1(1959-Norlen)-Atomic Rabbit, Atomic Mouse	4.00	11.00	22.00

WOTALIFE COMICS
1957 - No. 5, 1957
Green Publications

	GD25	FN65	NM94
1	3.20	8.00	16.00
2-5	2.40	6.00	12.00

WOW COMICS
July, 1936 - No. 4, Nov, 1936 (52 pgs., magazine size)
Henle Publishing Co.

	GD25	FN65	NM94
1-Fu Manchu; Eisner-a; Briefer-c	200.00	500.00	1200.00
2-Ken Maynard, Fu Manchu, Popeye by Segar plus article on Popeye; Eisner-a	125.00	315.00	750.00
3-Eisner-c/a(3); Popeye by Segar, Fu Manchu, Hiram Hick by Bob Kane, Space Limited app.; Jimmy Dempsey talks about Popeye's punch; Briefer-a	125.00	315.00	750.00
4-Flash Gordon by Raymond, Mandrake, Popeye by Segar, Tillie The Toiler, Fu Manchu, Hiram Hick by Bob Kane; Eisner-a(3); Briefer-c/a	158.00	395.00	950.00

WOW COMICS (Real Western Hero #70 on)(See XMas Comics)
Winter, 1940-41; No. 2, Summer, 1941 - No. 69, Fall, 1948
Fawcett Publications

	GD25	FN65	VF82	NM94
nn(#1)-Origin Mr. Scarlet by S&K; Atom Blake, Boy Wizard, Jim Dolan, & Rick O'Shay begin; Diamond Jack, The White Rajah, & Shipwreck Roberts, only app.; 1st mention of Gotham City in comics; the cover was printed on unstable paper stock and is rarely found in fine or mint condition; blank inside-c; bondage-c by Beck	800.00	2400.00	4800.00	8000.00

(Estimated up to 100 total copies exist, 3 in NM/Mint)

	GD25	FN65	NM94
2 (Scarce)-The Hunchback begins	108.00	325.00	650.00
3 (Fall, 1941)	67.00	200.00	400.00
4-Origin Pinky	75.00	225.00	450.00
5	50.00	150.00	300.00
6-Origin The Phantom Eagle; Commando Yank begins	42.00	125.00	250.00
7,8,10: 10-Swayze-c/a on Mary Marvel	38.00	115.00	230.00
9 (1/6/43)-Capt. Marvel, Capt. Marvel Jr., Shazam app.; Scarlet & Pinky x-over; Mary Marvel-c/stories begin (cameo #9)	75.00	225.00	450.00
11-17,19,20: 15-Flag-c	25.00	75.00	150.00
18-1st app. Uncle Marvel (10/43); infinity-c	30.00	90.00	180.00
21-30: 28-Pinky x-over in Mary Marvel	14.00	42.00	85.00
31-40: 32-68-Phantom Eagle by Swayze	10.00	30.00	60.00
41-50	8.35	25.00	50.00
51-58: Last Mary Marvel	7.50	22.50	45.00
59-69: 59-Ozzie begins. 62-Flying Saucer gag-c (1/48). 65-69-Tom Mix stories	6.70	20.00	40.00

WRATH OF THE SPECTRE, THE
May, 1988 - No. 4, Aug, 1988 ($2.50, color, mini-series)
DC Comics

	GD25	FN65	NM94
1-4: Aparo-r/Adventure #431-440	.50	1.25	2.50

WRECK OF GROSVENOR (See Superior Stories #3)

WRINGLE WRANGLE (See 4-Color #821)

WULF THE BARBARIAN
Feb, 1975 - No. 4, Sept, 1975

World War III #1, © ACE

Wow Comics #3, © Henle Publ.

Wow Comics #9, © FAW

Wyatt Earp #10, © MEG

X-Factor #62, © MEG

XMas Comics #2 (1942), © FAW

GD25 FN65 NM94

Atlas/Seaboard Publ.
1-4: 1-Origin. 2-Intro. Berithe the Swordswoman; Neal Adams, Wood, Reese-a assists .50 1.00

WYATT EARP
Nov, 1955 - #29, June, 1960; #30, Oct, 1972 - #34, June, 1973
Atlas Comics/Marvel No. 23 on (IPC)
1 11.50 34.00 80.00
2-Williamson-a, 4 pgs. 7.50 22.50 45.00
3-6,8-11: 3-Black Bart app. 8-Wild Bill Hickok app. 5.85 17.50 35.00
7,12-Williamson-a, 4 pgs. ea.; #12 with Mayo 6.35 19.00 38.00
13-20: 17-1st app. Wyatt's deputy, Grizzly Grant 5.00 15.00 30.00
21-Davis-c 4.00 11.00 22.00
22-24,26-29: 22-Ringo Kid app. 23-Kid From Texas app. 29-Last 10 cent issue 3.20 8.00 16.00
25-Davis-a 3.60 9.00 18.00
30-Williamson-r (1972) .40 1.00 2.00
31-34-Reprints. 32-Torres-a(r) .50 1.00
NOTE: ***Ayers** a-8, 10(2), 17, 20(4). **Berg** a-9. **Everett** c-6. **Kirby** c-25, 29. **Maneely** a-1; c-1-4, 8, 12, 17, 20. **Maurer** a-2(2), 3(4), 4(4), 8(4). **Severin** a-4, 9(4), 10; c-2, 9, 10, 14. **Wildey** a-5, 17, 24, 28.*

WYATT EARP (Hugh O'Brian Famous Marshal)
No. 860, Nov, 1957 - No. 13, Dec-Feb, 1960-61 (Photo-c)
Dell Publishing Co.
4-Color 860 (#1)-Manning-a 10.00 30.00 70.00
4-Color 890,921(6/58)-All Manning-a 6.70 20.00 40.00
4 (9-11/58) - 12-Manning-a 5.00 15.00 30.00
13-Toth-a 5.85 17.50 35.00

WYATT EARP FRONTIER MARSHAL (Formerly Range Busters)
No. 12, Jan, 1956 - No. 72, Dec, 1967 (Also see Blue Bird)
Charlton Comics
12 4.20 12.50 25.00
13-19 2.40 6.00 12.00
20-(68 pgs.)-Williamson-a(4), 8,5,5,& 7 pgs. 6.35 19.00 38.00
21-30 1.60 4.00 8.00
31-50: 31-Crandall-r 1.20 3.00 6.00
51-72 .80 2.00 4.00

XANADU COLOR SPECIAL (Eclipse) (Value: cover or less)

XENON (Eclipse) (Value: cover or less)

XENOZOIC TALES (Kitchen Sink) (Value: cover or less)

X-FACTOR (Also see The Avengers #263 & Fantastic Four #286)
Feb, 1986 - Present
Marvel Comics Group
1-($1.25, 52 pgs)-Story recaps 1st app. from Avengers #263; story cont'd from F.F. #286; return of original X-Men (now X-Factor); Guice/Layton-a; Baby Nathan app. (2nd after X-Men #201) 2.40 6.00 12.00
2,3 1.20 3.00 6.00
4,5: 5-1st app. Apocalypse 1.00 2.50 5.00
6-10 .80 2.00 4.00
11-20: 13-Baby Nathan app. in flashback. 15-Intro wingless Angel .60 1.50 3.00
21-23: 23-1st app. Archangel (cameo) .50 1.25 2.50
24-1st full app. Archangel (now in Uncanny X-Men); Fall Of The Mutants begins; origin Apocalypse 3.00 7.50 15.00
25,26: Fall Of The Mutants; 26-New outfits .80 2.00 4.00
27-30 .40 1.00 2.00
31-37,39,41-49: 35-Origin Cyclops .30 .75 1.50
38,50-($1.50, 52 pgs.): 50-Liefeld/McFarlane-c .40 1.00 2.00
40-Rob Liefeld-c/a (4/88, 1st at Marvel?) 1.20 3.00 6.00
51-53-Sabretooth app. 52-Liefeld-c(p) 1.00 2.50 5.00
54-59: 54-Intro Crimson .50 1.00

GD25 FN65 NM94

60-X-Tinction Agenda x-over; New Mutants (w/Cable) x-over in #60-62; Wolverine in #62 1.60 4.00 8.00
60-Gold 2nd printing .50 1.25 2.50
61,62-X-Tinction Agenda. 62-Jim Lee-c 1.20 3.00 6.00
63-Whilce Portacio-c/a(p) begins, ends #69 1.20 3.00 6.00
64-67,69,70: 65-68-Lee co-plots. 67-Inhumans app. 69,70-X-Men (w/ Wolverine) x-over .40 1.00 2.00
68-Baby Nathan is sent into future to save his life 1.00 2.50 5.00
71-New team begins (Havok, Polaris, Wolfsbane & Madrox); Stroman-c/a begins 1.20 3.00 6.00
71-2nd printing ($1.25) .60 1.25
72-74: 74-Last $1.00-c .30 .75 1.50
75-($1.75, 52 pgs.) .35 .90 1.75
76-83,87-90: 77-Cannonball (of X-Force) app. 87-Quesada-c/a(p) begins .60 1.25
84-86 ($1.50)-X-Cutioner's Song x-overs; polybagged with trading card in each. 84-Jae Lee-a(p). 85-Jae Lee-c/a(p) .40 1.00 2.00
Annual 1-5: 1-(10/86). 2-(10/87). 3-(1988, $1.75)-Evolutionary War x-over. 4-(1989, $2.00, 68 pgs.)-Atlantis Attacks; Byrne/Simonson-a; Byrne-c, 5-(1990, $2.00, 68 pgs.)-Fantastic Four, New Mutants x-over .50 1.25 2.50
Annual 6 (1991, $2.00, 68 pgs.)-New Warriors app.; 5th app. X-Force cont'd from X-Men Annual #15 .50 1.25 2.50
Annual 7 (1992, $2.25, 68 pgs.)-1st Quesada-a(p) on X-Factor plus-c(p) .45 1.15 2.25
...Prisoner of Love nn (1990, $4.95, 52 pgs.)-Starlin scripts; Guice-a 1.00 2.50 5.00
NOTE: ***Art Adams** a-41p, 42p. **Buckler** a-50p. **Liefeld** a-40; c-40, 50i, 52p. **McFarlane** c-50i. **Brandon Peterson** a-78p(part). **Whilce Portacio** c/a(p)-63-69. **Quesada** c(p)-78, 79, 82. **Simonson** c/a-10, 11, 13-15, 17-19, 21, 23-31, 33, 34, 36-39; c-16. **Paul Smith** a-44-48; c-43. **Stroman** a(p)-71-75, 77, 78(part), 80, 81; c(p)-71-77, 80, 81, 84.*

X-FORCE (Also see The New Mutants #100 & 1992 X-Men Annuals)
Aug, 1991 - Present ($1.00/$1.25, color)
Marvel Comics
1-($1.50, 52 pgs.)-Sealed in plastic bag with 1 of 5 diff. Marvel Universe trading cards inside(1 each); 6th app. of X-Force; Liefeld-c/a begins, ends #9 .80 2.00 4.00
1-1st printing with Cable trading card inside 1.20 3.00 6.00
1-2nd printing; metallic ink-c (no bag or card) .30 .75 1.50
2,3: 2-Deadpool-c/story. 3-New Brotherhood of Evil Mutants app. .40 1.00 2.00
4-Spider-Man x-over; cont'd from Spider-Man #16; reads sideways .60 1.50 3.00
5-10: 6-Last $1.00-c. 7,9-Weapon X back-ups. 10-Weapon X full-length story (part 3). 11-1st Weapon Prime (cameo) .30 .75 1.50
11-15,19-22: 15-Cable leaves X-Force .60 1.25
16-18-($1.50)-Polybagged w/trading card in each .40 1.00 2.00
Annual 1 (1992, $2.25, 68 pgs.)-1st Greg Capullo-a(p) on X-Force .45 1.15 2.25
NOTE: ***Capullo** a(p)-15-19, Annual 1; c(p)-14-17. **Rob Liefeld** a-1-7, 9p; c-1-9, 110; plots-1-12. **Mignola** a-8p.*

XMAS COMICS
12?/1941 - No. 2, 12?/1942 (324 pgs.) (50 cents)
No. 3, 12?/1943 - No. 7, 12?/1947 (132 pgs.)
Fawcett Publications GD25 FN65 VF82 NM94
1-Contains Whiz #21, Capt. Marvel #3, Bulletman #2, Wow #3, & Master #18; Raboy back-c. Not rebound, remaindered comics; printed at same time as originals 170.00 500.00 1000.00 1700.00
(Estimated up to 110 total copies exist, 5 in NM/Mint)
GD25 FN65 NM94
2-Capt. Marvel, Bulletman, Spy Smasher 83.00 250.00 500.00
3-7-Funny animals 30.00 90.00 180.00

XMAS COMICS
No. 4, Dec, 1949 - No. 7, Dec, 1952 (50 cents, 196 pgs.)

The X-Men #6, © MEG

The X-Men #18, © MEG

The X-Men #53, © MEG

	GD25	FN65	NM94
Fawcett Publications			
4-Contains Whiz, Master, Tom Mix, Captain Marvel, Nyoka, Capt. Video, Bob Colt, Monte Hale, Hot Rod Comics, & Battle Stories. Not rebound, remaindered comics; printed at the same time as originals	37.00	110.00	220.00
5-7-Same as above. 7-Bill Boyd app.; stocking on cover is made of green felt (novelty cover)	32.00	95.00	190.00

XMAS FUNNIES
No date (paper cover) (36 pgs.?)
Kinney Shoes (Giveaway)

	GD25	FN65	NM94
Contains 1933 color strip-r; Mutt & Jeff, etc.	29.00	85.00	200.00

X-MEN, THE (See Amazing Adventures, Capt. America #172, Classic X-Men, Giant-Size..., Heroes For Hope..., Kitty Pryde &..., Marvel & DC Present, Marvel Fanfare, Marvel Graphic Novel, Marvel Super Heroes, Marvel Team-up, Marvel Triple Action, Nightcrawler, Official Marvel Index To..., Special Edition..., The Uncanny..., X-Factor & X-Terminators)

X-MEN, THE (X-Men #94-141; The Uncanny X-Men on-c only #114-141; The Uncanny X-Men #142 on)
Sept, 1963 - No. 66, Mar, 1970; No. 67, Dec, 1970 - Present
Marvel Comics Group

	GD25	FN65	NM94
1-Origin/1st app. X-Men; 1st app. Magneto & Professor X	360.00	1075.00	2150.00
2-1st app. The Vanisher	115.00	345.00	800.00
3-1st app. The Blob	50.00	150.00	350.00
4-1st Quick Silver & Scarlet Witch & Brotherhood of the Evil Mutants; 1st app. Toad; Magneto app.	38.00	115.00	265.00
5	27.00	80.00	185.00
6-10: 6-Sub-Mariner app. 8-1st Unus the Untouchable. 9-Early Avengers app.; 1st Lucifer. 10-1st S.A. app. Ka-Zar	20.00	60.00	140.00
11,13-15: 11-1st app. The Stranger. 14-1st app. Sentinels. 15-Origin Beast	14.00	43.00	100.00
12-Origin Prof. X; Origin/1st app. Juggernaut	20.00	60.00	140.00
16-20: 19-1st app. The Mimic	10.00	30.00	60.00
21-27,29,30: 27-Re-enter The Mimic (r-in #75)	8.35	25.00	50.00
28-1st app. The Banshee (r-in #76)	10.00	30.00	70.00
31-34,36,37,39,40: 39-New costumes	5.85	17.50	35.00
35-Spider-Man x-over (8/67)(r-in #83); 1st app. Changeling	10.00	30.00	60.00
38-Origins of the X-Men series begins, ends #57	9.15	27.50	55.00
41-49: 42-Death of Prof. X (Changeling disguised as). 44-1st S.A. app. G.A. Red Raven. 49-Steranko-c; 1st Polaris	4.70	14.00	28.00
50,51-Steranko-c/a	5.85	17.50	35.00
52	4.00	11.00	22.00
53-Barry Smith-c/a (1st comic book work)	5.85	17.50	35.00
54,55-B. Smith-c. 54-1st app. Alex Summers who later becomes Havok. 55-Summers discovers he has mutant powers	5.00	15.00	30.00
56,57,59-63,65-Neal Adams-a(p). 56-Intro Havoc without costume. 65-Return of Professor X	5.35	16.00	32.00
58-1st app. Havoc in costume; N. Adams-a(p)	8.35	25.00	50.00
64-1st app. Sunfire	5.85	17.50	35.00
66-Last new story w/original X-Men; battles Hulk	3.60	9.00	18.00
67-70,72: (52 pgs.). 67-Reprints begin, end #93	3.00	7.50	15.00
71,73-93: 71-Last 15 cent issue. 73-86-r/#25-38 w/new-c. 87-93-r/#39-45 with covers	2.60	6.50	13.00
94(8/75)-New X-Men begin (See Giant-Size X-Men for 1st app.); Colossus, Nightcrawler, Thunderbird, Storm, Wolverine, & Banshee join; Angel, Marvel Girl, & Iceman resign	26.00	77.00	180.00
95-Death of Thunderbird	7.50	22.50	45.00
96-99: 98,99-25 cent & 30 cent-c exist	5.85	17.50	35.00
100-Old vs. New X-Men; part origin Phoenix; last 25 cent issue (8/76)	6.35	19.00	38.00
101-Phoenix origin concludes	5.00	15.00	30.00
102-107: 102-Origin Storm. 104-1st app. Starjammers (brief cameo); Magneto-c/story. 106-Old vs. New X-Men; 30 & 35 cent issues exist. 107-1st full app. Starjammers; last 30 cent issue	3.00	7.50	15.00
108-Byrne-a begins (see Marvel Team-Up #53)	5.00	15.00	30.00
109-1st Vindicator	4.20	12.50	25.00
110,111: 110-Phoenix joins	3.00	7.50	15.00
112-119: 117-Origin Professor X	2.40	6.00	12.00
120-1st app. Alpha Flight (cameo), story line begins; last 35 cent issue	4.70	14.00	28.00
121-1st full Alpha Flight story	5.00	15.00	30.00
122-128: 123-Spider-Man x-over. 124-Colossus becomes Proletarian	2.20	5.50	11.00
129-Intro Kitty Pryde; last Banshee	2.60	6.50	13.00
130-1st app. The Dazzler by Byrne	2.80	7.00	14.00
131-135: 131-Dazzler app. 132-1st White Queen. 133-Wolverine app. 134-Phoenix becomes Dark Phoenix	2.00	5.00	10.00
136,138: 138-Dazzler app.; Cyclops leaves	1.70	4.25	8.50
137-Giant; death of Phoenix	2.20	5.50	11.00

X-Men #104, © MEG

X-Men #130, © MEG

The Uncanny X-Men #173, © MEG

The Uncanny X-Men #258, © MEG

The Uncanny X-Men Annual #15, © MEG

X-Men #1 (10/91, cover c), © MEG

	GD25	FN65	NM94
139-Alpha Flight app.; Kitty Pryde joins; new costume for Wolverine	4.00	10.00	20.00
140-Alpha Flight app.	3.60	9.00	18.00
141-Intro Future X-Men & The New Brotherhood of Evil Mutants; 1st app. Rachel (Phoenix II); death of Frank Richards	4.00	10.00	20.00
142-Rachel app.; deaths of Wolverine, Storm & Colossus	3.00	7.50	15.00
143-Last Byrne issue	1.40	3.50	7.00
144-150: 144-Man-Thing app. 145-Old X-Men app. 148-Spider-Woman, Dazzler app. 150-Double size	1.20	3.00	6.00
151-157,159-161,163,164: 161-Origin Magneto. 163-Origin Binary. 164-1st app. Binary as Carol Danvers	.80	2.00	4.00
158-1st app. Rogue in X-Men (see Avengers Annual #10)	1.00	2.50	5.00
162-Wolverine solo story	1.60	4.00	8.00
165-Paul Smith-c/a begins, ends #175	1.20	3.00	6.00
166-Double size; Paul Smith-a	1.00	2.50	5.00
167-170: 167-New Mutants app. (3/83); same date as New Mutants #1; 1st meeting w/X-Men; ties into N.M. #3,4; Starjammers app.; contains skin "Tattooz" decals. 168-1st app. Madelyne Pryor (last pg. cameo) in X-Men (see Avengers Annual #10)	.80	2.00	4.00
171-Rogue joins X-Men; Simonson-c/a	1.40	3.50	7.00
172-174: 172,173-Two part Wolverine solo story. 173-Two cover variations, blue & black. 174-Phoenix cameo	.80	2.00	4.00
175-(52 pgs.)-Anniversary issue; Phoenix returns	1.00	2.50	5.00
176-185: 181-Sunfire app. 182-Rogue solo story. 184-1st app. Forge	.60	1.50	3.00
186-Double-size; Barry Smith/Austin-a	.80	2.00	4.00
187-192,194-199: 190,191-Spider-Man & Avengers x-over. 195-Power Pack x-over	.60	1.50	3.00
193-Double size; 100th app. New X-Men; 1st app. Warpath in costume (see New Mutants #16)	1.00	2.50	5.00
200-(12/85, $1.25, 52 pgs.)	1.60	4.00	8.00
201-(1/86)-1st app. Cable? (as baby Nathan; see X-Factor #1); 1st Whilce Portacio-c/a(i) on X-Men (guest artist)	4.00	10.00	20.00
202-204,206-209: 204-Nightcrawler solo story; Portacio-a(i). 207-Wolverine/ Phoenix story	1.00	2.50	5.00
205-Wolverine solo story by Barry Smith	3.00	7.50	15.00
210,211-Mutant Massacre begins	3.60	9.00	18.00
212,213-Wolverine vs. Sabretooth (Mutant Mass.)	5.35	16.00	32.00
214-221,223,224: 219-Havok joins (7/87); brief app. Sabretooth	.80	2.00	4.00
222-Wolverine battles Sabretooth	3.00	7.50	15.00
225-227: Fall Of The Mutants. 226-Double size	1.60	4.00	8.00
228-239,241: 229-$1.00 begin	.80	2.00	4.00
240-Sabretooth app.	1.00	2.50	5.00
242-Double size, X-Factor app., Inferno tie-in	.80	2.00	4.00
243,245-247: 245-Rob Liefeld-a(p)	.60	1.50	3.00
244-1st app. Jubilee	1.60	4.00	8.00
248-1st Jim Lee art on X-Men (1989)	4.70	14.00	28.00
248-2nd printing (1992, $1.25)	.30	.75	1.50
249-252: 252-Lee-c	.40	1.00	2.00
253-255: 253-All new X-men begin. 254-Lee-c	.80	2.00	4.00
256,257-Jim Lee-c/a begins	2.00	5.00	10.00
258-Wolverine solo story; Lee-c/a	2.40	6.00	12.00
259-Sylvestri-a; no Lee-a	1.00	2.50	5.00
260-265-No Lee-a. 260,261,264-Lee-c	.40	1.00	2.00
266-1st full app. Gambit (see Ann. #14)-No Lee-a	4.20	12.50	25.00
267-Jim Lee-c/a resumes	2.40	6.00	12.00
268-Capt. America, Black Widow & Wolverine team-up; Lee-a	4.00	10.00	20.00
269-Lee-a	1.20	3.00	6.00
270-X-Tinction Agenda begins	2.00	5.00	10.00
270-Gold 2nd printing	.60	1.50	3.00

	GD25	FN65	NM94
271,272-X-Tinction Agenda	1.40	3.50	7.00
273-New Mutants (Cable) & X-Factor x-over; Golden, Byrne & Lee part pencils	1.20	3.00	6.00
274	1.00	2.50	5.00
275-($1.50, 52 pgs.)-Tri-fold-c by Jim Lee (p)	1.20	3.00	6.00
275-Gold 2nd printing	.40	1.00	2.00
276-280: 277-Last Lee-c/a. 280-X-Factor x-over	.30	.75	1.50
281-New team begins (Storm, Archangel, Colossus, Iceman & Marvel Girl); Whilce Portacio-c/a begins; Byrne scripts begin; wraparound-c (white logo)	1.20	3.00	6.00
281-2nd printing with red metallic ink logo w/o UPC box ($1.00-c); does not say 2nd printing inside		.50	1.00
282-1st app. Bishop (cover & 1 pg. cameo)	1.20	3.00	6.00
282-Gold 2nd printing ($1.00-c)		.50	1.00
283-1st full app. Bishop	1.80	4.50	9.00
284-293,297-299: 284-Last $1.00-c. 286,287-Lee plots. 287-Bishop joins team. 288-Lee/Portacio plots. 290-Last Portacio-c/a. 294-Brandon Peterson-a(p) begins (#292 is 1st Peterson-c)		.60	1.25
294-296 ($1.50)-X-Cutioner's Song x-overs; polybagged w/trading card in each; all have Peterson/Austin-c/a	.40	1.00	2.00
300-($3.95, 68 pgs.)-Holo-grafx foil-c; Magneto app.	.80	2.00	4.00
Special 1(12/70)-Kirby-c/a; origin The Stranger	5.85	17.50	35.00
Special 2(11/71)	5.00	15.00	30.00
Annual 3(1979, 52pgs.)-New story; Miller/Austin-c	2.40	6.00	12.00
Annual 4(1980, 52 pgs.)-Dr. Strange guest stars	1.40	3.50	7.00
Annual 5(1981, 52 pgs.)	1.00	2.50	5.00
Annual 6(1982, 52 pgs.)	.80	2.00	4.00
Annual 7,8: 7-(1983, 52 pgs.). 8-(1984, 52 pgs.)	.80	2.00	4.00
Annual 9(1985)-New Mutants x-over cont'd from New Mutants Special Ed. #1; Art Adams-a	2.40	6.00	12.00
Annual 10(1986)-Art Adams-a	2.00	5.00	10.00
Annual 11(1987)	.60	1.50	3.00
Annual 12(1988, $1.75)-Evolutionary War app.	.80	2.00	4.00
Annual 13(1989, $2.00, 68 pgs.)-Atlantis Attacks	.60	1.50	3.00
Annual 14(1990, $2.00, 68 pgs.)-1st app. Gambit (minor app., 5 pgs.); Fantastic Four, New Mutants (Cable) & X-Factor x-over; Arthur Adams-c/a(p)	1.60	4.00	8.00
Annual 15 (1991, $2.00, 68 pgs.)-4 pg. origin; New Mutants x-over; 4 pg. Wolverine solo back-up story; 4th app. X-Force cont'd from New Warriors Annual #1	.80	2.00	4.00
Annual 16 (1992, $2.25, 68 pgs.)	.45	1.15	2.25

NOTE: ***Art Adams*** *a-Annual 9, 10p, 12p, 14p; c-218p.* ***Neal Adams*** *a-56-63p, 65p; c-56-63.* ***Adkins*** *c-34.* ***Austin*** *a-108i, 109i, 111-117i, 119-143i, 186i, 204i, 228i, Annual 3i, 7i, 9i, 13; c-109-111i, 114-122i, 123, 124-141i, 142, 143, 196i, 204i, 228i, 294i, Annual 3i.* ***J. Buscema*** *c-42, 43p, 45p.* ***Byrne*** *a(p)-108, 109, 111-143, 273; c(p)-113-116, 127, 129, 131-141.* ***Ditko*** *r-86, 90.* ***Everett*** *c-73.* ***Golden*** *a-273, Annual 7p.* ***Guice*** *a-216p, 217p.* ***G. Kane*** *c(p)-33, 74-76, 79, 80, 94, 95.* ***Kirby*** *a(p)-1-17 (#12-17, 24, 27-29, 32, 67r-layouts); c(p)-1-22, 25, 26, 30, 31, 35.* ***Layton*** *a-105i; c-112i, 113i.* ***Jim Lee*** *a(p)-248, 256-258, 267-277; c(p)-252, 254, 256-261, 264, 267, 270, 275-277, 286.* ***Perez*** *a-Annual 3p; c(p)-112, 128, Annual 3.* ***Peterson/Austin*** *c/a-294-297.* ***Whilce Portacio*** *a(p)-281-286, 289, 290; c-281-285p, 289p, 290.* ***Roussos*** *a-84i.* ***Simonson*** *a-171p; c-171, 217.* ***B. Smith*** *a-53, 186p, 198p, 205, 214; c-53-55, 186p, 198, 205, 212, 214, 216.* ***Paul Smith*** *a(p)-165-170, 172-175, 278; c-165-170, 172-175, 278.* ***Sparling*** *a-78p.* ***Steranko*** *a-50p, 51p; c-49-51.* ***Sutton*** *a-106i.* ***Toth*** *a-12p, 67p(r).* ***Tuska*** *a-40-42i, 44-46p, 88i(r); c-39-41, 77p, 78p.* ***Williamson*** *a-202i, 203i, 211i; c-202i, 203i, 206i.* ***Wood*** *c-14i.*

X-MEN (2nd series)
Oct, 1991 - Present ($1.00-$1.25, color)
Marvel Comics

	GD25	FN65	NM94
1-($1.50, 52 pgs.)-Jim Lee-c/a begins; new team begins (Cyclops, Beast, Wolverine, Gambit, Psylocke & Rogue); new Uncanny X-Men & Magneto app.; cover 1a-Beast & Storm-c	.40	1.00	2.00
1-b-Colossus & Gambit-c	.40	1.00	2.00
1-c-Wolverine & Cyclops-c	.40	1.00	2.00
1-d-Magneto-c	.40	1.00	2.00

1-e-($3.95)-Double gate-fold-c consisting of all four covers from 1a-d by Jim Lee; contains all pin-ups from #1a-d plus inside-c foldout poster; no

ads; printed on coated stock 1.00 2.50 5.00
2 .40 1.00 2.00
3,5,7: 5-Byrne scripts .30 .75 1.50
4-Wolverine back to old yellow costume (same date as Wolverine #50); last $1.00-c .40 1.00 2.00
6-Sabretooth-c/story .40 1.00 2.00
8-Gambit vs. Bishop-c/story; last Lee-a; Ghost Rider cameo cont'd in Ghost Rider #26 .40 1.00 2.00
9-Wolverine vs. Ghost Rider; cont'd/G.R. #26 .40 1.00 2.00
10-Return of Longshot .40 1.00 2.00
11-13,17-20: 12,13-Art Thibert-c/a .60 1.25
14-16-($1.50)-X-Cutioner's Song x-overs; polybagged with trading card in each. 14-Andy Kubert-c/a begins .40 1.00 2.00
Annual 1 (1992, $2.25, 68 pgs.)-Lee-c & layouts .45 1.15 2.25

NOTE: ***Jim Lee** a-5-11p; c-5p, 6p, 7, 8, 9p, 10, 11p. **Art Thibert** a-6-9i, 12, 13; c-6i, 12, 13.*

X-MEN ADVENTURES (TV)
Nov, 1992 - Present ($1.25, color)
Marvel Comics

1-Wolverine, Cyclops, Jubilee, Rogue, Gambit .30 .75 1.50
2-8 .60 1.25

X-MEN/ALPHA FLIGHT
Dec, 1985 - No. 2, Dec, 1985 ($1.50, mini-series)
Marvel Comics Group

1,2: 1-Intro The Berserkers; Paul Smith-a .70 1.75 3.50

X-MEN AND THE MICRONAUTS, THE
Jan, 1984 - No. 4, April, 1984 (Mini-series)
Marvel Comics Group

1-4: Guice-c/a(p) in all .30 .75 1.50

X-MEN CLASSIC (Formerly Classic X-Men)
No. 46, Apr, 1990 - Present ($1.25, color)
Marvel Comics

46-69,71-84: Reprints from X-Men. 54-($1.25, 52 pgs.). 57,60-63,65-Russell-c(i); 62-r/X-Men #158(Rogue). 66-r/#162(Wolverine). 69-Begins-r of Paul Smith issues (#165 on) .60 1.25
70-($1.75, 52 pgs.)-r/X-Men #166 .35 .90 1.75

X-MEN CLASSICS
Dec, 1983 - No. 3, Feb, 1984 ($2.00; Baxter paper)
Marvel Comics Group

1-3: X-Men-r by Neal Adams .60 1.50 3.00

X-MEN SPOTLIGHT ON... STARJAMMERS (Marvel)(Value: cover or less)(See X-Men #104)

X-MEN VS. THE AVENGERS, THE
Apr, 1987 - No. 4, July, 1987 ($1.50, mini-series, Baxter paper)
Marvel Comics Group

1 .70 1.75 3.50
2-4 .50 1.25 2.50

X-O MANOWAR
Feb, 1992 - Present ($1.95/$2.25, color, high quality)
Valiant

1-Barry Windsor-Smith/Layton-a; Layton-c 5.00 15.00 30.00
2-B. Smith/Layton-c; Layton part inks 3.00 7.50 15.00
3-Layton-c(i) 2.00 5.00 10.00
4-6: 5-B. Smith-c; last $1.95-c. 6-Ditko-a(p) 1.20 3.00 6.00
7,8-Unity x-overs. 7-Miller-c. 8-Simonson-c 1.00 2.50 5.00
9,10 .70 1.75 3.50
11-18: 14-Turok app. .45 1.10 2.25

NOTE: ***Layton** a-1i, 2i(part); c-1, 2i, 3i, 6i. **Reese** a-4i(part).*

X-TERMINATORS
Oct, 1988 - No. 4, Jan, 1989 ($1.00, color, mini-series)
Marvel Comics

1-1st app.; X-Men/X-Factor tie-in; Williamson-i .60 1.50 3.00

GD25 FN65 NM94

2 .35 .90 1.75
3,4 .60 1.25

X, THE MAN WITH THE X-RAY EYES (See Movie Comics)

X-VENTURE
July, 1947 - No. 2, Nov, 1947 (Super heroes)
Victory Magazines Corp.

1-Atom Wizard, Mystery Shadow, Lester Trumble begin 47.00 140.00 280.00
2 30.00 90.00 180.00

XYR (See Eclipse Graphic Album Series #21)

YAK YAK (See 4-Color #1186, 1348)

YAKKY DOODLE & CHOPPER (TV) (Also see Spotlight #3)
Dec, 1962 (Hanna-Barbera)
Gold Key

1 4.20 12.50 25.00

YALTA TO KOREA (Also see Korea My Home)
1952 (8 pgs.) (Giveaway) (paper cover)
M. Phillip Corp. (Republican National Committee)

nn-Anti-communist propaganda book 14.00 43.00 100.00

YANG (See House of Yang)
Nov, 1973 - No. 13, May, 1976; V14#14, Sept, 1985 - No. 17, Jan, 1986
Charlton Comics

1-Origin .60 1.50 3.00
2-13(1976) .30 .75 1.50
14-17(1986) .50 1.00
3,10,11(Modern Comics-r, 1977) .50 1.00

YANKEE COMICS
Sept, 1941 - No. 4, Mar, 1942
Harry 'A' Chesler

1-Origin The Echo, The Enchanted Dagger, Yankee Doodle Jones, The Firebrand, & The Scarlet Sentry; Black Satan app. 62.00 188.00 375.00
2-Origin Johnny Rebel; Major Victory app.; Barry Kuda begins 38.00 115.00 230.00
3,4 32.00 95.00 190.00
4 (nd, 1940s; 7-1/4x5", 68 pgs, distr. to the service)-Foxy Grandpa, Tom, Dick & Harry, Impy, Ace & Deuce, Dot & Dash, Ima Slooth by Jack Cole (Remington Morse publ.) 1.70 5.00 12.00

YANKS IN BATTLE
Sept, 1956 - No. 4, Dec, 1956; 1963
Quality Comics Group

1-Cuidera-c(i) 5.00 15.00 30.00
2-4: Cuidera-c(i) 3.00 7.50 15.00
I.W. Reprint #3(1963)-r/#?; exist? .60 1.50 3.00

YARDBIRDS, THE (G. I. Joe's Sidekicks)
Summer, 1952
Ziff-Davis Publishing Co.

1-By Bob Oskner 5.85 17.50 35.00

YARNS OF YELLOWSTONE
1972 (36 pages) (50 cents)
World Color Press

nn-Illustrated by Bill Chapman .60 1.50 3.00

YELLOW CLAW (Also see Giant Size Master of Kung Fu)
Oct, 1956 - No. 4, April, 1957
Atlas Comics (MjMC)

1-Origin by Joe Maneely 47.00 140.00 325.00
2-Kirby-a 36.00 107.00 250.00
3,4-Kirby-a; 4-Kirby/Severin-a 31.00 92.00 215.00

NOTE: ***Everett** c-3. **Maneely** c-1. **Reinman** a-2i, 3. **Severin** c-2, 4.*

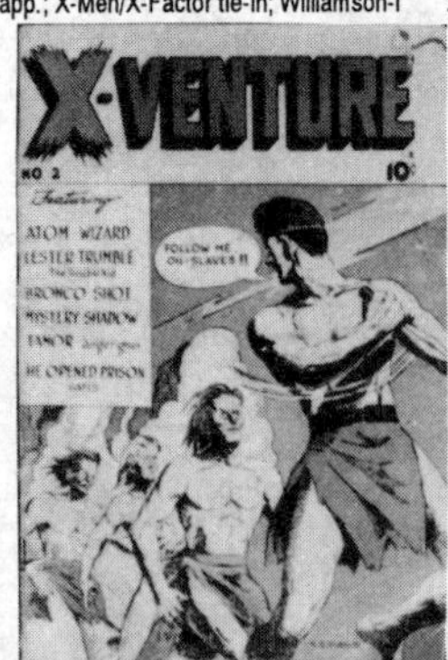

X-Venture #2, © Victory Mag.

Yakky Doodle & Chopper #1, © Hanna-Barbera

Yellow Claw #2, © MEG

Yellowjacket Comics #1, © F. Comunale

Yogi Bear #5 (Dell), © Hanna-Barbera

Young Allies Comics #6, © MEG

	GD25	FN65	NM94

YELLOWJACKET COMICS (Jack in the Box #11 on)(See TNT Comics)
Sept, 1944 - No. 10, June, 1946
E. Levy/Frank Comunale/Charlton

	GD25	FN65	NM94
1-Origin Yellowjacket; Diana, the Huntress begins; E.A. Poe's "The Black Cat" adaptation	28.00	85.00	170.00
2	17.00	50.00	100.00
3,5	15.00	45.00	90.00
4-E.A. Poe's "Fall Of The House Of Usher" adaptation; Palais-a	17.00	50.00	100.00
6-10: 1,3,4,6-10-Have stories narrated by old witch in "Tales of Terror"	13.00	40.00	80.00

YELLOWSTONE KELLY (See 4-Color #1056)

YELLOW SUBMARINE (See Movie Comics)

YIN FEI THE CHINESE NINJA (Leung)(Value: cover or less)

YOGI BEAR (TV) (Hanna-Barbera)
No. 1067, 12-2/59-60 - No. 9, 7-9/62; No. 10, 10/62 - No. 42, 10/70
Dell Publishing Co./Gold Key No. 10 on

	GD25	FN65	NM94
4-Color 1067 (#1)	10.00	30.00	60.00
4-Color 1104,1162 (5-7/61)	6.70	20.00	40.00
4(8-9/61) - 6(12-1/61-62)	5.00	15.00	30.00
4-Color 1271(11/61)	5.00	15.00	30.00
4-Color 1349(1/62)-Photo-c	10.00	30.00	60.00
7(2-3/62) - 9(7-9/62)-Last Dell	5.00	15.00	30.00
10(10/62-G.K.), 11(1/63)-titled "Yogi Bear Jellystone Jollies"-80 pgs.; 11-Xmas-c	3.75	11.50	30.00
12(4/63), 14-20	4.00	10.00	20.00
13(7/63)-Surprise Party, 68 pgs.	4.70	14.00	28.00
21-30	2.40	6.00	12.00
31-42	1.60	4.00	8.00
Giveaway ('84, '86)-City of Los Angeles, "Creative First Aid" & "Earthquake Preparedness for Children"	.40	1.00	2.00

YOGI BEAR (See Dell Giant #41, Kite Fun Book, March of Comics #253, 265, 279, 291, 309, 319, 337, 344, Movie Comics under "Hey There It's..." & Whitman Comic Books)

YOGI BEAR (TV)
Nov, 1970 - No. 35, Jan, 1976 (Hanna-Barbera)
Charlton Comics

	GD25	FN65	NM94
1	3.60	9.00	18.00
2-6,8-35: 28-31-partial-r	2.00	5.00	10.00
7-Summer Fun (Giant, 52 pgs.)	2.40	6.00	12.00

YOGI BEAR (TV)(See The Flintstones, 3rd series & Spotlight #1)
Nov, 1977 - No. 9, Mar, 1979 (Hanna-Barbera)
Marvel Comics Group

	GD25	FN65	NM94
1-Flintstones begin		.60	1.20
2-9		.50	1.00

YOGI BEAR (TV)
Sept, 1992 - Present ($1.25, color)
Harvey Comics

	GD25	FN65	NM94
V2#1,2		.65	1.25
...Big Book V2#1,2: 1-(11/92, $1.95, 52 pgs)	.40	1.00	2.00
...Giant Size V2#1,2: 1-(10/92, $2.25, 68 pgs.)	.45	1.15	2.25

YOGI BEAR'S EASTER PARADE (See The Funtastic World of Hanna-Barbera #2)

YOGI BERRA (Baseball hero)
1951 (Yankee catcher)
Fawcett Publications

	GD25	FN65	NM94
nn-Photo-c	43.00	130.00	300.00

YOSEMITE SAM (...& Bugs Bunny)
Dec, 1970 - No. 81, Feb, 1984
Gold Key/Whitman

	GD25	FN65	NM94
1	2.00	5.00	10.00
2-10	.80	2.00	4.00
11-30	.60	1.50	3.00
31-81: 81-r(1/3)	.40	1.00	2.00

(See March of Comics #363, 380, 392)

YOUNG ALLIES COMICS (All-Winners #21; see Kid Komics #2)
Summer, 1941 - No. 20, Oct, 1946
Timely Comics (USA 1-7/NPI 8,9/YAI 10-20)

	GD25	FN65	VF82	NM94
1-Origin/1st app. The Young Allies; 1st meeting of Captain America & Human Torch; Red Skull app.; S&K-c/splash; Hitler-c	400.00	1200.00	2200.00	3200.00

(Estimated up to 165 total copies exist, 9 in NM/Mint)

	GD25	FN65	NM94
2-Captain America & Human Torch app.; Simon & Kirby-c	150.00	450.00	900.00
3-Fathertime, Captain America & Human Torch app.	121.00	362.00	725.00
4-The Vagabond & Red Skull, Capt. America, Human Torch app.	125.00	375.00	750.00
5-Captain America & Human Torch app.	67.00	200.00	400.00
6-10: 9-Hitler, Tojo, Mussolini-c. 10-Origin Tommy Tyme & Clock of Ages; ends #19	54.00	162.00	325.00
11-20: 12-Classic decapitation story	42.00	125.00	250.00

NOTE: *Brodsky* c-15. *Gabrielle* c-3, 4. *S&K* c-1, 2. *Schomburg* c-5-14, 16-19. *Shores* c-20.

YOUNG ALL-STARS (DC)(Value: cover or less)

YOUNGBLOOD (See Megaton Explosion)
Apr, 1992 - No. 4, 1992 ($2.50, color, mini-series)
Image Comics

	GD25	FN65	NM94
1-Liefeld-c/a/scripts in all; flip book format with 2 trading cards	1.40	3.50	7.00
1-2nd printing	.50	1.25	2.50
2-1st app. Shadowhawk in solo back-up story; 2 trading cards inside; flip book format	1.00	2.50	5.00
2-2nd printing (1.95)	.40	1.00	2.00
3-Contains 2 trading cards inside (flip book); 1st app. Supreme in back-up story	.40	1.25	2.50
4-Glow-in-the-dark-c w/2 trading cards; 1st app. Dale Keown's The Pitt	.40	1.25	2.50
0-(8/92)-Contains 2 trading cards	.40	1.25	2.50

YOUNG BRIDES
Sept-Oct, 1952 - No. 30, Nov-Dec, 1956 (Photo-c: 1-3)
Feature/Prize Publications

	GD25	FN65	NM94
V1#1-Simon & Kirby-a	11.50	34.00	80.00
2-S&K-a	6.70	20.00	40.00
3-6-S&K-a	5.85	17.50	35.00
V2#1,3-7,10-12 (#7-18)-S&K-a	4.70	14.00	28.00
2,8,9-No S&K-a	2.40	6.00	12.00
V3#1-3(#19-21)-Last precode (3-4/55)	2.00	5.00	10.00
4,6(#22,24), V4#1,3(#25,27)	1.60	4.00	8.00
V3#5(#23)-Meskin-c	2.40	6.00	12.00
V4#2(#26)-All S&K issue	4.70	14.00	28.00
V4#4(#28)-S&K-a, V4#5,6(#29,30)	3.60	9.00	18.00

YOUNG DEATH (Fleetway/Quality)(Value: cover or less)

YOUNG DR. MASTERS (See The Adventures of Young Dr. Masters)

YOUNG DOCTORS, THE
January, 1963 - No. 6, Nov, 1963
Charlton Comics

	GD25	FN65	NM94
V1#1	1.20	3.00	6.00
2-6	.60	1.50	3.00

YOUNG EAGLE
12/50 - No. 10, 6/52; No. 3, 7/56 - No. 5, 4/57 (Photo-c: 1-10)

	GD25	FN65	NM94

Fawcett Publications/Charlton

	GD25	FN65	NM94
1	11.00	32.00	75.00
2	6.35	19.00	38.00
3-9	5.00	15.00	30.00
10-Origin Thunder, Young Eagle's Horse	4.00	12.00	24.00
3-5(Charlton)-Formerly Sherlock Holmes?	3.00	7.50	15.00

YOUNG HEARTS
Nov, 1949 - No. 2, Feb, 1950
Marvel Comics (SPC)

	GD25	FN65	NM94
1-Photo-c	6.70	20.00	40.00
2	4.20	12.50	25.00

YOUNG HEARTS IN LOVE
1964
Super Comics

	GD25	FN65	NM94
17,18: 17-r/Young Love V5#6 (4-5/62)	.60	1.60	3.00

YOUNG HEROES (Formerly Forbidden Worlds #34)
No. 35, Feb-Mar, 1955 - No. 37, June-July, 1955
American Comics Group (Titan)

	GD25	FN65	NM94
35-37-Frontier Scout	5.35	16.00	32.00

YOUNG INDIANA JONES CHRONICLES, THE
Feb, 1992 - Present ($2.50, color)
Dark Horse Comics

	GD25	FN65	NM94
1-12: Dan Barry scripts in all	.50	1.25	2.50

NOTE: ***Dan Barry** a(p)-1, 2, 5, 6, 10; c-1-10. **Morrow** a-3, 4, 5p, 6p. **Springer** a-1i, 2i.*

YOUNG INDIANA JONES CHRONICLES, THE
1992 - Present ($3.95, color, squarebound, 68 pgs.)
Hollywood Comics (Disney)

	GD25	FN65	NM94
1-3: 1-r/YIJC #1,2 by D. Horse. 2-r/#3,4. 3-r/#5,6	.80	2.00	4.00

YOUNG KING COLE (Becomes Criminals on the Run)
Fall, 1945 - V3#12, July, 1948
Premium Group/Novelty Press

	GD25	FN65	NM94
V1#1-Toni Gayle begins	12.00	36.00	85.00
2	7.50	22.50	45.00
3-6	5.85	17.50	35.00
V2#1-7(7/47)	4.70	14.00	28.00
V3#1,3-6,12: 5-McWilliams-c/a	4.00	11.00	22.00
2-L.B. Cole-a	4.70	14.00	28.00
7-L.B. Cole-c/a	6.35	19.00	38.00
8-11-L.B. Cole-c	5.85	17.50	35.00

YOUNG LAWYERS, THE (TV)
Jan, 1971 - No. 2, April, 1971
Dell Publishing co.

	GD25	FN65	NM94
1,2	2.40	6.00	12.00

YOUNG LIFE (Teen Life #3 on)
Spring, 1945 - No. 2, Summer, 1945
New Age Publ./Quality Comics Group

	GD25	FN65	NM94
1-Skip Homeier, Louis Prima stories	7.50	22.50	45.00
2-Frank Sinatra photo on-c plus story	7.50	22.50	45.00

YOUNG LOVE
2-3/49 - No. 73, 12-1/56-57; V3#5, 2-3/60 - V7#1, 6-7/63
Prize(Feature)Publ.(Crestwood)

	GD25	FN65	NM94
V1#1-S&K-c/a(2)	18.00	54.00	125.00
2-Photo-c begin; S&K-a	10.00	30.00	60.00
3-S&K-a	7.50	22.50	45.00
4-5-Minor S&K-a	5.00	15.00	30.00
V2#1(#7)-S&K-a	7.50	22.50	45.00
2-5(#8-11)-Minor S&K-a	4.00	11.00	22.00
6,8(#12,14)-S&K-c only	4.70	14.00	28.00
7,9-12(#13,15-18)-S&K-c/a	7.50	22.50	45.00
V3#1-4(#19-22)-S&K-c/a	5.00	15.00	30.00
5-7,9-12(#23-25,27-30)-Photo-c resume; S&K-a	4.20	12.50	25.00
8(#26)-No S&K-a	2.80	7.00	14.00
V4#1,6(#31,36)-S&K-a	4.20	12.50	25.00
2-5,7-12(#32-35,37-42)-Minor S&K-a	4.00	10.00	20.00
V5#1-12(#43-54), V6#1-9(#55-63)-Last precode; S&K-a in some	2.80	7.00	14.00
V6#10-12(#64-66)	2.00	5.00	10.00
V7#1-7(#67-73)	1.60	4.00	8.00
V3#5(2-3/60),6(4-5/60)(Formerly All For Love)	1.20	3.00	6.00
V4#1(6-7/60)-6(4-5/61)	1.00	2.50	5.00
V5#1(6-7/61)-6(4-5/62)	1.00	2.50	5.00
V6#1(6-7/62)-6(4-5/63), V7#1	.80	2.00	4.00

NOTE: ***Meskin** a-27, 42. **Powell** a-V4#6. **Severin/Elder** a-V1#3. S&K art not in #53, 57, 58, 61, 63-65. Photo c-V3#5-V5#11.*

YOUNG LOVE
#39, 9-10/63 - #120, Wint./75-76; #121, 10/76 - #126, 7/77
National Periodical Publ.(Arleigh Publ. Corp #49-60)/DC Comics

	GD25	FN65	NM94
39	2.40	6.00	12.00
40-50	1.40	3.50	7.00
51-70: 64-Simon & Kirby-a	1.00	2.50	5.00
71,72,74-77,80	.80	2.00	4.00
73,78,79-Toth-a	.60	1.50	3.00
81-126: 107-114-(100 pgs.)	.30	.75	1.50

NOTE: ***Bolle** a-117. **Colan** a-107r. **Nasser** a-123, 124. **Orlando** a-122. **Simonson** c-125. **Toth** a-73, 78, 79, 122-125r. **Wood** a-107r(4 pgs.).*

YOUNG LOVER ROMANCES (Formerly & becomes Great Lover...)
No. 4, June, 1952 - No. 5, Aug, 1952
Toby Press

	GD25	FN65	NM94
4,5-Photo-c	3.60	9.00	18.00

YOUNG LOVERS (My Secret Life #19 on)(Formerly Brenda Starr?)
No. 16, July, 1956 - No. 18, May, 1957
Charlton Comics

	GD25	FN65	NM94
16,17('56): 16-Marcus Swayze-a	2.80	7.00	14.00
18-Elvis Presley picture-c, text story (biography)(Scarce)	36.00	107.00	250.00

YOUNG MARRIAGE
June, 1950
Fawcett Publications

	GD25	FN65	NM94
1-Powell-a; photo-c	7.50	22.50	45.00

YOUNG MEN (Formerly Cowboy Romances)(...on the Battlefield #12-20 (4/53); ...In Action #21)
No. 4, 6/50 - No. 11, 10/51; No. 12, 12/51 - No. 28, 6/54
Marvel/Atlas Comics (IPC)

	GD25	FN65	NM94
4-(52 pgs.)	10.00	30.00	60.00
5-11	5.85	17.50	35.00
12-23: 15-Colan, Pakula-a	5.00	15.00	30.00
24-Origin Captain America, Human Torch, & Sub-Mariner which are revived thru #28. Red Skull app.	50.00	150.00	350.00
25-28: 25-Romita-c/a	39.00	120.00	275.00

NOTE: ***Berg** a-7, 14, 17, 18, 20; c-17? **Brodsky** c-4-9, 13, 14, 16, 17, 21-25. **Burgos** c-26-28. **Colan** a-14, 15. **Everett** a-18-20. **Heath** a-13, 14. **Maneely** c-10, 12, 15. **Pakula** a-14. **Robinson** c-18. Captain America by **Romita**-#24?, 25, 26?, 27, 28. Human Torch by **Burgos**-#25, 27, 28. Sub-Mariner by **Everett**-#24-28.*

YOUNG REBELS, THE (TV)
January, 1971
Dell Publishing Co.

	GD25	FN65	NM94
1-Photo-c	2.00	5.00	10.00

YOUNG ROMANCE COMICS (The 2nd romance comic)
Sept-Oct, 1947 - V16#4, June-July, 1963 (#1-33: 52 pgs.)
Prize/Headline (Feature Publ.)

	GD25	FN65	NM94
V1#1-S&K-c/a(2)	20.00	60.00	140.00
2-S&K-c/a(2-3)	11.00	32.00	75.00

Young Eagle #6, © FAW

Young King Cole V1#2, © NOVP

Young Men #24, © MEG

Young Romance #43, © PRIZE

Zago, Jungle Prince #1, © FOX

Ziggy Pig-Silly Seal Comics #5, © MEG

	GD25	FN65	NM94
3-6-S&K-c/a(2-3) each	10.00	30.00	60.00
V2#1-6(#7-12)-S&K-c/a(2-3) each	9.15	27.50	55.00
V3#1-3(#13-15): V3#1-Photo-c begin; S&K-a	5.85	17.50	35.00
4-12(#16-24)-Photo-c; S&K-a	5.85	17.50	35.00
V4#1-11(#25-35)-S&K-a	5.00	15.00	30.00
12(#36)-S&K, Toth-a	7.50	22.50	45.00
V5#1-12(#37-48), V6#4-12(#52-60)-S&K-a	5.00	15.00	30.00
V6#1-3(#49-51)-No S&K-a	3.60	9.00	18.00
V7#1-11(#61-71)-S&K-a in most	4.20	12.50	25.00
V7#12(#72), V8#1-3(#73-75)-Last precode (12-1/54-55)-No S&K-a	2.00	5.00	10.00
V8#4(#76, 4-5/55), 5(#77)-No S&K-a	1.80	4.50	9.00
V8#6-8(#78-80, 12-1/55-56)-S&K-a	3.20	8.00	16.00
V9#3,5,6(#81, 2-3/56, 83,84)-S&K-a	3.20	8.00	16.00
4, V10#1(#82,85)-All S&K-a	4.00	11.00	22.00
V10#2-6(#86-90, 10-11/57)-S&K-a	3.20	8.00	16.00
V11#1,2,5,6(#91,92,95,96)-S&K-a	3.20	8.00	16.00
3,4(#93,94), V12#2,4,5(#98,100,101)-No S&K	1.60	4.00	8.00
V12#1,3,6(#97,99,102)-S&K-a	3.20	8.00	16.00
V13#1(#103)-S&K, Powell-a	3.20	8.00	16.00
2-6(#104-108)	1.20	3.00	6.00
V14#1-6, V15#1-6, V16#1-4(#109-124)	1.00	2.50	5.00

*NOTE: **Meskin** a-16, 24(2), 33, 47, 50. **Robinson/Meskin** a-6. **Leonard Starr** a-11. Photo c-13-32, 34-65.*

YOUNG ROMANCE COMICS (Continued from Prize series)
No. 125, Aug-Sept, 1963 - No. 208, Nov-Dec, 1975
National Periodical Publ.(Arleigh Publ. Corp. No. 127)

	GD25	FN65	NM94
125	2.80	7.00	14.00
126-162: 154-Neal Adams-c	1.40	3.50	7.00
163,164-Toth-a	1.20	3.00	6.00
165-196: 170-Michell from Young Love ends; Lily Martin, the Swinger begins	.60	1.50	3.00
197 (100 pgs.)-208	.60	1.50	3.00

YOUR DREAMS (See Strange World of...)

YOUR TRIP TO NEWSPAPERLAND
June, 1955 (12 pgs.; 14x11-1/2")
Philadelphia Evening Bulletin (Printed by Harvey Press)

	GD25	FN65	NM94
nn-Joe Palooka takes kids on tour through newspaper	4.00	11.00	22.00

YOUR UNITED STATES
1946
Lloyd Jacquet Studios

	GD25	FN65	NM94
nn-Used in **SOTI**, pg. 309,310; Sid Greene-a	16.00	48.00	110.00

YOUTHFUL HEARTS (Daring Confessions #4 on)
May, 1952 - No. 3, Sept, 1952
Youthful Magazines

	GD25	FN65	NM94
1-"Monkey on Her Back" swipes E.C. drug story from Shock SuspenStories #12; Doug Wildey-a in all	12.00	36.00	85.00
2,3	10.00	30.00	60.00

YOUTHFUL LOVE (Truthful Love #2)
May, 1950
Youthful Magazines

	GD25	FN65	NM94
1	5.85	17.50	35.00

YOUTHFUL ROMANCES
8-9/49 - No. 5, 4/50; No. 6, 2/51; No. 7, 5/51 - #14, 10/52; #15, 1/53 - #18, 7/53; #5, 9/53 - #8, 5/54
Pix-Parade #1-14/Ribage #15 on

	GD25	FN65	NM94
1-(1st series)-Titled Youthful Love-Romances	11.50	34.00	80.00
2	7.50	22.50	45.00
3-5	5.85	17.50	35.00
6,7,9-14(10/52, Pix-Parade; becomes Daring Love #15); 7-Tony Martin photo on-c	4.70	14.00	28.00
8-Wood-c	11.00	32.00	75.00
15-18 (Ribage)	4.00	11.00	22.00
5(9/53, Ribage)	3.20	8.00	16.00
6,7(#7, 2/54), 8(5/54)	2.80	7.00	14.00

YUPPIES FROM HELL (Marvel) (Value: cover or less) (See Sex, Lies, &..., Son of...)

ZAGO, JUNGLE PRINCE (My Story #5 on)
Sept, 1948 - No. 4, March, 1949
Fox Features Syndicate

	GD25	FN65	NM94
1-Blue Beetle app.; partial-r/Atomic #4 (Toni Luck)	24.00	70.00	165.00
2,3-Kamen-a	17.00	52.00	120.00
4-Baker-c	16.00	48.00	110.00

ZANE GREY'S STORIES OF THE WEST
No. 197, 9/48 - No. 996, 5-7/59; 11/64 (All painted-c)
Dell Publishing Co./Gold Key 11/64

	GD25	FN65	NM94
4-Color 197(#1)(9/48)	9.15	27.50	55.00
4-Color 222,230,236('49)	6.70	20.00	40.00
4-Color 246,255,270,301,314,333,346	4.70	14.00	28.00
4-Color 357,372,395,412,433,449,467,484	4.00	12.00	24.00
4-Color 511-Kinstler-a	4.35	13.00	26.00
4-Color 532,555,583,604,616,632(5/55)	4.00	12.00	24.00
27(9-11/55) - 39(9-11/58)	3.60	9.00	18.00
4-Color 996(5-7/59)	3.60	9.00	18.00
10131-411-(11/64-G.K.)-Nevada; r/4-Color #996	2.00	5.00	10.00

ZANY (Magazine)(Satire)(See Frantic & Ratfink)
Sept, 1958 - No. 4, May, 1959
Candor Publ. Co.

	GD25	FN65	NM94
1-Bill Everett-c	5.85	17.50	35.00
2-4: 4-Everett-c	4.00	11.00	22.00

ZATANNA SPECIAL (DC) (Value: cover or less) (See Adventure Comics #413, Justice League of America #161, Supergirl #1, & World's Finest Comics #274)

ZAZA, THE MYSTIC (Formerly Charlie Chan; This Magazine Is Haunted V2#12 on)
No. 10, April, 1956 - No. 11, Sept, 1956
Charlton Comics

	GD25	FN65	NM94
10,11	6.70	20.00	40.00

ZEGRA JUNGLE EMPRESS (Formerly Tegra)(My Love Life #6 on)
No. 2, Oct, 1948 - No. 5, April, 1949
Fox Features Syndicate

	GD25	FN65	NM94
2	26.00	77.00	180.00
3-5	19.00	57.00	130.00

ZEN, INTERGALACTIC NINJA
Sept, 1992 - Present ($1.25, color)(Formerly a B&W comic by Zen Comics)
Zen Comics/Archie Comics

	GD25	FN65	NM94
1-4: 1-Origin Zen; contains mini-poster		.60	1.25

ZERO PATROL, THE (Continuity) (Value: cover or less)

ZERO TOLERANCE
Oct, 1990 - No. 4, Jan, 1991 ($2.25, color, limited series)
First Comics

	GD25	FN65	NM94
1-4: Tim Vigil-c/a(p) (his 1st color mini-series)	.45	1.15	2.25

ZIGGY PIG-SILLY SEAL COMICS (See Animated Movie-Tunes, Comic Capers, Krazy Komics & Silly Tunes)
Fall, 1944 - No. 6, Fall, 1946
Timely Comics (CmPL)

	GD25	FN65	NM94
1-Vs. the Japs	13.00	40.00	90.00
2	7.50	22.50	45.00

	GD25	FN65	NM94
3-5	6.35	19.00	38.00
6-Infinity-c	9.15	27.50	55.00
I.W. Reprint #1('58)-r/Krazy Komics	.80	2.00	4.00
I.W. Reprint #2,7,8	.60	1.50	3.00

ZIP COMICS
Feb, 1940 - No. 47, Summer, 1944
MLJ Magazines

	GD25	FN65	NM94
1-Origin Kalathar the Giant Man, The Scarlet Avenger, & Steel Sterling; Mr. Satan, Nevada Jones (masked hero) & Zambini, the Miracle Man, War Eagle, Captain Valor begins	200.00	600.00	1200.00
2-Nevada Jones adds mask & horse Blaze	100.00	300.00	600.00
3	75.00	225.00	450.00
4,5	60.00	180.00	360.00
6-9: 9-Last Kalathar & Mr. Satan	50.00	150.00	300.00
10-Inferno, the Flame Breather begins, ends #13	56.00	167.00	335.00
11,12: 11-Inferno without costume	44.00	132.00	265.00
13-17,19: 17-Last Scarlet Avenger	44.00	132.00	265.00
18-Wilbur begins (1st app.)	47.00	142.00	285.00
20-Origin Black Jack (1st app.); Hitler-c	62.00	188.00	375.00
21-26: 25-Last Nevada Jones. 26-Black Witch begins; last Captain Valor	42.00	125.00	250.00
27-Intro. Web	62.00	188.00	375.00
28-Origin Web	62.00	188.00	375.00
29,30: 29-The Hyena app.	33.00	100.00	200.00
31-38: 34-1st Applejack app. 35-Last Zambini, Black Jack. 38-Last Web issue	25.00	75.00	150.00
39-Red Rube begins (origin, 8/43)	25.00	75.00	150.00
40-47: 45-Wilbur ends	18.00	55.00	110.00

NOTE: *Biro a-5, 9, 17; c-3-17.* ***Meskin*** *a-1-3, 5-7, 9, 10, 12, 13, 15, 16 at least.* ***Montana*** *c-29, 30, 32-35.* ***Novick*** *c-18-28, 31. Bondage c-8, 9, 33, 34.* ***Sahle*** *c-37, 38, 40-46.*

ZIP-JET (Hero)
Feb, 1953 - No. 2, Apr-May, 1953
St. John Publishing Co.

	GD25	FN65	NM94
1,2-Rocketman-r from Punch Comics; #1-c from splash in Punch #10	28.00	85.00	170.00

ZIPPY THE CHIMP (CBS TV Presents...)
No. 50, March, 1957; No. 51, Aug, 1957
Pines (Literary Ent.)

	GD25	FN65	NM94
50,51	4.20	12.50	25.00

ZODY, THE MOD ROB
July, 1970
Gold Key

	GD25	FN65	NM94
1	1.40	3.50	7.00

ZOMBIE 3-D (3-D Zone) (Value: cover or less)

ZONE (Dark Horse) (Value: cover or less)

ZOO ANIMALS
No. 8, 1954 (36 pages; 15 cents)
Star Publications

	GD25	FN65	NM94
8-(B&W for coloring)	3.20	8.00	16.00

ZOO FUNNIES (Tim McCoy #16 on)
Nov, 1945 - No. 15, 1947
Charlton Comics/Children Comics Publ.

	GD25	FN65	NM94
101(#1)(1945; 1st Charlton comic book?)-Funny animal; Al Fago-c	10.00	30.00	65.00
2(12/45, 52 pgs.)	5.35	16.00	32.00
3-5	4.20	12.50	25.00
6-15: 8-Diana the Huntress app.	3.60	9.00	18.00

ZOO FUNNIES (Becomes Nyoka, The Jungle Girl #14 on?)
July, 1953 - No. 13, Sept, 1955; Dec, 1984
Capitol Stories/Charlton Comics

	GD25	FN65	NM94
1-1st app.? Timothy The Ghost; Fago-c/a	5.85	17.50	35.00
2	4.00	10.00	20.00
3-7 (8/46)	3.20	8.00	16.00
8-13-Nyoka app.	5.00	15.00	30.00
1(1984)		.50	1.00

ZOONIVERSE (Eclipse) (Value: cover or less)

ZOO PARADE (See 4-Color #662)

ZOOM COMICS
December, 1945 (One Shot)
Carlton Publishing Co.

	GD25	FN65	NM94
nn-Dr. Mercy, Satannas, from Red Band Comics; Capt. Milksop origin retold	27.00	82.00	165.00

ZOOT (Rulah Jungle Goddess #17 on)
nd (1946) - No. 16, July, 1948 (Two #13s & 14s)
Fox Features Syndicate

	GD25	FN65	NM94
nn-Funny animal only	11.00	32.00	75.00
2-The Jaguar app.	10.00	30.00	65.00
3(Fall, 1946) - 6-Funny animals & teen-age	5.85	17.50	35.00
7-(6/47)-Rulah, Jungle Goddess begins (origin & 1st app.)	43.00	130.00	300.00
8-10	32.00	95.00	220.00
11-Kamen bondage-c	35.00	105.00	245.00
12-Injury-to-eye panels, torture scene	20.00	60.00	140.00
13(2/48)	20.00	60.00	140.00
14(3/48)-Used in **SOTI**, pg. 104, "One picture showing a girl nailed by her wrists to trees with blood flowing from the wounds, might be taken straight from an ill. ed. of the Marquis deSade"	24.00	73.00	170.00
13(4/48),14(5/48)-Becomes Western True Crime #15 on?	20.00	60.00	140.00
15,16	20.00	60.00	140.00

ZORRO (Walt Disney with #882)(TV)(See Eclipse Graphic Album)
May, 1949 - No. 15, Sept-Nov, 1961 (Photo-c 882 on)
Dell Publishing Co.

	GD25	FN65	NM94
4-Color 228	19.00	57.00	135.00
4-Color 425,497,617,732	11.50	34.00	80.00
4-Color 538,574-Kinstler-a	12.00	36.00	85.00
4-Color 882-Photo-c begin; Toth-a	10.00	30.00	70.00
4-Color 920,933,960,976-Toth-a in all	10.00	30.00	70.00
4-Color 1003('59)-Toth-a	10.00	30.00	60.00
4-Color 1037-Annette Funicello photo-c	11.00	32.00	75.00
8(12-2/59-60)	8.35	25.00	50.00
9,12-Toth-a. 12-Last 10 cent issue	9.15	27.50	55.00
10,11,13-15-Last photo-c	6.70	20.00	40.00

NOTE: ***Warren Tufts*** *a-4-Color 1037, 8, 9, 10, 13.*

ZORRO (Walt Disney)(TV)
Jan, 1966 - No. 9, March, 1968 (All photo-c)
Gold Key

	GD25	FN65	NM94
1-Toth-a	6.70	20.00	40.00
2,4,5,7-9-Toth-a. 5-r/F.C. #1003 by Toth	4.35	13.00	26.00
3,6-Tufts-a	4.00	11.00	22.00

NOTE: *#1-9 are reprinted from Dell issues.* ***Tufts*** *a-3, 4. #1-r/F.C. #882. #2-r/F.C. #960. #3-r/#12-c & #8 inside. #4-r/#9-c & insides. #6-r/#11(all); #7-r/#14-c. #8-r/F.C. #933 inside & back-c & #976-c. #9-r/F.C. #920.*

ZORRO (TV)
Dec, 1990 - No. 12, Nov, 1991 ($1.00, color)
Marvel Comics

	GD25	FN65	NM94
1-12: Based on new TV show. 12-Toth-c		.50	1.00

ZOT! (Eclipse) (Value: cover or less)

Z-2 COMICS (Secret Agent...) (See Holyoke One-Shot #7)

ZULU (See Movie Classics)

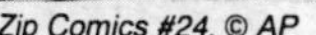
Zip Comics #24, © AP

Zoot #9, © FOX

Zorro #11 (Dell), © WDC

ANNOUNCING!!

The OVERSTREET COMIC BOOK PHOTO GRADING GUIDE!!

INTRODUCING NEW 100 POINT GRADING SYSTEM!!

THIS FIRST EDITION IS LOADED WITH PHOTOS SHOWING ALL GRADES

ORDER YOUR COPY TODAY!

FEATURING

- Over 300 pages!
- 16 page Color Section!
- Exclusive articles on restoration!
- Detailed glossary of terms!
- Comic books from most major collections included as examples!
- Exclusive tips on grading!
- Special Defect Sections to aid in grading!

ONLY $12.00ppd.

Tennessee residents include 7¾ per cent sales tax

— Available through all regular outlets —

or send payment to:

OVERSTREET PUBLICATIONS, INC.

780 Hunt Cliff Drive NW, Dept. G, Cleveland, TN 37311

Foreign: Please send International Money Order payable in U.S funds and on a U.S. bank

COMIC RELIEF
In Berkeley, CA.
We Mail Order Anywhere!
West Coast's Largest Selection of Gold and Silver-Age Collectibles!
Over 7,000 Graphic Novels, Art Books, and Movie/TV Books in Stock!
Computerized Want-list Service!
COMIC RELIEF
2138 University Avenue
Berkeley, CA 94704
(510) 843-5002
1597 Haight Street
San Francisco, CA 94117
(415) 552-9010
COMIC RELIEF TM.

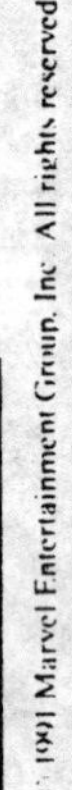
TM & © 1991 Marvel Entertainment Group, Inc. All rights reserved.

DAVID T. ALEXANDER

P.O. BOX 273086 • TAMPA, FLORIDA 33618 • (813) 968-1805
FAX (813) 264-6226
"CONTACT US FIRST"

ALL CATALOG COSTS ARE REFUNDABLE ON YOUR ORDER

Offering the Following Fine Catalogs:

☆ ALL NEW FOR 1993 ☆

A COMIC BOOK PRICE LIST SERIES......................EACH...**$1.00**
- **#103** 1950'S COMICS: CRIME, WESTERN, GOOD GIRL ART, E.C., AVON, HORROR, ETC.
- **#104** GOLDEN AGE COMICS, CLASSICS, ETC.
- **#105** UNDERGROUNDS, MISC. OLD COMICS, MOVIE & TV COMICS
- **#106** FUNNY COMICS, DISNEY, ARCHIE, HARVEY, DELL, GOLD KEY, ETC.
- **#107** INDEPENDENT PUBLISHERS 1960'S TO 1993

B MARVEL AND D.C. LIST................**$1.00**
ALSO INCLUDES INDEPENDENT TITLES, GOLD KEY, AND THE SMALLER PUBLISHERS FROM THE 60'S TO DATE.

C THE SPECIAL BLEND...................**$1.00**
WE NEVER KNOW WHAT'S ON THIS LIST — CONSISTS OF NEW ARRIVALS MIXED IN WITH SOME OLD FAVORITES — GOLDEN AGE, EARLY MARVELS, PULPS, ART, COMIC BOOK-RELATED COLLECTABLES, WHO KNOWS WHAT WE WILL GET, COULD BE ANYTHING, BUT WE GUARANTEE YOU'LL LIKE THIS SELECTION AND THE PRICES.

D PULP MAGAZINE LIST #15...........**$1.00**
HOT OFF THE PRESS: SHADOW, WEIRD TALES, SPICY DETECTIVE, AMAZING, BLACK MASK, G-8, DOC SAVAGE, WESTERNS, ARGOSY, ETC.

E THE CATALOG OF GLAMOUR........ **$2.00**
THIS PHOTO ILLUSTRATED LARGE CATALOG FEATURES THE WORLDS LARGEST COLLECTION OF PIN-UP MAGAZINES, MOVIE AND TV MAGAZINES, MEN'S ADVENTURE, TRUE DETECTIVE, MARILYN MONROE, BETTY PAGE, JAYNE MANSFIELD, ETC. - MANY RARE AND OBSCURE TITLES FROM -1900 TO THE 90'S.

F MAGAZINE LIST..........................**$1.00**
ALL VARIETIES INCLUDING MAD, FAMOUS MONSTERS, SAVAGE TALES, MARVELS, HEAVY METAL, FANZINES, WARREN TITLES, D.C., COMIC BOOK AND HUMOR — HUGE SELECTION.

G PAPERBACK BOOK LIST...............**$1.00**
SOON TO BE PUBLISHED . . . AVON, MAPBACKS, DUST JACKETS, POPULAR LIBRARY, ACE, DELL, ETC.— OVER 20,000 VINTAGE PAPERBACKS AVAILABLE.

H EDGAR RICE BURROUGHS LIST....**$1.00**
TARZAN 1ST EDITION, HARDBACKS, PULPS, COMICS, BIG LITTLE BOOKS, VINTAGE MOVIE POSTERS, ORIGINAL ART, PAPERBACKS AND OTHER SCARCE ITEMS.

I THE ART CATALOG.......................**$1.00**
ORIGINAL COMIC BOOK AND NEWSPAPER ART, COLOR MAGAZINE AND PULP COVERS, PORTFOLIOS, PRINTS, POSTERS, LIMITED EDITIONS.

J BIG LITTLE BOOKS.......................**$1.00**
MICKEY MOUSE, FLASH GORDON, POPEYE, SHADOW, DICK TRACY, GENE AUTRY, ETC. ALL TYPES — TREMENDOUS VARIETY.

K MOVIE POSTERS..........................**$1.00**
HORROR, WESTERN, FIILM NOIR, SCIENCE FICTION, EXPLOITATION, CLASSICS — 1930's to 1990's — ONE SHEETS, LOBBY CARDS, PRESS BOOKS, MAGAZINES, MOVIE/TV COMICS, BOOKS, ETC.

L SPORTS COLLECTORS ITEMS.......**$2.00**
PROGRAMS, YEARBOOKS, SPORT MAGAZINE, SPORTS ILLUSTRATED, BASEBALL, FOOTBALL, BOXING, YANKEES, DODGERS, METS, RAMS, AUTOGRAPHS, OLYMPICS, SPORTING NEWS, MEDIA GUIDES — POPULAR AND UNIQUE ITEMS FROM 1910 TO 1993.

M BASEBALL CARDS.......................**$1.00**
THE HOT TICKET TO THE NINETIES — TOPS, FLEER, DONRUSS, UPPER DECK, OLD JUDGE, T-CARDS, ETC. — SINGLES, SETS, UNOPENED MATERIAL PLUS FOOTBALL, BASKETBALL, ETC.

N AUTO RACING MEMORABILIA.......**$1.00**
A NEW RAGE IN COLLECTING, THIS CATALOG FEATURES: INDY 500, DAYTONA 500, FORMULA ONE, DRAG RACING, SPRINT CARS, DIRT TRACKS, SUPER-SPEEDWAYS, PROGRAMS, YEAR-BOOKS, POST CARDS, DRIVER AUTOGRAPHS, MAGAZINES AND MUCH MORE—MUCH MORE—THE ONLY CATALOG OF ITS KIND IN THE WORLD INCLUDES ITEMS FROM 1906 TO 1993.

WANT ALL CATALOGS? SEND $15.00

CATALOGING IS A CONTINUAL PROCESS FOR US SINCE WE HAVE A CONSTANT INFLUX OF COLLECTORS ITEMS INTO OUR INVENTORY. AS WE GET NEW MATERIAL, OUR CATALOGS ARE CONSTANTLY BEING UPDATED. IF YOU DO NOT RECEIVE A CATALOG SHORTLY AFTER SENDING FOR IT, THAT MEANS WE ARE UPDATING THAT PARTICULAR CATALOG AND WE WILL RUSH YOU THE LATEST EDITION WHEN IT IS PRINTED.

— AND FOR UP-TO-THE-MINUTE QUOTES ON THE PRICE AND AVAILABILITY OF CERTAIN SPECIFIC OR "HOT" ITEMS, PLUG INTO OUR

RADICAL WANT LIST SYSTEM

- IF YOU ARE INTERESTED IN QUICKLY LOCATING SPECIFIC COMIC BOOKS, PULPS, OR RELATED GOODS, FOLLOW THESE STEPS:
  1. MAKE A LIST OF THE ITEMS YOU WANT TO IMMEDIATELY OBTAIN.
  2. SEND THE LIST AND $5.00 (TO COVER HANDLING) TO US.
- YOUR WANT LIST WILL BE CHECKED AGAINST OUR ENTIRE STOCK, INCLUDING NEW ARRIVALS THAT MAY NOT BE ON OUR CURRENT LISTS.
- YOUR $5.00 SERVICE CHARGE IS THEN REFUNDABLE WITH YOUR FIRST ORDER.
- WE ALSO FILE ALL WANT LISTS UNTIL WE LOCATE THE ITEMS YOU'VE REQUESTED.

LBCole
JOIN THE PARADE TO. . .

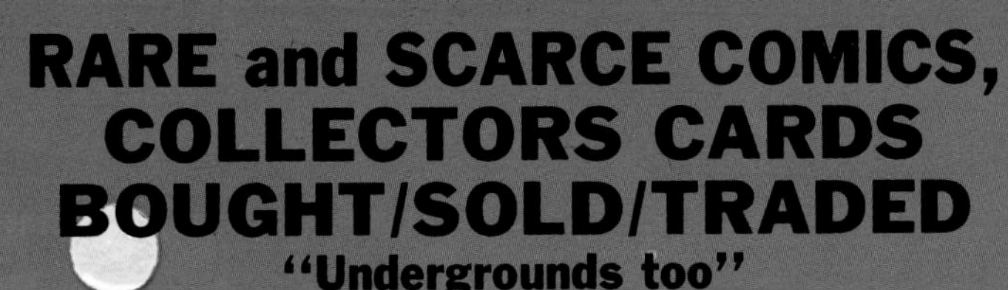
RARE and SCARCE COMICS,
COLLECTORS CARDS
BOUGHT/SOLD/TRADED
"Undergrounds too"
NO COLLECTION TOO LARGE OR SMALL!
REDBEARD'S BOOK DEN
P.O. Box 217
Crystal Bay, NV. 89402-0217
(702) 831-4848

INTRODUCING A LINE OF CLASSICS...

DC Comics Archives are beautiful, high-quality hardcover books reprinting the most collectible and sought-after comics ever published. They are authentic recreations of the originals, reproduced and re-colored from the original pages.

BATMAN ARCHIVES VOLUME 1

The original Golden Age adventures from DETECTIVE COMICS #27-50. Included are the first appearances of both BATMAN and ROBIN, THE BOY WONDER and classic confrontations with The Joker, Clayface, and Hugo Strange.
306-page Hardcover $39.95

BATMAN ARCHIVES VOLUME 2

Featuring stories from DETECTIVE COMICS #51-70, this volume of early Batman tales includes the debut of the Penguin, the first appearance of Two-Face, and four exciting Joker tales.
288-page Hardcover $39.95

ALL STAR ARCHIVES

Re-presented in their entirety from the Golden Age of comics are issues #3-6 of ALL STAR COMICS, showcasing the early adventures of the Justice Society of America. Among the characters featured in this historic team book are the Flash, Green Lantern, Hawkman, Sandman, Dr. Fate, and the Atom.
272-page Hardcover $49.95

LEGION ARCHIVES

This book collects the earliest stories of THE LEGION OF SUPER-HEROES in chronological order. It includes Legion appearances in ADVENTURE COMICS, SUPERBOY, ACTION COMICS, and SUPERMAN. This is a must-have for all loyal LEGION OF SUPER-HEROES readers.
256-page Hardcover $39.95

DC Comics are available at comic shops nationwide

SUPERMAN ARCHIVES VOLUME 1

These are the stories that started it all! The original Golden Age SUPERMAN #1-4 by Jerry Siegel and Joe Shuster. These stories portray Superman as a Depression-era champion who was rough and tough and strong in his quest for social justice.

272-page Hardcover $39.95

SUPERMAN ARCHIVES VOLUME 2

More comic book history is preserved in this volume which reprints SUPERMAN #5-8. The stories are classic adventure strips with emphasis on the mystery/ detective genre where Superman tackles crooked politicians and racketeers. Also featured are Perry White and Lex Luthor.

272-page Hardcover $39.95

SUPERMAN ARCHIVES VOLUME 3

This third volume collects SUPERMAN #9-12 with an introduction by landmark Superman artist Jack Burnley. The stories include Superman smashing a spy ring and apprehending a gangster who commits murders for hire.

272-page Hardcover $39.95

Don't forget: You can also call our toll-free number weekdays from 8am-6pm EST for Mastercard and VISA orders. Just dial 1-800-753-7300.

TITLE	PRICE	Quantity GIFT	YOURSELF
BATMAN ARCHIVES VOLUME 1	$39.95		
BATMAN ARCHIVES VOLUME 2	$39.95		
SUPERMAN ARCHIVES VOLUME 1	$39.95		
SUPERMAN ARCHIVES VOLUME 2	$39.95		
SUPERMAN ARCHIVES VOLUME 3	$39.95		
LEGION ARCHIVES VOLUME 1	$39.95		
ALL STAR ARCHIVES	$49.95		

☐ Check enclosed payable to NECA Sales
Charge my ☐ VISA ☐ MASTERCARD

Subtotal
Shipping ($4.00)
Grand Total

Cardnumber Expiration Date

Cardholder Signature

Name ______

Address ______
(no P.O. boxes, please)

City______ State ______ Zip______

Titles: ______

Please make check or money order payable to NECA Sales. Sorry, U.S. orders only. Mail to Archives Offer * NECA Sales * P. O. Box 7551 Dept. DM-40 * Warwick, RI, 02887. Offer expires December 31, 1993.

Jungle Comics #21, 1941, © FH

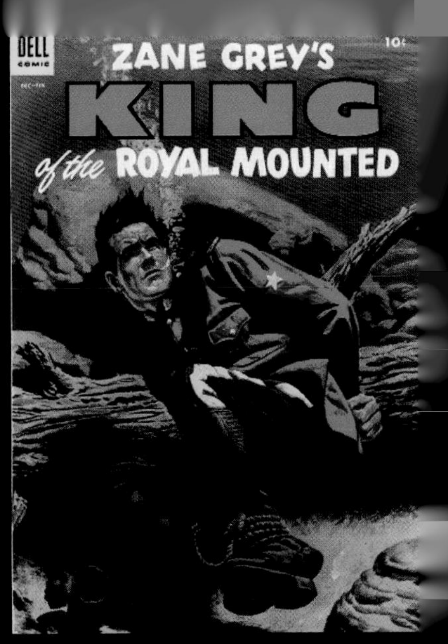

King of the Royal Mounted #11, 1954, © Stephen Slesinger

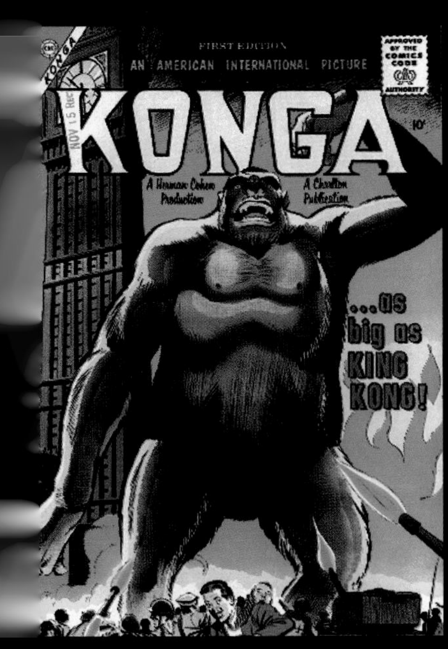

Konga #1, 1960, © American International

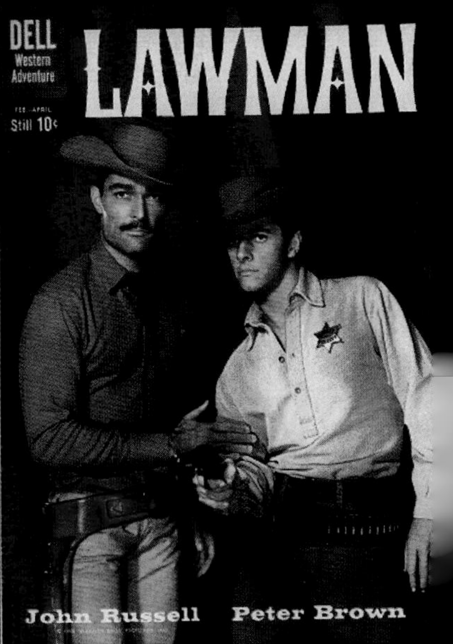

Lawman #3, 1959, © Warner Bros.

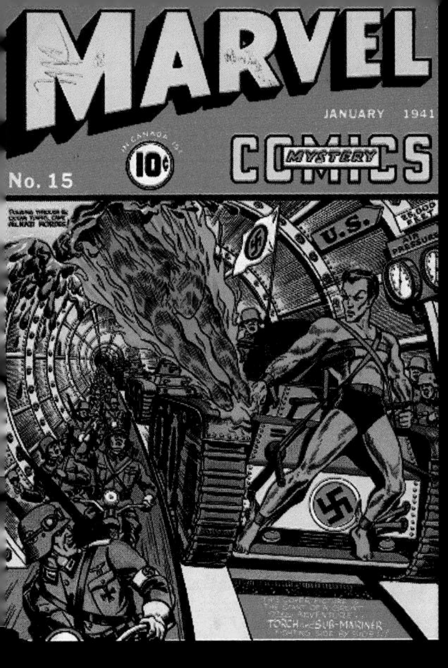

Marvel Mystery Comics #15, 1941, © Marvel

Master Comics #8, 1940, © Fawcett
Red Gaucho, Capt. Venture, & the Planet Princess begin.

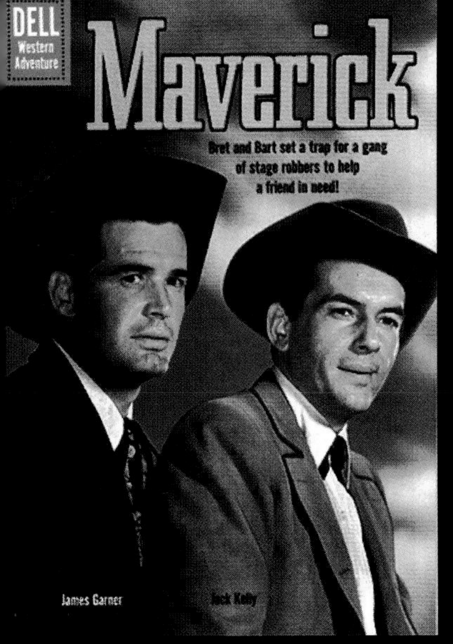

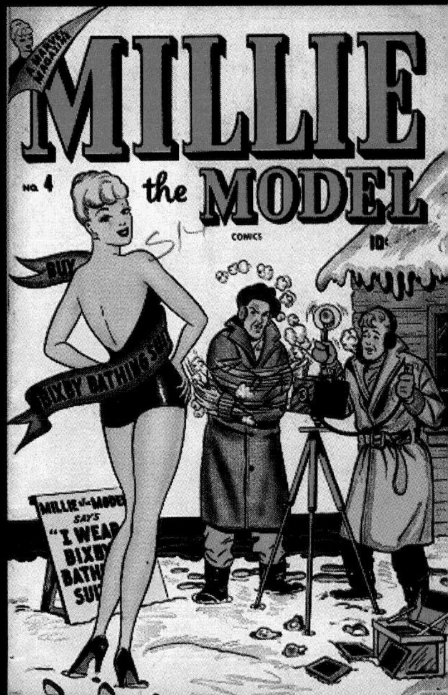

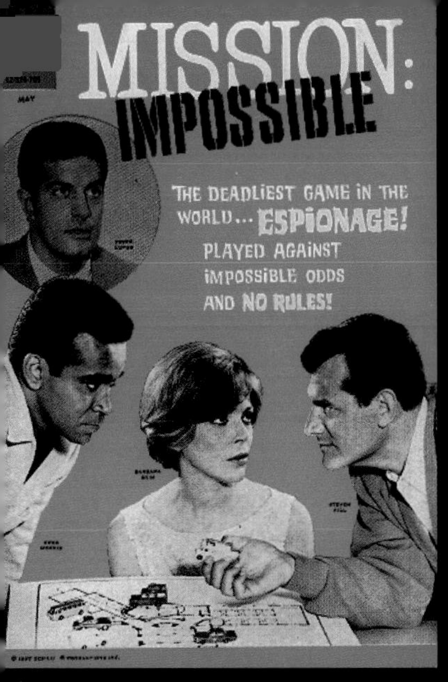

Mission Impossible #1, 1967, © Desilu

Mod Squad #1, 1969, © Thomas-Spelling Prod.

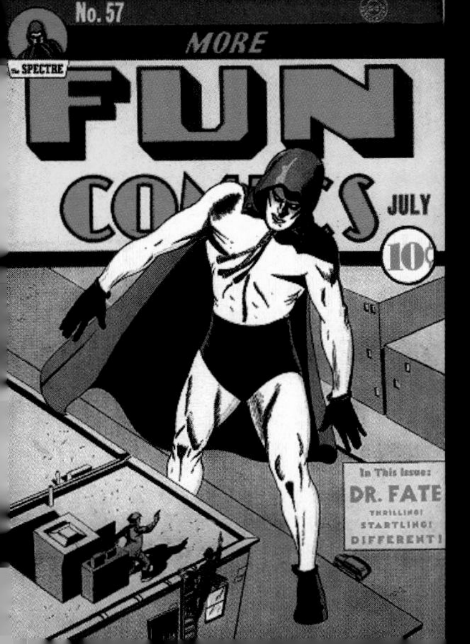

Mystery In Space #45, 1958, © DC

Perry Mason Mystery Magazine #1, 1964, © Atlantic Publishing Corp.

Punch Comics #20, 1947, © Chesler
Unique cover.

Rawhide Kid #4, 1955, © Marvel

Red Ryder #11, 1943, © King Features Syndicate

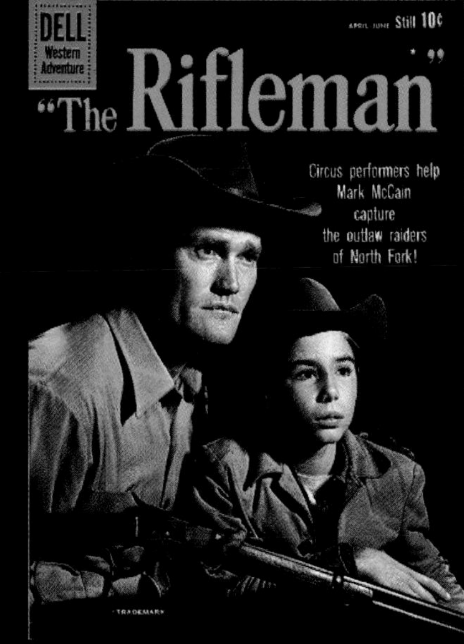

The Rifleman #3, 1960, © Four Star-Sussex

Rin Tin Tin #523, 1953, © Lee Duncan

Rip Hunter. . .Time Master #2, 1961, © DC

Room 222 #1, 1970, © Twentieth Century Fox Film Corp.

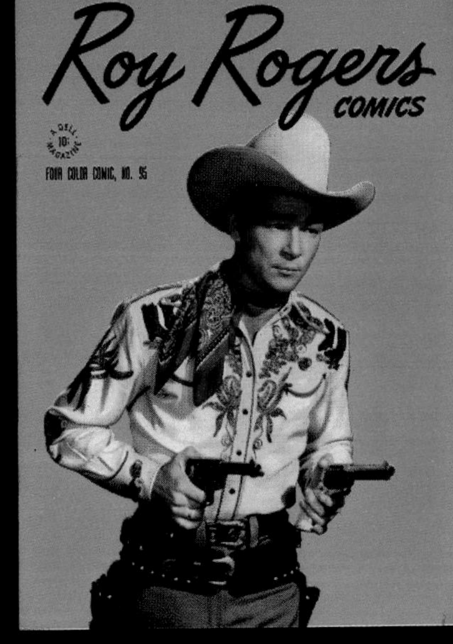

Roy Rogers #95, 1945, © Roy Rogers

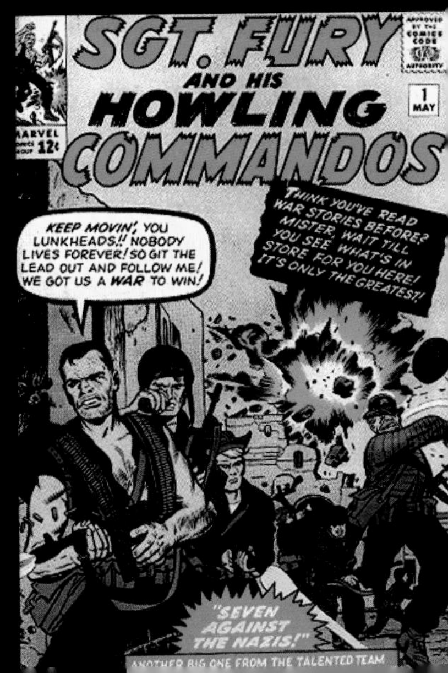

Showcase #6, 1957, © DC
Origin/1st app. Challengers of the Unknown. 1st Silver Age superhero team.

Star Spangled War Stories #90, 1960, © DC. 1st dinosaur issue.

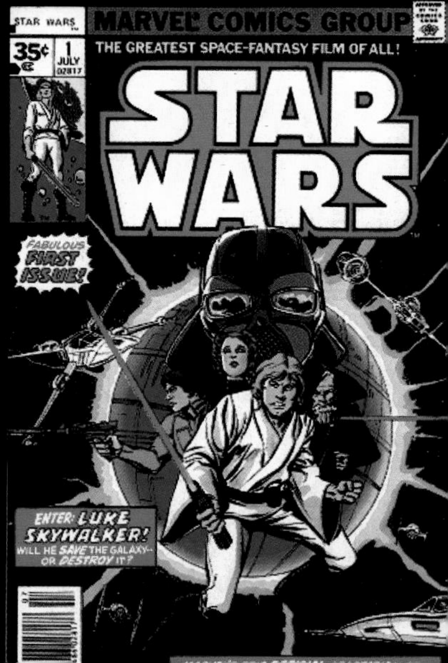

Strange Adventures #121, 1960, © DC

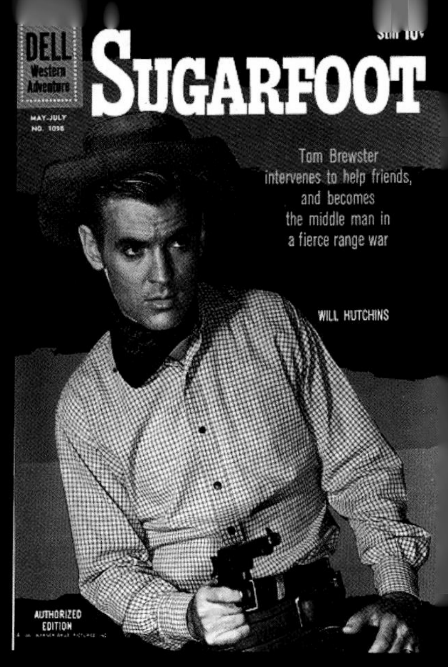

Sugarfoot (Four Color) #1098, 1960, © Warner Bros.

Superman #146, 1961, © DC
Superman's life story.

Tales of the Unexpected #43, 1959, © DC
1st Space Ranger cover & story.

MEANWHILE, IN THE BACK STOCKROOM...
HEE! HEE!
FOX+CROW
MUTT and JEFF
SEA DEVILS
DC's
SILVER AND
GOLDEN AGE
MORE FUN
ALL STAR
FLASH
ALL FLASH
UT!
ACTION
ADVENTURE
GREEN LANT.
ALL AMERICAN
COMIC CAVAL.
BATMAN
DETECTIVE
WORLD'S FINEST

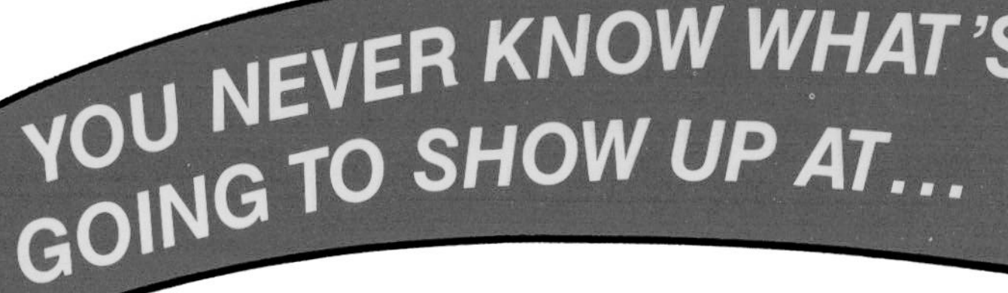

GEPPI'S COMIC WORLD

ACE... THE BATHOUND SAYS...

For the best in comics and related material, visit **Geppi's Comic World**. Specializing in everything, from the Golden Age comics to the latest hits hot off the presses, you can find it here.

We are always anxiously seeking to buy collections and guarantee to pay the highest prices the market will bear whether it's to a long time collector or someone who's found a dusty old box of comics in the attic.

Send for our free mail order catalog or get our subscription service by writing:

Geppi's Comic World
Mail Order & Subscription Service
1722 N. Rolling Road
Baltimore, MD 21244
401-298-1758

Also available are Harvey and Dell file copies. Send to the above address for mail order (Attn. Doug Gratz)

8317 Fenton Street
Silver Spring, MD 20910
301-588-2546

Harbor Place
Upper Level, Dept. 14
301 Light St. Pavillion
Baltimore, MD 21202
410-547-0910

Anything Else Is Incomplete

This catalog offers over 2000 items for shipping in January.

Now...Better than ever. If you're looking for selection, *Advance Comics*® is the only place to go. Month after month, *Advance Comics* offers more great products than any other source. And *Advance Comics* is designed to be easy to use. It's organized into categories that reflect your areas of interest. More products and easier to use–there's really no better choice.

Advance Comics and the convenient *Advance Comics Order Book* are available through the finest comics retailers worldwide for ordering all the best new comics, games, cards, videos, and more.

Released the last Thursday of every month.

Available to retailers only from Capital City. Call 608/223-2000 to order yours.

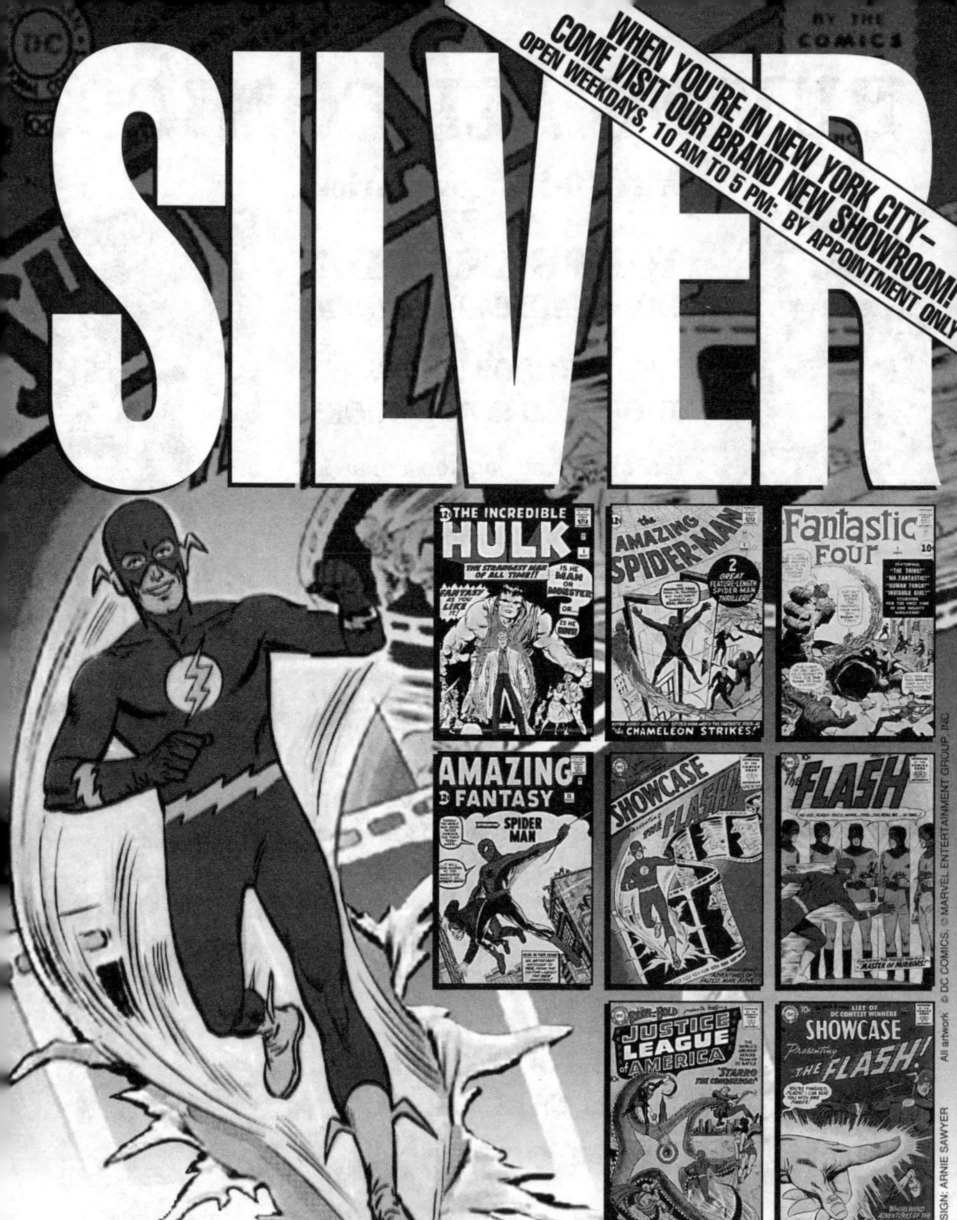

WHY YOU SHOULD CALL US BEFORE YOU SELL YOUR COLLECTION OF COMICS, ARTWORK OR MEMORABILIA:
We make it easy! No waiting for payment, No song and dance about grading. We'll come to you; anywhere, anytime! Four Color Comics takes the risk out of selling. Treat yourself to an honest, straight-forward experience—Sell your collection to us and walk away with more money in your pocket and a smile on r face

FOUR COLOR
COMICS

NEW YORK SHOWROOM:
115 West 27th Street, New York, NY 10001
TEL: (212) 675-6990

WHEN YOU'RE IN NEW YORK CITY–
COME VISIT OUR BRAND NEW SHOWROOM!
OPEN WEEKDAYS, 10 AM TO 5 PM: BY APPOINTMENT ONLY
GOLD
BATMAN
SENSATION COMICS
Detective COMICS
ACTION COMICS
64 Pages of New CAPTAIN MARVEL Adventures
ALL STAR Comics
SILVER STREAK
ALL-AMERICAN COMICS
DESIGN: ARNIE SAWYER
All artwork : © DC COMICS, © MARVEL ENTERTAINMENT GROUP, INC

© DON MARIS 1986

BIG-D SUPER COMIC & COLLICTIBLE SHOWS

July 9-10-11
<u>and</u>
Nov. 12-13-14

2 Great Shows for 1993

300 Tables of the Best Pre-1974 Comics, Movie Posters, Comic Character Items, Play Sets, BLB's, Western Collectibles, Premiums, Toy Soldiers, etc.

Sheraton Park Central
Coit Rd. & Hwy, 635
Dallas, Texas

Come Join the Fun!!

Don Maris
Box 200725
Arlington, Texas 76006
(817) 261-8745

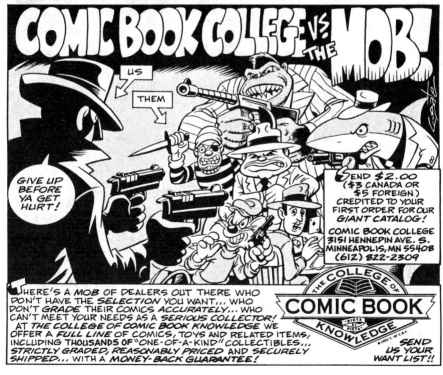

HOW TO ORDER: Simply list on any sheet of paper what you would like. Add $3.00 for postage. Print your name and address clearly. Payment with order please. All orders are securely packaged, insured and sent out promptly (Overseas customers please add extra for postage and specify air or surface delivery. Unused postage shall be refunded).

CONDITION: Very Fine to Mint. 90% Near Mint to Mint. Satisfaction guaranteed or money refunded.

Refunds are sent when an item is out of stock. Alternate choices are appreciated. We sell First Printings only. Prices good through March 31, 1994. Minimum order $12.00.

SPECIAL 10% DISCOUNT-You may deduct 10% when your order is over $50.

SORRY-no phone orders-but we're quick to fill mail orders. ORDER TODAY!!

–Ed Kalb

MARVEL COMICS

ADVENTURES ON THE PLANET OF THE APES
1-11 .... 1.50
ALPHA FLIGHT
1,13,17 .... 4.50
2-12,14-16,18-32 .... 1.25
33,34 .... 3.00
35-50 .... 1.25
51-53 .... 4.50
54,63,65-86 .... 1.25
55-62,64 .... 2.00
87-90,100,Ann 1 up 2.50
91-99,101-105,107-up 1.25
AMAZING ADVENTURES (1970)
20-39 .... 2.50
AMAZING ADVENTURES (X-MEN)
1-14 .... 1.50
AMAZING SPIDER-MAN
160,164,168,169 .... 4.00
161 .... 15.00
162 .... 22.00
182-184,188,190,192,193 .... 3.00
240-243,246-248 .... 2.50
244,245,249-251,253 .... 5.50
252,259,265 .... 9.00
254,255,263,264 .... 2.00
256-258,260-262 .... 5.00
266-273 .... 2.00
274-277,281,287 .... 4.50
278-280,282,283 .... 2.00
284 .... 7.00
285 .... 10.00
286,288 .... 5.00
289 .... 15.00
290-292,295-297 .... 2.00
293,294 .... 6.50
298 .... 20.00
299 .... 12.00
300 .... 25.00
301-305 .... 9.00
306-311 .... 7.00
312-317 .... 8.00
318-323 .... 4.50
324 .... 9.00
325 .... 7.00
326,327,329,330 .... 2.50
328,332,333 .... 5.00
331,334,335 .... 2.50
336-343,348-360 .... 1.25
344-347,362 .... 4.00
361 .... 5.50
363-up 1.25
Annual 10-13 .... 4.00
16-20,23-25 .... 2.50
21 .... 9.00
22 .... 5.00
Giant Size 1-3,5 .... 5.00
ASTONISHING TALES (1970)
11,12 .... 5.00
13-24 .... 3.00
AVENGERS
136-150 .... 4.00
151-168 .... 3.00
169-199 .... 2.00
200,214,263 .... 4.00
201-213,215-229 .... 1.50
230-262,264-up 1.25
Annual 6,10 .... 4.00
8,9 .... 3.00
11-20 .... 2.00
Giant Size 1-5 .... 4.50
AVENGERS SPOTLIGHT
21-up 1.25
AVENGERS WEST COAST
47-up 1.25
Annual 4-up 2.00
BLACK GOLIATH
1-5 .... 2.50
BLACK KNIGHT
1-4 .... 1.50
BLACK PANTHER (1977)
3,4,6,10-15 .... 2.50
1-4(1988) 1.25

CAPTAIN AMERICA
183-199,201-219 .... 2.00
220-240,242,246 .... 1.50
247-255 .... 2.50
256-281,283-285 .... 1.25
289-331 .... 1.25
332 .... 6.00
333-340 .... 2.00
341-343,346-349 .... 1.25
344,345,350,354 .... 2.00
351-353,355-365 .... 1.25
366,372,383,400 .... 2.00
367-371,373-382,384-399, 401-up 1.25
Annual 4 .... 4.00
6,7,9-up 2.00
CAPTAIN MARVEL
35-62 .... 2.00
CHAMPIONS
1 .... 6.00
2-5,7-11,13-16 .... 2.50
CLASSIC X-MEN
1,2,10,17,26,39 .... 3.00
3-9,11-16,18-25,27-38,40-72 .... 1.25
CLOAK AND DAGGER
1-4(1983) 1.25
1-11(1985) 1.25
CONAN
26,37 .... 5.00
27-36 .... 4.00
38-60 .... 3.00
61-69 .... 2.50
70-99 .... 2.00
101-231,233-240,242-249, 251-up 1.25
232,241,250 .... 2.50
King Size 1 .... 7.00
Annual 2-4 .... 3.00
5-12 .... 2.00
Giant Size 1,3,4 .... 4.50
CONAN THE KING/KING CONAN
1 .... 4.50
2-51,54,55 .... 1.50
COYOTE
1,12-14 .... 3.00
2-9,15,16 .... 1.25
CREATURES ON THE LOOSE
16-29,34,35,37 .... 3.00
DAREDEVIL
124-126,128-130 .... 2.50
133-137,139-157,162 .... 2.50
159 .... 10.00
160,169,170 .... 7.50
163-167,175,196 .... 6.00
171-174 .... 3.50
176-180 .... 2.50
181-184 .... 4.50
185-195,197-226 .... 1.50
227 .... 4.50
228-233,238,241 .... 2.50
234-237,239,240,242-247, 250-253 .... 1.25
248,249,255 .... 5.00
254 .... 9.00
256,258,259,270 .... 2.00
260-269,271 .... 1.25
272,292,300 .... 2.00
273-291,293-299,301-up 1.25
Annual 4(1976) 3.00
4-up 2.00
DAZZLER
1,38 .... 4.00
2-37,39-42 .... 1.50
DEATHLOK
1 .... 3.00
2-12,14 .... 1.25
DEFENDERS
12-19 .... 4.00
20-25 .... 3.00
30-60 .... 2.00
61-72 .... 1.50
73-75,96,100 .... 4.00
76-95,97-99,101-152 .... 1.25
Annual 1 .... 4.00
Giant Size 1-5 .... 5.00

DOC SAVAGE
1-8,Giant 1 .... 3.00
DR. STRANGE (1974-87)
3-5 .... 4.50
6,7 .... 3.00
10-20 .... 2.00
21-40 .... 1.50
41-81 .... 1.25
DR. STRANGE (1988)
2,3,11-13,16-22,31-42 .... 1.25
DR. WHO (1984)
1-18 .... 1.50
DREADSTAR
6-21 .... 1.25
ELEKTRA ASSASSIN
1-7 .... 2.00
ETERNALS (1ST)
1 .... 3.00
2-19,Annual 1 .... 1.50
EXCALIBUR
1(1987) 6.00
1(1988) 5.00
2-5 .... 2.00
6-up 1.25
FALCON
1-4 .... 1.50
FALLEN ANGELS
1-8 .... 1.25
FANTASTIC FOUR
163-199,201-267 .... 2.00
268-336,339-346 .... 1.25
337,338,347-350 .... 3.00
351-up 1.25
Annual 11-14 .... 4.00
15-up 2.00
Vs. X-Men 1-4 .... 2.50
FEAR
6,12-18 .... 3.00
22-31 .... 10.00
FIRESTAR
1-4 .... 2.00
FOOLKILLER
1 .... 3.00
2-4 .... 1.25
FURTHER ADVENTURES OF INDIANA JONES
3-20 .... 1.25
GARGOYLE
1-4 .... 1.25
GHOST RIDER (1990)
14,16-up 1.50
G.I. JOE
1 .... 20.00
3-12 .... 7.50
13-27 .... 6.00
28-50 .... 2.00
51-74,76-80,99,100,102,112, 123-125 .... 1.25
Year Book 1-4 .... 1.50
Special Mission 1-25 .... 1.25
GODZILLA
1 .... 4.50
2-24 .... 2.00
HAWKEYE (1983)
1-4 .... 1.25
HERCULES
1-4(1982) 1.25
1-4(1984) 1.25
HOWARD THE DUCK
1 .... 10.00
2-33 .... 2.00
HUMAN TORCH
1-8(1974) 3.00
ICEMAN
1 .... 4.00
2-4 .... 3.00
IMPOSSIBLE MAN
1,2(1990) 2.00
INCREDIBLE HULK
183-199,201-219 .... 2.00
220-249,251-270 .... 1.50
250,272,273,314 .... 4.50
271,274-299,301-313,315-323,325-329,335 .... 1.25
324,332-334 .... 6.00
330 .... 15.00
331 .... 10.00
336-339,341-346 .... 4.50
347-366 .... 1.25
367,368,372,377 .... 6.50
369-371,373-376 .... 4.50
378,380-392,394-up 1.25
379,393 .... 4.00
Annual 3,7,8 .... 4.50
5,6,9-up 2.00
INHUMANS (1975)
1 .... 4.50
2-12 .... 2.50
INVADERS (1975)
1 .... 8.00
2-41 .... 2.00
Giant 1 .... 4.50
Annual 1 .... 3.00
IRON MAN
90,92,94,95,99,101-128 .... 2.50
129-149 .... 2.00
151-168,171-199 .... 1.25
150,170,200,225 .... 4.00
201-224,233-up 1.25
226-232 .... 2.00
Annual 3,4 .... 4.00
5-up 2.00
JACK OF HEARTS
1-4 .... 1.50
JOHN CARTER WARLORD OF MARS
1,18 .... 3.00
2-17,19-28 .... 1.50
Annual 1,3 .... 2.00
JUNGLE ACTION (1972)
1,5-24 .... 2.00
JUSTICE
1-32 .... 1.25
KAZAR (1974)
1 .... 3.00
2-20 .... 1.25
KAZAR THE SAVAGE
1 .... 3.00
2-34 .... 1.25
KID COLT
140-142,149,160,162-165, 169,170 .... 2.00
KITTY PRYDE AND WOLVERINE
1-3 .... 2.00
4-6 .... 3.00
KULL (1974)
5-11,13-15,29 .... 2.00
LOGANS RUN
1-5 .... 2.00
LONGSHOT
1,6 .... 15.00
2-5 .... 12.00
MACHINE MAN (1978)
1 .... 3.00
2-17 .... 1.25
1-4(1984) 1.25
MAGIK
1-4 .... 2.00
MAN THING (1974)
2,5,6,8,9,11-22 .... 2.00
MARC SPECTOR MOON KNIGHT
1,8,9,19-21 .... 3.00
2-7,22-39 .... 1.25
MARVEL CLASSICS
1-4,6-8,10,11,21,22,24-27,29 31-34 .... 2.00
MARVEL COMICS PRESENTS
1 .... 4.00
2-37,39-47,51-61,63,65-71, 75,77-84,86-UP 1.25
38,48-50,62,64,72-74,76,85 .... 3.00
MARVEL FANFARE
1,2 .... 8.00
3,4 .... 4.50
5-54,56 .... 1.25
MARVEL FEATURE (RED SONJA)
1-7 .... 2.50
MARVEL PREMIERE
6-14,17-24 .... 4.50
15 .... 22.50
16,25 .... 10.00
26,27,29-49,51-61 .... 1.50
MARVEL PRESENTS (1975)
1,2 .... 2.00
4-9,12 .... 4.00
MARVEL SAGA
1 .... 2.50
2-24 .... 1.25
MARVEL SPOTLIGHT
13,14 .... 10.00
15-24,28 .... 6.00
25-27,30,31 .... 2.50
32,33 .... 4.50
MARVEL SUPERHEROES
1-8(1990) 2.50
MARVEL TALES
35-100 .... 1.50
MARVEL TEAM UP
16-19 .... 4.50
20-31 .... 4.00
32-45 .... 3.00
46,53,55,58 .... 7.50
47-52 .... 2.00
54,56,57,59-70 .... 2.00
71-85,87-90 .... 1.50
86,91,93,100 .... 5.00
92,94-99 .... 1.50
101-116,118-150 .... 1.25
Annual 2-7 .... 2.00
MARVEL TWO IN ONE
2-4,6,7,9,10 .... 4.50
11-14,16-20 .... 2.50
21-26,28-53 .... 2.00
27,54,69 .... 6.00
55-68 .... 1.50
70-79,81-100 .... 1.25
Annual 1,3-7 .... 2.00
MARVEL UNIVERSE
4-15(1983) 1.50
1-20(1985) 1.50
MASTER OF KUNG FU
18,21-39 .... 2.50
40-51 .... 2.00
52-125 .... 1.25
MEPHISTO VS. FOUR HEROES
1-4 .... 1.50
MICRONAUTS
1 .... 3.00
2-59,Annual 1,2 .... 1.25
MOON KNIGHT (1980)
1 .... 4.00
2-38 .... 1.50
MS MARVEL
1 .... 4.50
2-23 .... 2.00
'NAM
2-52 .... 1.25
NAMOR THE SUB-MARINER
4-6,9-27 .... 1.25
NEW MUTANTS
1 .... 8.00
2,16,18,21 .... 4.00
3-15,17 .... 2.00
19,20,22-85 .... 1.50
100 .... 5.00
Annual 1,4,6 .... 4.00
2,3,7 .... 2.00
5 .... 6.00
NEW WARRIORS
8,9,12-26 .... 1.25
NICK FURY AGENT OF SHIELD (1989)
1 .... 2.50
2-6,10,11 .... 1.25
NICK FURY VS. SHIELD
1 .... 7.50
2 .... 12.00
3-6 .... 3.00
NIGHTCRAWLER
1 .... 4.00
2-4 .... 2.00
NIGHTMASK
1 .... 2.00
2-5,7-12 .... 1.25
NOVA
1 .... 7.50
2 .... 4.00
3-25 .... 2.00
OMEGA THE UNKNOWN
1-7,10 .... 2.50

PETER PARKER (SPECTACULAR SPIDER-MAN)
9-26,29 .... 4.00
27,28 .... 12.00
30-37 .... 2.50
38,56 .... 6.00
39-55,57-63,65-68 .... 2.50
64 .... 8.00
69,70 .... 4.50
71-80 .... 2.25
81-83 .... 6.50
84-99 .... 2.00
100,116,119,130 .... 4.00
101-115,117,118,120-129, 134-139 .... 1.25
131-133 .... 4.50
140-143,147 .... 4.00
144-146,148-157 .... 1.25
158-160,189 .... 4.50
161-188,190-up 1.25
Annual 4-up 2.50
POWER MAN/HERO FOR HIRE/AND IRON FIST
10-16,18,19 .... 4.00
20-29 .... 2.50
30-47 .... 2.00
48-50 .... 4.00
51-56,58-65 .... 1.50
67-77,79-83 .... 1.25
85-125 .... 1.25
POWER PACK
1,12,46 .... 3.00
2-11,13-18,20-26,28-44,50, 52,53,57,61,62 .... 1.25
PUNISHER (MINI)
2,3 .... 15.00
4,5 .... 7.50
PUNISHER (1987)
1 .... 17.50
2-7 .... 6.00
11-15 .... 4.00
16-25 .... 3.00
26-29 .... 2.00
30-up 1.25
Annual 1 .... 6.00
2 .... 3.00
3-up 2.00
PUNISHER WAR JOURNAL
1 .... 12.00
2,6,7 .... 7.00
3-5,8 .... 5.00
9-12,14,15 .... 3.00
13,16-up 1.50
QUASAR
1 .... 2.50
2-6,10,12,22,27,35-37 .... 1.25
RAWHIDE KID
68-82,84-86,92,94 .... 2.00
RED SONJA (1977)
1 .... 4.50
2-14 .... 2.00
ROBOCOP
1 .... 3.00
2-23 .... 1.25
ROM
1,17,18 .... 4.00
2-16,19-75 .... 1.25
Annual 1-4 .... 2.00
SAGA OF THE SUB-MARINER
1-12 .... 1.25
SECRET WARS I
1 .... 4.00
2-7,9-12 .... 2.00
SECRET WARS II
1-9 .... 1.50
SENSATIONAL SHE HULK
1 .... 4.00
2-8,16,19,22,26,29,35 .... 1.25
SILVER SURFER (1987)
1 .... 7.00
2-14 .... 2.00
16-33 .... 1.50
37-44,47-49 .... 2.00
51-up 1.25
Annual 1-up 2.50
1 (1982) 4.50
1,2 (Epic) 3.00
SKULL THE SLAYER

1-8 .... 2.50
SOLARMAN
1,2 .... 1.25
SOLO AVENGERS
1 .... 2.50
2-20 .... 1.25
SON OF SATAN
1 .... 7.50
2-7 .... 4.00
SPIDER-MAN
1 purple 4.00
1 silver 5.00
2-5 .... 4.00
6-8 .... 3.50
9,10 .... 3.00
11-up 1.50
SPIDER WOMAN
1 .... 5.00
2-36,39-50 .... 1.25
37,38 .... 4.00
SQUADRON SUPREME
1-12 .... 1.25
STAR TREK
1 .... 4.00
STAR WARS
1 .... 7.50
2-4 .... 4.00
5-10 .... 3.00
11-21 .... 2.50
22-50 .... 2.00
51-107 .... 1.50
Annual 1-3 .... 2.50
STRANGE TALES (1987)
1 .... 2.50
2-11,14,15,17,19 .... 1.25
STRIKE FORCE MORITURI
1-11,18-26 .... 1.25
SUB-MARINER (1968)
41-72 .... 3.00
Annual 1,2 .... 4.00
SUPER VILLAIN TEAM UP
1 .... 6.00
2-17 .... 3.00
Giant 1,2 .... 4.50
THING
2-36 .... 1.25
THOR
211-238 .... 2.00
239-269 .... 1.50
270-299,301-336 .... 1.25
300,338 .... 3.00
339-372,375-383 .... 1.25
373,374,384,400 .... 2.50
385-410 .... 1.25
413-428,431,434-449 .... 1.25
429,430,432,433,450 .... 2.00
451-up 1.25
Annual 5-7 .... 4.00
8-up 2.00
TOMB OF DRACULA (1987)
15-21 .... 4.00
22-51 .... 2.50
52-70 .... 2.00
TOXIC AVENGER
1 .... 2.50
2-5 .... 1.25
2001 A SPACE ODYSSEY
1-10 .... 2.00
VISION & THE SCARLET WITCH
1-4 (1982) 1.25
1-12 (1985) 1.25
WEB OF SPIDER-MAN
1 .... 15.00
2 .... 5.00
3,4 .... 4.00
5-15 .... 3.00
16-28,33-38 .... 2.00
29 .... 14.00
30 .... 8.00
31,32 .... 6.00
39-46,49 .... 1.50
47,50,60 .... 3.00
48,59,61,90 .... 5.00
51-58,62-89,91-up 1.25
Annual 1-up 2.50
WEREWOLF BY NIGHT
6-28,30,34,35,38,41,43 .. 4.00
WEST COAST AVENGERS (MINI)
1 .... 4.00
2-4 .... 2.50
WEST COAST AVENGERS (1985)
1 .... 4.50
2-10 .... 1.50
11-46 .... 1.25
Annual 1-3 .... 2.00
WHAT IF? (1977)
1 .... 15.00
2-13,17 .... 4.00
14-16,18-26 .... 3.00
29,30 .... 3.00
32-47 .... 2.00
WHAT IF? (1988)
1,4,7,9,10,16 .... 2.50
11-15,17-28,32,35-38 .... 1.25
WOLVERINE
1,10 .... 14.00
2-5 .... 5.00
6-9 .... 3.50
11-17 .... 2.50
18-29 .... 2.00
30-40 .... 1.50
41,42 .... 4.50
43-up 1.50
WONDER MAN (1986)
1 .... 2.00
WONDER MAN (1991)
1 .... 2.00
2-4,6-10 .... 1.25
X-FACTOR
1 .... 8.00
2-11 .... 2.50
12-22 .... 1.50
23,25,26 .... 3.00
24,40 .... 6.00
27-39,41-49 .... 1.25
50-53,60-62 .... 3.00
54-59 .... 1.25
63 .... 8.50
64,68 .... 5.50
65-67,69,71 .... 3.00
70,72-up 1.25
Annual 1-up 2.50
X-FORCE
1 (set of all 5 w/cards) .. 13.50
2-up 1.25
X-MEN
123-128,131-138 .... 7.50
143 .... 5.00
144-150 .... 4.50
151-161,163-170 .... 4.00
162,171,172 .... 6.00
173-192,194-199 .... 2.50
193,200,205 .... 5.00
202-204,206-209 .... 2.50
214-221,223,224 .... 2.00
225-227 .... 5.00
228-247 .... 1.50
249-255,259-265 .... 1.25
256-258,269,271-273 .... 4.50
266,267,270 .... 8.00
268 .... 12.00
274,278-280,284-up 1.25
275 .... 6.50
276,277,281-283 .... 3.50
Annual 4 .... 6.00
5,6 .... 4.00
7,8,11-up 2.50
9 .... 5.00
X-MEN (1991)
1 (set of all 5 editions) .. 15.00
2-up 1.25
X-MEN & ALPHA FLIGHT
1,2 .... 3.00
X-MEN & THE MICRONAUTS
1-4 .... 2.00
X-MEN VS THE AVENGERS
1-4 .... 3.00

DC COMICS

ACTION COMICS/WEEKLY
413-436,438,439 .... 2.00
442,444-499,501-551 .... 1.50
500 .... 4.00
554-582,584-597 .... 1.25
598,600 .... 4.00
599,601-649,651-653 .... 1.25
ADVENTURE COMICS
425-441 .... 3.00
442-490 .... 1.25
ADVENTURES OF THE OUTSIDERS
33-43 .... 1.25
ALL STAR
58 .... 4.00
59,60,63,65,66,68,71-73
.... 2.50
ALL STAR SQUADRON
1,25,26,47 .... 3.00
2-24,28-46,48-67 .... 1.25
Annual 1-3 .... 2.00
AMERICA VS. THE JUSTICE SOCIETY
1-4 .... 2.00
ANIMAL MAN
4,6-9 .... 2.50
16,19,20,22-46 .... 1.25
AQUAMAN
57-63 .... 2.00
1 (1986) 3.00
2-4 .... 2.00
BATMAN
336-348,351-356,360,361,
363-365,367 .... 3.00
406-408,410 .... 3.00
409,411,412,414-416,421,
422,424,425 .... 1.50
429,433,436,442 .... 3.00
431,432,434,435,437-441
.... 1.50
443-447,449-454,463-474
.... 1.25
Annual 9-14 .... 2.00
Cult 2-4 .... 5.00
BATMAN AND THE OUTSIDERS
1 .... 3.00
2-32 .... 1.25
Annual 1,2 .... 2.00
BATMAN FAMILY
1,6,8,9 .... 6.00
2-5,7,10,11,13-16,18,19
.... 4.50
BLACKHAWK
244-273 .... 1.25
1-3 (1988) 2.00
3-16, Annual 1 (1989) 1.25
BLACK LIGHTNING
1 .... 4.00
2-11 .... 1.50
BLUE BEETLE
1 .... 3.00
2-24 .... 1.25
BLUE DEVIL
1 .... 3.00
2-31,Annual 1 .... 1.25
BOOSTER GOLD
1 .... 3.00
2-25 .... 1.25
BRAVE & THE BOLD
112,113,115-118 .... 4.50
142-190,192-195,196,198,
199 .... 1.50
CAMELOT 3000
1-11 .... 1.50
CAPTAIN ATOM
1 .... 3.00
2-56,Annual 1,2 .... 1.25
CATWOMAN
4 .... 3.00
CHALLENGERS OF THE UNKNOWN
78-87 .... 2.00
CHECKMATE
1 .... 3.00
2-28 .... 1.25
CLAW THE UNCONQUERED
1 .... 4.00
2-12 .... 2.00
COSMIC ODYSSEY
1-4 .... 2.50
CRISIS ON INFINITE EARTHS
1,7 .... 4.00
2-6,9-12 .... 1.50
DC CHALLENGE
1-12 .... 1.25
DC COMICS PRESENTS
1 .... 4.50
2-25 .... 1.50
27-40,42-97 .... 1.25
Annual 1-3 .... 2.00
DC SPECIAL (REPRINTS)
1 .... 6.00
5,7-9,12-15 .... 3.50
16-20,22-29 .... 2.50
DC SUPERSTARS
2,4-8,11-16,18 .... 2.50
DEADMAN
2-7 (1985) 2.00
1-4 (1986) 1.50
DEMON (1972)
1 .... 6.00
2-16 .... 3.00
DETECTIVE COMICS
447,449,451-455,457-460,
462-464,469,470 .... 3.00
466,468,471,473,474,
479-482 .... 6.00
475,476 .... 8.00
500 .... 5.00
502,503,506,511-525,
527-531 .... 2.50
571-574 .... 2.50
575-578 .... 7.50
579-597,599,601-640 .... 1.25
598,600 .... 4.00
Annual 1-4 .... 2.00
DOC SAVAGE
1-4 (1987) 1.50
1 (1988) 3.00
2-14, Annual 1 .... 1.25
DOCTOR FATE
1-4 (1987) 1.25
DOOM PATROL
122-124 .... 4.00
DOOM PATROL
1 .... 3.00
2-13,15,16 .... 1.25
22,23,29 .... 3.00
32-35,37,41,44,48,50,Annual
1, Special 1 .... 1.25
FLASH
239-288, 290-299 .... 1.50
300,305,306,309,350 .... 3.50
301-304,307,308,310-349
.... 1.25
FLASH (1987)
2-59 .... 1.25
Annual 1-3 .... 2.00
FLASH GORDON
1-8 .... 1.25
FOREVER PEOPLE (1971)
2-9 .... 5.00
10,11 .... 4.00
1-6 (1988) 1.25
FREEDOM FIGHTERS
1 .... 4.00
2-15 .... 1.50
FURY OF FIRESTORM
1,100 .... 4.00
2-99,Annual 1-5 .... 1.25
GREEN ARROW
1-4 (1983) 1.50
GREEN ARROW (1988)
1 .... 5.00
4,6-11 .... 1.50
12-48,50,56,62 .... 1.25
Annual 1-3 .... 2.00
Long Bow Hunters 2,3 .. 5.00
GREEN LANTERN
120,121,124-137 .... 2.00
122,123,138,139,141 .... 4.50
140,142-164 .... 1.50
165-193,197,198 .... 1.25
199-224 .... 1.25
GREEN LANTERN (1990)
1,3 .... 3.00
2,4-31 .... 1.25
GREEN LANTERN EMERALD DAWN
1 .... 9.00
2 .... 7.50
3-6 .... 3.50
1 (series II) 3.00
2-6 .... 1.25
HAWK & THE DOVE
1-3(1988) 2.00
1 (1989) 2.50
2-28,Annual 1,2 .... 1.25
HAWKMAN (1986)
1 .... 2.50
2-17, Special 1 .... 1.25
HAWKWORLD (1989)
1 .... 5.50
2,3 .... 3.50
1 (1990) 3.00
2-20, Annual 1 .... 1.25
HISTORY OF THE DC UNIVERSE
1,2 .... 3.00
HUNTRESS
1 .... 2.50
2-19 .... 1.25
IMMORTAL DR. FATE
1-3 (1985) 2.00
INFINITY INC.
1 .... 3.00
2-13,15-37 .... 1.50
38-53 .... 1.25
INVASION!
1-3 .... 2.50
JIMMY OLSEN
134,136-148 .... 4.50
149-163 .... 2.50
JONAH HEX
1 .... 4.00
3,8,10,11,18-50 .... 1.50
51-92 .... 1.25
JUSTIC LEAGUE EUROPE
1 .... 3.00
2-41,Annual 1,2 .... 1.25
JUSTIC LEAGUE AMERICA
118-122,125-127,129-131,
134,138,140-146,149-160
.... 2.50
161-200 .... 1.50
201-261 .... 1.25
Annual 1-3 .... 2.00
JUSTICE LEAGUE AMERICA (1987)
1 .... 7.50
2 .... 6.00
3 .... 3.50
4-7,18,19,24 .... 1.50
8-17,20-23,25-59,63 .... 1.25
Annual 1-5 .... 2.00
KAMANDI
1 .... 6.00
2-59 .... 2.00
KORAK
46-59 .... 2.00
LEGENDS (1986)
1-5 .... 1.25
6 .... 3.00
LEGENDS OF THE DARK KNIGHT
2-9,15,26,Annual 1 .... 1.25
LEGION OF SUPERHEROES
259 .... 4.00
260-290,300 .... 2.00
291-299,301-354 .... 1.25
Annual 1-5 .... 1.50
LEGION OF SUPERHEROES (1984)
1 .... 4.00
2-36,39-63 .... 1.25
Annual 1-4 .... 1.50
LOIS LANE
124-137 .... 2.50
MANHUNTER
1 (1984) 2.50
1 (1988) 2.50
2-22 .... 1.25
MAN OF STEEL
1,1-6 .... 1.25
MARTIAN MANHUNTER
1-4 .... 1.25
MILLENIUM
1-8 .... 1.25
MISTER MIRACLE (1971)
2-8 .... 5.00
9-19 .... 2.50
20-25 .... 2.00
1,13,14 (1988) 3.00
2-12,15-28,Special 1 .... 1.25
NEW GODS (1971)
2,3,5-9 .... 5.00
10,11 .... 4.00
12-19 .... 2.00
1 (1989) 2.50
2-28 .... 1.25
NEW TEEN TITANS (1980)
1 .... 4.00
2-49,54-59 .... 1.25
60-65,75,79 .... 3.00
66-68,76-78 .... 1.25
Annual 1-6 .... 1.50
NEW TEEN TITANS/NEW TITANS (1984)
1 .... 4.00
2-49,54-59 .... 1.25
60-65,75,79 .... 3.00
66-68,76-78 .... 1.25
Annual 1-6 .... 1.50
OMEGA MEN
1,5,6,9,20,37 .... 3.50
2,4,7,8,11-19,21-36,38,
Annual 1,2 .... 1.25
3,10 .... 6.50
OUTCASTS (1987)
1-7,9,10,12 .... 1.25
OUTSIDERS
1 .... 3.00
2-28,Special 1 .... 1.25
PHANTOM STRANGER (1969)
13-41 .... 2.00
POWER OF THE ATOM
1 .... 2.50
2-7,11,14-18 .... 1.25
QUESTION
1, Annual 1 .... 2.50
2-32 .... 1.25
RAGMAN (1976)
1,2,4,5 .... 2.00
RED TORNADO
1-4 .... 1.25
RIMA THE JUNGLE GIRL
1 .... 3.00
4 .... 1.50
RONIN
1-5 .... 2.50
SANDMAN (1974)
1-6 .... 2.50
SECRET ORIGINS (1986)
1,5,6,44,50,Special 1 .... 3.00
2-4,7-43,45-47 .... 1.25
SECRET SOCIETY OF SUPER VILLAINS
1 .... 4.00
2-15 .... 1.50
SHADE THE CHANGING MAN (1977)
1 .... 3.00
2-8 .... 2.00
SHADOW (1973)
1,3 .... 6.00
2,4-12 .... 4.50
3,4 (1986) 2.50
SHADOW (1987)
1 .... 2.50
2-15,17,Annual 1 .... 1.25
SHADOW OF THE BATMAN
3-5 .... 4.50
SHADOW WAR OF HAWKMAN
1-4 .... 1.25
SHAZAM (1973)
1,12-14 .... 4.00
2-7,11,19-21,27,35 .... 1.50
SHOWCASE
94,96 .... 3.00
97,98,100-104 .... 1.25
SPECTRE (1987)
1 .... 2.50
2-31,Annual 1 .... 1.25
STEEL THE INDESTRUCTIBLE MAN
1-5 .... 1.50
SUICIDE SQUAD
1 .... 3.00
2-21,26-59,Annual 1 .... 1.25
SUPERBOY
211,213-242 .... 2.50
243-258 .... 1.50
SUPERGIRL (1972)
1-5,7-10 .... 3.00
SUPERMAN
281-283,285-299,301-350
.... 1.50
351-399,401-422,424-462,
465,480 .... 1.25
Annual 9-12 .... 2.00
Special 1-3 .... 2.00
SUPERMAN (1987)
1,9 .... 2.50
2-8,10-45 .... 1.25
Annual 1-3 .... 1.50
SUPERMAN FAMILY
172-174,176-179 .... 2.50
180-222 .... 1.50
SUPER TEAM FAMILY
2,4,6-8,10-15 .... 2.50
SWAMP THING (1972)
5-10 .... 4.50
11-20 .... 2.50
SWAMP THING (1982)
1 .... 4.00
2-19 .... 1.50
23 .... 6.00
28,29 .... 3.00
30-33,38-40 .... 2.00
35,36,41-49,51,54-81 .... 1.25
50,52,53 .... 3.00
SWORD OF SORCERY
3-5 (1973) 3.00
SWORD OF THE ATOM
1-4, Special 1-3 .... 1.25
TALES OF THE NEW TEEN TITANS
1-4 .... 1.25
TARZAN
207-209,230-235 .... 4.00
210-229 .... 2.00
236-258 .... 1.50
TARZAN FAMILY
60-66 .... 2.00
TEEN TITANS
45-53 .... 2.50
TEEN TITANS SPOTLIGHT
1-21 .... 1.25
TOR
1-6 .... 2.00
VIGILANTE
1 .... 3.00
2-50, Annual 1,2 .... 1.25
WANTED THE WORLDS MOST DANGEROUS VILLAINS
1-9 (1972) 3.00
WARLORD
1 .... 15.00
2 .... 5.00
3-10 .... 4.00
11-20 .... 2.50
21-52 .... 1.50
53-130 .... 1.25
Annual 1-3,5,6 .... 1.50
WATCHMEN
1-6,10-12 .... 2.00
WEIRD WESTERN TALES
42-44,46,48-50,52-57,59-
65,67,69,70 .... 1.50
WEIRD WORLD OF E.R.B.
1 .... 4.00
4-8,10 .... 2.50
WONDER WOMAN
203,205,207,209,210,212,
215,218,221,224-251 .... 1.50
252-266,269-299 .... 1.25
301-329 .... 1.25
WONDER WOMAN (1987)
1 .... 4.00
2-58,65 .... 1.25
WORLD'S FINEST
213-222 .... 2.00
223-228,230 .... 4.00
229,231-243 .... 1.50
245,250,252,253,256,257,
259,260 .... 2.50
262,264-282,300 .... 2.00
283-323 .... 1.25
YOUNG ALL STARS
1 .... 2.50
2-31,Annual 1 .... 1.25

$50. Each
23" x 18" COPY OF WALLY WOOD'S ORIGINAL ART OF 1971 AS APPEARED IN OVERSEAS WEEKLY. LIMITED EDITION OF 100 NUMBERED PRINTS WITH AUTHENTIC PUBLISHERS SEAL. SEND PAYMENT TO GUS KROESEN, INC., PO BOX 8721, EMERYVILLE, CALIFORNIA 94608.

COMICS- NEW & OLD, A-Z, CAREFULLY GRADED

CARDS- NON-SPORT BOXES, SETS & PEMIUMS

TOYS- ACTION FIGURES, VEHICLES, MODELS

ART- S/N PRINTS, PORTFOLIOS, LITHOS

SERVICE- *FAST, FRIENDLY, HONEST, SMART*

BUY/SELL/TRADE
RETAIL/WHOLESALE **CALL US FIRST!**
WALK-IN/MAIL-ORDER/ADVANCE ORDER

DEPRESSED?

If you're an unhappy general collector check this out:

30% to 75% off Overstreet. All types old to recent.

FAST SERVICE: Orders out in one to two days. NO holding for personal check.

STRICT GRADING: BEA's Fine is most dealers' Mint.

NO MINIMUM ORDER: Free postage and extra discounts on orders over $50.00.

Send $1.00 for next 3 monthly catalogs; refunded with order

BEA

P.O. BOX 811X, TEMPLE CITY, CA 91780

HIGH QUALITY COMICS
Presents:
• OVER 200,000 COMICS FOR COLLECTORS
• THOUSANDS OF HOT SILVER AGE COMICS IN HIGH TO MEDIUM GRADES
• A HUGE INVENTORY OF RECENT ('75-'90) COMICS
• BUYING - SELLING - TRADING ! !
• SEND $ 1.00 FOR OUR GIANT CATALOG
• SEND YOUR WANT LIST W/S.A.S.E. FOR REPLIES
• BUYING COLLECTIONS - LARGE & SMALL OLD & NEW
PAYING TOP PRICES ! ! ! !
WRITE OR CALL:
(619) 723-7269
HIGH QUALITY COMICS
1106 2nd St.
SUITE 110
ENCINITAS, CA
92024

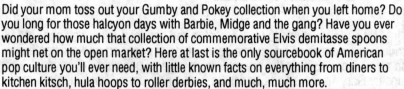

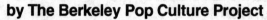

ORIGINAL ART

BUY - SELL - TRADE

Specializing in ORIGINAL COMIC BOOK & COMIC STRIP ART I have a selection of THOUSANDS of ORIGINALS in stock. Possibly the LARGEST SELECTION of classic, quality comic art IN THE WORLD!

From ALEX RAYMOND's "Flash Gordon" & HAL FOSTER's "Prince Valiant" & "Tarzan", to JACK KIRBY's "Fantastic Four" or DITKO's "Spider-man". SEGAR's "Popeye", WAYNE BORING or CURT SWAN's "Superman", SCHULZ's "Peanuts", GEORGE HERRIMAN's "Krazy Kat", CANIFF's "Terry" or "Steve Canyon". WILL EISNER, LOU FINE, BERNI WRIGHTSON, JOE KUBERT, CARMINE INFANTINO, WALLY WOOD, FRANK FRAZETTA, AL WILLIAMSON, R. CRUMB, STERRETT, SPRANG, FINLAY, BOK and on and on....

If original comic art & other graphic media are your hobby, then you should call or write me. If you are interested in buying, trading or selling fine quality originals, I HAVE MORE THAN ANYONE ELSE!! Contact me today....

My interests are: SILVER AGE DC & MARVEL; CLASSIC COMIC STRIPS; PIN-UP, PULP & PAPERBACK ART; MOVIE POSTER ART and UNDERGROUND COMIC ART.

Send $2. in stamps for my current catalog, $4. Foreign & Canada.

above: JACK KIRBY DC splash. One of 2 known, inked by WALLY WOOD. below: HERRIMAN's Krazy Kat

RICHARD HALEGUA
P.O.BOX 8256 CINCINNATI, OHIO 45208
phone 513-321-4208

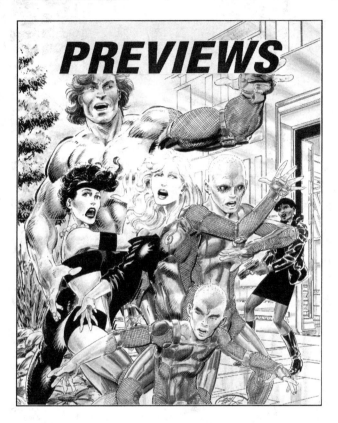

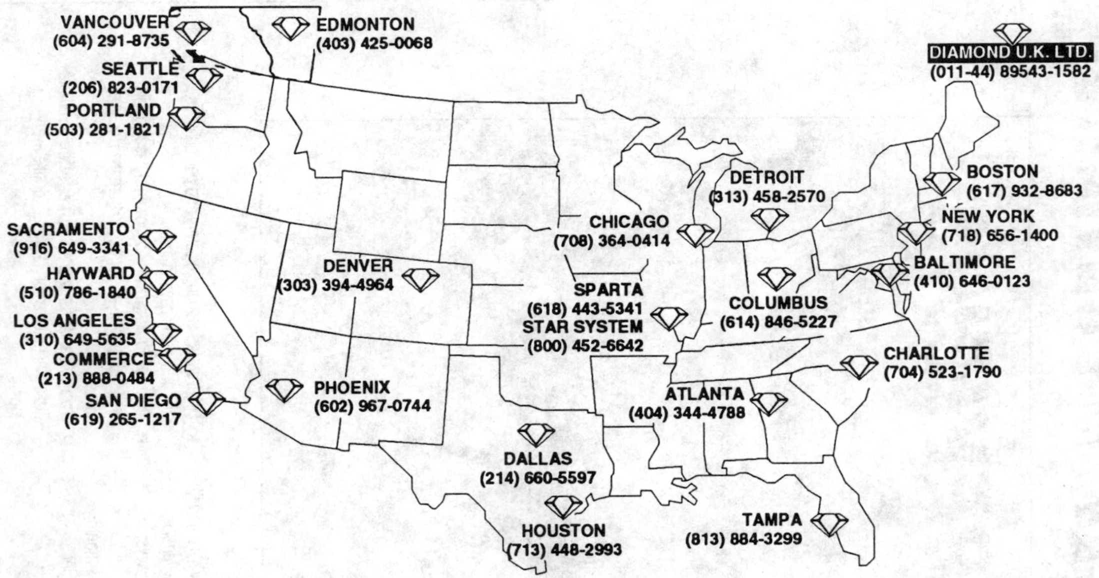

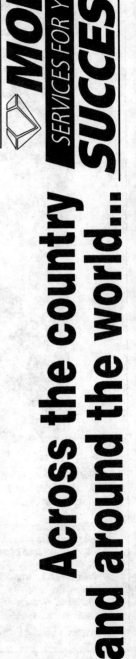

Domestic and international service from 24 strategically located Distribution Centers, delivering new products to your store as quickly and economically as possible.

Local management and staffs—rated as "Knowledgeable, Friendly, and Helpful" by over 90% of our customers—who bring local commitment to your store's needs!

Straightforward discounts that let you know exactly what you're ordering and how much it will cost!

The Diamond Star System, which provides you with the industry's only centralized, constantly-updated source for hundreds of best-selling backlist items! Always convenient with toll-free ordering, Diamond's QuickShip Guarantee, and free-freight delivery options!

Our computerized reorder system, which cross-matches your orders against the inventories of all of our Distribution Centers to find what you need (and automatically notifies you of its availability)!

Clear and simple computerized billing and account statements from our Credit Department Staff, which is rated as "Professional, Friendly, and Fair" by over 95% of our customers!

The finest ordering tools and information services available, including *Diamond Dateline*, *Diamond Dialogue*, and *Previews*—the industry's most comprehensive, colorful, and convenient wholesale catalog, featuring the widest selection of merchandise available to your store!

Strong retailer support programs, including "Instant" Co-op Credit, consumer editions of *Previews*, the industry's most comprehensive returns program, our annual Diamond Seminar, *Previews* on Disk, and more!

The peace of mind that comes from building your business on the strength and stability of the Industry Leader. More locations. More convenience. More services for your success!

For more information on Diamond Comic Distributors, call the Diamond Distribution Center nearest you, or contact our Customer Service Dept. at **(800) 783-2981.**

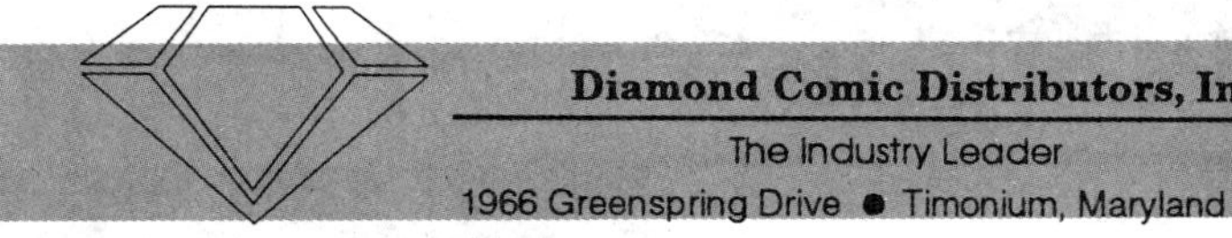

Diamond Comic Distributors, Inc.

The Industry Leader

1966 Greenspring Drive • Timonium, Maryland 21093

HEROES CONVENTION
CHARLOTTE™

Top Representatives From Marvel, DC, Valiant, Aardvark-Vanaheim and Many More!!!
Plus Art Contests, Comic Art Seminars & Workshops, Exhibits, and Lots More!!!

JUNE 11, 12 & 13, 1993

Show Location:
Charlotte International Trade Center
(formerly Charlotte Apparel Center)
200 North College Street • Charlotte NC

Host Hotel ($55 Rate)
Holiday Inn Center City
230 North College Street
Charlotte NC

Sponsored By:

HEROES AREN'T HARD TO FIND

Midwood Corners Shopping Center
Corner of Central Avenue & The Plaza
Charlotte NC
(704) 375 7462

Silas Creek Crossing Shopping Center
3204 Silas Creek Parkway
Winston-Salem NC 27103
(919) 765 4370 (HERØ)

Heroes Plaza Shopping Center
1415-A Laurens Road
Greenville SC 29607
(803) 235 3488

Westgate Mall
At The Intersection Of I-26 & U.S. 29
Spartanburg SC 29301
(803) 574 1713

For Dealer & Ticket Info: PO Box 9181, Charlotte NC 28299-9181 or 1-800-321-4370 (HERØ)

For The Latest Information About New Comics, Special Events, & Other Surprises, Call The HEROES HOTLINE!!!
Dial 704 372 4370 (HERØ) Around The Clock In Charlotte, After-Hours At The Regular Numbers Everywhere Else!!

COMIC-ART
INVESTMENTS

GEM
COMICS
Chicagoland's Finest
serving our customers for 10 years
COMIC BOOKS
-OLD & NEW-
T-SHIRTS
GAMES
TOYS
& MORE
GEM Comics
156 N. York Rd.
Elmhurst, Ill. 60126
(708) 833-8787

RARE COMIC ART IS MY BAG
. . .and I love to trade bags of money, or other art for items of special interest to me.
I'll pay top dollar for original artwork by Carl Barks, E.C. Segar, and other classic cartoonists, as well as paintings, cartoon movie posters from the '30s and '40s, and other rare comic oriented esoterica.
If you have rare material for sale contact me first. If you don't, you may be selling your collection short.
Bruce Hamilton
P.O. Box 4235
Prescott, AZ 86302
(602)776-1300

Send Inquires To:

Richard Muchin

P.O. Box 925

Commack, NY 11725

Phone: (516) 543-7574

Fax:(516) 543-5737

EEP?
SHUFFLE ON DOWN TO
THE
AMERICAN COMIC BOOK COMPANY
IN FABULOUS
LONG BEACH, CA 90807
3972 ATLANTIC BLVD.
(310)-426-0393
OPEN SEVEN DAYS
©1977 BY SCOTT SHAW!

AT YOUR SERVICE SUBSCRIPTIONS

✻ Mention **Overstreet Price Guide** #23 for an added discount!

17815 Davenport Rd. Suite 120 Dallas, TX 75252
Ph: 214-931-3393/FAX: 214-931-3789

Tired of not knowing what's coming out this month? Sick of missing all those '**hot**' books? Compare your supplier to our **mail-order** service, with the **At Your Service** checklist:

✓ Huge discounts on all new comics!!!
✓ 30% OFF ALL comic-related merchandise!!!
✓ Collector's supplies and Back issues!!!!
✓ MasterCard/VISA and C.O.D. orders welcome!!
✓ Friendly and knowledgable staff!!
✓ Monthly contests for subscribers!!! Recent prizes have included **Magnus #0w/card**, **Gold Valiants** and **Wizard Gold Cards**!!!!!

SO CHECK US OUT:
1-214-931-3393

Office Hours 9am - 5pm Central, or leave a message.

"Times are changing, don't get caught in the Darque!"

SHOW-OFF YOUR COLLECTION!

Efficient! Create a display adapted to your needs! Attach it to the wall or ceiling! Ideal for decoration and exhibitions! Does not dammage your comic collection or protective bags!

IT'S MORE ATTRACTIVE THAN A BOX!

The module AM-18 allows you to display 18 comics! **AM-18↑**

ORDER NOW!

______AM-18 $18.00(Can.) $16.00(U.S.)	______
Orders of $75.00 or more add $4.00......................	______
Shipping and handling, add $5.00	$5.00
Foreign orders, add $5.00 for shipping	______
Total..	______

Name ____________________
Address ____________________
City ____________ State ____________
Zip Code ____________ Phone ____________

Send cheque or money order. All taxes included. Allow three to six weeks for delivery. The module ACOMIK is designed for comics approx. 17cm. X 26cm.(6.7" X 10.5"). Comics and protective bags not included.

Write to:

ACOMIK (O)
CP 47062
Sillery, Qc, Canada
G1S 4X1

ACOMIK MODULE

Pat. Pend. 9214737.0

F-A-S-T SERVICE (309) 833-1809 VISA/MC

NOW AVAILABLE!
TV GUIDE COLLECTING VIDEO

TV Guide Specialists 1993

TV GUIDES FOR SALE 1948-1993

Now Ready 1993
15th Edition TV GUIDE SPECIALISTS CATALOG

Special CHRISTMAS COVER issue. Includes over 65 rare Christmas cover photos including a special color centerfold. Plus over 100 other cover photos are also pictured.

All TV GUIDES 1949-1992 listed and available.
68 pages • Only $3.00
THE MOST COMPLETE, MOST UP-TO-DATE, MOST AUTHORITATIVE TV GUIDE LISTING AVAILABLE. THE ESSENTIAL REFERENCE FOR TV GUIDE COLLECTORS.

TV GUIDE SPECIALISTS
Box 20 — O
Macomb, IL 61455

14 PGS. OF NEWSPAPER SUPPLEMENTS, ETC.

LOW PRICES---LOW PRICES

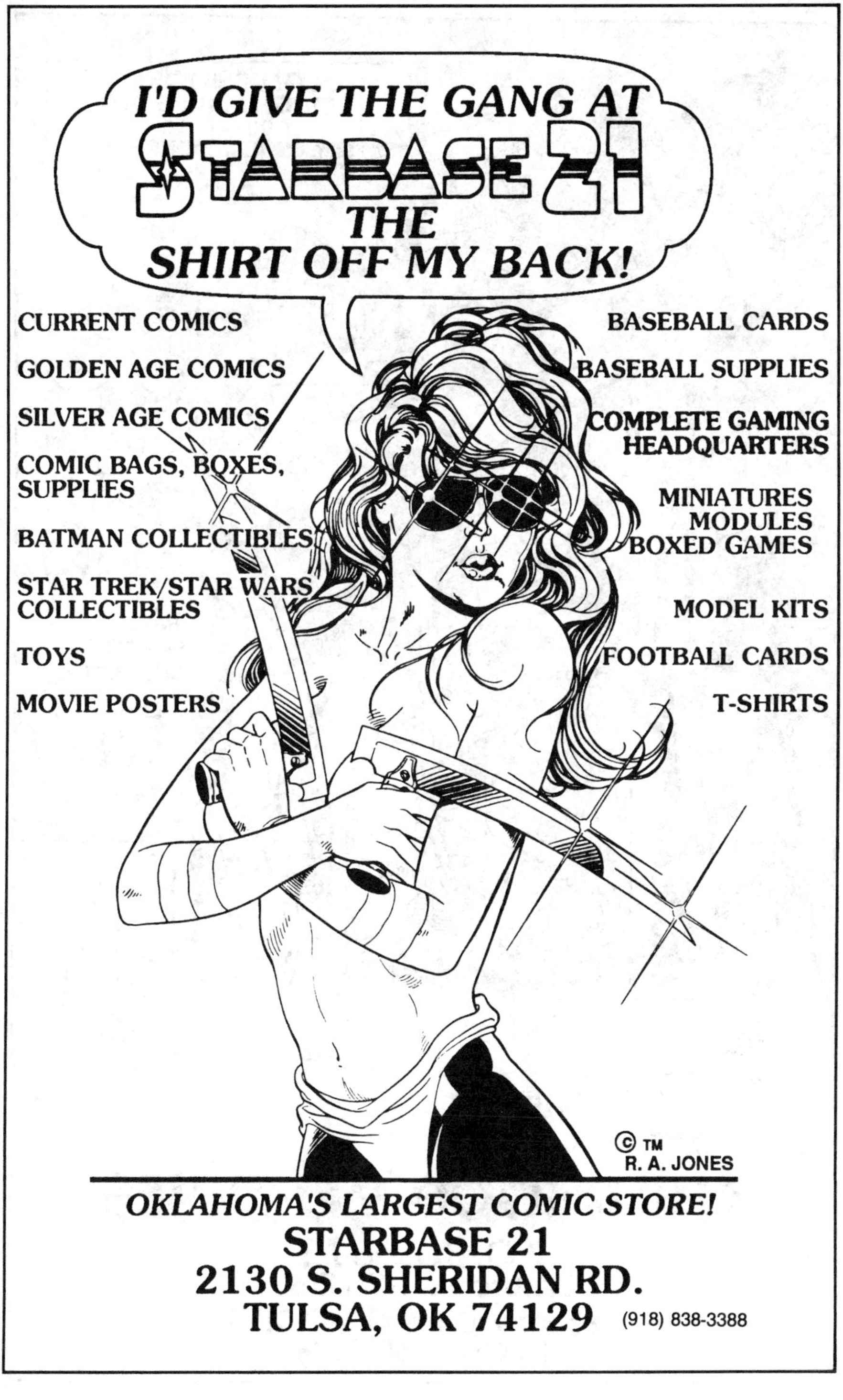

COMIC BOOKS
BOUGHT and SOLD
1933-1970
THAT'S MY FAVORITE SUPERHERO!
SHELDON "SHELLY" MOLDOFF

COLLECTOR'S WORLD OFFERS 20% OFF TO CLUB MEMBERS

CBG
Customer Service
Award - 1991
PHILIP M. LEVINE AND SONS
RARE AND ESOTERIC BOOKS
P. O. Box 246
Three Bridges, NJ 08887
Phone (908) 788-0532
FAX (908) 788-1028
CUSTOMER SERVICE AWARD
Toy Shop
1991
ON
SEND US ALL OF YOUR PRE-
1970 COMIC BOOKS TODAY!
We will make you an immediate cash offer. If we don't buy your books, we will pay the "book rate postage" both ways. We are always buying and selling comics, giveaway comics, Big Little books, old paperbacks, MAD memorabilia, Seduction of the Innocent and related censorship material, radio premiums, early crime magazines, "Cardboard Age" comics, antediluvian comics and related material, pulps, Catechetical Guild comics and related material, Golden Age comics, Silver Age comics, old toys and Gum Cards. We have the largest inventory of old "TV Guides" in North America. Send us your name & address today to get on our mailing list.
YOU CAN COME AND SEE US AT ALL NEW YORK AREA COLLECTIBLE SHOWS, ALL WES-REX SHOWS, CHICAGO COMIC-CON, ALLENTOWN PAPER FAIR, & SAN DIEGO COMIC-CON.
Don't forget to send us your books. We have been buying and selling comic books for 39 years.
SEND US YOUR WANT LIST
TODAY!

CLASSIFIED ADVERTISING

Need Silver Age Marvels
and ALL comics from the 1940's and 50's
Low and High grade. Darren 908-495-5629.

Robert J. La Tremouille
Attorney at Law
875 Massachusetts Avenue, Suite 31
Cambridge, Massachusetts 02139
Telephone 617-864-8055 / 617-491-7181

FREE Comic Catalogue. LOW PRICES. Golden-Silver Age, Marvels, DCs, Disneys, All Kinds. I like to TRADE too. Money Back Guarantee. SPECIAL BONUS WITH PURCHASE. Send an EXTRA 1st Class Stamp to: DAVE YARUSS, 7916 BLUE LAKE DR., SAN DIEGO, CALIF. 92119. WANTED: Disney Animation Art.

SAVE ON COMICS! Key issues/top artists! All priced to sell! Marvel, DC, Disney, Archie, EC, Gold, Silver, more! Trades (comics, games) welcomed! Huge Catalog only $2 (+SASE). HM Levy, Box 197-S, East Meadow, NY 11554.

COMIC BOOKS FOR SALE! 50,000 IN STOCK. SEND WANT LISTS. ALL PRICED WELL BELOW GUIDE! 607-648-4025. RICK SEMOWICH, 56 JOHN SMITH ROAD, BINGHAMTON, NY 13901.

WANT LISTS FILLED—It's my hobby! 99% can be found if not in stock! Write/call for info: (712) 295-6222. Jeff Dilocker, PO Box 167 Peterson, Iowa 51047.

COMIC BOOKS FOR SALE
ONE OF THE WORLD'S LARGEST CATALOGUES SELLING GOLDEN AGE, DC, MARVEL, DELL AND CLASSICS ILLUSTRATED COMICS PLUS BIG LITTLE BOOKS, SUNDAY PAGES, ORIGINAL ART. WE SUPPLY CANADIAN COLLECTORS AND COMIC STORES WITH ALL SIZES AND TYPES OF PLASTIC BAGS, ACID FREE BOXES AND BACKING BOARDS, ETC. SEND $1.00 FOR CATALOGUE.
COMIC BOOKS WANTED
HIGHEST PRICES PAID FOR COMIC BOOKS, BIG LITTLE BOOKS, NEWSPAPER COMICS BEFORE 1965. NO COLLECTION TOO LARGE OR SMALL. 40 YEARS EXPERIENCE AS A COLLECTOR AND DEALER. CONTACT US BEFORE SELLING.
INTERNATIONAL COMIC BOOK COMPANY
CALVIN AND ELEANOR SLOBODIAN
859 - 4TH AVE., RIVERS, MANITOBA
CANADA R0K 1X0. PHONE:204-328-7846

WANTED! Anything by or about HOWARD CHAYKIN, especially obscure and unusual material and not just comic books. Also wanted: syndicated work by FRAZETTA, and live tapes and printed collectibles relating to RANDY CALIFORNIA/SPIRIT. Write me: TIM BARNES, 103 Tredworth Road, Gloucester, Glos. GL1 4QU ENGLAND. Fifth Glorious Year!

SEND TO: E.K. Wong, 4282 10th Ave., Port Alberni, BC

FREE CARTOONS! For a free sample of a delightful new comic strip, send a SASE to: SpringTime, 11641 Decatur St, Westminster, CO, 80234.

Prices 15-50% below Guide. 15% discount on all orders $40 or more–Comicbook Hotline Inc. P.O. Box 8230, North Bergen, NJ 07047. (201) 656-3228. SEND SASE.

$400,000 SEARCH!!!
OLD COMIC BOOKS WANTED!! 1933-1973
HIGHEST PRICES PAID!
Send lists or call. Generally paying 40%-70% of guide. Golden Age and early Silver Age books our specialty. Rick Semowich, 56 John Smith Rd., Binghamton, NY 13901. Phone: 607-648-4025.

Disney comics by **Dell** wanted, dealers please **send lists** to Mr. A. Köhne, Bosschestraat 180, 2587 HJ Den Haag, Holland. **Selling**: MARVEL and DC Plastic **PVC figures** made by Comic Spain, $4 each (Size: 5" high) Trade too!

Buying Classics Illustrated and Classic Comics – Call or write Phil Gaudino, 84 - 19 106 St., Richmond Hill, NY 11418 - 718-847-6850.

Buying Comics
Any comic, any condition
D.F., 6 Annette Ct., Hazlet, NJ, 07730

COMIC BOOKS WANTED - 1930's thru 1990's. Dealer needs stock. Our buying catalog lists prices we pay for thousands. Send 2 stamps to Ed Kalb 1353 S. Los Alamos St. Mesa, Arizona 85204.

PENTHOUSE MAGAZINES. VOLUME 1#1 SEPT. 1969 200 DOLLARS MINT CONDITION OR $300 FOR 1ST 4 ISSUES ALL UNOPENED. STORE BOUGHT. NO FINGERNAIL PRINTS. $350 FIRST 7 MINT. COVER PRICE WAS 75¢. WE PAY UPS 2ND DAY AIR. 30 DAY MONEY BACK. DuMONT, 836 EDGEWATER CIRCLE, EUSTIS, FLA. 1-800-426-9889.

COMIC SOFTWARE!!

Organize your comics with COMIC BOOK III.
Send $27.95 plus $1.75 for S/H to: Data Loggers, PO Box 434, Burlington, IA 52601.
(see full page ad in front of catalog)

COMICS - Thousands of Marvels, DCs & others, late 70s to present! Many Superhero role playing games available as well! For list, write to: A. Christians, 75 Wynford Heights Cres. Apt #1507, Don Mills, Ont. Canada M3C 3H9.

Wanted character related toys and items from the 50's, 60's, and early 70's. Also plastic figure model kits. Buy sell trade, sales catalog $2.00. Gordy Dutt, PO Box 201, Sharon Center, Ohio 44274-0201.

Wanted Star Wars toys, dolls, plates, bed items, watches, etc. also GI Joe, Raiders, 007, UNCLE, Thunderbirds, Fireball XL5, 1999, Supercar, Capt. Action, Superman, Munsters, Add. Family & all TV, Movie etc. D. Wilson, 14 Berryman St., North Ryde, NSW Australia.

"AMERICA'S FAVORITE COMIC BOOK DEALER"

GARY DOLGOFF COMICS

Brooklyn Navy Yard / Building 280 / Suite 608/609
Brooklyn, NY 11205
PH: 718-596-5719
M-F 10 a.m.-5 p.m.

Tight grading satisfaction guaranteed!

Strictly Graded

ALL TREASURY ORDERS PLEASE DOUBLE POSTAGE RATES

ALL MAGAZINE ADD 50¢ TO RATES

POSTAGE:
East U.S. - add 3¢/Bk (Insured)
West U.S. - add 6¢/Bk (Insured)
Outside U.S. - add 8¢/Bk (Uninsured)
Outside U.S. - add 16¢/Bk (Insured)
Orders shipped within 7-days of receipt: however cks must clear our banks.

In The "Biz" For 20 Years!

WELCOME TO THE WORLD OF GARY DOLGOFF COMICS!

A World of Honesty, Tough Grading & Satisfaction Guaranteed"

800,000 Comics, Mags & Art In Stock! (1940s-1990s)

New, or Expanding Store-Owners: Call Me & I'll Advise You "Right!!!"

"Chock-Full" of bargains galore; make 2x - 3x your money, easy . . .

Please note my "across the board" deals...stock it right (in one shot)!

All Prices Do Not Include Postage (Unless o/w Stated)

Good Deals For Dealers!!

Note! P.G. = Latest Overstreet Publication

CONTINUED FROM PAGE "A-2" & INSIDE F.C. OF THIS PRICE GUIDE . . .

DEAL #1

1940s (Early) 1960s Priced & Graded Books

• Hero, Western, Funny, Dell, Gold-Key, WDC&S, Movie & TV-Comics, etc., etc. • 80% "GVG" or better • Value Per Book: $4-$30 Range • Strictly Graded!

PRICE:
$200.00 Worth of Bks .... $150.00 (25% Off P.G.)
$750.00 Worth of Bks .... 500.00 (33⅓% off P.G.)
$2,000.00 Worth of Bks .... 1,200.00 (40% off P.G.)
Postage on Deal #1 $6.00 (U.S.), $15.00 • (Outside U.S. Insured)

DEAL #1½

80s "Decent" Superhero Marvel & DC/cs

• 1982-1990 • 80-90% Marvel & DC Hero Stuff • No "Junk" ie No N. Talent, Showcase, No "New Universe" etc. • 90% VFNM, Unread, etc. • TITLE EXAMPLES Action, Alpha-Flight, Batman, Dazzler, Elementals, Moon-Knights, Superman, T, Titans, Vis & Sc. Witch, Vigilante, Flash, JLA, Conan, Demon, Robin, Detective, Wamor, etc.

PRICE
400 Books (3 each) .... $140.00 (comes to **35¢**/Bk)
800 Books (3-5 each) .... 240.00 (comes to **30¢**/Bk)
1,600 Books (5-6 each) .... 400.00 (comes to **25¢**/Bk)
3,000 Books (5-10 each .... 750.00 (comes to **25¢**/Bk)

DEAL #2

60s "Warehouse-Sharp" Marvels (80-90% 12¢ Cover, o/w 15¢ Cover)

• Strictly Graded! • 1-3 Of An issue # (mostly 1-2 of an ish #!) • 90% Superhero Titles (ie Avengers, D.D., F. Four, Hulk, S. Tales, T.O.S., T.T.A., Thor, Sub-Mariner, Capt. Marvel, X-Men, Shield, etc.) • 1965-1971 (mostly '65-70)

PRICE VFNM Shape
$200.00 in NM "PG" .... $120.00 | $1,500.00 in NM "PG" 900.00
$500.00 in NM "PG" .... 300.00 | $2,500.00 in NM "PG" 1,500.00

FVF Shape: (VFNM w/slight ding on corner, or some other "minor imperfection)
$250.00 in NM "PG" .... 100.00 | $1,500.00 in NM "PG" 600.00
$500.00 in NM "PG" .... 200.00 | $2,500.00 in NM "PG" 1,000.00

VG-F Shape: (still nice, slightly larger dings, many call many of these FN+, but what I guarantee is a nice VG/F)
$400.00 in NM "PG" .... 100.00 | $2,000.00 in "PG" 500.00
$800.00 in NM "PG" 200.00

Postage on Deal #2: U.S. $6.00, Outside U.S. $15.00 Insured

DEAL #3

70s Marvels

• 1974-1982 (90% Superhero) • All Books Strictly Graded! • TITLES - SAMPLES: Cap. Amer., D. Devil, F. Four, Hulk, Thor, M Team Up, Defender, Kung-Fu, Invaders, Bl. Panther, Iron-Fist, M. Spotlight, Hero-For-Hire, Werewolf, M's Greatest, M Tales, etc., etc.

PRICE: VFNM
$200.00 in NM "PG" ... $100.00 (2-3 each) | $1,000 in NM "PG" ...... 500.00 (3-5 each)
$500 in NM "PG" .... 250.00 (3-4 each)

FVF
$300.00 in NM "PG" .... 120.00 (2-3 each) | $1,500.00 in NM "PG" .. 600.00 (3-6 each)
$600.00 in NM "PG" .... 240.00 (3-4 each)

VGF
$400.00 in NM "PG" .... 100.00 (2-3 each) | $2,000.00 in NM "PG" .. 500.00 (3-6 each)
$800.00 in NM "PG" .... 200.00 (3-5 each)

Postage On Deal #3: Assume Value Of Each "Deal #3" Bk in NM PG to be $2.50/Bk, then use postage rate on top of this pg.

DEAL #4

80s Mainline Marvels (Good, Solid, "Long-Running", Titles Only - No "Dogs")

• 90% VFNM, Clean & "Unread" • TITLE - SAMPLES: Avengers, D. D., F. Four (#233-Up) Hulk, Iron-Man, New Mutants, Cap, Hulk, Thor, P. Parker, Batman, Detective, Etc.

PRICE:
400 Comics .... $180.00 (3 Each Max) (comes to 45¢/Bk)
1,000 Comics .... 400.00 (3-5 Each Max) (comes to 40¢/Bk)
2,000 Comics .... 750.00 (5-8 Each Max) (comes to 37½¢/Bk)
4,000 Comics .... 1,400.00 (10-15 Each Max) (comes to 35¢/Bk)

DEAL #5

80s Mainline & "Sideline" Marvel & DC!
(A-Combo of deal #1½ & 4)

A nice, **well-balanced** combo of "Superhero Stuff" for the **new (or "Expanding) store, owner** or "Convention" **Dealer**

• 90% VFNM, "Unread" • 1982-1990 Books • SAMPLES - TITLES: Avengers, D.D., Action, Alpha Fi., F.F., Cab, Hulk, Batman, Dazzler, Superman, Iron-Man, Thor, T.Titans, Vis & Sc. Witch, Vigilante, P. Parker, etc. etc.

400 Bks (3 Each) .... $160.00 (comes to **40¢**/Bk)
1,000 Bks (3-5 Each) .... 350.00 (comes to **35¢**/Bk)
2,000 Bks (4-6 Each) .... 650.00 (comes to **32¢**/Bk)
4,000 Bks (5-8 Each) .... 1,200.00 (comes to **30¢**/BK)

DEAL #6

Big Bulk Occasionally, I have 10,000 to 100,000 VFNM (mostly) DC & Marvel (Lesser titles) (50-150 of a #): **15¢** Each. Independents: **10¢** each

DEAL #7

Treasuries ("Oversize" Comics)

• All Marvel & DC 1975-1981 • All clean, bright, warehouse copies (VGF, FVF, Graded Real Strict! • Inexpensive, Pretty "Space Fillers" • Includes Spider-Man, F.F., Legion, Thor, Dr. Strange, Conan, (B Smith) etc. • Cover price 90% mostly $1.50

PRICE: **8-Treasuries in Set!**
3-Sets (24 Treasuries) .... 30.00 (comes to **$1.25**/Treasury)
10-Sets (80 Treasuries) .... 80.00 (comes to **$1.10**/Treasury)
50-Sets (400 Treasuries) .... 300.00 (comes to **75¢**/Treasury)

DEAL #8

Marvel & Warren Monsters & Hero Magazines (1968-1982)

• All clean warehouse copies • Max 3-5 of a # • 90% VGF-FVF • TITLE - SAMPLES: Creepy, Eerie, Kung-Fu, Hulk, Epic-Illustrated, Monsters, Unleased, etc., etc.

PRICE:
100 Books .... $100.00 | 1,000 Books 900.00
300 Books 300.00

DEAL #9

80s & 90s Hot, Strong, Titles!

EX:
Punisher, Pun, W. Jour, X-Men, Spider-Man, Web #3-9, G.H. Rider, Pun, & Wolv. Appearances, X-Force, etc., etc.

PRICE:
$500.00 + in "PG" .... $200.00 (Max 3 of a #)
$1,000.00 in "PG" .... 400.00 (Max 5-6 of a #)
$2,000.00 + in "PG" .... 750.00 (Max 5-8 of a #)
$2,700.00 in Overstreet .... 1,000.00 (Max 6-10 of a #)

DEAL #10

80s & Decent Titles

EX:
Fantastic Four, Batman, Detective, Watchmen, Daredevil, Deathlok, Baxter Warlock, X-Factor, etc. (Mostly DC & Marvel Superheroes & most worth $2-6.00)

PRICE:
$500.00 in "PG" .... $150.00 (Max of 3 of a #)
$1,000.00 in "PG" .... 300.00 (Max of 3-5 of a #)
$2,000.00 in "PG" .... 500.00 (Max of 4-6 of a #)